2020年 Import and Export Tariff of the People's Republic of China and a Declaration Guidebook

中华人民共和国海关进出口税则

及申报指南

汉英对照

进出口关税税率　出口退税率　十位商品编码　监管证件

Import & Export Tariff Rates　Export Tax Rebate Rate　Ten HS Code　Control Documents

中华人民共和国海关进出口税则及申报指南编委会　编

Compiled by the Editorial Committee of the Import and Export Tariff of the People's Republic of China and a Declaration Guidebook

中国商务出版社
CCTP
CHINA COMMERCE AND TRADE PRESS

图书在版编目（CIP）数据

2020 年中华人民共和国海关进出口税则及申报指南：汉英对照 / 中华人民共和国海关进出口税则及申报指南编委会编．-- 北京：中国商务出版社，2019.12

ISBN 978-7-5103-3101-5

Ⅰ．①2… Ⅱ．①中… Ⅲ．①海关税则－中国－2020－指南－英、汉 Ⅳ．① F752.53-62

中国版本图书馆 CIP 数据核字 (2019) 第 275634 号

2020 年中华人民共和国海关进出口税则及申报指南

2020 NIAN ZHONGHUA RENMIN GONGHEGUO HAIGUAN JINCHUKOU SHUIZE JI SHENBAO ZHINAN

中华人民共和国海关进出口税则及申报指南编委会　编

出　　版：中国商务出版社
地　　址：北京市东城区安定门外大街东后巷 28 号　**邮　编**：100710
责任部门：数字出版事业部（010-64515140）
总 发 行：中国商务出版社发行部（010-51393396　64515150）
网　　址：http://www.cctpress.com
邮　　箱：cctp@cctpress.com
印　　刷：大厂回族自治县益利印刷有限公司
开　　本：880　毫米 ×1230　毫米　　1/16
印　　张：75　　**字　数**：2100　千字
版　　次：2020 年 1 月第 1 版　　**印　次**：2020 年 1 月第 1 次印刷
书　　号：ISBN 978-7-5103-3101-5
定　　价：360.00 元

凡所购本版图书有印装质量问题，请与本社总编室联系。（电话：010-85843626）

关于增值服务的说明

为答谢本版《税则》的新老用户，我们为您花重金统一购买了易通网(www. i—tong. cn)通关查询服务及权威专家归类、关务咨询服务等增值服务。

2020 年新增服务栏目：

税号定制服务：客户通过关注易通网公众号，在税号定制栏目下输入您关注的税号，当该税号项下品名、申报要素、最惠国、普通、增值、协定、特惠、暂定、消费、信息技术、反倾销反补贴等税率、3C 认证、出口退税、监管条件、报检等信息发生变动都会主动推送给用户。

增值服务内容包括：

1. 提供包括申报要素填写实例、反倾销反补贴税、检验检疫类别、报检查询、3C 认证、危险化学品目录等增值查询服务。

2. 网站对特惠、普通、最惠国、出口退税、检验检疫类别、监管条件等信息将进行实时维护更，新保证您查询的税率的准确性。

3. 免费提供三次权威专家线上归类咨询和关务咨询服务。

4. 提供与海关计算结果一致的模拟计税服务。

5. 提供通关状态查询等。

增值服务的使用方法：

1. 刮开封面上的防伪标涂层，可以得到两行数字（第一行是登录账号，第二行是密码）。

2. 激活账号，登录（www. i—tong. cn)后，在网站的左上角注册页面找到激活按钮，点击激活，按照提示填写相关信息，完成后提交。

3. 提交激活信息后，系统会给您的注册邮箱中发送一封邮件，打开后点击激活，完成激活程序。

4. 在登录页面输入账号和密码即可登录使用。

特别申明：

凡是图书上未贴增值服务防伪标，或不能正常激活提供数据更新查询服务的一律为盗版图书。

提　　示：

此二维码为易通网微信公众服务号，您只需要添加关注，并将防伪标上的账号进行绑定，即可使用微信端进行查询使用。(此账号必须先在网站上激活后才能正常使用)

对照表编排图例及说明

该税号没有做拆分，填报时需补齐两个“0”，即“2205.1000 00”。

出入境检验检疫划入海关后，需填报3位CIQ扩展码，具体见品名后的“〔 〕”，T2即附表“CIQ扩展编码及品名”。

假设该列某商品最惠国税率为20%，“部分信息技术产品最惠国税率表”税率为“15/0”，按从低原则显示为“15/0”。即2020年1月1日至6月30日最惠国税率为15%，2020年7月1日至12月31日最惠国税率为0。

该税号商品增值税率为13%，消费税率为10%。

退税率表对该货品做了进一步拆分，分别适用9%、13%的退税率。

税则号列		货品名称〔CIQ扩展编码及品名－T2表示见附表2〕	最惠(%)	暂定税率	普通	增值/消费	出口退税	计量单位	监管条件	检验检疫	特殊证件对美关税
22.05		味美思酒及其他加植物或香料的用鲜葡萄酿造的酒：									
2205.1000		-装入2升及以下容器的〔101 发酵酒配制酒，102 未列出的其他酒〕	T2	14	180	13/10	9, 13	升/千克	AB	RS	/45
2205.9000		-其他〔102〕	65		180	13/10	13	升/千克	AB	RS	
……											
2207.2000		-任何浓度的改性乙醇及其他酒精									
2207.2000	10	任何浓度的改性乙醇[301 属于危险化学品的食品添加剂，302 无检疫要求食品添加剂，303 一般化学品，需申报仅用于工业用途不用于食品添加剂无检疫要求，304 易燃液体，需申报仅用于工业用途不用于食品添加剂无检疫要求]	T1		80	13/	0	升/千克	ABG	MRNS	
2207.2000	90	任何浓度的其他酒精[食用酒精，102 其他原酒，301 属于危险化学品的食品添加剂，302 无检疫要求食品添加剂，303 一般化学品，需申报仅用于工业用途不用于食品添加剂无检疫要求，304 易燃液	30		80	13/	0	升/千克	ABG	MRNS	

T2即附表“2020年进口从量、复合税税率表”。

T1即附表“2020年关税配额商品税目、税率表”。

第一法定计量单位为“升”，第二为“千克”。

说明需办理相应检验检疫手续，代码含义具体见附表“检验检疫证件代码表”。

具体4种代码含义见附表“特殊证件代码表”。对美关税率为45%。

（注：本图例仅作示范，具体数据以内文查询为准。）

适用国家包括：韩国、印度、斯里兰卡、孟加拉、老挝。

即东盟、冰岛、格鲁吉亚。东盟适用国家包括：越南、泰国、新加坡、马来西亚、印度尼西亚、文莱、缅甸、老挝、柬埔寨、菲律宾。

即新西兰、新加坡、智利。

即中国香港、中国澳门、中国台湾。

适用国家包括：埃塞俄比亚联邦民主共和国、布隆迪共和国、刚果民主共和国、吉布提共和国、几内亚共和国、几内亚比绍共和国、莱索托王国、马达加斯加共和国、马拉维共和国、马里共和国、莫桑比克共和国、南苏丹共和国、塞拉利昂共和国、塞内加尔共和国、苏丹共和国、索马里联邦共和国、坦桑尼亚联合共和国、乌干达共和国、乍得共和国、中非共和国、阿富汗伊斯兰共和国、也门共和国、瓦努阿图共和国、科摩罗联盟、毛里塔尼亚伊斯兰共和国、多哥共和国、利比里亚共和国、卢旺达共和国、安哥拉共和国、赞比亚共和国、尼泊尔联邦民主共和国、尼日尔共和国、厄立特里亚国、柬埔寨王国、冈比亚共和国、圣多美和普林西比民主共和国。

协定税率 %										特惠税率 %			
亚太5国	东/冰/格	巴基斯坦	韩国	瑞士	哥达	秘鲁	澳大利亚	新西/坡/智	港/澳/台	亚太2国	老/柬/缅	36/3/1	Article Description
													Vermouth and other wine of fresh grapes flavoured with plants or aromatic substances:
	0//0		48.7		0	10.8	0	0/0/0	0/ /				-In containers holding 2L or less
	0//0		48.7		0	10.8	0	0/0/0	0/0/				-Other
													-Ethyl alcohol and other spirits, denatured, of any strength
	0/0/0	0	22.5		0	0	0	0/0/0	0/0/			0/0/	Ethyl alcohol, denatured of any strength
	0/0/0	0	22.5		0	0	0	0/0/0	0/0/			0/0/	Other spirits, of any strength

即哥斯达黎加

说明该税号项下商品与中国香港的协定税率为“0”，没有与中国澳门、中国台湾的协定税率。

适用国家包括：孟加拉、老挝。

即老挝、柬埔寨、缅甸。

适用国家包括：贝宁共和国、东帝汶民主共和国、缅甸。

适用国家包括：孟加拉。

勘误表

注：因政策最新调整，上述税号参数以本表为准。

新增税则号列		货品名称〔CIQ 扩展编码及品名—T2 表示见附表 2〕	最惠(%)	暂定税率	普通	增值/消费	出口退税	计量单位	监管条件	检验检疫	特殊证件对美关税
2843.9000	91	贵金属汞齐(不论是否已有化学定义)	5.5		30	13/	0	克	4Xxy		3/15.5
2843.9000	99	其他贵金属化合物(不论是否已有化学定义)	5.5		30	13/	0	克	4xy		3/15.5
2853.9090	23	铅汞齐	5.5		30	13/	0	千克	X		3/15.5
2853.9090	24	其他汞齐	5.5		30	13/	0	千克	X		3/15.5
3001.9090	92	人类腺体、器官、组织(供治疗或预防疾病用)	3		30	13/	13	千克	AB	PVQW	3/
3404.9000	10	短链氯化石蜡(具有人造蜡特性)	10		70	13/	0	千克	X		3/20
3404.9000	90	其他人造蜡及调制蜡	10		70	13/	0	千克			3/20
3824.9999	91	短链氯化石蜡(不具有人造蜡特性)	6.5		35	13/	0,6	千克	X		3/
3824.9999	99	其他编号未列名的化工产品(包括水解物或水解料、DMC(六甲基环三硅氧烷，八甲基环四硅氧烷，十甲基环五硅氧烷，十二甲基环六硅氧烷中任何 2 种，3 种或 4 种组成的混合物))	6.5		35	13/	0,6	千克			3/
8517.6910	91	卫星地球站(含终端地球站)无线电发射设备	3/1.5		14	13/	13	台/千克	AO	LM	/10
8517.6910	99	其他无线通信设备	3/1.5		14	13/	13	台/千克	A	LM	/10
8703.8000	10	旧的仅装有驱动电动机的其他载人车辆	15		270	13/	13	辆/千克	46AOxy	LM	/
8703.8000	90	其他仅装有驱动电动机的其他载人车辆	15		270	13/	13	辆/千克	6AO	LM	/

税号	项目	修改为
2606000000	监管条件	4xy
2818200000	监管条件	
2922160000	监管条件	X
2923300000	监管条件	X
2923400000	监管条件	X
2935100000	监管条件	X
2935200000	监管条件	X
2935300000	监管条件	X
2935400000	监管条件	X
3004320022	监管条件	
3004909092	监管条件	L
3002903010	计量单位	千克 /株
8429590000	计量单位	台 /千克
8711202000	计量单位	辆 /千克
9002909010	计量单位	千克 /个
9006599010	计量单位	台 /千克
2932190030	暂定税率	0
3901200011	暂定税率	3
3901200091	暂定税率	3
2843900090	税号已经取消	
3824999990	税号已经取消	
8517691090	税号已经取消	

协定税率 %										特惠税率 %			Article Description
亚太5国	东/冰/格	巴基斯坦	韩国	瑞士	哥达	秘鲁	澳大利亚	新西/坡/智	港/澳/台	亚太2国	老/柬/缅	36/3/1	
	0/0/0	0	0		0	0	0	0//0	0/0/		//	0/0/	Precious metal amalgam (whether or not chemically defined)
	0/0/0	0	0		0	0	0	0//0	0/0/		//	0/0/	Other precious metal compounds (whether or not chemically defined)
	0/0/0	0	0	0	0	0	0	0//0	0/0/		//	0/0/	Lead amalgam
	0/0/0	0	0	0	0	0	0	0//0	0/0/		//	0/0/	Other amalgam
	0/0/0	0	0	0	0	0	0	0//0	0/0/		//	0/0/	Human glands, organs, tissues (for the treatment or prevention of diseases)
	0/0/0	0	0	0	0	0	0	0//0	0/0/		//	0/0/0	SCCPs (with artificial wax properties)
	0/0/0	0	0	0	0	0	0	0//0	0/0/		//	0/0/0	Other artificial waxes and formulated waxes
4.2	0/0/0	0	3.9		0	0	0	0/0/0	0/0/		//	0/0/0	SCCPs (no artificial wax properties)
4.2	0/0/0	0	3.9		0	0	0	0/0/0	0/0/		//	0/0/0	Other chemical products not listed (including hydrolysate or hydrolysate, DMC (any mixture of 2, 3 or 4 kinds of hexamethylcyclotrisiloxane, octamethylcyclotetrasiloxane, decamethylcyclopentasiloxane and dodecylcyclohexasiloxane))
	0/0/0	0	0	0	0	0	0	0//0	0/0/		//	0/0/0	Radio transmitting equipment of satellite earth station (including terminal earth station)
	0/0/0	0	0	0	0	0	0	0//0	0/0/		//	0/0/0	Other wireless communication equipment
13.5	0/0/10	22.5	22.5		0	0	0	0/0/0	0/0/		//	0/0/	Old other manned vehicles with drive motor only
13.5	0/0/10	22.5	22.5		0	0	0	0/0/0	0/0/		//	0/0/	Other manned vehicles with drive motor only

编者按

为方便海关等有关管理部门、从事进出口的企业、报关企业、预录入企业和其他单位及个人了解最新的进出口税则税率、进口环节代征税税率和海关监管条件，准确地将外贸单证中的英文商品名称翻译成规范的中文名称，及时办理报关手续，我们编写了2020版《中华人民共和国海关进出口税则》（中英文对照版）（以下简称《税则》）。

2020版《税则》内容根据国务院关税税则委员会2020年最新调整的进出口关税税率编制而成。最惠国税率方面，自2020年1月1日起，我国对859项商品（不含关税配额商品）实施进口暂定税率；自2020年7月1日起，取消7项信息技术产品进口暂定税率。对《中华人民共和国加入世界贸易组织关税减让表修正案》附表所列信息技术产品最惠国税率自2020年7月1日起实施第五步降税。协定税率和特惠税率方面，自2020年1月1日起，对我国与新西兰、秘鲁、哥斯达黎加、瑞士、冰岛、新加坡、澳大利亚、韩国、智利、格鲁吉亚、巴基斯坦的双边贸易协定以及亚太贸易协定的协定税率进一步降低。自2020年1月1日起，赤道几内亚停止享受零关税特惠待遇，等等。

我们对上述变化涉及的最新税率及商品编码等进行了认真修订。在此基础上，为了便于读者使用，我们还增加了检验检疫CIQ扩展编码及品名，收录了"进口反倾销、反补贴税清单"、《进出口商品规范申报目录》等。此外，还对增值税、退税税率，以及最新对美关税税率进行了修改和补充。

由于作者水平的限制和时间仓促，本书不足之处在所难免，恳请社会各界和广大读者批评指正。其中不准确和不全面之处敬请以发布的规范性文件为准！

Editor's Note

Aiming at assisting Customs and other governing bodies, enterprises participating import and export, Customs brokers, other trading partners and persons to query up-to-date tariff rates, other rates related to import and Custom supervision conditions, translate English commodity names in trade documents into standard Chinese names and go through declaring procedures to Customs, this Press compiles this Customs Import and Export Tariff of the People's Republic of China (Chinese-English Version , referred to as Chinese-English Tariff later)

2020 Tariff Regulations are compiled according to the latest import and export tariff rate adjusted by the Tariff Commission of the State Council in 2020. In terms of MFN tariff rate, since January 1, 2020, China has implemented provisional import tariff rate for 859 goods (excluding tariff quota goods); since July 1, 2020, it has cancelled the provisional import tariff rate for 7 information technology products. The fifth step of tax reduction shall be implemented from July 1, 2020 for the most favored nation tax rate of information technology products listed in the schedule of amendment to tariff schedule of the people's Republic of China's accession to the world trade organization. In terms of the agreement tax rate and preferential tax rate, since January 1, 2020, the agreement tax rate of China's bilateral trade agreements with New Zealand, Peru, Costa Rica, Switzerland, Iceland, Singapore, Australia, South Korea, Chile, Georgia, Pakistan and the Asia Pacific trade agreement has been further reduced. From January 1, 2020, Equatorial Guinea will stop enjoying zero tariff preferential treatment., etc.

We have carefully revised the latest tax rates and HS codes involved in these changes. On this basis, in order to facilitate the reader's use, we have also added the CIQ expansion code and the article Description , including the "import anti—dumping, countervailing duty list" and the " Index Catalogue on Essential Standard Data Required by China Customs for the Declaration of Import and Export Goods ", etc. In addition, VAT, rebate rates and the latest US to China tariff rates have been revised and supplemented.

Due to limits of time and the knowledge of the author, some weaknesses in this book should be inevitable. Here I am open to readers' corrections and comments with great sincerity. If there is any inaccuracy and inadequacy, the official documents prevail.

总目录

Table of Contents

1

中华人民共和国海关进口税则

（2020 年 1 月 1 日起实施）

Customs Import Tariff of the People's Republic of China

（Enforced from January 1，2020）

目　录

INDEX

第九类　木及木制品；木炭；软木及软木制品；稻草、秸秆、针茅或其他编结材料制品；篮筐及柳条编结品

第十类　木浆及其他纤维状纤维素浆；回收(废碎)纸或纸板；纸、纸板及其制品

第十一类　纺织原料及纺织制品

第十二类　鞋、帽、伞、杖、鞭及其零件；已加工的羽毛及其制品；人造花；人发制品

SECTION Ⅸ WOOD AND ARTICLES OF WOOD; WOOD CHARCOAL; CORK AND ARTICLES OF CORK; MANUFACTURES OF STRAW, OF ESPARTO OR OF OTHER PLAITING MATERIALS; BASKETWARE AND WICKERWORK

SECTION Ⅹ PULP OF WOOD OR OF OTHER FIBROUS CELLULOSIC MATERIAL; RECOVERED (WASTE AND SCRAP) PAPER OR PAPERBOARD; PAPER AND PAPERBOARD AND ARTICLES THEREOF

SECTION Ⅺ TEXTILES AND TEXTILE ARTICLES

SECTION Ⅻ FOOTWEAR, HEADGEAR, UMBRELLAS, SUN UMBRELLAS, WALKING-STICKS, SEAT-STICKS, WHIPS, RIDING-CROPS AND PARTS THEREOF; PREPARED FEATHERS AND ARTICLES MADETHEREWITH; ARTIFICIAL FLOWERS; ARTICLES OF HUMAN HAIR

归类总规则

货品在本税则目录上的归类,应遵循以下原则:

规则一 类、章及分章的标题,仅为查找方便而设;具有法律效力的归类,应按税目条文和有关类注或章注确定,如税目、类注或章注无其他规定,按以下规则确定。

规则二 (一)税目所列货品,应视为包括该项货品的不完整品或未制成品,只要在进口或出口时该项不完整品或未制成品具有完整品或制成品的基本特征;还应视为包括该项货品的完整品或制成品(或按本款可作为完整品或制成品归类的货品)在进口或出口时的未组装件或拆散件。

(二)税目中所列材料或物质,应视为包括该种材料或物质与其他材料或物质混合或组合的物品。税目所列某种材料或物质构成的货品,应视为包括全部或部分由该种材料或物质构成的货品。由一种以上材料或物质构成的货品,应按规则三归类。

规则三 当货品按规则二(二)或由于其他原因看起来可归入两个或两个以上税目时,应按以下规则归类:

(一)列名比较具体的税目,优先于列名一般的税目。但是,如果两个或两个以上税目都仅述及混合或组合货品所含的某部分材料或物质,或零售的成套货品中的某些货品,即使其中某个税目对该货品描述得更为全面、详细,这些货品在有关税目的列名应视为同样具体。

(二)混合物、不同材料构成或不同部件组成的组合物以及零售的成套货品,如果不能按照规则三(一)归类时,在本款可适用的条件下,应按构成货品基本特征的材料或部件归类。

(三)货品不能按照规则三(一)或(二)归类时,应按号列顺序归入其可归入的最末一个税目。

规则四 根据上述规则无法归类的货品,应归入与其最相类似的货品的税目。

规则五 除上述规则外,本规则适用于下列货品的归类:

(一)制成特殊形状,适用于盛装某个或某套物品并适合长期使用的照相机套、乐器盒、枪套、绘图仪器盒、项链盒及类似容器,如果与所装物品同时进口或出口,并通常与所装物品一同出售的,应与所装物品一并归类。但本款不适用于本身构成整个货品基本特征的容器。

(二)除规则五(一)规定的以外,与所装货品同时进口或出口的包装材料或包装容器,如果通常是用来包装这类货品的,应与所装货品一并归类。但明显可重复使用的包装材料和包装容器可不受本款限制。

规则六 货品在某一税目项下各子目的法定归类,应按子目条文或有关的子目注释以及以上各条规则来确定,但子目的比较只能在同一数级上进行。除本税则目录条文另有规定的以外,有关的类注、章注也适用于本规则。

第一类
活动物;动物产品

注释:

一、本类所称的各属种动物,除条文另有规定的以外,均包括其幼仔在内。

二、除条文另有规定的以外,本协调制度所称干的产品,均包括经脱水、蒸发或冷冻干燥的产品。

GENERAL RULES FOR THE INTERPRETATION OF THE HARMONIZED SYSTEM

Classification of goods in the Nomenclature shall be governed by the following Ruks：

1. The titles of Sections，Chapters and sub-Chapters are provided for easeof reference only；for legal purposes，classification shall be determined according to the terms of the headings and any relative Section or Chapter Notes andprovided such headings or Notes do not otherwise require，according to the following provisions.
2. (a) Any reference in a heading to an article shall be taken to include a reference to that article incomplete or unfinished，provided that，as presented，the incomplete or unfinished article has the essential character of the complete or finished article. It shall also be taken to include a reference to that article complete or finished (or falling to be classified as complete or finished by virtue of this Rule)，presented unassembled or disassembled.

   (b) Any reference in a heading to a material or substance shall be taken toinclude a reference to mixtures or combinations of that material or substance with other materials or substances. Any reference to goods of a given material orsubstance shall be taken to include a reference to goods consisting wholly or partly of such material or substance. The classification of goods consisting ofmore than one material or substance shall be according to the principles of Rule3.
3. When by application of Rule 2(b) or for any other reason，goods are，*prima facie*，classifiable under two or more headings，classification shall beeffected as follows：

   (a) The heading which provides the most specific description shall be preferred to headings providing a more general description. However，when two or moreheadings each refer to part only of the materials or substances contained in mixed or composite goods or to part only of the items in a set put up for retail sale，those headings are to be regarded as equally specific in relation to thosegoods，even if one of them gives a more complete or precise description of the goods.

   (b) Mixtures，composite goods consisting of different materials or made up of different components，and goods put up in sets for retail sale，which cannot be classified by reference to Rule 3(a)，shall be classified as they consisted of the material or component which gives them their essential character，insofar as this criterion is applicable.

   (c) When goods cannot be classified by reference to Rule 3(a) or Rule 3(b)，they shall be classified under the heading which occurs last in numerical order among those which equally merit consideration.
4. Goods which cannot be classified in accordance with the above Rules shall be classified under the heading appropriate to the goods to which they are most akin.
5. In addition to the foregoing Rules，the following Rules shall applyin respect of the goods referred to therein：

   (a) Camera cases，musical instrument cases，gun cases，drawing instrument cases，necklace cases and similar containers，specially shaped or fitted to contain a specific article or set of articles，suitable for long-term use and presented with the articles for which they are intended，shall be classified with sucharticles when of a kind normally sold therewith. This Rule does not，however，apply to containers which give the whole its essential character；

   (b) Subject to the provisions of Rule 5(a) above，packing materials and packing containers presented with the goods therein shall be classified with the goods if they are of a kind normally used for packing such goods. However，this provision is not binding when such packing materials or packing containers are clearly suitable for repetitive use.
6. For legal purposes，the classification of goods in the subheadings of aheading shall be determined according to the terms of those subheadings and anyrelated Subheading Notes and，*mutatis mutandis*，to the above Rules，on the understanding that only subheadings at the same level are comparable. For the purposes of this Rule the relative Section and Chapter Notes also apply，unless the context otherwise requires.

SECTION Ⅰ
LIVE ANIMALS；ANIMAL PRODUCTS

Notes：

1. Any reference in this Section to a particular genus or species of ananimal，except where the context otherwise requires，includes a reference to theyoung of that genus or species.
2. Except where the context otherwise requires，throughout the Nomenclature any reference to "dried" products also covers products which have beendehydrated，evaporated or freeze-dried.

第一章
活动物

注释：

本章包括所有活动物，但下列各项除外：

一、税目03.01、03.06、03.07或03.08的鱼、甲壳动物、软体动物及其他水生无脊椎动物；

二、税目30.02的培养微生物及其他产品；

三、税目95.08的动物。

税则号列		货品名称〔CIQ扩展编码及品名－T2表示见附表2〕	最惠(%)	暂定税率	普通	增值/消费	出口退税	计量单位	监管条件	检验检疫	特殊证件对美关税
01.01		马、驴、骡：									
		-马：									
0101.2100		--改良种用									
0101.2100	10	改良种用的濒危野马〔999〕	0		0	9/	0	千克/头	ABEF	PQ	/
0101.2100	90	其他改良种用马〔999〕	0		0	9/	6	千克/头	AB	PQ	/
0101.2900		--其他									
0101.2900	10	非改良种用濒危野马〔999〕	10		30	9/	0	千克/头	ABEF	PQ	/45
0101.2900	90	非改良种用其他马〔101屠宰马，102赛马，103其他用途马〕	10		30	9/	6	千克/头	AB	PQ	/45
		-驴：									
0101.3010		---改良种用									
0101.3010	10	改良种用的濒危野驴〔999〕	0		0	9/	0	千克/头	ABEF	PQ	/
0101.3010	90	改良种用的其他驴〔999〕	0		0	9/	6	千克/头	AB	PQ	/
0101.3090		---其他									
0101.3090	10	非改良种用濒危野驴〔999〕	10		30	9/	0	千克/头	ABEF	PQ	/15
0101.3090	90	非改良种用其他驴〔999〕	10		30	9/	6	千克/头	AB	PQ	/15
0101.9000		-其他〔999〕	10		30	9/	6	千克/头	AB	PQ	/15
01.02		牛：									
		-家牛：									
0102.2100		--改良种用〔101种牛，102屠宰牛，103其他用途牛〕	0		0	9/	6	千克/头	AB	PQ	/
0102.2900		--其他〔101种牛，102屠宰牛，103其他用途牛〕	10		30	9/	6	千克/头	4xAB	PQ	/15
		-水牛：									
0102.3100		--改良种用									
0102.3100	10	改良种用濒危水牛〔999〕	0		0	9/	0	千克/头	ABEF	PQ	/
0102.3100	90	改良种用其他水牛〔999〕	0		0	9/	6	千克/头	AB	PQ	/
0102.3900		--其他									
0102.3900	10	非改良种用濒危水牛〔999〕	10		30	9/	0	千克/头	4ABEFx	PQ	/15
0102.3900	90	非改良种用其他水牛〔999〕	10		30	9/	6	千克/头	4ABx	PQ	/15
		-其他：									
0102.9010		---改良种用									
0102.9010	10	改良种用濒危野牛〔999〕	0		0	9/	0	千克/头	ABEF	PQ	/
0102.9010	90	其他改良种用牛〔101种牛，102屠宰牛，103其他用途牛，104水牛，105牦牛〕	0		0	9/	6	千克/头	AB	PQ	/
0102.9090		---其他									
0102.9090	10	非改良种用濒危野牛〔999〕	10		30	9/	0	千克/头	4ABEFx	PQ	/15
0102.9090	90	非改良种用其他牛〔101种牛，102屠宰牛，103其他用途牛，104水牛，105牦牛〕	10		30	9/	6	千克/头	4ABx	PQ	/15
01.03		猪：									
0103.1000		-改良种用									
0103.1000	10	改良种用的鹿豚、姬猪〔999〕	0		0	9/	6	千克/头	AFEB	PQ	/
0103.1000	90	其他改良种用的猪〔999〕	0		0	9/	6	千克/头	AB	PQ	/
		-其他：									
		--重量在50千克以下：									
0103.9110		---重量在10千克以下									
0103.9110	10	重量在10千克以下的其他野猪(改良种用的除外)〔999〕	10		50	9/	6	千克/头	4xABFE	PRQ	/15
0103.9110	90	重量在10千克以下的其他猪(改良种用的除外)〔101屠宰猪，102其他用途猪〕	10		50	9/	6	千克/头	4xAB	PRQ	/15
0103.9120		---重量在10千克及以上，但在50千克以下									
0103.9120	10	10千克≤重量<50千克的其他野猪(改良种用的除外)〔999〕	10		50	9/	6	千克/头	4xABFE	PRQ	/15
0103.9120	90	10千克≤重量<50千克的其他猪(改良种用的除外)〔102其他用途猪，101屠宰猪〕	10		50	9/	6	千克/头	4xAB	PRQ	/15
0103.9200		--重量在50千克及以上									
0103.9200	10	重量在50千克及以上的其他野猪(改良种用的除外)〔999〕	10		50	9/	6	千克/头	4xABFE	PRQ	/15

Chapter 1
Live animals

Notes:

This Chapter covers all live animals except:

1. Fish and crustaceans, molluscs and other aquatic invertebrates, of heading No. 03.01,03.06,03.07 or 03.08
2. Cultures of micro-organisms and other products of heading No. 30.02;
3. Animals of heading No. 95.08.

协定税率 %										特惠税率 %			Article Description
亚太5国	东/冰/格	巴基斯坦	韩国	瑞士	哥达	秘鲁	澳大利亚	新西/坡/智	港/澳/台	亚太2国	老/柬/缅	36/3/1	
													Live horses, asses, mules and hinnies:
													-Horses:
													--Pure-bred breeding
												0/0/0	Endangered wild horses, pure-bred breeding
												0/0/0	Other horses, pure-bred breeding
													--Other
	0/0/0	4.5	4	0	0	0	0	0//0	0/0/			0/0/0	Endangered wild horses, not for breeding
	0/0/0	4.5	4	0	0	0	0	0//0	0/0/			0/0/0	Other horses, not for breeding
													-Asses:
													---Pure-bred breeding
												0/0/0	Endangered wild asses, pure-bred breeding
												0/0/0	Other asses, pure-bred breeding
													---Other
	0/0/0	4.5	4	0	0	0	0	0//0	0/0/			0/0/0	Endangered wild asses, not for breeding
	0/0/0	4.5	4	0	0	0	0	0//0	0/0/			0/0/0	Other asses, not for breeding
	0/0/0	4.5	4	0	0	0	0	0//0	0/0/			0/0/0	-Other
													Live bovine animals:
													-Cattle:
												0/0/0	--Pure-bred breeding
	0/0/0	4.5	4	0	0	0	0	0//0	0/0/		0/0/0	0/0/0	--Other
													-Buffalo:
													--Pure-bred breeding
												0/0/0	Endangered buffalo, pure-bred breeding
												0/0/0	Other buffalo, prue-bred breeding
													--Other
	0/0/0	4.5	4	0	0	0	0	0//0	0/0/		0/0/0	0/0/0	Endangered buffalo, not for breeding
	0/0/0	4.5	4	0	0	0	0	0//0	0/0/		0/0/0	0/0/0	Other buffalo, not for breeding
													-Other:
													---Pure-bred breeding
												0/0/0	Endangered wild bovine, pure-bred breeding
												0/0/0	Other bovine pure-bred breeding
													---Other
	0/0/0	4.5	4	0	0	0	0	0//0	0/0/		0/0/0	0/0/0	Endangered wild bovine, not for breeding
	0/0/0	4.5	4	0	0	0	0	0//0	0/0/		0/0/0	0/0/0	Other bovine not for breeding
													Live swine:
													-Pure-bred breeding
												0/0/0	Pig-deer (*Babyrousa*)、pygmy pig (*Porcula*), pure-bred breeding
												0/0/0	Other swine, pure-bred breeding
													-Other:
													--Weighing less than 50kg:
													---Weighing less than 10kg
	0/0/0	4.5	4	0	0	0	0	0//0	0/0/		/0/0	0/0/0	Other wild swine, weighing<10kg (other than pure-bred breeding)
	0/0/0	4.5	4	0	0	0	0	0//0	0/0/		/0/0	0/0/0	Other swine, weighing<10kg (other than pure-bred breeding)
													---Weighing 10kg or more, but less than 50kg
	0/0/0	4.5	4	0	0	0	0	0//0	0/0/		/0/0	0/0/0	Other wild swine, 10kg≤weighing<50kg (other than pure-bred breeding)
	0/0/0	4.5	4	0	0	0	0	0//0	0/0/		/0/0	0/0/0	Other swine, 10kg≤weighing<50kg (other than pure-bred breeding)
													--Weighing 50kg or more
	0/0/0	4.5	4	0	0	0	0	0//0	0/0/		0/0/0	0/0/0	Other wild swine, weighing≥50kg (other than pure-bred breeding)

税则号列	货品名称〔CIQ扩展编码及品名—T2表示见附表2〕	最惠(%)	暂定税率	普通	增值/消费	出口退税	计量单位	监管条件	检验检疫	特殊证件对美关税
0103.9200 90	重量在50千克及以上的其他猪(改良种用的除外)〔101屠宰猪,102其他用途猪〕	10		50	9/	6	千克/头	4xAB	PRQ	/15
01.04	绵羊、山羊:									
	-绵羊:									
0104.1010	---改良种用〔999〕	0		0	9/	6	千克/头	AB	PQ	/
0104.1090	---其他〔101屠宰绵羊,102其他用途绵羊〕	10		50	9/	6	千克/头	AB	PRQ	/15
	-山羊:									
0104.2010	---改良种用〔101种山羊,102种野山羊〕	0		0	9/	6	千克/头	AB	PQ	/
0104.2090	---其他〔101屠宰山羊,102其他用途山羊,103屠宰野山羊,104其他用途野山羊〕	10		50	9/	6	千克/头	AB	PQ	/15
01.05	家禽,即鸡、鸭、鹅、火鸡及珍珠鸡:									
	-重量不超过185克:									
	--鸡:									
0105.1110	---改良种用〔101肉种鸡,102蛋种鸡〕	0		0	9/	6	千克/只	AB	PQ	/
0105.1190	---其他〔101屠宰鸡,102其他用途鸡〕	10		50	9/	6	千克/只	AB	PRQ	/15
	--火鸡:									
0105.1210	---改良种用〔999〕	0		0	9/	6	千克/只	AB	PQ	/
0105.1290	---其他〔999〕	10		50	9/	6	千克/只	AB	PRQ	/15
	--鸭:									
0105.1310	---改良种用〔999〕	0		0	9/	6	千克/只	AB	PQ	/
0105.1390	---其他〔999〕	10		50	9/	6	千克/只	AB	PRQ	/15
	--鹅:									
0105.1410	---改良种用〔999〕	0		0	9/	6	千克/只	AB	PQ	/
0105.1490	---其他〔999〕	10		50	9/	6	千克/只	AB	PRQ	/15
	--珍珠鸡:									
0105.1510	---改良种用〔999〕	0		0	9/	6	千克/只	AB	PQ	/
0105.1590	---其他〔999〕	10		50	9/	6	千克/只	AB	PRQ	/15
	-其他:									
	--鸡:									
0105.9410	---改良种用〔101肉种鸡,102蛋种鸡〕	0		0	9/	6	千克/只	4xAB	PQ	/
0105.9490	---其他〔101屠宰鸡,102其他用途鸡〕	10		50	9/	6	千克/只	4xAB	PRQ	/15
	--其他:									
0105.9910	---改良种用〔101珍珠鸡,102其他饲养鸡形目禽鸟,103鹅,104鸭,105其他饲养雁形目禽鸟,106鸽,107其他饲养禽鸟〕	0		0	9/	6	千克/只	AB	PQ	/
	---其他:									
0105.9991	----鸭〔999〕	10		50	9/	6	千克/只	AB	PQ	/15
0105.9992	----鹅〔999〕	10		50	9/	6	千克/只	AB	PQ	/15
0105.9993	----珍珠鸡〔999〕	10		50	9/	6	千克/只	4xAB	PQ	/15
0105.9994	----火鸡〔999〕	10		50	9/	6	千克/只	AB	PQ	/15
01.06	其他活动物:									
	-哺乳动物:									
	--灵长目:									
0106.1110	---改良种用〔101猴,102猿,103猩猩,104狒狒,105山魈,106其他野生灵长动物〕	0		0	9/	6	千克/只	AFEB	PQ	/
0106.1190	---其他〔101猴,102猿,103猩猩,104狒狒,105山魈,106其他野生灵长动物〕	10		50	9/	6	千克/只	AFEB	PQ	/15
	--鲸、海豚及鼠海豚(鲸目哺乳动物);海牛及儒艮(海牛目哺乳动物);海豹、海狮及海象(鳍足亚目哺乳动物):									
	---鲸、海豚及鼠海豚(鲸目哺乳动物);海牛及儒艮(海牛目哺乳动物):									
0106.1211	----改良种用〔101海豚,102鲸,103海牛,104其他野生哺乳动物〕	10	0	50	9/	6	千克/只	ABEF	PQ	/
0106.1219	----其他〔101海豚,102鲸,103海牛,104其他野生哺乳动物〕	10		50	9/	6	千克/只	ABEF	PQ	/15
	---海豹、海狮及海象(鳍足亚目哺乳动物):									
0106.1221	----改良种用〔101海豹,102海狮,103海象,104其他野生哺乳动物〕	0		0	9/	6	千克/只	ABEF	PQ	/
0106.1229	----其他〔102海狮,101海豹,103海象,104其他野生哺乳动物〕	10		50	9/	6	千克/只	ABEF	PQ	/15
	--骆驼及其他骆驼科动物:									
0106.1310	---改良种用									
0106.1310 10	改良种用濒危骆驼及其他濒危骆驼科动物(包括人工驯养、繁殖的)〔101骆驼,102其他野生偶蹄动物〕	0		0	9/	0	千克/只	ABFE	PQ	/
0106.1310 90	其他改良种用骆驼及其他骆驼科动物〔101骆驼,102其他饲养偶蹄动物〕	0		0	9/	6	千克/只	AB	PQ	/
0106.1390	---其他									

协定税率 %										特惠税率 %			
亚太5国	东/冰/格	巴基斯坦	韩国	瑞士	哥达	秘鲁	澳大利亚	新西/坡/智	港/澳/台	亚太2国	老/柬/缅	36/3/1	Article Description
	0/0/0	4.5	4	0	0	0	0	0//0	0/0/		0/0/0	0/0/0	Other swine, weighing≥50kg (other than pure-bred breeding)
													Live sheep and goats:
													-Sheep:
												0/0/0	---Pure-bred breeding
	0/0/0	5	4	0	0	0	0	0//0	0/0/			0/0/0	---Other
													-Goats:
												0/0/0	---Pure-bred breeding
	0/0/0	5	4	0	0	0	0	0//0	0/0/			0/0/0	---Other
													Live poultry, that is to say, fowls of the species *Gallus domesticus*, ducks, geese, turkeys and guinea fowls:
													-Weighing not more than 185g:
													--Fowls of the species *Gallus domesticus*:
												0/0/0	---Pure-bred breeding
	0/0/0	4.5	4	0	0	0	0	0//0	0/0/		0//0	0/0/0	---Other
													–Turkeys:
												0/0/0	---Pure-bred breeding
	0/0/0	4.5	4	0	0	0	0	0//0	0/0/			0/0/0	---Other
													--Ducks:
												0/0/0	---Pure-bred breeding
	0/0/0	4.5	4	0	0	0	0	0//0	0/0/		0//	0/0/0	---Other
													--Geese:
												0/0/0	---Pure-bred breeding
	0/0/0	4.5	4	0	0	0	0	0//0	0/0/		0//	0/0/0	---Other
													--Guinea fowls:
												0/0/0	---Pure-bred breeding
	0/0/0	4.5	4	0	0	0	0	0//0	0/0/		0//	0/0/0	---Other
													-Other:
													--Fowls of the species *Gallus domesticus*:
												0/0/0	---Pure-bred breeding
	0/0/0	4.5	4	0	0	0	0	0//0	0/0/			0/0/0	---Other
													--Other:
												0/0/0	---Pure-bred breeding
													---Other:
	0/0/0	4.5	4	0	0	0	0	0//0	0/0/			0/0/0	----Ducks
	0/0/0	4.5	4	0	0	0	0	0//0	0/0/			0/0/0	----Geese
	0/0/0	4.5	4	0	0	0	0	0//0	0/0/			0/0/0	----Guinea fowls
	0/0/0	4.5	4	0	0	0	0	0//0	0/0/			0/0/0	----Turkeys
													Other live animals:
													-Mammals:
													--Primates:
												0/0/0	---pure-bred breeding
	0/0/0	4.5	4	0	0	0	0	0//0	0/0/			0/0/0	---Other
													--Whales, dolphins and porpoises(mammals of the order Cetacea); manatees and dugongs(mammals of the order Sirenia); seal, sea lion and walrus(Pinnipedia mammal):
													---Whales, dolphins and porpoises(mammals of the order Cetacea); manatees and dugongs(mammals of the order Sirenia):
	0/0/0	4.5	0	0	0	0	0	0//0	0/0/			0/0/0	----Pure-bred breeding
	0/0/0	4.5	4	0	0	0	0	0//0	0/0/			0/0/0	----Other
													---Seal、sea lion and walrus(mammals of the suborder Pinnipedia):
												0/0/0	----Pure-bred breeding
	0/0/0	4.5	4	0	0	0	0	0//0	0/0/			0/0/0	----Other
													--Camel and other camelids(camelidae):
													---Pure-bred breeding
												0/0/0	Endangered camel and other endangered camel familia animals, pure-bred breeding(including domesticated and artificially bred)
												0/0/0	Other camel and other camel familia animals, pure-bred brdding
													---Other

税则号列	货品名称〔CIQ扩展编码及品名－T2表示见附表2〕	最惠(%)	暂定税率	普通	增值/消费	出口退税	计量单位	监管条件	检验检疫	特殊证件对美关税
0106.1390 10	其他濒危骆驼及其他濒危骆驼科动物（包括人工驯养、繁殖的）〔101骆驼，102其他饲养偶蹄动物〕	10		50	9/	0	千克/只	AFEB	PRQ	/15
0106.1390 90	其他骆驼及其他骆驼科动物〔101骆驼，102其他饲养偶蹄动物〕	10		50	9/	6	千克/只	AB	PRQ	/15
	--家兔及野兔：									
0106.1410	---改良种用									
0106.1410 10	改良种用濒危野兔（包括人工驯养、繁殖的）〔999〕	0		0	9/	0	千克/只	ABEF	PQ	/
0106.1410 90	改良种用家兔及其他改良种用野兔〔999〕	0		0	9/	6	千克/只	AB	PQ	/
0106.1490	---其他									
0106.1490 10	其他濒危野兔（包括人工驯养、繁殖的）〔999〕	10		50	9/	0	千克/只	ABEF	PRQ	/15
0106.1490 90	其他家兔及野兔〔999〕	10		50	9/	6	千克/只	AB	PRQ	/15
	--其他：									
0106.1910	---改良种用									
0106.1910 10	其他改良种用濒危哺乳动物（包括人工驯养、繁殖的）[T2]	0		0	9/	0	千克/只	ABFE	PQ	/
0106.1910 90	其他改良种用哺乳动物[T2]	0		0	9/	6	千克/只	AB	PQ	/
0106.1990	---其他									
0106.1990 10	其他濒危哺乳动物（包括人工驯养、繁殖的）[T2]	10		50	9/	0	千克/只	AFEB	PRQ	/25
0106.1990 90	其他哺乳动物[T2]	10		50	9/	6	千克/只	AB	PRQ	/25
	-爬行动物（包括蛇及龟鳖）：									
	---改良种用：									
0106.2011	----鳄鱼苗〔999〕	0		0	9/	6	千克/只	AFEB	PQ	/
0106.2019	----其他[T2]	0		0	9/	6	千克/只	FEAB	PQ	/
0106.2020	---食用									
0106.2020 10	食用蛇（包括人工驯养、繁殖的）〔999〕	10		50	9/	6	千克/只	AFEB	PRQ	/15
0106.2020 21	食用濒危龟鳖（包括人工驯养、繁殖的）〔101乌龟，102草龟，103绿毛龟，104鳖（甲鱼、团鱼）、团鱼，105玳瑁，106鳄龟，107其他龟鳖〕	10		50	9/	0	千克/只	ABFE	PRQ	/15
0106.2020 29	其他食用龟鳖（包括人工驯养、繁殖的）〔101乌龟，102草龟，103绿毛龟，104鳖（甲鱼、团鱼）、团鱼，105玳瑁，106鳄龟，107其他龟鳖〕	10		50	9/	6	千克/只	AB	PRQ	/15
0106.2020 91	其他食用濒危爬行动物（包括人工驯养、繁殖的）〔999〕	10		50	9/	0	千克/只	FEAB	PRQ	/15
0106.2020 99	其他食用爬行动物（包括人工驯养、繁殖的）〔999〕	10		50	9/	6	千克/只	AB	PRQ	/15
0106.2090	---其他									
0106.2090 10	其他濒危爬行动物（包括人工驯养、繁殖的）〔999〕	10		50	9/	0	千克/只	FEAB	PQ	/25
0106.2090 90	其他爬行动物（包括人工驯养、繁殖的）[T2]	10		50	9/	6	千克/只	AB	PQ	/25
	-鸟：									
	--猛禽：									
0106.3110	---改良种用〔101鹰，102其他野生禽鸟〕	0		0	9/	6	千克/只	AFEB	PQ	/
0106.3190	---其他〔101鹰，102其他野生禽鸟〕	10		50	9/	6	千克/只	ABFE	PQ	/15
	--鹦形目（包括普通鹦鹉、长尾鹦鹉、金刚鹦鹉及美冠鹦鹉）：									
0106.3210	---改良种用[999]	0		0	9/	6	千克/只	ABFE	PQ	/
0106.3290	---其他[999]	10		50	9/	6	千克/只	ABFE	PQ	/15
	--鸵鸟；鸸鹋：									
0106.3310	---改良种用									
0106.3310 10	改良种用濒危鸵鸟（包括人工驯养、繁殖的）〔999〕	0		0	9/	0	千克/只	ABFE	PQ	/
0106.3310 90	其他改良种用鸵鸟和改良种用鸸鹋〔101鸵鸟，102鸸鹋〕	0		0	9/	6	千克/只	AB	PQ	/
0106.3390	---其他									
0106.3390 10	其他濒危鸵鸟（包括人工驯养、繁殖的）〔999〕	10		50	9/	0	千克/只	ABFE	PRQ	/15
0106.3390 90	其他鸵鸟、鸸鹋〔101鸵鸟，102鸸鹋〕	10		50	9/	6	千克/只	AB	PRQ	/15
	--其他：									
0106.3910	---改良种用									
0106.3910 10	其他改良种用濒危鸟（包括人工驯养、繁殖的）[T2]	0		0	9/	0	千克/只	ABFE	PQ	/
0106.3910 90	其他改良种用的鸟〔999〕	0		0	9/	6	千克/只	AB	PQ	/
	---食用：									
0106.3921	----乳鸽〔999〕	10		50	9/	6	千克/只	AB	PRQ	/15
0106.3923	----野鸭〔999〕	10		50	9/	6	千克/只	FEAB	PRQ	/15

协定税率 %										特惠税率 %			Article Description
亚太5国	东/冰/格	巴基斯坦	韩国	瑞士	哥达	秘鲁	澳大利亚	新西/坡/智	港/澳/台	亚太2国	老/柬/缅	36/3/1	
	0/0/0	4.5	4	0	0	0	0	0//0	0/0/			0/0/0	Endangered camel and other endangered camel familia animals(including domesticated and artificially bred)
	0/0/0	4.5	4	0	0	0	0	0//0	0/0/			0/0/0	Other camel and other camel familia animals
													--Rabbits and hares:
													---Pure-bred breeding
												0/0/0	Endangered hares,pure-bred breeding(including donesticatd and artificiauy bred)
												0/0/0	Rabbits and Other hares,pure-bred breeding
													---Other
	0/0/0	4.5	4	0	0	0	0	0//0	0/0/			0/0/0	Other endangered hares(including domes ticatedandan tificiauy bred)
	0/0/0	4.5	4	0	0	0	0	0//0	0/0/			0/0/0	Other rabbits and hares
													--Other:
													---Pure-bred breeding
												0/0/0	Other endangered mammals, pure-bred breeding(including domesticated and artificially bred)
												0/0/0	Other mammals, pure-bred breeding
													---Other
	0/0/0	4.5	4	0	0	0	0	0//0	0/0/			0/0/0	Other endangered mammals, including domesticated and artificially bred
	0/0/0	4.5	4	0	0	0	0	0//0	0/0/			0/0/0	Other mammals
													-Reptiles(including snakes and turtles):
													---Pure-bred breeding:
												0/0/0	----Crocodiles for cultivation
												0/0/0	----Other
													---For human consumption
	0/0/0	4.5	4	0	0	0	0	0//0	0/0/		//0	0/0/0	Snakes, for human consumption(including domesticated and artificially bred)
	0/0/0	4.5	4	0	0	0	0	0//0	0/0/		//0	0/0/0	Endangered turtle (including domestication and artificial breeding)
	0/0/0	4.5	4	0	0	0	0	0//0	0/0/		//0	0/0/0	Other eating a turtle (including domestication and artificial breeding)
	0/0/0	4.5	4	0	0	0	0	0//0	0/0/		//0	0/0/0	Other endangered reptiles, for human consumption (including domesticated and artificially propagated)
	0/0/0	4.5	4	0	0	0	0	0//0	0/0/		//0	0/0/0	Other reptiles, for human consumption (including domesticated and artificially propagated)
													---Other
	0/0/0	4.5	4	0	0	0	0	0//0	0/0/			0/0/0	Other endangered reptiles (including domesticated and artificially propagated)
	0/0/0	4.5	4	0	0	0	0	0//0	0/0/			0/0/0	Other reptiles (including domesticated and artificially propagated)
													-Birds:
													--Birds of prey:
												0/0/0	---Pure-bred breeding
	0/0/0	4.5	4	0	0	0	0	0//0	0/0/			0/0/0	---Other
													--Psittaciformes(including parrots, parakeets, macaws and cockatoos):
												0/0/0	---Pure-bred breeding
	0/0/0	4.5	4	0	0	0	0	0//0	0/0/			0/0/0	---Other
													--Ostriches;emus:
													---Pure-bred breeding
												0/0/0	Endangered ostriches, pure-bred breeding (including domesticated and artificially bred)
												0/0/0	Other ostriches and emus,pure-bred breeding
													---Other
	0/0/0	4.5	4	0	0	0	0	0//0	0/0/			0/0/0	Other endangered ostriches(including domesticated and artificially bred)
	0/0/0	4.5	4	0	0	0	0	0//0	0/0/			0/0/0	Other ostriches and emus
													--Other:
													---Pure-bred breeding
												0/0/0	Other endangered birds, pure-bred breeding(including domesticated and artificially bred)
												0/0/0	Other birds, pure-bred breeding
													---For human consumption:
	0/0/0	4.5	4	0	0	0	0	0//0	0/0/		//0	0/0/0	----Squabs
	0/0/0	4.5	4	0	0	0	0	0//0	0/0/		//0	0/0/0	----Teals

税则号列	货品名称〔CIQ 扩展编码及品名－T2 表示见附表 2〕	最惠(%)	暂定税率	普通	增值/消费	出口退税	计量单位	监管条件	检验检疫	特殊证件对美关税
0106.3929	----其他									
0106.3929 10	其他食用濒危鸟(包括人工驯养、繁殖的)〔101 鹌鹑,102 鹧鸪,103 雉(山鸡),104 乌骨鸡,105 其他野生鸡形目禽鸟〕	10		50	9/	0	千克/只	ABFE	PRQ	/15
0106.3929 90	其他食用鸟〔101 其他饲养鸡形目禽鸟,102 其他饲养雁形目禽鸟,103 其他饲养禽鸟〕	10		50	9/	6	千克/只	AB	PRQ	/15
0106.3990	---其他									
0106.3990 10	其他濒危鸟(包括人工驯养、繁殖的)[T2]	10		50	9/	0	千克/只	ABFE	PRQ	/15
0106.3990 90	其他鸟〔101 其他饲养鸡形目禽鸟,102 其他饲养雁形目禽鸟,103 其他饲养禽鸟〕	10		50	9/	6	千克/只	AB	PRQ	/15
	-昆虫:									
	--蜂:									
0106.4110	---改良种用〔999〕	0		0	9/	6	千克/只	AB	PQ	/
0106.4190	---其他									
0106.4190 01	赤眼蜂〔999〕	10		50	9/	6	千克/只	ABS	PQ	/15
0106.4190 90	其他蜂〔101 蜜蜂,102 其他动物〕	10		50	9/	6	千克/只	AB	PQ	/15
	--其他:									
0106.4910	---改良种用									
0106.4910 10	其他改良种用濒危昆虫(包括人工驯养、繁殖的)〔101 有害昆虫,102 媒介昆虫,103 害虫〕	0		0	9/	0	千克/只	ABFE	PQ	/
0106.4910 90	其他改良种用非濒危昆虫〔101 有害昆虫,102 媒介昆虫,103 害虫〕	0		0	9/	6	千克/只	AB	PQ	/
0106.4990	---其他									
0106.4990 01	捕食螨〔999〕	10		50	9/	6	千克/只	ABS	PQ	/25
0106.4990 10	其他濒危昆虫(包括人工驯养、繁殖的)〔999〕	10		50	9/	0	千克/只	ABFE	PQ	/25
0106.4990 90	其他非濒危昆虫〔101 有害昆虫,102 媒介昆虫,103 害虫〕	10		50	9/	6	千克/只	AB	PQ	/25
	-其他:									
	---改良种用:									
0106.9011	----蛙苗									
0106.9011 10	改良种用濒危蛙苗〔101 牛蛙苗,102 青蛙苗,103 金线蛙苗,104 棘胸蛙苗,105 其他蛙苗〕	0		0	9/	0	千克/只	ABFE	PQ	/
0106.9011 90	其他改良种用蛙苗〔101 牛蛙苗,102 青蛙苗,103 金线蛙苗,104 棘胸蛙苗,105 其他蛙苗〕	0		0	9/	6	千克/只	AB	PQ	/
0106.9019	----其他									
0106.9019 10	其他改良种用濒危动物(包括人工驯养、繁殖的)[T2]	0		0	9/	0	千克/只	ABFE	PQ	/
0106.9019 90	其他改良种用动物[T2]	0		0	9/	6	千克/只	AB	PQ	/
0106.9090	---其他									
0106.9090 10	其他濒危动物(包括人工驯养、繁殖的)[T2]	10		50	9/	0	千克/只	ABFE	PQ	/40
0106.9090 90	其他动物[T2]	10		50	9/	6	千克/只	AB	PQ	/40

协定税率 %										特惠税率 %			Article Description
亚太5国	东/冰/格	巴基斯坦	韩国	瑞士	哥达	秘鲁	澳大利亚	新西/坡/智	港/澳/台	亚太2国	老/柬/缅	36/3/1	
													----Other
	0/0/0	4.5	4	0	0	0	0	0//0	0/0/		//0	0/0/0	Other endangered birds, for human consumption(including domesticated and artificially bred)
	0/0/0	4.5	4	0	0	0	0	0//0	0/0/		//0	0/0/0	Other birds for human consumption
													---Other
	0/0/0	4.5	4	0	0	0	0	0//0	0/0/			0/0/0	Other endangered bird, including domesticated and artificially bred
	0/0/0	4.5	4	0	0	0	0	0//0	0/0/			0/0/0	Other birds
													-Insects:
													--Bees:
												0/0/0	---Pure-bred breeding
													---Other
9	0/0/0	4.5	0	0	0	0	0	0//0	0/0/			0/0/0	Trichogramma
9	0/0/0	4.5	0	0	0	0	0	0//0	0/0/			0/0/0	Other bees
													--Other:
													---Pure-bred breeding
												0/0/0	Other endangered insects, pure-bred breeding(including domesticated and artificially bred)
												0/0/0	Other insects, pure-bred breeding
													---Other
9	0/0/0	4.5	0	0	0	0	0	0//0	0/0/			0/0/0	Predatory mites
9	0/0/0	4.5	0	0	0	0	0	0//0	0/0/			0/0/0	Other endangered insects (including domesticated and artificially bred)
9	0/0/0	4.5	0	0	0	0	0	0//0	0/0/			0/0/0	Other insects
													-Other:
													---Pure-bred breeding:
													----Tadpole and young frogs
												0/0/0	Endangered tadpole and young frogs, pure-bred breeding
												0/0/0	Other tadpole and young frogs, pure-bred breeding
													----Other
												0/0/0	Other endangered animals, pure-bred breeding(including domesticated and artificially bred)
												0/0/0	Other animals, pure-bred breeding
													---Other
9	0/0/0	4.5	4	0	0	0	0	0//0	0/0/			0/0/0	Other endangered animals, purebred breeding(including domesticated and artificially bred)
9	0/0/0	4.5	4	0	0	0	0	0//0	0/0/			0/0/0	Other animals

第二章
肉及食用杂碎

注释：

本章不包括：

一、税目 02.01 至 02.08 或 02.10 的不适合供人食用的产品；

二、动物的肠、膀胱、胃(税目 05.04)或动物血(税目 05.11、30.02)；

三、税目 02.09 所列产品以外的动物脂肪(第十五章)。

税则号列		货品名称〔CIQ 扩展编码及品名－T2 表示见附表 2〕	最惠(%)	暂定税率	普通	增值/消费	出口退税	计量单位	监管条件	检验检疫	特殊证件对美关税
02.01		**鲜、冷牛肉：**									
0201.1000		-整头及半头									
0201.1000	10	整头及半头鲜或冷藏的野牛肉〔101 鲜的，102 冷藏〕	20		70	9/	6	千克	4xABFE	PRQS	/45
0201.1000	90	其他整头及半头鲜或冷藏的牛肉〔101 鲜的，102 冷藏，103 冰鲜(冷藏 30 月龄以下)〕	20		70	9/	6	千克	4xAB	PRQS	/45
0201.2000		-带骨肉									
0201.2000	10	鲜或冷藏的带骨野牛肉〔101 鲜的，102 冷藏〕	12		70	9/	6	千克	47ABEFx	PRQ	/47
0201.2000	90	其他鲜或冷藏的带骨牛肉〔101 鲜的，102 冷藏，103 冰鲜(冷藏 30 月龄以下)〕	12		70	9/	6	千克	47xAB	PRQ	/47
0201.3000		-去骨肉									
0201.3000	10	鲜或冷藏的去骨野牛肉〔101 鲜的，102 冷藏〕	12		70	9/	6	千克	47xABFE	PRQS	/47
0201.3000	90	其他鲜或冷藏的去骨牛肉〔101 鲜的，102 冷藏，103 鲜的(冷藏 12 月龄以下)，104 鲜的(冷藏 30 月龄以下)，105 鲜的(冷藏牛绞肉 30 月龄以下)〕	12		70	9/	9	千克	47xAB	PRQS	/47
02.02		**冻牛肉：**									
0202.1000		-整头及半头									
0202.1000	10	冻藏的整头及半头野牛肉〔999〕	25		70	9/	6	千克	4xABFE	PRQS	/50
0202.1000	90	其他冻藏的整头及半头牛肉〔101 冰鲜(12 月龄以下)，102 冰鲜(不含脊柱和头骨)，103 冰鲜(不含脊柱和头骨，30 月龄以下)，104 冻牛肉〕	25		70	9/	6	千克	4xAB	PRQS	/50
0202.2000		-带骨肉									
0202.2000	10	冻藏的带骨野牛肉〔999〕	12		70	9/	6	千克	47xABFE	PRQS	/47
0202.2000	90	其他冻藏的带骨牛肉〔101 冰鲜(12 月龄以下)，102 冰鲜(不含脊柱和头骨)，103 冰鲜(不含脊柱和头骨，30 月龄以下)，104 冻牛肉〕	12		70	9/	6	千克	47xAB	PRQS	/47
0202.3000		-去骨肉									
0202.3000	10	冻藏的去骨野牛肉〔999〕	12		70	9/	6	千克	47xABFE	PRQS	/47
0202.3000	90	其他冻藏的去骨牛肉〔101 冰鲜(12 月龄以下)，102 冰鲜(不含脊柱和头骨)，103 冰鲜(不含脊柱和头骨，30 月龄以下)，104 冻牛肉〕	12		70	9/	9	千克	47xAB	PRQS	/47
02.03		**鲜、冷、冻猪肉：**									
		-鲜或冷的：									
		--整头及半头：									
0203.1110		---乳猪									
0203.1110	10	鲜或冷藏的整头及半头野乳猪肉〔101 鲜的，102 冷藏〕	20		70	9/	6	千克	4ABEFx	PRQS	/45
0203.1110	90	其他鲜或冷藏的整头及半头乳猪肉〔101 鲜的，102 冷藏〕	20		70	9/	6	千克	4ABx	PRQS	/45
0203.1190		---其他									
0203.1190	10	其他鲜或冷藏的整头及半头野猪肉〔101 鲜的，102 冷藏〕	20		70	9/	6	千克	4ABEFx	PRQS	/45
0203.1190	90	其他鲜或冷藏的整头及半头猪肉〔101 鲜的，102 冷藏〕	20		70	9/	6	千克	4ABx	PRQS	/45
0203.1200		--带骨的前腿、后腿及其肉块									
0203.1200	10	鲜或冷的带骨野猪前腿、后腿及肉块〔101 鲜的，102 冷藏〕	20		70	9/	6	千克	47ABEFx	PRQS	/80
0203.1200	90	鲜或冷的带骨猪前腿、后腿及其肉块〔101 鲜的，102 冷藏〕	20		70	9/	6	千克	47ABx	PRQS	/80
0203.1900		--其他									
0203.1900	10	其他鲜或冷藏的野猪肉〔101 鲜的，102 冷藏〕	20		70	9/	6	千克	47ABEFx	PRQS	/80
0203.1900	90	其他鲜或冷藏的猪肉〔101 鲜的，102 冷藏〕	20		70	9/	6	千克	47ABx	PRQS	/80
		-冻的：									
		--整头及半头：									
0203.2110		---乳猪									
0203.2110	10	冻整头及半头野乳猪肉〔999〕	12		70	9/	6	千克	4ABEFx	PRQS	/37
0203.2110	90	冻整头及半头乳猪肉〔999〕	12		70	9/	6	千克	4ABx	PRQS	/37
0203.2190		---其他									
0203.2190	10	其他冻整头及半头野猪肉〔999〕	12		70	9/	6	千克	47ABEFx	PRQS	/62
0203.2190	90	其他冻整头及半头猪肉〔999〕	12		70	9/	6	千克	47ABx	PRQS	/62
0203.2200		--带骨的前腿、后腿及其肉块									

Chapter 2
Meat and edible meat offal

Notes:

This Chapter does not cover:

1. Products of the kinds described in headings No. 02. 01 to 02. 08 or 02. 10, unfit or unsuitable for human consumption;
2. Guts, bladders or stomachs of animals (heading No. 05. 04) or animal blood (heading No. 05. 11 or 30. 02);
3. Animal fat, other than products of heading No. 02. 09(Chapter15).

协定税率 %										特惠税率 %			Article Description
亚太5国	东/冰/格	巴基斯坦	韩国	瑞士	哥达	秘鲁	澳大利亚	新西/坡/智	港/澳/台	亚太2国	老/柬/缅	36/3/1	
													Meat of bovine animals, fresh or chilled:
													-Carcasses and half-carcasses
	0/0/8		12	6	6.7	5.3	8	0//0	0/0/		0/0/	0/0/0	Meat of wild bovine animals, carcasses and half-carcasses, fresh or chilled
	0/0/8		12	6	6.7	5.3	8	0//0	0/0/		0/0/	0/0/0	Other meat of bovine animals, carcasses and half-carcasses, fresh or chilled
													-Other cuts with bone in
	0/0/4.8	0	7.2	3.6	4	4.2	4.8	0//0	0/0/		0/0/	0/0/0	Meat of wild bovine animals, with bone in, fresh or chilled
	0/0/4.8	0	7.2	3.6	4	4.2	4.8	0//0	0/0/		0/0/	0/0/0	Other meat of bovine animals, with bone in, fresh or chilled
													-Boneless
	0/0/4.8	0	7.2	3.6	4	4.2	4.8	0//0	0/0/		/0/	0/0/0	Meat of wild bovine animals, boneless, fresh or chilled
	0/0/4.8	0	7.2	3.6	4	4.2	4.8	0//0	0/0/		/0/	0/0/0	Other meat of bovine animals, boneless, fresh or chilled
													Meat of bovine animals, frozen:
													-Carcasses and half-carcasses
	0/0/	0	17.5	7.5	0	6.7	10	0//0	0/0/		0/0/	0/0/0	Meat of wild bovine animals, carcasses and half-carcasses, frozen
	0/0/	0	17.5	7.5	0	6.7	10	0//0	0/0/		0/0/	0/0/0	Other meat of bovine animals, carcasses and half-carcasses, frozen
													-Other cuts with bone in
	0/0/	0	7.2	3.6	0	4.2	4.8	0//0	0/0/		0/0/	0/0/0	Meat of wild bovine animals, with bone in, frozen
	0/0/	0	7.2	3.6	0	4.2	4.8	0//0	0/0/		0/0/	0/0/0	Other meat of bovine animals, with bone in, frozen
													-Boneless
	0/0/	0	7.2	3.6	0	4.2	4.8	0//0	0/0/		/0/	0/0/0	Meat of wild bovine animals, boneless, frozen
	0/0/	0	7.2	3.6	0	4.2	4.8	0//0	0/0/		/0/	0/0/0	Other meat of bovine animals, boneless, frozen
													Meat of swine, fresh, chilled or frozen:
													-Fresh or chilled:
													--Carcasses and half-carcasses:
													---Sucking pig
	0/0/0		12	6	0	0	0	0//0	0/0/		0/0/	0/0/0	Meat of wild sucking pig, carcasses and half-carcasses, fresh or chilled
	0/0/0		12	6	0	0	0	0//0	0/0/		0/0/	0/0/0	Meat of other sucking pig, carcasses and half-carcasses, fresh or chilled
													---Other
	0/0/0		12	6	0	0	0	0//0	0/0/		0/0/	0/0/0	Other meat of wild swine, carcasses and half-carcasses, fresh or chilled
	0/0/0		12	6	0	0	0	0//0	0/0/		0/0/	0/0/0	Other meat of swine, carcasses and half-carcasses, fresh or chilled
													--Hams, shoulders and cuts thereof, with bone in
	0/0/0		12	6	0	0	0	0//0	0/0/		0/0/	0/0/0	Hams, shoulders and cuts thereof, with bone in, of wild swine, fresh or chilled
	0/0/0		12	6	0	0	0	0//0	0/0/		0/0/	0/0/0	Hams, shoulders and cuts thereof, with bone in, of swine, fresh or chilled
													--Other
	0/0/0		12	6	0	0	0	0//0	0/0/		0/0/	0/0/0	Other meat of wild swine, fresh or chilled
	0/0/0		12	6	0	0	0	0//0	0/0/		0/0/	0/0/0	Other meat of swine, fresh or chilled
													-Frozen:
													--Carcasses and half-carcasses:
													---Sucking pig
	0/0/0	6	4.8	3.6	0	0	0	0//0	0/0/		0/0/	0/0/0	Meat of wild sucking pig, carcasses and half-carcasses, frozen
	0/0/0	6	4.8	3.6	0	0	0	0//0	0/0/		0/0/	0/0/0	Meat of sucking pig, carcasses and half-carcasses, frozen
													---Other
	0/0/4.8	6	4.8	3.6	0	0	0	0//0	0/0/		0/0/	0/0/0	Other meat of wild swine, carcasses and half-carcasses, frozen
	0/0/4.8	6	4.8	3.6	0	0	0	0//0	0/0/		0/0/	0/0/0	Other meat of swine, carcasses and half-carcasses, frozen
													--Hams, shoulders and cuts thereof, with bone in

税则号列	货品名称〔CIQ 扩展编码及品名－T2 表示见附表 2〕	最惠(%)	暂定税率	普通	增值/消费	出口退税	计量单位	监管条件	检验检疫	特殊证件对美关税
0203.2200　10	冻带骨野猪前腿、后腿及肉〔999〕	12	8	70	9/	6	千克	47ABEFx	PRQS	/68
0203.2200　90	冻藏的带骨猪前腿、后腿及其肉块〔999〕	12	8	70	9/	6	千克	47ABx	PRQS	/68
0203.2900	--其他									
0203.2900　10	冻藏野猪其他肉〔999〕	12	8	70	9/	9	千克	47ABEFx	PRQS	/68
0203.2900　90	其他冻藏猪肉〔999〕	12	8	70	9/	9	千克	47ABx	PRQS	/68
02.04	**鲜、冷、冻绵羊肉或山羊肉：**									
0204.1000	-鲜或冷的整头及半头羔羊〔101 鲜的绵羊肉，102 冷藏绵羊肉，103 鲜的山羊肉，104 冷藏山羊肉，105 鲜的野羊肉，106 冷藏野羊肉，107 冷藏绵羊肉，6 月龄以下，108 冷藏山羊肉，6 月龄以下〕	15		70	9/	6	千克	7AB	PRQS	/
	-其他鲜或冷的绵羊肉：									
0204.2100	--整头及半头〔101 鲜的绵羊肉，102 冷藏绵羊肉，103 鲜的野羊肉，104 冷藏野羊肉，105 冷藏绵羊肉，6 月龄以下〕	23		70	9/	6	千克	7AB	PRQ	/
0204.2200	--带骨肉〔101 鲜的绵羊肉，102 冷藏绵羊肉，103 鲜的野羊肉，104 冷藏野羊肉，105 冷藏绵羊肉，6 月龄以下〕	15		70	9/	6	千克	7AB	PRQS	/50
0204.2300	--去骨肉〔101 鲜的绵羊肉，102 冷藏绵羊肉，103 鲜的野羊肉，104 冷藏野羊肉，105 冷藏绵羊肉，6 月龄以下〕	15		70	9/	6	千克	7AB	PRQS	/
0204.3000	-冻的整头及半头羔羊〔101 绵羊肉，102 山羊肉，103 野羊肉，104 绵羊肉，6 月龄以下 105 山羊肉，6 月龄以下〕	15		70	9/	6	千克	7AB	PRQS	/
	-其他冻的绵羊肉：									
0204.4100	--整头及半头〔101 绵羊肉，102 野羊肉，103 绵羊肉，6 月龄以下〕	23		70	9/	6	千克	7AB	PRQS	/
0204.4200	--带骨肉〔101 绵羊肉，102 野羊肉，103 绵羊肉，6 月龄以下〕	12		70	9/	6	千克	7AB	PRQS	/
0204.4300	--去骨肉〔101 绵羊肉，102 野羊肉，103 绵羊肉，6 月龄以下〕	15		70	9/	9	千克	7AB	PRQS	/
0204.5000	-山羊肉[T2]	20		70	9/	9	千克	7AB	PRQS	/
02.05	**鲜、冷、冻马、驴、骡肉：**									
0205.0000	鲜、冷、冻马、驴、骡肉									
0205.0000　10	鲜、冷或冻的濒危野马、野驴肉[T2]	20		70	9/	0	千克	ABFE	PRQS	/
0205.0000　90	鲜、冷或冻的马、驴、骡肉[T2]	20		70	9/	6	千克	AB	PRQS	/
02.06	**鲜、冷、冻牛、猪、绵羊、山羊、马、驴、骡的食用杂碎：**									
0206.1000	-鲜、冷牛杂碎[T2]	12		70	9/	9	千克	4xAB	PRQS	/
	-冻牛杂碎：									
0206.2100	--舌〔101 冻牛舌，102 冻野牛舌，103 冻牛舌(30 月龄以下)〕	12		70	9/	6	千克	47xAB	PRQS	/
0206.2200	--肝〔101 冻牛肝，102 冻野牛肝，103 冻牛肝(30 月龄以下)〕	12		70	9/	6	千克	47xAB	PRQS	/
0206.2900	--其他[T2]	12		70	9/	6	千克	47xAB	PRQS	/47
0206.3000	-鲜、冷猪杂碎[T2]	20		70	9/	6	千克	4ABx	PRQS	/55
	-冻猪杂碎：									
0206.4100	--肝〔101 冻猪肝，102 冻野猪肝〕	20		70	9/	6	千克	47ABx	PRQS	/80
0206.4900	--其他[T2]	12		70	9/	6	千克	47ABx	PRQS	/72
0206.8000	-其他鲜或冷杂碎									
0206.8000　10	鲜或冷的羊杂碎[T2]	20		70	9/	6	千克	AB	PRQS	/
0206.8000　90	鲜或冷的马、驴、骡杂碎[T2]	20		70	9/	6	千克	AB	PRQS	/
0206.9000	-其他冻杂碎									
0206.9000　10	冻藏的羊杂碎[T2]	18		70	9/	6	千克	7AB	PRQS	/
0206.9000　90	冻藏的马、驴、骡杂碎[T2]	18		70	9/	6	千克	AB	PRQS	/
02.07	**税目 01.05 所列家禽的鲜、冷、冻肉及食用杂碎：**									
	-鸡：									
0207.1100	--整只，鲜或冷的〔101 鲜的整只鸡，102 冷藏整只鸡〕	20		70	9/	6	千克	4ABx	PRQS	/55
0207.1200	--整只，冻的〔101 冻的整只鸡(不包括内脏及胃肠等消化道器官)，102 冻的整只鸡〕	T3		T3	9/	6	千克	4x7AB	PRQS	/35
	--块及杂碎，鲜或冷的：									
	---块：									
0207.1311	----带骨的〔101 鲜的带骨的鸡块，102 冷藏带骨的鸡块〕	20		70	9/	9	千克	4xAB	PRQS	/55
0207.1319	----其他〔101 其他鲜的鸡块，102 其他冷藏鸡块〕	20		70	9/	9	千克	4xAB	PRQS	/55
	---杂碎：									
0207.1321	----翼(不包括翼尖)〔101 鲜的鸡翼，102 冷藏鸡翼〕	20		70	10/	10	千克	4xAB	PRQS	
0207.1321　01	鲜或冷的整翅(翼)〔101：鲜的整翅，102：冷藏的整翅〕	20		70	9/	9	千克	4xAB	PRQS	/55
0207.1321　02	鲜或冷的翅(翼)根〔101：鲜的翼根，102：冷藏翼根〕	20		70	9/	9	千克	4xAB	PRQS	/55
0207.1321　03	鲜或冷的翅(翼)中〔101：鲜的翼中，102：冷藏翼中〕	20		70	9/	9	千克	4xAB	PRQS	/55
0207.1321　04	鲜或冷的两节翅(翼)〔101：鲜的两节翼，102：冷藏两节翼〕	20		70	9/	9	千克	4xAB	PRQS	/55
0207.1329	----其他[T2]	20		70	10/	6	千克	AB4x	PRQS	
0207.1329　01	鲜或冷的翅(翼)尖〔101：鲜的翼尖；102：冷藏翼尖〕	20		70	9/	6	千克	AB4x	PRQS	/55
0207.1329　02	鲜或冷的鸡膝软骨〔101：鲜的鸡膝软骨，102：冷藏鸡膝软骨〕	20		70	9/	6	千克	AB4x	PRQS	/55

协定税率 %										特惠税率 %			Article Description
亚太5国	东/冰/格	巴基斯坦	韩国	瑞士	哥达	秘鲁	澳大利亚	新西/坡/智	港/澳/台	亚太2国	老/柬/缅	36/3/1	
	0/0/4.8	6	4.8	3.6	0	0	0	0//0	0/0/		0/0/	0/0/0	Hams, shoulders and cuts thereof, with bone in, of wild swine, frozen
	0/0/4.8	6	4.8	3.6	0	0	0	0//0	0/0/		0/0/	0/0/0	Hams, shoulders and cuts thereof, with bone in, of swine, frozen
													--Other
	0/0/4.8	6	4.8	3.6	0	3.2	0	0//0	0/0/		/0/	0/0/0	Other meat of wild swine, frozen
	0/0/4.8	6	4.8	3.6	0	3.2	0	0//0	0/0/		/0/	0/0/0	Other meat of swine, frozen
													Meat of sheep or goats, fresh, chilled or frozen:
	0/0/6	12	6	4.5	5	4	5	0//0	0/0/			0/0/	-Carcasses and half-carcasses of lamb, fresh or chilled
													-Other meat of sheep, fresh or chilled:
	0/0/9.2		16.1	6.9	7.7	6.1	7.7	0//0	0/0/			0/0/	--Carcasses and half-carcasses
	0/0/6	12	6	4.5	5	4	5	0//0	0/0/			0/0/	--Other cuts with bone in
	0/0/6	12	6	4.5	5	1.3	5	0//0	0/0/			0/0/	--Boneless
	0/0/6	12	6	4.5	5	5.3	5	0//0	0/0/			0/0/	-Carcasses and half-carcasses of lamb, frozen
													-Other meat of sheep, frozen:
	0/0/9.2		16.1	6.9	7.7	8.1	7.7	0//0	0/0/			0/0/	--Carcasses and half-carcasses
	0/0/4.8	6	4.8	3.6	4	4.2	4	0//0	0/0/			0/0/	--Other cuts with bone in
	0/0/6	12	6	4.5	5	5.3	5	0//0	0/0/			0/0/	--Boneless
	0/0/8	0	12	6	6.7	1.7	6.7	0//0	0/0/			0/0/	-Meat of goats
													Meat of horses, asses, mules or hinnies, fresh, chilled or frozen:
													Meat of horses, asses, mules or hinnies, fresh, chilled or frozen
	0/0/0		12	6	0	0	0	0//0	0/0/			0/0/	Meat of endangered wild horses and asses, fresh, chilled or frozen
	0/0/0		12	6	0	0	0	0//0	0/0/			0/0/	Other meat of horses, asses, mules or hinnies, fresh, chilled or frozen
													Edible offal of bovine animals, swine, sheep, goats, horses, asses, mules or hinnies, fresh, chilled or frozen:
	0/0/4.8	6	4.8	3.6	0	1	0	0//0	0/0/		0/0/	0/0/0	-Of bovine animals, fresh or chilled
													-Of bovine animals, frozen:
	0/0/4.8	6	4.8	3.6	0	0	0	0//0	0/0/		0/0/	0/0/0	--Tongues
	0/0/4.8	6	4.8	3.6	0	0	0	0//0	0/0/		0/0/	0/0/0	--Livers
	0/0/4.8	0	4.8	3.6	0	0	3	0//0	0/0/		0/0/	0/0/0	--Other
	0/0/8		12	6	0	0	0	0//0	0/0/		0/0/0	0/0/0	-Of swine, fresh or chilled
													-Of swine, frozen:
	0/0/8		12	6	0	0	0	0//0	0/0/		0/0/	0/0/0	--Livers
	0/0/4.8	6	4.8	3.6	0	0	0	0//0	0/0/		0/0/	0/0/0	--Other
													-Other, fresh or chilled
	0/0/8		12	6	0	1.7	8	0//0	0/0/		/0/	0/0/0	Edible offal of sheep or goats, fresh or chilled
	0/0/8		12	6	0	1.7	8	0//0	0/0/		/0/	0/0/0	Edible offal of horses, asses, mules or hinnies, fresh or chilled
													-Other, frozen
	0/0/7.2	14.4	10.8	5.4	0	6.4	4.5	0//0	0/0/		/0/	0/0/0	Edible offal of sheep or goats, frozen
	0/0/7.2	14.4	10.8	5.4	0	6.4	4.5	0//0	0/0/		/0/	0/0/0	Edible offal of horses, asses, mules or hinnies, frozen
													Meat and edible offal, of the poultry of heading No. 01.05, fresh, chilled or frozen:
													-Of fowls of the species *Gallus domesticus*:
	0/0/0		12	6	0	0	0	0//0	0/0/		0/0/0	0/0/0	--Not cut in pieces, fresh or chilled
	0/0/0		0.7元/千克	6	0	0	0	0//0	0/0/		0/0/0	0/0/0	--Not cut in pieces, frozen
													--Chicken cuts and offal, fresh or chiued:
													---Cuts:
	0/0/0		12	6	0	0	0	0//0	0/0/		0/0/0	0/0/0	----With bone
	0/0/0		12	6	0	0	0	0//0	0/0/		0/0/0	0/0/0	----Other
													---Offal:
	0/0/12		13.3	8	0	0	0	0//0	0/0/		0/0/0	0/0/0	----Midjoint wing
	0/0/8		12	6	0	0	0	0//0	0/0/		0/0/0	0/0/0	Whole Wings, fresh or chilled
	0/0/8		12	6	0	0	0	0//0	0/0/		0/0/0	0/0/0	Wing root, fresh or chilled
	0/0/8		12	6	0	0	0	0//0	0/0/		0/0/0	0/0/0	Midjoint wing, fresh or chilled
	0/0/8		12	6	0	0	0	0//0	0/0/		0/0/0	0/0/0	2—joint wings, fresh or chilled
	0/0/12		13.3	8	0	0	0	0//0	0/0/		0/0/0	0/0/0	----Other
	0/0/8		12	6	0	0	0	0//0	0/0/		0/0/0	0/0/0	chicken wing tips, fresh or chilled
	0/0/8		12	6	0	0	0	0//0	0/0/		0/0/0	0/0/0	Chicken knee cartilage, fresh or chilled

税则号列		货品名称〔CIQ扩展编码及品名－T2表示见附表2〕	最惠(%)	暂定税率	普通	增值/消费	出口退税	计量单位	监管条件	检验检疫	特殊证件对美关税
0207.1329	90	其他鲜或冷的杂碎〔101鲜的鸡胸、鸡腿,102冷藏的鸡胸、鸡腿,103鲜的鸡爪,104冷藏鸡爪,105鲜的鸡肫、胃,106冷藏鸡肫、胃,107其他鲜的鸡杂碎,108其他冷藏鸡杂碎〕	20		70	9/	6	千克	AB4x	PRQS	/55
		--块及杂碎,冻的:									
		---块:									
0207.1411		----带骨的〔101冷冻带骨鸡肉,除鸡胸、鸡腿,102鸡胸、鸡腿〕	T3		T3	9/	9	千克	7AB4x	PRQS	/35
0207.1419		----其他〔101冷冻不带骨鸡肉,除鸡胸、鸡腿,102鸡胸、鸡腿〕	T3		T3	9/	9	千克	7AB4x	PRQS	/35
		---杂碎:									
0207.1421		----翼(不包括翼尖)〔999〕									
0207.1421	01	冻的整翅(翼)〔999〕	T3		T3	9/	9	千克	7AB4x	PRQS	/35
0207.1421	02	冻的翅(翼)根〔999〕	T3		T3	9/	9	千克	7AB4x	PRQS	/35
0207.1421	03	冻的翅(翼)中〔999〕	T3		T3	9/	9	千克	7AB4x	PRQS	/35
0207.1421	04	冻的两节翅(翼)〔999〕	T3		T3	9/	9	千克	7AB4x	PRQS	/35
0207.1422		----鸡爪〔999〕	T3		T3	9/	6	千克	7AB4x	PRQS	/35
0207.1429		----其他〔103鸡肝,101鸡翼,包括翼尖,102鸡翼翼尖,104其他鸡杂碎〕									
0207.1429	01	冻的翅(翼)尖	T3		T3	9/	6	千克	7AB4x	PRQS	/35
0207.1429	02	冻的鸡膝软骨	T3		T3	9/	6	千克	7AB4x	PRQS	/35
0207.1429	90	其他冻的食用杂碎	T3		T3	9/	6	千克	7AB4x	PRQS	/35
		-火鸡:									
0207.2400		--整只,鲜或冷的〔101鲜的整只火鸡,102冷藏整只火鸡〕	20		70	9/	6	千克	AB	PRQS	/55
0207.2500		--整只,冻的〔101冻的整只火鸡(不包括内脏及胃肠等消化道器官),102冻的整只火鸡〕	20		70	9/	6	千克	AB	PRQS	/55
0207.2600		--块及杂碎,鲜或冷的[T2]	20		70	9/	6,9	千克	AB	PRQS	/55
0207.2700		--块及杂碎,冻的[T2]	10		70	9/	6,9	千克	AB	PRQS	/45
		-鸭:									
0207.4100		--整只,鲜或冷的〔101鲜的,102冷的〕	20		70	9/	6	千克	AB	PRQS	/55
0207.4200		--整只,冻的〔999〕	20		70	9/	6	千克	AB	PRQS	/55
0207.4300		--肥肝,鲜或冷的〔101鲜的,102冷的〕	20		70	9/	6	千克	AB	PRQS	/55
0207.4400		--其他,鲜或冷的[T2]	20		70	9/	6,9	千克	AB	PRQS	/55
0207.4500		--其他,冻的[T2]	20		70	9/	6,9	千克	AB	PRQS	/55
		-鹅:									
0207.5100		--整只,鲜或冷的〔101鲜的,102冷藏〕	20		70	9/	6	千克	AB	PRQS	/55
0207.5200		--整只,冻的〔999〕	20		70	9/	6	千克	AB	PRQS	/55
0207.5300		--肥肝,鲜或冷的〔101鲜的,102冷藏〕	20		70	9/	6	千克	AB	PRQS	/55
0207.5400		--其他,鲜或冷的[T2]	20		70	9/	6,9	千克	AB	PRQS	/55
0207.5500		--其他,冻的[T2]	20		70	9/	6,9	千克	AB	PRQS	/55
0207.6000		-珍珠鸡〔101鲜的,饲养的;102冷藏,饲养的;103冻藏,饲养的〕	20		70	9/	6,9	千克	AB	PRQS	/
02.08		其他鲜、冷、冻肉及食用杂碎:									
		-家兔或野兔的:									
0208.1010		---鲜、冷家兔肉,兔头除外〔101鲜的家兔肉,102冷藏家兔肉〕	20		70	9/	9	千克	AB	PRQS	/
0208.1020		---冻家兔肉,兔头除外〔999〕	20		70	9/	9	千克	AB	PRQS	/
0208.1090		---其他									
0208.1090	10	鲜、冷或冻濒危野兔肉及其食用杂碎(不包括兔头)〔101鲜的野兔肉,102冷藏野兔肉,103冻藏野兔肉,104鲜的野兔杂碎,105冷藏野兔杂碎,106冻藏野兔杂碎〕	20		70	9/	0	千克	ABFE	PRQS	/
0208.1090	90	鲜、冷或冻家兔食用杂碎〔101鲜的,102冷藏,103冻藏〕	20		70	9/	9	千克	AB	PRQS	/
0208.3000		-灵长目的〔101鲜的,102冷藏,103冻藏〕	23		70	9/	6	千克	ABFE	PRQS	/
0208.4000		-鲸、海豚及鼠海豚(鲸目哺乳动物)的;海牛及儒艮(海牛目哺乳动物)的;海豹、海狮及海象(鳍足亚目哺乳动物)的〔101鲜、冷的,102冻的〕	23		70	9/	6	千克	ABEF	PRQS	/
0208.5000		-爬行动物(包括蛇及龟鳖)的[T2]	23		70	9/	6	千克	ABFE	PRQS	/
0208.6000		-骆驼及其他骆驼科动物的									
0208.6000	10	鲜、冷或冻的濒危野生骆驼及其他濒危野生骆驼科动物的肉及食用杂碎〔101鲜的,102冷藏,103冻藏〕	23		70	9/	0	千克	ABFE	PRQS	/

协定税率 %										特惠税率 %			Article Description
亚太5国	东/冰/格	巴基斯坦	韩国	瑞士	哥达	秘鲁	澳大利亚	新西/坡/智	港/澳/台	亚太2国	老/柬/缅	36/3/1	
	0/0/8		12	6	0	0	0	0//0	0/0/		0/0/0	0/0/0	Other chicken edible offal ,fresh or chilled
													--Cuts and offal, frozen:
													---Cuts:
	0/0/0	0	0.2元/千克	0	0	0	0	0//0	0/0/		0/0/0	0/0/0	----With bone
	0/0/0	0	0.2元/千克	0	0	0	0	0//0	0/0/		0/0/0	0/0/0	----Other
													---Offal:
													----Midjoint wing
	0/0/4	0	0.3元/千克	0	0	0	0	0//0	0/0/		0/0/0	0/0/0	Whole Wings,frozen
	0/0/4	0	0.3元/千克	0	0	0	0	0//0	0/0/		0/0/0	0/0/0	Drumettes,frozen
	0/0/4	0	0.3元/千克	0	0	0	0	0//0	0/0/		0/0/0	0/0/0	Midjoint Wings,frozen
	0/0/4	0	0.3元/千克	0	0	0	0	0//0	0/0/		0/0/0	0/0/0	2—Joint Wings,frozen
	0/0/4	0	0.2元/千克	0	0	0	0	0//0	0/0/		0/0/0	0/0/0	----Chicken claw
													----Other
	0/0/4	0	0.2元/千克	0	0	0	0	0//0	0/0/		0/0/0	0/0/0	Wing Tips,frozen
	0/0/4	0	0.2元/千克	0	0	0	0	0//0	0/0/		0/0/0	0/0/0	Chicken knee cartilage,frozen
	0/0/4	0	0.2元/千克	0	0	0	0	0//0	0/0/		0/0/0	0/0/0	Other chicken edible offal,frozen
													-Of turkeys:
	0/0/0		12	6	0	0	0	0//0	0/0/		0//	0/0/0	--Not cut in pieces, fresh or chilled
	0/0/0		12	6	0	0	0	0//0	0/0/		0//	0/0/0	--Not cut in pieces, frozen
	0/0/0		12	6	0	0	0	0//0	0/0/		0//	0/0/0	--Cuts and offal, fresh or chilled
	0/0/0	4.5	4	0	0	0	0	0//0	0/0/		0//	0/0/0	--Cuts and offal, frozen
													-Ducks:
	0/0/0		12	6	0	0	0	0//0	0/0/		0/0/0	0/0/0	--Not cut in pieces,fresh or chilled
	0/0/0		12	6	0	0	0	0//0	0/0/		0/0/0	0/0/0	--Not cut in pieces,frozen
	0/0/0		12	6	0	0	0	0//0	0/0/		0/0/	0/0/0	--Fatty livers(foie gras),fresh chilled
	0/0/0		12	6	0	0	0	0//0	0/0/		0/0/0	0/0/0	--Other,fresh or chilled
	0/0/0		14	6	0	0	0	0//0	0/0/		0/0/0	0/0/0	--Other,frozen
													-Geeses:
	0/0/0		12	6	0	0	0	0//0	0/0/		0/0/0	0/0/0	--Not cut in pieces,fresh or chilled
	0/0/0		12	6	0	0	0	0//0	0/0/		0/0/0	0/0/0	--Not cut in pieces,frozen
	0/0/0		12	6	0	0	0	0//0	0/0/		0/0/	0/0/0	--Fatty livers(foie gras),fresh or chilled
	0/0/0		12	6	0	0	0	0//0	0/0/		0/0/0	0/0/0	--Other,fresh or chilled
	0/0/0		12	6	0	0	0	0//0	0/0/		0/0/0	0/0/0	--Other,frozen
	0/0/0		12	6	0	0	0	0//0	0/0/		0/0/	0/0/0	-Guinea fowls
													Other meat and edible meat offal, fresh, chilled or frozen:
													-Of rabbits or hares:
	0/0/0		12	6	0	0	0	0//0	0/0/			0/0/	---Meat of rabbits, fresh or chilled,other than head
	0/0/0		12	6	0	0	0	0//0	0/0/			0/0/	---Meat of rabbits, frozen,other than head
													---Other
	0/0/0		12	6	0	0	0	0//0	0/0/			0/0/	Meat and offal,of endangered wild hares (other than head), fresh、chilled or frozen
	0/0/0		12	6	0	0	0	0//0	0/0/			0/0/	Edible offal of rabbits,fresh、chilled or frozen
	0/0/0		9.2	6.9	0	0	0	0//0	0/0/			0/0/	-Of primates
	0/0/0		9.2	6.9	0	0	0	0//0	0/0/			0/0/	-Of whales,dolphins and porpoises(mammals of the order Cetacea); manatees and dugongs(mammals of the order Sirenia);seal、sea lion and walrus(mammals of the suborder Pinnipedia)
	0/0/0		9.2	6.9	0	0	0	0//0	0/0/			0/0/	-Of reptiles(including snakes and turtles)
													-Of camel and other camelids(camelidae):
	0/0/0		9.2	6.9	0	0	0	0//0	0/0/			0/0/	Meat and offal of endangered wild camel and other endangered camel familia animals,fresh,chilled or fro zen

税则号列		货品名称〔CIQ扩展编码及品名—T2表示见附表2〕	最惠(%)	暂定税率	普通	增值/消费	出口退税	计量单位	监管条件	检验检疫	特殊证件对美关税
0208.6000	90	其他鲜、冷或冻骆驼及其他骆驼科动物的肉及食用杂碎〔101鲜的，102冷藏，103冻藏〕	23		70	9/	6	千克	AB	PRQS	/
		-其他：									
0208.9010		---乳鸽的〔101鲜的乳鸽肉，102冷藏的乳鸽肉，103冻藏的乳鸽肉，104鸽杂碎，105其它鸽肉及杂碎〕	20		70	9/	6	千克	AB	PRQS	/
0208.9090		---其他									
0208.9090	10	其他鲜、冷或冻的濒危野生动物肉[T2]	23		70	9/	0	千克	ABFE	PRQS	/
0208.9090	90	其他鲜、冷或冻肉及食用杂碎[T2]	23		70	9/	9	千克	AB	PRQS	/
02.09		**未炼制或用其他方法提取的不带瘦肉的肥猪肉、猪脂肪及家禽脂肪，鲜、冷、冻、干、熏、盐腌或盐渍的：**									
0209.1000		-猪的[T2]	20		70	9/	6	千克	AB	PRQ	/45
0209.9000		-其他[T2]	20		70	9/	6	千克	AB	PRQ	/
02.10		**肉及食用杂碎，干、熏、盐腌或盐渍的；可供食用的肉或杂碎的细粉、粗粉：**									
		-猪肉：									
		--带骨的前腿、后腿及其肉块：									
0210.1110		---带骨的腿									
0210.1110	10	干、熏、盐制的带骨鹿豚、姬猪腿〔101猪蹄，102带骨熟制猪肉制品〕	25		80	9/	6	千克	ABFE	PRQS	/60
0210.1110	90	其他干、熏、盐制的带骨猪腿〔101猪蹄，102带骨熟制猪肉制品〕	25		80	9/	6	千克	AB	PRQS	/60
0210.1190		---其他									
0210.1190	10	干、熏、盐制的带骨鹿豚、姬猪腿肉块〔101猪蹄，102带骨熟制猪肉制品〕	25		80	9/	6	千克	ABFE	PRQS	/60
0210.1190	90	其他干、熏、盐制的带骨猪腿肉〔101猪蹄，102带骨熟制猪肉制品〕	25		80	9/	6	千克	AB	PRQS	/60
0210.1200		--腹肉(五花肉)									
0210.1200	10	干、熏、盐制的鹿豚、姬猪腹肉(指五花肉)〔101干、熏制鹿豚腹肉，102去骨熟制猪肉制品，103盐制鹿豚腹肉〕	25		80	9/	6	千克	ABFE	PRQS	/60
0210.1200	90	其他干、熏、盐制的猪腹肉(指五花肉)〔101其他盐制猪腹肉、腌制猪腹肉，102去骨熟制猪肉制品〕	25		80	9/	6	千克	AB	PRQS	/60
0210.1900		--其他									
0210.1900	10	干、熏、盐制的鹿豚、姬猪其他肉〔101干、熏、盐制姬猪其他肉，102干、熏鹿豚其他肉，103盐制鹿豚其他肉〕	25		80	9/	9	千克	ABFE	PRQS	/60
0210.1900	90	其他干、熏、盐制的其他猪肉〔101其他干制其他猪肉，102去骨熟制猪肉制品〕	25		80	9/	9	千克	AB	PRQS	/60
0210.2000		-牛肉									
0210.2000	10	干、熏、盐制的濒危野牛肉〔101干、熏制野牛肉，102盐制带骨野牛肉、腌制带骨牛肉，103盐制去骨野牛肉、腌制去骨牛肉，104去骨熟制牛肉制品〕	25		80	9/	0	千克	ABFE	PRQS	/60
0210.2000	90	干、熏、盐制的其他牛肉〔101干、熏制牛肉，102盐制带骨牛肉、腌制带骨牛肉，103盐制去骨牛肉、腌制去骨牛肉，104去骨熟制牛肉制品〕	25		80	9/	6	千克	AB	PRQS	/60
		-其他，包括可供食用的肉或杂碎的细粉、粗粉：									
0210.9100		--灵长目的〔101干、熏、盐制灵长目动物肉，102干、熏、盐制灵长目动物食用杂碎〕	25		80	9/	6	千克	ABFE	PRQS	/
0210.9200		--鲸、海豚及鼠海豚(鲸目哺乳动物)的；海牛及儒艮(海牛目哺乳动物)的；海豹、海狮及海象(鳍足亚目哺乳动物)的〔101干、熏、盐制鲸目海牛目动物肉，102干、熏、盐制鲸目海牛目动物食用杂碎，103熏拷的灌肠类熟肉制品，104腌制的灌肠类熟肉制品〕	25		80	9/	6	千克	ABEF	PRQS	/
0210.9300		--爬行动物(包括蛇及龟鳖)的〔105养殖干制，106野生干制，107养殖盐腌及盐渍等，108野生盐腌及盐渍等，109养殖其他制作及保藏，110野生其他制作及保藏〕	25		80	9/	6	千克	ABFE	PRQS	/
0210.9900		--其他									
0210.9900	10	干、熏、盐制的其他濒危动物肉及杂碎(包括可供食用的肉或杂碎的细粉、粗粉)〔101干、熏、盐制其他濒危动物肉，102干、熏、盐制其他濒危动物食用杂碎〕	25		80	9/	0	千克	ABFE	PRQS	/50
0210.9900	90	干、熏、盐制的其他肉及食用杂碎(包括可供食用的肉或杂碎的细粉、粗粉)〔101腌制马肉，102腌制绵羊肉，103腌制山羊肉，104腌制鹿肉，105干、熏、盐制其他肉，106干、熏、盐制其他食用杂碎，107去骨熟制猪肉制品〕	25		80	9/	6	千克	AB	PRQS	/50

协定税率 %										特惠税率 %			Article Description
亚太5国	东/冰/格	巴基斯坦	韩国	瑞士	哥达	秘鲁	澳大利亚	新西/坡/智	港/澳/台	亚太2国	老/柬/缅	36/3/1	
	0/0/0		9.2	6.9	0	0	0	0//0	0/0/			0/0/	Meat and offal of other camel and other camel familia animals, fresh, chilled or frozen
													-Other:
	0/0/0		12	6	0	0	0	0//0	0/0/			0/0/	---Of squabs
													---Other
	0/0/9.2		16.1	6.9	0	0	0	0//0	0/0/			0/0/	Other meat of endangered wild animals, fresh, chilled or frozen
	0/0/9.2		16.1	6.9	0	0	0	0//0	0/0/			0/0/	Other meat and edible offal, fresh、chilled or frozen
													Pig fat free of lean meat and poultry fat not rendered or otherwise extracted, fresh, chilled, frozen, salted, in brine, dried or smoked:
	0/0/0		12	6	0	0	0	0//0	0/0/			0/0/	-Of swine
	0/0/0		12	6	0	0	0	0//0	0/0/			0/0/	-Other
													Meat and edible meat offal, salted, in brine, dried or smoked; edible flours and meals of meat or meat offal:
													-Meat of swine:
													--Hams, shoulders and cuts thereof, with bone in:
													---Hams and shoulders, with bone in
	0/0/0		17.5		0	0	0	0//0	0/0/		0/0/	0/0/0	Hams and shoulders of pig-deer (*Babyrousa*), pygmy pig (*Porcula*), with bone in, salted, in brine, dried or smoked
	0/0/0		17.5		0	0	0	0//0	0/0/		0/0/	0/0/0	Other hams and shoulders of swine, with bone in, salted, in brine, dried or smoked
													---Other
	0/0/0		17.5		0	0	0	0//0	0/0/		0/0/	0/0/0	Cuts of pig-deer (*Babyrousa*), pygmy pig (*Porcula*), with bone in, salted, in brine, dried or smoked
	0/0/0		17.5		0	0	0	0//0	0/0/		0/0/	0/0/0	Other meat of hams and shoulders, with bone in, salted, in brine, dried or smoked
													--Bellies (streaky) and cuts thereof
	0/0/0		17.5		0	0	0	0//0	0/0/		0/0/	0/0/0	Bellies (streaky) and cuts thereof, of pig-deer (*Babyrousa*), pygmy pig (*Porcula*), salted, in brine, dried or smoked
	0/0/0		17.5		0	0	0	0//0	0/0/		0/0/	0/0/0	Other bellies (streaky) and cuts thereof of swine, salted, in brine, dried or smoked
													--Other
	0/0/0		17.5		0	0	0	0//0	0/0/		/0/0	0/0/0	Other meat of pig-deer(*Babyrousa*), pygmy pig(*porcula*), salted, in brine, dried or smoked
	0/0/0		17.5		0	0	0	0//0	0/0/		/0/0	0/0/0	Other meat of swine, salted, in brine, dried or smoked
													-Meat of bovine animals
	0/0/0		17.5	0	0	0	10	0//0	0/0/		0/0/	0/0/0	Meat of endangered wild bovine animals, salted, in brine, dried or smoked
	0/0/0		17.5	0	0	0	10	0//0	0/0/		0/0/	0/0/0	Other meat of bovine animals, salted, in brine, dried or smoked
													-Other, including edible flours and meals of meat and meat offal:
	0/0/0		10	7.5	0	0	0	0//0	0/0/		0/0/	0/0/0	--Of primates
	0/0/0	22.5	10	7.5	0	0	0	0//0	0/0/		0/0/	0/0/0	--Of whales, dolphins and porpoises (mammals of the order Cetacea); manatees and dugongs (mammals of the order Sirenia); seal, sea lion and walrus (mammals of the suborder Pinnipedia)
	0/0/0		10	7.5	0	0	0	0//0	0/0/		0/0/	0/0/0	--Of reptiles(including snakes and turtles)
													--Other
	0/0/0		17.5	7.5	0	0	0	0//0	0/0/		0/0/	0/0/0	Meat and edible offal of other endangered wild animals(including edible flours and meals of meat and meat offal), salted, in brine, dried or smoked
	0/0/0		17.5	7.5	0	0	0	0//0	0/0/		0/0/	0/0/0	Other meat and edible offal (including edible flours and meals of meat and meat offal), salted, in brine, dried or smoked

第三章
鱼、甲壳动物，软体动物及其他水生无脊椎动物

注释：

一、本章不包括：

(一)税目 01.06 的哺乳动物；

(二)税目 01.06 的哺乳动物的肉(税目 02.08 或 02.10)；

(三)因品种或鲜度不适合供人食用的死鱼(包括鱼肝、鱼卵及鱼精等)、死甲壳动物、死软体动物及其他死水生无脊椎动物(第五章)；不适合供人食用的鱼、甲壳动物、软体动物、其他水生无脊椎动物的粉、粒(税目 23.01)；或

(四)鲟鱼子酱及用鱼卵制成的鲟鱼子酱代用品(税目 16.04)。

二、本章所称"团粒"，是指直接挤压或加入少量黏合剂制成的粒状产品。

税则号列		货品名称〔CIQ 扩展编码及品名—T2 表示见附表 2〕	最惠(%)	暂定税率	普通	增值/消费	出口退税	计量单位	监管条件	检验检疫	特殊证件对美关税
03.01		活鱼：									
		-观赏鱼：									
0301.1100		--淡水鱼									
0301.1100	10	观赏用濒危淡水鱼〔101 淡水养殖热带鱼，102 淡水捕捞热带鱼，103 其他观赏鱼〕	10		80	9/	0	千克	ABEF	PQ	/35
0301.1100	90	观赏用其他淡水鱼〔101 淡水养殖热带鱼，102 淡水捕捞热带鱼，103 其他观赏鱼〕	10		80	9/	6	千克	AB	PQ	/35
0301.1900		--其他									
0301.1900	10	观赏用濒危非淡水鱼〔101 海水养殖热带鱼，102 海水捕捞热带鱼，103 其他观赏鱼〕	10		80	9/	0	千克	ABFE	PQ	/35
0301.1900	90	其他观赏用非淡水鱼〔101 海水养殖热带鱼，102 海水捕捞热带鱼，103 其他观赏鱼〕	10		80	9/	9	千克	AB	PQ	/35
		-其他活鱼：									
		--鳟鱼(河鳟、虹鳟、克拉克大麻哈鱼、阿瓜大麻哈鱼、吉鱼大麻哈鱼、亚利桑那大麻哈鱼、金腹大麻哈鱼)：									
0301.9110		---鱼苗〔999〕	0		0	9/	9	千克	AB	PQ	/
0301.9190		---其他〔999〕	10		40	9/	9	千克	AB	PRQ	/20
		--鳗鱼(鳗鲡属)：									
0301.9210		---鱼苗									
0301.9210	10	花鳗鲡鱼苗〔999〕	0		0	9/	0	千克	ABE	PNQ	/
0301.9210	20	欧洲鳗鲡鱼苗〔999〕	0		0	9/	0	千克	ABEF	PNQ	/
0301.9210	90	其他鳗鱼(鳗鲡属)苗〔101 种用鳗鲡，102 海鳗〕	0		0	9/	0	千克	AB	PNQ	/
0301.9290		---其他									
0301.9290	10	花鳗鲡〔999〕	7		40	9/	9	千克	ABE	PRQS	/17
0301.9290	20	欧洲鳗鲡〔999〕	7		40	9/	9	千克	ABEF	PRQS	/17
0301.9290	90	其他活鳗鱼(鳗鲡属)〔101 种用鳗鲡，102 食用鳗鲡，103 海鳗〕	7		40	9/	9	千克	AB	PRQS	/17
		--鲤科鱼(鲤属、鲫属、草鱼、鲢属、鲮属、青鱼、卡特拉鲃、野鲮属、哈氏纹唇鱼、何氏细须鲃、鲂属)									
0301.9310		---鱼苗〔999〕	0		0	9/	9	千克	AB	PQ	/
0301.9390		---其他〔999〕	7		40	9/	9	千克	AB	PRQS	/17
		--大西洋及太平洋蓝鳍金枪鱼：									
0301.9410		---鱼苗〔999〕	0		0	9/	9	千克	AB	PQ	/
		---其他：	10.5								
0301.9491		----大西洋蓝鳍金枪鱼〔999〕	7		40	9/	9	千克	AB	PNQ	/17
0301.9492		----太平洋蓝鳍金枪鱼〔999〕	7		40	9/	9	千克	AB	PNQ	/17
		--南方蓝鳍金枪鱼：									
0301.9510		---鱼苗〔999〕	0		0	9/	9	千克	AB	PQ	/
0301.9590		---其他〔999〕	7		40	9/	9	千克	AB	PNQ	/17
		--其他：									
		---鱼苗：									
0301.9911		----鲈鱼〔101 淡水鲈鱼，102 海水鲈鱼〕	0		0	9/	9	千克	AB	PQ	/
0301.9912		----鲟鱼〔999〕	0		0	9/	9	千克	ABFE	PQ	/
0301.9919		----其他									
0301.9919	10	其他濒危鱼苗〔101 其他淡水鱼，102 其他海水鱼，103 其他观赏鱼，104 其他鱼〕	0		0	9/	0	千克	ABFE	PQ	/

Chapter 3
Fish and crustaceans, molluscs and other aquatic invertebrates

Notes:

1. This Chapter does not cover:
   (a) Mammals of heading No. 01. 06;
   (b) Meat of mammals of heading No. 01. 06 (heading No. 02. 08 or 02. 10);
   (c) Fish (including livers, roes thereof and milt) or crustaceans, molluscs or other aquatic invertebrates, dead and unfit or unsuitable for human consumption by reason of either their species or their condition (Chapter 5); flours, meals or pellets of fish or of crustaceans, molluscs or other aquatic invertebrates, unfit for human consumption (heading No. 23. 01); or
   (d) Caviar or caviar substitutes prepared from fish eggs (heading No. 16. 04).
2. In this Chapter the term "pellets" means products which have been agglomerated either directly by compression or by the addition of a small quantity of binder.

协定税率 %										特惠税率 %			Article Description
亚太5国	东/冰/格	巴基斯坦	韩国	瑞士	哥达	秘鲁	澳大利亚	新西/坡/智	港/澳/台	亚太2国	老/柬/缅	36/3/1	
													Live fish:
													-Ornamental fish:
													--Freshwater fish
	0/0/0	14	10.5	5.3	0	0	0	0//0	0/0/			0/0/0	Ornamental endangered freshwater fish
	0/0/0	14	10.5	5.3	0	0	0	0//0	0/0/			0/0/0	Ornamental other freshwater fish
													--Other
	0/0/0	14	10.5	5.3	0	0	0	0//0	0/0/			0/0/0	Ornamental endangered not freshwater fish
	0/0/0	14	10.5	5.3	0	0	0	0//0	0/0/			0/0/0	Ornamental other not freshwater fish
													-Other live fish:
													--Trout (*Salmo trutta*, *Oncorhynchus my kiss*, *Oncorhynchus clarki*, *Oncorhynchus aguabonita*, *Oncorhynchus gilae*, *Oncorhynchus apache* and *Oncorhynchus chrysogaster*):
												0/0/0	---Fry
7.6	0/0/0	4.5	4.2	3.2	0	0	0	0//0	0/0/			0/0/0	---Other
													--Eels (*Anguilla spp.*):
													---Fry
												0/0/0	Fry of marbled eels (*Anguilla marmorata*)
												0/0/0	Fry eruopean eels
												0/0/0	Other fry of eels (*Anguilla marmorata*)
													---Other
4.7	0/0/0	4.5	4	0	0	0	0	0//0	0/0/		/0/0	0/0/0	Marbled eels (*Anguilla marmorata*)
4.7	0/0/0	4.5	4	0	0	0	0	0//0	0/0/		/0/0	0/0/0	European eels
4.7	0/0/0	4.5	4	0	0	0	0	0//0	0/0/		/0/0	0/0/0	Other live eels (*Anguilla marmorata*)
													--Carp (*Cyprinus spp.*, *Caras — sius spp.*, *Ctenopharyngodon idellus*, *Hypophthalmichthys spp.*, *Cirrhinus spp.*, *Mylo — pharyngodon piceus*, *Catla catla*, *Labeo spp.*, *Osteochi — lus hasselti*, *Leptobarbus ho — eveni*, *Megalobrama spp.*)
												0/0/0	---Fry
5.3	0/0/0	4.5	4.2	3.2	0	0	0	0//0	0/0/		/0/0	0/0/0	---Other
													--Atlantic and pacific bluefin tunas (Thunnus thynnus, Thunnus orientalis):
												0/0/0	---Fry
													---Other:
5.3	0/0/0	4.5	4.2	3.2	0	0	0	0//0	0/0/		/0/0	0/0/0	----Atlantic bluefin tunas
5.3	0/0/0	4.5	4.2	3.2	0	0	0	0//0	0/0/0		/0/0	0/0/0	----Pacific bluefin tunas
													--Southern bluefin tunas (*thunnus maccoyii*):
												0/0/0	---Fry
5.3	0/0/0	4.5	4.2	3.2	0	0	0	0//0	0/0/		/0/0	0/0/0	---Other
													--Other:
													---Fry:
												0/0/0	----Of perches
												0/0/0	----Of sturgeon
													----Other
												0/0/0	Other endangered fry

税则号列	货品名称〔CIQ 扩展编码及品名—T2 表示见附表 2〕	最惠(%)	暂定税率	普通	增值/消费	出口退税	计量单位	监管条件	检验检疫	特殊证件对美关税
0301.9919 90	其他鱼苗[T2]	0		0	9/	9	千克	AB	PQ	/
	---其他：									
0301.9991	----罗非鱼〔999〕	7		40	9/	9	千克	AB	PRQS	/17
0301.9992	----鲀〔101 其他淡水鱼，102 其他海水鱼，103 其他观赏鱼〕	10		40	9/	9	千克	AB	PNQ	/20
0301.9993	----其他鲤科鱼									
0301.9993 10	活的濒危鲤科鱼〔999〕	7		40	9/	0	千克	ABFE	PNQ	/17
0301.9993 90	活的其他鲤科鱼(鲤科鱼(鲤属、鲫属、草鱼、鲢属、鳙属、青鱼、卡特拉鲃、野鲮属、哈氏纹唇鱼、何氏细须鲃、鲂属)除外)〔999〕	7		40	9/	9	千克	AB	PRQS	/17
0301.9999	----其他									
0301.9999 10	其他濒危活鱼〔101 其他淡水鱼，102 其他海水鱼，103 其他观赏鱼，104 其他鱼〕	7		40	9/	0	千克	ABFE	PNQ	/17
0301.9999 90	其他活鱼[T2]	7		40	9/	9	千克	AB	PRQS	/17
03.02	**鲜、冷鱼，但税目 03.04 的鱼片及其他鱼肉除外：**									
	-鲑科鱼，但子目 0302.91 至 0302.99 的可食用鱼杂碎除外：									
0302.1100	--鳟鱼(河鳟、虹鳟、克拉克大麻哈鱼、阿瓜大麻哈鱼、吉鱼大麻哈鱼、亚利桑那大麻哈鱼、金腹大麻哈鱼)[T2]	10		40	9/	9	千克	AB	PRQS	/
0302.1300	--大麻哈鱼[红大麻哈鱼、细鳞大麻哈鱼、大麻哈鱼(种)、大鳞大麻哈鱼、银大麻哈鱼、马苏大麻哈鱼、玫瑰大麻哈鱼][T2]	10		40	9/	9	千克	ABU	PRQS	/
	--大西洋鲑鱼及多瑙哲罗鱼：									
0302.1410	---大西洋鲑鱼〔101 养殖(非生食)，102 养殖(可能用于生食)，103 野生(非生食)，104 野生(可能用于生食)〕	10		40	9/	9	千克	AB	PRQS	/
0302.1420	---多瑙哲罗鱼〔102 野生，101 养殖〕	7		40	9/	9	千克	AB	PRQS	/
0302.1900	--其他									
0302.1900 10	鲜或冷川陕哲罗鲑(子目 0302.91 至 0302.99 的可食用鱼杂碎除外)〔101 养殖，102 野生〕	10		40	9/	9	千克	AB	PRQS	/
0302.1900 20	鲜或冷秦岭细鳞鲑(子目 0302.91 至 0302.99 的可食用鱼杂碎除外)〔101 养殖，102 野生〕	10		40	9/	9	千克	AB	PRQS	/
0302.1900 90	其他鲜或冷鲑科鱼(子目 0302.91 至 0302.99 的可食用鱼杂碎除外)〔101 养殖，102 野生〕	10		40	9/	9	千克	AB	PRQS	/
	-比目鱼(鲽科、鲆科、舌鳎科、鳎科、菱鲆科、刺鲆科)，但子目 0302.91 至 0302.99 的可食用鱼杂碎除外：									
0302.2100	--庸鲽鱼(马舌鲽、庸鲽、狭鳞庸鲽)									
0302.2100 10	鲜或冷大西洋庸鲽(庸鲽)(子目 0302.91 至 0302.99 的可食用鱼杂碎除外)〔101 养殖，102 野生〕	7		40	9/	9	千克	ABU	PRQS	/
0302.2100 20	鲜或冷马舌鲽(子目 0302.91 至 0302.99 的可食用鱼杂碎除外)〔101 养殖，102 野生〕	7		40	9/	9	千克	ABU	PRQS	/
0302.2100 90	其他鲜或冷庸鲽鱼(子目 0302.91 至 0302.99 的可食用鱼杂碎除外)〔101 养殖，102 野生〕	7		40	9/	9	千克	AB	PRQS	/
0302.2200	--鲽鱼(鲽)〔101 养殖，102 野生〕	7		40	9/	9	千克	AB	PRQS	/
0302.2300	--鳎鱼(鳎属)〔101 养殖，102 野生〕	7		40	9/	9	千克	AB	PRQS	/
0302.2400	--大菱鲆(瘤棘鲆)〔101 养殖，102 野生〕	7		40	9/	9	千克	AB	PRQS	/
0302.2900	--其他									
0302.2900 10	鲜或冷的亚洲箭齿鲽(子目 0302.91 至 0302.99 的可食用鱼杂碎除外)〔101 养殖，102 野生〕	7		40	9/	9	千克	ABU	PRQS	/
0302.2900 90	其他鲜或冷比目鱼(鲽科、鲆科、舌鳎科、鳎科、菱鲆科、刺鲆科)(子目 0302.91 至 0302.99 的可食用鱼杂碎除外)〔101 养殖，102 野生〕	7		40	9/	9	千克	AB	PRQS	/
	-金枪鱼(金枪鱼属)、鲣鱼或狐鲣(鲣)，但子目 0302.91 至 0302.99 的可食用鱼杂碎除外：									
0302.3100	--长鳍金枪鱼〔101 非生食，102 可能用于生食〕	7		40	9/	9	千克	AB	PRQS	/
0302.3200	--黄鳍金枪鱼〔101 非生食，102 可能用于生食〕	7		40	9/	9	千克	AB	PRQS	/
0302.3300	--鲣鱼或狐鲣〔999〕	7		40	9/	9	千克	AB	PRQS	/
0302.3400	--大眼金枪鱼〔101 非生食，102 可能用于生食〕	7		40	9/	9	千克	AB	PRQS	/
	--大西洋及太平洋蓝鳍金枪鱼：									
0302.3510	---大西洋蓝鳍金枪鱼〔102 可能用于生食，101 非生食〕	7		40	9/	9	千克	ABU	PRQS	/

协定税率 %										特惠税率 %			Article Description
亚太5国	东/冰/格	巴基斯坦	韩国	瑞士	哥达	秘鲁	澳大利亚	新西/坡/智	港/澳/台	亚太2国	老/柬/缅	36/3/1	
												0/0/0	Other fry
													---Other:
	0/0/0	4.5	4.2	3.2	0	0	0	0//0	0/0/		/0/0	0/0/0	----Tilapia
7.6	0/0/0	4.5	4.2	3.2	0	0	0	0//0	0/0/		/0/0	0/0/0	----Puffer fish
													----Other cyprinidae fish
5.3	0/0/0	4.5	4.2	3.2	0	0	0	0//0	0/0/		/0/0	0/0/0	Other endangered live carp
5.3	0/0/0	4.5	4.2	3.2	0	0	0	0//0	0/0/		/0/0	0/0/0	Other live carp (Carp (excluding Cyprinus spp., Carassius spp., Ctenopharyngodon idellus, Hypophthalmichthys spp., Cirrhinus spp., Mylopharyngodon piceus, Catla catla, Labeo spp., Osteochilus hasselti, Leptobarbus hoeveni, Megalobrama spp.)
													----Other
5.3	0/0/0	4.5	4.2	3.2	0	0	0	0//0	0/0/0		/0/0	0/0/0	Other endangered live fish
5.3	0/0/0	4.5	4.2	3.2	0	0	0	0//0	0/0/0		/0/0	0/0/0	Other live fish
													Fish, fresh or chilled, excluding fish fillets and other fish meat of heading No. 03.04:
													-Salmonoid, excluding edible fish offal of subheading 0302.91to 0302.99.
	0/0/0	6	4.8	3.6	0	0	0	0//0	0/0/			0/0/0	--Trout (*Salmo trutta*, *Oncorhynchus my-kiss*, *Oncorhynchus clarki*, *Oncorhynchus aguabonita*, *Oncorhynchus gilae*, *Oncorhynchus apache* and *Oncorhynchus chrysogaster*)
	0/0/0	4.5	4	0	0	0	0	0//0	0/0/			0/0/0	--Pacific salmon (Oncorhynchus nerka, Oncorhynchus gorbuscha, Oncorhynchus keta, Oncorhynchus tschawytscha, Oncorhynchus kisutch, Oncorhynchus masou and Oncorhynchus rhodurus)
													--Atlantic salmon(salmo salar)and Danube salmon(Hucho hucho):
	0/0/0	4.5	4	0	0	0	0	0//0	0/0/			0/0/0	---Atlantic salmon
	0/0/0	4.5	4	0	0	0	0	0//0	0/0/			0/0/0	---Danube salmon
													--Other
6.7	0/0/0	4.5	4.8	3.6	0	0	0	0//0	0/0/			0/0/0	Hucho bleekeri, fresh or chilled(excluding edible fish offal of subheading 0302.91 t0 0302.99)
6.7	0/0/0	4.5	4.8	3.6	0	0	0	0//0	0/0/			0/0/0	Brachymystax lenck(Tslinling lenok), fresh or chilled(excluding edible fish offal of subheading 0302.91 t0 0302.99)
6.7	0/0/0	4.5	4.8	3.6	0	0	0	0//0	0/0/			0/0/0	Other salmon, fresh or chilled (excluding edible fish offal of subheading 0302.91 t0 0302.99)
													-Carp (Cyprinus spp., Caras-sius spp., Ctenopharyngodon idellus, Hypophthalmichthys spp., Cirrhinus spp., Mylo-pharyngodon piceus, Catla catla, Labeo spp., Osteochilus hasselti, Leptobarbus hoeveni, Megalobrama spp.)
													--Halibut (*Reinhardtius hippo-glossoides*, *Hippoglossush ippoglossus*, *Hippoglossus stenole-pis*)
5.3	0/0/0	4.5	4.8	3.6	0	0	0	0//0	0/0/			0/0/0	Atlantic halibut(halibut), fresh or chilled(excluding edible fish offal of subheading 0302.91 t0 0302.99)
5.3	0/0/0	4.5	4.8	3.6	0	0	0	0//0	0/0/			0/0/0	Reinhardtius, fresh or chilled (excluding edible fish offal of subheading 0302.91 t0 0302.99)
5.3	0/0/0	4.5	4.8	3.6	0	0	0	0//0	0/0/			0/0/0	Other halibut, fresh or chilled (excluding edible fish offal of subheading 0302.91 t0 0302.99)
5.3	0/0/0	4.5	4.8	3.6	0	0	0	0//0	0/0/			0/0/0	--Plaice (*Pleuronectes platessa*)
5.3	0/0/0	4.5	4.8	3.6	0	0	0	0//0	0/0/			0/0/0	--Sole (*Solea spp.*)
3.5	0/0/0	4.5	4.8	3.6	0	0	0	0//0	0/0/		/0/	0/0/0	--Turbot(Psetta maxima)
													--Other
3.5	0/0/0	4.5	4.8	3.6	0	0	0	0//0	0/0/		/0/	0/0/0	Arrowtooth halibut, fresh or chilled (excluding edible fish offal of subheading 0302.91 t0 0302.99)
3.5	0/0/0	4.5	4.8	3.6	0	0	0	0//0	0/0/		/0/	0/0/0	Other flat fish , fresh or chilled(excluding edible fish offal of subheading 0302.91 t0 0302.99)
													--Tunas (*of the genus Thun-mus*), skipjack or stripe-bellied bonito (*Euthynnus*(*Katsuwo-nus*) *pelamis*), excluding edi-ble fish offal of subheading 0302. 91 t0 0302. 99:
5.3	0/0/0	4.5	4.8	3.6	0	0	0	0//0	0/0/		/0/	0/0/0	--Albacore or longfinned tunas (*Thunnus alalunga*)
5.3	0/0/0	4.5	4.8	3.6	0	0	0	0//0	0/0/			0/0/0	--Yellowfin tunas (*Thunnus albacares*)
4.7	0/0/0	4.5	4.8	3.6	0	0	0	0//0	0/0/			0/0/0	--Skipjack or stripe-bellied bonito
	0/0/0	6	4.8	3.6	0	0	0	0//0	0/0/		/0/0	0/0/0	--Bigeye tunas (*Thunnus obesus*)
													--Atlantic and pacific bluefin tunas:
	0/0/0	6	4.8	3.6	0	0	0	0//0	0/0/		/0/0	0/0/0	---Atlantic bluefin tunas

税则号列	货品名称〔CIQ扩展编码及品名—T2表示见附表2〕	最惠(%)	暂定税率	普通	增值/消费	出口退税	计量单位	监管条件	检验检疫	特殊证件对美关税
0302.3520	---太平洋蓝鳍金枪鱼〔101 非生食,102 可能用于生食。〕	7		40	9/	9	千克	AB	PRQS	/
0302.3600	--南方蓝鳍金枪鱼〔101 非生食,102 可能用于生食〕	7		40	9/	9	千克	AB	PRQS	/
0302.3900	--其他〔101 非生食,102 可能用于生食,103 养殖〕	7		40	9/	9	千克	AB	PRQS	/
	-鲱鱼(大西洋鲱鱼、太平洋鲱鱼)、鳀鱼(鳀属)、沙丁鱼(沙丁鱼、沙瑙鱼属)、小沙丁鱼属、黍鲱或西鲱、鲭鱼[大西洋鲭、澳洲鲭(鲐)、日本鲭(鲐)]、印度鲭(羽鳃鲐属)、马鲛鱼(马鲛属)、对称竹荚鱼、新西兰竹荚鱼及竹荚鱼(竹荚鱼属)、鲹鱼(鲹属)、军曹鱼、银鲳(鲳属)、秋刀鱼、圆鲹(圆鲹属))、多春鱼(毛鳞鱼)、剑鱼、鲔鱼、狐鲣(狐鲣属)、枪鱼 、旗鱼、四鳍旗鱼(旗鱼科),但子目 0302.91 至 0302.99 的可食用鱼杂碎除外:									
0302.4100	--鲱鱼(大西洋鲱鱼、太平洋鲱鱼)									
0302.4100 10	鲜或冷太平洋鲱鱼(子目 0302.91 至 0302.99 的可食用鱼杂碎除外)〔101 养殖,102 野生〕			40	9/	9	千克	ABU	PRQS	/
0302.4100 90	鲜或冷大西洋鲱鱼(子目 0302.91 至 0302.99 的可食用鱼杂碎除外)〔101 养殖,102 野生〕	7 7		40	9/	9	千克	AB	PRQS	/
0302.4200	--鳀鱼(鳀属)〔101 饲料用其他海水鱼,102 鲜或冷养殖鳀鱼(鳀属),103 鲜或冷野生鳀鱼(鳀属)〕	7		40	9/	9	千克	AB	PRQS	/
0302.4300	--沙丁鱼(沙丁鱼、沙瑙鱼属)、小沙丁鱼属、黍鲱或西鲱[T2]	7		40	9/	9	千克	AB	PRQS	/
0302.4400	--鲭鱼[大西洋鲭、澳洲鲭(鲐)、日本鲭(鲐)]〔101 饲料用鲭鱼,102 养殖日本鲭(鲐),103 大西洋鲭,104 澳洲鲭(鲐) ,105 野生日本鲭(鲐)〕	7		40	9/	9	千克	AB	PRQS	/
0302.4500	--对称竹荚鱼、新西兰竹荚鱼及竹荚鱼(竹荚鱼属)〔101 饲料用其他海水鱼,102 养殖对称竹荚鱼,103 养殖新西兰竹荚鱼及竹荚鱼(竹荚鱼属),104 野生对称竹荚鱼,105 野生新西兰竹荚鱼及竹荚鱼(竹荚鱼属)〕	7		40	9/	9	千克	AB	PRQS	/
0302.4600	--军曹鱼〔101 饲料用其他海水鱼,102 食用〕	7		40	9/	9	千克	AB	PRQS	/
0302.4700	--剑鱼〔999〕	7		40	9/	9	千克	ABU	PRQS	/
0302.4900	--其他[T2]	7		40	9/	9	千克	AB	PRQS	/
	-犀鳕科、多丝真鳕科、鳕科、长尾鳕科、黑鳕科、无须鳕科、深海鳕科及南极鳕科鱼,但子目 0302.91 至 0302.99 的可食用鱼杂碎除外:									
0302.5100	--鳕鱼(大西洋鳕鱼、格陵兰鳕鱼、太平洋鳕鱼)〔101 大西洋鳕鱼,102 太平洋鳕鱼,103 格陵兰鳕鱼〕	7		40	9/	9	千克	AB	PRQS	/
0302.5200	--黑线鳕鱼(黑线鳕)〔999〕	7		40	9/	9	千克	AB	PRQS	/
0302.5300	--绿青鳕鱼〔999〕	7		40	9/	9	千克	AB	PRQS	/
0302.5400	--狗鳕鱼(无须鳕属、长鳍鳕属)〔101 饲料用其他海水鱼,102 无须鳕属,103 长鳍鳕属〕	7		40	9/	9	千克	AB	PRQS	/
0302.5500	--狭鳕鱼〔101 饲料用其他海水鱼,102 食用〕	7		40	9/	9	千克	ABU	PRQS	/
0302.5600	--蓝鳕鱼(小鳍鳕、南蓝鳕)〔101 饲料用其他海水鱼,102 小鳍鳕,103 南蓝鳕〕	7		40	9/	9	千克	AB	PRQS	/
0302.5900	--其他[T2]	7		40	9/	9	千克	AB	PRQS	/
	-罗非鱼(口孵非鲫属)、鲶鱼(𩷶鲶属、鲶属、胡鲶属、真鮰属)、鲤科鱼(鲤属、鲫属、草鱼、鲢属、鲮属、青鱼、卡特拉鲃、野鲮属、哈氏纹唇鱼、何氏细须鲃、鲂属)、鳗鱼(鳗鲡属)、尼罗河鲈鱼(尼罗尖吻鲈)及黑鱼(鳢属),但子目 0302.91 至 0302.99 的可食用鱼杂碎除外:									
0302.7100	--罗非鱼(口孵非鲫属)〔101 养殖罗非鱼(口孵非鲫属),102 野生罗非鱼(口孵非鲫属)〕	7		40	9/	9	千克	AB	PRQS	/
0302.7200	--鲶鱼(𩷶鲶属、鲶属、胡鲶属、真鮰属)〔101 饲料用其他海水鱼,102 养殖𩷶鲶属,103 养殖胡鲶属,104 养殖真鮰属,105 野生𩷶鲶属,106 野生胡鲶属,107 野生真鮰属〕	10		40	9/	9	千克	AB	PRQS	/

协定税率 %										特惠税率 %			Article Description
亚太5国	东/冰/格	巴基斯坦	韩国	瑞士	哥达	秘鲁	澳大利亚	新西/坡/智	港/澳/台	亚太2国	老/柬/缅	36/3/1	
4.7	0/0/0	4.5	4.8	3.6	0	0	0	0//0	0/0/		/0/0	0/0/0	---Pacific bluefin tunas
	0/0/0	6	4.8	3.6	0	0	0	0//0	0/0/		/0/0	0/0/0	--Southern bluefin tunas(Thunnus maccoyii)
4.7	0/0/0	4.5	4.8	3.6	0	0	0	0//0	0/0/		/0/0	0/0/0	--Other
													-Herrings (*Clupea harengus*, *Clupea pallasii*), *anchovies* (*Engraulis spp.*), sardines (*Sardina pilchardus*, *Sardi-nops spp*), sardinella (*sardinella spp.*), brisling or sprats (*Sprattus Sprattus*), mackerel (*Scomber Scombrus*, *Scomber australasicus*, *Scomber japonicus*), Indian macker-els (*Rastrelliger spp.*), seerfi-shes (*Scomberomorus spp.*), jack and horse mackerel (*Tra-churus spp.*), jacks, crevalles (*Caranx spp.*), cobia (*Rachy-centron canadum*), silver pom-frets (*Pampus spp.*), Pacific saury (*Cololabis saira*), scad s (*Decapterus spp.*), capelin (*Mallotus villosus*), swordfish (*Xiphias gladius*), Kawakawa (*Euthynnus affinis*), bonitos (*Sarda spp.*), marlins, sail-fishes, spearfish (*Istiophoridae*), excluding edible fish offalof subheading 0302. 91 to 0302. 99:
													--Herring(Clupea harengus,clupea pallasii)
4.7	0/0/0	4.5	4.8	3.6	0	0	0	0//0	0/0/			0/0/0	Clupea pallasii, fresh or chilled(excluding edible fish offal of subheading 0302.91 t0 0302.99)
4.7	0/0/0	4.5	4.8	3.6	0	0	0	0//0	0/0/			0/0/0	Herrings(Clupea harengus), fresh or chilled(excluding edible fish offal of subheading 0302.91 t0 0302.99)
4.7	0/0/0	4.5	4.8	3.6	0	0	0	0//0	0/0/0		/0/0	0/0/0	--anchovies(Engraulis spp.)
4.7	0/0/0	4.5	4.8	3.6	0	0	0	0//0	0/0/			0/0/0	--sardines(Sardina pilchardus, Sardinops spp.), sardinella(Sardinella spp.), brisling or sprats(Sprattus sprattus)
4.7	0/0/0	4.5	4.8	3.6	0	0	0	0//0	0/0/			0/0/0	--mackerel(Scomber scombrus, Scomber australasicus, Scomber japonicus)
4.7	0/0/0	4.5	4.8	3.6	0	0	0	0//0	0/0/0		/0/0	0/0/0	--jack and horse mackerel (Trachurus spp.), cobia (Rachycentron canadum)
4.7	0/0/0	4.5	4.8	3.6	0	0	0	0//0	0/0/0		/0/0	0/0/0	--Cobia(Rachycentron canadum)
4.7	0/0/0	4.5	4.8	3.6	0	0	0	0//0	0/0/			0/0/0	--Swordfish(Xiphias gladius)
4.7	0/0/0	4.5	4.8	3.6	0	0	0	0//0	0/0/0		/0/0	0/0/0	-Other
													-Fish of the families Bregmacer-otidae, Euclichthyidae, Ga-didae, Macrouridae, Melanoni-dae, Merlucciidae, Moridae and Muraenolepididae, excluding edible fish offal of subheading 0303.91 to 0303. 99:
4.7	0/0/0	4.5	4.8	3.6	0	0	0	0//0	0/0/			0/0/0	--Cod(Gadus morhua, Gadus ogac, Gadus macrocephalus)
4.7	0/0/0	4.5	4.8	3.6	0	0	0	0//0	0/0/			0/0/0	--Haddock(Melanogrammus aeglefinus)
4.7	0/0/0	4.5	4.8	3.6	0	0	0	0//0	0/0/			0/0/0	--Coalfish(Pollachius virens)
4.7	0/0/0	4.5	4.8	3.6	0	0	0	0//0	0/0/0		/0/0	0/0/0	--Hake(Merluccius spp., Urophycis spp.)
4.7	0/0/0	4.5	4.8	3.6	0	0	0	0//0	0/0/0		/0/0	0/0/0	--Alaska Pollack(Theragra chalcogramma)
4.7	0/0/0	4.5	4.8	3.6	0	0	0	0//0	0/0/0		/0/0	0/0/0	--Blue whitings(Micromesistius poutassou, Micromesistius australis)
4.7	0/0/0	4.5	4.8	3.6	0	0	0	0//0	0/0/0		/0/0	0/0/0	--Other
													-Tilapias (*Oreochromis spp.*), catfish (*Pangasius spp.*, *Silu-rus spp.*, *Clarias spp.*, *Icta-lurus spp.*), carp (*Cyprinus spp.*, *Carassius spp.*, *Cteno-pharyngodon idellus*, *Hypo-phthalmichthys spp.*, *Cirrhi-nus spp.*, *Mylopharyngodon piceus*, *Catla catla*, *Labeo spp*,. *Osteochilus hasselti*, *Leptobarbus hoeveni*, *Megalo-brama spp*), eels (*Anguilla spp.*), Nile perch (*Lates niloticus*) and snakeheads (*Chamma spp.*), excluding edi-ble fish offal of subheading 0303.91 to 0303.99:
	0/0/0	6	4.8	3.6	0	0	0	0//0	0/0/		/0/0	0/0/0	--Tilapia(oreochromis spp.)
6.7	0/0/0	4.5	4.8	3.6	0	0	0	0//0	0/0/0		/0/0	0/0/0	--catfish(Pangasius spp., Silurus spp., Clarias spp., Ictalurus spp.)

税则号列		货品名称〔CIQ扩展编码及品名－T2表示见附表2〕	最惠(%)	暂定税率	普通	增值/消费	出口退税	计量单位	监管条件	检验检疫	特殊证件对美关税
0302.7300		--鲤科鱼(鲤属、鲫属、草鱼、鲢属、鲮属、青鱼、卡特拉鲃、野鲮属、哈氏纹唇鱼、何氏细须鲃、鲂属)[T2]	7		40	9/	9	千克	AB	PRQS	/
0302.7400		--鳗鱼(鳗鲡属)									
0302.7400	10	鲜或冷花鳗鲡(子目0302.91至0302.99的可食用鱼杂碎除外)〔101养殖非生食,102养殖可能用于生食,103野生非生食,104野生可能用于生食〕	7		40	9/	9	千克	ABE	PRQS	/
0302.7400	20	鲜或冷欧洲鳗鲡(子目0302.91至0302.99的可食用鱼杂碎除外)〔101养殖非生食,102养殖可能用于生食,103野生非生食,104野生可能用于生食〕	7		40	9/	9	千克	ABEF	PRQS	/
0302.7400	90	其他鲜或冷鳗鱼(鳗鲡属)(子目0302.91至0302.99的可食用鱼杂碎除外)〔101养殖非生食,102养殖可能用于生食,103野生非生食,104野生可能用于生食〕	7		40	9/	9	千克	AB	PRQS	/
0302.7900		--其他									
0302.7900	01	鲜或冷尼罗河鲈鱼(尼罗尖吻鲈)(子目0302.91至0302.99的可食用鱼杂碎除外)〔101养殖非生食,102养殖可能用于生食,103野生非生食,104野生可能用于生食〕	7		40	9/	9	千克	AB	PRQS	/
0302.7900	90	鲜或冷的黑鱼(鳢属)(子目0302.91至0302.99的可食用鱼杂碎除外)〔101养殖非生食,102养殖可能用于生食,103野生非生食,104野生可能用于生食〕	7		40	9/	9	千克	AB	PRQS	/
		-其他鱼,但子目0302.91至0302.99的可食用鱼杂碎除外:									
0302.8100		--角鲨及其他鲨鱼									
0302.8100	10	鲜或冷濒危鲨鱼(子目0302.91至0302.99的可食用鱼杂碎除外)〔999〕	7		40	9/	0	千克	ABEF	PRQS	/
0302.8100	90	鲜或冷其他鲨鱼(子目0302.91至0302.99的可食用鱼杂碎除外)〔999〕	7		40	9/	9	千克	AB	PRQS	/
0302.8200		--魟鱼及鳐鱼(鳐科)〔101饲料用其他海水鱼,102食用〕	7		40	9/	9	千克	AB	PRQS	/
0302.8300		--南极犬牙鱼(南极犬牙鱼属)〔999〕	7		40	9/	9	千克	ABU	PRQS	/
0302.8400		--尖吻鲈鱼(舌齿鲈属)〔999〕	7		40	9/	9	千克	AB	PRQS	/
0302.8500		--菱羊鲷(鲷科)〔应为:101饲料用其他海水鱼,102养殖非生食,103养殖可能用于生食,104野生非生食,105野生可能用于生食〕	7		40	9/	9	千克	AB	PRQS	/
		--其他:									
0302.8910		---带鱼〔999〕	7		40	9/	6	千克	AB	PRQS	/
0302.8920		---黄鱼〔101养殖,102野生〕	7		40	9/	6	千克	AB	PRQS	/
0302.8930		---鲳鱼〔101养殖,102野生〕	7		40	9/	6	千克	AB	PRQS	/
0302.8940		---鲀〔999〕	10		40	9/	6	千克	AB	PRQS	/
0302.8990		---其他									
0302.8990	01	鲜或冷的其他鲈鱼(子目0302.91至0302.99的可食用鱼杂碎除外)〔101养殖非生食,102养殖可能用于生食,103野生非生食,104野生可能用于生食〕	7		40	9/	9	千克	AB	PRQS	/
0302.8990	10	其他未列名濒危鲜或冷鱼(子目0302.91至0302.99的可食用鱼杂碎除外)〔999〕	7		40	9/	0	千克	ABFE	PRQS	/
0302.8990	20	鲜或冷的平鲉属(子目0302.91至0302.99的可食用鱼杂碎除外)〔101养殖,102野生〕	7		40	9/	9	千克	ABU	PRQS	/
0302.8990	30	鲜或冷的鲪鲉属(叶鳍鲉属)(子目0302.91至0302.99的可食用鱼杂碎除外)〔101养殖,102野生〕	7		40	9/	9	千克	ABU	PRQS	/
0302.8990	90	其他鲜或冷鱼(子目0302.91至0302.99的可食用鱼杂碎除外)[T2]	7		40	9/	9	千克	AB	PRQS	/
		-鱼肝、鱼卵、鱼精、鱼鳍、鱼头、鱼尾、鱼鳔及其他可食用鱼杂碎:									
0302.9100		--鱼肝、鱼卵及鱼精									
0302.9100	10	鲜或冷濒危鱼种的肝、鱼卵及鱼精[T2]	7		50	9/	0	千克	ABFE	PRQS	/
0302.9100	90	其他鲜或冷鱼肝、鱼卵及鱼精[T2]	7		50	9/	9	千克	AB	PRQS	/
0302.9200		--鲨鱼翅									
0302.9200	10	鲜或冷濒危鲨鱼翅〔999〕	12		40	9/	0	千克	ABFE	PRQS	/
0302.9200	90	其他鲜或冷鲨鱼翅〔999〕	12		40	9/	9	千克	AB	PRQS	/
0302.9900		--其他									
0302.9900	10	其他鲜或冷可食用濒危鱼杂碎〔101养殖,102野生〕	7		40	9/	0	千克	ABFE	PRQS	/
0302.9900	20	鲜或冷的大菱鲆、比目鱼、鲱鱼、鲭鱼、鲳鱼、带鱼、尼罗河鲈鱼、尖吻鲈鱼、其他鲈鱼的可食用其他鱼杂碎〔101养殖,102野生〕	7		40	9/	9	千克	AB	PRQS	/
0302.9900	90	其他鲜或冷可食用其他鱼杂碎〔101养殖,102野生〕	7		40	9/	9	千克	AB	PRQS	/

协定税率 %										特惠税率 %			Article Description
亚太5国	东/冰/格	巴基斯坦	韩国	瑞士	哥达	秘鲁	澳大利亚	新西/坡/智	港/澳/台	亚太2国	老/柬/缅	36/3/1	
4.7	0/0/0	4.5	4.8	3.6	0	0	0	0//0	0/0/0		/0/0	0/0/0	--Carp (*Cyprinus spp.*, *Caras- sius spp.*, *Ctenopharyngodon idellus*, *Hypophthalmichthys spp.*, *Cirrhinus spp.*, *Mylo- pharyngodon piceus*, *Catla catla*, *Labeo spp.*, *Osteochi-lus hasselti*, *Leptobarbus ho-eveni*, *Megalobrama spp.*)
													--Eel(anguilla spp.)
4.7	0/0/0	4.5	4.8	3.6	0	0	0	0//0	0/0/		//0	0/0/C	Marbled eels, fresh or chilled(excluding edible fish offal of subheading 0302.91 t0 0302.99)
4.7	0/0/0	4.5	4.8	3.6	0	0	0	0//0	0/0/		//0	0/0/0	European eels, fresh or chilled(excluding edible fish offal of subheading 0302.91 t0 0302.99)
4.7	0/0/0	4.5	4.8	3.6	0	0	0	0//0	0/0/		//0	0/C/0	Other eels, fresh or chilled(excluding edible fish offal of subheading 0302.91 t0 0302.99)
													--Other
4.7	0/0/0	4.5	4.8	3.6	0	0	0	0//0	0/0/0		/0/0	0/0/0	Nile perch(Lates niloticus) , fresh or chilled(excluding edible fish offal of subheading 0302.91 t0 0302.99)
4.7	0/0/0	4.5	4.8	3.6	0	0	0	0//0	0/0/0		/0/0	0/0/0	Snakeheads(Channa spp.), fresh or chilled(excluding edible fish offal of subheading 0302.91 t0 0302.99)
													-Other fish excluding edible fish offal of subheading 0302. 91 to 0302. 99:
													--Dogfish and other sharks
5.3	0/0/0	4.5	4.8	3.6	0	0	0	0//0	0/0/			0/0/0	Endangered shark, fresh or chilled(excluding edible fish offal of subheading 0302.91 t0 0302.99)
5.3	0/0/0	4.5	4.8	3.6	0	0	0	0//0	0/0/			0/0/0	Other sharks, fresh or chilled excluding livers and roes
4.7	0/0/0	4.5	4.8	3.6	0	0	0	0//0	0/0/0		/C/0	0/0/0	--Rays and skates(Rajidae)
4.7	0/0/0	4.5	4.8	3.6	0	0	0	0//0	0/0/		/0/0	0/0/0	--Toothfish(dissostichus spp.)
4.7	0/0/0	4.5	4.8	3.6	0	0	0	0//0	0/0/0		/0/0	0/0/0	--Seabass(Dicentrarchus spp.)
4.7	0/0/0	4.5	4.8	3.6	0	0	0	0//0	0/0/0		/0/0	0/0/0	--Seabream(Sparidae)
													--Other:
4.7	0/0/0	0	4.8	3.6	0	0	0	0//0	0/0/			0/0/0	---Scabber fish(Trichurius)
4.7	0/0/0	4.5	4.8	3.6	0	0	0	0//0	0/0/			0/0/0	---Yellow croaker(Pseudosicaena)
4.7	0/0/0	4	4.8	3.6	0	0	0	0//0	0/0/			0/0/0	---Tilapia
6.7	0/0/0	4.5	4.8	3.6	0	0	0	0//0	0/0/		/0/0	0/0/0	---Puffer fish
													---Other
4.7	0/0/0	4.5	4.8	3.6	0	0	0	0//0	0/0/0		/0/0	0/0/0	Other perch, fresh or chilled(excluding edible fish offal of subheading 0302.91 t0 0302.99)
4.7	0/0/0	4.5	4.8	3.6	0	0	0	0//0	0/0/0		/0/0	0/0/0	Other endangered fish, fresh or chilled(excluding edible fish offal of subheading 0302.91 t0 0302.99)
4.7	0/0/0	4.5	4.8	3.6	0	0	0	0//0	0/0/0		/0/0	0/0/0	Fresh and cold flat scorpionfish genera(excluding edible fish offal of subheading 0302.91 t0 0302.99)
4.7	0/0/0	4.5	4.8	3.6	0	0	0	0//0	0/0/0		/0/0	0/0/0	Fresh and cold Jun scorpionfish genera (leaf scorpionfish fins)(excluding edible fish offal of subheading 0302.91 t0 0302.99)
4.7	0/0/0	4.5	4.8	3.6	0	0	0	0//0	0/0/C		/0/0	0/0/0	Other fish, fresh or chilled(excluding edible fish offal of subheading 0302.91 t0 0302.99)
													Lvers, roes, milt, fins, fish head, fish tail, swim bladder, other edible fish offals of other fish
													--Livers, roes, milt
	0/0/0	6	4.8	3.6	0	0	0	0//0	0/0/		/0/	0/0/0	Livers, roes and milt of endangered fish, cold or chilled
	0/0/0	6	4.8	3.6	0	0	0	0//0	0/0/		/0/	0/0/0	Other fish livers, roes and milt, cold or chilled
													--Shark fins
9	0/0/0	4.5	4.8	3.6	0	0	0	0//0	0/0/			0/0/0	Endangered Shark fins, cold or chilled
9	0/0/0	4.5	4.8	3.6	0	0	0	0//0	0/0/			0/0/0	Other Shark fins, cold or chilled
													--Ohter
	0/0/0	4.5	4	0	0	0	0	0//0	0/0/			0/0/0	Other edible endangered fish offals, cold or chilled
	0/0/0	4.5	4	0	0	0	0	0//0	0/0/			0/0/0	Other edible fish offals of Turbots, flatfish, herring, mackerel, Pomfret, hairtail, Nile perch and other perch, fresh or chilled
	0/0/0	4.5	4	0	0	0	0	0//0	0/0/			0/0/0	Other edible fish offals of other fish , cold or chilled

税则号列		货品名称〔CIQ扩展编码及品名－T2表示见附表2〕	最惠(%)	暂定税率	普通	增值/消费	出口退税	计量单位	监管条件	检验检疫	特殊证件对美关税
03.03		**冻鱼，但税目03.04的鱼片及其他鱼肉除外：**									
		-鲑科鱼，但子目0303.91至0303.99的可食用鱼杂碎除外：									
0303.1100		--红大麻哈鱼〔101 冻养殖红大麻哈鱼，102 冻野生红大麻哈鱼〕	7		40	9/	9	千克	AB	PRQS	/42
0303.1200		--其他大麻哈鱼[细鳞大麻哈鱼、大麻哈鱼(种)、大鳞大麻哈鱼、银大麻哈鱼、马苏大麻哈鱼、玫瑰大麻哈鱼][T2]	7		40	9/	9	千克	ABU	PRQS	/42
0303.1300		--大西洋鲑鱼及多瑙哲罗鱼〔101 养殖大西洋鲑鱼(非生食)，102 养殖大西洋鲑鱼(可能用于生食)，103 养殖多瑙哲罗鱼，104 野生大西洋鲑鱼(非生食)，105 野生大西洋鲑鱼(可能用于生食)，106 野生多瑙哲罗鱼〕	7	5	40	9/	9	千克	AB	PRQS	/40
0303.1400		--鳟鱼(河鳟、虹鳟、克拉克大麻哈鱼、阿瓜大麻哈鱼、吉雨大麻哈鱼、亚利桑那大麻哈鱼、金腹大麻哈鱼)[T2]	12		40	9/	9	千克	AB	PRQS	/47
0303.1900		--其他									
0303.1900	10	冻川陕哲罗鲑(但子目0303.91至0303.99的可食用鱼杂碎除外)〔101 养殖，102 野生〕	10		40	9/	9	千克	AB	PRQS	/45
0303.1900	20	冻秦岭细鳞鲑(但子目0303.91至0303.99的可食用鱼杂碎除外)〔101 养殖，102 野生〕	10		40	9/	9	千克	AB	PRQS	/45
0303.1900	90	其他冻鲑科鱼(但子目0303.91至0303.99的可食用鱼杂碎除外)〔101 养殖，102 野生〕	10		40	9/	9	千克	AB	PRQS	/45
		-罗非鱼(口孵非鲫属)、鲶鱼(𩷶鲶属、鲶属、胡鲶属、真鮰属)、鲤科鱼(鲤属、鲫属、草鱼、鲢属、鲮属、青鱼、卡特拉鲃、野鲮属、哈氏纹唇鱼、何氏细须鲃、鲂属)、鳗鱼(鳗鲡属)、尼罗河鲈鱼(尼罗尖吻鲈)及黑鱼(鳢属)，但子目0303.91至0303.99的可食用鱼杂碎除外：									
0303.2300		--罗非鱼(口孵非鲫属)〔101 养殖，102 野生〕	7		40	9/	9	千克	AB	PRQS	/42
0303.2400		--鲶鱼(𩷶鲶属、鲶属、胡鲶属、真鮰属)[T2]	10		40	9/	9	千克	AB	PRQS	/45
0303.2500		--鲤科鱼(鲤属、鲫属、草鱼、鲢属、鲮属、青鱼、卡特拉鲃、野鲮属、哈氏纹唇鱼、何氏细须鲃、鲂属)[T2]	10		40	9/	9	千克	AB	PRQS	/45
0303.2600		--鳗鱼(鳗鲡属)									
0303.2600	10	冻花鳗鲡(但子目0303.91至0303.99的可食用鱼杂碎除外)〔101 养殖，102 野生〕	10		40	9/	9	千克	ABE	PRQS	/45
0303.2600	20	冻欧洲鳗鲡(但子目0303.91至0303.99的可食用鱼杂碎除外)〔101 养殖，102 野生〕	10		40	9/	9	千克	ABEF	PRQS	/45
0303.2600	90	其他冻鳗鱼(鳗鲡属)(但子目0303.91至0303.99的可食用鱼杂碎除外)〔101 养殖，102 野生〕	10		40	9/	9	千克	AB	PRQS	/45
0303.2900		--其他									
0303.2900	01	冻尼罗河鲈鱼(尼罗尖吻鲈)(但子目0303.91至0303.99的可食用鱼杂碎除外)〔101 养殖，102 野生〕	7		40	9/	9	千克	AB	PRQS	/42
0303.2900	90	冻黑鱼(鳢属)(但子目0303.91至0303.99的可食用鱼杂碎除外)〔101 养殖，102 野生〕	7		40	9/	9	千克	AB	PRQS	/42
		-比目鱼(鲆科、鲽科、舌鳎科、鳎科、菱鲆科、刺鲆科)，但子目0303.91至0303.99的可食用鱼杂碎除外：									
		--庸鲽鱼(马舌鲽、庸鲽、狭鳞庸鲽)：									
0303.3110		---格陵兰庸鲽鱼〔999〕	7	5	40	9/	9	千克	ABU	PRQS	/40
0303.3190		---其他									
0303.3190	10	冻大西洋庸鲽(庸鲽)(但子目0303.91至0303.99的可食用鱼杂碎除外)〔101 养殖，102 野生〕	10		40	9/	9	千克	ABU	PRQS	/45
0303.3190	90	其他冻庸鲽鱼(但子目0303.91至0303.99的可食用鱼杂碎除外)〔101 养殖，102 野生〕	10		40	9/	9	千克	AB	PRQS	/45
0303.3200		--鲽鱼(鲽)〔101 养殖，102 野生〕	7	2	40	9/	9	千克	AB	PRQS	/37
0303.3300		--鳎鱼(鳎属)〔101 养殖，102 野生〕	7		40	9/	9	千克	AB	PRQS	/42
0303.3400		--大菱鲆(瘤棘鲆)〔101 养殖，102 野生〕	7		40	9/	9	千克	AB	PRQS	/42
0303.3900		--其他									

协定税率 %										特惠税率 %			
亚太5国	东/冰/格	巴基斯坦	韩国	瑞士	哥达	秘鲁	澳大利亚	新西/坡/智	港/澳/台	亚太2国	老/柬/缅	36/3/1	Article Description
													Fish, frozen, excluding fish fillets and other fish meat of heading No. 03.04:
													-Salmonidae, excluding edible fish offal of subheading 0303.91 to 0303.99:
4.7	0/0/0	4.5	4	0	0	0	0	0//0	0/0/		/0/	0/0/0	--Sockeye salmon(red salmon)(*Oncorhynchus nerka*)
4.7	0/0/0	4.5	4	0	0	0	0	0//0	0/0/		/0/	0/0/0	--Other Pacific salmon(Oncorhynchus gorbuscha, Oncorhynchus keta, Oncorhynchus tschawytscha, Oncorhynchus kisutch, Oncorhynchus masou and Oncorhynchus rhodurus)
	0/0/0	4.5	4	0	0	0	0	0//0	0/0/			0/0/0	--Atlantic salmon(Salmo salar) and Danube salmon(Hucho hucho)
	0/0/0	6	4.8	3.6	0	0	0	0//0	0/0/			0/0/0	--Trout(Salmo trutta, Oncorhynchus mykiss, Oncorhynchus clarki, Oncorhynchus aguabonita, Oncorhynchus gilae, Oncorhynchus apache and Oncorhynchus chrysogaster)
													--Other
6.7	0/0/0	4.5	4	0	0	0	0	0//0	0/0/			0/0/0	Hucho bleekeri(excluding edible fish offal of subheading 0302.91 t0 0302.99), frozen
6.7	0/0/0	4.5	4	0	0	0	0	0//0	0/0/			0/0/0	Tslinling lenok(Brachymystax lenck)(excluding edible fish offal of subheading 0302.91 t0 0302.99), frozen
6.7	0/0/0	4.5	4	0	0	0	0	0//0	0/0/			0/0/0	Other salmon, frozen(excluding edible fish offal of subheading 0302.91 t0 0302.99)
													-Tilapias (*Oreochromis spp.*), catfish (*Pangasius spp.*, *Silu-rus spp.*, *Clarias spp.*, *Icta-lurus spp.*), carp (*Cyprinus spp.*, *Carassius spp.*, *Cteno-pharyngodon idellus*, *Hypo-phthalmichthys spp.*, *Cirrhi-nus spp.*, *Mylopharyngodon piceus*, *Catla catla*, *Labeo spp.*. *Osteochilus hasselti*, *Leptobarbus hoeveni*, *Megalo-brama spp*), eels (*Anguilla spp.*), Nile perch (*Lates niloticus*) and snakeheads (*Chamma spp.*), excluding edi-ble fish offal of subheading 0303.91 to 0303.99:
3.5	0/0/0	4.5	4	0	0	0	0	0//0	0/0/	0	/0/0	0/0/0	--Tilapia(oreochromis spp.)
5	0/0/0	5	0	0	0	0	0	0//0	0/0/0	0	/0/0	0/0/0	--Catfish(Pangasius spp., Silurus spp., Clarias spp., Ictalurus spp.)
5	0/0/0	0	0	0	0	0	0	0//0	0/0/0	0	/0/0	0/0/0	--Carp (*Cyprinus spp.*, *Caras- sius spp.*, *Ctenopharyngodon idellus*, *Hypophthalmichthys spp.*, *Cirrhinus spp.*, *Mylo- pharyngodon piceus*, *Catla catla*, *Labeo spp.*, *Osteochi-lus hasselti*, *Leptobarbus ho-eveni*, *Megalobrama spp.*)
													--Eel(anguilla spp.)
6.7	0/0/0	8	4.8	3.6	0	0	0	0//0	0/0/			0/0/0	Marbled eels(Anguilla marmorata), frozen(excluding edible fish offal of subheading 0302.91 t0 0302.99)
6.7	0/0/0	8	4.8	3.6	0	0	0	0//0	0/0/			0/0/0	European eels, frozen(excluding edible fish offal of subheading 0302.91 t0 0302.99)
6.7	0/0/0	8	4.8	3.6	0	0	0	0//0	0/0/			0/0/0	Other eels(Anguilla spp.(excluding edible fish offal of subheading 0302.91 t0 0302.99); frozen
													--Other
3.5	0/0/0	5	0	0	0	0	0	0//0	0/0/0	0	/0/0	0/0/0	Nile perch(Lates niloticus), frozen(excluding edible fish offal of subheading 0302.91 t0 0302.99)
3.5	0/0/0	5	0	0	0	0	0	0//0	0/0/0	0	/0/0	0/0/0	Snakeheads(Channa spp.), frozen(excluding edible fish offal of subheading 0302.91 t0 0302.99)
													-Flat fish (*Pleuronectidae*, *Bothidae*, *Cynoglossidae*, *So-leidae*, *Scophthalmidae and Citharidae*), excluding edible fish offal of subheading 0303.91 to 0303.99:
													--Halibut (*Reinhardtius hippo-glossoides*, *Hippoglossus hip-poglossus*, *Hippoglossus stenolepis*):
4.7	0/0/0	4.5	4	0	0	0	0	0//0	0/0/			0/0/0	---Greenland halibut
													---Other
6.7	0/0/0	4.5	4	0	0	0	0	0//0	0/0/			0/0/0	Frozen Atlantic agent sole (commonplace sole)(excluding edible fish offal of subheading 0302.91 t0 0302.99)
6.7	0/0/0	4.5	4	0	0	0	0	0//0	0/0/			0/0/0	Frozen horse tongue sole(excluding edible fish offal of subheading 0302.91 t0 0302.99)
4.7	0/0/0	8	4.8	3.6	0	0	0	0//0	0/0/			0/0/0	--Plaice (*Pleuronectes platessa*)
4.7	0/0/0	8	4.8	3.6	0	0	0	0//0	0/0/			0/0/0	--Sole (*Solea spp.*)
5.6	0/0/0	8	4	0	0	0	0	0//0	0/0/			0/0/0	--Turbots(Psetta maxima)
													--Other

税则号列		货品名称〔CIQ 扩展编码及品名—T2 表示见附表 2〕	最惠(%)	暂定税率	普通	增值/消费	出口退税	计量单位	监管条件	检验检疫	特殊证件对美关税
0303.3900	10	冻亚洲箭齿鲽(但子目 0303.91 至 0303.99 的可食用鱼杂碎除外)〔101 养殖,102 野生〕	7		40	9/	9	千克	ABU	PRQS	/42
0303.3900	90	其他冻比目鱼(鲽科、鲆科、舌鳎科、鳎科、菱鲆科、刺鲆科)(但子目 0303.91 至 0303.99 的可食用鱼杂碎除外)〔T2〕	7		40	9/	9	千克	AB	PRQS	/42
		-金枪鱼(金枪鱼属)、鲣鱼或狐鲣(鲣),但子目 0303.91 至 0303.99 的可食用鱼杂碎除外:									
0303.4100		--长鳍金枪鱼〔999〕	7	6	40	9/	9	千克	AB	PRQS	/41
0303.4200		--黄鳍金枪鱼〔999〕	7	6	40	9/	9	千克	AB	PRQS	/41
0303.4300		--鲣鱼或狐鲣〔999〕	7		40	9/	9	千克	AB	PRQS	/42
0303.4400		--大眼金枪鱼〔999〕	7	6	40	9/	9	千克	ABU	PRQS	/41
		--大西洋及太平洋蓝鳍金枪鱼:									
0303.4510		---大西洋蓝鳍金枪鱼〔999〕	7	6	40	9/	9	千克	ABU	PRQS	/41
0303.4520		---太平洋蓝鳍金枪鱼〔999〕	7	6	40	9/	9	千克	AB	PRQS	/41
0303.4600		--南方蓝鳍金枪鱼〔999〕	7	6	40	9/	9	千克	AB	PRQS	/41
0303.4900		--其他〔101 养殖,102 野生〕	7		40	9/	9	千克	AB	PRQS	/42
		-鲱鱼(大西洋鲱鱼、太平洋鲱鱼)、鳀鱼(鳀属)、沙丁鱼(沙丁鱼、沙瑙鱼属)、小沙丁鱼属、黍鲱或西鲱、鲭鱼[大西洋鲭、澳洲鲭(鲐)、日本鲭(鲐)]、印度鲭(羽鳃鲐属)、马鲛鱼(马鲛属)、对称竹荚鱼、新西兰竹荚鱼及竹荚鱼(竹荚鱼属)、鲹鱼(鲹属)、军曹鱼、银鲳(鲳属)、秋刀鱼、圆鲹(圆鲹属)、多春鱼(毛鳞鱼)、剑鱼、鲔鱼、狐鲣(狐鲣属)、枪鱼、旗鱼、四鳍旗鱼(旗鱼科),但子目 0303.91 至 0303.99 的可食用鱼杂碎除外:									
0303.5100		--鲱鱼(大西洋鲱鱼、太平洋鲱鱼)									
0303.5100	10	冻太平洋鲱鱼(但子目 0303.91 至 0303.99 的可食用鱼杂碎除外:)〔101 养殖,102 野生〕	7	2	40	9/	9	千克	ABU	PRQS	/37
0303.5100	90	冻大西洋鲱鱼(但子目 0303.91 至 0303.99 的可食用鱼杂碎除外:)〔101 养殖,102 野生〕	7	2	40	9/	9	千克	AB	PRQS	/37
0303.5300		--沙丁鱼(沙丁鱼、沙瑙鱼属)、小沙丁鱼属、黍鲱或西鲱[T2]	7		40	9/	9	千克	AB	PRQS	/42
0303.5400		--鲭鱼[大西洋鲭、澳洲鲭(鲐)、日本鲭(鲐)]〔101 饲料用鲭鱼,102 养殖日本鲭(鲐),103 野生日本鲭(鲐),104 大西洋鲭,105 澳洲鲭(鲐)〕	7		40	9/	9	千克	AB	PRQS	/42
0303.5500		--对称竹荚鱼、新西兰竹荚鱼及竹荚鱼(竹荚鱼属)[T2]	7		40	9/	9	千克	AB	PRQS	/42
0303.5600		--军曹鱼〔101 饲料用其他海水鱼,102 食用鱼〕	7		40	9/	9	千克	AB	PRQS	/42
0303.5700		--剑鱼〔999〕	7		40	9/	9	千克	ABU	PRQS	/42
0303.5900		--其他							AB		
0303.5900	10	冻毛鳞鱼,但食用杂碎除外〔999〕	7	5	40	9/	9	千克	AB	PRQS	/40
0303.5900	90	其他冻 0303.5 项下的鱼(鳀鱼(鳀属)、印度鲭(羽鳃鲐属)、马鲛鱼(马鲛属)、鲹鱼(鲹属)、银鲳(鲳属)、秋刀鱼、圆鲹(圆鲹属)、鲔鱼、狐鲣(狐鲣属)、枪鱼 、旗鱼、四鳍旗鱼(旗鱼科),但子目 0303.91 至 0303.99 的可食用鱼杂碎除外:)〔T2〕	7		40	9/	9	千克	AB	PRQS	/42
		-犀鳕科、多丝真鳕科、鳕科、长尾鳕科、黑鳕科、无须鳕科、深海鳕科及南极鳕科鱼,但子目 0303.91 至 0303.99 的可食用鱼杂碎除外:									
0303.6300		--鳕鱼(大西洋鳕鱼、格陵兰鳕鱼、太平洋鳕鱼)〔101 大西洋鳕鱼,102 太平洋鳕鱼,103 格陵兰鳕鱼〕	7	2	40	9/	9	千克	AB	PRQS	/37
0303.6400		--黑线鳕鱼(黑线鳕)〔999〕	7		40	9/	9	千克	AB	PRQS	/42
0303.6500		--绿青鳕鱼〔999〕	7		40	9/	9	千克	AB	PRQS	/42
0303.6600		--狗鳕鱼(无须鳕属、长鳍鳕属)〔101 无须鳕属,102 长鳍鳕属〕	7		40	9/	9	千克	AB	PRQS	/42
0303.6700		--狭鳕鱼〔101 饲料用其他海水鱼,102 食用鱼〕	7	5	40	9/	9	千克	ABU	PRQS	/40

协定税率 %										特惠税率 %			Article Description
亚太5国	东/冰/格	巴基斯坦	韩国	瑞士	哥达	秘鲁	澳大利亚	新西/坡/智	港/澳/台	亚太2国	老/柬/缅	36/3/1	
5.6	0/0/0	0	4	0	0	0	0	0//0	0/0/			0/0/0	Frozen arrow tooth sole in Asia(excluding edible fish offal of subheading 0302.91 t0 0302.99)
5.6	0/0/0	0	4	0	0	0	0	0//0	0/0/			0/0/0	Other flatfish(Pleuronectidae, Bothidae, Cynoglossidae, Soleidae, Scophthalmidae and Citharidae) frozen(excluding edible fish offal of subheading 0302.91 t0 0302.99)
													-Tunas (*of the genus Thun-nus*), skipjack or stripe-bellied bonito (*Euthynnus*(*Katsuwo-nus*)*pelamis*), excluding edible fish offal of subheading 0303.91 to 0303.99:
5.3	0/0/0	4.5	4.8	3.6	0	0	0	0//0	0/0/			0/0/0	--Albacore or longfinned tunas (*Thunnus alalunga*)
5.3	0/0/0	4.5	4.8	3.6	0	0	0	0//0	0/0/			0/0/0	--Yellowfin tunas (*Thunnus albacares*)
5.3	0/0/0	4.5	8.4	3.6	0	0	0	0//0	0/0/			0/0/0	--Skipjack or belted bonito
	0/0/0	6	4.8	3.6	0	0	0	0//0	0/0/		/0/0	0/0/0	--Bigeye tunas(*Thunnus obesus*)
													--Atlantic and pacific bluefin tunas(Thunnus thynnus, Thunnus orientalis):
	0/0/0	6	4.8	3.6	0	0	0	0//0	0/0/		/0/0	0/0/0	---Atlantic bluefin tunas
5.3	0/0/0	4.5	4.8	3.6	0	0	0	0//0	0/0/		/0/0	0/0/0	---pacific bluefin tunas
	0/0/0	6	4.8	3.6	0	0	0	0//0	0/0/		/0/0	0/0/0	--Southern bluefin tunas(*Thunnus maccoyii*)
5.3	0/0/0	4.5	4.8	3.6	0	0	0	0//0	0/0/		/0/0	0/0/0	--Other
													-Herrings (*Clupea harengus*, *Clupea pallasii*), anchovies (*Engraulis spp.*), sardines (*Sardina pilchardus*, *Sardi-nops spp.*), sardinella (*Sardinella spp.*), brisling or sprats (*Sprattus sprattus*), mackerel (*Scomber scombrus*, *Scomber australasicus*, *Scomber japonicus*), Indian macker-els (*Rastrelliger spp.*), seerfi-shes (*Scomberomorus spp.*), jack and horse mackerel (*Tra-churus spp.*), jacks, crevalles(*Caranx spp.*), cobia(*Rachy-centron canadum*), silver pom-frets(*Pampus spp.*), Pacific saury(*Cololabis saira*), scads(*Decapterus spp.*), capelin(*Mallotus villosus*), swordfish(*Xiphias gladius*), Kawakawa(*Euthymus affinis*), bonitos (*Sarda spp.*), marlins, sail-fishes, spearfish(*Istiophori-dae*), excluding edible fish offal of subheadin9 0303.91 to 0303.99:
													--Herrings(Clupea harengus, Clupea pallosii)
4.7	0/0/0	4.5	4	0	0	0	0	0//0	0/0/			0/0/0	Frozen Pacific herring(excluding edible fish offal of subheading 0302.91 t0 0302.99)
4.7	0/0/0	4.5	4	0	0	0	0	0//0	0/0/			0/0/0	Herrings(Clupea harengus) Frozen(excluding edible fish offal of subheading 0302.91 t0 0302.99)
4.7	0/0/0	0	4.8	3.6	0	0	0	0//0	0/0/			0/0/0	--Sardines(Sardina pilchardus, Sardinops spp.), sardinella (Sardinella spp.), brisling or sprats(Sprattus sprattus)
4.7	0/0/0	0	4	0	0	0	0	0//0	0/0/			0/0/0	--Mackerel(Scomber scombrus, Scomber australasicus, Scomber japonicus)
3.5	0/0/0	5	0	0	0	0	0	0//0	0/0/0	0	/0/0	0/0/0	-Jack and horse mackerel(Trachurus spp.)
3.5	0/0/0	5	0	0	0	0	0	0//0	0/0/0	0	/0/0	0/0/0	--Cobia(Rachycentron canadum)
3.5	0/0/0	5	4	0	0	0	0	0//0	0/0/	0		0/0/0	--Swordfish(Xiphias gladius)
													--Other
3.5	0/0/0	0	6	0	0	0	0	0//0	0/0/0	0	/0/0	0/0/0	Frozen capelin, but edible offal except
3.5	0/0/0	0	6	0	0	0	0	0//0	0/0/0	0	/0/0	0/0/0	Other frozen fish of the subheading 0303.5 , including anchovies $ (Engraulis spp.) $ $, Indian mackerel (feather gill danio genus), mackerel, horse mackerel (mackerel) (trevally), pomfret, saury, round trevally (butterfish) trevally (circle), spring (capelin), tuna fish, bonito (bonito) four fin sailfish, marlin, swordfish (swordfish), excluding the edible fish offal of the subheading 0303.91 to 0303.99
													-Fish of the families Bregmacer-otidae, Euclichthyidae, Ga-didae, Macrouridae, Melanoni-dae, Merlucciidae, Moridae and Muraenolepididae, excluding edible fish offal of subheading 0303.91 to 0303.99:
4.7	0/0/0	4.5	4	0	0	0	0	0//0	0/0/			0/0/0	--Cod(Gadus morhua, Gadus ogac, Gadus macrocep halus)
4.7	0/0/0	4.5	4.8	3.6	0	0	0	0//0	0/0/			0/0/0	--Haddock(melanogrammus aeglefinus)
4.7	0/0/0	4.5	4.8	3.6	0	0	0	0//0	0/0/			0/0/0	--Coalfish(Pollachius virens)
	0/0/0	6	4.8	3.6	0	0	0	0//0	0/0/			0/0/0	--Hake(Merluccius spp. ,urophycis spp.)
3.5	0/0/0	5	4	0	0	0	0	0//0	0/0/0	0	/0/0	0/0/0	--Alaska pollack(Theragra chalcogramma)

税则号列	货品名称〔CIQ 扩展编码及品名－T2 表示见附表 2〕	最惠(%)	暂定税率	普通	增值/消费	出口退税	计量单位	监管条件	检验检疫	特殊证件对美关税
0303.6800	--蓝鳕鱼(小鳍鳕、南蓝鳕)〔101 饲料用其他海水鱼,102 小鳍鳕,103 南蓝鳕,104 蓝鳕〕	7		40	9/	9	千克	AB	PRQS	/42
0303.6900	--其他〔101 饲料用其他海水鱼,102 犀鳕科,103 多丝真鳕科,104 鳕科,105 长尾鳕科,106 黑鳕科,107 无须鳕科,108 深海鳕科,109 南极鳕科鱼〕	7		40	9/	9	千克	AB	PRQS	/42
	-其他鱼,但子目 0303.91 至 0303.99 的可食用鱼杂碎除外:									
0303.8100	--角鲨及其他鲨鱼									
0303.8100 10	冻濒危鲨鱼(但子目 0303.91 至 0303.99 的可食用鱼杂碎除外:)〔999〕	7		40	9/	0	千克	ABEF	PRQS	/42
0303.8100 90	冻其他鲨鱼(但子目 0303.91 至 0303.99 的可食用鱼杂碎除外:)〔999〕	7		40	9/	9	千克	AB	PRQS	/42
0303.8200	--魟鱼及鳐鱼(鳐科)〔101 饲料用其他海水鱼,102 食用鱼〕	7		40	9/	9	千克	AB	PRQS	/42
0303.8300	--南极犬牙鱼(南极犬牙鱼属)〔999〕	7		40	9/	9	千克	ABU	PRQS	/42
0303.8400	--尖吻鲈鱼(舌齿鲈属)〔999〕	7		40	9/	9	千克	AB	PRQS	/42
	--其他:									
0303.8910	---带鱼〔999〕	7	5	40	9/	9	千克	AB	PRQS	/40
0303.8920	---黄鱼〔101 养殖,102 野生〕	7		40	9/	9	千克	AB	PRQS	/42
0303.8930	---鲳鱼〔101 养殖,102 野生〕	7		40	9/	9	千克	AB	PRQS	/42
0303.8990	---其他									
0303.8990 01	其他冻鲈鱼(但子目 0303.91 至 0303.99 的可食用鱼杂碎除外:)〔101 养殖,102 野生〕	7		40	9/	9	千克	AB	PRQS	/42
0303.8990 10	其他未列名濒危冻鱼(但子目 0303.91 至 0303.99 的可食用鱼杂碎除外:)〔999〕	7		40	9/	0	千克	ABFE	PRQS	/42
0303.8990 20	冻平鲉属(但子目 0303.91 至 0303.99 的可食用鱼杂碎除外:)〔101 养殖,102 野生〕	7		40	9/	9	千克	ABU	PRQS	/42
0303.8990 30	冻鲪鲉属(叶鳍鲉属)(但子目 0303.91 至 0303.99 的可食用鱼杂碎除外:)〔101 养殖,102 野生〕	7		40	9/	9	千克	ABU	PRQS	/42
0303.8990 90	其他未列名冻鱼(但子目 0303.91 至 0303.99 的可食用鱼杂碎除外:)[T2]	7		40	9/	9	千克	AB	PRQS	/42
	-鱼肝、鱼卵、鱼精、鱼鳍、鱼头、鱼尾、鱼鳔及其他可食用鱼杂碎:									
0303.9100	--鱼肝、鱼卵及鱼精									
0303.9100 10	冻濒危鱼种的肝、鱼卵及鱼精[T2]	7		50	9/	0	千克	ABFE	PRQS	/42
0303.9100 90	其他冻鱼肝、鱼卵及鱼精[T2]	7		50	9/	9	千克	AB	PRQS	/42
0303.9200	--鲨鱼翅									
0303.9200 10	冻濒危鲨鱼翅〔999〕	12		40	9/	0	千克	ABFE	PRQS	/47
0303.9200 90	其他冻鲨鱼翅〔999〕	12		40	9/	9	千克	AB	PRQS	/47
0303.9900	--其他									
0303.9900 10	其他冻可食用濒危鱼杂碎〔101 其他养殖冷冻鱼,102 其他野生冷冻鱼〕	7		40	9/	0	千克	ABFE	PRQS	/42
0303.9900 20	冻的大菱鲆、比目鱼、鲱鱼、鲭鱼、鲳鱼、带鱼、尼罗河鲈鱼、尖吻鲈鱼、其他鲈鱼的可食用其他鱼杂碎〔101 其他养殖冷冻鱼,102 其他野生冷冻鱼〕	7		40	9/	9	千克	AB	PRQS	/42
0303.9900 90	其他冻可食用其他鱼杂碎〔101 其他养殖冷冻鱼,102 其他野生冷冻鱼〕	7		40	9/	9	千克	AB	PRQS	/42
03.04	**鲜、冷、冻鱼片及其他鱼肉(不论是否绞碎):**									
	-鲜或冷的罗非鱼(口孵非鲫属)、鲶鱼(鲑鲶属、鲶属、胡鲶属、真鮰属)、鲤科鱼(鲤属、鲫属、草鱼、鲢属、鲮属、青鱼、卡特拉鲃、野鲮属、哈氏纹唇鱼、何氏细须鲃、鲂属)、鳗鱼(鳗鲡属)、尼罗河鲈鱼(尼罗尖吻鲈)及黑鱼(鳢属)的鱼片:									
0304.3100	--罗非鱼(口孵非鲫属)〔101 养殖,102 野生〕	7		70	9/	9	千克	AB	PRQS	/
0304.3200	--鲶鱼(鲑鲶属、鲶属、胡鲶属、真鮰属)〔101 养殖鲑鲶属,102 养殖胡鲶属,103 养殖真鮰属,104 野生鲑鲶属,105 野生胡鲶属,106 野生真鮰属〕	7		70	9/	9	千克	AB	PRQS	/
0304.3300	--尼罗河鲈鱼(尼罗尖吻鲈)〔999〕	7		70	9/	9	千克	AB	PRQS	/
0304.3900	--其他									
0304.3900 10	鲜或冷的花鳗鲡鱼片〔101 养殖,102 野生〕	7		70	9/	9	千克	ABE	PRQS	/
0304.3900 20	鲜或冷的欧洲鳗鲡鱼片〔101 养殖,102 野生〕	7		70	9/	9	千克	ABEF	PRQS	/

协定税率 %										特惠税率 %			Article Description
亚太5国	东/冰/格	巴基斯坦	韩国	瑞士	哥达	秘鲁	澳大利亚	新西/坡/智	巷/澳/台	亚太2国	老/柬/缅	36/3/1	
3.5	0/0/0	5	0	0	0	0	0	0//0	0/0/0	0	/0/0	0/0/0	--Blue whitings(Micromesistius poutassou, Micromesistius australis)
3.5	0/0/0	5	0	0	0	0	0	0//0	0/0/0	0	/0/0	0/0/0	--Other
													-Other fish, excluding edible fish offal of subheading 0303.91 to 0303.99:
													--Dogfish and other sharks
5.3	0/0/0	9	4.8	3.6	0	0	0	0//0	0/0/			0/0/0	Endangered shark(excluding edible fish offal of subheading 0302.91 t0 0302.99), frozen
5.3	0/0/0	9	4.8	3.6	0	0	0	0//0	0/0/			0/0/0	Other sharks(excluding edible fish offal of subheading 0302.91 t0 0302.99), frozen
3.5	0/0/0	5	0	0	0	0	0	0//0	0/0/0	0	/0/0	0/0/0	--Rays and skates(Rajidae)
3.5	0/0/0	5	4	0	0	0	0	0//0	0/0/	0	/0/0	0/0/0	--Toothfish(Dissostichus spp.)
4.7	0/0/0	4.5	4.8	3.6	0	0	0	0//0	0/0/			0/0/0	--Seabass(Dicentrarchus spp.)
													--Other:
3.5	0/3.6/0	0	4	0	0	0	0	0//0	0/0/	0	/0/0	0/0/0	---Scabber fish(Trichurius)
3.5	0/0/0	0	4	0	0	0	0	0//0	0/0/	0	/0/0	0/0/0	--－Yellow croaker(Pseudosicaena)
3.5	0/0/0	0	4	0	0	0	0	0//0	0/0/	0	/0/0	0/0/0	---Tilapia
													---Other
3.5	0/0/0	0	6	0	0	0	0	0//0	0/0/0	0	/0/0	0/0/0	Other perch, frozen (excluding edible fish offal of subheading 0302.91 t0 0302.99)
3.5	0/0/0	0	6	0	0	0	0	0//0	0/0/0	0	/0/0	0/0/0	Other endangered fish frozen, not elsewhere specified or included (excluding edible fish offal of subheading 0302.91 t0 0302.99)
3.5	0/0/0	0	6	0	0	0	0	0//0	0/0/0	0	/0/0	0/0/0	Frozen flat scorpionfish genera (excluding edible fish offal of subheading 0302.91 t0 0302.99)
3.5	0/0/0	0	6	0	0	0	0	0//0	0/0/0	0	/0/0	0/0/0	Frozen Jun scorpionfish belongs to fin (leaf scorpionfish)(excluding edible fish offal of subheading 0302.91 t0 0302.99)
3.5	0/0/0	0	6	0	0	0	0	0//0	0/0/0	0	/0/0	0/0/0	Other fish frozen, not elsewhere specified or included(excluding edible fish offal of subheading 0302.91 t0 0302.99)
													-Livers, roes, milt, fish fins, heads, tails, maws and other edible fish offal:
													--Livers, roes, milt
6.3	0/0/0	4.5	4	0	0		0	0//0	0/0/			0/0/0	Forzen livers, roes and milt of endangered fish
6.3	0/0/0	4.5	4	0	0		0	0//0	0/0/			0/0/0	Other forzen livers, roes and milt
													--Shark fins
9	0/0/0	9	4.8	3.6	0	0	0	0//0	0/0/			0/0/0	Frozen endangered Shark fins
9	0/0/0	9	4.8	3.6	0	0	0	0//0	0/0/			0/0/0	Other frozen Shark fins
													--Ohter
4.7	0/0/0	0	4	0	0	0	0	0//0	0/0/		/0/	0/0/0	Other edible offals of endangered fish
4.7	0/0/0	0	4	0	0	0	0	0//0	0/0/		/0/	0/0/0	Frozen edible fish offals of Turbots, flatfish, herring, mackerel, Pomfret, hairtail, Nile perch and other perch?
4.7	0/0/0	0	4	0	0	0	0	0//0	0/0/		/0/	0/0/0	Other frozen edible offals of other fish
													Fish fillets and other fish meat (whether or not minced), fresh, chilled or frozen:
													-Fresh or chilled fillets of tilapias (*Oreochromis spp.*), catfish (*Pangasius spp.*, *Silurus spp.*, *Clarias spp.*, *Ictalurus spp.*), carp (*Cyprin us spp.*, *Carassius spp.*, *Ctenopharyn-godon idellus* , *Hypophthal-michthys spp.* , *Cirrhins spp.* , *Mylopharyngodon piceus* , *Catla catla* , *Labeo spp.* , *Osteochilus hasselti* , *Leptobar-bus hoeveni* , *Megalobrama spp.*), eels (*Anguilla spp.*) , Nile perch (*Lates niloticus*) and snakeheads (*Channa spp.*) :
5.3	0/0/0	4.5	4.8	3.6	0	0	0	0//0	0/0/		//0	0/0/0	--Tilapia(oreochromis spp.)
5.3	0/0/0	4.5	4.8	3.6	0	0	0	0//0	0/0/		//0	0/0/0	--Catfish(pangasius spp.、silurus spp.、clarias spp.、ictalurus spp.)
5.3	0/0/0	4.5	4.8	3.6	0	0	0	0//0	0/0/		//0	0/0/0	--Nile perch(lates niloticus)
													--Other
5.3	0/0/0	4.5	4.8	3.6	0	0	0	0//0	0/0/		//0	0/0/0	Fresh or chilled fillets of marbled eels
5.3	0/0/0	4.5	4.8	3.6	0	0	0	0//0	0/0/		//0	0/0/0	Fresh or chilled fillets of european eels

税则号列	货品名称〔CIQ 扩展编码及品名－T2 表示见附表 2〕	最惠(%)	暂定税率	普通	增值/消费	出口退税	计量单位	监管条件	检验检疫	特殊证件对美关税
0304.3900 90	鲜或冷的鲤科鱼(鲤属、鲫属、草鱼、鲢属、鳙属、青鱼、卡特拉鲃、野鲮属、哈氏纹唇鱼、何氏细须鲃、鲂属)、其他鳗鱼(鳗鲡属)及黑鱼(鳢属)的鱼片[T2]	7		70	9/	9	千克	AB	PRQS	/
	-鲜或冷的其他鱼片：									
0304.4100	--大麻哈鱼[红大麻哈鱼、细鳞大麻哈鱼、大麻哈鱼(种)、大鳞大麻哈鱼、银大麻哈鱼、马苏大麻哈鱼、玫瑰大麻哈鱼]、大西洋鲑鱼及多瑙哲罗鱼〔101 非生食,102 可能用于生食〕	7		70	9/	9	千克	AB	PRQS	/
0304.4200	--鳟鱼(河鳟、虹鳟、克拉克大麻哈鱼、阿瓜大麻哈鱼、吉雨大麻哈鱼、亚利桑那大麻哈鱼、金腹大麻哈鱼)〔999〕	7		70	9/	9	千克	AB	PRQS	/
0304.4300	--比目鱼(鲽科、鲆科、舌鳎科、鳎科、菱鲆科、刺鲆科)[T2]	7		70	9/	9	千克	AB	PRQS	/
0304.4400	--犀鳕科、多丝真鳕科、鳕科、长尾鳕科、黑鳕科、无须鳕科、深海鳕科及南极鳕科鱼〔101 犀鳕科,102 多丝真鳕科,103 鳕科,104 长尾鳕科,105 黑鳕科,106 无须鳕科,107 深海鳕科,108 南极鳕科鱼〕	7		70	9/	9	千克	AB	PRQS	/
0304.4500	--剑鱼〔999〕	7		70	9/	9	千克	ABU	PRQS	/
0304.4600	--南极犬牙鱼(南极犬牙鱼属)〔999〕	7		70	9/	9	千克	ABU	PRQS	/
0304.4700	--角鲨及其他鲨鱼									
0304.4700 10	鲜或冷的濒危鲨鱼的鱼片〔999〕	7		70	9/	0	千克	ABFE	PRQS	/
0304.4700 90	鲜或冷的其他鲨鱼的鱼片〔999〕	7		70	9/	9	千克	AB	PRQS	/
0304.4800	--魟鱼及鳐鱼(鳐科)									
0304.4800 10	鲜或冷的濒危魟鱼及鳐鱼的鱼片〔999〕	7		70	9/	0	千克	ABFE	PRQS	/
0304.4800 90	鲜或冷的其他魟鱼及鳐鱼的鱼片〔999〕	7		70	9/	9	千克	AB	PRQS	/
0304.4900	--其他									
0304.4900 10	鲜或冷的其他濒危鱼的鱼片〔999〕	7		70	9/	0	千克	ABFE	PRQS	/
0304.4900 90	鲜或冷的其他鱼的鱼片〔999〕	7		70	9/	9	千克	AB	PRQS	/
	-其他,鲜或冷的：									
0304.5100	--罗非鱼(口孵非鲫属)、鲶鱼(𩽾鲶属、鲶属、胡鲶属、真鮰属)、鲤科鱼(鲤属、鲫属、草鱼、鲢属、鳙属、青鱼、卡特拉鲃、野鲮属、哈氏纹唇鱼、何氏细须鲃、鲂属)、鳗鱼(鳗鲡属)、尼罗河鲈鱼(尼罗尖吻鲈)及黑鱼(鳢属)									
0304.5100 10	鲜或冷的花鳗鲡的鱼肉(不论是否绞碎)〔101 养殖,102 野生〕	7		70	9/	9	千克	ABE	PRQS	/
0304.5100 20	鲜或冷的欧洲鳗鲡的鱼肉(不论是否绞碎)〔101 养殖,102 野生〕	7		70	9/	9	千克	ABEF	PRQS	/
0304.5100 90	鲜或冷的罗非鱼(口孵非鲫属)、鲶鱼(𩽾鲶属、鲶属、胡鲶属、真鮰属)、鲤科鱼(鲤属、鲫属、草鱼、鲢属、鳙属、青鱼、卡特拉鲃、野鲮属、哈氏纹唇鱼、何氏细须鲃、鲂属)、其他鳗鱼(鳗鲡属)、尼罗河鲈鱼(尼罗尖吻鲈)及黑鱼(鳢属)的鱼肉[T2]	7		70	9/	9	千克	AB	PRQS	/
0304.5200	--鲑科鱼〔101 养殖,102 野生〕	7		70	9/	9	千克	AB	PRQS	/
0304.5300	--犀鳕科、多丝真鳕科、鳕科、长尾鳕科、黑鳕科、无须鳕科、深海鳕科及南极鳕科鱼[T2]	7		70	9/	9	千克	AB	PRQS	/
0304.5400	--剑鱼〔999〕	7		70	9/	9	千克	ABU	PRQS	/
0304.5500	--南极犬牙鱼(南极犬牙鱼属)〔999〕	7		70	9/	9	千克	ABU	PRQS	/
0304.5600	--角鲨及其他鲨鱼									
0304.5600 10	鲜或冷的濒危鲨鱼肉(不论是否绞碎)〔999〕	7		70	9/	0	千克	ABEF	PRQS	/
0304.5600 90	鲜或冷的其他鲨鱼肉(不论是否绞碎)〔999〕	7		70	9/	9	千克	AB	PRQS	/
0304.5700	--魟鱼及鳐鱼(鳐科)									
0304.5700 10	鲜或冷的濒危魟鱼及鳐鱼的鱼肉(不论是否绞碎)〔999〕	7		70	9/	0	千克	ABEF	PRQS	/
0304.5700 90	鲜或冷的其他魟鱼及鳐鱼的鱼肉(不论是否绞碎)〔999〕	7		70	9/	9	千克	AB	PRQS	/
0304.5900	--其他									
0304.5900 10	鲜或冷的其他濒危鱼的鱼肉(不论是否绞碎)〔999〕	7		70	9/	0	千克	ABEF	PRQS	/
0304.5900 90	鲜或冷的其他鱼的鱼肉(不论是否绞碎)[T2]	7		70	9/	9	千克	AB	PRQS	/

协定税率 %										特惠税率 %			Article Description
亚太5国	东/冰/格	巴基斯坦	韩国	瑞士	哥达	秘鲁	澳大利亚	新西/坡/智	港/澳/台	亚太2国	老/柬/缅	36/3/1	
5.3	0/0/0	4.5	4.8	3.6	0	0	0	0//0	0/0/		//0	0/0/0	Fresh or chilled fillets of Carp (Cyprinus spp., Carassius spp., Ctenopharyngodon idellus, Hypophthalmichthys spp., Cirrhinus spp., Mylopharyngodon piceus, Catla catla, Labeo spp., Osteochilus hasselti, Leptobarbus hoeveni, Megalobrama spp.), Mylopharyngodon piceus) and snakeheads(Channa spp).
													-Other fish fillets, fresh and chilled:
5.3	0/0/0	4.5	4.8	3.6	0	0	0	0//0	0/0/		//0	0/0/0	--Pacific salmon (Oncorhynchus nerka, Oncorhynchus gorbuscha, Oncorhynchus keta, Oncorhynchus tschawytscha, Oncorhynchus kisutch, Oncorhynchus masou and Oncorhynchus rhodurus), Atlantic salmon(Salmo salar) and Danube salmon(Hucho hucho)
5.3	0/0/0	4.5	4.8	3.6	0	0	0	0//0	0/0/		//0	0/0/0	--Trout(Salmo trutta, Oncorhynchus mykiss, Oncorhynchus clarki, Oncorhynchus aguabonita, Oncorhynchus gilae, Oncorhynchus apache and Oncorhynchus chrysogaster)
5.3	0/0/0	4.5	4.8	3.6	0	0	0	0//0	0/0/		//0	0/0/0	--Flat fish(Pleuronectidae, Bothidae, Cynoglossidae, Soleidae, Scophthalmidae and Citharidae)
5.3	0/0/0	4.5	4.8	3.6	0	0	0	0//0	0/0/		//0	0/0/0	--Fish of the families Bregmacerotidae, Euclichthyidae, Gadidae, Macrouridae, Melanonidae, Merlucciidae, Moridae and Muraenolepididae
5.3	0/0/0	4.5	4.8	3.6	0	0	0	0//0	0/0/		//0	0/0/0	--Swordfish(Xiphias gladius)
5.3	0/0/0	4.5	4.8	3.6	0	0	0	0//0	0/0/		//0	0/0/0	--Toothfish(Dissostichus spp.)
													--Dogfish and other sharks
5.3	0/0/0	4.5	4.8	3.6	0	0	0	0//0	0/0/		//0	0/0/0	Fresh or chilled fillets of endangered Shark
5.3	0/0/0	4.5	4.8	3.6	0	0	0	0//0	0/0/		//0	0/0/0	Fresh or chilled fillets of other Shark
													--Ray and skates(*Rajidae*)
5.3	0/0/0	4.5	4.8	3.6	0	0	0	0//0	0/0/		//0	0/0/0	Fresh or chilled fillets of endangered Ray and skates
5.3	0/0/0	4.5	4.8	3.6	0	0	0	0//0	0/0/		//0	0/0/0	Fresh or chilled fillets of other Ray and skates
													--Other
5.3	0/0/0	4.5	4.8	3.6	0	0	0	0//0	0/0/		//0	0/0/0	Fresh or chilled fillets of Other endangered fish
5.3	0/0/0	4.5	4.8	3.6	0	0	0	0//0	0/0/		//0	0/0/0	Fresh or chilled fillets of fish
													-Other, fresh and chilled:
													--Tilapias (*Oreochromis spp.*), catfish (*Pangasius spp., Si-lurus spp., Cla rias spp., Ic-talurus spp.*), carp (*Cypri-nus spp., Carassius spp., Ctenopharyngodon idellus, Hypophthalmichthys spp., Cirrhinus spp., Mylopharyn-godon piceus, Catla catla, Labeo spp., Osteochilus hasselti, Leptobarbus hoeveni, Megalobrama spp.*), eels (*Anguilla spp.*), Nile perch (*Lates niloticus*) and snake-heads (*Channa spp.*)
5.3	0/0/0	4.5	4.8	3.6	0	0	0	0//0	0/0/		//0	0/0/0	Marbled eels, fresh or chilled (whether or not minced)
5.3	0/0/0	4.5	4.8	3.6	0	0	0	0//0	0/0/		//0	0/0/0	Meat of european eels, fresh or chilled (whether or not minced)
5.3	0/0/0	4.5	4.8	3.6	0	0	0	0//0	0/0/		//0	0/0/0	Fresh or chilled fish meat of Tilapias (*Oreochromis spp.*), catfish (*Pangasius spp., Silurus spp., Clarias spp., Ictalurus spp.*), carp (*Cyprinus spp., Carassius spp., Ctenopharyngodon idellus Hypophthalmichthys spp., Cirrhinus spp., Mylopharyngodon piceus, Catla catla, Labeo spp., Osteochilus hasselti, Leptobarbus hoeveni, Megalobrama spp.*), eels (*Anguilla spp.*), Nile perch (*Lates niloticus*) and snakeheads (*Channa spp.*)
5.3	0/0/0	4.5	4.8	3.6	0	0	0	0//0	0/0/		//0	0/0/0	--Salmonoids
5.3	0/0/0	4.5	4.8	3.6	0	0	0	0//0	0/0/		//0	0/0/0	--Fish of the families bregmacerotidae、euclichthyidae、gadidae、macrouridae、melanonidae、merluccidae、moridae and Muraenolepididae
5.3	0/0/0	4.5	4.8	3.6	0	0	0	0//0	0/0/		//0	0/0/0	--Swordfish(Xiphias gladius)
5.3	0/0/0	4.5	4.8	3.6	0	0	0	0//0	0/0/		//0	0/0/0	--Toothfish(Dissostichus spp.)
													--Dogfish and other sharks
5.3	0/0/0	4.5	4.8	3.6	0	0	0	0//0	0/0/		//0	0/0/0	Fresh or chilled fish meat of endangered Shark, whether or not minced
5.3	0/0/0	4.5	4.8	3.6	0	0	0	0//0	0/0/		//0	0/0/0	Fresh or chilled fish meat of other Shark, whether or not minced
													--Ray and skates(*Rajidae*)
5.3	0/0/0	4.5	4.8	3.6	0	0	0	0//0	0/0/		//0	0/0/0	Fresh or chilled fish meat of endangered Ray and skates, whether or not minced
5.3	0/0/0	4.5	4.8	3.6	0	0	0	0//0	0/0/		//0	0/0/0	Fresh or chilled fish meat of other Ray and skates, whether or not minced
													--Other
5.3	0/0/0	4.5	4.8	3.6	0	0	0	0//0	0/0/		//0	0/0/0	Other endangered fish meat, fresh or chilled(whether or not minced)
5.3	0/0/0	4.5	4.8	3.6	0	0	0	0//0	0/0/		//0	0/0/0	Other fish meat, fresh or chilled (whether or not minced)

税则号列		货品名称〔CIQ扩展编码及品名—T2表示见附表2〕	最惠(%)	暂定税率	普通	增值/消费	出口退税	计量单位	监管条件	检验检疫	特殊证件对美关税
		-冻的罗非鱼(口孵非鲫属)、鲶鱼(鲃鲶属、鲶属、胡鲶属、真鮰属)、鲤科鱼(鲤属、鲫属、草鱼、鲢属、鲮属、青鱼、卡特拉鲃、野鲮属、哈氏纹唇鱼、何氏细须鲃、鲂属)、鳗鱼(鳗鲡属)、尼罗河鲈鱼(尼罗尖吻鲈)及黑鱼(鳢属)的鱼片:									
0304.6100		--罗非鱼(口孵非鲫属)〔999〕	7		70	9/	9	千克	AB	PRQS	/42
		--鲶鱼(鲃鲶属、鲶属、胡鲶属、真鮰属):									
		---叉尾鮰鱼(真鮰属):									
0304.6211		----斑点叉尾鮰鱼〔101 养殖,102 野生〕	7		70	9/	9	千克	AB	PRQS	/42
0304.6219		----其他〔101 养殖,102 野生〕	7		70	9/	9	千克	AB	PRQS	/42
0304.6290		---其他[T2]	7		70	9/	9	千克	AB	PRQS	/42
0304.6300		--尼罗河鲈鱼(尼罗尖吻鲈)〔999〕	7		70	9/	9	千克	AB	PRQS	/42
0304.6900		--其他									
0304.6900	10	冻的花鳗鲡鱼片〔101 养殖,102 野生〕	7		70	9/	9	千克	ABE	PRQS	/42
0304.6900	20	冻的欧洲鳗鲡鱼片〔101 养殖,102 野生〕	7		70	9/	9	千克	ABEF	PRQS	/42
0304.6900	90	冻的鲤科鱼(鲤属、鲫属、草鱼、鲢属、鲮属、青鱼、卡特拉鲃、野鲮属、哈氏纹唇鱼、何氏细须鲃、鲂属)、其他鳗鱼(鳗鲡属)及黑鱼(鳢属)的鱼片[T2]	7		70	9/	9	千克	AB	PRQS	/42
		-冻的犀鳕科、多丝真鳕科、鳕科、长尾鳕科、黑鳕科、无须鳕科、深海鳕科及南极鳕科鱼的鱼片:									
0304.7100		--鳕鱼(大西洋鳕鱼、格陵兰鳕鱼、太平洋鳕鱼)〔101 大西洋鳕鱼,102 太平洋鳕鱼,103 格陵兰鳕鱼〕	7		70	9/	9	千克	AB	PRQS	/42
0304.7200		--黑线鳕鱼(黑线鳕)〔999〕	7		70	9/	9	千克	AB	PRQS	/42
0304.7300		--绿青鳕鱼〔999〕	7		70	9/	9	千克	AB	PRQS	/42
0304.7400		--狗鳕鱼(无须鳕属、长鳍鳕属)〔101 无须鳕属,102 长鳍鳕属〕	7		70	9/	9	千克	AB	PRQS	/42
0304.7500		--狭鳕鱼〔999〕	7		70	9/	9	千克	AB	PRQS	/42
0304.7900		--其他〔101 犀鳕科,102 多丝真鳕科,103 鳕科,104 长尾鳕科,105 黑鳕科,106 无须鳕科,107 深海鳕科,108 南极鳕科〕	7		70	9/	9	千克	AB	PRQS	/42
		-其他冻鱼片:									
0304.8100		--大麻哈鱼[红大麻哈鱼、细鳞大麻哈鱼、大麻哈鱼(种)、大鳞大麻哈鱼、银大麻哈鱼、马苏大麻哈鱼、玫瑰大麻哈鱼]、大西洋鲑鱼及多瑙哲罗鱼[T2]	7		70	9/	9	千克	AB	PRQS	/42
0304.8200		--鳟鱼(河鳟、虹鳟、克拉克大麻哈鱼、阿瓜大麻哈鱼、吉雨大麻哈鱼、亚利桑那大麻哈鱼、金腹大麻哈鱼)[T2]	7		70	9/	9	千克	AB	PRQS	/42
0304.8300		--比目鱼(鲽科、鲆科、舌鳎科、鳎科、菱鲆科、刺鲆科)[T2]	7		70	9/	9	千克	AB	PRQS	/42
0304.8400		--剑鱼〔999〕	7		70	9/	9	千克	ABU	PRQS	/42
0304.8500		--南极犬牙鱼(南极犬牙鱼属)〔999〕	7		70	9/	9	千克	ABU	PRQS	/42
0304.8600		--鲱鱼(大西洋鲱鱼、太平洋鲱鱼)〔101 大西洋鲱鱼,102 太平洋鲱鱼〕	7		70	9/	9	千克	AB	PRQS	/42
0304.8700		--金枪鱼(金枪鱼属)、鲣鱼或狐鲣(鲣)〔101 金枪鱼属,102 鲣〕	7		70	9/	9	千克	AB	PRQS	/42
0304.8800		--角鲨、其他鲨鱼、魟鱼及鳐鱼(鳐科)									
0304.8800	10	冻的濒危鲨鱼、魟鱼及鳐鱼的鱼片〔999〕	7		70	9/	0	千克	ABEF	PRQS	/42
0304.8800	90	冻的其他鲨鱼、魟鱼及鳐鱼的鱼片〔999〕	7		70	9/	9	千克	AB	PRQS	/42
0304.8900		--其他									
0304.8900	10	冻的其他濒危鱼片〔999〕	7		70	9/	0	千克	ABEF	PRQS	/42
0304.8900	90	冻的其他鱼片〔999〕	7		70	9/	9	千克	AB	PRQS	/42
		-其他,冻的:									
0304.9100		--剑鱼〔999〕	7		70	9/	9	千克	ABU	PRQS	/42
0304.9200		--南极犬牙鱼(南极犬牙鱼属)〔999〕	7		70	9/	9	千克	ABU	PRQS	/42

协定税率 %										特惠税率 %			Article Description
亚太5国	东/冰/格	巴基斯坦	韩国	瑞士	哥达	秘鲁	澳大利亚	新西/坡/智	港/澳/台	亚太2国	老/柬/缅	36/3/1	
													-Frozen fillets of tilapias (*Oreo-chromis spp.*), catfish(*Pan-gasi us spp., Silurus spp., Clarias spp., Ictalurus spp.*), carp(*Cyp rin us spp., Carassius spp., Ctenopharyn-godon idellus, Hypophthal-michthys spp., Cirrh inus spp., Mylopharyngodon pi-ceus, Catla catla, Labeo spp., Osteochilus hasselti, Leptobar-bus hoeveni, Meg-alobrama spp.*), eels (*Anguilla spp.*), Nile perch (*Lares nilotic-us*) and snakeheads (*Channa spp.*):
	0/0/0	4.5	4	0	0	0	0	0//0	0/0/		/0/0	0/0/0	--Tilapia(oreochromis spp.)
													--catfish(Pangasius spp., Silurus spp., Clarias spp., Ictalurus spp.):
													---Of Ictalurus:
	0/0/0	4.5	4	0	0	0	0	0//0	0/0/			0/0/0	----Channel catfish(ictaluru punctatus)
	0/0/0	4.5	4	0	0	0	0	0//0	0/0/			0/0/0	----Other
	0/0/0	4.5	4	0	0	0	0	0//0	0/0/0		/0/0	0/0/0	---Other
	0/0/0	4.5	4	0	0	0	0	0//0	0/0/0		/0/0	0/0/0	--Nile perch(Lates niloticus)
													--Other
	0/0/0	4.5	4	0	0	0	0	0//0	0/0/0		/0/0	0/0/0	Frozen fillets of marbled eels
	0/0/0	4.5	4	0	0	0	0	0//0	0/0/0		/0/0	0/0/0	Frozen fillets of european eels
	0/0/0	4.5	4	0	0	0	0	0//0	0/0/0		/0/0	0/0/0	Frozen fillets of Carp(Cyprinus spp., Carassius spp., Ctenopharyng-odon idellus, Hypophthalmichthys spp., Cirrhinus spp., Mylopharyngodon piceus, Catla catla, Labeo spp., Osteochilus hasselti, Leptobarbus hoeveni, Megalobrama spp.), Mylopharyngodon piceus) and snakeheads(Channa spp).
													-Frozen fillets of fish of the families Bregmacerotidae, Euclichthyidae, Gadidae, Macrouridae, Melanonidae, Merlucciidae, Moridae and Muraenolepididae:
	0/0/0	4.5	4	0	0	0	0	0//0	0/0/0		/0/0	0/0/0	--Cod(Gadus morhua, Gadus ogac, Gadus macrocephalus)
	0/0/0	4.5	4	0	0	0	0	0//0	0/0/0		/0/0	0/0/0	--Haddock(Melanogrammus aeglefinus)
	0/0/0	4.5	4	0	0	0	0	0//0	0/0/0		/0/0	0/0/0	--Coalfish(Pollachius virens)
	0/0/0	4.5	4	0	0	0	0	0//0	0/0/0		/0/0	0/0/0	--Hake(Merluccius spp. Urophycis spp.)
	0/0/0	4.5	4	0	0	0	0	0//0	0/0/0		/0/0	0/0/0	--Alaska pollack(Theragra chalcogramma)
	0/0/0	4.5	4	0	0	0	0	0//0	0/0/0		/0/0	0/0/0	--Other
													-Other fish fillets, frozen:
	0/0/0	4.5	4	0	0	0	0	0//0	0/0/0		/0/0	0/0/0	--Pacific salmon(Oncorhynchus nerka, Oncorhynchus gorbuscha, Oncorhynchus keta, Oncorhynchus tschawytscha, Oncorhynchus kisutch, Oncorhynchus masou and Oncorhynchus rhodurus), Atlantic salmon(Salmo salar) and Danube salmon(Hucho hucho)
	0/0/0	4.5	4	0	0	0	0	0//0	0/0/0		/0/0	0/0/0	--Trout(Salmo trutta, Oncorhynchus mykiss, Oncorhynchus clarki, Oncorhynchus aguabonita, Oncorhynchus gilae, Oncorhynchus apache and Oncorhynchus chrysogaster)
	0/0/0	4.5	4	0	0	0	0	0//0	0/0/0		/0/0	0/0/0	--Flat fish(Pleuronectidae, Bothidae, Cynoglossidae, Soleidae, Scophthalmidae and Citharidae)
	0/0/0	4.5	4	0	0	0	0	0//0	0/0/		/0/0	0/0/0	--Swordfish(Xiphias gladius)
	0/0/0	4.5	4	0	0	0	0	0//0	0/0/		/0/0	0/0/0	--Toothfish(Dissostichus spp.)
	0/0/0	4.5	4	0	0	0	0	0//0	0/0/0		/0/0	0/0/0	--Herring(Clupea harengus, clupea pallasii)
	0/0/0	4.5	4	0	0	0	0	0//0	0/0/0		/0/0	0/0/0	--Tunas(of the genus Thunnus), skipjack or stripe-bel-lied bonito (Euthynnus(Katsuwonus) pelamis)
													--Dogfish, other sharks, rays and skates(*Rajidae*)
	0/0/0	4.5	4	0	0	0	0	0//0	0/0/0		/0/0	0/0/0	Frozen fillets of endangered Shark, Ray and skates
	0/0/0	4.5	4	0	0	0	0	0//0	0/0/0		/0/0	0/0/0	Frozen fillets of other Shark, Ray and skates
													--Other
	0/0/0	4.5	4	0	0	0	0	0//0	0/0/0		/0/0	0/0/0	Other endangered fish fillets
	0/0/0	4.5	4	0	0	0	0	0//0	0/0/0		/0/0	0/0/0	Other fish fillets
													-Other, frozen:
	0/0/0	4.5	4	0	0	0	0	0//0	0/0/	0	//0	0/0/0	--Swordfish(Xiphias gladius)
	0/0/0	4.5	4	0	0	0	0	0//0	0/0/	0	//0	0/0/0	--Toothfish(Dissostichus spp.)

税则号列	货品名称〔CIQ 扩展编码及品名－T2 表示见附表 2〕	最惠(%)	暂定税率	普通	增值/消费	出口退税	计量单位	监管条件	检验检疫	特殊证件对美关税
0304.9300	--罗非鱼(口孵非鲫属)、鲶鱼(鲢鲶属、鲶属、胡鲶属、真鮰属)、鲤科鱼(鲤属、鲫属、草鱼、鲢属、鲮属、青鱼、卡特拉鲃、野鲮属、哈氏纹唇鱼、何氏细须鲃、鲂属)、鳗鱼(鳗鲡属)、尼罗河鲈鱼(尼罗尖吻鲈)及黑鱼(鳢属)									
0304.9300 10	冻的花鳗鲡鱼肉(不论是否绞碎)〔101 养殖,102 野生〕	7		70	9/	9	千克	ABE	PRQS	/42
0304.9300 20	冻的欧洲鳗鲡鱼肉(不论是否绞碎)〔101 养殖,102 野生〕	7		70	9/	9	千克	ABEF	PRQS	/42
0304.9300 90	冻的罗非鱼(口孵非鲫属)、鲶鱼(鲢鲶属、鲶属、胡鲶属、真鮰属)、鲤科鱼(鲤属、鲫属、草鱼、鲢属、鲮属、青鱼、卡特拉鲃、野鲮属、哈氏纹唇鱼、何氏细须鲃、鲂属)、其他鳗鱼(鳗鲡属)、尼罗河鲈鱼(尼罗尖吻鲈)及黑鱼(鳢属)鱼肉(不论是否绞碎)[T2]	7		70	9/	9	千克	AB	PRQS	/42
0304.9400	--狭鳕鱼〔999〕	7		70	9/	9	千克	AB	PRQS	/42
0304.9500	--犀鳕科、多丝真鳕科、鳕科、长尾鳕科、黑鳕科、无须鳕科、深海鳕科及南极鳕科鱼,狭鳕鱼除外〔101 犀鳕科,102 多丝真鳕科,103 鳕科,104 长尾鳕科,105 黑鳕科,106 无须鳕科,107 深海鳕科,108 南极鳕科鱼〕	7		70	9/	9	千克	AB	PRQS	/42
0304.9600	--角鲨及其他鲨鱼									
0304.9600 10	冻的濒危鲨鱼肉(不论是否绞碎)〔999〕	7		70	9/	0	千克	ABFE	PRQS	/42
0304.9600 90	冻的其他鲨鱼肉(不论是否绞碎)〔999〕	7		70	9/	9	千克	AB	PRQS	/42
0304.9700	--魟鱼及鳐鱼(鳐科)									
0304.9700 10	冻的濒危魟鱼及鳐鱼的鱼肉(不论是否绞碎)〔999〕	7		70	9/	0	千克	ABFE	PRQS	/42
0304.9700 90	冻的其他魟鱼及鳐鱼的鱼肉(不论是否绞碎)〔999〕	7		70	9/	9	千克	AB	PRQS	/42
0304.9900	--其他									
0304.9900 10	冻的其他濒危鱼的鱼肉(不论是否绞碎)	7		70	9/	0	千克	ABFE	PRQS	/42
0304.9900 90	其他冻鱼肉(不论是否绞碎)[T2]	7		70	9/	9	千克	AB	PRQS	/42
03.05	**干、盐腌或盐渍的鱼;熏鱼,不论在熏制前或熏制过程中是否烹煮;适合供人食用的鱼的细粉、粗粉及团粒:**									
0305.1000	-适合供人食用的鱼的细粉、粗粉及团粒〔101 养殖,102 野生〕	7		80	9/	9,13	千克	AB	PRQS	/42
0305.2000	-干、熏、盐腌或盐渍的鱼肝、鱼卵及鱼精									
0305.2000 10	干、熏、盐制的濒危鱼种肝、卵及鱼精[T2]	7		80	9/	0	千克	ABFE	PRQS	/42
0305.2000 90	其他干、熏、盐制的鱼肝、鱼卵及鱼精[T2]	7		80	9/	9,13	千克	AB	PRQS	/42
	-干、盐腌或盐渍的鱼片,但熏制的除外:									
0305.3100	--罗非鱼(口孵非鲫属)、鲶鱼(鲢鲶属、鲶属、胡鲶属、真鮰属)、鲤科鱼(鲤属、鲫属、草鱼、鲢属、鲮属、青鱼、卡特拉鲃、野鲮属、哈氏纹唇鱼、何氏细须鲃、鲂属)、鳗鱼(鳗鲡属)、尼罗河鲈鱼(尼罗尖吻鲈)及黑鱼(鳢属)									
0305.3100 10	干、盐腌或盐渍的花鳗鲡鱼片(熏制的除外)〔101 干制的养殖花鳗鲡,102 盐腌或盐渍的养殖花鳗鲡,103 干制的野生花鳗鲡,104 盐腌或盐渍的野生花鳗鲡〕	7		80	9/	9,13	千克	ABE	PRQS	/
0305.3100 20	干、盐腌或盐渍的欧洲鳗鲡鱼片(熏制的除外)〔101 干制的养殖欧洲鳗鲡,102 盐腌或盐渍的养殖欧洲鳗鲡,103 干制的野生欧洲鳗鲡,104 熏制的除外〕	7		80	9/	9,13	千克	ABEF	PRQS	/
0305.3100 90	干、盐腌或盐渍的罗非鱼(口孵非鲫属)、鲶鱼(鲢鲶属、鲶属、胡鲶属、真鮰属)、鲤科鱼(鲤属、鲫属、草鱼、鲢属、鲮属、青鱼、卡特拉鲃、野鲮属、哈氏纹唇鱼、何氏细须鲃、鲂属)、鳗鱼(鳗鲡属)、尼罗河鲈鱼(尼罗尖吻鲈)及黑鱼(鳢属)的鱼片(熏制的除外)〔161 干制的养殖鱼,162 干制的野生鱼,163 盐腌或盐渍的养殖鱼,164 盐腌或盐渍的野生鱼〕	7		80	9/	9,13	千克	AB	PRQS	/

协定税率 %										特惠税率 %			Article Description
亚太5国	东/冰/格	巴基斯坦	韩国	瑞士	哥达	秘鲁	澳大利亚	新西/坡/智	港/澳/台	亚太2国	老/柬/缅	36/3/1	
													--Tilapias (*Oreochromis spp.*), catfish (*Pangasius spp.*, *Si-lurus spp.*, *Clarias spp.*, *Ictalurus spp.*), carp (*Cypri-nus spp.*, *Carassius spp.*, *Ctenopharyngodon idellus Hypophthalmichthys spp.*, *Cirrhinus spp.*, *Mylopharyn-godon piceus* , *Catla catla*, *Labeo spp.*, *Osteochilus has-selti*, *Leptobarbus hoeveni*, *Megalobrama spp.*), eels (*Anguilla spp.*), Nile perch (*Lates niloticus*) and snake-heads (*Channa spp.*)
	0/0/0	0	4	0	0	0	0	0//0	0/0/	0	//0	0/0/0	Frozen meat of marbled eels(whether or not minced)
	0/0/0	0	4	0	0	0	0	0//0	0/0/	0	//0	0/0/0	Frozen meat of european eels(whether or not minced)
	0/0/0	0	4	0	0	0	0	0//0	0/0/	0	//0	0/0/0	Fresh or chilled fish meat of Tilapias (*Oreochromis spp.*), catfish (*Pangasius spp.*, *Silurus spp.*, *Clarias spp.*, *Ictalurus spp.*), carp (*Cyprinus spp.*, *Carassius spp.*, *Ctenopharyngodon idellus Hypophthalmichthys spp.*, *Cirrhinus spp.*, *Mylopharyngodon piceus* , *Catla catla*, *Labeo spp.*, *Osteochilus hasselti*, *Leptobarbus hoeveni*, *Megalobrama spp.*), eels (*Anguilla spp.*), Nile perch (*Lates niloticus*) and snakeheads (*Channa spp.*)
	0/0/0	4.5	4	0	0	0	0	0//0	0/0/	0	//0	0/0/0	--Alaska Pollack(Theragra chalcogramma)
	0/0/0	4.5	4	0	0	0	0	0//0	0/0/	0	//0	0/0/0	--Fish of the families Bregmacerotidae, Euclichthyidae, Gadidae, Macrouridae, Melanonidae, Merlucciidae, Moridae and Muraenolepididae, other than Alaska Pollack(Theragra chalcogramma)
													--Dogfish and other sharks
	0/0/0	0	4	0	0	0	0	0//0	0/0/	0	//0	0/0/0	Forzen endangered Shark meat, whether or not minced
	0/0/0	0	4	0	0	0	0	0//0	0/0/	0	//0	0/0/0	Forzen other Shark meat, whether or not minced
													--Ray and skates(*Rajidae*)
	0/0/0	0	4	0	0	0	0	0//0	0/0/	0	//0	0/0/0	Forzen meat of endangered Ray and skates, whether or not minced
	0/0/0	0	4	0	0	0	0	0//0	0/0/	0	//0	0/0/0	Forzen meat of other Ray and skates, whether or not minced
													--Other
	0/0/0	0	4	0	0	0	0	0//0	0/0/	0	//0	0/0/0	Other meat of endangered fish(whether or not minced) frozen
	0/0/0	0	4	0	0	0	0	0//0	0/0/	0	//0	0/0/0	Other fish meat(whether or not minced) frozen
													Fish, dried, salted or in brine; smoked fish, whether or not cooked before or during the smoking process; flours, meals and pellets of fish, fit for human consumption:
	0/0/0	4.5	4	0	0	0	0	0//0	0/0/			0/0/0	-Flours, meals and pellets of fish, fit for human consumption
													-Livers and roes, dried, smoked, salted or in brine
	0/0/0	4.5	4		0		0	0//0	0/0/			0/0/0	Livers, roes and milt of endangered fish, dried, smoked, salted or in brine
	0/0/0	4.5	4		0		0	0//0	0/0/			0/0/0	Livers, roes and milt of other fish, dried, smoked, salted or in brine
													-Fish fillets, dried, salted or in brine, but not smoked:
													--Tilapias (*Oreochromis spp.*), catfish (*Pangasius spp.*, *Si-lurus spp.*, *Clarias spp.*, *Ictalurus spp.*), carp (*Cypri-nus spp.*, *Carassius spp.*, *Ctenopharyngodon idellus Hypophthalmichthys spp.*, *Cirrhinus spp.*, *Mylopharyn-godon piceus* , *Catla catla*, *Labeo spp.*, *Osteochilus has-selti*, *Leptobarbus hoeveni*, *Megalobrama spp.*), eels (*Anguilla spp.*), Nile perch (*Lates niloticus*) and snake-heads (*Channa spp.*)
5.5	0/0/0	4.5	4		0	0	0	0//0	0/0/	0	//0	0/0/0	Fillets of marbled eels(Anguilla marmorata), dried, smoked, salted or in brine(excluding smoked)
5.5	0/0/0	4.5	4		0	0	0	0//0	0/0/	0	//0	0/0/0	Fillets of Tilapias (*Oreochromis spp.*), catfish (*Pangasius spp.*, *Silurus spp.*, *Clarias spp.*, *Ictalurus spp.*), carp (*Cyprinus spp.*, *Carassius spp.*, *Ctenopharyngodon idellus Hypophthalmichthys spp.*, *Cirrhinus spp.*, *Mylopharyngodon piceus* , *Catla catla*, *Labeo spp.*, *Osteochilus hasselti*, *Leptobarbus hoeveni*, *Megalobrama spp.*), eels (*Anguilla spp.*), Nile perch (*Lates niloticus*) and snakeheads (*Channa spp.*), dried, salted or in brine (excluding smoked)
5.5	0/0/0	4.5	4		0	0	0	0//0	0/0/	0	//0	0/0/0	Fish fillets of tilapia(oreochromis spp.), catfish(Pangasius spp., Silurus spp., Clarias spp., Ictalurus spp.), carp(Cyprinus carpio, Carassius carassius, Ctenopharyngodon idellus, Hypophthalmichthys spp., Cirrhinus spp., Mylopharyngodon piceus), eels(Aguilla spp.), nile perch(Lates niloticus) and snakeheads(Channa spp.), dried, salted or in brine, but not smoked

税则号列		货品名称〔CIQ扩展编码及品名－T2表示见附表2〕	最惠(%)	暂定税率	普通	增值/消费	出口退税	计量单位	监管条件	检验检疫	特殊证件对美关税
0305.3200		--犀鳕科、多丝真鳕科、鳕科、长尾鳕科、黑鳕科、无须鳕科、深海鳕科及南极鳕科鱼[T2]	7		80	9/	9,13	千克	AB	PRQS	/
0305.3900		--其他									
0305.3900	10	干、盐腌或盐渍的濒危鱼类的鱼片(熏制的除外)〔999〕	7		80	9/	0	千克	FEAB	PRQS	/
0305.3900	90	其他干、盐腌或盐渍的鱼片(熏制的除外)[T2]	7		80	9/	9,13	千克	AB	PRQS	/
		-熏鱼,包括鱼片,但食用杂碎除外:									
		--大麻哈鱼[红大麻哈鱼、细鳞大麻哈鱼、大麻哈鱼(种)、大鳞大麻哈鱼、银大麻哈鱼、马苏大麻哈鱼、玫瑰大麻哈鱼]、大西洋鲑鱼及多瑙哲罗鱼:									
0305.4110		---大西洋鲑鱼〔101养殖,102野生〕	14		80	9/	9	千克	AB	PRQ	/
0305.4120		---大麻哈鱼及多瑙哲罗鱼〔101养殖大麻哈鱼,102养殖多瑙哲罗鱼,103野生大麻哈鱼,104野生多瑙哲罗鱼〕	7		80	9/	9	千克	AB	PRQ	/42
0305.4200		--鲱鱼(大西洋鲱鱼、太平洋鲱鱼)[T2]	7		80	9/	9	千克	AB	PRQ	/
0305.4300		--鳟鱼(河鳟、虹鳟、克拉克大麻哈鱼、阿瓜大麻哈鱼、吉雨大麻哈鱼、亚利桑那大麻哈鱼、金腹大麻哈鱼)[T2]	14		80	9/	9	千克	AB	PRQS	/
0305.4400		--罗非鱼(口孵非鲫属)、鲶鱼(鲑鲶属、鲶属、胡鲶属、真鮰属)、鲤科鱼(鲤属、鲫属、草鱼、鲢属、鲮属、青鱼、卡特拉鲃、野鲮属、哈氏纹唇鱼、何氏细须鲃、鲂属)、鳗鱼(鳗鲡属)、尼罗河鲈鱼(尼罗尖吻鲈)及黑鱼(鳢属)									
0305.4400	10	熏制花鳗鲡及鱼片(食用杂碎除外)〔101养殖,102野生〕	7		80	9/	9	千克	ABE	PRQS	/
0305.4400	20	熏制欧洲鳗鲡及鱼片(食用杂碎除外)〔101养殖,102野生〕	7		80	9/	9	千克	ABEF	PRQS	/
0305.4400	90	熏制罗非鱼(口孵非鲫属)、鲶鱼(鲑鲶属、鲶属、胡鲶属、真鮰属)、鲤科鱼(鲤属、鲫属、草鱼、鲢属、鲮属、青鱼、卡特拉鲃、野鲮属、哈氏纹唇鱼、何氏细须鲃、鲂属)、鳗鱼(鳗鲡属)、尼罗河鲈鱼(尼罗尖吻鲈)及黑鱼(鳢属)(食用杂碎除外)〔131熏制的养殖鱼,132熏制的野生鱼〕	7		80	9/	9	千克	AB	PRQS	/
0305.4900		--其他									
0305.4900	20	熏制其他濒危鱼及鱼片(食用杂碎除外)〔999〕	7		80	9/	0	千克	ABEF	PRQS	/
0305.4900	90	其他熏鱼及鱼片(食用杂碎除外)[T2]	7		80	9/	9	千克	AB	PRQS	/
		-干鱼(不包括食用杂碎),不论是否盐腌,但熏制的除外:									
0305.5100		--鳕鱼(大西洋鳕鱼、格陵兰鳕鱼、太平洋鳕鱼)〔101干制的大西洋鳕鱼,102干制的太平洋鳕鱼,103干制的格陵兰鳕鱼〕	7		80	9/	9	千克	AB	PRQS	/
0305.5200		--罗非鱼(口孵非鲫属)、鲶鱼(鲑鲶属、鲶属、胡鲶属、真鮰属)、鲤科鱼(鲤属、鲫属、草鱼、鲢属、鲮属、青鱼、卡特拉鲃、野鲮属、哈氏纹唇鱼、何氏细须鲃、鲂属)、鳗鱼(鳗鲡属)、尼罗河鲈鱼(尼罗尖吻鲈)及黑鱼(鳢属)〔101养殖干制鱼类制品,102野生干制鱼类制品〕	7		80	9/	9	千克	AB	PRQS	/
0305.5300		--犀鳕科、多丝真鳕科、鳕科、长尾鳕科、黑鳕科、无须鳕科、深海鳕科及南极鳕科鱼,鳕鱼(大西洋鳕鱼、格陵兰鳕鱼、太平洋鳕鱼)除外〔101大西洋鳕鱼、格陵兰鳕鱼、太平洋鳕鱼除外〕	7		80	9/	9	千克	AB	PRQS	/

协定税率 %										特惠税率 %			
亚太5国	东/冰/格	巴基斯坦	韩国	瑞士	哥达	秘鲁	澳大利亚	新西/坡/智	港/澳/台	亚太2国	老/柬/缅	36/3/1	Article Description
5.5	0/0/0	4.5	4		0	0	0	0//0	0/0/	0	//0	0/0/0	--Fish of the families Bregmacerotidae, Euclichthyidae, Gadidae, Macrouridae, Melanonidae, Merlucciidae, Moridae and Muraenolepididae
													--Other
5.5	0/0/0	4.5	4		0	0	0	0//0	0/0/	0	//0	0/0/0	Endangered fish fillets, dried, salted or in brine (other than smoked)
5.5	0/0/0	4.5	4		0	0	0	0//0	0/0/	0	//0	0/0/0	Fish fillets, dried, salted or in brine (excluding smoked)
													-Smoked fish, including fillets, but excluding offal for human consumption:
													--Pacific salmon (Oncorhynchus nerka, Oncorhynchus gorbuscha, Oncorhynchus keta, Oncorhynchus tschawytscha, Oncorhynchus kisutch, Oncorhynchus masou and Oncorhynchus rhodurus), Altantic salmon(salmo salar) and Danube salmon(hucho hucho):
	0/0/0	7	5.6		0	0	0	0//0	0/0/			0/0/	---Atlantic salmon
	0/0/0	11.2	5.6		0	0	0	0//0	0/0/			0/0/	---Pacific salmon and Danube salmon
	0/0/0	12.8	9.6		0	0	0	0//0	0/0/			0/0/	--Herrings (Atlantic herring, Pacific herring)
	0/0/0	11.2	5.6		0	0	0	0//0	0/0/	0	//0	0/0/0	--Trout (Salmo trutta, Oncorhynchus mykiss, Oncorhynchus clarki, Oncorhynchus aguabonita, Oncorhynchus gilae, Oncorhynchus apache and Oncorhynchus chrysogaster)
													--Tilapias (*Oreochromis spp.*), catfish (*Pangasius spp.*, *Si-lurus spp.*, *Clarias spp.*, *Ictalurus spp.*), carp (*Cypri-nus spp.*, *Carassius spp.*, *Ctenopharyngodon idellus* *Hypophthalmichthys spp.*, *Cirrhinus spp.*, *Mylopharyn-godon piceus* , *Catla catla*, *Labeo spp.*, *Osteochilus has-selti*, *Leptobarbus hoeveni*, *Megalobrama spp.*), eels (*Anguilla spp.*), Nile perch (*Lates niloticus*) and snake-heads (*Channa spp.*)
	0/0/0	11.2	5.6		0	0	0	0//0	0/0/	0	//0	0/0/0	Marbled eels and fillets, smoked (other than edible for human consumption)
	0/0/0	11.2	5.6		0	0	0	0//0	0/0/	0	//0	0/0/0	European eels and fillets, smoked (other than edible for human consumption)
	0/0/0	11.2	5.6		0	0	0	0//0	0/0/	0	//0	0/0/0	smoked Tilapias (*Oreochromis spp.*), catfish (*Pangasius spp.*, *Silurus spp.*, *Clarias spp.*, *Ictalurus spp.*), carp (*Cyprinus spp.*, *Carassius spp.*, *Ctenopharyngodon idellus* *Hypophthalmichthys spp.*, *Cirrhinus spp.*, *Mylopharyngodon piceus* , *Catla catla*, *Labeo spp.*, *Osteochilus hasselti*, *Leptobarbus hoeveni*, *Megalobrama spp.*), eels (*Anguilla spp.*), Nile perch (*Lates niloticus*) and snakeheads (*Channa spp.*), dried, salted or in brine (excluding smoked) (other than edible fish offal)
													--Other
	0/0/0	11.2	5.6		0	0	0	0//0	0/0/	0	//0	0/0/0	Other endangered fish and its fillets, smoked
	0/0/0	11.2	5.6		0	0	0	0//0	0/0/	0	//0	0/0/0	Other fish and their fillets, smoked
													-Dried fish, other than edible fish offal, whether or not salted but not smoked:
	0/0/0	12.8	9.6	4.8	0	0	0	0//0	0/0/			0/0/	--Cod (Gadus morhua, Gadus ogac, Gadus macrocephalus)
	0/0/0		9.6	4.8	0	0	0	0//0	0/0/	0	//0	0/0/0	--Tilapias (*Oreochromis spp.*), catfish (*Pangasius spp.*, *Si-lurus spp.*, *Clarias spp.*, *Ictalurus spp.*), carp (*Cypri-nus spp.*, *Carassius spp.*, *Ctenopharyngodon idellus* *Hypophthalmichthys spp.*, *Cirrhinus spp.*, *Mylopharyn-godon piceus* , *Catla catla*, *Labeo spp.*, *Osteochilus has-selti*, *Leptobarbus hoeveni*, *Megalobrama spp.*), eels (*Anguilla spp.*), Nile perch (*Lates niloticus*) and snake-heads (*Channa spp.*)
	0/0/0		9.6	4.8	0	0	0	0//0	0/0/	0	//0	0/0/0	--Fish of the families Bregmacerotidae, Euclichthyidae, Gadidae, Macrouridae, Melanonidae, Merlucciidae, Moridae and Muraenolepididae, other than cod (*Gadusmorhua*, *Gadus ogac*, *Gadus macrocephalus*)

税则号列		货品名称〔CIQ 扩展编码及品名—T2 表示见附表 2〕	最惠(%)	暂定税率	普通	增值/消费	出口退税	计量单位	监管条件	检验检疫	特殊证件对美关税
0305.5400		--鲱鱼(大西洋鲱鱼、太平洋鲱鱼)、鳀鱼(鳀属)、沙丁鱼(沙丁鱼、沙瑙鱼属)、小沙丁鱼属、黍鲱或西鲱、鲭鱼[大西洋鲭、澳洲鲭(鲐)、日本鲭(鲐)]、印度鲭(羽鳃鲐属)、马鲛鱼(马鲛属)、对称竹荚鱼、新西兰竹荚鱼及竹荚鱼(竹荚鱼属)、鲹鱼(鲹属)、军曹鱼、银鲳(鲳属)、秋刀鱼、圆鲹(圆鲹属)、多春鱼(毛鳞鱼)、剑鱼、鲔鱼、狐鲣(狐鲣属)、枪鱼、旗鱼、四鳍旗鱼(旗鱼科)〔101 养殖干制鱼类制品，102 野生干制鱼类制品〕	7		80	9/	9	千克	AB	PRQS	/
		--其他：									
0305.5910		---海龙、海马〔101 干制的海马，102 干制的海龙，103 药用海马，104 药用海龙〕	2		20	9/	9	千克	FEAB	PRQ	/
0305.5990		---其他									
0305.5990	10	其他濒危干鱼，食用杂碎除外(不论是否盐腌，但熏制的除外)〔999〕	7		80	9/	0	千克	AFEB	PRQS	/
0305.5990	90	其他干鱼，食用杂碎除外(不论是否盐腌，但熏制的除外)[T2]	7		80	9/	9	千克	AB	PRQS	/
		-盐腌及盐渍的鱼(不包括食用杂碎)，但干或熏制的除外：									
0305.6100		--鲱鱼(大西洋鲱鱼、太平洋鲱鱼)〔101 盐腌及盐渍的大西洋鲱鱼，102 盐腌及盐渍的太平洋鲱鱼〕	7		80	9/	9	千克	AB	PRQ	/
0305.6200		--鳕鱼(大西洋鳕鱼、格陵兰鳕鱼、太平洋鳕鱼)〔101 盐腌及盐渍的大西洋鳕鱼，102 盐腌及盐渍的太平洋鳕鱼，103 盐腌及盐渍的格陵兰鳕鱼〕	7		80	9/	9	千克	AB	PRQS	/
0305.6300		--鳀鱼(鳀属)〔999〕	7		80	9/	9	千克	AB	PRQ	/
0305.6400		--罗非鱼(口孵非鲫属)、鲶鱼(鲑鲶属、鲶属、胡鲶属、真鮰属)、鲤科鱼(鲤属、鲫属、草鱼、鲢属、鲮属、青鱼、卡特拉鲃、野鲮属、哈氏纹唇鱼、何氏细须鲃、鲂属)、鳗鱼(鳗鲡属)、尼罗河鲈鱼(尼罗尖吻鲈)及黑鱼(鳢属)									
0305.6400	10	盐腌及盐渍的花鳗鲡，食用杂碎除外(干或熏制的除外)〔101 盐腌及盐渍的养殖花鳗鲡，102 盐腌及盐渍的野生花鳗鲡〕	10		80	9/	9	千克	ABE	PRQS	/
0305.6400	20	盐腌及盐渍的欧洲鳗鲡，食用杂碎除外(干或熏制的除外)〔101 盐腌及盐渍的养殖，102 盐腌及盐渍的野生〕	10		80	9/	9	千克	ABEF	PRQS	/
0305.6400	90	盐腌及盐渍的罗非鱼(口孵非鲫属)、鲶鱼(鲑鲶属、鲶属、胡鲶属、真鮰属)、鲤科鱼(鲤属、鲫属、草鱼、鲢属、鲮属、青鱼、卡特拉鲃、野鲮属、哈氏纹唇鱼、何氏细须鲃、鲂属)、其他鳗鱼(鳗鲡属)、尼罗河鲈鱼(尼罗尖吻鲈)及黑鱼(鳢属)，食用杂碎除外(干或熏制的除外)〔131 盐腌及腌渍的养殖鱼类制品，132 盐腌及腌渍的野生鱼类制品〕	10		80	9/	9	千克	AB	PRQS	/
		--其他：									
0305.6910		---带鱼〔999〕	7		80	9/	9	千克	AB	PRQS	/
0305.6920		---黄鱼〔101 盐腌及盐渍的养殖黄鱼，102 盐腌及盐渍的野生黄鱼〕	10		80	9/	9	千克	AB	PRQS	/
0305.6930		---鲳鱼〔102 盐腌及盐渍的野生鲳鱼，101 盐腌及盐渍的养殖鲳鱼外〕	7		80	9/	9	千克	AB	PRQS	/
0305.6990		---其他									
0305.6990	10	盐腌及盐渍的其他濒危鱼，食用杂碎除外(干或熏制的除外)〔999〕	7		80	9/	0	千克	ABFE	PRQS	/
0305.6990	90	盐腌及盐渍的其他鱼，食用杂碎除外(干或熏制的除外)[T2]	7		80	9/	9	千克	AB	PRQS	/
		-鱼鳍、鱼头、鱼尾、鱼鳔及其他可食用杂碎：									
0305.7100		--鲨鱼翅									
0305.7100	10	濒危鲨鱼鱼翅(不论是否干制、盐腌、盐渍和熏制)〔999〕	15		80	9/	0	千克	ABEF	PRQS	/

协定税率 %										特惠税率 %			Article Description
亚太5国	东/冰/格	巴基斯坦	韩国	瑞士	哥达	秘鲁	澳大利亚	新西/坡/智	港/澳/台	亚太2国	老/柬/缅	36/3/1	
	0/0/0		9.6	4.8	0	0	0	0//0	0/0/	0	//0	0/0/0	--Herrings (*Clupea harengus*, *Clupea pallasii*), anchovies (*Engraulis spp.*), sardines (*Sardina pilchardus*, *Sardi-nops spp.*), sardinella (*Sardinella spp.*), brisling or sprats (*Sprattus sprattus*), mackerel (*Scomber scombrus*, *Scomber australasicus*, *Scomber japonicus*), Indian macker-els (*Rastrelliger spp.*), seerfi-shes (*Scomberomorus spp.*), jack and horse mackerel(*Tra-churus spp.*), jacks, crevalles(*Caranx spp.*), cobia(*Rachy-centron canadum*), silver pom-frets(*Pampus spp.*), Pacific saury(*Cololabis saira*), scads (*Decapterus spp.*), capelin(*Mallotus villosus*), swordfish(*Xiphias gladius*), Kawakawa(*Euthymus affinis*), bonitos(*Sarda spp.*), marlins, sail-fishes, spearfish(*Istiophori-dae*)
													--Other:
	0/0/0	0	0	0	0	0	0	0//0	0/0/	0	/0/0	0/0/0	---Pipefish and hippocampi
													---Other
	0/0/0		9.6	4.8	0	0	0	0//0	0/0/	0	//0	0/0/0	Other endangered fish other than edible for human consumption, dried (whether or not salted but not smoked)
	0/0/0		9.6	4.8	0	0	0	0//0	0/0/	0	//0	0/0/0	Other fish other than edible for human consumption, dried (whether or not salted but not smoked)
													-Fish(excluding offal for human consumptior), salted but not dried nor smoked and fish in brine:
4.8	0/0/0	8	9.6	4.8	0	0	0	0//0	0/0/			0/0/	--Herrings (Atlantic herring, pacific herring)
5.3	0/0/0	8	9.6	4.8	0	0	0	0//0	0/0/			0/0/0	--Cod(Atlantic cod、Pacific cod、Greenland cod)
5.3	0/0/0	8	9.6	4.8	0	0	0	0//0	0/0/			0/0/	--Anchovies (*Engraulis spp.*)
													--Tilapias (*Oreochromis spp.*), catfish (*Pangasius spp.*, *Si-lurus spp.*, *Cia rias spp.*, *Ic-talurus spp.*), carp (*Cypri-nus spp.*, *Carassius spp.*, *Ctenopharyngodon idellus*, *Hypophthalmichthys spp.*, *Cirrhinus spp.*, *Mylopharyn-godon piceus*, *Catla catla*, *Labeo spp.*, *Osteochilus hasselti*, *Leptobarbus hoeveni*, *Megalobrama spp.*), eels (*Anguilla spp.*), Nile perch (*Lates niloticus*) and snake-heads (*Channa spp.*)
	0/0/0	12.8	9.6	4.8	0	0	0	0//0	0/0/	0	//0	0/0/0	Marbled eels, dried, salted or in brine, other than deible for human consumption, but not smoked
	0/0/0	12.8	9.6	4.8	0	0	0	0//0	0/0/	0	//0	0/0/0	European eels, dried, salted or in brine, other than deible for human consumption, but not smoked
	0/0/0	12.8	9.6	4.8	0	0	0	0//0	0/0/	0	//0	0/0/0	Tilapias (*Oreochromis spp.*), catfish (*Pangasius spp.*, *Silurus spp.*, *Clarias spp.*, *Ictalurus spp.*), carp (*Cyprinus spp.*, *Carassius spp.*, *Ctenopharyngodon idellus Hypophthalmichthys spp.*, *Cirrhinus spp.*, *Mylopharyngodon piceus*, *Catla catla*, *Labeo spp.*, *Osteochilus hasselti*, *Leptobarbus hoeveni*, *Megalobrama spp.*), eels (*Anguilla spp.*), Nile perch (*Lates niloticus*) and snake-heads (*Channa spp.*), dried, salted or in brine(excluding smoked) (other than edible fish offal), salted or in brine
													--Other:
	0/0/0	12.8	9.6	4.8	0	0	0	0//0	0/0/	0	//0	0/0/0	---Scabber fish (*Trichurius*)
	0/0/0	12.8	9.6	4.8	0	0	0	0//0	0/0/	0	//0	0/0/0	---Yellow croaker (*Pseudosicaena*)
	0/0/0	12.8	9.6	4.8	0	0	0	0//0	0/0/	0	//0	0/0/0	---Butterfish (*Pampus*)
													---Other
	0/0/0	12.8	9.6	4.8	0	0	0	0//0	0/0/	0	//0	0/0/0	Other endangered fish, other than edible for human consuption, salted or in brine (not dried nor smoked)
	0/0/0	12.8	9.6	4.8	0	0	0	0//0	0/0/	0	//0	0/0/0	Other fish, other than edible for human consuption salted or in brine (not dried nor smoked)
													-Fish head、tail、maws and other edible fish offal, for human consumption:
													--Shark fin
	0/0/0			4.5	0	0		0//0	0/0/	0	/0/0	0/0/0	Sharks fins of whale(Rhincodon), man-eating shark(Cacharodon), basking shark(Cetorhinus), whether or not dried, salted, in brine and smoked

税则号列		货品名称〔CIQ 扩展编码及品名—T2 表示见附表 2〕	最惠(%)	暂定税率	普通	增值/消费	出口退税	计量单位	监管条件	检验检疫	特殊证件对美关税
0305.7100	90	其他的鲨鱼鱼翅(不论是否干制、盐腌、盐渍和熏制)〔999〕	15		80	9/	9	千克	AB	PRQS	/
0305.7200		--鱼头、鱼尾、鱼鳔									
0305.7200	10	濒危鱼的鱼头、鱼尾、鱼鳔(不论是否干制、盐腌、盐渍和熏制)〔999〕	7		80	9/	0	千克	ABEF	PRQS	/
0305.7200	90	其他鱼的鱼头、鱼尾、鱼鳔(不论是否干制、盐腌、盐渍和熏制)〔101 养殖,102 野生〕	7		80	9/	9	千克	AB	PRQS	/
0305.7900		--其他									
0305.7900	10	其他濒危可食用鱼杂碎(不论是否干制、盐腌、盐渍和熏制)〔999〕	7		80	9/	0	千克	ABEF	PRQS	/
0305.7900	90	其他可食用鱼杂碎(不论是否干制、盐腌、盐渍和熏制)〔101 养殖,102 野生〕	7		80	9/	9	千克	AB	PRQS	/
03.06		**带壳或去壳的甲壳动物,活、鲜、冷、冻、干、盐腌或盐渍的;熏制的带壳或去壳甲壳动物,不论是在熏制前或熏制过程中是否烹煮;蒸过或用水煮过的带壳甲壳动物,不论是否冷、冻、干、盐腌或盐渍的;适合供人食用的甲壳动物的细粉、粗粉及团粒:**									
		-冻的:									
0306.1100		--岩礁虾和其他龙虾(真龙虾属、龙虾属、岩龙虾属)〔101 养殖大螯虾,102 养殖小龙虾,103 野生大螯虾,104 野生小龙虾〕	7		70	9/	9	千克	AB	PRQS	/42
0306.1200		--螯龙虾(螯龙虾属)〔101 养殖,102 野生〕	7		70	9/	9	千克	AB	PRQS	/42
		--蟹:									
0306.1410		---梭子蟹〔101 饲料用梭子蟹,102 养殖,103 野生〕	7		70	9/	9	千克	AB	PRQS	/42
0306.1490		---其他									
0306.1490	11	冻的金霸王蟹(帝王蟹)〔101 养殖,102 野生〕	7	5	70	9/	9	千克	ABU	PRQS	/40
0306.1490	19	冻的毛蟹、仿石蟹(仿岩蟹)、堪察加拟石蟹、短足拟石蟹、扁足拟石蟹、雪蟹、日本雪蟹[T2]	7	5	70	9/	9	千克	ABU	PRQS	/40
0306.1490	90	其他冻蟹[T2]	7	5	70	9/	9	千克	AB	PRQS	/40
0306.1500		--挪威海螯虾〔101 养殖,102 野生〕	7		70	9/	9	千克	AB	PRQS	/42
		--冷水小虾及对虾(长额虾属、褐虾):									
		---冷水小虾:									
0306.1611		----虾仁〔101 养殖,102 野生〕	7		70	9/	9	千克	AB	PRQS	/42
0306.1612		----其他,北方长额虾(虾仁除外)〔101 养殖,102 野生〕	5	2	70	9/	13,9	千克	AB	PRQS	/37
0306.1619		----其他〔101 养殖,102 野生〕	5		70	9/	9	千克	AB	PRQS	/40
		---冷水对虾:									
0306.1621		----虾仁〔101 养殖,102 野生〕	7		70	9/	9	千克	AB	PRQS	/42
0306.1629		----其他〔101 养殖,102 野生〕	5		70	9/	9	千克	AB	PRQS	/40
		--其他小虾及对虾:									
		---小虾:									
0306.1711		----虾仁[T2]	7		70	9/	9	千克	AB	PRQS	/42
0306.1719		----其他[T2]	5	2	70	9/	9	千克	AB	PRQS	/37
		---对虾:									
0306.1721		----虾仁〔101 养殖,102 野生〕	7		70	9/	9	千克	AB	PRQS	/42
0306.1729		----其他〔101 养殖斑节对虾(虎虾),102 养殖南美白对虾,103 养殖草虾,104 养殖其他对虾,105 野生斑节对虾(虎虾),106 野生南美白对虾,107 野生草虾,108 野生其他对虾〕	5		70	9/	9	千克	AB	PRQS	/40
		--其他,包括适合供人食用的甲壳动物的细粉、粗粉及团粒:									
		---淡水小龙虾:									
0306.1911		----虾仁〔101 养殖,102 野生〕	7		70	9/	9	千克	AB	PRQS	/42
0306.1919		----其他〔101 养殖,102 野生〕	7		70	9/	9	千克	AB	PRQS	/42
0306.1990		---其他〔101 养殖,102 野生〕	7		70	9/	9	千克	AB	PRQS	/42
		-活、鲜或冷的:									
		--岩礁虾及其他龙虾(真龙虾属、龙虾属、岩龙虾属):									
0306.3110		---种苗〔999〕	0		0	9/	9	千克	AB	PQ	/25
0306.3190		---其他[T2]	7	5	70	9/	9	千克	AB	PRQS	/40
		--螯龙虾(螯龙虾属):									
0306.3210		---种苗〔999〕	0		0	9/	9	千克	AB	PQ	/25
0306.3290		---其他〔101 活螯虾,102 鲜或冷的带壳或去壳养殖螯龙虾(螯龙虾属),103 鲜或冷的带壳或去壳野生螯龙虾(螯龙虾属)〕	7		70	9/	9	千克	AB	PRQS	/42
		--蟹:									

协定税率 %										特惠税率 %			Article Description
亚太5国	东/冰/格	巴基斯坦	韩国	瑞士	哥达	秘鲁	澳大利亚	新西/坡/智	港/澳/台	亚太2国	老/柬/缅	36/3/1	
	0/0/0			4.5	0	0		0//0	0/0/	0	/0/0	0/0/0	Other sharks fins, whether or not dried, salted, in brine and smoked, whether or not dried, salted, in brine and smoked
													--Fish head, tail and maws
	0/0/0	12.8	9.6		0	0	0	0//0	0/0/			0/0/	Endangered fish of fish head, tail and maws, whether or not dried, salted, in brine and smoked
	0/0/0	12.8	9.6		0	0	0	0//0	0/C/			0/0/	Other fish of fish head, tail and maws, whether or not dried, salted, in brine and smoked
													--Other
	0/0/0	12.8	9.6		0	0	0	0//0	0/0/			0/0/	Other endangered fish edible for human consumption, whether or not dried, salted, in brine and smoked
	0/0/0	12.8	9.6		0	0	0	0//0	0/0/			0/0/	Other fish edible for human consumption, whether or not dried, salted, in brine and smoked
													Crustaceans, whether in shell or not, live, fresh, chilled, frozen, dried, salted or in brine; smoked crustaceans, whether or not cooked before or during the smoking process; crustaceans, in shell, cooked by steaming or by boiling in water, whether or not chilled, frozen, dried, salted or in brine; flours, meals and pellets of crustaceans, fit for human consumption
													-Frozen:
	0/0/0	4.5	4	0	0	0	0	0//0	0/0/		/0/0	0/0/0	--Reef shrimp and shrimp(Palinurus、Lobster genus、Rock lobster genus)
5	0/0/0	4.5	4	0	0	0	0	0//0	0/0/		/0/	0/0/0	--Ao lobster(Ao lobster genus)
													--Crabs:
	0/0/0	4.5	4	0	0	0	0	0//0	0/0/	0	/0/0	0/0/0	---Swimming crab
													---Other
	0/0/0	4.5	6	0	0	0	0	0//0	0/0/	0	/0/0	0/0/0	Frozen Lithodes aequispinus
	0/0/0	4.5	6	0	0	0	0	0//0	0/0/	0	/0/0	0/0/0	Frozen Eriocheir sinensis, Lithodes, Paralithodes camtschaticus, Paralithodes brevipes, Paralithodes platypus, Snow Crab
	0/0/0	4.5	6	0	0	0	0	0//0	0/0/	0	/0/0	0/0/0	Other crab, frozen
	0/0/0	12.8	9.6	4.8	0	0	0	0//0	0/0/		/0/	0/0/0	--Norway Lobsters(Nehrops norvegicus)
													--Cold-water shrimp and prawns(pandalus, spp., Crangon crangon):
													---Cold-water shrimp:
3.5	0/0/0	0	0	0	0	0	0	0//0	0/0/		/0/0	0/0/0	----Shelled
2.5	0/0/0	0	0	0	0	0	0	0//0	0/0/		/0/0	0/0/0	----Frozen Northem pandalus(Pandalus), excluding shrimps
2.5	0/0/0	0	0	0	0	0	0	0//0	0/0/		/0/0	0/0/0	----Other
													---Cold-water prawns:
3.5	0/0/0	0	0	0	0	0	0	0//0	0/0/		/0/0	0/0/0	----Shelled
2.5	0/0/0	0	0	0	0	0	0	0//0	0/0/		/0/0	0/0/0	----Other
													--Other shrimps and prawns:
													---Shrimps:
3.5	0/0/0	0	0	0	0	0	0	0//0	0/0/		/0/0	0/0/0	----Shelled
2.5	0/0/0	0	0	0	0	0	0	0//0	0/0/		/0/0	0/0/0	----Other
													---Prawns:
3.5	0/0/0	0	0	0	0	0	0	0//0	0/0/		/0/0	0/0/0	----Shelled
2.5	0/0/0	0	0	0	0	0	0	0//0	0/0/		/0/0	0/0/0	----Other
													--Other, including flours, meals and pellets of crustaceans, fit for human consumption:
													---Freshwater crawfish:
	0/0/0	12.8	9.6	4.8	0	0	0	0//0	0/0/		/0/	0/0/0	----Shelled
	0/0/0	12.8	9.6	4.8	0	0	0	0//0	0/0/		/0/	0/0/0	----Other
	0/0/0	0	9.6	4.8	0	0	0	0//0	0/0/		/0/	0/0/0	---Other
													--Live, fresh or chilled:
													--Rock lobster and other seacrawfish (*Palinurus spp.* , *Panulirus spp.* , *Jasus spp.*):
												0/0/0	---For cultivation
	0/0/0	0	6	4.5	0	0	0	0//0	0/0/		/0/0	0/0/0	---Other
													--Lobsters (*Homarus spp.*):
												0/0/0	---For cultivation
	0/0/0	12	6	4.5	0	0	0	0//0	0/0/		/0/0	0/0/0	---Other
													--Crabs:

税则号列	货品名称〔CIQ 扩展编码及品名—T2 表示见附表 2〕	最惠(%)	暂定税率	普通	增值/消费	出口退税	计量单位	监管条件	检验检疫	特殊证件对美关税
0306.3310	---种苗〔105 其他淡水虾蟹,103 其他海水虾蟹,101 青蟹,102 梭子蟹,104 中华绒螯蟹(大闸蟹)〕	0		0	9/	9	千克	AB	PQ	/25
	---其他:									
0306.3391	----中华绒螯蟹〔103 野生鲜或冷中华绒螯蟹,102 其他野生鲜或冷蟹,101 大闸蟹〕	7		70	9/	9	千克	AB	PRQS	/42
0306.3392	----梭子蟹〔103 鲜或冷的养殖梭子蟹,104 鲜或冷的野生梭子蟹,101 活的梭子蟹,102 饲料用梭子蟹〕	14		70	9/	9	千克	AB	PRQS	/49
0306.3399	----其他									
0306.3399 11	活金霸王蟹(帝王蟹)〔101〕	7		70	9/	9	千克	ABU	PRQS	/42
0306.3399 19	活、鲜或冷的毛蟹、仿石蟹(仿岩蟹)、堪察加拟石蟹、短足拟石蟹、扁足拟石蟹、雪蟹、日本雪蟹,鲜或冷的金霸王蟹(帝王蟹)[T2]	7		70	9/	9	千克	ABU	PRQS	/42
0306.3399 90	其他活、鲜或冷的带壳或去壳蟹[T2]	7		70	9/	9	千克	AB	PRQS	/42
	--挪威海螯虾:									
0306.3410	---种苗〔999〕	0		0	9/	9	千克	AB	PQ	/25
0306.3490	---其他〔102 养殖,103 野生,101 活挪威海螯虾〕	7		70	9/	9	千克	AB	PRQS	/42
	--冷水小虾及对虾(长额虾属、褐虾):									
0306.3510	---种苗〔102 褐虾种苗,101 长额虾属种苗〕	0		0	9/	9	千克	AB	PQ	/25
0306.3520	---鲜、冷对虾〔101 养殖,102 野生〕	10		70	9/	9	千克	AB	PRQS	/45
0306.3590	---其他									
0306.3590 01	活、鲜或冷的其他冷水小虾〔103 养殖,104 野生,102 饲料用淡水虾,101 饲料用海水虾〕	10		70	9/	9	千克	AB	PRQS	/45
0306.3590 90	其他活的冷水对虾[T2]	10		70	9/	9	千克	AB	PRQS	/45
	--其他小虾及对虾:									
0306.3610	---种苗〔102 斑节对虾,101 南美白对虾,103 其他对虾,104 其他海水虾蟹〕	0		0	9/	9	千克	AB	PQ	/
0306.3620	---鲜、冷对虾〔101 其他养殖鲜或冷虾,102 其他野生鲜或冷虾〕	10		70	9/	9	千克	AB	PRQS	/45
0306.3690	---其他									
0306.3690 01	其他鲜、冷小虾〔103 其他养殖鲜或冷虾,104 其他野生鲜或冷虾,102 饲料用淡水虾,101 饲料用海水虾〕	12		70	9/	9	千克	AB	PRQS	/47
0306.3690 90	其他活的小虾及对虾[T2]	12		70	9/	9	千克	AB	PRQS	/47
	--其他,包括适合供人食用的甲壳动物的细粉、粗粉及团粒:									
0306.3910	---种苗[T2]	0		0	9/	9	千克	AB	PQ	/25
0306.3990	---其他〔103 养殖,104 野生,101 活的其他淡水虾蟹,102 未列出的饲料用其他淡水产品〕	7		70	9/	9	千克	AB	PRQS	/42
	-其他:									
0306.9100	--岩礁虾及其他龙虾(真龙虾属、龙虾属、岩龙虾属)〔101 养殖干制虾类制品,102 野生干制虾类制品,103 养殖盐腌及盐渍虾类制品,104 野生盐腌及盐渍虾类制品〕	7		70	9/	9	千克	AB	PRQS	/42
0306.9200	--螯龙虾(螯龙虾属)〔101 养殖干制虾类制品,102 野生干制虾类制品,103 养殖盐腌及盐渍虾类制品,104 野生盐腌及盐渍虾类制品〕	7		70	9/	9	千克	AB	PRQS	/42
	--蟹:									
0306.9310	---中华绒螯蟹[T2]	7		70	9/	9	千克	AB	PRQS	/42
0306.9320	---梭子蟹[T2]	7		70	9/	9	千克	AB	PRQS	/42
0306.9390	---其他〔101 养殖干制蟹类制品,102 野生干制蟹类制品,103 养殖盐腌及盐渍蟹类制品,104 野生盐腌及盐渍蟹类制品〕	7		70	9/	9	千克	AB	PRQS	/42
0306.9400	--挪威海螯虾[T2]	7		70	9/	9,13	千克	AB	PRQS	/42
	--小虾及对虾:									
0306.9510	---冷水小虾及对虾(长额虾属、褐虾)〔101 养殖干制虾类制品,102 野生干制虾类制品,103 养殖盐腌及盐渍虾类制品,104 野生盐腌及盐渍虾类制品〕	10		70	9/	9	千克	AB	PRQS	/45
0306.9590	---其他小虾及对虾[T2]	10		70	9/	9	千克	AB	PRQS	/45
0306.9900	--其他,包括适合供人食用的甲壳动物的细粉、粗粉及团粒[T2]	7		70	9/	9,13	千克	AB	PRQS	/42
03.07	**带壳或去壳的软体动物,活、鲜、冷、冻、干、盐腌或盐渍的;熏制的带壳或去壳软体动物,不论在熏制前或熏制过程中是否烹煮;适合供人食用的软体动物的细粉、粗粉及团粒:**									
	-牡蛎(蚝):									
	--活、鲜或冷的:									
0307.1110	---种苗〔999〕	0		0	9/	9	千克	AB	PQ	/25

协定税率 %										特惠税率 %			Article Description
亚太5国	东/冰/格	巴基斯坦	韩国	瑞士	哥达	秘鲁	澳大利亚	新西/坡/智	港/澳/台	亚太2国	老/柬/缅	36/3/1	
												0/0/0	---For cultivation
													--Other:
	0/0/0	6.3	5.6	4.2	0	0	0	0//0	0/0/		/0/	0/0/0	----Freshwater crabs, live
	0/0/0	0	5.6	4.2	0	0	0	0//0	0/0/		/0/	0/0/0	----Swimming crab
													----Other
	0/0/0	0	5.6	4.2	0	0	0	0//0	0/0/		/0/	0/0/0	Live Lithodes aequispinus
	0/0/0	0	5.6	4.2	0	0	0	0//0	0/0/		/0/	0/0/0	Eriocheir sinensis, Lithodes, Paralithodes camtschaticus, Paralithodes brevipes, Paralithodes platypus, Snow Crab, live, fresh or cold
	0/0/0	0	5.6	4.2	0	0	0	0//0	0/0/		/0/	0/0/0	Other live, fresh or cold crab, in shell or not
													--Norway lobsters (*Nephrops norvegicus*)
												0/0/0	---For cultivation
	0/0/0	11.2	5.6	4.2	0	0	0	0//0	0/0/		/0/0	0/0/0	---Other
													--Cold— water shrimps and prawns (*Pandalus spp.* , *Crangon crangon*):
												0/0/0	---For cultivation
	0/0/0	12	6	4.5	0	0	0	0//0	0/0/		/0/0	0/0/0	---Cold-water prawns, fresh or chilled
													---Other
	0/0/0	5.4	4.8	3.6	0	0	0	0//0	0/0/		/0/0	0/0/0	Other Cold water shrimps, live, fresh or cold
	0/0/0	5.4	4.8	3.6	0	0	0	0//0	0/0/		/0/0	0/0/0	Other live cold water prawns
													--Other shrimps and prawns:
												0/0/0	---For cultivation
	0/0/0	12	6	4.5	0	0	0	0//0	0/0/		/0/0	0/0/0	---Cold-water prawns, fresh or chilled
													---Other
	0/0/0	5.4	4.8	3.6	0	0	0	0//0	0/0/		/0/0	0/0/0	Other fresh or cold shrimps
	0/0/0	5.4	4.8	3.6	0	0	0	0//0	0/0/		/0/0	0/0/0	Other live shrimps and prawns
													--Other, including flours, meals and pellets of crustaceans, fit for human consumption:
												0/0/0	---For cultivation
	0/0/0	11.2	5.6	4.2	0	0	0	0//0	0/0/		/0/0	0/0/0	---Other
													-Other:
	0/0/0	0	6	4.5	0	0	0	0//0	0/0/		/0/0	0/0/0	--Rock lobster and other sea crawfish (*Palinurus spp.* , *Panulirus spp.* , *Jasus spp.*)
	0/0/0	12	6	4.5	0	0	0	0//0	0/0/		/0/0	0/0/0	--Lobsters (*Homarus spp.*)
													--Crabs:
	0/0/0	6.3	5.6	4.2	0	0	0	0//0	0/0/		/0/	0/0/0	---Freshwater crabs, live
	0/0/0	0	5.6	4.2	0	0	0	0//0	0/0/		/0/	0/0/0	---Swimming crab
	0/0/0	0	5.6	4.2	0	0	0	0//0	0/0/		/0/	0/0/0	---Other
	0/0/0	11.2	5.6	4.2	0	0	0	0//0	0/0/		/0/0	0/0/0	--Norway lobsters (*Nephrops norvegicus*)
													--Shrimps and prawns:
	0/0/0	5.4	4.8	3.6	0	0	0	0//0	0/0/		/0/0	0/0/0	---Cold-water shrimps and prawns (*Pandalus spp.* , *Crangon crangon*):
	0/0/0	5.4	4.8	3.6	0	0	0	0//0	0/0/		/0/0	0/0/0	---Other shrimps and prawns
	0/0/0	11.2	5.6	4.2	0	0	0	0//0	0/0/		/0/0	0/0/0	--Other, including flours, meals and pellets of crustaceans, fit for human consumption
													molluscs, whether in shell or not, live, fresh, chilled, frozen, dried, salted or in brine; smoked molluscs, whether in shell or not, whether or not cooked before or during the smoking pracess; flours, meals and pellets of mollusks, fit for human consumption:
													-Oysters:
													--Live, fresh or chilled:
												0/0/0	---For cultivation

税则号列		货品名称〔CIQ扩展编码及品名—T2表示见附表2〕	最惠(%)	暂定税率	普通	增值/消费	出口退税	计量单位	监管条件	检验检疫	特殊证件对美关税
0307.1190		---其他〔101 活的牡蛎(蚝),102 非生食的鲜、冷的养殖牡蛎(蚝),103 可用于生食的鲜、冷的养殖牡蛎(蚝),104 非生食的鲜、冷的野生牡蛎(蚝),105 可用于生食的鲜、冷的野生牡蛎(蚝)〕	7		70	9/	9	千克	AB	PRQS	/42
0307.1200		--冻的〔101 养殖,102 野生〕	10		70	9/	9	千克	AB	PRQS	/45
0307.1900		--其他〔101 干制的养殖牡蛎(蚝),102 干制的野生牡蛎(蚝),103 盐腌或盐渍的养殖牡蛎(蚝),104 盐腌或盐渍的野生牡蛎(蚝)〕	10		70	9/	6	千克	AB	PRQS	/45
		-扇贝,包括海扇:									
		--活、鲜或冷的:									
0307.2110		---种苗									
0307.2110	10	大珠母贝种苗	0		0	9/	9	千克	ABE	PQ	/25
0307.2110	90	其他扇贝种苗(包括海扇种苗)〔999〕	0		0	9/	9	千克	AB	PQ	/25
0307.2190		---其他									
0307.2190	10	其他活、鲜、冷大珠母贝〔101 活的扇贝,102 鲜、冷的养殖大珠母贝,103 鲜、冷的野生大珠母贝〕	10		70	9/	9	千克	ABE	PRQS	/45
0307.2190	90	其他活、鲜、冷扇贝(包括海扇,种苗除外)[T2]	10		70	9/	9	千克	AB	PRQS	/45
0307.2200		--冻的									
0307.2200	10	冻的大珠母贝〔101 其他养殖冷冻双壳贝,102 其他野生冷冻双壳贝〕	10		80	9/	9	千克	ABE	PRQS	/45
0307.2200	90	其他冻的扇贝(包括海扇)〔101 养殖冷冻扇贝,102 野生冷冻扇贝〕	10		80	9/	9	千克	AB	PRQS	/45
0307.2900		--其他									
0307.2900	10	其他干、盐腌或盐渍的大珠母贝(包括熏制的带壳或去壳的,不论在熏制前或熏制过程中是否烹煮)〔101 干制的养殖大珠母贝,102 干制的野生大珠母贝,103 盐腌或盐渍的养殖大珠母贝,104 盐腌或盐渍的野生大珠母贝〕	10		80	9/	9	千克	ABE	PRQS	/45
0307.2900	90	其他干、盐腌或盐渍的扇贝〔101 干制的养殖扇贝,102 干制的野生扇贝,103 盐腌或盐渍的养殖扇贝,104 盐腌或盐渍的野生扇贝〕	10		80	9/	9	千克	AB	PRQS	/45
		-贻贝:									
		--活、鲜或冷的:									
0307.3110		---种苗〔999〕	0		0	9/	9	千克	AB	PQ	/25
0307.3190		---其他									
0307.3190	01	鲜、冷贻贝〔101 养殖,102 野生〕	10		70	9/	9	千克	AB	PRQS	/45
0307.3190	90	其他活贻贝〔999〕	10		70	9/	9	千克	AB	PRQS	/45
0307.3200		--冻的〔101 养殖冷冻贻贝,102 其他野生冷冻双壳贝〕	10		70	9/	9	千克	AB	PRQS	/45
0307.3900		--其他〔101 养殖干制贝类制品,102 野生干制贝类制品,103 养殖盐腌及盐渍贝类制品,104 野生盐腌及盐渍贝类制品〕	10		70	9/	9	千克	AB	PRQS	/45
		-墨鱼及鱿鱼:									
		--活、鲜或冷的:									
0307.4210		---种苗〔101 乌贼(墨鱼),102 鱿鱼〕	0		0	9/	9	千克	AB	PQ	/25
		---其他:									
0307.4291		----墨鱼(乌贼属、巨粒僧头乌贼、耳乌贼属)及鱿鱼(柔鱼属、枪乌贼属、双柔鱼属、拟乌贼属)[T2]	12		70	9/	9	千克	AB	PRQS	/47
0307.4299		----其他[T2]	14		70	9/	9	千克	AB	PRQS	/49
		--冻的:									
0307.4310		---墨鱼(乌贼属、巨粒僧头乌贼、耳乌贼属)及鱿鱼(柔鱼属、枪乌贼属、双柔鱼属、拟乌贼属)[T2]	12		70	9/	9	千克	AB	PRQS	/47
0307.4390		---其他〔101 其他冻的养殖墨鱼,102 其他冻的野生墨鱼,103 其他冻的养殖鱿鱼,104 其他冻的野生鱿鱼〕	10		70	9/	9	千克	AB	PRQS	/45
		--其他:									
0307.4910		---墨鱼(乌贼属、巨粒僧头乌贼、耳乌贼属)及鱿鱼(柔鱼属、枪乌贼属、双柔鱼属、拟乌贼属)[T2]	12		70	9/	9	千克	AB	PRQS	/47
0307.4990		---其他[T2]	10		70	9/	9,13	千克	AB	PRQS	/45
		-章鱼:									
0307.5100		--活、鲜或冷的〔101 活的章鱼,102 饲料用章鱼,103 非生食的,104 可用于非生食的〕	7		70	9/	9	千克	AB	PRQS	/42
0307.5200		--冻的〔101 养殖,102 野生〕	7		70	9/	9	千克	AB	PRQS	/42
0307.5900		--其他〔101 饲料用章鱼,102 干制的章鱼,103 盐制的章鱼〕	7		70	9/	9	千克	AB	PRQS	/42

协定税率 %										特惠税率 %			
亚太5国	东/冰/格	巴基斯坦	韩国	瑞士	哥达	秘鲁	澳大利亚	新西/坡/智	港/澳/台	亚太2国	老/柬/缅	36/3/1	Article Description
	0/0/0	11.2	5.6	4.2	0	0	0	0//0	0/0/		//0	0/0/0	---Other
	0/0/0	11.2	5.6	4.2	0	0	0	0//0	0/0/		//0	0/0/0	--Frozen
	0/0/0	11.2	5.6	4.2	0	0	0	0//0	0/0/		//0	0/0/0	--Other
													-Scallops, including queen scallops, of the genera *Pecten*, *Chlamys or Placopecten*: --Live, fresh or chilled: ---For cultivation
	//							//	//		//	0/0/0	Pearl oyster seedlings
												0/0/0	Other scallops(including queen scallops) for cultivation) ---Other
	0/0/0	11.2	5.6	4.2	0	0	0	0//0	0/0/		//0	0/0/0	Other pearloyster(*Pinctada maxima*), live, fresh or chilled
	0/0/0	11.2	5.6	4.2	0	0	0	0//0	0/0/		//0	0/0/0	Other scallops (including queen scallops, excluding for cultivation) live, fresh or chilled --Frozen
	0/0/0	11.2	5.6	4.2	0	0	0	0//0	0/0/		//0	0/0/0	Frozen pearl oysters(Pinctada maxima)
	0/0/0	11.2	5.6	4.2	0	0	0	0//0	0/0/		//0	0/0/0	Other frozen scallops , including queen scallops --Other
	0/0/0	11.2	5.6	4.2	0	0	0	0//0	0/0/		//0	0/0/0	Other dried, salted or in brine, smoked pearl oysters(Pinctada maxima), whether in shell or not (including smoked, whether in shell or not, whether or not cooked before or during the smoking process)
	0/0/0	11.2	5.6	4.2	0	0	0	0//0	0/0/		//0	0/0/0	Other dried, salted or in brine, smoked scallops(including queen scallops), whether in shell or not(including smoked, whether in shell or not, whether or not cooked before or during the smoking process) -Mussels (*Mytilus spp.*, *Perna spp.*): --Live, fresh or chilled:
												0/0/0	---For cultivation ---Other
	0/0/0	11.2	5.6	4.2	0	0	0	0//0	0/0/		/0/0	0/0/0	Mussels fresh or chilled
	0/0/0	11.2	5.6	4.2	0	0	0	0//0	0/0/		/0/0	0/0/0	Other mussels ,live
7	0/0/0	6.3	5.6	4.2	0	0	0	0//0	0/0/		/0/0	0/0/0	--Frozen
7	0/0/0	6.3	5.6	4.2	0	0	0	0//0	0/0/		/0/0	0/0/0	--Other
													-Cuttle fish (*Sepia officinalis*, *Rossia macrosoma*, *Sepiola spp.*) and squid (*Ommastrephes spp.*, *Loligo spp.*, *Nototodarus spp.*, *Sepioteuthis spp.*): --Live, fresh or chilled:
												0/0/0	--For cultivation ---Other
	0/0/0	5.4	4.8	3.6	0	0	0	0//0	0/0/		/0/0	0/0/0	----Cuttle fish (*Sepia of fici-nalis*, *Rossia macrosoma*, *Sepiola spp.*) and squid (*Ommastrephes spp.*, *Loli-go spp.*, *Nototodarus spp.*, *Sepioteuthis spp.*)
	0/0/0	11.2	5.6	4.2	0	0	0	0//0	0/0/		/0/0	0/0/0	----Other --Frozen:
10	0/0/0	10	8.4	3.6	0	0	0	0//0	0/0/		/0/0	0/0/0	---Cuttle fish (*Sepia of ficina-lis*, *Rossia macrosoma*, *Sepi-ola spp.*) and squid (*Om-mastrephes spp.*, *Loligo spp.*, *Nototodarus spp.*, *Se-proteuthis spp.*)
	0/0/0		7	0	0	0	0	0//0	0/0/		/0/0	0/0/0	---Other --Other
10	0/0/0	10	8.4	3.6	0	0	0	0//0	0/0/		/0/0	0/0/0	---Cuttle fish (*Sepia of fici-nalis*, *Rossia macrosoma*, *Sepiola spp.*) and squid (*Ommastrephes spp.*, *Loli-go spp.*, *Nototodarus spp.*, *Sepioteuthis spp.*)
	0/0/0		7	0	0	0	0	0//0	0/0/		/0/0	0/0/0	---Other -Octopus (*Octopus spp.*):
	0/0/0	13.6	10.2	5.1	0	0	0	0//0	0/0/			0/0/	--Live, fresh or chilled
	0/0/0	13.6	10.2	5.1	0	0	0	0//0	0/0/			0/0/0	--Frozen
	0/0/0	13.6	10.2	5.1	0	0	0	0//0	0/0/			0/0/0	--Other

税则号列		货品名称〔CIQ 扩展编码及品名－T2 表示见附表 2〕	最惠(%)	暂定税率	普通	增值/消费	出口退税	计量单位	监管条件	检验检疫	特殊证件对美关税
		-蜗牛及螺，海螺除外：									
0307.6010		---种苗									
0307.6010	10	濒危蜗牛及螺种苗，海螺除外〔101 田螺，102 蜗牛〕	0		0	9/	0	千克	ABFE	PQ	/25
0307.6010	90	其他蜗牛及螺种苗，海螺除外〔101 田螺，102 蜗牛〕	0		0	9/	9	千克	AB	PQ	/25
0307.6090		---其他									
0307.6090	10	其他濒危蜗牛及螺，海螺除外〔101 田螺，102 蜗牛，103 其他软体〕	7		70	9/	0	千克	ABFE	PRQS	/42
0307.6090	90	其他活、鲜、冷、冻、干、盐腌或盐渍的蜗牛及螺，海螺除外（包括熏制的带壳或去壳的，不论在熏制前或熏制过程中是否烹煮）[T2]	7		70	9/	9	千克	AB	PRQS	/42
		-蛤、鸟蛤及舟贝（蚶科、北极蛤科、鸟蛤科、斧蛤科、缝栖蛤科、蛤蜊科、中带蛤科、海螂科、双带蛤科、截蛏科、竹蛏科、砗磲科、帘蛤科）：									
		--活、鲜或冷的：									
0307.7110		---种苗									
0307.7110	10	砗磲的种苗〔999〕	0		0	9/	9	千克	ABEF	PQ	/25
0307.7110	90	蛤、鸟蛤及舟贝（蚶科、北极蛤科、鸟蛤科、斧蛤科、缝栖蛤科、蛤蜊科中带蛤科、海螂科、双带蛤科、截蛏科、竹蛏科、帘蛤科）的种苗〔999〕	0		0	9/	9	千克	AB	PQ	/25
		---其他：									
0307.7191		----蛤[T2]	10		70	9/	9	千克	AB	PRQS	/45
0307.7199		----其他									
0307.7199	10	活、鲜、冷砗磲〔101 活的砗磲，102 鲜、冷的养殖砗磲，103 鲜、冷的野生砗磲〕	10		70	9/	9	千克	ABEF	PRQS	/45
0307.7199	20	活、鲜、冷的粗饰蚶〔101 活的，102 鲜、冷的〕	10		70	9/	9	千克	ABU	PRQS	/45
0307.7199	90	活、鲜、冷鸟蛤及舟贝（蚶科、北极蛤科、鸟蛤科、斧蛤科、缝栖蛤科、蛤蜊科中带蛤科、海螂科、双带蛤科、截蛏科、竹蛏科、帘蛤科）[T2]	10		70	9/	9	千克	AB	PRQS	/45
0307.7200		--冻的									
0307.7200	10	冻的砗磲〔999〕	10		70	9/	9	千克	ABEF	PRQS	/45
0307.7200	20	冻的粗饰蚶〔999〕	10		70	9/	9	千克	ABU	PRQS	/45
0307.7200	90	冻的其他蛤、鸟蛤及舟贝（蚶科、北极蛤科、鸟蛤科、斧蛤科、缝栖蛤科、蛤蜊科、中带蛤科、海螂科、双带蛤科、截蛏科、竹蛏科、帘蛤科）[T2]	10		70	9/	9	千克	AB	PRQS	/45
0307.7900		--其他									
0307.7900	10	干、盐制的砗磲（包括熏制的带壳或去壳的，不论在熏制前或熏制过程中是否烹煮）〔101 干制的砗磲，102 盐制的砗磲〕	10		70	9/	9,13	千克	ABEF	PRQS	/45
0307.7900	20	干、盐制的粗饰蚶（包括熏制的带壳或去壳的，不论在熏制前或熏制过程中是否烹煮）〔101 干制的粗饰蚶，102 盐制的粗饰蚶〕	10		70	9/	9,13	千克	AB	PRQS	/45
0307.7900	90	干、盐制其他蛤、鸟蛤及舟贝（蚶科、北极蛤科、鸟蛤科、斧蛤科、缝栖蛤科、蛤蜊科、中带蛤科、海螂科、双带蛤科、截蛏科、竹蛏科、帘蛤科）（包括熏制的带壳或去壳的，不论在熏制前或熏制过程中是否烹煮）[T2]	10		70	9/	9,13	千克	AB	PRQS	/45
		-鲍鱼（鲍属）及凤螺（凤螺属）：									
		--活、鲜或冷的凤螺（鲍属）：									
0307.8110		---种苗〔999〕	0		0	9/	9	千克	AB	PQ	/25
0307.8190		---其他〔101 活的鲍鱼鲍鱼，102 鲜、冷养殖的鲍鱼，103 鲜、冷野生的鲍鱼〕	10	7	80	9/	9	千克	AB	PRQS	/42
		--活、鲜或冷的凤螺（凤螺属）：									
0307.8210		---种苗〔999〕	0		0	9/	9	千克	AB	PQ	/25
0307.8290		---其他〔101 活的，102 鲜或冷的其他养殖凤螺（凤螺属），103 鲜或冷的其他野生凤螺（凤螺属）〕	10		70	9/	9	千克	AB	PRQS	/45
0307.8300		--冻的鲍鱼（鲍属）〔101 养殖，102 野生〕	10		80	9/	9	千克	AB	PRQS	/45
0307.8400		--冻的凤螺（凤螺属）〔101 养殖，102 野生〕	10		70	9/	9	千克	AB	PRQS	/45
0307.8700		--其他鲍鱼（鲍属）〔101 干制的养殖鲍鱼（鲍属），102 干制的野生鲍鱼（鲍属），103 盐腌或盐渍的养殖鲍鱼（鲍属），104 盐腌或盐渍的野生鲍鱼（鲍属）〕	10		80	9/	9	千克	AB	PRQS	/45
0307.8800		--其他凤螺（凤螺属）〔101 干制的养殖凤螺（凤螺属），102 干制的野生凤螺（凤螺属）），103 盐腌或盐渍的养殖凤螺（凤螺属），104 盐腌或盐渍的野生凤螺（凤螺属）〕	10		70	9/	9,13	千克	AB	PRQS	/45

协定税率 %										特惠税率 %			
亚太5国	东/冰/格	巴基斯坦	韩国	瑞士	哥达	秘鲁	澳大利亚	新西/坡/智	港/澳/台	亚太2国	老/柬/缅	36/3/1	Article Description
													-Snails, other than sea snails:
													---For cultivation
												0/0/0	Endangered snails, other than sea snails, for cultivation
												0/0/0	Other snails, other than sea snails, for cultivation
													---Other
	0/0/0	11.2	5.6	4.2	0	0	0	0//0	0/0/		/0/	0/0/0	Other endangered snails, other than sea snails
	0/0/0	11.2	5.6	4.2	0	0	0	0//0	0/0/		/0/	0/0/0	Other snails, other than sea snails, live, fresh, chilled, frozen, dried, salted or in brine (including smoked , in whether in shell or not, whether or not cooked before or during the smoking process)
													-Clam、cockle and ark shell (families arcidae、arcticidae、cardiidae、donacidae、hiatellidae、mactridae、mesodesmatidae、myidae、semelidae、sclecurtidae、solenidae、tridacnidae、veneridae):
													--Live, fresh or chilled:
													---For cultivation
												0/0/0	Tridacindae for cultivation
												0/0/0	Clam, cockles and ark shells(famillies Arcidae, Arcticidae, Cardiidae, Donacidae, Hiatellidae, Mactridae, Mesodesmatidae, Myidae, Semelidae, Solecutidae, Solenidae, Tridacnidae and Veneridae), for cultivation
													---Other
	0/0/0	11.2	5.6	4.2	0	0	0	0//0	0/0/			0/0/	----Clam
													----Other
	0/0/0	11.2	5.6	4.2	0	0	0	0//0	0/0/		/0/0	0/0/0	Tridacna stone , live, fresh or chilled
	0/0/0	11.2	5.6	4.2	0	0	0	0//0	0/0/		/0/0	0/0/0	Live, fresh, cold coarse act the role of cockle
	0/0/0	11.2	5.6	4.2	0	0	0	0//0	0/0/		/0/0	0/0/0	Clam、cockle and ark shell (arcidae、arcticidae、cardiidae、donacidae、hiatellidae、mactridae、mesodesmatidae、myidae、mesodesmatidae、solecurtidae、solenidae、tridacnidae、veneridae), live, fresh or chilled
													--Frozen
	0/0/0		4	0	0		0	0//0	0/0/			0/0/0	Frozen Tridacindae
	0/0/0		4	0	0		0	0//0	0/0/			0/0/0	Frozen Anadara
	0/0/0		4	0	0		0	0//0	0/0/			0/0/0	Other frozen Clam, cockles and ark shells(famillies Arcidae, Arcticidae, Cardiidae, Donacidae, Hiatellidae, Mactridae, Mesodesmatidae, Myidae, Semelidae, Solecutidae, Solenidae, Tridacnidae and Veneridae)
													--Other
	0/0/0		6	0	0	0	0	0//0	0/0/		/0/0	0/0/0	Tridacindae, dried, salted or in brine
	0/0/0		6	0	0	0	0	0//0	0/0/		/0/0	0/0/0	Anadara, dried, salted or in brine (smoked crustaceans, whether in shell or not, whether or not cooked before or during the smoking processother crustaceans, in shell, cooked by steaming or boiling in water)
	0/0/0		6	0	0	0	0	0//0	0/0/		/0/0	0/0/0	Other Clam, cockles and ark shells(famillies Arcidae, Arcticidae, Cardiidae, Donacidae, Hiatellidae, Mactridae, Mesodesmatidae, Myidae, Semelidae, Solecutidae, Solenidae, Tridacnidae and Veneridae), dried or salted
													-Abalone(*Haliotis spp.*) and stromboid conchs(*Strombus spp*):
													--Stromboid conchs (*Haliotis spp.*), live, fresh or chillde:
												0/0/0	---For cultivation
	0/0/0	11.2	5.6	4.2	0	0	0	0//0	0/0/		/0/0	0/0/0	---Other
													--Stromboid conchs (*Haliotis spp.*), live, fresh or chillde:
												0/0/0	---For cultivation
	0/0/0	11.2	5.6	4.2	0	0	0	0//0	0/0/		/0/0	0/0/0	---Other
	0/0/0	4.5	4	0	0		0	0//0	0/0/		/0/0	0/0/0	--Abalone (*Haliotis spp.*), fro-zen
	0/0/0		7	0	0	0	0	0//0	0/0/		/0/0	0/0/0	--Stromboid conchs (*Strombus spp.*), frozen
	0/0/0	4.5	4	0	0		0	0//0	0/0/		/0/0	0/0/0	--Other abalone (*Haliotis spp.*)
	0/0/0		7	0	0	0	0	0//0	0/0/		/0/0	0/0/0	--Other stromboid conchs (*Strombus spp.*)

税则号列	货品名称〔CIQ扩展编码及品名—T2表示见附表2〕	最惠(%)	暂定税率	普通	增值/消费	出口退税	计量单位	监管条件	检验检疫	特殊证件对美关税
	-其他,包括适合供人食用的的细粉、粗粉及团粒:									
	--活、鲜或冷的:									
0307.9110	---种苗									
0307.9110 10	濒危软体动物的种苗〔101 其他海水贝,102 其他淡水贝,103 其他棘皮动物,104 其他软体及其他水生无脊椎动物〕	0		0	9/	0	千克	AFEB	PQ	/25
0307.9110 90	其他软体动物的种苗[T2]	0		0	9/	6	千克	AB	PQ	/25
0307.9190	---其他									
0307.9190 10	其他活、鲜、冷的濒危软体动物〔999〕	7		70	9/	0	千克	ABEF	PRQS	/42
0307.9190 20	活、鲜、冷蚬属〔101 活的,102 鲜、冷的蚬属〕	7		70	9/	9	千克	ABU	PRQS	/42
0307.9190 30	活、鲜、冷的象拔蚌〔101 活的,102 非生食的养殖象拔蚌,103 可用于生食的养殖象拔蚌,104 非生食的野生象拔蚌,105 可用于生食的野生象拔蚌〕	7		70	9/	9	千克	AB	PRQS	/42
0307.9190 90	其他活、鲜、冷的软体动物[T2]	7		70	9/	9	千克	AB	PRQS	/42
0307.9200	--冻的									
0307.9200 10	其他冻的濒危软体动物〔101 养殖,102 野生〕	7		70	9/	0	千克	ABEF	PRQS	/42
0307.9200 20	冻的蚬属〔101 养殖,102 野生〕	7		70	9/	9	千克	ABU	PRQS	/42
0307.9200 90	其他冻的软体动物〔101 养殖,102 野生〕	7		70	9/	9	千克	AB	PRQS	/42
0307.9900	--其他									
0307.9900 10	其他干、盐腌或盐渍的濒危软体动物(包括供人食用的软体动物粉、团粒,甲壳动物除外;包括熏制的带壳或去壳的,不论在熏制前或熏制过程中是否烹煮)〔999〕	7		70	9/	0	千克	ABEF	PRQS	/42
0307.9900 20	干、盐腌或盐渍蚬属(包括供人食用的软体动物粉、团粒,甲壳动物除外;包括熏制的带壳或去壳的,不论在熏制前或熏制过程中是否烹煮)〔101 冻的,102 干的,103 盐腌或盐渍〕	7		70	9/	9,13	千克	ABU	PRQS	/42
0307.9900 90	其他干、盐腌或盐渍软体动物(包括供人食用的软体动物粉、团粒,甲壳动物除外;包括熏制的带壳或去壳的,不论在熏制前或熏制过程中是否烹煮)〔101 干制的养殖软体动物,102 干制的野生软体动物,103 盐腌或盐渍的养殖软体动物,104 盐腌或盐渍的野生软体动物〕	7		70	9/	9,13	千克	AB	PRQS	/42
03.08	**不属于甲壳动物及软体动物的水生无脊柱动物,活、鲜、冷、冻、干、盐腌或盐渍的;熏制的不属于甲壳动物及软体动物的水生无脊柱动物,不论在熏制前或熏制过程中是否烹煮;适合供人食用的不属于甲壳动物及软体动物的水生无脊柱动物的细粉、粗粉及团粒:**									
	-海参(仿刺参、海参纲):									
	--活、鲜或冷的:									
0308.1110	---种苗									
0308.1110 10	暗色刺参的种苗〔999〕	0		0	9/	9	千克	ABEF	PQ	/25
0308.1110 90	其他海参(仿刺参、海参纲)的种苗〔999〕	0		0	9/	9	千克	AB	PQ	/25
0308.1190	---其他									
0308.1190 10	活、鲜或冷的暗色刺参〔101 活的暗色刺参,102 鲜或冷的养殖暗色刺参,103 鲜或冷的野生暗色刺参〕	10		70	9/	9	千克	ABEF	PRQS	/45
0308.1190 20	活、鲜或冷的刺参(暗色刺参除外)〔101 活的其他海参,102 鲜或冷的养殖其他海参,103 鲜或冷的野生其他海参〕	10		70	9/	9	千克	ABU	PRQS	/45
0308.1190 90	活、鲜或冷的其他海参(仿刺参、海参纲)〔101 活的其他海参,102 鲜或冷的养殖其他海参,103 鲜或冷的野生其他海参〕	10		70	9/	9	千克	AB	PRQS	/45
0308.1200	--冻的									
0308.1200 10	冻的暗色刺参〔101 养殖冷冻海参,102 野生冷冻海参〕	10		80	9/	9	千克	ABEF	PRQS	/45
0308.1200 20	冻的其他刺参〔101 养殖冷冻海参,102 野生冷冻海参〕	10		80	9/	9	千克	ABU	PRQS	/45
0308.1200 90	冻的其他海参(仿刺参、海参纲)〔101 养殖冷冻海参,102 野生冷冻海参〕	10		80	9/	9	千克	AB	PRQS	/45
0308.1900	--其他									
0308.1900 10	干、盐腌或盐渍暗色刺参(包括熏制的,不论在熏制前或熏制过程中是否烹煮;适合供人食用的细粉、粗粉及团粒)〔101 干制的养殖暗色刺参,102 干制的野生暗色刺参,103 盐腌或盐渍的养殖暗色刺参,104 盐腌或盐渍的野生暗色刺参〕	10		80	9/	9	千克	ABEF	PRQS	/45

协定税率 %										特惠税率 %			
亚太5国	东/冰/格	巴基斯坦	韩国	瑞士	哥达	秘鲁	澳大利亚	新西/坡/智	港/澳/台	亚太2国	老/柬/缅	36/3/1	Article Description
													-Other, including flours, meals and pellets, fit for human consumption:
													--Live, fresh or chilled:
													---For cultivation
												0/0/0	Endangered molluscs, for cultivation
												0/0/0	Other molluscs, for cultivation
													---Other
	0/0/0	11.2	5.6	4.2	0	0	0	0//0	0/0/		/0/0	0/0/0	Other endangered molluscs, live, fresh, chilled
	0/0/0	11.2	5.6	4.2	0	0	0	0//0	0/0/		/0/0	0/0/0	Live, fresh, cold clam
	0/0/0	11.2	5.6	4.2	0	0	0	0//0	0/0/		/0/0	0/0/0	Live, fresh, cold geoduck
	0/0/0	11.2	5.6	4.2	0	0	0	0//0	0/0/		/0/0	0/0/0	Other molluscs, live, fresh, chilled
													--Frozen
	0/0/0		7	0	0	0	0	0//0	0/0/		/0/0	0/0/0	Other frozen endangered Molluscs
	0/0/0		7	0	0	0	0	0//0	0/0/		/0/0	0/0/0	Frozen clam
	0/0/0		7	0	0	0	0	0//0	0/0/		/0/0	0/0/0	Other frozen Molluscs
													--Other
	0/0/0		7	0	0	0	0	0//0	0/0/		/0/0	0/0/0	Other endangered molluscs, dried, salted or in brine (including flours, meals and pellets of molluscs, fit for human consumption; including smoked, whether in shell or not, whether or not cooked before or during the smoking process)
	0/0/0		7	0	0	0	0	0//0	0/0/		/0/0	0/0/0	dried, salted or in brine clam(including flours, meals and pellets of molluscs, fit for human consumption; including smoked, whether in shell or not, whether or not cooked before or during the smoking process)
	0/0/0		7	0	0	0	0	0//0	0/0/		/0/0	0/0/0	dried, salted or in brine Other molluscs(including flours, meals and pellets of molluscs, fit for human consumption; including smoked, whether in shell or not, whether or not cooked before or during the smoking process)
													Aquatic invertebrates other than crustaceans and molluscs, live, fresh, chilled, frozen, dried, salted or in brine; smoked aquatic invertebrates other than crustaceans and molluscs, whether or not cooked before or during the smoking process; flours, meals and pellets of aquatic invertebrates other than crustaceans and molluscs, fit for human consumption:
													-Sea cucumbers(Stichopus japonicus、holothurioidea):
													--Live, fresh and chilled:
													---For cultivation
												0/0/0	Isostichopus fuscus, for cultivation
												0/0/0	Other sea cucumbers (Stichopus japonicus, Holothurioidea), for cultivation
													---Other
	0/0/0	11.2	5.6	4.2	0	0	0	0//0	0/0/		/0/0	0/0/0	Isostichopus fuscus, live, fresh or chilled
	0/0/0	11.2	5.6	4.2	0	0	0	0//0	0/0/		/0/0	0/0/0	Live, fresh trepang or cold(exceptisostichopus fuscus)
	0/0/0	11.2	5.6	4.2	0	0	0	0//0	0/0/		/0/0	0/0/0	Other sea cucumbers (Stichopus japonicus, holothurioidea), live, fresh or chilled
													--Frozen
	0/0/0		4	0	0	0	0	0//0	0/0/		/0/0	0/0/0	Frozen Isostichopus fuscus
	0/0/0		4	0	0	0	0	0//0	0/0/		/0/0	0/0/0	Other frozen sea cucumbers
	0/0/0		4	0	0	0	0	0//0	0/0/		/0/0	0/0/0	Other frozensea cucumbers (Stichopus japonicus, Holothurioidea)
													--Other
	0/0/0		4	0	0	0	0	0//0	0/0/		/0/0	0/0/0	Isostichopus fuscus, frozen, dried, salted or in brine, smoked(including flours, meals and pellets, fit for human consumption; including smoked, whether or not cooked before or during the smoking process)

税则号列		货品名称〔CIQ 扩展编码及品名—T2 表示见附表 2〕	最惠(%)	暂定税率	普通	增值/消费	出口退税	计量单位	监管条件	检验检疫	特殊证件对美关税
0308.1900	20	干、盐腌或盐渍的其他刺参(包括熏制的,不论在熏制前或熏制过程中是否烹煮;适合供人食用的细粉、粗粉及团粒)〔101 干制的其他养殖刺参,102 干制的其他野生刺参,103 盐腌或盐渍的其他养殖刺参,104 盐腌或盐渍的其他野生刺参〕	10		80	9/	9	千克	ABU	PRQS	/45
0308.1900	90	干、盐腌或盐渍的其他海参(仿刺参、海参纲)(包括熏制的,不论在熏制前或熏制过程中是否烹煮;适合供人食用的细粉、粗粉及团粒)〔101 干制的其他养殖海参(仿刺参、海参纲),102 干制的其他野生海参(仿刺参、海参纲),103 盐腌或盐渍的其他养殖海参(仿刺参、海参纲),104 盐腌或盐渍的其他野生海参(仿刺参、海参纲)〕	10		80	9/	9	千克	AB	PRQS	/45
		-海胆(球海胆属、拟球海胆、智利海胆、食用正海胆):									
		--活、鲜或冷的:									
0308.2110		---种苗〔999〕	0		0	9/	9	千克	AB	PQ	/25
0308.2190		---其他									
0308.2190	10	活、鲜或冷的食用海胆纲〔101 活的海胆纲,102 鲜或冷的养殖海胆纲,103 鲜或冷的野生海胆纲〕	10		70	9/	9	千克	ABU	PRQS	/45
0308.2190	90	其他活、鲜或冷的海胆〔101 活的海胆,102 鲜或冷的养殖海胆,103 鲜或冷的野生海胆〕	10		70	9/	9	千克	AB	PRQS	/45
0308.2200		--冻的									
0308.2200	10	冻食用海胆纲〔101 养殖冷冻海胆,102 野生冷冻海胆〕	10		70	9/	9	千克	ABU	PRQS	/45
0308.2200	90	其他冻海胆〔101 养殖冷冻海胆,102 野生冷冻海胆〕	10		70	9/	9	千克	AB	PRQS	/45
0308.2900		--其他									
0308.2900	10	干、盐制食用海胆纲(包括熏制的,不论在熏制前或熏制过程中是否烹煮;适合供人食用的细粉、粗粉及团粒)〔101 干制的养殖海胆纲,102 干制的野生海胆纲,103 盐制的养殖海胆纲,104 盐制的野生海胆纲〕	10		70	9/	9,13	千克	ABU	PRQS	/45
0308.2900	90	其他干、盐制海胆(包括熏制的,不论在熏制前或熏制过程中是否烹煮;适合供人食用的细粉、粗粉及团粒)〔101 干制的养殖海胆,102 干制的野生海胆,103 盐制的养殖海胆,104 盐制的野生海胆〕	10		70	9/	9,13	千克	AB	PRQS	/45
		-海蜇(海蜇属):									
		---活、鲜或冷的:									
0308.3011		----种苗〔999〕	0		0	9/	9	千克	AB	PQ	/25
0308.3019		----其他〔101 活的海蜇,102 鲜或冷的养殖海蜇,103 鲜或冷的野生海蜇〕	7		70	9/	9	千克	AB	PRQS	/42
0308.3090		---其他〔101 冻的养殖海蜇(海蜇属),102 冻的野生海蜇(海蜇属),103 干制的养殖海蜇(海蜇属),104 干制的野生海蜇(海蜇属)),105 盐制的养殖海蜇(海蜇属),106 盐制的野生海蜇(海蜇属)〕	10		70	9/	9,13	千克	AB	PRQS	/45
		-其他:									
		---活、鲜或冷的:									
0308.9011		----种苗									
0308.9011	10	活、鲜或冷的其他濒危水生无脊椎动物的种苗(甲壳动物及软体动物除外)〔999〕	0		0	9/	0	千克	ABFE	PQ	/25
0308.9011	90	其他水生无脊椎动物的种苗(甲壳动物及软体动物除外)〔999〕	0		0	9/	9	千克	AB	PQ	/25
0308.9012		----沙蚕,种苗除外〔999〕	7		70	9/	6	千克	AB	PRQS	/42
0308.9019		----其他									
0308.9019	10	活、鲜或冷的其他濒危水生无脊椎动物(甲壳动物及软体动物除外)〔999〕	7		70	9/	0	千克	ABFE	PRQS	/42
0308.9019	90	活、鲜或冷的其他水生无脊椎动物(甲壳动物及软体动物除外)[T2]	7		70	9/	9	千克	AB	PRQS	/42
0308.9090		---其他									
0308.9090	10	其他冻、干、盐制濒危水生无脊椎动物,包括供人食用的水生无脊椎动物粉、团粒(包括熏制的,不论在熏制前或熏制过程中是否烹煮)[T2]	7		70	9/	0	千克	ABFE	PRQS	/42
0308.9090	90	其他冻、干、盐制水生无脊椎动物,包括供人食用的水生无脊椎动物粉、团粒(包括熏制的,不论在熏制前或熏制过程中是否烹煮)[T2]	7		70	9/	9,13	千克	AB	PRQS	/42

协定税率 %										特惠税率 %			
亚太5国	东/冰/格	巴基斯坦	韩国	瑞士	哥达	秘鲁	澳大利亚	新西/坡/智	巷/澳/台	亚太2国	老/柬/缅	36/3/1	Article Description
	0/0/0		4	0	0	0	0	0//0	0/0/		/0/0	0/0/0	Frozen, dried, salted or pickled trepang(including flours, meals and pellets, fit for human consumption; including smoked, whether or not cooked before or during the smoking process)
	0/0/0		4	0	0	0	0	0//0	0/0/		/0/0	0/0/0	Other sea cucumbers (Stichopus japonicus, Holothurioidea), frozen, dried, salted or in brine, smoked(including flours, meals and pellets, fit for human consumption; including smoked, whether or not cooked before or during the smoking process)
													-Sea urchin(strongylocentrotus spp. ,paracentrotus lividus, Loxechinus albus, Echichinus esculentus):
													--Live, fresh or chilled:
												0/0/0	---For cultivation
													---Other
	0/0/0	11.2	5.6	4.2	0	0	0	0//0	0/0/		/0/0	0/0/0	Live, fresh and cold edible echinoidea
	0/0/0	11.2	5.6	4.2	0	0	0	0//0	0/0/		/0/0	0/0/0	OtherSea urchins, live, fresh, chilled, not for cultivation.
													--Frozen
	0/0/0		6	0	0	0	0	0//0	0/0/		/0/0	0/0/0	Frozen edible echinoidea
	0/0/0		6	0	0	0	0	0//0	0/0/		/0/0	0/0/0	Other frozen Sea urchins
													--Other
	0/0/0		6	0	0	0	0	0//0	0/0/		/0/0	0/0/0	Frozen, dried, edible salt echinoidea (including flours, meals and pellets, fit for human consumption; including smoked, whether or not cooked before or during the smoking process)
	0/0/0		6	0	0	0	0	0//0	0/0/		/0/0	0/0/0	Other frozen, dry, salt sea urchin (ball sea urchins, sea urchins, sea urchins, Chile is sea urchins) (including flours, meals and pellets. fit for human consumption; including smoked, whether or not cooked before or during the smoking process)
													-Jellyfish(Rhopilema spp.):
													---Live, fresh or chilled:
												0/0/0	----For cultivation
	0/0/0	9	5.6	4.2	0	0	0	0//0	0/0/		/0/0	0/0/0	----Other
	0/0/0		6	0	0	0	0	0//0	0/0/		/0/0	0/0/0	---Other
													-Other:
													---Live, fresh or chilled:
													----For cultivation
												0/0/0	Other endangered aquatic invertebrates, other than crustaceans and molluscs, for cultivation
												0/0/0	Other aquatic invertebrates other than crustaceans and molluscs, for cultivation
	0/0/0	9	5.6	4.2	0	0	0	0//0	0/0/		/0/0	0/0/0	----Clamworm, other than for cultivation
													----Other
	0/0/0	11.2	5.6	4.2	0	0	0	0//0	0/0/		/0/0	0/0/0	Other endangered aquatic invertebrates, live, fresh or chilled (other than crustaceans and molluscs)
	0/0/0	11.2	5.6	4.2	0	0	0	0//0	0/0/		/0/0	0/0/0	Other aquatic invertebrates, live, fresh or chilled(other than crustaceans and molluscs)
													---Other
	0/0/0		6	0	0	0	0	0//0	0/0/		/0/0	0/0/0	Other endangered aquatic invertebrates, frozen, dried, salted, including flours, meals and pellets of aquatic invertebrates, fit for human consumption (other than crustaceans and molluscs, including smoked, whether in shell or not, whether or not cooked ebfore or during the smoking proccess; flours, meals and pellets fit for human consumption)
	0/0/0		6	0	0	0	0	0//0	0/0/		/0/0	0/0/0	Other aquatic invertebrates, frozen, dried, salted, including flours, meals and pellets of aquatic invertebrates, fit for human consumption (other than crustaceans and molluscs, including smoked, whether in shell or not, whether or not cooked ebfore or during the smoking proccess; flours, meals and pellets fit for human consumption)

第四章
乳品;蛋品;天然蜂蜜;其他食用动物产品

注释:

一、所称"乳",是指全脂乳及半脱脂或全脱脂的乳。

二、税目04.05所称:

(一)"黄油",仅指从乳中提取的天然黄油、乳清黄油及调制黄油(新鲜的、加盐或酸败的,包括罐装黄油),按重量计乳脂含量在80%及以上,但不超过95%,乳的无脂固形物最大含量不超过2%,以及水的最大含量不超过16%。黄油中不含添加的乳化剂,但可含有氯化钠、食用色素、中和盐及无害乳酸菌的培养物。

(二)"乳酱"是一种油包水型可涂抹的乳状物,乳脂是该制品所含的唯一脂肪,按重量计其含量在39%及以上,但小于80%。

三、乳清经浓缩并加入乳或乳脂制成的产品,若同时具有下列三种特性,则视为乳酪归入税目04.06:

(一)按干重计乳脂含量在5%及以上的;

(二)按重量计干质成分至少为70%,但不超过85%的;

(三)已成形或可以成形的。

四、本章不包括:

(一)按重量计乳糖含量(以干燥无水乳糖计)超过95%的乳清制品(税目17.02);

(二)以一种物质(例如,油酸酯)代替乳中一种或多种天然成分(例如,丁酸酯)而制得的产品(税目19.01或21.06);

(三)白蛋白(包括按重量计干质成分的乳清蛋白含量超过80%的两种或两种以上的乳清蛋白浓缩物)(税目35.02)及球蛋白(税目35.04)。

子目注释:

一、子目号0404.10所称"改性乳清",是指由乳清成分构成的制品,即全部或部分去除乳糖、蛋白或矿物质的乳清、加入天然乳清成分的乳清及由混入天然乳清成分制成的产品。

二、子目0405.10所称"黄油",不包括脱水黄油及印度酥油(子目号0405.90)。

税则号列	货品名称〔CIQ扩展编码及品名－T2表示见附表2〕	最惠(%)	暂定税率	普通	增值/消费	出口退税	计量单位	监管条件	检验检疫	特殊证件对美关税
04.01	**未浓缩及未加糖或其他甜物质的乳及奶油:**									
0401.1000	-按重量计脂肪含量不超过1%〔101巴氏杀菌乳,102超高温灭菌乳,103保持灭菌乳,104巴氏杀菌工艺调制乳,105其他乳与乳制品,106灭菌工艺调制乳,107其他调制乳〕	15		40	9/	13,6	千克	7AB	PRQS	/45
0401.2000	-按重量计脂肪含量超过1%,但不超过6%[T2]	15		40	9/	13,6	千克	7AB	PRQS	/45
0401.4000	-按重量计脂肪含量超过6%,但不超过10%[T2]	15		40	13/	6,13	千克	7AB	PRQS	/45
0401.5000	-按重量计脂肪含量超过10%[T2]	15		40	13/	6,13	千克	7AB	PRQS	/45
04.02	**浓缩、加糖或其他甜物质的乳及奶油:**									
0402.1000	-粉状、粒状或其他固体形状,按重量计脂肪含量不超过1.5%〔101脱脂乳粉,102儿童调制乳粉,103其他乳与乳制品,104孕产妇调制乳粉,105其他调制乳粉〕	10		40	13/	13	千克	7AB	MPRQS	/35
	-粉状、粒状或其他固体形状,按重量计脂肪含量超过1.5%:									
0402.2100	--未加糖或其他甜物质[T2]	10		40	13/	13	千克	7AB	MPRQS	/35
0402.2900	--其他〔101儿童调制乳粉,102其他乳与乳制品,103孕产妇调制乳粉,104其他调制乳粉〕	10		40	13/	13	千克	7AB	PRQS	/35
	-其他:									
0402.9100	--未加糖或其他甜物质[T2]	10		90	13/	6,13	千克	AB	PRQS	/35
0402.9900	--其他[T2]	10		90	13/	6,13	千克	AB	PRQS	/35
04.03	**酪乳、结块的乳及奶油、酸乳、酸乳酒及其他发酵或酸化的乳和奶油,不论是否浓缩、加糖、加其他甜物质、加香料、加水果、加坚果或加可可:**									
0403.1000	-酸乳〔101发酵乳,102其他乳与乳制品,103风味发酵乳〕	10		90	13/	13	千克	AB	PRQS	/40
0403.9000	-其他〔101风味发酵乳,102奶油,103无水奶油,104其他乳与乳制品〕	20		90	13/	13	千克	AB	PRQ	/50
04.04	**乳清,不论是否浓缩、加糖或其他甜物质;其他税目未列名的含天然乳的产品,不论是否加糖或其他甜物质:**									
0404.1000	-乳清及改性乳清,不论是否浓缩、加糖或其他甜物质[T2]	6	2	30	13/	13	千克	AB	PRQ	/27
0404.1000 10	饲料用乳清(按重量计蛋白含量2－7%,乳糖含量76－88%)(不论是否浓缩、加糖或其他甜物质)〔101饲料用乳粉,102饲料用乳清粉〕	6	2	30	13/	13	千克	AB	PRW	/

Chapter 4

Dairy produce; birds eggs; natural honey; edible products of animal origin, not elsewhere specified or included

Notes:

1. The expression "milk" means full cream milk or partially or completely skimmed milk.
2. For the purposes of heading No. 04.05:
   (a) The term "butter" means natural butter, whey butter or recombined butter (fresh, salted or rancid, including canned butter) derived exclusively from milk, with a milkfat content of 80% or more but not more than 95% by weight, a maximum milk solids-not-fvat content of 2% by weight and a maximum water content of 16% by weight. Butter does not contain added emulsifiers, but may contain sodium chloride, food colours, neutralising salts and cultures of harmless lactic-acid-producing bacteria.
   (b) The expression "dairy spreads" means a spreadable emulsion of the water-in-oil type, containing milkfat as the only fat in the product, with a milkfat content of 39% or more but less than 80% by weight.
3. Products obtained by the concentration of whey and with the addition of milk or milkfat are to be classified as cheese in heading No. 04.06. Provided that they have the three following characteristics:
   (a) A milkfat content, by weight of the dry matter, of 5% or more;
   (b) A dry matter content, by weight, of at least 70% but not exceeding 85%; and
   (c) They are moulded or capable of being moulded.
4. This Chapter does not cover:
   (a) Products obtained from whey, containing by weight more than 95% lactose, expressed as anhydrous lactose calculated on the dry matter (heading No. 17.02);
   (b) A product made of a substance (e.g., oleic acid ester) instead of one or more natural ingredients (e.g., butyrate) in milk.
   (c) Albumins (including concentrates of two or more whey proteins, containing by weight more than 80% whey proteins, calculated on the dry matter) (heading No. 35.02) or globulins (heading No. 35.04)

Subheading Notes:

1. For the purpose of subheading No. 0404.10, the expression "modified whey" means products consisting of whey constituents, that is, whey from which all or part of the lactose, proteins or minerals have been removed, whey to which natural whey constituents have been added and products obtained by mixing natural whey constituents.
2. For the purposes of subheading No. 0405.10 the term "butter" does not include dehydrated butter or ghee (subheading No. 0405.90).

协定税率 %										特惠税率 %			Article Description
亚太5国	东/冰/格	巴基斯坦	韩国	瑞士	哥达	秘鲁	澳大利亚	新西/坡/智	港/澳/台	亚太2国	老/柬/缅	36/3/1	
													Milk and cream, not concentrated nor containing added sugar or other sweetening matter:
	0/0/6	12		4.5	5	0	6	0//0	0/0/			0/0/0	-Of a fat content, by weight, not exceeding 1%
	0/0/6	0		4.5	5	0	6	0//0	0/0/			0/0/0	-Of a fat content, by weight, exceeding 1% but not exceeding 6%
	0/0/6	12		4.5	5	0	6	0//0	0/0/			0/0/0	-Of a fat content, by weight, exceeding 6%, but not exceeding 10%
	0/0/6	12		4.5	5	0	6	0//0	0/0/			0/0/0	-Of a fat content, by weight, exceeding 10%
													Milk and cream, concentrated or containing added sugar or other sweetening matter:
7	0/0/4	5		0	3.3	3.5	5	0//0	0/0/			0/0/0	-In powder, granules or other solid forms, of a fat content, by weight, not exceeding 1.5%
													-In powder, granules or other solid forms, of a fat content, by weight, exceeding 1.5%:
7	0/0/4	0			3.3	3.5	5	0//0	0/0/			0/0/0	--Not containing added sugar or other sweetening matter
	0/0/4	5		0	3.3	3.5	5	0//0	0/0/			0/0/0	--Other
													-Other:
	0/0/4	5			3.3	0	5	0//0	0/0/			0/0/0	--Not containing added sugar or other sweetening matter
	0/0/4	5			3.3	3.5	5	0//0	0/0/			0/0/0	--Other
													Buttermilk, curdled milk and cream, yogurt, kephir and other fermented or acidified milk and cream, whether or not concentrated or containing added sugar or other sweetening matter or flavoured or containing added fruit, nuts or cocoa:
	0/0/4	5		4.2	3.3	0	4	0//0	0/0/			0/0/0	-Yogurt
	0/0/8				6.7	0	8	0//0	0/0/			0/0/	-Other
													Whey, whether or not concentrated or containing added sugar or other sweetening matter; products consisting of natural milk constituents, whether or not containing added sugar or other sweetening matter, not elsewhere specified or included:
	0/0/3.6	5	4		2.4	0	0	0//0	0/0/			0/0/	-Whey and modified whey, whether or not concentrated or containing added sugar or other sweetening matter
	0/0/2.4	5	3.6		2	0	0	0//0	0/0/		//	0/0/	Whey for feed (2－7% protein by weight, 76－88% lactose) (whether or not concentrated, sweetened or otherwise)

税则号列	货品名称〔CIQ 扩展编码及品名－T2 表示见附表 2〕	最惠(%)	暂定税率	普通	增值/消费	出口退税	计量单位	监管条件	检验检疫	特殊证件对美关税
0404.1000 90	其他乳清及改性乳清(不论是否浓缩、加糖或其他甜物质)〔101 脱盐乳清粉,102 非脱盐乳清粉,103 乳清蛋白粉,104 其他乳清粉,105 其他乳与乳制品,106 饲料用乳粉,107 饲料用乳清粉〕	6	2	30	13/	13	千克	AB	PRW	/27
0404.9000	-其他〔999〕	20		90	13/	13	千克	AB	PRQ	/45
04.05	**黄油及其他从乳中提取的脂和油;乳酱:**									
0405.1000	-黄油〔101 奶油,102 无水奶油,103 其他奶油〕	10		90	13/	13	千克	AB	PRQS	/35
0405.2000	-乳酱〔101 调制淡炼乳,102 其他乳与乳制品〕	10		90	13/	13	千克	AB	PRQS	/35
0405.9000	-其他〔101 其他奶油,102 其他乳与乳制品〕	10		90	13/	13	千克	AB	PRQS	/35
04.06	**乳酪及凝乳:**									
0406.1000	-鲜乳酪(未熟化或未固化的),包括乳清乳酪;凝乳〔101 非熟化干酪,102 其他干酪〕	12		90	13/	13	千克	AB	PRQ	/42
0406.2000	-各种磨碎或粉化的乳酪〔101 霉菌成熟干酪,102 其他熟化干酪,103 非熟化干酪,104 其他干酪〕	12	8	90	13/	13	千克	AB	PRQS	/38
0406.3000	-经加工的乳酪,但磨碎或粉化的除外〔101 再制干酪,102 其他干酪〕	12	8	90	13/	13	千克	AB	PRQ	/38
0406.4000	-蓝纹乳酪和娄地青霉生产的带有纹理的其他乳酪〔101 霉菌成熟干酪,102 其他干酪〕	15	8	90	13/	13	千克	AB	PRQ	/38
0406.9000	-其他乳酪〔999〕	12	8	90	13/	13	千克	AB	PRQ	/38
04.07	**带壳禽蛋,鲜、腌制或煮过的:**									
	-孵化用受精禽蛋:									
0407.1100	--鸡的									
0407.1100 10	孵化用受精的濒危鸡的蛋〔999〕	0		0	9/	0	千克/个	AFEB	PQ	/
0407.1100 90	孵化用受精的其他鸡的蛋〔999〕	0		0	9/	6	千克/个	AB	PQ	/
0407.1900	--其他									
0407.1900 10	其他孵化用受精濒危禽蛋〔101 鸭种蛋,102 鹅种蛋,103 鸵鸟种蛋,104 火鸡种蛋,105 鸽种蛋,106 其他种蛋〕	0		0	9/	0	千克/个	AFEB	PQ	/
0407.1900 90	其他孵化用受精禽蛋〔101 鸭种蛋,102 鹅种蛋,103 鸵鸟种蛋,104 火鸡种蛋,105 鸽种蛋,106 其他种蛋〕	0		0	9/	9	千克/个	AB	PQ	/
	-其他鲜蛋:									
0407.2100	--鸡的〔999〕	20		80	9/	9	千克/个	AB	PRQS	/
0407.2900	--其他									
0407.2900 10	其他鲜的带壳濒危禽蛋〔999〕	20		80	9/	0	千克/个	ABFE	PRQS	/
0407.2900 90	其他鲜的带壳禽蛋[T2]	20		80	9/	9	千克/个	AB	PRQS	/
	-其他:									
0407.9010	---咸蛋〔999〕	20		90	9/	6	千克/个	AB	PRQS	/
0407.9020	---皮蛋〔999〕	20		90	9/	6	千克/个	AB	PRQS	/
0407.9090	---其他									
0407.9090 10	其他腌制或煮过的带壳濒危野鸟蛋〔999〕	20		90	9/	0	千克/个	ABFE	PRQS	/
0407.9090 90	其他腌制或煮过的带壳禽蛋〔999〕	20		90	9/	9,13	千克/个	AB	PRQS	/
04.08	**去壳禽蛋及蛋黄,鲜、干、冻、蒸过或水煮、制成型或用其他方法保藏的,不论是否加糖或其他甜物质:**									
	-蛋黄:									
0408.1100	--干的〔999〕	20		90	9/	9,13	千克	AB	PRQS	/
0408.1900	--其他〔101 咸蛋黄,102 食用蛋黄粉〕	20		90	9/	9	千克	AB	PRQS	/35
	-其他:									
0408.9100	--干的〔101 食用全蛋粉,102 片,103 干的其他食用蛋制品〕	20		90	9/	6,13	千克	AB	PRQS	/
0408.9900	--其他[T2]	20		90	9/	9,13	千克	AB	PRQS	/
04.09	**天然蜂蜜:**									
0409.0000	天然蜂蜜〔101 药用蜂蜜,102 食用蜂蜜〕	15		80	9/	9	千克	AB	PRQS	/50
04.10	**其他税目未列名的食用动物产品:**									
0410.0010	---燕窝〔101 毛燕,102 食用燕窝,103 燕窝制品,104 具有保健食品批准文号〕	25		80	13/	9	千克	AB	PRQS	/
	---蜂产品:									
0410.0041	----鲜蜂王浆〔999〕	15		70	9/	9	千克	AB	PRQS	/
0410.0042	----鲜蜂王浆粉〔999〕	15		70	13/	9	千克	AB	PRQS	/
0410.0043	----蜂花粉〔999〕	20		70	13/	9	千克	AB	PRQS	/
0410.0049	----其他〔101 药用蜂房,102 药用蜂胶,103 蜂胶,104 其他蜂产品,105 蜂胶乙醇提取物〕	20		70	13/	9	千克	AB	PRQS	/55
0410.0090	---其他									
0410.0090 10	其他编号未列名濒危野生动物产品(食用)〔101 批准为新食品原料,102 其他未列出的动物源性食品〕	20		70	13/	0	千克	ABFE	PRQS	/55
0410.0090 90	其他编号未列名的食用动物产品[T2]	20		70	13/	9	千克	AB	PRQS	/55

协定税率 %										特惠税率 %			Article Description
亚太5国	东/冰/格	巴基斯坦	韩国	瑞士	哥达	秘鲁	澳大利亚	新西/坡/智	港/澳/台	亚太2国	老/柬/缅	36/3/1	
	0/0/2.4	5	3.6		2	0	0	0//0	0/0/		//	0/0/	Other whey and modified whey (whether concentrated, sweetened or otherwise)
	0/0/8		12		6.7	0	8	0//0	0/0/			0/0/	-Other
													Butter and other fats and oils derived from milk; dairy spreads:
	0/0/4	5	6	0	3.3	0	4	0//0	0/0/			0/0/0	-Butter
8.1	0/0/4	5	6	0	3.3	0	0	0//0	0/0/			0/0/0	-Dairy spreads
	0/0/4	5	6		3.3	0	4	0//0	0/0/			0/0/0	-Other
													Cheese and curd:
	0/0/4.8	6	7.2	6.2	4	0	4.8	0//0	0/0/			0/0/0	-Fresh (unripened or uncured) cheese, including whey cheese, and curd
	0/0/4.8	6	7.2	6.2	4	3.2	4.8	0//0	0/0/			0//	-Grated or powdered cheese, of all kinds
	0/0/4.8	6	7.2	6.2	4	3.2	4.8	0//0	0/0/			0/0/	-Processed cheese, not grated or powdered
	0/0/6	12	9		5	0	0	0//0	0/0/			0/0/	-Blue-veined cheese and other cheese containing veins produced by *Penicillium roqueforti*
	0/0/4.8	6	7.2	6.2	4	0	4.8	0//0	0/0/			0/0/0	-Other cheese
													Birds' eggs, in shell, fresh, preserved or cooked:
													-Fertilised eggs for incubation:
													--Of fowls of the species Gallus domesticus
												0/0/0	Of endangered hen's fertilised eggs for incubation
												0/0/0	Of hen's fertilised eggs for incubation
													--Other
												0/0/0	Other fertilised endangered eggs for incubation
												0/0/0	Other fertilised eggs for incubation
													-Other eggs, fresh:
	0/0/0		12	6	0	0	0	0//0	0/0/		/0/0	0/0/0	--Of fowls of the species Gallus domesticus
													--Other
	0/0/0		12	6	0	0	0	0//0	0/0/		/0/0	0/0/0	Other endangered birds' eggs, in shell, fresh
	0/0/0		12	6	0	0	0	0//0	0/0/		/0/0	0/0/0	Other birds' eggs, in shell, fresh
													-Other:
	0/0/0		12	6	0	0	0	0//0	0/0/		//0	0/0/0	---Salted eggs
	0/0/0		12	6	0	0	0	0//0	0/0/			0/0/	---Lime-preserved eggs
													---Other
	0/0/0		12	6	0	0	0	0//0	0/0/			0/0/	Other endangered wild birds' eggs, in shell, preserved or cooked
	0/0/0		12	6	0	0	0	0//0	0/0/			0/0/	Other birds' eggs, in shell, preserved or cooked
													Birds' eggs, not in shell, and egg yolks, fresh, dried, cooked by steaming or by boiling in water, moulded, frozen or otherwise preserved, whether or not containing added sugar or other sweetening matter:
													-Egg yolks:
	0/0/0		12	6	0	0	0	0//0	0/0/			0/0/	--Dried
	0/0/0		12	6	0	0	0	0//0	0/0/			0/0/	--Other
													-Other:
	0/0/0		12	6	0	0	0	0//0	0/0/			0/0/	--Dried
	0/0/0		12	6	0	0	0	0//0	0/0/			0/0/	--Other
													Natural honey:
	0/0/0	0	9	4.5	0	0	0	0//0	0/0/		0/0/	0/0/0	Natural honey
													Edible products of animal origin, not elsewhere specified or included:
	0/0/0		10	7.5	0	0	0	0//0	0/0/		/0/0	0/0/0	---Salanganes' nests
													---Bee products:
	0/0/0	12	6	4.5	0	0	0	0//0	0/0/			0/0/	----Pure royal jelley
	0/0/0	12	6	4.5	0	0	0	0//0	0/0/			0/0/	----Pure royal jelley, in powder
	0/0/0		12	6	0	0	0	0//0	0/0/			0/0/	----Bee pollen
	0/0/0		12	6	0	0	0	0//0	0/0/			0/0/	----Other
													---Other
	0/0/0		12	6	0	0	0	0//0	0/0/0		//0	0/0/0	Other edible products of endangered wild animals origin, not elsewhere specified or included
	0/0/0		12	6	0	0	0	0//0	0/0/0		//0	0/0/0	Other edible products of animals origin, not elsewhere specified or included

第五章
其他动物产品

注释：

一、本章不包括：

(一)食用产品(整个或切块的动物肠、膀胱和胃以及液态或干制的动物血除外)；

(二)生皮或毛皮(第四十一章、第四十三章)，但税目 05.05 的货品及税目 05.11 的生皮或毛皮的边角废料仍归入本章；

(三)马毛及废马毛以外的动物纺织原料(第十一类)；

(四)供制帚、制刷用的成束、成簇的材料(税目 96.03)。

二、仅按长度而未按发根和发梢整理的人发，视为未加工品，归入税目 05.01。

三、本协调制度所称“兽牙”，是指象、河马、海象、一角鲸和野猪的长牙、犀角及其他动物的牙齿。

四、本协调制度所称“马毛”，是指马科、牛科动物的鬃毛和尾毛。税目 05.11 主要包括马毛及废马毛，不论是否制成带衬垫或不带衬垫的毛片。

税则号列	货品名称〔CIQ 扩展编码及品名—T2 表示见附表 2〕	最惠(%)	暂定税率	普通	增值/消费	出口退税	计量单位	监管条件	检验检疫	特殊证件对美关税
05.01	**未经加工的人发，不论是否洗涤；废人发：**									
0501.0000	未经加工的人发，不论是否洗涤；废人发〔999〕	15		90	13/	13	千克	B9	VW	/20
05.02	**猪鬃、猪毛；獾毛及其他制刷用兽毛；上述鬃毛的废料：**									
	-猪鬃、猪毛及其废料：									
0502.1010	---猪鬃〔999〕	20		90	9/	9,13	千克	AB	PQ	/30
0502.1020	---猪毛〔999〕	20		90	9/	6,13	千克	AB	PQ	/30
0502.1030	---废料〔101 猪毛，102 猪鬃〕	20		90	9/	6	千克	B9	PQ	/30
	-其他：									
	---獾毛及其他制刷用兽毛：									
0502.9011	----山羊毛〔999〕	20		90	9/	9,13	千克	AB	PQ	/30
0502.9012	----黄鼠狼尾毛〔999〕	20		90	9/	9,13	千克	ABEF	PQ	/30
0502.9019	----其他									
0502.9019 10	濒危獾毛及其他制刷用濒危兽毛〔T2〕	20		90	9/	0	千克	ABFE	PQ	/30
0502.9019 90	其他獾毛及其他制刷用兽毛〔T2〕	20		90	9/	9,13	千克	AB	PQ	/30
0502.9020	---废料									
0502.9020 10	濒危獾毛及其他制刷濒危兽毛废料〔T2〕	20		90	9/	0	千克	BEF	PQ	/30
0502.9020 90	其他獾毛及其他制刷用兽毛的废料〔T2〕	20		90	9/	6	千克	9B	PQ	/30
05.04	**整个或切块的动物(鱼除外)的肠、膀胱及胃，鲜、冷、冻、干、熏、盐腌或盐渍的：**									
	---肠衣：									
0504.0011	----盐渍猪肠衣(猪大肠头除外)〔999〕	20		90	9/	9	千克	AB	PRQS	/55
0504.0012	----盐渍绵羊肠衣〔999〕	18		90	9/	9	千克	AB	PRQS	/53
0504.0013	----盐渍山羊肠衣〔999〕	18		90	9/	9	千克	AB	PRQS	/28
0504.0014	----盐渍猪大肠头〔999〕	20		90	9/	9	千克	AB	PRQS	/30
0504.0019	----其他〔T2〕	18		90	9/	9	千克	AB	PRQS	/28
	---胃：									
0504.0021	----冷、冻的鸡胗〔101 冷藏的鸡胗、胃，102 冻藏的鸡胗、胃〕	T3		T3	9/	6	千克	7AB	PRQS	/35
0504.0029	----其他〔T2〕	20		90	9/	6	千克	AB	PRQS	/55
0504.0090	---其他〔T2〕	20		80	9/	6	千克	AB	PRQS	/30
05.05	**带有羽毛或羽绒的鸟皮及鸟体其他部分；羽毛及不完整羽毛(不论是否修边)、羽绒，仅经洗涤、消毒或为了保藏而作过处理，但未经进一步加工；羽毛或不完整羽毛的粉末及废料：**									
0505.1000	-填充用羽毛；羽绒									
0505.1000 10	填充用濒危野生禽类羽毛、羽绒(仅经洗涤、消毒等处理，未进一步加工)〔999〕	10	2	100	9/	0	千克	ABFE	PQ	/27
0505.1000 90	其他填充用羽毛；羽绒(仅经洗涤、消毒等处理，未进一步加工)〔999〕	10	2	100	9/	13,9	千克	AB	PQ	/27
	-其他：									
0505.9010	---羽毛或不完整羽毛的粉末及废料〔T2〕	10		35	9/	6	千克	9AB	PQ	/15
0505.9090	---其他									
0505.9090 10	其他濒危野生禽类羽毛、羽绒(包括带有羽毛或羽绒的鸟皮及鸟体的其他部分)〔101 绒(未经加工鸭毛除外)，102 其他禽鸟羽毛，103 未经加工鸭毛〕	10		90	9/	0	千克	AFEB	PQ	/25

Chapter 5
Products of animal origin, not elsewhere specified or included

Notes:

1. This Chapter does not cover:
   (a) Edible products (other than guts, bladders and stomachs of animals, whole and pieces thereof, and animal blood, liquid or dried);
   (b) Hides or skins (including furskins) other than goods of heading No. 05.05 and parings and similar waste of raw hides or skins of heading No. 05.11 (Chapter 41 or 43)
   (c) Animal textile materials, other than horsehair and horsehair waste (Section Ⅺ); or
   (d) Prepared knots or tufts for broom or brush making (heading No. 96.03).
2. For the purposes of heading No. 05.01, the sorting of human hair by length (provided the root ends and tip ends respectively are not arranged together) shall be deemed not to constitute working.
3. Throughout the Nomenclature, elephant, hippopotamus, walrus, narwhal and wild boar tusks, rhinoceros horns and the teeth of all animals are regarded as "ivory".
4. Throughout the Nomenclature, the expression"horsehair" means hair of the manes or tails of equine or bovine animals. Heading No.05. 11 mainly include horsehair and horsehair waster,whether or not put up as a layer with or without supporting material.

协定税率 %										特惠税率 %			
亚太5国	东/冰/格	巴基斯坦	韩国	瑞士	哥达	秘鲁	澳大利亚	新西/坡/智	港/澳/台	亚太2国	老/柬/缅	36/3/1	Article Description
													Human hair, unworked, whether or not washed or scoured; waste of human hair:
	0/0/0	10.8	6	4.5	0	0	0	0//0	0/0/			0/0/	Human hair, unworked, whether or not washed or scoured; waste of human hair
													Pigs', hogs', or boars', bristles and hair; badger hair and other brush making hair; waste of such bristles or hair:
													-Pigs', hogs', or boars', bristles and hair and waste thereof:
	0/0/0	18	12	6	0	0	0	0//0	0/0/			0/0/	---Bristles
	0/0/0	18	12	6	0	0	0	0//0	0/0/			0/0/	---Hair
	0/0/0	18	12	6	0	0	0	0//0	0/0/			0/0/	---Waste
													-Other:
													---Badger hair and other brush making hair:
	0/0/0		12	6	0	0	0	0//0	0/0/			0/0/	----Goat hair
	0/0/0		12	6	0	0	0	0//0	0/0/			0/0/	----Weasel tail hair
													----Other
	0/0/0		12	6	0	0	0	0//0	0/0/			0/0/	Endangered badger hair and other brush making hair of endangered animals
	0/0/0		12	6	0	0	0	0//0	0/0/			0/0/	Other badger hair and other brush making hair of other animal
													---Waste
	0/0/0		12	6	0	0	0	0//0	0/0/			0/0/	Waste of endangered badger hair and other brush making hair of endangered animals
	0/0/0		12	6	0	0	0	0//0	0/0/			0/0/	Waste of badger hair and other brush making hair of other animals
													Guts, bladders and stomachs of animals (other than fish), whole and pieces thereof, fresh, chilled, frozen, salted, in brine, dried or smoked:
													---Casings:
10	0/0/0	10	12	0	0	0	0	0//0	0/0/			0/0/	----Hog casings, salted(excluding hog fat-ends)
9	0/0/0	9	10.8	5.4	0	0	0	0//0	0/0/			0/0/	----Sheep casings, salted
9	0/0/0	9	10.8	5.4	0	0	0	0//0	0/0/			0/0/	----Goat casings, salted
10	0/0/0	10	12	6	0	0	0	0//0	0/0/			0/0/	----Hog fat-ends, salted
9	0/0/0	9	10.8	5.4	0	0	0	0//0	0/0/			0/0/	----Other
													---Gizzard:
10	0/0/0	0.65元/千克	0.7元/千克	6	0	0	0	0//0	0/0/			0/0/	----Cold, frozen gizzard
10	0/0/0	10	12	6	0	0	0	0//0	0/0/			0/0/0	----Other
10	0/0/0	10	12	0	0	0	0	0//0	0/0/			0/0/	---Other
													Skins and other parts of birds, with their feathers or down; feathers and parts of feathers (whether or not with trimmed edges) and down, not further worked than cleaned, disinfected or treated for preservation; powder and waste of feathers or parts of feathers:
													-Feathers of a kind used for stuffing; down
7.5	0/0/0	4.5	4	0	0	0	0	0//0	0/0/			0/0/0	Feathers of endangered wild birds, of a kind used for stuffing; down(not further worked than cleaned, disinfected or treated for preservation)
7.5	0/0/0	4.5	4	0	0	0	0	0//0	0/0/			0/0/0	Feathers of other birds, of a kind used for stuffing; down(not further worked than cleaned, disinfected or treated for preservation)
													-Other:
	0/0/0	4.5	4	0	0	0	0	0//0	0/0/			0/0/0	---Powder and waste of feathers or parts of feathers
													---Other
	0/0/0	4.5	4	0	0	0	0	0//0	0/0/			0/0/0	Feathers and down of endangered wild birds (including skins and other parts of birds, with their feathers or down)

税则号列		货品名称〔CIQ 扩展编码及品名－T2 表示见附表 2〕	最惠(%)	暂定税率	普通	增值/消费	出口退税	计量单位	监管条件	检验检疫	特殊证件对美关税
0505.9090	90	其他羽毛、羽绒(包括带有羽毛或羽绒的鸟皮及鸟体的其他部分)[T2]	10		90	9/	9,13	千克	AB	PQ	/25
05.06		**骨及角柱,未经加工或经脱脂、简单整理(但未切割成形)、酸处理或脱胶;上述产品的粉末及废料:**									
0506.1000		-经酸处理的骨胶原及骨[T2]	12		50	13/	0	千克	AB	PQ	/17
		-其他:									
		---骨粉、骨废料:									
0506.9011		----含牛羊成分的									
0506.9011	10	含牛羊成分的骨废料(未经加工或仅经脱脂等加工的)〔999〕	12		35	13/	0	千克	9AB	MPQ	/17
0506.9011	90	含牛羊成分的骨粉(未经加工或仅经脱脂等加工的)[T2]	12		35	13/	0	千克	AB	MPQ	/17
0506.9019		----其他									
0506.9019	10	其他骨废料(未经加工或仅经脱脂等加工的)〔999〕	12		35	13/	0	千克	9AB	MPQ	/17
0506.9019	90	其他骨粉(未经加工或仅经脱脂等加工的)[T2]	12		35	13/	0	千克	AB	MPQ	/17
0506.9090		---其他									
0506.9090	11	已脱胶的虎骨(指未经加工或经脱脂等加工的)〔999〕	12	12	50	9/	0	千克	89	PQ	/17
0506.9090	19	未脱胶的虎骨(指未经加工或经脱脂等加工的)〔999〕	12		50	9/	0	千克	89	PQ	/17
0506.9090	21	已脱胶的豹骨(指未经加工或经脱脂等加工的)〔999〕	12	12	50	9/	0	千克	ABFE	PQ	/17
0506.9090	29	未脱胶的豹骨(指未经加工或经脱脂等加工的)〔999〕	12		50	9/	0	千克	ABFE	PQ	/17
0506.9090	31	已脱胶的濒危野生动物的骨及角柱(不包括虎骨、豹骨,指未经加工或经脱脂等加工的)〔101 其他野生偶蹄动物骨、蹄、角,102 未列出的其他动物骨、蹄、角,103 工业用牛软骨,104 工业用羊软骨,105 工业用猪软骨,106 工业用烘干鹿骨〕	12	12	50	9/	0	千克	AFEB	PQ	/17
0506.9090	39	未脱胶的濒危野生动物的骨及角柱(不包括虎骨、豹骨,指未经加工或经脱脂等加工的)〔101 工业用牛软骨,102 工业用羊软骨,103 工业用猪软骨,104 工业用烘干鹿骨,105 未列出的其他动物骨、蹄、角	12		50	9/	0	千克	AFEB	PQ	/17
0506.9090	91	已脱胶的其他骨及角柱(不包括虎骨、豹骨,指未经加工或经脱脂等加工的)〔101 工业用牛软骨,102 工业用羊软骨,103 工业用猪软骨,104 工业用烘干鹿骨,105 未列出的其他动物骨、蹄、角〕	12	12	50	9/	0	千克	AB	PQ	/17
0506.9090	99	未脱胶的其他骨及角柱(不包括虎骨、豹骨,指未经加工或经脱脂等加工的)〔101 工业用牛软骨,102 工业用羊软骨,103 工业用猪软骨,104 工业用烘干鹿骨,105 未列出的其他动物骨、蹄、角〕	12		50	9/	0	千克	AB	PQ	/17
05.07		**兽牙、龟壳、鲸须、鲸须毛、角、鹿角、蹄、甲、爪及喙,未经加工或仅简单整理但未切割成形;上述产品的粉末及废料:**									
0507.1000		-兽牙;兽牙粉末及废料									
0507.1000	10	犀牛角〔999〕	10		30	9/	6	千克	89	PQ	/15
0507.1000	20	其他濒危野生兽牙、兽牙粉末及废料〔101 其他野生偶蹄动物骨、蹄、角(河马牙除外),102 象牙,103 未列出的其他动物骨、蹄、角,104 河马牙〕	10		30	9/	0	千克	AFEB	PQ	/15
0507.1000	30	其他兽牙[T2]	10		30	9/	6	千克	AB	PQ	/15
0507.1000	90	其他兽牙粉末及废料[T2]	10		30	9/	6	千克	9AB	PQ	/15
		-其他:									
0507.9010		---羚羊角及其粉末和废料〔101 羚羊角,102 药用羚羊角〕	3		14	9/	6	千克	ABFE	PQ	/
0507.9020		---鹿茸及其粉末[T2]	11		30	9/	6	千克	ABFE	PQ	/16
0507.9090		---其他									
0507.9090	10	龟壳、鲸须、鲸须毛、鹿角及其他濒危动物角(包括蹄,甲,爪及喙及其粉末和废料)[T2]	10		50	9/	0	千克	AFEB	PQ	/15
0507.9090	90	其他动物角(包括蹄,甲,爪及喙及其粉末和废料)[T2]	10		50	9/	6	千克	AB	PQ	/15
05.08		**珊瑚及类似品,未经加工或仅简单整理但未经进一步加工;软体动物壳、甲壳动物壳、棘皮动物壳、墨鱼骨,未经加工或仅简单整理但未切割成形,上述壳、骨的粉末及废料:**									
0508.0010		---粉末及废料									
0508.0010	10	珊瑚及濒危水产品的粉末、废料(包括介、贝、棘皮动物壳,不包括墨鱼骨的粉末及废料)〔999〕	12		35	9/	0	千克	AFEB	PQ	/42
0508.0010	90	其他水产品壳、骨的粉末及废料(包括介、贝、棘皮动物壳、墨鱼骨的粉末及废料)[T2]	12		35	9/	9	千克	AB	PQ	/42
0508.0090		---其他									

协定税率 %										特惠税率 %			
亚太5国	东/冰/格	巴基斯坦	韩国	瑞士	哥达	秘鲁	澳大利亚	新西/坡/智	浐/澳/台	亚太2国	老/柬/缅	36/3/1	Article Description
	0/0/0	4.5	4	0	0	0	0	0//0	0/0/			0/0/0	Feathers and down of other birds (including skins and other parts of birds, with their feathers or down)
													Bones and horn-cores, unworked, defatted, simply prepared (but not cut to shape), treated with acid or degelatinized; powder and waste of these products:
	0/0/0	5.4	4.8	3.6	0	0	0	0//0	0/0/		0//	0/0/0	-Ossein and bones treated with acid
													-Other:
													---Powder and waste of bones:
													----Of bovine and sheep
	0/0/0	5.4	4.8	3.6	0	0	0	0//0	0/0/		0//	0/0/0	Waste of bones, containing bovine composition or sheep and goats composition(unworked, defatted, simply prepared)
	0/0/0	5.4	4.8	3.6	0	0	0	0//0	0/0/		0//	0/0/0	Powder of bones, containing bovine composition or sheep and goats composition(unworked, defatted, simply prepared)
													----Other
	0/0/0	5.4	4.8	3.6	0	0	0	0//0	0/0/		0//	0/0/0	Other waste of bones(unworked, defatted, simply prepared)
	0/0/0	5.4	4.8	3.6	0	0	0	0//0	0/0/		0//	0/0/0	Other powder of bones(unworked, defatted, simply prepared)
													---Other
	0/0/0	4.8	4.8	3.6	0	0	0	0//0	0/0/		0//	0/0/0	Tiger-bone (*as tigris*), degelatinized(unworked, defatted, simply prepared)
	0/0/0	4.8	4.8	3.6	0	0	0	0//0	0/0/		0//	0/0/0	Tiger-bone (*as tigirs*), not degelatinized(unworked, defatted, simply prepared)
	0/0/0	4.8	4.8	3.6	0	0	0	0//0	0/0/		0//	0/0/0	Leopard-bone, degelatinized(unworked, defatted, simply prepared)
	0/0/0	4.8	4.8	3.6	0	0	0	0//0	0/0/		0//	0/0/0	Leopard-bone, not degelatinized(unworked, defatted, simply prepared)
	0/0/0	4.8	4.8	3.6	0	0	0	0//0	0/0/		0//	0/0/0	Bones and horn-cores of endangered wild animals, degelatinized (other than tiger-bone, leopard-bone, unworked, defatted, simply prepared)
	0/0/0	4.8	4.8	3.6	0	0	0	0//0	0/0/		0//	0/0/0	Bones and horn-cores of endangered wild animals, not degelatinized (other than tiger-bone, leopard-bone, unworked, defatted, simply prepared)
	0/0/0	4.8	4.8	3.6	0	0	0	0//0	0/0/		0//	0/0/0	Bones and horn-cores of other animals, degelatinized (other than tiger-bone, leopard-bone, unworked, defatted, simply prepared)
	0/0/0	4.8	4.8	3.6	0	0	0	0//0	0/0/		0//	0/0/0	Bones and horn-cores of other animals, not degelatinized (other than tiger-bone, leopard-bone, unworked, defatted, simply prepared)
													Ivory, tortoise-shell, whalebone and whalebone hair, horns, antlers, hooves, nails, claws and beaks, unworked or simply prepared but not cut to shape; powder and waste of these products:
													-Ivory; ivory powder and waste
	0/0/0	4.5	4	0	0	0	0	0//0	0/0/			0/0/0	Rhinocerus horn (*cornu rhinocerotis*)
	0/0/0	4.5	4	0	0	0	0	0//0	0/0/			0/0/0	Ivory, ivory powder and waste thereof of other endangered wild animals
	0/0/0	4.5	4	0	0	0	0	0//0	0/0/			0/0/0	Other ivory
	0/0/0	4.5	4	0	0	0	0	0//0	0/0/			0/0/0	Other ivory powedr and waste thereof
													-Other:
	0/0/0	0	0	0	0	0	0	0//0	0/0/			0/0/0	---Antelope horns and powder or waste thereof
	0/0/0	4.5	4.4	3.3	0	0	0	0//0	0/0/			0/0/0	---Pilose antlers and powder thereof
													---Other
	0/0/0	4.5	4	0	0	0	0	0//0	0/0/			0/0/0	Tortoise-shell, whalebone and whalebone hair, horns and other endangered antlers, hooves, nails, claws and beaks, unworked or simply prepared but not cut to shape; powder and waste of these products
	0/0/0	4.5	4	0	0	0	0	0//0	0/0/			0/0/0	Other animal antlers, hooves, nails, claws and beaks, unworked or simply prepared but not cut to shape; powder and waste of these products
													Coral and similar materials, unworked or simply prepared but not otherwise worked; shells of molluscs, crustaceans or echinoderms and cuttle-bone, unworked or simply prepared but not cut to shape, powder and waste thereof:
													---Powder and waste
	0/0/0		4.8	3.6	0	0	0	0//0	0/0/			0/0/0	Powder and waste of endangered aquatic product(including shells of molluscs, crustaceans or echinoderms and cuttle-bone)
	0/0/0		4.8	3.6	0	0	0	0//0	0/0/			0/0/0	Powder and waste of other aquatic products (including shells of molluscs, crustaceans or echinoderms and cuttle-bone)
													---Other

税则号列		货品名称〔CIQ 扩展编码及品名－T2 表示见附表 2〕	最惠(%)	暂定税率	普通	增值/消费	出口退税	计量单位	监管条件	检验检疫	特殊证件对美关税
0508.0090	10	珊瑚及濒危水产品的壳、骨(包括介、贝、棘皮动物的壳,不包括墨鱼骨)〔101 未经加工虾蟹壳,102 除未经加工虾蟹壳外〕	12		50	9/	0	千克	AFEB	PQ	/42
0508.0090	90	其他水产品的壳、骨(包括介、贝、棘皮动物的壳,墨鱼骨)〔101 未经加工虾蟹壳,102 除未经加工虾蟹壳外〕	12		50	9/	9	千克	AB	PQ	/42
05.10		**龙涎香、海狸香、灵猫香及麝香;斑蝥;胆汁,不论是否干制;供配制药用的腺体及其他动物产品,鲜、冷、冻或用其他方法暂时保藏的:**									
0510.0010		---黄药									
0510.0010	10	牛黄[T2]	3		14	9/	6	千克	8A	PQ	/
0510.0010	20	猴枣〔999〕	3		14	9/	6	千克	QAFEB	PQ	/
0510.0010	90	其他黄药(不包括牛黄)〔999〕	3		14	9/	6	千克	AFEB	PQ	/
0510.0020		---龙涎香、海狸香、灵猫香									
0510.0020	10	海狸香、灵猫香〔999〕	7		50	9/	6	千克	ABEF	PQ	/12
0510.0020	20	龙涎香〔999〕	7		50	9/	6	千克	AB	PQ	/12
0510.0030		---麝香〔999〕	7		20	9/	0	千克	8AF	PQ	/12
0510.0040		---斑蝥〔999〕	7		50	9/	6	千克	QAB	PQ	/12
0510.0090		---其他									
0510.0090	10	其他濒危野生动物胆汁及其他产品(不论是否干制;鲜、冷、冻或用其他方法暂时保藏的)〔101〕	6		20	9/	0	千克	AFEB	PQ	/11
0510.0090	90	胆汁,配药用腺体及其他动物产品(不论是否干制;鲜、冷、冻或用其他方法暂时保藏的)[T2]	6		20	9/	6	千克	AB	PQ	/11
05.11		**其他税目未列名的动物产品;不适合供人食用的第一章或第三章的死动物:**									
0511.1000		-牛的精液									
0511.1000	10	濒危野生牛的精液〔999〕	0		0	9/	0	千克	ABFE	PQ	/
0511.1000	90	其他牛的精液〔101 牛精液,102 其他精液〕	0		0	9/	9	千克	AB	PQ	/
		-其他:									
		--鱼、甲壳动物、软体动物、其他水生无脊椎动物的产品;第三章的死动物:									
		---鱼的:									
0511.9111		----受精鱼卵									
0511.9111	10	濒危鱼的受精卵〔999〕	12	0	35	9/	0	千克	ABFE	PQ	/
0511.9111	90	其他受精鱼卵[T2]	12	0	35	9/	6	千克	AB	PQ	/
0511.9119		----其他									
0511.9119	10	濒危鱼的非食用产品(包括鱼肚)〔101 受精卵,102 用作鱼饵的海水鱼,103 用作鱼饵的淡水鱼〕	12		35	9/	0	千克	ABFE	PQ	/17
0511.9119	90	其他鱼的非食用产品(包括鱼肚)〔101 受精卵,102 用作鱼饵的海水鱼,103 用作鱼饵的淡水鱼〕	12		35	9/	6	千克	AB	PQ	/17
0511.9190		---其他									
0511.9190	10	濒危水生无脊椎动物产品(包括甲壳动物、软体动物、第三章死动物)〔101 头索类,102 头索类以外〕	12		35	9/	0	千克	ABFE	PQ	/27
0511.9190	90	其他水生无脊椎动物产品(包括甲壳动物、软体动物、第三章死动物)〔101 头索类,102 头索类以外〕	12		35	9/	9	千克	AB	PQ	/27
		--其他:									
0511.9910		---动物精液(牛的精液除外)									
0511.9910	10	濒危野生动物精液(牛的精液除外)〔999〕	0		0	9/	0	千克	AFEB	PQ	/
0511.9910	90	其他动物精液(牛的精液除外)[T2]	0		0	9/	6	千克	AB	PQ	/
0511.9920		---动物胚胎									
0511.9920	10	濒危野生动物胚胎〔999〕	0		0	9/	0	千克	AFEB	PQ	/
0511.9920	90	其他动物胚胎[T2]	0		0	9/	6	千克	AB	PQ	/
0511.9930		---蚕种〔999〕	0		0	9/	6	千克	AB	PQ	/
0511.9940		---马毛及废马毛,不论是否制成有或无衬垫的毛片									
0511.9940	10	废马毛(不论是否制成有或无衬垫的毛片)[T2]	15		90	9/	6,13	千克	9B	PQ	/20
0511.9940	90	其他马毛(不论是否制成有或无衬垫的毛片)[T2]	15		90	9/	6,13	千克	AB	PQ	/20
0511.9990		---其他									
0511.9990	10	其他编号未列名濒危野生动物产品(包括不适合供人食用的第一章的死动物)[T2]	12		35	9/	0	千克	AFEB	PQ	/42
0511.9990	90	其他编号未列名的动物产品(包括不适合供人食用的第一章的死动物)[T2]	12		35	9/	6	千克	AB	PQ	/42

协定税率 %										特惠税率 %			Article Description
亚太5国	东/冰/格	巴基斯坦	韩国	瑞士	哥达	秘鲁	澳大利亚	新西/坡/智	港/澳/台	亚太2国	老/柬/缅	36/3/1	
	0/0/0	6	4.8	3.6	0	0	0	0//0	0/0/			0/0/0	Shells , bone of endangered coral and endangered aquatic products (including shells of molluscs, crustaceans or echinoderms and cuttle-bone)
	0/0/0	6	4.8	3.6	0	0	0	0//0	0/0/			0/0/0	Shells and bone of other aquatic products (including shells of molluscs, crustaceans or echinoderms and cuttle-bone)
													Ambergris, castoreum, civet and musk; cantharides; bile, whether of not dried; glands and other animal products used in the preparation of pharmaceutical products, fresh, chilled, frozen or otherwise provisionally preserved:
													---Bezoar
	0/0/0	0	0	0	0	0	0	0//0	0/0/			0/0/0	Calculus bovis
	0/0/0	0	0	0	0	0	0	0//0	0/0/			0/0/0	Calculus macaca mulatta
	0/0/0	0	0	0	0	0	0	0//0	0/0/			0/0/0	Other bezoar (excluding calculus bovis)
													---Ambergris, castoreum and civet
	0/0/0	4	0	0	0	0	0	0//0	0/0/			0/0/	castoreum and civet
	0/0/0	4	0	0	0	0	0	0//0	0/0/			0/0/	Ambergris
	0/0/0	4	0	0	0	0	0	0//0	0/0/			0/0/	---Musk
	0/0/0	4	0	0	0	0	0	0//0	0/0/			0/0/0	---Cantharides
													---Other
	0/0/0	4	0	0	0	0	0	0//0	0/0/			0/0/0	Bile and other products of other endangered wild animals (whether or not dried, fresh, chilled, frozen or otherwise provisionally preserved)
	0/0/0	4	0	0	0	0	0	0//0	0/0/			0/0/0	Bile, glands and other animal products used in the preparation of pharmaceutical products (whether or not dried, fresh, chilled, frozen or otherwise provisionally preserved)
													Animal products not elsewhere specified or included; dead animals of Chapter 1 or 3, unfit for human consumption:
													-Bovine semen
												0/0/0	Semen of endangered wild bovine
												0/0/0	Other bovine semen
													-Other:
													--Products of fish or crustaceans, molluscs or other aquatic invertebrates; dead animals of Chapter 3:
													---Fish:
													----Fertilized fish eggs
	0/0/0	6	0	3.6	0	0	0	0//0	0/0/			0/0/0	Fertilized eggs of endangered fish
	0/0/0	6	0	3.6	0	0	0	0//0	0/0/			0/0/0	Other fertilized fish eggs
													----Other
	0/4.4/0		4.8	3.6	0	0	0	0//0	0/0/			0/0/0	Products of endangered fish (including fish maw) unfit for human consumption
	0/4.4/0		4.8	3.6	0	0	0	0//0	0/0/			0/0/0	Products of other fish (including fish maw) unfit for human consumption
													---Other
	0/0/0	5.4	4.8	3.6	0	0	0	0//0	0/0/			0/0/0	Products of endangererd crustaceans molluscs or other aquatic invertebrates; dead animals of Chapter 3
	0/0/0	5.4	4.8	3.6	0	0	0	0//0	0/0/			0/0/0	Other products of crustaceans, molluscs or other aquatic invertebrates; dead animals of Chapter 3
													--Other:
													---Animal semen, other than bovine semen
												0/0/0	Semen of endangered wild animals (other than bovine semen)
												0/0/0	Semen of other animals (other than bovine semen)
													---Animal embryo
												0/0/0	Embryo of endangered wild animals
												0/0/0	Embryo of other animals
												0/0/0	---Silkworm graine
													---Horsehair and horsehair waster, whether or not put up as a layer with or without supporting material
	0/0/0	10.8	6	4.5	0	0	0	0//0	0/0/			0/0/	Horsehair waster (whether or not put up as a lalyer with or without supporting material)
	0/0/0	10.8	6	4.5	0	0	0	0//0	0/0/			0/0/	Other horsehair (whether or not put up as a lalyer with or without supporting material)
													---Other
	0/0/0	5.4	4.8	3.6	0	0	0	0//0	0/0/			0/0/0	Products of endangered wild animals, not elsewhere specified or included (including dead animals of Chapter 1, unfit for human consumption)
	0/0/0	5.4	4.8	3.6	0	0	0	0//0	0/0/			0/0/0	Animal products not elsewhere specified or included (including dead animals of Chapter 1, unfit for human consumption)

第二类
植 物 产 品

注释：

本类所称“团粒”，是指直接挤压或加入按重量计比例不超过3%的黏合剂制成的粒状产品。

第六章
活树及其他活植物；鳞茎、根及类似品；插花及装饰用簇叶

注释：

一、除税号06.01的菊苣植物及其根以外，本章包括通常由苗圃或花店供应为种植或装饰用的活树及其他货品(包括植物秧苗)；但不包括马铃薯、洋葱、青葱、大蒜及其他第七章的产品。

二、税号06.03、06.04的各种货品，包括全部或部分用这些货品制成的花束、花篮、花圈及类似品，不论是否有其他材料制成的附件。但这些货品不包括税号97.01的拼贴画或类似的装饰板。

税则号列	货品名称〔CIQ扩展编码及品名—T2表示见附表2〕	最惠(%)	暂定税率	普通	增值/消费	出口退税	计量单位	监管条件	检验检疫	特殊证件对美关税
06.01	**鳞茎、块茎、块根、球茎、根颈及根茎，休眠、生长或开花的；菊苣植物及其根，但税目12.12的根除外：**									
	-休眠的鳞茎、块茎、块根、球茎、根颈及根茎：									
0601.1010	---番红花球茎〔999〕	4		14	9/	6	个/千克	AB	PQ	/9
	---百合球茎：									
0601.1021	----种用〔999〕	0		0	9/	0	个/千克	AB	PQ	/
0601.1029	----其他〔999〕	5		40	9/	0	个/千克	AB	PQ	/10
	---其他：									
0601.1091	----种用									
0601.1091 10	种用休眠的兰花块茎(包括球茎、根颈及根茎)〔999〕	0		0	9/	6	个/千克	AFEB	PQ	/5
0601.1091 91	种用休眠其他濒危植物鳞茎等(包括球茎、根颈、根茎、鳞茎、块茎、块根)〔999〕	0		0	9/	0	个/千克	ABFE	PQ	/5
0601.1091 99	种用休眠的其他鳞茎、块茎、块根(包括球茎、根颈及根茎)[T2]	0		0	9/	6	个/千克	AB	PQ	/5
0601.1099	----其他									
0601.1099 10	其他休眠的兰花块茎(包括球茎、根颈及根茎)〔999〕	5		40	9/	6	个/千克	AFEB	PQ	/10
0601.1099 91	其他休眠濒危植物鳞茎等(包括球茎、根颈、根茎、鳞茎、块茎、块根)〔999〕	5		40	9/	0	个/千克	AFEB	PQ	/10
0601.1099 99	其他休眠的其他鳞茎、块茎、块根(包括球茎、根颈及根茎)〔101水仙花球茎，102其他鳞球块根茎〕	5		40	9/	6	个/千克	AB	PQ	/10
0601.2000	-生长或开花的鳞茎、块茎、块根、球茎、根颈及根茎；菊苣植物及其根									
0601.2000 10	生长或开花的兰花块茎(包括球茎、根颈及根茎)〔999〕	15		80	9/	6	个/千克	AFEB	PQ	/25
0601.2000 20	生长或开花的仙客来鳞茎〔999〕	15		80	9/	6	个/千克	AFEB	PQ	/25
0601.2000 91	生长或开花的其他濒危植物鳞茎等(包括球茎、根颈、根茎、鳞茎、块茎、块根、菊苣植物)〔999〕	15		80	9/	0	个/千克	AFEB	PQ	/25
0601.2000 99	生长或开花的其他鳞茎及菊苣植物(包括块茎、块根、球茎、根颈及根茎，税目12.12根除外)[T2]	15		80	9/	6	个/千克	AB	PQ	/25
06.02	**其他活植物(包括其根)、插枝及接穗；蘑菇菌丝：**									
0602.1000	-无根插枝及接穗									
0602.1000 10	濒危植物的无根插枝及接穗〔101营养体，102其他组培苗〕	0		0	9/	0	株/千克	ABFE	PQ	/5
0602.1000 90	其他无根插枝及接穗〔101其他观赏花木，102营养体〕	0		0	9/	6	株/千克	AB	PQ	/5
	-食用水果或食用坚果的树、灌木，不论是否嫁接：									
0602.2010	---种用苗木[T2]	0		0	9/	0	株/千克	AB	PQ	/5
0602.2090	---其他〔999〕	10		80	9/	6	株/千克	AB	PQ	/35
	-杜鹃，不论是否嫁接：									
0602.3010	---种用〔101观赏花木，102其他组培苗，103营养体〕	0		0	9/	6	株/千克	AB	PQ	/5
0602.3090	---其他〔999〕	15		80	9/	6	株/千克	AB	PQ	/20
	-玫瑰，不论是否嫁接：									
0602.4010	---种用〔101玫瑰，102其他组培苗，103营养体〕	0		0	9/	6	株/千克	AB	PQ	/
0602.4090	---其他〔999〕	15		80	9/	6	株/千克	AB	PQ	/20

SECTION Ⅱ
VEGETABLE PRODUCTS

Notes:

In this Section the term "pellets" means products which have been agglomerated either directly by compression or by the addition of a binder in a proportion not exceeding 3% by weight.

Chapter 6
Live trees and other plants; bulbs, roots and the like; cut flowers and ornamental foliage

Notes:

1. Subject to the second part of heading No. 06.01 this Chapter covers only live trees and goods (including seeding vegetables) of a kind commonly supplied by nursery gardeners or florists for planting or for ornamental use; nevertheless it does not include potatoes, onions, shallots, garlic or other products of Chapter 7.
2. Any reference in heading No. 06.03 or 06.04 to goods of any kind shall be construed as including a reference to bouquets, floral baskets, wreaths and similar articles made wholly or partly of goods of that kind, account not being taken of accessories of other materials. However, these headings do not include collages or similar decorative plaques of heading No. 97.01.

协定税率 %										特惠税率 %			Article Description
亚太5国	东/冰/格	巴基斯坦	韩国	瑞士	哥达	秘鲁	澳大利亚	新西/坡/智	港/澳/台	亚太2国	老/柬/缅	36/3/1	
													Bulbs, tubers, tuberous roots, corms, crowns and rhizomes, dormant, in growth or in flower; chicory plants and roots other than roots of heading No. 12.12:
													-Bulbs, tubers, tuberous roots, corms, crowns and rhizomes, dormant:
2	0/0/0	0	0	0	0	0	0	0//0	0/0/		0//	0/0/0	---Stigma croci corms
													---lily corms:
												0/0/0	----Seed
2.5	0/0/0	0	0	0	0	0	0	0//0	0/0/		0//	0/0/0	----Other
													---Other:
													----Seed
												0/0/0	Orchid tubers, dormant, seed (including corms, crowns and rhizomes)
												0/0/0	Bulbs, tubers, tuberous roots, dormant, seed (including corms, crowns and rhizomes) of endaergered plants
												0/0/0	Other bulbs, tubers, tuberous roots, dormant, seed (including corms, crowns and rhizomes)
													----Other
2.5	0/0/0	0	0	0	0	0	0	0//0	0/0/		0//	0/0/0	Other orchid tubers, dormant(including corms, crowns and rhizomes)
2.5	0/0/0	0	0	0	0	0	0	0//0	0/0/		0//	0/0/0	Other endangered plants bulbs (including corms, crowns, rhizomes, bulbs, tuber, tuberous roots, dormant)
2.5	0/0/0	0	0	0	0	0	0	0//0	0/0/		0//	0/0/0	Other bulbs, tubers, tuberous roots, dormant, seed (including corms, crowns and rhizomes), dormant
													-Bulbs, tubers, tuberous roots, corms, crowns and rhizomes, in growth or in flower; chicory plants and roots
7.5	0/0/0	6.8	6	4.5	0	0	0	0//0	0/0/			0/0/	Orchid tubers, in growth or in flower (in-cluding corms, crowns and rhizomes)
7.5	0/0/0	6.8	6	4.5	0	0	0	0//0	0/0/			0/0/	Cyclamen tubers, in growth or in flower
7.5	0/0/0	6.8	6	4.5	0	0	0	0//0	0/0/			0/0/	Other endangered plants bulbs (including corms, crowns, rhizomes, bulbs, tubers, tuberous roots, chicory plants) in growth or in flower
7.5	0/0/0	6.8	6	4.5	0	0	0	0//0	0/0/			0/0/	Other bulbs and chicory plants (including tubers, tuberous roots, corms, crowns and rhizomes, other than roots of heading No. 12.12) in growth or in flower
													Other live plants (including their roots) cuttings and slips; mushroom spawn:
													-Unrooted cuttings and slips
												0/0/0	Unrooted cuttings and slips of endangered pl-ants
												0/0/0	Other unrooted cuttings and slips
													-Trees, shrubs and bushes, grafted or not, of kinds which bear edible fruit or nuts:
												0/0/0	---Seedlings
5	0/0/0	4.5	4	0	0	0	0	0//0	0/0/			0/0/0	---Other
													-Rhododendrons and azaleas, grafted or not:
												0/0/0	---Seedlings
	0/0/0	9.6	6	4.5	0	0	0	0//0	0/0/			0/0/	---Other
													-Roses, grafted or not:
												0/0/0	---Seedlings
	0/0/0	9.6	6	4.5	0	0	0	0//0	0/0/			0/0/	---Other

税则号列	货品名称〔CIQ 扩展编码及品名－T2 表示见附表 2〕	最惠(%)	暂定税率	普通	增值/消费	出口退税	计量单位	监管条件	检验检疫	特殊证件对美关税
	-其他：									
0602.9010	---蘑菇菌丝〔999〕	0		0	9/	6	千克	AB	PQ	/
	---其他：									
0602.9091	----种用苗木									
0602.9091 10	种用兰花［T2］	0		0	9/	0	株/千克	AFEB	PQ	/5
0602.9091 20	种用红豆杉苗木〔999〕	0		0	9/	0	株/千克	AFEB	PQ	/5
0602.9091 91	其他濒危植物种用苗木［T2］	0		0	9/	0	株/千克	AFEB	PQ	/5
0602.9091 99	其他种用苗木［T2］	0		0	9/	0	株/千克	AB	PQ	/5
0602.9092	----兰花〔101 蝴蝶兰，102 兰花〕	10		80	9/	6	株/千克	ABFE	PQ	/15
0602.9093	----菊花〔999〕	10		80	9/	0，6	株/千克	AB	PQ	/15
0602.9094	----百合									
0602.9094 10	芦荟（种用除外）〔999〕	10		80	9/	6	株/千克	ABFEQ	PQ	/15
0602.9094 90	其他百合（种用除外）〔101 观赏花木，102 药用百合〕	10		80	9/	0	株/千克	AB	PQ	/15
0602.9095	----康乃馨〔999〕	10		80	9/	6	株/千克	AB	PQ	/15
0602.9099	----其他									
0602.9099 10	苏铁（铁树）类〔999〕	10		80	9/	6	株/千克	ABFE	PQ	/40
0602.9099 20	仙人掌（包括仙人球、仙人柱、仙人指）〔999〕	10		80	9/	6	株/千克	ABFE	PQ	/40
0602.9099 30	红豆杉（种用除外）〔999〕	10		80	9/	0	株/千克	ABFE	PQ	/40
0602.9099 91	其他濒危活植物（种用除外）［T2］	10		80	9/	0	株/千克	AFEB	PQ	/40
0602.9099 99	其他活植物（种用除外）［T2］	10		80	9/	6	株/千克	AB	PQ	/40
06.03	**制花束或装饰用的插花及花蕾，鲜、干、染色、漂白、浸渍或用其他方法处理的：**									
	-鲜的：									
0603.1100	--玫瑰〔999〕	10		100	9/	6	千克/枝	AB	PQ	/15
0603.1200	--康乃馨〔999〕	10		100	9/	6	千克/枝	AB	PQ	/15
0603.1300	--兰花〔101 洋兰切花，102 鹤望兰切花，103 其他切花〕	10		100	9/	6	千克/枝	ABEF	PQ	/15
0603.1400	--菊花〔999〕	10		100	9/	6	千克/枝	AB	PQ	/15
0603.1500	--百合花（百合属）〔999〕	10		100	9/	6	千克/枝	AB	PQ	/15
0603.1900	--其他									
0603.1900 10	鲜的濒危植物插花及花蕾（制花束或装饰用的）〔999〕	10		100	9/	0	千克/枝	ABFE	PQ	/40
0603.1900 90	其他鲜的插花及花蕾（制花束或装饰用的）〔999〕	10		100	9/	6	千克/枝	AB	PQ	/40
0603.9000	-其他									
0603.9000 10	干或染色等加工濒危植物的插花及花蕾（制花束或装饰用的，鲜的除外）〔999〕	23		100	13/	0	千克/枝	ABFE	PQ	/58
0603.9000 90	其他干或染色等加工的插花及花蕾（制花束或装饰用的，鲜的除外）〔999〕	23		100	13/	6	千克/枝	AB	PQ	/58
06.04	**制花束或装饰用的不带花及花蕾的植物枝、叶或其他部分，草、苔藓及地衣，鲜、干、染色、漂白、浸渍或用其他方法处理的：**									
	-鲜的：									
0604.2010	---苔藓及地衣〔101 苔藓及地衣，102 苔藓（栽培介质），103 泥炭藓（栽培介质）〕	23		100	9/	6	千克	AB	PQ	/58
0604.2090	---其他									
0604.2090 10	其他鲜濒危植物枝、叶或其他部分，草（枝、叶或其他部分是指制花束或装饰用并且不带花及花蕾）〔999〕	10		100	9/	0	千克	ABFE	PQ	/40
0604.2090 90	其他鲜植物枝、叶或其他部分，草（枝、叶或其他部分是指制花束或装饰用并且不带花及花蕾）〔101 其他林木苗木，102 其他观赏花木，103 富贵竹切花，104 未列出的其他植物〕	10		100	9/	6	千克	AB	PQ	/40
	-其他：									
0604.9010	---苔藓及地衣［T2］	23		100	9/	6	千克	AB	PQ	/33
0604.9090	---其他									
0604.9090 10	其他染色或经加工濒危植物枝、叶、草等（枝、叶或其他部分是指制花束或装饰用并且不带花及花蕾）〔999〕	10		100	13/	0	千克	ABFE	PQ	/40
0604.9090 90	其他染色或加工的植物枝、叶、草等（枝、叶或其他部分是指制花束或装饰用并且不带花及花蕾）〔102 未列出的其他植物产品，101 干花〕	10		100	13/	6	千克	AB	PQ	/40

协定税率 %										特惠税率 %			Article Description
亚太5国	东/冰/格	巴基斯坦	韩国	瑞士	哥达	秘鲁	澳大利亚	新西/坡/智	港/澳/台	亚太2国	老/柬/缅	36/3/1	
													-Other:
												0/0/0	---Mushroom spawn
													---Other:
													----Seedlings
												0/0/0	Orchid, seedlings
												0/0/0	Chinese yew, seeding
												0/0/0	Other seedlings of endangered plants
												0/0/0	Other nursery stock, seedlings
	0/0/0	4.5	4	0	0	0	0	0//0	0/0/			0/0/0	----Orchid
	0/0/0	4.5	4	0	0	0	0	0//0	0/0/			0/0/0	----Chrysathemum
													----Lily
	0/0/0	4.5	4	0	0	0	0	0//0	0/0/			0/0/0	Aloe(other than seedlings)
	0/0/0	4.5	4	0	0	0	0	0//0	0/0/			0/0/0	Other lily(other than seedling)
	0/0/0	4.5	4	0	0	0	0	0//0	0/0/			0/0/0	----Carnation
													----Other
5	0/0/0	4.5	4	0	0	0	0	0//0	0/0/			0/0/0	Sago cycas (*Cycas revoluta*)
5	0/0/0	4.5	4	0	0	0	0	0//0	0/0/			0/0/0	Cactus (including ball cactus, column cactus, finger cactus)
5	0/0/0	4.5	4	0	0	0	0	0//0	0/0/			0/0/0	Chinese yew(other than seeding)
5	0/0/0	4.5	4	0	0	0	0	0//0	0/0/			0/0/0	Other live endangered plants(other than seedlings)
5	0/0/0	4.5	4	0	0	0	0	0//0	0/0/			0/0/0	Other live plants (other than seedlings)
													Cut flowers and flower buds of a kind suitable for bouquets or for ornamental purposes, fresh, dried, dyed, bleached, impregnated or otherwise prepared:
													-Fresh:
5	0/0/0	4.5	4	0	0	0	0	0//0	0/0/		0//	0/0/0	--Roses
5	0/0/0	4.5	4	0	0	0	0	0//0	0/0/		0//	0/0/0	--Carnations
5	0/0/0	4.5	4	0	0	0	0	0//0	0/0/0		0//	0/0/0	--Orchids
5	0/0/0	4.5	4	0	0	0	0	0//0	0/0/		0//	0/0/0	--Chrysanthemums
5	0/0/0	4.5	4	0	0	0	0	0//0	0/0/		0//	0/0/0	--Lily(Lilium spp.)
													--Other
5	0/0/0	4.5	4	0	0	0	0	0//0	0/0/		0//	0/0/0	Cut flowers and flower buds of endangered plants(of a kind suitable for bouquets or for ornamental purposes)fresh
5	0/0/0	4.5	4	0	0	0	0	0//0	0/0/		0//	0/0/0	Other cut flower and flower buds(of a kind suitable for bouquets or for ornamental purposes)fresh
													-Other
11.5	0/0/0	10.4	16.1	6.9	0	0	0	0//0	0/0/		0//	0/0/0	Cut flowers and flower buds of endangered plants(of a kind suitable for bouquets or for ornamental purposes), other than fresh dried, dyed or otherwise prepared, other than fresh
11.5	0/0/0	10.4	16.1	6.9	0	0	0	0//0	0/0/		0//	0/0/0	Other cut flowers and flower buds(of a kind suitable for bouquets or for ornamental purposes) dried, dyed or otherwise prepared, other than fresh
													Foliage, branches and other parts of plants, without flowers or flower-buds, and grasses, mosses and lichens, being goods of a kind suitable for bouquets or for ornamental purposes, fresh, dried, dyed, bleached, impregnated or otherwise prepared:
													-Fresh:
	0/0/0	23	9.2	6.9	0	0	0	0//0	0/0/			0/0/	---Mosses and lichens
													---Other
	0/0/0	4.5	4	0	0	0	0	0//0	0/0/			0/0/0	Other foliage, branches and other parts of endangered plants, fresh, and grasses, without flowers or flower buds(being goods of a kind suitable for bouquets or for ornamental purposes)
	0/0/0	4.5	4	0	0	0	0	0//0	0/0/			0/0/0	Other foliage, branches or other parts of plants, fresh, and grasses, without flowers or flower buds(being good of a kind suitable for bouquets or for ornamental prposes)
													-Other:
	0/0/0	23	9.2	6.9	0	0	0	0//0	0/0/			0/0/	---Mosses and hiehens:
													---Other
	0/0/0	4.5	4	0	0	0	0	0//0	0/0/			0/0/0	Other foliage, branches and other parts of endangered plants, and grasses without flowers or flower buds, (being goods of a kind suitable for bouquets or for ornamental purposes)
	0/0/0	4.5	4	0	0	0	0	0//0	0/0/			0/0/0	Other foliage, branches and other parts of plants, and grasses without flowers or flower buds, (being goods of a kind sitable for banquets or for ornamental purposes)

第七章
食用蔬菜、根及块茎

注释：

一、本章不包括税号 12.14 的草料。

二、税号 07.09、07.10、07.11 及 07.12 所称"蔬菜"，包括食用的蘑菇、块菌、油橄榄、刺山柑、菜葫芦、南瓜、茄子、甜玉米、辣椒、茴香菜、欧芹、细叶芹、龙蒿、水芹、甜茉乔栾那。

三、税号 07.12 包括干制的归入税号 07.01 至 07.11 的各种蔬菜，但下列各项除外：

(一)作蔬菜用的脱荚干豆(税号 07.13)；

(二)税目 11.02 至 11.04 所列形状的甜玉米；

(三)马铃薯细粉、粗粉、粉末、粉片、颗粒及团粒(税号 11.05)；

(四)用税目 07.13 的干豆制成的细粉、粗粉及粉末(税目 11.06)。

四、本章不包括辣椒干及辣椒粉(税目 09.04)。

税则号列	货品名称〔CIQ 扩展编码及品名－T2 表示见附表 2〕	最惠(%)	暂定税率	普通	增值/消费	出口退税	计量单位	监管条件	检验检疫	特殊证件对美关税
07.01	**鲜或冷藏的马铃薯：**									
0701.1000	-种用〔999〕	13		70	9/	0	千克	AB	PQ	/43
0701.9000	-其他〔999〕	13		70	9/	0	千克	AB	PRQS	/48
07.02	**鲜或冷藏的番茄：**									
0702.0000	鲜或冷藏的番茄〔999〕	13		70	9/	0	千克	AB	PRQS	/48
07.03	**鲜或冷藏的洋葱、青葱、大蒜、韭葱及其他葱属蔬菜：**									
	-洋葱及青葱：									
0703.1010	---洋葱〔999〕	13		70	9/	0	千克	AB	PRQS	/48
0703.1020	---青葱〔999〕	13		70	9/	0	千克	AB	PRQS	/48
	-大蒜：									
0703.2010	---蒜头〔101 大蒜，102 药用大蒜(蒜头)〕	13		70	9/	0	千克	AB	PRQS	/48
0703.2020	---蒜苔及蒜苗(青蒜)〔101 蒜苔，102 蒜苗，103 青蒜〕	13		70	9/	0	千克	AB	PRQS	/48
0703.2090	---其他〔999〕	13		70	9/	0	千克	AB	PRQS	/48
	-韭葱及其他葱属蔬菜：									
0703.9010	---韭葱〔999〕	13		70	9/	0	千克	AB	PRQS	/48
0703.9020	---大葱〔999〕	13		70	9/	0	千克	AB	PRQS	/48
0703.9090	---其他〔101 分葱，102 荞头，103 分葱、荞头除外〕	13		70	9/	0	千克	AB	PRQS	/48
07.04	**鲜或冷藏的卷心菜、菜花、球茎甘蓝、羽衣甘蓝及类似的食用芥菜类蔬菜：**									
0704.1000	-菜花及硬花甘蓝									
0704.1000 01	鲜、冷硬花甘蓝〔101 羽衣甘蓝，102 羽衣甘蓝除外〕	10		70	9/	0	千克	AB	PRQS	/45
0704.1000 02	鲜、冷花椰菜(花椰菜也叫菜花)〔999〕	10		70	9/	0	千克	AB	PRQS	/45
0704.2000	-抱子甘蓝〔999〕	13		70	9/	0	千克	AB	PRQS	/48
	-其他：									
0704.9010	---卷心菜〔999〕	13		70	9/	0	千克	AB	PRQS	/48
0704.9020	---西兰花〔999〕	13		70	9/	0	千克	AB	PRQS	/48
0704.9090	---其他									
0704.9090 01	鲜、冷其他甘蓝〔101 芥蓝，102 芥蓝除外〕	13		70	9/	0	千克	AB	PRQS	/48
0704.9090 90	鲜或冷藏的其他食用芥菜类蔬菜〔101 芥蓝，102 芥蓝除外〕	13		70	9/	0	千克	AB	PRQS	/48
07.05	**鲜或冷藏的莴苣及菊苣：**									
	-莴苣：									
0705.1100	--结球莴苣(包心生菜)〔999〕	10		70	9/	0	千克	AB	PRQS	/45
0705.1900	--其他〔101 莴苣，102 莴苣除外〕	10		70	9/	0	千克	AB	PRQS	/45
	-菊苣：									
0705.2100	--维特罗夫菊苣〔999〕	13		70	9/	0	千克	AB	PRQ	/48
0705.2900	--其他〔101 莴苣，102 莴苣除外〕	13		70	9/	0	千克	AB	PRQ	/48
07.06	**鲜或冷藏的胡萝卜、萝卜、色拉甜菜根、婆罗门参、块根芹、小萝卜及类似的食用根茎：**									
0706.1000	-胡萝卜及萝卜									
0706.1000 01	鲜、冷胡萝卜〔999〕	13		70	9/	0	千克	AB	PRQS	/48
0706.1000 90	鲜或冷藏的萝卜〔999〕	13		70	9/	0	千克	AB	PRQS	/48
0706.9000	-其他〔101 小萝卜，102 小萝卜类似食用根茎(芜菁)，103 其他鲜或冷藏的小萝卜及类似食用根茎〕	13		70	9/	0	千克	AB	PRQS	/48
07.07	**鲜或冷藏的黄瓜及小黄瓜：**									
0707.0000	鲜或冷藏的黄瓜及小黄瓜〔999〕	13		70	9/	0	千克	AB	PRQS	/48
07.08	**鲜或冷藏的豆类蔬菜，不论是否脱荚：**									
0708.1000	-豌豆〔999〕	13		70	9/	0	千克	AB	PRQS	/48

Chapter 7
Edible vegetables and certain roots and tubers

Notes:

1. This Chapter does not cover forage products of heading 12.14.
2. In headings No. 07.09, 07.10, 07.11 and 07.12 the word "vegetables" includes edible mushrooms, truffles, olives, capers, marrows, pumpkins, aubergines, sweet corn (*Zea mays var. saccharata*), fruits of the genus *Capsicum* or of the genus *Pimenta*, fennel, parsley, chervil, tarragon, cress and sweet marjoram (*Majorana hortensis or Origanum majorana*).
3. Heading No. 07.12 covers all dried vegetables of the kinds falling in headings No. 07.01 to 07.11, other than:
   (a) dried leguminous vegetables, shelled (heading No. 07.13);
   (b) sweet corn in the forms specified in headings No. 11.02 to 11.04;
   (c) flour, meal, powder, flakes, granules and pellets of potatoes (heading No. 11.05);
   (d) flour, meal and powder of the dried leguminous vegetables of heading No. 07.13 (heading No. 11.06).
4. However, dried or crushed or ground fruits of the genus *Capsicum* or of the genus *Pimenta* are excluded from this Chapter (heading No. 09.04).

协定税率 %										特惠税率 %			
亚太5国	东/冰/格	巴基斯坦	韩国	瑞士	哥达	秘鲁	澳大利亚	新西/坡/智	港/澳/台	亚太2国	老/柬/缅	36/3/1	Article Description
													Potatoes, fresh or chilled:
	0//0	5.9	5.2	3.9	0	0	0	0//0	0/0/			0/0/0	-Seeds
9	0/0/0	4.5	5.2	3.9	0	0	0	0//0	0/0/		/0/	0/0/0	-Other
													Tomatoes, fresh or chilled:
	0/0/0	5.9	5.2	3.9	0	0	0	0//0	0/0/			0/0/0	Tomatoes, fresh or chilled
													Onions, shallots, garlic, leeks and other alliaceous vegetables, fresh or chilled:
													-Onions and shallots:
6.5	0/0/0	4.5	5.2	3.9	0	0	0	0//0	0/0/		/0/0	0/0/0	---Onions
6.5	0/0/0	4.5	5.2	3.9	0	0	0	0//0	0/0/		/0/0	0/0/0	---Shallots
													-Garlic:
6.5	0/0/0	0	5.2	3.9	0	0	0	0//0	0/0/			0/0/	---Garlic bulbs
6.5	0/0/0	0	5.2	3.9	0	0	0	0//0	0/0/			0/0/	---Garlic stems, garlic seedlings
6.5	0/0/0	0	5.2	3.9	0	0	0	0//0	0/0/			0/0/	---Other
													-Leeks and other alliaceous vegetables:
	0/0/0	5.9	5.2	3.9	0	0	0	0//0	0/0/		/0/	0/0/0	---Leeks
	0/0/0	5.9	5.2	3.9	0	0	0	0//0	0/0/		/0/	0/0/0	---Scallion
	0/0/0	5.9	5.2	3.9	0	0	0	0//0	0/0/		/0/	0/0/0	---Other
													Cabbages, cauliflowers, kohlrabi, kale and similar edible brassicas, fresh or chilled:
													-Cauliflowers and headed broccoli
	0//0	4.5	4	0	0	0	0	0//0	0/0/			0/0/0	Headed broccoli, fresh or chilled
	0//0	4.5	4	0	0	0	0	0//0	0/0/			0/0/0	Cauliflowers, fresh or chilled
	0/0/0	5.9	5.2	3.9	0	0	0	0//0	0/0/			0/0/	-Brussels sprouts
													-Other:
	0/0/0	5.9	5.2	3.9	0	0	0	0//0	0/0/		0//	0/0/0	---Cabbage (Brassica oleracea var. capitata)
	0/0/0	5.9	5.2	3.9	0	0	0	0//0	0/0/		0//	0/0/0	---Broccolis (Brassica oleracea var italica)
													---Other
	0/0/0	5.9	5.2	3.9	0	0	0	0//0	0/0/		0//	0/0/0	Other Cabbage, fresh or chilled
	0/0/0	5.9	5.2	3.9	0	0	0	0//0	0/0/		0//	0/0/0	Other edible brassicas, fresh or chilled
													Lettuce (*laetuca sativa*) and chicory (*Cichorium spp.*), fresh or chilled:
													-Lettuce:
	0/0/0	0	4	0	0	0	0	0//0	0/0/			0/0/0	--Cabbage lettuce (head lettuce)
	0/0/0	0	4	0	0	0	0	0//0	0/0/			0/0/0	--Other
													-Chicory:
	0/0/0	0	5.2	3.9	0	0	0	0//0	0/0/			0/0/	--Witloof chicory (*Cichoriym intybus var. foliosum*)
	0/0/0	0	5.2	3.9	0	0	0	0//0	0/0/			0/0/	--Other
													Carrots, turnips, salad beetroot, salsify, celeriac, radishes and similar edible roots, fresh or chilled:
													-Carrots and turnips
	0//0	5.9	5.2	3.9	0	0	0	0//0	0/0/			0/0/	Carrots, fresh or chilled
	0//0	5.9	5.2	3.9	0	0	0	0//0	0/0/			0/0/	Turnips, fresh or chilled
	0/0/0	5.9	5.2	3.9	0	0	0	0//0	0/0/			0/0/	-Other
													Cucumbers and gherkins, fresh or chilled:
6.5	0/0/0	4.5	5.2	3.9	0	0	0	0//0	0/0/		/0/	0/0/0	Cucumbers and gherkins, fresh or chilled
													Leguminous vegetables, shelled or unshelled, fresh or chilled:
6.5	0/0/0	0	5.2	3.9	0	0	0	0//0	0/0/		/0/	0/0/0	-Peas (*Pisum sativum*)

税则号列	货品名称〔CIQ扩展编码及品名—T2表示见附表2〕	最惠(%)	暂定税率	普通	增值/消费	出口退税	计量单位	监管条件	检验检疫	特殊证件对美关税
0708.2000	-豇豆及菜豆〔101 豇豆,102 菜豆〕	13		70	9/	0	千克	AB	PRQS	/48
0708.9000	-其他豆类蔬菜〔103 四棱豆,104 豆苗,105 豆芽,106 其他豆科蔬菜,101 蚕豆,102 毛豆〕	13		70	9/	0	千克	AB	PRQS	/48
07.09	**鲜或冷藏的其他蔬菜:**									
0709.2000	-芦笋〔999〕	13		70	9/	0	千克	AB	PRQS	/48
0709.3000	-茄子〔999〕	13		70	9/	0	千克	AB	PRQS	/48
0709.4000	-芹菜,但块根芹除外〔101 欧芹,102 欧芹除外〕	10		70	9/	0	千克	AB	PRQS	/45
	-蘑菇及块菌:									
0709.5100	--伞菌属蘑菇〔999〕	13		90	9/	0	千克	AB	PRQS	/48
	--其他:									
0709.5910	---松茸〔999〕	13		90	9/	0	千克	ABE	PRQS	/48
0709.5920	---香菇〔999〕	13		90	9/	0	千克	AB	PRQS	/48
0709.5930	---金针菇〔999〕	13		90	9/	0	千克	AB	PRQS	/48
0709.5940	---草菇〔999〕	13		90	9/	0	千克	AB	PRQS	/48
0709.5950	---口蘑〔999〕	13		90	9/	0	千克	AB	PRQS	/48
0709.5960	---块菌〔101 银耳,102 木耳,103 其他块菌〕	13		90	9/	9	千克	AB	PRQS	/48
0709.5990	---其他〔101 杏鲍菇,102 猴头菇,103 姬菇,104 平菇,105 秀珍菇,106 牛肝菌,107 其他食用菌〕	13		90	9/	0	千克	AB	PRQS	/48
0709.6000	-辣椒,包括甜椒〔999〕	13		70	9/	0	千克	AB	PRQS	/48
0709.7000	-菠菜〔999〕	13		70	9/	0	千克	AB	PRQS	/48
	-其他:									
0709.9100	--洋蓟〔999〕	13		70	9/	6	千克	AB	PRQS	/48
0709.9200	--油橄榄〔999〕	13		70	9/	6	千克	AB	PRQS	/48
0709.9300	--南瓜、笋瓜及瓠瓜(南瓜属)〔101 南瓜,102 笋瓜,103 瓠瓜〕	13		70	9/	0	千克	AB	PRQS	/48
	--其他:									
0709.9910	---竹笋									
0709.9910 10	鲜或冷藏的酸竹笋〔999〕	13		70	9/	0	千克	ABE	PRQS	/48
0709.9910 90	鲜或冷藏的其他竹笋〔999〕	13		70	9/	0	千克	AB	PRQS	/48
0709.9990	---其他									
0709.9990 01	鲜或冷藏的丝瓜〔999〕	13		70	9/	0	千克	AB	PRQS	/48
0709.9990 02	鲜或冷藏的青江菜〔999〕	13		70	9/	0	千克	AB	PRQS	/48
0709.9990 03	鲜或冷藏的小白菜〔999〕	13		70	9/	0	千克	AB	PRQS	/48
0709.9990 04	鲜或冷藏的苦瓜〔999〕	13		70	9/	0	千克	AB	PRQS	/48
0709.9990 05	鲜或冷藏的山葵〔999〕	13		70	9/	0	千克	AB	PRQS	/48
0709.9990 10	鲜或冷藏的莼菜〔999〕	13		70	9/	0	千克	ABE	PRQS	/48
0709.9990 90	鲜或冷藏的其他蔬菜[T2]	13		70	9/	0	千克	AB	PRQS	/48
07.10	**冷冻蔬菜(不论是否蒸煮):**									
0710.1000	-马铃薯〔999〕	13		70	9/	0,9	千克	AB	PRQS	/33
	-豆类、蔬菜,不论是否脱荚:									
0710.2100	--豌豆〔999〕	13		70	9/	0,9	千克	AB	PRQS	/48
	--豇豆属及菜豆属:									
0710.2210	---红小豆(赤豆)〔999〕	13		70	9/	0,6	千克	AB	PRQS	/18
0710.2290	---其他〔101 豇豆,102 菜豆〕	13		70	9/	0,9	千克	AB	PRQS	/33
0710.2900	--其他〔999〕	13		70	9/	0,9	千克	AB	PRQS	/48
0710.3000	-菠菜〔999〕	13		70	9/	0,9	千克	AB	PRQS	/48
0710.4000	-甜玉米〔999〕	10		70	9/	0,9	千克	AB	PRQS	/30
	-其他蔬菜:									
0710.8010	---松茸〔999〕	13		70	9/	0,9	千克	ABE	PRQS	/18
0710.8020	---蒜苔及蒜苗(青蒜)〔101 蒜苔,102 蒜苗,103 青蒜〕	13		70	9/	0,6	千克	AB	PRQS	/18
0710.8030	---蒜头〔999〕	13		70	9/	0,6	千克	AB	PRQS	/18
0710.8040	---牛肝菌〔999〕	13		70	9/	0,9	千克	AB	PRQS	/18
0710.8090	---其他									
0710.8090 10	冷冻的大蒜瓣(不论是否蒸煮)〔999〕	13		70	9/	0,9	千克	AB	PRQS	/33
0710.8090 20	冷冻的香菇(不论是否蒸煮)〔999〕	13		70	9/	0,9	千克	AB	PRQS	/33
0710.8090 30	冷冻莼菜(不论是否蒸煮)〔999〕	13		70	9/	0,9	千克	ABE	PRQS	/33
0710.8090 90	冷冻的未列名蔬菜(不论是否蒸煮)[T2]	13		70	9/	0,9	千克	AB	PRQS	/33
0710.9000	-什锦蔬菜〔999〕	10		70	9/	0,9	千克	AB	PRQS	/30
07.11	**暂时保藏(例如,使用二氧化硫气体、盐水、亚硫酸水或其他防腐液)的蔬菜,但不适于直接食用的:**									

协定税率 %										特惠税率 %			Article Description
亚太5国	东/冰/格	巴基斯坦	韩国	瑞士	哥达	秘鲁	澳大利亚	新西/坡/智	港/澳/台	亚太2国	老/柬/缅	36/3/1	
6.5	0/0/0	0	5.2	3.9	0	0	0	0//0	0/0/		0/0/	0/0/0	-Beans (*Vigna spp.*, *Phaseolus spp.*)
6.5	0/0/0	0	5.2	3.9	0	0	0	0//0	0/0/		/0/	0/0/0	-Other leguminous vegetables
													Other vegetables, fresh or chilled:
6.5	0/0/0	0	5.2	3.9	0	0	0	0//0	0/0/			0/0/0	-Asparagus
6.5	0/0/0	0	5.2	3.9	0	0	0	0//0	0/0/			0/0/0	-Aubergines (egg-plants)
	0/0/0	0	4	0	0	0	0	0//0	0/0/			0/0/0	-Celery, other than celeriac
													-Mushrooms and truffles:
	0/0/0	0	5.2	3.9	0	0	0	0//0	0/0/		/0/	0/0/0	--Mushrooms of the genus *Agaricus*
													--Other:
	0/0/0	0	5.2	3.9	0	0	0	0//0	0/0/		/0/	0/0/0	---Sungmo
	0/0/0	0	5.2	3.9	0	0	0	0//0	0/0/		/0/	0/0/0	---shiitake
	0/0/0	0	5.2	3.9	0	0	0	0//0	0/0/0		/0/	0/0/0	---Winter mushroom
	0/0/0	0	5.2	3.9	0	0	0	0//0	0/0/		/0/	0/0/0	---Paddy straw mushroom
	0/0/0	0	5.2	3.9	0	0	0	0//0	0/0/		/0/	0/0/0	---Tricholoma mongolicum Imai
	0/0/0	0	5.2	3.9	0	0	0	0//0	0/0/			0/0/	---Truffle
	0/0/0	0	5.2	3.9	0	0	0	0//0	0/0/		/0/	0/0/0	---Other
6.5	0/0/0	0	5.2	3.9	0	0	0	0//0	0/0/		/0/	0/0/0	-Fruits of the genus *Capsicum* or of the genus *Pimenta*
	0/0/0	0	5.2	3.9	0	0	0	0//0	0/0/			0/0/0	-Spinach, New Zealand spinach and orache spinach (garden spinach)
													-Other:
	0/0/0	0	5.2	3.9	0	0	0	0//0	0/0/		/0/	0/0/0	--Globe artichokes
	0/0/0	0	5.2	3.9	0	0	0	0//0	0/0/		/0/	0/0/0	--Olives
	0/0/0	0	5.2	3.9	0	0	0	0//0	0/0/		/0/	0/0/0	--Pumpkin, squash and gourd (cucurbita spp.)
													--Other:
													---Bamboo shoots
	0/0/0	0	5.2	3.9	0	0	0	0//0	0/0/		0/0/	0/0/0	Acidosasa shoots, fresh or chilled
	0/0/0	0	5.2	3.9	0	0	0	0//0	0/0/		0/0/	0/0/0	Other bamboo shoots, fresh or chilled
													---Other
	0/0/0	0	5.2	3.9	0	0	0	0//0	0/0/		/0/	0/0/0	Loofah, fresh or chilled
	0/0/0	0	5.2	3.9	0	0	0	0//0	0/0/		/0/	0/0/0	Bok choy, fresh or chilled
	0/0/0	0	5.2	3.9	0	0	0	0//0	0/0/		/0/	0/0/0	Pakchoi, fresh or chilled
	0/0/0	0	5.2	3.9	0	0	0	0//0	0/0/		/0/	0/0/0	Balsum pear, fresh or chilled
	0/0/0	0	5.2	3.9	0	0	0	0//0	0/0/		/0/	0/0/0	Horseradish, fresh or chilled
	0/0/0	0	5.2	3.9	0	0	0	0//0	0/0/		/0/	0/0/0	Water shield, fresh or chilled
	0/0/0	0	5.2	3.9	0	0	0	0//0	0/0/		/0/	0/0/0	Other vegetables, fresh or chilled
													Vegetables (uncooked or cooked by steaming or boiling in water), frozen:
	0//0	5.9	5.2	3.9	0	0	0	0//0	0/0/			0/0/	-Potatoes
													-Leguminous vegetables, shelled or unshelled:
	0/0/0	5.9	5.2	3.9	0	0	0	0//0	0/0/			0/0/	--Peas (*Pisum sativum*)
													--Beans (*Vigna spp.*, *Phaseolus spp.*):
	0/0/0	5.9	5.2	3.9	0	0	0	0//0	0/0/		/0/	0/0/0	---Small red (Adzuki) beans (*Phaseolus* or *Vigna angularis*)
	0/0/0	5.9	5.2	3.9	0	0	0	0//0	0/0/		/0/	0/0/0	---Other
	0/0/0	5.9	5.2	3.9	0	0	0	0//0	0/0/		/0/	0/0/0	--Other
	0/0/0	5.9	5.2	3.9	0	0	0	0//0	0/0/			0/0/	-Spinach, New Zealand spinach and orache spinach (garden spinach)
	0/0/0	4.5	4	0	0	0	0	0//0	0/0/			0/0/0	-Sweet corn
													-Other vegetables:
	0/0/0	5.9	5.2	3.9	0	0	0	0//0	0/0/		/0/	0/0/0	---Sungmo
	0/0/0	5.9	5.2	3.9	0	0	0	0//0	0/0/		/0/	0/0/0	---Garlic stems, garlic seedlings
	0/0/0	5.9	5.2	3.9	0	0	0	0//0	0/0/		/0/	0/0/0	---Garlic bulbs
	0/0/0	5.9	5.2	3.9	0	0	0	0//0	0/0/		/0/	0/0/0	---Boletus
													---Other
	0/0/0	5.9	5.2	3.9	0	0	0	0//0	0/0/		/0/	0/0/0	Garlic cloves, frozen (uncooked or cooked by steaming or boiling in water)
	0/0/0	5.9	5.2	3.9	0	0	0	0//0	0/0/		/0/	0/0/0	Shiitake, frozen (uncooked or cooked by steaming or boiling in water)
	0/0/0	5.9	5.2	3.9	0	0	0	0//0	0/0/		/0/	0/0/0	Water shield, frozen (uncooked or cooked by steaming or boiling in water)
	0/0/0	5.9	5.2	3.9	0	0	0	0//0	0/0/		/0/	0/0/0	Vegetables, frozen, not elsewhere specified or included (uncooked or cooked by steaming or boiling in water)
	0/0/0	4.5	4	0	0	0	0	0//0	0/0/		/0/	0/0/0	-Mixtures of vegetables
													Vegetables provisionally preserved (for example, by sulphur dioxide gas, in brine, in suphur water or in other preservative solutions), but unsuitable in that state for immediate consumption:

税则号列	货品名称〔CIQ扩展编码及品名—T2表示见附表2〕	最惠(%)	暂定税率	普通	增值/消费	出口退税	计量单位	监管条件	检验检疫	特殊证件对美关税
0711.2000	-油橄榄〔999〕	13		70	9/	6	千克	AB	PRQS	/18
0711.4000	-黄瓜及小黄瓜〔999〕	13		70	9/	9	千克	AB	PRQS	/18
	-蘑菇及块菌：									
	--伞菌属蘑菇：									
	---盐水的：									
0711.5112	----白蘑菇〔999〕	13		90	9/	9	千克	AB	PRQS	/18
0711.5119	----其他〔101 腌渍草菇，102 腌渍姬菇，103 腌渍口蘑，104 腌渍其他食用菌〕	13		90	9/	9	千克	AB	PRQS	/18
0711.5190	---其他〔101 腌渍草菇，102 腌渍姬菇，103 腌渍口蘑，104 腌渍其他食用菌〕	13		90	9/	9	千克	AB	PRQS	/18
	--其他：									
	---盐水的：									
0711.5911	----松茸〔999〕	13		90	9/	9	千克	EAB	PRQS	/18
0711.5919	----其他									
0711.5919 10	盐水的香菇(不适于直接食用的)〔999〕	13		90	9/	9	千克	AB	PRQS	/18
0711.5919 90	盐水的其他非伞菌属蘑菇及块菌(不适于直接食用的)〔101 腌渍牛肝菌，102 腌渍其他块菌〕	13		90	9/	9	千克	AB	PRQS	/18
0711.5990	---其他									
0711.5990 10	暂时保藏的香菇(用二氧化硫气体等物质处理，但不适于直接食用的)〔999〕	13		90	9/	6	千克	AB	PRQS	/18
0711.5990 90	暂时保藏的蘑菇及块菌(用二氧化硫气体等物质处理，但不适于直接食用的)〔101 腌渍蘑菇，102 腌渍其他块菌〕	13		90	9/	6	千克	AB	PRQS	/18
	-其他蔬菜；什锦蔬菜：									
	--盐水的：									
0711.9031	----竹笋									
0711.9031 10	盐水酸竹笋(不适于直接食用的)〔999〕	13		70	9/	6	千克	ABE	PRQS	/18
0711.9031 90	其他盐水竹笋(不适于直接食用的)〔999〕	13		70	9/	6	千克	AB	PRQS	/18
0711.9034	----大蒜									
0711.9034 10	盐水简单腌制的大蒜头、大蒜瓣(无论是否去皮，但不适于直接食用)〔999〕	13		70	9/	6	千克	AB	PRQS	/18
0711.9034 90	盐水简单腌制的其他大蒜(不含蒜头、蒜瓣，无论是否去皮，但不适于直接食用)〔999〕	13		70	9/	6	千克	AB	PRQS	/18
0711.9039	----其他[T2]	13		70	9/	6	千克	AB	PRQS	/18
0711.9090	---其他[T2]	13		90	9/	9	千克	AB	PRQS	/18
07.12	**干蔬菜，整个、切块、切片、破碎或制成粉状，但未经进一步加工的：**									
0712.2000	-洋葱〔999〕	13		80	9/	0,9	千克	AB	PRQS	/48
	-蘑菇、木耳、银耳及块菌：									
0712.3100	--伞菌属蘑菇〔101 脱水杏鲍菇，102 脱水姬菇，103 脱水秀珍菇，104 脱水姬松茸〕	13		80	9/	0,9	千克	AB	PRQS	/48
0712.3200	--木耳〔999〕	13		100	9/	0,9,13	千克	AB	PRQS	/48
0712.3300	--银耳〔999〕	13		90	9/	0,9,13	千克	AB	PRQS	/48
	--其他：									
0712.3910	---香菇〔999〕	13		100	9/	0,9,13	千克	AB	PRQS	/48
0712.3920	---金针菇〔999〕	13		100	9/	0,9	千克	AB	PRQS	/48
0712.3950	---牛肝菌〔999〕	13		100	9/	0,9	千克	AB	PRQS	/48
	---其他：									
0712.3991	----羊肚菌〔999〕	13		100	9/	0,9	千克	AB	PRQS	/48
0712.3999	----其他									
0712.3999 10	干制松茸(整个，切块，切片，破碎或制成粉状，但未经进一步加工的)〔999〕	13		100	9/	0,9	千克	ABE	PRQS	/48
0712.3999 90	其他干制蘑菇及块菌(整个，切块，切片，破碎或制成粉状，但未经进一步加工的)〔101 脱水蘑菇，102 脱水猴头菇，103 脱水平菇，104 脱水其他块菌，105 脱水竹荪，106 脱水其他食用菌，107 干制榛蘑〕	13		100	9/	0,9	千克	AB	PRQS	/48
	-其他蔬菜；什锦蔬菜：									
0712.9010	---笋干丝									
0712.9010 10	酸竹笋干丝〔999〕	13		80	9/	0	千克	ABE	PRQS	/48
0712.9010 90	其他笋干丝〔999〕	13		80	9/	0	千克	AB	PRQS	/48

协定税率 %										特惠税率 %			Article Description
亚太5国	东/冰/格	巴基斯坦	韩国	瑞士	哥达	秘鲁	澳大利亚	新西/坡/智	港/澳/台	亚太2国	老/柬/缅	36/3/1	
	0/0/0	0	5.2	3.9	0	0	0	0//0	0/0/			0/0/	-Olives
	0/0/0	0	5.2	3.9	0	0	0	0//0	0/0/			0/0/	-Cucumbers and gherkins
													-Mushrooms and truffles:
													--Mushrooms of the genus *Agaricus*:
													---In brine:
	0/0/0	0	5.2	3.9	0	0	0	0//0	0/0/			0/0/	----White mushroom
	0/0/0	0	5.2	3.9	0	0	0	0//0	0/0/			0/0/	----Other
	0/0/0	0	5.2	3.9	0	0	0	0//0	0/0/			0/0/	---Other
													--Other:
													---In brine:
	0/0/0	0	5.2	3.9	0	0	0	0//0	0/0/			0/0/	----Sungmo
													----Other
	0/0/0	0	5.2	3.9	0	0	0	0//0	0/0/			0/0/	Shiitake, in brine(unsuitable in that state for immediate consumption)
	0/0/0	0	5.2	3.9	0	0	0	0//0	0/0/			0/0/	Other mushroom except the genus *Agaricus* and truffles, in brine, (unsuitable in that state for immediate consumption)
													---Other
	0/0/0	0	5.2	3.9	0	0	0	0//0	0/0/			0/0/	Shiitake, provisionally preserved(by sulphur dioxide gas, or other wise prepared, but unsuitable in that state for immediate consumption)
	0/0/0	0	5.2	3.9	0	0	0	0//0	0/0/			0/0/	Mushrooms and truffles(by sulphur dioxide gas or other wise prepared, but unsuitable in that state for immediate consumption)
													-Other vegetables; mixtures of vegetables:
													---In brine:
													----Bamboo shoots
6.5	0/0/0	0	5.2	3.9	0	0	0	0//0	0/0/			0/0/	Acidosasa chinensis shoots, in brine(unsuitable in that state for immediate consumption)
6.5	0/0/0	0	5.2	3.9	0	0	0	0//0	0/0/			0/0/	Other bamboo shoots, in brine(unsuitable in that state for immediate consumption)
													----Garlic
6.5	0/0/0	0	5.2	3.9	0	0	0	0//0	0/0/			0/0/	Garlic bulbs and garlic cloves, in brine(but unsuitable in that state for immediate consumption, whether skinned or not)
6.5	0/0/0	0	5.2	3.9	0	0	0	0//0	0/0/			0/0/	Other garlic in brine (other than garlic bulbs, garlic cloves, whether or not skinned, but unsuitable in that state for immediate consumption)
6.5	0/0/0	0	5.2	3.9	0	0	0	0//0	0/0/			0/0/	----Other
6.5	0/0/0	0	5.2	3.9	0	0	0	0//0	0/0/			0/0/	---Other
													Dried vegetables, whole, cut, sliced, broken or in powder, but not further prepared:
	0/0/0	5.9	5.2	3.9	0	0	0	0//0	0/0/			0/0/0	-Onions
													-Mushrooms, wood ears(*Auricularia spp.*), jelly fungi(*Tremella spp.*) and truffles:
9	0/0/0	4.5	5.2	3.9	0	0	0	0//0	0/0/			0/0/0	--Mushrooms of the genus *Agaricus*
	0/0/0	5.9	5.2	3.9	0	0	0	0//0	0/0/			0/0/	--Wood ears(*Auricularia spp.*)
	0/0/0	5.9	5.2	3.9	0	0	0	0//0	0/0/			0/0/	--Jelly fungi (*Tremella spp.*)
													--Other:
9	0/0/0	4.5	5.2	3.9	0	0	0	0//0	0/0/			0/0/	---Shiitake
9	0/0/0	4.5	5.2	3.9	0	0	0	0//0	0/0/			0/0/	---Winter mushroom
9	0/0/0	4.5	5.2	3.9	0	0	0	0//0	0/0/			0/0/	---Boletus
													---Other:
9	0/0/0	9	5.2	3.9	0	0	0	0//0	0/0/			0/0/	----Toadsiool
													----Other
9	0/0/0	9	5.2	3.9	0	0	0	0//0	0/0/			0/0/	Dried sungmo (whole, cut, sliced, broken or in powder, but not further prepared)
9	0/0/0	9	5.2	3.9	0	0	0	0//0	0/0/			0/0/	Other dried Mushrooms and truffles (whole, cut, sliced, broken or in powder, but not further prepared)
													-Other vegetables; mixtures of vegetables:
													---Bamboo shoots
	0/0/0	5.9	5.2	3.9	0	0	0	0//0	0/0/			0/0/0	Dried acidosasa chinensis shoots
	0/0/0	5.9	5.2	3.9	0	0	0	0//0	0/0/			0/0/0	Other bamboo shoots

税则号列	货品名称〔CIQ 扩展编码及品名—T2 表示见附表 2〕	最惠(%)	暂定税率	普通	增值/消费	出口退税	计量单位	监管条件	检验检疫	特殊证件对美关税
0712.9020	---紫萁(薇菜干)〔999〕	13		80	9/	0,6	千克	AB	PRQS	/48
0712.9030	---金针菜(黄花菜)〔999〕	13		80	9/	0,6	千克	AB	PRQS	/48
0712.9040	---蕨菜〔999〕	13		80	9/	0,6	千克	AB	PRQS	/48
0712.9050	---大蒜									
0712.9050 10	干燥或脱水的大蒜头、大蒜瓣(无论是否去皮)〔999〕	13		80	13/	0	千克	AB	PRQS	/48
0712.9050 90	干燥或脱水的其他大蒜(不含蒜头、蒜瓣,无论是否去皮)〔999〕	13		80	13/	0,9,13	千克	AB	PRQS	/48
	---其他:									
0712.9091	----辣根〔999〕	13		80	9/	0,6,13	千克	AB	PRQS	/48
0712.9099	----其他									
0712.9099 10	干莼菜(整个、切块、切片、破碎或制成粉状,但未经进一步加工的)〔999〕	13		80	9/	0,9	千克	ABE	PRQS	/48
0712.9099 90	干制的其他蔬菜及什锦蔬菜(整个、切块、切片、破碎或制成粉状,但未经进一步加工的)〔T2〕	13		80	9/	0,9,13	千克	AB	PRQS	/48
07.13	**脱荚的干豆,不论是否去皮或分瓣:**									
	-豌豆:									
0713.1010	---种用〔999〕	0		0	9/	0	千克	AB	PNQ	/25
0713.1090	---其他〔101 食用,102 饲用〕	5		20	9/	0	千克	AB	PRQS	/35
	-鹰嘴豆:									
0713.2010	---种用〔999〕	0		0	9/	9	千克	AB	PNQ	/25
0713.2090	---其他〔999〕	7		20	9/	9	千克	AB	PRQS	/37
	-豇豆属及菜豆属:									
	--绿豆:									
0713.3110	---种用〔999〕	0		0	9/	9	千克	AB	PNQ	/25
0713.3190	---其他〔999〕	3		11	9/	9	千克	AB	PRQS	/33
	--红小豆(赤豆):									
0713.3210	---种用〔999〕	0		0	9/	9	千克	AB	PNQ	/25
0713.3290	---其他〔101 干赤豆,102 药用赤小豆〕	3		14	9/	9	千克	AB	PRQS	/33
	--芸豆:									
0713.3310	---种用〔999〕	0		0	9/	0	千克	AB	PNQ	/25
0713.3390	---其他〔999〕	7.5		20	9/	0	千克	AB	PRQS	/42.5
0713.3400	--巴姆巴拉豆〔999〕	7		20	9/	9	千克	AB	PRQS	/37
0713.3500	--牛豆(豇豆)〔101 豇豆,102 脱水豇豆〕	7		20	9/	9	千克	AB	PRQS	/37
0713.3900	--其他〔101 豇豆,102 脱水豇豆,103 脱水菜豆〕	7		20	9/	0	千克	AB	PRQS	/37
	-扁豆:									
0713.4010	---种用〔999〕	0		0	9/	0	千克	AB	PNQ	/25
0713.4090	---其他〔101 干扁豆,102 药用白扁豆〕	7		20	9/	0	千克	AB	PRQS	/37
	-蚕豆:									
0713.5010	---种用〔999〕	0		0	9/	9	千克	AB	PNQ	/25
0713.5090	---其他〔999〕	7		20	9/	9	千克	AB	PRQS	/37
	-木豆(木豆属):									
0713.6010	---种用〔999〕	0		0	9/	6	千克	AB	PNQ	/25
0713.6090	---其他〔999〕	7		20	9/	9	千克	AB	PRQS	/37
	-其他:									
0713.9010	---种用干豆〔999〕	0		0	9/	0	千克	AB	PNQ	/25
0713.9090	---其他〔101 其他实用豆类,102 药用黑豆,103 红腰豆,104 角豆,105 眉豆,106 饭豆,107 黑豆,108 竹豆,109 珍珠豆,110 白豆,111 瓜尔豆〕	7		20	9/	0,9	千克	AB	PRQS	/37
07.14	**鲜、冷、冻或干的木薯、竹芋、兰科植物块茎、菊芋、甘薯及含有高淀粉或菊粉的类似根茎,不论是否切片或制成团粒;西谷茎髓:**									
	-木薯:									
0714.1010	---鲜的〔999〕	10		30	9/	9	千克	AB7	PRQS	/40
0714.1020	---干的〔101 饲用,102 食品加工,103 工业用〕	5		30	9/	9	千克	AB7	PRQS	/30
0714.1030	---冷或冻的〔999〕	10		80	9/	9	千克	AB7	PRQ	/15
	-甘薯:									
	---鲜的:									
0714.2011	----种用〔999〕	0		50	9/	0	千克	AB	PQ	/25
0714.2019	----其他〔999〕	13		50	9/	0	千克	AB	PRQS	/48
0714.2020	---干的〔999〕	13		50	9/	0	千克	AB	PRQS	/48
0714.2030	---冷或冻的〔101 冷藏甘薯,102 冻藏甘薯〕	13		80	9/	0	千克	AB	PRQS	/43

协定税率 %										特惠税率 %			
亚太5国	东/冰/格	巴基斯坦	韩国	瑞士	哥达	秘鲁	澳大利亚	新西/坡/智	港/澳/台	亚太2国	老/柬/缅	36/3/1	Article Description
	0/0/0	5.9	5.2	3.9	0	0	0	0//0	0/0/			0/0/	---Osmund
	0/0/0	5.9	5.2	3.9	0	0	0	0//0	0/0/			0/0/	---Day lily flowers
	0/0/0	5.9	5.2	3.9	0	0	0	0//0	0/0/			0/0/	---Wild brake
													---Garlic
	0/0/0	5.9	5.2	3.9	0	0	0	0//0	0/0/			0/0/	Dried or dewatered garlic bulbs or garlic cloves (whether or not skinned)
	0/0/0	5.9	5.2	3.9	0	0	0	0//0	0/0/			0/0/	Other dried or dewatered garlic (other than garlic bulbs garlic cloves, whether or not skinned)
													---Other:
	0/0/0	5.9	5.2	3.9	0	0	0	0//0	0/0/			0/0/0	----Cochlearia
													----Other
	0/0/0	5.9	5.2	3.9	0	0	0	0//0	0/0/			0/0/0	Dried water shield (whole, cut, sliced, broken or in powder, but not further prepared)
	0/0/0	5.9	5.2	3.9	0	0	0	0//0	0/0/			0/0/0	Other dried vegetable and mixtures of vegetables (whole, cut, sliced, broken or in powder, but not further prepared)
													Dried leguminous vegetables, shelled, whether or not skinned or split:
													-Peas (*Pisum sativum*):
												0/0/0	---Seed
	0/0/0	0	0	0	0	0	0	0//0	0/0/			0/0/0	---Other
													-Chickpeas (garbanzos):
												0/0/0	---Seed
	0/0/0	4	0	0	0	0	0	0//0	0/0/			0/0/0	---Other
													-Vigna and lunatus:
													--Beans of the species *Vigna mungo* (*L.*) *Hepper or Vigna radiata* (*L.*) *Wilczek*:
												0/0/0	---Seed
1.5	0/0/0	0	0	0	0	0	0	0//0	0/0/		/0/0	0/0/0	---Other
													--Small red (Adzuki) beans (*Phaseolus* or *Vigna angularis*):
												0/0/0	---Seed
	0/0/0	0	0	0	0	0	0	0//0	0/0/		/0/	0/0/0	---Other
													--Kidney beans, including white pea-beans (*Phaseolus vulgaris*):
												0/0/0	---Seed
	0/0/0	4	0	0	0	0	0	0//0	0/0/		/0/	0/0/0	---Other
3.5	0/0/0	0	0	0	0	0	0	0//0	0/0/		/0/	0/0/0	--Bambara beans (Vigna subterranea or Voandzeia subterranea)
3.5	0/0/0	0	0	0	0	0	0	0//0	0/0/		/0/	0/0/0	--Cow peas (Vigna unguiculata)
3.5	0/0/0	0	0	0	0	0	0	0//0	0/0/		/0/	0/0/0	--Other
													-Lentils:
												0/0/0	---Seed
	0/0/0	4	0	0	0	0	0	0//0	0/0/			0/0/0	---Other
													-Broad beans (*Vicia faba var. Major*) and horse beans (*Vicia faba var. equina*, *Vicia faba var. minor*):
												0/0/0	---Seed
	0/0/0	4	0	0	0	0	0	0//0	0/0/			0/0/0	---Other
													-Pigeon peas (Cajanus cajan):
												0/0/0	---For cultivation
	0/0/0	4	0	0	0	0	0	0//0	0/0/			0/0/0	---Other
													-Other:
												0/0/0	---Seed
	0/0/0	5	0	0	0	0	0	0//0	0/0/			0/0/0	---Other
													Manioc, arrowroot, salep, Jerusalem artichokes, sweet potatoes and similar roots and tubers with high starch or inulin content, fresh, chilled, frozen or dried, whether or not sliced or in the form of pellets; sago pith:
													-Manioc (cassava):
	0/0/0	4.5	0	0	0	0	0	0//0	0/0/		0/0/	0/0/0	---Fresh
	0/0/0	0	0	0	0	0	0	0//0	0/0/		0/0/	0/0/0	---Dried
	0/0/0	4.5	4	0	0	0	0	0//0	0/0/		0/0/	0/0/0	---Chilled or frozen
													-Sweet potatoes:
													---Fresh:
											0/0/	0/0/0	----For Cultivation
6.5	0/0/0	4.5	5.2	3.9	0	0	0	0//0	0/0/		0/0/	0/0/0	----Other
6.5	0/0/0	4.5	5.2	3.9	0	0	0	0//0	0/0/		0/0/	0/0/0	---Dried
6.5	0/0/0	4.5	5.2	3.9	0	0	0	0//0	0/0/		0/0/	0/0/0	---Chilled or frozen

税则号列		货品名称〔CIQ扩展编码及品名—T2表示见附表2〕	最惠(%)	暂定税率	普通	增值/消费	出口退税	计量单位	监管条件	检验检疫	特殊证件对美关税
0714.3000		-山药〔101鲜、冷的山药,102冷冻山药,103脱水山药,104药用山药〕	13		50	9/	0	千克	AB	PRQ	/48
0714.4000		-芋头(芋属)									
0714.4000	01	鲜、冷的芋头(芋属)(不论是否切片或制成团粒;芋头又称芋艿,为天南星科芋属植物,分旱芋、水芋)〔999〕	13		50	9/	0	千克	AB	PRQ	/48
0714.4000	90	冻、干的芋头(芋属)(不论是否切片或制成团粒;芋头又称芋艿,为天南星科芋属植物,分旱芋、水芋)〔101冷冻芋头,102脱水芋头〕	13		50	9/	0	千克	AB	PRQ	/48
0714.5000		-箭叶黄体芋(黄肉芋属)〔101鲜、冷箭叶黄体芋,102冷冻箭叶黄体芋,103脱水箭叶黄体芋〕	13		50	9/	9	千克	AB	PRQ	/48
		-其他:									
0714.9010		---荸荠〔101鲜、冷的马蹄(荸荠),102冷冻马蹄(荸荠),103脱水马蹄(荸荠)〕	13		50	9/	0	千克	AB	PRQS	/48
		---藕:									
0714.9021		----种用〔999〕	0		0	9/	0	千克	AB	PNQ	/25
0714.9029		----其他〔101鲜、冷的莲藕,102冷冻莲藕,103脱水莲藕〕	13		50	9/	0	千克	AB	PRQS	/48
0714.9090		---其他									
0714.9090	10	鲜、冷、冻、干的兰科植物块茎〔999〕	13		50	9/	0	千克	ABFE	PRQ	/48
0714.9090	91	含高淀粉或菊粉其他濒危类似根茎(包括西谷茎髓,不论是否切片或制成团粒,鲜、冷、冻或干的)〔999包括西谷茎髓,不论是否切片或制成团粒,鲜、冷、冻或干的,101鲜、冷的,102冷冻的,103干的,104腌渍的,105其他鳞球块根茎〕	13		50	9/	0	千克	ABFE	PRQ	/48
0714.9090	99	含有高淀粉或菊粉的其他类似根茎(包括西谷茎髓,不论是否切片或制成团粒,鲜、冷、冻或干的)〔999包括西谷茎髓,不论是否切片或制成团粒,鲜、冷、冻或干的,101鲜、冷的,102冷冻的,103干的,104腌渍的,105其他鳞球块根茎〕	13		50	9/	0	千克	AB	PRQ	/48

协定税率 %										特惠税率 %			
亚太5国	东/冰/格	巴基斯坦	韩国	瑞士	哥达	秘鲁	澳大利亚	新西/坡/智	港/澳/台	亚太2国	老/柬/缅	36/3/1	Article Description
6.5	0/0/0	4.5	5.2	3.9	0	0	0	0//0	0/0/		0/0/	0/0/0	-Yams(*dioscoreae spp.*)
													-Taros(*colocasia spp.*)
6.5	0/0/0	4.5	5.2	3.9	0	0	0	0//0	0/0/			0/0/	Fresh, chilled taros(colocasia spp.)(whether or not sliced or made granule; taros are also called yunai belong to Spath hyttum of the Araceae vegetables, classified into ground taros and river taros)
6.5	0/0/0	4.5	5.2	3.9	0	0	0	0//0	0/0/			0/0/	Frozen, dried taros(colocasia spp.)(whether or not sliced or made granule; taros are also called yunai belong to Spath hyttum of the Araceae vegetables, classified into ground taros and river taros)
6.5	0/0/0	4.5	5.2	3.9	0	0	0	0//0	0/0/		0/0/	0/0/0	-Yautia(Xanthosoma spp.)
													-Other:
6.5	0/0/0	4.5	5.2	3.9	0	0	0	0//0	0/0/		0/0/	0/0/0	---Water chestnut
													---Lotus(*Nelumbo nucifera*) rootstock:
												0/0/0	----For cultivation
6.5	0/0/0	4.5	5.2	3.9	0	0	0	0//0	0/0/		0/0/	0/0/0	----Other
													---Other
6.5	0/0/0	4.5	5.2	3.9	0	0	0	0//0	0/0/		0/0/	0/0/0	Tubers of orchid family, fresh, chilled, frozen or dried
6.5	0/0/0	4.5	5.2	3.9	0	0	0	0//0	0/0/		0/0/	0/0/0	Other endangered similar roots and tubers with high starch or inulin content(including sago pith, whether or not sliced or made gramule, fresh, chilled, frozen, dried)
6.5	0/0/0	4.5	5.2	3.9	0	0	0	0//0	0/0/		0/0/	0/0/0	Other similar roots and tubers with high starch or inulin content(including sago pith whether or not sliced or in the form of pellets fresh, chilled, frozen, dried)

第八章
食用水果及坚果;
柑橘属水果或甜瓜的果皮

注释:

一、本章不包括非供食用的坚果或水果。

二、冷藏的水果和坚果应按相应的鲜果税目归类。

三、本章的干果可以部分复水或为下列目的进行其他处理,但必须保持干果的特征。

(一)为保藏或保持其稳定性(例如,经适度热处理或硫化处理、添加山梨酸或山梨酸钾);

(二)为改进或保持其外观(例如,添加植物油或少量葡萄糖浆)。

税则号列	货品名称〔CIQ 扩展编码及品名－T2 表示见附表 2〕	最惠(%)	暂定税率	普通	增值/消费	出口退税	计量单位	监管条件	检验检疫	特殊证件对美关税
08.01	**鲜或干的椰子、巴西果及腰果,不论是否去壳或去皮:**									
	-椰子:									
0801.1100	--干的〔101 坚果,102 蜜饯〕	12	7	80	9/	9	千克	AB	PRQS	/57
0801.1200	--未去内壳(内果皮)〔101 椰青,102 加工用去皮老椰子,103 椰青和加工用去皮老椰子除外〕	12		80	9/	9	千克	AB	PRQS	/62
	--其他:									
0801.1910	---种用〔999〕	0		0	9/	9	千克	AB	PQN	/25
0801.1990	---其他〔999〕	12		80	9/	9	千克	AB	PRQS	/62
	-巴西果:									
0801.2100	--未去壳〔101 提取(晒干的除外)、压榨、烹制、烘焙、冻干、脱水、裹糖屑、发酵、冷冻(经漂汤和杀青,并在－18 度以下冷冻)、浸酸、腌渍、炒制等工艺进行加工处理的,102 其他工艺〕	10	7	80	9/	6	千克	AB	PRQ	/57
0801.2200	--去壳〔101 提取(晒干的除外)、压榨、烹制、烘焙、冻干、脱水、裹糖屑、发酵、冷冻(经漂汤和杀青,并在－18 度以下冷冻)、浸酸、腌渍、炒制等工艺进行加工处理的,102 其他工艺〕	10	7	80	9/	6	千克	AB	PRQ	/57
	-腰果:									
0801.3100	--未去壳〔101 提取(晒干的除外)、压榨、烹制、烘焙、冻干、脱水、裹糖屑、发酵、冷冻(经漂汤和杀青,并在－18 度以下冷冻)、浸酸、腌渍、炒制等工艺进行加工处理的,102 其他工艺〕	20	7	70	9/	9	千克	AB	PRQS	/57
0801.3200	--去壳〔101 提取(晒干的除外)、压榨、烹制、烘焙、冻干、脱水、裹糖屑、发酵、冷冻(经漂汤和杀青,并在－18 度以下冷冻)、浸酸、腌渍、炒制等工艺进行加工处理的,102 其他工艺〕	10	7	70	9/	9	千克	AB	PRQS	/57
08.02	**鲜或干的其他坚果,不论是否去壳或去皮:**									
	-扁桃核及仁:									
0802.1100	--未去壳〔101 提取(晒干的除外)、压榨、烹制、烘焙、冻干、脱水、裹糖屑、发酵、冷冻(经漂汤和杀青,并在－18 度以下冷冻)、浸酸、腌渍、炒制等工艺进行加工处理的,102 其他工艺〕	24	10	70	9/	9	千克	AB	PRQS	/60
0802.1200	--去壳〔101 提取(晒干的除外)、压榨、烹制、烘焙、冻干、脱水、裹糖屑、发酵、冷冻(经漂汤和杀青,并在－18 度以下冷冻)、浸酸、腌渍、炒制等工艺进行加工处理的,102 其他工艺〕	10		70	9/	9	千克	AB	PRQS	/60
	-榛子:									
0802.2100	--未去壳〔101 提取(晒干的除外)、压榨、烹制、烘焙、冻干、脱水、裹糖屑、发酵、冷冻(经漂汤和杀青,并在－18 度以下冷冻)、浸酸、腌渍、炒制等工艺进行加工处理的,102 其他工艺〕	25		70	9/	6	千克	AB	PRQS	/65
0802.2200	--去壳〔101 提取(晒干的除外)、压榨、烹制、烘焙、冻干、脱水、裹糖屑、发酵、冷冻(经漂汤和杀青,并在－18 度以下冷冻)、浸酸、腌渍、炒制等工艺进行加工处理的,102 其他工艺〕	10		70	9/	9	千克	AB	PRQS	/60
	-核桃:									
0802.3100	--未去壳〔101 提取(晒干的除外)、压榨、烹制、烘焙、冻干、脱水、裹糖屑、发酵、冷冻(经漂汤和杀青,并在－18 度以下冷冻)、浸酸、腌渍、炒制等工艺进行加工处理的,102 其他工艺〕	25		70	9/	9	千克	AB	PRQS	/75
0802.3200	--去壳〔101 提取(晒干的除外)、压榨、烹制、烘焙、冻干、脱水、裹糖屑、发酵、冷冻(经漂汤和杀青,并在－18 度以下冷冻)、浸酸、腌渍、炒制等工艺进行加工处理的,102 其他工艺〕	20		70	9/	9	千克	AB	PRQS	/70
	-栗子:									
	--未去壳:									
0802.4110	---板栗〔101 提取(晒干的除外)、压榨、烹制、烘焙、冻干、脱水、裹糖屑、发酵、冷冻(经漂汤和杀青,并在－18 度以下冷冻)、浸酸、腌渍、炒制等工艺进行加工处理的,102 其他工艺〕	25		70	9/	9	千克	AB	PRQS	/75

Chapter 8
Edible fruit and nuts; peel of citrus fruit or melons

Notes:

1. This Chapter does not cover inedible nuts or fruits.
2. Chilled fruits and nuts are to be classified in the same headings as the corresponding fresh fruits and nuts.
3. Dried fruit or dried nuts of this Chapter may be partially rehydrated, or treated for the following purposes, provided that they retain the character of dried fruit or dried nuts.
   (a) For additional preservation or stabilization (for example, bymoderate heat treatment, sulphuring, the addition of sorbic acid or potassium sorbate).
   (b) To improve or maintain their appearance (for example., bythe addition of vegetable oil or small quantities of glucose syrup),

协定税率 %										特惠税率 %			
亚太5国	东/冰/格	巴基斯坦	韩国	瑞士	哥达	秘鲁	澳大利亚	新西/坡/智	港/澳/台	亚太2国	老/柬/缅	36/3/1	Article Description
													Coconuts, Brazil nuts and cashew- nuts, fresh or dried, whether or not shelled or peeled:
													-Coconuts:
6	0/0/0	4.5	0	3.6	4	0	0	0//0	0/0/		/0/	0/0/0	--Desiccated
6	0/0/0	4.5	0	3.6	4	0	0	0//0	0/0/		/0/	0/0/0	--In the inner shell(endocarp)
													--Other:
												0/0/0	---Seedlings
6	0/0/0	4.5	0	3.6	4	0	0	0//0	0/0/		/0/	0/0/0	---Other
													-Brazil nuts:
	0/0/0	4.5	0	0	3.3	0	0	0//0	0/0/			0/0/0	--In shell
	0/0/0	4.5	0	0	3.3	0	0	0//0	0/0/			0/0/0	--Shelled
													-Cashew nuts:
	0/0/0		8	6	6.7	0	0	0//0	0/0/		/0/	0/0/0	--In shell
	0/0/0	4.5	4	0	3.3	0	0	0//0	0/0/		/0/0	0/0/0	--Shelled
													Other nuts, fresh or dried, whether or not shelled or peeled:
													-semen amygdalae:
	0/0/0		9.6	7.2	8	0	0	0//0	0/0/			0/0/	--In shell
	0/0/0	4.5	4	0	3.3	0	0	0//0	0/0/			0/0/0	--Shelled
													-Hazelnuts or filberts (*Corylus spp.*):
	0/0/0		17.5	7.5	8.3	0	0	0//0	0/0/			0/0/	--In shell
	0/0/0	4.5	4	0	3.3	0	0	0//0	0/0/			0/0/0	--Shelled
													-Walnuts:
	0/0/0		17.5	7.5	8.3	0	0	0//0	0/0/			0/0/	--In shell
	0/0/0		12	6	6.7	0	0	0//0	0/0/			0/0/	--Shelled
													-Chestnuts (*Castanea spp.*):
													-In shell:
	0/0/0			7.5	8.3	0	0	0//0	0/0/			0/0/	---Chinese chestnuts

税则号列		货品名称〔CIQ扩展编码及品名—T2表示见附表2〕	最惠(%)	暂定税率	普通	增值/消费	出口退税	计量单位	监管条件	检验检疫	特殊证件对美关税
0802.4190		---其他〔101 栗子(板栗除外)(提取(晒干的除外)、压榨、烹制、烘焙、冻干、脱水、裹糖屑、发酵、冷冻(经漂汤和杀青,并在-18度以下冷冻)、浸酸、腌渍、炒制等工艺进行加工处理的),102 栗子(不论是否去壳或去皮)(其他工艺)〕	25	20	70	9/	9	千克	AB	PRQS	/55
		--去壳:									
0802.4210		---板栗〔101 板栗(提取(晒干的除外)、压榨、烹制、烘焙、冻干、脱水、裹糖屑、发酵、冷冻(经漂汤和杀青,并在-18度以下冷冻)、浸酸、腌渍、炒制等工艺进行加工处理的),102 板栗(其他工艺)〕	25		70	9/	9	千克	AB	PRQS	/60
0802.4290		---其他〔101 栗子(板栗除外)(提取(晒干的除外)、压榨、烹制、烘焙、冻干、脱水、裹糖屑、发酵、冷冻(经漂汤和杀青,并在-18度以下冷冻)、浸酸、腌渍、炒制等工艺进行加工处理的),102 栗子(板栗除外)(其他工艺)〕	25	20	70	9/	6	千克	AB	PRQS	/70
		-阿月浑子果(开心果):									
0802.5100		--未去壳〔101 提取(晒干的除外)、压榨、烹制、烘焙、冻干、脱水、裹糖屑、发酵、冷冻(经漂汤和杀青,并在-18度以下冷冻)、浸酸、腌渍、炒制等工艺进行加工处理的,102 其他工艺〕	10	5	70	9/	9	千克	AB	PRQS	/55
0802.5200		--去壳〔101 提取(晒干的除外)、压榨、烹制、烘焙、冻干、脱水、裹糖屑、发酵、冷冻(经漂汤和杀青,并在-18度以下冷冻)、浸酸、腌渍、炒制等工艺进行加工处理的,102 其他工艺〕	10	5	70	9/	9	千克	AB	PRQS	/55
		-马卡达姆坚果(夏威夷果):									
		--未去壳:									
0802.6110		---种用〔999〕	0		70	9/	6	千克	AB	PQ	/25
0802.6190		---其他〔101 提取(晒干的除外)、压榨、烹制、烘焙、冻干、脱水、裹糖屑、发酵、冷冻(经漂汤和杀青,并在-18度以下冷冻)、浸酸、腌渍、炒制等工艺进行加工处理的,102 其他工艺〕	24	12	70	9/	6	千克	AB	PRQS	/62
0802.6200		--去壳〔101 提取(晒干的除外)、压榨、烹制、烘焙、冻干、脱水、裹糖屑、发酵、冷冻(经漂汤和杀青,并在-18度以下冷冻)、浸酸、腌渍、炒制等工艺进行加工处理的,102 其他工艺〕	24	12	70	9/	9	千克	AB	PRQS	/62
0802.7000		-可乐果(可乐果属)〔101 提取(晒干的除外)、压榨、烹制、烘焙、冻干、脱水、裹糖屑、发酵、冷冻(经漂汤和杀青,并在-18度以下冷冻)、浸酸、腌渍、炒制等工艺进行加工处理的,102 其他工艺〕	24		70	9/	6	千克	AB	PRQS	/59
0802.8000		-槟榔果									
0802.8000	01	鲜的槟榔果(不论是否去壳或去皮)〔999〕	10		30	9/	6	千克	AB	PRQS	/60
0802.8000	90	干的槟榔果(不论是否去壳或去皮)〔101 其他工艺,102 其他蜜饯,103 提取(晒干的除外)、压榨、烹制、烘焙、冻干、脱水、裹糖屑、发酵、冷冻(经漂汤和杀青,并在-18度以下冷冻)、浸酸、腌渍、炒制等工艺进行加工处理的〕	10		30	9/	6	千克	AB	PRQS	/60
		-其他:									
0802.9020		---白果〔101 药用白果,102 白果(其他工艺),103 白果(提取(晒干的除外)、压榨、烹制、烘焙、冻干、脱水、裹糖屑、发酵、冷冻(经漂汤和杀青,并在-18度以下冷冻)、浸酸、腌渍、炒制等工艺进行加工处理〕	25	20	70	9/	6	千克	ABE	PRQ	/55
0802.9030		---松子仁									
0802.9030	10	鲜或干的红松子仁〔101 提取(晒干的除外)、压榨、烹制、烘焙、冻干、脱水、裹糖屑、发酵、冷冻(经漂汤和杀青,并在-18度以下冷冻)、浸酸、腌渍、炒制等工艺进行加工处理的,102 其他工艺〕	25		70	9/	9	千克	ABE	PRQS	/75
0802.9030	20	鲜或干的其他濒危松子仁〔101 提取(晒干的除外)、压榨、烹制、烘焙、冻干、脱水、裹糖屑、发酵、冷冻(经漂汤和杀青,并在-18度以下冷冻)、浸酸、腌渍、炒制等工艺进行加工处理的,102 其他工艺〕	25		70	9/	0	千克	ABEF	PRQS	/75
0802.9030	90	鲜或干的其他松子仁〔101 提取(晒干的除外)、压榨、烹制、烘焙、冻干、脱水、裹糖屑、发酵、冷冻(经漂汤和杀青,并在-18度以下冷冻)、浸酸、腌渍、炒制等工艺进行加工处理的,102 其他工艺〕	25		70	9/	9	千克	AB	PRQS	/75
0802.9090		---其他									
0802.9090	10	鲜或干的榧子、红松子(不论是否去壳或去皮)〔101 药用榧子,102 松子(其他工艺),103 榧子(其他工艺),104 松子(提取(晒干的除外)、压榨、烹制、烘焙、冻干、脱水、裹糖屑、发酵、冷冻(经漂汤和杀青,并在-18度以下冷冻)、浸酸、腌渍、炒制等工艺进行加工处理的),105 榧子(提取(晒干的除外)、压榨、烹制、烘焙、冻干、脱水、裹糖屑、发酵、冷冻(经漂汤和杀青,并在-19度以下冷冻)、浸酸、腌渍、炒制等工艺进行加工处理的)〕	24		70	9/	9	千克	ABE	PRQS	/74

协定税率 %										特惠税率 %			
亚太5国	东/冰/格	巴基斯坦	韩国	瑞士	哥达	秘鲁	澳大利亚	新西/坡/智	港/澳/台	亚太2国	老/柬/缅	36/3/1	Article Description
	0/0/0		17.5	7.5	8.3	0	0	0//0	0/0/			0/0/	---Other
													--Shelled:
	0/0/0		17.5	7.5	8.3	0	0	0//0	0/0/			0/0/	---Chinese chestnuts
	0/0/0		17.5	7.5	8.3	0	0	0//0	0/0/			0/0/	---Other
													-Pistachios:
	0/0/0	4.5	4	0	3.3	0	0	0//0	0/0/			0/0/	--In shell
	0/0/0	4.5	4	0	3.3	0	0	0//0	0/0/			0/0/	--Shelled
													-Macadamia nuts:
													--In shell:
												0/0/0	---Seedlings
	0/0/0		9.6	7.2	8	0	0	0//0	0/0/			0/0/	---Other
	0/0/0		9.6	7.2	8	0	0	0//0	0/0/			0/0/	--Shelled
	0/0/0		16.8	7.2	8	0	0	0//0	0/0/			0/0/	-Cola nut(Cola spp.)
													-Areca nut
5	0/0/0	4.5	4	0	3.3	0	0	0//0	0/0/			0/0/0	Areca nuts, fresh(whether or not shelled or peeled)
5	0/0/0	4.5	4	0	3.3	0	0	0//0	0/0/			0/0/0	Areca nuts, dried(whether or not shelled or peeled)
													-Other:
	0/0/0		17.5	7.5	8.3	0	0	0//0	0/0/			0/0/	---Gingko nuts
													---Pine-nuts, shelled
	0/0/0	0	17.5	7.5	8.3	0	0	0//0	0/0/			0/0/	Korean pine-nuts, shelled, fresh or dried
	0/0/0	0	17.5	7.5	8.3	0	0	0//0	0/0/			0/0/	Other endangered pine-nuts, shelled, fresh or dried
	0/0/0	0	17.5	7.5	8.3	0	0	0//0	0/0/			0/0/	Other pine-nuts, shelled, fresh or dried
													---Other
	0/0/0	0	16.8	7.2	8	0	0	0//0	0/0/			0/0/	semen torreyae or korean pine, fresh or dried(whether or not shelled or peeled)

税则号列	货品名称〔CIQ扩展编码及品名—T2表示见附表2〕	最惠(%)	暂定税率	普通	增值/消费	出口退税	计量单位	监管条件	检验检疫	特殊证件对美关税
0802.9090 20	鲜或干的其他濒危松子(不论是否去壳或去皮)〔101 提取(晒干的除外)、压榨、烹制、烘焙、冻干、脱水、裹糖屑、发酵、冷冻(经漂汤和杀青,并在－18度以下冷冻)、浸酸、腌渍、炒制等工艺进行加工处理的,102 其他工艺〕	24		70	9/	0	千克	ABEF	PRQS	/74
0802.9090 30	鲜或干的巨籽棕(海椰子)果仁〔101 提取(晒干的除外)、压榨、烹制、烘焙、冻干、脱水、裹糖屑、发酵、冷冻(经漂汤和杀青,并在－18度以下冷冻、浸酸、腌渍、炒制等工艺进行加工处理的,102 其他工艺〕	24		70	9/	9	千克	ABEF	PRQS	/74
0802.9090 40	鲜或干的碧根果(不论是否去壳或去皮)〔101 核桃(其他工艺),102 核桃仁(其他工艺),103 药用核桃仁,104 核桃或核桃仁(提取(晒干的除外)、压榨、烹制、烘焙、冻干、脱水、裹糖屑、发酵、冷冻(经漂汤和杀青,并在－18度以下冷冻、浸酸、腌渍、炒制等工艺进行加工处理的)〕	24	7	70	9/	9	千克	AB	PRQS	/57
0802.9090 90	鲜或干的其他坚果(不论是否去壳或去皮)〔101 干的其他瓜子,102 其他坚果(其他工艺),103 巴西坚果(其他工艺),104 鲍鱼果(其他工艺),105 干橡子仁(其他工艺),106 白皮松子(其他工艺),107 提取(晒干的除外)、压榨、烹制、烘焙、冻干、脱水、裹糖屑、发酵、冷冻(经漂汤和杀青,并在－18度以下冷冻、浸酸、腌渍、炒制等工艺进行加工处理的)〕	24		70	9/	9	千克	AB	PRQS	/74
08.03	**鲜或干的香蕉,包括芭蕉:**									
0803.1000	-芭蕉〔101 鲜芭蕉,102 干的芭蕉(其他工艺),103 其他蜜饯,104 干的芭蕉(提取(晒干的除外)、压榨、烹制、烘焙、冻干、脱水、裹糖屑、发酵、冷冻(经漂汤和杀青,并在－18度以下冷冻、浸酸、腌渍、炒制等工艺进行加工处理的)〕	10		40	9/	9	千克	AB	PRQS	/60
0803.9000	-其他〔101 鲜香蕉,102 干的香蕉(其他工艺),103 其他蜜饯,104 干的香蕉(提取(晒干的除外)、压榨、烹制、烘焙、冻干、脱水、裹糖屑、发酵、冷冻(经漂汤和杀青,并在－18度以下冷冻)、浸酸、腌渍、炒制等工艺进行加工处理的)〕	10		40	9/	9	千克	AB	PRQS	/60
08.04	**鲜或干的椰枣、无花果、菠萝、鳄梨、番石榴、芒果及山竹果:**									
0804.1000	-椰枣〔101 提取(晒干的除外)、压榨、烹制、烘焙、冻干、脱水、裹糖屑、发酵、冷冻(经漂汤和杀青,并在－18度以下冷冻)、浸酸、腌渍、炒制等工艺进行加工处理的,102 其他工艺〕	15		40	9/	9	千克	AB	PRQ	/65
0804.2000	-无花果〔101 提取(晒干的除外)、压榨、烹制、烘焙、冻干、脱水、裹糖屑、发酵、冷冻(经漂汤和杀青,并在－18度以下冷冻)、浸酸、腌渍、炒制等工艺进行加工处理的,102 其他工艺〕	30		70	9/	9	千克	AB	PRQ	/80
0804.3000	-菠萝									
0804.3000 01	鲜菠萝〔999〕	12		80	9/	9	千克	AB	PRQS	/62
0804.3000 90	干菠萝〔101 其他工艺,102 其他蜜饯,103 提取(晒干的除外)、压榨、烹制、烘焙、冻干、脱水、裹糖屑、发酵、冷冻(经漂汤和杀青,并在－18度以下冷冻)、浸酸、腌渍、炒制等工艺进行加工处理的〕	12		80	9/	9	千克	AB	PRQS	/62
0804.4000	-鳄梨〔101 鲜的鳄梨,102 干的鳄梨(其他工艺),103 其他蜜饯,104 干的鳄梨(提取(晒干的除外)、压榨、烹制、烘焙、冻干、脱水、裹糖屑、发酵、冷冻(经漂汤和杀青,并在－18度以下冷冻)、浸酸、腌渍、炒制等工艺进行加工处理的)〕	25	7	80	9/	6	千克	AB	PRQ	/57
	-番石榴、芒果及山竹果:									
0804.5010	---番石榴									
0804.5010 01	鲜番石榴〔999〕	15		80	9/	6	千克	AB	PRQ	/65
0804.5010 90	干番石榴〔101 其他工艺,102 其他蜜饯,103 提取(晒干的除外)、压榨、烹制、烘焙、冻干、脱水、裹糖屑、发酵、冷冻(经漂汤和杀青,并在－18度以下冷冻)、浸酸、腌渍、炒制等工艺进行加工处理的〕	15		80	9/	6	千克	AB	PRQ	/65
0804.5020	---芒果									
0804.5020 01	鲜芒果〔999〕	15		80	9/	6	千克	AB	PRQ	/65
0804.5020 90	干芒果〔101 其他工艺,102 其他蜜饯,103 提取(晒干的除外)、压榨、烹制、烘焙、冻干、脱水、裹糖屑、发酵、冷冻(经漂汤和杀青,并在－18度以下冷冻)、浸酸、腌渍、炒制等工艺进行加工处理的〕	15		80	9/	6	千克	AB	PRQ	/65
0804.5030	---山竹果〔101 鲜的,102 干的(其他工艺),103 其他蜜饯,104 提取(晒干的除外)、压榨、烹制、烘焙、冻干、脱水、裹糖屑、发酵、冷冻(经漂汤和杀青,并在－18度以下冷冻)、浸酸、腌渍、炒制等工艺进行加工处理的〕	15		80	9/	6	千克	AB	PRQ	/65
08.05	**鲜或干的柑橘属水果:**									

协定税率 %										特惠税率 %			Article Description
亚太5国	东/冰/格	巴基斯坦	韩国	瑞士	哥达	秘鲁	澳大利亚	新西/坡/智	港/澳/台	亚太2国	老/柬/缅	36/3/1	
	0/0/0	0	16.8	7.2	8	0	0	0//0	0/0/			0/0/	Endangered pine nut, fresh or dried (whether or not shelled or peeled)
	0/0/0	0	16.8	7.2	8	0	0	0//0	0/0/			0/0/	Lodoicea maldivica nut, fresh or dried
	0/0/0	0	16.8	7.2	8	0	0	0//0	0/0/			0/0/	Pecan fresh or dried(whether or not shelled or peeled)
	0/0/0	0	16.8	7.2	8	0	0	0//0	0/0/			0/0/	Other nuts, fresh or dried(whether or not shelled or peeled)
													Bananas, including plantains, fresh or dried:
6.9	0/0/0	4.5	4	0	3.3	0	0	0//0	0/0/0		0/0/	0/0/0	-Plantains
6.9	0/0/0	4.5	4	0	3.3	0	0	0//0	0/0/0		0/0/	0/0/0	-Other
													Dates, figs, pineapples, avocados, guavas, mangoes and mangosteens, fresh or dried:
	0/0/0	0	6	4.5	5	0	0	0//0	0/0/			0/0/	-Dates
	0/0/0	0	21	15.6	10	0	0	0//0	0/0/			0/0/	-Figs
													-Pineapples
7.9	0/0/0	0	4.8	3.6	4	0	0	0//0	0/0/		/0/	0/0/0	Pineapples, fresh
7.9	0/0/0	0	4.8	3.6	4	0	0	0//0	0/0/		/0/	0/0/0	Pineapples, dried
12.5	0/0/0	0	17.5	7.5	8.3	0	0	0//0	0/0/		/0/	0/0/0	-Avocados
													-Guavas, mangoes and mangosteens:
													---Guavas
7.5	0/0/0	0	6	4.5	5	0	0	0//0	0/0/			0/0/	Guavas, fresh
7.5	0/0/0	0	6	4.5	5	0	0	0//0	0/0/			0/0/	Guavas, dried
													---Mangoes
10.7	0/0/0	0	6	4.5	5	0	0	0//0	0/0/			0/0/0	Mangoes, fresh
10.7	0/0/0	0	6	4.5	5	0	0	0//0	0/0/			0/0/0	Mangoes, dried
7.5	0/0/0	0	6	4.5	5	0	0	0//0	0/0/			0/0/	---Mangosteens
													Citrus fruit, fresh or dried:

税则号列	货品名称〔CIQ 扩展编码及品名－T2 表示见附表 2〕	最惠(%)	暂定税率	普通	增值/消费	出口退税	计量单位	监管条件	检验检疫	特殊证件对美关税
0805.1000	-橙〔101 鲜的橙,102 其他工艺,103 其他蜜饯,104 干的橙(提取(晒干的除外)、压榨、烹制、烘焙、冻干、脱水、裹糖屑、发酵、冷冻(经漂汤和杀青,并在－18 度以下冷冻)、浸酸、腌渍、炒制等工艺进行加工处理的)〕	11		100	9/	9	千克	AB	PRQS	/61
	-柑橘(包括小蜜橘及萨摩蜜柑橘);克里曼丁橘、韦尔金橘及类似的杂交柑橘:									
	--柑橘(包括小蜜橘及萨摩蜜柑橘):									
0805.2110	---蕉柑〔101 鲜的蕉柑,102 干的蕉柑(提取(晒干的除外)、压榨、烹制、烘焙、冻干、脱水、裹糖屑、发酵、冷冻(经漂汤和杀青,并在－18 度以下冷冻)、浸酸、腌渍、炒制等工艺进行加工处理的),103 干的蕉柑(其他工艺)〕	12		100	9/	6	千克	AB	PRQS	/47
0805.2190	---其他〔101 鲜的柑橘,102 干的柑橘(提取(晒干的除外)、压榨、烹制、烘焙、冻干、脱水、裹糖屑、发酵、冷冻(经漂汤和杀青,并在－18 度以下冷冻)、浸酸、腌渍、炒制等工艺进行加工处理的),103 干的柑橘(其他工艺)〕	12		100	9/	9	千克	AB	PRQS	/62
0805.2200	--克里曼丁橘〔101 鲜的克里曼丁橘,102 干的克里曼丁橘(提取(晒干的除外)、压榨、烹制、烘焙、冻干、脱水、裹糖屑、发酵、冷冻(经漂汤和杀青,并在－18 度以下冷冻)、浸酸、腌渍、炒制等工艺进行加工处理的),103 干的克里曼丁橘(其他工艺)〕	12		100	9/	6	千克	AB	PRQS	/62
0805.2900	--其他〔101 鲜的,102 干的(提取(晒干的除外)、压榨、烹制、烘焙、冻干、脱水、裹糖屑、发酵、冷冻(经漂汤和杀青,并在－18 度以下冷冻)、浸酸、腌渍、炒制等工艺进行加工处理的),103 干的(其他工艺)〕	12		100	9/	9	千克	AB	PRQS	/62
0805.4000	-葡萄柚,包括柚									
0805.4000 01	鲜葡萄柚,包括鲜柚〔101 柚,102 葡萄柚〕	12		100	9/	6	千克	AB	PRQS	/62
0805.4000 90	干葡萄柚,包括干柚〔101 其他工艺,102 其他蜜饯,103 提取(晒干的除外)、压榨、烹制、烘焙、冻干、脱水、裹糖屑、发酵、冷冻(经漂汤和杀青,并在－18 度以下冷冻)、浸酸、腌渍、炒制等工艺进行加工处理的〕	12		100	9/	6	千克	AB	PRQS	/62
0805.5000	-柠檬及酸橙〔101 鲜的柠檬,102 鲜的酸橙,103 干的酸橙(其他工艺),104 其他蜜饯,105 柠檬干(其他工艺),106 干的酸橙(提取(晒干的除外)、压榨、烹制、烘焙、冻干、脱水、裹糖屑、发酵、冷冻(经漂汤和杀青,并在－18 度以下冷冻)、浸酸、腌渍、炒制等工艺进行加工处理的),107 柠檬干(提取(晒干的除外)、压榨、烹制、烘焙、冻干、脱水、裹糖屑、发酵、冷冻(经漂汤和杀青,并在－19 度以下冷冻)、浸酸、腌渍、炒制等工艺进行加工处理的)〕	11		100	9/	6	千克	AB	PRQS	/61
0805.9000	-其他〔101 鲜的榅桲,102 鲜的其他柑桔,103 干的其他柑桔属水果(其他工艺),104 其他蜜饯,105 干的其他柑桔属水果(提取(晒干的除外)、压榨、烹制、烘焙、冻干、脱水、裹糖屑、发酵、冷冻(经漂汤和杀青,并在－18 度以下冷冻)、浸酸、腌渍、炒制等工艺进行加工处理的)〕	30		100	9/	9	千克	AB	PRQS	/80
08.06	**鲜或干的葡萄:**									
0806.1000	-鲜的〔999〕	13		80	9/	6	千克	AB	PRQS	/63
0806.2000	-干的〔101 提取(晒干的除外)、压榨、烹制、烘焙、冻干、脱水、裹糖屑、发酵、冷冻(经漂汤和杀青,并在－18 度以下冷冻)、浸酸、腌渍、炒制等工艺进行加工处理的,102 其他工艺〕	10		80	9/	9	千克	AB	PRQS	/60
08.07	**鲜的甜瓜(包括西瓜)及木瓜:**									
	-甜瓜,包括西瓜:									
0807.1100	--西瓜〔999〕	25		70	9/	6	千克	AB	PRQS	/75
	--其他:									
0807.1910	---哈蜜瓜〔999〕	12		70	9/	6	千克	AB	PRQS	/62
0807.1920	---罗马甜瓜及加勒比甜瓜〔999〕	12		70	9/	6	千克	AB	PRQS	/47
0807.1990	---其他〔101 其他甜瓜,102 香瓜〕	12		70	9/	6	千克	AB	PRQS	/47
0807.2000	-木瓜〔101 鲜番木瓜除外,102 鲜番木瓜〕	25		70	9/	6	千克	AB	PRQS	/75
08.08	**鲜的苹果、梨及榅桲:**									
0808.1000	-苹果〔999〕	10		100	9/	9	千克	AB	PRQS	/60
	-梨:									
0808.3010	---鸭梨及雪梨〔101 鸭梨,102 其它梨〕	12		100	9/	9	千克	AB	PRQS	/62
0808.3020	---香梨〔999〕	12		100	9/	6	千克	AB	PRQS	/47
0808.3090	---其他〔101 砂梨属,102 中国梨,103 其它梨〕	10		100	9/	9	千克	AB	PRQS	/60
0808.4000	-榅桲〔999〕	16		100	9/	9	千克	AB	PRQ	/51
08.09	**鲜的杏、樱桃、桃(包括油桃)、梅及李:**									
0809.1000	-杏〔999〕	25		70	9/	6	千克	AB	PRQ	/60

协定税率 %										特惠税率 %			
亚太5国	东/冰/格	巴基斯坦	韩国	瑞士	哥达	秘鲁	澳大利亚	新西/坡/智	港/澳/台	亚太2国	老/柬/缅	36/3/1	Article Description
	0/0/0	0	4.4	3.3	3.7	0	3.7	0//0	0/0/0			0/0/0	-Oranges
													-Mandarins (*including tange-rines and satsumas*); clemen-tines, wilkings and similar cit-rus hybrids:
													--Mandarins (*including tange-rines and satsumas*):
	0/0/0	0	4.8	3.6	4	0	4	0//0	0/0/			0/0/	---Chiao-Kan
	0/0/0	0	4.8	3.6	4	0	4	0//0	0/0/			0/0/	---Other
	0/0/0	0	4.8	3.6	4	0	4	0//0	0/0/			0/0/	--Clementines
	0/0/0	0	4.8	3.6	4	0	4	0//0	0/0/			0/0/	--Other
													-Grapefruit, including pomelos
	0/0/0	0	4.8	3.6	4	0	4	0//0	0/0/			0/0/0	Grapefruit fresh, including pomelos
	0/0/0	0	4.8	3.6	4	0	4	0//0	0/0/			0/0/0	Grapefruit dried, including pomelos
5.5	0/0/0	0	4.4	3.3	3.7	0	3.7	0//0	0/0/0			0/0/0	-Lemons (*Citrus limon*, *Citrus limonum*) and limes (*Citrus aurantifolia*)
15	0/0/0	0	21	15.6	10	0	10	0//0	0/0/			0/0/	-Other
													Grapes, fresh or dried:
	0/0/0	5.9	5.2	3.9	0	0	0	0//0	0/0/			0/0/	-Fresh
	0/0/0	4.5	4	0	0	0	0	0//0	0/0/			0/0/	-Dried
													Melons (including watermelons) and papaws (papayas), fresh:
													-Melons (including watermelons):
12.5	0/0/0	11.3	17.5	7.5	0	0	0	0//0	0/0/			0//	--Watermelons
													--Other:
6	0/0/0	4.5	4.8	3.6	0	0	0	0//0	0/0/0			0/0/0	---Hami melons
6	0/0/0	4.5	4.8	3.6	0	0	0	0//0	0/0/			0/0/0	---Cantaloupe and Galia melons
6	0/0/0	4.5	4.8	3.6	0	0	0	0//0	0/0/			0/0/0	---Other
	0/0/0	22.5	10	7.5	0	0	0	0//0	0/0/		/0/	0/0/0	-Papaws(papayas)
													Apples, pears and quinces, fresh:
	0/0/0	4.5	4	0	0	0	0	0//0	0/0/			0/0/0	-Apples
													-Pears:
10	0/0/0	4.5	4.8	3.6	0	0	0	0//0	0/0/			0/0/	---Ya pears and snowy pearwhite
10	0/0/0	4.5	4.8	3.6	0	0	0	0//0	0/0/			0/0/	---Fragrant pear
	0/0/0	4.5	4	0	0	0	0	0//0	0/0/			0/0/	---Other
	0/0/0	10.2	9.6	4.8	0	0	0	0//0	0/0/			0/0/	-Quinces
													Apricots, cherries, peaches (including nectarines), plums and sloes, fresh:
	0/0/0	25	17.5	7.5	0	0	0	0//0	0/0/			0/0/	-Apricots

税则号列		货品名称〔CIQ 扩展编码及品名—T2 表示见附表 2〕	最惠(%)	暂定税率	普通	增值/消费	出口退税	计量单位	监管条件	检验检疫	特殊证件对美关税
		-樱桃:									
0809.2100		--欧洲酸樱桃〔999〕	10		70	9/	6	千克	AB	PRQ	/60
0809.2900		--其他〔999〕	10		70	9/	9	千克	AB	PRQ	/60
0809.3000		-桃,包括油桃〔999〕	10		70	9/	9	千克	AB	PRQS	/60
0809.4000		-梅及李									
0809.4000	01	鲜梅〔999〕	10		70	9/	6	千克	AB	PRQS	/60
0809.4000	90	鲜李子〔999〕	10		70	9/	6	千克	AB	PRQS	/60
08.10		**其他鲜果:**									
0810.1000		-草莓〔999〕	14		80	9/	9	千克	AB	PRQ	/64
0810.2000		-木莓、黑莓、桑葚及罗甘莓〔101 木莓,102 其他瓜果〕	25		80	9/	9	千克	AB	PRQ	/75
0810.3000		-黑、白或红的穗醋栗(加仑子)及醋栗〔999〕	25		80	9/	9	千克	AB	PRQ	/60
0810.4000		-蔓越橘及越橘									
0810.4000	10	鲜蔓越橘〔101〕	30	15	80	9/	9	千克	AB	PRQ	/65
0810.4000	90	越橘〔101 蓝莓,102 蓝莓除外〕	30		80	9/	9	千克	AB	PRQ	/80
0810.5000		-猕猴桃〔999〕	20		80	9/	6	千克	AB	PRQS	/70
0810.6000		-榴莲〔999〕	20		80	9/	6	千克	AB	PRQ	/70
0810.7000		-柿子〔999〕	20		80	9/	9	千克	AB	PRQS	/70
		-其他:									
0810.9010		---荔枝〔999〕	30		80	9/	6	千克	AB	PRQS	/80
0810.9030		---龙眼〔999〕	12		80	9/	6	千克	AB	PRQS	/62
0810.9040		---红毛丹〔999〕	20		80	9/	6	千克	AB	PRQS	/70
0810.9050		---蕃荔枝〔999〕	20		80	9/	6	千克	AB	PRQS	/70
0810.9060		---杨桃〔999〕	20		80	9/	6	千克	AB	PRQS	/70
0810.9070		---莲雾〔999〕	20		80	9/	6	千克	AB	PRQS	/70
0810.9080		---火龙果〔999〕	20		80	9/	6	千克	AB	PRQS	/70
0810.9090		---其他									
0810.9090	01	鲜枣〔999〕	20		80	9/	9	千克	AB	PRQS	/70
0810.9090	02	鲜枇杷〔999〕	20		80	9/	9	千克	AB	PRQS	/70
0810.9090	10	鲜的翅果油树果〔999〕	20		80	9/	9	千克	ABE	PRQS	/70
0810.9090	90	其他鲜果〔101 杨梅,102 椰青,103 椰子,104 巴旦杏(水果),105 槟榔,106 山楂,107 余甘子,108 西番莲,109 石榴,110 菱角,111 橄榄,112 菠萝蜜,113 蓝莓,114 其他瓜果,115 罗望子,116 人心果,117 蛇皮果,118 椰色果,119 蓝靛果〕	20		80	9/	9	千克	AB	PRQS	/70
08.11		**冷冻水果及坚果,不论是否蒸煮、加糖或其他甜物质:**									
0811.1000		-草莓〔999〕	30		80	9/	9	千克	AB	PRQS	/75
0811.2000		-木莓、黑莓、桑葚、罗甘莓、黑、白或红的穗醋栗(加仑子)及醋栗〔999〕	30		80	9/	9	千克	AB	PRQ	/80
		-其他:									
0811.9010		---栗子,未去壳〔999〕	30		80	9/	9	千克	AB	PRQS	/
0811.9090		---其他									
0811.9090	10	冷冻的白果〔999〕	30		80	9/	9	千克	ABE	PRQS	/80
0811.9090	21	冷冻的红松子(不论是否去壳或去皮)〔999〕	30		80	9/	9	千克	ABE	PRQS	/80
0811.9090	22	冷冻的其他濒危松子(不论是否去壳或去皮)〔999〕	30		80	9/	0	千克	ABEF	PRQS	/80
0811.9090	30	冷冻的榧子〔999〕	30		80	9/	9	千克	ABE	PRQS	/80
0811.9090	40	冷冻的翅果油树果〔999〕	30		80	9/	9	千克	ABE	PRQS	/80
0811.9090	50	冷冻的巨籽棕(海椰子)果仁〔999〕	30		80	9/	9	千克	ABEF	PRQS	/80
0811.9090	60	冷冻的鳄梨	30	7	80	9/	9	千克	AB	PRQS	/57
0811.9090	90	其他未列名冷冻水果及坚果〔T2〕	30		80	9/	9	千克	AB	PRQS	/80
08.12		**暂时保藏(例如,使用二氧化硫气体、盐水、亚硫酸水或其他防腐液)的水果及坚果,但不适于直接食用的:**									
0812.1000		-樱桃〔999〕	30		80	9/	6	千克	AB	PRQ	/45
0812.9000		-其他									
0812.9000	10	暂时保存的白果(用二氧化硫气体、盐水等物质处理,但不适于直接食用的)〔999〕	25		80	9/	9	千克	ABE	PRQS	/40
0812.9000	21	暂时保存的红松子(用二氧化硫气体、盐水等物质处理,但不适于直接食用的)〔999〕	25		80	9/	9	千克	ABE	PRQS	/40
0812.9000	22	暂时保存的其他濒危松子(用二氧化硫气体,盐水等物质处理,但不适于直接食用的)〔999〕	25		80	9/	0	千克	ABFE	PRQS	/40

协定税率 %										特惠税率 %			
亚太5国	东/冰/格	巴基斯坦	韩国	瑞士	哥达	秘鲁	澳大利亚	新西/坡/智	港/澳/台	亚太2国	老/柬/缅	36/3/1	Article Description
													-Cherries:
	0/0/0	4.5	4	0	0	0	0	0//0	0/0/			0/0/0	--Sour cherries(*Prunus cerasus*)
	0/0/0	0	4	0	0	0	0	0//0	0/0/			0/0/0	--Other
	0/0/0	4.5	4	0	0	0	0	0//0	0/0/			0/0/0	-Peaches, including nectarines
													-Plums and sloes
	0/0/0	4.5	4	0	0	0	0	0//0	0/0/			0/0/	Plums, fresh
	0/0/0	4.5	4	0	0	0	0	0//0	0/0/			0/0/	Sloes, fresh
													Other fruit, fresh:
	0/0/0	12.6	5.6	4.2	0	0	0	0//0	0/0/			0/0/0	-Strawberries
	0/0/0	25	17.5	7.5	0	0	0	0//0	0/0/			0/0/	-Raspberries, blackberries, mulberries and loganberries
	0/0/0	25	17.5	7.5	0	0	0	0//0	0/0/			0/0/	-Black, white or red currant and gooseberries
													-Cranberries, bilberries and other fruits of the genus *Vaccinium*
	0/0/0	30	21	15.6	0	0	0	0//0	0/0/			0//	Cranberries, fresh
	0/0/0	30	21	15.6	0	0	0	0//0	0/0/			0//	Cranberries
16.4	0/0/0	16	12	6	0	0	0	0//0	0/0/			0/0/	-Kiwifruit
	0/0/0	18	8	6	0	0	0	0//0	0/0/		/0/	0/0/0	-Durian
16.4	0/0/0	12.8	12	6	0	0	0	0//0	0/0/			0/0/	-Persimmons
													-Other:
20.1	0/0/0	18	21	15.6	0	0	0	0//0	0/0/			0/0/	---Lychee
	0/0/0	5.4	4.8	3.6	0	0	0	0//0	0/0/		/0/	0/0/0	---Longan
	0/0/0	18	8	6	0	0	0	0//0	0/0/			0/0/	---Rambutan
	0/0/0	18	8	6	0	0	0	0//0	0/0/			0/0/	---Sugar apple
	0/0/0	18	12	6	0	0	0	0//0	0/0/			0/0/	---Carambola
16.4	0/0/0	14.4	8	6	0	0	0	0//0	0/0/			0/0/	---Wax apple
16.4	0/0/0	12.8	8	6	0	0	0	0//0	0/0/0			0/0/	---Dragon fruit
													---Other
16.4	0/0/0	0	12	6	0	0	0	0//0	0/0/			0/0/	Chinese date, fresh
16.4	0/0/0	0	12	6	0	0	0	0//0	0/0/			0/0/	Loquat, fresh
16.4	0/0/0	0	12	6	0	0	0	0//0	0/0/			0/0/	Fruit of elaeagnus mollis diels
16.4	0/0/0	0	12	6	0	0	0	0//0	0/0/			0/0/	Other fruit, fresh
													Fruit and nuts, uncooked or cooked by steaming or boiling in water, frozen, whether or not containing added sugar or other sweetening matter:
	0/0/0	0	21		0	0	0	0//0	0/0/			0/0/	-Strawberries
	0/0/0		21		0	0	0	0//0	0/0/			0/0/	-Raspberries, blackberries, mulberries, loganberries, black, white or red currants and gooseberries
													-Other:
	0/0/0		21		0	0	0	0//0	0/0/			0/0/	---Chestnuts, in shell
													---Other
	0/0/0		21		0	0	0	0//0	0/0/			0//	Ginkgo, frozen
	0/0/0		21		0	0	0	0//0	0/0/			0//	Korean pine-nuts, shelled, frozen(whethe or not shelled or peeled)
	0/0/0		21		0	0	0	0//0	0/0/			0//	Other endangered pine-nuts, shelled (whethe or not shelled or peeled)
	0/0/0		21		0	0	0	0//0	0/0/			0//	Semen torreyae, frozen
	0/0/0		21		0	0	0	0//0	0/0/			0//	Fruit of wingfruit elaeagus (Elaeagus mollis Diels), frozen
	0/0/0		21		0	0	0	0//0	0/0/			0//	Lodoicea maldivica nut, frozen
	0/0/0		21		0	0	0	0//0	0/0/		//	0//	Frozen avocado
	0/0/0		21		0	0	0	0//0	0/0/			0//	Other fruit and nuts, frozen, not elsewhere specified or included
													Fruit and nuts, provisionally preserved (for example, by sulphur dioxide gas, in brine, in sulphur water or in other preservative solutions), but unsuitable in that state for immediate consumption:
	0/0/0		21		0	0	0	0//0	0/0/			0//	-Cherries
													-Other
	0/0/0		17.5	7.5	0	0	0	0//0	0/0/			0/0/	Ginkgo, provisionally preserved (by sulphur dioxide gas, in brine or in other preservative solutions but unsuitable in that state for immediate consumption)
	0/0/0		17.5	7.5	0	0	0	0//0	0/0/			0/0/	Korean pine-nuts, provisionally preserved (by sulphur dioxide gas, in brine or in other wise prepared, but unsuitable in that state for immediate consumption)
	0/0/0		17.5	7.5	0	0	0	0//0	0/0/			0/0/	Other endangered pine-nuts, provisionally preserved (by sulphur dioxide gas, in brine or in otherwise prepared, but unsuitable in that state for immediate consumption)

税则号列		货品名称〔CIQ扩展编码及品名－T2表示见附表2〕	最惠(%)	暂定税率	普通	增值/消费	出口退税	计量单位	监管条件	检验检疫	特殊证件对美关税
0812.9000	30	暂时保存的榧子(用二氧化硫气体、盐水等物质处理,但不适于直接食用的)〔999〕	25		80	9/	9	千克	ABE	PRQS	/40
0812.9000	40	暂时保存的翅果油树果(用二氧化硫气体、盐水等物质处理,但不适于直接食用的)〔999〕	25		80	9/	9	千克	ABE	PRQS	/40
0812.9000	50	暂时保存的巨籽棕(海椰子)果仁(用二氧化硫气体、盐水等物质处理,但不适于直接食用的)〔999〕	25		80	9/	9	千克	ABEF	PRQS	/40
0812.9000	90	暂时保存的其他水果及坚果(用二氧化硫气体,盐水等物质处理,但不适于直接食用的)〔999〕	25		80	9/	9	千克	AB	PRQS	/40
08.13		**税目08.01至08.06以外的干果;本章的什锦坚果或干果:**									
0813.1000		-杏〔101杏干,102其他蜜饯〕	25		70	9/	9	千克	AB	PRQS	/75
0813.2000		-梅及李〔101药用乌梅,102李干,103梅干,104话梅,105其他蜜饯〕	25		70	9/	9	千克	AB	PRQS	/75
0813.3000		-苹果〔999〕	25		70	9/	9	千克	AB	PRQS	/75
		-其他:									
0813.4010		---龙眼干、肉〔101药用龙眼肉,102龙眼干,103其他蜜饯〕	20		70	9/	6	千克	AB	PRQS	/70
0813.4020		---柿饼〔101柿饼,102其他蜜饯〕	25		70	9/	6	千克	AB	PRQS	/75
0813.4030		---红枣〔101药用大枣,102干枣,103其他蜜饯〕	25		70	9/	6	千克	AB	PRQS	/75
0813.4040		---荔枝干〔999〕	25		70	9/	6	千克	AB	PRQS	/75
0813.4090		---其他									
0813.4090	10	翅果油树干果〔999〕	25		70	9/	9	千克	ABE	PRQS	/75
0813.4090	20	蔓越橘干〔999〕	25	15	70	9/	9	千克	AB	PRQS	/65
0813.4090	90	其他干果(税目08.01至08.06的干果除外)〔101药用芡实,102药用薏米(薏苡仁),103薏米,104山楂干,105其他干(坚)果,106桑葚干,107其他蜜饯,108菠萝蜜干,109草莓干,110橄榄干,111哈密瓜干,112蓝莓干,113榴莲干,114甜角,115蔓越桔干果,116蔓越莓干,117玫瑰果干,118樱桃干,119猕猴桃干,120木瓜干,121酸角,122蔷薇果干,123桃干,124甜瓜干,125西西果干,126罗望子干〕	25		70	9/	9	千克	AB	PRQS	/75
0813.5000		-本章的什锦坚果或干果〔999〕	18		70	9/	9	千克	AB	PRQS	/68
08.14		**柑橘属水果或甜瓜(包括西瓜)的果皮,鲜、冻、干或用盐水、亚硫酸水或其他防腐液暂时保藏的:**									
0814.0000		柑橘属水果或甜瓜(包括西瓜)的果皮鲜、冻、干或用盐水、亚硫酸水或其他防腐液暂时保藏的〔101果脯,102其他蜜饯,103药用陈皮(橘皮),104冻的、干的,105橘子皮,106柠檬皮,107蓝莓皮,108山竹果皮〕	25		70	9/	9	千克	AB	PRQS	/50

协定税率 %										特惠税率 %			Article Description
亚太5国	东/冰/格	巴基斯坦	韩国	瑞士	哥达	秘鲁	澳大利亚	新西/坡/智	港/澳/台	亚太2国	老/柬/缅	36/3/1	
	0/0/0		17.5	7.5	0	0	0	0//0	0/0/			0/0/	Semen torreyae provisionally preserved (by sulphur dioxide gas, in brine or in otherwise prepared, but unsuitable in that state for immediate consumption)
	0/0/0		17.5	7.5	0	0	0	0//0	0/0/			0/0/	Fruit of elaeagnus mollis diels(*Elaeagus mollis Diels*) provisionally preserved (by sulphur dioxide gas, in brine or in otherwise prepared, but unsuitable in that state for immediate consumption)
	0/0/0		17.5	7.5	0	0	0	0//0	0/0/			0/0/	Lodoicea maldivica nut, provisionally preserved (by sulphur dioxide gas, in brine or in other preservative solutions, but unsuitable in that state for immediate consumoption)
	0/0/0		17.5	7.5	0	0	0	0//0	0/0/			0/0/	Other fruit and nuts, provisionally preserved (by sulphur dioxide gas, in brine or in otherwise prepared, but unsuitable in that state for immediate consumption)
													Fruit, dried, other than that of headings No. 08.01 to 08.06; mixtures of nuts or dried fruits of this Chapter:
	0/0/0		17.5	7.5	0	0	0	0//0	0/0/			0/0/	-Apricots
	0/0/0		17.5	7.5	0	0	0	0//0	0/0/			0/0/	-Prunes
	0/0/0		17.5	7.5	0	0	0	0//0	0/0/			0/0/	-Apples
													-Other:
	0/0/0	0	8	6	0	0	0	0//0	0/0/		/0/	0/0/0	---Longans and longan pulps
	0/0/0	0	17.5	7.5	0	0	0	0//0	0/0/		/0/	0/0/0	---Persimmons
	0/0/0		17.5	7.5	0	0	0	0//0	0/0/		/0/	0/0/0	---Red jujubes
	0/0/0		10	7.5	0	0	0	0//0	0/0/		/0/	0/0/0	---Preserved litchi
													---Other
	0/0/0	0	17.5	7.5	0	0	0	0//0	0/0/		/0/	0/0/0	Fruit of wingfruit elaeagus (*Elaeagus mollis Diels*), dried
	0/0/0	0	17.5	7.5	0	0	0	0//0	0/0/		/0/	0/0/0	Driec Cranberry
	0/0/0	0	17.5	7.5	0	0	0	0//0	0/0/		/0/	0/0/0	Other fruit, dried(other than that of headings No. 08.01 to 08.06)
	0/0/0	14.4	10.8	5.4	0	0	0	0//0	0/0/			0/0/	-Mixtures of nuts or dried fruits of this Chapter
													Peel of citrus fruit or melons (including watermelons), fresh, frozen, dried or provisionally preserved in brine, in sulphur water or in other preservative solutions:
	0/0/0		17.5	7.5	0	0	0	0//0	0/0/			0/0/	Peel of citrus fruit or melons (including watermelons), fresh, frozen, dried or provisionally preserved in brine, in sulphur water or in other preservative solutions

第九章
咖啡、茶、马黛茶及调味香料

注释：

一、税目 09.04 至 09.10 所列产品的混合物，应按下列规定归类：

(一)同一税目的两种或两种以上产品的混合物仍应归入该税目；

(二)不同税目的两种或两种以上产品的混合物应归入税目 09.10。

税目 09.04 至 09.10 的产品[或上述(一)或(二)项的混合物]如添加了其他物质，只要所得的混合物保持了原产品的基本特性，其归类应不受影响。基本特性已经改变的，则不应归入本章；构成混合调味品的，应归入税目 21.03。

二、本章不包括荜澄茄椒或税目 12.11 的其他产品。

税则号列	货品名称〔CIQ 扩展编码及品名－T2 表示见附表 2〕	最惠(%)	暂定税率	普通	增值/消费	出口退税	计量单位	监管条件	检验检疫	特殊证件对美关税
09.01	**咖啡，不论是否焙炒或浸除咖啡碱；咖啡豆荚及咖啡豆皮；含咖啡的咖啡代用品：**									
	-未焙炒的咖啡：									
0901.1100	--未浸除咖啡碱〔101 提取(晒干的除外)、压榨、烹制、烘焙、冻干、脱水、裹糖屑、发酵、冷冻(经漂汤和杀青，并在－18 度以下冷冻)、浸酸、腌渍、炒制等工艺进行加工处理的，102 其他工艺〕	8		50	13/	6	千克	AB	PRQS	/33
0901.1200	--已浸除咖啡碱〔101 提取(晒干的除外)、压榨、烹制、烘焙、冻干、脱水、裹糖屑、发酵、冷冻(经漂汤和杀青，并在－18 度以下冷冻)、浸酸、腌渍、炒制等工艺进行加工处理的，102 其他工艺〕	8		50	13/	6	千克	AB	PRQS	/33
	-已焙炒的咖啡：									
0901.2100	--未浸除咖啡碱〔101 咖啡粉，102 经焙烤后的咖啡豆〕	15		80	13/	13	千克	AB	PRQS	/40
0901.2200	--已浸除咖啡碱〔999〕	15		80	13/	13	千克	AB	PRQS	/40
	-其他：									
0901.9010	---咖啡豆荚及咖啡豆皮〔999〕	10		30	13/	6	千克	AB	PRQS	/25
0901.9020	---含咖啡的咖啡代用品〔999〕	30		80	13/	13	千克	AB	PRQ	/
09.02	**茶，不论是否加香料：**									
	-绿茶(未发酵)，内包装每件净重不超过 3 千克：									
0902.1010	---花茶〔999〕	15		100	9/	6,13	千克	AB	PRS	/40
0902.1090	---其他〔101 绿茶，102 白茶〕	15		100	9/	6,13	千克	AB	PRS	/40
	-其他绿茶(未发酵)：									
0902.2010	---花茶〔999〕	15		100	9/	6,13	千克	AB	PRS	/
0902.2090	---其他〔101 绿茶，102 白茶〕	15		100	9/	6,13	千克	AB	PRS	/40
	-红茶(已发酵)及半发酵茶，内包装每件净重不超过 3 千克：									
0902.3010	---乌龙茶〔999〕	15		100	9/	6,13	千克	AB	PRS	/40
0902.3020	---普洱茶〔999〕	15		100	9/	6,13	千克	AB	PRS	/
0902.3090	---其他〔999〕	15		100	9/	6,13	千克	AB	PRS	/40
	-其他红茶(已发酵)及半发酵茶：									
0902.4010	---乌龙茶〔999〕	15		100	9/	6,13	千克	AB	PRS	/
0902.4020	---普洱茶〔999〕	15		100	9/	6,13	千克	AB	PRS	/
0902.4090	---其他〔999〕	15		100	9/	6,13	千克	AB	PRS	/40
09.03	**马黛茶：**									
0903.0000	马黛茶〔999〕	10		100	9/	13	千克	AB	PRQ	/
09.04	**胡椒；辣椒干及辣椒粉：**									
	-胡椒：									
0904.1100	--未磨									
0904.1100 10	毕拨〔101 药用荜茇，102 调味料〕	20		70	9/	6	千克	QAB	PRQS	/45
0904.1100 90	未磨胡椒(毕拨除外)〔101 药用未磨胡椒，102 调味料〕	20		70	9/	6	千克	AB	PRQS	/45
0904.1200	--已磨〔101 药用已磨胡椒，102 调味料〕	20		70	9/	13	千克	AB	PRQS	/45
	-辣椒：									
0904.2100	--干，未磨〔101 药用辣椒(干)，102 辣椒干〕	20		70	9/	0	千克	AB	PRQS	/
0904.2200	--已磨〔999〕	20		70	9/	6,13	千克	AB	PRQS	/45
09.05	**香子兰豆：**									
0905.1000	-未磨〔999〕	15		50	9/	6	千克	AB	PRQ	/
0905.2000	-已磨〔999〕	15		50	9/	6	千克	AB	PRQ	/
09.06	**肉桂及肉桂花：**									
	-未磨：									
0906.1100	--锡兰肉桂〔999〕	5		50	9/	6	千克	AB	PRQS	/
0906.1900	--其他〔101 药用未磨肉桂(桂枝)，102 调味料〕	5		50	9/	6	千克	AB	PRQS	/30

Chapter 9
Coffee, tea, mate and spices

Notes:

1. Mixtures of the products of headings No. 09.04 to 09.10 are to be classified as follows:
   (a) Mixtures of two or more of the products of the same heading are to be classified in that heading;
   (b) Mixtures of two or more of the products of different headings are to be classified in heading No. 09.10.
   The addition of other substances to the products of headings No. 09.04 to 09.10 (or to the mixtures referred to in paragraph (a) or (b) above) shall not affect their classification provided the resulting mixtures retain the essential character of the goods of those headings. Otherwise such mixtures are not classified in this Chapter; those constituting mixed condiments or mixed seasonings are classified in heading No. 21.03.
2. This Chapter does not cover Cubeb pepper (*Piper cubeba*) or other products of heading No. 12.11.

协定税率 %										特惠税率 %			Article Description
亚太5国	东/冰/格	巴基斯坦	韩国	瑞士	哥达	秘鲁	澳大利亚	新西/坡/智	港/澳/台	亚太2国	老/柬/缅	36/3/1	
													Coffee, whether or not roasted or decaffeinated; coffee husks and skins; coffee substitutes containing coffee in any proportion:
													-Coffee, not roasted:
	5/0/		0	0	0		0	0//0	0/0/		0/0/	0/0/0	--Not decaffeinated
	5/0/		0	0			0	0//0	0/0/		0/0/	0/0/0	--Decaffeinated
													-Coffee, roasted:
	5/0/		6	8.7	0		0	0//0	0/0/		0/0/	0/0/0	--Not decaffeinated
	0/0/	12	6	4.5			0	0//0	0/0/		0/0/	0/0/0	--Decaffeinated
													-Other:
	0/0/	4.5	4	0	0	0	0	0/0/0	0/0/		0/0/	0/0/0	---Coffee husks and skins
	0/0/		21				0	0/0/0	0/0/		0/0/	0/0/0	---Coffee substitutes containing coffee
													Tea, whether or not flavoured:
													-Green tea (not fermented) in immediate packings of a content not exceeding 3kg:
7.5	0/0/0	7.5	6	4.5	0	0	0	0/0/0	0/0/			0/0/	---Flavoured
7.5	0/0/0	7.5	6	4.5	0	0	0	0/0/0	0/0/0			0/0/0	---Other
													-Other green tea (not fermented):
7.5	0/0/0	7.5	6	4.5	0	0	0	0/0/0	0/0/			0/0/	---Flavoured
7.5	0/0/0	7.5	6	4.5	0	0	0	0/0/0	0/0/0			0/0/0	---Other
													-Black tea (fermented) and partly fermented tea, in immediate packings of a content not exceeding 3 kg:
7.5	0/0/0	7.5	6	4.5	0	0	0	0/0/0	0/0/0			0/0/	---Oolong tea
7.5	0/0/0	7.5	6	4.5	0	0	0	0/0/0	0/0/			0/0/	---Pu-er tea
7.5	0/0/0	7.5	6	4.5	0	0	0	0/0/0	0/0/0			0/0/0	---Other
													-Other black tea (fermented) and other partly fermented tea:
7.5	0/0/0	7.5	6	4.5	0	0	0	0/0/0	0/0/0		0/0/0	0/0/0	---Oolong tea
7.5	0/0/0	7.5	6	4.5	0	0	0	0/0/0	0/0/		0/0/0	0/0/0	---Pu-er tea
7.5	0/0/0	7.5	6	4.5	0	0	0	0/0/0	0/0/0		0/0/0	0/0/0	---Other
													Mate:
	0/0/0	4.5	4	0	0	0	0	0/0/0	0/0/			0/0/0	Mate
													Pepper of the genus Piper; dried or crushed or ground fruits of the genus Capsicum or of the genus Pimenta:
													-Pepper:
													--Neither crushed nor ground
	5/0/0		12	6	0	0	0	0//0	0/0/			0/0/	Piper longum
	5/0/0		12	6	0	0	0	0//0	0/0/			0/0/	Pepper of the genus *Piper*, neither crushed nor ground (other than piper longum)
10	5/0/0	10	12	6	0	0	0	0//0	0/0/			0/0/	--Crushed or ground
													-Chili:
10	0/0/0	10	12	6	0	0	0	0/0/0	0/0/			0/0/	--Dried, neither crushed nor ground
10	0/0/0	10	12	6	0	0	0	0/0/0	0/0/			0/0/	--Crushed or ground
													Vanilla:
	0/0/0	12	6	4.5	0	0	0	0/0/0	0/0/			0/0/0	-Neither crushed nor ground
	0/0/0	12	6	4.5	0	0	0	0/0/0	0/0/			0/0/0	-Crushed or ground
													Cinnamon and cinnamon-tree flowers:
													-Neither crushed nor ground:
	0/0/0	0	0	0	0	0	0	0//0	0/0/			0/0/0	--Cinnamon(*Cinnamomum zeylan-icum blume*)
	0/0/0	0	0	0	0	0	0	0//0	0/0/			0/0/0	--Other

税则号列	货品名称〔CIQ扩展编码及品名—T2表示见附表2〕	最惠(%)	暂定税率	普通	增值/消费	出口退税	计量单位	监管条件	检验检疫	特殊证件对美关税
0906.2000	-已磨〔101 药用已磨肉桂(桂枝),102 调味料,103 调味料(玉桂)〕	15		50	9/	13	千克	QAB	PRQS	/
09.07	**丁香(母丁香、公丁香及丁香梗):**									
0907.1000	-未磨〔101 药用未磨丁香,102 调味料〕	3		14	9/	6	千克	QAB	PRQ	/
0907.2000	-已磨〔101 药用已磨丁香,102 调味料〕	3		14	9/	6	千克	QAB	PRQ	/
09.08	**肉豆蔻、肉豆蔻衣及豆蔻:**									
	-肉豆蔻:									
0908.1100	--未磨〔101 药用未磨肉豆蔻,102 调味料〕	8		30	9/	6	千克	QABE	PRQ	/
0908.1200	--已磨〔101 药用已磨肉豆蔻,102 调味料〕	8		30	9/	6	千克	QABE	PRQ	/
	-肉豆蔻衣:									
0908.2100	--未磨〔999〕	8		30	9/	6	千克	ABE	PRQ	/
0908.2200	--已磨〔999〕	8		30	9/	6	千克	ABE	PRQ	/
	-豆蔻:									
0908.3100	--未磨〔101 药用未磨豆蔻,102 调味料〕	3		14	9/	6	千克	QABE	PRQ	/
0908.3200	--已磨〔101 药用已磨豆蔻,102 调味料〕	3		14	9/	13	千克	QABE	PRQ	/
09.09	**茴芹子、八角茴香、小茴香子、芫荽子、枯茗子及黄蒿子;杜松果:**									
	-芫荽子:									
0909.2100	--未磨〔999〕	15		50	9/	6	千克	AB	PRQ	/
0909.2200	--已磨〔999〕	15		50	9/	13	千克	AB	PRQ	/
	-枯茗子:									
0909.3100	--未磨〔999〕	15		50	9/	6	千克	AB	PRQ	/
0909.3200	--已磨〔999〕	15		50	9/	13	千克	AB	PRQ	/40
	-茴芹子或八角茴香、页蒿子或小茴香子;杜松果:									
	--未磨:									
0909.6110	---八角茴香〔101 药用未磨八角茴香,102 调味料〕	20		90	9/	6	千克	QAB	PRQS	/
0909.6190	---其他									
0909.6190 10	未磨的小茴香子;未磨的杜松果〔101 药用未磨小茴香,102 调味料〕	15		50	9/	6	千克	QAB	PRQS	/
0909.6190 90	未磨的茴芹子;未磨的页蒿子〔101 茴芹子,102 页蒿子〕	15		50	9/	6	千克	AB	PRQ	/
	--已磨:									
0909.6210	---八角茴香〔101 药用已磨八角茴香,102 调味料〕	20		90	9/	13	千克	QAB	PRQS	/
0909.6290	---其他									
0909.6290 10	已磨的小茴香子;已磨的杜松果〔101 药用已磨小茴香,102 调味料〕	15		50	9/	13	千克	QAB	PRQS	/30
0909.6290 90	已磨的茴芹子;已磨的页蒿子〔101 茴芹子,102 页蒿子〕	15		50	9/	13	千克	AB	PRQ	/30
09.10	**姜、番红花、姜黄、麝香草、月桂叶、咖喱及其他调味香料:**									
	-姜:									
0910.1100	--未磨〔101 药用未磨干姜,102 药用未磨生姜,103 调味料〕	15		50	9/	0	千克	AB	PRQS	/
0910.1200	--已磨〔101 药用已磨干姜,102 调味料〕	15		50	9/	6	千克	AB	PRQS	/40
0910.2000	-番红花〔101 西红花,102 调味料〕	2		14	9/	6,13	千克	QAB	PRQS	/
0910.300C	-姜黄〔102 药用姜黄,103 调味料,104 有检疫要求食品添加剂〕	15		50	9/	6	千克	QAB	PRQS	/
	-其他调味香料:									
0910.9100	--本章注释一(二)所述的混合物〔101 五香,102 五香除外〕	15		50	13/	13	千克	AB	PRQS	/40
0910.9900	--其他〔101 药用花椒,102 调味料,103 奥勒岗,104 龙嵩,105 咖喱粉,106 百里香叶、百里香叶粉,107 干薄荷叶,108 香草,109 花椒,110 芥末粉,111 多香果,112 罗勒粉,113 莳萝子粉,114 芹菜子,115 葫芦巴子,116 牛至叶 、牛至叶粉,117 月桂,118 众香子,119 洋苏叶,120 墨角兰,121 迷迭香,122 香叶,123 草果〕	15		50	13/	6,13	千克	AB	PRQS	/40

协定税率 %										特惠税率 %			Article Description
亚太5国	东/冰/格	巴基斯坦	韩国	瑞士	哥达	秘鲁	澳大利亚	新西/坡/智	港/澳/台	亚太2国	老/柬/缅	36/3/1	
	0/0/0	12	6	4.5	0	0	0	0/0/0	0/0/			0/0/	-Crushed or ground
													Cloves (whole fruit, cloves and stems):
	0/0/0	0	0	0	0	0	0	0//0	0/0/		/0/	0/0/0	-Neither crushed nor ground
	0/0/0	0	0	0	0	0	0	0//0	0/0/		/0/	0/0/0	-Crushed or ground
													Nutmeg, mace and cardamoms:
													-Nutmeg:
	0/0/0	4	0	0	0	0	0	0//0	0/0/		0/0/	0/0/0	--Neither crushed nor ground
	0/0/0	4	0	0	0	0	0	0//0	0/0/		0/0/	0/0/0	--Crushed or ground
													-Mace:
	0/0/0	4	0	0	0	0	0	0//0	0/0/		0/0/	0/0/0	--Neither crushed nor ground
	0/0/0	4	0	0	0	0	0	0//0	0/0/		0/0/	0/0/0	--Crushed or ground
													-Cardamoms:
	0/0/0	0	0	0	0	0	0	0//0	0/0/		0/0/	0/0/0	--Neither crushed nor ground
	0/0/0	0	0	0	0	0	0	0//0	0/0/		0/0/	0/0/0	--Crushed or ground
													Seeds of anise, star anise, fennel, coriander, cumin or caraway; juniper berries:
													-Seeds of coriander:
	0/0/0	12	6	4.5	0	0	0	0/0/0	0/0/			0/0/	--Neither crushed nor ground
	0/0/0	12	6	4.5	0	0	0	0/0/0	0/0/			0/0/	--Crushed or ground
													-Seeds of cumin:
7.5	0/0/0	6.8	6	4.5	0	0	0	0/0/0	0/0/			0/0/	--Neither crushed nor ground
7.5	0/0/0	6.8	6	4.5	0	0	0	0/0/0	0/0/			0/0/	--Crushed nor ground
													-Seeds of pimpinella or star anise、seeds of caraway or seeds of fennel;juniper berries:
													--Neither crushed nor ground:
	0/0/0		12	6	0	0	0	0/0/0	0/0/			0/0/	---Star anises
													---Other
	0/0/0	12	6	4.5	0	0	0	0/0/0	0/0/			0/0/	Seed of fennel,seed of juniper berries, neither crushed nor ground
	0/0/0	12	6	4.5	0	0	0	0/0/0	0/0/			0/0/	Seed of pimpinella,seed of caraway, neither crushed nor ground
													--Crushed nor ground:
	0/0/0		12	6	0	0	0	0/0/0	0/0/			0/0/	---Star anises
													---Other
	0/0/0	12	6	4.5	0	0	0	0/0/0	0/0/			0/0/	Seed of fennel,seed of juniper berries, crushed or ground
	0/0/0	12	6	4.5	0	0	0	0/0/0	0/0/			0/0/	Seed of pimpinella,seed of caraway,crushed or ground
													Ginger, saffron, turmeric (curcuma), thyme, bay leaves, curry and other spices:
													-Ginger:
7.5	0/0/0	6.8	6	4.5	0	0	0	0/0/0	0/0/		0/0/	0/0/0	--Neither crushed nor ground
7.5	0/0/0	6.8	6	4.5	0	0	0	0/0/0	0/0/		0/0/	0/0/0	--Crushed or ground
	0/0/0	0	0	0	0	0	0	0//0	0/0/			0/0/0	-Saffron
7.5	0/0/0	6.8	6	4.5	0	0	0	0/0/0	0/0/		/0/	0/0/0	-Turmeric (curcuma)
													-Other spices:
7.5	0/0/0	0	6	4.5	0	0	0	0/0/0	0/0/			0/0/0	--Mixtures referred to in Note 1(b) to this Chapter
	0/0/0	0	6	4.5	0	0	0	0/0/0	0/0/			0/0/0	--Other

第十章
谷　　物

注释：

一、（一）本章各税目所列产品必须带有谷粒，不论是否成穗或带秆。

（二）本章不包括已去壳或经其他加工的谷物。但去壳、碾磨、磨光、上光、半熟或破碎的稻米仍应归入税目10.06。

二、税目10.05不包括甜玉米（第七章）。

子目注释：

所称“硬粒小麦”，是指硬粒小麦属的小麦及以该属具有相同染色体数目(28)的小麦种间杂交所得的小麦。

税则号列		货品名称〔CIQ扩展编码及品名－T2表示见附表2〕	最惠(%)	暂定税率	普通	增值/消费	出口退税	计量单位	监管条件	检验检疫	特殊证件对美关税
10.01		小麦及混合麦：									
		-硬粒小麦：									
1001.1100		--种用									
1001.1100	01	种用硬粒小麦(配额内)〔999〕	1		180	9/	0	千克	4xABty	MPNQ	/
1001.1100	90	种用硬粒小麦(配额外)〔999〕	65		180	9/	0	千克	4xABy	MPNQ	/
1001.1900		--其他									
1001.1900	01	其他硬粒小麦(配额内)〔101食用小麦，102工业用小麦，103饲用小麦〕	1		180	9/	0	千克	4xABty	MPRQS	/26
1001.1900	90	其他硬粒小麦(配额外)〔101食用小麦，102工业用小麦，103饲用小麦〕	65		180	9/	0	千克	4xABy	MPRQS	/90
		-其他：									
1001.9100		--种用									
1001.9100	01	其他种用小麦及混合麦(配额内)〔999〕	1		180	9/	0	千克	4xABty	MPNQ	/
1001.9100	90	其他种用小麦及混合麦(配额外)〔999〕	65		180	9/	0	千克	4xABy	MPNQ	/
1001.9900		--其他									
1001.9900	01	其他小麦及混合麦(配额内)〔101食用小麦，102工业用小麦，103饲用小麦〕	1		180	9/	0	千克	4xABty	MPRQS	/26
1001.9900	90	其他小麦及混合麦(配额外)〔101食用小麦，102工业用小麦，103饲用小麦〕	65		180	9/	0	千克	4xABy	MPRQS	/90
10.02		黑麦：									
1002.1000		-种用〔999〕	0		0	9/	0	千克	AB	PQ	/10
1002.9000		-其他〔999〕	3		8	9/	0	千克	AB	PRQ	/13
10.03		大麦：									
1003.1000		-种用〔999〕	0		160	9/	0	千克	AB7	MPNQ	/10
1003.9000		-其他〔101食用，102饲料用〕	3		160	9/	0	千克	AB7	MPRQS	/13
10.04		燕麦：									
1004.1000		-种用〔999〕	0		0	9/	0	千克	AB	PQ	/10
1004.9000		-其他〔999〕	2		8	9/	0	千克	AB	PRQ	/12
10.05		玉米：									
1005.1000		-种用									
1005.1000	01	种用玉米(配额内)〔999〕	1		180	9/	0	千克	4xAByt	PQ	/
1005.1000	90	种用玉米(配额外)〔999〕	20		180	9/	0	千克	4xABy	PQ	/
1005.9000		-其他									
1005.9000	01	其他玉米(配额内)〔101食用玉米，102工业用玉米，103饲用玉米〕	1		180	9/	0	千克	4xAByt	PRQS	/26
1005.9000	90	其他玉米(配额外)〔101食用玉米，102工业用玉米，103饲用玉米〕	65		180	9/	0	千克	4xABy	PRQS	/90
10.06		稻谷、大米：									
		-稻谷：									
		---种用：									
1006.1021		----长粒米									
1006.1021	01	种用长粒米稻谷(配额内)〔999〕	1		180	9/	0	千克	4xAByt	PNQ	/26
1006.1021	90	种用长粒米稻谷(配额外)〔999〕	65		180	9/	0	千克	4xABy	PNQ	/90
1006.1029		----其他									
1006.1029	01	其他种用稻谷(配额内)〔999〕	1		180	9/	0	千克	4xAByt	PNQ	/26
1006.1029	90	其他种用稻谷(配额外)〔999〕	65		180	9/	0	千克	4xABy	PNQ	/90
		---其他：									
1006.1081		----长粒米									
1006.1081	01	其他长粒米稻谷(配额内)〔999〕	1		180	9/	0	千克	4xAByt	PRQS	/26
1006.1081	90	其他长粒米稻谷(配额外)〔999〕	65		180	9/	0	千克	4xABy	PRQS	/90
1006.1089		----其他									
1006.1089	01	其他稻谷(配额内)〔999〕	1		180	9/	0	千克	4xAByt	PRQS	/26
1006.1089	90	其他稻谷(配额外)〔999〕	65		180	9/	0	千克	4xABy	PRQS	/90
		-糙米：									

Chapter 10
Cereals

Notes:

1. (a) The products specified in the headings of this Chapter are to be classified in those headings only if grains are present, whether or not in the ear or on the stalk.

   (b) The Chapter does not cover grains which have been hulled or otherwise worked. However, rice, husked, milled, polished, glazed, parboiled or broken remains classified in heading No. 10.06

2. Heading No. 10.05 does not cover sweet corn (Chapter 7).

Subheading Note:

The term "durum wheat" means wheat of the *Triticum durum* species and the hybrids derived from the inter-specific crossing of *Triticum durum* which have the same number (28) of chromosomes as that species.

协定税率 %										特惠税率 %			
亚太5国	东/冰/格	巴基斯坦	韩国	瑞士	哥达	秘鲁	澳大利亚	新西/坡/智	港/澳/台	亚太2国	老/柬/缅	36/3/1	Article Description
													Wheat and maslin:
													-Durum wheat:
													--Seed
	5//								0/0/				Durum wheat, seed(in-quota)
	5//								0/0/				Durum wheat, seed(out-quota)
													--Other
	5//								0/0/				Other durum wheat(in-quota)
	5//								0/0/				Other durum wheat(out-quota)
													-Other:
													--Seed
	5//								0/0/				Other wheat, seed and maslin(in-quota)
	5//								0/0/				Other wheat, seed and maslin(out-quota)
													--Other
	5//								0/0/				Other wheat and maslin (in-quota)
	5//								0/0/				Other wheat and maslin (out-quota)
													Rye:
												0/0/0	-Seed
	0/0/1.2	0	0	0	0	0	0	0//0	0/0/			0/0/0	-Other
													Barley:
												0/0/0	-Seed
0	0/0/1.2	0	0	0	0	0	0	0//0	0/0/			0/0/0	-Other
													Oats:
												0/0/0	-Seed
	0/0/0.8	0	0	0	0	0	0	0//0	0/0/			0/0/0	-Other
													Maize (corn):
													-Seed
									0/0/				Maize (corn) seed (in-quota)
									0/0/				Maize (corn) seed (out-quota)
													-Other
	50//								0/0/				Other maize (corn) (in-quota)
	50//								0/0/				Other maize (corn) (out-quota)
													Rice:
													-Rice in husk (paddy or rough):
													---Seed:
													----Long grain rice
	50//								0/0/				rice in husk(paddy or rough), Long grain rice, seed(in-quota)
	50//								0/0/				rice in husk(paddy or rough), Long grain rice, seed(out-quota)
													----Other
	50//								0/0/				Other rice in husk(paddy or rough), seed(in-quota)
	50//								0/0/				Other rice in husk(paddy or rough), seed(out-quota)
													---Other:
													----Long grain rice
	50//								0/0/				Other rice in husk(paddy or rough), Long grain rice(in-quota)
	50//								0/0/				Other rice in husk(paddy or rough), Long grain rice(out-quota)
													----Other
	50//								0/0/				Other rice in husk(paddy or rough)(in-quota)
	50//								0/0/				Other rice in husk(paddy or rough), (out-quota)
													-Husked (brown) rice:

税则号列		货品名称〔CIQ 扩展编码及品名—T2 表示见附表 2〕	最惠(%)	暂定税率	普通	增值/消费	出口退税	计量单位	监管条件	检验检疫	特殊证件对美关税
1006.2020		---长粒米									
1006.2020	01	长粒米糙米(配额内)〔999〕	1		180	9/	0	千克	4xAByt	MPRQS	/26
1006.2020	90	长粒米糙米(配额外)〔999〕	65		180	9/	0	千克	4xABy	MPRQS	/90
1006.2080		---其他									
1006.2080	01	其他糙米(配额内)〔999〕	1		180	9/	0	千克	4xAByt	MPRQS	/26
1006.2080	90	其他糙米(配额外)〔999〕	65		180	9/	0	千克	4xABy	MPRQS	/90
		-精米,不论是否磨光或上光:									
1006.3020		---长粒米									
1006.3020	01	长粒米精米(不论是否磨光或上光(配额内))〔201 食用白米,202 食用蒸煮米,203 食用其他加工米〕	1		180	9/	0	千克	4xAByt	MPRQS	/26
1006.3020	90	长粒米精米(不论是否磨光或上光(配额外))〔201 食用白米,202 食用蒸煮米,203 食用其他加工米〕	65		180	9/	0	千克	4xABy	MPRQS	/90
1006.3080		---其他									
1006.3080	01	其他精米(不论是否磨光或上光(配额内))〔201 食用白米,202 食用蒸煮米,203 食用其他加工米〕	1		180	9/	0	千克	4xAByt	MPRQS	/26
1006.3080	90	其他精米(不论是否磨光或上光(配额外))〔201 食用白米,202 食用蒸煮米,203 食用其他加工米〕	65		180	9/	0	千克	4xABy	MPRQS	/90
		-碎米:									
1006.4020		---长粒米									
1006.4020	01	长粒米碎米(配额内)〔201 食用白米,202 食用蒸煮米,203 食用其他加工米〕	1		180	9/	0	千克	4xAByt	MPRQS	/26
1006.4020	90	长粒米碎米(配额外)〔201 食用白米,202 食用蒸煮米,203 食用其他加工米〕	10		180	9/	0	千克	4xABy	MPRQS	/35
1006.4080		---其他									
1006.4080	01	其他碎米(配额内)〔201 食用白米,202 食用蒸煮米,203 食用其他加工米〕	1		180	9/	0	千克	4xAByt	MPRQS	/26
1006.4080	90	其他碎米(配额外)〔201 食用白米,202 食用蒸煮米,203 食用其他加工米〕	10		180	9/	0	千克	4xABy	MPRQS	/35
10.07		**食用高粱:**									
1007.1000		-种用〔101 种用,102 食用、带壳,103 食用、去壳〕	0		0	9/	0	千克	AB7	PNQ	/10
1007.9000		-其他〔101 饲用,102 食用、带壳,103 食用、去壳〕	2		8	9/	0	千克	AB7	PRQS	/27
10.08		**荞麦、谷子及加那利草子;其他谷物:**									
1008.1000		-荞麦〔101 食用、带壳,102 食用、去壳〕	2		8	9/	0	千克	AB	PRQS	/12
		-谷子:									
1008.2100		--种用〔999〕	2		8	9/	0	千克	AB	PQ	/12
1008.2900		--其他〔101 食用、带壳,102 食用、去壳〕	2		8	9/	0	千克	AB	PRQS	/12
1008.3000		-加那利草子〔999〕	2		8	9/	9	千克	AB	PRQ	/12
		-直长马唐(马唐属):									
1008.4010		---种用〔999〕	0		0	9/	0	千克	AB	PNQ	/10
1008.4090		---其他〔999〕	3		8	9/	0	千克	AB	PRQS	/13
		-昆诺阿藜:									
1008.5010		---种用〔999〕	0		0	9/	0	千克	AB	PNQ	/10
1008.5090		---其他〔999〕	3		8	9/	0	千克	AB	PRQS	/13
		-黑小麦:									
1008.6010		---种用〔999〕	0		0	9/	0	千克	AB	PNQ	/10
1008.6090		---其他〔101 食用,102 工业用,103 饲用〕	3		80	9/	0	千克	AB	PRQS	/13
		-其他谷物:									
1008.9010		---种用〔101 粟种子,102 荞麦种子,103 其他谷物种子〕	0		0	9/	0	千克	AB	PNQ	/10
1008.9090		---其他〔101 饲用其他粮谷,102 食用、去壳黍子,103 食用、带壳黍子,104 食用谷穗,105 食用其他粮谷,106 野米,107 薏米,108 藜麦〕	3		8	9/	0	千克	AB	PRQS	/13

协定税率 %										特惠税率 %			Article Description
亚太5国	东/冰/格	巴基斯坦	韩国	瑞士	哥达	秘鲁	澳大利亚	新西/坡/智	港/澳/台	亚太2国	老/柬/缅	36/3/1	
													---Long grain rice
	50//								0/0/				Husked(brown) rice, long grain rice(in-quota)
	50//								0/0/				Husked(brown) rice, long grain rice(out-quota)
													---Other
	50//								0/0/				Other husked(brown) rice(in-quota)
	50//								0/0/				Other husked(brown) rice(out-quota)
													-Semi-milled or wholly missed rice, whether or not polished or glazed:
													---Long grain rice
	50//								0/0/				Semi-milled or wholly milled rice, long grain rice(whether or not polished or glazed(in-quota))
	50//								0/0/				Semi-milled or wholly milled rice, long grain rice(whether or not polished or glazed(out-quota))
													---Other
	50//								0/0/				Other semi-milled or wholly milled rice(whether or not polished or glazed(in-quota))
	50//								0/0/				Other semi-milled or wholly milled rice(whether or not polished or glazed(out-quota))
													-Broken rice:
													---Long grain rice
	5//								0/0/				Broken rice, long grain rice(in-quota)
	5//								0/0/				Broken rice, long grain rice(out-quota)
													---Other
	5//								0/0/				Other broken rice(in-quota)
	5//								0/0/				Other broken rice(out-quota)
													Grain sorghum:
												0/0/0	-Seed
	0/0/0.8	0	0	0	0	0	0	0//0	0/0/			0/0/	-Other
													Buckwheat, millet and canary seed; other cereals:
	0/0/0.8	0	0	0	0	0	0	0//0	0/0/			0/0/0	-Buckwheat
													-Millet:
	0/0/0	0	0	0	0	0	0	0//0	0/0/		0//	0/0/0	--Seed
	0/0/0.8	0	0	0	0	0	0	0//0	0/0/		0//	0/0/0	--Other
	0/0/0	0	0	0	0	0	0	0//0	0/0/		0//	0/0/0	-Canary seed
													-Fonio(Digitaria spp.):
												0/0/0	---Seed
	0/0/0	0	0	0	0	0	0	0//0	0/0/		0//	0/0/0	---Other
													-Quinoa(Chenopodium quinoa):
												0/0/0	---Seed
	0/0/0	0	0	0	0	0	0	0//0	0/0/		0//	0/0/0	---Other
													-Triticale:
												0/0/0	---Seed
	0/0/0	0	0	0	0	0	0	0//0	0/0/		0//	0/0/0	---Other
													-Other cereals:
												0/0/0	---Seed
	0/0/1.2	0	0	0	0	0	0	0//0	0/0/		0//	0/0/0	---Other

第十一章
制粉工业产品；麦芽；淀粉；菊粉；面筋

注释：

一、本章不包括：

（一）作为咖啡代用品的焙制麦芽（税目09.01或21.01）；

（二）税目19.01的经制作的细粉、粗粒、粗粉或淀粉；

（三）税目19.04的玉米片及其他产品；

（四）税目20.01、20.04或20.05的经加工或保藏的蔬菜；

（五）药品（第三十章）；

（六）具有芳香料制品或化妆盥洗品性质的淀粉（第三十三章）。

二、（一）下表所列谷物碾磨产品按干制品重量计如果同时符合以下两个条件，应归入本章；但是，整粒、滚压、制片或磨碎的谷物胚芽均应归入税目11.04：

1. 淀粉含量（按修订的尤艾斯旋光法测定）超过表列第（2）栏的比例；以及

2. 灰分含量（除去任何添加的矿物质）不超过表列第（3）栏的比例。

否则，应归入税目23.02。

（二）符合上述规定归入本章的产品，如果用表列第（4）或第（5）栏规定孔径的金属丝网筛过筛，其通过率按重量计不低于表列比例的，应归入税目11.01或11.02。

否则，应归入税目11.03或11.04。

谷　物 （1）	淀粉含量 （2）	灰分含量 （3）	通过下列孔径筛子的比率	
			315微米 （4）	500微米 （5）
小麦及黑麦	45％	2.5％	80％	—
大　麦	45％	3％	80％	—
燕　麦	45％	5％	80％	—
玉米及高粱	45％	2％	—	90％
大　米	45％	1.6％	80％	—
荞　麦	45％	4％	80％	—

三、税目11.03所称"粗粒"及"粗粉"，是指谷物经碾碎所得的下列产品：

（一）玉米产品，用2毫米孔径的金属丝网筛过筛后通过率按重量计不低于95％的；

（二）其他谷物产品，用1.25毫米孔径的金属丝网筛过筛，通过率按重量计不低于95％的。

税则号列		货品名称〔CIQ扩展编码及品名－T2表示见附表2〕	最惠(%)	暂定税率	普通	增值/消费	出口退税	计量单位	监管条件	检验检疫	特殊证件对美关税
11.01		**小麦或混合麦的细粉：**									
1101.0000		小麦或混合麦的细粉									
1101.0000	01	小麦或混合麦的细粉（配额内）〔999〕	6		130	9/	9	千克	4ABtxy	PRQS	/31
1101.0000	90	小麦或混合麦的细粉（配额外）〔999〕	65		130	9/	9	千克	4ABxy	PRQS	/90
11.02		**其他谷物细粉，但小麦或混合麦的细粉除外：**									
1102.2000		-玉米细粉									
1102.2000	01	玉米细粉（配额内）〔999〕	9		130	9/	0	千克	4ABtxy	PRQS	/34
1102.2000	90	玉米细粉（配额外）〔999〕	40		130	9/	0	千克	4ABxy	PRQS	/65
		-其他：									
		---大米细粉：									
1102.9021		----长粒米的									
1102.9021	01	长粒米大米细粉（配额内）〔999〕	9		130	9/	0	千克	4ABtxy	PRQS	/34
1102.9021	90	长粒米大米细粉（配额外）〔999〕	40		130	9/	0	千克	4ABxy	PRQS	/65
1102.9029		----其他									

Chapter 11
Products of the milling industry; malt; starches; inulin; wheat gluten

chorpterr Notes:

1. This Chapter does not cover:
   (a) Roasted malt put up as coffee substitutes (heading No. 09.01 or 21.01);
   (b) Prepared flours, groats, meals or starches of heading No. 19.01;
   (c) Corn flakes or other products of heading No. 19.04;
   (d) Vegetables, prepared or preserved, of heading No. 20.01, 20.04 or 20.05;
   (e) Pharmaceutical products (Chapter 30);
   (f) Starches having the character of perfumery, cosmetic or toilet preparations (Chapter 33).
2. (A) Products from the milling of the cereals listed in the table below fall in this Chapter if they have, by weight on the dry product. However, germ of cereals, whole, rolled. flaked or ground is always classified in heading No. 11.04.
   (ⅰ) a starch content (determined by the modified Ewers polarimetric method) exceeding that indicated in Column (2); and
   (ⅱ) an ash content (after deduction of any added minerals) not exceeding that indicated in Column (3).
   Otherwise, they fall in heading No. 23.02

   (B) Products falling in this Chapter under the above provisions shall be classified in heading No. 11.01 or 11.02 if the percentage passing through a woven metal wire cloth sieve with the aperture indicated in Column (4) or (5) is not less, by weight, than that shown against the cereal concerned.
   Otherwise, they fall in heading No. 11.03 or 11.04.

Cereal (1)	Starch content (2)	Ash content (3)	Rate of passage through a sieve with an aperture of	
			315 micrometres (microns) (4)	500 micrometres (microns) (5)
Wheat and rye	45%	2.5%	80%	-
Barley	45%	3%	80%	-
Oats	45%	5%	80%	-
Maize(corn) and grain Sorghum	45%	2%	-	90%
Rice	45%	1.6%	80%	-
Buckwheat	45%	4%	80%	-

3. For the purposes of heading No. 11.03, the terms "groats" and "meal" mean products obtained by the fragmentation of cereal grains, of which:
   (a) in the case of maize (corn) products, at least 95% by weight passes through a woven metal wire cloth sieve with an aperture of 2mm.
   (b) in the case of other cereal products, at least 95% by weight passes through a woven metal wire cloth sieve with an aperture of 1.25mm.

协定税率 %										特惠税率 %			Article Description
亚太5国	东/冰/格	巴基斯坦	韩国	瑞士	哥达	秘鲁	澳大利亚	新西/坡/智	港/澳/台	亚太2国	老/柬/缅	36/3/1	
													Wheat or maslin flour:
													Wheat or maslin flour
	50//								0/0/				Wheat or maslin flour (in-quota)
	50//								0/0/				Wheat or maslin flour (out-quota)
													Cereal flours other than of wheat or maslin:
													-Maize (corn) flour
									0/0/				Maize (corn) flour (in-quota)
									0/0/				Maize(corn) flour(out-quota)
													-Other:
													---Rice flour
													----Long grain rice
									0/0/				Long grain rice flour(in-quota)
									0/0/				Long grain rice flour(out-quota)
													----Other

税则号列	货品名称〔CIQ 扩展编码及品名－T2 表示见附表 2〕	最惠(%)	暂定税率	普通	增值/消费	出口退税	计量单位	监管条件	检验检疫	特殊证件对美关税
1102.9029 01	其他大米细粉(配额内)〔201 食用米粉,202 食用其他粮食加工产品〕	9		130	9/	0	千克	4ABtxy	PRQS	/34
1102.9029 90	其他大米细粉(配额外)〔201 食用米粉,202 食用其他粮食加工产品〕	40		130	9/	0	千克	4ABxy	PRQS	/65
	-其他:									
	--大米细粉:									
1102.9090	---其他〔101 食用荞麦仁、粉,102 食用其他面粉类,103 食用其他粮食加工产品,105 黑麦粉〕	5		14	9/	0	千克	AB	PRQS	/30
11.03	**谷物的粗粒、粗粉及团粒:**									
	-粗粒及粗粉:									
1103.1100	--小麦的									
1103.1100 01	小麦粗粒及粗粉(配额内)〔999〕	9		130	9/	9	千克	4ABtxy	PRQS	/34
1103.1100 90	小麦粗粒及粗粉(配额外)〔999〕	65		130	9/	9	千克	4ABxy	PRQS	/90
1103.1300	--玉米的									
	--其他:									
1103.1300 01	玉米粗粒及粗粉(配额内)〔999〕	9		130	9/	0	千克	4ABtxy	PRQS	/19
1103.1300 90	玉米粗粒及粗粉(配额外)〔999〕	65		130	9/	0	千克	4ABxy	PRQS	/75
1103.1910	---燕麦的	5		14	9/	0	千克	AB	PRQ	/15
	--其他:									
	---大米的:									
1103.1931	----长粒米的									
1103.1931 01	长粒米大米粗粒及粗粉(配额内)〔999〕	9		70	9/	0	千克	4ABtxy	PRQS	/34
1103.1931 90	长粒米大米粗粒及粗粉(配额外)〔999〕	10		70	9/	0	千克	4ABxy	PRQS	/35
1103.1939	----其他									
1103.1939 01	其他大米粗粒及粗粉(配额内)〔201 食用米粉,202 食用其他粮食加工产品〕	9		70	9/	0	千克	4ABtxy	PRQS	/34
1103.1939 90	其他大米粗粒及粗粉(配额外)〔201 食用,202 食用米粉,203 食用其他粮食加工产品〕	10		70	9/	0	千克	4ABxy	PRQS	/35
	---大米的:									
1103.1990	---其他〔101 食用荞麦仁、粉,102 食用黑麦粉,103 食用其他粮食加工产品〕	5		14	9/	0	千克	AB	PRQS	/15
	-团粒:									
1103.2010	---小麦的									
1103.2010 01	小麦团粒(配额内)〔999〕	10		180	9/	9	千克	4ABtxy	PRQ	/20
1103.2010 90	小麦团粒(配额外)〔999〕	65		180	9/	9	千克	4ABxy	PRQ	/75
1103.2090	---其他〔101 食用荞麦仁、粉,102 食用黑麦粉,103 食用燕麦粉,104 食用其他面粉类〕	20		50	9/	0	千克	AB	PRQ	/30
11.04	**经其他加工的谷物(例如,去壳、滚压、制片、制成粒状、切片或粗磨),但税目 10.06 的稻谷、大米除外;谷物胚芽,整粒、滚压、制片或磨碎的:**									
	-滚压或制片的谷物:									
1104.1200	--燕麦的〔999〕	20		50	13/	0	千克	AB	PRQ	/50
	--其他:									
1104.1910	---大麦的〔999〕	20		50	13/	0	千克	AB	PRQ	/30
1104.1990	---其他									
1104.1990 10	滚压或制片的玉米〔999〕	20		50	13/	0	千克	4ABxy	PRQ	/30
1104.1990 90	滚压或制片的其他谷物〔999〕	20		50	13/	0	千克	AB	PRQ	/30
	-经其他加工的谷物(例如,去壳、制成粒状、切片或粗磨):									
1104.2200	--燕麦的〔999〕	20		50	13/	0	千克	AB	PRQ	/45
1104.2300	--玉米的									
1104.2300 01	经其他加工的玉米(配额内)〔101 食用玉米粉,102 食用其他粮食加工产品〕	10		180	9/	0	千克	4xAByt	PRQ	/20
1104.2300 90	经其他加工的玉米(配额外)〔101 食用玉米粉,102 食用其他粮食加工产品〕	65		180	9/	0	千克	4xABy	PRQ	/75
	--其他:									
1104.2910	---大麦的〔999〕	65		114	9/	0	千克	AB	PRQS	/75
1104.2990	---其他〔101 食用小麦粉,102 食用荞麦仁、粉,103 食用燕麦粉,104 食用其他粮食加工产品,105 黑麦粉,106 野米,107 薏仁米〕	20		50	9/	0	千克	AB	PRQS	/45
1104.3000	-谷物胚芽,整粒、滚压、制片或磨碎的〔101 食用其他麦芽,102 食用其他粮食加工产品〕	20		50	9/	0	千克	AB	MPRQ	/40
11.05	**马铃薯的细粉、粗粉、粉末、粉片、颗粒及团粒:**									
1105.1000	-细粉、粗粉及粉末〔999〕	15		50	13/	13	千克	AB	PRQ	/30
1105.2000	-粉片、颗粒及团粒〔999〕	15		50	13/	13	千克	AB	PRQ	/40

协定税率 %										特惠税率 %			
亚太5国	东/冰/格	巴基斯坦	韩国	瑞士	哥达	秘鲁	澳大利亚	新西/坡/智	港/澳/台	亚太2国	老/柬/缅	36/3/1	Article Description
	5//								0/0/				Other rice flour(in－quota)
	5//								0/0/				Other rice flour(out－quota)
													-Other:
													--Rice flour:
	0/0/2	0	0	0	0	0	0	0//0	0/0/		/0/	0/0/0	---Other
													Cereal groats, meal and pellets:
													-Groats and meal:
													--Of wheat
	50//								0/0/				Wheat groats and meal (in-quota)
	50//								0/0/				Wheat groats and meal (out-quota)
													--Of maize (corn)
													--Other:
	50//								0/0/				Maize (corn) groats and meal (in-quota)
	50//								0/0/				Maize (corn) groats and meal (out-quota)
	0/0/2	0	0	0	0	0	0	0//0	0/0/		//	0/0/0	---Of oat
													---Other:
													---Of rice
													----Of long grain rice
	5//								0/0/				long grain rice groats and meal(in－quota)
	5//								0/0/				long grain rice groats and meal(out－quota)
													----Other
	5//								0/0/				Other rice groats and meal(in－quota)
	5//								0/0/				Other rice groats and meal(out－quota)
													---Of rice:
	0/0/2	0	0	0	0	0	0	0//0	0/0/		/0/	0/0/0	---Other
													-Pellets:
													---Of wheat
	50//								0/0/				Wheat pellets (in-quota)
	50//								0/0/				Wheat pellets (out-quota)
	0/0/		12	6	0	0	0	0/0/0	0/0/			0/0/	---Of other cereals
													Cereal grains otherwise worked (for example, hulled, rolled, flaked, pearled, sliced or kibbled), except rice of heading No. 10.06; germ of cereals, whole, rolled, flaked or ground:
													-Rolled or flaked grains:
	0/0/		12	6	0	0	0	0/0/0	0/0/			0/0/	--Of oats
													--Other:
	0/0/		12	6	0	0	0	0/0/0	0/0/			0/0/	---Of barley
													---Other
	0/0/		12	6	0	0	0	0/0/0	0/0/			0/0/	Rolled or flaked maize
	0/0/		12	6	0	0	0	0/0/0	0/0/			0/0/	Rolled or flaked other corns
													-Other worked grains (for example, hulled, pearled, sliced or kibbled):
	0/0/		12	6	0	0	0	0/0/0	0/0/			0/0/	--Of oats
													--Of maize (corn)
	50//								0/0/				Maize (corn) otherwise worked (in-quota)
	50//								0/0/				Maize (corn) otherwise worked (out-quota)
													--Other:
	0//				0	0	0	0/0/0	0/0/			0/0/	---Of barley
	0/0/		12	6	0	0	0	0/0/0	0/0/			0/0/	---Other
	0/0/0		12	6	0	0	0	0/0/0	0/0/			0/0/	-Germ of cereals, whole, rolled, flaked or ground
													Flour, meal, powder, flakes, granules and pellets of potatoes:
	0/0/	12	6	4.5	0	0	0	0/0/0	0/0/			0/0/	-Flour, meal and powder
	0/0/	12	6	4.5	0	0	0	0/0/0	0/0/			0/0/	-Flakes, granules and pellets

税则号列	货品名称〔CIQ扩展编码及品名—T2表示见附表2〕	最惠(%)	暂定税率	普通	增值/消费	出口退税	计量单位	监管条件	检验检疫	特殊证件对美关税
11.06	**用税目07.13的干豆或税目07.14的西谷茎髓及植物根茎、块茎制成的细粉、粗粉及粉末;用第八章的产品制成的细粉、粗粉及粉末:**									
1106.1000	-用税目07.13的干豆制成的〔999〕	10		30	13/	13	千克	AB	PRQS	/25
1106.2000	-用税目07.14的西谷茎髓及植物根茎、块茎制成的〔999〕	20		50	13/	13	千克	AB	PRQS	/30
1106.3000	-用第八章的产品制成的〔999 其他籽仁为皮或衣等包被的籽实,998 其他籽仁为坚硬外壳包被的籽实〕	20		80	13/	9,13	千克	AB	PRQS	/45
11.07	**麦芽,不论是否焙制:**									
1107.1000	-未焙制〔101 食用,102 药用未焙制麦芽〕	10		50	13/	13	千克	AB	PRQS	/35
1107.2000	-已焙制〔101 食用,102 食用其他粮食加工产品,103 药用已焙制麦芽,104 其他粮食制品〕	10		50	13/	13	千克	AB	PRQS	/35
11.08	**淀粉;菊粉:**									
	-淀粉:									
1108.1100	--小麦淀粉〔999〕	20		50	13/	0	千克	AB	PRQS	/30
1108.1200	--玉米淀粉〔101 饲用,102 工业用,103 食用〕	20		50	13/	9,13	千克	AB	PRQS	/30
1108.1300	--马铃薯淀粉〔999〕	15		50	13/	13	千克	AB	PRQS	/40
1108.1400	--木薯淀粉〔999〕	10		50	13/	13	千克	AB	PRQS	/35
1108.1900	--其他〔101 其他粮食加工产品,102 其他粮食制品,103 其他淀粉制品,104 淀粉〕	20		50	13/	13	千克	AB	PRQ	/45
1108.2000	-菊粉〔999〕	20		50	13/	13	千克	AB	PRQS	/30
11.09	**面筋,不论是否干制:**									
1109.0000	面筋,不论是否干制〔101 面筋,102 其他粮食制品〕	18		80	13/	13	千克	AB	PRQS	/43

协定税率 %										特惠税率 %			Article Description
亚太5国	东/冰/格	巴基斯坦	韩国	瑞士	哥达	秘鲁	澳大利亚	新西/坡/智	港/澳/台	亚太2国	老/柬/缅	36/3/1	
													Flour, meal and powder of the dried leguminous vegetables of heading No. 07. 13, of sago or of roots or tubers of heading No. 07. 14; or of the products of Chapter 8:
	0/0/0		4	0	0	0	0	0/0/0	0/0/		/0/	0/0/0	-Of the dried leguminous vegetables of heading No. 07. 13
	0/0/0		12	6	0	0	0	0/0/0	0/0/		0/0/0	0/0/0	-Of sago or of roots or tubers of heading No. 07. 14
10	0/0/0	10	12	6	0	0	0	0/0/0	0/0/			0/0/	-Of the products of Chapter 8
													Malt, whether or not roasted:
	0/0/0	4.5	4	0	0	0	0	0/0/0	0/0/			0/0/	-Not roasted
	0/0/0	4.5	4	0	0	0	0	0/0/0	0/0/			0/0/	-Roasted
													Starches; inulin:
													-Starches:
	0/0/		12	6	0	0	0	0/0/0	0/0/			0/0/	--Wheat starch
	0/0/		12	6	0	0	0	0/0/0	0/0/			0/0/	--Maize (corn) starch
	0/0/	12	6	4.5	0	0	0	0/0/0	0/0/			0/0/	--Potato starch
	0/0/	5	4	0	0	0	0	0/0/0	0/0/			0/0/0	--Manioc (cassava) starch
	0/0/		12	6	0	0	0	0/0/0	0/0/			0/0/	--Other starches
	0/0/0		8	6	0	0	0	0/0/0	0/0/			0/0/	-Inulin
													Wheat gluten, whether or not dried:
	0/0/0	14.4	10.8	5.4	0	0	0	0/0/0	0/0/			0/0/	Wheat gluten, whether or not dried

第十二章
含油子仁及果实;杂项子仁及果实;工业用或药用植物;稻草、秸秆及饲料

注释:

一、税目12.07主要包括油棕果及油棕仁、棉子、蓖麻子、芝麻、芥子、红花子、罂粟子、牛油树果。但不包括税目08.01或08.02的产品及油橄榄(第七章或第二十章)。

二、税目12.08不仅包括未脱脂的细粉和粗粉,而且包括部分或全部脱脂以及用其本身的油料全部或部分复脂的细粉和粗粉。但不包括税目23.04至23.06的残渣。

三、甜菜子、草子及其他草本植物种子、观赏用花的种子、蔬菜种子、林木种子、果树种子、巢菜子(蚕豆除外)、羽扇豆属植物种子,可一律视为种植用种子,归入税目12.09。

但下列各项即使用作种子用,也不归入税目12.09:

(一)第七章作蔬菜用的豆类或甜玉米;

(二)第九章的调味香料及其他产品;

(三)第十章的谷物;

(四)税目12.01至12.07或12.11的产品。

四、税目12.11主要包括下列植物或这些植物的某部分:

罗勒、琉璃苣、人参、海索草、甘草、薄荷、迷迭香、芸香、鼠尾草及苦艾。

但税目12.11不包括:

(一)第三十章的药品;

(二)第三十三章的芳香料制品及化妆盥洗品;

(三)税目38.08的杀虫剂、杀菌剂、除草剂、消毒剂及类似产品。

五、税目12.12的"海草及其他藻类"不包括:

(一)税目21.02的已死的单细胞微生物;

(二)税目30.02的培养微生物;

(三)税目31.01或31.05的肥料。

子目注释:

子目1205.10所称"低芥子酸油菜子",是指所获取的固定油中芥子酸含量按重量计低于2%,以及所得的固体成分每克葡萄糖苷酸(酯)含量低于30微摩尔的油菜子。

税则号列	货品名称〔CIQ扩展编码及品名—T2表示见附表2〕	最惠(%)	暂定税率	普通	增值/消费	出口退税	计量单位	监管条件	检验检疫	特殊证件对美关税
12.01	**大豆,不论是否破碎:**									
1201.1000	-种用〔999〕	0		180	9/	0	千克	7AB	MPNQ	/10
	-其他:									
1201.9010	---黄大豆〔101榨油用,102饲料用,103食品加工用〕	3		180	9/	0	千克	7AB	MPRQS	/33
1201.9020	---黑大豆〔101榨油用,102饲料用,103食品加工用〕	3		180	9/	0	千克	7AB	MPRQS	/28
1201.9030	---青大豆〔101榨油用,102饲料用,103食品加工用〕	3		180	9/	0	千克	7AB	MPRQS	/13
1201.9090	---其他〔101榨油用,102饲料用,103食品加工用〕	3		180	9/	0	千克	7AB	MPRQS	/13
12.02	**未焙炒或未烹煮的花生,不论是否去壳或破碎:**									
1202.3000	-种用〔999〕	0		0	9/	0	千克	AB	PNQ	/10
	-其他:									
1202.4100	--未去壳〔999〕	15		70	9/	0	千克	AB	PRQS	/25
1202.4200	--去壳,不论是否破碎〔999〕	15		70	9/	0	千克	AB	PRQS	/45
12.03	**干椰子肉:**									
1203.0000	干椰子肉〔999〕	15		30	9/	6	千克	AB	PRQ	/25
12.04	**亚麻子,不论是否破碎:**									
1204.0000	亚麻子,不论是否破碎〔999〕	15		70	9/	9	千克	AB	PRQ	/45
12.05	**油菜子,不论是否破碎:**									
	-低芥子酸油菜子:									
1205.1010	---种用〔999〕	0		80	9/	0	千克	7AB	PNQ	/10
1205.1090	---其他〔999〕	9		80	9/	9	千克	7AB	PRQS	/19
	-其他:									
1205.9010	---种用〔999〕	0		80	9/	0	千克	7AB	PNQ	/10
1205.9090	---其他〔999〕	9		80	9/	9	千克	7AB	PRQS	/19
12.06	**葵花子,不论是否破碎:**									
1206.0010	---种用〔999〕	0		0	9/	9	千克	AB	PNQ	/
1206.0090	---其他〔101非熟制,102熟制〕	15		70	9/	9	千克	AB	PRQS	/40
12.07	**其他含油子仁及果实,不论是否破碎:**									
	-棕榈果及棕榈仁:									

Chapter 12
Oil seeds and oleaginous fruits; miscellaneous grains, seeds and fruit; industrial or medicinal plants; straw and fodder

Notes:

1. Heading No. 12.07 applies, *inter alia*, to palm nuts and kernels, cotton seeds, castor oil seeds, sesamum seeds, mustard seeds, safflower seeds, poppy seeds and shea nuts (karite nuts). It does not apply to products of heading No. 08.01 or 08.02 or to olives (Chapter 7 or Chapter 20).
2. Heading No. 12.08 applies not only to non-defatted flours and meals but also to flours and meals which have been partially defatted or defatted and wholly or partially refatted with their original oils. It does not, however, apply to residues of headings No. 23.04 to 23.06
3. For the purposes of heading No. 12.09, beet seeds, grass and other herbage seeds, seeds of ornamental flowers, vegetable seeds, seeds of forest trees, seeds of fruit trees, seeds of vetches (other than those of the species *Vicia faba*) or of lupines are to be regarded as "seeds of a kind used for sowing".
   Heading No. 12.09 does not, however, apply to the following even if for sowing:
   (a) Laguminous vegetables or sweet corn(Chapter 7);
   (b) Spices or other products of Chapter 9;
   (c) Cereals (Chapter 10); or
   (d) Products of headings No. 12.01 to 12.07 or 12.11
4. Heading No. 12.11 applies, *inter alia*, to the following plants or parts thereof:
   Basil, borage, ginseng, hyssop, liquorice, all species of mint, rosemary, rue, sage and wormwood.
   Heading No. 12.11 does not, however, apply to:
   (a) Medicaments of Chapter 30;
   (b) Perfumery, cosmetic or toilet preparations of Chapter 33;
   (c) Insecticides, fungicides, herbicides, disinfectants or similar products of heading No. 38.08.
5. For the purposes of heading No. 12.12, the term "seaweeds and other algae" does not include:
   (a) Dead single-cell micro-organisms of heading No. 21.02;
   (b) Cultures of micro-organisms of heading No. 30.02;
   (c) Fertilizers of heading No. 31.01 or 31.05.

Subheading Notes:

For the purposes of subheading No. 1205.10, the expression "low erucic acid rape or colza seeds" means rape or colza seeds yielding a fixed oil which has an erucic acid content of less than 2% by weight and yielding a solid component which contains less than 30 micromoles of glucosinolates per gram.

协定税率 %										特惠税率 %			
亚太5国	东/冰/格	巴基斯坦	韩国	瑞士	哥达	秘鲁	澳大利亚	新西/坡/智	港/澳/台	亚太2国	老/柬/缅	36/3/1	Article Description
													Soya beans, whether or not broken:
												0/0/0	-Seed
													-Other:
0	0/0/	0	0	0	0	0		0//0	0/0/		0/0/	0/0/0	---Yellow soya beans
0	0/0/	0	0	0	0	0		0//0	0/0/		0/0/	0/0/0	---Black soya beans
0	0/0/	0	0	0	0	0		0//0	0/0/		0/0/	0/0/0	---Green soya beans
0	0/0/	0	0	0	0	0		0//0	0/0/			0/0/0	---Other
													Ground-nuts, not roasted or otherwise cooked, whether or not shelled or broken:
												0/0/0	-Seed
													-Other:
	0/0/	0	6	4.5	0	0	0	0/0/0	0/0/		0//	0/0/0	--In shell
	0/0/	0	6	4.5	0	0	0	0/0/0	0/0/		0//	0/0/0	--Shell, whether or not broken
													Copra:
7.5	0/0/0	6.8	6	4.5	0	0	0	0/0/0	0/0/		/0/	0/0/0	Copra
													Linseed, whether or not broken:
	0/0/	12	6	4.5	0	0	0	0/0/0	0/0/			0/0/	Linseed, whether or not broken
													Rape or colza seeds, whether or not broken:
													-Low erucic acid rape or colza seeds:
												0/0/0	---Seed
0	0/0/	0	0	0	0	0		0//0	0/0/			0/0/	---Other
													-Other:
												0/0/0	---Seed
0	0/0/	0	0	0	0	0		0//0	0/0/			0/0/	---Other
													Sunflower seeds, whether or not broken:
												0/0/0	---Seed
	0/0/	12	6	4.5	0	0	0	0/0/0	0/0/			0/0/	---Other
													Other oil seeds and oleaginous fruits, whether or not broken:
													-Palm fruit and palm nut:

税则号列	货品名称〔CIQ扩展编码及品名—T2表示见附表2〕	最惠(%)	暂定税率	普通	增值/消费	出口退税	计量单位	监管条件	检验检疫	特殊证件对美关税
1207.1010	---种用									
1207.1010 10	种用濒危棕榈果及棕榈仁〔999〕	0		0	9/	0	千克	ABEF	PNQ	/10
1207.1010 90	其他种用棕榈果及棕榈仁〔999〕	0		0	9/	6	千克	AB	PNQ	/10
1207.1090	---其他									
1207.1090 10	其他濒危棕榈果及棕榈仁(不论是否破碎)〔999〕	10		70	9/	0	千克	ABEF	PRQS	/20
1207.1090 90	其他棕榈果及棕榈仁(不论是否破碎)〔999〕	10		70	9/	6	千克	AB	PRQS	/20
	-棉子:									
1207.2100	--种用〔999〕	0		0	9/	6	千克	AB	PNQ	/10
1207.2900	--其他〔999〕	15		70	9/	6	千克	AB	PRQS	/25
	-蓖麻子:									
1207.3010	---种用〔999〕	0		0	9/	6	千克	AB	PNQ	/10
1207.3090	---其他〔999〕	15		70	9/	6	千克	AB	PRQS	/25
	-芝麻:									
1207.4010	---种用〔999〕	0		0	9/	9	千克	AB	PNQ	/10
1207.4090	---其他〔101 食用,102 药用黑芝麻〕	10		70	9/	9	千克	AB	PRQS	/20
	-芥子:									
1207.5010	---种用〔999〕	0		0	9/	9	千克	AB	PNQ	/10
1207.5090	---其他〔999〕	15		70	9/	9	千克	AB	PRQ	/40
	-红花子:									
1207.6010	---种用〔999〕	0		0	9/	9	千克	AB	PNQ	/10
1207.6090	---其他〔999〕	20		70	9/	9	千克	AB	PRQS	/30
	-甜瓜的子:									
1207.7010	---种用〔101 西瓜种子,102 哈密瓜种子,103 甜瓜种子〕	0		0	9/	0	千克	AB	PQ	/
	---其他:									
1207.7091	----黑瓜子〔101 非熟制,102 熟制〕	20		80	9/	9	千克	AB	PRQS	/30
1207.7092	----红瓜子〔999〕	20		80	9/	9	千克	AB	PRQS	/30
1207.7099	----其他〔999〕	30		70	9/	9	千克	AB	PRQS	/40
	-其他:									
1207.9100	--罂粟子〔999〕	20		70	9/	9	千克	AB	PQ	/30
	--其他:									
1207.9910	---种用〔101 亚麻种子,102 蓖麻种子,103 油棕果种子,104 红花籽,105 其他油料种子〕	0		0	9/	9	千克	AB	PNQ	/10
	---其他:									
1207.9991	----牛油树果〔999〕	20		70	9/	6	千克	AB	PRQ	/30
1207.9999	----其他[T2]	10		70	9/	6	千克	AB	PRQS	/35
12.08	**含油子仁或果实的细粉及粗粉,但芥子粉除外:**									
1208.1000	-大豆粉〔999〕	9		70	13/	0	千克	AB	PRQS	/19
1208.9000	-其他〔999〕	15		80	13/	13	千克	AB	PRQS	/25
12.09	**种植用的种子、果实及孢子:**									
1209.1000	-糖甜菜子〔999〕	0		0	9/	9	千克	AB	PQ	/10
	-饲料植物种子:									
1209.2100	--紫苜蓿子〔999〕	0		0	9/	0	千克	AB	PQ	/
1209.2200	--三叶草子〔999〕	0		0	9/	0	千克	AB	PQ	/
1209.2300	--羊茅子〔999〕	0		0	9/	0	千克	AB	PQ	/
1209.2400	--草地早熟禾子〔999〕	0		0	9/	0	千克	AB	PQ	/
1209.2500	--黑麦草种子〔999〕	0		0	9/	0	千克	AB	PQ	/
	--其他:									
1209.2910	---甜菜子,糖甜菜子除外〔999〕	0		0	9/	9	千克	AB	PQ	/
1209.2990	---其他[T2]	0		0	9/	0	千克	AB	PQ	/10
1209.3000	-草本花卉植物种子									
1209.3000 10	濒危草本花卉植物种子〔999〕	0		0	9/	0	千克	ABFE	PQ	/
1209.3000 90	其他草本花卉植物种子〔101 地毯草种子,102 散尾葵种子,103 唐倡蒲种子,104 鸢尾种子,105 兔尾草种子,106 鹤望兰种子,107 其他花卉种子〕	0		0	9/	0	千克	AB	PQ	/
	-其他:									
1209.9100	--蔬菜种子[T2]	0		0	9/	0	千克	AB	PQ	/
1209.9900	--其他									
1209.9900 10	其他种植用濒危种子、果实及孢子〔101 其他花卉种子,102 其他林木种子,103 其他经济类植物种子〕	0		0	9/	0	千克	AFEB	PQ	/
1209.9900 90	其他种植用的种子、果实及孢子[T2]	0		0	9/	0	千克	AB	PQ	/
12.10	**鲜或干的啤酒花,不论是否研磨或制成团粒;蛇麻腺:**									
1210.1000	-啤酒花,未经研磨也未制成团粒〔999〕	20		50	13/	13	千克	AB	PRQS	/30

协定税率 %										特惠税率 %			Article Description
亚太5国	东/冰/格	巴基斯坦	韩国	瑞士	哥达	秘鲁	澳大利亚	新西/坡/智	港/澳/台	亚太2国	老/柬/缅	36/3/1	
													---Seed
												0/0/0	Endangered palm fruit and palm nut, seed
												0/0/0	Other palm fruit and palm nut, seed
													---Other
	0/0/0	4.5	4	0	0	0	0	0/0/0	0/0/		/0/	0/0/0	Other endangered palm fruit and palm nut(whether or not broken)
	0/0/0	4.5	4	0	0	0	0	0/0/0	0/0/		/0/	0/0/0	Other palm fruit and palm nut(whether or not broken)
													-Cotton seeds:
												0/0/0	--Seeds
	0/0/	12	6	4.5	0	0	0	0/0/0	0/0/			0/0/	--Other
													-Castor oil seeds:
												0/0/0	---Seed
	0/0/		6	4.5	0	0	0	0/0/0	0/0/		0/0/0	0/0/0	---Other
													-Sesamum seeds:
												0/0/0	---Seeds for cultivation
9	0/0/	0	4	0	0	0	0	0/0/0	0/0/		0/0/0	0/0/0	---Other
													-Mustard seeds:
												0/0/0	---Seeds for cultivation
	0/0/0	12	6	4.5	0	0	0	0/0/0	0/0/			0/0/	---Other
													-Safflower seeds:
												0/0/0	---Seed
	0/0/0		12	6	0	0	0	0/0/0	0/0/			0/0/	---Other
													-Melon seeds:
												0/0/0	---Seed
													---Other:
	0/0/0		12	6	0	0	0	0/0/0	0/0/			0/0/	----Black melon seeds
	0/0/0		12	6	0	0	0	0/0/0	0/0/			0/0/	----Red melon seeds
	0/0/0		21		0	0	0	0//0	0/0/			0/0/0	----Other
													-Other:
	0/0/0		12	6	0	0	0	0/0/0	0/0/			0/0/	--Poppy seeds
													--Other:
												0/0/0	---Seed
													---Other:
	0/0/0		12	6	0	0	0	0/0/0	0/0/		//0	0/0/0	----Shea nuts(*karite nuts*)
	0/0/	5	4	0	0	0	0	0/0/0	0/0/		0/0/0	0/0/0	----Other
													Flours and meals of oil seeds or oleaginous fruits, other than those of mustard:
	0/0/3.6	5	0	0	0	0	0	0//0	0/0/		/0/	0/0/0	-Of soya beans
	0/0/	12	6	4.5	0	0	0	0/0/0	0/0/		/0/	0/0/0	-Other
													Seeds, fruit and spores, of a kind used for sowing:
												0/0/0	-Sugar beet seed
													-Seeds of forage plants:
												0/0/0	--Lucerne (alfalfa) seed
												0/0/0	--Clover (*Trifolium spp.*) seed
												0/0/0	--Fescue seed
												0/0/0	--Kentucky blue grass (*Poa-pratensis L.*) seed
												0/0/0	--Rye grass (*Lolium multiflorum Lam.*, *Lolium perenne L.*) seed
													--Other:
												0/0/0	---Beet seed, excluding sugar beet seed
												0/0/0	---Other
													-Seeds of herbaceous plants cultivated principally for their flowers
												0/0/0	Seeds of endangered herbaceous plants cultivated principally for their flowers
												0/0/0	Other seeds of herbaceous plants cultivated principally for their flowers
													-Other:
												0/0/0	--Vegetable seeds
													--Other
												0/0/0	Other endangered seeds, fruit and spores, of a kind used for sowing
												0/0/0	Other seeds, fruit and spores, of a kind used for sowing
													Hop cones, fresh or dried, whethr or not ground, powdered or in the form of pellets; lupulin:
	0/0/0	20	12	6	0	0	0	0/0/0	0/0/			0/0/	-Hop cones, neither ground nor powdered nor in the form of pellets

税则号列	货品名称〔CIQ扩展编码及品名－T2表示见附表2〕	最惠(%)	暂定税率	普通	增值/消费	出口退税	计量单位	监管条件	检验检疫	特殊证件对美关税
1210.2000	-啤酒花,经研磨或制成团粒;蛇麻腺〔999〕	10		50	13/	13	千克	AB	PRQS	/30
12.11	**主要用作香料、药料、杀虫、杀菌或类似用途的植物或这些植物的某部分(包括子仁及果实),鲜、冷、冻或干的,不论是否切割、压碎或研磨成粉:**									
	-人参:									
1211.2010	---西洋参〔999〕	7.5		70	9/	9	千克	AQBFE	MPRQS	/32.5
1211.2020	---野山参(西洋参除外)〔101 药用野山参,102 食用野山参〕	20		90	9/	9	千克	ABFE	PRQS	/30
1211.2020 10	鲜、冷、冻或干的野山参(不论是否切割,压碎或研磨成粉,仅限俄罗斯属)	20		90	9/	9	千克	ABEF	PRQS	/30
1211.2020 90	鲜、冷、冻或干的野山参(不论是否切割,压碎或研磨成粉,非俄罗斯属)	20		90	9/	9	千克	AB	PRQS	/30
	---其他:									
1211.2091	----鲜的〔101 药用鲜人参,102 食用鲜人参〕	20		50	9/	9	千克	AB	PRQS	/45
1211.2091 10	其他鲜人参(不论是否切割,压碎或研磨成粉,仅限俄罗斯属)	20		50	9/	9	千克	ABEF	PRQS	/45
1211.2091 90	其他鲜人参(不论是否切割,压碎或研磨成粉,非俄罗斯属)	20		50	9/	9	千克	AB	PRQS	/45
1211.2099	----其他〔101 药用人参,102 药用红参,103 食用人参〕	20		50	9/	9	千克	ABQ	PRQS	/45
1211.2099 10	其他冷、冻或干的人参(不论是否切割,压碎或研磨成粉,仅限俄罗斯属)	20		50	9/	9	千克	ABEFQ	PRQS	/45
1211.2099 90	其他冷、冻或干的人参(不论是否切割,压碎或研磨成粉,非俄罗斯属)	20		50	9/	9	千克	ABQ	PRQS	/45
1211.3000	-古柯叶									
1211.3000 10	药用古柯叶(不论是否切割、压碎或研磨成粉)〔999〕	9		50	9/	9	千克	ABI	PQ	/19
1211.3000 20	做香料用古柯叶(不论是否切割、压碎或研磨成粉)〔999〕	9		50	9/	9	千克	AB	PQ	/19
1211.3000 90	杀虫杀菌用古柯叶(不论是否切割、压碎或研磨成粉)〔999〕	9		50	9/	9	千克	AB	PQ	/19
1211.4000	-罂粟秆									
1211.4000 10	药用罂粟秆(不论是否切割、压碎或研磨成粉)〔999〕	9		50	9/	9	千克	AB	PQ	/19
1211.4000 20	做香料用罂粟秆(不论是否切割、压碎或研磨成粉)〔999〕	9		50	9/	9	千克	AB	PQ	/19
1211.4000 90	杀虫杀菌用罂粟秆(不论是否切割、压碎或研磨成粉)〔999〕	9		50	9/	9	千克	AB	PQ	/19
1211.5000	-麻黄									
1211.5000 11	药料用麻黄草粉〔999〕	9		30	9/	9	千克	23AQB	PQ	/19
1211.5000 19	药料用麻黄草〔999〕	9		30	9/	9	千克	4AQ	PQ	/19
1211.5000 21	香料用麻黄草粉〔999〕	9		30	9/	9	千克	23AB	PRQ	/19
1211.5000 29	香料用麻黄草〔999〕	9		30	9/	9	千克	8A	R	/19
1211.5000 91	其他用麻黄草粉〔999〕	9		30	9/	9	千克	23AB	PQ	/19
1211.5000 99	其他用麻黄草〔999〕	9		30	9/	9	千克	8A	PQ	/19
	-其他:									
	---主要用作药料的植物及其某部分:									
1211.9011	----当归〔101 药用当归,102 药用三七〕	6		30	9/	9	千克	AQB	PRQ	/16
1211.9012	----三七(田七)〔101 药用田七,102 药用党参〕	6		20	9/	9	千克	AQB	PRQ	/16
1211.9013	----党参〔999〕	6		20	9/	9	千克	AQB	PRQ	/16
1211.9014	----黄连〔999〕	6		20	9/	9	千克	AQB	PQ	/16
1211.9015	----菊花〔101 药用野菊花,102 药用菊花,103 食用菊花〕	6		20	9/	0,9	千克	AQB	PRQS	/16
1211.9016	----冬虫夏草〔999〕	6		20	9/	9	千克	AQBE	PQ	/16
1211.9017	----贝母〔999〕	6		20	9/	9	千克	AQB	PRQ	/16
1211.9018	----川芎〔999〕	6		20	9/	9	千克	AQB	PRQ	/16
1211.9019	----半夏〔999〕	6		20	9/	9	千克	AQB	PQ	/16
1211.9021	----白芍〔999〕	6		20	9/	9	千克	AQB	PRQ	/16
1211.9022	----天麻〔999〕	6		20	9/	9	千克	AQBFE	PRQ	/16
1211.9023	----黄芪〔999〕	6		30	9/	9	千克	AQB	PRQ	/16
1211.9024	----大黄、籽黄〔999〕	6		20	9/	9	千克	AQB	PRQ	/16
1211.9025	----白术〔999〕	6		20	9/	9	千克	AQB	PRQ	/16
1211.9026	----地黄〔999〕	6		20	9/	9	千克	AQB	PRQ	/16
1211.9027	----槐米〔101 药用槐米,102 食用槐米〕	6		20	9/	9	千克	AQB	PRQS	/16
1211.9028	----杜仲〔999〕	6		20	9/	9	千克	AQB	PRQ	/16
1211.9029	----茯苓〔101 药用茯苓,102 食用茯苓〕	6		20	9/	9	千克	AQB	PRQS	/16

协定税率 %										特惠税率 %			
亚太5国	东/冰/格	巴基斯坦	韩国	瑞士	哥达	秘鲁	澳大利亚	新西/坡/智	港/澳/台	亚太2国	老/柬/缅	36/3/1	Article Description
	0/0/0	4.5	4	0	0	0	0	0/0/0	0/0/			0/0/0	-Hop cones, ground, powdered or in the form of pellets; lupulin
													Plants and parts of plants (including seeds and fruits), of a kind used primarily in perfumery, in pharmacy or for insecticidal, fungicidal or similar purposes, fresh or dried, whether or not cut, crushed or powdered:
													-Ginseng roots:
	0/0/0	4	0	0	0	0	0	0/0/0	0/0/			0/0/0	---American ginseng
16.4	0/0/0	16	12	6	0	0	0	0/0/0	0/0/			0/0/	---Wild ginseng (other than American ginseng)
	0/0/0	16	12	6	0	0	0	0/0/0	0/0/		//	0/0/	Wild ginseng, fresh, cold, frozen or dried (whether or not cut, crushed or ground to powder, of genera Russian only)
	0/0/0	16	12	6	0	0	0	0/0/0	0/0/		//	0/0/	Wild ginseng, fresh, cold, frozen or dried (whether or not cut, crushed or ground to powder, not of genera Russian)
													---Other:
	0/0/0		12	6	0	0	0	0/0/0	0/0/			0/0/	----Fresh
	0/0/0		12	6	0	0	0	0/0/0	0/0/		//	0/0/	Other fresh ginseng (whether or not cut, crushed or ground into powder, of genera Russian only)
	0/0/0		12	6	0	0	0	0/0/0	0/0/		//	0/0/	Other fresh ginseng (whether or not cut, crushed or ground into powder, not of genera Russian)
	0/0/0			6	0	0	0	0/0/0	0/0/			0/0/	----Other
	0/0/0			6	0	0	0	0/0/0	0/0/		//	0/0/	Other cold, frozen or dried ginseng (whether or not cut, crushed or ground to powder, of genera Russian only)
	0/0/0			6	0	0	0	0/0/0	0/0/		//	0/0/	Other cold, frozen or dried ginseng (whether or not cut, crushed or ground to powder, not of genera Russian)
													-Coca leaf
	0/0/0	4	0	0	0	0	0	0//0	0/0/		/0/	0/0/0	Coca leaf of a kind used primarily in pharmacy(whether or not cut, crushed or powdered)
	0/0/0	4	0	0	0	0	0	0//0	0/0/		/0/	0/0/0	Coca leaf of a kind used primarily in perfumery(whether or not cut, crushed or powdered)
	0/0/0	4	0	0	0	0	0	0//0	0/0/		/0/	0/0/0	Coca leaf of a kind used for insecticidal(fungicidal, whether or not cut, crushed or powdered)
													-Poppy straw
	0/0/0	4	0	0	0	0	0	0//0	0/0/		/0/	0/0/0	Poppy straw of a kind used primarily in pharmacy(whether or not cut, crushed or powdered)
	0/0/0	4	0	0	0	0	0	0//0	0/0/		/0/	0/0/0	Poppy straw of a kind used primarily in perfumery(whether or not cut, crushed or powdered)
	0/0/0	4	0	0	0	0	0	0//0	0/0/		/0/	0/0/0	Poppy straw of a kind used for insecticidal, fungicidal(whether or not cut, crushed or powdered)
													-Ephedra
4.5	0/0/0	0	0	0	0	0	0	0//0	0/0/		/0/	0/0/0	Ephedra powder, used in pharmacy
4.5	0/0/0	0	0	0	0	0	0	0//0	0/0/		/0/	0/0/0	Ephedra sinica, used in pharmacy
4.5	0/0/0	0	0	0	0	0	0	0//0	0/0/		/0/	0/0/0	Ephedra powder, of a kind used in perfumery
4.5	0/0/0	0	0	0	0	0	0	0//0	0/0/		/0/	0/0/0	Ephedra sinica, of a kind used in perfumery
4.5	0/0/0	0	0	0	0	0	0	0//0	0/0/		/0/	0/0/0	Other ephedra powder
4.5	0/0/0	0	0	0	0	0	0	0//0	0/0/		/0/	0/0/0	Other ephedra
													-Other:
													---Of a kind used primarily in pharmacy:
3	0/0/0	0	0	0	0	0	0	0//0	0/0/		/0/	0/0/0	----Radix angelicae sinensis
3	0/0/0	0	0	0	0	0	0	0//0	0/0/		/0/	0/0/0	----Radix pseudoginseng
3	0/0/0	0	0	0	0	0	0	0//0	0/0/			0/0/0	----Radix codonopsitis
3	0/0/0	0	0	0	0	0	0	0//0	0/0/			0/0/0	----Rhizoma coptidis
3	0/0/0	0	0	0	0	0	0	0//0	0/0/		/0/	0/0/0	----Flos chrysanthemi
3	0/0/0	0	0	0	0	0	0	0//0	0/0/		/0/	0/0/0	----Cordyceps sinensis
3	0/0/0	0	0	0	0	0	0	0//0	0/0/		/0/	0/0/0	----Bulbs fritillariae thunbergii
3	0/0/0	0	0	0	0	0	0	0//0	0/0/		/0/	0/0/0	----Rhizoma ligustici
3	0/0/0	0	0	0	0	0	0	0//0	0/0/		/0/	0/0/0	----Rhizoma pinelliae
3	0/0/0	0	0	0	0	0	0	0//0	0/0/		/0/	0/0/0	----Radix paeoniae lactiflorae
3	0/0/0	0	0	0	0	0	0	0//0	0/0/		/0/	0/0/0	----Rhizoma gastrodiae
3	0/0/0	0	0	0	0	0	0	0//0	0/0/		/0/	0/0/0	----Radix astragali
3	0/0/0	0	0	0	0	0	0	0//0	0/0/		/0/	0/0/0	----Rhubarb
3	0/0/0	0	0	0	0	0	0	0//0	0/0/		/0/	0/0/0	----Rhizoma atractylodis macrocephalae
3	0/0/0	0	0	0	0	0	0	0//0	0/0/		/0/	0/0/0	----Radix rehmanniae
3	0/0/0	0	0	0	0	0	0	0//0	0/0/		/0/	0/0/0	----Flos sophorae
3	0/0/0	0	0	0	0	0	0	0//0	0/0/		/0/	0/0/0	----Cortex eucommiae
3	0/0/0	0	0	0	0	0	0	0//0	0/0/		0/0/0	0/0/0	----Poria

税则号列	货品名称〔CIQ扩展编码及品名—T2表示见附表2〕	最惠(%)	暂定税率	普通	增值/消费	出口退税	计量单位	监管条件	检验检疫	特殊证件对美关税
1211.9031	----枸杞〔101药用枸杞子,102食用枸杞子〕	6		30	9/	9	千克	AQB	PRQS	/16
1211.9032	----大海子〔101药用大海子(胖大海),102食用大海子(胖大海)〕	6		20	9/	9	千克	AQB	PRQS	/16
1211.9033	----沉香〔999〕	3		20	9/	9	千克	AQFEB	PQ	/13
1211.9034	----沙参〔999〕	6		20	9/	9	千克	AQB	PRQ	/16
1211.9035	----青蒿〔999〕	6		20	9/	0	千克	AB	PQ	/16
1211.9036	----甘草〔101药用甘草,103食用甘草〕	6	0	30	9/	9	千克	AQB4xy	PRQS	/10
1211.9037	----黄芩〔999〕	6		20	9/	9	千克	ABQ	PQ	/16
1211.9038	----椴(欧椴)花及叶子									
1211.9038 10	海南椴、紫椴(籽椴)花及叶(不论是否切割、压碎或研磨成粉)〔999〕	6		30	9/	9	千克	ABEQ	PQ	/16
1211.9038 90	其他椴树(欧椴)花及叶〔999〕	6		30	9/	9	千克	ABQ	PQ	/16
1211.9039	----其他									
1211.9039 30	大麻〔999〕	6		20	9/	9	千克	ABI	PQ	/31
1211.9039 40	罂粟壳〔999〕	6		20	9/	9	千克	ABI	PQ	/31
1211.9039 50	鲜、冷、冻或干的木香(不论是否切割,压碎或研磨成粉)〔999〕	6		20	9/	9	千克	ABFE	PQ	/31
1211.9039 60	鲜、冷、冻或干的黄草及枫斗(石斛)(不论是否切割,压碎或研磨成粉)〔101〕	6		20	9/	9	千克	ABFE	PQ	/31
1211.9039 70	鲜、冷、冻或干的苁蓉(不论是否切割,压碎或研磨成粉)〔999〕	6		20	9/	9	千克	ABFE	PQ	/31
1211.9039 81	鲜或干的红豆杉皮、枝叶等(不论是否切割,压碎或研磨成粉)〔999〕	6	0	20	9/	9	千克	ABFE	PQ	/25
1211.9039 89	冷或冻的红豆杉皮、枝叶等(不论是否切割,压碎或研磨成粉)〔999〕	6		20	9/	9	千克	ABFE	PQ	/31
1211.9039 91	其他主要用作药料鲜、冷、冻或干的濒危植物(包括其某部分,不论是否切割,压碎或研磨成粉)〔101其他药用濒危植物中药材,102食用濒危植物中药材,103药用黄柏〕	6		20	9/	0	千克	ABFE	PQ	/31
1211.9039 92	加纳籽、车前子壳粉、育亨宾皮(包括其某部分,不论是否切割、压碎或研磨成粉)〔999〕	6		20	9/	9	千克	AB	PQ	/31
1211.9039 93	恰特草(Cathaedulis Forssk;包括其某部分,不论是否切割、压碎或研磨成粉)〔999〕	6		20	9/	9	千克	ABI	PQ	/31
1211.9039 99	其他主要用作药料的鲜、冷、冻或干的植物(包括其某部分,不论是否切割,压碎或研磨成粉)[T2]	6		20	9/	9	千克	ABQ	PQ	/31
1211.9050	---主要用作香料的植物及其某部分									
1211.9050 30	香料用沉香木及拟沉香木(包括其某部分,不论是否切割、压碎或研磨成粉)〔999〕	8		50	9/	0	千克	ABFE	PRQ	/33
1211.9050 91	其他主要用作香料的濒危植物(包括其某部分,不论是否切割、压碎或研磨成粉)〔101香辛料,102其他调味料〕	8		50	9/	0	千克	ABFE	PRQ	/33
1211.9050 99	其他主要用作香料的植物(包括其某部分,不论是否切割、压碎或研磨成粉)〔101香辛料,102其他调味料,103干薄荷叶,104罗勒粉,105香叶,106香叶,107洋苏叶,108野生墨角兰,109迷迭香〕	8		50	9/	9	千克	AB	MPRNQ	/33
	---其他:									
1211.9091	----鱼藤根、除虫菊〔999〕	3		11	9/	9	千克	ABS	MPNQ	/13
1211.9099	----其他									
1211.9099 91	其他鲜、冷、冻或干的杀虫、杀菌用濒危植物(不论是否切割,压碎或研磨成粉)〔999〕	9		30	9/	0	千克	ABFE	PQ	/34
1211.9099 99	其他鲜、冷、冻或干的杀虫、杀菌用植物(不论是否切割,压碎或研磨成粉)〔999〕	9		30	9/	9	千克	AB	PQ	/34
12.12	**鲜、冷、冻或干的刺槐豆、海草及其他藻类、甜菜及甘蔗,不论是否碾磨;主要供人食用的其他税目未列名的果核、果仁及植物产品(包括未焙制的菊苣根):**									
	-海草及其他藻类:									
	--适合供人食用的:									
1212.2110	---海带〔101鲜、冷的养殖海带,102冻的养殖海带,103干的养殖海带,104鲜、冷的野生海带,105冻的野生海带,106干的野生海带,107药用昆布〕	20		70	9/	0	千克	AB	PRQS	/30
1212.2120	---发菜〔101鲜、冷的养殖发菜,102冻的养殖发菜,103干的养殖发菜,104鲜、冷的野生发菜,105冻的野生发菜,106干的野生发菜〕	20		70	9/	9	千克	8A	PRQS	/30
	---裙带菜:									
1212.2131	----干的〔101干的养殖裙带菜,102干的野生裙带菜〕	15		70	9/	9	千克	AB	PRQS	/25

协定税率 %										特惠税率 %			Article Description
亚太5国	东/冰/格	巴基斯坦	韩国	瑞士	哥达	秘鲁	澳大利亚	新西/坡/智	港/澳/台	亚太2国	老/柬/缅	36/3/1	
3	0/0/0	0	0	0	0	0	0	0//0	0/0/		/0/	0/0/0	---Fructus lycii
3	0/0/0	0	0	0	0	0	0	0//0	0/0/		/0/	0/0/0	---Bantaroi seeds
1.5	0/0/0	0	0	0	0	0	0	0//0	0/0/		/0/	0/0/0	----Aloes wood
3	0/0/0	0	0	0	0	0	0	0//0	0/0/		/0/	0/0/0	----Adenophora axilliflora
	0/0/0	5	0	0	0	0	0	0//0	0/0/		/0/	0/0/0	----Southernwood
	0/0/2.4	0	0	0	0	0	0	0//0	0/0/			0/0/0	----Liquorice roots
3	0/0/0	0	0	0	0	0	0	0//0	0/0/		0/0/0	0/0/0	----scutellaria root
													----Flower and leaves of linden tree (lindens)
3	0/0/0	0	0	0	0	0	0	0//0	0/0/		0/0/0	0/0/0	Flower and leaves of hainan linden, amur linden(whether or not cut, crushed or powdered)
3	0/0/0	0	0	0	0	0	0	0//0	0/0/		0/0/0	0/0/0	Flower and leaves of other linden tree(lindens)
													----Other
3	0/0/0	0	0	0	0	0	0	0//0	0/0/		0/0/0	0/0/0	Hemp
3	0/0/0	0	0	0	0	0	0	0//0	0/0/		0/0/0	0/0/0	Poppy pod
3	0/0/0	0	0	0	0	0	0	0//0	0/0/		0/0/0	0/0/0	Costustoot, fresh, chilled, frozen or dried, whether or not cut, crushed or powdered
3	0/0/0	0	0	0	0	0	0	0//0	0/0/		0/0/0	0/0/0	Herba dendrobii and Dendrobium, fresh, chilled, frozen or dried, whether or not cut, crushed or powdered
3	0/0/0	0	0	0	0	0	0	0//0	0/0/		0/0/0	0/0/0	Cistanche, fresh, chilled, frozen or dried, whether or not cut, crushed or powdered
3	0/0/0	0	0	0	0	0	0	0//0	0/0/		0/0/0	0/0/0	Bark, branch and leaf of Chinese yew (Taxus chinensis) , fresh or dried, whether or not cut, crushed or powdered
3	0/0/0	0	0	0	0	0	0	0//0	0/0/		0/0/0	0/0/0	Bark, branch and leaf of Chinese yew (Taxus chinensis) , cold or frozen, whether or not cut, crushed or powdered
3	0/0/0	0	0	0	0	0	0	0//0	0/0/		0/0/0	0/0/0	Other endangered plants and parts of plants, of a kind used primarily in pharmacy, fresh, chilled, frozen or dried, whether or not cut, crushed or powdered
3	0/0/0	0	0	0	0	0	0	0//0	0/0/		0/0/0	0/0/0	Carbon Ghana seeds, plantago shell powder, yohimbe bark (including part of its, whether or not cut, crushed or ground to powder)
3	0/0/0	0	0	0	0	0	0	0//0	0/0/		0/0/0	0/0/0	Catha edulis forssk(Cathaedulis Forssk; including part of its, whether or not cut, ccrushed or powdered)
3	0/0/0	0	0	0	0	0	0	0//0	0/0/		0/0/0	0/0/0	Other plants and parts of plants, of a kind used primarily in pharmacy, fresh, chilled, frozen or drie, whether or not cut, crushed or powdered
													---Of a kind used primarily in perfumery
4	0/0/0	0	0	0	0	0	0	0//0	0/0/		/0/	0/0/0	Spices(including part of its, whether or not cutccrushed or powdered)
4	0/0/0	0	0	0	0	0	0	0//0	0/0/		/0/	0/0/0	Other endangered plants, of a kind used primarily in perfumery(including parts of its, whether or not cut, crushed or powdered)
4	0/0/0	0	0	0	0	0	0	0//0	0/0/		/0/	0/0/0	Other plants, of a kind used primarily in perfumery(including parts of its, whether or not cut, crushed or powdered)
													---Other:
1.5	0/0/0	0	0	0	0	0	0	0//0	0/0/		/0/	0/0/0	---Derris roots and pyrethrum
													----Other
4.5	0/0/0	3.6	0	0	0	0	0	0//0	0/0/		/0/	0/0/0	Other endangered plants of a kind used for insecticidal or fungicidal, fresh, chilled, frozen or drie, whether or not cut, crushed or powdered
4.5	0/0/0	3.6	0	0	0	0	0	0//0	0/0/		/0/	0/0/0	Other plants, of a kind used for insecticidal or fungicidal, fresh, chilled, frozen or drie, whether or not cut, crushed or powdered
													Locust beans, seaweeds and other algae, sugar beet and sugar cane, fresh, chilled, frozen or dried, whether or not ground; fruit stones and kernels and other vegetable products(including unroasted chicory roots of the variety *Cichorium intybus sativum*) of a kind used primarily for human consumption, not elsewhere specified or included:
													-Seaweeds and other algae:
													--Fit for human consumption:
10	0/0/0	9	12	6	0	0	0	0/0/0	0/0/			0/0/	---Sea tangle
10	0/0/0	9	12	6	0	0	0	0/0/0	0/0/			0/0/	---Black moss
													---Pinnatifida:
7.5	0/0/0	6.8	6	4.5	0	1.3	0	0/0/0	0/0/			0/0/	----Dried

税则号列		货品名称〔CIQ扩展编码及品名－T2表示见附表2〕	最惠(%)	暂定税率	普通	增值/消费	出口退税	计量单位	监管条件	检验检疫	特殊证件对美关税
1212.2132		----鲜的〔101 鲜的养殖裙带菜，102 鲜的野生裙带菜〕	15		70	9/	9	千克	AB	PRQS	/25
1212.2139		----其他〔101 冷藏养殖裙带菜，102 冻藏养殖裙带菜，103 冷藏野生裙带菜，104 冻藏野生裙带菜〕	15		70	9/	9	千克	AB	PRQS	/25
		---紫菜：									
1212.2141		----干的〔101 干的养殖紫菜，102 干的野生紫菜〕	15		70	9/	0	千克	AB	PRQS	/25
1212.2142		----鲜的〔101 鲜的养殖紫菜，102 鲜的野生紫菜〕	15		70	9/	0	千克	AB	PRQS	/25
1212.2149		----其他〔101 冷藏养殖紫菜，102 冻藏养殖紫菜，103 冷藏野生紫菜，104 冻藏野生紫菜〕	15		70	9/	0	千克	AB	PRQS	/25
		---麒麟菜：									
1212.2161		----干的〔101 干的养殖麒麟菜，102 干的野生麒麟菜〕	15		70	9/	9	千克	AB	PRQS	/25
1212.2169		----其他〔101 鲜、冷的养殖麒麟菜，102 冻藏养殖麒麟菜，103 鲜、冷的野生麒麟菜，104 冻藏野生麒麟菜〕	15		70	9/	9	千克	AB	PRQS	/25
		---江蓠：									
1212.2171		----干的〔101 干的养殖江蓠，102 干的野生江蓠〕	15		70	9/	9	千克	AB	PRQS	/25
1212.2179		----其他〔101 鲜、冷的养殖江蓠，102 冻藏养殖江蓠，103 鲜、冷的野生江蓠，104 冻藏野生江蓠〕	15		70	9/	9	千克	AB	PRQS	/25
1212.2190		---其他〔101 鲜、冷的养殖海草及藻类，102 冻藏养殖海草及藻类，103 干的养殖海草及藻类，104 鲜、冷的野生海草及藻类，105 冻藏野生海草及藻类，106 干的野生海草及藻类〕	15	2	70	9/	9	千克	AB	PRQS	/27
		--其他：									
1212.2910		---马尾藻〔999〕	15	2	70	9/	9	千克	AB	PQ	/12
1212.2990		---其他〔999〕	15	2	70	9/	9	千克	AB	PQ	/12
		-其他：									
1212.9100		--甜菜〔999〕	20		70	9/	6	千克	AB	PRQ	/30
1212.9200		--刺槐豆〔999〕	20		70	9/	9	千克	AB	PRQ	/30
1212.9300		--甘蔗〔999〕	20		70	9/	6	千克	AB	PRQ	/30
1212.9400		--菊苣根〔101 药用菊苣(干)〕	20		70	9/	6	千克	AB	PRQS	/30
		--其他：									
		---杏、桃(包括油桃)、梅或李的核及核仁：									
1212.9911		----苦杏仁〔101 药用苦杏仁，102 非药用〕	20		80	9/	9	千克	QAB	PRQS	/30
1212.9912		----甜杏仁〔999〕	20		80	9/	9	千克	AB	PRQS	/45
1212.9919		----其他〔101 药用桃仁，102 非熟制，103 熟制〕	20		80	9/	9	千克	AB	PRQS	/30
		---其他：									
1212.9993		----白瓜子〔101 非熟制，102 熟制，103 饲用〕	20		80	9/	9	千克	AB	PRQS	/30
1212.9994		----莲子〔101 药用莲子心，102 药用莲子，103 非药用〕	20		80	9/	9	千克	AB	PRQS	/30
1212.9996		----甜叶菊叶〔999〕	30		70	9/	9	千克	AB	PRQS	/40
1212.9999		----其他									
1212.9999	10	其他供人食用濒危植物产品(包括未焙制的菊苣根，包括果核、仁等)〔101 坚果，102 供制食品或医药用的植物产品，103 批准为新食品原料〕	30		70	9/	0	千克	ABFE	PRQS	/55
1212.9999	90	其他供人食用果核、仁及植物产品(包括未焙制的菊苣根)〔101 瓜子，102 坚果，103 供制食品或医药用的植物产品，104 批准为新食品原料〕	30		70	9/	9	千克	AB	PRQS	/55
12.13		**未经处理的谷类植物的茎、秆及谷壳，不论是否切碎、碾磨、挤压或制成团粒：**									
1213.0000		---未经处理的谷类植物的茎、秆及谷壳，不论是否切碎、碾磨、挤压或制成团粒〔101 其他饲用粮谷，102 稻草及其制品，103 其他草及草制品，104 饲用燕麦草，105 饲用稻草，106 其他饲草，107 饲用其他淀粉，108 饲用植物颗粒和植物粉，109 其他植物饲料〕	12		35	9/	9	千克	AB	PQ	/22
12.14		**芜菁甘蓝、饲料甜菜、饲料用根、干草、紫苜蓿、三叶草、驴喜豆、饲料羽衣甘蓝、羽扇豆、巢菜及类似饲料，不论是否制成团粒：**									
1214.1000		-紫苜蓿粗粉及团粒〔101 苜蓿草，102 苜蓿草颗粒，103 除苜蓿草和苜蓿草颗粒外〕	5		35	0/	0	千克	AB	MPQ	/
1214.9000		-其他									
1214.9000	01	其他紫苜蓿(粗粉及团粒除外)〔101 其他饲草，102 饲用其他淀粉，103 饲用植物颗粒和植物粉，104 其他植物饲料〕	9	7	35	0/	0	千克	AB	MPQ	/
1214.9000	02	以除紫苜蓿外的禾本科和豆科为主的多种混合天然饲草〔101 其他饲草(天然饲草除外)，102 饲用其他淀粉，103 饲用植物颗粒和植物粉，104 其他植物饲料，105 天然饲草〕	9	4	35	0/	0	千克	AB	MPQ	/29
1214.9000	90	芜菁甘蓝、饲料甜菜、其他植物饲料(包括饲料用根、干草、三叶草、驴喜豆等，不论是否制成团粒)〔101 其他饲草，102 饲用其他淀粉，103 饲用植物颗粒和植物粉，104 其他植物饲料，105 黑麦草，106 梯牧草，107 羊草，108 小叶章，109 狼尾草，110 稻草，111 碱草〕	9		35	0/	0	千克	AB	MPQ	/34

协定税率 %										特惠税率 %			Article Description
亚太5国	东/冰/格	巴基斯坦	韩国	瑞士	哥达	秘鲁	澳大利亚	新西/坡/智	港/澳/台	亚太2国	老/柬/缅	36/3/1	
7.5	0/0/0	6.8	6	4.5	0	1.3	0	0/0/0	0/0/			0/0/	----Fresh
7.5	0/0/0	6.8	6	4.5	0	1.3	0	0/0/0	0/0/			0/0/	----Other
													---Laver:
7.5	0/0/0	6.8	6	4.5	0	1.3	0	0/0/0	0/0/			0/0/	----Dried
7.5	0/0/0	6.8	6	4.5	0	1.3	0	0/0/0	0/0/			0/0/	----Fresh
7.5	0/0/0	6.8	6	4.5	0	1.3	0	0/0/0	0/0/			0/0/	----Other
													---Eucheuma:
7.5	0/0/0	6.8	6	4.5	0	1.3	0	0//0	0/0/			0/0/0	----Dried
7.5	0/0/0	6.8	6	4.5	0	1.3	0	0//0	0/0/			0/0/	----Other
													----Garcilaria:
7.5	0/0/0	6.8	6	4.5	0	1.3	0	0//0	0/0/			0/0/	----Dried
7.5	0/0/0	6.8	6	4.5	0	1.3	0	0//0	0/0/			0/0/	----Other
7.5	0/0/0	6.8	6	4.5	0	1.3	0	0/0/0	0/0/			0/0/0	---Other
													-Other:
7.5	0/0/0	6.8	0	4.5	0	1.3	0	0/0/0	0/0/			0/0/0	---Sargass
7.5	0/0/0	6.8	0	4.5	0	1.3	0	0/0/0	0/0/			0/0/0	---Other
													-Other:
	0/0/0		12	6	0	0	0	0/0/0	0/0/			0/0/	--Sugar beet
10	0/0/0	10	12	6	0	0	0	0/0/0	0/0/			0/0/	--Locust beans
	0/0/0		8	6	0	0	0	0//0	0/0/		0/0/0	0/0/0	--Sugar cane
	0/0/0		12		0	0	0	0//0	0/0/			0/0/0	--Chicory roots
													--Other:
													---Apricot, peach(including nectarine) or plum stones and kernels:
	0/0/0		12	6	0	0	0	0/0/0	0/0/			0/0/	----Bitter apricot kernels
	0/0/0		12	6	0	0	0	0/0/0	0/0/			0/0/	----Sweet apricot kernels
	0/0/0		12	6	0	0	0	0/0/0	0/0/			0/0/	----Other
													---Other:
	0/0/0		12	6	0	0	0	0/0/0	0/0/			0/0/	----Pumpkin seeds
	0/0/0		12	6	0	0	0	0/0/0	0/0/			0/0/	----Lotus seeds(*Semen Nelumbinis*)
	0/0/0				0	0	0	0/0/0	0/0/			0/0/0	----leaf of steviol
													----Other
	0/0/0				0	0	0	0/0/0	0/0/			0/0/0	Other endangered vegetable products (including unroasted chicory roots of the variety *Cichorium intybus sativum*) of a kind used primarily for human consumption
	0/0/0				0	0	0	0/0/0	0/0/			0/0/0	Other fruit stones and kernels and vegetable products (including unroasted chicory roots of the variety *Cichorium intybus sativum*) of a kind used primarily for human consumption
													Cereal straw and husks, unprepared, whether or not chopped, ground, pressed or in the form of pellets:
	0/0/0	5.4	4.8	3.6	0	0	0	0/0/0	0/0/		/0/	0/0/0	---Unprepared cereal straw and husks
													Swedes, mangolds, fodder roots, hay, lucerne (alfalfa), clover, sainfoin, forage kale, lupines, vetches and similar forage products, whether or not in the form of pellets:
	0/0/0	0	0	0	0	0	0	0//0	0/0/		/0/	0/0/0	-Lucerne (alfalfa) meal and pellets
													-Other
	0/0/0	4	0	0	0	0	0	0//0	0/0/		/0/	0/0/0	Other lucerne(other than meal and pellets)
	0/0/0	4	0	0	0	0	0	0//0	0/0/		/0/	0/0/0	In addition to alfalfa variety of graminaceous and leguminous based mixed natural forage grass
	0/0/0	4	0	0	0	0	0	0//0	0/0/		/0/	0/0/0	Swedes, mangolds, other vegetable fodder (including fodder roots, hay, clover, sainfoin, whether or not in the form of pellets)

第十三章
虫胶;树胶、树脂
及其他植物液、汁

注释:

税目 13.02 主要包括甘草、除虫菊、啤酒花、芦荟的浸膏及鸦片,但不包括:

一、按重量计蔗糖含量在10%以上或制成糖食的甘草浸膏(税目 17.04);
二、麦芽膏(税目 19.01);
三、咖啡精、茶精、马黛茶精(税目 21.01);
四、构成含酒精饮料的植物汁、液(第二十二章);
五、樟脑、甘草甜及税目 29.14 或 29.38 的其他产品;
六、按重量计生物碱含量不低于 50%的罂粟秆的浓缩物(税目 29.39);
七、税目 30.03 或 30.04 的药品及税目 30.06 的血型试剂;
八、鞣料或染料的浸膏(税目 32.01 或 32.03);
九、精油、浸膏、净油、香膏提取的油树脂或精油的水质馏出液或其水溶液;饮料制造业用的以芳香物质为基料的制剂(第三十三章);
十、天然橡胶、巴拉塔胶、古塔波胶、银胶菊胶、糖胶树胶或类似的天然树胶(税目 40.01)。

本国注释:

子目 1302.1100 的鸦片,我国禁止进口。

税则号列	货品名称〔CIQ扩展编码及品名－T2 表示见附表 2〕	最惠(%)	暂定税率	普通	增值/消费	出口退税	计量单位	监管条件	检验检疫	特殊证件对美关税
13.01	**虫胶;天然树胶、树脂、树胶脂及油树脂(例如,香树脂):**									
1301.2000	-阿拉伯胶〔101 饲料添加剂,102 有检疫要求食品添加剂,301 需申报仅用于工业用途不用于食品添加剂有检疫要求的化学品〕	15		40	9/	6	千克	AB	PRQ	/35
	-其他:									
1301.9010	---胶黄耆树胶(植物产品),〔999〕	15		40	9/	6	千克	AB	PQ	/
1301.9020	---乳香、没药及血竭〔101 植物产品,102 药用乳香,103 药用没药,104 药用血竭〕	3		17	9/	6	千克	ABQ	PQ	/13
1301.9030	---阿魏〔101 植物产品,102 药用阿魏〕	3		17	9/	6	千克	AB	PQ	/13
1301.9040	---松脂									
1301.9040 10	濒危松科植物的松脂[999,301 属于危险化学品的食品添加剂,302 一般化学品,需申报仅用于工业用途不用于食品添加剂有检疫要求,303 易燃液体,需申报仅用于工业用途不用于食品添加剂有检疫要求,304 有检疫要求食品添加剂〕	15		45	9/	0	千克	ABE	MPNQ	/
1301.9040 90	其他松脂[999,301 属于危险化学品的食品添加剂,302 一般化学品,需申报仅用于工业用途不用于食品添加剂有检疫要求,303 易燃液体,需申报仅用于工业用途不用于食品添加剂有检疫要求,304 有检疫要求食品添加剂〕	15		45	9/	6	千克	AB	MPRNQ	/
1301.9090	---其他									
1301.9090 10	龙血树脂、大戟脂、愈疮树脂〔999〕	15		45	9/	6	千克	ABFE	PQ	/35
1301.9090 20	大麻脂〔999〕	15		45	9/	6	千克	ABI	PQ	/35
1301.9090 91	其他濒危植物的天然树胶、树脂[包括天然树胶、树脂及其他油树脂(例如:香树脂)]〔999 例如香树脂,301 属于危险化学品的食品添加剂〕	15		45	9/	0	千克	ABFE	PQ	/35
1301.9090 99	其他天然树胶、树脂[包括天然树胶、树脂及其他油树脂(例如:香树脂)]〔101 药用干漆,102 药用安息香,103 药用苏合香,104 药用枫香脂,117 其他植物产品,301 属于危险化学品的食品添加剂〕	15		45	9/	6	千克	AB	PQ	/35
13.02	**植物液汁及浸膏;果胶、果胶酸盐及果胶酸酯;从植物产品制得的琼脂、其他胶液及增稠剂,不论是否改性:**									
	-植物液汁及浸膏:									
1302.1100	--鸦片〔101 供制食品或医药用的植物提取物,301 其他危险化学品〕	0		0	0/	13	千克	9BI	MPNQ	/10
1302.1200	--甘草的〔101 供制食品或医药用的植物提取物,102 甘草提取物(粉)(有检疫要求食品添加剂)103 甘草流浸膏(有检疫要求食品添加剂)〕	6	0	20	13/	13	千克	4xAy	R	/25
1302.1300	--啤酒花的〔999,301 有检疫要求食品添加剂〕	10		80	13/	13	千克	AB	PRQS	/25
1302.1400	--麻黄的									
1302.1400 11	供制农药用麻黄浸膏及浸膏粉〔999〕	9.5		80	13/	13	千克	23AB	PQ	/14.5

Chapter 13
Lac; gums, resins and other vegetable saps and extracts

Notes:

Heading No. 13. 02 applies, *inter alia*, to liquorice extract and extract of pyrethrum, extract of hops, extract of aloes and opium. The heading does not apply to:

(1) Liquorice extract containing more than 10% by weight of sucrose or putup as confectionery (heading No. 17. 04);
(2) Malt extract (heading No. 19. 01);
(3) Extracts of coffee, tea or mate (heading No. 21. 01);
(4) Vegetable saps or extracts constituting alcoholic beverages (Chapter22);
(5) Camphor, glycyrrhizin or other products of heading No. 29. 14 or 29. 38;
(6) Concentrates of poppy straw containing not less than 50% by weight of alkaloids(heading No. 29. 39);
(7) Medicaments of heading No. 30. 03 or 30. 04 or bloodgrouping reagents (heading No. 30. 06);
(8) Tanning or dyeing extracts (heading No. 32. 01 or 32. 03);
(9) Essential oils, concretes, absolutes, resinoids, extracted oleoresins, aqueous distillates or aqueous solutions of essential oils or preparations basedon odoriferous substances of a kind used for the manufacture of beverages (Chapter 33);
(10) Natural rubber, balata, gutta-percha, guayule, chicle or similar natural gums (heading No. 40. 01).

National note:

Opium of Subheading No. 1302. 1100 is subject to import ban.

协定税率 %										特惠税率 %			Article Description
亚太5国	东/冰/格	巴基斯坦	韩国	瑞士	哥达	秘鲁	澳大利亚	新西/坡/智	港/澳/台	亚太2国	老/柬/缅	36/3/1	
													Lac; natural gums, resins, gum-resins and oleoresins (for example, balsams):
	0/0/0	0	6	4.5	0	0	0	0/0/0	0/0/			0/0/0	-Gum Arabic
													-Other:
	0/0/0	0	6	4.5	0	0	0	0/0/0	0/0/			0/0/	---Gum tragacanth
	0/0/0	0	0	0	0	0	0	0//0	0/0/			0/0/0	---Olibanum, myrrh and dragon's blood
	0/0/0	0	0	0	0	0	0	0//0	0/0/			0/0/0	---Asafoetida
													---Pine-resin
	0/0/0	0	6	4.5	0	0	0	0/0/0	0/0/			0/0/0	Pine-resin of endangered plants of pine family
	0/0/0	0	6	4.5	0	0	0	0/0/0	0/0/			0/0/0	Other pine-resin
													---Other
	0/0/0	0	6	4.5	0	0	0	0/0/0	0/0/			0/0/0	Resin of daemonorops draco, resin of euphorbia, resin of lignum vitae
	0/0/0	0	6	4.5	0	0	0	0/0/0	0/0/			0/0/0	Charas, churrus
	0/0/0	0	6	4.5	0	0	0	0/0/0	0/0/			0/0/0	Other natural gums, resins, gum-resins and oleoresins (for example, balsams) of endangered plants
	0/0/0	0	6	4.5	0	0	0	0/0/0	0/0/			0/0/0	Other natural gums, resins, gum-resins and oleoresins (for example, balsams)
													Vegetable saps and extracts; pectic substances, pectinates and pectates; agar-agar and other mucilages and thickeners, whether or not modified, derived from vegetable products:
													-Vegetable saps and extracts:
												0/0/0	--Opium
	0/0/0	0	0	0	0	0	0	0//0	0/0/			0/0/0	--Of liquorice
	0/0/0	4.5	4	0	0	0	0	0/0/0	0/0/			0/0/0	--Of hops
													--Of ephedra
7.1	0/0/0	0	12	0	0	0	0	0/0/0	0/0/			0/0/	Ephedra extracts powder used in pesticide

税则号列	货品名称〔CIQ 扩展编码及品名—T2 表示见附表 2〕	最惠(%)	暂定税率	普通	增值/消费	出口退税	计量单位	监管条件	检验检疫	特殊证件对美关税
1302.1400 12	供制医药用麻黄浸膏及浸膏粉〔101 供工业用的植物及植物提取物〕	9.5		80	13/	13	千克	Q23AB	PQ	/14.5
1302.1400 19	其他麻黄浸膏及浸膏粉〔101 供工业用的植物及植物提取物〕	9.5		80	13/	13	千克	23AB	PQ	/14.5
1302.1400 20	麻黄液汁〔101 供工业用的植物及植物提取物〕	9.5		80	13/	13	千克	Q23AB	PQ	/14.5
	--其他:									
1302.1910	---生漆〔101 植物产品,102 毒害品,301 其他危险化学品〕	20		90	13/	6	千克	AB	MPNQ	/
1302.1920	---印楝素〔999〕	3		11	13/	6	千克	ABS	PQ	/13
1302.1930	---除虫菊的或含鱼藤酮植物根茎的〔101 供工业用的植物及植物提取物〕	3		11	13/	13	千克	ABS	MPNQ	/13
1302.1940	---银杏的〔999〕	9.5		80	13/	13	千克	ABE	PQ	/14.5
1302.1990	---其他									
1302.1990 01	苦参碱〔999〕	9.5		80	13/	13	千克	ABS	PQ	/29.5
1302.1990 13	供制农药用的濒危植物液汁及浸膏〔999〕	9.5		80	13/	0	千克	ABFE	PQ	/29.5
1302.1990 19	供制农药用的其他植物液汁及浸膏〔101 供工业用的植物及植物提取物〕	9.5		80	13/	13	千克	AB	PRQ	/29.5
1302.1990 95	红豆杉液汁及浸膏〔101 供工业用的植物及植物提取物,102 供制食品或医药用的植物提取物〕	9.5		80	13/	13	千克	ABFE	PQ	/29.5
1302.1990 96	黄草汁液及浸膏〔101 供工业用的植物及植物提取物,102 供制食品或医药用的植物提取物〕	9.5		80	13/	13	千克	ABFE	PQ	/29.5
1302.1990 97	其他濒危植物液汁及浸膏〔101 供工业用的植物及植物提取物,102 供制食品或医药用的植物提取物,103 批准为新食品原料〕	9.5		80	13/	0	千克	ABFE	PQ	/29.5
1302.1990 99	其他植物液汁及浸膏[T2]	9.5		80	13/	13	千克	AB	MPRNQS	/29.5
1302.2000	-果胶、果胶酸盐及果胶酸酯〔999〕	20		80	13/	13	千克	A	R	/45
	-从植物产品制得的胶液及增稠剂,不论是否改性:									
1302.3100	--琼脂〔101 饲料添加剂,102 有检疫要求食品添加剂〕	10		80	13/	13	千克	A	R	/40
1302.3200	--从刺槐豆、刺槐豆子或瓜尔豆制得的胶液及增稠剂,不论是否改性〔101 饲料添加剂,301 有检疫要求食品添加剂〕	10		80	13/	13	千克	A	R	/35
	--其他:									
	---海草及其他藻类制品:									
1302.3911	----卡拉胶〔101 有检疫要求食品添加剂,102 有检疫要求食品添加剂,301 需申报仅用于工业用途不用于食品添加剂有检疫要求的化学品〕	8		80	13/	13	千克	A	R	/18
1302.3912	----褐藻胶〔999〕	8		80	13/	13	千克	AB	PQ	/13
1302.3919	----其他〔103〕	8		80	13/	13	千克	AB	PQ	/28
1302.3990	---其他									
1302.3990 10	未列名濒危植物胶液及增稠剂(有机过氧化物)〔101〕	8		80	13/	0	千克	ABFE	PQ	/33
1302.3990 90	其他未列名植物胶液及增稠剂〔101 土荆芥油,301 有检疫要求食品添加剂〕	8		80	13/	13	千克	AB	MPRQ	/33

协定税率 %										特惠税率 %			
亚太5国	东/冰/格	巴基斯坦	韩国	瑞士	哥达	秘鲁	澳大利亚	新西/坡/智	港/澳/台	亚太2国	老/柬/缅	36/3/1	**Article Description**
7.1	0/0/0	0	12	0	0	0	0	0/0/0	0/0/			0/0/	Ephedra extracts powder used in medical
7.1	0/0/0	0	12	0	0	0	0	0/0/0	0/0/			0/0/	Other Ephedra extracts powder
7.1	0/0/0	0	12	0	0	0	0	0/0/0	0/0/			0/0/	Saps and extracts of Ephedra
													--Other:
	0/0/0		12	6	0	0	0	0/0/0	0/0/			0/0/	---Crude lacquer
	0/0/0	0	0	0	0	0	0	0//0	0/0/			0/0/0	---Azadirachtin
	0/0/0	0	0	0	0	0	0	0//0	0/0/			0/0/0	---Of pyrethrum or of the roots of plants containing rotenone
7.1	0/0/0	15	12	0	0	0	0	0/0/0	0/0/			0/0/	---Gingko
													---Other
7.1	0/0/0	0	12	0	0	0	0	0/0/0	0/0/			0/0/	Matrine
7.1	0/0/0	0	12	0	0	0	0	0/0/0	0/0/			0/0/	Endangered vegetable saps and extracts for used primarily in pesticide
7.1	0/0/0	0	12	0	0	0	0	0/0/0	0/0/			0/0/	Other vegetable saps and extracts used primarily in pharmacy
7.1	0/0/0	0	12	0	0	0	0	0/0/0	0/0/			0/0/	Saps and extracts of taxusl
7.1	0/0/0	0	12	0	0	0	0	0/0/0	0/0/			0/0/	Saps and extracts of herba dendroii
7.1	0/0/0	0	12	0	0	0	0	0/0/0	0/0/			0/0/	Saps and extracts of other endangered vegetable
7.1	0/0/0	0	12	0	0	0	0	0/0/0	0/0/			0/0/	Other vegetable saps and extracts
	0/0/0		12	6	0	0	0	0/0/0	0/0/			0/0/	-Pectic substances, pectinates and pectates
													-Mucilages and thickeners, whether or not modified, derived from vegetable products:
	0/0/0	4.5	4	0	0	0	0	0/0/0	0/0/			0/0/0	--Agar-agar
6.7	0/0/0	0	6	4.5	0	0	0	0/0/0	0/0/			0/0/	--Mucilages and thickeners, whether or not modified, derived from locust beans, locust bean seeds or guar seeds
													--Other:
													---Preparations of seaweeds and other algae:
	0/0/0	12	6	4.5	0	0	0	0/0/0	0/0/			0/0/	----Carrageenan
	0/0/0	12	6	4.5	0	0	0	0/0/0	0/0/			0/0/	----Algin
	0/0/0	12	6	4.5	0	5.3	0	0/0/0	0/0/			0/0/	----Other
													---Other
	0/0/0	12	6	4.5	0	1.3	0	0/0/0	0/0/			0/0/	Mucilages and thickeners, derived from endangered vegetable products, not elsewhere specified or included
	0/0/0	12	6	4.5	0	1.3	0	0/0/0	0/0/			0/0/	Other mucilages and thickeners, derived from vegetable products, not elsewhere specified or included

第十四章
编结用植物材料；
其他植物产品

注释：

一、本章不包括归入第十一类的下列产品：

主要供纺织用的植物材料或植物纤维，不论其加工程度如何；或经过处理使其只能作为纺织原料用的其他植物材料。

二、税目14.01主要包括竹（不论是否劈开、纵锯、切段、圆端、漂白、磨光、染色或进行不燃处理）、劈开的柳条、芦苇及类似品和藤心、藤丝、藤片。但不包括木片条（税目44.04）。

三、税目14.04不包括木丝（税目44.05）及供制帚、制刷用成束、成簇的材料（税目96.03）。

税则号列		货品名称〔CIQ扩展编码及品名—T2表示见附表2〕	最惠(%)	暂定税率	普通	增值/消费	出口退税	计量单位	监管条件	检验检疫	特殊证件对美关税
14.01		**主要作编结用的植物材料（例如，竹、藤、芦苇、灯芯草、柳条、酒椰叶，已净、漂白或染色的谷类植物的茎秆，椴树皮）：**									
1401.1000		-竹									
1401.1000	10	酸竹〔999〕	10		70	9/	9	千克	ABE	PQ	/35
1401.1000	90	其他竹〔101原竹，102其他竹及竹制品〕	10		70	9/	9	千克	AB	PQ	/35
1401.2000		-藤									
1401.2000	10	濒危藤〔999〕	10		35	9/	0	千克	ABFE	PQ	/20
1401.2000	90	其他藤〔999〕	10		35	9/	9	千克	AB	PQ	/20
		-其他：									
1401.9010		---谷类植物的茎秆（麦秸除外）〔999〕	10		70	9/	9	千克	AB	PQ	/20
1401.9020		---芦苇〔999〕	10		70	9/	9	千克	AB	PQ	/20
		---灯芯草属：									
1401.9031		----蔺草〔999〕	10		70	9/	9	千克	AB4xy	PQ	/20
1401.9039		----其他〔999〕	10		70	9/	9	千克	AB	PQ	/20
1401.9090		---其他〔999〕	10		70	9/	9	千克	AB	PQ	/20
14.04		**其他税目未列名的植物产品：**									
1404.2000		-棉短绒〔999〕	4		30	9/	9	千克	AB	PQ	/29
		-其他：									
1404.9010		---主要供染料、鞣料用的植物原料〔999〕	5		45	9/	9	千克	AB	PQ	/15
1404.9090		---其他									
1404.9090	10	椰糠（条/块）〔999〕	15	4	70	9/	9	千克	AB	PQ	/29
1404.9090	90	其他编号未列名植物产品〔101其他竹及竹制品，102藤及藤制品，103柳及柳制品，104其他草及草制品，105芦苇及芦苇制品，106棕及棕制品，107葵及葵制品，108其他竹藤柳草类，109软木（栽培介质），110木屑（栽培介质），111稻壳（栽培介质），112花生壳（栽培介质），113棉子壳（栽培介质），114其他有机栽培介质，115植物标本，116未列出的其他植物产品〕	15		70	9/	9	千克	AB	PQ	/40

Chapter 14
Vegetable plaiting materials; vegetable products not elsewhere specified or included

Notes:

1. This Chapter does not cover the following products which are to be classified in Section Ⅺ:
Vegetable materials or fibres of vegetable materials of a kind used primarily in the manufacture of textiles, however prepared, or other vegetable materials which have undergone treatment so as to render them suitable for use only as textile materials.
2. Heading No. 14. 01 applies, *inter alia*, to bamboos (whether or not split, sawn lengthwise, cut to length, rounded at the ends, bleached, rendered non-inflammable, polished or dyed), split osier, reeds and the like, to rattan cores and to drawn or split rattans. The heading does not apply to chipwood (heading No. 44. 04).
3. Heading No. 14. 04 does not apply to wood wool (heading No. 44. 05) and prepared knots or tufts for broom or brush making (heading No.96. 03).

协定税率 %										特惠税率 %			Article Description
亚太5国	东/冰/格	巴基斯坦	韩国	瑞士	哥达	秘鲁	澳大利亚	新西/坡/智	港/澳/台	亚太2国	老/柬/缅	36/3/1	
													Vegetable materials of a kind used primarily for plaiting (for example, bamboos, rattans, reeds, rushes, osier, raffia, cleaned, bleached or dyed cereal straw, and lime bark):
													-Bamboos
	0/0/0	4.5	4	0	0	0	0	0/0/0	0/0/		0/0/	0/0/0	Acidosasa chinensis(*Raphia vinifera*)
	0/0/0	4.5	4	0	0	0	0	0/0/0	0/0/		0/0/	0/0/0	Other bamboos
													-Rattans
	0/0/0	4.5	4	0	0	0	0	0/0/0	0/0/		0/0/	0/0/0	Endangered rattans
	0/0/0	4.5	4	0	0	0	0	0/0/0	0/0/		0/0/	0/0/0	Other rattans
													-Other:
	0/0/0	4.5	4	0	0	0	0	0/0/0	0/0/		/0/	0/0/0	---Cereal straw (other than wheat straw)
	0/0/0	4.5	4	0	0	0	0	0/0/0	0/0/		/0/	0/0/0	---Reeds
													---Rushes:
	0/0/0	4.5	4	0	0	0	0	0/0/0	0/0/		/0/	0/0/0	----Mat rush
	0/0/0	4.5	4	0	0	0	0	0/0/0	0/0/		/0/	0/0/0	----Other
	0/0/0	4.5	4	0	0	0	0	0/0/0	0/0/		/0/	0/0/0	---Other
													Vegetable products not elsewhere specified or included:
	0/0/0	0	0	0	0	0	0	0//0	0/0/			0/0/0	-Cotton linters
													-Other:
4.3	0/0/0	0	0	0	0	0.4	0	0//0	0/0/			0/0/0	---Raw vegetable materials of a kind used primarily in dyeing or tanning
													---Other
	0/0/0	0	6	4.5	0	0	0	0/0/0	0/0/			0/0/0	coco coir(sripe/piece)
	0/0/0	0	6	4.5	0	0	0	0/0/0	0/0/			0/0/0	Other vegetable products not elsewhere specified or included

第三类
动、植物油、脂及其分解产品;精制的食用油脂;动、植物蜡

第十五章
动、植物油、脂及其分解产品;精制的食用油脂;动、植物蜡

注释:

一、本章不包括:

(一)税目 02.09 的猪脂肪及家禽脂肪;

(二)可可脂、可可油(税目 18.04);

(三)按重量计税目 04.05 所列产品的含量超过 15%的食品(通常归入第二十一章);

(四)税目 23.01 的油渣或税目 23.04 至 23.06 的残渣;

(五)第六类的脂肪酸、精制蜡、药品、油漆、清漆、肥皂、芳香料制品、化妆品、盥洗品、磺化油及其他货品;

(六)从油类提取的油膏(税目 40.02)。

二、税目 15.09 不包括用溶剂提取的橄榄油(税目 15.10)。

三、税目 15.18 不包括变性的油、脂及其分离品,这些货品应归入其相应的未变性油、脂及其分离品的税目。

四、皂料、油脚、硬脂沥青、甘油沥青及羊毛脂残渣,归入税目 15.22。

子目注释:

子目 1514.11 及 1514.19 所称"低芥子酸菜子油",是指按重量计芥子酸含量低于 2%的固定油。

税则号列	货品名称〔CIQ 扩展编码及品名—T2 表示见附表 2〕	最惠(%)	暂定税率	普通	增值/消费	出口退税	计量单位	监管条件	检验检疫	特殊证件对美关税
15.01	**猪脂肪(包括已炼制的猪油)及家禽脂肪,但税目 02.09 及 15.03 的货品除外:**									
1501.1000	-猪油〔101 工业用猪油脂,102 饲料用猪油脂,103 饲料用野生猪、牛、羊油脂,104 未炼制的食用猪油(脂),105 已炼制的食用猪油(脂)〕	10		35	13/	13	千克	AB	MPRQS	/20
1501.2000	-其他猪脂肪〔101 工业用猪油脂,102 饲料用猪油脂,103 饲料用野生猪、牛、羊油脂,104 未炼制的食用猪油(脂),105 已炼制的食用猪油(脂)〕	10		35	13/	13	千克	AB	MPRQS	/20
1501.9000	-其他〔101 工业用禽油脂,102 饲料用禽油脂,103 未炼制的食用家禽油(脂),104 已炼制的食用家禽油(脂)〕	10		35	13/	13	千克	AB	MPRQS	/20
15.02	**牛、羊脂肪,但税目 15.03 的货品除外:**									
1502.1000	-牛、羊油脂[101 工业用牛油脂,102 工业用羊油脂,103 工业用野生猪、牛、羊油脂,104 饲料用牛油脂,105 饲料用羊油脂,106 饲料用野生猪、牛、羊油脂,107 未炼制的食用牛油(脂),108 未炼制的食用羊油(脂),109 已炼制的食用牛油(脂),110 已炼制的食用羊油(脂)]	8	2	30	13/	13	千克	AB	MPRQS	/12
1502.9000	-其他[T2][109 已炼制的食用牛油(脂),110 已炼制的食用羊油(脂)]	8	4	70	13/	6	千克	AB	MPRQS	/14
15.03	**猪油硬脂、液体猪油、油硬脂、食用或非食用脂油,未经乳化、混合或其他方法制作:**									
1503.0000	猪油硬脂、液体猪油、油硬脂、食用或非食用脂油,未经乳化、混合或其他方法制作[101 工业用猪油脂,102 工业用其他野生偶蹄动物油脂,103 未列出的工业用其他动物油脂,104 饲料用猪油脂,105 饲料用其他野生偶蹄动物油脂,106 未炼制的食用猪油(脂))〕	10		30	13/	13	千克	AB	PRQS	/20
15.04	**鱼或海生哺乳动物的油、脂及其分离品,不论是否精制,但未经化学改性:**									
1504.1000	-鱼肝油及其分离品									
1504.1000 10	濒危鱼鱼肝油及其分离品〔101〕	12		30	13/	0	千克	ABEF	PRQS	/37
1504.1000 90	其他鱼鱼肝油及其分离品〔101 工业用鱼油脂,102 未列出的工业用其他动物油脂,103 饲料用鱼油脂,104 未列出的饲料用其他动物油脂,201 保健食品〕	12		30	13/	13	千克	AB	PRQS	/37
1504.2000	-除鱼肝油以外的鱼油、脂及其分离品									
1504.2000 11	濒危鱼油软胶囊(鱼肝油除外)〔101 保健食品,102 除保健食品以外〕	12	6	50	13/	0	千克	ABEF	PRQS	/26

SECTION Ⅲ
ANIMAL OR VEGETABLE FATS AND OILS AND THEIR CLEAVAGE PRODUCTS; PREPARED EDIBLE FATS; ANIMAL OR VEGETABLE WAXES

Chapter 15

Animal or vegetable fats and oils and their cleavage products; prepared edible fats; animal or vegetable waxes

Notes:

1. This Chapter does not cover:
   (a) Pig fat or poultry fat of heading No. 02. 09;
   (b) Cocoa butter, fat or oil (heading No. 18. 04);
   (c) Edible preparations containing by weight more than 15% of the products of heading No. 04. 05 (generally Chapter 21);
   (d) Greaves (heading No. 23. 01) or residues of headings No. 23. 04 to 23. 06;
   (e) Fatty acids, prepared waxes, medicaments, paints, varnishes, soap, perfumery, cosmetic or toilet preparations, sulphonated oils or other goods of Section Ⅵ;
   (f) Factice derived from oils (heading No. 40. 02).
2. Heading No. 15. 09 does not apply to oils obtained from olives by solvent extraction (heading No. 15. 10).
3. Heading No. 15. 18 does not cover fats or oils or their fractions, merely denatured, which are to be classified in the heading appropriate to the corresponding undenatured fats and oils and their fractions.
4. Soap-stocks, oil foots and dregs, stearin pitch, glycerol pitch and wool grease residues fall in heading No. 15. 22.

Subheading Note:

For the purposes of subheadings No. 1514. 11 and 1514. 19, the expression "low erucic acid rape or colza oil" means the fixed oil which has an erucic acid content of less than 2% by weight.

协定税率 %										特惠税率 %			Article Description
亚太5国	东/冰/格	巴基斯坦	韩国	瑞士	哥达	秘鲁	澳大利亚	新西/坡/智	港/澳/台	亚太2国	老/柬/缅	36/3/1	
													Pig fat (including lard) and poultry fat, other than that of heading No. 02. 09 or 15. 03:
	0/0/0		4	0	0	0	0	0/0/0	0/0/			0/0/0	-Lard
	0/0/0		4	0	0	0	0	0/0/0	0/0/			0/0/0	-Other pig fat
	0/0/0		4	0	0	0	0	0/0/0	0/0/			0/0/0	-Other
													Fats of bovine animals, sheep or goats, other than those of heading No. 15. 03:
0	0/0/0	0	0	0	0	0	0	0//0	0/0/			0/0/0	-Tallow
0	0/0/0	0	0	0	0	0	0	0//0	0/0/			0/0/0	-Other
													Lard stearin, lard oil, oleostearin, oleooil and tallow oil, not emulsified or mixed or otherwise prepared:
	0/0/0		4	0	0	0	0	0/0/0	0/0/			0/0/0	Lard stearin, lard oil, oleostearin, oleooil and tallow oil, not emulsified or mixed or otherwise prepared
													Fats and oils and their fractions, of fish or marine mammals, whether or not refined, but not chemically modified:
													-Fish-liver oils and their fractions
	0/0/0		4.8	3.6	0	0	0	0/0/0	0/0/			0/0/	Endangered species of fish cod-liver oil and its fractions
	0/0/0		4.8	3.6	0	0	0	0/0/0	0/0/			0/0/	Other fish cod-liver oil and its fractions
													-Fats and oils and their fractions, of fish, other than liver oils
	0/0/0		4.8	6.2	0	0	0	0/0/0	0/0/			0/0/	Endangered fish oil capsules, other than liver oils

税则号列		货品名称〔CIQ扩展编码及品名—T2表示见附表2〕	最惠(%)	暂定税率	普通	增值/消费	出口退税	计量单位	监管条件	检验检疫	特殊证件对美关税
1504.2000	19	濒危鱼其他鱼油、脂及其分离品(鱼肝油除外)〔101工业用鱼油脂,102未列出的工业用其他动物油脂,103饲料用鱼油脂,104未列出的饲料用其他动物油脂,105养殖鱼鱼油,106野生鱼鱼油,107保健食品〕	12		50	13/	0	千克	ABEF	PRQS	/32
1504.2000	91	其他鱼油软胶囊(鱼肝油除外)〔101保健食品,102除保健食品以外〕	12	6	50	13/	13	千克	AB	PRQS	/26
1504.2000	99	其他鱼油、脂及其分离品(鱼肝油除外)〔101工业用鱼油脂,102未列出的工业用其他动物油脂,103饲料用鱼油脂,104未列出的饲料用其他动物油脂,105养殖鱼鱼油,106野生鱼鱼油,107保健食品〕	12		50	13/	13	千克	AB	PRQS	/32
1504.3000		-海生哺乳动物的油、脂及其分离品									
1504.3000	10	濒危哺乳动物的油、脂及其分离品(仅指海生)〔101工业用海生哺乳动物油脂,102未列出的工业用其他动物油脂,103饲料用海生哺乳动物油脂,104野生鱼鱼油〕	14		50	13/	0	千克	ABFE	PRQS	/19
1504.3000	90	其他海生哺乳动物油、脂及其分离品〔101工业用海生哺乳动物油脂,102未列出的工业用其他动物油脂,103饲料用海生哺乳动物油脂,104野生鱼鱼油〕	14		50	13/	13	千克	AB	PRQS	/19
15.05		**羊毛脂及从羊毛脂制得的脂肪物质(包括纯净的羊毛脂):**									
1505.0000		羊毛脂及从羊毛制得的脂肪物质(包括纯净的羊毛脂)〔101工业用羊毛脂,102饲料用羊毛脂〕	20		70	13/	13	千克	AB	PQS	/30
15.06		**其他动物油、脂及其分离品,不论是否精制,但未经化学改性:**									
1506.0000		其他动物油、脂及其分离品,不论是否精制,但未经化学改性									
1506.0000	10	其他濒危动物为原料制取的脂肪(包括河马、熊、野兔、海龟为原料的及海龟蛋油)〔101工业用其他野生偶蹄动物油脂,102未列出的工业用其他动物油脂,103饲料用其他野生偶蹄动物油脂,104未列出的饲料用其他动物油脂,105未炼制的食用濒危动物油(脂),106已炼制的食用濒危动物油(脂)〕	20		70	13/	0	千克	ABFE	PRQS	/45
1506.0000	90	其他动物油、脂及其分离品(不论是否精制,但未经化学改性)〔T2〕	20		70	13/	13	千克	AB	PRQS	/45
15.07		**豆油及其分离品,不论是否精制,但未经化学改性:**									
1507.1000		-初榨的,不论是否脱胶〔999〕	9		190	9/	0	千克	7AB	MPRQS	/34
1507.9000		-精制的豆油及其分离品(包括初榨豆油的分离品,但未经化学改性)〔101初榨食用大豆油,102食用豆油〕	9		190	9/	0	千克	7AB	MRS	/34
15.08		**花生油及其分离品,不论是否精制,但未经化学改性:**									
1508.1000		-初榨的〔999〕	10		100	9/	0	千克	AB	PRQS	/35
1508.9000		-精制的花生油及其分离品(包括初榨花生油的分离品,但未经化学改性)〔999〕	10		100	9/	0	千克	AB	MRS	/35
15.09		**油橄榄油及其分离品,不论是否精制,但未经化学改性:**									
1509.1000		-初榨的〔999〕	10		30	9/	0	千克	7AB	PRQS	/35
1509.9000		-精制的油橄榄油及其分离品(包括初榨油橄榄油的分离品,但未经化学改性)〔999〕	10		30	13/	0	千克	7AB	RS	/35
15.10		**其他橄榄油及其分离品,不论是否精制,但未经化学改性,包括掺有税目15.09的油或分离品的混合物:**									
1510.0000		其他橄榄油及其分离品,不论是否精制,但未经化学改性,包括掺有税目15.09的油或分离品的混合物〔101初榨食用橄榄油,102其他初榨植物食用油,103食用橄榄油〕	10		30	13/	0	千克	7AB	PRQS	/20
15.11		**棕榈油及其分离品,不论是否精制,但未经化学改性:**									
1511.1000		-初榨的〔999〕	9		60	9/	0	千克	7AB	MPRQS	/19
		-其他:									
1511.9010		---棕榈液油(熔点19～24度)〔999〕	9		60	9/	0	千克	7AB	MRS	/19
1511.9020		---棕榈硬脂(熔点44～56度)									
1511.9020	01	固态棕榈硬脂(50度≤熔点≤56度)(未经化学改性)〔999〕	8	2	60	9/	0	千克	7AB	MRS	/12
1511.9020	90	棕榈硬脂(44度≤熔点<50度,未经化学改性)〔999〕	8		60	9/	0	千克	AB	MRS	/18
1511.9090		---其他〔999〕	9		60	13/	0	千克	7AB	MRS	/19

协定税率 %										特惠税率 %			Article Description
亚太5国	东/冰/格	巴基斯坦	韩国	瑞士	哥达	秘鲁	澳大利亚	新西/坡/智	港/澳/台	亚太2国	老/柬/缅	36/3/1	
	0/0/0		4.8	6.2	0	0	0	0/0/0	0/0/			0/0/	Fats and oils and their fractions, of endangerd fish, other than liver oils
	0/0/0		4.8	6.2	0	0	0	0/0/0	0/0/			0/0/	Other fish oil capsules, other than liver oils
	0/0/0		4.8	6.2	0	0	0	0/0/0	0/0/			0/0/	Fats and oils and their fractions, of other fish, other than liver oils
													-Fats and oils and their fractions, of marine mammals
	0/0/0		5.7	4.3	0	0	0	0/0/0	0/0/			0/0/	Fats and oils and their fractions, of endangered marine mammals
	0/0/0		5.7	4.3	0	0	0	0/0/0	0/0/			0/0/	Other fats and oils and their fractions of marine mammals
													Wool grease and fatty substances derived therefrom (including lanolin):
	0/0/0		12	6	0	0	0	0/0/0	0/0/			0/0/	Wool grease and fatty substances derived therefrom (including lanolin)
													Other animal fats and oils and their fractions, whether or not refined, but not chemically modified:
													Other animal fats and oils and their fractions, whether or not refined, but not chemically modified
	0/0/0		12	6	0	0	0	0/0/0	0/0/			0/0/	Fats made of materials of endangered wild animals (including hippo, bear, hare, green turtle and green turtle egg)
	0/0/0		12	6	0	0	0	0/0/0	0/0/			0/0/	Fats and oils and their fractions, of other animals(whether or not refined, but not chemically modified)
													Soya-bean oil and its fractions, whether or not refined, but not chemically modified:
									0/0/				-Crude oil whether or not degummed
									0/0/				-Other
													Ground-nut oil and its fractions, whether or not refined, but not chemically modified:
	0//							/0/	0/0/				-Crude oil
	0//							/0/	0/0/				-Other
													Olive oil and its fractions, whether or not refined, but not chemically modified:
	0/0/		4	0	0	0		0/0/0	0/0/			0/0/	-Crude oil
	0/0/		4	0	0	0		0/0/0	0/0/			0/0/	-Other
													Other oils and their fractions, obtained solely from olives, whether or not refined, but not chemically modified, including blends of these oils or fractions with oils or fractions of heading No.15.09:
	0/0/		4	0	0	0		0/0/0	0/0/			0/0/	Other oils and their fractions, obtained solely from olives, whether or not refined, but not chemically modified, including blends of these oils or fractions with oils or fractions of heading No. 15.09
													Palm oil and its fractions, whether or not refined, but not chemically modified:
									0/0/				-Crude oil
													-Other:
									0/0/				---Palm olein(cmelting point 19℃~24℃)
													---Palm stearin(cmelting point 44℃~56℃)
									0/0/				Solid plam stearin(cmelting point 50℃~56℃, not chemically modified)
									0/0/				Palm Stearin(melting point 44℃~50℃, not chemically modified)
									0/0/				---Other

税则号列	货品名称〔CIQ 扩展编码及品名－T2 表示见附表 2〕	最惠(%)	暂定税率	普通	增值/消费	出口退税	计量单位	监管条件	检验检疫	特殊证件对美关税
15.12	**葵花油、红花油或棉子油及其分离品，不论是否精制，但未经化学改性：**									
	-葵花油或红花油及其分离品：									
1512.1100	--初榨的〔101 初榨食用葵花油，102 初榨食用红花油，103 其他食用植物油〕	9		160	9/	0	千克	AB	PRQS	/34
1512.1900	--其他〔101 食用葵花籽油，102 其他食用植物油〕	9		160	13/	0	千克	AB	RS	/34
	-棉子油及其分离品：									
1512.2100	--初榨的，不论是否去除棉子酚〔999〕	10		70	9/	0	千克	AB	PRQS	/20
1512.2900	--其他〔999〕	10		70	13/	0	千克	AB	RS	/20
15.13	**椰子油、棕榈仁油或巴巴苏棕榈果油及其分离品，不论是否精制，但未经化学改性：**									
	-椰子油及其分离品：									
1513.1100	--初榨的〔999〕	9		40	9/	0	千克	AB	MPRQS	/34
1513.1900	--其他〔999〕	9		40	9/	0	千克	AB	MPRQS	/34
	-棕榈仁油或巴巴苏棕榈果油及其分离品：									
1513.2100	--初榨的〔101 初榨食用棕榈油，102 其他初榨植物食用油〕	9		40	9/	0	千克	AB	MPRQS	/19
1513.2900	--其他〔999〕	9		40	13/	0	千克	AB	MRS	/19
15.14	**菜子油或芥子油及其分离品，不论是否精制，但未经化学改性：**									
	-低芥子酸菜子油及其分离品：									
1514.1100	--初榨的〔999〕	9		170	9/	0	千克	7AB	MPRQS	/34
1514.1900	--其他〔999〕	9		170	9/	0	千克	7AB	MPRQS	/19
	-其他：									
	--初榨的：									
1514.9110	---菜子油〔999〕	9		170	9/	0	千克	7AB	MPRQS	/19
1514.9190	---芥子油〔999〕	9		170	9/	0	千克	7AB	MPRQS	/19
1514.9900	--其他〔101 食用菜籽油，102 其他食用植物油〕	9		170	13/	0	千克	7AB	MRS	/34
15.15	**其他固定植物油、脂(包括希蒙得木油)及其分离品，不论是否精制，但未经化学改性：**									
	-亚麻子油及其分离品：									
1515.1100	--初榨的〔999〕	15		30	9/	0	千克	AB	MPRQS	/45
1515.1900	--其他〔999〕	15		30	13/	0	千克	AB	RS	/25
	-玉米油及其分离品：									
1515.2100	--初榨的〔999〕	10		160	9/	0	千克	AB	PRQS	/20
1515.2900	--其他〔999〕	10		160	13/	0	千克	AB	RS	/35
1515.3000	-蓖麻油及其分离品〔101〕	10		70	13/	6	千克	AB	MPQS	/35
1515.5000	-芝麻油及其分离品〔101 初榨食用芝麻油，102 食用芝麻油〕	12		20	9/	0	千克	AB	PRQS	/37
	-其他：									
1515.9010	---希蒙得木油(霍霍巴油)及其分离品〔101 初榨食用桐油，102 其他初榨植物食用油〕	20		70	13/	6	千克	AB	PRQS	/50
1515.9020	---印楝油及其分离品〔101 其他初榨植物食用油，102 食用茶油，103 其他食用植物油〕	20		70	13/	6	千克	ABS	PRQS	/30
1515.9030	---桐油及其分离品〔101 初榨食用桐油，102 其他初榨植物食用油，103 其他食用植物油〕	20		70	13/	6	千克	AB	PRQS	/30
1515.9090	---其他									
1515.9090 10	红松子油(不论是否精制，但未经化学改性)〔101 其他初榨植物食用油，102 其他食用植物油〕	20		70	13/	0	千克	ABE	PRQS	/40
1515.9090 90	其他固定植物油、脂及其分离品(不论是否精制，但未经化学改性)［T2］	20		70	13/	0	千克	AB	MPRNQS	/40
15.16	**动、植物油、脂及其分离品，全部或部分氢化、相互酯化、再酯化或反油酸化，不论是否精制，但未经进一步加工：**									
1516.1000	-动物油、脂及其分离品〔999〕	5		70	13/	13	千克	AB	RS	/30
1516.2000	-植物油、脂及其分离品〔101 其他食用植物油，103 食用起酥油，104 食用其他加工油脂，301 氢化植物油(无检疫要求食品添加剂)〕	25		70	13/	0	千克	AB	RS	/50
15.17	**人造黄油；本章各种动、植物油、脂及其分离品混合制成的食用油、脂或制品，但税目 15.16 的食用油、脂及其分离品除外：**									
1517.1000	-人造黄油，但不包括液态的〔101 食用植物奶油，102 食用其他加工油脂，301 无检疫要求食品添加剂〕	30		80	13/	0	千克	AB	MRS	/55
	-其他：									
1517.9010	---起酥油									

协定税率 %										特惠税率 %			Article Description
亚太5国	东/冰/格	巴基斯坦	韩国	瑞士	哥达	秘鲁	澳大利亚	新西/坡/智	港/澳/台	亚太2国	老/柬/缅	36/3/1	
													Sunflower-seed, safflower or cotton-seed oil and fractions thereof, whether or not refined, but not chemically modified:
													-Sunflower-seed or safflower oil and fractions thereof:
	0//								0/0/				--Crude oil
	0//								0/0/				--Other
													-Cotton-seed oil and its fractions:
	0//							/0/	0/0/				--Crude oil, whether or not gossypol has been removed
	0//							/0/	0/0/				--Other
													Coconut (copra), palm kernel or babassu oil and fractions thereof, whether or not refined, but not chemically modified:
													-Coconut (copra) oil and its fractions:
4.5	0/0/	4.5	0	0	0	0		0//0	0/0/			0/0/	--Crude oil
4.5	0/0/	4.5	0	0	0	0		0//0	0/0/			0/0/0	--Other
													-Palm kernel or babassu oil and fractions thereof:
	0/0/		0	0	0	0		0//0	0/0/			0/0/	--Crude oil
	0/0/		0	0	0	0		0//0	0/0/			0/0/	--Other
													Rape, colza or mustard oil and fractions thereof, whether or not refined, but not chemically modified:
													-Low erucic acid rape of colza oil and its fractions:
									0/0/				--Crude oil
									0/0/				--Other
													-Other:
													--Crude oil:
	5//								0/0/				---Rape oil
									0/0/				---Mustard oil
	5//								0/0/				--Other
													Other fixed vegetable fats and oils (including jojoba oil) and fractions thereof, whether or not refined, but not chemically modified:
													-Linseed oil and its fractions:
	0/0/		6	4.5	0	0		0/0/0	0/0/			0/0/	--Crude oil
	0/0/		6	4.5	0	0		0/0/0	0/0/			0/0/	--Other
													-Maize (corn) oil and its fractions:
	0//							/0/	0/0/		0/0/	0/0/0	--Crude oil
	0//							/0/	0/0/		0/0/	0/0/0	--Other
	0/0/		4	0	0	0	0	0/0/0	0/0/		0/0/	0/0/0	-Castor oil and its fractions
	0/0/		4.8	3.6	0	0	0	0/0/0	0/0/		0/0/	0/0/0	-Sesame oil and its fractions
													-Other:
	0/0/		12	6	0		0	0/0/0	0/0/		/0/	0/0/0	---Jojoba oil and its fractions
	0/0/		12	6	0		0	0/0/0	0/0/			0/0/	---Neem oil and its fractions
	0/0/		12	6	0		0	0/0/0	0/0/		/0/	0/0/0	---Tung oil and its fractions
													---Other
	0/0/			6	0		0	0/0/0	0/0/		0/0/0	0/0/0	Korean pine seed oil (whether or not refined, but not chemical modified)
	0/0/			6	0		0	0/0/0	0/0/		0/0/0	0/0/0	Other fixed vegetable fats and oils and fraction thereof oil (whether or not refined, but not chemically modified)
													Animal or vegetable fats and oil and fractions thereof, partly or wholly hydrogenated, inter-esterified, reesterified or elaidinized, whether or not refined, but not further prepared:
	0/0/0		0	0	0	0	0	0//0	0/0/			0/0/0	-Animal fats and oils and fractions thereof
	0/0/	0			0	0	0	0//0	0/0/			0/0/	-Vegetable fats and oils and fractions thereof
													Margarine; edible mixtures or preparations of animal or vegetable fats or oils or of fractions of different fats or oils of this Chapter, other than edible fats or oils or their fractions of heading No. 15.16:
	0//				0		0	0/0/0	0/0/				-Margarine, excluding liquid margarine
													-Other:
													---Shortening

税则号列		货品名称〔CIQ 扩展编码及品名—T2 表示见附表 2〕	最惠(%)	暂定税率	普通	增值/消费	出口退税	计量单位	监管条件	检验检疫	特殊证件对美关税
1517.9010	01	动物油脂制造的起酥油(税目 15.16 的食用油、脂及其分离品除外)〔999 品目 1516 的食用油、脂及其分离品除外,301 无检疫要求食品添加剂〕	25		70	13/	13	千克	AB	RS	/50
1517.9010	90	植物油脂制造的起酥油(税目 15.16 的食用油、脂及其分离品除外)〔101 食用植物调和油,102 食用其他加工油脂,301 无检疫要求食品添加剂〕	25		70	9/	0	千克	AB	RS	/50
1517.9090		---其他									
1517.9090	01	其他混合制成的动物质食用油脂或制品(税目 15.16 的食用油、脂及其分离品除外)〔101 脂或制品,102 食用其他加工油脂,301 无检疫要求食品添加剂〕	25		70	13/	13	千克	AB	RS	/50
1517.9090	90	其他混合制成的植物质食用油脂或制品(税目 15.16 的食用油、脂及其分离品除外)〔101 食用植物调和油,102 其他食用植物油,103 食用其他加工油脂,301 无检疫要求食品添加剂〕	25		70	9/	0	千克	AB	RS	/50
15.18		**动、植物油、脂及其分离品,经过熟炼、氧化、脱水、硫化、吹制或在真空、惰性气体中加热聚合及用其他化学方法改性的,但税目 15.16 的产品除外;本章各种油、脂及其分离品混合制成的其他税目未列名的非食用油、脂或制品:**									
1518.0000		动、植物油、脂及其分离品,经过熟炼、氧化、脱水、硫化、吹制或在真空、惰性气体中加热聚合及用其他化学方法改性的,但税目 15.16 的产品除外;本章各种油、脂及其分离品混合制成的其他税目未列名的非食用油、脂或制品〔101 脂,102 食用植物奶油,104 食用起酥油,105 食用其他加工油脂,106 饲用棕榈脂肪粉,107 棕榈油,301 无检疫要求食品添加剂,302 属于危险化学品的食品添加剂,303 一般化学品,需申报仅用于工业用途不用于食品添加剂无检疫要求,304 易燃液体,需申报仅用于工业用途不用于食品添加剂无检疫要求〕	10		70	13/	13	千克	AB	MRS	/30
15.20		**粗甘油;甘油水及甘油碱液:**									
1520.0000		粗甘油,甘油水及甘油碱液〔301 无检疫要求食品添加剂,302 需申报仅用于工业用途不用于食品添加剂无检疫要求的化学品〕	20	6	50	13/	13	千克	AB	MRS	/31
15.21		**植物蜡(甘油三酯除外)、蜂蜡、其他虫蜡及鲸蜡,不论是否精制或着色:**									
1521.1000		-植物蜡									
1521.1000	10	小烛树蜡〔999〕	20		80	13/	13	千克	ABEF	PRQ	/40
1521.1000	90	其他植物蜡〔101 琳脂肪酸盐(果蜡),102 巴西棕榈蜡〕	20		80	13/	13	千克	AB	PRQS	/40
		-其他:									
1521.9010		---蜂蜡〔101 其他动物产品,102 工业用未经加工蜂蜡〕	20		80	13/	13	千克	AB	PRQS	/30
1521.9090		---其他									
1521.9090	10	鲸蜡(不论是否精制或着色)〔999〕	20		80	13/	13	千克	AFEB	PQ	/30
1521.9090	90	其他虫蜡(不论是否精制或着色)〔101 其他动物产品,102 药用五倍子〕	20		80	13/	13	千克	AB	PQ	/30
15.22		**油鞣回收脂;加工处理油脂物质及动、植物蜡所剩的残渣:**									
1522.0000		油鞣回收脂;加工处理油脂物质及动、植物蜡所剩的残渣〔999〕	20		50	13/	13	千克	9		/30

协定税率 %										特惠税率 %			Article Description
亚太5国	东/冰/格	巴基斯坦	韩国	瑞士	哥达	秘鲁	澳大利亚	新西/坡/智	港/澳/台	亚太2国	老/柬/缅	36/3/1	
	0/0/			7.5	0	0	0	0//0	0/0/			0/0/	Shortening made of animal grease(other than edible fats or oils or their fractions of heading No.1516)
	0/0/			7.5	0	0	0	0//0	0/0/			0/0/	Shortening made of plant oil(other than edible fats or oils or their fractions of heading No.1516)
													---Other
	0/0/			13	0	0		0//0	0/0/			0/0/	Edible mixtures or preparations of animal fats or oil or of fractions (Other than edible fats or oil or their fractions of heading No. 15.16)
	0/0/			13	0	0		0//0	0/0/			0/0/	Edible mixtures or preparations of vegetable fats or oil or of fractions(Other than edible fats or oil or their fractions of heading No. 15.16)
													Animal or vegetable fats and oils and fractions thereof, boiled, oxidized, dehydrated, sulphurized, blown, polymerized by heat in vacuum or in inert gas or otherwise chemically modified, excluding those of heading No. 15. 16; inedible mixtures or preparations of animal or vegetable fats or oils or of fractions of different fats or oils of this Chapter, not elsewhere specified or included:
	0/0/		7	0	0	0		0/0/0	0/0/			0/0/0	Animal or vegetable fats and oils and fractions thereof, boiled, oxidized, dehydrated, sulphurized, blown, polymerized by heat in vacuum or in inert gas or otherwise chemically modified, excluding those of heading No. 15. 16; inedible mixtures or preparations of animal or vegetable fats or oils or of fractions of different fats or oils of this Chapter, not elsewhere specified or included
													Glycerol, crude; glycerol waters and glycerol lyes:
	0/0/0		12	6	0	0	0	0/0/0	0/0/			0/0/	Glycerol, crude; glycerol waters and glycerol lyes
													Vegetable waxes (other than triglycerides), beeswax, other insect waxes and spermaceti, whether or not refined or coloured:
													-Vegetable waxes
	0/0/0		12	6	0	0	0	0/0/0	0/0/			0/0/	Candelilla waxes
	0/0/0		12	6	0	0	0	0/0/0	0/0/			0/0/	Other vegetable waxes
													-Other:
	0/0/0		12	6	0	0	0	0/0/0	0/0/			0/0/	---Beeswax
													---Other
	0/0/0		12	6	0	0	0	0/0/0	0/0/			0/0/	Spermaceti(whether or not refined or coloured)
	0/0/0		12	6	0	0	0	0/0/0	0/0/			0/0/	Other insect waxes(whether or not refined or coloured)
													Degras; residues resulting from the treatment of fatty substances of animal or vegetable waxes:
	0/0/0		12	6	0	0	0	0/0/0	0/0/			0/0/	Degras; residues resulting from the treatment of fatty substances of animal or vegetable waxes

第四类
食品;饮料、酒及醋;烟草、烟草及烟草代用品的制品

注释:

本类所称"团粒",是指直接挤压或加入按重量计比例不超过3%的黏合剂制成的粒状产品。

第十六章
肉、鱼、甲壳动物,软体动物及其他水生无脊椎动物的制品

注释:

一、本章不包括用第二章、第三章及税目05.04所列方法制作或保藏的肉、食用杂碎、鱼、甲壳动物、软体动物或其他水生无脊椎动物。

二、本章的食品按重量计必须含有20%以上的香肠、肉、食用杂碎、动物血、鱼、甲壳动物、软体动物或其他水生无脊椎动物及其混合物。对于含有两种或两种以上前述产品的食品,则应按其中重量最大的产品归入第十六章的相应税目。但本条规定不适用于税目19.02的包馅食品和税目21.03及21.04的食品。

子目注释:

一、子目1602.10的"均化食品",是指用肉、食用杂碎或动物血经精细均化制成适合供婴幼儿食用或营养用的零售包装食品(每件净重不超过250克)。为了调味、保藏或其他目的,均化食品中可以加入少量其他配料,还可以含有少量可见的肉粒或食用杂碎粒。归类时该子目优先于税目16.02的其他子目。

二、税目16.04或16.05项下各子目所列的是鱼、甲壳动物、软体动物及其他水生无脊柱动物的俗名,它们与第三章中相同名称的鱼、甲壳动物、软体动物及其水生无脊柱动物种类范围相同。

税则号列		货品名称〔CIQ扩展编码及品名—T2表示见附表2〕	最惠(%)	暂定税率	普通	增值/消费	出口退税	计量单位	监管条件	检验检疫	特殊证件对美关税
16.01		**肉、食用杂碎或动物血制成的香肠及类似产品;用香肠制成的食品:**									
1601.0010		---用天然肠衣做外包装的香肠及类似产品									
1601.0010	10	濒危野生动物肉、杂碎,血制天然肠衣香肠(含税目02.08的野生动物,包括类似品)〔101 动物肉及杂碎,102 其他熟制禽肉制品,103 其他熟制畜肉制品〕	5		90	13/	0	千克	ABFE	PRQS	/35
1601.0010	90	其他动物肉,杂碎及血制天然肠衣香肠(包括类似品)[T2]	5		90	13/	13	千克	AB	PRQS	/35
1601.0020		---其他香肠及类似产品									
1601.0020	10	濒危野生动物肉,杂碎,血制其他肠衣香肠(含编号0208的野生动物,包括类似品)〔101 动物肉及杂碎,102 其他熟制禽肉制品,103 其他熟制畜肉制品〕	5		90	13/	0	千克	ABFE	PRQS	/35
1601.0020	90	其他动物肉、杂碎及血制其他肠衣香肠(包括类似品)[T2]	5		90	13/	13	千克	AB	PRQS	/35
1601.0030		---用香肠制成的食品									
1601.0030	10	用含濒危野生动物成分的香肠制的食品(含税目02.08的野生动物)〔101 其他熟制禽肉制品,102 其他熟制畜肉制品〕	5		90	13/	0	千克	ABFE	PRQS	/10
1601.0030	90	用含其他动物成分的香肠制的食品〔101 其他熟制禽肉制品,102 其他熟制畜肉制品〕	5		90	13/	6,13	千克	AB	PRQS	/10
16.02		**其他方法制作或保藏的肉、食用杂碎或动物血:**									
1602.1000		-均化食品									
1602.1000	10	含濒危野生动物成分的均化食品(指用肉、食用杂碎或动物血经精细均化制成,零售包装)〔101 其他熟制禽肉制品,102 其他去骨熟制畜肉制品,103 其他带骨熟制畜肉制品,104 未列出的其他动物肉脏及杂碎制品〕	5		90	13/	0	千克	ABFE	RS	/30
1602.1000	90	其他动物肉或食用杂碎的均化食品(指用肉、食用杂碎或动物血经精细均化制成,零售包装)〔101 其他熟制禽肉制品,102 其他去骨熟制畜肉制品,103 其他带骨熟制畜肉制品,104 未列出的其他动物肉脏及杂碎制品〕	5		90	13/	13	千克	AB	RS	/30
1602.2000		-动物肝									
1602.2000	10	制作或保藏的濒危动物肝(第二、三章所列方法制作或保藏的除外)[T2]	5		90	13/	0	千克	ABFE	PRQS	/10

SECTION Ⅳ
PREPARED FOODSTUFFS; BEVERAGES, SPIRITS AND VINEGAR, TOBACCO AND MANUFACTURED TOBACCO SUBSTITUTES

Note:

In this Section the term "pellets" means products which have been agglomerated either directly by compression or by the addition of a binder in a proportion not exceeding 3% by weight.

Chapter 16
Preparations of meat, of fish or of crustaceans, molluscs or other aquatic invertebrates

Notes:

1. This Chapter does not cover meat, meat offal, fish, crustaceans, molluscs or other aquatic invertebrates, prepared or preserved by the processes specified in Chapter 2 or 3 or heading No. 05. 04.
2. Food preparations fall in this Chapter provided that they contain more than 20% by weight of sausage, meat, meat offal, blood, fish or crustaceans, molluscs or other aquatic invertebrates, or any combination thereof. In cases where the preparation contains two or more of the products mentioned above, it is classified in the heading of Chapter 16 corresponding to the component or components which predominate by weight. These provisions do not apply to the stuffed products of heading No. 19. 02 or to the preparations of heading No. 21. 03 or 21. 04.

Subheading Notes:

1. For the purposes of subheading No. 1602. 10, the expression "homogenized preparations" means preparations of meat, meat offal or blood, finely homogenized, put up for retail sale Suitable for infants to eat or for dietetic purposes, in containers of a net weight content not exceeding 250g. For the application of this definition no account is to be taken of small quantities of any ingredients which may have been added to the preparation for seasoning, preservation or other purposes. These preparations may contain a small quantity of visible pieces of meat or meat offal. This subheading takes precedence over all other subheadings of heading No.16. 02.
2. Ther fish、crustaceans、Molluscs and other aquatic invertebrates specified in the subheadings of heading No.16.04 or 16.05 under their common names only, are of the same species as those mentionde in Chpapter 3 under the same name.

协定税率 %										特惠税率 %			Article Description
亚太5国	东/冰/格	巴基斯坦	韩国	瑞士	哥达	秘鲁	澳大利亚	新西/坡/智	港/澳/台	亚太2国	老/柬/缅	36/3/1	
													Sausages and similar products, of meat, meat offal or blood; food preparations based on these products:
													---Sausages and similar products, with a natural casing
	0/0/0	12	6	4.5	0	0	0	0/0/0	0/0/			0/0/	Sausages packed with natural casing of meat, meat offal or blood of endangered wild animals(including wild animals of heading No. 0208 and similar products)
	0/0/0	12	6	4.5	0	0	0	0/0/0	0/0/			0/0/	Sausages packed with natural casing of meat, meat offal or blood of other aminals(including similar products)
													---Other sausages and similar products
	0/0/0	12	6	4.5	0	0	0	0/0/0	0/0/			0/0/	Sausages packed with other casing of meat, meal offal or blood of endangered wild animals(including wild animals of heading No. 0208 and similar products)
	0/0/0	12	6	4.5	0	0	0	0/0/0	0/0/			0/0/	Sauages packed with other cosing of meat, meat offal or blood of other animals(including simiple products)
													---Food preparations basd on sausages food products
	0/0/0	12	6	4.5	0	0	0	0/0/0	0/0/			0/0/	Food preparations based on sauages, containing compositions of endangered wild animals (including endangered wild animals of heading No. 0208)
	0/0/0	12	6	4.5	0	0	0	0/0/0	0/0/			0/0/	Food preparation based on other sauages, containing compositions of other animals
													Other Prepared or preserved meat, meat offal or blood:
													-Homogenized preparations
	0/0/0	12	6	4.5	0	0	0	0/0/0	0/0/			0/0/	Homogenized preparations, with containing compositions of endangered wild animals(prepared or preserved meat, meat offal or blood, put up for retail sale)
	0/0/0	12	6	4.5	0	0	0	0/0/0	0/0/			0/0/	Homogenized preparations, with containing compositions of other animals (prepared or preserved meat, meat offal or blood, put up for retail sale)
													-Of liver of any animal
	0/0/0	12	6	4.5	0	0	0	0/0/0	0/0/			0/0/	Liver of endangered animal, prepared or preserved(other than prepared or preserved of Chapter 2 and 3)

税则号列	货品名称〔CIQ扩展编码及品名—T2表示见附表2〕	最惠(%)	暂定税率	普通	增值/消费	出口退税	计量单位	监管条件	检验检疫	特殊证件对美关税
1602.2000 90	制作或保藏的其他动物肝(第二、三章所列方法制作或保藏的除外)[T2]	5		90	13/	13	千克	AB	PRQS	/10
	-税目01.05的家禽的:									
1602.3100	--火鸡的[T2]	5		90	13/	13	千克	AB	PRQS	/15
	--鸡的:									
1602.3210	---罐头〔999〕	5		90	13/	13	千克	AB	PRQS	/10
	---其他:									
1602.3291	----鸡胸肉[T2]	5		90	13/	13	千克	AB	PRQS	/15
1602.3292	----鸡腿肉[T2]	5		90	13/	13	千克	AB	PRQS	/10
1602.3299	----其他[T2]	5		90	13/	13	千克	AB	PRQS	/10
	--其他:									
1602.3910	---罐头[T2]	5		90	13/	13	千克	AB	PRQS	/10
	---其他:									
1602.3991	----鸭的[T2]	5		90	13/	6,13	千克	AB	PRQS	/10
1602.3999	----其他[T2]	5		90	13/	13	千克	AB	PRQS	/10
	-猪的:									
1602.4100	--后腿及其肉块									
1602.4100 10	制作或保藏的鹿豚、姬猪后腿及肉块〔101猪蹄,102去骨熟制猪肉制品,103带骨熟制猪肉制品〕	5		90	13/	13	千克	ABFE	PRQS	/30
1602.4100 90	制作或保藏的猪后腿及其肉块〔101猪蹄,102去骨熟制猪肉制品,103带骨熟制猪肉制品〕	5		90	13/	13	千克	AB	PRQS	/30
1602.4200	--前腿及其肉块									
1602.4200 10	制作或保藏的鹿豚,姬猪前腿及其肉块〔101猪蹄,102去骨熟制猪肉制品,103带骨熟制猪肉制品〕	5		90	13/	13	千克	ABFE	PRQS	/10
1602.4200 90	制作或保藏的猪前腿及其肉块[T2]	5		90	13/	13	千克	AB	PRQS	/10
	--其他,包括混合的肉:									
1602.4910	---罐头									
1602.4910 10	其他含鹿豚、姬猪肉及杂碎的罐头〔999〕	5		90	13/	13	千克	ABFE	PRQS	/10
1602.4910 90	其他猪肉及杂碎的罐头〔101猪肉罐头,102午餐肉罐头,103火腿午餐肉罐头,104火腿罐头,105云腿罐头〕	5		90	13/	13	千克	AB	PRQS	/10
1602.4990	---其他									
1602.4990 10	制作或保藏的其他鹿豚、姬猪肉、杂碎(包括血等)〔101其他猪杂碎,102去骨熟制猪肉制品,103带骨熟制猪肉制品〕	5		90	13/	13	千克	ABFE	PRQS	/10
1602.4990 90	制作或保藏的其他猪肉、杂碎、血〔101猪杂碎,102去骨熟制猪肉制品,103带骨熟制猪肉制品〕	5		90	13/	13	千克	AB	PRQS	/10
	-牛的:									
1602.5010	---罐头									
1602.5010 10	含濒危野牛肉的罐头〔999〕	5		90	13/	0	千克	ABFE	PRQS	/10
1602.5010 90	其他牛肉及牛杂碎罐头(含野牛肉的除外)〔999〕	5		90	13/	13	千克	AB	PRQS	/10
1602.5090	---其他									
1602.5090 10	其他制作或保藏濒危野牛肉、杂碎(包括血等)〔101野牛肉及杂碎,102去骨熟制牛肉制品,103带骨熟制牛肉制品〕	5		90	13/	0	千克	ABFE	PRQS	/30
1602.5090 90	其他制作或保藏的牛肉、杂碎、血〔101其他牛杂碎,102去骨熟制牛肉制品,103带骨熟制牛肉制品〕	5		90	13/	13	千克	AB	PRQS	/30
	-其他,包括动物血的食品:									
1602.9010	---罐头									
1602.9010 10	其他濒危野生动物肉及杂碎罐头〔999〕	5		90	13/	0	千克	ABFE	PRQS	/10
1602.9010 90	其他肉及杂碎罐头〔101鸟肉罐头,102香肠罐头,103羊肉罐头,104鹿肉罐头,105袋鼠肉罐头,106马肉罐头,107食用〕	5		90	13/	13	千克	AB	PRQS	/10
1602.9090	---其他									
1602.9090 10	制作或保藏其他濒危野生动物肉(包括杂碎、血)〔101其他动物肉脏及杂碎,102其他熟制禽肉制品,103其他去骨熟制畜肉制品,104其他带骨熟制畜肉制品〕	5		90	13/	0	千克	ABFE	PRQS	/10
1602.9090 90	经制作或保藏的其他肉、杂碎及血[T2]	5		90	13/	13	千克	AB	PRQS	/10
16.03	**肉、鱼、甲壳动物、软体动物或其他水生无脊椎动物的精及汁:**									
1603.0000	肉、鱼、甲壳动物、软体动物或其他水生无脊椎动物的精及汁									
1603.0000 10	含濒危野生动物及鱼类成分的肉(指税目02.08及子目0301.92野生动物及鱼类)〔101水产制品,102鱼类罐头〕	5		90	13/	0	千克	ABFE	PRQS	/30

协定税率 %										特惠税率 %			Article Description
亚太5国	东/冰/格	巴基斯坦	韩国	瑞士	哥达	秘鲁	澳大利亚	新西/坡/智	港/澳/台	亚太2国	老/柬/缅	36/3/1	
	0/0/0	12	6	4.5	0	0	0	0/0/0	0/0/			0/0/	Liver of other animals, prepared or preserved(other than prepared or preserved of Chapter 2 and 3)
													-Of poultry of heading No. 01. 05:
	0/0/0	12	6	4.5	0	0	0	0/0/0	0/0/			0/0/	--Of turkeys
													--Of fowls of the species *Gallus domesticus*:
	0/0/0	12	6	4.5	0	0	0	0/0/0	0/0/			0/0/	---In airtight containers
													---Other:
	0/0/0	12	6	4.5	0	0	0	0/0/0	0/0/			0/0/	----Chicken breast filets
	0/0/0	12	6	4.5	0	0	0	0/0/0	0/0/			0/0/	----Chicken leg meat
	0/0/0	12	6	4.5	0	0	0	0/0/0	0/0/			0/0/	----Other
													--Other:
	0/0/0	12	6	4.5	0	0	0	0/0/0	0/0/			0/0/	---In airtight containers
													---Other:
	0/0/0	12	6	4.5	0	0	0	0/0/0	0/0/			0/0/	----Of duck
	0/0/0	12	6	4.5	0	0	0	0/0/0	0/0/			0/0/	----Other
													-Of swine:
													--Hams and cuts thereof
	0/0/0	12	6	4.5	0	0	0	0/0/0	0/0/			0/0/	Prepared or preserved hams and cuts of pig-deer (*Babyrousa*)、pygmy pig (*Porcula*)
	0/0/0	12	6	4.5	0	0	0	0/0/0	0/0/			0/0/	Prepared or preserved hams and cuts of swine
													--Shoulders and cuts thereof
	0/0/0	12	6	4.5	0	0	0	0/0/0	0/0/			0/0/	Prepared or preserved shoulders and cuts of pig-deer (*Babyrousa*)、pygmy pig (*Porcula*)
	0/0/0	12	6	4.5	0	0	0	0/0/0	0/0/			0/0/	Prepared or preserved shoulders and cuts of swine
													--Other, including mixtures:
													---In airtight containers
	0/0/0	12	6	4.5	0	0	0	0/0/0	0/0/			0/0/	Other meat, meat offal of pig-deer (*Babyrousa*)、pygmy pig (*Porcula*), tinned
	0/0/0	12	6	4.5	0	0	0	0/0/0	0/0/			0/0/	Other meat, meat offal of swine, tinned
													---Other
	0/0/0	12	6	4.5	0	0	0	0/0/0	0/0/			0/0/	Prepared or preserved meat, meat offal or blood of pig-deer (*Babyrousa*)、pygmy pig (*Porcula*)
	0/0/0	12	6	4.5	0	0	0	0/0/0	0/0/			0/0/	Prepared or preserved meat, meat offal or blood of swine
													-Of bovine animals:
													---In airtight containers
	0/0/0	6	4.8	3.6	0	0	0	0/0/0	0/0/			0/0/	Meat of endangered wild bovine animals, tinned
	0/0/0	6	4.8	3.6	0	0	0	0/0/0	0/0/			0/0/	Other meat, meat offal of bovine animals, tinned(other than meat of wild bovine animals)
													---Other
	0/0/0	6	4.8	3.6	0	0	0	0/0/0	0/0/			0/0/	Other prepared or preserved meat, meat offal or blood of endangered wild bovine animals
	0/0/0	6	4.8	3.6	0	0	0	0/0/0	0/0/			0/0/	Other prepared or preserved meat, meat offal or blood of bovine animals
													-Other, including preparations of blood of any animal:
													---In airtight containers
	0/0/0	12	6	4.5	0	0	0	0/0/0	0/0/			0/0/	Other meat, meat offal of endangered wild animals, tinned
	0/0/0	12	6	4.5	0	0	0	0/0/0	0/0/			0/0/	Other meat, meat offal of other animals, tinned
													---Other
	0/0/0	12	6	4.5	0	0	0	0/0/0	0/0/			0/0/	Other prepared or preserved meat, meat offal or blood of endangered wild animals
	0/0/0	12	6	4.5	0	0	0	0/0/0	0/0/			0/0/	Other prepared or preserved meat, meat offal or blood of other animals
													Extracts and juices of meat, fish or crustaceans, molluscs or other aquatic invertebrates:
													Extracts and juices of meat, fish or crustaceans, molluscs or other aquatic invertebrates
	0/0/0		16.1	5	0	0	0	0/0/0	0/0/			0/0/	Meat containing compositions of endangered wild animals and fish of heading No. 0208 or of subheading No. 030192

税则号列	货品名称〔CIQ扩展编码及品名—T2表示见附表2〕	最惠(%)	暂定税率	普通	增值/消费	出口退税	计量单位	监管条件	检验检疫	特殊证件对美关税
1603.0000 90	肉及水产品的精、汁(水产品指鱼、甲壳动物、软体动物或其他水生无脊椎动物)〔101 养殖水产制品,102 野生水产制品〕	5		90	13/	13	千克	AB	PRQS	/30
16.04	**制作或保藏的鱼;鲟鱼子酱及鱼卵制的鲟鱼子酱代用品:**									
	-鱼,整条或切块,但未绞碎:									
	--鲑鱼:									
1604.1110	---大西洋鲑鱼[T2]	10		90	13/	13	千克	AB	PRQS	/35
1604.1190	---其他									
1604.1190 10	制作或保藏的川陕哲罗鲑鱼(整条或切块,但未绞碎)〔101 水产制品,102 鱼类罐头〕	10		90	13/	13	千克	AB	PRQS	/35
1604.1190 20	制作或保藏的秦岭细鳞鲑鱼(整条或切块,但未绞碎)〔101 水产制品,102 鱼类罐头〕	10		90	13/	13	千克	AB	PRQS	/35
1604.1190 90	制作或保藏的其他鲑鱼〔101 水产制品,102 鱼类罐头〕	10		90	13/	13	千克	AB	PRQS	/35
1604.1200	--鲱鱼〔101 水产制品,102 鱼类罐头〕	5		90	13/	13	千克	AB	PRQS	/30
1604.1300	--沙丁鱼、小沙丁鱼属、黍鲱或西鲱[T2]	5		90	13/	13	千克	AB	PRQS	/30
1604.1400	--金枪鱼、鲣鱼及狐鲣(狐鲣属)[T2]	5		90	13/	13	千克	AB	PRQS	/30
1604.1500	--鲭鱼〔101 养殖水产制品,102 野生水产制品,103 养殖鱼类罐头,104 野生鱼类罐头〕	5		90	13/	13	千克	AB	PRQS	/30
1604.1600	--鳀鱼〔101 养殖水产制品,102 野生水产制品,103 养殖鱼类罐头,104 野生鱼类罐头〕	5		90	13/	13	千克	AB	PRQS	/30
1604.1700	--鳗鱼									
1604.1700 10	制作或保藏的花鳗鲡(整条或切块,但未绞碎)[T2]	5		90	13/	13	千克	ABE	PRQS	/30
1604.1700 20	制作或保藏的欧洲鳗鲡(整条或切块,但未绞碎)[T2]	5		90	13/	13	千克	ABEF	PRQS	/30
1604.1700 90	其他制作或保藏的鳗鱼(整条或切块,但未绞碎)[T2]	5		90	13/	13	千克	AB	PRQS	/30
1604.1800	--鲨鱼翅									
1604.1800 10	制作或保藏的濒危鲨鱼鱼翅(整条或切块,但未绞碎)〔999〕	12		90	13/	0	千克	AFEB	PRQS	/37
1604.1800 90	制作或保藏的其他鲨鱼鱼翅(整条或切块,但未绞碎)〔999〕	12		90	13/	13	千克	AB	PRQS	/37
	--其他:									
1604.1920	---罗非鱼〔101 养殖水产制品,102 野生水产制品,103 养殖鱼类罐头,104 野生鱼类罐头〕	5		90	13/	13	千克	AB	PRQS	/30
	---叉尾鮰鱼:									
1604.1931	----斑点叉尾鮰鱼〔101 养殖水产制品,102 野生水产制品,103 养殖鱼类罐头,104 野生鱼类罐头〕	5		90	13/	13	千克	AB	PRQS	/30
1604.1939	----其他〔101 养殖水产制品,102 野生水产制品,103 养殖鱼类罐头,104 野生鱼类罐头〕	5		90	13/	13	千克	AB	PRQS	/30
1604.1990	---其他									
1604.1990 10	制作或保藏的濒危鱼类(整条或切块,但未绞碎)〔101 野生水产制品,102 野生鱼类罐头〕	5		90	13/	0	千克	AFEB	PRQS	/30
1604.1990 90	制作或保藏的其他鱼(整条或切块,但未绞碎)[T2]	5		90	13/	13	千克	AB	PRQS	/30
	-其他制作或保藏的鱼:									
	---罐头:									
1604.2011	----鱼翅									
1604.2011 10	濒危鲨鱼鱼翅罐头〔999〕	12		90	13/	0	千克	ABFE	PRQS	/37
1604.2011 90	其他鲨鱼鱼翅罐头〔999〕	12		90	13/	13	千克	AB	PRQS	/37
1604.2019	----其他									
1604.2019 10	非整条或切块的濒危鱼罐头(鱼翅除外)〔999〕	5		90	13/	0	千克	ABFE	PRQS	/30
1604.2019 90	非整条或切块的其他鱼罐头(鱼翅除外)[T2]	5		90	13/	13	千克	AB	PRQS	/30
	---其他:									
1604.2091	----鱼翅									
1604.2091 10	制作或保藏的濒危鲨鱼鱼翅(非整条、非切块、非罐头)〔999〕	12		90	13/	0	千克	ABFE	PRQS	/37
1604.2091 90	制作或保藏其他鲨鱼鱼翅(非整条、非切块、非罐头)〔999〕	12		90	13/	13	千克	AB	PRQS	/37
1604.2099	----其他									
1604.2099 10	其他制作或保藏的濒危鱼(非整条、非切块、非罐头,鱼翅除外)〔999〕	5		90	13/	0	千克	ABFE	PRQS	/30
1604.2099 90	其他制作或保藏的鱼(非整条、非切块、非罐头,鱼翅除外)[T2]	5		90	13/	13	千克	AB	PRQS	/30

协定税率 %										特惠税率 %			
亚太5国	东/冰/格	巴基斯坦	韩国	瑞士	哥达	秘鲁	澳大利亚	新西/坡/智	港/澳/台	亚太2国	老/柬/缅	36/3/1	Article Description
	0/0/0		16.1	5	0	0	0	0/0/0	C/0/			0/0/	Extracts and juices of meat, fish or crustaceans, molluscs or other aquatic invertebrates
													Prepared or preserved fish; caviar and caviar substitutes prepared from fish eggs:
													-Fish, whole or in pieces, but not minced:
													--Salmon:
	0/0/0	5.4	4.8		0		0	0/0/0	0/0/			0/0/	---Atlantic Salmon
													---Other
	0/0/0	5.4	4.8		0		0	0/0/0	0/Ɔ/			0/0/	Prepared or preserved sichuan tamen(*Hucho taimen*)(whole or in pieces, but not minced)
	0/0/0	5.4	4.8		0		0	0/0/0	0/0/			0/0/	Prepared or preserved Qinling lenok (*Brachymystax lenok*)(whole or in pieces, but not minced)
	0/0/0	5.4	4.8		0		0	0/0/0	0/C/			0/0/	Prepared or preserved other salmon
	0/0/0	5.4	4.8	3.6	0	0	0	0/0/0	0/0/			0/0/	--Herrings
	0/0/0	0	0	0	0	0	0	0//0	0/0/		/0/	0/0/0	--sardines, sardinella, brisling or sprats
	0/0/0	0	0	0	0	0	0	0//0	0/0/		/0/	0/0/0	--Tuna、bonito or belted bonito(bonito)
	0/0/0	5.4	4.8	3.6	0	0	0	0/0/0	0/0/			0/0/	--Mackerel
	0/0/0	5.4	4.8	3.6	0	0	0	0/0/0	0/0/			0/0/	--Anchovies
													--Eels
4.1	0/0/0	4.5	4.8	3.6	0		0	0/0/0	0/0/			0/0/0	Preared or preserved marbled eels (whole or in pieces, but not minced)
4.1	0/0/0	4.5	4.8	3.6	0		0	0/0/0	0/0/			0/0/0	Preared or preserved europea eels (whole or in pieces, but not minced)
4.1	0/0/0	4.5	4.8	3.6	0		0	0/0/0	0/0/			0/0/0	Preared or preserved other eels(whole or in pieces, but not minced)
													--Shark fins
9.8	0/0/0	4.5	4.8	3.6	0		0	0/0/0	0/0/			0/0/0	Endangered shark's fins, prepared or preserved, whole nor in pieces, not not minced
9.8	0/0/0	4.5	4.8	3.6	0		0	0/0/0	0/0/			0/0/0	Other shark's fins, prepared or preserved, whole nor in pieces, not not minced
													--Other:
	0/0/0	5.4	4.8	3.6	0		0	0/0/0	0/0/			0/0/	---Tilapia
													---Ictalurus:
4.1	0/0/0	4.5	4.8	3.6	0		0	0/0/0	0/0/			0/0/0	----Channel catfish(*Ictalurus punctatus*)
4.1	0/0/0	4.5	4.8	3.6	0		0	0/0/0	0/0/			0/0/0	----Other
													---Other
4.1	0/0/0	4.5	4.8	3.6	0		0	0/0/0	0/0/			0/0/0	Prepared or preserved endangered fish(whole or in pieces, but not minced)
4.1	0/0/0	4.5	4.8	3.6	0		0	0/0/0	0/0/			0/0/0	Prepared or preserved other fish(whole or in pieces, but not minced)
													-Other prepared or preserved fish:
													---In airtight containers:
													----Shark's fin
9.8	0/0/0	4.5		3.6	0	0		0/0/0	0/0/			0/0/	Shark's fins of endangered shark (Cetorhinus) in airtight containers
9.8	0/0/0	4.5		3.6	0	0		0/0/0	0/0/			0/0/	Other shark's of shark fins in airtight containers
													----Other
4.1	0/0/0	4.5	4.8	3.6	0	0	0	0/0/0	0/0/			0/0/	Endangered fish in airtight containers, other than whole or in pieces (other than shark's fins)
4.1	0/0/0	4.5	4.8	3.6	0	0	0	0/0/0	0/0/			0/0/	Other fish in airtight containers, other than whole or in pieces(other than shark's fins)
													---Other:
													----Shark's fin
9.8	0/0/0	4.5		3.6	0	0		0/0/0	0/0/			0/0/	Prepared or preserved shark's fins of endangered shark(Cetorhinus)(other than whole or in pieces, not in airtight containers)
9.8	0/0/0	4.5		3.6	0	0		0/0/0	0/0/			0/0/	Prepared or preserved other shark's fins (other than whole or in pieces, not in airtight containers)
													----Other
4.1	0/0/0	4.5	4.8	3.6	0	0	0	0/0/0	0/0/			0/0/	Prepared or preserved engdangered fish (other than whole or in pieces, not in airtight containers, other than shark's fins)
4.1	0/0/0	4.5	4.8	3.6	0	0	0	0/0/0	0/0/			0/0/	Other prepared or preserved fish(other than whole or in pieces, not in airtight containers, other than shark's fins)

税则号列	货品名称〔CIQ 扩展编码及品名－T2 表示见附表 2〕	最惠(%)	暂定税率	普通	增值/消费	出口退税	计量单位	监管条件	检验检疫	特殊证件对美关税
	-鲟鱼子酱及鲟鱼子酱代用品：									
1604.3100	--鲟鱼子酱〔999〕	5		90	13/	13	千克	ABFE	PRQS	/30
1604.3200	--鲟鱼子酱代用品〔999〕	5		90	13/	13	千克	AB	PRQS	/30
16.05	**制作或保藏的甲壳动物、软体动物及其他水生无脊椎动物：**									
1605.1000	-蟹〔101 养殖水产制品，102 野生水产制品，103 养殖甲壳类罐头，104 野生甲壳类罐头〕	5		90	13/	13	千克	AB	PRQS	/40
	-小虾及对虾：									
1605.2100	--非密封包装〔101 养殖水产制品，102 野生水产制品，103 养殖甲壳类罐头，104 野生甲壳类罐头〕	5		90	13/	13	千克	AB	PRQS	/30
1605.2900	--其他〔101 养殖水产制品，102 野生水产制品，103 养殖甲壳类罐头，104 野生甲壳类罐头〕	5		90	13/	13	千克	AB	PRQS	/30
1605.3000	-龙虾〔101 养殖水产制品，102 野生水产制品，103 养殖甲壳类罐头，104 野生甲壳类罐头〕	5		90	13/	13	千克	AB	PRQS	/30
	-其他甲壳动物：									
	---淡水小龙虾：									
1605.4011	----虾仁[T2]	5		90	13/	13	千克	AB	PRQS	/30
1605.4019	----其他[T2]	5		90	13/	13	千克	AB	PRQS	/40
1605.4090	---其他[T2]	5		90	13/	13	千克	AB	PRQS	/30
	-软体动物：									
1605.5100	--牡蛎(蚝)〔101 养殖水产制品，102 野生水产制品，103 养殖贝类罐头，104 野生贝类罐头〕	5		90	13/	13	千克	AB	PRQS	/30
1605.5200	--扇贝，包括海扇									
1605.5200 10	制作或保藏的大珠母贝〔101 养殖水产制品，102 野生水产制品，103 养殖贝类罐头，104 野生贝类罐头〕	5		90	13/	13	千克	ABE	PRQS	/30
1605.5200 90	其他制作或保藏的扇贝，包括海扇〔101 养殖水产制品，102 野生水产制品，103 养殖贝类罐头，104 野生贝类罐头〕	5		90	13/	13	千克	AB	PRQS	/30
1605.5300	--贻贝〔101 养殖水产制品，102 野生水产制品，103 养殖贝类罐头，104 野生贝类罐头〕	5		90	13/	13	千克	AB	PRQS	/30
1605.540C	--墨鱼及鱿鱼〔101 养殖水产制品，102 野生水产制品，103 养殖水产罐头，104 野生水产罐头〕	5		90	13/	13	千克	AB	PRQS	/30
1605.5500	--章鱼〔101 养殖水产制品，102 野生水产制品，103 养殖水产罐头，104 野生水产罐头〕	5		90	13/	13	千克	AB	PRQS	/30
	--蛤、鸟蛤及舟贝：									
1605.5610	---蛤〔101 养殖水产制品，102 野生水产制品，103 养殖贝类罐头，104 野生贝类罐头〕	5		90	13/	9,13	千克	AB	PRQS	/30
1605.5620	---鸟蛤及舟贝									
1605.5620 10	制作或保藏的砗磲〔101 养殖水产制品，102 野生水产制品，103 养殖贝类罐头，104 野生贝类罐头〕	5		90	13/	13	千克	ABEF	PRQS	/30
1605.5620 90	其他制作或保藏的鸟蛤及舟贝〔101 养殖水产制品，102 野生水产制品，103 养殖贝类罐头，104 野生贝类罐头〕	5		90	13/	13	千克	AB	PRQS	/30
1605.5700	--鲍鱼〔101 养殖水产制品，102 野生水产制品，103 养殖贝类罐头，104 野生贝类罐头〕	5		90	13/	13	千克	AB	PRQS	/30
1605.5800	--蜗牛及螺，海螺除外									
1605.5300 10	制作或保藏的濒危蜗牛及螺，海螺除外[T2]	5		90	13/	0	千克	ABFE	PRQS	/30
1605.5800 90	其他制作或保藏的蜗牛及螺，海螺除外[T2]	5		90	13/	13	千克	AB	PRQS	/30
1605.5900	--其他									
1605.5900 10	其他制作或保藏的濒危软体动物〔101 野生水产制品，102 野生水产罐头〕	5		90	13/	0	千克	ABFE	PRQS	/30
1605.5900 90	其他制作或保藏的软体动物〔101 养殖水产制品，102 野生水产制品，103 养殖水产罐头，104 野生水产罐头〕	5		90	13/	13	千克	AB	PRQS	/30
	-其他水生无脊柱动物：									
1605.6100	--海参									
1605.6100 10	制作或保藏的暗色刺参〔101 养殖水产制品，102 野生水产制品，103 养殖水产罐头，104 野生水产罐头〕	5		90	13/	13	千克	ABFE	PRQS	/40
1605.6100 90	其他制作或保藏的海参〔101 养殖水产制品，102 野生水产制品，103 养殖水产罐头，104 野生水产罐头〕	5		90	13/	13	千克	AB	PRQS	/40
1605.6200	--海胆〔101 野生水产制品，102 野生水产罐头〕	5		90	13/	13	千克	AB	PRQS	/30
1605.6300	--海蜇[T2]	5		90	13/	9,13	千克	AB	PRQS	/30
1605.6900	--其他									
1605.6900 10	其他制作或保藏的濒危水生无脊椎动物[T2]	5		90	13/	0	千克	ABFE	PRQS	/30
1605.6900 90	其他制作或保藏的水生无脊椎动物[T2]	5		90	13/	13	千克	AB	PRQS	/30

协定税率 %										特惠税率 %			Article Description
亚太5国	东/冰/格	巴基斯坦	韩国	瑞士	哥达	秘鲁	澳大利亚	新西/坡/智	港/澳/台	亚太2国	老/柬/缅	36/3/1	
													-Caviar and caviar substitutes:
	0/0/0	5.4	4.8	3.6	0	0	0	0/0/0	0/0/			0/0/	--Caviar
	0/0/0	5.4	4.8	3.6	0	0	0	0/0/0	0/0/			0/0/	--Caviar substiutes
													Crustaceans, molluscs and other aquatic invertebrates, prepared or preserved:
	0/0/0	0	0	0	0	0	0	0//0	0/0/			0/0/0	-Crab
													-Shrimps and prawns:
	0/0/0	0	0	0	0	0	0	0//0	0/0/		/0/	0/0/0	--Not in airtight container
	0/0/0	0	0	0	0	0	0	0//0	0/0/		/0/	0/0/0	--Other
	0/0/0	0	0	0	0	0	0	0//0	0/0/		/0/	0/0/0	-Lobster
													-Other crustaceans:
													---Freshwater crawfish:
	0/0/0	0	0	0	0	0	0	0//0	0/0/		/0/	0/0/0	----Shelled
	0/0/0	0	0	0	0	0	0	0//0	0/0/		/0/	0/0/0	----Other
	0/0/0	0	0	0	0	0	0	0//0	0/0/		/0/	0/0/0	---Other
													-Molluscs:
3.9	0/0/0	0	0	0	0	0	0	0//0	0/0/			0/0/0	--Oysters
													--Scallops, including queen scallops
3.9	0/0/0	0	0	0	0	0	0	0//0	0/0/			0/0/0	Pinctada maxima, prepared or preserved
3.9	0/0/0	0	0	0	0	0	0	0//0	0/0/			0/0/0	Other scallops, including queen scallops, prepared or preserved
3.9	0/0/0	0	0	0	0	0	0	0//0	0/0/			0/0/0	--Mussels
3.9	0/0/0	0	0	0	0	0	0	0//0	0/0/			0/0/0	--Cuttle fish and squid
3.9	0/0/0	0	0	0	0	0	0	0//0	0/0/			0/0/0	--Octopus
													--Clams, cockles and arkshells:
3.9	0/0/0	0	0	0	0		0	0//0	0/0/			0/0/0	---Clam
													---Cockles and ark shells
3.9	0/0/0	0	0	0	0	0	0	0//0	0/0/			0/0/0	Tridacna stone, prepared or preserved
3.9	0/0/0	0	0	0	0	0	0	0//0	0/0/			0/0/0	Other cockles and ark shells, prepared or preserved
3.9	0/0/0	0	0	0	0	0	0	0//0	0/0/			0/0/0	--Abalone
													--Snails, other than sea snails
3.9	0/0/0	0	0	0	0	0	0	0//0	0/0/			0/0/0	Endangered snails, other than sea snails, prepared or preserved
3.9	0/0/0	0	0	0	0	0	0	0//0	0/0/			0/0/0	Other snails, other than sea snails, prepared or preserved
													--Other
3.9	0/0/0	0	0	0	0	0	0	0//0	0/0/			0/0/0	Endangered molluscs, prepared or preserved
3.9	0/0/0	0	0	0	0	0	0	0//0	0/0/			0/0/0	Other molluscs, prepared or preserved
													-Other aquatic invertebrates:
													--Sea cucumbers
3.9	0/0/0	0	0	0	0	0	0	0//0	0/0/			0/0/0	Isostichopus fuscus, prepared or preserved
3.9	0/0/0	0	0	0	0	0	0	0//0	0/0/			0/0/0	Other sea cucumbers, prepared or preserved
3.9	0/0/0	0	0	0	0	0	0	0//0	0/0/			0/0/0	--Sea urchin
	0/0/0	12	6	4.5	0		0	0/0/0	0/0/			0/0/0	--Jellyfish
													--Other
3.9	0/0/0	0	0	0	0	0	0	0//0	0/0/			0/0/0	Endangered aquatic invertebrates, prepared or preserved
3.9	0/0/0	0	0	0	0	0	0	0//0	0/0/			0/0/0	Other aquatic invertebrates, prepared or preserved

第十七章
糖及糖食

注释：

本章不包括：

一、含有可可的糖食(税目18.06)；

二、税目29.40的化学纯糖(蔗糖、乳糖、麦芽糖、葡萄糖及果糖除外)及其他产品；

三、第三十章的药品及其他产品。

子目注释：

一、子目号1701.12、1701.13及1701.14所称“原糖”，是指按重量计干燥状态的蔗糖含量对应的旋光读数低于99.5°的糖。

二、子目1701.13仅包括非离心甘蔗糖，其按重量计干燥状态的蔗糖含量对应的旋光读数不低于69°但低于93°。该产品仅含肉眼不可见的不规则形状天然他形微晶，外被糖蜜残余及其他甘蔗成分。

税则号列	货品名称〔CIQ扩展编码及品名—T2表示见附表2〕	最惠(%)	暂定税率	普通	增值/消费	出口退税	计量单位	监管条件	检验检疫	特殊证件对美关税
17.01	**固体甘蔗糖、甜菜糖及化学纯蔗糖：**									
	-未加香料或着色剂的原糖：									
1701.1200	--甜菜糖									
1701.1200　01	未加香料或着色剂的甜菜原糖[按重量计干燥状态的糖含量低于旋光读数99.5度(配额内)]〔999〕	15		125	13/	13	千克	ABt	MPRQS	/25
1701.1200　90	未加香料或着色剂的甜菜原糖[按重量计干燥状态的糖含量低于旋光读数99.5度(配额外)]〔999〕	50		125	13/	13	千克	7AB	MPRQS	/60
1701.1300	--本章子目注释二所述的甘蔗糖									
1701.1300　01	未加香料或着色剂的本章子目注释二所述的甘蔗原糖[按重量计干燥状态的蔗糖含量对应的旋光读数不低于69度，但低于93度(配额内)]〔101冰糖，102冰片糖，103原糖〕	15		125	13/	13	千克	ABt	MPRQS	/25
1701.1300　90	未加香料或着色剂的本章子目注释二所述的甘蔗原糖[按重量计干燥状态的蔗糖含量对应的旋光读数不低于69度，但低于93度(配额外)]〔101冰糖，102冰片糖，103原糖〕	50		125	13/	13	千克	7AB	MPRQS	/60
1701.1400	--其他甘蔗糖									
1701.1400　01	未加香料或着色剂其他甘蔗原糖[按重量计干燥状态的糖含量低于旋光读数99.5度(配额内)]〔101冰糖，102冰片糖，103原糖〕	15		125	13/	13	千克	ABt	MPRQS	/40
1701.1400　90	未加香料或着色剂其他甘蔗原糖[按重量计干燥状态的糖含量低于旋光读数99.5度(配额外)]〔101冰糖，102冰片糖，103原糖〕	50		125	13/	13	千克	7AB	MPRQS	/75
	-其他：									
1701.9100	--加有香料或着色剂									
1701.9100　01	加有香料或着色剂的糖[指甘蔗糖、甜菜糖及化学纯蔗糖(配额内)]〔999〕	15		125	13/	13	千克	ABt	RS	/25
1701.9100　90	加有香料或着色剂的糖[指甘蔗糖、甜菜糖及化学纯蔗糖(配额外)]〔999〕	50		125	13/	13	千克	7AB	RS	/60
	--其他：									
1701.9910	---砂糖									
1701.9910　10	砂糖(配额内)〔101白砂糖，102冰砂糖〕	15		125	13/	13	千克	ABt	MRS	/40
1701.9910　90	砂糖(配额外)〔101白砂糖，102冰砂糖〕	50		125	13/	13	千克	7AB	MRS	/75
1701.9920	---绵白糖									
1701.9920　01	绵白糖(配额内)〔999〕	15		125	13/	13	千克	BAt	RS	/25
1701.9920　90	绵白糖(配额外)〔999〕	50		125	13/	13	千克	7BA	RS	/60
1701.9990	---其他									
1701.9990　01	其他精制糖(配额内)〔101方糖，102冰糖，103红塘，104冰片糖内，105糖浆，106糖霜，107其他食糖〕	15		125	13/	13	千克	ABt	RS	/35
1701.9990　90	其他精制糖(配额外)〔101方糖，102冰糖，103红塘，104冰片糖内，105糖浆，106糖霜，107其他食糖〕	50		125	13/	13	千克	7AB	RS	/70
17.02	**其他固体糖，包括化学纯乳糖、麦芽糖、葡萄糖及果糖；未加香料或着色剂的糖浆；人造蜜，不论是否掺有天然蜂蜜；焦糖：**									
	-乳糖及乳糖浆：									

Chapter 17
Sugars and sugar confectionery

Note:

This Chapter does not cover:

(1) Sugar confectionery containing cocoa (heading No. 18.06);

(2) Chemically pure sugars (other than sucrose, lactose, maltose, glucose and fructose) or other products of heading No.29.40;

(3) Medicaments or other products of Chapter 30.

Subheading Note:

1. For the purposes of subheadings No. 1701.12、1701.13 及 1701.14, "raw sugar" means sugar whose content of sucrose by weight, in the dry state, corresponds to a polarimeter reading of less than 99.5°.
2. Subheading 1701.13 covers only cane sugar obtained without centrifugation, whose content of sucrose by weight, in the dry state, corresponds to a polarimeter reading of 69° or more but less than 93°. The product contains only natural anhedral microcrystals, of irregular shape, not visible to the naked eye, which are surrouded by residues of molasses and other constituents of sugar cane

协定税率 %										特惠税率 %			
亚太5国	东/冰/格	巴基斯坦	韩国	瑞士	哥达	秘鲁	澳大利亚	新西/坡/智	港/澳/台	亚太2国	老/柬/缅	36/3/1	Article Description
													Cane or beet sugar and chemically pure sucrose, in solid form:
													-Raw sugar not containing added flavouring or colouring matter:
													--Beet sugar
									0/0/				Raw beet sugar not containing added flavouring or colouring matter [sugar whose content of sucrose by weight, in the dry state, corresponds to a polarimeter reading of less than 99.5° (in-quota)]
									0/0/				Raw beet sugar not containing added flavouring or colouring matter [sugar whose content of sucroseby weight, in the dry state, corresponds to a polarimeter reading of less than 99.5° (out-quota)]
													--Cane sugar in subheading Note 2 to this chapter
									0/0/				Of cane sugar in subheading Note 2 to this chapter not containing added flavouring or colouring matter [whose content of sucrose by weight, in the dry state, corresponds to a polarimeter reading of 69° or more but less 93° (in-quota)]
									0/0/				Of cane sugar in subheading Note 2 to this chapter not containing added flavouring or colouring matter [whose content of sucrose by weight, in the dry state, corresponds to a polarimeter reading of 69° or more but less 93° (out-quota)]
													--Other cane sugar
									0/0/				Other cane sugar not containing added flavouring or colouring matter [sugar whose content of sucrose by weight, in the dry state, corresponds to a polarimeter reading of less than 99.5° (in-quota)]
									0/0/				Other cane sugar not containing added flavouring or colouring matter [sugar whose content of sucrose by weight, in the dry state, corresponds to a polarimeter reading of less than 99.5° (out-quota)]
													-Other:
													--Containing added flavouring or colouring matter
									0/0/				Cane or beet sugar and chemically pure sucrose, containing added flavouring or colouring matter (in-quota)
									0/0/				Cane or beet sugar and chemically pure sucrose, containing added flavouring or colouring matter (out-quota)
													--Other:
													---Granulated sugar
									0/0/				Granulated sugar (in-quota)
									0/0/				Granulated sugar (out-quota)
													---Superfine sugar
									0/0/				Superfine sugar (in-quota)
									0/0/				Superfine sugar (out-quota)
													---Other
									0/0/				Other refined sugar (in-quota)
									0/0/				Other refined sugar (out-quota)
													Other sugars, including chemically pure lactose, maltose, glucose and fructose, in solid form; sugar syrups not containing added flavouring or colouring matter; artificial honey, whether or not mixed with natural honey; caramel:
													-Lactose and lactose syrup:

税则号列	货品名称〔CIQ扩展编码及品名—T2表示见附表2〕	最惠(%)	暂定税率	普通	增值/消费	出口退税	计量单位	监管条件	检验检疫	特殊证件对美关税
1702.1100	--按重量计干燥无水乳糖含量在99%及以上〔999〕	10		80	13/	13	千克	AB	RS	/20
1702.1900	--其他〔111其他乳糖及乳糖浆,301可溶性大豆多糖(无检疫要求食品添加剂),302异构化乳糖液(无检疫要求食品添加剂)〕	10		80	13/	13	千克	AB	RS	/20
1702.2000	-槭糖及槭糖浆〔101槭糖浆,102槭糖,301需申报仅用于工业用途不用于食品添加剂无检疫要求的化学品〕	30		80	13/	13	千克	AB	RS	/55
1702.3000	-葡萄糖及葡萄糖浆,不含果糖或按重量计干燥状态的果糖含量在20%以下〔101葡萄糖浆,102葡萄糖,103变性淀粉,301无检疫要求食品添加剂〕	30		80	13/	13	千克	BA	RS	/55
1702.4000	-葡萄糖及葡萄糖浆,按重量计干燥状态的果糖含量在20%及以上,但在50%以下,转化糖除外〔101葡萄糖浆,102葡萄糖〕	30		80	13/	13	千克	BA	RS	/40
1702.5000	-化学纯果糖〔101合成糖,102无检疫要求食品添加剂,301需申报仅用于工业用途不用于食品添加剂无检疫要求的化学品〕	30		80	13/	13	千克	AB	RS	/55
1702.6000	-其他果糖及果糖浆,按重量计干燥状态的果糖含量在50%以上,转化糖除外〔101冰糖,102糖浆,103其他食糖,104合成糖,105其他糖果,106无检疫要求食品添加剂〕	30		80	13/	13	千克	BA	RS	/50
1702.9000	-其他,包括转化糖及其他按重量计干燥状态的果糖含量在50%以上的糖及糖浆混合物									
1702.9000　10	人造蜜〔101人造糖浆,102合成糖,103无检疫要求食品添加剂〕	30		80	13/	13	千克	AB	RS	/50
1702.9000　90	其他固体糖、焦糖(包括转化糖及按重量计干燥状态果糖含量为50%的糖、糖浆)〔101合成糖,103其他糖果,301无检疫要求食品添加剂〕	30		80	13/	13	千克	AB	RS	/50
17.03	**制糖后所剩的糖蜜:**									
1703.1000	-甘蔗糖蜜〔101冰片糖,102糖浆,103糖霜,104其他食糖,105废糖蜜,301需申报仅用于工业用途不用于食品添加剂无检疫要求的化学品〕	8		50	13/	13	千克	9B	RS	/18
1703.9000	-其他〔101冰片糖,102糖浆,103糖霜,104其他食糖,106废糖蜜,301无检疫要求食品添加剂,302需申报仅用于工业用途不用于食品添加剂无检疫要求的化学品〕	8		50	13/	13	千克	9B	RS	/18
17.04	**不含可可的糖食(包括白巧克力):**									
1704.1000	-口香糖,不论是否裹糖〔102凝胶口香糖,103胶基口香糖〕	12		50	13/	13	千克	AB	RS	/42
1704.9000	-其他〔101合成糖,107胶基糖果,111其他糖果,112巧克力,不适用非可可脂添加量超过5%的产品,113其他糖与糖果,巧克力与可可制品〕	10		50	13/	13	千克	AB	RS	/40

协定税率 %										特惠税率 %			
亚太5国	东/冰/格	巴基斯坦	韩国	瑞士	哥达	秘鲁	澳大利亚	新西/坡/智	港/澳/台	亚太2国	老/柬/缅	36/3/1	Article Description
	0//0	5	4	0	0	0	0	0/0/0	0/0/			0/0/0	--Containing by weight 99% or more lactose, expressed as anhydrous lactose, calculated on the dry matter
	0//0	5	4	0	0	0	0	0/0/0	0/0/			0/0/0	--Other
	0//		21		0	0	0	0/0/0	0/0/			0//	-Maple sugar and maple syrup
	0//	0			0	0	0	0/0/0	0/0/			0//	-Glucose and glucose syrup, not containing fructose or containing in the dry state less than 20% by weight of fructose
	0//				0	0	0	0/0/0	0/0/			0//	-Glucose and glucose syrup, containing in the dry state at least 20% but less than 50% by weight of fructose
	0/0/				0	0	0	0/0/0	0/0/			0//	-Chemically pure fructose
	0/0/				0	0	0	0/0/0	0/0/			0//	-Other fructose and fructose syrup, containing in the dry state more than 50% by weight of fructose
													-Other, including invert sugar
	0/0/			15.6	0	10.6	0	0/0/0	0/0/			0/0/0	Artificial honey
	0/0/			15.6	0	10.6	0	0/0/0	0/0/			0/0/0	Other sugars, caramel (including invert sugar, in the dry state 50% by weight of fructose)
													Molasses resulting from the extraction or refining or sugar:
	0/0/0	5	0	0	0	0	0	0//0	0/0/			0/0/0	-Cane molasses
	0/0/0	5	0	0	0	0	0	0//0	0/0/			0/0/0	-Other
													Sugar confectionery (including white chocolate), not containing cocoa:
9.5	0/0/0	0		3.6	0	4.2	0	0/0/0	0/0/			0/0/0	-Chewing gum, whether or not sugarcoated
8.2	0/0/0	0	7	0	0	0	0	0/0/0	0/0/			0/0/0	-Other

第十八章
可可及可可制品

注释：

一、本章不包括税目 04.03、19.01、19.04、19.05、21.05、22.02、22.08、30.03、30.04 的制品。

二、税目 18.06 包括含有可可的糖食及注释一以外的其他含可可的食品。

税则号列	货品名称〔CIQ 扩展编码及品名－T2 表示见附表 2〕	最惠(%)	暂定税率	普通	增值/消费	出口退税	计量单位	监管条件	检验检疫	特殊证件对美关税
18.01	**整颗或破碎的可可豆，生的或焙炒的：**									
1801.0000	整颗或破碎的可可豆，生的或焙炒的〔101 生的（提取（晒干的除外）、压榨、烹制、烘焙、冻干、脱水、裹糖屑、发酵、冷冻（经漂汤和杀青，并在－18 度以下冷冻）、浸酸、腌渍、炒制等工艺进行加工处理的），102 焙炒的，103 生的（其他工艺）〕	8	2	30	13/	13,6	千克	AB	MPRQS	/27
18.02	**可可荚、壳、皮及废料：**									
1802.0000	可可荚、壳、皮及废料〔999〕	10		30	13/	6	千克	AB	PQS	/20
18.03	**可可膏，不论是否脱脂：**									
1803.1000	-未脱脂〔999〕	10		30	13/	13	千克	AB	RS	/35
1803.2000	-全脱脂或部分脱脂〔999〕	10		30	13/	13	千克	AB	RS	/20
18.04	**可可脂、可可油：**									
1804.0000	可可脂、可可油〔101 可可油，102 可可壳酊（无检疫要求食品添加剂），103 可可酊（无检疫要求食品添加剂）〕									
1804.0000 10	可可脂〔999〕	22		70	13/	13	千克	AB	RS	/47
1804.0000 90	可可油〔101 可可油，102 可可壳酊（无检疫要求食品添加剂），103 可可酊（无检疫要求食品添加剂）〕	22		70	13/	13	千克	AB	RS	/47
18.05	**未加糖或其他甜物质的可可粉：**									
1805.0000	未加糖或其他甜物质的可可粉〔101〕	15		40	13/	13	千克	AB	PRQS	/40
18.06	**巧克力及其他含可可的食品：**									
1806.1000	-加糖或其他甜物质的可可粉〔101 可可粉，102 可可粉固体饮料〕	10		50	13/	13	千克	AB	PRQS	/20
1806.2000	-其他重量超过 2 千克的块状或条状含可可食品，或液状、膏状、粉状、粒状或其他散装形状的含可可食品，容器包装或内包装每件净重超过 2 千克的〔102 巧克力，不适用非可可脂添加量超过 5％的产品，103 可可粉固体饮料，104 巧克力〕	10		50	13/	13	千克	AB	RS	/35
	-其他块状或条状的含可可食品：									
1806.3100	--夹心〔102 巧克力，不适用非可可脂添加量超过 5％的产品，103 巧克力，适用非可可脂添加量超过 5％的产品〕	8		50	13/	13	千克	AB	RS	/38
1806.3200	--不夹心〔101 巧克力，不适用非可可脂添加量超过 5％的产品，102 其他糖与糖果，巧克力与可可制品，103 巧克力，适用非可可脂添加量超过 5％的产品〕	10		50	13/	13	千克	AB	RS	/35
1806.9000	-其他〔101 巧克力，不适用非可可脂添加量超过 5％的产品，102 其他可可制品，103 其他糖与糖果，巧克力与可可制品，104 巧克力，适用非可可脂添加量超过 5％的产品〕	8		50	13/	13	千克	AB	RS	/38

Chapter 18
Cocoa and cocoa preparations

Notes:

1. This Chapter does not cover the preparations of heading No. 04.03, 19.01, 19.04, 19.05, 21.05, 22.02, 22.08, 30.03, or 30.04.
2. Heading No. 18.06 includes sugar confectionery containing cocoa and, subject to Note 1 to this Chapter, other food preparations containing cocoa.

协定税率 %										特惠税率 %			
亚太5国	东/冰/格	巴基斯坦	韩国	瑞士	哥达	秘鲁	澳大利亚	新西/坡/智	港/澳/台	亚太2国	老/柬/缅	36/3/1	Article Description
													Cocoa beans, whole or broken, raw or roasted:
	0/0/0	4	0	0	0	0	0	0//0	0/0/			0/0/0	Cocoa beans, whole or broken, raw or roasted
													Cocoa shells, husks, skins and other cocoa waste:
	0/0/0	4.5	4	0	0	0	0	0/0/0	0/0/			0/0/0	Cocoa shells, husks, skins and other cocoa waste
													Cocoa paste, whether or not defatted:
	0/0/0	4.5	4	0	0	0	0	0//0	0/0/			0/0/	-Not defatted
	0/0/0	4.5	4	0	0	0	0	0//0	0/0/			0/0/	-Wholly or partly defatted
													Cocoa butter, fat and oil:
													Cocoa butter, fat and oil
	0/0/0		15.4	6.6	0	0	0	0//0	0/0/			0/0/0	Cocoa fat
	0/0/0		15.4	6.6	0	0	0	0//0	0/0/			0/0/0	Cocoa oil
													Cocoa powder, not containing added sugar or other sweetening matter:
	0/0/0	12	6	4.5	0	0	0	0//0	0/0/			0/0/	Cocoa powder, not containing added sugar or other sweetening matter
													Chocolate and other food preparations containing cocoa:
	0/0/0	4.5	4	0	0	0	0	0//0	0/0/			0/0/	-Cocoa powder, containing added sugar or other sweetening matter
7.7	0/0/0	4.5	4	0	0	0	0	0/0/0	0/0/			0/0/	-Other preparations in blocks, slabs or bars weighing more than 2kg or in liquid, paste, powder, granular or other bulk form in containers or immediate packings, of a content exceeding 2kg
													-Other, in blocks, slabs or bars:
6.4	0/0/0	4	4.8	0	0	0	0	0//0	0/0/			0/0/0	--Filled
7.7	0/0/0	4	6	0	0	0	0	0/0/0	0/0/			0/0/	--Not filled
6.4	0/0/0	4	4.8	2.4	0	0	0	0//0	0/0/			0/0/0	-Other

第十九章
谷物、粮食粉、淀粉或乳的制品;糕饼点心

注释:

一、本章不包括:

(一)按重量计含香肠、肉、食用杂碎、动物血、鱼、甲壳动物、软体动物、其他水生无脊椎动物及其混合物超过20%的食品(第十六章),但税目19.02的包馅食品除外;

(二)用粮食粉或淀粉制的专作动物饲料用的饼干及其他制品(税目23.09);

(三)第三十章的药品及其他产品。

二、税目19.01所称:

(一)"粗粒"是指第十一章谷物的粗粒;

(二)"细粉"及"粗粉",是指:

1. 第十一章谷物的细粉及粗粉;
2. 其他章植物的细粉、粗粉及粉末,但不包括干蔬菜、马铃薯和干豆类的细粉、粗粉及粉末(应分别归入税目07.12、11.05和11.06)。

三、税目19.04不包括按重量计全脱脂可可含量超过6%或用巧克力完全包裹的食品以及税目18.06的其他含可可食品(税目18.06)。

四、税目19.04所称"其他方法制作的",是指制作或加工程度超过第十章或第十一章各税目或注释所规定范围的。

税则号列	货品名称〔CIQ扩展编码及品名—T2表示见附表2〕	最惠(%)	暂定税率	普通	增值/消费	出口退税	计量单位	监管条件	检验检疫	特殊证件对美关税
19.01	**麦精;细粉、粗粒、粗粉、淀粉或麦精制的其他税目未列名的食品,不含可可或按重量计全脱脂可可含量低于40%;税目04.01至04.04所列货品制的其他税目未列名的食品,不含可可或按重量计全脱脂可可含量低于5%:**									
	-供婴幼儿食用的零售包装食品:									
1901.1010	---配方奶粉〔101乳基婴儿配方食品,102乳基较大婴儿配方食品,103早产/低出生体重婴儿配方食品,104乳基幼儿配方食品〕	15	5	40	13/	13	千克	7AB	RS	/30
1901.1090	---其他〔101其他含肉速冻粮食制品,102其他不含肉速冻粮食制品,103其他不含馅速冻粮食制品,104豆基婴儿配方食品,105豆基较大婴儿和幼儿配方食品,106婴幼儿谷类辅助食品,107婴幼儿罐装辅助食品,108婴幼儿配方液态乳〕	15	2	40	13/	13	千克	AB	RS	/12
1901.2000	-供烘焙税目19.05所列面包糕饼用的调制品及面团〔101速食粮食产品,102其他粮食制品,103其他含肉速冻粮食制品,104其他不含肉速冻粮食制品,105其他不含馅速冻粮食制品〕	10		80	13/	6,13	千克	AB	RS	/40
1901.9000	-其他[T2]	10	5	80	13/	13	千克	AB	RS	/30
19.02	**面食,不论是否煮熟、包馅(肉馅或其他馅)或其他方法制作,例如,通心粉、意大利面条、面条、汤团、馄饨、饺子、奶油面卷;古斯古斯面食,不论是否制作:**									
	-生的面食,未包馅或未经其他方法制作:									
1902.1100	--含蛋〔101生面食,102如挂面等,103通心粉,104速食粮食产品,105其他粮食制品〕	10		80	13/	6	千克	AB	PRQS	/35
1902.1100 10	未包馅或未制作的含蛋生面食,非速冻的〔101生面食102面条(如挂面等)103通心粉104速食粮食产品105其他粮食制品〕	10		80	9/	6	千克	AB	PRQS	/35
1902.1100 90	其他未包馅或未制作的含蛋生面食〔101生面食102面条(如挂面等)103通心粉104速食粮食产品105其他粮食制品〕	10		80	13/	6	千克	AB	PRQS	/35
1902.1900	--其他〔101生面食,102如挂面等,103通心粉,104湿面,105速食粮食产品,106其他粮食制品,107馒头〕	10	8	80	13/	13,9	千克	AB	PRQS	/28
1902.1900 10	其他未包馅或未制作的生面食,非速冻的〔101生面食102面条(如挂面等)103通心粉104湿面105速食粮食产品106其他粮食制品107馒头〕	10	8	80	9/	9	千克	AB	PRQS	/38
1902.1900 90	其他未包馅或未制作的生面食〔101生面食102面条(如挂面等)103通心粉104湿面105速食粮食产品106其他粮食制品107馒头〕	10	8	80	13/	13	千克	AB	PRQS	/38

Chapter 19
Preparations of cereals, flour, starch or milk; pastrycooks' products

Notes:

1. This Chapter does not cover:
   (a) Except in the case of stuffed products of heading No. 19.02, food preparations containing more than 20% by weight of sausage, meat, meat offal, blood, fish or crustaceans, molluscs or other aquatic invertebrates, or any combination thereof (Chapter 16);
   (b) Biscuits or other articles made from flour or from starch, specially prepared for use in animal feeding (heading No. 23.09);
   (c) Medicaments or other products of Chapter 30.
2. For the purposes of heading No. 19.01:
   (a) The term "groats" means cereal groats of Chapter 11;
   (b) The terms "flour" and "meal" mean:
      (1) Cereal flour and meal of Chapter 11, and
      (2) Flour, meal and powder of vegetable origin of any Chapter, other than flour, meal or powder of driedvegetables (heading No. 07.12), of potatoes(heading No. 11.05) or of dried leguminous vegetables (heading No. 11.06).
3. Heading No. 19.04 does not cover preparations containing more than 6% by weight of cocoa calculated on a totally defatted basis or completely coated with chocolate or other food preparations containing cocoa of heading 18.06 (heading No.18.06).
4. For the purposes of heading No.19.04, the expression "otherwise prepared" means preparedor or processed to an extent beyond that provided for in the headings of or Notes to Chapter 10 or 11.

协定税率 %										特惠税率 %			
亚太5国	东/冰/格	巴基斯坦	韩国	瑞士	哥达	秘鲁	澳大利亚	新西/坡/智	港/澳/台	亚太2国	老/柬/缅	36/3/1	Article Description
													Malt extract; food preparations of flour, groats, meal, starch or malt extract, not containing cocoa or containing less than 40% by weight of cocoa calculated on a totally defatted basis, not elsewhere specified or included; food preparations of goods of headings No. 04.01 to 04.04, not containing cocoa or containing less than 5%by weight of cocoa calculated on a totally defatted basis, not elsewhere specified or included:
													-Preparations for infant use, put up for retail sale:
	0/0/	0		4.5	0	0	0	0/0/0	0/0/			0/0/	---Powdered formulas
	0/0/	0		4.5	0	0	0	0/0/0	0/0/			0/0/	---Other
	0/0/10		17.5	7.5	0	0	0	0/0/0	0/0/			0/0/	-Mixes and doughs for the preparation of bakers' wares of heading No. 19.05
	0/0/4	0	6	0	0	0	0	0/0/0	0/0/			0/0/	-Other
													Pasta, whether or not cooked or stuffed (with meat or other substances) or otherwise prepared, such as spaghetti, macaroni, noodles, lasagne, gnocchi, ravioli, cannelloni; couscous, whether or not prepared:
													-Uncooked pasta, not stuffed or otherwise prepared:
	0//0	12	7.5	6	0	0	0	0/0/0	0/0/			0/0/0	--Containing eggs
	0//0	12	6	4.5	0	0	0	0/0/0	0/0/		//	0/0/0	Uncooked or unmade pasta with eggs, not frozen
	0//0	12	6	4.5	0	0	0	0/0/0	0/0/		//	0/0/0	Uncooked or unmade pasta with eggs
	0//9	12	10	6	0	0	0	0/0/0	0/0/			0/0/0	--Other
	0//6	0	9	4.5	0	0	0	0/0/0	0/0/		//	0/0/0	Other uncooked or unmade pasta, not frozen
	0//6	0	9	4.5	0	0	0	0/0/0	0/0/		//	0/0/0	Other uncooked or unmade pasta with eggs

税则号列	货品名称〔CIQ扩展编码及品名—T2表示见附表2〕	最惠(%)	暂定税率	普通	增值/消费	出口退税	计量单位	监管条件	检验检疫	特殊证件对美关税
1902.2000	-包馅面食,不论是否烹煮或经其他方法制作[101月饼,102蛋糕,103其他糕点,104饼干,107面包,108膨化食品,109生面食,110其他糕点饼干,111速食粮食产品,112其他粮食制品,113含肉包子,114不含肉包子,115含肉饺子,116不含肉饺子,117含肉春卷,118不含肉春卷,119其他含肉速冻粮食制品,120其他不含肉速冻粮食制品〕	10		80	13/	9,13	千克	AB	PRQS	/35
	-其他面食:									
1902.3010	---米粉干〔101方便米、粉,102米粉,103其他粮食制品,104其他不含馅速冻粮食制品〕	10		80	13/	9	千克	AB	PRQS	/20
1902.3020	---粉丝〔101粉丝,102其他粮食制品〕	10		80	13/	13	千克	AB	PRQS	/15
1902.3030	---即食或快熟面条〔101快熟面条,102即食面条,103如挂面等,104方便面,105方便米、粉,106速食通粉〕	10		80	13/	9,13	千克	AB	RS	/35
1902.3090	---其他[101面食罐头,102其他糕点饼干,103如挂面等,104方便面,105方便米、粉,106通心粉,107即食通粉沙律,108湿面,109速食粮食产品,110其他粮食制品,111馒头,112其他含肉速冻粮食制品,113其他不含肉速冻粮食制品,114其他不含馅速冻粮食制品〕	10		80	13/	9,13	千克	AB	PRQS	/40
1902.4000	-古斯古斯面食〔101其他糕点饼干,102速食粮食产品,103其他粮食制品〕	10		80	13/	6,13	千克	AB	RS	/15
19.03	**珍粉及淀粉制成的珍粉代用品,片、粒、珠、粉或类似形状的:**									
1903.0000	珍粉及淀粉制成的珍粉代用品,片、粒、珠、粉或类似形状的〔101其他糕点饼干,102速食粮食产品,103其他粮食制品,104其他淀粉制品〕	10		80	13/	13	千克	AB	RS	/15
19.04	**谷物或谷物产品经膨化或烘炒制成的食品(例如,玉米片);其他税目未列名的预煮或经其他方法制作的谷粒(玉米除外),谷物片或经其他加工的谷粒(细粉粗粒及粗粉除外):**									
1904.1000	-谷物或谷物产品经膨化或烘炒制成的食品[101熟制谷物坚果炒货,102膨化食品,103纯麦片,104速食粮食产品,105其他粮食制品,106其他纯谷物的冲调谷物制品,107含其他原料的谷物类冲调谷物制品,108淀粉质类冲调谷物制品〕	10		80	13/	13	千克	AB	RS	/40
1904.2000	-未烘炒谷物片制成的食品及未烘炒的谷物片与烘炒的谷物片或膨化的谷物混合制成的食品[101其他糕点饼干,102纯麦片,103湿粉,104速食粮食产品,105其他粮食制品,106其他含肉速冻粮食制品,107其他不含肉速冻粮食制品,108其他不含馅速冻粮食制品,109其他纯谷物的冲调谷物制品,110含其他原料的谷物类冲调谷物制品,111淀粉质类冲调谷物制品〕	10		80	13/	13	千克	AB	PRQS	/35
1904.3000	-碾碎的干小麦〔101食用小麦粉,102其他粮食制品〕	10		80	13/	13	千克	AB	PRQS	/20
1904.9000	-其他[T2]	10		80	13/	13	千克	AB	PRQS	/40
19.05	**面包、糕点、饼干及其他烘焙糕饼,不论是否含可可;圣餐饼、装药空囊、封碱、糯米纸及类似制品:**									
1905.1000	-黑麦脆面包片〔999〕	10		80	13/	13	千克	AB	RS	/15
1905.2000	-姜饼及类似品〔101姜饼,102姜饼类似品〕	10		80	13/	13	千克	AB	RS	/15
	-甜饼干;华夫饼干及圣餐饼:									
1905.3100	--甜饼干〔999〕	10		80	13/	13	千克	AB	RS	/35
1905.3200	--华夫饼干及圣餐饼〔101华夫饼干,102圣餐饼,103饼干〕	10		80	13/	13	千克	AB	RS	/35
1905.4000	-面包干、吐司及类似的烤面包〔999〕	10		80	13/	13	千克	AB	RS	/35
1905.9000	-其他[101未列出的其他熟制坚果炒货,103月饼,104蛋糕,105其他糕点,106饼干,109面包,110膨化食品,111其他糕点饼干,112发酵豆制品,113其他含肉速冻粮食制品,114其他不含肉速冻粮食制品,115其他不含馅速冻粮食制品,116其他淀粉制品,117非发酵豆制品〕	10		80	13/	13	千克	AB	RS	/40

协定税率 %										特惠税率 %			
亚太5国	东/冰/格	巴基斯坦	韩国	瑞士	哥达	秘鲁	澳大利亚	新西/坡/智	港/澳/台	亚太2国	老/柬/缅	36/3/1	Article Description
	0/0/6	12	9		0	0	0	0/0/0	0/0/			0/0/0	-Stuffed pasta, whether or not cooked or otherwise prepared
													-Other pasta:
	0/0/0	12	6	4.5	0	0	0	0/0/0	0/0/			0/0/	---Rice vermicelli, cooked
	0/0/0	12	6	4.5	0	0	0	0/0/0	0/0/			0/0/	---Bean vermicelli, cooked
8.7	0/0/6	7.5	10.5	4.5	0	0	0	0/0/0	0/0/			0/0/0	---Instant noodle
8.7	0/0/6	7.5	9		0	0	0	0/0/0	0/0/			0/0/	---Other
	0/0/10		17.5	7.5	0	0	0	0/0/0	0/0/			0/0/	-Couscous
													Tapioca and substitutes therefor prepared from starch, in the form of flakes, grains, pearls, siftings or in similar forms:
	0/0/6	12	6	4.5	0	0	0	0/0/0	0/0/			0/0/0	Tapioca and substitutes therefor prepared from starch, in the form of flakes, grains, pearls, siftings or in similar forms
													Prepared foods obtained by the swelling or roasting of cereals or cereal products (for example, corn flakes); cereals (other than maize (corn)) in grain form or in the form of flakes or other worked grains (except flour, groats and meal), precooked or otherwise prepared, not elsewhere specified or included:
	0/0/0		17.5	10	0	0	0	0/0/0	0/0/			0/0/	-Prepared foods obtained by the swelling or roasting of cereals or cereal products
	0/0/0		21	0	0	8	0	0/0/0	0/0/			0//	-Prepared foods obtained from unroasted cereal flakes or from mixtures of unroasted cereal flakes and roasted cereal flakes or swelled cereals
	0/0/12		21		0	8	0	0/0/0	0/0/			0//	-Bulgur wheet
	0/0/12		21	0	0	2.5	0	0/0/0	0/0/			0//	-Other
													Bread, pastry, cakes, biscuits and other bakers' wares, whether or not containing cocoa; communion wafers, empty cachets of a kind suitable for pharmaceutical use, sealing wafers, rice paper and similar products:
	0/0/0		12	6	0	0	0	0/0/0	0/0/			0/0/	-Crispbread
	0/0/0		12	6	0	0	0	0/0/0	0/0/			0/0/	-Gingerbread and the like
													-Sweet biscuits; waffles and wafers:
8.2	0/0/0	0	9	6.3	0	0	0	0/0/0	0/0/	5		0/0/0	--Sweet biscuits
8.2	0/0/0	7.5	9	0	0	0	0	0/0/0	0/0/	5		0/0/0	--Waffles and wafers
	0//0		12	6	0	0	0	0/0/0	0/0/			0/0/	-Rusks, toasted bread and similar toasted products
8.6	0/0/8	0	14	6	0	0	0	0/0/0	0/0/	5		0/0/	-Other

第二十章
蔬菜、水果、坚果或植物其他部分的制品

注释：

一、本章不包括：

(一)用第七章、第八章或第十一章所列方法制作或保藏的蔬菜、水果或坚果；

(二)按重量计含香肠、肉、食用杂碎、动物血、鱼、甲壳动物、软体动物、其他水生无脊椎动物及其混合物超过20%的食品(第十六章)；

(三)税目19.05的烘焙糕饼及其他制品；

(四)税目21.04的均化混合食品。

二、税目20.07及20.08不包括制成糖食的果冻、果膏、糖衣杏仁或类似品(税目17.04)及巧克力糖食(税目18.06)。

三、税目20.01、20.04及20.05仅分别包括用本章注释一(一)以外的方法制作或保藏的第七章或税目11.05、11.06的产品(第八章产品的细粉、粗粉除外)。

四、干重量在7%及以上的番茄汁归入税目20.02。

五、税目20.07所称"烹煮的"，是指在常压或减压下，通过减少水分或其他方法增加产品粘稠度的热处理制得的。

六、税目20.09所称"未发酵及未加酒精的水果汁"，是指按容量计酒精浓度(标准见第二十二章注释二)不超过0.5%的水果汁。

子目注释：

一、子目2005.10所称"均化蔬菜"，是指蔬菜经精细均化制成适合供婴幼儿食用或营养用的零售包装食品(每件净重不超过250克)。为了调味、保藏或其他目的，均化蔬菜中可以加入少量其他配料，还可以含有少量可见的蔬菜粒。归类时，子目2005.10优先于税目20.05的其他子目。

二、子目2007.10所称"均化食品"，是指果实经精细均化制成适合供婴幼儿食用或营养用的零售包装食品(每件净重不超过250克)。为了调味、保藏或其他目的，均化食品中可以加入少量其他配料，还可以含有少量可见的果粒。归类时，子目2007.10优先于税目20.07的其他子目。

三、子目2009.12、2009.21、2009.31、2009.41、2009.61及2009.71所称"白利糖度值"，是指在20℃时直接从白利糖度计读取的度数或从折射计读取的以蔗糖百分比含量计的折射率，在其他温度下读取的数值应折算为20℃时的折射率。

税则号列	货品名称〔CIQ扩展编码及品名—T2表示见附表2〕	最惠(%)	暂定税率	普通	增值/消费	出口退税	计量单位	监管条件	检验检疫	特殊证件对美关税
20.01	蔬菜、水果、坚果及植物的其他食用部分，用醋或醋酸制作或保藏的：									
2001.1000	-黄瓜及小黄瓜〔999〕	5		70	13/	9,13	千克	AB	RS	/30
	-其他：									
2001.9010	---大蒜									
2001.9010 10	用醋或醋酸腌制的大蒜头、大蒜瓣(无论是否加糖或去皮)〔999〕	5		70	13/	9,13	千克	AB	RS	/15
2001.9010 90	用醋或醋酸腌制的其他大蒜(不含蒜头、蒜瓣，无论是否加糖或去皮)〔999〕	5		70	13/	9,13	千克	AB	RS	/15
2001.9090	---其他									
2001.9090 10	用醋或醋酸制作或保藏的松茸〔999〕	5		70	13/	9	千克	ABE	RS	/30
2001.9090 20	用醋或醋酸制作或保藏的酸竹笋〔999〕	5		70	13/	9	千克	ABE	RS	/30
2001.9090 30	用醋或醋酸制作或保藏的芦荟〔999〕	5		70	13/	9	千克	ABFE	RS	/30
2001.9090 40	用醋或醋酸制作或保藏的仙人掌植物〔999〕	5		70	13/	9	千克	ABFE	RS	/30
2001.9090 50	用醋或醋酸制作或保藏的莼菜〔999〕	5		70	13/	9	千克	ABE	RS	/30
2001.9090 90	用醋制作的其他果、菜及食用植物(包括用醋酸制作或保藏的)〔101腌渍蘑菇，102腌渍其他未列出蔬菜〕	5		70	13/	9,13	千克	AB	RS	/30
20.02	番茄，用醋或醋酸以外的其他方法制作或保藏的：									
	-番茄，整个或切片：									
2002.1010	---罐头〔999〕	5		80	13/	13	千克	AB	RS	/30
2002.1090	---其他〔101冷冻番茄，102脱水番茄〕	5		70	13/	9,13	千克	AB	PRQ	/15
	-其他：									
	---番茄酱罐头：									

Chapter 20
Preparations of vegetables, fruit, nuts or other parts of plants

Notes:

1. This Chapter does not cover:
   (a) Vegetables, fruit or nuts, prepared or preserved by the processes specified in Chapter 7,8 or 11;
   (b) Food preparations containing more than 20% by weight of sausage, meat, meat offal, blood, fish or crustaceans, molluscs or other aquatic invertebrates, or any combination thereof (Chapter 16)
   (c) Bakers' wares and other products of heading No. 19.05;
   (d) Homogenized composite food preparations of heading No. 21.04.
2. Headings No. 20.07 and 20.08 do not apply to fruit jellies, fruit pastes, sugar-coated almonds or the like in the form of sugar confectionery (heading No. 17.04) or chocolate confectionery (heading No. 18.06).
3. Headings No. 20.01,20.04 and 20.05 cover, as the case may be, only those products of Chapter 7 or of heading No. 11.05 or 11.06 (other than flour, meal and powder of the products of Chapter 8) which have been prepared or preserved by processes other than those referred to in Note 1 (a).
4. Tomato juice the dry weight content of which is 7% or more, is to be classified in heading No. 20.02.
5. For the purposes of heading No. 20.07, the expression "obtained by cooking" means obtained by heat treatment at atmospheric pressure or under reduced pressure to increase the viscosity of a product through reduction of water content or other means.
6. For the purposes of heading No. 20.09, the expression "juices, unfermented and not containing added spirit" means juices of an alcoholic strength by volume (see Note 2 to Chapter 22) not exceeding 0.5% vol.

Subheading Notes:

1. For the purposes of subheading No. 2005.10, the expression "homogenized vegetables" means preparations of vegetables, finely homogenized, put up for retail sale Suitable for infants to eat or for dietetic purposes, in containers of a net weight content not exceeding 250g. For the application of this definition no account is to be taken of small quantities of any ingredients which may have been added to the preparation for seasoning, preparation or other purposes. These preparations may contain a small quantity of visible pieces of vegetables. Subheading No. 2005.10 takes precedence over all other subheadings of heading No. 20.05.
2. For the purposes of subheading No. 2007.10, the expression "homogenized preparations" means preparations of fruit, finely homogenized, put up for retail sale Suitable for infants to eat or for dietetic purposes, in containers of a net weight content not exceeding 250g. For the application of this definition no account is to be taken of small quantities of any ingredients which may have been added to the preparation for seasoning, preservation or other purposes. These preparations may contain a small quantity of visible pieces of fruit. Subheading No. 2007.10 takes precedence over all other subheadings of heading No. 20.07.
3. For the purposes of subheadings No. 2009.12, 2009.21,2009.31,2009.41,2009.61 and 2009.71, the expression "Brix value" means the direct reading of degrees Brix obtained from a Brix hydrometer or of refractive index expressed in terms of percentage sucrose content obtained from a refractometer, at a temperature of 20℃ or corrected for 20℃ if the reading is made at a different temperature.

协定税率 %										特惠税率 %			
亚太5国	东/冰/格	巴基斯坦	韩国	瑞士	哥达	秘鲁	澳大利亚	新西/坡/智	港/澳/台	亚太2国	老/柬/缅	36/3/1	Article Description
													Vegetagbles, fruit, nuts and other edible parts of plants, prepared or preserved by vinegar or acetic acid:
	0/0/0	22.5	17.5	5	0	0	0	0/0/0	0/0/			0/0/	-Cucumbers and gherkins
													-Other:
													---Garlic
	0/0/0	25	17.5	5	0	0	0	0/0/0	0/0/	2.5		0/0/	Garlic bulbs, garlic cloves, prepared by vinegar or acetic acid (whether or not added sugars or skinned)
	0/0/0	25	17.5	5	0	0	0	0/0/0	0/0/	2.5		0/0/	Other garlic prepared by vinegar or acetic acid(whether or not added sugars or skinned other than garlic bulbs, galic cloves)
													---Other
	0/0/0		17.5	5	0	0	0	0/0/0	0/0/	2.5		0/0/	Matsutske, prepared or preserved by vinegar or acetic acid
	0/0/0		17.5	5	0	0	0	0/0/0	0/0/	2.5		0/0/	Acidosasa chinensis shoots, prepared or preserved by vinegar or acetic acid
	0/0/0		17.5	5	0	0	0	0/0/0	0/0/	2.5		0/0/	Aloe, prepared or preserved by vinegar or acetic acid
	0/0/0		17.5	5	0	0	0	0/0/0	0/0/	2.5		0/0/	Cactus, prepared or preserved by vinegar or acetic acid
	0/0/0		17.5	5	0	0	0	0/0/0	0/0/	2.5		0/0/	Water shield, prepared or preserved by vinegar or acetic acid
	0/0/0		17.5	5	0	0	0	0/0/0	0/0/	2.5		0/0/	Vegetagbles, fruit, nuts and other edible parts of plants, prepared or preserved by vinegar or acetic acid
													Tomatoes prepared or preserved otherwise than by vinegar or acetic acid:
													-Tomatoes, whole or in pieces:
	0/0/0	19	11.4	5	0	0	0	0/0/0	0/0/			0/0/	---In airtight containers
	0/0/0	25	17.5	5	0	0	0	0/0/0	0/0/			0/0/	---Other
													-Other:
													---Tomato paste, in airtight containers:

税则号列	货品名称〔CIQ 扩展编码及品名－T2 表示见附表 2〕	最惠(%)	暂定税率	普通	增值/消费	出口退税	计量单位	监管条件	检验检疫	特殊证件对美关税
2002.9011	----重量不超过 5 千克的〔999〕	5		80	13/	13	千克	AB	RS	/20
2002.9019	----重量超过 5 千克的〔999〕	5		80	13/	13	千克	AB	RS	/20
2002.9090	---其他〔101 冷冻番茄，102 脱水番茄〕	5		70	13/	9,13	千克	AB	PRQS	/15
20.03	**蘑菇及块菌，用醋或醋酸以外的其他方法制作或保藏的：**									
	-伞菌属蘑菇：									
	---罐头：									
2003.1011	----小白蘑菇〔999〕	5		90	13/	13	千克	AB	RS	/30
2003.1019	----其他〔101 草菇罐头，102 金针菇罐头，103 其他食用菌罐头〕	5		90	13/	13	千克	AB	RS	/15
2003.1090	---其他〔101 冷冻其他伞菌属蘑菇，102 脱水其他伞菌属蘑菇，103 腌渍蘑菇，104 腌渍其他伞菌属蘑菇〕	5		90	13/	9,13	千克	AB	RS	/15
	-其他：									
2003.9010	---罐头									
2003.9010 10	非用醋制作的香菇罐头［用醋或醋酸以外其他方法制作或保藏的(非伞菌属蘑菇)］〔999〕	5		90	13/	13	千克	AB	RS	/30
2003.9010 20	非用醋制作的松茸罐头(用醋或醋酸以外其他方法制作或保藏的)〔999〕	5		90	13/	13	千克	ABE	RS	/30
2003.9010 90	非用醋制作的其他蘑菇罐头［用醋或醋酸以外其他方法制作或保藏的(非伞菌属蘑菇)］〔101 滑子蘑罐头，102 猴头菇罐头，103 鸡油菌罐头，104 牛肝菌罐头，105 姬菇罐头，106 鲍鱼菇罐头，107 白灵菇罐头，108 平菇罐头，109 茶树菇罐头，110 凤尾菇罐头，111 灰树花菇罐头，112 黑木耳罐头，113 球盖菇罐头，114 鸡腿菇罐头，115 松茸罐头，116 什锦菇罐头，117 其他蘑菇类罐头，118 其他木耳类罐头，119 其他食用菌罐头〕	5		90	13/	13	千克	AB	RS	/30
2003.9090	---其他									
2003.9090 10	非用醋制作的其他香菇［用醋或醋酸以外其他方法制作或保藏的(非伞菌属蘑菇)］〔101 冷冻香菇，102 脱水香菇，103 腌渍香菇〕	5		90	13/	9,13	千克	AB	PRQS	/15
2003.9090 20	非用醋制作的其他松茸(用醋或醋酸以外其他方法制作或保藏的)〔101 冷冻松茸，102 脱水松茸，103 腌渍松茸〕	5		90	13/	9,13	千克	ABE	PRQS	/15
2003.9090 90	非用醋制作的其他蘑菇［用醋或醋酸以外其他方法制作或保藏的(非伞菌属蘑菇)］〔101 冷冻其他非伞菌属蘑菇，102 脱水其他非伞菌属蘑菇，103 腌渍其他非伞菌属蘑菇〕	5		90	13/	9,13	千克	AB	PRQS	/15
20.04	**其他冷冻蔬菜，用醋或醋酸以外的其他方法制作或保藏的，但税目 20.06 的产品除外：**									
2004.1000	-马铃薯〔999〕	5		70	13/	9,13	千克	AB	PRQS	/15
2004.9000	-其他蔬菜及什锦蔬菜									
2004.9000 10	非用醋制作的冷冻松茸〔999〕	5		70	13/	9,13	千克	ABE	PRQS	/30
2004.9000 20	非用醋制作的冷冻酸竹笋〔999〕	5		70	13/	9,13	千克	ABE	PRQS	/30
2004.9000 30	非用醋制作的冷冻芦荟〔999〕	5		70	13/	9,13	千克	ABFE	PRQS	/30
2004.9000 40	非用醋制作的冷冻仙人掌植物〔999〕	5		70	13/	9,13	千克	ABFE	PRQS	/30
2004.9000 90	非用醋制作的其他冷冻蔬菜(税目 20.06 的货品除外)〔101 其它冷冻植物产品，102 其他含肉速冻粮食制品，103 其他不含肉速冻粮食制品，104 冷冻其他未列出蔬菜〕	5		70	13/	9,13	千克	AB	PRQS	/30
20.05	**其他未冷冻蔬菜，用醋或醋酸以外的其他方法制作或保藏的，但税目 20.06 的产品除外：**									
2005.1000	-均化蔬菜〔999〕	5		70	13/	13	千克	AB	PRQS	/15
2005.2000	-马铃薯〔999〕	5		70	13/	9,13	千克	AB	PRQS	/30
2005.4000	-豌豆〔101 青豆罐头，102 即食豌豆沙律，103 熟制豌豆炒货，104 发酵豆制品，105 非发酵豆制品〕	5		70	13/	9,13	千克	AB	PRQS	/30
	-豇豆及菜豆：									
	--脱荚的：									
	---罐头：									
2005.5111	----赤豆馅〔101 红豆罐头，102 豆类罐头〕	5		80	13/	13	千克	AB	RS	/15
2005.5119	----其他〔999〕	5		80	13/	13	千克	AB	RS	/30
	---其他：									
2005.5191	----赤豆馅〔101 红豆馅，102 其他粮食制品〕	5		70	13/	13	千克	AB	PRQS	/15
2005.5199	----其他〔101 冷冻脱荚豇豆，102 冷冻脱荚菜豆〕	5		70	13/	9,13	千克	AB	PRQS	/15
	--其他：									
2005.5910	---罐头〔999〕	5		80	13/	13	千克	AB	RS	/30
2005.5990	---其他〔101 腌渍豇豆，102 腌渍菜豆〕	5		70	13/	9,13	千克	AB	PRQS	/15
	-芦笋：									
2005.6010	---罐头〔999〕	5		80	13/	13	千克	AB	RS	/

协定税率 %										特惠税率 %			Article Description
亚太5国	东/冰/格	巴基斯坦	韩国	瑞士	哥达	秘鲁	澳大利亚	新西/坡/智	港/澳/台	亚太2国	老/柬/缅	36/3/1	
	0/0/0	20	12	5	0	0	0	0/0/0	0/0/			0/0/	----Weighing not more than 5kg
	0/0/0	20	8	5	0	0	0	0/0/0	0/0/			0/0/	----Weighing more than 5kg
	0/0/0	11.5	10.8	5	0	0	0	0/0/0	0/0/			0/0/	---Other
													Mushrooms and truffles, prepared or preserved otherwise than by vinegar or acetic acid:
													-Mushrooms:
													---In airtight containers:
	0/0/0		10	5	0	0	0	0/0/0	0/0/			0/0/	----Small white agaric
	0/0/0		10	5	0	0	0	0/0/0	0/0/			0/0/	----Other
	0/0/0		10	5	0	0	0	0/0/0	0/0/			0/0/	---Other
													-Other:
													---In airtight containers
	0/0/0		10	5	0	0	0	0/0/0	0/0/			0/0/	Shiitake in airtight containiers, not prepared by vinegar [prepared or preserved otherwise than by vinegar or acetic(not mushrooms of the genera agaricus)]
	0/0/0		10	5	0	0	0	0/0/0	0/0/			0/0/	Matsutske in airtight containiers, not prepared by vinegar [prepared or preserved otherwise than by vinegar or acetic(not mushrooms of the genera agaricus)]
	0/0/0		10	5	0	0	0	0/0/0	0/0/			0/0/	Other mushrooms in airtight containiers, not prepared by vinegar [prepared or preserved otherwise than by vinegar or acetic (not mushrooms of the genera agaricus)]
													---Other
	0/0/0		10	5	0	0	0	0/0/0	0/0/			0/0/	Other Matsutske mushroom, prepared or preserved otherwise than by vinegar(not mushrooms of the genera agaricus)
	0/0/0		10	5	0	0	0	0/0/0	0/0/			0/0/	Other sungmo, not prepared by vinegar(prepared or preserved otherwise than by vinegar or acetic)
	0/0/0		10	5	0	0	0	0/0/0	0/0/			0/0/	Other mushrooms, not prepared by vinegar or [prepared or preserved otherwise than by vinegar or acetic(not mushrooms of the genera agaricus)]
													Other vegetables prepared or preserved otherwise than by vinegar or acetic acid, other than products of heading No. 20.06:
	0//0	5.9	5.2	3.9	0	0	0	0/0/0	0/0/			0/0/0	-Potatoes
													-Other vegetables and mixtures of vegetables
	0/0/0		10	5	0	0	0	0/0/0	0/0/			0/0/	Sungmo, not prepared by vinegar or acetic acid, frozen
	0/0/0		10	5	0	0	0	0/0/0	0/0/			0/0/	Acidosasa chinensis shoots, frozen, not prepared by vinegar
	0/0/0		10	5	0	0	0	0/0/0	0/0/			0/0/	Aloe, frozen, not prepared by vinegar
	0/0/0		10	5	0	0	0	0/0/0	0/0/			0/0/	Cactus, frozen, not prepared by vinegar
	0/0/0		10	5	0	0	0	0/0/0	0/0/			0/0/	Other vegetables, not prepared by vinegar(other than products of heading No. 2006)
													Other vegetables prepared or preserved otherwise than by vinegar or acetic acid, not frozen, other than products of heading No. 20.06:
	0/0/0		10	5	0	0	0	0/0/0	0/0/			0/0/	-Homogenized vegetables
	0//0	0	6	4.5	0	0	0	0/0/0	0/0/			0/0/	-Potatoes
	0/0/0		10	5	0	0	0	0/0/0	0/0/			0/0/	-Peas (*Pisum sativum*)
													-Beans (*Vigna spp.*, *Phaseolus spp.*):
													--Beans, shelled:
													---In airtight containers:
	0/0/0		10	5	0	0	0	0/0/0	0/0/			0/0/	----Red bean paste
	0/0/0		17.5	5	0	0	0	0/0/0	0/0/			0/0/	----Other
													---Other:
	0/0/0		10	5	0	0	0	0/0/0	0/0/			0/0/	----Red bean paste
	0//0		17.5	5	0	0	0	0/0/0	0/0/			0/0/	----Other
													--Other:
	0//0		10	5	0	0	0	0/0/0	0/0/			0/0/	---In airtight containers
	0//0		10	5	0	0	0	0/0/0	0/0/			0/0/	---Other
													-Asparagus:
	0//0		10	5	0	0	0	0/0/0	0/0/			0/0/	---In airtight containers

税则号列		货品名称〔CIQ扩展编码及品名—T2表示见附表2〕	最惠(%)	暂定税率	普通	增值/消费	出口退税	计量单位	监管条件	检验检疫	特殊证件对美关税
2005.6090		---其他〔101 冷冻芦笋,102 脱水芦笋,103 腌渍芦笋〕	5		70	13/	9,13	千克	AB	PRQS	/15
2005.7000		-油橄榄〔999〕	5		70	13/	9,13	千克	AB	PRQS	/30
2005.8000		-甜玉米〔101〕	5		80	13/	9,13	千克	AB	PRQS	/30
		-其他蔬菜及什锦蔬菜:									
		--竹笋:									
2005.9110		---竹笋罐头									
2005.9110	10	非用醋制作的酸竹笋罐头〔999〕	5		80	13/	13	千克	ABE	RS	/15
2005.9110	90	非用醋制作的其他竹笋罐头〔999〕	5		80	13/	13	千克	AB	RS	/15
2005.9190		---其他									
2005.9190	10	非用醋制作的酸竹笋〔999〕	5		70	13/	9,13	千克	ABE	PRQS	/15
2005.9190	90	非用醋制作的其他竹笋〔101 冷冻竹笋,102 腌渍竹笋,103 脱水竹笋〕	5		70	13/	9,13	千克	AB	PRQS	/15
		--其他:									
2005.9920		---蚕豆罐头〔999〕	5		80	13/	13	千克	AB	RS	/15
2005.9940		---榨菜〔999〕	5		70	13/	9,13	千克	AB	RS	/15
2005.9950		---咸蕨菜〔999〕	5		70	13/	9,13	千克	AB	RS	/15
2005.9960		---咸葍头〔999〕	5		70	13/	9,13	千克	AB	RS	/15
		---其他:									
2005.9991		----罐头[T2]	5		70	13/	13	千克	AB	RS	/35
2005.9999		----其他									
2005.9999	10	非用醋制作的仙人掌〔101 冷冻仙人掌,102 脱水仙人掌,103 腌渍仙人掌〕	5		70	13/	9,13	千克	ABFE	PRQS	/30
2005.9999	20	非用醋制作的芦荟〔101 冷冻芦荟,102 脱水芦荟,103 腌渍芦荟〕	5		70	13/	9,13	千克	ABFE	PRQS	/30
2005.9999	90	非用醋制作的其他蔬菜及什锦蔬菜〔999〕	5		70	13/	9,13	千克	AB	PRQS	/30
20.06		**糖渍蔬菜、水果、坚果、果皮及植物的其他部分(沥干、糖渍或裹糖的):**									
2006.0010		---蜜枣〔999〕	5		90	13/	13	千克	AB	RS	/
2006.0020		---橄榄〔999〕	5		90	13/	13	千克	AB	RS	/30
2006.0090		---其他									
2006.0090	10	糖渍制松茸〔999〕	5		90	13/	13	千克	ABE	RS	/30
2006.0090	90	其他糖渍蔬菜、水果、坚果、果皮(包括糖渍植物的其他部分)〔101 红豆馅,102 果脯,103 话梅,104 其他蜜饯〕	5		90	13/	13	千克	AB	RS	/30
20.07		**烹煮的果酱、果冻、柑橘酱、果泥及果膏,不论是否加糖或其他甜物质:**									
2007.1000		-均化食品〔999 果酱罐头,201 非罐头工艺生产的果酱〕	5		80	13/	13	千克	AB	RS	/30
		-其他:									
2007.9100		--柑橘属水果的〔999 果酱罐头,201 非罐头工艺生产的果酱〕	5		80	13/	13	千克	AB	RS	/30
		--其他:									
2007.9910		---罐头〔101 什锦果酱罐头,102 杏酱罐头,103 菠萝酱罐头,104 苹果酱罐头,105 西瓜酱罐头,106 猕猴桃酱罐头,107 其他果酱罐头,108 果冻罐头〕	5		80	13/	13	千克	AB	RS	/30
2007.9990		---其他〔999 包括果泥、果膏,201 非罐头工艺生产的果酱〕	5		80	13/	13	千克	AB	RS	/30
20.08		**用其他方法制作或保藏的其他品目未列名水果、坚果及植物的其他食用部分,不论是否加酒、加糖或其他甜物质:**									
		-坚果、花生及其他子仁,不论是否混合:									
		--花生:									
2008.1110		---花生米罐头〔999〕	5		90	13/	13	千克	AB	RS	/30
2008.1120		---烘焙花生〔999〕	5		80	13/	13	千克	AB	PRQS	/25
2008.1130		---花生酱〔999〕	5		90	13/	13	千克	AB	RS	/25
2008.1190		---其他〔101 熟制,102 花生罐头〕	5		80	13/	9,13	千克	AB	PRQS	/30
		--其他,包括什锦坚果及其他子仁:									
2008.1910		---核桃仁罐头〔999〕	5		90	13/	13	千克	AB	RS	/10
2008.1920		---其他果仁罐头〔999〕	5		90	13/	13	千克	AB	RS	/15
		---其他:									
2008.1991		----栗仁〔999〕	5		80	13/	9,13	千克	AB	PRQS	/10
2008.1992		----芝麻〔101 芝麻罐头,102 即食芝麻沙律,103 熟制芝麻炒货,104 芝麻酱〕	5		80	13/	9,13	千克	AB	PRQS	/10
2008.1999		----其他									
2008.1999	10	其他方法制作保藏的红松子仁(用醋或醋酸以外其他方法制作或保藏的)〔101 熟制红松子仁,102 其他红松子仁炒货〕	5		80	13/	0	千克	ABE	PRQS	/30

协定税率 %										特惠税率 %			Article Description
亚太5国	东/冰/格	巴基斯坦	韩国	瑞士	哥达	秘鲁	澳大利亚	新西/坡/智	港/澳/台	亚太2国	老/柬/缅	36/3/1	
	0/0/0		10	5	0	0	0	0/0/0	0/0/			0/0/	---Other
	0/0/0	4.5	4	0	0	0	0	0/0/0	0/0/			0/0/	-Olives
	0/0/0	4.5	4	0	0	0	0	0/0/0	0/0/			0/0/	-Sweet corn (*Zea mays var. saccharata*)
													-Other vegetables and mixtures of vegetables:
													--Bamboo shoots:
													---Bamboo shoots in airtight containers
	0/0/0		10	5	0	0	0	0/0/0	0/0/			0/0/	Acidosasa chinensis shoots in airtight containers, not preserved by vinegar
	0/0/0		10	5	0	0	0	0/0/0	0/0/			0/0/	Other bamboo shoots in airtight containers, not preserved by vinegar
													---Other
	0/0/0		10	5	0	0	0	0/0/0	0/0/			0/0/	Acicosasa chinensis shoots, not preserved by vinegar
	0/0/0		10	5	0	0	0	0/0/0	0/0/			0/0/	Other bamboo shoots, not prepared or preserved by vinegar
													--Other:
	0/0/0	22.5	10	5	0	0	0	0/0/0	0/0/			0/0/	---Broad beans, in airtight containers
	0/0/0	22.5	10	5	0	0	0	0/0/0	0/0/			0/0/	---Hot pickled mustard tubers
	0/0/0	22.5	10	5	0	0	0	0/0/0	0/0/			0/0/	---Chueh tsai (fiddle-head), salted
	0/0/0	22.5	10	5	0	0	0	0/0/0	0/0/			0/0/	---Scallion, salted
													---Other:
	0/0/0		17.5	5	0	0	0	0/0/0	0/0/			0/0/	----In airtight containers
													----Other
	0/0/0		17.5	5	0	0	0	0/0/0	0/0/			0/0/	Cactus, not preserved by vinegar
	0/0/0		17.5	5	0	0	0	0/0/0	0/0/			0/0/	Aloe, not preserved by vinegar
	0/0/0		17.5	5	0	0	0	0/0/0	0/0/			0/0/	Other vegetables and mixtures of vegetables, not preserved by vinegar
													Vegetables, fruit, nuts, fruit-peel and other parts of plants, preserved by sugar (drained, glac or crystallized):
	0/0/0		21		0	0	0	0/0/0	0/0/		//0	0/0/0	---Preserved jujubes
	0/0/0		21		0	10.6	0	0/0/0	0/0/		//0	0/0/0	---Preserved olives
													---Other
	0/0/0		21	0	0	10.6	0	0/0/0	0/0/		//0	0/0/0	Matsutske, preserved by sugar
	0/0/0		21	0	0	10.6	0	0/0/0	0/0/		//0	0/0/0	Other vegetables, fruit, nuts, fruit-peel (including other parts of plants) preserved by sugar
													Jams, fruit jellies, marmalades, fruit or nut pure and fruit or nut pastes, being cooked preparations, whether or not containing added sugar or other sweetening matter:
	0/0/0		21	0	0	10.6	0	0/0/0	0/0/			0//	-Homogenized preparations
													-Other:
	0/0/0		21	0	0	0	0	0/0/0	0/0/		//0	0/0/0	--Citrus fruit
													--Other:
	0/0/0	0	0	0	0	0	0	0//0	0/0/	2.5		0/0/0	---In airtight containers
	0/0/0	0	0	0	1.7	0	0	0//0	0/0/	2.5		0/0/0	---Other
													Fruit, nuts and other edible parts of plants, otherwise prepared or preserved, whether or not containing added sugar or other sweetening matter or spirit, not elsewhere specified or included:
													-Nuts, groundnuts and other seeds, whether or not mixed together:
													--Ground-nuts:
	0/0/0		21		0		0	0/0/0	0/0/			0//	---Ground-nuts kernels, in airtight containers
	0/0/0		21		0		0	0/0/0	0/0/		/0/	0/0/0	---Roasted ground-nuts
	0/0/0		21		0		0	0/0/0	0/0/			0//	---Ground-nut butter
	0/0/0		21		0		0	0/0/0	0/0/			0//	---Other
													--Other, including mixtures:
2.5	0/0/0	10	12	5	0	0	0	0/0/0	0/0/		0/0/	0/0/0	---Walnut meats, in airtight containers
2.5	0/0/0	4.5	5.2	3.9	0	0	0	0/0/0	0/0/		0/0/	0/0/0	---Other nuts, in airtight containers
													---Other:
2.5	0/0/0	4.5	4	5	0	0	0	0/0/0	0/0/		0/0/	0/0/0	----Chestnut seed
2.5	0//0	4.5	4	0	0	0	0	0/0/0	0/0/			0/0/	----Sesame
													----Other
2.5	0/0/0	4.5	4	0	0	0	0	0/0/0	0/0/		0/0/	0/0/0	Korean pine-nuts, shelled, (not prepared or preserved by vinegar or acetic acid)

税则号列		货品名称〔CIQ扩展编码及品名－T2表示见附表2〕	最惠(%)	暂定税率	普通	增值/消费	出口退税	计量单位	监管条件	检验检疫	特殊证件对美关税
2008.1999	90	未列名制作或保藏坚果及其他子仁(用醋或醋酸以外其他方法制作或保藏的)[101 杏仁罐头,102 银杏罐头,103 板栗罐头,104 腰果罐头,105 其他坚果罐头,106 熟制杏仁,107 熟制开心果,108 熟制松子,109 熟制夏威夷果,110 熟制南瓜子,111 熟制西瓜子,112 未列名的即食坚果沙律,113 未列出的其他熟制坚果炒货,114 榛子酱,115 扁桃仁酱,116 其他坚果及籽类的泥(酱)]	5		80	13/	9,13	千克	AB	PRQS	/30
		-菠萝:									
2008.2010		---罐头〔101 马口铁菠萝罐头,102 玻璃瓶菠萝罐头,103 复合塑料袋菠萝罐头,104 其他材质菠萝罐头〕	5		90	13/	13	千克	AB	RS	/10
2008.2090		---其他〔999〕	5		80	13/	9,13	千克	AB	PRQ	/10
		-柑橘属水果:									
2008.3010		---罐头〔101 桔子罐头,102 糖水橘子罐头,103 橘子囊胞罐头,104 其他橘子罐头〕	5		90	13/	13	千克	AB	RS	/10
2008.3090		---其他〔999 用醋或醋酸以外其他方法制作或保藏的,101 食品工业用浓缩液(汁、浆),102 果脯〕	5		80	13/	9,13	千克	AB	PRQS	/15
		-梨:									
2008.4010		---罐头〔101 梨罐头,102 糖水梨罐头,103 糖水洋梨罐头,104 其他梨罐头〕	5		90	13/	13	千克	AB	RS	/10
2008.4090		---其他〔999〕	5		80	13/	9,13	千克	AB	PRQ	/10
2008.5000		-杏〔101 杏子罐头,102 果脯〕	5		90	13/	9,13	千克	AB	PRQS	/30
		-樱桃:									
2008.6010		---罐头〔101 樱桃罐头,102 果脯〕	5		90	13/	13	千克	AB	PRQS	/35
2008.6090		---其他〔101 果脯,102 其他蜜饯〕	5		90	13/	6,13	千克	AB	PRQS	/20
		-桃,包括油桃:									
2008.7010		---罐头〔999〕	5		90	13/	13	千克	AB	RS	/30
2008.7090		---其他〔101 其他桃罐头,102 果脯〕	5		80	13/	9,13	千克	AB	PRQS	/10
2008.8000		-草莓〔101 果脯,102 其他蜜饯〕	5		90	13/	9,13	千克	AB	PRQS	/35
		-其他,包括子目号 2008.19 以外的什锦果实:									
2008.9100		--棕榈芯〔999〕	5		80	13/	6,13	千克	AB	PRQS	/15
2008.9300		--蔓越橘(大果蔓越橘,小果蔓越橘,越橘)〔999〕	15		80	13/	9,13	千克	AB	PRQS	/50
2008.9700		--什锦果实〔101 马口铁什锦水果罐头,102 玻璃瓶什锦水果罐头,103 复合塑料袋什锦水果罐头,104 其他材质什锦水果罐头,105 果脯〕	5		80	13/	9,13	千克	AB	PRQS	/30
		--其他:									
2008.9910		---荔枝罐头〔101 马口铁荔枝罐头,102 玻璃瓶荔枝罐头,103 复合塑料袋荔枝罐头,104 其他材质荔枝罐头〕	5		90	13/	13	千克	AB	RS	/10
2008.9920		---龙眼罐头〔101 马口铁龙眼罐头,102 玻璃瓶龙眼罐头,103 复合塑料袋龙眼罐头,104 其他材质龙眼罐头〕	5		80	13/	13	千克	AB	RS	/10
		---海草及其他藻类制品:									
2008.9931		----调味紫菜〔101 养殖,102 野生〕	15		90	13/	13	千克	AB	RS	/40
2008.9932		----盐腌海带〔101 养殖,102 野生〕	10		80	13/	6,13	千克	AB	PRQS	/15
2008.9933		----盐腌裙带菜〔101 养殖,102 野生〕	10		80	13/	6,13	千克	AB	PRQS	/15
2008.9934		----烤紫菜〔101 养殖,102 野生〕	10		80	13/	13	千克	AB	RS	/15
2008.9939		----其他〔104 养殖水产制品,105 野生水产制品〕	10		80	13/	6,13	千克	AB	PRQS	/15
2008.9940		---清水荸荠(马蹄)罐头〔999〕	5		80	13/	13	千克	AB	RS	/15
2008.9990		---其他〔T2〕	5		80	13/	9,13	千克	AB	PRQS	/15
20.09		**未发酵及未加酒精的水果汁(包括酿酒葡萄汁)、蔬菜汁,不论是否加糖或其他甜物质:**									
		-橙汁:									
2009.1100		--冷冻的〔999〕	7.5		90	13/	13	千克	AB	PRQS	/32.5
2009.1200		--非冷冻的,白利糖度值不超过 20 的〔101 可直接饮用的蔬菜果汁类饮料,102 浓缩蔬菜果汁饮料(包括冷冻的),103 食品工业用浓缩液(汁、浆)〕	30		90	13/	13	千克	AB	PRQS	/55
2009.1200	10	白利糖度值不超过 20 的非冷冻橙汁,最小独立包装净重≥180 千克(未发酵及未加酒精的,不论是否加糖或其他甜物质)	30	15	90	13/	13	千克	AB	PRQS	/40
2009.1200	90	其他非冷冻白利糖浓度不超过 20 的橙汁(未发酵及未加酒精的,不论是否加糖或其他甜物质)	30		90	13/	13	千克	AB	PRQS	/55

协定税率 %										特惠税率 %			
亚太5国	东/冰/格	巴基斯坦	韩国	瑞士	哥达	秘鲁	澳大利亚	新西/坡/智	港/澳/台	亚太2国	老/柬/缅	36/3/1	Article Description
2.5	0/0/0	4.5	4	0	0	0	0	0/0/0	0/0/		0/0/	0/0/0	Nuts and other seeds,(not prepared or preserved by vinegar or acetic acid)not elsewhere specified or included
													-Pineapples:
	5/0/0		6	4.5	5	0	0	0//0	0/0/		0//	0/0/0	---In airtight containers
	5/0/0		6	4.5	5	0	0	0//0	0/0/		0//	0/0/0	---Other
													-Citrus fruit:
	0/0/0		12	5	6.7	0	0	0/0/0	0/0/		0//	0/0/0	---In airtight containers
	0/0/0		14	5	0	0	0	0/0/0	0/0/		0//	0/0/0	---Other
													-Pears:
	0/0/0		12	5	0	0	0	0/0/0	0/0/		0//	0/0/0	---In airtight containers
	0/0/0		12	5	0	0	0	0/0/0	0/0/		0//	0/0/0	---Other
	0/0/0		12	5	0	0	0	0/0/0	0/0/			0/0/	-Apricots
													-Cherries:
	0/0/0		12	5	0	0	0	0/0/0	0/0/			0/0/	---In airtight containers
	0/0/0		12	5	0	0	0	0/0/0	0/0/			0/0/	---Other
													-Peaches:
	0/0/0	4.5	4	0	0	0	0	0/0/0	0/0/		0//	0/0/0	---In airtight containers
	0/0/0		12	5	0	0	0	0/0/0	0/0/		0//	0/0/0	---Other
	0/0/0	12	6	4.5	0	0	0	0/0/0	0/0/			0/0/	-Strawberries
													-Other, including mixtures other than those of subheading No. 2008. 19:
	0/0/0	0	0	0	0	0	0	0//0	0/0/		/0/	0/0/0	--Palm hearts
	0/0/0	12	6	0	0	0	0	0/0/0	0/0/		/0/	0/0/0	--Cranberry(Vaccinium macrocarpon vaccinium oxycoccos, vaccinium vitis-idaea.)
	0/0/0	4.5	4	0	0	0	0	0/0/0	0/0/		/0/	0/0/0	--Mixtures
													--Other:
	0/0/0		12	5	0	0	0	0/0/0	0/0/			0/0/	---Lychee can
	5/0/0		6	4.5	0	0	0	0//0	0/0/		/0/	0/0/0	---Longan can
													---Preparations of seaweeds and other alga:
13.8	0/0/0	0	10.5	4.5	0	0	0	0/0/0	0/0/		/0/	0/0/0	----Seasoned laver
	0/0/0	12	6	4.5	0	0	0	0//0	0/0/		/0/	0/0/0	----Salted, sea tangle
	0/0/0	0	6	4.5	0	0	0	0//0	0/0/		/0/	0/0/0	----Pinnatifida, salted
	0/0/0	10.8	6	4.5	0	0	0	0//0	0/0/		/0/	0/0/0	----Roasted laver
	0/0/0	10.8	6	4.5	0	0	0	0//0	0/0/		/0/	0/0/0	----Other
	0/0/0	22.5	10	5	0	0	0	0/0/0	0/0/			0/0/	---Water chestnut, in airtight containers
	0/0/0	0	6	0	0	0	0	0/0/0	0/0/		/0/	0/0/0	---Other
													Fruit juices (including grape must) and vegetable juices, unfermented and not containing added spirit, whether or not containing added sugar or other sweetening matter:
													-Orange juice:
	0/0/0	4	0	0	0	0	1.9	0//0	0/0/		0/0/	0/0/0	--Frozen
	0/0/0		22.5	0		0	11.3	0/0/0	0/0/		0/0/	0/0/0	--Not frozen, of a Brix value not exceeding 20
	0/0/0		21	0		0	7.5	0/0/0	0/0/		0/0/	0/0/0	Non frozen orange juice with Brix value no more than 20, with minimum net weight of independent package ≥ 180kg (unfermented and without alcohol, whether or not added with sugar or other sweet substances)
	0/0/0		21	0		0	7.5	0/0/0	0/0/		0/0/	0/0/0	Other orange juices (unfermented and not containing alcohol, whether or not containing sugar or other sweet substances) of not more than 20 unfrozen Brix concentrations

税则号列		货品名称〔CIQ 扩展编码及品名－T2 表示见附表 2〕	最惠(%)	暂定税率	普通	增值/消费	出口退税	计量单位	监管条件	检验检疫	特殊证件对美关税
2009.1900		--其他〔101 可直接饮用的蔬菜果汁类饮料，102 浓缩蔬菜果汁饮料(包括冷冻的)，103 食品工业用浓缩液(汁、浆)〕	30		90	13/	13	千克	AB	RS	/40
2009.1900	10	白利糖度值超过 20 的非冷冻橙汁，最小独立包装净重≥180 千克(未发酵及未加酒精的，不论是否加糖或其他甜物质)	30	15	90	13/	13	千克	AB	RS	/25
2009.1900	90	非冷冻白利糖浓度超过 20 的橙汁(未发酵及未加酒精的，不论是否加糖或其他甜物质)	30		90	13/	13	千克	AB	RS	/40
		-葡萄柚(包括柚)汁：									
2009.2100		--白利糖度值不超过 20 的〔101 可直接饮用的蔬菜果汁类饮料，102 浓缩蔬菜果汁饮料(包括冷冻的)，103 食品工业用浓缩液(汁、浆)〕	5		90	13/	13	千克	AB	PRQS	/30
2009.2900		--其他〔101 可直接饮用的蔬菜果汁类饮料，102 浓缩蔬菜果汁饮料(包括冷冻的)，103 食品工业用浓缩液(汁、浆)〕	5		90	13/	13	千克	AB	RS	/30
		-其他未混合的柑橘属水果汁：									
		--白利糖度值不超过 20 的：									
2009.3110		---柠檬汁〔101 可直接饮用的蔬菜果汁类饮料，102 浓缩蔬菜果汁饮料(包括冷冻的)，103 食品工业用浓缩液(汁、浆)〕	5		90	13/	13	千克	AB	PRQS	/30
2009.3190		---其他〔101 可直接饮用的蔬菜果汁类饮料，102 包括冷冻的，103 汁、浆〕	5		90	13/	13	千克	AB	PRQS	/10
		--其他：									
2009.3910		---柠檬汁〔101 包括冷冻的，102 可直接饮用的蔬菜果汁类饮料，103 汁、浆〕	5		90	13/	13	千克	AB	RS	/30
2009.3990		---其他〔999〕	5		90	13/	13	千克	AB	RS	/10
		-菠萝汁：									
2009.4100		--白利糖度值不超过 20 的〔102 浓缩蔬菜果汁饮料(包括冷冻的)，103 食品工业用浓缩液(汁、浆)〕	5		90	13/	13	千克	AB	PRQS	/30
2009.4900		--其他〔101 可直接饮用的蔬菜果汁类饮料，102 浓缩蔬菜果汁饮料(包括冷冻的)〕	5		90	13/	13	千克	AB	RS	/30
2009.5000		-番茄汁〔101 可直接饮用的蔬菜果汁类饮料，102 浓缩蔬菜果汁饮料(包括冷冻的)〕	5		80	13/	13	千克	AB	RS	/25
		-葡萄汁，包括酿酒葡萄汁：									
2009.6100		--白利糖度值不超过 30 的〔101 浓缩蔬菜果汁饮料(包括冷冻的)，102 未发酵葡萄酒，103 可直接饮用的蔬菜果蔬汁类饮料〕	5		90	13/	13	千克	AB	PRQS	/30
2009.6900		--其他〔101 包括冷冻的，102 未发酵葡萄酒〕	5		90	13/	13	千克	AB	RS	/35
		-苹果汁：									
2009.7100		--白利糖度值不超过 20 的〔101 可直接饮用的蔬菜果汁类饮料，102 包括冷冻的〕	5		90	13/	13	千克	AB	PRQS	/35
2009.7900		--其他〔101 可直接饮用的蔬菜果汁类饮料，102 包括冷冻的〕	10		90	13/	13	千克	AB	RS	/35
		-其他未混合的水果汁或蔬菜汁：									
2009.8100		--蔓越橘汁(大果蔓越橘，小果蔓越橘、越橘)〔101 可直接饮用的蔬菜果汁类饮料，102 浓缩蔬菜果汁饮料(包括冷冻的)，103 食品工业用浓缩液(汁、浆)〕	5		90	13/	13	千克	AB	PRQS	/20
		--其他：									
		---水果汁：									
2009.8912		----芒果汁〔101 可直接饮用的蔬菜果汁类饮料，102 包括冷冻的，103 汁、浆〕	5		90	13/	13	千克	AB	PRQS	/30
2009.8913		----西番莲果汁〔101 可直接饮用的蔬菜果汁类饮料，102 包括冷冻的，103 汁、浆〕	5		90	13/	13	千克	AB	PRQS	/30
2009.8914		----番石榴果汁〔101 可直接饮用的蔬菜果汁类饮料，102 包括冷冻的，103 汁、浆〕	5		90	13/	13	千克	AB	PRQS	/30
2009.8915		----梨汁〔101 可直接饮用的蔬菜果汁类饮料，102 包括冷冻的，103 汁、浆〕	5		90	13/	13	千克	AB	PRQS	/10
2009.8919		----其他〔101 可直接饮用的蔬菜果汁类饮料，102 包括冷冻的，103 汁、浆〕	5		90	13/	13	千克	AB	PRQS	/20
2009.8920		---蔬菜汁〔101 可直接饮用的蔬菜果汁类饮料，102 包括冷冻的，103 汁、浆〕	5		80	13/	13	千克	AB	PRQS	/30
		-混合汁：									
2009.9010		---水果汁〔101 可直接饮用的蔬菜果汁类饮料，102 浓缩蔬菜果汁饮料(包括冷冻的)，103 食品工业用浓缩液(汁、浆)〕	5		90	13/	13	千克	AB	PRQS	/30
2009.9090		---其他〔101 可直接饮用的蔬菜果汁类饮料，102 包括冷冻的，103 汁、浆〕	5		80	13/	13	千克	AB	PRQS	/30

协定税率 %										特惠税率 %			
亚太5国	东/冰/格	巴基斯坦	韩国	瑞士	哥达	秘鲁	澳大利亚	新西/坡/智	港/澳/台	亚太2国	老/柬/缅	36/3/1	**Article Description**
	0/0/0		22.5			0	11.3	0/0/0	0/0/		0/0/	0/0/0	--Other
	0/0/0		21			0	7.5	0/0/0	0/0/		0/0/	0/0/0	Non frozen orange juice with a Brix value of more than 20, with a minimum net weight of independent packaging ≥ 180 kg (unfermented and non－alcoholic, with or without sugar or other sweet substances)
	0/0/0		21			0	7.5	0/0/0	0/0/		0/0/	0/0/0	Orange juice (unfermented and not containing alcohol, whether or not containing sugar or other sweet substances) with a concentration of non frozen Baili sugar exceeding 20
													-Grapefruit (including pomelo) juice:
	0/0/0	12	6	4.5	0	0	0	0/0/0	0/0/		0//	0/0/0	--Of a Brix value not exceeding 20
	0/0/0	12	6	4.5	0	0	0	0/0/0	0/0/		0//	0/0/0	--Other
													-Juice of any other single citrus fruit:
													--Of a Brix value not exceeding 20:
4.7	0/0/0	14.4	10.8	5	0	0	0	0/0/0	0/0/	2.5	/0/	0/0/0	---Lemon Juice
4.7	0/0/0	14.4	10.8	5	0	0	0	0/0/0	0/0/	2.5	/0/	0/0/0	---Other
													--Other:
4.7	0/0/0	14.4	10.8	5	0	0	0	0/0/0	0/0/	2.5	/0/	0/0/0	---Lemon juice
4.7	0/0/0	14.4	10.8	5	0	0	0	0/0/0	0/0/	2.5	/0/	0/0/0	---Other
													-Pineapple juice:
	5/0/0		4	0	0	0	0	0//0	0/0/		0/0/	0/0/0	--Of a Brix value not exceeding 20
	5/0/0		4	0	0	0	0	0//0	0/0/		0/0/	0/0/0	--Other
	0/0/0		21		0	0	0	0/0/0	0/0/	2.5	0//	0/0/0	-Tomato juice
													-Grape juice(including grape must):
	0/0/0		12	5	0	1.7	0	0/0/0	0/0/			0/0/	--Of a Brix value not exceeding 30
	0/0/0		12	5	0	1.7	0	0/0/0	0/0/			0/0/	--Other
													-Apple juice:
	0/0/0		12	5	0	0	0	0/0/0	0/0/			0/0/	--Of a Brix value not exceeding 20
	0/0/0		12	6	0	0	0	0/0/0	0/0/			0/0/	--Other
													-Juice of any other single fruit or vegetable:
2.5	0/0/0	10	12	5	0	0	0	0/0/0	0/0/		0//0	0/0/0	--Cranberry juice
													--Other:
													---Fruit juice:
4.4	0/0/0	0	12	5	0	0	0	0/0/0	0/0/		0//0	0/0/0	----Mango juice
4.4	0/0/0	16	12	5	0	0	0	0/0/0	0/0/		0//0	0/0/0	----Passion-fruit juice
4.4	0/0/0	16	12	5	0	0	0	0/0/0	0/0/		0//0	0/0/0	----Guva juice
2.5	0/0/0	0	12	5	0	0	0	0/0/0	0/0/		0//0	0/0/0	----Pear Juice
2.5	0/0/0	0	12	5	0	0	0	0/0/0	0/0/		0//0	0/0/0	----Other
2.5	0/0/0	10	12	5	0	0	0	0/0/0	0/0/		//0	0/0/0	---Vegetable juice
													-Mixtures of juices:
4.4	0/0/0	0	12	5	0	0	0	0/0/0	0/0/	2.5	0/0/	0/0/0	--Of fruit juices
	0/0/0	0	12	5	0	0	0	0/0/0	0/0/	2.5	0/0/	0/0/0	--Other

第二十一章
杂项食品

注释：

一、本章不包括：

(一)税目07.12的什锦蔬菜；

(二)含咖啡的焙炒咖啡代用品(税目09.01)；

(三)加香料的茶(税目09.02)；

(四)税目09.04至09.10的调味香料或其他产品；

(五)按重量计含香肠、肉、食用杂碎、动物血、鱼、甲壳动物、软体动物、其他水生无脊椎动物及其混合物超过20%的食品(第十六章)，但税目21.03或21.04的产品除外；

(六)税目30.03或30.04的药用酵母及其他产品；

(七)税目35.07的酶制品。

二、上述注释一(二)所述咖啡代用品的精汁归入税目21.01。

三、税目21.04所称"均化混合食品"，是指两种或两种以上的基本配料，例如，肉、鱼、蔬菜或果实等，经精细均化制成适合供婴幼儿食用或营养用的零售包装食品(每件净重不超过250克)。为了调味、保藏或其他目的，可以加入少量其他配料，还可以含有少量可见的小块配料。

税则号列	货品名称〔CIQ扩展编码及品名－T2表示见附表2〕	最惠(%)	暂定税率	普通	增值/消费	出口退税	计量单位	监管条件	检验检疫	特殊证件对美关税
21.01	**咖啡、茶、马黛茶的浓缩精汁及以其为基本成分或以咖啡、茶、马黛茶为基本成分的制品；烘焙菊苣和其他烘焙咖啡代用品及其浓缩精汁：**									
	-咖啡浓缩精汁及以其为基本成分或以咖啡为基本成分的制品：									
2101.1100	--浓缩精汁〔101速溶咖啡，102其他咖啡，103咖啡伴侣，104未列出的其他饮料、冷冻饮品、咖啡、果冻〕	12		130	13/	13	千克	AB	RS	/37
2101.1200	--以浓缩精汁或咖啡为基本成分的制品〔101茶饮料，102咖啡粉，103速溶咖啡，104其他咖啡，105未列出的其他饮料、冷冻饮品、咖啡、果冻〕	12		130	13/	13	千克	AB	RS	/37
2101.2000	-茶、马黛茶浓缩精汁及以其为基本成分或以茶、马黛茶为基本成分的制品〔999〕	12		130	13/	13	千克	AB	RS	/37
2101.3000	-烘焙菊苣和其他烘焙咖啡代用品及其浓缩精汁〔101其他咖啡，102植脂末(咖啡伴侣)，103未列出的其他饮料、冷冻饮品、咖啡、果冻〕	12		130	13/	13	千克	AB	RS	/22
21.02	**酵母(活性或非活性)；已死的其他单细胞微生物(不包括税目30.02的疫苗)；发酵粉：**									
2102.1000	-活性酵母〔101饲料添加剂，104活性酵母〕	25		80	13/	13	千克	AB	PRQS	/50
2102.2000	-非活性酵母；已死的其他单细胞微生物〔999，301有检疫要求食品添加剂，201非活性酵母〕	25		70	9/	13	千克	AB	PRQS	/50
2102.3000	-发酵粉〔101饲料添加剂，102其他粮食制品，103活性酵母，104非活性酵母，105食品加工用酵母衍生制品，106食品加工用其他酵母产品〕	25		70	13/	13	千克	AB	PRQS	/55
21.03	**调味汁及其制品；混合调味品；芥子粉及其调制品：**									
2103.1000	-酱油〔101酿造酱油，102配制酱油，103鲜味汁，104其他酱油〕	12		90	13/	13	千克	AB	RS	/37
2103.2000	-番茄沙司及其他番茄调味汁〔101番茄沙司，102番茄调味汁〕	12		90	13/	13	千克	AB	RS	/22
2103.3000	-芥子粉及其调制品〔999香辛料，998未列出的其他调味品〕	12		70	13/	13	千克	AB	PRQS	/22
	-其他：									
2103.9010	---味精〔999〕	12		130	13/	13	千克	AB	RS	/17
2103.9020	---别特酒(Aromatic bitters)，按体积计酒精含量44.2%～49.2%，按重量计含1.5%～6%的香料、各种配料以及4%～10%的糖〔999〕	12		90	13/	13	千克	AB	RS	/17
2103.9090	---其他[T2]	12		90	13/	9,13	千克	AB	RS	/42
21.04	**汤料及其制品；均化混合食品：**									
2104.1000	-汤料及其制品〔101制汤调料，102其他含肉速冻粮食制品，103其他不含肉速冻粮食制品〕	12		90	13/	13	千克	AB	PRQS	/42

Chapter 21
Miscellaneous edible preparations

Notes:

1. This Chapter does not cover:
   (a) Mixed vegetables of heading No. 07.12;
   (b) Roasted coffee substitutes containing coffee in any proportion (heading No. 09.01);
   (c) Flavoured tea (heading No. 09.02);
   (d) Spices or other products of headings No. 09.04 to 09.10;
   (e) Food preparations, other than the products described in heading No. 21.03 or 21.04, containing more than 20% by weight of sausage, meat, meat offal, blood, fish or crustaceans, molluscs or other aquatic invertebrates, or any combination thereof (Chapter 16);
   (f) Yeast put up as a medicament or other products of heading No. 30.03 or 30.04; or
   (g) Prepared enzymes of heading No. 35.07.
2. Extracts of the substitutes referred to in Note 1(b) above are to be classified in heading No. 21.01.
3. For the purposes of heading No. 21.04, the expression "homogenized composite food preparations" means preparations consisting of a finely homogenized mixture of two or more basic ingredients such as meat, fish, vegetables or fruit, put up for retail sale Suitable for infants to eat or for dietetic purposes, in containers of a net weight content not exceeding 250g. For the application of this definition, no account is to betaken of small quantities of any ingredients which may be added to the mixture for seasoning, preservation or other purposes. Such preparations may contain a small quantity of visible pieces of ingredients.

协定税率 %									特惠税率 %				
亚太5国	东/冰/格	巴基斯坦	韩国	瑞士	哥达	秘鲁	澳大利亚	新西/坡/智	港/澳/台	亚太2国	老/柬/缅	36/3/1	Article Description
													Extracts, essences and concentrates, of coffee, tea or maté and preparations with a basis of these products or with a basis of coffee, tea or maté; roasted chicory and other roasted coffee substitutes, and extracts, essences and concentrates thereof:
													-Extracts, essences and concentrates of coffee, and preparations with a basis of these extracts, essences or concentrates or with a basis of coffee:
	0/0/0	13.6	10.2		0		0	0/0/0	0/0/			0/0/0	--Extracts, essences and concentrates
	0/0/0		21		0		0	0/0/0	0/0/			0//	--Preparations with a basis of extracts, essences or concentrates or with a basis of coffee
6	0/0/0	16		0	0	0	0	0/0/0	0/0/			0/0/	-Extracts, essences and concentrates, of tea or maté, and preparations with a basis of these extracts, essences or concentrates or with a basis of tea or mate
	0//0		22.4		0		0	0/0/0	0/0/			0/0/	-Roasted chicory and other roasted coffee substitutes, and extracts, essences and concentrates thereof
													Yeasts (active or inactive); other singlecell micro-organisms, dead (but not including vaccines of heading No. 30.02); prepared baking powders:
	0/0/0	25	17.5	0	0	0	0	0/0/0	0/0/			0/0/	-Active yeasts
	0/0/0	22.5	17.5	0	0	0	0	0/0/0	0/0/			0/0/	-Inactive yeasts; other single-cell microorganisms, dead
	0/0/0	22.5	17.5		0	0	0	0/0/0	0/0/			0/0/	-Prepared baking powders
													Sauces and preparations therefor; mixed condiments and mixes seasonings; mustard flour and meal and prepared mustard:
	0/0/0	25.2	19.6	8.4	0	0	0	0/0/0	0/0/		/0/	0/0/0	-Soya sauce
	0//0	12	6	4.5	0	0	0	0/0/0	0/0/		/0/	0/0/0	-Tomato ketchup and other tomato sauces
	0//0	12	6	4.5	0	0	0	0/0/0	0/0/		/0/	0/0/0	-Mustard flour and meal and prepared mustard
													-Other:
10.4	0/0/0	16.4	14.7	6.3	0	0	0	0/0/0	0/0/			0/0/	---Gourmet powder
	0/0/0		14.7	6.3	0	7.4	0	0/0/0	0/0/			0/0/	---Aromatic bitters, 44.2%～49.2% of which is alcoholic strength by volume, 1.5%～6% of which is spiles and various ingredients by weight and 4%～10% of which is sugar by weight
10.6	0/0/0	18.4	14.7	8.8	0	1.8	0	0/0/0	0/0/			0/0/0	---Other
													Soups and broths and preparations therefor; homogenized composite food preparations:
	0/0/0	12	6	4.5	0	0	0	0/0/0	0/0/			0/0/	-Soups and broths and preparations therefor

税则号列	货品名称〔CIQ扩展编码及品名—T2表示见附表2〕	最惠(%)	暂定税率	普通	增值/消费	出口退税	计量单位	监管条件	检验检疫	特殊证件对美关税
2104.2000	-均化混合食品〔101 汤料,102 混合调味品,103 未列出的其他调味品,104 具有保健食品批准文号〕	12		90	13/	13	千克	AB	RS	/22
21.05	**冰淇淋及其他冰制食品,不论是否含可可:**									
2105.0000	冰淇淋及其他冰制食品,不论是否含可可〔101 冰淇淋,102 冷冻饮品制作料,104 食用冰,105 其他冷冻饮品〕	12		90	13/	13	千克	AB	RS	/37
21.06	**其他税目未列名的食品:**									
2106.1000	-浓缩蛋白质及人造蛋白物质[T2]	10		90	13/	6,13	千克	AB	RS	/20
	-其他:									
2106.9010	---制造碳酸饮料的浓缩物〔102 如菊花精、柠檬茶、果珍,103 未列出的其他饮料、冷冻饮品、咖啡、果冻〕	12		100	13/	13	千克	AB	RS	/
2106.9020	---制造饮料用的复合酒精制品〔999〕	12		180	13/5	13	千克	AB	RS	/17
2106.9030	---蜂王浆制剂									
2106.9030 10	含濒危植物成分的蜂王浆制剂〔101 具有保健食品批准文号,102 蜂王浆及制品〕	3		80	13/	0	千克	ABFE	RS	/13
2106.9030 90	其他蜂王浆制剂〔101 具有保健食品批准文号,102 蜂王浆及制品〕	3		80	13/	13	千克	AB	RS	/13
2106.9040	---椰子汁〔999〕	10		90	13/	13	千克	AB	PRQS	/35
2106.9050	---海豹油胶囊									
2106.9050 10	濒危海豹油胶囊〔999〕	5		90	13/	0	千克	ABEF	RS	/10
2106.9050 90	其他海豹油胶囊〔999〕	5		90	13/	13	千克	AB	RS	/10
2106.9090	---其他									
2106.9090 01	乳蛋白部分水解配方,乳蛋白深度水解配方、氨基酸配方、无乳糖配方特殊婴幼儿奶粉[101 乳基婴儿配方食品,102 乳基较大婴儿配方食品,103 氨基酸代谢障碍配方特殊医学用途婴儿配方食品,104 无乳糖配方特殊医学用途婴儿配方食品,105 乳蛋白部分水解配方特殊医学用途婴儿配方食品,106 乳蛋白深度水解配方特殊医学用途婴儿配方食品,107 乳基幼儿配方食品]	12	0	90	13/	13	千克	AB	RS	/10
2106.9090 11	含濒危鱼软骨素胶囊〔999〕	12		90	13/	0	千克	ABEF	RS	/22
2106.9090 19	含濒危动植物成分的其他编号未列名食品[101 蛋白型固体饮料,102 如菊花精、柠檬茶、果珍,103 未列出的其他饮料、冷冻饮品、咖啡、果冻,104 发酵豆制品,105 红豆馅,106 其他粮食制品,107 具有保健食品批准文号,108 非发酵豆制品,109 婴幼儿谷类辅助食品,110 婴幼儿罐装辅助食品,111 特殊医学用途配方食品]	12		90	13/	0	千克	ABEF	RS	/22
2106.9090 90	其他编号未列名的食品[T2]	12		90	13/	6,13	千克	AB	RS	/22

协定税率 %										特惠税率 %			Article Description
亚太5国	东/冰/格	巴基斯坦	韩国	瑞士	哥达	秘鲁	澳大利亚	新西/坡/智	港/澳/台	亚太2国	老/柬/缅	36/3/1	
	0//0		22.4		0	0	0	0/0/0	0/0/			0/0/	-Homogenized composite food preparations
													Ice cream and other edible ice, whether or not containing cocoa:
	0/0/0	0		0	0	0	0	0/0/0	0/0/			0/0/	Ice cream and other edible ice, whether or not containing cocoa
													Food preparations not elsewhere specified or included:
	0/0/0	4.5	4	0	0	0	0	0/0/0	0/0/			0/0/	-Protein concentrates and textured protein substances
													-Other:
	0/0/0		24.5		0	0	0	0/0/0	0/0/			0/0/	---Beverage bases
	0/0/0		12	6	0	0	0	0/0/0	0/0/			0/0/	---Compound alcoholic preparations of a kind used for the manufacture of beverages
													---Royal jelly, put up as tonic essences
	0/0/0	0	0	0	0	0	0	0//0	0/0/		0//	0/0/0	Royal jelly, put up as tonic essences containing composition of endangered plants
	0/0/0	0	0	0	0	0	0	0//0	0/0/		0//	0/0/0	Other royal jelly, put up as tonic essences
9	5/0/0	9	4	0	0	0	0	0//0	0/0/		0//0	0/0/0	---Coconut juice
													---Seal oil capsules
4.6	0/0/0	18.4	18.4	5	0	0	0	0/0/0	0/0/			0/0/	Endangered seal oil capsules
4.6	0/0/0	18.4	18.4	5	0	0	0	0/0/0	0/0/			0/0/	Other seal oil capsules
													---Other
11	0/0/	0	18.4	8.3	0	0	0	0/0/0	0/0/			0/0/	Milk protein partial hydrolysate formula, milk protein hydrolysis amino acid formula special depth formula, infant milk powder
11	0/0/	0	18.4	8.3	0	0	0	0/0/0	0/0/			0/0/	Endangered species of fish cartilage capsules
11	0/0/	0	18.4	8.3	0	0	0	0/0/0	0/0/			0/0/	Other food preparations containing composition of endangered plants, not eleswhere specified or included
11	0/0/	0	18.4	8.3	0	0	0	0/0/0	0/0/			0/0/	Other food preparations, not eleswhere specified or included

第二十二章
饮料、酒及醋

注释：

一、本章不包括：

(一)本章的产品(税目22.09的货品除外)经配制后，用于烹饪而不适于作为饮料的制品(通常归入税目21.03)；

(二)海水(税目25.01)；

(三)蒸馏水、导电水及类似的纯净水(税目28.53)；

(四)按重量计浓度超过10%的醋酸(税目29.15)；

(五)税目30.03或30.04的药品；

(六)芳香料制品及盥洗品(第三十三章)。

二、本章及第二十章和第二十一章所称"按容量计酒精浓度"，应是温度在20℃时测得的浓度。

三、税目22.02所称"无酒精饮料"，是指按容量计酒精浓度不超过0.5%的饮料。含酒精饮料应分别归入税目22.03至22.06或税目22.08。

子目注释：

子目2204.10所称"汽酒"，是指温度在20℃时装在密封容器中超过大气压力3巴及以上的酒。

税则号列	货品名称〔CIQ扩展编码及品名－T2表示见附表2〕	最惠(%)	暂定税率	普通	增值/消费	出口退税	计量单位	监管条件	检验检疫	特殊证件对美关税
22.01	**未加糖或其他甜物质及未加味的水，包括天然或人造矿泉水及汽水；冰及雪：**									
	-矿泉水及汽水：									
2201.1010	---矿泉水〔999〕	5		90	13/	0	升/千克	AB	RS	/35
2201.1020	---汽水〔101〕	5		90	13/	13	升/千克	AB	RS	/30
	-其他：									
	---天然水：									
2201.9011	----已包装〔999〕	5		30	13/	0	千升/千克	AB	RS	/30
2201.9019	----其他〔999〕	5		30	13/	0	千升/千克			/30
2201.9090	---其他〔T2〕	5		30	13/	0	千升/千克	AB	RS	/30
22.02	**加味、加糖或其他甜物质的水，包括矿泉水及汽水，其他无酒精饮料，但不包括税目20.09的水果汁或蔬菜汁：**									
2202.1000	-加味、加糖或其他甜物质的水，包括矿泉水及汽水									
2202.1000 10	含濒危动植物成分的加味、加糖或其他甜物质的水(包括矿泉水及汽水)〔T2〕	5		100	13/	0	升/千克	ABEF	RS	/35
2202.1000 90	其他加味、加糖或其他甜物质的水(包括矿泉水及汽水)〔T2〕	5		100	13/	13	升/千克	AB	RS	/35
	-其他：									
2202.9100	--无醇啤酒									
2202.9100 11	含濒危动植物成份散装无醇啤酒〔999〕	5		100	13/	0	升/千克	ABEF	RS	/35
2202.9100 19	其他散装无醇啤酒〔999〕	5		100	13/	13	升/千克	AB	RS	/35
2202.9100 91	含濒危动植物成份其他包装无醇啤酒〔999〕	5		100	13/	0	升/千克	ABEF	RS	/35
2202.9100 99	其他包装无醇啤酒〔999〕	5		100	13/	13	升/千克	AB	RS	/35
2202.9900	--其他									
2202.9900 11	其他含濒危动植物成份散装无酒精饮料(不包括品目20.09的水果汁或蔬菜汁)〔101碳酸饮料，102含乳饮料，103植物蛋白饮料，104茶饮料，105运动饮料，106其他软饮料，107未列出的其他饮料、冷冻饮品、咖啡、果冻，108具有保健食品批准文号，109植物饮料，110乳酸菌饮料〕	5		100	13/	0	升/千克	ABEF	RS	/35

Chapter 22
Beverages, spirits and vinegar

Notes:

1. This Chapter does not cover:
   (a) Products of this Chapter (other than those of heading No. 22.09) prepared for culinary purposes and thereby rendered unsuitable for consumption as beverages (generally heading No. 21.03);
   (b) Sea water (heading No. 25.01);
   (c) Distilled or conductivity water or water of similar purity (heading No. 28.53);
   (d) Acetic acid of a concentration exceeding 10% by weight of acetic acid (heading No. 29.15);
   (e) Medicaments of heading No. 30.03 or 30.04; or
   (f) Perfumery or toilet preparations (Chapter 33).
2. For the purposes of this Chapter and of Chapter 20 and 21, the "alcoholic strength by volume" shall be determined at a temperature of 20℃.
3. For the purposes of heading No. 22.02, the term "non-alcoholic beverages" means beverages of an alcoholic strength by volume not exceeding 0.5% vol. Alcoholic beverages are classified in headings No. 22.03 to 22.06 or heading No. 22.08 as appropriate.

Subheading Note:

For the purposes of subheading No. 2204.10, the expression "sparkling wine" means wine which, when kept at a temperature of 20℃ in closed containers, has an excess pressure of not less than 3 bars.

协定税率 %										特惠税率 %			
亚太5国	东/冰/格	巴基斯坦	韩国	瑞士	哥达	秘鲁	澳大利亚	新西/坡/智	港/澳/台	亚太2国	老/柬/缅	36/3/1	Article Description
													Waters, including natural or artificial mineral waters and aerated waters, not containing added sugar or other sweetening matter or flavoured; ice and snow:
													-Mineral waters and aerated waters:
	0/0/0	20	14	5	0	0	0	0/0/0	0/0/			0/0/0	---Mineral waters
	0/0/0	18	12	5	0	0	0	0/0/0	0/0/			0/0/0	---Aerated waters
													-Other:
													---Natural waters:
	0/0/0	4.5	4	0	0	0	0	0/0/0	0/0/				----Packaged
	0/0/0	4.5	4	0	0	0	0	0/0/0	0/0/				----Other
	0/0/0	4.5	4	0	0	0	0	0/0/0	0/0/			0/0/	---Other
													Waters, including mineral waters and aerated waters, containing added sugar or other sweetening matter or flavoured, and other non-alcoholic beverages, not including fruit or vegetable juices of heading No. 20.09:
													-Waters, including mineral waters and aerated waters, containing added sugar or other sweetening matter or flavoured
	0/0/0	0	14	5	0	0	0	0/0/0	0/0/			0/0/	Waters, containing added sugar or other sweetening matter or flavoured of endangered animals and plant (including mineral waters and aerated water)
	0/0/0	0	14	5	0	0	0	0/0/0	0/0/			0/0/	Other waters, containing added sugan or other sweetening matter or flavoured(including mineral waters and aerated waters)
													-Other:
													--Non-alcoholic beer
4.2	0/0/0	29.5	24.5	5	0	0	0	0/0/0	0/0/			0/0/0	Non alcoholic bulk beer containing endangered animal and plant ingredients
4.2	0/0/0	29.5	24.5	5	0	0	0	0/0/0	0/0/			0/0/0	Other Non alcoholic bulk beer
4.2	0/0/0	29.5	24.5	5	0	0	0	0/0/0	0/0/			0/0/0	Non alcoholic beer containing endangered animal and plant ingredients, in other package
4.2	0/0/0	29.5	24.5	5	0	0	0	0/0/0	0/0/			0/0/0	Other non alcoholic bulk beverages containing endangered animal and plant ingredients, excluding the fruit and vebatable juice of heading No.2009
													--Ohter
4.2	0/0/0	29.5	24.5	5	0	0	0	0/0/0	0/0/			0/0/0	Other non alcoholic bulk beverages , excluding the fruit and vebatable juice of heading No.2009

税则号列	货品名称〔CIQ扩展编码及品名—T2表示见附表2〕	最惠(%)	暂定税率	普通	增值/消费	出口退税	计量单位	监管条件	检验检疫	特殊证件对美关税
2202.9900 19	其他散装无酒精饮料(不包括品目2009的水果汁或蔬菜汁)[999保健食品,101碳酸饮料,102含乳饮料,103植物蛋白饮料,104茶饮料,105运动饮料,106其他软饮料,107未列出的其他饮料、冷冻饮品、咖啡、果冻,108植物饮料,109乳酸菌饮料]	5		100	13/	13	升/千克	AB	RS	/35
2202.9900 91	其他含濒危动植物成份其他包装无酒精饮料(不包括品目20.09的水果汁或蔬菜汁)[101碳酸饮料,102含乳饮料,103植物蛋白饮料,104茶饮料,105运动饮料,106其他软饮料,107未列出的其他饮料、冷冻饮品、咖啡、果冻,108具有保健食品批准文号,109植物饮料,110乳酸菌饮料]	5		100	13/	0	升/千克	ABEF	RS	/35
2202.9900 99	其他包装无酒精饮料(不包括品目2009的水果汁或蔬菜汁)[T2]	5		100	13/	13	升/千克	AB	RS	/35
22.03	**麦芽酿造的啤酒:**									
2203.0000	麦芽酿造的啤酒〔999〕	T3		T3	13/①	13	升/千克	AB	RS	/25
22.04	**鲜葡萄酿造的酒,包括加酒精的;税目20.09以外的酿酒葡萄汁:**									
2204.1000	-汽酒〔999〕	14		180	13/10	13	升/千克	AB	RS	/54
	-其他酒;加酒精抑制发酵的酿酒葡萄汁:									
2204.2100	--装入2升及以下容器的〔999〕	14		180	13/10	13	升/千克	AB	RS	/54
2204.2200	--装入2升以上但不超过10升容器的〔101葡萄酒,102未发酵葡萄酒,103其他原酒〕	20		180	13/10	13	升/千克	AB	RS	/45
2204.2900	--其他〔101葡萄酒,102未发酵葡萄酒,103其他原酒〕	20		180	13/10	13	升/千克	AB	RS	/60
2204.3000	-其他酿酒葡萄汁〔101未发酵葡萄酒,102其他原酒,301需申报仅用于工业用途不用于食品添加剂无检疫要求的化学品〕	30		90	13/10	13	升/千克	AB	RS	/55
22.05	**味美思酒及其他加植物或香料的用鲜葡萄酿造的酒:**									
2205.1000	-装入2升及以下容器的〔101发酵酒配制酒,102未列出的其他酒〕	65	14	180	13/10	13	升/千克	AB	RS	/39
2205.9000	-其他〔102未列出的其他酒〕	65		180	13/10	13	升/千克	AB	RS	/75
22.06	**其他发酵饮料(例如,苹果酒、梨酒、蜂蜜酒、清酒);其他品目未列名的发酵饮料的混合物及发酵饮料与无酒精饮料的混合物:**									
2206.0010	---黄酒〔999〕	40		180	13/0.2495元/升	13	升/千克	AB	RS	/50
2206.0090	---其他〔101含乳饮料,102未列出的其他饮料、冷冻饮品、咖啡、果冻,103果酒,104清酒,105其他发酵酒,106发酵酒配制酒〕	40		180	13/10	13	升/千克	AB	RS	/65
22.07	**未改性乙醇,按容量计酒精浓度在80%及以上;任何浓度的改性乙醇及其他酒精:**									
2207.1000	-未改性乙醇,按容量计酒精浓度在80%及以上〔101食用酒精,102其他原酒,301易燃液体,需申报仅用于工业用途不用于食品添加剂无检疫要求,302属于危险化学品的食品添加剂〕	40		100	13/	13	升/千克	ABG	MRNS	/65
2207.2000	-任何浓度的改性乙醇及其他酒精									
2207.2000 10	任何浓度的改性乙醇[301属于危险化学品的食品添加剂,302无检疫要求食品添加剂,303一般化学品,需申报仅用于工业用途不用于食品添加剂无检疫要求,304易燃液体,需申报仅用于工业用途不用于食品添加剂无检疫要求]	30		80	13/	0	升/千克	ABG	MRNS	/70
2207.2000 90	任何浓度的其他酒精[101食用酒精,102其他原酒,301属于危险化学品的食品添加剂,302无检疫要求食品添加剂,303一般化学品,需申报仅用于工业用途不用于食品添加剂无检疫要求,304易燃液体,需申报仅用于工业用途不用于食品添加剂无检疫要求]	30		80	13/	0	升/千克	ABG	MRNS	/70
22.08	**未改性乙醇,按容量计酒精浓度在80%以下;蒸馏酒、利口酒及其他酒精饮料:**									
2208.2000	-蒸馏葡萄酒制得的烈性酒									
2208.2000 10	装入200升及以上容器的蒸馏葡萄酒制得的烈性酒〔101白兰地,102其他蒸馏酒〕	10	5	180	13/②	13	升/千克	AB	RS	/30
2208.2000 90	其他蒸馏葡萄酒制得的烈性酒〔101白兰地,102其他蒸馏酒〕	10	5	180	13/②	13	升/千克	AB	RS	/30
2208.3000	-威士忌酒〔999〕	10	5	180	13/②	13	升/千克	AB	RS	/30

① 进口完税价格≥0.3745美元/升的麦芽酿造啤酒,税率为0.253元/升;进口完税价格<0.3745美元/升的麦芽酿造啤酒,税率为0.2227元/升。

② 消费税:从价20%,从量0.912元每升。

协定税率 %										特惠税率 %			Article Description
亚太5国	东/冰/格	巴基斯坦	韩国	瑞士	哥达	秘鲁	澳大利亚	新西/坡/智	港/澳/台	亚太2国	老/柬/缅	36/3/1	
4.2	0/0/0	29.5	24.5	5	0	0	0	0/0/0	0/0/			0/0/0	Other non alcoholic bulk beverages, excluding the fruit and vebatable juice of heading No.2009
4.2	0/0/0	29.5	24.5	5	0	0	0	0/0/0	0/0/			0/0/0	Other non alcoholic beverages containing endangered animal and plant ingredients in other package, excluding the fruit and vebatable juice of heading No.2009
4.2	0/0/0	29.5	24.5	5	0	0	0	0/0/0	0/0/			0/0/0	Other non alcoholic beverages in other package, excluding the fruit and vebatable juice of heading No.2009
													Beer made from malt:
												0/0/0	Beer made from malt
													Wine of fresh grapes, including fortified wines; grape must other than that of heading No. 20.09:
	0/0/0	11.2	5.6	4.2	0	0	0	0/0/0	0/0/			0/0/	-Sparkling wine
													-Other wine; grape must with fermentation prevented or arrested by the addition of alcohol:
	0/0/0	11.2	5.6	4.2	0	3.7	0	0/0/0	0/0/			0/0/	--In containers holding 2L or less
	0/0/0		12	6	0	5.3	0	0/0/0	0/0/			0/0/	--In containers holding more than 2L but not more than 10L
	0/0/0		12	6	0	5.3	0	0/0/0	0/0/			0/0/	--Other
	0/0/12		21		0	2.5	0	0/0/0	0/0/				-Other grape must
													Vermouth and other wine of fresh grapes flavoured with plants or aromatic substances:
	0//0		45.5		0	5.4	0	0/0/0	0/0/				-In containers holding 2L or less
	0//0		45.5		0	5.4	0	0/0/0	0/0/				-Other
													Other fermented beverages (for example, cider, perry, mead); mixtures of fermented beverages and mixtures of fermented beverages and non-alcoholic beverages, not elsewhere specified or included:
	0/0/0		28		0	0	0	0/0/0	0/0/		//	0/0/	---Yellow rice wine
	0/0/0		28		0	0	0	0/0/0	0/0/			0/0/	---Other
													Undenatured ethyl alcohol of an alcoholic strength by volume of 80% vol or higher; ethyl alcohol and other spirits, denatured, of any strength:
	0/0/0	0	28		0	0	0	0/0/0	0/0/			0/0/	-Undenatured ethyl alcohol of an alcoholic strength by volume of 80% vol or higher
													-Ethyl alcohol and other spirits, denatured, of any strength
	0/0/0	0	21		0	0	0	0/0/0	0/0/			0/0/	Ethyl alcohol, denatured of any strength
	0/0/0	0	21		0	0	0	0/0/0	0/0/			0/0/	Other spirits, of any strength
													Undenatured ethyl alcohol of an alcoholic strength by volume of less than 80% vol; spirits, liqueurs and other spirituous beverages:
													-Spirits obtained by distilling grape wine or grape marc
	0/0/0	5	4	0	0	0	0	0/0/0	0/0/			0/0/0	In more than 200 litres and containers of alcohol distillation wine
	0/0/0	5	4	0	0	0	0	0/0/0	0/0/			0/0/0	Other wine of liquor distillation
	0/0/0	5	4	0	0	0	0	0/0/0	0/0/			0/0/0	-Whiskies

税则号列		货品名称〔CIQ扩展编码及品名－T2表示见附表2〕	最惠(%)	暂定税率	普通	增值/消费	出口退税	计量单位	监管条件	检验检疫	特殊证件对美关税
2208.4000		-朗姆酒及蒸馏已发酵甘蔗产品制得的其他烈性酒〔101 朗姆酒，102 其他蒸馏酒〕	10		180	13/①	13	升/千克	AB	RS	/40
2208.5000		-杜松子酒〔999〕	10		180	13/①	13	升/千克	AB	RS	/35
2208.6000		-伏特加酒〔999〕	10		180	13/①	13	升/千克	AB	RS	/40
2208.7000		-利口酒及柯迪尔酒〔999〕	10		180	13/①	13	升/千克	AB	RS	/35
		-其他：									
2208.9010		---龙舌兰酒									
2208.9010	10	濒危龙舌兰酒〔999〕	10		180	13/①	0	升/千克	ABFE	RS	/35
2208.9010	90	其他龙兰舌酒〔999〕	10		180	13/①	13	升/千克	AB	RS	/35
2208.9020		---白酒〔999〕	10		180	13/①	13	升/千克	AB	RS	/35
2208.9090		---其他									
2208.9090	01	酒精浓度在80%以下的未改性乙醇〔101 食用酒精，102 其他原酒，301 属于危险化学品的食品添加剂，302 无检疫要求食品添加剂，303 一般化学品，需申报仅用于工业用途不用于食品添加剂无检疫要求，304 易燃液体，需申报仅用于工业用途不用于食品添加剂无检疫要求〕	10		180	13/	13	升/千克	AB	RS	/35
2208.9090	21	含濒危野生动植物成分的薯类蒸馏酒〔101 中国白酒，102 其他蒸馏酒，103 蒸馏酒配制酒，104 未列出的其他酒，105 具有保健食品批准文号〕	10		180	13/①	0	升/千克	ABEF	RS	/35
2208.9090	29	其他薯类蒸馏酒〔101 中国白酒，102 其他蒸馏酒，103 蒸馏酒配制酒，104 未列出的其他酒〕	10		180	13/①	13	升/千克	AB	RS	/35
2208.9090	91	含濒危野生动植物成分的其他蒸馏酒及酒精饮料〔101 中药酒，102 其他蒸馏酒，103 蒸馏酒配制酒，104 其他蒸馏配制酒，105 未列出的其他酒，106 具有保健食品批准文号〕	10		180	13/①	0	升/千克	ABEF	RS	/35
2208.9090	99	其他蒸馏酒及酒精饮料〔101 其他蒸馏酒，102 蒸馏酒配制酒，103 其他蒸馏配制酒，104 未列出的其他酒，105 按体积比乙醇≥24%，每一容器盛装＞5L 的〕	10		180	13/①	13	升/千克	AB	MRNS	/35
22.09		**醋及用醋酸制得的醋代用品：**									
2209.0000		醋及用醋酸制得的醋代用品〔101 配制食醋，102 其他食醋，103 未列出的其他调味品，104 具有保健食品批准文号〕	5		70	13/	13	升/千克	AB	RS	/30

① 消费税：从价 20%，从量 0.912 元每升。

协定税率 %										特惠税率 %			
亚太5国	东/冰/格	巴基斯坦	韩国	瑞士	哥达	秘鲁	澳大利亚	新西/坡/智	港/澳/台	亚太2国	老/柬/缅	36/3/1	Article Description
	0/0/4	5	4	0	0	0	0	0/0/0	0/0/			0/0/0	-Rum and other spirit obtained by distilling fermented sugarcane products
	0//4	4.5	4	0	0	0	0	0/0/0	0/0/			0/0/0	-Gin and geneva
8.8	0//0	4.5	4	0	0	0	0	0/0/0	0/0/			0/0/0	-Vodka
8.8	0/0/0	4.5	4	0	0	0	0	0/0/0	0/0/			0/0/0	-Liqueurs and cordials
													-Other:
													---Tequila,Mezcal
8.8	0/0/4	4.5	4	0	0	0	0	0/0/0	0/0/			0/0/	Endangered Tequila
8.8	0/0/4	4.5	4	0	0	0	0	0/0/0	0/0/			0/0/	Other Tequila
8.8	0/0/4	4.5	4	0	0	0	0	0/0/0	0/0/			0/0/0	---Chinese distilled spirits
													---Other
8.8	0/0/0	5	7	0	0	0	0	0/0/0	0/0/			0/0/0	Undenatured ethyl alcohol of an alcoholic strength by volume of less than 80% vol
8.8	0/0/0	5	7	0	0	0	0	0/0/0	0/0/			0/0/0	Potato spirits, endangered wild animals and plants
8.8	0/0/0	5	7	0	0	0	0	0/0/0	0/0/			0/0/0	Other spirits by distilling potatoes
8.8	0/0/0	5	7	0	0	0	0	0/0/0	0/0/			0/0/0	Spirits and spirituous beverages, containins endangered wild animals and plants
8.8	0/0/0	5	7	0	0	0	0	0/0/0	0/0/			0/0/0	Other spirits and spirituous beverages
													Vinegar and substitutes for vinegar obtained from acetic acid:
	0/0/0		12	5	0	0	0	0/0/0	0/0/			0/0/	Vinegar and substitutes for vinegar obtained from acetic acid

第二十三章
食品工业的残渣及废料；配制的动物饲料

注释：

税目23.09包括其他税目未列号的配制动物饲料，这些饲料是由动、植物原料加工而成的，并且已改变了原料的基本特性，但加工过程中的植物废料、植物残渣及副产品除外。

子目注释：

子目2306.41所称“低芥子酸油菜子”，是指第十二章子目注释一所定义的油菜子。

税则号列	货品名称〔CIQ扩展编码及品名－T2表示见附表2〕	最惠(%)	暂定税率	普通	增值/消费	出口退税	计量单位	监管条件	检验检疫	特殊证件对美关税
23.01	**不适于供人食用的肉、杂碎、鱼、甲壳动物、软体动物或其他水生无脊椎动物的渣粉及团粒；油渣：**									
	-肉、杂碎的渣粉及团粒；油渣：									
	---肉骨粉：									
2301.1011	----含牛羊成分的〔101 饲料用牛肉粉(肉成分67%以上)，102 饲料用牛肉骨粉，103 饲料用牛血粉，104 饲料用羊肉粉(肉成分67%以上)，105 饲料用羊肉骨粉，106 饲料用羊血粉，107 饲料用混合型饲养偶蹄动物肉骨粉，108 饲料用野生偶蹄猪、牛、羊肉骨粉，109 饲料用野生偶蹄猪、牛、羊血粉〕	2		11	9/	13	千克	AB	MPQ	/12
2301.1019	----其他〔T2〕	2		11	9/	13	千克	AB	MPQ	/12
2301.1020	---油渣〔101 工业用其他动物油脂，102 饲料用动物油渣，103 其他饲用加工植物蛋白〕	5		50	9/	0	千克	AB	PQ	/15
2301.1090	---其他〔999〕	5		30	9/	0	千克	AB	PQ	/15
	-鱼、甲壳动物、软体动物或其他水生无脊椎动物的渣粉及团粒：									
2301.2010	---饲料用鱼粉〔101 饲料用红鱼粉，102 饲料用白鱼粉〕	2		11	0/	0	千克	AB	MPQ	/
2301.2090	---其他〔999〕	5		30	0/	0	千克	AB	PQ	/30
23.02	**谷物或豆类植物在筛、碾或其他加工过程中所产生的糠、麸及其他残渣，不论是否制成团粒：**									
2302.1000	-玉米的〔999〕	5		30	0/	0	千克	AB	MPQ	/25
2302.3000	-小麦的〔101 饲用麦麸，102 其他饲用加工植物蛋白〕	3		30	0/	0	千克	AB	PQ	/13
2302.4000	-其他谷物的〔101 饲用米糠，102 其他饲用加工植物蛋白〕	5		30	0/	0	千克	AB	PQ	/15
2302.5000	-豆类植物的〔999〕	5		30	9/	0	千克	AB	PQ	/15
23.03	**制造淀粉过程中的残渣及类似的残渣，甜菜渣、甘蔗渣及制糖过程中的其他残渣，酿造及蒸馏过程中的糟粕及残渣，不论是否制成团粒：**									
2303.1000	-制造淀粉过程中的残渣及类似的残渣〔101 其他饲用加工植物蛋白，木薯渣除外，102 饲用植物颗粒和植物粉，103 其他植物饲料，104 木薯渣〕	5		30	9/	9,13	千克	AB	PQ	/15
2303.2000	-甜菜渣、甘蔗渣及制糖过程中的其他残渣〔101 饲用甜菜粕，102 其他饲用加工植物蛋白，103 甘蔗渣(栽培介质)〕	5		30	9/	0,6	千克	AB	PQ	/15
2303.3000	-酿造及蒸馏过程中的糟粕及残渣									
2303.3000 11	干玉米酒糟〔999〕	5		30	0/	0	千克	7AB	PQ	/30
2303.3000 19	其他玉米酒糟〔999〕	5		30	9/	0	千克	7AB	PQ	/30
2303.3000 90	其他酿造及蒸馏过程中的糟粕及残渣〔999〕	5		30	9/	0	千克	AB	PQ	/30
23.04	**提炼豆油所得的油渣饼及其他固体残渣，不论是否碾磨或制成团粒：**									
2304.0010	---油渣饼〔999〕	5		30	9/	0	千克	7AB	PNQ	/
2304.0090	---其他〔999〕	5		30	9/	0	千克	7AB	PNQ	/30
23.05	**提炼花生油所得的油渣饼及其他固体残渣，不论是否碾磨或制成团粒：**									
2305.0000	花生饼及类似油渣〔999〕	5	5	30	0/	0	千克	AB	PNQ	/
23.06	**税目23.04或23.05以外的提炼植物油脂所得的油渣饼及其他固体残渣，不论是否碾磨或制成团粒：**									
2306.1000	-棉子的〔999〕	5	0	30	0/	9	千克	AB	PNQ	/
2306.2000	-亚麻子的〔999〕	5	0	30	0/	9	千克	AB	PNQ	/
2306.3000	-葵花子的〔999〕	5	0	30	0/	9	千克	AB	PNQ	/

Chapter 23
Residues and waste from the food industries; prepared animal fodder

Note:

Heading No. 23.09 includes products of a kind used in animal feeding not elsewhere specified or included, obtained by processing vegetable or animal materials to such an extent that they have lost the essential characteristics of the original material, other than vegetable waste, vegetable residues and by-products of such processing.

Subheading Note:

For the purposes of subheading No. 2306.41, the expression "low erucic acid rape or colza seeds" means seeds as defined in Subheading Note 1 to Chapter 12.

协定税率 %										特惠税率 %			
亚太5国	东/冰/格	巴基斯坦	韩国	瑞士	哥达	秘鲁	澳大利亚	新西/坡/智	港/澳/台	亚太2国	老/柬/缅	36/3/1	Article Description
													Flours, meals and pellets, of meat or meat offal, of fish or of crustaceans, molluscs or other aquatic invertebrates, unfit for human consumption; greaves:
													-Flours, meals and pellets, of meat or meat offal; greaves:
													---Flours and meals, of meat bones:
	0/0/0	0	0	0	0	0	0	0//0	0/0/			0/0/0	----Of bovine and sheep
	0/0/0	0	0	0	0	0	0	0//0	0/0/			0/0/0	----Other
	0/0/0	0	0	0	0	0	0	0//0	0/0/			0/0/0	---Greaves
	0/0/0	0	0	0	0	0	0	0//0	0/0/			0/0/0	---Other
													-Flours, meals and pellets, of fish or of crustaceans, molluscs or other aquatic invertebrates:
0	0/0/0	0	0	0	0	0	0	0//0	0/0/			0/0/0	---Flours and meals of fish, of a kind used in animal feeding
0	0/0/0	0	0	0	0	0	0	0//0	0/0/			0/0/0	---Other
													Bran, sharps and other residues, whether or not in the form of pellets, derived from the sifting, milling or other working of cereals or of leguminous plants:
	0/0/2	0	0	0	0	0	0	0//0	0/0/			0/0/0	-Of maize (corn)
	0/0/1.2	0	0	0	0	0	0	0//0	0/0/			0/0/0	-Of wheat
	0/0/2	0	0	0	0	0	0	0//0	0/0/			0/0/0	-Of other cereals
	0/0/2	0	0	0	0	0	0	0//0	0/0/			0/0/0	-Of leguminous plants
													Residues of starch manufacture and similar residues, beet-pulp, bagasses and other waste of sugar manufacture, brewing or distilling dregs and waste, whether or not in the form of pellets:
	0/0/2	0	0	0	0	0	0	0//0	0/0/			0/0/0	-Residues of starch manufacture and similar residues
	0/0/2	0	0	0	0	0	0	0//0	0/0/			0/0/0	-Beet-pulp, bagasses and other waste of sugar manufacture
													-Brewing or distilling dregs and waste
	0/0/2	0	0	0	0	0	0	0//0	0/0/			0/0/0	Corn distillers solubles
	0/0/2	0	0	0	0	0	0	0//0	0/0/			0/0/0	Corn distillers solubles
	0/0/2	0	0	0	0	0	0	0//0	0/0/			0/0/0	Other brewing or distilling dregs and waste
													Oil-cake and other solid residues, whether or not ground or in the form of pellets, resulting from the extraction of soyabean oil:
0	0/0/2	0	0	0	0	0	0	0//0	0/0/			0/0/0	---Oil-cake
0	0/0/2	0	0	0	0	0	0	0//0	0/0/			0/0/0	---Other
													Oil-cake and other solid residues, whether or not ground or in the form of pellets, resulting from the extraction of groundnut oil:
	0/0/2	0	0	0	0	0	0	0//0	0/0/			0/0/0	Oil-cake and other solid residues, whether or not ground or in the form of pellets, resulting from the extraction of groundnut oil
													Oil-Cake and other solid residues, whether or not ground or in the form of pellets, resulting from the extraction of vegetable fats or oils, other than those of heading No. 23.04 or 23.05:
	0/0/2	0	0	0	0	0	0	0//0	0/0/			0/0/0	-Of cotton seeds
	0/0/2	0	0	0	0	0	0	0//0	0/0/		0//	0/0/0	-Of linseed
	0/0/2	0	0	0	0	0	0	0//0	0/0/			0/0/0	-Of sunflower seeds

税则号列	货品名称〔CIQ扩展编码及品名－T2表示见附表2〕	最惠(%)	暂定税率	普通	增值/消费	出口退税	计量单位	监管条件	检验检疫	特殊证件对美关税
	-油菜子的：									
2306.4100	--低芥子酸的〔999〕	5	0	30	0/	9	千克	AB	PNQ	/
2306.4900	--其他〔999〕	5	0	30	0/	9	千克	AB	PNQ	/
2306.5000	-椰子或干椰肉的〔999〕	5	0	30	9/	9	千克	AB	PNQ	/10
2306.6000	-棕榈果或棕榈仁的									
2306.6000 10	濒危棕榈果或濒危棕榈仁油渣饼及固体残渣(税目23.04或23.05以外提炼植物油脂所得的)〔999〕	5	0	30	9/	0	千克	ABEF	PNQ	/10
2306.6000 90	其他棕榈果或其他棕榈仁油渣饼及固体残渣(税目23.04或23.05以外提炼植物油脂所得的)〔999〕	5	0	30	9/	9	千克	AB	PNQ	/10
2306.9000	-其他〔101 饲用芝麻饼、粕，102 其他饲用加工植物蛋白〕	5	0	30	9/	13,9,0	千克	AB	PNQ	/25
23.07	**葡萄酒渣；粗酒石：**									
2307.0000	葡萄酒渣；粗酒石〔999，301 需申报仅用于工业用途不用于食品添加剂无检疫要求的化学品〕	5		30	0/	0	千克	AB	RS	/15
23.08	**动物饲料用的其他税目未列名的植物原料、废料、残渣及副产品，不论是否制成团粒：**									
2308.0000	动物饲料用的其他税目未列名的植物原料、废料、残渣及副产品，不论是否制成团粒〔101 饲用苜蓿草，102 饲用燕麦草，103 其他饲草，104 饲用其他淀粉，105 饲用青贮，106 饲用植物颗粒和植物粉，107 其他植物饲料，108 辣椒粕，109 橄榄粕，110 榴莲粕，111 扁桃仁粕〕	5	0	35	9/	9,13,0	千克	AB	PQ	/10
23.09	**配制的动物饲料：**									
	-零售包装的狗食或猫食：									
2309.1010	---罐头〔999〕	15	4	90	9/	9	千克	AB	PQ	/39
2309.1090	---其他〔101 非罐装宠物食品，102 咀嚼物〕	15	4	90	9/	9	千克	AB	PQ	/29
	-其他：									
2309.9010	---制成的饲料添加剂〔101 含动物源性饲料添加剂，102 含植物源性饲料添加剂，103 其他饲料添加剂〕	5		14	13/	9,13	千克	AB	MPQ	/15
2309.9090	---其他〔101 饲料用乳粉、蛋粉、乳清粉，102 未列出的饲料用其他动物粉，103 添加剂预混合饲料，104 浓缩饲料，105 全价配合饲料，106 精料补充料，107 其他配制的动物饲料，108 其他宠物食品，109 饲用蛋粉〕	6.5	4	14	9/	13,9,0	千克	AB	MPQ	/14

协定税率 %										特惠税率 %			Article Description
亚太5国	东/冰/格	巴基斯坦	韩国	瑞士	哥达	秘鲁	澳大利亚	新西/坡/智	港/澳/台	亚太2国	老/柬/缅	36/3/1	
													-Of rape or colza seeds:
	0/0/2	0	0	0	0	0	0	0//0	0/0/			0/0/	--Of low erucic acid rape or colza seeds
	0/0/2	0	0	0	0	0	0	0//0	0/0/			0/0/	--Other
2.5	0/0/0	0	0	0	0	0	0	0//0	0/0/		/0/	0/0/0	-Of coconut or copra
													-Of palm nuts or kernels3
	0/0/0	0	0	0	0	0	0	0//0	0/0/		/0/	0/0/0	Endangered oil-cake and other solid residues of palm nuts or dernels (other than those of heading No. 23. 04 or 23. 05)
	0/0/0	0	0	0	0	0	0	0//0	0/0/		/0/	0/0/0	Other oil-cake and other solid residues of palm nuts or dernels(other than those of heading No. 23. 04 or 23. 05)
	0/0/2	0	0	0	0	0	0	0//0	0/0/		0//	0/0/0	-Other
													Wine lees; argol:
	0/0/0	0	0	0	0	0	0	0//0	0/0/			0/0/0	Wine lees; argol
													Vegetable materials and vegetable waste, vegetable residues and by-products, whether or not in the form of pellets, of a kind used in animal feeding, not elsewhere specified or included:
	0/0/0	0	0	0	0	0	0	0//0	0/0/			0/0/	Vegetable materials and vegetable waste, vegetable residues and by-products, whether or not in the form of pellets, of a kind used in animal feeding, not elsewhere specified or included
													Preparations of a kind used in animal feeding:
													-Dog or cat food, put up for retail sale:
	0/0/0	12	6	4.5	0	0	0	0/0/0	0/0/			0/0/	---In airtight containers
	0/0/0	12	6	4.5	0	0	0	0/0/0	0/0/			0/0/	---Other
													-Other:
2.5	0/0/0	0	0	0	0	0	0	0//0	0/0/			0/0/0	---Preparations for use in making the complete feeds or supplementary feeds
3.3	0/0/0	0	2.6	0	0	0	0	0//0	0/0/			0/0/0	---Other

第二十四章
烟草及烟草代用品的制品

注释：

本章不包括药用卷烟（第三十章）。

子目注释：

子目2403.11所称"水烟料"，是指由烟草和甘油混合而成用水烟筒吸用的烟草，不论是否含有芳香油及提取物、糖蜜或糖，也不论是否用水果调味，但供在水烟筒中吸用的非烟草产品除外。

税则号列		货品名称〔CIQ扩展编码及品名—T2表示见附表2〕	最惠(%)	暂定税率	普通	增值/消费	出口退税	计量单位	监管条件	检验检疫	特殊证件对美关税
24.01		**烟草；烟草废料：**									
		-未去梗的烟草：									
2401.1010		---烤烟〔999〕	10		70	13/	9,13	千克	7AB	PMQS	/35
2401.1090		---其他〔101香料烟，102白肋烟〕	10		70	13/	9	千克	7AB	PMQS	/35
		-部分或全部去梗的烟草：									
2401.2010		---烤烟〔999〕	10		70	13/	9,13	千克	7AB	PQS	/35
2401.2090		---其他〔101香料烟，102白肋烟〕	10		70	13/	13	千克	7AB	PQS	/35
2401.3000		-烟草废料〔999〕	10		70	13/	9,13	千克	AB7	PQS	/35
24.02		**烟草或烟草代用品制成的雪茄烟及卷烟：**									
2402.1000		-烟草制的雪茄烟〔999〕	25		180	13/36	0	千克/千支	7		/50
2402.2000		-烟草制的卷烟〔999〕	25		180	13/①	0	千克/千支	7		/50
2402.9000		-其他									
2402.9000	01	烟草代用品制的卷烟〔999〕	25		180	13/①	0	千克/千支	7		/50
2402.9000	09	烟草代用品制的雪茄烟〔999〕	25		180	13/36	0	千克/千支	7		/50
24.03		**其他烟草及烟草代用品的制品；"均化"或"再造"烟草；烟草精汁：**									
		-供吸用的烟草，不论是否含有任何比例的烟草代用品：									
2403.1100		--本章子目注释所述的水烟料〔999〕	57		180	13/30	13	千克	7AB	PQS	/82
2403.1900		--其他〔999〕	57		180	13/30	13	千克	7AB	PQS	/82
		-其他：									
2403.9100		--"均化"或"再造"烟草									
2403.9100	10	再造烟草〔999〕	57	40	180	13/30	13	千克	AB7	PQ	/65
2403.9100	90	均化烟草〔999〕	57		180	13/30	13	千克	AB7	PQ	/82
2403.9900		--其他									
2403.9900	10	烟草精汁〔999〕	57		180	13/	13	千克	7AB	MPNQS	/82
2403.9900	90	其他烟草及烟草代用品的制品〔101其他烟草及烟草代用品的制品，102烟用香精〕	57		180	13/30	13	千克	AB	PQS	/82

① 每标准条进口完税价格≥50元人民币，45%+150元/标准箱；每标准条进口完税价格＜50元人民币，30%+150元/标准箱。

Chapter 24
Tobacco and manufactured tobacco substitutes

Note:

This Chapter does not cover medicinal cigarettes (Chapter 30).

Subheading Note:

For the purposes of Subheading 2403. 11, the expression"water pipe tobacco"means tobacco intended for smoking in a water pipe and which consists of a mixture of tobacco and glycerol, whether or not containing aromatic oils and extracts, molasses or sugar, and whether or not flavoured with fruit. However, tobacco-free products intended for smoking in a water pipe are excluded from this Subheading

协定税率 %										特惠税率 %			
亚太5国	东/冰/格	巴基斯坦	韩国	瑞士	哥达	秘鲁	澳大利亚	新西/坡/智	港/澳/台	亚太2国	老/柬/缅	36/3/1	Article Description
													Unmanufactured tobacco; tobacco refuse:
													-Tobacco, not stemmed/stripped:
9.4	5//	9.4						0//0	0/0/				---Flue-cured
	5//							0//0	0/0/				---Other
													-Tobacco, partly or wholly stemmed/stripped:
	5//							0//0	0/0/				---Flue-cured
	5//							0//0	0/0/				---Other
	5//					0		0//0	0/0/			0/0/0	-Tobacco refuse
													Cigars, cheroots, cigarillos and cigarettes, of tobacco or of tobacco substitutes:
								0//0	0/0/				-Cigars, cheroots and cigarillos, containing tobacco
								0//0	0/0/				-Cigarettes containing tobacco
													-Other
								0//0	0/0/				Cigarettes containing tobacco substitutes
								0//0	0/0/				Cigars, cheroots and cigarillos, containing tobacco substitutes
													Other manufactured tobacco and manufactured tobacco substitutes; "homogenized" or "reconstituted" tobacco; tobacco extracts and essences:
													-Smoking tobacco, whether or not containing tobacco substitutes in any proportion:
50.2	50//	50						0//0	0/0/				--Water pipe tobacco specified in Subheading Note to this Chapter
50.2	50//	50						0//0	0/0/				--Other
													-Other:
													--"Homogenized" or "reconstituted" tobacco
	50//							0//0	0/0/				Reconstituted tobacco
	50//							0//0	0/0/				Homogenized tobacco
													--Other
	50//							0//0	0/0/				Tobacco extracts and essences
	50//							0//0	0/0/				Other manufactured tobacco and manufactured tobacco substitutes

第五类
矿　产　品

第二十五章
盐;硫磺;泥土及石料;石膏料、石灰及水泥

注释:

一、除条文及注释四另有规定的以外,本章各税目只包括原产状态的矿产品,或只经过洗涤(包括用化学物质清除杂质而未改变产品结构的)、破碎、磨碎、研粉、淘洗、筛分以及用浮选、磁选和其他机械物理方法(不包括结晶法)精选过的货品,但不得经过焙烧、煅烧、混合或超过税目所列的加工范围。

本章产品可含有添加的抗尘剂,但所加剂料并不使原产品改变其一般用途而适合于某些特殊用途。

二、本章不包括:

(一)升华硫磺、沉淀硫磺及胶态硫磺(税目28.02);

(二)土色料,按重量计三氧化二铁含量在70%及以上(税目28.21);

(三)第三十章的药品及其他产品;

(四)芳香料制品及化妆盥洗品(第三十三章);

(五)长方砌石、路缘石、扁平石(税目68.01)、镶嵌石或类似石料(税目68.02)及铺屋顶、饰墙面或防潮用的板石(税目68.03);

(六)宝石或半宝石(税目71.02或71.03);

(七)每颗重量不低于2.5克的氧化钠或氧化镁培养晶体(光学元件除外)(税目38.24);氯化钠或氧化镁制的光学元件(税目90.01);

(八)台球用粉块(税目95.04);或

(九)书写或绘画用粉笔及裁缝划粉(税目96.09)。

三、既可归入税目25.17又可归入本章其他税目的产品,应归入税目25.17。

四、税目25.30主要包括:未膨胀的蛭石、珍珠岩及绿泥石;不论是否煅烧或混合的土色料;天然云母氧化铁;海泡石(不论是否磨光成块);琥珀;模制后未经进一步加工的片、条、杆或类似形状的粘聚海泡石及粘聚琥珀;黑玉;菱锶矿(不论是否煅烧),但不包括氧化锶;破碎陶器;砖或混凝土的碎块。

税则号列		货品名称〔CIQ扩展编码及品名－T2表示见附表2〕	最惠(%)	暂定税率	普通	增值/消费	出口退税	计量单位	监管条件	检验检疫	特殊证件对美关税
25.01		**盐(包括精制盐及变性盐)及纯氯化钠,不论是否为水溶液,也不论是否添加抗结块剂或松散剂;海水:**									
		---盐:									
2501.0011		----食用盐〔101饲料用盐,102食盐〕	0		0	9/	9	千克	AB	RS	/25
2501.0019		----其他[T2]	0		0	13/	13	千克	AB	RS	/25
2501.0020		---纯氯化钠〔101矿物源性饲料添加剂,102其他盐〕	3		35	13/	13	千克			/18
2501.0030		---海水〔999〕	0		0	13/	0	千克			/10
25.02		**未焙烧的黄铁矿:**									
2502.0000		未焙烧的黄铁矿〔999〕	3	2	20	13/	0	千克			/32
25.03		**各种硫磺,但升华硫磺、沉淀硫磺及胶态硫磺除外:**									
2503.0000		各种硫磺,但升华硫磺、沉淀硫磺及胶态硫磺除外[T2]	3	1	17	13/	0	千克	AB	MRNS	/31
25.04		**天然石墨:**									
		-粉末或粉片:									
2504.1010		---粉片〔999〕	3	1	30	13/	0	千克			/16
		---其他:									
2504.1091		----球化石墨〔999〕	3		30	13/	13	千克			/33
2504.1099		----其他〔999〕	3		30	13/	0	千克			/28
2504.9000		-其他〔999〕	3		30	13/	0	千克			/33
25.05		**各种天然砂,不论是否着色,但第二十六章的含金属矿砂除外:**									
2505.1000		-硅砂及石英砂〔101栽培介质,102硅砂〕	3	1	40	13/	0	千克	48xy		/26
2505.9000		-其他									
2505.9000	10	标准砂(不论是否着色,第二十六章的金属矿砂除外)〔101栽培介质,102硅砂〕	3	1	40	13/	0	千克	4xy		/31
2505.9000	90	其他天然砂(不论是否着色,第二十六章的金属矿砂除外)〔101栽培介质,102硅砂〕	3	1	40	13/	0	千克	48xy		/31

SECTION Ⅴ
MINERAL PRODUCTS

Chapter 25
Salt; sulphur; earths and stone; plastering materials, lime and cement

Notes:

1. Except where their context or Note 4 to this Chapter otherwise requires, the headings of this Chapter cover only products which are in the crude state or which have been washed (even with chemical substances eliminating the impurities without changing the structure of the product), crushed, ground, powdered, levigated, sifted, screened, concentrated by flotation, magnetic separation or other mechanical or physical processes (except crystallization), but not products which have been roasted, calcined, obtained by mixing or subjected to processing beyond that mentioned in each heading.
   The products of this Chapter may contain an added antidusting agent, provided that such addition does not render the product particularly suitable for specific use rather than for general use.
2. This Chapter does not cover:
   (a) Sublimed sulphur, precipitated sulphur or colloidal sulphur (heading No. 28.02);
   (b) Earth colours containing 70% or more by weight of combined iron evaluated as Fe_2O_3 (heading No. 28.21);
   (c) Medicaments or other products of Chapter 30;
   (d) Perfumery, cosmetic or toilet preparations (Chapter 33);
   (e) Setts, curbstones or flagstones (heading No. 68.01); mosaic cubes or the like (heading No. 68.02); roofing, facing or damp course slates (heading No. 68.03);
   (f) Precious or semi-precious stones (heading No. 71.02 or 71.03);
   (g) Cultured crystals (other than optical elements) weighing not less than 2.5g each, of sodium chloride or of magnesium oxide, of heading No. 38.24; optical elements of sodium chloride or of magnesium oxide (heading No. 90.01);
   (h) Billiard chalks (heading No. 95.04); or
   (i) Writing or drawing chalks or tailors' chalks (heading No. 96.09).
3. Any products classifiable in heading No. 25.17 and any other heading of this Chapter are to be classified in heading No. 25.17.
4. Heading No. 25.30 applies, *inter alia*, to: vermiculite, perlite and chlorites, unexpanded; earth colours, whether or not calcined or mixed together; natural micaceous iron oxides; meerschaum (whether or not in polished pieces); amber; agglomerated meerschaum and agglomerated amber, in plates, rods, sticks or similar forms, not worked after moulding; jet; strontianite (whether or not calcined), other than strontium oxide; broken pieces of pottery, brick or concrete.

协定税率 %										特惠税率 %			Article Description
亚太5国	东/冰/格	巴基斯坦	韩国	瑞士	哥达	秘鲁	澳大利亚	新西/坡/智	港/澳/台	亚太2国	老/柬/缅	36/3/1	
													Salt (including table salt and denatured salt) and pure sodium chloride, whether or not in aqueous solution or containing added anticaking or free-flowing agents; sea water:
													---Salt:
												0/0/0	----Edible salt
												0/0/0	----Other
1.5	0/0/0	0	0	0	0	0	0	0//0	0/0/		0//	0/0/0	---Pure sodium chloride
												0/0/0	---Sea water
													Unroasted iron pyrites:
1.5	0/0/0	0	0	0	0	0	0	0//0	0/0/			0/0/0	Unrcasted iron pyrite
													Sulphur of all kinds, other than sublimed sulphur, precipitated sulphur and colloidal sulphur:
1.5	0/0/0	0	0	0	0	0	0	0//0	0/0/			0/0/	Sulphur of all kinds, other than sublimed sulphur, precipitated sulphur and colloidal sulphur
													Natural graphite:
													-In powder or in flakes:
1.5	0/0/0	0	0	0.9	0	0	0	0//0	0/0/			0/0/0	---In flakes
													---Other:
	0/0/0	0	0	0	0	0	0	0//0	0/0/			0/0/0	----Spheroidized graphite
1.5	0/0/0	0	0	0	0	0	0	0//0	0/0/			0/0/0	----Other
1.5	0/0/0	0	0	0	0	0	0	0//0	0/0/			0/0/0	-Other
													Natural sands of all kinds, whether or not coloured, other than metal-bearing sands of Chapter 26:
	0/0/0	0	0	0	0	0	0	0//0	0/0/			0/0/0	-Silica sands and quartz sands
													-Other
1.5	0/0/0	0	0	0	0	0	0	0//0	0/0/			0/0/0	Standard sands (whether or not coloured, other than metal-bearing sands of Chapter 26)
1.5	0/0/0	0	0	0	0	0	0	0//0	0/0/			0/0/0	Other natural sands of all kinds (whether or not coloured, other than metal-bearing sands of Chapter 26)

税则号列	货品名称〔CIQ 扩展编码及品名－T2 表示见附表 2〕	最惠(%)	暂定税率	普通	增值/消费	出口退税	计量单位	监管条件	检验检疫	特殊证件对美关税
25.06	**石英(天然砂除外);石英岩,不论是否粗加修整或仅用锯或其他方法切割成矩形(包括正方形)的板、块:**									
2506.1000	-石英〔T2〕	3	1	40	13/	0	千克			/16
2506.2000	-石英岩〔101 栽培介质,102 石英岩〕	3	1	40	13/	0	千克			/31
25.07	**高岭土及类似土,不论是否煅烧:**									
	高岭土及类似土,不论是否煅烧:									
2507.0010	---高岭土〔999〕	3	1	50	13/	0	千克			/16
2507.0090	---其他〔999〕	3	1	50	13/	0	千克			/31
25.08	**其他黏土(不包括税目 68.06 的膨胀黏土)、红柱石、蓝晶石及硅线石,不论是否煅烧;富铝红柱石;火泥及第纳斯土:**									
2508.1000	-膨润土〔101 无检疫要求食品添加剂,102 膨润土〕	3		50	13/	0	千克			/18
2508.3000	-耐火黏土〔999〕	3	1	20	13/	0	千克	4xy		/26
2508.4000	-其他黏土〔102〕	3		50	13/	0	千克			/28
2508.5000	-红柱石、蓝晶石及硅线石〔999〕	3		40	13/	0	千克			/18
2508.6000	-富铝红柱石〔999〕	3		40	13/	0	千克			/18
2508.7000	-火泥及第纳斯土〔998 火泥,999 第纳斯土〕	3		20	13/	0	千克			/8
25.09	白垩:									
2509.0000	白垩〔999〕	3		45	13/	0	千克			/33
25.10	**天然磷酸钙、天然磷酸铝钙及磷酸盐白垩:**									
	-未碾磨:									
2510.1010	---磷灰石〔999〕	3	0	11	13/	0	千克	4xy		/5
2510.1090	---其他〔999〕	3		20	13/	0	千克	4xy		/8
	-已碾磨:									
2510.2010	---磷灰石〔999〕	3	0	11	13/	0	千克	4xy		/30
2510.2090	---其他〔999〕	3		20	13/	0	千克	4xy		/8
25.11	**天然硫酸钡(重晶石);天然碳酸钡(毒重石),不论是否煅烧,但税目 28.16 的氧化钡除外:**									
2511.1000	-天然硫酸钡(重晶石)〔101 重晶石块,102 重晶石粉〕	3		45	13/	0	千克			/18
2511.2000	-天然碳酸钡(毒重石)〔999〕	3		45	13/	0	千克			/8
25.12	**硅质化石粗粉(例如各种硅藻土)及类似的硅质土,不论是否煅烧,其表观比重不超过 1:**									
2512.0010	---硅藻土〔101 无检疫要求食品添加剂,102 硅藻土〕	3		40	13/	0	千克	A	R	/18
2512.0090	---其他〔999〕	3		40	13/	0	千克			/33
25.13	**浮石;刚玉岩;天然刚玉砂;天然石榴石及其他天然磨料,不论是否热处理:**									
2513.1000	-浮石〔999〕	3		35	13/	0	千克			/33
2513.2000	-刚玉岩、天然刚玉砂、天然石榴石及其他天然磨料〔101 刚玉岩,102 天然刚玉砂,103 天然石榴石〕	3		17	13/	0	千克			/18
25.14	**板岩,不论是否粗加修整或仅用锯或其他方法切割成矩形(包括正方形)的板、块:**									
2514.0000	板岩,不论是否粗加修整或仅用锯或其他方法切割成矩形(包括正方形)的板、块〔999〕	3		50	13/	0	千克			/8
25.15	**大理石、石灰华及其他石灰质碑用或建筑用石,表观比重为 2.5 及以上,蜡石,不论是否粗加修整或仅用锯或其他方法切割成矩形(包括正方形)的板、块:**									
	-大理石及石灰华:									
2515.1100	--原状或粗加修整〔999〕	4	0	80	13/	0	千克			/30
2515.1200	--用锯或其他方法切割成矩形,包括正方形〔999〕	4	0	80	13/	0	千克			/30
2515.2000	-其他石灰质碑用或建筑用石,蜡石〔999〕	3	0	50	13/	0	千克			/30
25.16	**花岗石、斑岩、玄武岩、砂岩以及其他碑用或建筑用石,不论是否粗加修整或仅用锯或其他方法切割成矩形(包括正方形)的板、块:**									
	-花岗岩:									

协定税率 %										特惠税率 %			Article Description
亚太5国	东/冰/格	巴基斯坦	韩国	瑞士	哥达	秘鲁	澳大利亚	新西/坡/智	港/澳/台	亚太2国	老/柬/缅	36/3/1	
													Quartz (other than natural sands); quartzite, whether or not roughly trimmed or merely cut, by sawing or otherwise, intoblocks or slabs of a rectangular (including square) shape:
1.5	0/0/0	0	0	0	0	0	0	0//0	0/0/			0/0/0	-Quartz
1.5	0/0/0	0	0	0	0	0	0	0//0	0/0/			0/0/0	-Quartzite
													Kaolin and other kaolinic clays, whether or not calcined:
													Kaolin and other kaolinic clays, whether or not calcined:
	0/0/0	0	0	0	0	0	0	0//0	0/0/			0/0/0	---Kaolin
	0/0/0	0	0	0	0	0	0	0//0	0/0/			0/0/0	---Other
													Other clays (not including expanded clays of heading No. 68.06), andalusite, kyanite and sillimanite, whether or not calcined; mullite; chamotte or dinas earths:
1.5	0/0/0	0	0	0	0	0	0	0//0	0/0/			0/0/0	-Bentonite
1.5	0/0/0	0	0	0	0	0	0	0//0	0/0/			0/0/0	-Fire-clay
	0/0/0	0	0	0	0	0	0	0//0	0/0/			0/0/0	-Other clays
1.5	0/0/0	0	0	0	0	0	0	0//0	0/0/			0/0/0	-Andalusite, kyanite and sillimanite
	0/0/0	0	0	0	0	0	0	0//0	0/0/			0/0/0	-Mullite
	0/0/0	0	0	0.9	0	0	0	0//0	0/0/			0/0/0	-Chamotte or dinas earths
													Chalk:
	0/0/0	0	0	0	0	0	0	0//0	0/0/			0/0/0	Chalk
													Natural calcium phosphates, natural aluminium calcium phosphates and phosphatic chalk:
													-Unground:
	0/0/0	0	0	0	0	0	0	0//0	0/0/			0/0/0	---Apatite
	0/0/0	0	0	0	0	0	0	0//0	0/0/			0/0/0	---Other
													-Ground:
	0/0/0	0	0	0	0	0	0	0//0	0/0/			0/0/0	---Apatite
	0/0/0	0	0	0	0	0	0	0//0	0/0/			0/0/0	---Other
													Natural barium sulphate (barytes); natural barium carbonate (witherite), whether or not calcined, other than barium oxide of heading No. 28.16:
1.5	0/0/0	0	0	0	0	0	0	0//0	0/0/			0/0/	-Natural barium sulphate (barytes)
	0/0/0	0	0	0	0	0	0	0//0	0/0/			0/0/	-Natural barium carbonate (witherite)
													Siliceous fossil meals (for example, kieselguhr, tripolite and diatomite) and similar siliceous earths, whether or not calcined, of an apparent specific gravity of 1 or less:
1.5	0/0/0	0	0	0	0	0	0	0//0	0/0/			0/0/0	---Kieselguhr
1.5	0/0/0	0	0	0	0	0	0	0//0	0/0/			0/0/0	---Other
													Pumice stone; emery; natural corundum, natural garnet and other natural abrasives, whether or not heat-treated:
	0/0/0	0	0	0	0	0	0	0//0	0/0/			0/0/0	-Pumice stone
1.5	0/0/0	0	0	0	0	0	0	0//0	0/0/			0/0/0	-Emery, natural corundum, narural garnet and other natural abrasives
													Slate, whether or not roughly trimmed or merely cut, by sawing or otherwise, into blocks or slabs of a rectangular (including square) shape:
1.5	0/0/0	0	0	0	0	0	0	0//0	0/0/			0/0/0	Slate, whether or not roughly trimmed or merely cut, by sawing or otherwise, into blocks or slabs of a rectangular (including square) shape
													Marble, travertine, ecaussine and other calcareous monumental or building stone of an apparent specific gravity of 2.5 or more, and alabaster, whether or not roughly trimmed or merely cut, by sawing or otherwise, into blocks or slabs of a rectangular (including square) shape:
													-Marble and travertine:
2	0/0/0	0	0	0	0	0	0	0//0	0/0/			0/0/0	--Crude or roughly trimmed Marble crude or roughly trimmed
2	0/0/0	0	0	0	0	0	0	0//0	0/0/			0/0/0	--Merely cut, by sawing or otherwise, into blocks or slabs of a rectangular (including square) shape
	0/0/1.2	0	0	0	0	0	0	0//0	0/0/			0/0/0	-Ecaussine and other calcareous monumental or building stone; alabaster
													Granite, porphyry, basalt, sandstone and other monumental or building stone, whether or not building stone whether or not roughly trimmed or merely cut, by sawing or otherwise, into blocks or slabs of a rectangular (including square) shape:
													-Granite:

税则号列	货品名称〔CIQ扩展编码及品名—T2表示见附表2〕	最惠(%)	暂定税率	普通	增值/消费	出口退税	计量单位	监管条件	检验检疫	特殊证件对美关税
2516.1100	--原状或粗加修整〔999〕	4	0	50	13/	0	千克	A	M	/30
2516.1200	--仅用锯或其他方法切割成矩形,包括正方形〔999〕	4	0	50	13/	0	千克	A	M	/30
2516.2000	-砂岩									
2516.2000 01	原状或粗加修整砂岩〔999〕	3	0	50	13/	0	千克	A	M	/30
2516.2000 90	矩形(包括正方形)砂岩(用锯或其他方法切割成矩形的板、块)〔999〕	3	0	50	13/	0	千克			/30
2516.9000	-其他碑用或建筑用石〔999〕	3	0	50	13/	0	千克			/30
25.17	**通常作混凝土粒料、铺路、铁道路基或其他路基用的卵石、砾石及碎石,圆石子及燧石,不论是否热处理;矿渣、浮渣及类似的工业残渣,不论是否混有本税目第一部分所列的材料;沥青碎石;税目25.15、25.16所列各种石料的碎粒、碎屑及粉末,不论是否热处理:**									
2517.1000	-通常作混凝土粒料、铺路、铁道路基或其他路基用的卵石、砾石及碎石,圆石子及燧石,不论是否热处理〔999〕	4		50	13/	0	千克			/34
2517.2000	-矿渣、浮渣及类似的工业残渣,不论是否混有子目号2517.10所列的材料〔999〕	3		50	13/	0	千克	9		/
2517.3000	-沥青碎石〔999〕	3		50	13/	0	千克	9		/8
	-税目25.15及25.16所列各种石料的碎粒、碎屑及粉末,不论是否热处理:									
2517.4100	--大理石的〔999〕	3		50	13/	0	千克			/18
2517.4900	--其他〔999〕	3		50	13/	0	千克			/33
25.18	**白云石,不论是否煅烧或烧结、粗加修整或仅用锯或其他方法切割成矩形(包括正方形)的板、块;夯混白云石:**									
2518.1000	-未煅烧或烧结的白云石〔999〕	3	0	40	13/	0	千克			/30
2518.2000	-已煅烧或烧结的白云石〔999〕	3	0	40	13/	0	千克			/5
2518.3000	-夯混白云石〔999〕	3	0	40	13/	0	千克			/5
25.19	**天然碳酸镁(菱镁矿);熔凝镁氧矿;烧结镁氧矿,不论烧结前是否加入少量其他氧化物;其他氧化镁,不论是否纯净:**									
2519.1000	-天然碳酸镁(菱镁矿)〔999〕	3	1	40	13/	0	千克	y4x		/
	-其他:									
2519.9010	---熔凝镁氧矿〔999〕	3	1	40	13/	0	千克	y4x		/31
2519.9020	---烧结镁氧矿(重烧镁)〔999〕	3	1	40	13/	0	千克	y4x		/31
2519.9030	---碱烧镁(轻烧镁)〔999〕	3	1	40	13/	0	千克	y4x		/31
	---其他:									
2519.9091	----化学纯氧化镁[T2]	3		35	13/	0	千克	A	R	/28
2519.9099	----其他									
2519.9099 10	其他氧化镁含量在70%及以上的矿产品〔101矿物源性饲料添加剂,102氧化镁〕	3	1	40	13/	0	千克	4xy		/26
2519.9099 90	其他氧化镁〔101矿物源性饲料添加剂,102氧化镁〕	3		40	13/	0	千克			/28
25.20	**生石膏;硬石膏;熟石膏(由煅烧的生石膏或硫酸钙构成),不论是否着色,也不论是否带有少量促凝剂或缓凝剂:**									
2520.1000	-生石膏;硬石膏〔999〕	5		80	13/	0	千克			/35
	-熟石膏:									
2520.2010	---牙科用〔999〕	5		40	13/	0	千克			/20
2520.2090	---其他〔999〕	5		80	13/	0	千克			/20
25.21	**石灰石助熔剂;通常用于制造石灰或水泥的石灰石及其他钙质石:**									
2521.0000	石灰石助熔剂;通常用于制造石灰或水泥的石灰石及其他钙质石〔999〕	5		50	13/	0	千克			/30
25.22	**生石灰、熟石灰及水硬石灰,但税目28.25的氧化钙及氢氧化钙除外:**									
2522.1000	-生石灰〔999〕	5		80	13/	0	千克			/35
2522.2000	-熟石灰〔999〕	5		80	13/	0	千克			/35
2522.3000	-水硬石灰〔999〕	5		80	13/	0	千克			/10
25.23	**硅酸盐水泥、矾土水泥、矿渣水泥、富硫酸盐水泥及类似的水凝水泥,不论是否着色,包括水泥熟料:**									

协定税率 %										特惠税率 %			Article Description
亚太5国	东/冰/格	巴基斯坦	韩国	瑞士	哥达	秘鲁	澳大利亚	新西/坡/智	港/澳/台	亚太2国	老/柬/缅	36/3/1	
2	0/0/0	0	0	0	0	0	0	0//0	0/0/			0/0/0	--Crude or roughly trimmed
2	0/0/0	0	0	0	0	0	0	0//0	0/0/			0/0/0	--Merely cut, by sawing or otherwise, into blocks or slabs of a rectangular (including square) shape
													-Sandstone
2.1	0/0/0	0	0	0	0	0	0	0//0	0/0/			0/0/0	Crude or roughly trimmed sandstone
2.1	0/0/0	0	0	0	0	0	0	0//0	0/0/			0/0/0	Rectangular(including square) sandstone(cut, by sawing or otherwise, into blocks or slabs of a rectangular)
2.1	0/0/0	0	0	0	0	0	0	0//0	0/0/			0/0/0	-Other monumental or building stone
													Pebbles, gravel, broken or crushed stone, of a kind commonly used for concrete aggregates, for road metalling or for railway or other ballast, shingle and flint, whether or not heat-treated; macadam of slag, dross or similar industrial waste, whether or not incorporating the materials cited in the first part of the heading; tarred macadam; granules, chippings and powder, of stones of heading No. 25.15 or 25.16, whether or not heat-treated:
2	0/0/0	0	0	0	0	0	0	0//0	0/0/			0/0/0	-Pebbles, gravel, broken or crushed stone, of a kind commonly used for concrete aggregates, for road metalling or for railway or other ballast, shingle and flint, whether or not heat-treated
	0/0/0	0	0	0	0	0	0	0//0	0/0/			0/0/0	-Macadam of slag, dross or similar industrial waste, whether or not incorporating the materials cited in subheading No. 2517.10
	0/0/0	0	0	0	0	0	0	0//0	0/0/			0/0/0	-Tarred macadam
													-Granules, chippings and powder, stones of heading No. 25.15 or 25.16, whether or not heat-treated:
1.5	0/0/0	0	0	0	0	0	0	0//0	0/0/			0/0/0	--Of marble
	0/0/0	0	0	0	0	0	0	0//0	0/0/			0/0/0	--Other
													Dolomite, whether or not calcined, including dolomite roughly trimmed or merely cut, by sawing or otherwise, into blocks or slabs of a rectangular (including square) shape; dolomite ramming mix:
1.5	0/0/0	0	0	0	0	0	0	0//0	0/0/			0/0/0	-Dolomite, not calcined or sintered
	0/0/0	0	0	0	0	0	0	0//0	0/0/			0/0/0	-Calcined or sintered dolomite
	0/0/0	0	0	0	0	0	0	0//0	0/0/			0/0/0	-Dolomite ramming mix
													Natural magnesium carbonate (magnesite); fused magnesia; dead-burned (sintered) magnesia, whether or not containing small quantities of other oxides added before sintering; other magnesium oxide, whether or not pure:
	0/0/0	0	0	0	0	0	0	0//0	0/0/			0/0/0	-Natural magnesium carbonate (magnesite)
													-Other:
	0/0/0	0	0	0	0	0	0	0//0	0/0/			0/0/0	---Fused magnesia
	0/0/0	0	0	0	0	0	0	0//0	0/0/			0/0/0	---Dead-burned (sintered) magnesia
	0/0/0	0	0	0	0	0	0	0//0	0/0/			0/0/0	---Light-burned magnesia
													---Other:
	0/0/0	0	0	0	0	0	0	0//0	0/0/			0/0/0	----Magnesium oxide, chemically pure
													----Other
	0/0/0	0	0	0	0	0	0	0//0	0/0/			0/0/0	Other mineral products containing ≥70% by weight of magnesium oxide
	0/0/0	0	0	0	0	0	0	0//0	0/0/			0/0/0	Other magnesium oxide
													Gypsum; anhydrite; plasters (consisting of calcined gypsum or calcium sulphate) whether or not coloured, with or without small quantities of accelerators or retarders:
2.5	0/0/2	0	0	0	0	0	0	0//0	0/0/		0//	0/0/0	-Gypsum; anhydrite
													-Plasters:
	0/0/0	0	0	0	0	0	0	0//0	0/0/		0//	0/0/0	---For dental use
	0/0/0	0	2	0	0	0	0	0//0	0/0/		0//	0/0/0	---Other
													Limestone flux; limestone and other calcareous stone, of a kind used for the manufacture of lime or cement:
2.5	0/0/0	0	0	0	0	0	0	0//0	0/0/			0/0/0	Limestone flux; limestone and other calcareous stone, of a kind used for the manufacture of lime or cement
													Quicklime, slaked lime and hydraulic lime, other than calcium oxide and hydroxide of heading No. 28.25:
2.5	0/0/0	0	0	0	0	0	0	0//0	0/0/			0/0/0	-Quicklime
2.5	0/0/0	0	0	0	0	0	0	0//0	0/0/			0/0/0	-Slaked lime
	0/0/0	0	0	0	0	0	0	0//0	0/0/			0/0/0	-Hydraulic lime
													Portland cement, aluminous cement, slag cement, supersulphate cement and similar hydraulic cements, whether or not coloured or in the form of clinkers:

税则号列	货品名称〔CIQ扩展编码及品名—T2表示见附表2〕	最惠(%)	暂定税率	普通	增值/消费	出口退税	计量单位	监管条件	检验检疫	特殊证件对美关税
2523.1000	-水泥熟料〔999〕	5		30	13/	0	千克			/35
	-硅酸盐水泥：									
2523.2100	--白水泥，不论是否人工着色〔999〕	5		30	13/	0	千克			/20
2523.2900	--其他〔999〕	5		30	13/	0	千克	A	M	/20
2523.3000	-矾土水泥〔999〕	5		30	13/	0	千克			/35
2523.9000	-其他水凝水泥〔101矿渣水泥，102其他水泥〕	5		30	13/	0	千克	A	M	/20
25.24	石棉：									
2524.1000	-青石棉〔101栽培介质，301杂项物质〕	5		30	13/	0	千克	89		/10
	-其他：									
2524.9010	---长纤维的									
2524.9010 10	长纤维阳起石石棉（包括长纤维铁石棉、透闪石石棉及直闪石石棉）〔T2〕	5		30	13/	0	千克	89		/10
2524.9010 90	其他长纤维石棉〔T2〕	5		30	13/	0	千克			/10
2524.9090	---其他的									
2524.9090 10	其他阳起石石棉（包括其他铁石棉、透闪石石棉及直闪石石棉）〔101栽培介质，102石棉，301杂项物质〕	5		35	13/	0	千克	89		/35
2524.9090 90	其他石棉〔101栽培介质，102石棉，301杂项物质〕	5		35	13/	0	千克			/35
25.25	云母，包括云母片；云母废料：									
2525.1000	-原状云母及劈开的云母片〔999〕	5	1	30	13/	0	千克			/31
2525.2000	-云母粉〔999〕	5		30	13/	0	千克			/20
2525.3000	-云母废料〔101其他云母，102废矿〕	5		30	13/	0	千克	9	M	/10
25.26	**天然冻石，不论是否粗加修整或仅用锯或其他方法切割成矩形（包括正方形）的板、块；滑石：**									
	-未破碎及未研粉：									
2526.1010	---冻石〔999〕	3		50	13/	0	千克			/8
2526.1020	---滑石〔999〕	3	1	50	13/	0	千克	y4x		/6
	-已破碎或已研粉：									
2526.2010	---冻石〔999〕	3		50	13/	0	千克			/8
2526.2020	---滑石									
2526.2020 01	滑石粉（体积百分比90%及以上的产品颗粒度小于等于18微米的）〔999〕	3	1	50	13/	0	千克	4Axy	R	/16
2526.2020 90	已破碎或已研粉的其他天然滑石〔999〕	3	1	50	13/	0	千克	4xy		/16
25.28	**天然硼酸盐及其精矿（不论是否煅烧），但不包括从天然盐水析离的硼酸盐；天然粗硼酸，含硼酸干重不超过85%：**									
2528.0010	-天然硼砂及其精矿（不论是否煅烧）〔999〕	3	0	30	13/	0	千克	A	M	/30
2528.0090	---其他〔999〕	5	0	30	13/	0	千克			/30
25.29	**长石；白榴石；霞石及霞石正长岩；萤石（氟石）：**									
2529.1000	-长石〔101栽培介质，102长石〕	3	1	50	13/	0	千克			/31
	-萤石：									
2529.2100	--按重量计氟化钙含量在97%及以下〔999〕	3		50	13/	0	千克	4xy		/8
2529.2200	--按重量计氟化钙含量在97%以上〔999〕	3		50	13/	0	千克	4xy		/8
2529.3000	-白榴石；霞石及霞石正长岩〔101栽培介质，102石材〕	5		50	13/	0	千克			/35
25.30	**其他税目未列名的矿产品：**									
	-未膨胀的蛭石、珍珠岩及绿泥石：									
2530.1010	---绿泥石〔999〕	5		30	13/	0	千克			/10
2530.1020	---未膨胀的蛭石和珍珠岩〔T2〕	5		30	13/	0	千克			/35
2530.2000	-硫镁矾矿及泻盐矿（天然硫酸镁）〔999〕	3		30	13/	0	千克			/18
	-其他：									
2530.9010	---矿物性药材〔999〕	3		30	13/	0	千克			/8
2530.9020	---稀土金属矿〔999〕	0		0	13/	0	千克	4Bxy	N	/25
	---其他：									
2530.9091	----硅灰石〔999〕	3		50	13/	0	千克			/18
2530.9099	----其他									
2530.9099 01	天青石〔999〕	3	1	50	13/	0	千克			/31
2530.9099 02	锂辉石矿〔999〕	3	0	50	13/	0	千克			/30
2530.9099 10	废镁砖〔999〕	3		50	13/	0	千克	49xy		/33
2530.9099 20	叶蜡石〔999〕	3		50	13/	0	千克			/33
2530.9099 30	未煅烧的水镁石〔999〕	3	1	50	13/	0	千克	4xy		/31
2530.9099 40	钟乳石	3		50	13/	0	千克	u		/33
2530.9099 92	其他品目未列名氧化镁含量在70%及以上的矿产品〔999〕	3		50	13/	0	千克			/33
2530.9099 99	其他矿产品〔999〕	3		50	13/	0	千克			/33

协定税率 %										特惠税率 %			Article Description
亚太5国	东/冰/格	巴基斯坦	韩国	瑞士	哥达	秘鲁	澳大利亚	新西/坡/智	港/澳/台	亚太2国	老/柬/缅	36/3/1	
2.5	0/0/0	4	0	0	0	0	0	0//0	0/0/0			0/0/0	-Cement clinkers
													-Portland cement:
3.8	0/0/0	0	0	0	0	0	0	0//0	0/0/0			0/0/0	--White cement, whether or not artificially coloured
3.8	0/0/0	0	0	0	0	0	0	0//0	0/0/0			0/0/0	--Other
2.5	0/0/0	4	0	0	0	0	0	0//0	0/0/			0/0/0	-Aluminous cement
	0/0/0	4	0	0	0	0	0	0//0	0/0/			0/0/0	-Other hydraulic cements
													Asbestos:
	0/0/0	0	0	0	0	0	0	0//0	0/0/			0/0/	-Grocidlite
													-Other:
													---Of long staple
	0/0/0	0	0	0	0	0	0	0//0	0/0/			0/0/	Actinolite asbestas of long fibre(including amosite asbestos、tremolite asbestos or anthopylite asbestos)
	0/0/0	0	0	0	0	0	0	0//0	0/0/			0/0/	Other asbestos of long fibre
													---Other
	0/0/0	0	0	0	0	0	0	0//0	0/0/			0/0/	Other actinolite asbestas(including other amosa asbestos、tremolite asbestos or anthopylite asbestos)
	0/0/0	0	0	0	0	0	0	0//0	0/0/			0/0/	Other asbestos
													Mica, including splittings; mica waste:
2.5	0/0/0	0	0	0	0	0	0	0//0	0/0/			0/0/0	-Crude mica and mica rifted into sheets or splittings
2.5	0/0/0	0	0	0	0	0	0	0//0	0/0/			0/0/0	-Mica powder
	0/0/0	0	0	0	0	0	0	0//0	0/0/			0/0/0	-Mica waste
													Natural steatite, whether or not roughly trimmed or merely cut, by sawing or otherwise, into blocks or slabs or a rectangular (including square) shape; talc:
													-Not crushed, not powdered:
	0/0/0	0	0	0	0	0	0	0//0	0/0/			0/0/0	---Natural steatite
1.5	0/0/0	0	0	0	0	0	0	0//0	0/0/			0/0/0	---Talc
													-Crushed or powdered:
	0/0/0	0	0	0	0	0	0	0//0	0/0/			0/0/0	---Natural steatite
													---Talc
	0/0/0	0	0	0	0	0	0	0//0	0/0/			0/0/0	Talc Fowder(volume percent ≥90% ,granularity≤18 micron)
	0/0/0	0	0	0	0	0	0	0//0	0/0/			0/0/0	Other natural talc, crushed or powdered
													Natural borates and concentrates thereof (whether or not calcined), but not including borates separated from natural brine; natural boric acid containing not more than 85% of H_3BO_3 calulated on the dry weight:
	0/0/0	0	0	0	0	0	0	0//0	0/0/			0/0/0	-Natural borates and concentrates thereof (whether or not calcined)
	0/0/0	0	0	0	0	0	0	0//0	0/0/			0/0/0	---Other
													Feldspar; leucite; nepheline and nepheline syenite; fluorspar:
1.5	0/0/0	0	0	0	0	0	0	0//0	0/0/			0/0/0	-Feldspar
													-Fluorspar:
1.5	0/0/0	0	0	0	0	0	0	0//0	0/0/			0/0/0	--Containing by weight 97% or less of calcium fluoride
	0/0/0	0	0	0	0	0	0	0//0	0/0/			0/0/0	--Containing by weight more than 97% of calcium fluoride
	0/0/0	0	0	0	0	0	0	0//0	0/0/			0/0/0	-Leucite; nepheline and nepheline syenite
													Mineral substances not elsewhere specified or included:
													-Vermiculite, perlite and chlorites, unexpanded:
	0/0/0	0	0	0	0	0	0	0//0	0/0/			0/0/0	---Chlorites
2.5	0/0/0	0	0	0	0	0	0	0//0	0/0/			0/0/0	---Vermiculite, perlite unexpanded
	0/0/0	0	0	0	0	0	0	0//0	0/0/			0/0/0	-Kieserite, epsomite (natural magnesium sulphates)
													-Other:
	0/0/0	0	0	0	0	0	0	0//0	0/0/			0/0/0	---Mineral medicinal substances
												0/0/0	---Ores of rare earth metals
													---Other:
1.5	0/0/0	0	0	0	0	0	0	0//0	0/0/			0/0/0	----Wollastonite
													----Other
1.5	0//0	0	0	0	0	0	0	0//0	0/0/			0/0/0	Celestite
1.5	0//0	0	0	0	0	0	0	0//0	0/0/			0/0/0	Spodumene
1.5	0//0	0	0	0	0	0	0	0//0	0/0/			0/0/0	Bricks of magnesia waste
1.5	0//0	0	0	0	0	0	0	0//0	0/0/			0/0/0	Pyrophyllite
1.5	0//0	0	0	0	0	0	0	0//0	0/0/			0/0/0	Brucite
1.5	0//0	0	0	0	0	0	0	0//0	0/0/		//	0/0/0	Stalactite
1.5	0//0	0	0	0	0	0	0	0//0	0/0/			0/0/0	Mianeral products with 70% or more of magnesia which are not listed in other items
1.5	0//0	0	0	0	0	0	0	0//0	0/0/			0/0/0	Other mineral products

第二十六章
矿砂、矿渣及矿灰

注释：

一、本章不包括：

(一)铺路用的矿渣及类似的工业废渣(税目25.17)；

(二)天然碳酸镁(菱镁矿)，不论是否煅烧(税目25.19)；

(三)主要含有石油的石油储罐的淤渣(品目27.10)

(四)第三十一章的碱性熔渣；

(五)矿物棉(税目68.06)；

(六)贵金属或包贵金属的废碎料；主要用于回收贵金属的含贵金属或贵金属化合物的其他废碎料(税目71.12)；

(七)通过熔炼所产生的铜锍、镍锍或钴锍(第十五类)。

二、税目26.01至26.17所称"矿砂"，是指冶金工业中提炼汞，税目28.44的金属以及第十四类、第十五类金属的矿物，即使这些矿物不用于冶金工业，也包括在内。但税目26.01至26.17不包括不是以冶金工业正常加工方法处理的各种矿物。

三、税目26.20只适用于：

(一)在工业上提炼金属或作为生产金属化合物基本原料的矿渣、矿灰及残渣，但焚化城市垃圾所产生的灰、渣除外(税目26.21)；

(二)含有砷的矿渣、矿灰及残渣，不论其是否含有金属，用于提取、生产砷、金属及其化合物。

子目注释：

一、子目2620.21所称"含铅汽油的淤渣及含铅抗震化合物的淤渣"，是指含铅汽油及含铅抗震化合物(例如，四乙基铅)储罐的淤渣，主要含有铅、铅化合物以及铁的氧化物。

二、含有砷、汞、铊及其混合物的矿渣，矿灰及残渣，用于提取或生产砷、汞、铊及其化合物，归入子目2620.60。

税则号列	货品名称〔CIQ扩展编码及品名—T2表示见附表2〕	最惠(%)	暂定税率	普通	增值/消费	出口退税	计量单位	监管条件	检验检疫	特殊证件对美关税
26.01	**铁矿砂及其精矿，包括焙烧黄铁矿：**									
	-铁矿砂及其精矿，但焙烧黄铁矿除外：									
	--未烧结：									
2601.1110	---平均粒度小于0.8毫米的〔999〕	0		0	13/	0	千克	7A	M	/
2601.1120	---平均粒度不小于0.8毫米，但不大于6.3毫米的〔999〕	0		0	13/	0	千克	7A	M	/
2601.1190	---其他〔999〕	0		0	13/	0	千克	7A	M	/
2601.1200	--已烧结〔999〕	0		0	13/	0	千克	7A	M	/25
2601.2000	-焙烧黄铁矿〔999〕	0		0	13/	0	千克	7A	M	/
26.02	**锰矿砂及其精矿，包括以干重计含锰量在20%及以上的锰铁矿及其精矿：**									
2602.0000	锰矿砂及其精矿，包括以干重计含锰量在20%及以上的锰铁矿及其精矿〔999〕	0		0	13/	0	千克	A	M	/25
26.03	**铜矿砂及其精矿：**									
2603.0000	铜矿砂及其精矿									
2603.0000 10	铜矿砂及其精矿(黄金价值部分)〔999铜矿，998铜精矿〕	0		0	0/	0	千克	7A	M	/25
2603.0000 90	铜矿砂及其精矿(非黄金价值部分)〔999铜矿，998铜精矿〕	0		0	13/	0	千克	7A	M	/25
26.04	**镍矿砂及其精矿：**									
2604.0000	镍矿砂及其精矿									
2604.0000 01	镍矿砂及其精矿(黄金价值部分)〔999〕	0		0	0/	0	千克			/25
2604.0000 90	镍矿砂及其精矿(非黄金价值部分)〔999〕	0		0	13/	0	千克			/25
26.05	**钴矿砂及其精矿：**									
2605.0000	钴矿砂及其精矿									
2605.0000 01	钴矿砂及其精矿(黄金价值部分)〔999〕	0		0	0/	0	千克			/
2605.0000 90	钴矿砂及其精矿(非黄金价值部分)〔999〕	0		0	13/	0	千克			/
26.06	**铝矿砂及其精矿：**									
2606.0000	铝矿砂及其精矿〔999〕	0		0	13/	0	千克	4xy		/
26.07	**铅矿砂及其精矿：**									
2607.0000	铅矿砂及其精矿									
2607.0000 01	铅矿砂及其精矿(黄金价值部分)〔999铅矿，998铅精矿〕	0		0	0/	0	千克	A	M	/10
2607.0000 90	铅矿砂及其精矿(非黄金价值部分)〔999铅矿，998铅精矿〕	0		0	13/	0	千克	A	M	/10
26.08	**锌矿砂及其精矿：**									
2608.0000	锌矿砂及其精矿									

Chapter 26
Ores, slag and ash

Notes:

1. This Chapter does not cover:
   (a) Slag or similar industrial waste prepared as macadam (heading No. 25.17);
   (b) Natural magnesium carbonate (magnesite), whether or not calcined (heading No. 25.19);
   (c) Sludges from the storage tanks of petroleum oils, consisting mainly of such oils (heading No. 27.10);
   (d) Basic slag of Chapter 31;
   (e) Slag wool, rock wool or similar mineral wools (heading No. 68.06);
   (f) Waste or scrap of precious metal or of metal clad with precious metal; other waste or scrap containing precious metal or precious metal compounds, of a kind used principally for the recovery of precious metal (heading No. 71.12);
   (g) Copper, nickel or cobalt mattes produced by any process of smelting (Section XV).
2. For the purposes of headings No. 26.01 to 26.17, the term "ores" means minerals of mineralogical species actually used in the metallurgical industry for the extraction of mercury, of the metals of heading No. 28.44 or of the metals of Section XIV or XV, even if they are intended for non-metallurgical purposes. Headings No. 26.01 to 26.17 do not, however, include minerals which have been submitted to processes not normal to the metallurgical industry.
3. Heading No. 26.20 applies only to:
   (a) Slag, ash and residues of a kind used in industry either for the extraction of metals or as a basis for the manufacture of chemical compounds of metals, excluding ash and residues from the incineration of municipal waste (heading No. 26.21);
   (b) Slag, ash and residues containing arsenic, whether or not containing metals, of a kind used either for the extraction of arsenic or matals or for the manufacture of their chemical compounds.

Subheading Notes:

1. For the purposes of subheading No. 2620.21, "leaded gasoline sludges and leaded anti-knock compound sludges" mean slud-ges obtained from storage tanks of leaded gasoline and leaded anti-knock compounds (for example, tetraethyl lead), and consisting essentially of lead, lead compounds and iron oxide.
2. Slag ash and residues containing arsenic, mercury, thallium or their mixtures, of a kind used for the extraction of arsenic or those metals or for the manufacture of their chemical compounds, are to be classified in subheading No. 2620.60.

协定税率 %										特惠税率 %			Article Description
亚太5国	东/冰/格	巴基斯坦	韩国	瑞士	哥达	秘鲁	澳大利亚	新西/坡/智	港/澳/台	亚太2国	老/柬/缅	36/3/1	
													Iron ores and concentrates, including roasted iron pyrites:
													-Iron ores and concentrates, other than roasted iron pyrites:
													--Non-agglomerated:
												0/0/0	---The average grain size less than 0.8mm
												0/0/0	---The average grain size not less than 0.8mm, but not more than 6.3 mm
												0/0/0	---Other
												0/0/0	--Agglomerated
												0/0/0	-Roasted iron pyrites
													Manganese ores and concentrates, including ferruginous manganese ores and concentrates with a manganese content of 20% or more, calculated on the dry weight:
												0/0/0	Manganese ores and concentrates, including ferruginous manganese ores and concentrates with a manganese content of 20% or more, calculated on the dry weight
													Copper ores and concentrates:
													Copper ores and concentrates
												0/0/0	Copper ores and concentrates (part of gold value)
												0/0/0	Copper ores and concentrates (part of non-gold value)
													Nickel ores and concentrates:
													Nickel ores and concentrates
												0/0/0	Nickel ores and concentrates(Part gold value part)
												0/0/0	Nickel ores and concen trates(Part of non-gold Value)
													Cobalt ores and concentrates:
													Cobalt ores and concentrates
												0/0/0	Cobalt ores and concentrates(Part gold value part)
												0/0/0	Cobalt ores and concen trates(Part of non-gold value)
													Aluminium ores and concentrate:
												0/0/0	Aluminium ores and concentrate
													Lead ores and concentrates:
													Lead ores and concentrates
												0/0/0	Lead ores and concentrates(Gold value part)
												0/0/0	Lead ores and con centrates(Non-gold value part)
													Zinc ores and concentrates:
													Zinc ores and concentrates

税则号列	货品名称〔CIQ扩展编码及品名—T2表示见附表2〕	最惠(%)	暂定税率	普通	增值/消费	出口退税	计量单位	监管条件	检验检疫	特殊证件对美关税
2608.0000 01	灰色饲料氧化锌(氧化锌 ZnO 含量大于 80%)〔999〕	0	0	0	13/	0	千克	A	M	/25
2608.0000 90	其他锌矿砂及其精矿〔999 锌矿,998 锌精矿〕	0		0	13/	0	千克	A	M	/25
26.09	**锡矿砂及其精矿:**									
2609.0000	锡矿砂及其精矿〔999〕	0	0	0	13/	0	千克	4xy		/
26.10	**铬矿砂及其精矿:**									
2610.0000	铬矿砂及其精矿〔999〕	0		0	13/	0	千克	A	M	/
26.11	**钨矿砂及其精矿:**									
2611.0000	钨矿砂及其精矿〔999〕	0		0	13/	0	千克	4xy		/
26.12	**铀或钍矿砂及其精矿:**									
2612.1000	-铀矿砂及其精矿〔999〕	0		0	13/	0	千克			/
2612.2000	-钍矿砂及其精矿〔999〕	0		0	13/	0	千克	4xy		/
26.13	**钼矿砂及其精矿:**									
2613.1000	-已焙烧〔999〕	0		0	13/	0	千克	4xy		/10
2613.9000	-其他〔999〕	0		0	13/	0	千克	4xy		/10
26.14	**钛矿砂及其精矿:**									
2614.0000	钛矿砂及其精矿〔999〕	0		0	13/	0	千克			/25
26.15	**铌、钽、钒或锆矿砂及其精矿:**									
2615.1000	-锆矿砂及其精矿〔101 悬浮于易燃液体中的,102 锆英砂矿〕	0		0	13/	0	千克			/25
	-其他:									
2615.9010	---水合钽铌原料(钽铌矿富集物)〔999〕	0		0	13/	0	千克			/
2615.9090	---其他									
2615.9090 10	铌,钽精矿及其矿砂〔999〕	0		0	13/	0	千克			/25
2615.9090 90	钒矿砂;钒精矿〔999〕	0		0	13/	0	千克			/25
26.16	**贵金属矿砂及其精矿:**									
2616.1000	-银矿砂及其精矿〔999〕	0		0	13/	0	千克			/20
2616.9000	-其他									
2616.9000 01	黄金矿砂〔999〕	0		0	0/	0	千克			/25
2616.9000 09	其他贵金属矿砂及其精矿〔999〕	0		0	13/	0	千克			/25
26.17	**其他矿砂及其精矿:**									
	-锑矿砂及其精矿:									
2617.1010	---生锑(锑精矿,选矿产品)〔999〕	0		0	13/	0	千克	4xy		/
2617.1090	---其他									
2617.1090 01	其他锑矿砂及其精矿(黄金价值部分)〔999〕	0		0	0/	0	千克	4xy		/
2617.1090 90	其他锑矿砂及其精矿(非黄金价值部分)〔999〕	0		0	13/	0	千克	4xy		/
	-其他:									
2617.9010	---朱砂(辰砂)〔999 辰砂,301 毒性物质和感染性物质〕	3		14	13/	0	千克			/8
2617.9090	---其他〔999〕	0		0	13/	0	千克			/25
26.18	**冶炼钢铁所产生的粒状熔渣(熔渣砂):**									
2618.0010	---主要含锰									
2618.0010 01	主要含锰的冶炼钢铁产生的粒状熔渣,含锰量＞25 %(包括熔渣砂)〔999〕	4		35	13/	0	千克	9A	M	/29
2618.0010 90	其他主要含锰的冶炼钢铁产生的粒状熔渣(包括熔渣砂)〔999〕	4		35	13/	0	千克	9A	M	/29
2618.0090	---其他〔999〕	4		35	13/	0	千克	9A	M	/
26.19	**冶炼钢铁所产生的熔渣、浮渣(粒状熔渣除外)、氧化皮及其他废料:**									
2619.0000	冶炼钢铁所产生的熔渣、浮渣(粒状熔渣除外)、氧化皮及其他废料									
2619.0000 10	轧钢产生的氧化皮〔999〕	4		35	13/	0	千克	9A	M	/29
2619.0000 21	冶炼钢铁所产生的含钒浮渣、熔渣,五氧化二钒含量＞20%(冶炼钢铁所产生的粒状熔渣除外)〔999〕	4		35	13/	0	千克	9	M	/29
2619.0000 29	其他冶炼钢铁所产生的含钒浮渣、熔渣(冶炼钢铁所产生的粒状熔渣除外)〔999〕	4		35	13/	0	千克	9	M	/29
2619.0000 30	含铁大于 80%的冶炼钢铁产生的渣钢铁〔999〕	4		35	13/	0	千克	9A	M	/29
2619.0000 90	冶炼钢铁产生的其他熔渣、浮渣及其他废料(冶炼钢铁所产生的粒状熔渣除外)〔101 炉渣(栽培介质),102 矿渣(栽培介质)〕	4		35	13/	0	千克	9A	M	/29
26.20	**含有金属、砷及其化合物的矿渣、矿灰及残渣(冶炼钢铁所产生的灰、渣除外):**									
	-主要含锌:									
2620.1100	--含硬锌〔999〕	4		35	13/	0	千克	9		/
2620.1900	--其他〔999〕	4		35	13/	0	千克	9	M	/

协定税率 %										特惠税率 %			
亚太5国	东/冰/格	巴基斯坦	韩国	瑞士	哥达	秘鲁	澳大利亚	新西/坡/智	港/澳/台	亚太2国	老/柬/缅	36/3/1	Article Description
												0/0/0	Grey feed grade zinc oxide(containing>80% by weight of ZnO)
												0/0/0	Other zinc ores and concentrates
													Tin ores and concentrates:
												0/0/0	Tin ores and concentrates
													Chromium ores and concentrates:
												0/0/0	Chromium ores and concentrates
													Tungsten ores and concentrates:
												0/0/0	Tungsten ores and concentrates
													Uranium or thorium ores and concentrates:
												0/0/0	-Uranium ores and concentrates
												0/0/0	-Thorium ores and concentrates
													Molybdenum ores and concentrates:
												0/0/0	-Roasted
												0/0/0	-Other
													Titanium ores and concentrates:
												0/0/0	Titanium ores and concentrates
													Niobium, tantalum, vanadium or zirconium ores and concentrates:
												0/0/0	-Zirconium ores and concentrates
													-Other:
												0/0/0	---Hydrated Tantalum-Niobium materials or enriched materials from Tantalum/Niobium ores
													---Other
												0/0/0	Tantalum and niobium concentrates and ores thereof
												0/0/0	Vanadium ores and concentrates
													Precious metal ores and concentrates:
												0/0/0	-Silver ores and concentrates
													-Other
												0/0/0	Gold ores and concentrates
												0/0/0	Other precious metal ores and concentrates
													Other ores and concentrates:
													-Antimony ores and concentrates:
												0/0/0	---Crude antimony(Antimony concentrates which are mineral products)
													---Other
												0/0/0	Other antimony ores and concentrates(parts of gold value)
												0/0/0	Other antimony ores and concentrates(parts of non-gold value)
													-Other:
	0/0/0	0	0	0	0	0	0	0//0	0/0/			0/0/0	---Cinnabar
												0/0/0	---Other
													Granulated slag (slag sand) from the manufacture of iron or steel:
													---Containing mainly Manganese
	0/0/0	0	0	0	0	0	0	0//0	0/0/			0/0/	Manganese slag from the manufacture of iron or steel, more than 25% of manganese(including slag sand)
	0/0/0	0	0	0	0	0	0	0//0	0/0/			0/0/	Other granulated slag(slag sand) from the manufacture of iron or steel, containing mainly Manganese
3.2	0/0/0	0	0	0	0	0	0	0//0	0/0/			0/0/	---Other
													Slag, dross (other than granulated slag), scalings and other waste from the manufacture of iron or steel:
													Slag, dross (other than granulated slag), scalings and other waste from the manufacture of iron or steel
	0/0/0	0	0	0	0	0	0	0//0	0/0/			0/0/	Scalings from the manufacture of steel
	0/0/0	0	0	0	0	0	0	0//0	0/0/			0/0/	Slag, drog, scalings and other waste from the manufacture of iron or steel, more than 20% vanadium pentoxide(other than granulated slag)
	0/0/0	0	0	0	0	0	0	0//0	0/0/			0/0/	Slap, dross from the manufaceure of iron or steel, containing vanadium(Other than granulated slag)
	0/0/0	0	0	0	0	0	0	0//0	0/0/			0/0/	Steel slag with more than 80% of steel form the manufaceure of steel and iron
	0/0/0	0	0	0	0	0	0	0//0	0/0/			0/0/	Slap, dross and other waster from the manufacture of iron or steel (Other than granulated slag)
													Slag, ash and residues (other than from the manufacture of iron or steel), containing metals arsenic, or their compounds:
													-Containing mainly zinc:
	0/0/0	0	0	0	0	0	0	0//0	0/0/			0/0/0	--Hard zinc spelter
	0/0/0	0	0	0	0	0	0	0//0	0/0/			0/0/0	--Other

税则号列	货品名称〔CIQ扩展编码及品名—T2表示见附表2〕	最惠(%)	暂定税率	普通	增值/消费	出口退税	计量单位	监管条件	检验检疫	特殊证件对美关税
	-主要含铅：									
2620.2100	--含铅汽油的淤渣及含铅抗震化合物的淤渣〔999〕	4		35	13/	0	千克	9		/
2620.2900	--其他〔999〕	4		35	13/	0	千克	9		/
2620.3000	-主要含铜〔999〕	4		35	13/	0	千克	9		/
2620.4000	-主要含铝〔999〕	4		35	13/	0	千克	9		/
2620.6000	-含砷、汞、铊及其混合物，用于提取或生产砷、汞、铊及其化合物〔999〕	4		35	13/	0	千克	9		/
	-其他：									
2620.9100	--含锑、铍、镉、铬及其混合物〔999〕	4		35	13/	0	千克	9		/
	--其他：									
2620.9910	---主要含钨〔999〕	4		35	13/	0	千克	y4x9		/
2620.9990	---其他									
2620.9990 11	含其他金属及其化合物的矿渣、矿灰及残渣，五氧化二钒＞20％(冶炼钢铁所产生的除外)〔999〕	4		35	13/	0	千克	9	M	/29
2620.9990 19	含其他金属及其化合物的矿渣、矿灰及残渣，10％＜五氧化二钒≤20％的(冶炼钢铁所产生的及含钒废催化剂除外)〔999〕	4		35	13/	0	千克	9	M	/29
2620.9990 20	含铜大于10％的铜冶炼转炉渣及火法精炼渣，其他铜冶炼渣〔101用作铜冶炼的原料，102用作除锈磨料的其他铜冶炼渣〕	4		35	13/	0	千克	9	M	/29
2620.9990 90	含其他金属及其化合物的矿渣、矿灰及残渣(冶炼钢铁所产生灰、渣的除外)〔999〕	4		35	13/	0	千克	9		/29
26.21	**其他矿渣及矿灰，包括海藻灰(海草灰)；焚化城市垃圾所产生的灰、渣：**									
2621.1000	-焚化城市垃圾所产生的灰、渣〔999〕	4		35	13/	0	千克	9		/
2621.9000	-其他									
2621.9000 10	海藻灰及其他植物灰(包括稻壳灰)〔999〕	4		35	13/	0	千克	9		/14
2621.9000 90	其他矿渣及矿灰〔999〕	4		35	13/	0	千克	9		/14

协定税率 %										特惠税率 %			Article Description
亚太5国	东/冰/格	巴基斯坦	韩国	瑞士	哥达	秘鲁	澳大利亚	新西/坡/智	港/澳/台	亚太2国	老/柬/缅	36/3/1	
													-Containing mainly lead:
	0/0/0	0	0	0	0	0	0	0//0	0/0/			0/0/0	--Leaded gasoline sludges and leaded anti-knock compound sludges
	0/0/0	0	0	0	0	0	0	0//0	0/0/			0/0/0	--Other
	0/0/0	0	0	0	0	0	0	0//0	0/0/			0/0/0	-Containing mainly copper
	0/0/0	0	0	0	0	0	0	0//0	0/0/			0/0/0	-Containing mainly aluminium
	0/0/0	0	0	0	0	0	0	0//0	0/0/			0/0/0	-Containing arsenic, mercury, thallium or their mixtures, of a kind used for the extraction of arsenic or those metals or for the manufacture of their chemical compounds
													-Other:
	0/0/0	0	0	0	0	0	0	0//0	0/0/			0/0/0	--Containing antimony, beryllium, cadmium, chromium or their mixtures
													--Other:
	0/0/0	0	0	0	0	0	0	0//0	0/0/			0/0/0	---Containing mainly tungsten
													---Other
	0/0/0	0	0	0	0	0	0	0//0	0/0/			0/0/0	Slag, ash and residues, containing other metals or their compounds, more than 20% vanadium pentoxide (other than from the manufacture of iron or steel)
	0/0/0	0	0	0	0	0	0	0//0	0/0/			0/0/0	Slag, ash and residues, containing other metals or their compounds, 10%< containing vanadium pentoxide≤20% (other than from the manufacture of iron or steel and including vanadium spent catalyst)
	0/0/0	0	0	0	0	0	0	0//0	0/0/			0/0/0	Copper converter slag fire refining slag from copper smelter, containing copper>10%
	0/0/0	0	0	0	0	0	0	0//0	0/0/			0/0/0	Slag, ash and residues, containing other metals or their compounds (other than from the manufacture of iron or steel)
													Other slag and ash, including seaweed ash (kelp); ash and residues from the incineration of municipal waste:
	0/0/0	0		0	0	0	0	0//0	0/0/			0/0/0	-Ash and residues from the incineration of municipal waste
													-Other
	0/0/0	0	0	0	0	0	0	0//0	0/0/			0/0/0	Algae ash and other plant ash (including rice husk ash)
	0/0/0	0	0	0	0	0	0	0//0	0/0/			0/0/0	Other ore slag and ore ash

第二十七章
矿物燃料、矿物油及其蒸馏产品；沥青物质；矿物蜡

注释：

一、本章不包括：

(一)单独的已有化学定义的有机化合物，但纯甲烷及纯丙烷应归入税目 27.11；

(二)税目 30.03 及 30.04 的药品；或

(三)税目 33.01、33.02 及 38.05 的不饱和烃混合物。

二、税目 27.10 所称"石油及从沥青矿物提取的油类"，不仅包括石油、从沥青矿物提取的油及类似油，还包括那些用任何方法提取的主要含有不饱和烃混合物的油，但其非芳族成分的重量必须超过芳族成分。然而，它不包括温度在 300℃ 时，压力转为 1013 毫巴后减压蒸镏出的以体积计小于 60% 的液体合成聚烯烃(第三十九章)。

三、税目 27.10 所称"废油"，是指主要含石油及从沥青矿物提取的油类(参见本章注释二)的废油，不论其是否与水混合。它们包括：

(一)不再适于作为原产品使用的废油(例如，用过的润滑油、液压油及变压器油)；

(二)石油储罐的淤渣油，主要含有废油及高浓度的在生产原产品时使用的添加剂(例如，化学品)；

(三)水乳浊液状或与水混合的废油，例如，浮油、清洗油罐所得的油或机械加工中已用过的切削油。

子目注释：

一、子目 2701.11 所称"无烟煤"，是指含挥发物(以干燥、无矿物质计)不超过 14% 的煤。

二、子目 2701.12 所称"烟煤"，是指含挥发物(以干燥、无矿物质计)超过 14%，并且热值(以潮湿、无矿物质计)等于或大于 5833 大卡/千克的煤。

三、子目 2707.10、2707.20、2707.30 及 2707.40 所称"粗苯""粗甲苯""粗二甲苯""萘"，分别指按重量计苯、甲苯、二甲苯、萘的含量在 50% 以上的产品。

四、子目 2710.12 所称"轻油及其制品"，是指根据 ISO 3405 方法(等同于 ASTMD 86 方法)，温度在 210℃ 时以体积计馏出量(包括损耗)在 90% 及以上的产品。

五、税目 27.10 的子目所称"生物柴油"，是指从动物植物油脂(不论是否使用过)得到的用作燃料的脂肪酸单烷基酯。

税则号列	货品名称〔CIQ 扩展编码及品名—T2 表示见附表 2〕	最惠(%)	暂定税率	普通	增值/消费	出口退税	计量单位	监管条件	检验检疫	特殊证件对美关税
27.01	**煤；煤砖、煤球及用煤制成的类似固体燃料：**									
	-煤，不论是否粉化，但未制成型：									
2701.1100	--无烟煤									
2701.1100 10	无烟煤(不论是否粉化，但未制成型)〔999〕	3		20	13/	0	千克	47Axy	M	/28
2701.1100 90	无烟煤滤料〔999〕	3		20	13/	0	千克	7A	M	/28
	--烟煤：									
2701.1210	---炼焦煤〔999〕	3		20	13/	0	千克	47Axy	M	/33
2701.1290	---其他〔999〕	6		20	13/	0	千克	47Axy	M	/31
2701.1900	--其他煤〔999〕	5		20	13/	0	千克	47Axy	M	/30
2701.2000	-煤砖、煤球及用煤制成的类似固体燃料〔999〕	5		50	13/	0	千克			/30
27.02	**褐煤，不论是否制成型，但不包括黑玉：**									
2702.1000	-褐煤，不论是否粉化，但未制成型〔999〕	3		20	13/	0	千克	A4xy	M	/28
2702.2000	-制成型的褐煤〔999〕	3		20	13/	0	千克	A	M	/28
27.03	**泥煤(包括肥料用泥煤)，不论是否制成型：**									
2703.0000	泥煤(包括肥料用泥煤)，不论是否制成型									
2703.0000 10	泥炭(草炭)[沼泽(湿地)中，地上植物枯死、腐烂堆积而成的有机矿体(不论干湿)]〔101 栽培介质，102 化工产品〕	5		20	13/	0	千克	8AB	PQ	/30
2703.0000 90	泥煤(包括肥料用泥煤)(不论是否制成型)〔101 栽培介质，102 泥煤〕	5		20	13/	0	千克	AB	PQ	/30
27.04	**煤、褐煤或泥煤制成的焦炭及半焦炭，不论是否制成型；甑炭：**									
2704.0010	---焦炭及半焦炭〔999〕	5	0	11	13/	0	千克	4xy		/25
2704.0090	---其他〔999〕	5	0	11	13/	0	千克			/25
27.05	**煤气、水煤气、炉煤气及类似气体，但石油气及其他烃类气除外**									
2705.0000	煤气、水煤气、炉煤气及类似气体，但石油气及其他烃类气除外									
2705.0000 10	煤气〔999〕	5	1	20	9/	0	千克	AB	MN	/26
2705.0000 90	水煤气、炉煤气及类似气体(石油气及其他烃类气除外)〔999 其他化工产品，998 其他危险化学品〕	5	1	20	9/	0	千克			/26

Chapter 27
Mineral fuels, mineral oils and products of their distillation; bituminous substances; mineral waxes

Notes:

1. This Chapter does not cover:
   (a) Separate chemically defined organic compounds, other than pure methane and propane which are to be classified in heading No. 27.11;
   (b) Medicaments of heading No. 30.03 or 30.04; or
   (c) Mixed unsaturated hydrocarbons of heading No. 33.01, 33.02 or 38.05.
2. References in heading No. 27.10 to "petroleum oils and oils obtained from bituminous minerals" include not only petroleum oils and oils obtained from bituminous minerals but also similar oils, as well as those consisting mainly of mixed unsaturated hydrocarbons, obtained by any process, provided that the weight of the non-aromatic constituents exceeds that of the aromatic constituents. However, the references do not include liquid synthetic polyolefins of which less than 60% by volume distils at 300℃, after conversion to 1,013 millibars when a reduced-pressure distillation method is used (Chapter 39).

   (a) Such oils no longer fit for use as primary products (for example, used lubricating oils, used hydraulic oils and used transformer oils);
   (b) Sludge oils from the storage tanks of petroleum oils, mainly containing such oils and a high concentration of additives (for example, chemicals) used in the manufacture of the primary products; and
   (c) Such oils in the form of emulsions in water or mixtures with water, such as those resulting from oil spills or storage tank washings, or from the use of cutting oils for machining operations.

Subheading Notes:

1. For the purposes of subheading No. 2701.11, "anthracite" means coal having a volatile matter limit (on a dry, mineral-matter-free basis) not exceeding 14%.
2. For the purposes of subheading No. 2701.12, "bituminous coal" means coal having a volatile matter limit (on a dry, mineral-matter-free basis) exceeding 14% and a calorific value limit (on a moist, mineral-matter-free basis) equal to or greater than 5,833kcal/kg.
3. For the purposes of subheadings. 2707.10, 2707.20, 2707.30 and 2707.40, the terms "benzole"(benzene), "toluole"(toluene), "xylole"(xylenes) and "naphthalene" apply to products which contain more than 50% by weight of benzene, toluene, xylene, or naphthalene, respectively.
4. For the purposes of subheading No. 2710.11, "light oils and preparations" are those of which according to ISO 3405 method (ASTMD 86 method to identify), 90% or more by volume (including losses) distil at 210℃.
5. For the purposes of the Subheadings of heading 27.10, the term "biodiesel" means mono-alkyl esters of fatty acids of a kind used as a fuel, derived from animal or vegetable fats and oils whether or not used

协定税率 %										特惠税率 %			
亚太5国	东/冰/格	巴基斯坦	韩国	瑞士	哥达	秘鲁	澳大利亚	新西/坡/智	港/澳/台	亚太2国	老/柬/缅	36/3/1	Article Description
													Coal; briquettes, ovoids and similar solid fuels manufactured from coal:
													-Coal, whether or not pulverized, but not agglomerated:
													--Anthracite
	0/0/0	0	0	0	0	0	0	0//0	0/0/		0//	0/0/0	Anthracite (whether or not pulverized, but not agglomerated)
	0/0/0	0	0	0	0	0	0	0//0	0/0/		0//	0/0/0	Anthracite filter medium
													--Bituminous coal:
	0/0/0	0	0	0	0	0	0	0//0	0/0/		0//	0/0/0	---Coking coal
	0/0/0	0	0	0	0	0	0	0//0	0/0/		0//	0/0/0	---Other
3.5	0/0/0	0	0	0	0	0	0	0//0	0/0/		0//	0/0/0	--Other coal
	0/0/0	0	0	0	0	0	0	0//0	0/0/		0//	0/0/0	-Briquettes, ovoids and similar solid fuels manufactured from coal
													Lignite, whether or not agglomerated, excluding jet:
	0/0/0	0	0	0	0	0	0	0//0	0/0/			0/0/0	-Lignite, whether or not pulverized, but not agglomerated
	0/0/0	0	0	0	0	0	0	0//0	0/0/			0/0/0	-Agglomerated lignite
													Peat (including peat litter), whether or not agglomerated:
													Peat (including peat litter), whether or not agglomerated
2.5	0/0/0	0	0	0	0	0	0	0//0	0/0/			0/0/	In peat and swamp (wetland), organic ore bodies formed by dried and rotten plants on the ground (whether dry or wet)
2.5	0/0/0	0	0	0	0	0	0	0//0	0/0/			0/0/	Peat (including peat used as fertilizer), whether shaped or not
													Coke and semi-coke of coal, of lignite or of peat, whether or not agglomerated; retort carbon:
2.5	0/0/0	0	0	0	0	0	0	0//0	0/0/			0/0/	---Coke and semi-coke
2.5	0/0/0	0	0	0	0	0	0	0//0	0/0/			0/0/	---Other
													Coal gas, water gas, producer gas and similar gases, other than petroleum gases and other gaseous hydrocarbons:
													Coal gas, water gas, producer gas and similar gases, other than petroleum gases and other gaseous hydrocarbons
	0/0/0	0	0	0	0	0	0	0//0	0/0/			0/0/	Coal gas
	0/0/0	0	0	0	0	0	0	0//0	0/0/			0/0/	Water gas, producer gas and similar gases, other than petroleum gases and other gaseous hydrocarbons

税则号列		货品名称〔CIQ扩展编码及品名－T2表示见附表2〕	最惠(%)	暂定税率	普通	增值/消费	出口退税	计量单位	监管条件	检验检疫	特殊证件对美关税
27.06		**从煤、褐煤或泥煤蒸馏所得的焦油及其他矿物焦油，不论是否脱水或部分蒸馏，包括再造焦油：**									
2706.0000		从煤、褐煤或泥煤蒸馏所得的焦油及其他矿物焦油，不论是否脱水或部分蒸馏，包括再造焦油									
2706.0000	01	含蒽油≥50％及沥青≥40％的"炭黑油"〔999其他化工产品，998其他危险化学品〕	6	1	30	13/	0	千克			/26
2706.0000	90	其他从煤、褐煤或泥煤蒸馏所得的焦油及矿物焦油（不论是否脱水或部分蒸馏，包括再造焦油）〔101煤焦油，102其他焦油，103煤焦沥青，104蒽油乳剂（其他危险化学品），105蒽油乳膏（其他危险化学品）〕	6	1	30	13/	0	千克	AB	MN	/26
27.07		**蒸馏高温煤焦油所得的油类及其他产品；芳族成分重量超过非芳族成分的类似产品：**									
2707.1000		-粗苯〔999〕	6		20	13/	0	千克	AB	MN	/31
2707.2000		-粗甲苯〔999〕	6		30	13/	0	千克			/31
2707.3000		-粗二甲苯〔999〕	6	2	20	13/	0	千克			/27
2707.4000		-萘〔301〕	7		30	13/	0	千克	AB	MN	/32
2707.5000		-其他芳烃混合物，根据ISO3405方法（等同于ASTMD86方法），温度在250℃时的馏出量以体积计（包括损耗）在65％及以上〔999其他化工产品，998其他危险化学品〕	7		30	13/	0	千克			/32
		-其他：									
2707.9100		--杂酚油〔999其他化工产品，998其他危险化学品〕	7		30	13/	0	千克			/32
		--其他：									
2707.9910		---酚〔999其他化工产品，998其他危险化学品〕	7		30	13/	0	千克			/32
2707.9990		---其他〔101分离焦油，102塑料印油，103偶氮紫苯溶液，104塑料薄膜油墨，105闪烁液〕	7		30	13/	0	千克			/32
27.08		**从煤焦油或其他矿物焦油所得的沥青及沥青焦：**									
2708.1000		-沥青〔999其他化工产品，998其他危险化学品〕	7		35	13/	0	千克			/32
2708.2000		-沥青焦									
2708.2000	01	针状沥青焦〔999其他化工产品，998其他危险化学品〕	6	3	11	13/	0	千克			/28
2708.2000	90	其他沥青焦〔999其他化工产品，998其他危险化学品〕	6		11	13/	0	千克			/31
27.09		**石油原油及从沥青矿物提取的原油：**									
2709.0000		石油原油及从沥青矿物提取的原油〔999〕	T3		T3	13/	0	千克	4x7AByv	MN	/5
27.10		**石油及从沥青矿物提取的油类，但原油除外；以上述油为基本成分（按重量计不低于70％）的其他税目未列名制品；废油：**									
		-石油及从沥青矿物提取的油类（但原油除外）；以及以上述油为基本成分（按重量计不低于70％）的其他税目未列名制品；不含有生物柴油，但废油除外：									
		--轻油及其制品：									
2710.1210		---车用汽油及航空汽油〔301〕	5	1	14	13/1.52元/升	13	千克/升	47ABvy	MN	2/26
2710.1220		---石脑油〔999〕	6	0	20	13/1.52元/升	0	千克/升	47ABvy	MN	2/25
2710.1230		---橡胶溶剂油、油漆溶剂油、抽提溶剂油〔999〕	6		30	13/1.52元/升	0	千克/升			2/31
		---其他：									
2710.1291		----壬烯									
2710.1291	01	壬烯，不含生物柴油（碳九异构体混合物含量高于90％）〔999其他化工产品，301易燃液体〕	9	4	20	13/	0	千克	4Ay	M	2/29
2710.1291	90	其他壬烯，不含生物柴油〔999其他化工产品，301易燃液体〕	9		20	13/	0	千克	4Ay	M	2/34
2710.1299		----其他									
2710.1299	10	异戊烯同分异构体混合物，不含生物柴油〔999其他化工产品，301易燃液体〕	9	5	20	13/	0	千克	4Ay	M	2/30
2710.1299	20	脱模剂（包括按重量计含油≥70％的制品）〔301其他化工产，302易燃液体〕	9.5		25	13/	0	千克	4Ay	M	2/
2710.1299	90	其他轻油及制品，不含生物柴油（包括按重量计含油≥70％的制品）〔999易燃液体，301其他化工产品〕	9		20	13/	0	千克	4Ay	M	2/34
		--其他：									
		---煤油馏分：									
2710.1911		----航空煤油〔999其他化工产品，301易燃液体〕	9	0	14	13/	13	千克/升	47ABvy	MN	2/25

协定税率 %										特惠税率 %			Article Description
亚太5国	东/冰/格	巴基斯坦	韩国	瑞士	哥达	秘鲁	澳大利亚	新西/坡/智	港/澳/台	亚太2国	老/柬/缅	36/3/1	
													Tar distilled from coal, from lignite or from peat, and other mineral tars, whether or not dehydrated or partially distilled, including reconstituted tars:
													Tar distilled from coal, from lignite or from peat, and other mineral tars, whether or not dehydrated or partially distilled, including reconstituted tars
	0/0/0	4.5	0	0	0	0	0	0//0	0/0/			0/0/	Containing anthracene oil≥ 50% and asphalt ≥ 40%, carbon"black oil"
	0/0/0	4.5	0	0	0	0	0	0//0	0/0/			0/0/	Other tars and mineral tars, distelled from coal, lignite or peat, whether or not dehydrated or partially distilled, including reconstituted tars
													Oils and other products of the distillation of high temperature coal tar; similar products in which the weight of the aromatic constituents exceeds that of the non-aromatic constituents:
	0/0/0	4.5	3.6	0	0	0	0	0//0	0/0/			0/0/0	-Benzole
	0/0/0	4.5	0	0	0	0	0	0//0	0/0/			0/0/0	-Toluole
	0/0/0	4.5	3.6	0	0	0	0	0/0/0	0/0/			0/0/0	-Xylole
6	0/0/0	4	4.2	0	0	0	0	0/0/0	0/0/			0/0/0	-Naphthalene
	0/0/0	4	4.2	0	0	0	0	0/0/0	0/0/			0/0/0	-Other aromatic hydrocarbon mixtures of which 65% or more by volume (including losses) distils at 250℃ by the ISO3405 method (ASTMD86 method)
													-Other:
	0/0/0	4	2.8	0	0	0	0	0//0	0/0/			0/0/0	--Creosote oils
													--Other:
	0/0/0	4	0	0	0	0	0	0/0/0	0/0/			0/0/0	---Phenols
	0/0/0	4	4.2	0	0	0	0	0/0/0	0/0/			0/0/0	---Other
													Pitch and pitch coke, obtained from coal tar or from other mineral tars:
	0/0/0	4	0	0	0	0	0	0//0	0/0/			0/0/	-Pitch
													-Pitch coke
	0/0/0	4.5	2.4	0	0	0	0	0//0	0/0/			0/0/	Needle-shaped pitch coke
	0/0/0	4.5	2.4	0	0	0	0	0//0	0/0/			0/0/	Other Needle-shaped pitch coke
													Petroleum oils and oils obtained from bituminous minerals, crude:
												0/0/0	Petroleum oils and oils obtained from bituminous minerals, crude
													Petroleum oils and oils obtained from bituminous minerals, other than crude; preparations not elsewhere specified or included, containing by weight 70% or more of petroleum oils or of oils obtained from bituminous minerals, these oils being the basic constituents of the preparations; waste oils:
													-Petroleum oils and oils obtained from bituminous minerals (other than crude) and preparations not elsewhere specified or included, containing by weight 70% or more of petroleum oils or of oils obtained from bituminous minerals, these oils being the basic constituents of the preparations; excluding biodiesel, other than waste oils:
													--Light oils and preparations:
	0/0/0	0	3	0	0		0	0/0/0	0/0/			0/0/	---Motor gasoline, aviation gasoline
5.4	0/0/0	0	3.6	0	0		0	0/0/0	0/0/			0/0/	---Naphtha
	5/0/0		3.6	0	0		0	0//0	0/0/			0//	---Rubber solvent, paint solvent, extractive solvent
													---Other:
													----Nonene
	5/0/3.6		5.4	0	0		0	0//0	0/0/			0//	Nonene, excluding biodiesel, excluding biodiesel (Carbon 9 isomer mixtures containing >90%)
	5/0/3.6		5.4	0	0		0	0//0	0/0/			0//	Other nonene exctuding biodiesel
													----Other
	5/0/3.6		5.4	0	0		0	0//0	0/0/			0//	Mixture of isomers of isoamylene, excluding biodiesel
	5/0/3.6		5.4	0	0		0	0//0	0/0/		//	0//	Release agent (including products with oil content ≥ 70% by weight)
	5/0/3.6		5.4	0	0		0	0//0	0/0/			0//	Other light oils and preparations, excluding biodiesel (containing≥ 70% by weight of oils)
													--Other:
													---Kerosene distillages:
	0/0/0	4	0	0	0	0	0	0/0/0	0/0/0			0/0/	----Aviation kerosene

税则号列		货品名称〔CIQ 扩展编码及品名－T2 表示见附表 2〕	最惠(%)	暂定税率	普通	增值/消费	出口退税	计量单位	监管条件	检验检疫	特殊证件对美关税
2710.1912		----灯用煤油〔999 其他化工产品,301 易燃液体〕	9		14	13/1.2元/升	0	千克/升	47ABvy	MN	2/34
2710.1919		----其他									
2710.1919	10	正构烷烃(C9～C13),不含生物柴油〔999 其他化工产品,998 其他危险化学品〕	6	2	20	13/1.2元/升	0	千克/升	4y		2/27
2710.1919	20	异构烷烃溶剂,不含生物柴油(初沸点 225℃,闪点 92℃,密度 0.79g/cm3,粘度 3.57mm2/s)〔301〕	6		25	13/	0	千克/升	4ABy	MN	2/
2710.1919	90	其他煤油馏分的油及制品,不含生物柴油〔301 其他化工产品,302 易燃液体〕	6		20	13/1.2元/升	0	千克/升	4yAB	MN	2/31
		---柴油及其他燃料油:									
2710.1922		----5～7 号燃料油〔999 其他化工产品,998 其他危险化学品〕	6	1	20	13/1.2元/升	0	千克/升	7ABv	MN	2/26
2710.1923		----柴油〔999〕	6	1	11	13/1.2元/L	13	千克/升	47ABvy	MN	2/26
2710.1929		----其他									
2710.1929	10	蜡油,不含生物柴油(350℃以下馏出物体积＜20%,550℃以下馏出物体积＞80%)〔999 其他化工产品,998 其他危险化学品〕	6	0	20	13/1.2元/升	0	千克/升	7ABv	MN	2/25
2710.1929	90	其他燃料油,不含生物柴油〔999 其他化工产品,301 易燃液体〕	6		20	13/1.2元/升	0	千克/升	7ABv	MN	2/31
		---润滑油、润滑脂及其他重油:									
2710.1991		----润滑油〔999 其他化工产品,998 其他危险化学品〕	6		17	13/1.52元/升	0	千克/升	4Ayx	M	2/
2710.1992		----润滑脂〔999 其他化工产品,998 其他危险化学品〕	6		17	13/1.52元/升	0	千克/升	4Ayx	M	2/
2710.1993		----润滑油基础油〔999 其他化工产品,998 其他危险化学品〕	6		17	16/1.52元/升	0	千克/升	4yx		2/31
2710.1993	10	润滑油基础油,不含生物柴油(产品粘度 100℃时 37－47,粘度指数 80 及以上,颜色实测 2.0 左右,倾点实测－8℃左右)〔301 其他化工品,302 易燃液体〕	6		17	13/	0	千克/升	4xy		2/
2710.1993	90	其他润滑油基础油,不含生物柴油〔301 其他化工品,302 其他危险化学品〕	6		17	13/	0	千克/升	4xy		/31
2710.1994		----液体石蜡和重质液体石蜡[301 属于危险化学品的食品添加剂,302 无检疫要求食品添加剂,303 一般化学品,需申报仅用于工业用途不用于食品添加剂无检疫要求,304 易燃液体,需申报仅用于工业用途不用于食品添加剂无检疫要求〕	6		20	13/	0	千克	AB	MRNS	2/31
2710.1999		----其他〔999〕	6		20	16/1.2元/升	0	千克/升	B	N	2/31
2710.1999	10	白油(液体烃类混合物组成的无色透明油状液体,由原油分馏所得)(商品成分为100%白矿油,40℃时该产品粘度为 65mm? /s,闪点为 225℃,倾点为－10℃,比重(20℃/20℃)为 0.885)〔999〕	6		20	13/	0	千克/升	B	N	2/
2710.1999	90	其他重油;其他重油制品,不含生物柴油(包括按重量计含油≥70%的制品)〔999〕	6		20	13/	0	千克/升	B	N	2/31
2710.2000		-石油及从沥青矿物提取的油类(但原油除外)以及以上述油为基本成分(按重量计不低于 70%)的其他税目未列名制品,含生物柴油＜30%,废油除外〔999 其他化工产品,301 易燃液体〕	6		20	13/1.2元/升	0	千克/升	4Ay	M	2/31
		-废油:									
2710.9100		--含多氯联苯(PCBs)、多氯三联苯(PCTs)或多溴联苯(PBBs)的〔999 其他化工产品,998 其他危险化学品〕	6		20	13/	0	千克	9		2/31
2710.9900		--其他〔999 其他化工产品,998 其他危险化学品〕	6		20	13/	0	千克	9		2/31
27.11		石油气及其他烃类气:									
		-液化的:									
2711.1100		--天然气〔301〕	0		20	9/	0	千克	4ABy	MN	/25
2711.1200		--丙烷〔301〕	5	1	20	9/	0	千克	AB	MN	/26
		--丁烷:									
2711.1310		---直接灌注香烟打火机及类似打火器用,其包装容器的容积超过 300 立方厘米〔999〕	5		80	13/	0	千克			/30
2711.1390		---其他〔301〕	5	1	20	9/	0	千克			/31
2711.1400		--乙烯、丙烯、丁烯及丁二烯									
2711.1400	10	液化的乙烯〔999〕	5		20	13/	0	千克	AB	MN	/30

协定税率 %										特惠税率 %			
亚太5国	东/冰/格	巴基斯坦	韩国	瑞士	哥达	秘鲁	澳大利亚	新西/坡/智	港/澳/台	亚太2国	老/柬/缅	36/3/1	Article Description
	5/0/3.6		5.4	0	0	0	0	0//0	0/0/			0//	----Lamp-kerosene
													----Other
	0/0/0	0	0	0	0	0	0	0/0/0	0/0/0			0/0/	Normal paraffin hydrocarbon ($C_9 \sim C_{13}$), excluding biodiesel
	0/0/0	0	0	0	0	0	0	0/0/0	0/0/0		//	0/0/	Isoalkane solvent, without biodiesel (initial boiling point 225 ℃, flash point 92 ℃, density 0.79g/cm3, viscosity 3.57mm2 / s)
	0/0/0	0	0	0	0	0	0	0/0/0	0/0/0			0/0/	Other kerosene distillages oils and preparations, excluding biodiesel
													---Diesel oils and other fuel oils:
	0/0/0	4.5	0	0	0	0	0	0/0/0	0/0/			0/0/	----Fuel oils No. 5～No. 7
	5/0/0		3.6	0	0	0	0	0//0	0/0/				----Diesel engine
													----Other
	0/0/0	4.5	3.6	0	0	0	0	0/0/0	0/0/			0//	Paraffin oils excluding biodiesel (which＜20% by volume distil＜350℃, which＞80% by volume distil＜550℃)
	0/0/0	4.5	3.6	0	0	0	0	0/0/0	0/0/			0//	Other fuel oils, excluding biodiesel
													---Lubricating oils, lubricating greases and other heavy oils:
5.4	0/0/0	0	3.6	0	0	0	0	0/0/0	0/0/			0/0/0	----Lubricating grease
5.4	0/0/0	0	3.6	0	0	0	0	0/0/0	0/0/			0/0/	----Lubricating oils
	0/0/0	5	4	0	0	0	0	0//0	0/0/0			0/0/	----Basic oils for lubricating oils
	0/0/0	4	3.6	0	0	0	0	0/0/0	0/0/0		//	0/0/	Lubricating oil base oil, excluding biodiesel (product viscosity: 37—47 at 100 ℃, viscosity index: 80 or above, measured color: about 2.0, measured pour point: about － 8 ℃)
	0/0/0	4	3.6	0	0	0	0	0/0/0	0/0/0		//	0/0/	Base oil of other lubricants, excluding biodiesel
5.4	0/0/0	0	0	0	0	0	0	0/0/0	0/0/0			0/0/	----Liquid paraffin and heavy liquid paraffin
	0/0/0	5	4.5	0	0	0	0	0//0	0/0/			0/0/	----Other
	0/0/0	0	4.2	0	0	0	0	0/0/0	0/0/		//	0/0/	White oil (a colorless and transparent oil like liquid composed of liquid hydrocarbon mixture, obtained from crude oil fractionation) (the commercial component is 100% white mineral oil, the viscosity of the product is 65mm? / s at 40 ℃, the flash point is 225 ℃, the pour point is － 10 ℃, and the specific gravity (20 ℃ / 20 ℃) is 0.885)
	0/0/0	0	4.2	0	0	0	0	0/0/0	0/0/		//	0/0/	Other heavy oil; other heavy oil products, excluding biodiesel (including products with oil content ≥ 70% by weight)
	0/0/0	0	3.6	0	0		0	0/0/0	0/0/0			0/0/	-Petroleum oils and oils obtained from bituminous minerals, other than crude; preparations not elsewhere specified or included, containing by weight 70% or more of petroleum oils or of oils obtained from bituminous minerals, these oils being the basic constituents of thepreparations; containing biodiesel＜30%, other than waste oils
													-Waste oils:
	0/0/0	4		0	0	0	0	0//0	0/0/			0/0/	--Containing polychlorinated biphenyls(PCBs), polychlorinated terphenyls(PCTs) or polybrominated biphenyls(PBBs)
	0/0/0	4	0	0	0	0	0	0/0/0	0/0/			0/0/	--Other
													Petroleum gases and other gaseous hydrocarbons:
													-Liquefied:
												0/0/0	--Natural gas
3.5	0/0/0	0	0	0	0	0	0	0/0/0	0/0/			0/0/	--Propane
													--Butanes:
	0/0/0	4.5	4.4	3.3	0	0	0	0/0/0	0/0/			0/0/	---Liquid or liquefied-gas fuels in containers of a kind used for filling or refilling cigarette or similar lighters and of a capacity exceeding 300cm^3
	0/0/0	0	2	0	0	0	0	0/0/0	0/0/			0//	---Other
													--Ethylene, propylene, butylene and butadiene
	0/0/0	0	3	0	0	0	0	0/0/0	0/0/			0/0/	Liquefied ethylene,

税则号列	货品名称〔CIQ 扩展编码及品名－T2 表示见附表 2〕	最惠(%)	暂定税率	普通	增值/消费	出口退税	计量单位	监管条件	检验检疫	特殊证件对美关税
2711.1400　90	液化的丙烯、丁烯及丁二烯〔999〕	5		20	13/	0	千克			/30
	--其他：									
2711.1910	---直接灌注香烟打火机及类似打火器用的燃料，其包装容器的容积超过 300 立方厘米〔999〕	5		80	13/	0	千克			/30
2711.1990	---其他									
2711.1990　10	其他液化石油气〔999〕	3		20	9/	0	千克	AB	MN	/28
2711.1990　90	其他液化烃类气〔999〕	3		20	9/	0	千克			/28
	-气态的：									
2711.2100	--天然气〔301〕	0		20	9/	0	千克	AB	MN	/25
2711.2900	--其他									
2711.2900　10	其他气态石油气〔999〕	5		20	9/	0	千克	AB	MN	/30
2711.2900　90	其他气态烃类气〔999〕	5		20	9/	0	千克			/30
27.12	**凡士林；石蜡、微晶石蜡、疏松石蜡、地蜡、褐煤蜡、泥煤蜡、其他矿物蜡及用合成或其他方法制得的类似产品，不论是否着色：**									
2712.1000	-凡士林〔999〕	8		45	13/	0	千克	A	R	/38
2712.2000	-石蜡，按重量计含油量小于 0.75%〔999 其他化工产品，301 需申报仅用于工业用途不用于食品添加剂无检疫要求的化学品，998 其他危险化学品〕	8		45	13/	0	千克	4Ax	R	/38
	-其他：									
2712.9010	---微晶石蜡〔101 微晶蜡（无检疫要求食品添加剂），102 无检疫要求食品添加剂，103 需申报仅用于工业用途不用于食品添加剂无检疫要求的化学品〕	8		45	13/	0	千克	4Ax	R	/33
2712.9010　10	食品级微晶石蜡（相应指标符合《食品级微晶石蜡》（GB22160－2008）的要求）〔101 微晶蜡（无检疫要求食品添加剂）102 无检疫要求食品添加剂〕	8		45	13/	0	千克	4Ax	R	/
2712.9010　90	其他微晶石蜡〔999〕	8		45	13/	0	千克	4Ax	R	/38
2712.9090	---其他〔999 其他化工产品，998 其他危险化学品〕	8		45	13/	0	千克			/38
27.13	**石油焦、石油沥青及其他石油或从沥青矿物提取的油类的残渣：**									
	-石油焦：									
	--未煅烧：									
2713.1110	---硫的重量百分比小于 3%的〔999 其他化工产品，998 其他危险化学品〕	3		11	13/	0	千克			/28
2713.1190	---其他〔999 其他化工产品，998 其他危险化学品〕	3		11	13/	0	千克			/33
	--已煅烧：									
2713.1210	---硫的重量百分比小于 0.8%的〔999 其他化工产品，998 其他危险化学品〕	3		11	13/	0	千克			/33
2713.1290	---其他〔999 其他化工产品，998 其他危险化学品〕	3		11	13/	0	千克			/28
2713.2000	-石油沥青〔999 其他化工产品，998 其他危险化学品〕	8		35	13/	0	千克			/38
2713.9000	-其他石油或从沥青矿物提取的油类的残渣〔999 其他化工产品，998 其他危险化学品〕	6		35	13/	0	千克	9		/36
27.14	**天然沥青（地沥青）；沥青页岩、油页岩及焦油砂；沥青岩：**									
2714.1000	-沥青页岩、油页岩及焦油砂〔999 其他化工产品，998 其他危险化学品〕	6		20	13/	0	千克			/36
	-其他：									
2714.9010	---天然沥青（地沥青）〔999 其他化工产品，998 其他危险化学品〕	8	4	35	13/	0	千克			/34
2714.9020	---乳化沥青〔999 其他化工产品，998 其他危险化学品〕	0		20	13/	0	千克			/25
2714.9090	---其他〔999 其他化工产品，998 其他危险化学品〕	3		20	13/	0	千克			/33
27.15	**以天然沥青（地沥青）、石油沥青、矿物焦油或矿物焦油沥青为基本成分的沥青混合物（例如，沥青胶粘剂、稀释沥青）：**									
2715.0000	以天然沥青（地沥青）、石油沥青、矿物焦油或矿物焦油沥青为基本成分的沥青混合物（例如，沥青胶粘剂、稀释沥青）〔999〕	8		35	13/	0	千克			/33
27.16	**电力：**									
2716.0000	电力〔999〕	0		8	13/	13	千瓦时			/

协定税率 %										特惠税率 %			
亚太5国	东/冰/格	巴基斯坦	韩国	瑞士	哥达	秘鲁	澳大利亚	新西/坡/智	港/澳/台	亚太2国	老/柬/缅	36/3/1	Article Description
	0/0/0	0	3	0	0	0	0	0/0/0	0/0/			0/0/	Liquefied propylene, butylene and butadiene,
													--Other:
3.5	0/0/0	4.5	4	0	0	0	0	0/0/0	0/0/			0/0/	---Liquid or liquefied-gas fuels in containers of a kind used for filling or refilling cigarette or similar lighters and of a capacity exceeding 300cm³
													---Other
2.1	0/0/0	0	0	0	0	0	0	0/0/0	0/0/			0//	Other liquefied petroleum gases
2.1	0/0/0	0	0	0	0	0	0	0/0/0	0/0/			0//	Other liquefied gaseous hydrocar
													-In gaseous state:
												0/0/0	--Natural gas
													--Other
	0/0/0	0	0	0	0	0	0	0/0/0	0/0/			0/0/	Other petroleum gases, in gaseous state
	0/0/0	0	0	0	0	0	0	0/0/0	0/0/			0/0/	Other gaseous hydrocar, in gaseous state
													Petroleum jelly; paraffin wax, microcrystalline petroleum wax, slack wax, ozokerite, lignite wax, peat wax, other mineral waxes, and similar products obtained by synthesis or by other processes, whether or not coloured:
	0/0/0	4	0	0	0	0	0	0//0	0/0/			0/0/0	-Petroleum jelly
	0/0/0	4	3.2	0	0	0	0	0//0	0/0/			0/0/0	-Paraffin wax containing by weight less than 0.75% of oil
													-Other:
	0/0/0	5	4	0	0	0	0	0//0	0/0/			0/0/0	---Microcrystalline petroleum wax
	0/0/0	4	3.2	0	0	0	0	0/0/0	0/0/		//	0/0/0	Food grade microcrystalline paraffin (corresponding indexes meet the requirements of food grade microcrystalline paraffin (GB22160—2008))
	0/0/0	4	3.2	0	0	0	0	0/0/0	0/0/		//	0/0/0	Other microcrystalline paraffin
	0/0/0	4	3.2	0	0	0	0	0/0/0	0/0/			0/0/0	---Other
													Petroleum coke, petroleum bitumen and other residues of petroleum oils or of oils obtained from bituminous minerals:
													-Petroleum coke:
													--Not calcined:
	0/0/0	0	1.8	0	0	0	0	0//0	0/0/			0/0/0	---Containing by weight less than 3% of Sulphur
	0/0/0	0	1.8	0	0	0	0	0//0	0/0/			0/0/0	---Other
													--Calcined:
	0/0/0	0	1.8	0	0	0	0	0//0	0/0/			0/0/0	---Containing by weight less than 0.8% of Sulphur
	0/0/0	0	1.8	0	0	0	0	0//0	0/0/			0/0/0	---Other
5.6	0/0/0	4	4.8	0	0	0	0	0/0/0	0/0/			0/0/0	-Petroleum bitumen
	0/0/0	0	0	0	0	0	0	0/0/0	0/0/			0/0/0	-Other residues of petroleum oils or of oils obtained from bituminous minerals
													Bitumen and asphalt, natural; bituminous or oil shale and tar sands; asphaltites and asphaltic rocks:
	0/0/0	4.5	0	0	0	0	0	0/0/0	0/0/			0/0/0	-Bituminous or oil shale and tar sands
													-Other:
	0/0/0	4	4.8	0	0	0	0	0/0/0	0/0/			0/0/0	---Natural bitumen and asphalt
												0/0/0	---Emulsified bitumen and asphalt
	0/0/0	0	0	0	0	0	0	0/0/0	0/0/			0/0/0	---Other
													Bituminous mixtures based on natural asphalt, on natural bitumen, on petroleum bitumen, on mineral tar or on mineral tar pitch (for example, bituminous mastics, cut-backs):
	0/0/0	4	3.2	0	0	0	0	0/0/0	0/0/			0/0/0	Bituminous mixtures based on natural asphalt, on natural bitumen, on petroleum bitumen, on mineral tar or on mineral tar pitch (for example, bituminous mastics, cut-backs)
													Electrical energy:
												0/0/0	Electrical energy

第六类
化学工业及其相关工业的产品

注释：

一、(一)凡符合税目28.44或28.45规定的货品(放射性矿砂除外)，应分别归入这两个税目而不归入本协调制度的其他税号。

(二)除上述(一)款另有规定的以外，凡符合税目28.43、28.46或28.52规定的货品，应分别归入这两个税目而不归入本类的其他税目。

二、除上述注释一另有规定的以外，凡由于按一定剂量或作为零售包装而可归入税目30.04、30.05、30.06、32.12、33.03、33.04、33.05、33.06、33.07、35.06、37.07或38.08的货品，应分别归入以上税目，而不归入本协调制度的其他税目。

三、由两种或两种以上单独成分配套的货品，其部分或全部成分属于本类范围以内，混合后则构成第六类或第七类的货品，应按混合后产品归入相应的税目，但其组成成分必须同时符合下列条件：

(一)其包装形式足以表明这些成分不需经过改装就可一起使用的；

(二)一起报验的；以及

(三)这些成分的属性及相互比例足以表明是相互配用的。

第二十八章
无机化学品；贵金属、稀土金属、放射性元素及其同位素的有机及无机化合物

注释：

一、除条文另有规定的以外，本章各税目只适用于：

(一)单独的化学元素及单独的已有化学定义的化合物，不论是否含有杂质；

(二)上述(一)款产品的水溶液；

(三)溶于其他溶剂的上述(一)款产品，但该产品处于溶液状态只是为了安全或运输所采取的正常必要方法，其所用溶剂并不使该产品改变其一般用途而适合于某些特殊用途；

(四)为了保存或运输需要，加入稳定剂(包括抗结块剂)的上述(一)、(二)、(三)款产品；

(五)为了便于识别或安全起见，加入抗尘剂或着色剂的上述(一)、(二)、(三)、(四)款产品，但所加剂料并不使原产品改变其一般用途而适合于某些特殊用途。

二、除以有机物质稳定的连二亚硫酸盐及次硫酸盐(税目28.31)，无机碱的碳酸盐及过碳酸盐(税目28.36)，无机碱的氰化物、氧氰化物及氰络合物(税目28.37)，无机碱的雷酸盐、氰酸盐及硫氰酸盐(税目28.42)，税目28.43至28.46及28.52的有机产品，以及碳化物(税目28.49)之外，本章仅包括下列碳化合物：

(一)碳的氧化物，氰化氢及雷酸、异氰酸、硫氰酸及其他简单或络合氰酸(税目28.11)；

(二)碳的卤氧化物(税目28.12)；

(三)二硫化碳(税目28.13)；

(四)硫代碳酸盐、硒代碳酸盐、碲代碳酸盐、硒代氰酸盐、碲代氰酸盐、四氰硫基二氨基络酸盐及其他无机碱络合氰酸盐(税目28.42)；

(五)用尿素固化的过氧化氢(税目28.47)、氧硫化碳、硫代羰基卤化物、氰、卤化氰、氨基氰及其金属衍生物(税目28.53)，不论是否纯净，但氰氨化钙除外(第三十一章)。

三、除第六类注释一另有规定的以外，本章不包括：

(一)氯化钠或氧化镁(不论是否纯净)及第五类的其他产品；

(二)上述注释二所述以外的有机——无机化合物；

(三)第三十一章注释二、三、四或五所述的产品；

(四)税目32.06的用作发光剂的无机产品；税目32.07的搪瓷玻璃料及其他玻璃，呈粉、粒或粉片状的；

(五)人造石墨(税目38.01)；税目38.13的灭火器的装配药及已装药的灭火弹；税目38.24的零售包装的除墨剂；税目38.24的每颗重量不少于2.5克的碱金属或碱土金属卤化物的培养晶体(光学元件除外)；

(六)宝石或半宝石(天然、合成或再造)及这些宝石、半宝石的粉末(税目71.02至71.05)，第七十一章的贵金属及贵金属合金；

(七)第十五类的金属(不论是否纯净)、金属合金或金属陶瓷，包括硬质合金(与金属烧结的金属碳化物)；

(八)光学元件，例如用碱金属或碱土金属卤化物制成的(税目90.01)。

四、由本章第二分章的非金属酸和第四分章的金属酸所构成的已有化学定义的络酸，应归入税目28.11。

五、税目28.26至28.42只适用于金属盐、铵盐及过氧酸盐。除条文另有规定的以外，复盐及络盐应归入税目28.42。

六、税目28.44只适用于：

(一)锝(原子序数43)、钷(原子序数61)、钋(原子序数84)及原子序数大于84的所有化学元素；

(二)天然或人造放射性同位素(包括第十四类及第十五类的贵金属和贱金属的放射性同位素)，不论是否混合；

(三)上述元素或同位素的无机或有机化合物，不论是否已有化学定义或是否混合；

SECTION Ⅵ
PRODUCTS OF THE CHEMICAL OR ALLIED INDUSTRIES

Notes:

1. (a) Goods (other than radioactive ores) answering to a description in heading No. 28.44 or 28.45 are to be classified in those headings and in no other heading of the Nomenclature.
   (b) Subject to paragraph (a) above, goods answering to a description in heading No. 28.43, 28.46 or 28.52 are to be classified in those headings and in no other heading of this Seciton.
2. Subject to Note 1 above, goods classifiable in heading No. 30.04, 30.05, 30.06, 32.12, 33.03, 33.04, 33.05, 33.06, 33.07, 35.06, 37.07, or 38.08 by reason of being put up in measured doses or for retail sale are to be classified in those headings and in no other headings of the Nomenclature.
3. Goods put up in sets consisting of two or more separate constituents, some or all of which fall in this Section and are intended to be mixed together to obtain a product of Section Ⅵ or Ⅶ, are to be classified in the heading appropriate to that product, provided that the constituents are:
   (a) having regard to the manner in which they are put up, clearly identifiable as being intended to be used together without first being repacked;
   (b) presented together; and
   (c) identifiable, whether by their nature or by the relative proportions in which they are present, as being complementary one to another.

Chapter 28
Inorganic chemicals; organic or inorganic compounds of precious metals, of rare-earth metals of radioactive elements or of isotopes

Notes:

1. Except where the context otherwise requires, the headings of this Chapter apply only to:
   (a) Separate chemical elements and separate chemically defined compounds, whether or not containing impurities;
   (b) The products mentioned in (a) above dissolved in water;
   (c) The products mentioned in (a) above dissolved in other solvents, provided that the solution constitutes a normal and necessary method of putting up these products adopted solely for reasons of safety or for transport, and that the solvent does not render the product particularly suitable for specific use rather than for general use;
   (d) The products mentioned in (a), (b) or (c) above with an added stabilizer (including an anti-caking agent) necessary for their preservation or transport;
   (e) The products mentioned in (a), (b), (c) or (d) above with an added antidusting agent or a colouring substance added to facilitate their identification or for safety reasons, provided that the additions do not render the product particularly suitable for specific use rather than for general use.
2. In addition to dithionites and sulphoxylates, stabilized with organic substances (heading No. 28.31), carbonates and peroxocarbonates of inorganic bases (heading No. 28.36), cyanides, cyanide oxides and complex cyanides of inorganic bases (heading No. 28.37), fulminates, cyanates and thiocyanates, of inorganic bases (heading No. 28.42), organic products included in headings No. 28.43 to 28.46 and 28.52 and carbides (heading No. 28.49), only the following compounds of carbon are to the classified in this Chapter:
   (a) Oxides of carbon, hydrogen cyanide and fulminic, isocyanic, thiocyanic and other simple or complex cyanogen acids (heading No. 28.11);
   (b) Halide oxides of carbon (heading No. 28.12);
   (c) Carbon disulphide (heading No. 28.13);
   (d) Thiocarbonates, selenocarbonates, tellurocarbonates, selenocyanates, tellurocyanates, tetrathiocyanatodiamminochromates (reineckates) and other complex cyanates, of inorganic bases (heading No. 28.42);
   (e) Hydrogen peroxide, solidified with urea (heading No. 28.47), carbon oxysulphide, thiocarbonyl halides, cyanogen, cyanogen halides and cyanamide and its metal derivatives (heading No. 28.53) other than calcium cyanamide, whether or not pure (Chapter 31).
3. Subject to the provisions of Note 1 to Section Ⅵ, this Chapter does not cover:
   (a) Sodium chloride or magnesium oxide, whether or not pure, or other products of Section Ⅴ;
   (b) Organo-inorganic compounds other than those mentioned in Note 2 above;
   (c) Products mentioned in Note 2, 3, 4 or 5 to Chapter 31;
   (d) Inorganic products of a kind used as luminophores, of heading No. 32.06; glass frit and other glass in the form of powder, granules of flakes, of heading No. 32.07;
   (e) Artificial graphite (heading No. 38.01); products put up as charges for fire-extinguishers or put up in fire-extinguishing grenades, of heading No. 38.13; ink removers put up in packings for retail sale, of heading No. 38.24, cultured crystals (other than optical elements) weighing not less than 2.5g each, of the halides of the alkali or alkaline-earth metals, of heading No. 38.24;
   (f) Precious or semi-precious stones (natural, synthetic or reconstructed) or dust or powder of such stones (headings Nos. 71.02 to 71.05), or precious metals or precious metal alloys of Chapter 71;
   (g) The metals, whether or not pure, metal alloys or cermets, including sintered metal carbides (metal carbides sintered with a metal), of Section ⅩⅤ; or
   (h) Optical elements, for example, of the halides of the alkali or alkaline-earth metals (heading No. 90.01).
4. Chemically defined complex acids consisting of a nonmetal acid of sub-Chapter Ⅱ and a metal acid of sub-Chapter Ⅳ are to be classified in heading No. 28.11.
5. Headings Nos. 28.26 to 28.42 apply only to metal or ammonium salts or peroxysalts. Except where the context otherwise requires, double or complex salts are to be classified in heading No. 28.42.
6. Heading No. 28.44 applies only to:
   (a) Technetium (atomic No. 43), promethium (atomic No. 61), polonium (atomic No. 84) and all elements with an atomic number greater than 84;
   (b) Natural or artificial radioactive isotopes (including those of the precious metals or of the base metals of Sections ⅩⅣ and ⅩⅤ), whether or not mixed together;
   (c) Compounds, inorganic or organic, of these elements or isotopes, whether or not chemically defined, whether or not mixed together;

(四)含有上述元素或同位素及其无机或有机化合物并且具有某种放射性强度超过74贝克勒尔/克(0.002微居里/克)的合金、分散体(包括金属陶瓷)、陶瓷产品及混合物;

(五)核反应堆已耗尽(已辐照)的燃料元件(释热元件);

(六)放射性的残渣,不论是否有用。

税目28.44、28.45及本注释所称"同位素",是指:

1. 单独的核素,但不包括自然界中以单一同位素状态存在的核素;

2. 同一元素的同位素混合物,其中一种或几种同位素已被浓缩,即人工地改变了该元素同位素的自然构成。

七、税目28.53包括按重量计含磷量超过15%的磷化铜(磷铜)。

八、经掺杂用于电子工业的化学元素(例如,硅、硒),如果拉制后未经加工或呈圆筒形、棒形,应归入本章;如果已切成圆片、薄片或类似形状,则归入税目38.18。

子目注释:

子目2812.10所称"已有化学定义"是指符合第二十八章注释一(一)至(五)或第二十九章注释一(一)至(八)规定的汞的无机或有化合物。

税则号列	货品名称〔CIQ扩展编码及品名—T2表示见附表2〕	最惠(%)	暂定税率	普通	增值/消费	出口退税	计量单位	监管条件	检验检疫	特殊证件对美关税
	第一分章　化学元素									
28.01	**氟、氯、溴及碘:**									
2801.1000	-氯〔999〕	5		80	13/	0	千克	AB	MN	1/35
2801.2000	-碘〔999〕	5		30	13/	0	千克	G		1/30
	-氟;溴:									
2801.3010	---氟〔999〕	5		30	13/	0	千克	AB	MN	1/
2801.3020	---溴〔999〕	5	1	30	13/	0	千克	23AB	MN	1/31
28.02	**升华硫磺、沉淀硫磺;胶态硫磺:**									
2802.0000	升华硫磺、沉淀硫磺;胶态硫磺〔101胶体硫,102硫磺〕	5	1	17	13/	0	千克	AB	MN	1/26
28.03	**碳(碳黑及其他税目未列名的其他形态的碳):**									
2803.0000	碳(包括碳黑及其他税号未列名的其他形态的碳)〔999〕	5		35	13/	0	千克			1/20
28.04	**氢、稀有气体及其他非金属:**									
2804.1000	-氢〔101氢气和甲烷混合物(压缩的),102压缩或液化的氢气,103氢气和甲烷混合物(压缩的),301压缩或液化的氢气〕	5		30	13/	0	千克/立方米	AB	MN	1/30
	-稀有气体:									
2804.2100	--氩〔301〕	5		30	13/	0	千克/立方米	AB	MN	1/35
2804.2900	--其他〔109稀有气体混合物,如氦氖混合气,301〕	5		30	13/	0	千克/立方米			1/15
2804.3000	-氮〔301〕	5		30	13/	0	千克/立方米	AB	MN	1/15
2804.4000	-氧〔301〕	5		80	13/	0	千克/立方米	AB	MN	1/15
2804.5000	-硼;碲									
2804.5000 01	碲〔999〕	5	0	17	13/	13	千克			1/30
2804.5000 10	颗粒＜500μm的硼及其合金(含量≥97%,不论球形、椭球体、雾化、片状、研碎金属燃料)〔999〕	5		17	13/	13	千克	3		1/35
2804.5000 20	能量密度＞40MJ/kg的硼浆(硼溶于溶剂形成的硼浆)〔999〕	5		17	13/	13	千克	3		1/35
2804.5000 90	其他硼〔999〕	5		17	13/	13	千克			1/35
	-硅:									
	--按重量计含硅量不少于99.99%:									
	---经掺杂用于电子工业的直径在7.5厘米及以上的单晶硅棒:									
2804.6117	----直径在30厘米及以上的〔999〕	4		11	13/	13	千克			1/14
2804.6119	----其他〔999〕	4		11	13/	0	千克			1/24
2804.6120	---经掺杂用于电子工业的其他单晶硅棒〔999〕	4		17	13/	0	千克			1/34
2804.6190	---其他									
2804.6190 11	含硅量≥99.9999999%的多晶硅废碎料(太阳能级多晶硅除外)〔101多晶硅,102硅废碎料〕	4		30	13/	0	千克	9	M	1/29
2804.6190 12	含硅量≥99.9999999%的太阳能级多晶硅〔999〕	4		30	13/	0	千克			1/29
2804.6190 13	含硅量≥99.9999999%的太阳能级多晶硅废碎料〔999〕	4		30	13/	0	千克	AP	M	1/29
2804.6190 19	其他含硅量≥99.9999999%的多晶硅(太阳能极多晶硅除外)〔999〕	4		30	13/	0	千克			1/29
2804.6190 91	其他含硅量≥99.99%的硅废碎料(太阳能级多晶硅除外)〔101其他硅,102硅废碎料〕	4		30	13/	0	千克	9	M	1/29
2804.6190 92	含硅量≥99.99%的太阳能级多晶硅〔999〕	4		30	13/	0	千克			1/29
2804.6190 93	含硅量≥99.99%的太阳能级多晶硅废碎料〔999〕	4		30	13/	0	千克	AP	M	1/29
2804.6190 99	其他含硅量≥99.99%的硅(太阳能级多晶硅除外)〔999〕	4		30	13/	0	千克			1/29

(d) Alloys, dispersions (including cermets), ceramic products and mixtures containing these elements or isotopes or inorganic or organic compounds thereof and having a specific radioactivity exceeding 74 Bq/g (0.002μ Ci/g);
(e) Spent (irradiated) fuel elements (cartridges) of nuclear reactors;
(f) Radioactive residues whether or not usable.

The term "isotopes", for the purposes of this Note and of the wording of headings No. 28.44 and 28.45, refers to:
(i) individual nuclides, excluding, however, those existing in nature in the monoisotopic state;
(ii) mixtures of isotopes of one and the same element, enriched in one or several of the said isotopes, that is, elements of which the natural isotopic composition has been artificially modified.

7. Heading No. 28.53 includes copper phosphide (phosphor copper) containing more than 15% by weight of phosphorus.
8. Chemical elements (for example, silicon and selenium) doped for use in electronics are to be classified in this Chapter, provided that they are in forms unworked as drawn, or in the form of cylinders or rods. When cut in the form of discs, wafers or similar forms, they fall in heading No. 38.18.

Subheading Note:

For the purposes of Subheading 2812.10, the expression "chemically defined" means all organic or inorganic compounds of mercury meeting the requirements of paragraphs (a) to (e) of Note 1 to Chapter 28 or paragraphs (a) to (h) of Note 1 to Chapter 29

协定税率 %										特惠税率 %			
亚太5国	东/冰/格	巴基斯坦	韩国	瑞士	哥达	秘鲁	澳大利亚	新西/坡/智	港/澳/台	亚太2国	老/柬/缅	36/3/1	Article Description
													Ⅰ. CHEMICAL ELEMENTS
													Fluorine, chlorine, bromine and iodine:
	0/0/0	0	0	0	0	0	0	0//0	0/0/			0/0/	-Chlorine
	0/0/0	0	0	0	0		0	0//	0/0/			0/0/	-Iodine
													-Fluorine; bromine:
4.5	0/0/0	0	0	0	0	0	0	0//0	0/0/			0/0/	---Fluorine
	0/0/0	0	0	0	0	0	0	0//0	0/0/			0/0/	---Bromine
													Sulphur, sublimed or precipitated; colloidal sulphur:
	0/0/0	0	0	0	0	0	0	0//0	0/0/			0/0/	Sulphur, sublimed or precipitated; colloidal sulphur
													Carbon (carbon blacks and other forms of carbon not elsewhere specified or included):
3.3	0//0	0	3.3	0	0	0	0	0//0	0/0/0			0/0/0	Carbon (carbon blacks and other forms of carbon not elsewhere specified or included)
													Hydrogen, rare gases and other non-metals:
	0/0/0	0	2.2	0	0	0	0	0//0	0/0/			0/0/0	-Hydrogen
													-Rare gases:
	0/0/0	0	0	0	0	0	0	0//0	0/0/			0/0/0	--Argon
	0/0/0	0	0	0	0	0	0	0//0	0/0/			0/0/0	--Other
	0/0/0	0	0	0	0	0	0	0//0	0/0/			0/0/0	-Nitrogen
	0/0/0	0	0	0	0	0	0	0//0	0/0/			0/0/0	-Oxygen
													-Boron; tellurium
	0/0/0	0	0	0	0	0	0	0//0	0/0/			0/0/0	tellurium
	0/0/0	0	0	0	0	0	0	0//0	0/0/			0/0/0	Boron and its alloys, granularity<500μm (containing boron≥97%, whether in the form of spheroid, ellipsoid, flakes, atomized or pulverized metallic fuel)
	0/0/0	0	0	0	0	0	0	0//0	0/0/			0/0/0	Boron paste, energy density>4 Mega J/kg, boron dissolved in solvent
	0/0/0	0	0	0	0	0	0	0//0	0/0/			0/0/0	Other boron
													-Silicon:
													--Containing by weight not less than 99.99% of silicon:
													---Monocrystals doped for use in electronics, in the form of cylinders or rods, 7.5cm or more in diameter:
	0/0/0	0	0	0	0	0	0	0//0	0/0/			0/0/0	----30cm or more in diameter
	0/0/0	0		0	0	0	0	0//0	0/0/			0/0/0	----Other
3.6	0/0/0	0	0	0	0	0	0	0//0	0/0/			0/0/0	---Other monocrystals doped for use in electronics, in the form of cylinders or rods
													---Other
	0/0/0	0	2.4	0	0	0	0	0//0	0/0/			0/0/0	Waste and scrape of polycrystalline silicon, containing by weight not less than 99.9999999% (excluding solar-grade polysilicon)
	0/0/0	0	2.4	0	0	0	0	0//0	0/0/			0/0/0	Solar grade polysilicon silicon content ≥99.9999999%
	0/0/0	0	2.4	0	0	0	0	0//0	0/0/			0/0/0	Solar grade polysilicon silicon content ≥ 99.9999999% of waste and scrap
	0/0/0	0	2.4	0	0	0	0	0//0	0/0/			0/0/0	Other polycrystalline silicon, containing by weight not less than 99.9999999% (excluding solay-grade poly silicon)
	0/0/0	0	2.4	0	0	0	0	0//0	0/0/			0/0/0	Waste and scrape of silicon, containing by weight not less than 99.99% (excluding solar-grade polysilicon)
	0/0/0	0	2.4	0	0	0	0	0//0	0/0/			0/0/0	Solar grade polysilicon silicon content ≥ 99.99%
	0/0/0	0	2.4	0	0	0	0	0//0	0/0/			0/0/0	Solar grade polysilicon silicon content ≥ 99.99% of waste and scrap
	0/0/0	0	2.4	0	0	0	0	0//0	0/0/			0/0/0	Other silicon, containing by weight not less than 99.99% (excluding solar-grade polysilicon)

税则号列	货品名称〔CIQ 扩展编码及品名－T2 表示见附表 2〕	最惠(%)	暂定税率	普通	增值/消费	出口退税	计量单位	监管条件	检验检疫	特殊证件对美关税
2804.6900	--其他〔101 化工产品，102 金属硅，103 其他硅〕	4		30	13/	0	千克			1/34
	-磷：									
2804.7010	---黄磷（白磷）〔999〕	5		30	13/	0	千克	AB	MN	1/
2804.7090	---其他									
2804.7090 10	红磷〔301〕	5	5	30	13/	0	千克	ABG	MN	1/30
2804.7090 90	其他磷〔999 其他化工产品，998 其他危险化学品〕	5	5	30	13/	0	千克			1/30
2804.8000	-砷〔101，301 毒性物质和感染性物质〕	5		30	13/	0	千克	AB	MN	1/35
	-硒：									
2804.9010	---经掺杂用于电子工业的硒晶体棒〔999〕	4		17	13/	0	千克			1/
2804.9090	---其他〔999 其他化工产品，998 其他危险化学品〕	5	0	30	13/	13	千克			1/30
28.05	**碱金属、碱土金属；稀土金属、钪及钇，不论是否相互混合或相互熔合；汞：**									
	-碱金属及碱土金属：									
2805.1100	--钠〔101 碱金属、碱土金属，102 金属钠〕	5		30	13/	0	千克	AB	MN	1/15
2805.1200	--钙									
2805.1200 10	高纯度钙[金属杂质（除镁外）含量<1‰，硼含量小于十万分之一]〔101 碱金属、碱土金属，102 金属钙〕	5	1	30	13/	0	千克	3A	M	1/31
2805.1200 90	其他钙〔301〕	5	1	30	13/	0	千克			1/31
	--其他：									
2805.1910	---锂〔999〕	5	1	30	13/	0	千克	AB	MN	1/11
2805.1990	---其他〔T2〕	5	1	30	13/	0	千克			1/11
	-稀土金属、钪及钇，不论是否相互混合或相互熔合：									
	---稀土金属、钪及钇，未相互混合或相互熔合：									
2805.3011	----钕〔301〕	5	0	30	13/	0	千克	4Bxy	N	1/
2805.3012	----镝〔999〕	5	0	30	13/	0	千克	4Bxy	N	1/10
2805.3013	----铽〔999〕	5	0	30	13/	0	千克	4Bxy	N	1/
2805.3014	----镧〔999〕	5	0	30	13/	0	千克	4Bxy	N	1/10
2805.3015	----铈									
2805.3015 10	颗粒<500μm 的铈及其合金（含量≥97%，不论球形，椭球体，雾化，片状，研碎金属燃料；未相互混合或相互熔合）〔301〕	5	0	30	13/	0	千克	3B	N	1/10
2805.3015 90	其他金属铈（未相互混合或相互熔合）〔999〕	5	0	30	13/	0	千克	4Bxy	N	1/10
2805.3016	----镨〔999〕	5	0	30	13/	0	千克	4Bxy	N	1/
2805.3017	----钇〔999〕	5	0	30	13/	0	千克	4Bxy	N	1/10
2805.3019	----其他〔101 金属钐，102 金属铕，103 金属钪，104 稀土金属，105 金属镧（浸在煤油中的），106 金属铈（浸在煤油中的）〕	5	0	30	13/	0	千克	4Bxy	N	1/10
	---稀土金属、钪及钇，相互混合或相互熔合：									
2805.3021	----电池级〔301〕	5	0	30	13/	0	千克	4Bxy	N	1/
2805.3029	----其他〔301 米许合金，属于危险化学品的稀土，302 不属于危险化学品的稀土〕	5	0	30	13/	0	千克	4Bxy	N	1/30
2805.4000	-汞〔999〕	5		17	13/	0	千克	ABX	MN	1/

第二分章　无机酸及非金属；
无机氧化物

税则号列	货品名称	最惠(%)	暂定税率	普通	增值/消费	出口退税	计量单位	监管条件	检验检疫	特殊证件对美关税
28.06	**氯化氢（盐酸）；氯磺酸：**									
2806.1000	-氯化氢（盐酸）〔T2〕	5		80	13/	0	千克	23AB	MRNS	1/20
2806.2000	-氯磺酸〔999〕	5		40	13/	0	千克	AB	MN	1/
28.07	**硫酸；发烟硫酸：**									
2807.0000	硫酸；发烟硫酸									
2807.0000 10	硫酸〔101 废硫酸，102 电池液（酸性的），103 危险化学品，104 属于危险化学品的食品添加剂〕	5	1	35	13/	0	千克	32		1/31
2807.0000 90	发烟硫酸〔999〕	5	1	35	13/	0	千克	AB	MN	1/31
28.08	**硝酸；磺硝酸：**									
2808.0000	硝酸；磺硝酸									
2808.0000 10	红发烟硝酸〔999〕	5		40	13/	0	千克	3A	M	1/35
2808.0000 90	磺硝酸及其他硝酸〔101 硝酸，102 废硝酸〕	5		40	13/	0	千克			1/35
28.09	**五氧化二磷；磷酸；多磷酸，不论是否已有化学定义：**									
2809.1000	-五氧化二磷〔999〕	1		8	13/	0	千克	AB	MN	1/6
	-磷酸及多磷酸：									
	---磷酸及偏磷酸、焦磷酸：									
2809.2011	----食品级磷酸〔101 饲料添加剂，102 属于危险化学品的食品添加剂〕	1		8	13/	0	千克	AB	RNS	1/

协定税率 %										特惠税率 %			Article Description
亚太5国	东/冰/格	巴基斯坦	韩国	瑞士	哥达	秘鲁	澳大利亚	新西/坡/智	巷/澳/台	亚太2国	老/柬/缅	36/3/1	
	0/0/0	0	0	0	0	0	0	0//0	0/0/			0/0/0	--Other
													-Phosphorus:
	0/0/0	0	0	0	0	0	0	0//0	0/0/			0/0/0	---Yellow phosphorus (white phosphorus)
													---Other
	0/0/0	0	2.2	0	0	0	0	0//0	0/0/			0/0/0	Red phosphorus
	0/0/0	0	2.2	0	0	0	0	0//0	0/0/			0/0/0	Other phosphorus
	0/0/0	0	0	0	0	0	0	0//0	0/0/			0/0/0	-Arsenic
													-Selenium:
3.2	0/0/0	0	0	0	0	0	0	0//0	0/0/			0/0/0	---Crystals doped for use in electronics, in the form of cylinders or rods
	0/0/0	0	0	0	0	1.9	0	0//0	0/0/			0/0/	---Other
													Alkali or alkaline-earth metals; rare-earth metals, scandium and yttrium, whether or not intermixed or interalloyed; mercury:
													-Alkali metals or alkaline-earth metals:
	0/0/0	0	0	0	0	0	0	0//0	0/0/			0/0/	--Sodium
													--Calcium
	0/0/0	0	0	0	0	0	0	0//0	0/0/			0/0/	Calcium, with a high purity, metallic impurity(other than Magnesium)<1‰, containing boron<$1/10^5$
	0/0/0	0	0	0	0	0	0	0//0	0/0/			0/0/	Other Calcium
													--Other:
	0/0/0	0	0	0	0	0	0	0//0	0/0/			0/0/	---Lithium
	0/0/0	0	0	0	0	0	0	0//0	0/0/			0/0/	---Other
													-Rare-earth metals, scandium and yttrium, whether or not intermixed or interalloyed:
													---Not intermixed or interalloyed:
	0/0/0	0	0	0	0	0	0	0//0	0/0/			0/0/	----Neodymium
	0/0/0	0	0	0	0	0	0	0//0	0/0/			0/0/	----Dysprosium
	0/0/0	0	0	0	0	0	0	0//0	0/0/			0/0/	----Terbium
	0/0/0	0	0	0	0	0	0	0//0	0/0/			0/0/	----Lanthanum
													----Cerium
	0/0/0	0	0	0	0	0	0	0//0	0/0/			0/0/	Cerium and its alloys, granularity < 500μm, containing cerium ≥ 97%, whether in the form of spheroid, ellipsoid, flakes, atomized or pulverized metallic fuel
	0/0/0	0	0	0	0	0	0	0//0	0/0/			0/0/	Other metalic cerium, not intermixed or interalloyed
	0/0/0	0	0	0	0	0	0	0//0	0/0/			0/0/	----Praseodymium
	0/0/0	0	0	0	0	0	0	0//0	0/0/			0/0/	----Yttrium
	0/0/0	0	0	0	0	0	0	0//0	0/0/			0/0/	----Other
													---intermixed or interalloyed:
	0/0/0	0	0	0	0	0	0	0//0	0/0/			0/0/	----Battery grade
	0/0/0	0	0	0	0	0	0	0//0	0/0/			0/0/	----Other
	0/0/0	0	0	0	0	0	0	0//0	0/0/			0/0/	-Mercury
													Ⅱ. INORGANIC ACIDS AND INORGANIC OXYGEN COMPOUNDS OF NON-METALS
													Hydrogen chloride (hydrochloric acid); chorosulphuric acid:
	0/0/0	0	0	0	0	0	0	0//0	0/0/			0/0/	-Hydrogen chloride (hydrochloric acid)
	0/0/0	0	0	0	0	0	0	0//0	0/0/			0/0/	-Chlorosulphuric acid
													Sulphuric acid; oleum:
													Sulphuric acid; oleum
	0/0/0	0	0	0	0	0	0	0//0	0/0/			0/0/	Sulphuric acid
	0/0/0	0	0	0	0	0	0	0//0	0/0/			0/0/	Oleum
													Nitric acid; sulphonitric acids:
													Nitric acid; sulphonitric acids
	0/0/0	0	0	0	0	0	0	0//0	0/0/			0/0/	Red fuming nitric acid
	0/0/0	0	0	0	0	0	0	0//0	0/0/			0/0/	Sulphonitric acids, other nitric acids
													Diphosphorus pentaoxide; phosphoric acid; polyphosphoric acids, whether or not chemically defined:
	0/0/0	0	0	0	0	0	0	0//0	0/0/			0/0/	-Diphosphorus pentaoxide
													-Phosphoric acid and polyphosphoric acids:
													---Phosphoric acid, metaphosphoric acid and pyrophosphoric acid:
	0/0/0	0	0	0	0	0	0	0//0	0/0/			0/0/	----Phosphoric acid, food grade

税则号列	货品名称〔CIQ 扩展编码及品名—T2 表示见附表 2〕	最惠(%)	暂定税率	普通	增值/消费	出口退税	计量单位	监管条件	检验检疫	特殊证件对美关税
2809.2019	----其他〔101 饲料添加剂,102 正磷酸(酸性腐蚀品),301 腐蚀性物质,302 需申报仅用于工业用途不用于食品添加剂无检疫要求的化学品,303 其他化工产品〕	1		8	13/	0	千克	B	N	1/26
2809.2090	---其他〔101 饲料添加剂,102 化工产品〕	5		35	13/	0	千克			1/15
28.10	**硼的氧化物;硼酸:**									
2810.0010	---硼的氧化物〔999〕	5		30	13/	0	千克			1/15
2810.0020	---硼酸〔999〕	5		30	13/	0	千克	AB	MN	1/25
28.11	**其他无机酸及非金属无机氧化物:**									
	-其他无机酸:									
2811.1110	---电子级氢氟酸〔301〕	5.5		35	13/	0	千克	3AB	MN	1/
2811.1190	--氟化氢(氢氟酸)〔301〕	5		35	13/	0	千克	3AB	MN	1/30
2811.1200	--氰化氢(氢氰酸)〔999〕	5		35	13/	0	千克	23		1/
	--其他:									
2811.1920	---硒化氢〔999〕	5		35	13/	0	千克	AB	MN	1/
2811.1990	---其他									
2811.1990 10	氢碘酸〔999〕	5		35	13/	0	千克	ABG	MN	1/30
2811.1990 20	砷酸、焦砷酸、偏砷酸〔301〕	5		35	13/	0	千克			1/30
2811.1990 90	其他无机酸[T2]	5		35	13/	0	千克	AB	MRNS	1/30
	-其他非金属无机氧化物:									
2811.2100	--二氧化碳[T2]	5		30	13/	0	千克	AB	MRNS	1/35
	--二氧化硅:									
2811.2210	---硅胶〔999〕	5		30	13/	10	千克	A	R	1/15
2811.2290	---其他〔101 饲料添加剂,102 硅粉(非晶形的),301 需申报仅用于工业用途不用于食品添加剂无检疫要求的化学品,302 无检疫要求食品添加剂〕	5		30	13/	10	千克	A	R	1/30
2811.2900	--其他									
2811.2900 10	三氧化二砷、五氧化二砷[亚砷(酸)酐、砒霜、白砒、氧化亚砷、砷(酸)酐、三氧化砷]〔301〕	5		30	13/	0	千克			1/20
2811.2900 20	四氧化二氮〔999〕	5		30	13/	0	千克	3A	M	1/20
2811.2900 90	其他非金属无机氧化物〔301 易燃气体,302 非易燃无毒气体,303 毒性气体,304 氧化性物质,305 毒性物质和感染性物质,306 腐蚀性物质,307 其他化工产品〕	5		30	13/	0	千克			1/20
	第三分章 非金属卤化物及硫化物*									
28.12	**非金属卤化物及卤氧化物:**									
	-氯化物及氯氧化物:									
2812.1100	--碳酰二氯〔999〕	5		30	13/	0	千克	23		1/
2812.1200	--氧氯化磷〔999〕	5		30	13/	0	千克	23		1/15
2812.1300	--三氯化磷〔999〕	5		30	13/	0	千克	23AB	MN	1/
2812.1400	--五氯化磷〔999〕	5		30	13/	0	千克	23AB	MN	1/
2812.1500	--一氯化硫〔999〕	5		30	13/	0	千克	23AB	MN	1/
2812.1600	--二氯化硫〔999〕	5		30	13/	0	千克	23AB	MN	1/
2812.1700	--亚硫酰氯〔999〕	5		30	13/	0	千克	23AB	MN	1/
2812.1900	--其他									
2812.1900 20	三氯化砷〔999〕	5		30	13/	0	千克	23AB	MN	1/35
2812.1900 91	其他非金属氯化物〔999 毒性物质和感染性物质,301 易燃气体,302 毒性气体,303 腐蚀性物质,304 其他化工产品〕	5		30	13/	0	千克			1/35
2812.1900 99	其他非金属氯氧化物〔999 其他化工产品,301 毒性气体,302 腐蚀性物质〕	5		30	13/	0	千克			1/35
	-其他:									
	---氟化物及氟氧化物:									
2812.9011	----三氟化氮〔999〕	5		30	13/	10	千克	AB	MN	1/30
2812.9019	----其他									
2812.9019 10	三氟化氯〔999〕	5		30	13/	0	千克	3A	M	1/15
2812.9019 20	三氟化砷(氟化亚砷)〔999〕	5		30	13/	0	千克			1/15
2812.9019 30	硫酰氟〔999〕	5		30	13/	0	千克	S		1/15
2812.9019 90	其他氟化物及氟氧化物〔301 非易燃无毒气体,302 毒性气体,303 氧化性物质,304 毒性物质和感染性物质,305 其他化工产品〕	5		30	13/	0	千克			1/15
2812.9090	---其他									
2812.9090 10	三溴化砷,三碘化砷(溴化亚砷,碘化亚砷)〔301〕	5		30	13/	0	千克			1/15
2812.9090 90	其他非金属卤化物及卤氧化物〔301 易于自燃的物质,302 氧化性物质,303 毒性物质和感染性物质,304 腐蚀性物质,305 其他化工产品〕	5		30	13/	0	千克			1/15
28.13	**非金属硫化物;商品三硫化二磷:**									

协定税率 %										特惠税率 %			Article Description
亚太5国	东/冰/格	巴基斯坦	韩国	瑞士	哥达	秘鲁	澳大利亚	新西/坡/智	港/澳/台	亚太2国	老/柬/缅	36/3/1	
	0/0/0	0	0.4	0	0	0	0	0//0	0/0/			0/0/	----Other
	0/0/0	0	0	0	0	0	0	0//0	0/0/			0/0/	---Other
													Oxides of boron; boric acids:
4.5	0/0/0	0	0	0	0	0	0	0//0	0/0/			0/0/	---Oxides of boron
	0/0/0	0	0	0	0	0	0	0//0	0/0/			0/0/	---Boric acids
													Other inorganic acids and other inorganic oxygen compounds of non-metals:
													-Other inorganic acids:
	0/0/0	0	0	0	0	0	0	0//0	0/0/			0/0/0	---Electronic grade hydrofluoric acid
	0/0/0	0	0	0	0	0	0	0//0	0/0/			0/0/0	--Hydrofluoric acid
4	0/0/0	0	0	0	0	0	0	0//0	0/0/			0/0/0	--Hydrocyanic acid
													--Other:
	0/0/0	0	2.2	0	0	0	0	0//0	0/0/			0/0/0	---Hydrogen selenide
													---Other
	0/0/0	0	2.2	0	0	0	0	0//0	0/0/			0/0/0	Hydroiodic acid
	0/0/0	0	2.2	0	0	0	0	0//0	0/0/			0/0/0	Arsenic acid, pyroarsenic acid, metaardsenic acid
	0/0/0	0	2.2	0	0	0	0	0//0	0/0/			0/0/0	Other inorganic acids
													-Other inorganic oxygen compounds of non-metals:
	0/0/0	0	0	0	0	0	0	0//0	0/0/			0/0/0	--Carbon dioxide
													--Silicon dioxide:
	0/0/0	0	0	0	0	0	0	0//0	0/0/			0/0/0	---Silica gel
	0/0/0	0	0	0	0	0	0	0//0	0/0/			0/0/0	---Other
													--Other
	0/0/0	0	0	0	0	0	0	0//0	0/0/			0/0/0	Arsenous oxide (*arsenic trioxide*), arsenic pentoxide(including arsenic trioxide, arsenous anhydride, arsenic white)
	0/0/0	0	0	0	0	0	0	0//0	0/0/			0/0/0	Dinitrogen tetroxide
	0/0/0	0	0	0	0	0	0	0//0	0/0/			0/0/0	Other inorganic oxygen compounds of non-metals
													Ⅲ. HALOGEN OR SULPHUR COMPOUNDS OF NON-METALS
													Halides and halide oxides of non-metals:
													-Chlorides and chloride oxides:
	0/0/0	0	0	0	0	0	0	0//0	0/0/			0/0/	--Carbonyl dichiloride (*phosgene*)
	0/0/0	0	0	0	0	0	0	0//0	0/0/			0/0/	--Phosphorus oxychloride (*phosphoryl monochloride*; *phosphorus oxytrichloride*)
	0/0/0	0	0	0	0	0	0	0//0	0/0/			0/0/	--Phosphorus trichloride
	0/0/0	0	0	0	0	0	0	0//0	0/0/			0/0/	--Phosphorus pentachloride
	0/0/0	0	0	0	0	0	0	0//0	0/0/			0/0/	--Sulfur monochloride
	0/0/0	0	0	0	0	0	0	0//0	0/0/			0/0/	--Sulfur dichloride
	0/0/0	0	0	0	0	0	0	0//0	0/0/			0/0/	--Thionyl chloride
													--Other
	0/0/0	0	0	0	0	0	0	0//0	0/0/			0/0/	Arsenic trichloride
	0/0/0	0	0	0	0	0	0	0//0	0/0/			0/0/	Other chlorides of non-metals
	0/0/0	0	0	0	0	0	0	0//0	0/0/			0/0/	Other chloride oxides of non-metals
													-Other:
													---Fluoride and oxyfluoride:
	0/0/0	0	3.3	0	0	0	0	0//0	0/0/			0/0/	----Nitrogen trifluoride
													----Other
	0/0/2.2	0	0	0	0	0	0	0//0	0/0/			0/0/	Chlorine trifluoride
	0/0/2.2	0	0	0	0	0	0	0//0	0/0/			0/0/	Arsenic trifluoride
	0/0/2.2	0	0	0	0	0	0	0//0	0/0/			0/0/	Sulphurylfluoride
	0/0/2.2	0	0	0	0	0	0	0//0	0/0/			0/0/	Other fluoride and oxyfluoride
													---Other
	0/0/0	0	2.2	0	0	0	0	0//0	0/0/			0/0/	Arsenic tribromide, arsenic triiodide
	0/0/0	0	2.2	0	0	0	0	0//0	0/0/			0/0/	Other halides and halide oxides of non-metals
													Sulphides of non-metals; commercial phosphorus trisulphides:

税则号列		货品名称〔CIQ 扩展编码及品名—T2 表示见附表 2〕	最惠(%)	暂定税率	普通	增值/消费	出口退税	计量单位	监管条件	检验检疫	特殊证件对美关税
2813.1000		-二硫化碳〔999〕	5		30	13/	0	千克	AB	MN	1/
2813.9000		-其他									
2813.9000	10	五硫化二磷〔999〕	5		30	13/	0	千克	23		1/20
2813.9000	20	三硫化二磷〔999〕	5		30	13/	0	千克	AB	MN	1/20
2813.9000	90	其他非金属硫化物〔301 毒性物质和感染性物质,302 其他化工产品〕	5		30	13/	0	千克			1/20
		第四分章　无机碱和金属氧化物、氢氧化物及过氧化物									
28.14		**氨及氨水:**									
2814.1000		-氨〔101 饲料添加剂,301 毒性气体〕	5	0	35	13/	0	千克	AB	MN	1/25
2814.2000		-氨水									
2814.2000	10	氨水(含量≥10%)〔101 饲料添加剂,301 腐蚀性物质〕	5	0	35	13/	0	千克	AB	MN	1/30
2814.2000	90	其他氨水〔101 饲料添加剂,102 化工产品〕	5	0	35	13/	0	千克			1/30
28.15		**氢氧化钠(烧碱);氢氧化钾(苛性钾);过氧化钠及过氧化钾:**									
		-氢氧化钠(烧碱):									
2815.1100		--固体〔101 饲料添加剂,103 属于危险化学品的食品添加剂,301 腐蚀性物质,需申报仅用于工业用途不用于食品添加剂无检疫要求〕	5		35	13/	0	千克	ABG	MRNS	1/35
2815.1200		--水溶液(氢氧化钠浓溶液及液体烧碱)〔101 饲料添加剂,301 腐蚀性物质〕	5		35	13/	0	千克	ABG	MN	1/20
2815.2000		-氢氧化钾(苛性钾)〔301 腐蚀性物质,需申报仅用于工业用途不用于食品添加剂无检疫要求,302 属于危险化学品的食品添加剂〕	5		30	13/	13	千克	AB	MRNS	1/15
2815.3000		-过氧化钠及过氧化钾〔301〕	5		30	13/	0	千克	AB	MN	1/35
28.16		**氢氧化镁及过氧化镁;锶或钡的氧化物、氢氧化物及过氧化物:**									
2816.1000		-氢氧化镁及过氧化镁									
2816.1000	10	过氧化镁〔999〕	5		30	13/	0	千克	AB	MN	1/35
2816.1000	90	氢氧化镁〔999〕	5		30	13/	0	千克			1/35
2816.4000		-锶或钡的氧化物、氢氧化物及过氧化物〔301 氧化性物质,302 腐蚀性物质,303 其他化工产品〕	5	2	30	13/	0	千克			1/12
28.17		**氧化锌及过氧化锌:**									
2817.0010		---氧化锌〔101 矿物源性饲料添加剂,102 无检疫要求食品添加剂,301 需申报仅用于工业用途不用于食品添加剂无检疫要求的化学品〕	5		40	13/	0	千克	A	R	1/30
2817.0090		---过氧化锌〔999〕	5		30	13/	0	千克	AB	MN	1/20
28.18		**人造刚玉,不论是否已有化学定义;氧化铝;氢氧化铝:**									
		-人造刚玉,不论是否已有化学定义:									
2818.1010		---棕刚玉〔999〕	5		20	13/	0	千克			1/35
2818.1090		---其他〔101 化工产品,102 人造刚玉,103 白刚玉,104 黑刚玉,105 锆刚玉〕	5		20	13/	0	千克			1/20
2818.2000		-氧化铝,但人造刚玉除外〔101 饲料添加剂,102 化工产品〕	5	0	30	13/	0	千克	7		1/30
2818.3000		-氢氧化铝〔999〕	5		30	13/	0	千克			1/30
28.19		**铬的氧化物及氢氧化物:**									
2819.1000		-三氧化铬〔999〕	5		20	13/	0	千克	AB	MN	1/10
2819.9000		-其他〔999 其他化工产品,998 其他危险化学品〕	5		30	13/	0	千克			1/20
28.20		**锰的氧化物:**									
2820.1000		-二氧化锰〔101 矿物源性饲料添加剂,102 化工产品〕	5		40	13/	0	千克			1/15
2820.9000		-其他〔101 矿物源性饲料添加剂,102 化工产品〕	5		30	13/	0	千克			1/30
28.21		**铁的氧化物及氢氧化物;土色料,按重量计三氧化二铁含量在 70% 及以上:**									
2821.1000		-铁的氧化物及氢氧化物〔101 矿物源性饲料添加剂〕	5		30	13/	0	千克			1/25
2821.2000		-土色料〔101 矿物源性饲料添加剂,102 化工产品〕	5		45	13/	0	千克			1/20
28.22		**钴的氧化物及氢氧化物;商品氧化钴:**									
2822.0010		---四氧化三钴〔999〕	5	2	30	13/	13	千克	4xy		1/
2822.0090		---其他〔999 其他化工产品,998 其他危险化学品〕	5	2	30	13/	0	千克	4xy		1/32
28.23		**钛的氧化物:**									
2823.0000		钛的氧化物〔999〕	5		30	13/	0	千克			1/35
28.24		**铅的氧化物;铅丹及铅橙:**									
2824.1000		---一氧化铅(铅黄、黄丹)〔301〕	5		30	13/	0	千克	AB	MN	1/
		-其他:									
2824.9010		---铅丹及铅橙〔999〕	5		45	13/	0	千克	AB	MN	1/
2824.9090		---其他〔999,301 其他化工产品〕	5		30	13/	0	千克			1/15
28.25		**肼(联氨)、胲(羟胺)及其无机盐;其他无机碱;其他金属氧化物、氢氧化物及过氧化物:**									
		-肼(联氨)、胲(羟胺)及其无机盐:									

协定税率 %										特惠税率 %			Article Description
亚太5国	东/冰/格	巴基斯坦	韩国	瑞士	哥达	秘鲁	澳大利亚	新西/坡/智	港/澳/台	亚太2国	老/柬/缅	36/3/1	
	0/0/0	0	0	0	0	0	0	0//0	0/0/			0/0/	-Carbon disulphide
													-Other
	0/0/0	0	0	0	0	0	0	0//0	0/0/			0/0/	Phosphorus pentasulfide
	0/0/0	0	0	0	0	0	0	0//0	0/0/			0/0/	Phosphorus trisulfide
	0/0/0	0	0	0	0	0	0	0//0	0/0/			0/0/	Other sulphides of non-metals
													Ⅳ. INORGANIC BASES AND OXIDES, HYDROXIDES AND PEROXIDES OF METALS
													Ammonia, anhydrous or in aqueous solution:
	0/0/0	0	0	0	0	0	0	0//0	0/0/			0/0/0	-Anhydrous ammonia
													-Ammonia in aqueous solution
	0/0/0	0	0	0	0	0	0	0//0	0/0/			0/0/0	Ammonia in aqueous solution
	0/0/0	0	0	0	0	0	0	0//0	0/0/			0/0/0	Other ammonia in aqueous solution
													Sodium hydroxide (caustic soda); potassium hydroxide (caustic potash); peroxides or sodium or potassium:
													-Sodium hydroxide (caustic soda):
3.3	5/0/0	7	4	0	0	0	0	0//0	0/0/			0/0/0	--Solid
3.3	5/0/0	5.6	3.2	0	0	0	0	0//0	0/0/			0/0/0	--In aqueous solution (soda lye or liquid soda)
	0/0/0	0	0	0	0	0	0	0//0	0/0/			0/0/0	-Potassium hydroxide (caustic potash)
	0/0/0	0	0	0	0	0	0	0//0	0/0/			0/0/0	-Peroxides of sodium or potassium
													Hydroxide and peroxide of magnesium; oxides, hydroxides and peroxides, of strontium or barium:
													-Hydroxide and peroxide of magnesium
	0/0/0	0	2.2	0	0	0	0	0//0	0/0/			0/0/	Peroxide of magnesium
	0/0/0	0	2.2	0	0	0	0	0//0	0/0/			0/0/	Hydroxide
	0/0/0	0	0	0	0	0	0	0//0	0/0/			0/0/	-Oxides, hydroxides and peroxides, of strontium or barium
													Zinc oxide; Zinc peroxide:
	0/0/0	0	0	0	0	0	0	0//0	0/0/			0/0/0	---Zinc oxide
4.5	0/0/0	0	0	0	0	0	0	0//0	0/0/			0/0/0	---Zinc peroxide
													Artificial corundum, whether or not chemically defined; aluminium oxide; aluminium hydroxide:
													-Artificial corundum, whether or not chemically defined:
	0/0/0	0	2.2	0	0	0	0	0//0	0/0/			0/0/0	---Brown fused alumina
	0/0/0	0	0	0	0	0	0	0//0	0/0/			0/0/0	---Other
	0/0/0	4	0	0	0	0	0	0/0/0	0/0/			0/0/0	-Aluminium oxide, other than artificial corundum
	0/0/0	0	0	0	0	0	0	0//0	0/0/			0/0/0	-Aluminium hydroxide
													Chromium oxides and hydroxides:
	0/0/0	0	2.2	0	0	0	0	0//0	0/0/			0/0/0	-Chromium trioxide
	0/0/0	0	0	0	0	0	0	0//0	0/0/			0/0/0	-Other
													Manganese oxide:
	0/0/0	0	0	0	0	0	0	0//0	0/0/			0/0/0	-Manganese dioxide
	0/0/0	0	0	0	0	0	0	0//0	0/0/			0/0/0	-Other
													Iron oxides and hydroxides; earth colours containing 70% or more by weight of combined iron evaluated as Fe_2O_3:
	0/0/0	0	3.3	0	0	0	0	0//0	0/0/			0/0/0	-Iron oxides and hydroxides
	0/0/0	0	2.2	0	0	0	0	0//0	0/0/			0/0/0	-Earth colours
													Cobalt oxides and hydroxides; commercial cobalt oxides:
	0/0/0	0	0	0	0	0	0	0//0	0/0/			0/0/	---Cobalt tetroxide
	0/0/0	0	0	0	0	0	0	0//0	0/0/			0/0/	---Other
													Titanium oxides:
	0/0/0	0	0	0	0	0	0	0//0	0/0/			0/0/	Titanium oxides
													Lead oxides; red lead and orange lead:
	0/0/0	0	0	0	0	0	0	0//0	0/0/			0/0/	-Lead monoxide (litharge, massicot)
													-Other:
	0/0/0	0	0	0	0	0	0	0//0	0/0/			0/0/	---Red lead and orange lead
	0/0/0	0	0	0	0	0	0	0//0	0/0/			0/0/	---Other
													Hydrazine and hydroxylamine and their inorganic salts; other inorganic bases; other metal oxides, hydroxides and peroxides:
													-Hydrazine and hydroxylamine and their inorganic salts:

税则号列	货品名称〔CIQ 扩展编码及品名—T2 表示见附表 2〕	最惠(%)	暂定税率	普通	增值/消费	出口退税	计量单位	监管条件	检验检疫	特殊证件对美关税
2825.1010	---水合肼									
2825.1010　10	纯度 70%及以上的水合肼〔999〕	5		30	13/	0	千克	3A	M	1/10
2825.1010　90	纯度 70%以下的水合肼〔301〕	5		30	13/	0	千克	AB	MN	1/10
2825.1020	---硫酸羟胺〔999〕	5		30	13/	0	千克	AB	MN	1/10
2825.1090	---其他〔301 爆炸品，302 其他化工产品〕	5		30	13/	0	千克			1/30
	-锂的氧化物及氢氧化物：									
2825.2010	---氢氧化锂〔301〕	5		30	13/	0	千克	AB	MN	1/30
2825.2090	---其他〔999〕	5		30	13/	0	千克			1/
	-钒的氧化物及氢氧化物：									
2825.3010	---五氧化二钒〔999〕	5		30	13/	0	千克	4ABxy	MN	1/35
2825.3090	---其他〔999〕	5		30	13/	0	千克	4xy		1/35
2825.4000	-镍的氧化物及氢氧化物〔999〕	5	2	30	13/	13	千克			1/
2825.5000	-铜的氧化物及氢氧化物〔101 矿物源性饲料添加剂，102 化工产品〕	5		30	13/	0	千克			1/15
2825.6000	-锗的氧化物及二氧化锆									
2825.6000　01	锗的氧化物〔999〕	5		30	13/	0	千克	4xy		1/15
2825.6000　90	二氧化锆〔999〕	5		30	13/	0	千克	3		1/15
2825.7000	-钼的氧化物及氢氧化物〔999〕	5		30	13/	0	千克	4xy		1/20
2825.8000	-锑的氧化物〔999 其他化工产品，301 毒性物质和感染性物质〕	5		30	13/	0	千克	4xBy	N	1/35
	-其他：									
	---钨的氧化物及氢氧化物：									
2825.9011	----钨酸〔999〕	5		30	13/	0	千克	4xy		1/
2825.9012	----三氧化钨〔999〕	5		30	13/	0	千克	4xy		1/35
2825.9019	----其他									
2825.9019　10	蓝色氧化钨〔999〕	5		30	13/	0	千克	4xy		1/
2825.9019　90	其他钨的氧化物及氢氧化物〔999〕	5		30	13/	0	千克			1/
	---铋的氧化物及氢氧化物：									
2825.9021	----三氧化二铋〔301 需申报仅用于工业用途不用于食品添加剂无检疫要求的化学品〕	5		30	13/	13	千克	4Axy	R	1/30
2825.9029	----其他〔301 需申报仅用于工业用途不用于食品添加剂无检疫要求的化学品〕	5		30	13/	0	千克	4Axy	R	1/
	---锡的氧化物及氢氧化物：						千克			
2825.9031	----二氧化锡〔301 需申报仅用于工业用途不用于食品添加剂无检疫要求的化学品〕	5		30	13/	0	千克	4Axy	R	1/35
2825.9039	----其他〔301 需申报仅用于工业用途不用于食品添加剂无检疫要求的化学品〕	5		30	13/	0	千克	4Axy	R	1/
	---铌的氧化物及氢氧化物：									
2825.9041	----一氧化铌〔999〕	5		30	13/	0	千克	A	M	1/
2825.9049	----其他〔301 需申报仅用于工业用途不用于食品添加剂无检疫要求的化学品〕	5		30	13/	0	千克	AB	MRN	1/
2825.9090	---其他[T2]	5		30	13/	0	千克	AB	MRNS	1/30
	第五分章　无机酸盐、无机过氧酸盐及金属酸盐、金属过氧酸盐									
28.26	**氟化物；氟硅酸盐、氟铝酸盐及其他氟络盐：**									
	-氟化物：									
	--氟化铝：									
2826.1210	---无水氟化铝〔999〕	5.5		30	13/	0	千克			1/30.5
2826.1290	---其他〔999〕	5		30	13/	0	千克			1/
	--其他：									
2826.1910	---铵的氟化物									
2826.1910　10	氟化氢铵〔999〕	5		30	13/	0	千克	3A	M	1/
2826.1910　90	其他铵的氟化物〔999 毒性物质和感染性物质，301 其他化工产品〕	5		30	13/	0	千克			1/
2826.1920	---钠的氟化物									
2826.1920　10	氟化钠〔999〕	5		30	13/	0	千克	3AB	MRNS	1/30
2826.1920　20	氟化氢钠〔999〕	5		30	13/	0	千克	3A	M	1/30
2826.1920　90	其他钠的氟化物〔999〕	5		30	13/	0	千克			1/30
2826.1990	---其他									
2826.1990　10	氟化钾〔999〕	5		30	13/	0	千克	3A	M	1/20
2826.1990　20	氟化氢钾〔999〕	5		30	13/	0	千克	3A	M	1/20
2826.1990　30	氟化铅，四氟化铅，氟化镉〔301 毒性物质和感染性物质，302 杂项物质〕	5		30	13/	0	千克			1/20
2826.1990　90	其他氟化物〔301 毒性物质和感染性物质，302 腐蚀性物质，303 杂项物质，304 其他危险化学品，305 其他化工产品〕	5		30	13/	0	千克			1/20
2826.3000	-六氟铝酸钠(人造冰晶石)〔999〕	5		30	13/	13	千克			1/
	-其他：									
2826.9010	---氟硅酸盐〔301 毒性物质和感染 性物质，302 其他化工产品〕	5		30	13/	0	千克			1/35

协定税率 %										特惠税率 %			Article Description
亚太5国	东/冰/格	巴基斯坦	韩国	瑞士	哥达	秘鲁	澳大利亚	新西/坡/智	港/澳/台	亚太2国	老/柬/缅	36/3/1	
													---Hydrazine hydrate
	0/0/0	0	2.2	0	0	0	0	0//0	0/0/			0/0/0	Hydrazine hydrate，purity≥70%
	0/0/0	0	2.2	0	0	0	0	0//0	0/0/			0/0/0	Hydrazine hydrate，purity<70%
	0/0/0	0	2.2	0	0	0	0	0//0	0/0/			0/0/0	---Hydroxylamine sulphate
	0/0/0	0	0	0	0	0	0	0//0	0/0/			0/0/0	---Other
													-Lithium oxide and hydroxide：
	0/0/0	0	0	0	0	0	0	0//0	0/0/			0/0/0	---Lithium hydroxide
	0/0/0	0	0	0	0	0	0	0//0	0/0/			0/0/0	---Other
													-Vanadium oxides and hydroxides：
	0/0/0	0	2.2	0	0	0	0	0//0	0/0/			0/0/0	---Divanadium pentaoxide
	0/0/0	0	0	0	0	0	0	0//0	0/0/			0/0/0	---Other
	0/0/0	0	0	0	0	0	0	0//0	0/0/			0/0/0	-Nickel oxides and hydroxides
	0/0/0	0	0	0	0	0	0	0//0	0/0/			0/0/0	-Copper oxides and hydroxides
													-Germanium oxides and zirconium dioxide
	0/0/0	0	0	0	0	0	0	0//0	0/0/			0/0/0	Cermaniurn oxides
	0/0/0	0	0	0	0	0	0	0//0	0/0/			0/0/0	Zirconium dioxide
	0/0/0	0	0	0	0		0	0//0	0/0/			0/0/0	-Molybdenum oxides and hydroxides
	0/0/0	0	0	0	0	0	0	0//0	0/0/			0/0/0	-Antimony oxides
													-Other：
													---Tungsten oxides and hydroxides：
	0/0/0	0	0	0	0	0	0	0//0	0/0/			0/0/0	----Tungstic acid
	0/0/0	0	0	0	0	0	0	0//0	0/0/			0/0/0	----Tungstic oxide
													----Other
	0/0/0	0	0	0	0	0	0	0//0	0/0/			0/0/0	Blue tungsten oxides
	0/0/0	0	0	0	0	0	0	0//0	0/0/			0/0/0	Other tungsten oxides and hydroxides
													---Bismuth oxdes and hydroxides：
	0/0/0	0	0	0	0	0	0	0//0	0/0/			0/0/0	----Bismuth trioxide
	0/0/0	0	0	0	0	0	0	0//0	0/0/			0/0/0	----Other
													---Tin oxides and hydroxides：
	0/0/0	0	0	0	0	0	0	0//0	0/0/			0/0/0	----Tin dioxide
	0/0/0	0	0	0	0	0	0	0//0	0/0/			0/0/0	----Other
													---Niobium oxdes and hydroxides：
	0/0/0	0	0	0	0	0	0	0//0	0/0/			0/0/0	----Columbium monoxide
	0/0/0	0	0	0	0	0	0	0//0	0/0/			0/0/0	----Other
	0/0/0	0	0	0	0	0	0	0//0	0/0/			0/0/0	---Other
													V. SALTS AND PEROXYSALTS，OF INORGANIC ACIDS AND METALS
													Fluorides；fluorosilicates，fluoroaluminates and other complex fluorine salts：
													-Fluorides：
													--Of aluminium：
	0/0/0	0	0	0	0	0	0	0//0	0/0/			0/0/0	---Anhydrous aluminium chloride
	0/0/0	0	0	0	0	0	0	0//0	0/0/			0/0/0	---Other
													--Other：
													---Of ammonium
	0/0/0	0	0	0	0	0	0	0//0	0/0/			0/0/0	Ammonium hydrogen fluoride
	0/0/0	0	0	0	0	0	0	0//0	0/0/			0/0/0	Other ammonium fluorid
													---Of sodium
	0/0/0	0	0	0	0	0	0	0//0	0/0/			0/0/0	Sodium fluoride
	0/0/0	0	0	0	0	0	0	0//0	0/0/			0/0/0	Sodium hydrogen fluoride
	0/0/0	0	0	0	0	0	0	0//0	0/0/			0/0/0	Other sodium fluorid
													---Other
	0/0/0	0	0	0	0	0	0	0//0	0/0/			0/0/0	Potassium fluoride
	0/0/0	0	0	0	0	0	0	0//0	0/0/			0/0/0	Potassium hydrogen fluoride
	0/0/0	0	0	0	0	0	0	0//0	0/0/			0/0/0	Lead fluoride，lead tetrafluoried ，cadmium fluoride
	0/0/0	0	0	0	0	0	0	0//0	0/0/			0/0/0	Other fluorides
	0/0/0	0	0	0	0	0	0	0//0	0/0/			0/0/0	-Sodium hexafluoroaluminate (synthetic cryolite)
													-Other：
	0/0/0	0	2.2	0	0	0	0	0//0	0/0/			0/0/0	---Fluorosilicates

税则号列	货品名称〔CIQ 扩展编码及品名—T2 表示见附表 2〕	最惠(%)	暂定税率	普通	增值/消费	出口退税	计量单位	监管条件	检验检疫	特殊证件对美关税
2826.9020	---六氟磷酸锂〔999〕	5.5		30	13/	13	千克			1/30.5
2826.9090	---其他									
2826.9090 10	氟钽酸钾〔999〕	5		30	13/	0	千克			1/35
2826.9090 30	氟硼酸铅，氟硼酸镉〔301〕	5		30	13/	0	千克			1/35
2826.9090 90	氟铝酸盐及其他氟络盐〔301 毒性物质和感染性物质，302 腐蚀性物质，303 其他化工产品〕	5		30	13/	0	千克			1/35
28.27	**氯化物、氯氧化物及氢氧基氯化物；溴化物及溴氧化物；碘化物及碘氧化物：**									
	-氯化铵：									
2827.1010	---肥料用〔999〕	4		11	13/	0	千克	G		1/9
2827.1090	---其他〔999〕	5		30	13/	0	千克	G		1/35
2827.2000	-氯化钙〔101 矿物源性饲料添加剂，102 无检疫要求食品添加剂，103 需申报仅用于工业用途不用于食品添加剂无检疫要求的化学品〕	5		50	13/	10	千克	A	R	1/35
	-其他氯化物：									
2827.3100	--氯化镁〔101 矿物源性饲料添加剂，102 无检疫要求食品添加剂，103 需申报仅用于工业用途不用于食品添加剂无检疫要求的化学品〕	5		30	13/	0	千克	A	R	1/15
2827.3200	--氯化铝〔101 无水，102 三氯化铝溶液〕	5		30	13/	0	千克			1/20
2827.3500	--氯化镍〔999〕	5		30	13/	0	千克	AB	MN	1/35
	--其他：									
2827.3910	---氯化锂〔999〕	5		30	13/	0	千克			1/35
2827.3920	---氯化钡〔999〕	5		30	13/	0	千克	AB	MN	1/30
2827.3930	---氯化钴〔101 矿物源性饲料添加剂，102 危险化学品，需申报仅用于工业用途不用于食品添加剂无检疫要求〕	5		30	13/	0	千克	4ABxy	MRNS	1/20
2827.3990	---其他[T2]	5		30	13/	0	千克	AB	MRNS	1/15
	-氯氧化物及氢氧基氯化物：									
2827.4100	--铜的氯氧化物及氢氧基氯化物〔999〕	5		30	13/	0	千克			1/15
	--其他：									
2827.4910	---锆的氯氧化物及氢氧基氯化物〔999〕	5		30	13/	0	千克			1/35
2827.4990	---其他〔301 氧化性物质，302 毒性物质和感染性物中，303 其他化工产品〕	5		30	13/	0	千克			1/15
	-溴化物及溴氧化物：									
2827.5100	--溴化钠及溴化钾〔999〕	5		30	13/	0	千克			1/35
2827.5900	--其他〔301 毒性物质和感染性物质，302 腐蚀性物质，303 其他化工产品〕	5		30	13/	0	千克			1/35
2827.6000	-碘化物及碘氧化物[T2]	5		30	13/	0	千克	AB	MRNS	1/35
28.28	**次氯酸盐；商品次氯酸钙；亚氯酸盐；次溴酸盐：**									
2828.1000	-商品次氯酸钙及其他钙的次氯酸盐〔301〕	5		80	13/	6	千克			1/10
2828.9000	-其他[T2]	5		30	13/	0	千克	AB	MRNS	1/35
28.29	**氯酸盐及高氯酸盐；溴酸盐及过溴酸盐；碘酸盐及高碘酸盐：**									
	-氯酸盐：									
2829.1100	--氯酸钠〔301〕	5		30	13/	0	千克	AB	MN	1/15
	--其他：									
2829.1910	---氯酸钾(洋硝)〔301〕	5		20	13/	0	千克	9B	N	1/
2829.1990	---其他〔301 氧化性物质，302 其他化工产品〕	5		30	13/	0	千克			1/
2829.9000	-其他									
2829.9000 10	颗粒<500μm 的球形高氯酸铵〔301 爆炸品，302 氧化性物质〕	5		30	13/	0	千克	3A	M	1/20
2829.9000 90	其他高氯酸盐、溴酸盐等(包括过溴酸盐、碘酸盐及高碘酸盐)〔101 矿物源性饲料添加剂，301 氧化性物质，302 其他化工产品〕	5		30	13/	0	千克			1/20
28.30	**硫化物；多硫化物，不论是否已有化学定义：**									
	-钠的硫化物：									
2830.1010	---硫化钠〔101 无水或含结晶水<30%，102 含结晶水≥30%〕	5		40	13/	0	千克	3AB	MN	1/15
2830.1090	---其他〔301 易于自燃的物质，302 其他化工产品〕	5		30	13/	0	千克			1/15
	-其他：									
2830.9020	---硫化锑〔999 硫化锑及其精矿，301 毒性物质和感染性物质〕	5		45	13/	0	千克	B	N	1/
2830.9030	---硫化钴〔999〕	5		30	13/	0	千克			1/15
2830.9090	---其他〔301 易燃液体，302 易于自燃的物质，303 腐蚀性物质，304 杂项物质，305 其他危险化学品，306 其他化工产品〕	5		30	13/	0	千克			1/30
28.31	**连二亚硫酸盐及次硫酸盐：**									
	-钠的连二亚硫酸盐及次硫酸盐：									
2831.1010	---钠的连二亚硫酸盐[T2]	5		30	13/	0	千克	AB	MRNS	1/35
2831.1020	---钠的次硫酸盐〔999〕	5		30	13/	0	千克			1/
2831.9000	-其他〔301 易于自燃的物质，302 其他化工产品〕	5		30	13/	0	千克			1/

协定税率 %										特惠税率 %			Article Description
亚太5国	东/冰/格	巴基斯坦	韩国	瑞士	哥达	秘鲁	澳大利亚	新西/坡/智	港/澳/台	亚太2国	老/柬/缅	36/3/1	
	0/0/0	0	3.3	0	0	0	0	0//0	0/0/			0/0/0	---Lithium Hexafluoroarsenate
													---Other
	0/0/0	0	3.3	0	0	0	0	0//0	0/0/			0/0/0	Potassium tantalifluoride
	0/0/0	0	3.3	0	0	0	0	0//0	0/0/			0/0/0	lead fluoboriate, cadmium fluoboriate
	0/0/0	0	3.3	0	0	0	0	0//0	0/0/			0/0/0	Fluoroaluminates and other complex fluorine salts
													Chlorides, chloride oxides and chloride hydroxides; bromides and bromide oxides; iodides and iodide oxides:
													-Ammonium chloride:
	0/0/1.6	0	0	0	0	0	0	0//0	0/0/			0/0/0	--For use as fertilizer
	0/0/0	0	0	0	0	0	0	0//0	0/0/			0/0/0	--Other
	0/0/0	0	0	0	0	0	0	0//0	0/0/			0/0/0	-Calcium chloride
													-Other chlorides:
	0/0/0	0	2.2	0	0	0	0	0//0	0/0/			0/0/0	--Of magnesium
	0/0/0	0	0	0	0	0	0	0//0	0/0/			0/0/0	--Of aluminium
	0/0/0	0	0	0	0	0	0	0//0	0/0/			0/0/0	--Of nickel
													--Other:
3.3	0/0/0	0	0	0	0		0	0//0	0/0/			0/0/0	---Lithium chloride
3.3	0/0/0	0	0		0		0	0//0	0/0/			0/0/0	---Barium chleride
3.3	0/0/0	0	0	0	0	0	0	0//0	0/0/			0/0/0	---Cobalt chleride
3.3	0/0/0	0	0	0	0		0	0//0	0/0/			0/0/0	---Other
													-Chloride oxides and chloride hydroxides:
	0/0/0	0	0	0	0	0	0	0//0	0/0/			0/0/0	--of copper
													--Other:
	0/0/0	0	0	0	0	0	0	0//0	0/0/			0/0/0	---of zirconium
	0/0/0	0	0	0	0	0	0	0//0	0/0/			0/0/0	---Other
													-Eromides and bromide oxides:
	0/0/0	0	0	0	0	0	0	0//0	0/0/			0/0/0	--Bromides of sodium or of potassium
	0/0/0	0	2.2	0	0	0	0	0//0	0/0/			0/0/0	--Other
	0/0/0	0	0	0	0		0	0//0	0/0/			0/0/0	-Iodides and iodide oxides
													Hypochlorites; commercial calcium hypochlorite; chlorites; hypobromites:
3.3	0/0/0	4.5	4.8	3.6	0	0	0	0/0/0	0/0/			0/0/	-Commercial calcium hypochlorite and other calcium hypochlorites
	0/0/0	0	0	0	0	0	0	0//0	0/0/			0/0/	-Other
													Chlorates and perchlorates; bromates and perbromates; iodates and periodates:
													-Chlorates:
	0/0/0	6	4.8	3.6	0	0	0	0/0/0	0/0/			0/0/	--Of sodium
													--Other:
	0/0/0	0	0	0	0	0	0	0//0	0/0/			0/0/	---Potassium chlorate
	0/0/0	0	0	0	0	0	0	0//0	0/0/			0/0/	---Other
													-Other
	0/0/0	0	0	0	0	0	0	0//0	0/0/			0/0/	Ammonium perchlorate, spheroids. Granularity $<500\mu m$
	0/0/0	0	0	0	0	0	0	0//0	0/0/			0/0/	Other perchlorates, bromates (Including perbromates iodates and periodates)
													Sulphides; polysulphides, whether or not chemically defined:
													-Sodium sulphides:
	0/0/0	0	0	0	0	0	0	0//0	0/0/			0/0/0	---Sodium sulphide
	0/0/0	0	0	0	0	0	0	0//0	0/0/			0/0/0	---Other
													-Other:
	0/0/0	0	0	0	0	0	0	0//0	0/0/			0/0/0	---Antimony sulphide
	0/0/0	0	2.2	0	0	0	0	0//0	0/0/			0/0/0	---Cobalt sulphide
	0/0/0	0	0	0	0	0	0	0//0	0/0/			0/0/0	---Other
													Dithionites and sulphoxylates:
													-of sodium:
	0/0/0	0	0	0	0	0	0	0//0	0/0/			0/0/	---Sodium Dithionites
	0/0/0	0	0	0	0	0	0	0//0	0/0/			0/0/	---Sodium Sulphoxylates
	0/0/0	0	0	0	0	0	0	0//0	0/0/			0/0/	-Other

税则号列		货品名称〔CIQ 扩展编码及品名—T2 表示见附表 2〕	最惠(%)	暂定税率	普通	增值/消费	出口退税	计量单位	监管条件	检验检疫	特殊证件对美关税
28.32		**亚硫酸盐；硫代硫酸盐：**									
2832.1000		-钠的亚硫酸盐〔101 危险化学品，104 属于危险化学品的食品添加剂〕	5		30	13/	0	千克			1/35
2832.2000		-其他亚硫酸盐[T2]	5		30	13/	0	千克	AB	MRNS	1/30
2832.3000		-硫代硫酸盐〔999〕	5		30	13/	0	千克			1/30
28.33		**硫酸盐；矾；过硫酸盐：**									
		-钠的硫酸盐：									
2833.1100		--硫酸钠〔101 矿物源性饲料添加剂，102 化工产品〕	5		40	13/	0	千克	4xy		1/35
2833.1900		--其他〔301 其他危险化学品，302 其他化工产品〕	5		30	13/	0	千克			1/15
		-其他硫酸盐：									
2833.2100		--硫酸镁〔101 矿物源性饲料添加剂，102 无检疫要求食品添加剂，103 需申报仅用于工业用途不用于食品添加剂无检疫要求的化学品〕	5		30	13/	0	千克	A	R	1/35
2833.2200		--硫酸铝〔999〕	5		30	13/	0	千克			1/35
2833.2400		--镍的硫酸盐〔999〕	5	2	30	13/	0	千克			1/27
2833.2500		--铜的硫酸盐〔101 矿物源性饲料添加剂，102 硫酸铜(危险化学品)，103 硫酸铜(属于危险化学品的食品添加剂)〕	5		30	13/	0	千克			1/20
2833.2700		--硫酸钡〔999〕	5		30	13/	0	千克	G		1/35
		--其他：									
2833.2910		---硫酸亚铁〔101 矿物源性饲料添加剂，102 无检疫要求食品添加剂，103 需申报仅用于工业用途不用于食品添加剂无检疫要求的化学品〕	5		45	13/	0	千克	A	R	1/35
2833.2920		---铬的硫酸盐〔999〕	5		30	13/	0	千克			1/35
2833.2930		---硫酸锌〔101 矿物源性饲料添加剂，102 无检疫要求食品添加剂，103 需申报仅用于工业用途不用于食品添加剂无检疫要求的化学品〕	5		30	13/	6	千克	A	R	1/20
2833.2990		---其他									
2833.2990	10	硫酸钴〔101 矿物源性饲料添加剂，301 其他危险化学品，需申报仅用于工业用途不用于食品添加剂无检疫要求〕	5	2	30	13/	0	千克	4ABxy	RS	1/17
2833.2990	20	其他钴的硫酸盐〔101 矿物源性饲料添加剂，301 其他危险化学品，需申报仅用于工业用途不用于食品添加剂无检疫要求〕	5	2	30	13/	0	千克	AB	MRNS	1/17
2833.2990	90	其他硫酸盐[T2]	5		30	13/	0	千克	AB	MRN	1/20
		-矾：									
2833.3010		---钾铝矾〔999〕	5		45	13/	0	千克			1/
2833.3090		---其他〔101 硫酸氧钒，102 硫酸铝铵(铵明矾)(无检疫要求食品添加剂)，301 毒性物质和感染性物质〕	5		30	13/	0	千克			1/15
2833.4000		-过硫酸盐〔301 氧化性物质〕	5		30	13/	0	千克			1/20
28.34		**亚硝酸盐；硝酸盐：**									
2834.1000		-亚硝酸盐[T2]	5		30	13/	0	千克	AB	MRNS	1/20
		-硝酸盐：									
		--硝酸钾：									
2834.2110		---肥料用〔999 其他化工产品，998 其他危险化学品〕	4	1	11	13/	0	千克	AB	MN	1/6
2834.2190		---其他〔102 无检疫要求食品添加剂，301 氧化性物质〕	5		30	13/	0	千克	AB	MN	1/35
		--其他：									
2834.2910		---硝酸钴〔999〕	5		30	13/	0	千克	AB	MN	1/15
2834.2990		---其他									
2834.2990	01	硝酸钡〔999〕	5	2	30	13/	0	千克	AB	MN	1/12
2834.2990	90	其他硝酸盐〔301 爆炸品，302 氧化性物质，303 硝酸钠(无检疫要求食品添加剂)，304 其他化工产品〕	5		30	13/	0	千克			1/15
28.35		**次磷酸盐、亚磷酸盐、磷酸盐及多磷酸盐，无论是否已有化学定义：**									
2835.1000		-次磷酸盐及亚磷酸盐〔999〕	5		20	13/	0	千克			1/35
		-磷酸盐：									
2835.2200		--磷酸一钠及磷酸二钠〔101 矿物源性饲料添加剂，102 化工产品〕	5		20	13/	0	千克			1/30
2835.2400		--钾的磷酸盐〔101 矿物源性饲料添加剂〕	5		20	13/	0	千克			1/30
		--正磷酸氢钙(磷酸二钙)：									
2835.2510		---饲料级的〔101 矿物源性饲料添加剂，102 化工产品〕	5		20	13/	0	千克	AB	RS	1/
2835.2520		---食品级的〔101 矿物源性饲料添加剂，102 无检疫要求食品添加剂〕	5		20	13/	6	千克	A	R	1/35
2835.2590		---其他〔999〕	5		20	13/	0	千克			1/15
2835.2600		--其他磷酸钙〔101 矿物源性饲料添加剂，104 无检疫要求食品添加剂〕	5		20	13/	0	千克			1/15
		--其他：									
2835.2910		---磷酸三钠〔999，301 需申报仅用于工业用途不用于食品添加剂无检疫要求的化学品〕	5		20	13/	0	千克	A	R	1/35
2835.2990		---其他[T2]	5		20	13/	0	千克	A	MR	1/30

协定税率 %										特惠税率 %			Article Description
亚太5国	东/冰/格	巴基斯坦	韩国	瑞士	哥达	秘鲁	澳大利亚	新西/坡/智	港/澳/台	亚太2国	老/柬/缅	36/3/1	
													Sulphites; thiosulphates:
	0/0/0	0	0	0	0	0	0	0//0	0/0/			0/0/	-Sodium sulphites
	0/0/0	0	0	0	0	0	0	0//0	0/0/			0/0/	-Other sulphites
	0/0/0	0	0	0	0	0	0	0//0	0/0/			0/0/	-Thiosulphates
													Sulphates; alums; peroxosulphates (persulphates):
													-Sodium sulphates:
2.5	0/0/0	0	0	1.7	0	0	0	0//0	0/0/			0/0/	--Disodium sulphate
	0/0/0	0	0	0	0	0	0	0//0	0/0/			0/0/	--Other
													-Other sulphates:
	0/0/0	0	0	0	0	0	0	0//0	0/0/			0/0/0	--Of magnesium
	0/0/0	0	0	0	0	0	0	0//0	0/0/			0/0/0	--Of aluminium
	0/0/0	0	0	0	0	0	0	0//0	0/0/			0/0/0	--Of nickel
	0/0/0	0	0	0	0	0	0	0//0	0/0/			0/0/0	--Of copper
	0/0/0	0	2.2	0	0	0	0	0//0	0/0/			0/0/0	--Of barium
													--Other:
	0/0/0	0	0	0	0	0	0	0//0	0/0/			0/0/0	---Ferrous sulphate
	0/0/0	0	0	0	0	0	0	0//0	0/0/			0/0/0	---Chromium sulphate
	0/0/0	0	2.2	0	0	0	0	0//0	0/0/			0/0/0	---Zinc sulphates
													---Other
	0/0/0	0	0	1.7	0	0	0	0//0	0/0/			0/0/0	Cobalt sulphate
	0/0/0	0	0	1.7	0	0	0	0//0	0/0/			0/0/0	Other cobalt sulfate
	0/0/0	0	0	1.7	0	0	0	0//0	0/0/			0/0/0	Other sulphates
													-Alums:
	0/0/0	0	2.2	0	0	0	0	0//0	0/0/			0/0/0	---Potassium aluminum sulfate
	0/0/0	0	2.2	0	0	0	0	0//0	0/0/			0/0/0	---Other
	0/0/0	0	2.2	0	0	0	0	0//0	0/0/			0/0/0	-Peroxosulphates (persulphates)
													Nitrites; nitrates:
	0/0/0	0	0	0	0	0	0	0//0	0/0/			0/0/0	-Nitrites
													-Nitrates:
													--Of potassium:
	0/0/	0	0	0	0	0	0	0//0	0/0/			0/0/0	---For use as fertilizer
	0/0/0	0	0	0	0	0	0	0//0	0/0/			0/0/0	---Other
													--Other:
	0/0/0	0	0	0	0	0	0	0//0	0/0/			0/0/0	---Of cobalt
													---Other
	0/0/0	0	0	0	0	0	0	0//0	0/0/			0/0/0	Barium nitrate
	0/0/0	0	0	0	0	0	0	0//0	0/0/			0/0/0	Other nitrates
													Phosphinates (hypophosphites), phosphonates (phosphites), phosphates and polyphosphates, whether or not chemically defined:
	0/0/0	0	0	0	0	0	0	0//0	0/0/			0/0/0	-Phosphinates (hypophosphites) and phosphonates (phosphites)
													-Phosphates:
	0/0/0	0	2.2	0	0	0	0	0//0	0/0/			0/0/0	--Of mono- or disodium
	0/0/0	0	0	0	0	0	0	0//0	0/0/			0/0/0	--Of potassium
													--Calcium hydrogenorthophosphate (dicalcium phosphate):
	0/0/0	0	0	0	0	0	0	0//0	0/0/			0/0/0	---Feed grade
	0/0/0	0	0	0	0	0	0	0//0	0/0/			0/0/0	---Food grade
	0/0/0	0	0	2.9	0	0	0	0//0	0/0/			0/0/0	---Other
	0/0/0	0	2.2	0	0	0	0	0//0	0/0/			0/0/0	--Other phosphates of calcium
													--Other:
	0/0/0	0	0	0	0	0	0	0//0	0/0/			0/0/0	---Trisodium phosphate
	0/0/0	0	2.2	0	0	0	0	0//0	0/0/			0/0/0	---Other

税则号列	货品名称〔CIQ 扩展编码及品名－T2 表示见附表 2〕	最惠(%)	暂定税率	普通	增值/消费	出口退税	计量单位	监管条件	检验检疫	特殊证件对美关税
	-多磷酸盐：									
	--三磷酸钠(三聚磷酸钠)：									
2835.3110	---食品级的〔301 无检疫要求食品添加剂〕	5		20	13/	13	千克	A	R	1/35
2835.3190	---其他〔999〕	5		20	13/	13	千克			1/15
	--其他：									
	---六偏磷酸钠：									
2835.3911	----食品级的〔301 无检疫要求食品添加剂〕	5		20	13/	10	千克	A	R	1/15
2835.3919	----其他〔999〕	5		20	13/	0	千克			1/15
2835.3990	---其他〔101 矿物源性饲料添加剂〕	5		20	13/	0	千克			1/20
28.36	**碳酸盐；过碳酸盐；含氨基甲酸铵的商品碳酸铵：**									
2836.2000	-碳酸钠(纯碱)〔101 矿物源性饲料添加剂，102 无检疫要求食品添加剂，301 需申报仅用于工业用途不用于食品添加剂无检疫要求的化学品〕	5		35	13/	10	千克	AG	MR	1/15
2836.3000	-碳酸氢钠(小苏打)〔101 矿物源性饲料添加剂，301 碳酸氢钠(无检疫要求食品添加剂)，302 应为：复合膨松剂(无检疫要求食品添加剂)，303 需申报仅用于工业用途不用于食品添加剂无检疫要求的化学品〕	5		45	13/	10	千克	AG	R	1/15
2836.4000	-钾的碳酸盐〔101 碳酸氢钾，102 碳酸钾〕	5		30	13/	0	千克			1/15
2836.5000	-碳酸钙[T2]	5		45	13/	0	千克	A	R	1/30
2836.6000	-碳酸钡〔999〕	5	1	40	13/	0	千克			1/31
	-其他：									
2836.9100	--锂的碳酸盐〔999〕	5	2	30	13/	0	千克			1/32
2836.9200	--锶的碳酸盐〔999〕	5	2	30	13/	0	千克			1/32
	--其他：									
2836.9910	---碳酸镁〔301 无检疫要求食品添加剂，302 需申报仅用于工业用途不用于食品添加剂无检疫要求的化学品〕	5		45	13/	0	千克	A	R	1/35
2836.9930	---碳酸钴〔101 矿物源性饲料添加剂，102 化工产品〕	5	2	30	13/	0	千克	4xy		1/
2836.9940	---商品碳酸铵及其他铵的碳酸盐〔101 矿物源性饲料添加剂〕	5		30	13/	0	千克			1/35
2836.9950	---碳酸锆〔999〕	5		30	13/	0	千克	AB	RS	1/
2836.9990	---其他[T2]	5		30	13/	13	千克	A	MR	1/20
28.37	**氰化物、氧氰化物及氰络合物：**									
	-氰化物及氧氰化物：									
	--氰化钠及氧氰化钠：									
2837.1110	---氰化钠〔999〕	5		20	13/	0	千克	23AB	MN	1/
2837.1120	---氧氰化钠〔999〕	5		30	13/	0	千克			1/
	--其他：									
2837.1910	---氰化钾〔999〕	5		20	13/	0	千克	23AB	MN	1/35
2837.1990	---其他									
2837.1990 11	氰化锌、氰化亚铜、氰化铜(氰化高铜)〔301〕	5		30	13/	0	千克			1/35
2837.1990 12	氰化镍、氰化钙(氰化亚镍)〔103 氰化镍钾，301 氰化亚镍〕	5		30	13/	0	千克			1/35
2837.1990 13	氰化钡、氰化镉、氰化铅〔301〕	5		30	13/	0	千克			1/35
2837.1990 14	氰化钴[氰化钴(Ⅱ)、氰化钴(Ⅲ)]〔999〕	5		30	13/	0	千克			1/35
2837.1990 90	其他氰化物及氧氰化物〔999 其他化工产品，998 其他危险化学品〕	5		30	13/	0	千克			1/35
2837.2000	-氰络合物									
2837.2000 11	氰化镍钾、氰化钠铜锌(氰化钾镍、镍氰化钾、铜盐)〔999〕	5		30	13/	0	千克			1/35
2837.2000 12	氰化亚铜(三)钠、氰化亚铜(三)钾(紫铜盐、紫铜矾、氰化铜钠、氰化亚铜钾、亚铜氰化钾)〔101〕	5		30	13/	0	千克			1/35
2837.2000 90	其他氰络合物〔999 其他化工产品，998 其他危险化学品〕	5		30	13/	0	千克			1/35
28.39	**硅酸盐；商品碱金属硅酸盐：**									
	-钠盐：									
2839.1100	--偏硅酸钠〔999〕	5		40	13/	0	千克	AB	MN	1/15
	--其他：									
2839.1910	---硅酸钠〔999〕	5		30	13/	0	千克	A	M	1/20
2839.1990	---其他钠盐〔999〕	5		30	13/	0	千克			1/35
2839.9000	-其他									
2839.9000 01	锆的硅酸盐〔999〕	5	2	30	13/	0	千克			1/12
2839.9000 10	硅酸铅〔999〕	5		30	13/	0	千克			1/15
2839.9000 90	其他硅酸盐；商品碱金属硅酸盐〔101 硅酸镁，102 硅酸钙铝〕	5		30	13/	0	千克			1/15
28.40	**硼酸盐及过硼酸盐：**									
	-四硼酸钠(精炼硼砂)：									
2840.1100	--无水四硼酸钠〔999〕	5	2	20	13/	0	千克			1/12

协定税率 %										特惠税率 %			Article Description
亚太5国	东/冰/格	巴基斯坦	韩国	瑞士	哥达	秘鲁	澳大利亚	新西/坡/智	港/澳/台	亚太2国	老/柬/缅	36/3/1	
													-Polyphosphates:
													--Sodium triphosphate (sodium tripolyphosphate):
	0/0/0	0	0	0	0	0	0	0//0	0/0/			0/0/0	---Food grade
	0/0/0	0	2.2	0	0	0	0	0//0	0/0/			0/0/0	---Other
													--Other:
													---Sodium hexametaphosphate:
	0/0/0	0	0	0	0	0	0	0//0	0/0/			0/0/0	----Food grade
	0/0/0	0	2.2	0	0	0	0	0//0	0/0/			0/0/0	----Other
	0//0	0	0	0	0	0	0	0//0	0/0/			0/0/0	---Other
													Carbonates; peroxocarbonates (percarbonates); commercial ammonium carbonate containing ammonium carbamate:
	0/0/0	0	0	0	0	0	0	0//0	0/0/			0/0/0	-Disodium carbonate
	0/0/0	0	2.2	0	0	0	0	0//0	0/0/			0/0/0	-Sodium hydrogencarbonate (sodium bicarbonate)
	0/0/0	0	0	0	0	0	0	0//0	0/0/			0/0/0	-Potassium carbonates
	0/0/0	0	0	0	0	0	0	0//0	0/0/			0/0/0	-Calcium carbonate
	0/0/0	0	0	0	0	0	0	0//0	0/0/			0/0/0	-Barium carbonate
													-Other:
	0/0/0	0	0	0			0	0//0	0/0/			0/0/0	--Lithium carbonates
	0/0/0	0	0	0	0	0	0	0//0	0/0/			0/0/0	--Strontium carbonate
													--Other:
	0/0/0	0	2.2	0	0	0	0	0//0	0/0/			0/0/0	---Magnesium carbonate
4	0/0/0	0	0	0	0	0	0	0//0	0/0/			0/0/0	---Cobalt carbonate
	0/0/0	0	0	0	0	0	0	0//0	0/0/			0/0/0	---Commericial ammonium carbonate and other ammonium carbonates
	0/0/0	0	0	0	0	0	0	0//0	0/0/			0/0/0	---Zirconium carbonate
	0/0/0	0	0	0	0	0	0	0//0	0/0/			0/0/0	---Other
													Cyanides, cyanide oxides and complex cyanides:
													-Cyanides and cyanide oxides:
													--Of sodium:
	0/0/0	0	3.3	0	0	0	0	0//0	0/0/			0/0/	---Sodium cyanide
3.3	0/0/0	0	0	0	0	0	0	0//0	0/0/			0/0/	---Sodium cyanide oxide
													--Other:
4	0/0/0	0	0	0	0	0	0	0//0	0/0/			0/0/	---Potassium cyanide
													---Other
	0/0/0	0	3.3	0	0	0	0	0//0	0/0/			0/0/	Znic cyanide, cuprous cyanide, copper cyanide (cupric cyanide)
	0/0/0	0	3.3	0	0	0	0	0//0	0/0/			0/0/	Nickel cyanide, calcium cyanide(Nickelous cygnide)
	0/0/0	0	3.3	0	0	0	0	0//0	0/0/			0/0/	Barium cyanide, cadmium cyanide, lead cyanide
	0/0/0	0	3.3	0	0	0	0	0//0	0/0/			0/0/	Cobalt cyanide [Cobalt cyanide (Co(CN)3), Cobalt cyanide (Co(CN)2)]
	0/0/0	0	3.3	0	0	0	0	0//0	0/0/			0/0/	Other cyanides and cyanide oxides
													-Complex cyanides
	0/0/0	0	0	0	0	0	0	0//0	0/0/			0/0/	Potassium nickel cyanide, sodium coopper - zinc cyanide (nickel potassium cyanide, nantokite)
	0/0/0	0	0	0	0	0	0	0//0	0/0/			0/0/	Cuprous cyanide (c) sodium, cuprous cyanide (c) potassium (copper salt, copper alum, sodium cyanide copper, cuprous potassium cyanide, cuprous potassium cyanide)
	0/0/0	0	0	0	0	0	0	0//0	0/0/			0/0/	Other complex cyanide
													Silicates; commercial alkali metal silicates:
													-Of sodium:
	0/0/0	0	2.2	0	0	0	0	0//0	0/0/			0/0/	--Sodium metasilicates
													--Other:
	0/0/0	0	2.2	0	0	0	0	0//0	0/0/			0/0/	---Sodium silicate
	0/0/0	0	2.2	0	0	0	0	0//0	0/0/			0/0/	---Other Sodium salts
													-Other
	0/0/0	0	0	1.7	0	0	0	0//0	0/0/			0/0/	Zirconium silicate
	0/0/0	0	0	1.7	0	0	0	0//0	0/0/			0/0/	Lead silicate
	0/0/0	0	0	1.7	0	0	0	0//0	0/0/			0/0/	Other silicate, commercial alkali metal silicates
													Borates; peroxoborates (perborates):
													-Disodium tetraborate (refined borax):
	0/0/0	0	0	0	0	0	0	0//0	0/0/			0/0/	--Anhydrous

税则号列		货品名称〔CIQ 扩展编码及品名—T2 表示见附表 2〕	最惠(%)	暂定税率	普通	增值/消费	出口退税	计量单位	监管条件	检验检疫	特殊证件对美关税
2840.1900		--其他〔999〕	5	2	20	13/	0	千克			1/12
2840.2000		-其他硼酸盐									
2840.2000	10	硼酸锌〔999〕	5		30	13/	0	千克	S		1/15
2840.2000	90	其他硼酸盐〔999〕	5		30	13/	0	千克			1/15
2840.3000		-过硼酸盐〔999〕	5		30	13/	0	千克			1/20
28.41		**金属酸盐及过金属酸盐：**									
2841.3000		-重铬酸钠〔999〕	5.5		20	13/	0	千克	AB	MN	1/10.5
2841.5000		-其他铬酸盐及重铬酸盐；过铬酸盐〔301〕	5.5		30	13/	0	千克			1/35.5
		-亚锰酸盐、锰酸盐及高锰酸盐：									
2841.6100		--高锰酸钾〔101 氧化性物质，102 属于危险化学品的食品添加剂〕	5.5		30	13/	0	千克	23AB	MRNS	1/20.5
		--其他：									
2841.6910		---锰酸锂〔999〕	5.5		30	13/	13	千克			1/10.5
2841.6990		---其他〔301 氧化性物质，302 其他化工产品〕	5.5		30	13/	0	千克			1/20.5
		-钼酸盐：									
2841.7010		---钼酸铵〔999〕	5.5		30	13/	0	千克	4xy		1/15.5
2841.7090		---其他〔101 矿物源性饲料添加剂，102 化工产品〕	5.5		30	13/	0	千克	4xy		1/30.5
		-钨酸盐：									
2841.8010		---仲钨酸铵〔999〕	5.5		30	13/	0	千克	4xy		1/10.5
2841.8020		---钨酸钠〔999〕	5.5		30	13/	0	千克	4xy		1/15.5
2841.8030		---钨酸钙〔999〕	5.5		30	13/	0	千克	4xy		1/10.5
2841.8040		---偏钨酸铵〔999〕	5.5		30	13/	0	千克	4xy		1/10.5
2841.8090		---其他〔999〕	5.5		30	13/	0	千克			1/20.5
2841.9000		-其他									
2841.9000	10	钴酸锂〔999〕	5.5	2	30	13/	13	千克			1/32
2841.9000	20	铼酸盐及高铼酸盐〔999〕	5.5	0	30	13/	0	千克			1/30
2841.9000	90	其他金属酸盐及过金属酸盐〔301 毒性物质和感染性物质，302 腐蚀性物质，303 其他化工产品〕	5.5		30	13/	0	千克			1/35.5
28.42		**其他无机酸盐或过氧酸盐(包括不论是否已有化学定义的硅铝酸盐)，但叠氮化物除外：**									
2842.1000		-硅酸复盐及硅酸络盐(包括不论是否已有化学定义的硅铝酸盐)〔T2〕	5.5		30	13/	0	千克	AB	MRNS	1/30.5
		-其他：									
		---雷酸盐、氰酸盐及硫氰酸盐：									
2842.9011		----硫氰酸钠〔101 硫氰酸钙，102 硫氰酸汞，103 硫氰酸汞钾，104 硫氰酸汞铵，105 其他一级其他液态农药〕	5.5		30	13/	0	千克			1/10.5
2842.9019		----其他									
2842.9019	10	其他硫氰酸盐〔301 其他危险化学品，302 其他化工产品〕	5.5		30	13/	0	千克	AB	MN	1/10.5
2842.9019	90	雷酸盐及氰酸盐〔999 其他化工产品，998 其他危险化学品〕	5.5		30	13/	0	千克			1/10.5
2842.9020		---碲化镉〔999〕	5.5		30	13/	0	千克	AB	MN	1/10.5
2842.9030		---锂镍钴锰氧化物〔999〕	5.5		30	13/	13	千克	AB	RS	1/35.5
2842.9040		---磷酸铁锂〔999〕	5.5		30	13/	0	千克	A	M	1/35.5
2842.9050		---硒酸盐及亚硒酸盐〔T2〕	5.5		30	13/	0	千克	AB	MRNS	1/30.5
2842.9060		---锂镍钴铝氧化物〔999〕	5.5		30	13/	13	千克	AB	MRNS	1/
2842.9090		---其他									
2842.9090	13	亚砷酸钠、亚砷酸钾、亚砷酸钙(偏亚砷酸钠)〔301〕	5.5		30	13/	13	千克			1/30.5
2842.9090	14	亚砷酸锶、亚砷酸钡、亚砷酸铁〔301〕	5.5		30	13/	13	千克			1/30.5
2842.9090	15	亚砷酸铜、亚砷酸锌、亚砷酸铅(亚砷酸氢铜)〔301 毒性物质和感染性物质〕	5.5		30	13/	13	千克			1/30.5
2842.9090	16	亚砷酸锑、砷酸铵、砷酸氢二铵〔999〕	5.5		30	13/	13	千克			1/30.5
2842.9090	17	砷酸钠、砷酸氢二钠、砷酸二氢钠(砷酸三钠)〔301〕	5.5		30	13/	13	千克			1/30.5
2842.9090	18	砷酸钾、砷酸二氢钾、砷酸镁〔301〕	5.5		30	13/	13	千克			1/30.5
2842.9090	19	砷酸钙、砷酸钡、砷酸铁(砷酸三钙)〔301〕	5.5		30	13/	13	千克			1/30.5
2842.9090	21	砷酸亚铁、砷酸铜、砷酸锌〔301〕	5.5		30	13/	13	千克			1/30.5
2842.9090	22	砷酸铅、砷酸锑、偏砷酸钠〔301〕	5.5		30	13/	13	千克			1/30.5
2842.9090	23	硒化铅、硒化镉〔301 毒性物质和感染性物质，302 杂项物质〕	5.5		30	13/	13	千克			1/30.5
2842.9090	90	其他无机酸盐及过氧酸盐(迭氮化物除外)〔T2〕	5.5		30	13/	13	千克	AB	MRNS	1/30.5
		第六分章　杂项产品									
28.43		**胶态贵金属；贵金属的无机或有机化合物，不论是否已有化学定义；贵金属汞齐：**									
2843.1000		-胶态贵金属〔999〕	5.5		30	13/	0	克			1/35.5
		-银化合物：									

协定税率 %										特惠税率 %			Article Description
亚太5国	东/冰/格	巴基斯坦	韩国	瑞士	哥达	秘鲁	澳大利亚	新西/坡/智	港/澳/台	亚太2国	老/柬/缅	36/3/1	
	0/0/0	0	0	0	0	0	0	0//0	0/0/			0/0/	--Other
													-Other borates
	0/0/0	0	2.2	0	0	0	0	0//0	0/0/			0/0/	Zinc borate
	0/0/0	0	2.2	0	0	0	0	0//0	0/0/			0/0/	Other borate
	0/0/0	0	0	0	0	0	0	0//0	0/0/			0/0/	-Peroxoborates (perborates)
													Salts of oxometallic or peroxometallic acids:
	0/0/0	0	0	0	0	0	0	0//0	0/0/			0/0/0	-Sodium dichromate
	0/0/0	0	0	0	0	0	0	0//0	0/0/			0/0/0	-Other chromates and dichromates; peroxochromates
													-Manganites, manganates and permanganates:
	0/0/0	0	0	0	0	0	0	0//0	0/0/			0/0/0	--Potassium permanganate
													--Other:
	0/0/0	0	0	0	0	0	0	0//0	0/0/			0/0/0	---Lithium manganate
	0/0/0	0	0	0	0	0	0	0//0	0/0/			0/0/0	---Other
													-Molybdates:
2.8	0/0/0	0	0	0	0	0	0	0//0	0/0/			0/0/0	---Ammonium molybdates
	0/0/0	0	0	0	0	0	0	0//0	0/0/			0/0/0	---Other
													-Tungstates (wolframates):
	0/0/0	0	0	0	0	0	0	0//0	0/0/			0/0/0	---Ammonium paratungstate
	0/0/0	0	0	0	0	0	0	0//0	0/0/			0/0/0	---Sodium tungstate
	0/0/0	0	0	0	0	0	0	0//0	0/0/			0/0/0	---Calcium wolframate
	0/0/0	0	0	0	0	0	0	0//0	0/0/			0/0/0	---Ammonium metatungstate
2.8	0/0/0	0	0	0	0	0	0	0//0	0/0/			0/0/0	---Other
													-Other
	0/0/0	0	2.2	0	0	0	0	0//0	0/0/			0/0/0	Lithium cobaltate
	0/0/0	0	2.2	0	0	0	0	0//0	0/0/			0/0/0	Rhenate
	0/0/0	0	2.2	0	0	0	0	0//0	0/0/			0/0/0	Other salts of oxometallic or peroxometallic acids
													Other salts of inorganic acids or peroxoacids(including aluminosilicates whether or not chemically defined), other than azides:
	0/0/0	0	0	2.9	0	0	0	0//0	0/0/			0/0/	-Double or complex silicates, including aluminosilicates whether or not chemically defined
													-Other:
													---Fulminates, cyanates and thiocyanates:
	0/0/0	0	0	0	0	0	0	0//0	0/0/			0/0/	----Sodium sulfocyanate
													----Other
	0/0/0	0	0	0	0	0	0	0//0	0/0/			0/0/	Other thiocyanates
	0/0/0	0	0	0	0	0	0	0//0	0/0/			0/0/	Fulminates and cyanates
	0/0/0	0	0	0	0	0	0	0//0	0/0/			0/0/	---Cadmium telluride
	0/0/0	0	0	0	0	0	0	0//0	0/0/			0/0/	---Lithium nickel cobalt manganese oxides
	0/0/0	0	2.2	0	0	0	0	0//0	0/0/			0/0/	---Lithium iron phosphate
	0/0/0	0	0	0	0	0	0	0//0	0/0/			0/0/	---Colloidal selenium and selenite
	0/0/0	0	0	0	0	0	0	0//0	0/0/			0/0/	---Lithium nickel cobalt aluminum oxide
													---Other
	0/0/0	0	0	0	0	0	0	0//0	0/0/			0/0/	Sodium arsenite, potassium arsenite, calcium arsenite
	0/0/0	0	0	0	0	0	0	0//0	0/0/			0/0/	Strontium arsenite, barium arsenite, Arsenous acid
	0/0/0	0	0	0	0	0	0	0//0	0/0/			0/0/	Copper arsonate, arsenen ous acrd, lead arsenite
	0/0/0	0	0	0	0	0	0	0//0	0/0/			0/0/	Antimony arsenite, ammonium arsenate, diammonium hydrogen arsenate
	0/0/0	0	0	0	0	0	0	0//0	0/0/			0/0/	Sodium arsenate, sodium arsenate dibasic, sodium arsenate monobasic
	0/0/0	0	0	0	0	0	0	0//0	0/0/			0/0/	Potassium arsenate, potassium dihyrogwn arsenate, magnesium arsenate
	0/0/0	0	0	0	0	0	0	0//0	0/0/			0/0/	Calcium arsenate, barium arsenate, ferric arsenate (tricalcium arsenate)
	0/0/0	0	0	0	0	0	0	0//0	0/0/			0/0/	Ferrous arsenate, cupric arsenate, zinc arsenate
	0/0/0	0	0	0	0	0	0	0//0	0/0/			0/0/	Lead arsenate, antimony arsenate, sodium metaarsenate
	0/0/0	0	0	0	0	0	0	0//0	0/0/			0/0/	Lead selenide, cadmium selenide
	0/0/0	0	0	0	0	0	0	0//0	0/0/			0/0/	Other salts of inorganic acids or peroxoacids
													Ⅵ. MISCELLANEOUS
													Colloidal precious metals; inorganic or organic compounds of precious metals, whether or not chemically defined; amalgams of precious metals:
	0/0/0	0	0	0	0	0	0	0//0	0/0/			0/0/	-Colloidal precious metals
													-Silver compounds:

税则号列		货品名称〔CIQ 扩展编码及品名－T2 表示见附表 2〕	最惠(%)	暂定税率	普通	增值/消费	出口退税	计量单位	监管条件	检验检疫	特殊证件对美关税
2843.2100		--硝酸银〔999〕	5.5		30	13/	0	克	AB	MN	1/15.5
2843.2900		--其他									
2843.2900	10	氰化银、氰化银钾、亚砷酸银(银氰化钾、砷酸银)〔301〕	5.5		30	13/	0	克			1/15.5
2843.2900	90	其他银化合物(不论是否已有化学定义)〔301 氧化性物质,302 腐蚀性物质,303 其他化工产品〕	5.5		30	13/	0	克			1/15.5
2843.3000		-金化合物									
2843.3000	10	氰化金、氰化金钾(含金 40%)等[包括氰化亚金(Ⅰ)钾(含金 68.3%)、氰化亚金(Ⅲ)钾(含金 57%)]〔999〕	5.5		30	13/	0	克	J		1/25.5
2843.3000	90	其他金化合物(不论是否已有化学定义)〔999〕	5.5		30	13/	0	克			1/25.5
2843.9000		-其他贵金属化合物;贵金属汞齐									
2843.9000	10	氯化钯〔999〕	5.5		30	13/	0	克	G		1/15.5
2843.9000	20	氯化铂〔999〕	5.5		30	13/	0	克	4xy		1/15.5
2843.9000	31	奥沙利铂、卡铂、奈达铂、顺铂〔999〕	5.5	0	30	3/	0	克	4xy		1/10
2843.9000	39	其他铂化合物(因拆分抗癌药品原料药产生的兜底税号)〔999〕	5.5		30	13/	0	克	4xy		1/15.5
2843.9000	90	其他贵金属化合物,贵金属汞齐(不论是否已有化学定义)〔101 其他碱金属汞齐,102 硝酸铑,103 硝酸钯〕	5.5		30	13/	0	克	4xy		1/15.5
28.44		**放射性化学元素及放射性同位素(包括可裂变或可转换的化学元素及同位素)及其化合物;含上述产品的混合物及残渣:**									
2844.1000		-天然铀及其化合物;含天然铀或天然铀化合物的合金、分散体(包括金属陶瓷)、陶瓷产品及混合物							23		
2844.1000	10	天然铀及其化合物〔999〕	5	0	30	13/	0	克/百万贝可	23		1/30
2844.1000	90	含天然铀或天然铀化合物的合金、分散体(包括金属陶瓷)、陶瓷产品及混合物〔999〕	5		30	13/	0	克/百万贝可	23		1/35
2844.2000		-U235浓缩铀及其化合物;钚及其化合物;含U235浓缩铀、钚或它们的化合物的合金、分散体(包括金属陶瓷)、陶瓷产品及混合物									
2844.2000	10	含 U235 浓度低于 5%的低浓铀及其化合物〔999〕	5	0	30	13/	0	克/百万贝可	23		1/30
2844.2000	90	其他 U235 浓缩铀,钚及其化合物(包括其合金,分散体,陶瓷产品及混合物)〔999〕	5		30	13/	0	克/百万贝可	23		1/35
2844.3000		-U235贫化铀及其化合物;钍及其化合物;含U235贫化铀、钍或它们的化合物的合金、分散体(包括金属陶瓷)、陶瓷产品及混合物〔999〕	5		30	13/	0	克/百万贝可	23		1/15
		-除子目 2844.10、2844.20 及 2844.30 以外的放射性元素、同位素及其化合物;含这些元素、同位素及其化合物的合金、分散体(包括金属陶瓷)、陶瓷产品及混合物:									
2844.4010		---镭及镭盐									
2844.4010	10	镭－226 及其化合物、混合物(两用物项管制商品)〔999〕	4		14	13/	0	克/百万贝可	23		1/29
2844.4010	90	其他镭及镭盐〔999〕	4		14	13/	0	克/百万贝可	2		1/29
2844.4020		---钴及钴盐〔999〕	4		14	13/	0	克/百万贝可	2		1/34
2844.4090		---其他									
2844.4090	10	铀-233 及其化合物(包括呈金属、合金、化合物或浓缩物形态的各种材料)〔999〕	5		30	13/	0	克/百万贝可	23		1/20
2844.4090	20	氚、氚化物和氚的混合物,以及含有上述任何一种物质的产品(氚－氢原子比超过千分之一的,不包括含氚(任何形态)量小于 1.48 $\times10^{-3}$GBq 的产品)〔999〕	5		30	13/	0	克/百万贝可	23		1/20
2844.4090	30	氦-3(3He)、含有氦-3 的混合物(不包括氦-3 的含量＜1g 的产品)〔999〕	5		30	13/	0	克/百万贝可	3		1/20
2844.4090	40	发射 α 粒子,其 α 半衰期为 10 天或更长但小于 200 年的放射性核素(1. 单质;2. 含有 α 总活度为 37GBq/kg 或更大的任何这类放射性核素的化合物;3. 含有 α 总活度为 37GBq/kg 或更大的任何这类放射性核素的混合物;4. 含有任何上述物质的产品,不包括所含 α 活度小于3.7GBq的产品)〔999〕	5		30	13/	0	克/百万贝可	23		1/20

协定税率 %										特惠税率 %			Article Description
亚太5国	东/冰/格	巴基斯坦	韩国	瑞士	哥达	秘鲁	澳大利亚	新西/坡/智	港/澳/台	亚太2国	老/柬/缅	36/3/1	
	0/0/0	0	0	0	0	0	0	0//0	0/0/			0/0/	--Silver nitrate
													--Other
	0/0/0	0	0	0	0	0	0	0//0	0/0/			0/0/	Silver cyanide, potassium arsentocyanide, silverarsenite (potassium silver(Ⅰ)cyanide, slilver arsenate)
	0/0/0	0	0	0	0	0	0	0//0	0/0/			0/0/	Other silver compounds (whether or not chemically defined)
													-Gold compounds
4.4	0/0/0	0	0	0	0	0	0	0//0	0/0/			0/0/	Gold cyanide, potassium cyanide gold(gold content 40%) (containing 40% of gold)(including subcyanide gold(Ⅰ)(gold content 68.3%)postassium subcyanide gold(Ⅲ)(gold content 57%))
4.4	0/0/0	0	0	0	0	0	0	0//0	0/0/			0/0/	Other gold compounds (whether or not chemically defined)
													-Other compounds; amalgams
	0/0/0	0	0		0	0	0	0//0	0/0/			0/0/	Palladium chloride
	0/0/0	0	0		0	0	0	0//0	0/0/			0/0/	Platinum chloride
	0/0/0	0	0		0	0	0	0//0	0/0/			0/0/	Oxaliplatin, carboplatin, nedaplatin, cisplatin and other platinum－containing anticancer drug preparations and APIs
	0/0/0	0	0		0	0	0	0//0	0/0/			0/0/	Other platinum compounds(tax number of Separating anti－cancer pharmaceutical raw materials)
	0/0/0	0	0		0	0	0	0//0	0/0/			0/0/	Other precious metal compounds or precious amalgam (whether chemical definition exists or not)
													Radioactive chemical elements and radioactive isotopes (including the fissile or fertile chemical elements and isotopes) and their compounds; mixtures and residues containing these products:
													-Natural uranium and its compounds; alloys, dispersions (including cermets), ceramic products and mixtures containing natural uranium or natural uranium compouds
	0/0/0	0	0	0	0	0	0	0//0	0/0/			0/0/0	Natural uranium and its compounds
	0/0/0	0	0	0	0	0	0	0//0	0/0/			0/0/0	Contains natural uranium alloy or natural uranium compounds, dispersions (including metal ceramic), ceramic products and mixture
													-Uranium enriched in U235 and its compounds; plutonium and its compounds; alloys dispersion (including cermets), ceramic products and mixtures containing uranium enriched in U235, plutonium or compounds of these products
	0/0/0	0	0	0	0	0	0	0//0	0/0/			0/0/0	Containing U235 concentration less than 5% of low-enriched uranium and its compounds
	0/0/0	0	0	0	0	0	0	0//0	0/0/			0/0/0	Other U235 enriched uranium and plutonium and its compounds (including its alloy, dispersions, ceramic products and mixture)
	0/0/0	0	0	0	0	0	0	0//0	0/0/			0/0/0	-Uranium depleted in U235and its compounds; thorium and its compounds; alloys, dispersions (including cermets), ceramic products and mixtures containing uranium depleted in U235, thorium or compounds of these products
													-Radioactive elements and isotopes and compounds other than those of subheading No. 2844.10, 2844.20 or 2844.30; alloys, dispersions (including cermets), ceramic products and mixtures containing these elements, isotopes or compounds; radioactive residues:
													---Radium and its salts
	0/0/0	0	0	0	0	0	0	0//0	0/0/			0/0/0	Radium-226 and its compounds
	0/0/0	0	0	0	0	0	0	0//0	0/0/			0/0/0	Other radium and its salts
	0/0/0	0	0	0	0	0	0	0//0	0/0/			0/0/0	---Cobalt and its salts
													---Other
	0/0/0	0	0	0	0	0	0	0//0	0/0/			0/0/0	Uranium-233 and its compounds (including metallic material, alloys, compounds or enriched materials)
	0/0/0	0	0	0	0	0	0	0//0	0/0/			0/0/0	A mixture of tritium, tritium compound and tritium, and of material contains any of these products (tritium - more than one over one thousand of the hydrogen atom, does not include the content of tritium (any form) less than 1.48×10^{3} GBq products)
	0/0/0	0	0	0	0	0	0	0//0	0/0/			0/0/0	helium (he) 3, 3 a mixture containing helium - 3 (not including the content of helium 3 < 1 g)
	0/0/0	0	0	0	0	0	0	0//0	0/0/			0/0/0	Emission of alpha particles, the alpha half-life of 10 days or more but less than 200 years of radionuclides (1. single matter; 2. Containing a total activity of 37GBq/ kg or greater in any of these types of radioactive compounds; 3. Containing a total activity of 37GBq/ kg or greater in any of these types of radioactive mixture; 4. Containing any of the above substances in products, not including the alpha activity less than 3.7GBq products)

税则号列		货品名称〔CIQ 扩展编码及品名－T2 表示见附表 2〕	最惠(%)	暂定税率	普通	增值/消费	出口退税	计量单位	监管条件	检验检疫	特殊证件对美关税
2844.4090	90	其他放射性元素、同位素及其化合物（编号 2844.10，2844.20，2844.30 以外的放射性元素、同位素）〔999〕	5		30	13/	0	克/百万贝可	2		1/20
2844.5000		-核反应堆已耗尽（已辐照）的燃料元件（释热元件）〔999〕	5		30	13/	0	克			1/10
28.45		**税目 28.44 以外的同位素；这些同位素的无机或有机化合物，不论是否已有化学定义：**									
2845.1000		-重水（氧化氘）〔999〕	5		30	13/	0	克	3		1/20
2845.9000		-其他									
2845.9000	10	除重水外的氘及氘化物〔999〕	5		30	13/	0	克	3		1/15
2845.9000	20	硼-10 同位素及其化合物、混合物（硼-10 同位素占硼总量＞20％的硼及其化合物、混合物）〔999〕	5		30	13/	0	克	3		1/15
2845.9000	30	富集锂-6 同位素及其化合物，混合物［富集锂-6 同位素指锂-6 同位素富集度＞7.5％（按原子数计）］〔999〕	5		30	13/	0	克	3		1/15
2845.9000	90	其他同位素及其他化合物（编号 28.44 以外的同位素）〔999〕	5		30	13/	0	克			1/15
28.46		**稀土金属、钇、钪及其混合物的无机或有机化合物：**									
		-铈的化合物：									
2846.1010		---氧化铈〔999〕	5	0	30	13/	0	千克	4Bxy	N	1/25
2846.1020		---氢氧化铈〔999〕	5	0	30	13/	0	千克	4Bxy	N	1/10
2846.1030		---碳酸铈〔999〕	5	0	30	13/	0	千克	4Bxy	N	1/
2846.1090		---其他									
2846.1090	10	氰化铈〔999〕	5	0	30	13/	0	千克	4Bxy	N	1/10
2846.1090	90	铈的其他化合物〔101 矿物源性饲料添加剂，103 不属于危险化学品的稀土，301 属于危险化学品的稀土〕	5	0	30	13/	0	千克	4Bxy	N	1/10
		-其他：									
		---氧化稀土（氧化铈除外）：									
2846.9011		----氧化钇〔999〕	5	0	30	13/	0	千克	4xBy	N	1/30
2846.9012		----氧化镧〔999〕	5	0	30	13/	0	千克	4Bxy	N	1/25
2846.9013		----氧化钕〔999〕	5	0	30	13/	0	千克	4Bxy	N	1/
2846.9014		----氧化铕〔999〕	5	0	30	13/	0	千克	4Bxy	N	1/
2846.9015		----氧化镝〔999〕	5	0	30	13/	0	千克	4Bxy	N	1/
2846.9016		----氧化铽〔999〕	5	0	30	13/	0	千克	4Bxy	N	1/
2846.9017		----氧化镨〔999〕	5	0	30	13/	0	千克	4Bxy	N	1/30
2846.9019		----其他									
2846.9019	20	氧化铒〔999〕	5	0	30	13/	0	千克	4Bxy	N	1/30
2846.9019	30	氧化钆〔999〕	5	0	30	13/	0	千克	4Bxy	N	1/30
2846.9019	40	氧化钐〔999〕	5	0	30	13/	0	千克	4Bxy	N	1/30
2846.9019	70	氧化镱〔999〕	5	0	30	13/	0	千克	4Bxy	N	1/30
2846.9019	80	氧化钪〔999〕	5	0	30	13/	0	千克	4Bxy	N	1/30
2846.9019	91	灯用红粉〔999〕	5	0	30	13/	0	千克	4Bxy	N	1/30
2846.9019	92	按重量计中重稀土总含量≥30％的其他氧化稀土（灯用红粉、氧化铈除外）〔999〕	5	0	30	13/	0	千克	4Bxy	N	1/30
2846.9019	99	其他氧化稀土（灯用红粉、氧化铈除外）〔999〕	5	0	30	13/	0	千克	4Bxy	N	1/30
		---氯化稀土：									
2846.9021		----氯化铽〔999〕	5	0	30	13/	0	千克	4Bxy	N	1/10
2846.9022		----氯化镝〔999〕	5	0	30	13/	0	千克	4Bxy	N	1/
2846.9023		----氯化镧〔999〕	5	0	30	13/	0	千克	4Bxy	N	1/10
2846.9024		----氯化钕〔999〕	5	0	30	13/	0	千克	4Bxy	N	1/
2846.9025		----氯化镨〔999〕	5	0	30	13/	0	千克	4Bxy	N	1/
2846.9026		----氯化钇〔999〕	5	0	30	13/	0	千克	4Bxy	N	1/10
2846.9028		----混合氯化稀土〔999〕	5	0	30	13/	0	千克	4Bxy	N	1/
2846.9029		----其他〔999〕	5	0	30	13/	0	千克	4Bxy	N	1/15
		---氟化稀土：									
2846.9031		----氟化铽〔999〕	5	0	30	13/	0	千克	4Bxy	N	1/
2846.9032		----氟化镝〔999〕	5	0	30	13/	0	千克	4Bxy	N	1/
2846.9033		----氟化镧〔999〕	5	0	30	13/	0	千克	4ABxy	MN	1/
2846.9034		----氟化钕〔999〕	5	0	30	13/	0	千克	4Bxy	N	1/
2846.9035		----氟化镨〔999〕	5	0	30	13/	0	千克	4Bxy	N	1/
2846.9036		----氟化钇〔999〕	5	0	30	13/	0	千克	4Bxy	N	1/
2846.9039		----其他〔301 不属于危险化学品的稀土，302 属于危险化学品的稀土〕	5	0	30	13/	0	千克	4Bxy	N	1/
		---碳酸稀土：									
2846.9041		----碳酸镧〔999〕	5	0	30	13/	0	千克	4Bxy	N	1/

协定税率 %										特惠税率 %			Article Description
亚太5国	东/冰/格	巴基斯坦	韩国	瑞士	哥达	秘鲁	澳大利亚	新西/坡/智	港/澳/台	亚太2国	老/柬/缅	36/3/1	
	0/0/0	0	0	0	0	0	0	0//0	0/0/			0/0/0	Other radioactive elements and isotopes and their compounds (radioactive elements and isotopes other than those of subheading No. 2844.10, 2844.20 or 2844.30)
	0/0/0	0	0	0	0	0	0	0//0	0/0/			0/0/	-Spent (irradiated) fuel elements (cartridges) of nuclear reactors
													Isotopes other than those of heading No. 28.44; compounds, inorganic or organic, of such isotopes, whether or not chemically defined:
	0/0/0	0	0	0	0	0	0	0//0	0/0/			0/0/	-Heavy water (deuterium oxide)
													-Other
	0/0/0	0	0	0	0	0	0	0//0	0/0/			0/0/	Deuterium and deuterides, other than heavy water
	0/0/0	0	0	0	0	0	0	0//0	0/0/			0/0/	Boron-10 and its compounds (boron and its compounds and mixtures with a containing of boron-10>20% of the total boron content)
	0/0/0	0	0	0	0	0	0	0//0	0/0/			0/0/	Lithium enriched in lithium-6 and its compounds and mixtures (lithium enriched in lithium-6 refers to enrichment of lithium-6 isotope>7.5% (atomicity))
	0/0/0	0	0	0	0	0	0	0//0	0/0/			0/0/	Other isotopes and other compounds (other than isotopes of heading No. 28.44)
													Compounds, inorganic or organic, of rareearth metals, of yttrium or of scandium or of mixtures of these metals:
													-Ceric compounds:
2.5	0/0/0	0	0	0	0	0	0	0//0	0/0/			0/0/	---Cerium oxide
2.5	0/0/0	0	0	0	0	0	0	0//0	0/0/			0/0/	---Cerium hydroxide
2.5	0/0/0	0	0	0	0	0	0	0//0	0/0/			0/0/	---Cerium carbonate
													---Other
2.5	0/0/0	0	0	0	0	0	0	0//0	0/0/			0/0/	Cerium cyanide
2.5	0/0/0	0	0	0	0	0	0	0//0	0/0/			0/0/	Other cerium compounds with
													-Other:
													---Rare-earth oxides (other than cerium oxide):
	0/0/0	0	0	0	0	0	0	0//0	0/0/			0/0/	----Yttrium oxide
	0/0/0	0	0	0	0	0	0	0//0	0/0/			0/0/	----Lanthanum oxide
	0/0/0	0	0	0	0	0	0	0//0	0/0/			0/0/	----Neodymium oxide
	0/0/0	0	0	0	0	0	0	0//0	0/0/			0/0/	----Europium oxide
	0/0/0	0	0	0	0	0	0	0//0	0/0/			0/0/	----Dysprosium oxide
	0/0/0	0	0	0	0	0	0	0//0	0/0/			0/0/	----Terbium oxide
	0/0/0	0	0	0	0	0	0	0//0	0/0/			0/0/	----Praseodymium oxide
													----Other
	0/0/0	0	0	0	0	0	0	0//0	0/0/			0/0/	Erbium oxide
	0/0/0	0	0	0	0	0	0	0//0	0/0/			0/0/	Gadolinium oxide
	0/0/0	0	0	0	0	0	0	0//0	0/0/			0/0/	Samarium oxide
	0/0/0	0	0	0	0	0	0	0//0	0/0/			0/0/	Ytterbium oxide
	0/0/0	0	0	0	0	0	0	0//0	0/0/			0/0/	Scandium oxide
	0/0/0	0	0	0	0	0	0	0//0	0/0/			0/0/	Red powder for lumination
	0/0/0	0	0	0	0	0	0	0//0	0/0/			0/0/	Other rare-earth oxide, containing by weihgt ≥30% of middle heavy rare-earth(other than red powder for lumination, cerium cyanide)
	0/0/0	0	0	0	0	0	0	0//0	0/0/			0/0/	Other rare-earth oxide(other than red powder for lumination, cerium cyanide)
													---Rare-earth chlorides:
	0/0/0	0	0	0	0	0	0	0//0	0/0/			0/0/	----Terbium chlorinates
	0/0/0	0	0	0	0	0	0	0//0	0/0/			0/0/	----Dysprosium chlorinates
	0/0/0	0	0	0	0	0	0	0//0	0/0/			0/0/	----Lan thanum chloride
	0/0/0	0	0	0	0	0	0	0//0	0/0/			0/0/	----Neodymium chlorinates
	0/0/0	0	0	0	0	0	0	0//0	0/0/			0/0/	----Praseodymium chlorinates
	0/0/0	0	0	0	0	0	0	0//0	0/0/			0/0/	----Yttrium chlorinates
	0/0/0	0	0	0	0	0	0	0//0	0/0/			0/0/	----Mixture of rareearth chlorides
	0/0/0	0	0	0	0	0	0	0//0	0/0/			0/0/	----Other
													---Rare-earth fluorides:
	0/0/0	0	0	0	0	0	0	0//0	0/0/			0/0/	----Terbium fluoride
	0/0/0	0	0	0	0	0	0	0//0	0/0/			0/0/	----Dysprosium fluoride
	0/0/0	0	0	0	0	0	0	0//0	0/0/			0/0/	----Lanthanum fluoride
	0/0/0	0	0	0	0	0	0	0//0	0/0/			0/0/	----Neodymium fluoride
	0/0/0	0	0	0	0	0	0	0//0	0/0/			0/0/	----Praseodymium fluoride
	0/0/0	0	0	0	0	0	0	0//0	0/0/			0/0/	----Yttrium fluoride
	0/0/0	0	0	0	0	0	0	0//0	0/0/			0/0/	----Other
													---Rare-earth carbonate:
	0/0/0	0	0	0	0	0	0	0//0	0/0/			0/0/	----Lanthanum carbonates

税则号列	货品名称〔CIQ扩展编码及品名－T2表示见附表2〕	最惠(%)	暂定税率	普通	增值/消费	出口退税	计量单位	监管条件	检验检疫	特殊证件对美关税
2846.9042	----碳酸铽〔999〕	5	0	30	13/	0	千克	4Bxy	N	1/
2846.9043	----碳酸镝〔999〕	5	0	30	13/	0	千克	4Bxy	N	1/
2846.9044	----碳酸钕〔999〕	5	0	30	13/	0	千克	4Bxy	N	1/
2846.9045	----碳酸镨〔999〕	5	0	30	13/	0	千克	4Bxy	N	1/
2846.9046	----碳酸钇〔999〕	5	0	30	13/	0	千克	4Bxy	N	1/
2846.9048	----混合碳酸稀土									
2846.9048 10	按重量计中重稀土总含量≥30%的混合碳酸稀土〔999〕	5	0	30	13/	0	千克	4Bxy	N	1/25
2846.9048 90	其他混合碳酸稀土〔999〕	5	0	30	13/	0	千克	4Bxy	N	1/25
2846.9049	----其他〔999〕	5	0	30	13/	0	千克	4Bxy	N	1/
	---其他：									
2846.9091	----镧的其他化合物〔301不属于危险化学品的稀土，302属于危险化学品的稀土〕	5	0	30	13/	0	千克	4Bxy	N	1/10
2846.9092	----钕的其他化合物〔301不属于危险化学品的稀土，302属于危险化学品的稀土〕	5	0	30	13/	0	千克	4Bxy	N	1/10
2846.9093	----铽的其他化合物〔999〕	5	0	30	13/	0	千克	4Bxy	N	1/30
2846.9094	----镝的其他化合物〔301不属于危险化学品的稀土，302属于危险化学品的稀土〕	5	0	30	13/	0	千克	4Bxy	N	1/
2846.9095	----镨的其他化合物〔301不属于危险化学品的稀土，302属于危险化学品的稀土〕	5	0	30	13/	0	千克	4Bxy	N	1/
2846.9096	----钇的其他化合物							4Bxy		
2846.9096 01	LED用荧光粉(成分含钇的其他化合物)〔999〕	5	0	30	13/	0	千克	B	N	1/30
2846.9096 90	钇的其他化合物〔301不属于危险化学品的稀土，302属于危险化学品的稀土〕	5	0	30	13/	0	千克	4Bxy	N	1/30
2846.9099	----其他									
2846.9099 01	LED用荧光粉(成分含稀土金属、钪的其他化合物，铈的化合物除外)〔999〕	5	0	30	13/	0	千克	B	N	1/25
2846.9099 10	按重量计中重稀土总含量≥30%的稀土金属、钪的其他化合物(铈的化合物除外)〔999〕	5	0	30	13/	0	千克	4Bxy	N	1/25
2846.9099 90	其他稀土金属、钪的其他化合物(铈的化合物除外)〔101饲料添加剂，301不属于危险化学品的稀土，302属于危险化学品的稀土〕	5	0	30	13/	0	千克	4Bxy	N	1/25
28.47	**过氧化氢，不论是否用尿素固化：**									
2847.0000	过氧化氢，不论是否用尿素固化〔301氧化性物质，需申报仅用于工业用途不用于食品添加剂无检疫要求，302属于危险化学品的食品添加剂〕	5.5		30	13/	0	千克	AB	MRNS	1/35.5
28.49	**碳化物，不论是否已有化学定义：**									
2849.1000	-碳化钙〔999〕	5.5		45	13/	0	千克	AB	MN	1/10.5
2849.2000	-碳化硅〔999〕	5.5		30	13/	0	千克	4xy		1/30.5
	-其他：									
2849.9010	---碳化硼〔999〕	5.5		30	13/	0	千克			1/10.5
2849.9020	---碳化钨〔999〕	5.5		30	13/	0	千克	4xy		1/15.5
2849.9090	---其他〔999遇水放出易燃气体的物质，301其他化工产品〕	5.5		30	13/	0	千克			1/30.5
28.50	**氢化物、氮化物、叠氮化物、硅化物及硼化物，不论是否已有化学定义，但可归入税目28.49的碳化物除外：**									
	---氮化物：									
2850.0011	----氮化锰〔999〕	5.5		30	13/	0	千克			1/10.5
2850.0012	----氮化硼〔999〕	5.5		30	13/	0	千克			1/15.5
2850.0019	----其他〔301爆炸品，302易燃气体，303毒性气体，304易燃固体，305遇水放出易燃气体的物质，306毒性物质和感染性物质，307其他化工产品〕	5.5		30	13/	0	千克			1/30.5
2850.0090	---其他									
2850.0090 10	砷化氢(砷烷、砷化三氢、胂)〔999〕	5.5		30	13/	0	千克			1/15.5
2850.0090 90	其他氢化物、硅化物等(包括硼化物，可归入税目28.49的碳化物除外)〔301易燃气体，302毒性气体，303易燃固体，304易于自燃的物质，305遇水放出易燃气体的物质，306其他化工产品〕	5.5		30	13/	0	千克			1/15.5
28.52	**汞的无机或有机化合物，汞齐除外：**									
2852.1000	-已有化学定义的〔301毒性物质和感染性物质?，302不属于危险化学品的金属?〕	5.5		30	13/	0	千克			1/10.5
2852.9000	-其他〔999其他化工产品，998其他危险化学品〕	5.5		30	13/	0	千克			1/10.5
28.53	**磷化物，不论是否已有化学定义，但磷铁除外；其他无机化合物(包括蒸馏水、导电水及类似的纯净水)；液态空气(不论是否除去稀有气体)；压缩空气；汞齐，但贵金属汞齐除外：**									
2853.1000	-氯化氰〔999〕	5.5		30	13/	0	千克	23AB	MN	1/10.5

协定税率 %										特惠税率 %			
亚太5国	东/冰/格	巴基斯坦	韩国	瑞士	哥达	秘鲁	澳大利亚	新西/坡/智	港/澳/台	亚太2国	老/柬/缅	36/3/1	Article Description
	0/0/0	0	0	0	0	0	0	0//0	0/0/			0/0/	----Terbium carbonates
	0/0/0	0	0	0	0	0	0	0//0	0/0/			0/0/	----Dysprosium carbonates
	0/0/0	0	0	0	0	0	0	0//0	0/0/			0/0/	----Neodymium carbonates
	0/0/0	0	0	0	0	0	0	0//0	0/0/			0/0/	----Praseodymium carbonates
	0/0/0	0	0	0	0	0	0	0//0	0/0/			0/0/	----Yttrium carbonates
													----Mixture of rare earth carbonate
	0/0/0	0	0	0	0	0	0	0//0	0/0/			0/0/	Other mixed rare-earth carbonates, containing by weihgt ≥30% of middle heavy rare-earth,
	0/0/0	0	0	0	0	0	0	0//0	0/0/			0/0/	Other mixed rare-earth carbonates
	0/0/0	0	0	0	0	0	0	0//0	0/0/			0/0/	----Other
													---Other:
	0/0/0	0	0	0	0	0	0	0//0	0/0/			0/0/	----Other compounds ,of lanthanum
	0/0/0	0	0	0	0	0	0	0//0	0/0/			0/0/	----Other compounds ,of lanthanum
	0/0/0	0	0	0	0	0	0	0//0	0/0/			0/0/	----Other compounds ,of neodymium
	0/0/0	0	0	0	0	0	0	0//0	0/0/			0/0/	----Other compounds ,of dysprosium
	0/0/0	0	0	0	0	0	0	0//0	0/0/			0/0/	----Other compounds ,of praseodymium
													----Other compounds ,of yttrium
	0/0/0	0	0	0	0	0	0	0//0	0/0/			0/0/	LED phosphor(other compounds containing yttrium)
	0/0/0	0	0	0	0	0	0	0//0	0/0/			0/0/	Other compounds containing yttrium
													----Other
	0/0/0	0	0	0	0	0	0	0//0	0/0/			0/0/	LED phosphor(other compounds containing rare earth metals, scandium, except for cerium compounds)
	0/0/0	0	0	0	0	0	0	0//0	0/0/			0/0/	Other rare-earth metals, other compounds of scandium , containing by weihgt ≥30% of middle heavy rare-earth,
	0/0/0	0	0	0	0	0	0	0//0	0/0/			0/0/	Other rare-earth metals, compounds of scandium
													Hydrogen peroxide, whether or not solidified with urea:
	0/0/0	0	3.3	0	0	0	0	0//0	0/0/			0/0/	Hydrogen peroxide, whether or not solidified with urea
													Carbides, whether or not chemically defined:
	0/0/0	0	0	0	0	0	0	0//0	0/0/			0/0/	-Of calcium
	0/0/0	0	2.2	0	0	0	0	0//0	0/0/			0/0/	-Of silicon
													-Other:
	0/0/0	0	0	0	0	0	0	0//0	0/0/			0/0/	---Of boron
	0/0/0	0	0	0	0	0	0	0//0	0/0/			0/0/	---Of tungsten
	0/0/0	0	0	0	0	0	0	0//0	0/0/			0/0/	---Other
													Hydrides, nitrides, azides, silicides and borides, whether or not chemically defined, other than compounds which are also carbides of heading No. 28.49:
													---Nitride:
3.6	0/0/0	0	0	0	0	0	0	0//0	0/0/			0/0/	----Manganese nitride
3.6	0/0/0	0	0	0	0	0	0	0//0	0/0/			0/0/	----Boron Nitride
3.6	0/0/0	0	0	0	0	0	0	0//0	0/0/			0/0/	----Other
													---Other
3.6	0/0/0	0	3.3	0	0	0	0	0//0	0/0/			0/0/	Arsenic hydride(arsine, hydride; arsine)
3.6	0/0/0	0	3.3	0	0	0	0	0//0	0/0/			0/0/	Other hydrides, silicides (including borides, other than compounds which qre also carbides of heading No. 28.49)
													Compounds, inorganic or organic, of mercury, whether or not chemically defined, excluding amalgams:
	0/0/0	0	0	0	0	0	0	0//0	0/0/			0/0/	-Chemically defined
	0/0/0	0	0	0	0	0	0	0//0	0/0/			0/0/0	-Other
													Phosphides, whether or not chemically defined, excluding ferrophosphorus; Other inorganic compounds (including distilled or conductivity water and water of similar purity); liquid air (whether or not rare gases have been removed); compressed air; amalgams, other than amalgams of precious metals:
	0/0/0	0	0	0	0	0	0	0//0	0/0/			0/0/	-Cyanogen chlorde(*chlorcyan*)

税则号列	货品名称〔CIQ扩展编码及品名－T2表示见附表2〕	最惠(%)	暂定税率	普通	增值/消费	出口退税	计量单位	监管条件	检验检疫	特殊证件对美关税
	-其他：									
2853.9010	---饮用蒸馏水〔998 食用,999 实验用〕	5.5		70	13/	0	千克	AB	RS	1/35.5
2853.9030	---镍钴锰氢氧化物〔999〕	6.5		30	13/	13	千克			1/11.5
2853.9040	---磷化物,不论是否已有化学定义,但不包括磷铁									
2853.9040 10	磷化铝,磷化锌〔999〕	5.5		20	13/	0	千克	S		1/15.5
2853.9040 90	其他磷化物(不论是否已有化学定义,但不包括磷铁)〔999 不论是否已有化学定义,但不包括磷铁,301 毒性气体,302 遇水放出易燃气体的物质,303 其他化工产品〕	5.5		20	13/	0	千克			1/15.5
2853.9050	---镍钴铝氢氧化物〔999〕	5.5		30	13/	13	千克			1/10.5
2853.9090	---其他									
2853.9090 10	饮用纯净水〔998 食用,999 实验用〕	5.5		30	13/	0	千克	AB	MN	1/15.5
2853.9090 21	氰,氰化碘,氰化溴,铅汞齐(包括氰气,碘化氰,溴化氰)〔999 包括氰气,碘化氰,溴化氰,301 毒性气体,302 毒性物质和感染性物质,303 遇水放出易燃气体的物质〕	5.5		30	13/	0	千克			1/15.5
2853.9090 22	砷化锌,砷化镓〔999〕	5.5		30	13/	0	千克			1/15.5
2853.9090 90	其他无机化合物、压缩空气等(包括单氰胺、导电水、液态空气、汞齐等,贵金属汞齐除外)[T2]	5.5		30	13/	0	千克			1/15.5

协定税率 %										特惠税率 %			
亚太5国	东/冰/格	巴基斯坦	韩国	瑞士	哥达	秘鲁	澳大利亚	新西/坡/智	港/澳/台	亚太2国	老/柬/缅	36/3/1	Article Description
													-Other:
	0/0/0	0	0	0	0	0	0	0//0	0/0/			0/0/	---Distilled water for human consumption
	0/0/0	4.5	0	0	0	0	0	0//0	0/0/			0/0/	---Nickel cobalt manganese composite hydroxide
													---Phosphides, whether or not chemically defined, excluding ferrophosphorus
	0/0/0	0	2.2	0	0	0	0	0//0	0/0/			0/0/	Aluminium phosphide, zinc phosphide
	0/0/0	0	2.2	0	0	0	0	0//0	0/0/			0/0/	Other phosphides, whether or not chemieally defined, excluding ferrophosphorus
	0/0/0	0	0	0	0	0	0	0//0	0/0/			0/0/	---Nickel cobalt aluminum hydroxide
													---Other
	0/0/0	0	0	0	0	0	0	0//0	0/0/			0/0/	Purified water for human consumption
	0/0/0	0	0	0	0	0	0	0//0	0/0/			0/0/	Mercury Arsenide, Cyanogen, Cyanogen iodide, Bromine cyanide (including Cyanogen Dicyanogen, iodine cyanide, Bromine cyanide)
	0/0/0	0	0	0	0	0	0	0//0	0/0/			0/0/	Zinc arsenide, gallium arsenide
	0/0/0	0	0	0	0	0	0	0//0	0/0/			0/0/	Other inorganic compounds, compressed air (including conductivity water, liquid air, amalgams, other than amalgamms of precious metals)

第二十九章
有机化学品

注释：

一、除条文另有规定的以外，本章各税目只适用于：

(一)单独的已有化学定义的有机化合物，不论是否含有杂质；

(二)同一有机化合物的两种或两种以上异构体的混合物(不论是否含有杂质)，但无环烃异构体的混合物(立体异构体除外)，不论是否饱和，应归入第二十七章；

(三)税目29.36至29.39的产品，税目29.40的糖醚、糖缩醛、糖酯及其盐类和税目29.41的产品，不论是否已有化学定义；

(四)上述(一)、(二)、(三)款产品的水溶液；

(五)溶于其他溶剂的上述(一)、(二)、(三)款的产品，但该产品处于溶液状态只是为了安全或运输所采取的正常必要方法，其所用溶剂并不使该产品改变其一般用途而适合于某些特殊用途；

(六)为了保存或运输的需要，加入稳定剂(包括抗结块剂)的上述(一)、(二)、(三)、(四)、(五)各款产品；

(七)为了便于识别或安全起见，加入抗尘剂、着色剂或气味剂的上述(一)、(二)、(三)、(四)、(五)、(六)各款产品，但所加剂料并不使原产品改变其一般用途而适合于某些特殊用途；

(八)为生产偶氮染料而稀释至标准浓度的下列产品：重氮盐，用于重氮盐、可重氮化的胺及其盐类的耦合剂。

二、本章不包括：

(一)税目15.04的货品及税目15.20的粗甘油；

(二)乙醇(税目22.07或22.08)；

(三)甲烷及丙烷(税目27.11)；

(四)第二十八章注释二所述的碳化合物；

(五)税目30.02的免疫制品。

(六)尿素(税目31.02或31.05)；

(七)植物性或动物性着色料(税目32.03)、合成有机着色料、用作荧光增白剂或发光体的合成有机产品(税目32.04)及零售包装的染料或其他着色料(税目32.12)；

(八)酶(税目35.07)；

(九)聚乙醛、六亚甲基四胺(乌洛托品)及类似物质，制成片、条或类似形状作为燃料用的，以及包装容器的容积不超过300立方厘米的直接灌注香烟打火机及类似打火器用的液体燃料或液化气体燃料(税目36.06)；

(十)灭火器的装配药及已装药的灭火弹(税目38.13)；零售包装的除墨剂(税目38.24)；或

(十一)光学元件，例如用酒石酸乙二胺制成的(税目90.01)。

三、可以归入本章两个或两个以上税目的货品，应归入有关税目中的最后一个税目。

四、税目29.04至29.06、29.08至29.11及29.13至29.20的卤化、磺化、硝化或亚硝化衍生物均包括复合衍生物，例如，卤磺化、卤硝化、磺硝化及卤磺硝化衍生物。

硝基及亚硝基不作为税目29.29的含氮基官能团。

税目29.11、29.12、29.14、29.18及29.22所称"含氧基"，仅限于税目29.05至29.20的各种含氧基(其特征为有机含氧基)。

五、(一)本章第一分章至第七分章的酸基有机化合物与这些分章的有机化合物构成的酯，应归入有关税号中的最后一个税号。

(二)乙醇与本章第一分章至第七分章的酸基有机化合物所构成的酯，应按有关酸基化合物归类。

(三)除第六类注释一及第二十八章注释二另有规定的以外：

1. 第一分章至第十分章及税目29.42的有机化合物的无机盐，例如，含酸基、酚基或烯醇基的化合物及有机碱的无机盐，应归入相应的有机化合物的税目；
2. 第一分章至第十分章及税目29.42的有机化合物之间生成的盐，应按生成该盐的碱或酸(包括酚基或烯醇基化合物)归入本章有关税目中的最后一个税目；以及
3. 除第十一分章或税目29.41的产品外，配位化合物应按该化合物所有金属键(金属-碳键除外)"断开"所形成的片段归入第二十九章有关税目中的最后一个税目。

(四)除乙醇外，金属醇化物应按相应的醇归类(税目29.05)。

(五)羧酸酰卤化物应按相应的酸归类。

六、税目29.30及29.31的化合物是指有机化合物，其分子中除含氢、氧或氮原子外，还含有与碳原子直接连接的其他非金属或金属原子(例如，硫、砷或铅)。

税目29.30(有机硫化合物)及税目29.31(其他有机-无机化合物)不包括某些磺化或卤化衍生物(含复合衍生物)。这些衍生物分子中除氢、氧、氮之外，只有具有磺化或卤化衍生物(或复合衍生物)性质的硫原子或卤素原子与碳原子直接连接。

七、税目29.32、29.33及29.34不包括三节环环氧化物、过氧化酮、醛或硫醛的环聚合物、多元羧酸酐、多元醇或酚与多元酸构成的环酯及多元酸酰亚胺。

Chapter 29
Organic chemicals

Notes:

1. Except where the context otherwise requires, the headings of this Chapter apply only to:
   (a) Separate chemically defined organic compounds, whether or not containing impurities;
   (b) Mixtures of two or more isomers of the same organic compound (whether or not containing impurities), except mixtures of acyclic hydrocarbon isomers (other than stereoisomers), whether or not saturated (Chapter 27);
   (c) The products of headings No 29.36 to 29.39 or the sugar ethers, sugar acetals and sugar esters, and their salts, of heading No. 29.40, or the products of heading No. 29.41, whether or not chemically defined;
   (d) The products mentioned in (a), (b) or (c) above dissolved in water;
   (e) The products mentioned in (a), (b) or (c) above dissolved in other slovents provided that the solution constitutes a normal and necessary method of putting up these products adopted solely for reasons of safety or for transport and that the solvent does not render the product particularly suitable for specific use rather than for general use;
   (f) The products mentioned in (a), (b), (c), (d) or (e) above with an added stabilizer (including an anti-caking agent) necessary for their preservation or transport;
   (g) The products mentioned in (a), (b), (c), (d), (e) or (f) above with an added anti-dusting agent or a colouring or odoriferous substance added to facilitate their identification or for safety reasons, provided that the additions do not render the product particularly suitable for specific use rather than for general use;
   (h) The following products, diluted to standard strengths, for the production of azo dyes: diazonium salts, couplers used for these salts and diazotisable amines and their salts.
2. This Chapter does not cover:
   (a) Goods of heading No. 15.04 or crude glycerol of heading No. 15.20;
   (b) Ethyl alcohol (heading No. 22.07 or 22.08);
   (c) Methane or propane (headng No. 27.11);
   (d) The compounds of carbon mentioned in Note 2 to Chapter 28;
   (e) Immunological products of heading No. 30.02
   (f) Urea (heading No. 31.02 or 31.05);
   (g) Colouring matter of vegetable or animal origin (heading No. 32.03), synthetic organic colouring matter, synthetic organic products of a kind used as fluorescent brightening agents or as luminophores (heading No. 32.04) or dyes or other colouring matter put up in forms or packings for retail sale (heading No. 32.12);
   (h) Enzymes (heading No. 35.07);
   (i) Metaldehyde, hexamethylenetetramine or similar substances, put up in forms (for example, tablets, sticks or similar forms) for use as fuels, or liquid or liquefied-gas fuels in containers of a kind used for filling or refilling cigarette or similar lighters and of a capacity not exceeding 300 cm^3 (heading No. 36.06);
   (j) Products put up as charges for fire-extinguishers or put up in fire-extinguishing grenades, of heading No. 38.13; ink removers put up in packings for retail sale, of heading No. 38.24; or
   (k) Optical elements, for example, of ethylenediamine tartrate (heading No. 90.01)
3. Goods which could be included in two or more of the headings of this Chapter are to be classified in that one of those headings which occurs last in numerical order.
4. In headings No. 29.04 to 29.06, 29.08 to 29.11 and 29.13 to 29.20, any reference to halogenated, sulphonated, nitrated or nitrosated derivatives includes a reference to compound derivatives, such as sulphohalogenated, nitrohalogenated, nitrosulphonated or nitrosulphohalogenated derivatives.
   Nitro or nitroso groups are not to be taken a "nitrogen-functions" for the purpose of heading No. 29.29.
   For the purposes of headings No. 29.11, 29.12, 29.14, 29.18 and 29.22, "oxygen-function" is to be restricted to the functions (the characteristic organic oxygen-containing groups) referred to in headings No. 29.05 to 29.20.
5. (a) The esters of acid-function organic compounds of sub-Chapters Ⅰ to Ⅶ with organic compounds of these sub-Chapters are to be classified with that compound which is classified in the heading which occurs last in numerical order in these sub-Chapters.
   (b) Esters of ethyl alcohol with acid-function organic compounds of sub-Chapters Ⅰ to Ⅶ are to be classified in the same heading as the corresponding acid-function compounds.
   (c) Subject to Note 1 to Section Ⅵ and Note 2 to Chapter 28:
      (i) Inorganic salts of organic compounds such as acid, phenol or enol-function compounds or organic bases, of sub-Chapters Ⅰ to Ⅹ or heading No. 29.42, are to be classified in the heading appropriate to the organic compound;
      (ii) Salts formed between organic compounds of sub-Chapters Ⅰ to Ⅹ or heading No. 29.42 are to be classified in the heading appropriate to the base or to the acid (including phenol or enol-function compounds) from which they are formed, whichever occurs last in numerical order in the Chapter;
      (iii) Co-ordination compounds, other than products classifiable in sub-Chapter Ⅺ or heading 29.41, are to be classified in the heading which occurs last in numberical order in chapter 29. among those appropriate to the fragments formed by "cleaving" of all metal bonds, other than metal carbon bonds.
   (d) Metal alcoholates are to be classified in the same heading as the corresponding alcohols except in the case of ethanol (heading No. 29.05).
   (e) Halides of carboxylic acids are to be classified in the same heading as the corresponding acids.
6. The compounds of headings No. 29.30 and 29.31 are organic compounds the molecules of which contain, in addition to atoms of hydrogen, oxygen or nitrogen, atoms of other non-metals or of metals (such ass ulphur, arsenic or lead) directly linked to carbon atoms. Heading No. 29.30 (organo-sulphur compounds) and heading No. 29.31 (other organo-inorganic compounds) do not include sulphonated or halogenated derivatives (including compound derivatives) which, apart from hydrogen, oxygen and nitrogen, only have directly linked to carbon the atoms of sulphur or of a halogen which give them their nature of sulphonated or halogenated derivatives (or compound derivatives).
7. Headings No. 29.32, 29.33 and 29.34 do not include epoxides with a three-membered ring, ketone peroxides, cyclic polymers of aldehydes or of thioaldehydes, anhydrides of polybasic carboxylic acids, cyclic esters of polyhydric alcohols or phenols with polybasic acids, or imides of polybasic acids.

本条规定只适用于由本条所列环化功能形成环内杂原子的化合物。

八、税目 29.37 所称：

（一）“激素”包括激素释放因子、激素刺激和释放因子、激素抑制剂以及激素抗体；

（二）“主要起激素作用的”，不仅适用于激素衍生物以及主要起激素作用的结构类似物，也适用于在本税目所列产品合成过程中主要用作中间体的激素衍生物及结构类似物。

子目注释：

一、属于本章任一税目项下的一种（组）化合物的衍生物，如果该税目其他子目未明确将其包括在内，而且有关的子目中又无列名为“其他”的子目，则应与该种（组）化合物归入同一子目。

二、第二十九章注释三不适用于本章的子目。

税则号列	货品名称〔CIQ 扩展编码及品名—T2 表示见附表 2〕	最惠(%)	暂定税率	普通	增值/消费	出口退税	计量单位	监管条件	检验检疫	特殊证件对美关税
	第一分章　烃类及其卤化、磺化、硝化或亚硝化衍生物									
29.01	无环烃：									
2901.1000	-饱和〔301 易燃气体，302 易燃液体，303 其他化工产品〕	2		30	13/	10	千克			1/7
	-不饱和：									
2901.2100	--乙烯〔999〕	2	1	20	13/	10	千克	AB	MN	1/26
2901.2200	--丙烯〔999〕	2	1	20	13/	10	千克	AB	MN	1/26
	--丁烯及其异构体：									
2901.2310	---1-丁烯〔999〕	2		20	13/	10	千克	AB	MN	1/
2901.2320	---2-丁烯〔301〕	2		20	13/	10	千克	AB	MN	1/7
2901.2330	---2-甲基丙烯〔999〕	2		20	13/	10	千克			1/27
	--1,3-丁二烯及异戊二烯：									
2901.2410	---1.3-丁二烯〔301〕	2		20	13/	13	千克	AB	MN	1/27
2901.2420	---异戊二烯〔999〕	2		20	13/	10	千克			1/27
	--其他：									
2901.2910	---异戊烯〔301〕	2		30	13/	10	千克	AB	MN	1/
2901.2920	---乙炔〔999〕	2		45	13/	10	千克	AB	MN	1/27
2901.2990	---其他									
2901.2990 10	诱虫烯〔999〕	2		30	13/	9,10	千克	S		1/7
2901.2990 90	其他不饱和无环烃〔301 易燃气体，302 易燃液体，303 其他化工产品〕	2		30	13/	10	千克			1/7
29.02	环烃：									
	-环烷烃、环烯及环萜烯：									
2902.1100	--环已烷〔301〕	2		30	13/	10	千克	AB	MN	1/27
	--其他：									
2902.1910	---蒎烯〔101：α-蒎烯，102：β-蒎烯〕	2		30	13/	10	千克			1/7
2902.1920	---4-烷基-4'-烷基双环已烷〔999〕	2		30	13/	10	千克			1/
2902.1990	---其他									
2902.1990 11	1-甲基环丙烯〔999〕	2		30	13/	9,10	千克	S		1/27
2902.1990 12	d-柠檬烯〔999〕	2		30	13/	9,10	千克			1/27
2902.1990 90	其他环烷烃、环烯及环萜稀〔301 易燃液体，302 易燃固体，303 其他化工产品〕	2		30	13/	10	千克			1/27
2902.2000	-苯〔102〕	2	2	20	13/	0	千克	AB	MN	1/27
2902.3000	-甲苯〔999〕	2		30	13/	13	千克	23AB	MN	1/27
	-二甲苯：									
2902.4100	--邻二甲苯〔999〕	2		20	13/	10	千克			1/27
2902.4200	--间二甲苯〔999〕	2		20	13/	10	千克			1/27
2902.4300	--对二甲苯〔301〕	2		20	13/	13	千克			1/27
2902.4400	--混合二甲苯异构体〔999〕	2		20	13/	13	千克			1/27
2902.5000	-苯乙烯〔301〕	2		30	13/	10	千克	AB	MN	1/27
2902.6000	-乙苯〔999〕	2		30	13/	10	千克	AB	MN	1/27
2902.7000	-异丙基苯〔301〕	2		30	13/	10	千克	AB	MN	1/27
	-其他：									
2902.9010	---四氢萘〔999〕	2		11	13/	10	千克			1/12
2902.9020	---精萘〔999〕	2		35	13/	10	千克	AB	MN	1/22
2902.9030	---十二烷基苯〔999〕	2		30	13/	10	千克			1/
2902.9040	---4-(4'-烷基环已基)环已基乙烯〔999〕	2		30	13/	13	千克			1/
2902.9050	---1-烷基-4-(4-烷烯基-1,1'-双环已基)苯〔999〕	2		30	13/	9,13	千克			1/
2902.9090	---其他〔101 易燃液体，102 易燃固体，105 其他化工产品〕	2		30	13/	9,10	千克			1/22
29.03	**烃的卤化衍生物：**									
	-无环烃的饱和氯化衍生物：									
2903.1100	---一氯甲烷及氯乙烷〔999〕	5.5		30	13/	10	千克			1/10.5

These provisions apply only when the ring-position hetero-atoms are those resulting solely form the cyclising function or functions here listed.

8. For the purposes of heading No. 29.37:
   (a) the term "hormones" includes hormone-releasing or hormone-stimulating factors, hormone inhibitors and hormone antagonists (anti-hormones);
   (b) the expression "used primarily as hormones" applies not only to hormone derivatives and structural analogues used primarily for their hormonal effect, but also to those derivatives and structural analogues used primarily as intermediates in the synthesis of products of this heading.

Subheading Notes:

1. Within any one heading of this Chapter, derivatives of a chemical compound (or group of chemical compounds) are to be classified in the same subheading as that compound (or group of compounds) provided that they are not more specifically covered by any other subheading and that there is no residual subheading named "other" in the series of subheadings concerned.
2. Note 3 of Chapter 29 does not apply to the subheading of this Chapter.

协定税率 %										特惠税率 %			Article Description
亚太5国	东/冰/格	巴基斯坦	韩国	瑞士	哥达	秘鲁	澳大利亚	新西/坡/智	港/澳/台	亚太2国	老/柬/缅	36/3/1	
													Ⅰ. HYDROCARBONS AND THEIR HALOGENATED, SULPHONATED, NITRATED OR NITROSATED DERIVATIVES
													Acyclic hydrocarbons:
	0/0/0	0	0	0	0	0	0	0//0	0/0/			0/0/	-Saturated
													-Unsaturated:
	0/0/0	0	0.8	0	0	0	0	0/0/0	0/0/			0/0/	--Ethylene
	0/0/0	0	0.8	0	0	0	0	0//0	0/0/0			0/0/	--Propene (propylene)
													--Butene (butylene) and isomers thereof:
	0/0/0	0	0.8	0	0	0	0	0//0	0/0/			0/0/	---1-butene
1.6	0/0/0	0	0	0	0	0	0	0//0	0/0/			0/0/	---2-butene
	0/0/0	0	0	0	0	0	0	0//0	0/0/			0/0/	---2-methyl-propene
													--Buta-1, 3-diene and isoprene:
	0/0/0	0	0.8	0	0	0	0	0//0	0/0/0			0/0/	---Buta-1,3-diene
	0/0/0	0	1.2	0	0	0	0	0//0	0/0/0			0/0/	---Isoprene
													--Other:
1.6	0/0/0	0	0	0	0	0	0	0//0	0/0/			0/0/	---Isopentene
1.6	0/0/0	0	0	0	0	0	0	0//0	0/0/			0/0/	---Acetylene
													---Other
	0/0/0	0	0.8	0	0	0	0	0//0	0/0/			0/0/	Muscalure
	0/0/0	0	0.8	0	0	0	0	0//0	0/0/			0/0/	Other unsaturated acyclic hydrocarbon
													Cyclic hydrocarbons:
													-Cyclanes, cyclenes and cycloterpenes:
	0/0/0	0	0	0	0	0	0	0//0	0/0/			0/0/	--Cyclohexane
													--Other:
	0/0/0	0	0	0	0	0	0	0//0	0/0/			0/0/	---Pinene
	0/0/0	0	0	0	0	0	0	0//0	0/0/			0/0/	---4-alkyl-4'-alkyl-bicyclohexane
													---Other
	0/0/0	0	0	0	0	0	0	0//0	0/0/			0/0/	1-methyl cyclopropene
	0/0/0	0	0	0	0	0	0	0//0	0/0/			0/0/	D-limonene
	0/0/0	0	0	0	0	0	0	0//0	0/0/			0/0/	Other cyclanes, cyclenes and cycloterpenes
	0/0/0	0	1.2	0	0	0	0	0//0	0/0/			0/0/	-Benzene
	0/0/0	0	1.2	0	0	0	0	0/0/0	0/0/			0/0/	-Toluene
													-Xylenes:
	0/0/0.8	0	0.8	0	0	0	0	0//0	0/0/0			0/0/	--*o*-Xylene
	0/0/0.8	0	0	0	0	0	0	0//0	0/0/0			0/0/	--*m*-Xylene
	0/0/	0		0.6	0	0	0	0/0/0	0/0/0			0/0/	--*p*-Xylene
	0/0/0.8	0	0	0	0	0	0	0//0	0/0/0			0/0/	--Mixed xylene isomers
1.3	/0/0	0	1.4	0.6	0	0	0	0//0	0/0/				-Styrene
	0/0/0	0	0.8	0	0	0	0	0//0	0/0/			0/0/	-Ethylbenzene
	0/0/0	0	0	0	0	0	0	0/0/0	0/0/			0/0/	-Cumene
													-Other:
	0/0/0	0	0	0	0	0	0	0//0	0/0/			0/0/	---Tetrahydronaphthalene (tetralin)
1.6	0/0/0	0	1.2	0	0	0	0	0//0	0/0/			0/0/	---Naphthalene
	0/0/0	0		0	0	0	0	0//0	0/0/0			0/0/	---Dodecylbenzene
	0/0/0	0	0	0	0	0	0	0//0	0/0/			0/0/	---4-(4'-alkyl cyclohexyl) cyclohexyl ethylene
	0/0/0	0	0	0	0	0	0	0//0	0/0/			0/0/	---1-Alkyl-4- (4-alkeny-1,1'-dicyclohexyl) benzene
	0/0/0	0	0	0	0	0	0	0//0	0/0/			0/0/	---Other
													Halogenated derivatives of hydrocarbons:
													-Saturated chlorinated derivatives of acyclic hydrocarbons:
	0/0/0	0	0	0	0	0	0	0//0	0/0/			0/0/	--Chloromethane (methyl chloride) and chloroethane (ethyl chloride)

税则号列	货品名称〔CIQ扩展编码及品名—T2表示见附表2〕	最惠(%)	暂定税率	普通	增值/消费	出口退税	计量单位	监管条件	检验检疫	特殊证件对美关税
2903.1200	--二氯甲烷									
2903.1200 01	纯度在99%及以上的二氯甲烷〔999〕	8		30	13/	10	千克			1/18
2903.1200 90	其他二氯甲烷〔999〕	8		30	13/	10	千克			1/18
2903.1300	--氯仿(三氯甲烷)〔999〕	10		30	13/	10	千克	23AB	MN	1/
2903.1400	--四氯化碳									
2903.1400 10	非用于清洗剂的四氯化碳〔999〕	8		30	13/	10	千克	49Bxy	N	1/
2903.1400 90	用于清洗剂的四氯化碳〔999〕	8		30	13/	10	千克	89		1/
2903.1500	--1,2-二氯乙烷(ISO)〔301易燃液体,需申报仅用于工业用途不用于食品添加剂无检疫要求,302属于危险化学品的食品添加剂〕	5.5	1	30	13/	0	千克	AB	MRNS	1/26
	--其他:									
2903.1910	---1,1,1-三氯乙烷(甲基氯仿)									
2903.1910 10	1,1,1-三氯乙烷(甲基氯仿)(用于清洗剂的除外)〔999〕	8		30	13/	10	千克	ABy14x	MN	14/
2903.1910 90	1,1,1-三氯乙烷(甲基氯仿)(用于清洗剂的)〔999〕	8		30	13/	10	千克	18A	M	14/
2903.1990	---其他〔301易燃液体,302毒性物质和感染性物质,303杂项物质,304其他化工产品〕	5.5		30	13/	10	千克			1/30.5
	-无环烃的不饱和氯化衍生物:									
2903.2100	--氯乙烯〔999〕	5.5	1	30	13/	10	千克	AB	MN	1/
2903.2200	--三氯乙烯〔999〕	8		30	13/	10	千克	AB	MN	1/13
2903.2300	--四氯乙烯(全氯乙烯)〔999〕	5.5		30	13/	10	千克	AB	MN	1/30.5
	--其他:									
2903.2910	---3-氯-1-丙烯(氯丙烯)〔999〕	5.5		30	13/	10	千克			1/10.5
2903.2990	---其他									
2903.2990 10	1,1-二氯乙烯〔999〕	5.5		30	13/	10	千克			1/10.5
2903.2990 90	其他无环烃的不饱和氯化衍生物〔301易燃气体,302毒性气体,303易燃液体,304其他化工产品〕	5.5		30	13/	10	千克			1/10.5
	-无环烃的氟化、溴化或碘化衍生物:									
2903.3100	--1,2-二溴乙烷(ISO)〔999〕	5.5		30	13/	0	千克	89		1/
	--其他:									
2903.3910	---1,1,3,3,3-五氟-2-三氟甲基-1-丙烯(全氟异丁烯;八氟异丁烯)〔999〕	5.5		30	13/	10	千克	23		1/
2903.3990	---其他									
2903.3990 10	二溴甲烷〔999〕	5.5		30	13/	10	千克	AB	MN	1/10.5
2903.3990 20	溴甲烷(别名甲基溴)〔102三溴甲烷,103四溴甲烷,301一溴甲烷〕	5.5		30	13/	0	千克	AB14xy	MN	14/10.5
2903.3990 30	碘甲烷〔999〕	5.5		30	13/	13	千克	AB	MN	1/10.5
2903.3990 90	其他无环烃的氟化、溴化或碘化衍生物[T2]	5.5		30	13/	13	千克			1/10.5
	-含有两种或两种以上不同卤素的无环烃卤化衍生物:									
2903.7100	---一氯二氟甲烷〔999〕	5.5		30	13/	13	千克	AB14xy	MN	14/
2903.7200	--二氯三氟乙烷〔999〕	5.5		30	13/	10	千克	14xy		14/
2903.7300	--二氯一氟乙烷〔999〕	5.5		30	13/	10	千克	14xy		14/
2903.7400	---一氯二氟乙烷〔999〕	5.5		30	13/	10	千克	14xy		14/
2903.7500	--二氯五氟丙烷									
2903.7500 10	1,1,1,2,2-五氟-3,3-二氯丙烷〔999〕	5.5		30	13/	10	千克	14xy		14/
2903.7500 20	1,1,2,2,3-五氟-1,3-二氯丙烷〔999〕	5.5		30	13/	10	千克	14xy		14/
2903.7500 90	其他二氯五氟丙烷〔999〕	5.5		30	13/	10	千克	14xy		14/
2903.7600	--溴氯二氟甲烷、溴三氟甲烷及二溴四氟乙烷									
2903.7600 10	溴氯二氟甲烷(Halon-1211)〔999〕	5.5		30	13/	10	千克	14xy		14/
2903.7600 20	溴三氟甲烷(Halon-1301)〔999〕	5.5		30	13/	10	千克	14ABxy	MN	14/
2903.7600 30	二溴四氟乙烷〔999〕	5.5		30	13/	10	千克			1/
	--其他,仅含氟和氯的全卤化物:									
2903.7710	---三氯氟甲烷〔999〕	5.5		30	13/	10	千克	14xy		14/
2903.7720	---其他仅含氟和氯的甲烷、乙烷及丙烷的全卤化物									
2903.7720 11	二氯二氟甲烷(CFC-12)〔101不燃气体,102二氯二氟甲烷和环氧乙烷混合物(含环氧乙烷≤12%)〕	5.5		30	13/	10	千克	14ABxy	MN	14/
2903.7720 12	三氯三氟乙烷,用于清洗剂除外(CFC-113)〔999〕	5.5		30	13/	10	千克	14xy		14/
2903.7720 13	三氯三氟乙烷,用于清洗剂(CFC-113)〔999〕	5.5		30	13/	10	千克	89		1/
2903.7720 14	二氯四氟乙烷(CFC-114)〔999〕	5.5		30	13/	10	千克	14ABxy	MN	14/
2903.7720 15	一氯五氟乙烷(CFC-115)〔999〕	5.5		30	13/	10	千克	14ABxy	MN	14/
2903.7720 16	一氯三氟甲烷(CFC-13)〔999〕	5.5		30	13/	10	千克	14ABxy	MN	14/

协定税率 %										特惠税率 %			
亚太5国	东/冰/格	巴基斯坦	韩国	瑞士	哥达	秘鲁	澳大利亚	新西/坡/智	港/澳/台	亚太2国	老/柬/缅	36/3/1	Article Description
													--Dichloromethane (methylene chloride)
	0/0/0	4	4.8	0	0	0	0	0//0	0/0/			0/0/	Dichloromethane (methylene chloride) (purity≥99%)
	0/0/0	4	4.8	0	0	0	0	0//0	0/0/			0/0/	Other dichloromethane (methylene chloride)
9	0/0/0	4.5	4	0	0	0	0	0//0	0/0/0			0/0/	--Chloroform (trichloromethane)
													--Carbon tetrachloride
	0/0/0	4	0	0	0	0	0	0//0	0/0/			0/0/	Carbon tetrachloride, other than for cleaner preparation
	0/0/0	4	0	0	0	0	0	0//0	0/0/			0/0/	Carbon tetrachloride, for cleaner preparation
	5/0/0		0	0	0		0	0//0	0/0/			0//	--1,2-Dichloroethane (ISO) (ethylene dichloride)
													--Other:
													---1,1,1-Trichloroethane (methylchloro form)
	0/0/0	4	0	0	0	0	0	0//0	0/0/			0/0/	1,1,1-Trichloroethane (methylchloro form) (other than for cleaner preparation)
	0/0/0	4	0	0	0	0	0	0//0	0/0/			0/0/	1,1,1-Trichloroethane (methylchloro form) (for cleaner preparation)
	0/0/0	4	2.2	0	0	0	0	0//0	0/0/			0/0/	---Other
													-Unsaturated chlorinated derivatives of acyclic hydrocarbons:
3.6	0/0/0	0	0	0	0	0	0	0//0	0/0/0			0/0/	--Vinyl chloride (chloroethylene)
	0/0/0	4	4.8	0	0	0	0	0//0	0/0/			0/0/	--Trichloroethylene
4.4	0/0/0	0	0	0	0	0	0	0//0	0/0/			0/0/	--Tetrachloroethylene (perchloroethylene)
													--Other:
	0/0/0	0	0	0	0	0	0	0//0	0/0/			0/0/	---3-Chloro-1-propene (chloropropene)
													---Other
	0/0/0	0	0	0	0	0	0	0//0	0/0/			0/0/	1,1-dichloroethylene
	0/0/0	0	0	0	0	0	0	0//0	0/0/			0/0/	Other unsaturated chlorinated derivatives of acyclic hydrocarbons
													-Fluorinated, brominated or iodinated derivatives of acyclic hydrocarbons:
	0/0/0	4.5	0	0	0	0	0	0//0	0/0/			0/0/	--Ethylene dibromide (ISO)
													--Other:
	0/0/0	0	0	0	0	0	0	0//0	0/0/			0/0/	---1, 1, 3, 3, 3-Pentafluro-2-trifluromethyl-1-propene (Perfluorolisobutylene, isobutylene octafluoride)
													---Other
	0/0/0	4.5	0	0	0	0	0	0//0	0/0/			0/0/	Dibromomethane
	0/0/0	4.5	0	0	0	0	0	0//0	0/0/			0/0/	Methyl bromide
	0/0/0	4.5	0	0	0	0	0	0//0	0/0/			0/0/	Methyl iodide
	0/0/0	4.5	0	0	0	0	0	0//0	0/0/			0/0/	Other fluorinated, brominated or iodinated derivatives of acyclic hydrocarbons
													-Halogenated derivatives of acyclic hydrocarbons containing two or more different halogens:
	0/0/0	4.5	0	0	0	0	0	0//0	0/0/			0/0/	--Chlorodifluoromethane
	0/0/0	4.5	0	0	0	0	0	0//0	0/0/			0/0/	--Dichlorotrifluoroethane
	0/0/0	4.5	0	0	0	0	0	0//0	0/0/			0/0/	--Dichlorofluoroethane
	0/0/0	4.5	0	0	0	0	0	0//0	0/0/			0/0/	--Chlorodifluoroethane
													--Dichloropentafluoropropane
	0/0/0	4.5	0	0	0	0	0	0//0	0/0/			0/0/	1,1,1,2,2-Pentafluoro-3,3-dichloropropane
	0/0/0	4.5	0	0	0	0	0	0//0	0/0/			0/0/	1,1,1,2,2-Pentafluoro-1,3-dichloropropane
	0/0/0	4.5	0	0	0	0	0	0//0	0/0/			0/0/	Other Dichloropentafluoropropane
													--Bromochlorodifluoromethane, bromotrifluoromethane, dibromotetrafluoroethane
	0/0/0	0	0	0	0	0	0	0//0	0/0/			0/0/	Bromochlorodifluoromethane (Halon-1211)
	0/0/0	0	0	0	0	0	0	0//0	0/0/			0/0/	Bromotrifluoromethane (Halon-1301)
	0/0/0	0	0	0	0	0	0	0//0	0/0/			0/0/	Dibromotetrafluoroethane
													--Other, perhalogenated, only with fluorine and chlorine:
	0/0/0	4.5	0	0	0	0	0	0//0	0/0/			0/0/	---Trichlorofluoromethane
													---Other, methane, ethane and propane halogenide, only with fluorine and chlorine
	0/0/0	0	0	0	0	0	0	0//0	0/0/			0/0/	Dichlorodifluoromethane (CFC-12)
	0/0/0	0	0	0	0	0	0	0//0	0/0/			0/0/	Trichlorotrifluoroethanes, other than for cleaner preparation (CFC-113)
	0/0/0	0	0	0	0	0	0	0//0	0/0/			0/0/	Trichlorotrifluoroethanes, for cleaner preparation (CFC-113)
	0/0/0	0	0	0	0	0	0	0//0	0/0/			0/0/	Dichlorotetrafluoroethane (CFC-114)
	0/0/0	0	0	0	0	0	0	0//0	0/0/			0/0/	Chloropentafluoroethane (CFC-115)
	0/0/0	0	0	0	0	0	0	0//0	0/0/			0/0/	Chlorotrifluoromethane (CFC-13)

税则号列		货品名称〔CIQ 扩展编码及品名—T2 表示见附表 2〕	最惠(%)	暂定税率	普通	增值/消费	出口退税	计量单位	监管条件	检验检疫	特殊证件对美关税
2903.7720	90	其他仅含氟和氯的甲烷、乙烷及丙烷的全卤化物〔999 其他化工产品,998 其他危险化学品〕	5.5		30	13/	10	千克			1/
2903.7790		---其他〔999 其他化工产品,998 其他危险化学品〕	5.5		30	13/	13	千克			1/
2903.7800		--其他全卤化衍生物〔999 其他化工产品,998 其他危险化学品〕	5.5		30	13/	10	千克			1/10.5
		--其他:									
2903.7910		---其他仅含氟和氯的甲烷、乙烷及丙烷的全卤化衍生物									
2903.7910	11	一氟二氯甲烷〔999〕	5.5		30	13/	10	千克	14xy		14/
2903.7910	12	1,1,1,2-四氟-2-氯乙烷〔999〕	5.5		30	13/	10	千克	14xy		14/
2903.7910	13	三氟一氯乙烷〔999〕	5.5		30	13/	10	千克	14xy		14/
2903.7910	14	1-氟-1,1-二氯乙烷〔999〕	5.5		30	13/	10	千克	14xy		14/
2903.7910	15	1,1-二氟-1-氯乙烷〔999〕	5.5		30	13/	10	千克	14xy		14/
2903.7910	90	其他仅含氟和氯的甲烷、乙烷及丙烷的卤化衍生物〔999〕	5.5		30	13/	10	千克	14xy		14/
2903.7990		---其他									
2903.7990	10	二溴氯丙烷(1,2-二溴-3-氯丙烷)〔999〕	5.5		30	13/	10	千克	89		1/15.5
2903.7990	21	其他仅含溴、氟的甲烷、乙烷和丙烷〔999,301 非易燃无毒气体〕	5.5		30	13/	10	千克	14xy		14/15.5
2903.7990	90	其他无环烃卤化衍生物(含二种或二种以上不同卤素的其他无环烃卤化衍生物)〔T2〕	5.5		30	13/	10	千克			1/15.5
		-环烷烃、环烯烃或环萜烯烃的卤化衍生物:									
2903.8100		--1,2,3,4,5,6-六氯环已烷〔六六六(ISO)〕,包括林丹(ISO,INN)									
2903.8100	10	林丹(ISO,INN)〔301〕	5.5		30	13/	0	千克	89		1/
2903.8100	20	α-六氯环已烷、β-六氯环已烷〔999〕	5.5		30	13/	0	千克	89		1/
2903.8100	90	其他 1,2,3,4,5,6 六氯环已烷{六六六(ISO)}(混合异构体)〔301〕	5.5		30	13/	0	千克			1/
2903.8200		--艾氏剂(ISO)、氯丹(ISO)及七氯(ISO)									
2903.8200	10	艾氏剂(ISO)及七氯(ISO)〔T2〕	5.5		30	13/	0	千克	89		1/
2903.8200	90	氯丹(ISO)(别名八氯化甲桥茚)〔301〕	5.5		30	13/	0	千克	89		1/
2903.8300		--灭蚁灵(ISO)〔999〕	5.5		30	13/	0	千克	89		1/
2903.8900		--其他									
2903.8900	10	毒杀芬〔301〕	5.5		30	13/	0	千克	89		1/30.5
2903.8900	20	六溴环十二烷〔999〕	5.5		30	13/	13	千克	X		1/30.5
2903.8900	90	其他环烷烃、环烯烃或环萜烯烃的卤化衍生物〔301 非易燃无毒气体,302 易燃液体,303 毒性物质和感染性物质,304 其他化工产品〕	5.5		30	13/	13	千克			1/30.5
		-芳烃卤化衍生物:									
		--氯苯、邻二氯苯及对二氯苯:									
2903.9110		---邻二氯苯〔999〕	5.5		30	13/	10	千克			1/
2903.9190		---其他									
2903.9190	10	1,4-二氯苯(对二氯苯)〔999〕	5.5		30	13/	9,10	千克	S		1/30.5
2903.9190	90	氯苯〔999〕	5.5		30	13/	10	千克	AB	MN	1/30.5
2903.9200		--六氯苯(ISO)及滴滴涕(ISO,INN)〔1,1,1-三氯-2,2-双(4-氯苯基)乙烷〕〔101 滴滴涕(含量＞20%),102 滴滴涕乳剂,103 滴滴混剂,104 其他〕	5.5		30	13/	0	千克	89		1/
2903.9300		--五氯苯(ISO)〔999〕	5.5		30	13/	10	千克	89		1/
2903.9400		--六溴联苯〔999〕	5.5		30	13/	10	千克			1/
		--其他:									
2903.9910		---对氯甲苯〔999〕	5.5		30	13/	10	千克	AB	MN	1/
2903.9920		---3,4-二氯三氟甲苯〔999〕	5.5		30	13/	10	千克			1/
2903.9930		---4-(4'-烷基苯基)-1-(4'-烷基苯基)-2-氟苯〔999〕	5.5		30	13/	13	千克			1/
2903.9990		---其他									
2903.9990	10	多氯联苯,多溴联苯〔101 多氯联苯,102α,α,α-三氯甲(基)苯〕	5.5		30	13/	10	千克	89		1/10.5
2903.9990	30	多氯三联苯(PCT)〔999〕	5.5		30	13/	10	千克	X		1/10.5
2903.9990	40	稗草烯〔999〕	5.5		30	13/	0	千克	S		1/10.5
2903.9990	90	其他芳烃卤化衍生物〔301 易燃液体,302 毒性物质和感染性物质,303 杂项物质,304 其他化工产品〕	5.5		30	13/	10	千克			1/10.5
29.04		**烃的磺化、硝化或亚硝化衍生物,不论是否卤化:**									
2904.1000		-仅含磺基的衍生物及其盐和乙酯〔301 腐蚀性物质,302 其他化工产品〕	5.5		30	13/	10	千克			1/15.5
		-仅含硝基或亚硝基的衍生物:									
2904.2010		---硝基苯〔101:1,3,5—三硝基苯(干的或含水＜30%),102:毒性物质和感染性物质〕	5.5		20	13/	10	千克	AB	MN	1/
2904.2020		---硝基甲苯〔101:2—硝基甲苯,102:3—硝基甲苯,103:4—硝基甲苯〕	5.5		30	13/	10	千克			1/
2904.2030		---二硝基甲苯〔301〕	5.5		20	13/	10	千克	AB	MN	1/

协定税率 %										特惠税率 %			Article Description
亚太5国	东/冰/格	巴基斯坦	韩国	瑞士	哥达	秘鲁	澳大利亚	新西/坡/智	港/澳/台	亚太2国	老/柬/缅	36/3/1	
	0/0/0	0	0	0	0	0	0	0//0	0/0/			0/0/	Other methane, ethane and propane halogenated derivatives only with fluorine and bromine
	0/0/0	4.5	2.2	0	0	0	0	0//0	0/0/			0/0/	---Other
	0/0/0	0	0	0	0	0	0	0//0	0/0/			0/0/	--Other perhalogenated derivatives
													--Other:
													---Other methane, ethane and propane halogenated derivatives only with fluorine and chlorine
	0/0/0	4.5	0	0	0	0	0	0//0	0/0/			0/0/	Dichlorofluoromethane
	0/0/0	4.5	0	0	0	0	0	0//0	0/0/			0/0/	1,1,1,2-Tetrafluoro-2,2-dichloroethane
	0/0/0	4.5	0	0	0	0	0	0//0	0/0/			0/0/	Trifluoromonochloroethane
	0/0/0	4.5	0	0	0	0	0	0//0	0/0/			0/0/	1,1-dichloro-1-fluoroethane
	0/0/0	4.5	0	0	0	0	0	0//0	0/0/			0/0/	1,1-Difluoro--1-chloroethane
	0/0/0	4.5	0	0	0	0	0	0//0	0/0/			0/0/	Other methane, ethane and propane halogenated derivatives with fluorine and chlorine
													---Other
	0/0/0	0	0	0	0	0	0	0//0	0/0/			0/0/	Dibromochloropropane(1,2-dibromo-3chloropropane)
	0/0/0	0	0	0	0	0	0	0//0	0/0/			0/0/	Other methane, ethane and propane only with fluorine and bromine
	0/0/0	0	0	0	0	0	0	0//0	0/0/			0/0/	Other Halogenated derivatives of acyclic hydro- carbons containing two or more different halogens
													-Halogenated derivatives of cyclanic, cyclenic or cycloterpenic hydrocarbons:
													--1,2,3,4,5,6-Hexachlorocyclohexane clohexane[HCH(ISO)], including lindane(ISO, INN)
	0/0/0	0	0	0	0	0	0	0//0	0/0/			0/0/	Lindan(ISO,INN)
	0/0/0	0	0	0	0	0	0	0//0	0/0/			0/0/	α-hexachlorocyclohexane, β-hexachlorocyclohexane
	0/0/0	0	0	0	0	0	0	0//0	0/0/			0/0/	1,2,3,4,5,6-hexachlorocyclohexane
													--Aldrin(ISO) chlordane(ISO) and heptachlor(ISO)
	0/0/0	0	0	0	0	0	0	0//0	0/0/			0/0/	Aldrin(ISO), haptachlor(ISO)
	0/0/0	0	0	0	0	0	0	0//0	0/0/			0/0/	Chlordane(ISO)
	0/0/0	0	0	0	0	0	0	0//0	0/0/			0/0/	--Mirex(ISO)
													--Other
	0/0/0	0	0	0	0	0	0	0//0	0/0/			0/0/	Camphechlor
	0/0/0	0	0	0	0	0	0	0//0	0/0/			0/0/	Hexabromocyclododecane
	0/0/0	0	0	0	0	0	0	0//0	0/0/			0/0/	Other halogenatives of acycanlic, cyclenic or cycloterpenic hydrocarbons
													-Halogenated derivatives of aromatic hydrocarbons:
													--Chlorobenzene, o-dichlorobenzene and p-dichlorobenzene:
	0/0/0	0	2.2	0	0	0	0	0//0	0/0/			0/0/	---o-Dichlorobenzene
													---Other
	0/0/0	0	0	0	0	0	0	0//0	0/0/			0/0/	1,4-dichlorobenzene
	0/0/0	0	0	0	0	0	0	0//0	0/0/			0/0/	Cldorobenzene
	0/0/0	0	0	0	0	0	0	0//0	0/0/			0/0/	--Hexachlorobenzene(ISO) and DDT(ISO) clofenotane(INN)[1,1,1-trichloro-2,2-bis(p-chlorophenyl)ethane]
	0/0/0	0	0	0	0	0	0	0//0	0/0/			0/0/	--Pentachlcrobenzene
	0/0/0	0	0	0	0	0	0	0//0	0/0/			0/0/	--Hexabromobiphenyls
													--Other:
	0/0/0	0	0	0	0	0	0	0//0	0/0/			0/0/	---p-Chlorotoluene
4.4	0/0/0	0	0	0	0	0	0	0//0	0/0/			0/0/	---3,4-Dichlorotrifluoride toluene
	0/0/0	0	0	0	0	0	0	0//0	0/0/			0/0/	---4-(4'-alkyl phenyl)-1-(4'-alkyl phenyl)-2-fluorobenzene
													---Other
	0/0/0	0	0	0	0	0	0	0//0	0/0/			0/0/	Polychlorinated biphenyls, polybromobiphenyl
	0/0/0	0	0	0	0	0	0	0//0	0/0/			0/0/	Polychlorinated terphenyl(pct)
	0/0/0	0	0	0	0	0	0	0//0	0/0/			0/0/	Tavron
	0/0/0	0	0	0	0	0	0	0//0	0/0/			0/0/	Other halogen derivatives of aromatic hydrocarbons
													Sulphonated, nitrated or nitrosated derivatives of hydrocarbons, whether or not halogenated:
	0/0/0	0	0	0	0	0	0	0//0	0/0/			0/0/	-Derivatives containing only sulpho groups, their salts and ethyl esters
													-Derivatives containing only nitro or only nitroso groups:
4.4	0/0/0	0	0	0	0	0	0	0//0	0/0/			0/0/	---Nitrobenzene
	0/0/0	0	0	0	0	0	0	0//0	0/0/			0/0/	---Nitrotoluene and nitrochlorobenzene
4.4	0/0/0	0	0	0	0	0	0	0//0	0/0/			0/0/	---Dinitrotoluene and dinitrochlorobenzene

税则号列	货品名称〔CIQ 扩展编码及品名－T2 表示见附表 2〕	最惠(%)	暂定税率	普通	增值/消费	出口退税	计量单位	监管条件	检验检疫	特殊证件对美关税
2904.2040	---三硝基甲苯(TNT)〔101(2,4,6－三硝基甲苯(干的或含水<30%)),102(2,4,6－三硝基二甲苯),103(2,4,6－三硝基甲苯(含水≥30%))〕	5.5		40	13/	10	千克	ABk	MN	1/
2904.2090	---其他									
2904.2090 10	六硝基芪〔999〕	5.5		30	13/	10	千克	3		1/10.5
2904.2090 20	4-硝基联苯〔999〕	5.5		30	13/	10	千克			1/10.5
2904.2090 90	其他仅含硝基或亚硝基衍生物〔301 爆炸品,302 易燃液体,303 易燃固体,304 毒性物质和感染性物质,305 杂项物质,306 其他化工产品〕	5.5		30	13/	10	千克			1/10.5
	-全氟辛基磺酸及其盐和全氟辛基磺酰氟:									
2904.3100	--全氟辛基磺酸〔999〕	5.5		30	13/	10	千克	X		1/
2904.3200	--全氟辛基磺酸铵〔999〕	5.5		30	13/	10	千克	X		1/
2904.3300	--全氟辛基磺酸锂〔999〕	5.5		30	13/	10	千克	X		1/
2904.3400	--全氟辛基磺酸钾〔999〕	5.5		30	13/	10	千克	X		1/
2904.3500	--其他全氟辛基磺酸盐〔999,301 其他危险化学品,302 其他化工产品,303 杂项物质〕	5.5		30	13/	10	千克	X		1/
2904.3600	--全氟辛基磺酰氟〔999〕	5.5		30	13/	10	千克	X		1/
	-其他:									
2904.9100	--三氯硝基甲烷(氯化苦)〔999〕	5.5		30	13/	0	千克	23S		1/
2904.9900	--其他									
2904.9900 11	氯硝丙烷〔999〕	5.5		30	13/	0	千克	S		1/25.5
2904.9900 12	四氯硝基苯〔999〕	5.5		30	13/	0	千克	S		1/25.5
2904.9900 13	五氯硝基苯〔999〕	5.5		30	13/	0	千克	S		1/25.5
2904.9900 90	其他烃的磺化、硝化、亚硝化衍生物(不论是否卤化)〔999 不论是否卤化,301 爆炸品,302 毒性物质和感染性物质,303 腐蚀性物质,304 杂项物质,305 其他化工产品〕	5.5		30	13/	10	千克			1/25.5
	第二分章　醇类及其卤化、磺化、硝化或亚硝化衍生物									
29.05	**无环醇及其卤化、磺化、硝化或亚硝化衍生物:**									
	-饱和一元醇:									
2905.1100	--甲醇〔301〕	5.5		30	13/	13	千克	AB	MN	1/30.5
	--丙醇及异丙醇:									
2905.1210	---正丙醇〔301〕	5.5	3	30	13/	10	千克	AB	MN	1/8
2905.1220	---异丙醇〔301〕	5.5		30	13/	10	千克	ABG	MN	1/30.5
2905.1300	--正丁醇〔301 易燃液体,需申报仅用于工业用途不用于食品添加剂无检疫要求,302 属于危险化学品的食品添加剂〕	5.5		30	13/	13	千克	AB	MRNS	1/15.5
	--其他丁醇:									
2905.1410	---异丁醇〔999〕	5.5		30	13/	10	千克			1/15.5
2905.1420	---仲丁醇〔999〕	5.5		30	13/	10	千克			1/
2905.1430	---叔丁醇〔999〕	5.5		30	13/	10	千克			1/25.5
	--辛醇及其异构体:									
2905.1610	---正辛醇〔101:2－辛醇,102:非工业用无检疫要求食品添加剂〕	5.5		30	13/	13	千克			1/30.5
2905.1690	---其他〔999〕	5.5		30	13/	10	千克			1/30.5
2905.1700	--十二醇、十六醇及十八醇〔999〕	7		30	13/	10	千克			1/32
	--其他:									
2905.1910	---3,3-二甲基丁-2-醇(频哪基醇)〔999〕	5.5		30	13/	10	千克	23		1/
2905.1990	---其他									
2905.1990 10	三十烷醇〔999〕	5.5		30	13/	9,13	千克	S		1/25.5
2905.1990 90	其他饱和一元醇〔301 易燃液体,302 毒性物质和感染性物质,303 其他化工产品〕	5.5		30	13/	13	千克			1/25.5
	-不饱和一元醇:									
	--无环萜烯醇:									
2905.2210	---香叶醇、橙花醇(3,7-二甲基-2,6-辛二烯-1-醇)〔101 反式－3－己烯醇,102 香叶醇,103 橙花醇〕	5.5		30	13/	13	千克			1/10.5
2905.2220	---香茅醇(3,7-二甲基-6 辛烯-1-醇)〔999〕	5.5		30	13/	13	千克			1/10.5
2905.2230	---芳樟醇〔102 无检疫要求食品添加剂,301 需申报仅用于工业用途不用于食品添加剂无检疫要求的化学品〕	5.5		30	13/	13	千克	A	R	1/10.5
2905.2290	---其他〔301 易燃液体,302 毒性物质和感染性物质,303 腐蚀性物质,304 其他化工产品〕	5.5		30	13/	10	千克			1/30.5
2905.2900	--其他[T2]	5.5		30	13/	13	千克			1/30.5
	-二元醇:									
2905.3100	--1,2-乙二醇〔999〕	5.5		30	13/	10	千克			1/30.5
2905.3200	--1,2-丙二醇〔101 饲料添加剂〕	5.5	3	30	13/	10	千克			1/13

协定税率 %										特惠税率 %			Article Description
亚太5国	东/冰/格	巴基斯坦	韩国	瑞士	哥达	秘鲁	澳大利亚	新西/坡/智	港/澳/台	亚太2国	老/柬/缅	36/3/1	
4.4	0/0/0	0	0	0	0	0	0	0//0	0/0/			0/0/	---Trinitrotoluene(TNT)
													---Other
	0/0/0	0	0	0	0	0	0	0//0	0/0/			0/0/	Hexanitrostilbene
	0/0/0	0	0	0	0	0	0	0//0	0/0/			0/0/	4-Nitrobiphenyl
	0/0/0	0	0	0	0	0	0	0//0	0/0/			0/0/	Other derivatives containing only nitro or only nitroso groups
													-Perfluorooctane sulphonic acid, its salts and perfluorooctane sulphonyl fluoride:
	0/0/0	0	0	0	0	0	0	0//0	0/0/			0/0/	--Perfluorooctane sulphonic acid
	0/0/0	0	0	0	0	0	0	0//0	0/0/			0/0/	--Ammonium perfluorooctane sulphonate
	0/0/0	0	0	0	0	0	0	0//0	0/0/			0/0/	--Lithium perfluorooctane sul-phonate
	0/0/0	0	0	0	0	0	0	0//0	0/0/			0/0/	--Potassium perfluorooctane sul-phonate
	0/0/0	0	0	0	0	0	0	0//0	0/0/			0/0/	--Other salts of perfluorooctane sulphonic acid
	0/0/0	0	0	0	0	0	0	0//0	0/0/			0/0/	--Perfluorooctane sulphonyl flu-oride
													-Other:
	0/0/0	0	0	0	0	0	0	0//0	0/0/			0/0/	--Trichloronitromethane (*chloropicrin*)
													--Other
	0/0/0	0	0	0	0	0	0	0//0	0/0/			0/0/	Sodium chloride Propane
	0/0/0	0	0	0	0	0	0	0//0	0/0/			0/0/	Tecnazene
	0/0/0	0	0	0	0	0	0	0//0	0/0/			0/0/	Quintozene
	0/0/0	0	0	0	0	0	0	0//0	0/0/			0/0/	Other sulphonated, nitrated, nitrosalted derivatives of hydrocarbons, whether or not halogenated
													Ⅱ. ALCOHOLS AND THEIR HALO-GENATED, SULPHONATED, NITRATED OR NITROSATED DERIVATIVES
													Acyclic alcohols and their halogenated, sulphonated, nitrated or nitrosated derivatives:
													-Saturated monohydric alcohols:
	0/0/0	0		0	0		0	0//0	0/0/				--Methanol (methyl alcohol)
													--Propan-1-ol (propyl alcohol) and propan-2-ol (isopropyl alcohol):
	0/0/0	0	3.3	0	0	0	0	0//0	0/0/			0/0/	---Propan-1-ol (propyl alcohol)
	0/0/0	0	3.3	0	0	0	0	0//0	0/0/0			0/0/	---Propan-2-ol (isopropyl alcohol)
	0/0/0	0	3.3	0	0	0	0	0//0	0/0/0			0/0/	--Butan-1-ol (*n*-butyl alcohol)
													--Other butanols:
	0/0/0	0	3.3	0	0	0	0	0//0	0/0/0			0/0/	---iso-Butyl alcohol
	0/0/0	0	3.3	0	0	0	0	0//0	0/0/			0/0/	---sec-Butyl alcohol
	0/0/0	0	3.3	0	0	0	0	0//0	0/0/			0/0/	---tert-Butgl alcohol
													--Octanol (octyl alcohol) and isomors thereof:
	0/0/0	0		0	0		0	0//0	0/0/				---n-Octanol
	0/0/0	0		0	0		0	0//0	0/0/				---Other
	0/0/0	4	4.2	0	0	0	0	0//0	0/0/			0/0/	--Dodecan-1-ol (lauryl alcohol), hexadecan-1-ol (cetyl alcohol) and octadecan-1-ol (stearyl alcohol)
													--Other:
4.4	0/0/0	0	0	0	0	0	0	0//0	0/0/			0/0/	---3,3-Dimethyl-2-butanol (pinacolyl alcohol)
													---Other
	0/0/0	0	0	1.7	0	0	0	0//0	0/0/			0/0/	Triacontanol
	0/0/0	0	0	1.7	0	0	0	0//0	0/0/			0/0/	Other saturated monohydric alcohols
													-Unsaturated monohydric alcohols:
													--Acyclic terpene alcohols:
	0/0/0	0	0	0	0	0	0	0//0	0/0/			0/0/	---Geraniol, nerol (cis-3,7-Dimethyl-2,6-octadien-1-ol)
	0/0/0	0	0	0	0	0	0	0//0	0/0/			0/0/	---Citronellol (3,7-Dimethyl-6-octen-1-ol)
	0/0/0	0	0		0	0	0	0//0	0/0/			0/0/	---Linalool
	0/0/0	0	0	2.9	0	0	0	0//0	0/0/			0/0/	---Other
	0/0/0	0	0	0	0	0	0	0//0	0/0/			0/0/	--Other
													-Diols:
	5/0/			0			0	0//0	0/0/				--Ethylene glycol (ethanediol)
	0/0/0	0	2.2	0	0	0	0	0//0	0/0/			0/0/	--Propylene glycol (propane-1,2-diol)

税则号列	货品名称〔CIQ 扩展编码及品名—T2 表示见附表 2〕	最惠(%)	暂定税率	普通	增值/消费	出口退税	计量单位	监管条件	检验检疫	特殊证件对美关税
	--其他:									
2905.3910	---2,5-二甲基己二醇〔999〕	4		11	13/	10	千克			1/24
2905.3990	---其他									
2905.3990 01	1,3-丙二醇〔101 饲料添加剂,102 化工产品〕	5.5	3	30	13/	10	千克	AB	RS	1/13
2905.3990 02	1,4-丁二醇〔999〕	5.5		30	13/	10	千克	AB	RS	1/15.5
2905.3990 10	驱蚊醇〔999〕	5.5		30	13/	9,10	千克	S		1/15.5
2905.3990 91	白消安〔301 无检疫要求食品添加剂,302 需申报仅用于工业用途不用于食品添加剂无检疫要求的化学品〕	5.5	0	30	3/	10	千克	AB	MRNS	1/10
2905.3990 99	其他二元醇(因拆分抗癌药品原料药产生的兜底税号)〔301 无检疫要求食品添加剂,302 需申报仅用于工业用途不用于食品添加剂无检疫要求的化学品,303 属于危险化学品的食品添加剂〕	5.5		30	13/	10	千克	AB	MRNS	1/15.5
	-其他多元醇:									
2905.4100	--2-乙基-2-(羟甲基)丙烷-1,3-二醇(三羟甲基丙烷)〔999〕	5.5		30	13/	10	千克			1/30.5
2905.4200	--季戊四醇〔999〕	5.5		30	13/	13	千克			1/30.5
2905.4300	--甘露糖醇〔101 饲料添加剂,102 无检疫要求食品添加剂,103 需申报仅用于工业用途不用于食品添加剂无检疫要求的化学品〕	8		30	13/	13	千克	A	R	1/33
2905.4400	--山梨醇〔101 饲料添加剂,102 非工业用无检疫要求食品添加剂〕	8		40	13/	13	千克			1/18
2905.4500	--丙三醇(甘油)〔101 饲料添加剂,102 无检疫要求食品添加剂,103 需申报仅用于工业用途不用于食品添加剂无检疫要求的化学品〕	8	3	50	13/	13	千克	A	R	1/28
	--其他:									
2905.4910	---木糖醇〔301 无检疫要求食品添加剂〕	5.5		30	13/	10	千克	A	R	1/10.5
2905.4990	---其他[T2]	5.5		30	13/	10	千克			1/10.5
	-无环醇的卤化、磺化、硝化或亚硝化衍生物:									
2905.5100	--乙氯维诺(INN)〔999〕	5.5		30	13/	10	千克	I		1/
2905.5900	--其他									
2905.5900 10	乙氯维诺的盐〔999〕	5.5		30	13/	10	千克	I		1/25.5
2905.5900 20	2—氯乙醇〔999〕	5.5		30	13/	10	千克	3A	M	1/25.5
2905.5900 40	鼠甘伏〔999〕	5.5		30	13/	9,10	千克	S		1/25.5
2905.5900 90	其他无环醇的卤化、磺化等衍生物〔301 易燃液体,302 遇水放出易燃气体的物质,303 毒性物质和感染性物质,304 腐蚀性物质,305 其他化工产品〕	5.5		30	13/	10	千克			1/25.5
29.06	**环醇及其卤化、磺化、硝化或亚硝化衍生物:**									
	-环烷醇、环烯醇及环萜烯醇:									
2906.1100	--薄荷醇〔301 无检疫要求食品添加剂〕	5		70	13/	13	千克			1/30
2906.1200	--环己醇、甲基环己醇及二甲基环己醇									
2906.1200 10	甲基环己醇〔999〕	5.5		30	13/	10	千克	AB	MN	1/15.5
2906.1200 90	环己醇,二甲基环己醇〔999〕	5.5		30	13/	10	千克			1/15.5
	--固醇及肌醇:									
2906.1310	---固醇〔999〕	5.5	3	30	13/	10	千克			1/8
2906.1320	---肌醇〔101 饲料添加剂,102 无检疫要求食品添加剂,103 需申报仅用于工业用途不用于食品添加剂无检疫要求的化学品〕	5.5		30	13/	10	千克	A	R	1/25.5
	--其他:									
2906.1910	---萜品醇〔101 松油醇,102α-松油醇〕	5.5		30	13/	10	千克			1/15.5
2906.1990	---其他									
2906.1990 11	5α 雄烷 3α, 17α 二醇(阿法雄烷二醇)(包括 5α 雄烷 3β, 17β 二醇(倍他雄烷二醇))〔999〕	5.5		30	13/	13	千克	L		1/25.5
2906.1990 12	雄甾 4 烯 3α, 17α 二醇(4 雄烯二醇(3α, 17α))(包括雄甾 4 烯 3α, 17β 二醇(4 雄烯二醇(3α, 17β)))〔999〕	5.5		30	13/	13	千克	L		1/25.5
2906.1990 13	雄甾 5 烯 3α, 17α 二醇(5 雄烯二醇(3α, 17α))(包括雄甾 5 烯 3α, 17β 二醇(5 雄烯二醇(3α, 17β)))〔999〕	5.5		30	13/	13	千克	L		1/25.5
2906.1990 14	2—雄烯醇(5α-雄甾-2-烯-17—醇)	5.5		30	13/	13	千克	L		/25.5
2906.1990 15	3—雄烯醇(5α-雄甾-3-烯-17-醇)	5.5		30	13/	13	千克	L		/25.5
2906.1990 90	其他环烷醇,环烯醇及环萜烯醇〔301 易燃固体,302 毒性物质和感染性物质,303 其他化工产品〕	5.5		30	13/	13	千克			1/25.5
	-芳香醇:									
2906.2100	--苄醇〔999〕	5		30	13/	10	千克			1/30
	--其他:									
2906.2910	---2-苯基乙醇〔999〕	5.5		30	13/	10	千克			1/10.5
2906.2990	---其他									
2906.2990 10	三氯杀螨醇、杀螨醇〔999〕	5.5		30	13/	9,10	千克	S		1/30.5
2906.2990 90	其他芳香醇〔301 毒性物质和感染性物质,302 其他化工产品〕	5.5		30	13/	10	千克			1/30.5
	第三分章 酚、酚醇及其卤化、磺化、硝化或亚硝化衍生物									

协定税率 %										特惠税率 %			
亚太5国	东/冰/格	巴基斯坦	韩国	瑞士	哥达	秘鲁	澳大利亚	新西/坡/智	港/澳/台	亚太2国	老/柬/缅	36/3/1	Article Description
													--Other:
	0/0/0	0	0	0	0	0	0	0//0	0/0/			0/0/	---2,5-dimethyl hexandiol
													---Other
	0/0/0	0		0	0	0	0	0//0	0/0/			0/0/	1,3-Propanediol
	0/0/0	0		0	0	0	0	0//0	0/0/			0/0/	1,4-Butanediol
	0/0/0	0		0	0	0	0	0//0	0/0/			0/0/	Ethohexadiol
	0/0/0	0		0	0	0	0	0//0	0/0/			0/0/	Busulfan and Other Anticancer Drugs
	0/0/0	0		0	0	0	0	0//0	0/0/			0/0/	Other diatomic alcohols (tax number of Separating anti－cancer pharmaceutical raw materials)
													-Other polyhydric alcohols:
	0/0/0	0	0	0	0	0	0	0//0	0/0/			0/0/	--2-Ethyl-2-(hydroxymethyl) propane-1,3-diol (trimethylolpropane)
	0/0/0	0	2.2	0	0	0	0	0//0	0/0/			0/0/	--Pentaerythritol
	0/0/0	4	0	0	0	0	0	0//0	0/0/			0/0/0	--Mannitol
	0/0/0	11.2	5.6	4.2	0	0	0	0/0/0	0/0/			0/0/	--D-glucitol (sorbitol)
5.2	0/0/0	7	5.6	4.2	0	0	0	0/0/0	0/0/			0/0/	--Glycerol
													--Other:
	0/0/0	0	0	0	0	0	0	0//0	0/0/			0/0/	---Xylitol
	0/0/0	0	0	0	0	0	0	0//0	0/0/			0/0/	---Other
													-Halogenated, sulphonated, nitrated or nitrosated derivatives of acyclic alcohols:
	0/0/0	0	0	0	0	0	0	0//0	0/0/			0/0/	--Ethchlorvynol (INN)
													--Other
	0/0/0	0	2.2	0	0	0	0	0//0	0/0/			0/0/	Salts of Ethchlorvynol (INN)
	0/0/0	0	2.2	0	0	0	0	0//0	0/0/			0/0/	2-Chloroethanol
	0/0/0	0	2.2	0	0	0	0	0//0	0/0/			0/0/	Geftor
	0/0/0	0	2.2	0	0	0	0	0//0	0/0/			0/0/	Other halogenated, sulphonated derivatives, of acyclic alcohol
													Cyclic alcohols and their halogenated, sulphonated, nitrated or nitrosated derivatives:
													-Cyclanic, cyclenic or cycloterpenic:
	0/0/0	0	0	0	0	0	0	0//0	0/0/			0/0/	--Menthol
													--Cyclohexanol, methylcyclohexanols and dimethylcyclohexanols
	0/0/0	0	0	0	0	0	0	0//0	0/0/			0/0/	Methylcyclohexanol
	0/0/0	0	0	0	0	0	0	0//0	0/0/			0/0/	Cyclohexanol, Dimethylcyclohexanol
													--Sterols and inositols:
	0/0/0	0	2.2	0	0	0	0	0//0	0/0/			0/0/	---Sterol
	0/0/0	0	0	0	0	0	0	0//0	0/0/			0/0/	---Inositol
													--Other:
	0/0/0	0	0	0	0	0	0	0//0	0/0/			0/0/	---Terpineols
													---Other
	0/0/0	0	0		0	0	0	0//0	0/0/			0/0/	5 α - androstane -3 α, 17 α - diol (including 5 α - androstane -3 β, 17 β - estradiol
	0/0/0	0	0		0	0	0	0//0	0/0/			0/0/	Androst -4- allyl -3 α, 17 α - diol {including androst -4- allyl -3 α, 17 β - estrad [4-androstendione(3α,17β)]}
	0/0/0	0	0		0	0	0	0//0	0/0/			0/0/	Androst -5- allyl -3α,17α-diol [5-androstendione(3α,17α)]{including androst -5 -allyl -3α, 17β-estra}
	0/0/0	0	0		0	0	0	0//0	0/0/		//	0/0/	2-androstenol (5a-androsterol-2-ene-17-ol)
	0/0/0	0	0		0	0	0	0//0	0/0/		//	0/0/	3－androstenol (5a－androsterol－3－ene－17－ol)
	0/0/0	0	0		0	0	0	0//0	0/0/			0/0/	Other cyclanic, cyclenic or cycloterpenic
													-Aromatic:
	0/0/0	0	0	0	0	0	0	0//0	0/0/			0/0/	--Benzyl alcohol
													--Other:
	0/0/0	0	0	0	0	0	0	0//0	0/0/			0/0/	---2-Phenyl alcohol
													---Other
	0/0/0	0	2.2	2.9	0	0	0	0//0	0/0/			0/0/	Dicofol, chlorfenethol
	0/0/0	0	2.2	2.9	0	0	0	0//0	0/0/			0/0/	Other aromatic alcohols
													Ⅲ. PHENOLS, PHENOLALCOHOLS, AND THEIR HALOGENATED, SULPHONATED, NITRATED OR NITROSATED DERIVATIVES

税则号列		货品名称〔CIQ 扩展编码及品名—T2 表示见附表 2〕	最惠(%)	暂定税率	普通	增值/消费	出口退税	计量单位	监管条件	检验检疫	特殊证件对美关税
29.07		**酚;酚醇:**									
		-一元酚:									
		--苯酚及其盐:									
2907.1110		---苯酚〔301 毒性物质和感染性物质〕	5.5		30	13/	13	千克	AB	MN	1/15.5
2907.1190		---其他〔301 腐蚀性物质,302 其他化工产品〕	5.5		30	13/	10	千克			1/10.5
		--甲酚及其盐:									
		---甲酚:									
2907.1211		----间甲酚〔101:2—甲(苯)酚,102:2,5—二甲(苯)酚,103:2,6—二甲(苯)酚,104:,5—二甲(苯)酚〕	5.5	3	30	13/	10	千克			1/8
2907.1212		----邻甲酚〔101:3—甲(苯)酚,102:3,4—二甲(苯)酚〕	5.5	3	30	13/	10	千克			1/28
2907.1219		----其他[T2]	5.5		30	13/	10	千克	AB	MRNS	1/30.5
2907.1290		---其他〔101〕	5.5		30	13/	10	千克			1/
		--辛基酚、壬基酚及其异构体以及它们的盐:									
2907.1310		---壬基酚〔999〕	5.5		30	13/	10	千克	AB	MN	1/
2907.1390		---其他〔999〕	5.5		30	13/	10	千克			1/
		--萘酚及其盐:									
2907.1510		---2-萘酚(β-萘酚)〔999〕	5.5		30	13/	10	千克			1/
2907.1590		---其他[T2]	5.5		30	13/	10	千克	AB	RS	1/15.5
		--其他:									
2907.1910		---邻仲丁基酚、邻异丙基酚									
2907.1910	10	邻异丙基(苯)酚〔999〕	4	2	11	13/	10	千克	AB	MN	1/7
2907.1910	90	邻仲丁基酚〔999〕	4	2	11	13/	10	千克			1/7
2907.1990		---其他									
2907.1990	12	邻烯丙基苯酚及盐〔301 腐蚀性物质,302 其他化工产品〕	5.5		30	13/	0	千克	S		1/15.5
2907.1990	90	其他一元酚〔301 腐蚀性物质,302 杂项物质,303 其他化工产品〕	5.5		30	13/	10	千克			1/15.5
		-多元酚;酚醇:									
2907.2100		--间苯二酚及其盐									
2907.2100	01	间苯二酚〔301 毒性物质和感染性物质〕	5.5		30	13/	10	千克			1/25.5
2907.2100	90	间苯二酚盐〔101 属于危险化学品的食品添加剂,102 化工产品〕	5.5		30	13/	10	千克			1/25.5
		--对苯二酚及其盐:									
2907.2210		---对苯二酚〔301〕	5.5		30	13/	10	千克			1/10.5
2907.2290		---其他〔999〕	5.5		30	13/	10	千克			1/10.5
2907.2300		--4,4'-异亚丙基联苯酚(双酚 A,二苯基酚丙烷)及其盐									
2907.2300	01	双酚 A(4,4-异亚丙基联苯酚)〔999〕	5.5		30	13/	10	千克			1/30.5
2907.2300	90	双酚 A 的盐(4,4-异亚丙基联苯酚的盐)〔999〕	5.5		30	13/	10	千克			1/30.5
		--其他:									
2907.2910		---邻苯二酚〔999〕	4		11	13/	10	千克			1/14
2907.2990		---其他									
2907.2990	01	特丁基对苯二酚〔999〕	5.5		30	13/	10	千克	AB	MRNS	1/10.5
2907.2990	10	毒菌酚〔999〕	5.5		30	13/	0	千克	S		1/10.5
2907.2990	90	其他多元酚;酚醇[T2]	5.5		30	13/	10	千克	AB	MRNS	1/10.5
29.08		**酚及酚醇的卤化、磺化、硝化或亚硝化衍生物:**									
		-仅含卤素取代基的衍生物及其盐:									
2908.1100		--五氯苯酚(ISO)〔301〕	5.5		30	13/	0	千克	AB	MN	1/
		--其他:									
2908.1910		---对氯苯酚〔999〕	4		11	13/	10	千克			1/
2908.1990		---其他									
2908.1990	21	格螨酯〔999〕	5.5		30	13/	0	千克	S		1/15.5
2908.1990	22	双氯酚〔999〕	5.5		30	13/	0	千克	S		1/15.5
2908.1990	23	五氯酚钠〔999〕	5.5		30	13/	0	千克	S		1/15.5
2908.1990	90	其他仅含卤素取代基的衍生物及盐〔301 毒性物质和感染性物质,302 其他化工产品〕	5.5		30	13/	10	千克			1/15.5
		-其他:									
2908.9100		--地乐酚(ISO)及其盐〔301 毒性物质和感染性物质,302 其他化工产品〕	5.5		30	13/	0	千克	89		1/
2908.9200		--4,6-二硝基邻甲酚[二硝酚(ISO)]及其盐〔999〕	5.5		30	13/	10	千克	89		1/
		--其他:									
2908.9910		---对硝基酚、对硝基酚钠									
2908.9910	10	4-硝基苯酚(对硝基苯酚)〔101:2—硝基—4—甲(苯)酚,102:4—硝基(苯)酚〕	5.5		30	13/	10	千克			1/
2908.9910	90	对硝基苯酚钠〔301 腐蚀性物质〕	5.5		30	13/	0	千克	S		1/
2908.9990		---其他									
2908.9990	21	芬螨酯〔999〕	5.5		30	13/	0	千克	S		1/30.5
2908.9990	22	消螨酚〔999〕	5.5		30	13/	0	千克	S		1/30.5

协定税率 %										特惠税率 %			
亚太5国	东/冰/格	巴基斯坦	韩国	瑞士	哥达	秘鲁	澳大利亚	新西/坡/智	巷/澳/台	亚太2国	老/柬/缅	36/3/1	Article Description
													Phenols; phenol-alcohols:
													-Monophenols:
													--Phenol (hydroxybenzene) and its salts:
	0/0/0	0		0	0	0	0	0//0	0/0/			0/0/0	---Phenol
	0/0/0	0		1.7	0	0	0	0//0	0/0/			0/0/0	---Other
													--Cresol and its salts:
													---Cresol:
	0/0/0	0	0	0	0	0	0	0//0	0/0/			0/0/0	----*m*-Cresol
	0/0/0	0	0	0	0	0	0	0//0	0/0/			0/0/0	----*o*-Cresol
	0/0/0	0	2.2	0	0	0	0	0//0	0/0/			0/0/0	----Other
	0/0/0	0	0	0	0	0	0	0//0	0/0/			0/0/0	---Other
													--Octylphenol, nonylphenol and their isomers; salts thereof:
	0/0/0	0		0	0	0	0	0//0	0/0/			0/0/0	---Nonylphenol
	0/0/0	0	3.3	0	0	0	0	0//0	0/0/			0/0/0	---Other
													--Naphthols and their salts:
	0/0/0	0	0	0	0	0	0	0//0	0/0/			0/0/0	---2-Naphthols (*β*-naphthol)
	0/0/0	0	0	0	0	0	0	0//0	0/0/			0/0/0	---Other
													--Other:
													---*o*-Sec-butyl phenol, *o*-isopropyl phenol
	0/0/0	0	0	1.2	0	0	0	0//0	0/0/			0/0/0	o-Isopropyl phenol
	0/0/0	0	0	1.2	0	0	0	0//0	0/0/			0/0/0	*o*-sec-buyl phenol
													---Other
	0/0/0	0	0	1.7	0	0	0	0//0	0/0/			0/0/0	*o*-Allylphenol and its salt
	0/0/0	0	0	1.7	0	0	0	0//0	0/0/			0/0/0	Other monophenols
													-Polyphenols; phenol-alcohols:
													--*m*-Dihydroxybenzene (resorcinol) and its salts
	0/0/0	0	2.2	0	0	0	0	0//0	0/0/			0/0/0	*m*-Dihydroxybenzene
	0/0/0	0	2.2	0	0	0	0	0//0	0/0/			0/0/0	*m*-Dihydroxybenzene salts
													--*p*-Dihydroxybenzene (hydroquinone) and its salts:
	0/0/0	0	0	0	0	0	0	0//0	0/0/			0/0/0	---Hydroquinone
	0/0/0	0	0	0	0	0	0	0//0	0/0/			0/0/0	---Other
													--4,4′-Isopropylidenediphenol (bisphenol A, diphenylolpropane) and its salts
	0/0/0	0		0	0	0	0	0//0	0/0/			0/0/0	Bisphenol-A(4,4′-Isopropylidenediphenol)
	0/0/0	0		0	0	0	0	0//0	0/0/			0/0/0	Salts of bisphenol-A(salts of 4,4′-Isopropylidenediphenol)
													--Other:
	0/0/0	0		0	0	0	0	0//0	0/0/			0/0/0	---*o*-Dihydroxybenzene (catechol, pyrocatechol)
													---Other
	0/0/0	0	3.3	0	0	0	0	0//0	0/0/			0/0/0	tert-Butylhydroquinone
	0/0/0	0	3.3	0	0	0	0	0//0	0/0/			0/0/0	Hexachlorophene
	0/0/0	0	3.3	0	0	0	0	0//0	0/0/			0/0/0	Other polyphenols, phenol-alcohol
													Halogenated, sulphonated, nitrated or nitrosated derivatives of phenols or phenolalcohols:
													-Derivatives containing only halogen substituents and their salts:
	0/0/0	0	0	0	0	0	0	0//0	0/0/			0/0/	--Pentachlorophenol(ISO)
													--Other:
	0/0/0	0	0	0	0	0	0	0//0	0/0/			0/0/	---*p*-Chlorophenol
													---Other
	0/0/0	0	0	0	0	0	0	0//0	0/0/			0/0/	Genit
	0/0/0	0	0	0	0	0	0	0//0	0/0/			0/0/	Dichlorophen
	0/0/0	0	0	0	0	0	0	0//0	0/0/			0/0/	Sodium pentachlorophenate
	0/0/0	0	0	0	0	0	0	0//0	0/0/			0/0/	Other derivatives containing only halogen substituents and their salts
													-Other:
	0/0/0	0	0	0	0	0	0	0//0	0/0/			0/0/	--Dinoseb(ISO)and its salts
	0/0/0	0	0	0	0	0	0	0//0	0/0/			0/0/	--4,6-Dinitro-o-cresol [DNOC(ISO)]and its salts
													--Other:
													---*p*-Nitrophenol, sodium *p*-nitro-phenolate
	0/0/0	0	0	0	0	0	0	0//0	0/0/			0/0/	4-Nitrophenol(P-nitrophenol)
	0/0/0	0	0	0	0	0	0	0//0	0/0/			0/0/	Sodium P-nitro-phenolate
													---Other
	0/0/0	0	2.2	0	0	0	0	0//0	0/0/			0/0/	Fenson
	0/0/0	0	2.2	0	0	0	0	0//0	0/0/			0/0/	Dinex

税则号列	货品名称〔CIQ扩展编码及品名—T2表示见附表2〕	最惠(%)	暂定税率	普通	增值/消费	出口退税	计量单位	监管条件	检验检疫	特殊证件对美关税
2908.9990 23	戊硝酚〔999〕	5.5		30	13/	0	千克	S		1/30.5
2908.9990 24	特乐酚〔999〕	5.5		30	13/	0	千克	S		1/30.5
2908.9990 30	苦味酸(2,4,6—三硝基苯酚)	5.5		30	13/	10	千克	k		1/30.5
2908.9990 90	其他酚及酚醇的卤化等衍生物(包括其磺化、硝化或亚硝化衍生物)〔301爆炸品,302易燃液体,303易燃固体,304毒性物质和感染性物质,305腐蚀性物质,306杂项物质,307其他化工产品〕	5.5		30	13/	10	千克			1/30.5
	第四分章　醚、过氧化醇、过氧化醚、过氧化酮、三节环环氧化物、缩醛及半缩醛及其卤化、磺化、硝化或亚硝化衍生物									
29.09	**醚、醚醇、醚酚、醚醇酚、过氧化醇、过氧化醚、过氧化酮(不论是否已有化学定义)及其卤化、磺化、硝化或亚硝化衍生物:**									
	-无环醚及其卤化、磺化、硝化或亚硝化衍生物:									
2909.1100	--乙醚〔301〕	5.5		30	13/	10	千克	23AB	MN	1/10.5
	--其他:									
2909.1910	---甲醚〔999〕	5.5		30	13/	9	千克			1/10.5
2909.1990	---其他									
2909.1990 11	八氯二丙醚〔999〕	5.5		30	13/	9,13	千克	S		1/25.5
2909.1990 12	二氯异丙醚〔999〕	5.5		30	13/	9,13	千克	S		1/25.5
2909.1990 90	其他无环醚及其卤化等衍生物(包括其磺化、硝化或亚硝化衍生物)〔301易燃气体,302易燃液体,303毒性物质和感染性物质,304腐蚀性物质,305其他化工产品〕	5.5		30	13/	9,13	千克			1/25.5
2909.2000	-环烷醚、环烯醚或环萜烯醚及其卤化、磺化、硝化或亚硝化衍生物〔101:1,2—环氧丙烷(抑制了的),102:1,2—环氧—3—乙氧基丙烷〕	5.5		30	13/	10	千克			1/25.5
	-芳香醚及其卤化、磺化、硝化或亚硝化衍生物:									
2909.3010	---1-烷氧基-4-(4-乙烯基环已基)-2,3-二氟苯〔999〕	5.5		30	13/	10	千克			1/
2909.3020	---4-(4-烷氧基苯基)-4'-烷烯基-1,1'-双环已烷及其氟代衍生物〔999〕	5.5		30	13/	13	千克			1/
2909.3090	---其他									
2909.3090 11	甲氧滴滴涕、除草醚〔999〕	5.5		30	13/	0	千克	S		1/25.5
2909.3090 12	醚菊酯、苄螨醚、三氟醚〔999〕	5.5		30	13/	9,10	千克	S		1/25.5
2909.3090 13	氯苯甲醚、甲氧除草醚〔999〕	5.5		30	13/	9,10	千克	S		1/25.5
2909.3090 14	三氟硝草醚、草枯醚〔999〕	5.5		30	13/	9,10	千克	S		1/25.5
2909.3090 15	氟除草醚、乙氧氟草醚〔999〕	5.5		30	13/	9,10	千克	S		1/25.5
2909.3090 16	四溴二苯醚、五溴二苯醚、六溴二苯醚、七溴二苯醚〔999〕	5.5		30	13/	10	千克	89		1/25.5
2909.3090 90	其他芳香醚及其卤化、磺化、硝化衍生物(包括其亚硝化衍生物)〔101饲料添加剂,301爆炸品,302易燃气体,303易燃固体,304毒性物质和感染性物质,305杂项物质,306其他化工产品〕	5.5		30	13/	10	千克			1/25.5
	-醚醇及其卤化、磺化、硝化或亚硝化衍生物:									
2909.4100	--2,2'-氧联二乙醇(二甘醇)〔999〕	5.5	3	30	13/	10	千克			1/28
2909.4300	--乙二醇或二甘醇的单丁醚〔101:1,2—二甲氧基乙烷,102:2,2—二甲氧基丙烷〕	5.5		30	13/	10	千克			1/10.5
2909.4400	--乙二醇或二甘醇的其他单烷基醚〔301易燃液体,302其他化工产品〕	5.5		30	13/	10	千克			1/10.5
	--其他:									
2909.4910	---间苯氧基苄醇〔999〕	4		11	13/	10	千克			1/
2909.4990	---其他〔301易燃液体,302毒性物质和感染性物质,303其他化工产品〕	5.5		30	13/	10	千克			1/15.5
2909.5000	-醚酚、醚醇酚及其卤化、磺化、硝化或亚硝化衍生物〔301其它危险化学品,302其他化工产品〕	5.5		30	13/	10	千克			1/30.5
2909.6000	-过氧化醇、过氧化醚、过氧化酮及其卤化、磺化、硝化或亚硝化衍生物〔301自反应物质,302有机过氧化物,303其他化工品〕	5.5		30	13/	10	千克			1/10.5
29.10	**三节环环氧化物、环氧醇、环氧酚、环氧醚及其卤化、磺化、硝化或亚硝化衍生物:**									
2910.1000	-环氧乙烷(氧化乙烯)〔301〕	5.5		30	13/	13	千克	AB	MN	1/
2910.2000	-甲基环氧乙烷(氧化丙烯)〔101:1,2—环氧丙烷(抑制了的),102含环氧乙烷≤30%〕	5.5		30	13/	0	千克			1/15.5

协定税率 %										特惠税率 %			Article Description
亚太5国	东/冰/格	巴基斯坦	韩国	瑞士	哥达	秘鲁	澳大利亚	新西/坡/智	港/澳/台	亚太2国	老/柬/缅	36/3/1	
	0/0/0	0	2.2	0	0	0	0	0//0	C/0/			0/0/	Dinosam
	0/0/0	0	2.2	0	0	0	0	0//0	0/0/			0/0/	Dinoterb
	0/0/0	0	2.2	0	0	0	0	0//0	0/0/		//	0/0/	Picric acid (2,4,6－trinitrophenol)
	0/0/0	0	2.2	0	0	0	0	0//0	0/0/			0/0/	Other halogenated, sulphonated, nitrated or nitrosated derivatives of hpenols or phenolalcohols
													Ⅳ. ETHERS, ALCOHOL PEROXIDES, ETHER PEROXIDES, KETONE PEROXIDES, EPOXIDES WITH A THREE-MEMBERED RING, ACETALS AND HEMIACETALS, AND THEIR HALOGENATED, SULPHONATED, NITRATED OR NITROSATED DERIVATIVES
													Ethers, ether-alcohols, ether-phenols, ether-alcohol-phenols, alcohol peroxides, ether peroxides, ketone peroxides (whether or not chemically defined), and their halogenated, sulphonated, nitrated or nitrosated derivatives:
													-Acyclic ethers and their halogenated, sulphonated, nitrated or nitrosated derivatives:
	0/0/0	0	0	0	0	0	0	0//0	0/0/			0/0/0	--Diethyl ether
													--Other
	0/0/0	0	3.3	0	0		0	0//0	0/0/			0//	---Methyl ether
													---Other:
	0/0/0	0	3.3	0	0		0	0//0	0/0/			0//	Octachlorodipropyl ether
	0/0/0	0	3.3	0	0		0	0//0	0/C/			0//	Nemamort(DCIP)
	0/0/0	0	3.3	0	0		0	0//0	0/C/			0//	Other acyclic ethers and their halogenated(including sulphonated, nitrated or nitrosated derivatives and their halogenated)
	0/0/0	0	0	0	0	0	0	0//0	0/0/			0/0/0	-Cyclanic, cyclenic or cycloterpenic ethers and their halogenated, sulphonated, nitrated or nitrosated derivatives
													-Aromatic ethers and their halogenated, sulphonated, nitrated or nitrosated derivatives:
	0/0/0	0	0	0	0	0	0	0//0	0/0/			0/0/0	---1-alkoxylate-4-(4-vingl cyclohexyl)-2,3-difluoro benzene
	0/0/0	0	0	0	0	0	0	0//0	0/0/			0/0/0	---4- (4- alkoxy phenyl) -4 ′alkenyl -1, 1′- dicyclohexane and its fluorinated derivatives
													---Other
	0/0/0	0	0	0	0	0	0	0//0	0/0/			0/0/0	Methoxychlor, nitrofen
	0/0/0	0	0	0	0	0	0	0//0	0/0/			0/0/0	Ethofenprox, halfenprox, trifluoro
	0/0/0	0	0	0	0	0	0	0//0	0/0/			0/0/0	Chloroanisole, chlomethoxyfen
	0/0/0	0	0	0	0	0	0	0//0	0/0/			0/0/0	Fluorodifen, chlomitrofen
	0/0/0	0	0	0	0	0	0	0//0	0/0/			0/0/0	Fluoronitrofen, oxyfluorfen
	0/0/0	0	0	0	0	0	0	0//0	0/0/			0/0/0	Tetrabromodiphenyl ether, Pentabromodiphenyl ether, Hexabromodiphenyl ether, Heptabromodiphenyl ether
	0/0/0	0	0	0	0	0	0	0//0	0/0/			0/0/0	Other aromatic ethers and its halogenated, sulphonated, nitrated or nitrosated derivatives
													-Ether-alcohols and their halogenated, sulphonated, nitrated or nitrosated derivatives:
	0/0/0	0	0	0	0		0	0//0	0/0/0			0//	--2,2′-Oxydiethanol (diethylene glycol, digol)
	0/0/0	0	0	0	0	0	0	0//0	0/0/0			0/0/0	--Monobutyl ethers of ethylene glycol or of diethylene glycol
	0/0/0	0	3.3	0	0	0	0	0//0	0/0/			0/0/0	--Other monoalkylethers of ethylene glycol or of diethylene glycol
													--Other:
	0/0/0	0	0	0	0	0	0	0//0	0/0/			0/0/0	---*m*-Phenoxy benzalcohol
	0/0/0	0	3.3	0	0	0	0	0//0	0/0/			0/0/0	---Other
	0//0	0	3.3	0	0	0	0	0//0	0/0/			0/0/0	-Ether-phenols, ether-alcohol-phenols and their halogenated, sulphonated, nitrated or nitrosated derivatives
	0/0/0	0	3.3	0	0	0	0	0//0	0/0/			0/0/0	-Alcohol peroxides, ether peroxides, ketone peroxides and their halogenated, sulphonated, nitrated or nitrosated derivatives
													Epoxides, epoxyalcohols, epoxyphenols and epoxyethers, with a three-membered ring, and their halogenated, sulphonated, nitrated or nitrosated derivatives:
	0/0/0	0	3.3	0	0	0	0	0//0	0/0/			0/0/	-Oxirane (ethylene oxide)
	0/0/0	0	3.3	0	0	0	0	0//0	0/0/			0/0/	-Methyloxirane (propylene oxide)

税则号列	货品名称〔CIQ 扩展编码及品名－T2 表示见附表 2〕	最惠(%)	暂定税率	普通	增值/消费	出口退税	计量单位	监管条件	检验检疫	特殊证件对美关税
2910.3000	-1-氯-2,3-环氧丙烷(表氯醇)〔999〕	5.5		30	13/	0	千克	AB	MN	1/30.5
2910.4000	-狄氏剂(ISO,INN)〔101 狄氏剂粉剂、颗粒剂(含量 10%～90%),102 狄氏剂乳剂(含量 2%～90%),103 其他〕	5.5		30	13/	0	千克	89		1/
2910.5000	-异狄氏剂(ISO)〔999〕	5.5		30	13/	0	千克	89		1/
2910.9000	-其他									
2910.9000 20	灭草环〔999〕	5.5		30	13/	9,13	千克	S		1/15.5
2910.9000 90	三节环环氧化物、环氧醇(酚、醚)(包括其卤化、磺化、硝化或亚硝化的衍生物)〔301 有机过氧化物,302 毒性物质和感染性物质,303 其他化工产品〕	5.5		30	13/	13	千克			1/15.5
29.11	**缩醛及半缩醛,不论是否含有其他含氧基,及其卤化、磺化、硝化或亚硝化衍生物:**									
2911.0000	缩醛及半缩醛,不论是否含有其他含氧基,及其卤化、磺化、硝化或亚硝化衍生物〔301 易燃液体,302 其他化工产品〕	5.5		30	13/	10	千克			1/30.5
	第五分章　醛基化合物									
29.12	**醛,不论是否含有其他含氧基;环聚醛;多聚甲醛:**									
	-不含其他含氧基的无环醛:									
2912.1100	--甲醛〔301 易燃液体,302 腐蚀性物质〕	5.5		30	13/	10	千克	AB	MN	1/10.5
2912.1200	--乙醛〔301〕	5.5		30	13/	10	千克	AB	MN	1/
2912.1900	--其他									
2912.1900 01	乙二醛〔999〕	5.5	3	30	13/	13	千克			1/13
2912.1900 30	丙烯醛〔999〕	5.5		30	13/	13	千克			1/15.5
2912.1900 90	其他无环醛(指不含其他含氧基)[T2]	5.5		30	13/	13	千克			1/15.5
	-不含其他含氧基的环醛:									
2912.2100	--苯甲醛(101:2－羰基－4－甲基苯甲醛,102:非工业用无检疫要求食品添加剂)	5.5		30	13/	10	千克			1/30.5
	--其他:									
2912.2910	---铃兰醛(对叔丁基-α-甲基-氧化肉桂醛)〔999〕	5.5		30	13/	10	千克			1/15.5
2912.2990	---其他〔101:1,2,3,6－四氢化苯甲醛,301:易燃液体,302:毒性物质和感染性物质,303:其他化工产品〕	5.5		30	13/	13	千克			1/10.5
	-醛醇、醛酚及含其他含氧基的醛:									
2912.4100	--香草醛(3-甲氧基-4-羟基苯甲醛)〔101 双香兰素,102 香兰素〕	5.5		30	13/	13	千克			1/25.5
2912.4200	--乙基香草醛(3-乙氧基-4-羟基苯甲醛)〔999〕	5.5		30	13/	13	千克			1/10.5
	--其他:									
2912.4910	---醛醇〔999〕	5.5		30	13/	13	千克			1/30.5
2912.4990	---其他									
2912.4990 10	间苯氧基苯甲醛〔301 易燃液体〕	5.5		30	13/	10	千克			1/30.5
2912.4990 90	其他醛醚、醛酚(包括含其他含氧基的醛)〔301:2,3－环氧－1－丙醛〕	5.5		30	13/	10	千克			1/30.5
2912.5000	-环聚醛									
2912.5000 10	四聚乙醛〔999〕	5.5		30	13/	9,10	千克	S		1/
2912.5000 90	其他环聚醛〔301 易燃固体,302 其他化工产品〕	5.5		30	13/	10	千克			1/
2912.6000	-多聚甲醛〔999〕	5.5		30	13/	10	千克	AB	MN	1/15.5
29.13	**税目 29.12 所列产品的卤化、磺化、硝化或亚硝化衍生物:**									
2913.0000	税目 29.12 所列产品的卤化、磺化、硝化或亚硝化衍生物									
2913.0000 10	三氯乙醛〔999〕	5.5		30	13/	10	千克	ABG	MN	1/30.5
2913.0000 90	税目 29.12 所列产品的其他衍生物(指卤化、磺化、硝化或亚硝化的衍生物)〔301 毒性物质和感染性物质,302 腐蚀性物质,303 其他化工产品〕	5.5		30	13/	10	千克			1/30.5
	第六分章　酮基化合物及醌基化合物									
29.14	**酮及醌,不论是否含有其他含氧基,及其卤化、磺化、硝化或亚硝化衍生物:**									
	-不含其他含氧基的无环酮:									
2914.1100	--丙酮〔301 二甲基甲酮、二甲酮、醋酮、木酮〕	5.5		20	13/	13	千克	23AB	MN	1/30.5
2914.1200	--丁酮〔甲基乙基(甲)酮(甲乙酮)(2－丁酮)〕〔101〕	5.5		30	13/	10	千克	23		1/30.5
2914.1300	--4-甲基-2-戊酮〔甲基异丁基(甲)酮〕〔999〕	5.5		30	13/	10	千克	AB	MN	1/25.5
2914.1900	--其他									
2914.1900 10	频哪酮〔999〕	5.5		30	13/	10	千克	23		1/10.5
2914.1900 90	其他不含其他含氧基的无环酮〔301 易燃液体,302 其他化工产品〕	5.5		30	13/	10,13	千克			1/10.5

协定税率 %										特惠税率 %			Article Description
亚太5国	东/冰/格	巴基斯坦	韩国	瑞士	哥达	秘鲁	澳大利亚	新西/坡/智	港/澳/台	亚太2国	老/柬/缅	36/3/1	
	0/0/0	0	2.2	0	0	0	0	0//0	0/0/0			0/0/	-1-Chloro-2,3-epoxypropane (epichlorohydrin)
	0/0/0	0	0	0	0	0	0	0//0	0/0/			0/0/	-Dieldrin(ISO,INN)
	0/0/0	0	0	2.9	0	0	0	0//0	0/0/			0/0/	-Endrin(ISO)
													-Other
	0/0/0	0	0	2.9	0	0	0	0//0	0/0/			0/0/	Tridiphane
	0/0/0	0	0	2.9	0	0	0	0//0	0/0/			0/0/	Three-ring epoxide, epoxy alcohol (phenols, ether) (including their halogenated, sulphonated, nitration or nitrosated derivatives)
													Acetals and hemiacetals, whether or not with other oxygen function, and their halogenated, sulphonated, nitrated or nitrosated derivatives:
	0/0/0	0	2.2	2.9	0	0	0	0//0	0/0/			0/0/	Acetals and hemiacetals, whether or not with other oxygen function, and their halogenated, sulphonated, nitrated or nitrosated derivatives
													Ⅴ. ALDEHYDE-FUNCTION COMPOUNDS
													Aldehydes, whether or not with other oxygen function; cyclic polymers of aldehydes; paraformaldehyde:
													-Acyclic aldehydes without other oxygen function:
	0/0/0	0	0	0	0	0	0	0//0	0/0/			0/0/	--Methanal (formaldehyde)
	0/0/0	0	0	0	0	0	0	0//0	0/0/			0/0/	--Ethanal (acetaldehyde)
													--Other
	0/0/0	0	3.3	1.7	0	0	0	0//0	0/0/			0/0/	Glyoxal (ethanedial)
	0/0/0	0	3.3	1.7	0	0	0	0//0	0/0/			0/0/	Acrolein
	0/0/0	0	3.3	1.7	0	0	0	0//0	0/0/			0/0/	Other acyclic aldehydes(without other oxygen function)
													-Cyclic aldehydes without other oxygen function:
	0/0/0	0	0	0	0	0	0	0//0	0/0/			0/0/	--Benzaldehyde
													--Other:
4.4	0/0/0	0	0	0	0	0	0	0//0	0/0/			0/0/	---Lilial (p-tert-butyl-α-methyl-oxocinn amaldehyde)
	0/0/0	0	0	2.9	0	0	0	0//0	0/0/			0/0/	---Other
													-Aldehyde-alcohols, aldehyde-phenols and aldehydes with other oxygen function:
	0/0/0	0	0	0	0	0	0	0//0	0/0/			0/0/	--Vanillin (4-hydroxy-3-methoxybenzaldehyde)
	0/0/0	0	0	0	0	0	0	0//0	0/0/			0/0/	--Ethylvanillin (3-ethoxy-4-hydroxybenzaldehyde)
													--Other:
	0/0/0	0	0	0	0	0	0	0//0	0/0/			0/0/	---Aldehyde-alcohols
													---Other
	0/0/0	0	0	0	0	0	0	0//0	0/0/			0/0/	M—phenoxybenzaldehyde
	0/0/0	0	0	0	0	0	0	0//0	0/0/			0/0/	Other aldehyde ethers, aldehyde phenols (including other oxygen—containing aldehydes)
													-Cyclic polymers of aldehydes
	0/0/0	0	3.3		0	0	0	0//0	0/0/			0/0/	Metaldehyde
	0/0/0	0	3.3		0	0	0	0//0	0/0/			0/0/	Other cyclic polymers of aldehydes
	0/0/0	0	3.3	0	0	0	0	0//0	0/0/			0/0/	-Paraformaldehyde
													Halogenated, sulphonated, nitrated or nitrosated derivatives of products of heading No. 29.12:
													Halogenated, sulphonated, nitrated or nitrosated derivatives of products of heading No. 29.12
	0/0/0	4	0	0	0	0	0	0//0	0/0/			0/0/	Chloral
	0/0/0	4	0	0	0	0	0	0//0	0/0/			0/0/	Halogenated, sulphonated, nitrated or nitrosated derivatives of products of heading No. 29.12
													Ⅵ. -KETONE-FUNCTION COMPOUNDS AND QUINONE-FUNCTION COMPOUNDS
													Ketones and quinones, whether or not with other oxygen function, and their halogenated, sulphonated, nitrated or nitrosated derivatives:
													-Acyclic ketones without other oxygen function:
	0/0/0	0		0	0	0	0	0//0	0/0/			0/0/	--Acetone
	0/0/0	0		0	0	0	0	0//0	0/0/			0/0/	--Butanone (methyl ethyl ketone)
	0/0/0	0	3.3	0	0	0	0	0//0	0/0/			0/0/	--4-Methyl-2-pentanone (isobutyl methyl ketone)
													--Other
	0/0/0	0	3.3	0	0	0	0	0//0	0/0/			0/0/	Pinacolone
	0/0/0	0	3.3	0	0	0	0	0//0	0/0/			0/0/	Other acyclic ketones, without other oxygen function

税则号列	货品名称〔CIQ扩展编码及品名－T2表示见附表2〕	最惠(%)	暂定税率	普通	增值/消费	出口退税	计量单位	监管条件	检验检疫	特殊证件对美关税
	-不含其他含氧基的环烷酮、环烯酮或环萜烯酮：									
2914.2200	--环已酮及甲基环乙酮〔301易燃液体〕	5.5		30	13/	10	千克	AB	MN	1/15.5
2914.2300	--芷香酮及甲基芷香酮〔999〕	5.5		30	13/	13	千克			1/30.5
	--其他：									
2914.2910	---樟脑〔301易燃固体〕	5.5		40	13/	9,10	千克	B	N	1/10.5
2914.2990	---其他									
2914.2990 10	5α-雄烷-2-烯-17-酮〔301易燃液体,302毒性物质和感染性物质,303腐蚀性物质,304其他化工产品〕	5.5		30	13/	13	千克	L		1/15.5
2914.2990 11	3－雄烯酮(5α-雄甾-3-烯-17-酮)	5.5		30	13/	13	千克	L		/15.5
2914.2990 90	其他环烷酮.环烯酮或环萜烯酮(指不含其他含氧基的)〔301易燃液体,302毒性物质和感染性物质,303腐蚀性物质,304其他化工产品〕	5.5		30	13/	13	千克			1/15.5
	-不含其他含氧基的芳香酮：									
2914.3100	--苯丙酮(苯基丙-2-酮)〔999〕	5.5		30	13/	10	千克	23		1/15.5
	--其他：									
2914.3910	---苯乙酮〔1014－甲基苯乙酮,102非工业用无检疫要求食品添加剂〕	4		11	13/	10	千克			1/29
2914.3990	---其他									
2914.3990 11	杀鼠酮〔999〕	5.5		30	13/	9,10	千克	S		1/30.5
2914.3990 12	鼠完〔999〕	5.5		30	13/	0	千克	S		1/30.5
2914.3990 13	敌鼠〔101含量＜2%,102敌鼠乳剂(含量＜2%)〕	5.5		30	13/	9,10	千克	S		1/30.5
2914.3990 14	邻氯苯基环戊酮〔999〕	5.5		30	13/	9,10	千克	23		1/30.5
2914.3990 15	1－苯基－1－丙酮	5.5		30	13/	10,9	千克	23		/30.5
2914.3990 90	其他不含其他含氧基的芳香酮〔101:2－甲基苯乙酮,102:二苯甲酮〕	5.5		30	13/	13	千克			1/30.5
2914.4000	-酮醇及酮醛									
2914.4000 10	敌鼠钠〔999〕	5.5		30	13/	0	千克	S		1/30.5
2914.4000 20	表雄酮(3β－羟基－5α－雄烷－17－酮)、表睾酮〔999〕	5.5		30	13/	10	千克	L		1/30.5
2914.4000 30	1－表雄酮(3β－羟基－5α－雄甾－1－烯－17－酮)	5.5		30	13/	10	千克	L		/30.5
2914.4000 90	其他酮醇及酮醛〔101:4－羟基－4－甲基－2－戊酮,102:3－羟基－2－丁酮,103:5－羟基－2－戊酮,301易燃液体,302其他化工产品〕	5.5		30	13/	10	千克			1/30.5
	-酮酚及含有其他含氧基的酮：									
	---酮酚：									
2914.5011	----覆盆子酮〔101悬钩子酮,102复盆子酮?〕	5.5		30	13/	13	千克			1/15.5
2914.5019	----其他〔999〕	5.5		30	13/	10	千克			1/30.5
2914.5020	---2-羟基-4-甲氧基二苯甲酮〔999〕	5.5		30	13/	10	千克			1/30.5
2914.5090	---其他									
2914.5090 11	苯草酮,双炔酰菌胺〔999〕	5.5		30	13/	9,10	千克	S		1/30.5
2914.5090 12	甲氧虫酰肼〔999〕	5.5		30	13/	9,10	千克	S		1/30.5
2914.5090 90	含其他含氧基的酮〔1014－甲氧基－4－甲基－2－戊酮,301易燃液体,302其他化工产品〕	5.5		30	13/	10	千克			1/30.5
	-醌：									
2914.6100	--蒽醌〔999〕	5.5		30	13/	10	千克			1/30.5
2914.6200	--辅酶Q10(癸烯醌(INN))〔999〕	5.5		30	13/	13	千克			1/10.5
2914.6900	--其他									
2914.6900 10	大黄素甲醚〔999〕	5.5		30	13/	10	千克	S		1/30.5
2914.6900 90	其他醌〔999〕	5.5		30	13/	10	千克			1/30.5
	-卤化、磺化、硝化或亚硝化衍生物：									
2914.7100	--十氯酮(ISO)〔301毒性物质和感染性物质〕	5.5		30	13/	10	千克	89		1/15.5
2914.7900	--其他									
2914.7900 11	氯鼠酮、苯茵酮、茚草酮〔999〕	5.5		30	13/	0	千克	S		1/10.5
2914.7900 12	二氯萘醌〔999〕	5.5		30	13/	0	千克	S		1/10.5
2914.7900 13	四氯对醌〔999〕	5.5		30	13/	0	千克	S		1/10.5
2914.7900 14	六氯丙酮〔999〕	5.5		30	13/	0	千克	S		1/10.5
2914.7900 15	氯敌鼠钠盐〔999〕	5.5		30	13/	9,10	千克	S		1/10.5
2914.7900 16	1-苯基-2-溴-1-丙酮〔999〕	5.5		30	13/	10	千克	23		1/10.5
2914.7900 90	其他酮及醌的卤化、磺化衍生物(包括硝化或亚硝化衍生物)〔301爆炸品,302毒性气体,303易燃液体,304易燃固体,305毒性物质和感染性物质,306腐蚀性物质,307其他化工产品〕	5.5		30	13/	10	千克			1/10.5
	第七分章　羧酸及其酸酐、酰卤化物、过氧化物和过氧酸以及它们的卤化、磺化、硝化或亚硝化衍生物									

协定税率 %										特惠税率 %			Article Description
亚太5国	东/冰/格	巴基斯坦	韩国	瑞士	哥达	秘鲁	澳大利亚	新西/坡/智	港/澳/台	亚太2国	老/柬/缅	36/3/1	
													-Cyclanic, cyclenic or cycloterpenic ketones without other oxygen function:
	0/0/0	0	3.3	0	0	0	0	0//0	0/0/			0/0/	--Cyclohexanone and methylcyclohexanone
	0/0/0	0	0		0	0	0	0//0	0/0/			0/0/	--Ionones and methylionones
													--Other:
	0/0/0	0	0	0	0	0	0	0//0	0/0/			0/0/	---Camphor
													---Other
	0/0/0	0	2.2		0	0	0	0//0	0/0/			0/0/	5α-androstane-2-ene-17-ketone
	0/0/0	0	2.2		0	0	0	0//0	0/0/		//	0/0/	3—androstenone (5a—androsterone—3—ene—17—one)
	0/0/0	0	2.2		0	0	0	0//0	0/0/			0/0/	Other cyclanic, cyclenic or cycloterpenic ketones without other oxygen function
													-Aromatic ketones without other oxygen function:
	0/0/0	0	0	0	0	0	0	0//0	0/0/			0/0/	--Propiophenone (phenylpropan-2-one)
													--Other:
	0/0/0	0	0	0	0	0	0	0//0	0/0/			0/0/	---Acetophenone
													---Other
	0/0/0	0	0	1.7	0	0	0	0//0	0/0/			0/0/	Duocide
	0/0/0	0	0	1.7	0	0	0	0//0	0/0/			0/0/	Pindone
	0/0/0	0	0	1.7	0	0	0	0//0	0/0/			0/0/	Diphacinone
	0/0/0	0	0	1.7	0	0	0	0//0	0/0/			0/0/	*o*-Chlorophenyl Cyclopentyl Ketone
	0/0/0	0	0	1.7	0	0	0	0//0	0/0/		//	0/0/	1—phenyl—1—acetone
	0/0/0	0	0	1.7	0	0	0	0//0	0/0/			0/0/	Other aromatic ketones without other oxygen function
													-Ketone-alcohols and ketone-aldehydes
	0/0/0	0	0	1.7	0	0	0	0//0	0/0/			0/0/	Natrium diphacinone
	0/0/0	0	0	1.7	0	0	0	0//0	0/0/			0/0/	androsterone(3β-Hydroxy-5α-androstane-17-ketone), epitestosterone
	0/0/0	0	0	1.7	0	0	0	0//0	0/0/		//	0/0/	1—epiandrone (3 β — hydroxy—5 α — androsterol—1—ene—17—one)
	0/0/0	0	0	1.7	0	0	0	0//0	0/0/			0/0/	Other ketone-alcohols and ketone-aldehydes
													-Ketone-phenols and ketones with other oxygen function:
													---Ketone-phenols:
	0/0/0	0	0	0	0	0	0	0//0	0/0/			0/0/	----Raspberry ketone
	0/0/0	0	0	1.7	0	0	0	0//0	0/0/			0/0/	----Other
	0/0/0	0	0	0	0	0	0	0//0	0/0/			0/0/	---2-Hydroxy-4-methoxybenzophenone
													---Other
	0/0/0	0	2.2	0	0	0	0	0//0	0/0/			0/0/	Tralkoxydim, mandipropamid
	0/0/0	0	2.2	0	0	0	0	0//0	0/0/			0/0/	Methoxyfenoxide
	0/0/0	0	2.2	0	0	0	0	0//0	0/0/			0/0/	Other ketone with other oxygen function
													-Quinones:
	0/0/0	0	2.2	0	0	0	0	0//0	0/0/			0/0/	--Anthraquinone
	0/0/0	0	2.2	0	0	0	0	0//0	0/0/			0/0/	--Coenzyme Q10(*ubidecarenone*(*INN*))
													--Other
	0/0/0	0	2.2	0	0	0	0	0//0	0/0/			0/0/	Physcione
	0/0/0	0	2.2	0	0	0	0	0//0	0/0/			0/0/	Other quinones
													-halogenated, sulphonated, nitrated or nitrosated derivatives:
	0/0/0	0	2.2		0	0	0	0//0	0/0/			0/0/	--Chlordecone (*ISO*)
													--Other
	0/0/0	0	2.2		0	0	0	0//0	0/0/			0/0/	Chlorophacinone
	0/0/0	0	2.2		0	0	0	0//0	0/0/			0/0/	Dichlone
	0/0/0	0	2.2		0	0	0	0//0	0/0/			0/0/	Chloranil
	0/0/0	0	2.2		0	0	0	0//0	0/0/			0/0/	Hexachloroacetone
	0/0/0	0	2.2		0	0	0	0//0	0/0/			0/0/	Chlorophacinone
	0/0/0	0	2.2		0	0	0	0//0	0/0/			0/0/	1-Bromo-1-phenyl-2-propanone?
	0/0/0	0	2.2		0	0	0	0//0	0/0/			0/0/	Halogenated, sulphonated, nitrated or nitrosated derivatives of other ketones and quinones
													Ⅷ. CARBOXYLIC ACIDS AND THEIR ANHYDRIDES, HALIDES, PEROXIDES AND PEROXYACIDS AND THEIR HALOGENATED, SULPHONATED, NITRATED OR NITROSATED DERIVATIVES

税则号列		货品名称〔CIQ扩展编码及品名—T2表示见附表2〕	最惠(%)	暂定税率	普通	增值/消费	出口退税	计量单位	监管条件	检验检疫	特殊证件对美关税
29.15		**饱和无环一元羧酸及其酸酐、酰卤化物、过氧化物和过氧酸以及它们的卤化、磺化、硝化或亚硝化衍生物:**									
		-甲酸及其盐和酯:									
2915.1100		--甲酸〔101饲料添加剂,301腐蚀性物质〕	5.5		40	13/	10	千克	AB	MN	1/25.5
2915.1200		--甲酸盐〔101饲料添加剂,102甲酸亚铊,103甲酸钡,301毒性物质和感染性物质,302其他化工产品〕	5.5		30	13/	10	千克			1/30.5
2915.1300		--甲酸酯[T2]	5.5		30	13/	10	千克			1/30.5
		-乙酸及其盐;乙酸酐:									
		--乙酸:									
		---冰乙酸:									
2915.2111		----食品级的〔101饲料添加剂,301属于危险化学品的食品添加剂〕	5.5		30	13/	10	千克	ABG	MRNS	1/15.5
2915.2119		----其他〔101冰醋酸饲料添加剂,102化工产品〕	5.5		30	13/	10	千克	G		1/30.5
2915.2190		---其他									
2915.2190	10	乙酸溶液,80≥含量>10%〔101饲料添加剂,301腐蚀性物质〕	5.5		50	13/	10	千克	ABG	MN	1/30.5
2915.2190	20	乙酸,含量>80%〔301腐蚀性物质〕	5.5		50	13/	10	千克	ABG	MN	1/30.5
2915.2190	90	其他乙酸[T2]	5.5		50	13/	10	千克	ABG	MRNS	1/30.5
2915.2400		--乙酸酐〔999〕	5.5		50	13/	10	千克	23AB	MN	1/25.5
		--其他:									
2915.2910		---乙酸钠〔101饲料添加剂,301无检疫要求食品添加剂,302需申报仅用于工业用途不用于食品添加剂无检疫要求的化学品〕	5.5		50	13/	10	千克	AG	R	1/15.5
2915.2990		---其他									
2915.2990	11	乙酸铜〔999〕	5.5		50	13/	9,10	千克			1/15.5
2915.2990	23	乙酸铅(醋酸铅)〔999〕	5.5		50	13/	10	千克			1/15.5
2915.2990	90	其他乙酸盐[T2]	5.5		50	13/	10	千克	AB	MRNS	1/15.5
		-乙酸酯:									
2915.3100		--乙酸乙酯〔301易燃液体,需申报仅用于工业用途不用于食品添加剂无检疫要求,302属于危险化学品的食品添加剂〕	5.5		30	13/	10	千克	ABG	MRNS	1/25.5
2915.3200		--乙酸乙烯酯〔999〕	5.5		30	13/	13	千克	AB	MN	1/30.5
2915.3300		--乙酸(正)丁酯〔301〕	5.5		30	13/	10	千克	AB	MN	1/15.5
2915.3600		--地乐酚(ISO)乙酸酯〔999〕	5.5		30	13/	0	千克	S		1/15.5
2915.3900		--其他									
2915.3900	11	三氯杀虫酯〔999〕	5.5		30	13/	9,13	千克	S		1/10.5
2915.3900	13	特乐酯〔999〕	5.5		30	13/	9,13	千克	S		1/10.5
2915.3900	14	灭螨醌〔999〕	5.5		30	13/	0	千克	S		1/10.5
2915.3900	15	信铃酯〔999〕	5.5		30	13/	9,13	千克	S		1/10.5
2915.3900	16	种衣酯〔999〕	5.5		30	13/	9,13	千克	S		1/10.5
2915.3900	90	其他乙酸酯[T2]	5.5		30	13/	13	千克	AB	MRNS	1/10.5
2915.4000		-一氯代乙酸、二氯乙酸或三氯乙酸及其盐和酯									
2915.4000	10	一氯醋酸钠〔999〕	5.5		30	13/	0	千克			1/30.5
2915.4000	90	其他一氯代乙酸的盐和酯(包括二氯乙酸或三氯乙酸的盐和酯)〔301毒性物质和感染性物质,302腐蚀性物质,303其他危险化学品,304其他化工产品〕	5.5		30	13/	10	千克			1/30.5
		-丙酸及其盐和酯:									
2915.5010		---丙酸〔101饲料添加剂,103危险化学品&食品添加剂,301腐蚀性物质,302属于危险化学品的食品添加剂〕	5.5	3	30	13/	10	千克	AB	MRNS	1/8
2915.5090		---其他[T2]	5.5		30	13/	10	千克	AB	MRNS	1/30.5
2915.6000		-丁酸、戊酸及其盐和酯〔101饲料添加剂,301易燃液体,302腐蚀性物质,303杂项物质,304其他化工产品〕	5.5		30	13/	10	千克			1/10.5
		-棕榈酸、硬脂酸及其盐和酯:									
2915.7010		---硬脂酸〔101饲料添加剂,102化工产品,301无检疫要求食品添加剂,302需申报仅用于工业用途不用于食品添加剂无检疫要求的化学品〕	7		50	13/	10	千克	A	R	1/32
2915.7090		---其他〔101饲料添加剂,102十二酸钡〕	5.5		30	13/	13	千克			1/25.5
2915.9000		-其他									
2915.9000	11	茅草枯〔999〕	5.5		30	13/	0	千克	S		1/25.5
2915.9000	12	抑草蓬〔999〕	5.5		30	13/	0	千克	S		1/25.5
2915.9000	13	四氟丙酸〔999〕	5.5		30	13/	9,10	千克	S		1/25.5
2915.9000	20	氟乙酸钠〔999〕	5.5		30	13/	10	千克	89		1/25.5
2915.9000	90	其他饱和无环一元羧酸及其酸酐[(酰卤、过氧)化物,过氧酸及其卤化、硝化、磺化、亚硝化衍生物][T2]	5.5		30	13/	10	千克	AB	MRNS	1/25.5
29.16		**不饱和无环一元羧酸、环一元羧酸及其酸酐、酰卤化物、过氧化物和过氧酸以及它们的卤化、磺化、硝化或亚硝化衍生物:**									

协定税率 %										特惠税率 %			Article Description
亚太5国	东/冰/格	巴基斯坦	韩国	瑞士	哥达	秘鲁	澳大利亚	新西/坡/智	港/澳/台	亚太2国	老/柬/缅	36/3/1	
													Saturated acyclic monocarboxylic acids and their anhydrides, halides, peroxides and peroxyacids; their halogenated, sulphonated, nitrated or nitrosated derivatives:
													-Formic acid, its salts and esters:
	0/0/0	4	2.2	0	0	0	0	0//0	0/0/			0/0/0	--Formic acid
	0/0/0	4	2.2	0	0	0	0	0//0	0/0/			0/0/0	--Salts of formic acid
	0/0/0	4	0	0	0	0	0	0//0	0/0/			0/0/0	--Esters of formic acid
													-Acetic acid and its salts; acetic anhydride:
													--Acetic acid:
													---Acetic acid, glacial:
	0/0/0	4	0	0	0	0	0	0//0	0/0/0			0/0/0	----food-grade
	0/0/0	4	0	0	0	0	0	0//0	0/0/0			0/0/0	----Other
													---Other
	0/0/0	4	0	0	0	0	0	0//0	0/0/			0/0/0	Acetic acid solution, 80%≥content>10%
	0/0/0	4	0	0	0	0	0	0//0	0/0/			0/0/0	Acetic acid ,content>80%
	0/0/0	4	0	0	0	0	0	0//0	0/0/			0/0/0	Other acetic acid
4.4	0/0/0	0	0	0	0	0	0	0//0	0/0/			0/0/0	--Acetic anhydride
													--Other:
	0/0/0	4	0	0	0	0	0	0//0	0/0/			0/0/0	---Sodium acetate
													---Other
	0/0/0	4	2.2	0	0	0	0	0//0	0/0/			0/0/0	Copper acetate
	0/0/0	4	2.2	0	0	0	0	0//0	0/0/			0/0/0	Lead acetate
	0/0/0	4	2.2	0	0	0	0	0//0	0/0/			0/0/0	Other Salts of acetate acid
													-Esters of acetic acid:
	0/0/0	4	0	0	0	0	0	0//0	0/0/			0/0/0	--Ethyl acetate
	0/0/0	4	0	0	0	0	0	0//0	0/0/0			0/0/0	--Vinyl acetate
	0/0/0	0	3.3	0	0	0	0	0//0	0/0/			0/0/0	--*n*-Butyl acetate
	0/0/0	4	0	0	0	0	0	0//0	0/0/			0/0/0	--Dinoseb (ISO) acetate acid
													--Other
	0/0/0	4	3.3	1.7	0	0	0	0//0	0/0/			0/0/0	Acetofenate
	0/0/0	4	3.3	1.7	0	0	0	0//0	0/0/			0/0/0	Dinoterb acetate
	0/0/0	4	3.3	1.7	0	0	0	0//0	0/0/			0/0/0	Acequinocy
	0/0/0	4	3.3	1.7	0	0	0	0//0	0/0/			0/0/0	11-Hexadecadien-l-Yl acetate
	0/0/0	4	3.3	1.7	0	0	0	0//0	0/0/			0/0/0	Fenitropan
	0/0/0	4	3.3	1.7	0	0	0	0//0	0/0/			0/0/0	Other esters of acetic acid
													-Mono-, di- or trichloroacetic acids, their salts and esters
	0/0/0	4	0	0	0	0	0	0//0	0/0/			0/0/0	Sodium monochloracetate
	0/0/0	4	0	0	0	0	0	0//0	0/0/			0/0/0	Other mono-, di-or trichloroacetic acids, their salts and esters
													-Propionic acid, its salts and esters:
	0/0/0	4	0	0	0	0	0	0//0	0/0/			0/0/0	---Propionic acid
	0/0/0	4	3.3	0	0	0	0	0//0	0/0/			0/0/0	---Other
	0/0/0	4	2.2	0	0	0	0	0//0	0/0/			0/0/0	-Butanoic acids, pentanoic acids, their salts and esters
													-Palmitic acid, stearic acid, their salts and esters:
	0/0/0	4	0	0	0	0	0	0//0	0/0/			0/0/0	---Stearic acid
	0/0/0	4	3.3	0	0	0	0	0//0	0/0/			0/0/0	---Other
													-Other
	0/0/0	0	0	1.7	0	0	0	0//0	0/0/			0/0/0	Dalapon
	0/0/0	0	0	1.7	0	0	0	0//0	0/0/			0/0/0	Erbon
	0/0/0	0	0	1.7	0	0	0	0//0	0/0/			0/0/0	Flupropanate
	0/0/0	0	0	1.7	0	0	0	0//0	0/0/			0/0/0	Sodium fluoroacetate
	0/0/0	0	0	1.7	0	0	0	0//0	0/0/			0/0/0	Other saturaed acyclic monocarboxylic acids and their anhydrides, halides, peroxides and peroxyacids; their halogenated, sulphonated, nitrated or nitrosated derivatives
													Unsaturated acyclic monocarboxylic acids, cyclic monocarboxylic acids, their anhydrides, halides, peroxides and peroxyacids; their halogenated, sulphonated, nitrated or nitrosated derivatives:

税则号列		货品名称〔CIQ扩展编码及品名－T2表示见附表2〕	最惠(%)	暂定税率	普通	增值/消费	出口退税	计量单位	监管条件	检验检疫	特殊证件对美关税
		-不饱和无环一元羧酸及其酸酐、酰卤化物、过氧化物和过氧酸以及它们的衍生物：									
2916.1100		--丙烯酸及其盐〔301 腐蚀性物质,302 其他化工产品〕	6.5		30	13/	10	千克			1/31.5
		--丙烯酸酯：									
2916.1210		---丙烯酸甲酯〔999〕	6.5		30	13/	10	千克	AB	MN	1/
2916.1220		---丙烯酸乙酯〔301〕	6.5		30	13/	10	千克	AB	MN	1/16.5
2916.1230		---丙烯酸丁酯									
2916.1230	01	丙烯酸正丁酯〔999〕	6.5		30	13/	10	千克	AB	MN	1/11.5
2916.1230	90	丙烯酸异丁酯〔999〕	6.5		30	13/	10	千克	AB	MN	1/11.5
2916.1240		---丙烯酸异辛酯〔999〕	6.5		30	13/	10	千克			1/31.5
2916.1290		---其他〔301 易燃液体,302 腐蚀性物质,303 杂项物质,304 其他化工产品〕	6.5		30	13/	10	千克			1/26.5
2916.1300		--甲基丙烯酸及其盐									
2916.1300	10	甲基丙烯酸〔999〕	6.5		80	13/	13	千克	AB	MN	1/31.5
2916.1300	90	甲基丙烯酸盐〔999〕	6.5		80	13/	13	千克			1/31.5
2916.1400		--甲基丙烯酸酯									
2916.1400	10	甲基丙烯酸甲酯〔301 爆炸品,302 易燃液体〕	6.5		80	13/	13	千克			1/31.5
2916.1400	90	其他甲基丙烯酸酯〔301 爆炸品,302 易燃液体〕	6.5		80	13/	13	千克			1/31.5
2916.1500		--油酸、亚油酸或亚麻酸及其盐和酯〔101 亚麻酸,102 亚油酸,103:亚油酸甲酯(48%)、亚麻酸甲酯(52%)混合物,104 亚油酸乙酯,105 油酸乙酯,106 单,双甘油脂肪酸酯〕	6.5		30	13/	10	千克			1/16.5
2916.1600		--乐杀螨(ISO)〔301〕	6.5		30	13/	0	千克	S		1/
2916.1900		--其他									
2916.1900	11	烯虫乙酯〔999〕	6.5		30	13/	9,10	千克	S		1/16.5
2916.1900	12	烯虫炔酯〔999〕	6.5		30	13/	9,10	千克	S		1/16.5
2916.1900	13	消螨普〔999〕	6.5		30	13/	9,10	千克	S		1/16.5
2916.1900	90	其他不饱和无环一元羧酸(包括其酸酐、酰卤化物、过氧化物和过氧酸及它们的衍生物)[T2]	6.5		30	13/	10	千克	AB	MRNS	1/16.5
		-环烷一元羧酸、环烯一元羧酸或环萜烯一元羧酸及其酸酐、酰卤化物、过氧化物和过氧酸以及它们的衍生物：									
2916.2010		---二溴菊酸、DV 菊酸甲酯〔999〕	4		11	13/	10	千克			1/
2916.2090		---其他									
2916.2090	21	苄菊酯、苯醚菊酯(包括右旋苯醚菊酯、富右旋反式苯醚菊酯)〔999〕	6.5		30	13/	9,10	千克	S		1/31.5
2916.2090	22	苄烯菊酯、氯菊酯(包括生物氯菊酯)〔101 苄氯菊酯乙醇溶液,102 氯氰菊酯,103 丙烯菊酯(含量>30%)〕	6.5		30	13/	9,10	千克	S		1/31.5
2916.2090	23	氯烯炔菊酯、联苯菊酯〔999〕	6.5		30	13/	9,10	千克	S		1/31.5
2916.2090	24	七氟菊酯、四氟苯菊酯、五氟苯菊酯、七氟甲醚酯(包括甲氧苄菊酯、氯氟醚菊酯)〔999〕	6.5		30	13/	9,10	千克	S		1/31.5
2916.2090	25	戊菊酯、环螨酯〔999〕	6.5		30	13/	9,10	千克	S		1/31.5
2916.2090	26	四氟甲醚菊酯、烯炔菊酯、四氟醚菊酯(包括右旋烯炔菊酯、富右旋反式烯炔菊酯)〔999〕	6.5		30	13/	9,10	千克	S		1/31.5
2916.2090	27	炔丙菊酯(包括右旋炔丙菊酯、富右旋反式炔丙菊酯)〔999〕	6.5		30	13/	9,10	千克	S		1/31.5
2916.2090	28	氯丙炔菊酯(包括右旋反式氯丙炔菊酯)〔999〕	6.5		30	13/	9,10	千克	S		1/31.5
2916.2090	90	其他(环烷、环烯、环萜烯)一元羧酸(包括酸酐、酰卤化物、过氧化物和过氧酸及该编号的衍生物)[T2]	6.5		30	13/	10	千克	AB	MRNS	1/31.5
		-芳香一元羧酸及其酸酐、酰卤化物、过氧化物和过氧酸以及它们的衍生物：									
2916.3100		--苯甲酸及其盐和酯[T2]	6.5		30	13/	10	千克	AB	MRNS	1/26.5
2916.3200		--过氧化苯甲酰及苯甲酰氯〔301 其他危险化学品,需申报仅用于工业用途不用于食品添加剂无检疫要求,302 属于危险化学品的食品添加剂〕	6.5		30	13/	10	千克	AB	MRNS	1/31.5
2916.3400		--苯乙酸及其盐									
2916.3400	10	苯乙酸〔101〕	6.5		30	13/	10	千克	23		1/26.5
2916.3400	90	苯乙酸盐〔999〕	6.5		30	13/	10	千克			1/26.5
		--其他：									
2916.3910		---邻甲基苯甲酸〔999〕	6.5		30	13/	10	千克			1/11.5
2916.3920		---布洛芬〔999〕	6.5		30	13/	10	千克			1/16.5
2916.3930		---2-(3-碘-4-乙基苯基)-2-甲基丙酸〔999〕	6.5		30	13/	13	千克			1/
2916.3990		---其他									
2916.3990	12	草芽畏、燕麦酯〔999〕	6.5		30	13/	9,10	千克	S		1/16.5
2916.3990	13	5-硝基邻甲氧基苯酸钠〔999〕	6.5		30	13/	0	千克	S		1/16.5
2916.3990	14	对氯苯氧乙酸及其盐〔999〕	6.5		30	13/	9,10	千克	S		1/16.5
2916.3990	15	三碘苯甲酸〔999〕	6.5		30	13/	0	千克	S		1/16.5

协定税率 %										特惠税率 %			Article Description
亚太5国	东/冰/格	巴基斯坦	韩国	瑞士	哥达	秘鲁	澳大利亚	新西/坡/智	港/澳/台	亚太2国	老/柬/缅	36/3/1	
													-Unsaturated acyclic monocarboxylic acids, their anhydrides, halides, peroxides, peroxyacids and their derivatives:
	0/0/0		3.9	0	0	0	0	0//0	0/0/			0/0/	--Acrylic acid and its salts
													--Esters of acrylic acid:
	0/0/0	4	3.9	3.4	0	0	0	0/0/0	C/0/			0/0/	---Methyl acrylate
	0/0/0	4	3.9	0	0	0	0	0/0/0	0/0/			0/0/	---Ethyl acrylate
													---Butyl achylate
	0/0/0	4		0	0	0	0	0/0/0	0/0/			0/0/	N-butyl acrylate
	0/0/0	4		0	0	0	0	0/0/0	0/0/			0/0/	Iscbutyl acrylate
	0/0/0	4	3.9	0	0	0	0	0/0/0	0/0/			0/0/	---Isooctyl acrylate
	0/0/0	4		0	0	0	0	0/0/0	0/0/			0/0/	---Other
													--Methacrylic acid and its salts
	0/0/0	4	0	0	0	0	0	0//0	0/0/0			0/0/	Methacrylic acid
	0/0/0	4	0	0	0	0	0	0//0	0/C/0			0/0/	Salts of methacrylic acid
													--Esters of methacrylic acid
	0/0/0	0	0	0	0	0	0	0//0	0/0/0			0/0/	Methyl methacrylate
	0/0/0	0	0	0	0	0	0	0//0	0/0/0			0/0/	Other esters of methacrylic acid
	0/0/0	4	3.9	0	0	0	0	0//0	0/C/			0/0/	--Oleic, linoleic or linolenic acids, their salts and esters
	0/0/0	4	0	0	0	0	0	0//0	0/0/			0/0/	--Binapacryl(ISO)
													--Other
	0/0/0	4	0		0	0	0	0//0	0/0/			0/0/	Hydroprene
	0/0/0	4	0		0	0	0	0//0	0/0/			0/0/	Kinoprene
	0/0/0	4	0		0	0	0	0//0	0/0/			0/0/	Dinocap
	0/0/0	4	0		0	0	0	0//0	0/0/			0/0/	Other unsaturated acyclic monocarboxylic acids, their anhydrides, halides, peroxides, peroxyacids and their derivatives
													-Cyclanic, cyclenic or cycloterpenic monocarboxylic acids, their anhydrides, halides, peroxides, peroxyacids and their derivatives:
	0/0/0	0	0	0	0	0	0	0//0	0/0/			0/0/	---Dibromochrysanthemicacid, DV chrysanthemimono carboxylate
													---Other
	0/0/0	4	0	3.4	0	0	0	0//0	0/0/			0/0/	Dimethirn , Phenothrin (including d-phenothrin, rich-d-trans-phenothrin)
	0/0/0	4	0	3.4	0	0	0	0//0	0/0/			0/0/	Butethrin, Permethrin(including biopermethrin)
	0/0/0	4	0	3.4	0	0	0	0//0	0/0/			0/0/	Chlorempenthrin , Bifenthrin
	0/0/0	4	0	3.4	0	0	0	0//0	0/0/			0/0/	Tefluthrin, transfluthrin, fenfluthrin, methothrin heptafluoride (including matofluthrin)
	0/0/0	4	0	3.4	0	0	0	0//0	0/0/			0/0/	Valerate, cyclopropate
	0/0/0	4	0	3.4	0	0	0	0//0	0/0/			0/0/	Dimefluthrin, empenthrin Four fluorine ethofenprox(including d-empenthrin, rich-d-empenthrin)
	0/0/0	4	0	3.4	0	0	0	0//0	0/0/			0/0/	Prallethrin(including d-prallethrin、rich-d-t-prallethrin)
	0/0/0	4	0	3.4	0	0	0	0//0	0/0/			0/0/	Chlorpromazine acetylene permethrin (including d-trans-permethrin chlorpromazine acetylene)
	0/0/0	4	0	3.4	0	0	0	0//0	0/0/			0/0/	Other cyclanic, cyclenic or cycloterpenic monocarboxylic acids, their anhydrides, halides, peroxides, peroxyacids and their derivatives
													-Aromatic monocarboxylic acids, their anhydrides, halides, peroxides, peroxyacids and their derivatives:
	0/0/0	4	2.6		0	0	0	0//0	0/0/			0/0/	--Benzoic acid, its salts and esters
	0/0/0	4	2.6	0	0	0	0	0//0	0/0/			0/0/	--Benzoyl peroxide and benzoyl chloride
													--Phenylacetic acid and its salts
	0/0/0	4	0		0	0	0	0//0	0/0/			0/0/	Phenylacetic acid
	0/0/0	4	0		0	0	0	0//0	0/0/			0/0/	Salts of phenylacetic acid
													--Other:
	0/0/0	4	0	0	0	0	0	0//0	0/0/			0/0/	---*m*-Methylbenzoic acid
	0/0/0	4	0	0	0	0	0	0//0	0/0/			0/0/	---Brufen (Ibuprofen)
	0/0/0	4	0	3.4	0	0	0	0//0	0/0/			0/0/	---4- (4-Alkoxyphenyl) -4'-alkenyne-1, 1'-bicyclohexane and its fluorinated derivatives
													---Other
	0/0/0	4	0	3.4	0	0	0	0//0	0/0/			0/0/	2,3,6-TAB, methachlorphenprop
	0/0/0	4	0	3.4	0	0	0	0//0	0/0/			0/0/	5-Sodium nitro-o-methoxy-benzene
	0/0/0	4	0	3.4	0	0	0	0//0	0/0/			0/0/	p-Chlorophenoxyacetic acid and its salt
	0/0/0	4	0	3.4	0	0	0	0//0	0/0/			0/0/	Triiodobenzoic acid

税则号列	货品名称〔CIQ 扩展编码及品名－T2 表示见附表 2〕	最惠(%)	暂定税率	普通	增值/消费	出口退税	计量单位	监管条件	检验检疫	特殊证件对美关税
2916.3990 16	萘乙酸〔999〕	6.5		30	13/	9,10	千克	S		1/16.5
2916.3990 17	伐草克〔999〕	6.5		30	13/	9,10	千克	S		1/16.5
2916.3990 18	α-萘乙酸及其盐〔999〕	6.5		30	13/	9,10	千克	S		1/16.5
2916.3990 90	其他芳香一元羧酸[T2]	6.5		30	13/	10	千克			1/16.5
29.17	**多元羧酸及其酸酐、酰卤化物、过氧化物和过氧酸以及它们的卤化、磺化、硝化或亚硝化衍生物：**									
	-无环多元羧酸及其酸酐、酰卤化物、过氧化物和过氧酸以及它们的衍生物：									
	--草酸及其盐和酯：									
2917.1110	---草酸〔999〕	6.5		40	13/	10	千克			1/26.5
2917.1120	---草酸钴〔999〕	9		30	13/	10	千克	4xy		1/
2917.1190	---其他〔301 其他危险化学品，302 需申报仅用于工业用途不用于食品添加剂无检疫要求的化学品〕	6.5		30	13/	10	千克			1/11.5
2917.1200	--己二酸及其盐和酯									
2917.1200 01	己二酸〔301 无检疫要求食品添加剂〕	6.5		30	13/	13	千克	A	R	1/31.5
2917.1200 90	己二酸盐和酯〔999，301 无检疫要求食品添加剂，302 需申报仅用于工业用途不用于食品添加剂无检疫要求的化学品，303 其他化工产品〕	6.5		30	13/	13	千克	A	R	1/31.5
	--壬二酸、癸二酸及其盐和酯：									
2917.1310	---癸二酸及其盐和酯〔999〕	6.5		30	13/	10	千克			1/31.5
2917.1390	---其他〔999〕	6.5		30	13/	10	千克			1/11.5
2917.1400	--马来酐〔999〕	6.5		30	13/	10	千克			1/31.5
2917.1900	--其他									
2917.1900 10	驱虫特、硝苯菌酯〔999〕	6.5		30	13/	0	千克	S		1/16.5
2917.1900 90	其他无环多元羧酸〔101 饲料添加剂，301 有机过氧化物，302 毒性物质和感染性物质，303 其他化工产品〕	6.5		30	13/	10	千克			1/16.5
	-环烷多元羧酸、环烯多元羧酸、环萜烯多元羧酸及其酸酐、酰卤化物、过氧化物和过氧酸以及它们的衍生物：									
2917.2010	---四氢苯酐〔999〕	4		11	13/	10	千克			1/29
2917.2090	---其他									
2917.2090 10	驱蚊灵〔999〕	6.5		30	13/	0	千克	S		1/26.5
2917.2090 90	其他(环烷、环烯、环萜烯)多元羧酸[T2]	6.5		30	13/	10	千克	AB	MRNS	1/26.5
	-芳香多元羧酸及其酸酐、酰卤化物、过氧化物和过氧酸以及它们的衍生物：									
2917.3200	--邻苯二甲酸二辛酯〔999〕	6.5		30	13/	10	千克			1/31.5
2917.3300	--邻苯二甲酸二壬酯及邻苯二甲酸二癸酯〔999〕	6.5		30	13/	10	千克			1/16.5
	--其他邻苯二甲酸酯：									
2917.3410	---邻苯二甲酸二丁酯									
2917.3410 10	驱蚊叮〔999〕	6.5		30	13/	0	千克	S		1/26.5
2917.3410 90	其他邻苯二甲酸二丁酯〔301 杂项物质，302 其他化工产品〕	6.5		30	13/	10	千克			1/26.5
2917.3490	---其他〔999〕	6.5		30	13/	10	千克			1/16.5
2917.3500	--邻苯二甲酸酐〔301 腐蚀性物质，302 其他化工产品〕	6.5		30	13/	10	千克	AB	MN	1/
	--对苯二甲酸及其盐：									
	---对苯二甲酸：									
2917.3611	----精对苯二甲酸〔999〕	6.5		30	13/	13	千克			1/31.5
2917.3619	----其他〔999〕	6.5		30	13/	10	千克			1/31.5
2917.3690	---其他〔999〕	6.5		30	13/	10	千克			1/11.5
2917.3700	--对苯二甲酸二甲酯〔999〕	6.5		30	13/	10	千克			1/31.5
	--其他：									
2917.3910	---间苯二甲酸〔999〕	6.5		30	13/	10	千克			1/31.5
2917.3990	---其他									
2917.3990 11	酞菌酯〔999〕	6.5		30	13/	9,10	千克	S		1/26.5
2917.3990 12	氯酞酸甲酯〔999〕	6.5		30	13/	9,10	千克	S		1/26.5
2917.3990 13	氯酞酸〔999〕	6.5		30	13/	9,10	千克	S		1/26.5
2917.3990 90	其他芳香多元羧酸〔301 易燃固体，302 腐蚀性物质，303 其他危险化学品，304 其他化工产品〕	6.5		30	13/	10	千克			1/26.5
29.18	**含附加含氧基的羧酸及其酸酐、酰卤化物、过氧化物和过氧酸以及它们的卤化、磺化、硝化或亚硝化衍生物：**									
	-含醇基但不含其他含氧基的羧酸及其酸酐、酰卤化物、过氧化物和过氧酸以及它们的衍生物：									
2918.1100	--乳酸及其盐和酯[T2]	6.5		30	13/	13	千克	AB	MRNS	1/26.5
2918.1200	--酒石酸〔101 饲料添加剂，301 无检疫要求食品添加剂，302 需申报仅用于工业用途不用于食品添加剂无检疫要求的化学品〕	6.5		35	13/	10	千克	A	R	1/31.5

协定税率 %										特惠税率 %			
亚太5国	东/冰/格	巴基斯坦	韩国	瑞士	哥达	秘鲁	澳大利亚	新西/坡/智	港/澳/台	亚太2国	老/柬/缅	36/3/1	Article Description
	0/0/0	4	0	3.4	0	0	0	0//0	0/0/			0/0/	Naphthylacetic acid
	0/0/0	4	0	3.4	0	0	0	0//0	0/0/			0/0/	Chlorfenac
	0/0/0	4	0	3.4	0	0	0	0//0	0/0/			0/0/	α-Naphthylacetic acid and its salt
	0/0/0	4	0	3.4	0	0	0	0//0	0/0/			0/0/	Other aromatic monocarboxylic acids
													Polycarboxylic acids, their anhydrides, halides, peroxides and peroxyacids; their halogenated, sulphonated, nitrated or nitrosated derivatives:
													-Acyclic polycarboxylic acids, their anhydrides, halides, peroxides, peroxyacids and their derivatives:
													--Oxalic acid, its salts and esters:
	0/0/0	4	2.6	0	0	0	0	0//0	0/0/			0/0/	---Oxalic acid
	0/0/0	4	0	0	0	0	0	0//0	0/0/			0/0/	---Cobalt oxalate
	0/0/0	4	2.6	0	0	0	0	0//0	0/0/			0/0/	---Other
													--Adipic acid, its salts and esters
	0/0/0	4		0	0	0	0	0//0	0/0/			0/0/	Adipic acid
	0/0/0	4		0	0	0	0	0//0	0/0/			0/0/	Adipic acid, its salts and esters
													--Azelaic acid, sebacic acid, their salts and esters:
	0/0/0	4	3.9	0	0	0	0	0//0	C/0/			0/0/	---Sebacic acid, its salts and esters
5.2	0/0/0	4	0	0	0	0	0	0//0	C/0/			0/0/	---Other
	0/0/0	4	2.6	0	0	0	0	0//0	C/0/			0/0/	--Maleic anhydride
													--Other
	0/0/0	4	0	0	0	0	0	0//0	C/0/			0/0/	Dibutyl succinate, nifedipinestrobin
	0/0/0	4	0	0	0	0	0	0//0	C/0/			0/0/	Other acyclic pohycarboxylic acid
													-Cyclanic, cyclenic or cycloterpenic polycarboxylic acids, their anhydrides, halides, peroxides, peroxyacids and their derivatives:
	0/0/0	0	2.4	0	0	0	0	0//0	C/0/			0/0/	---Tetrahydro benzoic anhydride
													---Other
	0/0/0	4	3.9	0	0	0	0	0//0	C/0/			0/0/	Dimethyl carbate
	0/0/0	4	3.9	0	0	0	0	0//0	C/0/			0/0/	Other cyclanic, cyclenic or cycloterpenic) polycarboxylic acids
													-Aromatic polycarboxylic acids, their anhydrides, halides, peroxides, peroxyacids and their derivatives:
	0/0/0	0		0	0	0	0	0//0	0/0/0			0/0/	--Dioctyl orthophthalates
	0/0/0	4	0	0	0	0	0	0//0	0/0/0			0/0/	--Dinonyl or didecyl orthophthalates
													--Other esters of orthaphthalic acid:
													---Dibutyl orthophthalates
	0/0/0	4	2.6	0	0	0	0	0//0	C/0/			0/0/	Dinbutyl phthalate
	0/0/0	4	2.6	0	0	0	0	0//0	C/0/			0/0/	Other phthalic acid dibutyl ester
	0/0/0	4	0	0	0	0	0	0//0	0/0/0			0/0/	---Other
	0/0/0	0		0	0	0	0	0//0	C/0/			0/0/	--Phthalic anhydride
													--Terephthalic acid and its salts:
													---Tere phthalic acid:
6	0/0/	0		3.4	0		0	0/0/0	C/0/			0/0/	----Purified terephthalic acid
6	0/0/2.6	0		3.4	0	0	0	0/0/0	C/0/			0/0/	----Other
	0/0/0	4		0	0	0	0	0//0	C/0/			0/0/	---Other
	0/0/0	4	3.9	0	0	0	0	0//0	C/0/			0/0/	--Dimethyl terephthalate
													--Other:
	0/0/0	0		0	0	0	0	0//0	C/0/			0/0/	---*m*-Phthalic acid
													---Other
	0/0/0	0	3.9	0	0	0	0	0//0	C/0/			0/0/	Nitrotalisopropyl
	0/0/0	0	3.9	0	0	0	0	0//0	C/0/			0/0/	Chlorthal-dimethyl
	0/0/0	0	3.9	0	0	0	0	0//0	C/0/			0/0/	Chlorthal
	0/0/0	0	3.9	0	0	0	0	0//0	C/0/			0/0/	Other aromatic polycarboxylic acid
													Carboxylic acids with additional oxygen function and their anhydrides, halides, peroxides and peroxyacids; their halogenated, sulphonated, nitrated or nitrosated derivatives:
													-Carboxylic acids with alcohol function but without other oxygen function, their anhydrides, halides, peroxides, peroxyacids and their derivatives:
	0/0/0	4	2.6	0	0	0	0	0//0	C/0/			0/0/	--Lactic acid, its salts and esters
	0/0/0	4	0	0	0	0	0	0//0	C/0/			0/0/	--Tartaric acid

税则号列	货品名称〔CIQ扩展编码及品名—T2表示见附表2〕	最惠(%)	暂定税率	普通	增值/消费	出口退税	计量单位	监管条件	检验检疫	特殊证件对美关税
2918.1300	--酒石酸盐及酒石酸酯〔301 毒性物质和感染性物质,302 无检疫要求食品添加剂,303 属于危险化学品的食品添加剂,304 一般化工品〕	6.5		30	13/	10	千克	AB	MRNS	1/31.5
2918.1400	--柠檬酸〔101 饲料添加剂,102 无检疫要求食品添加剂,103 需申报仅用于工业用途不用于食品添加剂无检疫要求的化学品〕	6.5		35	13/	13	千克	4Axy	R	1/26.5
2918.1500	--柠檬酸盐及柠檬酸酯〔101 饲料添加剂,301 无检疫要求食品添加剂,302 需申报仅用于工业用途不用于食品添加剂无检疫要求的化学品〕	6.5		30	13/	13	千克	4Axy	R	1/16.5
2918.1600	--葡糖酸及其盐和酯〔101 葡萄糖酸钙,102 葡萄糖酸锌,103 葡萄糖酸亚铁,104 葡萄糖酸钠〕	6.5		30	13/	13	千克			1/16.5
2918.1700	--2,2-二苯基-2-羟基乙酸(二苯基乙醇酸)〔999〕	6.5		30	13/	10	千克	23		1/
2918.1800	--乙酯杀螨醇(ISO)〔301 毒性物质和感染性物质〕	6.5		30	13/	0	千克	S		1/
2918.1900	--其他									
2918.1900 10	二苯乙醇酸甲酯(包括其酸酐,酰卤化物,过氧化物和过氧酸及其衍生物)〔999〕	6.5		30	13/	10	千克	23		1/16.5
2918.1900 30	γ-羟基丁酸及其盐〔999〕	6.5		30	13/	10	千克	I		1/16.5
2918.1900 41	丙酯杀螨醇〔999〕	6.5		30	13/	0	千克	S		1/16.5
2918.1900 42	溴螨酯〔999〕	6.5		30	13/	9,10	千克	S		1/16.5
2918.1900 43	莠丁酯〔999〕	6.5		30	13/	9,10	千克	S		1/16.5
2918.1900 44	整形醇〔999〕	6.5		30	13/	9,10	千克	S		1/16.5
2918.1900 90	其他含醇基但不含其他含氧基羧酸(包括其酸酐,酰卤化物,过氧化物和过氧酸及其衍生物)〔999 毒害品,101 饲料添加剂〕	6.5		30	13/	10	千克			1/16.5
	-含酚基但不含其他含氧基的羧酸及其酸酐、酰卤化物、过氧化物和过氧酸以及它们的衍生物:									
	--水杨酸及其盐:									
2918.2110	---水杨酸、水杨酸钠〔999〕	6.5		20	13/	10	千克			1/26.5
2918.2190	---其他〔999〕	6.5		30	13/	10	千克			1/16.5
	--邻乙酰水杨酸及其盐和酯:									
2918.2210	---邻乙酰水杨酸(阿司匹林)〔999〕	6		20	13/	10	千克			1/11
2918.2290	---其他〔999〕	6.5		30	13/	10	千克			1/
2918.2300	--水杨酸的其他酯及其盐〔101 水杨酸苯乙酯,102 水杨酸苯酯,103 水杨酸苄酯(柳酸苄酯),104 水杨酸甲酯(柳酸甲酯),105 水杨酸乙酯(柳酸乙酯),106 水杨酸异丁酯,107 水杨酸异戊酯(柳酸异戊酯),108 柳酸丁酯(水杨酸丁酯)〕	6.5		30	13/	13	千克			1/11.5
2918.2900	--其他〔301 无检疫要求食品添加剂,302 需申报仅用于工业用途不用于食品添加剂无检疫要求的化学品〕	6.5		30	13/	10	千克	A	R	1/31.5
2918.3000	-含醛基或酮基但不含其他含氧基的羧酸及其酸酐、酰卤化物、过氧化物和过氧酸以及它们的衍生物									
2918.3000 11	除虫菊素 I、除虫菊素 II〔999〕	6.5		30	13/	9,13	千克	S		1/16.5
2918.3000 12	瓜叶菊素 I、瓜叶菊素 II〔999〕	6.5		30	13/	9,13	千克	S		1/16.5
2918.3000 13	茉酮菊素 I、茉酮菊素 II〔999〕	6.5		30	13/	9,13	千克	S		1/16.5
2918.3000 14	环戊烯丙菊酯〔999〕	6.5		30	13/	9,13	千克	S		1/16.5
2918.3000 15	调环酸、抗倒酯、环虫菊酯〔999〕	6.5		30	13/	9,13	千克	S		1/16.5
2918.3000 16	烯丙菊酯等(包括右旋烯丙菊酯、富右旋反式烯丙菊酯,右旋反式烯丙菊酯)〔999〕	6.5		30	13/	9,13	千克	S		1/16.5
2918.3000 17	Es-生物烯丙菊酯、生物烯丙菊酯等(包括 S-生物烯丙菊酯)〔999〕	6.5		30	13/	9,13	千克	S		1/16.5
2918.3000 18	乙酰氟菊酯〔999〕	6.5		30	13/	9,13	千克	S		1/16.5
2918.3000 90	其他含醛基或酮基不含其他含氧基羧酸(包括酸酐、酰卤化物、过氧化物和过氧酸及其衍生物)[T2]	6.5		30	13/	13	千克			1/16.5
	-其他:									
2918.9100	--2,4,5-涕(ISO)(2,4,5-三氯苯氧乙酸)及其盐或酯〔301 毒性物质和感染性物质〕	6.5		30	13/	0	千克	89		1/
2918.9900	--其他									
2918.9900 21	2,4-滴、2,4-滴丙酸、2,4-滴丁酸等(包括精 2,4-滴丙酸、苯醚菌酯)〔301 毒性物质和感染性物质〕	6.5		30	13/	9,13	千克	S		1/16.5
2918.9900 22	2 甲 4 氯、2 甲 4 氯丙酸等(包括精 2 甲 4 氯丙酸)〔101:2 甲 4 氯,102:2 甲 4 氯丙酸,103:除草佳,104:2 甲 4 氯乳剂(含量＞35%,105:2 甲 4 氯丙酸乳剂(含量＞30%)〕	6.5		30	13/	9,13	千克	S		1/16.5
2918.9900 23	2 甲 4 氯丁酸〔999〕	6.5		30	13/	9,13	千克	S		1/16.5
2918.9900 24	麦草畏、杀草畏〔101 杀草畏(含量＞60%),102 麦草畏,103 杀草畏乳剂(含量＞50%),104 麦草畏乳剂(含量＞50%)〕	6.5		30	13/	9,13	千克	S		1/16.5
2918.9900 25	禾草灵、乳氟禾草灵〔999〕	6.5		30	13/	9,13	千克	S		1/16.5

亚太5国	东/冰/格	巴基斯坦	韩国	瑞士	哥达	秘鲁	澳大利亚	新西/坡/智	港/澳/台	亚太2国	老/柬/缅	36/3/1	Article Description
协定税率 %										特惠税率 %			
	0/0/0	4	0	0	0	0	0	0//0	0/0/			0/0/	--Salts and esters of tartaric acid
	0/0/0	4	2.6	0	0	0	0	0//0	0/0/			0/0/	--Citric acid
	0/0/0	4	0	0	0	0	0	0//0	0/0/			0/0/	--Salts and esters of citric acid
	0/0/0	4	0	0	0	0	0	0//0	0/0/			0/0/	--Gluconic acid, its salts and esters
	0/0/0	4	0	0	0	0	0	0//0	0/0/			0/0/	--2, 2-Dipheny1-2-hydroxyacetic acid (*benzilic acid*)
	0/0/0	4	0	0	0	0	0	0//0	0/0/			0/0/	--Chlorobenzilate(ISO)
													--Other
	0/0/0	4	0	0	0	0	0	0//0	0/0/			0/0/	Methyl benzilate (including their anhydrides, halides, peroxides, peroxyacids and their derivatives)
	0/0/0	4	0	0	0	0	0	0//0	0/0/			0/0/	γ-hydroxybutyric acid and its salts
	0/0/0	4	0	0	0	0	0	0//0	0/0/			0/0/	Acaralate
	0/0/0	4	0	0	0	0	0	0//0	0/0/			0/0/	Bromopropylate
	0/0/0	4	0	0	0	0	0	0//0	0/0/			0/0/	Fluorenol butyl ester
	0/0/0	4	0	0	0	0	0	0//0	0/0/			0/0/	Chlorflurenol
	0/0/0	4	0	0	0	0	0	0//0	0/0/			0/0/	Other carboxylic acids with alcohol function but without other oxygen function(including their anhydrides, etheride, peroxides, peroxyacids and their derivatives
													-Carboxylic acids with phenol function but without other oxygen function, their anhydrides, halides, peroxides, peroxyacids and their derivatives:
													--Salicylic acid and its salts:
	0/0/0	4	2.6	3.4	0	0	0	0//0	0/0/			0/0/	---Salicylic acid and sodium salicylate
	0/0/0	4	0	0	0	0	0	0//0	0/0/			0/0/	---Other
													--*o*-Acetylsalicylic acid, its salts and esters:
	0/0/0	5	0	0	0	0	0	0//0	0/0/			0/0/	---Acetylsalicylic acid
	0/0/0	5	0	0	0	0	0	0//0	0/0/			0/0/	---Other
	0/0/0	4.5	0		0	0	0	0//0	0/0/			0/0/	--Other esters of salicylic acid and their salts
	0/0/0	5	3.9	0	0	0	0	0//0	0/0/			0/0/	--Other
													-Carboxylic acids with aldehyde or ketone function but without other oxygen function, their anhydrides, halides, peroxides, peroxyacids and their derivatives
	0/0/0	5	0	3.4	0	0	0	0//0	0/0/			0/0/	Pyrethrum Ⅰ,Pyrethrum Ⅱ
	0/0/0	5	0	3.4	0	0	0	0//0	0/0/			0/0/	Cinerin Ⅰ,cinerin Ⅱ
	0/0/0	5	0	3.4	0	0	0	0//0	0/0/			0/0/	Jasmplin Ⅰ,Jasmolin Ⅱ
	0/0/0	5	0	3.4	0	0	0	0//0	0/0/			0/0/	Terallethrin
	0/0/0	5	0	3.4	0	0	0	0//0	0/0/			0/0/	Prohexadione, trinexapac-ethyl, cyclethrin
	0/0/0	5	0	3.4	0	0	0	0//0	0/0/			0/0/	Allethrin(including d-allethrin、rich-d-t-allethrin、d-t-allethrin)
	0/0/0	5	0	3.4	0	0	0	0//0	0/0/			0/0/	Es-bioallethrin, bioallethrin(including S-bioallethrin)
	0/0/0	5	0	3.4	0	0	0	0//0	0/0/			0/0/	acetyl-fluthrinate
	0/0/0	5	0	3.4	0	0	0	0//0	0/0/			0/0/	Other carboxylic acid with aldehyde or ketone function but without other oxygen function, their anhydrides, halides, peroxides, peroxyacids and their derivatives
													-Other:
	0/0/0	5	0	0	0	0	0	0//0	0/0/			0/0/	--2,4,5-T(ISO) (2,4,5-trichlorophenoxy acetic acid), ist salts and esters
													--Other
	0/0/0	5	0	3.4	0	0	0	0//0	0/0/			0/0/	2,4-d, 2,4-dichlorprop-p, 2,4-embutox(including J-2,4-ichlorprop-p)
	0/0/0	5	0	3.4	0	0	0	0//0	0/0/			0/0/	MCPA, Mecoprop (including mecoprop-P)
	0/0/0	5	0	3.4	0	0	0	0//0	0/0/			0/0/	MCPA butyric acid
	0/0/0	5	0	3.4	0	0	0	0//0	0/0/			0/0/	Dicamba, tricamba
	0/0/0	5	0	3.4	0	0	0	0//0	0/0/			0/0/	Diclofop, lactofen

税则号列	货品名称〔CIQ扩展编码及品名—T2表示见附表2〕	最惠(%)	暂定税率	普通	增值/消费	出口退税	计量单位	监管条件	检验检疫	特殊证件对美关税
2918.9900 26	氟萘禾草灵、甲羧除草醚〔999〕	6.5		30	13/	9,13	千克	S		1/16.5
2918.9900 27	三氟羧草醚、乙羧氟草醚〔999〕	6.5		30	13/	9,13	千克	S		1/16.5
2918.9900 28	氟乳醚、调果酸、座果酸〔999〕	6.5		30	13/	9,13	千克	S		1/16.5
2918.9900 29	增糖酯、S—诱抗素(包括烯虫酯)〔999〕	6.5		30	13/	9,13	千克	S		1/16.5
2918.9900 30	调环酸钙〔999〕	6.5		30	13/	13	千克	S		1/16.5
2918.9900 41	2甲4氯异辛酯〔999〕	6.5		30	13/	9,13	千克	S		1/16.5
2918.9900 90	其他含其他附加含氧基羧酸(包括其酸酐、酰卤化物、过氧化物和过氧酸及其衍生物)〔301有机过氧化物〕	6.5		30	13/	13	千克			1/16.5
	第八分章 非金属无机酸酯及其盐以及它们的卤化、磺化、硝化或亚硝化衍生物									
29.19	**磷酸酯及其盐,包括乳磷酸盐,以及它们的卤化、磺化、硝化或亚硝化衍生物:**									
2919.1000	-三(2,3-二溴丙基)磷酸酯〔999〕	6.5		30	13/	10	千克	89		1/
2919.9000	-其他									
2919.9000 20	磷酸三丁酯〔999〕	6.5		30	13/	10	千克	3		1/26.5
2919.9000 31	敌敌钙,敌敌畏〔301毒性物质和感染性物质〕	6.5		30	13/	9,10	千克	S		1/26.5
2919.9000 32	速灭磷、二溴磷〔301毒性物质和感染性物质〕	6.5		30	13/	9,10	千克	S		1/26.5
2919.9000 33	巴毒磷、杀虫畏〔301毒性物质和感染性物质〕	6.5		30	13/	0	千克	S		1/26.5
2919.9000 34	毒虫畏、甲基毒虫畏〔301毒性物质和感染性物质〕	6.5		30	13/	0	千克	S		1/26.5
2919.9000 35	庚烯磷、特普〔999〕	6.5		30	13/	0	千克	S		1/26.5
2919.9000 36	三乙膦酸铝、乙膦酸〔999〕	6.5		30	13/	9,10	千克	S		1/26.5
2919.9000 37	氯瘟磷、伐草磷〔999〕	6.5		30	13/	0	千克	S		1/26.5
2919.9000 90	其他磷酸酯及其盐(包括乳磷酸盐)(包括它们的卤化、磺化、硝化或亚硝化衍生物)[T2]	6.5		30	13/	9,10	千克	AB	MRNS	1/26.5
29.20	**其他非金属无机酸酯(不包括卤化氢的酯)及其盐,以及它们的卤化、磺化、硝化或亚硝化衍生物:**									
	-硫代磷酸酯及其盐,以及它们的卤化、磺化、硝化或亚硝化衍生物:									
2920.1100	--对硫磷(ISO)及甲基对硫磷(ISO)〔301毒性物质和感染性物质〕	6.5		30	13/	0	千克			1/
2920.1900	--其他									
2920.1900 12	氯氧磷、虫螨畏〔999〕	6.5		30	13/	0	千克	S		1/26.5
2920.1900 13	杀螟硫磷、除线磷〔101杀螟硫磷粉剂、可湿性粉剂,102除线磷(含量＞50%),103杀螟硫磷(含量＞10%),104除线磷乳剂(含量＞10%)〕	6.5		30	13/	9,10	千克	S		1/26.5
2920.1900 14	异氯磷、皮蝇磷〔101异氯磷粉剂、可湿性粉剂,102皮蝇磷粉剂、丸剂、可湿性粉剂,103皮蝇磷乳剂、水混悬剂〕	6.5		30	13/	9,10	千克	S		1/26.5
2920.1900 15	溴硫磷、乙基溴硫磷、硝虫硫磷〔301毒性物质和感染性物质,302其他化工产品〕	6.5		30	13/	9,10	千克	S		1/26.5
2920.1900 17	碘硫磷、苯稻瘟净〔999〕	6.5		30	13/	0	千克	S		1/26.5
2920.1900 18	甲基立枯磷、克菌磷〔999〕	6.5		30	13/	9,10	千克	S		1/26.5
2920.1900 19	速杀硫磷、丰丙磷〔301毒性物质和感染性物质〕	6.5		30	13/	9,10	千克	S		1/26.5
2920.1900 90	其他硫代磷酸酯及其盐(包括它们的卤化、磺化、硝化或亚硝化衍生物)〔301毒性物质和感染性物质,302其他化工产品〕	6.5		30	13/	10	千克			1/26.5
	-亚磷酸酯及其盐,以及它们的卤化、磺化、硝化或亚硝化衍生物:									
2920.2100	--亚磷酸二甲酯〔999〕	6.5		30	13/	10	千克	23		1/
2920.2200	--亚磷酸二乙酯〔999〕	6.5		30	13/	10	千克	23		1/
2920.2300	--亚磷酸三甲酯〔999〕	6.5		30	13/	10	千克	23AB	MN	1/11.5
2920.2400	--亚磷酸三乙酯〔999〕	6.5		30	13/	10	千克	23AB	MN	1/
	--其他:									
2920.2910	---其他亚磷酸酯〔999,301易燃液体,302杂项物质,303其他化工产品,304毒性物质和感染性物质〕	6.5		30	13/	9,10	千克			1/16.5
2920.2990	---其他									
2920.2990 10	浸种磷〔999〕	6.5		30	13/	0	千克	S		1/11.5
2920.2990 90	其他亚磷酸酯及其盐以及它们的卤化、磺化、硝化或亚硝化衍生物〔999,301其他危险化学品,302其他化工产品,303毒性物质和感染性物质〕	6.5		30	13/	10	千克			1/11.5
2920.3000	-硫丹(ISO)〔999〕	6.5		30	13/	0	千克	89		1/
2920.9000	-其他									
2920.9000 11	碳酸二苯酯〔999〕	6.5	2	30	13/	10	千克			1/12
2920.9000 12	治螟磷〔301毒性物质和感染性物质,302其他化工产品〕	6.5		30	13/	0	千克	S		1/16.5
2920.9000 13	消螨通〔999〕	6.5		30	13/	0	千克	S		1/16.5

协定税率 %										特惠税率 %			Article Description
亚太5国	东/冰/格	巴基斯坦	韩国	瑞士	哥达	秘鲁	澳大利亚	新西/坡/智	巷/澳/台	亚太2国	老/柬/缅	36/3/1	
	0/0/0	5	0	3.4	0	0	0	0//0	0/0/			0/0/	Fluoro-naphthalene diclofop, bifenox
	0/0/0	5	0	3.4	0	0	0	0//0	0/0/			0/0/	Acifluorfen, benzofluorfen
	0/0/0	5	0	3.4	0	0	0	0//0	0/0/			0/0/	Ethoxycarbofen, cloprop, cloxyfonac
	0/0/0	5	0	3.4	0	0	0	0//0	0/0/			0/0/	Dicamba-methyl-ester, abscisic acid, ethoxyfen-ethyl (including methoprene)
	0/0/0	5	0	3.4	0	0	0	0//0	0/0/			0/0/	Adjustable calcium sulfonate
	0/0/0	5	0	3.4	0	0	0	0//0	0/0/			0/0/	2 a 4 chloride isooctyl
	0/0/0	5	0	3.4	0	0	0	0//0	0/0/			0/0/	Other carboxylic acids with other additional oxygen function and their anhydrides, halides, peroxides and peroxyacids; their derivatives
													Ⅷ. ESTERS OF INORGANIC ACIDS OF NON-METALS AND THEIR SALTS, AND THEIR HALOGENATED, SULPHONATED, NITRATED OR NITROSATED DERIVATIVES
													Phosphoric esters and their salts, including lactophosphates; their halogenated, sulphonated, nitrated or nitrosated derivatives:
	0/0/0	5	0	0	0	0	0	0//0	0/0/			0/0/	-Tris(2,3-dibromopropyl)phosphate
													-Other
	0/0/0	5	0	0	0	0	0	0//0	0/0/			0/0/	Tributyl phosphate
	0/0/0	5	0	0	0	0	0	0//0	0/0/			0/0/	Calvinphos, dichlorvos
	0/0/0	5	0	0	0	0	0	0//0	0/0/			0/0/	Mevinphos, dibron
	0/0/0	5	0	0	0	0	0	0//0	0/0/			0/0/	Crotoxyphos, tetrachlorvinphos
	0/0/0	5	0	0	0	0	0	0//0	0/0/			0/0/	Chlorfenvinphos, dimethylvinphos
	0/0/0	5	0	0	0	0	0	0//0	0/0/			0/0/	Heptenophos, tepp
	0/0/0	5	0	0	0	0	0	0//0	0/0/			0/0/	Fosetyl-aluminium, phosphonoacetic acid
	0/0/0	5	0	0	0	0	0	0//0	0/0/			0/0/	Phosdiphen, grass-killing phosphate
	0/0/0	5	0	0	0	0	0	0//0	0/0/			0/0/	Other phosphoric esters and their salts, including lactophosphates; their halogenated, sulphonated, nitrated or nitrosated derivatives
													Esters of other inorganic acids of non-metals (excluding esters of hydrogen halides) and their salts; their halogenated, sulphonated, nitrated or nitrosated derivatives:
													-Thiophosphoric esters (phosphorothioates) and their salts; their halogenated, sulphonated, nitrated or nitrosated derivatives:
	0/0/0	5	0	0	0	0	0	0//0	0/0/			0/0/	--Parathion(ISO) and parathion-metlyl(ISO)(methyl-parathion)
													--Other
	0/0/0	5	0	0	0	0	0	0//0	0/0/			0/0/	Chlorethoxyfos, methacrifos
	0/0/0	5	0	0	0	0	0	0//0	0/0/			0/0/	Fenitrothion, dichlofention
	0/0/0	5	0	0	0	0	0	0//0	0/0/			0/0/	Isochlorthion, fenchlorphos
	0/0/0	5	0	0	0	0	0	0//0	0/0/			0/0/	Bromophos, bromofos-ethyl, xiaochongthion
	0/0/0	5	0	0	0	0	0	0//0	0/0/			0/0/	Idofenphos, Benzene rice blast net
	0/0/0	5	0	0	0	0	0	0//0	0/0/			0/0/	Tolclofos-methyl, pyrazophos
	0/0/0	5	0	0	0	0	0	0//0	0/0/			0/0/	Heterophos, apidan
	0/0/0	5	0	0	0	0	0	0//0	0/0/			0/0/	Other thiophosphoric esters (phosphorothioates) and their salts; their halogenated, sulphonated, nitrated or nitrosated derivatives
													-Phosphite esters and their salts; their halogenated, sulphonated, nitrated or nitrosated derivatives:
5.2	0/0/0	5	0	0	0	0	0	0//0	0/0/			0/0/	--Dimethyl phosphite
5.2	0/0/0	5	0	0	0	0	0	0//0	0/0/			0/0/	--Diethyl phosphite
5.2	0/0/0	5	0	0	0	0	0	0//0	0/0/			0/0/	--Trimethyl phosphite
5.2	0/0/0	5	0	0	0	0	0	0//0	0/0/			0/0/	--Triethyl phosphite
													--Other:
	0/0/0	5	0	0	0	0	0	0//0	0/0/			0/0/	---Other Phosphite esters
													---Other
	0/0/0	5	0	0	0	0	0	0//0	0/0/			0/0/	Izopamfos
	0/0/0	5	0	0	0	0	0	0//0	0/0/			0/0/	Phosphite esters and their salts; their halogenated, sulphonated, nitrated or nitrosated derivatives
	0/0/0	5	0	0	0	0	0	0//0	0/0/			0/0/	-Endosulfan (*ISO*)
													-Other
	0/0/0	5	0	0	0	0	0	0//0	0/0/			0/0/	Diphenyl carbonate
	0/0/0	5	0	0	0	0	0	0//0	0/0/			0/0/	Sulfotepp
	0/0/0	5	0	0	0	0	0	0//0	0/0/			0/0/	Dinobuton

税则号列	货品名称〔CIQ 扩展编码及品名—T2 表示见附表 2〕	最惠(%)	暂定税率	普通	增值/消费	出口退税	计量单位	监管条件	检验检疫	特殊证件对美关税
2920.9000　14	炔螨特〔999〕	6.5		30	13/	9,10	千克	S		1/16.5
2920.9000　15	赛松〔999〕	6.5		30	13/	0	千克	S		1/16.5
2920.9000　16	三乙基砷酸酯〔999〕	6.5		30	13/	10	千克			1/16.5
2920.9000　20	太安(PETN)(季戊四醇四硝酸酯)	6.5		30	13/	10	千克	k		1/16.5
2920.9000　90	其他无机酸酯(不包括卤化氢的酯)(包括其盐以及它们的卤化,磺化,硝化或亚硝化衍生物)〔T2〕	6.5		30	13/	10	千克			1/16.5
	第九分章　含氮基化合物									
29.21	**氨基化合物:**									
	-无环单胺及其衍生物,以及它们的盐:									
2921.1100	--甲胺、二甲胺或三甲胺及其盐									
2921.1100　10	二甲胺〔301 易燃气体,302 易燃液体〕	6.5		30	13/	10	千克	23		1/26.5
2921.1100　20	二甲胺盐酸盐〔999〕	6.5		30	13/	10	千克	23		1/26.5
2921.1100　30	甲胺盐〔999〕	6.5		30	13/	10	千克			1/26.5
2921.1100　90	甲胺,三甲胺及其盐,其他二甲胺盐〔301 易燃气体,302 易燃液体,303 其他化工产品〕	6.5		30	13/	10	千克	AB	MN	1/26.5
2921.1200	--2-(N,N-二甲基氨基)氯乙烷盐酸盐〔999〕	6.5		30	13/	10	千克			1/11.5
2921.1300	--2-(N,N-二乙基氨基)氯乙烷盐酸盐〔999〕	6.5		30	13/	10	千克			1/
2921.1400	--2-(N,N-二异丙基氨基)氯乙烷盐酸盐〔999〕	6.5		30	13/	10	千克			1/
	--其他:									
2921.1910	---二正丙胺〔301 易燃液体〕	4		11	13/	10	千克	AB	MN	1/
2921.1920	---异丙胺〔999〕	6.5	2	30	13/	10	千克			1/
2921.1930	---N,N-二(2-氯乙基)乙胺〔999〕	6.5		30	13/	10	千克	32		1/
2921.1940	---N,N-二(2-氯乙基)甲胺〔999〕	6.5		30	13/	10	千克	32		1/
2921.1950	---三(2-氯乙基)胺〔999〕	6.5		30	13/	10	千克	32		1/
2921.1960	---二烷(甲、乙、正丙或异丙)氨基乙基-2-氯及其质子化盐〔999〕	6.5		30	13/	10	千克	23		1/
2921.1990	---其他									
2921.1990　11	三乙胺(单一成分,用做点火剂)〔301〕	6.5		30	13/	10	千克	3A	M	1/16.5
2921.1990　20	二异丙胺〔999〕	6.5		30	13/	10	千克	3		1/16.5
2921.1990　31	2-氨基丁烷〔999〕	6.5		30	13/	0	千克	S		1/16.5
2921.1990　33	胺鲜酯〔999〕	6.5		30	13/	9,10	千克	S		1/16.5
2921.1990　90	其他无环单胺及其衍生物及其盐〔301 易燃气体,302 易燃液体,303 易燃固体,304 毒性物质和感染性物质,305 腐蚀性物质,306 其他化工产品〕	6.5		30	13/	10	千克			1/16.5
	-无环多胺及其衍生物以及它们的盐:									
	--乙二胺及其盐:									
2921.2110	---乙二胺〔999〕	6.5		30	13/	10	千克			1/11.5
2921.2190	---其他〔301〕	6.5		30	13/	10	千克			1/16.5
	--六亚甲基二胺及其盐:									
2921.2210	---己二酸己二胺盐(尼龙-6,6 盐)〔999〕	6.5		20	13/	10	千克			1/
2921.2290	---其他〔301 易燃液体,302 腐蚀性物质〕	6.5		30	13/	10	千克			1/11.5
2921.2900	--其他									
2921.2900　10	辛菌胺〔101 饲料添加剂,301 易燃液体,302 毒性物质和感染性物质,303 腐蚀性物质,304 其他化工产品〕	6.5		30	13/	10	千克	S		1/16.5
2921.2900　90	其他无环多胺及其衍生物(包括它们的盐)〔101 饲料添加剂,301 易燃液体,302 毒性物质和感染性物质,303 腐蚀性物质,304 其他化工产品〕	6.5		30	13/	10	千克			1/16.5
2921.3000	-环烷单胺或多胺、环烯单胺或多胺、环萜烯单胺或多胺及其衍生物以及它们的盐									
2921.3000　10	丙己君及其盐〔999〕	6.5		30	13/	10	千克	I		1/26.5
2921.3000　30	氨基羧酸环丙烷〔999〕	6.5		30	13/	9,10	千克	S		1/26.5
2921.3000　40	乙撑亚胺〔999〕	6.5		30	13/	10	千克	AB	MN	1/26.5
2921.3000　90	其他环(烷、烯、萜烯)单胺或多胺(包括其衍生物及它们的盐)〔301 易燃液体,302 易燃固体,303 毒性物质和感染性物质,304 腐蚀性物质,305 其他化工产品〕	6.5		30	13/	10	千克			1/26.5
	-芳香单胺及其衍生物以及它们的盐:									
	--苯胺及其盐:									
2921.4110	---苯胺〔999〕	6.5		20	13/	10	千克	AB	MN	1/
2921.4190	---其他〔999〕	6.5		30	13/	10	千克			1/
2921.4200	--苯胺衍生物及其盐									
2921.4200　12	敌锈钠〔999〕	6.5		30	13/	9,10	千克	S		1/31.5
2921.4200　13	苯草醚〔999〕	6.5		30	13/	9,10	千克	S		1/31.5
2921.4200　20	邻氯对硝基苯胺〔999〕	6.5		30	13/	10	千克			1/31.5

协定税率 %										特惠税率 %			
亚太5国	东/冰/格	巴基斯坦	韩国	瑞士	哥达	秘鲁	澳大利亚	新西/坡/智	港/澳/台	亚太2国	老/柬/缅	36/3/1	Article Description
	0/0/0	5	0	0	0	0	0	0//0	0/0/			0/0/	Propargite
	0/0/0	5	0	0	0	0	0	0//0	0/0/			0/0/	Sesone
	0/0/0	5	0	0	0	0	0	0//0	0/0/			0/0/	Triethyl arsenate
	0/0/0	5	0	0	0	0	0	0//0	0/0/		//	0/0/	PETN (Pentaerythritol Tetranitrate)
	0/0/0	5	0	0	0	0	0	0//0	0/0/			0/0/	Other Esters of other inorganic acids(excluding esters of hydrogen halides(and their salts; their halogenated, ulphonated, nitrated or nitrosated derivatives
													Ⅸ. NITROGEN-FUNCTION COMPOUNDS
													Amine-function compounds:
													-Acyclic monoamines and their derivatives; salts thereof:
													--Methylamine, di- or trimethylamine and their salts
	0/0/0	5	0	0	0	0	0	0//0	0/0/			0/0/	Dimethylamine
	0/0/0	5	0	0	0	0	0	0//0	0/0/			0/0/	Dimethylamine hydrochloride
	0/0/0	5	0	0	0	0	0	0//0	0/0/			0/0/	Salts of methylamine
	0/0/0	5	0	0	0	0	0	0//0	0/0/			0/0/	Methylamine, trimethylamine and their salts
	0/0/0	5	0	0	0	0	0	0//0	0/0/			0/0/	--2-(*N,N-Dimethylamino*)ethylchloride hydrochloride
	0/0/0	5	0	0	0	0	0	0//0	0/0/			0/0/	--2-(*N,N-Diethylamino*)ethylchloride hydrochloride
	0/0/0	5	0	0	0	0	0	0//0	0/0/			0/0/	--2-(*N,N-Diisopropylamino*)ehylchloride hydrochloride
													--Other:
3.6	0/0/0	0	0	0	0	0	0	0//0	0/0/			0/0/	---Di-*n*-propylamine
	0/0/0	5	0	0	0	0	0	0//0	0/0/			0/0/	---Isopropyl amine
5.2	0/0/0	5	0	0	0	0	0	0//0	0/0/			0/0/	---N,N-Bis(2-chloroethyl) ethylamine
5.2	0/0/0	5	0	0	0	0	0	0//0	0/0/			0/0/	---N,N-Bis(2-chloroethyl) methylamine
5.2	0/0/0	5	0	0	0	0	0	0//0	0/0/			0/0/	---Tri-(2-chloroethyl) amine
5.2	0/0/0	5	0	0	0	0	0	0//0	0/0/			0/0/	---N,N-Dialkyl (Me, Et, n-Pr or i-Pr) aminoethyl-2-chlorides and corresponking protonated salts
													---Other
	0/0/0	5	0	0	0	0	0	0//0	0/0/			0/0/	Triethylamine(Single component, used for igniter)
	0/0/0	5	0	0	0	0	0	0//0	0/0/			0/0/	Diisopropylamine
	0/0/0	5	0	0	0	0	0	0//0	0/0/			0/0/	2-Amidobutane
	0/0/0	5	0	0	0	0	0	0//0	0/0/			0/0/	Diethyl aminoethyl hexanoate
	0/0/0	5	0	0	0	0	0	0//0	0/0/			0/0/	Other acyclic monoamines and their derivatives; salts thereof
													-Acyclic polyamines and their derivatives; salts thereof:
													--Ethylenediamine and its salts:
	0/0/0	5	3.9	0	0	0	0	0//0	0/0/			0/0/	---Ethylenediamine
	0/0/0	5	2.6	3.4	0	0	0	0//0	0/0/			0/0/	---Other
													--Hexamethylenediamine and its salts:
5.2	0/0/0	5	0	0	0	0	0	0//0	0/0/			0/0/	---Hexamethylene adipamide(nylon-6,6 salt)
	0/0/0	5	2.6	0	0	0	0	0//0	0/0/			0/0/	---Other
													--Other
	0/0/0	0	2.6	0	0	0	0	0//0	0/0/			0/0/	N-octyl-N-[2-(octylamino)]ethyl (lnendiamine)]
	0/0/0	0	2.6	0	0	0	0	0//0	0/0/			0/0/	Other acyclic polyamines and their derivatives (including salts thereof)
													-Cyclanic, cyclenic or cycloterpenic monoor polyamines, and their derivatives; salts thereof
	0/0/0	5	0	0	0	0	0	0//0	0/0/			0/0/	Propylhexedrine and its salts
	0/0/0	5	0	0	0	0	0	0//0	0/0/			0/0/	1-Aminocy-clopropane-1-carboxylic acid(ACC)
	0/0/0	5	0	0	0	0	0	0//0	0/0/			0/0/	Ethylenimine
	0/0/0	5	0	0	0	0	0	0//0	0/0/			0/0/	Other cyclanic, cyclenic or cycloterpenic monoor polyamines, and their derivatives; salts thereof
													-Aromatic monoamines and their derivatives; salts thereof:
													--Aniline and its salts:
5.2	0/0/0	5	0	0	0	0	0	0//0	0/0/			0/0/	---Aniline
	0/0/0	5	0		0	0	0	0//0	0/0/			0/0/	---Other
													--Aniline derivatives and their salts
	0/0/0	0	2.6		0	0	0	0//0	0/0/			0/0/	Sodium-p-aminbenzene sulfonate
	0/0/0	0	2.6		0	0	0	0//0	0/0/			0/0/	Dicloran
	0/0/0	0	2.6		0	0	0	0//0	0/0/			0/0/	OrthoChloro? Para? Nitro? Aniline

税则号列		货品名称〔CIQ 扩展编码及品名－T2 表示见附表 2〕	最惠(%)	暂定税率	普通	增值/消费	出口退税	计量单位	监管条件	检验检疫	特殊证件对美关税
2921.4200	90	其他苯胺衍生物及其盐〔301 爆炸品,302 易燃液体,303 易于自燃的物质,304 毒性物质和感染性物质,305 杂项物质,306 其他危险化学品,307 其他化工产品〕	6.5		30	13/	10	千克			1/31.5
2921.4300		--甲苯胺及其衍生物以及它们的盐									
2921.4300	01	间甲苯胺或对甲苯胺〔999〕	6.5		30	13/	10	千克			1/26.5
2921.4300	10	氟乐灵〔999〕	6.5		30	13/	9,10	千克	S		1/26.5
2921.4300	20	邻甲苯胺〔999〕	6.5		30	13/	10	千克			1/26.5
2921.4300	31	溴鼠胺〔999〕	6.5		30	13/	0	千克	S		1/26.5
2921.4300	32	乙丁氟灵〔999〕	6.5		30	13/	9,10	千克	S		1/26.5
2921.4300	33	氯乙氟灵〔999〕	6.5		30	13/	9,10	千克	S		1/26.5
2921.4300	34	环丙氟灵〔999〕	6.5		30	13/	9,10	千克	S		1/26.5
2921.4300	35	乙丁烯氟灵〔999〕	6.5		30	13/	9,10	千克	S		1/26.5
2921.4300	36	地乐灵〔999〕	6.5		30	13/	9,10	千克	S		1/26.5
2921.4300	37	氯乙灵〔999〕	6.5		30	13/	9,10	千克	S		1/26.5
2921.4300	38	氟节胺〔999〕	6.5		30	13/	9,10	千克	S		1/26.5
2921.4300	90	甲苯胺盐、甲苯胺衍生物及其盐〔301 毒性物质和感染性物质,302 其他危险化学品,303 其他化工产品〕	6.5		30	13/	10	千克			1/26.5
2921.4400		--二苯胺及其衍生物以及它们的盐〔301 毒性物质和感染性物质,302 腐蚀性物质,303 其他化工产品〕	6.5		30	13/	13	千克			1/31.5
2921.4500		--1-萘胺(α-萘胺)、2-萘胺(β-萘胺)及其衍生物以及它们的盐									
2921.4500	10	2-萘胺〔999〕	6.5		30	13/	10	千克			1/31.5
2921.4500	90	1-萘胺和 2-萘胺的衍生物及盐(包括 1-萘胺)〔111 盐酸－1－萘乙二胺,301 杂项物质,302 其他危险化学品,303 其他化工产品〕	6.5		30	13/	10	千克			1/31.5
2921.4600		--安非他明(INN)、苄非他明(INN)、右苯丙胺(INN)、乙非他明、芬坎法明(INN)、利非他明、左苯丙胺(INN)、美芬雷司(INN)、苯丁胺(INN)以及它们的盐									
2921.4600	11	安非他明、苄非他明、右苯丙胺(包括它们的盐)〔999〕	6.5		30	13/	10	千克	I		1/11.5
2921.4600	12	乙非他明、芬坎法明、利非他明(包括它们的盐)〔999〕	6.5		30	13/	10	千克	I		1/11.5
2921.4600	13	左苯丙胺、美芬雷司、芬特明(包括它们的盐)〔999〕	6.5		30	13/	10	千克	I		1/11.5
		--其他:									
2921.4910		---对异丙基苯胺〔999〕	4		11	13/	13	千克			1/
2921.4920		---二甲基苯胺〔301 毒性物质和感染性物质,302 杂项物质〕	6.5		20	13/	13	千克			1/26.5
2921.4930		---2,6-甲基乙基苯胺〔999〕	4		11	13/	13	千克			1/9
2921.4940		---2,6-二乙基苯胺〔999〕	6.5		20	13/	13	千克			1/
2921.4990		---其他									
2921.4990	11	异丙乐灵〔999〕	6.5		30	13/	9,13	千克	S		1/26.5
2921.4990	12	仲丁灵〔999〕	6.5		30	13/	9,13	千克	S		1/26.5
2921.4990	13	二甲戊灵〔999〕	6.5		30	13/	9,13	千克	S		1/26.5
2921.4990	20	4-氨基联苯〔999〕	6.5		30	13/	13	千克			1/26.5
2921.4990	31	乙环利定,二甲基安非他明(以及它们的盐)〔999〕	6.5		30	13/	13	千克	I		1/26.5
2921.4990	32	芬氟拉明、右旋芬氟拉明(以及它们的盐)〔999〕	6.5		30	13/	13	千克	I		1/26.5
2921.4990	90	其他芳香单胺及衍生物及它们的盐〔301 爆炸品,302 腐蚀性物质,303 杂项物质,304 其他危险化学品,305 其他化工产品〕	6.5		30	13/	13	千克			1/26.5
		-芳香多胺及其衍生物以及它们的盐:									
		--邻-、间-、对-苯二胺、二氨基甲苯及其衍生物以及它们的盐:									
2921.5110		---邻苯二胺〔999〕	4		11	13/	10	千克			1/9
2921.5190		---其他									
2921.5190	11	氨氟灵〔999〕	6.5		30	13/	9,10	千克	S		1/31.5
2921.5190	12	氨氟乐灵〔999〕	6.5		30	13/	9,10	千克	S		1/31.5
2921.5190	20	2,4-二氨基甲苯〔999〕	6.5		30	13/	13	千克			1/31.5
2921.5190	90	间-、对-苯二胺、二氨基甲苯等(包括衍生物及它们的盐)〔301 毒性物质和感染性物质,302 杂项物质,303 其他危险化学品,304 其他化工产品〕	6.5		30	13/	13	千克			1/31.5
2921.5900		--其他									
2921.5900	10	三氨基三硝基苯〔999〕	6.5		30	13/	10	千克	3		1/31.5
2921.5900	20	联苯胺(4,4'-二氨基联苯)〔999〕	6.5		30	13/	10	千克	89		1/31.5
2921.5900	31	4,4'-二氨基-3,3'-二氯二苯基甲烷〔999〕	6.5		30	13/	10	千克			1/31.5
2921.5900	32	3,3'-二氯联苯胺〔999〕	6.5		30	13/	10	千克			1/31.5
2921.5900	33	4,4'-二氨基二苯基甲烷〔999〕	6.5		30	13/	13	千克			1/31.5

协定税率 %										特惠税率 %			
亚太5国	东/冰/格	巴基斯坦	韩国	瑞士	哥达	秘鲁	澳大利亚	新西/坡/智	港/澳/台	亚太2国	老/柬/缅	36/3/1	Article Description
	0/0/0	0	2.6		0	0	0	0//0	0/0/			0/0/	Other aniline derivatives and their salts
													--Toluidines and their derivatives; salts thereof
	0/0/0	5	3.9	0	0	0	0	0//0	0/0/			0/0/	M-toluidine or p-toluidine
	0/0/0	5	3.9	0	0	0	0	0//0	0/0/			0/0/	Trifluralin (TC)
	0/0/0	5	3.9	0	0	0	0	0//0	0/0/			0/0/	*O*-Toluidine
	0/0/0	5	3.9	0	0	0	0	0//0	0/0/			0/0/	Bromethalin
	0/0/0	5	3.9	0	0	0	0	0//0	0/0/			0/0/	Benfluralin
	0/0/0	5	3.9	0	0	0	0	0//0	0/0/			0/0/	Fluchloraline
	0/0/0	5	3.9	0	0	0	0	0//0	0/0/			0/0/	Profluralin
	0/0/0	5	3.9	0	0	0	0	0//0	0/0/			0/0/	Ethalfluralin
	0/0/0	5	3.9	0	0	0	0	0//0	0/0/			0/0/	Dipropalin
	0/0/0	5	3.9	0	0	0	0	0//0	0/0/			0/0/	Chlornidine
	0/0/0	5	3.9	0	0	0	0	0//0	0/0/			0/0/	Flumetralin
	0/0/0	5	3.9	0	0	0	0	0//0	0/0/			0/0/	Toluidines, toluidine derivatives and salts thereof
	0/0/0	5	2.6		0	0	0	0//0	0/0/			0/0/	--Diphenylamine and its derivatives; salts thereof
													--1-Naphthylamine (α-naphthylamine), 2-naphthylamine (β-naphthylamine) and their derivatives; salts thereof
	0/0/0	5	0		0	0	0	0//0	0/0/			0/0/	2-Naphthylamine
	0/0/0	5	0		0	0	0	0//0	0/0/			0/0/	1-Naphthylamine and 2-Naphthylamine and its derivatires salis thereof
													--Amfetamine(INN), benzfetamine(INN), dexamfetamine(INN), etilamfetamine(INN), fencamfamin(INN), lefetamine(INN), levamfetamine(INN), mefenorex(INN) and phentermine(INN); salts thereof
	0/0/0	5	0	0	0	0	0	0//0	0/0/			0/0/	Amfetamine(INN), benzfetamine(INN), dexamfetamine(INN) (salts thereof)
	0/0/0	5	0	0	0	0	0	0//0	0/0/			0/0/	Etilamfetamine(INN), fencamfamin(INN), lefetamine(INN)(salts thereof)
	0/0/0	5	0	0	0	0	0	0//0	0/0/			0/0/	levamfetamine(INN), mefenorex(INN) and phentermine(INN) (salts thereof)
													--Other:
	0/0/0	0	0	0	0	0	0	0//0	0/0/			0/0/	---*p*-Isopropyl-aniline
	0/0/0	5	2.6	0	0	0	0	0//0	0/0/			0/0/	---Dimethylanilines
3.2	0/0/0	0	0	0	0	0	0	0//0	0/0/			0/0/	---2,6-Methyl ethyl aniline
	0/0/0	5	0		0	0	0	0//0	0/0/			0/0/	---2,6-Diethylaniline
													---Other
	0/0/0	5	0		0	0	0	0//0	0/0/			0/0/	Isopropalin
	0/0/0	5	0		0	0	0	0//0	0/0/			0/0/	Butralin
	0/0/0	5	0		0	0	0	0//0	0/0/			0/0/	Pendimethalin
	0/0/0	5	0		0	0	0	0//0	0/0/			0/0/	4-Aminobiphenyl
	0/0/0	5	0		0	0	0	0//0	0/0/			0/0/	Eticyclidine, dimethylamphetamine (and their salt)
	0/0/0	5	0		0	0	0	0//0	0/0/			0/0/	Fenfluramine, d-fenfluramine (and their salt)
	0/0/0	5	0		0	0	0	0//0	0/0/			0/0/	Other aromatic monoamine and derivants and their salt
													-Aromatic polyamines and their derivatives; salts thereof:
													--*o*-, *m*-, *p*-Phenylenediamine, diaminotoluenes, and their derivatives; salts thereof:
3.2	0/0/0	0	0	0	0	0	0	0//0	0/0/			0/0/	---*o*-Phenylenediamine
													---Other
	0/0/0	5	0	0	0	0	0	0//0	0/0/			0/0/	Dinitamine
	0/0/0	5	0	0	0	0	0	0//0	0/0/			0/0/	Prodiamine
	0/0/0	5	0	0	0	0	0	0//0	0/0/			0/0/	2,4-Diaminotoluene
	0/0/0	5	0	0	0	0	0	0//0	0/0/			0/0/	*o*-, *m*-, *p*-Phenylene diamine, diaminotoluene(including and their derivatives; salts thereof)
													--Other
	0/0/0	5	2.6		0	0	0	0//0	0/0/			0/0/	Triamino trinitrobenzene
	0/0/0	5	2.6		0	0	0	0//0	0/0/			0/0/	Benzidine(4,4′-diaminobiphenyl)
	0/0/0	5	2.6		0	0	0	0//0	0/0/			0/0/	4,4′-Diamino-3,3′-dicophane
	0/0/0	5	2.6		0	0	0	0//0	0/0/			0/0/	3,3′-Dichlorobenzidine
	0/0/0	5	2.6		0	0	0	0//0	0/0/			0/0/	4,4′-Methylenedianiline

税则号列		货品名称〔CIQ 扩展编码及品名－T2 表示见附表 2〕	最惠(%)	暂定税率	普通	增值/消费	出口退税	计量单位	监管条件	检验检疫	特殊证件对美关税
2921.5900	90	其他芳香多胺及衍生物及它们的盐〔301 毒性物质和感染性物质，302 腐蚀性物质，303 杂项物质，304 其他危险化学品，305 其他化工产品〕	6.5		30	13/	13	千克			1/31.5
29.22		**含氧基氨基化合物：**									
		-氨基醇(但含有一种以上含氧基的除外)及其醚和酯，以及它们的盐：									
2922.1100		--单乙醇胺及其盐									
2922.1100	01	单乙醇胺[T2]	6.5		30	13/	10	千克	AB	MRNS	1/11.5
2922.1100	90	单乙醇胺盐〔999〕	6.5		30	13/	10	千克			1/11.5
2922.1200		--二乙醇胺及其盐〔 999 〕									
2922.1200	01	二乙醇胺〔999〕	6.5		30	13/	10	千克			1/16.5
2922.1200	90	二乙醇胺盐〔 301 毒性物质和感染性物质，302 腐蚀性物质，303 其他化工产品〕	6.5		30	13/	10	千克			1/16.5
2922.1400		--右丙氧吩(INN)及其盐〔999〕	6.5		30	13/	10	千克	I		1/
2922.1500		--三乙醇胺〔999〕	6.5		30	13/	10	千克	23A	R	1/11.5
2922.1600		--全氟辛基磺酸二乙醇铵〔999〕	6.5		30	13/	10	千克			1/
2922.1700		--甲基二乙醇胺和乙基二乙醇胺〔999〕	6.5		30	13/	10,13	千克	23		1/11.5
2922.1800		--2-(N,N-二异丙基氨基)乙醇〔999〕	6.5		30	13/	13	千克			1/
		--其他：									
2922.1910		---乙胺丁醇〔999〕	6.5		30	13/	13	千克			1/
		---二烷(甲、乙、正丙或异丙)氨基乙-2-醇及其质子化盐：									
2922.1921		----二甲氨基乙醇及其质子化盐〔999，301 腐蚀性物质，302 其他化工产品〕	6.5		30	13/	13	千克			1/11.5
2922.1922		----二乙氨基乙醇及其质子化盐									
2922.1922	10	2-二乙氨基乙醇(或称 N,N-二乙基乙醇胺)〔999〕	6.5		30	13/	10	千克	3		1/16.5
2922.1922	90	二乙氨基乙醇的质子化盐〔999〕	6.5		30	13/	10	千克			1/16.5
2922.1929		----其他〔301 腐蚀性物质，302 其他化工产品〕	6.5		30	13/	10	千克	23		1/
2922.1930		---乙基二乙醇胺的盐〔999〕	6.5		30	13/	10	千克			1/
2922.1940		---甲基二乙醇胺的盐〔999〕	6.5		30	13/	13	千克			1/11.5
2922.1950		---本芴醇〔999〕	6.5		30	13/	13	千克			1/26.5
2922.1990		---其他									
2922.1990	10	增产胺〔999〕	6.5		30	13/	9,13	千克	S		1/11.5
2922.1990	20	克仑特罗〔999〕	6.5		30	13/	9,13	千克	L		1/11.5
2922.1990	31	醋美沙朵、阿醋美沙朵、阿法美沙朵(以及它们的盐)〔999〕	6.5		30	13/	9,13	千克	I		1/11.5
2922.1990	32	倍醋美沙多、倍他美沙朵(以及它们的盐)〔999〕	6.5		30	13/	9,13	千克	I		1/11.5
2922.1990	33	地美沙多、地美庚醇、诺美沙朵(以及它们的盐)〔999〕	6.5		30	13/	9,13	千克	I		1/11.5
2922.1990	41	三乙醇胺盐酸盐〔999〕	6.5		30	13/	10	千克	23		1/11.5
2922.1990	49	其他三乙醇胺的盐〔999〕	6.5		30	13/	10	千克			1/11.5
2922.1990	90	其他氨基醇及其醚、酯和它们的盐(但含有一种以上含氧基的除外)〔301 易燃液体，302 腐蚀性物质，303 其他危险化学品，304 其他化工产品〕	6.5		30	13/	9,13	千克			1/11.5
		-氨基萘酚和其他氨基酚(但含有一种以上含氧基的除外)及其醚和酯，以及它们的盐：									
2922.2100		--氨基羟基萘磺酸及其盐〔301 毒性物质和感染性物质，302 其他化工产品〕	6.5		30	13/	13	千克			1/16.5
		--其他：									
2922.2910		---茴香胺、二茴香胺、氨基苯乙醚及其盐〔999〕	6.5		30	13/	13	千克			1/
2922.2990		---其他									
2922.2990	11	布苯丙胺、二甲氧基乙基安非他明(以及它们的盐)〔999〕	6.5		30	13/	13	千克	I		1/31.5
2922.2990	12	二甲氧基安非他明、副甲氧基安非他明(以及它们的盐)〔999〕	6.5		30	13/	13	千克	I		1/31.5
2922.2990	13	二甲氧基甲苯异丙胺、三甲氧基安非他明(以及它们的盐)〔999〕	6.5		30	13/	13	千克	I		1/31.5
2922.2990	14	2,5-二甲氧基-4-溴苯乙胺、地佐辛(以及它们的盐)〔999〕	6.5		30	13/	13	千克	I		1/31.5
2922.2990	15	他喷他多(Tapentadol;CAS 号:175591238)〔999〕	6.5		30	13/	13	千克	I		1/31.5
2922.2990	16	2,5－二甲氧基 4 碘苯乙胺(2,5Dimethoxy4iodophenethylamine;CAS 号:69587117)〔999〕	6.5		30	13/	13	千克	I		1/31.5
2922.2990	17	2,5－二甲氧基苯乙胺(2,5Dimethoxyphenethylamine;CAS 号:3600860)〔999〕	6.5		30	13/	13	千克	I		1/31.5
2922.2990	90	其他氨基(萘酚、酚)及醚、酯(包括它们的盐，但含有一种以上含氧基的除外)〔301 毒性物质和感染性物质，302 其他化工产品〕	6.5		30	13/	13	千克			1/31.5

协定税率 %										特惠税率 %			
亚太5国	东/冰/格	巴基斯坦	韩国	瑞士	哥达	秘鲁	澳大利亚	新西/坡/智	港/澳/台	亚太2国	老/柬/缅	36/3/1	Article Description
	0/0/0	5	2.6		0	0	0	0//0	0/0/			0/0/	Other aromatic polyamines and their derivatives; salts thereof
													Oxygen-function amino-compounds:
													-Amino-alcohols, other than those containing more than one kind of oxygen function, their ethers and esters; salts thereof:
													--Monoethanolamine and its salts
	0/0/0	5		0	0	0	0	0//0	0/0/			0/0/	Monoethanolamine
	0/0/0	5		0	0	0	0	0//0	0/0/			0/0/	Salts of monoethanolamine
													--Diethanolamine and its salts
	0/0/0	5		0	0	0	0	0//0	0/0/			0/0/	Diethanolamine
	0/0/0	5		0	0	0	0	0//0	0/0/			0/0/	Diethanolamine salt
	0/0/0	5	0	0	0	0	0	0//0	0/0/			0/0/	--Dextropropoxyphene(INN) and its salts
	0/0/0	5	3.9	0	0	0	0	0//0	0/0/			0/0/	--Triethanolamine
	0/0/0	5	0	0	0	0	0	0//0	0/0/			0/0/	--Diethanolammonium perfluorooctane sulphonate
	0/0/0	5	0	0	0	0	0	0//0	0/0/			0/0/	--Methyldiethanolamine and ethyldiethanolamine
	0/0/0	5	0	0	0	0	0	0//0	0/0/			0/0/	--2-(*N*, *N-Diisopropylamino*) ethanol
													--Other:
	0/0/0	5	0	0	0	0	0	0//0	0/0/			0/0/	---Ethylamino butanol (Ethambutol)
													---N, N-Dialkyl-(Me, Et, n-Pr or i-Pr) aminoethane-2-ols and cornesponding protonated salts:
	0/0/0	5	0	0	0	0	0	0//0	0/0/			0/0/	----N,N-Dimethylaminoethanol and corresponding protonated salts
													----N,N-Diethylaminoethanol and corresponding protonated salts
	0/0/0	5	0	0	0	0	0	0//0	0/0/			0/0/	2-Diethylaminoethanol(N,N-Diethylethanolamine)
	0/0/0	5	0	0	0	0	0	0//0	0/0/			0/0/	Protonated salts of 2-Diethylaminoethanol
5.2	0/0/0	5	0	0	0	0	0	0//0	0/0/			0/0/	----Other
5.2	0/0/0	5	0	0	0	0	0	0//0	0/0/			0/0/	---Ethyldiethanolamine
5.2	0/0/0	5	0	0	0	0	0	0//0	0/0/			0/0/	---Methyldiethanolamine
	0/0/0	5	0	0	0	0	0	0//0	0/0/			0/0/	---Benflumelol
													---Other
	0/0/0	5	0	0	0	0	0	0//0	0/0/			0/0/	Ethanamine
	0/0/0	5	0	0	0	0	0	0//0	0/0/			0/0/	Clenbuterol
	0/0/0	5	0	0	0	0	0	0//0	0/0/			0/0/	Acetylmethadol, alphacetylmethadol, alphamethadol(and its salts)
	0/0/0	5	0	0	0	0	0	0//0	0/0/			0/0/	Betacetylmethadol, betamethadol (and their salt)
	0/0/0	5	0	0	0	0	0	0//0	0/0/			0/0/	Dimenoxadol, dimepheptanol, noracymethadol (and their salt)
	0/0/0	5	0	0	0	0	0	0//0	0/0/			0/0/	Triethanolamine hydrochloride
	0/0/0	5	0	0	0	0	0	0//0	0/0/			0/0/	Other salts of triethanolamine
	0/0/0	5	0	0	0	0	0	0//0	0/0/			0/0/	Other alkamine and their ethers, esters and their salt (other than those containing more than one kind of Oxygen function)
													-Amino-naphthols and amino-phenols, other than those containing more than one kind of oxygen function, their ethers and esters; salts thereof:
	0/0/0	5	2.6	0	0	0	0	0//0	0/0/			0/0/	--Aminohydroxynaphthal-ene-sulphonic acid and their salts
													--Other:
	0/0/0	5	2.6	0	0	0	0	0//0	0/0/			0/0/	---Anisidine, dianisidine, phenetidine and their salts
													---Other
	0/0/0	5	0	0	0	0	0	0//0	0/0/			0/0/	Brolamfetamine, dimethoxy-4-ethyl, amphetamine (and their salt)
	0/0/0	5	0	0	0	0	0	0//0	0/0/			0/0/	12, 5Dimethoxyamfetamine, paramethoxyamfetamine (and their salt)
	0/0/0	5	0	0	0	0	0	0//0	0/0/			0/0/	Domdimethoxy-methyl-amphetamine, trimethoxyamfetamine (and their salt)
	0/0/0	5	0	0	0	0	0	0//0	0/0/			0/0/	4-bromo-2,5-dimethoxyphenethylamine, dezocine (and their salt)
	0/0/0	5	0	0	0	0	0	0//0	0/0/			0/0/	Tapentadol(CAS:175591-23-8)
	0/0/0	5	0	0	0	0	0	0//0	0/0/			0/0/	2,5-Dimethoxy-4-iodophenethylamine(CAS:69587-11-7)
	0/0/0	5	0	0	0	0	0	0//0	0/0/			0/0/	2,5-Dimethoxy-phenethylamine(CAS:3600-86-0)
	0/0/0	5	0	0	0	0	0	0//0	0/0/			0/0/	Other amino (naphthol, hydroxybenzene) and aether, ester (including their salt, but with the exception of those containing one or more oxygen containing groups

税则号列	货品名称〔CIQ 扩展编码及品名－T2 表示见附表 2〕	最惠(%)	暂定税率	普通	增值/消费	出口退税	计量单位	监管条件	检验检疫	特殊证件对美关税
	-氨基醛、氨基酮和氨基醌,但含有一种以上含氧基的除外,以及它们的盐:									
2922.3100	--安非拉酮(INN)、美沙酮(INN)和去甲美沙酮(INN),以及它们的盐									
2922.3100 10	安非拉酮及其盐〔999〕	6.5		30	13/	10	千克	I		1/11.5
2922.3100 20	美沙酮、去甲美沙酮及它们的盐〔999〕	6.5		30	13/	10	千克	I		1/11.5
	--其他:									
2922.3910	---4-甲基甲卡西酮〔999〕	6.5		30	13/	10	千克	I		1/
2922.3920	---安非他酮及其盐〔999〕	6.5		30	13/	9,13	千克			1/
2922.3990	---其他									
2922.3990 10	氯胺酮及其盐〔999〕	6.5		30	13/	10	千克	I		1/31.5
2922.3990 20	灭藻醌〔999〕	6.5		30	13/	9,10	千克	S		1/31.5
2922.3990 30	异美沙酮及其盐〔999〕	6.5		30	13/	10	千克	I		1/31.5
2922.3990 40	甲卡西酮及其盐〔999〕	6.5		30	13/	10	千克	I		1/31.5
2922.3990 50	4－甲基乙卡西酮(4MEC)(4Methylethcathinone;CAS 号:1225617184)〔999〕	6.5		30	13/	10	千克	I		1/31.5
2922.3990 90	其他氨基醛、氨基酮及其盐(包括氨基醌及其盐,但含有一种以上含氧基除外)〔101〕	6.5		30	13/	10	千克			1/31.5
	-氨基酸(但含有一种以上含氧基的除外)及其酯,以及它们的盐:									
	--赖氨酸及其酯,以及它们的盐:									
2922.4110	---赖氨酸〔101 饲料添加剂,301:L－赖氨酸(有检疫要求食品添加剂),302:L－盐酸赖氨酸(有检疫要求食品添加剂)〕	5		20	13/	13	千克	AB	MPQ	1/30
2922.4190	---其他〔101 饲料添加剂,102:L－赖氨酸盐酸盐(有检疫要求食品添加剂)〕	6	5	30	13/	13	千克	AB	MPRQ	1/10
	--谷氨酸及其盐:									
2922.4210	---谷氨酸〔101 饲料添加剂,102 有检疫要求食品添加剂〕	5		90	13/	10	千克	A	MP	1/30
2922.4220	---谷氨酸钠〔101 饲料添加剂,102 有检疫要求食品添加剂〕	5		130	13/	13	千克	A	MP	1/30
2922.4290	---其他〔101 饲料添加剂,102:L－谷氨酰胺(有检疫要求食品添加剂)〕	6.5		30	13/	10	千克	A	MP	1/26.5
	--邻氨基苯甲酸(氨茴酸)及其盐:									
2922.4310	---邻氨基苯甲酸(氨茴酸)〔101 饲料添加剂,102 化工产品〕	6.5		20	13/	10	千克	23		1/
2922.4390	---其他〔101〕	6.5		30	13/	10	千克			1/11.5
2922.4400	--替利定(INN)及其盐〔999〕	6.5		30	13/	10	千克	I		1/
	--其他:									
	---其他氨基酸:									
2922.4911	----氨甲环酸〔101 饲料添加剂,102 化工产品〕	6.5		20	13/	13	千克	AB	MRS	1/31.5
2922.4919	----其他									
2922.4919 10	安咪奈丁〔101 饲料添加剂,102 化工产品〕	6.5		20	13/	13	千克	I		1/16.5
2922.4919 90	其他氨基酸[T2]	6.5		20	13/	13	千克	AB	MPRQ	1/16.5
	---其他:									
2922.4991	----普鲁卡因〔999〕	6		20	13/	13	千克			1/11
2922.4999	----其他									
2922.4999 11	草灭畏〔999〕	6.5		30	13/	9,10	千克	AS	MP	1/11.5
2922.4999 12	灭杀威、灭除威、混灭威等(害扑威、速灭威、残杀威、猛杀威)〔301 毒性物质和感染性物质,302 其他化工产品〕	6.5		30	13/	9,10	千克	ABS	MN	1/11.5
2922.4999 13	兹克威、除害威〔101 灭多威(含量＞30%),102 灭害威粉剂(含量＞6%～60%),103 自克威粉剂(含量 2%～25%),104 除害威,105 灭害威乳剂(含量 1%～60%),106 自克威乳剂(含量＜25%),107 除害威乳剂〕	6.5		30	13/	0	千克	ABS	MN	1/11.5
2922.4999 14	异丙威〔301〕	6.5		30	13/	9,10	千克	ABS	MN	1/11.5
2922.4999 15	仲丁威、畜虫威、合杀威〔101 仲丁威,102 合杀威,103 仲丁威乳剂,104 合杀威乳剂〕	6.5		30	13/	9,10	千克	ABS	MN	1/11.5
2922.4999 16	甲萘威、地麦威、蜱虱威〔999〕	6.5		30	13/	9,10	千克	AS	MP	1/11.5
2922.4999 17	除线威〔999〕	6.5		30	13/	9,10	千克	AS	MP	1/11.5
2922.4999 18	氨酰丙酸(盐酸盐)〔101 饲料添加剂,102 化工产品〕	6.5		30	13/	9,10	千克	AS	MP	1/11.5
2922.4999 19	安咪奈丁的盐〔999〕	6.5		20	13/	13	千克	I		1/11.5
2922.4999 90	其他氨基酸及其酯及它们的盐(含有一种以上含氧基的除外)[T2]	6.5		30	13/	10	千克	AB	MRNQ	1/11.5
	-氨基醇酚、氨基酸酚及其他含氧基氨基化合物:									
2922.5010	---对羟基苯甘氨酸及其邓钾盐〔999〕	6.5		30	13/	13	千克	A	R	1/
2922.5020	---莱克多巴胺和盐酸莱克多巴胺〔999〕	6.5		30	13/	10	千克	89		1/
2922.5090	---其他									
2922.5090 10	曲马多〔999〕	6.5		30	13/	13	千克	I		1/31.5

协定税率 %										特惠税率 %			Article Description
亚太5国	东/冰/格	巴基斯坦	韩国	瑞士	哥达	秘鲁	澳大利亚	新西/坡/智	港/澳/台	亚太2国	老/柬/缅	36/3/1	
													-Amino-aldehydes, amino-ketones and amino-quinones, other than those containing more than one kind of oxygen function; salts thereof:
													--Amfepramone(INN), methadone(INN) and normethadone(INN); salts thereof
	0/0/0	5	0	0	0	0	0	0//0	0/0/			0/0/	Amfepramone(INN) and salts thereof
	0/0/0	5	0	0	0	0	0	0//0	0/0/			0/0/	Methadone(INN), normethadone(INN) and salts thereof
													--Other:
	0/0/0	5	0	0	0	0	0	0//0	0/0/			0/0/	---4-Methcathinone
	0/0/0	5	0	0	0	0	0	0//0	0/0/			0/0/	---Bupropion and salt
													---Other
	0/0/0	5	0	0	0	0	0	0//0	0/0/			0/0/	Ketamine and salts thereof
	0/0/0	5	0	0	0	0	0	0//0	0/0/			0/0/	Quinoclamine
	0/0/0	5	0	0	0	0	0	0//0	0/0/			0/0/	Isomethadone and salts thereof
	0/0/0	5	0	0	0	0	0	0//0	0/0/			0/0/	Methcathinone and salts thereof
	0/0/0	5	0	0	0	0	0	0//0	0/0/			0/0/	4-Methylethcathinone(CAS:1225617-18-4)
	0/0/0	5	0	0	0	0	0	0//0	0/0/			0/0/	Other amino-aldehydes, amino-ketones and amino-quinones, other than those containing more than one kind of oxygen function and salts thereof
													-Amino-acids, other than those containing more than one kind of oxygen function, and their esters, salts thereof:
													--Lysine and its esters; salts thereof:
	0/0/0	0	3	0	0	0	0	0//0	0/0/			0/0/	---Lysine
	0/0/0	5	0	0	0	0	0	0//0	0/0/			0/0/	---Other
													--Glutamic acid and its salts:
3.3	0/0/0	4.5	4	0	0	0	0	0/0/0	0/0/			0/0/	---Glutamic acid
	0/0/0	4.5	4	0	0	0	0	0/0/0	0/0/			0/0/	---Sodium glutamate
	0/0/0	5	0	0	0	0	0	0//0	0/0/			0/0/	---Other
													--Anthranilic acid and its salts:
	0/0/0	5	0	0	0	0	0	0//0	0/0/			0/0/	---Anthranilic acids
	0/0/0	5	0	0	0	0	0	0//0	0/0/			0/0/	---Other
	0/0/0	5	0	0	0	0	0	0//0	0/0/			0/0/	--Tilidine(INN) and its salts
													--Other:
													---Amino acids:
	0/0/0	5	3.9	0	0	0	0	0//0	0/0/			0/0/	----Tranexamic acid
													----Other
	0/0/0	5	3.9	0	0	0	0	0//0	0/0/			0/0/	Amineptine
	0/0/0	5	3.9	0	0	0	0	0//0	0/0/			0/0/	Other amino acids
													---Other:
3.6	0/0/0	5	0	0	0	0	0	0//0	0/0/			0/0/	----Procaine
													----Other
	0/0/0	5	0	0	0	0	0	0//0	0/0/			0/0/	Chloramben
	0/0/0	5	0	0	0	0	0	0//0	0/0/			0/0/	Meobal, XMC, dimethacarb (etrofol, metolcarb, propoxur, promecarb)
	0/0/0	5	0	0	0	0	0	0//0	0/0/			0/0/	Mexacarbate, allyxycarb
	0/0/0	5	0	0	0	0	0	0//0	0/0/			0/0/	Isoprocarb
	0/0/0	5	0	0	0	0	0	0//0	0/0/			0/0/	Fenobucarb, butacarb, bufencarb
	0/0/0	5	0	0	0	0	0	0//0	0/0/			0/0/	Carbaryl, dimetan, promacyl
	0/0/0	5	0	0	0	0	0	0//0	0/0/			0/0/	cloethocarb
	0/0/0	5	0	0	0	0	0	0//0	0/0/			0/0/	Hydrochlorate
	0/0/0	5	0	0	0	0	0	0//0	0/0/			0/0/	Salts of amineptine
	0/0/0	5	0	0	0	0	0	0//0	0/0/			0/0/	Other amino-acids and their esters; their salt(Other than those containing more than one kind of oxygen function)
													-Amino-alcohol-phenols, amino-acid-phenols and other amino-compounds with oxygen function:
	0/0/0	5	0	0	0	0	0	0//0	0/0/			0/0/	---D-p-hydroxyphenylglycine and deng sylvite
	0/0/0	5	3.9	0	0	0	0	0//0	0/0/			0/0/	---Ractopamine and ractopamine hydrochloride
													---Other
	0/0/0	5	2.6	0	0	0	0	0//0	0/0/			0/0/	Tramadol

税则号列		货品名称〔CIQ 扩展编码及品名－T2 表示见附表 2〕	最惠(%)	暂定税率	普通	增值/消费	出口退税	计量单位	监管条件	检验检疫	特殊证件对美关税
2922.5090	20	苏氨酸〔999,101 饲用,301 有检疫要求食品添加剂,302 其他化工产品〕	6.5	5	20	13/	13	千克	A	R	1/30
2922.5090	91	盐酸米托蒽醌〔301 无检疫要求食品添加剂,302 需申报仅用于工业用途不用于食品添加剂无检疫要求的化学品〕	6.5	0	30	3/	13	千克	A	R	1/25
2922.5090	99	其他氨基醇酚、氨基酸酚(包括其他含氧基氨基化合物)(因拆分抗癌药品原料药产生的兜底税号)〔301 无检疫要求食品添加剂,302 需申报仅用于工业用途不用于食品添加剂无检疫要求的化学品〕	6.5		30	13/	13	千克	A	R	1/31.5
29.23		**季铵盐及季铵碱;卵磷脂及其他磷氨基类脂,不论是否已有化学定义:**									
2923.1000		-胆碱及其盐〔101 饲料添加剂,102 无检疫要求食品添加剂,103 需申报仅用于工业用途不用于食品添加剂无检疫要求的化学品〕	6.5		30	13/	10	千克	A	R	1/16.5
2923.2000		-卵磷脂及其他磷氨基类脂[T2]	6.5		30	13/	10	千克	A	R	1/16.5
2923.3000		-全氟辛基磺酸四乙基铵〔999 其他化工产品,301 毒性物质和感染性物质〕	6.5		30	13/	10	千克			1/
2923.4000		-全氟辛基磺酸二癸基二甲基铵〔999 其他化工产品,301 其他危险化学品〕	6.5		30	13/	10	千克			1/
2923.9000		-其他									
2923.9000	11	矮壮素〔101 矮壮素水剂(含量＞30%),102 其他〕	6.5		30	13/	9,10	千克	S		1/16.5
2923.9000	12	菊胺酯〔999〕	6.5		30	13/	9,10	千克	S		1/16.5
2923.9000	90	其他季铵盐及季铵碱〔101 饲料添加剂,301 易燃液体,302 毒性物质和感染性物质,303 腐蚀性物质,304 其他化工产品,305 无检疫要求食品添加剂〕	6.5		30	13/	10	千克			1/16.5
29.24		**羧基酰胺基化合物;碳酸酰胺基化合物:**									
		-无环酰胺(包括无环氨基甲酸酯)及其衍生物以及它们的盐:									
2924.1100		--甲丙氨酯(INN)〔999〕	6.5		30	13/	10	千克	I		1/
2924.1200		--氟乙酰胺(ISO)久效磷(ISO)及磷胺(ISO)									
2924.1200	10	氟乙酰胺(ISO)(氟乙酰胺别名敌蚜胺)〔301 毒性物质和感染性物质〕	6.5		30	13/	0	千克	89		1/
2924.1200	90	久效磷(ISO)及磷胺(ISO)〔301〕	6.5		30	13/	0	千克			1/
		--其他(INN):									
2924.1910		---二甲基甲酰胺〔999〕	6.5		30	13/	10	千克			1/11.5
2924.1990		---其他									
2924.1990	12	百治磷〔301〕	6.5		30	13/	0	千克	S		1/26.5
2924.1990	13	溴乙酰胺〔999〕	6.5		30	13/	0	千克	S		1/26.5
2924.1990	14	霜霉威〔999〕	6.5		30	13/	9,10	千克	S		1/26.5
2924.1990	15	叶枯炔〔999〕	6.5		30	13/	0	千克	S		1/26.5
2924.1990	16	二丙烯草胺〔101 草毒死颗粒剂(含量＞35%),102 草毒死(含量＞35%)〕	6.5		30	13/	9,10	千克	S		1/26.5
2924.1990	18	驱蚊酯〔999〕	6.5		30	13/	9,10	千克	S		1/26.5
2924.1990	30	甲丙氨酯的盐〔999〕	6.5		30	13/	10	千克	I		1/26.5
2924.1990	40	丙烯酰胺〔999〕	6.5		30	13/	10	千克			1/26.5
2924.1990	90	其他无环酰胺(包括无环氨基甲酸酯)(包括其衍生物及其盐)〔101 饲料添加剂,301 爆炸品,302 易燃液体,303 易燃固体,304 毒性物质和感染性物质,305 其他危险化学品,306 其他化工产品〕	6.5		30	13/	13	千克			1/26.5
		-环酰胺(包括环氨基甲酸酯)及其衍生物以及它们的盐:									
2924.2100		--酰脲及其衍生物以及它们的盐									
2924.2100	10	氟环脲〔999〕	6.5		30	13/	9,10	千克	S		1/31.5
2924.2100	20	绿麦隆〔999〕	6.5		30	13/	10	千克	S		1/31.5
2924.2100	90	其他酰脲及其衍生物以及它们的盐〔101 饲料添加剂,301 杂项物质,302 其他化工产品〕	6.5		30	13/	10	千克			1/31.5
2924.2300		--2-乙酰氨基苯甲酸(N-乙酰邻氨基苯甲酸)及其盐									
2924.2300	10	2-乙酰氨基苯甲酸、N-乙酰邻氨基苯酸(包括 N-乙酰邻氨基苯甲酸)〔999〕	6.5		30	13/	10	千克	23		1/
2924.2300	90	2-乙酰氨基苯甲酸的盐〔999〕	6.5		30	13/	10	千克			1/
2924.2400		--炔己蚁胺(INN)〔999〕	6.5		30	13/	10	千克	I		1/
2924.2500		--甲草胺(ISO)〔999〕	6.5		30	13/	9,13	千克	S		1/
		--其他:									
2924.2910		---对乙酰氨基苯乙醚(非那西丁)〔999〕	6		30	13/	10	千克	Q		1/
2924.2920		---对乙酰氨基酚(扑热息痛)〔999〕	6		30	13/	10	千克	Q		1/26
2924.2930		---阿斯巴甜〔999〕	6.5		30	13/	13	千克			1/31.5
2924.2990		---其他									

协定税率 %										特惠税率 %			Article Description
亚太5国	东/冰/格	巴基斯坦	韩国	瑞士	哥达	秘鲁	澳大利亚	新西/坡/智	港/澳/台	亚太2国	老/柬/缅	36/3/1	
	0/0/0	5	2.6	0	0	0	0	0//0	0/0/			0/0/	threonine
	0/0/0	5	2.6	0	0	0	0	0//0	0/0/			0/0/	Mitoxantrone hydrochloride and other anticancer drug substances
	0/0/0	5	2.6	0	0	0	0	0//0	0/0/			0/0/	Other amino alcohol phenols, amino acid phenols (including other amino—compounds with oxygen function)(tax number of Separating anti—cancer pharmaceutical raw materials)
													Quaternary ammonium salts and hydroxides; lecithins and other phosphoaminolipids, whether or not chemically defined:
	0/0/0	5	0	0	0	0	0	0//0	0/0/			0/0/	-Choline and its salts
	0/0/0	5	2.6	0	0	0	0	0//0	0/0/			0/0/	-Lecithins and other phosphoaminolipids
	0/0/0	5	0	0	0	0	0	0//0	0/0/			0/0/	-Tetraethylammonium perfluorooctane sulphonate
	0/0/0	5	0	0	0	0	0	0//0	0/0/			0/0/	-Didecyldimethylammonium perfluorooctane sulphonate
													-Other
	0/0/0	5	0	0	0	0	0	0//0	0/0/			0/0/	Chlorocholine chloride
	0/0/0	5	0	0	0	0	0	0//0	0/0/			0/0/	Tetramethrin
	0/0/0	5	0	0	0	0	0	0//0	0/0/			0/0/	Other quaternary ammonium salts and hydroxides
													Carboxyamide-function compounds; amide-function compounds of carbonic acid:
													-Acyclic amides (including acyclic carbamates) and their derivatives; salts thereof:
	0/0/0	5	0	0	0	0	0	0//0	0/0/			0/0/	--Meprobamate(INN)
													--Fluoroacetamide(ISO), monocrotophos (ISO). and phophamidon (ISO)
	0/0/0	5	0	0	0	0	0	0//0	0/0/			0/0/	Fluoroacetamide(ISO)
	0/0/0	5	0	0	0	0	0	0//0	0/0/			0/0/	Monocrotophos(ISO), phosphamidon(ISO)
													--Other:
	0/0/0	5	0	0	0	0	0	0//0	0/0/0			0/0/	---N,N-dimethylformamide
													---Other
	0/0/0	5	3.9	0	0	0	0	0//0	0/0/			0/0/	Dicrotophos
	0/0/0	5	3.9	0	0	0	0	0//0	0/0/			0/0/	Bromoacetamide
	0/0/0	5	3.9	0	0	0	0	0//0	0/0/			0/0/	Propamocarb
	0/0/0	5	3.9	0	0	0	0	0//0	0/0/			0/0/	Cellocidin
	0/0/0	5	3.9	0	0	0	0	0//0	0/0/			0/0/	Allicochlor
	0/0/0	5	3.9	0	0	0	0	0//0	0/0/			0/0/	Dimethyl phthalate
	0/0/0	5	3.9	0	0	0	0	0//0	0/0/			0/0/	Salts of meprobamate (INN)
	0/0/0	5	3.9	0	0	0	0	0//0	0/0/			0/0/	Acrylamide
	0/0/0	5	3.9	0	0	0	0	0//0	0/0/			0/0/	Other acyclic amides (including acyclic carbamates) (and their derivatives; salts thereof)
													-Cyclic amides (including cyclic carbamates) and their derivatives; salts thereof:
													--Ureides and their derivatives; salts thereof
	0/0/0	5	0	0	0	0	0	0//0	0/0/			0/0/	Flucycloxuron
	0/0/0	5	0	0	0	0	0	0//0	0/0/			0/0/	chlortoluron
	0/0/0	5	0	0	0	0	0	0//0	0/0/			0/0/	Other ureides and its derivants and their salt
													--2-Acetamidobenzoic acid(N-Acetylanthranilic acid) and its salts
	0/0/0	5	0		0	0	0	0//0	0/0/			0/0/	2-Acetamidobenzoic acid; N-acetylanthranilicacid (including N-acetamidobenzoic acid)
	0/0/0	5	0		0	0	0	0//0	0/0/			0/0/	Salts of 2-acetamidobenzoic acid
	0/0/0	5	0	0	0	0	0	0//0	0/0/			0/0/	--Ethinamate(INN)
	0/0/0	0	0	2	0	0	0	0//0	0/0/			0/0/	--Alachlor(ISO)
													--Other:
4.8	0/0/0	0	0	0	0	0	0	0//0	0/0/			0/0/	---Phenacetin
4.8	0/0/0	0	0	0	0	0	0	0//0	0/0/			0/0/	---*p*-Acetaminophenol (paracetanol)
	0/0/0	0	0	2	0	0	0	0//0	0/0/			0/0/	---Aspartame
													---Other

税则号列		货品名称〔CIQ 扩展编码及品名—T2 表示见附表 2〕	最惠(%)	暂定税率	普通	增值/消费	出口退税	计量单位	监管条件	检验检疫	特殊证件对美关税
2924.2990	11	避蚊胺、灭锈胺、叶枯酞、水杨菌胺、氟丁酰草胺(包括苯酰菌胺)〔999〕	6.5		30	13/	9,13	千克	S		1/31.5
2924.2990	12	萘草胺、新燕灵、非草隆、氯炔灵、苄草隆〔301 杂项物质,302 其他化工产品〕	6.5		30	13/	9,13	千克	S		1/31.5
2924.2990	13	燕麦灵、苄胺灵、特草灵、特胺灵、环丙酰亚胺〔301 杂项物质,302 其他化工产品〕	6.5		30	13/	9,13	千克	S		1/31.5
2924.2990	14	毒草胺、丁烯草胺、二氯己酰草胺〔301 杂项物质,302 其他化工产品〕	6.5		30	13/	9,13	千克	S		1/31.5
2924.2990	15	萘丙胺、牧草胺、溴丁酰草胺〔999〕	6.5		30	13/	9,13	千克	S		1/31.5
2924.2990	16	氯甲酰草胺、麦草伏 M、麦草伏〔999〕	6.5		30	13/	9,13	千克	S		1/31.5
2924.2990	17	氯虫酰肼、异丙甲草胺、苯肽胺酸等(包括精异丙甲草胺、缬霉威)〔999〕	6.5		30	13/	9,13	千克	S		1/31.5
2924.2990	18	灭害威〔999〕	6.5		30	13/	9,13	千克	S		1/31.5
2924.2990	19	苯氧威〔999〕	6.5		30	13/	9,13	千克	S		1/31.5
2924.2990	20	氟酰脲、环丙酰草胺、烯草胺〔999〕	6.5		30	13/	9,13	千克	S		1/31.5
2924.2990	31	苯胺灵、苯霜灵、丙草胺、敌稗等(包括丙炔草胺、草不隆、草完隆、除虫脲、除幼脲)〔101 敌稗,102 敌稗乳剂(含量＞25％)〕	6.5		30	13/	9,13	千克	S		1/31.5
2924.2990	32	敌草胺、敌草隆、二甲苯草胺等(包括丁草胺、丁酰草胺、二甲草胺、氟苯脲、氟草隆)〔999〕	6.5		30	13/	9,13	千克	S		1/31.5
2924.2990	33	庚酰草胺、环丙草胺、环酰草胺等(包括氟虫脲、氟铃脲、氟酰胺、氟蚁灵、氟幼脲)〔999〕	6.5		30	13/	9,13	千克	S		1/31.5
2924.2990	34	甲氯酰草胺、甲霜灵、环草隆等(包括环莠隆、甲氧隆、克草胺、枯草隆)〔101 杂项物质,102 其他化工产品〕	6.5		30	13/	9,13	千克	S		1/31.5
2924.2990	35	甲基杀草隆、枯莠隆、邻酰胺等(包括氯苯胺灵、麦草氟甲酯、麦草氟异丙酯)〔999〕	6.5		30	13/	9,13	千克	S		1/31.5
2924.2990	36	灭草隆、灭幼脲、炔苯酰草胺等(包括麦锈灵、棉胺宁、灭草灵、炔草隆、杀草胺)〔101 灭草灵,102 灭草灵乳剂〕	6.5		30	13/	9,13	千克	S		1/31.5
2924.2990	37	虱螨脲、双苯酰草胺、双酰草胺等(包括杀草隆、杀铃脲、杀螺胺、莎稗磷)〔101 草乃敌(含量＞55％),102 草乃敌乳剂(含量＞10％)〕	6.5		30	13/	9,13	千克	S		1/31.5
2924.2990	38	甜菜安、特丁草胺、乙氧苯草胺等(包括甜菜宁、戊菌隆、酰草隆、乙草胺、乙霉威)〔301 杂项物质,302 其他化工产品〕	6.5		30	13/	9,13	千克	S		1/31.5
2924.2990	39	乙酰甲草胺、异丙隆、异草完隆等(包括异丙草胺、异丁草胺)〔999〕	6.5		30	13/	9,13	千克	S		1/31.5
2924.2990	40	炔己蚁胺的盐〔999〕	6.5		30	13/	13	千克	I		1/31.5
2924.2990	50	地恩丙胺及其盐〔999〕	6.5		30	13/	13	千克	I		1/31.5
2924.2990	91	氟他胺及其他抗癌药品原料药〔999〕	6.5	0	30	3/	13	千克			1/25
2924.2990	99	其他环酰胺(包括环氨基甲酸酯)(包括其衍生物以及它们的盐)(因拆分抗癌药品原料药产生的兜底税号)〔301 易燃固体、自反应物质及固态退敏爆炸品,302 毒性物质和感染性物质,303 其他危险化学品,304 其他化工产品〕	6.5		30	13/	13	千克			1/31.5
29.25		**羧基酰亚胺化合物(包括糖精及其盐)及亚胺基化合物:**									
		-酰亚胺及其衍生物以及它们的盐:									
2925.1100		--糖精及其盐〔101 饲料添加剂,102 无检疫要求食品添加剂,103 需申报仅用于工业用途不用于食品添加剂无检疫要求的化学品〕	9		90	13/	10	千克	A	R	1/34
2925.1200		--格鲁米特(INN)〔999〕	6.5		30	13/	10	千克	I		1/
2925.1900		--其他									
2925.1900	10	格鲁米特的盐〔999〕	6.5		30	13/	10	千克	I		1/11.5
2925.1900	21	腐霉利〔999〕	6.5		30	13/	9,10	千克	S		1/11.5
2925.1900	22	菌核净、菌核利、甲菌利、乙菌利〔999〕	6.5		30	13/	9,10	千克	S		1/11.5
2925.1900	23	氟烯草酸〔999〕	6.5		30	13/	9,10	千克	S		1/11.5
2925.1900	24	胺菊酯(包括右旋胺菊酯、右旋反式胺菊酯、富右旋反式胺菊酯)〔999〕	6.5		30	13/	9,10	千克	S		1/11.5
2925.1900	90	其他酰亚胺及其衍生物、盐〔999〕	6.5		30	13/	10	千克			1/11.5
		-亚胺及其衍生物以及它们的盐:									
2925.2100		--杀虫脒(ISO)〔301 毒性物质和感染性物质,302 杂项物质〕	6.5		30	13/	0	千克	89		1/
2925.2900		--其他									
2925.2900	11	杀螨特、杀螨脒〔999〕	6.5		30	13/	9,10	千克	S		1/31.5
2925.2900	12	单甲脒、伐虫脒、丙烷脒〔301 毒性物质和感染性物质,302 其他化工产品〕	6.5		30	13/	9,10	千克	S		1/31.5
2925.2900	13	烯肟菌胺、烯肟菌酯、醚菌酯〔999〕	6.5		30	13/	9,10	千克	S		1/31.5
2925.2900	14	双胍辛胺、多果啶、双胍辛胺乙酸盐等(包括双胍三辛烷基苯磺酸盐)〔999〕	6.5		30	13/	9,10	千克	S		1/31.5
2925.2900	15	禾草灭、氟草醚、增产肟〔999〕	6.5		30	13/	9,10	千克	S		1/31.5
2925.2900	16	氯代水杨胺、双胍辛乙酸盐、顺己烯醇〔999〕	6.5		30	13/	9,10	千克	S		1/31.5
2925.2900	20	羟亚胺及其盐〔999〕	6.5		30	13/	10	千克	23		1/31.5

协定税率 %										特惠税率 %			
亚太5国	东/冰/格	巴基斯坦	韩国	瑞士	哥达	秘鲁	澳大利亚	新西/坡/智	港/澳/台	亚太2国	老/柬/缅	36/3/1	Article Description
	0/0/0	0	0	2	0	0	0	0//0	0/0/			0/0/	Deet, mepronil, tecloftalam, trichlamide, buflubutamid(including zoxamide)
	0/0/0	0	0	2	0	0	0	0//0	0/0/			0/0/	Naptalam, benzoylprop-ethyl , fenuron , chlorbufam chlorbufam
	0/0/0	0	0	2	0	0	0	0//0	0/0/			0/0/	Barban dichlormate, terbutol , karbutilate
	0/0/0	0	0	2	0	0	0	0//0	0/0/			0/0/	Propachlor, butenachlor, dichloro acetyl thenylchlor
	0/0/0	0	0	2	0	0	0	0//0	0/0/			0/0/	Naproanilide, tebutam, bromobutide
	0/0/0	0	0	2	0	0	0	0//0	0/0/			0/0/	Clomeprop, flamprop M, flamprop
	0/0/0	0	0	2	0	0	0	0//0	0/0/			0/0/	Halofenozide, metolachlor, phthalanillic (including s-metolachlor, iprovalicarb)
	0/0/0	0	0	2	0	0	0	0//0	0/0/			0/0/	aminocarb
	0/0/0	0	0	2	0	0	0	0//0	0/0/			0/0/	fenoxycarb
	0/0/0	0	0	2	0	0	0	0//0	0/0/			0/0/	Fluoylureas, cyclanilide, pethoxamid
	0/0/0	0	0	2	0	0	0	0//0	0/0/			0/0/	Propham, benalaxyl, pretilachlor, propanil (including prynachlor、neburon, noruron diful Benzuron, penfluron, dichlorbenzuron)
	0/0/0	0	0	2	0	0	0	0//0	0/0/			0/0/	Napropamide, diuron, xylachlor (including Butachlor, chloranocryl dimethachlor , teflubenzuron, fluometuron)
	0/0/0	0	0	2	0	0	0	0//0	0/0/			0/0/	Monalide, cyclanilide, cypromid, flufenoxuron (including fluorobenzamide, hexaflumuron, flutolanil nifluridide, penfluron)
	0/0/0	0	0	2	0	0	0	0//0	0/0/			0/0/	Pentanochlor metalaxyl, siduron (including cycluron, alachlor, metoxuron, kecaoan, chloroxuron)
	0/0/0	0	0	2	0	0	0	0//0	0/0/			0/0/	Methyldymron, difenoxuron, mebenil (including chlortoluron, chlorpropham, flamprop-methyl, flamprop-isopropyl)
	0/0/0	0	0	2	0	0	0	0//0	0/0/			0/0/	Monuron, chlorbenzuron, propyzamide(including benodanil, phenisopham , swep, buturon, ethaprochlor)
	0/0/0	0	0	2	0	0	0	0//0	0/0/			0/0/	Lufenuron diphenamide, carbetamide (includaimuron, triflumuron, niclosamide, anilofos, dichlormide)
	0/0/0	0	0	2	0	0	0	0//0	0/0/			0/0/	Desmedipham, terbuchlor, ethobenzanid (including Phenmedipham, Pencycuron, Acetochlor, Polystyrene resin)
	0/0/0	0	0	2	0	0	0	0//0	0/0/			0/0/	Diethatyl, isoproturon, isonoruron (including propisochlor, delachlor)
	0/0/0	0	0	2	0	0	0	0//0	0/0/			0/0/	Salts of ethinamate(INN)
	0/0/0	0	0	2	0	0	0	0//0	0/0/			0/0/	Diampromide and its salts
	0/0/0	0	0	2	0	0	0	0//0	0/0/			0/0/	Flutamide and Other Anticancer Drugs
	0/0/0	0	0	2	0	0	0	0//0	0/0/			0/0/	Other cyclic amides (including cyclic carbamates) (including their derivatives and their salts) (tax number of Separating anti－cancer pharmaceutical raw materials)
													Carboxyimide-function compounds (including saccharin and its salts) and imine-function compounds:
													-Imides and their derivatives; salts thereof:
	0/0/	4	3.6	0	0	0	0	0//0	0/0/			0/0/	--Saccharin and its salts
	0/0/0	5	0	0	0	0	0	0//0	0/0/			0/0/	--Glutethimide(INN)
													--Other
	0/0/0	5	0	3.4	0	0	0	0//0	0/0/			0/0/	Salts of glutethimide (INN)
	0/0/0	5	0	3.4	0	0	0	0//0	0/0/			0/0/	Procymidone
	0/0/0	5	0	3.4	0	0	0	0//0	0/0/			0/0/	Dimetachlone, dichlozoline, myclozolin, chlozolinate
	0/0/0	5	0	3.4	0	0	0	0//0	0/0/			0/0/	Flumiclorac-pentyl
	0/0/0	5	0	3.4	0	0	0	0//0	0/0/			0/0/	Tetramethrin (including d-tetramethrin, d-t-tetramethrin, rich-d-t-tetramethrin
	0/0/0	5	0	3.4	0	0	0	0//0	0/0/			0/0/	Other imides and their derivatives; salts thereof
													-Imines and their derivatives; salts thereof:
	0/0/0	5	0	0	0	0	0	0//0	0/0/			0/0/	--Chlordimeform(ISO)
													--Other
	0/0/0	5	0	0	0	0	0	0//0	0/0/			0/0/	Aramite, semiamitraz
	0/0/0	5	0	0	0	0	0	0//0	0/0/			0/0/	Semiamitraz, formetanate, propamidine
	0/0/0	5	0	0	0	0	0	0//0	0/0/			0/0/	Trichlamide, enostroburin, kresoxim-methyl
	0/0/0	5	0	0	0	0	0	0//0	0/0/			0/0/	Iminoctadine, dodine, iminoctadine triacetate (including iminoctadinris)
	0/0/0	5	0	0	0	0	0	0//0	0/0/			0/0/	Alloxydim-sodium, ethoxyfen-ethyl, heptopargil
	0/0/0	5	0	0	0	0	0	0//0	0/0/			0/0/	LDS, Iminoctadine triacetate, cis-hexenyl
	0/0/0	5	0	0	0	0	0	0//0	0/0/			0/0/	Oxyamino and its salts

税则号列		货品名称〔CIQ 扩展编码及品名—T2 表示见附表 2〕	最惠(%)	暂定税率	普通	增值/消费	出口退税	计量单位	监管条件	检验检疫	特殊证件对美关税
2925.2900	30	双甲脒〔999〕	6.5		30	13/	9,10	千克	S		1/31.5
2925.2900	90	其他亚胺及其衍生物以及它们的盐〔301 易燃液体,302 易燃固体,303 氧化性物质,304 其他化工产品〕	6.5		30	13/	10	千克			1/31.5
29.26		**腈基化合物:**									
2926.1000		-丙烯腈〔999〕	6.5	3	30	13/	13	千克			1/28
2926.2000		-1-氰基胍(双氰胺)〔999〕	6.5		30	13/	13	千克			1/16.5
2926.3000		-芬普雷司(INN)及其盐;美沙酮(INN)中间体(4-氰基-2-二甲氨基-4,4-二苯基丁烷)									
2926.3000	10	美沙酮中间体(4-氰基-2-二甲氨基-4,4-二苯基丁烷)〔999〕	6.5		30	13/	10	千克	I		1/
2926.3000	20	芬普雷司及其盐〔999〕	6.5		30	13/	10	千克	I		1/
2926.4000		-α-苯基乙酰基乙腈〔999〕	6.5		30	13/	10	千克			1/
		-其他:									
2926.9010		---对氯氰苄〔999〕	4		11	13/	10	千克			1/
2926.9020		---间苯二甲腈〔999〕	6.5		30	13/	10	千克			1/
2926.9090		---其他									
2926.9090	10	甲氰菊酯、S-氰戊菊酯、氯氟氰菊酯(包括氰氟虫腙)〔999〕	6.5		30	13/	9,10	千克	S		1/11.5
2926.9090	20	己二腈〔999〕	6.5	1	30	13/	10	千克			1/6
2926.9090	31	氯氰菊酯、氟氯氰菊酯等(包括高效氯氰菊酯、高效反式氯氰菊酯、高效氟氯氰菊酯)〔301 杂项物质,302 其他化工产品〕	6.5		30	13/	9,10	千克	S		1/11.5
2926.9090	32	杀螟腈、甲基辛硫磷等(包括敌草腈、碘苯腈、辛酰碘苯腈、溴苯腈、辛酰溴苯腈)〔301 毒性物质和感染性物质,302 其他化工产品〕	6.5		30	13/	9,10	千克	S		1/11.5
2926.9090	33	氯辛硫磷、戊氰威、苯醚氰菊酯等(包括稻瘟酰胺、丙螨氰、右旋苯醚氰菊酯)〔999〕	6.5		30	13/	9,10	千克	S		1/11.5
2926.9090	34	戊烯氰氯菊酯、溴氯氰菊酯(包括高效氯氟氰菊酯、精高效氯氟氰菊酯)〔999〕	6.5		30	13/	9,10	千克	S		1/11.5
2926.9090	35	溴氰菊酯、四溴菊酯、氟丙菊酯〔999〕	6.5		30	13/	9,10	千克	S		1/11.5
2926.9090	36	氟氯苯菊酯、氰戊菊酯、乙氰菊酯〔999〕	6.5		30	13/	9,10	千克	S		1/11.5
2926.9090	37	氟氰戊菊酯、溴氟菊酯、溴灭菊酯〔999〕	6.5		30	13/	9,10	千克	S		1/11.5
2926.9090	38	氰菌胺、百菌清、霜脲氰、溴菌腈〔999〕	6.5		30	13/	9,10	千克	S		1/11.5
2926.9090	39	氟胺氰菊酯、氰氟草酯(包括富右旋反式苯氰菊酯)〔999〕	6.5		30	13/	9,10	千克	S		1/11.5
2926.9090	41	氰烯菌酯〔999〕	6.5		30	13/	10	千克	S		1/11.5
2926.9090	50	辛硫磷〔999〕	6.5		30	13/	10	千克	S		1/11.5
2926.9090	60	丁氟螨酯〔999〕	6.5		30	13/	10	千克	S		1/11.5
2926.9090	70	3-氧-2-苯基丁腈〔999〕	6.5		30	13/	10	千克	23		1/11.5
2926.9090	90	其他腈基化合物〔301 易燃液体,302 毒性物质和感染性物质,303 杂项物质,304 其他危险化学品,305 其他化工产品〕	6.5		30	13/	10	千克			1/11.5
29.27		**重氮化合物、偶氮化合物及氧化偶氮化合物:**									
2927.0000		重氮化合物、偶氮化合物及氧化偶氮化合物									
2927.0000	10	敌磺钠(包括氧化偶氮化合物)〔999〕	6.5		30	13/	9,10	千克	S		1/31.5
2927.0000	90	其他重氮化合物、偶氮化合物等(包括氧化偶氮化合物)[T2]	6.5		30	13/	10	千克			1/31.5
29.28		**肼(联氨)及胲(羟胺)的有机衍生物:**									
2928.0000		肼(联氨)及胲(羟胺)的有机衍生物									
2928.0000	10	偏二甲肼〔999〕	6.5		20	13/	10	千克	3		1/26.5
2928.0000	20	甲基肼〔999〕	6.5		20	13/	10	千克	3A	M	1/26.5
2928.0000	31	抑食肼、虫酰肼、丁酰肼、联苯肼酯(包括肟菌酯,苯氧菌胺)〔999〕	6.5		20	13/	9,10	千克	S		1/26.5
2928.0000	32	绿谷隆、溴谷隆、利谷隆、氯溴隆〔999〕	6.5		20	13/	9,10	千克	S		1/26.5
2928.0000	33	溴酚肟、乙二肟〔999〕	6.5		20	13/	9,10	千克	S		1/26.5
2928.0000	34	苯螨特〔999〕	6.5		20	13/	9,10	千克	S		1/26.5
2928.0000	35	醌肟腙〔999〕	6.5		20	13/	9,10	千克	S		1/26.5
2928.0000	36	三甲苯草酮〔999〕	6.5		20	13/	9,10	千克	S		1/26.5
2928.0000	90	其他肼(联氨)及胲(羟胺)的有机衍生物[T2]	6.5		20	13/	10	千克			1/26.5
29.29		**其他含氮基化合物:**									
		-异氰酸酯:									
2929.1010		---2,4-和 2,6-甲苯二异氰酸酯混合物(甲苯二异氰酸酯 TDI)〔999〕	6.5		30	13/	10	千克	AB	MN	1/31.5
2929.1020		---二甲苯二异氰酸酯(TODI)〔999〕	6.5		30	13/	10	千克			1/
2929.1030		---二苯基甲烷二异氰酸酯(纯 MDI)〔999〕	6.5		30	13/	13	千克			1/31.5
2929.1040		六亚基甲烷二异氰酸酯〔999〕	6.5		30	13/	10	千克			1/
2929.1090		---其他〔301 易燃液体,302 毒性物质和感染性物质,303 腐蚀性物质,304 其他危险化学品,305 其他化工产品〕	6.5		30	13/	13	千克			1/16.5
		-其他:									

协定税率 %										特惠税率 %			
亚太5国	东/冰/格	巴基斯坦	韩国	瑞士	哥达	秘鲁	澳大利亚	新西/坡/智	港/澳/台	亚太2国	老/柬/缅	36/3/1	Article Description
	0/0/0	5	0	0	0	0	0	0//0	0/0/			0/0/	Amitraz
	0/0/0	5	0	0	0	0	0	0//0	0/0/			0/0/	Other imines and their derivatives; salts thereof
													Nitrile-function compounds:
	5/0/			0	0	0	0	0//0	0/0/			0/0/	-Acrylonitrile
	0/0/0	5	2.6	0	0	0	0	0//0	0/0/			0/0/	-1-Cyanoguanidine (dicyandiamide)
													-Fenproporex(INN) and its salts; methadone(INN) intermediate(4-cyano-2-dimethylamino-4,4-diphenylbutane)
	0/0/0	5	0	0	0	0	0	0//0	0/0/			0/0/	Methadone (INN) intermediate (4-cyano-2-dimethylamino-4, 4-diphenylbutane)
	0/0/0	5	0	0	0	0	0	0//0	0/0/			0/0/	Fenproporex (INN) and salts thereof
	0/0/0	0	0	2	0	0	0	0//0	0/0/			0/0/	-alpha-Phenylacetoacetonitrile
													-Other:
	0/0/0	0	0	0	0	0	0	0//0	0/0/			0/0/	---*p*-Chlorobenzyl cyanide
5.2	0/0/0	5	0	0	0	0	0	0//0	0/0/			0/0/	---*m*-Phthalonitrile
													---Other
	0/0/0	0	0	2	0	0	0	0//0	0/0/			0/0/	Fenpropathrin, s-fenvalerate, cyhalothrin (including insect hydrazone)
	0/0/0	0	0	2	0	0	0	0//0	0/0/			0/0/	Hexanedinitrile
	0/0/0	0	0	2	0	0	0	0//0	0/0/			0/0/	Cypermethrin, cynuthrin (including beta-cypermethrin, theta-cypermethrin, beta-cyfluthrin)
	0/0/0	0	0	2	0	0	0	0//0	0/0/			0/0/	Cyanophos Phoxim-methyl (including dichlobenil, ioxynil, ioxynil octanoate, bromooxynil, bromoxynil octanoate)
	0/0/0	0	0	2	0	0	0	0//0	0/0/			0/0/	Chlorphoxim, nitrilacarb, cyphenothrin(including fenoxanil, malonoben, d-cyphenothrin)
	0/0/0	0	0	2	0	0	0	0//0	0/0/			0/0/	Pentmethrin, tralocythrin (including lambda-cyhalothrin, gamma-cyhalothrin)
	0/0/0	0	0	2	0	0	0	0//0	0/0/			0/0/	Deltamethrin, tralomerhrin, acrinathrin
	0/0/0	0	0	2	0	0	0	0//0	0/0/			0/0/	Flumethrin, fenvalerate, cycloprothrin
	0/0/0	0	0	2	0	0	0	0//0	0/0/			0/0/	Flucythrinate, brofluthrinate, brofenvalerate
	0/0/0	0	0	2	0	0	0	0//0	0/0/			0/0/	Fenoxanil, chlorothalonil, cymoxanil, bromothalonil
	0/0/0	0	0	2	0	0	0	0//0	0/0/			0/0/	Tau-fluralinate cyhalofop-butyl, cyphenothrin (including rich-d-t-cyphenothrin)
	0/0/0	0	0	2	0	0	0	0//0	0/0/			0/0/	js399-19
	0/0/0	0	0	2	0	0	0	0//0	0/0/			0/0/	Phoxim
	0/0/0	0	0	2	0	0	0	0//0	0/0/			0/0/	Cyflumetofen
	0/0/0	0	0	2	0	0	0	0//0	0/0/			0/0/	3-Methyl-2-phenylbutyronitrile
	0/0/0	0	0	2	0	0	0	0//0	0/0/			0/0/	Other nitrile-function compounds
													Diazo-, azo-. or azoxy-compounds:
													Diazo-, azo-. or azoxy-compounds
	0/0/0	5	0	0	0	0	0	0//0	0/0/			0/0/	Dexon(including azoxy-compounds)
	0/0/0	5	0	0	0	0	0	0//0	0/0/			0/0/	Other diazo-azo-compounds(including azoxy compounds)
													Organic derivatives of hydrazine or of hydroxylamine:
													Organic derivatives of hydrazine or of hydroxylamine
	0/0/0	5	2.6	0	0	0	0	0//0	0/0/			0/0/	Dimethylhydrazine
	0/0/0	5	2.6	0	0	0	0	0//0	0/0/			0/0/	Methylhydrazine
	0/0/0	5	2.6	0	0	0	0	0//0	0/0/			0/0/	RH-5849, tebufenozide, daminozide, bifenazate (including, trifloxystrobin, metomiuostrobin)
	0/0/0	5	2.6	0	0	0	0	0//0	0/0/			0/0/	Monolinuron, metobromuron, linuron, chlorbromuron
	0/0/0	5	2.6	0	0	0	0	0//0	0/0/			0/0/	Bromofenoxim, glyoxime
	0/0/0	5	2.6	0	0	0	0	0//0	0/0/			0/0/	Benzoximate
	0/0/0	5	2.6	0	0	0	0	0//0	0/0/			0/0/	Benquinox
	0/0/0	5	2.6	0	0	0	0	0//0	0/0/			0/0/	Tralkoxydim
	0/0/0	5	2.6	0	0	0	0	0//0	0/0/			0/0/	Organic derivatives of hydrazine or of hydroxylamine
													Compounds with other nitrogen function:
													-Isocyanates:
	0/0/0	0	3.9	0	0	0	0	0//0	0/0/0			0/0/	---Toluene diisocyanate
	0/0/0	5	0		0	0	0	0//0	0/0/			0/0/	---*o*-Xylene diisocyanate
	0/0/0	0		2	0	0	0	0//0	0/0/			0/0/	---Diphenylmethane diisocyanate
	0/0/0	5	2.6	0	0	0	0	0//0	0/0/			0/0/	---Hexamethylene diisocyanate
	0/0/0	0	0	0	0	0	0	0//0	0/0/			0/0/	---Other
													-Other:

税则号列	货品名称〔CIQ 扩展编码及品名—T2 表示见附表 2〕	最惠(%)	暂定税率	普通	增值/消费	出口退税	计量单位	监管条件	检验检疫	特殊证件对美关税
2929.9010	---环己基氨基磺酸钠(甜蜜素)〔301 无检疫要求食品添加剂,302 无检疫要求食品添加剂,303 需申报仅用于工业用途不用于食品添加剂无检疫要求的化学品〕	9		90	13/	10	千克	A	R	1/
2929.9020	---二烷(甲、乙、正丙或异丙)氨基膦酰二卤〔999〕	6.5		30	13/	10	千克	23		1/
2929.9030	---二烷(甲、乙、正丙或异丙)氨基膦酸二烷(甲、乙、正丙或异丙)酯〔999〕	6.5		30	13/	10	千克	23		1/
2929.9040	---乙酰甲胺磷〔999〕	6.5		30	13/	9,10	千克	S		1/
2929.9090	---其他									
2929.9090 11	胺丙畏、胺草磷、抑草磷,丁苯草酮等(包括甲基胺草磷)〔999〕	6.5		30	13/	9,10	千克	S		1/26.5
2929.9090 12	异柳磷、甲基异柳磷、丙胺氟磷等〔301 毒性物质和感染性物质,302 其他危险化学品,303 其他化工产品〕	6.5		30	13/	0	千克	S		1/26.5
2929.9090 13	八甲磷、育畜磷、甘氨硫磷等(包括甲氟磷、毒鼠磷、水胺硫磷)〔301 毒性物质和感染性物质,302 其他化工产品〕	6.5		30	13/	9,10	千克	S		1/26.5
2929.9090 90	其他含氮基化合物〔301 爆炸品,302 毒性物质和感染性物质,303 其他化工产品〕	6.5		30	13/	10	千克			1/26.5
	第十分章　有机—无机化合物、杂环化合物、核酸及其盐以及磺(酰)胺									
29.30	**有机硫化合物:**									
2930.2000	-硫代氨基甲酸盐(或酯)及二硫代氨基甲酸盐									
2930.2000 11	禾草丹、杀螟丹〔101 巴丹,102 杀草丹颗粒剂,103 杀草丹〕	6.5		30	13/	9,10	千克	S		1/11.5
2930.2000 12	威百亩、代森钠、丙森锌、福美铁等(包括福美锌、代森福美锌、安百亩)〔301 毒性物质和感染性物质,302 杂项物质,303 其他化工产品〕	6.5		30	13/	9,10	千克	S		1/11.5
2930.2000 13	燕麦敌、野麦畏、硫草敌〔101 野麦畏(含量>30%),102 燕麦敌粉剂(含量>80%),103 燕麦敌二号,104 燕麦敌乳剂(含量>20%),105 燕麦敌二号乳剂,106 燕麦敌二号蒽油乳油〕	6.5		30	13/	9,10	千克	S		1/11.5
2930.2000 14	苄草丹、戊草丹、坪草丹、仲草丹〔999〕	6.5		30	13/	9,10	千克	S		1/11.5
2930.2000 15	丁草敌、克草敌、茵草敌、灭草敌等(包括环草敌)〔999〕	6.5		30	13/	9,10	千克	S		1/11.5
2930.2000 16	硫茵威、莱草畏〔301 杂项物质,302 其他化工产品〕	6.5		30	13/	9,10	千克	S		1/11.5
2930.2000 90	其他硫代氨基甲酸盐(或酯)(包括二硫代氨基甲酸盐)〔101〕	6.5		30	13/	10	千克			1/11.5
2930.3000	-一硫化二烃氨基硫羰、二硫化二烃氨基硫羰及四硫化二烃氨基硫羰									
2930.3000 10	福美双〔102〕	6.5		30	13/	9,10	千克	S		1/26.5
2930.3000 90	其他一硫化二烃氨基硫羰等(包括二硫化二烃氨基硫羰及四硫化二烃氨基硫羰)〔999〕	6.5		30	13/	10	千克			1/26.5
2930.4000	-甲硫氨酸(蛋氨酸)〔101 饲料添加剂〕	6.5	5	30	13/	13	千克	A	MP	1/30
2930.6000	-2-(N,N-二乙基氨基)乙硫醇〔999〕	6.5		30	13/	13	千克			1/
2930.7000	-二(2-羟乙基)硫醚[硫二甘醇(INN)]〔999〕	6.5		30	13/	10	千克	23		1/
2930.8000	-涕灭威(ISO)、敌菌丹(ISO)及甲胺磷(ISO)									
2930.8000 10	甲胺磷(ISO)〔999〕	6.5		30	13/	0	千克			1/
2930.8000 20	敌菌丹(ISO)〔999〕	6.5		30	13/	0	千克	S		1/
2930.8000 30	涕灭威(ISO)〔999〕	6.5		30	13/	0	千克	S		1/
	-其他:									
2930.9010	---双巯丙氨酸(胱氨酸)〔101 饲料添加剂〕	6.5		30	13/	10	千克	A	MP	1/31.5
2930.9020	---二硫代碳酸酯(或盐)[黄原酸酯(或盐)]〔999〕	6.5		30	13/	13	千克			1/31.5
2930.9090	---其他									
2930.9090 11	烯禾啶,双环磺草酮,氟虫酰胺,氟苯虫酰胺〔999〕	6.5		30	13/	9,10	千克	S		1/11.5
2930.9090 13	2-氯乙基氯甲基硫醚〔999〕	6.5		30	13/	10	千克	32		1/11.5
2930.9090 14	二(2-氯乙基)硫醚(即芥子气)〔999〕	6.5		30	13/	10	千克	32		1/11.5
2930.9090 15	二(2-氯乙硫基)甲烷〔999〕	6.5		30	13/	10	千克	32		1/11.5
2930.9090 16	1,2-二(2-氯乙硫基)乙烷(倍半芥气)〔999〕	6.5		30	13/	10	千克	32		1/11.5
2930.9090 17	1,3-二(2-氯乙硫基)正丙烷〔999〕	6.5		30	13/	10	千克	32		1/11.5
2930.9090 18	1,4-二(2-氯乙硫基)正丁烷〔999〕	6.5		30	13/	10	千克	32		1/11.5
2930.9090 19	1,5-二(2-氯乙硫基)正戊烷〔999〕	6.5		30	13/	10	千克	32		1/11.5
2930.9090 21	二(2-氯乙硫基甲基)醚〔999〕	6.5		30	13/	10	千克	32		1/11.5
2930.9090 22	二(2-氯乙硫基乙基)醚(氧芥气)〔999〕	6.5		30	13/	10	千克	32		1/11.5
2930.9090 23	胺吸膦(硫代磷酸二乙基-S-2-二乙氨基乙酯及烷基化或质子化盐)〔999〕	6.5		30	13/	10	千克	23		1/11.5
2930.9090 24	烷基氨基乙-2-硫醇及相应质子盐〔999〕	6.5		30	13/	10	千克	23		1/11.5
2930.9090 26	烷基硫代膦酸烷 S-2-二烷氨基乙酯(包括相应烷基化盐、质子化盐,烷基指甲、乙、正丙、异丙基)〔999〕	6.5		30	13/	10	千克	23		1/11.5

协定税率 %										特惠税率 %			
亚太5国	东/冰/格	巴基斯坦	韩国	瑞士	哥达	秘鲁	澳大利亚	新西/坡/智	港/澳/台	亚太2国	老/柬/缅	36/3/1	Article Description
7.2	0/0/0	4	0	0	0	0	0	0//0	0/0/			0/0/	---Sodium cyclamate
5.2	0/0/0	5	0	0	0	0	0	0//0	0/0/			0/0/	---N,N-Dialkyl (Me, Et, n-Pr or i-Pr) phosphoramidic dihalides
5.2	0/0/0	5	0	0	0	0	0	0//0	0/0/			0/0/	---Dialkyl (Me, Et, n-Pr or i-Pr) N,N-dialkyl(Me, Et, n-Pr or i-Pr)-phosphoramidates
	0/0/0	5	0	0	0	0	0	0//0	0/0/			0/0/	---Acephate
													---Other
	0/0/0	5	3.9	0	0	0	0	0//0	0/0/			0/0/	Propetamaphos, amiprophos, butamifos (including amiprophos-methl)
	0/0/0	5	3.9	0	0	0	0	0//0	0/0/			0/0/	Isofenphos , isofenphos-methy, mipafox
	0/0/0	5	3.9	0	0	0	0	0//0	0/0/			0/0/	Schradan, crufomate, phosglycin (including dimefox, phosazetim, isocarbophos)
	0/0/0	5	3.9	0	0	0	0	0//0	0/0/			0/0/	Compounds with other nitrogen function
													Ⅹ. ORGANO-INORGANIC COMPOUNDS, HETEROCYCLIC COMPOUNDS, NUCLEIC ACIDS AND THEIR SALTS, AND SULPHONAMIDES
													Organo-sulphur compounds:
													-Thiocarbamates and dithiocarbamates
	0/0/0	5	0	0	0	0	0	0//0	0/0/			0/0/	Thiobencarb, cartap
	0/0/0	5	0	0	0	0	0	0//0	0/0/			0/0/	Metam-sodium, nabam, propineb, ferbam (including ziram, poly-carbamate, meta-ammonium
	0/0/0	5	0	0	0	0	0	0//0	0/0/			0/0/	Diallate, triallate, ethiolate
	0/0/0	5	0	0	0	0	0	0//0	0/0/			0/0/	Prosulfocarb, esprocarb, orbencarb, tiocarbazil
	0/0/0	5	0	0	0	0	0	0//0	0/0/			0/0/	Butylate, pebulate, eradicane, vernolate (including cycloate)
	0/0/0	5	0	0	0	0	0	0//0	0/0/			0/0/	Prothiocarb, sulfallate
	0/0/0	5	0	0	0	0	0	0//0	0/0/			0/0/	Other thiocarbamates and dithiocarbamates(or ester) (including salt dithiocarbamate)
													-A sulfur dialkyl amino carbonyl sulphide, dialkyl disulfide and sulfur amino carbonyl sulfide dialkyl amino carbonyl sulfur
	0/0/0	5	0	0	0	0	0	0//0	0/0/			0/0/	Thiram
	0/0/0	5	0	0	0	0	0	0//0	0/0/			0/0/	Other thiuram mono-, (including dihydrocarbon-sulfur vulcanization carbonylation and thiuram tetrasulphides)
	0/0/0	0	0	0	0	0	0	0//0	0/0/			0/0/	-Methionine
	0/0/0	5	0	0	0	0	0	0//0	0/0/			0/0/	-2-(*N*,*N-Diethylamino*) ethanethiol
	0/0/0	5	0	0	0	0	0	0//0	0/0/			0/0/	-Bis (2-*hydroxyethyl*) sulfide (*thiodiglycol*(*INN*))
													-Aldicarb(*ISO*), captafol (*ISO*)and methamidophos (*ISO*)
	0/0/0	5	0	0	0	0	0	0//0	0/0/			0/0/	Methamidophos (ISO)
	0/0/0	5	0	0	0	0	0	0//0	0/0/			0/0/	Coptafol(ISO)
	0/0/0	5	0	0	0	0	0	0//0	0/0/			0/0/	Aldicarb(ISO)
													-Other:
	0/0/0	5	0	0	0	0	0	0//0	0/0/			0/0/	---Cystine
	0/0/0	5	0	0	0	0	0	0//0	0/0/			0/0/	---Dithiocarbonates (Xanth-ates)
													---Other
	0/0/0	5	0	0	0	0	0	0//0	0/0/			0/0/	Sethoxydinm, benzobicylon, flubendiamide
	0/0/0	5	0	0	0	0	0	0//0	0/0/			0/0/	2-chloroethyl chloromethyl sulfide
	0/0/0	5	0	0	0	0	0	0//0	0/0/			0/0/	Bis (2-chloroethyl) sulfide
	0/0/0	5	0	0	0	0	0	0//0	0/0/			0/0/	Bis (2-chloroethyl sulfide) methane
	0/0/0	5	0	0	0	0	0	0//0	0/0/			0/0/	1,2-Bis(2-chloroethyl sulfide) ethane
	0/0/0	5	0	0	0	0	0	0//0	0/0/			0/0/	1,3-Bis(2-chloroethyl sulfide) propane
	0/0/0	5	0	0	0	0	0	0//0	0/0/			0/0/	1,4-Bis(2-chloroethyl sulfide) butane
	0/0/0	5	0	0	0	0	0	0//0	0/0/			0/0/	1,5-Bis(2-chloroethyl sulfide) pentane
	0/0/0	5	0	0	0	0	0	0//0	0/0/			0/0/	Bis (2-chloroethyl sulfide methyl) ester
	0/0/0	5	0	0	0	0	0	0//0	0/0/			0/0/	Bis (2-chloroethyl sulfide ethyl) ester
	0/0/0	5	0	0	0	0	0	0//0	0/0/			0/0/	Amiton O, O-Diethyl S-2-(diethy lamino) ethyl phosphorothilolate and corresponding alkylated or protonated salts
	0/0/0	5	0	0	0	0	0	0//0	0/0/			0/0/	N, N-dialkyl aminoethane-2-thiols and corresponding protonated salts
	0/0/0	5	0	0	0	0	0	0//0	0/0/			0/0/	Alkyl alkane thiophosphate-S-2-aminoethyl, including cyclo alkane-S-2-dialkane (Me, Et, n-Pr or i-Pr) aminoethyl and corresponding alkylated or protonated salts

税则号列	货品名称〔CIQ扩展编码及品名—T2表示见附表2〕	最惠(%)	暂定税率	普通	增值/消费	出口退税	计量单位	监管条件	检验检疫	特殊证件对美关税
2930.9090 27	含一磷原子与甲、乙、丙基结合化合物(不包括地虫磷)〔999〕	6.5		30	13/	10	千克	23		1/11.5
2930.9090 28	内吸磷〔999〕	6.5		30	13/	10	千克			1/11.5
2930.9090 31	4-甲基硫基安非他明〔999〕	6.5		30	13/	10	千克	I		1/11.5
2930.9090 32	莫达非尼〔999〕	6.5		30	13/	10	千克	I		1/11.5
2930.9090 51	甲基硫菌灵、硫菌灵、苯螨醚等(包括乙蒜素、敌灭生、丁酮威、丁酮砜威、棉铃威)〔999〕	6.5		30	13/	9,10	千克	S		1/11.5
2930.9090 52	灭多威、乙硫苯威等(包括杀线威、甲硫威、多杀威、涕灭砜威、硫双威)〔301毒性物质和感染性物质,302杂项物质,303其他化工产品〕	6.5		30	13/	0	千克	S		1/11.5
2930.9090 53	丁醚脲、久效威、苯硫威等(包括敌螨特、2甲4氯乙硫酯)〔301毒性物质和感染性物质,302杂项物质,303其他化工产品〕	6.5		30	13/	9,10	千克	S		1/11.5
2930.9090 54	杀虫双、杀虫单、灭虫脲等(包括避虫醇、烯虫硫酯、三氯杀螨砜、杀螨醚、杀螨酯)〔101一氯杀螨砜,102杀螨酯,103一氯杀螨砜乳剂,104杀螨酯乳剂〕	6.5		30	13/	9,10	千克	S		1/11.5
2930.9090 55	代森锌、代森锰、代森锰锌等(包括福美胂、福美甲胂、代森铵、代森联)〔301易于自燃的物质,302其他化工产品〕	6.5		30	13/	9,10	千克	S		1/11.5
2930.9090 56	烯草酮、磺草酮、嗪草酸甲酯、硝磺草酮等(包括苯氟磺胺、甲磺乐灵、氯硫酰草胺、脱叶磷)〔301毒性物质和感染性物质,302杂项物质,303其他化工产品〕	6.5		30	13/	9,10	千克	S		1/11.5
2930.9090 57	灭菌丹、克菌丹、杀螨硫醚等(包括氟杀螨、硫肟醚、莠不生)〔999〕	6.5		30	13/	9,10	千克	S		1/11.5
2930.9090 58	稻瘟净、异稻瘟净、稻丰散等(包括敌瘟磷)〔301毒性物质和感染性物质,302其他化工产品〕	6.5		30	13/	9,10	千克	S		1/11.5
2930.9090 59	安妥、灭鼠特、二硫氰基甲烷等(包括灭鼠肼、氟硫隆)〔301毒性物质和感染性物质,302其他化工产品〕	6.5		30	13/	9,10	千克	S		1/11.5
2930.9090 61	马拉硫磷、苏硫磷、赛硫磷等(包括丙虫磷、双硫磷、亚砜磷、异亚砜磷)〔301杂项物质,302其他化工产品〕	6.5		30	13/	9,10	千克	S		1/11.5
2930.9090 62	丙溴磷、田乐磷、特丁硫磷等(包括硫丙磷、地虫硫膦、乙硫磷、丙硫磷、甲基乙拌磷)〔301毒性物质和感染性物质,302其他化工产品〕	6.5		30	13/	9,10	千克	S		1/11.5
2930.9090 63	乐果、益硫磷、氧乐果等(包括甲拌磷、乙拌磷、虫螨磷、果虫磷)〔301毒性物质和感染性物质,302其他化工产品〕	6.5		30	13/	9,10	千克	S		1/11.5
2930.9090 64	氯胺磷、家蝇磷、灭蚜磷等(包括安硫磷、四甲磷、丁苯硫磷、苯线磷、蚜灭磷)〔301毒性物质和感染性物质,302其他化工产品〕	6.5		30	13/	9,10	千克	S		1/11.5
2930.9090 65	硫线磷、氯甲硫磷、杀虫磺等(包括砜吸磷、砜拌磷、异拌磷、三硫磷、芬硫磷)〔301毒性物质和感染性物质,302其他化工产品〕	6.5		30	13/	9,10	千克	S		1/11.5
2930.9090 66	倍硫磷、甲基内吸磷、乙酯磷等(包括丰索磷、内吸磷、发硫磷)〔301毒性物质和感染性物质,302其他化工产品〕	6.5		30	13/	9,10	千克	S		1/11.5
2930.9090 67	灭线磷〔999〕	6.5		30	13/	9,10	千克	S		1/11.5
2930.9090 68	青霉胺	6.5	0	30	3/	13	千克			/5
2930.9090 91	DL-羟基蛋氨酸〔101饲料添加剂,102化工产品〕	6.5		30	13/	13	千克	A	MP	1/11.5
2930.9090 92	比卡鲁胺〔999〕	6.5	0	30	3/	13	千克			1/5
2930.9090 99	其他有机硫化合物[T2]	6.5		30	13/	13	千克			1/11.5
29.31	**其他有机—无机化合物:**									
2931.1000	-四甲基铅及四乙基铅〔101四甲基铅,102四乙基铅〕	6.5		30	13/	10	千克	XAB	MN	1/
2931.2000	-三丁基锡化合物〔999〕	6.5		30	13/	0	千克	X		1/
	-其他有机磷衍生物:									
2931.3100	--甲基膦酸二甲酯〔999〕	6.5		30	13/	10	千克	23		1/
2931.3200	--丙基膦酸二甲酯〔999〕	6.5		30	13/	10	千克	AB	MRNS	1/
2931.3300	--乙基膦酸二乙酯〔999〕	6.5		30	13/	10	千克	23		1/
2931.3400	--3-(三羟基硅烷基)丙基甲基膦酸钠〔999〕	6.5		30	13/	10	千克	AB	MRNS	1/
2931.3500	--1-丙基磷酸环酐〔999〕	6.5		30	13/	10	千克	AB	MRNS	1/
2931.3600	--(5-乙基-2-甲基-2-氧代-1,3,2-二氧磷杂环己-5-基)甲基膦酸二甲酯(CAS号:41203—81—0)〔999〕	6.5		30	13/	10	千克	23		1/
2931.3700	--双[(5-乙基-2-甲基-2-氧代-1,3,2-二氧磷杂环己-5-基)甲基]甲基膦酸酯(阻燃剂FRC-1)(CAS号:42595—45—9)〔999〕	6.5		30	13/	10	千克	AB	MRNS	1/
2931.3800	--甲基膦酸和脒基尿素(1:1)生成的盐〔999〕	6.5		30	13/	10	千克	AB	MRNS	1/
	---其他									
2931.3910	---双甘膦〔301需申报仅用于工业用途不用于食品添加剂无检疫要求的化学品〕	6.5		30	13/	0	千克	AB	RS	1/
2931.3990	---其他									
2931.3990 11	烷基亚膦酰烷基-2-二烷氨基乙酯(包括相应烷基化盐或质子化盐)〔999〕	6.5		30	13/	10	千克	23		1/31.5
2931.3990 12	氯沙林、氯梭曼(氯沙林即甲基氯膦酸异丙酯,氯梭曼即甲基氯膦酸频那酯)〔999〕	6.5		30	13/	10	千克	23		1/31.5
2931.3990 13	烷基氟膦酸烷酯,10碳原子以下(烷基指甲,乙,正丙,异丙基,例如沙林,梭曼)〔999〕	6.5		30	13/	10	千克	23		1/31.5

协定税率 %										特惠税率 %			Article Description
亚太5国	东/冰/格	巴基斯坦	韩国	瑞士	哥达	秘鲁	澳大利亚	新西/坡/智	港/澳/台	亚太2国	老/柬/缅	36/3/1	
	0/0/0	5	0	0	0	0	0	0//0	0/0/			0/0/	Chemicals, containing a phosphorus atom to which is boned one methyl, ethyl or propyl group
	0/0/0	5	0	0	0	0	0	0//0	0/0/			0/0/	Demeton
	0/0/0	5	0	0	0	0	0	0//0	0/0/			0/0/	4-methylthioamfetamine
	0/0/0	5	0	0	0	0	0	0//0	0/0/			0/0/	Modafinil
	0/0/0	5	0	0	0	0	0	0//0	0/0/			0/0/	Thiophanate-methyl, thiophanate, phenproxide. (including ethylicin, dimexano , butocarboxim, butoxycarboxim, alanycarb)
	0/0/0	5	0	0	0	0	0	0//0	0/0/			0/0/	Methomyl, aldicarb, ethiofencarb, (including oxamyl, methiocarb, toxisamate, aldoxycarb, thiodicarb)
	0/0/0	5	0	0	0	0	0	0//0	0/0/			0/0/	Diafenthiuron, thiofanox, fenothiocarb (including chlorfensulphide, MCPA-thioethyl)
	0/0/0	5	0	0	0	0	0	0//0	0/0/			0/0/	Disosultap, monosultap, chloromethiuron(including (octylthio) ethanol, triprene, tetradifon, chlorbenside, chlorfenson)
	0/0/0	5	0	0	0	0	0	0//0	0/0/			0/0/	Zineb, maneb, mancozeb, (including asomate , urbacide(JMAP) , amobam, metiram)
	0/0/0	5	0	0	0	0	0	0//0	0/0/			0/0/	Clethodim, sulcotrione, fluthiacet-methyl mesotrione (including dichlofluanid, nitralin, chlorthiamide, tribuphons)
	0/0/0	5	0	0	0	0	0	0//0	0/0/			0/0/	Folpet, captan, tetrasul (including fluorbenside, sulfoxime, EXD)
	0/0/0	5	0	0	0	0	0	0//0	0/0/			0/0/	Kitazine, iprobenfos phenthoate(including edifenphos)
	0/0/0	5	0	0	0	0	0	0//0	0/0/			0/0/	Antu, thiosemicarbazide, dithiocyano-methane (including promurit, flurothiuron)
	0/0/0	5	0	0	0	0	0	0//0	0/0/			0/0/	Malathion, sophamide, amidithion (including propaphos, temephos, oxydemeton-methyl, oxydeprofos)
	0/0/0	5	0	0	0	0	0	0//0	0/0/			0/0/	Profenofos, demephion, terbufos(including sulprofos, fonofos, ethion, prothiofos, thiometon)
	0/0/0	5	0	0	0	0	0	0//0	0/0/			0/0/	Dimethoate, ethoate-methyl, omethoate(including phorate, disulfoton, chlorthiophos, cyanthoate)
	0/0/0	5	0	0	0	0	0	0//0	0/0/			0/0/	Chloramine phosphorus, acethion mecarbam(including formothion, mecarphon, fosmethilan, fenamiphos, vamidothion)
	0/0/0	5	0	0	0	0	0	0//0	0/0/			0/0/	Cadusafos, chlormephos, bensultap (including oxydemetonmethyl, oxydisulfoton, isothioate, carbophenothion, phenkapton)
	0/0/0	5	0	0	0	0	0	0//0	0/0/			0/0/	Fenthion, demeton-s-methyl, acetophos (including fensulfothion, demeton , prothoate, methylacetophos)
	0/0/0	5	0	0	0	0	0	0//0	0/0/			0/0/	Ethoprophos
	0/0/0	5	0	0	0	0	0	0//0	0/0/		//	0/0/	penicillamine
	0/0/0	5	0	0	0	0	0	0//0	0/0/			0/0/	DL- hydroxy methionine
	0/0/0	5	0	0	0	0	0	0//0	0/0/			0/0/	Bicalutamide, Mesna, Sulindac and Other Anticancer Drugs
	0/0/0	5	0	0	0	0	0	0//0	0/0/			0/0/	Other organic sulfur compounds
													Other organo-inorganic compounds:
	0/0/0	5	0	0	0	0	0	0//0	0/0/			0/0/	-Tetramethyl lead and tetraethyl lead
	0/0/0	5	0	0	0	0	0	0//0	0/0/			0/0/	-Tributyltin compounds:
													-Other organo-phosphorous derivatives:
	0/0/0	5	0	0	0	0	0	0//0	0/0/			0/0/	--Dimethyl methylphosphonate
	0/0/0	5	0	0	0	0	0	0//0	0/0/			0/0/	--Dimethyl propylphosphonate
	0/0/0	5	0	0	0	0	0	0//0	0/0/			0/0/	--Diethyl ethylphosphonate
	0/0/0	5	0	0	0	0	0	0//0	0/0/			0/0/	--Sodium 3-(*trihydroxysilyl*) propyl methylphosphonate
	0/0/0	5	0	0	0	0	0	0//0	0/0/			0/0/	--2,4,6-Tripropyl-1,3,5,2,4,6-trioxatriphosphinane 2,4,6-trioxide
	0/0/0	5	0	0	0	0	0	0//0	0/0/			0/0/	--(5-*Ethyl-2-methyl-2-oxido*-1, 3, 2-*dioxaphosphinan*-5-*Yl*) methyl methyl methylphosphonate
	0/0/0	5	0	0	0	0	0	0//0	0/0/			0/0/	--Bis [5-*ethyl-2-methyl-2-ox-ido*-1, 3, 2-*dioxaphosphinan*-5-*Yl*) *methyl*] methylphosphonate
	0/0/0	5	0	0	0	0	0	0//0	0/0/			0/0/	--Salt of methylphosphonic acid and (*aminoiminomethyl*) urea (1:1)
													---Other
	0/0/0	5	0	0	0	0	0	0//0	0/0/			0/0/	---N-(*Phosphonomethyl*) iminodiacetic acid
													---Other
	0/0/0	5	0	0	0	0	0	0//0	0/0/			0/0/	Alkyl-phosphonic alkyl 2-n-diethyl(including corresponding alkylated salt or protonated salt)
	0/0/0	5	0	0	0	0	0	0//0	0/0/			0/0/	Chlorosarin(O-Isopropylmethylphosphonochloridate); Chlorosoman (O-Pinacolylmethylphosphonochloridate)
	0/0/0	5	0	0	0	0	0	0//0	0/0/			0/0/	Alkyl(Me, Et, n-Pr, i-Pr) alkane fluorophosphate esters, below 10-carbon atoms, for example, sarin, Soman

税则号列	货品名称〔CIQ 扩展编码及品名－T2 表示见附表 2〕	最惠(%)	暂定税率	普通	增值/消费	出口退税	计量单位	监管条件	检验检疫	特殊证件对美关税
2931.3990 14	二烷氨基氰膦酸烷酯 10 碳原子以下(烷基指甲,乙,正丙,异丙基,例如塔崩)〔999〕	6.5		30	13/	10	千克	23		1/31.5
2931.3990 15	烷基膦酰二氟(烷基指甲,乙,正丙,异丙基,例如,DF:甲基膦酰二氟)〔999〕	6.5		30	13/	10	千克	23		1/31.5
2931.3990 16	草甘膦〔999〕	6.5		30	13/	0	千克	S		1/31.5
2931.3990 17	草铵膦,草硫膦,杀木膦等(包括双丙氨膦,增甘膦及其盐)〔999〕	6.5		30	13/	9,10	千克	S		1/31.5
2931.3990 18	三丁氯苄鏻〔999〕	6.5		30	13/	9,10	千克	S		1/31.5
2931.3990 19	乙烯利〔999〕	6.5		30	13/	9,10	千克	S		1/31.5
2931.3990 21	敌百虫,氟硅菊酯,毒壤膦等(包括苯硫膦,溴苯膦,苯腈膦,丁酯膦)〔999〕	6.5		30	13/	9,10	千克	S		1/31.5
2931.3990 22	甲基膦酰二氯、丙基膦酸、甲基膦酸、甲基膦酸二聚乙二醇酯(CAS 号:294675-51-7)(甲基膦酸二[5-(5-乙基-2-甲基-2-氧代-1,3,2-二氧磷杂环己基)甲基]酯(CAS 号:42595-45-9),地虫磷除外)〔999〕	6.5		30	13/	9,10	千克	23		1/31.5
2931.3990 90	其他含磷原子的有机-无机化合物[T2]	6.5		30	13/	9,10	千克	AB	MRNS	1/31.5
2931.9000	--其他									
2931.9000 01	六甲基环三硅氧烷(包括八甲基环四硅氧烷,十甲基环五硅氧烷,十二甲基环六硅氧烷)〔999〕	6.5		30	13/	10	千克			1/11.5
2931.9000 11	2-氯乙烯基二氯胂〔999〕	6.5		30	13/	0	千克	23		1/11.5
2931.9000 12	二(2-氯乙烯基)氯胂〔999〕	6.5		30	13/	0	千克	23		1/11.5
2931.9000 13	三(2-氯乙烯基)胂〔999〕	6.5		30	13/	0	千克	23		1/11.5
2931.9000 14	锆试剂,二甲胂酸等(包括 4 二甲氨基偶氮苯 4'胂酸,卡可基酸,二甲基胂酸钠)〔999〕	6.5		30	13/	0	千克			1/11.5
2931.9000 15	4-氨基苯胂酸钠,二氯化苯胂(对氨基苯胂酸钠,二氯苯胂,苯胂化二氯)〔999〕	6.5		30	13/	0	千克			1/11.5
2931.9000 16	蒽醌-1-胂酸、三环锡(普特丹)等(包括月桂酸三丁基锡、醋酸三丁基锡)〔999〕	6.5		30	13/	0	千克			1/11.5
2931.9000 17	硫酸三乙基锡,二丁基氧化锡等(包括氧化二丁基锡,乙酸三乙基锡,三乙基乙酸锡)〔999〕	6.5		30	13/	10	千克			1/11.5
2931.9000 18	四乙基锡,乙酸三甲基锡(四乙锡,醋酸三甲基锡)〔999〕	6.5		30	13/	10	千克			1/11.5
2931.9000 19	毒菌锡(三苯基羟基锡(含量＞20%))〔999〕	6.5		30	13/	10	千克			1/11.5
2931.9000 21	乙酰亚砷酸铜,二苯(基)胺氯胂(祖母绿;翡翠绿;醋酸亚砷酸铜,吩吡嗪化氯;亚当氏气)〔999〕	6.5		30	13/	0	千克			1/11.5
2931.9000 22	3-硝基-4-羟基苯胂酸(4-羟基-3-硝基苯胂酸)〔999〕	6.5		30	13/	0	千克			1/11.5
2931.9000 23	乙基二氯胂,二苯(基)氯胂(包括二氯化乙基胂,氯化二苯胂)〔999〕	6.5		30	13/	0	千克			1/11.5
2931.9000 24	甲(基)胂酸,丙(基)胂酸,二碘化苯胂(苯基二碘胂)〔999〕	6.5		30	13/	0	千克			1/11.5
2931.9000 25	苯胂酸,2-硝基苯胂酸等(包括邻硝基苯胂酸,3-硝基苯胂酸,间硝基苯胂酸等)〔999〕	6.5		30	13/	0	千克			1/11.5
2931.9000 26	4-硝基苯胂酸,2-氨基苯胂酸(对硝基苯胂酸,邻氨基苯胂酸)〔999〕	6.5		30	13/	0	千克			1/11.5
2931.9000 27	3－氨基苯胂酸、4－氨基苯胂酸(间氨基苯胂酸、对氨基苯胂酸)〔999〕	6.5		30	13/	0	千克			1/11.5
2931.9000 28	三苯锡,三苯基乙酸锡等(包括三苯基氯化锡,三苯基氢氧化锡,苯丁锡,三唑锡)〔999〕	6.5		30	13/	9,10	千克	S		1/11.5
2931.9000 29	田安〔999〕	6.5		30	13/	9,13	千克	S		1/11.5
2931.9000 31	乙烯硅〔999〕	6.5		30	13/	9,10	千克	S		1/11.5
2931.9000 90	其他有机-无机化合物〔999,301 其他危险化学品,302 无检疫要求的食品添加剂,303 属于危险化学品的食品添加剂,304 毒性物质和感染性物质〕	6.5		30	13/	13	千克	AB	MRNS	1/11.5
29.32	**仅含有氧杂原子的杂环化合物:**									
	-结构上含有一个非稠合呋喃环(不论是否氢化)的化合物:									
2932.1100	--四氢呋喃〔101:2－甲基四氢呋喃,301:易燃液体,302:2,5－二乙基四氢呋喃(无检疫要求食品添加剂),303:2－甲基－3－四氢呋喃硫醇(无检疫要求食品添加剂)〕	6		20	13/	10	千克	AB	MN	1/26
2932.1200	--2-糠醛〔301〕	6		20	13/	9,10	千克	B	N	1/31
2932.1300	--糠醇及四氢糠醇〔101〕	6		20	13/	10	千克			1/16

协定税率 %										特惠税率 %			
亚太5国	东/冰/格	巴基斯坦	韩国	瑞士	哥达	秘鲁	澳大利亚	新西/坡/智	港/澳/台	亚太2国	老/柬/缅	36/3/1	Article Description
	0/0/0	5	0	0	0	0	0	0//0	0/0/			0/0/	Dialkyl (Me, Et, n-Pr, i-Pr) cyanamide alkane phosphate esters, below 10-carbon atoms, for example, tabun
	0/0/0	5	0	0	0	0	0	0//0	0/0/			0/0/	Alkyl(Me, Et, n-Pr, i-Pr) phosphoryl difluoride, for example, DF: Methylphosphonic dichloride
	0/0/0	5	0	0	0	0	0	0//0	0/0/			0/0/	Glyphosate
	0/0/0	5	0	0	0	0	0	0//0	0/0/			0/0/	Glufosinate-ammonium, glyphosate-trimesium, fosamine-ammonium etc.(including bialaphos, glyphosine and its salt)
	0/0/0	5	0	0	0	0	0	0//0	0/0/			0/0/	Chlorphonium(BSI, ISO)
	0/0/0	5	0	0	0	0	0	0//0	0/0/			0/0/	Ethephon
	0/0/0	5	0	0	0	0	0	0//0	0/0/			0/0/	Trichlorfon, silafluofen, trichloronat etc.(including EPN(ESA), leptophos, cyan-ofenphos, butonate
	0/0/0	5	0	0	0	0	0	0//0	0/0/			0/0/	Methyl phosphonic acid, two chlorine methyl phosphonic acid two methyl ester, propyl phosphonic acid, methyl phosphonic acid, ethyl phosphonic acid ethyl ester two, methyl phosphonic acid polyethylene glycol two (CAS: 294678-51-7) [including methyl phosphonic acid, methyl 5-(5-ethyl-2-methyl-2-oxo-1, 3, 2-two oxygen phosphorus heterocyclic methyl ester (2-ethylhexyl) CAS NO. 41203-81-0]. methyl phosphonic acid[two 5-(5-ethyl-2-methyl-2-oxo-1, 3, 2-two oxygen phosphorus heterocyclic hexyl) methy] ester(CAS NO. 42595-45-9), except the fonofos
	0/0/0	5	0	0	0	0	0	0//0	0/0/			0/0/	Other organo-inorganic compounds containing Phosphorus atoms
													-Other
	0/0/0	5	0	0	0	0	0	0//0	0/0/			0/0/	Hexamethylcyclotrisiloxane (including octamethylcyotetrasiloxane, decamethylcyclotrisiloxane, decamethylcyclotrisiloxane)
	0/0/0	5	0	0	0	0	0	0//0	0/0/			0/0/	2-chlorovinyl dichloroarsine
	0/0/0	5	0	0	0	0	0	0//0	0/0/			0/0/	Di(2-Chlorovinyl)chloroarsine
	0/0/0	5	0	0	0	0	0	0//0	0/0/			0/0/	Tri(2-Chlorovinyl)arsine
	0/0/0	5	0	0	0	0	0	0//0	0/0/			0/0/	Zirconin, cacodylic acid, etc.(including 4- dimethyl- aminoazobenzene-4'- arsonic acid, cacodylic acid, sodium cacodylate)
	0/0/0	5	0	0	0	0	0	0//0	0/0/			0/0/	4-sodium arsanilate, phenyldichloroarsine (sodium rho-aminophenylarsonate, dichlorophenarsine, phenylarsine dichloride)
	0/0/0	5	0	0	0	0	0	0//0	0/0/			0/0/	Anthraquinone-1-arsonic acid, cyhexatin etc.(including lauric acid tributyltin, acetic acid tributyltin)
	0/0/0	5	0	0	0	0	0	0//0	0/0/			0/0/	Triethyltin sulphate, Dibutyltin oxide etc.(including oxidation dibutyltin? Acetoxytriethylstannane, triethyl ethyl stannic acid)
	0/0/0	5	0	0	0	0	0	0//0	0/0/			0/0/	Tetraethyltin, trimethyltin acetate
	0/0/0	5	0	0	0	0	0	0//0	0/0/			0/0/	Fentin hydroxide[Triphenyltin hydroxide(content>20%)]
	0/0/0	5	0	0	0	0	0	0//0	0/0/			0/0/	Copper acetoarsenite, phenarsazinechloride
	0/0/0	5	0	0	0	0	0	0//0	0/0/			0/0/	4-Hydroxy-3-nitro phenylarsonic acid
	0/0/0	5	0	0	0	0	0	0//0	0/0/			0/0/	Ethyldichloroarsine diphenylchloroarsine etc.(including dichloroethyl arsenic, diphenylarsine chloride)
	0/0/0	5	0	0	0	0	0	0//0	0/0/			0/0/	Methanearsonic acid, propylarsonic acid , phenyl diiodoarsine etc.(including phenylarsine diiondide)
	0/0/0	5	0	0	0	0	0	0//0	0/0/			0/0/	Phenylarsonic acid, 2-nitrophenylarsonic acid(including o-nitrophenyl arsonic acid, 3- nitrophenylarsonic acid, m-nitrophenol arsonic acid etc.)
	0/0/0	5	0	0	0	0	0	0//0	0/0/			0/0/	4-Nitrophenylarsonic acid, 2-aminophenylarsonic acid(para-nitrotoluene arsonic acid, o-phenetidine arsonic acid)
	0/0/0	5	0	0	0	0	0	0//0	0/0/			0/0/	3-Aminophenylarsonic acid, Aminophenylars- onic acid(m-aminophenol arsonic acid , pamin- ophenylarsonic acid)
	0/0/0	5	0	0	0	0	0	0//0	0/0/			0/0/	Fentin, fentin acetate etc.(including fentinCh- loride, fentin hydroxide, fenbutatin oxide, azocy- clotin)
	0/0/0	5	0	0	0	0	0	0//0	0/0/			0/0/	Neoasozin
	0/0/0	5	0	0	0	0	0	0//0	0/0/			0/0/	Etacelasil
	0/0/0	5	0	0	0	0	0	0//0	0/0/			0/0/	Other organo-inorganic compound
													Heterocyclic compounds with oxygen hetero-atom(s) only:
													-Compounds containing an unfused furan ring (whether or not hydrogenated) in the structure:
	0/0/0	5	0	0	0	0	0	0//0	0/0/0			0/0/	--Tetrahydrofuran
	0/0/0	5	0	0	0	0	0	0//0	0/0/			0/0/	--2-Furaldehyde (furfuraldehyde)
	0/0/0	5	0	0	0	0	0	0//0	0/0/			0/0/	--Furfuryl alcohol and tetrahydrofurfuryl alcohol

税则号列		货品名称〔CIQ扩展编码及品名—T2表示见附表2〕	最惠(%)	暂定税率	普通	增值/消费	出口退税	计量单位	监管条件	检验检疫	特殊证件对美关税
2932.1400		--三氯蔗糖〔999〕	6.5		20	13/	13	千克			1/11.5
2932.1900		--其他									
2932.1900	11	喃烯菊酯、炔呋菊酯等(包括甲呋炔菊酯、溴苄呋菊酯、右旋炔呋菊酯)〔999〕	6.5		20	13/	9,10	千克	S		1/16.5
2932.1900	12	呋菌胺、酯菌胺、抑霉胺等(包括环菌胺、甲呋酰胺、二甲呋酰胺)〔999〕	6.5		20	13/	9,10	千克	S		1/16.5
2932.1900	13	呋氧草醚、环庚草醚、呋草酮等(包括茵多酸)〔999〕	6.5		20	13/	9,10	千克	S		1/16.5
2932.1900	14	楝素、呋霜灵等(包括呋菌隆、螺螨酯)〔999〕	6.5		20	13/	9,10	千克	S		1/16.5
2932.1900	15	苄呋菊酯(包括右旋苄呋菊酯、生物苄呋菊酯)〔999〕	6.5		20	13/	9,10	千克	S		1/16.5
2932.1900	16	呋虫胺〔999〕	6.5		20	13/	9,10	千克	S		1/16.5
2932.1900	20	呋芬雷司〔999〕	6.5		20	13/	10	千克	I		1/16.5
2932.1900	30	恩格列净	6.5	6.5	20	13/	10	千克			/10
2932.1900	90	其他结构上有非稠合呋喃环化合物〔301易燃液体〕	6.5		20	13/	10	千克			1/16.5
		-内酯:									
2932.2010		--香豆素、甲基香豆素及乙基香豆素〔301无检疫要求食品添加剂,302其他化工产品〕	6.5		20	13/	13	千克			1/26.5
2932.2090		--其他内酯									
2932.2090	11	杀鼠灵、克鼠灵、敌鼠灵、溴鼠灵等(包括氯灭鼠灵、氟鼠灵、鼠得克、杀鼠醚)〔301其他危险化学品,302毒性物质和感染性物质〕	6.5		20	13/	0	千克	S		1/26.5
2932.2090	12	赤霉酸〔999〕	6.5		20	13/	9,13	千克	S		1/26.5
2932.2090	13	蝇毒磷、茴蒿素、溴敌隆、呋酰胺等(包括四氯苯酞,畜虫磷)〔301毒性物质和感染性物质〕	6.5		20	13/	0	千克	S		1/26.5
2932.2090	14	丁香菌酯〔999〕	6.5		20	13/	9,13	千克	S		1/26.5
2932.2090	15	甲氨基阿维菌素苯甲酸盐〔999〕	6.5		20	13/	9,13	千克	S		1/26.5
2932.2090	16	阿维菌素〔999〕	6.5		20	13/	9,13	千克	S		1/26.5
2932.2090	20	鬼臼毒素〔999〕	6.5		20	13/	13	千克	EF		1/26.5
2932.2090	90	其他内酯〔301毒性物质和感染性物质,302无检疫要求食品添加剂,303其他化工产品〕	6.5		20	13/	13	千克			1/26.5
		-其他:									
2932.9100		--4-丙烯基-1,2-亚甲二氧基苯(即异黄樟脑)〔999〕	6.5		20	13/	10	千克	23		1/
2932.9200		--1-(1,3-苯并二噁茂-5基)丙烷-2酮〔999〕	6.5		20	13/	10	千克	23		1/
2932.9300		--3,4-亚甲二氧基苯甲醛(胡椒醛)〔999〕	6.5		20	13/	13	千克	23		1/
2932.9400		--4-烯丙基-1,2-亚甲二氧基苯(黄樟脑)〔999〕	6.5		20	13/	13	千克	23		1/
2932.9500		--四氢大麻酚(所有异构体)〔999〕	6.5		20	13/	10	千克	I		1/11.5
		--其他:									
2932.9910		---7-羟基苯并呋喃(呋喃酚)〔999〕	4		11	13/	13	千克			1/
2932.9920		---2,2′-双甲氧羰基-4,4′-双甲氧基-5,6,5′,6′-双亚甲二氧基联苯(联苯双酯)〔999〕	6.5		20	13/	13	千克			1/
2932.9930		---蒿甲醚〔999〕	6.5		20	13/	13	千克			1/11.5
2932.9990		---其他									
2932.9990	11	克百威〔301毒性物质和感染性物质〕	6.5		20	13/	9,13	千克	S		1/26.5
2932.9990	12	二氧威、恶虫威、丙硫克百威等(包括丁硫克百威、呋线威)〔101丁硫威粉剂,102恶虫威粉剂(含量5%～65%),103二氧威乳剂(含量＞3%),104丁硫威,105二氧威粉剂(含量＞10%)〕	6.5		20	13/	9,13	千克	S		1/26.5
2932.9990	13	因毒磷、敌恶磷、碳氯灵〔301〕	6.5		20	13/	9,13	千克	S		1/26.5
2932.9990	14	增效特、增效砜、增效醚、增效酯等(包括增效环、增效散)〔999〕	6.5		20	13/	9,13	千克			1/26.5
2932.9990	15	吡喃灵、吡喃隆、乙氧呋草黄等(包括呋草黄、氟草肟)〔999〕	6.5		20	13/	9,13	千克	S		1/26.5
2932.9990	16	避蚊酮、苯虫醚、鱼藤酮〔999〕	6.5		20	13/	9,13	千克	S		1/26.5
2932.9990	17	调呋酸、芸苔素内酯〔999〕	6.5		20	13/	9,13	千克	S		1/26.5
2932.9990	21	紫杉醇〔999〕	6.5	0	20	3/	0	千克	QFE		1/20
2932.9990	22	三尖杉宁碱〔999〕	6.5		20	13/	13	千克	FE		1/26.5
2932.9990	23	十去乙酰基巴卡丁三(红豆杉提取物10-DAB)〔999〕	6.5		20	13/	13	千克	FE		1/26.5
2932.9990	24	十去乙酰基紫杉醇(红豆杉提取物10-DAT)〔999〕	6.5		20	13/	0	千克	FE		1/26.5
2932.9990	25	巴卡丁三〔999〕	6.5		20	13/	13	千克	FE		1/26.5
2932.9990	26	7-表紫杉醇〔999〕	6.5		20	13/	0	千克	FE		1/26.5
2932.9990	27	10-去乙酰7-表紫杉醇〔999〕	6.5		20	13/	0	千克	FE		1/26.5
2932.9990	28	7,10-双(三氯乙酰基)-10-去乙酰基巴卡丁三类似物〔999〕	6.5		20	13/	13	千克	EF		1/26.5
2932.9990	29	多烯紫杉醇(多西他赛)〔999〕	6.5	0	20	3/	0	千克	EF		1/20
2932.9990	31	7,10-双(三氯乙酰基)-多西他赛〔999〕	6.5		20	13/	13	千克	EF		1/26.5
2932.9990	40	替苯丙胺及其盐〔999〕	6.5		20	13/	13	千克	I		1/26.5
2932.9990	51	(1,2-二甲基庚基)羟基四氢甲基二苯吡喃(包括六氢大麻酚)〔999〕	6.5		20	13/	13	千克	I		1/26.5
2932.9990	52	甲羟芬胺,乙芬胺,羟芬胺〔999〕	6.5		20	13/	13	千克	I		1/26.5
2932.9990	53	二亚甲基双氧安非他明及其盐(IMDMA)〔999〕	6.5		20	13/	13	千克	I		1/26.5

协定税率 %										特惠税率 %			
亚太5国	东/冰/格	巴基斯坦	韩国	瑞士	哥达	秘鲁	澳大利亚	新西/坡/智	港/澳/台	亚太2国	老/柬/缅	36/3/1	Article Description
	0/0/0	5	0		0	0	0	0//0	0/0/			0/0/	--Sucralose
													--Other
	0/0/0	5	0		0	0	0	0//0	0/0/			0/0/	Japothrins, furamethrin (JMAF) (including proparthrin, bromethrin, d-furamethrin)
	0/0/0	5	0		0	0	0	0//0	0/0/			0/0/	Metomedan, cyprofuram, vangard (including cyprodinil, fenfuram, furcarbanil)
	0/0/0	5	0		0	0	0	0//0	0/0/			0/0/	Furyloxyfen, cinmethylin, flurtamone (including endothal)
	0/0/0	5	0		0	0	0	0//0	0/0/			0/0/	Toosendanin, furalaxyl(including furophanat, spirodiclofen
	0/0/0	5	0		0	0	0	0//0	0/0/			0/0/	Resmethrin (including d-resmethrin, bioresmethrin)
	0/0/0	5	0		0	0	0	0//0	0/0/			0/0/	Dinotefuran;
	0/0/0	5	0		0	0	0	0//0	0/0/			0/0/	Furfennorex
	0/0/0	5	0		0	0	0	0//0	0/0/		//	0/0/	Empagliflozin
	0/0/0	5	0		0	0	0	0//0	0/0/			0/0/	Other compounds containing an unfused furaning in the structure
													-Lactones:
	0/0/0	5	0	0	0	0	0	0//0	0/0/			0/0/	--Coumarin, methylcoumarins and ethyl-coumarins
													--Other lactones
	0/0/0	5	0	2	0	0	0	0//0	0/0/			0/0/	warfarin, coumafuryl, melitoxin, brodifacoum (including coumachlor, flocoumafen, difenacoum, coumatetralyl)
	0/0/0	5	0	2	0	0	0	0//0	0/0/			0/0/	Gibberellic acid
	0/0/0	5	0	2	0	0	0	0//0	0/0/			0/0/	Coumaphos, saneonin, bromadiolone, ofurace(including phthalide, coumithoate)
	0/0/0	5	0	2	0	0	0	0//0	0/0/			0/0/	Coumoxystrobin
	0/0/0	5	0	2	0	0	0	0//0	0/0/			0/0/	Emamectin benzoate
	0/0/0	5	0	2	0	0	0	0//0	0/0/			0/0/	Avermectin
	0/0/0	5	0	2	0	0	0	0//0	0/0/			0/0/	Podophyllotoxin
	0/0/0	5	0	2	0	0	0	0//0	0/0/			0/0/	Other lactones
													-Other:
	0/0/0	5	0	0	0	0	0	0//0	0/0/			0/0/	--2-methoxy-4-(1-propenyl)-pheno benzoate(Isosafrole)
	0/0/0	5	0	0	0	0	0	0//0	0/0/			0/0/	--1-(1,3-Benzodioxol-5-Yl)propan-2-one
	0/0/0	5	0	0	0	0	0	0//0	0/0/			0/0/	--Piperonal
	0/0/0	5	0	0	0	0	0	0//0	0/0/			0/0/	--Safrole
	0/0/0	5	0	0	0	0	0	0//0	0/0/			0/0/	--Tetrahydrocannabinols(all is omers)
													--Other:
3.6	0/0/0	0	2.4	0	0	0	0	0//0	0/0/			0/0/	---Furan phenol
5.2	0/0/0	5	0	0	0	0	0	0//0	0/0/			0/0/	---Bifendate
	0/0/0	5	0	2	0	0	0	0//0	0/0/			0/0/	---Artemether
													---Other
	0/0/0	0	0	2	0	0	0	0//0	0/0/			0/0/	Carbofuran
	0/0/0	0	0	2	0	0	0	0//0	0/0/			0/0/	Dioxocarb, bendiocarb, benfuracarb(including carbosulfan, furathiocarb)
	0/0/0	0	0	2	0	0	0	0//0	0/0/			0/0/	Endothion, dioxathion, isobenzan
	0/0/0	0	0	2	0	0	0	0//0	0/0/			0/0/	Bucarpolate, sufoxide, piperonyl butoxide, propylisorne (including piperonyl cyclonene, sesamex)
	0/0/0	0	0	2	0	0	0	0//0	0/0/			0/0/	Pyracarbolin, metobenzuron, ethofumesate (including benfuresate, fluxofenim)
	0/0/0	0	0	2	0	0	0	0//0	0/0/			0/0/	Butopyronoxyl, difenolan, rotenone
	0/0/0	0	0	2	0	0	0	0//0	0/0/			0/0/	Dikegulac, brassinolide
	0/0/0	0	0	2	0	0	0	0//0	0/0/			0/0/	Taxinol
	0/0/0	0	0	2	0	0	0	0//0	0/0/			0/0/	Cephalomanine
	0/0/0	0	0	2	0	0	0	0//0	0/0/			0/0/	10-Deacetyl-baccatin Ⅲ(Extracts of taxus chinensis 10-DAB)
	0/0/0	0	0	2	0	0	0	0//0	0/0/			0/0/	10-Deacetyl-paclitaxel(Extracts of taxus chinensis 10-DAB)
	0/0/0	0	0	2	0	0	0	0//0	0/0/			0/0/	Baccatin Ⅲ
	0/0/0	0	0	2	0	0	0	0//0	0/0/			0/0/	7-Epitaxinol
	0/0/0	0	0	2	0	0	0	0//0	0/0/			0/0/	10-Deacetyl-7-epi-taxinol
	0/0/0	0	0	2	0	0	0	0//0	0/0/			0/0/	Analogues of 7,10-double(3-trichloroacetyl)-10-deacetyl Baccatin
	0/0/0	0	0	2	0	0	0	0//0	0/0/			0/0/	Docetaxel
	0/0/0	0	0	2	0	0	0	0//0	0/0/			0/0/	7,10-couble(3-trichloroacetyl)-taxotere
	0/0/0	0	0	2	0	0	0	0//0	0/0/			0/0/	Tenamfetamine and its salts
	0/0/0	0	0	2	0	0	0	0//0	0/0/			0/0/	(1,2-Dimetol)hydroxytetrahydrobiopterin(including parahexyl)
	0/0/0	0	0	2	0	0	0	0//0	0/0/			0/0/	MMDA, N-ethyl MDA, N-hydroxy MDA.
	0/0/0	0	0	2	0	0	0	0//0	0/0/			0/0/	2-methylenedioxy-n-methylamphetamine and its salts

税则号列	货品名称〔CIQ扩展编码及品名－T2表示见附表2〕	最惠(%)	暂定税率	普通	增值/消费	出口退税	计量单位	监管条件	检验检疫	特殊证件对美关税
2932.9990 54	3,4－亚甲二氧基甲卡西酮(3,4methylenedioxyNmethylcathinone;CAS号:186028795)〔999〕	6.5		20	13/	9,13	千克	I		1/26.5
2932.9990 60	二噁英,呋喃(多氯二苯并对二噁英,多氯二苯并呋喃)〔999〕	6.5		20	13/	13	千克	89		1/26.5
2932.9990 70	1,4－二噁烷〔999〕	6.5		20	13/	13	千克			1/26.5
2932.9990 80	二氢黄樟素〔999〕	6.5		20	13/	13	千克	G		1/26.5
2932.9990 91	其他濒危植物提取的仅含氧杂原子的杂环化合物〔999〕	6.5		20	13/	0	千克	EF		1/26.5
2932.9990 92	阿卡波糖水合物〔999〕	6.5	0	20	13/	13	千克			1/20
2932.9990 99	其他仅含氧杂原子的杂环化合物〔301易燃液体,302毒性物质和感染性物质〕	6.5		20	13/	9,13	千克			1/26.5
29.33	**仅含有氮杂原子的杂环化合物:**									
	-结构上含有一个非稠合吡唑环(不论是否氢化)的化合物:									
2933.1100	--二甲基苯基吡唑酮(安替比林)及其衍生物〔999〕	6.5		20	13/	10	千克			1/31.5
	--其他:									
2933.1920	---安乃近〔999〕	6		20	13/	10	千克	Q		1/
2933.1990	---其他									
2933.1990 11	吡硫磷、吡唑硫磷、敌蝇威、乙虫腈等(包括异索威、吡唑威)〔101异索威粉剂(含量2%～20%),102敌蝇威粉剂(含量5%～50%),103异索威乳剂(含量0.5%～20%),104敌蝇威乳剂(含量1%～50%)〕	6.5		20	13/	9,13	千克	S		1/31.5
2933.1990 12	氟虫腈、唑螨酯、吡螨胺等(包括吡唑醚菌酯)〔999〕	6.5		20	13/	9,13	千克	S		1/31.5
2933.1990 13	吡草醚、吡唑草胺、氟氯草胺等(包括野燕枯、苄草唑、吡唑特、吡草酮)〔999〕	6.5		20	13/	9,13	千克	S		1/31.5
2933.1990 14	吡唑萘菌胺(包括氟唑菌胺、乙唑螨腈、异丙吡草酯、唑虫酰胺)〔999〕	6.5		20	13/	9,13	千克	S		1/31.5
2933.1990 15	苯并烯氟菌唑〔999〕	6.5		20	13/	13	千克	S		1/31.5
2933.1990 90	其他结构上有非稠合吡唑环化合物〔999〕	6.5		20	13/	13	千克			1/31.5
	-结构上含有一个非稠合咪唑环(不论是否氢化)的化合物:									
2933.2100	--乙内酰脲及其衍生物〔999〕	6.5		30	13/	10	千克			1/11.5
2933.2900	--其他									
2933.2900 11	异菌脲〔999〕	6.5		20	13/	9,13	千克	S		1/26.5
2933.2900 12	抑霉唑、咪菌腈、咪菌酮、咪鲜胺等(包括克霉唑、咪鲜胺锰盐)〔999〕	6.5		20	13/	9,13	千克	S		1/26.5
2933.2900 13	咪草酸、丁咪酰胺〔999〕	6.5		20	13/	9,13	千克	S		1/26.5
2933.2900 14	果绿啶〔999〕	6.5		20	13/	9,13	千克	S		1/26.5
2933.2900 15	氟菌唑〔999〕	6.5		20	13/	9,13	千克	S		1/26.5
2933.2900 90	其他结构上有非稠合咪唑环化合物〔999〕	6.5		20	13/	13	千克			1/26.5
	-结构上含有一个非稠合吡啶环(不论是否氢化)的化合物:									
2933.3100	--吡啶及其盐									
2933.3100 10	吡啶〔301易燃液体〕	6		20	13/	10	千克	AB	MN	1/11
2933.3100 90	吡啶盐〔999〕	6		20	13/	10	千克			1/11
	--六氢吡啶(哌啶)及其盐:									
2933.3210	---六氢吡啶(哌啶)〔301腐蚀性物质〕	4		11	13/	10	千克	23		1/29
2933.3220	---六氢吡啶(哌啶)盐〔999〕	6.5		20	13/	10	千克			1/
2933.3300	--阿芬太尼(INN)、阿尼利定(INN)、苯氰米特(INN)、溴西泮(INN)、地芬诺新(INN)、地芬诺酯(INN)、地匹哌酮(INN)、芬太尼(INN)、凯托米酮(INN)、哌醋甲酯(INN)、喷他左辛(INN)、哌替啶(INN)、哌替啶中间体A(INN)、苯环利定(INN)、苯哌利定(INN)、哌苯甲醇(INN)、哌氰米特(INN)、哌丙吡胺(INN)及三甲利定(INN),以及它们的盐									
2933.3300 11	阿芬太尼、芬太尼(以及它们的盐)〔999〕	6.5		20	13/	10	千克	I		1/11.5
2933.3300 12	哌替啶、地芬诺酯(以及它们的盐)〔999〕	6.5		20	13/	10	千克	I		1/11.5
2933.3300 13	哌腈(氰)米特、丙吡兰(哌丙吡胺)(以及它们的盐)〔999〕	6.5		20	13/	10	千克	I		1/11.5
2933.3300 21	哌醋甲酯、喷他左辛、溴西泮(以及它们的盐)〔999〕	6.5		20	13/	10	千克	I		1/11.5
2933.3300 22	苯环利定、哌苯甲醇(以及它们的盐)〔999〕	6.5		20	13/	10	千克	I		1/11.5
2933.3300 31	地匹哌酮、凯托米酮、地芬诺新(以及它们的盐)〔999〕	6.5		20	13/	10	千克	I		1/11.5

协定税率 %										特惠税率 %			
亚太5国	东/冰/格	巴基斯坦	韩国	瑞士	哥达	秘鲁	澳大利亚	新西/坡/智	港/澳/台	亚太2国	老/柬/缅	36/3/1	Article Description
	0/0/0	0	0	2	0	0	0	0//0	0/0/			0/0/	3,4-methylenedioxy-N-methylcathinone(CAS:186028-79-5)
	0/0/0	0	0	2	0	0	0	0//0	0/0/			0/0/	Dioxin, Furan (Polychrorinate. dibenzo-p-dioxins, polychlorinated dibenzofurans)
	0/0/0	0	0	2	0	0	0	0//0	0/0/			0/0/	1,4-Diaxane
	0/0/0	0	0	2	0	0	0	0//0	0/0/			0/0/	Dihydrosafrol
	0/0/0	0	0	2	0	0	0	0//0	0/0/			0/0/	Other heterocyclic compounds with oxygen hetero-atom only, distilled from endangered plants
	0/0/0	0	0	2	0	0	0	0//0	0/0/			0/0/	Acarbose hydrate
	0/0/0	0	0	2	0	0	0	0//0	0/0/			0/0/	Other heterocyclic compounds with oxygen hetero-atom(s) only
													Heterocyclic compounds with nitrogen hetero-atom(s) only:
													-Compounds containing an unfused pyrazole ring (whether or not hydrogenated) in the structure:
4.2	0/0/0	5	0	0	0	0	0	0//0	0/0/			0/0/	--Phenazone (antipyrin) and its derivatives
													--Other:
4.8	0/0/0	5	0	0	0	0	0	0//0	0/0/			0/0/	---Analgin
													---Other
	0/0/0	5	0	0	0	0	0	0//0	0/0/			0/0/	Pyrazothion, pyraclofos, dimetilan(includins isolan, pyrolan)
	0/0/0	5	0	0	0	0	0	0//0	0/0/			0/0/	Fipronil, fenpyroximate, tebufenpyrad(including pyraclost)
	0/0/0	5	0	0	0	0	0	0//0	0/0/			0/0/	Pyraflufen-ethyl, metazachlor, nipyralo fen (indnding difenzoquat, pyrazoxyfen, pyrazolate, benzofenap)
	0/0/0	5	0	0	0	0	0	0//0	0/0/			0/0/	Isopyrazam(penflufen, fluazolate, tolfenpyrad)
	0/0/0	5	0	0	0	0	0	0//0	0/0/			0/0/	Benzene and olefin triflumizole
	0/0/0	5	0	0	0	0	0	0//0	0/0/			0/0/	Other compounds containing an unfused pyrazole ring in the structure
													-Compounds containing an unfused imidazole ring (whether or not hydrogenated) in the structure:
	0/0/0	5	0	0	0	0	0	0//0	0/0/			0/0/	--Hydantoin and its derivatives
													--Other
	0/0/0	5	2.6	3.4	0	0	0	0//0	0/0/			0/0/	Iprodine
	0/0/0	5	2.6	3.4	0	0	0	0//0	0/0/			0/0/	Imazalil, fenapanil, climbazole, prochloraz(including clotrimazole prochloraz-manganese)
	0/0/0	5	2.6	3.4	0	0	0	0//0	0/0/			0/0/	Imazamethabenz-methyl, isocarbamide
	0/0/0	5	2.6	3.4	0	0	0	0//0	0/0/			0/0/	Glyodin
	0/0/0	5	2.6	3.4	0	0	0	0//0	0/0/			0/0/	Triflumizole
	0/0/0	5	2.6	3.4	0	0	0	0//0	0/0/			0/0/	Other compounds containing an unfused imidazole ring in the structure
													-Compounds containing an unfused pyridine ring (whether or not hydrogenated) in the structure:
													--Pyridine and its salts
	0/0/0	5	0	0	0	0	0	0//0	0/0/0			0/0/	Pyridine
	0/0/0	5	0	0	0	0	0	0//0	0/0/0			0/0/	Pyridine salt
													--Piperidine and its salts:
	0/0/0	0	0	0	0	0	0	0//0	0/0/			0/0/	---Hexahydropyridine (piperidine)
	0/0/0	5	0	0	0	0	0	0//0	0/0/			0/0/	---Isoniazidum
													--Alfentanil(INN)、anileridine(INN)、bezitramide(INN)、bromazepam(INN)、difenoxin(INN)、diphenoxylate(INN)、dipipanone(INN)、fentanyl(INN)、ketobemidone(INN)、methylphenidate(INN)、pentazocine(INN)、pethidine(INN)、pethidine(INN) intermediate A、phencyclidine(INN)(PCP)、phenoperidine(INN)、pipradrol(INN)、piritramide(INN)、propiram(INN) and trimeperidine(INN); salts thereof
	0/0/0	5	3.9	0	0	0	0	0//0	0/0/			0/0/	Alfentanil(INN)、fentanyl(INN); salts thereof
	0/0/0	5	3.9	0	0	0	0	0//0	0/0/			0/0/	Pethidine(INN)、diphenoxylate(INN); salts thereof
	0/0/0	5	3.9	0	0	0	0	0//0	0/0/			0/0/	Bezitramide(INN)、propiram(INN); salts thereof
	0/0/0	5	3.9	0	0	0	0	0//0	0/0/			0/0/	Methylphenidate(INN)、pentazocine(INN)、bromazepam(INN); salts thereof
	0/0/0	5	3.9	0	0	0	0	0//0	0/0/			0/0/	Phencyclidine(INN)(PCP), pipradrol(INN), salts thereof
	0/0/0	5	3.9	0	0	0	0	0//0	0/0/			0/0/	Dipipanone(INN), ketobemidone(INN), difenoxin(INN); salts thereof

税则号列	货品名称〔CIQ扩展编码及品名－T2表示见附表2〕	最惠(%)	暂定税率	普通	增值/消费	出口退税	计量单位	监管条件	检验检疫	特殊证件对美关税
2933.3300 32	哌替啶中间体A、苯哌利定、三甲利定(以及它们的盐)〔999〕	6.5		20	13/	10	千克	I		1/11.5
2933.3300 33	阿尼利定、苯氰米特(以及它们的盐)〔999〕	6.5		20	13/	10	千克	I		1/11.5
	--其他:									
2933.3910	---二苯乙醇酸-3-奎宁环酯〔999〕	6.5		20	13/	10	千克	23		1/
2933.3920	---奎宁环-3-醇〔999〕	6.5		20	13/	10	千克	23		1/
2933.3990	---其他									
2933.3990 21	精吡氟禾草灵、毒死蜱、二氯氨基吡啶羧酸(包括二氟吡隆、三氟甲吡醚、氯虫苯甲酰胺)〔101毒死蜱粉剂、颗粒剂(含量＞15%)、102毒死蜱乳剂(含量＞4%)〕	6.5		20	13/	9,13	千克	S		1/16.5
2933.3990 22	百草枯、啶虫脒〔101百草枯(含量＞4%)),102百草枯水剂(含量4%～40%)〕	6.5		20	13/	9,13	千克	S		1/16.5
2933.3990 23	精喹禾灵〔999〕	6.5		20	13/	9,13	千克	S		1/16.5
2933.3990 24	喹禾灵、氟吡禾灵、吡氟禾草灵等(包括炔禾灵、氟吡乙禾灵、氟吡胺、卤草啶)〔999〕	6.5		20	13/	9,13	千克	S		1/16.5
2933.3990 25	高效氟吡甲禾灵、氟吡甲禾灵等(包括鼠特灵、灭鼠优、灭鼠安、氟鼠啶)〔101:RH－908,102:敌鼠(含量＞2%)〕	6.5		20	13/	9,13	千克	S		1/16.5
2933.3990 26	甲基毒死蜱、吡虫啉等(包括吡氯氰菊酯、啶蜱脲、氟啶脲、哒幼酮、吡丙醚)〔999〕	6.5		20	13/	9,13	千克	S		1/16.5
2933.3990 27	驱蝇啶、烯啶虫胺〔999〕	6.5		20	13/	9,13	千克	S		1/16.5
2933.3990 28	咪唑烟酸、甲咪唑烟酸、咪唑乙烟酸等(包括氨氯吡啶酸、三氯吡氧乙酸、氯氟吡氧乙酸、二氯吡啶酸)〔999〕	6.5		20	13/	9,13	千克	S		1/16.5
2933.3990 29	炔草酸、哌草磷、哌草丹、稗草丹等(包括吡氟酰草胺、氟啶草酮、氟硫草啶、甲氧咪草烟)〔999〕	6.5		20	13/	9,13	千克	S		1/16.5
2933.3990 30	3-羟基-1-甲基哌啶〔999〕	6.5		20	13/	13	千克	23		1/16.5
2933.3990 40	3-奎宁环酮〔999〕	6.5		20	13/	13	千克	23		1/16.5
2933.3990 51	甲哌翁、抗倒胺、氯吡脲、吡啶醇〔999〕	6.5		20	13/	9,13	千克	S		1/16.5
2933.3990 52	啶菌噁唑、苯锈啶、啶斑肟等(包括啶菌腈)〔999〕	6.5		20	13/	9,13	千克	S		1/16.5
2933.3990 53	氟啶胺、氟啶虫酰胺、三氯甲基吡啶〔999〕	6.5		20	13/	9,13	千克	S		1/16.5
2933.3990 54	咪唑嗪、丁硫啶、氯苯吡啶、哌丙灵〔999〕	6.5		20	13/	9,13	千克	S		1/16.5
2933.3990 55	氟吡菌酰胺〔999〕	6.5		20	13/	9,13	千克	S		1/16.5
2933.3990 56	氯啶菌酯〔999〕	6.5		20	13/	13	千克	S		1/16.5
2933.3990 57	氯氨吡啶酸〔999〕	6.5		20	13/	13	千克	S		1/16.5
2933.3990 58	哌壮素〔999〕	6.5		20	13/	9,13	千克	S		1/16.5
2933.3990 60	啶氧菌酯(包括氟啶虫胺腈、环啶菌胺、四氯虫酰胺、溴氰虫酰胺、玉雄杀、氟吡菌胺)〔999〕	6.5		20	13/	9,13	千克	S		1/16.5
2933.3990 71	乙酰阿法甲基芬太尼、烯丙罗定、阿法美罗定(以及它们的盐)〔999〕	6.5		20	13/	13	千克	I		1/16.5
2933.3990 72	阿法甲基芬太尼、阿法罗定、苄替啶(以及它们的盐)〔999〕	6.5		20	13/	13	千克	I		1/16.5
2933.3990 73	倍他羟基芬太尼、倍他羟基-3-甲基芬太尼、倍他美罗定(以及它们的盐)〔999〕	6.5		20	13/	13	千克	I		1/16.5
2933.3990 74	倍他罗啶、依托利啶、羟哌替定、美他佐辛(以及它们的盐)〔999〕	6.5		20	13/	13	千克	I		1/16.5
2933.3990 75	3-甲基芬太尼、1-甲基4-苯基-4-哌啶丙酸酯、诺匹哌酮(以及它们的盐)〔999〕	6.5		20	13/	13	千克	I		1/16.5
2933.3990 76	对氟芬太尼、1-苯乙基-4-苯基-4-哌啶乙酸酯(以及它们的盐)〔999〕	6.5		20	13/	13	千克	I		1/16.5
2933.3990 77	哌替啶中间体B、哌替啶中间体C(以及它们的盐)〔999〕	6.5		20	13/	13	千克	I		1/16.5
2933.3990 78	非那丙胺、非那佐辛、匹米诺定、丙哌利定(以及它们的盐)〔999〕	6.5		20	13/	13	千克	I		1/16.5
2933.3990 80	瑞太尼及其盐〔999〕	6.5		20	13/	13	千克	I		1/16.5
2933.3990 91	吉美嘧啶、甲磺酸阿帕替尼、西达本胺〔999〕	6.5	0	20	3/	13	千克			1/10
2933.3990 92	N－苯乙基－4－哌啶酮、4－苯胺基－N－苯乙基哌啶	6.5		20	13/	13	千克	23		/16.5
2933.3990 99	其他结构上含有一个非稠合吡啶环(不论是否氢化)的化合物(因拆分抗癌药品原料药产生的兜底税号)〔301易燃液体,302易燃固体、自反应物质及固态退敏爆炸品,303毒性物质和感染性物质,304其他危险化学品〕	6.5		20	13/	9,13	千克			1/16.5
	-结构上含有一个喹啉或异喹啉环系(不论是否氢化)的化合物,但未经进一步稠合的:									
2933.4100	--左非诺(INN)及其盐〔999〕	6.5		20	13/	10	千克	I		1/11.5
2933.4900	--其他									
2933.4900 11	丙烯酸喹啉酯,苯氧喹啉〔999〕	6.5		20	13/	9,13	千克	S		1/31.5
2933.4900 12	咯喹酮〔999〕	6.5		20	13/	9,13	千克	S		1/31.5
2933.4900 13	氯甲喹啉酸、乙氧喹啉〔101饲料添加剂,102化工产品〕	6.5		20	13/	9,13	千克	S		1/31.5

协定税率 %										特惠税率 %			Article Description
亚太5国	东/冰/格	巴基斯坦	韩国	瑞士	哥达	秘鲁	澳大利亚	新西/坡/智	港/澳/台	亚太2国	老/柬/缅	36/3/1	
	0/0/0	5	3.9	0	0	0	0	0//0	0/0/			0/0/	Pethidine(INN), phenoperidine(INN); trimeperidine(INN); salts thereof
	0/0/0	5	3.9	0	0	0	0	0//0	0/0/			0/0/	Anileridine(INN), piritramide(INN), salts thereof
													—Other:
5.2	0/0/0	5	0	0	0	0	0	0//0	0/0/			0/0/	---Benzilic acid-3-quinuclidinate
5.2	0/0/0	5	0	0	0	0	0	0//0	0/0/			0/0/	---Quinuclidine-3-ol
													---Other
	0/0/0	0	0	2	0	0	0	0//0	0/0/			0/0/	Fluazifop-p-butyl, chlorpyrifos, dichloro-aminoacetophen-one-carboxylic acid(including diflufenzopyr, pyridalyl, chlorantraniliprole)
	0/0/0	0	0	2	0	0	0	0//0	0/0/			0/0/	Paraquat, acetamiprid
	0/0/0	0	0	2	0	0	0	0//0	0/0/			0/0/	Quizalofop-p-ethyl
	0/0/0	0	0	2	0	0	0	0//0	0/0/			0/0/	Quizalofop-ethyl, heptenophos, fluazifop, (including chloroazifop-propyny, haloxyfop-methyl picolinafen, haloxydin)
	0/0/0	0	0	2	0	0	0	0//0	0/0/			0/0/	Haloxyfop-P-methyl, haloxyfop-methy1(including norbormide, pyrimuron, flupropadine)
	0/0/0	0	0	2	0	0	0	0//0	0/0/			0/0/	Chlorpyrifos-methyl, imidacloprid(including fenpyrithrin, fluazuron, chlorfluazuron, pyridaben, pyriproxyfen)
	0/0/0	0	0	2	0	0	0	0//0	0/0/			0/0/	Dipropyl pyridine, nitenpyram
	0/0/0	0	0	2	0	0	0	0//0	0/0/			0/0/	Imazapyr, imazameth, imazethapyr(including picloram, fluroxypyr, clopyralid)
	0/0/0	0	0	2	0	0	0	0//0	0/0/			0/0/	Clodinafop-propargyl, piperophos, dimepiperate, pyributicarb(including diflufenican, fluridon, dithiopyr, imazamox)
	0/0/0	0	0	2	0	0	0	0//0	0/0/			0/0/	3-hydroxy-1-methyl piperidine
	0/0/0	0	0	2	0	0	0	0//0	0/0/			0/0/	3-Quinuclidone
	0/0/0	0	0	2	0	0	0	0//0	0/0/			0/0/	Mepiquate chloride, inabenfide, forchlorfenuron, pyripropanol
	0/0/0	0	0	2	0	0	0	0//0	0/0/			0/0/	SYP-Z048, fenpropidin, pyrifenox(includins pyridintril)
	0/0/0	0	0	2	0	0	0	0//0	0/0/			0/0/	Fluazinam, flonicamid, nitrapyrin
	0/0/0	0	0	2	0	0	0	0//0	0/0/			0/0/	Triazoxide, buthiobate, parinol, piperlin
	0/0/0	0	0	2	0	0	0	0//0	0/0/			0/0/	Fluopyram
	0/0/0	0	0	2	0	0	0	0//0	0/0/			0/0/	Carbamate
	0/0/0	0	0	2	0	0	0	0//0	0/0/			0/0/	Picloram
	0/0/0	0	0	2	0	0	0	0//0	0/0/			0/0/	Piproctanyl
	0/0/0	0	0	2	0	0	0	0//0	0/0/			0/0/	Picoxystrobin(including fluorine organism worm amine nitrile, ring organism bacteria amine, four chlorine worm amide, bromine cyanide worm amide, jade males kill, fluorine bacteria amine)
	0/0/0	0	0	2	0	0	0	0//0	0/0/			36/0/	Acetyl-alpha-methylfentanyl, allylprodine, alphameprodine (and their salt)
	0/0/0	0	0	2	0	0	0	0//0	0/0/			0/0/	Alpha-methylfentanyl, alphaprodine, benzethidine
	0/0/0	0	0	2	0	0	0	0//0	0/0/			0/0/	Betahydroxyfentanyl, betahydroxy-3-methylfentanyl, betameprodine (and their salt)
	0/0/0	0	0	2	0	0	0	0//0	0/0/			0/0/	Betaprodine, etoxeridine, hydroxypethidine, metazocine (and their salt)
	0/0/0	0	0	2	0	0	0	0//0	0/0/			0/0/	3-methylfentanyl, 1-methyl-4-phenyl-4-piperidine propionate, norpipanone (and their salt)
	0/0/0	0	0	2	0	0	0	0//0	0/0/			0/0/	Parafluorofentanyl, 1-phenylethyl-4-phenyl-4-piperidine acetate (and their salt)
	0/0/0	0	0	2	0	0	0	0//0	0/0/			0/0/	Pethidine intermediate B, pethidine intermediate C (and their salt)
	0/0/0	0	0	2	0	0	0	0//0	0/0/			0/0/	Phenampromide, phenazocine, piminodine, porperidine (and their salt)
	0/0/0	0	0	2	0	0	0	0//0	0/0/			0/0/	Ramifentanil and salts thereof
	0/0/0	0	0	2	0	0	0	0//0	0/0/			0/0/	Gempirim, apatinib mesylate, sirodine, and other anticancer drug substances
	0/0/0	0	0	2	0	0	0	0//0	0/0/		//	0/0/	N—phenethyl—4—piperidine, 4—anilino—n—phenethyl piperidine
	0/0/0	0	0	2	0	0	0	0//0	0/0/			0/0/	Other compounds containing a non—fused pyridine ring (whether hydrogenated or not)(tax number of Separating anti—cancer pharmaceutical raw materials)
													-Compounds containing a quinoline or isoquinoline ringsystem (whether or not hydrogenated), not further fused:
	0/0/0	5	0	0	0	0	0	0//0	0/0/			0/0/	--Levorpharol(INN) and its salts
													--Other
	0/0/0	5	0	0	0	0	0	0//0	0/0/			0/0/	Halacrinate, quinoxyfen
	0/0/0	5	0	0	0	0	0	0//0	0/0/			0/0/	Pyroquilon
	0/0/0	5	0	0	0	0	0	0//0	0/0/			0/0/	Quinmerac, quinmerac, ethoxyquin

税则号列	货品名称〔CIQ 扩展编码及品名－T2 表示见附表 2〕	最惠(%)	暂定税率	普通	增值/消费	出口退税	计量单位	监管条件	检验检疫	特殊证件对美关税
2933.4900 14	二氯喹啉酸〔999〕	6.5		20	13/	9,13	千克	S		1/31.5
2933.4900 15	FG-4592(CAS 号:808118-40-3)(一种缺氧诱导因子—脯氨酸羟化酶抑制剂)〔999〕	6.5		20	13/	13	千克			1/31.5
2933.4900 21	羟蒂巴酚、左美沙芬、左芬啡烷〔999〕	6.5		20	13/	13	千克	I		1/31.5
2933.4900 22	去甲左啡诺、非诺啡烷、消旋甲啡烷、消旋啡烷〔999〕	6.5		20	13/	13	千克	I		1/31.5
2933.4900 30	布托啡诺〔999〕	6.5		20	13/	13	千克	I		1/31.5
2933.4900 90	其他含喹啉或异喹啉环系的化合物(但未进一步稠合的)〔301 易燃液体,302 毒性物质和感染性物质,303 其他危险化学品,304 其他化工产品〕	6.5		20	13/	13	千克			1/31.5
	-结构上含有一个嘧啶环(不论是否氢化)或哌嗪环的化合物:									
2933.5200	--丙二酰脲(巴比妥酸)及其盐〔999〕	6.5		20	13/	10	千克			1/11.5
2933.5300	--阿洛巴比妥(INN)、异戊巴比妥(INN)、巴比妥(INN)、布他比妥(INN)、正丁巴比妥(INN)、环己巴比妥(INN)、甲苯巴比妥(INN)、戊巴比妥(INN)、苯巴比妥(INN)、仲丁巴比妥(INN)、司可巴比妥(INN)及和乙烯比妥(INN)以及它们的盐									
2933.5300 11	阿洛巴比妥、仲丁巴比妥(以及它们的盐)〔999〕	6.5		20	13/	10	千克	I		1/26.5
2933.5300 12	乙烯比妥、布他比妥、丁巴比妥(以及它们的盐)〔999〕	6.5		20	13/	10	千克	I		1/26.5
2933.5300 13	环己巴比妥、甲苯巴比妥(以及它们的盐)〔999〕	6.5		20	13/	10	千克	I		1/26.5
2933.5300 14	司可巴比妥、异戊巴比妥(以及它们的盐)〔999〕	6.5		20	13/	10	千克	I		1/26.5
2933.5300 15	戊巴比妥、苯巴比妥、巴比妥(以及它们的盐)〔999〕	6.5		20	13/	10	千克	I		1/26.5
2933.5400	--其他丙二酰脲(巴比妥酸)的衍生物以及它们的盐〔999〕	6.5		20	13/	10	千克			1/
2933.5500	--氯普唑仑(INN),甲氯喹酮(INN),甲喹酮(INN)和齐培丙醇(INN)以及它们的盐									
2933.5500 11	甲氯喹酮、甲喹酮(以及它们的盐)〔999〕	6.5		20	13/	10	千克	I		1/
2933.5500 12	氯普唑仑、齐培丙醇(以及它们的盐)〔999〕	6.5		20	13/	10	千克	I		1/
	--其他:									
2933.5910	---胞嘧啶〔999〕	6.5		20	13/	13	千克			1/11.5
2933.5920	---环丙氟哌酸〔999〕	6.5		20	13/	10	千克			1/
2933.5990	---其他									
2933.5990 11	嘧啶磷、甲基嘧啶磷、二嗪磷、双苯嘧草酮等(包括嘧啶氧磷、乙嘧硫磷)〔101 嘧啶氧磷粉剂,102 嘧啶氧磷〕	6.5		20	13/	9,13	千克	S		1/31.5
2933.5990 12	烯腺嘌呤、苄腺嘌呤、丁基嘧啶磷、嘧啶肟草醚等(包括苄氨基嘌呤、羟烯腺嘌呤)〔999〕	6.5		20	13/	9,13	千克	S		1/31.5
2933.5990 13	嘧草醚、双草醚、除草啶、环草啶等(包括异草啶、异丙酯草醚、嘧草硫醚、特草啶)〔999〕	6.5		20	13/	9,13	千克	S		1/31.5
2933.5990 14	吡菌磷、嘧霉胺、嘧菌胺、嘧菌酯等(包括嘧菌环胺、嘧菌腙)〔999〕	6.5		20	13/	9,13	千克	S		1/31.5
2933.5990 15	嘧啶威、抗蚜威、环虫腈、嘧螨醚等(包括嘧螨酯)〔101 抗蚜威粉剂(含量＞75%),102 嘧啶威可湿性粉剂、颗粒剂,103 嘧啶威〕	6.5		20	13/	9,13	千克	S		1/31.5
2933.5990 16	氯苯嘧啶醇、环丙嘧啶醇、呋嘧醇等(包括氟苯嘧啶醇)〔999〕	6.5		20	13/	9,13	千克	S		1/31.5
2933.5990 17	氟蚁腙、鼠立死〔999〕	6.5		20	13/	9,13	千克	S		1/31.5
2933.5990 18	二甲嘧酚、乙嘧酚、乙嘧酚磺酸酯〔999〕	6.5		20	13/	9,13	千克	S		1/31.5
2933.5990 19	嗪氨灵、咪唑喹啉酸、丙酯草醚〔999〕	6.5		20	13/	9,13	千克	S		1/31.5
2933.5990 20	氟丙嘧草酯、氯丙嘧啶酸〔999〕	6.5		20	13/	9,13	千克	S		1/31.5
2933.5990 30	溴嘧草醚〔999〕	6.5		20	13/	9	千克	S		1/31.5
2933.5990 40	唑嘧菌胺〔999〕	6.5		20	13/	13	千克	S		1/31.5
2933.5990 51	依他喹酮(Etaqualone;CAS 号:7432259)〔999〕	6.5		20	13/	13	千克	I		1/31.5
2933.5990 52	苄基哌嗪(Benzylpiperazine;CAS 号:2759286)〔999〕	6.5		20	13/	13	千克	I		1/31.5
2933.5990 53	恩替卡韦	6.5	0	20	13/	13	千克			/25
2933.5990 60	利格列汀	6.5	0	20	13/	13	千克			/25
2933.5990 91	甲磺酸伊马替尼、硫唑嘌呤、培美曲塞二钠、左亚叶酸钙〔999〕	6.5	0	20	3/	13	千克			1/25
2933.5990 99	其他结构上有嘧啶环等的化合物(包括其他结构上有哌嗪环的化合物)(因拆分抗癌药品原料药产生的兜底税号)〔301 腐蚀性物质,302 其他化工产品〕	6.5		20	13/	13	千克			1/31.5
	-结构上含有一个非稠合三嗪环(不论是否氢化)的化合物:									
2933.6100	--三聚氰胺(蜜胺)〔999〕	6.5		20	13/	10	千克	A	M	1/31.5
	--其他:									
2933.6910	---三聚氰氯〔999〕	6		20	13/	10	千克			1/
	---异氰脲酸氯化衍生物:									

协定税率 %										特惠税率 %			Article Description
亚太5国	东/冰/格	巴基斯坦	韩国	瑞士	哥达	秘鲁	澳大利亚	新西/坡/智	港/澳/台	亚太2国	老/柬/缅	36/3/1	
	0/0/0	5	0	0	0	0	0	0//0	0/0/			0/0/	Quinclorac
	0/0/0	5	0	0	0	0	0	0//0	0/0/			0/0/	FG-4592 (CAS: 808118-40-3) (a kind of hypoxia inducible factor - prolinehydroxylase inhibitor)
	0/0/0	5	0	0	0	0	0	0//0	0/0/			0/0/	Drotebanol, levomethorphan, levophenacylmorphan.
	0/0/0	5	0	0	0	0	0	0//0	0/0/			0/0/	Norlevorphanol, phenomorphan, racemethorphan, racemorphan
	0/0/0	5	0	0	0	0	0	0//0	0/0/			0/0/	Butorphanol
	0/0/0	5	0	0	0	0	0	0//0	0/0/			0/0/	Other compounds containingan quinoline or isoquinoline ringsysterm (not further fused)
													-Compounds containing a pyrimidine ring (whether or not hydrogenated) or piperazine ring in the structure:
	0/0/0	5	0	0	0	0	0	0//0	0/0/			0/0/	--Malonylurea (barbituric acid) and its salts
													--Allobarbital(INN), amobarbital(INN), barbital(INN), butalbital (INN), butobarbital(INN), cyclobarbital(INN), methylphenobarbital(INN), pentobarbital(INN), phenobarbital(INN), secbutabarbital(INN), secobarbital(INN) and vinylbital(INN); salts thereof
	0/0/0	5	0	0	0	0	0	0//0	0/0/			0/0/	Allobarbital (INN), secbutabarbital (INN); salts thereof
	0/0/0	5	0	0	0	0	0	0//0	0/0/			0/0/	Vinylbital(INN), butalbital(INN), butobarbital(INN); salts thereof
	0/0/0	5	0	0	0	0	0	0//0	0/0/			0/0/	Cyclobarbital (INN), methylphenobarbital (INN); salts thereof
	0/0/0	5	0	0	0	0	0	0//0	0/0/			0/0/	Secobarbital (INN), amobarbital (INN), salts thereof
	0/0/0	5	0	0	0	0	0	0//0	0/0/			0/0/	Pentobarbital (INN), phenobarbital (INN), barbital (INN); salts thereof
	0/0/0	5	0	0	0	0	0	0//0	0/0/			0/0/	--Other derivatives of malonylurea(barbituric acid); salts thereof
													--Loprazolam (INN), mecloqualone (INN), methaqualone (INN) and zipeprol (INN); salts thereof
	0/0/0	5	0	0	0	0	0	0//0	0/0/			0/0/	Mecloqualone (INN), methaqualone (INN); salts thereof
	0/0/0	5	0	0	0	0	0	0//0	0/0/			0/0/	Loprazolam(INN), zipeprol(INN); salts thereof
													--Other:
4.2	0/0/0	0	0	0	0	0	0	0//0	0/0/			0/0/	---Cytosine
4.2	0/0/0	5	0	0	0	0	0	0//0	0/0/			0/0/	---Ciprofloxacin
													---Other
4.2	0/0/0	0	0	2	0	0	0	0//0	0/0/			0/0/	Pyrimithate, pirimiphos-methyl, diazinon (including midinyangrin, etrimfos)
4.2	0/0/0	0	0	2	0	0	0	0//0	0/0/			0/0/	Enadenine, 6-benzylaminopurine tebupirimfos, pyribenzonxim (including benzolaminopurine, oxyenadenine)
4.2	0/0/0	0	0	2	0	0	0	0//0	0/0/			0/0/	Pyriminobac-methl, bispyribac-sodium, bromacil, lenacil (including isocil, pyribambenz isoprop pyrithiobac-sodium, terbacil)
4.2	0/0/0	0	0	2	0	0	0	0//0	0/0/			0/0/	Pyrazophos, pyrimethanil, mepampyrim, azoxystrobin (including cyprodinil, ferimzone)
4.2	0/0/0	0	0	2	0	0	0	0//0	0/0/			0/0/	Pyramat, pirimicarb, dicyclanil, pyrimidifen (including fluacrypyrim)
4.2	0/0/0	0	0	2	0	0	0	0//0	0/0/			0/0/	Fenarimol, ancymidol, flurprimidol(including nuarimol)
4.2	0/0/0	0	0	2	0	0	0	0//0	0/0/			0/0/	Hydramethylnon, crimidine
4.2	0/0/0	0	0	2	0	0	0	0//0	0/0/			0/0/	Dimethirimol, ethirmol, bupirimate
4.2	0/0/0	0	0	2	0	0	0	0//0	0/0/			0/0/	Triforin, imazquin, pyribambenz-propyl
4.2	0/0/0	0	0	2	0	0	0	0//0	0/0/			0/0/	Butafenacil
4.2	0/0/0	0	0	2	0	0	0	0//0	0/0/			0/0/	Bromide-pyriminobac-methyl
4.2	0/0/0	0	0	2	0	0	0	0//0	0/0/			0/0/	Mepanipyrim
4.2	0/0/0	0	0	2	0	0	0	0//0	0/0/			0/0/	Etaqualone(CAS:7432-25-9)
4.2	0/0/0	0	0	2	0	0	0	0//0	0/0/			0/0/	Benzylpiperazine(CAS 号:2759-28-6)
4.2	0/0/0	0	0	2	0	0	0	0//0	0/0/		//	0/0/	entecavir
4.2	0/0/0	0	0	2	0	0	0	0//0	0/0/		//	0/0/	Trajenta
4.2	0/0/0	0	0	2	0	0	0	0//0	0/0/			0/0/	Imatinib mesylate, azathioprine, pemetrexed disodium, calcium levalinate and other anticancer drug substances
4.2	0/0/0	0	0	2	0	0	0	0//0	0/0/			0/0/	Other compounds containing pyrimidine rings in the structre(including other compounds containing piperazine rings in the strcture) (tax number of Separating anti－cancer pharmaceutical raw materials)
													-Compounds containing an unfused triazine ring (whether or not hydrogenated) in the structure:
	0/0/0	5	0	0	0	0	0	0//0	0/0/			0/0/	--Melamine
													--Other:
5.4	0/0/0	5	0	0	0	0	0	0//0	0/0/			0/0/	---Cyanuric chloride
													---Chloroisocyanurate:

税则号列		货品名称〔CIQ 扩展编码及品名－T2 表示见附表 2〕	最惠(%)	暂定税率	普通	增值/消费	出口退税	计量单位	监管条件	检验检疫	特殊证件对美关税
2933.6921		----二氯异氰脲酸〔999〕	6.5		20	13/	10	千克			1/
2933.6922		----三氯异氰脲酸〔999〕	6.5		20	13/	10	千克	AB	MN	1/
2933.6929		----其他									
2933.6929	10	二氯异氰尿酸钠〔999〕	6.5		20	13/	10	千克	A	R	1/31.5
2933.6929	90	其他异氰脲酸氯化衍生物〔301 腐蚀性物质〕	6.5		20	13/	10	千克			1/31.5
2933.6990		---其他									
2933.6990	11	西玛津、莠去津、扑灭津、草达津等(包括特丁津、氰草津、环丙津、甘扑津、甘草津)〔999〕	6.5		20	13/	9,10	千克	S		1/16.5
2933.6990	12	西草净、扑草净、敌草净、莠灭净等(包括特丁净、异丙净、异戊乙净、氰草净、氟草净、甲氧丙净)〔101 扑草灭颗粒剂,102 扑草灭(含量＞80％),103 西草净,104 莠灭净,105 敌草净〕	6.5		20	13/	9,10	千克	S		1/16.5
2933.6990	13	扑灭通、仲丁通〔999〕	6.5		20	13/	9,10	千克	S		1/16.5
2933.6990	14	丁嗪草酮、环嗪酮、嗪草酮等(包括苯嗪草酮、乙嗪草酮)〔999〕	6.5		20	13/	9,10	千克	S		1/16.5
2933.6990	15	灭蚜硫磷、灭蝇胺、吡蚜酮等(包括敌菌灵)〔999〕	6.5		20	13/	9,10	千克	S		1/16.5
2933.6990	16	三嗪氟草胺〔999〕	6.5		20	13/	9,10	千克	S		1/16.5
2933.6990	91	奥替拉西钾〔301 其他危险化学品,302 其他化工产〕	6.5	0	20	3/	10	千克			1/10
2933.6990	99	其他结构上含非稠合三嗪环化合物(因拆分抗癌药品原料药产生的兜底税号)〔999〕	6.5		20	13/	10	千克			1/16.5
		-内酰胺:									
2933.7100		--6-己内酰胺〔999〕	9		35	13/	10	千克	A	M	1/
2933.7200		--氯巴占(INN)和甲乙哌酮(INN)〔999〕	9		15	13/	10	千克	I		1/
2933.7900		--其他内酰胺									
2933.7900	10	氯巴占和甲乙哌酮的盐〔999〕	9		20	13/	10	千克	I		1/19
2933.7900	20	灭菌磷、螺虫乙酯〔999〕	9		20	13/	9,10	千克	S		1/19
2933.7900	30	佐匹克隆(Zopiclone;CAS 号:43200802)〔999〕	9		20	13/	10	千克	I		1/19
2933.7900	42	吡非尼酮	9	0	20	3/	10	千克			/10
2933.7900	91	来那度胺	9	0	20	3/	10	千克			/10
2933.7900	99	其他内酰胺	9		20	13/	10	千克			/19
		-其他:									
2933.9100		--阿普唑仑(INN)、卡马西泮(INN)、氯氮卓(INN)、氯硝西泮(INN)、氯拉卓酸、地洛西泮(INN)、地西泮(INN)、艾司唑仑(INN)、氯氟卓乙酯(INN)、氟地西泮(INN)、氟硝西泮(INN)、氟西泮(INN)、哈拉西泮(INN)、劳拉西泮(INN)、氯甲西泮(INN)、马吲哚(INN)、美达西泮(INN)、咪达唑仑(INN)、硝甲西泮(INN)、去甲西泮(INN)、奥沙西泮(INN)、匹那西泮(INN)、普拉西泮(INN)、吡咯戊酮(INN)、替马西泮(INN)、四氢西泮(INN)及三唑仑(INN)以及它们的盐									
2933.9100	11	阿普唑仑、卡马西泮、氯氮卓(以及它们的盐)〔999〕	6.5		20	13/	13	千克	I		1/11.5
2933.9100	12	氯硝西泮、氯拉卓酸、地洛西泮(以及它们的盐)〔999〕	6.5		20	13/	13	千克	I		1/11.5
2933.9100	13	地西泮、艾司唑仑、氯氟卓乙酯(以及它们的盐)〔999〕	6.5		20	13/	13	千克	I		1/11.5
2933.9100	14	氟地西泮、氟硝西泮、氟西泮(以及它们的盐)〔999〕	6.5		20	13/	13	千克	I		1/11.5
2933.9100	15	哈拉西泮、劳拉西泮、氯甲西泮(以及它们的盐)〔999〕	6.5		20	13/	13	千克	I		1/11.5
2933.9100	16	马吲哚、咪达唑仑、硝西泮(以及它们的盐)〔999〕	6.5		20	13/	13	千克	I		1/11.5
2933.9100	17	奥沙西泮、匹那西泮、普拉西泮(以及它们的盐)〔999〕	6.5		20	13/	13	千克	I		1/11.5
2933.9100	18	去甲西泮、三唑仑(以及它们的盐)〔999〕	6.5		20	13/	13	千克	I		1/11.5
2933.9100	21	硝甲西泮、美达西泮(以及它们的盐)〔999〕	6.5		20	13/	13	千克	I		1/11.5
2933.9100	22	吡咯戊酮、替马西泮、四氢西泮(以及它们的盐)〔999〕	6.5		20	13/	13	千克	I		1/11.5
2933.9200		--甲基谷硫磷(ISO)〔999〕	6.5		20	13/	13	千克			1/
2933.9900		--其他									
2933.9900	11	抑芽丹、三唑磷、虫线磷、喹硫磷、唑啶草酮等(包括哒嗪硫磷、亚胺硫磷、氯亚胺硫磷、保棉磷、益棉磷、威菌磷)〔301〕	6.5		20	13/	9,13	千克	S		1/31.5
2933.9900	12	氯唑磷、炔咪菊酯、吲哚酮草酯等(包括呋喃虫酰肼、唑蚜威、不育胺、虫螨腈、抗螨唑、四螨嗪)〔999〕	6.5		20	13/	9,13	千克	S		1/31.5
2933.9900	13	多菌灵、苯菌灵、氰菌灵、麦穗宁、氟哒嗪草酯等(包括咪菌威、丙硫多菌灵、氟氯菌核利、哒菌酮、拌种咯、杀草强)〔999〕	6.5		20	13/	9,13	千克	S		1/31.5

协定税率 %										特惠税率 %			Article Description
亚太5国	东/冰/格	巴基斯坦	韩国	瑞士	哥达	秘鲁	澳大利亚	新西/坡/智	港/澳/台	亚太2国	老/柬/缅	36/3/1	
5.2	0/0/0	5	0	0	0	0	0	0//0	0/0/			0/0/	----Dichloroisocyanurate acid
	0/0/0	5	0	0	0	0	0	0//0	0/0/			0/0/	----Trichloroisooyanurate acid
													----Other
	0/0/0	5	0	0	0	0	0	0//0	0/0/			0/0/	Sodium dichloro isocyanurate
	0/0/0	5	0	0	0	0	0	0//0	0/0/			0/0/	Other chloroisocyanuric acid derivatives
													---Other
	0/0/0	5	2.6	0	0	0	0	0//0	0/0/			0/0/	Simazine, atrazine, propazine, trietazine(including terbuthylazine, cyanazine, cyprazine, proglinazine, eglinazine)
	0/0/0	5	2.6	0	0	0	0	0//0	0/0/			0/0/	Simetryn, prometryn, desmetryn, ametryn (including terbutryn, dipropetryn, dimethametryn, cyanatryn, SSH-108, methoprotryne)
	0/0/0	5	2.6	0	0	0	0	0//0	0/0/			0/0/	Prometon, secbumeton
	0/0/0	5	2.6	0	0	0	0	0//0	0/0/			0/0/	Isomethiozin, hexazinone, metribuzin (including metamitron, ethiozin)
	0/0/0	5	2.6	0	0	0	0	0//0	0/0/			0/0/	Memazon, cyromazine, pymetrozime (including anilazine)
	0/0/0	5	2.6	0	0	0	0	0//0	0/0/			0/0/	Triaziflam
	0/0/0	5	2.6	0	0	0	0	0//0	0/0/			0/0/	Otlasexi Potassium and Other Anticancer Drugs
	0/0/0	5	2.6	0	0	0	0	0//0	0/0/			0/0/	Other compounds containing non-fused triazine ring in the structure(tax number of Separating anti-cancer pharmaceutical raw materials)
													-Lactams:
	5/0/3.6			0	0		0	0//0	0/0/				--6-Hexanolactam (epsilon-caprolactam)
	0/0/3.6	4	0	0	0	0	0	0//0	0/0/			0/0/	--Clobazam(INN) and methyprylon(INN)
													--Other lactams
	0/0/0	4	0		0	0	0	0//0	0/0/			0/0/	Salts of clobazam(INN) and methyprylon(INN)
	0/0/0	4	0		0	0	0	0//0	0/0/			0/0/	Ditalimfos, spirotetramat
	0/0/0	4	0		0	0	0	0//0	0/0/			0/0/	Zopiclone(CAS: 43200-80-2)
	0/0/0	4	0		0	0	0	0//0	0/0/		//	0/0/	pirfenidone
	0/0/0	4	0		0	0	0	0//0	0/0/		//	0/0/	Lenalidomide
	0/0/0	4	0		0	0	0	0//0	0/0/		//	0/0/	Other lactams
													-Other:
													--Alprazolam(INN), camazepam(INN), chlordiazepoxide(INN), clonazepam(INN), clorazepate, delorazepam(INN), diazepam(INN), estazolam(INN), ethyl loflazepate(INN), fludiazepam(INN), flunitrazepam(INN), flurazepam(INN), halazepam(INN), lorazepam(INN), lormetazepam(INN), mazindol(INN), medazepam(INN), midazolam(INN), nimetazepam(INN), nitrazepam(INN), nordazepam(INN), oxazepam(INN), pinazepam(INN), prazepam(INN), pyrovalerone(INN), temazepam(INN), tetrazepam(INN) and triazolam(INN); salts thereof
	0/0/0	5	0	0	0	0	0	0//0	0/0/			0/0/	Alprazolam(INN), camazepam(INN), chlordiazepoxide(INN); salts thereof
	0/0/0	5	0	0	0	0	0	0//0	0/0/			0/0/	Clonazepam(INN), clorazepate, delorazepam(INN); salts thereof
	0/0/0	5	0	0	0	0	0	0//0	0/0/			0/0/	Diazepam(INN), estazolam(INN), ethyl loflazepate(INN); salts thereof
	0/0/0	5	0	0	0	0	0	0//0	0/0/			0/0/	Fludiazepam(INN), flunitrazepam(INN), flurazepam(INN); salts thereof
	0/0/0	5	0	0	0	0	0	0//0	0/0/			0/0/	Halazepam(INN), lorazepam(INN), lormetazepam(INN); salts thereof
	0/0/0	5	0	0	0	0	0	0//0	0/0/			0/0/	Mazindol(INN), midazolam(INN), nimetazepam(INN); salts thereof
	0/0/0	5	0	0	0	0	0	0//0	0/0/			0/0/	Oxazepam(INN), pinazepam(INN), prazepam(INN); salts thereof
	0/0/0	5	0	0	0	0	0	0//0	0/0/			0/0/	Nordazepam(INN), triazolam(INN); salts thereof
	0/0/0	5	0	0	0	0	0	0//0	0/0/			0/0/	Nimetazepam(INN), medazepam(INN); salts thereof
	0/0/0	5	0	0	0	0	0	0//0	0/0/			0/0/	Pyrovalerone(INN), temazepam(INN), tetrazepam(INN); salts thereof
	0/0/0	0	0	3.4	0	0	0	0//0	0/0/			0/0/	--Azinphos-methyl(ISO)
													--Other
	0/0/0	0	0	3.4	0	0	0	0//0	0/0/			0/0/	Maleic hydrazide, triazophos, thionazin, quinalphos, azafenidin(including pyridaphenthione(JMAF), phosmet, dialifos, azinphos-methyl, azinphos-ethyl, triamiphos)
	0/0/0	0	0	3.4	0	0	0	0//0	0/0/			0/0/	Isazofos, imiprothrin, cinidon-ethyl(including furan-tebufenozide triaamate, metepa, fenazaflor, clofentezine, chlorfenapyr)
	0/0/0	0	0	3.4	0	0	0	0//0	0/0/			0/0/	Carbendazim, benomyl, cypendazole, fuberidazole (including debacarb, albendazole TOP, fluoromide(JMAF), pyridinitril, amitrole)

税则号列		货品名称〔CIQ扩展编码及品名—T2表示见附表2〕	最惠(%)	暂定税率	普通	增值/消费	出口退税	计量单位	监管条件	检验检疫	特殊证件对美关税
2933.9900	14	三唑酮、醚草敏、三唑醇、唑草酮等(包括四氯喹恶啉、己唑醇、腈苯唑、亚胺唑、四氟醚唑、氟环唑)〔101三唑酮,102三唑醇〕	6.5		20	13/	9,13	千克	S		1/31.5
2933.9900	15	苄氯三唑醇、戊菌唑、粉唑醇等(包括联苯三唑醇、腈菌唑、环丙唑醇、烯唑醇、戊唑醇、氟硅唑)〔999〕	6.5		20	13/	9,13	千克	S		1/31.5
2933.9900	16	环菌唑、叶菌唑、灭菌唑、种菌唑等(包括申嗪霉素、氟喹唑、哒螨灵、喹螨醚、氟草敏、氟咯草酮)〔999〕	6.5		20	13/	9,13	千克	S		1/31.5
2933.9900	17	唑草酯、四环唑、恶草酸等(包括喹禾糠酯、哒草特、咯草隆、禾草敌、唑草胺、敌草快、氯草敏)〔101草达灭颗粒剂,102草达灭(含量＞25%),103敌草快(含量＞45%),104敌草快浓水剂(含量＞10%)〕	6.5		20	13/	9,13	千克	S		1/31.5
2933.9900	18	氟胺草唑,氨唑草酮,三氟苯唑等(包括吲哚丁酸,溴莠敏,吲熟酯,三唑磺,四唑酰草胺)〔999〕	6.5		20	13/	9,13	千克	S		1/31.5
2933.9900	19	多效唑,烯效唑,抑芽唑等(包括叶枯净,叶锈特,吡喃草酮,吲哚乙酸)〔999〕	6.5		20	13/	9,13	千克	S		1/31.5
2933.9900	21	氯尼他秦〔999〕	6.5		20	13/	13	千克	I		1/31.5
2933.9900	22	依托尼秦〔999〕	6.5		20	13/	13	千克	I		1/31.5
2933.9900	23	普罗庚嗪,布桂嗪〔999〕	6.5		20	13/	13	千克	I		1/31.5
2933.9900	30	扎莱普隆、唑吡坦(以及它们的盐)〔999〕	6.5		20	13/	13	千克	I		1/31.5
2933.9900	40	齐帕特罗〔999〕	6.5		20	13/	13	千克	L		1/31.5
2933.9900	51	二甲基色胺、二乙基色胺〔999〕	6.5		20	13/	13	千克	I		1/31.5
2933.9900	52	乙色胺,咯环利定〔999〕	6.5		20	13/	13	千克	I		1/31.5
2933.9900	53	[1—(5—氟戊基)—1H—吲哚—3—基](2—碘苯基)甲酮(1—[(5—Fluoropentyl)—1H—indol—3—yl]—(2—iodophenyl) methanone;CAS号:335161—03—0)〔999〕	6.5		20	13/	13	千克	I		1/31.5
2933.9900	54	1—(5—氟戊基)—3—(1—萘甲酰基)—1H—吲哚(1—(5—Fluoropentyl)—3—(1—naphthoyl) indole;CAS号:335161—24—5)〔999〕	6.5		20	13/	13	千克	I		1/31.5
2933.9900	55	1—戊基—3—(1—萘甲酰基)吲哚(1—Pentyl—3—(1—naphthoyl) indole;CAS号:209414—07—3)〔999〕	6.5		20	13/	13	千克	I		1/31.5
2933.9900	56	1—丁基—3—(1—萘甲酰基)吲哚(1—Butyl—3—(1—naphthoyl) indole;CAS号:208987—48—8)〔999〕	6.5		20	13/	13	千克	I		1/31.5
2933.9900	57	2—(2—甲氧基苯基)—1—(1—戊基—1H—吲哚—3—基)乙酮(2—(2—Methoxyphenyl)—1—(1—pentyl—1H—indol—3—yl) ethanone;CAS号:864445—43—2)〔999〕	6.5		20	13/	13	千克	I		1/31.5
2933.9900	60	(环)四亚甲基四硝胺(俗名奥托金HMX)〔999〕	6.5		20	13/	13	千克	3k		1/31.5
2933.9900	70	(环)三亚甲基三硝基胺(俗名黑索金RDX)〔999〕	6.5		20	13/	13	千克	3k		1/31.5
2933.9900	80	丁羟咯酮(包括杀雄啉、杀雄嗪酸、双唑草腈、唑酮草酯)〔999〕	6.5		20	13/	13	千克	S		1/31.5
2933.9900	91	阿托伐他汀钙〔999〕	6.5	0	20	13/	13	千克			1/25
2933.9900	92	阿那曲唑、来曲唑、硼替佐米、替莫唑胺〔999〕	6.5	0	20	3/	13	千克			1/25
2933.9900	93	维格列汀	6.5	0	20	13/	13	千克			1/25
2933.9900	99	其他仅含氮杂原子的杂环化合物〔301爆炸品,302易燃液体,303易燃固体,304杂项物质,305一般化工产品〕	6.5		20	13/	13	千克			1/31.5
29.34		**核酸及其盐;无论是否已有化学定义;其他杂环化合物:**									
		-结构上含有一个非稠合噻唑环(不论是否氢化)的化合物:									
2934.1010		---三苯甲基氨噻肟酸〔999〕	6.5		20	13/	9,13	千克			1/
2934.1090		---其他									
2934.1090	11	噻螨酮〔999〕	6.5		20	13/	9,10	千克	S		1/31.5
2934.1090	12	噻唑膦,噻唑硫磷〔999〕	6.5		20	13/	9,10	千克	S		1/31.5
2934.1090	13	噻唑烟酸,噻唑菌胺〔999〕	6.5		20	13/	9,10	千克	S		1/31.5
2934.1090	14	氯噻啉,氟螨噻〔999〕	6.5		20	13/	9,10	千克	S		1/31.5
2934.1090	15	噻菌灵,噻菌胺,噻丙腈〔999〕	6.5		20	13/	9,10	千克	S		1/31.5
2934.1090	16	噻呋酰胺、噻虫胺、噻虫嗪、噻虫啉〔999〕	6.5		20	13/	9,10	千克	S		1/31.5
2934.1090	17	辛噻酮,拌种灵〔999〕	6.5		20	13/	9,10	千克	S		1/31.5
2934.1090	18	稻瘟灵〔999〕	6.5		20	13/	9,10	千克	S		1/31.5
2934.1090	19	甲噻诱胺〔999〕	6.5		20	13/	9,10	千克	S		1/31.5
2934.1090	91	达沙替尼〔301其他危险化学品,302其他化工产品〕	6.5	0	20	3/	10	千克			1/25
2934.1090	99	其他结构上含有非稠合噻唑环的化合物(非稠合噻唑环不论是否氢化)(因拆分抗癌药品原料药产生的兜底税号)〔301麦草净,302:2—氨基噻唑硫酸盐,303:2—氨基噻唑盐酸盐〕	6.5		20	13/	10	千克			1/31.5

协定税率 %										特惠税率 %			Article Description
亚太5国	东/冰/格	巴基斯坦	韩国	瑞士	哥达	秘鲁	澳大利亚	新西/坡/智	港/澳/台	亚太2国	老/柬/缅	36/3/1	
	0/0/0	0	0	3.4	0	0	0	0//0	0/0/			0/0/	Triadimefo, credazine, triadimeno, carfentrazone-ethyl (including 4-chloroquinoxaline, hexaconazole, fenbuconazole, imbenconazole, tetraconazole, epoxiconazole)
	0/0/0	0	0	3.4	0	0	0	0//0	0/0/			0/0/	Diclobutrazol, penconzole, flutriafol (including bitertanol, myclobutanil, cyproconazole, diniconazole, tebuconazole, flusilazole)
	0/0/0	0	0	3.4	0	0	0	0//0	0/0/			0/0/	Cyproconazole, metconazole, triticonazole, ipconazole(including shenqinmycin, fluquinconazole, pyridaben, fenazaquin, norflurazon, fluorochloridone)
	0/0/0	0	0	3.4	0	0	0	0//0	0/0/			0/0/	Carfentrazone-ethyl, tetcyclacis, propaquizafop(including quizalofop-P-tefuryl, pyridate, cisanilide, molinate, cafenstrole, diquat, chloridazon)
	0/0/0	0	0	3.4	0	0	0	0//0	0/0/			0/0/	Flupoxam, foramsulfuron, fluotrimazole (including indole-butytic-acid), brompyrazon, piproctanly, ethychlozate(JMAF), fentrazamide)
	0/0/0	0	0	3.4	0	0	0	0//0	0/0/			0/0/	Paclobutrazol, uniconazole, triapenthenol, bifenthrin (including phenazineoxide, butrizol, tepraloxydim, heteroauxin)
	0/0/0	0	0	3.4	0	0	0	0//0	0/0/			0/0/	Clonitazene
	0/0/0	0	0	3.4	0	0	0	0//0	0/0/			0/0/	Etonitazene
	0/0/0	0	0	3.4	0	0	0	0//0	0/0/			0/0/	Proheptazine, bucinnazine
	0/0/0	0	0	3.4	0	0	0	0//0	0/0/			0/0/	Zaleplon zolpidem(salts thereof)
	0/0/0	0	0	3.4	0	0	0	0//0	0/0/			0/0/	Zilpaterol
	0/0/0	0	0	3.4	0	0	0	0//0	0/0/			0/0/	Dimethyltryptamine, diethyltryptamine
	0/0/0	0	0	3.4	0	0	0	0//0	0/0/			0/0/	Etryptamine, rolicyclidine
	0/0/0	0	0	3.4	0	0	0	0//0	0/0/			0/0/	1-[(5-Fluoropentyl)-1H-indol-3-Yl]-(2-iodophenyl) methanone (CAS:335161-03-0)
	0/0/0	0	0	3.4	0	0	0	0//0	0/0/			0/0/	1-(5-Fluoropentyl)-3-(1-naphthoyl)indole(CAS:335161-24-5)
	0/0/0	0	0	3.4	0	0	0	0//0	0/0/			0/0/	1-Pentyl-3-(1-naphthoyl)indole(CAS:209414-07-3)
	0/0/0	0	0	3.4	0	0	0	0//0	0/0/			0/0/	1-Butyl-3-(1-naphthoyl)indole(CAS:208987-48-8)
	0/0/0	0	0	3.4	0	0	0	0//0	0/0/			0/0/	2-(2-Methoxyphenyl)-1-(1-pentyl-1H-indol-3-Yl) ethanone (CAS:864445-43-2)
	0/0/0	0	0	3.4	0	0	0	0//0	0/0/			0/0/	Cyclotetramethylene tetranitramine(octogen)
	0/0/0	0	0	3.4	0	0	0	0//0	0/0/			0/0/	Cycltrimethylene-trinitramine(hexogen)
	0/0/0	0	0	3.4	0	0	0	0//0	0/0/			0/0/	Tepraloxydim(including sintofen, clofencet, pyraclonil, carfentrazone-ethyl)
	0/0/0	0	0	3.4	0	0	0	0//0	0/0/			0/0/	Atorvastatin calcium
	0/0/0	0	0	3.4	0	0	0	0//0	0/0/			0/0/	Anastrozole, letrozole, bortezomib, temozolomide and other anti-cancer drug substances
	0/0/0	0	0	3.4	0	0	0	0//0	0/0/		//	0/0/	Veglding
	0/0/0	0	0	3.4	0	0	0	0//0	0/0/			0/0/	Nitrogen containing heterocyclic compounds other atoms
													Nucleic acids and their salts, whether or not chemically defined; other heterocyclic compounds:
													-The structure contains a compound of non fused thiazole ring, whether or not hydrogenated:
	0/0/0	5	3.9	0	0	0	0	0//0	0/0/			0/0/	---Three benzothiothiotaxime acid
													---Other
	0/0/0	5	3.9	0	0	0	0	0//0	0/0/			0/0/	Hexythiazox
	0/0/0	5	3.9	0	0	0	0	0//0	0/0/			0/0/	Thiazolidazole
	0/0/0	5	3.9	0	0	0	0	0//0	0/0/			0/0/	Thiazolidic acid, thiazolamide
	0/0/0	5	3.9	0	0	0	0	0//0	0/0/			0/0/	Chlorothiazoline
	0/0/0	5	3.9	0	0	0	0	0//0	0/0/			0/0/	Thiabendazole, Sai Fluopicolide, Sai propanenitrile
	0/0/0	5	3.9	0	0	0	0	0//0	0/0/			0/0/	Thioacetamide, thiamide, thiamoxin and thiamidine
	0/0/0	5	3.9	0	0	0	0	0//0	0/0/			0/0/	Essien Thiazone, Seedvax
	0/0/0	5	3.9	0	0	0	0	0//0	0/0/			0/0/	Isoprothiolane
	0/0/0	5	3.9	0	0	0	0	0//0	0/0/			0/0/	Methiadinil
	0/0/0	5	3.9	0	0	0	0	0//0	0/0/			0/0/	Dasatinib and Other Anticancer Drugs
	0/0/0	5	3.9	0	0	0	0	0//0	0/0/			0/0/	Other compounds that contain unfused thiazole rings in their structure (non—condensed thiazole rings, whether or not they are hydrogenated)(tax number of Separating anti—cancer pharmaceutical raw materials)

税则号列	货品名称〔CIQ扩展编码及品名－T2表示见附表2〕	最惠(%)	暂定税率	普通	增值/消费	出口退税	计量单位	监管条件	检验检疫	特殊证件对美关税
2934.2000	-结构上含有一个苯并噻唑环系(不论是否氢化)的化合物,但未经进一步稠合的									
2934.2000 11	噻螨威,噻霉酮〔999〕	6.5		20	13/	9,10	千克	S		1/26.5
2934.2000 12	苯噻硫氰〔999〕	6.5		20	13/	9,10	千克	S		1/26.5
2934.2000 13	烯丙苯噻唑〔999〕	6.5		20	13/	9,10	千克	S		1/26.5
2934.2000 14	草除灵〔999〕	6.5		20	13/	9,10	千克	S		1/26.5
2934.2000 15	噻唑禾草灵〔999〕	6.5		20	13/	9,10	千克	S		1/26.5
2934.2000 16	苯噻隆〔999〕	6.5		20	13/	9,10	千克	S		1/26.5
2934.2000 17	甲基苯噻隆〔999〕	6.5		20	13/	9,10	千克	S		1/26.5
2934.2000 18	苯噻酰草胺〔999〕	6.5		20	13/	9,10	千克	S		1/26.5
2934.2000 19	苯噻菌酯〔999〕	6.5		20	13/	9,13	千克	S		1/26.5
2934.2000 21	利鲁唑	6.5	0	20	3/	13	千克			/20
2934.2000 90	其他含一个苯并噻唑环系的化合物〔999〕	6.5		20	13/	13	千克			1/26.5
2934.3000	-结构上含有一个吩噻嗪环系(不论是否氢化)的化合物,但未经进一步稠合的〔999〕	6.5		20	13/	13	千克			1/26.5
	-其他:									
2934.9100	--阿米雷司(INN),溴替唑仑(INN),氯噻西泮(INN),氯恶唑仑(INN),右吗拉胺(INN),卤恶唑仑(INN),凯他唑仑(INN),美索卡(INN),恶唑仑(INN),匹莫林(INN),苯甲曲嗪(INN),芬美曲嗪(INN)和舒芬太尼(INN)及它们的盐									
2934.9100 11	阿米雷司、溴替唑仑、氯噻西泮(以及它们的盐)〔999〕	6.5		20	13/	13	千克	I		1/11.5
2934.9100 12	氯恶唑仑、卤沙(恶)唑仑(以及它们的盐)〔999〕	6.5		20	13/	13	千克	I		1/11.5
2934.9100 13	凯他唑仑、美索卡、奥沙(恶)唑仑(以及它们的盐)〔999〕	6.5		20	13/	13	千克	I		1/11.5
2934.9100 14	匹莫林、苯甲曲嗪、芬美曲嗪(以及它们的盐)〔999〕	6.5		20	13/	13	千克	I		1/11.5
2934.9100 20	右吗拉胺、舒芬太尼(以及它们的盐)〔999〕	6.5		20	13/	13	千克	I		1/11.5
	--其他:									
2934.9910	---磺内酯及磺内酰胺〔999〕	6.5		30	13/	13	千克			1/31.5
2934.9920	---呋喃唑酮〔999〕	6		20	13/	13	千克	A	M	1/
2934.9930	---核酸及其盐〔104〕									
2934.9930 10	人类核酸及其盐	6.5		35	13/	13	千克	V		1/11.5
2934.9930 90	其他核酸及其盐〔101医学或生命科学用途,102非医学或生命科学用途〕	6.5		35	13/	13	千克			1/11.5
2934.9940	---奈韦拉平、依发韦仑、利托那韦及它们的盐〔999〕	6.5		20	13/	13	千克			1/
2934.9950	---克拉维酸及其盐〔999〕	6.5		20	13/	13	千克			1/
2934.9960	---7-苯乙酰氨基-3-氯甲基-4-头孢烷酸对甲氧基苄酯、7-氨基头孢烷酸、7-氨基脱乙酰氧基头孢烷酸〔999〕	6		20	13/	10,13	千克			1/
2934.9990	---其他									
2934.9990 01	核苷酸类食品添加剂〔301无检疫要求食品添加剂,302需申报仅用于工业用途不用于食品添加剂无检疫要求的化学品〕	6.5		20	13/	13	千克	A	R	1/36.5
2934.9990 10	恶草酮、氟噻草胺、活化酯、高效二甲吩草胺(包括吡噻菌胺)〔999〕	6.5		20	13/	9,13	千克	S		1/36.5
2934.9990 21	恶唑磷、蔬果磷、茂硫磷、除害磷等(包括甲基吡恶磷、丁硫环磷、硫环磷、杀扑磷、伏杀硫磷、地胺磷)〔301毒性物质和感染性物质〕	6.5		20	13/	9,13	千克	S		1/36.5
2934.9990 22	环线威、杀虫环、杀虫钉、多噻烷等(包括甲基硫环磷、噻嗯菊酯、噻嗪酮、恶虫酮、茚虫威)〔101甲基硫环磷颗粒剂〕	6.5		20	13/	9,13	千克	S		1/
2934.9990 23	恶唑禾草灵、毒鼠硅、噻鼠灵等(包括福拉比、噻节因、糠菌唑、精恶唑禾草灵)〔999〕	6.5		20	13/	9,13	千克	S		1/36.5
2934.9990 24	代森硫、代森环、福吗啉、咯菌腈等(包括稻瘟酯、烯酰吗啉、噻菌腈、土菌灵、恶霜灵、恶霉灵)〔101代森硫,102代森环〕	6.5		20	13/	9,13	千克	S		1/36.5
2934.9990 25	噻霉酮、丙环唑、乙环唑等(包括恶唑菌酮、金核霉素、呋菌唑、叶枯唑、呋醚唑、苯醚甲环唑)〔999〕	6.5		20	13/	9,13	千克	S		1/36.5
2934.9990 26	嗪草酸、噻氟隆、丁噻隆、异恶隆等(包括噻苯隆、磺噻隆、恶唑隆、异恶草醚、噻吩草胺、二甲吩草胺)〔999〕	6.5		20	13/	9,13	千克	S		1/36.5
2934.9990 27	苯草灭、灭草松、灭草唑等(包括异恶草松、恶嗪草酮、环苯草酮、丙炔氟草胺)〔999〕	6.5		20	13/	9,13	千克	S		1/36.5
2934.9990 28	丙炔恶草酮,噻草酮等(包括糖氨基嘌呤,苯螨噻,异恶酰草胺,异恶唑草酮)〔999〕	6.5		20	13/	9,13	千克	S		1/36.5

协定税率 %										特惠税率 %			Article Description
亚太5国	东/冰/格	巴基斯坦	韩国	瑞士	哥达	秘鲁	澳大利亚	新西/坡/智	港/澳/台	亚太2国	老/柬/缅	36/3/1	
													-Compounds containing in the structure a benzothiazole ring-system (whether or not hydrogenated), not further fused
	0/0/0	5	2.6	0	0	0	0	0//0	0/0/			0/0/	Tazimcarb, benziothiazolinone
	0/0/0	5	2.6	0	0	0	0	0//0	0/0/			0/0/	Benthiozole
	0/0/0	5	2.6	0	0	0	0	0//0	0/0/			0/0/	Probenazole
	0/0/0	5	2.6	0	0	0	0	0//0	0/0/			0/0/	Benazolin ethyl
	0/0/0	5	2.6	0	0	0	0	0//0	0/0/			0/0/	Fenthiaprop-ethyl
	0/0/0	5	2.6	0	0	0	0	0//0	0/0/			0/0/	Benzthiazuron
	0/0/0	5	2.6	0	0	0	0	0//0	0/0/			0/0/	Methabenzthiazuron
	0/0/0	5	2.6	0	0	0	0	0//0	0/0/			0/0/	Mefenacet
	0/0/0	5	2.6	0	0	0	0	0//0	0/0/			0/0/	Benzothiostrobin
	0/0/0	5	2.6	0	0	0	0	0//0	0/0/		//	0/0/	Riluzole
	0/0/0	5	2.6	0	0	0	0	0//0	0/0/			0/0/	Other compounds containing in the structure a benzothiazole ring-system
	0/0/0	5	0	0	0	0	0	0//0	0/0/			0/0/	-Compounds containing in the structure a phenothiazine ring-system (whether or not hydrogenated), not further fused
													-Other:
													--Aminorex(INN), brotizolam(INN), clotiazepam(INN), cloxazolam(INN), dextromoramide(INN), haloxazolam(INN), ketazolam(INN), mesocarb(INN), oxazolam(INN), pemoline(INN), phendimetrazine (INN), phenmetrazine (INN) and sufentanil (INN); salts thereof
	0/0/0	5	0	0	0	0	0	0//0	0/0/			0/0/	Aminorex(INN), brotizolam(INN), clotiazepam(INN)(salts thereof)
	0/0/0	5	0	0	0	0	0	0//0	0/0/			0/0/	Cloxazolam(INN), haloxazolam(INN); (salts thereof)
	0/0/0	5	0	0	0	0	0	0//0	0/0/			0/0/	Ketazolam(INN), mesocarb(INN), oxazolam(INN)(salts thereof)
	0/0/0	5	0	0	0	0	0	0//0	0/0/			0/0/	Pemoline (INN), phendimetrazine (INN), phenmetrazine (INN) (salts thereof)
	0/0/0	5	0	0	0	0	0	0//0	0/0/			0/0/	Dextromoramide(INN), sufentanil(INN)(salts thereof)
													--Other:
	0/0/0	5	0	0	0	0	0	0//0	0/0/			0/0/	---Sultones and sultams
4.8	0/0/0	5	0		0	0	0	0//0	0/0/			0/0/	---Furazolidone
	0/0/0	4.5	0	0	0	0	0	0//0	0/0/		//	0/0/	Human nucleic acids and their salts
	0/0/0	4.5	0	0	0	0	0	0//0	0/0/		//	0/0/	Other nucleic acids and their salts
	0/0/0	5	0	0	0	0	0	0//0	0/0/			0/0/	---Nevirapine, Efavirenz, Ritonavir and their salts
	0/0/0	5	0	0	0	0	0	0//0	0/0/			0/0/	---Clavulante acid and its salt
5	0/0/0	0	0	0	0	0	0	0//0	0/0/			0/0/	---7-phenylacetamido-3-chloromethylcephem-4-carbonicacidp-methoxybenzylester; 2, 0) oct-2-ene-2-carboxylicacid, 7-Aminocephalosporanic acid, 7-amido acetoxy eicosanoic acid removal
													---Other
	0/0/0	0	0	0	0	0	0	0//0	0/0/			0/0/	Nucleotides food additives, hgslmof
	0/0/0	0	0	0	0	0	0	0//0	0/0/			0/0/	Oxadiazon, flufenacet, acibenzolar, dimethenamid (including penthiopyrad)
	0/0/0	0	0	0	0	0	0	0//0	0/0/			0/0/	Isoxathion, salithion dioxabenzofos, morphothion, (including azamethiphos, fosthietan, phosfolan, methidathion , phosalone , mephosfolan)
	0/0/0	0	0	0	0	0	0	0//0	0/0/			0/0/	Tirpate , thiocyclam, trithialan, polythialan (including phosfolan-methyl, kadethrin, buprofezin, metoxadiazone, indoxacarb)
	0/0/0	0	0	0	0	0	0	0//0	0/0/			0/0/	Fenoxaprop-ethyl, silatrane, difethialone(including furametpyr, dimethipin , bromuconazole, fenoxaprop-p-ethyl)
	0/0/0	0	0	0	0	0	0	0//0	0/0/			0/0/	Etem (BSI), milmeb (BSI) , flumorph fludioxonil (including pefurazoate, dimethomoph, thicyofen, etridiazole, oxadixyl , hymexazol)
	0/0/0	0	0	0	0	0	0	0//0	0/0/			0/0/	Benziothiazolinone, propiconazole, etaconazole (including famoxadone, aureonuclemycin, furconazole bismerthiazol, furconazole-cis, difenoconazole)
	0/0/0	0	0	0	0	0	0	0//0	0/0/			0/0/	Fluthiacet thiazfluron, tebuthiuron, isoproturon (including thidiazuron, ethidimuron, dimefuron, isoxapyrifop, thenychlor, dimethachlor)
	0/0/0	0	0	0	0	0	0	0//0	0/0/			0/0/	Bentranil, bentazone, methazole (including, clomazone, oxaziclomefone, cloproxydim, flumioxazin)
	0/0/0	0	0	0	0	0	0	0//0	0/0/			0/0/	Fulthiacet-methyl, oxakiargyl, cycloxydim (including kinetin, triarathene , ixoxaben, isoxaflutole)

税则号列		货品名称〔CIQ 扩展编码及品名—T2 表示见附表 2〕	最惠(%)	暂定税率	普通	增值/消费	出口退税	计量单位	监管条件	检验检疫	特殊证件对美关税
2934.9990	29	炔丙恶唑草,噻唑锌等(包括噻菌茂,硅丰环)〔999〕	6.5		20	13/	9,13	千克	S		1/36.5
2934.9990	31	多抗霉素、灰瘟素〔301 毒性物质和感染性物质〕	6.5		20	13/	9,13	千克	S		1/36.5
2934.9990	32	三环唑、氧环唑〔999〕	6.5		20	13/	9,13	千克	S		1/36.5
2934.9990	33	灭螨猛、克杀螨、螨蜱胺〔999〕	6.5		20	13/	9,13	千克	S		1/36.5
2934.9990	34	二氰蒽醌、吗菌威〔101 二噻农,102 二噻农乳剂(含量>50%)〕	6.5		20	13/	9,13	千克	S		1/36.5
2934.9990	35	十二环吗啉、十三吗啉〔999〕	6.5		20	13/	9,13	千克	S		1/36.5
2934.9990	36	杀螺吗啉、丁苯吗啉〔101 蜗螺净粉剂、颗粒剂,102 蜗螺净乳剂〕	6.5		20	13/	9,13	千克	S		1/36.5
2934.9990	37	喹菌酮、肼菌酮〔999〕	6.5		20	13/	9,13	千克	S		1/36.5
2934.9990	38	萎锈灵、氧化萎锈灵〔999〕	6.5		20	13/	9,13	千克	S		1/36.5
2934.9990	39	棉隆、乙烯菌核利〔999〕	6.5		20	13/	9,13	千克	S		1/36.5
2934.9990	41	环酯草醚〔999〕	6.5		20	13/	9,13	千克	S		1/36.5
2934.9990	42	噻菌铜〔999〕	6.5		20	13/	9,13	千克	S		1/36.5
2934.9990	43	苯唑草酮〔999〕	6.5		20	13/	9,13	千克	S		1/36.5
2934.9990	44	丁吡吗啉〔999〕	6.5		20	13/	9,13	千克	S		1/36.5
2934.9990	45	环戊噁草酮〔999〕	6.5		20	13/	13	千克	S		1/36.5
2934.9990	50	恶唑酰草胺(包括环氧虫啶、噻恩菊酯、双苯恶唑酸、乙螨唑、异恶氯草酮、唑啉草酯)〔999〕	6.5		20	13/	9,13	千克	S		1/36.5
2934.9990	61	甲米雷司及其盐〔999〕	6.5		20	13/	13	千克	I		1/36.5
2934.9990	62	替诺环定及其盐〔999〕	6.5		20	13/	13	千克	I		1/36.5
2934.9990	71	硫代芬太尼、阿法甲基硫代芬太尼(以及它们的盐)〔999〕	6.5		20	13/	13	千克	I		1/36.5
2934.9990	72	二乙噻丁、二甲噻丁、吗苯丁酯、乙甲噻丁(以及它们的盐)〔999〕	6.5		20	13/	13	千克	I		1/36.5
2934.9990	73	呋替啶、左吗拉胺、3-甲基硫代芬太尼(以及它们的盐)〔999〕	6.5		20	13/	13	千克	I		1/36.5
2934.9990	74	吗拉胺中间体、吗哌利定、苯吗庚酮、消旋吗拉胺(以及它们的盐)〔999〕	6.5		20	13/	13	千克	I		1/36.5
2934.9990	75	亚甲基二氧吡咯戊酮(Methylenedioxypyrovalerone;CAS 号:687603663)〔999〕	6.5		20	13/	13	千克	I		1/36.5
2934.9990	91	地西他滨、氟脲苷、环磷酰胺、吉非替尼、卡培他滨、雷替曲塞、磷酸氟达拉滨、替加氟、盐酸阿糖胞苷、盐酸吉西他滨、盐酸埃克替尼、异环磷酰胺及其他抗癌药品原料药〔999〕	6.5	0	20	3/	13	千克			1/
2934.9990	99	其他杂环化合物(因拆分抗癌药品原料药产生的兜底税号)〔301 易燃液体,302 毒性物质和感染性物质,303 腐蚀性物质,304 其他化工产品〕	6.5		20	13/	13	千克			1/36.5
29.35		磺(酰)胺:									
2935.1000		-N-甲基全氟辛基磺酰胺〔999〕	6.5		35	13/	9,10	千克			1/
2935.2000		-N-乙基全氟辛基磺酰胺〔999〕	6.5		35	13/	9,10	千克			1/
2935.3000		-N-乙基-N-(2-羟乙基)全氟辛基磺酰胺〔999〕	6.5		35	13/	9,10	千克			1/
2935.4000		-N-(2-羟乙基)-N-甲基全氟辛基磺酰胺〔999〕	6.5		35	13/	9,10	千克			1/
2935.5000		-其他全氟辛基磺酰胺〔999〕	6.5		35	13/	10	千克			1/
2935.9000		-其他									
2935.9000	11	氟唑磺隆,氟吡磺隆,磺酰磺隆,氯酯磺草胺等(包括甲酰氨基嘧磺隆,乙氧磺隆,氯磺隆,甲磺隆,苯磺隆,胺苯磺隆)〔999〕	6.5		35	13/	9,10	千克	S		1/26.5
2935.9000	12	醚苯磺隆,噻吩磺隆,醚磺隆,氟啶嘧磺隆等(包括氟胺磺隆,氟磺隆,甲嘧磺隆,氯嘧磺隆,氟嘧磺隆)〔999〕	6.5		35	13/	9,10	千克	S		1/26.5
2935.9000	13	苄嘧磺隆,吡嘧磺隆,烟嘧磺隆,双氯磺草胺等(包括啶嘧磺隆,砜嘧磺隆,唑嘧磺隆)〔999〕	6.5		35	13/	9,10	千克	S		1/26.5
2935.9000	14	四唑嘧磺隆,唑吡嘧磺隆,三氟甲磺隆等(包括氯吡嘧磺隆,酰嘧磺隆,环丙嘧磺隆,甲基二磺隆)〔999〕	6.5		35	13/	9,10	千克	S		1/26.5
2935.9000	15	氟磺酰草胺,甲磺草胺,嘧苯胺磺隆等(包括唑嘧磺草胺,双氟磺草胺,五氟磺草胺)〔999〕	6.5		35	13/	9,10	千克	S		1/26.5
2935.9000	16	氟磺胺草醚,磺草灵,吲唑磺菌胺等(包括单嘧磺酯,磺草唑胺,三氟啶磺隆钠)〔999〕	6.5		35	13/	9,10	千克	S		1/26.5
2935.9000	17	磺草膦,氨磺乐灵,三氟啶磺隆,啶磺草胺等(包括甲基碘磺隆钠盐)〔999〕	6.5		35	13/	9,10	千克	S		1/26.5
2935.9000	18	磺菌胺,增糖胺等(包括甲苯氟磺胺,氟虫胺)〔999〕	6.5		35	13/	9,10	千克	S		1/26.5
2935.9000	19	畜蜱磷,伐灭磷,地散磷等(包括磺菌威,氰霜唑)〔999〕	6.5		35	13/	9,10	千克	S		1/26.5
2935.9000	20	环氧嘧磺隆〔999〕	6.5		35	13/	9,10	千克	S		1/26.5
2935.9000	31	苯嘧磺草胺〔999〕	6.5		35	13/	9,10	千克	S		1/26.5
2935.9000	32	噻酮磺隆〔999〕	6.5		35	13/	9,10	千克	S		1/26.5

协定税率 %										特惠税率 %			Article Description
亚太5国	东/冰/格	巴基斯坦	韩国	瑞士	哥达	秘鲁	澳大利亚	新西/坡/智	港/澳/台	亚太2国	老/柬/缅	36/3/1	
	0/0/0	0	0	0	0	0	0	0//0	0/0/			0/0/	Oxadiargyl, ethaboxam, zinc thiazole(including Saijunmao, silatrane)
	0/0/0	0	0	0	0	0	0	0//0	0/0/			0/0/	Polyoxin, blasticidin
	0/0/0	0	0	0	0	0	0	0//0	0/0/			0/0/	Tricyclazole, azaconazole
	0/0/0	0	0	0	0	0	0	0//0	0/0/			0/0/	Chinomethionate, thioquino, tifatol
	0/0/0	0	0	0	0	0	0	0//0	0/0/			0/0/	Dithianon, carbamorph
	0/0/0	0	0	0	0	0	0	0//0	0/0/			0/0/	Dodemorph, tridemorph
	0/0/0	0	0	0	0	0	0	0//0	0/0/			0/0/	Trifenmorph, fenpropimorph
	0/0/0	0	0	0	0	0	0	0//0	0/0/			0/0/	Oxolinic acid, drazoxolon
	0/0/0	0	0	0	0	0	0	0//0	0/0/			0/0/	Carboxin, oxycarboxin
	0/0/0	0	0	0	0	0	0	0//0	0/0/			0/0/	Dazomet, vinclozolin
	0/0/0	0	0	0	0	0	0	0//0	0/0/			0/0/	Pyriftalid
	0/0/0	0	0	0	0	0	0	0//0	0/0/			0/0/	Thiodiazole-copper
	0/0/0	0	0	0	0	0	0	0//0	0/0/			0/0/	Carfentrazone-ethyl
	0/0/0	0	0	0	0	0	0	0//0	0/0/			0/0/	Pyrimorph
	0/0/0	0	0	0	0	0	0	0//0	0/0/			0/0/	Pentoxazone
	0/0/0	0	0	0	0	0	0	0//0	0/0/			0/0/	Metamifop (including kadethrin, isoxadifen ethyletoxazole, clomazone, pinoxaden)
	0/0/0	0	0	0	0	0	0	0//0	0/0/			0/0/	4-methylaminorex and its salt
	0/0/0	0	0	0	0	0	0	0//0	0/0/			0/0/	Tenocyclidine and its salt
	0/0/0	0	0	0	0	0	0	0//0	0/0/			0/0/	Thiofentanyl, alpha-methylthiofentanyl (and their salt)
	0/0/0	0	0	0	0	0	0	0//0	0/0/			0/0/	Diethylthiambutene, dimethylthiambutene, dioxaphetylbutyrate, ethyl-methylthiambutene(and their salts)
	0/0/0	0	0	0	0	0	0	0//0	0/0/			0/0/	Furethidine, levomoramide, 3-methylthiofentanyl(and their salts)
	0/0/0	0	0	0	0	0	0	0//0	0/0/			0/0/	Moramide intermediate, morpheridine, benmaliangtong, racemoramide(and their salts)
	0/0/0	0	0	0	0	0	0	0//0	0/0/			0/0/	Methylenedioxypyrovalerone(CAS:687603-66-3)
	0/0/0	0	0	0	0	0	0	0//0	0/0/			0/0/	Decitabine, fluorouridine, cyclophosphamide, gefitinib, capecitabine, raltitrexed, fludarabine phosphate, tegafur, cytarabine hydrochloride, gemcitabine hydrochloride, acetic acid hydrochloride Tinglitin, Ifosfamide and Other Anticancer Drugs
	0/0/0	0	0	0	0	0	0	0//0	0/0/			0/0/	Other heterocyclic compounds(tax number of Separating anti—cancer pharmaceutical raw materials)
													Sulphonamides:
	0/0/0	0	0	3.4	0	0	0	0//0	0/0/			0/0/	-N-Methylperfluorooctane sulphonamide
	0/0/0	0	0	3.4	0	0	0	0//0	0/0/			0/0/	-N-Ethylperfluorooctane sulphonamide
	0/0/0	0	0	3.4	0	0	0	0//0	0/0/			0/0/	-N-Ethyl-N- (2-*hydroxyethyl*) perfluorooctane sulphonamide
	0/0/0	0	0	3.4	0	0	0	0//0	0/0/			0/0/	-N-(2-*Hydroxyethyl*) -N-methylperfluorooctane sulphonamide
	0/0/0	0	0	3.4	0	0	0	0//0	0/0/			0/0/	-Other perfluorooctane sulphonamides
													-Other
	0/0/0	0	0	3.4	0	0	0	0//0	0/0/			0/0/	Flucarbazone, flucetosulfuron, sulfosulfuron, cloransulam-methy etc(including formamide-sulfometuron, ethoxysulfuron, chlorsulfuron, metsulfuron-methyl, tribenuronmethyl, ethametsulfuron-methyl)
	0/0/0	0	0	3.4	0	0	0	0//0	0/0/			0/0/	Triasulfuron, thifensulfuron-methyl, cinosulfuron, flupyrsulfuron-methyl-sodium etc(including triflusulfuronmethyl, prosulfuron, sulfometuron-methyl, chlorimuron-ethyl, primisulfuron-methy)
	0/0/0	0	0	3.4	0	0	0	0//0	0/0/			0/0/	Bensulfuron-methyl, pyrazosulfuron-ethyl, nicosulfuron, diclosulam etc(including flazasulfuron, rimsulfuron, imazosulfuron)
	0/0/0	0	0	3.4	0	0	0	0//0	0/0/			0/0/	Azimsulfuron, mazosulfuron, tritosulfuron etc.(including halosulfuron-methyl, amidosulfuron, cyclosulfamuron, 爛 esosulfuron-methyl)
	0/0/0	0	0	3.4	0	0	0	0//0	0/0/			0/0/	Mefluidide, sulfentrazone, orthosulfamuron etc.(including flumetsulam, florasulam, penoxsulam)
	0/0/0	0	0	3.4	0	0	0	0//0	0/0/			0/0/	Fomesafen, asulam, amisulbrom etc.(including monosulfuron ester, metosulam)
	0/0/0	0	0	3.4	0	0	0	0//0	0/0/			0/0/	Mesyl (methyl) caramoylmethyla-minome-thyl phosphonic acid, oryzalin, trifloxysulfuron, pyroxsulam etc.(including iodosulfuron methyl sodium)
	0/0/0	0	0	3.4	0	0	0	0//0	0/0/			0/0/	Flusulfamide, flucridamid etc.(including toly- lfluanid, sulfluramid)
	0/0/0	0	0	3.4	0	0	0	0//0	0/0/			0/0/	Cythioate, famphur(ESA), bensulide etc.(including methasulfocarb, cyazofamid)
	0/0/0	0	0	3.4	0	0	0	0//0	0/0/			0/0/	Oxasulfuron
	0/0/0	0	0	3.4	0	0	0	0//0	0/0/			0/0/	Saflufenacil
	0/0/0	0	0	3.4	0	0	0	0//0	0/0/			0/0/	Thiencarbazone-methyl

税则号列	货品名称〔CIQ 扩展编码及品名－T2 表示见附表 2〕	最惠(%)	暂定税率	普通	增值/消费	出口退税	计量单位	监管条件	检验检疫	特殊证件对美关税
2935.9000 33	磺胺嘧啶〔999〕	6.5		35	13/	10	千克			1/26.5
2935.9000 34	磺胺双甲基嘧啶〔999〕	6.5		35	13/	10	千克	A	M	1/26.5
2935.9000 35	磺胺甲噁唑(磺胺甲基异噁唑,新诺明、新明磺)〔999〕	6.5		35	13/	10	千克			1/26.5
2935.9000 36	波生坦	6.5	0	35	3/	10	千克			/20
2935.9000 90	其他磺(酰)胺〔101 偶氮甲酰胺,102:4－甲基－5－(β－羟乙基)噻唑〕	6.5		35	13/	10	千克			1/26.5
	第十一分章 维生素原、维生素及激素									
29.36	**天然或合成再制的维生素原和维生素(包括天然浓缩物)及其主要用作维生素的衍生物,上述产品的混合物,不论是否溶于溶剂:**									
	-未混合的维生素及其衍生物:									
2936.2100	--维生素 A 及其衍生物〔101 饲料添加剂,301 无检疫要求食品添加剂,302 需申报仅用于工业用途不用于食品添加剂无检疫要求的化学品〕	4		20	13/	13	千克	A	R	1/29
2936.2200	--维生素 B_1 及其衍生物〔101 饲料添加剂,102 维生素 B1(无检疫要求食品添加剂)),103 盐酸硫胺素(无检疫要求食品添加剂),301 需申报仅用于工业用途不用于食品添加剂无检疫要求的化学品〕	4		20	13/	13	千克	A	R	1/29
2936.2300	--维生素 B_2 及其衍生物〔101 饲料添加剂,301 维生素 B2(无检疫要求食品添加剂)),302 核黄素 5′—磷酸钠(无检疫要求食品添加剂),303 需申报仅用于工业用途不用于食品添加剂无检疫要求的化学品〕	4		20	13/	13	千克	A	R	1/29
2936.2400	--D 或 DL-泛酸(维生素 B_3 或维生素 B_5)及其衍生物[T2]	4		20	13/	13	千克	A	R	1/29
2936.2500	--维生素 B_6 及其衍生物〔101 饲料添加剂,301 无检疫要求食品添加剂,302 需申报仅用于工业用途不用于食品添加剂无检疫要求的化学品〕	4		20	13/	13	千克	A	R	1/24
2936.2600	--维生素 B_{12} 及其衍生物〔101 饲料添加剂,301 维生素 B12(氰钴铵或羟钴铵)(无检疫要求食品添加剂),302:氰钴胺(无检疫要求食品添加剂),303 需申报仅用于工业用途不用于食品添加剂无检疫要求的化学品〕	4		20	13/	13	千克	A	R	1/29
2936.2700	--维生素 C 及其衍生物									
2936.2700 10	未混合的维生素 C 原粉(不论是否溶于溶剂)〔301 无检疫要求食品添加剂,302 需申报仅用于工业用途不用于食品添加剂无检疫要求的化学品〕	4		20	13/	13	千克	A	R	1/24
2936.2700 20	未混合的维生素 C 钙、维生素 C 钠(不论是否溶于溶剂)[T2]	4		20	13/	13	千克	A	R	1/24
2936.2700 30	颗粒或包衣维生素 C(不论是否溶于溶剂)[T2]	4		20	13/	13	千克	A	R	1/24
2936.2700 90	维生素 C 酯类及其他(不论是否溶于溶剂)[T2]	4		20	13/	13	千克	A	R	1/24
2936.2800	--维生素 E 及其衍生物[T2]	4		20	13/	13	千克	A	R	1/14
2936.2900	--其他维生素及其衍生物									
2936.2900 10	胆钙化醇(不论是否溶于溶剂)〔101 饲料添加剂,301 无检疫要求食品添加剂,302 需申报仅用于工业用途不用于食品添加剂无检疫要求的化学品〕	4		20	13/	13	千克	AS	R	1/14
2936.2900 90	其他未混合的维生素及其衍生物(不论是否溶于溶剂)[T2]	4		20	13/	13	千克	A	R	1/14
	-其他,包括天然浓缩物:									
2936.9010	---维生素 AD3〔101 饲料添加剂,102 具有保健食品批准文号,103 无检疫要求食品添加剂〕	4		20	13/	13	千克	A	R	1/
2936.9090	---其他〔101 饲料添加剂,102 具有保健食品批准文号,301 叶酸(无检疫要求食品添加剂),302 需申报仅用于工业用途不用于食品添加剂无检疫要求的化学品〕	4		20	13/	13	千克	A	R	1/14
29.37	**天然或合成再制的激素、前列腺素、血栓烷、白细胞三烯及其衍生物和结构类似物,包括主要用作激素的改性链多肽:**									
	-多肽激素、蛋白激素、糖蛋白激素及其衍生物和结构类似物:									
2937.1100	--生长激素及其衍生物和结构类似物									
2937.1100 10	生长激素(GH)〔999〕	4		20	13/	13	千克	L		1/
2937.1100 90	生长激素的衍生物和结构类似物〔999〕	4		20	13/	13	千克	L		1/
	--胰岛素及其盐:									
2937.1210	---重组人胰岛素及其盐〔999〕	4	0	20	13/	13	千克	L		1/25
2937.1290	---其他〔999〕	4	0	20	13/	13	千克	L		1/25
2937.1900	--其他									

协定税率 %									特惠税率 %			
亚太5国	东/冰/格	巴基斯坦	韩国	瑞士	哥达	秘鲁	澳大利亚	新西/坡/智	港/澳/台	亚太2国	老/柬/缅	36/3/1	Article Description
	0/0/0	0	0	3.4	0	0	0	0//0	0/0/			0/0/	Sulphadiazine
	0/0/0	0	0	3.4	0	0	0	0//0	0/0/			0/0/	Sulfadimidine
	0/0/0	0	0	3.4	0	0	0	0//0	0/0/			0/0/	Sulfamethoxazole
	0/0/0	0	0	3.4	0	0	0	0//0	0/0/		//	0/0/	Bosentan
	0/0/0	0	0	3.4	0	0	0	0//0	0/0/			0/0/	Other sulphonamides
													Ⅺ. PROVITAMINS, VITAMINS AND HORMONES
													Provitamins and vitamins, natural or reproduced by synthesis (including natural concentrates), derivatives thereof used primarily as vitamins, and intermixtures of the foregoing, whether or not in any solvent:
													-Vitamins and their derivatives, unmixed:
	0/0/0	0	0	2.1	0	0	0	0//0	0/0/			0/0/0	--Vitamins A and their derivatives
	0/0/0	0	0	0	0	0	0	0//0	0/0/			0/0/0	--Vitamin B_1 and its derivatives
	0/0/0	0	0	0	0	0	0	0//0	0/0/			0/0/0	--Vitamin B_2 and its derivatives
	0/0/0	0	0	0	0	0	0	0//0	0/0/			0/0/0	--D-or DL-Pantothenic acid (Vitamin B_3 or Vitamin B_5) and its derivatives
	0/0/0	0	0	0	0	0	0	0//0	0/0/			0/0/0	--Vitamin B_6 and its derivatives
	0/0/0	0	0	1.2	0	0	0	0//0	0/0/			0/0/0	--Vitamin B_{12} and its derivatives
													--Vitamin C and its derivatives
	0/0/0	0	0	0	0	0	0	0//0	0/0/			0/0/0	Not mixed vitamin C of original powder(whether or not in any solvent)
	0/0/0	0	0	0	0	0	0	0//0	0/0/			0/0/0	Not mixed Calcium ascorbate, odiumascorbate(whether or not in orny solvent)
	0/0/0	0	0	0	0	0	0	0//0	0/0/			0/0/0	Particles or coated vitamin C(whether or not in any solvent)
	0/0/0	0	0	0	0	0	0	0//0	0/0/			0/0/0	vitamin c of ester and other(whether or not in any solvent)
	0/0/0	0	0	1.2	0	0	0	0//0	0/0/			0/0/0	--Vitamin E and its derivatives
													--Other
	0/0/0	0	0	1.2	0	0	0	0//0	0/0/			0/0/0	Cholecalciferol(whether or not in any solvent)
	0/0/0	0	0	1.2	0	0	0	0//0	0/0/			0/0/0	Other vitamins and their derivatives, unmixed(whether or not in any solvent)
													-Other, including natural concentrates:
	0/0/0	0	0	0	0	0	0	0//0	0/0/			0/0/0	---Vitamin AD3
	0/0/0	0	0	0	0	0	0	0//0	0/0/			0/0/0	---Other
													Hormones, prostaglandins, thromboxanes and leukotrienes, natural or reproduced by synthesis; derivatives and structural analogues thereof, including chain modified polypeptides, used primarily as hormones:
													-Polypeptide hormones, protein hormones and glycoprotein hormones, their derivatives and structural analogues:
													--Somatotropin, its derivatives and structural analogues
	0/0/0	0	0	0	0	0	0	0//0	0/0/			0/0/	Growth hormone(GH)
	0/0/0	0	0	0	0	0	0	0//0	0/0/			0/0/	Growth hormone derivatives and structural analogues
													--Insulin and its salts:
	0/0/0	0	0	0	0	0	0	0//0	0/0/			0/0/	---Recombinant human insulin and its salts
	0/0/0	0	0	0	0	0	0	0//0	0/0/			0/0/	---Other
													--Other

税则号列		货品名称〔CIQ 扩展编码及品名—T2 表示见附表 2〕	最惠(%)	暂定税率	普通	增值/消费	出口退税	计量单位	监管条件	检验检疫	特殊证件对美关税
2937.1900	13	绒促性素、促黄体生成素等(包括生长激素释放肽类(GHRPs)、普拉莫瑞林(生长激素释放肽—2)、CJC—1295(CAS 号 863288340)、生长激素释放肽—6、生长激素释放激素及其类似物、生长激素促分泌剂)〔999〕	4		20	13/	13	千克	L		1/29
2937.1900	15	促皮质素类等肽类激素(包括艾瑞莫瑞林、阿那瑞林、布舍瑞林、可的瑞林、海沙瑞林、伊莫瑞林、舍莫瑞林、替莫瑞林、戈那瑞林、葛瑞林(脑肠肽)及葛瑞林模拟物类)〔999〕	4		20	13/	13	千克	L		1/29
2937.1900	16	亮丙瑞林〔999〕	4		20	13/	13	千克	L		1/29
2937.1900	91	醋酸曲普瑞林〔999〕	4	0	20	3/	13	千克	Q		1/25
2937.1900	93	卵泡抑素	4		20	13/	13	千克	L		/29
2937.1900	99	其他多肽激素及衍生物和结构类似物(包括蛋白激素、糖蛋白激素及其衍生物和结构类似物)(因拆分抗癌药品原料药产生的兜底税号)〔999〕	4		20	13/	13	千克	Q		1/29
		-甾族激素及其衍生物和结构类似物:									
2937.2100		--可的松、氢化可的松、脱氢可的松及脱氢皮质醇〔999〕	4		20	13/	10	千克	Q		1/
		--皮质(甾)类激素的卤化衍生物:									
2937.2210		---地塞米松〔999〕	4		30	13/	10	千克	Q		1/
2937.2290		---其他〔999〕	4		30	13/	10	千克	Q		1/29
		--雌(甾)激素和孕激素:									
		---动物源的:									
2937.2311		----孕马结合雌激素〔999〕	4		30	13/	13	千克	Q		1/
2937.2319		----其他									
2937.2319	10	福美坦〔999〕	4	0	30	3/	13	千克	Q		1/
2937.2319	90	其他动物源雌(甾)激素和孕激素(因拆分抗癌药品原料药产生的兜底税号)〔999〕	4		30	13/	13	千克	Q		1/
2937.2390		---其他									
2937.2390	10	泽仑诺;孕三烯酮;替勃龙(包括四氢孕三烯酮)〔999〕	4		30	13/	13	千克	L		1/29
2937.2390	90	其他雌(甾)激素及孕激素(因拆分抗癌药品原料药产生的兜底税号)〔999〕	4		30	13/	13	千克	Q		/29
2937.2900		--其他									
2937.2900	11	1—雄烯二醇;1—雄烯二酮(包括雄甾—4—烯—3β, 17α—二醇(4—雄烯二醇(3β, 17α));雄甾—5—烯—3β, 17α—二醇(5—雄烯二醇(3β, 17α))〔999〕	4		30	13/	13	千克	L		1/29
2937.2900	12	4 雄烯二醇;5 雄烯二酮(包括 5α 雄烷 3α, 17β 二醇(雄烷二醇(3α, 17β));5α 雄烷 3β, 17α 二醇(雄烷二醇(3β, 17α));勃拉睾酮;5β 雄烷 3α, 17β 二醇(5β 雄烷二醇(3α, 17β)))〔999〕	4		30	13/	13	千克	L		1/29
2937.2900	13	勃地酮;卡芦睾酮(包括勃二酮;氯司替勃)〔999〕	4		30	13/	13	千克	L		1/29
2937.2900	14	达那唑;脱氢氯甲睾酮(包括普拉睾酮;去氧甲睾酮)〔999〕	4		30	13/	13	千克	L		1/29
2937.2900	15	双氢睾酮;屈他雄酮(包括表双氢睾酮;乙雌烯醇;氟甲睾酮;甲酰勃龙)〔999〕	4		30	13/	13	千克	L		1/29
2937.2900	16	夫拉扎勃(包括 4-羟基睾酮;3α-羟基-5α-雄烷-17-酮)〔999〕	4		30	13/	13	千克	L		1/29
2937.2900	17	美雄诺龙;美睾酮;美雄酮(包括甲基屈他雄酮)〔999〕	4		30	13/	13	千克	L		1/29
2937.2900	18	甲基-1-睾酮;甲睾酮;甲诺睾酮(包括甲二烯诺龙;去甲雄酮)〔999〕	4		30	13/	13	千克	L		1/29
2937.2900	19	美替诺龙;美雄醇(包括美曲勃龙)〔999〕	4		30	13/	13	千克	L		1/29
2937.2900	21	米勃酮;诺龙;诺勃酮;诺司替勃(包括 19-去甲雄烯二醇;诺乙雄龙)〔999〕	4		30	13/	13	千克	L		1/29
2937.2900	22	19—去甲本胆烷醇酮(包括羟勃龙;氧雄龙)	4		30	13/	13	千克	L		1/29
2937.2900	23	羟甲睾酮;羟甲烯龙(包括前列他唑)〔999〕	4		30	13/	13	千克	L		1/29
2937.2900	24	奎勃龙;司坦唑醇;司腾勃龙(包括 1-睾酮;睾酮;群勃龙)〔999〕	4		30	13/	13	千克	L		1/29
2937.2900	25	7α-羟基-普拉睾酮〔999〕	4		30	13/	13	千克	L		1/29
2937.2900	26	7β-羟基-普拉睾酮〔999〕	4		30	13/	13	千克	L		1/29
2937.2900	27	7-羰基-普拉睾酮〔999〕	4		30	13/	13	千克	L		1/29
2937.2900	28	胆烷醇酮〔999〕	4		30	13/	13	千克	L		1/29
2937.2900	31	雄甾—5—烯—3β,17β—二醇(5—雄烯二醇(3β, 17β))〔999〕	4		30	13/	13	千克	L		1/29
2937.2900	32	雄甾—4—烯—3,17—二酮(4—雄烯二酮)〔999〕	4		30	13/	13	千克	L		1/29
2937.2900	34	雄酮〔999〕	4		30	13/	13	千克	L		1/29
2937.2900	35	1,4—雄烯二酮(雄甾—1,4—二烯—3,17 —二酮)〔999〕	4		30	13/	13	千克	L		/29
2937.2900	91	依西美坦〔999〕	4	0	30	3/	13	千克	Q		1/25

协定税率 %										特惠税率 %			Article Description
亚太5国	东/冰/格	巴基斯坦	韩国	瑞士	哥达	秘鲁	澳大利亚	新西/坡/智	港/澳/台	亚太2国	老/柬/缅	36/3/1	
	0/0/0	0	0	1.2	0	0	0	0//0	0/0/			0/0/	HCG and luteinizing hormone[Including growth hormone releasing peptide (GHRPs), Plummer Relin (growth hormone releasing peptide -2), CJC-1295 (CAS No. 863288-34-0), growth hormone releasing peptide -6, growth hormone releasing hormone and its analogues, growth hormone secretagogue]
	0/0/0	0	0	1.2	0	0	0	0//0	0/0/			0/0/	Adrenocoticotropin [including Ai Rui, A Bernard Relin, Bushrui Lin, Mo Ruilin corticorelin, sea Sha Ruilin, Iraq, Mo Ruilin, Mo Ruilin, Gore Bernard Relin, for Mo Ruilin Ge Ruilin (triptorelin, brain gut peptide) and its analogue]
	0/0/0	0	0	1.2	0	0	0	0//0	0/0/			0/0/	Lightc gonadorelin
	0/0/0	0	0	1.2	0	0	0	0//0	0/0/			0/0/	Trichoretin acetate and other anticancer medicines
	0/0/0	0	0	1.2	0	0	0	0//0	0/0/		//	0/0/	follstatin
	0/0/0	0	0	1.2	0	0	0	0//0	0/0/			0/0/	Other polypeptide hormones and derivatives and structural analogues (including protein hormones, glycoprotein hormones and their derivatives and structural analogues) (tax number of Separating anti－cancer pharmaceutical raw materials)
													-Steroidal hormones, their derivatives and structural analogues:
	0/0/0	0	0	0	0	0	0	0//0	0/0/			0/0/	--Cortisone, hydrocortisone, prednisone (dehydrocortisone) and prednisolone(dehydrohydrocortisone)
													--Halogenated derivatives of corticosteroidal hormones:
	0/0/0	0	0	0	0	0	0	0//0	0/0/			0/0/	---Dexamethasone
	0/0/0	0	0	0	0	0	0	0//0	0/0/			0/0/	---Other
													--Oestrogens and progestogens:
													---Animal source:
	0/0/0	0	0	0	0	0	0	0//0	0/0/			0/0/	----Pregnant mare conjugated estrogens
													----Other
	0/0/0	0	0	0	0	0	0	0//0	0/0/			0/0/	Formestane and Other Anticancer Drugs
	0/0/0	0	0	0	0	0	0	0//0	0/0/			0/0/	Other animal sources of estrogen and progesterone(tax number of Separating anti－cancer pharmaceutical raw materials)
													---Other
	0/0/0	0	0	0	0	0	0	0//0	0/0/			0/0/	Zearalanol, gestrinone, tibolone(including tetrahydrogestrinone)
	0/0/0	0	0	0	0	0	0	0//0	0/0/		//	0/0/	Other estrogen (steroid) hormones and progesterone
													--Other
	0/0/0	0	0	0	0	0	0	0//0	0/0/			0/0/	1- androstenediol; 1- androstene two ketone (including androst -4- allyl -3 β, 17 α - glycol; androst -5- allyl -3 β, 17 α - gly
	0/0/0	0	0	0	0	0	0	0//0	0/0/			0/0/	Including 5 α - androstane -3 α, 17 β - estradiol; 5 α - androstane -3 β, 17 α - glycol; bolas
	0/0/0	0	0	0	0	0	0	0//0	0/0/			0/0/	Boldenone; calusterone (including clostebol) Boldenone, calusterone (including 1,4-amdrostodiene-3;17-dione; clostebol)
	0/0/0	0	0	0	0	0	0	0//0	0/0/			0/0/	Danazol; dehydrochloromethy (including prasterone; desoxymethyltestosterone)
	0/0/0	0	0	0	0	0	0	0//0	0/0/			0/0/	Dihydrotestosterone; drostanolone (including epi-dihydrotestosterone; ethylestrenol; fluoxymesterone, formebolone)
	0/0/0	0	0	0	0	0	0	0//0	0/0/			0/0/	Furazabol(including 4-hydroxy-testosterone; 4-hydroxy-nandrolone; 3α-hydroxy-5α-androstan-17-ketone)
	0/0/0	0	0	0	0	0	0	0//0	0/0/			0/0/	Mestanolone; mesterolone; methandienone(including methyl drostanolone)
	0/0/0	0	0	0	0	0	0	0//0	0/0/			0/0/	Methyl-1-testosterone, methyltestosterone; Kanok testosterone (including ciene nandrolone; 19-norandrosterone)
	0/0/0	0	0	0	0	0	0	0//0	0/0/			0/0/	Methenolone; methandriol(including methyltrienolone)
	0/0/0	0	0	0	0	0	0	0//0	0/0/			0/0/	Mibolerone; nandrolone; norbolethone; norclostebol (including 19-norandrostenediol, norethandrolone)
	0/0/0	0	0	0	0	0	0	0//0	0/0/			0/0/	19-noretiocholanolone(including oxandrolone; oxymesterone)
	0/0/0	0	0	0	0	0	0	0//0	0/0/			0/0/	Oxymesterone, oxymetholone(including prostanozol)
	0/0/0	0	0	0	0	0	0	0//0	0/0/			0/0/	Quinbolone, stanozolol, stenbolone(including 1-testosterone, testosterone, trenbolone)
	0/0/0	0	0	0	0	0	0	0//0	0/0/			0/0/	7α-Hydroxy-DHEA
	0/0/0	0	0	0	0	0	0	0//0	0/0/			0/0/	7β-Hydroxy-DHEA
	0/0/0	0	0	0	0	0	0	0//0	0/0/			0/0/	7-Keto-prasterone
	0/0/0	0	0	0	0	0	0	0//0	0/0/			0/0/	Androstane
	0/0/0	0	0	0	0	0	0	0//0	0/0/			0/0/	Androst -5- allyl -3 β, 17 β - estradi
	0/0/0	0	0	0	0	0	0	0//0	0/0/			0/0/	Androst -4- allyl -3, 17- two ketone
	0/0/0	0	0	0	0	0	0	0//0	0/0/			0/0/	androsterone
	0/0/0	0	0	0	0	0	0	0//0	0/0/		//	0/0/	1,4－androstenedione (androsterone－1,4－diene－3,17－dione)
	0/0/0	0	0	0	0	0	0	0//0	0/0/			0/0/	Exemestane and Other Anticancer Drugs

税则号列		货品名称〔CIQ 扩展编码及品名一T2 表示见附表 2〕	最惠(%)	暂定税率	普通	增值/消费	出口退税	计量单位	监管条件	检验检疫	特殊证件对美关税
2937.2900	99	其他甾类激素及其衍生物和结构类似物(因拆分抗癌药品原料药产生的兜底税号)〔999〕	4		30	13/	13	千克	Q		1/29
2937.5000		-前列腺素、血栓烷和白细胞三烯及其衍生物和结构类似物〔999〕	4		30	13/	10	千克			1/29
2937.9000		-其他									
2937.9000	10	氨基酸衍生物〔301 需申报仅用于工业用途不用于食品添加剂无检疫要求的化学品〕	4		30	13/	10	千克	AQ	R	1/9
2937.9000	11	马昔瑞林	4		30	13/	10	千克	L		/9
2937.9000	90	其他激素及其衍生物和结构类似物〔999〕	4		30	13/	10	千克	Q		1/9
		第十二分章　天然或合成再制的苷(配糖物)、生物碱及其盐、醚、酯和其他衍生物									
29.38		**天然或合成再制的苷(配糖物)及其盐、醚、酯和其他衍生物:**									
2938.1000		-芸香苷及其衍生物〔999〕	6.5		20	13/	13	千克	Q		1/
		-其他:									
2938.9010		---齐多夫定、拉米夫定、司他夫定、地达诺新及它们的盐〔999〕	6.5		20	13/	13	千克			1/
2938.9090		---其他									
2938.9090	10	甘草酸粉〔999〕	6.5	3	20	13/	13	千克	y4x		1/28
2938.9090	20	甘草酸盐类〔301 需申报仅用于工业用途不用于食品添加剂无检疫要求的化学品,302 无检疫要求食品添加剂〕	6.5		20	13/	13	千克	4Axy	R	1/31.5
2938.9090	30	甘草次酸及其衍生物〔999〕	6.5		20	13/	13	千克	y4x		1/31.5
2938.9090	40	其他甘草酸	6.5	3	20	13/	13	千克			/28
2938.9090	90	其他天然或合成再制的苷及其盐等(包括醚、酯和其他衍生物)〔301 毒性物质和感染性物质,302 无检疫要求食品添加剂,303 其他化工产品〕	6.5		20	13/	13	千克			1/31.5
29.39		**天然或合成再制的生物碱及其盐、醚、酯和其他衍生物:**									
		-鸦片碱及其衍生物,以及它们的盐:									
2939.1100		--罂粟秆浓缩物、丁丙诺啡(INN)、可待因、双氢可待因(INN)、乙基吗啡、埃托啡(INN)、海洛因、氢可酮(INN)、氢吗啡酮(INN)、吗啡、尼可吗啡(INN)、羟考酮(INN)、羟吗啡酮(INN)、福尔可定(INN)、醋氢可酮(INN)和蒂巴因,以及它们的盐									
2939.1100	11	罂粟秆浓缩物〔999〕	4		50	13/	13	千克	I		1/24
2939.1100	12	可待因、双氢可待因、乙基吗啡(以及它们的盐)〔999〕	4		50	13/	13	千克	I		1/24
2939.1100	13	埃托啡、海洛因、氢可酮(以及它们的盐)〔999〕	4		50	13/	13	千克	I		1/24
2939.1100	14	氢吗啡酮、吗啡、尼可吗啡(以及它们的盐)〔999〕	4		50	13/	13	千克	I		1/24
2939.1100	15	羟考酮、羟吗啡酮、福尔可定(以及它们的盐)〔999〕	4		50	13/	13	千克	I		1/24
2939.1100	16	醋氢可酮、蒂巴因(以及它们的盐)〔999〕	4		50	13/	13	千克	I		1/24
2939.1100	20	丁丙诺啡及其盐〔999〕	4		50	13/	13	千克	I		1/24
2939.1900		--其他									
2939.1900	10	二氢埃托啡及其盐〔999〕	4		50	13/	13	千克	I		1/29
2939.1900	21	苄吗啡、可多克辛、地索吗啡、酯托啡(以及它们的盐)〔999〕	4		50	13/	13	千克	I		1/29
2939.1900	22	双氢吗啡、氢吗啡醇、甲地索啡、甲二氢吗啡(以及它们的盐)〔999〕	4		50	13/	13	千克	I		1/29
2939.1900	23	美托酮、吗啡-N-氧化物、麦罗啡、去甲吗啡(以及它们的盐)〔999〕	4		50	13/	13	千克	I		1/29
2939.1900	24	醋氢可待因、尼可待因、尼二氢可待因、去甲可待因(以及它们的盐)〔999〕	4		50	13/	13	千克	I		1/29
2939.1900	25	吗啡甲溴化物及其盐〔999〕	4		50	13/	13	千克	I		1/29
2939.1900	30	纳布啡及其盐〔999〕	4		50	13/	13	千克	I		1/29
2939.1900	40	奥列巴文(Oripavine;CAS 号:467049)〔999〕	4		50	13/	13	千克	I		1/29
2939.1900	90	其他鸦片碱及其衍生物及它们的盐〔999〕	4		50	13/	13	千克	Q		1/29
2939.2000		-金鸡纳生物碱及其衍生物以及它们的盐〔999〕	4		20	13/	13	千克	Q		1/
2939.3000		-咖啡因及其盐									
2939.3000	10	咖啡因〔301 无检疫要求食品添加剂,302 需申报仅用于工业用途不用于食品添加剂无检疫要求的化学品〕	4		20	13/	10	千克	AI	R	1/9
2939.3000	90	咖啡因的盐〔999,301 需申报仅用于工业用途不用于食品添加剂无检疫要求的化学品〕	4		20	13/	10	千克	AI	R	1/9
		-麻黄碱类及其盐:									
2939.4100		--麻黄碱及其盐									
2939.4100	10	麻黄碱(麻黄素,盐酸麻黄碱)〔999〕	4		20	13/	13	千克	23Q		1/
2939.4100	20	硫酸麻黄碱〔999〕	4		20	13/	13	千克	23Q		1/
2939.4100	30	消旋盐酸麻黄碱〔999〕	4		20	13/	13	千克	23Q		1/

协定税率 %										特惠税率 %			Article Description
亚太5国	东/冰/格	巴基斯坦	韩国	瑞士	哥达	秘鲁	澳大利亚	新西/坡/智	港/澳/台	亚太2国	老/柬/缅	36/3/1	
	0/0/0	0	0	0	0	0	0	0//0	0/0/			0/0/	Other somatotropin and their derivatives and structural analogs(tax number of Separating anti—cancer pharmaceutical raw materials)
	0/0/0	0	0	0	0	0	0	0//0	0/0/			0/0/	-Prostaglandins, thromboxanes and leukotrienes, their derivatives and structural analogues
													-Other
	0/0/0	0	0	0	0	0	0	0//0	0/0/			0/0/	Amino-acid dervatives
	0/0/0	0	0	0	0	0	0	0//0	0/0/		//	0/0/	Ma Xiruilin
	0/0/0	0	0	0	0	0	0	0//0	0/0/			0/0/	Other hormone its derivatives and structural analogues
													Ⅻ. GLYCOSIDES AND VEGETABLE ALKALOIDS, NATURAL OR REPRODUCED BY SYNTHESIS, AND THEIR SALTS, ETHERS, ESTERS AND OTHER DERIVATIVES
													Glycosides, natural or reproduced by synthesis, and their salts, ethers, esters and other derivatives:
	0/0/0	5	0	0	0	0	0	0//0	0/0/			0/0/	-Rutoside (rutin) and its derivatives
													-Other:
	0/0/0	5	0	0	0	0	0	0//0	0/0/			0/0/	---Zidovudine, lamivudine, Stavudine, didanosine and their salts
													---Other
	0/0/0	5	0	0	0	0	0	0//0	0/0/			0/0/	Glycyrrhizic acid powder
	0/0/0	5	0	0	0	0	0	0//0	0/0/			0/0/	Salts of glycyrrhizic acid
	0/0/0	5	0	0	0	0	0	0//0	0/0/			0/0/	Glycyrrhetic acid and its derivatives
	0/0/0	5	0	0	0	0	0	0//0	0/0/		//	0/0/	Other glycyrrhizic acid
	0/0/0	5	0	0	0	0	0	0//0	0/0/			0/0/	Other glycosides, natural or reproduced by synthesis, and their salts, ethers, esters and other derivatives
													Vegetable alkaloids, natural or reproduced by synthesis, and their salts, ethers, esters and other derivatives:
													-Alkaloids of opium and their derivatives; salts thereof:
													--Concentrates of poppy straw; buprenorphine(INN), codeine, dihydrocodeine(INN), ethylmorphine, etorphine(INN), heroin, hydrocodone(INN), hydromorphone(INN), morphine, nicomorphine(INN), oxycodone(INN), oxymorphone(INN), pholcodine (INN), thebacon(INN) and thebaine; salts thereof
	0/0/0	0	0	0	0	0	0	0//0	0/0/			0/0/0	Concentrates of poppy straw
	0/0/0	0	0	0	0	0	0	0//0	0/0/			0/0/0	Codeine, dihydrocodeine (INN), ethylmorphine (salts thereof)
	0/0/0	0	0	0	0	0	0	0//0	0/0/			0/0/0	Etorphine(INN), heroin, hydrocodone(INN)(salts thereof)
	0/0/0	0	0	0	0	0	0	0//0	0/0/			0/0/0	Hydromorphone (INN), morphine, nicomorphine (INN) (salts thereof)
	0/0/0	0	0	0	0	0	0	0//0	0/0/			0/0/0	Oxycodone(INN), oxymorphone(INN), pholcodine(INN)(salts thereof)
	0/0/0	0	0	0	0	0	0	0//0	0/0/			0/0/0	Thebacon(INN) and thebaine(salts thereof)
	0/0/0	0	0	0	0	0	0	0//0	0/0/			0/0/0	Buprenorphine and salts thereof
													--Other
	0/0/0	0	0	0	0	0	0	0//0	0/0/			0/0/0	Dihydroetorphine and its salts
	0/0/0	0	0	0	0	0	0	0//0	0/0/			0/0/0	Benzylmorphine, codoxime, desomorphine, acteorphinp (and their salt)
	0/0/0	0	0	0	0	0	0	0//0	0/0/			0/0/0	Dihydromorphine, hydromorphinol, methyldesorphine, methyldihydromorphine (and their salt)
	0/0/0	0	0	0	0	0	0	0//0	0/0/			0/0/0	Metopon, morphine-N-oxide, myrophine, normorphine (and their salt)
	0/0/0	0	0	0	0	0	0	0//0	0/0/			0/0/0	Acetyldihydrocodeine, nicocodine, nicomorphine, norcodeine (and their salt)
	0/0/0	0	0	0	0	0	0	0//0	0/0/			0/0/0	Morphine methobromide and its salt
	0/0/0	0	0	0	0	0	0	0//0	0/0/			0/0/0	Nalbuphine and its salt
	0/0/0	0	0	0	0	0	0	0//0	0/0/			0/0/0	Oripavine(CAS:467-04-9)
	0/0/0	0	0	0	0	0	0	0//0	0/0/			0/0/0	Other alkaloids of opium and their derivatives; salts thereof
	0/0/0	0	0	0	0	0	0	0//0	0/0/			0/0/0	-Alkaloids of cinchona and their derivatives; salts thereof
													-Caffeine and its salts
	0/0/0	0	0	0	0	0	0	0//0	0/0/			0/0/0	Caffeine
	0/0/0	0	0	0	0	0	0	0//0	0/0/			0/0/0	Salts of caffeine
													-Ephedrines and their salts:
													--Ephedrine and its salts
	0/0/0	0	0	0	0	0	0	0//0	0/0/			0/0/0	Ephedrine (ephedrine, ephedrine-hydrochloride)
	0/0/0	0	0	0	0	0	0	0//0	0/0/			0/0/0	Ephedrine sulfate
	0/0/0	0	0	0	0	0	0	0//0	0/0/			0/0/0	Racephedrine hydrochloride

税则号列		货品名称〔CIQ扩展编码及品名－T2表示见附表2〕	最惠(%)	暂定税率	普通	增值/消费	出口退税	计量单位	监管条件	检验检疫	特殊证件对美关税
2939.4100	40	草酸麻黄碱〔999〕	4		20	13/	13	千克	23Q		1/
2939.4100	90	麻黄碱盐〔999〕	4		20	13/	13	千克	Q		1/
2939.4200		--假麻黄碱及其盐									
2939.4200	10	伪麻黄碱(伪麻黄素、盐酸伪麻黄碱)〔999〕	4		20	13/	13	千克	23Q		1/9
2939.4200	20	硫酸伪麻黄碱〔999〕	4		20	13/	13	千克	23Q		1/9
2939.4200	90	假麻黄碱盐(D-2-甲胺基-1-苯基丙醇)〔999〕	4		20	13/	13	千克	Q		1/9
2939.4300		--d-去甲假麻黄碱(INN)及其盐〔999〕	4		20	13/	13	千克	I		1/
2939.4400		--去甲麻黄碱及其盐〔999〕	4		20	13/	13	千克	23		1/
2939.4900		--其他									
2939.4900	10	盐酸甲基麻黄碱〔999〕	4		20	13/	13	千克	Q23		1/
2939.4900	20	消旋盐酸甲基麻黄碱〔999〕	4		20	13/	13	千克	Q23		1/
2939.4900	90	其他麻黄碱及其盐〔999〕	4		20	13/	13	千克	Q		1/
		-茶碱和氨茶碱及其衍生物以及它们的盐：									
2939.5100		芬乙茶碱及其盐〔999〕	4		20	13/	13	千克	I		1/
2939.5900		--其他〔999〕	4		20	13/	13	千克	Q		1/
		-麦角生物碱及其衍生物以及它们的盐：									
2939.6100		--麦角新碱(INN)及其盐									
2939.6100	10	麦角新碱(INN)〔999〕	4		20	13/	13	千克	3Q2		1/
2939.6100	90	麦角新碱盐(INN)〔999〕	4		20	13/	13	千克	Q		1/
2939.6200		--麦角胺(INN)及其盐									
2939.6200	10	麦角胺〔999〕	4		20	13/	13	千克	3Q2		1/
2939.6200	90	麦角胺盐〔999〕	4		20	13/	13	千克	Q		1/
2939.6300		--麦角酸及其盐									
2939.6300	10	麦角酸〔999〕	4		20	13/	13	千克	3Q2		1/
2939.6300	90	麦角酸盐〔999〕	4		20	13/	13	千克	Q		1/
2939.6900		--其他									
2939.6900	10	麦角二乙胺及其盐〔999〕	4		20	13/	13	千克	I		1/
2939.6900	90	其他麦角生物碱及其衍生物(包括它们的盐)〔999〕	4		20	13/	13	千克	Q		1/
		-其他，植物来源的：									
		--可卡因、芽子碱、左甲苯丙胺、去氧麻黄碱(INN)、去氧麻黄碱外消旋体，它们的盐、酯及其他衍生物：									
2939.7110		---可卡因及其盐〔999〕	4		20	13/	13	千克	I		1/
2939.7190		---其他									
2939.7190	11	左甲苯丙胺(以及它们的盐、酯及其他衍生物)〔999〕	4		20	13/	13	千克	I		1/9
2939.7190	12	去氧麻黄碱(以及它们的盐、酯及其他衍生物)〔999〕	4		20	13/	13	千克	I		1/9
2939.7190	13	去氧麻黄碱外消旋体(以及它们的盐、酯及其他衍生物)〔999〕	4		20	13/	13	千克	I		1/9
2939.7190	14	氯代麻黄碱	4		20	13/	13	千克	23I		/9
2939.7190	20	芽子碱(以及它们的盐、酯及其他衍生物)〔999〕	4		20	13/	13	千克	I		1/9
		--其他：									
2939.7910		---烟碱及其盐									
2939.7910	10	烟碱〔999〕	4		20	13/	13	千克	ABQ	MN	1/
2939.7910	90	烟碱盐〔999〕	4		20	13/	13	千克	Q		1/
2939.7920		---番木鳖碱(士的年)及其盐									
2939.7920	10	番木鳖碱〔999〕	4		17	13/	13	千克	ABQ	MN	1/
2939.7920	90	番木鳖碱盐〔999〕	4		17	13/	13	千克	Q		1/
2939.7990		---其他									
2939.7990	11	卡西酮、麦司卡林(以及它们的盐)〔999〕	4		20	13/	13	千克	I		1/
2939.7990	12	赛洛新、赛洛西宾(以及它们的盐)〔999〕	4		20	13/	13	千克	I		1/
2939.7990	91	酒石酸长春瑞滨、硫酸长春新碱、盐酸托泊替康、盐酸伊立替康[T2]	4	0	20	3/	13	千克	ABQ	MRN	1/
2939.7990	99	其他植物碱及其衍生物(包括植物碱的盐、酯及其他衍生物)(因拆分抗癌药品原料药产生的兜底税号)〔301 毒性物质和感染性物质，302 其他危险化学品，303 需申报仅用于工业用途不用于食品添加剂无检疫要求的化学品〕	4		20	13/	13	千克	ABQ	MRN	1/
2939.8000		-其他〔999 毒性物质和感染性物质，301 需申报仅用于工业用途不用于食品添加剂无检疫要求的化学品〕	4		20	13/	13	千克	ABQ	MRN	1/29
		第十三分章　其他有机化合物									
29.40		**化学纯糖，但蔗糖、乳糖、麦芽糖、葡萄糖及果糖除外；糖醚、糖缩醛、糖酯及其盐，但不包括税目29.37、29.38及29.39的产品：**									
2940.0010		---木糖[T2]	6		30	13/	13	千克	AQ	R	1/
2940.0090		---其他[T2]	6		30	13/	13	千克	AQ	R	1/26
29.41		**抗菌素：**									
		-青霉素和具有青霉烷酸结构的青霉素衍生物及其盐：									
		---氨苄青霉素及其盐：									

协定税率 %										特惠税率 %			Article Description
亚太5国	东/冰/格	巴基斯坦	韩国	瑞士	哥达	秘鲁	澳大利亚	新西/坡/智	港/澳/台	亚太2国	老/柬/缅	36/3/1	
	0/0/0	0	0	0	0	0	0	0//0	0/0/			0/0/0	Ephedrine oxalate
	0/0/0	0	0	0	0	0	0	0//0	0/0/			0/0/0	Salts of ephedrine
													--Pseudoephedrine (INN) and its salts
	0/0/0	0	0	0	0	0	0	0//0	0/0/			0/0/0	Pseudoephedrine(pseudoephedrine, pseudoephedrine hydrochloride)
	0/0/0	0	0	0	0	0	0	0//0	0/0/			0/0/0	Pseudoephedrine sulfate
	0/0/0	0	0	0	0	0	0	0//0	0/0/			0/0/0	Salts of pseudoephedrine(D-2-methylamino-1-phenylethyl carbinol)
	0/0/0	0	0	0	0	0	0	0//0	0/0/			0/0/0	--d-Norpseudoephedrine and its salts
	0/0/0	0	0	0	0	0	0	0//0	0/0/			0/0/0	--Norephedrine and its salts
													--Other
	0/0/0	0	0	0	0	0	0	0//0	0/0/			0/0/0	Methylephedrine hydrochloride
	0/0/0	0	0	0	0	0	0	0//0	0/0/			0/0/0	DL-methylephedrine hydrochloride
	0/0/0	0	0	0	0	0	0	0//0	0/0/			0/0/0	Other ephedrines and their salts
													-Theophylline and aminophylline (theophylline-ethylenediamine) and their derivatives; salts thereof:
	0/0/0	0	0	0	0	0	0	0//0	0/0/			0/0/0	--Fenetylline(INN) and its salts
	0/0/0	0	0	0	0	0	0	0//0	0/0/			0/0/0	--Other
													-Alkaloids of rye ergot and their derivatives; salts thereof:
													--Ergometrine (INN) and its salts
	0/0/0	0	0	0	0	0	0	0//0	0/0/			0/0/0	Ergometrine (INN)
	0/0/0	0	0	0	0	0	0	0//0	0/0/			0/0/0	Salt of ergometrine (INN)
													--Ergotamine (INN) and its salts
	0/0/0	0	0	0	0	0	0	0//0	0/0/			0/0/0	Ergotamine (INN)
	0/0/0	0	0	0	0	0	0	0//0	0/0/			0/0/0	Salts of ergotamine (INN)
													--Lysergic acid and its salts
	0/0/0	0	0	0	0	0	0	0//0	0/0/			0/0/0	Lysergic acid
	0/0/0	0	0	0	0	0	0	0//0	0/0/			0/0/0	Salts of lysergic acid
													--Other
	0/0/0	0	0	1.2	0	0	0	0//0	0/0/			0/0/0	Lysergide and its salts
	0/0/0	0	0	1.2	0	0	0	0//0	0/0/			0/0/0	Other alkaloids of rye ergot and their derivatives(salts thereof)
													-Other, of vegetal origin:
													--Cocaine, ecgonine, levometamfe-tamine, metamfetamine (*INN*), metamfetamineracemate; salts, eaters and other derivatives thereof:
	0/0/0	0	0	0	0	0	0	0//0	0/0/			0/0/0	---Cacaine and its salts
													---Other
	0/0/0	0	0	0	0	0	0	0//0	0/0/			0/0/0	Levometamfet-amine (and their salts, esters and other derivatives)
	0/0/0	0	0	0	0	0	0	0//0	0/0/			0/0/0	Metamfetamine(INN)(and their salts, esters and other derivatives)
	0/0/0	0	0	0	0	0	0	0//0	0/0/			0/0/0	Metamfetamine racemate (and their salts, esters and other derivatives)
	0/0/0	0	0	0	0	0	0	0//0	0/0/		//	0/0/0	Ephedrine chloride
	0/0/0	0	0	0	0	0	0	0//0	0/0/			0/0/0	Ecgonine and its salts
													--Other:
													---Nicotine and its salts
	0/0/0	0	0	0	0	0	0	0//0	0/0/			0/0/0	Nicotine
	0/0/0	0	0	0	0	0	0	0//0	0/0/			0/0/0	Salts of nicotine
													---Strychnine and its salts
	0/0/0	0	0	0	0	0	0	0//0	0/0/			0/0/0	Strychnine
	0/0/0	0	0	0	0	0	0	0//0	0/0/			0/0/0	Salts of strychnine
													---Other
	0/0/0	0	0	1.2	0	0	0	0//0	0/0/			0/0/0	Cathinone, mescaline (and their salts)
	0/0/0	0	0	1.2	0	0	0	0//0	0/0/			0/0/0	Psilocine, psilocybin (and their salts)
	0/0/0	0	0	1.2	0	0	0	0//0	0/0/			0/0/0	Vinorelbine tartrate, vincristine sulfate, topotecan hydrochloride, irinotecan hydrochloride, and other anticancer drug substances
	0/0/0	0	0	1.2	0	0	0	0//0	0/0/			0/0/0	Other vegetable alkaliods and their derivatives (including salts, esters and other derivatives of vegetable alkaliods)(tax number of Separating anti—cancer pharmaceutical raw materials)
	0/0/0	0	0	1.2	0	0	0	0//0	0/0/			0/0/0	-Other
													XIII. OTHER ORGANIC COMPOUNDS
													Sugars, chemically pure, other than sucrose, lactose, maltose, glucose and fructose, sugar ethers, sugar acetals and sugar esters, and their salts, other than products of heading No. 29.37, 29.38 or 29.39:
	0/0/	5	2.4	0	0	0	0	0//0	0/0/			0/0/0	---Xylose
	0/0/	5	2.4	0	0	0	0	0//0	0/0/			0/0/0	---Other
													Antibiotics:
													-Penicillins and their derivatives with a penicillanic acid structure; salts thereof:
													---Ampicillin and its salts:

税则号列	货品名称〔CIQ 扩展编码及品名—T2 表示见附表 2〕	最惠(%)	暂定税率	普通	增值/消费	出口退税	计量单位	监管条件	检验检疫	特殊证件对美关税
2941.1011	----氨苄青霉素〔999〕	6		20	13/	13	千克	Q		1/
2941.1012	----氨苄青霉素三水酸〔999〕	6		20	13/	13	千克	Q		1/
2941.1019	----其他〔999〕	6		20	13/	13	千克	Q		1/11
	---其他:									
2941.1091	----羟氨苄青霉素〔999〕	4		20	13/	13	千克	Q		1/
2941.1092	----羟氨苄青霉素三水酸〔999〕	4		20	13/	13	千克	Q		1/
2941.1093	----6 氨基青霉烷酸(6APA)〔999〕	4		20	13/	13	千克			1/29
2941.1094	----青霉素 V〔999〕	4		20	13/	13	千克	Q		1/
2941.1095	----磺苄青霉素〔999〕	4		20	13/	13	千克	Q		1/
2941.1096	----邻氯青霉素〔999〕	4		20	13/	13	千克	Q		1/
2941.1099	----其他〔999〕	4		20	13/	13	千克	Q		1/
2941.2000	-链霉素及其衍生物以及它们的盐									
2941.2000　11	硫酸链霉素〔999〕	4		20	13/	13	千克	QS		1/9
2941.2000　90	其他链霉素及其衍生物、盐〔999〕	4		20	13/	13	千克	Q		1/9
	-四环素及其衍生物以及它们的盐:									
	---四环素及其盐:									
2941.3011	----四环素〔999〕	4		20	13/	13	千克	Q		1/
2941.3012	----四环素盐〔999〕	4		20	13/	13	千克	Q		1/
2941.3020	---四环素衍生物及其盐〔999〕	4		20	13/	13	千克	Q		1/
2941.4000	-氯霉素及其衍生物以及它们的盐〔999〕	4		20	13/	13	千克	Q		1/
2941.5000	-红霉素及其衍生物以及它们的盐〔999〕	4		20	13/	13	千克	Q		1/
	-其他:									
2941.9010	---庆大霉素及其衍生物以及它们的盐〔999〕	4		20	13/	13	千克	Q		1/29
2941.9020	---卡那霉素及其衍生物以及它们的盐〔999〕	4		20	13/	13	千克	Q		1/
2941.9030	---利福平及其衍生物以及它们的盐〔999〕	4		20	13/	13	千克	Q		1/
2941.9040	---林可霉素及其衍生物以及它们的盐〔999〕	4		20	13/	13	千克	Q		1/
	---头孢菌素及其衍生物以及它们的盐:									
2941.9052	----头孢氨苄及其盐〔999〕	6		20	13/	13	千克	Q		1/
2941.9053	----头孢唑啉及其盐〔999〕	6		20	13/	13	千克	Q		1/
2941.9054	----头孢拉啶及其盐〔999〕	6		20	13/	13	千克	Q		1/
2941.9055	----头孢三嗪(头孢曲松)及其盐〔999〕	6		20	13/	13	千克	Q		1/
2941.9056	----头孢哌酮及其盐〔999〕	6		20	13/	13	千克	Q		1/
2941.9057	----头孢噻肟及其盐〔999〕	6		20	13/	13	千克	Q		1/
2941.9058	----头孢克罗及其盐〔999〕	6		20	13/	13	千克	Q		1/11
2941.9059	----其他									
2941.9059　10	放线菌酮〔999〕	6		20	13/	13	千克	QS		1/31
2941.9059　90	其他头孢菌素及其衍生物(包括它们的盐)〔999〕	6		20	13/	13	千克	Q		1/31
2941.9060	---麦迪霉素及其衍生物以及它们的盐〔999〕	6		20	13/	13	千克	Q		1/11
2941.9070	---乙酰螺旋霉素及其衍生物以及它们的盐〔999〕	4		20	13/	13	千克	Q		1/
2941.9090	---其他									
2941.9090　11	中生菌素〔101 无检疫要求食品添加剂〕	6		20	13/	13	千克	QS		1/11
2941.9090　12	春雷霉素〔101 无检疫要求食品添加剂〕	6		20	13/	13	千克	QS		1/11
2941.9090　13	吗替麦考酚酯〔999〕	6	0	20	13/	13	千克	Q		1/5
2941.9090　14	盐酸阿柔比星	6	0	20	13/	13	千克	Q		/5
2941.9090　91	吡柔比星、丝裂霉素、盐酸表柔比星、盐酸多柔比星、盐酸平阳霉素、盐酸柔红霉素、盐酸伊达比星〔999〕	6	0	20	3/	13	千克	Q		1/5
2941.9090　99	其他抗菌素(因拆分抗癌药品原料药产生的兜底税号)〔999〕	6		20	13/	13	千克	Q		1/11
29.42	**其他有机化合物:**									
2942.0000	其他有机化合物〔T2〕	6.5		30	13/	10	千克			1/11.5

协定税率 %										特惠税率 %			Article Description
亚太5国	东/冰/格	巴基斯坦	韩国	瑞士	哥达	秘鲁	澳大利亚	新西/坡/智	港/澳/台	亚太2国	老/柬/缅	36/3/1	
3	0/0/0	0	0	0	0	0	0	0//0	0/0/			0/0/0	----Ampicillin
3	0/0/0	0	0	0	0	0	0	0//0	0/0/			0/0/0	----Ampicillin trihydrate
3	0/0/0	0	0	0	0	0	0	0//0	0/0/			0/0/0	---Other
													---Other:
	0/0/0	0	0	0	0	0	0	0//0	0/0/			0/0/0	----Amoxycillin
3.2	0/0/0	0	0	0	0	0	0	0//0	0/0/			0/0/0	----Amoxycillin trihydrate
	0/0/0	0	0	0	0	0	0	0//0	0/0/			0/0/0	----6-Aminopenicillanic acid
	0/0/0	0	0	0	0	0	0	0//0	0/0/			0/0/0	----Penicillin V
	0/0/0	0	0	0	0	0	0	0//0	0/0/			0/0/0	----Sulfobenzylpenicillin
	0/0/0	0	0	0	0	0	0	0//0	0/0/			0/0/0	----Cloxacillin
	0/0/0	0	0	0	0	0	0	0//0	0/0/			0/0/0	----Other
													-Streptomycins and their derivatives; salts thereof
	0/0/0	0	0	0	0	0	0	0//0	0/0/			0/0/0	Streptomycin sulfate
	0/0/0	0	0	0	0	0	0	0//0	0/0/			0/0/0	Other streptomycin and its derivatives, salt
													-Tetracyclines and their derivatives; salts thereof:
													---Tetracyclines and their salts:
	0/0/0	0	0	0	0	0	0	0//0	0/0/			0/0/0	----Tetracyclines
	0/0/0	0	0	0	0	0	0	0//0	0/0/			0/0/0	----Salts of tetracyclines
	0/0/0	0	0	0	0	0	0	0//0	0/0/			0/0/0	---Tetracyclines derivatives and their salts:
	0/0/0	0	0	0	0	0	0	0//0	0/0/			0/0/0	-Chloramphenicol and its derivatives; salts thereof
	0/0/0	0	0	0	0	0	0	0//0	0/0/			0/0/0	-Erythromycin and its derivatives; salts thereof
													-Other:
	0/0/0	0	0	0	0	0	0	0//0	0/0/			0/0/0	---Gentamycin and its derivatives; salts thereof
	0/0/0	0	0	0	0	0	0	0//0	0/0/			0/0/0	---Kanamycin and its derivatives; salts thereof
	0/0/0	0	0	0	0	0	0	0//0	0/0/			0/0/0	---Rifampicin (RFP); salts thereof
	0/0/0	0	0	0	0	0	0	0//0	0/0/			0/0/0	---Lincomycin and its derivatives; salts thereof
													---Cephamycin and its derivatives; salts thereof:
3.9	0/0/0	0	0	0	0	0	0	0//0	0/0/			0/0/0	----Cefalexin and its salts
3	0/0/0	0	0	0	0	0	0	0//0	0/0/			0/0/0	----Cefazolin and its salts
3	0/0/0	0	0	0	0	0	0	0//0	0/0/			0/0/0	----Cefradine and its salts
3	0/0/0	0	0	3.1	0	0	0	0//0	0/0/			0/0/0	----Ceftriaxone and its salts
3	0/0/0	0	0	0	0	0	0	0//0	0/0/			0/0/0	----Cefoperazone and its salts
3	0/0/0	0	0	0	0	0	0	0//0	0/0/			0/0/0	----Cefotaxime and its salts
5	0/0/0	0	0	0	0	0	0	0//0	0/0/			0/0/0	----Cefaclor and its salts
													----Other
5	0/0/0	0	2.4	0	0	0	0	0//0	0/0/			0/0/0	Actidione
5	0/0/0	0	2.4	0	0	0	0	0//0	0/0/			0/0/0	Other cephamycin and its derivaatives;salts thereof
3	0/0/0	0	0	0	0	0	0	0//0	0/0/			0/0/0	---Midecamycin and its derivatives; salts thereof
	0/0/0	0	0	0	0	0	0	0//0	0/0/			0/0/0	---Acetyl-spiramycin and its derivatives; salts thereof
													---Other
3.9	0/0/0	0	0	0	0	0	0	0//0	0/0/			0/0/0	Zhongshengmycin
3.9	0/0/0	0	0	0	0	0	0	0//0	0/0/			0/0/0	Kasugamycin
3.9	0/0/0	0	0	0	0	0	0	0//0	0/0/			0/0/0	Mycophenolate mofetil
3.9	0/0/0	0	0	0	0	0	0	0//0	0/0/		//	0/0/0	Arubicin Hydrochloride
3.9	0/0/0	0	0	0	0	0	0	0//0	0/0/			0/0/0	Pirarubicin, Actinomycin D, Mitomycin, Epirubicin Hydrochloride, Doxorubicin Hydrochloride, Pingyangmycin Hydrochloride, Daunorubicin Hydrochloride, Idarubicin Hydrochloride, and Other Anticancer Drug Raw Materials medicine
3.9	0/0/0	0	0	0	0	0	0	0//0	0/0/			0/0/0	Other antibiotics(tax number of Separating anti—cancer pharmaceutical raw materials)
													Other organic compounds:
	0/0/0	5	0	0	0	0	0	0//0	0/0/			0/0/0	Other organic compounds

第三十章
药　品

注释：

一、本章不包括：

(一)食品及饮料（例如，营养品、糖尿病食品、强化食品、保健食品、滋补饮料及矿泉水），但不包括供静脉摄入用的滋养品(第四类)；

(二)用于帮助吸烟者戒烟的制剂，例如，片剂、咀嚼胶或透皮贴片(税目21.06或38.24)；

(三)经特殊煅烧或精细研磨的牙科用熟石膏(税目25.20)；

(四)适合医药用的精油水馏液及水溶液(税目33.01)；

(五)税目33.03至33.07的制品，不论是否具有治疗及预防疾病的作用；

(六)加有药料的肥皂及税目34.01的其他产品；

(七)以熟石膏为基本成分的牙科用制品(税目34.07)；或

(八)不作治疗及预防疾病用的血清蛋白(税目35.02)。

二、税目30.02所称的"免疫制品"是指直接参与免疫过程调节的多肽及蛋白质(税目29.37的货品除外)，例如，单克隆抗体(MAB)、抗体片段、抗体偶联物及抗体片段偶联物、白介素、干扰素(IFN)、趋化因子及特定的肿瘤坏死因子(TNF)、生长因子(GF)、促红细胞生成素及集落刺激因子(CSF)。

三、税目30.03及30.04以及本章注释四(四)所述的非混合产品及混合产品，按下列规定处理：

(一)非混合产品：

1. 溶于水的非混合产品；

2. 第二十八章及第二十九章的所有货品；以及

3. 税目13.02的单一植物浸膏，只经标定或溶于溶剂的。

(二)混合产品：

1. 胶体溶液及悬浮液(胶态硫磺除外)；

2. 从植物性混合物加工所得的植物浸膏；

3. 蒸发天然矿质水所得的盐及浓缩物。

四、税目30.06仅适用于下列物品(这些物品只能归入税目30.06而不得归入本目录其他税目)：

(一)无菌外科肠线、类似的无菌缝合材料(包括外科或牙科用无菌可吸收缝线)及外伤创口闭合用的无菌粘合胶布；

(二)无菌昆布及无菌昆布塞条；

(三)外科或牙科用无菌吸收性止血材料；外科或牙科用无菌抗粘连阻隔材料，不论是否可吸收；

(四)用于病人的X光检查造影剂及其他诊断试剂，这些药剂是由单一产品配定剂量或由两种以上成分混合而成的；

(五)血型试剂；

(六)牙科粘固剂及其他牙科填料；骨骼粘固剂；

(七)急救药箱、药包；

(八)以激素、税目29.37的其他产品或杀精子剂为基本成分的化学避孕药物；

(九)专用于人类或作兽药用的凝胶制品，作为外科手术或体检时躯体部位的润滑剂，或者作为躯体和医疗器械之间的耦合剂；

(十)废药物，即那些因超过有效保存期等原因而不适于作原用途的药品；

(十一)可确定用于造口术的用具，即裁切成型的结肠造口术，回肠造口术、尿道造口术用袋及其具有黏性的片或底盘。

子目注释：

一、子目3002.13及3002.14所述的非混合产品、纯物质及混合产品，按下列规定处理：

(一)非混合产品或纯物质，不论是否含有杂质；

(二)混合产品：

1.上述(一)款所述的产品溶于水或其他溶剂的；

2.为保存或运输需要，上述(一)款及(二)1.项所述的产品加入稳定剂的；

3.上述(一)款、(二)1.项及(二)2.项所述的产品添加其他添加剂的。

二、子目3003.60和3004.60包括的药品含有与其他药用活性成分配伍的口服用青蒿素(INN)，或者含有下列任何一种活性成分，不论是否与其他药用活性成分配伍：阿莫地喹(INN)、蒿醚林酸及其盐(INN)、双氢青蒿素(INN)、蒿乙醚(INN)、蒿甲醚(INN)、青蒿琥酯(INN)、氯喹(INN)、二氢青蒿素(INN)、苯芴醇(INN)、甲氟喹(INN)、哌喹(INN)、乙胺嘧啶(INN)或磺胺多辛(INN)。

Chapter 30
Pharmaceutical products

Notes:

1. This Chapter does not cover:
   (a) Foods or beverages (such as dietetic, diabetic or fortified foods, food supplements, tonic beverages and mineral waters), other than nutritional preparations for intraverwas administration (Section Ⅳ);
   (b) Preparations, such as tablets, chewing gum or patches (transdermal systems), intended to assist smokers to stop smoking (heading 21.06 or 38.24);
   (c) Plasters specially calcined or finely ground for use in dentistry (heading No. 25.20);
   (d) Aqueous distillates or aqueous solutions of essential oils, suitable for medicinal uses (heading No. 33.01);
   (e) Preparations of headings No. 33.03 to 33.07, even if they have therapeutic or prophylactic properties;
   (f) Soap or other products of heading No. 34.01 containing added medicaments;
   (g) Preparations with a basis of plaster for use in dentistry (heading No. 34.07); or
   (h) Blood albumin not prepared for therapeutic or prophylactic uses (heading No. 35.02).
2. For the purposes of heading 30.02, the expression "immunological products" applies to peptides and proteins (other than goods of heading 29.37) which are directly involved in the regulation of immunological processes, such as monoclonal antibodies (MAB), antibody fragments, antibody conjugates and antibody fragment conjugates, interleukins, interferons (IFN), chemodines and certain tumor necrosis factors (TNF), growth factors (GF), hematopoietins and colony stimulating factors (CSF)
3. For the purposes of headings No. 30.03 and 30.04 and of Note 4 (d) to this Chapter, the following are to be treated:
   (a) As unmixed products:
      (1) Unmixed products dissolved in water;
      (2) All goods of Chapter 28 or 29;
      (3) Simple vegetable extracts of heading No. 13.02, merely standardised or dissolved in any solvent;
   (b) As products which have been mixed:
      (1) Colloidal solutions and suspensions (other than colloidal sulphur);
      (2) Vegetable extracts obtained by the treatment of mixtures of vegetable materials;
      (3) Salts and concentrates obtained by evaporating natural mineral waters.
4. Heading No. 30.06 applies only to the following, which are to be classified in that heading and in no other heading of the Nomenclature:
   (a) Sterile surgical catgut, similar sterile suture materials (including sterile absorbable surgical or denfal yams) and sterile tissue adhesives for surgical wound closure;
   (b) Sterile laminaria and sterile laminaria tents;
   (c) Sterile absorbable surgical or dental haemostatics; sterile surgical or dental adhesion barriers, whether or not absorbable
   (d) Opacifying preparations for X-ray examinations and diagnostic reagents designed to be administered to the patient, being unmixed products put up in measured doses or products consisting of two or more ingredients which have been mixed together for such uses;
   (e) Blood-grouping reagents;
   (f) Dental cements and other dental fillings; bone reconstruction cements;
   (g) First-aid boxes and kits;
   (h) Chemical contraceptive preparations based on hormones, on other products of heading No. 29.37 or on spermicides;
   (i) Gel preparations designed to be used in human or veterinary medicine as a lubricant for parts of the body for surgical operations or physical examinations or as a coupling agent between the body and medical instruments;
   (j) Waste pharmaceuticals, that is, pharmaceutical products which are unfit for their original intended purpose due to, for example, expiry of shelf life;
   (k) Appliances identifiable for ostomy use, that is, cdostomy, ileostomy and utosto my pouches cut to shape and their adhesive wafers or faceplates.

Subheading Notes:

a. Un-mixed products, pure substances heading and mixed products of No. 3002.13 and heading No.3002.14, according to the following regulations:
   (a) un-mixed products and Pure substances, Whether or not containing impurities;
   (b) Mixed products;
      i. The products mentioned in the preceding
      (a) paragraph are dissolved in water or other solvents;
      (ii) The products referred to in paragraph (a) and (b) above are added to the stabilizer for preservation or transport;
      iii. The products mentioned in i of (a) or ii of (b) add other additives.

a. Subheading No. 3003.60 and Subheading No.3004.60 include medicines containing oral and other medicinal active ingredients combined with artemisinins (INN), or contain any of the following active ingredients, whether or not with other medicinal active ingredient compatibility: amodiaquine (INN), Artelinic acid and its salts (INN), dihydroartemisinine (INN), artemotil (INN), artemether (INN), artesunate (INN), chloroquine (INN), dihydroartemisinin (INN), lumefantrine (INN), mefloquine (INN), piperaquine (INN), pyrimethamine (INN) or sulfadoxine (INN)

税则号列		货品名称〔CIQ扩展编码及品名—T2表示见附表2〕	最惠(%)	暂定税率	普通	增值/消费	出口退税	计量单位	监管条件	检验检疫	特殊证件对美关税
30.01		**已干燥的器官疗法用腺体及其他器官,不论是否制成粉末;器官疗法用腺体、其他器官及其分泌物的提取物;肝素及其盐;其他供治疗或预防疾病用的其他税目未列名的人体或动物制品:**									
3001.2000		-腺体、其他器官及其分泌物的提取物									
3001.2000	10	其他濒危野生动物腺体、器官(包括分泌物)〔101动物培养器官,102动物培养细胞,103动物微生物培养培养基,104其他动物器官、细胞、培养基,105未列出的其他动物产品,106其他化工产品〕	3		30	13/	0	千克	AQFEB	PQ	1/
3001.2000	21	含有人类遗传资源的人类腺体、器官及其分泌物提取物〔101人体器官,102人体组织,103人体细胞,104人源细胞系,105人体胚胎、人胚活细胞,106人体排泄物、分泌物,107殡葬目的的人类尸体、骸骨,108其他人体组织器官〕	3		30	13/	13	千克	ABV	VW	1/
3001.2000	29	其他人类的腺体、器官及其分泌物提取物	3		30	13/	13	千克	ABV	VW	1/
3001.2000	90	其他腺体、器官及其分泌物提取物[T2]	3		30	13/	13	千克	AB	PQ	1/
		-其他:									
3001.9010		---肝素及其盐〔999〕	3		30	13/	13	千克	Q		1/
3001.9090		---其他									
3001.9090	10	蛇毒制品(供治疗或预防疾病用)〔999〕	3		30	13/	13	千克	AQFEB	PVQW	1/
3001.9090	20	含有人类遗传资源的人体制品〔101供治疗或预防疾病用、药用血余炭,102供治疗或预防疾病用、药用紫河车,103供治疗或预防疾病用、医用抗体,104供治疗或预防疾病用、医用抗原,105供治疗或预防疾病用、其他医用生物制品〕	3		30	13/	13	千克	ABQV	VW	1/
3001.9090	91	其他濒危动物制品(供治疗或预防疾病用)〔101动物性血液制品,102其他化工产品〕	3		30	13/	0	千克	ABFEQ	PQ	1/
3001.9090	99	其他未列名的人体或动物制品(供治疗或预防疾病用)〔101动物性血液制品,102药用血余炭,103医用抗体,104医用抗原,105诊疗目的的组织标本、手术样本,106其他化工产品,107其他医用生物制品〕	3		30	13/	9,13	千克	ABQ	PVQW	1/
30.02		**人血;治病、防病或诊断用的动物血制品;抗血清、其他血份及免疫制品,不论是否修饰或通过生物工艺加工制得;疫苗、毒素、培养微生物(不包括酵母)及类似产品:**									
		-抗血清、其他血份及免疫制品,不论是否修饰或通过生物工艺加工制得:									
3002.1100		--疟疾诊断试剂盒〔101医用诊断试剂,999其他化工产品〕	3	0	20	13/	13	千克	AB	PVQW	1/
3002.1200		--抗血清及其他血份									
3002.1200	11	唾液酸促红素、促红素衍生肽、氨甲酰促红素、达促红素、促红素(EPO)类等促红素〔101医用细胞因子,999其他化工产品〕	3	0	20	13/	13	千克	ABL	PVQW	1/
3002.1200	12	胰岛素样生长因子1(IGF-1)及其类似物〔101医用细胞因子,999其他化工产品〕	3	0	20	13/	13	千克	ABL	PVQW	1/
3002.1200	13	机械生长因子类〔101医用细胞因子,999其他化工产品〕	3	0	20	13/	13	千克	ABL	PVQW	1/
3002.1200	14	成纤维细胞生长因子类(FGFs)〔101医用细胞因子,999其他化工产品〕	3	0	20	13/	13	千克	ABL	PVQW	1/
3002.1200	15	肝细胞生长因子(HGF)〔101医用细胞因子,999其他化工产品〕	3	0	20	13/	13	千克	ABL	PVQW	1/
3002.1200	16	血小板衍生生长因子(PDGF)〔101医用细胞因子,999其他化工产品〕	3	0	20	13/	13	千克	ABL	PVQW	1/
3002.1200	17	血管内皮生长因子(VEGF)〔101医用细胞因子,999其他化工产品〕	3	0	20	13/	13	千克	ABL	PVQW	1/
3002.1200	18	转化生长因子-β(TGF-β)抑制剂类〔101医用细胞因子,999其他化工产品〕	3	0	20	13/	13	千克	ABL	PVQW	1/
3002.1200	19	培尼沙肽、罗特西普〔101其他医用蛋白,999其他化工产品〕	3	0	20	13/	13	千克	ABL	PVQW	1/
3002.1200	21	缺氧诱导因子(HIF)激活剂类、缺氧诱导因子(HIF)稳定剂类〔101其他医用蛋白,999其他化工产品〕	3	0	20	13/	13	千克	ABL	PVQW	1/
3002.1200	22	EPO-Fc(IgG4)融合蛋白、EPO-Fc融合蛋白〔101其他医用蛋白,999其他化工产品〕	3	0	20	13/	13	千克	ABL	PVQW	1/
3002.1200	91	抗(防)癌药品制剂(不含癌症辅助治疗药品)〔301其他化工产品,401其他人血制品〕	3	0	20	3/	13	千克	AB	PVQW	1/

协定税率 %										特惠税率 %			
亚太5国	东/冰/格	巴基斯坦	韩国	瑞士	哥达	秘鲁	澳大利亚	新西/坡/智	港/澳/台	亚太2国	老/柬/缅	36/3/1	Article Description
													Glands and other organs for organo-therapeutic uses, dried, whether or not powdered; extracts of glands or other organs or of their secretions for organo-therapeutic uses; heparin and its salts; other human or animal substances prepared for therapeutic or prophylactic uses, not elsewhere specified or included:
													-Extracts of glands or other organs or of their secretions
	0/0/0	0	0	0	0	0	0	0//0	0/0/			0/0/	Extracts of glands or other organs or of their secretions of endangered wild animals
	0/0/0	0	0	0	0	0	0	0//0	0/0/		//	0/0/	Human glands, organs and secretions containing human genetic resources
	0/0/0	0	0	0	0	0	0	0//0	0/0/		//	0/0/	Extracts from other human glands, organs and secretions
	0/0/0	0	0	0	0	0	0	0//0	0/0/			0/0/	Other extracts of glands of other organs or of their secretions
													-Other:
	0/0/0	0	0	0	0	0	0	0//0	0/0/			0/0/	---Heparin and its salts
													---Other
	0/0/0	0	0	0	0	0	0	0//0	0/0/			0/0/	Venom substances prepared (for therapeutic or prophylactic uses)
	0/0/0	0	0	0	0	0	0	0//0	0/0/		//	0/0/	Human products containing human genetic resources
	0/0/0	0	0	0	0	0	0	0//0	0/0/			0/0/	Other substances of endangered animals for therapeutic or prophylactic uses
	0/0/0	0	0	0	0	0	0	0//0	0/0/			0/0/	Other human or animal substances prepared (for therapeutic or prophylactic uses) not elsewhere specified or included
													Human blood; animal blood prepared for therapeutic, prophylactic or diagnostic uses; antisera, other blood fractions and immunological products, whether or not modified or obtained by means of biotechnological processes; vaccines, toxins, cultures of micro-organisms (other than yeasts) and similar products:
													-Antisera and other blood fractions and immunological products, whether or not modified or obtained by means of biotechnological processes::
	0/0/0	0	0	1.6	0	0	0	0//0	0/0/			0/0/0	--Malaria diagnostic tesk kits
													--Antisera and other blood fractions
	0/0/0	0	0	1.6	0	0	0	0//0	0/0/			0/0/0	Erythropoietin(EPO)
	0/0/0	0	0	1.6	0	0	0	0//0	0/0/			0/0/0	Type-1 insulin like growth factor
	0/0/0	0	0	1.6	0	0	0	0//0	0/0/			0/0/0	Mechano Growth Factor
	0/0/0	0	0	1.6	0	0	0	0//0	0/0/			0/0/0	Fibroblast growth factor
	0/0/0	0	0	1.6	0	0	0	0//0	0/0/			0/0/0	Hepatocyte growth factor
	0/0/0	0	0	1.6	0	0	0	0//0	0/0/			0/0/0	Platelet derived growth factor
	0/0/0	0	0	1.6	0	0	0	0//0	0/0/			0/0/0	Vascular endothelial growth factor
	0/0/0	0	0	1.6	0	0	0	0//0	0/0/			0/0/0	Transforming growth factor -β (TGF-β) inhibitors
	0/0/0	0	0	1.6	0	0	0	0//0	0/0/			0/0/0	Peinisha peptide, Roth Heap
	0/0/0	0	0	1.6	0	0	0	0//0	0/0/			0/0/0	Hypoxia inducible factor (HIF) activator, hypoxia inducible factor (HIF) stabilizer
	0/0/0	0	0	1.6	0	0	0	0//0	0/0/			0/0/0	EPO-Fc (IgG4) fusion protein, EPO-Fc fusion protein
	0/0/0	0	0	1.6	0	0	0	0//0	0/0/			0/0/0	Anti—cancer drug preparations (excluding cancer adjuncts)

税则号列	货品名称〔CIQ 扩展编码及品名－T2 表示见附表 2〕	最惠(%)	暂定税率	普通	增值/消费	出口退税	计量单位	监管条件	检验检疫	特殊证件对美关税
3002.1200 92	人凝血因子Ⅷ、注射用重组人凝血因子Ⅷ、注射用重组人凝血因子Ⅸ、注射用重组人凝血因子Ⅶa、人凝血酶原复合物〔301 其他化工产品,401 其他人血制品〕	3	0	20	3/	13	千克	AB	PVQW	/
3002.1200 23	含有人类遗传资源的抗血清及其他血份	3	0	20	13/	13	千克	ABV	PVQW	1/
3002.1200 99	其他抗血清及其他血份(因拆分抗癌药产生的兜底税号)〔301 其他化工产品,401 其他人血制品〕	3	0	20	13/	13	千克	AB	PVQW	1/
3002.1300	--非混合的免疫制品,未配定剂量或制成零售包装〔101 其他医用生物制品,999 其他化工产品〕	3	0	20	13/	13	千克	AB	PVQW	1/
3002.1400	--混合的免疫制品,未配定剂量或制成零售包装〔101 其他医用生物制品,999 其他化工产品〕	3	0	20	13/	13	千克	AB	PVQW	1/
3002.1500	--免疫制品,已配定剂量或制成零售包装									
3002.1500 10	抗(防)癌药品制剂(不含癌症辅助治疗药品)〔301 其他化工产品,401 其他医用生物制品〕	3	0	20	3/	13	千克	AB	PVQW	1/
3002.1500 20	重组人干扰素β1a 注射液(注射剂)〔301 其他化工产品,401 其他医用生物制品〕	3	0	20	3/	13	千克	AB	PVQW	/
3002.1500 90	其他免疫制品,已配定剂量或制成零售包装(因拆分抗癌药产生的兜底税号)〔301 其他化工产品,401 其他医用生物制品〕	3	0	20	13/	13	千克	AB	PVQW	1/
3002.1900	--其他									
3002.1900 10	抗(防)癌药品制剂(不含癌症辅助治疗药品)〔301 其他化工产品,401 其他医用生物制品〕	3	0	20	3/	13	千克	AB	PVQW	1/
3002.1900 90	其他抗血清、其他血份及免疫制品,不论是否修饰或通过生物工艺加工制得(因拆分抗癌药产生的兜底税号)[T2]	3	0	20	13/	13	千克	AB	PVQW	1/
3002.2000	-人用疫苗〔999〕	3	0	20	13/	13	千克	QAB	VW	1/
3002.3000	-兽用疫苗〔101 动检灭活疫苗,102 动检强毒疫苗,103 动检弱毒疫苗,104 动检基因疫苗,105 动检菌苗,106 其他动物疫苗〕	3		20	13/	13	千克	R		1/
	-其他:									
3002.9010	---石房蛤毒素〔999〕	3		20	13/	13	千克	23Q		1/
3002.9020	---蓖麻毒素〔999〕	3		20	13/	13	千克	23Q		1/
3002.9030	---细菌及病毒									
3002.9030 10	两用物项管制细菌及病毒[T2]	3		20	13/	13	千克	3AB	PVQW	1/
3002.9030 20	苏云金杆菌〔999〕	3		20	13/	13	千克	ABS	PQ	1/
3002.9030 30	枯草芽孢杆菌〔999〕	3		20	13/	13	千克	ABS	PVQW	1/
3002.9030 90	其他细菌及病毒[T2]	3		20	13/	13	千克	AB	PVQW	1/
3002.9040	---遗传物质和基因修饰生物体									
3002.9040 10	两用物项管制遗传物质和基因修饰生物体[T2]	3	0	20	13/	13	千克	3AB	PVQW	1/
3002.9040 90	其他遗传物质和基因修饰生物体[T2]	3	0	20	13/	13	千克	AB	PVQW	1/
3002.9090	---其他									
3002.9090 11	濒危动物血制品[T2]	3	0	20	13/	0	千克	ABQFE	PQ	1/
3002.9090 19	其他人血制品、动物血制品[T2]	3	0	20	13/	13	千克	ABQ	PVQW	1/
3002.9090 21	噬菌核霉〔101 用于非医学、环保领域,102 用于医学、环保领域〕	3	0	20	13/	13	千克	ABS	PVQW	1/
3002.9090 22	淡紫拟青霉〔101 用于非医学、环保领域,102 用于医学、环保领域〕	3	0	20	13/	13	千克	ABS	PVQW	1/
3002.9090 23	哈茨木霉菌〔101 用于非医学、环保领域,102 用于医学、环保领域〕	3	0	20	13/	13	千克	ABS	PVQW	1/
3002.9090 24	寡雄腐霉〔101 用于非医学、环保领域,102 用于医学、环保领域〕	3	0	20	13/	13	千克	ABS	PVQW	1/
3002.9090 91	两用物项管制毒素[T2]	3	0	20	13/	13	千克	3AB	PVQW	1/
3002.9090 92	人血〔101 人源全血,102 人源血浆,103 人源血清,104 血细胞、人源血细胞、红细胞、白细胞、血小板,105 脐带血,106 其他人血制品〕	3	0	20	13/	13	千克	ABV	PVQW	1/
3002.9090 99	其他毒素等(包括培养微生物(不包括酵母)及类似产品)[T2]	3	0	20	13/	13	千克	AB	PVQW	1/
30.03	**两种或两种以上成分混合而成的治病或防病用药品(不包括税目 30.02、30.05 或 30.06 的货品),未配定剂量或制成零售包装:**									
	-含有青霉素及具有青霉烷酸结构的青霉素衍生物或链霉素及其衍生物:									
	---青霉素:									
3003.1011	----氨苄青霉素〔101 其他化工产品,999 未配定剂量或非零售包装〕	0		30	13/	13	千克	Q		1/
3003.1012	----羟氨苄青霉素〔101 其他化工产品,999 未配定剂量或非零售包装〕	0		30	13/	13	千克	Q		1/

协定税率 %										特惠税率 %			Article Description
亚太5国	东/冰/格	巴基斯坦	韩国	瑞士	哥达	秘鲁	澳大利亚	新西/坡/智	港/澳/台	亚太2国	老/柬/缅	36/3/1	
	0/0/0	0	0	1.6	0	0	0	0//0	0/0/		//	0/0/0	Human coagulation factor Ⅷ, Recombinant human coagulation factor for injection Ⅷ, Recombinant human coagulation factor for injection Ⅸ, Recombinant human coagulation factor for injection Ⅶa, Human prothrombin complex
	0/0/0	0	0	1.6	0	0	0	0//0	0/0/		//	0/0/0	Antiserum and other blood components containing human genetic resources
	0/0/0	0	0	1.6	0	0	0	0//0	0/0/			0/0/0	Other antisera, other blood fractions and immunological products (Tax number due to separation of anticancer drugs)
	0/0/0	0	0	1.6	0	0	0	0//0	0/0/			0/0/0	--Immunological products, unmixed, not put up in measured doses or in forms or packings for retail sale
	0/0/0	0	0	1.6	0	0	0	0//0	0/0/			0/0/0	--Immunological products, mixed, not put up in measured doses or in forms or packings for retail sale
													--Immunological products, put up in measured doses or in forms or packings for retail sale
	0/0/0	0	0	1.6	0	0	0	0//0	0/0/			0/0/0	Anti-cancer drug preparations (excluding cancer adjuncts)
	0/0/0	0	0	1.6	0	0	0	0//0	0/0/		//	0/0/0	Recombinant human interferon β1a injection, injection
	0/0/0	0	0	1.6	0	0	0	0//0	0/0/			0/0/0	Other immunological products, put up in measured doses or in forms or packings for retail sale (Tax number due to separation of anticancer drugs)
													--Other
	0/0/0	0	0	1.6	0	0	0	0//0	0/0/			0/0/0	Anti-cancer drug preparations (excluding cancer adjuncts)
	0/0/0	0	0	1.6	0	0	0	0//0	0/0/			0/0/0	Other antisera, other blood and immune products, whether modified or processed through bioprocessing (Tax number due to separation of anticancer drugs)
	0/0/0	0	0	0.9	0	0	0	0//0	0/0/			0/0/0	-Vaccines for human medicine
	0/0/0	0	0	0	0	0	0	0//0	0/0/			0/0/0	-Vaccines for veterinary medicine
													-Other:
	0/0/0	0	0	0	0	0	0	0//0	0/0/			0/0/0	---Saxitoxin
	0/0/0	0	0	0	0	0	0	0//0	0/0/			0/0/0	---Ricitoxin
													---Bacteria and virus
	0/0/0	0	0	0.9	0	0	0	0//0	0/0/			0/0/0	Bacteria and virus under sensitive items control
	0/0/0	0	0	0.9	0	0	0	0//0	0/0/			0/0/0	Bacillus thurinsiensis
	0/0/0	0	0	0.9	0	0	0	0//0	0/0/			0/0/0	Bacillus subtilis
	0/0/0	0	0	0.9	0	0	0	0//0	0/0/			0/0/0	Other bacteria and virus
													---Genetics material and gene-modified or ganism
	0/0/0	0	0	0	0	0	0	0//0	0/0/			0/0/0	Genetics material and gene-modified or ganism under sensitive items control
	0/0/0	0	0	0	0	0	0	0//0	0/0/			0/0/0	Other genetics material and gene-modified or ganism
													---Other
	0/0/0	0	0	0	0	0	0	0//0	0/0/			0/0/0	Blood preparations of endangered animals
	0/0/0	0	0	0	0	0	0	0//0	0/0/			0/0/0	Other human or animal blood preparations
	0/0/0	0	0	0	0	0	0	0//0	0/0/			0/0/0	Sclerotinia Rot mildew bite
	0/0/0	0	0	0	0	0	0	0//0	0/0/			0/0/0	Paecilomyces lilacinus
	0/0/0	0	0	0	0	0	0	0//0	0/0/			0/0/0	Trichoderma harzianum
	0/0/0	0	0	0	0	0	0	0//0	0/0/			0/0/0	Pythium oligandrum
	0/0/0	0	0	0	0	0	0	0//0	0/0/			0/0/0	Toxin under sensitive items control
	0/0/0	0	0	0	0	0	0	0//0	0/0/		//	0/0/0	Human blood
	0/0/0	0	0	0	0	0	0	0//0	0/0/			0/0/0	Other human blood, other toxins, [including cultures of micro-organisms (excluding yeasts) and similar products]
													Medicaments (excluding goods of heading No. 30.02, 30.05 or 30.06) consisting of two or more constituents which have been mixed together for therapeutic or prophylactic uses, not put up in measured doses or in forms or packings for retail sale:
													-Containing penicillins or derivatives thereof, with a penicillanic acid structure or streptomycins or their derivatives:
													---Containing penicillins:
	0//							//				0/0/0	----Ampicillin
	0//							//				0/0/0	----Amoxycillin

税则号列	货品名称〔CIQ 扩展编码及品名－T2 表示见附表 2〕	最惠(%)	暂定税率	普通	增值/消费	出口退税	计量单位	监管条件	检验检疫	特殊证件对美关税
3003.1013	----青霉素 V〔101 其他化工产品,999 未配定剂量或非零售包装〕	0		30	13/	13	千克	Q		1/
3003.1019	----其他〔101 其他化工产品,999 未配定剂量或非零售包装〕	0		30	13/	13	千克	Q		1/
3003.1090	---其他〔101 其他化工产品,999 未配定剂量或非零售包装,混合指含两种或两种以上成分〕	0		30	13/	13	千克	Q		1/
	-其他,含有抗菌素:									
	--头孢菌素:									
3003.2011	----头孢噻肟〔999〕	0		30	13/	13	千克	Q		1/
3003.2012	----头孢他啶〔999〕	0		30	13/	13	千克	Q		1/
3003.2013	----头孢西丁〔999〕	0		30	13/	13	千克	Q		1/
3003.2014	----头孢替唑〔999〕	0		30	13/	13	千克	Q		1/
3003.2015	----头孢克罗〔999〕	0		30	13/	13	千克	Q		1/
3003.2016	----头孢呋辛〔999〕	0		30	13/	13	千克	Q		1/
3003.2017	----头孢三嗪(头孢曲松)〔999〕	0		30	13/	13	千克	Q		1/
3003.2018	----头孢哌酮〔999〕	0		30	13/	13	千克	Q		1/
3003.2019	----其他〔999〕	0		30	13/	13	千克	Q		1/
3003.2090	---其他〔999〕	0		30	13/	13	千克	Q		1/
	-其他,含有激素或税目 29.37 的其他产品:									
3003.3100	--含有胰岛素〔999〕	0		30	13/	13	千克	Q		1/5
3003.3900	--其他〔101 其他化工产品,999 不含抗菌素且未配定剂量或非零售包装,混合指含两种或两种以上成分〕	0		30	13/	13	千克	Q		1/
	-其他,含有生物碱及其衍生物:									
3003.4100	--含有麻黄碱及其盐〔998 药品,999 其他化工产品〕	5		35	13/	13	千克	Q		1/
3003.4200	--含有伪麻黄碱(INN)及其盐〔998 药品,999 其他化工产品〕	5		30	13/	13	千克	Q		1/
3003.4300	--含有去甲麻黄碱及其盐〔998 药品,999 其他化工产品〕	5		35	13/	13	千克	Q		1/
3003.4900	--其他									
3003.4900 10	含奎宁或其盐的混合药品(未配定剂量或非零售包装,混合指含两种或两种以上成分)〔998 药品,999 其他化工产品〕	5		35	13/	13	千克	Q		1/
3003.4900 90	含其他生物碱及衍生物的混合药品(未配定剂量或非零售包装,混合指含两种或两种以上成分)〔998 药品,999 其他化工产品〕	5		30	13/	13	千克	Q		1/
	--其他,含有本章子目注释二所列抗疟疾活性成分的:									
3003.6010	---含有青蒿素及其衍生物〔998 药品,999 其他化工产品〕	0		30	13/	13	千克	Q		1/5
3003.6090	---其他									
3003.6090 10	含有磺胺类的混合药品(未配定剂量或非零售包装,混合指含两种或两种以上成分)〔998 药品,999 其他化工产品〕	0		30	13/	13	千克	Q		1/5
3003.6090 20	含濒危动植物的混合药品(未配定剂量或非零售包装,混合指含两种或两种以上成分)〔998 药品,999 其他化工产品〕	0		30	13/	0	千克	EFQ		1/5
3003.6090 90	其他含有本章子目注释二所列抗疟疾活性成分的混合药品(未配定剂量或非零售包装,混合指含两种或两种以上成分)〔998 药品,999 其他化工产品〕	0		30	13/	13	千克	Q		1/5
3003.9000	-其他									
3003.9000 10	含紫杉醇的混合药品(未配定剂量或非零售包装,混合指含两种或两种以上成分)〔998 药品,999 其他化工产品〕	0		30	13/	0	千克	EFQ		1/
3003.9000 20	其他含未列名濒危动植物混合药品(未配定剂量或非零售包装,混合指含两种或两种以上成分)〔998 药品,999 其他化工产品〕	0		30	13/	0	千克	EFQ		1/
3003.9000 30	其他含磺胺类的混合药品(未配定剂量或非零售包装,混合指含两种或两种以上成分)〔998 药品,999 其他化工产品〕	0		30	13/	13	千克	Q		1/
3003.9000 90	其他含未列名成分混合药品(未配定剂量或非零售包装,混合指含两种或两种以上成分)〔998 药品,999 其他化工产品〕	0		30	13/	13	千克	Q		1/
	-其他:									

协定税率 %										特惠税率 %			Article Description
亚太5国	东/冰/格	巴基斯坦	韩国	瑞士	哥达	秘鲁	澳大利亚	新西/坡/智	港/澳/台	亚太2国	老/柬/缅	36/3/1	
	0//							//				0/0/0	----Penicillin V
	0//							//				0/0/0	----Other
	0//							//				0/0/0	---Other
													-Other, containing antibiotics:
													---Containing cephamycins:
	0//							//				0/0/0	----Cefotaxime
	0//							//				0/0/0	----Ceftazidime
	0//							//				0/0/0	----Cefoxitin
	0//							//				0/0/0	----Ceftezole
	0//							//				0/0/0	----Cefaclor
	0//							//				0/0/0	----Cefuroxime
	0//							//				0/0/0	----Ceftriaxone
	0//							//				0/0/0	----Cefoperazone
	0//							//				0/0/0	----Other
	0//							//				0/0/0	---Other
													-Other, containing hormones or other products of heading 29.37:
	0//							//				0/0/0	--Containing insulin
	0//							//				0/0/0	--Other
													-Other, containing alkaloids or derivatives thereof:
	0/0/0	0	0	0	0	0	0	0//0	0/0/			0/0/0	--Containing ephedrine or its salts
	0/0/0	0	0	0	0	0	0	0//0	0/0/			0/0/0	--Containing pseudoephedrine (*INN*) or its salts
	0/0/0	0	0	0	0	0	0	0//0	0/0/			0/0/0	--Containing norephedrine or its salts
													--Other
	0/0/0	0	0	0	0	0	0	0//0	0/0/			0/0/0	Medicaments containing quinine or its salts (consisting of two or more constituents which have been mixed together, not put up in measured doses or in forms or packings for retail sale)
	0/0/0	0	0	0	0	0	0	0//0	0/0/			0/0/0	Other medicaments containing alkaloids or derivatives thereof (consisting of two or more constituents which have been mixed together, but not containing hormones or other prouducts of heading 29.37 or antibiotics, not put up in measured doses or in forms or packings for retail sale)
													-Other, containing antimalarial active principles described in Subheading Note 2 to this Chapter:
	0//							//	//			0/0/0	---Containing artemisinins and their derivatives
													---Other
	0//							//	//			0/0/0	Medicaments containing sulfa drugs (consisting of two or more constituents which have been mixed together, not put up in measured doses or in forms or packings for retail sale)
	0//							//	//			0/0/0	Medicaments containing endangered animals and plants (consisting of two or more constituents which have been mixed together, not put up in measured doses or in forms or packings for retail sale)
	0//							//	//			0/0/0	Other, containing antimalarial active principles described in Subheading Note 2 to this Chapter (consisting of two or more constituents which have been mixed together, but not containing hormones or other prouducts of heading 29.37 or antibiotics, not put up in measured doses or in forms or packings for retail sale)
													-Other
	0//							//	//			0/0/0	Other medicaments containing sulfa drugs (consisting of two or more constituents which have been mixed together, not put up in measured doses or in forms or packings for retail sale)
	0//							//	//			0/0/0	Other medicaments containing endangered animals and plants (consisting of two or more constituents which have been mixed together, not put up in measured doses or in forms or packings for retail sale)
	0//							//	//			0/0/0	Other medicaments containing sulfa drugs (consisting of two or more constituents which have been mixed together, not put up in measured doses or in forms or packings for retail sale)
	0//							//	//			0/0/0	Other medicaments, containing other two or more constituents, not elsewhere specified or included, not put up in measured doses or in forms of packings for retail sale
													-Other:

税则号列	货品名称〔CIQ 扩展编码及品名—T2 表示见附表 2〕	最惠(%)	暂定税率	普通	增值/消费	出口退税	计量单位	监管条件	检验检疫	特殊证件对美关税
30.04	**由混合或非混合产品构成的治病或防病用药品(不包括税目 30.02、30.05 或 30.06 的货品),已配定剂量或(包括制成皮肤摄入形式的)或制成零售包装:**									
	-含有青霉素及具有青霉烷酸结构的青霉素衍生物或链霉素及其衍生物:									
	---青霉素:									
3004.1011	----氨苄青霉素制剂									
3004.1011　10	兽用普鲁卡因青霉素、奈夫西林钠制剂(包括制成零售包装)〔999〕	0		30	13/	13	千克	R		1/
3004.1011　90	氨苄青霉素制剂(包括制成零售包装)〔101 其他化工产品,999 包括制成零售包装〕	0		30	13/	13	千克	Q		1/
3004.1012	----羟氨苄青霉素制剂〔101 其他化工产品,999 包括制成零售包装〕	0		30	13/	13	千克	Q		1/
3004.1013	----青霉素 V 制剂〔101 其他化工产品,999 包括制成零售包装〕	0		30	13/	13	千克	Q		1/
3004.1019	----其他〔999〕	0		30	13/	13	千克	Q		1/
3004.1090	---其他									
3004.1090　10	抗(防)癌药品制剂(不含癌症辅助治疗药品)〔999〕	0		30	3/	13	千克	Q		1/
3004.1090　90	其他已配剂量含有青霉素或链霉素药品(因拆分抗癌药产生的兜底税号)〔999〕	0		30	13/	13	千克	Q		1/
	-其他,含有抗菌素:									
	---头孢菌素:									
3004.2011	----头孢噻肟制剂〔999〕	0		30	13/	13	千克	Q		1/
3004.2012	----头孢他啶制剂〔999〕	0		30	13/	13	千克	Q		1/
3004.2013	----头孢西丁制剂〔999〕	0		30	13/	13	千克	Q		1/
3004.2014	----头孢替唑制剂〔999〕	0		30	13/	13	千克	Q		1/
3004.2015	----头孢克罗制剂〔999〕	0		30	13/	13	千克	Q		1/
3004.2016	----头孢呋辛制剂〔999〕	0		30	13/	13	千克	Q		1/
3004.2017	----头孢三嗪(头孢曲松)制剂〔999〕	0		30	13/	13	千克	Q		1/
3004.2018	----头孢哌酮制剂〔999〕	0		30	13/	13	千克	Q		1/
3004.2019	----其他									
3004.2019　11	兽用已配剂量的头孢氨苄,头孢噻呋钠制剂(包括零售包装的制成品)〔999〕	0		30	13/	13	千克	R		1/
3004.2019　12	兽用已配剂量的头孢噻呋晶体,硫酸头孢喹肟制剂(包括零售包装的制成品)〔999〕	0		30	13/	13	千克	R		1/
3004.2019　90	其他已配剂量头孢菌素制剂(包括零售包装的制成品)〔999〕	0		30	13/	13	千克	Q		1/
3004.2090	---其他									
3004.2090　11	兽用已配剂量的土霉素,延胡索酸泰妙菌素,泰拉霉素制剂(包括制成零售包装)〔999〕	0		30	13/	13	千克	R		1/
3004.2090　12	兽用已配剂量的氟苯尼考,多拉菌素,硫酸庆大霉素制剂(包括制成零售包装)〔999〕	0		30	13/	13	千克	R		1/
3004.2090　13	兽用已配剂量的硫酸双羟链霉素制剂(包括制成零售包装)〔999〕	0		30	13/	13	千克	R		1/
3004.2090　91	抗(防)癌药品制剂(不含癌症辅助治疗药品)〔999〕	0		30	3/	13	千克	Q		1/
3004.2090　99	其他已配剂量含有其他抗菌素的药品(包括制成零售包装)(因拆分抗癌药产生的兜底税号)〔999〕	0		30	13/	13	千克	Q		1/
	-其他,含有激素或税目 29.37 的其他产品:									
	--含有胰岛素:									
3004.3110	---含有重组人胰岛素的									
3004.3110　10	已配剂量含重组人胰岛素的单方制剂(包括零售包装)〔999〕	0		30	13/	13	千克	L		1/
3004.3110　90	已配剂量含重组人胰岛素的其他药品(不含抗菌素,包括零售包装)〔999〕	0		30	13/	13	千克	Q		1/
3004.3190	---其他									
3004.3190　10	其他已配剂量含胰岛素的单方制剂(包括零售包装)〔999〕	0		30	13/	13	千克	L		1/
3004.3190　90	其他已配剂量含胰岛素的其他药品(不含抗菌素,包括零售包装)〔999〕	0		30	13/	13	千克	Q		1/

协定税率 %										特惠税率 %			Article Description
亚太5国	东/冰/格	巴基斯坦	韩国	瑞士	哥达	秘鲁	澳大利亚	新西/坡/智	港/澳/台	亚太2国	老/柬/缅	36/3/1	
													Medicaments (excluding goods of heading No. 30.02, 30.05 or 30.06) consisting of mixed or unmixed products for therapeutic or prophylactic uses, put up in measured doses (including those in the form of transdermal administration systems) or in forms or packings for retail sale:
													-Containing penicillins or derivatives thereof, with a penicillanic acid structure, or streptomycins or their derivatives:
													---Containing penicillins:
													----Ampicillin
	0//							//	//			0/0/0	Procaine benzylpenicillin, nafcillin sodium for veterinary purposes (including in forms or packing for retail sale)
	0//							//	//			0/0/0	Ampicillin(including in forms or packings for retail sale)
	0//							//	//			0/0/0	----Amoxycillin
	0//							//	//			0/0/0	----Penicillin V
	0//							//	//			0/0/0	----Other
													---Other
	0//							//	//			0/0/0	Anti—cancer drug preparations (excluding cancer adjuncts)
	0//							//	//			0/0/0	Other medicines containing penicillin or streptomycin (Tax number due to separation of anticancer drugs)
													-Other, containing antibiotics:
													---Containing cephamycins:
	0//							//	//			0/0/0	----Cefotaxime
	0//							//	//			0/0/0	----Ceftazidime
	0//							//	//			0/0/0	----Cefoxitin
	0//							//	//			0/0/0	----Ceftezole
	0//							//	//			0/0/0	----Cefaclor
	0//							//	//			0/0/0	----Cefuroxime
	0//							//	//			0/0/0	----Ceftriaxone
	0//							//	//			0/0/0	----Cefoperazone
													----Other
	0//		2.4					//	//			0/0/0	Cefalexin, ceftiofur sodium, for veterinary purposes, put up in measured doses(including in forms or packings for retail sale)
	0//		2.4					//	//			0/0/0	Cefliofur crystalline, cefquinome sulfate, for veterinary purposes, put up in measured doses (including in forms of packing for retail sale)
	0//		2.4					//	//			0/0/0	Other cephalosporin preparations, put up in measured doses(including in forms of packing for retail sale)
													---Other
	0//							//	//			0/0/0	Teramycin, tiamulin fumarate, tulathromycin for veterinarypurposes, put up in measured doses(including in forms or packing for retail sale)
	0//							//	//			0/0/0	Florfenicol, doramectin, gentamycin sulfate for veterinary purposes, put up in measured dose(including in forms or packing for retail sale)
	0//							//	//			0/0/0	Streptomycin sulfate for veterinary purposes, put up in measured dose(including in forms or packing for retail sale)
	0//							//	//			0/0/0	Anti—cancer drug preparations (excluding cancer adjuncts)
	0//							//	//			0/0/0	Containing other antibiotics of drugs, put up in measured dose(including in forms or packing for retail sale)(Tax number due to separation of anticancer drugs)
													-Other, containing hormones or other products of heading 29.37:
													--Containing insulin:
													---Containing recombinant human insulin
	0//							//				0/0/0	Simple preparation with recombinant human insulin, put up in measured doses(including in forms or packing for retail sale)
	0//							//				0/0/0	Containing recombinant human insulin of other drugs, put up in measured doses(excluding antibiotics, including in forms or packing for retail sale)
													---Other
	0//							//				0/0/0	Other single preparations, containing insulin, put up in measured dose(including in forms or packing for retail sale)
	0//							//				0/0/0	Other medicaments, containing insulin, put up in measured doses (excluding antibiotics, including in forms or packing for retail sale)

税则号列	货品名称〔CIQ扩展编码及品名—T2表示见附表2〕	最惠(%)	暂定税率	普通	增值/消费	出口退税	计量单位	监管条件	检验检疫	特殊证件对美关税
3004.3200	--含有皮质甾类激素及其衍生物或结构类似物									
3004.3200 11	已配剂量含1-雄烯二醇或1-雄烯二酮的单方制剂(包括其衍生物及结构类似物,包括零售包装)〔999〕	0		30	13/	13	千克	L		1/
3004.3200 12	已配剂量含甲酰勃龙的单方制剂(包括其衍生物及结构类似物,包括零售包装)〔999〕	0		30	13/	13	千克	L		1/
3004.3200 13	已配剂量含雄甾-4-烯-3β,17α-二醇[4-雄烯二醇(3β,17α)]的单方制剂(包括其衍生物及结构类似物,包括零售包装)〔999〕	0		30	13/	13	千克	L		1/
3004.3200 14	已配剂量含雄甾-5-烯-3β,17α-二醇[5-雄烯二醇(3β,17α)]的单方制剂(包括其衍生物及结构类似物,包括零售包装)〔999〕	0		30	13/	13	千克	L		1/
3004.3200 15	已配剂量含4-雄烯二醇或乙雌烯醇的单方制剂(包括其衍生物及结构类似物,包括零售包装)〔999〕	0		30	13/	13	千克	L		1/
3004.3200 16	已配剂量含5-雄烯二酮的单方制剂(包括其衍生物及结构类似物,包括零售包装)〔999〕	0		30	13/	13	千克	L		1/
3004.3200 17	已配剂量含5α—雄烷—3α, 17β—二醇(雄烷二醇(3α, 17β))或5β—雄烷—3α, 17β—二醇(5β—雄烷二醇(3α, 17β))的单方制剂(包括其衍生物及其结构类似物,包括零售包装)〔999〕	0		30	13/	13	千克	L		1/
3004.3200 18	已配剂量5α—雄烷—3β, 17α—二醇(雄烷二醇(3β, 17α))的单方制剂(包括其衍生物及结构类似物,包括零售包装)〔999〕	0		30	13/	13	千克	L		1/
3004.3200 19	已配剂量含勃拉睾酮的单方制剂(包括其衍生物及结构类似物,包括零售包装)〔999〕	0		30	13/	13	千克	L		1/
3004.3200 21	已配剂量含勃地酮的单方制剂(包括其衍生物及结构类似物,包括零售包装)〔999〕	0		30	13/	13	千克	L		1/
3004.3200 22	已配剂量含勃二酮的单方制剂(包括其衍生物及结构类似物,包括零售包装)〔999〕	0		30	13/	13	千克	L		1/
3004.3200 23	已配剂量含卡芦睾酮或达那唑的单方制剂(包括其衍生物及结构类似物,包括零售包装)〔999〕	0		30	13/	13	千克	L		1/
3004.3200 24	已配剂量含氯司替勃的单方制剂(包括其衍生物及结构类似物,包括零售包装)〔999〕	0		30	13/	13	千克	L		1/
3004.3200 25	已配剂量含去氢氯甲睾酮的单方制剂(包括其衍生物及结构类似物,包括零售包装)〔999〕	0		30	13/	13	千克	L		1/
3004.3200 26	已配剂量含甲基氯司替勃的单方制剂(包括其衍生物及结构类似物,包括零售包装)	0		30	13/	13	千克	L		/
3004.3200 28	已配剂量含普拉睾酮或屈他雄酮的单方制剂(包括其衍生物及结构类似物,包括零售包装)〔999〕	0		30	13/	13	千克	L		1/
3004.3200 29	已配剂量含去氧甲睾酮或双氢睾酮的单方制剂(包括其衍生物及结构类似物,包括零售包装)〔999〕	0		30	13/	13	千克	L		1/
3004.3200 31	已配剂量含表双氢睾酮或氟甲睾酮的单方制剂(包括其衍生物及结构类似物,包括零售包装)〔999〕	0		30	13/	13	千克	L		1/
3004.3200 32	已配剂量含夫拉扎勃的单方制剂(包括其衍生物及结构类似物,包括零售包装)〔999〕	0		30	13/	13	千克	L		1/

协定税率 %										特惠税率 %			
亚太5国	东/冰/格	巴基斯坦	韩国	瑞士	哥达	秘鲁	澳大利亚	新西/坡/智	港/澳/台	亚太2国	老/柬/缅	36/3/1	Article Description
													--Containing corticosteroid hormones, their derivatives and structural analogues
	0//							//	//			0/0/0	Single preparations, containing androstenediol or androstenedione, put up in measured doses (including in forms or packing for retail sale)
	0//							//	//			0/0/0	Single preparations, containing formebolone, put up in measured dose (including their derivatives and structural analogues, in forms or packing for retail sale)
	0//							//	//			0/0/0	Single preparations, containing androst-4-ene-3β, 17α-diol [4-androstenediol (3β,17α)], put up in measured dose (including their derivatives and structural analogues, in forms or packing for retail sale)
	0//							//	//			0/0/0	Single peparations, containing androst-5-ene-3β, 17α-diol [5-androstenediol (3β,17α)], put up in measured dose (including their derivatives and structural analogues, in forms or packing for retail sale)
	0//							//	//			0/0/0	Single preparations, containing 4-androstenediol or ethylestrenol, put up in measured dose (including their derivatives and structural analogues, in froms or packing for retail sale)
	0//							//	//			0/0/0	Single preparations, containing androstenedione isomer, put up in measured doses (including their derivatives and structural analogues, in forms or packing for retail sale)
	0//							//	//			0/0/0	Single preparations, containing 5α-androstane-3α, 17β-estrad [dihydroandrosterone (3β, 17α)] or 5β-androstane-3α, 17β-glycol [5β-dihydroandrosterone (3α, 17β)], put up in measured doses (including their derivatives and structural analogues, in forms or packing for retail sale)
	0//							//	//			0/0/0	Single preparations, containing 5α-androstane-3α, 17β-estrad [dihydroandrosterone (3β, 17α)], put up in measured doses (including their derivatives and structural analogues, in forms or packing for retail sale)
	0//							//	//			0/0/0	Single preparations, containing bolasterone, put up in measured doses (including their derivatives and structural analogues, in forms or packing for retail sale)
	0//							//	//			0/0/0	Single preparations, containing boldenone, put up in measured doses (including their derivatives and structural analogues, in forms or packing for retail sale)
	0//							//	//			0/0/0	Single preparations, containing androstadien-3, 17-dione, put up in measured doses (including their derivatives and structural analogues, in forms or packing for retail sale)
	0//							//	//			0/0/0	Single preparations, containing calusterone or danazol, put up in measured doses (including their derivatives and structural analogues, in forms or packing for retail sale)
	0//							//	//			0/0/0	Single preparations, containing clostebol, put up in measured doses (including their derivatives and structural analogues, in forms or packing for retail sale)
	0//							//	//			0/0/0	Single preparations, containing dehydrochloro-methyltestosterone, put up in measured doses (including their derivatives and structural analogues, in forms or packing for retail sale)
	0//							//	//		//	0/0/0	Single dose preparations (including derivatives and structural analogues, including retail packaging) with methylchlorostilbestrol
	0//							//	//			0/0/0	Single preparations, containing prasterone or dormostanolone, put up in measured doses (including their derivatives and structural analogues, in forms or packing for retail sale)
	0//							//	//			0/0/0	Single preparations, containing deoxymethyltestosterone or dihydrotestosterone, put up in measured doses (including their derivatives and structural analogues, in forms or packing for retail sale)
	0//							//	//			0/0/0	Single preparations, containing epi-dihydrotestosterone or fluoxymesterone, put up in measured doses (including their derivatives and structural analogues, in forms or packing for retail sale)
	0//							//	//			0/0/0	Single preparations, containing furazabol, put up in measured doses (including their derivatives and structural analogues, in forms or packing for retail sale)

税则号列		货品名称〔CIQ 扩展编码及品名－T2 表示见附表 2〕	最惠(%)	暂定税率	普通	增值/消费	出口退税	计量单位	监管条件	检验检疫	特殊证件对美关税
3004.3200	33	已配剂量含孕三烯酮或 4-羟基睾酮的单方制剂(包括其衍生物及结构类似物,包括零售包装)〔999〕	0		30	13/	13	千克	L		1/
3004.3200	34	含 3α-羟基-5α-雄烷-17-酮的单方制剂(包括其衍生物及结构类似物,已配剂量或制成零售包装)〔999〕	0		30	13/	13	千克			1/
3004.3200	35	已配剂量含美睾酮或美雄酮的单方制剂(包括其衍生物及结构类似物,包括零售包装)〔999〕	0		30	13/	13	千克	L		1/
3004.3200	36	已配剂量含甲基屈他雄酮的单方制剂(包括其衍生物及结构类似物,包括零售包装)〔999〕	0		30	13/	13	千克	L		1/
3004.3200	37	已配剂量含甲二烯诺龙的单方制剂(包括其衍生物及结构类似物,包括零售包装)〔999〕	0		30	13/	13	千克	L		1/
3004.3200	38	已配剂量含甲基－1－睾酮或甲诺睾酮的单方制剂(包括其衍生物及结构类似物,包括零售包装)〔999〕	0		30	13/	13	千克	L		1/
3004.3200	39	已配剂量含美曲勃龙的单方制剂(包括其衍生物及结构类似物,包括零售包装)〔999〕	0		30	13/	13	千克	L		1/
3004.3200	41	已配剂量含美雄诺龙或美替诺龙的单方制剂(包括其衍生物及结构类似物,包括零售包装)〔999〕	0		30	13/	13	千克	L		1/
3004.3200	42	已配剂量含美雄醇或甲睾酮或米勃酮的单方制剂(包括其衍生物及结构类似物,包括零售包装)〔999〕	0		30	13/	13	千克	L		1/
3004.3200	43	已配剂量含诺龙或诺勃酮或诺司替勃的单方制剂(包括其衍生物及结构类似物,包括零售包装)〔999〕	0		30	13/	13	千克	L		1/
3004.3200	44	已配剂量含 19-去甲雄烯二酮的单方制剂(包括其衍生物及结构类似物,包括零售包装)〔999〕	0		30	13/	13	千克	L		1/
3004.3200	45	已配剂量含去甲雄酮或诺乙雄龙的单方制剂(包括其衍生物及结构类似物,包括零售包装)〔999〕	0		30	13/	13	千克	L		1/
3004.3200	46	已配剂量含 19－去甲本胆烷醇酮的单方制剂(包括其衍生物及结构类似物,包括零售包装)〔999〕	0		30	13/	13	千克	L		1/
3004.3200	47	已配剂量含羟勃龙或氧雄龙的单方制剂(包括其衍生物及结构类似物,包括零售包装)〔999〕	0		30	13/	13	千克	L		1/
3004.3200	48	已配剂量含羟甲睾酮或羟甲烯龙的单方制剂(包括其衍生物及结构类似物,包括零售包装)〔999〕	0		30	13/	13	千克	L		1/
3004.3200	49	已配剂量含前列他唑的单方制剂(包括其衍生物及结构类似物,包括零售包装)〔999〕	0		30	13/	13	千克	L		1/
3004.3200	51	含奎勃龙或替勃龙或群勃龙的单方制剂(包括其衍生物及结构类似物,已配剂量或制成零售包装)〔999〕	0		30	13/	13	千克	L		1/
3004.3200	52	已配剂量含司坦唑醇或司腾勃龙的单方制剂(包括其衍生物及结构类似物,包括零售包装)〔999〕	0		30	13/	13	千克	L		1/
3004.3200	53	已配剂量含 1-睾酮或睾酮的单方制剂(包括其衍生物及结构类似物,包括零售包装)〔999〕	0		30	13/	13	千克	L		1/
3004.3200	54	已配剂量含四氢孕三烯酮或泽仑诺的单方制剂(包括其衍生物及结构类似物,包括零售包装)〔999〕	0		30	13/	13	千克	L		1/
3004.3200	60	兽用已配剂量倍他米松戊酸酯制剂(包括其衍生物及结构类似物,包括零售包装)〔999〕	0		30	13/	13	千克	R		1/

协定税率 %										特惠税率 %			
亚太5国	东/冰/格	巴基斯坦	韩国	瑞士	哥达	秘鲁	澳大利亚	新西/坡/智	港/澳/台	亚太2国	老/柬/缅	36/3/1	Article Description
	0//							//	//			0/0/0	Single preparations, containing gestrinone or 4-hydroxyltestosterone, put up in measured doses (including their derivatives and structural analogues, in forms or packing for retail sale)
	0//							//	//			0/0/0	Single preparations, containing 3α-hydroxide-5α-androstane-17-ketone, put up in measured doses (including their derivatives and structural analogues, in forms or packing for retail sale)
	0//							//	//			0/0/0	Single preparations, containing mesterolone or methandienone, put up in measured doses (including their derivatives and structural analogues, in forms or packing for retail sale)
	0//							//	//			0/0/0	Single preparations, containing 2α, 17α-dimethyl-5α-androstane-3-ketone-17β-alcohol, put up in measured doses (including their derivatives and structural analogues, in forms or packing for retail sale)
	0//							//	//			0/0/0	Single preparations, containing 17α-methyl-17β- hydroxy-estr-4, 9(10)-di-3-ketone, put up in measured doses (including their derivatives and structural analogues, in forms or packing for retail sale)
	0//							//	//			0/0/0	Single preparations, containing Methyl-1-testosterone or methylnortestosterone, put up in measured doses (including their derivatives and structural analogues, in forms or packing for retail sale)
	0//							//	//			0/0/0	Single preparations, containing 17α-methyl-17β- hydroxy-estr-4, 9, 11triene-3-ketone, put up in measured doses (including their derivatives and structural analogues, in forms or packing for retail sale)
	0//							//	//			0/0/0	Single preparations, containing mestanolone or methenolone, put up in measured doses (including their derivatives and structural analogues, in forms or packing for retail sale)
	0//							//	//			0/0/0	Single preparations, containing methandriol or methyltestosterone or mibolerone, put up in measured doses (including their derivatives and structural analogues , in forms or packing for retail sale)
	0//							//	//			0/0/0	Single preparations, containing nandrolone or norboletone or norclostebol, put up in measured doses (including their derivatives and structural analogues, in forms or packing for retail sale)
	0//							//	//			0/0/0	Single preparations, containing 19-norandrostenedion or 19-norandrostenedione, put up in measured doses (including their derivatives and structural analogues, in forms or packing for retail sale)
	0//							//	//			0/0/0	Single preparations, containing norandrosterone or norethandrolone, put up in measured doses (including their derivatives and structural analogues, in forms or packing for retailsale)
	0//							//	//			0/0/0	Single preparations, containing 19-noretiocholanolone, put up in measured doses (including their derivatives and structural analogues, in forms or packing for retail sale)
	0//							//	//			0/0/0	Single preparations, containing oxabolone or oxandrolone, put up in measured doses (including their derivatives and structural analogues, in forms or packing for retail sale)
	0//							//	//			0/0/0	Single preparations, containing Oxymesterone or oxymetholone, put up in measured doses (including their derivatives and structural analogues, in forms or packing for retailsale)
	0//							//	//			0/0/0	Single preparations, containing 17β-hydroxy-5α-androstane[3, 2-c] pyrazole, put up in measured doses (including their derivatives and structural analogues, in forms or packing for retail sale)
	0//							//	//			0/0/0	Single preparations, containing quinbolone or tibolone or trenbolone, put up in measured doses (including their derivatives andstructural analogues, in forms or packing for retail sale)
	0//							//	//			0/0/0	Single preparations, containing stanozolol or stenbolone, put up in measured doses (including their derivatives and structural analogues, in forms or packing for retail sale)
	0//							//	//			0/0/0	Single preparations, containing 1-testosterone or testosterone, put up in measured doses (including their derivatives and structural analogues, in forms or packing for retail sale)
	0//							//	//			0/0/0	Single preparations, containing tetrahydrogestrinone or zeranol, put up in measured doses (including their derivatives and structural analogues, in forms or packing for retail sale)
	0//							//	//			0/0/0	Betamethasone valerate for veterinary, put up in measured doses (including their derivatives and Structural analogues, in forms or packing for retail sale)

税则号列	货品名称〔CIQ扩展编码及品名—T2表示见附表2〕	最惠(%)	暂定税率	普通	增值/消费	出口退税	计量单位	监管条件	检验检疫	特殊证件对美关税
3004.3200 71	已配剂量含雄甾-5-烯-3β,17β-二醇[5-雄烯二醇(3β,17β)]的单方制剂(包括其衍生物及结构类似物,不含抗菌素,包括零售包装)〔999〕	0		30	13/	13	千克	L		1/
3004.3200 72	已配剂量含雄甾-4-烯-3,17-二酮(4-雄烯二酮)的单方制剂(包括其衍生物及结构类似物,不含抗菌素,包括零售包装)〔999〕	0		30	13/	13	千克	L		1/
3004.3200 74	已配剂量含7α-羟基-普拉睾酮的单方制剂(包括其衍生物及结构类似物,不含抗菌素,包括零售包装)〔999〕	0		30	13/	13	千克	L		1/
3004.3200 75	已配剂量含7β-羟基-普拉睾酮的单方制剂(包括其衍生物及结构类似物,不含抗菌素,包括零售包装)〔999〕	0		30	13/	13	千克	L		1/
3004.3200 76	已配剂量含7-羰基-普拉睾酮的单方制剂(包括其衍生物及结构类似物,不含抗菌素,包括零售包装)〔999〕	0		30	13/	13	千克	L		1/
3004.3200 77	已配剂量含胆烷醇酮的单方制剂(包括其衍生物及结构类似物,不含抗菌素,包括零售包装)〔999〕	0		30	13/	13	千克	L		1/
3004.3200 78	已配剂量含1,4雄烯二酮(雄甾1,4二烯3,17二酮)的单方制剂(包括其衍生物及结构类似物,不含抗菌素,包括零售包装)〔999〕	0		30	13/	13	千克	L		/
3004.3200 91	抗(防)癌药品制剂(不含癌症辅助治疗药品)〔999〕	0		30	3/	13	千克	Q		1/
3004.3200 99	其他已配剂量含其他皮质甾类激素的药品(包括其衍生物及结构类似物,不含抗菌素,包括零售包装)(因拆分抗癌药产生的兜底税号)〔301易燃液体,999包括其衍生物及结构类似物,不含抗菌素,包括零售包装〕	0		30	13/	13	千克	Q		1/
3004.3900	--其他									
3004.3900 11	已配剂量含克仑特罗的单方制剂(包括零售包装)〔999〕	0		30	13/	13	千克	L		1/
3004.3900 25	已配剂量含绒促性素、促黄体生成素等的单方制剂(包括含生长激素释放肽类(GHRPs)、普拉莫瑞林(生长激素释放肽2)、CJC1295(CAS号863288340)、生长激素释放肽6、生长激素释放激素及其类似物、生长激素促分泌剂,零售包装)〔999〕	0		30	13/	13	千克	L		1/
3004.3900 26	已配剂量含促皮质素类等肽类激素的单方制剂(包括零售包装,以及已配剂量或零售包装的艾瑞莫瑞林、阿那瑞林、布舍瑞林、可的瑞林、海沙瑞林、伊莫瑞林、舍莫瑞林、替莫瑞林、戈那瑞林、葛瑞林(脑肠肽)及其模拟物类的单方制剂)〔999〕	0		30	13/	13	千克	L		1/
3004.3900 27	已配剂量含亮丙瑞林的单方制剂〔999〕	0		30	13/	13	千克	L		1/
3004.3900 28	已配剂量含雄酮的单方制剂〔999〕	0		30	13/	13	千克	L		1/
3004.3900 30	兽用血促性素、绒促性素制剂(包括零售包装)〔999〕	0		30	13/	13	千克	R		1/
3004.3900 91	抗(防)癌药品制剂(不含癌症辅助治疗药品)〔999〕	0		30	3/	13	千克	Q		1/
3004.3900 92	其他已配剂量含卵泡抑素的单方制剂	0		30	13/	13	千克	L		/
3004.3900 93	其他已配剂量含马昔瑞林的单方制剂	0		30	13/	13	千克	L		/
3004.3900 94	吸入用伊洛前列素溶液、曲前列尼尔注射液或重组人生长激素注射液(已配定计量或制成零售包装)	0		30	3/	13	千克	Q		/
3004.3900 99	其他已配剂量含激素或品目2937产品的药品(不含抗菌素,包括零售包装)(因拆分抗癌药产生的兜底税号)〔999〕	0		30	13/	13	千克	Q		1/
	-其他,含有生物碱及其衍生物:							Q		
3004.4100	--含有麻黄碱及其盐									
3004.4100 10	盐酸麻黄碱片、盐酸麻黄碱注射剂、硫酸麻黄碱片〔998药品,999其他化工产品〕	5		30	13/	13	千克	23Q		1/
3004.4100 20	其他含麻黄碱及其盐的单方制剂(已配定剂量或制成零售包装)〔998药品,999其他化工产品〕	5		30	13/	13	千克	I		1/
3004.4100 90	其他含有麻黄碱及其盐的药品(已配定剂量或制成零售包装)〔998药品,999其他化工产品〕	5		30	13/	13	千克	Q		1/
3004.4200	--含有伪麻黄碱(INN)及其盐									
3004.4200 10	盐酸伪麻黄碱片〔998药品,999其他化工产品〕	5		30	13/	13	千克	23Q		1/
3004.4200 20	其他含伪麻黄碱及其盐的单方制剂(已配定剂量或制成零售包装)〔998药品,999其他化工产品〕	5		30	13/	13	千克	I		1/

协定税率 %										特惠税率 %			
亚太5国	东/冰/格	巴基斯坦	韩国	瑞士	哥达	秘鲁	澳大利亚	新西/坡/智	港/澳/台	亚太2国	老/柬/缅	36/3/1	Article Description
	0//							//	//			0/0/0	Single preparartions, 5-Androstenediol(3β,17β)[5-androstene-glycol (3β,17β)], put up in measured doses(including their derivatives and strutural analogues, in forms or packing for retailsale)
	0//							//	//			0/0/0	Single preparartions, androstenedione (4-androstene-glycol), put up in measured doses (including their derivatives and strutural analogues, in forms or packing for retailsale)
	0//							//	//			0/0/0	]Single preparartions, 7α-hydroxy-DHEA, put up in measured doses (including their derivatives and strutural analogues, in forms or packing for retailsale)
	0//							//	//			0/0/0	Single preparartions, 7β-hydroxy-DHEA, put up in measured doses (including their derivatives and strutural analogues, in forms or packing for retailsale)
	0//							//	//			0/0/0	Single preparartions, 7- carbonyl Prasterone(put up in measured doses and in forms or packing for retail sale)
	0//							//	//			0/0/0	Single preparartions, Androstane, put up in measured doses(including their derivatives and strutural analogues, in forms or packing for retailsale)
	0//							//	//		//	0/0/0	Formula containing 1,4 — androstenedione (androsterone — 1,4 — diene — 3,17 — dione)
	0//							//	//			0/0/0	Anti — cancer drug preparations (excluding cancer adjuncts)
	0//							//	//			0/0/0	Drugs containing corticosteroed hormone, put up in measured dose (excluding antibiotics, including their derivatives and structural analogues, in forms or packing for retail sale)(Tax number due to separation of anticancer drugs)
													--Other
	0//							//	//			0/0/0	Single preparations, containting clenbuterol, put up in measured doses(including packing for retail sale)
	0//							//	//			0/0/0	Single preparartions, HCG and luteinizing hormone put up in measured doses[including Growth hormone releasing peptide (GHRPs), Plummer Relin (growth hormone releasing peptide -2), CJC-1295 (CAS No. 863288-34-0), growth hormone releasing peptide -6, growth hormone releasing hormone and its analogues, growth Ji Sucu secretion agent, packing for retail sale]
	0//							//	//			0/0/0	Single preparations, peptide hormones[including retail packaging, and have dosage or retail packaging Ai Rui Mo Ruilin, A Bernard Relin, Bushrui Lin, Sha Ruilin, sea corticorelin, Iraq Mo Ruilin, Mo Ruilin, Mo Ruilin, Gore Bernard Relin, on behalf of triptorelin, Ge Ruilin (brain gut peptide) and its preparations) analogue.]
	0//							//	//			0/0/0	Monomer preparation dose containing leuprolide
	0//							//	//			0/0/0	Monomer preparation containing dose of DHEA therapy
	0//							//	//			0/0/0	Sera gonadotrophin, chorionic gonadotrophin for veterinary purposes (including in forms or packing for retail sale)
	0//							//	//			0/0/0	Anti — cancer drug preparations (excluding cancer adjuncts)
	0//							//	//		//	0/0/0	Other formulations containing follistatin in prescribed doses
	0//							//	//		//	0/0/0	Other prescribed doses containing maxillin
	0//							//	//		//	0/0/0	Inhalation of iloprost solution, tranquilizer injection or recombinant human growth hormone injection (measured doses or packings for retail sale)
	0//							//	//			0/0/0	Other medicines that have been dosed with hormones or products of heading 2937 (without antibiotics, including retail packaging)(Tax number due to separation of anticancer drugs)
													-Other, containing alkaloids or derivatives thereof:
													--Containing ephedrine or its salts
	0/0/0	0	0	0	0	0	0	0//0	0/0/			0/0/0	Ephedrine Hydrochloride Tablets, ephedrine hydrochloride injection, ephedrine sulfate tablets
	0/0/0	0	0	0	0	0	0	0//0	0/0/			0/0/0	Other preparations containing ephedrine and its salts, put up in measured doses or in forms or packings for retail sale
	0/0/0	0	0	0	0	0	0	0//0	0/0/			0/0/0	Other drugs containing ephedrine and its salts, put up in measured doses or in forms or packings for retail sale
													--Containing pseudoephedrine (*INN*) or its salts
	0/0/0	0	0	0	0	0	0	0//0	0/0/			0/0/0	Pseudoephedrine Hydrochloride Tablets
	0/0/0	0	0	0	0	0	0	0//0	0/0/			0/0/0	Other preparations containing pseudoephedrine and its salts, put up in measured doses or in forms or packings for retail sale

税则号列		货品名称〔CIQ扩展编码及品名—T2表示见附表2〕	最惠(%)	暂定税率	普通	增值/消费	出口退税	计量单位	监管条件	检验检疫	特殊证件对美关税
3004.4200	90	其他含有伪麻黄碱及其盐的药品(已配定剂量或制成零售包装)〔998药品,999其他化工产品〕	5		30	13/	13	千克	Q		1/
3004.4300		--含有去甲麻黄碱及其盐									
3004.4300	10	去甲麻黄碱及其盐的单方制剂(已配定剂量或制成零售包装)〔998药品,999其他化工产品〕	5		30	13/	13	千克	I		1/
3004.4300	90	其他含有去甲麻黄碱及其盐的药品(已配定剂量或制成零售包装)〔998药品,999其他化工产品〕	5		30	13/	13	千克	Q		1/
3004.4900		--其他									
3004.4900	10	含有奎宁或其盐的药品(已配定剂量或制成零售包装)〔998药品,999其他化工产品〕	5		35	13/	13	千克	Q		1/
3004.4900	20	含可待因及衍生物及盐的复方制剂(已配定剂量或制成零售包装)〔998药品,999其他化工产品〕	5		30	13/	13	千克	I		1/
3004.4900	31	丁丙诺啡透皮贴剂(包括其衍生物,已配定剂量或制成零售包装)〔998药品,999其他化工产品〕	5		30	13/	13	千克	I		1/
3004.4900	39	其他含生物碱类精神药品的单方制剂(包括其衍生物,已配定剂量或制成零售包装)〔998药品,999其他化工产品〕	5		30	13/	13	千克	I		1/
3004.4900	40	含生物碱类麻醉药品的单方制剂(包括其衍生物,已配定剂量或制成零售包装)〔998药品,999其他化工产品〕	5		30	13/	13	千克	I		1/
3004.4900	50	吗啡阿托品注射液〔998药品,999其他化工产品〕	5		30	13/	13	千克	I		1/
3004.4900	61	含有氨酚氢可酮片或其盐〔998药品,999其他化工产品〕	5		30	13/	13	千克	I		1/
3004.4900	62	含有麦角胺咖啡因片/安钠咖或其盐〔998药品,999其他化工产品〕	5		30	13/	13	千克	I		1/
3004.4900	63	阿桔片、复方甘草片(含阿片粉,已配定剂量或制成零售包装)〔998药品,999其他化工产品〕	5		30	13/	13	千克	I		1/
3004.4900	70	氨酚双氢可待因片〔998药品,999其他化工产品〕	5		30	13/	13	千克	I		1/
3004.4900	91	具有抗癌作用的含有生物碱及其衍生物的药品(混合或非混合,治病或防病用已配定剂量或零售包装)〔999〕	5	0	30	3/	13	千克	Q		1/
3004.4900	92	噻托溴铵粉吸入剂、噻托溴铵喷雾剂、吸入用复方异丙托溴铵溶液、异丙托溴铵气雾剂(已配定剂量或制成零售包装)	5	0	30	13/	13	千克	Q		/
3004.4900	99	其他含有生物碱及其衍生物的药品(已配定剂量或制成零售包装)〔301其他化工产品,999药品〕	5		30	13/	13	千克	Q		1/
3004.5000		-其他,含有维生素或税目29.36所列产品〔999〕	0		40	13/	13	千克	Q		1/
		-其他,含有本章子目注释二所列抗疟疾活性成分的:									
3004.6010		---含有青蒿素及其衍生物〔998药品,999其他化工产品〕	0		30	13/	13	千克	Q		1/5
3004.6090		---其他									
3004.6090	10	含有磺胺类的混合药品(已配定剂量或制成零售包装)〔998药品,999其他化工产品〕	0		30	13/	13	千克	Q		1/5
3004.6090	21	含濒危动植物成分的中式成药(已配定剂量或零售包装)〔998药品,999其他化工产品〕	0		30	13/	0	千克	EFQ		1/5
3004.6090	29	含其他成分的中式成药(已配定剂量或零售包装)〔998药品,999其他化工产品〕	0		30	13/	13	千克	Q		1/5
3004.6090	30	其他含濒危野生动植物成分的药品(已配定剂量或零售包装)〔998药品,999其他化工产品〕	0		30	13/	0	千克	EFQ		1/5
3004.6090	90	其他含有本章子目注释二所列抗疟疾活性成分的药品(已配定剂量或零售包装)〔998药品,999其他化工产品〕	0		30	13/	13	千克	Q		1/5
		-其他:									
3004.9010		---含有磺胺类〔999〕	0		40	13/	13	千克	Q		1/
3004.9020		---含有联苯双酯〔999〕	4		30	13/	13	千克	Q		1/
		---中式成药:									
3004.9051		----中药酒									
3004.9051	10	含濒危动植物成分的中药酒(已配定剂量或零售包装)〔101中药酒,102保健食品,999已配定剂量或零售包装〕	0		30	13/	0	千克	FE		1/5
3004.9051	90	含其他成分的中药酒(已配定剂量或零售包装)〔101中药酒,102具有保健食品批准文号,103其他化工产品,999已配定剂量或零售包装〕	0		30	13/	13	千克			1/5
3004.9052		----片仔癀〔101其他化工产品,999已配定剂量或零售包装〕	3		30	13/	13	千克	QFE		1/
3004.9053		----白药									

协定税率 %										特惠税率 %			Article Description
亚太5国	东/冰/格	巴基斯坦	韩国	瑞士	哥达	秘鲁	澳大利亚	新西/坡/智	港/澳/台	亚太2国	老/柬/缅	36/3/1	
	0/0/0	0	0	0	0	0	0	0//0	0/0/			0/0/0	Other drugs containing pseudoephedrine and its salts, put up in measured doses or in forms or packings for retail sale
													--Containing norephedrine or its salts
	0/0/0	0	0	0	0	0	0	0//0	0/0/			0/0/0	Preparations cathine and its salts, put up in measured doses, packings for retail sale
	0/0/0	0	0	0	0	0	0	0//0	0/0/			0/0/0	Other drugs containing norephedrine and salts, put up in measured doses, packings for retail sale
													--Other
	0/0/0	0	0	0	0	0	0	0//0	0/0/			0/0/0	Medicaments containing quinine or its salts, put up in measured doses, packings for retail sale
	0/0/0	0	0	0	0	0	0	0//0	0/0/			0/0/0	Compound preparations, containing codeine, its derivatives and salts, put up in measured doses, packings for retail sale
	0/0/0	0	0	0	0	0	0	0//0	0/0/			0/0/0	Buprenorphine Transdermal patch, and its salts, put up in measured doses, packings for retail sale
	0/0/0	0	0	0	0	0	0	0//0	0/0/			0/0/0	Other single preparations, containing alkaloids spirit drug and its derivatives, put up in measured doses, packings for retail
	0/0/0	0	0	0	0	0	0	0//0	0/0/			0/0/0	Single preparations, containing alkaloids narcotic drugs and its derivatives, put up in measured doses, packings for retail sale
	0/0/0	0	0	0	0	0	0	0//0	0/0/			0/0/0	Morphine and atropine sulfate injection
	0/0/0	0	0	0	0	0	0	0//0	0/0/			0/0/0	Medicaments containing paracetamol and hydrocodone bitartrate tablet or its salt
	0/0/0	0	0	0	0	0	0	0//0	0/0/			0/0/0	Medicaments containing ergotamine and caffeine tablet or caffeine and sodium benzoate or its salt
	0/0/0	0	0	0	0	0	0	0//0	0/0/			0/0/0	Compound Platycodon and Liquorice tablets? put up in measured doses or in forms of packings for retail sale
	0/0/0	0	0	0	0	0	0	0//0	0/0/			0/0/0	Paracetamol and Dihydrocodeine Tartrate Tablets
	0/0/0	0	0	0	0	0	0	0//0	0/0/			0/0/0	Drugs containing alkaloids and their derivatives that have an anticancer effect (mixed or non－mixed, administrated dose or retail package for treatment or prevention)
	0/0/0	0	0	0	0	0	0	0//0	0/0/		//	0/0/0	Tiotropium Bromide Powder for Inhalation, Tiotropium Bromide Spray, Compound Ipratropium Bromide Solution for Inhalation, Ipratropium Bromide Aerosol (fixed dose or made retail packaging)
	0/0/0	0	0	0	0	0	0	0//0	0/0/			0/0/0	Other medicines containing alkaloids and their derivatives (in formulated dose or in retail packaging)
	0//							//	//			0/0/0	-Other, containing vitamins or other products of heading 29.36
													--Other, containing antimalarial active principles described in Subheading Note 2 to this Chapter:
	0//							//	//			0/0/0	---Containing artemisinins and their derivatives
													---Other
	0//							//	//			0/0/	Medicaments containing sulfa drugs, put up in measured doses, packings for retail sale
	0//							//	//			0/0/	Medicaments of Chinese style, containing endangered animals or vegetables, put up in measured doses, packings for retail sale
	0//							//	//			0/0/	Medicaments of Chinese style, containing other composition, put up in measured doses, packings for retail sale
	0//							//	//			0/0/	Other medicaments of Chinese style, containing endangered animals or vegetables, put up in measured doses, packings for retail sale
	0//							//	//			0/0/	Other medicaments, containing antimalarial active principles described in Subheading Note 2 to this Chapter, put up in measured doses, packings for retail sale
													-Other:
	0//							//	//			0/0/0	---Containing sulfa drugs
2	0/0/0	0	0	0	0	0	0	0//0	0/0/			0/0/0	---Containing biphenyl dicarbxybte
													---Medicaments of Chinese type:
													----Medicated liquors or wines
	0//							//	//			0/0/0	Medicated liquors or wines, containing composition of endangered animals or plants, (put up in measured doses or in forms or packings for retail sale)
	0//							//	//			0/0/0	Medicated liquors or wines, containing other composition(put up in measured doses or in forms or packings for retail sale)
1.5	0/0/0	0	0	0	0	0	0	0//0	0/0/			0/0/0	----Pien Tzu Huang
													----Bai Yao

税则号列		货品名称〔CIQ 扩展编码及品名－T2 表示见附表 2〕	最惠(%)	暂定税率	普通	增值/消费	出口退税	计量单位	监管条件	检验检疫	特殊证件对美关税
3004.9053	10	含天然麝香的白药(已配定剂量或零售包装)〔999〕	3		30	13/	13	千克	FEQ		1/
3004.9053	90	含人工麝香的白药(已配定剂量或零售包装)〔999〕	3		30	13/	13	千克	Q		1/
3004.9054		----清凉油〔101 其他化工产品,999 已配定剂量或零售包装〕	0		30 0	13/	13	千克	Q		1/5
3004.9055		----安宫牛黄丸									
3004.9055	10	含天然麝香的安宫牛黄丸(已配定剂量或零售包装)〔999〕	3		30	13/	0	千克	QFE		1/
3004.9055	90	其他安宫牛黄丸(已配定剂量或零售包装)〔101 其他化工产品,999 已配定剂量或零售包装〕	3		30	13/	13	千克	Q		1/
3004.9059		----其他									
3004.9059	10	含濒危动植物成分的中式成药(已配定剂量或零售包装)〔999〕	0		30	13/	0	千克	QFE		1/
3004.9059	90	含其他成分的中式成药(已配定剂量或零售包装)〔101 其他化工产品,999 已配定剂量或零售包装〕	0		30	13/	13	千克	Q		1/
3004.9090		---其他									
3004.9090	10	含濒危野生动植物成分的药品(已配定剂量或零售包装,不含紫杉醇)〔999〕	0		30	13/	0	千克	FEQ		1/
3004.9090	20	含紫杉醇成分的药品(已配定剂量或制成零售包装)〔999〕	0		30	3/	0	千克	EFQ		1/
3004.9090	30	其他含第 29 章麻醉药品的单方制剂(已配定剂量或制成零售包装)〔101 其他化工产品,999 已配定剂量或制成零售包装〕	0		30	13/	13	千克	I		1/
3004.9090	41	地芬诺酯复方制剂(已配定剂量或制成零售包装)〔101 其他化工产品,999 已配定剂量或制成零售包装〕	0		30	13/	13	千克	I		1/
3004.9090	49	其他含第 29 章精神药品的单方制剂(已配定剂量或制成零售包装)〔101 其他化工产品,999 已配定剂量或制成零售包装〕	0		30	13/	13	千克	I		1/
3004.9090	50	含右丙氧芬及其盐的复方制剂(已配定剂量或制成零售包装)〔999〕	0		30	13/	13	千克	I		1/
3004.9090	60	复方樟脑酊(含阿片酊、樟脑、苯甲酸、八角茴香油等,包括零售包装)〔999〕	0		30	13/	13	千克	I		1/
3004.9090	71	已配剂量含雄甾-4-烯-3α,17β-二醇[4-雄烯二醇(3α,17β)]的单方制剂(包括零售包装)〔999〕	0		30	13/	13	千克	L		1/
3004.9090	72	已配剂量含雄甾-5-烯-3α,17α-二醇[5-雄烯二醇(3α,17α)]的单方制剂(包括零售包装)〔999〕	0		30	13/	13	千克	L		1/
3004.9090	73	已配剂量含雄甾-5-烯-3α,17β-二醇[5-雄烯二醇(3α,17β)]的单方制剂(包括零售包装)〔999〕	0		30	13/	13	千克	L		1/
3004.9090	74	已配剂量含 5α-雄烷-3α,17α-二醇(阿法雄烷二醇)或雄甾-4-烯-3α,17α-二醇[4-雄烯二醇(3α,17α)]的单方制剂(包括零售包装)〔999〕	0		30	13/	13	千克	L		1/
3004.9090	75	已配剂量含 5α-雄烷-3β,17β-二醇(倍他雄烷二醇)的单方制剂(包括零售包装)〔999〕	0		30	13/	13	千克	L		1/
3004.9090	77	含表雄酮(3β－羟基－5α－雄烷－17－酮)的单方制剂(已配剂量或制成零售包装)〔101 其他化工产品,999 已配剂量或制成零售包装〕	0		30	13/	13	千克	L		1/
3004.9090	78	已配剂量含齐帕特罗的单方制剂(包括零售包装)〔999〕	0		30	13/	13	千克	L		1/
3004.9090	79	已配剂量含表睾酮的单方制剂(包括零售包装)〔999〕	0		30	13/	13	千克	L		1/
3004.9090	81	兽用已配剂量含右旋糖苷铁、替泊沙林、布他磷制剂(包括零售包装)〔999〕	0		30	13/	13	千克	R		1/
3004.9090	82	兽用已配剂量含硝碘酚腈、氟尼辛葡甲胺、美洛昔康制剂(包括零售包装)〔999〕	0		30	13/	13	千克	R		1/
3004.9090	83	含 1－表雄酮(3β－羟基－5α－雄甾－1－烯－17－酮)的单方制剂(包括零售包装)	0		30	13/	13	千克	L		/

协定税率 %										特惠税率 %			Article Description
亚太5国	东/冰/格	巴基斯坦	韩国	瑞士	哥达	秘鲁	澳大利亚	新西/坡/智	港/澳/台	亚太2国	老/柬/缅	36/3/1	
1.5	0/0/0	0	0	0	0	0	0	0//0	0/0/			0/0/0	Bai Yao, containing natural musk (put up in measured doses or in form or packing for retail sale)
1.5	0/0/0	0	0	0	0	0	0	0//0	0/0/			0/0/0	Bai Yao, containing artificial musk (put up in measured doses or in form or packing for retail sale)
	0//							//	//			0/0/0	----Essential balm
													----Angong niuhuang pills
1.5	0/0/0	0	0	0	0	0	0	0//0	0/0/			0/0/0	Angongniuhuang pills, containing natural musk (put up in measured doses or in form or packings for retail sale)
1.5	0/0/0	0	0	0	0	0	0	0//0	0/0/			0/0/0	Other angongniuhuang pills, (put up in measured doses or in form or packings for retail sale)
													----Other
	0//							//	//			0/0/0	Medicaments of Chinese style, containing composition of endangered animals or plants (put up in measured doses or in forms or packings for retail sale)
	0//							//	//			0/0/0	Medicaments of Chinese style, containing other composition (put up in measured doses or in forms or packings for retail sale)
													---Other
	0//							//	//			0/0/	Medicaments containing composition of endangered animals or plants (not containing taxinol, put up in measured doses or in forms or packings for retail sale)
	0//							//	//			0/0/	Medicaments containing taxinol (put up in measured doses or in forms or packings for retail sale)
	0//							//	//			0/0/	Other single preparations containing narcotic drngs of Chapter 29 (put up in measured doses or in forms or packings for retail sale)
	0//							//	//			0/0/	Compound preparations, containing diphenoxylate (put up in measured doses and in forms or packing for retail sale)
	0//							//	//			0/0/	Other single preparations , containing psychotropic substances of Chapter 29 (put up in measured doses and in forms or packing for retail sale)
	0//							//	//			0/0/	Compound preparations, containing propoxyphene and its salts (put up in measured doses or in forms or packings for retail sale)
	0//							//	//			0/0/	Compound camphor tincture (containing opium tincture, camphor benzoic acid, star-anise oil, including in forms or packing for retail sale)
	0//							//	//			0/0/	Single preparartions, androst-4-allyl-3α, 17β-estradi [4-androstene-glycol(3α, 17β)], put up in measured doses (including in forms or packing for retail sale)
	0//							//	//			0/0/	Single preparartions, androst-5-allyl-3α, 17α-estradi [5-androstene-glycol(3α, 17α)], put up in measured doses (including in forms or packing for retail sale)
	0//							//	//			0/0/	Single preparartions, androst-5-allyl-3α, 17β-estradi [5-androstene-glycol(3α, 17β)], put up in measured doses (including in forms or packing for retail sale)
	0//							//	//			0/0/	Single preparations, containting 5α-androstane-3α, 17α-diol or androst-4-allyl-3α, 17α-estradi [4-androstene-glycol (3α, 17α)], put up in measured doses (including in forms or packing for retail sale)
	0//							//	//			0/0/	Single preparations, containting 5α-androstan-3β, 17β-estradi, put up in measured doses (including in forms or packing for retail sale)
	0//							//	//			0/0/	Single preparations, containting androsterone (3β-hydroxy-5α-androstane-17-ketone), put up in measured doses (including in forms or packing for retail sale)
	0//							//	//			0/0/	Single preparations, containting zilpaterol, put up in measured doses (including in forms or packing for retail sale)
	0//							//	//			0/0/	Single preparations, containting epitestosterone, put up in measured doses (including in forms or packing for retail sale)
	0//							//	//			0/0/	Preparations containting iron dextran, tepoxalin, butafosfan for veterinary purposes, put up in measured doses (including in forms or packing for retail sale)
	0//							//	//			0/0/	Preparations containting nitroxinil, flunixin meglumine, meloxicam for veterinary purposes, put up in measured doses (including in forms or packingfor retail sale)
	0//							//	//		//	0/0/	Single formulation containing 1－epiandrone (3 β － hydroxy－5 α － androsterol－1－ene－17－one) (including retail packaging)

税则号列		货品名称〔CIQ 扩展编码及品名－T2 表示见附表 2〕	最惠(%)	暂定税率	普通	增值/消费	出口退税	计量单位	监管条件	检验检疫	特殊证件对美关税
3004.9090	91	含 FG-4592(CAS 号 808118-40-3,一种缺氧诱导因子-脯氨酸羟化酶抑制剂)的已配定剂量的制剂(包括零售包装)〔999〕	0		30	13/	13	千克	Q		1/
3004.9090	92	已配剂量含 5α-雄烷-2-烯-17-酮的单方制剂(包括零售包装)〔999〕	0		30	13/	13	千克	Q		1/
3004.9090	93	抗(防)癌药品制剂(不含癌症辅助治疗药品)〔999〕	0		30	3/	13	千克	Q		1/
3004.9090	94	已配剂量含 2－雄烯醇(5α－雄甾－2－烯－17－醇)的单方制剂〔999〕	0		30	13/	13	千克	L		/
3004.9090	95	已配剂量含 3－雄烯醇(5α－雄甾－3－烯－17－醇)的单方制剂〔999〕	0		30	13/	13	千克	L		/
3004.9090	96	已配剂量含 3－雄烯酮(5α－雄甾－3－烯－17－酮)的单方制剂〔999〕	0		30	13/	13	千克	L		/
3004.9090	97	波生坦片、安立生坦片、利奥西呱片、马昔藤坦片、吡非尼酮胶囊、乙磺酸尼达尼布软胶囊、注射用伊米苷酶、注射用阿糖苷酶 α、麦格司他胶囊、盐酸沙丙蝶呤片、青霉胺片、利鲁唑片(已配定计量或制成零售包装)	0		30	3/		千克	Q		/
3004.9090	99	其他已配定剂量的药品(包括零售包装)〔101 鸡眼水,102 硫汞白癫疯擦药,999 包括零售包装〕	0		30	13/	13	千克	Q		1/
30.05		**软填料、纱布、绷带及类似物品(例如,敷料、橡皮膏、泥罨剂),经过药物浸涂或制成零售包装供医疗、外科、牙科或兽医用:**									
		-胶粘敷料及有胶粘涂层的其他物品:									
3005.1010		---橡皮膏〔101 其他化工产品,999 制成零售包装供医疗、外科、牙科或兽医用〕	5		70	13/	13	千克			1/35
3005.1090		---其他〔101 其他化工产品,999 经药物浸涂或制成零售包装,供医疗、外科、牙科或兽医用〕	5		35	13/	13	千克			1/15
		-其他:									
3005.9010		---药棉、纱布、绷带〔999〕	5		70	13/	13	千克			1/15
3005.9090		---其他〔101 其他化工产品,999 经药物浸涂或制成零售包装,供医疗、外科、牙科或兽医用〕	5		35	13/	13	千克			1/15
30.06		**本章注释四所规定的医药用品:**									
3006.1000		-无菌外科肠线、类似的无菌缝合材料(包括外科或牙科用无菌可吸收缝线)及外伤创口闭合用的无菌粘合胶布;无菌昆布及无菌昆布塞条;外科或牙科用无菌吸收性止血材料;外科或牙科用无菌抗粘连阻隔材料,不论是否可吸收〔101 其他化工产品,999 无菌吸收性止血材料,无菌抗粘连阻隔材料,外伤创口闭合用无菌粘合胶布〕	5		30	13/	13	千克			1/10
3006.2000		-血型试剂〔999〕	3		20	13/	13	千克	AB	VW	1/13
3006.3000		-X 光检查造影剂;用于病人的诊断试剂〔101 其他化工产品,102 医用诊断试剂〕	4		30	13/	13	千克	ABQ	VW	1/34
3006.4000		-牙科粘固剂及其他牙科填料;骨骼粘固剂〔101 其他化工产品,999 包括骨骼粘固剂〕	5		30	13/	13	千克			1/20
3006.5000		-急救药箱、药包〔101 其他化工产品,999〕	5		30	13/	13	千克			1/20
		-以激素,税目 29.37 的其他产品或杀精子剂为基本成分的化学避孕药物:									
3006.6010		---以激素为基本成分的避孕药〔101 其他化工产品,999〕	0		0	0/	0	千克	Q		1/25
3006.6090		---其他〔101 其他化工产品,999 以品目 2937 的其他产品或杀精子剂为基本成分〕	0		0	0/	0	千克	Q		1/
3006.7000		-专用于人类或作兽药用的凝胶制品,作为外科手术或体检时躯体部位的润滑剂,或者作为躯体和医疗器械之间的耦合剂〔999〕	6.5		30	13/	13	千克			1/21.5
		-其他:									
3006.9100		--可确定用于造口术的用具〔101 其他化工产品,999〕	10		80	13/	13	千克			1/40
3006.9200		--废药物〔101 其他化工产品,999 超过有效保存期等原因而不适于原用途的药品〕	5		30	13/	13	千克	9		1/

协定税率 %										特惠税率 %			Article Description
亚太5国	东/冰/格	巴基斯坦	韩国	瑞士	哥达	秘鲁	澳大利亚	新西/坡/智	港/澳/台	亚太2国	老/柬/缅	36/3/1	
	0//							//	//			0/0/	With FG-4592 (CAS 808118-40-3, a kind of hypoxia inducible factor - prolinehydroxylase inhibitors) have been preparations dosage (including retail wrapping)
	0//							//	//			0/0/	Medicaments containing 5α-androstane-2-ene-17-ketone, put up in measured doses(including in forms or packings for retail sale)
	0//							//	//			0/0/	Anti—cancer drug preparations (excluding cancer adjuncts)
	0//							//	//		//	0/0/	Formula containing 2—androstenol (5alpha—androsterol—2—ene—17—ol) in prescribed dose
	0//							//	//		//	0/0/	Formula containing 3—androstenol (5alpha—androsterol—3—ene—17—ol) in prescribed dose
	0//							//	//		//	0/0/	Formula containing 3—androstenone (5alpha—androsterone—3—ene—17—one) in prescribed dose
	0//							//	//		//	0/0/	Bosentan Tablets, Antibiotics Tablets, Leossie Tablets, Maxitengtan Tablets, Pifenidone Capsules, Nidanib Ethylsulfonate Soft Capsules, Imidase for Injection, Arabidase Alpha for Injection, Magistrate Capsules, Salpropterin Hydrochloride Tablets, Penicillamine Tablets and Riluzole Tablets(measured doses or packings for retail sale)
	0//							//	//			0/0/	Other equipped with fixed dose drug (including retail wrapping)
													Wadding, gauze, bandages and similar articles (for example, dressings, adhesive plasters, poultices), impregnated or coated with pharmaceutical substances or put up in forms or packings for retail sale for medical, surgical, dental or veterinary purposes:
													-Adhesive dressings and other articles having an adhesive layer:
4	0/0/0	0	0	0	0	0	0	0//0	0/0/			0/0/0	---Adhesive plasters
	0//0	0	0	0	0	0	0	0//0	0/0/			0/0/0	---Other
													-Other:
3	0/0/0	0	0	0	0	0	0	0//0	0/0/			0/0/0	---Absorbent cotton, gauze, bandages
	0//0	0	0	0	0	0	0	0//0	0/0/			0/0/0	---Other
													Pharmaceutical goods specified in Note 4 to this Chapter:
	0/0/0	0	0	0	0	0	0	0//0	0/0/			0/0/0	-Sterile surgical catgut, similar sterile suture materials (including sterile absorbable surgical or donfal yams) and sterile tissue adhesives for surgical wound closure; sterile laminaria and sterile laminaria tents; sterile absorbable surgical or dental haemostatics; sterile surgical or dontal adhesion borriers, whether or not absorbable
	0/0/0	0	0	0.9	0	0	0	0//0	0/0/			0/0/0	-Blood-grouping reagents
	0/0/0	0	0	0	0	0	0	0//0	0/0/			0/0/0	-Opacifying preparations for X-ray examinations; diagnostic reagents designed to be administered to the patient
	0/0/0	0	2	0	0	0	0	0//0	0/0/			0/0/0	-Dental cements and other dental fillings; bone reconstruction cements
	0/0/0	0	0	0	0	0	0	0//0	0/0/			0/0/0	-First-aid boxes and kits
													-Chemical contraceptive preparations based on hormones on other products of heading No. 29. 37 or on spermicides:
												0/0/0	---Contraceptive preparations based on hormones
												0/0/0	---Other
	0/0/0	4.5	0	0	0	0	0	0//0	0/0/			0/0/0	-Gel preparations designed to be used in human or veterinary medicine as a lubricant for parts of the body for surgical operations or physical examinations or as a coupling agent between the body and medical instruments
													-Other:
5	0/0/0	9.2	4	0	0	0	0	0/0/0	0/0/			0/0/0	--Appliamces identifiable for ostomy use
	0/0/0	0	0	0	0	0	0	0//0	0/0/			0/0/0	--Waste pharmaceuticals

第三十一章
肥　料

注释：

一、本章不包括：

(一)税目05.11的动物血；

(二)单独的已有化学定义的化合物(符合下列注释二(一)、三(一)、四(一)或五所规定的化合物除外)；

(三)税目38.24的每颗重量不低于2.5克的氯化钾培养晶体(光学元件除外)；氯化钾光学元件(税目90.01)。

二、税目31.02只适用于下列货品，但未制成税目31.05所述形状或包装：

(一)符合下列任何一条规定的货品：

1. 硝酸钠，不论是否纯净；
2. 硝酸铵，不论是否纯净；
3. 硫酸铵及硝酸铵的复盐，不论是否纯净；
4. 硫酸铵，不论是否纯净；
5. 硝酸钙及硝酸铵的复盐(不论是否纯净)或硝酸钙及硝酸铵的混合物；
6. 硝酸钙及硝酸镁的复盐(不论是否纯净)或硝酸钙及硝酸镁的混合物；
7. 氰氨化钙，不论是否纯净或用油处理；
8. 尿素，不论是否纯净。

(二)由上述(一)款任何货品相互混合的肥料。

(三)由氯化铵或上述(一)或(二)款任何货品与白垩、石膏或其他无肥效无机物混合而成的肥料。

(四)由上述(一)2或8项的货品或其混合物溶于水或液氨的液体肥料。

三、税目31.03只适用于下列货品，但未制成税目31.05所述形状或包装：

(一)符合下列任何一条规定的货品：

1. 碱性熔渣；
2. 税目25.10的天然磷酸盐，已焙烧或经过超出清除杂质范围的热处理；
3. 过磷酸钙(一过磷酸钙、二过磷酸钙或三过磷酸钙)；
4. 磷酸氢钙，按干燥无水产品重量计含氟量不低于0.2%。

(二)由上述(一)款的任何货品互相混合的肥料，不论含氟量多少。

(三)由上述(一)或(二)款的任何货品与白垩、石膏或其他无肥效无机物混合而成的肥料，不论含氟量多少。

四、税目31.04只适用于下列货品，但未制成税目31.05所述形状或包装：

(一)符合下列任何一条规定的货品：

1. 天然粗钾盐(例如，光卤石、钾盐镁矾及钾盐)；
2. 氯化钾，不论是否纯净，但上述注释一(三)所述的产品除外；
3. 硫酸钾，不论是否纯净；
4. 硫酸镁钾，不论是否纯净。

(二)由上述(一)款任何货品相互混合的肥料。

五、磷酸二氢铵及磷酸氢二铵(不论是否纯净)及其相互之间的混合物应归入税目31.05。

六、税目31.05所称"其他肥料"，仅适用于其基本成分至少含有氮、磷、钾中一种肥效元素的肥料用产品。

税则号列	货品名称〔CIQ扩展编码及品名—T2表示见附表2〕	最惠(%)	暂定税率	普通	增值/消费	出口退税	计量单位	监管条件	检验检疫	特殊证件对美关税
31.01	**动物或植物肥料，不论是否相互混合或经化学处理；动植物产品经混合或化学处理制成的肥料：**									
	---未经化学处理：									
3101.0011	----鸟粪〔999〕	3		11	9/	0	千克	AB	PQ	1/
3101.0019	----其他									
3101.0019　10	未经化学处理的森林凋落物(包括腐叶、腐根、树皮、树叶、树根等森林腐殖质)〔101栽培介质，102其他有机栽培介质，103植物有机肥，104其他动植物肥料〕	6.5		30	9/	0	千克	8AB	PQ	1/11.5
3101.0019　90	未经化学处理的其他动植物肥料〔101其他动物器官、细胞、培养基，102猪、牛、羊等偶蹄动物粪便，103马等奇蹄动物粪，104其他动物粪便，105动物性肥料、垃圾，106其他动物性废弃物，107植物有机肥，108其他动物源性肥料，109禽源性有机肥〕	6.5		30	9/	0	千克	AB	PQ	1/11.5
3101.0090	---其他									

Chapter 31
Fertilizers

Notes:

1. This Chapter does not cover:
   (a) Animal blood of heading No. 05.11;
   (b) Separate chemically defined compounds (other than those answering to the descriptions in Note 2(a), 3(a), 4(a) or 5 below); or
   (c) Cultured potassium chloride crystals (other than optical elements) weighing not less than 2.5g each, of heading No. 38.24; optical elements of potassium chloride (heading No. 90.01).
2. Heading No. 31.02 applies only to the following goods, provided that they are not put up in the forms or packages described in heading No. 31.05:
   (a) Goods which answer to one or other of the descriptions given below:
      (i) Sodium nitrate, whether or not pure;
      (ii) Ammonium nitrate, whether or not pure;
      (iii) Double salts, whether or not pure of ammonium sulphate and ammonium nitrate;
      (iv) Ammonium sulphate, whether or not pure;
      (v) Double salts (whether or not pure) or mixtures of calcium nitrate and ammonium nitrate;
      (vi) Double salts (whether or not pure) or mixtures of calcium nitrate and magnesium nitrate;
      (vii) Calcium cyanamide, whether or not pure or treated with oil;
      (viii) Urea, whether or not pure.
   (b) Fertilizers consisting of any of the goods described in (a) above mixed together.
   (c) Fertilizers consisting of ammonium chloride or of any of the goods described in (a) or (b) above mixed with chalk, gypsum or other inorganic nonfertilizing substances.
   (d) Liquid fertilizers consisting of the goods of subparagraph (a) (ii) or (viii) above, or of mixtures of those goods, in an aqueous or ammoniacal solution.
3. Heading No. 31.03 applies only to the following goods, provided that they are not put up in the forms or packages described in heading No. 31.05:
   (a) Goods which answer to one or other of the descriptions given below:
      (i) Basic slag;
      (ii) Natural phosphates of heading No. 25.10, calcined or further heat-treated than for the removal of impurities;
      (iii) Superphosphates (single, double or triple);
      (iv) Calcium hydrogenorthophosphate containing not less than 0.2% by weight of flourine calculated on the dry anhydrous product.
   (b) Fertilizers consisting of any of the goods described in (a) above mixed together, but with no account being taken of the fluorine content limit.
   (c) Fertilizers consisting of any of the goods described in (a) or (b) above, but with no account being taken of the fluorine content limit, mixed with chalk, gypsum or other inorganic non-fertilizing substances.
4. Heading No. 31.04 applies only to the following goods, provided that they are not put up in the forms or packages described in heading No. 31.05:
   (a) Goods which answer to one or other of the descriptions given below:
      (i) Crude natural potassium salts (for example, carnallite, kainite and sylvite);
      (ii) Potassium chloride, whether or not pure, except as provided in Note 1(c) above;
      (iii) Potassium sulphate, whether or not pure;
      (iv) Magnesium potassium sulphate, whether or not pure.
   (b) Fertilizers consisting of any of the goods described in (a) above mixed together.
5. Ammonium dihydrogenorthophosphate (monoammonium phosphate) and diammonium hydrogenorthophosphate (diammonium phosphate), whether or not pure, and intermixtures thereof, are to be classified in heading No. 31.05.
6. For the purposes of heading No. 31.05, the term "other fertilizers" applies only to products of a kind used as fertilizers and containing, as an essential constituent, at least one of the fertilizing elements nitrogen, phosphorus or potassium.

协定税率 %										特惠税率 %			
亚太5国	东/冰/格	巴基斯坦	韩国	瑞士	哥达	秘鲁	澳大利亚	新西/坡/智	港/澳/台	亚太2国	老/柬/缅	36/3/1	Article Description
													Animal or vegetable fertilizers, whether or not mixed together or chemically treated; fertilizers produced by the mixing or chemical treatment of animal or vegetable products:
													---Not chemically treated:
	0/0/0	0	0	0	0	0	0	0//0	0/0/			0/0/0	----Guano
													----Other
3.3	0/0/0	4.5	0	0	0	0	0	0//0	0/0/			0/0/0	Forest litter, not chemically treated (including rotten leaves, rotten roots, bark, leaves, roots and other forest humus)
3.3	0/0/0	4.5	0	0	0	0	0	0//0	0/0/			0/0/0	Other animal and vegetable fertilizer not chemically treated
													---Other

税则号列	货品名称〔CIQ扩展编码及品名－T2表示见附表2〕	最惠(%)	暂定税率	普通	增值/消费	出口退税	计量单位	监管条件	检验检疫	特殊证件对美关税
3101.0090 10	经化学处理的含动物源性成分(如粪、羽毛等)动植物肥料〔101其他动物器官、细胞、培养基,102猪、牛、羊等偶蹄动物粪便,103马等奇蹄动物粪,104其他动物粪便,105动物性肥料、垃圾,106其他动物性废弃物,107其他化工产品〕	4		11	9/	0	千克	AB	PQ	1/24
3101.0090 20	经化学处理的森林凋落物(包括腐叶、腐根、树皮、树叶、树根等森林腐殖质)〔101其他动物器官、细胞、培养基,102植物有机肥,103其他化工产品〕	4		11	9/	0	千克	8AB	PQ	1/24
3101.0090 90	经化学处理的其他动植物肥料〔101其他动物器官、细胞、培养基,102猪、牛、羊等偶蹄动物粪便,103马等奇蹄动物粪,104其他动物粪便,105动物性肥料、垃圾,106其他动物性废弃物,107植物有机肥,108其他动物源性肥料,109禽源性有机肥〕	4		11	9/	0	千克	AB	PQ	1/24
31.02	**矿物氮肥及化学氮肥:**									
3102.1000	-尿素,不论是否水溶液									
3102.1000 10	尿素(配额内,不论是否水溶液)〔101〕	T1	1	150	9/	0	千克	tA	M	1/26
3102.1000 90	尿素(配额外,不论是否水溶液)〔101饲料添加剂,102其他化工产品〕	50		150	9/	0	千克	A	M	1/75
	-硫酸铵,硫酸铵和硝酸铵的复盐及混合物:									
3102.2100	--硫酸铵〔101矿物源性饲料添加剂,102无检疫要求食品添加剂,103需申报仅用于工业用途不用于食品添加剂无检疫要求的化学品〕	4		11	9/	0	千克	7A	R	1/19
3102.2900	--其他〔999〕	4		11	9/	0	千克	7		1/9
3102.3000	-硝酸铵,不论是否水溶液〔301爆炸品,302氧化性物质〕	4		11	9/	0	千克	9k	M	1/9
3102.4000	-硝酸铵与碳酸钙或其他无肥效无机物的混合物〔999〕	4		11	9/	0	千克	7		1/9
3102.5000	-硝酸钠〔301氧化性物质,需申报仅用于工业用途不用于食品添加剂无检疫要求,302无检疫要求食品添加剂,303一般化学品,需申报仅用于工业用途不用于食品添加剂无检疫要求,304属于危险化学品的食品添加剂〕	4		11	9/	0	千克	7AB	MNS	1/34
3102.6000	-硝酸钙和硝酸铵的复盐及混合物〔999〕	4		11	9/	0	千克	7		1/9
3102.8000	-尿素及硝酸铵混合物的水溶液或氨水溶液〔999〕	4		11	9/	0	千克	7		1/9
	-其他,包括上述子目未列名的混合物:									
3102.9010	---氰氨化钙〔301遇水放出易燃气体的物质,302其他化工产品〕	4		11	9/	0	千克	7AB	MN	1/9
3102.9090	---其他〔999〕	4		11	9/	0	千克	7		1/34
31.03	**矿物磷肥及化学磷肥:**									
	-过磷酸钙:									
	--按重量计五氧化二磷(P205)含量在35%及以上:									
3103.1110	---重过磷酸钙〔999〕	4	1	11	9/	0	千克	7A	M	1/6
3103.1190	---其他〔999〕	4	1	11	9/	0	千克	7A	M	1/6
3103.1900	--其他〔999〕	4	1	11	9/	0	千克	7A	M	1/11
3103.9000	-其他〔999〕	4	1	11	9/	0	千克	7		1/6
31.04	**矿物钾肥及化学钾肥:**									
	-氯化钾:									
3104.2020	---纯氯化钾〔999〕	3		11	9/	0	千克	7A	M	1/33
3104.2090	---其他〔101矿物源性饲料添加剂,102化工产品,301需申报仅用于工业用途不用于食品添加剂无检疫要求的化学品〕	3	1	11	9/	0	千克	7A	R	1/31
3104.3000	-硫酸钾〔101矿物源性饲料添加剂,102化工产品〕	3	1	11	9/	0	千克	7A	M	1/31
	-其他:									
3104.9010	---光卤石、钾盐及其他天然粗钾盐〔999〕	3	1	11	9/	0	千克	7		1/6
3104.9090	---其他〔999〕	3	1	11	9/	0	千克	7		1/11
31.05	**含氮、磷、钾中两种或三种肥效元素的矿物肥料或化学肥料;其他肥料;制成片及类似形状或每包毛重不超过10千克的本章各项货品:**									
3105.1000	-制成片及类似形状或每包毛重不超过10千克的本章各项货品									
3105.1000 10	制成片状及类似形状或零售包装的硝酸铵(零售包装每包毛重不超过10千克)〔999〕	4	1	11	9/	0	千克	9		1/26
3105.1000 90	制成片状及类似形状或零售包装的第31章其他货品(零售包装每包毛重不超过10千克)〔999〕	4	1	11	9/	0	千克	7		1/26
3105.2000	-含氮、磷、钾三种肥效元素的矿物肥料或化学肥料									

协定税率 %										特惠税率 %			Article Description
亚太5国	东/冰/格	巴基斯坦	韩国	瑞士	哥达	秘鲁	澳大利亚	新西/坡/智	港/澳/台	亚太2国	老/柬/缅	36/3/1	
	0/0/0	0	2.4	0	0	0	0	0//0	0/0/			0/0/0	Animals or vegetable fertilizer, chemically treated, containing, compositions of animals' natural character
	0/0/0	0	2.4	0	0	0	0	0//0	0/0/			0/0/0	Forest litter, chemically treated (including rotten leaves, rotten roots, bark, leaves, roots and other forest humus)
	0/0/0	0	2.4	0	0	0	0	0//0	0/0/			0/0/0	Other vegetable fertilizere, chemical treated
													Mineral or chemical fertilizers, nitrogenous:
													-Urea, whether or not in aqueous solution
40	//	40							0/0/				Urea(whether or not in aqueous solution, in-quota)
40	//	40							0/0/				Urea(whether or not in aqueous solution, out -quota)
													-Ammonium sulphate; double salts and mixtures of ammonium sulphate and ammonium nitrate:
	0/0/0	0	0	0	0	0	0	0//0	0/0/			0/0/	--Ammonium sulphate
	0/0/0	0	0	0	0	0	0	0//0	0/0/			0/0/	--Other
	0/0/0	0	0	0	0	0	0	0//0	0/0/			0/0/	-Ammonium nitrate, whether or not in aqueous solution
	0/0/0	0	0	0	0	0	0	0//0	0/0/			0/0/	-Mixtures of ammonium nitrate with calcium carbonate or other inorganic nonfertilizing substances
	0/0/0	0	0	0	0	0	0	0//0	0/0/			0/0/	-Sodium nitrate
	0/0/0	0	0	0	0	0	0	0//0	0/0/			0/0/	-Double salts and mixtures of calcium nitrate and ammonium nitrate
	0/0/1.6	0	0	0	0	0	0	0//0	0/0/			0/0/	-Mixtures of urea and ammonium ni-trate in aqueous or ammoniacal solution
													-Other, including mixtures not specified in the foregoing subheadings:
	0/0/0	0	0	0	0	0	0	0//0	0/0/			0/0/	---Calcium cyanamide
	0/0/0	0	0	0	0	0	0	0//0	0/0/			0/0/	---Other
													Mineral or chemical fertilizers, phosphatic:
													-Superphosphates:
													--Phosphorus pentoxide (P205)≥35% by weight
	0/0/0	0	0	0	0	0	0	0//0	0/0/			0/0/	---Triple superphosphates
	0/0/0	0	0	0	0	0	0	0//0	0/0/			0/0/	---Other
	0/0/0	0	0	0	0	0	0	0//0	0/0/			0/0/	--Other
	0/0/1.6	0	0	0	0	0	0	0//0	0/0/			0/0/	-Other
													Mineral or chemical fertilizers, potassic:
													-Potassium chloride:
	0/0/0	0	0	0	0	0	0	0//0	0/0/			0/0/	---Pure potassium chloride(Potassium chloride≥99.5% by weigh)
	0/0/0	0	0	0	0	0	0	0//0	0/0/			0/0/	---Other
	0/0/0	0	1.8	0	0	0	0	0//0	0/0/			0/0/	-Potassium sulphate
													-Other:
	0/0/0	0	0	0	0	0	0	0//0	0/0/			0/0/	---Carnallite, sylvite and other crude natural potassium salts
	0/0/	0	0	0	0	0	0	0//0	0/0/			0/0/	---Other
													Mineral or chemical fertilizers containing two or three of the fertilizing elements nitrogen, phosphorus and potassium; other fertilizers; goods of this Chapter in tablets or similar forms or in packages of a gross weight not exceeding 10kg:
													-Goods of this Chapter in tablets or similar forms or in packages of a gross weight not exceeding 10kg
	0/0/0	0	0	0	0	0	0	0//0	0/0/			0/0/	Ammonium nitrate, goods of this in tablets or similar in forms or packages of a gross weight≤10kg
	0/0/0	0	0	0	0	0	0	0//0	0/0/			0/0/	Other goods of the chapter 31, in tablets or similar in forms or packages of a gross weight≤10kg
													-Mineral or chemical fertilizers containing the three fertilizing elements nitrogen, phosphorus and potassium

税则号列		货品名称〔CIQ 扩展编码及品名－T2 表示见附表 2〕	最惠(%)	暂定税率	普通	增值/消费	出口退税	计量单位	监管条件	检验检疫	特殊证件对美关税
3105.2000	10	化学肥料或矿物肥料(配额内,含氮、磷、钾三种肥效元素)〔999〕	T1	1	150	9/	0	千克	At	M	1/26
3105.2000	90	化学肥料或矿物肥料(配额外,含氮、磷、钾三种肥效元素)〔999〕	50		150	9/	0	千克	A	M	1/75
3105.3000		-磷酸氢二铵									
3105.3000	10	磷酸氢二铵(配额内)〔101 饲料添加剂,301 需申报仅用于工业用途不用于食品添加剂无检疫要求的化学品〕	T1	1	150	9/	0	千克	At	R	1/11
3105.3000	90	磷酸氢二铵(配额外)〔101 矿物源性饲料添加剂,102 化工产品,301 需申报仅用于工业用途不用于食品添加剂无检疫要求的化学品〕	50		150	9/	0	千克	A	R	1/60
3105.4000		-磷酸二氢铵及磷酸二氢铵与磷酸氢二铵的混合物〔101 矿物源性饲料添加剂,102 化工产品〕	4	1	11	9/	0	千克	7A	M	1/31
		-其他含氮、磷两种肥效元素的矿物肥料或化学肥料:									
3105.5100		--含有硝酸盐及磷酸盐〔301 其他危险化学品,302 无检疫要求的食品添加剂,303 属于危险化学品的食品添加剂〕	4	1	11	9/	0	千克	7A	M	1/6
3105.5900		--其他〔101 矿物源性饲料添加剂,102 化工产品〕	4	1	11	9/	0	千克	7A	M	1/11
3105.6000		-含磷、钾两种肥效元素的矿物肥料或化学肥料〔999〕	4	1	11	9/	0	千克	7A	M	1/26
		-其他:									
3105.9010		---有机-无机复混肥料〔999 其他化工产品,301 其他危险化学品〕	4	1	11	9/	0	千克	7A	M	1/11
3105.9090		---其他:〔999 其他化工产品,301 其他危险化学品〕	4	1	11	9/	0	千克	7A	M	1/26

协定税率 %										特惠税率 %			
亚太5国	东/冰/格	巴基斯坦	韩国	瑞士	哥达	秘鲁	澳大利亚	新西/坡/智	港/澳/台	亚太2国	老/柬/缅	36/3/1	Article Description
									0/0/				Mineral or chemical fertilizers containing the three fertilizing elemtnts nitrogen, phosphorus and potassium, in-quota
									0/0/				Mineral or chemical fertilizers (containing the three fertilizing elements nitrogen, phosphorus and potassium, out -quota)
													-Diammonium hydrogenorthophosphate (diammonium phosphate)
									0/0/				Diammonium hydrogenorthophosphate (diammonium phosphate), in-quota
									0/0/				Diammonium hydrogenorthophosphate (diammonium phosphate), out -quota
	0/0/0	0	0	0	0	0	0	0//0	0/0/			0/0/	-Ammonium dihydrogenorthophosphate (monoammonium phosphate) and mixtures thereof with diammonium hydrogenorthophosphate (diammonium phosphate)
													-Other mineral or chemical fertilizers containing the two fertilizing elements nitrogen and phosphorus:
	0/0/1.6	0	0	0	0	0	0	0//0	0/0/			0/0/	--Containing nitrates and phosphates
	0/0/1.6	0	0	0	0	0	0	0//0	0/0/			0/0/	--Other
	0/0/1.6	0	0	0	0	0	0	0//0	0/0/			0/0/	-Mineral or chemical fertilizers containing the two fertilizing elements phosphorus and potassium
													-Other:
	0/0/1.6	0	0	0	0	0	0	0//0	0/0/			0/0/	---Organic -iaorganic compound fertilizers.
	0/0/1.6	0	0	0	0	0	0	0//0	0/0/			0/0/	---Other:

第三十二章

鞣料浸膏及染料浸膏;鞣酸及其衍生物;染料、颜料及其他着色料;油漆及清漆;油灰及其他类似胶粘剂;墨水、油墨

注释:

一、本章不包括:

(一)单独的已有化学定义的化学元素及化合物(税目32.03及32.04的货品、税目32.06的用作发光体的无机产品、税目32.07所述形状的熔融石英或其他熔融硅石制成的玻璃及税目32.12的零售形状或零售包装的染料及其他着色料除外);

(二)税目29.36至29.39、29.41及35.01至35.04的鞣酸盐及其他鞣酸衍生物;

(三)沥青胶粘剂(税目27.15)。

二、税目32.04包括生产偶氮染料用的稳定重氮盐与偶合物的混合物。

三、税目32.03、32.04、32.05及32.06也包括以着色料为基本成分的制品(例如,税目32.06包括以税目25.30或第二十八章的颜料,金属粉片及金属粉末为基本成分的制品)。该制品是用作原材料着色剂的拼料。但以上税目不包括分散在非水介质中呈液状或浆状的制漆用颜料,例如,税目32.12的瓷漆及税目32.07、32.08、32.09、32.10、32.12、32.13及32.15的其他制品。

四、税目32.08包括由税目39.01至39.13所列产品溶于挥发性有机溶剂的溶液(胶棉除外),但溶剂重量必须超过溶液重量的50%。

五、本章所称"着色料",不包括作为油漆填料的产品,不论这些产品能否用于水浆涂料的着色。

六、税目32.12所称"压印箔",只包括用以压印诸如书本封面或帽带之类的薄片,这些薄片由以下材料构成:

(一)金属粉(包括贵金属粉)或颜料经胶水、明胶及其他黏合剂凝结而成的;或

(二)金属(包括贵金属)或颜料沉积于任何材料衬片上的。

税则号列	货品名称〔CIQ扩展编码及品名－T2表示见附表2〕	最惠(%)	暂定税率	普通	增值/消费	出口退税	计量单位	监管条件	检验检疫	特殊证件对美关税
32.01	**植物鞣料浸膏;鞣酸及其盐、醚、酯和其他衍生物:**									
3201.1000	-坚木浸膏〔999〕	5		35	13/	0	千克			1/30
3201.2000	-荆树皮浸膏〔999〕	6.5		35	13/	0	千克			1/11.5
	-其他:									
3201.9010	---其他鞣料浸膏									
3201.9010 10	其他濒危植物鞣料浸膏〔999〕	6.5		40	13/	0	千克	FE		1/36.5
3201.9010 90	其他植物鞣料浸膏〔999〕	6.5		40	13/	0	千克			1/36.5
3201.9090	---其他〔101食用单宁,102单宁酸,103固化单宁〕	6.5		35	13/	0	千克			1/36.5
32.02	**有机合成鞣料;无机鞣料;鞣料制剂,不论是否含有天然鞣料;预鞣用酶制剂:**									
3202.1000	-有机合成鞣料〔999〕	6.5		35	13/	0	千克			1/36.5
3202.9000	-其他									
3202.9000 10	无铬鞣料(不论是否含有天然鞣料,包括预鞣用酶制剂)〔999〕	6.5	3	35	13/	0	千克			1/33
3202.9000 90	其他无机鞣料、鞣料制剂等(不论是否含有天然鞣料,包括预鞣用酶制剂)〔999〕	6.5		35	13/	0	千克			1/36.5
32.03	**动植物质着色料(包括染料浸膏,但动物炭黑除外),不论是否已有化学定义;本章注释三所述的以动植物质着色料为基本成分的制品:**									
	---植物质着色料及以其为基本成分的制品:									
3203.0011	----天然靛蓝及以其为基本成分的制品〔301无检疫要求食品添加剂,302需申报仅用于工业用途不用于食品添加剂无检疫要求的化学品〕	6.5		80	13/	0	千克	A	R	1/16.5
3203.0019	----其他									
3203.0019 10	濒危植物质着色料及制品(制品是指以植物质着色料为基本成分的)〔101饲料添加剂,301其他危险化学品,需申报仅用于工业用途不用于食品添加剂无检疫要求,302无检疫要求食品添加剂,303一般化学品,需申报仅用于工业用途不用于食品添加剂无检疫要求,304属于危险化学品的食品添加剂〕	6.5		45	13/	0	千克	ABEF	RS	1/36.5

Chapter 32

Tanning or dyeing extracts; tannins and their derivatives; dyes, pigments and other colouring matter; paints and varnishes; putty and other mastics; inks

Notes:

1. This Chapter does not cover:
   (a) Separate chemically defined elements or compounds (except those of heading No. 32.03 or 32.04, inorganic products of a kind used as luminophores (heading No. 32.06), glass obtained from fused quartz or other fused silica in the forms provided for in heading No. 32.07, and also dyes and other colouring matter put up in forms or packings for retail sale, of heading No. 32.12);
   (b) Tannates or other tannin derivatives of products of headings No. 29.36 to 29.39, 29.41 or 35.01 to 35.04;
   (c) Mastics of asphalt or other bituminous mastics (heading No. 27.15).
2. Heading No. 32.04 includes mixtures of stabilized diazonium salts and couplers for the production of azo dyes.
3. Headings No. 32.03, 32.04, 32.05 and 32.06 apply also to preparations based on colouring matter (including, in the case of heading No. 32.06, colouring pigments of heading No. 25.30 or Chapter 28, metal flakes and metal powders), of a kind used for colouring any material or used as ingredi-ents in the manufacture of colouring preparations. The headings do not apply, however, to pigments dispersed in nonaqueous media, in liquid or paste form, of a kind used in the manufacture of paints, including enamels (heading No. 32.12), or to other preparations of heading No. 32.07, 32.08, 32.09, 32.10, 32.12, 32.13 or 32.15.
4. Heading No. 32.08 includes solutions (other than collodions) consisting of any of the products specified in headings No. 39.01 to 39.13 in volatile organic solvents when the weight of the solvent exceeds 50% of the weight of the solution.
5. The expression "colouring matter" in this Chapter does not include products of a kind used as extenders in oil paints, whether or not they are also suitable for colouring distempers.
6. The expression "stamping foils" in heading No. 32.12 applies only to thin sheets of a kind used for printing, for example, book covers or hat bands, and consisting of:
   (a) Metallic powder (including powder of precious metal) or pigment, agglomerated with glue, gelatin or other binder; or
   (b) Metal (including precious metal) or pigment, deposited on a supporting sheet of any material.

协定税率 %										特惠税率 %			Article Description
亚太5国	东/冰/格	巴基斯坦	韩国	瑞士	哥达	秘鲁	澳大利亚	新西/坡/智	港/澳/台	亚太2国	老/柬/缅	36/3/1	
													Tanning extracts of vegetable origin; tannins and their salts, ethers, esters and other derivatives:
	0/0/0	0	0	0	0	0	0	0//0	0/0/			0/0/	-Quebracho extract
	0/0/0	4.5	0	0	0	0	0	0//0	0/0/			0/0/	-Wattle extract
													-Other:
													---Other tanning extracts
	0/0/0	4.5	0	0	0	0	0	0//0	0/0/			0/0/	Other tanning extracts of endangered vegetable origin
	0/0/0	4.5	0	0	0	0	0	0//0	0/0/			0/0/	Other tanning extracts of vegetable origin
	0/0/0	4	0	0	0	0	0	0//0	0/0/			0/0/	---Other
													Synthetic organic tanning substances; inorganic tanning substances; tanning preparations, whether or not containing natural tanning substances; enzymatic preparations for pre-tanning:
	0/0/0	0	0	0	0	0	0	0//0	0/0/			0/0/	-Synthetic organic tanning substances
													-Other
	0/0/0	4	0	0	0	0	0	0//0	0/0/			0/0/	Chrome free tanning(whether or not containing natural substances, including enzyme preparation for pre tanning)
	0/0/0	4	0	0	0	0	0	0//0	0/0/			0/0/	Other inorganic tanning and tanning agents(whether or not containing natural substances, including enzyme preparation for pre tanning)
													Colouring matter of vegetable or animal origin (including dyeing extracts but excluding animal black), whether or not chemically defined; preparations as specified in Note 3 to this Chapter based on colouring matter of vegetable or animal origin:
													---Colouring matter of vegetable origin and preparations based thereon:
	0/0/0	4	0	0	0	2.3	0	0//0	0/0/			0/0/0	----Natural indigo and preparations based thereon
													----Other
	0/0/0	4	0	0	0	2.3	0	0//0	0/0/			0/0/0	Colouring matter and preparations based thereon of endangered vegetable origin

税则号列		货品名称〔CIQ 扩展编码及品名－T2 表示见附表 2〕	最惠(%)	暂定税率	普通	增值/消费	出口退税	计量单位	监管条件	检验检疫	特殊证件对美关税
3203.0019	90	其他植物质着色料及制品(制品是指以植物质着色料为基本成分的)〔101 饲料添加剂,301 其他危险化学品,需申报仅用于工业用途不用于食品添加剂无检疫要求,302 无检疫要求食品添加剂,303 一般化学品,需申报仅用于工业用途不用于食品添加剂无检疫要求,304 属于危险化学品的食品添加剂〕	6.5		45	13/	13	千克	AB	RS	1/36.5
3203.0020		---动物质着色料及以其为基本成分的制品[T2]	6.5		50	13/	13	千克	A	MR	1/11.5
32.04		**有机合成着色料,不论是否已有化学定义;本章注释三所述的以有机合成着色料为基本成分的制品;用作荧光增白剂或发光体的有机合成产品,不论是否已有化学定义:**									
		-有机合成着色料及本章注释三所述的以有机合成着色料为基本成分的制品:									
3204.1100		--分散染料及以其为基本成分的制品[T2]	6.5		35	13/	0	千克	AB	RS	1/36.5
3204.1200		--酸性染料(不论是否与金属络合)及以其为基本成分的制品;媒染染料及以其为基本成分的制品[T2]	6.5		35	13/	0	千克	AB	RS	1/36.5
3204.1300		--碱性染料及以其为基本成分的制品[T2]	6.5		35	13/	0	千克	AB	RS	1/36.5
3204.1400		--直接染料及以其为基本成分的制品[T2]	6.5		35	13/	0	千克	AB	RS	1/21.5
		--瓮染料(包括颜料用的)及以其为基本成分的制品:									
3204.1510		---合成靛蓝(还原靛蓝)〔101 靛蓝(无检疫要求食品添加剂),102 靛蓝铝色淀(无检疫要求食品添加剂),103 需申报仅用于工业用途不用于食品添加剂无检疫要求的化学品〕	6.5		35	13/	0	千克	A	R	1/16.5
3204.1590		---其他〔999〕	6.5		35	13/	0	千克			1/31.5
3204.1600		--活性染料及以其为基本成分的制品〔999〕	6.5		35	13/	0	千克			1/36.5
3204.1700		--颜料及以其为基本成分的制品〔999〕	6.5		35	13/	0	千克			1/26.5
3204.1700	10	彩色光刻胶用光刻胶颜料分散液	6.5	6.5	35	13/	0	千克			/28
3204.1700	90	其他颜料及以其为基本成分的制品	6.5		35	13/	0	千克			/31.5
		--其他,包括由子目号 3204.11 至 3204.19 中两个或多个子目所列着色料组成的混合物:									
		---硫化染料及以其为基本成分的制品:									
3204.1911		----硫化黑(硫化青)及以其为基本成分的制品〔999〕	6.5		35	13/	0	千克			1/36.5
3204.1919		----其他〔999〕	6.5		35	13/	0	千克			1/36.5
3204.1990		---其他[T2]	6.5		35	13/	0	千克	AB	RS	1/31.5
3204.2000		-用作荧光增白剂的有机合成产品〔301 其他危险化学品,302 其他化工产品〕	6.5		40	13/	13	千克	A	M	1/16.5
		-其他:									
3204.9010		---生物染色剂及染料指示剂〔999〕	6.5		20	13/	0	千克			1/31.5
3204.9020		---胡萝卜素及类胡萝卜素〔999 其他化工产品,998 无检疫要求食品添加剂〕	6.5		20	13/	13	千克			1/36.5
3204.9090		---其他〔999〕	6.5		40	13/	0	千克			1/31.5
32.05		**色淀;本章注释三所述的以色淀为基本成分的制品:**									
3205.0000		色淀;本章注释三所述的以色淀为基本成分的制品〔301 新红(无检疫要求食品添加剂),302 新红铝色淀(无检疫要求食品添加剂),303 需申报仅用于工业用途不用于食品添加剂无检疫要求的化学品〕	6.5		35	13/	0	千克	A	R	1/16.5
32.06		**其他着色料;本章注释三所述的制品,但税目 32.03、32.04 及 32.05 的货品除外;用作发光体的无机产品,不论是否已有化学定义:**									
		-以二氧化钛为基本成分的颜料及制品:									
		--以干物质计二氧化钛含量在 80%及以上的:									
3206.1110		---钛白粉〔999〕	6.5		30	13/	0	千克	4xy		1/21.5
3206.1190		---其他〔999〕	6.5		30	13/	0	千克			1/31.5
3206.1900		--其他〔999〕	10		30	13/	0	千克			1/25
3206.2000		-以铬化合物为基本成分的颜料及制品〔999〕	6.5		35	13/	0	千克			1/21.5
		-其他着色料及其他制品:									
3206.4100		--群青及以其为基本成分的制品〔999〕	6.5		35	13/	0	千克			1/36.5
		--锌钡白及以硫化锌为基本成分的其他颜料和制品:									
3206.4210		---锌钡白〔999〕	6.5		30	13/	0	千克			1/36.5
3206.4290		---其他〔999〕	6.5		30	13/	0	千克			1/31.5

协定税率 %										特惠税率 %			
亚太5国	东/冰/格	巴基斯坦	韩国	瑞士	哥达	秘鲁	澳大利亚	新西/坡/智	港/澳/台	亚太2国	老/柬/缅	36/3/1	Article Description
	0/0/0	4	0	0	0	2.3	0	0//0	0/0/			0/0/0	Other colouring matter of vegetable origin based thereon of vegetable origin
	0/0/0	4	0	0	0	2.3	0	0//0	0/0/			0/0/0	---Colouring matter of animal origin and preparations based thereon
													Synthetic organic colouring matter, whether or not chemically defined; preparations as specified in Note 3 to this Chapter based on synthetic organic colouring matter; synthetic organic products of a kind used as fluorescent brightening agents or as luminophores, whether or not chemically defined:
													-Synthetic organic colouring matter and preparations based thereon as specified in Note 3 to this Chapter:
4.2	0/0/0	0	0		0	0	0	0//0	0/0/			0/0/0	--Disperse dyes and preparations based thereon
4.2	0/0/0	0	0	3.4	0	0	0	0//0	0/0/0			0/0/0	--Acid dyes, whether or not premetallized, and preparations based thereon; mordant dyes and preparations based thereon
4.2	0/0/0	0	0	0	0	0	0	0//0	0/0/			0/0/0	--Basic dyes and preparations based thereon
4.2	0/0/0	0	0	2	0	0	0	0//0	0/0/0			0/0/0	--Direct dyes and preparations based thereon
													--Vat dyes (including those usable in that state as pigments) and preparations based thereon:
4.2	0/0/0	0	2.6	0	0	0	0	0//0	0/0/			0/0/0	---Synthetic indigo(reductive indigo)
4.2	0/0/0	0	2.6	0	0	0	0	0//0	0/0/			0/0/0	---Other
4.2	0/0/0	0	0	3.4	0	0	0	0//0	0/0/0			0/0/0	--Reactive dyes and preparations based thereon
4.2	0/0/0	0	0	2.6	0	0	0	0//0	0/0/0			0/0/0	--Pigments and preparations based thereon
4.2	0/0/0	0	0	2	0	0	0	0//0	0/0/0		//	0/0/0	Pigment dispersion of photoresist for color photoresist
4.2	0/0/0	0	0	2	0	0	0	0//0	0/0/0		//	0/0/0	Other pigments and products based on them
													--Other, including mixtures of colouring matter of two or more of the subheadings No. 3204. 11 to 3204. 19:
													---Sulphur dyes and preparations based thereon:
4.2	0/0/0	0	2.6	0	0	0	0	0//0	0/0/			0/0/0	----Sulphur black and preparations based thereon
4.2	0/0/0	0	2.6	0	0	0	0	0//0	0/0/			0/0/0	----Other
4.2	0/0/0	0	0		0	0	0	0//0	0/0/0			0/0/0	---Other
4.2	0/0/0	0	0	3.4	0	0	0	0//0	0/0/0			0/0/0	-Synthetic organic products of a kind used as flourescent brightening agents
													-Other:
4.2	0/0/0	0	0	2	0	0	0	0//0	0/0/			0/0/0	---Biological stains and dye indicators
4.2	0/0/0	0	0	0	0	0	0	0//0	0/0/			0/0/0	---Carotene and Carotenoid
4.2	0/0/0	0	0	0	0	0	0	0//0	0/0/			0/0/0	---Other
													Colour lakes; preparations as specified in Note 3 to this Chapter based on colour lakes:
	0/0/0	4	3.9	0	0	0	0	0//0	0/0/			0/0/0	Colour lakes; preparations as specified in Note 3 to this Chapter based on colour lakes
													Other colouring matter; preparations as specified in Note 3 to this Chapter, other than those of heading No. 32. 03, 32. 04 or 32. 05; inorganic products of a kind used as luminophores, whether or not chemically defined:
													-Pigments and preparations based on titanium dioxide:
													--Containing 80% or more by weight of titanium dioxide calculated on the dry matter:
	0/0/0	4	0	0	0	0	0	0//0	0/0/0			0/0/0	---Titanium White
	0/0/0	4	0	0	0	0	0	0//0	0/0/			0/0/0	---Other
	0/0/0	4.5	4	0	0	0	0	0/0/0	0/0/0			0/0/0	--Other
	0/0/0	4	0	0	0	0	0	0//0	0/0/			0/0/0	-Pigments and preparations based on chromium compounds
													-Other colouring matter and other preparations:
	0/0/0	4	0	0	0	0	0	0//0	0/0/			0/0/0	--Ultramarine and preparations based thereon
													--Lithopone and other pigments and preparations based on zinc sulphide:
	0/0/0	4	0	0	0	0	0	0//0	0/0/			0/0/0	---Lithopone
	0/0/0	4	2.6	0	0	0	0	0//0	0/0/			0/0/0	---Other

税则号列		货品名称〔CIQ扩展编码及品名—T2表示见附表2〕	最惠(%)	暂定税率	普通	增值/消费	出口退税	计量单位	监管条件	检验检疫	特殊证件对美关税
		--其他:									
		---以铋化合物为基本成分的颜料及制品:									
3206.4911		----以钒酸铋为基本成基本成分的颜料及制品〔999〕	6.5		35	13/	0	千克			1/36.5
3206.4919		----其他〔999〕	6.5		35	13/	0	千克			1/16.5
3206.4990		---其他〔999〕	6.5		35	13/	0	千克			1/21.5
3206.5000		-用作发光体的无机产品〔999〕	6.5		35	13/	0	千克			1/21.5
32.07		**陶瓷、搪瓷及玻璃工业用的调制颜料、遮光剂、着色剂、珐琅和釉料、釉底料(泥釉)、光瓷釉以及类似产品;搪瓷玻璃料及其他玻璃,呈粉、粒或粉片状的:**									
3207.1000		-调制颜料、遮光剂、着色剂及类似制品〔999〕	5		50	13/	0	千克			1/30
3207.2000		-珐琅和釉料、釉底料(泥釉)及类似制品〔999〕	5		50	13/	0	千克			1/30
3207.3000		-光瓷釉及类似制品〔999〕	5		50	13/	0	千克			1/30
3207.4000		-搪瓷玻璃料及其他玻璃,呈粉、粒或粉片状的〔999〕	5		50	13/	0	千克			1/15
32.08		**以合成聚合物或化学改性天然聚合物为基本成分的油漆及清漆(包括瓷漆及大漆),分散于或溶于非水介质的;本章注释四所述的溶液:**									
3208.1000		-以聚酯为基本成分									
3208.1000	10	分散于或溶于非水介质的聚酯油漆及清漆,施工状态下挥发性有机物含量大于420克/升(以聚酯为基本成分的(包括瓷漆及大漆))	10		50	13/4	0	千克	A	M	1/40
3208.1000	90	其他分散于或溶于非水介质的聚酯油漆及清漆;以聚酯为基本成分的本章注释四所述溶液(以聚酯为基本成分的(包括瓷漆及大漆))	10		50	13/	0	千克	A	M	1/40
		-以丙烯酸聚合物或乙烯聚合物为基本成分:									
3208.2010		---以丙烯酸聚合物为基本成分									
3208.2010	11	分散于或溶于非水介质的光导纤维用涂料,施工状态下挥发性有机物含量大于420克/升,主要成分为聚胺酯丙烯酸酯类化合物,以丙烯酸聚合物为基本成分〔999不属于危险化学品的涂料,998属于危险化学品的涂料〕	10	6	50	13/4	13	千克	A	M	1/31
3208.2010	19	其他分散于或溶于非水介质的光导纤维用涂料,主要成分为聚胺酯丙烯酸酯类化合物,以丙烯酸聚合物为基本成分〔999不属于危险化学品的涂料,998属于危险化学品的涂料〕	10	6	50	13/	13	千克	A	M	1/31
3208.2010	91	其他以丙烯酸聚合物为基本成分的油漆、清漆等,施工状态下挥发性有机物含量大于420克/升(分散于或溶于非水质的以丙烯酸聚合物为基本成分,包括瓷漆大漆)〔301〕	10		50	13/4	0	千克	A	M	1/35
3208.2010	99	其他以丙烯酸聚合物为基本成分的油漆、清漆等;以丙烯酸聚合物为基本成分的本章注释四所述溶液(分散于或溶于非水质的以丙烯酸聚合物为基本成分,包括瓷漆大漆)〔301〕	10		50	13/	0	千克	A	M	1/35
3208.2020		---以乙烯聚合物为基本成分									
3208.2020	10	溶于非水介质的聚乙烯油漆及清漆,施工状态下挥发性有机物含量大于420克/升,以乙烯聚合物为基本成分(包括瓷漆及大漆)〔301〕	10		50	13/4	0	千克	A	M	1/40
3208.2020	90	其他分散于或溶于非水介质的以乙烯聚合物为基本成分的油漆及清漆;以乙烯聚合物基本成分的本章注释四所述溶液(以乙烯聚合物为基本成分(包括瓷漆及大漆))〔301〕	10		50	13/	0	千克	A	M	1/40
		-其他:									
3208.9010		---以聚胺酯类化合物为基本成分									
3208.9010	11	分散于或溶于非水介质的光导纤维用涂料,施工状态下挥发性有机物含量大于420克/升,主要成分为聚胺酯丙烯酸酯类化合物,以聚胺酯类化合物为基本成分〔999〕	10	6	50	13/4	0	千克	A	M	1/31
3208.9010	19	其他分散于或溶于非水介质的光导纤维用涂料,主要成分为聚胺酯丙烯酸酯类化合物,以聚胺酯类化合物为基本成分〔999〕	10	6	50	13/	0	千克	A	M	1/31

协定税率 %										特惠税率 %			Article Description
亚太5国	东/冰/格	巴基斯坦	韩国	瑞士	哥达	秘鲁	澳大利亚	新西/坡/智	港/澳/台	亚太2国	老/柬/缅	36/3/1	
													--Other:
													---Pigmenlts and preparations based on bismuth compound:
3.3	0/0/0	0	2.6	0	0	0	0	0//0	0/0/0			0/0/0	----Pigmenlts and preparations based on pucherite
3.3	0/0/0	0	2.6	0	0	0	0	0//0	0/0/0			0/0/0	----Other
3.3	0/0/0	0	2.6	0	0	0	0	0//0	0/0/0			0/0/0	---Other
4.2	0/0/0	4	2.6	0	0	0	0	0//0	0/0/			0/0/0	-Inorganic products of a kind used as luminophores
													Prepared pigments, prepared opacifiers and prepared colours, vitrifiable enamels and glazes, engobes (slips), liquid lustres and similar preparations, of a kind used in the ceramic, enamelling or glass industry; glass frit and other glass, in the form of powder, granules or flakes:
	0/0/0	0	2	0	0	0	0	0//0	0/0/			0/0/0	-Prepared pigments, prepared opacifiers, prepared colours and similar preparations
	0/0/0	0	3	0	0	0	0	0//0	0/0/			0/0/0	-Vitrifiable enamels and glazes, engobes (slips) and similar preparations
	0/0/0	0	0	0	0	0	0	0//0	0/0/			0/0/0	-Liquid lustres and similar preparations
	0/0/0	0	0	0	0	0	0	0//0	0/0/			0/0/0	-Glass frit and other glass, in the form of powder, granules or flakes
													Paints and varnishes (including enamels and lacquers) based on synthetic polymers or chemically modified natural polymers, dispersed or dissolved in a nonaqueous medium; solutions as defined in Note 4 to this Chapter:
													-Based on polyesters
9	0/0/0	4.5	7	0	0	0	0	0/0/0	0/0/0			0/0/0	-Soluble in non-aqueous medium polyester paint and varnish and so on, the construction condition of volatile organic matter content is more than 420 grams/liter, polyester as the basic ingredients (including enamel and Chinese lacquer)
9	0/0/0	4.5	7	0	0	0	0	0/0/0	0/0/0			0/0/0	Other soluble in non-aqueous medium polyester paint and varnish and so on, with polyester as the basic ingredients (including enamel and Chinese lacquer)
													-Based on acrylic or vinyl polymers:
													---Based on acrylic polymers
9	0/0/0	4	7	0	0	0	0	0/0/0	0/0/0			0/0/	Scattered or dissolve in non-aqueous medium of optical fiber coating; Construction condition of volatile organic matter content is more than 420 grams/liter, main composition of polyurethane and acrylic ester compounds with acrylic polymer as the basic ingredients
9	0/0/0	4	7	0	0	0	0	0/0/0	0/0/0			0/0/	Other scattered or dissolve in non-aqueous medium of optical fiber coating Main composition of polyurethane and acrylic ester compounds with acrylic polymer as the basic ingredients
9	0/0/0	4	7	0	0	0	0	0/0/0	0/0/0			0/0/	Other poly acrylic paint, varnish, construction condition of volatile organic matter content is more than 420 g/l; Dissolve in the water quality of acrylic polymer as basic elements, including enamel Chinese lacquer
9	0/0/0	4	7	0	0	0	0	0/0/0	0/0/0			0/0/	Other poly acrylic paint, varnish, construction condition of volatile organic matter content is not more than 420 g/l; Dissolve in the water quality of acrylic polymer as basic elements, including enamel Chinese lacquer
													---Based on vinyl polymers
9	0/0/0	4.5	4	0	0	0	0	0//0	0/0/			0/0/	Soluble in non-aqueous medium PE paint and varnish, construction condition of volatile organic matter content is more than 420 g/l; Vinyl polymer as basic ingredients (including enamel and Chinese lacquer)
9	0/0/0	4.5	4	0	0	0	0	0//0	0/0/			0/0/	Other soluble in non-aqueous medium polyethylene paint and varnish; Vinyl polymer as basic ingredients (including enamel and Chinese lacquer)
													-Other:
													---Based on polyurethane polymers
9	0/0/0	4.5	4	0	0	0	0	0/0/0	0/0/			0/0/	Dispersion in optical fibre or dissolve in the water medium with coating, construction condition of volatile organic matter content is more than 420 g/l; Main composition of polyurethane and acrylic ester compounds with polyurethane compounds of the basic ingredients
9	0/0/0	4.5	4	0	0	0	0	0/0/0	0/0/			0/0/	Other scattered or dissolve in non-aqueous medium of optical fiber coating; Main composition of polyurethane and acrylic ester compounds with polyurethane compounds of the basic ingredients

税则号列		货品名称〔CIQ 扩展编码及品名—T2 表示见附表 2〕	最惠(%)	暂定税率	普通	增值/消费	出口退税	计量单位	监管条件	检验检疫	特殊证件对美关税
3208.9010	91	其他聚胺酯油漆清漆等,施工状态下挥发性有机物含量大于 420 克/升,溶于非水介质以聚胺酯类化合物为基本成分,含瓷漆大漆〔301 属于危险化学品的涂料〕	10		50	13/4	0	千克	A	LM	1/35
3208.9010	99	其他聚胺酯油漆清漆等;以聚氨酯类化合物为基本成分的本章注释四所述溶液(分散于或溶于非水介质以聚胺酯类化合物为基本成分,含瓷漆大漆)〔999〕	10		50	13/	0	千克	A	LM	1/35
3208.9090		---其他									
3208.9090	10	分散于或溶于非水介质其他油漆、清漆溶液,施工状态下挥发性有机物含量大于 420 克/升(包括以聚合物为基本成分的漆,本章注释四所述溶液)[T2]	10		50	13/4	0	千克	A	LM	1/35
3208.9090	90	分散于或溶于非水介质其他油漆、清漆溶液;其他本章注释四所述溶液(包括以聚合物为基本成分的漆,本章注释四所述溶液)〔301〕	10		50	13/	0	千克	A	LM	1/35
32.09		**以合成聚合物或化学改性天然聚合物为基本成分的油漆及清漆(包括瓷漆及大漆),分散于或溶于水介质的:**									
3209.1000		-以丙烯酸聚合物或乙烯聚合物为基本成分									
3209.1000	10	溶于水介质的聚丙烯酸油漆及清漆,施工状态下挥发性有机物含量大于 420 克/升,以聚丙烯酸或聚乙烯为基本成分的(包括瓷漆及大漆)〔301 不属于危险化学品的涂料,302 属于危险化学品的涂料〕	10		50	13/4	0	千克	A	M	1/25
3209.1000	90	其他溶于水介质的聚丙烯酸油漆及清漆,以聚丙烯酸或聚乙烯为基本成分的(包括瓷漆及大漆)〔301 不属于危险化学品的涂料,302 属于危险化学品的涂料〕	10		50	13/	0	千克	A	M	1/25
		-其他:									
3209.9010		---以环氧树脂为基本成分									
3209.9010	10	以环氧树脂为基本成分的油漆及清漆,施工状态下挥发性有机物含量大于 420 克/升,包括瓷漆及大漆,分散或溶于水介质〔301 不属于危险化学品的涂料,302 属于危险化学品的涂料〕	10		50	13/4	0	千克	A	M	1/35
3209.9010	90	其他以环氧树脂为基本成分的油漆及清漆,包括瓷漆及大漆,分散或溶于水介质〔301 不属于危险化学品的涂料,302 属于危险化学品的涂料〕	10		50	13/	0	千克	A	M	1/35
3209.9020		---以氟树脂为基本成分									
3209.9020	10	以氟树脂为基本成分的油漆及清漆,施工状态下挥发性有机物含量大于 420 克/升,包括瓷漆及大漆,分散于或溶于水介质〔301 不属于危险化学品的涂料,302 属于危险化学品的涂料〕	10		50	13/4	13	千克	A	M	1/40
3209.9020	90	其他以氟树脂为基本成分的油漆及清漆,包括瓷漆及大漆,分散于或溶于水介质〔301 不属于危险化学品的涂料,302 属于危险化学品的涂料〕	10		50	13/	13	千克	A	M	1/40
3209.9090		---其他									
3209.9090	10	溶于水介质其他聚合物油漆及清漆,施工状态下挥发性有机物含量大于 420 克/升,以合成聚合物或化学改性天然聚合物为基本成分的〔301 不属于危险化学品的涂料,302 属于危险化学品的涂料〕	10		50	13/4	0	千克	A	M	1/35
3209.9090	90	溶于水介质其他聚合物油漆及清漆,施工状态下挥发性有机物含量不大于 420 克/升,以合成聚合物或化学改性天然聚合物为基本成分的〔301 不属于危险化学品的涂料,302 属于危险化学品的涂料〕	10		50	13/	0	千克	A	M	1/35
32.10		**其他油漆及清漆(包括瓷漆、大漆及水浆涂料);加工皮革用的水性颜料:**									
3210.0000		其他油漆及清漆(包括瓷漆、大漆及水浆涂料);加工皮革用的水性颜料									
3210.0000	11	其他光导纤维用涂料,施工状态下挥发性有机物含量大于 420 克/升〔999 不属于危险化学品的涂料,998 属于危险化学品的涂料〕	10	6	50	13/4	0	千克			1/31
3210.0000	19	其他光导纤维用涂料,施工状态下挥发性有机物含量不大于 420 克/升〔999 不属于危险化学品的涂料,998 属于危险化学品的涂料〕	10	6	50	13/	0	千克			1/31

协定税率 %										特惠税率 %			Article Description
亚太5国	东/冰/格	巴基斯坦	韩国	瑞士	哥达	秘鲁	澳大利亚	新西/坡/智	港/澳/台	亚太2国	老/柬/缅	36/3/1	
9	0/0/0	4.5	4	0	0	0	0	0/0/0	0/0/			0/0/	Other polyurethane paint varnish, etc, the construction condition of volatile organic matter content is more than 420 g/l; With polyurethane compounds dissolve in the water as the basic composition, containing enamel Chinese lacquer
9	0/0/0	4.5	4	0	0	0	0	0/0/0	0/0/			0/0/	Other polyurethane paint varnish, etc, the construction condition of volatile organic matter content is not more than 420 g/l; With polyurethane compounds dissolve in the water as the basic composition, containing enamel Chinese lacquer
													---Other
9	0/0/0	4.5	7	3	0	0	0	0/0/0	0/0/0			0/0/	Soluble in non-aqueous medium other paint, varnish solution, construction condition of volatile organic matter content is more than 420 g/l; Including the polymer as the basic ingredients of paint, this chapter four mentioned solution comment
9	0/0/0	4.5	7	3	0	0	0	0/0/0	0/0/0			0/0/	Soluble in non-aqueous medium other paint, varnish solution, construction condition of volatile organic matter content is not more than 420 g/l; Including the polymer as the basic ingredients of paint, this chapter four mentioned solution comment
													Paints and varnishes (including enamels and lacquers) based on synthetic polymers or chemically modified natural polymers, dispersed or dissolved in an aqueous medium:
													-Based on acrylic or vinyl polymers
6.5	0/0/0	4.5	4	0	0	0	0	0/0/0	0/0/			0/0/0	Soluble in water medium poly acrylic paint and varnish, construction condition of volatile organic matter content is more than 420 g/l; With polyacrylic acid or polyethylene as basic ingredients (including Chinese lacquer and enamel)
6.5	0/0/0	4.5	4	0	0	0	0	0/0/0	0/0/			0/0/0	Other soluble in water medium of poly (acrylic paint and varnish; With polyacrylic acid or polyethylene as basic ingredients (including Chinese lacquer and enamel)
													-Other:
													---Based on epoxy resin
	0/0/0	4.5	7	0	0	0	0	0/0/0	0/0/0			0/0/	With epoxy resin as the basic composition of the paint and varnish, construction condition of volatile organic matter content is more than 420 g/l; Including enamel and Chinese lacquer, dispersed or dissolved in water medium
	0/0/0	4.5	7	0	0	0	0	0/0/0	0/0/0			0/0/	Other with epoxy resin as the basic composition of the paint and varnish; Including enamel and Chinese lacquer, dispersed or dissolved in water medium
													---Based on fluororesin
	0/0/0	4.5	4	0	0	0	0	0/0/0	0/0/			0/0/	Fluorine resin as the basic ingredients of paint, varnish, construction condition of volatile organic matter content is more than 420 g/l; Including enamel and Chinese lacquer, decentralised or dissolve in water medium
	0/0/0	4.5	4	0	0	0	0	0/0/0	0/0/			0/0/	Other fluorine resin as the basic composition of the paint and varnish; Including enamel and Chinese lacquer, decentralised or dissolve in water medium
													---Other
	0/0/0	4.5	7	3	0	0	0	0/0/0	0/0/0			0/0/	Soluble in water medium and other polymer paint varnish, construction condition of volatile organic matter content is more than 420 g/l; Synthetic polymer or chemical modification of natural polymers as basic elements
	0/0/0	4.5	7	3	0	0	0	0/0/0	0/0/0			0/0/	Soluble in water medium and other polymer paint varnish, construction condition of volatile organic matter content is not more than 420 g/l; Synthetic polymer or chemical modification of natural polymers as basic elements
													Other paints and varnishes (including enamels, lacquers and distempers); prepared water pigments of a kind used for finishing leather:
													Other paints and varnishes (including enamels, lacquers and distempers); prepared water pigments of a kind used for finishing leather
6.5	0/0/0	4	0	0	0	0	0	0/0/0	0/0/0			0/0/0	Other optical fiber coating, construction condition of volatile organic matter content is more than 420 grams/liter
6.5	0/0/0	4	0	0	0	0	0	0/0/0	0/0/0			0/0/0	Other optical fiber coating, construction condition of volatile organic matter content is not more than 420 grams/liter

税则号列		货品名称〔CIQ扩展编码及品名—T2表示见附表2〕	最惠(%)	暂定税率	普通	增值/消费	出口退税	计量单位	监管条件	检验检疫	特殊证件对美关税
3210.0000	91	其他油漆及清漆，皮革用水性颜料，施工状态下挥发性有机物含量大于420克/升，包括非聚合物为基料的瓷漆，大漆及水浆涂料[T2]	10		50	13/4	0	千克		L	1/35
3210.0000	99	其他油漆及清漆，皮革用水性颜料，施工状态下挥发性有机物含量不大于420克/升，包括非聚合物为基料的瓷漆，大漆及水浆涂料[T2]	10		50	13/	0	千克		L	1/35
32.11		配制的催干剂：									
3211.0000		配制的催干剂〔999〕	10		50	13/	0	千克			1/35
32.12		**制造油漆(含瓷漆)用的颜料(包括金属粉末或金属粉片)，分散于非水介质中呈液状或浆状的；压印箔；零售形状及零售包装的染料或其他着色料：**									
3212.1000		-压印箔〔999〕	15		80	13/	0	千克			1/35
3212.9000		-其他〔999 其他化工产品，998 其他危险化学品〕	10		50	13/	0	千克			1/25
32.13		**艺术家、学生和广告美工用的颜料、调色料、文娱颜料及类似品，片状、管装、罐装、瓶装、扁盒装以及类似形状或包装的：**									
3213.1000		-成套的颜料〔999 其他化工产品，998 其他危险化学品〕	6.5		70	13/	13	千克			1/16.5
3213.9000		-其他〔999 其他化工产品，998 其他危险化学品〕	6.5		70	13/	13	千克			1/11.5
32.14		**安装玻璃用油灰、接缝用油灰、树脂胶泥、嵌缝胶及其他类似胶粘剂；漆工用填料；非耐火涂面制剂，涂门面、内墙、地板、天花板等用：**									
		-安装玻璃用油灰、接缝用油灰、树脂胶泥、嵌缝胶及其他类似胶粘剂；漆工用填料：									
3214.1010		---半导体器件封装材料〔999〕	9		70	13/	13	千克			1/39
3214.1090		---其他〔101 贴胡胶，102 聚氨酯导电粘合剂，103 多用粘结胶，104FS203C 胶，105 压敏胶，106 嵌缝油膏〕	9		70	13/	13	千克			1/24
3214.9000		-其他									
3214.9000	10	非耐火涂面制剂，施工状态下挥发性有机物含量大于420克/升，涂门面、内墙、地板、天花板等用〔999〕	9		70	13/4	0	千克			1/24
3214.9000	90	其他非耐火涂面制剂；涂门面、内墙、地板、天花板等用〔999〕	9		70	13/	0	千克			1/24
32.15		**印刷油墨、书写或绘图墨水及其他墨类，不论是否固体或浓缩：**									
		-印刷油墨：									
3215.1100		--黑色									
3215.1100	10	黑色，用于装入税号8443.31、8443.32或8443.39所列设备的工程形态的固体油墨〔999 其他化工产品，998 其他危险化学品〕	2.2/1.1		45	13/	0	千克	AB	MN	1/27.2，26.1
3215.1100	90	其他黑色印刷油墨(不论是否固体或浓缩)〔999 其他化工产品，998 其他危险化学品〕	6.5		45	13/	0	千克	AB	MN	1/31.5
3215.1900		--其他									
3215.1900	10	其他用于装入税号8443.31、8443.32或8443.39所列设备的工程形态的固体油墨〔999 其他化工产品，998 其他危险化学品〕	2.2/1.1		45	13/	0	千克			1/27.2，26.1
3215.1900	90	其他印刷油墨(不论是否固体或浓缩)〔101 醇溶凹印油墨，102 其他塑料油墨，103 塑料凸板油墨，104 塑料喷涂油墨，105 影印油墨，106 氧化锌静电复印油墨〕	6.5		45	13/	0	千克			1/31.5
		-其他：									
3215.9010		---书写墨水〔999 其他化工产品，998 其他危险化学品〕	5		70	13/	13	千克			1/35
3215.9020		---水性喷墨墨水〔999〕	10		70	13/	13	千克			1/20
3215.9090		---其他〔101 软管滚涂油墨，102 软管白墨，103 其他化工产品〕	10		70	13/	13	千克			1/25

协定税率 %										特惠税率 %			Article Description
亚太5国	东/冰/格	巴基斯坦	韩国	瑞士	哥达	秘鲁	澳大利亚	新西/坡/智	港/澳/台	亚太2国	老/柬/缅	36/3/1	
6.5	0/0/0	4	0	0	0	0	0	0/0/0	0/0/0			0/0/0	Other paint and varnish, leather with acrylic paint, construction condition of volatile organic matter content is more than 420 g/l; Including the polymer materials for the enamel, Chinese lacquer and water slurry coating
6.5	0/0/0	4	0	0	0	0	0	0/0/0	0/0/0			0/0/0	Other paint and varnish, leather with acrylic paint, construction condition of volatile organic matter content is not more than 420g/l; Including the polymer materials for the enamel, Chinese lacquer and water slurry coating
													Prepared driers:
	0/0/0	4.5	6	3	0	0	0	0/0/0	0/0/			0/0/	Prepared driers
													Pigments (including metallic powders and flakes) dispersed in non-aqueous media, in liquid or paste form, of a kind used in the manufacture of paints (including enamels); stamping foils; dyes and other colouring matter put up in forms or packings for retail sale:
	0/0/0	12	6	4.5	0	0	0	0/0/0	0/0/			0/0/	-Stamping foils
	0/0/0	4.5	4	0	0	0	0	0/0/0	0/0/			0/0/	-Other
													Artists', students' or signboard painters' colours, modifying tints, amusement colours and the like, in tablets, tubes, jars, bottles, pans or in similar forms or packings:
	0/0/0	4.5	4	0	0	0	0	0//0	0/0/			0/0/	-Colours in sets
4.2	0/0/0	4.5	4	0	0	0	0	0//0	0/0/			0/0/0	-Other
													Glaziers' putty, graftig putty, resin cements, caulking compounds and other mastics; painters' fillings; non-refractory surfacing preparations for facades, indoor walls, floors, ceilings or the like:
													-Glaziers' putty, grafting putty, resin cements, caulking compounds and other mastics; painters' fillings:
	0/0/3.6	4		0	0	0	0	0//0	0/0/			0/0/0	---Encpackaging materials for semiconductor device
	0/0/0	4	0	2.7	0	0	0	0//0	0/0/			0/0/0	---Other
													-Other
	0/0/0	4	5.4	0	0	0	0	0//0	0/0/			0/0/0	The refractory coating preparation, the construction condition of volatile organic matter content is more than 420 g/l; Coated facade, interior wall, floor, ceiling, etc
	0/0/0	4	5.4	0	0	0	0	0//0	0/0/			0/0/0	Other, refractory coating agent; Coated facade, interior wall, floor, ceiling, etc
													Printing ink, writing or drawing ink and other inks, whether or not concentrated or solid:
													-Printing ink:
													--Black
4.2	0/0/0	0	0	0	0	0	0	0//0	0/0/			0/0/0	Black, solid ink, for the engineering equipment of subheading No. 8443.31, 8443.32 or 8443.39
4.2	0/0/0	0	0	0	0	0	0	0//0	0/0/			0/0/0	Other black printing oil, whether or not concentrated or solid
													--Other
4.6	0/0/0	0	2.6	2	0	0	0	0//0	0/0/0			0/0/0	Other sclid ink, for the engineering equipment of subheading No. 8443.31, 8443.32 or 8443.39
4.6	0/0/0	0	2.6	2	0	0	0	0//0	0/0/0			0/0/0	Other printing oil, whether or not concentrated or solid
													-Other:
	0/0/0	4	0	0	0	0	0	0//0	0/0/			0/0/0	---Writing or drawing inks
	0/0/0	4.5	0	3	0	0	0	0/0/0	0/0/			0/0/0	---Aqueous ink jet ink
	0/0/0	4.5	0	3	0	0	0	0/0/0	0/0/			0/0/0	---Other

第三十三章
精油及香膏;芳香料制品及化妆盥洗品

注释:

一、本章不包括:

(一)税目13.01及13.02的天然油树脂及植物浸膏;

(二)税目34.01的肥皂及其他产品;

(三)税目38.05的脂松节油、木松节油和硫酸盐松节油及其他产品。

二、税目33.02所称"香料"仅指税目33.01所列的物质,从这些物质离析出来的香料组分以及合成芳香剂。

三、税目33.03至33.07主要包括适合作这些税目所列用途的零售包装产品,不论其是否混合(精油水馏液及水溶液除外)。

四、税目33.07所称"芳香料制品及化妆盥洗品",主要适用于下列产品:香袋;通过燃烧散发香气的制品;香纸及用化妆品浸渍或涂布的纸;隐形眼镜片或假眼用的溶液;用香水或化妆品浸渍、涂布、包覆的絮胎、毡呢及无纺织物;动物用盥洗品。

税则号列	货品名称〔CIQ扩展编码及品名—T2表示见附表2〕	最惠(%)	暂定税率	普通	增值/消费	出口退税	计量单位	监管条件	检验检疫	特殊证件对美关税
33.01	**精油(无萜或含萜),包括浸膏及净油;香膏;提取的油树脂;用花香吸取法或浸渍法制成的含浓缩精油的脂肪、固定油、蜡及类似品;精油脱萜时所得的萜烯副产品;精油水馏液及水溶液:**									
	-柑橘属果实的精油:									
3301.1200	--橙油[T2]	20		80	13/	10	千克	A	R	1/30
3301.1300	--柠檬油[T2]	20		80	13/	13	千克	A	R	1/30
	--其他:									
3301.1910	---白柠檬油(酸橙油)[T2]	20		80	13/	10	千克	A	R	1/30
3301.1990	---其他〔111面部香精油,112发用香精精油,113体用香精精油,301无检疫要求食品添加剂〕	20		80	13/	10	千克	A	R	1/30
	-非柑橘属果实的精油:									
3301.2400	--胡椒薄荷油〔111面部香精油,112发用香精精油,113体用香精精油,301无检疫要求食品添加剂〕	20		90	13/	10	千克	A	R	1/30
3301.2500	--其他薄荷油[T2]	15	5	90	13/	13	千克	A	R	1/15
	--其他:									
3301.2910	---樟脑油[T2]	20		90	13/	10	千克	ABE	MRN	1/30
3301.2920	---香茅油〔111面部香精油,112发用香精精油,113体用香精精油,301无检疫要求食品添加剂〕	15		70	13/	10	千克	A	R	1/35
3301.2930	---茴香油〔111面部香精油,112发用香精精油,113体用香精精油,301无检疫要求食品添加剂〕	20		80	13/	9	千克	A	R	1/30
3301.2940	---桂油〔111面部香精油,112发用香精精油,113体用香精精油,301无检疫要求食品添加剂〕	20		80	13/	10	千克	A	R	1/50
3301.2950	---山苍子油〔111面部香精油,112发用香精精油,113体用香精精油,301无检疫要求食品添加剂〕	20		80	13/	10	千克	A	R	1/30
3301.2960	---桉叶油〔102桉叶油,111面部香精油,112发用香精精油,113体用香精精油,301无检疫要求食品添加剂〕	20		80	13/	10	千克	AB	MRN	1/30
	---其他:									
3301.2991	----老鹳草油(香叶油)〔101面部香精油,102发用香精精油,103体用香精精油,301无检疫要求食品添加剂〕	20		80	13/	10	千克	A	R	1/45
3301.2999	----其他									
3301.2999 10	黄樟油〔101面部香精油,102发用香精精油,103体用香精精油,301无检疫要求食品添加剂〕	15	7	80	13/	10	千克	23A	R	1/12
3301.2999 91	其他濒危植物精油(柑桔属果实除外)(包括浸膏及净油)〔111面部香精油,112发用香精精油,113体用香精精油,301无检疫要求食品添加剂〕	15		80	13/	0	千克	AFE	R	1/20
3301.2999 99	其他非柑橘属果实的精油(包括浸膏及净油)〔338工业用精油,401面部香精油,402发用香精精油,403体用香精精油,339无检疫要求食品添加剂〕	15		80	13/	10	千克	A	R	1/20
	-香膏:									
3301.3010	---鸢尾凝脂〔101〕	20	10	80	13/	13	千克			1/40
3301.3090	---其他									
3301.3090 10	其他濒危植物香膏〔999〕	20		80	13/	0	千克	FE		1/45
3301.3090 90	其他香膏[T2]	20		80	13/	10	千克			1/45
	-其他:									
3301.9010	---提取的油树脂									

Chapter 33
Essential oils and resinoids; perfumery, cosmetic or toilet preparations

Notes:

1. This Chapter does not cover:
   (a) Natural oleoresins or vegetable extracts of heading No. 13.01 or 13.02;
   (b) Soap or other products of heading No. 34.01; or
   (c) Gum, wood or sulphate turpentine or other products of heading No. 38.05.
2. The expression "odoriferous substances" in heading No. 33.02 refers only to the substances of heading No. 33.01, to odoriferous constituents isolated from those substances or to synthetic aromatics.
3. Headings No. 33.03 to 33.07 apply, *inter alia*, to products, whether or not mixed (other than aqueous distillates and aqueous solutions of essential oils), suitable for use as goods of these headings and put up in packings of a kind sold by retail for such use.
4. The expression "perfumery, cosmetic or toilet preparations" in heading No. 33.07 applies, *inter alia*, to the following products: scented sachets; odoriferous preparations which operate by burning; perfumed papers and papers impregnated or coated with cosmetics; contact lens or artificial eye solutions; wadding, felt and nonwovens, impregnated, coated or covered with perfume or cosmetics; animal toilet preparations.

协定税率 %										特惠税率 %			Article Description
亚太5国	东/冰/格	巴基斯坦	韩国	瑞士	哥达	秘鲁	澳大利亚	新西/坡/智	港/澳/台	亚太2国	老/柬/缅	36/3/1	
													Essential oils (terpeneless or not), including concretes and absolutes; resinoids; extracted oleoresins; concentrates of essential oils in fats, in fixed oils, in waxes or the like, obtained by enfleurage or maceration; terpenic byproducts of the deterpenation of essential oils; aqueous distillates and aqueous solutions of essential oils:
													-Essential oils of citrus fruit:
	0/0/8		12	8.3	0	0	0	0/0/0	0/0/			0/0/	--Of orange
	0/0/0		12	0	0	0	0	0/0/0	0/0/			0/0/0	--Of lemon
													--Other:
	0/0/0		12	6	0	0	0	0/0/0	0/0/			0/0/	---Of lime
	0/0/0		12	6	0	0	0	0/0/0	0/0/			0/0/	---Other
													-Essential oils other than those of citrus fruit:
	0/0/0		12	6	0	0	0	0/0/0	0/0/			0/0/	--Of peppermint (Mentha piperita)
14	0/0/0	12	6	4.5	0	0	0	0/0/0	0/0/			0/0/0	--Of other mints
													--Other:
	0/0/0		12	6	0	0	0	0/0/0	0/0/			0/0/	---Of camphor
	0/0/0	12	6	4.5	0	0	0	0/0/0	0/0/			0/0/0	---Of citronella
	0/0/0		12	6	0	0	0	0/0/0	0/0/			0/0/	---Of aniseed
	0/0/0		12	6	0	0	0	0/0/0	0/0/			0/0/	---Of cassia
	0/0/0		12	6	0	0	0	0/0/0	0/0/			0/0/	---Of litsea cubeba
	0/0/0		12	6	0	0	0	0/0/0	0/0/			0/0/	---Of eucalyptus
													---Other:
	0/0/0		12	6	0	0	0	0/0/0	0/0/			0/0/	----Of geranium
													----Other
	0/0/0	12	9	4.5	0	0	0	0/0/0	0/0/			0/0/0	Oil of sassafras
	0/0/0	12	9	4.5	0	0	0	0/0/0	0/0/			0/0/0	Other endangered essential (other than citrus fruit) (including concretes and absolutes)
	0/0/0	12	9	4.5	0	0	0	0/0/0	0/0/			0/0/0	Other essential oils other than those of citrus fruit (including concretes and absolutes)
													-Resinoids:
	0/0/0		12	6	0	0	0	0/0/0	0/0/			0/0/	---Balsam of irises
													---Other
	0/0/0		12	6	0	0	0	0/0/0	0/0/			0/0/	Other resinoids of endangered vegetable
	0/0/0		12	6	0	0	0	0/0/0	0/0/			0/0/	Other resinoids
													-Other:
													---Extracted oleoresins

税则号列		货品名称〔CIQ扩展编码及品名—T2表示见附表2〕	最惠(%)	暂定税率	普通	增值/消费	出口退税	计量单位	监管条件	检验检疫	特殊证件对美关税
3301.9010	10	濒危植物提取的油树脂〔999〕	20		80	13/	0	千克	FE		1/30
3301.9010	90	其他提取的油树脂[T2]	20		80	13/	10	千克			1/30
3301.9020		---柑橘属果实的精油脱萜的萜烯副产品〔101〕	20		80	13/	10	千克			1/30
3301.9090		---其他〔101 含固定油、蜡及类似品,精油水溶液及水馏液〕	20		80	13/	10	千克			1/45
33.02		**工业原料用的混合香料以及以一种或多种香料为基本成分的混合物(包括酒精溶液);生产饮料用的以香料为基本成分的其他制品:**									
		-食品或饮料工业用:									
3302.1010		---生产饮料用的以香料为基本成分的制品,按容量计酒精浓度不超过0.5%的〔999〕	15		90	13/	13	千克	A	R	1/40
3302.1090		---其他									
3302.1090	01	生产食品、饮料用混合香料及制品(含以香料为基本成分的混合物,按容量计酒精浓度>0.5%)[T2]	15		130	13/5	13	千克	A	R	1/20
3302.1090	90	其他生产食品用混合香料及制品(含以香料为基本成分的混合物)[T2]	15		130	13/	13	千克	A	R	1/20
3302.9000		-其他〔103〕	10		130	13/	13	千克			1/30
33.03		香水及花露水:									
3303.0000		香水及花露水									
3303.0000	10	包装标注含量以重量计的香水及花露水[T2]	3		150	13/15	13	千克/件	AB	MN	1/28
3303.0000	20	包装标注含量以体积计的香水及花露水[T2]	3		150	13/15	13	千克/件	AB	MN	1/28
33.04		**美容品或化妆品及护肤品(药品除外),包括防晒油或晒黑油;指(趾)甲化妆品:**									
3304.1000		-唇用化妆品									
3304.1000	11	包装标注含量以重量计的含濒危植物成分唇用化妆品[T2]	5		150	13/15	0	千克/件	ABEF	MN	1/30
3304.1000	12	包装标注含量以体积计的含濒危植物成分唇用化妆品[T2]	5		150	13/15	0	千克/件	ABEF	MN	1/30
3304.1000	13	包装标注规格为"片"或"张"的含濒危植物成分唇用化妆品〔101 成人口唇膜类化妆品〕	5		150	13/15	0	千克/件	ABEF	MN	1/30
3304.1000	91	包装标注含量以重量计的其他唇用化妆品[T2]	5		150	13/15	13	千克/件	AB	MN	1/30
3304.1000	92	包装标注含量以体积计的其他唇用化妆品[T2]	5		150	13/15	13	千克/件	AB	MN	1/30
3304.1000	93	包装标注规格为"片"或"张"的其他唇用化妆品〔101 成人口唇膜类化妆品〕	5		150	13/15	13	千克/件	AB	MN	1/30
3304.2000		-眼用化妆品									
3304.2000	11	包装标注含量以重量计的含濒危植物成分眼用化妆品[T2]	5		150	13/15	0	千克/件	ABEF	MN	1/30
3304.2000	12	包装标注含量以体积计的含濒危植物成分眼用化妆品[T2]	5		150	13/15	0	千克/件	ABEF	MN	1/30
3304.2000	13	包装标注规格为"片"或"张"的含濒危植物成分眼用化妆品〔101 成人眼部膜类化妆品〕	5		150	13/15	0	千克/件	ABEF	MN	1/30
3304.2000	91	包装标注含量以重量计的其他眼用化妆品[T2]	5		150	13/15	13	千克/件	AB	MN	1/30
3304.2000	92	包装标注含量以体积计的其他眼用化妆品[T2]	5		150	13/15	13	千克/件	AB	MN	1/30
3304.2000	93	包装标注规格为"片"或"张"的其他眼用化妆品[T2]	5		150	13/15	13	千克/件	AB	MN	1/30
3304.3000		-指(趾)甲化妆品									
3304.3000	01	包装标注含量以重量计的指(趾)甲化妆品[T2]	5		150	13/15	13	千克/件	AB	MN	1/30
3304.3000	02	包装标注含量以体积计的指(趾)甲化妆品[T2]	5		150	13/15	13	千克/件	AB	MN	1/30
3304.3000	03	包装标注规格为"片"或"张"的指(趾)甲化妆品〔101 趾甲护理化妆品,102 趾甲美容化妆品,103 趾甲化妆品〕	5		150	13/15	13	千克/件	AB	MN	1/30
		-其他:									
3304.9100		--粉,不论是否压紧[T2]	5		150	13/15	13	千克/件	AB	MN	1/30
3304.9900		--其他									
3304.9900	21	包装标注含量以重量计含濒危物种成分的美容品或化妆品及护肤品(包括防晒油或晒黑油,但药品除外)[T2]	1		150	13/15	0	千克/件	ABEF	MN	1/31
3304.9900	29	包装标注含量以重量计的其他美容品或化妆品及护肤品(包括防晒油或晒黑油,但药品除外)[T2]	1		150	13/15	13	千克/件	AB	MN	1/31
3304.9900	31	包装标注含量以体积计的含濒危物种成分美容品或化妆品及护肤品(包括防晒油或晒黑油,但药品除外)[T2]	1		150	13/15	0	千克/件	ABFE	MN	1/31
3304.9900	39	包装标注含量以体积计的其他美容品或化妆品及护肤品(包括防晒油或晒黑油,但药品除外)[T2]	1		150	13/15	13	千克/件	AB	MN	1/31

协定税率 %										特惠税率 %			Article Description
亚太5国	东/冰/格	巴基斯坦	韩国	瑞士	哥达	秘鲁	澳大利亚	新西/坡/智	港/澳/台	亚太2国	老/柬/缅	36/3/1	
13	0/0/0	18	12	6	0	0	0	0/0/0	0/0/			0/0/	Extracted oleoresins of endangered vegetable
13	0/0/0	18	12	6	0	0	0	0/0/0	0/0/			0/0/	Other extracted oleoresins
13	0/0/0	18	12	6	0	0	0	0/0/0	0/0/			0/0/	---Terpenic byproducts of the deterpenation of essential oils of citrus fruit
13	0/0/0	18	12	6	0	0	0	0/0/0	0/0/			0/0/0	---Other
													Mixtures of odoriferous substances and mixtures (including alcoholic solutions) with a basis of one or more of these substances, of a kind used as raw materials in industry; other preparations based on odoriferous substances, of a kind used for the manufacture of beverages:
													-Of a kind used in the food or drink industry:
9.8	0/0/6	0	6	4.5	0	0	0	0/0/0	0/0/			0/0/	---Preparations based on odoriferous substances, of a kind used for the manufacture of beverages, alcoholic strength by volume not ≤0.5% vol.
													---Other
	0/0/0	0	6	4.5	0	0	0	0/0/0	0/0/			0/0/0	Mixtures of odoriferous substances and products, alcoholic strength by vol>0.5%, of a kind used in the food or drink industry
	0/0/0	0	6	4.5	0	0	0	0/0/0	0/0/			0/0/0	Other mistures of odoriferous substances and preparations, based on oboriferous substances, of a kind used in the food industry
	0/0/0	4.5	4	0	0	0	0	0/0/0	0/0/			0/0/0	-Other
													Perfumes and toilet waters:
													Perfumes and toilet waters
2	0/0/0	4.5		0	0	0	0	0/0/0	0/0/			0/0/0	Perfumes and toilet waters
2	0/0/0	4.5		0	0	0	0	0/0/0	0/0/			0/0/0	Perfumes and toilet waters
													Beauty or make-up preparations and preparations for the care of the skin (other than medicaments), including sunscreen or suntan preparations; manicure or pedicure preparations:
													-Lip make-up preparations
	0/0/0	4.5		0	0	0	0	0/0/0	0/0/			0/0/	Lip make-up preparations
	0/0/0	4.5		0	0	0	0	0/0/0	0/0/			0/0/	Lip make-up preparations
	0/0/0	4.5		0	0	0	0	0/0/0	0/0/			0/0/	Lip make-up preparations
	0/0/0	4.5		0	0	0	0	0/0/0	0/0/			0/0/	Lip make-up preparations
	0/0/0	4.5		0	0	0	0	0/0/0	0/0/			0/0/	Lip make-up preparations
	0/0/0	4.5		0	0	0	0	0/0/0	0/0/			0/0/	Lip make-up preparations
													-Eye make-up preparations
	0/0/0	4.5		0	0	0	0	0/0/0	0/0/			0/0/	Eye make-up preparations
	0/0/0	4.5		0	0	0	0	0/0/0	0/0/			0/0/	Eye make-up preparations
	0/0/0	4.5		0	0	0	0	0/0/0	0/0/			0/0/	Eye make-up preparations
	0/0/0	4.5		0	0	0	0	0/0/0	0/0/			0/0/	Eye make-up preparations
	0/0/0	4.5		0	0	0	0	0/0/0	0/0/			0/0/	Eye make-up preparations
	0/0/0	4.5		0	0	0	0	0/0/0	0/0/			0/0/	Eye make-up preparations
													-Manicure or pedicure preparations
	0/0/0	0		4.5	0	0	0	0/0/0	0/0/			0/0/	Manicture or pedicure preparations
	0/0/0	0		4.5	0	0	0	0/0/0	0/0/			0/0/	Manicture or pedicure preparations
	0/0/0	0		4.5	0	0	0	0/0/0	0/0/			0/0/	Manicture or pedicure preparations
													-Other:
	0/0/4	4.5		0	0	0	0	0/0/0	0/0/			0/0/	--Powders, whether or not compressed
													--Other
	0/0/0	0	5.2	0	0	0	0	0/0/0	0/0/			0/0/	Packaging and labeling content containing by weight of endangered species composition of cosmetics or cosmetics and skin care products (including sunscreen or suntan oil, but the drugs except)
	0/0/0	0	5.2	0	0	0	0	0/0/0	0/0/			0/0/	Packaging and labeling content by weight of other cosmetics or cosmetics and skin care products (including sunscreen or suntan oil, but the drugs except)
	0/0/0	0	5.2	0	0	0	0	0/0/0	0/0/			0/0/	Packaging and labeling content by volume containing the endangered species components of cosmetics or cosmetic and skin care products (including sunscreen or suntan oil, but the drugs except)
	0/0/0	0	5.2	0	0	0	0	0/0/0	0/0/			0/0/	Packaging and labeling content by volume of other cosmetics or cosmetics and skin care products (including sunscreen or suntan oil, but the drugs except)

税则号列		货品名称〔CIQ 扩展编码及品名－T2 表示见附表 2〕	最惠(%)	暂定税率	普通	增值/消费	出口退税	计量单位	监管条件	检验检疫	特殊证件对美关税
3304.9900	41	包装标注规格为"片"或"张"的含濒危物种成分美容品或化妆品及护肤品(包括防晒油或晒黑油,但药品除外)〔201 成人面部膜类化妆品,202 成人眼部膜类化妆品,203 成人口唇膜类化妆品,204 成人体用膜类化妆品,205 美白化妆品〕	1		150	13/15	0	千克/件	ABFE	MN	1/31
3304.9900	49	包装标注规格为"片"或"张"的其他美容品或化妆品及护肤品(包括防晒油或晒黑油,但药品除外)〔201 成人面部膜类化妆品,202 成人眼部膜类化妆品,203 成人口唇膜类化妆品,204 成人体用膜类化妆品,205 美白化妆品〕	1		150	13/15	13	千克/件	AB	MN	1/31
3304.9900	91	其他包装标注规格的含濒危物种成分美容品或化妆品及护肤品(包括防晒油或晒黑油,但药品除外)[T2]	1		150	13/15	0	千克/件	ABFE	MN	1/31
3304.9900	99	其他包装标注规格的其他美容品或化妆品及护肤品(包括防晒油或晒黑油,但药品除外)[T2]	1		150	13/15	13	千克/件	AB	MN	1/31
33.05		**护发品:**									
3305.1000		-洗发剂(香波)									
3305.1000	10	含濒危植物成分的洗发剂〔102 婴幼儿淋洗类发用化妆品,107 成人淋洗类毛发用化妆品〕	3	2	150	13/	0	千克	ABFE	MN	1/27
3305.1000	90	其他洗发剂(香波)〔102 婴幼儿淋洗类发用化妆品,107 成人淋洗类毛发用化妆品〕	3	2	150	13/	13	千克	AB	MN	1/27
3305.2000		-烫发剂〔101 烫发化妆品,301 其他危险化学品〕	3		150	13/	13	千克	AB	MN	1/28
3305.3000		-定型剂〔107 婴幼儿驻留类发用化妆品,108 成人驻留类毛发用化妆品,301 其他危险化学品〕	3		150	13/	13	千克	AB	MN	1/28
3305.9000		-其他[T2]	3		150	13/	13	千克	AB	MN	1/28
33.06		**口腔及牙齿清洁剂,包括假牙模膏及粉;清洁牙缝用的纱线(牙线),单独零售包装的:**									
		-洁齿品:									
3306.1010		---牙膏									
3306.1010	10	含濒危植物成分牙膏〔104 成人牙膏,105 婴幼儿口腔类产品〕	3		150	13/	0	千克	ABEF	RS	1/33
3306.1010	90	其他牙膏〔104 成人牙膏,105 婴幼儿口腔类产品〕	3		150	13/	13	千克	AB	RS	1/33
3306.1090		---其他〔999〕	3		150	13/	10	千克			1/33
3306.2000		-清洁牙缝用的纱线(牙线)〔999〕	3		70	13/	10	千克			1/33
		-其他:									
3306.9010		---漱口剂(包括假牙模膏及粉)〔201 包括漱口水、口腔清新喷雾,202 包括牙粉、牙贴、假牙模膏,203 包括漱口水、口腔清新喷雾〕	3		70	13/	13	千克	AB	RS	1/33
3306.9090		---其他口腔及牙齿清洁剂(包括假牙模膏及粉)〔201 包括牙粉、牙贴、假牙模膏,202 婴幼儿口腔类产品,203 包括假牙模膏及粉〕	3		70	13/	13	千克	AB	RS	1/33
33.07		**剃须用制剂、人体除臭剂、沐浴用制剂、脱毛剂和其他税目未列名的芳香料制品及化妆盥洗品;室内除臭剂,不论是否加香水或消毒剂:**									
3307.1000		-剃须用制剂〔103 成人面部驻留类化妆品,104 成人淋洗类毛发用化妆品〕	3		150	13/	13	千克	AB	MN	1/33
3307.2000		-人体除臭剂及止汗剂〔106〕	3		150	13/	13	千克	AB	MN	1/33
3307.3000		-香浴盐及其他沐浴用制剂〔101 婴幼儿淋洗类肤用化妆品,112 成人体用淋洗类化妆品〕	3		150	13/	13	千克	AB	MN	1/33
		-室内散香或除臭制品,包括宗教仪式用的香:									
3307.4100		--神香及其他通过燃烧散发香气的制品〔999〕	3		150	13/	13	千克			1/33
3307.4900		--其他〔999〕	3		150	13/	13	千克			1/33
3307.9000		-其他〔999〕	3		150	13/	13	千克			1/33

协定税率 %										特惠税率 %			Article Description
亚太5国	东/冰/格	巴基斯坦	韩国	瑞士	哥达	秘鲁	澳大利亚	新西/坡/智	港/澳/台	亚太2国	老/柬/缅	36/3/1	
	0/0/0	0	5.2	0	0	0	0	0/0/0	0/0/			0/0/	Packaging and labeling specifications for the endangered species composition of cosmetics or cosmetic and skin care products containing " or" a "(including sunscreen or suntan oil, but the drugs except)
	0/0/0	0	5.2	0	0	0	0	0/0/0	0/0/			0/0/	Packaging and labeling specifications for the "slice" or "card" or other cosmetics cosmetics and skin care products (including sunscreen or suntan oil, but the drugs except)
	0/0/0	0	5.2	0	0	0	0	0/0/0	0/0/			0/0/	Other packaging labeling specifications containing endangered species composition of cosmetics or cosmetic and skin care products (including sunscreen or suntan oil, but the drugs except)
	0/0/0	0	5.2	0	0	0	0	0/0/0	0/0/			0/0/	Other packaging labeling specifications of other cosmetics or cosmetics and skin care products (including sunscreen or suntan oil, but the drugs except)
													Preparations for use on the hair:
													-Shampoos
2	0//0	4	4.2	0	0	0	0	0/0/0	0/0/			0/0/0	Shampoos containing composition of endangered vegetable
2	0//0	4	4.2	0	0	0	0	0/0/0	0/0/			0/0/0	Other shampoos
	0/0/0	12		3	0	0	0	0/0/0	0/0/			0/0/	-Preparations for permanent waving or straightening
	0/0/0	12		3	0	0	0	0/0/0	0/0/			0/0/	-Hair lacquers
2	0//0	4	6.5	0	0	0	0	0/0/0	0/0/			0/0/0	-Other
													Preparations for oral or dental hygiene, including denture fixative pastes and powders; yarn used to clean between the teeth (dental floss), in individual retail package:
													-Dentifrices:
													---Toothpastes
2	0/0/0	4.5	4	0	0	0	0	0/0/0	0/0/			0/0/0	Toothpastes containing composition of endangered vegetable
2	0/0/0	4.5	4	0	0	0	0	0/0/0	0/0/			0/0/0	Other toothpastes
2	0/0/0	4.5	4	0	0	0	0	0/0/0	0/0/			0/0/	---Other
2	0/0/0	4.5	4	0	0	0	0	0//0	0/0/			0/0/	-Yarn used to clean between the teeth (dental floss)
													-Other:
	0/0/0	4.5	4	0	0	0	0	0/0/0	0/0/			0/0/	---Mouthwash (including denture paste and powder)
	0/0/0	4.5	4	0	0	0	0	0/0/0	0/0/			0/0/	---Two chloroethylene - vinyl chloride copolymers
													Pre-shave, shaving or after-shave preparations, personal deodorants, bath preparations, depilatories and other perfumery, cosmetic or toilet preparations, not elsewhere specified or included; prepared room deodorizers, whether or not perfumed or having disinfectant properties:
2	0/0/0	4.5		0	0	0	0	0/0/0	0/0/			0/0/	-Pre-shave, shaving or after-shave preparations
2	0/0/0	4.5		0	0	0	0	0/0/0	0/0/			0/0/	-Personal deodorants and antiperspirants
2	0/0/0	4.5	6.5	0	0	0	0	0/0/0	0/0/			0/0/	-Perfumed bath salts and other bath preparations
													-Preparations for perfuming or deodorizing rooms, including odoriferous preparations used during religious rites:
	0/0/0	4	4	0	0	0	0	0/0/0	0/0/			0/0/0	--Agarbatti and other odoriferous preparations which operate by burning
	0/0/0	4.5	4	0	0	0	0	0/0/0	0/0/			0/0/0	--Other
2	0/0/0	4	5.8	0	0	0	0	0//0	0/0/			0/0/0	-Other

第三十四章
肥皂、有机表面活性剂、洗涤剂、润滑剂、人造蜡、调制蜡、光洁剂、蜡烛及类似品、塑型用膏、“牙科用蜡”及牙科用熟石膏制剂

注释：

一、本章不包括：

(一)用作脱模剂的食用动植物油、脂混合物或制品(税目15.17)；

(二)单独的已有化学定义的化合物；

(三)含肥皂或其他有机表面活性剂的洗发剂、洁齿品、剃须膏及沐浴用制剂(税目33.05、33.06及33.07)。

二、税目34.01所称“肥皂”，只适用于水溶性肥皂。税目34.01的肥皂及其他产品可以含有添加料(例如，消毒剂、磨料粉、填料或药料)。含磨料粉的产品，只有条状、块状或模制形状可以归入税目34.01。其他形状的应作为“去污粉及类似品”归入 税目34.05。

三、税目34.02所称“有机表面活性剂”，是指温度在20℃时与水混合配成0.5%浓度的 水溶液，并在同样温度下搁置一小时后与下列规定相符的产品：

(一)成为透明或半透明的液体或稳定的乳浊液而未离析出不溶解物质；

(二)将水的表面张力减低到每厘米45达因及以下。

四、税目34.03所称“石油及从沥青矿物提取的油类”，适用于第二十七章注释二所规定的产品。

五、税目34.04所称“人造蜡及调制蜡”，仅适用于：

(一)用化学方法生产的具有蜡质特性的有机产品，不论是否为水溶性的；

(二)各种蜡混合制成的产品；

(三)以一种或几种蜡为基本原料并含有油脂、树脂、矿物质或其他原料的具有蜡质特性的产品。

本税目不包括：

(一)税目15.16、34.02或38.23的产品，不论是否具有蜡质特性；

(二)税目15.21的未混合的动物蜡或未混合的植物蜡，不论是否精制或着色；

(三)税目27.12的矿物蜡或类似产品，不论是否相互混合或仅经着色；

(四)混合、分散或溶解于液体溶剂的蜡(税目34.05、38.09等)。

税则号列	货品名称〔CIQ扩展编码及品名—T2表示见附表2〕	最惠(%)	暂定税率	普通	增值/消费	出口退税	计量单位	监管条件	检验检疫	特殊证件对美关税
34.01	**肥皂；作肥皂用的有机表面活性产品及制品，条状、块状或模制形状的，不论是否含有肥皂；洁肤用的有机表面活性产品及制品，液状或膏状并制成零售包装的，不论是否含有肥皂；用肥皂或洗涤剂浸渍、涂面或包覆的纸、絮胎、毡呢及无纺织物：**									
	-肥皂及有机表面活性产品及制品，条状、块状或模制形状的，以及用肥皂或洗涤剂浸渍、涂面或包覆的纸、絮胎、毡呢及无纺织物：									
3401.1100	--盥洗用(包括含有药物的产品)〔101 婴幼儿淋洗类肤用化妆品，109 成人面部淋洗类化妆品，110 成人体用淋洗类化妆品，111 其他产品〕	6.5		130	13/	13	千克	AB	MN	1/31.5
	--其他：									
3401.1910	---洗衣皂〔999〕	6.5		80	13/	13	千克			1/31.5
3401.1990	---其他〔105〕	6.5		130	13/	13	千克			1/26.5
3401.2000	-其他形状的肥皂〔999〕	6.5		130	13/	13	千克			1/31.5
3401.3000	-洁肤用的有机表面活性产品及制品，液状或膏状并制成零售包装的，不论是否含有肥皂〔101 婴幼儿淋洗类肤用化妆品，109 成人面部淋洗类化妆品，110 成人体用淋洗类化妆品〕	6.5		130	13/	13	千克	AB	MN	1/16.5
34.02	**有机表面活性剂(肥皂除外)；表面活性剂制品、洗涤剂(包括助洗剂)及清洁剂，不论是否含有肥皂，但税目34.01的产品除外：**									
	-有机表面活性剂，不论是否零售包装：									
3402.1100	--阴离子型〔999〕	6.5		30	13/	13	千克			1/11.5
3402.1200	--阳离子型〔106〕	6.5		30	13/	13	千克			1/11.5
3402.1300	--非离子型									
3402.1300　10	含有壬基酚聚氧乙烯醚的有机表面活性剂(不论是否零售包装，肥皂除外)〔999〕	6.5		30	13/	13	千克			1/

Chapter 34

Soap, organic surface-active agents, washing preparations, lubricating preparations, artificial waxes, prepared waxes polishing or scouring preparations, candles and similar articles, modelling pastes, "dental waxes" and dental preparations with a basis of plaster

Notes:

1. This Chapter does not cover:
   (a) Edible mixtures or preparations of animal or vegetable fats or oils of a kind used as mould release preparations (heading No. 15. 17);
   (b) Separate chemically defined compounds; or
   (c) Shampoos, dentifrices, shaving creams and foams, or bath preparations, containing soap or other organic surface-active agents (heading No. 33. 05, 33. 06 or 33. 07).
2. For the purposes of heading No. 34. 01, the expression "soap" applies only to soap soluble in water. Soap and the other products of heading No. 34. 01 may contain added substances (for example, disinfectants, abrasive powders, fillers or medicaments). Products containing abrasive powders remain classified in heading No. 34. 01 only if in the form of bars, cakes or moulded pieces or shapes. In other forms they are to be classified in heading No. 34. 05 as "scouring powders and similar preparations".
3. For the purposes of heading No. 34. 02, "organic surface-active agents" are products which when mixed with water at a concentration of 0. 5% at 20℃ and left to stand for one hour at the same temperature:
   (a) give a transparent or translucent liquid or stable emulsion without separation of insoluble matter; and
   (b) reduce the surface tension of water to 4.5×10^{-2} N/m (45 dyne/cm) or less.
4. In heading No. 34. 03 the expression "petroleum oils and oils obtained from bituminous minerals" applies to the products defined in Note 2 to Chapter 27.
5. In heading No. 34. 04, subject to the exclusions provided below, the expression "artificial waxes and prepared waxes" applies only to:
   (a) Chemically produced organic products of a waxy character, whether or not water-soluble;
   (b) Products obtained by mixing different waxes;
   (c) Products of a waxy character with a basis of one or more waxes and containing fats, resins, mineral substances or other materials.
   The heading does not apply to:
   (a) Products of heading No. 15. 16, 34. 02 or 38. 23, even if having a waxy character;
   (b) Unmixed animal waxes or unmixed vegetable waxes, whether or not refined or coloured, of heading No. 15. 21;
   (c) Mineral waxes or similar products of heading No. 27. 12, whether or not intermixed or merely coloured;
   (d) Waxes mixed with, dispersed in or dissolved in a liquid medium (headings No. 34. 05, 38. 09, etc.).

协定税率 %										特惠税率 %			Article Description
亚太5国	东/冰/格	巴基斯坦	韩国	瑞士	哥达	秘鲁	澳大利亚	新西/坡/智	港/澳/台	亚太2国	老/柬/缅	36/3/1	
													Soap; organic surface-active products and preparations for use as soap, in the form of bars, cakes, moulded pieces or shapes, whether or not containing soap; organic surface-active products and preparations for washing the skin, in the form of liquid or cream and put up for retail sale, whether or not containing soap; paper, wadding, felt and nonwovens, impregnated, coated or covered with soap or detergent:
													-Soap and organic surface-active products and preparations, in the form of bars, cakes, moulded pieces or shapes, and paper, wadding, felt and nonwovens, impregnated, coated or covered with soap or detergent:
4.2	0/0/0	0	4	0	0	0	0	0/0/0	0/C/	0		0/0/0	--For toilet use (including medicated products)
													--Other:
	0/0/0	4.5		0	0	0	0	0/0/0	0/0/			0/0/0	---Laundry soap
	0/0/0	0	6	4.5	0	0	0	0//0	0/0/			0/0/	---Other
4.2	0/0/0	0	6	4.5	0	0	0	0//0	0/0/	0		0/0/0	-Soap in other forms
	0/0/0	4.5	4	0	0	0	0	0/0/0	0/0/			0/0/0	-Organic surface-active products and preparations for washing the skin, in the form of liquid or cream and put up for retail sale, whether or not containing soap
													Organic surface-active agents (other than soap); surface-active preparations, washing preparations (including auxiliary washing preparations) and cleaning preparations, whether or not containing soap, other than those of heading No. 34. 01:
													-Organic surface-active agents, whether or not put up for retail sale:
4.2	0/0/0	4	4.2	0	0	0	0	0//0	0/0/			0/0/0	--Anionic
4.2	0/0/0	4	4.2	0	0	0	0	0//0	0/0/			0/0/0	--Cationic
													--Non-ionic
4.2	0/0/0	0	3.9	2	0	0	0	0/0/0	0/0/0			0/0/0	Organic surface-active agents, containing polyoxy ethrlene nonyl phinyl ether(whether or not put up for retail sale, other than soap)

税则号列	货品名称〔CIQ扩展编码及品名—T2表示见附表2〕	最惠(%)	暂定税率	普通	增值/消费	出口退税	计量单位	监管条件	检验检疫	特殊证件对美关税
3402.1300　90	其他非离子型有机表面活性剂(不论是否零售包装,肥皂除外)〔999〕	6.5		30	13/	13	千克			1/
3402.1900	--其他〔999〕	6.5		30	13/	13	千克			1/16.5
	-零售包装的制品:									
3402.2010	---合成洗涤粉〔999〕	6.5		80	13/	13	千克			1/26.5
3402.2090	---其他〔999〕	6.5		80	13/	13	千克			1/16.5
3402.9000	-其他									
3402.9000　01	十二烷基苯磺酸钙甲醇溶液(非零售包装,十二烷基苯磺酸钙含量高于70%)〔999〕	6.5		80	13/	13	千克			1/16.5
3402.9000　90	非零售包装有机表面活性剂制品(包括洗涤剂及清洁剂,不论是否含有肥皂)〔103 煤炭浮选剂〕	6.5		80	13/	13	千克			1/16.5
34.03	**润滑剂(包括以润滑剂为基本成分的切削油制剂、螺栓或螺母松开剂、防锈或防腐蚀制剂及脱模剂)及用于纺织材料、皮革、毛皮或其他材料油脂处理的制剂,但不包括以石油或从沥青矿物提取的油类为基本成分(按重量计不低于70%)的制剂:**									
	-含有石油或从沥青矿物提取的油类:									
3403.1100	--处理纺织材料、皮革、毛皮或其他材料的制剂〔999〕	10	8	50	13/	13	千克			1/28
3403.1900	--其他〔999〕	10	8	50	13/	13	千克			1/
	-其他:									
3403.9100	--处理纺织材料、皮革、毛皮或其他材料的制剂〔999〕	10	8	50	13/	13	千克			1/33
3403.9900	--其他〔102 汽油稀型防锈油,103 半干型防锈油,104 溶剂稀释型防锈油,105 薄层防锈油,106 驻退液〕	10		50	13/	13	千克			1/
34.04	**人造蜡及调制蜡:**									
3404.2000	-聚氧乙烯(聚乙二醇)蜡〔999〕	10		70	13/	13	千克			1/15
3404.9000	-其他〔999 无检疫要求食品添加剂,301 其他化工产品〕	10		70	13/	0	千克			1/20
34.05	**鞋靴、家具、地板、车身、玻璃或金属用的光洁剂、擦洗膏、去污粉及类似制品(包括用这类制剂浸渍、涂面或包覆的纸、絮胎、毡呢、无纺织物、泡沫塑料或海绵橡胶),但不包括税目34.04的蜡:**									
3405.1000	-鞋靴或皮革用的上光剂及类似制品〔101 皮革光滑剂,102 皮革顶层涂饰剂,103 皮革光亮剂〕	6.5		80	13/	13	千克			1/26.5
3405.2000	-保养木制家具、地板或其他木制品用的上光剂及类似制品〔999〕	6.5		80	13/	13	千克			1/16.5
3405.3000	-车身用的上光剂及类似制品,但金属用的光洁剂除外〔999〕	6.5		80	13/	13	千克			1/16.5
3405.4000	-擦洗膏、去污粉及类似制品〔999〕	6.5		80	13/	13	千克			1/16.5
3405.9000	-其他〔102 修相油,103 油画上光油,104 油画色调合油,105 闪烁体材料〕	6.5		80	13/	13	千克			1/16.5
34.06	**各种蜡烛及类似品:**									
3406.0000	各种蜡烛及类似品									
3406.0000　10	含濒危动物成分的蜡烛及类似品〔101 含木制品,102 不含木制品〕	6.5		130	13/	0	千克	EF		1/16.5
3406.0000　90	其他各种蜡烛及类似品〔101 含木制品,102 不含木制品〕	6.5		130	13/	13	千克			1/16.5
34.07	**塑型用膏,包括供儿童娱乐用的在内;通称为"牙科用蜡"或"牙科造形膏"的制品,成套、零售包装或制成片状、马蹄形、条状及类似形状的;以熟石膏(煅烧石膏或硫酸钙)为基本成分的牙科用其他制品:**									
3407.0010	---牙科用蜡及造型膏〔999〕	6.5		30	13/	10	千克			1/16.5
3407.0020	---以熟石膏为基本成分的牙科用其他制品〔999〕	6.5		40	13/	10	千克			1/31.5
3407.0090	---其他〔999〕	10		100	13/	10	千克			1/30

协定税率 %										特惠税率 %			Article Description
亚太5国	东/冰/格	巴基斯坦	韩国	瑞士	哥达	秘鲁	澳大利亚	新西/坡/智	港/澳/台	亚太2国	老/柬/缅	36/3/1	
4.2	0/0/0	0	3.9	2	0	0	0	0/0/0	0/0/0			0/0/0	Other organic surface-active agents(whether or not put up for retail sale, other than soap)
4.2	0/0/0	4	4.2	0	0	0	0	0//0	0/0/			0/0/0	--Other
													-Preparations put up for retail sale:
4.2	0/0/0	4.5	6.5	0	0	0	0	0/0/0	0/0/			0/0/	---Synthetic detergents in powder form
4.2	0/0/0	4.5	6.5	0	0	0	0	0/0/0	0/0/			0/0/	---Other
													-Other
4.2	0/0/3.6	0	0	2.7	0	0	0	0/0/0	0/0/			0/0/0	Calcium dodecyl benzen sulfonate methanol solution (containing more than 70% of calcium dodecyl benzosulfonate, not put up for retail sale)
4.2	0/0/3.6	0	0	2.7	0	0	0	0/0/0	0/0/			0/0/0	Organic surface-active agents, including washing preparations and cleaning preparations, whether or not containing soap, not in forms or packing for retail sale
													Lubricating preparations (including cutting-oil preparations, bolt or nut release preparations, anti-rust or anticorrosion preparations and mould release preparations, based on lubricants) and preparations of a kind used for the oil or grease treatment of textile materials, leather, furskins or other materials, but excluding preparations containing, as basic constituents, 70% or more by weight of petroleum oils or of oils obtained from bituminous minerals:
													-Containing petroleum oils or oils obtained from bituminous minerals:
6.5	0/0/0	4.5	4	0	0	0	0	0/0/0	0/0/			0/0/	--Preparations for the treatment of textile materials, leather, furskins or other materials
	0/0/0	4	0	0	0	0	0	0/0/0	0/0/			0/0/0	--Other
													-Other:
	0/0/0	4.5	0	0	0	0	0	0/0/0	0/0/			0/0/	--Preparations for the treatment of textile materials, leather, furskins or other materials
	0/0/0	4.5	0	3	0	0	0	0/0/0	0/0/			0/0/	--Other
													Artificial waxes and prepared waxes:
	0/0/0	4.5		0	0	0	0	0//0	0/0/			0/0/	-Of poly(oxyethylene) (polyethylene glycol)
	0/0/0	0	0	0	0	0	0	0//0	0/0/			0/0/0	-Other
													Polishes and creams, for footwear, furniture, floors, coachwork, glass or metal, scouring pastes and powders and similar preparations (whether or not in the form of paper, wadding, felt, nonwovens, cellular plastics or cellular rubber, impregnated, coated or covered with such preparations), excluding waxes of heading No. 34.04:
	0/0/0	4.5	4	0	0	0	0	0/0/0	0/0/			0/0/	-Polishes, creams and similar preparations for footwear or leather
	0/0/0	4.5	4	0	0	0	0	0/0/0	0/0/			0/0/	-Polishes, creams and similar preparations for the maintenance of wooden furniture, floors or other woodwork
	0/0/0	4.5	4	0	0	0	0	0/0/0	0/0/			0/0/	-Polishes and similar preparations for coachwork, other than metal polishes
	0/0/0	4.5	4	0	0	0	0	0//0	0/0/			0/0/	-Scouring pastes and powders and other scouring preparations
4.2	0/0/0	4.5	0	0	0	0	0	0/0/0	0/0/			0/0/	-Other
													Candles, tapers and the like:
													Candles, tapers and the like
	0/0/0	4.5	4	0	0	0	0	0/0/0	0/0/			0/0/	Candle and gimilar products made from on endangered animals
	0/0/0	4.5	4	0	0	0	0	0/0/0	0/0/			0/0/	Other candles, tapers and the like
													Modelling pastes, including those put up for children's amusement; preparations known as "dental wax" or as "dental impression compounds", put up in sets, in packings for retail sale or in plates, horseshoe shapes, sticks or similar forms; other preparations for use in dentistry, with a basis of plaster (of calcined gypsum or calcium sulphate):
	0/0/0	4	2.6	2	0	0	0	0//0	0/0/			0/0/0	---Preparations of a kind known as "dental wax" or as "dental impression compounds"
	0/0/0	4	0	0	0	0	0	0//0	0/0/			0/0/0	---Other preparations for use in dentistry, with a basis of plaster
	0/0/0	4.5	4	0	0	0	0	0//0	0/0/			0/0/	---Other

第三十五章
蛋白类物质;改性淀粉;胶;酶

注释:

一、本章不包括:

(一)酵母(税目 21.02);

(二)第三十章的血份(非治病、防病用的血清白蛋白除外)、药品及其他产品;

(三)预鞣用酶制剂(税目 32.02);

(四)第三十四章的加酶的浸透剂、洗涤剂及其他产品;

(五)硬化蛋白(税目 39.13);

(六)印刷工业用的明胶产品(第四十九章)。

二、税目 35.05 所称"糊精",是指淀粉的降解产品,其还原糖含量以右旋糖的干重量计不超过 10%。

如果还原糖含量超过 10%,应归入税目 17.02。

税则号列	货品名称〔CIQ 扩展编码及品名－T2 表示见附表 2〕	最惠(%)	暂定税率	普通	增值/消费	出口退税	计量单位	监管条件	检验检疫	特殊证件对美关税
35.01	**酪蛋白、酪蛋白酸盐及其他酪蛋白衍生物;酪蛋白胶:**									
3501.1000	-酪蛋白〔999,101 食用,102 非食用性乳品,301 无检疫要求食品添加剂,302 需申报仅用于工业用途不用于食品添加剂无检疫要求的化学品〕	10		35	13/	13	千克	AB	RS	1/35
3501.9000	-其他〔101 非食用性乳品,102 无检疫要求食品添加剂,103 需申报仅用于工业用途不用于食品添加剂无检疫要求的化学品〕	10		35	13/	13	千克	A	R	1/30
35.02	**白蛋白(包括按重量计干质成分的乳清蛋白含量超过 80%的两种或两种以上的乳清蛋白浓缩物)、白蛋白盐及其他白蛋白衍生物:**									
	-卵清蛋白:									
3502.1100	--干的〔101 食用〕	10		80	13/	13	千克	AB	PQ	1/15
3502.1900	--其他〔101 食用〕	10		80	13/	13	千克	AB	PQ	1/20
3502.2000	-乳白蛋白(包括两种或两种以上的乳清蛋白浓缩物)〔999 动物白蛋白,101 食用浓缩乳清蛋白粉,102 乳清蛋白粉,301 无检疫要求食品添加剂,302 需申报仅用于工业用途不用于食品添加剂无检疫要求的化学品〕	10		35	13/	13	千克	AB	RS	1/15
3502.9000	-其他〔999 包括白蛋白衍生物,301 无检疫要求食品添加剂,302 需申报仅用于工业用途不用于食品添加剂无检疫要求的化学品〕	10		35	13/	13	千克	A	R	1/30
35.03	**明胶(包括长方形、正方形明胶薄片,不论是否表面加工或着色)及其衍生物;鱼鳔胶;其他动物胶,但不包括税目 35.01 的酪蛋白胶:**									
3503.0010	---明胶及其衍生物									
3503.0010　01	明胶〔101 饲用,102 工业用,103 有检疫要求食品添加剂〕	12	5	35	13/	13	千克	AB	PRQ	1/15
3503.0010　90	明胶的衍生物(包括长方形、正方形明胶薄片,不论是否表面加工或着色)〔101 饲用,102 工业用〕	12		35	13/	13	千克	AB	PQ	1/22
3503.0090	---其他〔101 药用龟甲胶,102 药用阿胶,103 药用鹿角胶,104 有检疫要求食品添加剂〕	12		50	13/	13	千克	AB	PRQ	1/17
35.04	**蛋白胨及其衍生物;其他税目未列名的蛋白质及其衍生物;皮粉,不论是否加入铬矾:**									
3504.0010	---蛋白胨〔101 具有保健食品批准文号,102 无检疫要求食品添加剂,103 工业用动物骨蛋白胨,301 需申报仅用于工业用途不用于食品添加剂无检疫要求的化学品〕	3		11	13/	13	千克	A	R	1/8
3504.0090	---其他[T2]	8		35	13/	13	千克	A	R	1/18
35.05	**糊精及其他改性淀粉(例如,预凝化淀粉或酯化淀粉);以淀粉、糊精或其他改性淀粉为基本成分的胶:**									
3505.1000	-糊精及其他改性淀粉〔101 饲料添加剂,102 变性淀粉,301 爆炸品,需申报仅用于工业用途不用于食品添加剂无检疫要求,302 无检疫要求食品添加剂,303 一般化学品,需申报仅用于工业用途不用于食品添加剂无检疫要求,304 属于危险化学品的食品添加剂〕	12	6	50	13/	13	千克	A	MR	1/21
3505.2000	-胶〔101 变性淀粉,301 其他危险化学品,需申报仅用于工业用途不用于食品添加剂无检疫要求,302 无检疫要求食品添加剂,303 一般化学品,需申报仅用于工业用途不用于食品添加剂无检疫要求,304 属于危险化学品的食品添加剂〕	20		50	13/	13	千克	A	MR	1/30

Chapter 35
Albuminoidal substances; modified starches; glues; enzymes

Notes:

1. This Chapter does not cover:
   (a) Yeasts (heading No. 21.02);
   (b) Blood fractions (other than blood albumin not prepared for therapeutic or prophylactic uses), medicaments or other products of Chapter 30;
   (c) Enzymatic preparations for pre-tanning (heading No. 32.02);
   (d) Enzymatic soaking or washing preparations or other products of Chapter 34;
   (e) Hardened proteins (heading No. 39.13); or
   (f) Gelatin products of the printing industry (Chapter 49).
2. For the purposes of heading No. 35.05, the term "dextrins" means starch degradation products with a reducing sugar content, expressed as dextrose on the dry substance, not exceeding 10%.
   Such products with a reducing sugar content exceeding 10% fall in heading No. 17.02.

协定税率 %										特惠税率 %			Article Description
亚太5国	东/冰/格	巴基斯坦	韩国	瑞士	哥达	秘鲁	澳大利亚	新西/坡/智	港/澳/台	亚太2国	老/柬/缅	36/3/1	
													Casein, caseinates and other casein derivatives; casein glues:
	0/0/0	4	4	0	0	0	0	0/0/0	0/0/			0/0/	-Casein
	0/0/0	4.5	4	0	0	0	0	0//0	0/0/			0/0/	-Other
													Albumins (including concentrates of two or more whey proteins, containing by weight more than 80% whey proteins, calculated on the dry matter), albuminates and other albumin derivatives:
													-Egg albumin:
	0/0/0	4.5	4	0	0	0	0	0//0	0/0/			0/0/	--Dried
	0/0/0	4.5	4	0	0	0	0	0//0	0/0/			0/0/	--Other
	0/0/0	4.5	4	0	0	0	0	0//0	0/0/			0/0/	-Milk albumin, including concentrates of two or more whey proteins
	0/0/0	4.5	4	0	0	0	0	0//0	0/0/			0/0/	-Other
													Gelatin (including gelatin in rectangular (including square) sheets, whether or not surface-worked or coloured) and gelatin derivatives; isinglass; other glues of animal origin, excluding casein glues of heading No. 35.01:
													---Gelatin and gelatin derivatives
9.6	0/0/0	0	4.8	3.6	0	0	0	0/0/0	0/0/			0/0/	Gelatin
9.6	0/0/0	0	4.8	3.6	0	0	0	0/0/0	0/0/			0/0/	Gelatin derivatives (including gelatin in rectangular, square sheets, whether or not surface-worked or coloured)
9.6	0/0/0	6	4.8	3.6	0	0	0	0/0/0	0/0/			0/0/	---Other
													Peptones and their derivatives; other protein substances and their derivatives, not elsewhere specified or included; hide powder, whether or not chromed:
	0/0/0	0	0	0	0	0	0	0//0	0/0/			0/0/0	---Peptones
	0/0/0	4	0	0	0	0	0	0//0	0/0/			0/0/0	---Other
													Dextrins and other modified starches (for example, pregelatinized or esterified starches); glues based on starches, or on dextrins or other modified starches:
	0/0/0	4.8	4.8	3.6	0	0	0	0/0/0	0/0/			0/0/	-Dextrins and other modified starches
	0/0/0		12	6	0	0	0	0/0/0	0/0/			0/0/	-Glues

税则号列		货品名称〔CIQ扩展编码及品名—T2表示见附表2〕	最惠(%)	暂定税率	普通	增值/消费	出口退税	计量单位	监管条件	检验检疫	特殊证件对美关税
35.06		**其他税目未列名的调制胶及其他调制黏合剂;适于作胶或黏合剂用的产品,零售包装每件净重不超过1千克:**									
3506.1000		-适于作胶或黏合剂用的产品,零售包装每件净重不超过1千克									
3506.1000	10	硅酮结构密封胶(零售包装每件净重不超过1千克)〔301其他危险化学品,302其他化工产品〕	10		90	13/	13	千克	A	M	1/20
3506.1000	90	其他适于作胶或粘合剂的零售产品(零售包装每件净重不超过1千克)〔301易燃液体,302腐蚀性物质,303其他危险化学品,304其他化工产品〕	10		90	13/	13	千克			1/20
		-其他:									
		--以橡胶或税目39.01至39.13的聚合物为基本成分的黏合剂:									
3506.9110		---以聚酰胺为基本成分的〔999〕	10		90	13/	13	千克			1/20
3506.9120		---以环氧树脂为基本成分的〔999〕	10		90	13/	13	千克			1/20
3506.9190		---其他									
3506.9190	10	非零售,硅酮结构密封胶〔301其他危险化学品,302其他化工产品〕	10		90	13/	13	千克	A	M	1/35
3506.9190	20	专门或主要用于显示屏或触摸屏制造的光学透明膜黏合剂和光固化液体黏合剂(包括以人造树脂(环氧树脂除外)为基本成分的)〔999〕	0		90	13/	13	千克			1/25
3506.9190	90	其他橡胶或塑料为基本成分粘合剂(包括以人造树脂(环氧树脂除外)为基本成分的)[T2]	10		90	13/	13	千克			1/35
3506.9900		--其他〔999〕	10		90	13/	13	千克			1/20
35.07		**酶;其他税目未列名的酶制品:**									
3507.1000		-粗制凝乳酶及其浓缩物〔999,101饲用酶制剂,301无检疫要求食品添加剂,302需申报仅用于工业用途不用于食品添加剂无检疫要求的化学品〕	6		30	13/	13	千克	A	R	1/
		-其他:									
3507.9010		---碱性蛋白酶〔999,101饲用酶制剂,301无检疫要求食品添加剂,302需申报仅用于工业用途不用于食品添加剂无检疫要求的化学品〕	6		30	13/	13	千克	A	R	1/11
3507.9020		---碱性脂肪酶〔999,101饲用酶制剂,301无检疫要求食品添加剂,302需申报仅用于工业用途不用于食品添加剂无检疫要求的化学品〕	6		30	13/	13	千克	A	R	1/16
3507.9090		---其他									
3507.9090	10	门冬酰胺酶〔301其他化工产品,401医用酶及酶制剂〕	6	0	30	3/	13	千克	AB	RVW	1/10
3507.9090	90	其他酶及酶制品(因拆分抗癌药品原料药产生的兜底税号)〔101饲用酶制剂 301无检疫要求食品添加剂 302需申报仅用于工业用途不用于食品添加剂无检疫要求的化学品 401医用诊断试剂 402医用检测试剂 403医用酶及酶制剂 404其他医用生物制品〕	6		30	13/	13	千克	AB	RVW	1/16

协定税率 %										特惠税率 %			
亚太5国	东/冰/格	巴基斯坦	韩国	瑞士	哥达	秘鲁	澳大利亚	新西/坡/智	港/澳/台	亚太2国	老/柬/缅	36/3/1	Article Description
													Prepared glues and other prepared adhesives, not elsewhere specified or included; products suitable for use as glues or adhesives, put up for retail sale as glues or adhesives, not exceeding a net weight of 1 kg:
													-Products suitable for use as glues or adhesives, put up for retail sale as glues or adhesives, not exceeding a net weight of 1kg
6.5	0//0	4.5	0	3	0	0	0	0/0/0	0/0/0			0/0/0	Structure silicone sealant (in forms or packing for retail sale as glues or adhesives, not exceeding a net weight of 1kg)
6.5	0//0	4.5	0	3	0	0	0	0/0/0	0/0/0			0/0/0	Other-products suitable for use as glues or adhesives, in forms or packing for retail sale as glues or adhesives, not exceeding a net weight of 1kg
													-Other:
													--Adhesives based on polymers of headings Nos. 39.01 to 39.13 or on rubber:
7	0/0/0	4.5	6	0	0	0	0	0/0/0	0/0/0			0/0/0	---Based on polyamide
6.5	0/0/0	4.5	7	3	0	0	0	0/0/0	0/0/0			0/0/0	---Based on epoxy resin
													---Other
7	0/0/4	4.5	4	3	0	0	0	0/0/0	0/0/0			0/0/0	Structure silicone sealant, not in forms or packing for retail sale
7	0/0/4	4.5	4	3	0	0	0	0/0/0	0/0/0			0/0/0	Specially built or is mainly used to display or touch screen optical transparent film adhesive and light curing liquid adhesive (including synthetic resin (epoxy resin except) as the basic component of)
7	0/0/4	4.5	4	3	0	0	0	0/0/0	0/0/0			0/0/0	Other adhesives based on rubber or plastic including[artificial resin (other than epoxy resin)]
6.5	0/0/0	4.5	7	3	0	0	0	0/0/0	0/0/0			0/0/0	--Other
													Enzymes; prepared enzymes not elsewhere specified or included:
	0/0/0	0	0	0	0	0	0	0//0	0/0/			0/0/0	-Rennet and concentrates thereof
													-Other:
	0/0/0	0	2.4	0	0	0	0	0//0	0/0/			0/0/0	---Basic proteinase
	0/0/0	0	2.4	0	0	0	0	0//0	0/0/			0/0/0	---Basic lipase
													---Other
	0/0/0	0	0	0	0	0	0	0//0	0/0/			0/0/0	
	0/0/0	0	0	0	0	0	0	0//0	0/0/			0/0/0	Other enzymes and enzyme products(tax number of Separating anti—cancer pharmaceutical raw materials)

第三十六章
炸药;烟火制品;火柴;引火合金;易燃材料制品

注释:

一、本章不包括单独的已有化学定义的化合物,但下列注释二(一)、(二)所述物品除外。

二、税目36.06所称"易燃材料制品",只适用于:

(一)聚乙醛、六亚甲基四胺(六甲撑四胺)及类似物质,已制成片、棒或类似形状作燃料用的;以酒精为基本成分的固体或半固体燃料及类似的配制燃料;

(二)直接灌注香烟打火机及类似打火器用的液体燃料或液化气体燃料,其包装容器的容积不超过300立方厘米;

(三)树脂火炬、引火物及类似品。

税则号列		货品名称〔CIQ扩展编码及品名—T2表示见附表2〕	最惠(%)	暂定税率	普通	增值/消费	出口退税	计量单位	监管条件	检验检疫	特殊证件对美关税
36.01		**发射药:**									
3601.0000		发射药									
3601.0000	10	模压的胶质推进剂〔999〕	9		50	13/	0	千克	3		1/19
3601.0000	20	含硝化粘接剂及铝粉>5%的推进剂〔999〕	9		50	13/	0	千克	3		1/19
3601.0000	30	黑火药	9		50	13/	0	千克	k		1/19
3601.0000	91	民用推进剂(限于购买、销售、运输管理)〔999〕	9		50	13/	0	千克	k		1/19
3601.0000	99	其他发射药	9		50	13/	0	千克			1/19
36.02		**配制炸药,但发射药除外:**									
3602.0010		---硝铵炸药									
3602.0010	10	符合特定标准的硝铵炸药(硝胺类物质超过2%,或密度>1.8g/cm^3、爆速>8000m/s)〔301〕	9		50	13/	0	千克	3		1/14
3602.0010	91	其他铵梯类炸药、铵油类炸药、膨化硝铵炸药、胶状乳化炸药、粉状乳化炸药、震源药柱、其他工业炸药	9		50	13/	0	千克	k		1/14
3602.0010	99	其他硝铵炸药,但发射药除外	9		50	13/	0	千克			1/14
3602.0090		---其他									
3602.0090	10	符合特定标准的其他配制炸药(含有超过2%(按重量计)的下述任何一种物质:(环)四亚甲基四硝胺(HMX);(环)三亚甲基三硝基胺(RDX);三氨基三硝基苯(TATB);氨基二硝基苯并氧化呋咱或7氨基4,6硝基苯并呋咱1氧化物;六硝基芪(HNS)等;或晶体密度大于1.8g/cm3、爆速超过8000m/s的各种炸药。)〔301〕	9		50	13/	0	千克	3k		1/14
3602.0090	91	民用的其他配置炸药,但发射药除外	9		50	13/	0	千克	k		1/14
3602.0090	99	其他配制炸药,但发射药除外	9		50	13/	0	千克			1/14
36.03		**安全导火索;导爆索;火帽或雷管;引爆器;电雷管:**									
3603.0000		安全导火索;导爆索;火帽或雷管;引爆器;电雷管									
3603.0000	10	爆炸桥〔999〕	9		50	13/	0	千克	3		1/24
3603.0000	20	爆炸桥丝〔999〕	9		50	13/	0	千克	3		1/24
3603.0000	30	冲击片〔999〕	9		50	13/	0	千克	3		1/24
3603.0000	40	爆炸箔起爆器〔999〕	9		50	13/	0	千克	3		1/24
3603.0000	50	使用单个或多个雷管的装置(由单一点火信号同时起爆,不包括仅使用起药的雷管)〔999〕	9		50	13/	0	千克	3		1/24
3603.0000	61	工业用炸药雷管点火装置(用于引爆上述品目3603各子目列名的爆炸配件的雷管)	9		50	13/	0	千克	3		1/24
3603.0000	69	其他炸药雷管点火装置(用于引爆上述品目3603各子目列名的爆炸配件的雷管)	9		50	13/	0	千克	3		1/24
3603.0000	91	民用的其他安全导火索、导爆索等引爆器件	9		50	13/	0	千克	k		1/24
3603.0000	99	其他安全导火索导爆索等引爆器件(包括火帽或雷管、引爆器、电雷管)	9		50	13/	0	千克			1/24
36.04		**烟花、爆竹、信号弹、降雨火箭、浓雾信号弹及其他烟火制品:**									
3604.1000		-烟花、爆竹[T2]	6		130	13/15	13	千克	AB	MN	1/16
3604.9000		-其他〔999〕									
3604.9000	10	人工影响天气用燃爆器材、海上救生烟火信号及其他特殊用途烟火制品	6		100	13/	13	千克	k		1/16
3604.9000	90	其他信号弹,降雨火箭及其他烟火制品	6		100	13/	13	千克			1/16

Chapter 36

Explosives; pyrotechnic products; matches; pyrophoric alloys; certain combustible preparations

Notes:

1. This Chapter does not cover separate chemically defined compounds other than those described in Note 2 (a) or (b) below.
2. The expression "articles of combustible materials" in heading No. 36. 06 applies only to:
   (a) Metaldehyde, hexamethylenetetramine and similar substances, put up in forms (for example, tablets, sticks or similar forms) for use as fuels; fuels with a basis of alcohol, and similar prepared fuels, in solid or semi-solid form;
   (b) Liquid or liquefied-gas fuels in containers of a kind used for filling or refilling cigarette or similar lighters and of a capacity not exceeding 300 cm^3;
   (c) Resin torches, firelighters and the like.

协定税率 %										特惠税率 %			Article Description
亚太5国	东/冰/格	巴基斯坦	韩国	瑞士	哥达	秘鲁	澳大利亚	新西/坡/智	港/澳/台	亚太2国	老/柬/缅	36/3/1	
													Propellent powders:
													Propellent powders
	0/0/0	4	0	0	0	0	0	0//0	0/0/			0/0/	Colloidal propellant, molded
	0/0/0	4	0	0	0	0	0	0//0	0/0/			0/0/	Propellant, containing cementing agent and aluminum powder>5%
	0/0/0	4	0	0	0	0	0	0//0	0/0/		//	0/0/	Black powder
	0/0/0	4	0	0	0	0	0	0//0	0/0/		//	0/0/	Other civil propellants
	0/0/0	4	0	0	0	0	0	0//0	0/0/		//	0/0/	Other propellants
													Prepared explosives, other than propellent powders:
													---Based on ammonals nitrate
	0/0/0	4	0	0	0	0	0	0//0	0/0/			0/0/	Meet specific standared of ammonium nitrate exploseives(containing of ammonium nitrate>2%, density>1. 8g/cm^3, explodingvelocity>8000m/s)
	0/0/0	4	0	0	0	0	0	0//0	0/0/		//	0/0/	Other ammonium ladder explosives, ammonium oil explosives, expanded ammonium nitrate explosives, gelatinous emulsion explosives, Powdered Emulsion explosives, source explosive columns, other industrial explosives
	0/0/0	4	0	0	0	0	0	0//0	0/0/		//	0/0/	Other ammonium nitrate explosives except propellants
													---Other
	0/0/0	4	0	0	0	0	0	0//0	0/0/			0/0/	Meet specific standared of explosives(containing hexanitrostilbene>2%, density>1. 8g/cm^3, exploding velocity>8000m/s)
	0/0/0	4	0	0	0	0	0	0//0	0/0/		//	0/0/	Other configurations of explosives for civil use, except for propellants
	0/0/0	4	0	0	0	0	0	0//0	0/0/		//	0/0/	Other compound explosives, except propellants
													Safety fuses; detonating fuses; percussion or detonating caps; igniters; electric detonators:
													Safety fuses; detonating fuses; percussion or detonating caps; igniters; electric detonators
	0/0/0	4	0	0	0	0	0	0//0	0/0/			0/0/0	Detonating bridge
	0/0/0	4	0	0	0	0	0	0//0	0/0/			0/0/0	Detonating bridge filaments
	0/0/0	4	0	0	0	0	0	0//0	0/0/			0/0/0	Percussion cap
	0/0/0	4	0	0	0	0	0	0//0	0/0/			0/0/0	Detonating foil igniter
	0/0/0	4	0	0	0	0	0	0//0	0/0/			0/0/0	Devices with one or more detonator (detonated by one electric firing signal at the same time, other than those used detonating powder only)
	0/0/0	4	0	0	0	0	0	0//0	0/0/		//	0/0/0	Industrial Explosive Detonator Ignition Device
	0/0/0	4	0	0	0	0	0	0//0	0/0/		//	0/0/0	Other Explosive Detonator Ignition Devices
	0/0/0	4	0	0	0	0	0	0//0	0/0/		//	0/0/0	Other safety fuses, detonating fuses and other detonating devices for civil use
	0/0/0	4	0	0	0	0	0	0//0	0/0/		//	0/0/0	Other detonating devices (including cap or detonator, detonator, electric detonator) such as safety fuse detonating cord
													Fireworks, signalling flares, rain rockets, fog signals and other pyrotechnic articles:
	0/0/0	0	0	0	0	0	0	0//0	0/0/			0/0/	-Fireworks
													-Other
	0/0/0	0	0	0	0	0	0	0//0	0/0/		//	0/0/	Fire and explosive devices for weather modification, marine life－saving pyrotechnic signals and other special－purpose pyrotechnic products
	0/0/0	0	0	0	0	0	0	0//0	0/0/		//	0/0/	Other signal bombs, rain rockets and other pyrotechnics

税则号列	货品名称〔CIQ 扩展编码及品名－T2 表示见附表 2〕	最惠(%)	暂定税率	普通	增值/消费	出口退税	计量单位	监管条件	检验检疫	特殊证件对美关税
36.05	**火柴，但税目 36.04 的烟火制品除外：**									
3605.0000	火柴，但税目 36.04 的烟火制品除外〔101 含木制品的其他轻工品，102 任何地方可擦燃〕	6		100	13/	0	千克			1/11
36.06	**各种形状的铈铁及其他引火合金；本章注释二所述的易燃材料制品：**									
3606.1000	-直接灌注香烟打火机及类似打火器用的液体燃料或液化气体燃料，其包装容器的容积不超过 300 立方厘米〔999〕	6		80	13/	0	千克			1/11
	-其他：									
	---铈铁及其他引火合金：									
3606.9011	----已切成形可直接使用〔999〕	6		80	13/	0	千克			1/11
3606.9019	----其他〔102〕	6		50	13/	0	千克			1/
3606.9090	---其他〔301 爆炸品〕	6		80	13/	0	千克			1/

协定税率 %										特惠税率 %			Article Description
亚太5国	东/冰/格	巴基斯坦	韩国	瑞士	哥达	秘鲁	澳大利亚	新西/坡/智	港/澳/台	亚太2国	老/柬/缅	36/3/1	
													Matches, other than pyrotechnic articles of heading No. 36. 04:
	0/0/0	0	0	0	0	0	0	0//0	0/0/			0/0/0	Matches, other than pyrotechnic articles of heading No. 36. 04
													Ferro-cerium and other pyrophoric alloys in all forms; articles of combustible materials as specified in Note 2 to this Chapter:
	0/0/0	4.5	4	0	0	0	0	0//0	0/0/			0/0/	-Liquid or liquefied-gas fuels in containers of a kind used for filling or refilling cigarette or similar lighters and of a capacity not exceeding 300 cm^3
													-Other:
													---Ferro-cerium and other pyrophoric alloys:
	0/0/0	4	0	0	0	0	0	0//0	0/0/			0/0/0	----Cut to shape, for immediate use
	0/0/0	4	0	0	0	0	0	0//0	0/0/			0/0/0	----Other
	0/0/0	4	0	0	0	0	0	0//0	0/0/			0/0/0	---Other

第三十七章
照相及电影用品

注释：

一、本章不包括废碎料。

二、本章所称“摄影”，是指光或其他射线作用于感光面上直接或间接形成可见影像的过程。

税则号列		货品名称〔CIQ 扩展编码及品名－T2 表示见附表 2〕	最惠(%)	暂定税率	普通	增值/消费	出口退税	计量单位	监管条件	检验检疫	特殊证件对美关税
37.01		**未曝光的摄影感光硬片及平面软片，用纸、纸板及纺织物以外任何材料制成；未曝光的一次成像感光平片，不论是否分装：**									
3701.1000		-X 光用〔999〕	20	10	40	13/	13	千克/平方米			1/25
3701.2000		---一次成像平片〔999〕	5		40	13/	13	千克			1/30
		-其他硬片及软片，任何一边超过 255 毫米：									
		---照相制版用：									
3701.3021		----激光照排片〔999〕	0		50	13/	13	千克/平方米			1/5
3701.3022		----PS 版〔999〕	0		50	13/	13	千克/平方米			1/30
3701.3024		----CTP 版〔999〕	0		50	13/	13	千克/平方米			1/30
3701.3025		----柔性印刷板〔999〕	0		50	13/	13	千克/平方米			1/10
3701.3029		----其他〔999〕	0		50	13/	13	千克/平方米			1/15
3701.3090		---其他〔999〕	0		70	13/	13	千克/平方米			1/25
		-其他：									
3701.9100		--彩色摄影用〔999〕	20		70	13/	13	千克			1/50
		--其他：									
3701.9920		---照相制版用									
3701.9920	01	石英玻璃基质的未曝光感光硬片〔999〕	5/3.8		40	13/	13	千克/平方米			1/35，33.8
3701.9920	90	照相制版用其他未曝光软片及硬片(非彩色摄影用，边长≤255mm)〔999〕	5/3.8		40	13/	13	千克/平方米			1/35,33.8
3701.9990		---其他〔999〕	12.5/9.4		70	13/	13	千克/平方米			1/22.5,19.4
37.02		**成卷的未曝光摄影感光胶片，用纸、纸板及纺织物以外任何材料制成；未曝光的一次成像感光卷片：**									
3702.1000		-X 光用〔999〕	10		40	13/	13	千克/平方米			1/35
		-无齿孔的其他胶片，宽度不超过 105 毫米：									
		--彩色摄影用：									
3702.3110		----一次成像卷片〔999〕	5		40	13/	13	个/平方米			1/
3702.3190		---其他〔999〕	T3		T3	13/	13	个/平方米			1/5
		--其他涂卤化银乳液的：									
3702.3210		----一次成像卷片〔999〕	5		40	13/	13	千克/平方米			1/
3702.3220		---照相制版用〔999〕	T3		T3	13/	13	千克/平方米			1/
3702.3290		---其他〔999〕	T3		T3	13/	13	千克/平方米			1/15
		--其他：									
3702.3920		---照相制版用〔999〕	T3		T3	13/	13	千克/平方米			1/10
3702.3990		---其他〔999〕	T3		T3	13/	13	千克/平方米			1/15
		-无齿孔的其他胶片，宽度超过 105 毫米：									
3702.4100		--彩色摄影用，宽度超过 610 毫米，长度超过 200 米〔999〕	T3		T3	13/	13	千克/平方米			1/
		--非彩色摄影用，宽度超过 610 毫米，长度超过 200 米：									
		---照相制版用：									
3702.4221		----印刷电路板制造用光致抗蚀干膜〔999〕	T3		T3	13/	13	千克/平方米			1/25

Chapter 37
Photographic or cinematographic goods

Chapter Notes:

1. This Chapter does not cover waste or scrap.
2. In this Chapter the word "photographic" relates to the process by which visible images are formed, directly or indirectly, by the action of light or other forms of radiation on photosensitive surfaces.

协定税率 %										特惠税率 %			
亚太5国	东/冰/格	巴基斯坦	韩国	瑞士	哥达	秘鲁	澳大利亚	新西/坡/智	港/澳/台	亚太2国	老/柬/缅	36/3/1	Article Description
													Photographic plates and film in the flat, sensitized, unexposed, of any material other than paper, paperboard or textiles; instant print film in the flat, sensitized, unexposed, whether or not in packs:
16	5/0/0		16	6	0	0	0	0//0	0/0/			0/0/	-For X-ray
	0/0/0	0	2	2.6	0	0	0	0//0	0/0/			0/0/0	-Instant print film
													-Other plates and film, with any side exceeding 255 mm:
													---For preparing printing plates or cylinders:
	5//		1.4元/平方米					//	0/0/			0/0/	----Laser phototypesetting film
	5//		3.2元/平方米					//	0/0/			0/0/	----Precoated sensitized plate
	0//	4	3.2元/平方米					//	0/0/			0/0/	----CTF plate
	//		6元/平方米					//	0/0/			0/0/	----Flexible printed board
	5//		0元/平方米					//	0/0/			0/0/	----Other
	0//		12					//	0/0/			0/0/	---Other
													-Other:
	0/0/0			6.6	0	0	0	0/0/0	0/0/			0/0/	--For colour photography (polychrome)
													--Other:
													---For preparing printing plates or cylinders
	0/0/0	4.5	4	0	0	0	0	0//0	0/0/			0/0/	Quartz glass matrix of photographic film, unexposed
	0/0/0	4.5	4	0	0	0	0	0//0	0/0/			0/0/	Other photographic plates and film in the flat sensitized for preparing printing plates or cylinders, with any side≤255mm, (other than ultrafine-grain plate, other than for colour photography)
	0/0/0			7.5	0	0	0	0/0/0	0/0/			0/0/	---Other
													Photographic film in rolls, sensitized, unexposed, of any material other than paper, paperboard or textiles; instant print film in rolls, sensitized, unexposed:
8	5/0/0		6	0	0	0	0	0//0	0/0/			0/0/	-For X-ray
													-Other film, without perforations, of a width not exceeding 105 mm:
													--For colour photography (polychrome):
	0/0/0	0	0	0	0	0	0	0//0	0/0/			0/0/0	---Instant print film
	0/0/0				0	0	0	0/0/0	0/0/			0/0/	---Other
													--Other, with silver halide emulsion:
	0/0/0	0	0	0	0	0	0	0//0	0/0/			0/0/0	---Instant print film
	0/0/0	1.8元/平方米	1.8元/平方米	0	0	0	0	0//0	0/0/			0/0/	---For preparing printing plates or cylinders
	0/0/0		14.7元/平方米	6.6	0	0	0	0/0/0	0/0/			0/0/	---Other
													--Other:
	0/0/0	4.8元/平方米	4.8元/平方米	0	0	0	0	0//0	0/0/			0/0/	---For preparing printing plates or cylinders
	0/0/0		16.8元/平方米	6.6	0	0	0	0/0/0	0/0/			0/0/	---Other
													-Other film, without perforations, of a width exceeding 105 mm:
	/0/0			4.8	0	0	0	0//0	0/0/			0/0/	--Of a width exceeding 610 mm and of a length exceeding 200 m, for colour photography (polychrome)
													--Of a width exceeding 610 mm and of a length exceeding 200 m, other than for colour photography:
													---For preparing printing plates or cylinders:
	0/0/0	0.2元/平方米		0	0	0	0	0/0/0	0/0/			0/0/	----Wide anticorrosive photographic plate for printed circuit processing

税则号列	货品名称〔CIQ扩展编码及品名—T2表示见附表2〕	最惠(%)	暂定税率	普通	增值/消费	出口退税	计量单位	监管条件	检验检疫	特殊证件对美关税
3702.4229	----其他〔999〕	T3	1.0元/平方米	T3	13/	13	千克/平方米			1/25
	---其他：									
3702.4292	----红色或红外激光胶片									
3702.4292　01	未曝光红色或红外激光胶片(宽长胶卷指宽度>800mm，长度>1000m)〔999〕	T3	0.5元/平方米	T3	13/	13	千克/平方米			1/30
3702.4292　90	其他未曝光红色或红外激光胶片(610mm<宽度≤800mm，200m<长度≤1000m)〔999〕	T3		T3	13/	13	千克/平方米			1/30
3702.4299	----其他〔999〕	T3		T3	13/	13	千克/平方米			1/35
	--宽度超过610毫米，长度不超过200米：									
	---照相制版用：									
3702.4321	----激光照排片〔999〕	T3		T3	13/	13	千克/平方米			1/
3702.4329	----其他〔999〕	T3		T3	13/	13	千克/平方米			1/15
3702.4390	---其他〔999〕	T3		T3	13/	13	千克/平方米			1/15
	--宽度超过105毫米，但不超过610毫米：									
	---照相制版用：									
3702.4421	----激光照排片〔999〕	T3		T3	13/	13	千克/平方米			1/
3702.4422	----印刷电路板制造用光致抗蚀干膜〔999〕	T3		T3	13/	13	千克/平方米			1/30
3702.4429	----其他〔999〕	T3		T3	13/	13	千克/平方米			1/30
3702.4490	---其他〔999〕	T3		T3	13/	13	千克/平方米			1/30
	-彩色摄影用的其他胶片：									
3702.5200	--宽度不超过16毫米〔999〕	T3		T3	13/	13	米/平方米			1/5
3702.5300	--幻灯片用，宽度超过16毫米，但不超过35毫米，长度不超过30米〔999〕	T3		T3	13/	13	米/平方米			1/10
	--非幻灯片用，宽度超过16毫米，但不超过35毫米，长度不超过30米：									
3702.5410	---宽度为35毫米，长度不超过2米〔999〕	T3		T3	13/	13	米/平方米			1/10
3702.5490	---其他〔999〕	T3		T3	13/	13	米/平方米			1/
	--宽度超过16毫米，但不超过35毫米，长度超过30米：									
3702.5520	---电影胶片〔999〕	T3		T3	13/	13	米/平方米			1/15
3702.5590	---其他〔999〕	T3		T3	13/	13	米/平方米			1/
	--宽度超过35毫米：									
3702.5620	---电影胶片〔999〕	T3		T3	13/	13	米/平方米			1/15
3702.5690	---其他〔999〕	T3		T3	13/	13	米/平方米			1/5
	-其他：									
3702.9600	--宽度不超过35毫米，长度不超过30米〔999〕	T3		T3	13/	13	米/平方米			1/15
3702.9700	--宽度不超过35毫米，长度超过30米〔101硝化纤维片基，999用纸、纸板及纺织物以外任何材料制成〕	T3		T3	13/	13	米/平方米			1/15
3702.9800	--宽度超过35毫米〔999〕	T3		T3	13/	13	米/平方米			1/
37.03	**未曝光的摄影感光纸、纸板及纺织物：**									
	-成卷，宽度超过610毫米：									
3703.1010	---感光纸及纸板〔999〕	18		100	13/	13	千克			1/23
3703.1090	---其他〔999〕	18		70	13/	13	千克			1/28
	-其他，彩色摄影用：									
3703.2010	---感光纸及纸板〔999〕	35		100	13/	13	千克			1/45
3703.2090	---其他〔999〕	18		70	13/	13	千克			1/28
	-其他：									
3703.9010	---感光纸及纸板〔999〕	35		100	13/	13	千克			1/45

协定税率 %										特惠税率 %			Article Description
亚太5国	东/冰/格	巴基斯坦	韩国	瑞士	哥达	秘鲁	澳大利亚	新西/坡/智	港/澳/台	亚太2国	老/柬/缅	36/3/1	
8	0/0/0	0.6元/平方米	0.6元/平方米	0	0	0	0	0//0	0/0/			0/0/	----Other
													---Other:
													----Red or infra-red laser film
12.8	0/0/0		0.9元/平方米	4.8	0	0	0	0/0/0	0/0/			0/0/	Red or infra-red laser film, unexposed, of a width＞800mm, of a length＞1000m,
12.8	0/0/0		0.9元/平方米	4.8	0	0	0	0/0/0	0/0/			0/0/	Other red or infra-red laser film, unexposed, 610mm＜ width≤800mm, 200m＜length≤1001m,
12.8	0/0/0		2.8元/平方米	4.8	0	0	0	0/0/0	0/0/			0/0/	----Other
													--Of a width exceeding 610 mm and of a length not exceeding 200 m:
													---For preparing printing plates or cylinders:
8	0/0/0	0.7元/平方米	0.7元/平方米	0	0	0	0	0//0	0/C/			0/0/	----Laser phototypesetting film
9	0/0/0	1.5元/平方米	1.4元/平方米	0	0	0	0	0//0	0/0/			0/0/	----Other
16	0/0/0		10.2元/平方米	6	0	0	0	0/0/0	0/0/			0/0/	---Other
													--Of a width exceeding 105 mm but not exceeding 610 mm:
													---For preparing printing plates or cylinders:
9	0/0/0	0.8元/平方米	0.8元/平方米	0	0	0	0	0//0	0/0/			0/0/	----Laser phototypesetting film
	0/0/0	0.4元/平方米		0	0	0	0	0//0	0/0/			0/0/	----Narrow anticorrosive photographic plate for printed circuit processing
	0/0/0	1.2元/平方米	1.1元/平方米	0	0	0	0	0//0	0/0/			0/0/	----Other
16	0/0/0		16.2元/平方米	6	0	0	0	0/0/0	0/0/			0/0/	---Other
													-Other film, for colour photography (polychrome):
	0/0/0				0	0	0	0/0/0	0/0/			0/0/	--Of a width not exceeding 16 mm
	0/0/0				0	0	0	0/0/0	0/0/			0/0/	--Of a width exceeding 16 mm but not exceeding 35 mm and of a length not exceeding 30 m, for slides
													--Of a width exceeding 16 mm but not exceeding 35 mm and of a length not exceeding 30 m, other than for slides:
8	5/0/0		13.2元/平方米	5.4	0	0	0	0//0	0/0/			0/0/	---Of a width 35 mm and of a length not exceeding 2 m
14.4	5/0/0		14.4元/平方米	5.4	0	0	0	0//0	0/0/			0/0/	---Other
													--Of a width exceeding 16 mm but not exceeding 35 mm and of a length exceeding 30 m:
20	5/0/0				0	0	0	0//0	0/0/			0/0/	---Cinematographic film
32	5/0/0				0		0	0//0	0/0/			0//	---Other
													--Of a width exceeding 35 mm:
	0/0/0		9.1元/平方米	7.2	0	0	0	0/0/0	0/0/			0/0/	---Cinematographic film
	0/0/0				0	0	0	0/0/0	0/0/			0/0/	---Other
													-Other:
	5/0/0		12.6元/平方米	6	0	0	0	0//0	0/0/			0/0/	--Of a width not exceeding 35 mm and of a length not exceeding 30 mm
	5/0/0		5.4元/平方米	5.4	0	0	0	0//0	0/0/			0/0/	--Of a width not exceeding 35 mm and of a length exceeding 30 mm
	0/0/0	8元/平方米	4元/平方米	5.4	0	0	0	0/0/0	0/0/			0/0/	--Of a width exceeding 35 mm
													Photographic paper, paperboard and textiles, sensitized, unexposed:
													-In rolls of a width exceeding 610 mm:
14.4	5/0/0		10.8	5.4	0	0	0	0//0	0/0/			0/0/	---Photographic paper and paperboard
14.4	5/0/0		10.8	5.4	0	0	0	0//0	0/0/			0/0/	---Other
													-Other, for colour photography (polychrome):
	5/0/0				0		0	0//0	0/0/			0//	---Photographic paper and paperboard
	5/0/0		10.8	5.4	0	0	0	0//0	0/0/			0/0/	---Other
													-Other:
	5/0/0				0		0	0//0	0/0/			0//	---Photographic paper and paperboard

税则号列	货品名称〔CIQ扩展编码及品名—T2表示见附表2〕	最惠(%)	暂定税率	普通	增值/消费	出口退税	计量单位	监管条件	检验检疫	特殊证件对美关税
3703.9090	---其他〔999〕	18		70	13/	13	千克			1/28
37.04	**已曝光未冲洗的摄影硬片、软片、纸、纸板及纺织物：**									
3704.0010	---电影胶片〔999〕									
3704.0010 10	含有人类遗传资源信息资料的电影胶片(已曝光但未冲洗)	6.5		30	13/	13	千克	V		1/11.5
3704.0010 20	录有广播电影电视节目的电影胶片(已曝光但未冲洗)	6.5		30	13/	13	千克	b		1/11.5
3704.0010 90	其他电影胶片(已曝光但未冲洗)	6.5		30	13/	13	千克			1/11.5
3704.0090	---其他〔999〕									
3704.0090 10	含有人类遗传资源信息资料的其他已曝光未冲洗的摄影硬、软片(包括已曝光未冲洗的感光纸、纸板及纺织物)〔999〕	18		70	13/	13	千克	V		1/33
3704.0090 90	其他已曝光未冲洗的摄影硬、软片(包括已曝光未冲洗的感光纸、纸板及纺织物)〔999〕	18		70	13/	13	千克			1/33
37.05	**已曝光已冲洗的摄影硬片及软片，但电影胶片除外：**									
3705.0010	---教学专用幻灯片〔999〕									
3705.0010 10	含有人类遗传资源信息资料的教学专用幻灯片(已曝光已冲洗)	0		0	13/	13	千克	V		1/5
3705.0010 20	录有广播电影电视节目的教学专用幻灯片(已曝光已冲洗)	0		0	13/	13	千克	b		1/5
3705.0010 90	其他教学专用幻灯片(已曝光已冲洗)	0		0	13/	13	千克			1/5
	---缩微胶片：									
3705.0021	----书籍、报刊的〔999〕									
3705.0021 10	含有人类遗传资源信息资料的书籍、报刊用缩微胶片(已曝光已冲洗)	0		0	13/	13	千克	V		1/5
3705.0021 90	其他书籍、报刊用缩微胶片(已曝光已冲洗)	0		0	13/	13	千克			1/5
3705.0029	----其他〔999〕									
3705.0029 10	含有人类遗传资源信息资料的其他缩微胶片(已曝光已冲洗)	0		14	13/	13	千克	V		1/5
3705.0029 90	其他缩微胶片(已曝光已冲洗)	0		14	13/	13	千克			1/5
3705.0090	---其他〔999〕									
3705.0090 10	含有人类遗传资源信息资料的其他摄影硬、软片(已曝光已冲洗)(电影胶片除外)〔999〕	0		70	13/	13	千克	V		1/10
3705.0090 90	其他摄影硬、软片(已曝光已冲洗)(电影胶片除外)〔999〕	0		70	13/	13	千克			1/10
37.06	**已曝光已冲洗的电影胶片，不论是否配有声道或仅有声道：**									
	-宽度在35毫米及以上：									
3706.1010	---教学专用〔999〕									
3706.1010 10	录有广播电影电视节目的已冲洗的教学专用中宽电影胶片	0		0	13/	13	千克/米	b		1/5
3706.1010 90	其他已冲洗的教学专用中宽电影胶片(中宽胶片指宽度≥35毫米，不论是否配有声道或仅有声道)	0		0	13/	13	千克/米			1/5
3706.1090	---其他〔999〕									
3706.1090 10	录有广播电影电视节目的已冲洗的其他中宽电影胶片	5		14	13/	13	千克/米	b		1/10
3706.1090 90	其他已冲洗的其他中宽电影胶片(中宽胶片指宽度≥35毫米，不论是否配有声道或仅有声道)	5		14	13/	13	千克/米			1/10
	-其他：									
3706.9010	---教学专用〔999〕									
3706.9010 10	录有广播电影电视节目的教学专用其他已冲洗的电影胶片	0		0	13/	13	千克/米	b		1/
3706.9010 90	其他教学专用其他已冲洗的电影胶片(宽度＜35毫米)	0		0	13/	13	千克/米			1/
3706.9090	---其他〔999〕									
3706.9090 10	录有广播电影电视节目的其他已冲洗的电影胶片	4		14	13/	13	千克/米	b		1/
3706.9090 90	其他已冲洗的电影胶片(宽度＜35毫米)	4		14	13/	13	千克/米			1/
37.07	**摄影用化学制剂(不包括上光漆、胶水、黏合剂及类似制剂)；摄影用未混合产品；定量包装或零售包装可立即使用的：**									
3707.1000	-感光乳液									
3707.1000 01	不含银的感光乳液剂〔999,301易燃液体〕	8	4	35	13/	13	千克			1/
3707.1000 90	其他感光乳液〔101尼龙丝网感光浆,999,102易燃液体〕	8		35	13/	13	千克			1/

协定税率 %										特惠税率 %			Article Description
亚太5国	东/冰/格	巴基斯坦	韩国	瑞士	哥达	秘鲁	澳大利亚	新西/坡/智	港/澳/台	亚太2国	老/柬/缅	36/3/1	
													-Other:
	0/0/0	12.8	9.6	4.8	0	0	0	0/0/0	0/0/			0/0/[illegible]	---For use in developing photographic film and photographs
	0/0/0	4.5	4	0	0	0	0	0/0/0	0/0/			0/0/0	---For use in photo-copying apparatus
	0/0/0	4	3.2	2.4	0	0	0	0//0	0/0/			0/0/0	---Other

第三十八章
杂项化学产品

注释：

一、本章不包括：

（一）单独的已有化学定义的元素及化合物，但下列各项除外：

1. 人造石墨（税目 38.01）；
2. 制成税目 38.08 所述的形状或包装的杀虫剂、杀鼠剂、杀菌剂、除草剂、抗萌剂、植物生长调节剂、消毒剂及类似产品；
3. 灭火器的装配药及已装药的灭火弹（税目 38.13）；
4. 下列注释二所规定的检定参照物；
5. 下列注释三（一）及三（三）所规定的产品。

（二）化学品与食品或其他营养物质的混合物，配制食品用的（一般归入税目 21.06）。

（三）符合第二十六章注释三（一）或三（二）的规定，含有金属，砷及其混合物的矿渣、矿灰及残渣（包括淤渣，但下水道淤泥除外）（税目 26.20）；

（四）药品（税目 30.03 及 30.04）。

（五）用于提取贱金属或生产贱金属化合物的废催化剂（税目 26.20），主要用于回收贵金属的废催化剂（税目 71.12），或某种形状（例如，精细粉末或纱网状）的金属或金属合金催化剂（第十四类或第十五类）。

二、（一）税目 38.22 所称的"检定参照物"，是指附有证书的参照物，该证书标明了参照物属性的指标、确定这些指标的方法以及与每一指标相关的确定度，这些参照物适用于分析、校准和比较。

（二）除第二十八章和二十九章的产品外，检定参照物在本目录中应优先归入税目 38.22。

三、税目 38.24 包括不归入本协调制度其他品目的下列货品：

（一）每颗重量不小于 2.5 克的氧化镁、碱金属或碱土金属卤化物制成的培养晶体（光学元件除外）；

（二）杂醇油；骨焦油；

（三）零售包装的除墨剂；

（四）零售包装的蜡纸改正液、其他改正液及改正带（税目 96.12 的产品除外）；

（五）可熔性陶瓷测温器（例如，塞格测温锥）。

四、本目录所称"城市垃圾"，是指一种从家庭、宾馆、餐馆、医院、商店、办公室等收集来的废物、马路和人行道的垃圾以及建筑垃圾或废墟废物。城市垃圾通常含有大量各种各样的材料，例如，塑料、橡胶、木材、纸张、纺织品、玻璃、金属、食物、破碎家具和其他已损坏或被丢弃的物品，但不包括：

（一）已从垃圾中分拣出来的单独的材料或物品，例如，塑料、橡胶、木材、纸张、纺织品、玻璃、金属的废品及用尽的电池，这些材料或物品应归入本目录中适当税目；

（二）工业废物；

（三）在第三十章注释四（十）所规定的废药物；

（四）本章注释六（一）所规定的医疗废物。

五、税目 38.25 所称"下水道淤泥"，是指城市污水处理厂产生的淤渣，包括预处理的废物、洗涤污垢和性质不稳定的淤泥。但适合作为肥料用的性质稳定的淤泥除外（第三十一章）。

六、税目 38.25 所称"其他废物"适用于：

（一）医疗废物，即医学研究、诊断、治疗以及其他内科、外科、牙科或兽医治疗所产生的被污染的废物，通常含有病菌和药物，需作专门处理（例如，脏的敷料、用过的手套及注射器）；

（二）废有机溶剂；

（三）废的金属酸洗液、液压油、制动油及防冻液；

（四）其他化学工业及相关工业的废物。

但不包括主要含有石油及从沥青矿物提取的油类的废油（税目 27.10）。

七、税目 38.26 所称的"生物柴油"是指从动植物油脂（不论是否使用过）得到的用作燃料的脂肪酸单烷基酯。

子目注释：

一、子目 3808.52 及 3808.59 仅包括税目 38.08 的货品，含有一种或多种下列物质：甲草胺（ISO）、涕灭威（ISO）、艾氏剂（ISO）、谷硫磷（ISO）、乐杀螨（ISO）、毒杀芬（ISO）、敌菌丹（ISO）、氯丹（ISO）、杀虫脒（ISO）、乙酯杀螨醇（ISO）、滴滴涕（ISO，INN）〔1，1，1-三氯-2，2-双（4-氯苯基）乙烷〕、狄氏剂（ISO，INN）、4，6-二硝基邻甲酚〔二硝酚（ISO）〕及其盐、地乐酚（ISO）及其盐或酯、硫丹（ISO）、1，2-二溴乙烷（ISO）、1，2-二氯乙烷（ISO）、氟乙酰胺（ISO）、七氯（ISO）、六氯苯（ISO）、1，2，3，4，5，6-六氯环己烷〔六六六（ISO）〕，包括林丹（ISO，INN）、汞化合物、甲胺磷（ISO）、久效磷（ISO）、环氧乙烷（氧化乙烯）、对硫磷（ISO）、甲基对硫磷（ISO）、五溴二苯醚及八溴二苯醚、五氯苯酚（ISO）及其盐或酯、全氟辛基磺酸及其盐、全氟辛基磺胺、全氟辛基磺酰氯、磷胺（ISO）、2，4，5-涕（ISO）（2，4，5-三氯苯氧基乙酸）及其盐或酯、三丁基锡化合物。

子目 3808.59 还包括含有苯菌灵（ISO）、克百威（ISO）及福美双（ISO）混合物的粉状制剂。

二、子目 3808.61 及 3808.69 仅包括品目 38.08 项下含有下列物质的货品：α-氯氰菊酯（ISO）、恶虫威（ISO）、联苯菊酯（ISO）、虫螨腈（ISO）、氟氯氰菊酯（ISO）、溴氰菊酯（INN，ISO）、醚菊酯（INN）、杀螟硫磷（ISO）、高效氯氟氰菊酯（ISO）、马拉硫磷（ISO）、甲基嘧啶磷（ISO）、或残杀威（ISO）。

Chapter 38
Miscellaneous chemical products

Notes:

1. This Chapter does not cover:
(a) Separate chemically defined elements or compounds with the exception of the following:
(i) Artificial graphite (heading No. 38.01);
(ii) Insecticides, rodenticides, fungicides, herbicides, anti-sprouting products and plant-growth regulators, disinfectants and similar products, put up as described in heading No. 38.08;
(iii) Products put up as charges for fire-extinguishers or put up in fire-extinguishing grenades (heading No. 38.13);
(iv) Certified reference materials specified in Note 2 below;
(v) Products specified in Note 3(a) or 3(c) below.
(b) Mixtures of chemicals with foodstuffs or other substances with nutritive value, of a kind used in the preparations of human foodstuffs (generally heading No. 21.06).
(c) Slag, ash and residues (including sludges, other than sewage sludge), containing metals, arsenic or their mixtures and meeting the requirements of Note 3(a) or (b) to Chapter 26 (heading No. 26.20).
(d) Medicaments (heading No. 30.03 or 30.04). or
(e) Spent catalysts of a kind used for the extraction of base metals or for the manufacture of chemical compounds of base metals (heading No. 26.20), spent catalysts of a kind used principally for the recovery of precious metal (heading No. 71.12) or catalysts consisting of metals or metal alloys in the form of, for example, finely divided powder or woven gauze (Section XIV or XV).
2. (a) For the purpose of heading No. 38.22, the expression "certified reference materials" means reference materials which are accompanied by a certificate which indicates the values of the certified properties, the methods used to detemine these values and the degree of certainty associated with each value and which are suitable for analytical, calibrating or referencing purposes.
(b) With the exception of the products of Chapter 28 or 29, for the classification of certified reference materials, heading No. 38.22 shall take precedence over any other heading in the Nomenclature.
3. Heading No. 38.24 includes the following goods which are not to be classified in any other heading of the Nomenclature:
(a) Cultured crystals (other than optical elements) weighing not less than 2.5 g each, of magnesium oxide or of the halides of the alkali or alkaline-earth metals;
(b) Fusel oil; Dippel's oil;
(c) Ink removers put up in packings for retail sale;
(d) Stencil correctors, other correcting fluids and correction tape, put up in packings for retail sale (other than those of heading, 96.12);
(e) Ceramic firing testers, fusible (for example, Seger cones).
4. Throughout the Nomenclature, "municipal waste" means waste of a kind collected from households, hotels, restaurants, hospitals, shops, offices, etc., road and pavement sweepings, as well as construction and demolition waste. Municipal waste generally contains a large variety of materials such as plastics, rubber, wood, paper, textiles, glass, metals, food materials, broken furniture and other damaged or discarded articles. The term "municipal waste", however, does not cover:
(a) Individual materials or articles segregated from the waste, such as wastes of plastics, rubber, wood, paper, textiles, glass or metals and spent batteries which fall in their appropriate headings of the Nomenclature;
(b) Industrial waste;
(c) Waste pharmaceuticals, as defined in Note 4(k) to Chapter 30; or
(d) Clinical waste, as defined in Note 6 (a) below.
5. For the purposes of heading 38.25, "sewage sludge" means sludge arising from urban effluent treatment plant and includes pretreatment waste, scourings and unstabilised sludge. Stabilised sludge when suitable for use as fertiliser is excluded (Chapter 31).
6. For the purposes of heading No. 38.25, the expression "other wastes" applies to:
(a) Clinical waste, that is, contaminated waste arising from medical research, diagnosis, treatment or other medical, surgical, dental or veterinary procedures, which often contain pathogens and pharmaceutical substances and require special disposal procedures (for example, soiled dressings, used gloves and used syringes);
(b) Waste organic solvents;
(c) Wastes of metal pickling liquors, hydraulic fluids, brake fluids and anti-freezing fluids; and
(d) Other wastes from chemical or allied industries.
The expression "other wastes" does not, however, cover wastes which contain mainly petroleum oils or oils obtained from bituminous minerals (heading No. 27.10).
7. For the purposes of heading 38.26, the term "biodiesel" means mono-alkyl esters of fatty acids of a kind used ao a fuel, derived from animal or vegetable fats and oils whether or not used

Subheading Note:

1. Subheading No. 3808.52 and 3808.59 covers only goods of heading No. 38.08, containing one or more of the following substances: alachlor(ISO)、aldicarb(ISO)、aldrin(ISO)、azinphos-methyl(ISO)、binapacryl(ISO)、toxaphene(ISO)、captafol(ISO)、chlordan(ISO)、chlordimeform hydrochloride(ISO)、chlorobenzilate(ISO)、DDT(ISO,INN)〔1,1,1 - three chloro - 2,2 - bis (4 chloro phenyl) ethane〕、compound(ISO,INN)、4,6 - two, dinitroorthocresol DNOC (ISO)及其盐、Dinoseb (ISO) and its salts or esters、endosulfan (ISO)、1,2 dibromethane(ISO)、1,2 - two chloride(ISO)、fluoroacetamide(ISO)、heptachlor(ISO)、hexachlorobenzene(ISO)、1,2,3,4,5,6 - 666 benzenehexachloride (ISO), including lindane(ISO,INN)、Mercuric compound、methamidophos(ISO)、Azodrin(ISO)、epoxyethane(ethylene oxide)、parathion(ISO)、methyl parathion(ISO)、[网络] PentaBDE and OctaBDE、chlorophenasic acid(ISO) and its salts or esters、Perfluorooctanesulfonic acid and its salts、Perfluorooctane sulfonamide、Perfluorooctane sulfonyl chloride、phosphamidon (ISO)、2,4,5 - t(ISO)(2,4,5-trichlorophenoxyacetic acid) and its salts or esters、tributyl tin compound.
Subheading 3808.50 also covers dustable powder formulations containing a mixture of benomyl(ISO), carbofuran(ISO) and thiram (ISO)
2. The following Subheading No.3808.61 and Subheading No.3808.69 only containing Heading No.38.08 under the goods: α-alpha cypermethrin (ISO), ficam (ISO), bifenthrin (ISO), chlorfenapyr (ISO), cyhalothrin, permethrin bromine (ISO) (INN, ISO), ethofenprox (INN), fenitrothion (ISO), lambda cyhalothrin (ISO), malathion (ISO) and pirimiphos methyl (ISO), or propoxur (ISO).

三、子目3824.81至3824.88仅包括含有下列一种或多种物质的混合物及制品：环氧乙烷（氧化乙烯）、多溴联苯（PBBs）、多氯联苯（PCBs）、多氯三联苯（PCTs）、三（2,3-二溴丙基）磷酸酯、艾氏剂（ISO）、毒杀芬（ISO）、氯丹（ISO）、十氯酮（ISO）、滴滴涕（ISO，INN）〔1,1,1-三氯-2,2-双（4-氯苯基）乙烷〕、狄氏剂（ISO，INN）、硫丹（ISO）、异狄氏剂（ISO）、七氯（ISO）、灭蚁灵（ISO）、1,2,3,4,5,6-六氯环己烷〔六六六（ISO）〕，包括林丹（ISO，INN）、五氯苯（ISO）、六氯苯（ISO）、全氟辛基磺酸及其盐、全氟辛基磺胺、全氟辛基磺酰氯，或四、五、六、七或八溴联苯醚。

四、子目3825.41和3825.49所称"废有机溶剂"，是指主要含有有机溶剂的废物，不适合再作原产品使用，不论其是否用于回收溶剂。

税则号列		货品名称〔CIQ扩展编码及品名—T2表示见附表2〕	最惠(%)	暂定税率	普通	增值/消费	出口退税	计量单位	监管条件	检验检疫	特殊证件对美关税
38.01		**人造石墨；胶态或半胶态石墨；以石墨或其他碳为基本成分的糊状、块状、板状制品或半制品：**									
3801.1000		-人造石墨									
3801.1000	10	核级石墨（纯度高于百万分之五硼当量，密度大于1.50g/cm^3）〔999〕	6.5	3	30	13/	0	千克	3		1/13
3801.1000	20	人造细晶粒整体石墨（20℃下的密度、拉伸断裂应变、热膨胀系数符合特殊要求）〔999〕	6.5	3	30	13/	0	千克	3		1/13
3801.1000	90	其他人造石墨〔999〕	6.5	3	30	13/	0	千克	3		1/13
3801.2000		-胶态或半胶态石墨〔101电子束管石墨乳，102电子数码管石墨乳，103胶体石墨乙醇制剂，104其他石墨〕	6.5		30	13/	0	千克			1/11.5
3801.3000		-电极用碳糊及炉衬用的类似糊〔999〕	6.5		35	13/	0	千克			1/16.5
		-其他：									
3801.9010		---表面处理的球化石墨〔999〕	6.5		35	13/	13	千克	3		1/31.5
3801.9090		---其他〔999〕	6.5		35	13/	0	千克	3		1/16.5
38.02		**活性碳；活性天然矿产品；动物炭黑，包括废动物炭黑：**									
		-活性碳：									
3802.1010		---木质的〔101自燃物品〕	6.5		20	13/	0	千克	G		1/16.5
3802.1090		---其他〔999〕	6.5		20	13/	0	千克	G		1/31.5
3802.9000		-其他									
3802.9000	10	濒危动物炭黑（包括废动物炭黑）〔999〕	10		45	13/	0	千克	FE		1/15
3802.9000	90	活性天然矿产品；其他动物炭黑（包括废动物炭黑）〔102〕	10		45	13/	0	千克			1/15
38.03		**妥尔油，不论是否精炼：**									
3803.0000		妥尔油，不论是否精炼〔999〕	6.5		35	13/	0	千克			1/11.5
38.04		**木浆残余碱液，不论是否浓缩、脱糖或经化学处理，包括木素磺酸盐，但不包括税目38.03的妥尔油：**									
3804.0000		木浆残余碱液，不论是否浓缩、脱糖或经化学处理，包括木素磺酸盐，但不包括税目38.03的妥尔油									
3804.0000	10	未经浓缩、脱糖或经过化学处理的木浆残余碱液（妥尔油除外）〔999〕	6.5		35	13/	0	千克	9		1/16.5
3804.0000	90	经浓缩、脱糖或经过化学处理的木浆残余碱液，包括木素磺酸盐（妥尔油除外）〔999〕	6.5		35	13/	0	千克			1/16.5
38.05		**脂松节油、木松节油和硫酸盐松节油及其他萜烯油，用蒸馏或其他方法从针叶木制得；粗制二聚戊烯；亚硫酸盐松节油及其他粗制对异丙基苯甲烷；以α萜品醇为基本成分的松油：**									
3805.1000		-脂松节油、木松节油和硫酸盐松节油〔301易燃液体，302其他化工产品〕	6.5		50	13/	0	千克	AB	MN	1/31.5
		-其他：									
3805.9010		---松油〔301易燃液体，302其他化工产品〕	6.5		50	13/	0	千克	AB	MN	1/31.5
3805.9090		---其他〔101松节油混合萜，102双戊烯，103萜品油烯〕	6.5		50	13/	0	千克			1/31.5
38.06		**松香和树脂酸及其衍生物；松香精及松香油；再熔胶：**									
		-松香及树脂酸：									
3806.1010		---松香〔999〕	10		70	13/	0	千克			1/35
3806.1020		---树脂酸〔999〕	10		70	13/	0	千克			1/

3.Subheading No.3824.81 to Subheading No.3824.88 including only mixtures and products containing one or more of the following materials: ethylene oxide (ethylene oxide), polybrominated biphenyls (PBBs), polychlorinated biphenyls (PCBs), polychlorinated biphenyl (PCTs three), three (2,3 - dibromopropyl) phosphate (ISO), aldrin, toxaphene (ISO), chlordanes (ISO), ten (ISO), ketamine (ISO, INN) DDT 1,1,1 - three - 2,2 - Double chlorine (4 - chloro phenyl) ethane, dieldrin (ISO, INN), endosulfan (ISO), endrin chloride (ISO), seven (ISO), mirex (ISO, 1,2,3,4,5,6) - benzenehexachloride 666 (ISO), including Lin Dan (ISO, INN), five - (ISO), six - (ISO), perfluorooctanesulfonic acid and its salts, perfluorooctane sulfonamide, perfluoro Xin Jihuang chloride, or 4-BDE,5-BDE,6-BDE,7-BDE or Octa-BDE

4. For the purposes of subheadings No. 3825. 41 and 3825. 49, "waste organic solvents" are wastes containing mainly organic solvents, not fit for further use as presented as primary products, whether or not intended for recovery of the solvents.

协定税率 %										特惠税率 %			
亚太5国	东/冰/格	巴基斯坦	韩国	瑞士	哥达	秘鲁	澳大利亚	新西/坡/智	港/澳/台	亚太2国	老/柬/缅	36/3/1	Article Description
													Artificial graphite; colloidal or semi-colloidal graphite; preparations based on graphite or other carbon in the form of pastes, blocks, plates or other semi-manufactures:
													-Artificial graphite
	0/0/0	0	2.6	2	0	0	0	0//0	0/0/			0/0/0	Nuclear graphite (purity＞5/million boron equivalent, density＞1. 50g/cm^3)
	0/0/0	0	2.6	2	0	0	0	0//0	0/0/			0/0/0	Artificial fine-grainedgraphite(density, temsile fracture strain, coefficient of thermal expansion in line with specific requirements at 20℃ or below)
	0/0/0	0	2.6	2	0	0	0	0//0	0/0/			0/0/0	Other artificial graphite
	0/0/0	4	3.9	0	0	0	0	0//0	0/0/			0/0/0	-Colloidal or semi-colloidal graphite
	0/0/0	4	0	2	0	0	0	0//0	0/0/			0/0/0	-Carbonaceous pastes for electrodes and similar pastes for furnace linings
													-Other:
	0/0/0	4	0	0	0	0	0	0//0	0/0/			0/0/0	---Surface treatment of spherical graphite
	0/0/0	0	0	0	0	0	0	0//0	0/0/			0/0/0	---Other
													Activated carbon; activated natural mineral products; animal black, including spent animal black:
													-Activated carbon:
4.2	0/0/0	4	0	0	0	0	0	0//0	0/0/			0/0/	---Of wood
4.2	0/0/0	4	0	0	0	0	0	0//0	0/0/			0/0/	---Other
													-Other
	0/0/0	4.5	4	0	0	0	0	0/0/0	0/0/			0/0/	Endangered animals black(including spent animal black)
	0/0/0	4.5	4	0	0	0	0	0/0/0	0/0/			0/0/	Activated natural mineral products; other animal black (including spent animal black)
													Tall oil, whether or not refined:
	0/0/0	4	0	0	0	0	0	0//0	0/0/			0/0/0	Tall oil, whether or not refined
													Residual lyes from the manufacture of wood pulp, whether or not concentrated, desugared or chemically treated, including lignin sulphonates, but excluding tall oil of heading No. 38. 03:
													Residual lyes from the manufacture of wood pulp, whether or not concentrated, desugared or chemically treated, including lignin sulphonates, but excluding tall oil of heading No. 38. 03
	0/0/0	4	2.6	0	0	0	0	0//0	0/0/			0/0/	Residual lyes from the manufactare of wood pulp, non-concentrated, non-desugared or non-chemically treated(exincluding tall oil)
	0/0/0	4	2.6	0	0	0	0	0//0	0/0/			0/0/	Residual lyes from the manufacture of wood pulp, concentrated, desugared or chemically treated, including lignin Sulp-honates (excluding tall oil)
													Gum, wood or sulphate turpentine and other terpenic oils produced by the distillation or other treatment of coniferous woods; crude dipentene; sulphite turpentine and other crude paracymene; pine oil containing alpha-terpineol as the main constituent:
	0/0/0	4	0	0	0	0	0	0//0	0/0/			0/0/0	-Gum, wood or sulphate turpentine oils
													-Other:
	0/0/0	4	0	0	0	0	0	0//0	0/0/			0/0/0	---Pine oil
	0/0/0	4	0	0	0	0	0	0//0	0/0/			0/0/0	---Other
													Rosin and resin acids, and derivatives thereof; rosin spirit and rosin oils; run gums:
													-Rosin and resin acids:
	0/0/0	4.5	4	0	0	0	0	0/0/0	0/0/			0/0/	---Rosin
	0/0/0	4.5	4	0	0	0	0	0//0	0/0/			0/0/	---Resin acides

税则号列		货品名称〔CIQ扩展编码及品名—T2表示见附表2〕	最惠(%)	暂定税率	普通	增值/消费	出口退税	计量单位	监管条件	检验检疫	特殊证件对美关税
		-松香盐、树脂酸盐及松香或树脂酸衍生物的盐，但松香加合物的盐除外：									
3806.2010		---松香盐及树脂酸盐〔301 易燃固体〕	6.5		40	13/	13	千克			1/11.5
3806.2090		---其他〔999〕	6.5		40	13/	13	千克			1/11.5
3806.3000		-酯胶〔301 其他危险化学品，302 无检疫要求的食品添加剂，303 属于危险化学品的食品添加剂〕	6.5		50	13/	0	千克	AB	PRQS	1/11.5
3806.9000		-其他〔999〕	6.5		40	13/	0	千克			1/16.5
38.07		**木焦油；精制木焦油；木杂酚油；粗木精；植物沥青；以松香、树脂酸或植物沥青为基本成分的啤酒桶沥青及类似制品：**									
3807.0000		木焦油；精制木焦油；木杂酚油；粗木精；植物沥青；以松香、树脂酸或植物沥青为基本成分的啤酒桶沥青及类似制品〔301〕	6.5		35	13/	0	千克			1/11.5
38.08		**杀虫剂、杀鼠剂、杀菌剂、除草剂、抗萌剂、植物生长调节剂、消毒剂及类似产品，零售形状、零售包装或制成制剂及成品(例如，经硫磺处理的带子、杀虫灯芯、蜡烛及捕蝇纸)：**									
		-本章子目注释一所列货品：									
3808.5200		--DDT(ISO)[滴滴涕(INN)]，每包净重不超过300克〔999 其他化工产品，301 其他危险化学品〕	9		35	9/	6	千克	S		1/
		--其他：									
3808.5910		---零售包装的									
3808.5910	10	零售包装含一种第38章子目注释一所列物质的货品〔999 其他化工产品，301 其他危险化学品〕	9		35	9/	6	千克	S		1/
3808.5910	90	零售包装含多种第38章子目注释一所列物质的货品〔999 其他化工产品，301 其他危险化学品〕	9		35	9/	6	千克			1/
3808.5990		---其他									
3808.5990	10	非零售包装的含有一种第38章子目注释一所列物质的货品〔999 其他化工产品，301 其他危险化学品〕	5		11	9/	6	千克	AS	M	1/
3808.5990	90	非零售包装含多种第38章子目注释一所列物质的货品〔999，301 其他危险化学品，302 其他化工产品〕	5		11	9/	6	千克			1/
		-本章子目注释二所列货品：									
3808.6100		--每包净重不超过300克〔999，301 其他危险化学品，302 其他化工产品〕	10		35	9/	6	千克	AS	M	1/
3808.6200		--每包净重超过300克，但不超过7.5千克〔999 其他化工产品，301 其他危险化学品〕	10		35	9/	6	千克	AS	M	1/
3808.6900		--其他〔999 其他化工产品，301 其他危险化学品〕	6		11	9/	6	千克	AS	M	1/31
		-其他：									
		--杀虫剂：									
		---零售包装：									
3808.9111		----蚊香〔301 其他危险化学品，302 其他化工产品〕	10		80	13/	6	千克	AS	M	1/
3808.9112		----生物杀虫剂〔301 其他危险化学品，302 其他化工产品〕	10		35	9/	6	千克	AS	M	1/
3808.9119		----其他〔301 其他危险化学品，302 其他化工产品〕	10		35	9/	6	千克	AS	M	1/35
3808.9190		---其他〔301 其他危险化学品，302 其他化工产品〕	6		11	9/	6	千克	AS	M	1/11
		--杀菌剂：									
3808.9210		---零售包装〔999〕	9		35	13/	6	千克	S		1/34
3808.9290		---其他									
3808.9290	10	非零售包装的医用杀菌剂〔999〕	6		11	13/	6	千克			1/26
3808.9290	21	经农药杀菌剂浸渍的纸质水果套袋〔999〕	6		11	13/	6	千克	S		1/26
3808.9290	29	非零售包装的其他农用杀菌剂成药〔999〕	6		11	9/	6	千克	S		1/26
3808.9290	90	非零售包装的非农用杀菌剂成药(包括非医用杀菌剂)〔999〕	6		11	9/	6	千克			1/26
		--除草剂、抗萌剂及植物生长调节剂：									
		---除草剂：									
3808.9311		----零售包装〔301 其他危险化学品，302 其他化工产品〕	9		35	9/	6	千克	AS	M	1/34
3808.9319		----其他									
3808.9319	10	非零售包装百草枯母液〔301 毒性物质和感染性物质〕	5		11	9/	6	千克	AS	M	1/15
3808.9319	90	其他非零售包装的除草剂成药〔301 其他危险化学品，302 其他化工产品〕	5		11	9/	6	千克	AS	M	1/15
		---其他：									
3808.9391		----零售包装〔999〕	9		35	9/	6	千克	S		1/14
3808.9399		----其他〔999〕	6		14	9/	6	千克	S		1/16

协定税率 %										特惠税率 %			Article Description
亚太5国	东/冰/格	巴基斯坦	韩国	瑞士	哥达	秘鲁	澳大利亚	新西/坡/智	港/澳/台	亚太2国	老/柬/缅	36/3/1	
													-Salts of rosin, of resin acids or of derivatives of rosin or resin acids, other than salts of rosin adducts:
	0/0/0	4	0	0	0	0	0	0//0	0/0/			0/0/	---Salts of rosin, of resin acids
	0/0/0	4	0	0	0	0	0	0//0	0/0/			0/0/	---Other
	0/0/0	4	0	0	0	0	0	0//0	0/0/			0/0/	-Ester gums
	0/0/0	4	0	0	0	0	0	0//0	0/0/			0/0/	-Other
													Wood tar; wood tar oils; wood creosote; wood naphtha; vegetable pitch; brewers pitch and similar preparations based on rosin, resin acids or on vegetable pitch:
	0/0/0	4	0	0	0	0	0	0//0	0/0/			0/0/	Wood tar; wood tar oils; wood creosote; wood naphtha; vegetable pitch; brewers' pitch and similar preparations based on rosin, resin acids or on vegetable pitch
													Insecticides, rodenticides, fungicides, herbicides, anti-sprouting products and plantgrowth regulators, disinfectants and similar products, put up in forms or packings for retail sale or as preparations or articles (for example, sulphur-treated bands, wicks and candles, and fly-papers):
													-Goods specified in Subheading Note 1 to this Chapter:
	0/0/0	4	0	0	0	0	0	0//0	0/0/			0/0/0	--DDT (ISO) (clofenotane (INN)), in packings of a net weight content not exceeding 300 g
													--Other:
													---Put up for retail sale
	0/0/0	4	0	0	0	0	0	0//0	0/0/			0/0/0	Goods put up for retail sale, containing one substance specified in Subheading Note 1 to Chapter 38
	0/0/0	4	0	0	0	0	0	0//0	0/0/			0/0/0	Goods put up for retail sale, containing more than one substance specified in Subheading Note 1 to Chapter 38
													---Other
	0/0/0	0	0	0	0	0	0	0//0	0/0/			0/0/0	Goods not put up for retail sale, containing one substance specified in Subheading Note 1 to Chapter 38
	0/0/0	0	0	0	0	0	0	0//0	0/0/			0/0/0	Goods not put up for retail sale, containing more than one substance specified in Subheading Note 1 to Chapter 38
													--Goods specified in Subheading Note 2 to this Chapter:
6.5	0/0/0	0	4	0	0	0	0	0//0	0/0/				--In packings of a net weight content not exceeding 300 g
6.5	0/0/0	0	4	0	0	0	0	0//0	0/0/			0/0/0	--In packings of a net weight content not exceeding 300 g but not exceeding 7.5 kg
3.9	0/0/0	0	0	1.8	0	0	0	0//0	0/0/			0/0/0	--Other
													-Other:
													--Insecticides:
													---Put up for retail sale:
0	0/0/0	0	0	0	0	0	0	0//0	0/0/			0/0/0	----Mosquito smudges
6.5	0/0/0	4.5	4	0	0	0	0	0//0	0/0/			0/0/0	----Biotic insecticide
6.5	0/0/0	4.5	4	0	0	0	0	0//0	0/0/			0/0/0	----Other
3.9	0/0/0	0	0	1.8	0	0	0	0//0	0/0/			0/0/0	---Other
													--Fungicides:
	0/0/0	4	0	2.7	0	0	0	0//0	0/0/			0/0/0	---Put up for retail sale
													---Other
	0/0/0	0	0	1.8	0	0	0	0//0	0/0/			0/0/0	Medical fungicides, not in forms or packing for retail sale
	0/0/0	0	0	1.8	0	0	0	0//0	0/0/			0/0/0	Paper bags for fruit protecion, agricultural fungicides scaked
	0/0/0	0	0	1.8	0	0	0	0//0	0/0/			0/0/0	Other agricultural fungicides medicine, not in forms or packing for retail sale
	0/0/0	0	0	1.8	0	0	0	0//0	0/0/			0/0/0	Non-agricultural fungicides medicine and non-medical fungicides, not in forms packing for retail sale
													--Herbicides anti-sprouting products and plantgrowth regulators:
													---Herbicides:
	0/0/0	4	0	0	0	0	0	0//0	0/0/			0/0/0	----Put up for retail sale
													----Other
3.3	0/0/0	0	0	1.5	0	0	0	0//0	0/0/			0/0/0	Paraquat liquor, not put up for retail sale
3.3	0/0/0	0	0	1.5	0	0	0	0//0	0/0/			0/0/0	Other herbicides Patent medicine, not put up for retail sale
													---Other:
5.9	0/0/0	4	0	0	0	0	0	0//0	0/0/			0/0/0	----Put up for retail sale
3.9	0/0/0	0	0	0	0	0	0	0//0	0/0/			0/0/0	----Other

税则号列	货品名称〔CIQ扩展编码及品名－T2表示见附表2〕	最惠(%)	暂定税率	普通	增值/消费	出口退税	计量单位	监管条件	检验检疫	特殊证件对美关税
3808.9400	--消毒剂									
3808.9400 10	医用消毒剂〔999〕	9		35	13/	6	千克			1/19
3808.9400 20	兽用已配剂量含戊二醛，癸甲溴铵消毒剂等(包括复方煤焦油酸溶液消毒防腐药)〔999〕	9		35	9/	6	千克	R		1/19
3808.9400 90	其他非医用消毒剂〔999〕	9		35	9/	6	千克			1/19
	--其他：									
3808.9910	---零售包装〔999〕	9		35	9/	6,13	千克	S		1/
3808.9990	---其他〔999包括类似品，301毒性物质和感染性物质〕	9		14	9/	6,13	千克	S		1/14
38.09	**纺织、造纸、制革及类似工业用的其他税目未列名的整理剂、染料加速着色或固色助剂及其他产品和制剂(例如，修整剂及媒染剂)：**									
3809.1000	-以淀粉物质为基本成分〔999〕	10		35	13/	0	千克			1/35
	-其他：									
3809.9100	--纺织工业及类似工业用〔101塑料增光剂，102硬脂酰氯化铬，999包括整理剂、染料加速着色或固色助剂及其他制剂〕	6.5		35	13/	0	千克			1/26.5
3809.9200	--造纸工业及类似工业用〔999〕	6.5		35	13/	0	千克			1/11.5
3809.9300	--制革工业及类似工业用〔999〕	6.5		35	13/	0	千克			1/26.5
38.10	**金属表面酸洗剂；焊接用的焊剂及其他辅助剂；金属及其他材料制成的焊粉或焊膏；作焊条芯子或焊条涂料用的制品：**									
3810.1000	-金属表面酸洗剂；金属及其他材料制成的焊粉或焊膏〔999〕	6.5		35	13/	13	千克			1/26.5
3810.9000	-其他〔101快干助焊剂，999包括作焊条芯子或焊条涂料用的制品〕	6.5		35	13/	0	千克			1/16.5
38.11	**抗震剂、抗氧剂、防胶剂、黏度改良剂、防腐蚀制剂及其他配制添加剂，用于矿物油(包括汽油)或与矿物油同样用途的其他液体：**									
	-抗震剂：									
3811.1100	--以铅化合物为基本成分〔999〕	6.5		35	13/	0	千克			1/
3811.1900	--其他〔999〕	6.5		35	13/	0	千克			1/16.5
	-润滑油添加剂：									
3811.2100	--含有石油或从沥青矿物提取的油类〔999〕	6.5		35	13/	0	千克			1/11.5
3811.2900	--其他〔999〕	6.5		35	13/	0	千克			1/
3811.9000	-其他〔999〕	6.5		35	13/	0	千克			1/11.5
38.12	**配制的橡胶促进剂；其他税目未列名的橡胶或塑料用复合增塑剂；橡胶或塑料用抗氧制剂及其他复合稳定剂：**									
3812.1000	-配制的橡胶促进剂〔999〕	6		20	13/	13	千克			1/26
3812.2000	-橡胶或塑料用复合增塑剂〔999〕	6.5		35	13/	6	千克			1/16.5
	-橡胶或塑料用抗氧制剂及其他复合稳定剂：									
3812.3100	--2,2,4-三甲基-1,2-二氢化喹啉(TMQ)低聚体混合物〔999〕	6		20	13/	6	千克			1/31
	--其他：									
3812.3910	---其他橡胶防老剂〔999其他化工产品，301易燃固体，302其他危险化学品〕	6		20	13/	6	千克			1/16
3812.3990	---其他〔999其他化工产品，301易燃固体，302其他危险化学品〕	6.5		35	13/	6	千克			1/16.5
38.13	**灭火器的装配药；已装药的灭火弹：**									
3813.0010	---灭火器的装配药〔101腐蚀性液体，999〕	6.5		35	13/	0	千克			1/11.5
3813.0020	---已装药的灭火弹〔999〕	10		70	13/	0	千克			1/15
38.14	**其他税目未列名的有机复合溶剂及稀释剂；除漆剂：**									
3814.0000	其他税目未列名的有机复合溶剂及稀释剂；除漆剂[T2]	10		50	13/	0	千克			1/20
38.15	**其他税目未列名的反应引发剂、反应促进剂、催化剂：**									
	-载体催化剂：									

协定税率 %										特惠税率 %			
亚太5国	东/冰/格	巴基斯坦	韩国	瑞士	哥达	秘鲁	澳大利亚	新西/坡/智	港/澳/台	亚太2国	老/柬/缅	36/3/1	Article Description
													--Disinfectants
	0/0/3.6	4.5	0	2.7	0	0	0	0//0	0/0/			0/0/0	Medical disinfectants
	0/0/3.6	4.5	0	2.7	0	0	0	0//0	0/0/			0/0/0	Disinfectant of glutaraldehyde, disinfectant of deciquan solution, for veterinary purposes (including disinfectant and antiseptics for compound coal tar acid solution)
	0/0/3.6	4.5	0	2.7	0	0	0	0//0	0/0/			0/0/0	Non-medical disinfectants
													–Other:
	0/0/0	4	0	0	0	0	0	0//0	0/0/			0/0/0	---Put up for retail sale
	0/0/0	4	0	0	0	0	0	0//0	0/0/			0/0/0	---Other
													Finishing agents, dye carriers to accelerate the dyeing or fixing of dyestuffs and other products and preparations (for example, dressings and mordants), of a kind used in the textile, paper, leather or like industries, not elsewhere specified or included:
	0/0/0	0	4	0	0	0	0	0/0/0	0/0/			0/0/0	-With a basis of amylaceous substances
													-Other:
6	0/0/0	0	0	2	0	0	0	0//0	0/0/			0/0/0	--Of a kind used in the textile or like industries
	0/0/0	0	2.6	0	0	0	0	0//0	0/0/			0/0/0	--Of a kind used in the paper or like industries
	0/0/0	0	0	0	0	0	0	0//0	0/0/			0/0/0	--Of a kind used in the leather or like industries
													Pickling preparations for metal surfaces; fluxes and other auxiliary preparations for soldering, brazing or welding; soldering, brazing or welding powders and pastes consisting of metal and other materials; preparations of a kind used as cores or coatings for welding electrodes or rods:
6	0/0/0	0	3.9	0	0	0	0	0//0	0/0/			0/0/0	-Pickling preparations for metal surfaces; soldering, brazing or welding powders and pastes consisting of metal and other materials
	0/0/0	0	3.9	0	0	0	0	0//0	0/0/			0/0/0	-Other
													Anti-knock preparations, oxidation inhibitors, gum inhibitors, viscosity improvers, anti-corrosive preparations and other prepared additives, for mineral oils (including gasoline) or for other liquids used for the same purposes as mineral oils:
													-Anti-knock preparations:
	0/0/0	4	0	0	0	0	0	0//0	0/0/			0/0/	--Based on lead compounds
	0/0/0	4	0	0	0	0	0	0//0	0/0/			0/0/	--Other
													-Additives for lubricating oils:
	0/0/0	0	0	0	0	0	0	0//0	0/0/			0/0/	--Containing petroleum oils or oils obtained from bituminous minerals
5.5	0/0/0	4	2.6	0	0	0	0	0//0	0/0/			0/0/	--Other
	0/0/2.6	4	0	0	0	0	0	0//0	0/0/			0/0/	-Other
													Prepared rubber accelerators; compounds plasticizers for rubber or plastics, not elsewhere specified or included; anti-oxidizing preparations and other compound stabilizers for rubber or plastics:
	0/0/0	0	3.6	0	0	0	0	0//0	0/0/			0/0/0	-Prepared rubber accelerators
	0/0/0	0	3.9	0	0	0	0	0//0	0/0/			0/0/0	-Compound plasticizers for rubber or plastics
													-Anti-oxidizing preparations and other compound stabilizers for rubber or plastics:
	0/0/0	0	3.6	0	0	0	0	0//0	0/0/			0/0/0	--Mixtures of oligomers of 2,2,4-trimethyl-1, 2-dihydroquino-line (*TMQ*)
													--Other
	0/0/0	0	3.6	0	0	0	0	0//0	0/0/			0/0/0	---Other rubber antioxidants
4.6	0/0/0	0	0	2	0	0	0	0//0	0/0/			0/0/0	---Other
													Preparations and charges for fire-extinguishers; charged fire-extinguishing grenades:
	0/0/0	4	2.6	0	0	0	0	0//0	0/0/			0/0/0	---Preparations and charges for fire-extinguishers
	0/0/0	4.5	4	0	0	0	0	0//0	0/0/			0/0/0	---Charged fire-extinguishing grenades
													Organic composite solvents and thinners, not elsewhere specified or included; prepared paint or varnish removers:
9	0/0/0	4.5	7	3	0	0	0	0/0/0	0/0/			0/0/0	Organic composite solvents and thinners, not elsewhere specified or included; prepared paint or varnish removers
													Reaction initiators, reaction accelerators and catalytic preparations, not elsewhere specified or included:
													-Supported catalysts:

税则号列	货品名称〔CIQ 扩展编码及品名一T2 表示见附表 2〕	最惠(%)	暂定税率	普通	增值/消费	出口退税	计量单位	监管条件	检验检疫	特殊证件对美关税
3815.1100	--以镍及其化合物为活性物的〔999 包括以镍化合物为活性物的,301 易燃固体〕	6.5		35	13/	13	千克			1/11.5
3815.1200	--以贵金属及其化合物为活性物的									
3815.1200 10	载铂催化剂(为了从重水中回收氚或为了生产重水而专门设计或制备,用于加速氢和水之间的氢同位素交换反应)〔999〕	6.5	4	35	13/	13	千克	3		1/
3815.1200 90	其他以贵金属为活性物的载体催化剂〔999〕	6.5	4	35	13/	13	千克			1/
3815.1900	--其他〔999〕	6.5		35	13/	13	千克			1/
3815.9000	-其他〔999 包括反应催化剂,302 易于自燃的物质,301 腐蚀性物质〕	6.5		35	13/	13	千克			1/
38.16	**耐火的水泥、灰泥、混凝土及类似耐火混合制品,但税目 38.01 的产品除外:**									
3816.0000	耐火的水泥、灰泥、混凝土及类似耐火混合制品,但税目 38.01 的产品除外〔999〕	6.5		35	13/	0	千克			1/16.5
38.17	**混合烷基苯及混合烷基萘,但税目 27.07 及 29.02 的货品除外:**									
3817.0000	混合烷基苯及混合烷基萘,但税目 27.07 及 29.02 的货品除外〔101 但马酸二甲苯溶液,102 环化橡胶二甲苯溶液,103 环庚亚胺二甲苯溶剂〕	6.5		35	13/	13	千克			1/31.5
38.18	**经掺杂用于电子工业的化学元素,已切成圆片、薄片或类似形状;经掺杂用于电子工业的化合物:**									
	---直径在 7.5 厘米及以上的单晶硅切片:									
3818.0011	----直径在 15.24 厘米及以下的〔999〕	0		11	13/	13	千克/片			1/10
3818.0019	----其他〔999〕	0		11	13/	13	千克/片			1/20
3818.0090	---其他〔999〕	0		17	13/	13	千克			1/20
38.19	**闸用液压油及其他液压传动用液体,不含石油或从沥青矿物提取的油类,或者按重量计石油或从沥青矿物提取的油类含量低于 70%:**									
3819.0000	闸用液压油及其他液压传动用液体,不含石油或从沥青矿物提取的油类,或者按重量计石油或从沥青矿物提取的油类含量低于 70%〔999〕	6.5		35	13/	0	千克			1/16.5
38.20	**防冻剂及解冻剂:**									
3820.0000	防冻剂及解冻剂〔999〕	10		35	13/	13	千克			1/20
38.21	**制成的供微生物(包括病毒及类似品)或植物、人体、动物细胞生长或维持用的培养基:**									
3821.0000	制成的供微生物(包括病毒及类似品)或植物,人体,动物细胞生长或维持用的培养基〔101 动物微生物培养培养基,102 其他医用生物制品〕	3	2	11	13/	0	千克			1/7
38.22	**附于衬背上的诊断或实验用试剂及不论是否附于衬背上的诊断或实验用配制试剂,但税目 30.02 及 30.06 的货品除外;检定参照物:**									
3822.0010	---附于衬背上的〔101 其他动物性血液制品,102 诊断用试剂及试剂盒,103 医用诊断试剂,104 医用检测试剂,105 其他医用生物制品,106 化学试剂〕	4		35	13/	13	千克	AB	VW	1/
3822.0090	---其他〔101 诊断用试剂及试剂盒,102 医用诊断试剂,103 医用检测试剂,104 其他医用生物制品,105 化学试剂〕	5		35	13/	13	千克	AB	VW	1/
38.23	**工业用单羧脂肪酸;精炼所得的酸性油;工业用脂肪醇:**									
	-工业用单羧脂肪酸;精炼所得的酸性油:									
3823.1100	--硬脂酸〔101 其他饲料添加剂,999〕	16		50	13/	13	千克			1/41
3823.1200	--油酸〔999,301 无检疫要求食品添加剂,302 需申报仅用于工业用途不用于食品添加剂无检疫要求的化学品〕	16	8	50	13/	10	千克	A	R	1/33
3823.1300	--妥尔油脂肪酸〔999〕	16		50	13/	0	千克			1/21
3823.1900	--其他									
3823.1900 01	植物酸性油(酸性油仅指精炼所得的)〔999〕	16	5	50	13/	0	千克			1/30
3823.1900 90	其他工业用单羧脂肪酸、酸性油(酸性油仅指精炼所得的)〔999〕	16		50	13/	0	千克			1/41
3823.7000	-工业用脂肪醇〔999〕	13	9	50	13/	0	千克			1/34

协定税率 %										特惠税率 %			
亚太5国	东/冰/格	巴基斯坦	韩国	瑞士	哥达	秘鲁	澳大利亚	新西/坡/智	港/澳/台	亚太2国	老/柬/缅	36/3/1	Article Description
	0/0/0	4	2.6	0	0	0	0	0//0	0/0/			0/0/C	--With nickel or nickel compounds as the active substance
													--With precious metal or precious metal compounds as the active substance
	0/0/0	0	2.6	0	0	0	0	0//0	0/0/			0/0/0	Platinum supported catalyst(in order to reclaim tritium from heavy water or design or prepare for production of heavy water for accelerate exchange reaction of hydrogen isotope between hydrogen and water)
	0/0/0	0	2.6	0	0	0	0	0//0	0/0/			0/0/0	Other supported catalysts with precious metal compounds as the active substance
4.6	0/0/0	0	0	0	0	0	0	0//0	0/0/			0/0/0	--Other
4.2	0/0/0	0	0	2	0	0	0	0//0	0/0/			0/0/0	-Other
													Refractory cements, mortars, concretes and similar compositions, other than products of heading No. 38. 01:
	0/0/0	4	0	0	0	0	0	0//0	0/0/			0/0/	Refractory cements, mortars, concretes and similar compositions, other than products of heading No. 38. 01
													Mixed alkylbenzenes and mixed alkylnaphthalenes, other than those of heading No. 27. 07 or 29. 02:
	0/0/0	4	3.9	0	0	0	0	0//0	0/0/0			0/0/0	Mixed alkylbenzenes and alkylnaphthalenes, other than those of heading N. 27. 07or 29. 02
													Chemical elements doped for use in electronics, in the form of discs, wafers or similar forms; chemical compouds doped for use in electronics:
													---Monocrystalline sillicon, in the form of discs, wafers or similar form, 7. 5 cm or more in diameter:
												0/0/0	----Diameter not exceeding 15. 24cm
												0/0/0	----Other
												0/0/0	---Other
													Hydraulic brake fluids and other prepared liquids for hydraulic transmission, not containing or containing less than 70% by weight of petroleum oils or oils obtained from bituminous minerals:
	0/0/0	4	0	0	0	0	0	0//0	0/0/			0/0/	Hydraulic brake fluids and other prepared liquids for hydraulic transmission, not containing or containing less than 70% by weight of petroleum oils or oils obtaines from bituminous minerals
													Anti-freezing preparations and prepared de-icing fluids:
	0/0/0	4.5	4	0	0	0	0	0/0/0	0/0/			0/0/0	Anti-freezing preparations and prepared de-icing fluids
													Prepared culture media for the development or maintenance of micro-organisms (including virus and the like) or of plant, human or animal cells:
	0/0/0	0	0	0	0	0	0	0//0	0/0/			0/0/	Prepared culture media for the development or maintenance of micro-organisms (including viruses and the like) or of plant, human or animal cells:
													Diagnostic or laboratory reagents on a backing and prepared diagnostic or laboratory reagents whether or not on a backing, other than those of heading No. 30. 02 or 30. 06; certified reference materials:
	0/0/0	0	0	0	0	0	0	0//0	0/0/			0/0/0	---On a backing
	0/0/0	0	0	0	0	0	0	0//0	0/0/			0/0/0	---Other
													Industrial monocarboxylic fatty acids; acid oils from refining; industrial fatty alcohols:
													-Industrial monocarboxylic fatty acids; acid oils from refining:
	0//0	12.8	9.6	4.8	0	0	0	0//0	0/0/			0/0/	--Stearic acid
	0//0	12.8	9.6	4.8	0	0	0	0/0/0	0/0/			0/0/	--Oleic acid
	0/0/0	12.8	9.6	4.8	0	0	0	0/0/0	0/0/			0/0/	--Tall oil fatty acids
													--Other
	0/0/0	12.8	9.6	4.8	0	0	0	0/0/0	0/0/			0/0/	Acid oils of plant(acid oils from refining)
	0/0/0	12.8	9.6	4.8	0	0	0	0/0/0	0/0/			0/0/	Other industrial monocarboxylic fatty acids, acid oils(acid oils from refining)
	0/0/0	6.5	7.8	3.9	0	0	0	0/0/0	0/0/			0/0/	-Industrial fatty alcohols

税则号列	货品名称〔CIQ 扩展编码及品名－T2 表示见附表 2〕	最惠(%)	暂定税率	普通	增值/消费	出口退税	计量单位	监管条件	检验检疫	特殊证件对美关税
38.24	铸模及铸芯用黏合剂;其他税目未列名的化学工业及其相关工业的化学产品及配制品(包括由天然产品混合组成的):									
3824.1000	-铸模及铸芯用黏合剂〔999〕	6.5		35	13/	6	千克			1/16.5
3824.3000	-自身混合或与金属黏合剂混合的未烧结金属碳化物									
3824.3000 10	混合的未烧结金属碳化钨(包括自身混合或与金属粘合剂混合的)〔999〕	6.5		35	13/	0	千克	4xy		1/11.5
3824.3000 90	其他混合的未烧结金属碳化物(包括自身混合或与金属粘合剂混合的)〔999〕	6.5		35	13/	0	千克			1/11.5
	-水泥、灰泥及混凝土用添加剂:									
3824.4010	---高效减水剂〔999〕	6.5		35	13/	13	千克			1/31.5
3824.4090	---其他〔999〕	6.5		35	13/	0	千克			1/16.5
3824.5000	-非耐火的灰泥及混凝土〔999〕	6.5		35	13/	0	千克			1/26.5
3824.6000	-子目号 2905.44 以外的山梨醇〔999〕	14		40	13/	0	千克			1/24
	-含有甲烷、乙烷或丙烷的卤化衍生物的混合物:									
3824.7100	--含全氯氟烃(CFCs)的,不论是否含氢氯氟烃(HCFCs)、全氟烃(PFCs)或氢氟烃(HFCs)									
3824.7100 11	二氯二氟甲烷和二氟乙烷的混合物(R-500)〔301 非易燃无毒气体〕	6.5		35	13/	0	千克	AB14xy	MN	14/11.5
3824.7100 12	一氯二氟甲烷和二氯二氟甲烷的混合物(R-501)〔999〕	6.5		35	13/	0	千克	14xy		14/11.5
3824.7100 13	一氯二氟甲烷和一氯五氟乙烷的混合物(R-502)〔301 非易燃无毒气体〕	6.5		35	13/	0	千克	AB14xy	MN	14/11.5
3824.7100 14	三氟甲烷和一氯三氟甲烷的混合物(R-503)〔301〕	6.5		35	13/	0	千克	AB14xy	MN	14/11.5
3824.7100 15	二氟甲烷和一氯五氟乙烷的混合物(R-504)〔999〕	6.5		35	13/	0	千克	14xy		14/11.5
3824.7100 16	二氯二氟甲烷和一氟一氯甲烷的混合物(R-505)〔999〕	6.5		35	13/	0	千克	14xy		14/11.5
3824.7100 17	一氟一氯甲烷和二氯四氟乙烷的混合物(R-506)〔999〕	6.5		35	13/	0	千克	14xy		14/11.5
3824.7100 18	二氯二氟甲烷和二氯四氟乙烷的混合物(R-400)〔999〕	6.5		35	13/	0	千克	14xy		14/11.5
3824.7100 90	其他含甲烷、乙烷或丙烷的全氯氟烃(CFCs)的混合物[不论是否含甲烷、乙烷或丙烷的氢氯氟烃(HCFCs)、全氟烃(PFCs)或氢氟烃(HFCs)]〔999〕	6.5		35	13/	0	千克			1/11.5
3824.7200	--含溴氯二氟甲烷、溴三氟甲烷或二溴四氟乙烷的混合物〔999〕	6.5		35	13/	0	千克			1/
3824.7300	--含氢溴氟烃(HBFCs)的〔999〕	6.5		35	13/	0	千克			1/
3824.7400	--含氢氯氟烃(HCFCs)的,不论是否含全氟烃(PFCs)或氢氟烃(HFCs),但不含全氯氟烃(CFCs)									
3824.7400 11	二氟一氯甲烷、二氟乙烷和一氯四氟乙烷的混合物(R-401)〔999〕	6.5		35	13/	13	千克	14xy		14/
3824.7400 12	五氟乙烷、丙烷和二氟一氯甲烷的混合物(R402)〔999〕	6.5		35	13/	13	千克	14xy		14/
3824.7400 13	丙烷、二氟一氯甲烷和八氟丙烷的混合物(R403)〔999〕	6.5		35	13/	13	千克	14xy		14/
3824.7400 14	二氟一氯甲烷、二氟乙烷、一氯二氟乙烷和八氟环丁烷的混合物(R405)〔999〕	6.5		35	13/	13	千克	14xy		14/
3824.7400 15	二氟一氯甲烷、2-甲基丙烷(异丁烷)和一氯二氟乙烷的混合物(R406)〔999〕	6.5		35	13/	13	千克	14xy		14/
3824.7400 16	五氟乙烷、三氟乙烷和二氟一氯甲烷的混合物(R408)〔999〕	6.5		35	13/	13	千克	14xy		14/
3824.7400 17	二氟一氯甲烷、一氯四氟乙烷和一氯二氟乙烷的混合物(R409)〔999〕	6.5		35	13/	13	千克	14xy		14/
3824.7400 18	丙烯、二氟一氯甲烷和二氟乙烷的混合物(R411)〔999〕	6.5		35	13/	13	千克	14xy		14/
3824.7400 19	二氟一氯甲烷、八氟丙烷和一氯二氟乙烷的混合物(R412)〔999〕	6.5		35	13/	13	千克	14xy		14/

协定税率 %										特惠税率 %			
亚太5国	东/冰/格	巴基斯坦	韩国	瑞士	哥达	秘鲁	澳大利亚	新西/坡/智	港/澳/台	亚太2国	老/柬/缅	36/3/1	Article Description
													Prepared binders for foundry moulds or cores; chemical products and preparations of the chemical or allied industries (including those consisting of mixtures of natural products), not elsewhere specified or included:
	0/0/0	4	2.6	0	0	0	0	0//0	0/0/			0/0/0	-Prepared binders for foundry moulds or cores
													-Non-agglomerated metal carbides mixed together or with metallic binders
	0/0/0	4	0	0	0	0	0	0//0	0/0/			0/0/0	Non-agglomerated metal carbonizded tungsten(containing mixed together or with metallic binders)
	0/0/0	4	0	0	0	0	0	0//0	0/0/			0/0/0	Other non-agglomerated metal carbides(containing mixed together or with metallic binders)
													-Prepared additives for cements, mortars or concretes:
	0/0/0	4	3.9	0	0	0	0	0//0	0/0/			0/0/0	---High efficiency water reducing agent
	0/0/0	4	0	0	0	0	0	0//0	0/0/			0/0/0	---Other
	0/0/0	4	0	0	0	0	0	0//0	0/0/			0/0/0	-Non-refraciory mortars and concretes
	0/0/0	11.2	5.6	4.2	0	0	0	0/0/0	0/0/			0/0/	-Sorbitol other than that of subheading No. 2905. 44
													-Mixtures containing halogenated dervatives of methane, ethane or propane:
													--Containing chorofluorocarbons(CFCs), whether or not containing hydrochlorofluorocarbons (HCFCs) perfluorocarbons (PFCs) orhydrofluorocarbons(HFCs)
	0/0/0	4	0	0	0	0	0	0//0	0/0/			0/0/0	Mixture of dichlorodifluoromethane and difluoroethane(R-500)
	0/0/0	4	0	0	0	0	0	0//0	0/0/			0/0/0	Mixture of difluorochloromethane and dichlorodifluoromethane(R-501)
	0/0/0	4	0	0	0	0	0	0//0	0/0/			0/0/0	Mixture of difluorochloromethane and Chloropentafluoroethane(R-502)
	0/0/0	4	0	0	0	0	0	0//0	0/0/			0/0/0	Mixture of trifluoromethane and monochlorotrifluoromethane (R-503)
	0/0/0	4	0	0	0	0	0	0//0	0/0/			0/0/0	Mixture of difluoromethane and Chloropentafluoroethane (R-504)
	0/0/0	4	0	0	0	0	0	0//0	0/0/			0/0/0	Mixture of dichlorodifluoromethane and fluouochlouomethane (R-505)
	0/0/0	4	0	0	0	0	0	0//0	0/0/			0/0/0	Mixture offluouochlouomethane and difluorotetrachloroethane (R-506)
	0/0/0	4	0	0	0	0	0	0//0	0/0/			0/0/0	Mixture of dichlorodifluoromethane and difluorotetrachloroethane (R-400)
	0/0/0	4	0	0	0	0	0	0//0	0/0/			0/0/0	Other mixtures containing chlorojluorocarbons of methane, ethane or propane. (whether or not containing) hydrochlorofluorocarbons, chorofluoro carbons or orhydrofluorocarbons of methane, ethane or propane
	0/0/0	4	0	0	0	0	0	0//0	0/0/			0/0/0	--Containing bromochlorodifluoromethane, bromotrifluoromethane or dibromotetrafluoroethanes
	0/0/0	4	0	0	0	0	0	0//0	0/0/			0/0/0	--Containing hydrobromofluocarbons(HBFCs)
													--Containing hydrochlorofluorocarbons (HCFCs), whether or not containing perfluorocarbons (PFCs) or hydrofluorocarbons (HFCs), but not containing chlorofluorocarbons(CFCs)
	0/0/0	4	0	0	0	0	0	0//0	0/0/			0/0/0	Mixture of Monochlorodifluoromethane, difluoroethane and chlorotetrafluoroethane (R-401)
	0/0/0	4	0	0	0	0	0	0//0	0/0/			0/0/0	Mixture of pentafluoroethane, propane and chlorodifluoromethane (R-402)
	0/0/0	4	0	0	0	0	0	0//0	0/0/			0/0/0	Mixture of propane, chlorotetrafluoroethane and octafluoropropane (R-403)
	0/0/0	4	0	0	0	0	0	0//0	0/0/			0/0/0	Mixture of chlorotetrafluoroethane, difluoroethane, chlordifluoroethane and octafluorocyclobutane (R-405)
	0/0/0	4	0	0	0	0	0	0//0	0/0/			0/0/0	Mixture of Chlorotetrafluoroethane, 2-methylpropane and chlordifluoroethane (R-406)
	0/0/0	4	0	0	0	0	0	0//0	0/0/			0/0/0	Mixture of pentafluoroethane, trifluoroethane and chlorodifluoromethane (R-408)
	0/0/0	4	0	0	0	0	0	0//0	0/0/			0/0/0	Mixture of chlorodifluoromethane, chlorotetrafluoroethane and difluoromonochloroethane (R-409)
	0/0/0	4	0	0	0	0	0	0//0	0/0/			0/0/0	Mixture of propene, chlorodifluoromethane and difluoroethane (R-411)
	0/0/0	4	0	0	0	0	0	0//0	0/0/			0/0/0	Mixture of chlorodifluoromethane, octafluoropropane and difluoromonochloroethane (R-412)

税则号列	货品名称〔CIQ扩展编码及品名－T2表示见附表2〕	最惠(%)	暂定税率	普通	增值/消费	出口退税	计量单位	监管条件	检验检疫	特殊证件对美关税
3824.7400 21	二氟一氯甲烷、一氯四氟乙烷、一氯二氟乙烷和2-甲基丙烷的混合物(R414)〔999〕	6.5		35	13/	13	千克	14xy		14/
3824.7400 22	二氟一氯甲烷和二氟乙烷的混合物(R415)〔999〕	6.5		35	13/	13	千克	14xy		14/
3824.7400 23	四氟乙烷、一氯四氟乙烷和丁烷的混合物(R416)〔999〕	6.5		35	13/	13	千克	14xy		14/
3824.7400 24	丙烷、二氟一氯甲烷和二氟乙烷的混合物(R418)〔999〕	6.5		35	13/	13	千克	14xy		14/
3824.7400 25	二氟一氯甲烷和八氟丙烷的混合物(R509)〔999〕	6.5		35	13/	13	千克	14xy		14/
3824.7400 26	二氟一氯甲烷和一氯二氟乙烷的混合物〔101 二氟一氯甲烷,氯二氟甲烷,999〕	6.5		35	13/	13	千克	14xy		14/
3824.7400 90	其他含甲烷、乙烷或丙烷的氢氯氟烃混合物(不论是否含甲烷、乙烷或丙烷的全氟烃或氢氟烃,但不含全氯氟烃)〔999〕	6.5		35	13/	13	千克	14xy		14/
3824.7500	--含四氯化碳的〔999〕	6.5		35	13/	0	千克			1/11.5
3824.7600	--含1,1,1-三氯乙烷(甲基氯仿)的〔101 汽油氯仿混合液,999 甲基氯仿的混合物〕	6.5		35	13/	0	千克			1/31.5
3824.7700	--含溴化甲烷(甲基溴)或溴氯甲烷的〔999〕	6.5		35	13/	0	千克			1/
3824.7800	--含全氟烃(PFCs)或氢氟烃(HFCs)的,但不含全氯氟烃(CFCs)或氢氯氟烃(HCFCs)的〔999〕	6.5		35	13/	13	千克			1/26.5
3824.7900	--其他〔101 氯甲烷和二氯甲烷混合物,999,301 遇水放出易燃气体的物质〕	6.5		35	13/	0	千克			1/31.5
	-本章子目注释三所列货品:									
3824.8100	--含环氧乙烷(氧化乙烯)的〔999〕	6.5		35	13/	0	千克			1/31.5
3824.8200	--含多氯联苯(PCB_S)、多氯三联苯(PCT_S)或多溴联苯(PBB_S)的〔999〕	6.5		35	13/	0	千克			1/
3824.8300	--含三(2,3-二溴丙基)磷酸酯的〔999〕	6.5		35	13/	0	千克			1/
3824.8400	--含艾氏剂(ISO)、毒杀芬(ISO)、氯丹(ISO)、十氯酮(ISO)、DDT(ISO)[滴滴涕(INN)、1,1,1-三氯-2,2-双(4-氯苯基)乙烷]、狄氏剂(ISO,INN)、硫丹(ISO)、异狄氏剂(ISO)、七氯(ISO)或灭蚁灵(ISO)的〔999 其他化工产品,301 其他危险化学品〕	6.5		35	13/	0	千克			1/
3824.8500	--含1,2,3,4,5,6-六氯环己烷〔六六六(ISO)〕,包括林丹(ISO,INN)的〔999:其他化工产品,301:ISO,INN的〕	6.5		35	13/	0	千克			1/
3824.8600	--含五氯苯(ISO)或六氯苯(ISO)的〔999 其他化工产品,301 其他危险化学品〕	6.5		35	13/	6	千克			1/
3824.8700	--含全氟辛基磺酸及其盐,全氟辛基磺胺或全氟辛基磺酰氯的〔999 其他化工产品,301 其他危险化学品〕	6.5		35	13/	6	千克			1/
3824.8800	--含四、五、六、七或八溴联苯醚的〔999 其他化工产品,301 其他危险化学品〕	6.5		35	13/	6	千克			1/
	-其他:									
3824.9100	--主要由(5-乙基-2-甲基-2 氧代-1,3,2-二氧磷杂环己-5-基)甲基膦酸二甲酯和双[(5-乙基-2-甲基-2 氧代-1,3,2-二氧磷杂环己-5-基)甲基]甲基膦酸酯(阻燃剂 FRC-1)组成的混合物及制品〔999 其他化工产品,301 其他危险化学品〕	6.5		35	13/	6	千克			1/
	--其他:									
3824.9910	---杂醇油〔999 其他化工产品,301 易燃液体〕	6.5		40	13/	0	千克			1/16.5
3824.9920	---除墨剂、蜡纸改正液及类似品〔999 其他化工产品,301 其他危险化学品〕	9		80	13/	0	千克			1/29
3824.9930	---增炭剂〔999 其他化工产品,301 其他危险化学品〕	6.5		35	13/	0	千克			1/
	---其他:									
3824.9991	----按重量计含滑石50%以上的混合物〔999〕	6.5		35	13/	0	千克	4xy		1/31.5
3824.9992	----按重量计含氧化镁70%以上的混合物〔999〕	6.5		35	13/	0	千克	4xy		1/
3824.9993	----表面包覆钴化物的氢氧化镍(掺杂碳)〔999 其他化工产品,301 其他危险化学品〕	6.5		35	13/	6	千克			1/
3824.9999	----其他									
3824.9999 10	粗制碳化硅(其中碳化硅含量大于15%(按重量计))〔999〕	6.5		35	13/	0	千克	y4x		1/
3824.9999 20	混胺(二甲胺和三乙胺混合物的水溶液)〔999〕	6.5		35	13/	0	千克	3		1/
3824.9999 30	氰化物的混合物〔999〕	6.5		35	13/	0	千克			1/
3824.9999 40	膨胀石墨〔999〕	6.5		35	13/	0	千克	3		1/

协定税率 %										特惠税率 %			Article Description
亚太5国	东/冰/格	巴基斯坦	韩国	瑞士	哥达	秘鲁	澳大利亚	新西/坡/智	港/澳/台	亚太2国	老/柬/缅	36/3/1	
	0/0/0	4	0	0	0	0	0	0//0	0/0/			0/0/0	Mixture of chlorodifluoromethane, chlorotetrafluoroethane, difluoromonochloroethane and 2-methylpropane (R-414)
	0/0/0	4	0	0	0	0	0	0//0	0/0/			0/0/0	Mixture of chlorodifluoromethane, difluoroethane (R-415)
	0/0/0	4	0	0	0	0	0	0//0	0/0/			0/0/0	Mixture of tetrafluoroethane, Chlorotetrafluoroethane and butane (R-416)
	0/0/0	4	0	0	0	0	0	0//0	0/0/			0/0/0	Mixture of propane, chlorodifluoromethane difluoroethane (R-418)
	0/0/0	4	0	0	0	0	0	0//0	0/0/			0/0/0	Mixture of chlorodifluoromethane and octafluoropropane (R-509)
	0/0/0	4	0	0	0	0	0	0//0	0/0/			0/0/0	Mixture of chlorodifluoromethane and difluoromonochloroethane
	0/0/0	4	0	0	0	0	0	0//0	0/0/			0/0/0	Other mixtures containing chorofluorocarbons of methane, ethane or propane(whether or not containing hydrofluorocarbons or perfluorocarbons, but not containing chlorofluorocarbons)
4.2	0/0/0	4	0	0	0	0	0	0//0	0/0/			0/0/0	--Containing Carbon tetrachloride
4.2	0/0/0	4	0	0	0	0	0	0//0	0/0/			0/0/0	--Containing 1,1,1-trichloroethane(methyl chloroform)
	0/0/0	4	0	0	0	0	0	0//0	0/0/			0/0/0	--Containing bromomethane(methyl bromide) or bromochloromethane
4.2	0/0/0	4	0	0	0	0	0	0//0	0/0/			0/0/0	--Containing perfluorocarbons (PFCs) or hydrofluorocarbons (HFCs), but not containing chlorofluorocarbons(CFCs) or hydrochlorofluorocarbons (HCFCs)
	0/0/0	4	0	0	0	0	0	0//0	0/0/			0/0/0	--Other
													-Goods specified in Subheading Note 3 to this Chapter:
4.2	0/0/0	4	0	0	0	0	0	0//0	0/0/			0/0/0	--Containing oxirane(ethylene oxide)
4.2	0/0/0	4	0	0	0	0	0	0//0	0/0/			0/0/0	--Containing polychlorinated biphenyls(PCBs), polychlorinoted terphenyls(PCTs) or polybrominated biphenyls(PBBs)
4.2	0/0/0	4	0	0	0	0	0	0//0	0/0/			0/0/0	--Contaning tris (2,3-dibromopopyl) phosphate
4.2	0/0/0	0	3.9		0	0	0	0/0/0	0/0/			0/0/0	--Containing aldrin (*ISO*), cam-phechlor (*ISO*) (*toxaphene*), chlordane (*ISO*), chlordecone (*ISO*), DDT (*ISO*) *clofeno-tane* (INN), 1,1,1-*trichloro*-2, 2-*bis* (p-chlorophenyl) *ethane*), dieldrin (*ISO*, *INN*), endosulfan (*ISO*), en-drin (*ISO*), heptachlor (*ISO*) or mirex (*ISO*)
4.2	0/0/0	0	3.9		0	0	0	0/0/0	0/0/			0/0/0	--Containing 1,2,3,4,5,6-hexa-chlorocyclohexane (*HCH* (ISO)), including lindane (*ISO*, *INN*)
4.2	0/0/0	0	3.9		0	0	0	0/0/0	0/0/			0/0/0	--Containing pentachlorobenzene (ISO) *or hexachlorobenzene* (*ISO*)
4.2	0/0/0	0	3.9		0	0	0	0/0/0	0/0/			0/0/0	--Containing perfluorooctane sulphonic acid, its salts, per-fluorooctane sulphonamides, or perfluorooctane sulphonyl fluoride
4.2	0/0/0	0	3.9		0	0	0	0/0/0	0/0/			0/0/0	--Containing tetra-, penta-, hexa-hepta-or octabromodiphe-nyl ethers
													-Other:
4.2	0/0/0	0	3.9		0	0	0	0/0/0	0/0/			0/0/0	--Mixtures and preparations consisting mainly of(5-ethyl-2-methyl-2-oxido-1,3,2-dioxaphosphinan-5－Yl) menthylmethyl methylphosphonate and bis[(5-ethyl-2-methyl-2-oxido-1,3,2-dioxaphosphinan-5－Yl) methyl]methylphosphonate
													--Other:
4.2	0/0/0	4	2.6	0	0	0	0	0/0/0	0/0/			0/0/0	---Fusel oil
5.9	0/0/0	4	0	0	0	0	0	0/0/0	0/0/			0/0/0	---Ink-removers, stencil correc-tors and the like
5.2	0/0/0	4	0	0	0	0	0	0/0/0	0/0/			0/0/0	---Carburetant
													---Other:
4.2	0/0/0	4	0	0	0	0	0	0/0/0	0/0/			0/0/0	----Mixtures containing more than 50% by weight of talc
4.2	0/0/0	4	0	0	0	0	0	0/0/0	0/0/			0/0/0	----Mixtures containing more than 70% by weight of mag＝nesium oxide
4.2	0/0/0	4	3.9		0	0	0	0/0/0	0/0/			0/0/0	----Nickelous hydroxide (*doped carbon*) covered on the face side with cobalt compound
													----Other
4.2	0/0/0	0	3.9		0	0	0	0/0/0	0/0/			0/0/0	Crude silicon carbide, containing more than 15% by weight of silicon carbide
4.2	0/0/0	0	3.9		0	0	0	0/0/0	0/0/			0/0/0	Mixed amine(dimethylamine and triethylamine mixture in aqueous solution)
4.2	0/0/0	0	3.9		0	0	0	0/0/0	0/0/			0/0/0	Mixtures of cyanide
4.2	0/0/0	0	3.9		0	0	0	0/0/0	0/0/			0/0/0	Expanded graphite

税则号列	货品名称〔CIQ扩展编码及品名－T2表示见附表2〕	最惠(%)	暂定税率	普通	增值/消费	出口退税	计量单位	监管条件	检验检疫	特殊证件对美关税
3824.9999 50	三乙醇胺混合物、甲基二乙醇胺混合物、环状膦酸酯A和环状膦酸酯B的混合物〔999〕	6.5		35	13/	6	千克	23		1/
3824.9999 60	高钛渣(二氧化钛质量百分含量＞70%的)〔999其他化工产品,301其他危险化学品〕	6.5	0	35	13/	0	千克			1/
3824.9999 70	核苷酸类食品添加剂〔999其他化工产品,301有检疫要求食品添加剂,302需申报仅用于工业用途不用于食品添加剂有检疫要求的化学品〕	6.5		35	13/	6	千克	AB	RS	1/
3824.9999 80	按重量计氧化锌含量在50%及以上的混合物〔999其他化工产品,301其他危险化学品〕	6.5	3	35	13/	0	千克			1/
3824.9999 90	其他编号未列名的化工产品(包括水解物或水解料、DMC(六甲基环三硅氧烷,八甲基环四硅氧烷,十甲基环五硅氧烷,十二甲基环六硅氧烷中任何2种,3种或4种组成的混合物))〔999其他化工产品,301其他危险化学品〕	6.5		35	13/	6	千克			1/
38.25	**其他税目未列名的化学工业及其相关工业的副产品;城市垃圾;下水道淤泥;本章注释六所规定的其他废物:**									
3825.1000	-城市垃圾〔999〕	6.5		35	13/	0	千克	9		1/
3825.2000	-下水道淤泥〔999〕	6.5		35	13/	0	千克	9		1/
3825.3000	-医疗废物〔999〕	6.5		35	13/	0	千克	9		1/
	-废有机溶剂:									
3825.4100	--卤化物的〔999〕	6.5		35	13/	0	千克	9		1/
3825.4900	--其他〔999〕	6.5		35	13/	0	千克	9		1/
3825.5000	-废的金属酸洗液、液压油、制动油及防冻液〔999〕	6.5		35	13/	0	千克	9		1/
	-其他化学工业及相关工业的废物:									
3825.6100	--主要含有有机成分的〔999〕	6.5		35	13/	0	千克	9		1/
3825.6900	--其他〔999〕	6.5		35	13/	0	千克	9		1/
3825.9000	-其他									
3825.9000 10	浓缩糖蜜发酵液〔999,301无检疫要求食品添加剂,302需申报仅用于工业用途不用于食品添加剂无检疫要求的化学品〕	6.5		35	13/	0	千克	A	R	1/31.5
3825.9000 90	其他商品编号未列名化工副产品及废物〔999〕	6.5		35	13/	0	千克	9		1/31.5
38.26	**生物柴油及其混合物,不含或含有按重量计低于70%的石油或从沥青矿物提取的油类:**									
3826.0000	生物柴油及其混合物,不含或含有按重量计低于70%的石油或从沥青矿物提取的油类									
3826.0000 01	纯生物柴油〔999〕	6.5		35	13/	0	千克/升			1/31.5
3826.0000 90	其他生物柴油及其混合物〔999〕	6.5		35	13/1.2元/升	0	千克/升			1/31.5

协定税率 %										特惠税率 %			
亚太5国	东/冰/格	巴基斯坦	韩国	瑞士	哥达	秘鲁	澳大利亚	新西/坡/智	港/澳/台	亚太2国	老/柬/缅	36/3/1	Article Description
4.2	0/0/0	0	3.9		0	0	0	0/0/0	0/0/			0/0/0	A mixture of methyl phosphonic acid (CAS NO. 170836-68-7) {by methyl phosphonic acid, methyl 5-(5-ethyl-2-methyl-2-oxo-1,3,2-two oxygen phosphorusheterocyclic hexyl) methyl ester(CAS NO. 41203-81-0) and methyl phosphonic acid two [5-(5-ethyl-2-methyl-2-oxo-1,3,2-two oxygen phosphorus heterocyclichexyl) methyl)] ester (CAS NO. 42595-45-9) and mixed}
4.2	0/0/0	0	3.9		0	0	0	0/0/0	0/0/			0/0/0	Titanium slag (containing more than 70% by weight of titanium dioxide)
4.2	0/0/0	0	3.9		0	0	0	0/0/0	0/0/			0/0/0	Nucleotide food additives
4.2	0/0/0	0	3.9		0	0	0	0/0/0	0/0/			0/0/0	Mixture containing more than 50% by weight of zinc oxide
4.2	0/0/0	0	3.9		0	0	0	0/0/0	0/0/			0/0/0	Other chemical products, not elsewhere specified or included, including Hydrolyzate or hydrolysis materials, DMC(the mixtures, composed of any 2, 3 or 4 kinds of 6-methyl siloxane ring 3, 8-methyl
													Residual products of the chemical or allied industries, not elsewhere specified or included; municipal waste; sewage sludge; other wastes specified in Note 6 to this Chapter:
	0/0/0	4	0	0	0	0	0	0//0	0/0/			0/0/	-Municipal waste
	0/0/0	4	0	0	0	0	0	0//0	0/0/			0/0/	-Sewage sludge
	0/0/0	4	0	0	0	0	0	0//0	0/0/			0/0/	-Clinical waste
													-Waste organic solvents:
	0/0/0	4	0	0	0	0	0	0//0	0/0/			0/0/	--Halogenated
	0/0/0	4	0	0	0	0	0	0//0	0/0/			0/0/	--Other
	0/0/0	4	0	0	0	0	0	0/0/0	0/0/			0/0/	-Wastes of metal pickling liquors, hydraulic fluids, brake fluids and anti-freeze fluids
													-Other wastes from chemical or allied industries:
	0/0/0	4	0	0	0	0	0	0//0	0/0/			0/0/	--Mainly containing organic constituents
	0/0/0	4	0	0	0	0	0	0//0	0/0/			0/0/	--Other
													-Other
	0/0/0	4	0	0	0	0	0	0//0	0/0/			0/0/	Condensed molasses fermented solubles
	0/0/0	4	0	0	0	0	0	0//0	0/0/			0/0/	Other chemical by-product or waste, not elsewhere specified or included
													Biodiesel and mixture thereof, not containing or containing less than 70% by weight of petroleum oils or oils obtaines from bituminous minerals:
													Biodiesel and mixture thereof, not containing or containingless than 70% by weight of petroleum oils or oils obtained from bituminous minerals
4.2	0/0/0	4	3.9		0	0	0	0//0	0/0/			0/0/0	Pure biodiesel
4.2	0/0/0	4	3.9		0	0	0	0//0	0/0/			0/0/0	Other biodiesel and mixture thereof

第七类
塑料及其制品;橡胶及其制品

注释:

一、由两种或两种以上单独成分配套的货品,其部分或全部成分属于本类范围以内,混合后则构成第六类或第七类的货品,应按混合后产品归入相应的税目,但其组成成分必须同时符合下列条件:

(一)其包装形式足以表明这些成分不需经过改装就可以一起使用的;

(二)一起报验;

(三)这些成分的属性及相互比例足以表明是相互配用的。

二、除税目39.18或39.19的货品外,印有花纹、文字、图画的塑料、橡胶及其制品,如果所印花纹、字画作为其主要用途,应归入第四十九章。

第三十九章
塑料及其制品

注释:

一、本协调制度所称"塑料",是指税目39.01至39.14的材料,这些材料能够在聚合时或聚合后在外力(一般是热力和压力,必要时加入溶剂或增塑剂)作用下通过模制、浇铸、挤压、滚轧或其他工序制成一定的形状,成形后除去外力,其形状仍保持不变。

本协调制度所称"塑料",还应包括钢纸,但不包括第十一类的纺织材料。

二、本章不包括:

(一)税目27.10或34.03的润滑油;

(二)税目27.12或34.04的蜡;

(三)单独的已有化学定义的有机化合物(第二十九章);

(四)肝素及其盐(税目30.01);

(五)税目39.01至39.13所列的任何产品溶于挥发性有机溶剂的溶液(火胶棉除外),但溶剂的重量必须超过溶液重量的50%(税目32.08);税目32.12的压印箔;

(六)有机表面活性剂或税目34.02的制剂;

(七)再熔胶及酯胶(税目38.06);

(八)配制的添加剂,用于矿物油(包括汽油)或与矿物油同样用途的其他液体(税目38.11);

(九)以第三十九章的聚乙二醇、聚硅氧烷或其他聚合物为基本成分的液压用液体;(税目38.19)

(十)有塑料衬背的诊断或实验用试剂(税号38.22);

(十一)第四十章规定的合成橡胶及其制品;

(十二)鞍具及挽具(税号42.01);税号42.02的衣箱、提箱、手提包及其他容器;

(十三)第四十六章的缏条、编结品及其他制品;

(十四)税号48.14的壁纸;

(十五)第十一类的货品(纺织原料及纺织制品);

(十六)第十二类的物品(例如,鞋靴、帽类、雨伞、阳伞、手杖、鞭子、马鞭及其零件);

(十七)税号71.17的仿首饰;

(十八)第十六类的物品(机器、机械器具或电气器具);

(十九)第十七类的航空器零件及车辆零件;

(二十)第九十章的物品(例如,光学元件、眼镜架及绘图仪器);

(二十一)第九十一章的物品(例如,钟壳及表壳);

(二十二)第九十二章的物品(例如,乐器及其零件);

(二十三)第九十四章的物品(例如,家具、灯具、照明装置、灯箱及活动房屋);

(二十四)第九十五章的物品(例如,玩具、游戏品及运动用品);

(二十五)第九十六章的物品(例如,刷子、纽扣、拉链、梳子、烟斗的嘴及柄、香烟嘴及类似品、保温瓶的零件及类似品、钢笔、活动铅笔、独脚架、双脚架、三脚架及类似品)。

三、税目39.01至39.11仅适用于化学合成的下列货品:

(一)温度在300℃时,压力转为1013毫巴后减压蒸馏出的以体积计小于60%的液体合成聚烯烃(税目39.01及39.02);

(二)非高度聚合的苯并呋喃-茚式树脂(税目39.11);

(三)平均至少有五个单体单元的其他合成聚合物;

(四)聚硅氧烷(税目39.10);

(五)甲阶酚醛树脂(税目39.09)及其他预聚物。

SECTION Ⅶ
PLASTICS AND ARTICLES THEREOF;
RUBBER AND ARTICLES THEREOF

Notes:

1. Goods put up in sets consisting of two or more separate constituents, some or all of which fall in this Section and are intended to be mixed together to obtain a product of Section Ⅵ or Ⅶ, are to be classified in the heading appropriate to that product, provided that the constituents are:
   (a) having regard to the manner in which they are put up, clearly identifiable as being intended to be used together without first being repacked;
   (b) presented together;
   (c) identifiable, whether by their nature or by the relative proportions in which they are present, as being complementary one to another.
2. Except for the goods of heading No. 39.18 or 39.19, plastics, rubber, and articles thereof, printed with motifs, characters or pictorial representations, which are not merely incidental to the primary use of the goods, fall in Chapter 49.

Chapter 39
Plastics and articles thereof

Notes:

1. Throughout the Nomenclature the expression "plastics" means those materials of headings No. 39.01 to 39.14 which are or have been capable, either at the moment of polymerization or at some subsequent stage, of being formed under external influence (usually heat and pressure, if necessary with a solvent or plasticizer) by moulding, casting, extruding, rolling or other process into shapes which are retained on the removal of the external influence.
   Throughout the Nomenclature any reference to "plastics" also includes vulcanized fibre. The expression, however, does not apply to materials regarded as textile materials of Section Ⅺ.
2. This Chapter does not cover:
   (a) Lubricating preparations of heading No. 27.10 or 34.03.
   (b) Waxes of heading No. 27.12 or 34.04;
   (c) Separate chemically defined organic compounds (Chapter 29);
   (d) Heparin or its salts (heading No. 30.01);
   (e) Solutions (other than collodions) consisting of any of the products specified in headings No. 39.01 to 39.13 in volatile organic solvents when the weight of the solvent exceeds 50% of the weight of the solution (heading No. 32.08); stamping foils of heading No. 32.12;
   (f) Organic surface-active agents or preparations of heading No 34.02;
   (g) Run gums or ester gums (heading No. 38.06);
   (h) Prepared additives for mineral oils (including gasoline) or for other liquids used for the same purposes as mineral oils (heading No. 38.11)
   (i) Prepared hydronlic fluids based on polyglycols silianes or other polymers of chapter 39(heading No. 38.19);
   (j) Diagnostic or laboratory reagents on a backing of plastics (heading No. 38.22);
   (k) Synthetic rubber, as defined for the purposes of Chapter 40, or articles thereof;
   (l) Saddlery or harness (heading No. 42.01) or trunks, suitcases, handbags or other containers of heading No. 42.02;
   (m) Plaits, wickerwork or other articles of Chapter 46;
   (n) Wall coverings of heading No. 48.14;
   (o) Goods of Section Ⅺ (textiles and textile articles);
   (p) Articles of Section Ⅻ (for example, footwear, headgear, umbrellas, sun umbrellas, walking-sticks, whips, riding-crops or parts thereof);
   (q) Imitation jewellery of heading No. 71.17;
   (r) Articles of Section XVI (machines and mechanical or electrical appliances);
   (s) Parts of aircraft or vehicles of Section ⅩⅦ;
   (t) Articles of Chapter 90 (for example, optical elements, spectacle frames, drawing instruments);
   (u) Articles of Chapter 91 (for example, clock or watch cases);
   (v) Articles of Chapter 92 (for example, musical instruments or parts thereof);
   (w) Articles of Chapter 94 (for example, furniture, lamps and lighting fittings. illuminated signs, prefabricated buildings);
   (x) Articles of Chapter 95 (for example, toys, games, sports requisites); or
   (y) Articles of Chapter 96 (for example, brushes, buttons, slide fasteners, combs, mouthpieces or stems for smoking pipes, cigaretteholders or the like, parts of vacuum flasks or the like, pens, propelling pencils unipod, bipod, trpod or the Like).
3. Headings No. 39.01 to 39.11 apply only to goods of a kind produced by chemical synthesis, falling in the following categories:
   (a) Liquid synthetic polyolefins of which less than 60% by volume distils at 300℃, after conversion to 1,013 millibars when a reduced-pressure distillation method is used (headings No. 39.01 and 39.02);
   (b) Resins, not highly polymerized, of the coumarone-indene type (heading No. 39.11);
   (c) Other synthetic polymers with an average of at least 5 monomer units;
   (d) Silicones (heading No. 39.10);
   (e) Resols (heading No. 39.09) and other prepolymers.

四、所称"共聚物",包括在整个聚合物中按重量计没有一种单体单元的含量在95%及以上的各种聚合物。

在本章中,除条文另有规定以外,共聚物(包括共缩聚物、共加聚物、嵌段共聚物及接枝共聚物)及聚合物混合体应按聚合物中重量最大的那种共聚单体单元所构成的聚合物归入相应税目。在本注释中,归入同一税目的聚合物的共聚单体单元应作为一种单体单元对待。

如果没有任何一种共聚单体单元重量为最大,共聚物或聚合物混合体应按号列顺序归入其可归入的最末一个税目。

五、化学改性聚合物,即聚合物主链上的支链通过化学反应发生了变化的聚合物,应按未改性的聚合物的相应税目归类。本规定不适用于接枝共聚物。

六、税目39.01至39.14所称"初级形状",只限于下列各种形状:

(一)液状及糊状,包括分散体(乳浊液及悬浮液)及溶液;

(二)不规则形状的块、团、粉(包括压型粉)、颗粒、粉片及类似的散装形状。

七、税目39.15不适用于已制成初级形状的单一的热塑材料废碎料及下脚料(税目39.01至39.14)。

八、税目39.17所称"管子",是指通常用于输送或供给气体或液体的空心制品或半制品(例如,肋纹浇花软管、多孔管),还包括香肠用肠衣及其他扁平管。除肠衣及扁平管外,内截面如果不呈圆形、椭圆形、矩形(其长度不超过宽度的1.5倍)或正几何形,则不能视为管子,而应作为异型材。

九、税目39.18所称"塑料糊墙品",适用于墙壁或天花板装饰用的宽度不小于45厘米的成卷产品,这类产品是将塑料牢固地附着在除纸张以外任何材料的衬背上,并且在塑料面起纹、压花、着色、印制图案或用其他方法装饰。

十、税目39.20及39.21所称"板、片、膜、箔、扁条",只适用于未切割或仅切割成矩形(包括正方形)(含切割后即可供使用的),但未经进一步加工的板、片、膜、箔、扁条(第五十四章的物品除外)及正几何形块,不论是否经过印制或其他表面加工。

十一、税目39.25只适用于第二分章以前各税目未包括的下列物品:

(一)容积超过300升的囤、柜(包括化粪池)、罐、桶及类似容器;

(二)用于地板、墙壁、隔墙、天花板或屋顶等方面的结构件;

(三)槽管及其附件;

(四)门、窗及其框架和门槛;

(五)阳台、栏杆、栅栏、栅门及类似品;

(六)窗板、百叶窗(包括威尼斯式百叶窗)或类似品及其零件、附件;

(七)商店、工棚、仓库等用的拼装式固定大型货架;

(八)建筑用的特色(例如,凹槽、圆顶及鸽棚式)装饰件;

(九)固定装于门窗、楼梯、墙壁或建筑物其他部位的附件及架座,例如,球形把手、拉手、挂钩、托架、毛巾架、开关板及其他护板。

子目注释:

一、属于本章任一税号项下的聚合物(包括共聚物)及化学改性聚合物应按下列规则归类:

(一)在同级子目中有一个"其他"子目的:

1. 子目所列聚合物名称冠有"聚(多)"的(例如,聚乙烯及聚酰胺-6,6),是指列名的该种聚合物单体单元一种式多种总量在整个聚合物中按重量计必须占95%及以上。

2. 子目3901.30、3901.40、3903.20、3903.30及3904.30所列的共聚物,如果该种共聚单体单元含量在整个聚合物中按重量计占95%及以上,即应归入上述子目。

3. 化学改性聚合物如未在其他子目具体列名,应归入列明为"其他"的子目内。

4. 不符合上述1、2、3款规定的聚合物,应按聚合物中重量最大的那种单体单元(与其他各种单一的共聚单体单元相比)所构成的聚合物归入该级其他相应子目。为此,归入同一子目的聚合物单体单元应作为一种单体单元对待。只有在同级子目中的聚合物共聚单体单元才可以进行比较。

(二)在同级子目中没有"其他"子目的:

1. 聚合物应按聚合物中重量最大的那种单体单元(与其他各种单一的共聚单体单元相比)所构成的聚合物归入该级相应子目。为此,归入同一子目的聚合物单体单元应作为一种单体单元对待。只有在同一组子目中的聚合物共聚单体单元才可以进行比较。

2. 化学改性聚合物应按相应的未改性聚合物的子目归类。聚合物混合体应按单体单元比例相等、种类相同的聚合物归入相应子目。

二、子目3920.43所称"增塑剂",包括"次级增塑剂"。

4. The expression "copolymers" covers all polymers in which no single monomer unit contributes 95% or more by weight to the total polymer content.

   For the purposes of this Chapter, except where the context otherwise requires, copolymers (including copolycondensates, co-polyaddition products, block copolymers and graft copolymers) and polymer blends are to be classified in the heading covering polymers of that comonomer unit which predominates by weight over every other single comonomer unit. For the purposes of this Note, constituent comonomer units of polymers falling in the same heading shall be taken together.

   If no single comonomer unit predominates, copolymers or polymer blends, as the case may be, are to be classified in the heading which occurs last in numerical order among those which equally merit consideration.
5. Chemically modified polymers, that is those in which only appendages to the main polymer chain have been changed by chemical reaction, are to be classified in the heading appropriate to the unmodified polymer. This provision does not apply to graft copolymers.
6. In headings No. 39.01 to 39.14, the expression "primary forms" applies only to the following forms:
   (a) Liquids and pastes, including dispersions (emulsions and suspensions) and solutions;
   (b) Blocks of irregular shape, lumps, powders (including moulding powders), granules, flakes and similar bulk forms.
7. Heading No. 39.15 does not apply to waste, parings and scrap of a single thermoplastic material, transformed into primary forms (headings No. 39.01 to 39.14).
8. For the purposes of heading No. 39.17, the expression "tubes, pipes and hoses" means hollow products, whether semi-manufactures or finished products, of a kind generally used for conveying, conducting or distributing gases or liquids (for example, ribbed garden hose, perforated tubes). This expression also includes sausage casings and other layflat tubing. However, except for the last-mentioned, those having an internal cross-section other than round, oval, rectangular (in which the length does not exceed 1.5 times the width) or in the shape of a regular polygon are not to be regarded as tubes, pipes and hoses but as profile shapes.
9. For the purposes of heading No. 39.18, the expression "wall or ceiling coverings of plastics" applies to products in rolls, of a width not less than 45 cm, suitable for wall or ceiling decoration, consisting of plastics fixed permanently on a backing of any material other than paper, the layer of plastics (on the face side) being grained, embossed, coloured, design-printed or otherwise decorated.
10. In headings No. 39.20 and 39.21, the expression "plates, sheets, film, foil and strip" applies only to plates, sheets, film, foil and strip (other than those of Chapter 54) and to blocks of regular geometric shape, whether or not printed or otherwise surface-woked, uncut or cut into rectangles (including squares) but not further worked (even if when so cut they become articles ready for use).
11. Heading No. 39.25 applies only to the following articles, not being products covered by any of the earlier headings of sub-Chapter Ⅱ:
    (a) Reservoirs, tanks (including septic tanks), vats and similar containers, of a capacity exceeding 300 L;
    (b) Structural elements used, for example, in floors, walls or partitions, ceilings or roofs;
    (c) Gutters and fittings therefor;
    (d) Doors, windows and their frames and thresholds for doors;
    (e) Balconies, balustrades, fencing, gates and similar barriers;
    (f) Shutters, blinds (including Venetian blinds) and similar articles and parts and fittings thereof;
    (g) Large-scale shelving for assembly and permanent installation, for example, in shops, workshops, warehouses;
    (h) Ornamental architectural features, for example, flutings, cupolas, dovecotes; and
    (i) Fittings and mountings intended for permanent installation in or on doors, windows, staircases, walls or other parts of buildings, for example, knobs, handles, hooks, brackets, towel rails, switch-plates and other protective plates.

Subheading Notes:

1. Within any one heading of this Chapter, polymers (including copolymers) and chemically modified polymers are to be classified according to the following provisions:
   (a) Where there is a subheading named "Other" in the same series:
      (i) The designation in a subheading of a polymer by the prefix "poly" (forexample, polyethylene and polyamide-6,6) means that the constituent monomer unit or monomer units of the named polymer taken together must contribute 95% or more by weight of the total polymer content.
      (ii) The copolymers named in subheadings Nos. 3901.30, 3901.40, 3903.20, 3903.30 and 3904.30 are to be classified in those subheadings, provided that the comonomer units of the named copolymers contribute 95% or more by weight of the total polymer content.
      (iii) Chemically modified polymers are to be classified in the subheading named "Other", provided that the chemically modified polymers are not more specifically covered by another subheading.
      (iv) Polymers not meeting (1), (2) or (3) above, are to be classified in the subheading, among the remaining subheadings in the series, covering polymers of that monomer unit which predominates by weight over every other single comonomer unit. For this purpose, constituent monomer units of polymers falling in the same subheading shall be taken together. Only the constituent comonomer units of the polymers in the series of subheadings under consideration are to be compared.
   (b) Where there is no subheading named "Other" in the same series:
      (i) Polymers are to be classified in the subheading covering polymers of that monomer unit which predominates by weight over every other single comonomer unit. For this purpose, constituent monomer units of polymers falling in the same subheading shall be taken together. Only the constituent comonomer units of the polymers in the series under consideration are to be compared.
      (ii) Chemically modified polymers are to be classified in the subheading appropriate to the unmodified polymer.

      Polymer blends are to be classified in the same subheading as polymers of the same monomer units in the same proportions.
2. For the purposes of subheading No. 3920.43, the term "plasticisers" includes "secondary plasticisers."

税则号列	货品名称〔CIQ扩展编码及品名—T2表示见附表2〕	最惠(%)	暂定税率	普通	增值/消费	出口退税	计量单位	监管条件	检验检疫	特殊证件对美关税
	第一分章　初级形状									
39.01	**初级形状的乙烯聚合物：**									
3901.1000	-聚乙烯，比重小于0.94									
3901.1000 01	初级形状比重<0.94的聚乙烯（进口CIF价高于3800美元/吨）〔999〕	6.5	3	45	13/	13	千克			/
3901.1000 90	初级形状比重<0.94的聚乙烯〔999〕	6.5		45	13/	13	千克			/
3901.2000	-聚乙烯，比重在0.94及以上			45	17	13	千克			
3901.2000 11	茂金属高密度聚乙烯（密度0.962g/cm^3，熔流率0.85g/10min）（进口CIF价高于3800美元/吨）〔301〕	6.5		45	13/	13	千克			/
3901.2000 19	茂金属高密度聚乙烯（密度0.962g/cm^3，熔流率0.85g/10min）〔301〕	6.5		45	13/	13	千克			/
3901.2000 91	其他初级形状比重≥0.94的聚乙烯（进口CIF价高于3800美元/吨）〔301〕	6.5		45	13/	13	千克			/33
3901.2000 99	其他初级形状比重≥0.94的聚乙烯〔301〕	6.5		45	13/	13	千克			/36.5
3901.3000	-乙烯-乙酸乙烯酯共聚物〔999〕	6.5		45	13/	10	千克			/36.5
	-乙烯-α-烯烃共聚物，比重小于0.94：									
3901.4010	---乙烯-丙烯共聚物（乙丙橡胶）〔999〕	6.5		45	13/	10	千克			/31.5
3901.4010 10	粘指剂，比重小于0.94（初级形状，乙烯单体单元65%，丙烯单体单元35%）〔301〕	6.5		45	13/	10	千克			/
3901.4010 90	乙烯—丙烯共聚物（乙丙橡胶），比重小于0.94（初级形状，乙烯单体单元的含量大于丙烯单体单元）〔301〕	6.5		45	13/	10	千克			/36.5
3901.4020	---线型低密度聚乙烯〔999〕	6.5		45	13/	13	千克			/31.5
3901.4020 10	线型低密度的乙烯与1—辛烃共聚物，比重小于0.94（初级形状的）〔301〕	6.5		45	13/	13	千克			/
3901.4020 90	线型低密度聚乙烯，比重小于0.94（初级形状的）〔301〕	6.5		45	13/	13	千克			/36.5
3901.4090	---其他〔999〕	6.5		45	13/	13	千克			/
	-其他：									
3901.9010	---乙烯-丙烯共聚物（乙丙橡胶）〔999〕	6.5		45	13/	10	千克			/36.5
3901.9090	---其他〔999〕	6.5		45	13/	13	千克			/
39.02	**初级形状的丙烯或其他烯烃聚合物：**									
3902.1000	-聚丙烯									
3902.1000 10	电工级初级形状聚丙烯树脂（灰分含量不大于30ppm）〔999〕	6.5	3	45	13/	13	千克			/33
3902.1000 20	共聚抗冲等级初级形状聚丙烯（熔融指数MI<0.5g/10min，UL认证黄卡中RTI（相当于长期工作温度）115℃，悬臂梁缺口冲击强度（测量方法ISO 180）：23℃时为64KJ/m^2，—40℃时为4.0KJ/m^2）〔301〕	6.5		45	13/	13	千克			/
3902.1000 90	其他初级形状的聚丙烯〔999〕	6.5		45	13/	13	千克			/36.5
3902.2000	-聚异丁烯〔101无检疫要求食品添加剂，999，301需申报仅用于工业用途不用于食品添加剂无检疫要求的化学品〕	6.5		45	13/	10	千克	A	R	/36.5
	-丙烯共聚物：									
3902.3010	---乙烯-丙烯共聚物（乙丙橡胶）〔999〕	6.5		45	13/	10	千克			/36.5
3902.3090	---其他〔999〕	6.5		45	13/	13	千克			/36.5
3902.9000	-其他									
3902.9000 10	端羧基聚丁二烯，CTPB（作粘接剂或燃料）〔999〕	6.5		45	13/	10	千克	3		/21.5
3902.9000 20	端羟基聚丁二烯，HTPB（作粘接剂或燃料）〔999〕	6.5		45	13/	10	千克	3		/21.5
3902.9000 90	其他初级形状的烯烃聚合物〔999〕	6.5		45	13/	10	千克			/21.5
39.03	**初级形状的苯乙烯聚合物：**									
	-聚苯乙烯：									
3903.1100	--可发性的〔301〕	6.5		45	13/	10	千克			/16.5
	--其他：									
3903.1910	---改性的〔999〕	6.5		45	13/	13	千克			/36.5
3903.1990	---其他〔999〕	6.5		45	13/	10	千克			/36.5
3903.2000	-苯乙烯-丙烯腈（SAN）共聚物〔999〕	12		45	13/	10	千克			/42
	-丙烯腈-丁二烯-苯乙烯（ABS）共聚物：									
3903.3010	---改性的〔999〕	6.5		45	13/	13	千克			/36.5
3903.3090	---其他〔999〕	6.5		45	13/	10	千克			/36.5
3903.9000	-其他〔999〕	6.5		45	13/	10	千克			/21.5

协定税率 %										特惠税率 %			
亚太5国	东/冰/格	巴基斯坦	韩国	瑞士	哥达	秘鲁	澳大利亚	新西/坡/智	港/澳/台	亚太2国	老/柬/缅	36/3/1	Article Description
													1. -PRIMARY FORMS
													Polymers of ethylene, in primary forms:
													-Polyethylene having a specific gravity of less than 0. 94
6	/0/	6	5.9	3.4	0		0	0//0	0/0/				Polyethylene having a sopecific gravity of less than 0. 94, in primary forms(CIF>USD3800/ton)
6	/0/	6	5.9	3.4	0		0	0//0	0/0/				Polyethylene having a specific gravity of less than 0. 94, in primary forms
													-Polyethylene having a specific gravity of 0. 94 or more
6	/0/	6	5.9	3.4	0		0	0//0	0/0/		//	//	Metallocene HDPE (density 0. 962g/cm 3, melting rate 0. 85g/10min) (CIF price of import is higher than 3800 USD / ton)
6	/0/	6	5.9	3.4	0		0	0//0	0/0/		//	//	Metallocene HDPE (density 0. 962g/cm ^ 3, melting rate 0. 85g/10min)
6	/0/	6	5.9	3.4	0		0	0//0	0/0/		//	//	Other polyethylene with the proportion of primary shape ≥ 0. 94 (CIF price of import is higher than 3800 USD / ton)
6	/0/	6	5.9	3.4	0		0	0//0	0/0/		//	//	Polyethylene with other primary shape specific gravity ≥ 0.94
6	0/0/	4	5.9	0	0	0	0	0/0/0	0/0/			0/0/	-Ethylene-vinyl acetate copolymers
													-Ethylene—alpha—olefin copoly—mers, having a specific gravity of less than 0. 94:
	0/0/0	5	4.3	0	0	0	0	0/0/0	0/0/			0/0/	---Ethylene-propylene copoly-mers
	0/0/0	0	3.9	0	0	0	0	0/0/0	0/0/		//	0/0/	Adhesive, specific gravity less than 0.94 (primary shape, ethylene monomer unit 65%, propylene monomer unit 35%)
	0/0/0	0	3.9	0	0	0	0	0/0/0	0/0/		//	0/0/	Ethylene propylene copolymer (ethylene propylene rubber), specific gravity less than 0.94 (primary shape, ethylene monomer unit content greater than propylene monomer unit)
	0/0/	5			0		0	0/0/0	0/0/			0/0/0	---Linearity low density polyeth—Ylene
	0/0/	0			0		0	0/0/0	0/0/		//	0/0/0	Linear low density ethylene and 1—octane copolymer, specific gravity less than 0.94 (primary shape)
	0/0/	0			0		0	0/0/0	0/0/		//	0/0/0	Linear low density polyethylene, specific gravity less than 0.94 (primary shape)
4.2	0/0/0	0	4.2	0	0	0	0	0/0/0	0/0/			0/0/	---Other
													-Other:
	0/0/0	0	3.9	0	0	0	0	0/0/0	0/0/			0/0/	---Ethylene-propylene copolymers
4.2	0/0/0	0	4.2	0	0	0	0	0/0/0	0/0/			0/0/	---Other
													Polymers of propylene or of other olefins, in primary forms:
													-Polypropylene
	0/0/	4		3.4	0		0	0/0/0	0/0/				Polypropylene resin, in primary forms, electrical grade (ash content ≤30ppm)
	0/0/	4		3.4	0		0	0/0/0	0/0/		//	//	Impact resistance grade of copolymerized polypropylene of primary shape (MI < 0.5g/10min, RTI (equivalent to long—term working temperature) in UL certified yellow card 115 ℃, impact strength of cantilever notch (Measurement Method ISO 180): 64kj / m ^ 2 at 23 ℃, 4.0kj/m ^ 2 at — 40 ℃)
	0/0/	4		3.4	0		0	0/0/0	0/0/				Other polypropylene, in primary forms
	0/0/0	4		0	0	0	0	0//0	0/0/			0/0/0	-Polyisobutylene
													-Propylene copolymers:
6	0/0/0	0	3.9	0	0	0	0	0/0/0	0/0/0			0/0/0	---Ethylene-propylene copolymers
6	0/0/	4	5.9	0	0	0	0	0/0/0	0/0/			0/0/0	---Other
													-Other
	0/0/0	0		0	0	0	0	0/0/0	0/0/0			0/0/0	Carboxyl-terminal polybutadiene, CTPB (used as adhesive or fuel)
	0/0/0	0		0	0	0	0	0/0/0	0/0/0			0/0/0	Hydroxyl-terminal polybutadiene, HTPB (used as adhesive or fuel)
	0/0/0	0		0	0	0	0	0/0/0	0/0/0			0/0/0	Other polymers of olefins, in primary forms
													Polymers of styrene, in primary forms:
													-Polystyrene:
6	0/0/2.6	0	5.9	0	0	0	0	0/0/0	0/0/			0/0/0	--Expansible
													--Other:
6	0/0/	0	4.5	0	0	0	0	0/0/0	0/0/			0/0/0	---Modified
6	0/0/	0	4.5	0	0	0	0	0/0/0	0/0/			0/0/0	---Other
	0/0/0	6	9.6	3.6	0	0	0	0/0/0	0/0/0			0/0/	-Styrene-acrylonitrile (SAN) copolymers
													-Acrylonitrile-butadiene-styrene (ABS) copolymers:
6	0/0/	4	4.5	3.4	0	0	0	0/0/0	0/0/			0/0/0	---Modified
6	0/0/	4	4.5	2	0	0	0	0/0/0	0/0/			0/0/0	---Other
6	0/0/0	0	3.9	0	0	0	0	0/0/0	0/0/0			0/0/0	-Other

税则号列	货品名称〔CIQ扩展编码及品名—T2表示见附表2〕	最惠(%)	暂定税率	普通	增值/消费	出口退税	计量单位	监管条件	检验检疫	特殊证件对美关税
39.04	**初级形状的氯乙烯或其他卤化烯烃聚合物:**									
	-聚氯乙烯,未掺其他物质:									
3904.1010	---糊树脂〔999〕	6.5		45	13/	13	千克			/36.5
3904.1090	---其他									
3904.1090 01	聚氯乙烯纯粉(纯指未掺其他物质)〔999〕	6.5		45	13/	13	千克			/
3904.1090 90	其他初级形状的纯聚氯乙烯(纯指未掺其他物质)〔999〕	6.5		45	13/	13	千克			/
	-其他聚氯乙烯:									
3904.2100	--未塑化〔999〕	6.5		45	13/	13	千克			/16.5
3904.2200	--已塑化〔999〕	6.5		45	13/	13	千克			/21.5
3904.3000	-氯乙烯-乙酸乙烯酯共聚物〔999〕	9		45	13/	10	千克			/34
3904.4000	-其他氯乙烯共聚物〔999〕	12		45	13/	10	千克			/37
3904.5000	-偏二氯乙烯聚合物									
3904.5000 10	偏二氯乙烯－氯乙烯共聚树脂〔999〕	6.5		45	13/	10	千克			/31.5
3904.5000 90	其他偏二氯乙烯聚合物〔999〕	6.5		45	13/	10	千克			/31.5
	-氟聚合物:									
3904.6100	--聚四氟乙烯〔999〕	10		45	13/	13	千克			/20
3904.6900	--其他〔999〕	6.5		45	13/	13	千克			/16.5
3904.9000	-其他〔999〕	10		45	13/	10	千克			/20
39.05	**初级形状的乙酸乙烯酯或其他乙烯酯聚合物;初级形状的其他乙烯基聚合物:**									
	-聚乙酸乙烯酯:									
3905.1200	--水分散体〔101:PM2035溶液,999〕	10		45	13/	10	千克			/20
3905.1900	--其他〔999〕	10		45	13/	10	千克			/40
	-乙酸乙烯酯共聚物:									
3905.2100	--水分散体〔999〕	10		45	13/	10	千克			/40
3905.2900	--其他〔999〕	10		45	13/	10	千克			/40
3905.3000	-聚乙烯醇,不论是否含有未水解的乙酸酯基〔101无检疫要求食品添加剂,999不论是否含有未水解的乙酸酯基,301需申报仅用于工业用途不用于食品添加剂无检疫要求的化学品〕	14		45	13/	10	千克	A	R	/34
	-其他:									
3905.9100	--共聚物〔999〕	10		45	13/	10	千克			/20
3905.9900	--其他〔999〕	10		45	13/	10	千克			/20
39.06	**初级形状的丙烯酸聚合物:**									
3906.1000	-聚甲基丙烯酸甲酯〔999〕	6.5		45	13/	13	千克			/36.5
	-其他:									
3906.9010	---聚丙烯酰胺〔999,301无检疫要求食品添加剂,302需申报仅用于工业用途不用于食品添加剂无检疫要求的化学品〕	6.5		45	13/	10	千克	A	R	/36.5
3906.9090	---其他〔999〕	6.5		45	13/	10,13	千克			/
39.07	**初级形状的聚缩醛、其他聚醚及环氧树脂;初级形状的聚碳酸酯、醇酸树脂、聚烯丙基酯及其他聚酯:**									
	-聚缩醛:									
3907.1010	---聚甲醛									
3907.1010 10	聚甲醛(均聚聚甲醛及改性聚甲醛除外)〔999〕	6.5		45	13/	13	千克			/31.5
3907.1010 90	其他聚甲醛〔999〕	6.5		45	13/	13	千克			/31.5
3907.1090	---其他									
3907.1090 10	共聚聚甲醛(改性聚甲醛除外)〔999〕	6.5		45	13/	10	千克			/31.5
3907.1090 90	其他聚缩醛〔999〕	6.5		45	13/	10	千克			/31.5
	-其他聚醚:									
3907.2010	---聚四亚甲基醚二醇〔999〕	6.5	3	45	13/	10	千克			/33
3907.2090	---其他〔101:－18℃≤闪点＜23℃,环氧树脂,999:〕	6.5		45	13/	13	千克			/
3907.3000	-环氧树脂									
3907.3000 01	初级形状溴质量≥18%或进口CIF价＞3800美元/吨的环氧树脂(如溶于溶剂,以纯环氧树脂折算溴百分比含量)〔999如溶于溶剂,以纯环氧树脂折算溴的百分比含量,301其他危险化学品〕	6.5	4	45	13/	10	千克	A	M	/
3907.3000 90	初级形状的环氧树脂(溴重量百分比含量在18%以下)〔999溴重量百分比含量在18%以下,301其他危险化学品〕	6.5		45	13/	10	千克	AB	MN	/
3907.4000	-聚碳酸酯〔999〕	6.5	3	45	13/	13	千克			/
3907.5000	-醇酸树脂〔999,301易燃液体〕	10		45	13/	10	千克	AB	MN	/40
	-聚对苯二甲酸乙二酯:									
	--粘数在78毫升/克或以上:									

协定税率 %										特惠税率 %			
亚太5国	东/冰/格	巴基斯坦	韩国	瑞士	哥达	秘鲁	澳大利亚	新西/坡/智	港/澳/台	亚太2国	老/柬/缅	36/3/1	Article Description
													Polymers of vinyl chloride or of other halogenated olefins, in primary forms:
													-Poly(vinyl chloride), not mixed with any other substances:
4.2	0/0/2.6	0	4.5	0	0	0	0	0/0/0	0/0/			0/0/C	---Paste resins
													---Other
4.2	0/0/	0	4.2	0	0	0	0	0/0/0	0/0/			0/0/0	Poly (vinyl chloride)(not mixed with any other substances) in powder
4.2	0/0/	0	4.2	0	0	0	0	0/0/0	0/0/			0/0/0	Other poly (vinyl chloride)(not mixed with any other substances)
													-Other poly(vinyl chloride):
	0/0/2.6	4	4.5	0	0	0	0	0/0/0	0/0/			0/0/0	--Non-plasticized
	0/0/		4.5	0	0	0	0	0/0/0	0/0/			0/0/0	--Plasticized
8.6	0/0/0	4	5.4	0	0	0	0	0//0	0/0/			0/0/0	-Vinyl chloride-vinyl acetate copolymers
7.8	0/0/0	6	7.2	3.6	0	0	0	0/0/0	0/0/			0/0/	-Other vinyl chloride copolymers
													-Vinylidene chloride polymers
	0/0/0	4	0	0	0	0	0	0//0	0/0/			0/0/0	Vinylidene Chloride—Vinyl Chloride Copolymer Resin
	0/0/0	4	0	0	0	0	0	0//0	0/0/			0/0/0	Other vinylidene chloride polymers, in primary forms
													-Fluoro-polymers:
	0/0/0	4.5	4	0	0	0	0	0/0/0	0/0/			0/0/0	--Polytetrafluoroethylene
	0/0/0	4	0	0	0	0	0	0//0	0/0/			0/0/0	--Other
	0/0/0	4.5	6	0	0	0	0	0//0	0/0/			0/0/0	-Other
													Polymers of vinyl acetate or of other vinyl esters, in primary forms; other vinyl polymers in primary forms:
													-Poly(vinyl acetate):
	0/0/0		6	0	0	0	0	0/0/0	0/0/			0/0/	--In aqueous dispersion
	0/0/0	4.5	6	0	0	0	0	0//0	0/0/			0/0/	--Other
													-Vinyl acetate copolymers:
	0/0/0	4.5	6	0	0	0	0	0/0/0	0/0/0			0/0/	--In aqueous dispersion
	0/0/0	4.5	6		0	0	0	0/0/0	0/0/			0/0/	--Other
	0/0/0	11.2	5.6	4.2	0	0	0	0/0/0	0/0/0			0/0/	-Poly(vinyl alcohol), whether or not containing unhydrolyzed acetate groups
													-Other:
	0/0/0	4.5	6	0	0	0	0	0//0	0/0/			0/0/	--Copolymers
	0/0/0		6	0	0	0	0	0//0	0/0/			0/0/	--Other
													Acrylic polymers in primary forms:
6	0/0/2.6	4	5.9	0	0	0	0	0//0	0/0/0			0/0/0	-Poly(methyl methacrylate)
													-Other:
6	0/0/0	0	5.9	0	0	0	0	0//0	0/0/0			0/0/0	---Polyacrylamide
6	0/0/0	0	2.6	2	0	0	0	0//0	0/0/0			0/0/0	---Other
													Polyacetals, other polyethers and epoxide resins, in primary forms; polycarbonates, alkyd resins, polyallyl esters and other polyesters, in primary forms:
													-Polyacetals:
													---Polyoxymethylene(POM)
6.1	0/0/0	0	3.9	0	0	0	0	0/0/0	0/0/0			0/0/0	Polyoxymethylene(POM), other than homoPOM and modification of POM
6.1	0/0/0	0	3.9	0	0	0	0	0/0/0	0/0/0			0/0/0	Other polyoxymethylene(POM)
													---Other
4.2	0/0/0	4	0	0	0	0	0	0/0/0	0/0/			0/0/0	Polyformaldehyde, other than modification of POM
4.2	0/0/0	4	0	0	0	0	0	0/0/0	0/0/			0/0/0	Other polyacetals
													-Other polyethers:
6.1	0/0/0	0	0	0	0	0	0	0/0/0	0/0/0			0/0/0	---Polytetramethylene ether glycol
6.1	0/0/0	0	3.9	2	0	0	0	0/0/0	0/0/			0/0/0	---Other
													-Epoxide resins
6.1	0/0/0	0	3.9	3.4	0	0	0	0/0/0	0/0/0			0/0/0	Epoxide resins, in primary forms, containing ≥18% by weight of bromine, or import CIF price >3800 USD/ton (If dissolved into solutions, convert the content percentage of bromine by pure epoxy resin)
6.1	0/0/0	0	3.9	3.4	0	0	0	0/0/0	0/0/0			0/0/0	Epoxide resins, in primary forms, containing <18% by weight of bromine
6.1	0/0/0	0	3.9	2	0	0	0	0/0/0	0/0/0			0/0/0	-Polycarbonates
6.5	0/0/0	4.5	4	0	0	0	0	0/0/0	0/0/0			0/0/0	-Alkyd resins
													-Poly(ethylene terephthalate):
													--Having a viscosity number of 78 ml/ g or higher:

税则号列	货品名称〔CIQ扩展编码及品名－T2表示见附表2〕	最惠(%)	暂定税率	普通	增值/消费	出口退税	计量单位	监管条件	检验检疫	特殊证件对美关税
3907.6110	---切片〔999 其他化工产品,301 易燃液体〕	6.5		45	13/	13	千克			/36.5
3907.6190	---其他〔999 其他化工产品,301 易燃液体〕	6.5		45	13/	13	千克			/31.5
	--其他:									
3907.6910	---切片〔999 其他化工产品,301 易燃液体〕	6.5		45	13/	13	千克			/21.5
3907.6990	---其他〔999 其他化工产品,301 易燃液体〕	6.5		45	13/	13	千克			/31.5
3907.7000	-聚乳酸〔999〕	6.5	3	45	13/	10	千克			/8
	-其他聚酯:									
3907.9100	--不饱和〔101:－18℃≤闪点＜23℃,不饱和聚酯树脂,999:〕	6.5		45	13/	10	千克			/31.5
	--其他:									
3907.9910	---聚对苯二甲酸丁二酯									
3907.9910 01	未经增强或改性的初级形状PBT树脂〔999〕	6.5		45	13/	13	千克			/31.5
3907.9910 90	其他聚对苯二甲酸丁二酯〔999〕	6.5		45	13/	13	千克			/31.5
	---其他:									
3907.9991	----聚对苯二甲酸-己二醇-丁二醇酯									
3907.9991 10	初级形状的热塑性液晶聚对苯二甲酸-己二醇-丁二醇酯〔999〕	2.2/1.1		45	13/	10	千克	AB	RS	/12.2,11.1
3907.9991 90	其他初级形状的聚对苯二甲酸-己二醇-丁二醇酯〔999〕	6.5		45	13/	10	千克	AB	RS	/16.5
3907.9999	----其他									
3907.9999 10	初级形状的热塑性液晶其他聚酯〔999〕	2.2/1.1		45	13/	10	千克	AB	RS	/
3907.9999 90	初级形状的其他聚酯〔999,301 无检疫要求食品添加剂,302 需申报仅用于工业用途不用于食品添加剂无检疫要求的化学品〕	6.5		45	13/	10	千克	AB	RS	/
39.08	**初级形状的聚酰胺:**									
	-聚酰胺-6、-11、-12、-6,6、-6,9、-6,10或-6,12:									
	---切片:									
3908.1011	----聚酰胺-6,6切片									
3908.1011 01	聚酰胺-6,6切片〔999〕	6.5		45	13/	13	千克			/
3908.1011 90	改性聚酰胺-6,6切片(经螺杆二次混炼加入玻璃纤维、矿物质、增韧剂、阻燃剂的改性聚酰胺-6,6切片)〔999〕	6.5		45	13/	13	千克			/
3908.1012	----聚酰胺-6切片〔999〕	6.5		45	13/	13	千克			/36.5
3908.1019	----其他〔999〕	6.5		45	13/	13	千克			/21.5
3908.1090	---其他〔999〕	6.5		45	13/	10	千克			/31.5
	-其他:									
3908.9010	---芳香族聚酰胺及其共聚物〔101:闭杯闪点≤60℃,102:－18℃≤闪点＜23℃,酚醛树脂,103:其他〕	10		45	13/	10	千克			/
3908.9020	---半芳香族聚酰胺及其共聚物〔101:闭杯闪点≤60℃,102:－18℃≤闪点＜23℃,酚醛树脂,103:其他〕	10		45	13/	10	千克			/
3908.9090	---其他〔101:闭杯闪点≤60℃,102:－18℃≤闪点＜23℃,酚醛树脂,103:其他〕	10		45	13/	10	千克			/
39.09	**初级形状的氨基树脂、酚醛树脂及聚氨酯类:**									
3909.1000	-尿素树脂;硫尿树脂〔999〕	6.5		45	13/	10	千克			/36.5
3909.2000	-蜜胺树脂:〔101:－18℃≤闪点＜23℃,三聚氰胺甲醛树酯,102:－18℃≤闪点＜23℃,三聚氰胺树酯,103:－18℃≤闪点＜23℃,甲醇改性三羟甲基三聚氰胺甲醛树脂,104:－18℃≤闪点＜23℃,苯代三聚氰胺甲醛树脂,999:〕	6.5		45	13/	10	千克			/21.5
	-其他氨基树脂:									
3909.3100	--聚(亚甲基苯基异氰酸酯)(粗MDI、聚合MDI)〔999〕	6.5		35	13/	13	千克			/31.5
3909.3900	--其他〔999 其他化工产品,301 易燃液体〕	6.5		45	13/	10	千克	AB	MN	/31.5
3909.4000	-酚醛树脂〔999,301 易燃液体〕	6.5		45	13/	10	千克	AB	MN	/31.5
3909.5000	-聚氨基甲酸酯〔102 含二级易燃溶剂的合成树脂,聚氨酯树脂,103 含二级易燃溶剂的合成树脂,潮气固化型聚氨基甲酸酯,301 易燃液体,302 其他化工产品〕	6.5		45	13/	13	千克	AB	MN	/31.5
39.10	**初级形状的聚硅氧烷:**									
3910.0000	初级形状的聚硅氧烷〔101:－18℃≤闪点＜23℃,有机硅树脂,999:〕	6.5		45	13/	13	千克			/
39.11	**初级形状的石油树脂、苯并呋喃-茚树脂、多萜树脂、多硫化物、聚砜及本章注释三所规定的其他税目未列名产品:**									
3911.1000	-石油树脂、苯并呋喃树脂、茚树脂、苯并呋喃-茚树脂及多萜树脂〔999〕	6.5		45	13/	10	千克			/21.5
3911.9000	-其他									
3911.9000 01	芳基酸与芳基胺预缩聚物〔999〕	6.5	3	45	13/	10	千克			/
3911.9000 03	改性三羟乙基脲酸酯类预缩聚物〔999〕	6.5	3	45	13/	10	千克			/
3911.9000 04	聚苯硫醚〔999〕	6.5		45	13/	13	千克			/

协定税率 %										特惠税率 %			Article Description
亚太5国	东/冰/格	巴基斯坦	韩国	瑞士	哥达	秘鲁	澳大利亚	新西/坡/智	港/澳/台	亚太2国	老/柬/缅	36/3/1	
	5/0/2.6		4.5	0	0	0	0	0//0	0/0/			0/0/0	--In the form of slices or chips
	0/0/0	0	3.9	0	0	0	0	0/0/0	0/0/			0/0/0	---Other
													--Other:
	5/0/	0	4.5	0	0	0	0	0//0	0/0/			0/0/0	---In the form of slices or chips
	0/0/0	0	3.9	0	0	0	0	0/0/0	0/0/			0/0/0	---Other
4.2	0/0/0	4	0	0	0	0	0	0//0	0/0/			0/0/0	-Poly(lactic acid)
													-Other polyesters:
	0/0/0	0	2.6	0	0	0	0	0/0/0	0/0/0			0/0/0	--Unsaturated
													--Other:
													---Poly butylene terephthalate
4.2	0/0/	0	3.9	0	0	0	0	0/0/0	0/0/			0/0/0	Not reinforced or modified PBT resins, in primary forms
4.2	0/0/	0	3.9	0	0	0	0	0/0/0	0/0/			0/0/0	Other Poly butylene terephthalate
													---Other:
													----Poly terephthalic acid hexylene glycol - butanediol ester
4.2	0/0/0	0	0	0	0	0	0	0/0/0	0/0/0			0/0/0	Poly terephthalic acid hexylene glycol - butanediol J28, thermoplastic liquid crystal, in primary forms
4.2	0/0/0	0	0	0	0	0	0	0/0/0	0/0/0			0/0/0	Poly terephthalic acid hexylene glycol - butanediol J28, in other forms
													----Other
4.2	0/0/0	0	0	0	0	0	0	0/0/0	0/0/0			0/0/0	Polyesters, thermoplastic liquid crystal, in primary forms
4.2	0/0/0	0	0	0	0	0	0	0/0/0	0/0/0			0/0/0	Other polyesters, in primary forms
													Polyamides in primary forms:
													-Polyamide-6, -11, -12, -6,6, -6,9, -6,10 or -6,12:
													---In the form of slices or chips:
													----Of polyamide-6,6
	0/0/	4		2	0	0	0	0/0/0	0/0/			0/0/0	Polyamide -6,6 slice
	0/0/	4		2	0	0	0	0/0/0	0/0/			0/0/0	Modification polyamide -6,6 slice (screw secondary mixing, adding glass fiber, minerals, plasticizer, flame retardant)
	0/0/	4		3.4	0	0	0	0/0/0	0/0/			0/0/0	----Of polyamide-6
	0/0/	4		3.4	0	0	0	0/0/0	0/0/			0/0/0	----Other
	0/0/	4		2	0	0	0	0/0/0	0/0/			0/0/0	---Other
													-Other:
	0/0/	4.5			0	0	0	0/0/0	0/0/			0/0/0	---Aromatic polyamide and copolymerl
	0/0/	4.5			0	0	0	0/0/0	0/0/			0/0/0	---Semi aromatic polyamide and copolymerl
	0/0/	4.5			0	0	0	0/0/0	0/0/			0/0/0	---Other
													Amino-resins, phenolic resins and polyurethanes, in primary forms:
4.2	0/0/0	4	0	0	0	0	0	0//0	0/0/0			0/0/0	-Urea resins; thiourea resins
4.2	0/0/0	4	0	0	0	0	0	0//0	0/0/0			0/0/0	-Melamine resins
													-Other amino-resins:
6.1	0/0/0	0	3.9	0	0	0	0	0/0/0	0/0/			0/0/0	--Poly (*methylene phenyl isocy-anate*) (*crude MDI*, *polymeric MDI*)
	0/0/0	4	0	0	0	0	0	0/0/0	0/0/0			0/0/0	--Other
6.1	0/0/0	0	2.6	0	0	0	0	0//0	0/0/0			0/0/0	-Phenolic resins
4.2	0/0/0	4	0	0	0	0	0	0/0/0	0/0/0			0/0/0	-Polyurethanes
													Silicones in primary forms:
6.1	0/0/0	4	2.6	0	0	0	0	0//0	0/0/0			0/0/0	Silicones in primary forms
													Petroleum resins, coumarone-indene resins, polyterpenes, polysulphides, polysulphones and other products specified in Note 3 to this Chapter, not elsewhere specified or included, in primary forms:
4.2	0/0/0	4	3.9	0	0	0	0	0//0	0/0/0			0/0/0	-Petroleum resins, coumarone, indene or coumarone-indene resins and polyterpenes
													-Other
	0/0/0	0	0	0	0	0	0	0//0	0/0/			0/0/0	Precondensed polymer of aromatic acid and aromatic amide
	0/0/0	0	0	0	0	0	0	0//0	0/0/			0/0/0	Precondensed polymer of modified trihydroxy acetate
	0/0/0	0	0	0	0	0	0	0//0	0/0/			0/0/0	Polyphenylene sulfide

税则号列	货品名称〔CIQ 扩展编码及品名—T2 表示见附表 2〕	最惠(%)	暂定税率	普通	增值/消费	出口退税	计量单位	监管条件	检验检疫	特殊证件对美关税
3911.9000 05	偏苯三酸酐和异氰酸预缩聚物〔999〕	6.5	3	45	13/	10	千克			/
3911.9000 90	其他初级形状的多硫化物、聚砜等(包括本章注释三所规定的其他编号未列名产品)〔999 等包括本章注释三所规定的其他编号未列名产品,301 无检疫要求食品添加剂〕	6.5		45	13/	13	千克			/
39.12	**初级形状的其他税目未列名的纤维素及其化学衍生物:**									
	-乙酸纤维素:									
3912.1100	--未塑化〔999〕	6.5		40	13/	0,10	千克			/
3912.1200	--已塑化〔999〕	6.5		40	13/	0	千克			/16.5
3912.2000	-硝酸纤维素(包括胶棉)〔999 包括棉胶,301 爆炸品,302 易燃液体,303 易燃固体〕	6.5		45	13/	0	千克			/36.5
	-纤维素醚:									
3912.3100	--羧甲基纤维素及其盐〔101 其他饲料添加剂,999〕	6.5		45	13/	0	千克			/21.5
3912.3900	--其他〔999〕	6.5		45	13/	0	千克			/16.5
3912.9000	-其他〔999 包括化学衍生物,301 易于自燃的物质,302 不易于自燃的物质〕	6.5		45	13/	0	千克			/16.5
39.13	**初级形状的其他税目未列名的天然聚合物(例如藻酸)及改性天然聚合物(例如,硬化蛋白、天然橡胶的化学衍生物):**									
3913.1000	-藻酸及其盐和酯〔101 其他饲料添加剂,301 其他危险化学品,需申报仅用于工业用途不用于食品添加剂无检疫要求,302 无检疫要求食品添加剂,303 一般化学品,需申报仅用于工业用途不用于食品添加剂无检疫要求,304 属于危险化学品的食品添加剂〕	10		45	13/	0	千克	AB	RS	/40
3913.9000	-其他									
3913.9000 11	香菇多糖〔101 其他饲料添加剂,999〕	6.5		50	13/	13	千克	S		/16.5
3913.9000 90	其他初级形状的未列名天然聚合物[包括改性天然聚合物(如硬化蛋白)]〔101 其他饲料添加剂,999 如硬化蛋白〕	6.5		50	13/	13	千克			/16.5
39.14	**初级形状的离子交换剂,以税目 39.01 至 39.13 的聚合物为基本成分的:**									
3914.0000	初级形状的离子交换剂,以税目 39.01 至 39.13 的聚合物为基本成分的〔999〕	6.5		45	13/	10	千克			/21.5
	第二分章　废碎料及下脚料;半制品;制成品									
39.15	**塑料的废碎料及下脚料:**									
3915.1000	-乙烯聚合物的〔101 不包括铝塑复合膜,102 铝塑复合膜〕	6.5		50	13/	0	千克	9A	M	/31.5
3915.2000	-苯乙烯聚合物的〔999〕	6.5		50	13/	0	千克	9A	M	/31.5
3915.3000	-氯乙烯聚合物的〔999〕	6.5		50	13/	0	千克	9A	M	/31.5
	-其他塑料的:									
3915.9010	---聚对苯二甲酸乙二酯的〔101 不包括废 PET 饮料瓶(砖),102 废 PET 饮料瓶(砖)〕	6.5		50	13/	0	千克	9A	M	/31.5
3915.9090	---其他〔101 不包括废光盘破碎料,102 废光盘破碎料〕	6.5		50	13/	0	千克	9A	M	/31.5
39.16	**塑料制的单丝(截面直径超过 1 毫米)、条、杆、型材及异型材,不论是否经表面加工,但未经其他加工:**									
3916.1000	-乙烯聚合物制〔999〕	10		45	13/	13	千克			/40
	-氯乙烯聚合物制:									
3916.2010	---异型材〔999〕	10		45	13/	13	千克			/40
3916.2090	---其他〔999〕	10		45	13/	13	千克			/40
	-其他塑料制:									
3916.9010	---聚酰胺制〔999〕	10		45	13/	13	千克			/40
3916.9090	---其他〔999〕	10		45	13/	13	千克			/25
39.17	**塑料制的管子及其附件(例如,接头、肘管、法兰):**									
3917.1000	-硬化蛋白或纤维素材料制的人造肠衣(香肠用肠衣)〔999〕	10		50	13/	13	千克	A	R	/40
	-硬管:									
3917.2100	--乙烯聚合物制〔999〕	10		45	13/	13	千克			/35
3917.2200	--丙烯聚合物制〔999〕	10		45	13/	13	千克			/40
3917.2300	--氯乙烯聚合物制〔999〕	10		45	13/	13	千克			/35
3917.2900	--其他塑料制〔999〕	10		45	13/	13	千克			/25
	-其他管:									
3917.3100	--软管,最小爆破压力为 27.6 兆帕斯卡〔999〕	10		45	13/	13	千克			/25

协定税率 %										特惠税率 %			Article Description
亚太5国	东/冰/格	巴基斯坦	韩国	瑞士	哥达	秘鲁	澳大利亚	新西/坡/智	港/澳/台	亚太2国	老/柬/缅	36/3/1	
	0/0/0	0	0	0	0	0	0	0//0	0/0/			0/0/0	Frecondensed polymer of trimelltic anhydride and isocyanic acid
	0/0/0	0	0	0	0	0	0	0//0	0/0/			0/0/0	Other polysulphides, polysulphones (including other products specified in Note 3 to this Chapter, not elsewhere specified or included) in primary forms
													Cellulose and its chemical derivatives, not elsewhere specified or included, in primary forms:
													-Cellulose acetates:
	0/0/0	4	2.6	0	0	0	0	0//0	0/0/			0/0/	--Non-plasticized
5.9	0/0/0	4	0	0	0	0	0	0//0	0/0/			0/0/	--Plasticized
	0/0/0	4	0	0	0	0	0	0//0	0/0/			0/0/	-Cellulose nitrates (including collodions)
													-Cellulose ethers:
	0/0/0	4	0	0	0	0	0	0//0	0/0/			0/0/	--Carboxymethylcellulose and its salts
	0/0/0	4	0	0	0	0	0	0//0	0/0/			0/0/	--Other
	0/0/0	0	0	0	0	0	0	0//0	0/0/			0/0/	-Other
													Natural polymers (for example, alginic acid) and modified natural polymers (for example, hardened proteins, chemical derivatives of natural rubber), not elsewhere specified or included, in primary forms:
	0/0/0	4.5	4	0	0		0	0/0/0	0/0/			0/0/0	-Alginic acid, its salts and esters
													-Other
	0/0/2.6	4	0	0	0	0	0	0//0	0/0/			0/0/0	Mushrooms polysaccharide
	0/0/2.6	4	0	0	0	0	0	0//0	0/0/			0/0/0	Other primary NES (including natural polymer modified natural polymer (such ashardening protein))
													Ion-exchangers based on polymers of headings No. 39. 01 to 39. 13, in primary forms:
	0//0	4	0	0	0	0	0	0//0	0/0/			0/0/0	Ion-exchangers based on polymers of headings Nos. 39. 01 to 39. 13, in primary forms
													Ⅱ-WASTE, PARINGS AND SCRAP; SEMI-MANUFACTURES; ARTICLES
													Waste, parings and scrap, of plastics:
	0/0/0	0	3.9	0	0	0	0	0/0/0	0/0/			0/0/0	-Of polymers of ethylene
	0/0/0	4	3.9	0	0	0	0	0/0/0	0/0/			0/0/0	-Of polymers of styrene
	0/0/0	4	3.9	0	0	0	0	0/0/0	0/0/			0/0/0	-Of polymers of vinyl chloride
													-Of other plastics:
	0/0/0	0	3.9	2	0	0	0	0/0/0	0/0/			0/0/0	---Of pdyethylene glycol terephthalate
	0/0/0	0	3.9	2	0	0	0	0/0/0	0/0/			0/0/0	---Other
													Monofilament of which any cross-sectional dimension exceeds 1 mm, rods, sticks and profile shapes, whether or not surface-worked but not otherwise worked, of plastics:
	0/0/0	4.5	4	0	0	0	0	0/0/0	0/0/			0/0/	-Of polymers of ethylene
													-Of polymers of vinyl chloride:
6.5	0/0/0	4.5	4	0	0	0	0	0//0	0/0/			0/0/	---Profile shapes
6.5	0/0/0	4.5	4	0	0	0	0	0//0	0/0/			0/0/	---Monofilament, rods, sticks and profile
													-Of other plastics:
	0/0/0	4.5	4	0	0	0	0	0/0/0	0/0/			0/0/	---Of polyamides
	0/0/0	4.5	4	0	0	0	0	0/0/0	0/0/			0/0/	---Other
													Tubes, pipes and hoses, and fittings therefor (for example, joints, elbows, flanges), of plastics:
8	0/0/0	4.5	4	0	0	0	0	0//0	0/0/			0/0/	-Artificial guts (sausage casings) of hardened protein or of cellulosic materials
													-Tubes, pipes and hoses, rigid:
	0/0/0	4.5	4	0	0	0	0	0/0/0	0/0/			0/0/0	--Of polymers of ethylene
	0/0/0	0	4	0	0	0	0	0//0	0/0/			0/0/0	--Of polymers of propylene
	0/0/0	4.5	4	0	0	0	0	0/0/0	0/0/			0/0/0	--Of polymers of vinyl chloride
	0/0/0	4.5	4	3	0	0	0	0/0/0	0/0/			0/0/0	--Of other plastics
													-Other tubes, pipes and hoses:
6.5	0/0/0	4.5	0	0	0	0	0	0/0/0	0/0/			0/0/0	--Flexible tubes, pipes and hoses, having a minimum burst pressure of 27. 6 MPa

税则号列		货品名称〔CIQ扩展编码及品名－T2表示见附表2〕	最惠(%)	暂定税率	普通	增值/消费	出口退税	计量单位	监管条件	检验检疫	特殊证件对美关税
3917.3200		--其他未装有附件的管子，未经加强也未与其他材料合制〔999〕	6.5		45	13/	13	千克			/21.5
3917.3300		--其他装有附件的管子，未经加强也未与其他材料合制〔999〕	6.5		45	13/	13	千克			/16.5
3917.3900		--其他〔999〕	6.5		45	13/	13	千克			/21.5
3917.4000		-管子附件〔999〕	10		45	13/	13	千克			/25
39.18		**块状或成卷的塑料铺地制品，不论是否胶粘；本章注释九所规定的塑料糊墙品：**									
		-氯乙烯聚合物制：									
3918.1010		---糊墙品〔999〕	10		45	13/	13	千克			/20
3918.1090		---其他〔999〕	10		45	13/	13	千克			/40
		-其他塑料制：									
3918.9010		---糊墙品〔999〕	10		45	13/	13	千克			/20
3918.9090		---其他〔999〕	10		45	13/	13	千克			/25
39.19		**自粘的塑料板、片、膜、箔、带、扁条及其他扁平形状材料，不论是否成卷：**									
		-成卷，宽度不超过20厘米：									
3919.1010		---丙烯酸树脂类为基本成分〔999〕	6.5		45	13/	13	千克			/21.5
		---其他：									
3919.1091		----胶囊型反光膜〔999〕	6.5		45	13/	13	千克			/36.5
3919.1099		----其他〔999〕	6.5		45	13/	13	千克			/21.5
		-其他：									
3919.9010		---胶囊型反光膜〔999〕	6.5		45	13/	13	千克			/36.5
3919.9090		---其他									
3919.9090	10	半导体晶圆制造用自粘式圆形抛光垫〔999〕	2.2/1.1		45	13/	13	千克			/
3919.9090	90	其他自粘塑料板、片、膜等材料（包括箔，带，扁条及其他扁平形状材料，不论是否成卷）〔101车身反光标识零部件，999包括箔，带，扁条及其他扁平形状材料，不论是否成卷〕	6.5		45	13/	13	千克			/
39.20		**其他非泡沫塑料的板、片、膜、箔及扁条，未用其他材料强化、层压、支撑或用类似方法合制：**									
		-乙烯聚合物制：									
3920.1010		---乙烯聚合物制电池隔膜〔999〕	6.5	3	45	13/	13	千克			/33
3920.1090		---其他									
3920.1090	10	农用非泡沫聚乙烯薄膜（未用其他材料强化、层压、支撑或用类似方法合制）〔999〕	6.5		45	9/	0	千克			/
3920.1090	90	其他非泡沫乙烯聚合物板、片、膜、箔及扁条（未用其他材料强化、层压、支撑或用类似方法合制，非农用）〔999〕	6.5		45	13/	13	千克			/
		-丙烯聚合物制：									
3920.2010		---丙烯聚合物制电池隔膜〔999〕	6.5		45	13/	13	千克			/16.5
3920.2090		---其他									
3920.2090	10	农用非泡沫聚丙烯薄膜（未用其他材料强化、层压、支撑或用类似方法合制）〔999〕	6.5		45	9/	0	千克			/31.5
3920.2090	90	非泡沫丙烯聚合物板、片、膜、箔及扁条（未用其他材料强化、层压、支撑或用类似方法合制，非农用）〔999〕	6.5		45	13/	10	千克			/31.5
3920.3000		-苯乙烯聚合物制〔999〕	6.5		45	13/	13	千克			/36.5
		-氯乙烯聚合物制：									
3920.4300		--按重量计增塑剂含量不小于6%									
3920.4300	10	农用软质聚氯乙烯薄膜（增塑剂含量≥6%，未用其他材料强化、层压、支撑）〔999〕	6.5		45	9/	0	千克			/31.5
3920.4300	90	氯乙烯聚合物板、片、膜、箔及扁条（增塑剂含量≥6%，未用其他材料强化、层压、支撑）〔999〕	6.5		45	13/	10	千克			/31.5
3920.4900		--其他									
3920.4900	10	其他农用软质聚氯乙烯薄膜（非泡沫料的，未用其他材料强化、层压、支撑）〔999〕	6.5		45	9/	0	千克			/21.5
3920.4900	90	其他氯乙烯聚合物板、片、膜、箔及扁条（非泡沫料的，未用其他材料强化、层压、支撑，非农用）〔999〕	6.5		45	13/	10	千克			/21.5

协定税率 %										特惠税率 %			Article Description
亚太5国	东/冰/格	巴基斯坦	韩国	瑞士	哥达	秘鲁	澳大利亚	新西/坡/智	港/澳/台	亚太2国	老/柬/缅	36/3/1	
4.6	0/0/0	0	0	2	0	0	0	0//0	0/0/			0/0/0	--Other, not reinforced or otherwise combined with other materials, without fittings
4.2	0/0/0	0	0	0	0	0	0	0//0	0/0/			0/0/0	--Other, not reinforced or otherwise combined with other materials, with fittings
4.2	0/0/0	0	3.9	0	0	0	0	0/0/0	0/0/			0/0/0	--Other
6.5	0/0/0	4.5	0	3	0	0	0	0/0/0	0/0/			0/0/0	-Fittings
													Floor coverings of plastics, whether or not self-adhesive, in rolls or in the form of tiles; wall or ceiling coverings of plastics, as defined in Note 9 to this Chapter:
													-Of polymers of vinyl chloride:
	0/0/0	4.5	4	0	0	0	0	0//0	0/0/			0/0/	---Wall or ceiling coverings
	0/0/0	4.5		3	0	0	0	0//0	0/0/			0/0/	---Other
													-Of other plastics:
	0/0/0	4.5	4	0	0	0	0	0//0	0/0/			0/0/	---Wall or ceiling coverings
	0/0/0	4.5	4	0	0	0	0	0//0	0/0/			0/0/	---Other
													Self-adhesive plates, sheets, film, foil, tape, strip and other flat shapes, of plastics, whether or not in rolls:
													-In rolls of a width not exceeding 20 cm:
	0/0/0	0	0	0	0	0	0	0//0	0/0/			0/0/0	---Based on acrylic resin
													---Other:
	0/0/0	0	0	0	0	0	0	0//0	0/0/			0/0/0	----Encapsulant reflective film
	0/0/0	0		2	0	0	0	0//0	0/0/0			0/0/0	----Other
													-Other:
4.2	0/0/0	0	3.9	0	0	0	0	0//0	0/0/			0/0/0	---Encapsulant reflective film
													---Other
4.6	0/0/0	0	3.9	0	0	0	0	0//0	0/0/0			0/0/0	Self-adhesive circular polishing pad for manufacturing semiconductor wafer
4.6	0/0/0	0	3.9	0	0	0	0	0//0	0/0/0			0/0/0	Other self-adhesive plates, sheets, film, foil, tape, strip and other flat shapes, of plastics, whether or not in rolls
													Other plates, sheets, film, foil and strip, of plastics, non-cellular and not reinforced, laminated, supported or similarly combined with other materials:
													-Of polymers of ethylene:
4.2	0/0/0	0	2.6	0	0	0	0	0//0	0/0/			0/0/0	---Battery separator, of polymers of ethylene
													---Other
4.6	0/0/0	0	3.9	2	0	0	0	0//0	0/0/0			0/0/0	Agricultural PE film, non-cellular (not reinforced, laminated, supported or similarly combined with other materials)
4.6	0/0/0	0	3.9	2	0	0	0	0//0	0/0/0			0/0/0	Plates, sheets, film, foil and strip, of PE film, non-cellular (not reinforced, laminated, supported or similarly combined with other materials, non-agricultural)
													-Of polymers of propylene:
	0/0/0	0		0	0	0	0	0//0	0/0/			0/0/0	---Battery separator, of polymers of propylene
													---Other
	0/0/0	0	2.6	2	0	0	0	0//0	0/0/0			0/0/0	Agricultural PP film, non-cellular (not reinforced, laminated, supported or similarly combined with other materials)
	0/0/0	0	2.6	2	0	0	0	0//0	0/0/0			0/0/0	Plates, sheets, film, foil and strip, of PP film, non-cellular (not reinforced, laminated, supported or similarly combined with other materials, non-agricultural)
4.2	0/0/0	0	2.6	0	0	0	0	0//0	0/0/0			0/0/0	-Of polymers of styrene
													-Of polymers of vinyl chloride:
													--Containing by weight not less than 6% of plasticisers
4.2	0/0/0	0	2.6	0	0	0	0	0/0/0	0/0/0			0/0/0	Agricultural PVC-P film (containing by weight not less than 6% of plasticisers, not reinforced, laminated, supported or similarly combined with other materials)
4.2	0/0/0	0	2.6	0	0	0	0	0/0/0	0/0/0			0/0/0	Plates, sheets, film (foil and strip, of PVC film containing by weight not less than 6% of plasticisers, not reinforced, laminated, supported or similarly combined with other materials)
													--Other
4.2	0/0/0	0	3.9	2	0	0	0	0//0	0/0/0			0/0/0	Other agricultural PVC-P film (non-cellular, not reinforced, laminated, supported or similarly combined with other materials)
4.2	0/0/0	0	3.9	2	0	0	0	0//0	0/0/0			0/0/0	Other plates, sheets, film, foil and strip, of PVC (non-cellular, not reinforced, laminated, supported or similarly combined with other materials, non-agricultural)

税则号列	货品名称〔CIQ 扩展编码及品名—T2 表示见附表 2〕	最惠(%)	暂定税率	普通	增值/消费	出口退税	计量单位	监管条件	检验检疫	特殊证件对美关税
	-丙烯酸聚合物制：									
3920.5100	--聚甲基丙烯酸甲酯制〔999〕	6.5		45	13/	13	千克			/31.5
3920.5900	--其他〔999〕	6.5		45	13/	13	千克			/31.5
	-聚碳酸酯、醇酸树脂、聚烯丙酯或其他聚酯制：									
3920.6100	--聚碳酸酯制〔999〕	6.5		45	13/	13	千克			/31.5
3920.6200	--聚对苯二甲酸乙二酯制〔999〕	6.5		45	13/	13	千克			/
3920.6300	--不饱和聚酯制〔999〕	10		45	13/	13	千克			/40
3920.6900	--其他聚酯制〔999〕	10		45	13/	13	千克			/25
	-纤维素及其化学衍生物制：									
3920.7100	--再生纤维素制〔999〕	6.5		45	13/	13	千克			/21.5
3920.7300	--乙酸纤维素制〔999〕	6.5		45	13/	13	千克			/36.5
3920.7900	--其他纤维素衍生物制〔999〕	10		45	13/	13	千克			/40
	-其他塑料制：									
3920.9100	--聚乙烯醇缩丁醛制									
3920.9100 01	聚乙烯醇缩丁醛膜(厚度不超过 3 毫米)(非泡沫料的，未用其他材料强化、层压、支撑)〔999〕	6.5	3	45	13/	13	千克			/28
3920.9100 90	聚乙烯醇缩丁醛板、片、箔、扁条及厚度超过 3 毫米的膜(非泡沫料的，未用其他材料强化、层压、支撑)〔999〕	6.5		45	13/	13	千克			/31.5
3920.9200	--聚酰胺制〔999〕	10		45	13/	13	千克			/35
3920.9300	--氨基树脂制〔999〕	6.5		45	13/	13	千克			/16.5
3920.9400	--酚醛树脂制〔999〕	10		45	13/	13	千克			/35
	--其他塑料制：									
3920.9910	---聚四氟乙烯制〔999〕	6.5		45	13/	13	千克			/16.5
3920.9990	---其他塑料制									
3920.9990 01	聚酰亚胺膜，厚度不超过 0.03 毫米(未用其他材料强化、层压、支撑)〔999〕	6.5	3	45	13/	13	千克			/
3920.9990 90	其他非泡沫塑料板、片、膜、箔、扁条(未用其他材料强化、层压、支撑)〔999〕	6.5		45	13/	13	千克			/
39.21	**其他塑料板、片、膜、箔、扁条：**									
	-泡沫塑料的：									
3921.1100	--苯乙烯聚合物制〔999〕	10		45	13/	13	千克			/20
	--氯乙烯聚合物制：									
3921.1210	---人造革及合成革〔999〕	9		70	13/	13	千克/米			/39
3921.1290	---其他〔999〕	6.5		45	13/	13	千克			/36.5
	--氨酯聚合物制：									
3921.1310	---人造革及合成革〔999〕	9		70	13/	13	千克/米			/39
3921.1390	---其他〔999〕	6.5		45	13/	13	千克			/21.5
3921.1400	--再生纤维素制〔999〕	10		45	13/	13	千克			/20
	--其他塑料制：									
3921.1910	---人造革及合成革〔999〕	9		45	13/	13	千克/米			/24
3921.1990	---其他〔999〕	6.5		45	13/	13	千克			/21.5
	-其他：									
3921.9020	---聚乙烯嵌有玻璃纤维的板、片〔999〕	6.5		45	13/	13	千克			/31.5
3921.9030	---聚异丁烯为基本成分的附有人造毛毡的板、片、卷材〔999〕	6.5		45	13/	13	千克			/31.5
3921.9090	---其他									
3921.9090 01	离子交换膜〔999〕	6.5	5	45	13/	13	千克			/
3921.9090 10	两用物项管制结构复合材料的层压板(用纤维和丝材增强而制成的各种预浸件和预成形件，其中增强材料的比拉伸强度大于 7.62 × 10^4 m 和比模量大于 3.18×10^6 m)〔999〕	6.5		45	13/	13	千克	3		/
3921.9090 90	未列名塑料板、片、膜、箔、扁条(离子交换膜，两用物项管制结构复合材料的层压板除外)〔999〕	6.5		45	13/	13	千克			/
39.22	**塑料浴缸、淋浴盘、洗涤槽、盥洗盆、坐浴盆、便盆、马桶座圈及盖、抽水箱及类似卫生洁具：**									
3922.1000	-浴缸、淋浴盘、洗涤槽及盥洗盆〔999〕	6.5		80	13/	13	千克			/36.5
3922.2000	-马桶座圈及盖〔999〕	6.5		80	13/	13	千克			/26.5
3922.9000	-其他〔999〕	6.5		80	13/	13	千克			/26.5
39.23	**供运输或包装货物用的塑料制品；塑料制的塞子、盖子及类似品：**									

协定税率 %										特惠税率 %			Article Description
亚太5国	东/冰/格	巴基斯坦	韩国	瑞士	哥达	秘鲁	澳大利亚	新西/坡/智	港/澳/台	亚太2国	老/柬/缅	36/3/1	
													-Of acrylic polymers:
4.6	0/0/0	0	2.6	0	0	0	0	0//0	0/0/0			0/0/0	--Of poly(methyl methacrylate)
	0/0/0	4	3.9	0	0	0	0	0//0	0/0/			0/0/0	--Other
													-Of polycarbonates, alkyd resins, polyallyl esters or other polyesters:
4.6	0/0/0	0	3.9	0	0	0	0	0//0	0/0/0			0/0/0	--Of polycarbonates
4.6	0/0/0	0	3.9	0	0	0	0	0//0	0/0/0			0/0/0	--Of poly(ethylene terephthalate)
	0/0/0	4.5	4	0	0	0	0	0//0	0/0/			0/0/0	--Of unsaturated polyesters
6.5	0/0/0	4.5	7	0	0	0	0	0/0/0	0/0/0			0/0/0	--Of other polyesters
													-Of cellulose or its chemical derivatives:
	0/0/0	4	2.6	0	0	0	0	0//0	0/0/			0/0/0	--Of regenerated cellulose
	0/0/0	4	0	0	0	0	0	0//0	0/0/			0/0/0	--Of cellulose acetate
	0/0/0	4.5	4	0	0	0	0	0//0	0/0/			0/0/0	--Of other cellulose derivatives
													-Of other plastics:
													--Of poly(vinyl butyral)
	0/0/0	0	3.9	0	0	0	0	0//0	0/0/			0/0/0	Film of poly vinyl butyral. (thieck ness≤3mm)(non-cellular, not reinforced, laminated, supported or similarly combined with other materials)
	0/0/0	0	3.9	0	0	0	0	0//0	0/0/			0/0/0	Plates, sheets, foil and strip, of poly vinyl butyral. (thickness≤3mm)(non-cellular, not reinforced, laminated, supported or similarly combined with other materials)
	0/0/0	4.5	0	0	0	0	0	0/0/0	0/0/			0/0/0	--Of polyamides
	0/0/0	4	0	0	0	0	0	0//0	0/0/			0/0/0	--Of amino-resins
6.5	0/0/0	4.5	4	0	0	0	0	0/0/0	0/0/			0/0/0	--Of phenolic resins
													--Of other plastics:
	0/0/0	0	3.9	0	0	0	0	0//0	0/0/			0/0/0	---Of polytetrafluoroethylene
													---Of other plastics
	0/0/0	0	2.6	0	0	0	0	0//0	0/0/0			0/0/0	Polyimide(PI) film, thickness≤0.03mm(not reinforced, laminated, supported or similarly combined with other materials)
	0/0/0	0	2.6	0	0	0	0	0//0	0/0/0			0/0/0	Other plates, sheets, foil and strip, non-cellular(not reinforced, laminated, supported or similarly combined with other materials)
													Other plates, sheets, film, foil and strip, of plastics:
													-Cellular:
6.5	0/0/0	4.5	4	0	0	0	0	0//0	0/0/			0/0/0	--Of polymers of styrene
													--Of polymers of vinyl chloride:
	0/0/0	4	5.4	0	0	0	0	0/0/0	0/0/0			0/0/0	---Combined with textile fabrics
	0/0/0	0	0	2	0	0	0	0//0	0/0/			0/0/0	---Other
													--Of polyurethanes:
5.9	0/0/0	4	5.4	0	0	0	0	0/0/0	0/0/0			0/0/0	---Combined with textile fabrics
4.6	0/0/0	0	2.6	0	0	0	0	0//0	0/0/			0/0/0	---Other
	0/0/0	4.5	4	0	0	0	0	0//0	0/0/			0/0/0	--Of regenerated cellulose
													--Of other plastics:
6.3	0/0/0	4	5.4	0	0	0	0	0//0	0/0/			0/0/0	---Combined with textile fabrics
4.2	0/0/0	0	3.9	2	0	0	0	0//0	0/0/0			0/0/0	---Other
													-Other:
4.2	0/0/0	0	0	2	0	0	0	0//0	0/0/			0/0/0	---Plates, sheets of polyethylene with glass fibres
4.2	0/0/0	0	2.6	0	0	0	0	0//0	0/0/			0/0/0	---Plates, sheets, coils of polyisobutylene with man-made felt
													---Other
4.6	0/0/0	0	3.9	2	0	0	0	0//0	0/0/0			0/0/0	Ion exchange membrane
4.6	0/0/0	0	3.9	2	0	0	0	0//0	0/0/0			0/0/0	Laminated structural board made of composite materials under sensitive items control (various persoaked and fabricated parts reinforced by fibers and threads, therein the specific tensile strength of reinforcing materials is greater than 7.62×10^4 m and specific modulus greater than 3.18×10^6 m)
4.6	0/0/0	0	3.9	2	0	0	0	0//0	0/0/0			0/0/0	Other plates, sheets, film, foil fiol and strip of plastic not elsewhere specified or in cluded(other than ion exchanging membrane and laminated structural board made of composite materials under sensitive product control)
													Baths, shower-baths, sinks, wash-basins, bidets, lavatory pans, seats and covers, flushing cisterns and similar sanitary ware, of plastics:
	0/0/0	4.5	4	0	0	0	0	0//0	0/0/		0//	0/0/0	-Baths, shower-baths, sinks and wash-basins
	0/0/0	4.5	4	0	0	0	0	0//0	0/0/		0//	0/0/0	-Lavatory seats and covers
	0/0/0	4.5	4	0	0	0	0	0//0	0/0/			0/0/0	-Other
													Articles for the conveyance or packing of goods, of plastics; stoppers, lids, caps and other closures, of plastics:

税则号列	货品名称〔CIQ扩展编码及品名－T2表示见附表2〕	最惠(%)	暂定税率	普通	增值/消费	出口退税	计量单位	监管条件	检验检疫	特殊证件对美关税
3923.1000	-盒、箱(包括板条箱)及类似品									
3923.1000 10	具有特定形状或装置,供运输或包装半导体晶圆、掩模或光罩的塑料盒、箱、板条箱及类似物品〔999〕	0		80	13/	13	千克			/25
3923.1000 90	其他塑料制盒,箱及类似品(包括塑料制板条箱,供运输或包装货物用的)〔101 食品用其他塑料包装,102 非食品用塑料制品〕	10		80	13/	13	千克			/35
	-袋及包(包括锥形的):									
3923.2100	--乙烯聚合物制〔101 食品用其他塑料包装,102 非食品用塑料制品〕	10		80	13/	13	千克			/25
3923.2900	--其他塑料制〔101 食品用其他塑料包装,999 供运输或包装货物用的〕	10		80	13/	13	千克			/25
3923.3000	-坛、瓶及类似品〔101 食品用其他塑料包装,999 供运输或包装货物用的〕	6.5		80	13/	13	千克			/21.5
3923.4000	-卷轴、纡子、筒管及类似品〔101 食品接触其他塑料产品,102 食品用其他塑料包装,103 非食品用塑料制品〕	10		35	13/	13	千克			/40
3923.5000	-塞子、盖子及类似品〔101 食品用其他塑料包装,102 非食品用塑料制品〕	10		80	13/	13	千克			/25
3923.9000	-其他〔101 食品用其他塑料包装,103 非食品用塑料制品〕	10		80	13/	13	千克			/35
39.24	**塑料制的餐具、厨房用具、其他家庭用具及卫生或盥洗用具:**									
3924.1000	-餐具及厨房用具[T2]	6.5		80	13/	13	千克	A	R	/26.5
3924.9000	-其他〔999〕	6.5		80	13/	13	千克	A	M	/36.5
39.25	**其他税目未列名的建筑用塑料制品:**									
3925.1000	-囤、柜、罐、桶及类似容器,容积超过 300 升〔101 食品用其他塑料包装,102 非食品用塑料制品〕	6.5		80	13/	13	千克			/36.5
3925.2000	-门、窗及其框架、门槛〔999〕	6.5		80	13/	13	千克			/11.5
3925.3000	-窗板、百叶窗(包括威尼斯式百叶窗)或类似制品及其零件〔999〕	6.5		80	13/	13	千克			/26.5
3925.9000	-其他〔999〕	6.5		80	13/	13	千克			/11.5
39.26	**其他塑料制品及税目 39.01 至 39.14 所列其他材料的制品:**									
3926.1000	-办公室或学校用品〔999〕	10		80	13/	13	千克			/40
	-衣服及衣着附件(包括分指手套、连指手套及露指手套):									
	---手套(包括分指手套、连指手套及露指手套):									
3926.2011	----聚氯乙烯制〔999〕	6.5		90	13/	13	千克/双			/26.5
3926.2019	----其他〔999〕	6.5		90	13/	13	千克/双			/26.5
3926.2090	---其他〔999〕	6.5		90	13/	13	千克			/26.5
3926.3000	-家具、车厢或类似品的附件〔101 车辆内饰零部件,999〕	10		80	13/	13	千克			/35
3926.4000	-小雕塑品及其他装饰品〔999〕	6.5		100	13/	13	千克			/26.5
	-其他:									
3926.9010	---机器及仪器用零件〔999〕	10		35	13/	13	千克			/30
3926.9090	---其他									
3926.9090 10	两用物项管制结构复合材料的预成形件和制品(用纤维和丝材增强而制成的各种预浸件和预成形件,其中增强材料的比拉伸强度大于 7.62×10^4 m 和比模量大于 3.18×10^6 m)〔999〕	10		80	13/	13	千克	3		/
3926.9090 20	聚氨酯制避孕套〔999〕	10	0	80	0/	0	千克			/
3926.9090 90	其他塑料制品(包括税目 39.01 至 39.14 所列材料的制品)〔101 含一级易燃溶剂的其他制品(－18℃≤闪点＜23℃),胶套,102 塑料沥青,103 其他〕	10		80	13/	13	千克			/

协定税率 %										特惠税率 %			Article Description
亚太5国	东/冰/格	巴基斯坦	韩国	瑞士	哥达	秘鲁	澳大利亚	新西/坡/智	港/澳/台	亚太2国	老/柬/缅	36/3/1	
													-Boxes, cases, crates and similar articles
6.5	0/0/0	4	7	0	0	0	0	0/0/0	0/0/0			0/0/0	Plastic boxes, boxes, crates and similar items ,with a specific shape or device ,for the conveyance or packing of semiconductor wafer and mask
6.5	0/0/0	4	7	0	0	0	0	0/0/0	0/0/0			0/0/0	Other plastic boxes, boxes and similar articles, including plastic crates, for transport or packaging of goods
													-Sacks and bags (including cones):
	0/0/0	0	0	0	0	0	0	0/0/0	0/0/			0/0/	--Of polymers of ethylene
	0/0/0	4.5	6	0	0	0	0	0/0/0	0/0/			0/0/0	--Of other plastics
	0/0/0	4	3.9	0	0		0	0/0/0	0/0/			0/0/0	-Carboys, bottles, flasks and similar articles
6.5	0/0/0	4.5	6	0	0	0	0	0/0/0	0/0/			0/0/	-Spools, cops, bobbins and similar supports
	0/0/0	4.5	4	3	0	0	0	0/0/0	0/0/0			0/0/0	-Stoppers, lids, caps and other closures
6.5	0/0/0	4.5	7	0	0	0	0	0/0/0	0/0/0			0/0/	-Other
													Tableware, kitchenware, other household articles and hygienic or toilet articles, of plastics:
	0/0/0	4.5	6	0	0	0	0	0/0/0	0/0/	0		0/0/0	-Tableware and kitchenware
	0/0/0	0	4	0	0	0	0	0/0/0	0/0/			0/0/0	-Other
													Builders' ware of plastics, not elsewhere specified or included:
	0/0/0	4.5	4	0	0	0	0	0//0	0/0/			0/0/0	-Reservoirs, tanks, vats and similar containers, of a capacity exceeding 300L
4.2	0/0/0	4.5	4	0	0	0	0	0//0	0/0/			0/0/	-Doors, windows and their frames and thresholds for doors
	0/0/0	4.5	4	0	0	0	0	0//0	0/0/			0/0/	-Shutters, blinds (including Venetian blinds) and similar articles and parts thereof
	0/0/0	4.5	4	5.2	0	0	0	0//0	0/0/			0/0/	-Other
													Other articles of plastics and articles of other materials of headings Nos. 39. 01 to 39. 14:
	0/0/0	4.5	4	0	0	0	0	0/0/0	0/0/			0/0/0	-Offices or school supplies
													-Articles of apparel and clothing accessories (including gloves, mittens and mitts):
													---Gloves(including gloves, mittens and mitts):
	0/0/0		4	0	0	0	0	0/0/0	0/0/			0/0/	----Of poly (vinyl chrlrride)
	0/0/0		4	0	0	0	0	0/0/0	0/0/			0/0/	----Other
	0/0/0		4	0	0	0	0	0/0/0	0/0/			0/0/0	---Other
	0/0/0	4.5	6	0	0	0	0	0/0/0	0/0/			0/0/0	-Fittings for furniture, coachwork or the like
4.2	0/0/0	4	4	0	0	0	0	0//0	0/0/			0/0/0	-Statuettes and other ornamental articles
													-Other:
6.5	0/0/0	0	4	3	0	0	0	0/0/0	0/0/0			0/0/0	---Of a kind for used in machines or instruments
													---Other
6.5	0/0/0	9.2	4	3	0	0	0	0/0/0	0/0/0			0/0/0	Laminated structural board made of composite materials under sensitive items control (various persoaked and fabricated parts reinforced by fibers and threads, therein the specific tensile strength of reinforcing materials is greater than 7. 62×10⁴ m and specific modulus greater than 3. 18×10⁶ m)
6.5	0/0/0	9.2	4	3	0	0	0	0/0/0	0/0/0			0/0/0	Polyurethane condom
6.5	0/0/0	9.2	4	3	0	0	0	0/0/0	0/0/0			0/0/0	Other articles of plastics (including articles of other materials of heading 39. 01 to 39. 14)

第四十章
橡胶及其制品

注释：

一、除条文另有规定的以外，本目录所称“橡胶”，是指不论是否硫化或硬化的下列产品：天然橡胶、巴拉塔胶、古塔波胶、银胶菊胶、糖胶树胶及类似的天然树胶、合成橡胶、从油类中提取的油膏以及上述物品的再生品。

二、本章不包括：

（一）第十一类的货品（纺织原料及纺织制品）；

（二）第六十四章的鞋靴及其零件；

（三）第六十五章的帽类及其零件（包括游泳帽）；

（四）第十六类的硬质橡胶制的机械器具、电气器具及其零件（包括各种电气用品）；

（五）第九十章、第九十二章、第九十四章或第九十六章的物品；

（六）第九十五章的物品（运动用分指手套、连指手套、露指手套及税目 40.11 至 40.13 的制品除外）。

三、税目 40.01 至 40.03 及 40.05 所称“初级形状”，只限于下列形状：

（一）液状及糊状，包括胶乳（不论是否预硫化）及其他分散体和溶液；

（二）不规则形状的块，团、包、粉、粒、碎屑及类似的散装形状。

四、本章注释一和税目 40.02 所称“合成橡胶”，适用于：

（一）不饱和合成物质，即用硫磺硫化能使其不可逆地变为非热塑物质，这种物质能在温度 18℃ 至 29℃ 之间被拉长到其原长度的三倍而不致断裂，拉长到原长度的两倍时，在五分钟内能回复到不超过原长度的一倍半。为了进行上述试验，可以加入交联所需的硫化活化剂或促进剂；也允许含有注释五（二）2 及 3 所述的物质。但不能加入非交联所需的物质，例如，增量剂、增塑剂及填料；

（二）聚硫橡胶（TM）；

（三）与塑料接枝共聚或混合而改性的天然橡胶、解聚天然橡胶以及不饱和合成物质与饱和合成高聚物的混合物，但这些产品必须符合以上（一）款关于硫化、延伸及回复的要求。

五、（一）税目 40.01 及 40.02 不适用于任何凝结前或凝结后与下列物质相混合的橡胶或橡胶混合物：

1. 硫化剂、促进剂、防焦剂或活性剂（为制造预硫胶乳所加入的除外）；

2. 颜料或其他着色料，但仅为易于识别而加入的除外；
3. 增塑剂或增量剂（用油增量的橡胶中所加的矿物油除外）、填料、增强剂、有机溶剂或其他物质，但以下（二）款所述的除外；

（二）含有下列物质的橡胶或橡胶混合物，只要仍具有原料的基本特性，应归入税目 40.01 或 40.02：

1. 乳化剂或防粘剂；
2. 少量的乳化剂分解产品；
3. 微量的下列物质：热敏剂（一般为制造热敏胶乳用）、阳离子表面活性剂（一般为制造阳性胶乳用）、抗氧剂、凝固剂、碎裂剂、抗冻剂、胶溶剂、保存剂、稳定剂、黏度控制剂或类似的特殊用途添加剂。

六、税目 40.04 所称“废碎料及下脚料”，是指在橡胶或橡胶制品生产或加工过程中由于切割、磨损或其他原因所造成没有使用价值的废橡胶及下脚料。

七、全部用硫化橡胶制成的线，其任一截面的尺寸超过 5 毫米的，应作为带、杆或型材及异型材归入税目 40.08。

八、税目 40.10 包括用橡胶浸渍、涂布、包覆或层压的织物制成的或用橡胶浸渍、涂布、包覆或套裹的纱线或绳制成的传动带、输送带。

九、税目 40.01、40.02、40.03、40.05 及 40.08 所称“板”、“片”、“带”，仅指未切割或只简单切割成矩形（包括正方形）的板、片、带及正几何形块，不论是否具有成品的特征，也不论是否经过印制或其他表面加工，但未切割成其他形状或进一步加工。

税目 40.08 所称“杆”或“型材及异型材”，仅指不论是否切割成一定长度或表面加工，但未经进一步加工的该类产品。

税则号列	货品名称〔CIQ 扩展编码及品名—T2 表示见附表 2〕	最惠(%)	暂定税率	普通	增值/消费	出口退税	计量单位	监管条件	检验检疫	特殊证件对美关税
40.01	**天然橡胶、巴拉塔胶、古塔波胶、银胶菊胶、糖胶树胶及类似的天然树胶，初级形状或板、片、带：**									
4001.1000	-天然胶乳，不论是否预硫化〔101 有检疫要求食品添加剂，999 不论是否预硫化〕	20	①	40	13/	9	千克	AB	MPQ	/
	-其他形状的天然橡胶：									
4001.2100	--烟胶片〔999〕	20	②	40	13/	9	千克	AB	MPQ	/
4001.2200	--技术分类天然橡胶（TSNR）〔999〕	20	②	40	13/	9	千克			/
4001.2900	--其他〔999〕	20		40	13/	9	千克			/45

① 10%或 900 元/吨，两者从低。
② 20%或 1500 元/吨，两者从低。

Chapter 40
Rubber and articles thereof

Notes:

1. Except where the context otherwise requires, throughout the Nomenclature the expression "rubber" means the following products, whether or not vulcanized or hard: natural rubber, balata, gutta-percha, guayule, chicle and similar natural gums, synthetic rubber, factice derived from oils, and such substances reclaimed.
2. This Chapter does not cover:
   (a) Goods of Section Ⅺ (texitils and textile articles);
   (b) Footwear or parts thereof of Chapter 64;
   (c) Headgear or parts thereof (including bathing caps) of Chapter 65;
   (d) Mechanical or electrical appliances or parts thereof of Section ⅩⅥ (including electrical goods of all kinds), of hard rubber;
   (e) Articles of Chapter 90, 92, 94 or 96;
   (f) Articles of Chapter 95 (other than sports gloves, mittens and mitts and articles of headings No. 40.11 to 40.13).
3. In headings No. 40.01 to 40.03 and 40.05, the expression "primary forms" applies only to the following forms:
   (a) Liquids and pastes (including latex, whether or not pre-vulcanized, and other dispersions and solutions);
   (b) Blocks of irregular shape, lumps, bales, powders, granules, crumbs and similar bulk forms.
4. In Note Ⅰ to this Chapter and in heading No. 40.02, the expression "synthetic rubber" applies to:
   (a) Unsaturated synthetic substances which can be irreversibly transformed by vulcanization with sulphur into non-thermoplastic substances which, at a temperature between 18℃ and 29℃, will not break on being extended to three times their original length and will return, after being extended to twice their original length, within a period of five minutes, to a length not greater than one and a half times their original length. For the purposes of this test, substances necessary for the cross-linking, such as vulcanisng activators or accelerators, may be added; the presence of substances as provided for by Note 5(b) (ii) and (iii) is also permitted. However, the presence of any substances not necessary for the cross-linking, such as extenders, plasticizers and fillers, is not permitted;
   (b) Thioplasts (TM); and
   (c) Natural rubber modified by grafting or mixing with plastics, depolymerized natural rubber, mixtures of unsaturated synthetic substances with saturated synthetic high polymers provided that all the above-mentioned products comply with the requirements concerning vulcanization, elongation and recovery in (a) above.
5. (a) Headings No. 40.01 and 40.02 do not apply to any rubber or mixture of rubbers which has been compounded, before or after coagulation, with:
   (i) vulcanizing agents, accelerators, retarders or activators (other than those added for the preparation of pre-vulcanized rubber latex);
   (ii) pigments or other colouring matter, other than those added solely for the purpose of identification;
   (iii) plasticizers or extenders (except mineral oil in the case of oil-extended rubber), fillers, reinforcing agents, organic solvents or any other substances, except those permitted under (b);
   (b) The presence of the following substances in any rubber or mixture of rubbers shall not affect its classification in heading No. 40.01 or 40.02, as the case may be, provided that such rubber or mixture of rubbers retains its essential character as a raw material:
   (i) emulsifiers or anti-tack agents;
   (ii) small amounts of breakdown products of emulsifiers;
   (iii) very small amounts of the following: heat-sensitive agents (generally for obtaining thermosensitive rubber latexes), cationic surface-active agents (generally for obtaining electro-positive rubber latexes), antioxidants, coagulants, crumbling agents, freeze-resisting agents, peptizers, preservatives, stabilizers, viscosity-control agents, or similar special-purpose additives.
6. For the purposes of heading No. 40.04, the expression "waste, parings and scrap" means rubber waste, parings and scrap from the manufacture or working of rubber and rubber goods definitely not usable as such because of cutting-up, wear or other reasons.
7. Thread wholly of vulcanized rubber, of which any cross-sectional dimension exceeds 5 mm, is to be classified as strip, rods or profile shapes, of heading No. 40.08.
8. Heading No. 40.10 includes conveyor or transmission belts or belting of textile fabric impregnated, coated, covered or laminated with rubber or made from textile yarn or cord impregnated, coated, covered or sheathed with rubber.
9. In headings No. 40.01, 40.02, 40.03, 40.05, and 40.08, the expressions "plates", "sheets" and "strip" apply only to plates, sheets and strip and to blocks of regular geometric shape, uncut or simply cut to rectangular (including square) shape, whether or not having the character of articles and whether or not printed or otherwise surface-worked, but not otherwise cut to shape or further worked. In heading No. 40.08 the expressions "rods" and "profile shapes" apply only to such products, whether or not cut to length or surface-worked but not otherwise worked.

协定税率 %										特惠税率 %			
亚太5国	东/冰/格	巴基斯坦	韩国	瑞士	哥达	秘鲁	澳大利亚	新西/坡/智	港/澳/台	亚太2国	老/柬/缅	36/3/1	**Article Description**
													Natural rubber, balata, gutta-percha, guayule, chicle and similar natural gums, in primary forms or in plates, sheets or strip:
	/0/		12	6	0		0	0//0	0/0/				-Natural rubber latex, whether or not prevulcanized
													-Natural rubber in other forms:
17	/0/	17	12	6	0		0	0//0	0/0/				--Smoked sheets
	/0/			6	0		0	0//0	0/0/				--Technically specified natural rubber (TSNR)
17	/0/	17		6	0		0	0//0	0/0/				--Other

税则号列	货品名称〔CIQ 扩展编码及品名一T2 表示见附表 2〕	最惠(%)	暂定税率	普通	增值/消费	出口退税	计量单位	监管条件	检验检疫	特殊证件对美关税
4001.3000	-巴拉塔胶、古塔波胶、银胶菊胶、糖胶树胶及类似的天然树胶〔101 杜仲胶溶液,999 包括古塔波胶,糖胶树胶等,胶乳外的初级形状或板,片,带〕	20		40	13/	9	千克			/
40.02	**合成橡胶及从油类提取的油膏,初级形状或板、片、带;税号 40.01 所列产品与本税号所列产品的混合物,初级形状或板、片、带:**									
	-丁苯橡胶(SBR);羧基丁苯橡胶(XSBR):									
	--胶乳:									
4002.1110	---羧基丁苯橡胶〔999〕	7.5		14	13/	10	千克			/32.5
4002.1190	---其他〔999〕	7.5		14	13/	10	千克			/17.5
	--其他:									
	---初级形状的:									
4002.1911	----未经任何加工的丁苯橡胶(溶聚的除外)〔999〕	7.5		14	13/	13	千克			/17.5
4002.1912	----充油丁苯橡胶(溶聚的除外)〔999〕	7.5		14	13/	10	千克			/32.5
4002.1913	----热塑丁苯橡胶〔999〕	7.5		14	13/	10	千克			/27.5
4002.1914	----充油热塑丁苯橡胶〔999〕	7.5		14	13/	10	千克			/27.5
4002.1915	----未经任何加工的溶聚丁苯橡胶〔999〕	7.5		14	13/	13	千克			/32.5
4002.1916	----充油溶聚丁苯橡胶〔999〕	7.5		14	13/	10	千克			/32.5
4002.1919	----其他〔999〕	7.5		14	13/	10	千克			/12.5
4002.1990	---其他									
4002.1990 01	简单处理的丁苯橡胶,热塑或充油热塑丁苯橡胶除外(指为便于运输,对初级形状进行压缩、挤压等简单成型处理)〔999〕	7.5		35	13/	10	千克			/27.5
4002.1990 90	其他丁苯橡胶及羧基丁苯橡胶板,片,带(4002199001 项下的除外)〔999〕	7.5		35	13/	0	千克			/27.5
	-丁二烯橡胶(BR):									
4002.2010	---初级形状的〔999〕	7.5		14	13/	10	千克			/32.5
4002.2090	---其他〔999〕	7.5		35	13/	0	千克			/27.5
	-异丁烯-异戊二烯(丁基)橡胶(IIR);卤代丁基橡胶(CIIR 或 BIIR):									
	--异丁烯-异戊二烯(丁基)橡胶(IIR):									
4002.3110	---初级形状的〔999〕	6		14	13/	10	千克			/26
4002.3190	---其他〔999〕	7.5		35	13/	0	千克			/17.5
	--其他:									
4002.3910	---初级形状的〔999〕	7.5		14	13/	10	千克			/12.5
4002.3990	---其他〔999〕	7.5		35	13/	0	千克			/32.5
	-氯丁二烯(氯丁)橡胶(CR):									
4002.4100	--胶乳〔999〕	7.5		14	13/	10	千克			/17.5
	--其他:									
4002.4910	---初级形状的〔999〕	7.5		14	13/	10	千克			/32.5
4002.4990	---其他〔999〕	7.5		35	13/	0	千克			/32.5
	-丁腈橡胶(NBR):									
4002.5100	--胶乳〔999〕	7.5		14	13/	10	千克			/32.5
	--其他:									
4002.5910	---初级形状的〔999〕	7.5		14	13/	10	千克			/27.5
4002.5990	---其他〔999〕	7.5		35	13/	0	千克			/27.5
	-异戊二烯橡胶(IR):									
4002.6010	---初级形状的〔999〕	3		14	13/	10	千克			/13
4002.6090	---其他〔999〕	5		35	13/	0	千克			/30
	-乙丙非共轭二烯橡胶(EPDM):									
4002.7010	---初级形状的〔999〕	7.5		14	13/	10	千克			/12.5
4002.7090	---其他〔999〕	7.5		35	13/	0	千克			/12.5
4002.8000	-税目 40.01 所列产品与本税目所列产品的混合物〔999〕	7.5		35	13/	0	千克			/32.5
	-其他:									
4002.9100	--胶乳〔999〕	7.5		14	13/	0	千克			/27.5
	--其他:									
	---其他合成橡胶:									
4002.9911	----初级形状的〔999〕	7.5		14	13/	13	千克			/12.5
4002.9919	----其他〔999〕	7.5		35	13/	0	千克			/17.5
4002.9990	---其他〔999〕	4		14	13/	13	千克			/29
40.03	**再生橡胶,初级形状或板、片、带:**									
4003.0000	再生橡胶,初级形状或板、片、带〔999〕	8		30	13/	13	千克			/28

协定税率 %										特惠税率 %			Article Description
亚太5国	东/冰/格	巴基斯坦	韩国	瑞士	哥达	秘鲁	澳大利亚	新西/坡/智	港/澳/台	亚太2国	老/柬/缅	36/3/1	
	0/0/0		12	6	0	0	0	0/0/0	0/0/			0/0/	-Balata, gutta-percha, guayule, chicle and similar natural gums
													Synthetic rubber and factice derived from oils, in primary forms or in plates, sheets or strip; mixtures of any products of heading No. 40. 01 with any product of this heading, in primary forms or in plates, sheets or strip:
													-Styrene-butadiene rubber (SBR); carboxylated styrene-butadiene rubber (XSBR):
													--Latex:
	0/0/0	4	4.5	0	0	0	0	0//0	0/0/			0/0/0	---Carboxylated styrene-butadiene rubber (XSBR)
	0/0/0	4	4.5	0	0	0	0	0//0	0/0/			0/0/0	---Other
													--Other:
													---In primary forms:
	0/0/0	4	4.5	0	0	0	0	0/0/0	0/0/			0/0/0	----SBR, not worked(except solution polymerized)
	0/0/0	4	4.5	0	0	0	0	0/0/0	0/0/			0/0/0	----SBR, oil-filled(except solution polymerized)
	0/0/0	4	4.5	0	0	0	0	0/0/0	0/0/			0/0/0	----SBR, thermo-plasticated
	0/0/0	4	4.5	0	0	0	0	0/0/0	0/0/			0/0/0	----SBR, oil-filled and thermo-plasticated
	0/0/0	4	4.5	0	0	0	0	0/0/0	0/0/			0/0/0	----SBR,Solution polymerized ,not worked
	0/0/0	4	4.5	0	0	0	0	0/0/0	0/0/			0/0/0	----SBR,Solution polymerized ,oil-filled
	5/0/0		4.5	0	0	0	0	0//0	0/0/			0/0/0	----Other
													---Other
4.9	0/0/0	4	4.5	0	0	0	0	0/0/0	0/0/			0/0/0	Except simple treatment of styrene-butadiene rubber or styrene-butadiene-styrene block copolymer (referring to compression, extrusicn in order to facilitate transportation)
4.9	0/0/0	4	4.5	0	0	0	0	0/0/0	0/0/			0/0/0	Other styrene-butadiene rubber and carboxy lated styrene-butadiene rubber, plates, sheets or strip (except those under item 4002199010)
													-Butadiene rubber (BR):
	0/0/0	4	4.5	0	0	0	0	0//0	0/0/			0/0/0	---In primary forms
7	0/0/0	4	4.5	0	0	0	0	0//0	0/0/			0/0/0	---Other
													-Isobutene-isoprene (butyl) rubber (IIR); halo-isobutene-isoprene rubber (CIIR or BIIR):
													--Isobutene-isoprene (butyl) rubber (IIR):
3.9	0/0/0	0	3.6	0	0	0	0	0//0	0/0/			0/0/0	---In primary forms
4.9	0/0/0	4	4.5	0	0	0	0	0//0	0/0/			0/0/0	---Other
													--Other:
	0/0/0	4	4.5	0	0	0	0	0//0	0/0/			0/0/0	---In pimary forms
4.9	0/0/0	4	4.5	0	0	0	0	0//0	0/0/			0/0/0	---Other
													-Chloroprene (ehlorobutadiene) rubber(CR):
4.9	0/0/0	4	0	0	0	0	0	0//0	0/0/			0/0/0	--Latex
													--Other:
	0/0/0	4		0	0	0	0	0//0	0/0/			0/0/0	---In primary forms
4.9	0/0/0	4	4.5	0	0	0	0	0//0	0/0/			0/0/0	---Other
													-Acrylonitrile-butadient rubber(NBR):
4.9	0/0/0	4	4.5	0	0	0	0	0//0	0/0/			0/0/0	--Latex
													--Other:
	0/0/0	4	4.5	0	0	0	0	0//0	0/0/			0/0/0	---In primary forms
	0/0/0	4	4.5	0	0	0	0	0//0	0/0/			0/0/0	---Other
													-Isoprene rubber (IR):
	0/0/0	0	1.8	0	0	0	0	0//0	0/0/			0/0/0	---In primary forms
3.3	0/0/0	0	3	0	0	0	0	0//0	0/0/			0/0/0	---Other
													-Ethylene-propylene-non-conjugated diene rubber (EPDM):
	0/0/0	4	4.5	0	0	0	0	0//0	0/0/			0/0/0	---In primary forms
7.1	0/0/0	4	4.5	0	0	0	0	0//0	0/0/			0/0/0	---Other
	0/0/0	4	4.5	0	0	0	0	0//0	0/0/			0/0/0	-Mixtures of any product of heading No. 40. 01 with any product of this heading
													-Other:
	0/0/0	4	4.5	0	0	0	0	0//0	0/0/			0/0/0	--Latex
													--Other
													---Other synthetic rubber:
	0/0/0	4	4.5	0	0	0	0	0//0	0/0/0			0/0/0	----In primary forms
	0/0/0	4	4.5	0	0	0	0	0//0	0/0/			0/0/0	----Other
	0/0/0	0	0	0	0	0	0	0//0	0/0/			0/0/0	---Other
													Reclaimed rubber in primary forms or in plates, sheets or strip:
	0/0/0	4	4.8	0	0	0	0	0//0	0/0/			0/0/0	Reclaimed rubber in primary forms or in plates, sheets or strip

税则号列	货品名称〔CIQ 扩展编码及品名－T2 表示见附表 2〕	最惠(%)	暂定税率	普通	增值/消费	出口退税	计量单位	监管条件	检验检疫	特殊证件对美关税
40.04	**橡胶(硬质橡胶的除外)的废碎料、下脚料及其粉、粒：**									
4004.0000	橡胶(硬质橡胶的除外)的废碎料、下脚料及其粉、粒									
4004.0000 10	废轮胎及其切块〔999〕	8		30	13/	0	千克	9		/
4004.0000 20	硫化橡胶废碎料、下脚料及其粉、粒(硬质橡胶的除外)(不包括符合 GB/T19208 标准的硫化橡胶粉产品)〔999〕	8		30	13/	0	千克	9		/
4004.0000 90	未硫化橡胶废碎料、下脚料及其粉、粒〔101 橡胶皮革废碎料,999〕	8		30	13/	0	千克	9	M	/
40.05	**未硫化的复合橡胶,初级形状或板、片、带：**									
4005.1000	-与炭黑或硅石混合〔999〕	8		35	13/	0	千克	A	M	/28
4005.2000	-溶液;子目号 4005.10 以外的分散体〔999〕	8		35	13/	0	千克	A	M	/33
	-其他：									
4005.9100	--板、片、带〔999〕	8		35	13/	0	千克	A	M	/18
4005.9900	--其他〔999〕	8		35	13/	0	千克	A	M	/28
40.06	**其他形状(例如,杆、管或型材及异型材)的未硫化橡胶及未硫化橡胶制品(例如,盘、环)：**									
4006.1000	-轮胎翻新用胎面补料胎条〔999〕	8		35	13/	0	千克			/33
	-其他：									
4006.9010	---其他形状的未硫化橡胶〔999〕	8		35	13/	0	千克			/18
4006.9020	---未硫化橡胶制品〔999〕	14		80	13/	0	千克			/19
40.07	**硫化橡胶线及绳：**									
4007.0000	硫化橡胶线及绳〔999〕	14		80	13/	13	千克			/39
40.08	**硫化橡胶(硬质橡胶除外)制的板、片、带、杆或型材及异型材：**									
	-海绵橡胶制：									
4008.1100	--板、片、带〔999〕	8		35	13/	13	千克			/28
4008.1900	--其他〔999〕	8		35	13/	13	千克			/18
	-非海绵橡胶制：									
4008.2100	--板、片、带〔999〕	8		35	13/	13	千克			/18
4008.2900	--其他〔999〕	8		35	13/	13	千克			/28
40.09	**硫化橡胶(硬质橡胶除外)制的管子,不论是否装有附件(例如,接头、肘管、法兰)：**									
	-未经加强或未与其他材料合制：									
4009.1100	--未装有附件〔999〕	10		40	13/	13	千克			/30
4009.1200	--装有附件〔999〕	10		40	13/	10	千克			/30
	-用金属加强或只与金属合制：									
4009.2100	--未装有附件〔999〕	10		40	13/	13	千克			/20
4009.2200	--装有附件〔999〕	10		40	13/	13	千克			/20
	-用纺织材料加强或只与纺织材料合制：									
4009.3100	--未装有附件〔999〕	10		40	13/	13	千克			/30
4009.3200	--装有附件〔999〕	10		40	13/	13	千克			/35
	-用其他材料加强或与其他材料合制：									
4009.4100	--未装有附件〔999〕	10		40	13/	13	千克			/20
4009.4200	--装有附件〔999〕	10		40	13/	10	千克			/20
40.10	**硫化橡胶制的传动带或输送带及带料：**									
	-输送带及带料：									
4010.1100	--仅用金属加强的〔999〕	10		35	13/	13	千克			/35
4010.1200	--仅用纺织材料加强的〔999〕	10		35	13/	13	千克			/20
4010.1900	--其他〔999〕	10		35	13/	13	千克			/20
	-传动带及带料：									
4010.3100	--梯形截面的环形传动带(三角带),V 形肋状的,外周长超过 60 厘米,但不超过 180 厘米〔999〕	8		35	13/	13	千克			/33
4010.3200	--梯形截面的环形传动带(三角带),外周长超过 60 厘米,但不超过 180 厘米,V 形肋状的除外〔999〕	8		35	13/	13	千克			/28
4010.3300	--梯形截面的环形传动带(三角带),V 形肋状的,外周长超过 180 厘米,但不超过 240 厘米〔999〕	8		35	13/	13	千克			/28
4010.3400	--梯形截面的环形传动带(三角带),外周长超过 180 厘米,但不超过 240 厘米,V 形肋状的除外〔999〕	8		35	13/	13	千克			/28

协定税率 %										特惠税率 %			
亚太5国	东/冰/格	巴基斯坦	韩国	瑞士	哥达	秘鲁	澳大利亚	新西/坡/智	港/澳/台	亚太2国	老/柬/缅	36/3/1	Article Description
													Waste, parings and scrap of rubber (other than hard rubber) and powders and granules obtained therefrom:
													Waste, parings and scrap of rubber (other than hard rubber) and powders and granules obtained therefrom
5.2	0/0/0	4	0	0	0	0	0	0//0	0/0/			0/0/	Waste rubber tyres and their cuts
5.2	0/0/0	4	0	0	0	0	0	0//0	0/0/			0/0/	Waste, parings and scrap of vulcanized rubber (other than hard rubber) and powders and granules obtained therefrom
5.2	0/0/0	4	0	0	0	0	0	0//0	0/0/			0/0/	Other waste, parings and scrap of rubber (other than hard rubber) and powders and granules obtained therefrom
													Compounded rubber, unvulcanized, in primary forms or in plates, sheets or strip:
	0/0/	4	4.8	0	0	0	0	0//0	0/0/			0/0/0	-Compounded with carbon black or silica
	0/0/	4	4.8	0	0	0	0	0//0	0/0/			0/0/0	-Solutions; dispersions other than those of subheading No. 4005. 10
													-Other:
	0/0/	4	0	0	0	0	0	0//0	0/0/			0/0/0	--Plates, sheets and strip
	0/0/	4	4.8	0	0	0	0	0//0	0/0/			0/0/0	--Other
													Other forms (for example, rods, tubes and profile shapes) and articles (for example, discs and rings), or unvulcanized rubber:
	0/0/0	4	0	0	0	0	0	0//0	0/0/			0/0/0	-"Camel-back" strips for retreading rubber tyres
													-Other:
	0/0/0	4	3.2	0	0	0	0	0//0	0/0/			0/0/0	---Other forms of unvulcanized rubber
	0/0/0	11.2	5.6	4.2	0	0	0	0/0/0	0/0/			0/0/	---Articles of unvulcanized rubber
													Vulcanized rubber thread and cord:
	0/0/0	11.2	5.6	4.2	0	0	0	0/0/0	0/0/			0/0/	Vulcanized rubber thread and cord
													Plates, sheets, strip, rods and profile shapes, of vulcanized rubber other than hard rubber:
													-Of cellular rubber:
	0/0/0	4	4.8	0	0	0	0	0//0	0/0/			0/0/0	--Plates, sheets and strip
	0/0/0	4	0	0	0	0	0	0//0	0/0/			0/0/0	--Other
													-Of non-cellular rubber:
	0/0/0	4	0	0	0	0	0	0//0	0/0/			0/0/0	--Plates, sheets and strip
	0/0/0	4	0	0	0	0	0	0//0	0/0/			0/0/0	--Other
													Tubes, pipes and hoses, of vulcanized rubber other than hard rubber, with or without their fittings (for example, joints, elbows, flanges):
													-Not reinforced or otherwise combined with other materials:
	0/0/0	4.5	4.2	3.2	0	0	0	0/0/0	0/0/			0/0/	--Without fittings
	0/0/0	4.5	4	0	0	0	0	0//0	0/0/			0/0/	--With fittings
													-Reinforced or otherwise combined only with metal:
	0/0/0	4.5	4.2	3.2	0	0	0	0/0/0	0/0/			0/0/	--Without fittings
	0/0/0	4.5	4	0	0	0	0	0/0/0	0/0/			0/0/	--With fittings
													-Reinforced or otherwise combined only with textile materials:
	0/0/0	4.5	7.3	3.2	0	0	0	0/0/0	0/0/			0/0/	--Without fittings
	0/0/4	4.5	4	0	0	0	0	0//0	0/0/			0/0/	--With fittings
													-Reinforced or otherwise combined with other materials:
	0/0/0	4.5	4.2	3.2	0	0	0	0/0/0	0/0/			0/0/	--Without fittings
	0/0/0	4.5	4	0	0	0	0	0/0/0	0/0/			0/0/	--With fittings
													Conveyor or transmission belts or belting, of vulcanized rubber:
													-Conveyor belts or belting:
	0/0/0	4.5	4	4.2	0	0	0	0//0	0/0/			0/0/	--Reinforced only with metal
	0/0/0	4.5	4	0	0	0	0	0//0	0/0/			0/0/	--Reinforced only with textile materials
	0/0/0	4.5	4	0	0	0	0	0//0	0/0/			0/0/	--Other
													-Transmission belts or belting:
	0/0/0	4	0	0	0	0	0	0//0	0/0/			0/0/0	--Endless transmission belts of trapezoidal cross-section (V-belts), whether or not groved of a circumference exceeding 60cm but not exceeding 180cm
	0/0/0	4	0	0	0	0	0	0//0	0/0/			0/0/0	--Endless transmission belts of trapezoidal cross-section (V-belts), V-ribbed, of an outside circumference exceeding 60cm but not exceeding 180cm
	0/0/0	4	0	0	0	0	0	0//0	0/0/			0/0/0	--Endless transmission belts of trapezoidal cross-section (V-belts), other than V-ribbed, of an outside circumference exceeding 180cm but not exceeding 240cm
	0/0/0	4	0	0	0	0	0	0//0	0/0/			0/0/0	--Endless transmission belts of trapezoidal cross-section (V-belts), V-ribbed, of an outside circumference exceeding 180cm but not exceeding 240cm

税则号列	货品名称〔CIQ扩展编码及品名－T2表示见附表2〕	最惠(%)	暂定税率	普通	增值/消费	出口退税	计量单位	监管条件	检验检疫	特殊证件对美关税
4010.3500	--环形同步带,外周长超过60厘米,但不超过150厘米〔999〕	10		35	13/	13	千克			/30
4010.3600	--环形同步带,外周长超过150厘米,但不超过198厘米〔999〕	10		35	13/	13	千克			/30
4010.3900	--其他〔999〕	8		35	13/	13	千克			/28
40.11	新的充气橡胶轮胎:									
4011.1000	-机动小客车(包括旅行小客车及赛车)用〔101有内胎,102无内胎,999橡胶轮胎,包括旅行小客车及赛车用〕	10		50	13/	13	千克/条	A	LM	/15
4011.2000	-客运机动车辆或货运机动车辆用									
4011.2000　10	断面宽≥30英寸客或货车用新充气橡胶轮胎(指机动车辆用橡胶轮胎,断面宽度≥30英寸)〔101轻型、微型载重汽车轮胎,102其他载重轮胎,999指机动车辆用橡胶轮胎,断面宽度≥30英寸〕	10	8	50	13/	13	千克/条	A	M	/13
4011.2000　90	其他客或货车用新充气橡胶轮胎(指机动车辆用橡胶轮胎)〔101轻型、微型载重汽车轮胎,102其他载重轮胎,999指机动车辆用橡胶轮胎〕	10		50	13/	13	千克/条	A	LM	/15
4011.3000	-航空器用〔999〕	1		11	13/	13	千克/条			/11
4011.4000	-摩托车用〔999〕	15		80	13/	13	千克/条	A	LM	/40
4011.5000	-自行车用〔999〕	20		80	13/	13	千克/条			/25
	-农业或林业车辆及机器用:									
4011.7010	---人字形胎面或类似胎面									
4011.7010　10	断面宽≥24英寸人字轮胎(新充气橡胶轮胎,含胎面类似人字形的,农林车辆及机器用)〔999〕	17	8	50	13/	13	千克/条	A	M	/38
4011.7010　90	其他人字形胎面轮胎(新充气橡胶轮胎,含胎面类似人字形的,农林车辆及机器用)〔999〕	17		50	13/	13	千克/条	A	M	/47
4011.7090	---其他〔999〕	25		50	13/	13	千克/条			/40
	-建筑业、采矿业或工业搬运车辆及机器用: ---人字形胎面或类似胎面:									
4011.8011	----辋圈尺寸不超过61厘米									
4011.8011　10	断面宽≥24英寸人字形轮胎(建筑业、采矿业或工业搬运车辆及机器用,辋圈≤61cm,新充气橡胶胎,含类似人字形)〔999〕	17		50	13/	13	千克/条	A	M	/47
4011.8011　90	其他人字形胎面轮胎(建筑业、采矿业或工业搬运车辆及机器用,辋圈≤61cm,新充气橡胶胎,含类似人字形)〔999〕	17		50	13/	13	千克/条	A	M	/47
4011.8012	----辋圈尺寸超过61厘米 ---其他:									
4011.8012　10	断面宽≥24英寸人字形子轮胎(建筑业、采矿业或工业搬运车辆及机器用,辋圈>61cm,新充气橡胶胎,含类人字形)〔999〕	17	8	50	13/	13	千克/条	A	M	/38
4011.8012　90	其他人字形胎面轮胎(建筑业、采矿业或工业搬运车辆及机器用,辋圈>61cm,新充气橡胶胎,含类人字形)〔999〕	17		50	13/	13	千克/条	A	M	/47
	---其他:									
4011.8091	----辋圈尺寸不超过61厘米〔999〕	25		50	13/	13	千克/条			/55
4011.8092	----辋圈尺寸超过61厘米									
4011.8092　10	其他断面宽度≥24英寸轮胎(建筑业、采矿业或工业搬运车辆及机器用,辋圈>61cm,新充气橡胶胎,非人字形胎面)〔999〕	25	8	50	13/	13	千克/条			/23
4011.8092　90	其他新的充气橡胶轮胎(建筑业、采矿业或工业搬运车辆及机器用,辋圈>61cm,新充气橡胶胎,非人字形胎面)〔999〕	25		50	13/	13	千克/条			/40
	-其他:									
4011.9010	---人字形胎面或类似胎面的									
4011.9010　10	断面宽≥30英寸人字形轮胎(其他用途,新充气橡胶轮胎,含胎面类似人字形的)〔999〕	17	8	50	13/	13	千克/条	A	M	/18
4011.9010　90	其他人字形胎面轮胎(其他用途,新充气橡胶轮胎,含胎面类似人字形的)〔999〕	17		50	13/	13	千克/条	A	M	/27
4011.9090	---其他									
4011.9090　10	其他断面宽度≥30英寸轮胎(其他用途,新充气橡胶轮胎,非人字形胎面)〔999〕	25	8	50	13/	13	千克/条			/38
4011.9090　90	其他新的充气橡胶轮胎(其他用途,新充气橡胶轮胎,非人字形胎面)〔999〕	25		50	13/	13	千克/条		L	/55
40.12	**翻新的或旧的充气橡胶轮胎;实心或半实心橡胶轮胎、橡胶胎面及橡胶轮胎衬带:** -翻新轮胎:									

协定税率 %										特惠税率 %			Article Description
亚太5国	东/冰/格	巴基斯坦	韩国	瑞士	哥达	秘鲁	澳大利亚	新西/坡/智	港/澳/台	亚太2国	老/柬/缅	36/3/1	
	0/0/0	4.5	4	0	0	0	0	0/0/0	0/0/			0/0/	--Endless transmission belts, of trapezodal crossseltionl (V-belts) other tlan V-ibbed, of an outside circumference exceeding 60cm but not exceeding 150cm
	0/0/0	4.5	4	0	0	0	0	0//0	0/0/			0/0/	--Endless synchronous belts, of an outside circumference exceeding 150cm but not exceeding 198cm
5.2	0/0/0	4	0	0	0	0	0	0//0	0/0/			0/0/0	--Other
													New pneumatic tyres, of rubber:
6.5	0/0/0	4	6	0	0		0	0/0/0	0/0/0			0/0/0	-Of a kind used on motor cars (including station wagons and racing cars)
													-Of a kind used on buses or lorries
6.5	0/0/0	4.5	6	0	0	0	0	0/0/0	0/0/0			0/0/	The section width is greater than or equal to 30 inches off or a truck with new rubber tyres (of a motor vehicle with rubber tires, section width is more than or equal to 30 inches)
6.5	0/0/0	4.5	6	0	0	0	0	0/0/0	0/0/0			0/0/	Other passengers or freight cars with new rubber tyres (refers to the rubber tirefor motor vehicles)
	0/0/0	0	0	0	0	0	0	0//0	0/0/			0/0/0	-Of a kind used on aircraft
	0/0/0	12	9	4.5	0	0	0	0/0/0	0/0/0			0/0/	-Of a kind used on motorcycles
	0/0/0		12	6	0	0	0	0/0/0	0/0/0			0/0/	-Of a kind used on bicycles
													-Of a kind used on agricultural or forestry vehicles and ma—chines:
													---Having a "herring-bone" or similar tread
	0/0/0	14	7	5.3	0	0	0	0/0/0	0/0/0			0/0/	New pneumatic tyres of rubber, with "herring-bone" tread, of a cross-section width ≥ 24 inches, of a kind used on agricultural or forestry vehicles and machines
	0/0/0	14	7	5.3	0	0	0	0/0/0	0/0/0			0/0/	Other new pneumatic tyres of rubber, with "herring-bone" tread, of a kind used on agricultural or forestry vehicles and machines
	0/0/0		17.5		0		0	0/0/0	0/0/0			0/0/0	---Other
													--Of a kind used on construction, mining or industrial handling:
													---Having a "herring—bone" or similar tread:
													----Rim size not exceeding 61cm
	0/0/0	14	7	5.3	0	0	0	0/0/0	0/0/			0/0/	New pneumatic tyres of rubber, with "herring-bone" tread, of a cross-section width ≥ 24 inches, on construction or industrial uses and having a rim size ≤ 61cm
	0/0/0	14	7	5.3	0	0	0	0/0/0	0/0/			0/0/	Other new pneumatic tyres of rubber, with "herring-bone" tread, on construction or industrial uses and having a rim size not exceeding 61cm
													----Rim size exceeding 61cm
													---Other:
	0/0/0	14	7	5.3	0	0	0	0/0/0	0/0/			0/0/	Other new pneumatic tyres of rubber, other than "herring-bone" tread, of a cross-section width ≥ 24 inches, on construction or industrial uses and having a rim size > 61cm
	0/0/0	14	7	5.3	0	0	0	0/0/0	0/0/			0/0/	New pneumatic tyres of rubber, with "herring-bone" tread, of a cross-section width ≥ 24 inches, on construction or industrial uses and having a rim size > 61cm
													---Other:
	0/0/0		17.5		0		0	0/0/0	0/0/			0//	----Rim size not exceeding 61cm
													----Rim size exceeding 61cm
	0/0/0		17.5		0		0	0/0/0	0/0/			0//	Other new pneumatic tyres of rubber, other than "herring-bone" tread, on construction or industrial uses and having a rim size not exceeding 61cm
	0/0/0		17.5		0		0	0/0/0	0/0/			0//	Other new pneumatic tyres of rubber, other than "herring-bone" tread, on construction or industrial uses and having a rim size > 61cm
													-Other:
													---Having a "herring-bone" or similar tread:
	0/0/0	14	7	5.3	0	0	0	0/0/0	0/0/0			0/0/	New pneumatic tyres of rubber, with "herring-bone" tread, of a cross-section width ≥ 30 inches, for other uses
	0/0/0	14	7	5.3	0	0	0	0/0/0	0/0/0			0/0/	Other new pneumatic tyres of rubber, "herring-bone" tread similiar, for other uses
													---Other
	0/0/0		17.5		0		0	0/0/0	0/0/			0//	Other new pneumatic tyres of rubber, other than "herring-bone" tread, of a cross-section width ≥ 30 inches, for other uses
	0/0/0		17.5		0		0	0/0/0	0/0/			0//	Other new pneumatic tyres of rubber, with "herring-bone" tread, for other uses
													Retreaded or used pneumatic tyres of rubber; solid or cushion tyres, tyre treads and tyre flaps, of rubber:
													-Retreaded tyres:

税则号列	货品名称〔CIQ 扩展编码及品名—T2 表示见附表 2〕	最惠(%)	暂定税率	普通	增值/消费	出口退税	计量单位	监管条件	检验检疫	特殊证件对美关税
4012.1100	--机动小客车(包括旅行小客车及赛车)用〔999〕	20		50	13/	13	千克/条	A	M	/
4012.1200	--机动大客车或货运机动车辆用〔999〕	20		50	13/	13	千克/条	A	M	/25
4012.1300	--航空器用〔999〕	20	4	50	13/	13	千克/条			/34
4012.1900	--其他〔999〕	20		50	13/	13	千克/条			/
	-旧的充气轮胎：									
4012.2010	---汽车用〔999〕	25		50	13/	13	千克/条	A	M	/50
4012.2090	---其他〔999〕	25		80	13/	13	千克/条			/50
	-其他：									
4012.9010	---航空器用〔999〕	3		11	13/	13	千克			/8
4012.9020	---汽车用〔101 充气轮胎轮辋实心轮胎，102 压配式实心轮胎，999〕	22		50	13/	13	千克	A	M	/32
4012.9090	---其他〔999〕	22		50	13/	13	千克			/52
40.13	**橡胶内胎：**									
4013.1000	-机动小客车(包括旅行小客车及赛车)、客运机动车辆或货运机动车辆用〔101 轿车轮胎，102 载重轮胎，999 包括旅行小客车及赛车、客运车或货运车用〕	15		50	13/3	13	千克/条	A	M	/20
4013.2000	-自行车用〔999〕	15		80	13/	13	千克/条			/
	-其他：									
4013.9010	---航空器用〔999〕	3		11	13/	13	千克/条			/8
4013.9090	---其他〔999〕	15		50	13/3	13	千克/条			/40
40.14	**硫化橡胶(硬质橡胶除外)制的卫生及医疗用品(包括奶嘴)，不论是否装有硬质橡胶制的附件：**									
4014.1000	-避孕套〔999〕	0		0	0/	0	千克			/25
4014.9000	-其他〔101 其他医疗器具，102 食品接触橡胶产品，103 食品用橡胶包装〕	17		50	13/	13	千克	A	M	/32
40.15	**硫化橡胶(硬质橡胶除外)制的衣着用品及附件(包括分指手套、连指手套及露指手套)：**									
	-分指手套、连指手套及露指手套：									
4015.1100	--外科用〔999〕	8		30	13/	13	千克/双			/33
4015.1900	--其他〔999〕	10		80	13/	13	千克/双			/35
	-其他：									
4015.9010	---医疗用〔999〕	8		30	13/	13	千克			/18
4015.9090	---其他〔999〕	10		90	13/	13	千克			/35
40.16	**硫化橡胶(硬质橡胶除外)的其他制品：**									
	-海绵橡胶制：									
4016.1010	---机器及仪器用零件〔999〕	8		30	13/	13	千克			/18
4016.1090	---其他〔999〕	15		80	13/	13	千克			/25
	-其他：									
4016.9100	--铺地制品及门垫〔999〕	10		80	13/	13	千克			/40
4016.9200	--橡皮擦〔999〕	10		80	13/	13	千克			/35
	--垫片、垫圈及其他密封垫：									
4016.9310	---机器及仪器用〔999〕	8		30	13/	13	千克			/18
4016.9390	---其他〔999〕	15		80	13/	13	千克			/25
4016.9400	--船舶或码头的碰垫，不论是否可充气〔999〕	18		80	13/	13	千克			/48
4016.9500	--其他可充气制品									
4016.9500 01	硫化橡胶制液压隔离式蓄能器用胶囊〔999〕	18	9	80	13/	13	千克			/24
4016.9500 90	硫化橡胶制其他可充气制品〔999〕	18		80	13/	13	千克			/33
	--其他：									
4016.9910	---机器及仪器用零件									
4016.9910 01	奶衬(硬质橡胶除外)〔999〕	8	4	30	13/	13	千克			/24
4016.9910 90	硫化橡胶制机器及仪器其他零件(硬质橡胶除外)〔999〕	8		30	13/	13	千克			/28
4016.9990	---其他									
4016.9990 01	动车组用胶囊、外风挡板，硬质橡胶除外〔101 硫化橡胶制品，102 食品接触橡胶产品，103 食品用橡胶包装〕	10	5	80	13/	13	千克			/15
4016.9990 90	其他未列名硫化橡胶制品(硬质橡胶除外)〔101 硫化橡胶制品，102 硫化橡胶制品，103 食品接触橡胶产品，104 食品用橡胶包装〕	10		80	13/	13	千克			/20
40.17	**各种形状的硬质橡胶(例如纯硬质胶)，包括废碎料；硬质橡胶制品：**									
4017.0010	---各种形状的硬质橡胶，包括废碎料									
4017.0010 10	各种形状的硬质橡胶废碎料〔999〕	8		35	13/	10	千克	9		/33
4017.0010 90	各种形状的硬质橡胶〔999〕	8		35	13/	10	千克			/33
4017.0020	---硬质橡胶制品〔999〕	15		90	13/	13	千克			/25

协定税率 %										特惠税率 %			Article Description
亚太5国	东/冰/格	巴基斯坦	韩国	瑞士	哥达	秘鲁	澳大利亚	新西/坡/智	港/澳/台	亚太2国	老/柬/缅	36/3/1	
	0/0/0		12	6	0	0	0	0/0/0	0/0/			0/0/	--Of a kind used on motor cars (including station wagons and racing cars)
	0/0/0		12	6	0	0	0	0/0/0	0/0/			0/0/	--Of a kind used on buses or lorries
	0/0/0		12	6	0	0	0	0/0/0	0/0/			0/0/	--Of a kind used on aircraft
	0/0/0		12	6	0	0	0	0/0/0	0/0/			0/0/	--Other
													-Used pneumatic tyres:
	0/0/0		17.5		0		0	0/0/0	0/0/				---Of a kind used on motor cars, buses or lorries
	0/0/0		17.5		0		0	0/0/0	0/0/				---Other
													-Other:
	0/0/0	0	0	0	0	0	0	0//0	0/0/			0/0/	---Of a kind used on aircraft
	0/0/0		15.4	6.6	0	0	0	0/0/0	0/0/			0/0/	---Of a kind used on motor cars, buses or lorries
	0/0/0		15.4	6.6	0	0	0	0/0/0	0/0/			0/0/	---Other
													Inner tubes, of rubber:
13.1	0/0/0	7.5	9	4.5	0	0	0	0/0/0	0/0/			0/0/	-Of a kind used on motor cars (including station wagons and racing cars), buses or lorries
	0/0/0	12	6	4.5	0	0	0	0/0/0	0/0/			0/0/	-Of a kind used on bicycles
													-Other:
1.8	0/0/0	0	0	0	0	0	0	0//0	0/0/			0/0/0	---Of a kind used on aircraft
	0/0/0	12	6	4.5	0	0	0	0/0/0	0/0/			0/0/	---Other
													Hygienic or pharmaceutical articles (including teats), of vulcanized rubber other than hard rubber, with or without fittings of hard rubber:
												0/0/0	-Sheath contraceptives
	0/0/0	14	7	5.3	0	0	0	0/0/0	0/0/			0/0/	-Other
													Articles of apparel and clothing accessories (including gloves), for all purposes, of vulcanized rubber other than hard rubber:
													-Gloves, mitens and mias:
	0/0/0	4	0	0	0	0	0	0//0	0/0/			0/0/0	--Surgical
	0/0/0		7.2	5.4	0	0	0	0/0/0	0/0/			0/0/0	--Other
													-Other:
	0//0	4	0	0	0	0	0	0//0	0/0/			0/0/0	---For medical purpose
	0/0/0		6	4.5	0	0	0	0/0/0	0/0/			0/0/	---Other
													Other articles of vulcanized rubber other than hard rubber:
													-Of cellular rubber:
	0/0/0	4	4.8	0	0	0	0	0//0	0/0/			0/0/0	---of a kind used in machines or instruments
	0/0/0	12	6	4.5	0	0	0	0/0/0	0/0/			0/0/	---Other
													-Other:
	0/0/0		7.2	5.4	0	0	0	0/0/0	0/0/			0/0/	--Floor coverings and mats
	0/0/0		7.2	5.4	0	0	0	0//0	0/0/			0/0/	--Erasers
													--Gaskets, washers and other seals:
	0/0/3.2	4	0	2.4	0	0	0	0//0	0/0/			0/0/0	---Of a kind used in machines or instruments
	0/0/0		0	4.5	0	0	0	0/0/0	0/0/			0/0/0	---Other
	0/0/0		7.2	5.4	0	0	0	0/0/0	0/0/			0/0/	--Boat or dock fenders, whether or not inflatable
													--Other inflatable articles
	0/0/0		7.2	5.4	0	0	0	0/0/0	0/0/			0/0/	Of a kind used on Hydraulic separator accumulator ,capsule
	0/0/0		7.2	5.4	0	0	0	0/0/0	0/0/			0/0/	Other inflatable articles,of vulcanized rubber
													--Other:
													---Of a kind used in machines or instruments
7.6	0/0/3.2	4	4.8	2.4	0	0	0	0//0	0/0/			0/0/0	Milk lining (other than hard rubber)
7.6	0/0/3.2	4	4.8	2.4	0	0	0	0//0	0/0/			0/0/0	Other machines or instruments of vulcanized rubbtrother than hard and its articles
													---Other
6.5	0/0/4	4	4	3	0	0	0	0/0/0	0/0/			0/0/0	Of a kind used on motor train set,capsule and External wind baffle
6.5	0/0/4	4	4	3	0	0	0	0/0/0	0/0/			0/0/0	Other articles of vulcanized rubber other than hard rubber
													Hard rubber (for example, ebonite) in all forms, including waste and scrap; articles of hard rubber:
													---Hard rubber in all forms, including waste and scrap
4.8	0/0/0	4	3.2	0	0	0	0	0//0	0/0/			0/0/	Waster and scrap of hard rubber in all forms
4.8	0/0/0	4	3.2	0	0	0	0	0//0	0/0/			0/0/	Hard rubber in all forms
	0/0/0	12	6	4.5	0	0	0	0/0/0	0/0/			0/0/	---Articles of hard rubber

第八类
生皮、皮革、毛皮及其制品;鞍具及挽具;旅行用品、手提包及类似容器;动物肠线(蚕胶丝除外)制品

第四十一章
生皮(毛皮除外)及皮革

注释:

一、本章不包括:

(一)生皮的边角废料(税目 05.11);

(二)税目 05.05 或 67.01 的带羽毛或羽绒的整张或部分鸟皮;

(三)带毛生皮或已鞣的带毛皮张(第四十三章);但下列动物的带毛生皮应归入第四十一章:牛(包括水牛)、马、绵羊及羔羊(不包括阿斯特拉罕、喀拉科尔、波斯羔羊或类似羔羊、印度、中国或蒙古羔羊)、山羊或小山羊(不包括也门或蒙古山羊及小山羊)、猪(包括野猪)、小羚羊、瞪羚、骆驼(包括单峰骆驼)、驯鹿、麋、鹿、狍或狗。

二、(一)税目 41.04 至 41.06 不包括经逆鞣(包括预鞣)加工的皮(酌情归入税目 41.01 至 41.03);

(二)税目 41.04 至 41.06 所称"坯革",包括在干燥前经复鞣、染色或加油(加脂)的皮。

三、本目录所称"再生皮革",仅指税目 41.15 的皮革。

税则号列	货品名称〔CIQ 扩展编码及品名—T2 表示见附表 2〕	最惠(%)	暂定税率	普通	增值/消费	出口退税	计量单位	监管条件	检验检疫	特殊证件对美关税
41.01	生牛皮(包括水牛皮)、生马科动物皮(鲜的、盐腌的、干的、石灰浸渍的、浸酸的或以其他方法保藏,但未鞣制、未经羊皮纸化处理或进一步加工的),不论是否去毛或剖层:									
	-未剖层的整张皮,简单干燥的每张重量不超过 8 千克,干盐腌的不超过 10 千克,鲜的、湿盐腌的或以其他方法保藏的不超过 16 千克:									
	---牛皮:									
4101.2011	----经逆鞣处理的									
4101.2011 10	规定重量退鞣未剖层整张濒危生野牛皮(指每张,简单干燥≤8kg,干盐渍≤10kg,鲜或湿盐≤16kg)〔999〕	8		17	9/	0	千克/张	ABFE	MPQ	/18
4101.2011 90	规定重量未剖层退鞣处理整张生牛皮(包括水牛皮)(指每张,简单干燥≤8kg,干盐渍≤10kg,鲜或湿盐≤16kg)〔101 牛皮,102 水牛皮,103 牦牛皮〕	8		17	9/	0	千克/张	AB	MPQ	/18
4101.2019	----其他									
4101.2019 10	规定重量非退鞣未剖层整张濒危生野牛皮(指每张,简单干燥≤8kg,干盐渍≤10kg,鲜或湿盐≤16kg)〔999〕	5		17	9/	0	千克/张	ABFE	MPQ	/30
4101.2019 90	规定重量非退鞣未剖层处理整张生牛皮(包括水牛皮)(指每张,简单干燥≤8kg,干盐渍≤10kg,鲜或湿盐≤16kg)〔101 牛皮,102 水牛皮,103 牦牛皮〕	5		17	9/	0	千克/张	AB	MPQ	/30
4101.2020	---马科动物皮									
4101.2020 11	规定重量未剖层整张濒危生野驴皮(指每张,简单干燥≤8 千克,干盐渍≤10 千克,鲜或湿盐≤16 千克)〔999〕	5	2	30	9/	0	千克/张	ABFE	MPQ	/12
4101.2020 19	规定重量未剖层整张其他濒危生野马科动物皮(指每张,简单干燥≤8 千克,干盐渍≤10 千克,鲜或湿盐≤16 千克)〔999〕	5		30	9/	0	千克/张	ABFE	MPQ	/15
4101.2020 91	规定重量未剖层整张生驴皮(指每张,简单干燥≤8 千克,干盐渍≤10 千克,鲜或湿盐≤16 千克)〔999〕	5	2	30	9/	0	千克/张	AB	MPQ	/12
4101.2020 99	规定重量未剖层整张其他生马科动物皮(指每张,简单干燥≤8 千克,干盐渍≤10 千克,鲜或湿盐≤16 千克)〔999〕	5		30	9/	0	千克/张	AB	MPQ	/15
	-整张皮,重量超过 16 千克:									
	---牛皮:									

SECTION Ⅷ
RAW HIDES AND SKINS, LEATHER, FURSKINS AND ARTICLES THEREOF; SADDLERY AND HARNESS; TRAVEL GOODS, HANDBAGS AND SIMILAR CONTAINERS; ARTICLES OF ANIMAL GUT(OTHER THAN SILK-WORM GUT)
Chapter 41
Raw hides and skins(other than furskins) and leather

Notes:

1. This Chapter does not cover:
   (a) Parings or similar waste, of raw hides or skins (heading No. 05. 11);
   (b) Birdskins or parts of birdskins, with their feathers or down, of heading No. 05. 05 or 67. 01; or
   (c) Hides or skins, with the hair or wool on, raw, tanned or dressed (Chapter 43); the following are, however, to be classified in Chapter 41, namely, raw hides and skins with the hair or wool on, of bovine animals (including buffalo), of equine animals, of sheep or lambs (except Astrakhan, Broadtail, Caracul, Persian or similar lambs, Indian, Chinese, Mongolian or Tibetan lambs), of goats or kids (except Yemen, Mongolian or Tibetan goats and kids), of swine (including peccary), of chamois, of gazelle, of camels(including dromedaries) of reindeer, of elk, of deer, of roebucks or of dogs.
2. (a) Headings No. 41. 04 to 41. 06 do not cover hides and skins which have undergone a tanning(including pre-tanning) process which is reversible(headings No. 41. 01 to 41. 03, as the case may be).
   (b) For the purposes of headings No. 41. 04 to 41. 06, the term "crust" includes hides and skins that have been retanned, coloured or fat-liquored(stuffed) prior to drying.
3. Throughout the Nomenclature the expression "composition leather" means only substances of the kind referred to in heading No. 41. 15.

协定税率 %										特惠税率 %			Article Description
亚太5国	东/冰/格	巴基斯坦	韩国	瑞士	哥达	秘鲁	澳大利亚	新西/坡/智	港/澳/台	亚太2国	老/柬/缅	36/3/1	
													Raw hides and skins of bovine (including buffalo) or equine animals (fresh, or salted, dried, limed, pickled or otherwise preserved, but not tanned, parchment-dressed or further prepared), whether or not dehaired or split:
													-Not split Whole hides and skins, unsplit, of a weight per skin not exceeding 8 kg when simply dried, 10 kg when dry-salted, or 16 kg when fresh, wet-salted or otherwise preserved:
													---Of bovine animals:
													----Have undergone a reversible tanning process
6	0/0/0	4	0	0	0	0	2	0//0	0/0/			0/0/0	Whole raw hides and skins of endangered wild bovine animals, not split, have undergone a reversible tanning, w≤8kg when simply dried, w≤10kg when dry-salted, w≤16kg when fresh, wet-salted
6	0/0/0	4	0	0	0	0	2	0//0	0/0/			0/0/0	Whole raw hides and skins of bovine animals, not split, have undergone a reversible tanning, w≤8kg when simply dried, w≤10kg when dry-salted, w≤16kg when fresh, wet-salted (including buffalo hides)
													----Other
	0/0/0	0	0	0	0	0	1.3	0//0	0/0/		0/0/	0/0/0	Whole raw hides and skins of endangered wild bovine animals, not split, not have undergone a reversible tanning, not split, w≤8kg when simply dried, w≤10kg when dry-salted, w≤16kg when fresh, wet-salted
	0/0/0	0	0	0	0	0	1.3	0//0	0/0/		0/0/	0/0/0	Whole raw hides and skins of bovine animals, not split, not have undergone a reversible tanning, w≤8kg when simply dried, w≤10kg when dry-salted, w≤16kg when fresh, wet-salted(including buffalo hides)
													---Of equine animals
	0/0/0	0	0	0	0	0	0	0//0	0/0/		0/0/	0/0/0	Provisions did not split the whole weight of endangered wild life (of each simple, dry skin is less than or equal to 8 kg, less than 10 kg of dry saline, fresh or wet salt is less than or equal to 16 kg)
	0/0/0	0	0	0	0	0	0	0//0	0/0/		0/0/	0/0/0	Provisions did not split the whole weight of other endangered animal skins, raw Mustang (refers to each, simple drying is less than or equal to 8 kg, less than 10 kg of dry saline, fresh or wet salt is less than or equal to 16 kg)
	0/0/0	0	0	0	0	0	0	0//0	0/0/		0/0/	0/0/0	Provisions did not split the whole weight of raw donkey skin (of each simple, less than 8 kg dry, dry saline is less than 10 kg, fresh or wet salt is less than or equal to 16 kg)
	0/0/0	0	0	0	0	0	0	0//0	0/0/		0/0/	0/0/0	Provisions did not split the whole weight of other equine animal skin (which is less than or equal to 8 kg each, easy drying, dry salted less than 10 kg, fresh or wet salt is less than or equal to 16 kg)
													-Whole hides and skins, of a weight exceeding 16 kg:
													---Of bovine animals:

税则号列	货品名称〔CIQ 扩展编码及品名—T2 表示见附表 2〕	最惠(%)	暂定税率	普通	增值/消费	出口退税	计量单位	监管条件	检验检疫	特殊证件对美关税
4101.5011	----经逆鞣处理的									
4101.5011 10	重＞16 千克退鞣整张濒危生野牛皮〔999〕	8		17	9/	0	千克/张	ABFE	MPQ	/
4101.5011 90	重＞16 千克退鞣处理整张生牛皮(包括水牛皮)〔101 牛皮,102 水牛皮,103 牦牛皮〕	8		17	9/	0	千克/张	AB	MPQ	/
4101.5019	----其他									
4101.5019 10	重＞16 千克非退鞣整张濒危生野牛皮〔999〕	5		17	9/	0	千克/张	ABFE	MPQ	/10
4101.5019 90	重＞16 千克非退鞣处理整张生牛皮(包括水牛皮)〔101 牛皮,102 水牛皮,103 牦牛皮〕	5		17	9/	0	千克/张	AB	MPQ	/10
4101.5020	---马科动物皮									
4101.5020 10	重＞16 千克整张濒危生野马科动物皮〔999〕	5		30	9/	0	千克/张	ABFE	MPQ	/15
4101.5020 90	重＞16 千克整张生马科动物皮〔999〕	5		30	9/	0	千克/张	AB	MPQ	/15
	-其他,包括整张或半张的背皮及腹皮:									
	---牛皮:									
4101.9011	----经逆鞣处理的									
4101.9011 10	其他退鞣处理濒危生野牛皮(包括整张或半张的背皮及腹皮)〔999〕	8		17	9/	0	千克	FEAB	MPQ	/
4101.9011 90	其他退鞣处理生牛皮(包括整张或半张的背皮及腹皮)〔101 牛皮,102 水牛皮,103 牦牛皮〕	8		17	9/	0	千克	AB	MPQ	/
4101.9019	----其他									
4101.9019 10	其他濒危生野牛皮(包括整张或半张的背皮及腹皮)〔999〕	5		17	9/	0	千克	FEAB	MPQ	/25
4101.9019 90	其他生牛皮(包括整张或半张的背皮及腹皮)〔101 牛皮,102 水牛皮,103 牦牛皮〕	5		17	9/	0	千克	AB	MPQ	/25
4101.9020	---马科动物皮									
4101.9020 10	其他濒危生野马科动物皮(包括整张或半张的背皮及腹皮)〔999〕	5		30	9/	0	千克	FEAB	PQ	/15
4101.9020 90	其他生马科动物皮(包括整张或半张的背皮及腹皮)〔999〕	5		30	9/	0	千克	AB	PQ	/15
41.02	**绵羊或羔羊生皮(鲜的、盐腌的、干的、石灰浸渍的、浸酸的或经其他方法保藏,但未鞣制、未经羊皮纸化处理或进一步加工的),不论是否带毛或剖层,但本章注释一(三)所述不包括的生皮除外:**									
4102.1000	-带毛〔999〕	7		30	9/	0	千克/张	AB	MPQ	/32
	-不带毛:									
	--浸酸的:									
4102.2110	---经逆鞣处理的〔999〕	14		30	9/	0	千克/张	AB	MPQ	/24
4102.2190	---其他〔999〕	9		30	9/	0	千克/张	AB	MPQ	/19
	--其他:									
4102.2910	---经逆鞣处理的〔999〕	14		30	9/	0	千克/张	AB	PQ	/24
4102.2990	---其他〔999〕	7		30	9/	0	千克/张	AB	PQ	/17
41.03	**其他生皮(鲜的、盐渍的、干的、石灰浸渍的、浸酸的或以其他方法保藏,但未鞣制、未经羊皮纸化处理或进一步加工的),不论是否去毛或剖层,但本章注释一(二)或(三)所述不包括的生皮除外:**									
4103.2000	-爬行动物皮									
4103.2000 10	濒危爬行动物的生皮〔101 鳄鱼皮,102 蜥蜴皮,103 蛇皮,104 蟒蛇皮,105 未列出的其他动物皮张〕	9		30	9/	0	千克/张	FEAB	PQ	/19
4103.2000 90	其他爬行动物的生皮〔101 鳄鱼皮,102 蜥蜴皮,103 蛇皮,104 蟒蛇皮,105 未列出的其他动物皮张〕	9		30	9/	0	千克/张	AB	PQ	/19
4103.3000	-猪皮									
4103.3000 10	生鹿豚、姬猪皮〔999〕	9		30	9/	0	千克/张	ABFE	MPQ	/14
4103.3000 90	生猪皮〔999〕	9		30	9/	0	千克/张	AB	MPQ	/14
	-其他:									
	---山羊板皮:									
4103.9011	----经逆鞣处理的〔101 山羊皮,102 野羊皮〕	14		35	9/	0	千克/张	AB	MPQ	/24
4103.9019	-----其他〔101 山羊皮,102 野羊皮〕	9		35	9/	0	千克/张	AB	MPQ	/19
	---其他山羊或小山羊皮:									
4103.9021	----经逆鞣处理的〔101 山羊皮,102 野羊皮〕	14		30	9/	0	千克/张	AB	MPQ	/24
4103.9029	----其他〔101 山羊皮,102 野羊皮〕	9		30	9/	0	千克/张	AB	MPQ	/19
4103.9090	---其他									

协定税率 %										特惠税率 %			
亚太5国	东/冰/格	巴基斯坦	韩国	瑞士	哥达	秘鲁	澳大利亚	新西/坡/智	港/澳/台	亚太2国	老/柬/缅	36/3/1	Article Description
													----Have undergone a reversible tanning process
6.6	0/0/0	4	0	0	0	0	2.1	0//0	0/0/			0/0/0	Whole raw hides and skins of endangered wild equine animals, have undergone a reversible tanning, W>16kg
6.6	0/0/0	4	0	0	0	0	2.1	0//0	0/0/			0/0/0	Whole raw hides and skins of equine animals, have undergone a tanning which is reversible, W>16kg
													----Other
	0/0/0	0	0	0	0	0	1.3	0//0	0/0/		0/0/	0/0/0	Whole raw hides and skins of endangered wild equine animals, not have undergone a reversible tanning, W>16kg
	0/0/0	0	0	0	0	0	1.3	0//0	0/0/		0/0/	0/0/0	Whole raw hides and skins of equine animals, not have undergone a reversible tanning, W>16kg(including buffalo hioles)
													---Of equine animals
	0/0/0	0	0	0	0	0	0	0//0	0/0/		0/0/	0/0/0	Whole raw hides and skins of endangered wild equine animals, W>16kg
	0/0/0	0	0	0	0	0	0	0//0	0/0/		0/0/	0/0/0	Whole raw hides and skins of equine animals, W>16kg
													-Other, including butts, bends and bollies:
													---Of bovine animals:
													----Have undergone a reversible tanning process
6.6	0/0/0	4	0	0	0	0	2.1	0//0	0/0/			0/0/0	Other whole raw hides and skins (including butts, bends and bellies), of endangered wild bovine animals, have undergone a reversible tanning
6.6	0/0/0	4	0	0	0	0	2.1	0//0	0/0/			0/0/0	Other whole raw hides and skins (including butts, bends and bellies), of bovine animals, have undergone a reversible tanning
													----Other
	0/0/0	0	0	0	0	0	1.3	0//0	0/0/		0/0/	0/0/0	Other whole raw hides and skins (including butts, bends and bellies), of endangered wild bovine animals
	0/0/0	0	0	0	0	0	1.3	0//0	0/0/		0/0/	0/0/0	Other whole raw hides and skins (including butts, bends and bellies), of bovine animals
													---of equine animals
	0/0/0	0	0	0	0	0	0	0//0	0/0/		0/0/	0/0/0	Other whole raw hides and skins (including butts, bends and bellies), of endangered wild equine animals
	0/0/0	0	0	0	0	0	0	0//0	0/0/		0/0/	0/0/0	Other whole raw hides and skins (including butts, bends and bellies), of equine animals
													Raw skins of sheep or lambs (fresh, or salted, dried, limed, pickled or otherwise preseved, but not tanned, parchment-dressed or further prepared), whether or not with wool on or split, other than those excluded by Note 1 (c) to this Chapter:
	0/0/0	4	0	0	0		0	0//0	0/0/			0/0/0	-With wool on
													-Without wool on:
													--Pickled:
	0/0/0	11.2	5.6	4.2	0		3.5	0/0/0	0/0/			0/0/	---Have undergone a reversible tanning process
8	0/0/0	4	0	0	0	0	2.3	0//0	0/0/			0/0/0	---Other
													--Other:
	0/0/0	7	5.6	4.2	0	0	3.5	0/0/0	0/0/			0/0/	---Have undergone a reversible tanning process
6	0/0/0	4	0	0	0	0	1.8	0//0	0/0/			0/0/0	---Other
													Other raw hides and skins (fresh, or salted, dried, limed, pickled or otherwise preserved, but not tanned, parchment-dressed or further prepared), whether or not dehaired or split, other than those excluded by Note 1 (b) or 1 (c) to this Chapter:
													-Of reptiles
	0/0/0	4	0	0	0	0	2.3	0//0	0/0/			0/0/0	Endangered raw hides and skins of reptiles
	0/0/0	4	0	0	0	0	2.3	0//0	0/0/			0/0/0	Other raw hides and skins of reptiles
													-Of swine
	0/0/0	4	0	0	0	0	0	0//0	0/0/		//0	0/0/0	Raw hides and skins of pig-deer (*Babyrousa*)、pygmy pig (*Porcula*)
	0/0/0	4	0	0	0	0	0	0//0	0/0/		//0	0/0/0	Raw hides and skins of swine
													-Other:
													---Of goats:
	0/0/0	7	5.6	4.2	0	0	3.5	0/0/0	0/0/			0/0/	----Have undergone a reversible tanning process
	0/0/0	4	0	0	0	0	0	0//0	0/0/			0/0/0	-----Other
													---Other of goats or kids:
	0/0/0	7	5.6	4.2	0	0	3.5	0/0/0	0/0/			0/0/	----Have undergone a reversible tanning process
	0/0/0	4	0	0	0	0	0	0//0	0/0/			0/0/0	----Other
													---Other

税则号列		货品名称〔CIQ 扩展编码及品名—T2 表示见附表 2〕	最惠(%)	暂定税率	普通	增值/消费	出口退税	计量单位	监管条件	检验检疫	特殊证件对美关税
4103.9090	10	其他濒危野生动物生皮[本章注释一(二)或(三)所述不包括的生皮除外]〔101 斑马皮,102 野驴皮,103 其他野生奇蹄动物皮张,104 野骆驼皮,105 野鹿皮,106 其他野生偶蹄动物皮张,107 其他禽鸟皮,108 象皮,109 袋鼠皮,110 海豹皮,111 蛇皮,112 貂皮,113 狐狸皮,114 未列出的其他动物皮张,115 艾鼬皮,116 臭鼬皮,117 短尾猫皮,118 负鼠皮,119 海狸皮,120 旱獭皮,121 貉子皮,122 浣熊皮,123 灰鼠皮,124 狼皮,125 猞猁皮,126 麝鼠皮,127 水獭皮,128 松鼠皮〕	9		30	9/	0	千克/张	ABEF	MPQ	/14
4103.9090	90	其他生皮[本章注释一(二)或(三)所述不包括的生皮除外]〔101 驴皮,102 骡皮,103 其他饲养奇蹄动物皮张,104 骆驼皮,105 鹿皮,106 其他饲养偶蹄动物皮张,107 其他禽鸟皮,108 象皮,109 袋鼠皮,110 海豹皮,111 蛇皮,112 貂皮,113 狐狸皮,114 未列出的其他动物皮张,115 艾鼬皮,116 臭鼬皮,117 短尾猫皮,118 负鼠皮,119 海狸皮,120 旱獭皮,121 貉子皮,122 浣熊皮,123 灰鼠皮,124 狼皮,125 猞猁皮,126 麝鼠皮,127 水獭皮,128 松鼠皮〕	9		30	9/	0	千克/张	AB	MPQ	/14
41.04		**经鞣制的不带毛牛皮(包括水牛皮)、马科动物皮及其坯革,不论是否剖层,但未经进一步加工:**									
		-湿革(包括蓝湿皮):									
		--全粒面未剖层革;粒面剖层革:									
		---牛皮:									
4104.1111		----蓝湿的									
4104.1111	10	蓝湿濒危野牛皮(全粒面未剖或粒面剖层,经鞣制不带毛)〔999〕	6	3	17	13/	0	千克	ABFE	MPQ	/8
4104.1111	90	全粒面未剖层或粒面剖层蓝湿牛皮(经鞣制不带毛)〔999〕	6	3	17	13/	0	千克	AB	MPQ	/8
4104.1119		----其他									
4104.1119	10	湿濒危野牛皮(全粒面未剖或粒面剖层,经鞣制不带毛)〔999〕	6		35	13/	0	千克	FE		/11
4104.1119	90	全粒面未剖层或粒面剖层湿牛皮(经鞣制不带毛)〔999〕	6		35	13/	0	千克			/11
4104.1120		---马科动物皮									
4104.1120	10	湿濒危野马科动物皮(全粒面未剖或粒面剖层,经鞣制不带毛)〔999〕	5		35	13/	0	千克	FE		/15
4104.1120	90	全粒面未剖层或粒面剖层湿马科动物皮(经鞣制不带毛)〔999〕	5		35	13/	0	千克			/15
		--其他:									
		---牛皮:									
4104.1911		----蓝湿的									
4104.1911	10	其他蓝湿濒危野牛皮(经鞣制不带毛)〔999〕	6	3	17	13/	0	千克	ABFE	MPQ	/28
4104.1911	90	其他蓝湿牛皮(经鞣制不带毛)〔999〕	6	3	17	13/	0	千克	AB	MPQ	/28
4104.1919		----其他									
4104.1919	10	其他湿濒危野牛皮(经鞣制不带毛)〔999〕	7		35	13/	0	千克	FE		/17
4104.1919	90	其他湿牛皮(经鞣制不带毛)〔999〕	7		35	13/	0	千克			/17
4104.1920		---马科动物皮									
4104.1920	10	其他湿濒危野马科动物皮(经鞣制不带毛)〔999〕	5		35	13/	0	千克	FE		/
4104.1920	90	其他湿马科动物皮(经鞣制不带毛)〔999〕	5		35	13/	0	千克			/
		-干革(坯革):									
4104.4100		--全粒面未剖层或粒面剖层革的									
4104.4100	10	濒危野牛马干革(全粒面未剖或粒面剖层,经鞣制不带毛)〔999〕	5	3	35	13/	0	千克	FE		/28
4104.4100	90	全粒面未剖层或粒面剖层干革(经鞣制不带毛)〔999〕	5	3	35	13/	0	千克			/28
		--其他:									
4104.4910		---机器带用牛、马皮革									
4104.4910	10	其他机器带用濒危野牛马皮革(经鞣制不带毛)〔999〕	5		20	13/	0	千克	FE		/15

协定税率 %										特惠税率 %			
亚太5国	东/冰/格	巴基斯坦	韩国	瑞士	哥达	秘鲁	澳大利亚	新西/坡/智	港/澳/台	亚太2国	老/柬/缅	36/3/1	Article Description
	0/0/0	4	0	0	0	0	0	0//0	0/0/		//0	0/0/0	Other raw hides and skins of endangered wild animals, other than those excluded by Note 1(b) or 1(c) to this Chapter
	0/0/0	4	0	0	0	0	0	0//0	0/0/		//0	0/0/0	Other raw hides and skins of animals, other than those excluded by Note 1 (b) or (c) to this Chapter
													Tanned or crust hides and skins of bovine (including buffalo) or equine animals, without hair on, whether or not split, but not further prepared:
													-In the wet state (including wet-blue):
													--Full grains, unsplit; grain splits:
													---Of bovine animals:
													----Wet-blue
3	0/0/0	0	0	0	0	0	0	0//0	0/0/	1.2		0/0/0	Tanned or crust hides and skins of endangered wild bovine animals, without hair on, in the wet-blue state, full grains, unsplit or grain splits
3	0/0/0	0	0	0	0	0	0	0//0	0/0/	1.2		0/0/0	Tanned or crust hides and skins of bovine animals, without hair on, in the wet-blue state, full grains, unsplit, grain splits
													----Other
3	0/0/0	0	0	0	0	0	0	0//0	0/0/	1.5		0/0/0	Tanned or crust hides and skins of endangered wild bovine animals, without hair on, full grains, unsplit or grain splits, in the wet state
3	0/0/0	0	0	0	0	0	0	0//0	0/0/	1.5		0/0/0	Tanned or crust hides and skins of bovine animals, without hair on, full grains, unsplit or grain splits, in the wet state
													---Of equine animals
2.5	0/0/0	0	0	0	0	0	0	0//0	0/0/	2		0/0/0	Tanned or crust hides and skins of endangered wild equine animals, without hair on, full grains, unsplit or grain splits, in the wet state
2.5	0/0/0	0	0	0	0	0	0	0//0	0/0/	2		0/0/0	Tanned or crust hides and skins of equine animals, without hair on, full grains, unsplit or grain splits, in the wet state
													--Other:
													---Of bovine animals:
													----Wet-blue
3	0/0/0	3	0	0	0	0	0	0//0	0/0/	1.5		0/0/0	Other tanned or crust hides and skins of endangered wild bovine animals, without hair on, in the wet-blue state
3	0/0/0	3	0	0	0	0	0	0//0	0/0/	1.5		0/0/0	Other tanned or crust hides and skins, of bovine animals, without hair on, in the wet-blue state
													----Other
3.5	0/0/0	0	0	0	0	0	0	0//0	0/0/	1.8		0/0/0	Other tanned or crust hides and skins of endangered wild bovine animals, without hair on, in the wet state
3.5	0/0/0	0	0	0	0	0	0	0//0	0/0/	1.8		0/0/0	Other tanned or crust hides and skins of bovine animals, without hair on, in the wet state
													---Of equine animals
2.5	0/0/0	0	0	0	0	0	0	0//0	0/0/	1.5		0/0/0	Other tanned or crust hides and skins of endangered wild equine animals, without hair on, in the wet state
2.5	0/0/0	0	0	0	0	0	0	0//0	0/0/	1.5		0/0/0	Other tanned or crust hides and skins of equine animals, without hair on, in the wet state
													-In the dry state (crust):
													--Full grain, unsplit; grain splits
3.5	0/0/0	0	0	0	0	0	0	0//0	0/0/	2		0/0/0	Tanned or crust hides and skins of endangered wild bovine or equine animals, without hair on, full grains, unsplit or grain splits, in the dry state (crust)
3.5	0/0/0	0	0	0	0	0	0	0//0	0/0/	2		0/0/0	Tanned or crust hides and skins, without hair on, full grains, unsplit; grain splits, in the dry state (crust)
													--Other:
													---For machinery belting
3.5	0/0/0	0	0	0	0	0	0	0//0	0/0/	0		0/0/0	Tanned or crust hides and skins of endangered wild bovine or equine animals, without hair on, for machinery belting

税则号列		货品名称〔CIQ 扩展编码及品名－T2 表示见附表 2〕	最惠(%)	暂定税率	普通	增值/消费	出口退税	计量单位	监管条件	检验检疫	特殊证件对美关税
4104.4910	90	其他机器带用牛马皮革(经鞣制不带毛)〔101 马皮革,102 牛皮革〕	5		20	13/	0	千克			/15
4104.4990		---其他									
4104.4990	10	其他濒危野牛马皮革(经鞣制不带毛)〔999〕	7		35	13/	0	千克	FE		/32
4104.4990	90	其他牛马皮革(经鞣制不带毛)〔101 马皮革,102 牛皮革〕	7		35	13/	0	千克			/32
41.05		**经鞣制的不带毛绵羊或者羔羊皮及其坯革,不论是否剖层,但未经进一步加工:**									
		-湿革(包括蓝湿皮):									
4105.1010		---蓝湿的〔999〕	14	10	50	13/	0	千克	AB	MPQ	/20
4105.1090		---其他〔999〕	10		50	13/	0	千克			/20
4105.3000		-干革(坯革)〔999〕	8		50	13/	0	千克			/18
41.06		**经鞣制的其他不带毛动物皮及其坯革,不论是否剖层,但未经进一步加工:**									
		-山羊或小山羊的:									
4106.2100		--湿革(包括蓝湿皮)									
4106.2100	01	蓝湿山羊皮(经鞣制不带毛)〔999〕	14	10	50	13/	0	千克			/20
4106.2100	90	其他山羊或小山羊湿革(经鞣制不带毛)〔101 山羊皮革,102 未列出的其他动物皮革〕	14		50	13/	0	千克			/24
4106.2200		--干革(坯革)〔101 山羊皮革,102 未列出的其他动物皮革〕	14		50	13/	0	千克			/24
		-猪的:									
		--湿革(包括蓝湿皮):									
4106.3110		---蓝湿的									
4106.3110	10	蓝湿鹿豚、姬猪皮(经鞣制不带毛)〔999〕	14	10	50	13/	0	千克	FEAB	PQ	/35
4106.3110	90	其他蓝湿猪皮(经鞣制不带毛)〔999〕	14	10	50	13/	0	千克	AB	PQ	/35
4106.3190		---其他									
4106.3190	10	鹿豚、姬猪湿革(经鞣制不带毛)〔999〕	14		50	13/	0	千克	FE		/24
4106.3190	90	其他猪湿革(经鞣制不带毛)〔999〕	14		50	13/	0	千克			/24
4106.3200		--干革(坯革)									
4106.3200	10	鹿豚、姬猪干革(经鞣制不带毛,坯革)〔999〕	14		50	13/	0	千克	FE		/24
4106.3200	90	其他猪干革(经鞣制不带毛,坯革)〔999〕	14		50	13/	0	千克			/24
4106.4000		-爬行动物的									
4106.4000	10	濒危爬行动物皮革(经鞣制不带毛)〔101 鳄鱼皮,102 鳄鱼皮革,103 蜥蜴皮,104 蟒蛇皮,105 蛇皮革,106 未列出的其他动物皮革〕	14		50	13/	0	千克	FE		/24
4106.4000	90	其他爬行动物皮革(经鞣制不带毛)〔101 鳄鱼皮,102 鳄鱼皮革,103 蜥蜴皮,104 蟒蛇皮,105 蛇皮革,106 未列出的其他动物皮革〕	14		50	13/	0	千克			/24
		-其他:									
4106.9100		--湿革(包括蓝湿皮)									
4106.9100	10	其他濒危野生动物湿革(经鞣制不带毛)〔999〕	14		50	13/	0	千克	FE		/24
4106.9100	90	其他动物湿革(经鞣制不带毛)〔999〕	14		50	13/	0	千克			/24
4106.9200		--干革(坯革)									
4106.9200	10	其他濒危野生动物干革(经鞣制不带毛)〔999〕	14		50	13/	0	千克	FE		/24
4106.9200	90	其他动物干革(经鞣制不带毛)〔999〕	14		50	13/	0	千克			/24
41.07		**经鞣制或半硝处理后进一步加工的不带毛的牛皮革(包括水牛皮革)及马科动物皮革,包括羊皮纸化处理的皮革,不论是否剖层,但税目 41.14 的皮革除外:**									
		-整张的:									
		--全粒面未剖层革:									
4107.1110		---牛皮									
4107.1110	10	全粒面未剖层整张濒危野牛皮(经鞣制或半硝后进一步加工,羊皮纸化处理)〔999〕	6		50	13/	0	千克/张	FE		/31

协定税率 %										特惠税率 %			Article Description
亚太5国	东/冰/格	巴基斯坦	韩国	瑞士	哥达	秘鲁	澳大利亚	新西/坡/智	港/澳/台	亚太2国	老/柬/缅	36/3/1	
3.5	0/0/0	0	0	0	0	0	0	0//0	0/0/	0		0/0/0	Tanned or crust hides and skins of bovine, equine animals, without hair on, for machinery belting
													---Other
4.9	0/0/0	0	4.2	0	0	0	0	0//0	0/0/	2.1		0/0/0	Other tanned or crust hides and skins of endangered wild bovine or equine animals, without hair on
4.9	0/0/0	0	4.2	0	0	0	0	0//0	0/0/	2.1		0/0/0	Other tanned or crust hides and skins of bovine, equine animals, without hair on
													Tanned or crust skins of sheep or lambs, without wool on, whether or not split, but not further prepared:
													-In the wet state(including wet-blue):
7	0/0/0	4	5.6	4.2	0		0	0/0/0	0/0/	2.1		0/0/0	---Wet-blue
5	0/0/0	4	4	0	0	0	0	0//0	0/0/	2		0/0/0	---Other
5.6	0/0/0	5.6	3.2	0	0	0	0	0//0	0/0/	4.8		0/0/0	-In the dry state(crust)
													Tanned or crust hides and skins of other animals, without wool or hair on, whether or not split, but not further prepared:
													-Of goats or kids:
													--In the wet state (including wet-blue)
12	0/0/0	12	5.6	4.2	0	0	0	0/0/0	0/0/	2.1		0/0/0	Tannde or crust hides and skins of goats in wet-blue, without hair on, in the wet state
12	0/0/0	12	5.6	4.2	0	0	0	0/0/0	0/0/	2.1		0/0/0	Other tanned or crust skins of goats or kids, in the dry state, without hair on, in the wet state
9.8	0/0/0	0	5.6	4.2	0		0	0/0/0	0/0/	8.4		0/0/0	--In the dry state(crust)
													-Of swine:
													--In the wet state(including wet-blue):
													---Wet-blue
	0/0/0	11.2	5.6	4.2	0	0	0	0/0/0	0/0/	4.2		0/0/	Tanned or crust hides and skins of pig-deer (*Babyrousa*)、pygmy pig (*Porcula*), without hair on, in the wet-blue state
	0/0/0	11.2	5.6	4.2	0	0	0	0/0/0	0/0/	4.2		0/0/	Other tanned or crust hides and skins of swine, without hair on, in the wet-blue state
													---Other
	0/0/0	7	5.6	4.2	0	0	0	0/0/0	0/0/	4.2		0/0/	Tanned or crust hides and skins of pig-deer (*Babyrousa*)、pygmy pig (*Porcula*), without hair on, in the wet state
	0/0/0	7	5.6	4.2	0	0	0	0/0/0	0/0/	4.2		0/0/	Other tanned or crust hides and skins of swine, without hair on, in the wet state
													--In the dry state(crust)
	0/0/0	11.2	5.6	4.2	0	0	0	0/0/0	0/0/	4.2		0/0/	Tanned or crust hides and skins of pig-deer (*Babyrousa*)、pygmy pig (*Porcula*), without hair on, in the dry state
	0/0/0	11.2	5.6	4.2	0	0	0	0/0/0	0/0/	4.2		0/0/	Other tanned or crust hides and skins of swine, without hair on, in the dry state
													-Of reptiles
	0/0/0	7	5.6	4.2	0	0	0	0/0/0	0/0/	0		0/0/0	Endangered tanned or crust hides and skins of reptiles, without wool or hair on
	0/0/0	7	5.6	4.2	0	0	0	0/0/0	0/0/	0		0/0/0	Other tanned or crust hides and skins of reptiles, without wool or hair on
													-Other:
													--In the wet state(including wet-blue)
	0/0/0	11.2	5.6	4.2	0	0	0	0/0/0	0/0/	0		0/0/0	Tanned or crust hides and skins of other endangered wild animals, without wool or hair on, in the wet state
	0/0/0	11.2	5.6	4.2	0	0	0	0/0/0	0/0/	0		0/0/0	Tanned or crust hides and skins of other animals, without wool or hair on, in the wet state
													--In the dry state(crust)
	0/0/0	0	5.6	4.2	0	0	0	0/0/0	0/0/	0		0/0/0	Tanned or crust hides and skins of other endangered wild animals, without wool or hair on, in the dry state
	0/0/0	0	5.6	4.2	0	0	0	0/0/0	0/0/	0		0/0/0	Tanned or crust hides and skins of other animals, without wool or hair on, in the dry state
													Leather further prepared after tanning or crusting, including parchment-dressed leather, of bovine(including buffalo) or equine animals, without hair on, whether or not split, other than leather of heading 41.14:
													-Whole hides and skins:
													--Full grains, unsplit:
													---Of bovine animals
	0/0/0	0	4.8	0	0		0	0//0	0/0/				Leather further prepared after tanning or crusting, including parchment-dressed leather, of endangered wild bovine animals, whole hides and skins, full grains, unsplit

税则号列		货品名称〔CIQ 扩展编码及品名－T2 表示见附表 2〕	最惠(%)	暂定税率	普通	增值/消费	出口退税	计量单位	监管条件	检验检疫	特殊证件对美关税
4107.1110	90	全粒面未剖层整张牛皮(经鞣制或半硝后进一步加工,羊皮纸化处理)〔999〕	6		50	13/	0	千克/张			/31
4107.1120		---马科动物皮									
4107.1120	10	全粒面未剖层整张濒危野马科动物皮(经鞣制或半硝后进一步加工,羊皮纸化处理)〔999〕	5		50	13/	0	千克/张	FE		/15
4107.1120	90	全粒面未剖层整张马科动物皮(经鞣制或半硝后进一步加工,羊皮纸化处理)〔999〕	5		50	13/	0	千克/张			/15
		--粒面剖层革:									
4107.1210		---牛皮									
4107.1210	10	粒面剖层整张濒危野牛皮(经鞣制或半硝后进一步加工,羊皮纸化处理)〔999〕	6		50	13/	0	千克/张	FE		/31
4107.1210	90	粒面剖层整张牛皮(经鞣制或半硝后进一步加工,羊皮纸化处理)〔999〕	6		50	13/	0	千克/张			/31
4107.1220		---马皮									
4107.1220	10	粒面剖层整张濒危野马科动物皮(经鞣制或半硝后进一步加工,羊皮纸化处理)〔999〕	5		50	13/	0	千克/张	FE		/10
4107.1220	90	粒面剖层整张马科动物皮(经鞣制或半硝后进一步加工,羊皮纸化处理)〔999〕	5		50	13/	0	千克/张			/10
		--其他:									
4107.1910		---机器带用									
4107.1910	10	其他机器带用整张濒危野牛马皮革(经鞣制或半硝后进一步加工,羊皮纸化处理)〔999〕	5		50	13/	0	千克/张	FE		/15
4107.1910	90	其他机器带用整张牛马皮革(经鞣制或半硝后进一步加工,羊皮纸化处理)〔101 马皮革,102 牛皮革〕	5		50	13/	0	千克/张			/15
4107.1990		---其他									
4107.1990	10	其他整张濒危野牛马皮革(经鞣制或半硝后进一步加工,羊皮纸化处理)〔999〕	7		50	13/	0	千克/张	FE		/32
4107.1990	90	其他整张牛马皮革(经鞣制或半硝后进一步加工,羊皮纸化处理)〔101 马皮革,102 牛皮革〕	7		50	13/	0	千克/张			/32
		-其他,包括半张的:									
4107.9100		--全粒面未剖层革									
4107.9100	10	全粒面未剖层非整张濒危野牛马皮(经鞣制或半硝后进一步加工,羊皮纸化处理)〔999〕	5		50	13/	0	千克	FE		/30
4107.9100	90	全粒面未剖层非整张革(经鞣制或半硝后进一步加工,羊皮纸化处理)〔101 马皮革,102 牛皮革,103 未列出的其他动物皮革〕	5		50	13/	0	千克			/30
4107.9200		--粒面剖层革									
4107.9200	10	粒面剖层非整张濒危野牛马皮革(经鞣制或半硝后进一步加工,羊皮纸化处理)〔999〕	5		50	13/	0	千克	FE		/30
4107.9200	90	粒面剖层非整张革(经鞣制或半硝后进一步加工,羊皮纸化处理)〔101 马皮革,102 牛皮革,103 未列出的其他动物皮革〕	5		50	13/	0	千克			/30
		--其他:									
4107.9910		---机器带用									
4107.9910	10	其他机器带用非整张濒危野牛马皮(经鞣制或半硝后进一步加工,羊皮纸化处理)〔999〕	5		50	13/	0	千克	FE		/15
4107.9910	90	其他机器带用非整张牛马皮革(经鞣制或半硝后进一步加工,羊皮纸化处理)〔101 马皮革,102 牛皮革〕	5		50	13/	0	千克			/15
4107.9990		---其他									

协定税率 %										特惠税率 %			
亚太5国	东/冰/格	巴基斯坦	韩国	瑞士	哥达	秘鲁	澳大利亚	新西/坡/智	港/澳/台	亚太2国	老/柬/缅	36/3/1	Article Description
	0/0/0	0	4.8	0	0		0	0//0	0/0/				Leather further prepared after tanning or crusting, including parchment-dressed leather, of bovine animals, whole hides and skins, full grains, unsplit
													---Of equine animals
	0/0/0	0	0	0	0	0	0	0//0	0/0/			0/0/0	Leather further prepared after tanning or crusting, including parchment-dressed leather, of endangered wild equine animals, whole hides and skins, full grains, unsplit
	0/0/0	0	0	0	0	0	0	0//0	0/0/			0/0/0	Leather further prepared after tanning or crusting, including parchment-dressed leather, of equine animals, whole hides and skins, full grains, unsplit
													--Grain splits:
													---Of bovine animals
	0/0/0	0	3.2	0	0		0	0//0	0/0/				Leather further prepared after tanning or crusting, including parchment-dressed leather, of endangered wild bovine animals, whole hides and skins, grain splits
	0/0/0	0	3.2	0	0		0	0//0	0/0/				Leather further prepared after tanning or crusting, including parchment-dressed leather, of bovine animals, whole hides and skins, grain splits
													---Of equine animals
	0/0/0	0	0	0	0	0	0	0//0	0/0/			0/0/0	Leather further prepared after tanning or crusting, including parchment-dressed leather, of endangered wild equine animals, whole hides and skins, grain splits
	0/0/0	0	0	0	0	0	0	0//0	0/0/			0/0/0	Leather further prepared after tanning or crusting, including parchment-dressed leather, of equine animals, whole hides and skins, grain splits
													--Other:
													---For machinery belting
	0/0/0	0	2	0	0	0	0	0//0	0/0/			0/0/0	Leather further prepared after tanning or crusting, including parchment-dressed leather, of endangered wild bovine or wild equine amimals, whole hides and skins, for machinery belting
	0/0/0	0	2	0	0	0	0	0//0	0/0/			0/0/0	Leather further prepared after tanning or crusting, including parchment-dressed leather, of bevine or equine animals, whole hides and skins, for machinery belting
													---Other
	0/0/0		0	0	0		0	0//0	0/0/				Cther leather further prepared after tanning or crusting, including parchment-dressed leather of endangered wild bovine or wild equine animals, whole hides and skins
	0/0/0		0	0	0		0	0//0	0/0/				Other leather further prepared after tanning or crusting, including parchment-dressed leather of bovine or equine animals, whole hides and skins
													-Other, including sides:
													--Full grains, unsplit
	0/0/0	0	2	0	0	0	0	0//0	0/0/			0/0/0	Leather further prepared after tanning or crusting, including parchment-dressed leather of endangered wild bovine or wild equine animals, other than whole hides and skins, full grains, unsplit
	0/0/0	0	2	0	0	0	0	0//0	0/0/			0/0/0	Leather further prepared after tanning or crusting, including parchment-dressed leather, other than whole hides and skins, full grains, unsplit
													--Grain splits
	0/0/0	0	3	0	0	0	0	0//0	0/0/			0/0/0	Leather further prepared after tanning or crusting, including parchment-dressed leather, of endangered wild bovine or wild equine animals, other than whole hides and skins, grain, splits
	0/0/0	0	3	0	0	0	0	0//0	0/0/			0/0/0	Leather further prepared after tanning or crusting, including parchment-dressed leather, other than whole hides and skins, grain, splits
													--Other:
													---For machinery belting
	0/0/0	0	0	0	0	0	0	0//0	0/0/			0/0/0	Leather further prepared after tanning or crusting, including parchment-dressed leather of endangered wild bovine or wild equine animals, other than whole hides and skins, for machinery belting
	0/0/0	0	0	0	0	0	0	0//0	0/0/			0/0/0	Leather further prepared after tanning or crusting, including parchment-dressed leather, of bovine or equine animals, other than whole hides and skins, for machinery belting
													---Other

税则号列		货品名称〔CIQ扩展编码及品名—T2表示见附表2〕	最惠(%)	暂定税率	普通	增值/消费	出口退税	计量单位	监管条件	检验检疫	特殊证件对美关税
4107.9990	10	其他非整张濒危野牛马皮革(经鞣制或半硝后进一步加工,羊皮纸化处理)〔999〕	7		50	13/	0	千克	FE		/32
4107.9990	90	其他非整张牛马皮革(经鞣制或半硝后进一步加工,羊皮纸化处理)〔101 马皮革,102 牛皮革〕	7		50	13/	0	千克			/32
41.12		**经鞣制或半硝处理后进一步加工的不带毛的绵羊或羔羊皮革,包括羊皮纸化处理的,不论是否剖层,但税目41.14的皮革除外:**									
4112.0000		经鞣制或半硝处理后进一步加工的不带毛的绵羊或羔羊皮革,包括羊皮纸化处理的,不论是否剖层,但税目41.14的皮革除外〔999〕	8		50	13/	0	千克			/33
41.13		**经鞣制或半硝处理后进一步加工的不带毛的其他动物皮革,包括羊皮纸化处理的,不论是否剖层,但税目41.14的皮革除外:**									
4113.1000		-山羊或小山羊皮的〔101 山羊皮革,102 未列出的其他动物皮革〕	14		50	13/	0	千克			/39
4113.2000		-猪皮的									
4113.2000	10	加工的鹿豚、姬猪皮革(经鞣制或半硝后进一步加工,不带毛,羊皮纸化处理)〔999〕	14		50	13/	0	千克	FE		/39
4113.2000	90	加工的猪皮革(经鞣制或半硝后进一步加工,不带毛,羊皮纸化处理)〔999〕	14		50	13/	0	千克			/39
4113.3000		-爬行动物皮的									
4113.3000	10	加工的濒危爬行动物皮革(经鞣制或半硝后进一步加工,不带毛,羊皮纸化处理)〔101 鳄鱼皮,102 鳄鱼皮革,103 蜥蜴皮,104 蟒蛇皮,105 蛇皮革,106 未列出的其他动物皮革〕	14		50	13/	0	千克	FE		/34
4113.3000	90	加工的其他爬行动物皮革(经鞣制或半硝后进一步加工,不带毛,羊皮纸化处理)〔101 鳄鱼皮,102 鳄鱼皮革,103 蜥蜴皮,104 蟒蛇皮,105 蛇皮革,106 未列出的其他动物皮革〕	14		50	13/	0	千克			/34
4113.9000		-其他									
4113.9000	10	加工的其他濒危野生动物皮革(经鞣制或半硝后进一步加工,不带毛,羊皮纸化处理)〔101 其他奇蹄动物皮革,102 骆驼皮革,103 鹿皮革,104 其他偶蹄动物皮革,105 象皮革,106 袋鼠皮革,107 兔皮革,108 海豹皮革,109 未列出的其他动物皮革〕	14		50	13/	0	千克	FE		/39
4113.9000	90	加工的其他动物皮革(经鞣制或半硝后进一步加工,不带毛,羊皮纸化处理)〔101 驴皮革,102 骡皮革,103 其他奇蹄动物皮革,104 骆驼皮革,105 鹿皮革,106 其他偶蹄动物皮革,107 象皮革,108 袋鼠皮革,109 兔皮革,110 未列出的其他动物皮革〕	14		50	13/	0	千克			/39
41.14		**油鞣皮革(包括结合鞣制的油鞣皮革);漆皮及层压漆皮;镀金属皮革:**									
4114.1000		-油鞣皮革(包括结合鞣制的油鞣皮革)									
4114.1000	10	油鞣其他濒危野生动物皮革(包括结合鞣制的油鞣皮革)〔999〕	14		50	13/	0	千克	FE		/34
4114.1000	90	油鞣其他动物皮革(包括结合鞣制的油鞣皮革;野生动物皮革除外)〔999〕	14		50	13/	0	千克			/34
4114.2000		-漆皮及层压漆皮;镀金属皮革〔999〕	10		50	13/	0	千克			/35
41.15		**以皮革或皮革纤维为基本成分的再生皮革,成块、成张或成条的,不论是否成卷;皮革或再生皮革的边角废料,不适宜作皮革制品用;皮革粉末:**									
4115.1000		-以皮革或皮革纤维为基本成分的再生皮革,成块、成张或成条,不论是否成卷〔999〕	14		50	13/	0	千克			/39
4115.2000		-皮革或再生皮革的边角废料,不适宜作皮革制品用;皮革粉末									
4115.2000	10	皮革废渣、灰渣、淤渣及粉末〔999〕	14		50	13/	0	千克	9		/24
4115.2000	90	成品皮革、皮革制品或再生皮革的边角料〔101 未列出的其他动物皮革,102 橡胶皮革废碎料〕	14		50	13/	0	千克	9		/24

协定税率 %										特惠税率 %			Article Description
亚太5国	东/冰/格	巴基斯坦	韩国	瑞士	哥达	秘鲁	澳大利亚	新西/坡/智	港/澳/台	亚太2国	老/柬/缅	36/3/1	
	0/0/0		4.2	0	0	0	0	0//0	0/0/			0/0/0	Other leather further prepared after tanning or crusting, including parchment-dressed leather, of endangered wild bovine or wild equine animals, other than whole hides and skins
	0/0/0		4.2	0	0	0	0	0//0	0/0/			0/0/0	Other leather further prepared after tanning or crusting, (including parchment-dressed leather, of bovine or equine animals, other than whole hides and skins)
													Leather further prepared after tanning or crusting, including parchment-dressed leather, of sheep or lamb, without wool on, whether or not split, other than leather of heading No. 41.14:
5.6	0/0/0	0	4.8	0	0	0	0	0//0	0/0/			0/0/0	Leather further prepared after tanning or crusting, including parchment-dressed leather, of sheep or lamb, without wool on, whether or not split, other than leather of heading No. 41.14
													Leather further prepared after tanning or crusting, including parchment-dressed leather, of other animals, without wool or hair on, whether or not split, other than leather of heading No. 41.14:
9.8	0//0	0	5.6	4.2	0		0	0/0/0	0/0/			0/0/0	-Of goats or kids
													-Of swine
	0/0/0		5.6	4.2	0	0	0	0/0/0	0/0/			0/0/	Leather further prepared after tanning or crusting, including parchment-dressed leather, of pig-deer (*Babyrousa*)、pygmy pig (*Porcula*), without hair on
	0/0/0		5.6	4.2	0	0	0	0/0/0	0/0/			0/0/	Leather further prepared after tanning or crusting, including parchment-dressed leather, of swine, without hair on
													-Of reptiles
	0//0	0	5.6	4.2	0	0	0	0/0/0	0/0/			0/0/0	Endangered leather further prepared after tanning or crusting, including parchment—dressed leather, of reptiles, without wool or hair on
	0//0	0	5.6	4.2	0	0	0	0/0/0	0/0/			0/0/0	Other leather further prepared after tanning or crusting, including parchment—dressed leather, of reptiles, without wool or hair on
													-Other
	0/0/0	0	5.6	4.2	0	0	0	0/0/0	0/0/			0/0/0	Leather further prepared after tanning or crusting, including parchment-dressed leather, of endangered wild animals, without wool or hair on
	0/0/0	0	5.6	4.2	0	0	0	0/0/0	0/0/			0/0/0	Leather further prepared after tanning or crusting, including parchment-dressed leather, of other animals, without wool or hair on
													Chamois(including combination chamois) leather; patent leather and patent laminated leather; metallised leather:
													-Chamois(including combination chamois) leather
	0/0/0		5.6	4.2	0	0	0	0/0/0	0/0/			0/0/	Chamois (including combination chamois) leather of endangered wild animals
	0/0/0		5.6	4.2	0	0	0	0/0/0	0/0/			0/0/	Chamois (including combination chamois) leather of other animals
9	0/0/0	9	7	0	0		0	0/0/0	0/0/				-Patent leather and patent laminated leather; metallised leather
													Composition leather with a basis of leather or leather fibre, in slabs, sheets or strip, whether or not in rolls; parings and other waste of leather or of composition leather, not suitable for the manufacture of leather articles; leather dust, powder and flour:
	0/0/0		5.6	4.2	0		0	0/0/0	0/0/				-Composition leather with a basis of leather or leather fibre, in slabs, sheets or strip, whether or not in rolls
													-Parings and other waste of leather or of composition leather, not suitable for the manufacture of leather articles; leather dust, powder and flour
	0/0/0		5.6	4.2	0	0	0	0/0/0	0/0/	4.2		0/0/	Waste residue, dust, powder and flour of leather or of composition leather
	0/0/0		5.6	4.2	0	0	0	0/0/0	0/0/	4.2		0/0/	The leftover bits and pieces of finished leather, leather or recycled leather products (after screening, area is larger than 200 square centimeters of leather scrap, used for processing gloves, accessories, toys, etc.)

第四十二章
皮革制品;鞍具及挽具;旅行用品、手提包及类似容器;动物肠线(蚕胶丝除外)制品

注释:

一、本章所称的"皮革"包括油鞣皮革(含结合鞣制的油鞣皮革)、漆皮、层压漆皮和镀金属皮革。

二、本章不包括:

(一)外科用无菌肠线或类似的无菌缝合材料(税目30.06);

(二)以毛皮或人造毛皮衬里或作面(仅饰边的除外)的衣服及衣着附件(分指手套、连指手套及露指手套除外)(税目43.03或43.04);

(三)网线袋及类似品(税目56.08);

(四)第六十四章的物品;

(五)第六十五章的帽类及其零件;

(六)税目66.02的鞭子、马鞭或其他物品;

(七)袖扣、手镯或其他仿首饰(税目71.17);

(八)单独报验的挽具附件或装饰物,例如,马镫、马嚼子、马铃铛及类似品、带扣(一般归入第十五类);

(九)弦线、鼓面皮或类似品及其他乐器零件(税目92.09);

(十)第九十四章的物品(例如,家具、灯具及照明装置);

(十一)第九十五章的物品(例如,玩具、游戏品及运动用品);

(十二)税目96.06的纽扣、揿扣、纽扣芯或这些物品的其他零件、纽扣坯。

三、(一)除上述注释二所规定的以外,税目42.02也不包括:

1. 非供长期使用的带把手塑料薄膜袋,不论是否印制(税目39.23);

2. 编结材料制品(税目46.02)。

(二)税目42.02、42.03的制品,如果装有用贵金属、包贵金属、天然或养殖珍珠、宝石或半宝石(天然、合成或再造)制的零件,即使这些零件不是仅作为小配件或小饰物的,只要其未构成物品的基本特征,仍应归入上述税号。但如果这些零件已构成物品的基本特征,则应归入第七十一章。

四、税目42.03所称"衣服及衣着附件",主要包括分指手套、连指手套及露指手套(包括运动及防护手套)、围裙及其他防护用衣着、裤吊带、腰带、子弹带及腕带,但不包括表带(税目91.13)。

税则号列		货品名称〔CIQ扩展编码及品名—T2表示见附表2〕	最惠(%)	暂定税率	普通	增值/消费	出口退税	计量单位	监管条件	检验检疫	特殊证件对美关税
42.01		**各种材料制成的鞍具及挽具(包括缰绳、挽绳、护膝垫、口套、鞍褥、马褡裢、狗外套及类似品),适合各种动物用:**									
4201.0000		各种材料制成的鞍具及挽具(包括缰绳、挽绳、护膝垫、口套、鞍褥、马褡裢、狗外套及类似品),适合各种动物用									
4201.0000	10	濒危野生动物材料制的鞍具及挽具(适合各种动物用)〔101含木制品,102不含木制品〕	10		100	13/	0	千克	FE		/35
4201.0000	90	各种材料制成的鞍具及挽具(野生动物材料制的除外;适合各种动物用)〔101含木制品,102不含木制品〕	10		100	13/	13	千克			/35
42.02		**衣箱、提箱、小手袋、公文箱、公文包、书包、眼镜盒、望远镜盒、照相机套、乐器盒、枪套及类似容器;旅行包、食品或饮料保温包、化妆包、帆布包、手提包、购物袋、钱夹、钱包、地图盒、烟盒、烟袋、工具包、运动包、瓶盒、首饰盒、粉盒、刀叉餐具盒及类似容器,用皮革或再生皮革、塑料片、纺织材料、钢纸或纸板制成,或者全部或主要用上述材料或纸包覆制成:**									
		-衣箱、提箱、小手袋、公文箱、公文包、书包及类似容器:									
		--以皮革或再生皮革作面:									
4202.1110		---衣箱									

Chapter 42
Articles of leather; saddlery and harness; travel goods, handbags and similar containers; articles of animal gut (other than silk-worm gut)

Notes:

1. For the purposes of this Chapter, the term "leather" includes chamois (including combination chamois) leather, patent leather, patent laminated leather and metallised leather
2. This Chapter does not cover:
   (a) Sterile surgical catgut or similar sterile suture materials (heading No. 30.06);
   (b) Articles of apparel or clothing accessories (except gloves, mittens and mitts), lined with furskin or artificial fur or to which furskin or artificial fur is attached on the outside except as mere trimming (heading No. 43.03 or 43.04);
   (c) Made up articles of netting (heading No. 56.08);
   (d) Articles of Chapter 64;
   (e) Headgear or parts thereof of Chapter 65;
   (f) Whips, riding-crops or other articles of heading No. 66.02;
   (g) Cuff-links, bracelets or other imitation jewellery (heading No. 71.17);
   (h) Fittings or trimmings for harness, such as stirrups, bits, horse brasses and buckles, separately presented (generally Section XV);
   (i) Strings, skins for drums or the like, or other parts of musical instruments (heading No. 92.09);
   (j) Articles of Chapter 94 (for example, furniture, lamps and lighting fittings);
   (k) Articles of Chapter 95 (for example, toys, games, sports requisites);
   (l) Buttons, press-fasteners, snap-fasteners, pres-sstuds, button moulds or other parts of these articles, button blanks, of heading No. 96.06.
3. (a) In addition to the provisions of Note 2 above, heading No. 42.02 does not cover:
   (ⅰ) Bags made of sheeting of plastics, whether or not printed, with handles, not designed for prolonged use (heading No. 39.23);
   (ⅱ) Articles of plaiting materials (heading No. 46.02).
   (b) Articles of headings No. 42.02 and 42.03 which have parts of precious metal or metal clad with precious metal, of natural or cultured pearls, of precious or semi-precious stones (natural, synthetic or reconstructed) remain classified in those headings even if such parts constitute more than minor fittings or minor ornamentation, provided that these parts do not give the articles their essential character. If, on the other hand, the parts give the articles their essential character, the articles are to be classified in Chapter 71.
4. For the purpose of heading No. 42.03, the expression "articles of apparel and clothing accessories" applies, *inter alia*, to gloves, mittens and mitts (including those for sport or for protection), aprons and other protective clothing, braces, belts, bandoliers and wrist straps, but excluding watch straps (heading No. 91.13).

协定税率 %										特惠税率 %			Article Description
亚太5国	东/冰/格	巴基斯坦	韩国	瑞士	哥达	秘鲁	澳大利亚	新西/坡/智	港/澳/台	亚太2国	老/柬/缅	36/3/1	
													Saddlery and harness for any animal (including traces, leads, knee pads, muzzles, saddle cloths, saddle bags, dog coats and the like), of any material:
													Saddlery and harness for any animal (including traces, leads, knee pads, muzzles, saddle cloths, saddle bags, dog coats and the like), of any material
6	0/0/0	10	12	6	0	0	0	0/0/0	0/0/	4		0/0/0	Saddlery and harness for any animal of material of endangered wild animals
6	0/0/0	10	12	6	0	0	0	0/0/0	0/0/	4		0/0/0	Saddlery and harness for any animal, of any material, other than the material of wild animals
													Trunks, suit-cases, vanity-cases, executive-cases, brief-cases, school satchels, spectacle cases, binocular cases, camera cases, musical instrument cases, gun cases, holsters and similar containers; travelling-bags, insulated food or beverages bags, toilet bags, rucksacks, handbags, shopping-bags, wallets, purses, map-cases, cigarett-cases, tobacco-pouches, tool bags, sports bags, bottle-cases, jewellery boxes, powder-boxes, cutlery cases and similar containers, of leather or of composition leather, of sheeting of plastics, of textile materials, of vulcanized fibre or of paperboard, or wholly or mainly covered with such materials or with paper:
													-Trunks, suit-cases, vanity-cases, executive-cases, brief-cases, school satchels and similar containers:
													--With outer surface of leather or of composition leather:
													---Trunks and suit-cases

税则号列	货品名称〔CIQ扩展编码及品名－T2表示见附表2〕	最惠(%)	暂定税率	普通	增值/消费	出口退税	计量单位	监管条件	检验检疫	特殊证件对美关税
4202.1110 10	以含濒危野生动物皮革或再生皮革作面的衣箱〔999〕	8		100	13/	0	千克/个	FE		/33
4202.1110 90	其他以皮革或再生皮革作面的衣箱〔999〕	8		100	13/	13	千克/个			/33
4202.1190	---其他									
4202.1190 10	以含濒危野生动物皮革或再生皮革作面的箱包(包括提箱、小手袋、公文包、书包及类似容器,但不包括衣箱)〔101皮箱,102皮包〕	6		100	13/	0	千克/个	FE		/31
4202.1190 90	其他以皮革或再生皮革作面的箱包(包括提箱、小手袋、公文包、书包及类似容器,但不包括衣箱)〔101皮箱,102儿童用皮包,103非儿童用皮包〕	6		100	13/	13	千克/个			/31
	--以塑料或纺织材料作面:									
4202.1210	---衣箱〔101塑料类,102纺织材料类〕	10		100	13/	13	千克/个			/40
4202.1290	---其他〔101塑料箱,102纺织材料箱,103儿童用塑料包,104非儿童用塑料包,105儿童用纺织材料包,106非儿童用纺织材料包〕	10		100	13/	13	千克/个			/40
4202.1900	--其他〔101其他箱,102其他包〕	10		100	13/	13	千克/个			/40
	-手提包,不论是否有背带,包括无把手的:									
4202.2100	--以皮革或再生皮革作面									
4202.2100 10	以含濒危野生动物皮革或再生皮革作面的手提包(不论是否有背带,包括无把手的)〔999〕	6		100	13/	0	千克/个	FE		/31
4202.2100 90	其他以皮革或再生皮革作面的手提包(不论是否有背带,包括无把手的)〔999〕	6		100	13/	13	千克/个			/31
4202.2200	--以塑料片或纺织材料作面〔101塑料包,102纺织材料包〕	6		100	13/	13	千克/个			/31
4202.2900	--其他〔999〕	10		100	13/	13	千克/个			/
	-通常置于口袋或手提包内的物品:									
4202.3100	--以皮革或再生皮革或作面									
4202.3100 10	以含濒危野生动物皮革或再生皮革作面的钱包等物品(指通常置于口袋或手提包内的物品)〔999〕	6		100	13/	0	千克/个	FE		/31
4202.3100 90	以皮革或再生皮革作面的钱包等物品(指通常置于口袋或手提包内的物品)〔999〕	6		100	13/	13	千克/个			/31
4202.3200	--以塑料片或纺织材料作面〔101塑料包,102纺织材料包〕	10		100	13/	13	千克/个			/40
4202.3900	--其他〔999〕	10		100	13/	13	千克/个			/40
	-其他:									
4202.9100	--以皮革或再生皮革或作面									
4202.9100 10	以含濒危野生动物皮革或再生皮革作面的其他容器〔999〕	6		100	13/	0	千克/个	FE		/31
4202.9100 90	其他皮革或再生皮革作面其他容器〔999〕	6		100	13/	13	千克/个			/31
4202.9200	--以塑料片或纺织材料作面〔101塑料包,102纺织材料包〕	6		100	13/	13	千克/个			/31
4202.9900	--其他〔999〕	10		100	13/	13	千克/个			/40
42.03	**皮革或再生皮革制的衣服及衣着附件:**									
4203.1000	-衣服									
4203.1000 10	含濒危野生动物皮革制的衣服(包括再生野生动物皮革制作的)〔999〕	6		100	13/	0	千克/件	FE		/31
4203.1000 90	皮革或再生皮革制的衣服(野生动物皮革制作的除外)〔999〕	6		100	13/	13	千克/件			/31
	-手套,包括连指或露指的:									
4203.2100	--专供运动用									
4203.2100 10	含濒危野生动物皮革制的运动手套(包括再生野生动物皮革制作的)〔999〕	10		100	13/	0	千克/双	FE		/35
4203.2100 90	皮革或再生皮革制专供运动用手套(包括连指或露指的,野生动物皮革制作的除外)〔999〕	10		100	13/	13	千克/双			/35
	--其他:									
4203.2910	---劳保手套									
4203.2910 10	含濒危野生动物皮革制的劳保手套(包括再生野生动物皮革制作的)〔999〕	10		100	13/	0	千克/双	FE		/35
4203.2910 90	皮革或再生皮革制的劳保手套(野生动物皮革制作的除外)〔999〕	10		100	13/	13	千克/双			/35
4203.2990	---其他									

协定税率 %										特惠税率 %			
亚太5国	东/冰/格	巴基斯坦	韩国	瑞士	哥达	秘鲁	澳大利亚	新西/坡/智	港/澳/台	亚太2国	老/柬/缅	36/3/1	**Article Description**
	0/0/0	12	6	4.5	0	0	0	0/0/0	0/0/	4.4		0/0/	Trunks with outer surface of leather, of composition leather or of patent leather, of endangered wild animals
	0/0/0	12	6	4.5	0	0	0	0/0/0	0/0/	4.4		0/0/	Trunks with outer surface of leather, of composition leather, other than of wild animals
													---Other
	0/0/0	4	4	3	0	0	0	0//0	0/0/	4.8		0/0/0	Cases with outer surface of leather, of composition leather, of wild animals, in imminent dangers(including trunks, suit-cases, vanity-cases, executive-cases, brief-cases, school satchels and similar containers)
	0/0/0	4	4	3	0	0	0	0//0	0/0/	4.8		0/0/0	Cases(suit-cases, brief-cases, school satchels and similar containers, other than trunks) with outer surface of leather, of composition leather
													--With outer surface of plastics or of textile materials:
6.5	0/0/0	0	12	6	0	0	0	0/0/0	0/0/0			0/0/	---Trunks and suit-cases
6.5	0/0/0	0	8	6	0	0	0	0/0/0	0/0/0			0/0/0	---Other
	0/0/0	0	12	6	0	0	0	0/0/0	0/0/0	4		0/0/0	--Other
													-Handbags, whether or not with shoulder strap, including those without handle:
													--With outer surface of leather or of composition leather
3.9	0/0/0	0	4	3	0	0	0	0//0	0/0/			0/0/0	Handbags with outer surface of leather, of composition leather, of endangered wild animals(whether or not with shoulder strap, including those without handle)
3.9	0/0/0	0	4	3	0	0	0	0//0	0/0/			0/0/0	Handbags, whether or not with shoulder strap, including those without handle, with outer surface of leather, of composition leather
3.9	0/0/0	0	4	3	0	0	0	0/0/0	0/0/0			0/0/0	--With outer surface of plastic sheeting or of textile materials
6.5	0/0/0	14	12	6	0	0	0	0/0/0	0/0/	4		0/0/	--Other
													-Articles of a kind normally carried in the pocket or in the handbag:
													--With outer surface of leather or of composition leather
3.9	0/0/0	4	4	3	0	0	0	0//0	0/0/			0/0/0	Wallets or purses, with outer surface of leather, of composition leather of endangered wild animals
3.9	0/0/0	4	4	3	0	0	0	0//0	0/0/			0/0/0	Wallets or purses, with outer surface of leather, of composition leather
6.5	0/0/0	14	8	6	0	0	0	0/0/0	0/0/			0/0/0	--With outer surface of plastic sheeting or of textile materials
6.5	0/0/0	14	12	6	0	0	0	0/0/0	0/0/	4		0/0/	--Other
													-Other:
													--With outer surface of leather or of composition leather
3.9	0/0/0	4.5	4	3	0	0	0	0//0	0/0/			0/0/0	Other containers with outer surface of leather, of composition leather, of endangered wild animals
3.9	0/0/0	4.5	4	3	0	0	0	0//0	0/0/			0/0/0	Other containers with outer surface of leather, of composition leather
3.9	0/0/0	0	4	0	0	0	0	0/0/0	0/0/			0/0/0	--With outer surface of plastic sheeting or of textile materials
	0/0/0		12	10	0	0	0	0/0/0	0/0/			0/0/	--Other
													Articles of apparel and clothing accessories, of leather or of composition leather:
													-Articles of apparel
	0/0/0	0	0	0	0	0	0	0//0	0/0/	4.8		0/0/0	Articles of apparel of leather or of composition leather, of endangered wild animals
	0/0/0	0	0	0	0	0	0	0//0	0/0/	4.8		0/0/0	Articles of apparel of leather or of composition leather (other than leather of wild animals)
													-Gloves, mittens and mitts:
													--Specially designed for use in sports
6.5	0//0	0	12	6	0	0	0	0/0/0	0/0/			0/0/	Gloves, specially designed for use in sports, of leather or of composition leather, of endangered wild animals
6.5	0//0	0	12	6	0	0	0	0/0/0	0/0/			0/0/	Gloves, mittens and mitts, specially designed for use in sports, of leather or of composition leather, other than leather of wild animals
													--Other:
													---Working gloves
	0//0	0	12	6	0	0	0	0/0/0	0/0/	4		0/0/	Working gloves, of leather or of composition leather, of endangered wild animals
	0//0	0	12	6	0	0	0	0/0/0	0/0/	4		0/0/	Working gloves, of leather or of composition leather, other than leather of wild animals
													---Other

税则号列		货品名称〔CIQ 扩展编码及品名－T2 表示见附表 2〕	最惠(%)	暂定税率	普通	增值/消费	出口退税	计量单位	监管条件	检验检疫	特殊证件对美关税
4203.2990	10	含濒危野生动物皮革制的其他手套(包括再生野生动物皮革制作的)〔999〕	10		100	13/	0	千克/双	FE		/35
4203.2990	90	皮革或再生皮革制的其他手套(包括连指或露指的)〔999〕	10		100	13/	13	千克/双			/35
		-腰带及子弹带:									
4203.3010		---腰带									
4203.3010	10	含濒危野生动物皮革制的腰带(包括再生野生动物皮革制作的)〔999〕	6		100	13/	0	千克	FE		/31
4203.3010	90	其他动物皮革制的腰带(包括再生动物皮革制作的)〔999〕	6		100	13/	13	千克			/31
4203.3020		---子弹带									
4203.3020	10	含濒危野生动物皮革制的子弹带(包括再生野生动物皮革制作的)〔999〕	6		100	13/	0	千克	FE		/
4203.3020	90	其他动物皮革制的子弹带(包括再生动物皮革制作的)〔999〕	6		100	13/	13	千克			/
4203.4000		-其他衣着附件									
4203.4000	10	含濒危野生动物皮革制的衣着附件(包括再生野生动物皮革制作的)〔999〕	10		100	13/	0	千克	FE		/35
4203.4000	90	皮革或再生皮革制的其他衣着附件〔999〕	10		100	13/	13	千克			/35
42.05		**皮革或再生皮革的其他制品:**									
		-皮革或再生皮革的其他制品:									
4205.0010		---坐具套									
4205.0010	10	含濒危野生动物皮革制的坐具套(包括再生野生动物皮革制作的)〔999〕	6		100	13/	0	千克	FE		/31
4205.0010	90	其他动物皮革制的坐具套(包括再生皮革制作的)〔999〕	6		100	13/	13	千克			/31
4205.0020		---机器、机械器具或其他专门技术用途的									
4205.0020	10	含濒危野生动物皮革制工业用皮革或再生皮革制品(工业用指机器、机械器具或其他专门技术用途的)〔999〕	6		35	13/	0	千克	FE		/31
4205.0020	90	其他工业用皮革或再生皮革制品(工业用指机器,机械器具或其他专门技术用途的)〔999〕	6		35	13/	13	千克			/31
4205.0090		---其他									
4205.0090	10	含濒危野生动物皮革的其他制品(包括再生野生动物皮革制作的)〔999〕	6		100	13/	0	千克	FE		/36
4205.0090	20	皮革或再生皮革制宠物用品〔999〕	6		100	13/	13	千克	AB	PQ	/36
4205.0090	90	皮革或再生皮革的其他制品〔999〕	6		100	13/	13	千克			/36
42.06		**肠线(蚕胶丝除外)、肠膜、膀胱或筋腱制品:**									
4206.0000		肠线(蚕胶丝除外)、肠膜、膀胱或筋腱制品(不包括外科用无菌肠线或制成乐器弦的肠线,蚕胶丝除外)〔999〕	10		90	13/	6	千克			/

协定税率 %										特惠税率 %			Article Description
亚太5国	东/冰/格	巴基斯坦	韩国	瑞士	哥达	秘鲁	澳大利亚	新西/坡/智	港/澳/台	亚太2国	老/柬/缅	36/3/1	
	0//0	0	12	6	0	0	0	0/0/0	0/0/	4		0/0/	Other gloves, mittens and mitts, of leather or of composition leather of endangered wild animals
	0//0	0	12	6	0	0	0	0/0/0	0/0/	4		0/0/	Other gloves, mittens and mitts, of leather or of composition leather
													-Belts and bandoliers:
													---Belts
	0/0/0	0	4	0	0	0	0	0//0	0/0/	4.8		0/0/0	Belts of leather or of composition leather of endangered wild animals
	0/0/0	0	4	0	0	0	0	0//0	0/0/	4.8		0/0/0	Belts of leather or of composition leather, of other animals
													---Bandoliers
5.4	0/0/0	0	4	0	0	0	0	0//0	0/0/	4.8		0/0/0	Bandoliers of leather or of composition leather of endangered wild animals
5.4	0/0/0	0	4	0	0	0	0	0//0	0/0/	4.8		0/0/0	Bandoliers of leather or of composition leather of other animals
													-Other clothing accessories
	0//0	0	12	6	0	0	0	0/0/0	0/0/	4		0/0/	Clothing accessories of leather or of composition leather, of endangered wild animals
	0//0	0	12	6	0	0	0	0/0/0	0/0/	4		0/0/	Other clothing accessories, of leather or of composition leather
													Other articles of leather or of composition leather:
													-Other articles of leather or of composition leather:
													---Cover of seat
	0/0/0	0		3.6	0	0	0	0/0/0	0/0/	3.9		0/0/0	Covering of seats, of leather or of composition leather, of endangered wild animals
	0/0/0	0		3.6	0	0	0	0/0/0	0/0/	3.9		0/0/0	Covering of seats, of leather or of composition leather, of other animals
													---Of a kind used in machinery or mechanical appilances or for other technical uses
	0/0/0	4	3.2	4.2	0	0	0	0//0	0/0/			0/0/0	Articles of leather or of composition leather of endangered animals, of a kind used in machinery or mechanial appilances or for other technical uses
	0/0/0	4	3.2	4.2	0	0	0	0//0	0/0/			0/0/0	Other articles of leather or of composition leather, of a kind used in machinery or mechanial appilances or for other technical uses
													---Other
	0/0/0	0	7.2	3.6	0	0	0	0/0/0	0/0/	3.9		0/0/0	Other articles, of leather or of composition leather, of endangered wild animals
	0/0/0	0	7.2	3.6	0	0	0	0/0/0	0/0/	3.9		0/0/0	Articles for pets, of leather or of compostition leather
	0/0/0	0	7.2	3.6	0	0	0	0/0/0	0/0/	3.9		0/0/0	Other articles of leather or of composition leather
													Articles of gut (other than silk-worm gut), of goldbeater's skin, of bladders or of tendons:
	0/0/0		12	6	0	0	0	0/0/0	0/0/			0/0/	Articles of gut (other than silk-worm gut), of goldbeater's skin, of bladders or of tendons

第四十三章
毛皮、人造毛皮及其制品

注释：

一、本目录所称“毛皮”，是指已鞣的各种动物的带毛毛皮，但不包括税目43.01的生毛皮。

二、本章不包括：

(一)带羽毛或羽绒的整张或部分鸟皮(税目05.05或67.01)；

(二)第四十一章的带毛生皮[见该章注释一(三)]；

(三)用皮革与毛皮或用皮革与人造毛皮制成的分指手套、连指手套及露指手套(税目42.03)；

(四)第六十四章的物品；

(五)第六十五章的帽类及其零件；

(六)第九十五章的物品(例如，玩具、游戏品及运动用品)。

三、税目43.03包括加有其他材料缝合的毛皮和毛皮部分品，以及缝合成衣服、衣服部分品、衣着附件或其他制品的毛皮和毛皮部分品。

四、以毛皮或人造毛皮衬里或作面(仅饰边的除外)的衣服及衣着附件(不包括注释二所述的货品)，应分别归入税目43.03或43.04，但毛皮或人造毛皮仅作为装饰的除外。

五、本目录所称“人造毛皮”，是指以毛、发或其他纤维粘附或缝合于皮革、织物或其他材料之上而构成的仿毛皮，但不包括以机织或针织方法制得的仿毛皮(一般应归入税目58.01或60.01)。

税则号列	货品名称〔CIQ扩展编码及品名－T2表示见附表2〕	最惠(%)	暂定税率	普通	增值/消费	出口退税	计量单位	监管条件	检验检疫	特殊证件对美关税
43.01	**生毛皮(包括适合加工皮货用的头、尾、爪及其他块、片)，但税目41.01、41.02或41.03的生皮除外：**									
4301.1000	-整张水貂皮，不论是否带头、尾或爪〔999〕	15	10	100	9/	0	千克	AB	PQ	/30
4301.3000	-下列羔羊的整张毛皮，不论是否带头、尾或爪：阿斯特拉罕、喀拉科尔、波斯羔羊及类似羔羊、印度、中国或蒙古羔羊〔101绵羊皮，102山羊皮〕	20		90	9/	0	千克	AB	PQ	/30
4301.6000	-整张狐皮，不论是否带头、尾或爪									
4301.6000　10	整张濒危生狐皮(不论是否带头、尾或爪)〔999〕	20	10	100	9/	0	千克/张	AFEB	PQ	/20
4301.6000　90	其他整张生狐皮(不论是否带头、尾或爪)〔999〕	20	10	100	9/	0	千克/张	AB	PQ	/20
	-整张的其他毛皮，不论是否带头、尾或爪：									
4301.8010	---整张兔皮，不论是否带头，尾或爪									
4301.8010　10	整张生濒危野兔皮(不论是否带头，尾或爪)〔999〕	20		90	9/	0	千克/张	AFEB	PQ	/30
4301.8010　90	整张生兔皮(不论是否带头，尾或爪)〔999〕	20		90	9/	0	千克/张	AB	PQ	/30
4301.8090	---其他									
4301.8090　10	整张的其他生濒危野生动物毛皮(不论是否带头，尾或爪，包括整张濒危生海豹皮)[T2]	20	15	90	9/	0	千克/张	ABEF	PQ	/20
4301.8090　90	整张的其他生毛皮(不论是否带头，尾或爪，包括整张生海豹皮)〔101驴皮，102骡皮，103其他饲养奇蹄动物皮张，104猪皮，105绵羊皮，106山羊皮，107骆驼皮，108鹿皮，109其他饲养偶蹄动物皮张，110鸡、鸭、鹅皮，111兔皮，112未列出的其他动物皮张，113艾鼬皮，114臭鼬皮，115短尾猫皮，116负鼠皮，117海狸皮，118旱獭皮，119貉子皮，120浣熊皮，121灰鼠皮，122狼皮，123猞猁皮，124麝鼠皮，125水獭皮，126松鼠皮〕	20	15	90	9/	0	千克/张	AB	PQ	/20
	-适合加工皮货用的头、尾、爪及其他块、片：									
4301.9010	---黄鼠狼尾〔999〕	20		50	9/	0	千克	EABF	PQ	/30
4301.9090	---其他									
4301.9090　10	其他濒危野生动物未鞣头尾(加工皮货用，包括爪及其他块、片)〔101松鼠尾，102松鼠尾除外〕	20		90	9/	0	千克	ABFE	PQ	/45
4301.9090　90	适合加工皮货用的其他未鞣头、尾(包括爪及其他块、片)〔101松鼠尾，102松鼠尾除外〕	20		90	9/	0	千克	AB	PQ	/45
43.02	**未缝制或已缝制(不加其他材料)的已鞣毛皮(包括头、尾、爪及其他块、片)，但税目43.03的货品除外：**									
	-未缝制的整张毛皮，不论是否带头、尾或爪：									
4302.1100	--水貂皮〔999〕	12		130	13/	6	千克/张			/37
	--其他：									

Chapter 43
Furskins and artificial fur; manufactures thereof

Notes:

1. Throughout the Nomenclature references to "furskins", other than to raw furskins of heading No. 43. 01, apply to hides or skins of all animals which have been tanned or dressed with the hair or wool on.
2. This Chapter does not cover:
   (a) Birdskins or parts of birdskins, with their feathers or down (heading No. 05. 05 or 67. 01);
   (b) Raw hides or skins, with the hair or wool on, of Chapter 41 (see Note 1 (c) to that Chapter);
   (c) Gloves, mittens and mitts, consisting of leather and furskin or of leather and artificial fur (heading No. 42. 03);
   (d) Articles of Chapter 64;
   (e) Headgear or parts thereof of Chapter 65;
   (f) Articles of Chapter 95 (for example, toys, games, sports requisites).
3. Heading No. 43. 03 includes furskins and parts thereof, assembled with the addition of other materials, and furskins and parts thereof, sewn together in the form of garments or parts or accessories of garments or in the form of other articles.
4. Articles of apparel and clothing accessories (except those excluded by Note 2) lined with furskin or artificial fur or to which furskin or artificial fur is attached on the outside except as mere trimming are to be classified in heading No. 43. 03 or 43. 04 as the case may be.
5. Throughout the Nomenclature the expression "artificial fur" means any imitation of furskin consisting of wool, hair or other fibres gummed or sewn on to leather, woven fabric or other materials, but does not include imitation furskins obtained by weaving or knitting (generally, heading No. 58. 01 or 60. 01).

协定税率 %										特惠税率 %			Article Description
亚太5国	东/冰/格	巴基斯坦	韩国	瑞士	哥达	秘鲁	澳大利亚	新西/坡/智	港/澳/台	亚太2国	老/柬/缅	36/3/1	
													Raw furskins (including heads, tails, paws and other pieces or cuttings, suitable for furriers' use), other than raw hides and skins of heading No. 41. 01, 41. 02 or 41. 03:
12	0/0/0	12	6	4.5	0	0	0	0/0/0	0/0/			0/0/	-Of mink, whole, with or without head, tail or paws
	0/0/0		12	6	0	0	0	0/0/0	0/0/			0/0/	-Of lamb, the following: Astrakhan, Broadtail, Caracul, Persian and similar lamb, Indian, Chinese, Mongolian or Tibetan lamb, whole, with or without head, tail or paws
													-Of fox, whole, with or without head, tail or paws
14	0/0/0		12	6	0	0	0	0/0/0	0/0/			0/0/	Raw furskins of endangered fox, whole, with or without head, tail or paws
14	0/0/0		12	6	0	0	0	0/0/0	0/0/			0/0/	Other raw furskins of fox, whole, with or without head, tail or paws
													-Other furskins, whole, with or without head, tail or paws:
													---Of rabbit or hare, whole, with or without head, tail or paws
14	0/0/0		12	6	0	0	0	0/0/0	0/0/			0/0/	Raw furskins of endangered wild rabbit or hare, whole, with or without head tail or paws
14	0/0/0		12	6	0	0	0	0/0/0	0/0/			0/0/	Raw furskins of rabbit or hare, whole, with or without head tail or paws
													---Other
14	0/0/0		12	6	0	0	0	0/0/0	0/0/			0/0/	Raw furskins of other endangered wild animals, whole, with or without head tail or paws including endangered raw sealskin
14	0/0/0		12	6	0	0	0	0/0/0	0/0/			0/0/	Raw furskins of other animals, whole, with or without head tail or paws including raw sealskin
													-Heads, tails, paws and other pieces or cuttings, suitable for furriers' use:
	0/0/0		12	6	0	0	0	0/0/0	0/0/			0/0/	---Weasel tails
													---Other
	0/0/0		12	6	0	0	0	0/0/0	0/0/			0/0/	Heads, tails, paws and other pieces or cuttings, of endangered wild animals, not tanned or dressed, suitable for furriers' use
	0/0/0		12	6	0	0	0	0/0/0	0/0/			0/0/	Other heads, tails, paws and other pieces or cuttings of animals, not tanned or dressed, suitable for furriers' use
													Tanned or dressed furskins (including heads, tails, paws and other pieces or cuttings), unassembled, or assembled (without the addition of other materials) other than those of heading No. 43. 03:
													-Whole skins, with or without head, tail or paws, not assembled:
8.4	0/0/0	6	4.8	3.6	0	0	0	0/0/0	0/0/			0/0/	--Of mink
													--Other:

税则号列		货品名称〔CIQ扩展编码及品名—T2表示见附表2〕	最惠(%)	暂定税率	普通	增值/消费	出口退税	计量单位	监管条件	检验检疫	特殊证件对美关税
4302.1910		---灰鼠皮、白鼬皮、其他貂皮、狐皮、水獭皮、旱獭皮及猞猁皮									
4302.1910	10	已鞣未缝制的濒危狐皮(兰狐皮、银狐皮除外)〔999〕	10		130	13/	0	千克/张	FE		/35
4302.1910	20	已鞣未缝制的兰狐皮、银狐皮〔999〕	10		130	13/	6	千克/张			/35
4302.1910	90	已鞣未缝制的其他贵重濒危动物毛皮(灰鼠皮、白鼬皮、其他貂皮、水獭皮、旱獭皮、猞猁皮)〔999〕	10		130	13/	0	千克/张	FE		/35
4302.1920		---兔皮									
4302.1920	10	已鞣未缝制的整张濒危野兔皮(不论是否带头、尾或爪)〔999〕	10		100	13/	0	千克/张	FE		/20
4302.1920	90	已鞣未缝制的整张兔皮(不论是否带头、尾或爪)〔999〕	10		100	13/	6	千克/张			/20
4302.1930		---下列羔羊皮:阿斯特拉罕、喀拉科尔、波斯羔羊及类似羔羊、印度、中国或蒙古羔羊〔999〕	20		100	13/	6	千克/张			/30
4302.1990		---其他									
4302.1990	10	已鞣未缝制的其他濒危野生动物毛皮〔999〕	10		100	13/	0	千克/张	FE		/35
4302.1990	90	已鞣未缝制的其他毛皮〔999〕	10		100	13/	6	千克/张			/35
4302.2000		-未缝制的头、尾、爪及其他块、片									
4302.2000	10	已鞣未缝濒危野生动物头、尾、爪等(包括块、片)〔999〕	20		100	13/	0	千克	FE		/45
4302.2000	90	已鞣未缝制的头、尾、爪及其他块、片〔999〕	20		100	13/	6	千克			/45
		-已缝制的整张毛皮及其块、片:									
4302.3010		---灰鼠、白鼬、貂、狐、水獭、旱獭及猞猁的整张毛皮及其块、片									
4302.3010	10	已鞣已缝制貂皮、狐皮及其块、片(兰狐银狐、水貂、艾虎的整张毛皮及块、片除外)〔999〕	20		130	13/	6	千克	FE		/30
4302.3010	90	已鞣已缝制的贵重濒危动物毛皮及其块、片(灰鼠皮、白鼬皮、其他貂皮、水獭皮、旱獭皮、猞猁皮及块、片)〔999〕	20		130	13/	0	千克	FE		/30
4302.3090		---其他									
4302.3090	10	已鞣缝的其他整张濒危野生毛皮(包括块、片)〔999〕	20		100	13/	0	千克	FE		/30
4302.3090	90	已鞣已缝制的其他整张毛皮及块、片〔999〕	20		100	13/	6	千克			/30
43.03		**毛皮制的衣服、衣着附件及其他物品:**									
		-衣服及衣着附件:									
4303.1010		---毛皮衣服									
4303.1010	10	含濒危野生动物毛皮衣服〔999〕	10		150	13/	0	千克/件	EF		/35
4303.1010	90	其他毛皮衣服〔999〕	10		150	13/	13	千克/件			/35
4303.1020		---毛皮衣着附件									
4303.1020	10	含濒危野生动物毛皮衣着附件〔999〕	10		150	13/	0	千克	EF		/40
4303.1020	90	其他毛皮衣着附件〔999〕	10		150	13/	13	千克			/40
4303.9000		-其他									
4303.9000	10	含濒危野生动物毛皮制其他物品〔999〕	10		150	13/	0	千克	EF		/35
4303.9000	90	其他毛皮制物品〔999〕	10		150	13/	13	千克			/35
43.04		**人造毛皮及其制品:**									
4304.0010		---人造毛皮〔999〕	10		130	13/	13	千克			/
4304.0020		---人造毛皮制品〔101 其他装饰用纺织制品,102 其他纺织制品〕	10		150	13/	13	千克			/35

协定税率 %										特惠税率 %			Article Description
亚太5国	东/冰/格	巴基斯坦	韩国	瑞士	哥达	秘鲁	澳大利亚	新西/坡/智	港/澳/台	亚太2国	老/柬/缅	36/3/1	
													---Of grey squirrel, ermine, other marten, fox, otter, marmot and lynx
7	0/0/0	4.5	4	0	0	0	0	0//0	0/0/			0/0/	Tanned or dressed furskins of endangered fox, unassembled(other than furskins of blue fox or silver fox)
7	0/0/0	4.5	4	0	0	0	0	0//0	0/0/			0/0/	Tanned or dressed furskins of blue fox, silver fox, unassembled
7	0/0/0	4.5	4	0	0	0	0	0//0	0/0/			0/0/	Tanned or dressed furskins precious furskins of endangered animals (grey squirrel, ermine, other marten, fox, otter, marmot and lynx) unassembled
													---Of rabbit or hare
	0/0/0	4.5	4	0	0	0	0	0//0	0/0/			0/0/0	Tanned or dressed furskins of endangered rabbit or hare, endangered whole, with or without head tail or paws, unassembled
	0/0/0	4.5	4	0	0	0	0	0//0	0/0/			0/0/0	Tanned or dressed furskins of rabbit or hare, whole, with or without head tail or paws, unassembled
	0//0		12	6	0	0	0	0/0/0	0/0/			0/0/0	---Of lamb, the following: Astrakhan, Broadtail, Caracul, Persian and similar lamb, Indian, Chinese Mongolian or Tibetan lamb
													---Other
	0/0/0		4	0	0	0	0	0//0	0/0/			0/0/0	Tanned or dressed furskins of other endangered wild animals, unassembled
	0/0/0		4	0	0	0	0	0//0	0/0/			0/0/0	Other tanned or dressed furskins of other animals, unassembled
													-Heads, tails, paws and other pieces or cuttings, not assembled
	0/0/0		12	6	0	0	0	0/0/0	0/0/			0/0/	Tanned or dressed heads, tails, paws and other pieces or cuttings, of endangered wild animals, unassembled
	0/0/0		12	6	0	0	0	0/0/0	0/0/			0/0/	Tanned or dressed heads, tails, paws and other pieces or cuttings of other animals, unassembled
													-Whole skins and pieces or cuttings thereof, assembled:
													---Of grey squirrel, ermine, other marten, fox, otter, marmot and lynx
	0/0/0		12	6	0	0	0	0/0/0	0/0/			0/0/	Tanned or dressed whole skins and pieces or cuttings thereof, of marten, fox, other than whole skins and pieces or cuttings of blue fox, silver fox, mink, perwitsky (ferret-polecat), assembled
	0/0/0		12	6	0	0	0	0/0/0	0/0/			0/0/	Tanned or dressed whole skins and pieces or cuttings thereof, of grey squirrel, ermine, other marten, fox, otter, marmot and lynx, endangered, assembled
													---Other
	0//0		12	6	0	0	0	0/0/0	0/0/			0/0/	Tanned or dressed whole skins and pieces or cuttings thereof, of other endangered wild animals, assembled
	0//0		12	6	0	0	0	0/0/0	0/0/			0/0/	Tanned or dressed whole skins and pieces or cuttings thereof, of other animals, assembled
													Articles of apparel, clothing accessories and other articles of furskin:
													-Articles of apparel and clothing accessories:
													---Articles of apparel
	0//0		16.1	6.9	0	0	0	0/0/0	0/0/	4.5		0/0/	Articles of apparel of endangered wild animals
	0//0		16.1	6.9	0	0	0	0/0/0	0/0/	4.5		0/0/	Articles of apparel of other animals
													---Clothing accessories
	0//0		7.2	5.4	0	0	0	0/0/0	0/0/	5.5		0/0/	Clothing accessories of endangered wild animals
	0//0		7.2	5.4	0	0	0	0/0/0	0/0/	5.5		0/0/	Clothing accessories of other animals
													-Other
	0//0	14.4	7.2	5.4	0	0	0	0/0/0	0/0/	5.5		0/0/	Other articles of furskin, of endangered wild animals
	0//0	14.4	7.2	5.4	0	0	0	0/0/0	0/0/	5.5		0/0/	Other articles of furskin, of other animals
													Artificial fur and articles thereof:
	0//0		7.2	5.4	0	0	0	0/0/0	0/0/	6		0/0/	---Artificial fur
	0//0	14.4	7.2	5.4	0	0	0	0/0/0	0/0/	6		0/0/	---Articles of artificial fur

第九类
木及木制品；木炭；软木及软木制品；稻草、秸秆、针茅或其他编结材料制品；篮筐及柳条编结品

第四十四章
木及木制品；木炭

注释：

一、本章不包括：

(一)主要作香料、药料、杀虫、杀菌或类似用途的木片、刨花、碎木、木粒或木粉(品目12.11)；

(二)竹或主要作编织用的其他木质材料呈原木状，不论是否经劈开，纵锯或切段(品目14.01)；

(三)主要作染料或鞣料用的木片、刨花、木粒或木粉(品目14.04)；

(四)活性炭(品目38.02)；

(五)品目42.02的物品；

(六)第四十六章的货品；

(七)第六十四章的鞋靴及其零件；

(八)第六十六章的货品(例如，伞、手杖及其零件)；

(九)税目68.08的货品；

(十)税目71.17的仿首饰；

(十一)第十六类或第十七类的货品(例如，机器零件，机器及器具的箱、罩、壳，车辆部件)；

(十二)第十八类的货品(例如，钟壳、乐器及其零件)；

(十三)火器的零件(税目93.05)；

(十四)第九十四章的物品(例如，家具、灯具及照明器具、活动房屋)；

(十五)第九十五章的物品(例如，玩具、游戏品及运动用品)；

(十六)第九十六章的物品(例如，烟斗及其零件、纽扣、铅笔、独脚架、双脚架、三脚架及类似品)，但税目96.03所列物品的木身及木柄除外；或

(十七)第九十七章的物品(例如，艺术品)。

二、本章所称“强化木”，是指经过化学或物理方法处理(对于多层粘合木材，其处理应超出一般粘合需要)，从而增加了密度或硬度并改善了机械强度、抗化学或抗电性能的木材。

三、税目44.14至44.21适用于木质碎料板或类似木质材料板、纤维板、层压板或强化木的制品。

四、税目44.10、44.11或44.12的产品，可以加工成税目44.09所述的各种形状，也可以加工成弯曲、瓦楞、多孔或其他形状(正方形或矩形除外)，以及经其他任何加工，但未具有其他税目所列制品的特性。

五、税目44.17不包括装有第八十二章注释一所述材料制成的刀片、工作刃、工作面或其他工作部件的工具。

六、除上述注释一及其他条文另有规定的以外，本章税目中所称“木”，也包括竹及其他木质材料。

子目注释：

一、子目4401.31所称“木屑棒”是指由木材加工业、家具制造业及其他木材加工活动中产生的副产品(例如，刨花、锯末及碎木片)直接压制而成或加入按重量计不超过3%的黏合剂后粘聚而成的产品。此类产品呈圆柱状，其直径不超过25毫米，长度不超过100毫米。

税则号列	货品名称〔CIQ扩展编码及品名－T2表示见附表2〕	最惠(%)	暂定税率	普通	增值/消费	出口退税	计量单位	监管条件	检验检疫	特殊证件对美关税
44.01	薪柴(圆木段、块、枝、成捆或类似形状)；木片或木粒；锯末、木废料及碎片，不论是否粘结成圆木段、块、片或类似形状：									
	-薪柴(圆木段、块、枝、成捆或类似形状)									
4401.1100	--针叶木〔999〕	0		70	13/	0	千克	AB	PQ	/
4401.1200	--非针叶木〔999〕	0		70	13/	0	千克	AB	PQ	/30
	-木片或木粒：									
4401.2100	--针叶木									
4401.2100　10	濒危针叶木木片或木粒〔999〕	0		8	13/	0	千克	ABFE	PQ	/30
4401.2100　90	其他针叶木木片或木粒〔999〕	0		8	13/	0	千克	AB	PQ	/30
4401.2200	--非针叶木									

SECTION Ⅸ
WOOD AND ARTICLES OF WOOD; WOOD CHARCOAL; CORK AND ARTICLES OF CORK; MANUFACTURES OF STRAW, OF ESPARTO OR OF OTHER PLAITING MATERIALS; BASKETWARE AND WICKERWORK

Chapter 44
Wood and articles of wood; wood charcoal

Notes:

1. This Chapter does not cover:
   (a) Wood, in chips, in shavings, crushed, ground or powdered, of a kind used primarily in perfumery, in pharmacy, or for insecticidal, fungicidal or similar purposes (heading No. 12.11);
   (b) Bamboos or other materials of a woody nature of a kind used primarily for plaiting, in the rough, whether or not split, sawn lengthwise or cut to length (heading No. 14.01);
   (c) Wood, in chips, in shavings, ground or powdered, of a kind used primarily in dyeing or in tanning (heading No. 14.04);
   (d) Activated charcoal (heading No. 38.02);
   (e) Articles of heading No. 42.02;
   (f) Goods of Chapter 46;
   (g) Footwear or parts thereof of Chapter 64;
   (h) Goods of Chapter 66 (for example, umbrellas and walking-sticks and parts thereof);
   (i) Goods of heading No. 68.08;
   (j) Imitation jewellery of heading No. 71.17;
   (k) Goods of Section ⅩⅥ or Section ⅩⅦ (for example, machine parts, cases, covers, cabinets for machines and apparatus and wheel wrights' wares);
   (l) Goods of Section ⅩⅧ (for example, clock cases and musical instruments and parts thereof);
   (m) Parts of firearms (heading No. 93.05);
   (n) Articles of Chapter 94 (for example, furniture, lamps and lighting fittings, prefabricated buildings);
   (o) Articles of Chapter 95 (for example, toys, games, sports requisites);
   (p) Articles of Chapter 96 (for example, smoking pipes and parts thereof, buttons, pencils unipod, bipod, trpod or the Like) excluding bodies and handles, of wood, for articles of heading No. 96.03;
   (q) Articles, of Chapter 97 (for example, works of art).

2. In this Chapter, the expression "densified wood" means wood which has been subjected to chemical or physical treatment (being, in the case of layers bonded together, treatment in excess of that needed to ensure a good bond), and which has thereby acquired increased density or hardness together with improved mechanical strength or resistance to chemical or electrical agencies.
3. Headings No. 44.14 to 44.21 apply to articles of the respective descriptions of particle board or similar board, fibreboard, laminated wood or densified wood as they apply to such articles of wood.
4. Products of heading No. 44.10, 44.11 or 44.12 may be worked to form the shapes provided for in respect of the goods of heading No. 44.09, curved, corrugated, perforated, cut or formed to shapes other than square or rectangular or submitted to any other operation provided it does not give them the character of articles of other headings.
5. Heading No. 44.17 does not apply to tools in which the blade, working edge, working surface or other working part is formed by any of the materials specified in Note 1 to Chapter 82.
6. Subject to Note 1 above and except where the context otherwise requires, any reference to "wood" in a heading of this Chapter applies also to bamboos and other materials of a woody nature.

Subheading Note:

1. For the purposes of Subheading 4401.31, the expression "wood pellets" means by-products such as cutter shavings, sawdust or chips, of the mechanical wood processing industry, furnitrue-mading industry or other wood transformation activities, which have been agglomerated either directly by compression or by the addition of a binder in a proportion not exceeding 3% by weight. Such pellets are cylindrical, with a diameter not exceeding 25mm and a length not exceeding 100mm

协定税率 %										特惠税率 %			Article Description
亚太5国	东/冰/格	巴基斯坦	韩国	瑞士	哥达	秘鲁	澳大利亚	新西/坡/智	港/澳/台	亚太2国	老/柬/缅	36/3/1	
													Fuel wood, in logs, in billets, in twigs, in faggots or in similar forms; wood in chips or particles; sawdust and wood waste and scrap, whether or not agglomerated in logs, briquettes, pellets or similar forms:
													-Fuel wood, in logs, in billets, in twigs, in faggots or in similar forms
												0/0/0	--Coniferous
												0/0/0	--Non-coniferous
													-Wood in chips or particles:
													--Coniferous
												0/0/0	Chips or particles of endangered coniferous wood
												0/0/0	Chips or particles of other coniferous wood
													--Non-coniferous

税则号列		货品名称〔CIQ 扩展编码及品名—T2 表示见附表 2〕	最惠(%)	暂定税率	普通	增值/消费	出口退税	计量单位	监管条件	检验检疫	特殊证件对美关税
4401.2200	10	濒危非针叶木木片或木粒〔999〕	0		8	13/	0	千克	ABFE	PQ	/25
4401.2200	90	其他非针叶木木片或木粒〔999〕	0		8	13/	0	千克	AB	PQ	/25
		-锯末、木废料及碎片,粘结成圆木段、块、片或类似形状:									
4401.3100		--木屑棒〔999〕	0		8	13/	0	千克	9AB	MPQ	/25
4401.3900		--其他〔102〕	0		8	13/	0	千克	9AB	MPQ	/25
4401.4000		-锯末、木废料及碎片,未粘结的〔999〕	0		8	13/	0	千克	AB	MPQ	/25
44.02		**木炭(包括果壳炭及果核炭),不论是否结块:**									
4402.1000		-竹炭的〔999〕	6	4	70	13/	0	千克			/
4402.9000		-其他									
4402.9000	10	以木材为原料直接烧制的木炭〔999〕	6	4	70	13/	0	千克	8		/29
4402.9000	90	其他木炭(包括果壳炭及果核炭,不论是否结块)〔999〕	6	4	70	13/	0	千克			/29
44.03		**原木,不论是否去皮、去边材或粗锯成方:**									
		-用油漆、着色剂、杂酚油或其他防腐剂处理:									
4403.1100		--针叶木									
4403.1100	10	油漆,着色剂等处理的红豆杉原木(包括用杂酚油或其他防腐剂处理)〔999〕	0		8	9/	0	千克/立方米	8AF	MPQ	/25
4403.1100	20	油漆,着色剂等处理的其他濒危针叶木原木(包括用杂酚油或其他防腐剂处理)〔999〕	0		8	9/	0	千克/立方米	8AF	MPQ	/25
4403.1100	90	其他油漆,着色剂等处理的针叶木原木(包括用杂酚油或其他防腐剂处理)〔999〕	0		8	9/	0	千克/立方米	8A	MPQ	/25
4403.1200		--非针叶木									
4403.1200	10	油漆,着色剂等处理的濒危非针叶木原木(包括用杂酚油或其他防腐剂处理)〔999〕	0		8	9/	0	千克/立方米	8AF	MPQ	/20
4403.1200	90	其他油漆,着色剂等处理的非针叶木原木(包括用杂酚油或其他防腐剂处理)〔999〕	0		8	9/	0	千克/立方米	8A	MPQ	/20
		-其他,针叶木:									
		--松木,截面尺寸在 15 厘米及以上:									
4403.2110		---红松和樟子松									
4403.2110	10	截面尺寸在 15 厘米及以上的红松原木(用油漆着色剂,杂酚油或其他防腐剂处理的除外)〔999〕	0		8	9/	0	千克/立方米	8AEF	MPQ	/25
4403.2110	90	截面尺寸在 15 厘米及以上的樟子松原木(用油漆着色剂,杂酚油或其他防腐剂处理的除外)〔999〕	0		8	9/	0	千克/立方米	8A	MPQ	/25
4403.2120		---辐射松〔999〕	0		8	9/	0	千克/立方米	8A	MPQ	/
4403.2130		---落叶松〔999〕	0		8	9/	0	千克/立方米	8A	MPQ	/25
4403.2140		---花旗松〔999〕	0		8	9/	0	千克/立方米	8A	MPQ	/5
4403.2190		---其他									
4403.2190	10	截面尺寸在 15 厘米及以上的濒危松木原木(用油漆着色剂,杂酚油或其他防腐剂处理的除外)〔999〕	0		8	9/	0	千克/立方米	8AF	MPQ	/25
4403.2190	90	截面尺寸在 15 厘米及以上的其他松木原木(用油漆着色剂,杂酚油或其他防腐剂处理的除外)〔999〕	0		8	9/	0	千克/立方米	8A	MPQ	/25
		--其他松木:									
4403.2210		---红松和樟子松									
4403.2210	10	截面尺寸在 15 厘米以下的红松原木(用油漆着色剂,杂酚油或其他防腐剂处理的除外)〔999〕	0		8	9/	0	千克/立方米	8AEF	MPQ	/
4403.2210	90	截面尺寸在 15 厘米以下的樟子松原木(用油漆着色剂,杂酚油或其他防腐剂处理的除外)〔999〕	0		8	9/	0	千克/立方米	8A	MPQ	/
4403.2220		---辐射松〔999〕	0		8	9/	0	千克/立方米	8A	MPQ	/
4403.2230		---落叶松〔999〕	0		8	9/	0	千克/立方米	8A	MPQ	/
4403.2240		---花旗松〔999〕	0		8	9/	0	千克/立方米	8A	MPQ	/20
4403.2290		---其他									

协定税率 %										特惠税率 %			
亚太5国	东/冰/格	巴基斯坦	韩国	瑞士	哥达	秘鲁	澳大利亚	新西/坡/智	港/澳/台	亚太2国	老/柬/缅	36/3/1	Article Description
												0/0/0	Chips or particles of endangered non-coniferous wood
												0/0/0	Chips or particles of other non-coniferous wood
													-Sawdust and wood waste and scrap, agglomerated in logs, briquettes, pellets or similar forms:
												0/0/0	--Wood pellets
												0/0/0	—Other
												0/0/0	-Sawdust and wood waste and sctap, whether or not agglomer-ated in logs, briquettes, pellets or similar
													Wood charcoal (including shell or nut charcoal), whether or not agglomerated:
	0/0/	4.5	4.2	3.2	0	0	0	0/0/0	0/0/			0/0/	-Of bamboo
													-Other
	0/0/	4.5	4.2	3.2	0	0	0	0/0/0	0/0/			0/0/	Wood charcoal, obtained by burning wood
	0/0/	4.5	4.2	3.2	0	0	0	0/0/0	0/0/			0/0/	Other wood charcoal (including shell or nut charcoal, whether or not agglomerated)
													Wood in the rough, whether or not stripped of bark or sapwood, or roughly squared:
													-Treated with paint, stains, creosote or other preservatives(treated with paint, stains, creosote or other preservatives)
													--Coniferous
												0/0/0	Rough wood of Taxaceae , treated with paint, stains, creosote or other preservatives
												0/0/0	Other endangered rough wood of coniferous, treated with paint, stains, creosote or other preservatives
												0/0/0	Other rough wood of coniferous, treated with paint, stains, creosote or other preservatives
													--Non-coniferous
												0/0/0	Endangered rough wood of non-coniferous, treated with paint, stains, creosote or other preservatives
												0/0/0	Rough wood of non-coniferous, treated with paint, stains, creosote or other preservatives
													-Other coniferous:
													--Of pine (Pinus spp.), *of which any cross—sectional di—mension is 15 cm or more*:
													---Korean pine and Mongolian scotch pine
												0/0/0	*Korean pine rough wood (other than that treated with paint, stains, creosote or other preservatives), of which cross-sectional dimension≥15cm*
												0/0/0	*Mongolian scotch pine rough wood (other than that treated with paint, stains, creosote or other preservatives), of which cross-sectional dimension≥15cm*
												0/0/0	*--Radiata pine*
												0/0/0	*---Larch*
												0/0/0	*---Douglas fir*
													---Other
												0/0/0	*Endangered pine rough wood (other than that treated with paint, stains, creosote or other preservatives), of which cross-sectional dimension≥15cm*
												0/0/0	*Other pine rough wood (other than that treated with paint, stains, creosote or other preservatives), of which cross-sectional dimension ≥15cm*
													--Of pine (Pinus spp.), *other*:
													---Korean pine and Mongolian scotch pine
												0/0/0	*Korean pine rough wood (other than that treated with paint, stains, creosote or other preservatives), of which cross-sectional dimension < 15cm*
												0/0/0	*Mongolian scotch pine rough wood (other than that treated with paint, stains, creosote or other preservatives), of which cross-sectional dimension < 15cm*
												0/0/0	*---Radiata pine*
												0/0/0	*--Of fir* (Abies spp.) *and spruce* (Picea spp.), *of which any cross-sectional dimension is 15 cm or more*
												0/0/0	*--Of fir* (Abies spp.) *and spruce* (Picea spp.), *other*
													---Other

税则号列		货品名称〔CIQ扩展编码及品名－T2表示见附表2〕	最惠(%)	暂定税率	普通	增值/消费	出口退税	计量单位	监管条件	检验检疫	特殊证件对美关税
4403.2290	10	截面尺寸在15厘米以下的濒危其他松木原木(用油漆着色剂,杂酚油或其他防腐剂处理的除外)〔999〕	0		8	9/	0	千克/立方米	8AF	MPQ	/20
4403.2290	90	截面尺寸在15厘米以下的其他松木原木(用油漆着色剂,杂酚油或其他防腐剂处理的除外)〔999〕	0		8	9/	0	千克/立方米	8A	MPQ	/20
4403.2300		--冷杉和云杉,截面尺寸在15厘米及以上									
4403.2300	10	截面尺寸在15厘米及以上的濒危云杉和冷杉原木(用油漆着色剂,杂酚油或其他防腐剂处理的除外)〔999〕	0		8	9/	0	千克/立方米	8AF	MPQ	/20
4403.2300	90	截面尺寸在15厘米及以上的其他云杉和冷杉原木(用油漆着色剂,杂酚油或其他防腐剂处理的除外)〔999〕	0		8	9/	0	千克/立方米	8A	MPQ	/20
4403.2400		--其他冷杉和云杉									
4403.2400	10	截面尺寸在15厘米以下的濒危云杉和冷杉原木(用油漆着色剂,杂酚油或其他防腐剂处理的除外)〔999〕	0		8	9/	0	千克/立方米	8AF	MPQ	/25
4403.2400	90	截面尺寸在15厘米以下的其他云杉和冷杉原木(用油漆着色剂,杂酚油或其他防腐剂处理的除外)〔999〕	0		8	9/	0	千克/立方米	8A	MPQ	/25
4403.2500		--其他,截面尺寸在15厘米及以上									
4403.2500	10	截面尺寸在15厘米及以上的红豆杉原木(用油漆着色剂,杂酚油或其他防腐剂处理的除外)〔999〕	0		8	9/	0	千克/立方米	8AF	MPQ	/5
4403.2500	20	截面尺寸在15厘米及以上的其他濒危针叶木原木(用油漆着色剂,杂酚油或其他防腐剂处理的除外)〔999〕	0		8	9/	0	千克/立方米	8AF	MPQ	/5
4403.2500	90	截面尺寸在15厘米及以上的其他针叶木原木(用油漆着色剂,杂酚油或其他防腐剂处理的除外)〔999〕	0		8	9/	0	千克/立方米	8A	MPQ	/5
4403.2600		--其他									
4403.2600	10	截面尺寸在15厘米以下的红豆杉原木(用油漆着色剂,杂酚油或其他防腐剂处理的除外)〔999〕	0		8	9/	0	千克/立方米	8AF	MPQ	/20
4403.2600	20	截面尺寸在15厘米以下的其他濒危针叶木原木(用油漆着色剂,杂酚油或其他防腐剂处理的除外)〔999〕	0		8	9/	0	千克/立方米	8AF	MPQ	/20
4403.2600	90	截面尺寸在15厘米以下的其他针叶木原木(用油漆着色剂,杂酚油或其他防腐剂处理的除外)〔999〕	0		8	9/	0	千克/立方米	8A	MPQ	/20
		-其他,热带木:									
4403.4100		--深红色红柳桉木、浅红色红柳桉木及巴栲红柳桉木〔999〕	0		8	9/	0	千克/立方米	8A	MPQ	/
		--其他:									
4403.4910		---柚木〔999〕	0		35	9/	0	千克/立方米	8A	MPQ	/
4403.4920		---奥克曼(奥克榄)〔999〕	0		35	9/	0	千克/立方米	8A	MPQ	/
4403.4930		---龙脑香木(克隆)〔999〕	0		35	9/	0	千克/立方米	8A	MPQ	/
4403.4940		---山樟(香木)〔999〕	0		35	9/	0	千克/立方米	8A	MPQ	/
4403.4950		---印加木(波罗格)〔999〕	0		35	9/	0	千克/立方米	8A	MPQ	/
4403.4960		---大干巴豆(门格里斯或康派斯)〔999〕	0		35	9/	0	千克/立方米	8A	MPQ	/
4403.4970		---异翅香木〔999〕	0		35	9/	0	千克/立方米	8A	MPQ	/
4403.4980		---红木									
4403.4980	10	濒危热带红木原木(用油漆着色剂,杂酚油或其他防腐剂处理的除外)〔999〕	0		35	9/	0	千克/立方米	8AEF	MPQ	/
4403.4980	90	其他热带红木原木(用油漆着色剂,杂酚油或其他防腐剂处理的除外)〔999〕	0		35	9/	0	千克/立方米	8A	MPQ	/
4403.4990		---其他									
4403.4990	10	南美蒺藜木(玉檀木)原木(用油漆,着色剂,杂酚油或其他防腐剂处理的除外)〔101〕	0		8	9/	0	千克/立方米	8AEF	MPQ	/
4403.4990	20	其他濒危热带原木(用油漆,着色剂,杂酚油或其他防腐剂处理的除外)〔999〕	0		8	9/	0	千克/立方米	8AF	MPQ	/

协定税率 %										特惠税率 %			Article Description
亚太5国	东/冰/格	巴基斯坦	韩国	瑞士	哥达	秘鲁	澳大利亚	新西/坡/智	港/澳/台	亚太2国	老/柬/缅	36/3/1	
												0/0/0	*Other endangered pine rough wood (other than that treated with paint, stains, creosote or other preservatives), of which cross-sectional dimension < 15cm*
												0/0/0	*Other pine rough wood (other than that treated with paint, stains, creosote or other preservatives), of which cross-sectional dimension ≥15cm*
													--Of fir (Abies spp.) *and spruce* (Picea spp.), *of which any cross-sectional dimension is 15 cm or more*
												0/0/0	*Endangered pine(spruce and fir)rough wood(other than that treated with paint, stains, creosote or other preservatives), of which cross-sectional dimension≥15cm*
												0/0/0	*Other pine(spruce and fir)rough wood(other than that treated with paint, stains, creosote or other preservatives), of which cross-sectional dimension≥15cm*
													--Of fir (Abies spp.) *and spruce* (Picea spp.), *other*
												0/0/0	*Endangered pine(spruce and fir)rough wood(other than that treated with paint, stains, creosote or other preservatives), of which cross-sectional dimension < 15cm*
												0/0/0	*Other pine(spruce and fir)rough wood(other than that treated with paint, stains, creosote or other preservatives), of which cross-sectional dimension < 15cm*
													--Other, of which any cross-sec-tional dimension is 15 cm or more
												0/0/0	*Taxaceae pine rough wood (other than that treated with paint, stains, creosote or other preservatives), of which cross-sectional dimension≥15cm*
												0/0/0	*Other endangered rough wood of coniferous(other than that treated with paint, stains, creosote or other preservatives), of which cross-sectional dimension≥15cm*
												0/0/0	*Rough wood of coniferous (other than that treated with paint, stains, creosote or other preservatives), of which cross-sectional dimension≥15cm*
													--Other
												0/0/0	*Taxaceae pine rough wood (other than that treated with paint, stains, creosote or other preservatives), of which cross-sectional dimension < 15cm*
												0/0/0	*Other endangered rough wood of coniferous(other than that treated with paint, stains, creosote or other preservatives), of which cross-sectional dimension < 15cm*
												0/0/0	*Other rough wood of coniferous(other than that treated with paint, stains, creosote or other preservatives), of which cross-sectional dimension < 15cm*
													-Other, of tropical wood:
												0/0/0	*--Dark Red Meranti, Light Red Meranti and Meranti Bakau*
													--Other(of tropical non-contiferous wood specified in subheading note 1 to this chapter):
												0/0/0	*---Teak*
												0/0/0	---Okoume(*Au koumed*)
												0/0/0	---Dipterocarpus spp. *Keruing*
												0/0/0	---*Kapur* (Dryobalanops spp.)
												0/0/0	---Intsia spp. (*Mengaris*)
												0/0/0	---*Koompassiaspp.* (Mengaris or Kempas)
												0/0/0	---Anisopter *spp.*
													---Of rosewood
												0/0/0	Endangered tropic rose wood(other than that treated with paint, stains, creosote or other preservatives)
												0/0/0	Other tropic rose wood(other than that treated with paint, stains, creosote or other preservatives)
													---Other
												0/0/0	Bulnesia sarmientoi log(paint, colorant, creosote or other preservative treatmentexcept)
												0/0/0	Other endangered tropic rough wood(other than that treated with paint, stains, creosote or other preservatives)

税则号列		货品名称〔CIQ 扩展编码及品名—T2 表示见附表 2〕	最惠(%)	暂定税率	普通	增值/消费	出口退税	计量单位	监管条件	检验检疫	特殊证件对美关税
4403.4990	90	其他热带原木(用油漆,着色剂,杂酚油或其他防腐剂处理的除外)〔T2〕	0		8	9/	0	千克/立方米	8A	MPQ	/
		-其他:									
4403.9100		--栎木(橡木)									
4403.9100	10	蒙古栎原木(用油漆、着色剂、杂酚油或其他防腐剂处理的除外)〔999〕	0		8	9/	0	千克/立方米	8AEF	MPQ	/25
4403.9100	90	其他栎木(橡木)原木(用油漆、着色剂、杂酚油或其他防腐剂处理的除外)〔999〕	0		8	9/	0	千克/立方米	8A	MPQ	/25
4403.9300		--水青冈木(山毛榉木),截面尺寸在 15 厘米及以上〔999〕	0		8	9/	0	千克/立方米	8A	MPQ	/
4403.9400		--其他水青冈木(山毛榉木)〔999〕	0		8	9/	0	千克/立方米	8A	MPQ	/
4403.9500		--桦木,截面尺寸在 15 厘米及以上									
4403.9500	10	濒危的桦木,截面尺寸在 15 厘米及以上(用油漆,着色剂,杂酚油或其他防腐剂处理的除外)〔999〕	0		8	9/	0	千克/立方米	8AF	MPQ	/25
4403.9500	90	其他桦木,截面尺寸在 15 厘米及以上(用油漆,着色剂,杂酚油或其他防腐剂处理的除外)〔999〕	0		8	9/	0	千克/立方米	8A	MPQ	/25
4403.9600		--其他桦木									
4403.9600	10	濒危的桦木,截面尺寸在 15 厘米及以下(用油漆,着色剂,杂酚油或其他防腐剂处理的除外)〔999〕	0		8	9/	0	千克/立方米	8AF	MPQ	/
4403.9600	90	其他桦木,截面尺寸在 15 厘米及以下(用油漆,着色剂,杂酚油或其他防腐剂处理的除外)〔999〕	0		8	9/	0	千克/立方米	8A	MPQ	/
4403.9700		--杨木〔999〕	0		8	9/	0	千克/立方米	8A	MPQ	/25
4403.9800		--桉木〔999〕	0		8	9/	0	千克/立方米	8A	MPQ	/25
		--其他:									
4403.9930		---红木,但税号 4403.4980 所列热带红木除外									
4403.9930	10	濒危红木原木,但税号 4403.4980 所列热带红木除外(用油漆,着色剂,杂酚油或其他防腐剂处理的除外)〔999〕	0		35	9/	0	千克/立方米	8AEF	MPQ	/
4403.9930	90	其他红木原木,但税号 4403.4980 所列热带红木除外(用油漆,着色剂,杂酚油或其他防腐剂处理的除外)〔999〕	0		35	9/	0	千克/立方米	8A	MPQ	/
4403.9940		---泡桐木〔999〕	0		8	9/	0	千克/立方米	8A	PQ	/
4403.9950		---水曲柳〔999〕	0		8	9/	0	千克/立方米	8AF	MPQ	/
4403.9960		---北美硬阔叶木(包括樱桃木、黑胡桃木、槭木)〔999〕	0		8	9/	0	千克/立方米	8A	MPQ	/20
4403.9980		---其他未列名的温带非针叶木									
4403.9980	10	其他未列名温带濒危非针叶木原木(用油漆、着色剂、杂酚油或其他防腐剂处理的除外)〔101 加蓬榄木、非洲白梧桐木等原木,102 白柳桉原木及其他柳桉原木,103 羯布罗香木等原木,104 安哥拉香桃花心木等原木,105 其他非针叶原木〕	0		8	9/	0	千克/立方米	8AF	MPQ	/25
4403.9980	90	其他未列名温带非针叶木原木(用油漆、着色剂、杂酚油或其他防腐剂处理的除外)〔101 加蓬榄木、非洲白梧桐木等原木,102 白柳桉原木及其他柳桉原木,103 羯布罗香木等原木,104 安哥拉香桃花心木等原木,105 其他非针叶原木〕	0		8	9/	0	千克/立方米	8A	MPQ	/25
4403.9990		---其他									
4403.9990	12	沉香木及拟沉香木原木(用油漆,着色剂,杂酚油或其他防腐剂处理的除外)〔999〕	0		8	9/	0	千克/立方米	8AEF	MPQ	/25
4403.9990	19	其他未列名濒危非针叶原木(用油漆、着色剂、杂酚油或其他防腐剂处理的除外)〔101 加蓬榄木、非洲白梧桐木等原木,102 白柳桉原木及其他柳桉原木,103 羯布罗香木等原木,104 安哥拉香桃花心木等原木,105 其他非针叶原木〕	0		8	9/	0	千克/立方米	8AEF	MPQ	/25
4403.9990	90	其他未列名非针叶原木(用油漆、着色剂、杂酚油或其他防腐剂处理的除外)〔101 加蓬榄木、非洲白梧桐木等原木,102 白柳桉原木及其他柳桉原木,103 羯布罗香木等原木,104 安哥拉香桃花心木等原木,105 其他非针叶原木〕	0		8	9/	0	千克/立方米	8A	MPQ	/25
44.04		**箍木;木劈条;已削尖但未经纵锯的木桩;粗加修整但未经车圆、弯曲或其他方式加工的木棒,适合制手杖、伞柄、工具把柄及类似品;木片条及类似品:**									
4404.1000		-针叶木的									

协定税率 %										特惠税率 %			
亚太5国	东/冰/格	巴基斯坦	韩国	瑞士	哥达	秘鲁	澳大利亚	新西/坡/智	港/澳/台	亚太2国	老/柬/缅	36/3/1	Article Description
												0/0/0	Ohter tropical wood(the wood treated with paint, stains, creosote or other preservatives)
													-Other:
													--Of oak (*Quercus spp.*)
												0/0/0	Mongolia oak logs (paint, colorant, creosote or other preservative treatmentexcept)
												0/0/0	Other oak (oak) log (paint, colorant, creosote or other preservative treatmentexcept)
												0/0/0	--Of beech (*Fagus spp.*), of which any cross-sectional di-mension is 15cm or more
												0/0/0	--Of beech (*Fagus spp.*), other
													--Of birch (*Betula spp.*), of which any cross-sectional di-mension is 15cm or more
												0/0/0	Of endangered birch (*Betula spp.*), (other than that treated with paint, stains, creosote or other preservatives) of which any cross-sectional di-mension is 15cm or more
												0/0/0	Of other birch (*Betula spp.*), (other than that treated with paint, stains, creosote or other preservatives) of which any cross-sectional di-mension is 15cm or more
													--Of birch (*Betula spp.*), other
												0/0/0	Of endangered birch (*Betula spp.*), (other than that treated with paint, stains, creosote or other preservatives) of which any cross-sectional di-mension is 15cm or less
												0/0/0	Of other birch (*Betula spp.*), (other than that treated with paint, stains, creosote or other preservatives) of which any cross-sectional di-mension is 15cm or less
												0/0/0	--Of poplar and aspen (*Populus spp.*)
												0/0/0	--Of eucalyptus (*Eucalyptus spp.*)
													--Other:
													---Of rosewood, other than tropical wood of Subheading 4403.4980
												0/0/0	Endangered rosewood, but excluding tropical rosewood of subheading No.4403.4980
												0/0/0	Ohter rosewood log, excluding tropical rosewood of subheading No. 4403.4980(the wood treated with paint, stains, creosote or other preservatives)
												0/0/0	---Of Kiri (*Paulownia*)
												0/0/0	---Ash
												0/0/0	---North American hard wood (including cherry, walnut and maple)
													---Other, temperate non-coniferous, not specified
												0/0/0	Other temperate zone endangered non-coniferous wood (other than the wood treated with paint, stains, creosote or other preservatives) not elsewhere specified or included
												0/0/0	Other temperate zone non-coniferous wood (other than the wood treated with paint, stains, creosote or other preservatives) not elsewhere specified or included
													---Other
												0/0/0	Chinese eaglewood and similar chinese eaglewood (other than the wood treated with paint, stains, creosote or other preservatives)
												0/0/0	Other endangered non-coniferous wood in the rough(other than the wood treated with paint, stains, creosote or other preservatives)
												0/0/0	Other non-coniferous wood in the rough(other than the wood treated with paint, stains, creosote or other preservatives) not elsewhere specified or included
													Hoopwood; split poles; piles, pickets and stakes of wood, pointed but not sawn lengthwise; wooden sticks, roughly trimmed but not turned, bent or otherwise worked, suitable for the manufacture of walking-sticks, umbrellas, tool handles or the like; chipwood and the like:
													-Coniferous

税则号列		货品名称〔CIQ 扩展编码及品名一T2 表示见附表 2〕	最惠(%)	暂定税率	普通	增值/消费	出口退税	计量单位	监管条件	检验检疫	特殊证件对美关税
4404.1000	10	濒危针叶木的箍木等及类似品(包括木劈条、棒及类似品)〔999〕	6	4	50	13/	0	千克	ABFE	PQ	/
4404.1000	90	其他针叶木的箍木等及类似品(包括木劈条、棒及类似品)〔999〕	6	4	50	13/	0	千克	AB	PQ	/
4404.2000		-非针叶木的									
4404.2000	10	濒危非针叶木箍木等(包括木劈条、棒及类似品)〔999〕	6	4	50	13/	0	千克	ABFE	PQ	/24
4404.2000	90	其他非针叶木箍木等(包括木劈条、棒及类似品)〔101 其他木制品,102 其他碎木料、锯末、刨花〕	6	4	50	13/	0	千克	AB	PQ	/24
44.05		**木丝;木粉:**									
4405.0000		木丝;木粉〔999〕	6	4	40	13/	0	千克	AB	PQ	/29
44.06		**铁道及电车道枕木:**									
		-未浸渍									
4406.1100		--针叶木〔999〕	0		14	13/	0	千克/立方米	4ABxy	PQ	/
4406.1200		--非针叶木〔999〕	0		14	13/	0	千克/立方米	4ABxy	PQ	/
		-其他:									
4406.9100		--针叶木									
4406.9100	10	濒危已浸渍针叶木铁道及电车道枕木〔999〕	0		14	13/	0	千克/立方米	FE		/5
4406.9100	90	其他已浸渍的针叶木铁道及电车道枕木〔999〕	0		14	13/	0	千克/立方米			/5
4406.9200		--非针叶木									
4406.9200	10	濒危已浸渍非针叶木铁道及电车道枕木〔999〕	0		14	13/	0	千克/立方米	FE		/
4406.9200	90	其他已浸渍的非针叶木铁道及电车道枕木〔999〕	0		14	13/	0	千克/立方米			/
44.07		**经纵锯、纵切、刨切或旋切的木材,不论是否刨平、砂光或端部接合,厚度超过 6 毫米:**									
		-针叶木:									
		--松木:									
4407.1110		---红松和樟子松									
4407.1110	11	端部接合的红松厚板材(经纵锯、纵切、刨切或旋切的,厚度超过 6mm)〔999〕	0		14	13/	0	千克/立方米	ABEF	MPQ	/25
4407.1110	19	端部接合的樟子松厚板材(经纵锯、纵切、刨切或旋切的,厚度超过 6mm)〔999〕	0		14	13/	0	千克/立方米	AB	MPQ	/25
4407.1110	91	非端部接合的红松厚板材(经纵锯、纵切、刨切或旋切的,厚度超过 6mm)〔999〕	0		14	13/	0	千克/立方米	4ABEFxy	MPQ	/25
4407.1110	99	非端部接合的樟子松厚板材(经纵锯、纵切、刨切或旋切的,厚度超过 6mm)〔999〕	0		14	13/	0	千克/立方米	4ABxy	MPQ	/25
4407.1120		---辐射松									
4407.1120	10	端部接合的辐射松厚板材(经纵锯、纵切、刨切或旋切的,厚度超过 6mm)〔999〕	0		14	13/	0	千克/立方米	AB	MPQ	/25
4407.1120	90	非端部接合的辐射松厚板材(经纵锯、纵切、刨切或旋切的,厚度超过 6mm)〔999〕	0		14	13/	0	千克/立方米	4ABxy	MPQ	/25
4407.1130		---花旗松									
4407.1130	10	端部接合的花旗松厚板材(经纵锯、纵切、刨切或旋切的,厚度超过 6mm)〔999〕	0		14	13/	0	千克/立方米	AB	MPQ	/20
4407.1130	90	非端部接合的花旗松厚板材(经纵锯、纵切、刨切或旋切的,厚度超过 6mm)〔999〕	0		14	13/	0	千克/立方米	4ABxy	MPQ	/20
4407.1190		---其他:									
4407.1190	11	端部接合其他濒危松木厚板材(经纵锯、纵切、刨切或旋切的,厚度超过 6mm)〔999〕	0		14	13/	0	千克/立方米	ABEF	MPQ	/30
4407.1190	19	端部接合其他松木厚板材(经纵锯、纵切、刨切或旋切的,厚度超过 6mm)〔999〕	0		14	13/	0	千克/立方米	AB	MPQ	/30
4407.1190	91	非端部接合其他濒危松木厚板材(经纵锯、纵切、刨切或旋切的,厚度超过 6mm)〔999〕	0		14	13/	0	千克/立方米	4ABEFxy	MPQ	/30
4407.1190	99	非端部接合的其他松木厚板材(经纵锯、纵切、刨切或旋切的,厚度超过 6mm)〔999〕	0		14	13/	0	千克/立方米	4ABxy	MPQ	/30
4407.1200		--冷杉及云杉									
4407.1200	11	端部接合的濒危云杉及冷杉厚板材(经纵锯、纵切、刨切或旋切的,厚度超过 6mm)〔999〕	0		14	13/	0	千克/立方米	ABEF	MPQ	/25
4407.1200	19	端部接合的其他云杉及冷杉厚板材(经纵锯、纵切、刨切或旋切的,厚度超过 6mm)〔999〕	0		14	13/	0	千克/立方米	AB	MPQ	/25

协定税率 %										特惠税率 %			Article Description
亚太5国	东/冰/格	巴基斯坦	韩国	瑞士	哥达	秘鲁	澳大利亚	新西/坡/智	港/澳/台	亚太2国	老/柬/缅	36/3/1	
	0/0/	4	0	0	0	0	0	0/0/0	0/0/			0/0/	Hoopwood; split poles; wooden sticks or the like; of endangered coniferous wood
	0/0/	4	0	0	0	0	0	0/0/0	0/0/			0/0/	Other hoopwood; split poles; wooden sticks or the like; of coniferous wood
													-Non-coniferous
	0/0/	4	0	0	0	0	0	0/0/0	0/0/			0/0/	Hoopwood; split poles, wooden sticks or the like, of endangered non-coniferous wood
	0/0/	4	0	0	0	0	0	0/0/0	0/0/			0/0/	Other hoopwood; split poles, wooden sticks or the like, of non-coniferous wood
													Wood wool; wood flour:
	0/0/	4	0	0	0	0	0	0/0/0	0/0/			0/0/0	Wood wool; wood flour
													Railway or tramway sleepers (cross-ties) of wood:
													-Not impregnated
												0/0/0	--Coniferous
												0/0/0	--Non-coniferous
													-Other:
													--Coniferous
												0/0/0	Railway or tramway sleepers (crossties) of endangered Coniferous wood, impregnated
												0/0/0	Railway or tramway sleepers (crossties) of other Coniferous wood, impregnated
													--Non-coniferous
												0/0/0	Railway or tramway sleepers (crossties) of endangered non-Coniferous wood, impregnated
												0/0/0	Railway or tramway sleepers (crossties) of other non-Coniferous wood, impregnated
													Wood sawn or chipped lengthwise, sliced or peeled, whether or not planed, sanded or finger-jointed, of a thickness exceeding 6 mm:
													-Coniferous:
													--Of pine (*Pinus spp.*):
													---Korean pine and Mongolian scotch pine
												0/0/0	Korean pine wood, sawn or chipped lengthwise, sliced or peeled, end-jointed, of a thickness exceeding 6mm
												0/0/0	Mongolian scotch pine wood sawn or chipped lengthwise, sliced or peeled, end-jointed, of a thickness exceeding 6mm
												0/0/0	Korean pine and Mongolian scotch pine wood, sawn or chipped lengthwise, sliced or peeled, not end-jointed, of a thickness exceeding 6mm
												0/0/0	Wood sawn or chipped lengthwise, sliced or peeled, not end jointed, of Mongolian scocth pine, of a thinkness exceeding 6mm
													---Rediata pine
												0/0/0	Radiata pine wood sawn or chipped lengthwise, sliced or peeled, end-jointed, of a thickness exceeding 6mm
												0/0/0	Radiata pine wood sawn or chipped lengthwise, sliced or peeled, end-jointed, of a thickness exceeding 6mm
													---Douglas fir
												0/0/0	Radiata pine wood sawn or chipped lengthwise, sliced or peeled, end-jointed, of a thickness exceeding 6mm
												0/0/0	Douglas fir wood sawn or chipped lengthwise, sliced or peeled, not end-jointed, of a thickness exceeding 6mm
													---Other:
												0/0/0	Other endangered spine wood of conifer, sawn or chipped lengthwise, sliced or peeled, end-jointed, of a thickness exceeding 6mm
												0/0/0	Other pine wood of conifes sawn or chipped lengthwise, sliced or peeled, end-jointed, of a thickness exceeding 6mm
												0/0/0	Other endangered pine wood sawn or chipped lengthwise, sliced or peeled, end-jointed, of a thickness exceeding 6mm
												0/0/0	Other pine wood, sawn or chipped lengthwise, sliced or peeled, not end-jointed, of a thickness exceeding 6mm
													--Of fir (*Abies spp.*) and sprue (*Picea spp.*)
												0/0/0	Endangered spruce and fir, sawn or chipped lengthwise, sliced or peeled, end-jointed, of a thickness exceeding 6mm
												0/0/0	Other spruce and fir, sawn or chipped lengthwise, sliced or peeled, end-jointed, of a thickness exceeding 6mm

税则号列	货品名称〔CIQ扩展编码及品名—T2表示见附表2〕	最惠(%)	暂定税率	普通	增值/消费	出口退税	计量单位	监管条件	检验检疫	特殊证件对美关税
4407.1200 91	非端部接合濒危云杉及冷杉厚板材(经纵锯、纵切、刨切或旋切的,厚度超过6mm)〔999〕	0		14	13/	0	千克/立方米	4ABEFxy	MPQ	/25
4407.1200 99	非端部接合其他云杉及冷杉厚板材(经纵锯、纵切、刨切或旋切的,厚度超过6mm)〔999〕	0		14	13/	0	千克/立方米	4ABxy	MPQ	/25
4407.1900	--其他									
4407.1900 11	端部接合其他濒危针叶木厚板材(经纵锯、纵切、刨切或旋切的,厚度超过6mm)〔999〕	0		14	13/	0	千克/立方米	ABEF	MPQ	/30
4407.1900 19	端部接合其他针叶木厚板材(经纵锯、纵切、刨切或旋切的,厚度超过6mm)〔999〕	0		14	13/	0	千克/立方米	AB	MPQ	/30
4407.1900 91	非端部接合其他濒危针叶木厚板材(经纵锯、纵切、刨切或旋切的,厚度超过6mm)〔999〕	0		14	13/	0	千克/立方米	4ABEFxy	MPQ	/30
4407.1900 99	非端部接合的其他针叶木厚板材(经纵锯、纵切、刨切或旋切的,厚度超过6mm)〔999〕	0		14	13/	0	千克/立方米	4ABxy	MPQ	/30
	-热带木:									
4407.2100	--美洲桃花心木									
4407.2100 10	端部接合美洲桃花心木(经纵锯、纵切、刨切或旋切的,厚度超过6mm)〔999〕	0		14	13/	0	千克/立方米	FEAB	MPQ	/
4407.2100 90	非端部接合美洲桃花心木(经纵锯、纵切、刨切或旋切的,厚度超过6mm)〔999〕	0		14	13/	0	千克/立方米	y4xAFEB	MPQ	/
4407.2200	--苏里南肉豆蔻木、细孔绿心樟及美洲轻木									
4407.2200 10	端部接合的苏里南肉豆蔻木、细孔绿心樟及美洲轻木(经纵锯、纵切、刨切或旋切的,厚度超过6mm)〔999〕	0		14	13/	0	千克/立方米	AB	MPQ	/
4407.2200 90	非端部接合的苏里南肉豆蔻木、细孔绿心樟及美洲轻木(经纵锯、纵切、刨切或旋切的,厚度超过6mm)〔999〕	0		14	13/	0	千克/立方米	4ABxy	MPQ	/
4407.2500	--深红色红柳桉木、浅红色红柳桉木及巴栲红柳桉木									
4407.2500 10	端部接合的红柳桉木板材(指深红色、浅红色及巴栲红柳桉木,厚度超过6mm)〔999〕	0		14	13/	0	千克/立方米	AB	MPQ	/
4407.2500 90	非端部接合的红柳桉木板材(指深红色、浅红色及巴栲红柳桉木,经纵锯、纵切、刨切或旋切的,厚度超过6mm)〔999〕	0		14	13/	0	千克/立方米	y4xAB	MPQ	/
4407.2600	--白柳桉木、白色红柳桉木、白色柳桉木、黄色红柳桉木及阿兰木									
4407.2600 10	端部接合的白柳桉,其他柳桉木和阿兰木板材(经纵锯、纵切、刨切或旋切的,厚度超过6mm)〔999〕	0		14	13/	0	千克/立方米	AB	MPQ	/
4407.2600 90	非端部接合的白柳桉,其他柳桉木和阿兰木板材(经纵锯、纵切、刨切或旋切的,厚度超过6mm)〔999〕	0		14	13/	0	千克/立方米	y4xAB	MPQ	/
4407.2700	--沙比利									
4407.2700 10	端部接合的沙比利木板材(经纵锯、纵切、刨切或旋切的,厚度超过6mm)〔999〕	0		40	13/	0	千克/立方米	AB	MPQ	/
4407.2700 90	非端部接合的沙比利木板材(经纵锯、纵切、刨切或旋切的,厚度超过6mm)〔999〕	0		40	13/	0	千克/立方米	4ABxy	MPQ	/
4407.2800	--伊罗科木									
4407.2800 10	端部接合的伊罗科木板材(经纵锯、纵切、刨切或旋切的,厚度超过6mm)〔999〕	0		14	13/	0	千克/立方米	AB	MPQ	/
4407.2800 90	非端部接合的伊罗科木板材(经纵锯、纵切、刨切或旋切的,厚度超过6mm)〔999〕	0		14	13/	0	千克/立方米	4ABxy	MPQ	/
	--其他:									
4407.2910	---柚木									
4407.2910 10	端部接合的柚木板材(经纵锯、纵切、刨切或旋切的,厚度超过6mm)〔999〕	0		40	13/	0	千克/立方米	AB	PQ	/25
4407.2910 90	非端部接合的柚木板材(经纵锯、纵切、刨切或旋切的,厚度超过6mm)〔999〕	0		40	13/	0	千克/立方米	y4xAB	PQ	/25
4407.2920	---非洲桃花心木									
4407.2920 10	端部接合的非洲桃花心木板材(经纵锯、纵切、刨切或旋切的,厚度超过6mm)〔999〕	0		40	13/	0	千克/立方米	AB	MPQ	/
4407.2920 90	非端部接合的非洲桃花心木板材(经纵锯、纵切、刨切或旋切的,厚度超过6mm)〔999〕	0		40	13/	0	千克/立方米	AB	MPQ	/
4407.2930	---波罗格									
4407.2930 10	端部接合的波罗格Merban板材(经纵锯、纵切、刨切或旋切的,厚度超过6mm)〔999〕	0		40	13/	0	千克/立方米	AB	MPQ	/25

协定税率 %										特惠税率 %			Article Description
亚太5国	东/冰/格	巴基斯坦	韩国	瑞士	哥达	秘鲁	澳大利亚	新西/坡/智	港/澳/台	亚太2国	老/柬/缅	36/3/1	
												0/0/0	Endangered spruce and fir, sawn or chipped lengthwise, sliced or peeled, not end-jointed, of a thickness exceeding 6mm
												0/0/0	Other spruce and fir, sawn or chipped lengthwise, sliced or peeled, not end-jointed, of a thickness exceeding 6mm
													--Other
												0/0/0	Endangered coniferous, sawn or chipped lengthwise, sliced or peeled, end-jointed, of a thickness exceeding 6mm
												0/0/0	Other coniferous and fir, sawn or chipped lengthwise, sliced or peeled, end-jointed, of a thickness exceeding 6mm
												0/0/0	Endangered coniferous, sawn or chipped lengthwise, sliced or peeled, not end-jointed, of a thickness exceeding 6mm
												0/0/0	Other coniferous and fir, sawn or chipped lengthwise, sliced or peeled, not end-jointed, of a thickness exceeding 6mm
													-Of tropical wood:
													--Mahogany (Swietenia spp.)
												0/0/0	Wood sawn or chipped lengthwise, sliced or peeled, of mashogany (swietenia spp.), end-jointed, thickness>6mm
												0/0/0	Wood sawn or chipped lengthwise, sliced or peeled, of mashogany (swietenia spp.), not-end-jointed, thickness>6mm
													--Virola, Imbuia and Balsa
												0/0/0	Wood sawn or chipped lengthwise, sliced or peeled, of virola, embuia and American light wood, end-jointed, thickness>6mm
												0/0/0	Wood sawn or chipped lengthwise, sliced or peeled, of virola, embuia and American light wood, not end-jointed
													--Dark Red Meranti, Light Red Meranti and Meranti Bakau
												0/0/0	Wood sawn or chipped lengthwise, sliced or peeled, of Dark Red Meranti, Light Red Meranti and Meranti Bakau, end-jointed, thickness>6mm
												0/0/0	Wood sawn or chipped lengthwise, sliced or peeled, of Dark Red Meranti, Light Red Meranti and Meranti Bakau, not end-jointed, thickness>6mm
													--White Lauan, White Meranti, White Seraya, Yellow Meranti and Alan
												0/0/0	Wood sawn or chipped lengthwise, sliced or peeled, of White Lauan, White Meranti, White Seraya, Yellow Meranti and Alan, end-jointed, thickness>6mm
												0/0/0	Wood sawn or chipped lengthwise, sliced or peeled, of White Lauan, White Meranti, White Seraya, Yellow Meranti and Alan, not end-jointed, thickness>6mm
													--Sapelli
												0/0/0	Wood sawn or chipped lengihwise, sliced or peeled, of sapelli, end-jointed, thinkness>6mm
												0/0/0	Wood sawn or chipped lengthwise, sliced or peeled, of sapelli, not end-jointed, thinkness>6mm
													--Iroko
												0/0/0	Wood sawn or chipped lengthwise, sliced or peeled, of Iroko, end-jointed, thickness>6mm
												0/0/0	Wood sawn or chipped lengthwise, sliced or peeled, of Iroko, not end-jointed, thickness>6mm
													--Other:
													---Teak
												0/0/0	Wood sawn or chipped lengthwise, sliced or peeled, of teak, end-jointed, thickness>6mm
												0/0/0	Wood sawn or chipped lengthwise, sliced or peeled, of teak, not end-jointed, thickness>6mm
													---Acajou
												0/0/0	Wood sawn or chipped lengthwise, sliced or peeled, of acajou, end-jointed, thickness>6mm
												0/0/0	Wood sawn or chipped lengthwise, sliced or peeled, of acajou, not end-jointed, thickness>6mm
													---Merban
												0/0/0	Wood sawn or chipped lengthwise, sliced or peeled, of merban, end-jointed, thickness>6mm

税则号列		货品名称〔CIQ 扩展编码及品名—T2 表示见附表 2〕	最惠(%)	暂定税率	普通	增值/消费	出口退税	计量单位	监管条件	检验检疫	特殊证件对美关税
4407.2930	90	非端部接合的波罗格 Merban 板材(经纵锯、纵切、刨切或旋切的,厚度超过 6mm)〔999〕	0		40	13/	0	千克/立方米	AB	MPQ	/25
4407.2940		---红木									
4407.2940	11	端部接合濒危热带红木厚板材(经纵锯、纵切、刨切或旋切的,厚度超过 6mm)〔999〕	0		40	13/	0	千克/立方米	FEAB	MPQ	/
4407.2940	19	端部接合其他热带红木厚板材(经纵锯、纵切、刨切或旋切的,厚度超过 6mm)〔999〕	0		40	13/	0	千克/立方米	AB	MPQ	/
4407.2940	91	非端部接合濒危热带红木厚板材(经纵锯、纵切、刨切或旋切的,厚度超过 6mm)〔999〕	0		40	13/	0	千克/立方米	4ABEFxy	MPQ	/
4407.2940	99	非端部接合其他热带红木厚板材(经纵锯、纵切、刨切或旋切的,厚度超过 6mm)〔999〕	0		40	13/	0	千克/立方米	4ABxy	MPQ	/
4407.2990		---其他									
4407.2990	11	端部接合拉敏木厚板材(经纵锯、纵切、刨切或旋切的,厚度超过 6mm)〔999〕	0		14	13/	0	千克/立方米	FEAB	MPQ	/25
4407.2990	12	端部接合的南美蒺藜木(玉檀木)厚板材(经纵锯、纵切、刨切或旋切的,厚度超过 6mm)〔101〕	0		14	13/	0	千克/立方米	FEAB	MPQ	/25
4407.2990	13	端部接合其他未列名濒危热带木厚板材(经纵锯、纵切、刨切或旋切的,厚度超过 6mm)〔999〕	0		14	13/	0	千克/立方米	FEAB	MPQ	/25
4407.2990	19	端部接合其他未列名热带木厚板材(经纵锯、纵切、刨切或旋切的,厚度超过 6mm)〔101〕	0		14	13/	0	千克/立方米	AB	MPQ	/25
4407.2990	91	非端部接合的南美蒺藜木(玉檀木)厚板材(经纵锯、纵切、刨切或旋切的,厚度超过 6mm)〔101〕	0		14	13/	0	千克/立方米	y4xAFEB	MPQ	/25
4407.2990	92	非端部接合其他未列名濒危热带木板材(经纵锯、纵切、刨切或旋切的,厚度超过 6mm)〔999〕	0		14	13/	0	千克/立方米	y4xAFEB	MPQ	/25
4407.2990	99	非端部接合其他未列名热带木板材(经纵锯、纵切、刨切或旋切的,厚度超过 6mm)[T2]	0		14	13/	0	千克/立方米	y4xAB	MPQ	/25
		-其他:									
4407.9100		--栎木(橡木)									
4407.9100	11	端部接合的蒙古栎厚板材(经纵锯、纵切、刨切或旋切的,厚度>6 毫米)〔999〕	0		14	13/	0	千克/立方米	ABEF	PQ	/25
4407.9100	19	端部接合的其他栎木(橡木)厚板材(经纵锯、纵切、刨切或旋切的,厚度超过 6mm)〔999〕	0		14	13/	0	千克/立方米	AB	PQ	/25
4407.9100	91	非端部接合的蒙古栎厚板材(经纵锯、纵切、刨切或旋切的,厚度>6 毫米)〔999〕	0		14	13/	0	千克/立方米	y4xAFEB	PQ	/25
4407.9100	99	非端部接合的其他栎木(橡木)厚板材(经纵锯、纵切、刨切或旋切的,厚度超过 6mm)〔999〕	0		14	13/	0	千克/立方米	y4xAB	PQ	/25
4407.9200		--水青冈(山毛榉木)									
4407.9200	10	端部接合的水青冈木(山毛榉木)厚板材(经纵锯、纵切、刨切或旋切的,厚度超过 6mm)〔999〕	0		14	13/	0	千克/立方米	ABE	PQ	/25
4407.9200	90	非端部接合的水青冈木(山毛榉木)厚板材(经纵锯、纵切、刨切或旋切的,厚度超过 6mm)〔999〕	0		14	13/	0	千克/立方米	4ABExy	PQ	/25
4407.9300		--槭木(枫木)									
4407.9300	10	端部接合的槭木(枫木)厚板材(经纵锯、纵切、刨切或旋切,厚度超过 6mm)〔999〕	0		14	13/	0	千克/立方米	AB	MPQ	/5
4407.9300	90	非端部接合的槭木(枫木)厚板材(经纵锯、纵切、刨切或旋切,厚度超过 6mm)〔999〕	0		14	13/	0	千克/立方米	4ABxy	MPQ	/5
4407.9400		--樱桃木									
4407.9400	10	端部接合的樱桃木厚板材(经纵锯、纵切、刨切或旋切的,厚度超过 6mm)〔999〕	0		14	13/	0	千克/立方米	AB	MPQ	/20
4407.9400	90	非端部接合的樱桃木厚板材(经纵锯、纵切、刨切或旋切的,厚度超过 6mm)〔999〕	0		14	13/	0	千克/立方米	4ABxy	MPQ	/20
4407.9500		--白蜡木									
4407.9500	11	端部接合的水曲柳厚板材(经纵锯、纵切、刨切或旋切的,厚度>6 毫米)〔999〕	0		14	13/	0	千克/立方米	ABEF	MPQ	/20
4407.9500	19	端部接合的白蜡木厚板材(经纵锯、纵切、刨切或旋切的,厚度超过 6mm)〔999〕	0		14	13/	0	千克/立方米	AB	MPQ	/20
4407.9500	91	非端部接合的水曲柳厚板材(经纵锯、纵切、刨切或旋切的,厚度>6 毫米)〔999〕	0		14	13/	0	千克/立方米	y4xAFEB	MPQ	/20
4407.9500	99	非端部接合的白蜡木厚板材(经纵锯、纵切、刨切或旋切的,厚度超过 6mm)〔999〕	0		14	13/	0	千克/立方米	4ABxy	MPQ	/20
4407.9600		--桦木									

协定税率 %										特惠税率 %			
亚太5国	东/冰/格	巴基斯坦	韩国	瑞士	哥达	秘鲁	澳大利亚	新西/坡/智	港/澳/台	亚太2国	老/柬/缅	36/3/1	Article Description
												0/0/0	Wood sawn or chipped lengthwise, sliced or peeled, of merban, not end-jointed, thickness>6mm
													---Other
												0/0/0	Endangered tropical rosewood, sawn or chipped lengthwise, sliced or peeled, end-jointed, of a thickness exceeding 6mm
												0/0/0	Other tropical rosewood, sawn or chipped lengthwise, sliced or peeled, end-jointed, of a thickness exceeding 6mm
												0/0/0	Endangered tropical rosewood, sawn or chipped lengthwise, sliced or peeled, not end-jointed, of a thickness exceeding 6mm
												0/0/0	Other tropical rosewood, sawn or chipped lengthwise, sliced or peeled, not end-jointed, of a thickness exceeding 6mm
													---Other
												0/0/0	Wood sawn or chipped lengthwise, sliced or peeled, of Ramin wood, end-jointed, thickness>6mm
												0/0/0	Wood sawn or chipped lengthwise, sliced or peeled, of bulnesia sarmientoi, end-jointed
												0/0/0	Endangered tropical wood, sawn or chipped lengthwise, not elsewhere specified or included, sliced or peeled, end-jointed, of a thickness exceeding 6mm
												0/0/0	wood sawn or chipped lengthwise , sliced or peeled , of other tropical wood, not elsewhere specified, endjointed , thicknese >6mm
												0/0/0	Wood sawn or chipped lengthwise, sliced or peeled, of bulnesia sarmientoi, not end-jointed
												0/0/0	Endangered tropical wood, sawn or chipped lengthwise, not elsewhere specified or included, sliced or peeled, not end-jointed, of a thickness exceeding 6mm
												0/0/0	Wood sawn or chipped lengthwise, sliced or peeled, of other tropical wood, not elsewhere specified, not end-jointed
													-Other:
													--Of oak (*Quercus spp.*)
												0/0/0	Mongolia oak planks end joining (sawn or chipped lengthwise, sliced or peeled, the thickness of >6 mm)
												0/0/0	Wood sawn or chipped lengthwise, sliced or peeled, of oak (*Quercus spp.*), end-jointed, thickness>6mm
												0/0/0	Mongolia oak planks - end joining (sawn or chipped lengthwise, sliced or peeled, the thickness of >6 mm)
												0/0/0	Wood sawn or chipped lengthwise, sliced or peeled, of oak (*Quercus spp.*), not end-jointed, thickness>6mm
													--Of beech (*Fagus spp.*)
												0/0/0	Beech(*Fagus spp.*) wood sawn or chipped lengthwise, sliced or peeled, end-jointed, of a thicknessthicknese >6mm
												0/0/0	Beech(*Fagus spp.*) wood sawn or chipped lengthwise, sliced or peeled, not end-jointed, of a thickness >6mm
													--Of maple(*Acer spp.*)
												0/0/0	Maple wood sawn or chipped lengthwise, sliced or peeled, end-jointed, of a thickness exceeding 6mm
												0/0/0	Maple wood sawn or chipped lengthwise, sliced or peeled, end-jointed, of a thickness >6mm
													--Of cherry (*Prunus spp.*)
												0/0/0	Wood sawn or chipped lengthwise, sliced or peeled, of cherry, end-jointed, thickness>6mm
												0/0/0	Wood sawn or chipped lengthwise, sliced or peeled, of cherry, not end-jointed, thickness>6mm
													--Of ash(Fraxinus *spp.*)
												0/0/0	Fraxinus mandshurica thick plate end joining (sawn or chipped lengthwise, sliced or peeled, the thickness of >6 mm)
												0/0/0	Wood sawn or chipped lengthwise, sliced or peeled, of ash, end-jointed, thickness>6mm
												0/0/0	Fraxinus mandshurica thick plate non end joining (sawn or chipped lengthwise, sliced or peeled, the thickness of >6 mm)
												0/0/0	Wood sawn or chipped lengthwise, sliced or peeled, of ash, not end-jointed, thickness>6mm
													--Of birch (*Betula spp.*)

税则号列		货品名称〔CIQ扩展编码及品名—T2表示见附表2〕	最惠(%)	暂定税率	普通	增值/消费	出口退税	计量单位	监管条件	检验检疫	特殊证件对美关税
4407.9600	11	端部接合的濒危桦木板材(经纵锯、纵切、刨切或旋切,厚度超过6mm)〔999〕	0		14	13/	0	千克/立方米	ABEF	MPQ	/25
4407.9600	19	端部接合的其他桦木厚板材(经纵锯、纵切、刨切或旋切,厚度超过6mm)〔999〕	0		14	13/	0	千克/立方米	AB	MPQ	/25
4407.9600	91	非端部结合的濒危桦木厚板材(经纵锯、纵切、刨切或旋切,厚度超过6mm)〔999〕	0		14	13/	0	千克/立方米	y4xAFEB	MPQ	/25
4407.9600	99	非端部接合的其他桦木厚板材(经纵锯、纵切、刨切或旋切,厚度超过6mm)〔999〕	0		14	13/	0	千克/立方米	4ABxy	MPQ	/25
4407.9700		--杨木									
4407.9700	10	端部接合的杨木厚板材(经纵锯、纵切、刨切或旋切,厚度超过6mm)〔999〕	0		14	13/	0	千克/立方米	AB	MPQ	/5
4407.9700	90	非端部接合的杨木厚板材(经纵锯、纵切、刨切或旋切,厚度超过6mm)〔999〕	0		14	13/	0	千克/立方米	4ABxy	MPQ	/5
		--其他:									
4407.9910		---红木,但税号4407.2940所列热带红木除外									
4407.9910	11	端部接合濒危红木厚板材,但税号4407.2940所列热带红木除外(经纵锯、纵切、刨切或旋切的,厚度超过6mm)〔999〕	0		40	13/	0	千克/立方米	AFEB	MPQ	/25
4407.9910	19	端部接合其他红木厚板材,但税号4407.2940所列热带红木除外(经纵锯、纵切、刨切或旋切的,厚度超过6mm)〔999〕	0		40	13/	0	千克/立方米	AB	MPQ	/25
4407.9910	91	非端部接合濒危红木厚板材,但税号4407.2940所列热带红木除外(经纵锯、纵切、刨切或旋切的,厚度超过6mm)〔999〕	0		40	13/	0	千克/立方米	y4xAFEB	MPQ	/25
4407.9910	99	非端部接合其他红木厚板材,但税号4407.2940所列热带红木除外(经纵锯、纵切、刨切或旋切的,厚度超过6mm)〔999〕	0		40	13/	0	千克/立方米	4ABxy	MPQ	/25
4407.9920		---泡桐木									
4407.9920	10	端部接合的泡桐木厚板材(经纵锯、纵切、刨切或旋切的,厚度超过6mm)〔999〕	0		14	13/	13	千克/立方米	AB	PQ	/
4407.9920	90	非端部接合的泡桐木厚板材(经纵锯、纵切、刨切或旋切的,厚度超过6mm)〔999〕	0		14	13/	13	千克/立方米	AB	PQ	/
4407.9930		---北美硬阔叶材(含黑胡桃木)									
4407.9930	10	端部接合的北美硬阔叶材厚板材(含黑胡桃木,经纵锯、纵切、刨切或旋切,厚度超过6mm)〔999〕	0		14	13/	0	千克/立方米	AB	MPQ	/5
4407.9930	90	非端部接合的北美硬阔叶材厚板材(含黑胡桃木,经纵锯、纵切、刨切或旋切,厚度超过6mm)〔999〕	0		14	13/	0	千克/立方米	AB	MPQ	/5
4407.9980		---其他温带非针叶木									
4407.9980	11	端部接合其他温带濒危非针叶板材(经纵锯、纵切、刨切或旋切的,厚度超过6mm)〔999〕	0		14	13/	0	千克/立方米	FEAB	MPQ	/30
4407.9980	19	端部接合的其他温带非针叶厚板材(纵锯、纵切、刨切或旋切的,厚度超过6mm)〔999〕	0		14	13/	0	千克/立方米	AB	MPQ	/30
4407.9980	91	非端部接合其他温带濒危非针叶厚板材(经纵锯、纵切、刨切或旋切的,厚度超过6mm)〔999〕	0		14	13/	0	千克/立方米	y4xAFEB	MPQ	/30
4407.9980	99	非端部接合的其他温带非针叶厚板材(经纵锯、纵切、刨切或旋切的,厚度超过6mm)〔999〕	0		14	13/	0	千克/立方米	4ABxy	MPQ	/30
4407.9990		---其他									
4407.9990	12	端部接合的沉香木及拟沉香木厚板材(经纵锯、纵切、刨切或旋切的,厚度超过6mm)〔999〕	0		14	13/	0	千克/立方米	AFEB	MPQ	/20
4407.9990	15	端部接合的其他濒危木厚板材(经纵锯、纵切、刨切或旋切的,厚度超过6mm)〔101针叶木木材,102其他非针叶木材〕	0		14	13/	0	千克/立方米	AFEB	MPQ	/20
4407.9990	19	端部接合的其他木厚板材(经纵锯、纵切、刨切或旋切的,厚度超过6mm)〔101针叶木木材,102其他非针叶木材〕	0		14	13/	0	千克/立方米	AB	MPQ	/20
4407.9990	92	非端部接合的沉香木及拟沉香木厚板材(经纵锯、纵切、刨切或旋切的,厚度超过6mm)〔999〕	0		14	13/	0	千克/立方米	y4xAFEB	MPQ	/20
4407.9990	95	非端部接合的其他濒危木厚板材(经纵锯、纵切、刨切或旋切的,厚度超过6mm)〔101针叶木木材,102其他非针叶木材〕	0		14	13/	0	千克/立方米	y4xAFEB	MPQ	/20
4407.9990	99	非端部接合的其他木厚板材(经纵锯、纵切、刨切或旋切的,厚度超过6mm)〔101针叶木木材,102其他非针叶木材〕	0		14	13/	0	千克/立方米	y4xAB	MPQ	/20

协定税率 %										特惠税率 %			Article Description
亚太5国	东/冰/格	巴基斯坦	韩国	瑞士	哥达	秘鲁	澳大利亚	新西/坡/智	港/澳/台	亚太2国	老/柬/缅	36/3/1	
												0/0/0	Endangered birch, sawn or chipped lengthwise, sliced or peeled, end-jointed, of a thickness exceeding 6mm
												0/0/0	Other birch, sawn or chipped lengthwise, sliced or peeled, end-jointed, of a thickness exceeding 6mm
												0/0/0	Endangered birch, sawn or chipped lengthwise, sliced or peeled, not end-jointed, of a thickness exceeding 6mm
												0/0/0	Other birch, sawn or chipped lengthwise, sliced or peeled, not end-jointed, of a thickness exceeding 6mm
													--Of poplar and aspen (*Populus spp.*)
												0/0/0	Poplar, sawn or chipped lengthwise, sliced or peeled, end-jointed, of a thickness exceeding 6mm
												0/0/0	Poplar, sawn or chipped lengthwise, sliced or peeled, not end-jointed, of a thickness exceeding 6mm
													--Other:
													---Of rosewood, other than tropical wood of Subheading 4407.2940
												0/0/0	Ohter endangered rosewood sawn or chipped lengthwise, sliced or peeled, end-jointed, of a thickness >6mm, excluding tropical rosewood of subheading No.4403.4980
												0/0/0	Ohter rosewood sawn or chipped lengthwise, sliced or peeled, end-jointed, of a thickness >6mm, excluding tropical rosewood of subheading No.4403.4980
												0/0/0	Ohter endangered rosewood sawn or chipped lengthwise, sliced or peeled, not end-jointed, of a thickness >6mm, excluding tropical rosewood of subheading No.4403.4980
												0/0/0	Ohter other rosewood sawn or chipped lengthwise, sliced or peeled, not end-jointed, of a thickness >6mm, excluding tropical rosewood of subheading No.4403.4980
													---Of paulownia
												0/0/0	Wood sawn or chipped lengthwise, sliced or peeled, of paulownia, end-jointed, thickness>6mm
												0/0/0	Wood sawn or chipped lengthwise, sliced or peeled, of paulownia, not end-jointed, thickness>6mm
													---North American hardwood(including walnut)
												0/0/0	Wood sawn or chipped lengthwise, sliced or peeled, of North American broadleaf hardwood (including walnut), end-jointed, thickness >6mm
												0/0/0	Wood sawn or chipped lengthwise, sliced or peeled, of North American broadleaf hardwood (including walnut), not end-jointed, thickness>6mm
													---Other temperate, non-coniferous wood
												0/0/0	Wood sawn or chipped lengthwise, sliced or peeled, endangered non-coniferous wood, of temperate, end-jointed, thickness>6mm
												0/0/0	Wood sawn or chipped lengthwise, sliced or peeled, of temperate zone, non-coniferous wood, end-jointed, thickness>6mm
												0/0/0	Wood sawn or chipped lengthwise, sliced or peeled, endangered non-coniferous wood of temperate, not end-jointed, thickness>6mm
												0/0/0	Wood sawn or chipped lengthwise, sliced or peeled, of temperate zone, non-coniferous wood, not end-jointed, thickness>6mm
													---Other
												0/0/0	Wood sawn or chipped lengthwise, sliced or peeled, of Chinese eaglewood and similar chinese eaglewood, end-jointed, thickness>6mm
												0/0/0	Wood sawn or chipped lengthwise, sliced or peeled, of other endangered wood , end-jointed, thickness>6mm
												0/0/0	Other wood sawn or chipped lengthwise, sliced or peeled, end-jointed thickness>6mm
												0/0/0	Wood sawn or chipped lengthwise, sliced or peeled, of Chinese eaglewood and similar chinese eaglewood , not end-jointed, thickness>6mm
												0/0/0	Wood sawn or chipped lengthwise, sliced or peeled, of other endangered wood , not end-jointed, thickness>6mm
												0/0/0	Other wood sawn or chipped lengthwise, sliced or peeled, not end-jointed, thickness>6mm

税则号列		货品名称〔CIQ 扩展编码及品名－T2 表示见附表 2〕	最惠(%)	暂定税率	普通	增值/消费	出口退税	计量单位	监管条件	检验检疫	特殊证件对美关税
44.08		**饰面用单板(包括刨切积层木获得的单板)、制胶合板或类似多层板用单板以及其他经纵锯、刨切或旋切的木材，不论是否刨平、砂光、拼接或端部结合，厚度不超过 6 毫米：**									
		-针叶木：									
		---饰面用单板：									
4408.1011		----用胶合板等多层板制的									
4408.1011	10	胶合板等多层板制濒危针叶木单板(厚度≤6mm，饰面用)〔999〕	6	3	40	13/	0	千克	ABFE	MPQ	/
4408.1011	90	其他胶合板等多层板制针叶木单板(厚度≤6mm，饰面用)〔999〕	6	6	40	13/	0	千克	AB	MPQ	/
4408.1019		----其他									
4408.1019	10	其他饰面濒危针叶木单板(厚度≤6mm)〔999〕	4	2	40	13/	0	千克	ABFE	MPQ	/22
4408.1019	90	其他饰面针叶木单板(厚度≤6mm)〔999〕	4	2	40	13/	0	千克	AB	MPQ	/22
4408.1020		---制胶合板用单板									
4408.1020	10	制胶合板用濒危针叶木单板(厚度≤6mm)〔999〕	4	2	17	13/	0	千克	ABFE	MPQ	/
4408.1020	90	其他制胶合板用针叶木单板(厚度≤6mm)〔999〕	4	2	17	13/	0	千克	AB	MPQ	/
4408.1090		---其他									
4408.1090	10	其他濒危针叶木单板材(经纵锯，刨切或旋切的，厚度≤6mm)〔999〕	4	2	30	13/	0	千克	ABFE	MPQ	/27
4408.1090	90	其他针叶木单板材(经纵锯，刨切或旋切的，厚度≤6mm)〔999〕	4	2	30	13/	0	千克	AB	MPQ	/27
		-热带木：									
		--深红色红柳桉木、浅红色红柳桉木及巴栲红柳桉木：									
		---饰面用单板：									
4408.3111		----用胶合板等多层板制的〔999〕	6	3	40	13/	0	千克	AB	MPQ	/
4408.3119		----其他〔999〕	4	2	40	13/	0	千克	AB	MPQ	/27
4408.3120		---制胶合板用单板〔999〕	4	2	17	13/	0	千克	AB	MPQ	/
4408.3190		---其他〔999〕	4	2	30	13/	0	千克	AB	MPQ	/
		--其他：									
		---饰面用单板：									
4408.3911		----用胶合板等多层板制的									
4408.3911	10	胶合板多层板制饰面桃花心木单板(厚度≤6mm)〔999〕	6	3	40	13/	0	千克	ABFE	MPQ	/
4408.3911	20	胶合板多层板制饰面拉敏木单板(厚度≤6mm)〔999〕	6	3	40	13/	0	千克	AB	MPQ	/
4408.3911	30	厚度≤6mm 胶合板多层板制饰面濒危热带木单板〔101 针叶木薄板，102 非针叶木薄板〕	6	3	40	13/	0	千克	ABFE	MPQ	/
4408.3911	90	厚度≤6mm 胶合板多层板制饰面热带木单板〔101 针叶木薄板，102 非针叶木薄板〕	6	3	40	13/	0	千克	AB	MPQ	/
4408.3919		----其他									
4408.3919	10	其他饰面用桃花心木单板(厚度≤6mm)〔999〕	4	3	40	13/	0	千克	ABFE	MPQ	/28
4408.3919	30	厚度≤6mm 其他濒危热带木制饰面用单板〔101 针叶木薄板，102 非针叶木薄板〕	4	3	40	13/	0	千克	ABFE	MPQ	/28
4408.3919	90	厚度≤6mm 其他热带木饰面用单板[T2]	4	3	40	13/	0	千克	AB	MPQ	/28
4408.3920		---制胶合板用单板									
4408.3920	10	其他桃花心木制的胶合板用单板(厚度≤6mm)〔999〕	4	2	17	13/	0	千克	ABFE	MPQ	/
4408.3920	20	其他拉敏木制的胶合板用单板(厚度≤6mm)〔999〕	4	2	17	13/	0	千克	AB	MPQ	/
4408.3920	30	其他濒危热带木制的胶合板用单板(厚度≤6mm)〔101 针叶木薄板，102 非针叶木薄板〕	4	2	17	13/	0	千克	ABFE	MPQ	/
4408.3920	90	其他列名热带木制的胶合板用单板(厚度≤6mm)〔101 针叶木薄板，102 非针叶木薄板〕	4	2	17	13/	0	千克	AB	MPQ	/
4408.3990		---其他									
4408.3990	10	其他桃花心木制的其他单板(厚度≤6mm)〔999〕	4	2	30	13/	0	千克	ABFE	MPQ	/27
4408.3990	30	其他列名濒危热带木制的其他单板(厚度≤6mm)〔101 针叶木薄板，102 非针叶木薄板〕	4	2	30	13/	0	千克	ABFE	MPQ	/27
4408.3990	90	其他列名的热带木制的其他单板(厚度≤6mm)〔101 针叶木薄板，102 非针叶木薄板〕	4	2	30	13/	0	千克	AB	MPQ	/27
		-其他：									
		---饰面用单板：									
4408.9011		----用胶合板等多层板制的									

协定税率 %										特惠税率 %			Article Description
亚太5国	东/冰/格	巴基斯坦	韩国	瑞士	哥达	秘鲁	澳大利亚	新西/坡/智	港/澳/台	亚太2国	老/柬/缅	36/3/1	
													Sheets for veneering (including those obtained by slicing laminated wood), for plywood or for other similar laminated wood and other wood, sawn lengthwise, sliced or peeled, whether or not planed, sanded, spliced or end-jointed, of a thickness not exceeding 6mm:
													-Coniferous:
													---Veneer sheets:
													----Of laminated plywood
	5/0/		4.8	0	0	0	0	0//0	0/0/			0//	Veneer sheets of endangered coniferous wood, of laminated wood of plywood, thickness≤6mm
	5/0/		4.8	0	0	0	0	0//0	0/0/			0//	Other veneer sheets of coniferous wood, of laminated wood of plywood, thickness≤6mm
													----Other
	0/0/	0	0	0	0	0	0	0/0/0	0/0/			0/0/	Other veneer sheets of endangered coniferous wood, thickness≤6mm
	0/0/	0	0	0	0	0	0	0/0/0	0/0/			0/0/	Other veneer sheets of coniferous wood, thickness≤6mm
													---Sheets for plywood
	0/0/	0	0	0	0	0	0	0/0/0	0/0/			0/0/	Sheets for plywood of coniferous endangered wood, thickness≤6mm
	0/0/	0	0	0	0	0	0	0/0/0	0/0/			0/0/	Other sheets for plywood of coniferous wood, thickness≤6mm
													---Other
	0/0/	0	0	0	0	0	0	0/0/0	0/0/			0/0/	Sheets for plywood of endangered coniferous wood, wood sawn or chipped lengthwise, sliced or peeled, thickness≤6mm
	0/0/	0	0	0	0	0	0	0/0/0	0/0/			0/0/	Sheets for plywood of coniferous wood, wood sawn or chipped lengthwise, sliced or peeled, thickness≤6mm
													-Of tropical wood:
													--Dark Red Meranti, Light Red Meranti and Meranti Bakau:
													---Veneer sheets:
	5/0/		6	0	0	0	0	0//0	0/0/			0//	----Of laminated plywood
	0/0/	0	0	0	0	0	0	0/0/0	0/0/			0/0/	----Other
	0/0/	0	0	0	0	0	0	0/0/0	0/0/			0/0/	---Sheets for plywood
	0/0/	0	0	0	0	0	0	0/0/0	0/0/			0/0/	---Other
													--Other:
													---Veneer sheets:
													----Of laminated plywood
4.2	5/0/		6	0	0	0	0	0//0	0/0/			0//	Veneer sheets, of acajou d'afrique, of laminated wood of plywood, thickness≤6mm
4.2	5/0/		6	0	0	0	0	0//0	0/0/			0//	Sheets for veneering, of Ramin wood, of laminated wood of plywood, thickness≤6mm
4.2	5/0/		6	0	0	0	0	0//0	0/0/			0//	Veneer sheets, of endangered tropical wood, of laminated plywood, of a thickness not exceeding 6mm
4.2	5/0/		6	0	0	0	0	0//0	0/0/			0//	Veneer sheets, of tropical wood, of laminated plywood, of a thickness not exceeding 6mm
													----Other
	0/0/	0	0	0	0	0	0	0/0/0	0/0/			0/0/	Other veneer sheets, of acajou d'afri-que, thickness≤6mm
	0/0/	0	0	0	0	0	0	0/0/0	0/0/			0/0/	Veneer sheets, of endangered tropical wood , of a thickness not exceeding 6mm
	0/0/	0	0	0	0	0	0	0/0/0	0/0/			0/0/	Veneer sheets, of tropical wood ,of a thickness not exceeding 6mm
													---Sheets for plywood
3.6	0/0/	0	0	0	0	0	0	0/0/0	0/0/			0/0/	Other sheets for plywood, of acajou d'afrique, thickness≤6mm
3.6	0/0/	0	0	0	0	0	0	0/0/0	0/0/			0/0/	Other sheets for plywood, of ramin wood, thickness≤6mm
3.6	0/0/	0	0	0	0	0	0	0/0/0	0/0/			0/0/	Other sheets for plywood, of endangered tropical wood, of a thickness not exceeding 6mm
3.6	0/0/	0	0	0	0	0	0	0/0/0	0/0/			0/0/	Other sheets for plywood, of tropical wood, of a thickness not exceeding 6mm
													---Other
	0/0/	0	0	0	0	0	0	0/0/0	0/0/			0/0/	Other sheets of other Acajou d'afrique, of tropical wood, of a thickness not exceeding 6mm
	0/0/	0	0	0	0	0	0	0/0/0	0/0/			0/0/	Other sheets of endangered specified tropical wood, of a thickness not exceeding 6mm
	0/0/	0	0	0	0	0	0	0/0/0	0/0/			0/0/	Other sheets of other specified tropical wood, of a thickness not exceeding 6mm
													-Other:
													---Veneer sheets:
													----Of laminated plywood

税则号列		货品名称〔CIQ扩展编码及品名－T2表示见附表2〕	最惠(%)	暂定税率	普通	增值/消费	出口退税	计量单位	监管条件	检验检疫	特殊证件对美关税
4408.9011	10	胶合板多层板制饰面濒危木单板(厚度≤6mm)〔101针叶木薄板,102非针叶木薄板〕	4	2	40	13/	0	千克	ABFE	MPQ	/22
4408.9011	90	胶合板多层板制饰面其他木单板(厚度≤6mm,针叶木、热带木除外)〔101针叶木薄板,102非针叶木薄板〕	4	2	40	13/	0	千克	AB	MPQ	/22
4408.9012		----温带非针叶木制									
4408.9012	10	温带濒危非针叶木制饰面用木单板(厚度≤6mm,针叶木、热带木除外)〔999〕	3	1	40	13/	0	千克	ABFE	MPQ	/21
4408.9012	90	其他温带非针叶木制饰面用木单板(厚度≤6mm,针叶木、热带木除外)〔999〕	3	1	40	13/	0	千克	AB	MPQ	/21
4408.9013		----竹制									
4408.9013	10	濒危竹制饰面用单板(厚度≤6mm)〔999〕	4	2	40	13/	0	千克	ABE	MPQ	/
4408.9013	90	其他竹制饰面用单板(厚度≤6mm)〔999〕	4	2	40	13/	0	千克	AB	MPQ	/
4408.9019		----其他									
4408.9019	11	家具饰面用濒危木单板(厚度≤6mm)[T2]	3	1	40	13/	0	千克	ABFE	MPQ	/6
4408.9019	19	其他家具饰面用单板(厚度≤6mm)[T2]	3	1	40	13/	0	千克	AB	MPQ	/6
4408.9019	91	其他饰面用濒危木单板(厚度≤6mm)[T2]	3	1	40	13/	0	千克	ABFE	MPQ	/6
4408.9019	99	其他饰面用单板(厚度≤6mm)[T2]	3	1	40	13/	0	千克	AB	MPQ	/6
		---胶合板用单板:									
4408.9021		----温带非针叶木制									
4408.9021	10	温带濒危非针叶木制胶合板用单板(厚度≤6mm)〔999〕	3	2	17	13/	0	千克	ABFE	MPQ	/27
4408.9021	90	其他温带非针叶木制胶合板用单板(厚度≤6mm)〔999〕	3	2	17	13/	0	千克	AB	MPQ	/27
4408.9029		----其他									
4408.9029	11	其他濒危木制胶合板用旋切单板(厚度≤6mm)〔101针叶木薄板,102非针叶木薄板〕	3	1	17	13/	0	千克	ABFE	MPQ	/
4408.9029	19	其他濒危木制胶合板用其他单板(厚度≤6mm,旋切单板除外)〔101针叶木薄板,102非针叶木薄板〕	3	1	17	13/	0	千克	ABFE	MPQ	/
4408.9029	91	其他木制胶合板用旋切单板(厚度≤6mm)〔101针叶木薄板,102非针叶木薄板〕	3	1	17	13/	0	千克	AB	MPQ	/
4408.9029	99	其他木制胶合板用其他单板(厚度≤6mm,旋切单板除外)〔101针叶木薄板,102非针叶木薄板〕	3	1	17	13/	0	千克	AB	MPQ	/
		---其他:									
4408.9091		----温带非针叶木制									
4408.9091	10	温带濒危非针叶木制其他单板材(经纵锯、刨切或旋切的,厚度≤6mm)〔999〕	3	2	30	13/	0	千克	ABFE	MPQ	/27
4408.9091	90	温带非针叶木制其他单板材(经纵锯、刨切或旋切的,厚度≤6mm)〔999〕	3	2	30	13/	0	千克	AB	MPQ	/27
4408.9099		----其他									
4408.9099	10	其他濒危木制的其他单板材(经纵锯、刨切或旋切的,厚度≤6mm)〔101针叶木薄板,102非针叶木薄板〕	3	2	30	13/	0	千克	ABFE	MPQ	/22
4408.9099	90	其他木材,但针叶木热带木除外(经纵锯、刨切或旋切的,厚度≤6mm)〔999〕	3	2	30	13/	0	千克	AB	MPQ	/22
44.09		**任何一边端或面制成连续形状(舌榫、槽榫、半槽榫、斜角、V形接头、珠榫、缘饰、刨圆及类似形状)的木材(包括未装拼的拼花地板用板条及缘板),不论是否刨平、砂光或端部结合:**									
		-针叶木:									
4409.1010		---地板条(块)									
4409.1010	10	一边或面制成连续形状的濒危针叶木制地板条、块(包括未装拼的拼花地板用板条及缘板)〔999〕	6	3	50	13/5	0	千克	ABFE	PQ	/
4409.1010	90	一边或面制成连续形状的其他针叶木地板条,块(包括未装拼的拼花地板用板条及缘板)〔999〕	6	3	50	13/5	0	千克	AB	PQ	/
4409.1090		---其他									
4409.1090	10	一边或面制成连续形状濒危针叶木材〔999〕	6	3	50	13/	0	千克	ABFE	PQ	/
4409.1090	90	其他一边或面制成连续形状的针叶木材〔999〕	6	3	50	13/	0	千克	AB	PQ	/
		-非针叶木:									
		--竹的:									
4409.2110		---地板条(块)									

协定税率 %										特惠税率 %			Article Description
亚太5国	东/冰/格	巴基斯坦	韩国	瑞士	哥达	秘鲁	澳大利亚	新西/坡/智	港/澳/台	亚太2国	老/柬/缅	36/3/1	
2.8	/0/		2.4	0	0	0	0	0//0	0/0/			0//	Veneer sheets, of wood, of laminatedr plywood of endangered wood, thickness≤6mm
2.8	/0/		2.4	0	0	0	0	0//0	0/0/			0//	Veneer sheets, of other wood, other than tropical coniferous wood, of laminated ply wood of plywood, thickness≤6mm
													----Of temperate non-coniferous wood
	0/0/	0	0	0	0	0	0	0/0/0	0/0/			0/0/	Venner sheets, of temperate zone non-coniferous endangered wood, other than tropical coniferous wood, thickness≤6mm
	0/0/	0	0	0	0	0	0	0/0/0	0/0/			0/0/	Venner sheets of temperate zone non-coniferous wood (other than tropical coniferous wood, thickness≤6mm)
													----Of bamboo
2.8	/0/		2.4	0	0	0	0	0//0	0/0/			0//	Veneer sheets of endangered bamboo(thickness≤6mm)
2.8	/0/		2.4	0	0	0	0	0//0	0/0/			0//	Veneer sheets of other bamboo(thickness≤6mm)
													----Other
	0/0/	0	0	0	0	0	0	0/0/0	0/0/			0/0/	Venner sheets of endangered wood(thickness≤6mm)
	0/0/	0	0	0	0	0	0	0/0/0	0/0/			0/0/	Other venner sheets of wood (thickness≤6mm)
	0/0/	0	0	0	0	0	0	0/0/0	0/0/			0/0/	Other venner sheets of endangered wood(thickness≤6mm)
	0/0/	0	0	0	0	0	0	0/0/0	0/0/			0/0/	Other veneer sheets(thickness≤6mm)
													---Sheets for plywood:
													----Of temperate non-coniferous wood
	0/0/	0	0	0	0	0	0	0/0/0	0/0/			0/0/	Sheets for plywood of temperate zone non-coniferous endangered wood (thickness≤6mm)
	0/0/	0	0	0	0	0	0	0/0/0	0/0/			0/0/	Other sheets for plywood of temperate zone non-coniferous wood (thickness ≤6mm)
													----Other
	0/0/	0	0	0	0	0	0	0/0/0	0/0/			0/0/	Other sheets for plywood of endangered wood, peeled sheets(thickness≤6mm)
	0/0/	0	0	0	0	0	0	0/0/0	0/0/			0/0/	Other sheets for plywood of endangered wood(thinckness≤6mm, other than peeled sheets)
	0/0/	0	0	0	0	0	0	0/0/0	0/0/			0/0/	Other sheets for plywood of wood, peeled sheets(thickness≤6mm)
	0/0/	0	0	0	0	0	0	0/0/0	0/0/			0/0/	Other sheets for plywood of wood (thiekness≤6mm, other than peeled sheets)
													---Other:
													----Of temperate non-coniferous wood
	0/0/	0	0	0	0	0	0	0/0/0	0/0/			0/0/	Sheets of temperate zone endangered non-coniferous wood(sawn or chipped lengthwise, sliced or peeled, thickness ≤6mm)
	0/0/	0	0	0	0	0	0	0/0/0	0/0/			0/0/	Other sheets of temperate zone non-coniferous wood (sawn or chipped lengthwise, sliced or peeled, thickness ≤6mm)
													----Other
	0/0/	0	0	0	0	0	0	0/0/0	0/0/			0/0/	Other sheets of endangered wood(sawn or chipped lengthwise, sliced or peeled, thickness≤6mm)
	0/0/	0	0	0	0	0	0	0/0/0	0/0/			0/0/	Other wood, other than tropical coniferous wood(sawn or chipped lengthwise, sliced or peeled, thickness≤6mm)
													Wood (including strips and friezes for parquet flooring, not assembled) continuously shaped (tongues, grooved, rebated, chamfered, V-jointed, beaded, moulded, rounded or the like) along any of its "edges, ends or faces, whether or not planed, sanded or end-jointed":
													-Coniferous:
													---Floor board strips
	0/0/	4	3	0	0	0	0	0/0/0	0/0/			0/0/0	Endangered coniferous wood(including strips and friezes for parquet flooring, not assembled) continuously shaped along any of its edges or faces
	0/0/	4	3	0	0	0	0	0/0/0	0/0/			0/0/0	Other coniferous wood (including strips and friezes for parquet flooring, not assembled) continuously shaped along any of its edges or faces
													---Other
	0/0/	4	0	0	0	0	0	0/0/0	0/0/			0/0/0	Endangered coniferous wood, continuously shaped along any of its edges or faces
	0/0/	4	0	0	0	0	0	0/0/0	0/0/			0/0/0	Coniferous wood, continuously shaped along any of its edges or faces
													-Non-coniferous:
													--Of bamboo:
													---Floor board strips

税则号列	货品名称〔CIQ扩展编码及品名－T2表示见附表2〕	最惠(%)	暂定税率	普通	增值/消费	出口退税	计量单位	监管条件	检验检疫	特殊证件对美关税
4409.2110　10	一边或面制成连续形状的濒危竹地板条(块)(包括未装拼的拼花竹地板用板条及缘板)〔999〕	4	2	50	13/	0	千克	ABE	PQ	/
4409.2110　90	一边或面制成连续形状的竹地板条(块)(包括未装拼的拼花竹地板用板条及缘板)〔999〕	4	2	50	13/	13	千克	AB	PQ	/
4409.2190	---其他									
4409.2190　10	一边或面制成连续形状的其他濒危竹材〔999〕	4	2	50	13/	0	千克	ABE	PQ	/
4409.2190　90	一边或面制成连续形状的其他竹材〔999〕	4	2	50	13/	13	千克	AB	PQ	/
	--热带木的：									
4409.2210	---地板条(块)									
4409.2210　20	一边或面制成连续形状的桃花心木地板条、块〔999〕	4	2	50	13/5	0	千克	ABFE	PQ	/
4409.2210　30	一边或面制成连续形状的其他濒危热带木地板条、块〔999〕	4	2	50	13/5	0	千克	ABFE	PQ	/
4409.2210　90	一边或面制成连续形状的其他热带木地板条、块〔999〕	4	2	50	13/5	0	千克	AB	PQ	/
4409.2290	---其他									
4409.2290　20	一边或面制成连续形状的桃花心木〔999〕	4	2	50	13/	0	千克	ABFE	PQ	/
4409.2290　30	一边或面制成连续形状的其他濒危热带木〔999〕	4	2	50	13/	0	千克	ABFE	PQ	/
4409.2290　90	一边或面制成连续形状的其他热带木〔999〕	4	2	50	13/	0	千克	AB	PQ	/
	--其他：									
4409.2910	---地板条(块)									
4409.2910　30	一边或面制成连续形状的其他濒危木地板条、块(包括未装拼的其他濒危木拼花地板用板条及缘板)〔999〕	4	2	50	13/5	0	千克	ABFE	PQ	/7
4409.2910　90	一边或面制成连续形状的其他非针叶木地板条、块(包括未装拼的其他非针叶木拼花地板用板条及缘板)〔999〕	4	2	50	13/5	0	千克	AB	PQ	/7
4409.2990	---其他									
4409.2990　30	一边或面制成连续形状的其他濒危木〔101 针叶木木材，102 其他非针叶木材〕	4	2	50	13/	0	千克	ABFE	PQ	/27
4409.2990　90	一边或面制成连续形状的其他非针叶木材〔999〕	4	2	50	13/	0	千克	AB	PQ	/27
44.10	**碎料板，定向刨花板(OSB)及类似板(例如，华夫板)，木或其他木质材料制，不论是否用树脂或其他有机黏合剂粘合：**									
	-木制：									
4410.1100	--碎料板〔101 其它胶合板，102 其他碎木料、锯末、刨花〕	4	2	40	13/	13	千克	AB	PQ	/27
4410.1200	--定向刨花板〔999〕	4	3	40	13/	13	千克	AB	PQ	/28
4410.1900	--其他〔999〕	4	2	40	13/	13	千克	AB	PQ	/27
	-其他：									
	---碎料板：									
4410.9011	----麦稻秸秆制〔999〕	6		40	13/	13	千克	AB	PQ	/
4410.9019	----其他〔999〕	6		40	13/	13	千克	AB	PQ	/11
4410.9090	---其他[T2]	6		40	13/	13	千克	AB	PQ	/
44.11	**木纤维板或其他木质材料纤维板，不论是否用树脂或其他有机黏合剂粘合：**									
	-中密度纤维板(MDF)：									
	--厚度不超过5毫米：									
	---密度超过每立方厘米0.8克：									
4411.1211	----未经机械加工或盖面的〔101 针叶木纤维板，102 非针叶木纤维板，103 其他纤维板〕	4	2	40	13/	13	千克	AB	PQ	/27
4411.1219	----其他[T2]	6	2	40	13/	13	千克	AB	PQ	/22
	---密度超过每立方厘米0.5克，但未超过每立方厘米0.8克：									
4411.1221	----辐射松制的〔999〕	4	2	40	13/	13	千克	AB	PQ	/
4411.1229	----其他[T2]	4	2	40	13/	13	千克	AB	PQ	/22
	---其他：									
4411.1291	----未经机械加工或盖面的[T2]	6	2	40	13/	13	千克	AB	PQ	/

协定税率 %										特惠税率 %			Article Description
亚太5国	东/冰/格	巴基斯坦	韩国	瑞士	哥达	秘鲁	澳大利亚	新西/坡/智	港/澳/台	亚太2国	老/柬/缅	36/3/1	
	0/0/	0	0	0	0	0	0	0/0/0	0/0/			0/0/0	Endangered bamboo(including strips and friezes for parquet flooring, not assembled) continuously shaped along any of its edges or faces
	0/0/	0	0	0	0	0	0	0/0/0	0/0/			0/0/0	Bamboo (including strips and friezes for parquet flooring, not assembled) continuously shaped along any of its edges or faces
													---Other
	0/0/0	0	0	0	0	0	0	0/0/0	0/0/			0/0/0	Other endangered bamboo, continuously shaped along any of its edges or faces
	0/0/0	0	0	0	0	0	0	0/0/0	0/0/			0/0/0	Other bamboo, continuously shaped along any of its edges or faces
													--Of tropical wood:
													---Floor board strips
	0/0/	0	0	0	0	0	0	0/0/0	0/0/			0/0/0	Floor board strips of mahogany wood(including strips and friezes for parquet flooring, not assembled) continuously shaped along any of its edges or faces
	0/0/	0	0	0	0	0	0	0/0/0	0/0/			0/0/0	Floor board strips of other endangered tropical wood(including strips and friezes for parquet flooring, not assembled) continuously shaped along any of its edges or faces
	0/0/	0	0	0	0	0	0	0/0/0	0/0/			0/0/0	Floor board strips of other tropical wood(including strips and friezes for parquet flooring, not assembled) continuously shaped along any of its edges or faces
													---Other
	0/0/	0	0	0	0	0	0	0/0/0	0/0/			0/0/	mahogany wood, continuously shaped along any of its edges or faces
	0/0/	0	0	0	0	0	0	0/0/0	0/0/			0/0/	Endangered tropical wood, continuously shaped along any of its edges or faces
	0/0/	0	0	0	0	0	0	0/0/0	0/0/			0/0/	Other tropical wood, continuously shaped along any of its edges or faces
													--Other:
													---Floor board strips
	0/0/	0	0	0	0	0	0	0/0/0	0/0/			0/0/0	Other endangered wood (including strips and friezes for parquet flooring, not assembled) continuously shaped along any of its edges or faces
	0/0/	0	0	0	0	0	0	0/0/0	0/0/			0/0/0	Other non-coniferous wood (including strips and friezes for parquet flooring, not assembled) continuously shaped along anyof its edges or faces
													---Other
	0/0/	0	0	0	0	0	0	0/0/0	0/0/			0/0/	Other endangered wood , continuously shaped along any of its edges or faces
	0/0/	0	0	0	0	0	0	0/0/0	0/0/			0/0/	Other non-coniferous wood, continuously sh-aped along any of its edges or faces
													Particle board and similar board of wood or other ligneous materials (for example, oriented strand board and waferboabd) where or not agglomerated with resins or other organic binging, substancec
													-Of wood:
				0				0//1.3	0/0/				--Particle board
				0				0//1.3	0/0/				--Oriented standard board (OSB)
				0				0//1.3	0/0/				--Other
													-Other:
													---Particle board:
													----Of wheat and rice straw
													----Other
													---Other
													Fibreboard of wood or other ligneous materials, whether or not bonded with resins or other organic substances:
													-Medium density fibreboand (MDF):
													--Of a thickness not exceeding 5mm:
													---Of a density exceeding 0.8/cm^3:
			2.4	0				0//1.3	0/0/				----Not mechanically worked or surface covered
			0	0				0//2	0/0/				----Other
													---Of a density exceeding 0.5 g/cm^3 but not exceeding 0.8 g/cm^3:
			2.4	0			0	0//1.3	0/0/			0//	----Of radiata pine
			2.4	0				0//1.3	0/0/				----Other
													---Other:
	5//		4.5	0				0//2	0/0/				----Not mechanically worked or surface covered

税则号列		货品名称〔CIQ 扩展编码及品名—T2 表示见附表 2〕	最惠(%)	暂定税率	普通	增值/消费	出口退税	计量单位	监管条件	检验检疫	特殊证件对美关税
4411.1299		----其他〔999〕	4	2	40	13/	13	千克	AB	PQ	/
		--厚度超过 5 毫米但未超过 9 毫米：									
		---密度超过每立方厘米 0.8 克：									
4411.1311		----未经机械加工或盖面的[T2]	4	2	40	13/	13	千克	AB	PQ	/22
4411.1319		----其他[T2]	6	3	40	13/	13	千克	AB	MPQ	/28
		---密度超过每立方厘米 0.5 克，但未超过每立方厘米 0.8 克：									
4411.1321		----辐射松制的〔999〕	4	2	40	13/	13	千克	AB	PQ	/
4411.1329		----其他[T2]	4	2	40	13/	13	千克	AB	PQ	/
		---其他：									
4411.1391		----未经机械加工或盖面的[T2]	6	3	40	13/	13	千克	AB	PQ	/
4411.1399		----其他[T2]	4	2	40	13/	13	千克	AB	PQ	/
		--厚度超过 9 毫米：									
		---密度超过每立方厘米 0.8 克：									
4411.1411		----未经机械加工或盖面的〔999〕	4	2	40	13/	13	千克	AB	PQ	/
4411.1419		----其他〔999〕	6	3	40	13/	13	千克	AB	MPQ	/28
		---密度超过每立方厘米 0.5 克，但未超过每立方厘米 0.8 克：									
4411.1421		----辐射松制的〔999〕	4	2	40	13/	13	千克	AB	PQ	/27
4411.1429		----其他[T2]	4	2	40	13/	13	千克	AB	PQ	/27
		---其他：									
4411.1491		----未经机械加工或盖面的〔999〕	6	3	40	13/	13	千克	AB	PQ	/
4411.1499		----其他[T2]	4	2	40	13/	13	千克	AB	PQ	/27
		-其他：									
		--密度超过每立方厘米 0.8 克：									
4411.9210		---未经机械加工或盖面的[T2]	4	2	40	13/	13	千克	AB	PQ	/27
4411.9290		---其他〔999〕	6	3	40	13/	13	千克	AB	MPQ	/28
		--密度超过每立方厘米 0.5 克，但未超过每立方厘米 0.8 克：									
4411.9310		---辐射松制的〔999〕	4	2	40	13/	13	千克	AB	PQ	/
4411.9390		---其他[T2]	4	2	40	13/	13	千克	AB	PQ	/27
		--密度未超过每立方厘米 0.5 克：									
4411.9410		---密度超过每立方厘米 0.35 克，但未超过每立方厘米 0.5 克〔999〕	6	3	40	13/	13	千克	AB	PQ	/28
		---密度未超过每立方厘米 0.35 克：									
4411.9421		----未经机械加工或盖面的[T2]	6	3	40	13/	13	千克	AB	PQ	/
4411.9429		----其他〔999〕	4	2	40	13/	13	千克	AB	PQ	/7
44.12		**胶合板、单板饰面板及类似的多层板：**									
		-竹制的：									
		---仅由薄板制的胶合板，每层厚度不超过 6 毫米：									
4412.1011		----至少有一表层是热带木									
4412.1011	11	至少有一表层为濒危热带木薄板制濒危竹胶合板（每层厚度≤6mm）〔999〕	6	3	30	13/	0	千克/立方米	ABFE	MPQ	/13
4412.1011	19	至少有一表层为濒危热带木薄板制其他竹胶合板（每层厚度≤6mm）〔999〕	6	3	30	13/	0	千克/立方米	ABFE	MPQ	/13
4412.1011	91	至少有一表层是其他热带木薄板制濒危竹胶合板（每层厚度≤6mm）〔999〕	6	3	30	13/	0	千克/立方米	ABEF	MPQ	/13
4412.1011	99	至少有一表层是其他热带木薄板制其他竹胶合板（每层厚度≤6mm）〔999〕	6	3	30	13/	13	千克/立方米	AB	MPQ	/13
4412.1019		----其他									
4412.1019	11	至少有一表层为濒危非针叶木薄板胶合板（至少有一表层为温带非针叶木制，每层厚度≤6mm）〔999〕	4	2	30	13/	0	千克/立方米	ABFE	MPQ	/27
4412.1019	19	其他至少有一表层为非针叶木薄板胶合板（至少有一表层为温带非针叶木制，每层厚度≤6mm）〔999〕	4	2	30	13/	13	千克/立方米	AB	MPQ	/27
4412.1019	21	濒危竹地板层叠胶合而成的多层板（每层厚度≤6mm）〔999〕	4	2	30	13/	0	千克/立方米	ABE	MPQ	/27
4412.1019	29	其他竹地板层叠胶合而成的多层板（每层厚度≤6mm）〔999〕	4	2	30	13/	13	千克/立方米	AB	MPQ	/27
4412.1019	91	其他濒危竹胶合板（每层厚度≤6mm）〔999〕	4	2	30	13/	0	千克/立方米	ABE	MPQ	/27
4412.1019	99	其他竹胶合板（每层厚度≤6mm）〔999〕	4	2	30	13/	13	千克/立方米	AB	MPQ	/27
4412.1020		---其他，至少有一表层是非针叶木									

协定税率 %										特惠税率 %			Article Description
亚太5国	东/冰/格	巴基斯坦	韩国	瑞士	哥达	秘鲁	澳大利亚	新西/坡/智	港/澳/台	亚太2国	老/柬/缅	36/3/1	
			2.4	0				0//	0/0/				----Other
													--Of a thickness exceeding 5mm but not exceeding 9mm:
													---Of a density exceeding 0.8g/cm³:
				0				0//	0/0/				----Not mechanically worked or surface covered
				3.9				3.9//					----Other
													---Of a density exceeding 0.5g/cm³ but not exceeding 0.8g/cm³:
				0			0	0//1.3	0/0/			0//	----Of radiata pine
				0				0//1.3	0/0/				----Other
													---Other:
	5//			0				0//2	0/0/				----Not mechanically worked or surface covered
			2.4	0				0//1.3	0/0/				----Other
													--Of a thickness exceeding 9mm:
													---Of a density exceeding 0.8g/cm³:
			2.4	0				0//	0/0/				----Not mechanically worked or surface covered
			4.5	3.9				3.9//					----Other
													---Of a density exceeding 0.5g/cm³ but not exceeding 0.8g/cm³:
			2.4	0			0	0//1.3	0/0/			0//	----Of radiata pine
			2.4	0				0//1.3	0/0/				----Other
													---Other:
	5//		4.5	0				0//2	0/0/				----Not mechanically worked or surface covered
			2.4	0				0//1.3	0/0/				----Other
													-Other:
													--Of a density exceeding 0.8g/cm³:
			2.4	0				0//1.3	0/0/				---Not mechanically worked or surface covered
			4.5	0				0//2	0/0/				---Other
													--Of a density exceeding 0.5g/cm³ but not exceeding 0.8g/cm³:
				0			0	0//	0/0/			0//	---Of radiata pine
				0				0//1.3	0/0/				---Other
													--Of a density not exceeding 0.5g/cm³:
	5//		4.5	0				0//2	0/0/				---Of a density exceeding 0.35g/cm³ but not exceeding 0.5g/cm³
													---Of a density not exceeding 0.35g/cm³:
			4.5	0				0//	0/0/				----Not mechanically worked or suface covered
			2.4	0				0//	0/0/				----Other
													Plywood, veneered panels and similar laminated wood:
													-Of bamboo:
													---Plywood consisting solely of sheets of wood, each ply not exceeding 6 mm thickness
													----With at least one outer ply of tropical wood
	5/0/		7.2	3.6	0	0	0	0//0	0/0/			0//	With at least one outer ply of endangered tropical wood, plywood consisting solely of sheets of endangered bamboo, each ply not exceeding 6mm thickness
	5/0/		7.2	3.6	0	0	0	0//0	0/0/			0//	With at least one outer ply of endangered tropical wood, plywood consisting solely of sheets of other bamboo, each ply not exceeding 6mm thickness
	5/0/		7.2	3.6	0	0	0	0//0	0/0/			0//	With at least one outer ply of other tropical wood, plywood consisting solely of sheets of endangered bamboo, each ply not exceeding 6mm thickness
	5/0/		7.2	3.6	0	0	0	0//0	0/0/			0//	With at least one outer ply of other tropical wood, plywood consisting solely of sheets of other bamboo, each ply not exceeding 6mm thickness
													----Other
			2.4	0				0//	0/0/				Plywood consisting solely of sheets of wood, with at least one outer ply of endangered non-coniferous wood, each ply thickness≤6mm
			2.4	0				0//	0/0/				Plywood consisting solely of sheets of wood, with at least one outer ply of non-coniferous wood each ply thickness≤6mm
			2.4	0				0//	0/0/				Plywood with two or more plies of endangered bamboo, each ply thickness≤6mm
			2.4	0				0//	0/0/				Plywood with two or more plies of bamboo, each ply thickness≤6mm
			2.4	0				0//	0/0/				Plywood consisting solely of sheets of endangered bamboo, each ply thickness≤6mm
			2.4	0				0//	0/0/				Other plywood consisting solely of sheets of other bamboo, each ply thickness≤6mm
													---Other, with at least one outer ply of non-coniferous wood

税则号列		货品名称〔CIQ 扩展编码及品名－T2 表示见附表 2〕	最惠(%)	暂定税率	普通	增值/消费	出口退税	计量单位	监管条件	检验检疫	特殊证件对美关税
4412.1020	11	至少有一表层是濒危非针叶木的濒危竹制多层板（每层厚度≤6mm）〔999〕	6	3	30	13/	0	千克/立方米	ABFE	MPQ	/
4412.1020	19	至少有一表层是其他非针叶木的其他濒危竹制多层板（每层厚度≤6mm）〔999〕	6	3	30	13/	0	千克/立方米	ABEF	MPQ	/
4412.1020	91	至少有一表层是濒危非针叶木的其他竹制多层板（每层厚度≤6mm）〔999〕	6	3	30	13/	0	千克/立方米	ABEF	MPQ	/
4412.1020	99	至少有一表层是其他非针叶木的其他竹制多层板（每层厚度≤6mm）〔999〕	6	3	30	13/	13	千克/立方米	AB	MPQ	/
		---其他：									
4412.1091		----至少有一层是热带木									
4412.1091	10	至少有一层是热带木的濒危竹制多层板〔999〕	6	3	30	13/	0	千克/立方米	ABEF	MPQ	/
4412.1091	90	至少有一层是热带木的其他竹制多层板〔999〕	6	3	30	13/	13	千克/立方米	AB	MPQ	/
4412.1092		----至少含有一层木碎料板									
4412.1092	10	至少含有一层木碎料板的濒危竹制多层板〔999〕	6	3	30	13/	0	千克/立方米	ABEF	MPQ	/
4412.1092	90	至少含有一层木碎料板的其他竹制多层板〔999〕	6	3	30	13/	13	千克/立方米	AB	MPQ	/
4412.1099		----其他									
4412.1099	10	其他濒危竹制多层板〔999〕	4	2	30	13/	0	千克/立方米	ABE	MPQ	/
4412.1099	90	其他竹制多层板〔999〕	4	2	30	13/	13	千克/立方米	AB	MPQ	/
		-其他仅由薄木板制的胶合板（竹制除外），每层厚度不超过 6 毫米：									
4412.3100		--至少有一表层是热带木									
4412.3100	10	至少有一表层为桃花心木薄板制胶合板（每层厚度≤6mm）〔999〕	6	3	30	13/	6	千克/立方米	ABFE	MPQ	/28
4412.3100	20	至少有一表层为拉敏木薄板制胶合板（每层厚度≤6mm）〔999〕	6	3	30	13/	6	千克/立方米	AB	MPQ	/28
4412.3100	30	至少有一表层为濒危热带木薄板制胶合板（每层厚度≤6mm）〔999〕	6	3	30	13/	0	千克/立方米	ABFE	MPQ	/28
4412.3100	90	至少有一表层是其他热带木制的胶合板（每层厚度≤6mm，竹制除外）〔999〕	6	3	30	13/	13	千克/立方米	AB	MPQ	/28
4412.3300		--其他，至少有一表层是下列非针叶木：桤木、白蜡木、水青冈木（山毛榉木）、桦木、樱桃木、栗木、榆木、桉木、山核桃、七叶树、椴木、槭木、栎木（橡木）、悬铃木、杨木、刺槐木、鹅掌楸或核桃木									
4412.3300	10	至少有一表层是濒危的下列非针叶木：桤木、白蜡木、水青冈木（山毛榉木）、桦木、樱桃木、栗木、榆木、桉木、山核桃、七叶树、椴木、槭木、栎木（橡木）、悬铃木、杨木、刺槐木、鹅掌楸或核桃木薄板制胶合板（每层厚度≤6mm，竹制除外）〔999〕	4	2	30	13/	0	千克/立方米	ABFE	MPQ	/27
4412.3300	90	至少有一表层是下列非针叶木：桤木、白蜡木、水青冈木（山毛榉木）、桦木、樱桃木、栗木、榆木、桉木、山核桃、七叶树、椴木、槭木、栎木（橡木）、悬铃木、杨木、刺槐木、鹅掌楸或核桃木薄板制胶合板〔999〕	4	2	30	13/	13	千克/立方米	AB	MPQ	/27
		--其他，至少有一表层为子目 4412.33 未具体列名的非针叶木：									
4412.3410		---其他，至少有一表层是温带非针叶木（子目 4412.33 的非针叶木除外）									
4412.3410	10	至少有一表层是濒危温带非针叶木薄板制胶合板〔999〕	4	2	30	13/	0	千克/立方米	*ABEF*	*MPQ*	/27
4412.3410	90	至少有一表层是其他温带非针叶木薄板制胶合板〔999〕	4	2	30	13/	13	千克/立方米	*AB*	*MPQ*	/27
4412.3490		---其他									
4412.3490	10	至少有一表层是濒危其他非针叶胶合板（每层厚度≤6*mm*，竹制除外）等待风景 16:58:09〔999〕	4	2	30	13/	0	千克/立方米	*ABEF*	*MPQ*	/27

协定税率 %										特惠税率 %			Article Description
亚太5国	东/冰/格	巴基斯坦	韩国	瑞士	哥达	秘鲁	澳大利亚	新西/坡/智	港/澳/台	亚太2国	老/柬/缅	36/3/1	
	5//	4.5	6	0	0	0	0	0//	0/0/			0//	Laminated wood of endangered bamboo, with at least one outer ply of endangered non-coniferous wood, each ply thickness≤6mm
	5//	4.5	6	0	0	0	0	0//	0/0/			0//	Laminated wood of endangered bamboo, with at least one outer ply of non-coniferous wood, each ply thickness≤6mm
	5//	4.5	6	0	0	0	0	0//	0/0/			0//	Laminated wood of bamboo, with at least one outer ply of endangered non-coniferous wood in imminent dangers, each ply thickness ≤6mm
	5//	4.5	6	0	0	0	0	0//	0/0/			0//	Laminated wood of bamboo, with at least one outer ply of non-coniferous wood, each ply thickness≤6mm
													---Other:
													----With at least one outer ply of tropical wood
			4.8	0				0//	0/0/				tropical wood of endangered bamboo, containing at least one layer of tropical wood
			4.8	0				0//	0/0/				tropical wood of other bamboo, containing at least one layer of tropical wood
													----Containing at least one layer of particle board
			6	0				0//	0/0/				Laminated wood, at least one outer ply of endangered bamboo, containing at least one layer of particle board
			6	0				0//	0/0/				Laminated wood, at least one outer ply of other bamboo, containing at least one layer of particle board
													----Other
	0/0/	0	0	0	0	0	0	0/0/0	0/0/			0/0/0	Other laminated wood of endangered bamboo
	0/0/	0	0	0	0	0	0	0/0/0	0/0/			0/0/0	Other laminated of bamboo
													-Other plywood consisting solely of sheets of wood(other than bamboo), each ply exceeding 6mm thickness:
													--With at least one outer ply of tropical wood
	5/0/		7.2	3.6	0	0	0	0//0	0/0/			0//	Plywood, with at least one outer ply of Acajou d'afrique, each ply thickness≤6mm
	5/0/		7.2	3.6	0	0	0	0//0	0/0/			0//	Plywood, with at least one outer ply of Ramin wood, each ply thickness≤6mm
	5/0/		7.2	3.6	0	0	0	0//0	0/0/			0//	Plywood, with at least one outer ply of tropical wood, each ply not exceeding 6mm thickness
	5/0/		7.2	3.6	0	0	0	0//0	0/0/			0//	Plywood, with at least one outer ply of other tropical wood, each ply not exceeding 6mm thickness, other than bamboo
													--Other, with at least one outer ply Of non-coniferous wood Of the species alder (*Alnus spp.*), ash (*Fraxinus spp.*), beech (*Fagus spp.*), birch (*Betula spp.*), *chestnut* (Castanea spp.), elm (*Ulmus spp.*), eucalyptus(*eucalyp-tus spp.*)
			2.4	0				0//	0/0/				At least one surface of the following endangered non coniferous wood: alder, Chinese ash, water wood (beech), birch, cherry, chestnut, elm, eucalyptus, hickory, chestnut, basswood, maple, oak (oak), sycamore, poplar, locust, Liriodendron or walnut plywood sheet, of a thickness not exceeding 6mm
			2.4	0				0//	0/0/				At least one surface of the following non coniferous wood: alder, Chinese ash, water wood (beech), birch, cherry, chestnut, elm, eucalyptus, hickory, chestnut, basswood, maple, oak (oak), sycamore, poplar, locust, Liriodendron or walnut plywood sheet, of a thickness not exceeding 6mm
													--Other, with at least one outer ply of non-coniferous wood not specified under subheading 4412.33:
													---With at least one outer ply of temperate non-coniferous wood(*other than non-conif-erous wood of subheading* 4412.33)
			2.4	0				0//	0/0/				*Plywood, with at least one outer ply of other endangered temperate non-coniferous wood, each ply not exceeding 6mm thickness (other than of bamboo)*
			2.4	0				0//	0/0/				*Plywood, with at least one outer ply of other temperate non-coniferous wood, each ply not exceeding 6mm thickness (other than of bamboo)*
													---Other
			2.4	0				0//	0/0/				*Plywood, with at least one outer ply of other endangered non-coniferous wood, each ply not exceeding 6mm thickness (other than of bamboo)*

税则号列	货品名称〔CIQ扩展编码及品名－T2表示见附表2〕	最惠(%)	暂定税率	普通	增值/消费	出口退税	计量单位	监管条件	检验检疫	特殊证件对美关税
4412.3490　90	至少有一表层是其他非针叶胶合板〔999〕	4	2	30	13/	13	千克/立方米	AB	MPQ	/27
4412.3900	--其他，上下表层均为针叶木									
4412.3900　10	其他濒危薄板制胶合板，上下表层均为针叶木（每层厚度≤6mm，竹制除外）〔101 针叶木胶合板，102 非针叶木胶合板，103 其它胶合板〕	4	2	30	13/	0	千克/立方米	ABFE	MPQ	/27
4412.3900　90	其他薄板制胶合板，上下表层均为针叶木（每层厚度≤6mm，竹制除外）〔101 针叶木胶合板，102 非针叶木胶合板，103 其它胶合板〕	4	2	30	13/	13	千克/立方米	AB	MPQ	/27
	-其他：									
	--木块芯胶合板，侧板条芯胶合板及板条芯胶合板：									
4412.9410	---至少有一表层是非针叶木									
4412.9410　10	至少有一表层是桃花心木的木块芯胶合板等（还包括侧板条芯胶合板及板条芯胶合板）〔999〕	6	3	30	13/	6	千克/立方米	ABFE	MPQ	/28
4412.9410　20	至少有一表层是拉敏木的木块芯胶合板等（还包括侧板条芯胶合板及板条芯胶合板）〔999〕	6	3	30	13/	6	千克/立方米	AB	MPQ	/28
4412.9410　30	至少有一表层是濒危热带木的木块芯胶合板等（还包括侧板条芯胶合板及板条芯胶合板）〔999〕	6	3	30	13/	0	千克/立方米	ABFE	MPQ	/28
4412.9410　40	至少有一表层是濒危非针叶木的木块芯胶合板等（还包括侧板条芯胶合板及板条芯胶合板）〔999〕	6	3	30	13/	0	千克/立方米	ABFE	MPQ	/28
4412.9410　90	至少有一表层是非针叶木的木块芯胶合板等（还包括侧板条芯胶合板及板条芯胶合板）〔999〕	6	3	30	13/	13	千克/立方米	AB	MPQ	/28
	---其他：									
4412.9491	----至少有一层是热带木									
4412.9491　10	至少有一层是濒危热带木的针叶木面木块芯胶合板等（还包括侧板条芯胶合板及板条芯胶合板）〔999〕	6	3	30	13/	0	千克/立方米	ABFE	MPQ	/
4412.9491　90	至少有一层是热带木的针叶木面木块芯胶合板等（还包括侧板条芯胶合板及板条芯胶合板）〔999〕	6	3	30	13/	13	千克/立方米	AB	MPQ	/
4412.9492	----其他，至少含有一层木碎料板									
4412.9492　10	至少含有一层木碎料板的濒危针叶木面木块芯胶合板等（还包括侧板条芯胶合板及板条芯胶合板）〔999〕	6	3	30	13/	0	千克/立方米	ABFE	MPQ	/
4412.9492　90	至少含有一层木碎料板的针叶木面木块芯胶合板等（还包括侧板条芯胶合板及板条芯胶合板）〔999〕	6	3	30	13/	13	千克/立方米	AB	MPQ	/
4412.9499	----其他									
4412.9499　10	其他濒危针叶木面木块芯胶合板等（还包括侧板条芯胶合板及板条芯胶合板）〔999〕	4	2	30	13/	0	千克/立方米	ABEF	MPQ	/
4412.9499　90	其他针叶木面木块芯胶合板等（还包括侧板条芯胶合板及板条芯胶合板）〔999〕	4	2	30	13/	13	千克/立方米	AB	MPQ	/
	--其他：									
4412.9910	---至少有一表层是非针叶木									
4412.9910　10	至少有一表层是桃花心木的多层板〔999〕	6	3	30	13/	6,0	千克/立方米	ABFE	MPQ	/28
4412.9910　20	至少有一表层是拉敏木的多层板〔999〕	6	3	30	13/	6,0	千克/立方米	ABFE	MPQ	/28
4412.9910　30	至少有一表层是濒危热带木的多层板〔999〕	6	3	30	13/	0	千克/立方米	ABFE	MPQ	/28
4412.9910　40	其他至少有一表层是濒危非针叶木的多层板〔999〕	6	3	30	13/	0	千克/立方米	ABFE	MPQ	/28
4412.9910　90	其他至少有一表层是非针叶木的多层板〔999〕	6	3	30	13/	13	千克/立方米	AB	MPQ	/28
	---其他：									
4412.9991	----至少有一层是热带木									
4412.9991　10	其他至少有一层是濒危热带木的针叶木面多层板〔999〕	6	3	30	13/	0	千克/立方米	ABFE	MPQ	/
4412.9991　90	其他至少有一层是热带木的针叶木面多层板〔999〕	6	3	30	13/	13	千克/立方米	AB	MPQ	/
4412.9992	----其他，至少含有一层木碎料板									
4412.9992　10	其他至少含有一层木碎料板的濒危针叶木面多层板〔999〕	6	3	30	13/	0	千克/立方米	ABFE	MPQ	/
4412.9992　90	其他至少含有一层木碎料板的针叶木面多层板〔999〕	6	3	30	13/	13	千克/立方米	AB	MPQ	/
4412.9999	----其他									
4412.9999　10	其他濒危针叶木面多层板〔999〕	4	2	30	13/	0	千克/立方米	ABFE	MPQ	/27
4412.9999　90	其他针叶木面多层板〔999〕	4	2	30	13/	13	千克/立方米	AB	MPQ	/27
44.13	**强化木，成块、板、条或异型的：**									
4413.0000	强化木（成块、板、条或异型的）〔999〕	6	3	20	13/	13	千克	AB	MPQ	/28

协定税率 %										特惠税率 %			Article Description
亚太5国	东/冰/格	巴基斯坦	韩国	瑞士	哥达	秘鲁	澳大利亚	新西/坡/智	港/澳/台	亚太2国	老/柬/缅	36/3/1	
			2.4	0				0//	0/0/				Plywood, with at least one outer ply of other non-coniferous wood, each ply not exceeding 6mm thickness (other than of bamboo)
													--Other, with both outer plies of coniferous wood
	0/0/	0	0	0	0	0	0	0/0/0	0/0/			0/0/0	Plywood, Plywood consisting solely of sheets of endangered wood, Upper and lower surface are needle leaf wood, each ply not exceeding 6mm thickness (other than of bamboo)
	0/0/	0	0	0	0	0	0	0/0/0	0/0/			0/0/0	Plywood consisting solely of sheets of other wood, Upper and lower surface are needle leaf wood, each ply not exceeding 6mm thickness (other than of bamboo)
													-Other:
													--Blockboard, laminboard and battenboard:
													---With at least one outer ply of non-coniferous wood
	5//	4.5	6	0				0//2	0/0/				Blockboard (including laminboard and battenboard) with at least one outer ply of acajou board
	5//	4.5	6	0				0//2	0/0/				Blockboard (including laminboard and battenboard) with at least one outer ply of Ramin board
	5//	4.5	6	0				0//2	0/0/				Blockboard (including laminboard and battenboard) with at least one outer ply of endangered tropical wood
	5//	4.5	6	0				0//2	0/0/				Blockboard (including laminboard and battenboard) with at least one outer ply of endangered non-coniferous wood
	5//	4.5	6	0				0//2	0/0/				Boockboard (including laminboard and battenboard) with at least one outer ply of non-coniferous wood
													---Other:
													----With at least one outer ply of tropical wood
			4.8	0				0//2	0/0/				Blockboard, laminboard and battenboard, with at least one outer ply of endangered tropical coniferous wood
			4.8	0				0//2	0/0/				Blockboard, laminboard and battenboard, with at least one outer ply of tropical coniferous wood
													----Other, containing at least one layer of particle board
			6	0				0//2	0/0/				Blockboard (including laminboard and battenboard), with at least one layer of particle board, sruface layer of endangered coniferous wood
			6	0				0//2	0/0/				Blockboard (including laminboard and battenboard), with at least one layer of particle board, sruface layer of coniferous wood
													----Other
	0/0/	0	0	0	0	0	0	0/0/0	0/0/			0/0/0	Other laminated wood, containing an least one layer of particle board, surface layer of endangered coniferous wood
	0/0/	0	0	0	0	0	0	0/0/0	0/0/			0/0/0	Other laminated wood, containing an least one layer of particle board, surface layer of coniferous wood
													--Other:
													---With at least one outer ply of non-coniferous wood
	5//	4.5	6	0				0//2	0/0/				Laminated wood with at least one outer ply of Acajou d'afrique
	5//	4.5	6	0				0//2	0/0/				Laminated wood with a least one outer ply of Ramin wood
	5//	4.5	6	0				0//2	0/0/				Laminated wood with at least one outer ply of endangered tropical wood
	5//	4.5	6	0				0//2	0/0/				Laminated wood with at least one outer ply of endangered non-coniferous wood
	5//	4.5	6	0				0//2	0/0/				Laminated wood with at least one outer ply of non-coniferous wood
													---Other:
													----With at least one outer ply of tropical wood
			4.8	0				0//2	0/0/				Other laminated wood, with at least one outer ply of tropical coniferous wood
			4.8	0				0//2	0/0/				Other laminated wood, with at least one outer ply of tropical coniferous wood
													----Other, containing at least one layer of particle board
			6	0				0//2	0/0/				Other laminated wood, containing at least one layer of particle bodrd, surface layer of endangered conirterus wood
			6	0				0//2	0/0/				Other laminated wood, containing at least one layer of particle board, surface layer of conirerous wood
													----Other
2.8	0/0/	0	0	0	0	0	0	0/0/0	0/0/			0/0/	The endangered coniferous board veneer particle board
2.8	0/0/	0	0	0	0	0	0	0/0/0	0/0/			0/0/	The coniferous board veneer particle board
													Densified wood, in blocks, plates, strips or profile shapes:
	0/0/	0	2.4	0	0	0	0	0/0/0	0/0/			0/0/0	Densified wood, in blocks, plates, strips or profile shapes

税则号列	货品名称〔CIQ 扩展编码及品名—T2 表示见附表 2〕	最惠(%)	暂定税率	普通	增值/消费	出口退税	计量单位	监管条件	检验检疫	特殊证件对美关税
44.14	**木制的画框、相框、镜框及类似品：**									
4414.0010	---辐射松制的〔999〕	7	3	100	13/	13	千克	AB	PQ	/23
4414.0090	---其他									
4414.0090 10	拉敏木制画框、相框、镜框及类似品〔999〕	7		100	13/	13	千克	ABFE	PQ	/27
4414.0090 20	濒危木制画框、相框、镜框及类似品〔999〕	7		100	13/	0	千克	ABFE	PQ	/27
4414.0090 90	其他木制的画框、相框、镜框及类似品〔999〕	7		100	13/	13	千克	AB	PQ	/27
44.15	**包装木箱、木盒、板条箱、圆桶及类似的包装容器；木制电缆卷筒；木托板、箱形托盘及其他装载用木板；木制的托盘护框：**									
4415.1000	-箱、盒、板条箱、圆桶及类似的包装容器；电缆卷筒									
4415.1000 10	拉敏木制木箱及类似包装容器(电缆卷筒)〔999〕	6	3	80	13/	6	千克/件	ABFE	PQ	/28
4415.1000 20	濒危木制木箱及类似包装容器(电缆卷筒)[T2]	6	3	80	13/	0	千克/件	ABFE	PQ	/28
4415.1000 90	木箱及类似的包装容器、电缆卷筒[T2]	6	3	80	13/	13	千克/件	AB	PQ	/28
	-木托板、箱形托盘及其他装载用木板；木制的托盘护框：									
4415.2010	---辐射松制的〔999〕	6	3	80	13/	10	千克/件	AB	PQ	/
4415.2090	---其他									
4415.2090 10	拉敏木托板、箱形托盘及装载木板(包括拉敏木制托盘护框)〔999〕	6	3	80	13/	6	千克/件	AB	PQ	/28
4415.2090 20	濒危木托板、箱形托盘及装载木板(包括濒危木制托盘护框)〔101 针叶木木质包装，102 非针叶木木质包装，103 其他木质包装〕	6	3	80	13/	0	千克/件	ABFE	PQ	/28
4415.2090 90	其他木制托板、箱形托盘及其他装载木板(包括其他木制托盘护框)[T2]	6	3	80	13/	13	千克/件	AB	PQ	/28
44.16	**木制大桶、琵琶桶、盆和其他木制箍桶及其零件，包括桶板：**									
4416.0010	---辐射松制的〔101 其他木制品，102 针叶木木质包装〕	12	9	80	13/	0	千克	AB	PQ	/
4416.0090	---其他									
4416.0090 10	拉敏木制大桶、琵琶桶、盆和其他箍桶及其零件(包括拉敏木制桶板)〔101 其他木制品，102 非针叶木木质包装〕	12		80	13/	0	千克	ABFE	PQ	/32
4416.0090 20	濒危木制大桶、琵琶桶、盆和其他箍桶及其零件(包括濒危木制桶板)〔101 其他木制品，102 针叶木木质包装，103 非针叶木木质包装，104 其他木质包装〕	12		80	13/	0	千克	ABFE	PQ	/32
4416.0090 90	其他木制大桶、琵琶桶、盆和其他箍桶及其零件(包括其他木制桶板)[T2]	12		80	13/	0	千克	AB	PQ	/32
44.17	**木制的工具、工具支架、工具柄、扫帚及刷子的身及柄；木制鞋靴楦及楦头：**									
4417.0010	---辐射松制的〔999〕	12	9	80	13/	0	千克	AB	PQ	/
4417.0090	---其他									
4417.0090 10	拉敏木制工具、工具支架、工具柄、扫帚及刷子的身及柄(包括拉敏木制鞋靴楦及楦头)〔999〕	12		80	13/	0	千克	ABFE	PQ	/37
4417.0090 20	濒危木制工具、工具支架、工具柄、扫帚及刷子的身及柄(包括濒危木制鞋靴楦及楦头)〔999〕	12		80	13/	0	千克	ABFE	PQ	/37
4417.0090 90	其他木制工具、工具支架、工具柄、扫帚及刷子的身及柄(包括其他木制鞋靴楦及楦头)〔999〕	12		80	13/	0	千克	AB	PQ	/37
44.18	**建筑用木工制品，包括蜂窝结构木镶板、已装拼的地板、木瓦及盖屋板：**									
	-窗、法兰西式(落地)窗及其框架：									
4418.1010	---辐射松制的〔999〕	4	2	70	13/	10	千克	AB	LPQ	/
4418.1090	---其他									
4418.1090 10	拉敏木制木窗、落地窗及其框架〔999〕	4		70	13/	6	千克	ABFE	LPQ	/29
4418.1090 20	濒危木制木窗、落地窗及其框架〔999〕	4		70	13/	0	千克	ABFE	LPQ	/29
4418.1090 90	其他木制木窗、落地窗及其框架〔999〕	4		70	13/	13	千克	AB	LPQ	/29
4418.2000	-门及其框架和门槛									
4418.2000 10	拉敏木制的木门及其框架和门槛〔999〕	4	2	70	13/	6	千克	ABFE	PQ	/27
4418.2000 20	濒危木制的木门及其框架和门槛〔999〕	4	2	70	13/	0	千克	ABFE	PQ	/27
4418.2000 90	木门及其框架和门槛〔101 木门，102 其他木制品〕	4	2	70	13/	13	千克	AB	LPQ	/27
4418.4000	-水泥构件的木模板〔999〕	4	2	70	13/	13	千克	AB	PQ	/

协定税率 %										特惠税率 %			
亚太5国	东/冰/格	巴基斯坦	韩国	瑞士	哥达	秘鲁	澳大利亚	新西/坡/智	港/澳/台	亚太2国	老/柬/缅	36/3/1	Article Description
													Wooden frames for paintings, photographs, mirrors or similar objects:
							0	0//23	0/0/			0//	---Of radiata pine
													---Other
													Frames for paintings, photographs, mirrors or similar objects, of Ramin wood
													Frames for paintings, photographs, mirrors or similar objects, of endangered wood
													Frames for paintings, photographs, mirrors or similar objects, of wood
													Packing cases, boxes, crates, drums and similar packings, of wood; cable-drums of wood; pallets, box pallets and other load boards, of wood; pallet collars of wood:
													-Cases, boxes, crates, drums and similar packing; cabledrums
	0/0/	4	3	0	0	0	0	0/0/0	0/0/			0/0/0	Cases and similar packing; cable-drums, of Ramin wood (*gonystylus. spp.*)
	0/0/	4	3	0	0	0	0	0/0/0	0/0/			0/0/0	Cases and similar packing; cable-drums, of endangered wood
	0/0/	4	3	0	0	0	0	0/0/0	0/0/			0/0/0	Cases and similar packing; cable-drums, of wood
													-Pallets, box pallets and other load boards; pallet collars:
	5//						0	0//2	0/0/			0//	---Of radiatat pine
													---Other
	5//							5//					Pallets, box pallets and other load boards; pallet collars, of Ramin wood (*gonystylus. spp.*)
	5//							5//					Fallets, box pallets and other load boards; pallet collars, of endangered wood
	5//							5//					Fallets, box pallets and other load boards; pallet collars, of wood
													Casks, barrels, vats, tubs and other coopers' products and parts thereof, of wood, including staves:
							0	0//4	0/0/			0//	---Of radiata pine
													---Other
													Coopers' products and parts thereof (including staves), of Ramin wood (*gonystylus. spp.*)
													Coopers' products and parts thereof (including staves), of endangered wood
													Coopers' products and parts thereof (including staves), of other wood
													Tools, tool bodies, tool handles, broom or brush bodies and handles, of wood; boot or shoe lasts and trees, of wood:
							0	0//4	0/0/			0//	---Of radiata pine
													---Other
													Tools, tool bodies, tool handles, broom or brush bodies and handles, of ramin wood (including boot or shoe lasts and trees, of ramin wood)
													Tools, tool bodies, tool handles, broom or brush bodies and handles, of endangered wood (including boot or shoe lasts and trees, of endangered wood)
													Tools, tool bodies, tool handles, broom or brush bodies and handles, of wood (including boot or shoe lasts and trees, of wood)
													Builders' joinery and carpentry of wood, including cellular wood panels, assembled flooring parquet panels, shingles and shakes:
													-Windows, French-windows and their frames:
							0	0//	0/0/			0//	---Of radiata pine
													---Other
									0/0/			0//	Windows, French-windows and their frames of Ramin wood (*gonystylus. spp.*)
									0/0/			0//	Windows, French-windows and their frames of endangered wood
									0/0/			0//	Windows, French-windows and their frames of other wood
													-Doors and their frames and thresholds
	0/0/	0	0	0	0	0	0	0/0/0	0/0/			0/0/0	Doors and their frames and thresholds of Ramin wood (*gonystylus. spp.*)
	0/0/	0	0	0	0	0	0	0/0/0	0/0/			0/0/0	Doors and their frames and thresholds of endangered wood
	0/0/	0	0	0	0	0	0	0/0/0	0/0/			0/0/0	Doors and their frames and thresholds of other wood
	0/0/	0	0	0	0	0	0	0//0	0/0/			0/0/0	-Shuttering for concrete constructional work

税则号列	货品名称〔CIQ扩展编码及品名－T2表示见附表2〕	最惠(%)	暂定税率	普通	增值/消费	出口退税	计量单位	监管条件	检验检疫	特殊证件对美关税
4418.5000	-木瓦及盖屋板〔101 木瓦,102 其他木制品〕	6	3	70	13/	13	千克	AB	PQ	/
4418.6000	-柱和梁									
4418.6000 10	濒危木制柱和梁〔999〕	4	2	70	13/	0	千克	FEAB	PQ	/27
4418.6000 90	其他木制柱和梁〔999〕	4	2	70	13/	13	千克	AB	PQ	/27
	-已装拼的地板:									
	--竹的或至少顶层(耐磨层)是竹的:									
4418.7310	---马赛克地板用〔999〕	4	2	70	13/	0	千克	AB	PQ	/
4418.7320	---其他,竹制多层的〔999〕	4	2	70	13/	13	千克	AB	PQ	/
4418.7390	---其他〔999〕	4	2	70	13/	13	千克	AB	PQ	/
4418.7400	--其他,马赛克地板用									
4418.7400 10	已装拼的拉敏木制马赛克地板〔999〕	4	2	70	13/	0	千克	ABFE	PQ	/
4418.7400 20	已装拼的其他濒危木制马赛克地板〔999〕	4	2	70	13/	0	千克	ABFE	PQ	/
4418.7400 90	已装拼的其他木制马赛克地板〔999〕	4	2	70	13/	0	千克	AB	PQ	/
4418.7500	--其他,多层的									
4418.7500 10	已装拼的拉敏木制多层地板〔999〕	4	2	70	13/	0	千克	ABFE	PQ	/27
4418.7500 20	已装拼的其他濒危木制多层地板〔999〕	4	2	70	13/	0	千克	ABFE	PQ	/27
4418.7500 90	已装拼的其他木制多层地板〔999〕	4	2	70	13/	0	千克	AB	PQ	/27
4418.7900	--其他									
4418.7900 10	已装拼的拉敏木制其他地板〔999〕	4	2	70	13/	0	千克	ABFE	PQ	/22
4418.7900 20	已装拼的其他濒危木制地板〔999〕	4	2	70	13/	0	千克	ABFE	PQ	/22
4418.7900 90	已装拼的木制其他地板〔999〕	4	2	70	13/	0	千克	AB	PQ	/22
	-其他:									
4418.9100	--竹的									
4418.9100 10	濒危竹制其他建筑用木工制品〔999〕	4	2	70	13/	0	千克	ABE	PQ	/
4418.9100 90	其他竹制其他建筑用木工制品〔999〕	4	2	70	13/	13	千克	AB	PQ	/
4418.9900	--其他									
4418.9900 10	拉敏木制其他建筑用木工制品〔999〕	4	2	70	13/	6	千克	FEAB	PQ	/27
4418.9900 20	濒危木制其他建筑用木工制品〔999〕	4	2	70	13/	0	千克	FEAB	PQ	/27
4418.9900 90	其他建筑用木工制品(包括蜂窝结构的木镶板)〔999〕	4	2	70	13/	13	千克	AB	PQ	/27
44.19	**木制餐具及厨房用具:**									
	-竹的:									
4419.1100	--切面包板、砧板及类似板〔999〕	0		100	13/	13	千克	AB	PRQ	/5
	--筷子:									
4419.1210	----次性筷子									
4419.1210 10	酸竹制一次性筷子〔999 食品接触木制产品,998 竹筷〕	0		100	13/	0	千克	ABE	PRQ	/10
4419.1210 90	其他竹制一次性筷子〔999 食品接触木制产品,998 竹筷〕	0		100	13/	13	千克	AB	PRQ	/10
4419.1290	---其他〔999 食品接触木制产品,998 竹筷〕	0		100	13/	13	千克	AB	PRQ	/10
4419.1900	--其他〔999〕	0		100	13/	13	千克	AB	PRQ	/10
	-其他:									
4419.9010	----次性筷子[T2]	0		100	13/5	0	千克	AB	PQ	/10
4419.9090	---其他									
4419.9090 10	拉敏木制的其他餐具及厨房用具〔999〕	0		100	13/	6	千克	FEAB	PRQ	/30
4419.9090 20	濒危木制的其他餐具及厨房用具〔999〕	0		100	13/	0	千克	FEAB	PRQ	/30
4419.9090 90	其他木制其他餐具及厨房用具〔999〕	0		100	13/	10	千克	AB	PRQ	/30
44.20	**镶嵌木(包括细工镶嵌木);装珠宝或刀具用的木制盒子和小匣子及类似品;木制小雕像及其他装饰品;第九十四章以外的木制家具:**									
	-木制小雕像及其他装饰品:									
	---木刻及竹刻:									
4420.1011	----木刻									
4420.1011 20	濒危木制的木刻〔999〕	0		100	13/	0	千克	FEAB	PQ	/25
4420.1011 90	其他木刻〔101 木制工艺品,102 其他木制品〕	0		100	13/	13	千克	AB	PQ	/25
4420.1012	----竹刻〔999〕	0		100	13/	13	千克	AB	PQ	/
4420.1020	---木扇									
4420.1020 20	濒危木制的木扇〔999〕	0		100	13/	0	千克	FEAB	PQ	/
4420.1020 90	木扇〔999〕	0		100	13/	13	千克	AB	PQ	/
4420.1090	---其他									

协定税率 %										特惠税率 %			
亚太5国	东/冰/格	巴基斯坦	韩国	瑞士	哥达	秘鲁	澳大利亚	新西/坡/智	港/澳/台	亚太2国	老/柬/缅	36/3/1	Article Description
	0/0/	4	0	0	0	0	0	0//0	0/0/			0/0/0	-Shingles and shakes
													-Poles and beams
	0/0/	0	0	0	0	0	0	0/0/0	0/0/			0/0/0	Endangered wood made poles and girder
	0/0/	0	0	0	0	0	0	0/0/0	0/0/			0/0/0	Other wood made poles and girder
													-Assembled flooring panels:
													--Of bamboo or with at least the top layer (*wear layer*) of bamboo:
	0/0/	0	0	0	0	0	0	0/0/0	0/0/			0/0/0	---For mosaic floors
	0/0/	0	0	0	0	0	0	0/0/0	0/0/			0/0/	---Other, multilayer of bamboo
	0/0/	0	0	0	0	0	0	0/0/0	0/0/			0/0/	---Other
													---Other, for mosaic floors
	0/0/	0	0	0	0	0	0	0/0/0	0/0/			0/0/0	Assembled flooring panels for mosaic floor, of Ramin wood
	0/0/	0	0	0	0	0	0	0/0/0	0/0/			0/0/0	Assembled flooring panels for mosaic floor, of other endangered wood
	0/0/	0	0	0	0	0	0	0/0/0	0/0/			0/0/0	Assembled flooring panels for mosaic floor, of other wood
													---Other, multilayer
	0/0/0	0	0	0	0	0	0	0/0/0	0/0/			0/0/	Assembled flooring panels, multilayer, of Ramin wood
	0/0/0	0	0	0	0	0	0	0/0/0	0/0/			0/0/	Assembled flooring panels, multilayer, of endangered wood
	0/0/0	0	0	0	0	0	0	0/0/0	0/0/			0/0/	Assembled flooring panels, multilayer, of other wood
													--Other
	0/0/	0	0	0	0	0	0	0/0/0	0/0/			0/0/	Other flooring panels of ramin wood , assembled
	0/0/	0	0	0	0	0	0	0/0/0	0/0/			0/0/	Other flooring panels of endangered wood , assembled
	0/0/	0	0	0	0	0	0	0/0/0	0/0/			0/0/	Other flooring panels of other wood , assembled
													-Other:
													--Of bamboo
	0/0/	0	0	0	0	0	0	0/0/0	0/0/			0/0/0	Other builder's joinery and carpentry of endangered bamboo(including cellular wood panels)
	0/0/	0	0	0	0	0	0	0/0/0	0/0/			0/0/0	Other builder's joinery and carpentry of other bamboo(including cellular wood panels)
													--Other
	0/0/	0	0	0	0	0	0	0/0/0	0/0/			0/0/0	Other builder's joinery and carpentry of Ramin wood(including cellular wood panels)
	0/0/	0	0	0	0	0	0	0/0/0	0/0/			0/0/0	Other builder's joinery and carpentry of other endangered wood(including cellular wood panels)
	0/0/	0	0	0	0	0	0	0/0/0	0/0/			0/0/0	Other builder's joinery and carpentry of other bamboo(including cellular wood panels)
													Tableware and kitchenware, of wood:
													-Of bamboo:
												0/0/0	--Bread boards, chopping boards and similar boards
													--Chopsticks:
													---One-time chopsticks
												0/0/0	One-time chopsticks, of acidosasa chinensis
												0/0/0	One-time chopsticks, of other bamboo
												0/0/0	---Other
												0/0/0	---Other
													-Other
												0/0/0	---One-time chopsticks
													---Other
												0/0/0	Other tableware and kitchenware, of Ramin wood
												0/0/0	Other tableware and kitchenware, of endangered wood
												0/0/0	Other tableware and kitchenware, of other wood
													Wood marquetry and inlaid wood; caskets and cases for jewellery or cutlery, and similar articles, of wood; statuettes and other ornaments, of wood; wooden articles or furniture not falling in Chapter 94:
													-Statuettes and other ornaments, of wood:
													---Wood or bamboo carvings:
													----wood carving
												0/0/0	Wood carving of endangered wood
												0/0/0	Other wood carving
												0/0/0	----Bamboo carving
													---Wooden fans
												0/0/0	Wooden fans of endangered wood
												0/0/0	Wooden fans
													---Other

税则号列	货品名称〔CIQ扩展编码及品名－T2表示见附表2〕	最惠(%)	暂定税率	普通	增值/消费	出口退税	计量单位	监管条件	检验检疫	特殊证件对美关税
4420.1090 30	沉香木及拟沉香木制其他小雕像及其他装饰品〔999〕	0		100	13/	0	千克	FEAB	PQ	/25
4420.1090 40	其他濒危木制其他小雕像及其他装饰品〔999〕	0		100	13/	0	千克	FEAB	PQ	/25
4420.1090 90	其他木制小雕像及其他装饰品〔999〕	0		100	13/	13	千克	AB	PQ	/25
	-其他：									
4420.9010	---镶嵌木									
4420.9010 10	拉敏木制的镶嵌木〔999〕	0		45	13/	10	千克	FEAB	PQ	/5
4420.9010 20	濒危木制的镶嵌木〔999〕	0		45	13/	0	千克	FEAB	PQ	/5
4420.9010 90	镶嵌木〔999〕	0		45	13/	13	千克	AB	PQ	/5
4420.9090	---其他									
4420.9090 10	拉敏木盒及类似品，非落地木家具（前者用于装珠宝或家具；后者不包括第九十四章的家具）〔999〕	0		100	13/	6	千克	FEAB	PQ	/25
4420.9090 20	濒危木盒及类似品，非落地木家具（前者用于装珠宝或家具；后者不包括第九十四章的家具）〔999〕	0		100	13/	0	千克	FEAB	PQ	/25
4420.9090 90	木盒子及类似品；非落地式木家具（前者用于装珠宝或家具；后者不包括第九十四章的家具）〔999〕	0		100	13/	13	千克	AB	PQ	/25
44.21	**其他木制品：**									
4421.1000	-衣架									
4421.1000 10	拉敏木制木衣架〔999〕	0		90	13/	6	千克	AB	PQ	/25
4421.1000 20	濒危木制木衣架〔999〕	0		90	13/	0	千克	FEAB	PQ	/25
4421.1000 90	木衣架〔999〕	0		90	13/	13	千克	AB	PQ	/25
	-其他：									
	--竹的：									
4421.9110	---圆签、圆棒、冰果棒、压舌片及类似一次性制品									
4421.9110 10	酸竹制圆签、圆棒、冰果棒、压舌片及类似一次性制品〔999食品接触竹制产品，998其他竹及竹制品〕	0		35	13/	0	千克	ABE	PQ	/25
4421.9110 90	其他竹制圆签、圆棒、冰果棒、压舌片及类似一次性制品〔999食品接触竹制产品，998其他竹及竹制品〕	0		35	13/	13	千克	AB	PQ	/25
4421.9190	---其他									
4421.9190 10	其他未列名的濒危竹制品〔999〕	0		90	13/	0	千克	FEAB	PQ	/20
4421.9190 90	其他未列名的竹制品〔999〕	0		35	13/	13	千克	AB	PQ	/20
	--其他：									
4421.9910	---木制圆签、圆棒、冰果棒、压舌片及类似一次性制品									
4421.9910 10	拉敏木制圆签、圆棒、冰果棒、压舌片及类似一次性制品〔999其他木制品，998其他木制品〕	0		35	13/	0	千克	FEAB	PQ	/
4421.9910 20	濒危木制圆签、圆棒、冰果棒、压舌片及类似一次性制品〔999食品接触木制产品，998其他木制品〕	0		35	13/	0	千克	FEAB	PQ	/
4421.9910 90	其他木制圆签、圆棒、冰果棒、压舌片及类似一次性制品〔999食品接触木制产品，998其他木制品〕	0		35	13/	0	千克	AB	PQ	/
4421.9990	---其他									
4421.9990 10	拉敏木制的未列名的木制品〔999〕	0		35	13/	10	千克	FEAB	PQ	/25
4421.9990 20	濒危木制的未列名的木制品〔999〕	0		35	13/	0	千克	FEAB	PQ	/25
4421.9990 90	未列名的木制品〔999〕	0		35	13/	13	千克	AB	PQ	/25

协定税率 %										特惠税率 %			
亚太5国	东/冰/格	巴基斯坦	韩国	瑞士	哥达	秘鲁	澳大利亚	新西/坡/智	港/澳/台	亚太2国	老/柬/缅	36/3/1	Article Description
												0/0/0	Statuettes and other ornaments of chinese eaglewood and quasi chinese eaglewood
												0/0/0	Statuettes and other ornaments of endangered wood
												0/0/0	Statuettes and other ornaments of other wood
													-Other:
													---Wood marquetry and inlaid wood
												0/0/0	Wood marquetry and inlaid wood of Ramin wood
												0/0/0	Wood marquetry and inlaid wood of endangered wood
												0/0/0	Wood marquetry and inlaid wood
													---Other
												0/0/0	Caskets and similar articles non-floor type furniture not falling, of Ramin wood (the former used for jewelry or furniture, the latter not including furniture falling in Chapter 94)
												0/0/0	Caskets and similar articles or non-floor type furniture of endangered wood in(the former used for jewelry or furniture, the latter not including furniture falling in Chapter 94)
												0/0/0	Caskets and similar articles or furniture not falling, of wood (the former used for jewelry or furniture, the latter not including furniture falling in Chapter 94)
													Other articles of wood:
													-Clothes hangers
												0/0/0	Clothes hangers of Ramin wood
												0/0/0	Clothes hangers of endangered wood
												0/0/0	Clothes hangers of wood
													-Other:
													--Of bamboo:
													---Circle sticks, cricle bars, pop-sicle sticks, spatula and the like
												0/0/0	Round picks and sticks, sticks for ice-sucker, spatulas and similar one time articles, of acidosasa chinensis
												0/0/0	Round picks and sticks, sticks for ice-sucker, spatulas and similar one time articles, of other bamboo
													---Other
												0/0/0	Other endangered bamboo products, not specified
												0/0/0	Other bamboo products, not specified
													--Other:
													---Of wood, circle sticks, cir-cle bars, popsicle sticks, spatula and the like
												0/0/0	Round picks and sticks, sticks for ice-sucker, spatulas and similar one time articles, of Ramin wood
												0/0/0	Round picks and sticks, sticks for ice-sucker, spatulas and similar one time articles, of endangered wood
												0/0/0	Round picks and sticks, sticks for ice-sucker, spatulas and similar one time articles, of other wood
													---Other
												0/0/0	Articles cf ramin wood, not specified
												0/0/0	Articles of endangered wood, not specified
												0/0/0	Articles of wood, not specified

第四十五章
软木及软木制品

注释：

本章不包括：

一、第六十四章的鞋靴及其零件；

二、第六十五章的帽类及其零件；

三、第九十五章的物品(例如，玩具、游戏品及运动用品)。

税则号列		货品名称〔CIQ扩展编码及品名—T2表示见附表2〕	最惠(%)	暂定税率	普通	增值/消费	出口退税	计量单位	监管条件	检验检疫	特殊证件对美关税
45.01		**未加工或简单加工的天然软木；软木废料；碎的、粒状的或粉状的软木：**									
4501.1000		-未加工或简单加工的天然软木〔999〕	6	1	17	13/	0	千克	AB	PQ	/
		-其他：									
4501.9010		---软木废料〔102〕	0		17	13/	0	千克	9AB	MPQ	/25
4501.9020		---碎的、粉粒状的或粉状的软木(软木碎，软木粒或软木粉)〔999〕	0		17	13/	0	千克	AB	PQ	/25
45.02		**天然软木，除去表皮或粗切成方形，或成长方块、正方块、板、片或条状(包括作塞子用的方块坯料)：**									
4502.0000		天然软木，除去表皮或粗切成方形，或成长方块、正方块、板、片或条状(包括作塞子用的方块坯料)〔999〕	8	4	30	13/	0	千克	AB	PQ	/
45.03		**天然软木制品：**									
4503.1000		-塞子〔101 软木、软木粒及软木制品，102 食品接触木制产品〕	8	4	50	13/	0	千克	AB	PQ	/29
4503.9000		-其他〔999〕	8	4	50	13/	0	千克	AB	PQ	/24
45.04		**压制软木(不论是否使用黏合剂压成)及其制品：**									
4504.1000		-块、板、片及条状压制软木(包括任何形状的压制软木的砖，瓦，实心圆柱体，圆片)									
4504.1000	10	压制软木塞〔999〕	8	4	30	13/	0	千克	AB	PQ	/29
4504.1000	90	块，板，片及条状压制软木，压制软木塞除外〔999〕	8	4	30	13/	0	千克	AB	PQ	/29
4504.9000		-其他〔999〕	0		50	13/	0	千克	AB	PQ	/25

Chapter 45
Cork and articles of cork

Notes:

This Chapter does not cover:

(a) Footwear or parts of footwear of Chapter 64;

(b) Headgear or parts of headgear of Chapter 65;

(c) Articles of Chapter 95 (for example, toys, games, sports requisites).

协定税率 %										特惠税率 %			
亚太5国	东/冰/格	巴基斯坦	韩国	瑞士	哥达	秘鲁	澳大利亚	新西/坡/智	港/澳/台	亚太2国	老/柬/缅	36/3/1	Article Description
													Natural cork, raw or simply prepared; waste cork; crushed, granulated or ground cork:
	0/0/	0	0	0	0	0	0	0//0	0/0/			0/0/	-Natrual cork, raw or simply prepared
													-Other:
												0/0/0	---Waste cork
												0/0/0	---Crushed, granulated or ground cork (Cork wood is broken, the cork wood granule or cork wood turns to powder)
													Natural cork, debarked or roughly squared, or in rectangular (including square) blocks, plates, sheets or strip, (including sharp-edged blanks for corks or stoppers):
	0/0/	4	0	0	0	0	0	0//0	0/0/			0/0/0	Natural cork, debarked or roughly squared, or in rectangular (including square) blocks, plates, sheets or strip, (including sharp-edged blanks for corks or stoppers)
													Articles of natural cork:
	0/0/	4	0	0	0	0	0	0//0	0/0/			0/0/0	-Corks and stoppers
	0/0/	4.5	4.2	3.2	0	0	0	0/0/0	0/0/			0/0/0	-Other
													Agglomerated cork (with or without a binding substance) and articles of agglomerated cork:
													-Blocks, plates, sheets and strip; tiles of any shape; solid cylinders, including discs
	0/0/	4	3.3	0	0	0	0	0//0	0/0/			0/0/0	Suppression of cork (including any shape of agglomerated cork brick and tile, solid cylinder, wafer)
	0/0/	4	3.3	0	0	0	0	0//0	0/0/			0/0/0	Blocks, plates, sheets and strips, excluding suppression of cork (including any shape of agglomerated cork brick and tile, solid cylinder, wafer)
												0/0/0	-Other

第四十六章
稻草、秸秆、针茅或其他编结材料制品;篮筐及柳条编结品

注释:

一、本章所称“编结材料”,是指其状态或形状适于编结、交织或类似加工的材料,包括稻草、秸秆、柳条、竹、藤灯芯草、芦苇、木片条、其他植物材料扁条(例如,树皮条、狭叶、酒椰叶纤维或其他从阔叶获取的条)、未纺的天然纺织纤维、塑料单丝及扁条、纸带,但不包括皮革、再生皮革、毡呢或无纺织物的扁条、人发、马毛、纺织粗纱或纱线以及第五十四章的单丝和扁条。

二、本章不包括:

(一)税目48.14的壁纸;

(二)不论是否编结而成的线、绳、索、缆(税目56.07);

(三)第六十四章和第六十五章的鞋靴、帽类及其零件;

(四)编结而成的车辆或车身(第八十七章);

(五)第九十四章的物品(例如,家具、灯及灯具)。

三、税目46.01所称“平行连结的成片编结材料、缏条或类似的编结材料产品”,是指编结材料、缏条及类似的编结材料产品平行排列连结成片的制品,其连结材料不论是否为纺制的纺织材料。

税则号列		货品名称〔CIQ扩展编码及品名－T2表示见附表2〕	最惠(%)	暂定税率	普通	增值/消费	出口退税	计量单位	监管条件	检验检疫	特殊证件对美关税
46.01		**用编结材料编成的缏条及类似产品,不论是否缝合成宽条;平行连结或编结的成片材料、缏条或类似的编结材料产品,不论是否制成品(例如,席子、席料、帘子):**									
		-植物材料制的席子、席料及帘子:									
4601.2100		--竹制的〔101竹帘,102竹席〕	7		90	13/	13	千克/张	AB	PQ	/32
4601.2200		--藤制的〔999〕	7		100	13/	13	千克/张	AB	PQ	/
		--其他:									
		---草制的:									
4601.2911		----灯心草属材料制的									
4601.2911	11	蔺草制的提花席、双首席、垫子(单位面积>1m²,不论是否包边)〔999〕	7		90	13/	13	千克/张	4ABxy	PQ	/
4601.2911	12	蔺草制的其他席子(单位面积>1m²,不论是否包边)〔999〕	7		90	13/	13	千克/张	4ABxy	PQ	/
4601.2911	19	蔺草制的其他席子、席料及帘子(单位面积≤1m²,不论是否包边)〔999〕	7		90	13/	13	千克/张	AB	PQ	/
4601.2911	90	其他灯芯草属材料制的席子等(包括席子、席料、帘子、垫子)〔999〕	7		90	13/	13	千克/张	AB	PQ	/
4601.2919		----其他〔101稻草及其制品,102其他草及草制品〕	7		90	13/	13	千克/张	AB	PQ	/
		---芦苇制的:									
4601.2921		----苇帘〔999〕	7		90	13/	13	千克/张	AB	PQ	/
4601.2929		----其他〔999〕	7		90	13/	13	千克/张	AB	PQ	/
4601.2990		---其他〔101其他草及草制品,102棕及棕制品,103葵及葵制品,104其他竹藤柳草类〕	7		90	13/	13	千克/张	AB	PQ	/
		-其他:									
		--竹制的:									
4601.9210		---缏条及类似产品,不论是否缝合成宽条〔101其他竹及竹制品,102其他竹藤柳草类〕	7		100	13/	13	千克	AB	PQ	/
4601.9290		---其他〔101其他竹及竹制品,102其他竹藤柳草类〕	7		90	13/	13	千克	AB	PQ	/
		--藤制的:									
4601.9310		---缏条及类似产品,不论是否缝合成宽条〔999〕	7		100	13/	13	千克	AB	PQ	/
4601.9390		---其他〔999〕	7		90	13/	13	千克	AB	PQ	/
		--其他植物材料制的:									
		---稻草制的:									
4601.9411		----缏条(绳)〔999〕	7		90	13/	13	千克	AB	PQ	/
4601.9419		----其他〔101稻草及其制品,102其他草及草制品〕	7		90	13/	13	千克	AB	PQ	/
		---其他:									
4601.9491		----缏条及类似产品,不论是否缝合成宽条〔101其他竹及竹制品,102藤及藤制品,103柳及柳制品,104其他草及草制品,105棕及棕制品,106葵及葵制品,107其他竹藤柳草类〕	7		100	13/	13	千克	AB	PQ	/
4601.9499		----其他〔101藤及藤制品,102柳及柳制品,103其他草及草制品,104棕及棕制品,105葵及葵制品,106其他竹藤柳草类〕	7		90	13/	13	千克	AB	PQ	/
		--其他:									

Chapter 46
Manufactures of straw, of esparto or of other plaiting materials; basketware and wickerwork

Notes:

1. In this Chapter the expression "plaiting materials" means materials in a state or form suitable for plaiting, interlacing or similar processes; it includes straw, osier or willow, bamboos, rattans rushes, reeds, strips of wood, strips of other vegetable material (for example, strips of bark, narrow leaves and raffia or other strips obtained from broad leaves), unspun natural textile fibres, monofilament and strip and the like of plastics and strips of paper, but not strips of leather or composition leather or of felt or nonwovens, human hair, horsehair, textile rovings or yarns, or monofilament and strip and the like of Chapter 54.
2. This Chapter does not cover:
   (a) Wall coverings of heading No. 48.14;
   (b) Twine, cordage, ropes or cables, plaited or not (heading No. 56.07);
   (c) Footwear or headgear or parts thereof of Chapter 64 or 65;
   (d) Vehicles or bodies for vehicles of basketware (Chapter 87);
   (e) Articles of Chapter 94 (for example, furniture, lamps).
3. For the purposes of heading No. 46.01, the expression "plaiting materials, plaits and similar products of plaiting materials, bound together in parallel strands" means plaiting materials, plaits and similar products of plaiting materials, placed side by side and bound together, in the form of sheets, whether or not the binding materials are of spun textile materials.

协定税率 %										特惠税率 %			
亚太5国	东/冰/格	巴基斯坦	韩国	瑞士	哥达	秘鲁	澳大利亚	新西/坡/智	港/澳/台	亚太2国	老/柬/缅	36/3/1	Article Description
													Plaits and similar products of plaiting materials, whether or not assembled into strips; plaiting materials, plaits and similar products of plaiting materials, bound together in parallel strands or woven, in sheet form, whether or not being finished articles (for example, mats, matting, screens):
													-Mats, matting and screens of vegetable materials:
	0/0/0	4	0	0	0	0	0	0//0	0/0/		0//	0/0/0	--Of bamboo
	0/0/0	4	0	0	0	0	0	0//0	0/0/		0//	0/0/0	--Of rattan
													--Other:
													---Of grass or straw:
													----Of rushes
	0/0/0	4	0	0	0	0	0	0//0	0/0/		0//	0/0/0	Juncaceae mats, pairs of clover mats, mat(ubit area $>1m^2$, whether or not edged)
	0/0/0	4	0	0	0	0	0	0//0	0/0/		0//	0/0/0	Other mats, matting and screens, of Juncaceae, area$>1m^2$, whether or not edged
	0/0/0	4	0	0	0	0	0	0//0	0/0/		0//	0/0/0	Jacquard mats, clover mats and cushion, of rush, of per unit area exceeding $1m^2$, whether or not deged
	0/0/0	4	0	0	0	0	0	0//0	0/0/		0//	0/0/0	Other mats, matting, of rushes(including mat, matting screens)
	0/0/0	4	0	0	0	0	0	0//0	0/0/		0//	0/0/0	---Other
													--Of reeds:
	0/0/0	4	0	0	0	0	0	0//0	0/0/		0//	0/0/0	---Screens of reeds
	0/0/0	4	0	0	0	0	0	0//0	0/0/		0//	0/0/0	---Other
	0/0/0	4	0	0	0	0	0	0//0	0/0/		0//	0/0/0	---Other
													-Other:
													--Of bamboo:
	0/0/0	4	0	0	0	0	0	0//0	0/0/		0//	0/0/0	---Plaits and similar products of plaiting materials, whether or not assembled into strips
	0/0/0	4	0	0	0	0	0	0//0	0/0/			0/0/0	---Other
													--Of rattan:
	0/0/0	4	0	0	0	0	0	0//0	0/0/		0//	0/0/0	---Plaits and similar products of plaiting materials, whether or not assembled into strips
	0/0/0	4	0	0	0		0	0//0	0/0/			0//	---Other
													--Of other vegetable materials:
													---Of straw:
	0/0/0	4.5	4	0	0	0	0	0//0	0/0/			0/0/	----Plaits
	0/0/0	4.5	4	0	0	0	0	0//0	0/0/			0/0/	----Other
													---Other:
	0/0/0	4	0	0	0	0	0	0//0	0/0/		0//	0/0/0	----Plaits and similar products of plaiting materials, whether or not assembled into strips
	0/0/0	4	0	0	0	0	0	0//0	0/0/			0/0/0	----Other
													--Other:

税则号列	货品名称〔CIQ扩展编码及品名—T2表示见附表2〕	最惠(%)	暂定税率	普通	增值/消费	出口退税	计量单位	监管条件	检验检疫	特殊证件对美关税
4601.9910	---缏条及类似产品,不论是否缝合成宽条〔999〕	7		90	13/	13	千克			/
4601.9990	---其他〔999〕	7		90	13/	13	千克			/27
46.02	**用编结材料直接编成或用税目46.01所列货品制成的篮筐、柳条编结品及其他制品;丝瓜络制品:**									
	-植物材料制:									
4602.1100	--竹制的〔101竹片、竹地板,102竹工艺品,103竹叶,104竹帘,105竹椅,106竹席,107竹篓,108其他竹及竹制品〕	7		100	13/	13	千克	AB	PQ	/
4602.1200	--藤制的〔101藤及藤制品,102其他竹藤柳草类〕	7		100	13/	13	千克	AB	PQ	/
	--其他:									
4602.1910	---草制的〔101蔺草及其制品,102稻草及其制品,103其他草及草制品,104其他竹藤柳草类〕	7		100	13/	13	千克	AB	PQ	/32
4602.1920	---玉米皮制的〔101其他草及草制品,102其他竹藤柳草类〕	7		100	13/	13	千克	AB	PQ	/
4602.1930	---柳条制的〔101柳及柳制品,102其他竹藤柳草类〕	7		100	13/	13	千克	AB	PQ	/
4602.1990	---其他〔101藤及藤制品,102其他草及草制品,103棕及棕制品,104葵及葵制品,105其他竹藤柳草类〕	7		100	13/	13	千克	AB	PQ	/32
4602.9000	-其他〔999〕	7		100	13/	13	千克			/32

协定税率 %										特惠税率 %			Article Description
亚太5国	东/冰/格	巴基斯坦	韩国	瑞士	哥达	秘鲁	澳大利亚	新西/坡/智	港/澳/台	亚太2国	老/柬/缅	36/3/1	
	0/0/0	4	0	0	0	0	0	0//0	0/0/		0//	0/0/0	---Plaits and similar products of plaiting materials, whether or not assembled into strips
	0/0/0	4	3.6	0	0	0	0	0//0	0/0/			0/0/	---Other
													Basketwork, wickerwork and other articles, made directly to shape from plaiting materials or made up from goods of heading No. 46. 01; articles of loofah:
													-Of vegetable materials:
4.2	0/0/0	4	0	0	0	0	0	0//0	0/0/		/0/	0/0/0	--Of bamboo
4.2	0/0/0	4	0	0	0		0	0//0	0/0/		/0/	0/0/0	--Of rattan
													--Other:
	0/0/0	4	0	0	0	0	0	0//0	0/0/		/0/	0/0/0	---Of grass or straw
	0/0/0	4	0	0	0	0	0	0//0	0/0/		/0/	0/0/0	---Of maize-shuck
	0/0/0	4	0	0	0	0	0	0//0	0/0/		/0/	0/0/0	---Of osier
	0/0/0	4	0	0	0		0	0//0	0/0/		/0/	0/0/0	---Other
4.6	0/0/0	4	0	0	0	0	0	0//0	0/0/		/0/	0/0/0	-Other

第十类
木浆及其他纤维状纤维素浆；回收(废碎)纸或纸板；纸、纸板及其制品

第四十七章
木浆及其他纤维状纤维素浆；回收(废碎)纸或纸板

注释：

税目47.02所称"化学木浆，溶解级"，是指温度在20℃时浸入含18%氢氧化钠的苛性碱溶液内，一小时后，按重量计含有92%及以上的不溶级分的碱木浆或硫酸盐木浆，或者含有88%及以上的不溶级分的亚硫酸盐木浆。对于亚硫酸盐木浆，按重量计灰分含量不得超过0.15%。

税则号列		货品名称〔CIQ扩展编码及品名－T2表示见附表2〕	最惠(%)	暂定税率	普通	增值/消费	出口退税	计量单位	监管条件	检验检疫	特殊证件对美关税
47.01		**机械木浆：**									
4701.0000		机械木浆〔999〕	0		8	13/	0	千克			/5
47.02		**化学木浆，溶解级：**									
4702.0000		化学木浆，溶解级									
4702.0000	01	用于生产粘胶等化学纤维(不含醋酸纤维)的化学木浆，溶解级(浆粕的粘度≧3.7dl/g，且＜6.4dl/g，或者≧350ml/g，且＜700ml/g，α纤维素含量(R18，硫酸盐法)＜95.5%，或者α纤维素含量(R18，亚硫酸盐法)＜94%，灰分≦0.15%)〔999〕	0		8	13/	0	千克			/5
4702.0000	90	其他化学木浆，溶解级〔999〕	0		8	13/	0	千克			/5
47.03		**碱木浆或硫酸盐木浆，但溶解级的除外：**									
		-未漂白：									
4703.1100		--针叶木的〔999〕	0		8	13/	0	千克			/5
4703.1900		--非针叶木的〔999〕	0		8	13/	0	千克			/5
		-半漂白或漂白：									
4703.2100		--针叶木的									
4703.2100	01	用于生产粘胶等化学纤维(不含醋酸纤维)的漂白针叶木碱木浆或硫酸盐木浆(包括半漂白的，溶解级的除外)(浆粕的黏度≥3.7dl/g，且＜6.4dl/g，或者≥350ml/g，且＜700ml/g，α纤维素含量(R18，硫酸盐法)≥88%，且＜95.5%，灰分≤0.15%)〔999〕	0		8	13/	0	千克			/5
4703.2100	90	其他漂白针叶木碱木浆或硫酸盐木浆(包括半漂白的，溶解级的除外)〔999〕	0		8	13/	0	千克			/5
4703.2900		--非针叶木的〔999〕	0		8	13/	0	千克			/5
47.04		**亚硫酸盐木浆，但溶解级的除外：**									
		-未漂白：									
4704.1100		--针叶木的〔999〕	0		8	13/	0	千克			/5
4704.1900		--非针叶木的〔999〕	0		8	13/	0	千克			/5
		-半漂白或漂白：									
4704.2100		--针叶木的〔999〕	0		8	13/	0	千克			/5
4704.2900		--非针叶木的〔999〕	0		8	13/	0	千克			/5
47.05		**用机械与化学联合制浆法制得的木浆：**									
4705.0000		用机械与化学联合制浆法制得的木浆〔999〕	0		8	13/	0	千克			/5
47.06		**从回收(废碎)纸或纸板提取的纤维浆或其他纤维状纤维素浆：**									
4706.1000		-棉短绒纸浆									

SECTION X
PULP OF WOOD OR OF OTHER FIBROUS CELLULOSIC MATERIAL; ZRCOVERED (WASTE AND SCRAP) PAPER OR PAPERBOARD; PAPER AND PAPERBOARD AND ARTICLES THEREOF

Chapter 47
Pulp of wood or of other fibrous cellulosic material; recovered (waste and scrap) paper or paperboard

Notes:

For the purposes of heading No. 47. 02, the expression "chemical wood pulp, dissolving grades" means chemical wood pulp having by weight an insoluble fraction of 92% or more for soda or sulphate wood pulp or of 88% or more for sulphite wood pulp after one hour in a caustic soda solution containing 18% sodium bydroxide (NaOH) at 20℃, and for sulphite wood pulp an ash content that does not exceed 0. 15% by weight.

协定税率 %										特惠税率 %			
亚太5国	东/冰/格	巴基斯坦	韩国	瑞士	哥达	秘鲁	澳大利亚	新西/坡/智	港/澳/台	亚太2国	老/柬/缅	36/3/1	Article Description
													Mechanical wood pulp:
												0/0/0	Mechanical wood pulp
													Chemical wood pulp, dissolving grades:
													Chemical wood pulp, dissolving grades
												0/0/0	For the production of viscose chemical fiber (not containing cellulose acetate) of chemical wood pulp, dissolving (content of alpha cellulose pulp viscosity is greater than or equal to 3.7dl/g, and <6.4dl/g, and ⩾ 350ml/g, and (<700ml/g, R18, sulfate) ⩾ 88%, and <95.5%, or the content of alpha cellulose (R18, sulfite) ⩾ 87%, and <94%, ash ⩽ 0.15%)
												0/0/0	Other chemical wood pulp,dissolving grades
													Chemical wood pulp, soda or sulphate, other than dissolving grades:
													-Unbleached:
												0/0/0	--Coniferous
												0/0/0	--Non-coniferous
													-Semi-bleached or bleached:
													--Coniferous
												0/0/0	For the production of viscose chemical fiber (not containing cellulose acetate) of bleached softwood pulp of wood or kraft pulp (including semi bleached, dissolving except) (content of alpha cellulose pulp viscosity is greater than or equal to 3.7dl/g, and <6.4dl/g, and ⩾ 350ml/g, and <700ml/g, (R18, sulfur acid salt) ⩾ 88%, and < 95.5%, ash ⩽ 0.15%)
												0/0/0	Other chemical wood pulp, soda or sulhate(including semi-bleached or bleached, other than dissolving grades)
												0/0/0	--Non-coniferous
													Chemical wood pulp, sulphite, other than dissolving grades:
													-Unbleached:
												0/0/0	--Coniferous
												0/0/0	--Non-coniferous
													-Semi-bleached or bleached:
												0/0/0	--Coniferous
												0/0/0	--Non-coniferous
													Wood pulp obtained by a combination of mechanical and chemical pulping processes:
												0/0/0	Wood pulp obtained by a combination of mechanical and chemical pulping processes
													Pulps of fibres derived from recovered (waste and scrap) paper or paperboard or of other fibrous cellulosic material:
													-Cotton linters pulp

税则号列		货品名称〔CIQ 扩展编码及品名－T2 表示见附表 2〕	最惠(%)	暂定税率	普通	增值/消费	出口退税	计量单位	监管条件	检验检疫	特殊证件对美关税
4706.1000	01	用于生产粘胶等化学纤维(不含醋酸纤维)的棉短绒浆粕(浆粕的粘度≧3.7dl/g,且＜6.4dl/g,或者≧350ml/g,且＜700ml/g,α纤维素含量(R18,硫酸盐法)＜95.5％,或者α纤维素含量(R18,亚硫酸盐法)＜94％,灰分≦0.15％)〔999〕	0		8	13/	13	千克			/5
4706.1000	90	其他棉短绒纸浆〔999〕	0		8	13/	13	千克			/5
4706.2000		-从回收(废碎)纸或纸板提取的纤维浆〔999〕	0		8	13/	0	千克			/20
4706.3000		-其他,竹浆									
4706.3000	01	-用于生产粘胶等化学纤维(不含醋酸纤维)的其他纤维状纤维素竹浆(包括机械浆、化学浆、半化学浆)(浆粕的粘度≧3.7dl/g,且＜6.4dl/g,或者≧350ml/g,且＜700ml/g,α纤维素含量(R18,硫酸盐法)＜95.5％,或者α纤维素含量(R18,亚硫酸盐法)＜94％,灰分≦0.15％)〔999〕	0		8	13/	0	千克			/
4706.3000	90	其他纤维状纤维素竹浆(包括机械浆、化学浆、半化学浆)〔999〕	0		8	13/	0	千克			/
		-其他:									
4706.9100		--机械浆〔999〕	0		8	13/	0	千克			/
4706.9200		--化学浆〔999〕	0		8	13/	0	千克			/25
4706.9300		--用机械和化学联合法制得的浆〔999〕	0		8	13/	0	千克			/
47.07		**回收(废碎)纸或纸板:**									
4707.1000		-未漂白的牛皮纸或纸板及瓦楞纸或纸板〔999〕	0		8	13/	0	千克	ABP	MPQ	/25
4707.2000		-主要由漂白化学木浆制成未经本体染色的其他纸和纸板〔999〕	0		8	13/	0	千克	ABP	MPQ	/25
4707.3000		-主要由机械浆制成的纸或纸板(例如,报纸、杂志及类似印刷品)〔999〕	0		8	13/	0	千克	ABP	MPQ	/25
4707.9000		-其他,包括未分选的废碎品									
4707.9000	10	回收(废碎)墙(壁)纸、涂蜡纸、浸蜡纸、复写纸(包括未分选的废碎品)〔999〕	0		8	13/	0	千克	AB9	MPQ	/25
4707.9000	90	其他回收纸或纸板(包括未分选的废碎品)〔999〕	0		8	13/	0	千克	9B	MPQ	/25

协定税率 %										特惠税率 %			
亚太5国	东/冰/格	巴基斯坦	韩国	瑞士	哥达	秘鲁	澳大利亚	新西/坡/智	港/澳/台	亚太2国	老/柬/缅	36/3/1	Article Description
												0/0/0	For the production of viscose chemical fiber (not containing cellulose acetate) of cotton linter pulp (content of alpha cellulose pulp viscosity is greater than or equal to 3.7dl/g, and ＜6.4dl/g, and ≥ 350ml/g, and (＜700ml/g, R18, sulfate) ≥ 88%, and ＜95.5%, or the content of alpha cellulose (R18, sulfurous acid salt) ≥ 87%, and ＜ 94%, ash ≤ 0.15%)
												0/0/0	Other cotton linters pulp
												0/0/0	-Pulps of fibres derived from recovered (waste and scrap) paper or paperboard
													-Other, of bamboo
												0/0/0	-For the production of viscose chemical fiber (not containing cellulose acetate) of cellulose pulp (including mechanical pulp, chemical pulp, semi chemical pulp) (content of alpha cellulose pulp viscosity is greater than or equal to 3.7dl/g, and ＜6.4dl/g, and ≥ 350ml/g, and (＜700ml/g, R18, sulfate) ≥ 88%, and ＜95.5%, or alpha the content of cellulose (R18, sulfite) ≥ 87%, and ＜94%, ash ≤ 0.15%)
												0/0/0	Other fibrous cellulosic material (including mechanical wood pulp, chemical pulp, semi-chemical)
													-Other:
												0/0/0	--Mechanical
												0/0/0	--Chemical
												0/0/0	--Pulp obtained by a combination of mechanical and chemical pulping processes
													Recovered (waste and scrap) paper or paperboard:
												0/0/0	-Unbleached kraft paper or paperboard or of corrugated paper or paperboard
												0/0/0	-Other paper or paperboard made mainly of bleached chemical pulp, not coloured in the mass
												0/0/0	-Paper or paperboard made mainly of mechanical pulp (for example, newspapers, journals and similar printed matter)
													-Other, including unsorted waste and scrap
												0/0/0	Recoverd (waste and scrap) wallpaper, mimeograph or waxed paper and carbon paper (including unsorted waste and scrap)
												0/0/0	Other recovered paper or paperboard (including unsorted waste and scrap)

第四十八章
纸及纸板;纸浆、纸或纸板制品

注释:

一、除条文另有规定的以外,本章所称"纸"包括"纸板"(不论其厚度或每平方米重量如何)。

二、本章不包括:
(一)第三十章的物品;
(二)税目32.12的压印箔;
(三)香纸及用化妆品浸渍或涂布的纸(第三十三章);
(四)用肥皂或洗涤剂浸渍、覆盖或涂布的纸或纤维素絮纸(税号34.01)和用光洁剂、擦光膏及类似制剂浸渍、覆盖或涂布的纸或纤维素絮纸(税目34.05);
(五)税目37.01至37.04的感光纸或感光纸板;
(六)用诊断或实验用试剂浸渍的纸(税目38.22);
(七)第三十九章的用纸强化的层压塑料板,用塑料覆盖或涂布的单层纸或纸板(塑料部分占总厚度的一半以上),以及上述材料的制品,但税目48.14的壁纸除外;

(八)税目42.02的物品(例如旅行用品);
(九)第四十六章的物品(编结材料制品);
(十)纸纱线或纸纱线纺织物(第十一类);
(十一)第六十四章或第六十五章的物品;
(十二)税目68.05的砂纸或税目68.14的用纸或纸板衬底的云母(但涂布云母粉的纸及纸板归入本章);

(十三)用纸或纸板衬底的金属箔(通常为第十四类或第十五类);
(十四)税目92.09的制品;
(十五)第九十五章的物品(例如,玩具、游戏品及运动用品);
(十六)第九十六章的物品[例如,纽扣、卫生巾(护垫)及止血塞、婴儿尿布及尿布衬里]。

三、除注释七另有规定的以外,税目48.01至48.05包括经砑光、高度砑光、釉光或类似处理、仿水印、表面施胶的纸及纸板;同时还包括用各种方法本体着色或染成斑纹的纸、纸板、纤维素絮纸及纤维素纤维网纸。除税目48.03另有规定的以外,上述税目不适用于经过其他方法加工的纸、纸板、纤维素絮纸或纤维素纤维网纸。

四、本章所称"新闻纸",是指所含用机械或化学一机械方法制得的木纤维不少于全部纤维重量的50%的未经涂布的报刊用纸,未施胶或微施胶,每面粗糙度〔帕克印刷表面粗糙度(1兆帕)〕超过2.5微米,每平方米重量不小于40克,但不超过65克,并且仅适用于下列规格的纸:
(一)成条或成卷,宽度超过28厘米;或
(二)成张矩形(包括正方形),一边超过28厘米,另一边超过15厘米(以未折叠计)。

五、税目48.02所称"书写、印刷或类似用途的纸及纸板"及"未打孔的穿孔卡片纸及穿孔纸带纸",是指主要用漂白纸浆或用机械或化学-机械方法制得的纸浆制成的纸及纸板,并且符合下列任一标准:

每平方米重量不超过150克的纸或纸板:
(一)用机械或化学—机械方法制得的纤维含量在10%及以上,并且
　1. 每平方米重量不超过80克;
　2. 本体着色;
(二)灰分含量在8%以上,并且
　1. 每平方米重量不超过80克;
　2. 本体着色;
(三)灰分含量在3%以上,亮度在60%及以上;
(四)灰分含量在3%以上,但不超过8%,亮度低于60%,耐破指数等于或小于2.5千帕斯卡·平方米/克;

(五)灰分含量在3%及以下,亮度在60% 及以上,耐破指数等于或小于2.5千帕斯卡·平方米/克。
每平方米重量超过150克的纸或纸板:
(一)本体着色;或
(二)亮度在60%及以上,并且
　1.厚度在225微米及以下;或
　2.厚度在225微米以上,但不超过508微米,灰分含量在3%以上;

(三)亮度低于60%,厚度不超过254微米,灰分含量在8%以上。
税目48.02不包括滤纸及纸板(含茶袋纸)或毡纸及纸板。

六、本章所称"牛皮纸及纸板",是指所含用硫酸盐法或烧碱法制得的纤维不少于全部纤维重量的80% 的纸及纸板。

七、除税目条文另有规定的以外,符合税目48.01至48.11中两个或两个以上税目所规定的纸、纸板、纤维素絮纸及纤维素纤维网纸,应按号列顺序归入有关税目中的最末一个税目。

八、税目48.03至48.09仅适用于下列规格的纸、纸板、纤维素絮纸及纤维素纤维网纸:
(一)成条或成卷,宽度超过36厘米;或
(二)成张矩形(包括正方形),一边超过36厘米,另一边超过15厘米(以未折叠计)。

Chapter 48
Paper and paperboard; articles of paper pulp, of paper or of paperboard

Notes:

1. For the purposes of this Chapter, except where the context otherwise requires, a reference to "paper" includes references to paperboard (irrespective of thickness or weight per m^2).
2. This Chapter does not cover:
   (a) Articles of Chapter 30;
   (b) Stamping foils of heading No. 32.12;
   (c) Perfumed papers or papers impregnated or coated with cosmetics (Chapter 33);
   (d) Paper or cellulose wadding impregnated, coated or covered with soap or detergent (heading No. 34.01), or with polishes, creams or similar preparations (heading No. 34.05);
   (e) Sensitized paper or paperboard of headings No. 37.01 to 37.04;
   (f) Paper impregnated with diagnostic or laboratory reagents (heading No. 38.22);
   (g) Paper-reinforced stratified sheeting of plastics, or one layer of paper or paperboard coated or covered with a layer of plastics, the latter constituting more than half the total thickness, or articles of such materials, other than wall coverings of heading No. 48.14 (Chapter 39);
   (h) Articles of heading No. 42.02 (for example, travel goods);
   (i) Articles of Chapter 46 (manufactures of plaiting material);
   (j) Paper yarn or textile articles of paper yarn (Section XI);
   (k) Articles of Chapter 64 or Chapter 65;
   (l) Abrasive paper or paperboard (heading No. 68.05) or paper backed or paperboard-backed mica (heading No. 68.14) (paper and paperboard coated with mica powder are, however, to be classified in this Chapter);
   (m) Metal foil backed with paper or paperboard (generally to be classified in Section XIV or XV);
   (n) Articles of heading No. 92.09;
   (o) Articles of Chapter 95 (for example, toys, games, sports requisites)
   (p) Chapter96(for example buttons、sanitary(sanitary napkin) and hemostatic plug、napkins and napkin liners for babies
3. Subject to the provisions of Note 7, headings Nos. 48.01 to 48.05 include paper and paperboard which have been subjected to calendering, super-calendering, glazing or similar finishing, false watermarking or surface sizing, and also paper, paperboard, cellulose wading and webs of cellulose fibres, coloured or marbled throughout the mass by any method. Except where heading No. 48.03 otherwise requires, these headings do not apply to paper, paperboard, cellulose wadding or webs of cellulose fibres which have been otherwise processed.
4. In this Chapter the expression "newsprint" means uncoated paper of a kind used for the printing of newspapers, of which not less than 50% by weight of the total fibre content consists of wood fibres obtained by a mechanical or chemi-mechanical process, unsized or very lightly sized, having a surface roughness Parker Print Surf (1 MPa) on each side exceeding 2.5 micrometres (microns), weighing not less than 40 g/m^2 and not more than 65 g/m^2, apply only to paper:
   (a) in strips or rolls of a width exceeding 28cm;
   (b) in rectangular(including square) sheets with one side exceeding 28cm and the other side exceeding 15cm in the unfolded state.
5. For the purposes of heading No. 48.02, the expressions "paper and paperboard, of a kind used for writing, printing or other graphic purposes" and "non perforated punch-cards and punch tape paper" mean paper and paperboard made mainly from bleached pulp or from pulp obtained by a mechanical or chemi-mechanical process and satisfying any of the following criteria:
   For paper or paperboard weighing not more than 150g/m^2:
   (a) containing 10% or more of fibres obtained by a mechanical or chemi-mechanical process, and
      (ⅰ)①weighing not more than 80 g/m^2,
      (ⅱ) coloured throughout the mass; or
   (b) containing more than 8% ash, and
      (ⅰ) weighing not more than 80 g/m^2,
      (ⅱ) coloured throughout the mass; or
   (c) containing more than 3% ash and having a brightness of 60% or more;
   (d) containing more than 3% but not more than 8% ash, having a brightness less than 60%, and a burst index equal to or less than 2.5 $kPa/m^2/g$;
   (e) containing 3% ash or less, having a brightness of 60% or more and a burst index equal to or less than 2.5 $kPa \cdot m^2/g$.
   For paper or paperboard weighing more than 150 g/m^2:
   (a) coloured throughout the mass; or
   (b) having a brightness of 60% or more, and
      (ⅰ) a caliper of 225 micrometres (microns) or less, or
      (ⅱ) a caliper more than 225 micrometres (microns) but not more than 508 micrometres (microns) and an ash content more than 3%; or
   (c) having a brightness of less than 60%, a caliper of 254 micrometres (microns) or less and an ash content of more than 8%.
   Heading No. 48.02 does not, however, cover filter paper and paperboard (including tea-bag paper) or felt paper or paperboard.
6. In this Chapter "kraft paper and paperboard" means paper and paperboard of which not less than 80% by weight of the total fibre content consists of fibres obtained by the chemical sulphate or soda processes.
7. Except where the terms of the headings otherwise require, paper, paperboard, cellulose wadding and webs of cellulose fibres answering to a description in two or more of the headings No. 48.01 to 48.11 are to be classified under that one of such headings which occurs last in numerical order in the Nomenclature.
8. Headings No. 48.01 to 48.09 apply only to paper, paperboard, cellulose wadding and webs of cellulose fibres:
   (a) in strips or rolls of a width exceeding 36 cm;
   (b) in rectangular (including square) sheets with one side exceeding 36 cm and the other side exceeding 15 cm in the unfolded state.

九、税目 48.14 所称"壁纸及类似品",仅限于:

(一)适合作墙壁或天花板装饰用的成卷纸张,宽度不小于 45 厘米,但不超过 160 厘米:

1. 起纹、压花、染面、印有图案或经其他装饰的(例如起绒),不论是否用透明的防护塑料涂布或覆盖;

2. 表面饰有木粒或草粒而凹凸不平的;

3. 表面用塑料涂布或覆盖并起纹、压花、染面、印有图案或经其他装饰的;

4. 表面用不论是否平行连结或编织的编结材料覆盖的;

(二)适于装饰墙壁或天花板用的经上述加工的纸边及纸条,不论是否成卷;

(三)由几幅拼成的壁纸,成卷或成张,贴到墙上可组成印制的风景或图案。

既可作铺地制品,也可作壁纸的以纸或纸板为底的产品,应归入税目 48.23。

十、税目 48.20 不包括切成一定尺寸的活页纸张或卡片,不论是否印制、压花、打孔。

十一、税目 48.23 主要适用于提花机或类似机器用的穿孔纸或卡片,以及纸花边。

十二、除税目 48.14 及 48.21 的货品外,印有图案、文字或图画的纸、纸板、纤维素絮纸及其制品,如果所印图案、文字或图画作为其主要用途,应归入第四十九章。

子目注释:

一、子目号 4804.11 及 4804.19 所称"牛皮挂面纸",是指所含用硫酸盐法或烧碱法制得的木纤维不少于全部纤维重量的 80% 的成卷机器上光或研光纸及纸板,每平方米重量超过 115 克,并且最低缪伦耐破度符合下表所示(其他重量的耐破度可参照下表换算):

重　量 克/平方米	最低耐破度 千帕斯卡
115	393
125	417
200	637
300	824
400	961

二、子目号 4804.21 及 4804.29 所称"袋用牛皮纸",是指所含用硫酸盐法或烧碱法制得的木纤维不少于全部纤维重量的 80% 的成卷机器上光纸,每平方米重量不小于 60 克,但不超过 115 克,并且符合下列一种规格:

(一)缪伦耐破指数不小于 3.7 千帕斯卡 · 平方米/克,并且横向伸长率大于 4.5%,纵向伸长率大于 2%;

(二)至少能达到下表所示的最小撕裂度和抗张强度(其他重量的可参照下表换算):

重　量	最小撕裂度 毫牛顿		最小抗张强度 千牛顿/米	
克/平方米	纵　向	纵向 加横向	横　向	纵向 加横向
60	700	1510	1.9	6
70	830	1790	2.3	7.2
80	965	2070	2.8	8.3
100	1230	2635	3.7	10.6
115	1425	3060	4.4	12.3

三、子目号 4805.11 所称"半化学的瓦楞纸",是指所含用机械和化学联合法制得的未漂白硬木纤维不少于全部纤维重量的 65% 的成卷纸张,并且在温度为 23℃ 和相对湿度为 50% 时,经过 30 分钟的瓦楞芯纸平压强度测定(CMT30),抗压强度超过 1.8 牛顿/克/平方米。

四、子目 4805.12 包括主要用机械和化学联合法制得的草浆制成的成卷纸张,每平方米重量在 130 克及以上,并且在温度为 23℃ 和相对湿度为 50% 时,经过 30 分钟的瓦楞芯纸平压强度测定(CMT30),抗压强度超过 1.4 牛顿/克/平方米。

五、子目 4805.24 及 4805.25 包括全部或主要用回收(废碎)纸及纸板制得的纸浆制成的纸及纸板。强韧箱纸板也可以有一面用染色纸或由漂白或未漂白的非再生浆制得的纸做表层。这些产品缪伦耐破指数不小于 2 千帕斯卡 · 平方米/克。

六、子目号 4805.30 所称"亚硫酸盐包装纸",是指所含用亚硫酸盐法制得的木纤维超过全部纤维重量的 40% 的机器研光纸,灰分含量不超过 8%,并且缪伦耐破指数不小于 1.47 千帕斯卡 · 平方米/克。

9. For the purposes of heading No. 48. 14, the expression "wallpaper and similar wall coverings" applies only to:
(a) Paper in rolls, of a width of not less than 45 cm and not more than 160 cm, suitable for wall or ceiling decoration:
(ⅰ) Grained, embossed, surface-coloured, designprinted or otherwise surface-decorated (for exanple, with textile flock), whether or not coated or covered with transparent protective plastics;
(ⅱ) With an uneven surface resulting from the incorporation ofparticles of wood, straw, etc.;
(ⅲ) Coated or covered on the face side with plastics, the layer of plastics being grained, embossed, coloured, design-printed or otherwise decorated;
(ⅳ) Covered on the face side with plaiting material, whether or not bound together in parallel strands or woven;
(b) Borders and friezes, of paper, treated as above, whether or not in rolls, suitable for wall or ceiling decoration;
(c) Wall coverings of paper made up of several panels, in rolls or sheets, printed so as to make up a scene, design or motif when applied to a wall.
Products on a base of paper or paperboard, suitable for use both as floor coverings and as wall coverings, are to be classified in heading No. 48. 23.
10. Heading No. 48. 20 does not cover loose sheets or cards, cut to size, whether or not printed, embossed or perforated.
11. Heading No. 48. 23 applies, *inter alia*, to perforated paper or paperboard cards for Jacquard or similar machines and paper lace.
12. Except for the goods of heading No. 48. 14 or 48. 21, paper, paperboard, cellulose wadding and articles thereof, printed with motifs, characters or pictorial representations, which are not merely incidental to the primary use of the goods, fall in Chapter 49.

Subheading Notes:

1. For the purposes of subheadings No. 4804. 11 and 4804. 19. "kraftliner" means machine-finished or machine-glazed paper and paperboard, of which not less than 80% by weight of the total fibre content consists of wood fibres obtained by the chemical sulphate or soda processes, in rolls, weighing more than 115 g/m^2 and having a minimum Mullen bursting strength as indicated in the following table or the linearly interpolated or extrapolated equivalent for any other weight.

Weight g/m^2	Minimum Mullen bursting strength kPa
115	393
125	417
200	637
300	834
400	961

2. For the puposes of subheadings Nos. 4804. 21 and 4804. 29, "sack kraft paper" means machine-finished paper, of which not less than 80% by weight of the total fibre content consists of fibres obtained by the chemical sulphate or soda processes, in rolls, weighing not less than 60 g/m^2 but not more than 115 g/m^2 and meeting one of the following sets of specifications:

(a) Having a Mullen burst index of not less than 3. 7 kPa · m^2/g and a stretch factor of more than 4. 5% in the cross direction and of more than 2% in the machine direction.
(b) Having minima for tear and tensile as indicated in the following table or the linearly interpolated equivalent for any other weight:

Weight g/m^2	Minimum tear mN		Minimum tensile kN/m	
	Machine direction	Machine direction plus cross direction	Cross direction	Machine direction plus cross direction
60	700	1,510	1. 9	6
70	830	1,790	2. 3	7. 2
80	2965	2070	2. 8	8. 3
100	1230	2635	3. 7	10. 6
115	1425	3060	4. 4	12. 3

3. For the purposes of subheading No. 4805. 11, "semi-chemical fluting paper" means paper, in rolls, of which not less than 65% by weight of the total fibre content consists of unbleached hardwood fibres obtained by a combination of mechanical and chemical pulping processes, and having a CMT 30 (Corrugated Medium Test with 30 minutes of conditioning) crush resistance exceeding 1. 8 $N/g/m^2$ at 50% relative humidity, at 23℃.
4. Subheading No. 4805. 12 covers paper, in rolls, made mainly of straw pulp obtained by a combination of mechanical and chemical process, weighing 130 g/m^2 or more, and having a CMT 30(Corrugated Medium Test with 30 minutes of conditioning) crush resistance exceeding 1. 4 newtons/g/m^2 at 50% relative humidity, at 23℃.
5. Subheadings 4805. 24 and 4805. 25 cover paper and paperboard made wholly or mainly of pulp of recovered(waste and scrap) paper or paperboard. Testliner may also have a surface layer of dyed paper or of paper made of bleached or unbleached non-recovered pulp. These products have a Mullen burst index of not less than 2 kPa · m^2/g.
6. For the purposes of subheading No. 4805. 30, "sulphite wrapping paper" means machine-glazed paper, of which more than 40% by weight of the total fibre content consists of wood fibres obtained by the chemical sulpohite process, having an ash content not exceeding 8% and having a Mullen burst index of not less than 1. 47 kPa · m^2/g.

七、子目号 4810.22 所称“轻质涂布纸”，是指双面涂布纸，其每平方米总重量不超过 72 克，每面每平方米的涂层重量不超过 15 克，原纸中所含用机械方法制得的木纤维不少于全部纤维重量的 50%。

税则号列	货品名称〔CIQ 扩展编码及品名－T2 表示见附表 2〕	最惠(%)	暂定税率	普通	增值/消费	出口退税	计量单位	监管条件	检验检疫	特殊证件对美关税
48.01	**成卷或成张的新闻纸：**									
4801.0010	---成卷的〔999〕	5		30	13/	0	千克			/30
4801.0090	---其他〔999〕	5		30	13/	0	千克			/30
48.02	**书写、印刷或类似用途的未经涂布的纸及纸板、未打孔的穿孔卡片纸及穿孔纸带纸，成卷或成张矩形(包括正方形)，任何尺寸，但税目 48.01 或 48.03 的纸除外；手工制纸及纸板：**									
	-手工制纸及纸板：									
4802.1010	---宣纸〔999〕	6	4	70	13/	13	千克			/
4802.1090	---其他〔999〕	6	5	70	13/	13	千克			/30
	-光敏、热敏、电敏纸及纸板的原纸和原纸板：									
4802.2010	---照相原纸〔999〕	6	5	40	13/	0	千克			/30
4802.2090	---其他〔999〕	6	5	40	13/	0	千克			/25
4802.4000	-壁纸原纸〔999〕	6		40	13/	0	千克			/
	-其他纸及纸板，不含用机械或化学—机械方法制得的纤维或所含前述纤维不超过全部纤维重量的 10%：									
4802.5400	--每平方米重量小于 40 克〔999〕	6		30	13/	0	千克			/31
4802.5500	--每平方米重量在 40 克及以上，但不超过 150 克，成卷									
4802.5500 10	40g<每平方米重≤150g 的胶版纸(成卷，机械或化学－机械法制得的纤维含量≤10%)〔999〕	5		30	13/	0	千克			/30
4802.5500 90	40g<每平方米重≤150g 未涂布中厚纸(书写印刷用，成卷，含机械或化学－机械法制纤维含量≤10%)〔999〕	5		30	13/	0	千克			/30
4802.5600	--每平方米重量在 40 克及以上，但不超过 150 克，一边不超过 435 毫米，另一边不超过 297 毫米(以未折叠计)，成张的									
4802.5600 10	成张 40g<每平方米重≤150g 胶版纸(长≤435mm，宽≤297mm 含机械或化学－机械法制纤维≤10%)〔999〕	5		30	13/	0	千克			/30
4802.5600 90	40g<每平方米重≤150g 未涂布纸，成张(书写印刷，长≤435mm，宽≤297mm 含机械或半化学浆≤10%)〔999〕	5		30	13/	0	千克			/30
4802.5700	--其他，每平方米重量在 40 克及以上，但不超过 150 克									
4802.5700 10	其他 40g<每平方米重≤150g 的胶版纸(机械或化学－机械法制得的纤维含量≤10%)〔999〕	5		30	13/	0	千克			/30
4802.5700 90	其他 40g<每平方米重≤150g 未涂中厚纸(书写印刷用，含机械或化学－机械法制纤维≤10%)〔999〕	5		30	13/	0	千克			/30
4802.5800	--每平方米重量超过 150 克〔999〕	5		30	13/	0	千克			/25
	-其他纸及纸板，所含用机械或化学－机械方法制得的纤维超过全部纤维重量的 10%：									
4802.6100	--成卷的〔999〕	5		30	13/	0	千克			/25
4802.6200	--成张的，一边不超过 435 毫米，另一边不超过 297 毫米(以未折叠计)〔999〕	5		30	13/	0	千克			/30
4802.6900	--其他〔999〕	5		30	13/	0	千克			/30
48.03	**卫生纸、面巾纸、餐巾纸以及家庭或卫生用的类似纸、纤维素絮纸和纤维素纤维网纸，不论是否起纹、压花、打孔、染面、饰面或印花，成卷或成张的：**									
4803.0000	卫生纸、面巾纸、餐巾纸以及家庭或卫生用的类似纸、纤维素絮纸和纤维素纤维网纸，不论是否起纹、压花、打孔、染面、饰面或印花，成卷或成张的〔101 卫生纸原纸、卫生纸，102 面巾纸、餐巾纸及类似纸，103 擦拭用纸〕	5		40	13/	0	千克	A	M	/35
48.04	**成卷或成张的未经涂布的牛皮纸及纸板，但不包括税目 48.02 或 48.03 的货品：**									

7. For the purposes of subheading No. 4810. 22, "lightweight coated paper" means paper, coated on both sides, of a total weight not exceeding 72 g/m^2, with a coating weight not exceeding 15 g/m^2 per side, on a base of which not less than 50% by weight of the total fibre content consists of wood fibres obtained by a mechanical process.

协定税率 %										特惠税率 %			Article Description
亚太5国	东/冰/格	巴基斯坦	韩国	瑞士	哥达	秘鲁	澳大利亚	新西/坡/智	港/澳/台	亚太2国	老/柬/缅	36/3/1	
													Newsprint, in rolls or sheets:
													---In rolls
													---Other
													Uncoated paper and paperboard, of a kind used for writing, printing or other graphic purposes, and non perforated punchcards and punch tape paper, in rolls or rectangular (including square) sheets, of any size, other than paper of heading No. 48. 01 or 48. 03; hand-made paper and paperboard:
													-Hand-made paper and paperboard:
	5//							5//					---Rice paper
	5//							5//					---Other
													-Paper and paperboard of a kind used as a base for photo-sensitive, heat-sensitive or electro-sensitive paper or paperboard:
									0/0/			0//	---Photo paper base
	5//							5//	0/0/			0//	---Other
									0/0/			0//	-Wallpaper base
													-Other paper and paperboard, not containing fibres obtained by a mechanical or chemi-mechanical process or of which not more than 10% by weight of the total fibre content consists of such fibres:
									0/0/			0//	--Weighing less than 40 g/m^2
													--Weighing 40 g/m^2 or more but not more than 150 g/m^2, in rolls
									0/0/			0//	Offset paper, in rolls, $40g/m^2 < w \leqslant 150g/m^2$, containing fibres ≤ 10%, obtained by a mechanical or chemi-mechanical process
									0/0/			0//	Paper, of a kind used for writing, printing or other graphic purposes, in rolls, $40g/m^2 < w \leqslant 150g/m^2$, containing fibres ≤ 10%, obtained by a mechanical or chemi-mechanical process
													--Weighing 40 g/m^2 or more but not more than 150 g/m^2, in sheets with one side not exceeding 435 mm and the other side not exceeding 297 mm in the unfolded state
									0/0/			0//	Offset paper, in sheets, $40g/m^2 < w \leqslant 150g/m^2$ (length ≤ 435mm, width ≤ 297mm, containing fibres ≤ 10%, obtained by a mechanical or chemi-mechanical process)
									0/0/			0//	Uncoated paper, $40g/m^2 < w \leqslant 150g/m^2$ (of a kind used for writing, printing or other graphic purposes, in sheets, length ≤ 435mm, width ≤ 297mm, containing fibres ≤ 10%, obtained by a mechanical or chemi-mechanical process)
													--Other, weighing 40 g/m^2 or more but not more than 150 g/m^2
									0/0/			0//	Other offset paper, $40g/m^2 < w \leqslant 150g/m^2$, containing fibres ≤ 10%, obtained by a mechanical or chemi-mechanical process
									0/0/			0//	Other uncoated paper, $40g/m^2 < w \leqslant 150g/m^2$, of a kind used for writing, printing or other graphic purposes, containing fibres ≤ 10%, obtained by a mechanical or chemi-mechanical process
									0/0/			0//	--Weighing more than 150 g/m^2
													-Other paper and paperboard, fibres obtaibed by a mechanical or chemi—mechanical process more than 10% by weight of the total fibre content:
									0/0/			0//	--In rolls
									0/0/			0//	--In sheets with one side not exceeding 435 mm and the other side not exceeding 297 mm in the unfolded state
									0/0/			0//	--Other
													Toilet or facial tissue stock, towel or napkin stock and similar paper of a kind used for household or sanitary purposes, cellulose wadding and webs of cellulose fibres, whether or not creped, crinkled, embossed, perforated, surface-coloured, surface-decorated or printed, in rolls or sheets:
													Toilet or facial tissue stock, towel or napkin stock and similar paper of a kind used for household or sanitary purposes, cellulose wadding and webs of cellulose fibres, whether or not creped, crinkled, embossed, perforated, surface-coloured, surface-decorated or printed, in rolls or sheets
													Uncoated kraft paper and paperboard, in rolls or sheets, other than that of heading No. 48. 02 or 48. 03:

税则号列	货品名称〔CIQ扩展编码及品名－T2表示见附表2〕	最惠(%)	暂定税率	普通	增值/消费	出口退税	计量单位	监管条件	检验检疫	特殊证件对美关税
	-牛皮挂面纸：									
4804.1100	--未漂白〔999〕	5		30	13/	0	千克			/10
4804.1900	--其他〔999〕	5		30	13/	0	千克			/25
	-袋用牛皮纸：									
4804.2100	--未漂白〔999〕	5		30	13/	0	千克			/10
4804.2900	--其他〔999〕	5		30	13/	0	千克			/35
	-其他牛皮纸及纸板，每平方米重量不超过150克：									
4804.3100	--未漂白									
4804.3100 20	未漂白的其他薄牛皮纸及纸板（抗张指数（横向＋纵向）大于等于69Nm/g，撕裂指数（纵向）大于等于10mNm^2/g，抗张能量吸收指数（横向）大于等于1.0J/g，抗张能量吸收指数（纵向）大于等于0.8J/g，透气度大于等于3.4um/(pa.s)，伸长率（纵向）大于等于2%。（薄纸指每平方米重≤150克，成卷或成张未经涂布的）〔999〕	2		30	13/	0	千克			/32
4804.3100 90	未漂白的其他薄牛皮纸及纸板（薄纸指每平米重≤150克，成卷或成张未经涂布的）〔999〕	2		30	13/	0	千克			/32
4804.3900	--其他〔999〕	2		30	13/	0	千克			/7
	-其他牛皮纸及纸板，每平方米重量超过150克，但小于225克：									
4804.4100	--未漂白〔999〕	2		30	13/	0	千克			/7
4804.4200	--本体均匀漂白，所含用化学方法制得的木纤维超过全部纤维重量的95%〔999〕	5		30	13/	0	千克			/35
4804.4900	--其他〔999〕	2		30	13/	0	千克			/32
	-其他牛皮纸及纸板，每平方米重量在225克及以上：									
4804.5100	--未漂白〔999〕	2		30	13/	0	千克			/7
4804.5200	--本体均匀漂白，所含用化学方法制得的木纤维超过全部纤维重量的95%〔999〕	5		30	13/	0	千克			/10
4804.5900	--其他〔999〕	2		30	13/	0	千克			/7
48.05	**成卷或成张的其他未经涂布的纸及纸板，加工程度不超过本章注释三所列范围：**									
	-瓦楞原纸：									
4805.1100	--半化学的瓦楞原纸〔999〕	6		30	13/	0	千克			/
4805.1200	--草浆瓦楞原纸〔999〕	6		30	13/	0	千克			/
4805.1900	--其他〔999〕	6	5	30	13/	0	千克			/30
	-强韧箱纸板（再生挂面纸板）：									
4805.2400	--每平方米重量在150克及以下〔999〕	6		30	13/	0	千克			/
4805.2500	--每平方米重量超过150克〔999〕	6		30	13/	0	千克			/31
4805.3000	-亚硫酸盐包装纸〔999〕	6		30	13/	0	千克			/36
4805.4000	-滤纸及纸板〔999〕	6		30	13/	0	千克			/11
4805.5000	-毡纸及纸板〔999〕	6		30	13/	0	千克			/
	-其他：									
	--每平方米重量在150克及以下：									
4805.9110	---电解电容器原纸〔999〕	6	5	30	13/	0	千克			/25
4805.9190	---其他〔999〕	6	5	30	13/	0	千克			/25
4805.9200	--每平方米重量超过150克以上，但小于225克〔999〕	6		30	13/	0	千克			/26
4805.9300	--每平方米重量在225克及以上〔999〕	6		30	13/	0	千克			/36
48.06	**成卷或成张的植物羊皮纸、防油纸、描图纸、半透明纸及其他高光泽透明或半透明纸：**									
4806.1000	-植物羊皮纸〔999〕	6	5	40	13/	0	千克			/30
4806.2000	-防油纸〔999〕	6	5	40	13/	0	千克			/30
4806.3000	-描图纸〔999〕	6	5	30	13/	0	千克			/10
4806.4000	-高光泽透明或半透明纸〔999〕	6	5	40	13/	0	千克			/25
48.07	**成卷或成张的复合纸及纸板（用黏合剂粘合各层纸或纸板制成），未经表面涂布或未浸渍，不论内层是否有加强材料：**									
4807.0000	成卷或成张的复合纸及纸板（用黏合剂粘合各层纸或纸板制成），未经表面涂布或未浸渍，不论内层是否有加强材料〔999〕	6	5	40	13/	0	千克			/30
48.08	**成卷或成张的瓦楞纸及纸板（不论是否与平面纸胶合）、皱纹纸及纸板、压纹纸及纸板、穿孔纸及纸板，但税目48.03的纸除外：**									

协定税率 %										特惠税率 %			Article Description
亚太5国	东/冰/格	巴基斯坦	韩国	瑞士	哥达	秘鲁	澳大利亚	新西/坡/智	港/澳/台	亚太2国	老/柬/缅	36/3/1	
													-Kraftliner:
													--Unbleached
													--Other
													-Sack kraft paper:
													--Unbleached
													--Other
													-Other kraft paper and paperboard weighing 150 g/m² or less:
													--Unbleached
													Uncoatde krafliner paper and paperboard(tensile index (vertical + lateral) is greater than or equal to 69 N. M/g, tear index (vertical) is greater than or equal to 10 mN2/ g, tensile energy absorption index (horizontal) is greater than or equal to 1.0 J/g, tensile energy absorption index (vertical) is greater than or equal to 0.8 J/g, porosity is greater than or equal to 3.4 um/(Pa. s), elongation (vertical) is greater than or equal to 2%. (tissue paper refers to the per square metre weighs≤150 grams or less, roll or into zhang without coating)
													Other uncoated kraft paper and paperboard, unbleached(w≤150g/m², in rolls or sheets)
													--Other
													-Other kraft paper and paperboard weighing more than 150 g/m² but less than 225g/m²:
													--Unbleached
													--Bleached uniformly throughout the mass and of which more than 95% by weight of the total fibre content consists of wood fibres obtained by a chemical process
													--Other
													-Other kraft paper and paperboard weighing 225 g/m² or more:
													--Unbleached
													--Bleached uniformly throughout the mass and of which more than 95% by weight of the total fibre content consists of wood fibres obtained by a chemical process
													--Other
													Other uncoated paper and paperboard, in rolls or sheets, not further worked or processed than as specified in Note 3 to this Chapter:
													-Fluting paper:
									0/0/			0//	--Semi-chemical fluting paper
									0/0/			0//	--Straw fluting paper
	5//								0/0/			0//	--Other
													-Testliner(recycled liner board):
									0/0/			0//	--Weighing 150 g/m² or less
									0/0/			0//	--Weighing more than 150 g/m²
													-Sulphite wrapping paper
													-Filter paper and paperboard
													-Felt paper and paperboard
													-Other:
													--Weighing 150 g/m² or less:
	5//							5//	0/0/			0//	---Paper for electrolytic capacitor
	5//							5//	0/0/			0//	---Other
													--Weighing more than 150 g/m² but less than 225 g/m²
									0/0/			0//	--Weighing 225 g/m² or more
													Vegetable parchment, greaseproof papers, tracing papers and glassine and other glazed transparent or translucent papers, in rolls or sheets:
	5//							5//					-Vegetable parchment
	5//							5//					-Greaseproof papers
	5//							5//					-Tracing papers
	5//							5//					-Glassine and other glazed transparent or translucent papers
													Composite paper and paperboard (made by sticking flat layers of paper or paperboard together with an adhesive), not surface-coated or impregnated, whether or not internally reinforced, in rolls or sheets:
													Composite paper and paperboard (made by sticking flat layers of paper or paperboard together with an adhesive), not surface-coated or impregnated, whether or not internally reinforced, in rolls or sheets
													Paper and paperboard, corrugated (with or without glued flat surface sheets), creped, crinkled, embossed or perforated, in rolls or sheets, other than paper of the kind described in heading No. 48. 03:

税则号列	货品名称〔CIQ扩展编码及品名—T2表示见附表2〕	最惠(%)	暂定税率	普通	增值/消费	出口退税	计量单位	监管条件	检验检疫	特殊证件对美关税
4808.1000	-瓦楞纸及纸板,不论是否穿孔〔999〕	6	5	30	13/	0	千克			/30
4808.4000	-皱纹牛皮纸,不论是否压花或穿孔〔999〕	6		40	13/	0	千克			/11
4808.9000	-其他〔999〕	6		40	13/	0	千克			/26
48.09	**复写纸、自印复写纸及其他拷贝或转印纸(包括涂布或浸渍的油印蜡纸或胶印版纸),不论是否印制,成卷或成张的:**									
4809.2000	-自印复写纸〔999〕	6		40	13/	0	千克			/11
4809.9000	-其他〔999〕	6		40	13/	0	千克			/26
48.10	**成卷或成张矩形(包括正方形)的任何尺寸的单面或双面涂布高岭土或其他无机物质(不论是否加黏合剂)的纸及纸板,未涂布其他涂料,不论是否染面、饰面或印花:**									
	-书写、印刷或类似用途的纸及纸板,不含用机械或化学—机械方法制得的纤维或所含前述纤维不超过全部纤维重量的10%:									
4810.1300	--成卷的									
4810.1300 01	成卷的铜版纸(所含用机械或化学—机械法制得的纤维≤10%)〔999〕	5		40	13/	0	千克			/10
4810.1300 90	涂无机物的其他书写/印刷或类似用途纸/纸板(成卷的,所含用机械或化学—机械法制得的纤维≤10%)〔999〕	5		40	13/	0	千克			/10
4810.1400	--成张的,一边不超过435毫米,另一边不超过297毫米(以未折叠计)〔999〕	5		40	13/	0	千克			/25
4810.1900	--其他〔999〕	5		40	13/	0	千克			/25
	-书写、印刷或类似用途的纸及纸板,所含用机械或化学—机械方法制得的纤维超过全部纤维重量的10%:									
4810.2200	--轻质涂布纸〔999〕	5		40	13/	0	千克			/25
4810.2900	--其他〔999〕	5		40	13/	0	千克			/35
	-牛皮纸及纸板,但书写、印刷或类似用途的除外:									
4810.3100	--本体均匀漂白,所含用化学方法制得的木纤维超过全部纤维重量的95%,每平方米重量不超过150克									
4810.3100 10	涂无机物的白板纸、白卡纸(薄纸指每平方米重≤150g,含用化学方法制得木纤维)〔999〕	5		40	13/	0	千克			/35
4810.3100 90	涂无机物的薄漂白牛皮纸及纸板(薄纸指每平方米重量≤150克,含用化学方法制得的木纤维)〔999〕	5		40	13/	0	千克			/35
4810.3200	--本体均匀漂白,所含用化学方法制得的木纤维超过全部纤维重量的95%,每平方米重量超过150克									
4810.3200 10	涂无机物的白板纸、白卡纸(厚纸指每平方米重量>150克,含用化学方法制得的木纤维)〔999〕	5		40	13/	0	千克			/10
4810.3200 90	涂无机物的厚漂白牛皮纸及纸板(厚纸指每平方米重量>150g,含用化学方法制得的木纤维)〔999〕	5		40	13/	0	千克			/10
4810.3900	--其他〔999〕	5		40	13/	0	千克			/10
	-其他纸及纸板:									
4810.9200	--多层的〔999〕	5		40	13/	0	千克			/30
4810.9900	--其他〔999〕	6	5	40	13/	0	千克			/25
48.11	**成卷或成张矩形(包括正方形)的任何尺寸的经涂布、浸渍、覆盖、染面、饰面或印花的纸、纸板、纤维素絮纸及纤维素纤维网纸,但税目48.03、48.09或48.10的货品除外:**									
4811.1000	-焦油纸及纸板、沥青纸及纸板〔999〕	6	5	40	13/	0	千克			/
	-胶粘纸及纸板:									
4811.4100	--自粘的〔999〕	6	5	40	13/	0	千克			/25
4811.4900	--其他〔999〕	6	5	40	13/	0	千克			/10

协定税率 %										特惠税率 %			Article Description
亚太5国	东/冰/格	巴基斯坦	韩国	瑞士	哥达	秘鲁	澳大利亚	新西/坡/智	港/澳/台	亚太2国	老/柬/缅	36/3/1	
				3.9				3.9//					-Corrugated paper and paperboard, whether or not perforated
													-Kraft paper, creped or crinkled, whether or not embossed or perforated
													-Other
													Carbon paper, self-copy paper and other copying or transfer papers (including coated or impregnated paper for duplicator stencils or offset plates), whether or not printed, in rolls or sheets:
													-Self-copy paper
													-Other
													Paper and paperboard, coated on one or both sides with kaolin(China clay) or other inorganic substances, with or without a binder, and with no other coating, whether or not surface-coloured, surface-decorated or printed, in rolls or rectangular(including square) sheets, of any size:
													-Paper and paperboard of a kind used for writing, printing or other graphic purposes, not containing fibres obtained by a mechanical or chemi-mechanical process or of which not more than 10% by weight of the total fibre content consists of such fibres:
													--In rolls
									0/0/			0//	Art paper, in rolls (containing fibres≤10%, obtained by a mechanical or chemi-mechanical process)
									0/0/			0//	Other paper and paperboard, coated with inorganic substances, of a kind used for writing, printing or other graphic purposes (containing fibres≤10%, obtained by a mechanical or chemi-mechanical process, in rolls)
									0/0/			0//	--In sheets with one side not exceeding 435 mm and the other side not exceeding 297 mm in the unfolded state
									0/0/			0//	--Other
													-Paper and paperboard of a kind used for writing, printing or other graphic purposes, of which more than 10% by weight of the total fibre content consists of fibres obtained by a mechanical or chemi-mechanical process:
													--Light-weight coated paper
									0/0/			0//	--Other
													-Kraft paper and paperboard, other than that of a kind used for writing, printing or other graphic purposes:
													--Bleached uniformly throughout the mass and of which more than 95% by weight of the total fibre content consists of wood fibres obtained by a chemical process, and weighing 150 g/m² or less
									0/0/			0//	White board and ivory board, bleached, coated with inarganic substances (w≤150g/m², consisting of wood fibres obtained by a chemical process)
									0/0/			0//	White kraft paper and paperboard, bleached, coated with inorganic substances, (w≤150g/m², consisting of wood fibres obtained by a chemical process)
													--Bleached uniformly throughout the mass and of which more than 95% by weight of the total fibre content consists of wood fibres obtained by a chemical process, and weighing more than 150g/m²
									0/0/			0//	White board and ivory board, bleached, coated with inorganic substances(w>150g/m² consisting of wood fibres obtained by a chemical process)
									0/0/			0//	White kraft paper and paperboard, bleached, coated with inorganic substances(w>150g/m², consisting of wood fibres obtained by a chemical process)
									0/0/			0//	--Other
													-Other paper and paperboard:
									0/0/			0//	--Multiply
	5//							5//	0/0/			0//	--Other
													Paper, paperboard, cellulose wadding and webs of cellulose fibres, coated, impregnated, covered, surface-coloured, surface-decorated or printed, in rolls or rectangular(including square)sheets, of any size, other than goods of the kind described in heading No. 48.03, 48.09or 48.10:
	5//							5//	0/0/			0//	-Tarred, bituminised or asphalted paper and paperboard
													-Gummed or adhesive paper and paperboard:
	5//							5//	0/0/			0//	--Self-adhesive
	5//							5//	0/0/			0//	--Other

税则号列	货品名称〔CIQ扩展编码及品名－T2表示见附表2〕	最惠(%)	暂定税率	普通	增值/消费	出口退税	计量单位	监管条件	检验检疫	特殊证件对美关税
	-用塑料(不包括黏合剂)涂布、浸渍或覆盖的纸及纸板：									
	--漂白的，每平方米重量超过150克：									
4811.5110	---彩色相纸用双面涂塑厚纸〔999〕	6	1	40	13/	0	千克			/26
	---其他：									
4811.5191	----纸塑铝复合材料〔999〕	6	5	40	13/	13	千克			/
4811.5199	----其他〔999〕	6		40	13/	0	千克			/26
	--其他：									
4811.5910	---绝缘纸及纸板〔999〕	6	5	30	13/	0	千克			/25
	---其他：									
4811.5991	----镀铝的〔999〕	6	5	40	13/	13	千克			/10
4811.5999	----其他〔999〕	6	5	40	13/	0	千克			/10
	-用蜡、石蜡、硬脂精、油或甘油涂布、浸渍、覆盖的纸及纸板：									
4811.6010	---绝缘纸及纸板〔999〕	6	5	30	13/	0	千克			/10
4811.6090	---其他〔999〕	6	5	40	13/	0	千克			/25
4811.9000	-其他纸、纸板、纤维素絮纸及纤维素纤维网纸〔999〕	6	5	40	13/	0	千克			/10
48.12	**纸浆制的滤块、滤板及滤片：**									
4812.0000	纸浆制的滤块、滤板及滤片〔999〕	6		40	13/	0	千克			/26
48.13	**卷烟纸，不论是否切成一定尺寸、成小本或管状：**									
4813.1000	-成小本或管状〔999〕	7.5		100	13/	0	千克	7		/
4813.2000	-宽度不超过5厘米成卷的〔999〕	7.5		100	13/	0	千克	7		/
4813.9000	-其他〔999〕	7.5		100	13/	0	千克	7		/
48.14	**壁纸及类似品；窗用透明纸：**									
4814.2000	-用塑料涂面或盖面的壁纸及类似品，起纹、压花、着色、印刷图案或经其他装饰〔999〕	6	5	50	13/	13	千克			/25
4814.9000	-其他									
4814.9000 10	用木粒或草粒等饰面的壁纸〔999〕	6	5	50	13/	0	千克			/25
4814.9000 90	其他壁纸及类似品，窗用透明纸〔999〕	6	5	50	13/	0	千克			/25
48.16	**复写纸、自印复写纸及其他拷贝或转印纸(不包括税目48.09的纸)、油印蜡纸或胶印版纸，不论是否盒装：**									
4816.2000	-自印复写纸〔999〕	6		70	13/	0	千克			/31
	-其他：									
4816.9010	小卷(张)热敏转印纸(宽度≤36cm)〔999〕	6		40	13/	0	千克			/11
4816.9090	---其他〔999〕	6		70	13/	0	千克			/26
48.17	**纸或纸板制的信封、封缄信片、素色明信片及通信卡片；纸或纸板制的盒子、袋子及夹子，内装各种纸制文具：**									
4817.1000	-信封〔999〕	5		80	13/	13	千克			/35
4817.2000	-封缄信片、素色明信片及通信卡片〔999〕	5		80	13/	13	千克			/35
4817.3000	-纸或纸板制的盒子、袋子及夹子，内装各种纸制文具〔999〕	5		80	13/	13	千克			/30
48.18	**卫生纸及类似纸，家庭或卫生用纤维素絮纸及纤维素纤维网纸，成卷宽度不超过36厘米或切成一定尺寸或形状的；纸浆、纸、纤维素絮纸或纤维素纤维网纸制的手帕、面巾、台布、餐巾、床单及类似的家庭、卫生或医院用品、衣服及衣着附件：**									
4818.1000	-卫生纸〔999〕	5		80	13/	6	千克	A	M	/35
4818.2000	-纸手帕及纸面巾〔101面巾纸、餐巾纸及类似纸，102擦拭用纸〕	5		90	13/	6	千克	A	M	/35
4818.3000	-纸台布及纸餐巾〔101面巾纸、餐巾纸及类似纸，102擦拭用纸〕	5		90	13/	6	千克	A	M	/35
4818.5000	-衣服及衣着附件〔101服装生产用纸板或衬里，102一次性生活用纸〕	5	4	90	13/	13	千克	A	M	/
4818.9000	-其他〔999〕	5		90	13/	13	千克	A	M	/10
48.19	**纸、纸板、纤维素絮纸或纤维素纤维网纸制的箱、盒、匣、袋及其他包装容器；纸或纸板制的卷宗盒、信件盘及类似品，供办公室、商店及类似场所使用的：**									
4819.1000	-瓦楞纸或纸板制的箱、盒、匣〔999〕	5		80	13/	13	千克			/35

协定税率 %										特惠税率 %			
亚太5国	东/冰/格	巴基斯坦	韩国	瑞士	哥达	秘鲁	澳大利亚	新西/坡/智	港/澳/台	亚太2国	老/柬/缅	36/3/1	Article Description
													-Paper and paperboard coated, impregnated or covered with plastics (excluding adhesives):
													--Bleached, weighing more than 150g/m^2:
	5//							5//	0/0/			0//	---Paper coated on both sides with plastics for colour photography
													---Other:
	5//							5//	0/0/			0//	----Paper-plastic compound material
									0/0/			0//	----Other
													--Other:
	5//							5//	0/0/			0//	---Insulating paper and paperboard
													---Other:
	5//							5//	0/0/			0//	----Aluminium plated
	5//							5//	0/0/			0//	----Other
													-Paper and paperboard, coated, impregnated or covered with wax, paraffin wax, stearin, oil or glyecrol:
	5//							5//	0/0/			0//	---Insulating paper and paperboard
	5//							5//	0/0/			0//	---Other
	5//							5//	0/0/			0//	-Other paper, paperboard, cellulose wadding and webs of cellulose fibres
													Filter blocks, slabs and plates, of paper pulp:
													Filter blocks, slabs and plates, of paper pulp
													Cigarette paper, whether or not cut to size or in the form of booklets or tubes:
													-In the form of booklets or tubes
													-In rolls of a width not exceeding 5 cm
													-Other
													Wallpaper and similar wall coverings; window transparencies of paper:
	5//							5//					-Wallpaper and similar wall coverings, consisting of paper coated or covered, on the face side, with a grained, embossed, coloured, design-printed or otherwise decorated layer of plastics
													-Other
	5//							5//					"Ingrain" paper
	5//							5//					Other wallpaper and similar wall coverings, window transparencies of paper
													Carbon paper, self-copy paper and other copying or transfer papers (other than those of heading No. 48.09), duplicator stencils and offset plates, of paper, whether or not put up in boxes:
													-Self-copy paper
													-Other:
													---Heat transfer paper
													---Other
													Envelopes, letter cards, plain postcards and correspondence cards, of paper or paperboard; boxes, pouches, wallets and writing compendiums, of paper or paperboard, containing an assortment of paper stationery:
	5//												-Envelopes
	5//												-Letter cards, plain postcards and correspondence cards
	5//												-Boxes, pouches, wallets and writing compendiums, of paper or paperboard, containing an assortment of paper stationery
													Toilet paper and similar paper, cellulose wadding or webs of cellulose fibres, of a kind used for household or sanitary purposes, in rolls of a width not exceeding 36 cm, or cut to size or shape; handkerchiefs, cleansing tissues, towels, tablecloths, serviettes, bed sheets and similar household, sanitary or hospital articles, articles of apparel and clothing accessories, of paper pulp, paper, cellulose wadding or webs of cellulose fibres:
													-Toilet paper
													-Handkerchiefs, cleansing or facial tissues and towels
	5//												-Tablecloths and serviettes
	0/0/	4	0	0	0	0	0	0//0	0/0/			0/0/0	-Articles of apparel and clothing accessories
													-Other
													Cartons, boxes, cases, bags and other packing containers, of paper, paperboard, cellulose wadding or webs of cellulose fibres; box files, letter trays and similar articles, of paper or paperboard of a kind used in offices, shops or the like:
									0/0/			0//	-Cartons, boxes and cases, of corrugated paper or paperboard

税则号列	货品名称〔CIQ 扩展编码及品名—T2 表示见附表 2〕	最惠(%)	暂定税率	普通	增值/消费	出口退税	计量单位	监管条件	检验检疫	特殊证件对美关税
4819.2000	-非瓦楞纸或纸板制的可折叠箱、盒、匣〔999〕	5		80	13/	13	千克			/35
4819.3000	-底宽 40 厘米及以上的纸袋〔999〕	6	5	80	13/	13	千克			/30
4819.4000	-其他纸袋,包括锥形袋〔999〕	5		80	13/	13	千克			/30
4819.5000	-其他包装容器,包括唱片套〔999〕	5		80	13/	13	千克	A	R	/35
4819.6000	-办公室、商店及类似场所使用的卷宗盒、信件盘、存储盒及类似品〔999〕	5		80	13/	13	千克			/30
48.20	**纸或纸板制的登记本、账本、笔记本、订货本、收据本、信笺本、记事本、日记本及类似品、练习本、吸墨纸本、活动封面(活页及非活页)、文件夹、卷宗皮、多联商业表格纸、页间夹有复写纸的本及其他文具用品;纸或纸板制的样品簿、粘贴簿及书籍封面:**									
4820.1000	-登记本、账本、笔记本、订货本、收据本、信笺本、记事本、日记本及类似品〔999〕	5		80	13/	13	千克			/35
4820.2000	-练习本〔999〕	5		80	13/	13	千克			/30
4820.3000	-活动封面(书籍封面除外)、文件夹及卷宗皮〔999〕	5		80	13/	13	千克			/35
4820.4000	-多联商业表格纸、本页间夹有复写纸的本〔999〕	5	4	80	13/	13	千克			/34
4820.5000	-样品簿及粘贴簿〔999〕	5		80	13/	13	千克			/10
4820.9000	-其他〔999〕	5		80	13/	13	千克			/35
48.21	**纸或纸板制的各种标签,不论是否印制:**									
4821.1000	-印制〔999〕	6	5	50	13/	13	千克			/25
4821.9000	-其他〔999〕	6	5	50	13/	13	千克			/25
48.22	**纸浆、纸或纸板(不论是否穿孔或硬化)制的筒管、卷轴、纡子及类似品:**									
4822.1000	-纺织纱线用〔999〕	6	5	35	13/	13	千克			/30
4822.9000	-其他〔999〕	6	5	70	13/	13	千克			/25
48.23	**切成一定尺寸或形状的其他纸、纸板、纤维素絮纸及纤维素纤维网纸;纸浆、纸、纸板、纤维素絮纸及纤维素纤维网纸制的其他物品:**									
4823.2000	-滤纸及纸板〔999〕	6		30	13/	13	千克			/26
4823.4000	-已印制的自动记录器用打印纸卷、纸张及纸盘〔999〕	6	5	30	13/	13	千克			/10
	-纸或纸板制的盘、碟、盆、杯及类似品:									
4823.6100	--竹浆纸制〔101 纸和塑料膜等其他材料复合,102 食品接触上蜡纸产品,103 食品接触其他纸产品,104 纸和塑料膜等其他材料复合,105 食品用上蜡纸包装,106 食品用其他纸包装〕	5	4	90	13/	13	千克	A	M	/
	--其他:									
4823.6910	---非木植物浆制〔101 纸和塑料膜等其他材料复合,102 食品接触上蜡纸产品,103 食品接触其他纸产品,104 纸和塑料膜等其他材料复合,105 食品用上蜡纸包装,106 食品用其他纸包装〕	5	4	90	13/	13	千克	A	M	/29
4823.6990	---其他〔101 食品接触原纸产品,102 纸和塑料膜等其他材料复合,103,104 食品接触其他纸产品,105,106 纸和塑料膜等其他材料复合,107 食品用上蜡纸包装,108 食品用其他纸包装〕	5	4	90	13/	13	千克	A	M	/34
4823.7000	-压制或模制纸浆制品〔999〕	6	5	90	13/	13	千克			/30
	-其他:									
4823.9010	---以纸或纸板为底制的铺地制品〔999〕	6	4	90	13/	0	千克			/29
4823.9020	---神纸及类似用品〔999〕	6	4	180	13/	13	千克			/
4823.9030	---纸扇〔999〕	5	4	90	13/	13	千克			/
4823.9090	---其他〔T2〕	6		90	13/	13	千克			/26

协定税率 %										特惠税率 %			
亚太5国	东/冰/格	巴基斯坦	韩国	瑞士	哥达	秘鲁	澳大利亚	新西/坡/智	港/澳/台	亚太2国	老/柬/缅	36/3/1	Article Description
									0/0/			0//	-Folding cartons, boxes and cases, of noncorrugated paper or paperboard
	0/0/	4	0	0	0	0	0	0/0/0	0/0/			0/0/0	-Sacks and bags, having a base of a width of 40 cm or more
	5//												-Other sacks and bags, including cones
	5//												-Other packing containers, including record sleeves
	5//												-Box files, letter trays, storage boxes and similar articles, of a kind used in offices, shops or the like
													Registers, account books, note books, order books, receipt books, letter pads, memorandum pads, diaries and similar articles, exercise books, blotting-pads, binders (loose-leaf or other), folders, file covers, manifold business forms, interleaved carbon sets and other articles of stationery, of paper or paperboard; albums for samples or for collections and book covers, of paper or paperboard:
	5//												-Registers, account books, note books, order books, receipt books, letter pads, memorandum pads, diaries and similar articles
	5//												-Exercise books
	5//												-Binders (other than book covers), folders and file covers
	0/0/	4.5	3	0	0	0	0	0//0	0/0/			0/0/0	-Manifold business forms and interleaved carbon sets
	5//												-Albums for samples or for collections
	5//												-Other
													Paper or paperboard labels of all kinds, whether or not printed:
	5//							5//	0/0/			0//	-Printed
	5//							5//					-Other
													Bobbins, spools, cops and similar supports of paper pulp, paper or paperboard (whether or not perforated or hardened):
	5//							5//					-Of a kind used for winding textile yarn
	5//							5//					-Other
													Other paper, paperboard, cellulose wadding and webs of cellulose fibres, cut to size or shape; other articles of paper pulp, paper, paperboard, cellulose wadding or webs of cellulose fibres:
													-Filter paper and paperboard
	5//												-Rolls, sheets and dials, printed for sel-frecording apparatus
													-Trays, dishes, plates, cups and the like, of paper or paperboard:
	0/0/	4	0	0	0	0	0	0//0	0/0/			0/0/0	--Of bamboo
													--Other:
	0/0/	4	3	0	0	0	0	0//0	0/0/			0/0/0	---Non woody plant pulp
	0/0/	4	3	0	0	0	0	0//0	0/0/			0/0/0	---Other
	5//							5//					-Moulded or pressed articles of paper pulp
													-Other:
	5//		4.5	0				0//	0/0/				---Floor coverings on a base of paper or of paperboard whether or not cut to size
	0/0/	4	0	0	0	0	0	0//0	0/0/			0/0/0	---Joss paper and the like
	0/0/	4	0	0	0	0	0	0//0	0/0/			0/0/0	---Paper fans
									0/0/			0//	---Other

第四十九章
书籍、报纸、印刷图画及其他印刷品；手稿、打字稿及设计图纸

注释：

一、本章不包括：

(一)透明基的照相负片或正片(第三十七章)；

(二)立体地图、设计图表或地球仪、天体仪，不论是否印刷(税目90.23)；

(三)第九十五章的扑克牌或其他物品；

(四)雕版画、印刷画、石印画的原本(税目97.02)，税目97.04的邮票、印花税票、纪念封、首日封、邮政信笺及类似品，以及第九十七章的超过一百年的古物或其他物品。

二、第四十九章所称"印刷"，也包括用胶版复印机、油印机印制，在自动数据处理设备控制下打印绘制，压印、冲印、感光复印、热敏复印或打字。

三、用纸以外材料装订成册的报纸、杂志和期刊，以及一期以上装订在同一封面里的成套报纸、杂志和期刊，应归入税目49.01，不论是否有广告材料。

四、税目49.01还包括：

(一)附有说明文字，每页编有号数以便装订成一册或几册的整集印刷复制品，例如，美术作品、绘画；

(二)随同成册书籍的图画附刊；

(三)供装订书籍或小册子用的散页、集页或书帖形式的印刷品，已构成一部作品的全部或部分。

但没有说明文字的印刷图画或图解，不论是否散页或书帖形式，应归入税目49.11。

五、除本章注释三另有规定的以外，税目49.01不包括主要作广告用的出版物(例如，小册子、散页印刷品、商业目录、同业公会出版的年鉴、旅游宣传品)，这类出版物应归入税目49.11。

六、税目49.03所称"儿童图画书"，是指以图画为主、文字为辅，供儿童阅览的书籍。

税则号列	货品名称〔CIQ扩展编码及品名－T2表示见附表2〕	最惠(%)	暂定税率	普通	增值/消费	出口退税	计量单位	监管条件	检验检疫	特殊证件对美关税
49.01	**书籍、小册子、散页印刷品及类似印刷品，不论是否单张：**									
4901.1000	-单张的，不论是否折叠〔999〕	0		0	9/	0,9,13	千克			/30
	-其他：									
4901.9100	--字典或百科全书及其连续出版的分册〔999〕	0		0	9/	0,9	千克			/30
4901.9900	--其他〔999〕	0		0	9/	0,9,13	千克			/5
49.02	**报纸、杂志及期刊，不论有无插图或广告材料：**									
4902.1000	-每周至少出版四次〔999〕	0		0	9/	9,13	千克			/5
4902.9000	-其他〔999〕	0		0	9/	9,13	千克			/5
49.03	**儿童图画书、绘画或涂色书：**									
4903.0000	儿童图画书、绘画或涂色书〔999〕	0		0	9/	0,9,13	千克			/5
49.04	**乐谱原稿或印本，不论是否装订或印有插图：**									
4904.0000	乐谱原稿或印本，不论是否装订或印有插图〔999〕	0		0	9/	0,9,13	千克			/5
49.05	**各种印刷的地图、水道图及类似图表，包括地图册、挂图、地形图及地球仪、天体仪：**									
4905.1000	-地球仪、天体仪〔999〕	0		0	13/	13	千克			/5
	-其他：									
4905.9100	--成册的〔999〕	0		0	13/	0,9,13	千克			/30
4905.9900	--其他〔999〕	0		0	13/	0,9,13	千克			/30
49.06	**手绘的建筑、工程、工业、商业、地形或类似用途的设计图纸原稿；手稿；用感光纸照相复印或用复写纸誊写的上述物品复制件：**									
4906.0000	手绘的建筑、工程、工业、商业、地形或类似用途的设计图纸原稿；手稿；用感光纸照相复印或用复写纸誊写的上述物品复制件〔999〕									
4906.0000 10	含有人类遗传资源信息的设计图纸原稿或手稿及其复制件(手绘的建筑、工程、工业、商业、地形或类似用途的)〔999〕	0		0	13/	13	千克	V		/25
4906.0000 90	其他设计图纸原稿或手稿及其复制件(手绘的建筑、工程、工业、商业、地形或类似用途的)〔999〕	0		0	13/	13	千克			/25

Chapter 49
Printed books, newspapers, pictures and other products of the printing industry; manuscripts, typescripts and plans

Notes:

1. This Chapter does not cover:
   (a) Photographic negatives or positives on transparent bases (Chapter 37);
   (b) Maps, plans or globes, in relief, whether or not printed (heading No. 90. 23);
   (c) Playing cards or other goods of Chapter 95;
   (d) Original engravings, prints or lithographs (heading No. 97. 02), postage or revenue stamps, stamp-postmarks, first-day covers, postal stationery or the like of heading No. 97. 04, antiques of an age exceeding one hundred years or other articles of Chapter 97.
2. For the purposes of Chapter 49, the term "printed" also means reproduced by means of a duplicating machine, produced under the control of an automatic data processing machine, embossed, photographed, photocopied, thermocopied or typewritten.
3. Newspapers, journals and periodicals which are bound otherwise than in paper, and sets of newspapers, journals or periodicals comprising more than one number under a single cover are to be classified in heading No. 49. 01, whether or not containing advertising material.
4. Heading No. 49. 01 also covers:
   (a) A collection of printed reproductions of, for example, works of art or drawings, with a relative text, put up with numbered pages in a form suitable for binding into one or more volumes;
   (b) A pictorial supplement accompanying, and subsidiary to, a bound volume;
   (c) Printed parts of books or booklets, in the form of assembled or separate sheets or signatures, constituting the whole or a part of a complete work and designed for binding.

   However, printed pictures or illustrations not bearing a text, whether in the form of signatures or separate sheets, fall in heading No. 49. 11.
5. Subject to Note 3 to this Chapter, heading No. 49. 01 does not cover publications which are essentially devoted to advertising (for example, brochures, pamphlets, leaflets, trade catalogues, year books published by trade associations, tourist propaganda). Such publications are to be classified in heading No. 49. 11.
6. For the purposes of heading No. 49. 03, the expression "children's picture books" means books for children in which the pictures form the principal interest and the text is subsidiary

协定税率 %										特惠税率 %			Article Description
亚太5国	东/冰/格	巴基斯坦	韩国	瑞士	哥达	秘鲁	澳大利亚	新西/坡/智	港/澳/台	亚太2国	老/柬/缅	36/3/1	
													Printed books, brochures, leaflets and similar printed matter, whether or not in single sheets:
												0/0/0	-In single sheets, whether or not folded
													-Other:
												0/0/0	--Dictionaries and encyclopaedias, and serial instalments thereof
												0/0/0	--Other
													Newspapers, journals and periodicals, whether or not illustrated or containing advertising material:
												0/0/0	-Appearing at least four times a week
												0/0/0	-Other
													Children's picture, drawing or colouring books:
												0/0/0	Children's picture, drawing or colouring books
													Music, printed or in manuscript, whether or not bound or illustrated:
												0/0/0	Music, printed or in manuscript, whether or not bound or illustrated
													Maps and hydrographic or similar charts of all kinds, including atlases, wall maps, topographical plans and globes, printed:
												0/0/0	-Globes
													-Other:
												0/0/0	--In book form
												0/0/0	--Other
													Plans and drawings for architectural, engineering, industrial, commercial, topographical or similar purposes, being originals drawn by hand; hand-written text; photographic reproductions on sensitized paper and carbon copies of the foregoing:
													Plans and drawings for architectural, engineering, industrial, commercial, topographical or similar purposes, being originals drawn by hand; hand-written text; photographic reproductions on sensitized paper and carbon copies of the foregoing
	//							//	//		//	0/0/0	Printed pictures, design drawings and photographs containing information on human genetic resources
	//							//	//		//	0/0/0	Other original or manuscript of design drawings and copies thereof

税则号列		货品名称〔CIQ扩展编码及品名—T2表示见附表2〕	最惠(%)	暂定税率	普通	增值/消费	出口退税	计量单位	监管条件	检验检疫	特殊证件对美关税
49.07		**在承认或将承认其面值的国家流通或新发行并且未经使用的邮票、印花税票及类似票证；印有邮票或印花税票的纸品；钞票；空白支票；股票、债券及类似所有权凭证：**									
4907.0010		---邮票〔999〕	6	5	50	13/	13	千克			/10
4907.0020		---钞票〔999〕	0		50	13/	13	千克			/20
4907.0030		---证券凭证〔999〕	0		50	13/	13	千克			/
4907.0090		---其他									
4907.0090	11	特许权使用凭证(包括软件升级许可证、软件用户许可证等，但游戏软件升级许可证、游戏软件用户许可证除外)〔999〕	6	0	50	13/	13	千克			/5
4907.0090	19	其他给予存取、安装、复制或使用软件(含游戏)、数据、互联网内容物(含游戏内或应用程序内内容物)、服务或电信服务(含移动服务)权利的印刷品(特许权使用凭证除外)〔999〕	2.5/1.3		50	13/	13	千克			/7.5,6.3
4907.0090	90	其他印有邮票等的其他纸品(包括印有印花税票的纸品)〔999〕	6		50	13/	13	千克			/11
49.08		**转印贴花纸(移画印花法用图案纸)：**									
4908.1000		-釉转印贴花纸(移画印花法用图案纸)〔999〕	6	5	50	13/	13	千克			/25
4908.9000		-其他〔999〕	6	4	50	13/	13	千克			/29
49.09		**印刷或有图画的明信片；印有个人问候、祝贺、通告的卡片，不论是否有图画、带信封或饰边：**									
4909.0010		---印刷或有图画的明信片〔999〕	6	5	50	13/	13	千克			/25
4909.0090		---其他〔999〕	6	5	50	13/	13	千克			/25
49.10		**印刷的各种日历，包括日历芯：**									
4910.0000		印刷的各种日历(包括日历芯)〔999〕	6	5	50	13/	13	千克			/30
49.11		**其他印刷品，包括印刷的图片及照片：**									
		-商业广告品、商品目录及类似印刷品：									
4911.1010		---无商业价值的〔999〕	0		0	13/	13	千克			/20
4911.1090		---其他〔999〕	6	5	50	13/	13	千克			/25
		-其他：									
4911.9100		--图片、设计图样及照片〔999〕									
4911.9100	10	含有人类遗传资源信息的印刷图片、设计图样及照片	6	5	50	13/	13	千克	V		/25
4911.9100	90	其他印刷的图片、设计图样及照片	6	5	50	13/	13	千克			/25
		--其他：									
4911.9910		---纸质的									
4911.9910	10	给予存取、安装、复制或使用软件(含游戏)、数据、互联网内容物(含游戏内或应用程序内内容物)、服务或电信服务(含移动服务)权利的印刷品〔999〕	2.5/1.3		50	13/	13	千克			/27.5,26.3
4911.9910	20	含有人类遗传资源信息的纸质印刷品	6	4	50	13/	13	千克	V		/29
4911.9910	90	其他纸质的印刷品〔999〕	6	4	50	13/	13	千克			/29
4911.9990		---其他									
4911.9990	10	给予存取、安装、复制或使用软件(含游戏)、数据、互联网内容物(含游戏内或应用程序内内容物)、服务或电信服务(含移动服务)权利的印刷品〔999〕	2.5/1.3		50	13/	13	千克			/22.5,21.3
4911.9990	20	含有人类遗传资源信息的其他印刷品	6	5	50	13/	13	千克	V		/25
4911.9990	90	其他印刷品〔999〕	6	5	50	13/	13	千克			/25

协定税率 %										特惠税率 %			Article Description
亚太5国	东/冰/格	巴基斯坦	韩国	瑞士	哥达	秘鲁	澳大利亚	新西/坡/智	港/澳/台	亚太2国	老/柬/缅	36/3/1	
													Unused postage, revenue or similar stamps of current or new issue in the country in which they have, or will have, a recognised face value; stamp-impressed paper; banknotes; cheque forms; stock, share or bond certificates and similar documents of title:
	5//		4.5	0				0//	0/0/			0/0/	---Postage
												0/0/0	---Banknotes
												0/0/0	---Documents of title
													---Other
	5//		4.5	0				0//	0/0/			0/0/	Presswork,ctificate of right of special permission (including software upgrade license , software user License, Unless the game software upgrade license, game software license)
	5//		4.5	0				0//	0/0/			0/0/	Fresswork,the other given access, install, copy or use the software (including games), data, Internet content (including games or applications within contents) services or telecommunications services (including mobile services) rights (royalty receipts except)
	5//		4.5	0				0//	0/0/			0/0/	Other stamp-impressed paper(including revenue stamps)
													Transfers (decalcomanias):
	5//		4.5	0				0//	0/0/			0/0/	-Transfers (decalcomanias), vitrifiable
	5//		4.5	0				0//	0/0/			0/0/	-Other
													Printed or illustrated postcards; printed cards bearing personal greetings, messages or announcements, whether or not illustrated, with or without envelopes or trimmings:
	5//		4.5	0				0//	0/0/			0/0/	---Printed or illustrated postcards
	5//		4.5	0				0//	0/0/			0/0/	---Other
													Calendars of any kind, printed, including calendar blocks:
	5//		4.5	2.3				2.3//	0/0/			0/0/0	Calendars of any kind, printed, including calendar blocks
													Other printed matter, including printed pictures and photographs:
													-Trade advertising material, commercial catalogues and the like:
												0/0/0	---No commercial value
	5//		4.5	2.3				2.3//	0/0/			0/0/	---Other
													-Other:
													--Pictures, designs and photographs
	5//		4.5	0				0//	0/0/		//	0/0/	Printed pictures, design drawings and photographs containing information on human genetic resources
	5//		4.5	0				0//	0/0/		//	0/0/	Other printed pictures, design drawings and photographs
													--Other:
													---Of paper
	5/0/		4.5	3.9				0//	0/0/			0/0/	Presswork,the given access, install, copy or use the software (including games), data, Internet content (including games or applications within contents) services or telecommunications services (including mobile services) rights
	5/0/		4.5	3.9				0//	0/0/		//	0/0/	Paper Prints Containing Information on Human Genetic Resources
	5/0/		4.5	3.9				0//	0/0/			0/0/	Other paper printing
													---Other
	5/0/		4.5	3.9				0//	0/0/			0/0/	Presswork,the given access, install, copy or use the software (including games), data, Internet content (including games or applications within contents) services or telecommunications services (including mobile services) rights
	5/0/		4.5	3.9				0//	0/0/		//	0/0/	Other printed materials containing information on human genetic resources
	5/0/		4.5	3.9				0//	0/0/			0/0/	Other printing

第十一类
纺织原料及纺织制品

注释：

一、本类不包括：

(一)制刷用的动物鬃、毛(税目05.02)；马毛及废马毛(税目05.11)；

(二)人发及人发制品(税目05.01、67.03或67.04)，但通常用于榨油机或类似机器的滤布除外(税目59.11)；

(三)第十四章的棉短绒或其他植物材料；

(四)税目25.24的石棉、税目68.12或68.13的石棉制品或其他产品；

(五)税目30.05或30.06的物品；税号33.06的用于清洁牙缝的纱线(牙线)，单独零售包装的；

(六)税目37.01至37.04的感光布；

(七)截面尺寸超过1毫米的塑料单丝和表面宽度超过5毫米的塑料扁条及类似品(例如，人造草)(第三十九章)，以及上述单丝或扁条的缏条、织物、篮筐或柳条编结品(第四十六章)；

(八)第三十九章的用塑料浸渍、涂布、包覆或层压的机织物、针织物或钩编织物、毡呢或无纺织物及其制品；

(九)第四十章的用橡胶浸渍、涂布、包覆或层压的机织物、针织物或钩编织物、毡呢或无纺织物及其制品；

(十)带毛皮张(第四十一章或第四十三章)、税目43.03或43.04的毛皮制品、人造毛皮及其制品；

(十一)税目42.01或42.02的用纺织材料制成的物品；

(十二)第四十八章的产品或物品(例如纤维素絮纸)；

(十三)第六十四章的鞋靴及其零件、护腿、裹腿及类似品；

(十四)第六十五章的发网、其他帽类及其零件；

(十五)第六十七章的货品；

(十六)涂有研磨料的纺织材料(税目68.05)以及税目68.15的碳纤维及其制品；

(十七)玻璃纤维及其制品，但可见底布的玻璃线刺绣品除外(第七十章)；

(十八)第九十四章的物品(例如，家具、寝具、灯具及照明装置)；

(十九)第九十五章的物品(例如，玩具、游戏品、运动用品及网具)；

(二十)第九十六章的物品(例如：刷子、旅行用成套缝纫用具、拉链及打字机色带、卫生巾(护垫)及止血塞、婴儿尿布及尿布衬里；

(二十一)第九十七章的物品。

二、(一)可归入第五十章至第五十五章及税目58.09或59.02的由两种或两种以上纺织材料混合制成的货品，应按其中重量最大的那种纺织材料归类。

当没有一种纺织材料的重量较大时，应按可归入的有关税目中最后一个税目所列的纺织材料归类。

(二)应用上述规定时：

1. 马毛粗松螺旋花线(税目51.10)和含金属纱线(税目56.05)均应作为一种单一的纺织材料，其重量应为它们在纱线中的合计重量；在机织物的归类中，金属线应作为一种纺织材料；

2. 在选择合适的税目时，应首先确定章，然后再确定该章的有关税目，至于不归入该章的其他材料可不予考虑；

3. 当归入第五十四章及第五十五章的货品与其他章的货品进行比较时，应将这两章作为一个单一的章对待；

4. 同一章或同一税目所列各种不同的纺织材料应作为单一的纺织材料对待。

(三)上述(一)、(二)两款规定亦适用于以下注释三、四、五或六所述纱线。

三、(一)本类的纱线(单纱、多股纱线或缆线)除下列(二)款另有规定的以外，凡符合以下规格的应作为“线、绳、索、缆”：

1. 丝或绢丝纱线，细度在20000分特以上；

2. 化学纤维纱线(包括第五十四章的用两根及以上单丝纺成的纱线)，细度在10000分特以上；

3. 大麻或亚麻纱线：

(1)加光或上光的，细度在1429分特及以上；

(2)未加光或上光的，细度在20000分特以上；

4. 三股或三股以上的椰壳纤维纱线；

5. 其他植物纤维纱线，细度在20000分特以上；

6. 用金属线加强的纱线。

(二)下列各项不按上述(一)款规定办理：

1. 羊毛或其他动物毛纱线及纸纱线，但用金属线加强的纱线除外；

2. 第五十五章的化学纤维长丝丝束以及第五十四章的未加捻或捻度每米少于5转的复丝纱线；

3. 税目50.06的蚕胶丝及第五十四章的单丝；

4. 税目56.05的含金属纱线；但用金属线加强的纱线按上述(一)款6项规定办理；

SECTION XI
TEXTILES AND TEXTILE ARTICLES

Notes:

1. This Section does not cover:
   (a) Animal brush making bristles or hair (heading No. 05. 02); horsehair orhorsehair waste (heading No. 05. 11);
   (b) Human hair or articles of human hair (heading No. 05. 01, 67. 03 or 67. 04), except straining cloth of a kind commonly used in oil presses or the like (heading No. 59. 11);
   (c) Cotton linters or other vegetable materials of Chapter 14;
   (d) Asbestos of heading No. 25. 24 or articles of asbestos or other products of heading No. 68. 12 or 68. 13;
   (e) Articles of heading No. 30. 05 or 30. 06; yarn used to clean between the teeth, in individual, retail packages dental floss, of heading No. 33. 06;
   (f) Sensitized textiles of headings No. 37. 01 to 37. 04;
   (g) Monofilament of which any cross-sectional dimensionexceeds 1mm or strip or the like (for example, artificial straw) of an apparent width exceeding 5mm, of plastics (Chapter 39), or plaits cr fabrics or other basketware or wickerwork of such monofilament or strip (Chapter 46);
   (h) Woven, knitted or crocheted fabrics, felt or nonwovens, impregnated, coated, covered or laminated with plastics, or articles thereof, ofChapter 39;
   (i) Woven, knitted or crocheted fabrics, felt or nonwovens, impregnated, coated, covered or laminated with rubber, or articles thereof, ofChapter 40;
   (j) Hides or skins with their hair or wool on (Chapter 41 or43) or artcles of furskin, artificial fur or articles thereof, of heading No. 43. 03 or 43. 04;
   (k) Articles of textile materials of heading No. 42. 01or42. 02;
   (l) Products or articles of Chapter 48 (for example, cellulose wadding);
   (m) Footwear or parts of footwear, gaiters or leggings or similar articles of Chapter 64;
   (n) Hair-nets or other headgear or parts thereof of Chapter65;
   (o) Goods of Chapter 67;
   (p) Abrasive-coated textile material (Heading No. 68. 05) and also carbon fibres or articles of carbon fibres of heading No. 68. 15;
   (q) Glass fibres or articles of glass fibres, other thanembroidery with glass thread on a visible ground of fabric (Chapter 70);
   (r) Articles of Chapter 94 (for example, furniture, bedding, lamps and lighting fittings);
   (s) Articles of Chapter 95 (for example, toys, games, sports requisites and nets);
   (t) Articles of Chapter 96 (for example, brushes, travelsets for sewing, slide fasteners and typewriter ribbons, Sanitary towels(pads) and napkin liners for babies);
   (u) Articles of Chapter 97.
2. (a) Goods classifiable in Chapters 50 to 55 or of headingNo. 58. 09 or 59. 02 and of a mixture of two or more textile materials are to be classified as if consisting wholly of that one textile material which predominates by weight over any other single textile material. When no one textile material predominates by weight, the goods are to be classified as if consisting wholly of that one textile material which is covered by the heading which occurs last in numerical order among those which equally merit consideration.
   (b) For the purposes of the above rule:
      (i) Gimped horsehair yarn (heading No. 51. 10) and metallized yarn (heading No. 56. 05) are to be treated as a single textile material the weight of which is to be taken as the aggregate of the weights of its components; for the classification of woven fabrics, metal thread is to be regarded as a textile material;
      (ii) The choice of appropriate heading shall be effected by determining first the Chapter and then the applicable heading within that Chapter, disregarding any materials not classified in that Chapter;
      (iii) When both Chapters 54 and 55 are involved with any otherChapter, Chapters 54 and 55 are to be treated as a single Chapter;
      (iv) Where a Chapter or a heading refers to goods of different textile materials, such materials are to be treated as a single textile material.
   (c) The provisions of paragraphs (A) and (B) above apply also to the yarns referred to in Notes 3, 4, 5 or 6 below.
3. (a) For the purposes of this Section, and subject to the exceptions in paragraph (B) below, yarns (single, multiple (folded) or cabled) of the following descriptions are to be treated as "twine, cordage, ropes and cables":
      (i) Of silk or waste silk, measuring more than 20,000 decitex;
      (ii) Of man-made fibres (including yarn of two or more monofilaments of Chapter 54), measuring more than 10,000 decitex;
      (iii) Of true hemp or flax:
         i) Polished or glazed, measuring 1,429 decitex or more;
         ii) Not polished or glazed, measuring more than 20,000 decitex;
      (iv) Of coir, consisting of three or more plies;
      (v) Of other vegetable fibres, measuring more than 20,000 decitex;
      (vi) Reinforced with metal thread.
   (b) Exceptions:
      (i) Yarn of wool or other animal hair and paper yarn, otherthan yarn reinforced with metal thread;
      (ii) Man-made filament tow of Chapter 55 and multifilament yarn without twist or with a twist of less than 5 turns per metre of Chapter 54;
      (iii) Silk worm gut of heading No. 50. 06, and monofilamentsofChapter 54;
      (iv) Metallized yarn of Heading No. 56. 05; yarn reinforcedwith metal thread is subject to paragraph (A) (f) above; and

5. 税目56.06的绳绒线、粗松螺旋花线及纵行起圈纱线。

四、(一)除下列(二)款另有规定的以外,第五十章、第五十一章、第五十二章、第五十四章和第五十五章所称"供零售用"纱线,是指以下列方式包装的纱线(单纱、股纱线或缆线):

1. 绕于纸板、线轴、纱管或类似芯子上,其重量(含线芯)符合下列规定:

(1)丝、绢丝或化学纤维长丝纱线,不超过85克;

(2)其他纱线,不超过125克。

2. 绕成团、绞或束,其重量符合下列规定:

(1) 细度在3000分特以下的化学纤维长丝纱线,丝或绢丝纱线,不超过85克;

(2)细度在2000分特以下的任何其他纱线,不超过125克;

(3)其他纱线,不超过500克。

3. 绕成绞或束,每绞或每束中有若干用线分开的小绞或小束,每小绞或小束的重量相等,并且符合下列规定:

(1)丝、绢丝或化学纤维长丝纱线,不超过85克;

(2)其他纱线,不超过125克。

(二)下列各项不按上述(一)款规定办理:

1. 各种纺织材料制的单纱,但下列两种除外:

(1)未漂白的羊毛或动物细毛单纱;

(2)漂白、染色或印色的羊毛或动物细毛单纱,细度在5000分特以上。

2. 未漂白的多股纱线或缆线:

(1)丝或绢丝制的,不论何种包装;

(2)除羊毛或动物细毛外其他纺织材料制,成绞或成束的。

3. 漂白、染色或印色丝或绢丝制的多股纱线或缆线,细度在133分特及以下;

4. 任何纺织材料制的单纱、多股纱线或缆线:

(1)交叉绕成绞或束的;

(2)绕于纱芯上或以其他方式卷绕,明显用于纺织工业的(例如,绕于纱管、加捻管、纬纱管、锥形筒管或锭子上的或者绕成蚕茧状以供绣花机使用的纱线)。

五、税目52.04、54.01及55.08所称"缝纫线",是指下列多股纱线或缆线:

(一)绕于芯子(例如,线轴、纱管)上,重量(包括纱芯)不超过1000克;

(二)作为缝纫线上过浆的;

(三)终捻为反手(Z)捻的。

六、本类所称"高强力纱",是指断裂强度大于下列标准的纱线:

尼龙、其他聚酰胺或聚酯制的单纱-60厘牛顿/特克斯;

尼龙、其他聚酰胺或聚酯制的多股纱线或缆线-53厘牛顿/特克斯;

粘胶纤维制的单纱、多股纱线或缆线-27厘牛顿/特克斯。

七、本类所称"制成的",是指:

(一)裁剪成除正方形或长方形以外的其他形状的;

(二)呈制成状态,无需缝纫或其他进一步加工(或仅需剪断分隔联线)即可使用的(例如,某些抹布、毛巾、台布、方披巾、毯子);

(三)裁剪成一定尺寸,至少有一边为带有可见的锥形或压平形的热封边,其余各边经本注释其他各项所述加工,但不包括为防止剪边脱纱而用热切法或其他简单方法处理的织物。

(四)已缝边或滚边,或者在任一边带有结制的流苏,但不包括为防止剪边脱纱而锁边或用其他简单方法处理的织物;

(五)裁剪成一定尺寸并经抽纱加工的;

(六)缝合、胶合或用其他方法拼合而成的(将两段或两段以上同样料子的织物首尾连接而成的匹头,以及由两层或两层以上的织物,不论中间有无胎料,层叠而成的匹头除外);

(七)针织或钩编成一定形状,不论报验时是单件还是以若干件相连成幅的。

八、对于第五十章至第六十章:

(一)第五十章至第五十五章和第六十章,以及除条文另有规定以外的第五十六章至第五十九章,不适用于上述注释七所规定的制成货品;

(二)第五十章至第五十五章及第六十章不包括第五十六章至第五十九章的货品。

九、第五十章至第五十五章的机织物包括由若干层平行纱线以锐角或直角相互层叠,在纱线交叉点用黏合剂或以热粘合法粘合而成的织物。

十、用纺织材料和橡胶线制成的弹性产品归入本类。

十一、本类所称"浸渍",包括"浸泡"。

十二、本类所称"聚酰胺",包括"芳族聚酰胺"。

十三、本类及本目录所称"弹性纱线",是指合成纤维纺织材料制成的长丝纱线(包括单丝但变形纱线除外)。这些纱线可拉伸至原长的三倍而不断裂,并可在拉伸至原长两倍后五分钟内回复到不超过原长度的一倍半。

十四、除条文另有规定的以外,各种服装即使成套包装供零售用,也应按各自税目分别归类。本注释所称"纺织服装",是指税目61.01至61.14及税目62.01至62.11所列的各种服装。

(Ⅴ)Chenille yarn, gimped yarn and loop wale—Yarn of heading 56.06.

4. (a)For the purposes of Chapters 50,51,52,54 and 55, the expression"put up for retail sale" in relation to yarn means, subject to the exceptionsin paragraph (B) below, yarn (single, multiple (folded) or cabled) put up:
   (ⅰ)On cards, reels,tubes or similar supports, of a weight (including support) not exceeding:
      ⅰ)85g in the case of silk, waste silk or man-made filaments; or
      ⅱ)125g in other cases;
   (ⅱ)In balls, hanks or skeins of a weight not exceeding:
      ⅰ)85g in the case of man-made filament yarn of less than 3,000 decitex, silk or silk waste;
      ⅱ)125g in the case of all other yarns of less than 2,000 decitex; or
      ⅲ)500g in other cases;
   (ⅲ)In hanks or skeins comprising several smaller hanks or skeins separated by dividing threads which render them independent one of the other, each of uniform weight not exceeding:
      ⅰ)85g in the case of silk, waste silk or man-made filament yarn; or
      ⅱ)125g in other cases.

   (b)Exceptions:
   (ⅰ)Single yarn of any textile material, except:
      ⅰ)Single yarn of wool or fine animal hair, unbleached; and
      ⅱ)Single yarn of wool or fine animal hair, bleached, dyed or printed, measuring more than 5,000 decitex;
   (ⅱ)Multiple (folded) or cabled yarn, unbleached:
      ⅰ)Of silk or waste silk, however put up;
      ⅱ)Of other textile material except wool or fineanimal hair in hanks or skeins;
   (ⅲ)Multiple (folded) or cabled yarn of silk or waste silk,bleached, dyed or printed, measuring 133 decitex or less; and
   (ⅳ)Single, multiple (folded) or cabled yarn of any textilematerial:
      ⅰ)In cross-reeled hanks or skeins;
      ⅱ)Put up on supports or in some other manner indicating its use in the textile industry (for example, on cops, twisting mill tubes, pirns, conical bobbins or spindles, or reeled in the form of cocoons for embroidery looms).

5. For the purposes of headings No. 52.04, 54.01 and 55.08the expression "sewing thread" means multiple (folded) or cabled yarn:
   (a)Put up on supports (for example, reels, tubes) of aweight (including support) not exceeding 1,000g;
   (b)Dressed for use as sewing thread;
   (c)With a final "Z" twist.

6. For the purposes of this Section, the expression "high tenacity yarn" means yarn having a tenacity, expressed in cN/tex (centinewton per tex), greater than the following:
   Single yarn of nylon or other polyamides, or of polyesters 60 cN/tex
   Multiple (folded) or cabled yarn of nylon or other polyamides, or of polyesters 53 cN/tex
   Single, multiple (folded) or cabled yarn of viscose rayon 27 cN/tex

7. For the purposes of this Section, the expression "made up" means:
   (a)Cut otherwise than into squares or rectangles;
   (b)Produced in the finished state, ready for use (or merely needing separation by cutting dividing threads) without sewing or other working (for example, certain dusters, towels, table cloths, scarf squares, blankets);
   (c)Cut to size and with at least one heatsealed edge with a visibly tapered or compressed border and the other edges treated as described in any other subparagraph of this Note,but excluding fabrics the cut edges of which have been prevented from unravelling by hot cutting or by other simple means;
   (d)Hemmed or with rolled edges, or with a knotted fringe atany of the edges, but excluding fabrics the cut edges of which have been prevented from unravelling by whipping or by other simple means;
   (e)Cut to size and having undergone a process of drawnthread work;
   (f)Assembled by sewing, gumming or otherwise (other than piece goods consisting of two or more lengths of identical material joined end toend and piece goods composed of two or more textiles assembled in layers, whether or not padded);
   (g)Knitted or crocheted to shape, whether presented asseparate items or in the form of a number of items in the length.

8. For the purposes of Chapters 50 to 60:
   (a)Chapters 50 to 55 and 60 and, except where the context otherwise requires, Chapters 56 to 59 do not apply to goods made up within the meaning of Note 7 above; and
   (b)Chapters 50 to 55 and 60 do not apply to goods of Chapters 56 to 59.

9. The woven fabrics of Chapters 50 to 55 include fabrics consisting of layers of parallel textile yarns superimposed on each other at acute or right angles. These layers are bonded at the intersections of the yarns by an adhesive or by thermal bonding.

10. Elastic products consisting of textile materials combined with rubber threads are classified in this Section.

11. For the purposes of this Section, the expression "impregnated" includes "dipped".

12. For the purposes of this Section, the expression "polyamides" includes "aramides".

13. For the purposes of this section and where applicaple throughout the nomeclature the expression"elastomencyarn"means Filament yarn,including monofilament,of synthetic textile material,other than textured yarn,which does not break on being extended to three times its original length and which returns,after being extended to twice its original length,within a period of five minutes,to a length not greater than one and a half times its original length.

14. Unless the context otherwise requires, textile garments of different headings are to be classified in their own headings even if put up in sets for retail sale. For the purposes of this Note, the expression "textile garments" means garments of headings No. 61.01 to 61.14 and headings No. 62.01 to 62.11.

子目注释：

一、本类及本目录所用有关名词解释如下：

（一）未漂白纱线

1. 带有纤维自然色泽并且未经漂染（不论是否整体染色）或印色的纱线；

2. 从回收纤维制得，色泽未定的纱线（本色纱）。

这种纱线可用无色浆料或易褪色染料（可轻易地用肥皂洗去）处理，如果是化学纤维纱线，则整体用消光剂（例如二氧化钛）进行处理。

（二）漂白纱线

1. 经漂白加工、用漂白纤维制得或经染白（除条文另有规定的以外）（不论是否整体染色）及用白浆料处理的纱线；

2. 用未漂白纤维和漂白纤维混纺制得的纱线；

3. 用未漂白纱和漂白纱纺成多股纱线或缆线。

（三）着色（染色或印色）纱线

1. 染成彩色（不论是否整体染色，但白色或易褪色除外）或印色的纱线，以及用染色或印色纤维纺制的纱线；

2. 用各色染色纤维混合纺制或用未漂白或漂白纤维与着色纤维混合制得的纱线（夹色纱或混色纱），以及用一种或几种颜色间隔印色而获得点纹印迹的纱线；

3. 用已经印色的纱条或粗纱纺制的纱线；

4. 用未漂白纱和漂白纱与着色纱纺成的多股纱线或缆线。

上述定义作相应调整后适用于第五十四章的单丝、扁条或类似产品。

（四）未漂白机织物

用未漂白纱线织成后未经漂白、染色或印花的机织物。这类织物可用无色浆料或易褪色染料处理。

（五）漂白机织物

1. 经漂白、染白或用白浆料处理（除条文另有规定的以外）的成匹机织物；

2. 用漂白纱线织成的机织物；

3. 用未漂白纱线和漂白纱线织成的机织物；

（六）染色机织物

1. 除条文另有规定的以外，染成白色以外的其他单一颜色或用白色以外的其他有色整理剂处理的成匹机织物；

2. 以单一颜色的着色纱线织成的机织物。

（七）色织机织物

除印花机织物以外的下列机织物：

1. 用各种不同颜色纱线或同一颜色不同深浅（纤维的自然色彩除外）纱线织成的机织物；

2. 用未漂白或漂白与着色纱线织成的机织物；

3. 用夹色纱线或混色纱线织成的机织物。

不论何种情况，布边或布头的纱线均可忽略不计。

（八）印花机织物

成匹印花的机织物，不论是否用各色纱线织成。

用刷子或喷枪，经转印纸转印、植绒或蜡防印花等方法印成花纹图案的机织物亦可视为印花机织物。

上述各类纱线或织物如经丝光工艺处理并不影响其归类。

上述（四）至（八）的定义在作必要修改后适用于针织或钩编织物。

（九）平纹织物

每根纬纱在并排的经纱间上下交错而过，而每根经纱也在并排的纬纱间上下交错而过的织物组织。

二、（一）含有两种或两种以上纺织材料的第五十六章至第六十三章的产品，应根据本类注释二对第五十章至第五十五章或税目 58.09 的此类纺织材料产品归类的规定来确定归类。

（二）运用本条规定时：

1. 应酌情考虑按归类总规则第三条来确定归类

2. 对由底布和绒面或毛圈面构成的纺织品，在归类时可不考虑底布的属性

3. 对税目 58.10 的刺绣品及其制品，归类时应只考虑底布的属性，但不见底布的刺绣品及其制品应根据绣线的属性确定归类。

Subheading Notes:

1. In the Section and, where applicable, throughout the Nomenclature, the following expressions have the meanings hereby assigned to them:

(a) Unbleached yarnYarn which:

(ⅰ) has the natural colour of its constituent fibres and hasnot been bleached, dyed (whether or not in the mass) or printed;

(ⅱ) is of indeterminate colour ("grey yarn"), manufactured from garnetted stock.

Such yarn may have been treated with a colourless dressing or fugitive dye(which disappears after simple washing with soap) and, in the case of man-made fibres, treated in the mass with delustring agent (for example, titanium dioxide).

(b) Bleached yarn Yarn which:

(ⅰ) has undergone a bleaching process, is made of bleached fibres or, unless the context otherwise requires, has been dyed white (whether or not in the mass) or treated with a white dressing;

(ⅱ) consists of a mixture of unbleached and bleachedfibres;

(ⅲ) is multiple (folded) or cabled and consists ofunbleached and bleached yarns.

(c) Coloured (dyed or printed) yarn Yarn which:

(ⅰ) is dyed (whether or not in the mass) other thanwhite or in a fugitive colour, or printed, or made from dyed or printed fibres;

(ⅱ) consists of a mixture of dyed fibres of different colours or of a mixture of unbleached or bleached fibres with coloured fibres (marl or mixture yarns), or is printed in one or more colours at intervals to givethe impression of dots;

(ⅲ) is obtained from slivers or rovings which havebeenprinted; or

(ⅳ) is multiple (folded) or cabled and consists ofunbleached or bleached yarn and coloured yarn.

The above definitions also apply, *mutatis mutandis*, to monofilament and to strip or the like of Chapter 54.

(d) Unbleached woven fabric

Woven fabric made from unbleached yarn and which has not been bleached, dyed or printed. Such fabric may have treated with a colourless dressing or a fugitive dye.

(e) Bleached woven fabricwoven fabric which:

(ⅰ) has been bleached or, unless the context otherwise requires, dyed white or treated with a white dressing, in the piece;

(ⅱ) consists of bleached yarn; or

(ⅲ) consists of unbleached and bleached yarn.

(f) Dyed woven fabricwoven fabric which:

(ⅰ) is dyed a single uniform colour other than white (unless the context otherwise requires) or has been treated with a coloured finishother than white (unless the context otherwise requires), in the piece; or

(ⅱ) consists of coloured yarn of a single uniform colour.

(g) Woven fabric of yarns of different colours

Woven fabric (other than printed woven fabric) which:

(ⅰ) consists of yarns of different colours or yarnsofdifferent shades of the same colour (other than the natural colour of the constituent fibres);

(ⅱ) consists of unbleached or bleached yarn and coloured yarn; or

(ⅲ) consists of marl or mixture yarns.

(In all cases, the yarn used in selvedges and pieceends is not taken into consideration.)

(h) Printed woven fabric

Woven fabric which has been printed in the piece, whether or not made from yarnsof differenent colours. (The following are also regarded as printed woven fabrics: woven fabrics bearing designs made, for example, with a brush or spray gun, by means of transfer paper, by flocking or by the batik process.)

The process of mercerization does not affect the classification of yarns or fabrics within the above categories.

The definitions at(d) to (h) above apply, *mutatis mutandis*, to knitted or crocheted fabrics.

(ij) Plain weave

A fabric construction in which each yarn of the weft passes alternately over andunder successive yarns of the warp and each yarn of the warp passes alternatelyover and under successive yarns of the weft.

2. (a) Products of Chapters 56 to 63 containing two or more textilematerials are to be regarded as consisting wholly of that textile material whichwould be selected under Note 2 to this Section for the classification of the product of Chapters 50 to 55 or of heading No. 58. 09 consisting of the same textile materials.

(b) For the application of this rule:

(ⅰ) where appropriate, only the part which determines the classification under interpretative Rule 3 shall be taken into account;

(ⅱ) in the case of textile products consisting of a ground fabric and a pile or looped surface, no account shall be taken of the ground fabric;

(ⅲ) in the case of embroidery of heading No. 58. 10 and goods thereof, only the ground fabric shall be taken into account. However, embroidery without visible ground, and goods thereof, shall be classified with reference to the embroidering threads alone.

第五十章
蚕　丝

税则号列	货品名称〔CIQ 扩展编码及品名—T2 表示见附表 2〕	最惠(%)	暂定税率	普通	增值/消费	出口退税	计量单位	监管条件	检验检疫	特殊证件对美关税
50.01	**适于缫丝的蚕茧:**									
5001.0010	---适于缫丝的桑蚕茧〔101 未经加工的蚕茧,102 未经加工的蚕茧除外〕	6		70	13/	9	千克	AB	PQ	/16
5001.0090	---其他〔999〕	6		70	13/	9	千克	AB	PQ	/16
50.02	**生丝(未加捻):**									
	---桑蚕丝:									
5002.0011	----厂丝〔101 生丝,102 粗丝,103 初级加工丝〕	9		80	13/	13	千克	AB	PQ	/
5002.0012	----土丝〔999〕	9		80	13/	13	千克	AB	PQ	/
5002.0013	----双宫丝〔999〕	9		80	13/	13	千克	AB	PQ	/
5002.0019	----其他〔999〕	9		80	13/	13	千克	AB	PQ	/
5002.0020	---柞蚕丝〔999〕	9		80	13/	13	千克	AB	PQ	/
5002.0090	---其他〔999〕	9		80	13/	13	千克	AB	PQ	/
50.03	**废丝(包括不适于缫丝的蚕茧、废纱及回收纤维):**									
	---未梳:									
5003.0011	----下茧、茧衣、长吐、滞头〔101 未经加工的蚕茧、削口茧,102 未经加工的长吐,滞头〕,103 未经加工的蚕茧、削口茧、长吐,滞头除外〕	9		70	13/	13	千克	AB	PQ	/
5003.0012	----回收纤维〔999〕	9		70	13/	13	千克	AB	PQ	/
5003.0019	----其他〔999〕	9		70	13/	13	千克	AB	PQ	/
	---其他:									
5003.0091	----绵球〔999〕	9		70	13/	13	千克	AB	PQ	/
5003.0099	----其他〔999〕	9		70	13/	13	千克	AB	PQ	/
50.04	**丝纱线(绢纺纱线除外),非供零售用:**									
5004.0000	丝纱线(绢纺纱线除外),非供零售用〔101 桑蚕捻线丝,102 双宫捻线丝,103 土丝捻线丝,104 特种加工丝〕	6		90	13/	13	千克			/
50.05	**绢纺纱线,非供零售用:**									
5005.0010	---䌷丝纱线〔999〕	6		90	13/	13	千克			/
5005.0090	---其他〔101 桑蚕绢丝,102 柞蚕绢丝,103 木薯绢丝〕	6		90	13/	13	千克			/
50.06	**丝纱线及绢纺纱线,供零售用;蚕胶丝:**									
5006.0000	零售用丝纱线,绢纺纱线;蚕胶丝(含丝及绢丝)〔999〕	6		100	13/	13	千克			/
50.07	**丝或绢丝机织物:**									
	-䌷丝机织物:									
5007.1010	---未漂白(包括未练白或练白)或漂白〔999〕	8		130	13/	13	米/千克			/
5007.1090	---其他〔999〕	8		130	13/	13	米/千克			/
	-其他机织物,按重量计丝或绢丝(䌷丝除外)含量在 85%及以上:									
	---桑蚕丝机织物:									
5007.2011	----未漂白(包括未练白或练白)或漂白〔999〕	8		130	13/	13	米/千克			/28
5007.2019	----其他〔999〕	8		130	13/	13	米/千克			/33
	---柞蚕丝机织物:									
5007.2021	----未漂白(包括未练白或练白)或漂白〔999〕	8		130	13/	13	米/千克			/
5007.2029	----其他〔999〕	8		130	13/	13	米/千克			/
	---绢丝机织物:									
5007.2031	----未漂白(包括未练白或练白)或漂白〔999〕	8		130	13/	13	米/千克			/
5007.2039	----其他〔999〕	8		130	13/	13	米/千克			/33
5007.2090	---其他〔999〕	8		130	13/	13	米/千克			/33
	-其他机织物:									
5007.9010	---未漂白(包括未练白或练白)或漂白〔999〕	8		130	13/	13	米/千克			/33
5007.9090	---其他〔999〕	8		130	13/	13	米/千克			/33

Chapter 50
Silk

协定税率 %										特惠税率 %			Article Description
亚太5国	东/冰/格	巴基斯坦	韩国	瑞士	哥达	秘鲁	澳大利亚	新西/坡/智	港/澳/台	亚太2国	老/柬/缅	36/3/1	
													Silk-worm cocoons suitable for reeling:
	0/0/0	4.5	0	0	0	0	0	0//0	0/0/			0/0/0	---Bombyx mori cocoons (Mulberry feeding silk-worm cocoons)
	0/0/0	5	0	0	0	0	0	0//0	0/0/			0/0/0	---Other
													Raw silk (not thrown):
													---Steam filature silk:
	0/0/0	4	0	0	0	0	0	0//0	0/0/			0/0/0	----Plant reeled (filature silk)
	0/0/0	4	0	0	0	0	0	0//0	0/0/			0/0/0	----Home reeled
	0/0/0	4	0	0	0	0	0	0//0	0/0/			0/0/0	----Doupion
	0/0/0	4	0	0	0	0	0	0//0	0/0/			0/0/0	----Other
	0/0/0	4	0	0	0	0	0	0//0	0/0/			0/0/0	---Tussah silk
	0/0/0	4	0	0	0	0	0	0//0	0/0/			0/0/0	---Other
													Silk waste (including cocoons unsuitable for reeling, yarn waste and garnetted stock):
													---Not carded or combed:
	0/0/0	4	0	0	0	0	0	0//0	0/0/			0/0/0	----Spoiled cocoon, cocoon outer floss, frison, frigon
	0/0/0	4	0	0	0	0	0	0//0	0/0/			0/0/0	----Garnetted stock
	0/0/0	4	0	0	0	0	0	0//0	0/0/			0/0/0	----Other
													---Other:
	0/0/0	4	0	0	0	0	0	0//0	0/0/			0/0/0	----Silk top
	0/0/0	4	0	0	0	0	0	0//0	0/0/			0/0/0	----Other
													Silk yarn (other than yarn spun from spun silk waste) not put up for retail sale:
	0/0/0	0	0	0	0	0	0	0//0	0/0/			0/0/0	Silk yarn (other than yarn spun from spun silk waste) not put up for retail sale
													Yarn spun from silk spum waste, not put up for retail sale:
	0/0/0	0	0	0	0	0	0	0//0	0/0/			0/0/0	---Spun from noil
	0/0/0	0	0	0	0	0	0	0//0	0/0/			0/0/0	---Other
													Silk yarn and yarn spun from silk waste, put up for retail sale; silk-worm gut:
	0/0/0	0	0	0	0	0	0	0//0	0/0/			0/0/0	Silk yarn and yarn spun from spun silk, put up for retail sale; silk-worm gut
													Woven fabrics of silk or of spun silk:
													-Fabrics of noil silk:
	0/0/0	4.5	0	0	0	0	0	0//0	0/0/		0//	0/0/0	---Unbleaded (unscoured or scoured) or bleached
	0/0/0	4.5	0	0	0	0	0	0//0	0/0/		0//	0/0/0	---Other
													-Other fabrics, containing 85% or more by weight of silk or of spun silk other than noil silk:
													---Of Bombyx mori silk:
5.2	0/0/0	4.5	0	0	0	0	0	0//0	0/0/		0//	0/0/0	----Unbleached (unscoured or scoured) or bleached
5.2	0/0/0	4.5	6	0	0	0	0	0//0	0/0/		0//	0/0/0	----Other
													---Of tussah silk:
5.2	0/0/0	4.5	0	0	0	0	0	0//0	0/0/		0//	0/0/0	
5.2	0/0/0	4.5	0	0	0	0	0	0//0	0/0/		0//	0/0/0	----Other
													---Of spun silk other than noil silk:
5.2	0/0/0	4.5	0	0	0	0	0	0//0	0/0/		0//	0/0/0	----Unbleached (unscoured or scoured) or bleached
5.2	0/0/0	4.5	0	0	0	0	0	0//0	0/0/		0//	0/0/0	----Other
5.2	0/0/0	4.5	0	0	0	0	0	0//0	0/0/		0//	0/0/0	---Other
													-Other fabrics:
5.2	0/0/0	4.5	0	0	0	0	0	0//0	0/0/		0//	0/0/0	---Unbleached (unscoured or scoured) or bleached
5.2	0/0/0	4.5	0	0	0	0	0	0//0	0/0/		0//	0/0/0	---Other

第五十一章
羊毛、动物细毛或粗毛;马毛纱线及其机织物

注释:

本协调制度所称:

一、"羊毛",是指绵羊或羔羊身上长的天然纤维;

二、"动物细毛",是指下列动物的毛:羊驼、美洲驼、驼马、骆驼(包括单峰骆驼)、牦牛、安哥拉山羊、西藏山羊、克什米尔山羊及类似山羊(普通山羊除外)、家兔(包括安哥拉兔)、野兔、海狸、河狸鼠或麝鼠;

三、"动物粗毛",是指以上未提及的其他动物的毛,但不包括制刷用鬃、毛(税目05.02)以及马毛(税目05.11)。

税则号列	货品名称〔CIQ扩展编码及品名—T2表示见附表2〕	最惠(%)	暂定税率	普通	增值/消费	出口退税	计量单位	监管条件	检验检疫	特殊证件对美关税
51.01	**未梳的羊毛:**									
	-含脂羊毛,包括剪前水洗毛:									
5101.1100	--剪羊毛									
5101.1100 01	未梳的含脂剪羊毛(配额内)〔101 绵羊毛,102 山羊毛〕	1		50	9/	9	千克	tAB	MPQ	/26
5101.1100 90	未梳的含脂剪羊毛(配额外)〔101 绵羊毛,102 山羊毛〕	38		50	9/	9	千克	AB	MPQ	/63
5101.1900	--其他									
5101.1900 01	未梳的其他含脂羊毛(配额内)〔101 绵羊毛,102 山羊毛〕	1		50	9/	9	千克	tAB	MPQ	/11
5101.1900 90	未梳的其他含脂羊毛(配额外)〔101 绵羊毛,102 山羊毛〕	38		50	9/	9	千克	AB	MPQ	/48
	-脱脂羊毛,未碳化:									
5101.2100	--剪羊毛									
5101.2100 01	未梳的脱脂剪羊毛(未碳化)(配额内)〔101 洗净绵羊毛,102 洗净山羊毛〕	1		50	13/	13	千克	tAB	MPQ	/11
5101.2100 90	未梳的脱脂剪羊毛(未碳化)(配额外)〔101 洗净绵羊毛,102 洗净山羊毛〕	38		50	13/	13	千克	AB	MPQ	/48
5101.2900	--其他									
5101.2900 01	未梳的其他脱脂羊毛(未碳化)(配额内)〔101 洗净绵羊毛,102 洗净山羊毛〕	1		50	13/	13	千克	tAB	MPQ	/11
5101.2900 90	未梳的其他脱脂羊毛(未碳化)(配额外)〔101 洗净绵羊毛,102 洗净山羊毛〕	38		50	13/	13	千克	AB	MPQ	/48
5101.3000	-碳化羊毛									
5101.3000 01	未梳碳化羊毛(配额内)〔999〕	1		50	13/	13	千克	tAB	MPQ	/11
5101.3000 90	未梳碳化羊毛(配额外)〔999〕	38		50	13/	13	千克	AB	MPQ	/48
51.02	**未梳的动物细毛或粗毛:**									
	-细毛:									
5102.1100	--克什米尔山羊的〔101 未洗净山羊毛,102 洗净山羊毛,103 山羊绒〕	9		45	13/	0	千克	AB	PQ	/19
	--其他:									
5102.1910	---兔毛									
5102.1910 10	未梳濒危野兔毛〔101 未洗净兔毛,102 洗净兔毛〕	9		50	13/	0	千克	ABFE	PQ	/19
5102.1910 90	其他未梳兔毛〔101 未洗净兔毛,102 洗净兔毛〕	9		50	13/	6	千克	AB	PQ	/19
5102.1920	---其他山羊绒〔101 未洗净山羊绒,102 未洗净野羊毛(绒),103 洗净山羊绒,104 洗净野山羊绒〕	9		45	13/	0	千克	AB	PQ	/19
5102.1930	---骆驼毛、骆驼绒									
5102.1930 10	未梳濒危野生骆驼科动物毛、绒〔101 未洗净驼毛,102 未洗净驼绒,103 未洗净其他野生偶蹄动物鬃毛,104 洗净驼毛(绒),105 洗净其他野生偶蹄动物鬃毛〕	9		45	13/	0	千克	FEAB	PQ	/19
5102.1930 90	其他未梳骆驼毛、绒〔101 未洗净驼毛,102 未洗净驼绒,103 洗净驼毛,104 洗净驼绒〕	9		45	13/	9	千克	AB	PQ	/19
5102.1990	---其他									
5102.1990 10	未梳的其他濒危野生动物细毛[T2]	9		45	13/	0	千克	FEAB	PQ	/19
5102.1990 90	未梳的其他动物细毛[T2]	9		45	13/	9	千克	AB	PQ	/19
5102.2000	-粗毛									
5102.2000 10	未梳的濒危野生动物粗毛[T2]	9		50	13/	0	千克	FEAB	PQ	/19
5102.2000 90	未梳的其他动物粗毛[T2]	9		50	13/	9	千克	AB	PQ	/19
51.03	**羊毛或动物细毛或粗毛的废料,包括废纱线,但不包括回收纤维:**									
	-羊毛及动物细毛的落毛:									
5103.1010	---羊毛落毛									
5103.1010 01	羊毛落毛(配额内)〔101 未洗净绵羊毛,102 未洗净山羊毛,103 未洗净山羊绒,104 未洗净野羊毛(绒),105 洗净羊毛〕	1		50	13/	9	千克	tAB	PQ	/26
5103.1010 90	羊毛落毛(配额外)〔101 未洗净绵羊毛,102 未洗净山羊毛,103 未洗净山羊绒,104 未洗净野羊毛(绒),105 洗净羊毛〕	38		50	13/	9	千克	AB	PQ	/63
5103.1090	---其他									
5103.1090 10	其他濒危野生动物细毛的落毛[T2]	9		50	13/	0	千克	FEAB	PQ	/34
5103.1090 90	其他动物细毛的落毛〔110〕	9		50	13/	6	千克	9B	MPQ	/34
	-羊毛或动物细毛的其他废料:									
5103.2010	---羊毛废料〔999〕	13.5		20	13/	6	千克	AB	PQ	/23.5
5103.2090	---其他									
5103.2090 10	其他濒危野生动物细毛废料(包括废纱线,不包括回收纤维)〔999〕	9		50	13/	0	千克	FEAB	PQ	/34
5103.2090 90	其他动物细毛废料(包括废纱线,不包括回收纤维)〔999〕	9		50	13/	6	千克	9B	MPQ	/34

Chapter 51
Wool, fine or coarse animal hair; horsehair yarn and woven fabric

Notes:

Throughout the Nomenclature:

1. "Wool" means the natural fibre grown by sheep or lambs;
2. "Fine animal hair" means the hair of alpaca, llama, vicuna, camel, (including dromedary) yak, Angora, Tibetan, Kashmir or similar goats (but not common goats), rabbit (including Angora rabbit), hare, beaver, nutria or muskrat;
3. "Coarse animal hair" means the hair of animals not mentioned above, excluding brush-making hair and bristles (heading No. 05.02) and horsehair (heading No. 05.11).

协定税率 %										特惠税率 %			Article Description
亚太5国	东/冰/格	巴基斯坦	韩国	瑞士	哥达	秘鲁	澳大利亚	新西/坡/智	港/澳/台	亚太2国	老/柬/缅	36/3/1	
													Wool, not carded or combed:
													-Greasy, including fleece-washed wool:
													—Shorn wool
	5//						T1	T1//	0/0/				Greasy shorn wool, not carded or combeb, in-quota
	5//						T1	T1//	0/0/				Greasy shorn wool, not carded or combeb, out-quota
													—Other
	5//						T1	T1//	0/0/				Other greasy wool, not carded or combed, in-quota
	5//						T1	T1//	0/0/				Other greasy wool, not carded or combed, out-quota
													-Degreased, not carbonized:
													--Shorn wool
	5//						T1	T1//	0/0/				Degreased shorn wool, not carded or combed, not carbonized, in-quota
	5//						T1	T1//	0/0/				Degreased shorn wool, not carded or combed, not carbonized, out-quota
													--Other
	5//						T1	T1//	0/0/				Other degreased wool, not carded or combeb, not carbonized, in-quota
	5//						T1	T1//	0/0/				Other degreased wool, not carded or combeb, not carbonized, out-quota
													-Carbonized
	5//						T1	T1//	0/0/				Carbonized wool, not carded or combed, in-quota
	5//						T1	T1//	0/0/				Carbonized wool, not carded or combed, out-quota
													Fine or coarse animal hair, not carded or combed:
													-Fine animal hair:
	0/0/0	4	0	0	0	0	0	0//0	0/0/			0/0/0	--Of Kashmir(cashmere) goats
													--Other:
													---Of rabbit and hare
	0/0/0	4	0	0	0	0	0	0//0	0/0/			0/0/0	Hair of endangered rabbit and hare, not carded or combed
	0/0/0	4	0	0	0	0	0	0//0	0/0/			0/0/0	Other hair of rabbit and hare, not carded or combed
	0/0/0	4	0	0	0	0	0	0//0	0/0/			0/0/0	---Of other goats
													---Of camel
	0/0/0	4	0	0	0	0	0	0//0	0/0/			0/0/0	Hair and down of endangered wild camel, not carded or combed
	0/0/0	4	0	0	0	0	0	0//0	0/0/			0/0/0	Other hair and down of camel, not carded or combed
													---Other
	0/0/0	4	0	0	0	0	0	0//0	0/0/			0/0/	Fine hair of other endangered wild animals dangers, not carded or combed
	0/0/0	4	0	0	0	0	0	0//0	0/0/			0/0/	Fine hair of other animals, not carded or combed
													-Coarse animal hair
	0/0/0	4	0	0	0	0	0	0//0	0/0/			0/0/0	Coarse hair of endangered wild animals not carded or combed
	0/0/0	4	0	0	0	0	0	0//0	0/0/			0/0/0	Coarse hair of other animals, not carded or combed
													Waste of wool or of fine or coarse animal hair, including yarn waste but excluding garnetted stock:
													-Noils of wool or of fine animal hair:
													---Of wool
	5//						T1	T1//	0/0/				Noils of wool(in-quota)
	5//						T1	T1//	0/0/				Noils of wool(out-quota)
													---Other
	0/0/0	4	0	0	0	0	0	0//0	0/0/			0/0/0	Other noils of fine hair of endangered wild animal
	0/0/0	4	0	0	0	0	0	0//0	0/0/			0/0/0	Other noils of fine hair of animal
													-Other waste of wool or of fine animal hair:
	0/0/0	6.8	5.4	4.1	0	0	0	0/0/0	0/0/			0/0/	---Of wool
													---Other
	0/0/0	4	0	0	0	0	0	0//0	0/0/			0/0/	Other waste of fine hair of endangered wild animal (including yarn waste, but excluding garnetted stock)
	0/0/0	4	0	0	0	0	0	0//0	0/0/			0/0/	Other waste of fine hair of other animals (including yarn waste, but excluding garnetted stock)

税则号列		货品名称〔CIQ扩展编码及品名－T2表示见附表2〕	最惠(%)	暂定税率	普通	增值/消费	出口退税	计量单位	监管条件	检验检疫	特殊证件对美关税
5103.3000		-动物粗毛废料									
5103.3000	10	濒危野生动物粗毛废料(包括废纱线,不包括回收纤维)〔999〕	9		50	13/	0	千克	FEAB	PQ	/34
5103.3000	90	其他动物粗毛废料(包括废纱线,不包括回收纤维)〔999〕	9		50	13/	6	千克	9B	MPQ	/34
51.04		**羊毛或动物细毛或粗毛的回收纤维:**									
5104.0010		---羊毛的回收纤维〔999〕	15		20	13/	6	千克	AB	PQ	/
5104.0090		---其他									
5104.0090	10	其他濒危野生动物细毛(包括粗毛回收纤维)〔101毛回收纤维,102用于纺织原料的其它动物纤维〕	5		50	13/	0	千克	FEAB	PQ	/30
5104.0090	90	其他动物细毛或粗毛的回收纤维〔103〕	5		50	13/	13	千克	9B	MPQ	/30
51.05		**已梳的羊毛及动物细毛或粗毛(包括精梳片毛):**									
5105.1000		-粗梳羊毛									
5105.1000	01	粗梳羊毛(配额内)〔999〕	3		50	13/	13	千克	tAB	MPQ	/
5105.1000	90	粗梳羊毛(配额外)〔999〕	38		50	13/	13	千克	AB	MPQ	/
		-羊毛条及其他精梳羊毛:									
5105.2100		--精梳片毛									
5105.2100	01	精梳羊毛片毛(配额内)〔999〕	3		50	13/	13	千克	tAB	MPQ	/
5105.2100	90	精梳羊毛片毛(配额外)〔999〕	38		50	13/	13	千克	AB	MPQ	/
5105.2900		--其他									
5105.2900	01	羊毛条及其他精梳羊毛(配额内)〔999〕	3		50	13/	13	千克	tAB	MPQ	/
5105.2900	90	羊毛条及其他精梳羊毛(配额外)〔999〕	38		50	13/	13	千克	AB	MPQ	/
		-已梳动物细毛:									
5105.3100		--克什米尔山羊的〔999〕	5		50	13/	0	千克	AB	PQ	/
		--其他:									
5105.3910		---兔毛									
5105.3910	10	已梳濒危兔毛〔999〕	5		70	13/	0	千克	ABFE	PQ	/
5105.3910	90	其他已梳兔毛〔999〕	5		70	13/	13	千克	AB	PQ	/
		---其他山羊绒:									
5105.3921		----无毛山羊绒〔999〕	5		50	13/	0	千克	AB	MPQ	/
5105.3929		----其他〔999〕	5		50	13/	0	千克	AB	PQ	/
5105.3990		---其他									
5105.3990	10	其他已梳濒危野生动物细毛〔999〕	5		50	13/	0	千克	ABEF	PQ	/
5105.3990	90	其他已梳动物细毛〔999〕	5		50	13/	13	千克	AB	PQ	/
5105.4000		-已梳动物粗毛									
5105.4000	10	其他已梳濒危野生动物粗毛〔999〕	5		50	13/	0	千克	FEAB	PQ	/
5105.4000	90	其他已梳动物粗毛〔999〕	5		50	13/	13	千克	AB	PQ	/
51.06		**粗梳羊毛纱线,非供零售用:**									
5106.1000		-按重量计羊毛含量在85%及以上〔999〕	5		70	13/	13	千克			/
5106.2000		-按重量计羊毛含量在85%以下〔999〕	5		70	13/	13	千克			/30
51.07		**精梳羊毛纱线,非供零售用:**									
5107.1000		-按重量计羊毛含量在85%及以上〔999〕	5		70	13/	13	千克			/30
5107.2000		-按重量计羊毛含量在85%以下〔999〕	5		70	13/	13	千克			/30
51.08		**动物细毛(粗梳或精梳)纱线,非供零售用:**									
		-粗梳:									
		---按重量计动物细毛含量在85%及以上的:									
5108.1011		----山羊绒的〔999〕	5		70	13/	13	千克			/30
5108.1019		----其他									
5108.1019	10	非供零售用粗梳其他濒危动物细毛纱线(按重量计其他动物细毛含量≥85%)〔999〕	5		70	13/	0	千克	FE		/
5108.1019	90	非供零售用粗梳其他动物细毛纱线(按重量计其他动物细毛含量≥85%)〔999〕	5		70	13/	13	千克			/
5108.1090		---其他									
5108.1090	10	非供零售用粗梳其他濒危动物细毛纱线(按重量计其他粗梳动物细毛含量<85%)〔999〕	5		70	13/	0	千克	FE		/30
5108.1090	90	非供零售用粗梳其他动物细毛纱线(按重量计其他粗梳动物细毛含量<85%)〔999〕	5		70	13/	13	千克			/30
		-精梳:									
		---按重量计动物细毛含量在85%及以上的:									
5108.2011		----山羊绒的〔999〕	5		70	13/	13	千克			/
5108.2019		----其他									
5108.2019	10	非供零售用精梳其他濒危动物细毛纱线(按重量计其他动物细毛含量≥85%)〔999〕	5		70	13/	0	千克	FE		/
5108.2019	90	非供零售用精梳其他动物细毛纱线(按重量计其他动物细毛含量≥85%)〔999〕	5		70	13/	13	千克			/
5108.2090		---其他									

协定税率 %										特惠税率 %			
亚太5国	东/冰/格	巴基斯坦	韩国	瑞士	哥达	秘鲁	澳大利亚	新西/坡/智	港/澳/台	亚太2国	老/柬/缅	36/3/1	Article Description
													-Waste of coarse animal hair
	0/0/0	4	0	0	0	0	0	0//0	0/0/			0/0/0	Waste of coarse hair of endangered wild animal (including yarn waste but excluding garnetted stock)
	0/0/0	4	0	0	0	0	0	0//0	0/0/			0/0/0	Other waste of coarse hair of animals (including yarn waste but excluding garnetted stock)
													Garnetted stock of wool or of fine or coarse animal hair:
	0/0/0	12	6	4.5	0	0	0	0/0/0	0/0/			0/0/	---Of wool
													---Other
	0/0/0	0	0	0	0	0	0	0//0	0/0/			0/0/0	Garnetted stock of other fine or coarse hair of endangered wild animal
	0/0/0	0	0	0	0	0	0	0//0	0/0/			0/0/0	Garnetted stock of other of fine or coarse animal hair
													Wool and fine or coarse animal hair, carded or combed (including combed wool in fragments):
													-Carded wool
								T1//	0/0/				Carded wool(in-quota)
								T1//	0/0/				Carded wool(out-quota)
													-Wool tops and other combed wool:
													--Combed wool in fragments
								T1//	0/0/				Combed wool in fragments(in-quota)
								T1//	0/0/				Combed wool in fragments(out-quota)
													--Other
								T1//	0/0/				Wool tops and other combed wool(in-quota)
								T1//	0/0/				Wool tops and other combed wool(out-quota)
													-Fine animal hair, Carded or combed:
	0/0/0	0	0	0	0	0	0	0//0	0/0/			0/0/0	--Of Kashmir(cashmere) goats
													--Other:
													---Of rabbit or hare
3.5	0/0/0	0	0	0	0		0	0//0	0/0/			0/0/0	Fine hair of endangered rabbit and hare, carded or combed
3.5	0/0/0	0	0	0	0		0	0//0	0/0/			0/0/0	Other fine hair of rabbit and hare, carded or combed
													---Of other goats:
3.5	0/0/0	0	0	0	0		0	0//0	0/0/			0/0/0	----Dehaired goats wool
3.5	0/0/0	0	0	0	0		0	0//0	0/0/			0/0/0	----Other
													---Other
3.5	0/0/0	0	0	0	0		0	0//0	0/0/			0/0/	Other fine hair of wild animals, carded or combed
3.5	0/0/0	0	0	0	0		0	0//0	0/0/			0/0/	Other fine hair of animals, carded or combed
													-Coarse animal hair, carded or combed
	0/0/0	0	0	0	0		0	0//0	0/0/			0/0/0	Other coarse hair of endangered wild animals, carded or combed
	0/0/0	0	0	0	0		0	0//0	0/0/			0/0/0	Other coarse hair of animals, carded or combed
													Yarn of carded wool, not put up for retailsale:
	0/0/0	0	0	0	0	0	0	0//0	0/0/			0/0/0	-Containing 85% or more by weight of wool
	0/0/0	0	0	0	0	0	0	0//0	0/0/			0/0/0	-Containing less than 85% by weight of wool
													Yarn of combed wool, not put up for retail sale:
2.5	0//0	0	0	0	0	0	0	0//0	0/0/			0/0/0	-Containing 85% or more by weight of wool
	0/0/0	0	0	0	0	0	0	0//0	0/0/			0/0/0	-Containing less than 85% by weight of wool
													Yarn of fine animal hair (carded or combed), not put up for retail-sale:
													-Carded:
													---Containing 85% or more by weight of fine animal hair
3.3	0/0/0	0	0	0	0	0	0	0//0	0/0/			0/0/0	----Of goats
													----Other
3.3	0/0/0	0	0	0	0	0	0	0//0	0/0/			0/0/0	Yarn of fine hair of endangered animals, carded, not in forms or packing for retail sale(containing≥85% by weight of other animals hair)
3.3	0/0/0	0	0	0	0	0	0	0//0	0/0/			0/0/0	Yarn of fine hair of animals, carded, not in forms or packing for retailsale(containing≥85% by weight of other fine animals hair)
													---Other
3.3	0/0/0	0	0	0	0	0	0	0//0	0/0/			0/0/0	Yarn of fine hair of endangered animals, carded, not in forms or packingfor retail sale(containing<85% by weight of other fine animals hair)
3.3	0/0/0	0	0	0	0	0	0	0//0	0/0/			0/0/0	Yarn of fine hair of animals, carded, not in forms or packing for retail sale(containing<85% by weight of other fine animals hair)
													-Combed:
													---Containing 85% or more by weight of fine animal hair:
	0/0/0	0	0	0	0		0	0//0	0/0/			0/0/0	----Of goats
													----Other
	0/0/0	0	0	0	0		0	0//0	0/0/			0/0/0	Yarn of fine hair of endangered animals, combed, not in formsorpacking for retail sale(containing≥85% by weight of other fine animals hair)
	0/0/0	0	0	0	0		0	0//0	0/0/			0/0/0	Yarn of fine hair of other animals, combed, not put up for retail sale (containing ≥85% by weight of other fine animals hair)
													---Other

税则号列	货品名称〔CIQ扩展编码及品名—T2表示见附表2〕	最惠(%)	暂定税率	普通	增值/消费	出口退税	计量单位	监管条件	检验检疫	特殊证件对美关税
5108.2090 10	非供零售用精梳其他濒危动物细毛纱线(按重量计其他精梳动物细毛含量＜85%)〔999〕	5		70	13/	0	千克	FE		/30
5108.2090 90	非供零售用精梳其他动物细毛纱线(按重量计其他精梳动物细毛含量＜85%)〔999〕	5		70	13/	13	千克			/30
51.09	**羊毛或动物细毛的纱线,供零售用:**									
	-按重量计羊毛或动物细毛含量在85%及以上:									
	---动物细毛:									
5109.1011	----山羊绒的〔999〕	6		80	13/	13	千克			/
5109.1019	----其他〔999〕	6		80	13/	13	千克			/
5109.1090	---其他〔999〕	6		80	13/	13	千克			/26
	-其他:									
	---动物细毛:									
5109.9011	----山羊绒的〔999〕	6		80	13/	13	千克			/
5109.9019	----其他〔999〕	6		80	13/	13	千克			/
5109.9090	---其他〔999〕	6		80	13/	13	千克			/31
51.10	**动物粗毛或马毛的纱线(包括马毛粗松螺旋花线),不论是否供零售用:**									
5110.0000	动物粗毛或马毛的纱线(包括马毛粗松螺旋花线),不论是否供零售用									
5110.0000 10	濒危动物粗毛的纱线(包括马毛粗松螺旋花线,不论是否供零售用)〔999〕	6		70	13/	0	千克	FE		/
5110.0000 90	其他动物粗毛或马毛的纱线(包括马毛粗松螺旋花线,不论是否供零售用)〔999〕	6		70	13/	13	千克			/
51.11	**粗梳羊毛或粗梳动物细毛的机织物:**									
	-按重量计羊毛或动物细毛含量在85%及以上:									
	--每平方米重量不超过300克:									
	---动物细毛的:									
5111.1111	----山羊绒的〔999〕	10		130	13/	13	米/千克			/
5111.1119	----其他〔999〕	10		130	13/	13	米/千克			/35
5111.1190	---其他〔999〕	10		130	13/	13	米/千克			/35
	--其他:									
	---动物细毛的:									
5111.1911	----山羊绒的〔999〕	10		130	13/	13	米/千克			/
5111.1919	----其他〔999〕	10		130	13/	13	米/千克			/35
5111.1990	---其他〔999〕	10		130	13/	13	米/千克			/35
5111.2000	-其他,主要或仅与化学纤维长丝混纺〔999〕	8		130	13/	13	米/千克			/33
5111.3000	-其他,主要或仅与化学纤维短纤混纺〔999〕	8		130	13/	13	米/千克			/33
5111.9000	-其他〔999〕	8		130	13/	13	米/千克			/33
51.12	**精梳羊毛或精梳动物细毛的机织物:**									
	-按重量计羊毛或动物细毛含量在85%及以上:									
5112.1100	--每平方米重量不超过200克〔999〕	8		130	13/	13	米/千克			/33
5112.1900	--其他〔999〕	8		130	13/	13	米/千克			/33
5112.2000	-其他,主要或仅与化学纤维长丝混纺〔999〕	8		130	13/	13	米/千克			/33
5112.3000	-其他,主要或仅与化学纤维短纤混纺〔999〕	8		130	13/	13	米/千克			/33
5112.9000	-其他〔999〕	8		130	13/	13	米/千克			/33
51.13	**动物粗毛或马毛的机织物:**									
5113.0000	动物粗毛或马毛的机织物〔999〕	8		130	13/	13	米/千克			/

协定税率 %										特惠税率 %			Article Description
亚太5国	东/冰/格	巴基斯坦	韩国	瑞士	哥达	秘鲁	澳大利亚	新西/坡/智	港/澳/台	亚太2国	老/柬/缅	36/3/1	
	0/0/0	0	0	0	0		0	0//0	0/0/			0/0/0	Yarn of fine hair of endangered animal, combed, not in forms or packing for retail sale(containing <85% by weight of other fine animals hair)
	0/0/0	0	0	0	0		0	0//0	0/0/			0/0/0	Yarn of fine hair of animal; combed, not in forms or packing for retail sale(containing <85% by weight of other animals, hair)
													Yarn of wool or of fine animal hair, put up for retail sale:
													-Containing 85% or more by weight of wool or of fine animal hair:
													---Of fine animal hair:
	0/0/0	0	0	0	0	0	0	0//0	0/0/			0/0/0	----Of goats
	0/0/0	0	0	0	0	0	0	0//0	0/0/			0/0/0	----Other
	0/0/0	0	0	0	0	0	0	0//0	0/0/			0/0/0	---Other
													-Other:
													---Of fine animal hair:
4.2	0/0/0	0	0	0	0		0	0//0	0/0/			0/0/0	----Of goats
4.2	0/0/0	0	0	0	0		0	0//0	0/0/			0/0/0	----Other
	0/0/0	0	0	0	0		0	0//0	0/0/			0/0/0	---Other
													Yarn of coarse animal hair or of horsehair (including gimped horsehair yarn), whether or not put up for retail sale:
													Yarn of coarse animal hair or of horsehair (including gimped horsehair yarn), whether or not put up for retail sale
	0/0/0	0	0	0	0	0	0	0//0	0/0/			0/0/0	Yarn of coarse hair of endangered animals hair (including gimped horsehair yarn, whether or not in forms or packing for retail sale)
	0/0/0	0	0	0	0	0	0	0//0	0/0/			0/0/0	Other yarn of coarse hair of animal or horsehair (including gimped horsehair yarn, whether or not put up for retail sale)
													Woven fabrics of carded wool or of carded fine animal hair:
													-Containing 85% or more by weight of wool or of fine animal hair:
													--Of a weight not exceeding 300 g/m^2:
													---Of fine animal hair:
6.5	0/0/0	4.5	0	0	0	0	0	0/0/0	0/0/			0/0/	----Of goats
6.5	0/0/0	4.5	0	0	0	0	0	0/0/0	0/0/			0/0/	----Other
6.5	0/0/0	4.5	0	0	0	0	0	0/0/0	0/0/			0/0/	---Other
													--Other:
													---Of fine animal hair:
6.5	0/0/0	4.5	0	0	0	0	0	0/0/0	0/0/			0/0/	----Of goats
6.5	0/0/0	4.5	0	0	0	0	0	0/0/0	0/0/			0/0/	----Other
6.5	0/0/0	4	0	0	0	0	0	0/0/0	0/0/			0/0/	---Other
	0/0/0	4.5	0	0	0	0	0	0/0/0	0/0/			0/0/	-Other, mixed mainly or solely with manmade filaments
5.2	0/0/0	4.5	0	0	0	0	0	0/0/0	0/0/			0/0/	-Other, mixed mainly or solely with man-made staple fibres
	0//0	4.5	0	0	0	0	0	0/0/0	0/0/			0/0/	-Other
													Woven fabrics of combed wool or of combed fine animal hair:
													-Containing 85% or more by weight of wool or of fine animal hair:
4	0/0/0	4.5	0	0	0	0	0	0/0/0	0/0/			0/0/0	--Of a weight not exceeding 200 g/m^2
4	0/0/0	4.5	0	0	0	0	0	0/0/0	0/0/		0/0/0	0/0/0	--Other
	0/0/0	4.5	0	0	0	0	0	0/0/0	0/0/			0/0/0	-Other, mixed mainly or solely with manmade filaments
	0/0/0	4.5	0	0	0	0	0	0/0/0	0/0/			0/0/0	-Other, mixed mainly or solely with man-made staple fibres
	0/0/0	4.5	0	0	0	0	0	0/0/0	0/0/			0/0/0	-Other
													Woven fabrics of coarse animal hair or of horsehair:
	0/0/0	4.5	0	0	0	0	0	0/0/0	0/0/			0/0/0	Woven fabrics of coarse animal hair or of horsehair

第五十二章
棉　花

子目注释：

子目号 5209.42 及 5211.42 所称“粗斜纹布(劳动布)”，是指用不同颜色的纱线织成的三线或四线斜纹织物，包括破斜纹组织的织物，这种织物以经纱为面，经纱染成一种相同的颜色，纬纱未漂白或经漂白、染成灰色或比经纱稍浅的颜色。

税则号列	货品名称〔CIQ 扩展编码及品名－T2 表示见附表 2〕	最惠(%)	暂定税率	普通	增值/消费	出口退税	计量单位	监管条件	检验检疫	特殊证件对美关税
52.01	**未梳的棉花：**									
5201.0000	未梳的棉花									
5201.0000　01	未梳的棉花[包括脱脂棉花(配额内)]〔999〕	1		125	9/	9	千克	t4xAB	MPQ	/26
5201.0000　80	未梳的棉花[包括脱脂棉花(关税配额外暂定)]〔999〕	0		0	9/	9	千克	4ABex	MPQ	/25
5201.0000　90	未梳的棉花[包括脱脂棉花(配额外)]〔999〕	T1		125	9/	9	千克	4xAB	MPQ	/65
52.02	**废棉(包括废棉纱线及回收纤维)：**									
5202.1000	-废棉纱线(包括废棉线)〔999〕	10		30	13/	13	千克	9	M	/35
	-其他：									
5202.9100	--回收纤维〔102〕	10		30	13/	13	千克	9B	MPQ	/35
5202.9900	--其他〔102〕	10		30	13/	9	千克	9B	MPQ	/35
52.03	**已梳的棉花：**									
5203.0000	已梳的棉花									
5203.0000　01	已梳的棉花(配额内)〔999〕	1		125	13/	9	千克	t4xAB	MPQ	/26
5203.0000　90	已梳的棉花(配额外)〔999〕	40		125	13/	9	千克	4xAB	MPQ	/65
52.04	**棉制缝纫线，不论是否供零售用：**									
	-非供零售用：									
5204.1100	--按重量计含棉量在 85%及以上〔999〕	5		40	13/	13	千克			/30
5204.1900	--其他〔999〕	5		40	13/	13	千克			/15
5204.2000	-供零售用〔999〕	5		50	13/	13	千克			/15
52.05	**棉纱线(缝纫线除外)，按重量计含棉量在 85%及以上，非供零售用：**									
	-未精梳纤维纺制的单纱：									
5205.1100	--细度在 714.29 分特及以上(不超过 14 公支)〔999〕	5		40	13/	13	千克			/30
5205.1200	--细度在 714.29 分特以下，但不细于 232.56 分特(超过 14 公支，但不超过 43 公支)〔999〕	5		40	13/	13	千克			/30
5205.1300	--细度在 232.56 分特以下，但不细于 192.31 分特(超过 43 公支，但不超过 52 公支)〔999〕	5		40	13/	13	千克			/25
5205.1400	--细度在 192.31 分特以下，但不细于 125 分特(超过 52 公支，但不超过 80 公支)〔999〕	5		40	13/	13	千克			/
5205.1500	--细度在 125 分特以下(超过 80 公支)〔999〕	5		40	13/	13	千克			/
	-精梳纤维纺制的单纱：									
5205.2100	--细度在 714.29 分特及以上(不超过 14 公支)〔999〕	5		40	13/	13	千克			/
5205.2200	--细度在 714.29 分特以下，但不细于 232.56 分特(超过 14 公支，但不超过 43 公支)〔999〕	5		40	13/	13	千克			/30
5205.2300	--细度在 232.56 分特以下，但不细于 192.31 分特(超过 43 公支，但不超过 52 公支)〔999〕	5		40	13/	13	千克			/
5205.2400	--细度在 192.31 分特以下，但不细于 125 分特(超过 52 公支，但不超过 80 公支)〔999〕	5		40	13/	13	千克			/30
5205.2600	--细度在 125 分特以下，但不细于 106.38 分特(超过 80 公支，但不超过 94 公支)〔999〕	5		40	13/	13	千克			/
5205.2700	--细度在 106.38 分特以下，但不细于 83.33 分特(超过 94 公支，但不超过 120 公支)〔999〕	5		40	13/	13	千克			/
5205.2800	--细度在 83.33 分特以下(超过 120 公支)〔999〕	5		40	13/	13	千克			/
	-未精梳纤维纺制的多股纱线或缆线：									
5205.3100	--每根单纱细度在 714.29 分特及以上(每根单纱不超过 14 公支)〔999〕	5		40	13/	13	千克			/25
5205.3200	--每根单纱细度在 714.29 分特以下，但不细于 232.56 分特(每根单纱超过 14 公支，但不超过 43 公支)〔999〕	5		40	13/	13	千克			/
5205.3300	--每根单纱细度在 232.56 分特以下，但不细于 192.31 分特(每根单纱超过 43 公支，但不超过 52 公支)〔999〕	5		40	13/	13	千克			/

Chapter 52
Cotton

Subheading Note:

For the purposes of subheadings Nos. 5209. 42 and 5211. 42, the expression "denim" means fabrics of yarns of different colours, of 3-thread or 4-thread twill, including broken twill, warp faced, the warp yarns of which are of one and the same colour and the weft yarns of which are unbleached, bleached, dyed grey or coloured a lighter shade of the colour of the warp yarns.

协定税率 %										特惠税率 %			
亚太5国	东/冰/格	巴基斯坦	韩国	瑞士	哥达	秘鲁	澳大利亚	新西/坡/智	港/澳/台	亚太2国	老/柬/缅	36/3/1	Article Description
													Cotton, not carded or combed:
													Cotton, not carded or combed
	5//								0/0/				Cotton, not carded or combed[including absorbent cotton(in-quota)]
	5//								0/0/				Cotton, not carded or combed[including absorben cotton (custom, out-guota, interim)]
	5//								0/0/				Cotton, not carded or combed[including absorbent cotton(out-quota)]
													Cotton waste (including yarn waste and garnetted stock):
	0/0/	0	4	0	0	0	0	0/0/0	0/0/			0/0/	—Yarn waste (including thread waste)
													-Other:
	0/0/		0	0	0	0	0	0/0/0	0/0/			0/0/0	--Garnetted stock
	0/0/	0	4	0	0		0	0/0/0	0/0/				--Other
													Cotton, carded or combed:
													Cotton, carded or combed
									0/0/				Cotton, carded or combed(in-quota)
									0/0/				Cotton, carded or combed(out-quota)
													Cotton sewing thread, whether or not put up for retail sale:
													-Not put up for retail sale:
	0/0/0	0	0	0	0	0	0	0//0	0/0/		0//	0/0/0	--Containing 85% or more by weight of cotton
	0/0/0	0	0	0	0	0	0	0//0	0/0/			0/0/0	--Other
	0/0/0	0	0	0	0	0	0	0//0	0/0/		0//	0/0/0	-Put up for retail sale
													Cotton yarn (other than sewing thread), containing 85% or more by weight of cotton, not put up for retail sale:
													-Single yarn, of uncombed fibres:
3.5	0/0/2	0	3	0	0	0	1.7	0//0	0/0/0		0/0/0	0/0/0	--Measuring 714. 29 decitex or more (not exceeding 14 metric number)
3.5	0/0/2	0	3	0	0	0	1.7	0//0	0/0/0		0/0/0	0/0/0	--Measuring less than 714. 29 decitex but not less than 232. 56 decitex (exceeding 14 metric number but not exceeding 43 metric number)
3.5	0/0/2	0	3	0	0	0	1.7	0//0	0/0/			0/0/0	--Measuring less than 232. 56 decitex but not less than 192. 31 decitex (exceeding 43 metric number but not exceeding 52 metric number)
3.5	0/0/2	0	3.5	0	0	0	1.7	0//0	0/0/		0//0	0/0/0	--Measuring less than 192. 31 decitex but not less than 125 decitex (exceeding 52 metric number but not exceeding 80 metric number)
3.5	0/0/2	3.5	3	0	0	0	1.7	0//0	0/0/			0/0/0	--Measuring less than 125 decitex (exceeding 80 metric number)
													-Single yarn, of combed fibres:
3.5	0/0/2	0	3	0	0	0	1.7	0//0	0/0/		//0	0/0/0	--Measuring 714. 29 decitex or more (not exceeding 14 metric number)
3.5	0/0/2	0	3	0	0	0	1.7	0//0	0/0/			0/0/0	--Measuring less than 714. 29 decitex but not less than 232. 56 decitex (exceeding 14 metric number but not exceeding 43 metric number)
3.5	0/0/2	0	2	0	0	0	1.7	0//0	0/0/			0/0/0	--Measuring less than 232. 56 decitex but not less than 192. 31 decitex (exceeding 43 metric number but not exceeding 52 metric number)
3.5	0/0/2	0	2	0	0	0	1.7	0//0	0/0/		0//0	0/0/0	--Measuring less than 192. 31 decitex but not less than 125 decitex (exceeding 52 metric number but not exceeding 80 metric number)
	0/0/2	0	3	0	0	0	1.7	0//0	0/0/			0/0/0	--Measuring less than 125 decitex but not less than 106. 38 decitex (exceeding 80 metric number but not exceeding 94 metric number)
	0/0/2		3	0	0	0	1.7	0//0	0/0/			0/0/0	--Measuring less than 106. 38 decitex but not less than 83. 33 decitex (exceeding 94 metric number but not exceeding 120 metric number)
	0/0/2		3	0	0	0	1.7	0//0	0/0/			0/0/0	--Measuring less than 83. 33 decitex (exceeding 120 metric number)
													-Multiple (folded) or cabled yarn, of uncombed fibres:
4.5	0/0/2	0	3	0	0		1.7	0//0	0/0/				--Measuring per single yarn 714. 29 decitex or more (not exceeding 14 metric number per single yarn)
3.5	0/0/2	0	3	0	0	0	1.7	0//0	0/0/			0/0/0	--Measuring per single yarn less than 714. 29 decitex but not less than 232. 56 decitex (exceeding 14 metric number but not exceeding 43 metric number per single yarn)
	0/0/2		3	0	0	0	1.7	0//0	0/0/			0/0/0	--Measuring per single yarn less than 232. 56 decitex but not less than 192. 31 decitex (exceeding 43 metric number but not exceeding 52 metric number per single yarn)

税则号列	货品名称〔CIQ扩展编码及品名—T2表示见附表2〕	最惠(%)	暂定税率	普通	增值/消费	出口退税	计量单位	监管条件	检验检疫	特殊证件对美关税
5205.3400	--每根单纱细度在192.31分特以下,但不细于125分特(每根单纱超过52公支,但不超过80公支)〔999〕	5		40	13/	13	千克			/
5205.3500	--每根单纱细度在125分特以下(每根单纱超过80公支)〔999〕	5		40	13/	13	千克			/
	-精梳纤维纺制的多股纱线或缆线:									
5205.4100	--每根单纱细度在714.29分特及以上(每根单纱不超过14公支)〔999〕	5		40	13/	13	千克			/
5205.4200	--每根单纱细度在714.29分特以下,但不细于232.56分特(每根单纱超过14公支,但不超过43公支)〔999〕	5		40	13/	13	千克			/
5205.4300	--每根单纱细度在232.56分特以下,但不细于192.31分特(每根单纱超过43公支,但不超过52公支)〔999〕	5		40	13/	13	千克			/30
5205.4400	--每根单纱细度在192.31分特以下,但不细于125分特(每根单纱超过52公支,但不超过80公支)〔999〕	5		40	13/	13	千克			/
5205.4600	--每根单纱细度在125分特以下,但不细于106.38分特(每根单纱超过80公支,但不超过94公支)〔999〕	5		40	13/	13	千克			/
5205.4700	--每根单纱细度在106.38分特以下,但不细于83.33分特(每根单纱超过94公支,但不超过120公支)〔999〕	5		40	13/	13	千克			/
5205.4800	--每根单纱细度83.33分特以下(每根单纱超过120公支)〔999〕	5		40	13/	13	千克			/
52.06	**棉纱线(缝纫线除外),按重量计含棉量在85%以下,非供零售用:**									
	-未精梳纤维纺制的单纱:									
5206.1100	--细度在714.29分特及以上(不超过14公支)〔999〕	5		40	13/	13	千克			/
5206.1200	--细度在714.29分特以下,但不细于232.56分特(超过14公支,但不超过43公支)〔999〕	5		40	13/	13	千克			/30
5206.1300	--细度在232.56分特以下,但不细于192.31分特(超过43公支,但不超过52公支)〔999〕	5		40	13/	13	千克			/15
5206.1400	--细度在192.31分特以下,但不细于125分特(超过52公支,但不超过80公支)〔999〕	5		40	13/	13	千克			/
5206.1500	--细度在125分特以下(超过80公支)〔999〕	5		40	13/	13	千克			/
	-精梳纤维纺制的单纱:									
5206.2100	--细度在714.29分特及以上(不超过14公支)〔999〕	5		40	13/	13	千克			/
5206.2200	--细度在714.29分特以下,但不细于232.56分特(超过14公支,但不超过43公支)〔999〕	5		40	13/	13	千克			/
5206.2300	--细度在232.56分特以下,但不细于192.31分特(超过43公支,但不超过52公支)〔999〕	5		40	13/	13	千克			/30
5206.2400	--细度在192.31分特以下,但不细于125分特(超过52公支,但不超过80公支)〔999〕	5		40	13/	13	千克			/
5206.2500	--细度在125分特以下(超过80公支)〔999〕	5		40	13/	13	千克			/
	-未精梳纤维纺制的多股纱线或缆线:									
5206.3100	--每根单纱细度在714.29分特及以上(每根单纱不超过14公支)〔999〕	5		40	13/	13	千克			/30
5206.3200	--每根单纱细度在714.29分特以下,但不细于232.56分特(每根单纱超过14公支,但不超过43公支)〔999〕	5		40	13/	13	千克			/
5206.3300	--每根单纱细度在232.56分特以下,但不细于192.31分特(每根单纱超过43公支,但不超过52公支)〔999〕	5		40	13/	13	千克			/
5206.3400	--每根单纱细度在192.31分特以下,但不细于125分特(每根单纱超过52公支,但不超过80公支)〔999〕	5		40	13/	13	千克			/
5206.3500	--每根单纱细度在125分特以下(每根单纱超过80公支)〔999〕	5		40	13/	13	千克			/
	-精梳纤维纺制的多股纱线或缆线:									

协定税率 %										特惠税率 %			
亚太5国	东/冰/格	巴基斯坦	韩国	瑞士	哥达	秘鲁	澳大利亚	新西/坡/智	港/澳/台	亚太2国	老/柬/缅	36/3/1	Article Description
	0/0/2	0	3	0	0	0	1.7	0//0	0/0/			0/0/0	--Measuring per single yarn less than 192. 31 decitex but not less than 125 decitex (exceeding 52 metric number but not exceeding 80 metric number per single yarn)
	0/0/2		3	0	0	0	1.7	0//0	0/0/			0/0/0	--Measuring per single yarn less than 125 decitex (exceeding 80 metric number per single yarn)
													-Multiple (folded) or cabled yarn, of combed fibres:
4.5	0/0/2	4.5	3	0	0		1.7	0//0	0/0/			0/0/	--Measuring per single yarn 714. 29 decitex or more (not exceeding 14 metric number per single yarn)
3.5	/0/2	0	3.5	0	0	0	1.7	0//0	0/0/			0/0/0	--Measuring per single yarn less than 714. 29 decitex but not less than 232. 56 decitex (exceeding 14 metric number but not exceeding 43 metric number per single yarn)
	0/0/2	4	3	0	0		1.7	0//0	0/0/			0/0/0	--Measuring per single yarn less than 232. 56 decitex but not less than 192. 31 decitex (exceeding 43 metric number but not exceeding 52 metric number per single yarn)
	0/0/2	0	3	0	0	0	1.7	0//0	0/0/			0/0/0	--Measuring per single yarn less than 192. 31 decitex but not less than 125 decitex (exceeding 52 metric number but not exceeding 80 metric number per single yarn)
4.5	0/0/2	3.6	3	0	0	0	1.7	0//0	0/0/			0/0/0	--Measuring per single yarn less than 125 decitex but not less than 106. 38 decitex (exceeding 80 metric number but not exceeding 94 metric number per single yarn)
4.5	0/0/2	3.6	3	0	0	0	1.7	0//0	0/0/			0/0/0	--Measuring per single yarn less than 106. 38 decitex but not less than 83. 33 decitex (exceeding 94 metric number but not exceeding 120 metric number per single yarn)
4.5	0/0/2	4.5	3	0	0	0	1.7	0//0	0/0/			0/0/0	--Measuring per single yarn less than 83. 33 decitex (exceeding 120 metric number per single yarn)
													Cotton yarn (other than sewing thread), containing less than 85% by weight of cotton, not put up for retail sale:
													-Single yarn, of uncombed fibres:
3.5	0/0/2	3.5	3	0	0		1.7	0//0	0/0/				--Measuring 714. 29 decitex or more (not exceeding 14 metric number)
3.5	0/0/2	0	3	0	0	0	1.7	0//0	0/0/0			0/0/	--Measuring less than 714. 29 decitex but not less than 232. 56 decitex (exceeding 14 metric number but not exceeding 43 metric number)
	0/0/2		3	0	0	0	1.7	0//0	0/0/			0/0/0	--Measuring less than 232. 56 decitex but not less than 192. 31 decitex (exceeding 43 metric number but not exceeding 52 metric number)
	0/0/2	4	3	0	0	0	1.7	0//0	0/0/			0/0/0	--Measuring less than 192. 31 decitex but not less than 125 decitex (exceeding 52 metric number but not exceeding 80 metric number)
3.5	0/0/2	3.5	3	0	0	0	1.7	0//0	0/0/			0/0/0	--Measuring less than 125 decitex (exceeding 80 metric number)
													-Single yarn, of combed fibres:
4.5	0/0/2	4.5	3	0	0	0	1.7	0//0	0/0/			0/0/	--Measuring 714. 29 decitex or more (not exceeding 14 metric number)
	0/0/2	0	3	0	0	0	1.7	0//0	0/0/0			0/0/	--Measuring less than 714. 29 decitex but not less than 232. 56 decitex (exceeding 14 metric number but not exceeding 43 metric number)
	0/0/2		3	0	0	0	1.7	0//0	0/0/			0/0/0	--Measuring less than 232. 56 decitex but not less than 192. 31 decitex (exceeding 43 metric number but not exceeding 52 metric number)
	0/0/2	4	3	0	0	0	1.7	0//0	0/0/0			0/0/0	--Measuring less than 192. 31 decitex but not less than 125 decitex (exceeding 52 metric number but not exceeding 80 metric number)
	0/0/2		3	0	0	0	1.7	0//0	0/0/			0/0/0	--Measuring less than 125 decitex (exceeding 80 metric number)
													-Multiple (folded) or cabled yarn, of uncombed fibres:
	0/0/2		3	0	0	0	1.7	0//0	0/0/			0/0/	--Measuring per single yarn 714. 29 decitex or more (not exceeding 14 metric number per single yarn)
	0/0/2	0	3	0	0	0	1.7	0//0	0/0/			0/0/	--Measuring per single yarn less than 714. 29 decitex but not less than 232. 56 decitex (exceeding 14 metric number but not exceeding 43 metric number per single yarn)
	0/0/2		3	0	0	0	1.7	0//0	0/0/			0/0/0	--Measuring per single yarn less than 232. 56 decitex but not less than 192. 31 decitex (exceeding 43 metric number but not exceeding 52 metric number per single yarn)
	0/0/2		3	0	0	0	1.7	0//0	0/0/			0/0/0	--Measuring per single yarn less than 192. 31 decitex but not less than 125 decitex (exceeding 52 metric number but not exceeding 80 metric number per single yarn)
	0/0/2		3	0	0	0	1.7	0//0	0/0/			0/0/0	--Measuring per single yarn less than 125 decitex (exceeding 80 metric number per single yarn)
													-Multiple (folded) or cabled yarn, of combed fibres:

税则号列	货品名称〔CIQ扩展编码及品名—T2表示见附表2〕	最惠(%)	暂定税率	普通	增值/消费	出口退税	计量单位	监管条件	检验检疫	特殊证件对美关税
5206.4100	--每根单纱细度在714.29分特及以上(每根单纱不超过14公支)〔999〕	5		40	13/	13	千克			/
5206.4200	--每根单纱细度在714.29分特以下,但不细于232.56分特(每根单纱超过14公支,但不超过43公支)〔999〕	5		40	13/	13	千克			/
5206.4300	--每根单纱细度在232.56分特以下,但不细于192.31分特(每根单纱超过43公支,但不超过52公支)〔999〕	5		40	13/	13	千克			/
5206.4400	--每根单纱细度在192.31分特以下,但不细于125分特(每根单纱超过52公支,但不超过80公支)〔999〕	5		40	13/	13	千克			/
5206.4500	--每根单纱细度在125分特以下(每根单纱超过80公支)〔999〕	5		40	13/	13	千克			/
52.07	**棉纱线(缝纫线除外),供零售用:**									
5207.1000	-按重量计含棉量在85%及以上〔999〕	5		50	13/	13	千克			/30
5207.9000	-其他〔999〕	5		50	13/	13	千克			/
52.08	**棉机织物,按重量计含棉量在85%及以上,每平方米重量不超过200克:**									
	-未漂白:									
5208.1100	--平纹机织物,每平方米重量不超过100克〔999〕	8		70	13/	13	米/千克			/33
5208.1200	--平纹机织物,每平方米重量超过100克〔999〕	8		70	13/	13	米/千克			/33
5208.1300	--三线或四线斜纹机织物,包括双面斜纹机织物〔999〕	8		70	13/	13	米/千克			/
5208.1900	--其他机织物〔999〕	8		70	13/	13	米/千克			/33
	-漂白:									
5208.2100	--平纹机织物,每平方米重量不超过100克									
5208.2100 10	漂白全棉平纹府绸及细平布(每平方米重≤100g,含棉量≥85%)〔999〕	8		70	13/	13	米/千克			/
5208.2100 20	漂白全棉平纹机织平布(每平方米重≤100g,68号及以下)〔999〕	8		70	13/	13	米/千克			/
5208.2100 30	漂白全棉平纹奶酪布(每平方米重≤100g,含棉量≥85%)〔999〕	8		70	13/	13	米/千克			/
5208.2100 40	漂白全棉平纹印染用布(每平方米重≤100g,43-68号)〔999〕	8		70	13/	13	米/千克			/
5208.2100 50	漂白全棉平纹巴里纱及薄细布(每平方米重量≤100g,69号及以上)〔999〕	8		70	13/	13	米/千克			/
5208.2100 60	漂白全棉医用纱布(每平方米重≤100g,含棉量≥85%)〔999〕	8		70	13/	13	米/千克			/
5208.2200	--平纹机织物,每平方米重量超过100克									
5208.2200 10	漂白全棉平纹府绸及细平布(100g<每平方米重量≤200g,含棉量≥85%)〔999〕	8		70	13/	13	米/千克			/33
5208.2200 20	漂白全棉平纹机织平布(100g<每平方米重≤200g,68号及以下)〔999〕	8		70	13/	13	米/千克			/33
5208.2200 30	漂白全棉平纹奶酪布(100g<每平方米重≤200g,含棉量≥85%)〔999〕	8		70	13/	13	米/千克			/33
5208.2200 40	漂白全棉平纹印染用布(100g<每平方米重≤200g,43-68号)〔999〕	8		70	13/	13	米/千克			/33
5208.2200 50	漂白全棉巴里纱及薄细布(100g<每平方米重≤200g,69号及以上)〔999〕	8		70	13/	13	米/千克			/33
5208.2300	--三线或四线斜纹机织物,包括双面斜纹机织物〔999〕	8		70	13/	13	米/千克			/
5208.2900	--其他机织物									
5208.2900 10	漂白其他全棉机织缎布(每平方米重≤200g,含棉量≥85%)〔999〕	8		70	13/	13	米/千克			/33
5208.2900 20	漂白其他全棉机织斜纹布(每平方米重≤200g,含棉量≥85%)〔999〕	8		70	13/	13	米/千克			/33
5208.2900 30	漂白其他全棉机织牛津布(每平方米重≤200g,含棉量≥85%)〔999〕	8		70	13/	13	米/千克			/33
5208.2900 90	漂白其他全棉机织物(每平方米重≤200g,含棉量≥85%)〔999〕	8		70	13/	13	米/千克			/33
	-染色:									
5208.3100	--平纹机织物,每平方米重量不超过100克									
5208.3100 10	染色全棉手工织布(每平方米重≤100g,含棉量≥85%)〔999〕	8		70	13/	13	米/千克			/33
5208.3100 91	染色全棉平纹府绸及细平布(每平方米重≤100g,含棉量≥85%)〔999〕	8		70	13/	13	米/千克			/33
5208.3100 92	染色全棉平纹机织平布(每平方米重≤100g,68号及以下)〔999〕	8		70	13/	13	米/千克			/33

协定税率 %										特惠税率 %			
亚太5国	东/冰/格	巴基斯坦	韩国	瑞士	哥达	秘鲁	澳大利亚	新西/坡/智	港/澳/台	亚太2国	老/柬/缅	36/3/1	Article Description
	0/0/2		3	0	0	0	1.7	0//0	0/0/			0/0/	--Measuring per single yarn 714.29 decitex or more (not exceeding 14 metric number per single yarn)
	0/0/2		3	0	0	0	1.7	0//0	0/0/			0/0/	--Measuring per single yarn less than 714.29 decitex but not less than 232.56 decitex (exceeding 14 metric number but not exceeding 43 metric number per single yarn)
	0/0/2		3	0	0	0	1.7	0//0	0/0/			0/0/0	--Measuring per single yarn less than 232.56 decitex but not less then 192.31 decitex (exceeding 43 metric number but not exceeding 52 metric number per single yarn)
	0/0/2		3	0	0	0	1.7	0//0	0/0/			0/0/0	--Measuring per single yarn less than 192.31 decitex but not less than 125 decitex (exceeding 52 metric number but not exceeding 80 metric number per single yarn)
	0/0/2		3	0	0	0	1.7	0//0	0/0/			0/0/0	--Measuring per single yarn less than 125 decitex (exceeding 80 metric number per single yarn)
													Cotton yarn (other than sewing thread) put up for retail sale:
4.2	0/0/0	4	0	0	0	0	0	0//0	0/0/			0/0/	-Containing 85% or more by weight of cotton
	0/0/0	4.5	0	0	0	0	0	0//0	0/0/			0/0/0	-Other
													Woven fabrics of cotton, containing 85% or more by weight of cotton, weighing not more than 200 g/m^2:
													-Unbleached:
	0/0/0	0	0	0	0	0	0	0//0	0/0/			0/0/	--Plain weave, weighing not more than 100 g/m^2
	0/0/0	0	0	0	0	0	0	0/0/0	0/0/			0/0/	--Plain weave, weighing more than 100 g/m^2
5.2	0/0/0	0	4	0	0	0	0	0//0	0/0/			0/0/	--3-thread or 4-thread twill, including cross twill
	0/0/0	0	0	0	0	0	0	0/0/0	0/0/			0/0/	--Other fabrics
													-Bleached:
													--Plain weave, weighing not more than 100 g/m^2
	0/0/0	0	0	0	0	0	0	0//0	0/0/			0/0/	Poplin and fine plain cloth of cotton, w≤100g/m^2, containing≥85% by weight of cotton, bleached
	0/0/0	0	0	0	0	0	0	0//0	0/0/			0/0/	Woven fabrics of cotton, plain weave, ≤No. 68, w≤100g/m^2, bleached
	0/0/0	0	0	0	0	0	0	0//0	0/0/			0/0/	Cheese cloth of cotton, plain weave, w≤100g/m^2, containing≥85% by weight of cotton, bleached
	0/0/0	0	0	0	0	0	0	0//0	0/0/			0/0/	Cloth for printing and dying of cotton, plain weave, No. 43～No. 68, w≤100g/m^2, bleached
	0/0/0	0	0	0	0	0	0	0//0	0/0/			0/0/	Voiles and swiss muslim of cotton, plain weave, w≤100g/m^2, containing≥85% by weight of cotton, ≥No. 69, bleached
	0/0/0	0	0	0	0	0	0	0//0	0/0/			0/0/	Medical gauze of cotton, w≤100g/m^2, containing≥85% by weight of cotton, bleached
													--Plain weave, weighing more than 100 g/m^2
	0/0/0	0	0	0	0	0	0	0/0/0	0/0/		0/0/0	0/0/0	Poplin and fine plain cloth of cotton, plain weave, 100g/m^2＜w≤200g/m^2, containing≥85% by weight of cotton, bleached
	0/0/0	0	0	0	0	0	0	0/0/0	0/0/		0/0/0	0/0/0	Plain cloth of cotton, plain weave, 100g/m^2＜w≤200g/m^2, ≤No. 68, bleached
	0/0/0	0	0	0	0	0	0	0/0/0	0/0/		0/0/0	0/0/0	Cheese cloth of cotton, plain weave, 100g/m^2＜w≤200g/m^2, containing≥85% by weight of cotton, bleached
	0/0/0	0	0	0	0	0	0	0/0/0	0/0/		0/0/0	0/0/0	Cloth for printing and dying, of cotton, plain weave, No. 43～No. 68, 100g/m^2＜w≤200g/m^2, bleached
	0/0/0	0	0	0	0	0	0	0/0/0	0/0/		0/0/0	0/0/0	Voiles and swiss muslin of cotton, 100g/m^2＜w≤200g/m^2, ≥No. 69, bleached
	0/0/0	0	0	6.2	0	0	0	0/0/0	0/0/			0/0/	--3-thread or 4-thread twill, including cross twill
													--Other fabrics
	0/0/0	0	0	0	0	0	0	0//0	0/0/			0/0/	Woven fabrics of cotton, satin weave, w≤200 g/m^2, containing≥85% by weight of cotton, bleached
	0/0/0	0	0	0	0	0	0	0//0	0/0/			0/0/	Woven fabrics of cotton, twill weave, w≤200 g/m^2, containing≥85% by weight of cotton, bleached
	0/0/0	0	0	0	0	0	0	0//0	0/0/			0/0/	Woven fabrics of cotton, oxford weave, w≤200 g/m^2, containing≥85% by weight of cotton, bleached
	0/0/0	0	0	0	0	0	0	0//0	0/0/			0/0/	Other woven fabrics of cotton, w≤200g/m^2, containing≥85% by weight of cotton, bleached
													-Dyed:
													--Plain weave, weighing not more than 100 g/m^2
	0/0/0	0	0	0	0	0	0	0//0	0/0/0			0/0/0	Handwoven plain cloth of cotton, w≤100g/m^2, containing≥85% by weight of cotton, dyed
	0/0/0	0	0	0	0	0	0	0//0	0/0/0			0/0/0	Popin and fine plain cloth of cotton, w≤100g/m^2, containing≥85% by weight of cotton, dyed
	0/0/0	0	0	0	0	0	0	0//0	0/0/0			0/0/0	Plain cloth of cotton, w≤100g/m^2, ≤No. 68, dyed

税则号列	货品名称〔CIQ 扩展编码及品名－T2 表示见附表 2〕	最惠(%)	暂定税率	普通	增值/消费	出口退税	计量单位	监管条件	检验检疫	特殊证件对美关税
5208.3100　93	染色全棉平纹奶酪布(每平方米重≤100g,含棉量≥85%)〔999〕	8		70	13/	13	米/千克			/33
5208.3100　94	染色全棉平纹印染用布(每平方米重≤100g,43-68 号)〔999〕	8		70	13/	13	米/千克			/33
5208.3100　95	染色全棉巴里纱及薄细布(每平方米重≤100g,69 号及以上)〔999〕	8		70	13/	13	米/千克			/33
5208.3200	--平纹机织物,每平方米重量超过 100 克									
5208.3200　10	染色全棉手工织布(100g＜每平方米重≤200g,含棉量≥85%)〔999〕	8		70	13/	13	米/千克			/33
5208.3200　91	染色全棉平纹府绸及细平布(100g＜每平方米重≤200g,含棉量≥85%)〔999〕	8		70	13/	13	米/千克			/33
5208.3200　92	染色全棉平纹机织平布(100g＜每平方米重≤200g,68 号及以下)〔999〕	8		70	13/	13	米/千克			/33
5208.3200　93	染色全棉平纹奶酪布(100g＜每平方米重≤200g,含棉量≥85%)〔999〕	8		70	13/	13	米/千克			/33
5208.3200　94	染色全棉平纹印染用布(100g＜每平方米重≤200g,43-68 号)〔999〕	8		70	13/	13	米/千克			/33
5208.3200　95	染色全棉巴里纱及薄细布(100g＜每平方米重≤200g,69 号及以上)〔999〕	8		70	13/	13	米/千克			/33
5208.3300	--三线或四线斜纹机织物,包括双面斜纹机织物〔999〕	8		70	13/	13	米/千克			/
5208.3900	--其他机织物									
5208.3900　10	染色其他全棉机织缎布(每平方米重≤200g,含棉量≥85%)〔999〕	8		70	13/	13	米/千克			/33
5208.3900　20	染色其他全棉机织斜纹布(每平方米重≤200g,含棉量≥85%)〔999〕	8		70	13/	13	米/千克			/33
5208.3900　30	染色其他全棉机织牛津布(每平方米重≤200g,含棉量≥85%)〔999〕	8		70	13/	13	米/千克			/33
5208.3900　90	染色其他全棉机织物(每平方米重≤200g,含棉量≥85%)〔999〕	8		70	13/	13	米/千克			/33
	-色织:									
5208.4100	--平纹机织物,每平方米重量不超过 100 克									
5208.4100　10	色织的全棉手工织布(每平方米重≤100g,含棉量≥85%)〔999〕	8		70	13/	13	米/千克			/
5208.4100　90	色织的全棉平纹机织物(每平方米重≤100g,含棉量≥85%)〔999〕	8		70	13/	13	米/千克			/
5208.4200	--平纹机织物,每平方米重 100 克									
5208.4200　10	色织的全棉手工织布(100g＜每平方米重≤200g,含棉量≥85%)〔999〕	8		70	13/	13	米/千克			/33
5208.4200　90	色织的全棉平纹机织物(100 克＜每平方米重≤200g,含棉量≥85%)〔999〕	8		70	13/	13	米/千克			/33
5208.4300	--三线或四线斜纹机织物,包括双面斜纹机织物〔999〕	8		70	13/	13	米/千克			/33
5208.4900	--其他机织物									
5208.4900　10	色织的其他全棉提花机织物(每平方米重≤200g,含棉量≥85%)〔999〕	8		70	13/	13	米/千克			/33
5208.4900　90	色织的其他全棉机织物(每平方米重≤200g,含棉量≥85%)〔999〕	8		70	13/	13	米/千克			/33
	-印花:									
5208.5100	--平纹机织物,每平方米重量不超过 100 克									
5208.5100　10	印花全棉手工织布(每平方米重≤100g,含棉量≥85%)〔999〕	8		70	13/	13	米/千克			/33
5208.5100　91	印花全棉平纹府绸及细平布(每平方米重≤100g,含棉量≥85%)〔999〕	8		70	13/	13	米/千克			/33
5208.5100　92	印花全棉平纹机织平布(每平方米重≤100g,68 号及以下)〔999〕	8		70	13/	13	米/千克			/33
5208.5100　93	印花全棉平纹奶酪布(每平方米重≤100g,含棉量≥85%)〔999〕	8		70	13/	13	米/千克			/33
5208.5100　94	印花全棉平纹印染用布(每平方米重≤100g,43-68 号)〔999〕	8		70	13/	13	米/千克			/33
5208.5100　95	印花全棉平纹巴里纱及薄细布(每平方米重≤100g,69 号及以上)〔999〕	8		70	13/	13	米/千克			/33
5208.5200	--平纹机织物,每平方米重量超过 100 克									
5208.5200　10	印花的全棉手工织布(100g＜每平方米重≤200g,含棉量≥85%)〔999〕	8		70	13/	13	米/千克			/33
5208.5200　91	印花的全棉平纹府绸及细平布(100g＜每平方米重≤200g,含棉量≥85%)〔999〕	8		70	13/	13	米/千克			/33
5208.5200　92	印花的全棉平纹机织平布(100g＜每平方米重≤200g,68 号及以下)〔999〕	8		70	13/	13	米/千克			/33

协定税率 %										特惠税率 %			
亚太5国	东/冰/格	巴基斯坦	韩国	瑞士	哥达	秘鲁	澳大利亚	新西/坡/智	港/澳/台	亚太2国	老/柬/缅	36/3/1	Article Description
	0/0/0	0	0	0	0	0	0	0//0	0/0/0			0/0/0	Cheese cloth of cotton, w≤100 g/m², containing≥85% by weight of cotton, dyed
	0/0/0	0	0	0	0	0	0	0//0	0/0/0			0/0/0	Cloth for printing and dying, of cotton, plain weave, No. 43～No. 68, w≤100g/m², dyed
	0/0/0	0	0	0	0	0	0	0//0	0/0/0			0/0/0	Voiles and fine thin cloth of cotton, w≤100g/m², ≥No. 69, dyed
													--Plain weave, weighing more than 100 g/m²
5.2	0/0/0	0	0	0	0	0	0	0/0/0	0/0/0			0/0/0	Handwoven plain cloth of cotton, 100g/m²<w≤200g/m², containing≥85% by weight of cotton, dyed
5.2	0/0/0	0	0	0	0	0	0	0/0/0	0/0/0			0/0/0	Poplin and fine plain cloth of cotton, 100g/m²<w≤200g/m², containing≥85% by weight of cotton, dyed
5.2	0/0/0	0	0	0	0	0	0	0/0/0	0/0/0			0/0/0	Plain cloth of cotton, 100g/m²<w≤200g/m², ≤No. 68, dyed
5.2	0/0/0	0	0	0	0	0	0	0/0/0	0/0/0			0/0/0	Cheese cloth of cotton, plain weave, 100g/m²<w≤200g/m², containing≥85% by weight of cotton, dyed
5.2	0/0/0	0	0	0	0	0	0	0/0/0	0/0/0			0/0/0	Cloth for printing and dying of cotton, plain weave, No. 43～No. 68, 100g/m²<w≤200g/m², dyed
5.2	0/0/0	0	0	0	0	0	0	0/0/0	0/0/0			0/0/0	Voiles and swiss muslin of cotton, 100g/m²<w≤200g/m², ≥No. 69, dyed
5.2	0/0/0	0	0	0	0	0	0	0//0	0/0/		0/0/0	0/0/0	—3-thread or 4-thread twill, including cross twill
													—Other fabrics
5.2	0/0/0	0	0	0	0	0	0	0/0/0	0/0/0			0/0/0	Woven fabrics of cotton, satin weave, w≤200 g/m², containing≥85% by weight of cotton, dyed
5.2	0/0/0	0	0	0	0	0	0	0/0/0	0/0/0			0/0/0	Woven fabrics of cotton, twill weave, w≤200 g/m², containing≥85% by weight of cotton, dyed
5.2	0/0/0	0	0	0	0	0	0	0/0/0	0/0/0			0/0/0	Woven fabrics of cotton, oxford weave, w≤200 g/m², containing≥85% by weight of cotton, dyed
5.2	0/0/0	0	0	0	0	0	0	0/0/0	0/0/0			0/0/0	Other woven fabrics of cotton, w≤200g/m², containing≥85% by weight of cotton, dyed
													-Of yarns of different colours:
													--Plain weave, weighing not more than 100 g/m²
	0/0/0	0	0	3	0	0	0	0/0/0	0/0/			0/0/	Handwoven cloth of cotton, w≤100g/m², containing≥85% by weight of cotton, of yarns of different colours
	0/0/0	0	0	3	0	0	0	0/0/0	0/0/			0/0/	Woven fabrics of cotton, plain weave, w≤100 g/m², containing≥85% by weight of cotton, of yarns of different colours
													--Plain weave, weighing more than 100 g/m²
5.2	0/0/0	0	0	3	0	0	0	0/0/0	0/0/0			0/0/0	Handwoven cloth of cotton, 100g/m²<w≤200 g/m², containing≥85% by weight of cotton, of yarns of different colours
5.2	0/0/0	0	0	3	0	0	0	0/0/0	0/0/0			0/0/0	Woven fabrics of cotton, plain weave, 100g/m²<w≤200g/m², containing≥85% by weight of cotton, of yarns of different colours
	0/0/0	0	0	3	0	0	0	0//0	0/0/			0/0/	--3-thread or 4-thread twill, including cross twill
													--Other fabrics
5.2	0/0/0	0	0	0	0	0	0	0/0/0	0/0/		0/0/0	0/0/0	Other woven fabrics of cotton, jacquard weave, w≤200g/m², containing≥85% by weight of cotton, of yarns of different colours
5.2	0/0/0	0	0	0	0	0	0	0/0/0	0/0/		0/0/0	0/0/0	Other woven fabrics of cotton, w≤200g/m², containing≥85% by weight of cotton, of yarns of different colours
													-Printed:
													--Plain weave, weighing not more than 100 g/m²
	0/0/0	0	0	0	0	0	0	0//0	0/0/			0/0/0	Handwoven cloth of cotton, w≤100g/m², containing≥85% by weight of cotton, printed
	0/0/0	0	0	0	0	0	0	0//0	0/0/			0/0/0	Poplin and fine plain cloth of cotton, w≤100g/m², containing≥85% by weight of cotton, printed
	0/0/0	0	0	0	0	0	0	0//0	0/0/			0/0/0	Plain cloth of cotton, plain weave, w≤100g/m², ≤No. 68, printed
	0/0/0	0	0	0	0	0	0	0//0	0/0/			0/0/0	Cheese cloth of cotton, plain weave, w≤100 g/m², containing≥85% by weight of cotton, printed
	0/0/0	0	0	0	0	0	0	0//0	0/0/			0/0/0	Cloth for printing and dying of cotton, plain weave, w≤100g/m², No. 43～No. 68, printed
	0/0/0	0	0	0	0	0	0	0//0	0/0/			0/0/0	Voiles and swiss muslin of cotton, w≤100g/m², ≥No. 69, printed
													--Plain weave, weighing more than 100 g/m²
5.2	0/0/0	0	7	0	0	0	0	0/0/0	0/0/			0/0/0	Handwoven cloth of cotton, 100g/m²<w≤200 g/m², containing≥85% by weight of cotton, printed
5.2	0/0/0	0	7	0	0	0	0	0/0/0	0/0/			0/0/0	Poplin and fine plain cloth of cotton, 100g/m²<w≤200g/m², containing≥85% by weight of cotton, printed
5.2	0/0/0	0	7	0	0	0	0	0/0/0	0/0/			0/0/0	Plain cloth of cotton, 100g/m²<w≤200g/m², ≤No. 68 printed

税则号列		货品名称〔CIQ 扩展编码及品名－T2 表示见附表 2〕	最惠(%)	暂定税率	普通	增值/消费	出口退税	计量单位	监管条件	检验检疫	特殊证件对美关税
5208.5200	93	印花的全棉平纹奶酪布(100g＜每平方米重量≤200g,含棉量≥85%)〔999〕	8		70	13/	13	米/千克			/33
5208.5200	94	印花的全棉平纹印染用布(100g＜每平方米重≤200g,43-68 号)〔999〕	8		70	13/	13	米/千克			/33
5208.5200	95	印花的全棉巴里纱及薄细布(100g＜每平方米重≤200g,69 号及以上)〔999〕	8		70	13/	13	米/千克			/33
		--其他机织物:									
5208.5910		---三线或四线斜纹机织物,包括双面斜纹机织物〔999〕	8		70	13/	13	米/千克			/
5208.5990		---其他									
5208.5990	10	印花其他全棉机织缎布(每平方米重≤200g,含棉量≥85%)〔999〕	8		70	13/	13	米/千克			/33
5208.5990	20	印花其他全棉机织斜纹布(每平方米重≤200g,含棉量≥85%)〔999〕	8		70	13/	13	米/千克			/33
5208.5990	30	印花其他全棉机织牛津布(每平方米重≤200g,含棉量≥85%)〔999〕	8		70	13/	13	米/千克			/33
5208.5990	90	印花其他全棉机织物(每平方米重≤200g,含棉量≥85%)〔999〕	8		70	13/	13	米/千克			/33
52.09		**棉机织物,按重量计含棉量在 85%及以上,每平方米重量超过 200 克:**									
		-未漂白:									
5209.1100		--平纹机织物〔999〕	8		70	13/	13	米/千克			/33
5209.1200		--三线或四线斜纹机织物,包括双面斜纹机织物〔999〕	8		70	13/	13	米/千克			/33
5209.1900		--其他机织物〔999〕	8		70	13/	13	米/千克			/33
		-漂白:									
5209.2100		--平纹机织物〔999〕	8		70	13/	13	米/千克			/33
5209.2200		--三线或四线斜纹机织物,包括双面斜纹机织物〔999〕	8		70	13/	13	米/千克			/33
5209.2900		--其他机织物〔999〕	8		70	13/	13	米/千克			/33
		-染色:									
5209.3100		--平纹机织物									
5209.3100	10	染色全棉手工织布(指每平方米重＞200 克,含棉量≥85%)〔999〕	8		70	13/	13	米/千克			/33
5209.3100	91	染色全棉平纹府绸及细平布(指每平方米重＞200 克,含棉量≥85%)〔999〕	8		70	13/	13	米/千克			/33
5209.3100	92	染色的全棉平纹机织平布(指每平方米重＞200 克,含棉量≥85%)〔999〕	8		70	13/	13	米/千克			/33
5209.3100	93	染色的全棉平纹机织帆布(指每平方米重＞200 克,含棉量≥85%)〔999〕	8		70	13/	13	米/千克			/33
5209.3200		--三线或四线斜纹机织物,包括双面斜纹机织物〔999〕	8		70	13/	13	米/千克			/33
5209.3900		--其他机织物									
5209.3900	10	染色的其他全棉机织缎布(指每平方米重＞200 克,含棉量≥85%)〔999〕	8		70	13/	13	米/千克			/33
5209.3900	20	染色的其他全棉机织斜纹布(指每平方米重＞200 克,含棉量≥85%)〔999〕	8		70	13/	13	米/千克			/33
5209.3900	30	染色的其他全棉机织帆布(指每平方米重量＞200 克,含棉量≥85%)〔999〕	8		70	13/	13	米/千克			/33
5209.3900	90	染色的其他全棉机织物(指每平方米重量＞200 克,含棉量≥85%)〔999〕	8		70	13/	13	米/千克			/33
		-色织:									
5209.4100		--平纹机织物									
5209.4100	10	色织的全棉手工织布(指每平方米重＞200 克,含棉量≥85%)〔999〕	8		70	13/	13	米/千克			/33
5209.4100	90	色织的全棉平纹机织物(指每平方米重＞200 克,含棉量≥85%)〔999〕	8		70	13/	13	米/千克			/33
5209.4200		--粗斜纹布(劳动布)									
5209.4200	10	色织全棉蓝粗斜纹布(劳动布)(指每平方米重＞200 克,含棉量≥85%)〔999〕	8		70	13/	13	米/千克			/33
5209.4200	90	色织其他全棉粗斜纹布(劳动布)(指每平方米重＞200 克,含棉量≥85%)〔999〕	8		70	13/	13	米/千克			/33
5209.4300		--其他三线或四线斜纹机织物,包括双面斜纹机织物〔999〕	8		70	13/	13	米/千克			/33
5209.4900		--其他机织物									
5209.4900	10	色织的其他全棉提花机织物(指每平方米重＞200 克,含棉量≥85%)〔999〕	8		70	13/	13	米/千克			/33
5209.4900	90	色织的其他全棉机织物(指每平方米重＞200 克,含棉量≥85%)〔999〕	8		70	13/	13	米/千克			/33
		-印花:									

协定税率 %										特惠税率 %			Article Description
亚太5国	东/冰/格	巴基斯坦	韩国	瑞士	哥达	秘鲁	澳大利亚	新西/坡/智	港/澳/台	亚太2国	老/柬/缅	36/3/1	
5.2	0/0/0	0	7	0	0	0	0	0/0/0	0/0/			0/0/0	Cheese cloth of cotton, plain weave, 100g/m^2<w≤200g/m^2, containing≥85% by weight of cotton, printed
5.2	0/0/0	0	7	0	0	0	0	0/0/0	0/0/			0/0/0	Cloth for printing and dying of cotton, plain weave, 100g/m^2<w≤200g/m^2, No. 43～No. 68, printed
5.2	0/0/0	0	7	0	0	0	0	0/0/0	0/0/			0/0/0	Voiles and swiss muslin of cotton 100g/m^2 < w ≤ 200g/m^2, ≥ No. 69, printed
													--Other fabrics:
	0/0/0	0	0	0	0	0	0	0//0	0/0/			0/0/	---3-thread or 4-thread twill, including cross twill
													---Other
5.2	0/0/0	0	0	0	0	0	0	0//0	0/0/0			0/0/	Woven fabrics of cotton, satin weave, w≤200g/m^2 containing≥85% by weight of cotton, printed
5.2	0/0/0	0	0	0	0	0	0	0//0	0/0/0			0/0/	Woven fabrics of cotton, twill weave, w≤200 g/m^2, containing≥85% by weight of cotton, printed
5.2	0/0/0	0	0	0	0	0	0	0//0	0/0/0			0/0/	Woven fabrics of cotton, oxford weave w≤200 g/m^2, containing≥85% by weight of cotton, printed
5.2	0/0/0	0	0	0	0	0	0	0//0	0/0/0			0/0/	Other woven fabrics of cotton, w≤200g/m^2, containing≥85% by weight of cotton, printed
													Woven fabrics of cotton, containing 85% or more by weight of cotton, weighing more than 200 g/m^2:
													-Unbleached:
	5/0/0	0	7	0	0		0	0//0	0/0/			0/0/0	--Plain weave
5.2	0/0/0	0	0	0	0	0	0	0/0/0	0/0/			0/0/	--3-thread or 4-thread twill, including cross twill
	0/0/0	0	0	0	0	0	0	0/0/0	0/0/			0/0/0	--Other fabrics
													-Bleached:
	0/0/0	0	0	3.6	0	0	0	0/0/0	0/0/			0/0/0	--Plain weave
	0/0/0	0	0	3.6	0	0	0	0/0/0	0/0/			0/0/	--3-thread or 4-thread twill, including cross twill
	0/0/0	0	0	3.6	0	0	0	0/0/0	0/0/			0/0/	--Other fabrics
													-Dyed:
													--Plain weave
5.2	0/0/0	0	0	0	0	0	0	0/0/0	0/0/0		0/0/0	0/0/0	Handwoven cloth of cotton, w > 200g/m^2, containing ≥ 85% by weight of cotton, dyed
5.2	0/0/0	0	0	0	0	0	0	0/0/0	0/0/0		0/0/0	0/0/0	Poplin and fine plain cloth of cotton, w>200g/m^2, containing≥85% by weight of cotton, dyed
5.2	0/0/0	0	0	0	0	0	0	0/0/0	0/0/0		0/0/0	0/0/0	Plain cloth of cotton, w>200g/m^2, containing≥85% by weight of cotton, dyed
5.2	0/0/0	0	0	0	0	0	0	0/0/0	0/0/0		0/0/0	0/0/0	Woven canvas of cotton, plain weave, w>200 g/m^2, containing≥85% by weight of cotton, dyed
5.2	0/0/0	0	0	0	0	0	0	0/0/0	0/0/0		0/0/0	0/0/0	--3-thread or 4-thread twill, including cross twill
													--Other fabrics
5.2	0/0/0	0	0	0	0	0	0	0/0/0	0/0/0		0/0/0	0/0/0	Other woven fabrics of cotton, satin weave, w>200g/m^2, containing≥85% by weight of cotton, dyed
5.2	0/0/0	0	0	0	0	0	0	0/0/0	0/0/0		0/0/0	0/0/0	Other woven fabrics of cotton, twill weave, w>200g/m^2, containing≥85% by weight of cotton, dyed
5.2	0/0/0	0	0	0	0	0	0	0/0/0	0/0/0		0/0/0	0/0/0	Other woren canvas of cotton, w>200g/m^2, containing≥85% by weight of cotton, dyed
5.2	0/0/0	0	0	0	0	0	0	0/0/0	0/0/0		0/0/0	0/0/0	Other woven fabrics of cotton, w>200g/m^2, containing≥85% by weight of cotton, dyed
													-Of yarns of different colours:
													--Plain weave
	0/0/0	0	0	0	0	0	0	0/0/0	0/0/0			0/0/	Handwoven cloth of cotton, w > 200g/m^2 containing ≥ 85% by weight of cotton, of yarns of different colours
	0/0/0	0	0	0	0	0	0	0/0/0	0/0/0			0/0/	Woven fabrics of cotton, plain weave, w>200g/m^2, containing≥85% by weight of cotton, of yarns of different colours
													--Denim
5.2	0/0/0	0	0	0	0	0	0	0/0/0	0/0/0		0/0/0	0/0/0	Blue denim of cotton, w>200g/m^2, containing≥85% by weight of cotton, of yarns of different colours
5.2	0/0/0	0	0	0	0	0	0	0/0/0	0/0/0		0/0/0	0/0/0	Other denim of cotton, w>200g/m^2, containing≥85% by weight of cotton, of yarns of different colours
5.2	0/0/0	0	0	0	0	0	0	0//0	0/0/			0/0/	--Other fabrics of 3-thread or 4-thread twill, including cross twill
													--Other fabrics
	0/0/0	0	6	0	0	0	0	0/0/0	0/0/			0/0/	Other woven fabrics of cotton, jacquad weave, w>200g/m^2, containing≥85% by weight of cotton, of yarns of different colours
	0/0/0	0	6	0	0	0	0	0/0/0	0/0/			0/0/	Other woven fabrics of cotton, w>200g/m^2, containing≥85% by weight of cotton, of yarns of different colours
													-Printed:

税则号列	货品名称〔CIQ扩展编码及品名—T2表示见附表2〕	最惠(%)	暂定税率	普通	增值/消费	出口退税	计量单位	监管条件	检验检疫	特殊证件对美关税
5209.5100	--平纹机织物									
5209.5100 10	印花全棉手工织布(指每平方米重＞200克,含棉量≥85%)〔999〕	8		70	13/	13	米/千克			/33
5209.5100 91	印花全棉平纹府绸及细平布(指每平方米重＞200克,含棉量≥85%)〔999〕	8		70	13/	13	米/千克			/33
5209.5100 92	印花全棉平纹机织平布(指每平方米重＞200克,含棉量≥85%)〔999〕	8		70	13/	13	米/千克			/33
5209.5100 93	印花全棉平纹机织帆布(指每平方米重＞200克,含棉量≥85%)〔999〕	8		70	13/	13	米/千克			/33
5209.5200	--三线或四线斜纹机织物,包括双面斜纹机织物〔999〕	8		70	13/	13	米/千克			/
5209.5900	--其他机织物									
5209.5900 10	印花的其他全棉机织缎布(指每平方米重＞200克,含棉量≥85%)〔999〕	8		70	13/	13	米/千克			/33
5209.5900 20	印花的其他全棉机织斜纹布(指每平方米重＞200克,含棉量≥85%)〔999〕	8		70	13/	13	米/千克			/33
5209.5900 30	印花的其他全棉机织帆布(指每平方米重＞200克,含棉量≥85%)〔999〕	8		70	13/	13	米/千克			/33
5209.5900 90	印花的其他全棉机织物(指每平方米重＞200克,含棉量≥85%)〔999〕	8		70	13/	13	米/千克			/33
52.10	**棉机织物,按重量计含棉量在85%以下,主要或仅与化学纤维混纺,每平方米重量不超过200克:**									
	-未漂白:									
5210.1100	--平纹机织物									
5210.1100 11	未漂白与聚酯短纤混纺的棉制府绸(指每平方米重≤200克,含棉量＜85%,含平细布)〔999〕	8	6	90	13/	13	米/千克			/31
5210.1100 12	未漂白与聚酯短纤混纺棉机织平布(指每平方米重≤200克,68号及以下,含棉量＜85%)〔999〕	8	6	90	13/	13	米/千克			/31
5210.1100 13	未漂白与聚酯短纤混纺棉奶酪布(指每平方米重≤200克,含棉量＜85%)〔999〕	8	6	90	13/	13	米/千克			/31
5210.1100 14	未漂白与聚酯短纤混纺棉印染用布(指每平方米重≤200克,43—68号,含棉量＜85%)〔999〕	8	6	90	13/	13	米/千克			/31
5210.1100 15	未漂白与聚酯短纤混纺棉巴里纱(指每平方米重≤200克,69号及以上,含棉量＜85%,含薄细布)〔999〕	8	6	90	13/	13	米/千克			/31
5210.1100 91	未漂白与其他化学纤维混纺棉府绸(指每平方米重≤200克,含棉量＜85%,含细平布)〔999〕	8	6	90	13/	13	米/千克			/31
5210.1100 92	未漂白与其他化学纤维混纺棉机织平布(指每平方米重≤200克,≤68号,含棉量＜85%)〔999〕	8	6	90	13/	13	米/千克			/31
5210.1100 93	未漂白与其他化学纤维混纺棉奶酪布(指每平方米重≤200克,含棉量＜85%)〔999〕	8	6	90	13/	13	米/千克			/31
5210.1100 94	未漂白与其他化学纤维混纺棉印染用布(指每平方米重≤200克,43—68号,含棉量＜85%)〔999〕	8	6	90	13/	13	米/千克			/31
5210.1100 95	未漂白与其他化学纤维混纺棉巴里纱(指每平方米重≤200克,69号及以上,含棉量＜85%,含薄细布)〔999〕	8	6	90	13/	13	米/千克			/31
	--其他机织物:									
5210.1910	---三线或四线斜纹机织物,包括双面斜纹机织物〔999〕	8		90	13/	13	米/千克			/
5210.1990	---其他									
5210.1990 11	其他未漂白与聚酯短纤混纺的缎布(每平方米重≤200克,含棉量＜85%)〔999〕	8	6	90	13/	13	米/千克			/31
5210.1990 12	其他未漂白与聚酯短纤混纺斜纹布(每平方米重≤200克,含棉量＜85%)〔999〕	8	6	90	13/	13	米/千克			/31
5210.1990 13	其他未漂白与聚酯短纤混纺牛津布(每平方米重≤200克,含棉量＜85%)〔999〕	8	6	90	13/	13	米/千克			/31
5210.1990 19	其他未漂白与聚酯短纤混纺棉布(每平方米重≤200克,含棉量＜85%)〔999〕	8	6	90	13/	13	米/千克			/31

协定税率 %										特惠税率 %			
亚太5国	东/冰/格	巴基斯坦	韩国	瑞士	哥达	秘鲁	澳大利亚	新西/坡/智	港/澳/台	亚太2国	老/柬/缅	36/3/1	Article Description
													--Plain weave
5.2	0/0/0	0	0	0	0	0	0	0/0/0	0/0/			0/0/0	Handwoven cloth of cotton, w>200g/m^2, containing≥85% by weight of cotton, printed
5.2	0/0/0	0	0	0	0	0	0	0/0/0	0/0/			0/0/0	Poplin and fine plain cloth of cotton, w>200g/m^2, containing≥85% by weight of cotton, printed
5.2	0/0/0	0	0	0	0	0	0	0/0/0	0/0/			0/0/0	Plain cloth of cotton, w>200g/m^2, containing≥85% by weight of cotton, printed
5.2	0/0/0	0	0	0	0	0	0	0/0/0	0/0/			0/0/0	Woven canvas of cotton, plain weave, w>200g/m^2, containing≥85% by weight of cotton, printed
	0/0/0	0	0	0	0	0	0	0//0	0/0/			0/0/	--3-thread or 4-thread twill, including cross twill
													--Other fabrics
5.2	0/0/0	0	0	0	0	0	0	0//0	0/0/			0/0/0	Other woven fabrics of cotton, satin weave, w>200g/m^2, containing≥85% by weight of cotton, printed
5.2	0/0/0	0	0	0	0	0	0	0//0	0/0/			0/0/0	Other woven fabrics of cotton, twill weave, w>200g/m^2, containing≥85% by weight of cotton, printed
5.2	0/0/0	0	0	0	0	0	0	0//0	0/0/			0/0/0	Otver canvas of cotton, w>200g/m^2, containing≥85% by weight of cotton, printed
5.2	0/0/0	0	0	0	0	0	0	0//0	0/0/			0/0/0	Other woven fabrics of cotton, w>200g/m^2, containing≥85% by weight of cotton, printed
													Woven fabrics of cotton, containing less than 85% by weight of cotton, mixed mainly or solely with man-made fibres, weighing not more than 200 g/m^2:
													-Unbleached:
													--Plain weave
5.2	0/0/0	0	0	3.6	0	0	0	0/0/0	0/0/			0/0/0	Poplin and fine plain cloth of cotton, mixed with polyester staple fibres, w≤200g/m^2, containing<85% by weight of cotton, unbleached
5.2	0/0/0	0	0	3.6	0	0	0	0/0/0	0/0/			0/0/0	Plain cloth of cotton, mixed with polyester staple fibres, w≤200g/m^2, ≤No. 68, containing<85% by weight of cotton, unbleached
5.2	0/0/0	0	0	3.6	0	0	0	0/0/0	0/0/			0/0/0	Cheese cloth of cotton, plain weave, mixed with polyester staple fibres, w≤200g/m^2, containing<85% by weight of cotton, unbleached
5.2	0/0/0	0	0	3.6	0	0	0	0/0/0	0/0/			0/0/0	Cloth for printing and dying of cotton, plain weave, mixed with polyester staple fibres, w≤200g/m^2, No. 43～No. 68, containing<85% by weight of cotton, unbleached
5.2	0/0/0	0	0	3.6	0	0	0	0/0/0	0/0/			0/0/0	Voiles and swiss muslin of cotton, plain weave, mixed with polyester staple fibres, w≤200g/m^2, containing<85% by weight of cotton, unbleached
5.2	0/0/0	0	0	3.6	0	0	0	0/0/0	0/0/			0/0/0	Poplin and fine plain cloth of cotton, mixed with other man-made fibres, w≤200g/m^2, containing<85% by weight of cotton, unbleached
5.2	0/0/0	0	0	3.6	0	0	0	0/0/0	0/0/			0/0/0	Plain cloth of cotton, mixed with other man-made fibres, w≤200g/m^2, ≤No. 68, containing<85% by weight of cotton, unbleached
5.2	0/0/0	0	0	3.6	0	0	0	0/0/0	0/0/			0/0/0	Cheese cloth of cotton, plain weave, mixed with other man-made fibres, w≤200g/m^2, containing<85% by weight of cotton, unbleached
5.2	0/0/0	0	0	3.6	0	0	0	0/0/0	0/0/			0/0/0	Cloth for printing and dying of cotton, plain weave, mixed with other man-made fibres, w≤200g/m^2, No. 43～No. 68, containing<85% by weight of cotton, unbleached
5.2	0/0/0	0	0	3.6	0	0	0	0/0/0	0/0/			0/0/0	Voiles and swiss muslin of cotton, mixed with man-made fibres, w≤200g/m^2, containing <85% by weight of cotton, ≥No. 69, unbleached
													--Other fabrics:
4.8	0/0/0	0	0	3.6	0	0	0	0/0/0	0/0/			0/0/	---3-thread or 4-thread twill, including cross twill
													---Other
	0/0/0	0	0	3.6	0	0	0	0/0/0	0/0/			0/0/0	Other woven fabrics of cotton, satin weave, mixed with polyester staple fibres, w≤200g/m^2, containing<85% by weight of cotton, unbleached
	0/0/0	0	0	3.6	0	0	0	0/0/0	0/0/			0/0/0	Other woven fabrics of cotton, twill weave, mixed with polyester staple fibres, w≤200g/m^2, containing<85% by weight of cotton, unbleached
	0/0/0	0	0	3.6	0	0	0	0/0/0	0/0/			0/0/0	Other woven fabrics of cotton, oxford weave, mixed with polyester staple fibres, w≤200g/m^2, containing<85% by weight of cotton, unbleached
	0/0/0	0	0	3.6	0	0	0	0/0/0	0/0/			0/0/0	Other woven fabrics of cotton, mixed with polyester staple fibres, w≤200g/m^2, containing<85% by weight of cotton, unbleached

税则号列	货品名称〔CIQ扩展编码及品名—T2表示见附表2〕	最惠(%)	暂定税率	普通	增值/消费	出口退税	计量单位	监管条件	检验检疫	特殊证件对美关税
5210.1990 91	其他未漂白与其他化学纤维混纺缎布(每平方米重≤200克,含棉量＜85%)〔999〕	8	6	90	13/	13	米/千克			/31
5210.1990 92	其他未漂白与其他化学纤维混纺斜纹布(每平方米重≤200克,含棉量＜85%)〔999〕	8	6	90	13/	13	米/千克			/31
5210.1990 93	其他未漂白与其他化学纤维混纺的牛津布(每平方米重≤200克,含棉量＜85%)〔999〕	8	6	90	13/	13	米/千克			/31
5210.1990 99	其他未漂白与其他化学纤维混纺棉布(每平方米重≤200克,含棉量＜85%)〔999〕	8	6	90	13/	13	米/千克			/31
	-漂白:									
5210.2100	--平纹机织物〔999〕	8		90	13/	13	米/千克			/
	--其他机织物:									
5210.2910	---三线或四线斜纹机织物,包括双面斜纹机织物〔999〕	8		90	13/	13	米/千克			/
5210.2990	---其他〔999〕	8		90	13/	13	米/千克			/
	-染色:									
5210.3100	--平纹机织物〔999〕	8		90	13/	13	米/千克			/33
5210.3200	--三线或四线斜纹机织物,包括双面斜纹机织物〔999〕	8		90	13/	13	米/千克			/33
5210.3900	--其他机织物〔999〕	8		90	13/	13	米/千克			/33
	-色织:									
5210.4100	--平纹机织物〔999〕	8		90	13/	13	米/千克			/33
	--其他机织物:									
5210.4910	---三线或四线斜纹机织物,包括双面斜纹机织物〔999〕	8		90	13/	13	米/千克			/33
5210.4990	---其他〔999〕	8		90	13/	13	米/千克			/33
5210.5100	--平纹机织物〔999〕	8		90	13/	13	米/千克			/33
	--其他机织物:									
5210.5910	---三线或四线斜纹机织物,包括双面斜纹机织物〔999〕	8		90	13/	13	米/千克			/
5210.5990	---其他〔999〕	8		90	13/	13	米/千克			/33
52.11	**棉机织物,按重量计含棉量在85%以下,主要或仅与化学纤维混纺,每平方米重量超过200克:**									
	-未漂白:									
5211.1100	--平纹机织物									
5211.1100 11	未漂白与聚酯短纤混纺棉府绸(每平方米重＞200克,含棉量＜85%,含细平布)〔999〕	8	6	90	13/	13	米/千克			/31
5211.1100 12	未漂白与聚酯短纤混纺棉机织平布(每平方米重＞200克,含棉量＜85%)〔999〕	8	6	90	13/	13	米/千克			/31
5211.1100 19	未漂白与聚酯短纤混纺棉平纹帆布(每平方米重＞200克,含棉量＜85%)〔999〕	8	6	90	13/	13	米/千克			/31
5211.1100 91	未漂白与其他化学纤维混纺棉府绸(每平方米重＞200克,含棉量＜85%,含细平布)〔999〕	8	6	90	13/	13	米/千克			/31
5211.1100 92	未漂白与其他化学纤维混纺棉机织平布(每平方米重＞200克,含棉量＜85%)〔999〕	8	6	90	13/	13	米/千克			/31
5211.1100 99	未漂白与其他化学纤维混纺棉平纹帆布(每平方米重＞200克,含棉量＜85%)〔999〕	8	6	90	13/	13	米/千克			/31
5211.1200	--三线或四线斜纹机织物,包括双面斜纹机织物									
5211.1200 10	未漂白聚酯短纤混纺斜纹棉布(每平方米重＞200克,含棉量＜85%,三、四线斜纹布,双面斜纹布)〔999〕	8	6	90	13/	13	米/千克			/31
5211.1200 90	未漂白其他化学纤维混纺斜纹棉布(每平方米重＞200克,含棉量＜85%,三、四线斜纹布,双面斜纹布)〔999〕	8	6	90	13/	13	米/千克			/31
5211.1900	--其他机织物〔999〕	8		90	13/	13	米/千克			/
5211.2000	-漂白〔999〕	8		90	13/	13	米/千克			/33
	-染色:									
5211.3100	--平纹机织物〔999〕	8		90	13/	13	米/千克			/33
5211.3200	--三线或四线斜纹机织物,包括双面斜纹机织物〔999〕	8		90	13/	13	米/千克			/33
5211.3900	--其他机织物〔999〕	8		90	13/	13	米/千克			/33
	-色织:									
5211.4100	--平纹机织物〔999〕	8		90	13/	13	米/千克			/33
5211.4200	--粗斜纹布(劳动布)									

协定税率 %										特惠税率 %			Article Description
亚太5国	东/冰/格	巴基斯坦	韩国	瑞士	哥达	秘鲁	澳大利亚	新西/坡/智	港/澳/台	亚太2国	老/柬/缅	36/3/1	
	0/0/0	0	0	3.6	0	0	0	0/0/0	0/0/			0/0/0	Other woven of cotton, stain weave, mixed with other man-made fibres, w ≤ 200g/m², containing < 85% by weight of cotton, unbleached
	0/0/0	0	0	3.6	0	0	0	0/0/0	0/0/			0/0/0	Other woven fabrics of cotton, twill weave, mixed with other man-made fibres, w≤200 g/m², containing<85% by weight of cotton, unbleached
	0/0/0	0	0	3.6	0	0	0	0/0/0	0/0/			0/0/0	Other woven fabrics of cotton, oxford weave, mixed with other man-made fibres, w≤200g/m², by weight of cotton, unbleached
	0/0/0	0	0	3.6	0	0	0	0/0/0	0/0/			0/0/0	Other woven fabrics of cotton, mixed with other man-made fibres. w ≤200g/m², containing<85% by weight of cotton, unbleached
													-Bleached:
	0/0/0	0	5.6	4.2	0	0	0	0/0/0	0/0/			0/0/0	--Plain weave
													--Other fabrics:
	0/0/0	0	5.6	4.2	0	0	0	0/0/0	0/0/			0/0/	---3-thread or 4-thread twill, including cross twill
	0/0/0	0	5.6	4.2	0	0	0	0/0/0	0/0/			0/0/	---Other
													-Dyed:
5.2	0/0/0	0	7	0	0	0	0	0/0/0	0/0/0			0/0/0	--Plain weave
5.2	0/0/0	0	0	0	0	0	0	0/0/0	0/0/			0/0/	--3-thread or 4-thread twill, including cross twill
5.2	0/0/0	0	6	0	0	0	0	0/0/0	0/0/0			0/0/	--Other fabrics
													-Of yarns of different colours:
	0/0/0	0	0	0	0	0	0	0/0/0	0/0/0			0/0/	--Plain weave
													--Other fabrics:
	0/0/0	0	0	0	0	0	0	0/0/0	0/0/			0/0/	---3-thread or 4-thread twill, including cross twill, including double twill
	0/0/0	0	0	0	0	0	0	0/0/0	0/0/0			0/0/0	---Other
	0/0/0	0	0	0	0	0	0	0//0	0/0/			0/0/0	--Plain weave
													--Other fabrics:
	0/0/0	0	0	0	0	0	0	0//0	0/0/			0/0/	---3-thread or 4-thread twill, including cross twill
	0/0/0	0	0	0	0	0	0	0//0	0/0/			0/0/0	---Other
													Woven fabrics of cotton, containing less than 85% by weight of cotton, mixed mainly or solely with man-made fibres, weighing more than 200 g/m²:
													-Unbleached:
													--Plain weave
	0/0/0	0	7.2	3.6	0	0	0	0/0/0	0/0/			0/0/0	Poplin and fine plain cloth of cotton, mixed with polyester staple fibres, w > 200g/m², containing < 85% by weight of cotton, unbleached
	0/0/0	0	7.2	3.6	0	0	0	0/0/0	0/0/			0/0/0	Plain cloth of cotton, mixed with polyester staple fibres, w>200g/m², containing<85% by weight of cotton, unbleached
	0/0/0	0	7.2	3.6	0	0	0	0/0/0	0/0/			0/0/0	Canvas of cotton, mixed with polyester staple fibres, plain weave, w>200g/m², containing<85% by weight of cotton, unbleached
	0/0/0	0	7.2	3.6	0	0	0	0/0/0	0/0/			0/0/0	Poplin and fine plain cloth of cotton, mixed with other man-made fibres, w > 200g/m², containing < 85% by weight of cotton, unbleached
	0/0/0	0	7.2	3.6	0	0	0	0/0/0	0/0/			0/0/0	Plain cloth of cotton, mixed with other man-made fibres, w>200g/m², containing<85% by weight of cotton, unbleached
	0/0/0	0	7.2	3.6	0	0	0	0/0/0	0/0/			0/0/0	Canvas of cotton, mixed with other man-made fibres, plain weave, w>200g/m², containing<85% by weight of cotton, unbleached
													--3-thread or 4-thread twill, including cross twill
	0/0/0	0	0	3.6	0	0	0	0/0/0	0/0/			0/0/0	Woven fabrics of cotton, twill weave (3-or 4-thread), mixed with polyester staple fibres, w>200g/m², containing<85% by weight of cotton, unbleached
	0/0/0	0	0	3.6	0	0	0	0/0/0	0/0/			0/0/0	Woven fabrics of cotton, twill weave (3-or 4-thread), mixed with other man-made fibres, w>200g/m², containing<85% by weight of cotton, unbleached
	0/0/0	0	0	3.6	0	0	0	0/0/0	0/0/			0/0/0	--Other fabrics
	0/0/0	0	5.6	4.2	0	0	0	0/0/0	0/0/			0/0/	-Bleached
													-Dyed:
6.8	0/0/0	0	8.5	0	0	0	0	0/0/0	0/0/			0/0/0	--Plain weave
5.2	0/0/0	0	0	0	0	0	0	0/0/0	0/0/			0/0/	--3-thread or 4-thread twill, including cross twill
5.2	0/0/0	0	6	0	0	0	0	0/0/0	0/0/0			0/0/0	--Other fabrics
													-Of yarns of different colours:
	0/0/0	0	0	0	0	0	0	0//0	0/0/			0/0/	--Plain weave
													--Denim

税则号列	货品名称〔CIQ扩展编码及品名—T2表示见附表2〕	最惠(%)	暂定税率	普通	增值/消费	出口退税	计量单位	监管条件	检验检疫	特殊证件对美关税
5211.4200 10	色织与化学纤维混纺蓝色粗斜纹棉布(每平方米重超过200克,含棉量＜85%)〔999〕	8		90	13/	13	米/千克			/33
5211.4200 90	色织与化学纤维混纺非蓝色粗斜纹棉布(每平方米重超过200克,含棉量＜85%)〔999〕	8		90	13/	13	米/千克			/33
5211.4300	--其他三线或四线斜纹机织物,包括双面斜纹机织物〔999〕	8		90	13/	13	米/千克			/33
5211.4900	--其他机织物〔999〕	8		90	13/	13	米/千克			/33
	-印花:									
5211.5100	--平纹机织物〔999〕	8		90	13/	13	米/千克			/33
5211.5200	--三线或四线斜纹机织物,包括双面斜纹机织物〔999〕	8		90	13/	13	米/千克			/28
5211.5900	--其他机织物〔999〕	8		90	13/	13	米/千克			/18
52.12	**其他棉机织物:**									
	-每平方米重量不超过200克:									
5212.1100	--未漂白〔999〕	8		80	13/	13	米/千克			/
5212.1200	--漂白〔999〕	8		80	13/	13	米/千克			/18
5212.1300	--染色〔999〕	8		80	13/	13	米/千克			/33
5212.1400	--色织〔999〕	8		80	13/	13	米/千克			/33
5212.1500	--印花〔999〕	8		80	13/	13	米/千克			/33
	-每平方米重量超过200克:									
5212.2100	--未漂白									
5212.2100 11	未漂白其他混纺棉布(每平方米重＞200克,与36%及以上精梳羊毛/动物细毛混纺)〔999〕	8	6	80	13/	13	米/千克			/31
5212.2100 19	未漂白其他混纺棉布(每平方米重＞200克,与36%及以下精梳羊毛/动物细毛混纺)〔999〕	8	6	80	13/	13	米/千克			/31
5212.2100 21	未漂白其他混纺棉布(每平方米重＞200克,与36%及以上其他羊毛/动物细毛混纺)〔999〕	8	6	80	13/	13	米/千克			/31
5212.2100 29	未漂白其他混纺棉布(每平方米重＞200克,与36%及以下其他羊毛/动物细毛混纺)〔999〕	8	6	80	13/	13	米/千克			/31
5212.2100 30	未漂白其他混纺府绸及平细布(每平方米重＞200克,与化学纤维以外其他纤维混纺)〔999〕	8	6	80	13/	13	米/千克			/31
5212.2100 40	未漂白其他混纺棉机织平布(每平方米重＞200克,与化学纤维以外其他纤维混纺)〔999〕	8	6	80	13/	13	米/千克			/31
5212.2100 50	未漂白其他混纺棉帆布(每平方米重＞200克,与化学纤维以外其他纤维混纺)〔999〕	8	6	80	13/	13	米/千克			/31
5212.2100 60	未漂白其他混纺棉缎布(每平方米重＞200克,与化学纤维以外其他纤维混纺)〔999〕	8	6	80	13/	13	米/千克			/31
5212.2100 70	未漂白其他混纺斜纹棉布(每平方米重＞200克,与化学纤维以外其他纤维混纺)〔999〕	8	6	80	13/	13	米/千克			/31
5212.2100 90	未漂白其他混纺棉布(每平方米重＞200克,与化学纤维以外其他纤维混纺)〔999〕	8	6	80	13/	13	米/千克			/31
5212.2200	--漂白〔999〕	8		80	13/	13	米/千克			/28
5212.2300	--染色〔999〕	8		80	13/	13	米/千克			/33
5212.2400	--色织〔999〕	8		80	13/	13	米/千克			/33
5212.2500	--印花〔999〕	8		80	13/	13	米/千克			/33

协定税率 %										特惠税率 %			
亚太5国	东/冰/格	巴基斯坦	韩国	瑞士	哥达	秘鲁	澳大利亚	新西/坡/智	港/澳/台	亚太2国	老/柬/缅	36/3/1	Article Description
	0/0/0	0	0	0	0	0	0	0/0/0	0/0/			0/0/	Blue denim of cotton, mixed with other man-made fibres, w>200g/m², containing<85% by weight of cotton, of yarns of different colours
	0/0/0	0	0	0	0	0	0	0/0/0	0/0/			0/0/	Denim of cotton, other than blue, w>200g/m², containing<85% by weight of cotton, of yarns of different colours
	0/0/0	0	0	0	0	0	0	0//0	0/0/			0/0/	--Other fabrics of 3-thread or 4-thread twill, including cross twill
	0/0/0	0	6	0	0	0	0	0/0/0	0/0/			0/0/	--Other fabrics
													-Printed:
	0/0/0	0	0	0	0	0	0	0//0	0/0/			0/0/	--Plain weave
	0/0/0	0	0	0	0	0	0	0//0	0/0/			0/0/	--3-thread or 4-thread twill, including cross twill, including double twill
5.2	0/0/0	0	0	0	0	0	0	0//0	0/0/			0/0/	--Other fabrics
													Other woven fabrics of cotton:
													-Weighing not more than 200 g/m²:
	0/0/0	0	0	3.6	0	0	0	0/0/0	0/0/			0/0/0	--Unbleached
	0/0/0	0	5.6	4.2	0	0	0	0/0/0	0/0/			0/0/	--Bleached
	0/0/0	0	0	0	0	0	0	0//0	0/0/			0/0/	--Dyed
	0/0/0	0	0	0	0	0	0	0//0	0/0/			0/0/	--Of yarns of different colours
	0/0/0	0	0	0	0	0	0	0//0	0/0/			0/0/	--Printed
													-Weighing more than 200 g/m²:
													--Unbleached
	0/0/0	0	0	3.6	0	0	0	0/0/0	0/0/			0/0/0	Other woven fabrics of cotton, mixed, containing≥36% by weight of combed wool or fine animal hair, w>200g/m², unbleached
	0/0/0	0	0	3.6	0	0	0	0/0/0	0/0/			0/0/0	Other woven fabrics of cotton, mixed, containing<36% by weight of combed wool or fine animal hair, w>200g/m², unbleached
	0/0/0	0	0	3.6	0	0	0	0/0/0	0/0/			0/0/0	Other woven fabrics of cotton, mixed, containing≥36% by weight of wool or fine animal hair, w>200g/m², unbleached
	0/0/0	0	0	3.6	0	0	0	0/0/0	0/0/			0/0/0	Other woven fabrics of cotton, mixed, containing<36% by weight of wool or fine animal hair, w>200g/m², unbleached
	0/0/0	0	0	3.6	0	0	0	0/0/0	0/0/			0/0/0	Poplin and fine plain cloth, mixed with other fibres, other than man-made fibres, w>200g/m², unbleached
	0/0/0	0	0	3.6	0	0	0	0/0/0	0/0/			0/0/0	Plain cloth of cotton, mixed with other fibres, other than man-made fibres, w>200g/m², unbleached
	0/0/0	0	0	3.6	0	0	0	0/0/0	0/0/			0/0/0	Canvas of cotton, mixed with other fibres, other than man-made fibres, w>200g/m², unbleached
	0/0/0	0	0	3.6	0	0	0	0/0/0	0/0/			0/0/0	Other woven fabrics of cotton, satin weave, mixed with other fibres, other than man-made fibres, w>200g/m², unbleached
	0/0/0	0	0	3.6	0	0	0	0/0/0	0/0/			0/0/0	Other woven fabrics of cotton, twill weave, mixed with other fibres, other than man-made fibres, w>200g/m², unbleached
	0/0/0	0	0	3.6	0	0	0	0/0/0	0/0/			0/0/0	Other woven fabrics of cotton, mixed with other fibres, other than man-made fibres, w>200g/m², unbleached
	0/0/0	0	5.6	4.2	0	0	0	0/0/0	0/0/			0/0/	--Bleached
	0/0/0	0	0	0	0	0	0	0//0	0/0/			0/0/	--Dyed
	0/0/0	0	0	0	0	0	0	0//0	0/0/			0/0/	--Of yarns of different colours
	0/0/0	0	0	0	0	0	0	0//0	0/0/			0/0/0	--Printed

第五十三章
其他植物纺织纤维;纸纱线及其机织物

税则号列	货品名称〔CIQ扩展编码及品名一T2表示见附表2〕	最惠(%)	暂定税率	普通	增值/消费	出口退税	计量单位	监管条件	检验检疫	特殊证件对美关税
53.01	**亚麻,生的或经加工但未纺制的;亚麻短纤及废麻(包括废麻纱线及回收纤维):**									
5301.1000	-生的或经沤制的亚麻〔101亚麻,102麻纤维〕	6		30	13/	9	千克	AB	PQ	/16
	-破开、打成、栉梳或经其他加工但未纺制的亚麻:									
5301.2100	--破开的或打成的〔101亚麻,102麻纤维〕	6	1	30	13/	9	千克	AB	PQ	/11
5301.2900	--其他〔101亚麻,102麻纤维〕	6		30	13/	9	千克	AB	PQ	/16
5301.3000	-亚麻短纤及废麻〔999〕	6	1	30	13/	9	千克	AB	PQ	/11
53.02	**大麻,生的或经加工但未纺制的;大麻短纤及废麻(包括废麻纱线及回收纤维):**									
5302.1000	-生的或经沤制的大麻〔101麻,102麻纤维〕	6		30	13/	9	千克	AB	PQ	/16
5302.9000	-其他〔999〕	6		30	13/	9	千克	AB	PQ	/16
53.03	**黄麻及其他纺织用韧皮纤维(不包括亚麻、大麻及苎麻),生的或经加工但未纺制的;上述纤维的短纤及废麻(包括废纱线及回收纤维):**									
5303.1000	-生的或经沤制的黄麻及其他纺织用韧皮纤维〔101麻,102麻纤维〕	5		20	9/	9	千克	AB	PQ	/
5303.9000	-其他〔999〕	5		30	13/	9	千克	AB	PQ	/
53.05	**椰壳纤维、蕉麻(马尼拉麻)、苎麻及其他税目未列名的纺织用植物纤维,生的或经加工但未纺制的;上述纤维的短纤、落麻及废料(包括废纱线及回收纤维):**									
	---苎麻:									
5305.0011	----生的〔101麻,102麻纤维〕	5		30	13/	9	千克	AB	PQ	/
5305.0012	----经加工但未纺制的〔101麻,102麻纤维〕	5		30	13/	9	千克	AB	PQ	/
5305.0013	----短纤及废麻〔999〕	5		30	13/	9	千克	AB	PQ	/
5305.0019	----其他〔999〕	5		20	13/	9	千克	AB	PQ	/
5305.0020	---蕉麻〔999〕	3		20	13/	9	千克	AB	PQ	/
	---其他:									
5305.0091	----西沙尔麻及其他纺织用龙舌兰纤维〔999〕	5		30	13/	9	千克	AB	PQ	/
5305.0092	----椰壳纤维〔999〕	5		30	13/	6	千克	AB	PQ	/
5305.0099	----其他〔999〕	5		30	13/	9	千克	AB	PQ	/
53.06	**亚麻纱线:**									
5306.1000	-单纱〔999〕	5		50	13/	13	千克			/
5306.2000	-多股纱线或缆线〔101麻纱线,102绳、索、缆〕	5		50	13/	13	千克			/30
53.07	**黄麻纱线或税目53.03的其他纺织用韧皮纤维纱线:**									
5307.1000	-单纱〔999〕	5		35	13/	13	千克			/
5307.2000	-多股纱线或缆线〔101麻纱线,102绳、索、缆〕	5		35	13/	13	千克			/
53.08	**其他植物纺织纤维纱线;纸纱线:**									
5308.1000	-椰壳纤维纱线〔999〕	5		45	13/	13	千克			/
5308.2000	-大麻纱线〔999〕	5		45	13/	13	千克			/
	-其他:									
	---苎麻纱线:									
5308.9011	----按重量计苎麻含量在85%及以上的未漂白或漂白纱线〔999〕	5		50	13/	13	千克			/
5308.9012	----按重量计苎麻含量在85%及以上的色纱线〔999〕	5		50	13/	13	千克			/
5308.9013	----按重量计苎麻含量在85%以下的未漂白或漂白纱线〔999〕	5		50	13/	13	千克			/
5308.9014	----按重量计苎麻含量在85%以下的色纱线〔999〕	5		50	13/	13	千克			/
	---其他:									
5308.9091	----纸纱线〔999〕	5		70	13/	13	千克			/
5308.9099	----其他〔999〕	5		45	13/	13	千克			/
53.09	**亚麻机织物:**									
	-按重量计亚麻含量在85%及以上:									
	--未漂白或漂白:									
5309.1110	---未漂白〔999〕	8		80	13/	13	米/千克			/33
5309.1120	---漂白〔999〕	8		80	13/	13	米/千克			/
5309.1900	--其他〔999〕	8		80	13/	13	米/千克			/33
	-按重量计亚麻含量在85%以下:									
	--未漂白或漂白:									
5309.2110	---未漂白〔101棉混纺坯布,102亚麻混纺织物〕	8		80	13/	13	米/千克			/33

Chapter 53
Other vegetable textile fibres; paper yarn and woven fabrics of paper yarn

协定税率 %										特惠税率 %			
亚太5国	东/冰/格	巴基斯坦	韩国	瑞士	哥达	秘鲁	澳大利亚	新西/坡/智	港/澳/台	亚太2国	老/柬/缅	36/3/1	Article Description
													Flax, raw or processed but not spun; flax tow and waste (including yarn waste and garnetted stock):
	0/0/0	0	0	0	0	0	0	0//0	0/0/			0/0/0	-Flax, raw or retted
													-Flax, broken, scutched, hackled or otherwise processed, but not spun:
	0/0/0	0	0	0	0	0	0	0//0	0/0/			0/0/0	--Broken or scutched
	0/0/0	0	0	0	0	0	0	0//0	0/0/			0/0/0	--Other
	0/0/0	0	0	0	0	0	0	0//0	0/0/			0/0/0	-Flax tow and waste
													True hemp (*Cannabis sativa L*), raw or processed but not spun; tow and waste of true hemp (including yarn waste and garnetted stock):
	0/0/0	0	0	0	0	0	0	0//0	0/0/			0/0/0	-True hemp, raw or retted
	0/0/0	0	0	0	0	0	0	0//0	0/0/			0/0/0	-Other
													Jute and other textile bast fibres (excluding flax, true hemp and ramie), raw or processed but not spun; tow and waste of these fibres (including yarn waste and garnetted stock):
	0/0/0	0	0	0	0	0	0	0//0	0/0/	0	0/0/0	0/0/0	-Jute and other textile bast fibres, raw or retted
	0/0/0	0	0	0	0	0	0	0//0	0/0/		0/0/0	0/0/0	-Other
													Coconut, abaca (Manila hemp or *Musatextilis Nee*), ramie and other vegetable textile fibres, not elsewhere specified or included, raw or processed but not spun; tow, noils and waste of these fibres (including yarn waste and garnetted stock):
													---Ramie:
	0/0/0	0	0	0	0	0	0	0//0	0/0/			0/0/0	----Raw
3	0/0/0	0	0	0	0	0	0	0//0	0/0/			0/0/0	----Processed but not spun
3	0/0/0	0	0	0	0	0	0	0//0	0/0/			0/0/0	----Tow and waste
	0/0/0	0	0	0	0	0	0	0//0	0/0/			0/0/0	----Other
1.8	0/0/0	0	0	0	0	0	0	0//0	0/0/			0/0/0	---Of Abaca
													---Other:
3	0/0/0	0	0	0	0	0	0	0//0	0/0/			0/0/0	----Sisal and other textile fabircs of the genus Agave
3.3	0/0/0	0	0	0	0	0	0	0//0	0/0/		0/0/0	0/0/0	----of Coconut(coir)
3	0/0/0	0	0	0	0	0	0	0//0	0/0/			0/0/0	----Other
													Flax yarn:
	0/0/0	0	0	0	0	0	0	0//0	0/0/			0/0/0	-Single
	0/0/0	4.5	0	0	0	0	0	0//0	0/0/			0/0/0	-Multiple (folded) or cabled
													Yarn of jute or of other textile bast fibres of heading No. 53.03:
	0/0/0	0	0	0	0	0	0	0//0	0/0/	2.5	/0/	0/0/0	-Single
	0/0/0	0	0	0	0	0	0	0//0	0/0/	2.5	/0/	0/0/0	-Multiple (folded) or cabled
													Yarn of other vegetable textile fibres; paper yarn:
	0/0/0	0	0	0	0	0	0	0//0	0/0/			0/0/0	-Coir yarn
	0/0/0	0	0	0	0	0	0	0//0	0/0/			0/0/0	-True hemp yarn
													-Other:
													---Ramie yarn:
3.5	0/0/0	0	0	0	0	0	0	0//0	0/0/			0/0/0	----Containing 85% or more by weight of ramie, unbleached or bleached yarn
3.5	0/0/0	0	0	0	0	0	0	0//0	0/0/			0/0/0	----Containing 85% or more by weight of ramie, coloured yarn
3.5	0/0/0	0	0	0	0	0	0	0//0	0/0/			0/0/0	----Containing less than 85% by weight of ramie, unbleached or bleached yarn
3.5	0/0/0	0	0	0	0	0	0	0//0	0/0/			0/0/0	----Containing less than 85% by weight of coloured yarn
													---Other:
3.5	0/0/0	0	0	0	0	0	0	0//0	0/0/			0/0/0	----Paper yarn
	0/0/0	0	0	0	0	0	0	0//0	0/0/			0/0/0	----Other
													Woven fabrics of flax:
													-Containing 85% or more by weight of flax:
													--Unbleached or bleached:
	0/0/0	0	0	0	0	0	0	0//0	0/0/			0/0/0	---Unbleached
	0/0/0	0	0	0	0	0	0	0//0	0/0/			0/0/0	---Bleached
5.2	0/0/0	0	0	0	0	0	0	0//0	0/0/			0/0/0	--Other
													-Containing less than 85% by weight of flax:
													--Unbleached or bleached:
	0/0/0	0	0	0	0	0	0	0//0	0/0/			0/0/0	---Unbleached

税则号列	货品名称〔CIQ扩展编码及品名—T2表示见附表2〕	最惠(%)	暂定税率	普通	增值/消费	出口退税	计量单位	监管条件	检验检疫	特殊证件对美关税
5309.2120	---漂白〔101 漂白棉混纺布,102 亚麻混纺织物〕	8		80	13/	13	米/千克			/
5309.2900	--其他〔999〕	8		80	13/	13	米/千克			/33
53.10	**黄麻或税目53.03的其他纺织用韧皮纤维机织物:**									
5310.1000	-未漂白〔999〕	8		40	13/	13	米/千克			/
5310.9000	-其他〔999〕	8		40	13/	13	米/千克			/
53.11	**其他纺织用植物纤维机织物;纸纱线机织物:**									
	---苎麻的:									
5311.0012	----按重量计苎麻含量在85%及以上的未漂白机织物〔999〕	8		80	13/	13	米/千克			/
5311.0013	----按重量计苎麻含量在85%及以上的其他机织物〔999〕	8		80	13/	13	米/千克			/
5311.0014	----按重量计苎麻含量在85%以下的未漂白机织物〔101 棉混纺坯布,102 苎麻混纺织物,103 其他麻织物〕	8		80	13/	13	米/千克			/
5311.0015	----按重量计苎麻含量在85%以下的其他机织物〔101 苎麻混纺织物,102 其他麻织物〕	8		80	13/	13	米/千克			/
5311.0020	---纸纱线的〔999〕	8		90	13/	13	米/千克			/
5311.0030	---大麻的〔999〕	8		50	13/	13	米/千克			/
5311.0090	---其他〔999〕	8		50	13/	13	米/千克			/

协定税率 %										特惠税率 %			
亚太5国	东/冰/格	巴基斯坦	韩国	瑞士	哥达	秘鲁	澳大利亚	新西/坡/智	港/澳/台	亚太2国	老/柬/缅	36/3/1	Article Description
	0/0/0	0	0	0	0	0	0	0//0	0/0/			0/0/0	---Bleached
5.2	0/0/0	0	0	0	0	0	0	0//0	0/0/			0/0/0	--Other
													Woven fabrics of jute or of other textilebast fibres of heading No. 53. 03:
	0/0/0	4.5	0	0	0	0	0	0//0	0/0/	4	/0/	0/0/0	-Unbleached
	0/0/0	4.5	0	0	0	0	0	0//0	0/0/	4	/0/	0/0/0	-Other
													Woven fabrics of other vegetable textile fibres; woven fabrics of paper yarn:
													---Of ramie:
	0/0/0	4.5	0	0	0	0	0	0//0	0/0/			0/0/0	----Containing 85% or more by weight of ramie, unbleached woven fabrics
	0/0/0	6	0	3.6	0	0	0	0/0/0	0/0/			0/0/0	----Containing 85% or more by weight of ramie, other woven fabrics
4.8	0/0/0	4.5	0	0	0	0	0	0//0	0/0/			0/0/0	----Containing less than 85% by weight of ramie, unbleached woven fabrics
	0/0/0	6	0	3.6	0	0	0	0/0/0	0/0/			0/0/	----Containing less than 85% by weight of ramie, other woven fabrics
4.8	0/0/0	4.5	0	0	0	0	0	0//0	0/0/			0/0/0	---Of paper yarn
5.2	0/0/0	4.5	0	0	0	0	0	0//0	0/0/			0/0/0	---Of true hemp
5.2	0/0/0	4.5	0	0	0	0	0	0//0	0/0/			0/0/0	---Other

第五十四章
化学纤维长丝,化学纤维纺织材料制扁条及类似品

注释:

一、本协调制度所称"化学纤维",是指通过下列任一方法加工制得的有机聚合物的短纤或长丝:

(一)将有机单体物质加以聚合而制成聚合物,例如,聚酰胺、聚酯、聚烯烃、聚氨基甲酸酯;或通过上述加工将聚合物经化学改性制得(例如,聚乙酸乙烯酯水解得的聚乙烯醇);

(二)将天然有机聚合物(例如,纤维素)溶解或化学处理制成聚合物,例如,铜铵纤维或粘胶纤维;或将天然有机聚合物(例如,纤维素、酪蛋白及其他蛋白质、或藻酸)经化学改性制成聚合物,例如,醋酸纤维素纤维或藻酸盐纤维。

对于化学纤维,所称"合成",是指(一)款所述的纤维;所称"人造",是指(二)款所述的纤维。税目54.04或54.05的扁条及类似品不视作化学纤维。

对于纺织材料,所称"化学纤维""合成纤维"及"人造纤维",其含义应与上述解释相同。

二、税目54.02及54.03不适用于第五十五章的合成纤维或人造纤维的长丝丝束。

税则号列		货品名称〔CIQ扩展编码及品名—T2表示见附表2〕	最惠(%)	暂定税率	普通	增值/消费	出口退税	计量单位	监管条件	检验检疫	特殊证件对美关税
54.01		**化学纤维长丝纺制的缝纫线,不论是否供零售用:**									
		-合成纤维长丝纺制:									
5401.1010		---非供零售用〔999〕	5		70	13/	13	千克			/25
5401.1020		---供零售用〔999〕	5		90	13/	13	千克			/30
		-人造纤维长丝纺制:									
5401.2010		---非供零售用〔999〕	5		35	13/	13	千克			/
5401.2020		---供零售用〔999〕	5		90	13/	13	千克			/
54.02		**合成纤维长丝纱线(缝纫线除外),非供零售用,包括细度在67分特以下的合成纤维单丝:**									
		-尼龙或其他聚酰胺纺制的高强力纱,不论是否经变形加工:									
		--芳香族聚酰胺纺制:									
5402.1110		---聚间苯二甲酰间苯二胺纺制〔999〕	5		70	13/	13	千克			/15
5402.1120		---聚对苯二甲酰对苯二胺纺制〔999〕	5		70	13/	13	千克			/15
5402.1190		---其他〔999〕	5		70	13/	13	千克			/30
		--其他:									
5402.1910		---聚酰胺-6(尼龙-6)纺制的〔999〕	5		70	13/	13	千克			/30
5402.1920		---聚酰胺-6,6(尼龙-6,6)纺制的〔999〕	5		70	13/	13	千克			/30
5402.1990		---其他〔999〕	5		70	13/	13	千克			/30
5402.2000		-聚酯高强力纱,不论是否经变形加工									
5402.2000	10	非零售聚酯高强力纱,不论是否经变形加工(单丝/未捻或捻度<5转/米的复丝单纱)〔999〕	5		70	13/	13	千克			/30
5402.2000	20	非零售聚酯高强力纱,不论是否经变形加工(捻度≥5转/米的复丝单纱)〔999〕	5		70	13/	13	千克			/30
5402.2000	90	非零售聚酯高强力多股纱,不论是否经变形加工〔999〕	5		70	13/	13	千克			/30
		-变形纱线:									
		--尼龙或其他聚酰胺纺制,每根单纱细度不超过50特:									
		---弹力丝:									
5402.3111		----聚酰胺-6(尼龙-6)纺制的〔999〕	5		80	13/	13	千克			/30
5402.3112		----聚酰胺-6,6(尼龙-6,6)纺制〔999〕	5		80	13/	13	千克			/30
5402.3113		----芳香族聚酰胺纺制〔999〕	5		80	13/	13	千克			/
5402.3119		----其他〔999〕	5		80	13/	13	千克			/30
5402.3190		---其他〔999〕	5		70	13/	13	千克			/30
		--尼龙或其他聚酰胺纺制,每根单纱细度超过50特:									
		---弹力丝:									
5402.3211		----聚酰胺-6(尼龙-6)纺制〔999〕	5		80	13/	13	千克			/15
5402.3212		----聚酰胺-6,6(尼龙-6,6)纺制〔999〕	5		80	13/	13	千克			/15
5402.3213		----芳香族聚酰胺纺制〔999〕	5		80	13/	13	千克			/

Chapter 54
Man-made filaments;strip and the like of man made textile materials

Notes:

1. Throughout the Nomenclature,the term"man-made fibres"means stapl fibres and filaments of organic polymers produced by manufacruring processes,either:
   (a) By polymerization of organic monomers to prduce polymers such as polyamides,polyesters,polyolefins or polyurethanes,or by chemical modification of polymers plrduced by this process(for example,poly(vinyl alcohol) prepared by the hydrolysis of poly (vinyl acetate);
   (b) By dissolution or chemical treatment of natural organic polymers(for example,cellulose) to produce polymers such as cuprammonium rayon(cupro) or viscose rayon,or by chemical modification of narural organic polymers(for example,cellulose,casein and other proteins,or alginic acid),to produce polymers such as cellulose acetate or alginates.

   The terms"synthetic"and "artificial",used in relation to fibres,mean:synthetic:fibres as defined at(a);artificial:fibres as defined at (b).Strip and the like of heading 50. 04 or 54. 05are not considered to be man made fibres.

   The tems"man-made","synthetic"and"artificial"shall have the same meanings when used in relation to"textile materials".
2. Headings 54. 02 and 54. 03 do not apply to synthetic or artificial filament tow of chapter 55.

协定税率 %										特惠税率 %			Article Description
亚太5国	东/冰/格	巴基斯坦	韩国	瑞士	哥达	秘鲁	澳大利亚	新西/坡/智	港/澳/台	亚太2国	老/柬/缅	36/3/1	
													Sewing thread of man-made filaments,whether or not put up for retail sale:
													-Of synthetic filaments:
	0/0/0	0	3	0	0	0	0	0//0	0/0/0			0/0/0	---Not put up for retail sale
	0/0/0	0	0	0	0	0	0	0//0	0/0/			0/0/0	---Put up for retail sale
													-Of artificial filaments:
	0/0/0	0	0	0	0	0	0	0//0	0/0/			0/0/0	---Not put up for retail sale
	0/0/0	0	0	0	0	0	0	0//0	0/0/			0/0/0	---Put up for retail sale
													Synthetic filament yarn (other than sewing thread),not put up for retail sale,including synthetic monofilament of less than 67 decitex:
													-High tenacity yarn of nylon or other polyamides,whether or not through texturing processing:
													--Of aramides:
	0/0/0	0	3	0	0	0	0	0//0	0/0/			0/0/0	---Of poly-isophthaloyl metaphenylene diamide
	0/0/0	0	3	0	0	0	0	0//0	0/0/			0/0/0	---Of poly-p-phenylene terephthalamide
	0/0/0	0	3	0	0	0	0	0//0	0/0/			0/0/0	---Other
													--Other:
	0/0/0	0		0	0	0	0	0//0	0/0/			0/0/0	---Of nylon-6
	0/0/0	0		0	0	0	0	0//0	0/0/			0/0/0	---Of nylon-6,6
	0/0/0	0	3	0	0	0	0	0//0	0/0/			0/0/0	---Other
													-High tenacity yarn of polyesters, whether or not through texturing processing:
	0/0/0	0	3	0	0	0	0	0//0	0/0/0			0/0/0	High tenacity yarn of polyesters (single filament/multi-filament single yarn not twisted or with a twist of less than 5 turns per meter) not put up for retail sale,whether or not through texturing processing
	0/0/0	0	3	0	0	0	0	0//0	0/0/0			0/0/0	High tenacity yarn of polyesters, multi-filament single yarn with a twist of 5 or more turns per meter, not put up for retail sale,whether or not through texturing processing
	0/0/0	0	3	0	0	0	0	0//0	0/0/0			0/0/0	High tenacity yarn of polyesters, multiple yarn, not put up for retail sale -Textured yarn,whether or not through texturing processing
													-Textured yarn:
													--Of nylon or other polyamides,measuring per single yarn not more than 50 tex:
													---Elastic filament:
	0/0/0	0		0	0	0	0	0//0	0/0/			0/0/0	----Of nylon-6
	0/0/0	0		0	0	0	0	0//0	0/0/			0/0/0	----Of nylon-6,6
3	0/0/0	0		0	0	0	0	0//0	0/0/			0/0/0	----Of aramides
	0/0/0	0	3	0	0	0	0	0//0	0/0/			0/0/0	----Other
	0/0/0	0	3	0	0	0	0	0//0	0/0/			0/0/0	---Other
													--Of nylon or other polyamides,measuring per single yarn more than 50tex:
													---Elastic filament:
	0/0/0	0		0	0	0	0	0//0	0/0/			0/0/0	----Of nylon-6
	0/0/0	0		0	0	0	0	0//0	0/0/			0/0/0	----Of nylon-6,6
	0/0/0	0	3	0	0	0	0	0//0	0/0/			0/0/0	----Of aramides

税则号列	货品名称〔CIQ 扩展编码及品名－T2 表示见附表 2〕	最惠(%)	暂定税率	普通	增值/消费	出口退税	计量单位	监管条件	检验检疫	特殊证件对美关税
5402.3219	---其他〔999〕	5		80	13/	13	千克			/30
5402.3290	---其他〔999〕	5		70	13/	13	千克			/15
	--聚酯纺制：									
5402.3310	---弹力丝〔999〕	5		90	13/	13	千克			/30
5402.3390	---其他〔999〕	5		70	13/	13	千克			/30
5402.3400	--聚丙烯纺制〔101 合成纤维纱线,102 绳、索、缆〕	5		70	13/	13	千克			/30
5402.3900	--其他〔999〕	5		70	13/	13	千克			/30
	-其他单纱,未加捻或捻度每米不超过 50 转：									
	--弹性纱线：									
5402.4410	---氨纶纱线〔101 合成纤维纱线,102 绳、索、缆〕	5		70	13/	13	千克			/30
5402.4490	---其他〔999〕	5		70	13/	13	千克			/
	--其他,尼龙或其他聚酰胺纱线：									
5402.4510	---聚酰胺-6(尼龙-6)纺制的〔101 合成纤维纱线,102 绳、索、缆〕	5		70	13/	13	千克			/30
5402.4520	---聚酰胺-6,6(尼龙-6,6)纺制的〔101 合成纤维纱线,102 绳、索、缆〕	5		70	13/	13	千克			/15
5402.4530	---芳香族聚酰胺纺制的〔101 合成纤维纱线,102 绳、索、缆〕	5		70	13/	13	千克			/15
5402.4590	---其他〔101 合成纤维纱线,102 绳、索、缆〕	5		70	13/	13	千克			/15
5402.4600	--其他,部分定向聚酯纱线〔999〕	5		70	13/	13	千克			/15
5402.4700	--其他,聚酯纱线〔999〕	5		70	13/	13	千克			/30
5402.4800	--其他,聚丙烯纱线〔101 合成纤维纱线,102 绳、索、缆〕	5		70	13/	13	千克			/30
	--其他：									
5402.4910	---断裂强度大于等于 22cN/dtex,且初始模量大于等于 750cN/dtex 的聚乙烯纱线〔999〕	5		70	13/	13	千克			/15
5402.4990	---其他									
5402.4990 01	非弹性氨纶单纱(非供零售用,未加捻或捻度每米不超过 50 转,缝纫线除外)〔999〕	5		70	13/	13	千克			/15
5402.4990 90	其他合成纤维长丝单纱(非供零售用,未加捻或捻度每米不超过 50 转,缝纫线除外)〔999〕	5		70	13/	13	千克			/15
	-其他单纱,捻度每米超过 50 转：									
	--尼龙或其他聚酰胺纱线：									
5402.5110	---聚酰胺-6(尼龙-6)制〔999〕	5		70	13/	13	千克			/30
5402.5120	---聚酰胺-6,6(尼龙-6,6)制〔999〕	5		70	13/	13	千克			/
5402.5130	---芳香族聚酰胺纺制〔999〕	5		70	13/	13	千克			/
5402.5190	---其他〔999〕	5		70	13/	13	千克			/
5402.5200	--聚酯纱线〔999〕	5		70	13/	13	千克			/30
5402.5300	--聚丙烯纱线〔999〕	5		70	13/	13	千克			/30
	--其他：									
5402.5920	---断裂强度大于等于 22cN/dtex,且初始模量大于等于 750cN/dtex 的聚乙烯纱线〔999〕	5		70	13/	13	千克			/15
5402.5990	---其他〔999〕	5		70	13/	13	千克			/15
	-其他纱线(多股纱线或缆线)：									
	--尼龙或其他聚酰胺纺制：									
5402.6110	---聚酰胺-6(尼龙-6)制〔101 合成纤维纱线,102 绳、索、缆〕	5		70	13/	13	千克			/30
5402.6120	---聚酰胺-6,6(尼龙-6,6)制〔101 合成纤维纱线,102 绳、索、缆〕	5		70	13/	13	千克			/30
5402.6130	---芳香族聚酰胺纺制〔101 合成纤维纱线,102 绳、索、缆〕	5		70	13/	13	千克			/25
5402.6190	---其他〔101 合成纤维纱线,102 绳、索、缆〕	5		70	13/	13	千克			/30
5402.6200	--聚酯纺制〔101 合成纤维纱线,102 绳、索、缆〕	5		70	13/	13	千克			/30
5402.6300	--聚丙烯纺制〔999〕	5		70	13/	13	千克			/30
	--其他：									
5402.6920	---氨纶纱线〔101 合成纤维纱线,102 绳、索、缆〕	5		70	13/	13	千克			/30
5402.6990	---其他〔101 合成纤维纱线,102 绳、索、缆〕	5		70	13/	13	千克			/25
54.03	**人造纤维长丝纱线(缝纫线除外),非供零售用,包括细度在 67 分特以下的人造纤维单丝：**									
5403.1000	-粘胶纤维纺制的高强力纱〔999〕	5		35	13/	13	千克			/15
	-其他单纱：									
	--粘胶纤维纺制,未加捻或捻度每米不超过 120 转：									
5403.3110	---竹制〔999〕	5		35	13/	13	千克			/
5403.3190	---其他〔999〕	5		35	13/	13	千克			/
	--粘胶纤维纺制,捻度每米超过 120 转：									
5403.3210	---竹制〔999〕	5		35	13/	13	千克			/
5403.3290	---其他〔999〕	5		35	13/	13	千克			/
	--醋酸纤维纺制：									
5403.3310	---二醋酸纤维纺制									

协定税率 %										特惠税率 %			Article Description
亚太5国	东/冰/格	巴基斯坦	韩国	瑞士	哥达	秘鲁	澳大利亚	新西/坡/智	港/澳/台	亚太2国	老/柬/缅	36/3/1	
	0/0/0	0		0	0	0	0	0//0	0/0/			0/0/0	----Other
3.3	0/0/0	0	3.2	0	0	0	0	0//0	0/0/			0/0/0	---Other
													--Of polyesters:
	0/0/0	0	0	0	0	0	0	0//0	0/0/0			0/0/0	---Elastic filament
	/0/0	0	2	0	0	0	0	0//0	0/0/			0/0/0	---Other
	0/0/0	0	2	0	0	0	0	0//0	0/0/			0/0/0	--Of polypropylene
	0/0/0	0	2	0	0	0	0	0//0	0/0/			0/0/0	--Other
													-Other yarn, single, untwisted or with a twist not exceeding 50 turns per metre:
													--Elastomeric:
	0/0/0	0		0	0	0	0	0//0	0/0/			0/0/0	---Of polyurethane
3.3	0/0/0	0	0	0	0	0	0	0//0	0/0/			0/0/0	---Other
													--Other, of nylon or other polyamides:
3.3	0/0/0	0	3.2	0	0	0	0	0//0	0/0/			0/0/0	---Of nylon-6
3.3	0/0/0	0	3.2	0	0	0	0	0//0	0/0/			0/0/0	---Of nylon-6,6
3.3	0/0/0	0	3	0	0	0	0	0//0	0/0/			0/0/0	---Of aramides
3.3	0/0/0	0	3.2	0	0	0	0	0//0	0/0/			0/0/0	---Other
	/0/0	0	2	0	0	0	0	0//0	0/0/			0/0/0	--Other, of polyesters, partially oriented
3.3	/0/0	0	3.2	1.5	0	0	0	0//0	0/0/			0/0/0	--Other, of polyesters
	0/0/0	0	0	0	0	0	0	0//0	0/0/			0/0/0	--Other, Of polypropylene
													--Other:
	0/0/0	0		0	0	0	0	0//0	0/0/			0/0/0	---Polyethylene filament yarn (yarn)
													---Other
	0/0/0	0		0	0	0	0	0//0	0/0/			0/0/0	Single yarn of polyurethane[untwisted or twist<50turns/m multiple (folded), not in forms or packing for retail sale]
	0/0/0	0		0	0	0	0	0//0	0/0/			0/0/0	Other single yarn of synthetic filaments [untwisted or twist<50turns/m multiple (folded), not in forms or packing for retail sale]
													-Other yarn, single, with a twist exceeding 50 turns per metre:
													—Of nylon or other polyamides:
	/0/0	0		0	0	0	0	0//0	0/0/			0/0/0	---Of nylon-6
4.5	0/0/0	0		0	0	0	0	0//0	0/0/			0/0/0	---Of nylon-6,6
3.5	0/0/0	0	3	0	0	0	0	0//0	0/0/			0/0/0	---Of aramides
	0/0/0	0	3	0	0	0	0	0//0	0/0/			0/0/0	---Other
3.3	/0/0	0	2	0	0	0	0	0//0	0/0/			0/0/0	—Of polyesters
	0/0/0	0	0	0	0	0	0	0//0	0/0/			0/0/0	—Of polypropylene
													--Other:
	0/0/0	0	0	0	0	0	0	0//0	0/0/			0/0/0	---Polyethy lene yarn with break strength ≥22cN/dtex, and initial modulus≥750cN/dtex
	0/0/0	0	0	0	0	0	0	0//0	0/0/			0/0/0	---Other
													-Other yarn, multiple (folded) or cabled:
													--Of nylon or other polyamides:
	0/0/0	0	3	0	0	0	0	0//0	0/0/			0/0/0	---Of nylon-6
	0/0/0	0	3	0	0	0	0	0//0	0/0/			0/0/0	---Of nylon-6,6
	0/0/0	0	3	0	0	0	0	0//0	0/0/			0/0/0	---Of aramides
	0/0/0	0	0	0	0	0	0	0//0	0/0/			0/0/0	---Other
	0/0/0	0	0	0	0	0	0	0//0	0/0/0			0/0/0	--Of polyesters
	0/0/0	0	3	0	0	0	0	0//0	0/0/			0/0/0	--Of polypropylene
													--Other:
	0/0/0	0		0	0	0	0	0//0	0/0/			0/0/0	—Of polyurethane
	0/0/0	0	2	0	0	0	0	0//0	0/0/			0/0/0	—Other
													Artificial filament yarn (other than sewing thread), not put up for retail sale, including artificial monofilament of less than 67 decitex:
	0/0/0	0	0	0	0	0	0	0//0	0/0/			0/0/0	-High tenacity yarn of viscose rayon
													-Other yarn, single:
													--Of viscose rayon, untwisted or with a twist not exceeding 120 turns per metre:
	0/0/0	0	0	0	0	0	0	0//0	0/0/			0/0/0	---Of bamboo
	0/0/0	0	0	0	0	0	0	0//0	0/0/			0/0/0	---Other
													--Of viscose rayon, with a twist exceeding 120 turns per metre:
	0/0/0	0	0	0	0	0	0	0//0	0/0/			0/0/0	---Of bomboo
	0/0/0	0	0	0	0	0	0	0//0	0/0/			0/0/0	---Other
													--Of cellulose acetate:
													---Of cellulose diacetate

税则号列		货品名称〔CIQ扩展编码及品名—T2表示见附表2〕	最惠(%)	暂定税率	普通	增值/消费	出口退税	计量单位	监管条件	检验检疫	特殊证件对美关税
5403.3310	10	非零售二醋酸纤维单纱(单丝/未捻或捻度5转/米以下的复丝单纱,包括变形纱线)〔999〕	5		40	13/	13	千克			/15
5403.3310	20	非零售二醋酸纤维单纱(捻度5转/米及以上不超过250转,包括变形纱线)〔999〕	5		40	13/	13	千克			/15
5403.3310	90	非零售二醋酸纤维单纱(捻度超过250转/米)〔999〕	5		40	13/	13	千克			/15
5403.3390		---其他〔999〕	5		35	13/	13	千克			/15
5403.3900		--其他〔999〕	5		35	13/	13	千克			/
		-其他纱线(多股纱线或缆线):									
5403.4100		--粘胶纤维纺制〔999〕	5		35	13/	13	千克			/
5403.4200		--醋酸纤维纺制〔999〕	5		35	13/	13	千克			/
5403.4900		--其他〔999〕	5		35	13/	13	千克			/30
54.04		**截面尺寸不超过1毫米,细度在67分特及以上的合成纤维单丝;表观宽度不超过5毫米的合成纤维纺织材料制扁条及类似品(例如人造草):**									
		-单丝:									
5404.1100		--弹性单丝									
5404.1100	10	细度≥67分特的涤纶纤维弹性单丝(截面尺寸≤1mm,细度<67分特的合成纤维单丝归入编号5402)〔999〕	5		80	13/	13	千克			/15
5404.1100	90	细度≥67分特的其他合成纤维弹性单丝(截面尺寸≤1mm,细度<67分特的合成纤维单丝归入编号5402)〔999〕	5		80	13/	13	千克			/15
5404.1200		--其他,聚丙烯制〔999〕	5		80	13/	13	千克			/
5404.1900		--其他									
5404.1900	10	细度≥67分特的涤纶纤维单丝(截面尺寸≤1mm,细度<67分特的合成纤维单丝归入税目54.02)〔999〕	5		80	13/	13	千克			/25
5404.1900	90	细度≥67分特的其他合成纤维单丝(截面尺寸≤1mm,细度<67分特的合成纤维单丝归入税目54.02)〔999〕	5		80	13/	13	千克			/25
5404.9000		-其他〔999〕	5		80	13/	13	千克			/25
54.05		**截面尺寸不超过1毫米,细度在67分特及以上的人造纤维单丝;表观宽度不超过5毫米的人造纤维纺织材料制扁条及类似品(例如人造草):**									
5405.0000		截面尺寸不超过1毫米,细度在67分特及以上的人造纤维单丝;表观宽度不超过5毫米的人造纤维纺织材料制扁条及类似品(例如人造草)〔999〕	5		80	13/	13	千克			/25
54.06		**化学纤维长丝纱线(缝纫线除外),供零售用:**									
5406.0010		--合成纤维长丝纱线〔999〕	5		90	13/	13	千克			/25
5406.0020		--人造纤维长丝纱线〔999〕	5		90	13/	13	千克			/
54.07		**合成纤维长丝纱线的机织物,包括税目54.04所列材料的机织物:**									
		-尼龙或其他聚酰胺高强力纱、聚酯高强力纱纺制的机织物:									
5407.1010		---尼龙或其他聚酰胺高强力纱纺制〔999〕	8		130	13/	13	米/千克			/33
5407.1020		---聚酯高强力纱纺制									
5407.1020	10	聚酯高强力纱纺制机织物(重量≤170克/平方米)〔999〕	8		130	13/	13	米/千克			/33
5407.1020	90	聚酯高强力纱纺制机织物(重量>170克/平方米)〔999〕	8		130	13/	13	米/千克			/33
5407.2000		-扁条及类似品的机织物〔999〕	8		130	13/	13	米/千克			/28
5407.3000		-第十一类注释九所列的机织物〔999〕	8		130	13/	13	米/千克			/28
		-其他机织物,按重量计尼龙或其他聚酰胺长丝含量在85%及以上:									
5407.4100		--未漂白或漂白〔999〕	8		130	13/	13	米/千克			/33
5407.4200		--染色〔999〕	8		130	13/	13	米/千克			/33
5407.4300		--色织〔999〕	8		130	13/	13	米/千克			/33
5407.4400		--印花〔999〕	8		130	13/	13	米/千克			/33

协定税率 %										特惠税率 %			Article Description
亚太5国	东/冰/格	巴基斯坦	韩国	瑞士	哥达	秘鲁	澳大利亚	新西/坡/智	港/澳/台	亚太2国	老/柬/缅	36/3/1	
	0/0/0	0	0	0	0	0	0	0//0	0/0/			0/0/0	Single yarn of cellulose diacetate, untwisted or twist＜5 turns/m multiple (folded), not in forms or packing for retail sale, including textured yarn
	0/0/0	0	0	0	0	0	0	0//0	0/0/			0/0/0	Single yarn of cellulose diacetate, 5 turns/m≤twist≤250 turns/m, not put up for retail sale, including Deformation yarn
	0/0/0	0	0	0	0	0	0	0//0	0/0/			0/0/0	Single yarn of cellulose diacetate, twist＞250 turns/m, not put up for retail sale
	0/0/0	0	0	0	0	0	0	0//0	0/0/			0/0/0	---Other
	0/0/0	0	0	0	0	0	0	0//0	0/0/			0/0/0	--Other
													-Other yarn, multiple (folded) or cabled:
	0/0/0	0	0	0	0	0	0	0//0	0/0/			0/0/0	--Of viscose rayon
	0/0/0	0	0	0	0	0	0	0//0	0/0/			0/0/0	--Of cellulose acetate
	0/0/0	0	0	0	0	0	0	0//0	0/0/			0/0/0	--Other
													Synthetic monofilament of 67 decitex or more and of which no cross-sectional dimension exceeds 1 mm; strip and the like (for example, artificial straw) of synthetic textile materials of an apparent width not exceeing 5 mm:
													-Monofilament:
													--Elastomeric
	0/0/0	0	3	0	0	0	0	0//0	0/0/			0/0/0	Elastomeric monofilament of polyester, fineness≥67 decitex (cross-sectional dimension≤1mm, fineness＜67 decitex, should be classified under No. 5402)
	0/0/0	0	3	0	0	0	0	0//0	0/0/			0/0/0	Other synthetic elastomeric monofilament, fineness ≥ 67 decitex (cross-sectional dimension≤1mm, fineness＜67 decitex, should be classified under No. 5402)
	0/0/0	0	0	0	0	0	0	0//0	0/0/			0/0/0	--Other, of polypropylene
													--Other
	0/0/0	0	2	0	0	0	0	0//0	0/0/			0/0/0	Monofilament of polyester, fineness≥67 decitex (cross-sectional dimension≤1mm, fineness＜67 decitex, should be classified under No. 5402)
	0/0/0	0	2	0	0	0	0	0//0	0/0/			0/0/0	Other synthetic monofilament, fineness≥67 decitex (cross-sectional dimension≤1mm, fineness＜67 decitex, should be classified under No. 5402)
	0/0/0	0	2	0	0	0	0	0//0	0/0/			0/0/0	-Other
													Artificial monofilament of 67 decitex or more and of which no cross-sectional dimension exceeds 1 mm; strip and the like (for example, artificial straw) of artificial textile materials of an apparent width not exceeding 5 mm:
	0/0/0	0	0	0	0	0	0	0//0	0/0/			0/0/0	Artificial monofilament of 67 decitex or more of whichno cross-sectional dimension exceeds 1 mm; strip and the like (for example, artificial straw) of artificial textile materials of an apparent width not exceeding 5 mm
													Man-made filament yarn (other than sewing thread), put up for retail sale:
	0/0/0	0	0	0	0	0	0	0//0	0/0/			0/0/0	--Synthetic filament yarn
	0/0/0	0	0	0	0	0	0	0//0	0/0/			0/0/0	--Artificial filament yarn
													Woven fabrics of synthetic filamentyarn, including woven fabrics obtained from materials of heading 54.04:
													-Woven fabrics obtained from high tenacity yarn of nylon or other polyamides or of polyesters:
	0/0/0	0	0	0	0	0	0	0/0/0	0/0/0			0/0/	---Of nylon or other polyamides
													---Of polyesters
	0/0/0	0	0	0	0	0	0	0/0/0	0/0/0			0/0/	Woven fabrics of high tenacity yarn of polyesters, weight≤$170g/m^2$
	0/0/0	0	0	0	0	0	0	0/0/0	0/0/0			0/0/	Woven fabrics of high tenacity yarn of polyesters, weight＞$170g/m^2$
	0/0/0	0	7	0	0	0	0	0/0/0	0/0/			0/0/	-Woven fabrics obtained from strip or the like
	0/0/0	0	0	0	0	0	0	0/0/0	0/0/			0/0/	-Fabrics specified in Note 9 to Section XI
													-Other woven fabrics, containing 85% or more by weight of filaments of nylon or other polyamides:
	0/0/0	0	0	0	0	0	0	0/0/0	0/0/0			0/0/	--Unbleached or bleached
5.2	0/0/0	0	7	0	0	0	0	0/0/0	0/0/0		0/0/0	0/0/0	--Dyed
5.2	0/0/0	0	0	0	0	0	0	0/0/0	0/0/0			0/0/	--Of yarns of different colours
	0/0/0	0	7	0	0	0	0	0/0/0	0/0/			0/0/	--Printed

税则号列	货品名称〔CIQ 扩展编码及品名—T2 表示见附表 2〕	最惠(%)	暂定税率	普通	增值/消费	出口退税	计量单位	监管条件	检验检疫	特殊证件对美关税
	-其他机织物，按重量计聚酯变形长丝含量在 85％及以上：									
5407.5100	--未漂白或漂白〔999〕	8		130	13/	13	米/千克			/33
5407.5200	--染色〔999〕	8		130	13/	13	米/千克			/33
5407.5300	--色织〔999〕	8		130	13/	13	米/千克			/33
5407.5400	--印花〔999〕	8		130	13/	13	米/千克			/33
	-其他机织物，按重量计聚酯长丝含量在 85％及以上：									
5407.6100	--按重量计聚酯非变形长丝含量在 85％及以上〔999〕	8		130	13/	13	米/千克			/33
5407.6900	--其他〔999〕	8		130	13/	13	米/千克			/33
	-其他机织物，按重量计其他合成纤维长丝含量在 85％及以上：									
5407.7100	--未漂白或漂白〔999〕	8		130	13/	13	米/千克			/33
5407.7200	--染色〔999〕	8		130	13/	13	米/千克			/33
5407.7300	--色织〔999〕	8		130	13/	13	米/千克			/33
5407.7400	--印花〔999〕	8		130	13/	13	米/千克			/33
	-其他机织物，按重量计其他合成纤维长丝含量在 85％以下，主要或仅与棉混纺：									
5407.8100	--未漂白或漂白〔101 棉混纺坯布，102 漂白棉混纺布，103 合成纤维混纺机织物〕	8		130	13/	13	米/千克			/33
5407.8200	--染色〔101 棉混纺染色布，102 合成纤维混纺机织物〕	8		130	13/	13	米/千克			/33
5407.8300	--色织〔101 色织棉混纺布，102 合成纤维混纺机织物〕	8		130	13/	13	米/千克			/33
5407.8400	--印花〔101 棉混纺印花布，102 合成纤维混纺机织物〕	8		130	13/	13	米/千克			/28
	-其他机织物：									
5407.9100	--未漂白或漂白〔999〕	8		130	13/	13	米/千克			/33
5407.9200	--染色〔999〕	8		130	13/	13	米/千克			/33
5407.9300	--色织〔999〕	8		130	13/	13	米/千克			/28
5407.9400	--印花〔999〕	8		130	13/	13	米/千克			/33
54.08	**人造纤维长丝纱线的机织物，包括品目 54.05 所列材料的机织物：**									
5408.1000	-粘胶纤维高强力纱的机织物〔999〕	8		130	13/	13	米/千克			/18
	-其他机织物，按重量计人造纤维长丝、扁条或类似品含量在 85％及以上：									
	--未漂白或漂白：									
5408.2110	---粘胶纤维制〔999〕	8		130	13/	13	米/千克			/33
5408.2120	---醋酸纤维制〔999〕	8		130	13/	13	米/千克			/
5408.2190	---其他〔999〕	8		130	13/	13	米/千克			/33
	--染色：									
5408.2210	---粘胶纤维制〔999〕	8		130	13/	13	米/千克			/33
5408.2220	---醋酸纤维制〔999〕	8		130	13/	13	米/千克			/
5408.2290	---其他〔999〕	8		130	13/	13	米/千克			/33
	--色织：									
5408.2310	---粘胶纤维制〔999〕	8		130	13/	13	米/千克			/33
5408.2320	---醋酸纤维制〔999〕	8		130	13/	13	米/千克			/
5408.2390	---其他〔999〕	8		130	13/	13	米/千克			/33
	--印花：									
5408.2410	---粘胶纤维制〔999〕	8		130	13/	13	米/千克			/
5408.2420	---醋酸纤维制〔999〕	8		130	13/	13	米/千克			/
5408.2490	---其他〔999〕	8		130	13/	13	米/千克			/
	-其他机织物：									
5408.3100	--未漂白或漂白〔999〕	8		130	13/	13	米/千克			/
5408.3200	--染色〔999〕	8		130	13/	13	米/千克			/33
5408.3300	--色织〔999〕	8		130	13/	13	米/千克			/33
5408.3400	--印花〔999〕	8		130	13/	13	米/千克			/33

协定税率 %										特惠税率 %			Article Description
亚太5国	东/冰/格	巴基斯坦	韩国	瑞士	哥达	秘鲁	澳大利亚	新西/坡/智	港/澳/台	亚太2国	老/柬/缅	36/3/1	
													-Other woven fabrics, containing 85% or more by weight of textured polyester filaments:
5.2	0/0/0	0	0	0	0	0	0	0/0/0	0/0/0			0/0/	--Unbleached or bleached
5.2	0/0/0	0	7	0	0	0	0	0/0/0	0/0/0		0/0/0	0/0/C	--Dyed
	0/0/0	0	0	0	0	0	0	0/0/0	0/0/0			0/0/	--Of yarns of different colours
	0/0/0	0	6	0	0	0	0	0/0/0	0/0/0			0/0/	--Printed
													-Other woven fabrics, containing 85% or more by weight of polyester filaments:
5.2	0/0/0	0	7	0	0	0	0	0/0/0	0/0/0			0/0/0	--Containing 85% or more by weight of non-textured polyester filaments
5.2	0/0/0	0	7	0	0	0	0	0/0/0	0/0/0			0/0/0	--Other
													-Other woven fabrics, containing 85% or more by weight of synthetic filaments:
5.2	0/0/0	0	0	0	0	0	0	0/0/0	0/0/0			0/0/	--Unbleached or bleached
5.2	0/0/0	0	7	0	0	0	0	0/0/0	0/0/0		0/0/0	0/0/0	--Dyed
	0/0/0	0	7	0	0	0	0	0/0/0	0/0/			0/0/	--Of yarns of different colours
5.2	0/0/0	0	0	0	0	0	0	0/0/0	0/0/			0/0/	--Printed
													-Other woven fabrics, containing less than 85% by weight of synthetic filaments, mixed mainly or solely with cotton:
	0/0/0	0	0	0	0	0	0	0/0/0	0/0/			0/0/	--Unbleached or bleached
	0/0/0	0	7	0	0	0	0	0/0/0	0/0/0			0/0/0	--Dyed
	0/0/0	0	0	0	0	0	0	0/0/0	0/0/0			0/0/	--Of yarns of different colours
	0/0/0	0	0	0	0	0	0	0/0/0	0/0/			0/0/	--Printed
													-Other woven fabrics:
	0/0/0	0	7	0	0	0	0	0/0/0	0/0/			0/0/	--Unbleached or bleached
	0/0/0	0	7	0	0	0	0	0/0/0	0/0/0		0/0/0	0/0/0	--Dyed
	0/0/0	0	0	0	0	0	0	0/0/0	0/0/0			0/0/	--Of yarns of different colours
	0/0/0	0	0	0	0	0	0	0/0/0	0/0/			0/0/	--Printed
													Woven fabrics of artificial filament yarn, including woven fabrics obtained from materials of heading No. 54. 05:
	0/0/0	0	0	0	0	0	0	0/0/0	0/0/			0/0/	-Woven fabrics obtained from high tenacity yarn of viscose rayon
													-Other woven fabrics, containing 85% or more by weight of artificial filament or strip or the like:
													--Unbleached or bleached:
	0/0/0	0	0	3.6	0	0	0	0/0/0	0/0/			0/0/	---Of yarns of viscose rayon
	0/0/0	0	8.4	3.6	0	0	0	0/0/0	0/0/			0/0/	---Of yarns of cellulose acetate
	0/0/0	0	0	3.6	0	0	0	0/0/0	0/0/			0/0/	---Other
													--Dyed:
	0/0/0	0	0	0	0	0	0	0/0/0	0/0/			0/0/	---Of yarns of viscose rayon
	0/0/0	0	0	0	0	0	0	0/0/0	0/0/0			0/0/	---Of yarns of cellulose acetate
	0/0/0	0	0	0	0	0	0	0/0/0	0/0/0			0/0/	---Other
													--Of yarns of different colours:
	0/0/0	0	0	0	0	0	0	0/0/0	0/0/			0/0/	---Of yarns of viscose rayon
	0/0/0	0	0	0	0	0	0	0/0/0	0/0/			0/0/	---Of yarns of cellulose acetate
	0/0/0	0	0	0	0	0	0	0/0/0	0/0/0			0/0/	---Other
													--Printed:
	0/0/0	0	0	0	0	0	0	0/0/0	0/0/			0/0/	---Of yarns of viscose rayon
	0/0/0	0	0	0	0	0	0	0/0/0	0/0/			0/0/	---Of yarns of cellulose acetate
	0/0/0	0	0	0	0	0	0	0/0/0	0/0/			0/0/	---Other
													-Other woven fabrics:
	0/0/0	0	0	0	0	0	0	0/0/0	0/0/			0/0/	--Unbleached or bleached
5.2	0/0/0	0	6	0	0	0	0	0/0/0	0/0/0			0/0/0	--Dyed
	0/0/0	0	0	0	0	0	0	0/0/0	0/0/			0/0/	--Of yarns of different colours
	0/0/0	0	0	0	0	0	0	0/0/0	0/0/			0/0/	--Printed

第五十五章
化学纤维短纤

注释：

税目55.01和55.02仅适用于每根与丝束长度相等的平行化学纤维长丝丝束。前述丝束应同时符合下列规格：

一、丝束长度超过2米；
二、捻度每米少于5转；
三、每根长丝细度在67分特以下；
四、合成纤维长丝丝束，须经拉伸处理，即本身不能被拉伸至超过本身长度的一倍；

五、丝束总细度大于20000分特。
丝束长度不超过2米的归入税目55.03或55.04。

税则号列		货品名称〔CIQ扩展编码及品名－T2表示见附表2〕	最惠(%)	暂定税率	普通	增值/消费	出口退税	计量单位	监管条件	检验检疫	特殊证件对美关税
55.01		**合成纤维长丝丝束：**									
5501.1000		-尼龙或其他聚酰胺制〔999〕	5		70	13/	13	千克			/30
5501.2000		-聚酯制〔999〕	5		70	13/	13	千克			/15
5501.3000		-聚丙烯腈或变性聚丙烯腈制									
5501.3000	10	聚丙烯腈制长丝丝束(不包括变性聚丙烯腈制)〔999〕	5		35	13/	13	千克			/30
5501.3000	90	变性聚丙烯腈长丝丝束〔999〕	5		35	13/	13	千克			/30
5501.4000		-聚丙烯制〔999〕	5		70	13/	13	千克			/
5501.9000		-其他〔999〕	5		70	13/	13	千克			/30
55.02		**人造纤维长丝丝束：**									
		-醋酸纤维丝束：									
5502.1010		---二醋酸纤维丝束〔999〕	3		40	13/	13	千克	7		/13
5502.1090		---其他〔999〕	5		35	13/	13	千克			/
5502.9000		-其他〔999〕	5		35	13/	13	千克			/
55.03		**合成纤维短纤，未梳或未经其他纺前加工：**									
		-尼龙或其他聚酰胺制：									
		--芳族聚酰胺纺制：									
5503.1110		---聚间苯二甲酰间苯二胺纺制〔999〕	5		70	13/	13	千克			/30
5503.1120		---聚对苯二甲酰对苯二胺纺制〔999〕	5		70	13/	13	千克			/15
5503.1190		---其他〔999〕	5		70	13/	13	千克			/30
5503.1900		--其他〔999〕	5		70	13/	13	千克			/15
5503.2000		-聚酯制〔999〕	5		70	13/	13	千克			/30
5503.3000		-聚丙烯腈或变性聚丙烯腈制									
5503.3000	10	未梳或未经其他纺前加工的聚丙烯腈制短纤维(不包括变性聚丙烯腈制)〔999〕	5		35	13/	13	千克			/30
5503.3000	90	未梳或未经其他纺前加工的变性聚丙烯腈制短纤维〔999〕	5		35	13/	13	千克			/30
5503.4000		-聚丙烯制〔999〕	5		70	13/	13	千克			/30
		-其他：									
5503.9010		---聚苯硫醚短纤〔999〕	5		70	13/	13	千克			/30
5503.9090		---其他〔999〕	5		70	13/	13	千克			/30
55.04		**人造纤维短纤，未梳或未经其他纺前加工：**									
		-粘胶纤维制：									
5504.1010		---竹制〔999〕	5		35	13/	13	千克			/
		---木制：									
5504.1021		----阻燃的〔999〕	5		35	13/	13	千克			/
5504.1029		----其他〔999〕	5		35	13/	13	千克			/
5504.1090		---其他〔999〕	5		35	13/	13	千克			/30
5504.9000		-其他〔999〕	5		35	13/	13	千克			/30
55.05		**化学纤维废料(包括落棉、废纱及回收纤维)：**									
5505.1000		-合成纤维的〔999〕	5		70	13/	13	千克	9	M	/30
5505.2000		-人造纤维的〔999〕	5		70	13/	13	千克	9	M	/30
55.06		**合成纤维短纤，已梳或经其他纺前加工：**									
		-尼龙或其他聚酰胺制：									
		---芳族聚酰胺纺制：									
5506.1011		----聚间苯二甲酰间苯二胺纺制〔999〕	5		70	13/	13	千克			/30
5506.1012		----聚对苯二甲酰对苯二胺纺制〔999〕	5		70	13/	13	千克			/15

Chapter 55
Man-made staple fibres

Notes:

Headings 55.01 and 55.02 apply only to man-made filament tow, consisting of parallel filaments of a uniform length equal to the length of the tow, meeting the following specifications:

1. Length of tow exceeding 2 m;
2. Twist less than 5 turns per metre;
3. Measuring per filament less than 67 decitex;
4. Synthetic filament tow only: the tow must be drawn, that is to say, be incapable of being stretched by more than 100% of its length;
5. Total measurement of tow more than 20,000 decitex.

Tow of a length not exceeding 2 m is to be classified in heading No.55.03 or 55.04.

协定税率 %										特惠税率 %			
亚太5国	东/冰/格	巴基斯坦	韩国	瑞士	哥达	秘鲁	澳大利亚	新西/坡/智	港/澳/台	亚太2国	老/柬/缅	36/3/1	Article Description
													Synthetic filament tow:
	0/0/0	0	0	0	0	0	0	0//0	0/0/			0/0/0	-Of nylon or other polyamides
	/0/0	0	2	0	0	0	0	0//0	0/0/			0/0/0	-Of polyesters
													-Acrylic or modacrylic
3.3	/0/0	0	3	0	0		0	0//0	0/0/			0/0/0	Filament tow of acrylic(other than modacrylic)
3.3	/0/0	0	3	0	0		0	0//0	0/0/			0/0/0	Filament tow of modacrylic
	0/0/0	0	0	0	0	0	0	0//0	0/0/			0/0/0	-Of polypropylene
	0/0/0	0	2	0	0	0	0	0//0	0/0/			0/0/0	-Other
													Artificial filament tow:
													-Cellulose acetate filament tow:
2	0/0/0	0	0	0	0	0	0	0//0	0/0/			0/0/0	---Cellulose diacetate filament tow
3.3	0/0/0	0	3	0	0	0	0	0//0	0/0/			0/0/0	---Other
3.3	0/0/0	0	3	0	0	0	0	0//0	0/0/			0/0/0	-Other
													Synthetic staple fibres, not carded, combed or otherwise processed for spinning:
													-Of nylon or other polyamides:
													--Of aramides:
	0/0/0	0		0	0	0	0	0//0	0/0/			0/0/0	---Of poly-isophthaloyl metaphenylene diamine
	0/0/0	0		0	0	0	0	0//0	0/0/			0/0/0	---Of poly-p-phenylene terephthalamide
	0/0/0	0		1.5	0	0	0	0//0	0/0/			0/0/0	---Other
	0/0/0	0	2	1.5	0	0	0	0//0	0/0/			0/0/0	--Other
3.3	/0/0	0	3	0	0	0	0	0//0	0/0/			0/0/0	-Of polyesters
													-Acrylic or modacrylic
3.3	/0/0	0	2	0	0	0	0	0//0	0/0/			0/0/0	Staple fibres of acrylic, not carded, combed or otherwise processed forspinning(other than modacrylic)
3.3	/0/0	0	2	0	0	0	0	0//0	0/0/			0/0/0	Staple fibres of modacrylic, not carded, combed or otherwise processed forspinning
	0/0/0	0	2	0	0	0	0	0//0	0/0/			0/0/0	-Of polypropylene
													-Other:
	0/0/0	0	2	0	0	0	0	0//0	0/0/0			0/0/0	---Polyphe-nylenesu staple fibres
	0/0/0	0	0	0	0	0	0	0//0	0/0/0			0/0/0	---Other[999]
													Artificial staple fibres, not carded, combed or otherwise processed for spinning:
													-Of viscose rayon:
4.5	0/0/0	0	0	0	0	0	0	0//0	0/0/			0/0/0	---Of bamboo
													---Of wood:
4	0/0/0	0	2	0	0	0	0	0//0	0/0/			0/0/0	----Flame retardancy
	0/0/0	0	2	0	0	0	0	0//0	0/0/			0/0/0	----Other
	0/0/0	0	2	0	0	0	0	0//0	0/0/			0/0/0	---Other
	0/0/0	0	0	0	0	0	0	0//0	0/0/0			0/0/0	-Other
													Waste (including noils, yarn waste and garnetted stock) of man-made fibres:
	0/0/0	0	2	0	0	0	0	0//0	0/0/			0/0/0	-Of synthetic fibres
3.5	0/0/0	0	2	0	0	0	0	0//0	0/0/			0/0/0	-Of artificial fibres
													Synthetic staple fibres, carded, combed or otherwise processed for spinning:
													-Of nylon or other polyamides:
													---Of aramides:
	0/0/0	0		0	0	0	0	0//0	0/0/			0/0/0	----Of poly isophthaloy polpamides:l metaphenylene diamine
	0/0/0	0		0	0	0	0	0//0	0/0/			0/0/0	----Of poly-p-phenylene terephthalamide

税则号列	货品名称〔CIQ扩展编码及品名—T2表示见附表2〕	最惠(%)	暂定税率	普通	增值/消费	出口退税	计量单位	监管条件	检验检疫	特殊证件对美关税
5506.1019	----其他〔999〕	5		70	13/	13	千克			/
5506.1090	---其他〔999〕	5		70	13/	13	千克			/30
5506.2000	-聚酯制〔999〕	5		70	13/	13	千克			/30
5506.3000	-聚丙烯腈或变性聚丙烯腈制									
5506.3000　10	已梳或经其他纺前加工的聚丙烯腈制短纤(不包括变性聚丙烯腈制)〔999〕	5		35	13/	13	千克			/25
5506.3000　90	已梳或经其他纺前加工的变性聚丙烯腈制短纤〔999〕	5		35	13/	13	千克			/25
5506.4000	-聚丙烯制〔999〕	5		70	13/	13	千克			/
	-其他：									
5506.9010	---聚苯硫醚制〔999〕	5		70	13/	13	千克			/
5506.9090	---其他〔999〕	5		70	13/	13	千克			/15
55.07	**人造纤维短纤，已梳或经其他纺前加工：**									
5507.0000	人造纤维短纤，已梳或经其他纺前加工〔999〕	5		35	13/	13	千克			/30
55.08	**化学纤维短纤纺制的缝纫线，不论是否供零售用：**									
5508.1000	-合成纤维短纤纺制〔999〕	5		90	13/	13	千克			/30
5508.2000	-人造纤维短纤纺制〔999〕	5		70	13/	13	千克			/
55.09	**合成纤维短纤纺制的纱线(缝纫线除外)，非供零售用：**									
	-按重量计尼龙或其他聚酰胺短纤含量在85%及以上：									
5509.1100	--单纱〔999〕	5		90	13/	13	千克			/15
5509.1200	--多股纱线或缆线〔999〕	5		90	13/	13	千克			/30
	-按重量计聚酯短纤含量在85%及以上：									
5509.2100	--单纱〔999〕	5		90	13/	13	千克			/30
5509.2200	--多股纱线或缆线〔999〕	5		90	13/	13	千克			/30
	-按重量计聚丙烯腈或变性聚丙烯腈短纤含量在85%及以上：									
5509.3100	--单纱〔999〕	5		90	13/	13	千克			/
5509.3200	--多股纱线或缆线〔999〕	5		90	13/	13	千克			/30
	-其他纱线，按重量计合成纤维短纤含量在85%及以上：									
5509.4100	--单纱〔999〕	5		90	13/	13	千克			/
5509.4200	--多股纱线或缆线〔999〕	5		90	13/	13	千克			/30
	-其他聚酯短纤纺制的纱线：									
5509.5100	--主要或仅与人造纤维短纤混纺〔999〕	5		90	13/	13	千克			/30
5509.5200	--主要或仅与羊毛或动物细毛混纺〔999〕	5		90	13/	13	千克			/30
5509.5300	--主要或仅与棉混纺〔999〕	5		90	13/	13	千克			/30
5509.5900	--其他〔999〕	5		90	13/	13	千克			/15
	-其他聚丙烯腈或变性聚丙烯腈短纤纺制的纱线：									
5509.6100	--主要或仅与羊毛或动物细毛混纺〔999〕	5		90	13/	13	千克			/30
5509.6200	--主要或仅与棉混纺〔999〕	5		90	13/	13	千克			/
5509.6900	--其他〔999〕	5		90	13/	13	千克			/
	-其他纱线：									
5509.9100	--主要或仅与羊毛或动物细毛混纺〔999〕	5		90	13/	13	千克			/
5509.9200	--主要或仅与棉混纺〔999〕	5		90	13/	13	千克			/
5509.9900	--其他〔999〕	5		90	13/	13	千克			/25
55.10	**人造纤维短纤纺制的纱线(缝纫线除外)，非供零售用：**									
	-按重量计人造纤维短纤含量在85%及以上：									
5510.1100	--单纱〔999〕	5		70	13/	13	千克			/
5510.1200	--多股纱线或缆线〔999〕	5		70	13/	13	千克			/30
5510.2000	-其他纱线，主要或仅与羊毛或动物细毛混纺〔999〕	5		70	13/	13	千克			/30
5510.3000	-其他纱线，主要或仅与棉混纺〔999〕	5		70	13/	13	千克			/
5510.9000	-其他〔999〕	5		70	13/	13	千克			/
55.11	**化学纤维短纤纺制的纱线(缝纫线除外)，供零售用：**									
5511.1000	-按重量计合成纤维短纤含量在85%及以上〔999〕	5		90	13/	13	千克			/25
5511.2000	-按重量计合成纤维短纤含量在85%以下〔999〕	5		90	13/	13	千克			/30
5511.3000	-人造纤维短纤纺制〔999〕	5		90	13/	13	千克			/

协定税率 %										特惠税率 %			
亚太5国	东/冰/格	巴基斯坦	韩国	瑞士	哥达	秘鲁	澳大利亚	新西/坡/智	港/澳/台	亚太2国	老/柬/缅	36/3/1	Article Description
	0/0/0	0	3	0	0	0	0	0//0	0/0/			0/0/0	----Other
	0/0/0	0	0	0	0	0	0	0//0	0/0/			0/0/0	---Other
3.3	/0/0	4.5	2	0	0	0	0	0//0	0/0/			0/0/0	-Of polyesters
													-Acrylic or modacrylic
3.3	/0/0	4.5	2	0	0	0	0	0//0	0/0/			0/0/0	Staple fibres of acrylic, carded, combed or otherwise processed forspinning(other than modacrylic)
3.3	/0/0	4.5	2	0	0	0	0	0//0	0/0/			0/0/0	Staple fibres of modacrylic, carded, combed or otherwise processed forspinning
	0/0/0	0	3	0	0	0	0	0//0	0/0/			0/0/0	-Of polyphenylene
													-Other:
	0/0/0	0	3	0	0	0	0	0//0	0/0/			0/0/0	Polyphe-nylenesu staple fibres
	0/0/0	0	3	0	0	0	0	0//0	0/0/			0/0/0	---Other
													Artificial staple fibres, carded, combed or otherwise processed for spinning:
	0/0/0	0	0	0	0	0	0	0//0	0/0/			0/0/0	Artificial staple fibres, carded, combed or otherwise processed for spinning
													Sewingthread of man-made staple fibres, whether or not put up for retail sale:
3.3	0/0/0	0	0	0	0	0	0	0//0	0/0/			0/0/0	-Of synthetic staple fibres
	0/0/0	0	0	0	0	0	0	0//0	0/0/			0/0/0	-Of artificial staple fibres
													Yarn (other than sewing thread) of synthetic staple fibres, not put up for retail sale:
													-Containing 85% or more by weight of staple fibres of nylon or other polyamides:
	0/0/0	0	0	0	0	0	0	0//0	0/0/			0/0/0	--Single yarn
	0/0/0	0	0	0	0	0	0	0//0	0/0/			0/0/0	--Multiple (folded) or cabled yarn
													-Containing 85% or more by weight of polyester staple fibres:
	0/0/0	0	0	0	0	0	0	0//0	0/0/			0/0/0	--Single yarn
	0/0/0	0	0	0	0	0	0	0//0	0/0/			0/0/0	--Multiple (folded) or cabled yarn
													-Containing 85% or more by weight of acrylic or modacrylic staple fibres:
	0/0/0	0	0	0	0	0	0	0//0	0/0/			0/0/0	--Single yarn
3.3	0/0/0	0	0	0	0	0	0	0//0	0/0/0			0/0/0	--Multiple (folded) or cabled yarn
													-Other yarn, containing 85% or more by weight of synthetic staple fibres:
	0/0/0	0	0	0	0	0	0	0//0	0/0/			0/0/0	--Single yarn
	0/0/0	0	2	0	0	0	0	0//0	0/0/			0/0/0	--Multiple (folded) or cabled yarn
													-Other yarn, of polyester staple fibres:
	0/0/0	0	2	0	0	0	0	0//0	0/0/			0/0/0	--Mixed mainly or solely with artificial staple fibres
	0/0/0	0	0	0	0	0	0	0//0	0/0/			0/0/0	--Mixed mainly or solely with wool or fine animal hair
3.3	0/0/0	0	0	0	0	0	0	0//0	0/0/0			0/0/0	--Mixed mainly or solely with cotton
	0/0/0	0	0	0	0	0	0	0//0	0/0/			0/0/0	--Other
													-Other yarn, of acrylic or modacrylic staple fibres:
	0/0/0	0	0	0	0	0	0	0//0	0/0/			0/0/0	--Mixed mainly or solely with wool or fine animal hair
3.3	0/0/0	0	0	0	0	0	0	0//0	0/0/			0/0/0	--Mixed mainly or solely with cotton
	0/0/0	0	0	0	0	0	0	0//0	0/0/			0/0/0	--Other
													-Other yarn:
	0//0	0	0	0	0	0	0	0//0	0/0/			0/0/0	--Mixed mainly or solely with wool or fine animal hair
	0/0/0	0	0	0	0	0	0	0//0	0/0/0			0/0/0	--Mixed mainly or solely with cotton
	0/0/0	0	0	0	0	0	0	0//0	0/0/			0/0/0	--Other
													Yarn (other than sewing thread) of artificial staple fibres, not put up for retail sale:
													-Containing 85% or more by weight of artificial staple fibres:
3.3	0/0/0	0	3	0	0	0	0	0//0	0/0/0			0/0/0	--Single yarn
	0/0/0	0	3	0	0	0	0	0//0	0/0/0			0/0/0	--Multiple (folded) or cabled yarn
	0/0/0	0	0	0	0	0	0	0//0	0/0/			0/0/0	-Other yarn, mixed mainly or solely with wool or fine animal hair
3.3	0/0/0	0	0	0	0	0	0	0//0	0/0/0			0/0/0	-Other yarn, mixed mainly or solely with cotton
3.3	0/0/0	0	2	0	0	0	0	0//0	0/0/			0/0/0	-Other yarn
													Yarn (other than sewing thread) of man-made staple fibres, put up for retail sale:
	0/0/0	0	0	0	0	0	0	0//0	0/0/			36/0/0	-Of synthetic staple fibres, containing 85% or more by weight of such fibres
	0/0/0	0	0	0	0	0	0	0//0	0/0/			0/0/0	-Of synthetic staple fibres, containing less than 85% by weight of such fibres
	0/0/0	0	0	0	0	0	0	0//0	0/0/			0/0/0	-Of artificial staple fibres

税则号列		货品名称〔CIQ 扩展编码及品名—T2 表示见附表 2〕	最惠(%)	暂定税率	普通	增值/消费	出口退税	计量单位	监管条件	检验检疫	特殊证件对美关税
55.12		**合成纤维短纤纺制的机织物，按重量计合成纤维短纤含量在 85%及以上：**									
		-按重量计聚酯短纤含量在 85%及以上：									
5512.1100		--未漂白或漂白〔999〕	8		130	13/	13	米/千克			/33
5512.1900		--其他〔999〕	8		130	13/	13	米/千克			/33
		-按重量计聚丙烯腈或变性聚丙烯腈短纤含量在 85%及以上：									
5512.2100		--未漂白或漂白〔999〕	8		130	13/	13	米/千克			/28
5512.2900		--其他〔999〕	8		130	13/	13	米/千克			/18
		-其他：									
5512.9100		--未漂白或漂白〔999〕	8		130	13/	13	米/千克			/33
5512.9900		--其他〔999〕	8		130	13/	13	米/千克			/33
55.13		**合成纤维短纤纺制的机织物，按重量计合成纤维短纤含量在 85%以下，主要或仅与棉混纺，每平方米重量不超过 170 克：**									
		-未漂白或漂白：									
		--聚酯短纤纺制的平纹机织物：									
5513.1110		---未漂白〔101 棉混纺坯布，102 合成纤维混纺机织物〕	8		130	13/	13	米/千克			/18
5513.1120		---漂白									
5513.1120	10	与棉混纺漂白聚酯短纤平纹府绸（聚酯短纤 85%以下，每平方米重≤170 克，含细平布）〔101 漂白棉混纺布，102 合成纤维混纺机织物〕	8		130	13/	13	米/千克			/18
5513.1120	20	与棉混纺漂白聚酯短纤机织平布（混纺为含聚酯短纤 85%以下，轻质指每平方米重≤170 克）〔101 漂白棉混纺布，102 合成纤维混纺机织物〕	8		130	13/	13	米/千克			/18
5513.1120	30	与棉混纺漂白聚酯平纹印染用布（混纺为含聚酯短纤 85%以下，轻质指每平方米重≤170 克）〔101 漂白棉混纺布，102 合成纤维混纺机织物〕	8		130	13/	13	米/千克			/18
5513.1120	40	与棉混纺漂白聚酯短纤平纹奶酪布等（聚酯短纤＜85%，每平方米重≤170 克，含薄细布、巴里纱）〔101 漂白棉混纺布，102 合成纤维混纺机织物〕	8		130	13/	13	米/千克			/18
		--聚酯短纤纺制的三线或四线斜纹机织物，包括双面斜纹机织物：									
5513.1210		---未漂白〔101 棉混纺坯布，102 漂白棉混纺布，103 合成纤维混纺机织物〕	8		130	13/	13	米/千克			/18
5513.1220		---漂白〔101 漂白棉混纺布，102 合成纤维混纺机织物〕	8		130	13/	13	米/千克			/18
		--其他聚酯短纤纺制的机织物：									
5513.1310		---未漂白〔101 棉混纺坯布，102 合成纤维混纺机织物〕	8		130	13/	13	米/千克			/18
5513.1320		---漂白〔101 漂白棉混纺布，102 合成纤维混纺机织物〕	8		130	13/	13	米/千克			/18
5513.1900		--其他机织物〔101 棉混纺坯布，102 漂白棉混纺布，103 合成纤维混纺机织物〕	8		130	13/	13	米/千克			/18
		-染色：									
5513.2100		--聚酯短纤纺制的平纹机织物〔101 棉混纺染色布，102 合成纤维混纺机织物〕	8		130	13/	13	米/千克			/33
		--其他聚酯短纤纺制的机织物：									
5513.2310		---聚酯短纤纺制的三线或四线斜纹机织物，包括双面斜纹机织物〔101 棉混纺染色布，102 合成纤维混纺机织物〕	8		130	13/	13	米/千克			/
5513.2390		---其他〔101 棉混纺染色布，102 合成纤维混纺机织物〕	8		130	13/	13	米/千克			/33
5513.2900		--其他机织物〔101 棉混纺染色布，102 合成纤维混纺机织物〕	8		130	13/	13	米/千克			/33
		-色织：									
5513.3100		--聚酯短纤纺制的平纹机织物〔101 色织棉混纺布，102 合成纤维混纺机织物〕	8		130	13/	13	米/千克			/33
		--其他机织物：									
5513.3910		---聚酯短纤纺制的三线或四线斜纹机织物，包括双面斜纹机织物〔101 色织棉混纺布，102 合成纤维混纺机织物〕	8		130	13/	13	米/千克			/
5513.3920		---其他聚酯短纤纺制的机织物〔101 色织棉混纺布，102 合成纤维混纺机织物〕	8		130	13/	13	米/千克			/
5513.3990		---其他〔101 色织棉混纺布，102 合成纤维混纺机织物〕	8		130	13/	13	米/千克			/
		-印花：									
5513.4100		--聚酯短纤纺制的平纹机织物〔101 棉混纺印花布，102 合成纤维混纺机织物〕	8		130	13/	13	米/千克			/
		--其他机织物：									

协定税率 %										特惠税率 %			
亚太5国	东/冰/格	巴基斯坦	韩国	瑞士	哥达	秘鲁	澳大利亚	新西/坡/智	港/澳/台	亚太2国	老/柬/缅	36/3/1	Article Description
													Woven fabrics of synthetic staple fibres, containing 85% or more by weight of synthetic staple fibres:
													-Containing 85% or more by weight of polyester staple fibres:
5.2	0/0/0	0	6	4.5	0	0	0	0/0/0	0/0/0			0/0/0	--Unbleached or bleached
	0/0/0	0	7	0	0	0	0	0/0/0	0/0/0			0/0/0	--Other
													-Containing 85% or more by weight of acrylic or modacrylic staple fibres:
	0/0/0	0	5.2	3.9	0	0	0	0/0/0	0/0/			0/0/0	--Unbleached or bleached
5.2	0/0/0	0	0	0	0	0	0	0/0/0	0/0/			0/0/	--Other
													-Other:
	0/0/0	0	7.2	5.4	0	0	0	0/0/0	0/0/			0/0/	--Unbleached or bleached
	0/0/0	0	6	0	0	0	0	0/0/0	0/0/0		0/0/0	0/0/0	--Other
													Woven fabrics of synthetic staple fibres, containing less than 85% by weight of such fibres, mixed mainly or solely with cotton, of a weight not exceeding 170 g/m²:
													-Unbleached or bleached:
													--Of polyester staple fibres, plain weave:
4.8	0/0/0	0	6.4	4.8	0	0	0	0/0/0	0/0/			0/0/	---Unbleached
													---Bleached
4.8	0/0/0	0	6	4.5	0	0	0	0/0/0	0/0/			0/0/	Poplin, plain weave, including fine plain cloth, mixed with cotton, containing＜85% by weight of polyester staple fibres, weight≤170g/m², bleached
4.8	0/0/0	0	6	4.5	0	0	0	0/0/0	0/0/			0/0/	Plain cloth, mixed with cotton, containing＜85% by weight of polyester staple fibres, weight≤170g/m², bleached
4.8	0/0/0	0	6	4.5	0	0	0	0/0/0	0/0/			0/0/	Woven fabrics for printing and dying, plain weave, mixed with cotton, containing＜85% by weight of polyesterstaple fibres, weight≤170g/m², bleached
4.8	0/0/0	0	6	4.5	0	0	0	0/0/0	0/0/			0/0/	Cheese cloth, plain weave, including voiles and fine thin cloth, mixed with cotton, containing＜85% by weight of polyester staple fibres, weight≤170g/m², bleached
													--3-thread or 4-thread twill, including cross twill, of polyester staple fibres:
	0/0/0	0	6.4	4.8	0	0	0	0/0/0	0/0/			0/0/	---Unbleached
	0/0/0	0	7.2	5.4	0	0	0	0/0/0	0/0/			0/0/	---Bleached
													--Other woven fabrics of polyester staple fibres:
7.2	0/0/0	0	6.4	4.8	0	0	0	0/0/0	0/0/			0/0/	---Unbleached
	0/0/0	0	7.2	5.4	0	0	0	0/0/0	0/0/			0/0/	---Bleached
4.8	0/0/0	0	7.2	5.4	0	0	0	0/0/0	0/0/			0/0/	--Other woven fabrics
													-Dyed:
5.2	0/0/0	0	0	0	0	0	0	0/0/0	0/0/0			0/0/	--Of polyester staple fibres, plain weave
													--Other woven fabrics of polyester staple fibres:
	0/0/0	0	0	0	0	0	0	0/0/0	0/0/			0/0/	---3-thread or 4-thread twill, including cross twill, of polyester staple fibres
	0/0/0	0	4	0	0	0	0	0/0/0	0/0/			0/0/	---Other
	0/0/0	0	0	0	0	0	0	0/0/0	0/0/			0/0/0	--Other woven fabrics
													-Of yarns of different colours:
	0/0/0	0	0	0	0	0	0	0/0/0	0/0/			0/0/	--Of polyester staple fibres, plain weave
													--Other woven fabrics:
5.2	0/0/0	0	0	0	0	0	0	0/0/0	0/0/			0/0/	---3-thread or 4-thread twill, including cross twill, of polyester staple fibres
	0/0/0	0	0	0	0	0	0	0/0/0	0/0/			0/0/	---Other woven fabrics of polyester staple fibres
	0/0/0	0	0	0	0	0	0	0/0/0	0/0/			0/0/	---Other
													-Printed:
	0/0/0	0	0	0	0	0	0	0/0/0	0/0/		0/0/0	0/0/0	--Of polyester staple fibres, plain weave
													--Other woven fabrics:

税则号列	货品名称〔CIQ扩展编码及品名—T2表示见附表2〕	最惠(%)	暂定税率	普通	增值/消费	出口退税	计量单位	监管条件	检验检疫	特殊证件对美关税
5513.4910	---聚酯短纤纺制的三线或四线斜纹机织物,包括双面斜纹机织物〔101 棉混纺印花布,102 合成纤维混纺机织物〕	8		130	13/	13	米/千克			/
5513.4920	---其他聚酯短纤纺制的机织物〔101 棉混纺印花布,102 合成纤维混纺机织物〕	8		130	13/	13	米/千克			/
5513.4990	---其他〔101 棉混纺印花布,102 合成纤维混纺机织物〕	8		130	13/	13	米/千克			/
55.14	**合成纤维短纤纺制的机织物,按重量计合成纤维短纤含量在85%以下,主要或仅与棉混纺,每平方米重量超过170克:**									
	-未漂白或漂白:									
	--聚酯短纤纺制的平纹机织物:									
5514.1110	---未漂白〔101 棉混纺坯布,102 合成纤维混纺机织物〕	8		130	13/	13	米/千克			/18
5514.1120	---漂白〔101 漂白棉混纺布,102 合成纤维混纺机织物〕	8		130	13/	13	米/千克			/33
	--聚酯短纤纺制的三线或四线斜纹机织物,包括双面斜纹机织物:									
5514.1210	---未漂白〔101 棉混纺坯布,102 合成纤维混纺机织物〕	8		130	13/	13	米/千克			/18
5514.1220	---漂白〔101 漂白棉混纺布,102 合成纤维混纺机织物〕	8		130	13/	13	米/千克			/18
	--其他机织物:									
	---聚酯短纤纺制的机织物:									
5514.1911	----未漂白〔101 棉混纺坯布,102 合成纤维混纺机织物〕	8		130	13/	13	米/千克			/18
5514.1912	----漂白〔101 漂白棉混纺布,102 合成纤维混纺机织物〕	8		130	13/	13	米/千克			/18
5514.1990	---其他〔101 棉混纺坯布,102 漂白棉混纺布,103 合成纤维混纺机织物〕	8		130	13/	13	米/千克			/33
	-染色:									
5514.2100	--聚酯短纤纺制的平纹机织物〔101 棉混纺染色布,102 合成纤维混纺机织物〕	8		130	13/	13	米/千克			/33
5514.2200	--聚酯短纤纺制的三线或四线斜纹机织物,包括双面斜纹机织物〔101 棉混纺染色布,102 合成纤维混纺机织物〕	8		130	13/	13	米/千克			/33
5514.2300	--其他聚酯短纤纺制的机织物〔101 棉混纺染色布,102 合成纤维混纺机织物〕	8		130	13/	13	米/千克			/33
5514.2900	--其他机织物〔101 棉混纺染色布,102 合成纤维混纺机织物〕	8		130	13/	13	米/千克			/33
	-色织:									
5514.3010	---聚酯短纤纺制的平纹机织物〔101 色织棉混纺布,102 合成纤维混纺机织物〕	8		130	13/	13	米/千克			/33
5514.3020	---聚酯短纤纺制的三线或四线斜纹机织物,包括双面斜纹机织物〔101 色织棉混纺布,102 合成纤维混纺机织物〕	8		130	13/	13	米/千克			/
5514.3030	---其他聚酯短纤纺制的机织物〔101 色织棉混纺布,102 合成纤维混纺机织物〕	8		130	13/	13	米/千克			/28
5514.3090	---其他机织物〔101 色织棉混纺布,102 合成纤维混纺机织物〕	8		130	13/	13	米/千克			/33
	-印花:									
5514.4100	--聚酯短纤纺制的平纹机织物〔101 棉混纺印花布,102 合成纤维混纺机织物〕	8		130	13/	13	米/千克			/18
5514.4200	--聚酯短纤纺制的三线或四线斜纹机织物,包括双面斜纹机织物〔101 棉混纺印花布,102 合成纤维混纺机织物〕	8		130	13/	13	米/千克			/
5514.4300	--其他聚酯短纤纺制的机织物〔101 棉混纺印花布,102 合成纤维混纺机织物〕	8		130	13/	13	米/千克			/18
5514.4900	--其他机织物〔101 棉混纺印花布,102 合成纤维混纺机织物〕	8		130	13/	13	米/千克			/
55.15	**合成纤维短纤纺制的其他机织物:**									
	-聚酯短纤纺制:									
5515.1100	--主要或仅与粘胶纤维短纤混纺〔999〕	8		130	13/	13	米/千克			/33
5515.1200	--主要或仅与化学纤维长丝混纺〔999〕	8		130	13/	13	米/千克			/33
5515.1300	--主要或仅与羊毛或动物细毛混纺〔999〕	8		130	13/	13	米/千克			/33
5515.1900	--其他〔999〕	8		130	13/	13	米/千克			/33
	-聚丙烯腈或变性聚丙烯腈短纤纺制:									
5515.2100	--主要或仅与化学纤维长丝混纺〔999〕	8		130	13/	13	米/千克			/18
5515.2200	--主要或仅与羊毛或动物细毛混纺〔999〕	8		130	13/	13	米/千克			/
5515.2900	--其他〔999〕	8		130	13/	13	米/千克			/33
	-其他机织物:									
5515.9100	--主要或仅与化学纤维长丝混纺〔999〕	8		130	13/	13	米/千克			/33
5515.9900	--其他〔999〕	8		130	13/	13	米/千克			/28
55.16	**人造纤维短纤纺制的机织物:**									
	-按重量计人造纤维短纤含量在85%及以上:									
5516.1100	--未漂白或漂白〔999〕	8		130	13/	13	米/千克			/33
5516.1200	--染色〔999〕	8		130	13/	13	米/千克			/28

协定税率 %										特惠税率 %			Article Description
亚太5国	东/冰/格	巴基斯坦	韩国	瑞士	哥达	秘鲁	澳大利亚	新西/坡/智	港/澳/台	亚太2国	老/柬/缅	36/3/1	
	0/0/0	0	0	0	0	0	0	0/0/0	0/0/			0/0/	---3-thread or 4-thread twill, including cross twill, of polyeste staple fibres
	0/0/0	0	0	0	0	0	0	0/0/0	0/0/			0/0/	---Other woven fabrics of polyester staple fibres
	0/0/0	0	0	0	0	0	0	0/0/0	0/0/			0/0/	---Other
													Woven fabrics of synthetic staple fibres, containing less than 85% by weight of such fibres, mixed mainly or solely with cotton, of a weight exceeding 170 g/m²:
													-Unbleached or bleached:
													--Of polyester staple fibres, plain weave:
5.2	0/0/0	0	6.4	4.8	0	0	0	0/0/0	0/0/			0/0/	---Unbleached
	0/0/0	0	7.2	5.4	0	0	0	0/0/0	0/0/			0/0/	---Bleached
													--3-thread or 4-thread twill, including cross twill, of polyester staple fibres:
	0/0/0	0	6.4	4.8	0	0	0	0/0/0	0/0/			0/0/	---Unbleached
	0/0/0	0	7.2	5.4	0	0	0	0/0/0	0/0/			0/0/	---Bleached
													--Other woven fabrics:
													---Other woven fabrics of polyester staple fibres:
	0/0/0	0	6.4	4.8	0	0	0	0/0/0	0/0/			0/0/	----Unbleached
	0/0/0	0	7.2	5.4	0	0	0	0/0/0	0/0/			0/0/	----Bleached
5.2	0/0/0	0	6.4	4.8	0	0	0	0/0/0	0/0/			0/0/	---Other
													-Dyed:
	0/0/0	0	0	0	0	0	0	0/0/0	0/0/			0/0/	--Of polyester staple fibres, plain weave
	0/0/0	0	0	0	0	0	0	0/0/0	0/0/			0/0/	--3-thread or 4-thread twill, including cross twill, of polyester staple fibres
	0/0/0	0	0	0	0	0	0	0/0/0	0/0/		0/0/0	0/0/0	--Other woven fabrics of polyester staple fibres
	0/0/0	0	0	0	0	0	0	0/0/0	0/0/			0/0/0	--Other woven fabrics
													-Of yarns of different colours:
	0/0/0	0	0	0	0	0	0	0/0/0	0/0/			0/0/	---Of polyester staple fibres, plain weave
	0/0/0	0	0	0	0	0	0	0/0/0	0/0/			0/0/	---3-thread or 4-thread twill, including cross twill, of polyester staple fibres
	0/0/0	0	0	0	0	0	0	0/0/0	0/0/			0/0/	---Other woven fabrics of polyester staple fibres
	0/0/0	0	0	0	0	0	0	0/0/0	0/0/			0/0/	---Other woven fabrics
													-Printed:
	0/0/0	0	0	0	0	0	0	0/0/0	0/0/			0/0/	--Of polyester staple fibres, plain weave
	0/0/0	0	0	0	0	0	0	0/0/0	0/0/			0/0/	--3-thread or 4-thread twill, including cross twill, of polyester staple fibres
	0/0/0	0	0	0	0	0	0	0/0/0	0/0/			0/0/	--Other woven fabrics of polyester staple fibres
	0/0/0	0	0	0	0	0	0	0/0/0	0/0/			0/0/	--Other woven fabrics
													Other woven fabrics of synthetic staple fibres:
													-Of polyester staple fibres:
5.2	0/0/0	0	0	0	0	0	0	0/0/0	0/0/0			0/0/	--Mixed mainly or solely with viscose rayon staple fibres
5.2	0/0/0	0	0	0	0	0	0	0/0/0	0/0/0			0/0/	--Mixed mainly or solely with man-made filaments
	0/0/0	0	0	0	0	0	0	0/0/0	0/0/			0/0/	--Mixed mainly or solely with wool or fine animal hair
5.2	0/0/0	0	0	0	0	0	0	0/0/0	0/0/			0/0/	--Other
													-Of acrylic or modacrylic staple fibres:
	0/0/0	0	0	0	0	0	0	0/0/0	0/0/			0/0/	--Mixed mainly or solely with man-made filaments
	0/0/0	0	0	3.6	0	0	0	0/0/0	0/0/			0/0/0	--Mixed mainly or solely with wool or fine animal hair
	0/0/0	0	0	0	0	0	0	0/0/0	0/0/			0/0/	--Other
													-Other woven fabrics:
	0/0/0	0	0	0	0	0	0	0/0/0	0/0/			0/0/	--Mixed mainly or solely with man-made filaments
5.2	0/0/0	0	0	0	0	0	0	0/0/0	0/0/			0/0/	--Other
													Woven fabrics of artificial staple fibres:
													-Containing 85% or more by weight of artificial staple fibres:
	0/0/0	0	0	3.6	0	0	0	0/0/0	0/0/			0/0/0	--Unbleached or bleached
	0/0/0	0	0	0	0	0	0	0/0/0	0/0/0			0/0/	--Dyed

税则号列	货品名称〔CIQ 扩展编码及品名－T2 表示见附表 2〕	最惠(%)	暂定税率	普通	增值/消费	出口退税	计量单位	监管条件	检验检疫	特殊证件对美关税
5516.1300	--色织〔999〕	8		130	13/	13	米/千克			/33
5516.1400	--印花〔999〕	8		130	13/	13	米/千克			/33
	-按重量计人造纤维短纤含量在85%以下，主要或仅与化学纤维长丝混纺：									
5516.2100	--未漂白或漂白〔999〕	8		130	13/	13	米/千克			/28
5516.2200	--染色〔999〕	8		130	13/	13	米/千克			/33
5516.2300	--色织〔999〕	8		130	13/	13	米/千克			/28
5516.2400	--印花〔999〕	8		130	13/	13	米/千克			/
	-按重量计人造纤维短纤含量在85%以下，主要或仅与羊毛或动物细毛混纺：									
5516.3100	--未漂白或漂白〔999〕	8		130	13/	13	米/千克			/
5516.3200	--染色〔999〕	8		130	13/	13	米/千克			/
5516.3300	--色织〔999〕	8		130	13/	13	米/千克			/33
5516.3400	--印花〔999〕	8		130	13/	13	米/千克			/
	-按重量计人造纤维短纤含量在85%以下，主要或仅与棉混纺：									
5516.4100	--未漂白或漂白〔101 棉混纺坯布，102 漂白棉混纺布，103 人造纤维混纺机织物〕	8		130	13/	13	米/千克			/33
5516.4200	--染色〔101 棉混纺染色布，102 人造纤维混纺机织物〕	8		130	13/	13	米/千克			/33
5516.4300	--色织〔101 色织棉混纺布，102 人造纤维混纺机织物〕	8		130	13/	13	米/千克			/28
5516.4400	--印花〔101 棉混纺印花布，102 人造纤维混纺机织物〕	8		130	13/	13	米/千克			/
	-其他：									
5516.9100	--未漂白或漂白〔999〕	8		130	13/	13	米/千克			/
5516.9200	--染色〔999〕	8		130	13/	13	米/千克			/33
5516.9300	--色织〔999〕	8		130	13/	13	米/千克			/33
5516.9400	--印花〔999〕	8		130	13/	13	米/千克			/33

协定税率 %										特惠税率 %			Article Description
亚太5国	东/冰/格	巴基斯坦	韩国	瑞士	哥达	秘鲁	澳大利亚	新西/坡/智	港/澳/台	亚太2国	老/柬/缅	36/3/1	
	0/0/0	0	0	0	0	0	0	0/0/0	0/0/			0/0/	--Of yarns of different colours
	0/0/0	0	0	0	0	0	0	0/0/0	0/0/			0/0/	--Printed
													-Containing less than 85% by weight of artificial staple fibres, mixed mainly or solely with man-made filaments:
	0/0/0	0	0	3.6	0	0	0	0/0/0	0/0/			0/0/	--Unbleached or bleached
5.2	0/0/0	0	6	0	0	0	0	0/0/0	0/0/0			0/0/	--Dyed
	0/0/0	0	0	0	0	0	0	0/0/0	0/0/			0/0/	--Of yarns of different colours
	0/0/0	0	0	0	0	0	0	0/0/0	0/0/			0/0/	--Printed
													-Containing less than 85% by weight of artficial staple fibres, mixed mainly or solely with wool or fine animal hair:
	0/0/0	0	0	3.6	0	0	0	0/0/0	0/0/			0/0/	--Unbleached or bleached
	0/0/0	0	0	0	0	0	0	0/0/0	0/0/			0/0/	--Dyed
	0/0/0	0	0	0	0	0	0	0/0/0	0/0/			0/0/	--Of yarns of different colours
	0/0/0	0	0	0	0	0	0	0/0/0	0/0/			0/0/	--Printed
													-Containing less than 85% by weight of artificial staple fibres, mixed mainly or solely with cotton:
	0/0/0	0	0	3.6	0	0	0	0/0/0	0/0/			0/0/	--Unbleached or bleached
	0/0/0	0	0	3.6	0	0	0	0/0/0	0/0/			0/0/	--Dyed
	0/0/0	0	0	0	0	0	0	0/0/0	0/0/			0/0/	--Of yarns of different colours
	0/0/0	0	0	0	0	0	0	0/0/0	0/0/			0/0/	--Printed
													-Other:
	0/0/0	0	0	3.6	0	0	0	0/0/0	0/0/			0/0/	—Unbleached or bleached
	0/0/0	0	6	0	0	0	0	0/0/0	0/0/			0/0/0	—Dyed
	0/0/0	0	0	0	0	0	0	0/0/0	0/0/			0/0/	—Of yarns of different colours
5.2	0/0/0	0	0	0	0	0	0	0/0/0	0/0/			0/0/	—Printed

第五十六章
絮胎、毡呢及无纺织物；特种纱线；线、绳、索、缆及其制品

注释：

一、本章不包括：

(一)用各种物质或制剂(例如，第三十三章的香水或化妆品、税目 34.01 的肥皂或洗涤剂、税目 34.05 的光洁剂及类似制剂、税目 38.09 的织物柔软剂)浸渍、涂布、包覆的絮胎、毡呢或无纺织物，其中的纺织材料仅作为承载介质；

(二)税目 58.11 的纺织产品；

(三)以毡呢或无纺织物为底的砂布及类似品(税目 68.05)；

(四)以毡呢或无纺织物为底的粘聚或复制云母(税目 68.14)；

(五)以毡呢或无纺织物为底的金属箔(通常归入第十四类或第十五类)。

(六)税目 96.19 的卫生巾(护垫)及止血塞、婴儿尿布及尿布衬里和类似品。

二、所称“毡呢”，包括针刺机制毡呢以及纤维本身通过缝编工序增强了抱合力的纺织纤维网状织物。

三、税目 56.02 及 56.03 分别包括用各种性质(紧密结构或泡沫状)的塑料或橡胶浸渍、涂布、包覆或层压的毡呢及无纺织物。

税目 56.03 还包括用塑料或橡胶作粘合材料的无纺织物。

但税目 56.02 及 56.03 不包括：

(一)用塑料或橡胶浸渍、涂布、包覆或层压，按重量计纺织材料含量在 50%及以下的毡呢或者完全嵌入塑料或橡胶之内的毡呢(第三十九章或第四十章)；

(二)完全嵌入塑料或橡胶之内的无纺织物，以及用肉眼可辨别出两面都用塑料或橡胶涂布、包覆的无纺织物，涂布或包覆所引起的颜色变化可不予考虑(第三十九章或第四十章)；

(三)与毡呢或无纺织物混制的泡沫塑料或海绵橡胶板、片或扁条，纺织材料仅在其中起增强作用(第三十九章或第四十章)。

四、税目 56.04 不包括用肉眼无法辨别出是否经过浸渍、涂布或包覆的纺织纱线或税目 54.04 或 54.05 的扁条及类似品(通常归入第五十章至第五十五章)；运用本条规定，可不考虑浸渍、涂布或包覆所引起的颜色变化。

税则号列	货品名称〔CIQ 扩展编码及品名—T2 表示见附表 2〕	最惠(%)	暂定税率	普通	增值/消费	出口退税	计量单位	监管条件	检验检疫	特殊证件对美关税
56.01	**纺织材料絮胎及其制品；长度不超过 5 毫米的纺织纤维(纤维屑)、纤维粉末及球结：**									
	-纺织材料制的絮胎及其制品：									
5601.2100	--棉制〔999〕	8		50	13/	13	千克			/33
	--化学纤维制：									
5601.2210	---卷烟滤嘴〔999〕	8		100	13/	13	千克	7		/
5601.2290	---其他〔999〕	8		100	13/	13	千克			/18
5601.2900	--其他〔999〕	8		90	13/	13	千克			/33
5601.3000	-纤维屑、纤维粉末及球结									
5601.3000 10	由两种或以上有机聚合物纺制的纤维(横截面为皮芯结构或并列结构或海岛结构，长度不超过 5mm)〔999〕	8	5	100	13/	13	千克			/15
5601.3000 90	纺织纤维屑，纤维粉末及球结(纺织纤维长度不超过 5mm)〔999〕	8		100	13/	13	千克			/18
56.02	**毡呢，不论是否浸渍、涂布、包覆或层压：**									
5602.1000	-针刺机制毡呢及纤维缝编织物〔999〕	8		100	13/	13	千克			/18
	-其他毡呢，未浸渍、涂布、包覆或层压：									
5602.2100	--羊毛或动物细毛制〔999〕	8		100	13/	13	千克			/33
5602.2900	--其他纺织材料制〔999〕	8		100	13/	13	千克			/28
5602.9000	-其他〔999〕	8		100	13/	13	千克			/28
56.03	**无纺织物，不论是否浸渍、涂布、包覆或层压：**									
	-化学纤维长丝制：									
	--每平方米重量不超过 25 克：									
5603.1110	---经浸渍、涂布、包覆或层压〔999〕	8		70	13/	13	千克			/33
5603.1190	---其他〔999〕	8		130	13/	13	千克			/33
	--每平方米重量超过 25 克，但不超过 70 克：									
5603.1210	---经浸渍、涂布、包覆或层压〔999〕	8		70	13/	13	千克			/18
5603.1290	---其他〔999〕	8		130	13/	13	千克			/18
	--每平方米重量超过 70 克，但不超过 150 克：									
5603.1310	---经浸渍、涂布、包覆或层压〔999〕	8		70	13/	13	千克			/18
5603.1390	---其他〔999〕	8		130	13/	13	千克			/18
	--每平方米重量超过 150 克：									

Chapter 56
Wadding, felt and nonwovens; special yarns; twine, cordage, ropes and cables and articles thereof

Notes:

1. This Chapter does not cover:

(a) Wadding, felt or nonwovens, impregnated, coated or covered with substances or preparations (for example, pefumes or cosmetics of Chapter 33, soaps or detergents of heading No.34. 01, polishes, creams or similar preparations of heading No.34. 05, fabric softeners of heading No.38. 09) where the textile material is present merely as a carrying medium;

(b) Textile products of heading No.58. 11;

(c) Natural or artificial abrasive powder or grain, on a backing of felt or nonwovens (heading No.68. 05);

(d) Agglomerated or reconstituted mica, on a backing of felt or nonwovens (heading No.68. 14);

(e) Metal foil on a backing of felt or nonwovens (Generelly section ⅩⅣ orsection ⅩⅤ).

(f) Sanitary towels(pads) and tampons, napkins and napkin liners for babies and similar articles of heading 96.19

2. The term "felt" includes needleloom felt and fabrics consisting of a web of textile fibres the cohesion of which has been enhanced by a stitch-bonding process using fibres from the web itself.

3. Headings No.56. 02 and 56. 03 cover respectively felt and nonwovens, impregnated, coated, covered or laminated with plastics or rubber whatever the nature of these materials (compact or cellular).

Heading No.56. 03 also includes nonwovens in which plastics or rubber forms the bonding substance.

Headings No.56. 02 and 56. 03 do not, however, cover:

(a) Felt impregnated, coated, covered or laminated with plastics or rubber, containing 50% or less by weight of textile material or felt completely embedded in plastics or rubber (Chapter 39 or 40);

(b) Nonwovens, either completely embedded in plastics or rubber, or entirely coated or covered on both sides with such materials, provided that such coating or covering can be seen with the naked eye with no account being taken of any resulting change of colour (Chapter 39 or 40); or

(c) Plates, sheets or strips of cellular plastics or cellular rubber combined with felt or nonwovens, where the textile material is present merely for reinforcing purposes (Chapter 39 or 40).

4. Heading No.56. 04 does not cover textile yarn, or strip or the like of heading No.54. 04 or 54. 05, in which the impregnation, coating or covering cannot be seen with the naked eye (usually Chapters 50 to 55); for the purpose of this provision, no account should be taken of any resulting change of colour.

协定税率 %										特惠税率 %			
亚太5国	东/冰/格	巴基斯坦	韩国	瑞士	哥达	秘鲁	澳大利亚	新西/坡/智	港/澳/台	亚太2国	老/柬/缅	36/3/1	Article Description
													Wadding of textile materials and articles thereof; textile fibres, not exceeding 5 mm in length (flock), textile dust and mill neps:
													-wadding of textile materials and articles thereof:
	0/0/0	4.5	0	0	0	0	0	0/0/0	0/0/			0/0/	--Of cotton
													--Of man-made fibres:
	0/0/	4.8		3.6	0	0		0/0/0	0/0/			0/0/	---Cigarette filter tips
	0/0/0		7.2	3.6	0	0	0	0/0/0	0/0/0			0/0/0	---Other
	0/0/0	4.5	0	0	0	0	0	0/0/0	0/0/			0/0/0	--Other
													-Textile flock and dust and mill neps
	0/0/0	4.5	0	0	0	0	0	0/0/0	0/0/			0/0/	Textile fibres of two or more organic polymers (skin/core, side-by-side or island-in-the-sea type cross-section, length ≤5mm)
	0/0/0	4.5	0	0	0	0	0	0/0/0	0/0/			0/0/	Textile flock and dust and mill neps, length≤5mm
													Felt, whether or not impregnated, coated, covered or laminated:
	0/0/0	4.5	0	0	0	0	0	0/0/0	0/0/			0/0/	-Needleloom felt and stitch-bonded fibre fabrics
													-Other felt, not impregnated, coated, covered or laminated:
	0/0/0	4.5	0	0	0	0	0	0/0/0	0/0/			0/0/	--Of wool or fine animal hair
	0/0/0	4.5	0	0	0	0	0	0/0/0	0/0/			0/0/	--Of other textile materials
	0/0/0	4.5	0	0	0	0	0	0/0/0	0/0/			0/0/0	-Other
													Nonwovens, whether or not impregnated, coated, covered or laminated:
													-Of man-made filaments:
													--Weighing not more than 25 g/m²
5.2	0/0/0	0	0	0	0	0	0	0/0/0	0/0/0		0/0/0	0/0/0	---Impregnated, coated, covered or laminated
6.8	0/0/0	0	4	0	0	0	0	0/0/0	0/0/			0/0/	---Other
													--Weighing more than 25 g/m² but not more than 70 g/m²:
5.2	0/0/0	0	6	0	0	0	0	0/0/0	0/0/		0/0/0	0/0/0	---Impregnated, coated, covered or laminated
	0/0/0	0	0	0	0	0	0	0/0/0	0/0/0			0/0/0	---Other
													--Weighing more than 70 g/m² but not more than 150 g/m²:
5.2	0/0/0	0	0	0	0	0	0	0/0/0	0/0/0			0/0/	---Impregnated, coated, covered or laminated
	0/0/0	0	0	0	0	0	0	0/0/0	0/0/0			0/0/0	---Other
													--Weighing more than 150 g/m²:

税则号列	货品名称〔CIQ 扩展编码及品名－T2 表示见附表 2〕	最惠(%)	暂定税率	普通	增值/消费	出口退税	计量单位	监管条件	检验检疫	特殊证件对美关税
5603.1410	---经浸渍、涂布、包覆或层压〔999〕	8		70	13/	13	千克			/28
5603.1490	---其他〔999〕	8		130	13/	13	千克			/28
	-其他：									
	--每平方米重量不超过 25 克：									
5603.9110	---经浸渍、涂布、包覆或层压									
5603.9110 10	每平方米重量≤25 克经浸渍的乙烯聚合物制电池隔膜基布(浸渍包括涂布、包覆或层压)〔999〕	8	5	70	13/	13	千克			/25
5603.9110 90	每平方米重量≤25 克经浸渍其他无纺布(浸渍包括涂布、包覆或层压)〔999〕	8		70	13/	13	千克			/28
5603.9190	---其他〔999〕	8		85	13/	13	千克			/33
	--每平方米重量超过 25 克，但不超过 70 克：									
5603.9210	---经浸渍、涂布、包覆或层压									
5603.9210 10	25 克＜每平方米重量≤70 克浸渍的乙烯聚合物制电池隔膜基布(浸渍包括涂布、包覆或层压)〔999〕	8	5	70	13/	13	千克			/15
5603.9210 90	25 克＜每平方米重量≤70 克经浸渍其他无纺布(浸渍包括涂布、包覆或层压)〔999〕	8		70	13/	13	千克			/18
5603.9290	---其他〔999〕	8		85	13/	13	千克			/18
	--每平方米重量超过 70 克，但不超过 150 克：									
5603.9310	---经浸渍、涂布、包覆或层压									
5603.9310 10	70＜每平方米重≤150 克浸渍的乙烯聚合物制电池隔膜基布(浸渍包括涂布、包覆或压层)〔999〕	8	5	70	13/	13	千克			/25
5603.9310 90	70＜每平方米重≤150 克浸渍其他无纺布(浸渍包括涂布、包覆或压层)〔999〕	8		70	13/	13	千克			/28
5603.9390	---其他〔999〕	8		85	13/	13	千克			/28
	--每平方米重量超过 150 克：									
5603.9410	---经浸渍、涂布、包覆或层压〔999〕	8		70	13/	13	千克			/28
5603.9490	---其他〔999〕	8		85	13/	13	千克			/28
56.04	**用纺织材料包覆的橡胶线及绳；用橡胶或塑料浸渍、涂布、包覆或套裹的纺织纱线及税目 54.04 或 54.05 的扁条及类似品：**									
5604.1000	-用纺织材料包覆的橡胶线及绳〔999〕	5		80	13/	13	千克			/15
5604.9000	-其他〔999〕	5		80	13/	13	千克			/15
56.05	**含金属纱线，不论是否螺旋花线，由纺织纱线或税目 54.04 或 54.05 的扁条及类似品与金属线、扁条或粉末混合制得或用金属包覆制得：**									
5605.0000	含金属纱线，不论是否螺旋花线，由纺织纱线或税目 54.04 或 54.05 的扁条及类似品与金属线、扁条或粉末混合制得或用金属包覆制得〔999〕	5		70	13/	13	千克			/30
56.06	**粗松螺旋花线，税目 54.04 或 54.05 的扁条及类似品制的螺旋花线(税目 56.05 的货品及马毛粗松螺旋花线除外)；绳绒线(包括植绒绳绒线)；纵行起圈纱线：**									
5606.0000	绳绒线及粗松螺旋花线(包括纵行起圈纱线，但品目 5605 的货品及马毛粗松线除外)〔999〕	5		70	13/	13	千克			/30
56.07	**线、绳、索、缆，不论是否编织或编结而成，也不论是否用橡胶或塑料浸渍、涂布、包覆或套裹：**									
	-西沙尔麻或其他纺织用龙舌兰类纤维纺制：									
5607.2100	--包扎用绳〔999〕	5		50	13/	13	千克			/
5607.2900	--其他〔999〕	5		50	13/	13	千克			/
	-聚乙烯或聚丙烯纺制：									
5607.4100	--包扎用绳〔999〕	5		100	13/	13	千克			/15
5607.4900	--其他〔999〕	5		100	13/	13	千克			/15
5607.5000	-其他合成纤维纺制〔999〕	5		100	13/	13	千克			/15
	-其他：									
5607.9010	---蕉麻(马尼拉麻)或其他硬质(叶)纤维纺制〔999〕	5		50	13/	13	千克			/

协定税率 %										特惠税率 %			Article Description
亚太5国	东/冰/格	巴基斯坦	韩国	瑞士	哥达	秘鲁	澳大利亚	新西/坡/智	港/澳/台	亚太2国	老/柬/缅	36/3/1	
5.2	0/0/0	0	6	0	0	0	0	0/0/0	0/0/0			0/0/	---Impregnated, coated, covered or laminated
5.2	0/0/0	0	0	0	0	0	0	0/0/0	0/0/0			0/0/0	---Other
													-Other:
													--Weighing not more than 25 g/m²:
													---Impregnated, coated, covered or laminated
5.2	0/0/0	0	4	0	0	0	0	0/0/0	0/0/			0/0/	The weight per square meter is less than or equal to 25 grams of the impregnated polymers of ethylene (including battery diaphragm base fabricimpregnated, coated or laminated coating)
5.2	0/0/0	0	4	0	0	0	0	0/0/0	0/0/			0/0/	The weight per square meter is less than or equal to 25 grams of impregnatedother non-woven (impregnated, coated or laminated including coating)
6.8	0/0/0	0	4	0	0	0	0	0/0/0	0/0/			0/0/	---Other
													--Weighing more than 25 g/m² but not more than 70 g/m²:
													---Impregnated, coated, covered or laminated
5.2	0/0/0	0	4	0	0	0	0	0/0/0	0/0/			0/0/	25 g < the weight per square meter is less than or equal to 70 grams ofimpregnated polymers of ethylene (including battery diaphragm base fabricimpregnated, coated or laminated coating)
5.2	0/0/0	0	4	0	0	0	0	0/0/0	0/0/			0/0/	25 g < the weight per square meter is less than or equal to 70 grams ofimpregnated other non-woven (impregnated, coated or laminated including coating)
5.2	0/0/0	0	0	0	0	0	0	0//0	0/0/0		0/0/0	0/0/0	---Other
													--Weighing more than 70 g/m² but not more than 150 g/m²:
													---Impregnated, coated, covered or laminated
5.2	0/0/0	0	4	0	0	0	0	0/0/0	0/0/			0/0/	70<per square metre weighs≤150 grams or less system of impregnation of the vinyl polymer battery diaphragm base cloth (dip coating, coating or laminating)
5.2	0/0/0	0	4	0	0	0	0	0/0/0	0/0/			0/0/	70<per square metre weighs≤150 grams or less other non-woven impregnated (dip coating, coating or laminating)
5.2	0/0/0	0	0	0	0	0	0	0/0/0	0/0/0			0/0/	---Other
													–Weighing more than 150 g/m²:
5.2	0/0/0	0	0	0	0	0	0	0/0/0	0/0/0			0/0/	---Impregnated, coated, covered or laminated
5.2	0/0/0	0	6	0	0	0	0	0/0/0	0/0/0		0/0/0	0/0/0	---Other
													Rubber thread and cord, textile covered; textile yarn, and strip and the like of heading No. 54. 04 or 54. 05, impregnated, coated, covered or sheathed with rubber or plastics:
	0/0/0	0	0	0	0	0	0	0//0	0/0/		0/0/0	0/0/0	-Rubber thread and cord, textile covered
	0/0/0	0	2	0	0	0	0	0//0	0/0/			0/0/0	-Other
													Metallized yarn, whether or not gimped, being textile yarn, or strip or the like of heading No. 54. 04 or 54. 05, combined with metal in the form of thread, strip or powder or covered with metal:
	0/0/0	0	0	0	0	0	0	0//0	0/0/			0/0/0	Metallzied yarn, whether or not gimped, being textile yarn, or strip or the like of heading No. 54. 04 or 54. 05, combined with metal in the form of thread, strip or powder or covered with metal
													Gimped yarn, and strip and the like of heading No. 54. 04 or 54. 05, gimped (other than those of heading No. 56, 05 and gimped horsehair yarn); chenille yarn (including flock chenille yarn); loop wale — Yarn:
	0/0/0	0	0	0	0	0	0	0//0	0/0/			0/0/0	Gimped yarn, and strip and the like of heading No. 54. 04 or 54. 05, gimped (other than those of heading No. 56. 05 and gimped horsehair yarn); chenille yarn (including flock chenille yarn); loopwale — Yarn
													Twine, cordage, ropes and cables, whether or not plaited or braided and whether or not impregnated, coated, covered or sheathed with rubber or plastics:
													-Of sisal or other textile fibres of the genus Agave:
	0/0/0	0	0	0	0	0	0	0//0	0/0/			0/0/0	--Binder or baler twine
	0/0/0	0	0	0	0	0	0	0//0	0/0/			0/0/0	--Other
													-Of polyethylene or polypropylene:
	0/0/0	0	0	0	0	0	0	0//0	0/0/			0/0/0	--Binder or baler twine
	0/0/0	0	0	0	0	0	0	0//0	0/0/			0/0/0	--Other
	0/0/0	0	0	0	0	0	0	0//0	0/0/0			0/0/0	-Of other synthetic fibres
													-Other:
	0/0/0	0	0	0	0	0	0	0//0	0/0/			0/0/0	---Of abaca (Manila hemp or *Musa textilis Nee*) or other hard (leaf) fibres

税则号列	货品名称〔CIQ 扩展编码及品名－T2 表示见附表 2〕	最惠(%)	暂定税率	普通	增值/消费	出口退税	计量单位	监管条件	检验检疫	特殊证件对美关税
5607.9090	---其他〔999〕	5		100	13/	13	千克			/25
56.08	**线、绳或索结制的网料；纺织材料制成的渔网及其他网：**									
	-化学纤维材料制：									
5608.1100	--制成的渔网〔999〕	8		50	13/	13	千克			/
5608.1900	--其他〔999〕	8		100	13/	13	千克			/28
5608.9000	-其他〔999〕	8		100	13/	13	千克			/28
56.09	**用纱线、税目 54.04 或 54.05 的扁条及类似品或线、绳、索、缆制成的其他税目未列名物品：**									
5609.0000	用纱线、税目 54.04 或 54.05 的扁条及类似品或线、绳、索、缆制成的其他税目未列名物品〔999〕	8		100	13/	13	千克			/33

协定税率 %									特惠税率 %			Article Description
亚太5国	东/冰/格	巴基斯坦	韩国	瑞士	哥达	秘鲁	澳大利亚	新西/坡/智	港/澳/台	亚太2国	老/柬/缅	36/3/1	
	0/0/0	0	0	0	0	0	0	0//0	0/0/	2.5	0/0/0	0/0/0	---Other
													Knotted netting of twine, cordage or rope; made up fishing nets and other made up nets, of textile materials:
													-Of man-made textile materials:
	0/0/0	4.5	0	0	0	0	0	0//0	0/0/			0/0/0	–Made up fishing nets
	0/0/0	0	0	3.6	0	0	0	0/0/0	0/0/0			0/0/	–Other
	0/0/0	4.5	0	0	0	0	0	0//0	0/0/			0/0/0	-Other
													Articles of yarn, strip or the like of heading No. 54. 04 or 54. 05, twine, cordage, rope or cables, not elsewhere specified or included:
	0/0/0	4	0	0	0	0	0	0//0	0/0/	0		0/0/0	Articles of yarn, strip or the like of heading No. 54. 04 or 54. 05, twine, cordage, rope or cables, not elsewhere specified or included

第五十七章
地毯及纺织材料的其他铺地制品

注释：

一、本章所称"地毯及纺织材料的其他铺地制品"，是指使用时以纺织材料作面的铺地制品，也包括具有纺织材料铺地制品特征但作其他用途的物品。

二、本章不包括铺地制品衬垫。

税则号列	货品名称〔CIQ 扩展编码及品名－T2 表示见附表 2〕	最惠(%)	暂定税率	普通	增值/消费	出口退税	计量单位	监管条件	检验检疫	特殊证件对美关税
57.01	**结织栽绒地毯及纺织材料的其他结织栽绒铺地制品，不论是否制成的：**									
5701.1000	-羊毛或动物细毛制〔999〕	6		130	13/	13	千克/平方米			/31
	-其他纺织材料制：									
5701.9010	---化学纤维制〔999〕	6		130	13/	13	千克/平方米			/36
5701.9020	---丝制〔999〕	6		100	13/	13	千克/平方米			/31
5701.9090	---其他〔999〕	6		100	13/	13	千克/平方米			/36
57.02	**机织地毯及纺织材料的其他机织铺地制品，未簇绒或未植绒，不论是否制成的，包括"开来姆"、"苏麦克"、"卡拉马尼"及类似的手织地毯：**									
5702.1000	-"开来姆"、"苏麦克"、"卡拉马尼"及类似的手织地毯〔999〕	6		130	13/	13	千克/平方米			/31
5702.2000	-椰壳纤维制的铺地制品〔999〕	6		100	13/	13	千克/平方米			/
	-其他起绒结构的铺地制品，未制成的：									
5702.3100	--羊毛或动物细毛制〔999〕	4		130	13/	13	千克/平方米			/34
5702.3200	--化学纤维制〔999〕	6		130	13/	13	千克/平方米			/31
5702.3900	--其他纺织材料制〔999〕	6		100	13/	13	千克/平方米			/
	-其他起绒结构的铺地制品，制成的：									
5702.4100	--羊毛或动物细毛制〔999〕	4		130	13/	13	千克/平方米			/34
5702.4200	--化学纤维制〔999〕	4		130	13/	13	千克/平方米			/29
5702.4900	--其他纺织材料制〔999〕	6		100	13/	13	千克/平方米			/
	-其他非起绒结构的铺地制品，未制成的：									
5702.5010	---羊毛或动物细毛制〔999〕	6		130	13/	13	千克/平方米			/
5702.5020	---化学纤维制〔999〕	6		130	13/	13	千克/平方米			/
5702.5090	---其他纺织材料制〔999〕	6		100	13/	13	千克/平方米			/
	-其他非起绒结构的铺地制品，制成的：									
5702.9100	--羊毛或动物细毛制〔999〕	6		130	13/	13	千克/平方米			/31
5702.9200	--化学纤维制〔999〕	6		130	13/	13	千克/平方米			/31
5702.9900	--其他纺织材料制〔999〕	6		100	13/	13	千克/平方米			/31
57.03	**簇绒地毯及纺织材料的其他簇绒铺地制品，不论是否制成的：**									
5703.1000	-羊毛或动物细毛制〔999〕	6		130	13/	13	千克/平方米			/16
5703.2000	-尼龙或其他聚酰胺制〔999〕	4		130	13/	13	千克/平方米			/14
5703.3000	-其他化学纤维制〔999〕	4		130	13/	13	千克/平方米			/29
5703.9000	-其他纺织材料制〔999〕	6		100	13/	13	千克/平方米			/16
57.04	**毡呢地毯及纺织材料的其他毡呢铺地制品，未簇绒或未植绒，不论是否制成的：**									
5704.1000	-最大表面面积不超过 0.3 平方米〔999〕	6		130	13/	13	千克/平方米			/
5704.2000	-最大表面面积超过 0.3 平方米但不超过 1 平方米〔999〕	4		130	13/	13	千克/平方米			/34
5704.9000	-其他〔999〕	4		130	13/	13	千克/平方米			/34
57.05	**其他地毯及纺织材料的其他铺地制品，不论是否制成的：**									
5705.0010	---羊毛或动物细毛制〔999〕	6		130	13/	13	千克/平方米			/36
5705.0020	---化学纤维制〔999〕	4		130	13/	13	千克/平方米			/14
5705.0090	---其他纺织材料制〔999〕	6		100	13/	13	千克/平方米			/36

Chapter 57
Carpets and other textile floor coverings

Notes:

1. For the purposes of this Chapter, the term "carpets and other textilefloor coverings" means floor coverings in which textile materials serve as the exposed surface of the article when in use and includes articles having the characteristics of textile floor coverings but intended for use for other purposes.
2. This Chapter does not cover floor covering underlays.

协定税率 %										特惠税率 %			Article Description
亚太5国	东/冰/格	巴基斯坦	韩国	瑞士	哥达	秘鲁	澳大利亚	新西/坡/智	港/澳/台	亚太2国	老/柬/缅	36/3/1	
													Carpets and other textile floor coverings, knotted, whether or not made up:
	0/0/0	0	5.6	4.2	0	0	0	0/0/0	0/0/			0/0/0	-Of wool or fine animal hair
													-Of other textile materials:
	0/0/0	12.8	6.4	4.8	0	0	0	0/0/0	0/0/			0/0/0	---Of man-made textile materials
	0/0/0	7	5.6	4.2	0	0	0	0/0/0	0/0/			0/0/	---Of silk
	0/0/0	7	5.6	4.2	0	0	0	0/0/0	0/0/			0/0/	---Other
													Carpets and other textile floor coverings, woven, not tufted or flocked, whether or not made up, including "Kelem", "Schumacks", "Karamanie' and similar handwoven rugs:
	0/0/0	0	5.6	4.2	0	0	0	0/0/0	0/0/	0		0/0/0	-"Kelem", "Schumacks", "Karamanie" and similar handwoven rugs
	0/0/0	0	5.6	4.2	0	0	0	0/0/0	0/0/			0/0/	-Floor coverings of coconut fibres (coir)
													-Other, of pile construction, not made up:
	0/0/0	0	0	3	0	0	0	0/0/0	0/0/			0/0/0	--Of wool or fine animal hair
	0/0/0	0	6.4	4.8	0	0	0	0/0/0	0/0/			0/0/	--Of man-made textile materials
	0/0/0	0	5.6	4.2	0	0	0	0/0/0	0/0/	0		0/0/0	--Of other textile materials
													-Other, of pile construction, made up:
	0/0/0	0	0	0	0	0	0	0/0/0	0/0/			0/0/0	--Of wool or fine animal hair
	0/0/0	0	0	0	0	0	0	0/0/0	0/0/			0/0/0	--Of man-made textile materials
4	0/0/0	0	5.6	4.2	0	0	0	0/0/0	0/0/			0/0/	--Of other textile materials
													-Other, not of pile construction, not made up:
	0/0/0	0	5.6	4.2	0	0	0	0/0/0	0/0/			0/0/	---Of wool or fine animal hair
	0/0/0	0	6.4	4.8	0	0	0	0/0/0	0/0/			0/0/	---Of man made textile materials
	0/0/0	0	5.6	4.2	0	0	0	0/0/0	0/0/			0/0/	---Of other textile materials
													-Other, not of pile construction, made up:
	0/0/0	0	5.6	4.2	0	0	0	0/0/0	0/0/			0/0/	--Of wool or fine animal hair
	0/0/0	0	6.4	4.8	0	0	0	0/0/0	0/0/			0/0/	--Of man-made textile materials
	0/0/0	0	5.6	4.2	0	0	0	0/0/0	0/0/			0/0/	--Of other textile materials
													Carpets and other textile floor coverings, tufted, whether or not made up:
	0/0/0		5.6	4.2	0	0	0	0/0/0	0/0/			0/0/0	-Of wool or fine animal hair
	0/0/0	4.5	7	0	0	0	0	0/0/0	0/0/			0/0/0	-Of nylon or other polyamides
	0/0/0		0	0	0	0	0	0/0/0	0/0/			0/0/0	-Of other man-made textile materials
	0/0/0	11.2	5.6	4.2	0	0	0	0/0/0	0/0/	0		0/0/0	-Of other textile materials
													Carpets and other textile floor coverings, of felt, not tufted or flocked, whether or not made up:
	0/0/0	7	5.6	4.2	0	0	0	0/0/0	0/0/			0/0/	-Tiles, having a maximum surface area of 0.3 m²
	0/0/0	4	0	0	0	0	0	0/0/0	0/0/			0/0/0	-Tiles, having a maximum sur-face area more then 0.3m2 but not more thern 1 m2
	0/0/0	4	0	0	0	0	0	0/0/0	0/0/			0/0/0	-Other
													Other carpets and other textile floor coverings, whether or not made up:
	0/0/0	11.2	5.6	4.2	0	0	0	0/0/0	0/0/	0		0/0/0	---Of wool or fine animal hair
	0/0/0	4	0	0	0	0	0	0/0/0	0/0/	0		0/0/0	---Of man-made textile materials
	0/0/0	11.2	5.6	4.2	0	0	0	0/0/0	0/0/	0		0/0/0	---Of other textile materialar

第五十八章
特种机织物;簇绒织物;花边;装饰毯;装饰带;刺绣品

注释:

一、本章不适用于经浸渍、涂布、包覆或层压的第五十九章注释一所述的纺织物或第五十九章的其他货品。

二、税目58.01也包括因未将浮纱割断而使表面无竖绒的纬起绒织物。

三、税目58.03所称"纱罗",是指经线全部或部分由地经纱和绞经纱构成的织物,其中绞经纱绕地经纱半圈、一圈或几圈而形成圈状,纬纱从圈中穿过。

四、税目58.04不适用于税目56.08的线、绳、索结制的网状织物。

五、税目58.06所称"狭幅机织物",是指:

(一)幅宽不超过30厘米的机织物,不论是否织成或从宽幅料剪成,但两侧必须有织成的、胶粘的或用其他方法制成的布边;

(二)压平宽度不超过30厘米的圆筒机织物;

(三)折边的斜裁滚条布,其未折边时的宽度不超过30厘米。

流苏状的狭幅织物归入税目58.08。

六、税目58.10所称"刺绣品",除了一般纺织材料绣线绣制的刺绣品外,还包括在可见底布上用金属线或玻璃线刺绣的刺绣品,也包括用珠片、饰珠或纺织材料或其他材料制的装饰用花纹图案所缝绣的贴花织物。但不包括手工针绣嵌花装饰毯(税目58.05)。

七、除税目号58.09的产品外,本章还包括金属线制的用于衣着、装饰及类似用途的物品。

税则号列	货品名称〔CIQ扩展编码及品名—T2表示见附表2〕	最惠(%)	暂定税率	普通	增值/消费	出口退税	计量单位	监管条件	检验检疫	特殊证件对美关税
58.01	**起绒机织物及绳绒织物,但税号58.02或58.06的织物除外:**									
5801.1000	-羊毛或动物细毛制〔999〕	8		130	13/	13	米/千克			/33
	-棉制:									
5801.2100	--不割绒的纬起绒织物〔101棉混纺坯布,102其他特种机织物〕	8		70	13/	13	米/千克			/
5801.2200	--割绒的灯芯绒〔999〕	8		70	13/	13	米/千克			/33
5801.2300	--其他纬起绒织物〔101棉混纺坯布,102其他特种机织物〕	8		70	13/	13	米/千克			/
5801.2600	--绳绒织物〔101棉混纺坯布,102其他特种机织物〕	8		70	13/	13	米/千克			/18
	--经起绒织物:									
5801.2710	---不割绒的(棱纹绸)〔999〕	8		70	13/	13	米/千克			/33
5801.2720	---割绒的〔101棉混纺坯布,102其他特种机织物〕	8		70	13/	13	米/千克			/33
	-化学纤维制:									
5801.3100	--不割绒的纬起绒织物〔999〕	8		130	13/	13	米/千克			/33
5801.3200	--割绒的灯芯绒〔999〕	8		130	13/	13	米/千克			/33
5801.3300	--其他纬起绒织物〔999〕	8		130	13/	13	米/千克			/33
5801.3600	--绳绒织物〔999〕	8		130	13/	13	米/千克			/28
	--经起绒织物:									
5801.3710	---不割绒的(棱纹绸)〔999〕	8		130	13/	13	米/千克			/28
5801.3720	---割绒的〔999〕	8		130	13/	13	米/千克			/28
	-其他纺织材料制:									
5801.9010	---丝及绢丝制〔999〕	8		130	13/	13	米/千克			/33
5801.9090	---其他〔101亚麻混纺织物,102其他特种机织物〕	8		80	13/	13	米/千克			/33
58.02	**毛巾织物及类似的毛圈机织物,但税目58.06的狭幅织物除外;簇绒织物,但税目57.03的产品除外:**									
	-棉制毛巾织物及类似毛圈机织物:									
5802.1100	--未漂白〔999〕	8		70	13/	13	米/千克			/
5802.1900	--其他〔999〕	8		70	13/	13	米/千克			/
	-其他纺织材料制的毛巾织物及类似的毛圈机织物:									
5802.2010	---丝及绢丝制〔999〕	8		130	13/	13	米/千克			/
5802.2020	---羊毛或动物细毛制〔999〕	8		130	13/	13	米/千克			/
5802.2030	---化学纤维制〔999〕	8		130	13/	13	米/千克			/18
5802.2090	---其他〔999〕	8		80	13/	13	米/千克			/
	-簇绒织物:									
5802.3010	---丝及绢丝制〔999〕	8		130	13/	13	米/千克			/
5802.3020	---羊毛或动物细毛制〔999〕	8		130	13/	13	米/千克			/

Chapter 58
Special woven fabrics; tufted textile fabrics; lace; tapestries; trimmings; embroidery

Notes:

1. This Chapter does not apply to textile fabrics referred to in Note 1 to Chapter 59, impregnated, coated, covered or laminated, or to other goods of Chapter 59.
2. Heading No. 58. 01 also includes woven weft pile fabrics which have not yet had the floats cut, at which stage they have no pile standing up.
3. For the purpose of heading No. 58. 03, "gauze" means a fabric with a warp composed wholly or in part of standing or ground threads and crossing or doup threads which cross the standing or ground threads making a half turn, a complete turn or more to form loops through which weft threads pass.
4. Heading No. 58. 04 does not apply to knotted net fabrics of twine, cordage or rope, of heading No. 56. 08.
5. For the purposes of heading No. 58. 06, the expression "narrow woven fabrics" means:
   (a) Woven fabrics of a width not exceeding 30 cm, whether woven as such or cut from wider pieces, provided with selvedges (woven, gummed or otherwise made) on both edges;
   (b) Tubular woven fabrics of a flattened width not exceeding 30 cm;
   (c) Bias binding with folded edges, of a width when unfolded not exceeding 30 cm.
   Narrow woven fabrics with woven fringes are to be classified in heading No. 58. 08.
6. In heading No.58. 10, the expression "embroidery" means, *inter alia*, embroidery with metal or glass thread on a visible ground of textile fabric, and sewn appliquè work of sequins, beads or ornamental motifs of textile or other materials. The heading does not apply to needlework tapestry (heading No. 58. 05).
7. In addition to the products of heading No. 58. 09, this Chapter also includes articles made of metal thread and of a kind used in apparel, as furnishing fabrics or for similar purposes.

协定税率 %										特惠税率 %			Article Description
亚太5国	东/冰/格	巴基斯坦	韩国	瑞士	哥达	秘鲁	澳大利亚	新西/坡/智	港/澳/台	亚太2国	老/柬/缅	36/3/1	
													Woven pile fabrics and chenille fabrics, other than fabrics of heading No 58. 02 or 58. 06:
	0/0/0	0	0	0	0	0	0	0/0/0	0/0/			0/0/0	-Of wool or fine animal hair
													-Of cotton:
	0/0/0	0	0	3.6	0	0	0	0/0/0	0/0/			0/0/	--Uncut weft pile fabrics
	0/0/0	0	0	0	0	0	0	0//0	0/0/0			0/0/0	--Cut corduroy
	0/0/0	0	4	0	0	0	0	0//0	0/0/			0/0/0	--Other weft pile fabrics
	0/0/0	0	0	0	0	0	0	0//0	0/0/			0/0/0	--Chenille fabrics
													--Warp pile fabrics:
	0/0/0	0	0	0	0	0	0	0//0	0/0/			0/0/0	---Warp pile fabrics(epingle)(nucut)
	0/0/0	0	0	0	0	0	0	0//0	0/0/			0/0/0	---Warp pile fabrics(epingle)(cut)
													-Of man-made fibres:
	0/0/0	0	6	0	0	0	0	0/0/0	0/0/			0/0/0	--Uncut weft pile fabrics
	0/0/0	0	0	0	0	0	0	0/0/0	0/0/			0/0/0	--Cut corduroy
	0/0/0	0	0	0	0	0	0	0/0/0	0/0/0		0/0/0	0/0/0	--Other weft pile fabrics
	0/0/0	0	0	0	0	0	0	0/0/0	0/0/			0/0/0	--Chenille fabrics
													--Warp pile fabrics:
	0/0/0	0	0	0	0	0	0	0/0/0	0/0/			0/0/0	---Warp pile fabrics(epingle)(nucut)
	0/0/0	0	0	0	0	0	0	0/0/0	0/0/			0/0/0	---Warp pile fabrics(epingle)(cut)
													-Of other textile materials:
	0/0/0	0	0	0	0	0	0	0/0/0	0/0/			0/0/0	---Of silk or spun silk
	0/0/0	0	0	0	0	0	0	0/0/0	0/0/			0/0/0	---Other
													Terry towelling and similar woven terry fabrics, other than narrow fabricsof heading No. 58. 06; tufted textile fabrics, other than products of heading No. 57. 03:
													-Terry towelling and similar woven terry fabrics, of cotton:
	0/0/0	0	0	3.6	0	0	0	0/0/0	0/0/	0		0/0/0	--Unbleached
	0/0/0	0	0	0	0	0	0	0//0	0/0/			0/0/0	--Other
													-Terry towelling and similar woven terry fabrics, of other textile materials:
	0/0/0	0	0	3.6	0	0	0	0/0/0	0/0/	0		0/0/0	---Of silk or spun silk
	0/0/0	0	0	3.6	0	0	0	0/0/0	0/0/	0		0/0/0	---Of wool or fine animal hair
	0/0/0	0	5.6	4.2	0	0	0	0/0/0	0/0/	0		0/0/0	---Of man-made fibres
	0/0/0	0	0	3.6	0	0	0	0/0/0	0/0/	0		0/0/0	---Other
													-Tufted textile fabrics:
	0/0/0	0	0	0	0	0	0	0/0/0	0/0/			0/0/0	---Of silk or spun silk
	0/0/0	0	0	0	0	0	0	0/0/0	0/0/			0/0/0	---Of wool or fine animal hair

税则号列	货品名称〔CIQ扩展编码及品名—T2表示见附表2〕	最惠(%)	暂定税率	普通	增值/消费	出口退税	计量单位	监管条件	检验检疫	特殊证件对美关税
5802.3030	---棉或麻制〔999〕	8		70	13/	13	米/千克			/
5802.3040	---化学纤维制〔999〕	8		130	13/	13	米/千克			/33
5802.3090	---其他纺织材料制〔999〕	8		80	13/	13	米/千克			/
58.03	**纱罗，但税目58.06的狭幅织物除外：**									
5803.0010	---棉制〔999〕	8		70	13/	13	米/千克			/
5803.0020	---丝及绢丝制〔999〕	8		130	13/	13	米/千克			/
5803.0030	---化学纤维制〔999〕	8		130	13/	13	米/千克			/
5803.0090	---其他纺织材料制〔999〕	8		80	13/	13	米/千克			/18
58.04	**网眼薄纱及其他网眼织物，但不包括机织物、针织物或钩编织物；成卷、成条或成小块图案的花边，但税目60.02的织物除外：**									
	-网眼薄纱及其他网眼织物：									
5804.1010	---丝及绢丝制〔999〕	8		130	13/	13	千克			/
5804.1020	---棉制〔999〕	8		70	13/	13	千克			/33
5804.1030	---化学纤维制〔999〕	8		130	13/	13	千克			/33
5804.1090	---其他纺织材料制〔999〕	8		90	13/	13	千克			/18
	-机制花边：									
5804.2100	--化学纤维制〔999〕	8		130	13/	13	千克			/33
	--其他纺织材料制：									
5804.2910	---丝及绢丝制〔999〕	8		130	13/	13	千克			/
5804.2920	---棉制〔999〕	8		70	13/	13	千克			/33
5804.2990	---其他〔999〕	8		90	13/	13	千克			/
5804.3000	-手工制花边〔999〕	8		100	13/	13	千克			/
58.05	**"哥白林"、"弗朗德"、"奥步生"、"波威"及类似式样的手织装饰毯，以及手工针绣嵌花装饰毯（例如，小针脚或十字绣），不论是否制成的：**									
5805.0010	---手工针绣嵌花装饰毯〔999〕	6		130	13/	13	平方米/千克			/
5805.0090	---其他〔999〕	6		130	13/	13	平方米/千克			/
58.06	**狭幅机织物，但税目58.07的货品除外；用黏合剂粘合制成的有经纱而无纬纱的狭幅织物（包扎匹头用带）：**									
	-起绒机织物（包括毛巾织物及类似的毛圈织物）及绳绒织物：									
5806.1010	---棉或麻制〔999〕	8		70	13/	13	千克			/33
5806.1090	---其他纺织材料制〔999〕	8		80	13/	13	千克			/18
5806.2000	-按重量计弹性纱线或橡胶线含量在5%及以上的其他机织物〔999〕	8		100	13/	13	千克			/33
	-其他机织物：									
5806.3100	--棉制〔999〕	8		70	13/	13	千克			/33
5806.3200	--化学纤维制〔999〕	8		130	13/	13	千克			/28
	--其他纺织材料制：									
5806.3910	---丝及绢丝制〔999〕	8		130	13/	13	千克			/18
5806.3920	---羊毛或动物细毛制〔999〕	8		130	13/	13	千克			/
5806.3990	---其他〔999〕	8		80	13/	13	千克			/33
	-用黏合剂粘合制成的有经纱而无纬纱的织物（包扎匹头用带）：									
5806.4010	---棉或麻制〔999〕	8		70	13/	13	千克			/
5806.4090	---其他纺织材料制〔999〕	8		80	13/	13	千克			/28
58.07	**非绣制的纺织材料制标签、徽章及类似品，成匹、成条或裁成一定形状或尺寸：**									
5807.1000	-机织〔999〕	8		100	13/	13	千克			/33
5807.9000	-其他〔999〕	8		100	13/	13	千克			/28
58.08	**成匹的编带；非绣制的成匹装饰带，但针织或钩编的除外；流苏、绒球及类似品：**									
5808.1000	-成匹的编带									
5808.1000 20	蕉麻或苎麻制成匹的编带（适合制造或装饰帽类用）〔999〕	8		100	13/	13	千克			/33
5808.1000 90	其他纺织材料制成匹的编带〔999〕	8		100	13/	13	千克			/33
5808.9000	-其他〔999〕	8		100	13/	13	千克			/33
58.09	**其他税目未列名的金属线机织物及税目56.05所列含金属纱线的机织物，用于衣着、装饰及类似用途：**									
5809.0010	---与棉混制〔999〕	8		90	13/	13	米/千克			/

协定税率 %										特惠税率 %			Article Description
亚太5国	东/冰/格	巴基斯坦	韩国	瑞士	哥达	秘鲁	澳大利亚	新西/坡/智	港/澳/台	亚太2国	老/柬/缅	36/3/1	
	0/0/0	0	0	0	0	0	0	0//0	0/0/			0/0/0	---Of cotton or bast fibres
	0/0/0	0	0	0	0	0	0	0/0/0	0/0/			0/0/0	---Of man-made fibres
	0/0/0	0	0	0	0	0	0	0/0/0	0/0/			0/0/0	---Of other textile materials
													Gauze, other than narrow fabrics of heading No. 58.06:
	0/0/0	4	0	0	0	0	0	0//0	0/0/			0/0/0	---Of cotton
	0/0/0	4	0	0	0	0	0	0/0/0	0/0/			0/0/0	---Of silk or spun silk
	0/0/0	5	0	0	0	0	0	0/0/0	0/0/			0/0/0	---Of man-made fibres
	0/0/0	4	0	0	0	0	0	0/0/0	0/0/			0/0/0	---Of other textile materials
													Tulles and other net fabrics, not including woven, knitted or crocheted fabrics; lace in the piece, in strips or in motifs, other than fabrics of headings No. 60.02:
													-Tulles and other net fabrics:
5.2	0/0/0	4	0	0	0	0	0	0/0/0	0/0/			0/0/0	---Of silk or spun silk
5.2	0/0/0	4	0	5.2	0	0	0	0//0	0/0/			0/0/0	---Of cotton
5.2	0/0/0	4.5	8.4	3.6	0	0	0	0/0/0	0/0/0		0/0/0	0/0/0	---Of man-made fibres
5.2	0/0/0	4	0	0	0	0	0	0/0/0	0/0/0			0/0/0	---Of other textile materials
													-Mechanically made lace:
	0/0/0	4	0	0	0	0	0	0/0/0	0/0/0			0/0/0	--Of man-made fibres
													--Of other textile materials:
	0/0/0	4	0	0	0	0	0	0/0/0	0/0/			0/0/0	---Of silk or spun silk
	0/0/0	4	0	0	0	0	0	0//0	0/0/		0/0/0	0/0/0	---Of cotton
	0/0/0	4	0	0	0	0	0	0/0/0	0/0/			0/0/0	---Other
	0/0/0	4	0	0	0	0	0	0/0/0	0/0/			0/0/0	-Hand-made lace
													Hand-woven tapestries of the type Gobelins, Flanders, Aubusson, Beauvais and the like, and needle-worked tapestries (for example, petit point, cross stitch), whether or not made up:
	0/0/0	6	0	3.6	0	0	0	0/0/0	0/0/			0/0/0	---Needle-worked tapestries
	0/0/0	6	0	3.6	0	0	0	0/0/0	0/0/			0/0/0	---Other
													Narrow woven fabrics, other than goods of heading No. 58.07; narrow fabrics consisting of warp without weft assembled by means of an adhesive (bolducs):
													-Woven pile fabrics (including terry towelling and similar terry fabris) and chenille fabrics:
6.4	0/0/0	4	0	0	0	0	0	0//0	0/0/			0/0/0	---Of cotton or bast fibres
5.2	0/0/0	4	0	0	0	0	0	0/0/0	0/0/0		0/0/0	0/0/0	---Of other textile materials
	0/0/0	4	0	0	0	0	0	0/0/0	0/0/0		0/0/0	0/0/0	-Other woven fabrics, containing by weight 5% or more of elastomeric yarn or rubber thread
													-Other woven fabrics:
	0/0/0	4	0	0	0	0	0	0//0	0/0/		0/0/0	0/0/0	--Of cotton
5.2	0/0/0	4	0	0	0	0	0	0/0/0	0/0/0		0/0/0	0/0/0	--Of man-made fibres
													--Of other textile materials:
	0/0/0	4	0	0	0	0	0	0/0/0	0/0/			0/0/0	---Of silk or spun silk
	0/0/0	4	0	0	0	0	0	0/0/0	0/0/			0/0/0	---Of wool or fine animal hair
	0/0/0	4	0	0	0	0	0	0/0/0	0/0/			0/0/0	---Other
													-Fabrics consisting of warp without weft assembled by means of an adhesive (bolducs):
4.8	0/0/0	4	0	0	0	0	0	0//0	0/0/			0/0/0	---Of cotton or bast fibres
	0/0/0	4	0	0	0	0	0	0/0/0	0/0/			0/0/0	---Of other textile materials
													Labels, badges and similar articles of textile materials, in the piece, in strips or cut to shape or size, not embroidered:
5.2	0/0/0	0	0	0	0	0	0	0/0/0	0/0/0		0/0/0	0/0/0	-Woven
	0/0/0	4	0	0	0	0	0	0/0/0	0/0/			0/0/0	-Other
													Braids in the piece; ornamental trimmings in the piece, without embroidery, other than knitted or crocheted; tassels, pompons and similar articles:
													-Braids in the piece
	0/0/0		0	0	0	0	0	0/0/0	0/0/			0/0/0	Braids in the piece, of abaca or ramie (suitable for manufacturing or decoration of head gear)
	0/0/0		0	0	0	0	0	0/0/0	0/0/			0/0/0	Braids in the piece, of other textile materials
	0/0/0	4	0	0	0	0	0	0/0/0	0/0/		0/0/0	0/0/0	-Other
													Woven fabrics of metal thread and woven fabrics of metallized yarn of heading No. 56.05, of a kind used in apparel, as furnishing fabrics or for similar purposes, not elsewhere specified or included:
	0/0/0	4	0	0	0	0	0	0/0/0	0/0/			0/0/0	---Combined with cotton

税则号列	货品名称〔CIQ 扩展编码及品名一T2 表示见附表 2〕	最惠(%)	暂定税率	普通	增值/消费	出口退税	计量单位	监管条件	检验检疫	特殊证件对美关税
5809.0020	---与化学纤维混制〔999〕	8		130	13/	13	米/千克			/18
5809.0090	---其他〔999〕	8		100	13/	13	米/千克			/18
58.10	**成匹、成条或成小块图案的刺绣品：**									
5810.1000	-不见底布的刺绣品〔999〕	8		130	13/	13	千克			/33
	-其他刺绣品：									
5810.9100	--棉制〔999〕	8		130	13/	13	千克			/
5810.9200	--化学纤维制〔999〕	8		130	13/	13	千克			/33
5810.9900	--其他纺织材料制〔999〕	8		130	13/	13	千克			/33
58.11	**用一层或几层纺织材料与胎料经绗缝或其他方法组合制成的被褥状纺织品，但税目 58.10 的刺绣品除外：**									
5811.0010	---丝及绢丝制〔101 被子，102 褥垫〕	8		130	13/	13	千克			/
5811.0020	---羊毛或动物细毛制〔101 被子，102 褥垫〕	8		130	13/	13	千克			/
5811.0030	---棉制〔101 被子，102 褥垫〕	8		80	13/	13	千克			/28
5811.0040	---化学纤维制〔101 被子，102 褥垫，103 毯子〕	8		130	13/	13	千克			/28
5811.0090	---其他纺织材料制〔101 被子，102 褥垫〕	8		90	13/	13	千克			/

协定税率 %										特惠税率 %			
亚太5国	东/冰/格	巴基斯坦	韩国	瑞士	哥达	秘鲁	澳大利亚	新西/坡/智	港/澳/台	亚太2国	老/柬/缅	36/3/1	Article Description
	0/0/0	4	0	0	0	0	0	0/0/0	0/0/			0/0/0	---Combined with man-made fibres
	0/0/0	4	0	0	0	0	0	0/0/0	0/0/			0/0/0	---Other
													Embroidery in the piece, in strips or in motifs:
	0/0/0	4	0	0	0	0	0	0/0/0	0/0/			0/0/0	-Embroidery without visible ground
													-Other embroidery:
	0/0/0		0	0	0	0	0	0/0/0	0/0/			0/0/0	--Of cotton
	0/0/0	4	6	0	0	0	0	0/0/0	0/0/0			0/0/0	--Of man-made fibres
	0/0/0	4	0	0	0	0	0	0/0/0	0/0/			0/0/0	--Of other textile materials
													Quilted textile products in the piece, composed of one or more layers of textile materials assembled with padding by stitching or otherwise, other than embroidery of heading No. 58.10:
5.6	0/0/0	0	0	0	0	0	0	0/0/0	0/0/			0/0/0	---Of silk or spun silk
	0/0/0	0	0	0	0	0	0	0/0/0	0/0/			0/0/0	---Of wool or fine animal hair
	0/0/0	0	0	0	0	0	0	0//0	0/0/			0/0/0	---Of cotton
	0/0/0	0	8.4	3.6	0	0	0	0/0/0	0/0/			0/0/0	---Of man-made fibres
	0/0/0	0	0	0	0	0	0	0/0/0	0/0/			0/0/0	---Of other textile materials

第五十九章 浸渍、涂布、包覆或层压的纺织物;工业用纺织制品

注释:

一、除条文另有规定的以外,本章所称"纺织物",仅适用于第五十章至第五十五章、税目58.03及58.06的机织物、税目58.08的成匹编带和装饰带及税目60.02至60.06的针织物或钩编织物。

二、税目59.03适用于:

(一)用塑料浸渍、涂布、包覆或层压的纺织物,不论每平方米重量多少以及塑料的性质如何(紧密结构或泡沫状的),但下列各项除外:

1. 用肉眼无法辨别出是否经过浸渍、涂布、包覆或层压的织物(通常归入第五十章至第五十五章、第五十八章或第六十章);但由于浸渍、涂布、包覆或层压所引起的颜色变化可不予考虑;

2. 温度在15℃至30℃时,用手工将其绕于直径7毫米的圆柱体上会发生断裂的产品(通常归入第三十九章);

3. 纺织物完全嵌入塑料内或在其两面均用塑料完全包覆或涂布,而这种包覆或涂布用肉眼是能够辨别出的产品(但由于包覆或涂布所引起的颜色变化可不予考虑)(第三十九章);

4. 用塑料部分涂布或包覆并由此而形成图案的织物(通常归入第五十章至第五十五章、第五十八章或第六十章);

5. 与纺织物混制而其中纺织物仅起增强作用的泡沫塑料板、片或带(第三十九章);

6. 税目58.11的纺织品;

(二)由税目56.04的用塑料浸渍、涂布、包覆或套裹的纱线、扁条或类似品制成的织物。

三、税目59.05所称"糊墙织物",是指以纺织材料作面,固定在一衬背上或在背面进行处理(浸渍或涂布以便于裱糊),适于装饰墙壁或天花板,且宽度不小于45厘米的成卷产品。

但本税目不适用于以纺织纤维屑或粉末直接粘于纸上(税目48.14)或布底上(通常归入税目59.07)的糊墙物品。

四、税目59.06所称"用橡胶处理的纺织物"是指:

(一)用橡胶浸渍、涂布、包覆或层压的纺织物:

1. 每平方米重量不超过1 500克;

2. 每平方米重量超过1 500克,按重量计纺织材料含量在50%以上。

(二)由税目56.04的用橡胶浸渍、涂布、包覆或套裹的纱线、扁条或类似品制成的织物;以及

(三)平行纺织纱线经橡胶粘合的织物,不论每平方米重量多少。

但本税目不包括与纺织物混制而其中纺织物仅起增强作用的海绵橡胶板、片或带(第四十章),也不包括税目58.11的纺织品。

五、税目59.07不适用于:

(一)用肉眼无法辨别出是否经过浸渍、涂布或包覆的织物(通常归入第五十章至第五十五章、第五十八章或第六十章),但由于浸渍、涂布或包覆所引起的颜色变化可不予考虑;

(二)绘有图画的织物(作为舞台、摄影布景或类似品的已绘制的画布除外);

(三)用短绒、粉末、软木粉或类似品部分覆面并由此而形成图案的织物,但仿绒织物仍归入本税目;

(四)以淀粉或类似物质为基本成分的普通浆料上浆整理的织物;

(五)以纺织物为底的木饰面板(税目44.08);

(六)以纺织物为底的砂布及类似品(税号68.05);

(七)以纺织物为底的粘聚或复制云母片(税号68.14);

(八)以纺织物为底的金属箔(通常为第十四类或第十五类)。

六、税目59.10不适用于:

(一)厚度小于3毫米的纺织材料制传动带或输送带;

(二)用橡胶浸渍、涂布、包覆或层压的织物制成的或用橡胶浸渍、涂布、包覆或套裹的纱线或绳制成的传动带及运输带(税目40.10)。

七、税目59.11适用于下列不能归入第十一类其他税目的货品:

(一)下列成匹的、裁成一定长度或仅裁成矩形(包括正方形)的纺织产品(具有税目59.08至59.10所列产品特征的产品除外):

1. 用橡胶、皮革或其他材料涂布、包覆或层压的作针布用的纺织物、毡呢及毡呢衬里机织物,以及其他专门技术用途的类似织物,包括用橡胶浸渍的用于包覆纺锤(织轴)的狭幅丝绒织物。

2. 筛布;

3. 用于榨油机器或类似机器的纺织材料制或人发制滤布;

4. 用多股经纱或纬纱平织而成的纺织物,不论是否毡化、浸渍或涂布,通常用于机械或其他专门技术用途;

5. 专门技术用途的增强纺织物;

Chapter 59

Impregnated, coated, covered or laminated textile fabrics; textile articles of a kind suitable for industrial use

Notes:

1. Except where the context otherwise requires, for the purposes of this Chapter the expression "textile fabrics" applies only to the woven fabrics of Chapters 50 to 55 and headings No.58.03 and 58.06, the braids and ornamental trimmings in the piece of heading No.58.08 and the knitted or crocheted fabrics of headings No.60.02 to 60.06.
2. Heading No. 59.03 applies to:
   (a) Textile fabrics, impregnated, coated, covered or laminated with plastics, whatever the weight per square metre and whatever the nature of the plastic material (compact or cellular), other than:
   (ⅰ) Fabrics in which the impregnation, coating, or covering cannot be seen with the naked eye (usually Chapters 50 to 55, 58 or 60); for the purpose of this provision, no account should be taken of any resulting change of colour;
   (ⅱ) Products which cannot, without fracturing, be bent manually around a cylinder of a diameter of 7 mm, at a temperature between 15℃ and 30℃ (usually Chapter 39);
   (ⅲ) Products in which the textile fabric is either completely embedded in plastics or entirely coated or covered on both sides with such material, provided that such coating or covering can be seen with the naked eye with no account being taken of any resulting change of colour (Chapter 39);
   (ⅳ) Fabrics partially coated or partially covered with plastics and bearing designs resulting from these treatments (usually Chapters 50 to 55, 58 or 60);
   (ⅴ) Plates, sheets or strip of cellular plastics, combined with textile fabric, where the textile fabric is present merely for reinforcing purposes (Chapter 39);
   (ⅵ) Textile products of heading No. 58.11;
   (b) Fabrics made from yarn, strip or the like, impregnated, coated, covered or sheathed with plastics, of heading No. 56.04.
3. For the purposes of heading No. 59.05, the expression "textile wall coverings" applies to products in rolls, of a width of not less than 45 cm, suitable for wall or ceiling decoration, consisting of a textile surface which has been fixed on a backing or has been treated on the back (impregnated or coated to permit pasting).
   This heading does not, however, apply to wall coverings consisting of textile flock or dust fixed directly on a backing of paper (heading No. 48.14) or on a textile backing (generally heading No. 59.07).
4. For the purposes of heading No. 59.06, the expression "rubberized textile fabrics" means:
   (a) Textile fabrics impregnated, coated, covered or laminated with rubber:
   (ⅰ) Weighing not more than 1,500 g/m^2; or
   (ⅱ) Weighing more than 1,500 g/m^2 and containing more than 50% by weight of textile material。
   (b) Fabrics made from yarn, strip or the like, impregnated, coated, covered or sheathed with rubber, of heading No. 56.04; and
   (c) Fabrics composed of parallel textile yarns agglomerated with rubber, irrespective of their weight per square metre.
   This heading does not, however, apply to plates, sheets or strip of cellular rubber, combined with textile fabric, where the textile fabric is present merely for reinforcing purposes (Chapter 40), or textile products of heading No. 58.11.
5. Heading No. 59.07 does not apply to:
   (a) Fabrics in which the impregnation, coating or covering cannot be seen with the naked eye (usually Chapters 50 to 55, 58 or 60); for the purpose of this provision, no account should be taken of any resulting change of colour;
   (b) Fabrics painted with designs (other than painted canvas being theatrical scenery, studio back-cloths or the like);
   (c) Fabrics partially covered with flock, dust, powdered cork or the like and bearing designs resulting from these treatments; however, imitation pile fabrics remain classified in this heading;
   (d) Fabrics finished with normal dressings having a basis of amylaceous or similar substances;
   (e) Wood veneered on a backing of textile fabrics (heading No. 44.08);
   (f) Natural or artificial abrasive powder or grain, on a backing of textile fabrics (heading No. 68.05);
   (g) Agglomerated or reconstituted mica, on a backing of textile fabrics (heading No. 68.14); or
   (h) Metal foil on a backing of textile fabrics (Generauy section XIV or XV).
6. Heading No. 59.10 does not apply to:
   (a) Transmission or conveyor belting, of textile material, of a thickness of less than 3 mm; or
   (b) Transmission or conveyor belts or belting of textile fabric impregnated, coated, covered or laminated with rubber or made from textile yarn or cord impregnated, coated, covered or sheathed with rubber (heading No. 40.10).
7. Heading No. 59.11 applies to the following goods, which do not fall in any other heading of Section XI:
   (a) Textile products in the piece, cut to length or simply cut to rectangular (including square) shape (other than those having the character of the products of headings No. 59.08 to 59.10), the following only:
   (ⅰ) Textile fabrics, felt and felt-lined woven fabrics, coated, covered or laminated with rubber, leather or other material, of a kind used for card clothing, and similar fabrics of a kind used for other technical purposes, including narrow fabrics made of velvet impregnated with rubber, for covering weaving spindles (weaving beams);
   (ⅱ) Bolting cloth;
   (ⅲ) Straining cloth of a kind used in oil presses or the like, of textile material or of human hair;
   (ⅳ) Flat woven textile fabrics with multiple warp or weft, whether or not felted, impregnated or coated, of a kind used in machinery or for other technical purposes;
   (ⅴ) Textile fabrics reinforced with metal, of a kind used for technical purposes;

6. 工业上作填塞或润滑材料的线绳、编带及类似品，不论是否涂布、浸渍或用金属加强。

（二）专门技术用途的纺织制品（税目59.08至59.10的货品除外），例如，造纸机器或类似机器（如制浆机或制石棉水泥的机器）用的环状或装有连接装置的纺织物或毛呢、密封垫、垫圈、抛光盘及其他机器零件。

税则号列		货品名称〔CIQ扩展编码及品名—T2表示见附表2〕	最惠(%)	暂定税率	普通	增值/消费	出口退税	计量单位	监管条件	检验检疫	特殊证件对美关税
59.01		**用胶或淀粉物质涂布的纺织物，作书籍封面及类似用途的；描图布；制成的油画布；作帽里的硬衬布及类似硬挺纺织物：**									
		-用胶或淀粉物质涂布的纺织物，作书籍封面及类似用途的：									
5901.1010		---棉或麻制									
5901.1010	10	胶或淀粉涂布的棉纺织物（作书籍封面，棉织物重≥50%，经漂染印花）〔101 棉混纺印花布，999 作书籍封面，棉织物重≥50%，经漂染印花〕	8		80	13/	13	千克			/18
5901.1010	90	胶或淀粉涂布的麻及其他棉纺织（作书籍封面及类似用途的）〔999〕	8		80	13/	13	千克			/18
5901.1020		---化学纤维制									
5901.1020	10	胶或淀粉涂布的涤棉短纤混纺织品（书籍封面及类似用途，聚酯短纤棉混纺漂染织物重＞50%）〔999〕	8		130	13/	13	千克			/33
5901.1020	90	胶或淀粉涂布的其他化学纤维纺织物（作书籍封面及类似用途的）〔999〕	8		130	13/	13	千克			/33
5901.1090		---其他									
5901.1090	10	用胶或淀粉涂布的精梳毛纺织物（书籍封面及类似用途，精梳羊毛或动物细毛织物重≥50%）〔999〕	8		100	13/	13	千克			/28
5901.1090	90	用胶或淀粉涂布的其他纺织物（作书籍封面及类似用途的）〔999〕	8		100	13/	13	千克			/28
		-其他：									
5901.9010		---制成的油画布〔999〕	8		50	13/	13	千克			/33
		---其他：									
5901.9091		----棉或麻制									
5901.9091	10	棉制描图布、帽里硬衬布等（包括类似硬挺纺织物，棉织物≥50%经漂染印花）〔101 棉混纺印花布，102 其他，999 包括类似硬挺纺织物，棉织物重≥50%经漂染印花〕	8		80	13/	13	千克			/33
5901.9091	90	麻及其他棉制描图布、帽里硬衬布（包括类似硬挺纺织物）〔101 服装衬布，102 其他〕	8		80	13/	13	千克			/33
5901.9092		----化学纤维制									
5901.9092	10	聚酯短纤与棉混纺织物制描图布（含帽里硬衬类似硬挺纺织物，织物重≥50%，经漂染印）〔101 服装衬布，102 其他〕	8		130	13/	13	千克			/
5901.9092	90	其他化学纤维制描图布，帽里硬衬布等（包括类似硬挺纺织物）〔101 服装衬布，102 其他〕	8		130	13/	13	千克			/
5901.9099		----其他									
5901.9099	10	精梳毛纺织物制描图布，帽里硬衬（包括类似硬挺纺织物，精梳羊毛或动物细毛织物重≥50%）〔101 服装衬布，102 其他〕	8		100	13/	13	千克			/33
5901.9099	90	其他纺织物制描图布，帽里硬衬布（包括类似硬挺纺织物）〔101 服装衬布，102 其他〕	8		100	13/	13	千克			/33
59.02		**尼龙或其他聚酰胺，聚酯或粘胶纤维高强力纱制的帘子布：**									
		-尼龙或其他聚酰胺制：									
5902.1010		---聚酰胺-6（尼龙-6）制〔999〕	8		40	13/	13	千克			/33
5902.1020		---聚酰胺-6，6（尼龙-6，6）制〔999〕	8		40	13/	13	千克			/33
5902.1090		---其他〔999〕	8		40	13/	13	千克			/33
5902.2000		-聚酯制〔999〕	8		40	13/	13	千克			/
5902.9000		-其他〔999〕	8		40	13/	13	千克			/33

(ⅵ) Cords, braids and the like, whether or not coated, impregnated or reinforced with metal, of a kind used in industry as packing or lubricating materials;

(b) Textile articles (other than those of headings No. 59.08 to 59.10) of a kind used for technical purposes, for example, textile fabrics and felts, endless or fitted with linking devicse, of a kind used in paper-making or similar machines (for example, for pulp or asbestos-cement), gaskets, washers, polishing discs and other machinery parts.

协定税率 %										特惠税率 %			
亚太5国	东/冰/格	巴基斯坦	韩国	瑞士	哥达	秘鲁	澳大利亚	新西/坡/智	港/澳/台	亚太2国	老/柬/缅	36/3/1	Article Description
													Textile fabrics coated with gum or amylaceous substances, of a kind used for the outer covers of books or the like; tracing cloth; prepared painting canvas; buckram and similar stiffened textile fabrics of a kind used for hat foundations:
													-Textile fabrics coated with gum or amylaceous substances, of a kind used for the outer covers of books or the like:
													---Of cotton or bast fibres
	0/0/0	4	4	0	0	0	0	0/0/0	0/0/			0/0/0	Textile fabrics coated with gum or amylaceous substances, of a kind used for the outer covers of books or the like, containing≥50% by weight of cotton, bleached, dyed, printed
	0/0/0	4	4	0	0	0	0	0/0/0	0/0/			0/0/0	Textile fabrics coated with gum or amylaceous substances, of a kind used for the outer covers of books or the like, of bast fibres and other cotton
													---Of man-made fibres
	0/0/0	4	0	0	0	0	0	0/0/0	0/0/			0/0/0	Textile fabrics coated with gum or amylaceous substances, of a kind used for the outer covers of books or the like, containing≥50% by weight of polyester staple fibres and cotton, bleached, dyed
	0/0/0	4	0	0	0	0	0	0/0/0	0/0/			0/0/0	Other man-made textile fabrics coated with gum or amylaceous substances, of a kind used for the outer covers of books or the like, of other textile fabrics
													---Other
	0/0/0	4	0	0	0	0	0	0/0/0	0/0/			0/0/0	Woollen textile fabrics coated with gum or amylaceous substances, of a kind used for the outer covers of books or the like, containing≥50% by weight of combed wool or fine animal hair
	0/0/0	4	0	0	0	0	0	0/0/0	0/0/			0/0/0	Other textile fabrics coated with gum or amylaceous substances, of a kind used for the outer covers of books or the like, of other textile fabrics
													-Other:
	0/0/0	4.5	0	0	0	0	0	0//0	0/0/			0/0/0	---Prepared painting canvas
													---Other:
													----Of cotton or bast fibres
	0/0/0	4.5	0	0	0	0	0	0//0	0/0/		0/0/0	0/0/0	Tracing cloth, buckram and similar stiffened textile fabrics, of a kind used for hat foundations, of cotton, containing≥50% by weight of cotton, bleached dyed printed
	0/0/0	4.5	0	0	0	0	0	0//0	0/0/		0/0/0	0/0/0	Tracing cloth, buckram and similar stiffened textile fabrics, of a kind used for hat foundations, of bast fibres and other cotton
													----Of man-made fibres
	0/0/0	4.5	0	0	0	0	0	0//0	0/0/			0/0/1	Tracing cloth, buckram and similar stiffened textile fabrics, of a kind used for hat foundations, mixed, containing≥50% by weight of polyester staple fibres and cotton, bleached, dyed, printed
	0/0/0	4.5	0	0	0	0	0	0//0	0/0/			0/0/0	Tracing cloth, buckram and similar stiffened textile fabrics, of a kind used for hat foundations, of other man-made fibres
													----Other
	0/0/0	4.5	0	0	0	0	0	0//0	0/0/			0/0/0	Tracing cloth, buckram and similar stiffened textile fabrics, of a kind used for hat foundations, containing≥50% by weight, of combed wool or combed fine animals hair
	0/0/0	4.5	0	0	0	0	0	0//0	0/0/			0/0/0	Tracing cloth, buckram and similar stiffened textile fabrics, of a kind used for hat foundations, of other textile fabrics
													Tyre cord fabric of high tenacity yarn of nylon or other polyamides, polyesters or viscose rayon:
													-Of nylon or other polyamides:
5.2	0/0/0	4	6.5	0	0	0	0	0/0/0	0/0/			0/0/0	---Of polyamides(nylon-6)
5.2	0/0/0	4	6.5	0	0	0	0	0/0/0	0/0/			0/0/0	---Of polyamides(nylon-6,6)
5.2	0/0/0	4	4	0	0	0	0	0/0/0	0/0/			0/0/0	---Other
5.2	0/0/0	4	7	0	0	0	0	0/0/0	0/0/			0/0/0	-Of polyesters
	0/0/0	4	0	3	0	0	0	0//0	0/0/			0/0/0	-Other

税则号列	货品名称〔CIQ扩展编码及品名—T2表示见附表2〕	最惠(%)	暂定税率	普通	增值/消费	出口退税	计量单位	监管条件	检验检疫	特殊证件对美关税
59.03	**用塑料浸渍、涂布、包覆或层压的纺织物,但税目59.02的货品除外:**									
	-用聚氯乙烯浸渍、涂布、包覆或层压的:									
5903.1010	---绝缘布或带〔999〕	8		40	13/	13	千克			/18
5903.1020	---人造革〔101棉混纺印花布,999〕	8		70	13/	13	千克/米			/33
5903.1090	---其他〔101棉混纺印花布,999包括用聚氯乙烯涂布,包覆或层压的〕	8		90	13/	13	千克			/28
	-用聚氨基甲酸酯浸渍、涂布、包覆或层压的:									
5903.2010	---绝缘布或带〔999〕	8		40	13/	13	千克			/18
5903.2020	---人造革〔999〕	8		70	13/	13	千克/米			/33
5903.2090	---其他〔999〕	8		90	13/	13	千克			/33
	-其他:									
5903.9010	---绝缘布或带〔999〕	8		40	13/	13	千克			/18
5903.9020	---人造革〔101棉混纺印花布,999〕	8		70	13/	13	千克/米			/28
5903.9090	---其他〔101棉混纺印花布,999包括用其他塑料涂布、包覆或层压的〕	8		90	13/	13	千克			/28
59.04	**列诺伦(亚麻油地毡),不论是否剪切成形;以织物为底布经涂布或覆面的铺地制品,不论是否剪切成形:**									
5904.1000	-列诺伦(亚麻油地毡)〔999〕	6		90	13/	13	千克/平方米			/
5904.9000	-其他〔999〕	6		90	13/	13	千克/平方米			/
59.05	**糊墙织物:**									
5905.0000	糊墙织物〔999〕	8		80	13/	13	千克/平方米			/28
59.06	**用橡胶处理的纺织物,但税目59.02的货品除外:**									
	-宽度不超过20厘米的胶粘带:									
5906.1010	---绝缘带〔999〕	8		40	13/	13	千克			/33
5906.1090	---其他〔999〕	8		100	13/	13	千克			/28
	-其他:									
5906.9100	--针织或钩编的〔999〕	8		130	13/	13	千克			/33
	--其他:									
5906.9910	---绝缘布或带〔101棉混纺印花布,999非针织或钩编,宽>20cm〕	8		40	13/	13	千克			/33
5906.9990	---其他〔101棉混纺印花布,999非针织或钩编.宽>20cm〕	8		100	13/	13	千克			/18
59.07	**用其他材料浸渍、涂布或包覆的纺织物;作舞台、摄影布景或类似用途的已绘制画布:**									
5907.0010	---绝缘布或带〔999〕	8		40	13/	13	千克			/33
5907.0020	---已绘制画布〔999〕	8		50	13/	13	千克			/28
5907.0090	---其他〔999〕	8		100	13/	13	千克			/18
59.08	**用纺织材料机织、编结或针织而成的灯芯、炉芯、打火机芯、烛芯或类似品;煤气灯纱筒及纱罩,不论是否浸渍:**									
5908.0000	用纺织材料机织、编结或针织而成的灯芯、炉芯、打火机芯、烛芯或类似品;煤气灯纱筒及纱罩,不论是否浸渍〔999〕	8		70	13/	13	千克			/18
59.09	**纺织材料制的水龙软管及类似的管子,不论有无其他材料作衬里、护套或附件:**									
5909.0000	纺织材料制的水龙软管及类似的管子,不论有无其他材料作衬里、护套或附件〔999〕	8		35	13/	13	千克		L	/18
59.10	**纺织材料制的传动带或输送带及带料,不论是否用塑料浸渍、涂布、包覆或压层,也不论是否用金属或其他材料加强:**									
5910.0000	纺织材料制的传动带或输送带及带料,不论是否用塑料浸渍、涂布、包覆或压层,也不论是否用金属或其他材料加强〔999〕	8		35	13/	13	千克			/28
59.11	**本章注释七所规定的作专门技术用途的纺织产品及制品:**									
	-用橡胶、皮革或其他材料涂布、包覆或层压的作针布用的纺织物、毡呢及毡呢衬里机织物,以及作专门技术用途的类似织物,包括用橡胶浸渍的、用于包覆纺锤(织轴)的狭幅丝绒织物:									
5911.1010	---用橡胶浸渍的、用于包覆纺锤(织轴)的狭幅丝绒织物〔999〕	8		75	13/	13	千克			/28
5911.1090	---其他〔999〕	8		35	13/	13	千克			/33
5911.2000	-筛布,不论是否制成的									

协定税率 %										特惠税率 %			
亚太5国	东/冰/格	巴基斯坦	韩国	瑞士	哥达	秘鲁	澳大利亚	新西/坡/智	港/澳/台	亚太2国	老/柬/缅	36/3/1	Article Description
													Textile fabrics impregnated, coated, covered or laminated with plastics, other than those of heading No. 59. 02:
													-With poly(vinyl chloride):
5.2	0/0/0	4	0	0	0	0	0	0//0	0/0/			0/0/0	---Insulating cloth or tape
5.2	0/0/0	4	7	0	0	0	0	0/0/0	0/0/0			0/0/0	---Imitation leather
5.2	0/0/0	4	7	0	0	0	0	0/0/0	0/0/0			0/0/0	---Other
													-With polyurethane:
5.2	0/0/0	4.5	0	0	0	0	0	0//0	0/0/			0/0/0	---Insulating cloth or tape
5.2	0/0/0	0	7	0	0	0	0	0/0/0	0/0/0			0/0/0	---Imitation leather
5.2	0/0/0	0	7	0	0	0	0	0/0/0	0/0/0			0/0/0	---Other
													-Other:
5.2	0/0/0	4	0	3	0	0	0	0//0	0/0/			0/0/0	---Insulating cloth or tape
5.2	0/0/0	4.5	6	0	0	0	0	0/0/0	0/0/0			0/0/0	---Imitation leather
5.2	0/0/0	8.5	7	0	0	0	0	0/0/0	0/0/0		0/0/0	0/0/0	---Other
													Linoleum, whether or not cut to shape; floor coverings consisting of a coating or covering applied on a textile backing, whether or not cut to shape:
	0/0/0	11.2	5.6	4.2	0	0	0	0/0/0	0/0/			0/0/	-Linoleum
	0/0/0	7	5.6	4.2	0	0	0	0/0/0	0/0/			0/0/	-Other
													Textile wall coverings:
	0/0/0	4	0	0	0	0	0	0/0/0	0/0/			0/0/0	Textile wall coverings
													Rubberized textile fabrics, other than those of heading No. 59. 02:
													-Adhesive tape of a width not exceeding 20 cm:
	0/0/0	4	0	0	0	0	0	0//0	0/0/			0/0/0	---Insulating tape
	0//0	4	0	0	0	0	0	0/0/0	0/0/			0/0/0	---Other
													-Other:
	0/0/0	4	0	0	0	0	0	0/0/0	0/0/0			0/0/0	--Knitted or crocheted
													--Other:
	0/0/0	4	0	0	0	0	0	0//0	0/0/			0/0/0	---Insulating cloth or tape
	0/0/0	4	0	0	0	0	0	0/0/0	0/0/0			0/0/0	---Other
													Textile fabrics otherwise impregnated, coated or covered; painted canvas being theatrical scenery, studio back-cloths or the like:
5.2	0/0/0	4.5	0	3	0	0	0	0//0	0/0/			0/0/0	---Insulating cloth or tape
5.2	0/0/0	4.5	0	0	0	0	0	0//0	0/0/			0/0/0	---Painted canvas
5.2	0/0/0	4.5	7	0	0	0	0	0/0/0	0/0/			0/0/0	---Other
													Textile wicks, woven, plaited or knitted, for lamps, stoves, lighters, candles or the like; incandescent gas mantles and tubular knitted gas mantle fabric therefor, whether or not impregnated:
	0/0/0	4	0	0	0	0	0	0//0	0/0/			0/0/0	Textile wicks, woven, plaited or knitted, for lamps, stoves, lighters, candles or the like; incandescent gas mantles and tubular knitted gas mantle fabric therefor, whether or not impregnated
													Textile hosepiping and similar textile tubing, with or without lining, armour or accessories of other materials:
	0/0/0	4	0	0	0	0	0	0//0	0/0/			0/0/0	Textile hosepiping and similar textile tubing, with or without lining, armour or accessories of other materials
													Transmission or conveyor belts or belting, of textile material, whether or not impregnated, coated, covered or laminated with plastics, or reinforced with metal or other material:
	0/0/0	4	0	0	0	0	0	0//0	0/0/0			0/0/0	Transmission or conveyor belts or belting, of textile material, whether or not impregnated, coated, covered or laminated with plastics, or reinforced with metal or other material
													Textile products and articles, for technical uses, specified in Note 7 to this Chapter:
													-Textile fabrics, felt and felt-lined woven fabrics, coated, covered or laminated with rubber, leather or other material, of a kind used for card clothing, and similar fabrics of a kind used for other technical purposes, including narrow fabrics made of velvet impregnated with rubber, for covering weaving spindles (weaving beams):
5.2	0/0/0	4	0	0	0	0	0	0//0	0/0/			0/0/0	---Narrow fabrics made of velvet impregnated with rubber, for covering weaving spindles (weaving beams)
	0/0/0	4	0	0	0	0	0	0//0	0/0/			0/0/0	---Other
													-Bolting cloth, whether or not made up

税则号列	货品名称〔CIQ 扩展编码及品名－T2 表示见附表 2〕	最惠(%)	暂定税率	普通	增值/消费	出口退税	计量单位	监管条件	检验检疫	特殊证件对美关税
5911.2000 10	丝制筛布(不论是否制成的)〔101 网料与筛布,999 不论是否制成的.〕	8		35	13/	13	千克			/28
5911.2000 90	其他纺织材料制筛布(不论是否制成的,刻版筛网印布除外)〔101 网料与筛布,999 不论是否制成的.刻版筛网印布除外〕	8		35	13/	13	千克			/28
	-环状或装有连接装置的纺织物及毡呢,用于造纸机器或类似机器(例如,制浆机或制石棉水泥的机器):									
5911.3100	--每平方米重量在 650 克以下〔101 毡呢,999 每平方米重量在 650 克以下,用于造纸机器或类似机器〕	8		35	13/	13	千克			/28
5911.3200	--每平方米重量在 650 克及以上〔101 毡呢,999 每平方米重量在 650 克及以上,用于造纸机器或类似机器〕	8		35	13/	13	千克			/28
5911.4000	-用于榨油机器或类似机器的滤布,包括人发制滤布〔101 网料与筛布,999 包括人发制滤布〕	8		35	13/	13	千克			/28
5911.9000	-其他									
5911.9000 10	半导体晶圆制造用自粘式圆形抛光垫(见第 59 章注释七)〔999〕	27/13		35	13/	13	千克			/12.7,11.3
5911.9000 90	其他专门技术用途纺织产品及制品(见第 59 章注释七)〔101 网料与筛布,102 其他产业用纺织制品〕	8		35	13/	13	千克			/18

协定税率 %										特惠税率 %			
亚太5国	东/冰/格	巴基斯坦	韩国	瑞士	哥达	秘鲁	澳大利亚	新西/坡/智	港/澳/台	亚太2国	老/柬/缅	36/3/1	**Article Description**
	0/0/0	4	0	0	0	0	0	0//0	0/0/			0/0/0	Bolting cloth of silk, whether or not made up
	0/0/0	4	0	0	0	0	0	0//0	0/0/			0/0/0	Bolting cloth of other textile materials, whether or not made up, other than stencil screen
													-Textile fabrics and felts, endless or fitted with linking devices, of a kind used in paper-making or similar machines (for example, for pulp or asbestos-cement):
	0/0/0	4	0	0	0	0	0	0//0	0/0/			0/0/0	--Weighing less than 650 g/m^2
	0/0/0	4	0	2.4	0	0	0	0//0	0/0/			0/0/0	--Weighing 650 g/m^2 or more
	0/0/3.2	4	0	0	0	0	0	0//0	0/0/			0/0/0	-Straining cloth of a kind used in oil presses or the like, including that of human hair
													-Other
	0/0/0	4		0	0	0	0	0//0	0/0/			0/0/0	With self-adhesive circular polishing pad manufacturing semiconductor wafer (Notes 7 of Chapter)
	0/0/0	4		0	0	0	0	0//0	0/0/			0/0/0	Other specialized technical purposes for textile products and products (Notes 7 of Chapter)

第六十章
针织物及钩编织物

注释：

一、本章不包括：

(一)税目 58.04 的钩编花边；

(二)税目 58.07 的针织或钩编的标签、徽章及类似品；或

(三)第五十九章的经浸渍、涂布、包覆或层压的针织物及钩编织物。但经浸渍、涂布、包覆或层压的起绒针织物及起绒钩编织物仍归入税目 60.01。

二、本章还包括用金属线制的用于衣着、装饰或类似用途的织物。

三、本协调制度所称“针织物”，包括由纺织纱线用链式针法构成的缝编织物。

子目注释：

一、子目 6005.35 包括由聚乙烯单丝或涤纶复丝制成的织物，重量不小于 30 克/平方米，但不超过 55 克/平方米，网眼尺寸不小于 20 孔/平方厘米，但不超过 100 孔/平方厘米，并且用 α-氯氰菊酯(ISO)、虫螨腈(ISO)、溴氰菊酯(INN,ISO)、高效氯氟氰菊酯(ISO)、除虫菊酯(ISO)或甲基嘧啶磷(ISO)浸渍或涂层。

税则号列	货品名称〔CIQ 扩展编码及品名－T2 表示见附表 2〕	最惠(%)	暂定税率	普通	增值/消费	出口退税	计量单位	监管条件	检验检疫	特殊证件对美关税
60.01	**针织或钩编的起绒织物，包括“长毛绒”织物及毛圈织物：**									
6001.1000	-“长毛绒”织物〔999〕	8		130	13/	13	米/千克			/33
	-毛圈绒头织物：									
6001.2100	--棉制〔999〕	8		70	13/	13	米/千克			/33
6001.2200	--化学纤维制〔999〕	8		130	13/	13	米/千克			/28
6001.2900	--其他纺织材料制〔999〕	8		130	13/	13	米/千克			/
	-其他：									
6001.9100	--棉制〔999〕	8		70	13/	13	米/千克			/33
6001.9200	--化学纤维制〔999〕	8		130	13/	13	米/千克			/33
6001.9900	--其他纺织材料制〔999〕	8		130	13/	13	米/千克			/33
60.02	**宽度不超过 30 厘米，按重量计弹性纱线或橡胶线含量在 5%及以上的针织物或钩编织物，但税目 60.01 的货品除外：**									
	-按重量计弹性纱线含量在 5%及以上，但不含橡胶线：									
6002.4010	---棉制〔999〕	8		70	13/	13	米/千克			/
6002.4020	---丝及绢丝制〔999〕	8		130	13/	13	米/千克			/
6002.4030	---合成纤维制〔999〕	8		130	13/	13	米/千克			/
6002.4040	---人造纤维制〔999〕	8		130	13/	13	米/千克			/
6002.4090	---其他〔999〕	8		130	13/	13	米/千克			/
	-其他：									
6002.9010	---棉制〔999〕	8		70	13/	13	米/千克			/18
6002.9020	---丝及绢丝制〔999〕	8		130	13/	13	米/千克			/
6002.9030	---合成纤维制〔999〕	8		130	13/	13	米/千克			/33
6002.9040	---人造纤维制〔999〕	8		130	13/	13	米/千克			/18
6002.9090	---其他〔999〕	8		130	13/	13	米/千克			/33
60.03	**宽度不超过 30 厘米的针织或钩编织物，但税目 60.01 或 60.02 的货品除外：**									
6003.1000	-羊毛或动物细毛制〔999〕	8		130	13/	13	米/千克			/
6003.2000	-棉制〔999〕	8		70	13/	13	米/千克			/33
6003.3000	-合成纤维制〔999〕	8		130	13/	13	米/千克			/33
6003.4000	-人造纤维制〔999〕	8		130	13/	13	米/千克			/
6003.9000	-其他〔999〕	8		130	13/	13	米/千克			/18
60.04	**宽度超过 30 厘米，按重量计弹性纱线或橡胶线含量在 5%及以上的针织物或钩编织物，但税目 60.01 的货品除外：**									
	-按重量计弹性纱线含量在 5%及以上，但不含橡胶线									
6004.1010	---棉制〔999〕	8		70	13/	13	米/千克			/33
6004.1020	---丝及绢丝制〔999〕	8		130	13/	13	米/千克			/
6004.1030	---合成纤维制〔999〕	8		130	13/	13	米/千克			/33
6004.1040	---人造纤维制〔999〕	8		130	13/	13	米/千克			/33
6004.1090	---其他〔999〕	8		130	13/	13	米/千克			/33
	-其他：									

Chapter 60
Knitted or crocheted fabrics

Notes:

1. This Chapter does not cover:
   (a) Crochet lace of heading No. 58.04;
   (b) Labels, badges or similar articles, knitted or crocheted, of heading No. 58.07; or
   (c) Knitted or crocheted fabrics, impregnated, coated, covered or laminated, of Chapter 59. However, knitted or crocheted pile fabrics, impregnated, coated, covered or laminated, remain classified in heading No. 60.01.
2. This Chapter also includes fabrics made of metal thread and of a kind used in apparel, as furnishing fabrics or for similar purposes.
3. Throughout the Nomenclature any reference to "knitted" goods includes a reference to stitch-bonded goods in which the chain stitches are formed of textile yarn.

Subheading Notes:

1. Subheading No. 6005.35 includes made of polyethylene monofilament or multifilament polyester fabric, the weight of not less than 30 g/ m2, but not more than 55 g/ m2, mesh size of not less than 20 holes per square centimeter, but not more than 100 holes per square centimeter, and alpha cypermethrin (ISO), insects and mites nitrile (ISO) and deltamethrin (INN, ISO), lambda cyhalothrin (ISO), pyrethrins (ISO) or pirimiphos methyl (ISO), impregnated or coated.

协定税率 %										特惠税率 %			Article Description
亚太5国	东/冰/格	巴基斯坦	韩国	瑞士	哥达	秘鲁	澳大利亚	新西/坡/智	港/澳/台	亚太2国	老/柬/缅	36/3/1	
													Pile fabrics, including "long pile" fabrics and terry fabrics, knitted or crocheted:
5.2	0/0/0	0	6	0	0	0	0	0/0/0	0/0/			0/0/0	-"Long pile" fabrics
													-Looped pile fabrics:
5.2	0/0/0	0	0	0	0	0	0	0//0	0/0/			0/0/0	--Of cotton
5.2	0/0/0	0	0	0	0	0	0	0/0/0	0/0/			0/0/0	--Of man-made fibres
	0/0/0	0	0	3.6	0	0	0	0/0/0	0/0/			0/0/	--Of other textile materials
													-Other:
5.2	0/0/0	0	0	0	0	0	0	0//0	0/0/			0/0/0	--Of cotton
5.2	0/0/0	0	7	0	0	0	0	0/0/0	0/0/0			0/0/0	--Of man-made fibres
	0/0/0	0	0	3.6	0	0	0	0/0/0	0/0/			0/0/	--Of other textile materials
													Knitted or crocheted fabrics of a width not exceeding 30 cm, containing by weight 5% or more of elastomeric yarn or rubber thread, other than those of heading No. 60.01:
													-Containing by weight 5% or more of elastomeric yarn but not containing rubber thread:
5.2	0/0/0	0	0	0	0	0	0	0//0	0/0/			0/0/0	---Of cotton
5.2	0/0/0	0	0	0	0	0	0	0/0/0	0/0/			0/0/0	---Of silk or spun silk
	0/0/0	0	0	0	0	0	0	0/0/0	0/0/			0/0/0	---Of synthetic fibres
	0/0/0	0	0	0	0	0	0	0/0/0	0/0/			0/0/0	---Of artificial fibres
5.2	0/0/0	0	0	0	0	0	0	0/0/0	0/0/			0/0/0	---Other
													-Other:
5.2	0/0/0	0	0	0	0	0	0	0//0	0/0/		0/0/0	0/0/0	---Of cotton
5.2	0/0/0	0	0	0	0	0	0	0/0/0	0/0/			0/0/0	---Of silk or spun silk
4	0/0/0	0	6	0	0	0	0	0/0/0	0/0/		0/0/0	0/0/0	---Of synthetic fibres
4	0/0/0	0	0	0	0	0	0	0/0/0	0/0/			0/0/0	---Of artificial fibres
5.2	0/0/0	0	0	0	0	0	0	0/0/0	0/0/			0/0/0	---Other
													Knitted or crocheted fabrics of a width not exceeding 30 cm, other than those of heading No. 60.01 or 60.02:
	0/0/0	0	0	0	0	0	0	0/0/0	0/0/			0/0/0	-Of wool or fine animal hair
	0/0/0	0	0	0	0	0	0	0//0	0/0/			0/0/0	-Of cotton
5.2	0/0/0	0	0	0	0	0	0	0/0/0	0/0/			0/0/0	-Of synthetic fibres
5.2	0/0/0	0	0	0	0	0	0	0/0/0	0/0/			0/0/0	-Of artificial fibres
	0/0/0	0	0	0	0	0	0	0/0/0	0/0/			0/0/0	-Other
													Knitted or crocheted fabrics of a width exceeding 30 cm, containing by weight 5% or more of elastomeric yarn or rubber thread, other than those of heading No. 60.01:
													-Containing by weight 5% or more of elastomeric yarn but not containing rubber thread:
5.2	0/0/0	0	0	0	0	0	0	0/0/0	0/0/		0/0/0	0/0/0	---Of cotton
5.2	0/0/0	0	0	0	0	0	0	0/0/0	0/0/			0/0/0	---Of silk or spun silk
	0/0/0	0	7	0	0	0	0	0/0/0	0/0/0			0/0/0	---Of synthetic fibres
	0/0/0	0	6	0	0	0	0	0/0/0	0/0/			0/0/0	---Of artificial fibres
5.2	0/0/0	0	0	0	0	0	0	0/0/0	0/0/0			0/0/0	---Other
													-Other:

税则号列	货品名称〔CIQ 扩展编码及品名—T2 表示见附表 2〕	最惠(%)	暂定税率	普通	增值/消费	出口退税	计量单位	监管条件	检验检疫	特殊证件对美关税
6004.9010	---棉制〔999〕	8		70	13/	13	米/千克			/33
6004.9020	---丝及绢丝制〔999〕	8		130	13/	13	米/千克			/
6004.9030	---合成纤维制〔999〕	8		130	13/	13	米/千克			/33
6004.9040	---人造纤维制〔999〕	8		130	13/	13	米/千克			/33
6004.9090	---其他〔999〕	8		130	13/	13	米/千克			/33
60.05	**经编针织物(包括由镶边针织机织成的),但税目 60.01 至 60.04 的货品除外:**									
	-棉制:									
6005.2100	--未漂白或漂白〔999〕	8		70	13/	13	米/千克			/
6005.2200	--染色〔999〕	8		70	13/	13	米/千克			/
6005.2300	--色织〔999〕	8		70	13/	13	米/千克			/
6005.2400	--印花〔999〕	8		70	13/	13	米/千克			/
	-合成纤维制:									
6005.3500	--本章子目注释一所列织物〔999〕	8		130	13/	13	米/千克			/33
6005.3600	--其他,未漂白或漂白〔999〕	8		130	13/	13	米/千克			/28
6005.3700	--其他,染色〔999〕	8		130	13/	13	米/千克			/33
6005.3800	--其他,色织〔999〕	8		130	13/	13	米/千克			/33
6005.3900	--其他,印花〔999〕	8		130	13/	13	米/千克			/
	-人造纤维制:									
6005.4100	--未漂白或漂白〔999〕	8		130	13/	13	米/千克			/
6005.4200	--染色〔999〕	8		130	13/	13	米/千克			/33
6005.4300	--色织〔999〕	8		130	13/	13	米/千克			/33
6005.4400	--印花〔999〕	8		130	13/	13	米/千克			/
	-其他:									
6005.9010	---羊毛或动物细毛制〔999〕	8		130	13/	13	米/千克			/
6005.9090	---其他〔999〕	8		130	13/	13	米/千克			/33
60.06	**其他针织或钩编织物:**									
6006.1000	-羊毛或动物细毛制〔999〕	8		130	13/	13	米/千克			/33
	-棉制:									
6006.2100	--未漂白或漂白〔999〕	8		70	13/	13	米/千克			/33
6006.2200	--染色〔999〕	8		70	13/	13	米/千克			/33
6006.2300	--色织〔999〕	8		70	13/	13	米/千克			/33
6006.2400	--印花〔999〕	8		70	13/	13	米/千克			/33
	-合成纤维制:									
6006.3100	--未漂白或漂白〔999〕	8		130	13/	13	米/千克			/33
6006.3200	--染色〔999〕	8		130	13/	13	米/千克			/33
6006.3300	--色织〔999〕	8		130	13/	13	米/千克			/33
6006.3400	--印花〔999〕	8		130	13/	13	米/千克			/33
	-人造纤维制:									
6006.4100	--未漂白或漂白〔999〕	8		130	13/	13	米/千克			/
6006.4200	--染色〔999〕	8		130	13/	13	米/千克			/33
6006.4300	--色织〔999〕	8		130	13/	13	米/千克			/33
6006.4400	--印花〔999〕	8		130	13/	13	米/千克			/
6006.9000	-其他〔999〕	8		130	13/	13	米/千克			/33

协定税率 %										特惠税率 %			Article Description
亚太5国	东/冰/格	巴基斯坦	韩国	瑞士	哥达	秘鲁	澳大利亚	新西/坡/智	港/澳/台	亚太2国	老/柬/缅	36/3/1	
5.2	0/0/0	0	0	0	0	0	0	0//0	0/0/			0/0/0	---Of cotton
5.2	0/0/0	0	0	0	0	0	0	0/0/0	0/0/			0/0/0	---Of silk or spun silk
	0/0/0	0	7	0	0	0	0	0/0/0	0/0/0			0/0/0	---Of synthetic fibres
	0/0/0	0	0	0	0	0	0	0/0/0	0/0/			0/0/0	---Of artificial fibres
5.2	0/0/0	0	0	0	0	0	0	0/0/0	0/0/0			0/0/0	---Other
													Warp knit fabrics (including those made on galloon knitting machines), other than those of headings Nos. 60. 01 to 60. 04:
													-Of cotton:
	0/0/0	0	0	0	0	0	0	0//0	0/0/			0/0/0	--Unbleached or bleached
	0/0/0	0	0	0	0	0	0	0//0	0/0/			0/0/0	--Dyed
	0/0/0	0	0	0	0	0	0	0//0	0/0/			0/0/0	--Of yarns of different colours
	0/0/0	0	0	0	0	0	0	0//0	0/0/			0/0/0	--Printed
													-Of synthetic fibres:
5.2	0/0/0	0	0	0	0	0	0	0/0/0	0/0/0			0/0/0	--Fabrics specified in Subheading Note 1 to this Chapter
5.2	0/0/0	0	0	0	0	0	0	0/0/0	0/0/0			0/0/0	--Other, unbleached or bleached
5.2	0/0/0	0	7	0	0	0	0	0/0/0	0/0/0		0/0/0	0/0/0	--Other, dyed
5.2	0/0/0	0	0	0	0	0	0	0/0/0	0/0/			0/0/0	--Other, of yarns of different colours
5.2	0/0/0	0	0	0	0	0	0	0/0/0	0/0/			0/0/0	--Other, printed
													-Of artificial fibres:
5.2	0/0/0	0	0	0	0	0	0	0/0/0	0/0/			0/0/0	--Unbleached or bleached
5.2	0/0/0	0	0	0	0	0	0	0/0/0	0/0/			0/0/0	--Dyed
5.2	0/0/0	0	0	0	0	0	0	0/0/0	0/0/			0/0/0	--Of yarns of different colours
5.2	0/0/0	0	0	0	0	0	0	0/0/0	0/0/			0/0/0	--Printed
													-Other:
	0/0/0	0	0	3.6	0	0	0	0/0/0	0/0/			0/0/	---Of wool or fine animal hair
	0/0/0	0	0	3.6	0	0	0	0/0/0	0/0/			0/0/	---Other
													Other knitted or crocheted fabrics:
	0/0/0	0	0	3.6	0	0	0	0/0/0	0/0/			0/0/	-Of wool or fine animal hair
													-Of cotton:
5.2	0/0/0	0	6	0	0	0	0	0//0	0/0/			0/0/0	--Unbleached or bleached
5.2	0/0/0	0	0	0	0	0	0	0/0/0	0/0/		0/0/0	0/0/0	--Dyed
5.2	0/0/0	0	0	0	0	0	0	0/0/0	0/0/		0/0/0	0/0/0	--Of yarns of different colours
5.2	0/0/0	0	0	0	0	0	0	0//0	0/0/0			0/0/0	--Printed
													-Of synthetic fibres:
5.2	0/0/0	0	0	0	0	0	0	0/0/0	0/0/0			0/0/0	--Unbleached or bleached
5.2	0/0/0	0	7	0	0	0	0	0/0/0	0/0/0			0/0/0	--Dyed
5.2	0/0/0	0	7	0	0	0	0	0/0/0	0/0/0			0/0/0	--Of yarns of different colours
5.2	0/0/0	0	7	0	0	0	0	0/0/0	0/0/0			0/0/0	--Printed
													-Of artificial fibres:
5.2	0/0/0	0	0	0	0	0	0	0/0/0	0/0/			0/0/0	--Unbleached or bleached
5.2	0/0/0	0	6	0	0	0	0	0/0/0	0/0/0			0/0/0	--Dyed
5.2	0/0/0	0	0	0	0	0	0	0/0/0	0/0/			0/0/0	--Of yarns of different colours
5.2	0/0/0	0	0	0	0	0	0	0/0/0	0/0/			0/0/0	--Printed
5.2	0/0/0	0	0	3.6	0	0	0	0/0/0	0/0/			0/0/	-Other

第六十一章
针织或钩编的服装及衣着附件

注释：

一、本章仅适用于制成的针织品或钩编织品。

二、本章不包括：

(一)税目62.12的货品；

(二)税目63.09的旧衣着或其他旧物品；

(三)矫形器具、外科手术带、疝气带及类似品(税目90.21)。

三、税目61.03及61.04所称：

(一)"西服套装"，是指面料用相同的织物制成的两件套或三件套的下列成套服装：

一件人体上半身穿着的外套或短上衣，除袖子外，其面料数为四片或四片以上；也可附带一件马甲(西服背心)，这件马甲(西服背心)的前片面料应与套装其他各件的面料相同，后片面料则应与外套或短上衣的衬里料相同；

以及一件人体下半身穿着的服装，即不带背带或护胸的长裤、马裤、短裤(游泳裤除外)、裙子或裙裤。

西服套装各件面料质地、颜色及构成必须相同，其款式也必须相同，尺寸大小还须相互般配，但可以用不同织物滚边(缝口上缝入长条织物)。

如果数件人体下半身穿着的服装同时报验或出口(例如，两条长裤、长裤与短裤、裙子或裙裤与长裤)，构成西服套装下装的应是一条长裤，而对于女式西服套装，则应是一条裙子或裙裤，其他服装应分别归类。

所称"西服套装"，包括不论是否完全符合上述条件的下列配套服装：

1.常礼服，由一件后襟下垂并下端开圆弧形叉的素色短上衣和一条条纹长裤组成；

2.晚礼服(燕尾服)，一般用黑色织物制成，上衣前襟较短且不闭合，背后有燕尾；

3.无燕尾套装夜礼服，其中上衣款式与普通上衣相似(可以更为显露衬衣前胸)，但有光滑丝质或仿丝质的翻领。

(二)"便服套装"，是指面料相同并作零售包装的下列成套服装(西服套装及税目61.07、61.08或61.09的物品除外)：

一件人体上半身穿着的服装，但套衫及背心除外，因为套衫可在两件套服装中作为内衣，背心也可作为内衣；以及一件或两件不同的人体下半身穿着的服装，即长裤、护胸背带工装裤、马裤、短裤(游泳裤除外)、裙子或裙裤。

便服套装各件面料质地、款式、颜色及构成必须相同；尺寸大小也须相互般配。所称"便服套装"，不包括税目61.12的运动服及滑雪服。

四、税目61.05及61.06不包括在腰围以下有口袋的服装、带有罗纹腰带及以其他方式收紧下摆的服装或其织物至少在10厘米×10厘米的面积内沿各方向的直线长度上平均每厘米少于10针的服装。税目61.05不包括无袖服装。

五、税目61.09不包括带有束带、罗纹腰带或其他方式收紧下摆的服装。

六、对于税目61.11：

(一)所称"婴儿服装及衣着附件"，是指用于身高不超过86厘米幼儿的服装；

(二)既可归入税目61.11，也可归入本章其他税目的物品，应归入税目61.11。

七、税目61.12所称"滑雪服"，是指从整个外观和织物质地来看，主要在滑雪(速度滑雪或高山滑雪)时穿着的下列服装或成套服装：

(一)"滑雪连身服"，即上下身连在一起的单件服装；除袖子和领子外，滑雪连身服可有口袋或脚带；或

(二)"滑雪套装"，即由两件或三件构成一套并作零售包装的下列服装：

一件用一条拉链扣合的带风帽的厚夹克、防风衣、防风短上衣或类似的服装，可以附带一件背心；以及一条不论是否过腰的长裤、一条马裤或一条护胸背带工装裤。

"滑雪套装"也可由一件类似以上(一)款所述的连身服和一件可套在连身服外面的有胎料背心组成。

"滑雪套装"各件颜色可以不同，但面料质地、款式及构成必须相同；尺寸大小也须相互般配。

八、既可归入税目61.13，也可归入本章其他税号的服装，除税目61.11所列的仍归入该税号外，其余的应一律归入税目61.13。

九、本章的服装，凡门襟为左压右的，应视为男式；右压左的，应视为女式。但本规定不适用于其式样已明显为男式或女式的服装。无法区别是男式还是女式的服装，应按女式服装归入有关税目。

Chapter 61
Articles of apparel and clothing accessories, knitted or crocheted6

Notes:

1. This Chapter applies only to made up knitted or crocheted articles.
2. This Chapter does not cover:
   (a) Goods of heading No.62.12;
   (b) Worn clothing or other worn articles of heading No.63.09; or
   (c) Orthopaedic appliances, surgical belts, trusses or the like (heaing No.90.21).
3. For the purposes of headings Nos.61.03 and 61.04:

(a) The term "suit" means a set of garments composed of two or three pieces made up, in respect of their outer surface, in identical fabric and comprising:

One suit coat or jacket the outer shell of which, exclusive of sleeves, consists of four or more panels, designed to cover the upper part of the body, possibly with a tailored waistcoat in addition whose front is made from the same fabric as the outer sulrace of the other components of the set and whose back is made from the same fabric as the lining of the suit coat or jacket, and one garment designed to cover the lower part of the body and consisting of trousers, breeches or shorts (other than swimwear), a skirt or a divided skirt, having neither braces nor bibs.

All of the components of a suit must be of the same fabric construction, style, colour and composition; they must also be of corresponding or compatible size. However, these components may have bindings of different fabric (the narrow fabric stitched to finish raw edges).

If several separate components to cover the lower part of the body are presented together (for example, trousers and shorts, or a skirt or divided skirt and trousers), the constituent lower part shall be one pair of trousers, or, in the case of women's or girls' suits, the skirt or divided skirt, the other garments being considered separately.

The term "suit" includes the following sets of garments, whether or not they fulfill all the above conditions:

(ⅰ) morning dress, comprising a plain jacket (cutaway) with rounded tails hanging well down at the back and striped trousers;

(ⅱ) evening dress (tailcoat), generally made of black fabric, the jacket of which is relatively short at the front, does not close and has narrow skirts cut in at the hips and hanging down behind;

(ⅲ) dinner jacket suits, in which the jacket is similar in style to an ordinary jacket (though perhaps revealing more of the shirt front), but has shiny silk or imitation silk lapels.

(b) The term "ensemble" means a set of garments (other than suits and articles of heading No.61.07, 61.08 or 61.09), composed of several pieces made up in identical fabric, put up for retail sale, and comprising:

One garment designed to cover the upper part of the body, with the exception of pullovers which may form a second upper garment in the sole context of twin sets, and of waistcoats which may also form a second upper garment, and

One or two different garments, designed to cover the lower part of the body and consisting of trousers, bib and brace overalls, breeches, shorts (other than swimwear), a skirt or a divided skirt.

All of the components of an ensemble must be of the same fabric construction, style, colour and composition; they also must be of corresponding or compatible size. The term "ensemble" does not apply to track suits or ski suits, of heading No.61.12.

4. Headings Nos.61.05 and 61.06 do not cover garments with pockets below the waist, with a ribbed waistband or other means of tightening at the bottom of the garment, or garments having an average of less than 10 stitches per linear centimetre in each direction counted on an area measuring at least 10cm×10cm. Heading No.61.05 does not cover sleeveless garments.
5. Heading No.61.09 does not cover garments with a drawstring, a ribbed waistband or other means of tightening at the bottom of the garment.
6. For the purposes of heading No.61.11:
   (a) The expression "babies' garments and clothing accessories" means articles for young children of a body height not exceeding 86cm;
   (b) Articles which are, *prima facie*, classifiable both in heading No.61.11 and in other headings of this Chapter are to be classified in heading No.61.11.
7. For the purposes of heading No.61.12, "ski suits" means garments or sets of garments which, by their general appearance and texture, are identifiable as intended to be worn principally for skiing (cross-country or alpine). They consist either of:
   (a) a " ski overall", that is, a one-piece garment designed to cover the upper and the lower parts of the body; in addition to sleeves and a collar the ski overall may have pockets or footstraps; or
   (b) a "ski ensemble", that is, a set of garments composed of two or three pieces, put up for retail sale and comprising:

   -One garment such as an anorak, wind-cheater, windjacket or similar article, closed by a slide fastener (zipper), possibly with a waistcoat in addition, and-one pair of trousers whether or not extending above waist-level, one pair of breeches or one bib and brace overall.

   The "ski ensemble" may also consist of an overall similar to the one mentioned in paragraph (a) above and a type of padded, sleeveless jacket worn over the overall.

   All the components of a "ski ensemble" must be made up in a fabric of the same texture, style and composition whether or not of the same colour; they also must be of corresponding or compatible size.
8. Garments which are, *prima facie*, classifiable both in heading No.61.13 and in other headings of this Chapter, excluding heading No.61.11, are to be classified in heading No.61.13.
9. Garments of this Chapter desinged for left over right closure at the front shall be regarded as men's or boys' garments, and those designed for right over left closure at the front as women's or girls' garments. These provisions do not apply where the cut of the garment clearly indicates that it is designed for one or other of the sexes. Garments which cannot be identified as either men's or boys' garments or as women's or girls' garments are to be classified in the headings covering women's or girls' garments.

十、本章物品可用金属线制成。

税则号列	货品名称〔CIQ 扩展编码及品名－T2 表示见附表 2〕	最惠(%)	暂定税率	普通	增值/消费	出口退税	计量单位	监管条件	检验检疫	特殊证件对美关税
61.01	**针织或钩编的男式大衣、短大衣、斗篷、短斗篷、带风帽的防寒短上衣(包括滑雪短上衣)、防风衣、防风短上衣及类似品,但税目 61.03 的货品除外:**									
6101.2000	-棉制〔999〕	8		90	13/	13	件/千克			/33
6101.3000	-化学纤维制〔999〕	8		130	13/	13	件/千克			/33
	-其他纺织材料制:									
6101.9010	---羊毛或动物细毛制									
6101.9010 10	毛制针织或钩编非手工制男式防风衣(包括防寒短上衣、防风短上衣及类似品)〔999〕	10		130	13/	13	件/千克			/
6101.9010 90	毛制针织或钩编其他男大衣、斗篷、防风衣等(包括防寒短上衣,防风短上衣、短大衣,短斗篷及类似品)〔999〕	10		130	13/	13	件/千克			/
6101.9090	---其他纺织材料制〔999〕	8		130	13/	13	件/千克			/33
61.02	**针织或钩编的女式大衣、短大衣、斗篷、短斗篷、带风帽的防寒短上衣(包括滑雪短上衣)、防风衣、防风短上衣及类似品,但税目 61.04 的货品除外:**									
6102.1000	-羊毛或动物细毛制									
6102.1000 10	毛制针织或钩编女式大衣等(包括短大衣、斗篷、短斗篷及类似品,雨衣除外)〔999〕	10		130	13/	13	件/千克			/40
6102.1000 21	毛制针织或钩编手工制女式防风衣(包括防寒短上衣、防风短上衣及类似品)〔999〕	10		130	13/	13	件/千克			/40
6102.1000 29	毛制针织或钩编女式防风衣(包括防寒短上衣,防风短上衣及类似品)〔999〕	10		130	13/	13	件/千克			/40
6102.1000 30	毛制针织或钩编女式雨衣〔999〕	10		130	13/	13	件/千克			/40
6102.2000	-棉制〔999〕	8		90	13/	13	件/千克			/33
6102.3000	-化学纤维制〔999〕	8		130	13/	13	件/千克			/33
6102.9000	-其他纺织材料制〔999〕	10		130	13/	13	件/千克			/
61.03	**针织或钩编的男式西服套装、便服套装、上衣、长裤、护胸背带工装裤、马裤及短裤(游泳裤除外):**									
	-西服套装:									
6103.1010	---羊毛或动物细毛制〔999〕	10		130	13/	13	套/千克			/
6103.1020	---合成纤维制〔999〕	10		130	13/	13	套/千克			/
6103.1090	---其他纺织材料制〔999〕	8		130	13/	13	套/千克			/
	-便服套装:									
6103.2200	--棉制〔999〕	10		90	13/	13	套/千克			/40
6103.2300	--合成纤维制〔999〕	10		130	13/	13	套/千克			/
	--其他纺织材料制:									
6103.2910	---羊毛或动物细毛制〔999〕	10		130	13/	13	套/千克			/
6103.2990	---其他纺织材料制〔999〕	10		130	13/	13	套/千克			/40
	-上衣:									
6103.3100	--羊毛或动物细毛制〔999〕	6		130	13/	13	件/千克			/31
6103.3200	--棉制〔999〕	6		90	13/	13	件/千克			/31
6103.3300	--合成纤维制〔999〕	8		130	13/	13	件/千克			/33
6103.3900	--其他纺织材料制〔999〕	6		130	13/	13	件/千克			/31
	-长裤、护胸背带工装裤、马裤及短裤:									
6103.4100	--羊毛或动物细毛制〔101 针织外衣,102 针织童装,103 针织裤子〕	6		130	13/	13	条/千克			/31
6103.4200	--棉制									
6103.4200 12	棉制针织钩编男童非保暖背带工装裤(2－7 号男童护胸背带工装裤)〔999〕	6		90	13/	13	条/千克	A	M	/31
6103.4200 21	棉制针织或钩编男童游戏套装长裤(指男童 8－18 号)〔999〕	6		90	13/	13	条/千克	A	M	/31
6103.4200 29	棉制针织或钩编其他男童游戏套装裤(包括长裤、马裤、短裤)〔999〕	6		90	13/	13	条/千克	A	M	/31
6103.4200 90	棉制针织或钩编其他男裤等(包括马裤、短裤及其他长裤)〔999〕	6		90	13/	13	条/千克			/31
6103.4300	--合成纤维制									
6103.4300 90	其他合纤制针织或钩编其他男裤(包括马裤、短裤及其他长裤)〔101 针织童装,999 包括马裤、短裤及其他长裤〕	8		130	13/	13	条/千克			/33

10. Articles of this Chapter may be made of metal thread.

协定税率 %										特惠税率 %			Article Description
亚太5国	东/冰/格	巴基斯坦	韩国	瑞士	哥达	秘鲁	澳大利亚	新西/坡/智	港/澳/台	亚太2国	老/柬/缅	36/3/1	
													Men's or boys' overcoats, car-coats, capes, cloaks, anoraks (including ski-jackets), wind-cheaters, wind-jackets and similar articles, knitted or crocheted, other than those of heading No.61. 03:
5.2	0/0/0	14	7	5.3	0	0	0	0/0/0	0/0/			0/0/0	-Of cotton
5.2	0/0/0	0	7	5.3	0	0	0	0/0/0	0/0/			0/0/0	-Of man-made fibres
													-Of other textile materials:
													---Of wool or fine animal hair
6.5	0/0/0	0	17.5	7.5	0	0	0	0/0/0	0/0/			0/0/	Men's or boys' wind-cheaters, anoraks, wind-jackets and similar articles, not hand-worked, knitted or crocheted, of wool or fine animal hair
6.5	0/0/0	0	17.5	7.5	0	0	0	0/0/0	0/0/			0/0/	Men's or boys' overcoats, capes, wind-cheaters, anoraks, wind-jackets, car-coats, cloak and similar articles, knitted or crocheted, of wool or fine animal hair
5.2	0/0/0	8.8	7	5.3	0	0	0	0/0/0	0/0/			0/0/	---Of other textile materials
													Women's or girls' overcoats, car-coats, capes, cloaks, anoraks (including ski-jackets), wind-cheaters, wind-jackets and similar articles, knitted or crocheted, other than those of heading No.61. 04:
													-Of wool or fine animal hair
6.5	0/0/0	18	17.5	7.5	0	0	0	0/0/0	0/0/			0/0/	Women's or girls' overcoats, car-coats, capes, cloak and similar articles, other than raincoats, knitted or crocheted, of wool or fine animal hair
6.5	0/0/0	18	17.5	7.5	0	0	0	0/0/0	0/0/			0/0/	Women's or girls' wind-cheaters, anoraks, wind-jackets and similar articles, hand-worked, knitted or crocheted, of wool or fine animal hair
6.5	0/0/0	18	17.5	7.5	0	0	0	0/0/0	0/0/			0/0/	Other women's or girls' wind-cheaters, anoraks, wind-jackets and similar articles, knitted or crocheted, of wool or fine animal hair
6.5	0/0/0	18	17.5	7.5	0	0	0	0/0/0	0/0/			0/0/	Women's or girls' raincoats, knitted or crocheted, of wool or fine animal hair
5.2	0/0/0	14	7	5.3	0		0	0/0/0	0/0/			0/0/0	-Of cotton
5.2	0/0/0	0	7	5.3	0	0	0	0/0/0	0/0/			0/0/0	-Of man-made fibres
6.5	0/0/0	10	12	6	0	0	0	0/0/0	0/0/			0/0/	-Of other textile materials
													Men's or boys' suits, ensembles, jackets, blazers, trousers, bib and brace overalls, breeches and shorts (other than swimwear), knitted or crocheted:
													-Suits:
6.5	0/0/0	18	17.5	7.5	0	0	0	0/0/0	0/0/			0/0/	---Of wool or fine animal hair
6.5	0/0/0	18	17.5	7.5	0	0	0	0/0/0	0/0/			0/0/	---Of synthetic fibres
5.2	0/0/0	8.8	7	5.3	0	0	0	0/0/0	0/0/		0//	0/0/0	---Of other textile materials
													-Ensembles:
6.5	0/0/0	14.8	12	6	0	0	0	0/0/0	0/0/		0//	0/0/0	--Of cotton
6.5	0/0/0	18	17.5	7.5	0	0	0	0/0/0	0/0/			0/0/	--Of synthetic fibres
													--Of other textile materials:
6.5	0/0/0	18	17.5	7.5	0	0	0	0/0/0	0/0/			0/0/	---Of wool or fine animal hair
6.5	0/0/0	18	17.5	7.5	0	0	0	0/0/0	0/0/		0//	0/0/0	---Of other textile materials
													-Jackets and blazers:
3.9	0/0/0	8	6.4	4.8	0	0	0	0/0/0	0/0/			0/0/	--Of wool or fine animal hair
3.9	0/0/0	0	6.4	4.8	0	0	0	0/0/0	0/0/		0/0/0	0/0/0	--Of cotton
5.2	0/0/0	0	7.6	5.7	0	0	0	0/0/0	0/0/		/0/	0/0/0	--Of synthetic fibres
3.9	0/0/0	0	6.4	4.8	0	0	0	0/0/0	0/0/		0/0/	0/0/0	--Of other textile materials
													-Trousers, bib and brace overalls, breeches and shorts:
3.9	0/0/0	8	6.4	4.8	0	0	0	0/0/0	0/0/	0		0/0/0	--Of wool or fine animal hair
													--Of cotton
3.9	0/0/0	0	6.4	4.8	0	0	0	0/0/0	0/0/	2.4	0/0/0	0/0/0	Boys' bib and brace overalls(not keep warm), No. 2～No. 7, knitted or crocheted, of cotton
3.9	0/0/0	0	6.4	4.8	0	0	0	0/0/0	0/0/	2.4	0/0/0	0/0/0	Boys' playsuit trousers No.8～No.18, knitted or crocheted, of cotton
3.9	0/0/0	0	6.4	4.8	0	0	0	0/0/0	0/0/	2.4	0/0/0	0/0/0	Other boys' playsuit, including trousers, breeches and shorts, knitted or crocheted, of cotton
3.9	0/0/0	0	6.4	4.8	0	0	0	0/0/0	0/0/	2.4	0/0/0	0/0/0	Other men's or boys' trousers, breeches and shorts, knitted or crocheted, of cotton
													--Of synthetic fibres
5.2	0/0/0	0	7	5.3	0	0	0	0/0/0	0/0/	0	/0/	0/0/0	Other men's or boys' trousers, breeches and shorts, of synthetic fibres, knitted or crocheted

税则号列	货品名称〔CIQ 扩展编码及品名—T2 表示见附表 2〕	最惠(%)	暂定税率	普通	增值/消费	出口退税	计量单位	监管条件	检验检疫	特殊证件对美关税
6103.4300　92	其他合成纤维制男童游戏套装长裤(针织或钩编,指男童 8—18 号)〔999〕	8		130	13/	13	条/千克	A	M	/33
6103.4300　93	其他合成纤维制男童游戏套装长裤(针织或钩编,包括马裤、短裤及其他长裤)〔999〕	8		130	13/	13	条/千克	A	M	/33
6103.4900	--其他纺织材料制									
6103.4900　13	丝制针织或钩编其他男童长裤、马裤(丝及绢丝含量在 70%及以上)〔999〕	6		130	13/	13	条/千克	A	M	/31
6103.4900　23	人造纤维制针织或钩编其他男童长裤、马裤(含毛 23%及以上)〔999〕	6		130	13/	13	条/千克	A	M	/31
6103.4900　26	其他人造纤维制针织或钩编其他男童长裤(包括马裤)〔999〕	6		130	13/	13	条/千克	A	M	/31
6103.4900　51	其他纺织材料制其他男童长裤、马裤(针织或钩编,棉限内)〔999〕	6		130	13/	13	条/千克	A	M	/31
6103.4900　52	其他纺织材料制其他男童长裤、马裤(针织或钩编,羊毛限内)〔999〕	6		130	13/	13	条/千克	A	M	/31
6103.4900　53	其他纺织材料制其他男童长裤、马裤(针织或钩编,化学纤维限内)〔999〕	6		130	13/	13	条/千克	A	M	/31
6103.4900　59	其他纺织材料制其他男童长裤、马裤(针织或钩编)〔999〕	6		130	13/	13	条/千克	A	M	/31
6103.4900　90	其他纺材制针织或钩编其他男式长裤、护胸背带工装裤、马裤及短裤〔101 针织童装,999〕	6		130	13/	13	条/千克			/31
61.04	**针织或钩编的女式西服套装、便服套装、上衣、连衣裙、裙子、裙裤、长裤、护胸背带工装裤、马裤及短裤(游泳服除外):**									
	-西服套装:									
6104.1300	--合成纤维制〔999〕	10		130	13/	13	套/千克			/
	--其他纺织材料制:									
6104.1910	---羊毛或动物细毛制〔999〕	8		130	13/	13	套/千克			/
6104.1920	---棉制〔999〕	8		90	13/	13	套/千克			/
6104.1990	---其他〔999〕	8		130	13/	13	套/千克			/
	-便服套装:									
6104.2200	--棉制〔999〕	8		90	13/	13	套/千克			/33
6104.2300	--合成纤维制〔999〕	10		130	13/	13	套/千克			/
	--其他纺织材料制:									
6104.2910	---羊毛或动物细毛制〔999〕	8		130	13/	13	套/千克			/
6104.2990	---其他〔999〕	6		130	13/	13	套/千克			/
	-上衣:									
6104.3100	--羊毛或动物细毛制〔999〕	6		130	13/	13	件/千克			/31
6104.3200	--棉制〔999〕	6		90	13/	13	件/千克			/31
6104.3300	--合成纤维制〔999〕	10		130	13/	13	件/千克			/35
6104.3900	--其他纺织材料制〔999〕	6		130	13/	13	件/千克			/31
	-连衣裙:									
6104.4100	--羊毛或动物细毛制〔999〕	6		130	13/	13	件/千克			/31
6104.4200	--棉制〔999〕	6		90	13/	13	件/千克			/31
6104.4300	--合成纤维制〔999〕	8		130	13/	13	件/千克			/33
6104.4400	--人造纤维制〔999〕	6		130	13/	13	件/千克			/31
6104.4900	--其他纺织材料制〔999〕	6		130	13/	13	件/千克			/31
	-裙子及裙裤:									
6104.5100	--羊毛或动物细毛制〔999〕	6		130	13/	13	件/千克			/31
6104.5200	--棉制〔999〕	6		90	13/	13	件/千克			/31
6104.5300	--合成纤维制〔999〕	6		130	13/	13	件/千克			/31
6104.5900	--其他纺织材料制〔999〕	6		130	13/	13	件/千克			/31
	-长裤、护胸背带工装裤、马裤及短裤:									
6104.6100	--羊毛或动物细毛制〔101 针织童装,999〕	6		130	13/	13	条/千克			/31
6104.6200	--棉制									
6104.6200　30	棉制针织或钩编女童游戏套装长裤(指女童 7—16 号,包括马裤)〔999〕	6		90	13/	13	条/千克	A	M	/31
6104.6200　40	棉针织或钩编其他女童游戏套装裤(包括马裤、短裤、非保暖护胸背带工装裤及其他长裤)〔999〕	6		90	13/	13	条/千克	A	M	/31
6104.6200　90	棉制针织或钩编其他女裤〔101 针织裤子,102 针织童装〕	6		90	13/	13	条/千克			/31
6104.6300	--合成纤维制									
6104.6300　90	其他合成纤维制针织或钩编女裤〔101 针织裤子,102 针织童装〕	8		130	13/	13	条/千克			/33
6104.6300　91	其他合成纤维制女童游戏套装长裤、马裤(针织或钩编,指女童 7—16 号)〔999〕	8		130	13/	13	条/千克	A	M	/33

协定税率 %										特惠税率 %			Article Description
亚太5国	东/冰/格	巴基斯坦	韩国	瑞士	哥达	秘鲁	澳大利亚	新西/坡/智	港/澳/台	亚太2国	老/柬/缅	36/3/1	
5.2	0/0/0	0	7	5.3	0	0	0	0/0/0	0/0/	0	/0/	0/0/0	Other boys' playsuit trousers No. 8～No.18, knitted or crocheted, of synthe3tic fibres
5.2	0/0/0	0	7	5.3	0	0	0	0/0/0	0/0/	0	/0/	0/0/0	Other boys' playsuit trousers, including breeches, shorts and other trousers, knitted or crocheted, of synthetic fibres
													--Of other textile materials
3.9	0/0/0	0	6.4	4.8	0	0	0	0/0/0	0/0/	0	0/0/	0/0/0	Boys' trousers and breeches, containing≥70% by weight of silk or spun silk knitted or crocheted
3.9	0/0/0	0	6.4	4.8	0	0	0	0/0/0	0/0/	0	0/0/	0/0/0	Other boys' trousers, breeches, of artificial fibres, containing≥23% by weight of wool or fine animal hair, knitted or crocheted
3.9	0/0/0	0	6.4	4.8	0	0	0	0/0/0	0/0/	0	0/0/	0/0/0	Other boys' trousers and breeches, of artificial fibres, knitted or crocheted
3.9	0/0/0	0	6.4	4.8	0	0	0	0/0/0	0/0/	0	0/0/	0/0/0	Other boys' trousers and breeches, cotton within limitations, knitted or crocheted, of other textile materials
3.9	0/0/0	0	6.4	4.8	0	0	0	0/0/0	0/0/	0	0/0/	0/0/0	Other boys' trousers and breeches, wool within limitations, knitted or crocheted, of other textile materials
3.9	0/0/0	0	6.4	4.8	0	0	0	0/0/0	0/0/	0	0/0/	0/0/0	Other boys' trousers and breeches, man-made fibres within limitations, knitted or crocheted, of other textile materials
3.9	0/0/0	0	6.4	4.8	0	0	0	0/0/0	0/0/	0	0/0/	0/0/0	Other boys' trousers and breeches, knitted or crocheted, of other textile materials
3.9	0/0/0	0	6.4	4.8	0	0	0	0/0/0	0/0/	0	0/0/	0/0/0	Men's knitted or crocheted trousers breeches, bib and brace overalls of other textile materials,
													Women's or girls' suits, ensembles, jackets, blazers, dresses, skirts, divided skirts, trousers, bib and brace overalls, breeches and shorts (otherthan swimwear), knitted or crocheted:
													-Suits:
6.5	0/0/0	18	17.5	7.5	0	0	0	0/0/0	0/0/			0/0/	--Of synthetic fibres
													--Of other textile materials:
5.2	0/0/0	8.8	7	5.3	0	0	0	0/0/0	0/0/			0/0/0	---Of wool or fine animal hair
5.2	0/0/0	14	7	5.3	0	0	0	0/0/0	0/0/		0//	0/0/0	---Of cotton
5.2	0/0/0	8.8	7	5.3	0	0	0	0/0/0	0/0/		0//	0/0/0	---Other
													-Ensembles:
5.2	0/0/0	14	7	5.3	0	0	0	0/0/0	0/0/		0//	0/0/0	--Of cotton
6.5	0/0/0	18	17.5	7.5	0	0	0	0/0/0	0/0/			0/0/	--Of synthetic fibres
													--Of other textile materials:
5.2	0/0/0	8.8	7	5.3	0	0	0	0/0/0	0/0/			0/0/	---Of wool or fine animal hair
3.9	0/0/0	7.5	6	4.5	0	0	0	0/0/0	0/0/			0/0/0	---Other
													-Jackets and blazers:
3.9	0/0/0	8	6.4	4.8	0	0	0	0/0/0	0/0/			0/0/0	--Of wool or fine animal hair
3.9	0/0/0	0	6.4	4.8	0	0	0	0/0/0	0/0/		0/0/0	0/0/0	--Of cotton
6.5	0/0/0	7.6	7.6	5.7	0	0	0	0/0/0	0/0/		/0/	0/0/0	--Of synthetic fibres
3.9	0/0/0	0	6.4	4.8	0	0	0	0/0/0	0/0/		/0/	0/0/0	--Of other textile materials
													-Dresses:
3.9	0/0/0	8	6.4	4.8	0	0	0	0/0/0	0/0/			0/0/	--Of wool or fine animal hair
3.9	0/0/0	0	6.4	4.8	0	0	0	0/0/0	0/0/			0/0/0	--Of cotton
5.2	0/0/0	7	7	5.3	0	0	0	0/0/0	0/0/		/0/	0/0/0	--Of synthetic fibres
3.9	0/0/0	8	6.4	4.8	0	0	0	0/0/0	0/0/		/0/	0/0/0	--Of artificial fibres
3.9	0/0/0	0	6.4	4.8	0	0	0	0/0/0	0/0/		/0/	0/0/0	--Of other textile materials
													-Skirts and divided skirts:
3.9	0/0/0	7	5.6	4.2	0	0	0	0/0/0	0/0/			0/0/	--Of wool or fine animal hair
3.9	0/0/0	5.6	5.6	4.2	0	0	0	0/0/0	0/0/			0/0/0	--Of cotton
3.9	0/0/0	8	6.4	4.8	0	0	0	0/0/0	0/0/		/0/	0/0/0	--Of synthetic fibres
3.9	0/0/0	7	5.6	4.2	0	0	0	0/0/0	0/0/		0/0/0	0/0/0	--Of other textile materials
													-Trousers, bib and brace overalls, breeches and shorts:
3.9	0/0/0	8	6.4	4.8	0	0	0	0/0/0	0/0/			0/0/0	--Of wool or fine animal hair
													--Of cotton
3.9	0/0/0	0	6.4	4.8	0	0	0	0/0/0	0/0/	2.4		0/0/0	Girls' playsuit trousers No. 7～No. 16, including breeches, knitted or crocheted, of cotton
3.9	0/0/0	0	6.4	4.8	0	0	0	0/0/0	0/0/	2.4		0/0/0	Other girls' playsuit, including breeches, shorts, bib and brace overalls and other trousers, knitted or crocheted, of cotton
3.9	0/0/0	0	6.4	4.8	0	0	0	0/0/0	0/0/	2.4		0/0/0	Other knitted or crocheted women's and girls's trousers, of cotton
													--Of synthetic fibres
5.2	0/0/0	0	7	5.3	0	0	0	0/0/0	0/0/			0/0/0	Other women's or girl' trousers, breeches and shorts, of synthetic fibres, knitted or crocheted
5.2	0/0/0	0	7	5.3	0	0	0	0/0/0	0/0/			0/0/0	Girls' playsuit trousers or breeches No.7～No.16, knitted or crocheted, of synthetic fibres

税则号列	货品名称〔CIQ 扩展编码及品名—T2 表示见附表 2〕	最惠(%)	暂定税率	普通	增值/消费	出口退税	计量单位	监管条件	检验检疫	特殊证件对美关税
6104.6300 92	其他合成纤维制女童游戏套装裤(针织或钩编,包括短裤及其他长裤)〔999〕	8		130	13/	13	条/千克	A	M	/33
6104.6900	--其他纺织材料制〔101 针织童装,999〕	6		130	13/	13	条/千克			/31
61.05	**针织或钩编的男衬衫:**									
6105.1000	-棉制									
6105.1000 11	棉制针织或钩编男童游戏套装衬衫(不带缝制领,指男童 8—18 号)〔999〕	6		90	13/	13	件/千克	A	M	/31
6105.1000 19	棉制其他男童游戏套装衬衫(针织或钩编)〔999〕	6		90	13/	13	件/千克	A	M	/31
6105.1000 90	其他棉制针织或钩编其他男衬衫〔101 针织童装,999〕	6		90	13/	13	件/千克			/31
6105.2000	-化学纤维制									
6105.2000 21	化学纤维制针织或钩编男童游戏套装衬衫(不带缝制领,指男童 8—18 号)〔999〕	8		130	13/	13	件/千克	A	M	/33
6105.2000 29	化学纤维制其他男童游戏套装衬衫(针织或钩编)〔999〕	8		130	13/	13	件/千克	A	M	/33
6105.2000 90	其他化纤制针织或钩编其他男衬衫〔101 针织童装,999〕	8		130	13/	13	件/千克			/33
6105.9000	-其他纺织材料制〔101 针织童装,102 针织或钩编,999〕	6		130	13/	13	件/千克			/31
61.06	**针织或钩编的女衬衫:**									
6106.1000	-棉制									
6106.1000 10	棉制针织或钩编女童游戏套装衬衫〔999〕	6		90	13/	13	件/千克	A	M	/31
6106.1000 90	棉制针织或钩编其他女衬衫〔999〕	6		90	13/	13	件/千克			/31
6106.2000	-化学纤维制									
6106.2000 20	其他化学纤维制女童游戏套装衬衫(针织或钩编)〔999〕	8		130	13/	13	件/千克	A	M	/33
6106.2000 90	其他化学纤维制针织或钩编未列名女衬衫(针织或钩编)〔999〕	8		130	13/	13	件/千克			/33
6106.9000	-其他纺织材料制〔101 毛衫,999〕	6		130	13/	13	件/千克			/31
61.07	**针织或钩编的男式内裤、三角裤、长睡衣、睡衣裤、浴衣、晨衣及类似品:**									
	-内裤及三角裤:									
6107.1100	--棉制〔999〕	6		90	13/	13	件/千克	A	M	/31
6107.1200	--化学纤维制〔999〕	6		130	13/	13	件/千克	A	M	/
	--其他纺织材料制:									
6107.1910	---丝及绢丝制									
6107.1910 10	丝及绢丝制男内裤及三角裤(含丝 70%及以上,针织或钩编)〔999〕	6		130	13/	13	件/千克	A	M	/
6107.1910 90	其他丝及绢丝制男内裤及三角裤(含丝 70%以下,针织或钩编)〔999〕	6		130	13/	13	件/千克	A	M	/
6107.1990	---其他									
6107.1990 10	羊毛或动物细毛制男内裤及三角裤(针织或钩编)〔999〕	6		130	13/	13	件/千克	A	M	/31
6107.1990 90	其他纺织材料制男内裤及三角裤(针织或钩编)〔999〕	6		130	13/	13	件/千克	A	M	/31
	-长睡衣及睡衣裤:									
6107.2100	--棉制〔999〕	6		90	13/	13	件/千克	A	M	/
6107.2200	--化学纤维制〔999〕	6		130	13/	13	件/千克	A	M	/
	--其他纺织材料制:									
6107.2910	---丝及绢丝制									
6107.2910 10	丝及绢丝制针织或钩编男睡衣裤(含丝 70%及以上,包括长睡衣)〔999〕	6		130	13/	13	件/千克	A	M	/
6107.2910 90	其他丝及绢丝制针织或钩编男睡衣裤(含丝 70%以下,包括长睡衣)〔999〕	6		130	13/	13	件/千克	A	M	/
6107.2990	---其他〔999〕	6		130	13/	13	件/千克	A	M	/
	-其他:									
6107.9100	--棉制									
6107.9100 10	棉制针织或钩编其他睡衣裤〔999〕	6		90	13/	13	件/千克	A	M	/
6107.9100 90	棉制针织或钩编男浴衣、晨衣等(包括类似品)〔999〕	6		90	13/	13	件/千克	A	M	/
	--其他纺织材料制:									
6107.9910	---化学纤维制〔999〕	6		130	13/	13	件/千克	A	M	/31
6107.9990	---其他〔999〕	6		130	13/	13	件/千克	A	M	/31
61.08	**针织或钩编的女式长衬裙、衬裙、三角裤、短衬裤、睡衣、睡衣裤、浴衣、晨衣及类似品:**									
	-长衬裙及衬裙:									

协定税率 %										特惠税率 %			Article Description
亚太5国	东/冰/格	巴基斯坦	韩国	瑞士	哥达	秘鲁	澳大利亚	新西/坡/智	港/澳/台	亚太2国	老/柬/缅	36/3/1	
5.2	0/0/0	0	7	5.3	0	0	0	0/0/0	0/0/			0/0/0	Other girls' playsuit, shorts and other trousers, knitted or crocheted, of synthetic fibres
3.9	0/0/0	0	6.4	4.8	0	0	0	0/0/0	0/0/	0		0/0/0	--Of other textile materials
													Men's or boys' shirts, knitted or crocheted:
													-Of cotton
3.9	0/0/0	0	6.4	4.8	0		0	0/0/0	0/0/0	4.2	0/0/0	0/0/0	Boys' playsuit shirts No. 8～No. 18, having no made-to-order collar, knitted or crocheted, of cotton
3.9	0/0/0	0	6.4	4.8	0		0	0/0/0	0/0/0	4.2	0/0/0	0/0/0	Other boys' playsuit shirts, knitted or crocheted, of cotton
3.9	0/0/0	0	6.4	4.8	0		0	0/0/0	0/0/0	4.2	0/0/0	0/0/0	Other knitted or crocheted men's or boys' shirts, of cotton
													-Of man-made fibres
5.2	0/0/0	0	7	5.3	0	0	0	0/0/0	0/0/	0		0/0/0	Boys' playsuit shirts No. 8～No. 18, having no made-to-order collar, knitted or crocheted, of man-made fibres
5.2	0/0/0	0	7	5.3	0	0	0	0/0/0	0/0/	0		0/0/0	Other boys' playsuit shirts, knitted or crocheted, of man-made fibres
5.2	0/0/0	0	7	5.3	0	0	0	0/0/0	0/0/	0		0/0/0	Other knitted or crocheted men's or boys' shirts, of man-made fibres
3.9	0/0/0	0	6.4	4.8	0	0	0	0/0/0	0/0/	0		0/0/0	-Of other textile materials
													Women's or girls' blouses, shirts and shirt-blouses, knitted or crocheted:
													-Of cotton
3.9	0/0/0	0	6.4	4.8	0	0	0	0/0/0	0/0/	2.4	0/0/0	0/0/0	Girls'playsuit shirts, knittedor crocheted, knitted or crocheted, of cotton
3.9	0/0/0	0	6.4	4.8	0	0	0	0/0/0	0/0/	2.4	0/0/0	0/0/0	Other women's or girls' shirts, knitted or crocheted, of cotton
													-Of man-made fibres
5.2	0/0/0	8.8	7	5.3	0	0	0	0/0/0	0/0/	0		0/0/0	Girls' playsuit shirts, knitted or crocheted, of man-made fibres
5.2	0/0/0	8.8	7	5.3	0	0	0	0/0/0	0/0/	0		0/0/0	Other women's or girls' shirts, knitted or crocheted, not elsewhere specified or included, of man-made fibres
3.9	0/0/0	0	6.4	4.8	0	0	0	0/0/0	0/0/0	0		0/0/0	-Of other textile materials
													Men's or boys' underpants, briefs, nightshirts, pyjamas, bathrobes, dressing gowns and similar articles, knitted or crocheted:
													-Underpants and briefs:
	0/0/0	0	5.6	4.2	0	0	0	0/0/0	0/0/	2.4	0/0/0	0/0/0	--Of cotton
3.9	0/0/0	6.4	6.4	4.8	0	0	0	0/0/0	0/0/			0/0/	--Of man-made fibres
													--Of other textile materials:
													---Of silk or spun silk
3.9	0/0/0	7	5.6	4.2	0	0	0	0/0/0	0/0/			0/0/	Men's or boys' underpants and briefs, knitted or crocheted, containing≥70% by weight of silk or spun silk
3.9	0/0/0	7	5.6	4.2	0	0	0	0/0/0	0/0/			0/0/	Men's or boys' underpants and briefs, knitted or crocheted, other, containing<70% by weight of silk or spun silk
													---Other
3.9	0/0/0	7	5.6	4.2	0	0	0	0/0/0	0/0/			0/0/	Men's or boys' underpants and briefs, knitted or crocheted, of wool or fine animal hair
3.9	0/0/0	7	5.6	4.2	0	0	0	0/0/0	0/0/			0/0/	Men's or boys' underpants and briefs, knitted or crocheted, of other textile fibres
													-Nightshirts and pyjamas:
	0/0/0	0	5.6	4.2	0		0	0/0/0	0/0/	2.4	0/0/0	0/0/0	--Of cotton
3.9	0/0/0	8	6.4	4.8	0	0	0	0/0/0	0/0/	0		0/0/0	--Of man-made fibres
													--Of other textile materials:
													---Of silk or spun silk
3.9	0/0/0	7	5.6	4.2	0	0	0	0/0/0	0/0/	0		0/0/0	Men's or boys' nightshirts, pyjamas, knitted or crocheted, containing ≥70% by weight of silk or spun silk
3.9	0/0/0	7	5.6	4.2	0	0	0	0/0/0	0/0/	0		0/0/0	Men's or boys' nightshirts, pyjamas, knitted or crocheted, containing <70% by weight of silk or spun silk
3.9	0/0/0	7	5.6	4.2	0	0	0	0/0/0	0/0/	0	0/0/0	0/0/0	---Other
													-Other:
													--Of cotton
	0/0/0	5.6	5.6	4.2	0	0	0	0/0/0	0/0/			0/0/	Other men's or boys' pyjamas, knitted or crocheted, of cotton
	0/0/0	5.6	5.6	4.2	0	0	0	0/0/0	0/0/			0/0/	Men's or boys' bathrobes, dressing gowns and similar articles, knitted or crocheted, of cotton
													--Of other textile materials:
3.9	0/0/0	8	6.4	4.8	0	0	0	0/0/0	0/0/			0/0/	---Of man-made fibres
3.9	0/0/0	7	5.6	4.2	0	0	0	0/0/0	0/0/			0/0/	---Of other
													Women's or girls' slips, petticoats, briefs, panties, nightdresses, pyjamas, nègligès, bathrobes, dressing gowns and similar articles, knitted or crocheted:
													-Slips and petticoats:

税则号列	货品名称〔CIQ 扩展编码及品名－T2 表示见附表 2〕	最惠(%)	暂定税率	普通	增值/消费	出口退税	计量单位	监管条件	检验检疫	特殊证件对美关税
6108.1100	--化学纤维制〔999〕	6		130	13/	13	件/千克			/
	--其他纺织材料制：									
6108.1910	---棉制〔999〕	6		90	13/	13	件/千克			/
6108.1920	---丝及绢丝制〔999〕	6		130	13/	13	件/千克			/
6108.1990	---其他〔999〕	6		130	13/	13	件/千克			/
	-三角裤及短衬裤：									
6108.2100	--棉制〔999〕	6		90	13/	13	件/千克	A	M	/31
6108.2200	--化学纤维制									
6108.2200 10	化学纤维制一次性女三角裤及短衬裤(针织或钩编)〔999〕	6		130	13/	13	件/千克	A	M	/31
6108.2200 90	化学纤维制其他女三角裤及短衬裤(针织或钩编)〔999〕	6		130	13/	13	件/千克	A	M	/31
	--其他纺织材料制：									
6108.2910	---丝及绢丝制									
6108.2910 10	丝及绢丝制女三角裤及短衬裤(针织或钩编,含丝 70%及以上)〔999〕	6		130	13/	13	件/千克	A	M	/
6108.2910 90	其他丝及绢丝制女三角裤及短衬裤(针织或钩编,含丝 70%以下)〔999〕	6		130	13/	13	件/千克	A	M	/
6108.2990	---其他									
6108.2990 10	羊毛制女三角裤及短衬裤(针织或钩编)〔999〕	6		130	13/	13	件/千克	A	M	/
6108.2990 90	其他纺织材料制女三角裤及短衬裤(针织或钩编)〔999〕	6		130	13/	13	件/千克	A	M	/
	-睡衣及睡衣裤：									
6108.3100	--棉制〔999〕	6		90	13/	13	件/千克	A	M	/31
6108.3200	--化学纤维制〔999〕	6		130	13/	13	件/千克	A	M	/31
	--其他纺织材料制：									
6108.3910	---丝及绢丝制									
6108.3910 10	丝及绢丝制女睡衣及睡衣裤(针织或钩编,含丝 70%及以上)〔999〕	6		130	13/	13	件/千克	A	M	/
6108.3910 90	其他丝及绢丝制女睡衣及睡衣裤(针织或钩编,含丝 70%以下)〔999〕	6		130	13/	13	件/千克	A	M	/
6108.3990	---其他									
6108.3990 10	羊毛或动物细毛制女睡衣及睡衣裤(针织或钩编)〔999〕	6		130	13/	13	件/千克	A	M	/
6108.3990 90	其他纺织材料制女睡衣及睡衣裤(针织或钩编)〔999〕	6		130	13/	13	件/千克	A	M	/
	-其他：									
6108.9100	--棉制									
6108.9100 10	棉制针织或钩编女内裤,内衣〔999〕	6		90	13/	13	件/千克	A	M	/31
6108.9100 90	其他棉制针织或钩编女浴衣、晨衣等(包括类似品)〔999〕	6		90	13/	13	件/千克	A	M	/31
6108.9200	--化学纤维制									
6108.9200 10	化学纤维制针织或钩编女内裤,内衣〔999〕	6		130	13/	13	件/千克	A	M	/31
6108.9200 90	其他化学纤维针织或钩编女浴衣、晨衣等(包括类似品)〔999〕	6		130	13/	13	件/千克	A	M	/31
6108.9900	--其他纺织材料制									
6108.9900 10	丝及绢丝制女浴衣、晨衣等(针织或钩编,包括类似品,含丝 70%及以上)〔999〕	6		130	13/	13	件/千克	A	M	/
6108.9900 20	羊毛或动物细毛制女浴衣、晨衣等(针织或钩编,包括类似品)〔999〕	6		130	13/	13	件/千克	A	M	/
6108.9900 90	其他纺织材料制女浴衣、晨衣等(针织或钩编,包括类似品)〔999〕	6		130	13/	13	件/千克	A	M	/
61.09	**针织或钩编的 T 恤衫、汗衫及其他背心：**									
6109.1000	-棉制									
6109.1000 10	棉制针织或钩编 T 恤衫、汗衫等(内衣式,包括其他背心)〔999〕	6		90	13/	13	件/千克	A	M	/31
6109.1000 21	其他棉制针织或钩编男式 T 恤衫(内衣除外)〔999〕	6		90	13/	13	件/千克	A	M	/31
6109.1000 22	其他棉制针织或钩编女式 T 恤衫(内衣除外)〔999〕	6		90	13/	13	件/千克	A	M	/31
6109.1000 91	其他棉制男式汗衫及其他背心(针织或钩编,内衣除外,包括男童 8－18 号)〔101 针织外衣,102 针织童装〕	6		90	13/	13	件/千克	A	M	/31

协定税率 %										特惠税率 %			Article Description
亚太5国	东/冰/格	巴基斯坦	韩国	瑞士	哥达	秘鲁	澳大利亚	新西/坡/智	港/澳/台	亚太2国	老/柬/缅	36/3/1	
3.9	0/0/0	8	6.4	4.8	0	0	0	0/0/0	0/0/			0/0/	--Of man-made fibres
													--Of other textile materials:
	0/0/0	7	5.6	4.2	0	0	0	0/0/0	0/0/			0/0/0	---Of cotton
	0/0/0	7	5.6	4.2	0	0	0	0/0/0	0/0/			0/0/	---Of silk or silk waste
3.9	0/0/0	7	5.6	4.2	0	0	0	0/0/0	0/0/			0/0/	---Other
													-Briefs and panties:
	0/0/0	0	5.6	4.2	0	0	0	0/0/0	0/0/		0/0/0	0/0/0	--Of cotton
													--Of man-made fibres
3.9	0/0/0	8	6.4	4.8	0	0	0	0/0/0	0/0/			0/0/0	Women's or girls' briefs and panties, knitted or crocheted, throw away, of man-made fibres
3.9	0/0/0	8	6.4	4.8	0	0	0	0/0/0	0/0/			0/0/0	Other women's or girls' briefs and panties, knitted or crocheted, of man-made fibres
													--Of other textile materials:
													---Of silk or silk waste
3.9	0/0/0	7	5.6	4.2	0	0	0	0/0/0	0/0/			0/0/	Women's or girls' briefs and panties, knitted or crocheted containing ≥70% by weight of silk or spun silk
3.9	0/0/0	7	5.6	4.2	0	0	0	0/0/0	0/0/			0/0/	Other women's or girls' briefs and panties, knitted or crocheted, containing <70% by weight of silk or spun silk
													---Other
3.9	0/0/0	7	5.6	4.2	0	0	0	0/0/0	0/0/			0/0/	Women's or girls' briefs and panties, knitted or crocheted, of wool
3.9	0/0/0	7	5.6	4.2	0	0	0	0/0/0	0/0/			0/0/	Women's or girls' briefs and panties, knitted or crocheted, of other textile materials
													-Nightdresses and pyjamas:
	0/0/0	0	5.6	4.2	0	0	0	0/0/0	0/0/	2.4	0/0/0	0/0/0	--Of cotton
3.9	0/0/0	8	6.4	4.8	0	0	0	0/0/0	0/0/	0		0/0/0	--Of man-made fibres
													--Of other textile materials:
													---Of silk or spun silk
3.9	0/0/0	7	5.6	4.2	0	0	0	0/0/0	0/0/	0		0/0/0	Women's or girls' nightshirts and pyjamas, knitted or crocheted, containing ≥70% by weight of silk or spun silk
3.9	0/0/0	7	5.6	4.2	0	0	0	0/0/0	0/0/	0		0/0/0	Other women's or girls' nightshirts and pyjamas, knitted or crocheted, containing <70% by weight of silk or spun silk
													---Other
3.9	0/0/0	7	5.6	4.2	0	0	0	0/0/0	0/0/	0		0/0/0	Women's or girls' nightshirts and pyjamas, knitted or crocheted, of wool or fine animal hair
3.9	0/0/0	7	5.6	4.2	0	0	0	0/0/0	0/0/	0		0/0/0	Women's or girls' nightshirts and pyjamas, knitted or crocheted, of other textile materials
													-Other:
													--Of cotton
	0/0/0	11.2	5.6	4.2	0	0	0	0/0/0	0/0/		0/0/0	0/0/0	Women's or girls' briefs, panties and underwear, knitted or crocheted, of cotton
	0/0/0	11.2	5.6	4.2	0	0	0	0/0/0	0/0/		0/0/0	0/0/0	Women's or girls' bathrobes, dressing gowns and similar articles, knitted or crocheted, of cotton
													--Of man-made fibres
3.9	0/0/0	8	6.4	4.8	0	0	0	0/0/0	0/0/			0/0/0	Women's or girls' briefs, panties and underwear, of man-made fibres
3.9	0/0/0	8	6.4	4.8	0	0	0	0/0/0	0/0/			0/0/0	Women's or girls' bathrobes, dressing gowns and similar articles, knitted or crocheted, of man-made fibres
													--Of other textile materials
3.9	0/0/0	7	5.6	4.2	0	0	0	0/0/0	0/0/			0/0/	Women's or girls' bathrobes, dressing gowns and similar articles, containing ≥70% by weight of silk or spun silk, knitted or crocheted
3.9	0/0/0	7	5.6	4.2	0	0	0	0/0/0	0/0/			0/0/	Women's or girls' bathrobes, dressing gowns and similar articles, of wool or fine animal hair, knitted or crocheted
3.9	0/0/0	7	5.6	4.2	0	0	0	0/0/0	0/0/			0/0/	Women's or girls' bathrobes, dressing gowns and similar articles, of other textile materials, knitted or crocheted
													T-shirts, singlets and other vests, knitted or crocheted:
													-Of cotton
3.9	0/0/0	0	0	4.2	0	0	0	0/0/0	0/0/		0/0/0	0/0/0	T-shirts, singlets, underwear style, including other vests, of cotton, knitted or crocheted
3.9	0/0/0	0	0	4.2	0	0	0	0/0/0	0/0/		0/0/0	0/0/0	Other men's or boys' T-shirts, other than underwear, of cotton, knitted or crocheted
3.9	0/0/0	0	0	4.2	0	0	0	0/0/0	0/0/		0/0/0	0/0/0	Other women's or girls' T-shirts other than underwear, of cotton, knitted or crocheted
3.9	0/0/0	0	0	4.2	0	0	0	0/0/0	0/0/		0/0/0	0/0/0	Other men's singlets and other vests, including boys' No. 8～No. 18, other than underwear, of cotton, knitted or crocheted

税则号列		货品名称〔CIQ 扩展编码及品名—T2 表示见附表 2〕	最惠(%)	暂定税率	普通	增值/消费	出口退税	计量单位	监管条件	检验检疫	特殊证件对美关税
6109.1000	92	其他棉制男式汗衫及其他背心(针织或钩编,内衣除外)〔999〕	6		90	13/	13	件/千克	A	M	/31
6109.1000	99	其他棉制女式汗衫及其他背心(针织或钩编,内衣除外)〔999〕	6		90	13/	13	件/千克	A	M	/31
		-其他纺织材料制:									
6109.9010		---丝及绢丝制									
6109.9010	11	丝及绢丝针织钩编 T 恤衫、汗衫、背心(内衣式,含丝≥70%)〔999〕	6		130	13/	13	件/千克	A	M	/31
6109.9010	19	其他丝及绢丝针织钩编 T 恤衫、背心(包括汗衫,内衣式,含丝 70%以下)〔999〕	6		130	13/	13	件/千克	A	M	/31
6109.9010	21	丝及绢丝针织钩编汗衫、背心(内衣除外,含丝≥70%,男童 8—18 号,女童 7—16 号)〔101 针织外衣,102 针织童装〕	6		130	13/	13	件/千克	A	M	/31
6109.9010	29	其他丝及绢丝针织或钩编汗衫、背心(内衣除外,含丝<70%,男童 8—18 号,女童 7—16 号)〔101 针织外衣,102 针织童装〕	6		130	13/	13	件/千克	A	M	/31
6109.9010	91	其他丝及绢丝针织或钩编 T 恤衫、汗衫(含丝≥70%,包括其他背心)〔999〕	6		130	13/	13	件/千克	A	M	/31
6109.9010	99	其他丝及绢丝针织或钩编 T 恤衫、汗衫(含丝<70%,包括其他背心)〔999〕	6		130	13/	13	件/千克	A	M	/31
6109.9090		---其他									
6109.9090	11	毛制针织或钩编 T 恤衫、汗衫等(内衣式,长袖衫)〔999〕	6		130	13/	13	件/千克	A	M	/31
6109.9090	12	毛制针织或钩编男式 T 恤衫、汗衫(内衣式,长袖衫除外)〔999〕	6		130	13/	13	件/千克	A	M	/31
6109.9090	13	毛制针织或钩编女式 T 恤衫、汗衫(内衣式,长袖衫除外)〔999〕	6		130	13/	13	件/千克	A	M	/31
6109.9090	21	毛制针织或钩编男式其他 T 恤衫(内衣除外)〔999〕	6		130	13/	13	件/千克	A	M	/31
6109.9090	22	毛制针织或钩编女式其他 T 恤衫(内衣除外)〔999〕	6		130	13/	13	件/千克	A	M	/31
6109.9090	31	毛制男式汗衫及其他背心(针织或钩编,内衣除外,含男童 8—18 号)〔101 毛衫,102 针织童装〕	6		130	13/	13	件/千克	A	M	/31
6109.9090	32	其他毛制男式汗衫及其他背心(针织或钩编,内衣除外)〔999〕	6		130	13/	13	件/千克	A	M	/31
6109.9090	33	其他毛制女式汗衫及其他背心(针织或钩编,内衣除外)〔999〕	6		130	13/	13	件/千克	A	M	/31
6109.9090	40	化学纤维制针织或钩编内衣〔999〕	6		130	13/	13	件/千克	A	M	/31
6109.9090	50	化纤制针织或钩编 T 恤衫(内衣除外)〔999〕	6		130	13/	13	件/千克	A	M	/31
6109.9090	60	化纤针织或钩编汗衫及其他背心(内衣除外)〔101 针织外衣,102 针织重装〕	6		130	13/	13	件/千克	A	M	/31
6109.9090	91	其他纺织材料制 T 恤衫.汗衫等(针织或钩编,内衣式,包括其他背心)〔999〕	6		130	13/	13	件/千克	A	M	/31
6109.9090	92	其他纺材针织钩编汗衫及其他背心(内衣除外,包括男童8—18 号,女童7—16 号)〔101 针织外衣,102 针织童装〕	6		130	13/	13	件/千克	A	M	/31
6109.9090	93	其他纺材制针织钩编 T 恤衫、汗衫(内衣除外,包括其他背心)〔999〕	6		130	13/	13	件/千克	A	M	/31
61.10		**针织或钩编的套头衫、开襟衫、背心及类似品:**									
		-羊毛或动物细毛制:									
6110.1100		--羊毛制〔999〕	6		130	13/	13	件/千克			/31
6110.1200		--克什米尔山羊细毛制									
6110.1200	11	克什米尔山羊细毛手工起绒男套头衫(针织或钩编,包括开襟衫、外穿背心及类似品)〔999〕	6	5	130	13/	13	件/千克			/35
6110.1200	19	克什米尔山羊细毛制起绒男套头衫(针织或钩编,包括开襟衫、外穿背心及类似品)〔999〕	6	5	130	13/	13	件/千克			/35
6110.1200	21	克什米尔山羊细毛手工起绒女套头衫(针织或钩编,包括开襟衫、外穿背心及类似品)〔999〕	6	5	130	13/	13	件/千克			/35
6110.1200	29	克什米尔山羊细毛制起绒女套头衫(针织或钩编,包括开襟衫、外穿背心及类似品)〔999〕	6	5	130	13/	13	件/千克			/35

协定税率 %										特惠税率 %			Article Description
亚太5国	东/冰/格	巴基斯坦	韩国	瑞士	哥达	秘鲁	澳大利亚	新西/坡/智	港/澳/台	亚太2国	老/柬/缅	36/3/1	
3.9	0/0/0	0	0	4.2	0	0	0	0/0/0	0/0/		0/0/0	0/0/0	Other men's or boys' singlets and other vests, other than underwear, of cotton, knitted or crocheted
3.9	0/0/0	0	0	4.2	0	0	0	0/0/0	0/0/		0/0/0	0/0/0	Other women's or girls' singlets and other vests, other than underwear, of cotton, knitted or crocheted
													-Of other textile materials:
													---Of silk or spun silk
3.9	0/0/0	0	5.6	4.2	0	0	0	0/0/0	0/0/	0		0/0/0	T-shirts, singlets and other vests, underwear, containing≥70% by weightof silk or spun silk, knitted or crocheted
3.9	0/0/0	0	5.6	4.2	0	0	0	0/0/0	0/0/	0		0/0/0	Other T-shirts, singlets and other vests, underwear, containing<70% by weight of silk or spun silk, knitted or crocheted
3.9	0/0/0	0	5.6	4.2	0	0	0	0/0/0	0/0/	0		0/0/0	Singlets, vests, including boys' No. 8～No. 18, girls' No. 7～No. 16, other than underwear, containing≥70% by weightof silk or spun silk, knitted or crocheted
3.9	0/0/0	0	5.6	4.2	0	0	0	0/0/0	0/0/	0		0/0/0	Other singlets, vests, including boys' No. 8～No. 18, girls' No. 7～No. 16, other than underwear, containing<70% by weight of silk or spun silk, knitted or crocheted
3.9	0/0/0	0	5.6	4.2	0	0	0	0/0/0	0/0/	0		0/0/0	Other T-shirts, singlets and other vests, including other vests, containing≥70% by weight of silk or spun silk, knitted or crocheted
3.9	0/0/0	0	5.6	4.2	0	0	0	0/0/0	0/0/	0		0/0/0	Other of other textile materials, including other vests, containing<70% by weight of silk or spun silk, knitted or crocheted
													---Other
3.9	0/0/0	0	5.6	4.2	0	0	0	0/0/0	0/0/	0	0/0/0	0/0/0	T-shirts, singlets and other vests, underwear style, long sleeve, of wool or fine animal hair, knitted or crocheted
3.9	0/0/0	0	5.6	4.2	0	0	0	0/0/0	0/0/	0	0/0/0	0/0/0	Men's or boys' T-shirts, singlets, underwear style, other than long sleeve, of wool or fine animal hair, knitted or crocheted
3.9	0/0/0	0	5.6	4.2	0	0	0	0/0/0	0/0/	0	0/0/0	0/0/0	Women's or grils' T-shirts, singlets, underwear style, other than long sleeve, of wool or fine animal hair, knitted or crocheted
3.9	0/0/0	0	5.6	4.2	0	0	0	0/0/0	0/0/	0	0/0/0	0/0/0	Men's or boys' T-shirts, other than underwear, of wool or fine animal hair, knitted or crocheted
3.9	0/0/0	0	5.6	4.2	0	0	0	0/0/0	0/0/	0	0/0/0	0/0/0	Women's or girls' T-shirts, other than underwear, of wool or fine animal hair, knitted or crocheted
3.9	0/0/0	0	5.6	4.2	0	0	0	0/0/0	0/0/	0	0/0/0	0/0/0	Men's singlets, vests, and boys' No. 8～No. 18, other than underwear, knitted or crocheted, of wool or fine animal hair
3.9	0/0/0	0	5.6	4.2	0	0	0	0/0/0	0/0/	0	0/0/0	0/0/0	Men's or boys' singlets, vests, other than underwear, of wool or fine animal hair, knitted or crocheted
3.9	0/0/0	0	5.6	4.2	0	0	0	0/0/0	0/0/	0	0/0/0	0/0/0	Women's or girls singlets vests, other than underwear, of wool or fine animal hair, knitted or crocheted
3.9	0/0/0	0	5.6	4.2	0	0	0	0/0/0	0/0/	0	0/0/0	0/0/0	Underwear, of man-made fibres, knitted or crocheted
3.9	0/0/0	0	5.6	4.2	0	0	0	0/0/0	0/0/	0	0/0/0	0/0/0	T-shirts, of man-made fibres, knitted or crocheted
3.9	0/0/0	0	5.6	4.2	0	0	0	0/0/0	0/0/	0	0/0/0	0/0/0	Other singlets, vests, of man-made fibres, knitted or crocheted
3.9	0/0/0	0	5.6	4.2	0	0	0	0/0/0	0/0/	0	0/0/0	0/0/0	Other T-shirts, singlets and other vests underwear style, of other textile materials, knitted or crocheted
3.9	0/0/0	0	5.6	4.2	0	0	0	0/0/0	0/0/	0	0/0/0	0/0/0	Other singlets, and other vests, other than underwear, of other textile materials, including boys' No. 8～No. 18 or girls' No. 7～No. 16, knitted or crocheted
3.9	0/0/0	0	5.6	4.2	0	0	0	0/0/0	0/0/	0	0/0/0	0/0/0	Other T-shirts, singlets and other vests, other than underwear, of other textile materials, knitted or crocheted
													Jerseys, pullovers, cardigans, waistcoats and similar articles, knitted or crocheted:
													-Of wool or fine animal hair:
3.9	0/0/0	0	0	4.2	0	0	0	0/0/0	0/0/0	0	0/0/0	0/0/0	--Of wool
													--Of Kashmir(cashmere) goats
3.9	0/0/0	0	5.6	4.2	0	0	0	0/0/0	0/0/			0/0/0	Men's or boys' pullovers, cardigans, waistcoats and similar articles, of fine hair of Kashmir (cashmere) goats, knitted or crocheted, piled, hand-worked
3.9	0/0/0	0	5.6	4.2	0	0	0	0/0/0	0/0/			0/0/0	Men's or boys' pullovers, cardigans, waistcoats and similar articles of fine hair of Kashmir (cashmere) goats, knitted or crocheted, piled
3.9	0/0/0	0	5.6	4.2	0	0	0	0/0/0	0/0/			0/0/0	Women's or girls' pullovers, cardigans, waistcoats and similar articles, of fine hair of Kashmir (cashmere) goats, knitted or crocheted, piled, hand-worked
3.9	0/0/0	0	5.6	4.2	0	0	0	0/0/0	0/0/			0/0/0	Women's or girls' pullovers, cardigans, waistcoats and similar articles, of fine hair of Kashmir (cashmere) goats, knitted or crocheted, piled

税则号列		货品名称〔CIQ扩展编码及品名—T2表示见附表2〕	最惠(%)	暂定税率	普通	增值/消费	出口退税	计量单位	监管条件	检验检疫	特殊证件对美关税
6110.1200	31	克什米尔山羊细毛手工非起绒男套头衫(针织或钩编,包括开襟衫、外穿背心及类似品)〔999〕	6	5	130	13/	13	件/千克			/35
6110.1200	39	克什米尔山羊细毛非起绒男套头衫(针织或钩编,包括开襟衫、外穿背心及类似品)〔999〕	6	5	130	13/	13	件/千克			/35
6110.1200	41	克什米尔山羊细毛手工非起绒女套头衫(针织或钩编,包括开襟衫、外穿背心及类似品)〔999〕	6	5	130	13/	13	件/千克			/35
6110.1200	49	克什米尔山羊细毛非起绒女套头衫(针织或钩编,包括开襟衫、外穿背心及类似品)〔999〕	6	5	130	13/	13	件/千克			/35
		--其他:									
6110.1910		---其他山羊细毛制〔999〕	6		130	13/	13	件/千克			/31
6110.1920		---兔毛制〔999〕	6		130	13/	13	件/千克			/
6110.1990		---其他〔999〕	6		130	13/	13	件/千克			/31
6110.2000		-棉制									
6110.2000	11	棉制儿童游戏套装紧身衫及套头衫(针织起绒,轻薄细针翻领、开领、高领,含亚麻36%以下)〔999〕	6		90	13/	13	件/千克	A	M	/31
6110.2000	12	棉制其他起绒儿童游戏套头衫等(针织或钩编,包括开襟衫、背心及类似品,含亚麻36%以下)〔999〕	6		90	13/	13	件/千克	A	M	/31
6110.2000	51	其他棉制儿童游戏套装紧身及套头衫(针织、非起绒、轻薄细针翻领、开领、高领)〔999〕	6		90	13/	13	件/千克	A	M	/31
6110.2000	52	其他棉制儿童游戏套装套头衫等(针织或钩编、非起绒、包括开襟衫、背心及类似品)〔999〕	6		90	13/	13	件/千克	A	M	/31
6110.2000	90	其他棉制针织或钩编的套头衫、开襟衫、马甲(背心)及类似品〔999〕	6		90	13/	13	件/千克			/31
6110.3000		-化学纤维制									
6110.3000	11	化学纤维儿童游戏套装紧身衫及套头衫(针织起绒,轻薄细针翻领、开领、高领毛<23%,丝<30%)〔999〕	6		130	13/	13	件/千克	A	M	/31
6110.3000	12	化学纤维起绒儿童游戏套装及套头衫等(针织或钩编包括开襟衫、背心及类似品含毛<23%,含丝<30%)〔999〕	6		130	13/	13	件/千克	A	M	/31
6110.3000	41	化学纤维其他儿童游戏套装紧身及套头衫(针织非起绒,轻薄细针翻领、开领、高领)〔999〕	6		130	13/	13	件/千克	A	M	/31
6110.3000	42	化学纤维制其他儿童游戏套装套头衫等(针织或钩编,非起绒,包括开襟衫、背心及类似品)〔999〕	6		130	13/	13	件/千克	A	M	/31
6110.3000	90	其他化纤制针织或钩编的套头衫、开襟衫、马甲(背心)及类似品〔999〕	6		130	13/	13	件/千克			/31
		-其他纺织材料制:									
6110.9010		---丝及绢丝制〔999〕	6		130	13/	13	件/千克			/31
6110.9090		---其他〔999〕	6		130	13/	13	件/千克			/31
61.11		**针织或钩编的婴儿服装及衣着附件:**									
6111.2000		-棉制									
6111.2000	10	棉制针织或钩编婴儿袜〔999〕	10		90	13/	13	千克	A	M	/35
6111.2000	20	棉制婴儿分指、连指、露指手套(针制或钩编)〔999〕	10		90	13/	13	千克	A	M	/35
6111.2000	40	棉制针织婴儿外衣、雨衣、滑雪装(针制或钩编,包括夹克类似品)〔999〕	10		90	13/	13	千克	A	M	/35
6111.2000	50	棉制针织钩编婴儿其他服装〔999〕	10		90	13/	13	千克	A	M	/35
6111.2000	90	棉制针织钩编婴儿衣着附件〔999〕	10		90	13/	13	千克	A	M	/35
6111.3000		-合成纤维制									
6111.3000	10	合成纤维制针织或钩编婴儿袜〔999〕	10		130	13/	13	千克	A	M	/35
6111.3000	20	合成纤维婴儿分指、连指及露指手套(针制或钩编)〔999〕	10		130	13/	13	千克	A	M	/35
6111.3000	40	合成纤维婴儿外衣、雨衣、滑雪装(针制或钩编,包括夹克类似服装)〔999〕	10		130	13/	13	千克	A	M	/35
6111.3000	50	合成纤维针织或钩编婴儿其他服装(包括衣着附件)〔999〕	10		130	13/	13	千克	A	M	/35

协定税率 %										特惠税率 %			Article Description
亚太5国	东/冰/格	巴基斯坦	韩国	瑞士	哥达	秘鲁	澳大利亚	新西/坡/智	港/澳/台	亚太2国	老/柬/缅	36/3/1	
3.9	0/0/0	0	5.6	4.2	0	0	0	0/0/0	0/0/			0/0/0	Men's or boys' pullovers, cardigans, waistcoats and similar articles, of fine hair of Kashmir (cashmere) goats, knitted or crocheted, not piled, hand-worked
3.9	0/0/0	0	5.6	4.2	0	0	0	0/0/0	0/0/			0/0/0	Men's or boys' pullovers, cardigans, waistcoats and similar articles, of fine hair of Kashmir (cashmere) goats, knitted or crocheted, not piled
3.9	0/0/0	0	5.6	4.2	0	0	0	0/0/0	0/0/			0/0/0	Women's or girls' pullovers, cardigans, waistcoats and similar articles, of fine hair of Kashmir (cashmere) goats, knitted or crocheted, not piled, hand-worked
3.9	0/0/0	0	5.6	4.2	0	0	0	0/0/0	0/0/			0/0/0	Women's or girls' pullovers, cardigans, waistcoats and similar articles, of fine hair of Kashmir (cashmere) goats, knitted or crocheted, not piled
													--Other:
3.9	0/0/0	0	5.6	4.2	0	0	0	0/0/0	0/0/			0/0/0	---Of other goats
3.9	0/0/0	0	5.6	4.2	0	0	0	0/0/0	0/0/			0/0/	---Of rabbit and hare
3.9	0/0/0	0	5.6	4.2	0	0	0	0/0/0	0/0/			0/0/0	---Other
													-Of cotton
3.9	0/0/0	0	5.6	4.2	0	0	0	0/0/0	0/0/0	2.4	0/0/0	0/0/0	Boys' or girls' playsuit, jerseys, pullovers, tricolette turn-down collar, open-necked collar, high-necked collar, containing < 36% by weight of flax, of cotton knitted, piled
3.9	0/0/0	0	5.6	4.2	0	0	0	0/0/0	0/0/0	2.4	0/0/0	0/0/0	Other boys' or girls' playsuit, pullovers, cardigans, waistcoats and similar articles, containing<36% by weight of flax, of cotton, knitted or crocheted
3.9	0/0/0	0	5.6	4.2	0	0	0	0/0/0	0/0/0	2.4	0/0/0	0/0/0	Other boys' or girls' playsuit, jerseys, pullovers, tricolette turn-down collar, open-necked collar, high-necked collar, not piled, of cotton, knitted
3.9	0/0/0	0	5.6	4.2	0	0	0	0/0/0	0/0/0	2.4	0/0/0	0/0/0	Other boys' or girls' playsuit pullovers, cardigans, waistcoats and similar articles, of cotton, knitted or crocheted not piled
3.9	0/0/0	0	5.6	4.2	0	0	0	0/0/0	0/0/0	2.4	0/0/0	0/0/0	Pullovers, cardigans, waistcoats and similar articles of cotton, knitted or crocheted
													-Of man-made fibres
3.9	0/0/0	0	9.6	4.8	0	0	0	0/0/0	0/0/0	0		0/0/0	Boys' or girls' playsuit, jerseys, pullovers, tricolette turn-down collar, open-necked collar, high-necked collar, containing < 23% by weight of wool or fine animal hair, containing<30% by weight of silk or silk waste, of man-made fibres, knitted, piled
3.9	0/0/0	0	9.6	4.8	0	0	0	0/0/0	0/0/0	0		0/0/0	Boys' or girls' playsuit, jerseys, pullovers, tricolette turn-down collar, open-necked collar, high-necked collar, containing < 23% by weight of wool or fine animal hair, containing<30% by weight of silk or silk waste, of man-made fibres knitted, piled
3.9	0/0/0	0	9.6	4.8	0	0	0	0/0/0	0/0/0	0		0/0/0	Other boys' or girls' playsuit, jerseys, pullovers, knitted, tricolette turn-down collar, open-necked collar, high-necked collar, not piled, of man-made fibres, knitted
3.9	0/0/0	0	9.6	4.8	0	0	0	0/0/0	0/0/0	0		0/0/0	Other boys' or girls' playsuit, including cardigans, waistcoats and similar articles, not piled, of man-made fibres, knitted or crocheted
3.9	0/0/0	0	9.6	4.8	0	0	0	0/0/0	0/0/0	0		0/0/0	Pullovers, cardigans, waistcoats and similar articles of synthetic fibres, knitted or crocheted
													-Of other textile materials:
3.9	0/0/0	0	5.6	4.2	0	0	0	0/0/0	0/0/	0		0/0/0	---Of silk or spun silk
3.9	0/0/0	0	5.6	4.2	0	0	0	0/0/0	0/0/	0		0/0/0	---Other
													Babies' garments and clothing accessories, knitted or crocheted:
													-Of cotton
	0/0/0	0	5.6	4.2	0	0	0	0/0/0	0/0/			0/0/0	Babies' hosiery of cotton, knitted or crocheted
	0/0/0	0	5.6	4.2	0	0	0	0/0/0	0/0/			0/0/0	Babies' gloves, mittens and mitts of cotton, knitted or crocheted
	0/0/0	0	5.6	4.2	0	0	0	0/0/0	0/0/			0/0/0	Babies' coat, raincoat, ski suit, including jacked and similar articles, of cotton, knitted or crocheted
	0/0/0	0	5.6	4.2	0	0	0	0/0/0	0/0/			0/0/0	Other babies' garments of cotton, knitted or crocheted
	0/0/0	0	5.6	4.2	0	0	0	0/0/0	0/0/			0/0/0	Babies' clothing accessories of cotton, knitted or crocheted
													-Of synthetic fibres
6.5	0/0/0	6.4	6.4	4.8	0	0	0	0/0/0	0/0/			0/0/0	Babies' hosiery of synthetic fibres, knitted or crocheted
6.5	0/0/0	6.4	6.4	4.8	0	0	0	0/0/0	0/0/			0/0/0	Babies' gloves, mittens and mitts of synthetic fibres, knitted or crocheted
6.5	0/0/0	6.4	6.4	4.8	0	0	0	0/0/0	0/0/			0/0/0	Babies' coat, raincoat, ski suit, jacked and similar articles, of synthetic fibres, knitted or crocheted
6.5	0/0/0	6.4	6.4	4.8	0	0	0	0/0/0	0/0/			0/0/0	Other babies' garments of synthetic fibres, knitted or crocheted

税则号列		货品名称〔CIQ扩展编码及品名—T2表示见附表2〕	最惠(%)	暂定税率	普通	增值/消费	出口退税	计量单位	监管条件	检验检疫	特殊证件对美关税
6111.3000	90	合成纤维针织或钩编婴儿衣着附件〔999〕	10		130	13/	13	千克	A	M	/35
		-其他纺织材料制：									
6111.9010		---羊毛或动物细毛制〔999〕	10		130	13/	13	千克	A	M	/
6111.9090		---其他									
6111.9090	10	人造纤维针织或钩编婴儿袜〔999〕	10		130	13/	13	千克	A	M	/
6111.9090	90	其他纺织材料制婴儿服装及衣着附件(针织或钩编)〔999〕	10		130	13/	13	千克	A	M	/
61.12		**针织或钩编的运动服、滑雪服及游泳服：**									
		-运动服：									
6112.1100		--棉制〔999〕	6		90	13/	13	套/千克			/31
6112.1200		--合成纤维制〔999〕	8		130	13/	13	套/千克			/33
6112.1900		--其他纺织材料制〔999〕	6		130	13/	13	套/千克			/31
		-滑雪服：									
6112.2010		---棉制〔999〕	6		90	13/	13	套/千克			/
6112.2090		---其他〔999〕	10		130	13/	13	套/千克			/
		-男式游泳服：									
6112.3100		--合成纤维制〔999〕	8		130	13/	13	件/千克			/
6112.3900		--其他纺织材料制〔999〕	6		130	13/	13	件/千克			/
		-女式游泳服：									
6112.4100		--合成纤维制〔999〕	8		130	13/	13	件/千克			/33
6112.4900		--其他纺织材料制〔999〕	6		130	13/	13	件/千克			/31
61.13		**用税目59.03、59.06或59.07的针织物或钩编织物制成的服装：**									
6113.0000		用税目59.03、59.06或59.07的针织物或钩编织物制成的服装〔999〕	6		130	13/	13	件/千克			/31
61.14		**针织或钩编的其他服装：**									
6114.2000		-棉制									
6114.2000	11	棉制针织或钩编儿童非保暖连身裤〔999〕	6		90	13/	13	件/千克	A	M	/31
6114.2000	21	棉制针织或钩编男成人及男童TOPS(指8－18号男童TOPS)〔101针织童装,102其他针织服装〕	6		90	13/	13	件/千克	A	M	/31
6114.2000	22	棉制针织或钩编其他男童TOPS〔101针织童装,102其他针织服装〕	6		90	13/	13	件/千克	A	M	/31
6114.2000	40	棉制针织或钩编夏服、水洗服(包括女成人、女童及男童)〔101针织外衣,102针织童装〕	6		90	13/	13	件/千克	A	M	/31
6114.2000	90	棉制针织或钩编其他服装〔999〕	6		90	13/	13	件/千克			/31
6114.3000		-化学纤维制									
6114.3000	21	化学纤维针织或钩编男成人及男TOPS(指8－18号男童TOPS)〔101针织童装,102其他针织服装〕	8		130	13/	13	件/千克	A	M	/33
6114.3000	22	化学纤维针织或钩编其他男童TOPS〔999〕	8		130	13/	13	件/千克	A	M	/33
6114.3000	90	化学纤维针织或钩编其他服装〔999,101针织外衣,102针织衬衫,103针织运动服,104针织童装〕	8		130	13/	13	件/千克			/33
		-其他纺织材料制：									
6114.9010		---羊毛或动物细毛制〔999〕	6		130	13/	13	件/千克			/31
6114.9090		---其他〔999〕	6		130	13/	13	件/千克			/31
61.15		**针织或钩编的连裤袜、紧身裤袜、长筒袜、短袜及其他袜类,包括渐紧压袜类(例如用以治疗静脉曲张的长筒袜)和无外绱鞋底的鞋类：**									
6115.1000		-渐紧压袜类(例如,用以治疗静脉曲张的长筒袜)〔999〕	6		130	13/	13	双/千克			/36
		-其他连裤袜及紧身裤袜：									
6115.2100		--每根单丝细度在67分特以下的合成纤维制〔999〕	6		130	13/	13	双/千克			/31
6115.2200		--每根单丝细度在67分特及以上的合成纤维制〔999〕	6		130	13/	13	双/千克			/31
		--其他纺织材料制：									
6115.2910		---棉制〔999〕	6		90	13/	13	双/千克			/
6115.2990		---其他〔999〕	6		130	13/	13	双/千克			/31
6115.3000		-其他女式长筒袜及中筒袜,每根单丝细度在67分特以下〔999〕	6		130	13/	13	双/千克			/31
		-其他：									
6115.9400		--羊毛或动物细毛制〔999〕	6		130	13/	13	双/千克			/16
6115.9500		--棉制									
6115.9500	11	棉制针织或钩编矫正袜(外科用带压缩刻度)〔999〕	6		90	13/	13	双/千克			/31
6115.9500	19	棉制针织或钩编短袜及其他袜类〔999〕	6		90	13/	13	双/千克			/31
6115.9600		--合成纤维制〔999〕	6		130	13/	13	双/千克			/31
6115.9900		--其他纺织材料制〔999〕	6		130	13/	13	双/千克			/

协定税率 %										特惠税率 %			Article Description
亚太5国	东/冰/格	巴基斯坦	韩国	瑞士	哥达	秘鲁	澳大利亚	新西/坡/智	港/澳/台	亚太2国	老/柬/缅	36/3/1	
6.5	0/0/0	6.4	6.4	4.8	0	0	0	0/0/0	0/0/			0/0/0	Babies' clothing accessories of synthetic fibres, knitted or crocheted
													-Of other textile materials:
6.5	0/0/0	7	5.6	4.2	0	0	0	0/0/0	0/0/			0/0/0	---Of wool or fine animal hair
													---Other
6.5	0/0/0	7	5.6	4.2	0	0	0	0/0/0	0/0/			0/0/	Babies' hosiery of artificial fibres, knitted or crocheted
6.5	0/0/0	7	5.6	4.2	0	0	0	0/0/0	0/0/			0/0/	Babies' garments and clothing accessories, of other textile materials, knitted or crocheted
													Track suits, ski suits and swimwear, knitted or crocheted:
													-Track suits:
3.9	0/0/0	6.4	6.4	4.8	0	0	0	0/0/0	0/0/			0/0/	--Of cotton
5.2	0/0/0	0	7	5.3	0	0	0	0/0/0	0/0/			0/0/0	--Of synthetic fibres
3.9	0/0/0	8	6.4	4.8	0	0	0	0/0/0	0/0/			0/0/	--Of other textile materials
													-Ski suits:
3.9	0/0/0	8	6.4	4.8	0	0	0	0/0/0	0/0/			0/0/0	---Of cotton
6.5	0/0/0	9.5	7.6	5.7	0	0	0	0/0/0	0/0/			0/0/	---Other
													-Men's or boys' swimwear:
5.2	0/0/0	8.8	7	5.3	0	0	0	0/0/0	0/0/			0/0/	--Of synthetic fibres
3.9	0/0/0	8	6.4	4.8	0	0	0	0/0/0	0/0/			0/0/	--Of other textile materials
													-Women's or girls' swimwear:
5.2	0/0/0	8.8	7	5.3	0	0	0	0/0/0	0/0/0			0/0/	--Of Synthetic fibres
3.9	0/0/0	8	6.4	4.8	0	0	0	0/0/0	0/0/			0/0/	--Of other textile materials
													Garments, made up of knitted or crocheted fabrics of heading No. 59.03, 59.06 or 59.07:
3.9	0/0/0	8	6.4	4.8	0	0	0	0/0/0	0/0/	0		0/0/0	Garments, made up of knitted or crocheted fabrics of heading No. 59.03, 59.06 or 59.07
													Other garments, knitted or crocheted:
													-Of cotton
	0/0/0	0	6.4	4.8	0		0	0/0/0	0/0/	2.4		0/0/0	Boys' or girls' overall, not thermal, knitted or crocheted, of cotton
	0/0/0	0	6.4	4.8	0		0	0/0/0	0/0/	2.4		0/0/0	Men's TOPS or boys' TOPS No.8～No.18, knitted or crocheted, of cotton
	0/0/0	0	6.4	4.8	0		0	0/0/0	0/0/	2.4		0/0/0	Other boys' TOPS, knitted or crocheted, of cotton
	0/0/0	0	6.4	4.8	0		0	0/0/0	0/0/	2.4		0/0/0	Women's or girls' and boys' summer wear, wash wear, knitted or crocheted, of cotton
	0/0/0	0	6.4	4.8	0		0	0/0/0	0/0/	2.4		0/0/0	Other garments, knitted or crocheted, of cotton
													-Of man-made fibres
	0/0/0	0	7	5.3	0	0	0	0/0/0	0/0/			0/0/0	Men's TOPS or boys' TOPS No.8～No.18, knitted or crocheted, of man-made fibres
	0/0/0	0	7	5.3	0	0	0	0/0/0	0/0/			0/0/0	Other boys' TOPS, knitted or crocheted, of man-made fibres
	0/0/0	0	7	5.3	0	0	0	0/0/0	0/0/			0/0/0	Other garments, knitted or crocheted, of man-made fibres
													-Of other textile materials:
	0/0/0	0	6.4	4.8	0	0	0	0/0/0	0/0/			0/0/	---Of wool or fine animal hair
	0/0/0	0	6.4	4.8	0	0	0	0/0/0	0/0/			0/0/	---Other
													Panty hose, tights, stockings, socks and other hosiery, including graduate compression hosiery (for example, stockings for varicose veins) and footwear without applied soles, knitted or crocheted:
3.5	0/0/0	0	6.4	6	0	0	0	0/0/0	0/0/			0/0/	-Graduated compression hosiery (for example, stockings for varicose veins)
													-Other panty hose and tights:
3.9	0/0/0	12.8	6.4	4.8	0	0	0	0/0/0	0/0/			0/0/	--Of synthetic fibres, measuring per single yarn less than 67 decitex
3.9	0/0/0	8	6.4	4.8	0	0	0	0/0/0	0/0/0			0/0/	--Of synthetic fibres, measuring per single yarn 67 decitex or more
													--Of other textile materials:
	0/0/0	11.2	5.6	4.2	0	0	0	0/0/0	0/0/			0/0/0	---Of cotton
3.9	0/0/0	7	5.6	4.2	0	0	0	0/0/0	0/0/0			0/0/	---Other
3.9	0/0/0	0	5.6	4.2	0	0	0	0/0/0	0/0/	0		0/0/0	-Women's full-length or knee-length hosiery, measuring per single yarn less than 67 decitex
													-Other:
	0/0/0	11.2	5.6	4.2	0	0	0	0/0/0	0/0/			0/0/	--Of wool or fine animal hair
													--Of cotton
	0/0/0	0	5.6	4.2	0	0	0	0/0/0	0/0/			0/0/0	Orthopedic stockings, with surgical restriction scale, of cotton, knitted or crocheted
	0/0/0	0	5.6	4.2	0	0	0	0/0/0	0/0/			0/0/0	Socks and other hosiery of cotton, knitted or crocheted
3.9	0/0/0	0	6.4	4.8	0	0	0	0/0/0	0/0/			0/0/0	--Of synthetic fibres
3.9	0/0/0	0	5.6	4.2	0	0	0	0/0/0	0/0/0			0/0/	--Of other textile materials

税则号列		货品名称〔CIQ 扩展编码及品名—T2 表示见附表 2〕	最惠(%)	暂定税率	普通	增值/消费	出口退税	计量单位	监管条件	检验检疫	特殊证件对美关税
61.16		**针织或钩编的分指手套、连指手套及露指手套：**									
6116.1000		-用塑料或橡胶浸渍、涂布或包覆的〔999〕	6		130	13/	13	双/千克			/31
		-其他：									
6116.9100		--羊毛或动物细毛制〔999〕	6		130	13/	13	双/千克			/
6116.9200		--棉制〔999〕	6		90	13/	13	双/千克			/16
6116.9300		--合成纤维制									
6116.9300	10	合成纤维制其他针织或钩编手套(含羊毛或动物细毛 23%及以上)〔999〕	6		130	13/	13	双/千克			/31
6116.9300	90	合成纤维制其他针织或钩编手套(含羊毛或动物细毛 23%以下)〔999〕	6		130	13/	13	双/千克			/31
6116.9900		--其他纺织材料制〔999〕	6		130	13/	13	双/千克			/36
61.17		**其他制成的针织或钩编的衣着附件；服装或衣着附件的针织或钩编的零件：**									
		-披巾、头巾、围巾、披纱、面纱及类似品：									
		---动物细毛制：									
6117.1011		----山羊绒制〔999〕	6		130	13/	13	条/千克			/31
6117.1019		----其他〔999〕	6		130	13/	13	条/千克			/31
6117.1020		---羊毛制〔999〕	6		130	13/	13	条/千克			/31
6117.1090		---其他〔999〕	6		130	13/	13	条/千克			/31
		-其他附件：									
6117.8010		---领带及领结〔999〕	6		130	13/	13	千克/条			/31
6117.8090		---其他〔999〕	6		130	13/	13	千克			/31
6117.9000		-零件〔999〕	6		130	13/	13	千克			/31

协定税率 %										特惠税率 %			Article Description
亚太5国	东/冰/格	巴基斯坦	韩国	瑞士	哥达	秘鲁	澳大利亚	新西/坡/智	港/澳/台	亚太2国	老/柬/缅	36/3/1	
													Gloves, mittens and mitts, knitted or crocheted:
	0/0/0	0	5.6	4.2	0	0	0	0/0/0	0/0/			0/0/0	-Gloves impregnated, coated or covered with plastics or rubber
													-Other:
	0/0/0	0	5.6	4.2	0	0	0	0/0/0	0/0/			0/0/0	--Of wool of fine animal hair
	0/0/0	0	5.6	4.2	0	0	0	0/0/0	0/0/			0/0/	--Of cotton
													--Of synthetic fibres
3.9	0/0/0	0	6.4	4.8	0	0	0	0/0/0	0/0/			0/0/0	Mittens and mitts, containing≥23% by weight of wool or fine animal hair, knitted or crocheted, of synthetic fibres
3.9	0/0/0	0	6.4	4.8	0	0	0	0/0/0	0/0/			0/0/0	Mittens and mitts, containing<23% by weight of wool or fine animal hair, knitted or crocheted, of synthetic fibres
3.9	0/0/0	0	5.6	4.2	0	0	0	0/0/0	0/0/			0/0/0	--Of other textile materials
													Other made up clothing accessories, knitted or crocheted; knitted or crocheted parts of garments or of clothing accessories:
													-Shawls, scarves, mufflers, mantillas, veils and the like:
													---Of fine animal hair:
3.9	0/0/0	0	5.6	4.2	0	0	0	0/0/0	0/0/			0/0/0	----Of goats
3.9	0/0/0	0	5.6	4.2	0	0	0	0/0/0	0/0/			0/0/0	----Other
3.9	0/0/0	0	5.6	4.2	0	0	0	0/0/0	0/0/			0/0/0	---Of wool
3.9	0/0/0	0	5.6	4.2	0	0	0	0/0/0	0/0/			0/0/0	---Other
													-Other accessories:
3.9	0/0/0	0	5.6	4.2	0	0	0	0/0/0	0/0/0			0/0/0	---Ties, bow ties and cravats
3.9	0/0/0	0	5.6	4.2	0	0	0	0/0/0	0/0/0			0/0/0	---Other
3	0/0/0	0	5.6	4.2	0	0	0	0/0/0	0/0/0			0/0/0	-Parts

第六十二章
非针织或非钩编的服装及衣着附件

注释：

一、本章仅适用于除絮胎以外任何纺织物的制成品，但不适用于针织品或钩编织品(税目62.12的除外)。

二、本章不包括：

(一)税目63.09的旧衣服及其他旧物品；

(二)矫形器具、外科手术带、疝气带及类似品(税目90.21)。

三、税目62.03及62.04所称：

(一)"西服套装"，是指面料用相同的织物制成的两件套或三件套的下列成套服装：

一件人体上半身穿着的外套或短上衣，除袖子外，应由四片或四片以上面料组成；也可附带一件马甲(西服背心)，这件马甲(西服背心)的前片面料应与套装其他各件的面料相同，后片料则应与外套或短上衣的衬里料相同；

以及一件人体下半身穿着的服装，即不带背带或护胸的长裤、马裤、短裤(游泳裤除外)、裙子或裙裤。

西服套装各件面料质地、颜色及构成必须完全相同，其款式、尺寸大小也须相互般配，但套装的各件可以用不同织物滚边(缝口上缝入长条织物)。

如果数件人体下半身穿着的服装同时进口或出口(例如，两条长裤、长裤与短裤、裙子或裙裤与长裤)，构成西服套装下装的应是一条长裤，而对于女式西服套装，则应是一条裙子或裙裤，其他服装应分别归类。

所称"西服套装"，包括不论是否完全符合上述条件的下列配套服装：

1.常礼服，由一件后襟下垂并下端开圆弧形叉的素色短上衣和一条条纹长裤组成；

2.晚礼服(燕尾服)，一般用黑色织物制成，上衣前襟较短且不闭合，背后有燕尾；

3.无燕尾套装夜礼服，其中上衣款式与普通上衣相似(可以更为显露衬衣前胸)，但有光滑丝质或仿丝质的翻领。

(二)"便服套装"，是指面料相同并作零售包装的下列成套服装(西服套装及税目62.07或62.08的物品除外)

一件人体上半身穿着的服装，但背心除外，因为背心可作为内衣；以及一件或两件不同的人体下半身穿着的服装，即长裤、护胸背带工装裤、马裤、短裤(游泳裤除外)、裙子或裙裤。

便服套装各件面料质地、款式、颜色及构成必须相同；尺寸大小也须相互般配。所称"便服套装"不包括税目62.11的运动服及滑雪服。

四、对于税目62.09：

(一)所称"婴儿服装及衣着附件"，是指用于身高不超过86厘米幼儿的服装；

(二)既可归入税目62.09，也可归入本章其他税目的物品，应归入税目62.09；

五、既可归入税目62.10，也可归入本章其他税目的服装，除税目62.09所列的仍归入该税目外，其余的应一律归入税目62.10。

六、税目62.11所称"滑雪服"，是指从整个外观和织物质地来看，主要在滑雪(速度滑雪和高山滑雪)时穿着的下列服装或成套服装：

(一)"滑雪连身服"，即上下身连在一起的单件服装；除袖子和领子外，滑雪连身服可有口袋或脚带；或

(二)"滑雪套装"，即由两件或三件构成一套并作零售包装的下列服装：

一件用一条拉链扣合的带风帽的厚夹克、防风衣、防风短上衣或类似的服装，可以附带一件背心；以及一条不论是否过腰的长裤、一条马裤或一条护胸背带工装裤。

"滑雪套装"也可由一件类似以上(一)款所述的类似连身服和一件可套在连身服外面的有胎料背心组成。

"滑雪套装"各件颜色可以不同，但面料质地、款式及构成必须相同；尺寸大小也须相互般配。

七、正方形或近似正方形的围巾及围巾式样的物品，如果每边均不超过60厘米，应作为手帕归类(税目62.13)。任何一边超过60厘米的手帕，应归入税目62.14。

八、本章的服装，凡门襟为左压右的，应视为男式；右压左的，应视为女式。但本规定不适用于其式样已明显为男式或女式的服装。无法区别是男式还是女式的服装，应按女式服装归入有关税目。

九、本章物品可用金属线制成。

Chapter 62
Articles of apparel and clothing accessories, not knitted or crocheted

Notes:

1. This Chapter applies only to made up articles of any textile fabric other than wadding, excluding knitted or crocheted articles (other than those of heading No.62.12).
2. This Chapter does not cover:
   (a) Worn clothing or other worn articles of heading No.63.09; or
   (b) Orthopaedic appliances, surgical belts, trusses or the like (heading No.90.21).
3. For the purposes of headings Nos.62.03 and 62.04:
   (a) The term "suit" means a set of garments composed of two or three pieces made up in hespect of their outer surface, in identical fabric and comprising:
   One suit coat or jacket the outer shell of which, exclusive of sleeves, consists of four or more panels, designed to cover the upper part of the body, possibly with a tailored waistcoat in addition whose front is made from the same fabric as the outer shell of the other components of the set and whose back is made from the same fabric as the lining of the suit coat or jacket, and
   One garment designed to cover the lower part of the body and consisting of trousers, breeches or shorts (other than swimwear), a skirt or a divided skirt, having neither braces nor bibs.
   All of the components of a suit must be of the same fabric construction, colour and composition; they must also be of the same style and of corresponding or compatible size. However, these components may have piping(a strip of fabric sewn into the seam) in a different fabric.
   If several separate components to cover the lower part of the body are presented together (for example two palls of trousers or, trousers and shorts, or a skirt or divided skirt and trousers), the constituent lower part shall be one pair of trousers, or, in the case of women's or girls' suits, the skirt or divided skirt, the other garments being considered separately.
   The term "suit" includes the following sets of garments, whether or not they fulfil all the above conditions:
   (i) Morning dress, comprising a plain jacket (cutaway) with rounded tails hanging well down at the back and striped trousers;
   (ii) Evening dress (tailcoat), generally made of black cloth, the jacket of which is relatively short at the front, does not close and has narrow skirts cut in at the hips and hanging down behind;
   (iii) Dinner jacket suits, in which the jacket is similar in style to an ordinary jacket (though perhaps revealing more of the shirt front), but has shiny silk or imitation silk lapels.
   (b) The term "ensemble" means a set of garments (other than suits and articles of heading No.62.07 or 62.08) composed of several pieces made up in identical fabric, put up for retail sale, and comprising:
   One garment designed to cover the upper part of the body, with the exception of waistcoats which may also form a second upper garment, and one or two different garments, designed to cover the lower part of the body and consisting of trousers, bib and brace overalls, breeches, shorts (other than swimwear), a skirt or a divided skirt.
   All of the components of an ensemble must be of the same fabric construction, style, colour and composition; they also must be of corresponding or compatible size. The term "ensemble" does not apply to track suits or ski suits, of heading No.62.11.
4. For the purposes of heading No.62.09:
   (a) The expression "babies' garments and clothing accessories" means articles for young children of a body height not exceeding 86cm;
   (b) Articles which are, *prima facie*, classifiable both in heading 62.09 and in other headings of this Chapter are to be classified in heading No.62.09.
5. Garments which are, *prima facie*, classifiable both in heading No.62.10 and in other headings of this Chapter, excluding heading No. 62.09, are to be classified in heading No.62.10.
6. For the purposes of heading No.62.11, "ski suits" means garments or sets of garments which, by their general appearance and texture, are identifiable as intended to be worn principally for skiing (cross-country or alpine).
   They consist either of:
   (a) A "ski overall", that is, a one-piece garment designed to cover the upper and the lower parts of the body; in addition to sleeves and a collar the ski overall may have pockets or footstraps; or
   (b) A "ski ensemble", that is, a set of garments composed of two or three pieces, put up for retail sale and comprising:
   One garment such as an anorak, wind-cheater, wind-jacket or similar article, closed by a slide fastener (zipper), possibly with a waistcoat in addition, and one pair of trousers whether or not extending above waist-level, one pair of breeches or one bib and brace overall.
   The "ski ensemble" may also consist of an overall similar to the one mentioned in paragraph (a) above and a type of padded, sleeveless jacket worn over the overall.
   All the components of a "ski ensemble" must be made up in a fabric of the same texture, style and composition whether or not of the same colour; they also must be of corresponding or compatible size.
7. Scarves and articles of the scarf type, square or approximately square, of which no side exceeds 60cm, are to be classified as handkerchiefs (heading No.62.13). Handkerchiefs of which any side exceeds 60cm are to be classified in heading No.62.14.
8. Garments of this Chapter designed for left over right closure at the front shall be regarded as men's or boys' garments, and those designed for right over left closure at the front as women's or girls' garments. these provisions do not apply where the cut of the garment clearly indicates that it is designed for one or other of the sexes. Garments which cannot be identified as either men's or boys' garments or as women's or girls' garments are to be classified in the headings covering women's or girls' garments.
9. Articles of this Chapter may be made of metal thread.

税则号列	货品名称〔CIQ 扩展编码及品名—T2 表示见附表 2〕	最惠(%)	暂定税率	普通	增值/消费	出口退税	计量单位	监管条件	检验检疫	特殊证件对美关税
62.01	**男式大衣、短大衣、斗篷、短斗篷、带风帽的防寒短上衣(包括滑雪短上衣)、防风衣、防风短上衣及类似品,但税号 62.03 的货品除外:**									
	-大衣、雨衣、短大衣、斗篷、短斗篷及类似品:									
6201.1100	--羊毛或动物细毛制									
6201.1100 10	毛制男式雨衣(羊毛或动物细毛制)〔999〕	6	5	130	13/	13	件/千克			/35
6201.1100 90	毛制男式大衣,斗篷及类似品(含短大衣、短斗篷,羊毛或动物细毛制)〔999〕	6	5	130	13/	13	件/千克			/35
	--棉制:									
6201.1210	---羽绒服〔999〕	6		90	13/	13	件/千克			/
6201.1290	---其他									
6201.1290 10	棉制男式雨衣〔999〕	6	5	90	13/	13	件/千克			/35
6201.1290 20	棉制男式连风帽派克大衣等(含带风帽的防寒短上衣、防风衣、防风短上衣及类似品)〔999〕	6	5	90	13/	13	件/千克			/35
6201.1290 90	棉制男式大衣、斗篷及类似品(包括短大衣、短斗篷)〔999〕	6	5	90	13/	13	件/千克			/35
	--化学纤维制:									
6201.1310	---羽绒服〔999〕	8		130	13/	13	件/千克			/33
6201.1390	---其他〔999〕	8		130	13/	13	件/千克			/33
6201.1900	--其他纺织材料制〔999〕	6		100	13/	13	件/千克			/31
	-其他:									
6201.9100	--羊毛或动物细毛制〔101 大衣、短大衣,102 上衣〕	6		130	13/	13	件/千克			/31
	--棉制:									
6201.9210	---羽绒服〔999〕	6		90	13/	13	件/千克			/31
6201.9290	---其他〔101 大衣、短大衣,102 上衣〕	6		90	13/	13	件/千克			/31
	--化学纤维制:									
6201.9310	---羽绒服〔999〕	8		130	13/	13	件/千克			/33
6201.9390	---其他〔101 大衣、短大衣,102 上衣〕	8		130	13/	13	件/千克			/33
6201.9900	--其他纺织材料制〔999〕	6		100	13/	13	件/千克			/31
62.02	**女式大衣、短大衣、斗篷、短斗篷、带风帽的防寒短上衣(包括滑雪短上衣)、防风衣、防风短上衣及类似品,但税目 62.04 的货品除外:**									
	-大衣、雨衣、短大衣、斗篷、短斗篷及类似品:									
6202.1100	--羊毛或动物细毛制									
6202.1100 10	毛制女式雨衣(羊毛或动物细毛制)〔999〕	6	5	130	13/	13	件/千克			/35
6202.1100 90	毛制女式大衣、斗篷及类似品等(包括短大衣、短斗篷,羊毛或动物细毛制)〔999〕	6	5	130	13/	13	件/千克			/35
	--棉制:									
6202.1210	---羽绒服〔999〕	6		90	13/	13	件/千克			/
6202.1290	---其他									
6202.1290 10	棉制女式雨衣〔999〕	6	5	90	13/	13	件/千克			/35
6202.1290 20	棉制女式连风帽派克大衣等(含带风帽的防寒短上衣、防风衣、防风短上衣及类似品)〔999〕	6	5	90	13/	13	件/千克			/35
6202.1290 90	棉制女式大衣、斗篷及类似品(包括短大衣、短斗篷)〔999〕	6	5	90	13/	13	件/千克			/35
	--化学纤维制:									
6202.1310	---羽绒服〔999〕	10		130	13/	13	件/千克			/35
6202.1390	---其他〔999〕	10		130	13/	13	件/千克			/35
6202.1900	--其他纺织材料制〔999〕	6		100	13/	13	件/千克			/31
	-其他:									
6202.9100	--羊毛或动物细毛制〔999〕	6		130	13/	13	件/千克			/31
	--棉制:									
6202.9210	---羽绒服〔999〕	6		90	13/	13	件/千克			/
6202.9290	---其他〔999〕	6		90	13/	13	件/千克			/31
	--化学纤维制:									
6202.9310	---羽绒服〔999〕	8		130	13/	13	件/千克			/33
6202.9390	---其他〔999〕	8		130	13/	13	件/千克			/33
6202.9900	--其他纺织材料制〔999〕	6		100	13/	13	件/千克			/31
62.03	**男式西服套装、便服套装、上衣、长裤、护胸背带工装裤、马裤及短裤(游泳裤除外):**									
	-西服套装:									
6203.1100	--羊毛或动物细毛制〔999〕	8	5	130	13/	13	套/千克			/25
6203.1200	--合成纤维制									
6203.1200 10	合成纤维制男式西服套装(含羊毛或动物细毛 36%及以上)〔999〕	8		130	13/	13	套/千克			/

协定税率 %										特惠税率 %			Article Description
亚太5国	东/冰/格	巴基斯坦	韩国	瑞士	哥达	秘鲁	澳大利亚	新西/坡/智	港/澳/台	亚太2国	老/柬/缅	36/3/1	
													Men's or boys' overcoats, car-coats, capes, cloaks, anoraks (including ski-jackets), wind-cheaters, wind-jackets and similar articles, other than those of heading No. 62. 03:
													-Overcoats, raincoats, car-coats, capes, cloaks and similar articles:
													--Of wool or fine animal hair
3.9	0/0/0	8	6.4	4.8	0	0	0	0/0/0	0/0/			0/0/0	Men's or boys' raincoats, of wool or fine animal hair
3.9	0/0/0	8	6.4	4.8	0	0	0	0/0/0	0/0/			0/0/0	Men's or boys' overcoats, car-coats, capes, cloak and similar articles, of wool or fine animal hair
													--Of cotton:
	0/0/0	12.8	6.4	4.8	0	0	0	0/0/0	0/0/			0/0/	---Padded with feathers or down
													---Other
	0/0/0	12.8	6.4	4.8	0	0	0	0/0/0	0/0/			0/0/0	Men's or boys' raincoats of cotton
	0/0/0	12.8	6.4	4.8	0	0	0	0/0/0	0/0/			0/0/0	Men's or boys' hooded parka, anoraks, wind-cheaters, wind-jackets and similar articles, of cotton
	0/0/0	12.8	6.4	4.8	0	0	0	0/0/0	0/0/			0/0/0	Men's or boys' overcoats, car-coats, capes, cloaks and similar articles, of cotton
													--Of man-made fibres:
5.2	0/0/	8.8	7	5.3	0	0	0	0/0/0	0/0/			0/0/0	---Padded with feathers or down
5.2	0/0/0	8.8	7	5.3	0	0	0	0/0/0	0/0/			0/0/0	---Other
3.9	0/0/0	8	6.4	4.8	0	0	0	0/0/0	0/0/			0/0/0	--Of other textile materials
													-Other:
3.9	0/0/0	8	6.4	4.8	0	0	0	0/0/0	0/0/			0/0/0	--Of wool or fine animal hair
													--Of cotton:
	0/0/0	12.8	6.4	4.8	0	0	0	0/0/0	0/0/			0/0/0	---Padded with feathers or down
	0/0/0	12.8	6.4	4.8	0	0	0	0/0/0	0/0/		0/0/0	0/0/0	---Other
													--Of man-made fibres:
5.2	0/0/0	0	7	5.3	0	0	0	0/0/0	0/0/			0/0/0	---Padded with feathers or down
5.2	0/0/0	0	7	5.3	0	0	0	0/0/0	0/0/			0/0/0	---Other
3.9	0/0/0	8	6.4	4.8	0	0	0	0/0/0	0/0/		//0	0/0/0	--Of other textile materials
													Women's or girls' overcoats, car-coats, capes, cloaks, anoraks (including ski-jackets), wind-cheaters, wind-jackets and similar articles, other than those of heading No.62. 04:
													-Overcoats, raincoats, car-coats, capes, cloaks and similar articles:
													--Of wool or fine animal hair
3.9	0/0/0	8	6.4	4.8	0	0	0	0/0/0	0/0/			0/0/0	Women's or girls' raincoats, of wool or fine animal hair
3.9	0/0/0	8	6.4	4.8	0	0	0	0/0/0	0/0/			0/0/0	Women's or girls' overcoats, car-coats, capes, cloak and similar articles, of wool or fine animal hair
													--Of cotton:
	0/0/0	12.8	6.4	4.8	0	0	0	0/0/0	0/0/			0/0/	---Padded with feathers or down
													---Other
	0/0/0	12.8	6.4	4.8	0	0	0	0/0/0	0/0/			0/0/0	Women's or girls' raincoats, of cotton
	0/0/0	12.8	6.4	4.8	0	0	0	0/0/0	0/0/			0/0/0	Women's or girls' hooded parka, wind-cheaters, wind-jackets and similar articles, of cotton
	0/0/0	12.8	6.4	4.8	0	0	0	0/0/0	0/0/			0/0/0	Women's or girls' overcoats, car-coats, capes, cloak and similar articles, of cotton
													--Of man-made fibres:
6.5	0/0/0	9.5	7.6	5.7	0	0	0	0/0/0	0/0/			0/0/0	---Padded with feathers or down
6.5	0/0/0	9.5	7.6	5.7	0	0	0	0/0/0	0/0/			0/0/0	---Other
3.9	0/0/0	8	6.4	4.8	0	0	0	0/0/0	0/0/			0/0/0	--Of other textile materials
													-Other:
3.9	0/0/0	8	6.4	4.8	0	0	0	0/0/0	0/0/			0/0/	--Of wool or fine animal hair
													--Of cotton:
	0/0/	12.8	6.4	4.8	0	0	0	0/0/0	0/0/			0/0/	---Padded with feathers or down
	0/0/0	12.8	6.4	4.8	0	0	0	0/0/0	0/0/			0/0/0	---Other
													--Of man-made fibres:
5.2	0/0/	8.8	7	5.3	0	0	0	0/0/0	0/0/			0/0/0	---Padded with feathers or down
5.2	0/0/0	7	7	5.3	0	0	0	0/0/0	0/0/			0/0/0	---Other
3.9	0/0/0	8	6.4	4.8	0	0	0	0/0/0	0/0/			0/0/0	--Of other textile materials
													Men's or boys' suits, ensembles, jackets, blazers, trousers, bib and brace overalls, breeches and shorts (other than swim wear):
													-Suits:
5.2	0/0/0	8.8	7	0	0	0	0	0/0/0	0/0/			0/0/0	--Of wool or fine animal hair
													--Of synthetic fibres
5.2	0/0/0	8.8	7	5.3	0	0	0	0/0/0	0/0/			0/0/0	Men's or boys' suits, containing≥36% by weight of wool or fine animal hair, of synthetic fibres

税则号列	货品名称〔CIQ扩展编码及品名－T2表示见附表2〕	最惠(%)	暂定税率	普通	增值/消费	出口退税	计量单位	监管条件	检验检疫	特殊证件对美关税
6203.1200 90	其他合成纤维制男式西服套装〔999〕	8		130	13/	13	套/千克			/
	--其他纺织材料制:									
6203.1910	---丝及绢丝制〔999〕	8		100	13/	13	套/千克			/
6203.1990	---其他〔999〕	8		100	13/	13	套/千克			/33
	-便服套装:									
6203.2200	--棉制〔999〕	8		90	13/	13	套/千克			/33
6203.2300	--合成纤维制〔999〕	8		130	13/	13	套/千克			/33
	--其他纺织材料制:									
6203.2910	---丝及绢丝制〔999〕	8		130	13/	13	套/千克			/
6203.2920	---羊毛或动物细毛制〔999〕	8		130	13/	13	套/千克			/
6203.2990	---其他〔999〕	8		100	13/	13	套/千克			/
	-上衣:									
6203.3100	--羊毛或动物细毛制									
6203.3100 10	毛制男式西服式上衣(羊毛或动物细毛制)〔999〕	6	5	130	13/	13	件/千克			/35
6203.3100 90	毛制男式其他上衣(羊毛或动物细毛制)〔999〕	6	5	130	13/	13	件/千克			/35
6203.3200	--棉制									
6203.3200 10	棉制工业及职业用男式上衣〔999〕	6		90	13/	13	件/千克			/31
6203.3200 90	棉制其他男式上衣〔999〕	6		90	13/	13	件/千克			/31
6203.3300	--合成纤维制〔999〕	12		130	13/	13	件/千克			/37
	--其他纺织材料制:									
6203.3910	---丝及绢丝制									
6203.3910 10	丝制男式上衣(含丝70%及以上)〔999〕	6		130	13/	13	件/千克			/31
6203.3910 90	丝制男式上衣(含丝70%以下)〔999〕	6		130	13/	13	件/千克			/31
6203.3990	---其他〔999〕	6		100	13/	13	件/千克			/31
	-长裤、护胸背带工装裤、马裤及短裤:									
6203.4100	--羊毛或动物细毛制									
6203.4100 22	毛制男式长裤、马裤(羊毛或动物细毛制,含8－18号男童)〔101裤子,102童装〕	6		130	13/	13	条/千克	A	M	/31
6203.4100 29	毛制其他男童长裤、马裤(羊毛或动物细毛制)〔999〕	6		130	13/	13	条/千克	A	M	/31
6203.4100 90	毛制其他男式长裤、护胸背带工装裤、马裤及短裤〔999〕	6		130	13/	13	条/千克			/31
	--棉制:									
6203.4210	---阿拉伯裤〔999〕	6		90	13/	13	条/千克			/
6203.4290	---其他									
6203.4290 15	棉制其他男童护胸背带工装裤(带防寒衬里)〔999〕	6		90	13/	13	条/千克	A	M	/31
6203.4290 19	棉制其他男童护胸背带工装裤〔999〕	6		90	13/	13	条/千克	A	M	/31
6203.4290 49	棉制其他男童长裤、马裤(游戏装,不带防寒衬里)〔999〕	6		90	13/	13	条/千克	A	M	/31
6203.4290 62	棉制男式长裤、马裤(非游戏装,不带防寒衬里,含8－18号男童)〔101裤子,102童装〕	6		90	13/	13	条/千克	A	M	/31
6203.4290 69	棉制其他男童长裤、马裤(非游戏装,不带防寒衬里)〔999〕	6		90	13/	13	条/千克	A	M	/31
6203.4290 90	棉制其他男式长裤、护胸背带工装裤、马裤及短裤〔101裤子,102童装〕	6		90	13/	13	条/千克			/31
	--合成纤维制:									
6203.4310	---阿拉伯裤〔999〕	8		130	13/	13	条/千克			/
6203.4390	---其他									
6203.4390 15	其他合成纤维制男童护胸背带工装裤(带防寒衬里)〔999〕	12		130	13/	13	条/千克	A	M	/37
6203.4390 19	其他合成纤维制男童护胸背带工装裤〔999〕	12		130	13/	13	条/千克	A	M	/37
6203.4390 49	其他合成纤维制男童长裤、马裤(不带防寒衬里,含羊毛或动物细毛36%及以上)〔999〕	12		130	13/	13	条/千克	A	M	/37
6203.4390 61	其他合成纤维制男式长裤、马裤(不带防寒衬里,游戏装,含8－18号男童)〔101裤子,102童装〕	12		130	13/	13	条/千克	A	M	/37
6203.4390 69	其他合成纤维制其他男童长裤、马裤(不带防寒衬里,游戏装)〔999〕	12		130	13/	13	条/千克	A	M	/37
6203.4390 82	其他合成纤维制男童长裤、马裤(不带防寒衬里,非游戏装和滑雪裤,指8-18号男童)〔999〕	12		130	13/	13	条/千克	A	M	/37
6203.4390 89	其他合成纤维制其他男童长裤、马裤(不带防寒衬里,非游戏装和滑雪裤)〔999〕	12		130	13/	13	条/千克	A	M	/37

协定税率 %										特惠税率 %			Article Description
亚太5国	东/冰/格	巴基斯坦	韩国	瑞士	哥达	秘鲁	澳大利亚	新西/坡/智	港/澳/台	亚太2国	老/柬/缅	36/3/1	
5.2	0/0/0	8.8	7	5.3	0	0	0	0/0/0	0/0/			0/0/0	Other men's or boys' suits of synthetic fibres
													--Of other textile materials:
5.2	0/0/0	0	7	5.3	0	0	0	0/0/0	0/0/			0/0/	---Of silk or spun silk
5.2	0/0/0	0	7	8	0	0	0	0/0/0	0/0/			0/0/	---Other
													-Ensembles:
	0/0/0	0	7	5.3	0	0	0	0/0/0	0/0/			0/0/0	--Of cotton
5.2	0/0/0	8.8	7	5.3	0	0	0	0/0/0	0/0/			0/0/0	--Of synthetic fibres
													--Of other textile materials:
5.2	0/0/0	8.8	7	5.3	0	0	0	0/0/0	0/0/			0/0/	---Of silk or spun silk
5.2	0/0/0	8.8	7	5.3	0	0	0	0/0/0	0/0/			0/0/	---Of wool or fine animal hair
5.2	0/0/0	8.8	7	5.3	0	0	0	0/0/0	0/0/			0/0/	---Other
													-Jackets and blazers:
													--Of wool or fine animal hair
3.9	0/0/0	8	6.4	4.8	0	0	0	0/0/0	0/0/	3.6	0/0/0	0/0/0	Men's or boys' suit jackets and blazers, of wool or fine animal hair
3.9	0/0/0	8	6.4	4.8	0	0	0	0/0/0	0/0/	3.6	0/0/0	0/0/0	Other men's or boys' jackets and blazers, of wool or fine animal hair
													--Of cotton
3.9	0/0/0	0	6.4	4.8	0	0	0	0/0/0	0/0/	4.2	0/0/0	0/0/0	Men's or boys' jackets and blazers of cotton, industrial and career apparel
3.9	0/0/0	0	6.4	4.8	0	0	0	0/0/0	0/0/	4.2	0/0/0	0/0/0	Men's or boys' jackets and blazers of cotton
7.8	0/0/0	0	0	5.3	0	0	0	0/0/0	0/0/			0/0/0	--Of synthetic fibres
													--Of other textile materials:
													---Of silk or spun silk
3.9	0/0/0	0	6.4	4.8	0	0	0	0/0/0	0/0/	3.6		0/0/0	Men's or boys' jackets and blazers of silk, containing ≥70% by weight of silk
3.9	0/0/0	0	6.4	4.8	0	0	0	0/0/0	0/0/	3.6		0/0/0	Men's or boys' jackets and blazers of silk, containing <70% by weight of silk
3.9	0/0/0	0	6.4	4.8	0	0	0	0/0/0	0/0/	3.6		0/0/0	---Other
													-Trousers, bib and brace overalls, breeches and shorts:
													--Of wool or fine animal hair
3.9	0/0/0	0	6.4	0	0	0	0	0/0/0	0/0/	0		0/0/0	Men's trousers, breeches, including boys' No.8～No.18, of wool or fine animal hair
3.9	0/0/0	0	6.4	0	0	0	0	0/0/0	0/0/	0		0/0/0	Other boys' trousers, breeches, of wool or fine animal hair
3.9	0/0/0	0	6.4	0	0	0	0	0/0/0	0/0/	0		0/0/0	Wool other men's trousers, bib and brace overalls, breeches and shorts
													--Of cotton:
3.9	0/0/0	0	6.4	4.8	0	0	0	0/0/0	0/0/	4.2		0/0/	---Arabian trousers
													---Other
3.9	0/0/0	0	6.4	4.8	0	0	0	0/0/0	0/0/	4.2	0/0/0	0/0/0	Other boys' bib and brace overalls, with thermal lining, of cotton
3.9	0/0/0	0	6.4	4.8	0	0	0	0/0/0	0/0/	4.2	0/0/0	0/0/0	Other boys' bib and brace overalls of cotton
3.9	0/0/0	0	6.4	4.8	0	0	0	0/0/0	0/0/	4.2	0/0/0	0/0/0	Other boys' trousers, breeches, of cotton, playsuit, without thermal lining
3.9	0/0/0	0	6.4	4.8	0	0	0	0/0/0	0/0/	4.2	0/0/0	0/0/0	Men's trousers, breeches, including boys' No.8～No.18, of cotton, other than playsuit, without thermal lining
3.9	0/0/0	0	6.4	4.8	0	0	0	0/0/0	0/0/	4.2	0/0/0	0/0/0	Other boys' trousers, breeches, of cotton, other than playsuit, without thermal lining
3.9	0/0/0	0	6.4	4.8	0	0	0	0/0/0	0/0/	4.2	0/0/0	0/0/0	Other men's or boys' trousers, breeches and shorts, of cotton, knitted or crocheted
													--Of synthetic fibres:
5.2	0/0/0	8.8	7	5.3	0	0	0	0/0/0	0/0/			0/0/	---Arabian trousers
													---Other
7.8	0/0/0	0	7	5.3	0	0	0	0/0/0	0/0/			0/0/0	Other boys' bib and brace overalls, with thermal lining of synthetic fibres
7.8	0/0/0	0	7	5.3	0	0	0	0/0/0	0/0/			0/0/0	Other boys' bib and brace overalls of synthetic fibres
7.8	0/0/0	0	7	5.3	0	0	0	0/0/0	0/0/			0/0/0	Boys' trousers, breeches, containing≥36% by weight of wool or fine animal hair, without thermal lining, of synthetic fibres
7.8	0/0/0	0	7	5.3	0	0	0	0/0/0	0/0/			0/0/0	Other men's trousers, breeches, of synthetic fibres, without thermal lining, including boys' No.8～No.18, playsuit
7.8	0/0/0	0	7	5.3	0	0	0	0/0/0	0/0/			0/0/0	Other boys' trousers, breeches, playsuit, of synthetic fibres, without thermal lining
7.8	0/0/0	0	7	5.3	0	0	0	0/0/0	0/0/			0/0/0	Other men's trousers, breeches, including boys' No.8～No.18, of synthetic fibres, other than playsuit or ski trousers without thermal lining
7.8	0/0/0	0	7	5.3	0	0	0	0/0/0	0/0/			0/0/0	Other boys' trousers, breeches of synthetic fibres, other than playsuit or ski trousers without thermal lining

税则号列		货品名称〔CIQ扩展编码及品名—T2表示见附表2〕	最惠(%)	暂定税率	普通	增值/消费	出口退税	计量单位	监管条件	检验检疫	特殊证件对美关税
6203.4390	90	合纤制其他男式长裤、护胸背带工装裤、马裤及短裤〔101 裤子,102 童装〕	12		130	13/	13	条/千克			/37
		--其他纺织材料制:									
6203.4910		---阿拉伯裤〔999〕	6		100	13/	13	条/千克			/
6203.4990		---其他									
6203.4990	12	人造纤维制男童护胸背带工装裤(带防寒衬里)〔999〕	6		100	13/	13	条/千克	A	M	/31
6203.4990	19	人造纤维制男童护胸背带工装裤〔999〕	6		100	13/	13	条/千克	A	M	/31
6203.4990	90	其他材料制其他男式长裤、护胸背带工装裤、马裤及短裤〔999〕	6		100	13/	13	条/千克			/31
62.04		女式西服套装、便服套装、上衣、连衣裙、裙子、裙裤、长裤、护胸背带工装裤、马裤及短裤(游泳服除外):									
		-西服套装:									
6204.1100		--羊毛或动物细毛制〔999〕	8	5	130	13/	13	套/千克			/
6204.1200		--棉制									
6204.1200	10	含裤子的棉制女式西服套装〔999〕	8		90	13/	13	套/千克			/
6204.1200	90	不含裤子的棉制女式西服套装〔999〕	8		90	13/	13	套/千克			/
6204.1300		--合成纤维制									
6204.1300	10	合成纤维制女式西服套装(含羊毛或动物细毛36%及以上)〔999〕	8		130	13/	13	套/千克			/
6204.1300	90	其他合成纤维制女式西服套装〔999〕	8		130	13/	13	套/千克			/
		--其他纺织材料制:									
6204.1910		---丝及绢丝制〔999〕	8		100	13/	13	套/千克			/
6204.1990		---其他〔999〕	8		100	13/	13	套/千克			/
		-便服套装:									
6204.2100		--羊毛或动物细毛制〔999〕	8		130	13/	13	套/千克			/
6204.2200		--棉制〔999〕	8		90	13/	13	套/千克			/
6204.2300		--合成纤维制〔999〕	10		130	13/	13	套/千克			/40
		--其他纺织材料制:									
6204.2910		---丝及绢丝制									
6204.2910	10	丝制女式便服套装(含丝及绢丝≥70%)〔999〕	10		130	13/	13	套/千克			/
6204.2910	90	丝制其他女式便服套装(含丝及绢丝<70%)〔999〕	10		130	13/	13	套/千克			/
6204.2990		---其他〔999〕	6		100	13/	13	套/千克			/
		-上衣:									
6204.3100		--羊毛或动物细毛制〔999〕	6	5	130	13/	13	件/千克			/35
6204.3200		--棉制									
6204.3200	10	棉制女式上衣(工业及职业用)〔999〕	6		90	13/	13	件/千克			/31
6204.3200	90	棉制其他女式上衣〔999〕	6		90	13/	13	件/千克			/31
6204.3300		--合成纤维制〔999〕	12		130	13/	13	件/千克			/37
		--其他纺织材料制:									
6204.3910		---丝及绢丝制									
6204.3910	10	丝制女式上衣(含丝及绢丝70%及以上)〔999〕	6		130	13/	13	件/千克			/31
6204.3910	90	丝制其他女式上衣(含丝及绢丝70%以下)〔999〕	6		130	13/	13	件/千克			/31
6204.3990		---其他〔999〕	6		100	13/	13	件/千克			/31
		-连衣裙:									
6204.4100		--羊毛或动物细毛制〔999〕	6		130	13/	13	件/千克			/31
6204.4200		--棉制〔999〕	6		90	13/	13	件/千克			/31
6204.4300		--合成纤维制									
6204.4300	10	合成纤维制女式连衣裙(含羊毛或动物细毛≥36%)〔999〕	8		130	13/	13	件/千克			/33
6204.4300	90	合成纤维制其他女式连衣裙〔999〕	8		130	13/	13	件/千克			/33
6204.4400		--人造纤维制									
6204.4400	10	人造纤维制女式连衣裙(含羊毛或动物细毛≥36%)〔999〕	6		130	13/	13	件/千克			/31
6204.4400	90	人造纤维制其他女式连衣裙〔999〕	6		130	13/	13	件/千克			/31
		--其他纺织材料制:									
6204.4910		---丝及绢丝制									
6204.4910	10	丝制女式连衣裙(含丝及绢丝70%及以上)〔999〕	6		130	13/	13	件/千克			/31

协定税率 %										特惠税率 %			Article Description
亚太5国	东/冰/格	巴基斯坦	韩国	瑞士	哥达	秘鲁	澳大利亚	新西/坡/智	港/澳/台	亚太2国	老/柬/缅	36/3/1	
7.8	0/0/0	0	7	5.3	0	0	0	0/0/0	0/0/			0/0/0	Men's knitted or crocheted trousers breeches, bib and brace overalls of woven fabrics
													--Of other textile materials:
3.9	0/0/0	8	6.4	4.8	0	0	0	0/0/0	0/0/	0		0/0/0	---Arabian trousers
													---Other
3.9	0/0/0	0	6.4	4.8	0	0	0	0/0/0	0/0/	0		0/0/0	Boys' bib and brace overalls, with thermal lining, of artificial fibres
3.9	0/0/0	0	6.4	4.8	0	0	0	0/0/0	0/0/	0		0/0/0	Boys' bib and brace overalls, of artificial fibres
3.9	0/0/0	0	6.4	4.8	0	0	0	0/0/0	0/0/	0		0/0/0	Other men's or boys' trousers, breeches and shorts, of other textile materials
													Women's or girls' suits, ensembles, jackets, blazers, dresses, skirts, divided skirts, trousers, bib and brace overalls, breeches and shorts (other than swimwear):
													-Suits:
5.2	0/0/0	8.8	7	5.3	0	0	0	0/0/0	0/0/			0/0/	--Of wool or fine animal hair
													--Of cotton
	0/0/0	14	7	5.3	0	0	0	0/0/0	0/0/			0/0/	Women's or girls' suits, including trousers, of cotton
	0/0/0	14	7	5.3	0	0	0	0/0/0	0/0/			0/0/	Women's or girls' suits, not including trousers, of cotton
													--Of synthetic fibres
5.2	0/0/0	8.8	7	5.3	0	0	0	0/0/0	0/0/			0/0/	Women's or girls' suits, containing≥36% by weight of wool or fine animal hair, of synthetic fibres
5.2	0/0/0	8.8	7	5.3	0	0	0	0/0/0	0/0/			0/0/	Other women's or girls' suits of synthetic fibres
													--Of other textile materials:
5.2	0/0/0	8.8	7	5.3	0	0	0	0/0/0	0/0/			0/0/	---Of silk or spun silk
5.2	0/0/0	8.8	7	5.3	0	0	0	0/0/0	0/0/			0/0/	---Other
													-Ensembles:
5.2	0/0/0	8.8	7	5.3	0	0	0	0/0/0	0/0/			0/0/	--Of wool or fine animal hair
	0/0/0	0	7	5.3	0	0	0	0/0/0	0/0/			0/0/	--Of cotton
6.5	0/0/0	10	12	6	0	0	0	0/0/0	0/0/			0/0/	--Of synthetic fibres
													--Of other textile materials:
													---Of silk or spun silk
6.5	0/0/0	10	12	6	0	0	0	0/0/0	0/0/			0/0/	Women's or girls' ensembles, containing≥70% by weight of silk or spun silk
6.5	0/0/0	10	12	6	0	0	0	0/0/0	0/0/			0/0/	Women's or girls' ensembles, containing<70% by weight of silk or spun silk
3.9	0/0/0	7	5.6	4.2	0	0	0	0/0/0	0/0/			0/0/	---Other
													-Jackets and blazers:
3.9	0/0/0	8	6.4	4.8	0	0	0	0/0/0	0/0/			0/0/0	--Of wool or fine animal hair
													--Of cotton
	0/0/0	0	6.4	4.8	0	0	0	0/0/0	0/0/	2.4	0/0/0	0/0/0	Women's or girls' jackets and blazers of cotton, industrial and career apparel
	0/0/0	0	6.4	4.8	0	0	0	0/0/0	0/0/	2.4	0/0/0	0/0/0	Women's or girls' jackets and blazers of cotton
7.8	0/0/0	7	10.5	5.3	0	0	0	0/0/0	0/0/	0		0/0/0	--Of synthetic fibres
													--Of other textile materials:
													---Of silk or spun silk
3.9	0/0/0	0	6.4	4.8	0	0	0	0/0/0	0/0/	0		0/0/0	Women's or girls' jackets and blazers of silk, containing≥70% by weight of silk or spun silk
3.9	0/0/0	0	6.4	4.8	0	0	0	0/0/0	0/0/	0		0/0/0	Women's or girls' jackets and blazers of silk, containing<70% by weight of silk or spun silk
3.9	0/0/0	0	6.4	4.8	0	0	0	0/0/0	0/0/	0		0/0/0	---Other
													-Dresses:
3.9	0/0/0	8	6.4	4.8	0	0	0	0/0/0	0/0/			0/0/0	--Of wool or fine animal hair
	0/0/0	0	6.4	4.8	0	0	0	0/0/0	0/0/		0/0/0	0/0/0	--Of cotton
													--Of synthetic fibres
5.2	0/0/0	0	10.5	5.3	0	0	0	0/0/0	0/0/			0/0/0	Women's or girls' dresses of synthetic fibres, containing≥36% by weight of wool or fine animal hair
5.2	0/0/0	0	10.5	5.3	0	0	0	0/0/0	0/0/			0/0/0	Other women's or girls' dresses of synthetic fibres
													--Of artificial fibres
3.9	0/0/0	6.4	6.4	4.8	0	0	0	0/0/0	0/0/			0/0/0	Women's or girls' dresses of artificial fibres, containing≥36% by weight of wool or fine animal hair
3.9	0/0/0	6.4	6.4	4.8	0	0	0	0/0/0	0/0/			0/0/0	Other women's or girls' dresses of artificial fibres
													--Of other textile materials:
													---Of silk or spun silk
3.9	0/0/0	0	6.4	4.8	0	0	0	0/0/0	0/0/			0/0/0	Women's or girls' dresses of silk, containing≥70% by weight of silk or spun silk

税则号列		货品名称〔CIQ扩展编码及品名一T2表示见附表2〕	最惠(%)	暂定税率	普通	增值/消费	出口退税	计量单位	监管条件	检验检疫	特殊证件对美关税
6204.4910	90	丝制其他女式连衣裙(含丝及绢丝70%以下)〔999〕	6		130	13/	13	件/千克			/31
6204.4990		---其他〔999〕	6		100	13/	13	件/千克			/31
		-裙子及裙裤:									
6204.5100		--羊毛或动物细毛制〔999〕	6		130	13/	13	件/千克			/31
6204.5200		--棉制〔999〕	6		90	13/	13	件/千克			/31
6204.5300		--合成纤维制									
6204.5300	10	合成纤维制女式裙子及裙裤(含羊毛或动物细毛≥36%)〔999〕	6		130	13/	13	件/千克			/31
6204.5300	90	合成纤维制其他女式裙子及裙裤〔999〕	6		130	13/	13	件/千克			/31
		--其他纺织材料制:									
6204.5910		---丝及绢丝制									
6204.5910	10	丝制女式裙子及裙裤(含丝70%及以上)〔999〕	6		130	13/	13	件/千克			/31
6204.5910	90	其他丝制女式裙子及裙裤(含丝70%以下)〔999〕	6		130	13/	13	件/千克			/31
6204.5990		---其他〔999〕	6		100	13/	13	件/千克			/31
		-长裤、护胸背带工装裤、马裤及短裤:									
6204.6100		--羊毛或动物细毛制〔999〕	6		130	13/	13	条/千克			/31
6204.6200		--棉制〔999〕	6		90	13/	13	条/千克			/31
6204.6300		--合成纤维制〔999〕	12		130	13/	13	条/千克			/37
6204.6900		--其他纺织材料制〔999〕	6		100	13/	13	条/千克			/31
62.05		男衬衫:									
6205.2000		-棉制									
6205.2000	10	不带特制领的棉制男成人衬衫(含男童8—18号衬衫)〔101衬衫,102童装〕	6		90	13/	13	件/千克	A	M	/31
6205.2000	91	其他棉制男童游戏套装衬衫(不包括长衬衫)〔999〕	6		90	13/	13	件/千克	A	M	/31
6205.2000	99	其他棉制男式衬衫〔999〕	6		90	13/	13	件/千克			/31
6205.3000		-化学纤维制									
6205.3000	11	不带特制领的化学纤维制男式衬衫(含羊毛或动物细毛36%及以上,含男童8—18号衬衫)〔101衬衫,102童装〕	6		130	13/	13	件/千克	A	M	/31
6205.3000	19	不带特制领的化学纤维制其他男童衬衫(含羊毛或动物细毛36%及以上)〔999〕	6		130	13/	13	件/千克	A	M	/31
6205.3000	91	化学纤维制其他男成人及男童衬衫(不带特制领,男童衬衫指8—18号)〔101衬衫,102童装〕	6		130	13/	13	件/千克	A	M	/31
6205.3000	92	化学纤维制其他男童游戏套装衬衫〔999〕	6		130	13/	13	件/千克	A	M	/31
6205.3000	99	化学纤维制其他男成人衬衫〔999〕	6		130	13/	13	件/千克			/31
		-其他纺织材料制:									
6205.9010		---丝及绢丝制									
6205.9010	11	不带特制领的丝制非针织男式衬衫(含丝70%及以上,含男童8—18号衬衫)〔101衬衫,102童装〕	6		130	13/	13	件/千克	A	M	/31
6205.9010	19	丝制非针织其他男式衬衫(含丝70%及以上)〔999〕	6		130	13/	13	件/千克	A	M	/31
6205.9010	21	丝制其他非针织男式衬衫(棉限内,不带特制领的,含男童8—18号衬衫)〔101衬衫,102童装〕	6		130	13/	13	件/千克	A	M	/31
6205.9010	29	丝制其他非针织其他男式衬衫(棉限内)〔999〕	6		130	13/	13	件/千克	A	M	/31
6205.9010	31	丝制其他非针织男式衬衫(羊毛限内,不带特制领的,含男童8—18号衬衫)〔101衬衫,102童装〕	6		130	13/	13	件/千克	A	M	/31
6205.9010	39	丝制其他非针织其他男式衬衫(羊毛限内)〔999〕	6		130	13/	13	件/千克	A	M	/31
6205.9010	41	丝制非针织男式衬衫(化学纤维限内,不带特制领的,含男童8—18号衬衫)〔101衬衫,102童装〕	6		130	13/	13	件/千克	A	M	/31
6205.9010	49	丝制其他非针织其他男式衬衫(化学纤维限内)〔999〕	6		130	13/	13	件/千克	A	M	/31
6205.9010	91	未列名丝制非针织男式衬衫(含丝70%以下,不带特制领的,含男童8—18号衬衫)〔101衬衫,102童装〕	6		130	13/	13	件/千克	A	M	/31
6205.9010	99	未列名丝制非针织其他男式衬衫(含丝70%以下)〔999〕	6		130	13/	13	件/千克	A	M	/31
6205.9020		---羊毛或动物细毛制〔101衬衫,102童装〕	6		100	13/	13	件/千克	A	M	/31
6205.9090		---其他									
6205.9090	11	其他纺织材料制男式衬衫(棉限内,不带特制领的,含男童8—18号衬衫)〔101衬衫,102童装〕	6		100	13/	13	件/千克	A	M	/31

协定税率 %										特惠税率 %			Article Description
亚太5国	东/冰/格	巴基斯坦	韩国	瑞士	哥达	秘鲁	澳大利亚	新西/坡/智	港/澳/台	亚太2国	老/柬/缅	36/3/1	
3.9	0/0/0	0	6.4	4.8	0	0	0	0/0/0	0/0/			0/0/0	Other women's or girls' dresses of silk, containing<70% by weight of silk or spun silk
3.9	0/0/0	8	6.4	4.8	0	0	0	0/0/0	0/0/			0/0/0	---Other
													-Skirts and divided skirts:
3.9	0/0/0	7	5.6	4.2	0	0	0	0/0/0	0/0/			0/0/0	--Of wool or fine animal hair
	0/0/0	0	5.6	4.2	0	0	0	0/0/0	0/0/			0/0/0	--Of cotton
													--Of synthetic fibres
3.9	0/0/0	6.4	6.4	4.8	0	0	0	0/0/0	0/0/			0/0/0	Women's or girls' skirts and divided skirts, of synthetic fibres, containing≥36% by weight of wool or fine animal hair
3.9	0/0/0	6.4	6.4	4.8	0	0	0	0/0/0	0/0/			0/0/0	Women's or girls' skirts and divided skirts, of synthetic fibres
													--Of other textile materials:
													---Of silk or spun silk
3.9	0/0/0	0	5.6	4.2	0	0	0	0/0/0	0/0/			0/0/0	Women's or girls' skirts and divided skirts, containing ≥ 70% by weight of silk
3.9	0/0/0	0	5.6	4.2	0	0	0	0/0/0	0/0/			0/0/0	Women's or girls' skirts and divided skirts, containing < 70% by weight of silk
3.9	0/0/0	0	5.6	4.2	0	0	0	0/0/0	0/0/			0/0/0	---Other
													-Trousers, bib and brace overalls, breeches and shorts:
3.9	0/0/0	8	6.4	4.8	0	0	0	0/0/0	0/0/			0/0/0	--Of wool or fine animal hair
3.9	0/0/0	0	0	4.8	0	0	0	0/0/0	0/0/	4.2	0/0/0	0/0/0	--Of cotton
7.8	0/0/0	0	7	5.3	0	0	0	0/0/0	0/0/			0/0/0	--Of synthetic fibres
3.9	0/0/0	0	6.4	4.8	0	0	0	0/0/0	0/0/			0/0/0	--Of other textile materials
													Men's or boys' shirts:
													-Of cotton
3	0/0/0	0	6.4	4.8	0	0	0	0/0/0	0/0/	2.4	0/0/0	0/0/0	Men's shirts and boys' No.8～No.18, without specially made collar, of cotton
3	0/0/0	0	6.4	4.8	0	0	0	0/0/0	0/0/	2.4	0/0/0	0/0/0	Boy's shirts, playsuit, other than long shirts, of cotton
3	0/0/0	0	6.4	4.8	0	0	0	0/0/0	0/0/	2.4	0/0/0	0/0/0	Other men's or boys' shirts, of cotton
													-Of man-made fibres
3.9	0/0/0	6.4	6.4	4.8	0	0	0	0/0/0	0/0/	0		0/0/0	Men's or boys' shirts, without specially made collar, containing≥36% by weight of wool or fine animal hair, including boys' No.8～No.18, of man-made fibres
3.9	0/0/0	6.4	6.4	4.8	0	0	0	0/0/0	0/0/	0		0/0/0	Boys' shirts, without specially made collar, containing ≥ 36% by weight of wool or fine animal hair, of man-made fibres
3.9	0/0/0	6.4	6.4	4.8	0	0	0	0/0/0	0/0/	0		0/0/0	Men's or boys' shirts without specially made collar, including boys' No.8～No.18, of man-made fibres
3.9	0/0/0	6.4	6.4	4.8	0	0	0	0/0/0	0/0/	0		0/0/0	Other boy's shirts of playsuit, of man-made fibres
3.9	0/0/0	6.4	6.4	4.8	0	0	0	0/0/0	0/0/	0		0/0/0	Other men's shirts of man-made fibres
													-Of other textile materials:
													---Of silk or spun silk
3.9	0/0/0	0	6.4	4.8	0	0	0	0/0/0	0/0/	0		0/0/0	Men's or boys' shirts of silk, without specially made collar, not knitted, containing≥70% by weight of silk, including boys' No.8～No.18
3.9	0/0/0	0	6.4	4.8	0	0	0	0/0/0	0/0/	0		0/0/0	Men's or boys' shirts of silk, not knitted, containing≥70% by weight of silk
3.9	0/0/0	0	6.4	4.8	0	0	0	0/0/0	0/0/	0		0/0/0	Men's or boys' shirts of silk, not knitted, without specially made collar, including boys' No.8～No.18, cotton within limitations
3.9	0/0/0	0	6.4	4.8	0	0	0	0/0/0	0/0/	0		0/0/0	Men's or boys' shirts of silk, not knitted, cotton within limitations
3.9	0/0/0	0	6.4	4.8	0	0	0	0/0/0	0/0/	0		0/0/0	Men's or boys' shirts of silk, not knitted, without specially made collar, including boys' No.8～No.18, wool within limitations
3.9	0/0/0	0	6.4	4.8	0	0	0	0/0/0	0/0/	0		0/0/0	Men's or boys' shirts of silk, not knitted, wool within limitations
3.9	0/0/0	0	6.4	4.8	0	0	0	0/0/0	0/0/	0		0/0/0	Men's or boys' shirts of silk, not knitted, without specially made collar, including boys' No.8～No.18, man-made fibres within limitations
3.9	0/0/0	0	6.4	4.8	0	0	0	0/0/0	0/0/	0		0/0/0	Men's or boys' shirts of silk, not knitted, man-made fibres within limitations
3.9	0/0/0	0	6.4	4.8	0	0	0	0/0/0	0/0/	0		0/0/0	Men's or boys' shirts of silk, not knitted, containing<70% by weight of silk, without specially made collar, including boys' No.8～No.18, not elsewhere specified or included
3.9	0/0/0	0	6.4	4.8	0	0	0	0/0/0	0/0/	0		0/0/0	Other men's or boys' shirts of silk, not knitted, containing<70% by weight of silk, not elsewhere specified or included
3.9	0/0/0	8	6.4	4.8	0	0	0	0/0/0	0/0/	0		0/0/0	---Of wool or fine animal hair
													---Other
3.9	0/0/0	0	6.4	4.8	0	0	0	0/0/0	0/0/	0		0/0/0	Men's or boys' shirts of other textile materials, without specially made collar, including boys' No.8～No.18, cotton within limitations

税则号列		货品名称〔CIQ 扩展编码及品名—T2 表示见附表 2〕	最惠(%)	暂定税率	普通	增值/消费	出口退税	计量单位	监管条件	检验检疫	特殊证件对美关税
6205.9090	19	其他纺织材料制其他男式衬衫(棉纤限内)〔999〕	6		100	13/	13	件/千克	A	M	/31
6205.9090	21	其他纺织材料制男式衬衫(羊毛限内,不带特制领的,含男童 8—18 号衬衫)〔101 衬衫,102 童装〕	6		100	13/	13	件/千克	A	M	/31
6205.9090	29	其他纺织材料制其他男式衬衫(羊毛限内)〔999〕	6		100	13/	13	件/千克	A	M	/31
6205.9090	31	其他纺织材料制男式衬衫(化学纤维限内,不带制特领的,含男童 8—18 号衬衫)〔101 衬衫,102 童装〕	6		100	13/	13	件/千克	A	M	/31
6205.9090	39	其他纺织材料制其他男式衬衫(化学纤维限内)〔999〕	6		100	13/	13	件/千克	A	M	/31
6205.9090	91	未列名纺织材料制男式衬衫(不带特制领的,含男童 8—18 号衬衫)〔101 衬衫,102 童装〕	6		100	13/	13	件/千克	A	M	/31
6205.9090	99	未列名纺织材料制其他男式衬衫〔999〕	6		100	13/	13	件/千克	A	M	/31
62.06		女衬衫:									
6206.1000		-丝及绢丝制									
6206.1000	11	丝及绢丝制女式衬衫(棉限内,成人及 7—16 号女童衬衫)〔101 衬衫,102 童装〕	6		130	13/	13	件/千克	A	M	/31
6206.1000	19	丝及绢丝制其他女童衬衫(棉限内)〔999〕	6		130	13/	13	件/千克	A	M	/31
6206.1000	21	丝及绢丝制女式衬衫(羊毛限内,成人及 7—16 号女童衬衫)〔101 衬衫,102 童装〕	6		130	13/	13	件/千克	A	M	/31
6206.1000	29	丝及绢丝制其他女童衬衫(羊毛限内)〔999〕	6		130	13/	13	件/千克	A	M	/31
6206.1000	31	丝及绢丝制女式衬衫(化学纤维限内,成人及 7—16 号女童衬衫)〔101 衬衫,102 童装〕	6		130	13/	13	件/千克	A	M	/31
6206.1000	39	丝及绢丝制其他女童衬衫(化学纤维限内)〔999〕	6		130	13/	13	件/千克	A	M	/31
6206.1000	41	丝制女成人及 7—16 号女童衬衫(含丝 70%及以上)〔101 衬衫,102 童装〕	6		130	13/	13	件/千克	A	M	/31
6206.1000	49	其他丝及绢丝制女童衬衫(含丝 70%及以上)〔999〕	6		130	13/	13	件/千克	A	M	/31
6206.1000	91	丝制女成人及 7—16 号女童衬衫(含丝 70%以下)〔101 衬衫,102 童装〕	6		130	13/	13	件/千克	A	M	/31
6206.1000	99	其他丝及绢丝制女童衬衫(含丝 70%以下)〔999〕	6		130	13/	13	件/千克	A	M	/31
6206.2000		-羊毛或动物细毛制									
6206.2000	10	毛制女成人及 7—16 号女童衬衫〔101 衬衫,102 童装〕	6		130	13/	13	件/千克	A	M	/31
6206.2000	90	其他羊毛或动物细毛制女童衬衫〔999〕	6		130	13/	13	件/千克	A	M	/31
6206.3000		-棉制									
6206.3000	10	棉制女成人及 7—16 号女童衬衫〔101 衬衫,102 童装〕	6		90	13/	13	件/千克	A	M	/31
6206.3000	20	棉制女童游戏套装衫(含游戏套装衬衫)〔999〕	6		90	13/	13	件/千克	A	M	/31
6206.3000	90	其他棉制女式衬衫〔999〕	6		90	13/	13	件/千克	A	M	/31
6206.4000		-化学纤维制									
6206.4000	11	化学纤维制女成人及女童衬衫(含羊毛或动物细毛 36%及以上,成人及 7—16 号女童衬衫)〔101 衬衫,102 童装〕	8		130	13/	13	件/千克	A	M	/33
6206.4000	19	化学纤维制女成人及女童衬衫(含羊毛或动物细毛 36%及以上)〔101 衬衫,102 童装〕	8		130	13/	13	件/千克	A	M	/33
6206.4000	20	化学纤维制女成人及 7—16 号女童衬衫〔101 衬衫,102 童装〕	8		130	13/	13	件/千克	A	M	/33
6206.4000	30	化学纤维制女童游戏套装衫〔999〕	8		130	13/	13	件/千克	A	M	/33
6206.4000	90	其他化学纤维制女式衬衫〔999〕	8		130	13/	13	件/千克	A	M	/33
6206.9000		-其他纺织材料制									
6206.9000	10	其他纺织材料制女式衬衫(棉限内)〔999〕	6		100	13/	13	件/千克	A	M	/
6206.9000	20	其他纺织材料制女式衬衫(羊毛限内)〔999〕	6		100	13/	13	件/千克	A	M	/
6206.9000	30	其他纺织材料制女式衬衫(化学纤维限内)〔999〕	6		100	13/	13	件/千克			/
6206.9000	91	其他纺织材料制女成人及女童衬衫(女童衬衫指 7—16 号)〔101 衬衫,102 童装〕	6		100	13/	13	件/千克	A	M	/
6206.9000	99	其他纺织材料制女成人及女童衬衫〔101 衬衫,102 童装〕	6		100	13/	13	件/千克	A	M	/
62.07		男式背心及其他内衣、内裤、三角裤、长睡衣、睡衣裤、浴衣、晨衣及类似品:									
		-内裤及三角裤:									

协定税率 %										特惠税率 %			Article Description
亚太5国	东/冰/格	巴基斯坦	韩国	瑞士	哥达	秘鲁	澳大利亚	新西/坡/智	港/澳/台	亚太2国	老/柬/缅	36/3/1	
3.9	0/0/0	0	6.4	4.8	0	0	0	0/0/0	0/0/	0		0/0/0	Men's or boys' shirts of other textile materials, cotton or man-made fibres within limitations
3.9	0/0/0	0	6.4	4.8	0	0	0	0/0/0	0/0/	0		0/0/0	Men's or boys' shirts of other textile materials, without specially made collar, including boys' No.8～No.18, wool within limitations
3.9	0/0/0	0	6.4	4.8	0	0	0	0/0/0	0/0/	0		0/0/0	Men's or boys' shirts of other textile materials, wool or man-made fibres within limitations
3.9	0/0/0	0	6.4	4.8	0	0	0	0/0/0	0/0/	0		0/0/0	Men's or boys' shirts of other textile materials, without specially made collar, including boys' No.8～No.18, man-made fibres within limitations
3.9	0/0/0	0	6.4	4.8	0	0	0	0/0/0	0/0/	0		0/0/0	Men's or boys' shirts of other textile materials, man-made fibres within limitations
3.9	0/0/0	0	6.4	4.8	0	0	0	0/0/0	0/0/	0		0/0/0	Men's or boys' shirts of other textile materials, without specially-made collar, including boys' No.8～No.18, not elsewhere specified or included
3.9	0/0/0	0	6.4	4.8	0	0	0	0/0/0	0/0/	0		0/0/0	Other men's or boys' shirts of other textile materials, not elsewhere specified or included
													Women's or girls' blouses, shirts and shirt-blouses:
													-Of silk or spun silk
3.9	0/0/0	8	6.4	4.8	0	0	0	0/0/0	0/0/			0/0/0	Women's or girls' shirts of silk or spun silk, cotton within limitations, including girls' No.7～No.16
3.9	0/0/0	8	6.4	4.8	0	0	0	0/0/0	0/0/			0/0/0	Other girls' shirts of silk or spun silk, cotton within limitations
3.9	0/0/0	8	6.4	4.8	0	0	0	0/0/0	0/0/			0/0/0	Women's or girls' shirts of silk or spun silk, wool within limitations, including girls' No.7～No.16
3.9	0/0/0	8	6.4	4.8	0	0	0	0/0/0	0/0/			0/0/0	Other girls' shirts of silk and spun silk, wool within limitations
3.9	0/0/0	8	6.4	4.8	0	0	0	0/0/0	0/0/			0/0/0	Women's or girls' shirts of silk and spun silk, including girls' No.7～No.16, man-made fibres within limitations
3.9	0/0/0	8	6.4	4.8	0	0	0	0/0/0	0/0/			0/0/0	Other girls' shirts of silk and spun silk, man-made fibres within limitations
3.9	0/0/0	8	6.4	4.8	0	0	0	0/0/0	0/0/			0/0/0	Women's shirts of silk, containing≥70% by weight of silk, including girls' No.7～No.16
3.9	0/0/0	8	6.4	4.8	0	0	0	0/0/0	0/0/			0/0/0	Other girls' shirts of silk and spun silk, containing≥70% by weight of silk
3.9	0/0/0	8	6.4	4.8	0	0	0	0/0/0	0/0/			0/0/0	Women's shirts of silk, containing<70% by weight of silk, including girls' No.7～No.16
3.9	0/0/0	8	6.4	4.8	0	0	0	0/0/0	0/0/			0/0/0	Other girls' shirts of silk and spun silk, containing<70% by weight of silk
													-Of wool or fine animal hair
3.9	0/0/0	8	6.4	4.8	0	0	0	0/0/0	0/0/			0/0/	Women's and girls No.7～No.16 shirts, of wool or fine animal hair
3.9	0/0/0	8	6.4	4.8	0	0	0	0/0/0	0/0/			0/0/	Other girls' shirts of wool or fine animal hair
													-Of cotton
3.9	0/0/0	0	6.4	4.8	0	0	0	0/0/0	0/0/	2.4	0/0/0	0/0/0	Women's and girls' No.7～No.16 shirts, of cotton
3.9	0/0/0	0	6.4	4.8	0	0	0	0/0/0	0/0/	2.4	0/0/0	0/0/0	Girls' shirt of playsuit, of cotton
3.9	0/0/0	0	6.4	4.8	0	0	0	0/0/0	0/0/	2.4	0/0/0	0/0/0	Other women's or girls' shirts of cotton
													-Of man-made fibres
5.2	0/0/0	8.8	7	5.3	0	0	0	0/0/0	0/0/			0/0/0	Women's and girls' No.7～No.16 shirts, containing≥36% by weight of wool or fine animal hair, of man-made fibres
5.2	0/0/0	8.8	7	5.3	0	0	0	0/0/0	0/0/			0/0/0	Other women's or girls' shirts, containing≥36% by weight of wool or fine animal hair, of man-made fibres
5.2	0/0/0	8.8	7	5.3	0	0	0	0/0/0	0/0/			0/0/0	Women's shirts and girls' No.7～No.16, of man-made fibres
5.2	0/0/0	8.8	7	5.3	0	0	0	0/0/0	0/0/			0/0/0	Girls' shirts, playsuit, of man-made fibres
5.2	0/0/0	8.8	7	5.3	0	0	0	0/0/0	0/0/			0/0/0	Other women's or girls' shirts of man-made fibres
													-Of other textile materials
3.9	0/0/0	0	6.4	4.8	0	0	0	0/0/0	0/0/	0		0/0/0	Women's or girls' shirts of other textile materials, cotton within limitations
3.9	0/0/0	0	6.4	4.8	0	0	0	0/0/0	0/0/	0		0/0/0	Women's or girls' shirts of other textile materials, wool within limitations
3.9	0/0/0	0	6.4	4.8	0	0	0	0/0/0	0/0/	0		0/0/0	Women's or girls' shirts of other textile materials, man-made fibres within limitations
3.9	0/0/0	0	6.4	4.8	0	0	0	0/0/0	0/0/	0		0/0/0	Women's and girls' No.7～No.16, shirts of other textile materials
3.9	0/0/0	0	6.4	4.8	0	0	0	0/0/0	0/0/	0		0/0/0	Other women's or girls' shirts of other textile materials
													Men's or boys' singlets and other vests, underpants, briefs, nightshirts, pyjamas, bathrobes, dressing gowns and similar articles:
													-Underpants and briefs:

税则号列		货品名称〔CIQ 扩展编码及品名—T2 表示见附表 2〕	最惠(%)	暂定税率	普通	增值/消费	出口退税	计量单位	监管条件	检验检疫	特殊证件对美关税
6207.1100		--棉制〔999〕	6		90	13/	13	件/千克	A	M	/31
		--其他纺织材料制：									
6207.1910		---丝及绢丝制									
6207.1910	10	含丝 70%及以上男式内裤及三角裤〔999〕	6		130	13/	13	件/千克	A	M	/
6207.1910	90	含丝 70%以下男式内裤及三角裤〔999〕	6		130	13/	13	件/千克	A	M	/
6207.1920		---化学纤维制〔999〕	6		130	13/	13	件/千克	A	M	/
6207.1990		---其他									
6207.1990	10	毛制男式内裤及三角裤〔999〕	6		100	13/	13	件/千克	A	M	/
6207.1990	90	其他材料制男式内裤及三角裤〔999〕	6		100	13/	13	件/千克	A	M	/
		-长睡衣及睡衣裤：									
6207.2100		--棉制〔101 内衣，102 内裤〕	6		90	13/	13	件/千克	A	M	/31
6207.2200		--化学纤维制〔101 内衣，102 内裤〕	6		130	13/	13	件/千克	A	M	/
		--其他纺织材料制：									
6207.2910		---丝及绢丝制									
6207.2910	11	含丝 70%及以上男式长睡衣、睡衣裤(含 8－18 号男童长睡衣、睡衣裤)〔101 内衣，102 内裤，103 童装〕	6		130	13/	13	件/千克	A	M	/
6207.2910	19	含丝 70%以下男式长睡衣、睡衣裤(含 8－18 号男童长睡衣、睡衣裤)〔101 内衣，102 内裤，103 童装〕	6		130	13/	13	件/千克	A	M	/
6207.2910	91	其他含丝≥70%男童长睡衣、睡衣裤〔999〕	6		130	13/	13	件/千克	A	M	/
6207.2910	99	其他含丝＜70%男童长睡衣、睡衣裤〔999〕	6		130	13/	13	件/千克	A	M	/
6207.2990		---其他									
6207.2990	10	毛制男式长睡衣及睡衣裤〔101 内衣，102 内裤〕	6		100	13/	13	件/千克	A	M	/
6207.2990	91	其他材料制男式长睡衣及睡衣裤(含8－18 号男童长睡衣及睡衣裤)〔101 内衣，102 内裤，103 童装〕	6		100	13/	13	件/千克	A	M	/
6207.2990	99	其他材料制男童长睡衣及睡衣裤〔999〕	6		100	13/	13	件/千克	A	M	/
		-其他：									
6207.9100		--棉制									
6207.9100	11	棉制男式内衣式背心〔999〕	6		90	13/	13	件/千克	A	M	/31
6207.9100	12	棉制男式非内衣式背心(男成人及 8－18 号男童背心)〔101 内衣，102 童装〕	6		90	13/	13	件/千克	A	M	/31
6207.9100	19	棉制其他男童非内衣式背心〔999〕	6		90	13/	13	件/千克	A	M	/31
6207.9100	91	棉制男式浴衣、晨衣及类似品〔999〕	6		90	13/	13	件/千克	A	M	/31
6207.9100	92	棉制男式睡衣、睡裤(男成人及 8－18 号男童背心)〔101 内衣，102 内裤，103 童装〕	6		90	13/	13	件/千克	A	M	/31
6207.9100	99	棉制男式其他内衣(男成人及 8－18 号男童背心)〔101 内衣，102 童装〕	6		90	13/	13	件/千克	A	M	/31
		--其他纺织材料制：									
6207.9910		---丝及绢丝制									
6207.9910	11	丝制男式内衣式背心(含丝 70%及以上)〔999〕	6		130	13/	13	件/千克	A	M	/
6207.9910	19	丝制其他男式内衣式背心〔999〕	6		130	13/	13	件/千克	A	M	/
6207.9910	21	丝制男式非内衣式背心(含丝 70%及以上)〔999〕	6		130	13/	13	件/千克	A	M	/
6207.9910	29	丝制其他男式非内衣式背心〔999〕	6		130	13/	13	件/千克	A	M	/
6207.9910	91	丝制男睡衣，浴衣，晨衣及类似品(含丝 70%及以上)〔999〕	6		130	13/	13	件/千克	A	M	/
6207.9910	99	丝制其他男睡衣，浴衣，晨衣(含类似品)〔999〕	6		130	13/	13	件/千克	A	M	/
6207.9920		---化学纤维制									
6207.9920	11	化学纤维制男式内衣式背心〔999〕	6		130	13/	13	件/千克	A	M	/31
6207.9920	12	化学纤维制男式非内衣式背心(男成人及 8－18 号男童背心)〔101 童装，102 其他服装〕	6		130	13/	13	件/千克	A	M	/31
6207.9920	19	化学纤维制其他男式非内衣式背心〔999〕	6		130	13/	13	件/千克	A	M	/31
6207.9920	21	化学纤维制男式浴衣、晨衣(含羊毛或动物细毛 36%及以上，含类似品)〔999〕	6		130	13/	13	件/千克	A	M	/31
6207.9920	29	其他化学纤维制男浴衣、晨衣(含类似品)〔999〕	6		130	13/	13	件/千克	A	M	/31

协定税率 %										特惠税率 %			Article Description
亚太5国	东/冰/格	巴基斯坦	韩国	瑞士	哥达	秘鲁	澳大利亚	新西/坡/智	港/澳/台	亚太2国	老/柬/缅	36/3/1	
3.9	0/0/0	7	5.6	4.2	0	0	0	0/0/0	0/0/			0/0/0	--Of cotton
													--Of other textile materials:
													---Of silk or spun silk
	0/0/0	7	5.6	4.2	0	0	0	0/0/0	0/0/			0/0/	Men's or boys' underpants and briefs, containing≥70% by weight of silk
	0/0/0	7	5.6	4.2	0	0	0	0/0/0	0/0/			0/0/	Men's or boys' underpants and briefs, containing<70% by weight of silk
	0/0/0	12.8	6.4	4.8	0	0	0	0/0/0	0/0/			0/0/	---Of man-made fibres
													---Other
	0/0/0	7	5.6	4.2	0	0	0	0/0/0	0/0/			0/0/	Men's or boys' underpants and briefs of wool or fine animal hair
	0/0/0	7	5.6	4.2	0	0	0	0/0/0	0/0/			0/0/	Men's or boys' underpants and briefs of other textile materials
													-Nightshirts and pyjamas:
	0/0/0	11.2	5.6	4.2	0	0	0	0/0/0	0/0/		0/0/0	0/0/0	--Of cotton
	0/0/0	12.8	6.4	4.8	0	0	0	0/0/0	0/0/			0/0/	--Of man-made fibres
													--Of other textile materials:
													---Of silk or spun silk
	0/0/0	7	5.6	4.2	0	0	0	0/0/0	0/0/			0/0/	Men's nightshirts and pyjamas containing≥70% by weight of silk, including boys' No.8～No.18
	0/0/0	7	5.6	4.2	0	0	0	0/0/0	0/0/			0/0/	Men's or boys' nightshirts and pyjamas, containing<70% by weight of silk, including boys' No.8～No.18
	0/0/0	7	5.6	4.2	0	0	0	0/0/0	0/0/			0/0/	Other boys' nightshirts and pyjamas, containing≥70% by weight of silk
	0/0/0	7	5.6	4.2	0	0	0	0/0/0	0/0/			0/0/	Other boys' nightshirts and pyjamas, containing<70% by weight of silk
													---Other
	0/0/0	7	5.6	4.2	0	0	0	0/0/0	0/0/		0/0/0	0/0/0	Men's or boys' nightshirts and pyjamas, of wool or fine animal hair
	0/0/0	7	5.6	4.2	0	0	0	0/0/0	0/0/		0/0/0	0/0/0	Men's or boys' nightshirts and pyjamas, of other textile materials, including boys' No.8～No.18
	0/0/0	7	5.6	4.2	0	0	0	0/0/0	0/0/		0/0/0	0/0/0	Boys' nightshirts and pyjamas of other textile materials
													-Other:
													--Of cotton
	0/0/0	0	5.6	4.2	0	0	0	0/0/0	0/0/			0/0/0	Men's or boys' singlets, vest style, of cotton
	0/0/0	0	5.6	4.2	0	0	0	0/0/0	0/0/			0/0/0	Men's and boys' No.8～No.18 singlets, of cotton, non-vest style
	0/0/0	0	5.6	4.2	0	0	0	0/0/0	0/0/			0/0/0	Other boy's singlets of cotton, non-vests style
	0/0/0	0	5.6	4.2	0	0	0	0/0/0	0/0/			0/0/0	Men's or boys' bathrobes, dressing gowns and similar articles of cotton
	0/0/0	0	5.6	4.2	0	0	0	0/0/0	0/0/			0/0/0	Men's or boys' nightshirts and pyjamas, men's and boy's No.8～No.18 singlets, of cotton
	0/0/0	0	5.6	4.2	0	0	0	0/0/0	0/0/			0/0/0	Other men's or boys' vests, men's and boys' No.8～No.18 singlets, of cotton
													--Of other textile materials:
													---Of silk or apun silk
3.9	0/0/0	7	5.6	4.2	0	0	0	0/0/0	0/0/			0/0/	Men's or boys' singlets of silk, vest style, containing ≥ 70% by weight of silk
3.9	0/0/0	7	5.6	4.2	0	0	0	0/0/0	0/0/			0/0/	Other men's or boys' singlets of sil, vest style
3.9	0/0/0	7	5.6	4.2	0	0	0	0/0/0	0/0/			0/0/	Men's or boys' singlets of silk, non-vest style, containing≥70% by weight of silk
3.9	0/0/0	7	5.6	4.2	0	0	0	0/0/0	0/0/			0/0/	Other men's or boys' singlets of silk, non-vests style
3.9	0/0/0	7	5.6	4.2	0	0	0	0/0/0	0/0/			0/0/	Men's or boys' bathrobes, dressing gowns and similar articles, of silk, containing≥70% by weight of silk
3.9	0/0/0	7	5.6	4.2	0	0	0	0/0/0	0/0/			0/0/	Other men's or boys' pyjamas, bathrobes, dressing gowns and similar articles, of silk
													---Of man-made fibres
	0/0/0	12.8	6.4	4.8	0	0	0	0/0/0	0/0/			0/0/0	Men's or boys' singlets, vest style, of man-made fibres
	0/0/0	12.8	6.4	4.8	0	0	0	0/0/0	0/0/			0/0/0	Men's or boys' singlets, non-vests style, men's and boys' No.8～No.18 singlets, of man-made fibres
	0/0/0	12.8	6.4	4.8	0	0	0	0/0/0	0/0/			0/0/0	Other men's or boys' singlets, non-vests style, of man-made fibres
	0/0/0	12.8	6.4	4.8	0	0	0	0/0/0	0/0/			0/0/0	Men's or boys' bathrobes, dressing gowns and similar articles, containing≥36% by weight of wool or fine animal hair, of man-made fibres
	0/0/0	12.8	6.4	4.8	0	0	0	0/0/0	0/0/			0/0/0	Other men's or boys' bathrobes, dressing gowns and similar articles, of man-made fibres

税则号列		货品名称〔CIQ扩展编码及品名－T2表示见附表2〕	最惠(%)	暂定税率	普通	增值/消费	出口退税	计量单位	监管条件	检验检疫	特殊证件对美关税
6207.9920	91	化学纤维制男睡衣、睡裤(含类似品)〔101内衣,102内裤〕	6		130	13/	13	件/千克	A	M	/31
6207.9920	99	化学纤维制男式其他内衣(含类似品)〔999〕	6		130	13/	13	件/千克	A	M	/31
6207.9990		---其他									
6207.9990	11	毛制男式内衣式背心〔999〕	6		100	13/	13	件/千克	A	M	/
6207.9990	12	毛制男式非内衣式背心(男成人及8－18号男童背心)〔101内衣,102童装〕	6		100	13/	13	件/千克	A	M	/
6207.9990	13	毛制其他男式非内衣式背心〔999〕	6		100	13/	13	件/千克	A	M	/
6207.9990	19	毛制男睡衣,浴衣,晨衣及类似品〔999〕	6		100	13/	13	件/千克	A	M	/
6207.9990	91	其他材料制男式内衣式背心〔999〕	6		100	13/	13	件/千克	A	M	/
6207.9990	92	其他材料制男式非内衣式背心〔999〕	6		100	13/	13	件/千克	A	M	/
6207.9990	99	其他材料制男睡衣、浴衣、晨衣(含类似品)〔999〕	6		100	13/	13	件/千克	A	M	/
62.08		**女式背心及其他内衣、长衬裙、衬裙、三角裤、短衬裤、睡衣、睡衣裤、浴衣、晨衣及类似品:**									
		-长衬裙及衬裙:									
6208.1100		--化学纤维制〔999〕	6		130	13/	13	件/千克			/31
		--其他纺织材料制:									
6208.1910		---丝及绢丝制〔101裙子,102童装〕	6		130	13/	13	件/千克			/
6208.1920		---棉制〔999〕	6		90	13/	13	件/千克			/
6208.1990		---其他									
6208.1990	10	毛制女式长衬裙及衬裙〔999〕	6		100	13/	13	件/千克			/
6208.1990	90	其他材料制女式长衬裙及衬裙〔999〕	6		100	13/	13	件/千克			/
		-睡衣及睡衣裤:									
6208.2100		--棉制〔101内衣,102内裤〕	6		90	13/	13	件/千克	A	M	/31
6208.2200		--化学纤维制〔101内衣,102内裤〕	6		130	13/	13	件/千克	A	M	/31
		--其他纺织材料制:									
6208.2910		---丝及绢丝制									
6208.2910	10	丝及绢丝≥70%女式睡衣及睡衣裤〔101内衣,102内裤〕	6		130	13/	13	件/千克	A	M	/31
6208.2910	90	丝及绢丝<70%女式睡衣及睡衣裤〔101内衣,102内裤〕	6		130	13/	13	件/千克	A	M	/31
6208.2990		---其他									
6208.2990	10	毛制女式睡衣及睡衣裤〔101内衣,102内裤〕	6		100	13/	13	件/千克	A	M	/
6208.2990	90	其他材料制女式睡衣及睡衣裤〔101内衣,102内裤〕	6		100	13/	13	件/千克	A	M	/
		-其他:									
6208.9100		--棉制									
6208.9100	10	棉制女式内衣式背心、三角裤等(包括短衬裤)〔101内衣,102内裤〕	6		90	13/	13	件/千克	A	M	/31
6208.9100	21	棉制女式非内衣式背心(女成人及7－16号女童背心)〔101内衣,102童装〕	6		90	13/	13	件/千克	A	M	/31
6208.9100	29	棉制其他女式非内衣式背心〔999〕	6		90	13/	13	件/千克	A	M	/31
6208.9100	90	棉制女式浴衣、晨衣及类似品〔999〕	6		90	13/	13	件/千克	A	M	/31
6208.9200		--化学纤维制									
6208.9200	10	化学纤维制女式内衣式背心、三角裤(含短衬裤)〔101内衣,102内裤〕	6		130	13/	13	件/千克	A	M	/31
6208.9200	21	化学纤维制女式非内衣式背心(女成人及7－16号女童背心)〔101内衣,102童装〕	6		130	13/	13	件/千克	A	M	/31
6208.9200	29	化学纤维制其他女式非内衣式背心〔999〕	6		130	13/	13	件/千克	A	M	/31
6208.9200	90	化学纤维制女式浴衣、晨衣及类似品〔999〕	6		130	13/	13	件/千克	A	M	/31
		--其他纺织材料制:									
6208.9910		---丝及绢丝制									
6208.9910	11	丝制女内衣式背心、三角裤等(含丝及绢丝≥70%,包括短衬裤)〔101内衣,102内裤〕	6		130	13/	13	件/千克	A	M	/
6208.9910	19	丝制女内衣式背心、三角裤等(含丝及绢丝<70%,包括短衬裤)〔101内衣,102内裤〕	6		130	13/	13	件/千克	A	M	/
6208.9910	21	丝制女式非内衣式背心(含丝及绢丝70%及以上)〔999〕	6		130	13/	13	件/千克	A	M	/

协定税率 %										特惠税率 %			Article Description
亚太5国	东/冰/格	巴基斯坦	韩国	瑞士	哥达	秘鲁	澳大利亚	新西/坡/智	港/澳/台	亚太2国	老/柬/缅	36/3/1	
	0/0/0	12.8	6.4	4.8	0	0	0	0/0/0	0/0/			0/0/0	Men's or boys' nightshirts, pyjamas and similar articles, of man-made fibres
	0/0/0	12.8	6.4	4.8	0	0	0	0/0/0	0/0/			0/0/0	Other men's or boys' vest and similar articles of man-made fibres
													---Other
3.9	0/0/0	7	5.6	4.2	0	0	0	0/0/0	0/0/			0/0/0	Men's or boys' singlets, vests style, of wool or fine animal hair
3.9	0/0/0	7	5.6	4.2	0	0	0	0/0/0	0/0/			0/0/0	Men's or boys' singlets, non-vests style, (men's and boys' No.8～No.18), of wool or fine animal hair
3.9	0/0/0	7	5.6	4.2	0	0	0	0/0/0	0/0/			0/0/0	Other men's or boys' singlets, non-vests style, of wool or fine animal hair
3.9	0/0/0	7	5.6	4.2	0	0	0	0/0/0	0/0/			0/0/0	Men's or boys' bathrobes, dressing gowns and similar articles, of wool or fine animal hair
3.9	0/0/0	7	5.6	4.2	0	0	0	0/0/0	0/0/			0/0/0	Men's or boys' singlets, vests style, of other textile materials
3.9	0/0/0	7	5.6	4.2	0	0	0	0/0/0	0/0/			0/0/0	Men's or boys' singlets, non-vests style, of other textile materials
3.9	0/0/0	7	5.6	4.2	0	0	0	0/0/0	0/0/			0/0/0	Other men's or boys' bathrobes, dressing gowns and similar articles, of other textile materials
													Women's or girls' singlets and other vests, slips, petticoats, briefs, panties, night-dresses, pyjamas, nègligès, bathrobes, dressing gowns and similar articles:
													-Slips and petticoats:
	0/0/0	12.8	6.4	4.8	0	0	0	0/0/0	0/0/			0/0/	--Of man-made fibres
													--Of other textile materials:
4.2	0/0/0	7	5.6	4.2	0	0	0	0/0/0	0/0/			0/0/	---Of silk or spun silk
	0/0/0	7	5.6	4.2	0	0	0	0/0/0	0/0/			0/0/0	---Of cotton
													---Other
	0/0/0	7	5.6	4.2	0	0	0	0/0/0	0/0/			0/0/	Women's or girls' slips and petticoats of wool or fine animal hair
	0/0/0	7	5.6	4.2	0	0	0	0/0/0	0/0/			0/0/	Women's or girls' slips and petticoats of other textile materials
													-Nightdresses and pyjamas:
3.9	0/0/0	5.6	5.6	4.2	0	0	0	0/0/0	0/0/		0/0/0	0/0/0	--Of cotton
	0/0/0	12.8	6.4	4.8	0	0	0	0/0/0	0/0/		0/0/0	0/0/0	--Of man-made fibres
													--Of other textile materials:
													---Of silk or spun silk
	0/0/0	7	5.6	4.2	0	0	0	0/0/0	0/0/			0/0/	Women's or girls' night-dresses and pyjamas, containing≥70% by weight of silk or spun silk
	0/0/0	7	5.6	4.2	0	0	0	0/0/0	0/0/			0/0/	Women's or girls' night-dresses and pyjamas, containing<70% by weight of silk or spun silk
													---Other
	0/0/0	7	5.6	4.2	0	0	0	0/0/0	0/0/			0/0/	Women's or girls' night-dresses and pyjamas, of wool or fine animal hair
	0/0/0	7	5.6	4.2	0	0	0	0/0/0	0/0/			0/0/	Women's or girls' nightdresses and pyjamas of other textile materials
													-Other:
													--Of cotton
	0/0/0	0	5.6	4.2	0	0	0	0/0/0	0/0/		0/0/0	0/0/0	Women's or girls' singlets, briefs, panties, vest style, of cotton
	0/0/0	0	5.6	4.2	0	0	0	0/0/0	0/0/		0/0/0	0/0/0	Women's or girls' singlets, non-vest style, (women's and girls No.7～No.16) of cotton
	0/0/0	0	5.6	4.2	0	0	0	0/0/0	0/0/		0/0/0	0/0/0	Other women's or girls' singlets, non-vest style, of cotton
	0/0/0	0	5.6	4.2	0	0	0	0/0/0	0/0/		0/0/0	0/0/0	Women's or girls' bathrobes, dressing gowns and similar articles, of cotton
													--Of man-made fibres
	0/0/0	12.8	6.4	4.8	0	0	0	0/0/0	0/0/0		0/0/0	0/0/0	Women's or girls' singlets, vest style, briefs, panties, of man-made fibres
	0/0/0	12.8	6.4	4.8	0	0	0	0/0/0	0/0/0		0/0/0	0/0/0	Women's or girls' singlets, non-vest style (women's and girls No.7～No.16), of man-made fibres
	0/0/0	12.8	6.4	4.8	0	0	0	0/0/0	0/0/0		0/0/0	0/0/0	Other women's or girls' singlets, non-vest style, of man-made fibres
	0/0/0	12.8	6.4	4.8	0	0	0	0/0/0	0/0/0		0/0/0	0/0/0	Women's or girls' bathrobes, dressing gowns and similar articles, of man-made fibres
													--Of other textile materials:
													---Of silk or spun silk
3.9	0/0/0	7	5.6	4.2	0	0	0	0/0/0	0/0/			0/0/	Women's or girls' singlets, vest style briefs, panties of silk, containing≥70% by weight of silk or spun silk
3.9	0/0/0	7	5.6	4.2	0	0	0	0/0/0	0/0/			0/0/	Women's or girls' singlets, vest style briefs, panties of silk, containing<70% by weight of silk or spun silk
3.9	0/0/0	7	5.6	4.2	0	0	0	0/0/0	0/0/			0/0/	Women's or girls' singlets of silk, non-vest style, containing≥70% by weight of silk or spun silk

税则号列		货品名称〔CIQ 扩展编码及品名－T2 表示见附表 2〕	最惠(%)	暂定税率	普通	增值/消费	出口退税	计量单位	监管条件	检验检疫	特殊证件对美关税
6208.9910	29	丝制女式非内衣式背心(含丝 70%以下)〔999〕	6		130	13/	13	件/千克	A	M	/
6208.9910	91	丝制女式浴衣、晨衣及类似品(含丝及绢丝 70%及以上)〔999〕	6		130	13/	13	件/千克	A	M	/
6208.9910	99	丝制女式浴衣、晨衣及类似品(含丝及绢丝 70%以下)〔999〕	6		130	13/	13	件/千克	A	M	/
6208.9990		---其他									
6208.9990	11	毛制女式内衣式背心、三角裤等(包括短衬裤)〔101 内衣,102 内裤〕	6		100	13/	13	件/千克	A	M	/31
6208.9990	12	毛制女式非内衣式背心(女成人及 7－16 号女童背心)〔101 内衣,102 童装〕	6		100	13/	13	件/千克	A	M	/31
6208.9990	13	毛制其他女式非内衣式背心〔999〕	6		100	13/	13	件/千克	A	M	/31
6208.9990	19	毛制女式浴衣、晨衣及类似品〔999〕	6		100	13/	13	件/千克	A	M	/31
6208.9990	90	其他材料制女式背心、三角裤、短衬裤、浴衣、晨衣及类似品〔101 内衣,102 内裤〕	6		100	13/	13	件/千克	A	M	/31
62.09		**婴儿服装及衣着附件:**									
6209.2000		-棉制〔999〕	10		90	13/	13	千克	A	M	/35
6209.3000		-合成纤维制									
6209.3000	10	合成纤维制婴儿手套、袜子(含分指、连指及露指手套,长袜、短袜及其他袜)〔999〕	10		130	13/	13	千克	A	M	/35
6209.3000	20	合成纤维婴儿外衣、雨衣、滑雪装(包括夹克类似服装)〔999〕	10		130	13/	13	千克	A	M	/35
6209.3000	30	合成纤维制婴儿其他服装(含裤子、衬衫、裙子、睡衣、内衣等)〔999〕	10		130	13/	13	千克	A	M	/35
6209.3000	90	合成纤维制婴儿衣着附件〔999〕	10		130	13/	13	千克	A	M	/35
		-其他纺织材料制:									
6209.9010		---羊毛或动物细毛制〔999〕	10		130	13/	13	千克	A	M	/
6209.9090		---其他纺织材料制〔999〕	10		100	13/	13	千克	A	M	/
62.10		**用税目 56.02、56.03、59.03、59.06 或 59.07 的织物制成的服装:**									
		-用税目 56.02 或 56.03 的织物制成的服装:									
6210.1010		---羊毛或动物细毛制〔999〕	6		130	13/	13	件/千克			/
6210.1020		---棉或麻制〔999〕	6		90	13/	13	件/千克			/31
6210.1030		---化学纤维制〔999〕	8		130	13/	13	件/千克			/38
6210.1090		---其他纺织材料制〔999〕	6		100	13/	13	件/千克			/16
6210.2000		-子目号 6201.11 至 6201.19 所列类型的其他服装〔999〕	6		100	13/	13	件/千克			/31
6210.3000		-子目号 6202.11 至 6202.19 所列类型的其他服装〔999〕	6		100	13/	13	件/千克			/
6210.4000		-其他男式服装〔999〕	6		100	13/	13	件/千克			/31
6210.5000		-其他女式服装〔999〕	6		100	13/	13	件/千克			/31
62.11		**运动服、滑雪服及游泳服;其他服装:**									
		-游泳服:									
6211.1100		--男式									
6211.1100	10	羊毛或动物细毛制男式游泳服〔999〕	6		130	13/	13	件/千克			/31
6211.1100	41	丝制男式游泳服(含丝 70%及以上)〔999〕	6		130	13/	13	件/千克			/31
6211.1100	49	丝制男式游泳服(含丝 70%以下)〔999〕	6		130	13/	13	件/千克			/31
6211.1100	90	其他纺织材料制男式游泳服〔999〕	6		130	13/	13	件/千克			/31
6211.1200		--女式									
6211.1200	10	羊毛或动物细毛制女式游泳服〔999〕	6		130	13/	13	件/千克			/31
6211.1200	41	丝制女式游泳服(含丝 70%及以上)〔999〕	6		130	13/	13	件/千克			/31
6211.1200	49	丝制女式游泳服(含丝 70%以下)〔999〕	6		130	13/	13	件/千克			/31
6211.1200	90	其他纺织材料制女式游泳服〔999〕	6		130	13/	13	件/千克			/31
		-滑雪服:									
6211.2010		---棉制〔999〕	6		90	13/	13	套/千克			/
6211.2090		---其他纺织材料制〔999〕	10		130	13/	13	套/千克			/35
		-其他男式服装:									
		--棉制:									
6211.3210		---阿拉伯袍〔999〕	6		90	13/	13	件/千克			/
6211.3220		---运动服〔999〕	6		90	13/	13	套/千克			/31

协定税率 %										特惠税率 %			Article Description
亚太5国	东/冰/格	巴基斯坦	韩国	瑞士	哥达	秘鲁	澳大利亚	新西/坡/智	港/澳/台	亚太2国	老/柬/缅	36/3/1	
3.9	0/0/0	7	5.6	4.2	0	0	0	0/0/0	0/0/			0/0/	Women's or girls' singlets of silk, non-vest style, containing<70% by weight of silk or spun silk
3.9	0/0/0	7	5.6	4.2	0	0	0	0/0/0	0/0/			0/0/	Women's or girls' bathrobes, dressing gowns and similar articles of silk, containing≥70% by weight of silk or spun silk
3.9	0/0/0	7	5.6	4.2	0	0	0	0/0/0	0/0/			0/0/	Women's or girls' bathrobes, dressing gowns and similar articles, of silk, containing<70% by weight of silk or spun silk
													---Other
3.9	0/0/0	7	5.6	4.2	0	0	0	0/0/0	0/0/			0/0/0	Women's or girls' singlets, vest style briefs, panties, of wool or fine animal hair
3.9	0/0/0	7	5.6	4.2	0	0	0	0/0/0	0/0/			0/0/0	Women's and girls' No. 7－No. 16 singlets, non-vest style, of wool or fine animal hair
3.9	0/0/0	7	5.6	4.2	0	0	0	0/0/0	0/0/			0/0/0	Other women's or girls' singlets, non-vest style, of wool or fine animal hair
3.9	0/0/0	7	5.6	4.2	0	0	0	0/0/0	0/0/			0/0/0	Women's or girls' bathrobes, dressing gowns and similar articles, of wool or fine animal hair
3.9	0/0/0	7	5.6	4.2	0	0	0	0/0/0	0/0/			0/0/0	Women's or girls' singlets, vest style briefs, panties, other textile materials
													Babies' garments and clothing accessories:
	0/0/0	0	5.6	4.2	0	0	0	0/0/0	0/0/			0/0/0	-Of cotton
													-Of synthetic fibres
	0/0/0	0	6.4	4.8	0	0	0	0/0/0	0/0/			0/0/0	Babies' gloves, mittens, mitts, stockings, socks and similar articles, of synthetic fibres
	0/0/0	0	6.4	4.8	0	0	0	0/0/0	0/0/			0/0/0	Babies' coats, raincoats, ski-suits, jackets and similar articles, of synthetic fibres
	0/0/0	0	6.4	4.8	0	0	0	0/0/0	0/0/			0/0/0	Babies' other garments, including trousers, shirt, skirt, night clothes, underwear, of synthetic fibres
	0/0/0	0	6.4	4.8	0	0	0	0/0/0	0/0/			0/0/0	Babies' clothing accessories, of synthetic fibres
													-Of other textile materials:
	0/0/0	7	5.6	4.2	0	0	0	0/0/0	0/0/			0/0/	---Of wool or fine animal hair
	0/0/0	5.6	5.6	4.2	0	0	0	0/0/0	0/0/			0/0/	---Other textile materials
													Garments, made up of fabrics of heading No. 56. 02, 56. 03, 59. 03, 59. 06 or 59. 07:
													-Of fabrics of heading No.56. 02 or 56. 03:
3.9	0/0/0	8	6.4	4.8	0	0	0	0/0/0	0/0/	0		0/0/0	---Of wool or fine animal hair
	0/0/0	12.8	6.4	4.8	0	0	0	0/0/0	0/0/	2.4		0/0/	---Of cotton or bast fibres
5.2	0/0/0	8.8	7	5.3	0	0	0	0/0/0	0/0/	0		0/0/0	---Of man-made fibres
	0/0/0	12.8	6.4	4.8	0	0	0	0/0/0	0/0/	0		0/0/0	---Of other textile materials
3.9	0/0/0	8	6.4	4.8	0	0	0	0/0/0	0/0/	0		0/0/0	-Other garments, made up of the type described in subheadings No. 6201. 11 to 6201. 19
3.9	0/0/0	8	6.4	4.8	0	0	0	0/0/0	0/0/			0/0/0	-Other garments, of the type described in subheadings No.6202. 11 to 6202. 19
3.9	0/0/0	0	6.4	4.8	0	0	0	0/0/0	0/0/	0		0/0/0	-Other men's or boys' garments
3.9	0/0/0	6.4	6.4	4.8	0	0	0	0/0/0	0/0/	0		0/0/0	-Other women's or girls' garments
													Track suits, ski suits and swimwear; other garments:
													-Swimwear:
													--Men's or boys'
3.9	0/0/0	8	6.4	4.8	0	0	0	0/0/0	0/0/			0/0/	Men's or boys' swimwear of wool or fine animal hair
3.9	0/0/0	8	6.4	4.8	0	0	0	0/0/0	0/0/			0/0/	Men's or boys' swimwear of silk, containing≥70% by weight of silk
3.9	0/0/0	8	6.4	4.8	0	0	0	0/0/0	0/0/			0/0/	Men's or boys' swimwear of silk, containing<70% by weight of silk
3.9	0/0/0	8	6.4	4.8	0	0	0	0/0/0	0/0/			0/0/	Men's or boys' swimwear of other textile materials
													--Women's or girls'
3.9	0/0/0	8	6.4	4.8	0	0	0	0/0/0	0/0/			0/0/0	Women's or girls' swimwear of wool or fine animal hair
3.9	0/0/0	8	6.4	4.8	0	0	0	0/0/0	0/0/			0/0/0	Women's or girls' swimwear of silk, containing≥70% by weight of silk
3.9	0/0/0	8	6.4	4.8	0	0	0	0/0/0	0/0/			0/0/0	Women's or girls' swimwear of silk, containing<70% by weight of silk
3.9	0/0/0	8	6.4	4.8	0	0	0	0/0/0	0/0/			0/0/0	Women's or girls' swimwear of other textile materials
													-Ski suits:
	0/0/0	12.8	6.4	4.8	0	0	0	0/0/0	0/0/			0/0/0	---Of cotton
6.5	0/0/0	9.5	7.6	5.7	0	0	0	0/0/0	0/0/			0/0/	---Of other textile materials
													-Other garments, men's or boys':
													--Of cotton:
	0/0/0	12.8	6.4	4.8	0	0	0	0/0/0	0/0/			0/0/	---Arabian robes
	0/0/0	0	6.4	4.8	0	0	0	0/0/0	0/0/			0/0/0	--- Track suits

税则号列	货品名称〔CIQ扩展编码及品名—T2表示见附表2〕	最惠(%)	暂定税率	普通	增值/消费	出口退税	计量单位	监管条件	检验检疫	特殊证件对美关税
6211.3290	---其他〔101 大衣、短大衣,102 上衣,103 裤子,104 衬衫,105 童装,106 其他梭织服装〕	6		90	13/	13	件/千克			/36
	--化学纤维制:									
6211.3310	---阿拉伯袍〔999〕	8		130	13/	13	件/千克			/33
6211.3320	---运动服〔999〕	8		130	13/	13	套/千克			/33
6211.3390	---其他〔101 大衣、短大衣,102 上衣,103 衬衫,104 童装,105 其他梭织服装〕	8		130	13/	13	件/千克			/33
	--其他纺织材料制:									
6211.3910	---丝及绢丝制〔101 大衣、短大衣,102 上衣,103 裤子,104 运动服,105 其他梭织服装〕	6		130	13/	13	件/千克			/
6211.3920	---羊毛或动物细毛制〔999〕	6		130	13/	13	件/千克			/31
6211.3990	---其他〔101 大衣、短大衣,102 上衣,103 裤子,104 运动服,105 其他梭织服装〕	6		100	13/	13	件/千克			/31
	-其他女式服装:									
	--棉制:									
6211.4210	---运动服〔999〕	6		90	13/	13	套/千克			/31
6211.4290	---其他〔999〕	6		90	13/	13	件/千克			/31
	--化学纤维制:									
6211.4310	---运动服〔999〕	8		130	13/	13	套/千克			/33
6211.4390	---其他〔999〕	8		130	13/	13	件/千克			/33
	--其他纺织材料制:									
6211.4910	---丝及绢丝制〔101 大衣、短大衣,102 上衣,103 裤子,104 运动服,105 其他梭织服装〕	6		130	13/	13	件/千克			/31
6211.4990	---其他〔101 运动服,102 其他梭织服装,103 其他服装〕	6		100	13/	13	件/千克			/31
62.12	**胸罩、束腰带、紧身胸衣、吊裤带、吊袜带、束袜带和类似品及其零件,不论是否针织或钩编的:**									
	-胸罩:									
6212.1010	---化学纤维制〔999〕	6		130	13/	13	件/千克	A	M	/31
6212.1090	---其他纺织材料制									
6212.1090 10	毛制其他胸罩(不论是否针织或钩编)〔999〕	6		100	13/	13	件/千克	A	M	/31
6212.1090 20	棉制其他胸罩(不论是否针织或钩编)〔999〕	6		100	13/	13	件/千克	A	M	/31
6212.1090 31	丝制胸罩(不论是否针织或钩编,含丝70%及以上)〔999〕	6		100	13/	13	件/千克	A	M	/31
6212.1090 39	丝制其他胸罩(不论是否针织或钩编,含丝70%以下)〔999〕	6		100	13/	13	件/千克	A	M	/31
6212.1090 90	其他纺织材料制其他胸罩(不论是否针织或钩编)〔999〕	6		100	13/	13	件/千克	A	M	/31
	-束腰带及腹带:									
6212.2010	---化学纤维制〔999〕	6		130	13/	13	件/千克	A	M	/31
6212.2090	---其他纺织材料制									
6212.2090 10	毛制束胸带及腹带(不论是否针织或钩编)〔999〕	6		100	13/	13	件/千克	A	M	/31
6212.2090 20	棉制束腰带及腹带(不论是否针织或钩编)〔999〕	6		100	13/	13	件/千克	A	M	/31
6212.2090 31	丝制束腰带及腹带(不论是否针织或钩编,含丝70%及以上)〔999〕	6		100	13/	13	件/千克	A	M	/31
6212.2090 39	丝制束腰带及腹带(不论是否针织或钩编,含丝70%以下)〔999〕	6		100	13/	13	件/千克	A	M	/31
6212.2090 90	其他材料制束胸带及腹带(不论是否针织或钩编)〔999〕	6		100	13/	13	件/千克	A	M	/31
	-束腰胸衣:									
6212.3010	---化学纤维制〔999〕	6		130	13/	13	件/千克	A	M	/31
6212.3090	---其他纺织材料制									
6212.3090 10	毛制紧身胸衣(不论是否针织或钩编)〔999〕	6		100	13/	13	件/千克	A	M	/31
6212.3090 20	棉制紧身胸衣(不论是否针织或钩编)〔999〕	6		100	13/	13	件/千克	A	M	/31
6212.3090 31	丝制紧身胸衣(不论是否针织或钩编,含丝70%及以上)〔999〕	6		100	13/	13	件/千克	A	M	/31
6212.3090 39	丝制其他紧身胸衣(不论是否针织或钩编,含丝70%以下)〔999〕	6		100	13/	13	件/千克	A	M	/31
6212.3090 90	其他材料制紧身胸衣(不论是否针织或钩编)〔999〕	6		100	13/	13	件/千克	A	M	/31
	-其他:									
6212.9010	---化学纤维制〔999〕	6		130	13/	13	件/千克			/31

协定税率 %										特惠税率 %			Article Description
亚太5国	东/冰/格	巴基斯坦	韩国	瑞士	哥达	秘鲁	澳大利亚	新西/坡/智	港/澳/台	亚太2国	老/柬/缅	36/3/1	
	0/0/0	0	6.4	4.8	0	0	0	0/0/0	0/0/			0/0/0	---Other
													--Of man-made fibres:
5.2	0/0/0	8.8	7	5.3	0	0	0	0/0/0	0/0/			0/0/	---Arabian robes
5.2	0/0/0	0	7.2	5.4	0	0	0	0/0/0	0/0/			0/0/0	---Track suits
5.2	0/0/0	0	7	5.3	0	0	0	0/0/0	0/0/			0/0/0	---Other
													--Of other textile materials:
3.9	0/0/0	8	6.4	4.8	0	0	0	0/0/0	0/0/			0/0/	---Of silk or spun silk
3.9	0/0/0	8	6.4	4.8	0	0	0	0/0/0	0/0/			0/0/	--Of wool or fine animal hair
3.9	0/0/0	6.4	6.4	4.8	0	0	0	0/0/0	0/0/			0/0/	---Other
													-Other garments, women's or girls':
													--Of cotton:
	0/0/0	12.8	6.4	4.8	0	0	0	0/0/0	0/0/			0/0/0	--- Track suits
	0/0/0	12.8	6.4	4.8	0	0	0	0/0/0	0/0/			0/0/0	---Other
													—Of man-made fibres:
5.2	0/0/0	8.8	7	5.3	0	0	0	0/0/0	0/0/			0/0/0	---Track suits
5.2	0/0/0	7	7	5.3	0	0	0	0/0/0	0/0/			0/0/0	---Other
													--Of other textile materials:
3.9	0/0/0	0	6.4	4.8	0	0	0	0/0/0	0/0/			0/0/	---Of silk or spun silk
3.9	0/0/0	0	6.4	4.8	0	0	0	0/0/0	0/0/			0/0/0	---Other
													Brassières, girdles, corsets, braces, suspenders, garters and similar articles and parts thereof, whether or not knitted or crocheted:
													-Brassières:
3.9	0/0/0	12.8	6.4	4.8	0	0	0	0/0/0	0/0/0		0/0/0	0/0/0	---Of man-made fibres
													---Of other textile materials
3.9	0/0/0	7	5.6	4.2	0	0	0	0/0/0	0/0/0			0/0/0	Brassieres of wool or fine animal hair(whether or not knitted or crocheted)
3.9	0/0/0	7	5.6	4.2	0	0	0	0/0/0	0/0/0			0/0/0	Brassières, whether or not knitted or crocheted, of cotton
3.9	0/0/0	7	5.6	4.2	0	0	0	0/0/0	0/0/0			0/0/0	Brassieres of silk, whether or not knitted or crocheted, containing≥70% by weight of silk
3.9	0/0/0	7	5.6	4.2	0	0	0	0/0/0	0/0/0			0/0/0	Brassières of silk, whether or not knitted or crocheted, containing<70% by weight of silk
3.9	0/0/0	7	5.6	4.2	0	0	0	0/0/0	0/0/0			0/0/0	Brassières, whether or not knitted or crocheted, of other textile materials
													-Girdles and panty-girdles:
	0/0/0	12.8	6.4	4.8	0	0	0	0/0/0	0/0/0			0/0/	---Of man-made fibres
													---Of other textile materials
	0/0/0	11.2	5.6	4.2	0	0	0	0/0/0	0/0/0			0/0/0	Girdles and panty-girdles, whether or not knitted or crocheted, of wool or fine animal hair
	0/0/0	11.2	5.6	4.2	0	0	0	0/0/0	0/0/0			0/0/0	Girdles and panty-girdles of cotton, whether or not knitted or crocheted
	0/0/0	11.2	5.6	4.2	0	0	0	0/0/0	0/0/0			0/0/0	Girdles and panty-girdles of silk, whether or not knitted or crocheted, containing≥70% by weight of silk
	0/0/0	11.2	5.6	4.2	0	0	0	0/0/0	0/0/0			0/0/0	Girdles and panty-girdles of silk, whether or not knitted or crocheted, containing<70% by weight of silk
	0/0/0	11.2	5.6	4.2	0	0	0	0/0/0	0/0/0			0/0/0	Girdles and panty-girdles, whether or not knitted or crocheted, of other textile materials
													-Corselettes:
	0/0/0	12.8	6.4	4.8	0	0	0	0/0/0	0/0/			0/0/	---Of man-made fibres
													---Of other textile materials
	0/0/0	7	5.6	4.2	0	0	0	0/0/0	0/0/			0/0/0	Croselettes, of wool or fine animal hair
	0/0/0	7	5.6	4.2	0	0	0	0/0/0	0/0/			0/0/0	Croselettes, whether or not knitted or crocheted, of cotton
	0/0/0	7	5.6	4.2	0	0	0	0/0/0	0/0/			0/0/0	Croselettes of silk, whether or not knitted or crocheted, containing≥70% by weight of silk
	0/0/0	7	5.6	4.2	0	0	0	0/0/0	0/0/			0/0/0	Croselettes of silk, whether or not knitted or crocheted, containing<70% by weight of silk
	0/0/0	7	5.6	4.2	0	0	0	0/0/0	0/0/			0/0/0	Croselettes of other textile materials, whether or not knitted or crocheted
													-Other:
3.9	0/0/0	12.8	6.4	4.8	0	0	0	0/0/0	0/0/0			0/0/	---Of man-made fibres

税则号列		货品名称〔CIQ 扩展编码及品名－T2 表示见附表 2〕	最惠(%)	暂定税率	普通	增值/消费	出口退税	计量单位	监管条件	检验检疫	特殊证件对美关税
6212.9090		---其他纺织材料制〔999〕	6		100	13/	13	件/千克			/
62.13		**手帕：**									
		-棉制：									
6213.2010		---刺绣的〔999〕	6		90	13/	13	条/千克			/
6213.2090		---其他〔999〕	6		90	13/	13	条/千克			/31
		-其他纺织材料制：									
6213.9020		---刺绣的〔999〕	6		100	13/	13	条/千克			/
6213.9090		---其他〔999〕	6		100	13/	13	条/千克			/31
62.14		**披巾、领巾、围巾、披纱、面纱及类似品：**									
6214.1000		-丝或绢丝制									
6214.1000	10	含丝 70%及以上的披巾、头巾、围巾(包括披纱、面纱等及类似品)〔999〕	6	5	130	13/	13	条/千克			/35
6214.1000	90	含丝 70%以下的披巾、头巾、围巾(包括披纱、面纱等及类似品)〔999〕	6	5	130	13/	13	条/千克			/35
		-羊毛或动物细毛制：									
6214.2010		---羊毛制〔999〕	6	5	130	13/	13	条/千克			/35
6214.2020		---山羊绒制〔999〕	6	5	130	13/	13	条/千克			/35
6214.2090		---其他〔999〕	6		130	13/	13	条/千克			/
6214.3000		-合成纤维制〔999〕	6		130	13/	13	条/千克			/31
6214.4000		-人造纤维制〔999〕	6		130	13/	13	条/千克			/
6214.9000		-其他纺织材料制									
6214.9000	10	棉制披巾、头巾及类似品(包括围巾、披纱、面纱)〔999〕	6		100	13/	13	条/千克			/31
6214.9000	90	其他材料制披巾、头巾及类似品(包括围巾、披纱、面纱及类似品)〔999〕	6		100	13/	13	条/千克			/31
62.15		**领带及领结：**									
6215.1000		-丝或绢丝制〔999〕	6		130	13/	13	条/千克			/31
6215.2000		-化学纤维制〔999〕	6		130	13/	13	条/千克			/31
6215.9000		-其他纺织材料制〔999〕	6		100	13/	13	条/千克			/31
62.16		**分指手套、连指手套及露指手套：**									
6216.0000		分指手套、连指手套及露指手套〔999〕	6		100	13/	13	双/千克			/31
62.17		**其他制成的衣着附件；服装或衣着附件的零件，但税目 62.12 的货品除外：**									
		-附件：									
6217.1010		---袜子及袜套〔999〕	6		130	13/	13	千克/双			/31
6217.1020		---和服腰带〔999〕	6		100	13/	13	千克/条			/
6217.1090		---其他〔999〕	6		100	13/	13	千克			/31
6217.9000		-零件〔999〕	6		100	13/	13	千克			/31

协定税率 %										特惠税率 %			
亚太5国	东/冰/格	巴基斯坦	韩国	瑞士	哥达	秘鲁	澳大利亚	新西/坡/智	港/澳/台	亚太2国	老/柬/缅	36/3/1	Article Description
3.9	0/0/0	7	5.6	4.2	0	0	0	0/0/0	0/0/0			0/0/	---Of other textile materials
													Handkerchiefs:
													-Of cotton:
	0/0/0	7	5.6	4.2	0	0	0	0/0/0	0/0/		0//	0/0/0	---Embroidered
	0/0/0	11.2	5.6	4.2	0	0	0	0/0/0	0/0/		0//	0/0/0	---Other
													-Of other textile materials:
	0/0/0	7	5.6	4.2	0	0	0	0/0/0	0/0/		0//	0/0/0	---Embroidered
	0/0/0	7	5.6	4.2	0	0	0	0/0/0	0/0/		0//	0/0/0	---Other
													Shawls, scarves, mufflers, mantillas, veils and the like:
													-Of silk or spun silk
	0/0/0	11.2	5.6	4.2	0	0	0	0/0/0	0/0/			0/0/0	Shawls, scarves, mufflers, mantillas, veils and the like, containing≥70% by weight of silk
	0/0/0	11.2	5.6	4.2	0	0	0	0/0/0	0/0/			0/0/0	Shawls, scarves, mufflers, mantillas, veils and the like, containing<70% by weight of silk
													-Of wool or fine animal hair:
	0/0/0	11.2	5.6	4.2	0	0	0	0/0/0	0/0/			0/0/0	---Of wool
	0/0/0	11.2	5.6	4.2	0	0	0	0/0/0	0/0/			0/0/0	---Of goats
	0/0/0	11.2	5.6	4.2	0	0	0	0/0/0	0/0/			0/0/0	---Other
	0/0/0	12.8	6.4	4.8	0	0	0	0/0/0	0/0/			0/0/0	-Of synthetic fibres
	0/0/0	11.2	5.6	4.2	0	0	0	0/0/0	0/0/			0/0/0	-Of artificial fibres
													-Of other textile materials
	0/0/0	0	5.6	4.2	0	0	0	0/0/0	0/0/			0/0/0	Shawls, scarves, mufflers, mantillas, veils and the like, of cotton
	0/0/0	0	5.6	4.2	0	0	0	0/0/0	0/0/			0/0/0	Shawls, scarves, mufflers, mantillas, veils and the like, of other textile materials
													Ties, bow ties and cravats:
	0/0/0	11.2	5.6	4.2	0	0	0	0/0/0	0/0/			0/0/0	-Of silk or spun silk
3.9	0/0/0	12.8	6.4	4.8	0	0	0	0/0/0	0/0/			0/0/0	-Of man-made fibres
	0/0/0	7	5.6	4.2	0	0	0	0/0/0	0/0/			0/0/0	-Of other textile materials
													Gloves, mittens and mitts:
	0/0/0	0	5.6	4.2	0	0	0	0/0/0	0/0/			0/0/0	Gloves, mittens and mitts
													Other made up clothing accessories; parts of garments or of clothing accessories, other than those of heading No. 62. 12:
													-Accessories:
3.9	0/0/0	7	5.6	4.2	0	0	0	0/0/0	0/0/0			0/0/	---Stocking, socks and sockettes
3.9	0/0/0	5.6	5.6	4.2	0	0	0	0/0/0	0/0/0			0/0/0	---Kimono belts
3.9	0/0/0	0	5.6	4.2	0	0	0	0/0/0	0/0/0		0/0/0	0/0/0	---Other
3.9	0/0/0	0	8.4	4.2	0	0	0	0/0/0	0/0/0		0/0/0	0/0/0	-Parts

第六十三章
其他纺织制成品;成套物品;旧衣着及旧纺织品;碎织物

注释:

一、第一分章仅适用于各种纺织物制成的物品。

二、第一分章不包括:

(一)第五十六章至第六十二章的货品;

(二)税目 63.09 的旧衣着或其他旧物品。

三、税目 63.09 仅适用于下列货品:

(一)纺织材料制品:

1.衣着和衣着附件及其零件;

2.毯子及旅行毯;

3.床上、餐桌、盥洗及厨房用的织物制品;

4.装饰用织物制品,但税目 57.01 至 57.05 的地毯及税目 58.05 的装饰毯除外。

(二)用石棉以外其他任何材料制成的鞋帽类。

上述物品只有同时符合下列两个条件才能归入本税目:

1.必须明显看得出穿用过;

2.必须以散装、捆装、袋装或类似的大包装形式进口或出口。

子目注释:

一、子目 6304.20 包括用 α-氯氰菊酯(ISO)、虫螨腈(ISO)、溴氰菊酯(INN,ISO)、高效氯氟氰菊酯(ISO)、除虫菊酯(ISO)或甲基嘧啶磷(ISO)浸渍或涂层的经编针织物制品。

税则号列	货品名称〔CIQ 扩展编码及品名－T2 表示见附表 2〕	最惠(%)	暂定税率	普通	增值/消费	出口退税	计量单位	监管条件	检验检疫	特殊证件对美关税
	第一分章　其他纺织制成品									
63.01	**毯子及旅行毯:**									
6301.1000	-电暖毯〔101 其它电热器具及其零件,102 毯子〕	6		100	13/	13	条/千克	A	M	/16
6301.2000	-羊毛或动物细毛制的毯子(电暖毯除外)及旅行毯									
6301.2000 10	毛制毯子及旅行毯(羊毛或动物细毛制,非电暖的,长度不超过 3 米)〔999〕	6	5	130	13/	13	条/千克			/35
6301.2000 20	其他毛制毯子及旅行毯(羊毛或动物细毛制,非电暖的,长度超过 3 米)〔999〕	6	5	130	13/	13	条/千克			/35
6301.3000	-棉制的毯子(电暖毯除外)及旅行毯〔999〕	6		90	13/	13	条/千克			/31
6301.4000	-合成纤维制的毯子(电暖毯除外)及旅行毯〔999〕	8		130	13/	13	条/千克			/33
6301.9000	-其他毯子及旅行毯〔999〕	6		90	13/	13	条/千克			/31
63.02	**床上、餐桌、盥洗及厨房用的织物制品:**									
	-针织或钩编的床上用织物制品:									
6302.1010	---棉制〔999〕	6		90	13/	13	条/千克			/
6302.1090	---其他纺织材料制〔999〕	6		130	13/	13	条/千克			/
	-其他印花的床上用织物制品:									
	--棉制:									
6302.2110	---床单〔999〕	6		90	13/	13	条/千克			/31
6302.2190	---其他〔101 枕芯、枕套,102 其他日用纺织制品〕	6		90	13/	13	条/千克			/31
	--化学纤维制:									
6302.2210	---床单〔999〕	6		130	13/	13	条/千克			/36
6302.2290	---其他〔101 枕芯、枕套,102 其他日用纺织制品〕	6		130	13/	13	条/千克			/31
	--其他纺织材料制:									
6302.2910	---丝及绢丝制〔999〕	6		130	13/	13	条/千克			/31
6302.2920	---麻制〔999〕	6		90	13/	13	条/千克			/16
6302.2990	---其他〔101 床单、床罩,102 其他日用纺织制品〕	6		100	13/	13	条/千克			/
	-其他床上用织物制品:									
	--棉制:									
6302.3110	---刺绣的〔999〕	6		90	13/	13	条/千克			/36
	---其他:									
6302.3191	----床单〔999〕	6		90	13/	13	条/千克			/31
6302.3192	----毛巾被〔999〕	6		90	13/	13	条/千克			/
6302.3199	----其他〔101 被子,102 枕芯、枕套,103 其他日用纺织制品〕	6		90	13/	13	条/千克			/31
	--化学纤维制:									
6302.3210	---刺绣的〔999〕	6		130	13/	13	条/千克			/
6302.3290	---其他〔101 床单、床罩,102 被子,103 枕芯、枕套,104 其他日用纺织制品〕	6		130	13/	13	条/千克			/36
	--其他纺织材料制:									

Chapter 63
Other made up textile articles; sets; worn clothing and worn textile articles; rags

Notes:

1. Sub-Chapter 1 applies only to made uparticles, of any textile fabric.
2. Sub-Chapter 1 does not cover:
   (a) Goods of Chapters 56 to 62; or
   (b) Worn clothing or other worn articles of heading No.63. 09.
3. Heading No.63. 09 applies only to the following goods:
   (a) Articles of textile materials:
      (ⅰ) Clothing and clothing accessories, and parts thereof;
      (ⅱ) Blankets and travelling rugs;
      (ⅲ) Bed linen, table linen, toilet lined and kitchen linen;
      (ⅳ) Furnishing articles, other than carpets of headings No.57. 01 to 57. 05 and tapestries of heading No.58. 05;
   (b) Footwear and headgear of any material other than asbestos.
   In order to be classified in this heading, the articles mentioned above must comply with both of the following requirements:
      (ⅰ) They must show signs of appreciable wear, and
      (ⅱ) They must be presented in bulk or in bales, sacks or similar packings.

Subheading Notes:

1. Subheading No. 6304.20 including the use of alpha cypermethrin (ISO), chlorfenapyr (ISO) and deltamethrin (INN, ISO), lambda cyhalothrin (ISO), pyrethrins (ISO) or pirimiphos methyl (ISO) warp knitted fabric impregnated or coated products.

协定税率 %										特惠税率 %			
亚太5国	东/冰/格	巴基斯坦	韩国	瑞士	哥达	秘鲁	澳大利亚	新西/坡/智	港/澳/台	亚太2国	老/柬/缅	36/3/1	Article Description
													Ⅰ.-OTHER MADE UP TEXTILE ARTICLES
													Blankets and travelling rugs:
	0/0/0	12.8	6.4	4.8	0	0	0	0/0/0	0/0/			0/0/	-Electric blankets
													-Blankets(other than electric blankets) and travelling rugs, of wool or of fine animal hair
	0/0/0	12.8	6.4	4.8	0	0	0	0/0/0	0/0/			0/0/0	Blankets (other than electric blankets) and travelling rugs, of wool or fine animal hair, length≤3m
	0/0/0	12.8	6.4	4.8	0	0	0	0/0/0	0/0/			0/0/0	Other blankets (other than electric blankets) and travelling rugs, of wool or of fine animal hair, length>3m
	0/0/0	12.8	6.4	4.8	0	0	0	0/0/0	0/0/			0/0/0	-Blankets (other than electric blankets) and travelling rugs, of cotton
	0/0/0	0	7	5.3	0	0	0	0/0/0	0/0/			0/0/0	-Blankets (other than electric blankets) and travelling rugs, of synthetic fibres
	0/0/0	12.8	6.4	4.8	0	0	0	0/0/0	0/0/0			0/0/0	-Other blankets and travelling rugs
													Bed linen, table linen, toilet linen and kitchen linen:
													-Bed linen, knitted or crocheted:
	0/0/0	0	5.6	4.2	0	0	0	0/0/0	0/0/			0/0/0	---Of cotton
	0/0/0	0	5.6	4.2	0	0	0	0/0/0	0/0/			0/0/	---Other
													-Other bed linen, printed:
													--Of cotton:
	0/0/0	0	5.6	6	0	0	0	0/0/0	0/0/			0/0/0	---Bed sheets
	0/0/0	0	5.6	4.2	0	0	0	0/0/0	0/0/			0/0/0	---Other
													--Of man-made fibres:
	0/0/0	0	6.4	4.8	0	0	0	0/0/0	0/0/			0/0/0	---Bed sheets
	0/0/0	0	6.4	4.8	0	0	0	0/0/0	0/0/			0/0/0	---Other
													--Of other textile materials:
	0/0/0	0	5.6	4.2	0	0	0	0/0/0	0/0/			0/0/	---Of silk or spun silk
	0/0/0	0	5.6	4.2	0	0	0	0/0/0	0/0/			0/0/	---Of bast fibres
	0/0/0	0	5.6	4.2	0	0	0	0/0/0	0/0/			0/0/	---Other
													-Other bed linen:
													--Of cotton:
	0/0/0	0	5.6	4.2	0	0	0	0/0/0	0/0/			0/0/0	---Embroidered
													---Other:
	0/0/0	0	5.6	4.2	0	0	0	0/0/0	0/0/			0/0/0	----Bed sheets
	0/0/0	0	5.6	4.2	0	0	0	0/0/0	0/0/			0/0/	----Towelling coverlets
	0/0/0	0	5.6	4.2	0	0	0	0/0/0	0/0/			0/0/0	----Other
													--Of man-made fibres:
	0/0/0	0	6.4	4.8	0	0	0	0/0/0	0/0/			0/0/0	---Embroidered
	0/0/0	0	6.4	4.8	0	0	0	0/0/0	0/0/			0/0/0	---Other
													--Of other textile materials:

税则号列	货品名称〔CIQ扩展编码及品名—T2表示见附表2〕	最惠(%)	暂定税率	普通	增值/消费	出口退税	计量单位	监管条件	检验检疫	特殊证件对美关税
6302.3910	---丝及绢丝制									
6302.3910 10	丝及绢丝制其他床上用织物制品(含丝85%及以上)〔999〕	6		130	13/	13	条/千克			/
6302.3910 90	丝及绢丝制其他床上用织物制品(含丝85%以下)〔999〕	6		130	13/	13	条/千克			/
	---麻制：									
6302.3921	----刺绣的									
6302.3921 10	亚麻或苎麻制其他床上用织物制品(刺绣的)〔999〕	6		90	13/	13	条/千克			/31
6302.3921 90	其他麻制其他床上用织物制品(刺绣的)〔999〕	6		90	13/	13	条/千克			/31
6302.3929	----其他									
6302.3929 10	亚麻或苎麻制其他床上用织物制品〔999〕	6		90	13/	13	条/千克			/16
6302.3929 90	其他麻制其他床上用织物制品〔999〕	6		90	13/	13	条/千克			/16
	---其他：									
6302.3991	----刺绣的									
6302.3991 10	毛制刺绣床上用织物制品〔999〕	6		100	13/	13	条/千克			/
6302.3991 90	其他材料制刺绣床上用织物制品〔999〕	6		100	13/	13	条/千克			/
6302.3999	----其他									
6302.3999 10	毛制非刺绣床上用织物制品〔999〕	6		100	13/	13	条/千克			/
6302.3999 90	其他材料制其他床上用织物制品〔999〕	6		100	13/	13	条/千克			/
	-针织或钩编的餐桌用织物制品：									
6302.4010	---手工制〔999〕	6		100	13/	13	件/千克			/
6302.4090	---其他〔999〕	6		100	13/	13	件/千克			/
	-其他餐桌用织物制品：									
	--棉制：									
6302.5110	---刺绣的〔999〕	6		90	13/	13	件/千克			/
6302.5190	---其他〔999〕	6		90	13/	13	件/千克			/31
	--化学纤维制：									
6302.5310	---刺绣的〔999〕	6		130	13/	13	件/千克			/
6302.5390	---其他									
6302.5390 10	化学纤维无纺织物制餐桌用织物制品〔999〕	6		130	13/	13	件/千克			/31
6302.5390 90	化学纤维制其他餐桌用织物制品〔999〕	6		130	13/	13	件/千克			/31
	--其他纺织材料制：									
	---亚麻制：									
6302.5911	----刺绣的〔999〕	6		90	13/	13	件/千克			/
6302.5919	----其他〔999〕	6		90	13/	13	件/千克			/
6302.5990	---其他									
6302.5990 10	羊毛或动物细毛制餐桌用织物制品〔999〕	6		100	13/	13	件/千克			/
6302.5990 90	其他纺织材料制餐桌用织物制品〔999〕	6		100	13/	13	件/千克			/
	-盥洗及厨房用棉制毛巾织物或类似的毛圈织物的制品：									
6302.6010	---浴巾									
6302.6010 10	棉制针织或钩编毛巾织物浴巾(含类似毛圈织物的制品)〔999〕	6		90	13/	13	条/千克			/31
6302.6010 90	棉制非针织或非钩编毛巾织物浴巾(含类似毛圈织物的制品)〔999〕	6		90	13/	13	条/千克			/31
6302.6090	---其他〔999〕	6		90	13/	13	条/千克			/31
	-其他：									
6302.9100	--棉制〔999〕	6		90	13/	13	条/千克			/31
6302.9300	--化学纤维制									
6302.9300 10	化学纤维无纺织物制盥洗及厨房制品〔999〕	6		130	13/	13	条/千克			/31
6302.9300 90	化学纤维制其他盥洗及厨房织物制品〔999〕	6		130	13/	13	条/千克			/31
	--其他纺织材料制：									
6302.9910	---亚麻制〔999〕	6		90	13/	13	条/千克			/
6302.9990	---其他									
6302.9990 10	毛制盥洗及厨房用织物制品〔999〕	6		100	13/	13	条/千克			/
6302.9990 90	其他材料制盥洗及厨房织物制品〔999〕	6		100	13/	13	条/千克			/
63.03	**窗帘(包括帷帘)及帐幔；帘帷或床帷：**									
	-针织或钩编的：									
	--合成纤维制：									
6303.1210	---针织的									
6303.1210 10	合成纤维制针织百叶窗、卷帘和窗幔〔999〕	6		130	13/	13	千克			/36
6303.1210 90	其他合成纤维制针织窗帘等(包括帷帘、帐幔、帘帷及床帷)〔999〕	6		130	13/	13	千克			/36
6303.1220	---钩编的									
6303.1220 10	合成纤维制钩编百叶窗、卷帘和窗幔〔999〕	6		130	13/	13	千克			/

协定税率 %										特惠税率 %			
亚太5国	东/冰/格	巴基斯坦	韩国	瑞士	哥达	秘鲁	澳大利亚	新西/坡/智	港/澳/台	亚太2国	老/柬/缅	36/3/1	Article Description
													---Of silk or spun silk
	0/0/0	0	5.6	4.2	0	0	0	0/0/0	0/0/			0/0/	Other bed linen of silk and spun silk, containing silk≥85%
	0/0/0	0	5.6	4.2	0	0	0	0/0/0	0/0/			0/0/	Other bed linen of silk and spun silk, containing silk<85%
													---Of bast fibres:
													----Embroidered
	0/0/0	0	5.6	4.2	0	0	0	0/0/0	0/0/			0/0/	Other bed linen of flax or ramie, embroidered
	0/0/0	0	5.6	4.2	0	0	0	0/0/0	0/0/			0/0/	Other bed linen of other bast fibres, embroidered
													----Other
	0/0/0	0	5.6	4.2	0	0	0	0/0/0	0/0/			0/0/	Other bed linen of flax or ramie
	0/0/0	0	5.6	4.2	0	0	0	0/0/0	0/0/			0/0/	Other bed linen of other bast fibres
													---Other:
													----Embroidered
	0/0/0	0	5.6	4.2	0	0	0	0/0/0	0/0/			0/0/	Other bed linen of wool or fine animal hair, embroidered
	0/0/0	0	5.6	4.2	0	0	0	0/0/0	0/0/			0/0/	Other bed linen of other textile materials, embroidered
													----Other
	0/0/0	0	5.6	4.2	0	0	0	0/0/0	0/0/			0/0/0	Other bed linen of wool or fine animal hair, embroidered
	0/0/0	0	5.6	4.2	0	0	0	0/0/0	0/0/			0/0/0	Other bed linen of other textile materials
													-Table linen, knitted or crocheted:
	0/0/0	0	5.6	4.2	0	0	0	0/0/0	0/0/			0/0/	---Hand-worked
	0/0/0	0	5.6	4.2	0	0	0	0/0/0	0/0/			0/0/0	---Other
													-Other table linen:
													--Of cotton:
	0/0/0	0	5.6	4.2	0	0	0	0/0/0	0/0/			0/0/	---Embroidered
	0/0/0	0	5.6	4.2	0	0	0	0/0/0	0/0/			0/0/0	---Other
													--Of man-made fibres:
	0/0/0	0	5.6	4.2	0	0	0	0/0/0	0/0/			0/0/	---Embroidered
													---Other
	0/0/0	0	6.4	4.8	0	0	0	0/0/0	0/0/			0/0/0	Table linen made up of nonwoven fabrics of man-made fibres
	0/0/0	0	6.4	4.8	0	0	0	0/0/0	0/0/			0/0/0	Other table linen of man-made fibres
													--Of other textile materials:
													---Of flax:
	0/0/0	0	5.6	4.2	0	0	0	0/0/0	0/0/			0/0/	----Embroidered
	0/0/0	0	5.6	4.2	0	0	0	0/0/0	0/0/			0/0/	----Other
													---Other
	0/0/0	0	5.6	4.2	0	0	0	0/0/0	0/0/			0/0/	Table linen of wool or other fine animal hair
	0/0/0	0	5.6	4.2	0	0	0	0/0/0	0/0/			0/0/	Table linen of other textile materials
													-Toilet linen and kitchen linen, of terry towelling or similar terry fabrics, of cotton:
													---Bath towels
	0/0/0	0	5.6	4.2	0	0	0	0/0/0	0/0/0			0/0/0	Bath towels, of terry towelling or similar terry fabrics, of cotton, knitted or crocheted
	0/0/0	0	5.6	4.2	0	0	0	0/0/0	0/0/0			0/0/0	Bath towels, of terry towelling or similar terry fabrics, of cotton, not knitted or crocheted
	0/0/0	0	5.6	4.2	0	0	0	0/0/0	0/0/0			0/0/0	---Other
													-Other:
	0/0/0	0	5.6	4.2	0	0	0	0/0/0	0/0/			0/0/0	--Of cotton
													--Of man-made fibres
	0/0/0	0	6.4	4.8	0	0	0	0/0/0	0/0/			0/0/	Toilet linen and kitchen linen of nonwoven fabrics of man-made fibres
	0/0/0	0	6.4	4.8	0	0	0	0/0/0	0/0/			0/0/	Other toilet linen and kitchen linen of man-made fibres
													--Of other textile materials:
	0/0/0	0	5.6	4.2	0	0	0	0/0/0	0/0/			0/0/	---Of flax
													---Other
	0/0/0	0	5.6	4.2	0	0	0	0/0/0	0/0/			0/0/	Other toilet linen and kitchen linen, of wool or fine animal hair
	0/0/0	0	5.6	4.2	0	0	0	0/0/0	0/0/			0/0/	Other toilet linen and kitchen linen of other textile materials
													Curtains (including drapes) and interior blinds; curtain or bed valances:
													-Knitted or crocheted:
													--Of synthetic fibres:
													---Knitted
	0/0/0	0	6.4	4.8	0	0	0	0/0/0	0/0/			0/0/	Shutter, valance, roller shutter, of knitted, of synthetic fibres
	0/0/0	0	6.4	4.8	0	0	0	0/0/0	0/0/			0/0/	Curtains, of knitted, of synthetic fibres (including drapes, interior blinds, curtain and bed valances)
													---Crocheted
	0/0/0	0	6.4	4.8	0	0	0	0/0/0	0/0/			0/0/	Shutter, valance, roller shutter, of crocheted, of synthetic fibres

税则号列		货品名称〔CIQ扩展编码及品名－T2表示见附表2〕	最惠(%)	暂定税率	普通	增值/消费	出口退税	计量单位	监管条件	检验检疫	特殊证件对美关税
6303.1220	90	其他合成纤维制钩编的窗帘等(包括帷帘、帐幔、帘帷及床帷)〔999〕	6		130	13/	13	千克			/
		--其他纺织材料制：									
		---棉制：									
6303.1931		----针织的〔999〕	6		90	13/	13	千克			/16
6303.1932		----钩编的〔999〕	6		90	13/	13	千克			/
		---其他纺织材料制：									
6303.1991		----针织的〔999〕	6		130	13/	13	千克			/16
6303.1992		----钩编的〔999〕	6		130	13/	13	千克			/
		-其他：									
6303.9100		--棉制									
6303.9100	10	棉制非针织网眼窗帘(包括帷帘、帐幔、帘帷及床帷)〔999〕	6		90	13/	13	千克			/31
6303.9100	90	棉制非针织非钩编窗帘(包括帷帘、帐幔、帘帷及床帷)〔999〕	6		90	13/	13	千克			/31
6303.9200		--合成纤维制									
6303.9200	10	合成纤维百叶窗、卷帘和窗幔(非针织非钩编)〔999〕	6		130	13/	13	千克		L	/36
6303.9200	90	其他合成纤维制非针织非钩编窗帘等(包括帷帘、帐幔、帘帷及床帷)〔999〕	6		130	13/	13	千克			/36
6303.9900		--其他纺织材料制〔999〕	6		100	13/	13	千克			/31
63.04		**其他装饰用织物制品，但税目94.04的货品除外：**									
		-床罩：									
		--针织或钩编的：									
		---针织的：									
6304.1121		----手工制〔999〕	6		100	13/	13	件/千克			/
6304.1129		----其他〔999〕	6		100	13/	13	件/千克			/31
		---钩编的：									
6304.1131		----手工制〔999〕	6		100	13/	13	件/千克			/
6304.1139		----其他〔999〕	6		100	13/	13	件/千克			/36
		--其他：									
6304.1910		---丝及绢丝制									
6304.1910	10	丝及绢丝制非针织非钩编床罩(含丝85%及以上)〔999〕	6		130	13/	13	件/千克			/
6304.1910	90	丝及绢丝制非针织非钩编床罩(含丝85%以下)〔999〕	6		130	13/	13	件/千克			/
		---棉或麻制：									
6304.1921		----刺绣的〔999〕	6		90	13/	13	件/千克			/
6304.1929		----其他〔999〕	6		90	13/	13	件/千克			/31
		---化学纤维制：									
6304.1931		----刺绣的〔999〕	6		130	13/	13	件/千克			/
6304.1939		----其他〔999〕	6		130	13/	13	件/千克			/
		---其他纺织材料制：									
6304.1991		----刺绣的									
6304.1991	10	毛制非针织非钩编刺绣床罩(羊毛或动物细毛制)〔999〕	6		100	13/	13	件/千克			/
6304.1991	90	其他纺织材料制非针织刺绣床罩(含非钩编的)〔999〕	6		100	13/	13	件/千克			/
6304.1999		----其他									
6304.1999	10	毛制其他非针织非钩编床罩(羊毛或动物细毛制)〔999〕	6		100	13/	13	件/千克			/
6304.1999	90	其他材料制非针织非钩编其他床罩〔999〕	6		100	13/	13	件/千克			/
		-本章子目注释一所列的蚊帐：									
6304.2010		---手工制〔999〕	6		100	13/	13	件/千克			/
6304.2090		---其他〔999〕	6		100	13/	13	件/千克			/
		-其他：									
		--针织或钩编的：									
		---针织的：									
6304.9121		----手工制〔999〕	6		100	13/	13	千克			/
6304.9129		----其他〔999〕	6		100	13/	13	千克			/31
		---钩编的：									
6304.9131		----手工制〔999〕	6		100	13/	13	千克			/
6304.9139		----其他〔999〕	6		100	13/	13	千克			/
		--非针织或非钩编的，棉制：									

协定税率 %										特惠税率 %			Article Description
亚太5国	东/冰/格	巴基斯坦	韩国	瑞士	哥达	秘鲁	澳大利亚	新西/坡/智	港/澳/台	亚太2国	老/柬/缅	36/3/1	
	0/0/0	0	6.4	4.8	0	0	0	0/0/0	0/0/			0/0/	Other curtains of crocheted, of synthetic fibres etc (including drapes, inter, or blinds, curtain and bed valances)
													--Of other textile materials:
													---Of cotton:
	0/0/0	0	5.6	4.2	0	0	0	0/0/0	0/0/			0/0/0	----Knitted
	0/0/0	0	5.6	4.2	0	0	0	0/0/0	0/0/			0/0/	----Crocheted
													---Of other textile materials:
	0/0/0	0	5.6	4.2	0	0	0	0/0/0	0/0/			0/0/	----Knitted
	0/0/0	0	5.6	4.2	0	0	0	0/0/0	0/0/			0/0/	----Crocheted
													-Other:
													--Of cotton
	0/0/0	0	5.6	4.2	0	0	0	0/0/0	0/0/			0/0/0	Curtains(including drapes, interior blinds, curtain or bed valances) of cotton, nets, not knitted
	0/0/0	0	5.6	4.2	0	0	0	0/0/0	0/0/			0/0/0	Curtains (including drapes, interior blinds, curtain or bed valances) of cotton, nets, not knitted or crocheted
													--Of synthetic fibres
	0/0/0	0	6.4	4.8	0	0	0	0/0/0	0/0/			0/0/0	Shutter, valance, roller shutter, of synthetic fibres, not knittedor crocheted
	0/0/0	0	6.4	4.8	0	0	0	0/0/0	0/0/			0/0/0	Curtains (including drapes) and interior blinds; curtain or bed valances, of synthetic fibres, not knitted or crocheted
	0/0/0	0	5.6	4.2	0	0	0	0/0/0	0/0/			0/0/0	--Of other textile materials
													Other furnishing articles, excluding those of heading No.94.04:
													-Bedspreads:
													--Knitted or crocheted:
													---Knitted:
	0/0/0	7	5.6	4.2	0	0	0	0/0/0	0/0/			0/0/	----Hand-worked
	0/0/0	5.6	5.6	4.2	0	0	0	0/0/0	0/0/			0/0/	----Other
													---Crocheted:
	0/0/0	7	5.6	4.2	0	0	0	0/0/0	0/0/			0/0/0	----Hand-worked
	0/0/0	7	5.6	4.2	0	0	0	0/0/0	0/0/			0/0/0	----Other
													--Other:
													---Of silk or spun silk
	0/0/0	0	5.6	4.2	0	0	0	0/0/0	0/0/			0/0/	Bedspreads of silk or spun silk, containing silk≥85%, not knitted or crocheted
	0/0/0	0	5.6	4.2	0	0	0	0/0/0	0/0/			0/0/	Bedspreads of silk or spun silk, containing silk<85%, not knitted or crocheted
													---Of cotton or bast fibres:
	0/0/0	0	5.6	4.2	0	0	0	0/0/0	0/0/			0/0/	----Embroidered
	0/0/0	0	5.6	4.2	0	0	0	0/0/0	0/0/			0/0/0	----Other
													---Of man-made fibres:
	0/0/0	12.8	6.4	4.8	0	0	0	0/0/0	0/0/			0/0/	----Embroidered
	0/0/0	12.8	6.4	4.8	0	0	0	0/0/0	0/0/			0/0/	----Other
													---Of other textile materials:
													----Embroidered
	0/0/0	7	5.6	4.2	0	0	0	0/0/0	0/0/			0/0/	Bedspreads, not knitted or crocheted, embroidered, of wool or fine animal hair
	0/0/0	7	5.6	4.2	0	0	0	0/0/0	0/0/			0/0/	Bedspreads, not knitted or crocheted, embroidered, of other textile materials
													----Other
	0/0/0	7	5.6	4.2	0	0	0	0/0/0	0/0/			0/0/	Bedspreads, not knitted or crocheted, embroidered, of wool or fine animal hair
	0/0/0	7	5.6	4.2	0	0	0	0/0/0	0/0/			0/0/	Bedspreads, not knitted or crocheted, embroidered, of other textile materials
													-Mosquito net in Subheading Note 1 to this chapter
	0/0/0	7	5.6	4.2	0	0	0	0/0/0	0/0/			0/0/0	---Hand-worked
	0/0/0	7	5.6	4.2	0	0	0	0/0/0	0/0/			0/0/0	---Other
													-Other:
													--Knitted or crocheted:
													---Knitted:
	0/0/0	7	5.6	4.2	0	0	0	0/0/0	0/0/			0/0/0	----Hand-worked
	0/0/0	7	5.6	4.2	0	0	0	0/0/0	0/0/			0/0/0	----Other
													---Crocheted:
	0/0/0	11.2	5.6	4.2	0	0	0	0/0/0	0/0/			0/0/	----Hand-worked
	0/0/0	5.6	5.6	4.2	0	0	0	0/0/0	0/0/			0/0/	----Other
													--Not knitted or crocheted, of cotton:

税则号列	货品名称〔CIQ扩展编码及品名－T2表示见附表2〕	最惠(%)	暂定税率	普通税率	增值/消费	出口退税	计量单位	监管条件	检验检疫	特殊证件对美关税
6304.9210	---刺绣的〔999〕	6		90	13/	13	千克			/31
6304.9290	---其他〔999〕	6		90	13/	13	千克			/36
	--非针织或非钩编的,合成纤维制:									
6304.9310	---刺绣的〔999〕	6		130	13/	13	千克			/
6304.9390	---其他〔999〕	6		130	13/	13	千克			/16
	--非针织或非钩编的,其他纺织材料制:									
6304.9910	---丝及绢丝制									
6304.9910 10	丝制非针织非钩编的装饰制品(含绢丝制品,含丝85%及以上)〔999〕	6		130	13/	13	千克			/
6304.9910 90	丝制非针织非钩编的装饰制品(含绢丝制品,含丝85%以下)〔999〕	6		130	13/	13	千克			/
	---麻制:									
6304.9921	----刺绣的									
6304.9921 10	亚麻或苎麻非针织其他刺绣装饰品(含非钩编制品)〔999〕	6		90	13/	13	千克			/
6304.9921 90	其他麻制非针织其他刺绣装饰品(包括非钩编的)〔999〕	6		90	13/	13	千克			/
6304.9929	----其他									
6304.9929 10	亚麻或苎麻制其他非针织的装饰品(含非钩编制品)〔999〕	6		90	13/	13	千克			/16
6304.9929 90	其他麻制其他非针织的装饰制品(含非钩编制品)〔999〕	6		90	13/	13	千克			/16
6304.9990	---其他〔999〕	6		100	13/	13	千克			/16
63.05	**货物包装用袋:**									
6305.1000	-黄麻或税目53.03的其他韧皮纺织纤维制									
6305.1000 10	黄麻制旧的货物包装袋(含税目53.03的其他韧皮纤维制)〔999〕	4		40	13/	13	条/千克			/
6305.1000 90	黄麻制其他货物包装袋(含税目53.03的其他韧皮纤维制)〔999〕	4		40	13/	13	条/千克			/
6305.2000	-棉制〔999〕	6		90	13/	13	条/千克			/31
	-化学纤维材料制:									
6305.3200	--散装货物储运软袋〔999〕	6		100	13/	13	条/千克			/31
6305.3300	--其他,聚乙烯、聚丙烯扁条或类似材料制									
6305.3300 10	聚乙烯或聚丙烯制其他货物包装袋(针织或钩编的,用扁条及类似材料制成)〔999〕	6		100	13/	13	条/千克			/31
6305.3300 90	聚乙烯或聚丙烯制其他货物包装袋(非针织或钩编的,用扁条及类似材料制成)〔999〕	6		100	13/	13	条/千克			/31
6305.3900	--其他〔999〕	6		100	13/	13	条/千克			/36
6305.9000	-其他纺织材料制〔999〕	6		90	13/	13	条/千克			/31
63.06	**油苫布、天篷及遮阳篷;帐篷;风帆;野营用品:**									
	-油苫布、天篷及遮阳篷:									
6306.1200	--合成纤维制〔999〕	6		130	13/	13	件/千克			/31
	--其他纺织材料制:									
6306.1910	---麻制〔999〕	6		80	13/	13	件/千克			/16
6306.1920	---棉制〔999〕	6		80	13/	13	件/千克			/
6306.1990	---其他									
6306.1990 10	人造纤维制油苫布、天篷及遮阳篷〔999〕	6		100	13/	13	件/千克			/16
6306.1990 90	其他材料制油苫布、天篷及遮阳篷〔999〕	6		100	13/	13	件/千克			/16
	-帐篷:									
6306.2200	--合成纤维制									
6306.2200 10	合成纤维制移动帐篷〔999〕	6		130	13/	13	件/千克			/31
6306.2200 90	合成纤维制帐篷〔999〕	6		130	13/	13	件/千克			/31
	--其他纺织材料制:									
6306.2910	---棉制〔999〕	6		80	13/	13	件/千克			/36
6306.2990	---其他〔999〕	6		100	13/	13	件/千克			/36
	-风帆:									
6306.3010	---合成纤维制〔999〕	6		130	13/	13	件/千克			/16
6306.3090	---其他纺织材料制〔999〕	6		100	13/	13	件/千克			/
	-充气褥垫:									
6306.4010	---棉制〔999〕	6		80	13/	13	件/千克			/
6306.4020	---化学纤维制〔999〕	6		130	13/	13	件/千克			/36
6306.4090	---其他〔999〕	6		100	13/	13	件/千克			/16
	-其他:									
6306.9010	---棉制〔999〕	6		80	13/	13	件/千克			/
6306.9020	---麻制〔999〕	6		80	13/	13	件/千克			/

协定税率 %										特惠税率 %			Article Description
亚太5国	东/冰/格	巴基斯坦	韩国	瑞士	哥达	秘鲁	澳大利亚	新西/坡/智	港/澳/台	亚太2国	老/柬/缅	36/3/1	
	0/0/0	7	5.6	4.2	0	0	0	0/0/0	0/0/			0/0/	---Embroidered
	0/0/0	0	5.6	4.2	0	0	0	0/0/0	0/0/			0/0/0	---Other
													--Not knitted or crocheted, of synthetic fibres:
	0/0/0	12.8	6.4	4.8	0	0	0	0/0/0	0/0/			0/0/	---Embroidered
	0/0/0	12.8	6.4	4.8	0	0	0	0/0/0	0/0/			0/0/0	---Other
													--Not knitted or crocheted, of other textile materials:
													---Of silk or spun silk
	0/0/0	7	5.6	4.2	0	0	0	0/0/0	0/0/			0/0/0	Other furnishing articles of silk or spun silk, not knitted or crocheted, containing silk≥85%
	0/0/0	7	5.6	4.2	0	0	0	0/0/0	0/0/			0/0/0	Other furnishing articles of silk or spun silk, not knitted or crocheted, containing silk<85%
													---Of bast fibres:
													----Embroidered
	0/0/0	7	5.6	4.2	0	0	0	0/0/0	0/0/			0/0/	Other furnishing articles, not knitted or crocheted, embroidered, of flax or ramie
	0/0/0	7	5.6	4.2	0	0	0	0/0/0	0/0/			0/0/	Other furnishing articles, not knitted or crocheted, embroidered, of other bast fibres
													----Other
	0/0/0	7	5.6	4.2	0	0	0	0/0/0	0/0/			0/0/	Other furnishing articles, not knitted or crocheted, of flax or ramie
	0/0/0	7	5.6	4.2	0	0	0	0/0/0	0/0/			0/0/	Other furnishing articles not knitted or crocheted, of other bast fibres
	0/0/0	0	5.6	4.2	0	0	0	0/0/0	0/0/			0/0/0	---Other
													Sacks and bags, of a kind used for the packing of goods:
													-Of jute or of other textile bast fibres of heading No.53.03
	0/0/0	4.5	0	0	0	0	0	0//0	0/0/	0		0/0/0	Sacks and bags, of a kind used for the packing of goods, of jute or of other textile bast fibres of heading No.53.03
	0/0/0	4.5	0	0	0	0	0	0//0	0/0/	0		0/0/0	Other sacks and bags, of a kind used for the packing of goods, of jute or of other textile bast fibres of heading No.53.03
	0/0/0	0	6.4	4.8	0	0	0	0/0/0	0/0/			0/0/0	-Of cotton
													-Of man-made textile materials:
	0/0/0	12.8	6.4	4.8	0	0	0	0/0/0	0/0/			0/0/0	--Flexible intermediate bulk containers
													--Other, of polyethylene or polypropylene strip or the like
3.9	0/0/0	0	6.4	4.8	0	0	0	0/0/0	0/0/			0/0/	Sacks and bags, of a kind used for the packing of goods, of PE or PP strip or the like, knitted or crocheted
3.9	0/0/0	0	6.4	4.8	0	0	0	0/0/0	0/0/			0/0/	Sacks and bags, of a kind used for the packing of goods, of PE or PP strip or the like, not knitted or crocheted
	0/0/0	0	6.4	4.8	0	0	0	0/0/0	0/0/			0/0/	--Other
	0/0/0	0	5.6	4.2	0	0	0	0/0/0	0/0/			0/0/0	-Of other textile materials
													Tarpaulins, awnings and sunblinds; tents; sails for boats, sailboards or landcraft; camping goods:
													-Tarpaulins, awnings and sunblinds:
	0/0/0	0	6.4	4.8	0	0	0	0/0/0	0/0/			0/0/	--Of synthetic fibres
													--Of other textile materials:
	0/0/0	0	5.6	4.2	0	0	0	0/0/0	0/0/			0/0/	---Of bast fibres
	0/0/0	0	5.6	4.2	0	0	0	0/0/0	0/0/			0/0/	---Of cotton
													---Other
	0/0/0	0	5.6	4.2	0	0	0	0/0/0	0/0/			0/0/	Tarpaulins, awnings and sunblinds, of artificial fibres
	0/0/0	0	5.6	4.2	0	0	0	0/0/0	0/0/			0/0/	Tarpaulins, awnings and sunblinds, of other textile materials
													-Tents:
													--Of synthetic fibres
	0/0/0	0	6.4	4.8	0	0	0	0/0/0	0/0/			0/0/0	Moveable, of synthetic fibres
	0/0/0	0	6.4	4.8	0	0	0	0/0/0	0/0/			0/0/0	Other tents of synthetic fibres:
													--Of other textile materials:
	0/0/0	0	5.6	4.2	0	0	0	0/0/0	0/0/			0/0/	---Of cotton
	0/0/0	0	5.6	4.2	0	0	0	0/0/0	0/0/			0/0/0	---Other
													-Sails:
	0/0/0	0	6.4	4.8	0	0	0	0/0/0	0/0/			0/0/	---Of synthetic fibres
	0/0/0	0	5.6	4.2	0	0	0	0/0/0	0/0/			0/0/	---Of other textile materials
													-Pneumatic mattresses:
	0/0/0	0	5.6	4.2	0	0	0	0/0/0	0/0/			0/0/	--Of cotton
	0/0/0	0	6.4	4.8	0	0	0	0/0/0	0/0/			0/0/0	---Of man-made fibres
	0/0/0	0	5.6	4.2	0	0	0	0/0/0	0/0/			0/0/	---Of other textile materials
													-Other:
	0/0/0	0	5.6	4.2	0	0	0	0/0/0	0/0/			0/0/0	---Of cotton
	0/0/0	0	5.6	4.2	0	0	0	0/0/0	0/0/			0/0/	---Of bast fibres

税则号列	货品名称〔CIQ扩展编码及品名—T2表示见附表2〕	最惠(%)	暂定税率	普通	增值/消费	出口退税	计量单位	监管条件	检验检疫	特殊证件对美关税
6306.9030	---化学纤维制〔999〕	6		130	13/	13	件/千克			/36
6306.9090	---其他〔999〕	6		100	13/	13	件/千克			/
63.07	**其他制成品,包括服装裁剪样:**									
6307.1000	-擦地布、擦碗布、抹布及类似擦拭用布〔999〕	6		130	13/	13	千克			/36
6307.2000	-救生衣及安全带〔999〕	6		70	13/	13	千克/件			/16
6307.9000	-其他〔999〕	6		100	13/	13	千克			/36
	第二分章　成套物品									
63.08	**由机织物及纱线构成的零售包装成套物品,不论是否带附件,用以制作小地毯、装饰毯、绣花台布、餐巾或类似的纺织物品:**									
6308.0000	由机织物及纱线构成的零售包装成套物品,不论是否带附件,用以制作小地毯、装饰毯、绣花台布、餐巾或类似的纺织物品〔998其他装饰用纺织制品,999其他纺织制品〕	6		130	13/	13	千克			/36
	第三分章　旧衣着及旧纺织品;碎织物									
63.09	**旧衣物:**									
6309.0000	旧衣物〔999〕	6		130	13/	0	千克	9		/
63.10	**新或旧的破、碎织物,线、绳、索、缆的废、碎料以及线、绳、索、缆或纺织材料的破旧制品:**									
6310.1000	-经分拣的									
6310.1000 10	新的或未使用过的纺织材料制经分拣的碎织物等(新的或未使用过的,包括废线、绳、索、缆及其制品)〔999〕	6		50	13/	13	千克	9		/31
6310.1000 90	其他纺织材料制经分拣的碎织物等(包括废线、绳、索、缆及其制品)〔999〕	6		50	13/	13	千克	9		/31
6310.9000	-其他									
6310.9000 10	新的或未使用过的纺织材料制其他碎织物等(新的或未使用过的,包括废线、绳、索、缆及其制品)〔999〕	6		50	13/	13	千克	9		/31
6310.9000 90	其他纺织材料制碎织物等(包括废线、绳、索、缆及其制品)〔999〕	6		50	13/	13	千克	9		/31

协定税率 %										特惠税率 %			Article Description
亚太5国	东/冰/格	巴基斯坦	韩国	瑞士	哥达	秘鲁	澳大利亚	新西/坡/智	港/澳/台	亚太2国	老/柬/缅	36/3/1	
	0/0/0	0	6.4	4.8	0	0	0	0/0/0	0/0/			0/0/	---Of man-made fibres
	0/0/0	0	5.6	4.2	0	0	0	0/0/0	0/0/			0/0/	---Other
													Other made up articles, including dress patterns:
3.9	0/0/0	0	5.6	4.2	0	0	0	0/0/0	0/0/0			0/0/	-Floor-cloths, dish-cloths, dusters and similar cleaning cloths
	0/0/0	11.2	5.6	4.2	0	0	0	0/0/0	0/0/			0/0/0	-Life-jackets and life-belts
	0/0/0	0	8.4	4.2	0	0	0	0/0/0	0/0/		0/0/0	0/0/0	-Other
													Ⅱ. SETS
													Sets consisting of woven fabric and yarn, whether or not with accessories, for making up into rugs, tapestries, embroidered table cloths or serviettes, or similar textile articles, put up in packings for retail sale:
	0/0/0	7	5.6	4.2	0	0	0	0/0/0	0/0/			0/0/	Sets consisting of woven fabric and yarn, whether or not with accessories, for making up into rugs, tapestries, embroidered table cloths or serviettes, or similar textile articles, put up in packings for retail sale
													Ⅲ. WORN CLOTHING AND WORN TEXTILE ARTICLES; RAGS
													Worn clothing and other worn articles:
	0/0/0	7	5.6	4.2	0	0	0	0/0/0	0/0/			0/0/	Worn clothing and other worn articles
													Used or new rags, scrap twine, cordage, rope and cables and worn out articles of twine, cordage, rope or cables, of textile materials:
													-Sorted
	0/0/0	0	5.6	4.2	0	0	0	0/0/0	0/0/			0/0/0	Not used or new rags, scrap twine, cordage, rope and cables and worn out articles of twine, cordage, rope or cables, of textile materials, sorted
	0/0/0	0	5.6	4.2	0	0	0	0/0/0	0/0/			0/0/0	Other sorted rags, including scrap twine, cordage, rope and cables and worn out articles of twine, of textile materials
													-Other
	0/0/0	0	5.6	4.2	0	0	0	0/0/0	0/0/		0/0/0	0/0/0	Not used or new rags, scrap twine, cordage, rope and cables and worn out articles of twine, cordage, rope or cables, of textile materials
	0/0/0	0	5.6	4.2	0	0	0	0/0/0	0/0/		0/0/0	0/0/0	Other rags, scrap twine, cordage, rope and cables and worn out articles of twine, cordage, rope or cables, of textile materials

第十二类
鞋、帽、伞、杖、鞭及其零件；已加工的羽毛及其制品；人造花；人发制品

第六十四章
鞋靴、护腿和类似品及其零件

注释：

一、本章不包括：

(一)易损材料(例如,纸、塑料薄膜)制的无外绱鞋底的一次性鞋靴罩或套,这些产品应按其构成材料归类；

(二)纺织材料制的鞋靴,没有用粘、缝或其他方法将外底固定或安装在鞋面上的(第十一类)；

(三)税目 63.09 的旧鞋靴；

(四)石棉制品(税目 68.12)；

(五)矫形鞋靴或其他矫形器具及其零件(税目 90.21)；

(六)玩具鞋及装有冰刀或轮子的滑冰鞋；护胫或类似的运动防护服装(第九十五章)。

二、税目 64.06 所称"零件",不包括鞋钉、护鞋铁掌、鞋眼、鞋钩、鞋扣、饰物、编带、鞋带、绒球或其他装饰带(应分别归入相应税目)及税目 96.06 的纽扣或其他货品。

三、本章所称：

(一)"橡胶"及"塑料",包括能用肉眼辨出其外表有一层橡胶或塑料的机织物或其他纺织产品,运用本款时,橡胶或塑料仅引起颜色变化的不计在内；

(二)"皮革",是指税目 41.07 及 41.12 至 41.14 的货品。

四、除本章注释三另有规定的以外：

(一)鞋面的材料应以占表面面积最大的那种材料为准,计算表面面积可不考虑附件及加固件,例如,护踝、裹边、饰物、扣子、拉襻、鞋眼或类似附属件。

(二)外底的主要材料应以与地面接触最广的那种材料为准,计算接触面时可不考虑鞋底钉、铁掌或类似附属件：

子目注释：

子目 6402.12、6402.19、6403.12、6403.19 及 6404.11 所称"运动鞋靴",仅适用于：

一、带有或可装鞋底钉、止滑柱、夹钳、马蹄掌或类似品的体育专用鞋靴。

二、滑冰靴,滑雪靴及越野滑雪用鞋靴、滑雪板靴、角力靴、拳击靴及赛车鞋。

税则号列	货品名称〔CIQ 扩展编码及品名－T2 表示见附表 2〕	最惠(%)	暂定税率	普通	增值/消费	出口退税	计量单位	监管条件	检验检疫	特殊证件对美关税
64.01	**橡胶或塑料制外底及鞋面的防水鞋靴,其鞋面不是用缝、铆、钉、旋、塞或类似方法固定在鞋底上的：**									
	-装有金属防护鞋头的鞋靴：									
6401.1010	---橡胶制鞋面的〔999〕	10		100	13/	13	千克/双			/
6401.1090	---塑料制鞋面的〔999〕	10		100	13/	13	千克/双			/40
	-其他鞋靴：									
	--中、短统靴(过踝但未到膝)：									
6401.9210	---橡胶制鞋面的〔999〕	10		100	13/	13	千克/双			/40
6401.9290	---塑料制鞋面的〔999〕	10		100	13/	13	千克/双			/
6401.9900	--其他〔999〕	10		100	13/	13	千克/双			/40
64.02	**橡胶或塑料制外底及鞋面的其他鞋靴：**									
	-运动鞋靴：									
6402.1200	--滑雪靴、越野滑雪鞋靴及滑雪板靴									
6402.1200 10	含濒危动物毛皮橡胶、塑料底及面滑雪靴(包括越野滑雪鞋靴及滑雪板靴)〔999〕	4		100	13/	0	千克/双	EF		/29
6402.1200 90	其他橡胶、塑料底及面滑雪靴(包括越野滑雪鞋靴及滑雪板靴)〔101 橡塑类鞋靴,102 运动类鞋靴〕	4		100	13/	13	千克/双			/29
6402.1900	--其他									
6402.1900 10	含濒危动物毛皮其他运动鞋靴(橡胶、塑料制底及面)〔999〕	10		100	13/	0	千克/双	EF		/35
6402.1900 90	橡胶、塑料制底及面的其他运动鞋靴〔999〕	10		100	13/	13	千克/双			/35

SECTION Ⅻ

FOOTWEAR, HEADGEAR, UMBRELLAS, SUN UMBRELLAS, WALKING-STICKS, SEAT-STICKS, WHIPS, RIDING-CROPS AND PARTS THEREOF; PREPARED FEATHERS AND ARTICLES MADE THEREWITH; ARTIFICIAL FLOWERS; ARTICLES OF HUMAN HAIR

Chapter 64

Footwear, gaiters and the like; parts of such articles

Notes:

1. This Chapter does not cover:

(a) Disposable foot or shoe coverings of flimsy material (for example, paper, sheeting of plastics) without applied soles. These products are classified according to their constituent material;

(b) Footwear of textile material, without an outer sole glued, sewn or otherwise affixed or applied to the upper (Section Ⅺ);

(c) Worn footwear of heading No.63.09;

(d) Articles of asbestos (heading No.68.12);

(e) Orthopaedic footwear or other orthopaedic appliances, or parts thereof (heading No.90.21) or;

(f) Toy footwear or skating boots with ice or roller skates attached; shin-guards or similar protective sportswear (Chapter 95).

2. For the purposes of heading No.64.06, the term "parts" does not include pegs, protectors, eyelets, hooks, buckles, ornaments, braid, laces, pompons or other trimmings (which are to be classified in their appropriate headings) or buttons or other goods of heading No. 96.06.

3. For the purposes of this Chapter:

(a) The terms "rubber" and "plastics" include woven fabrics or other textile products with an external layer of rubber or plastics being visible to the naked eye; for the purpose of this provision, no account should be taken of any resulting change of colour;

(b) The term "leather" refers to the goods of headings No.41.07 and 41.12 to 41.14.

4. Subject to Note 3 to this Chapter:

(a) The material of the upper shall be taken to be the constituent material having the greatest external surface area, no account being taken of accessories or reinforcements such as ankle patches, edging, ornamentation, buckles, tabs, eyelet stays or similar attachments;

(b) The constituent material of the outer sole shall be taken to be the material having the greatest surface area in contact with the ground, no account being taken of accessories or reinforcements such as spikes, bars, nails, protectors or similar attachments.

Subheading Notes:

For the purposes of subheadings No.6402.12, 6402.19, 6403.12, 6403.19 and 6404.11, the expression "sports footwear" applies only to:

1. Footwear which is designed for a sporting activity and has, or has provsion for the attachment of, spikes, sprigs, stops, clips, bars or the like;

2. Skating boots, ski-boots and cross-country ski footwear, snowboard boots, wrestling boots, boxing boots and cycling shoes.

协定税率 %										特惠税率 %			
亚太5国	东/冰/格	巴基斯坦	韩国	瑞士	哥达	秘鲁	澳大利亚	新西/坡/智	港/澳/台	亚太2国	老/柬/缅	36/3/1	Article Description
													Waterproof footwear with outer soles and uppers of rubber or of plastics, the uppers of which are neither fixed to the sole nor assembled by stitching, riveting, nailing, screwing, plugging or similar processes:
													-Footwear incorporating a protective metal toe-cap:
5	0/0/0	12	16.8	7.2	0	0	0	0/0/0	0/0/			0/0/	---With uppers of rubber
5	0/0/0	12	16.8	7.2	0	0	0	0/0/0	0/0/			0/0/	---With uppers of plastics
													-Other footwear:
													--Covering the ankle but not covering the knee:
5	0/0/0	12	16.8	7.2	0	0	0	0/0/0	0/0/			0/0/	---With uppers of rubber
5	0/0/0	12	16.8	7.2	0	0	0	0/0/0	0/0/			0/0/	---With uppers of plastics
5	0/0/0	12	16.8	7.2	0	0	0	0/0/0	0/0/			0/0/	--Other
													Other footwear with outer soles and uppers of rubber or plastics:
													-Sports footwear:
													--Ski-boots, cross-country ski footwear and snowboard boots
2	0/0/0	4	4	0	0	0	0	0//0	0/0/			0/0/0	Inverted skiing boot with rubber、plastic sole and hair of endangered animals(including cross-counory skiing boots and boots for skin)
2	0/0/0	4	4	0	0	0	0	0//0	0/0/			0/0/0	Other ski-boots cross-country ski footwear and snoroboard boots, with outer soles and upper of rubber or plastics
													--Other
5	0/0/0	12	16.8	7.2	0	0	0	0/0/0	0/0/			0/0/	Other sports shoes and boots containing endangered animal hair and hide (rubbor and plastic shoes and inverced)
5	0/0/0	12	16.8	7.2	0	0	0	0/0/0	0/0/			0/0/	Other sport footwear, with outer soles and uppers of rubber or plastics (rubber and plastic shoes and inverted)

税则号列		货品名称〔CIQ扩展编码及品名－T2表示见附表2〕	最惠(%)	暂定税率	普通	增值/消费	出口退税	计量单位	监管条件	检验检疫	特殊证件对美关税
6402.2000		-用栓塞方法将鞋面条带装配在鞋底上的鞋〔101 内底长度小于等于17cm,102 内底长度大于17cm〕	10		100	13/	13	千克/双			/35
		-其他鞋靴:									
6402.9100		--短筒靴(过踝)〔101 内底长度小于等于17cm,102 内底长度大于17cm的橡塑类鞋靴〕	10		100	13/	13	千克/双			/35
		--其他:									
6402.9910		---橡胶制鞋面的〔101 内底长度小于等于17cm,102 内底长度大于17cm〕	10		100	13/	13	千克/双			/35
		---塑料制鞋面的:									
6402.9921		----其他以机织物或其他纺织材料做衬底的〔101 内底长度小于等于17cm,102 内底长度大于17cm〕	10		100	13/	13	千克/双			/
6402.9929		----其他〔101 内底长度小于等于17cm,102 内底长度大于17cm〕	10		100	13/	13	千克/双			/35
64.03		**橡胶、塑料、皮革或再生皮革制外底,皮革制鞋面的鞋靴:**									
		-运动鞋靴:									
6403.1200		--滑雪靴、越野滑雪鞋靴及滑雪板靴									
6403.1200	10	含濒危野生动物皮革制鞋面的滑雪靴〔999〕	14		100	13/	0	千克/双	EF		/
6403.1200	90	其他皮革制鞋面的滑雪靴(包括橡胶、塑料、皮革制外底和越野滑雪鞋靴及板靴)〔999〕	14		100	13/	13	千克/双			/
6403.1900		--其他									
6403.1900	10	含濒危野生动物皮革制鞋面其他运动鞋靴〔999〕	10		100	13/	0	千克/双	EF		/35
6403.1900	90	皮革制鞋面的其他运动鞋靴(橡胶、塑料、皮革或再生皮革制外底)〔999〕	10		100	13/	13	千克/双			/35
6403.2000		-皮革制外底,由交叉于脚背并绕大脚趾的皮革条带构成鞋面的鞋									
6403.2000	10	含濒危野生动物皮革条带为鞋面的皮底鞋〔999〕	14		100	13/	0	千克/双	EF		/
6403.2000	90	其他皮革条带为鞋面的皮底鞋(皮革条带交叉于脚背并绕大脚趾的)〔999〕	14		100	13/	13	千克/双			/
6403.4000		-装有金属防护鞋头的其他鞋靴									
6403.4000	10	其他含濒危野生动物皮革面鞋靴(装有金属护鞋头的)〔999〕	14		100	13/	0	千克/双	FE		/24
6403.4000	90	装有金属护鞋头的其他皮革面鞋靴(橡胶、塑料、皮革或再生皮革制外底)〔999〕	14		100	13/	13	千克/双			/24
		-皮革制外底的其他鞋靴:									
		--短统靴(过踝):									
		---过脚踝但低于小腿的短统靴,按内底长度分类:									
6403.5111		----小于24cm的									
6403.5111	10	含濒危野生动物皮革制外底皮革面过脚踝但低于小腿的短筒靴(内底长度小于24cm,运动用靴除外)〔999〕	8		100	13/	0	千克/双	FE		/33
6403.5111	90	皮革制外底皮革面过脚踝但低于小腿的短筒靴(内底长度小于24cm,运动用靴除外)〔101 内底长度小于等于17cm,102 内底长度大于17cm,适用于14周岁及以下儿童穿用,103 内底长度大于17cm,不适用于14周岁及以下儿童穿用〕	8		100	13/	13	千克/双	A	M	/33
6403.5119		----其他									
6403.5119	10	其他含濒危野生动物皮革制外底皮革面过脚踝但低于小腿短筒靴(运动用靴除外)〔999〕	8		100	13/	0	千克/双	EF		/33
6403.5119	90	其他皮革制外底皮革面过脚踝但低于小腿短筒靴(运动用靴除外)〔101 内底长度小于等于17cm,102 内底长度大于17cm〕	8		100	13/	13	千克/双			/33
		---其他,按内底长度分类:									
6403.5191		----小于24cm的									
6403.5191	10	含濒危野生动物皮革制外底皮革面短筒靴(内底长度小于24cm,运动用靴除外)〔999〕	8		100	13/	0	千克/双	EF		/
6403.5191	90	皮革制外底的皮革面短筒靴(过踝)(内底长度小于24cm,运动用靴除外)〔101 内底长度小于等于17cm,102 内底长度大于17cm,适用于14周岁及以下儿童穿用,103 内底长度大于17cm,不适用于14周岁及以下儿童穿用〕	8		100	13/	13	千克/双	A	M	/
6403.5199		----其他									

协定税率 %										特惠税率 %			
亚太5国	东/冰/格	巴基斯坦	韩国	瑞士	哥达	秘鲁	澳大利亚	新西/坡/智	港/澳/台	亚太2国	老/柬/缅	36/3/1	Article Description
5	0/0/0	12	16.8	7.2	0	0	0	0/0/0	0/0/			0/0/	-Footwear with upper straps or thongs assembled to the sole by means of plugs
													-Other footwear:
5	0/0/0	12	16.8	7.2	0	0	0	0/0/0	0/0/			0/0/	--Covering the ankle
													--Other:
5	0/0/0	12	16.8	7.2	0	0	0	0/0/0	0/0/			0/0/0	---With uppers of rubber
													---With uppers of plastics:
5	0/0/0	0	16.8	7.2	0	0	0	0/0/0	0/0/			0/0/0	----With substrate of woven fabrics or other textile materials
5	0/0/9.6	0	16.8	7.2	0	0	0	0/0/0	0/0/			0/0/0	----Other
													Footwear with outer soles of rubber, plastics, leather or composition leather and upers of leather:
													-Sports footwear:
													--Ski-boots, cross-country ski footwear and snowboard boots
	0/0/0		16.8	7.2	0	0	0	0/0/0	0/0/		/0/	0/0/0	Ski-boots, with uppers of leather of wild animals
	0/0/0		16.8	7.2	0	0	0	0/0/0	0/0/		/0/	0/0/0	Ski-boots, cross-country sik footwear and snowboard boots, with outer soles of rubber, plastics, leather or composition leather and upers of leather
													—Other
	0/0/0	12	6	4.5	0	0	0	0/0/0	0/0/		/0/	0/0/0	Other sports footwear with uppers of leather of wild animals
	0/0/0	12	6	4.5	0	0	0	0/0/0	0/0/		/0/	0/0/0	Other sports footwear with outer soles of rubber, plastics, leather or composition leather and uppers of leather
													-Footwear with outer soles of leather, and uppers which consist of leather straps across the instep and around the big toe
	0/0/0	0	16.8	7.2	0	0	0	0/0/0	0/0/		/0/	0/0/0	Footwear with outer soles of leather and with uppers of leather straps of wild animals
	0/0/0	0	16.8	7.2	0	0	0	0/0/0	0/0/		/0/	0/0/0	Footwear with outer soles of leather and with uppers which consist of leather straps across the instep and around the big toe
													-Other footwear, incorporating a protective metal toe-cap
	0/0/0		16.8	7.2	0	0	0	0/0/0	0/0/		/0/	0/0/0	Other footwear, incorporating a protective metal toe-cap with uppers of leather of wild animals
	0/0/0		16.8	7.2	0	0	0	0/0/0	0/0/		/0/	0/0/0	Other footwear, incorporating a protective metal toe-cap, with outer soles of rubber, plastics, leather or composition leather and uppers of leather
													-Other footwear with outer soles of leather:
													--Covering the ankle:
													---Covering the ankle but not covering the calf, by length of inner soles:
													----Less than 24cm
	0/0/0	4	4	0	0	0	0	0//0	0/0/		/0/	0/0/0	Other footwear with outer soles of leather and uppers of leather, covering the ankle but lower than crus, with uppers of leather of wild animals(inner sole length<24cm, other than sports boots)
	0/0/0	4	4	0	0	0	0	0//0	0/0/		/0/	0/0/0	Footwear, with outer soles of leather and uppers of leather, covering the ankle but lower than crus, with uppers of leather(inner sole length<24cm, other than sports boots)
													----Other
	0/0/0	4	4	0	0	0	0	0//0	0/0/		/0/	0/0/0	Other footwear with outer soles of leather and uppers of leather, covering the ankle but lower than crus, with uppers of leather of wild animals, other than sports footwear
	0/0/0	4	4	0	0	0	0	0//0	0/0/		/0/	0/0/0	Other footwear with outer soles of leather and uppers of leather, covering the ankle but lower than crus, other than sports footwear
													---Other, by length of inner soles:
													----Less than 24cm
	0/0/0	4	4	0	0	0	0	0//0	0/0/		/0/	0/0/0	Footwear with outer soles of leather and uppers of leather, covering the ankle, with uppers of leather of wild animals(inner soles<24cm, other than sports footwear)
	0/0/0	4	4	0	0	0	0	0//0	0/0/		/0/	0/0/0	Footwear with outer soles of leather and uppers of leather, covering the ankle(inner soles<24cm other than sports footwear)
													----Other

税则号列		货品名称〔CIQ扩展编码及品名－T2表示见附表2〕	最惠(%)	暂定税率	普通	增值/消费	出口退税	计量单位	监管条件	检验检疫	特殊证件对美关税
6403.5199	10	含濒危野生动物皮革制外底皮革面短筒靴(运动用靴除外)〔999〕	8		100	13/	0	千克/双	FE		/33
6403.5199	90	皮革制外底的皮革面短筒靴(过踝)(运动用靴除外)〔101内底长度小于等于17cm,102内底长度大于17cm〕	8		100	13/	13	千克/双			/33
6403.5900		--其他									
6403.5900	10	含濒危野生动物皮革制外底皮革面其他鞋(包括靴,运动用鞋靴除外)〔999〕	8		100	13/	0	千克/双	EF		/33
6403.5900	90	皮革制外底的皮革面其他鞋靴(运动用鞋靴除外)〔101内底长度小于等于17cm,102内底长度大于17cm〕	8		100	13/	13	千克/双			/33
		-其他鞋靴:									
		--短筒靴(过踝):									
		---过脚踝但低于小腿的短筒靴,按内底长度分类:									
6403.9111		----小于24cm的									
6403.9111	10	其他含濒危野生动物皮革制面过脚踝但低于小腿的短筒靴(内底<24cm,橡胶、塑料、再生皮革制外底,运动用靴除外)〔999〕	8		100	13/	0	千克/双	EF		/33
6403.9111	90	其他皮革制面过脚踝但低于小腿的短筒靴(内底<24cm,橡胶、塑料、再生皮革制外底,运动用靴除外)〔101内底长度小于等于17cm,102内底长度大于17cm,适用于14周岁及以下儿童穿用,103内底长度大于17cm,不适用于14周岁及以下儿童穿用〕	8		100	13/	13	千克/双	A	M	/33
6403.9119		----其他									
6403.9119	10	其他含濒危野生动物皮革制面过脚踝但低于小腿的短筒靴(橡胶、塑料、再生皮革制外底,运动用靴除外)〔999〕	8		100	13/	0	千克/双	EF		/33
6403.9119	90	其他皮革制面过脚踝但低于小腿的短筒靴(橡胶、塑料、再生皮革制外底,运动用靴除外)〔101内底长度小于等于17cm,102内底长度大于17cm〕	8		100	13/	13	千克/双			/33
		---其他,按内底长度分类:									
6403.9191		----小于24cm的									
6403.9191	10	其他含濒危野生皮革制面的短筒靴(过踝)(内底<24cm,橡胶、塑料、再生皮革制外底,运动用靴除外)〔999〕	8		100	13/	0	千克/双	EF		/33
6403.9191	90	其他皮革制面的短筒靴(过踝)(内底<24cm,橡胶、塑料、再生皮革制外底,运动用靴除外)〔101内底长度小于等于17cm,102内底长度大于17cm,适用于14周岁及以下儿童穿用,103内底长度大于17cm,不适用于14周岁及以下儿童穿用〕	8		100	13/	13	千克/双	A	M	/33
6403.9199		----其他									
6403.9199	10	其他含濒危野生皮革制面的短筒靴(过踝)(橡胶、塑料、再生皮革制外底,运动用靴除外)〔999〕	8		100	13/	0	千克/双	EF		/33
6403.9199	90	其他皮革制面的短筒靴(过踝)(橡胶、塑料、再生皮革制外底,运动用靴除外)〔101内底长度小于等于17cm,102内底长度大于17cm〕	8		100	13/	13	千克/双			/33
6403.9900		--其他									
6403.9900	10	含濒危野生动物皮革制面的其他鞋靴(橡胶、塑料、再生皮革制外底,运动用鞋靴除外)〔999〕	8		100	13/	0	千克/双	FE		/33
6403.9900	90	其他皮革制面的其他鞋靴(橡胶、塑料、再生皮革制外底,运动用鞋靴除外)〔101内底长度小于等于17cm,102内底长度小于等于17cm〕	8		100	13/	13	千克/双			/33
64.04		**橡胶、塑料、皮革或再生皮革制外底,用纺织材料制鞋面的鞋靴:**									
		-橡胶或塑料制外底的鞋靴:									
6404.1100		--运动鞋靴;网球鞋、篮球鞋、体操鞋、训练鞋及类似鞋〔999〕	10		100	13/	13	千克/双			/35
		--其他:									
6404.1910		---拖鞋〔101内底长度小于等于17cm,102内底长度大于17cm〕	10		100	13/	13	千克/双			/35
6404.1990		---其他〔101内底长度小于等于17cm,102内底长度大于17cm〕	10		100	13/	13	千克/双			/35
		-皮革或再生皮革制外底的鞋靴:									
6404.2010		---拖鞋〔101内底长度小于等于17cm,102内底长度大于17cm,非运动鞋,103运动类鞋靴〕	10		100	13/	13	千克/双			/

协定税率 %										特惠税率 %			Article Description
亚太5国	东/冰/格	巴基斯坦	韩国	瑞士	哥达	秘鲁	澳大利亚	新西/坡/智	港/澳/台	亚太2国	老/柬/缅	36/3/1	
	0/0/0	4	4	0	0	0	0	0//0	0/0/		/0/	0/0/0	Footwear with outer soles of leather and uppers of leather, covering the ankle, with uppers of leather of wild animals(other than sports footwear)
	0/0/0	4	4	0	0	0	0	0//0	0/0/		/0/	0/0/0	Footwear with outer soles of leather and uppers of leather, covering the ankle, with uppers of leather(other than sports footwear)
													--Other
	0/0/0	4	4	3	0	0	0	0//0	0/0/		/0/	0/0/0	Other footwear with outer soles of leather and upers of leather of wild animals(other than sports footwear)
	0/0/0	4	4	3	0	0	0	0//0	0/0/		/0/	0/0/0	Other footwear with outer soles of leather and upers of leather of other animals(other than sports footwear)
													-Other footwear:
													--Covering the ankle:
													---Covering the ankle but not covering the calf, by length of inner soles
													----Less than 24cm
	0/0/0	4.5	4	3	0	0	0	0/0/0	0/0/		/0/	0/0/0	Footwear with outer uper of feather, covering the ankle but lower than crus, with upers of wild animal leather, inner soles of rubber or plastic and the length＜24cm, outer soles of composition leather, other than sports footwear
	0/0/0	4.5	4	3	0	0	0	0/0/0	0/0/		/0/	0/0/0	Footwear with outer uper of feather, lovering the ankle but lower than crus, with inner soles of rubber or plastic and the length＜24cm, outer soles of composition leather, other than sports footwear
													----Other
	0/0/0	0	4	0	0	0	0	0/0/0	0/0/		/0/	0/0/0	Footwear covering the ankle but lower than crus, with outer soles of rubber, plastics, leather of composition leather and upers of wild animal feather, other than sports footwear
	0/0/0	0	4	0	0	0	0	0/0/0	0/0/		/0/	0/0/0	Footwear covering the ankle but lower than crus, with outer soles of rubber, plastics, leather of composition leather and upers of leather, other than sports footwear
													---Other, by length of inner soles:
													----Less than 24cm
	0/0/0	0	4	0	0	0	0	0/0/0	0/0/		/0/	0/0/0	Footwear covering ankle, with outer upers of leather of wild animal, inner soles of rubber, plastic and the length＜24cm, outer soles of composition leather, other than sports footwear
	0/0/0	0	4	0	0	0	0	0/0/0	0/0/		/0/	0/0/0	Footwear covering ankle, with outer upers of leather, inner soles of rubber, plastic and the length＜24cm, outer soles of composition leather, other than sports footwear
													----Other
	0/0/0	0	4	0	0	0	0	0/0/0	0/0/		/0/	0/0/0	Footwear covering the ankle with outer soles of rubber, plastics, leather or composition leather and upers of leather, of wild animals, other than sports footwear
	0/0/0	0	4	0	0	0	0	0/0/0	0/0/		/0/	0/0/0	Footwear covering the ankle with outer soles of rubber, plastics, leather or composition leather and upers of leather, of other animals, other than sports footwear
													--Other
5.2	0/0/0	0	4	3	0	0	0	0/0/0	0/0/		/0/	0/0/0	Other footwear with outer soles of rubber, plastics, leather or composition leather and upers of leather of wild animals, other than sports footwear
5.2	0/0/0	0	4	3	0	0	0	0/0/0	0/0/		/0/	0/0/0	Other footwear with outer soles of rubber, plastics, leather or composition leather and upers of leather of other animals, other than sports footwear
													Footwear with outer soles of rubber, plastics, leather or composition leather and uppers of textile materials:
													-Footwear with outer soles of rubber or plastics:
5	0/0/0	0	16.8	7.2	0	0	0	0/0/0	0/0/			0/0/	--Sports footwear, tennis shoes, basketball shoes, gym shoes, training shoes and the like
													--Other:
5	0/0/0	9.6	16.8	7.2	0	0	0	0/0/0	0/0/				---Slippers
5	0/0/0	9.6	16.8	7.2	0	0	0	0/0/0	0/0/				---Other
													-Footwear with outer soles of leather or composition leather:
5	0/0/0	12	16.8	7.2	0	0	0	0/0/0	0/0/				---Slippers

税则号列		货品名称〔CIQ扩展编码及品名—T2表示见附表2〕	最惠(%)	暂定税率	普通	增值/消费	出口退税	计量单位	监管条件	检验检疫	特殊证件对美关税
6404.2090		---其他〔101内底长度小于等于17cm,102内底长度大于17cm,非运动鞋,103运动类鞋靴〕	10		100	13/	13	千克/双			/40
64.05		**其他鞋靴:**									
		-皮革或再生皮革制鞋面的:									
6405.1010		---橡胶、塑料、皮革及再生皮革制外底的〔101内底长度小于等于17cm,102内底长度大于17cm〕	12		100	13/	13	千克/双			/
6405.1090		---其他材料制外底的									
6405.1090	10	含濒危野生动物皮革制面的其他鞋靴(外底用橡胶、塑料、皮革及再生皮革以外材料制成)〔999〕	12		100	13/	0	千克/双	EF		/
6405.1090	90	其他皮革或再生皮革制面的其他鞋靴(外底用橡胶,塑料,皮革及再生皮革以外材料制成)〔101内底长度小于等于17cm,102内底长度大于17cm〕	12		100	13/	13	千克/双			/
6405.2000		-纺织材料制鞋面的									
6405.2000	10	羊毛毡呢制内底及鞋面的鞋靴(外底用橡胶,塑料,皮革或再生皮革制以外材料制成)〔101内底长度小于等于17cm,102内底长度大于17cm〕	10		100	13/	13	千克/双			/35
6405.2000	90	纺织材料制鞋面的其他鞋靴(外底用橡胶,塑料,皮革或再生皮革制以外材料制成)〔101内底长度小于等于17cm,102内底长度大于17cm〕	10		100	13/	13	千克/双			/35
		-其他:									
6405.9010		---橡胶、塑料、皮革及再生皮革制外底的〔101日常穿着用,102非日常穿着用〕	6		100	13/	13	千克/双			/31
6405.9090		---其他材料制外底的〔101日常穿着用,102非日常穿着用〕	6		100	13/	13	千克/双			/31
64.06		**鞋靴零件(包括鞋面,不论是否带有除外底以外的其他鞋底);活动式鞋内底、跟垫及类似品;护腿、裹腿和类似品及其零件:**									
6406.1000		-鞋面及其零件,但硬衬除外									
6406.1000	10	含濒危野生动物皮的鞋面及其零件〔999〕	6		90	13/	0	千克/双	FE		/31
6406.1000	90	其他鞋面及其零件(不包括硬衬及毡呢制品)〔999〕	6		90	13/	13	千克/双			/31
		-橡胶或塑料制的外底及鞋跟:									
6406.2010		---橡胶制的〔999〕	6		90	13/	13	千克/双			/31
6406.2020		---塑料制的〔999〕	6		90	13/	13	千克/双			/31
		-其他:									
6406.9010		---木制〔999〕	6		90	13/	13	千克/双			/
		---其他材料制:									
6406.9091		----活动式鞋内底、跟垫及类似品〔999〕	6		90	13/	13	千克/双			/31
6406.9092		----护腿、裹脚和类似品及其零件〔999〕	6		90	13/	13	千克/双			/31
6406.9099		----其他材料制其他鞋靴零件〔999〕	6		90	13/	13	千克/双			/16

协定税率 %										特惠税率 %			
亚太5国	东/冰/格	巴基斯坦	韩国	瑞士	哥达	秘鲁	澳大利亚	新西/坡/智	港/澳/台	亚太2国	老/柬/缅	36/3/1	Article Description
5	0/0/0	12	16.8	7.2	0	0	0	0/0/0	0/0/				---Other
													Other footwear:
													-With uppers of leather or composition leather:
6	0/0/0	12	16.8	7.2	0	0	0	0/0/0	0/0/			0/0/	---Outer soles of rubber, plastics, leather or composition leather
													---Outer soles of other materials
6	0/0/0	12	16.8	7.2	0	0	0	0/0/0	0/0/			0/0/	Other footwear with uppers of leather or composition leather of wid andimds(with outer soles of materials other than rubber, plastics, leather or composition leather)
6	0/0/0	12	16.8	7.2	0	0	0	0/0/0	0/0/			0/0/	Other footwear eieh uppers of leather or composition leather(with outer soles of materials other than rubber, plastics, leather or composition leather)
													-With uppers of textile materials
5	0/0/0	11	15.4	6.6	0	0	0	0/0/0	0/0/			0/0/	Footwear with inner soles and uppers of wool felt, outer soled of materials other than rubber, plastics, leather or composition leather
5	0/0/0	11	15.4	6.6	0	0	0	0/0/0	0/0/			0/0/	Other footwear with uppers of textile materials, outer soles of materials other than rubber, plastics, leather or composition leather
													-Other:
3.9	0/0/0	0	6	4.5	0	0	0	0/0/0	0/0/			0/0/	---With outer soles of rubber, plastics, leather or composition leather
3.9	0/0/0	7.5	6	4.5	0	0	0	0/0/0	0/0/			0/0/	---Outer soles of other materials
													Parts of footwear (including uppers whether or not attached to soles other than outer soles); removable in-soles, heel cushions and similar articles; gaiters, leggings and similar articles, and parts thereof:
													-Uppers and parts thereof, other than stiffeners
3.9	0/0/0	7.5	10.5	4.5	0	0	0	0/0/0	0/0/0			0/0/	Uppers and parts thereof, consist of leather of wild animals
3.9	0/0/0	7.5	10.5	4.5	0	0	0	0/0/0	0/0/0			0/0/	Other uppers and parts thereof(other than stiffeners and articles of felt)
													-Outer soles and heels, of rubber or plastics:
	0/0/0	12	6	4.5	0	0	0	0/0/0	0/0/0			0/0/0	---Of rubber
	0/0/0	12	6	4.5	0	0	0	0/0/0	0/0/			0/0/0	---Of plastics
													-Other:
3.9	0/0/0	7.5	6	4.5	0	0	0	0/0/0	0/0/			0/0/	---Of wood
													---Of other materials:
3.9	0/0/0	7.5	10.5	4.5	0	0	0	0/0/0	0/0/0			0/0/	----Removable in-soles, heel cushions and similar articles
3.9	0/0/0	6	10.5	4.5	0	0	0	0/0/0	0/0/0			0/0/	----Gaiters, leggings and similar articles, and parts thereof
3.9	0/0/0	6	10.5	4.5	0	0	0	0/0/0	0/0/0			0/0/	----Other parts of footwear of other materials

第六十五章
帽类及其零件

注释：

一、本章不包括：

(一)税目 63.09 的旧帽类；

(二)石棉制帽类(税目 68.12)；

(三)第九十五章的玩偶帽、其他玩具帽或狂欢节用品。

二、税目 65.02 不包括缝制的帽坯，但仅将条带缝成螺旋形的除外。

税则号列		货品名称〔CIQ 扩展编码及品名—T2 表示见附表 2〕	最惠(%)	暂定税率	普通	增值/消费	出口退税	计量单位	监管条件	检验检疫	特殊证件对美关税
65.01		**毡呢制的帽坯、帽身及帽兜，未楦制成形，也未加帽边；毡呢制的圆帽片及制帽用的毡呢筒(包括裁开的毡呢筒)：**									
6501.0000		毡呢制的帽坯、帽身及帽兜，未楦制成形，也未加帽边；毡呢制的圆帽片及制帽用的毡呢筒(包括裁开的毡呢筒)〔101 纤维素纤维制生活帽，102 动物纤维制生活帽，103 化学纤维制生活帽〕	10		100	13/	13	千克			/30
65.02		**编结的帽坯或用任何材料的条带拼制而成的帽坯，未楦制成形，也未加帽边、衬里或装饰物：**									
6502.0000		编结的帽坯或用任何材料的条带拼制成而的帽坯，未楦制成形，也未加帽边、衬里或装饰物〔101 皮革制生活帽，102 纤维素纤维制生活帽，103 动物纤维制生活帽，104 化学纤维制生活帽〕	8		100	13/	13	千克			/
65.04		**编结帽或用任何材料的条带拼制而成的帽类，不论有无衬里或装饰物：**									
6504.0000		编结帽或用任何材料的条带拼制而成的帽类，不论有无衬里或装饰物〔101 皮革制生活帽，102 纤维素纤维制生活帽，103 动物纤维制生活帽，104 化学纤维制生活帽〕	8		130	13/	13	个/千克			/28
65.05		**针织或钩编的帽类，用成匹的花边、毡呢或其他纺织物(条带除外)制成的帽类，不论有无衬里或装饰物；任何材料制的发网，不论有无衬里或装饰物：**									
6505.0010		---发网〔999〕	4		130	13/	13	个/千克			/29
6505.0020		---钩编的帽类〔101 纤维素纤维制生活帽，102 动物纤维制生活帽，103 化学纤维制生活帽〕	8		130	13/	13	个/千克			/33
		---其他：									
6505.0091		----用税目 65.01 的帽身、帽兜或圆帽片制成的毡呢帽类，无论有无衬里或装饰物〔101 纤维素纤维制生活帽，102 动物纤维制生活帽，103 化学纤维制生活帽〕	8		130	13/	13	个/千克			/18
6505.0099		----其他〔101 纤维素纤维制生活帽，102 动物纤维制生活帽，103 化学纤维制生活帽〕	8		130	13/	13	个/千克			/33
65.06		**其他帽类，不论有无衬里或装饰物：**									
6506.1000		-安全帽									
6506.1000	10	防护面罩(带有能够滤除生物因子滤器的面罩)〔999〕	4		100	13/	13	个/千克	3		/34
6506.1000	90	其他安全帽(不论有无衬里或饰物)〔101 工业用安全帽，102 非工业用安全帽〕	4		100	13/	13	个/千克			/34
		-其他：									
6506.9100		--橡胶或塑料制〔999〕	4		100	13/	13	个/千克			/14
		--其他材料制：									
6506.9910		---皮革制									
6506.9910	10	含濒危野生动物皮革制帽类〔999〕	8		130	13/	0	个/千克	EF		/28
6506.9910	90	其他皮革制帽类〔999〕	8		130	13/	13	个/千克			/28
6506.9920		---毛皮制									
6506.9920	10	含濒危野生动物毛皮制的帽类(无论有无衬里或饰物)〔999〕	4		130	13/	0	个/千克	EF		/14
6506.9920	90	其他毛皮制的帽类(无论有无衬里或饰物)〔999〕	4		130	13/	13	个/千克			/14
6506.9990		---其他〔999〕	10		100	13/	13	个/千克			/35
65.07		**帽圈、帽衬、帽套、帽帮、帽骨架、帽舌及帽颏带：**									
6507.0000		帽圈、帽衬、帽套、帽帮、帽骨架、帽舌及帽颏带	24		100	17	15	千克			
6507.0000	10	含濒危野生动物成分的帽类附件(指帽圈、衬、套、帮、骨架、舌及颏带)〔999〕	10		100	13/	0	千克	FE		/20
6507.0000	90	其他帽类附件(指帽圈、衬、套、帮、骨架、舌及颏带)〔999〕	10		100	13/	13	千克			/20

Chapter 65
Headgear and parts thereof

Notes:

1. This Chapter does not cover:
   (a) Worn headgear of heading No.63.09;
   (b) Asbestos headgear (Heading No.68.12) or;
   (c) Dolls' hats, other toy hats or carnival articles of Chapter 95.
2. Heading No.65.02 does not cover hat-shapes made by sewing, other than those obtained simply by sewing strips in spirals.

协定税率 %										特惠税率 %			
亚太5国	东/冰/格	巴基斯坦	韩国	瑞士	哥达	秘鲁	澳大利亚	新西/坡/智	港/澳/台	亚太2国	老/柬/缅	36/3/1	Article Description
													Hat-forms, hat bodies and hoods of felt, neither blocked to shape nor with made brims; plateaux and manchons (including slit manchons), of felt:
	0/0/0		15.4	6.6	0	0	0	0/0/0	0/0/			0/0/	Hat-forms, hat bodies and hoods of felt, neither blocked to shape nor with made brims; plateaux and manchons (including slit manchons), of felt
													Hat-shapes, plaited or made by assembling strips of any material, neither blocked to shape, nor with made brims, nor lined, nor trimmed:
	0/0/0		12	6	0	0	0	0/0/0	0/0/			0/0/	Hat-shapes, plaited or made by assembling strips of any material, neither blocked to shape, nor with made brims, nor lined, nor trimmed
													Hats and other headgear, plaited or made by assembling strips of any material, whether or not lined or trimmed:
	0/0/0		12	6	0	0	0	0/0/0	0/0/			0/0/	Hats and other headgear, plaited or made by assembling strips of any material, whether or not lined or trimmed
													Hats and other headgear, knitted or crocheted, or made up from lace, felt or other textile fabric, in the piece (but not in strips), whether or not lined or trimmed; hair-nets of any material, whether or not lined or trimmed:
	0/0/0	4	4	0	0	0	0	0//0	0/0/			0/0/0	---Hair-nets
5.2	0/0/0	19	12	6	0	0	0	0/0/0	0/0/			0/0/0	---Hats and other headgear, knitted or crocheted
													---Other:
4.8	0/0/0		15.4	6.6	0	0	0	0/0/0	0/0/			0/0/	----Felt hats and other felt headgear, made from the hat bodies, hoods or plateaux of heading No.65.01, whether or not lined or trimmed
5.2	0/0/0	19	8	6	0	0	0	0/0/0	0/0/			0/0/0	----Other
													Other headgear, whether or not lined or trimmed:
													-Safety headgear
	0/0/0	4	4	0	0	0	0	0//0	0/0/			0/0/	Protecting cover (with veil and colander that can screen biological elements)
	0/0/0	4	4	0	0	0	0	0//0	0/0/			0/0/	Other safety caps (whether or not lined or trimmed)
													-Other:
	0/0/0	4	4	0	0	0	0	0//0	0/0/			0/0/	--Of rubber or of plastics
													--Of other materials:
													---Of leather
	0/0/0	4	4	0	0	0	0	0//0	0/0/			0/0/	Other headgear, of leather of wild animals
	0/0/0	4	4	0	0	0	0	0//0	0/0/			0/0/	Other headgear, of leather of other animals
													---Of furskin
	0/0/0	4	4	0	0	0	0	0//0	0/0/			0/0/0	Other headgear, of leather of wild animals (whether or not lined or trimmed)
	0/0/0	4	4	0	0	0	0	0//0	0/0/			0/0/0	Other headgear, of leather of other animals (whether or not lined or trimmed)
	0/0/0		16.8	7.2	0	0	0	0/0/0	0/0/			0/0/0	---Other
													Head-bands, linings, covers, hat foundations, hat frames, peaks and chinstraps, for headgear:
													Head-bands, linings, covers, hat foundations, hat frames, peaks and chinstraps, for headgear
	0/0/0		16.8	7.2	0	0	0	0/0/0	0/0/			0/0/	Headwear accessories (including head-bands, linings, covers, hat foundations, hat frames, peaks and chinstraps) containing materials of wild animals
	0/0/0		16.8	7.2	0	0	0	0/0/0	0/0/			0/0/	Other headwear accessories (including head-bands, linings, covers, hat foundations, hat frames, peaks and chinstraps)

第六十六章
雨伞、阳伞、手杖、鞭子、马鞭及其零件

注释：

一、本章不包括：

(一)丈量用杖及类似品(税目90.17)；

(二)火器手杖、刀剑手杖、灌铅手杖及类似品(第九十三章)；

(三)第九十五章的货品(例如，玩具雨伞、玩具阳伞)。

二、税目66.03不包括纺织材料制的零件、附件及装饰品或者任何材料制的罩套、流苏、鞭梢、伞套及类似品。此类货品即使与税目66.01或66.02的物品一同进口或出口，只要未装配在一起，则不应视为上述税目所列物品的组成零件，而应分别归入各有关税目。

税则号列		货品名称〔CIQ扩展编码及品名－T2表示见附表2〕	最惠(%)	暂定税率	普通	增值/消费	出口退税	计量单位	监管条件	检验检疫	特殊证件对美关税
66.01		**雨伞及阳伞(包括手杖伞、庭园用伞及类似伞)：**									
6601.1000		-庭院用伞及类似伞〔101含木制品，102不含木制品〕	6		130	13/	13	千克/把			/16
		-其他：									
6601.9100		--折叠伞〔101含木制品，102不含木制品〕	4		130	13/	13	千克/把			/29
6601.9900		--其他〔101含木制品，102不含木制品〕	4		130	13/	13	千克/把			/29
66.02		**手杖、带座手杖、鞭子、马鞭及类似品：**									
6602.0000		手杖、带座手杖、鞭子、马鞭及类似品									
6602.0000	11	含濒危野生动物成分的手杖、带座手杖(包括马鞭、鞭子及类似品)〔999〕	4		130	13/	0	千克/把	EF		/29
6602.0000	19	动植物材料制手杖、鞭子及类似品(包括带座手杖)〔101含木制品，102不含木制品〕	4		130	13/	13	千克/把			/29
6602.0000	90	其他手杖、带座手杖、鞭子及类似品〔101含木制品，102不含木制品〕	4		130	13/	13	千克/把			/29
66.03		**税目66.01或66.02所列物品的零件及装饰品：**									
6603.2000		-伞骨，包括装在伞柄上的伞骨〔101含木制品，102不含木制品〕	6		130	13/	13	千克			/31
6603.9000		-其他									
6603.9000	10	含濒危野生动物成分的伞、手杖的零件及装饰品(包括鞭子的其他零件及饰品)〔999〕	6		130	13/	0	千克	EF		/31
6603.9000	90	伞、手杖及鞭子的其他零件及饰品(罩套、流苏、鞭梢及纺织材料制品除外)〔101含木制品，102不含木制品〕	6		130	13/	13	千克			/31

Chapter 66
Umbrellas, sun umbrellas, walking-sticks, seat-sticks, whips, riding-crops and parts thereof

Notes:

1. This Chapter does not cover:
   (a) Measure walking-sticks or the like (heading No.90.17);
   (b) Firearm-sticks, sword-sticks, loaded walking-sticks or the like (Chapter 93) or;
   (c) Goods of Chapter 95 (for example, toy umbrellas, toy sun umbrellas).
2. Heading No.66.03 does not cover parts, trimmings or accessories of textile material, or covers, tassels, thongs, umbrella cases or the like, of any material. Such goods presented with, but not fitted to, articles of heading No.66.01 or 66.02 are to be classified separately and not to be treated as forming part of those articles.

协定税率 %										特惠税率 %			
亚太5国	东/冰/格	巴基斯坦	韩国	瑞士	哥达	秘鲁	澳大利亚	新西/坡/智	港/澳/台	亚太2国	老/柬/缅	36/3/1	**Article Description**
													Umbrellas and sun umbrellas (including walking-stick umbrellas, garden umbrellas and similar umbrellas):
	0/0/0	7	5.6	4.2	0	0	0	0/0/0	0/0/			0/0/	-Garden or similar umbrellas
													-Other:
	0/0/0	4	4	0	0	0	0	0//0	0/0/			0/0/0	--Having a telescopic shaft
	0/0/0	4	4	0	0	0	0	0//0	0/0/			0/0/	--Other
													Walking-sticks, seat-sticks, whips, riding-crops and the like:
													Walking-sticks, seat-sticks, whips, riding-crops and the like
	0/0/0	4	4	0	0	0	0	0//0	0/0/			0/0/	Walking-sticks, seat-sticks, whips, riding-crops and the like, containing materials of wild animals
	0/0/0	4	4	0	0	0	0	0//0	0/0/			0/0/	Walking-sticks, seat-sticks, whips, riding-crops and the like, of plant materials or animal materials
	0/0/0	4	4	0	0	0	0	0//0	0/0/			0/0/	Other walking-sticks, seat-sticks, whips, riding-crops and the like
													Parts, trimmings and accessories of articles of heading No.66.01 or 66.02:
	0/0/0	11.2	5.6	4.2	0	0	0	0/0/0	0/0/			0/0/	-Umbrella frames, including frames mounted on shafts (sticks)
													-Other
	0/0/0	11.2	5.6	4.2	0	0	0	0/0/0	0/0/			0/0/0	Parts, trimmings and accessories of articles, containing materials of wild animals
	0/0/0	11.2	5.6	4.2	0	0	0	0/0/0	0/0/			0/0/0	Other parts, trimmings and accessories of articles, other than covers, tassels, thongs and other articles of textile material

第六十七章
已加工羽毛、羽绒及其制品；
人造花；人发制品

注释：

一、本章不包括：

(一)人发制滤布(税目 59.11)；

(二)花边、刺绣品或其他纺织物制成的花卉图案(第十一类)；

(三)鞋靴(第六十四章)；

(四)帽类及发网(第六十五章)；

(五)玩具、运动用品或狂欢节用品(第九十五章)；

(六)羽毛掸帚、粉扑及人发制的筛子(第九十六章)。

二、税目 67.01 不包括：

(一)羽毛或羽绒仅在其中作为填充料的物品(例如税目 94.04 的寝具)；

(二)羽毛或羽绒仅作为饰物或填充料的衣服或衣着附件；

(三)税目 67.02 的人造花、叶及其部分品，以及它们的制成品。

三、税目 67.02 不包括：

(一)玻璃制品(第七十章)；

(二)用陶器、石料、金属、木料或其他材料经模铸、锻造、雕刻、冲压或用其他方法整件制成形的人造花、叶或果实；用捆扎、胶粘及类似方法以外的其他方法将部分品组合而成的上述制品。

税则号列	货品名称〔CIQ 扩展编码及品名－T2 表示见附表 2〕	最惠(%)	暂定税率	普通	增值/消费	出口退税	计量单位	监管条件	检验检疫	特殊证件对美关税
67.01	**带羽毛或羽绒的鸟皮及鸟体其他部分、羽毛、部分羽毛、羽绒及其制品(税目 05.05 的货品和经加工的羽管及羽轴除外)：**									
6701.0000	带羽毛或羽绒的鸟皮及鸟体其他部分、羽毛、部分羽毛、羽绒及其制品(税目 05.05 的货品和经加工的羽管及羽轴除外)									
6701.0000　10	已加工野禽羽毛、羽绒及其制品〔999〕	8		130	13/	13	千克	AFEB	PQ	/18
6701.0000　90	其他已加工羽毛、羽绒及其制品(税目 05.05 的货品及经加工的羽管及羽轴除外)〔999〕	8		130	13/	13	千克	AB	PQ	/18
67.02	**人造花、叶、果实及其零件；用人造花、叶或果实制成的物品：**									
6702.1000	-塑料制〔101 含木制品，102 不含木制品〕	8		130	13/	13	千克			/18
	-其他材料制：									
6702.9010	--羽毛制									
6702.9010　10	野禽羽毛制花、叶、果实及其制品〔101 含木制品，102 不含木制品〕	8		130	13/	13	千克	AFEB	PQ	/
6702.9010　90	其他羽毛制花、叶、果实及其制品(包括花、叶、果实的零件)〔101 含木制品，102 不含木制品〕	8		130	13/	13	千克	AB	PQ	/
6702.9020	---丝及绢丝制〔101 含木制品，102 不含木制品〕	8		130	13/	13	千克			/33
6702.9030	---化学纤维制〔101 含木制品，102 不含木制品〕	8		130	13/	13	千克			/28
6702.9090	---其他〔101 含木制品，102 不含木制品〕	8		130	13/	13	千克			/33
67.03	**经梳理、稀疏、脱色或其他方法加工的人发；作假发及类似品用的羊毛、其他动物毛或其他纺织材料：**									
6703.0000	经梳理、稀疏、脱色或其他方法加工的人发或作假发及类似品用的羊毛、其他动物毛或其他纺织材料〔101 含木制品，102 不含木制品〕	8		100	13/	10	千克			/33
67.04	**人发、动物毛或纺织材料制的假发、假胡须、假眉毛、假睫毛及类似品；其他税目未列名的人发制品：**									
	-合成纤维纺织材料制：									
6704.1100	--整头假发〔101 含木制品，102 不含木制品〕	8		130	13/	10	千克			/28
6704.1900	--其他〔101 含木制品，102 不含木制品〕	8		130	13/	10	千克			/33
6704.2000	-人发制〔101 含木制品，102 不含木制品〕	6		130	13/	10	千克			/16
6704.9000	-其他材料制〔101 含木制品，102 不含木制品〕	8		130	13/	10	千克			/33

Chapter 67
Prepared feathers and down and articles made of feathers or of down; artificial flowers; articles of human hair

Notes:

1. This Chapter does not cover:
   (a) Straining cloth of human hair (heading No.59.11);
   (b) Floral motifs of lace, of embroidery or other textile fabric (Section XI);
   (c) Footwear (Chapter 64);
   (d) Headgear or hair-nets (Chapter 65);
   (e) Toys, sports requisites or carnival articles (Chapter 95); or
   (f) Feather dusters, powder-puffs or hair sieves (Chapter 96).
2. Heading No.67.01 does not cover:
   (a) Articles in which feathers or down constitute only filling or padding (for example, bedding of heading No.94.04);
   (b) Articles of apparel or clothing accessories in which feathers or down constitute no more than mere trimming or padding; or
   (c) Artificial flowers or foliage or parts thereof or made up articles of heading No.67.02.
3. Heading No.67.02 does not cover:
   (a) Articles of glass (Chapter 70); or
   (b) Artificial flowers, foliage or fruit of pottery, stone, metal, wood or other materials, obtained in one piece by moulding, forging, carving, stamping or other process, or consisting of parts assembled otherwise than by binding, glueing, fitting into one another or similar methods.

协定税率 %										特惠税率 %			
亚太5国	东/冰/格	巴基斯坦	韩国	瑞士	哥达	秘鲁	澳大利亚	新西/坡/智	港/澳/台	亚太2国	老/柬/缅	36/3/1	Article Description
													Skins and other parts of birds with their feathers or down, feathers, parts of feathers, down and articles thereof (other than goods of heading No. 05. 05 and worked quills and scapes):
													Skins and other parts of birds with their feathers or down, feathers, parts of feathers, down and articles thereof (other than goods of heading No.05.05 and worked quills and scapes)
	0/0/0		12	6	0	0	0	0/0/0	0/0/			0/0/	Worked feathers, down and articles thereof, of wild birds
	0/0/0		12	6	0	0	0	0/0/0	0/0/			0/0/	Other worked feathers, down and articles thereof (other than goods of heading No.0505 and worked quills and scapes)
													Artificial flowers, foliage and fruit and parts thereof; articles made of artificial flowers, foliage or fruit:
	0/0/0		12	6	0	0	0	0/0/0	0/0/			0/0/	-Of plastics
													-Of other materials:
													---Of feathers or down
4.8	0/0/0		12	6	0	0	0	0/0/0	0/0/			0/0/	Flowers, foliage and fruit and articles thereof, of feathers or down of wild birds
4.8	0/0/0		12	6	0	0	0	0/0/0	0/0/			0/0/	Flowers, foliage and fruit and parts thereof; articles made of artificial flowers, foliage or fruit, of other feathers or down
	0/0/0		16.8	7.2	0	0	0	0/0/0	0/0/			0/0/	---Of silk or spun silk
	0/0/0		16.8	7.2	0	0	0	0/0/0	0/0/			0/0/	---Of man-made fibres
	0/0/0		12	6	0	0	0	0/0/0	0/0/			0/0/	---Other
													Human hair, dressed, thinned, bleached or otherwise worked; wool or other animal hair or other textile materials, prepared for use in making wigs or the like:
5.2	0/0/0	18	8	6	0	0	0	0/0/0	0/0/			0/0/	Human hair, dressed, thinned, bleached or otherwise worked; wool or other animal hair or other textile materials, prepared for use in making wigs or the like
													Wigs, false beards, eyebrows and eyelashes, switches and the like, of human or animal hair or of textile materials; articles of human hair not elsewhere specified or included:
													-Of synthetic textile materials:
	0/0/0		17.5	8	0	0	0	0/0/0	0/0/			0/0/0	--Complete wigs
	0/0/0		17.5	8	0	0	0	0/0/0	0/0/			0/0/0	--Other
	0/0/0	12	6	4.5	0	0	0	0/0/0	0/0/			0/0/0	-Of human hair
	0/0/0		17.5	8	0	0	0	0/0/0	0/0/			0/0/0	-Of other materials

第十三类
石料、石膏、水泥、石棉、云母及类似材料的制品；陶瓷产品；玻璃及其制品

第六十八章
石料、石膏、水泥、石棉、云母及类似材料的制品

注释：

一、本章不包括：

(一)第二十五章的货品；

(二)税目 48.10 或 48.11 的经涂布、浸渍或覆盖的纸及纸板(例如，用云母粉或石墨涂布的纸及纸板、沥青纸及纸板)；

(三)第五十六章或第五十九章的经涂布、浸渍或包覆的纺织物(例如，用云母粉、沥青涂布或包覆的织物)；

(四)第七十一章的物品；

(五)第八十二章的工具及其零件；

(六)税目 84.42 的印刷用石板；

(七)绝缘子(税目 85.46)或绝缘材料制的零件(税目 85.47)；

(八)牙科用磨锉(税目 90.18)；

(九)第九十一章的物品(例如，钟及钟壳)；

(十)第九十四章的物品(例如，家具、灯具及照明装置、活动房屋)；

(十一)第九十五章的物品(例如，玩具、游戏品及运动用品)；

(十二)用第九十六章注释二(二)所述材料制成的税目 96.02 的物品或税目 96.06 的物品(例如纽扣)、税目 96.09 的物品(例如石笔)或税目 96.10 的物品(例如绘画石板)或税目 96.20 的物品(独脚架、双脚架、三脚架及类似品)；或

(十三)第九十七章的物品(例如艺术品)。

二、税目 68.02 所称"已加工的碑石或建筑用石"，不仅适用于已加工的税目 25.15、25.16 的各种石料，也适用于所有经类似加工的其他天然石料(例如，石英岩、燧石、白云石及冻石)，但不适用于板岩。

税则号列	货品名称〔CIQ 扩展编码及品名—T2 表示见附表 2〕	最惠(%)	暂定税率	普通	增值/消费	出口退税	计量单位	监管条件	检验检疫	特殊证件对美关税
68.01	**天然石料(不包括板岩)制的长方砌石、路缘石、扁平石：**									
6801.0000	天然石料(不包括板岩)制的长方砌石、路缘石、扁平石〔999〕	12		70	13/	0	千克			/
68.02	**已加工的碑石或建筑用石(不包括板岩)及其制品，但税目 68.01 的货品除外；天然石料(包括板岩)制的镶嵌石(马赛克)及类似品，不论是否有衬背；天然石料(包括板岩)制的人工染色石粒、石片及石粉：**									
	-砖、瓦、方块及类似品，不论是否为矩形(包括正方形)，其最大表面积以可置入边长小于 7 厘米的方格为限；人工染色的石粒、石片及石粉：									
6802.1010	---大理石〔999〕	15		90	13/	0	千克			/
6802.1090	---其他〔999〕	15		90	13/	0	千克			/
	-简单切削或锯开并具有一个平面的其他碑石或建筑用石及其制品：									
	--大理石、石灰华及蜡石：									
6802.2110	---大理石〔999〕	10		90	13/	0	千克			/35
6802.2120	---石灰华〔999〕	15		90	13/	13	千克			/
6802.2190	---其他〔999〕	15		90	13/	0	千克			/
6802.2300	--花岗岩〔999〕	10		90	13/	0	千克	A	M	/
	--其他石：									
6802.2910	---其他石灰石〔999〕	15		90	13/	0	千克			/
6802.2990	---其他〔999〕	15		90	13/	0	千克			/
	-其他：									
	--大理石、石灰华及蜡石：									
6802.9110	---石刻〔999〕	15		90	13/	13	千克			/40
6802.9190	---其他〔999〕	10		90	13/	13	千克			/35
	--其他石灰石：									
6802.9210	---石刻〔999〕	15		90	13/	13	千克			/25
6802.9290	---其他〔999〕	10		90	13/	13	千克			/30
	--花岗岩：									
	---石刻：									
6802.9311	----墓碑石〔999〕	15		90	13/	13	千克	A	M	/
6802.9319	----其他〔999〕	15		90	13/	13	千克	A	M	/
6802.9390	---其他〔999〕	10		90	13/	13	千克	A	M	/35
	--其他石：									
6802.9910	---石刻〔101 含木制品的工艺品，102 不含木制品的工艺品，103 其他石材、石料〕	15		90	13/	13	千克			/40
6802.9990	---其他〔999〕	15		90	13/	13	千克			/40
68.03	**已加工的板岩及板岩或粘聚板岩的制品：**									
6803.0010	---板岩制〔999〕	15		80	13/	10	千克			/

SECTION XIII
ARTICLES OF STONE,PLASTER,CEMENT,ASBESTOS,MICA OR SIMILAR MATERIALS;CERAMIC PRODUCTS;GLASS AND GLASSWARE
Chapter 68
Articles of stone,plaster,cement,asbestos,mica or similar materials

Notes:

1. This Chapter does not cover:
   (a)Goods of Chapter 25;
   (b)Coated,impregnated or covered paper and paperboard of heading No.48.10 or 48.11 (for example,paper and paperboard coated with mica powder or graphite,bituminized or asphalted paper and paperboard);
   (c)Coated,impregnated or covered textile fabric of Chapter 56 or 59 (for example,fabric coated or covered with mica powder,bituminized or asphalted fabric);
   (d)Articles of Chapter 71;
   (e)Tools or parts of tools,of Chapter 82;
   (f)Lithographic stones of heading No.84.42;
   (g)Electrical insulators (heading No.85.46) or fittings of insulating material of heading No.85.47;
   (h)Dental burrs (heading No.90.18);
   (ij)Articles of Chapter 91 (for example,clocks and clock cases);
   (k)Articles of Chapter 94 (for example,furniture,lamps and lighting fittings,prefabricated buildings);
   (l)Articles of Chapter 95 (for example,toys,games and sports requisites);
   (m)Articles of heading No.96.02,if made of materials specified in Note 2 (b) to Chapter 96,or of heading No.96.06 (for example,buttons),No.96.09(for example,slate pencils) or No.96.10 (for example,drawing slates);or of heading No.96.20(unipod,bipod,tripod or the like)
   (n)Articles of Chapter 97 (for example,works of art).
2. In heading No.68.02,the expression "worked monumental or building stone" applies not only to the varieties of stone referred to in heading No.25.15 or 25.16,but also to all other natural stone (for example,quartzite,flint,dolomite and steatite) similarly worked; it does not,however,apply to slate.

协定税率 %										特惠税率 %			Article Description
亚太5国	东/冰/格	巴基斯坦	韩国	瑞士	哥达	秘鲁	澳大利亚	新西/坡/智	港/澳/台	亚太2国	老/柬/缅	36/3/1	
													Setts,curbstones and flagstones,of natural stone (except slate):
	0/0/0	6	4.8	3.6	0	0	0	0/0/0	0/0/			0/0/	Setts,curbstones and flagstones,of natural stone (except slate)
													Worked monumental or building stone (except slate) and articles thereof,other than goods of heading No.68.01; mosaic cubes and the like,of natural stone (including slate),whether or not on a backing; artificially coloured granules,chippings and powder,of natural stone (including slate):
													-Tiles,cubes and similar articles,whether or not rectangular (including square),the largest surface area of which is capable of being enclosed in a square the side of which is less than 7cm; artificially coloured granules,chippings and powder:
9.8	0/0/0	0	16.8	7.2	0	0	0	0/0/0	0/0/			0/0/0	---Marble
9.8	0/0/0	0	12	6	0	0	0	0/0/0	0/0/			0/0/	---Other
													-Other monumental or building stone and articles thereof,simply cut or sawn,with a flat or even surface:
													--Marble,travertine and alabaster:
	0/0/0	0	4	0	0	0	0	0//0	0/0/			0/0/0	---Marble
10.5	0/0/0	0	16.8	7.2	0	0	0	0/0/0	0/0/			0/0/	---Travertine
10.5	0/0/0	0	16.8	7.2	0	0	0	0/0/0	0/0/			0/0/	---Other
6.5	0/0/0	0	4	0	0	0	0	0//0	0/0/			0/0/0	--Granite
													--Other stone:
	0/0/0	0	16.8	7.2	0	0	0	0/0/0	0/0/			0/0/	---Other calcareous stone
	0/0/0	0	6	4.5	0	0	0	0/0/0	0/0/			0/0/0	---Other
													-Other:
													--Marble,travertine and alabaster:
	0/0/0	0	16.8	7.2	0	0	0	0/0/0	0/0/			0/0/	---Carvings
	0/0/0	0	4	0	0	0	0	0//0	0/0/			0/0/0	---Other
													--Other calcareous stone:
	0/0/0	0	16.8	7.2	0	0	0	0/0/0	0/0/			0/0/	---Carvings
	0/0/0	0	4	0	0	0	0	0//0	0/0/			0/0/0	---Other
													--Granite:
													---Carvings:
	0/0/0	0	16.8	7.2	0	0	0	0/0/0	0/0/			0/0/	----Tombstone(gravestone)
10.5	0/0/0	0	16.8	7.2	0	0	0	0/0/0	0/0/			0/0/	----Other
6.5	0/0/0	0	4	0	0	0	0	0//0	0/0/			0/0/0	---Other
													--Other stone:
	0/0/0	0	16.8	7.2	0	0	0	0/0/0	0/0/			0/0/	---Carvings
	0/0/0	0	16.8	7.2	0	0	0	0/0/0	0/0/			0/0/0	---Other
													Worked slate and articles of slate or of agglomerated slate:
	0/0/0		12	6	0	0	0	0/0/0	0/0/			0/0/	---Of slate

税则号列	货品名称〔CIQ 扩展编码及品名—T2 表示见附表 2〕	最惠(%)	暂定税率	普通	增值/消费	出口退税	计量单位	监管条件	检验检疫	特殊证件对美关税
6803.0090	---其他〔999〕	15		80	13/	10	千克			/
68.04	**未装支架的石磨、石碾、砂轮和类似品及其零件，用于研磨、磨刃、抛光、整形或切割，以及手用磨石、抛光石及其零件，用天然石料、粘聚的天然磨料、人造磨料或陶瓷制成，不论是否装有其他材料制成的零件：**									
6804.1000	-碾磨或磨浆用石磨、石碾〔999〕	8		40	13/	10	千克			/18
	-其他石磨、石碾、砂轮及类似品：									
	--粘聚合成或天然金刚石制：	8		17	17	5	千克			
6804.2110	---砂轮〔999〕	8		17	13/	10	千克			/28
6804.2190	---其他〔101 石磨或石碾，102 其它磨具，103 其他石材、石料〕	8		17	13/	10	千克			/28
	--其他粘聚磨料制或陶瓷制：									
6804.2210	---砂轮〔999〕	8		17	13/	10	千克			/28
6804.2290	---其他〔999〕	8		40	13/	10	千克			/33
	--天然石料制：									
6804.2310	---砂轮〔999〕	8		17	13/	10	千克			/28
6804.2390	---其他〔999〕	8		40	13/	10	千克			/28
	-手用磨石及抛光石：									
6804.3010	---琢磨油石〔999〕	8		17	13/	10	千克			/18
6804.3090	---其他〔999〕	8		40	13/	10	千克			/28
68.05	**砂布、砂纸及以其他材料为底的类似品，不论是否裁切、缝合或用其他方法加工成形：**									
6805.1000	-砂布〔999〕	8		40	13/	10	千克			/18
6805.2000	-砂纸〔999〕	8		40	13/	10	千克			/18
6805.3000	-其他〔999〕	8		40	13/	10	千克			/18
68.06	**矿渣棉、岩石棉及类似的矿质棉；页状蛭石、膨胀黏土、泡沫矿渣及类似的膨胀矿物材料；具有隔热、隔音或吸音性能的矿物材料的混合物及制品，但税目 68.11、68.12 或第六十九章的货品除外：**									
	-矿渣棉、岩石棉及类似的矿质棉(包括其相互混合物)，块状、成片或成卷：									
6806.1010	---硅酸铝纤维及其制品〔999〕	10		40	13/	10	千克			/20
6806.1090	---其他									
6806.1090　01	其他矿物纤维，渣球含量小于 5%〔999〕	10	5	40	13/	10	千克			/25
6806.1090　90	其他矿渣棉，岩石棉及类似矿质棉(包括相互混合物，块状、成片或成卷)〔999〕	10		40	13/	10	千克			/30
6806.2000	-页状硅石、膨胀黏土、泡沫矿渣及类似的膨胀矿物材料(包括其相互混合物)〔999〕	10		40	13/	0	千克			/20
6806.9000	-其他〔999〕	10		50	13/	0	千克			/20
68.07	**沥青或类似原料(例如，石油沥青或煤焦油沥青)的制品：**									
6807.1000	-成卷〔999〕	10		50	13/	0	千克			/35
6807.9000	-其他〔301 杂项物质，302 其他沥青或类似原料的制品〕	10		50	13/	0	千克			/35
68.08	**镶板、平板、瓦、砖及类似品，用水泥、石膏及其他矿物粘合材料粘合植物纤维、稻草、刨花、木片屑、木粉、锯末或木废料制成：**									
6808.0000	镶板、平板、瓦、砖及类似品，用水泥、石膏及其他矿物粘合材料粘合植物纤维、稻草、刨花、木片屑、木粉、锯末或木废料制成〔999〕	8		40	13/	6	千克			/33
68.09	**石膏制品及以石膏为基本成分的混合材料制品：**									
	-未经装饰的板、片、砖、瓦及类似品：									
6809.1100	--仅用纸、纸板贴面或加强的〔999〕	15		100	13/	10	千克			/40
6809.1900	--其他〔999〕	15		100	13/	10	千克			/35
6809.9000	-其他制品〔999〕	15		100	13/	10	千克			/40
68.10	**水泥、混凝土或人造石制品，不论是否加强：**									
	-砖、瓦、扁平石及类似品：									
6810.1100	--建筑用砖及石砌块〔999〕	10		40	13/	10	千克			/20
	--其他：									
6810.1910	---人造石制〔999〕	10		70	13/	10	千克			/35
6810.1990	---其他〔999〕	10		70	13/	10	千克			/35
	-其他制品：									
	--建筑或土木工程用的预制结构件：									
6810.9110	---钢筋混凝土和预应力混凝土管、杆、板、桩等〔999〕	10		40	13/	10	千克			/
6810.9190	---其他〔999〕	10		40	13/	10	千克			/20

协定税率 %										特惠税率 %			
亚太5国	东/冰/格	巴基斯坦	韩国	瑞士	哥达	秘鲁	澳大利亚	新西/坡/智	港/澳/台	亚太2国	老/柬/缅	36/3/1	Article Description
	0/0/0		12	6	0	0	0	0/0/0	0/0/			0/0/	---Other
													Millstones, grindstones, grinding wheels and the like, without frameworks, for grinding, sharpening, polishing, trueing or cutting, hand sharpening or polishing stones, and parts thereof, of natural stone, of agglomerated natural or artificial abrasives, or of ceramics, with or without parts of other materials:
	0/0/0	4	0	0	0	0	0	0//0	0/0/			0/0/0	-Millstones and grindstones for milling, grinding or pulping
													-Other millstones, grindstones, grinding wheels and the like:
													--Of agglomerated synthetic or natural diamond:
	0/0/0	4	3.2	2.4	0	0	0	0//0	0/0/			0/0/0	---Grinding wheels
	0/0/0	4	3.2	2.4	0	0	0	0//0	0/0/			0/0/0	---Other
													--Of other agglomerated abrasives or of ceramics:
	0/0/0	4	0	2.4	0	0	0	0//0	0/0/			0/0/0	---Grinding wheels
	0/0/0	4	0	0	0	0	0	0//0	0/0/			0/0/0	---Other
													--Of natural stone:
	0/0/0	4	0	0	0	0	0	0//0	0/0/			0/0/0	---Grinding wheels
	0/0/0	4	3.2	0	0	0	0	0//0	0/0/			0/0/0	---Other
													-Hand sharpening or polishing stones:
5.2	0/0/0	4	0	0	0	0	0	0//0	0/0/			0/0/0	---Oilstones
6.4	0/0/0	4	3.2	0	0	0	0	0//0	0/0/			0/0/0	---Other
													Natural or artificial abrasive powder or grain, on a base of textile material, of paper, of paperboard or of other materials, whether or not cut to shape or sewn or otherwise made up:
	0/0/0	4	4.8	2.4	0	0	0	0//0	0/0/			0/0/0	-On a base of woven textile fabric only
	0/0/0	4	3.2	2.4	0	0	0	0//0	0/0/			0/0/0	-On a base of paper or paperboard only
	0/0/0	4	3.2	0	0	0	0	0//0	0/0/			0/0/0	-On a base of other materials
													Slag wool, rock wool and similar mineral wools; exfoliated vermiculite, expanded clays, foamed slag and similar expanded mineral materials; mixtures and articles of heat-insulating, sound-insulating or sound-absorbing mineral materials, other than those of heading No. 68. 11 or 68. 12 or of Chapter 69:
													-Slag wool, rock wool and similar mineral wools (including intermixtures thereof), in bulk, sheets or rolls:
	0/0/0	4.5	4.2	3.2	0	0	0	0/0/0	0/0/			0/0/0	---Aluminum silicate fiber and its products
													—Other
	0/0/0	4.5	4.2	3.2	0	0	0	0/0/0	0/0/			0/0/0	Other mineral fibre, containing slag, <5%
	0/0/0	4.5	4.2	3.2	0	0	0	0/0/0	0/0/			0/0/0	Slag wool, rock wool and similar mineral wools(including intermixtures thereof, inbulk, sheets or rolls)
	0/0/0	4.5	4.2	3.2	0	0	0	0/0/0	0/0/			0/0/0	-Exfoliated vermiculite, expanded clays, foamed slag and similar expanded mineral materials (including intermixtures thereof)
	0/0/0	4	6	0	0	0	0	0//0	0/0/			0/0/0	-Other
													Articles of asphalt or of similar material (for example, petroleum bitumen or coal tar pitch):
	0/0/0	6	4.8	3.6	0	0	0	0/0/0	0/0/			0/0/	-In rolls
8	0/0/0	4.5	4.8	3.6	0	0	0	0/0/0	0/0/			0/0/	-Other
													Panels, boards, tiles, blocks and similar articles of vegetable fibre, of straw or of shavings, chips, particles, sawdust or other waste, of wood, agglomerated with cement, plaster or other mineral binders:
	0/0/0	4.5	4.2	3.2	0	0	0	0/0/0	0/0/			0/0/	Panels, boards, tiles, blocks and similar articles of vegetable fibre, of straw or of shavings, chips, particles, sawdust or other waste, of wood, agglomerated with cement, plaster or other mineral binders
													Articles of plaster or of compositions based on plaster:
													-Boards, sheets, panels, tiles and similar articles, not ornamented:
	0/0/0			8.4	0	0	0	0/0/0	0/0/			0/0/	--Faced or reinforced with paper or paper-board only
	0/0/0		17.5		0	0	0	0/0/0	0/0/			0/0/	--Other
	0/0/0		17.5		0	0	0	0/0/0	0/0/			0/0/	-Other articles
													Articles of cement, of concrete or of artificial stone, whether or not reinforced:
													-Tiles, flagstones, bricks and similar articles:
6.5	0/0/0	4.5	4.2	3.2	0	0	0	0/0/0	0/0/			0/0/0	--Building blocks and bricks
													--Other:
6.5	0/0/0	4.5	4.2	3.2	0	0	0	0/0/0	0/0/			0/0/0	---Of artificial stone
6.5	0/0/0	4.5	4.2	3.2	0	0	0	0/0/0	0/0/			0/0/0	---Other
													-Other articles:
													--Prefabricated structural components for building or civil engineering:
	0/0/0	4.5	4.2	3.2	0	0	0	0/0/0	0/0/			0/0/0	---Reinforced concrete and prestressed concrete tubes, pipes, rods, plates, piles and similar articles
	0/0/0	4.5	4.2	3.2	0	0	0	0/0/0	0/0/			0/0/0	---Other

税则号列	货品名称〔CIQ 扩展编码及品名－T2 表示见附表 2〕	最惠(%)	暂定税率	普通	增值/消费	出口退税	计量单位	监管条件	检验检疫	特殊证件对美关税
	--其他：									
6810.9910	---铁道用水泥枕〔999〕	8		14	13/	10	千克			/
6810.9990	---其他〔999〕	10		70	13/	10	千克			/35
68.11	**石棉水泥、纤维素水泥或类似材料的制品：**									
	-含石棉的：									
6811.4010	---瓦楞板〔999〕	5		40	13/	10	千克			/
6811.4020	---其他片、板、砖、瓦及类似制品〔999〕	8		40	13/	10	千克			/33
6811.4030	---管子及管子附件〔999〕	8		40	13/	10	千克			/
6811.4090	---其他制品〔999〕	8		40	13/	10	千克			/18
	-不含石棉的：									
6811.8100	--瓦楞板〔999〕	5		40	13/	10	千克			/
6811.8200	--其他片、板、砖、瓦及类似制品〔999〕	8		40	13/	10	千克			/33
	--其他制品：									
6811.8910	---管子及管子附件〔999〕	8		40	13/	10	千克			/
6811.8990	---其他〔999〕	8		40	13/	10	千克			/33
68.12	**已加工的石棉纤维；以石棉为基本成分或以石棉和碳酸镁为基本成分的混合物；上述混合物或石棉的制品(例如，纱线、机织物、服装、帽类、鞋靴、衬垫)，不论是否加强，但税号 68.11 或 68.13 的货品除外：**									
6812.8000	-青石棉的〔999〕	10		40	13/	10	千克			/
	-其他：									
6812.9100	--服装、衣着附件、帽类及鞋靴〔999〕	10		40	13/	10	千克			/35
6812.9200	--纸、麻丝板及毡子〔999〕	10		40	13/	10	千克			/20
6812.9300	--成片或成卷的压缩石棉纤维接合材料〔999〕	10		40	13/	10	千克			/20
6812.9900	--其他〔999〕	10		40	13/	10	千克			/20
68.13	**以石棉、其他矿物质或纤维素为基本成分的未装配摩擦材料及其制品(例如，片、卷、带、盘、圈、垫及扇形)，适于作制动器、离合器及类似品，不论是否与织物或其他材料结合而成：**									
	-含石棉的：									
6813.2010	---闸衬、闸垫〔999〕	10		40	13/	10	千克			/20
6813.2090	---其他〔999〕	10		40	13/	10	千克			/20
	-不含石棉的：									
6813.8100	--闸衬、闸垫〔999〕	10		40	13/	10	千克			/35
6813.8900	--其他〔999〕	10		40	13/	10	千克			/20
68.14	**已加工的云母及其制品，包括粘聚或复制的云母，不论是否附于纸、纸板或其他材料上：**									
6814.1000	-粘聚或复制云母制的板、片、带，不论是否附于其他材料上〔999〕	8		35	13/	13	千克			/33
6814.9000	-其他〔999〕	8		35	13/	10	千克			/33
68.15	**其他税号未列名的石制品及其他矿物制品(包括碳纤维及其制品和泥煤制品)：**									
6815.1000	-非电器用的石墨或其他碳精制品〔999〕	10		70	13/	0	千克	3		/20
6815.2000	-泥煤制品〔999〕	10		70	13/	0	千克			/
	-其他制品：									
6815.9100	--含有菱镁矿、白云石或铬铁矿的〔999〕	10		70	13/	0	千克			/35
	--其他：									
6815.9920	---碳纤维									
6815.9920　10	两用物项管制的碳纤维(比模量≥12.7×10^6m，或比抗拉强度≥23.5×10^4m)〔999〕	17		70	13/	13	千克	3		/
6815.9920　90	其他碳纤维〔999〕	17		70	13/	13	千克			/
	---碳纤维制品：									
6815.9931	----碳布〔999〕	17		70	13/	13	千克			/27
6815.9932	----碳纤维预浸料(制品)									
6815.9932　10	两用物项管制的碳纤维预浸料(制品)〔999〕	17		70	13/	13	千克	3		/27
6815.9932　90	其他碳纤维预浸料(制品)〔999〕	17		70	13/	13	千克			/27
6815.9939	----其他〔999〕	17		70	13/	13	千克			/37
6815.9940	---玄武岩纤维及其制品〔999〕	17		70	13/	13	千克			/42
6815.9990	---其他〔999〕	10		70	13/	0	千克			/30

协定税率 %										特惠税率 %			
亚太5国	东/冰/格	巴基斯坦	韩国	瑞士	哥达	秘鲁	澳大利亚	新西/坡/智	港/澳/台	亚太2国	老/柬/缅	36/3/1	Article Description
													--Other:
	0/0/0	4	0	0	0	0	0	0//0	0/0/			0/0/0	---Railway sleepers of concrete
	0/0/0	4.5	4.2	3.2	0	0	0	0/0/0	0/0/			0/0/0	---Other
													Articles of asbestos-cement, of cellulose fibre-cement or the like:
													-Containing aspestos:
	0/0/0	0	0	0	0	0	0	0//0	0/0/			0/0/	---Corrugated sheets
	0/0/0	4.5	4.2	3.2	0	0	0	0/0/0	0/0/			0/0/	---Other sheets, panels, tiles and similar articles
	0/0/0	4	0	0	0	0	0	0//0	0/0/			0/0/	---Tubes, pipes and tube or pipe fittings
	0/0/0	4	3.3	0	0	0	0	0//0	0/0/			0/0/	---Other articles
													-Not containing asbestos:
	0/0/0	0	0	0	0	0	0	0//0	0/0/			0/0/	--Corrugated sheets
	0/0/0	4.5	4.2	5.5	0	0	0	0/0/0	0/0/			0/0/	--Other sheets, panels, tiles and similar articles
													--Other articles:
	0/0/0	4	0	0	0	0	0	0//0	0/0/			0/0/	---Tubes, pipes and tube or pipe fittings
	0/0/0	4	0	0	0	0	0	0//0	0/0/			0/0/	---Other
													Fabricated asbestos fibres; mixtures with a basis of asbestos or with a basis of asbestos and magnesium carbonate; articles of such mixtures or of asbestos (for example, thread, woven fabric, clothing, headgear, footwear, gaskets), whether or not reinforced, other than goods of heading No. 68. 11 or 68. 13:
	0/0/0	4.5	4.2	3.2	0	0	0	0/0/0	0/0/			0/0/0	-Of crocidolite
													-Other:
	0/0/0	4.5	4.2	3.2	0	0	0	0/0/0	0/0/			0/0/0	--Clothing, clothing accessories, footwear and headgear
	0/0/0	4.5	4.2	3.2	0	0	0	0/0/0	0/0/			0/0/0	--Paper, millboard and felt
	0/0/0	4.5	4.2	3.2	0	0	0	0/0/0	0/0/			0/0/0	--Compressed asbestos fibre jointing, in sheets or rolls
	0/0/0	4	4	0	0	0	0	0//0	0/0/			0/0/0	--Other
													Friction material and articles thereof (for example, sheets, rolls, strips, segments, discs, washers, pads), not mounted, for brakes, for clutches or the like, with a basis of asbestos, of other mineral substances or of cellulose, whether or not combined with textile or other materials:
													-Containing asbestos:
	0/0/0	4	4	0	0	0	0	0//0	0/0/			0/0/0	---Brake linings and pads
	0/0/0	6	4.8	3.6	0	0	0	0/0/0	0/0/			0/0/	---Other
													-Not containing asbestos:
	0/0/0	4	4	0	0	0	0	0//0	0/0/			0/0/0	--Brake linings and pads
	0/0/0	6	4.8	3.6	0	0	0	0/0/0	0/0/			0/0/	--Other
													Worked mica and articles of mica, including agglomerated or reconstituted mica, whether or not on a support of paper, paperboard or other meterials:
	0/0/0	4.5	4.2	0	0	0	0	0/0/0	0/0/			0/0/0	-Plates, sheets and strips of agglomerated or reconstituted mica, whether or not on a support
	0/0/0	4.5	4.2	3.2	0	0	0	0/0/0	0/0/			0/0/0	-Other
													Articles of stone or of other mineral substances (including carbon fibres, articles of carbon fibres and articles of peat), not elsewhere specified or included:
	0/0/0	12		4.5	0	0	0	0/0/0	0/0/			0/0/0	-Non-electrical articles of graphite or other carbon
	0/0/0	12	6	4.5	0	0	0	0/0/0	0/0/			0/0/	-Articles of peat
													-Other articles:
	0/0/0	12	6	4.5	0	0	0	0/0/0	0/0/			0/0/	--Containing magnesite, dolomite or chromite
													--Other:
													---Carbon fibres
	0/0/0			5.3	0	0	0	0/0/0	0/0/			0/0/0	Carbon fibres, fual-use items control, modulus atio≥12.7×106m, specific ultimate tensile strength≥23.5×104m
	0/0/0			5.3	0	0	0	0/0/0	0/0/			0/0/0	Other carbon fibres
													---Articles of carbon fibres:
	0/0/0			5.3	0	0	0	0/0/0	0/0/			0/0/0	----Carbon fabric
													----Carbon fiber prepreg(articles)
	0/0/0			5.3	0	0	0	0/0/0	0/0/			0/0/0	Carbon fiber pripreg(articles), fual-use items control
	0/0/0			5.3	0	0	0	0/0/0	0/0/			0/0/0	Other carbon fiber pripreg(articles)
	0/0/0			5.3	0	0	0	0/0/0	0/0/			0/0/0	----Other
	0/0/0	0	7	5.3	0	0	0	0/0/0	0/0/			0/0/0	---Basalt fiber and its products
	0/0/0	0	7	5.3	0	0	0	0/0/0	0/0/			0/0/0	---Other

第六十九章
陶瓷产品

注释：

一、本章仅适用于成形后经过烧制的陶瓷产品。税目 69.04 至 69.14 仅适用于不能归入税目 69.01 至 69.03 的产品。

二、本章不包括：

(一)税目 28.44 的产品；
(二)税目 68.04 的物品；
(三)第七十一章的物品(例如，仿首饰)；
(四)税目 81.13 的金属陶瓷；
(五)第八十二章的物品；
(六)绝缘子(税目 85.46)或绝缘材料制的零件(税目 85.47)；
(七)假牙(税目 90.21)；
(八)第九十一章的物品(例如，钟及钟壳)；
(九)第九十四章的物品(例如，家具、灯具及照明装置、活动房屋)；
(十)第九十五章的物品(例如，玩具、游戏品及运动用品)；
(十一)税目 96.06 的物品(例如，纽扣)或税目 96.14 的物品(例如，烟斗)；
(十二)第九十七章的物品(例如，艺术品)。

税则号列	货品名称〔CIQ 扩展编码及品名—T2 表示见附表 2〕	最惠(%)	暂定税率	普通	增值/消费	出口退税	计量单位	监管条件	检验检疫	特殊证件对美关税
	第一分章 硅化石粉或类似硅土及耐火材料制品									
69.01	**硅质化石粉(例如各种硅藻土)或类似硅土制的砖、块、瓦及其他陶瓷制品：**									
6901.0000	硅质化石粉(例如各种硅藻土)或类似硅土制的砖、瓦、块及其他陶瓷制品〔999〕	8		50	13/	0	千克			/33
69.02	**耐火砖、块、瓦及类似耐火陶瓷建材制品，但硅质化石粉及类似硅土制的除外：**									
6902.1000	-单独或同时含有按重量计超过 50%的镁、钙或铬(分别以氧化镁、氧化钙及三氧化二铬的含量计)〔999〕	8		30	13/	0	千克			/18
6902.2000	-含有按重量计超过 50%的三氧化二铝、二氧化硅或其混合物或化合物〔999〕	8		30	13/	0	千克			/18
6902.9000	-其他〔999〕	8		30	13/	0	千克			/33
69.03	**其他耐火陶瓷制品(例如，甑、坩埚、马弗罩、喷管、栓塞、支架、烤钵、管子、护套及棒条)，但硅质化石粉及类似硅土制的除外：**									
6903.1000	-含有按重量计超过 50%的石墨、其他碳或其混合物〔999〕	8		20	13/	0	千克			/18
6903.2000	-含有按重量计超过 50%的三氧化二铝或三氧化二铝和二氧化硅的混合物或化合物〔999〕	8		20	13/	0	千克			/28
6903.9000	-其他〔999〕	8		20	13/	13	千克			/18
	第二分章 其他陶瓷产品									
69.04	**陶瓷制建筑用砖、铺地砖、支撑或填充用砖及类似品：**									
6904.1000	-建筑用砖〔999〕	15		90	13/	13	千克/千块		L	/
6904.9000	-其他〔999〕	15		90	13/	13	千克		L	/35
69.05	**屋顶瓦、烟囱罩、通风帽、烟囱衬壁、建筑装饰物及其他建筑用陶瓷制品：**									
6905.1000	-屋顶瓦〔999〕	15		90	13/	13	千克			/25
6905.9000	-其他〔999〕	15		90	13/	13	千克		L	/35
69.06	**陶瓷套管、导管、槽管及管子附件：**									
6906.0000	陶瓷套管、导管、槽管及管子附件〔999〕	15	10	90	13/	13	千克			/30
69.07	**陶瓷贴面砖、铺面砖，包括炉面砖及墙面砖；陶瓷镶嵌砖(马赛克)及其类似品，不论是否有衬背；饰面陶瓷：**									
	-贴面砖、铺面砖，包括炉面砖及墙面砖，但子目 6907.30 和 6907.40 所列商品除外：									
	--按重量计吸水率不超过 0.5%：									

Chapter 69
Ceramic products

Notes:

1. This Chapter applies only to ceramic products which have been fired after shaping. Headings Nos.69. 04 to 69. 14 apply only to such products other than those classifiable in headings Nos.69. 01 to 69. 03.
2. This Chapter does not cover:
   (a) Products of heading No.28. 44;
   (b) Articles of heading No.68. 04;
   (c) Articles of Chapter 71 (for example, imitation jewellery);
   (d) Cermets of heading No.81. 13;
   (e) Articles of Chapter 82;
   (f) Electrical insulators (heading No.85. 46) or fittings of insulating material of heading No.85. 47;
   (g) Artificial teeth (heading No.90. 21);
   (h) Articles of Chapter 91 (for example, clocks and clock cases);
   (ij) Articles of Chapter 94 (for example, furniture, lamps and lighting fittings, prefabricated buildings);
   (k) Articles of Chapter 95 (for example, toys, games and sports requisites);
   (m) Articles of heading No.96. 06 (for example, buttons) or of heading No.96. 14 (for example, smoking pipes); or
   (l) Articles of Chapter 97 (for example, works of art).

协定税率 %										特惠税率 %			
亚太5国	东/冰/格	巴基斯坦	韩国	瑞士	哥达	秘鲁	澳大利亚	新西/坡/智	港/澳/台	亚太2国	老/柬/缅	36/3/1	Article Description
													Ⅰ. GOODS OF SILICEOUS FOSSIL MEALS OR OF SIMILAR SILICEOUS EARTHS, AND REFRACTORY GOODS
													Bricks, blocks, tiles and other ceramic goods of siliceous fossil meals (for example, kieselguhr, tripolite or diatomite) or of similar siliceous earths:
5.2	0/0/0	4	0	0	0	0	0	0//0	0/0/			0/0/	Bricks, blocks, tiles and other ceramic goods of siliceous fossil meals (for example, kieselguhr, tripolite or diatomite) or of similar siliceous earths
													Refractory bricks, blocks, tiles and similar refractory ceramic constructional goods, other than those of siliceous fossil meals or similar siliceous earths:
	0/0/0	4	0	0	0	0	0	0//0	0/0/			0/0/0	-Containing by weight, singly or together, more than 50% of the elements Mg, Ca or Cr, expressed as MgO, CaO or Cr_2O_3
	0/0/0	4	0	2.4	0	0	0	0//0	0/0/			0/0/0	-Containing by weight more than 50% of alumina (Al_2O_3), of silica (SiO_2) or of a mixture or compound of these products
	0/0/0	4	3.2	0	0	0	0	0//0	0/0/			0/0/0	-Other
													Other refractory ceramic goods (for example, retorts, crucibles, muffles, nozzles, plugs, supports, cupels, tubes, pipes, sheaths and rods), other than those of siliceous fossil meals or of similar siliceous earths:
	0/0/0	4	3.2	0	0	0	0	0//0	0/0/		0//	0/0/0	-Containing by weight more than 50% of graphite or other carbon or of a mixture of these products
	0/0/0	4	0	0	0	0	0	0//0	0/0/		0//	0/0/0	-Containing by weight more than 50% of alumina (AL_2O_3) or of a mixture of compound of alumina and of silica (SiO_2)
	0/0/0	4	0	0	0	0	0	0//0	0/0/		0//	0/0/0	-Other
													Ⅱ. -OTHER CERAMIC PRODUCTS
													Ceramic building bricks, flooring blocks, support or filler tiles and the like:
	0/0/0	12	6	4.5	0	0	0	0/0/0	0/0/			0/0/0	-Building bricks
	0/0/0		17.1	7.4	0	0	0	0/0/0	0/0/			0/0/	-Other
													Roofing tiles, chimney-pots, cowls, chimney liners, architectural ornaments and other ceramic constructional goods:
	0/0/0		17.1	7.4	0	0	0	0/0/0	0/0/			0/0/	-Roofing tiles
	0/0/0		17.1	7.4	0	0	0	0/0/0	0/0/			0/0/	-Other
													Ceramic pipes, conduits, guttering and pipe fittings:
	0/0/0	12	6	4.5	0	0	0	0/0/0	0/0/			0/0/	Ceramic pipes, conduits, guttering and pipe fittings
													Ceramic flags and paving, hearth or wall tiles; ceramic mosaic cubes and the like, whether or not on a backing; finished ceramic:
													-Ceramic flags and paving, hearth or wall tiles, other than that of subheading No.6907.30 or 6907.40:
													--Of water absorption coefficient by weight not exceeding 0.5%

税则号列	货品名称〔CIQ扩展编码及品名－T2表示见附表2〕	最惠(%)	暂定税率	普通	增值/消费	出口退税	计量单位	监管条件	检验检疫	特殊证件对美关税
6907.2110	---不论是否矩形,其最大表面积以可置入边长小于7厘米的方格为限〔999〕	7		100	13/	13	千克/平方米		L	/27
6907.2190	---其他〔999〕	7		100	13/	13	千克/平方米		L	/32
	--按重量计吸水率超过0.5%,但不超过10%:									
6907.2210	---不论是否矩形,其最大表面积以可置入边长小于7厘米的方格为限〔999〕	7		100	13/	13	千克/平方米			/32
6907.2290	---其他〔999〕	7		100	13/	13	千克/平方米			/32
	--按重量计吸水率超过10%:									
6907.2310	---不论是否矩形,其最大表面积以可置入边长小于7厘米的方格为限〔999〕	7		100	13/	13	千克/平方米			/
6907.2390	---其他〔999〕	7		100	13/	13	千克/平方米			/32
	-镶嵌砖(马赛克)及其类似品,但子目6907.40的货品除外:									
6907.3010	---不论是否矩形,其最大表面积以可置入边长小于7厘米的方格为限〔999〕	7		100	13/	13	千克/平方米		L	/
6907.3090	---其他〔999〕	7		100	13/	13	千克/平方米		L	/
	-饰面陶瓷:									
6907.4010	---不论是否矩形,其最大表面积以可置入边长小于7厘米的方格为限〔999〕	7		100	13/	13	千克/平方米		L	/
6907.4090	---其他〔999〕	7		100	13/	13	千克/平方米		L	/32
69.09	**实验室、化学或其他专门技术用途的陶瓷器;农业用陶瓷槽、缸及类似容器;通常供运输及盛装货物用的陶瓷罐、坛及类似品:**									
	-实验室、化学或其他专门技术用途的陶瓷器:									
6909.1100	--瓷制〔999〕	8		30	13/	13	千克			/18
6909.1200	--莫氏硬度为9或以上的物品〔999〕	8		30	13/	13	千克			/28
6909.1900	--其他〔999〕	8		30	13/	13	千克			/18
6909.9000	-其他〔999〕	15		90	13/	13	千克			/25
69.10	**陶瓷洗涤槽、脸盆、脸盆座、浴缸、坐浴盆、抽水马桶、水箱、小便池及类似的固定卫生设备:**									
6910.1000	-瓷制〔101洗涤槽,102面盆,103浴缸,104座便器,105小便器,106其他卫生瓷〕	7		100	13/	10	千克/件			/32
6910.9000	-其他〔101洗涤槽,102面盆,103浴缸,104座便器,105小便器,106其他卫生陶〕	7		100	13/	10	千克/件	A	M	/32
69.11	**瓷餐具、厨房器具及其他家用或盥洗用瓷器:**									
	-餐具及厨房器具:									
	---餐具:									
6911.1011	----骨瓷〔101食品接触陶瓷产品,102食品用陶瓷包装〕	7		100	13/	13	千克	A	R	/32
6911.1019	----其他〔101食品接触陶瓷产品,102食品用陶瓷包装〕	7		100	13/	13	千克	A	R	/32
	---厨房器具:									
6911.1021	----刀具〔101食品接触陶瓷产品,102食品用陶瓷包装〕	7		100	13/	13	千克	A	R	/
6911.1029	----其他〔101食品接触陶瓷产品,102食品用陶瓷包装〕	7		100	13/	13	千克	A	R	/32
6911.9000	-其他〔999〕	7		100	13/	13	千克			/32
69.12	**陶餐具、厨房器具及其他家用或盥洗用陶器:**									
6912.0010	---餐具〔101食品接触陶瓷产品,102食品用陶瓷包装〕	7		100	13/	13	千克	A	R	/32
6912.0090	---其他〔101食品接触陶瓷产品,102食品用陶瓷包装〕	7		100	13/	13	千克	A	R	/32
69.13	**塑像及其他装饰用陶瓷制品:**									
6913.1000	-瓷制〔999〕	7		100	13/	13	千克			/32
6913.9000	-其他〔999〕	7		100	13/	13	千克			/32
69.14	**其他陶瓷制品:**									
6914.1000	-瓷制〔101其他陶瓷及制品,102食品接触陶瓷产品,103食品用陶瓷包装〕	15		100	13/	13	千克			/35
6914.9000	-其他〔101其他陶瓷及制品,102食品接触陶瓷产品,103食品用陶瓷包装〕	10		100	13/	13	千克			/20

协定税率 %										特惠税率 %			Article Description
亚太5国	东/冰/格	巴基斯坦	韩国	瑞士	哥达	秘鲁	澳大利亚	新西/坡/智	港/澳/台	亚太2国	老/柬/缅	36/3/1	
4.6	0/0/0	4.5	4.8	3.6	0	0	0	0/0/0	0/0/			0/0/	--Tiles, cubes and similar arti-cles, whether or not rectan-gular, the largest surface area of which is capable of being enclosed in a square the side of which is less than 7 cm
	0/0/0	6	4.8	3.6	0	0	0	0/0/0	0/0/			0/0/	---Other
													--Of water absorption coefficient by weight exceeding 0.5% but not exceeding 10%
4.6	0/0/0	4.5	4.8	3.6	0	0	0	0/0/0	0/0/			0/0/	--Tiles, cubes and similar articles, whether or not rectan-gular, the largest surface area of which is capable of being enclosed in a square the side of which is less than 7 cm
	0/0/0	6	4.8	3.6	0	0	0	0/0/0	0/0/			0/0/	---Other
													--Of water absorption coefficient by weight exceeding 10%
4.6	0/0/0	4.5	4.8	3.6	0	0	0	0/0/0	0/0/			0/0/	--Tiles, cubes and similar arti-cles, whether or not rectan-gular, the largest surface area of which is capable of being enclosed in a square the side of which is less than 7 cm
	0/0/0	6	4.8	3.6	0	0	0	0/0/0	0/0/			0/0/	---Other
													-Mosaic cubes and the like, other than those of subheading No.6907.40:
4.6	0/0/0	4.5	4.8	3.6	0	0	0	0/0/0	0/0/			0/0/	---Tiles, cubes and similar articles, whether or not rectan-gular, the largest surface area of which is capable of being encolsed in a square the side of which is less than 7 cm
	0/0/0	6	4.8	3.6	0	0	0	0/0/0	0/0/			0/0/	---Other
													-Finishing ceramic:
4.6	0/0/0	4.5	4.8	3.6	0	0	0	0/0/0	0/0/			0/0/	---Tiles, cubes and similar arti-cles, whether or not rectan-gular, the largest surface area of which is capable of being encolsed in a square the side of which is less than 7 cm
	0/0/0	6	4.8	3.6	0	0	0	0/0/0	0/0/			0/0/	---Other
													Ceramic wares for laboratory, chemical or other technical uses; ceramic troughs, tubs and similar receptacles of a kind used in agriculture; ceramic pots, jars and similar articles of a kind used for the conveyance or packing of goods:
													-Ceramic wares for laboratory, chemical or other technical uses:
	0/0/0	4	0	0	0	0	0	0//0	0/0/			0/0/0	--Of porcelain or china
	0/0/0	4	0	0	0	0	0	0//0	0/0/			0/0/0	--Articles having a hardness equivalent to 9 or more on the Mohs scale
	0/0/0	4	0	0	0	0	0	0//0	0/0/			0/0/0	--Other
	0/0/0		14.7	6.3	0	0	0	0/0/0	0/0/			0/0/	-Other
													Ceramic sinks, wash basins, wash basin pedestals, baths, bidets, water closet pans, flushing cisterns, urinals and similar sanitary fixtures:
4.6	0/0/0	4	4	0	0	0	0	0/0/0	0/0/			0/0/0	-Of porcelain or china
	0/0/0	4	4	0	0	0	0	0/0/0	0/0/			0/0/0	-Other
													Tableware, kitchenware, other household articles and toilet articles, of porcelain or china:
													-Tableware and kitchenware:
													---Tableware:
4.6	0/0/0	4.5	4.8	3.6	0	0	0	0/0/0	0/0/			0/0/0	----Bone china
4.6	0/0/0	4.5	4.8	3.6	0	0	0	0/0/0	0/0/			0/0/0	----Other
													---Kitchenware:
4.6	0/0/0	7.5	6	4.5	0	0	0	0/0/0	0/0/			0/0/	----Knife tool
4.6	0/0/0	7.5	6	4.5	0	0	0	0/0/0	0/0/			0/0/	----Other
4.6	0/0/0	20	17.1	7	0	0	0	0/0/0	0/0/			0/0/	-Other
													Ceramic tableware, kitchenware, other household articles and toilet articles, other than of procelain or china:
	0/0/0	12	6	4.5	0	0	0	0/0/0	0/0/			0/0/0	---Tableware
	0/0/0	12	6	4.5	0	0	0	0/0/0	0/0/			0/0/	---Other
													Statuettes and other ornamental ceramic articles:
	0/0/0	12	6	4.5	0	0	0	0/0/0	0/0/			0/0/0	-Of porcelain or china
	0/0/0	12	6	4.5	0	0	0	0/0/0	0/0/			0/0/0	-Other
													Other ceramic articles:
	0/0/0		17.1	7.4	0	0	0	0/0/0	0/0/			0/0/	-Of porcelain or china
	0/0/0	4.5	6	3	0	0	0	0/0/0	0/0/			0/0/0	-Other

第七十章
玻璃及其制品

注释：

一、本章不包括：

（一）税目 32.07 的货品（例如，珐琅和釉料、搪瓷玻璃料及其他玻璃粉、粒或粉片）；

（二）第七十一章的物品（例如，仿首饰）；

（三）税目 85.44 的光缆、税目 85.46 的绝缘子或税目 85.47 所列绝缘材料制的零件；

（四）光导纤维、经光学加工的光学元件、注射用针管、假眼、温度计、气压计、液体比重计或第九十章的其他物品；

（五）有永久固定电光源的灯具及照明装置、灯箱标志或铭牌和类似品及其零件（税目94.05）；

（六）玩具、游戏品、运动用品、圣诞树装饰品及第九十五章的其他物品（供玩偶或第九十五章其他物品用的无机械装置的玻璃假眼珠除外）；

（七）纽扣、保温瓶、香水喷雾器和类似的喷雾器及第九十六章的其他物品。

二、对于税目 70.03、70.04 及 70.05：

（一）玻璃在退火前的各种处理都不视为"已加工"；

（二）玻璃切割成一定形状并不影响其作为板片归类；

（三）所称"吸收、反射或非反射层"，是指极薄的金属或化合物（例如金属氧化物）镀层，该镀层可以吸收红外线等光线或可以提高玻璃的反射性能，同时仍然使玻璃具有一定程度的透明性或半透明性；或者该镀层可以防止光线在玻璃表面的反射。

三、税目 70.06 所述产品，不论是否具有制成品的特性仍归入该税目。

四、税目 70.19 所称"玻璃棉"，是指：

（一）按重量计二氧化硅的含量在 60％及以上的矿质棉；

（二）按重量计二氧化硅的含量在 60％以下，但碱性氧化物（氧化钾或氧化钠）的含量在 5％以上或氧化硼的含量在 2％以上的矿质棉。

不符合上述规定的矿质棉归入税目 68.06。

五、本协调制度所称"玻璃"，包括熔融石英及其他熔融硅石。

子目注释：

子目号 7013.22、7013.33 及 7013.41 及 7013.91 所称"铅晶质玻璃"，仅指按重量计氧化铅含量不低于 24％的玻璃。

税则号列	货品名称〔CIQ 扩展编码及品名—T2 表示见附表 2〕	最惠(%)	暂定税率	普通	增值/消费	出口退税	计量单位	监管条件	检验检疫	特殊证件对美关税
70.01	**碎玻璃及废玻璃；玻璃块料：**									
7001.0000	碎玻璃及废玻璃；玻璃块料									
7001.0000 10	废碎玻璃〔999〕	12		50	13/	0	千克	9		/22
7001.0000 90	玻璃块料〔999〕	12		50	13/	0	千克			/22
70.02	**未加工的玻璃球、棒及管（税目 70.18 的微型玻璃球除外）：**									
7002.1000	-玻璃球〔999〕	12		50	13/	0	千克			/37
	-玻璃棒：									
7002.2010	---光导纤维预制棒〔999〕	6		50	13/	13	千克			/31
7002.2090	---其他〔999〕	12		50	13/	0	千克			/22
	-玻璃管：									
	--熔融石英或其他熔融硅石制：									
7002.3110	---光导纤维用波导级石英玻璃管〔999〕	5	1	17	13/	13	千克			/26
7002.3190	---其他〔999〕	12		50	13/	0	千克			/22
7002.3200	--温度在 0℃至 300℃时线膨胀系数不超过 5×10^{-6}/开尔文的其他玻璃制〔999〕	12		50	13/	13	千克			/32
7002.3900	--其他									
7002.3900 01	光通信用微光组件的玻璃毛细管、定位管（外径小于 3mm）〔999〕	12	3	50	13/	13	千克			/23
7002.3900 90	未列名、未加工的玻璃管〔999〕	12		50	13/	13	千克			/32
70.03	**铸制或轧制玻璃板、片或型材及异型材，不论是否有吸收、反射或非反射层，但未经其他加工：**									
	-非夹丝玻璃板、片：									
7003.1200	--整块着色、不透明、镶色或具有吸收、反射或非反射层的〔999〕	15		50	13/	0	千克/平方米			/40
7003.1900	--其他									

Chapter 70
Glass and glassware

Notes:

1. This Chapter does not cover:
   (a) Goods of heading No.32.07 (for example, vitrifiable enamels and glazes, glass frit, other glass in the form of powder, granules or flakes);
   (b) Articles of Chapter 71 (for example, imitation jewellery);
   (c) Optical fibre cables (heading No.85.44), electrical insulators (heading 85.46) or fitting of insulating material of heading No. 85.47;
   (d) Optical fibres, optically worked optical elements, hypodermic syringes, artificial eyes, thermometers, barometers, hydrometers or other articles of Chapter 90;
   (e) Lamps or lighting fittings, illuminated signs, illuminated nameplates or the like, having a permanently fixed light source, or parts thereof of heading No.94.05;
   (f) Toys, games, sports requisites, Christmas tree ornaments or other articles of Chapter 95 (excluding glass eyes without mechanisms for dolls or for other articles of Chapter 95); or
   (g) Buttons, fitted vacuum flasks, scent or similar sprays or other articles of Chapter 96.
2. For the purposes of headings Nos.70.03, 70.04 and 70.05:
   (a) glass is not regarded as "worked" by reason of any process it has undergone before annealing;
   (b) cutting to shape does not affect the classification of glass in sheets;
   (c) the expression "absorbent, reflecting or non-reflecting layer" means a microscopically thin coating of metal or of a chemical compound (for example, metal oxide) which absorbs, for example, infra-red light or improves the reflecting qualities of the glass while still allowing it to retain a degree of transparency or translucency; or which prevents light from being reflected on the surface of the glass.
3. The products referred to in heading No.70.06 remain classified in that heading whether or not they have the character of articles.
4. For the purposes of heading No.70.19, the expression "glass wool" means:
   (a) Mineral wools with a silica (SiO_2) content not less than 60% by weight;
   (b) Mineral wools with a silica (SiO_2) content less than 60% but with an alkaline oxide (K_2O or Na_2O) content exceeding 5% by weight or a boric oxide (B_2O_3) content exceeding 2% by weight.

   Mineral wools which do not comply with the above specifications fall in heading No.68.06.
5. Throughout the Nomenclature, the expression "glass" includes fused quartz and other fused silica.

Subheading Note:

For the purposes of subheadings Nos.7013.22, 7013.33, 7013, 41and 7013.91, the expression "lead crystal" means only glass having a minimum lead monoxide (PbO) content by weight of 24%.

协定税率 %										特惠税率 %			Article Description
亚太5国	东/冰/格	巴基斯坦	韩国	瑞士	哥达	秘鲁	澳大利亚	新西/坡/智	港/澳/台	亚太2国	老/柬/缅	36/3/1	
													Cullet and other waste and scrap of glass; glass in the mass:
													Cullet and other waste and scrap of glass; glass in the mass
	0/0/0	6	4.8	3.6	0	0	0	0/0/0	0/0/			0/0/	Waster and scrap of slass
	0/0/0	6	4.8	3.6	0	0	0	0/0/0	0/0/			0/0/	Glass in the mass
													Glass in balls (other than microspheres of heading No.70.18), rods or tubes, unworked:
	0/0/0	6	4.8	3.6	0	0	0	0/0/0	0/0/			0/0/	-Balls
													-Rods:
	0/0/0	0	0	0	0	0	0	0//0	0/0/			0/0/	---Preformed bars for drawing optical fibre
	0/0/0	6	4.8	3.6	0	0	0	0/0/0	0/0/			0/0/	---Other
													-Tubes:
													--Of fused quartz or other fused silica:
	0/0/0	0	0	0	0	0	0	0//0	0/0/			0/0/	---Waveguide quartz tubes for optical fibres use
	0/0/0	11.2	5.6	4.2	0	0	0	0/0/0	0/0/			0/0/	---Other
	0/0/0	6	4.8	3.6	0	0	0	0/0/0	0/0/			0/0/	--Of other glass having a linear coefficient of expansion not exceeding 5×10^{-6} per Kelvin within a temperature range of 0℃ to 300℃
													--Other
	0/0/0	6	4.8	3.6	0	0	0	0/0/0	0/0/			0/0/	Glass capillaries of micro-optical assemblies used in optical communications (external diameter<3mm)
	0/0/0	6	4.8	3.6	0	0	0	0/0/0	0/0/			0/0/	Glass tubes, not elsewhere specified or included, unworked
													Cast glass and rolled glass, in sheets or profiles, whether or not having an absorbent, reflecting or non-reflecting layer, but not otherwise worked:
													-Non-wired sheets:
	0/0/0	12	6	4.5	0	0	0	0/0/0	0/0/			0/0/	--Coloured throughout the mass (body tinted), opacified, flashed or having an absorbent, or non-reflecting reflecting layer
													--Other

税则号列	货品名称〔CIQ 扩展编码及品名—T2 表示见附表 2〕	最惠(%)	暂定税率	普通	增值/消费	出口退税	计量单位	监管条件	检验检疫	特殊证件对美关税
7003.1900 01	液晶或有机发光二极管(OLED)显示屏用原板玻璃,包括保护屏用含碱玻璃(铸、轧制的非夹丝玻璃板、片,未着色,透明及不具吸收层的,未经其他加工)〔999〕	15	3	50	13/	6	千克/平方米			/13
7003.1900 90	铸、轧制的其他非夹丝玻璃板、片(未着色,透明及不具吸收层的,未经其他加工)〔999〕	15		50	13/	0	千克/平方米			/25
7003.2000	-夹丝玻璃板、片〔999〕	15		50	13/	0	千克/平方米			/
7003.3000	-型材及异型材〔999〕	15		50	13/	0	千克/平方米			/25
70.04	**拉制或吹制玻璃板、片,不论是否有吸收、反射或非反射层,但未经其他加工:**									
7004.2000	-整块着色、不透明、镶色或具有吸收、反射或非反射层的〔999〕	15		50	13/	0	千克/平方米			/40
7004.9000	-其他玻璃									
7004.9000 01	光学平板玻璃,厚度 0.7mm 以下(未着色,透明及不具吸收层的,未经其他加工)〔999〕	15	9	50	13/	0	千克/平方米			/19
7004.9000 90	拉、吹制的其他玻璃板、片(未着色,透明及不具吸收层的,未经其他加工)〔999〕	15		50	13/	0	千克/平方米			/25
70.05	**浮法玻璃板、片及表面研磨或抛光玻璃板、片,不论是否有吸收、反射或非反射层,但未经其他加工:**									
7005.1000	-具有吸收、反射或非反射层的非夹丝玻璃〔999〕	15		50	13/	0	千克/平方米			/25
	-其他非夹丝玻璃:									
7005.2100	--整块着色、不透明、镶色或仅表面研磨的〔999〕	15		50	13/	0	千克/平方米			/35
7005.2900	--其他									
7005.2900 02	液晶或有机发光二极管(OLED)显示屏用原板玻璃,包括保护屏用含碱玻璃(非夹丝浮法玻璃板、片)〔999〕	10	3	50	13/	10	千克/平方米			/23
7005.2900 90	其他非夹丝浮法玻璃板、片〔999〕	10		50	13/	0	千克/平方米			/30
7005.3000	-夹丝玻璃〔999〕	15		50	13/	0	千克/平方米			/40
70.06	**经弯曲、磨边、镂刻、钻孔、涂珐琅或其他加工的税目 70.03、70.04 或 70.05 的玻璃,但未用其他材料镶框或装配:**									
7006.0000	经弯曲、磨边、镂刻、钻孔、涂珐琅或其他加工的税目 70.03、70.04 或 70.05 的玻璃,但未用其他材料镶框或装配									
7006.0000 01	液晶玻璃基板,6 代(1850mm×1500mm)以上,不含 6 代(经弯曲、磨边、镂刻、钻孔、涂珐琅等加工,款镶框或装配)〔999〕	10	4	50	13/	13	千克			/29
7006.0000 02	液晶玻璃基板,6 代(1850mm×1500mm)及以下(经弯曲、磨边、镂刻、钻孔、涂珐琅等加工,款镶框或装配)〔999〕	10	6	50	13/	13	千克			/31
7006.0000 90	经其他加工税目 70.03-70.05 的玻璃(经弯曲、磨边、镂刻、钻孔、涂珐琅等加工、未镶框或装配)〔999〕	10		50	13/	13	千克			/35
70.07	**钢化或层压玻璃制的安全玻璃:**									
	-钢化安全玻璃:									
	--规格及形状适于安装在车辆、航空器、航天器及船舶上:									
7007.1110	---航空器、航天器及船舶用									
7007.1110 01	空载重量≥25 吨飞机的挡风玻璃〔999〕	2	1	11	13/	13	千克			/11
7007.1110 90	航空航天器及船舶用钢化安全玻璃(其他规格及形状适于安装在航空航天器及船上的)〔999〕	2		11	13/	13	千克			/12
7007.1190	---其他〔101 其他车辆零部件,102 钢化玻璃〕	10		50	13/	13	千克	A	L	/20
7007.1900	--其他〔999〕	14		50	13/	13	千克/平方米		L	/39
	-层压安全玻璃:									

协定税率 %										特惠税率 %			
亚太5国	东/冰/格	巴基斯坦	韩国	瑞士	哥达	秘鲁	澳大利亚	新西/坡/智	港/澳/台	亚太2国	老/柬/缅	36/3/1	Article Description
	0/0/0	14	7	5.3	0	0	0	0/0/0	0/0/0			0/0/	Original plate glass using for liquid crystal or an organic light-emitting diode (OLED) displayincluding the protection screen containing alkali glass(cast and rolled other non-wired glass, in sheets or parcel, not colored, transparent and without absorbing layer, not processed in other way)
	0/0/0	14	7	5.3	0	0	0	0/0/0	0/0/0			0/0/	Cast and rolled other non-wired glass, in sheets or parcel (not colored, transparent and without absorbing layer, not processed in other way)
	0/0/0	12	6	4.5	0	0	0	0/0/0	0/0/			0/0/	-Wired sheets
	0/0/0	12	6	4.5	0	0	0	0/0/0	0/0/			0/0/	-Profiles
													Drawn glass and blown glass, in sheets, whether or not having an absorbent, reflecting or non-reflecting layer, but not otherwise worked:
	0/0/0	14	7	5.3	0	0	0	0/0/0	0/0/			0/0/0	-Glass, coloured throughout the mass (body tinted), opacified, flashed or having an absorbent, reflecting or non-reflecting layer
													-Other glass
	0/0/0	14	12.2	5.3	0	0	0	0/0/0	0/0/			0/0/	Optic plane glass, thickness<0.7mm (not coloured, transparent and not having an absorbent, not otherwise worked)
	0/0/0	14	12.2	5.3	0	0	0	0/0/0	0/0/			0/0/	Other glass plate and piece made by blowing and pulling (not colonred, transparent and not having an absorbent not othermie worked)
													Float glass and surface ground or polished glass, in sheets, whether or not having an absorbent, reflecting or non-reflecting layer, but not otherwise worked:
	0/0/0	12	6	4.5	0	0	0	0/0/0	0/0/			0/0/	-Non-wired glass, having an absorbent, reflecting or non-reflecting layer
													-Other non-wired glass:
	0/0/0	12	6	4.5	0	0	0	0/0/0	0/0/			0/0/	--Coloured throughout the mass (body tinted), opacified, flashed or merely surface ground
													--Other
	0/0/0	0	6	4.5	0	0	0	0/0/0	0/0/			0/0/	Lidquid cry stal or organic luminous diode (OLED) original plate glass used for display including the protection screen containing alkali glass(Non-wired float slass and piece
	0/0/0	0	6	4.5	0	0	0	0/0/0	0/0/			0/0/	Other float non-wired glass, in sheets
	0/0/0	14	7	5.3	0	0	0	0/0/0	0/0/			0/0/	-Wired glass
													Glass of heading No. 70.03, 70.04 or 70.05, bent, edge-worked, engraved, drilled, enamelled or otherwise worked, but not framed or fitted with other materials:
													Glass of heading No. 70.03, 70.04 or 70.05, bent, edge-worked, engraved, drilled, enamelled or otherwise worked, but not framed or fitted with other materials
	0/0/0	12	9	4.5	0	0	0	0/0/0	0/0/0			0/0/	LCD glass base plate, more than 6 generation, (1850mm × 1500mm), other than 6 generation (bent, edge-worked, engraved, drilled, enamelled or otherwise worked, but not framed or fitted)
	0/0/0	12	9	4.5	0	0	0	0/0/0	0/0/0			0/0/	LCD glass base plate, 6 generation and less than, (1850mm × 1500mm), other than 6 generation (bent, edge-worked, engraved, drilled, enamelled or otherwise worked, but not framed or fitted)
	0/0/0	12	9	4.5	0	0	0	0/0/0	0/0/0			0/0/	Glass in other process Nos. from 70.03 to 70.05 (after being bent, edged, carved, holed and painted with enamel, not mounted in cabinet or fixed)
													Safety glass, consisting of toughened (tempered) or laminated glass:
													-Toughened (tempered) safety glass:
													--Of size and shape suitable for incorporation in vehicles, aircraft, spacecraft or vessels:
													---For aircraft, spacecraft or vessels
	0/0/0	0	0	0	0	0	0	0//0	0/0/			0/0/0	Toughened (tempered) safety glass, of size and shape suitable for incorporation in aircraft, W≥25 tons
	0/0/0	0	0	0	0	0	0	0//0	0/0/			0/0/0	Toughened safety glass for aircraft, spacecraft and ships (other specs and forms suitable for installation in aircraft, spacecraft and ships)
	0/0/0	4	6	0	0	0	0	0//0	0/0/			0/0/0	---Other
	0/0/0	11.2	5.6	4.2	0	0	0	0/0/0	0/0/			0/0/	--Other
													-Laminated safety glass:

税则号列	货品名称〔CIQ扩展编码及品名—T2表示见附表2〕	最惠(%)	暂定税率	普通	增值/消费	出口退税	计量单位	监管条件	检验检疫	特殊证件对美关税
	--规格及形状适于安装在车辆、航空器、航天器及船舶上：									
7007.2110	---航空器、航天器及船舶用〔999〕	2		11	13/	13	千克			/12
7007.2190	---其他〔101其他车辆零部件，102钢化玻璃〕	14		50	13/	13	千克	A	L	/24
7007.2900	--其他〔999〕	14		50	13/	13	千克/平方米		L	/39
70.08	**多层隔温、隔音玻璃组件：**									
7008.0010	---中空或真空隔温、隔音玻璃〔101其他车辆零部件，102钢化玻璃，103其他玻璃及制品〕	14		50	13/	13	千克		L	/24
7008.0090	---其他〔101其他车辆零部件，102钢化玻璃，103其他玻璃及制品〕	14		50	13/	13	千克		L	/39
70.09	**玻璃镜(包括后视镜)，不论是否镶框：**									
7009.1000	-车辆后视镜〔101其他车辆零部件，102玻璃镜〕	10		100	13/	13	千克		L	/20
	-其他：									
7009.9100	--未镶框								L	
7009.9100 01	槽式太阳能抛物面反射镜〔999〕	14	10	70	13/	13	千克			/20
7009.9100 90	其他未镶框玻璃镜(包括后视镜)〔999〕	14		70	13/	13	千克			/24
7009.9200	--已镶框〔999〕	12		100	13/	13	千克			/37
70.10	**玻璃制的坛、瓶、缸、罐、安瓿及其他容器，用于运输或盛装货物；玻璃制保藏罐；玻璃塞、盖及类似的封口器：**									
7010.1000	-安瓿〔999〕	14		50	13/	13	千克			/39
7010.2000	-塞、盖及类似的封口器〔101非食品用玻璃器皿，102食品用玻璃包装〕	14		50	13/	13	千克			/39
	-其他：									
7010.9010	---超过1升〔101非食品用玻璃器皿，102食品用玻璃包装〕	14		50	13/	13	千克			/39
7010.9020	---超过0.33升，但不超过1升〔101非食品用玻璃器皿，102食品用玻璃包装〕	14		50	13/	13	千克			/24
7010.9030	---超过0.15升，但不超过0.33升〔101非食品用玻璃器皿，102食品用玻璃包装〕	14		50	13/	13	千克			/39
7010.9090	---不超过0.15升〔101非食品用玻璃器皿，102食品用玻璃包装〕	14		50	13/	13	千克			/39
70.11	**制灯泡、阴极射线管及类似品用的未封口玻璃外壳(包括玻璃泡及管)及其玻璃零件，但未装有配件：**									
7011.1000	-电灯用〔999〕	12		80	13/	0	千克			/37
	-阴极射线管用：									
7011.2010	---显像管玻壳及其零件〔101其它电光源及其零件，102其它显像管及其零件〕	10		35	13/	13	千克	6		/
7011.2090	---其他									
7011.2090 01	显示管玻壳及其零件(包括零件，但未装有配件)〔101其它电光源及其零件，102其它显像管及其零件〕	10	6	35	13/	10	千克	6		/16
7011.2090 90	其他阴极射线管用的未封口玻壳(包括零件，但未装有配件)〔101其它电光源及其零件，102其它显像管及其零件〕	10		35	13/	10	千克	6		/20
	-其他：									
7011.9010	---电子管用(阴极射线管用的除外)〔999〕	8		35	13/	10	千克			/28
7011.9090	---其他〔999〕	14		80	13/	0	千克			/24
70.13	**玻璃器，供餐桌、厨房、盥洗室、办公室、室内装饰或类似用途(税号70.10或70.18的货品除外)：**									
7013.1000	-玻璃陶瓷制〔999〕	7		100	13/	13	千克			/32
	-高脚杯，但玻璃陶瓷制的除外：									
7013.2200	--铅晶质玻璃制〔101非食品用玻璃器皿，102食品接触玻璃产品〕	7		100	13/	13	千克			/32
7013.2800	--其他〔101非食品用玻璃器皿，102食品接触玻璃产品〕	7		100	13/	13	千克	A	R	/32
	-其他杯子，但玻璃陶瓷制的除外：									
7013.3300	--铅晶质玻璃制〔101非食品用玻璃器皿，102食品接触玻璃产品，103食品用玻璃包装〕	7		100	13/	13	千克			/32
7013.3700	--其他〔101非食品用玻璃器皿，102食品接触玻璃产品，103食品用玻璃包装〕	7		100	13/	13	千克	A	R	/32
	-餐桌或厨房用玻璃器皿(不包括杯子)，但玻璃陶瓷制的除外：									
7013.4100	--铅晶质玻璃剂〔101非食品用玻璃器皿，102食品接触玻璃产品，103食品用玻璃包装〕	7		100	13/	13	千克	A	R	/32
7013.4200	--温度在0℃至300℃时线膨胀系数不超过5×10^{-6}/开尔文的其他玻璃制〔101非食品用玻璃器皿，102食品接触玻璃产品，103食品用玻璃包装〕	7		100	13/	13	千克	A	R	/27

协定税率 %										特惠税率 %			Article Description
亚太5国	东/冰/格	巴基斯坦	韩国	瑞士	哥达	秘鲁	澳大利亚	新西/坡/智	港/澳/台	亚太2国	老/柬/缅	36/3/1	
													--Of size and shape suitable for incorporation in vehicles, aircraft, spacecraft or vessels:
	0/0/0	0	0	0	0	0	0	0//0	0/0/			0/0/0	---for aircraft, spacecraft or vessels
	0/0/0	20	14	6	0	0	0	0/0/0	0/0/			0/0/0	---Other
	0/0/0	9	5.6	4.2	0	0	0	0/0/0	0/0/			0/0/	--Other
													Multiple-walled insulating units of glass:
	0/0/0	10.1	5.6	4.2	0	0	0	0/0/0	0/0/			0/0/	---Sealed or vacuum insulating glass
	0/0/0	10.1	5.6	4.2	0	0	0	0/0/0	0/0/			0/0/	---Other
													Glass mirrors, whether or not framed, including rear-view mirrors:
	0/0/0	4	7	0	0	0	0	0/0/0	0/0/0			0/0/0	-Rear-view mirrors for vehicles
													-Other:
													--Unframed
	0/0/0	21	14.7	6.3	0	0	0	0/0/0	0/0/			0/0/	Reflecting mirror of trench type solar paraboloid
	0/0/0	21	14.7	6.3	0	0	0	0/0/0	0/0/			0/0/	Other class mirrors, not framed(including rear-view mirrors)
7.8	0/0/0	4	4.8	3.6	0	0	0	0/0/0	0/0/			0/0/0	--Framed
													Carboys, bottles, flasks, jars, pots, phials, ampoules and other containers, of glass, of a kind used for the conveyance or packing of goods; preserving jars of glass; stoppers, lids and other closures, of glass:
	0/0/0	9	5.6	4.2	0	0	0	0/0/0	0/0/			0/0/	-Ampoules
	0/0/0	10.1	5.6	4.2	0	0	0	0/0/0	0/0/			0/0/	-Stoppers, lids and other closures
													-Other:
	0/0/0	10.1	5.6	4.2	0	0	0	0/0/0	0/0/			0/0/	---Exceeding 1L
	0/0/0	10.1	5.6	4.2	0	0	0	0/0/0	0/0/			0/0/	---Exceeding 0.33L but not exceeding 1L
	0/0/0	9	5.6	4.2	0	0	0	0/0/0	0/0/			0/0/	---Exceeding 0. 15L but not exceeding 0. 33L
	0/0/0	9	5.6	4.2	0	0	0	0/0/0	0/0/			0/0/0	---Nct exceeding 0. 15L
													Glass envelopes (including bulbs and tubes), open, and glass parts thereof, without fittings, for electric lamps, cathode-ray tubes or the like:
	0/0/0		14.7	6.3	0	0	0	0/0/0	0/0/			0/0/	-For electric lighting
													-For cathode-ray tubes:
6.5	0/0/0	4.5	4	0	0	0	0	0//0	0/0/			0/0/	---Glass envelopes for kinescope and glass parts thereof
													---Other
6.5	0/0/0	4.5		0	0	0	0	0//0	0/0/			0/0/	Glass envelopes for display tubes and glass parts (including parts thereof, without fittings)
6.5	0/0/0	4.5		0	0	0	0	0//0	0/0/			0/0/	Glass envelopes for cathode-ray tules open(including parts thereof, without fittings)
													-Other:
	0/0/0	4	0	0	0	0	0	0//0	0/0/			0/0/	---For electronic tubes and valves (other than cathode-ray tubes)
	0/0/0		14.7	6.3	0	0	0	0/0/0	0/0/			0/0/	---Other
													Glassware of a kind used for table, kitchen, toilet, office, indoor decoration or similar purposes (other than that of heading No. 70. 10 or 70. 18):
	0/0/0		17.1	7	0	0	0	0/0/0	0/0/			0/0/0	-Of glass-ceramics
													-Stemware drinking glasses, other than of glass-ceramics:
	0/0/0		17.1	7	0	0	0	0/0/0	0/0/			0/0/	--Of lead crystal
	0/0/0	4	0	0	0	0	0	0/0/0	0/0/			0/0/0	--Other
													-Other drinking glasses, other than of glass-ceramics:
	0/0/0		17.1	7	0	0	0	0/0/0	0/0/			0/0/	--Of lead crystal
	0/0/0	4	0	0	0	0	0	0/0/0	0/0/			0/0/0	--Other
													-Classware of a kind used for table (other than drinkings glasses) or kitchen purposes other than of glass-ceramics:
	0/0/0		17.1	7	0	0	0	0/0/0	0/0/			0/0/	--Of lead crystal
	0/0/0	4	4	0	0	0	0	0/0/0	0/0/			0/0/0	--Of glasc naving a linear coefficient of expansion not exceeding 5×10^{-6} perkelvin within a temperature range of 0℃ to 300℃

税则号列	货品名称〔CIQ 扩展编码及品名—T2 表示见附表 2〕	最惠(%)	暂定税率	普通	增值/消费	出口退税	计量单位	监管条件	检验检疫	特殊证件对美关税
7013.4900	--其他〔101 非食品用玻璃器皿,102 食品接触玻璃产品,103 食品用玻璃包装〕	7		100	13/	13	千克	A	R	/32
	-其他玻璃器:									
7013.9100	--铅晶质玻璃制〔101 非食品用玻璃器皿,102 食品接触玻璃产品,103 食品用玻璃包装〕	7		100	13/	13	千克			/32
7013.9900	--其他〔101 非食品用玻璃器皿,102 食品接触玻璃产品,103 食品用玻璃包装〕	7		100	13/	13	千克			/32
70.14	**未经光学加工的信号玻璃器及玻璃制光学元件(税目 70.15 的货品除外):**									
7014.0010	---光学仪器用光学元件毛坯〔999〕	10		40	13/	13	千克			/35
7014.0090	---其他									
7014.0090 01	滤波玻璃(带有抗红外和防反射薄膜的)〔999〕	15	9	80	13/	13	千克			/34
7014.0090 90	其他未经光学加工的信号玻璃器(包括玻璃制光学元件,编号 7015 的物品除外)〔999〕	15		80	13/	13	千克			/40
70.15	**钟表玻璃及类似玻璃、视力矫正或非视力矫正眼镜用玻璃,呈弧面、弯曲、凹形或类似形状但未经光学加工的;制造上述玻璃用的凹面圆形及扇形玻璃:**									
	-视力矫正眼镜用玻璃:									
7015.1010	---变色镜片坯件〔999〕	15		80	13/	13	千克			/25
7015.1090	---其他〔999〕	15		70	13/	13	千克			/
	-其他:									
7015.9010	---钟表玻璃〔999〕	15		70	13/	0	千克			/40
7015.9020	---平光变色镜片坯件〔999〕	15		80	13/	13	千克			/
7015.9090	---其他〔999〕	12		80	13/	0	千克			/37
70.16	**建筑用压制或模制的铺面用玻璃块、砖、片、瓦及其他制品,不论是否夹丝;供镶嵌或类似装饰用的玻璃马赛克及其他小件玻璃品,不论是否有衬背;花饰铅条窗玻璃及类似品;多孔或泡沫玻璃块、板、片及类似品:**									
7016.1000	-供镶嵌或类似装饰用的玻璃马赛克及其他小件玻璃品,不论是否有衬背〔999〕	15		100	13/	13	千克			/40
	-其他:									
7016.9010	---花饰铅条窗玻璃及类似品〔999〕	15		90	13/	13	千克			/40
7016.9090	---其他〔999〕	15		90	13/	13	千克			/25
70.17	**实验室、卫生及配药用的玻璃器,不论有无刻度或标量:**									
7017.1000	-熔融石英或其他熔融硅石制〔999〕	0		30	13/	13	千克			/10
7017.2000	-温度在 0℃至 300℃时线膨胀系数不超过 5×10^{-6}/开尔文的其他玻璃制〔999〕	8		30	13/	13	千克			/18
7017.9000	-其他〔999〕	8		30	13/	13	千克			/18
70.18	**玻璃珠、仿珍珠、仿宝石或仿半宝石和类似小件玻璃品及其制品,但仿首饰除外;玻璃假眼,但医用假眼除外;灯工方法制作的玻璃塑像及其他玻璃装饰品,但仿首饰除外;直径不超过 1 毫米的微型玻璃球:**									
7018.1000	-玻璃珠、仿珍珠、仿宝石或仿半宝石及类似小件玻璃品〔999〕	10		100	13/	13	千克			/35
7018.2000	-直径不超过 1 毫米的微型玻璃珠									
7018.2000 01	熔融球形二氧化硅微粉,直径≤100um〔999〕	15	5.5	100	13/	13	千克			/30.5
7018.2000 90	其他直径≤1 毫米的微型玻璃珠〔999〕	15		100	13/	13	千克			/40
7018.9000	-其他〔999〕	15	10	100	13/	13	千克			/30
70.19	**玻璃纤维(包括玻璃棉)及其制品(例如,玻璃纤维纱线及其织物):**									
	-梳条、粗纱、纱线及短切纤维:									
7019.1100	--长度不超过 50 毫米的短切纤维									
7019.1100 10	两用物项管制的长度不超过 50mm 的短切玻璃纤维(比模量≥3.18×10^{6} m,以及比抗拉强度≥7.62×10^{4} m)〔999〕	10		50	13/	10	千克	3		/30
7019.1100 90	其他长度不超过 50mm 的短切玻璃纤维〔999〕	10		50	13/	10	千克			/30
7019.1200	--粗纱									
7019.1200 20	两用物项管制的玻璃纤维粗纱(比模量≥3.18×10^{6} m,以及比抗拉强度≥7.62×10^{4} m)〔999〕	10		50	13/	10	千克	3		/35
7019.1200 90	其他玻璃纤维粗纱〔999〕	10		50	13/	10	千克			/35

协定税率 %										特惠税率 %			
亚太5国	东/冰/格	巴基斯坦	韩国	瑞士	哥达	秘鲁	澳大利亚	新西/坡/智	港/澳/台	亚太2国	老/柬/缅	36/3/1	Article Description
	0/0/0	4	4	0	0	0	0	0/0/0	0/0/			0/0/0	--Other
													-Other glassware:
	0/0/0	4	4	0	0	0	0	0/0/0	0/0/			0/0/0	--Of lead crystal
	0/0/0	4	4	0	0	0	0	0/0/0	0/0/			0/0/0	--Other
													Signalling glassware and optical elements of glass (other than thoseof heading No.70. 15), not optically worked:
	0/0/0	4	0	0	0	0	0	0/0/0	0/0/			0/0/0	---Blanks of optical elements, for optical instruments
													---Other
	0/0/0	14	7	5.3	0	0	0	0/0/0	0/0/			0/0/	Wave filtering glass (with anti-infrared and anti-radiation film)
	0/0/0	14	7	5.3	0	0	0	0/0/0	0/0/			0/0/	Other signaling glassware and optical elements of glass (including glass optical elements, other than thoseof heading No. 70. 15)
													Clock or watch glasses and similar glasses, glasses for non-corrective or corrective spectacles, curved, bent, hollowed or the like, not optically worked; hollow glass spheres and their segments, for the manufacture of such glasses:
													-Glasses for corrective spectacles:
	0/0/0		12.6	6.3	0	0	0	0/0/0	0/0/			0/0/	---Blanks for photochromic spectacles
	0/0/0	14	7	5.3	0	0	0	0/0/0	0/0/			0/0/	---Other
													-Other:
	0/0/0	14	7	5.3	0	0	0	0/0/0	0/0/			0/0/	---Clock and watch glasses
10.5	0/0/0	14.4	7.2	5.4	0	0	0	0/0/0	0/0/			0/0/	---Blanks for plane photochromic spectacles
10.8	0/0/0	5.4	4.8	6.2	0	0	0	0/0/0	0/0/			0/0/0	---Other
													Paving blocks, slabs, bricks, squares, tiles and other articles of pressed or moulded glass, whether or not wired, of a kind used for building or construction purposes; glass cubes and other glass smallwares, whether or not on a backing, for mosaics or similar decorative purposes; leaded lights and the like; multicellular or foam glass in blocks, panels, plates, shells or similar forms:
	0/0/0		15.4	6.6	0	0	0	0/0/0	0/0/			0/0/	-Glass cubes and other glass smallwares, whether or not on a backing, for mosaics or similar decorative purposes
													-Other:
10.5	0/0/0		16.8	7.2	0	0	0	0/0/0	0/0/			0/0/	---Leaded lights and the like
10.5	0/0/0		7.2	5.4	0	0	0	0/0/0	0/0/			0/0/	---Other
													Laboratory, hygienic or pharmaceutical glassware, whether or not graduated or calibrated:
												0/0/0	-Of fused quartz or other fused silica
	0/0/3.2	4	0	4.2	0	0	0	0//0	0/0/			0/0/0	-Of other glass having a linear coefficient of expansion not exceeding 5×10^{-6} per Kelvin within a temperature range of 0℃ to 300℃
	0/0/0	4	3.2	0	0	0	0	0//0	0/0/			0/0/0	-Other
													Glass beads, imitation pearls, imitation precious or semi-precious stones and similar glass smallwares, and articles thereof other than imitation jewellery; glass eyes other than prosthetic articles; statuettes and other ornaments of lampworked glass, other than imitation jewellery; glass microspheres not exceeding 1mm in diameter:
	0/0/0	4	0	0	0	0	0	0/0/0	0/0/			0/0/0	-Glass beads, imitation pearls, imitation precious or semi-precious stones and similar glass smallwares
													-Glass microspheres, diameter≤1mm
	0/0/0		12	6	0	0	0	0/0/0	0/0/			0/0/	Molten spherical silica powder, diameter ≤ 100um
	0/0/0		12	6	0	0	0	0/0/0	0/0/			0/0/	Other glass microspheres not exceeding lmm in diameler
	0/0/0		12	6	0	0	0	0/0/0	0/0/			0/0/	-Other
													Glass fibres (including glass wool) and articles thereof (for example, yarn, woven fabrics):
													-Slivers, rovings, yarn and chopped strands:
													--Chopped strands, of a length of not more than 50mm
	0/0/0	5.4	4.8	3.6	0	0	0	0/0/0	0/0/0			0/0/0	Chopped fibres, fual-use items control, length≤50mm, modulus atio ≥3.18×10^6 m, specific ultimate tensile strength≥7.62×10^4 m
	0/0/0	5.4	4.8	3.6	0	0	0	0/0/0	0/0/0			0/0/0	Other chopped fibres, fual-use items control, length≤50mm
													--Rovings
	0/0/0	5.4		3.6	0	0	0	0/0/0	0/0/			0/0/0	Glass fibres rovings, fual-use items control, modulus atio≥3.18×10^6 m, specific ultimate tensile strength≥7.62×10^4 m
	0/0/0	5.4		3.6	0	0	0	0/0/0	0/0/			0/0/0	Other glass fibres rovings

税则号列	货品名称〔CIQ 扩展编码及品名－T2 表示见附表 2〕	最惠(%)	暂定税率	普通	增值/消费	出口退税	计量单位	监管条件	检验检疫	特殊证件对美关税
7019.1900	--其他									
7019.1900 12	玻璃纤维或纤丝材料(其“比模量”为 3.18×10⁶ 米或更大和“比抗拉强度”为 7.62×10⁴ 米或更大的玻璃纤维或纤丝材料)〔999〕	8		50	13/	10	千克	3		/18
7019.1900 90	其他玻璃梳条、纱线及短切纤维〔999〕	8		50	13/	10	千克			/18
	-薄片(巴厘纱)、纤维网、席、垫、板及类似无纺产品：									
7019.3100	--席〔999〕	5		40	13/	10	千克			/15
7019.3200	--薄片(巴厘纱)〔999〕	10		40	13/	10	千克			/20
	--其他：						千克			
7019.3910	---垫〔999〕	10		40	13/	10	千克			/20
7019.3990	---其他〔999〕	10		40	13/	10	千克			/20
7019.4000	-粗纱机织物〔999〕	10		40	13/	10	千克			/20
	-其他机织物：									
7019.5100	--宽度不超过 30 厘米的									
7019.5100 10	两用物项管制的宽度≤15mm 的玻璃纤维机织物〔999〕	10		40	13/	10	千克	3		/20
7019.5100 90	其他宽度≤30cm 的玻璃纤维机织物〔999〕	10		40	13/	10	千克			/20
7019.5200	--宽度超过 30 厘米的长丝平纹织物，每平方米重量不超过 250 克，单根纱线细度不超过 136 特克斯									
7019.5200 01	覆铜板用玻璃纤维长丝平纹布，开纤或每平方米重≤180 克(宽度>30cm，单根纱线细度≤136 特)〔999〕	10		40	13/	10	千克			/35
7019.5200 90	其他平方米重≤250g 玻璃长丝平纹布(宽度超过 30cm，单根纱线细度不超过 136 特)〔999〕	10		40	13/	10	千克			/35
7019.5900	--其他〔999〕	10		40	13/	10	千克			/20
	-其他：						千克			
7019.9010	---玻璃棉及其制品〔999〕	7		40	13/	10	千克			/17
	---玻璃纤维布浸胶制品：									
7019.9021	----每平方米重量<450 克〔999〕	7		40	13/	10,13	千克			/17
7019.9029	----其他〔999〕	7		40	13/	10	千克			/17
7019.9090	---其他〔999〕	7		40	13/	13	千克			/17
70.20	**其他玻璃制品：**									
	---工业用：									
7020.0011	----导电玻璃〔999〕	10	7	40	13/	13	千克			/32
7020.0012	----绝缘子用玻璃伞盘〔999〕	10		40	13/	0	千克			/
7020.0013	----熔融石英或其他熔融硅石制									
7020.0013 01	半导体晶片生产用石英反应管及夹持器(熔融石英或其他熔融硅石制)(用于插入熔化和氧化炉内)〔999〕	0		40	13/	13	千克			/10
7020.0013 90	熔融石英或其他熔融硅石制工业用其他玻璃制品(导电玻璃及绝缘子用玻璃伞盘除外)〔999〕	10		40	13/	13	千克			/20
7020.0019	----其他									
7020.0019 01	半导体晶片生产用石英反应管及夹持器(用于插入熔化和氧化炉内)〔999〕	0		40	13/	0	千克			/10
7020.0019 90	其他工业用玻璃制品〔999〕	10		40	13/	0	千克			/20
	---其他：									
7020.0091	----保温瓶或其他保温容器用的玻璃胆〔999〕	20		100	13/	13	千克/个	A	R	/30
7020.0099	----其他									
7020.0099 01	石英玻璃，平整度小于等于 1 微米〔999〕	10	4	100	13/	0	千克			/14
7020.0099 90	其他非工业用玻璃制品〔999〕	10		100	13/	0	千克			/20

协定税率 %										特惠税率 %			
亚太5国	东/冰/格	巴基斯坦	韩国	瑞士	哥达	秘鲁	澳大利亚	新西/坡/智	港/澳/台	亚太2国	老/柬/缅	36/3/1	Article Description
													--Other
	0/0/0	4.5	4	0	0	0	0	0//0	0/0/0			0/0/0	Glass fibre or filaments(specific modulus ≥3.18×10^6 m, specific ultimate tensile strength≥7.62×10^4 m)
	0/0/0	4.5	4	0	0	0	0	0//0	0/0/0			0/0/0	Other glass comb, yarn and chopped fiber
													-Thin sheets (voiles), webs, mats, mattresses, boards and similar nonwoven products:
	0/0/0	0	0	0	0	0	0	0//0	0/0/			0/0/0	--Mats
	0/0/0	10.1	5.6	4.2	0	0	0	0/0/0	0/0/			0/0/	--Thin sheets (voiles)
													--Other:
	0/0/0	4.5	4.2	3.2	0	0	0	0/0/0	0/0/0			0/0/0	---Mattresses
	0/0/0	4.5	4.2	3.2	0	0	0	0/0/0	0/0/0			0/0/0	---Other
	0/0/0	5.4	4.8	3.6	0	0	0	0/0/0	0/0/			0/0/0	-Woven fabrics of rovings
													-Other woven fabrics:
													--Of a width not exceeding 30cm
	0/0/0	5.4	4.8	3.6	0	0	0	0/0/0	0/0/			0/0/0	Glass fibres woven fabrics, fual-use items control, width≤15mm
	0/0/0	5.4	4.8	3.6	0	0	0	0/0/0	0/0/			0/0/0	Other glass fibres woven fabrics, width≤30cm
													--Of a width exceeding 30cm, plain weave, weighing less than 250g/m^2, of filaments measuring per single yarn not more than 136 tex
	0/0/0	5.4		3.6	0	0	0	0/0/0	0/0/			0/0/0	Glass fibres filament plain weave for CCL (width >30cm, of filaments measuring per single yarn≤136 tex)
	0/0/0	5.4		3.6	0	0	0	0/0/0	0/0/			0/0/0	Other class fibrels filament plain weave (width>30cm, of filaments measuring per single yarn ≤ 136 tex)
6.5	0/0/0	4.5	7.8	3.6	0	0	0	0/0/0	0/0/			0/0/0	--Other
													-Other:
	0/0/0	4	4.2	0	0	0	0	0//0	0/0/			0/0/0	---Glass wool and its articles
													---Glass fiber cloth dipped articles:
	0/0/0	4	4.2	0	0	0	0	0//0	0/0/			0/0/0	----Weight<450g/m^2
	0/0/0	4	4.2	0	0	0	0	0//0	0/0/			0/0/0	----Other
	0/0/0	4	4.2	0	0	0	0	0//0	0/0/			0/0/0	---Other
													Other articles of glass:
													---For technical use:
	0/0/0	4.5		3.2	0	0	0	0/0/0	0/0/			0/0/0	----Conductivity glass
6.5	0/0/0	4.5	4.2	3.2	0	0	0	0/0/0	0/0/			0/0/0	----Glass umbrella for insulator
													----Of fused quartz or other fused silica
6.5	0/0/0	4.5	0	3.2	0	0	0	0/0/0	0/0/			0/0/0	Quartz reactor tubes and holders for production of semiconductor wafers, of fused quartz or other fused silica(for inserting in melting and oxidation)
6.5	0/0/0	4.5	0	3.2	0	0	0	0/0/0	0/0/			0/0/0	Other articles of fused quartz or other fused silica(other than glass umbrella for insulator)
													----Other
6.5	0/0/0	4.5	0	3.2	0	0	0	0/0/0	0/0/			0/0/0	Quartz reactor tubes and holders for production of semiconductor wafers (for inserting in melting and oxidation)
6.5	0/0/0	4.5	0	3.2	0	0	0	0/0/0	0/0/			0/0/0	Other galss articles for other technical use
													---Other:
	0/0/0		12.6	6.3	0	0	0	0/0/0	0/0/			0/0/	----Glass inners for vacuum flasks or for other vacuum vessels
													----Other
6.5	0/0/0	6.8	6	4.5	0	0	0	0/0/0	0/0/			0/0/0	Quartz glass, levelling degree ≤1 μm
6.5	0/0/0	6.8	6	4.5	0	0	0	0/0/0	0/0/			0/0/0	Other glass articles not for other technical use

第十四类
天然或养殖珍珠、宝石或半宝石、贵金属、包贵金属及其制品；仿首饰；硬币

第七十一章
天然或养殖珍珠、宝石或半宝石、贵金属、包贵金属及其制品；仿首饰；硬币

注释：

一、除第六类注释一(一)及下列各款另有规定的以外，凡制品的全部或部分由下列物品构成，均应归入本章：

(一)天然或养殖珍珠、宝石或半宝石(天然、合成或再造)；

(二)贵金属或包贵金属。

二、(一)税目71.13、71.14及71.15不包括带有贵金属或包贵金属制的小附件或小装饰品(例如，交织字母、套、圈、套环)的制品，上述注释一(二)也不适用于这类制品；

(二)税目71.16不包括含有贵金属或包贵金属(仅作为小附件或小装饰品的除外)的制品。

三、本章不包括：

(一)贵金属汞齐及胶态贵金属(税目28.43)；

(二)第三十章的外科用无菌缝合材料、牙科填料或其他货品；

(三)第三十二章的货品(例如光瓷釉)；

(四)载体催化剂(税目38.15)；

(五)第四十二章注释三(二)所述的税目42.02或42.03的物品；

(六)税目43.03或43.04的物品；

(七)第十一类的货品(纺织原料及纺织制品)；

(八)第六十四章或第六十五章的鞋靴、帽类及其他物品；

(九)第六十六章的伞、手杖及其他物品；

(十)税目68.04或68.05及第八十二章含有宝石或半宝石(天然或合成)粉末的研磨材料制品；第八十二章装有宝石或半宝石(天然、合成或再造)工作部件的器具；第十六类的机器、机械器具、电气设备及其零件。然而，完全以宝石或半宝石(天然、合成或再造)制成的物品及其零件，除未安装的唱针用已加工蓝宝石或钻石外(税目85.22)，其余仍应归入本章；

(十一)第九十章、第九十一章或第九十二章的物品(科学仪器、钟表及乐器)；

(十二)武器及其零件(第九十三章)；

(十三)第九十五章注释二所述物品；

(十四)根据第九十六章注释四应归入该章的物品；

(十五)雕塑品原件(税目97.03)、收藏品(税目97.05)或超过一百年的古物(税目97.06)，但天然或养殖珍珠、宝石及半宝石除外。

四、(一)所称"贵金属"，是指银、金及铂；

(二)所称"铂"，是指铂、铱、锇、钯、铑及钌；

(三)所称"宝石或半宝石"，不包括第九十六章注释二(二)所述任何物质。

五、含有贵金属的合金(包括烧结及化合的)，只要其中任何一种贵金属的含量达到合金重量的2%，即应视为本章的贵金属合金。贵金属合金应按下列规则归类：

(一)按重量计含铂量在2%及以上的合金，应视为铂合金；

(二)按重量计含金量在2%及以上，但不含铂或按重量计含铂量在2%以下的合金，应视为金合金；

(三)按重量计含银量在2%及以上的其他合金，应视为银合金。

六、除条文另有规定的以外，本协调制度所称贵金属应包括上述注释五所规定的贵金属合金，但不包括包贵金属或表面镀以贵金属的贱金属及非金属。

七、本协调制度所称"包贵金属"，是指以贱金属为底料，在其一面或多面用焊接、熔接、热轧或类似机械方法覆盖一层贵金属的材料。除条文另有规定的以外，也包括镶嵌贵金属的贱金属。

八、除第六类注释一(一)另有规定的以外，凡符合税目71.12规定的货品，应归入该税目而不归入本协调制度的其他税目。

九、税目71.13所称"首饰"，是指：

(一)个人用小饰物(例如，戒指、手镯、项圈、饰针、耳环 表链、表链饰物、垂饰、领带别针、袖扣、饰扣、宗教性或其他勋章及徽章)；

(二)通常放置在衣袋、手提包或佩戴在身上的个人用品(例如，雪茄盒、烟盒、鼻烟盒、口香糖或药丸盒、粉盒、链袋或念珠)。

这些物品可以和下列物品组合或镶嵌下列物品：例如，天然或养殖珍珠、宝石或半宝石、合成或再造的宝石或半宝石、玳瑁壳、珍珠母、兽牙、天然或再生琥珀、黑玉或珊瑚

SECTION XIV

NATURAL OR CULTURED PEARLS, PRECIOUS OR SEMI-PRECIOUS STONES, PRECIOUS METALS, METALS CLAD WITH PRECIOUS METAL, AND ARTICLES THEREOF; IMITATION JEWELLERY; COIN

Chapter 71

Natural or cultured pearls, precious or semi-precious stones, precious metals, metals clad with precious metal, and articles thereof; imitation jewellery; coin

Notes:

1. Subject to Note 1 (a) to Section VI and except as provided below, all articles consisting wholly or partly:
   (a) Of natural or cultured pearls or of precious or semi-precious stones (natural, synthetic or reconstructed), or
   (b) Of precious metal or of metal clad with precious metal, are to be classified in this Chapter.
2. (a) Headings Nos. 71.13, 71.14 and 71.15 do not cover articles in which precious metal or metal clad with precious metal is present as minor constituents only, such as minor fittings or minor ornamentation (for example, monograms, ferrules and rims), and paragraph Note 1(b) of the foregoing Note does not apply to such articles;
   (b) Heading No. 71.16 does not cover articles containing precious metal or metal clad with precious metal (other than as minor constituents).
3. This Chapter does not cover:
   (a) Amalgams of precious metal, or colloidal precious metal (heading No. 28.43);
   (b) Sterile surgical suture materials, dental fillings or other goods of Chapter 30;
   (c) Goods of Chapter 32 (for example, lustres);
   (d) Supported catalysts (heading No. 38.15);
   (e) Articles of heading No. 42.02 or 42.03 referred to in Note 3(B) to Chapter 42;
   (f) Articles of heading No. 43.03 or 43.04;
   (g) Goods of Section XI (textiles and textile articles);
   (h) Footwear, headgear or other articles of Chapter 64 or 65;
   (ij) Umbrellas, walking-sticks or other articles of Chapter 66;
   (k) Abrasive goods of heading 68.04 or 68.05 or Chapter 82, containing dust or powder of precious or semi-precious stones (natural or synthetic); articles of Chapter 82 with a working part of precious or semi-precious stones (natural, synthetic or reconsturcted); machinery, mechanical appliances or electrical goods, or parts thereof, of Section XVI. However, articles and parts thereof, wholly of precious or semi-precious stones (natural, synthetic or reconstructed) remain classified in this Chapter, except unmounted worked sapphires and diamonds for styli (heading No. 85.22)
   (l) Articles of Chapter 90, 91 or 92 (scientific instruments, clocks and watches, musical instruments);
   (m) Arms or parts thereof (Chapter 93);
   (n) Articles covered by Note 2 to Chapter 95;
   (o) Articles classified in Chapter 96 by virtue of Note 4 to that Chapter;
   (p) Original sculptures or statuary (heading No. 97.03), collectors' pieces (heading No. 97.05) or antiques of an age exceeding one hundred years (heading No. 97.06), other than natural or cultured pearls or precious or semi-precious stones.
4. (a) The expression "precious metal" means silver, gold and platinum.
   (b) The expression "platinum" means platinum, iridium, osmium, palladium, rhodium and ruthenium.
   (c) The expression "precious or semi-precious stones" does not include any of the substances specified in Note 2 (b) to Chapter 96.
5. For the purposes of this Chapter, any alloy (including a sintered mixture and an inter-metallic compound) containing precious metal is to be treated as an alloy of precious metal if any one precious metal constitutes as much as 2%, by weight, of the alloy. Alloys of precious metal are to be classified according to the following rules:
   (a) An alloy containing 2% or more, by weight, of platinum is to be treated as an alloy of platinum;
   (b) An alloy containing 2% or more, by weight, of gold but no platinum, or less than 2%, by weight, of platinum, is to be treated as an alloy of gold;
   (c) Other alloys containing 2% or more, by weight, of silver are to be treated as alloys of silver.
6. Except where the context otherwise requires, any reference in the Nomenclature to precious metal or to any particular precious metal includes a reference to alloys treated as alloys of precious metal or of the particular metal in accordance with the rules in Note 5 above, but not to metal clad with precious metal or to base metal or nonmetals plated with precious metal.
7. Throughout the Nomenclature the expression "metal clad with precious metal" means material made with a base of metal upon one or more surfaces of which there is affixed by soldering, brazing, welding, hot-rolling or similar mechanical means a covering of precious metal. Except where the context otherwise requires, the expression also covers base metal inlaid with precious metal.
8. Subject to Note 1 (a) to Section VI, goods answering to a description in heading No. 71.12 are to be classified in that heading and in no otherheading of the Nomenclature.
9. For the purposes of heading No. 71.13, the expression "articles of jewellery" means:
   (a) Any small objects of personal adornment (for example, rings, bracelets, necklaces, brooches, ear-rings, watch-chains, fobs, pendants, tie-pins, cuff-links, dress-studs, religious or other medals and insignia); and
   (b) Articles of personal use of a kind normally carried in the pocket, in the handbag or on the person (for example) cigar or cigarette cases snuffboxes cachou or pill boxes, powder boxes chain purses or prayer beads.
   These articles may be combined or set, for example, with natural or cultured pearls, precious or semiprecious stone, synthetic or reconstructed precious or semi-precious stones, tortoise shell, mother-of-pearl, ivory, natural or reconstituted amber, jet or coral.

十、税目71.14所称"金银器",包括装饰品、餐具、梳妆用具、吸烟用具及类似的家庭、办公室或宗教用的其他物品。

十一、税目71.17所称"仿首饰",是指不含天然或养殖珍珠、宝石或半宝石(天然、合成或再造)及贵金属或包贵金属(仅作为镀层或小附件、小装饰品的除外)的上述注释九(一)所述的首饰(不包括税目96.06的纽扣及其他物品或税目96.15的梳子、发夹及类似品)。

子目注释:

一、子目号7106.10、7108.11、7110.11、7110.21、7110.31及7110.41所称"粉末",是指按重量计90%及以上可从网眼孔径为0.5毫米的筛子通过的产品;

二、子目号7110.11及7110.19所称"铂",可不受本章注释四(二)的规定约束,不包括铱、锇、钯、铑及钌。

三、对于税目71.10项下的子目所列合金的归类,按其所含铂、钯、铑、铱、锇或钌中重量最大的一种金属归类。

税则号列	货品名称〔CIQ扩展编码及品名—T2表示见附表2〕	最惠(%)	暂定税率	普通	增值/消费	出口退税	计量单位	监管条件	检验检疫	特殊证件对美关税
	第一分章　天然或养殖珍珠、宝石或半宝石									
71.01	**天然或养殖珍珠,不论是否加工或分级,但未成串或镶嵌;天然或养殖珍珠,为便于运输而暂穿成串:**									
	-天然珍珠:									
	---未分级:									
7101.1011	----黑珍珠〔999〕	21	0	100	13/10	6	克	AB	PQ	/
7101.1019	----其他〔999〕	21		100	13/10	6	克	AB	PQ	/
	---其他:									
7101.1091	----黑珍珠〔999〕	21	0	130	13/10	6	克	AB	PQ	/
7101.1099	----其他〔101药用天然珍珠,102天然珍珠〕	21		130	13/10	6	克	AB	PQ	/
	-养殖珍珠:									
	--未加工:									
7101.2110	---未分级									
7101.2110 01	未分级、未加工的养殖黑珍珠(未制成制品)〔999〕	21	0	100	13/10	6	千克	AB	PQ	/
7101.2110 90	其他未分级、未加工的养殖珍珠(未制成制品)〔999〕	21		100	13/10	6	千克	AB	PQ	/
7101.2190	---其他									
7101.2190 01	其他未加工的养殖黑珍珠(未制成制品)〔999〕	21	0	130	13/10	6	千克	AB	PQ	/
7101.2190 90	其他未加工的养殖珍珠(未制成制品)〔101药用未加工养殖珍珠,102未加工养殖珍珠〕	21		130	13/10	6	千克	AB	PQ	/
	--已加工:									
7101.2210	---未分级									
7101.2210 01	未分级、已加工的养殖黑珍珠(未制成制品)〔999〕	21	0	100	13/10	6	千克			/
7101.2210 90	其他未分级、已加工的养殖珍珠(未制成制品)〔999〕	21		100	13/10	6	千克			/
7101.2290	---其他									
7101.2290 01	其他已加工的养殖黑珍珠(未制成制品)〔999〕	21	0	130	13/10	6	千克			/25
7101.2290 90	其他已加工的养殖珍珠(未制成制品)〔101药用已加工珍珠,102已加工养殖珍珠〕	21		130	13/10	6	千克			/46
71.02	**钻石,不论是否加工,但未镶嵌:**									
7102.1000	-未分级〔999〕	3		14	13/	0	克拉	D		/
	-工业用:									
7102.2100	--未加工或经简单锯开、劈开或粗磨〔999〕	0		14	13/	6	克拉	D		/25
7102.2900	--其他〔999〕	0		14	13/	6	克拉			/25
	-非工业用:									
7102.3100	--未加工或经简单锯开、劈开或粗磨〔999〕	3		14	13/	0	克拉	D		/28
7102.3900	--其他〔999〕	4		35	13/	0	克拉			/29
71.03	**宝石(钻石除外)或半宝石,不论是否加工或分级,但未成串或镶嵌;未分级的宝石(钻石除外)或半宝石,为便于运输而暂穿成串:**									
7103.1000	-未加工或经简单锯开或粗制成形〔999〕	3		14	13/10	6	千克			/28
	-经其他加工:									
7103.9100	--红宝石、蓝宝石、祖母绿〔999〕	4		35	13/10	6	克拉			/29
	--其他:									
7103.9910	---翡翠〔999〕	4		35	13/10	6	克拉			/
7103.9920	---水晶〔999〕	4		35	13/10	6	克拉			/29
7103.9930	---碧玺〔999〕	4		35	13/10	6	克拉			/
7103.9940	---软玉〔999〕	4		35	13/10	6	克拉			/

10. For the purposes of heading No.71. 14, the expression "articles of goldsmiths' or silversmiths' wares" includes such articles as ornaments, tableware, toilet-ware, smokers' requisites and other articles of household, office or religious use.
11. For the purposes of heading No.71. 17, the expression "imitation jewellery" means articles of jewellery within the meaning of Note 9 (a) above (but not including buttons or other articles of heading 96. 06, or dress-combs, hair-slides or the like, or hairpins, of heading No.96. 15), not incorporating natural or cultured pearls, precious or semi-precious stones (natural synthetic, or reconstructed) nor (except as plating or as minor constituents) precious metal or metal clad with precious metal.

Subheading Notes:

1. For the purposes of subheadings Nos.7106. 10, 7108. 11, 7110. 11, 7110. 21, 7110. 31 and 7110. 41, the expressions "powder" and "in powder form" mean products of which 90% or more by weight passes through a sieve having a mesh aperture of 0. 5mm.
2. Notwithstanding the provisions of Chapter Note 4 (b), for the purposes of subheadings Nos.7110. 11 and 7110. 19, the expression "platinum" does not include iridium, osmium, palladium, rhodium or ruthenium.
3. For the classification of alloys in the subheadings of heading No.71. 10, each alloy is to be classified with that metal, platinum, palladium, rhodium, iridium, osmium or ruthenium which predominates by weight over each other of these metals.

协定税率 %										特惠税率 %			
亚太5国	东/冰/格	巴基斯坦	韩国	瑞士	哥达	秘鲁	澳大利亚	新西/坡/智	港/澳/台	亚太2国	老/柬/缅	36/3/1	**Article Description**
													Ⅰ. NATURAL OR CULTURED PEARLS AND PRECIOUS OR SEMI-PRECIOUS STONES
													Pearls, natural or cultured, whether or not worked or graded but not strung, mounted or set; ungraded pearls, natural or cultured, temporarily strung for convenience of transport:
													-Natural pearls:
													---Ungraded:
	0/0/0		12.6	6.3	0	0	0	0/0/0	0/0/			0/0/	----Tahitian pearls
	0/0/0		12.6	6.3	0	0	0	0/0/0	0/0/			0/0/	----Other
													---Other:
	0/0/0		12.6	6.3	0	0	0	0/0/0	0/0/			0/0/	----Tahitan pearls
	0/0/0		12.6	6.3	0	0	0	0/0/0	0/0/			0/0/	----Other
													-Cultured pearls:
													--Unworked:
													---Ungraded
	0/0/0		12.6	6.3	0	0	0	0/0/0	0/0/			0/0/	Ungraded and unworked cultured tahitan pearls(semi-manufactured)
	0/0/0		12.6	6.3	0	0	0	0/0/0	0/0/			0/0/	Other uagraded and unworked cultured pearls(semi-manufactured)
													---Other
	0/0/0		12.6	6.3	0	0	0	0/0/0	0/0/			0/0/	Other unworked cultured tahitan pearls(semi-manufactured)
	0/0/0		12.6	6.3	0	0	0	0/0/0	0/0/			0/0/	Other unworked cultured pearls(semi-manufactured)
													--Worked:
													---Ungraded
	0/0/0		14.7	6.3	0	0	0	0/0/0	0/0/			0/0/	Cultured Tahitan pearls, ungraded, worlced (semi-manufactured)
	0/0/0		14.7	6.3	0	0	0	0/0/0	0/0/			0/0/	Other cultured pearls, ungraded, worked (semi-manufactured)
													---Other
	0/0/0		14.7	6.3	0	0	0	0/0/0	0/0/			0/0/	Other worked cultured tahitan pearls(semi-manufactured)
	0/0/0		14.7	6.3	0	0	0	0/0/0	0/0/			0/0/	Other worked cultured pearls(semi-manufactured)
													Diamonds, whether or not worked, but not mounted or set:
	0/0/0	0	0	0	0	0	0	0//0	0/0/			0/0/0	-Unsorted
													-Industrial:
												0/0/0	--Unworked or simply sawn, cleaved or bruted
												0/0/0	--Other
													-Non-industrial:
	0/0/0	0	0	0.9	0	0	0	0//0	0/0/			0/0/0	--Unworked or simply sawn, cleaved or bruted
0	0/0/0	0	0	2.4	0	0	0	0//0	0/0/			0/0/0	--Other
													Precious stones (other than diamonds) and semi-precious stones, whether or not worked or graded but not strung, mounted or set; ungraded precious stones (other than diamonds) and semi-precious stones, temporarily strung for covenience of transport:
2	0/0/1.2	0	0	0	0	0	0	0//0	0/0/		0//	0/0/0	-Unworked or simply sawn or roughly shaped
													-Otherwise worked:
2	0/0/0	0	0	2.4	0	0	0	0//0	0/0/		0//	0/0/0	--Rubies, sapphires and emeralds
													--Other:
2	0/0/0	0	0	0	0	0	0	0//0	0/0/			0/0/0	---Jadeite
2	0/0/0	0	3.2	2.4	0	0	0	0//0	0/0/			0/0/0	---Crystal
2	0/0/0	0	3.2	2.4	0	0	0	0//0	0/0/			0/0/0	---Tourmaline
2	0/0/0	0	3.2	2.4	0	0	0	0//0	0/0/			0/0/0	---Nephrite

税则号列	货品名称〔CIQ 扩展编码及品名－T2 表示见附表 2〕	最惠(%)	暂定税率	普通	增值/消费	出口退税	计量单位	监管条件	检验检疫	特殊证件对美关税
7103.9990	---其他〔999〕	4		35	13/10	6	克拉			/29
71.04	**合成或再造的宝石或半宝石，不论是否加工或分级，但未成串或镶嵌的；未分级的合成或再造的宝石或半宝石，为便于运输而暂穿成串：**									
7104.1000	-压电石英〔999〕	4		14	13/	6	克			/29
	-其他，未加工或经简单锯开或粗制成形：									
7104.2010	---钻石〔999〕	0		14	13/	0	克			/10
7104.2090	---其他〔999〕	0		14	13/10	6	克			/25
	-其他：									
	---工业用：									
7104.9011	----钻石〔999〕	4		14	13/	6	克			/24
7104.9012	----蓝宝石									
7104.9012 01	蓝宝石衬底（由人造刚玉加工而成，厚度＜0.5mm）〔999〕	4	1	14	13/10	13	克			/26
7104.9012 90	其他工业用蓝宝石（合成或再造宝石、半宝石）〔999〕	4		14	13/10	13	克			/29
7104.9019	----其他〔999〕	4		14	13/10	6	克			/14
	---其他：									
7104.9091	----钻石〔999〕	4		35	13/	0	克			/
7104.9099	----其他〔999〕	4		35	13/10	6	克			/29
71.05	**天然或合成的宝石或半宝石的粉末：**									
	-钻石的：									
7105.1010	---天然的〔999〕	0		17	13/	0	克拉			/
7105.1020	---人工合成的〔999〕	0		17	13/	6	克拉			/10
7105.9000	-其他〔999〕	0		17	13/10	6	克			/25
	第二分章　贵金属及包贵金属									
71.06	**银（包括镀金、镀铂的银），未锻造、半制成或粉末状：**									
	-银粉：									
	---非片状粉末：									
7106.1011	----平均粒径小于 3 微米〔999〕	0		0	13/	0	克	A4xy	M	/25
7106.1019	----其他〔101 银粉浆，102 银粉〕	0		0	13/	0	克	A4xy	M	/20
	---片状粉末：									
7106.1021	----平均粒径小于 10 微米〔999〕	0		0	13/	0	克	4xy		/10
7106.1029	----其他〔999〕	0		0	13/	0	克	4xy		/10
	-其他：									
	--未锻造：									
7106.9110	---纯度达 99.99％及以上〔999〕	0		0	13/	0	克	4xy		/25
7106.9190	---其他〔999〕	0		0	13/	0	克	4xy		/25
	--半制成：									
7106.9210	---纯度达 99.99％及以上〔999〕	0		50	13/	0	克	4xy		/25
7106.9290	---其他〔999〕	0		50	13/	0	克	4xy		/20
71.07	**以贱金属为底的包银材料：**									
7107.0000	以贱金属为底的包银材料〔999〕	8		50	13/	6	千克			/28
71.08	**金（包括镀铂的金），未锻造、半制成或粉末状：**									
	-非货币用：									
7108.1100	--金粉〔999〕	0		0	0/	0	克	J		/10
7108.1200	--其他未锻造形状〔999〕	0		0	0/	0	克	J		/20
7108.1300	--其他半制成形状〔999〕	0		50	0/	0	克	J		/25
7108.2000	-货币用〔999〕	0		0	0/	0	克	J		/
71.09	**以贱金属或银为底的包金材料：**									
7109.0000	以贱金属或银为底的包金材料〔999〕	8		50	13/	6	克			/33
71.10	**铂，未锻造、半制成或粉末状：**									
	-铂：									
7110.1100	--未锻造或粉末状〔999〕	0		0	0/	0	克	8x		/25
	--其他：									

协定税率 %										特惠税率 %			
亚太5国	东/冰/格	巴基斯坦	韩国	瑞士	哥达	秘鲁	澳大利亚	新西/坡/智	港/澳/台	亚太2国	老/柬/缅	36/3/1	Article Description
2	0/0/0	0	3.2	2.4	0	0	0	0//0	0/0/			0/0/0	---Other
													Synthetic or reconstructed precious or semi-precious stones, whether or not worked or graded but not strung, mounted or set; ungraded synthetic or reconstructed precious or semi-precious stones, temporarily strung for convenience of transport:
	0/0/0	0		0	0	0	0	0//0	0/0/			0/0/0	-Piezo-electric quartz
													-Other, unworked or simply sawn or roughly shaped:
												0/0/0	---Diamonds
									0//			0/0/0	---Other
													-Other:
													---For technical use:
	0/0/0	0	0	0	0	0	0	0//0	0/0/			0/0/0	----Diamonds
													----Sapphires
	0/0/0	0	0	0	0	0	0	0//0	0/0/			0/0/0	Precious or semi-precious stones underlay with sapphirel, made of man-made corundum(with thickness<0.5mm)
	0/0/0	0	0	0	0	0	0	0//0	0/0/			0/0/0	Other sapphire used for Industry(synthetic or reconstructed precious or semi-precious stones)
	0/0/0	0	2.4	0	0	0	0	0//0	0/0/			0/0/0	----Other
													---Other:
2.8	0/0/0	4	0	0	0	0	0	0//0	0/0/			0/0/0	----Diamonds
3.6	0/0/0	4	0	0	0	0	0	0//0	0/0/			0/0/0	----Other
													Dust and powder of natural orsynthetic precious or semi-precious stones:
													-Of diamonds:
												0/0/0	---Natural
												0/0/0	---Synthetic
												0/0/0	-Other
													Ⅱ. PRECIOUS METALS AND METALS CLAD WITH PRECIOUS METAL
													Silver (including silver plated with gold or platinum), unwrought or in semi-manufactured forms, or in powder form:
													-Powder:
													---Not Flake:
												0/0/0	----Average diameter less than 3 micron
												0/0/0	----Other
													---Flake:
												0/0/0	----Average diameter less than 10 micron
												0/0/0	----Other
													-Other:
													--Unwrought:
												0/0/0	---of a purity of 99.99 or more
												0/0/0	---Other
													--Semi-manufactured:
												0/0/0	---of a purity of 99.99 or more
												0/0/0	---Other
													Base metals clad with silver, not further worked than semi-manufactured:
	0/0/0	4.5	4.2	3.2	0	0	0	0/0/0	0/0/		0//	0/0/0	Base metals clad with silver, not further worked than semi-manufactured
													Gold (including gold plated with platinum) unwrought or in semi-manufactured forms, or in powder form:
													-Non-monetary:
												0/0/0	--Powder
												0/0/0	--Other unwrought forms
											0//	0/0/0	--Other semi-manufactured forms
												0/0/0	-Monetary
													Base metals or silver, clad with gold, not further worked than semi-manufactured:
	0/0/0	4.5	4.2	3.2	0	0	0	0/0/0	0/0/			0/0/0	Base metals or silver, clad with gold, not further worked than semi-manufactured
													Platinum, unwrought or in semi-manufactured forms, or in powder form:
													-Platinum:
												0/0/0	--Unwrought or in powder form
													--Other:

税则号列		货品名称〔CIQ扩展编码及品名—T2表示见附表2〕	最惠(%)	暂定税率	普通	增值/消费	出口退税	计量单位	监管条件	检验检疫	特殊证件对美关税
7110.1910		---板、片〔999〕	0		0	0/	0	克	8x		/25
7110.1990		---其他〔999〕	3		11	0/	0	克	4xy		/23
		-钯:									
7110.2100		--未锻造或粉末状〔999〕	0		10	13/	0	克	4xy		/25
		--其他:									
7110.2910		---板、片〔999〕	0		0	13/	0	克	4xy		/10
7110.2990		---其他〔999〕	3		11	13/	0	克	4xy		/23
		-铑:									
7110.3100		--未锻造或粉末状〔999〕	0		0	13/	0	克	4xy		/25
		--其他:									
7110.3910		---板、片〔999〕	0		0	13/	0	克	4xy		/25
7110.3990		---其他〔999〕	3		11	13/	0	克	4xy		/13
		-铱、锇及钌:									
7110.4100		--未锻造或粉末状〔999〕	0		0	13/	0	克	4xy		/25
		--其他:									
7110.4910		---板、片〔999〕	0		0	13/	0	克	4xy		/25
7110.4990		---其他〔999〕	3		11	13/	0	克	4xy		/28
71.11		**以贱金属、银或金为底的包铂材料:**									
7111.0000		以贱金属、银或金为底的包铂材料〔999〕	3		11	13/	0,6	克	4xy		/28
71.12		**贵金属或包贵金属的废碎料;含有贵金属或贵金属化合物的其他废碎料,主要用于回收贵金属:**									
		-含有贵金属或贵金属化合物的灰:									
7112.3010		---含有银或银化合物的〔999〕	8		50	13/	6	克	9		/
7112.3090		---其他〔999〕	6		50	13/	0	克	9		/
		-其他:									
		--金及包金的废碎料,但含有其他贵金属的除外:									
7112.9110		---金及包金的废碎料									
7112.9110	10	金的废碎料〔999〕	0		0	13/	0	克	A	M	/25
7112.9110	90	包金的废碎料(但含有其他贵金属的除外)〔999〕	0		0	13/	0	克	A	M	/25
7112.9120		---含有金或金化合物的废碎料〔999〕	6		35	13/	0	克	9		/
		--铂及包铂的废碎料,但含有其他贵金属的除外:									
7112.9210		---铂及包铂的废碎料〔999〕	0		0	13/	0	克	4Axy	M	/25
7112.9220		---含有铂或铂化合物的废碎料									
7112.9220	01	铂含量在3%以上的其他含有铂或铂化合物的废碎料(但含有其他贵金属除外,主要用于回收铂)〔999〕	6	0	35	13/	0	克	4xy		/10
7112.9220	90	其他含有铂及铂化合物的废碎料(但含有其他贵金属除外,主要用于回收铂)〔999〕	6		35	13/	0	克	4xy		/16
		--其他:									
7112.9910		---含有银或银化合物的废碎料〔999〕	8		35	13/	6	克	9		/
7112.9920		---含有其他贵金属或贵金属化合物的废碎料〔999〕	6		35	13/	0	克	9		/
7112.9990		---其他〔999〕	0		50	13/	0	克			/
		第三分章 珠宝首饰、金银器及其他制品									
71.13		**贵金属或包贵金属制的首饰及其零件:**									
		-贵金属制,不论是否包、镀贵金属:									
		--银制,不论是否包、镀其他贵金属:									
7113.1110		---镶嵌钻石的〔999〕	8		130	13/	0	克			/18
7113.1190		---其他									
7113.1190	10	镶嵌濒危物种制品的银首饰及零件(不论是否包、镀其他贵金属)〔999〕	8		130	13/	0	克	FE		/33
7113.1190	90	其他银首饰及其零件(不论是否包、镀其他贵金属)〔999〕	8		130	13/	6	克			/33
		--其他贵金属制,不论是否包、镀贵金属:									
		---金制:									
7113.1911		----镶嵌钻石的〔999〕	8		130	13/	0	克			/28

协定税率 %										特惠税率 %			Article Description
亚太5国	东/冰/格	巴基斯坦	韩国	瑞士	哥达	秘鲁	澳大利亚	新西/坡/智	港/澳/台	亚太2国	老/柬/缅	36/3/1	
												0/0/0	---Plates and sheets
	0/0/0	0	0	0	0	0	0	0//0	0/0/			0/0/0	---Other
													-Palladium:
												0/0/0	--Unwrought or in powder form
													--Other:
												0/0/0	---Plates and sheets
	0/0/0	0	0	0	0	0	0	0//0	0/0/			0/0/0	---Other
													-Rhodium:
												0/0/0	--Unwrought or in powder form
													--Other:
												0/0/0	---Plates and sheets
	0/0/0	0	0	0	0	0	0	0//0	0/0/			0/0/0	---Other
													-Iridium, osmium and ruthenium:
												0/0/0	--Unwrought or in powder form
													--Other:
												0/0/0	---Plates and sheets
	0/0/0	0	0	0	0	0	0	0//0	0/0/			0/0/0	---Other
													Base metals, silver or gold, clad with platinum, not further worked than semi-manufactured:
	0/0/0	0	0	0	0	0	0	0//0	0/0/			0/0/	Base metals, silver or gold, clad with platinum, not further worked than semi-manufactured
													Waste and scrap of precious metal or of metal clad with precious metal; other waste and scrap containing precious metal or precious metal compounds, of a kind used principally for the recovery of precious metal:
													-Ash containing precious metal or precious metal compounds:
	0/0/0	4	0	0	0	0	0	0//0	0/0/			0/0/0	---Of silver or silver compounds
	0/0/0	0	0	0	0	0	0	0//0	0/0/			0/0/0	---Other
													-Other:
													--Of gold, including metal clad with gold but excluding sweepings containing other precious metals:
													---Of gold, or gold compounds
												0/0/0	Waster and scrap of gold
												0/0/0	Waster and scrap of including metal clad with gold, but excluding sweepings containing other precious metals
	0/0/0	0	0	0	0	0	0	0//0	0/0/			0/0/0	---Waste and scrap with gold or gold compounds
													--Of platinum, including metal clad with platinum but excluding sweepings containing other precious metals:
												0/0/0	---Of platinum
													---Wastes and scrap with platinum
	0/0/0	0	0	0	0	0	0	0//0	0/0/			0/0/0	Other waste and scraps with platinum and its compounds, containing >3% of platinum(but excluding sweeping contcaining other precious metals, used for recycling platinum)
	0/0/0	0	0	0	0	0	0	0//0	0/0/			0/0/0	Other waste and scraps containing platinum(but excluding sweepings containing other precious metals, used for recycling platinum)
													--Other:
	0/0/0	4	0	0	0	0	0	0//0	0/0/			0/0/0	---Waste and scrap with silver or silver compounds
	0/0/0	0	0	0	0	0	0	0//0	0/0/			0/0/0	---Waste and scrap with other precious metals
												0/0/0	---Other
													Ⅲ. JEWELLERY, GOLDSMITHS' AND SILVERSMITHS' WARES AND OTHER ARTICLES
													Articles of jewellery and parts thereof, of precious metal or of metal chad with precious metal:
													-Of precious metal whether or not plated or clad with precious metal:
													--Of silver, whether or not plated or clad with other precious metal:
5.2	0/0/0	0	12	8	0	0	0	0/0/0	0/0/			0/0/	---Diamond mounted of set
													---Other
5.2	0/0/0	0	12	0	0	0	0	0/0/0	0/0/			0/0/0	Silver jewellery and parts thereof, inlaid with articles of endangered species(whether or not plated or clad with other precious metal)
5.2	0/0/0	0	12	0	0	0	0	0/0/0	0/0/			0/0/0	Other silver jewellery and parts thereof(whether or not plated or clad with other precious metal)
													--Of other precious metal, whether or not plated or clad with predious metal:
													---Of gold:
5.2	0/0/0	0	12	8	0	0	0	0/0/0	0/0/			0/0/	----Dicmond mounted

税则号列		货品名称〔CIQ扩展编码及品名—T2表示见附表2〕	最惠(%)	暂定税率	普通	增值/消费	出口退税	计量单位	监管条件	检验检疫	特殊证件对美关税
7113.1919		----其他									
7113.1919	10	镶嵌濒危物种制品的金首饰及零件(不论是否包、镀其他贵金属)〔999〕	8		130	13/	0	克	FE		/28
7113.1919	90	其他黄金制首饰及其零件(不论是否包、镀其他贵金属)〔999〕	8		130	13/	0	克	J		/28
		---铂制:									
7113.1921		----镶嵌钻石的〔999〕	10		130	13/	0	克			/20
7113.1929		----其他:									
7113.1929	10	镶嵌濒危物种制品的铂金首饰及零件(不论是否包、镀其他贵金属)〔999〕	10		130	13/	0	克	EF		/20
		--其他:									
7113.1929	90	其他铂金制首饰及其零件(不论是否包、镀其他贵金属)〔999〕	10		130	13/	0	克			/20
7113.1991		----镶嵌钻石的〔999〕	10		130	13/	0	克			/35
7113.1999		----其他									
7113.1999	10	镶嵌濒危物种制品的其他贵金属首饰(不论是否包、镀其他贵金属)〔999〕	10		130	13/	0	克	FE		/35
7113.1999	90	其他贵金属制首饰及其零件(不论是否包、镀其他贵金属)〔999〕	10		130	13/	0	克			/35
		-以贱金属为底的包贵金属制:									
7113.2010		---镶嵌钻石的〔999〕	10		130	13/	0	克			/35
7113.2090		---其他									
7113.2090	10	镶嵌濒危物种制品以贱金属为底的包贵金属制首饰(包括零件)〔999〕	10		130	13/10	0	克	FE		/35
7113.2090	90	其他以贱金属为底的包贵金属制首饰(包括零件)〔999〕	10		130	13/10	6	克			/35
71.14		**贵金属或包贵金属制的金银器及其零件:**									
		-贵金属制,不论是否包、镀贵金属:									
7114.1100		--银制,不论是否包、镀其他贵金属									
7114.1100	10	镶嵌濒危物种制品的银器及零件(不论是否包、镀贵金属)〔999〕	10		100	13/	0	克	FE		/20
7114.1100	90	其他银器及零件(不论是否包、镀贵金属)〔999〕	10		100	13/	6	克			/20
7114.1900		--其他贵金属制,不论是否包、镀贵金属									
7114.1900	10	镶嵌濒危物种制品的金银器及零件(不论是否包、镀贵金属)〔999〕	10		100	13/	0	克	FE		/35
7114.1900	20	其他贵金属制金器及零件(工艺金章,摆件等,不论是否包,镀贵金属)〔999〕	10		100	13/	0	克	J		/35
7114.1900	90	其他贵金属制银器及零件(不论是否包,镀贵金属)〔999〕	10		100	13/	0	克			/35
7114.2000		-以贱金属为底的包贵金属制									
7114.2000	10	以贱金属为底的包贵金属制金银器(镶嵌濒危物种制品,包括零件)〔999〕	10		100	13/	0	克	FE		/
7114.2000	90	其他贱金属为底包贵金属制金银器(包括零件)〔999〕	10		100	13/	0,6	克			/
71.15		**贵金属或包贵金属的其他制品:**									
7115.1000		-金属丝布或格栅形状的铂催化剂〔999〕	3		11	13/	0	克	4xy		/13
		-其他:									
7115.9010		---工业或实验室用									
7115.9010	10	银制工业、实验室用制品〔999〕	3	0	11	13/	6	克			/10
7115.9010	20	金制工业、实验室用制品〔999〕	3	0	11	13/	0	克			/10
7115.9010	90	其他工业、实验室用贵或包贵金制品〔999〕	3	0	11	13/	6,0	克			/10
7115.9090		---其他〔999〕	10		100	13/	0,6	克			/30
71.16		**用天然或养殖珍珠、宝石或半宝石(天然、合成或再造)制成的物品:**									

协定税率 %										特惠税率 %			
亚太5国	东/冰/格	巴基斯坦	韩国	瑞士	哥达	秘鲁	澳大利亚	新西/坡/智	港/澳/台	亚太2国	老/柬/缅	36/3/1	Article Description
													----Other
5.2	0/0/0	0	8	0	0	0	0	0/0/0	0/0/			0/0/	Gold jewellery and parts thereof, inlaid with articles of endangered species (whether or not plated or clad with other precious metal)
5.2	0/0/0	0	8	0	0	0	0	0/0/0	0/0/			0/0/	Other gold jewellery and parts thereof(whether or not plated or clad with other precious metal)
													---Of platinum
6.5	0/0/0	0			0	0	0	0/0/0	0/0/			0/0/	----Diomond mounted
													----Other:
6.5	0/0/0	0		0	0	0	0	0/0/0	0/0/			0/0/0	Platinum jewellery and parts thereof, inlaid with articles of endangered species, whether or not plated or clad with other precious metal
													--Other:
6.5	0/0/0	0		0	0	0	0	0/0/0	0/0/			0/0/0	Other platinum jewellery and parts thereof, whether or not plated or clad with other precious metal
6.5	0/0/0	0			0	0	0	0/0/0	0/0/			0/0/	----Diomond mounted or set
													----Other
6.5	0/0/0	0		0	0	0	0	0/0/0	0/0/			0/0/0	Jewellery and parts thereof, of precious metal, inlaid with articles of endangered species(whether or not plated or clad with other precious metal)
6.5	0/0/0	0		0	0	0	0	0/0/0	0/0/			0/0/0	Other jewellery and parts thereof of precious metal(whether or not plated or clad with other precious metal)
													-Of base metal clad with precious metal:
6.5	0//0	30		10	0	0	0	0/0/0	0/0/			0/0/	---Diamond mounted or set
													---Other
6.5	0/0/0	30			0	0	0	0/0/0	0/0/			0/0/	Jewellery and parts thereof, of base metal clad with precious metal, inlaid with articles of endangered species
6.5	0/0/0	30			0	0	0	0/0/0	0/0/			0/0/	Other jewellery and parts thereof, of base metal clad with precious metal
													Articles of goldsmiths' or silversmiths' wares and parts thereof, of precious metal or of metal clad with precious metal:
													-Of precious metal whether or not plated or clad with precious metal:
													--Of silver, whether or not plated or clad with other precious metal
	0/0/0			0	0	0	0	0/0/0	0/0/			0/0/0	Silversmiths' wares and parts thereof, inlaid with articles of endangered species(whether or not plated or clad with other precious metal)
	0/0/0			0	0	0	0	0/0/0	0/0/			0/0/0	Other silversmiths' wares and parts thereof(whether or not plated or clad with other precious metal)
													--Of other precious metal, whether or not plated or clad with precious metal
	0/0/0			10	0	0	0	0/0/0	0/0/			0/0/	Goldsmiths' or silversmiths' wares and parts thereof, inlaid with articles of endangered species(whether or not plated or clad with other precious metal)
	0/0/0			10	0	0	0	0/0/0	0/0/			0/0/	Of other precious metal gold and parts (regardless of whether the packet, plated with precious metal)
	0/0/0			10	0	0	0	0/0/0	0/0/			0/0/	Other goldsmiths' or silversmiths' wares and parts thereof, of precious metal(whether or not plated or clad with other precious metal)
													-Of base metal clad with precious metal
8	0/0/0			10	0	0	0	0/0/0	0/0/			0/0/0	Goldsmiths' or silversmiths' wares and parts thereof, inlaid with articles of endangered species, of base metal cald with precious metal
8	0/0/0			10	0	0	0	0/0/0	0/0/			0/0/0	Other goldsmiths' or silversmiths' wares and parts thereof, of base metal cald with precious metal
													Other articles of precious metal or of metal clad with precious metal:
	0/0/0	0	0	0	0	0	0	0//0	0/0/			0/0/0	-Catalysts in the form of wire cloth or grill, of platinum
													-Other:
													---For technical or laboratory use
	0/0/0	0	0	0	0	0	0	0//0	0/0/			0/0/0	Articles of silver for industrial or laboratory use
	0/0/0	0	0	0	0	0	0	0//0	0/0/			0/0/0	Articles of gold for industrial or laboratory use
	0/0/0	0	0	0	0	0	0	0//0	0/0/			0/0/0	Articles of precious metal or of metal clad with precious metal for industrial or laboratory use
	0/0/0				0	0	0	0/0/0	0/0/			0/0/	---Other
													Articles of natural or cultured pearls, precious or semi-precious stones (natural, synthetic or reconstructed):

税则号列	货品名称〔CIQ 扩展编码及品名—T2 表示见附表 2〕	最惠(%)	暂定税率	普通	增值/消费	出口退税	计量单位	监管条件	检验检疫	特殊证件对美关税
7116.1000	-天然或养殖珍珠制〔101 具有保健食品批准文号,102 珍珠宝石制品〕	10		130	13/10	6	千克			/35
7116.2000	-宝石或半宝石(天然、合成或再造)制〔999〕	10		130	13/10	0,6	千克			/35
71.17	**仿首饰:**									
	-贱金属制,不论是否镀贵金属:									
7117.1100	--袖扣、饰扣[101 锌合金制儿童用仿真首饰,102 铜合金制儿童用仿真首饰,103 不锈钢制儿童用仿真首饰,104 其他材料制儿童用仿真首饰,105 接触皮肤的成人用仿真首饰,106 非接触皮肤的成人用仿真首饰]	10		130	13/	10	千克	A	M	/35
7117.1900	--其他[101 锌合金制儿童用仿真首饰,102 铜合金制儿童用仿真首饰,103 不锈钢制儿童用仿真首饰,104 其他材料制儿童用仿真首饰,105 接触皮肤的成人用仿真首饰,106 非接触皮肤的成人用仿真首饰]	8		130	13/	10	千克	A	M	/33
7117.9000	-其他〔101 其他材料制儿童用仿真首饰,102 接触皮肤的成人用仿真首饰,103 非接触皮肤的成人用仿真首饰〕	18		130	13/	10	千克	A	M	/43
71.18	**硬币:**									
7118.1000	-非法定货币的硬币(金币除外)〔999〕	0		0	13/	6	千克			/20
7118.9000	-其他									
7118.9000　10	金质铸币(金质贵金属纪念币)〔999〕	0		0	13/	0	千克	J		/
7118.9000　90	其他硬币〔999〕	0		0	13/	0	千克			/

协定税率 %										特惠税率 %			Article Description
亚太5国	东/冰/格	巴基斯坦	韩国	瑞士	哥达	秘鲁	澳大利亚	新西/坡/智	港/澳/台	亚太2国	老/柬/缅	36/3/1	
	0/0/0			10	0	0	0	0/0/0	0/0/			0/0/	-Of natural or cultured pearls
	0/0/0	0		0	0	0	0	0/0/0	0/0/			0/0/0	-Of precious or semi-precious stones (natural, synthetic or reconstructed)
													Imitation jewellery:
													-Of base metal, whether or not plated with precious metal:
	0/0/0			10	0	0	0	0/0/0	0/0/			0/0/	--Cuff-links and studs
5.2	0/0/0	13.6	6.8	5.1	0	0	0	0/0/0	0/0/			0/0/0	--Other
11.7	0//0	30	22.7		0	0	0	0/0/0	0/0/			0/0/0	-Other
													Coin:
												0/0/0	-Coin (other than gold coin), not being legal tender
													-Other
												0/0/0	Gold coins (gold precious metal commemorative coins)
												0/0/0	Other coins

第十五类
贱金属及其制品

注释：

一、本类不包括：

(一)以金属粉末为基本成分的调制油漆、油墨或其他产品(税目 32.07 至 32.10、32.12、32.13 或 32.15)；

(二)铈铁或其他引火合金(税目 36.06)；

(三)税目 65.06 或 65.07 的帽类及其零件；

(四)税目 66.03 的伞骨及其他物品；

(五)第七十一章的货品(例如,贵金属合金、以贱金属为底的包贵金属、仿首饰)；

(六)第十六类的物品(机器、机械器具及电气设备)；

(七)已装配的铁路或电车轨道(税目 86.08)或第十七类的其他物品(车辆、船舶、航空器)；

(八)第十八类的仪器及器具,包括钟表发条；

(九)做弹药用的铅弹(税目 93.06)或第十九类的其他物品(武器、弹药)；

(十)第九十四章的物品(例如,家具、弹簧床垫、灯具及照明装置、发光标志、活动房屋)；

(十一)第九十五章的物品(例如,玩具、游戏品及运动用品)；

(十二)手用筛子、纽扣、钢笔、铅笔套、钢笔尖、独脚架、双脚架、三脚架及类似品或第九十六章的其他物品(杂项制品)；或

(十三)第九十七章的物品(例如,艺术品)。

二、本协调制度所称“通用零件”,是指：

(一)税目 73.07、73.12、73.15、73.17 或 73.18 的物品及其他贱金属制的类似品；

(二)贱金属制的弹簧及弹簧片,但钟表发条(税目 91.14)除外；

(三)税目 83.01、83.02、83.08、83.10 的物品及税目 83.06 的贱金属制的框架及镜子。

第七十三章至第七十六章(税目 73.15 除外)及第七十八章至第八十二章所列货品的零件,不包括上述的通用零件。

除上段及第八十三章注释一另有规定的以外,第七十二章至第七十六章及第七十八章至第八十一章不包括第八十二章、第八十三章的物品。

三、本协调制度所称“贱金属”是指:铁及钢、铜、镍、铝、铅、锌、锡、钨、钼、钽、镁、钴、铋、镉、钛、锆、锑、锰、铍、铬、锗、钒、镓、铪、铟、铌(钶)、铼及铊。

四、本协调制度所称“金属陶瓷”,是指金属与陶瓷成分的极细微粒不均匀结合而成的产品。“金属陶瓷”包括硬质合金(金属碳化物与金属烧结而成)。

五、合金的归类规则(第七十二章、第七十四章所规定的铁合金及母合金除外)：

(一)贱金属的合金按其所含重量最大的金属归类；

(二)由本类的贱金属和非本类的元素构成的合金,如果所含贱金属的总重量等于或超过所含其他元素的总重量,应作为本类贱金属合金归类；

(三)本类所称“合金”,包括金属粉末的烧结混合物、熔化而得的不均匀紧密混合物(金属陶瓷除外)及金属间化合物。

六、除条文另有规定的以外,本协调制度所称的贱金属包括贱金属合金,这类合金应按上述注释五的规则进行归类。

七、复合材料制品的归类规则：

除各税目另有规定的以外,贱金属制品(包括根据“归类总规则”作为贱金属制品的混合材料制品)如果含有两种或两种以上贱金属的,按其所含重量最大的贱金属的制品归类。为此：

(一)钢、铁或不同种类的钢铁,均视为一种金属；

(二)按照注释五的规定作为某一种金属归类的合金,应视为一种金属；

(三)税目 81.13 的金属陶瓷,应视为一种贱金属。

八、本类所用有关名词解释如下：

(一)废碎料

在金属生产或机械加工中产生的废料及碎屑以及因破裂、切断、磨损及其他原因而明显不能作为原物使用的金属货品。

(二)粉末

按重量计 90%及以上可从网眼孔径为 1 毫米的筛子通过的产品。

第七十二章
钢　铁

注释：

一、本章所述有关名词解释如下(本条注释(四)、(五)、(六)适用于本协调制度其他各章)：

SECTION XV
BASE METALS AND ARTICLES OF BASE METAL

Notes:

1. This Section does not cover:
   (a) Prepared paints, inks or other products with a basis of metallic flakes or powder (headings Nos.32.07 to 32.10, 32.12, 32.13 or 32.15);
   (b) Ferro-cerium or other pyrophoric alloys (heading No.36.06);
   (c) Headgear or parts thereof of heading No.65.06 or 65.07;
   (d) Umbrella frames or other articles of heading No.66.03;
   (e) Goods of Chapter 71 (for example, precious metal alloys, base metal clad with precious metal, imitation Jewelry);
   (f) Articles of Section XVI (machinery, mechanical appliances and electrical goods);
   (g) Assembled railway or tramway track (heading No.86.08) or other articles of Section XVII (vehicles, ships and boats, aircraft);
   (h) Instruments or apparatus of Section XVIII, including clock or watch springs;
   (ij) Lead shot prepared for anmmunition (heading No.93.06) or other articles of Section XIX (arms and ammunition);
   (k) Articles of Chapter 94 (for example, furniture, mattress supports, lamps and lighting fittings, illuminated signs, prefabricated buildings);
   (l) Articles of Chapter 95 (for example, toys, games, sports requ sites);
   (m) Hand sieves, buttons, pens, pencil-holders, pen nibs or other articles of Chapter 96 (miscellaneous manufactured articles); unipod, bipod, trpod or the Like
   (n) Articles of Chapter 97 (for example, works of art).
2. Throughout the Nomenclature, the expression "parts of general use" means:
   (a) Articles of heading No.73.07, 73.12, 73.15, 73.17 or 73.18 and similar articles of other base metal;
   (b) Springs and leaves for springs, of base metal, other than clock or watch springs (heading No.91.14); and
   (c) Articles of headings Nos.83.01, 83.02, 83.08, 83.10 and frames and mirrors, of base metal, of heading No.83.06.
   In Chapters 73 to 76 and 78 to 82 (but not in heading No.73.15) references to parts of goods do not include references to parts of general use as defined above.
   Subject to the preceding paragraph and to Note 1 to Chapter 83, the articles of Chapter 82 or 83 are excluded from Chapters 72 to 76 and 78 to 81.
3. Throughout the Nomenclature, the expression "base metals" means: iron and steel, copper, nickel, aluminium, lead, zinc, tin, tungsten (wolfram), molybdenum, tantalum, magnesium, cobalt, bismuth, cadmium, titanium, zirconium, antimony, manganese, beryllium, chromium, germanium, vanadium, gallium, hafnium, indium, niobium (columbium), rhenium and thallium.
4. Throughout the Nomenclature, the term "cermets" means products containing a microscopic heterogeneous combination of a metallic component and a ceramic component. The term "cermets" includes sintered metal carbides (metal carbides sintered with a metal).
5. Classification of alloys (other than ferro-alloys and master alloys as defined in Chapters 72 and 74):
   (a) An alloy of base metals is to be classified as an alloy of the metal which predominates by weight over each of the other metals;
   (b) An alloy composed of base metals of this Section and of elements not falling within this Section is to be treated as an alloy of base metals of this Section if the total weight of such metals equals or exceeds the total weight of the other elements present;
   (c) In this Section the term "alloys" includes sintered mixtures of metal powders, heterogeneous intimate mixtures obtained by melting (other than cermets) and intermetallic compounds.
6. Unless the context otherwise requires, any reference in the Nomenclature to a base metal includes a reference to alloys which, by virtue of Note 5 above, are to be classified as alloys of that metal.
7. Classification of composite articles:
   Except where the headings otherwise require, articles of base metal (including articles of mixed materials treated as articles of base metal under the Interpretative Rules) containing two or more base metals are to be treated as articles of the base metal predominating by weight over each of the other metals. For this purpose:
   (a) Iron and steel, or different kinds of iron or steel, are regarded as one and the same metal;
   (b) An alloy is regarded as being entirely composed of that metal as an alloy of which, by virtue of Note 5, it is classified; and
   (c) A cermet of heading No.81.13 is regarded as a single base metal.
8. In this Section, the following expressions have the meanings hereby assigned to them:
   (a) Waste and scrap
   Metal waste and scrap from the manufacture or mechanical working of metals, and metal goods definitely not usable as such because of breakage, cutting-up, wear or other reasons.
   (b) Powders
   Products of which 90% or more by weight passes through a sieve having a mesh aperture of 1mm.

Chapter 72
Iron and steel

Notes:

1. In this Chapter and, in the case of Notes (d), (e) and (f) throughout the Nomenclature, the following expressions have the meanings hereby assigned to them:

(一)生铁

无实用可锻性的铁碳合金,按重量计含碳量在2%以上并可含有一种或几种下列含量范围的其他元素:

铬不超过10%;
锰不超过6%;
磷不超过3%;
硅不超过8%;
其他元素合计不超过10%。

(二)镜铁

按重量计含锰量在6%以上,但不超过30%的铁碳合金,其他方面符合上述(一)款所列标准。

(三)铁合金

锭、块、团或类似初级形状、连续铸造而形成的各种形状及颗粒、粉末状的合金,不论是否烧结,通常用于其他合金生产过程中的添加剂或在黑色金属冶炼中作除氧剂、脱硫剂及类似用途,一般无实用可锻性,按重量计铁元素含量在4%及以上并含有下列一种或几种元素:

铬超过10%;
锰超过30%;
磷超过3%;
硅超过8%;
除碳以外的其他元素,合计超过10%,但最高含铜量不得超过10%。

(四)钢

除税目72.03以外的黑色金属材料(某些铸造而成的种类除外),具有实用可锻性,按重量计含碳量在2%及以下,但铬钢可具有较高的含碳量。

(五)不锈钢

按重量计含碳量在1.2%及以下,含铬量在10.5%及以上的合金钢,不论是否含有其他元素。

(六)其他合金钢

不符合以上不锈钢定义的钢,含有一种或几种按重量计符合下列含量比例的元素:

铝0.3%及以上;
硼0.0008%及以上;
铬0.3%及以上;
钴0.3%及以上;
铜0.4%及以上;
铅0.4%及以上;
锰1.65%及以上;
钼0.08%及以上;
镍0.3%及以上;
铌0.06%及以上;
硅0.6%及以上;
钛0.05%及以上;
钨0.3%及以上;
钒0.1%及以上;
锆0.05%及以上;

其他元素(硫、磷、碳及氮除外)单项含量在0.1%及以上。

(七)供再熔的碎料钢铁锭

粗铸成形无缩孔或冒口的锭块产品,表面有明显瑕疵,化学成分不同于生铁、镜铁及铁合金。

(八)颗粒

按重量计不到90%可从网眼孔径为1毫米的筛子通过,而90%及以上可从网眼孔径为5毫米的筛子通过的产品。

(九)半制成品

连续铸造的实心产品,不论是否初步热轧;其他实心产品,除经初步热轧或锻造粗制成形以外未经进一步加工,包括角材、型材及异型材的坯件。

本类产品不包括成卷的产品。

(十)平板轧材

截面为矩形(正方形除外)并且不符合以上第(九)款所述定义的下列形状实心轧制产品:

1. 层叠的卷材;
2. 平直形状,其厚度如果在4.75毫米以下,则宽度至少是厚度的十倍;其厚度如果在4.75毫米及以上,其宽度应超过150毫米,并且至少应为厚度的两倍。

(a) Pig iron

Iron-carbon alloys not usefully malleable, containing more than 2% by weight ofcarbon and which may contain by weight one or more other elements within the following limits:

Not more than 10% of chromium,

Not more than 6% of manganese,

Not more than 3% of phosphorus,

Not more than 8% of silicon,

A total of not more than 10% of other elements.

(b) Spiegeleisen

Iron-carbon alloys containing by weight more than 6% but not more than 30% of manganese and otherwise conforming to the specification at (a) above.

(c) Ferro-alloys

Alloys in pigs, blocks, lumps or similar primary forms, in forms obtained by continuous casting and also in granular or powder forms, whether or not agglomerated, commonly used as an additive in the manufacture of other alloys or as de-oxidants, de-sulphurizing agents or for similar uses in ferrous metal-lurgy and generally not usefully malleable, containing by weight 4% or more of the elementiron and one or more of the following:

More than 10% of chromium,

More than 30% of manganese,

More than 3% of phosphorus,

More than 8% of silicon,

A total of more than 10% of other elements, excluding carbon, subject to a maximum content of 10% in the case of copper.

(d) Steel

Ferrous materials other than those of heading 72.03 which (with the exception of certain types produced in the form of castings) are usefully malleable andwhich contain by weight 2% or less of carbon. However, chromium steels may contain higher proportions of carbon.

(e) Stainlesssteel

Alloy steels containing, by weight, 1.2% or less of carbon and 10.5% ormore of chromium, with or without other elements.

(f) Other alloy steel

Steels not complying with the definition of stainless steel and containing by weight one or more of the following elements in the proportion shown:

0.3% or more of aluminium,

0.0008% or more of boron,

0.3% or more of chromium,

0.3% or more of cobalt,

0.4% or more of copper,

0.4% or more of lead,

1.65% or more of manganese,

0.08% or more of molybdenum,

0.3% or more of nickel,

0.06% or more of niobium,

0.6% or more of silicon,

0.05% or more of titanium,

0.3% or more of tungsten (wolfram),

0.1% or more of vanadium,

0.05% or more of zirconium,

0.1% or more of other elements (except sulphur, phosphorus, carbon andnitrogen), taken separately.

(g) Remelting scrap ingots of iron or steel

Products roughly cast in the form of ingots without feeder-heads or hot tops, or of pigs, having obvious surface faults and not complying with the chemical composition of pig iron, spiegeleisen or ferro-alloys.

(h) Granules

Products of which less than 90% by weight passes through a sieve with a mesh aperture of 1mm and of which 90% or more by weight passes through a sieve with a mesh aperture of 5mm.

(ij) Semi-finished products

Continuous cast products of solid section, whether or not subjected to primary hot-rolling; and other products of solid section, which have not been further worked than subjected to primary hot-rolling or roughly shaped by forging, including blanks for angles, shapes or sections.

These products are not presented in coils.

(k) Flat-rolled products

Rolled products of solid rectangular (other than square) cross-section, which do not conform to the definition at (ij) above in the form of:

(i) Coils of successively superimposed layers; or

(ii) Straight lenghths, which if of athickness less than 4.75mm are of a width measuring at least ten times the thickness or if of a thickness of 4.75mm or more are of a width which exceeds 150mm and measures at least twice the thickness.

平板轧材包括直接轧制而成并有凸起式样(例如,凹槽、肋条形、格槽、珠粒、菱形)的产品以及穿孔、抛光或制成瓦楞形的产品,但不具有其他税目所列制品或产品的特征。

各种规格的平板轧材(矩形或正方形除外),但不具有其他税目所列制品或产品的特征,都应作为宽度为600毫米及以上的产品归类。

(十一)不规则盘绕的热轧条、杆

经热轧不规则盘绕的实心产品,其截面为圆形、扇形、椭圆形、矩形(包括正方形)、三角形及其他外凸多边形(包括"扁圆形"及"变形矩形",即相对两边为弧拱形,另外两边为等长平行直线形)。这类产品可带有在轧制过程中产生的凹痕、凸缘、槽沟或其他变形(钢筋)。

(十二)其他条、杆

不符合上述(九)、(十)、(十一)款或"丝"定义的实心产品,其全长截面均为圆形、扇形、椭圆形、矩形(包括正方形)三角形或其他外凸多边形(包括"扁圆形"及"变形矩形",即相对两边为弧拱形,另两边为等长平行直线形)。这些产品可以:

1. 带有在轧制过程中产生的凹痕、凸缘、槽沟或其他变形(钢筋);
2. 轧制后扭曲的。

(十三)角材、型材及异型材

不符合上述(九)、(十)、(十一)、(十二)款或"丝"定义,但其全长截面均为同样形状的实心产品。

第七十二章不包括税目73.01或73.02的产品。

(十四)丝

不符合平板轧材定义但全长截面均为同样形状的盘卷冷成形实心产品。

(十五)空心钻钢

适合钻探用的各种截面的空心条、杆,其最大外形尺寸超过15毫米但不超过52毫米,最大内孔尺寸不超过最大外形尺寸的二分之一。不符合本定义的钢铁空心条、杆应归入税目73.04。

二、用一种黑色金属包覆不同种类的黑色金属,应按其中重量最大的材料归类。

三、用电解沉积法、压铸法或烧结法所得的钢铁产品,应按其形状、成分及外观归入本章类似热轧产品的相应税目。

子目注释:

一、本章所用有关名词解释如下:

(一)合金生铁

按重量计含有一种或几种下列比例的元素的生铁:

铬0.2%以上;

铜0.3%以上;

镍0.3%以上;

0.1%以上的任何下列元素:

铝、钼、钛、钨、钒。

(二)非合金易切削钢

按重量计含有一种或几种下列比例的元素的非合金钢:

硫0.08%及以上;

铅0.1%及以上;

硒0.05%以上;

碲0.01%以上;

铋0.05%以上。

(三)硅电钢

按重量计含硅量至少为0.6%但不超过6%,含碳量不超过0.08%的合金钢。这类钢还可含有按重量计不超过1%的铝,但所含其他元素的比例并不使其具有其他合金钢的特性。

(四)高速钢

不论是否含有其他元素,但至少含有按重量计合计含量在7%及以上的钼、钨、钒中两种元素的合金钢,按重量计其含碳量在0.6%及以上,含铬量在3%~6%。

(五)硅锰钢

按重量计同时含有下列元素的合金钢:

碳不超过0.7%;

锰0.5%及以上,但不超过1.9%;

硅0.6%及以上,但不超过2.3%。但所含其他元素的比例并不使其具有其他合金钢的特性。

二、税目72.02项下的子目所列铁合金,应按照下列规则归类:

对于只有一种元素超出本章注释一(三)规定的最低百分比的铁合金,应作为二元合金归入相应的子目号。以此类推,如果有两种或三种合金元素超出了最低百分比的,则可分别作为三元或四元合金。

在运用本规定时,本章注释一(三)所述的未列名的"其他元素",按重量计单项含量必须超过10%。

Flat-rolled products include those with patterns in relief derived directly from rolling (for example, grooves, ribs, chequers, tears, buttons, lozenges) and those which have been perforated, corrugated or polished, provided that they do not thereby assume the character of articles or products of other headings.

Flat-rolled products of a shape other than rectangular or square, of any size, are to be classified as products of a width of 600mm or more, provided that theydo not assume the character of articles or products of other headings.

(l) Bars and rods, hot-rolled, in irregularly wound coils

Hot-rolled products in irregularly wound coils, which have a solid cross-section in the shape of circles, segments of circles, ovals, rectangles (including squares), triangles or other convex polygons (including "flattened circles" and modified rectangles of which two opposite sides are convex arcs, the other two sides being straight, of equal length and paralled). These products may have indentations, ribs, grooves or other deformations produced during the rolling process(reinforcing bars and rods).

(m) Other bars and rods

Products which do not conform to any of the definitions at (ij), (k) or (l) above or to the definition of wire, which have a uni-form solid cross-section alongtheir whole length in the shape of circles, segments of circles, ovals, rectangles (including squares), triangles or other convex polygons (including "flattened circles" and "modified rectangles", of which two opposite sides are convex-arcs, the other two sides being straight, of equal length and parallel). Theseproducts may:

(ⅰ) Have indentations, ribs, grooves or other deformations produced during the rolling process (reinforcing bars and rods);

(ⅱ) Be twisted after rolling.

(n) Angles, shapes and sections

Products having a uniform solid cross-section along their whole length which donot conform to any of the definitions at (ij), (k), (l) or (m) above or to thedefinition of wire.

Chapter 72 does not include products of heading No.73.01 or 73.02.

(o) Wire

Cold-formed products in coils, of any uniform solid cross-section along theirwhole length, which do not conform to the definition of flat-rolled products.

(p) Hollow drill bars and rods

Hollow bars and rods of any cross-section, suitable for drills, of which the greatest external dimension of the cross-section exceeds 15mm but does not exceed 52mm, and of which the greatest internal dimension does not exceed one half of the greatest external dimension. Hollow bars and rods of iron or steel not conforming to this definition are to be classified in heading No.73.04.

2. Ferrous metals clad with another ferrous metal are to be classified as products of the ferrous metal predominating by weight.

3. Iron or steel products obtained by electrolytic deposition, by pressure casting or by sintering are to be classified, according to their form, their composition and their appearance, in the headings of this Chapter appropriate to similar hot-rolled products.

Subheading Notes:

1. In this Chapter the followingexpressions have the meanings hereby assigned to them:

(a) Alloy pig iron

Pig iron containing, by weight, one or more of the following elements in the specified proportions:

More than 0.2% of chromium,

More than 0.3% of copper,

More than 0.3% of nickel,

More than 0.1% of any of the following elements:

Aluminium, molybdenum, titanium, tungsten (wolfram), vanadium.

(b) Non-alloy free-cutting steel

Non-alloy steel containing, by weight, one or more of the following elements inthe specified proportions:

0.08% or more of sulphur,

0.1% or more of lead,

More than 0.05% of selenium,

More than 0.01% of tellur, ium

More than 0.05% of bismuth.

(c) Silicon-electrical steel

Alloy steels containing by weight at least 0.6% but not more than 6% of siliconand not more than 0.08% of carbon. They may also contain by weight not more than 1% of aluminium but no other element in a proportion that would give the steel the characteristics of another alloy steel.

(d) High speed steel

Alloy steels containing, with or without other elements, at least two of the three elements molybdenum, tungsten and vanadium with a combined content by weight of 7% or more, 0.6% or more of carbon and 3% to 6% of chromium.

(e) Silico-manganese steel

Alloy steels containing by weight:

Not more than 0.7% of carbon,

0.5% or more but not more than 1.9% of manganese, and

0.6% or more but not more than 2.3% of silicon, but no other elementina proportion that would give the steel the characteristics of another alloy steel.

2. For the classification of ferro-alloys in the subheadings of heading 72.02 the following rule should be observed: A ferro-alloy is considered as binary and classified under the relevant subheading (if it exists) if only one of the alloy elements exceeds the minimum percentage laid down in Chapter Note 1 (c); by analogy, it is considered respectively as ternary or quaternary if two or three alloy elements exceed the minimum percentage.

For the application of this rule the unspecified "other elements" referred to in Chapter Note 1 (c) must each exceed 10% by weight.

税则号列	货品名称〔CIQ 扩展编码及品名－T2 表示见附表 2〕	最惠(%)	暂定税率	普通	增值/消费	出口退税	计量单位	监管条件	检验检疫	特殊证件对美关税
	第一分章　原料；粒状及粉状产品									
72.01	**生铁及镜铁，锭、块或其他初级形状：**									
7201.1000	-非合金生铁，按重量计含磷量在 0.5%及以下									
7201.1000　10	高纯生铁(含锰量<0.08%，含磷量<0.03%，含硫量<0.02%，含钛量<0.03%)〔999〕	1	1	8	13/	0	千克			/
7201.1000　90	非合金生铁，含磷量小于或等于 0.5%(含锰量<0.08%，含磷量<0.03%，含硫量<0.02%，含钛量<0.03%的高纯生铁除外)〔999〕	1		8	13/	0	千克			/
7201.2000	-非合金生铁，按重量计含磷量在 0.5%以上〔999〕	1		8	13/	0	千克			/
7201.5000	-合金生铁；镜铁									
7201.5000　10	合金生铁〔999〕	1		8	13/	0	千克			/26
7201.5000　90	镜铁〔999〕	1		8	13/	0	千克			/26
72.02	**铁合金：**									
	-锰铁：									
7202.1100	--按重量计含碳量在 2%以上〔999〕	2		11	13/	0	千克	4xy		/
7202.1900	--其他〔999〕	2		11	13/	0	千克	4xy		/27
	-硅铁：									
7202.2100	--按重量计含硅量在 55%以上									
7202.2100　10	硅铁，含硅量大于 55%，小于 90%〔999〕	2	2	11	13/	0	千克	4xy		/27
7202.2100　90	硅铁，含硅量大于 90%〔999〕	2	2	11	13/	0	千克	4xy		/27
7202.2900	--其他									
7202.2900　10	硅铁，含硅量大于等于 30%且不超过 55%〔999〕	2	2	11	13/	0	千克	4xy		/22
7202.2900　90	硅铁，含硅量小于 30%〔999〕	2	2	11	13/	0	千克	4xy		/22
7202.3000	-硅锰铁〔999〕	2		11	13/	0	千克	4xy		/
	-铬铁：									
7202.4100	--按重量计含碳量在 4%以上〔999〕	2	0	8	13/	0	千克	4xy		/
7202.4900	--其他〔999〕	2	1	8	13/	0	千克	4xy		/26
7202.5000	-硅铬铁〔999〕	2		11	13/	0	千克	4xy		/
7202.6000	-镍铁〔999〕	2	0	11	13/	0	千克	4xy		/25
7202.7000	-钼铁〔999〕	2	1	11	13/	0	千克	4xy		/
	-钨铁及硅钨铁：									
7202.8010	---钨铁〔999〕	2	1	11	13/	0	千克	4xy		/
7202.8020	---硅钨铁〔999〕	2		11	13/	0	千克	4xy		/
	-其他：									
7202.9100	--钛铁及硅钛铁〔101 硅钛铁，102 钛铁〕	2		11	13/	0	千克	4xy		/27
	--钒铁：									
7202.9210	---按重量计含钒量在 75%及以上〔999〕	5		30	13/	0	千克	4xy		/30
7202.9290	---其他〔999〕	5		30	13/	0	千克	4xy		/
7202.9300	--铌铁									
7202.9300　10	铁钽铌合金(钽含量<10%)〔999〕	2	0	11	13/	0	千克	4xy		/
7202.9300　90	其他铌铁〔101 铌铁，102 其他铁合金〕	2	0	11	13/	0	千克	4xy		/
	--其他：									
	---钕铁硼合金：									
7202.9911	----速凝永磁片〔999〕	2		11	13/	0	千克	4xy		/12
7202.9912	----磁粉〔999〕	2		11	13/	0	千克	4xy		/27
7202.9919	----其他〔999〕	2		11	13/	0	千克	4xy		/
	---其他：									
7202.9991	----按重量计稀土元素总含量在 10%以上的									
7202.9991　10	按重量计中重稀土总含量≥30%的铁合金(按重量计稀土元素总含量在 10%以上)〔104〕	2		11	13/	0	千克	4xy		/
7202.9991　91	稀土硅铁合金(按重量计稀土元素总含量在 10%以上)〔104〕	2		11	13/	0	千克	4xy		/
7202.9991　99	其他按重量计稀土元素总含量在 10%以上的铁合金〔104〕	2		11	13/	0	千克	4xy		/
7202.9999	----其他〔104〕	2		11	13/	0	千克	4xy		/12
72.03	**直接从铁矿还原所得的铁产品及其他海绵铁产品，块、团、团粒及类似形状；按重量计纯度在 99.94%及以上的铁，块、团、团粒及类似形状：**									
7203.1000	-直接从铁矿还原所得的铁产品									
7203.1000　10	热压铁块〔999〕	2	0	8	13/	0	千克			/25

协定税率 %										特惠税率 %			Article Description
亚太5国	东/冰/格	巴基斯坦	韩国	瑞士	哥达	秘鲁	澳大利亚	新西/坡/智	港/澳/台	亚太2国	老/柬/缅	36/3/1	
													Ⅰ. PRIMARY MATERIALS; PRODUCTS IN GRANULAR OR POWDER FORM
													Pig iron and spiegeleisen in pigs, blocks or other primary forms:
													-Non-alloy pig iron containing by weight 0.5% or less of phosphorus
	0/0/0	0	0	0	0	0	0	0//0	0/0/			0/0/0	High purity iron phosphorus content (<0.08%, manganese content <0.03%, sulfur content<0.02%, titanium content<0.02%)
	0/0/0	0	0	0	0	0	0	0//0	0/0/			0/0/0	Non alloy cast iron, phosphorus content is less than or equal to 0.5% (manganese content <0.08%, phosphorus content <0.03%, sulfur content <0.02%, containing high purity pig iron titanium content < 0.03% except)
	0/0/0	0	0	0	0	0	0	0//0	0/0/			0/0/0	-Non-alloy pig iron containing by weight more than 0.5% of phosphorus
													-Alloy pig iron; spiegeleisen
	0/0/0	0	0	0	0	0	0	0//0	0/0/			0/0/0	Alloy pig iron
	0/0/0	0	0	0	0	0	0	0//0	0/0/			0/0/0	Spiegeleisen
													Ferro-alloys:
													-Ferro-manganese:
	0/0/0	0	0	0	0	0	0	0//0	0/0/			0/0/0	--Containing by weight more than 2% of carbon
	0/0/0	0	0	0	0	0	0	0//0	0/0/			0/0/0	--Other
													-Ferro-silicon:
													--Containing by weight more than 55% of silicon
	0/0/0	0	0	0	0	0	0	0//0	0/0/			0/0/0	Ferro-silicon, containing more than 55% but less than 90% of silicon
	0/0/0	0	0	0	0	0	0	0//0	0/0/			0/0/0	Ferro-silicon, containing more than 90% of silicon
													--Other
	0/0/0	0	0	0	0	0	0	0//0	0/0/			0/0/0	Ferro-silicon, containing more than 30% but less than 55% of silicon
	0/0/0	0	0	0	0	0	0	0//0	0/0/			0/0/0	Ferro-silicon, containing less than 30% of silicon
	0/0/0	0	0	0	0	0	0	0//0	0/0/			0/0/0	-Ferro-silico-manganese
													-Ferro-chromium:
	0/0/0	0	0	0	0	0	0	0//0	0/0/			0/0/0	--Containing by weight more than 4% of carbon
	0/0/0	0	0	0	0	0	0	0//0	0/0/			0/0/0	--Other
	0/0/0	0	0	0	0	0	0	0//0	0/0/			0/0/0	-Ferro-silico-chromium
	0/0/0	0	0	0	0	0	0	0//0	0/0/			0/0/0	-Ferro-nickel
	0/0/0	0	0	0	0	0	0	0//0	0/0/			0/0/0	-Ferro-molybdenum
													-Ferro-tungsten and ferro-silico-tungsten:
	0/0/0	0	0	0	0	0	0	0//0	0/0/			0/0/0	---Ferro-tungsten
	0/0/0	0	0	0	0	0	0	0//0	0/0/			0/0/0	---Ferro-silico-tungsten
													-Other:
	0/0/0	0	0	0	0	0	0	0//0	0/0/			0/0/0	--Ferro-titanium and ferro-silico-titanium
													--Ferro-vanadium:
	0/0/0	4	0	0	0	0	0	0//0	0/0/			0/0/0	---Containing by weight more than 75% of ranadium
	0/0/0	4	0	0	0	0	0	0//0	0/0/			0/0/0	---Other
													--Ferro-niobium
	0/0/0	0	0	0	0	0	0	0//0	0/0/			0/0/0	Ferro-tantalum-niobium alloy(containing<10% by weight of tantalum)
	0/0/0	0	0	0	0	0	0	0//0	0/0/			0/0/0	Other ferro-niobium
													--Other:
													---Na-Fe-B alloy:
	0/0/0	0	0	0	0	0	0	0//0	0/0/			0/0/0	----Rapid setting permanent magnet film
	0/0/0	0	0	0	0	0	0	0//0	0/0/			0/0/0	----Magnetic powder
	0/0/0	0	0	0	0	0	0	0//0	0/0/			0/0/0	----Other
													---Other:
													----Containing by weight more than 10% of rate eath elements
	0/0/0	0	0	0	0	0	0	0//0	0/0/			0/0/0	Containing by weight more than 30% of middle heavy rare-earth, alloy iron(containing by weight more than 10% of rare-earth element)
	0/0/0	0	0	0	0	0	0	0//0	0/0/			0/0/0	Rare earth ferrosilicon alloy (containing by weight more than 10% of rare-earth element)
	0/0/0	0	0	0	0	0	0	0//0	0/0/			0/0/0	Containing weight by more than 10% of rare-earth element, alloy iron
	0/0/0	0	0	0	0	0	0	0//0	0/0/			0/0/0	----Other
													Ferrous products obtained by direct reduction of iron ore and other spongy ferrous products, in lumps, pellets or similar forms; iron having a minimum purity by weight of 99.94%, in lumps, pellets or similar forms:
													-Ferrous products obtained by direct reduction of iron ore
	0/0/0	0	0	0	0	0	0	0//0	0/0/			0/0/	Hot iron

税则号列		货品名称〔CIQ扩展编码及品名—T2表示见附表2〕	最惠(%)	暂定税率	普通	增值/消费	出口退税	计量单位	监管条件	检验检疫	特殊证件对美关税
7203.1000	90	直接从铁矿还原的铁产品(铁团、铁粒及类似形状)〔999〕	2		8	13/	0	千克			/27
7203.9000		-其他〔999〕	2		8	13/	0	千克			/22
72.04		**钢铁废碎料;供再熔的碎料钢铁锭:**									
7204.1000		-铸铁废碎料〔999〕	2	0	8	13/	0	千克	AP	M	/25
		-合金钢废碎料:									
7204.2100		--不锈钢废碎料〔999〕	0		8	13/	0	千克	9A	M	/25
7204.2900		--其他〔999〕	0		8	13/	0	千克	AP	M	/25
7204.3000		-镀锡钢铁废碎料〔999〕	2	0	8	13/	0	千克	AP	M	/25
		-其他废碎料:									
7204.4100		--车、刨、铣、磨、锯、锉、剪、冲加工过程中产生的废料,不论是否成捆〔999〕	2	0	8	13/	0	千克	AP	M	/25
7204.4900		--其他									
7204.4900	10	废汽车压件〔999〕	0		8	13/	0	千克	9A	M	/25
7204.4900	20	以回收钢铁为主的废五金电器〔999〕	0		8	13/	0	千克	9A	M	/25
7204.4900	90	未列名钢铁废碎料〔999〕	0		8	13/	0	千克	AP	M	/25
7204.5000		-供再熔的碎料钢铁锭〔999〕	0		8	13/	0	千克	AP	M	/25
72.05		**生铁、镜铁及钢铁的颗粒和粉末:**									
7205.1000		-颗粒〔101 非合金生铁,102 合金生铁,103 其他铁合金〕	2		30	13/	0	千克			/27
		-粉末:									
7205.2100		--合金钢的〔999〕	2		17	13/	10	千克			/12
7205.2900		--其他〔999〕	2		17	13/	0	千克			/22
		第二分章　铁及非合金钢									
72.06		**铁及非合金钢,锭状或其他初级形状(税目72.03的铁除外):**									
7206.1000		-锭状〔999〕	2		11	13/	0	千克			/27
7206.9000		-其他〔101 板坯,102 其他钢坯(锭)〕	2		11	13/	0	千克			/12
72.07		**铁及非合金钢的半制成品:**									
		-按重量计含碳量在0.25%以下:									
7207.1100		--矩形(包括正方形)截面,宽度小于厚度的两倍〔999〕	2		11	13/	0	千克			/27
7207.1200		--其他矩形(正方形除外)截面的									
7207.1200	10	其他矩形截面的厚度大于400MM的连铸板坯(含碳量小于0.25%(正方形截面除外))〔999〕	2		11	13/	0	千克			/
7207.1200	90	其他矩形截面钢坯(含碳量小于0.25%(正方形截面除外))〔999〕	2		11	13/	0	千克			/
7207.1900		--其他									
7207.1900	10	其他含碳量小于0.25%的厚度大于400MM的连铸板坯〔999〕	2		11	13/	0	千克			/27
7207.1900	90	其他含碳量小于0.25%的钢坯〔999〕	2		11	13/	0	千克			/27
7207.2000		-按重量计含碳量在0.25%及以上									
7207.2000	10	车轮用连铸圆坯(直径为380MM和450MM,公差±1.2%,含碳量:0.38%-0.85%,含锰量:0.68%-1.2%,含磷量≤0.012%,总氧化物含量≤0.0012%)〔999〕	2		11	13/	0	千克			/
7207.2000	90	其他含碳量不小于0.25%的钢坯〔999〕	2		11	13/	0	千克			/
72.08		**宽度在600毫米及以上的铁或非合金钢平板轧材,经热轧,但未经包覆、镀层或涂层:**									
7208.1000		-除热轧外未经进一步加工的卷材,已轧压花纹〔999〕	5		14	13/	0	千克			/30
		-其他经酸洗的卷材,除热轧外未经进一步加工:									
7208.2500		--厚度在4.75毫米及以上〔999〕	5		14	13/	0	千克			/30
		--厚度在3毫米及以上,但小于4.75毫米:									
7208.2610		---屈服强度大于355牛顿/平方毫米〔999〕	5		14	13/	0	千克	A	M	/15
7208.2690		---其他〔999〕	5		14	13/	0	千克	A	M	/30
		--厚度小于3毫米:									
7208.2710		---厚度小于1.5毫米〔999〕	5		14	13/	0	千克			/30
7208.2790		---其他〔999〕	5		14	13/	0	千克			/30
		-其他卷材,除热轧外未经进一步加工:									
7208.3600		--厚度超过10毫米〔999〕	6		14	13/	0	千克			/
7208.3700		--厚度在4.75毫米及以上,但不超过10毫米〔999〕	5		14	13/	0	千克			/15
		--厚度在3毫米及以上,但小于4.75毫米:									
7208.3810		---屈服强度大于355牛顿/平方毫米〔999〕	5		14	13/	0	千克	A	M	/15
7208.3890		---其他〔999〕	5		14	13/	0	千克	A	M	/15

亚太5国	东/冰/格	巴基斯坦	韩国	瑞士	哥达	秘鲁	澳大利亚	新西/坡/智	港/澳/台	亚太2国	老/柬/缅	36/3/1	Article Description
协定税率 %										特惠税率 %			
	0/0/0	0	0	0	0	0	0	0//0	0/0/			0/0/	Other ferrous products obtained by direct reduction of iron ore (in lumps, pellets or similar forms)
	0/0/0	0	0	0	0	0	0	0//0	0/0/			0/0/	-Other
													Ferrous waste and scrap; remelting scrap ingots of iron steel:
	0/0/0	0	0	0	0	0	0	0//0	0/0/			0/0/0	-Waste and scrap of cast iron
													-Waste and scrap of alloy steel:
												0/0/0	--Of stainless steel
												0/0/0	--Other
	0/0/0	0	0	0	0	0	0	0//0	0/0/			0/0/0	-Waste and scrap of tinned iron or steel
													-Other waste and scrap:
	0/0/0	0	0.8	0	0	0	0	0//0	0/0/			0/0/0	--Turnings, shavings, chips, milling waste, sawdust, filings, trimmings and stampings, whether or not in bundles
													--Other
												0/0/0	Compressed piece of scrap automobile
												0/0/0	Waste hardware and electric appliance mainly for recoverying steel and iron
												0/0/0	Other ferrous waste and scrap, not elsewhere specifiled or included
												0/0/0	-Remelting scrap ingots
													Granules and powders, of pig iron, spiegeleiseniron or steel:
	0/0/0	0	0	0	0	0	0	0//0	0/0/			0/0/0	-Granules
													-Powders:
	0/0/0	0	0	0	0	0	0	0//0	0/0/			0/0/0	--Of alloy steel
	0/0/0	0	0.8	0	0	0	0	0//0	0/0/			0/0/0	--Other
													Ⅱ. IRON AND NON-ALLOY STEEL
													Iron and non-alloy steel in ingots or other primary forms (excluding iron of heading No. 72.03):
	0/0/0	0	0	0	0	0	0	0//0	0/0/			0/0/	-Ingots
	0/0/0	0	0	0	0	0	0	0//0	0/0/			0/0/	-Other
													Semi-finished products of iron or non-alloy steel:
													-Containing by weight less than 0.25% of carbon:
	0/0/0	0	0	0	0	0	0	0//0	0/0/			0/0/	--Of rectangular (including square) cross-section, the width measuring less than twice the thickness
													--Other, of rectangular (other than square) cross-section
	0/0/0	0	0	0	0	0	0	0//0	0/0/			0/0/	Other continuous casting slab of other rectangular section with a thickness greater than 400MM (with a carbon content less than 0.25% (except for square cross section))
	0/0/0	0	0	0	0	0	0	0//0	0/0/			0/0/	Other rectangular section steel billets (with a carbon content less than 0.25% (except for square section))
													--Other
	0/0/0	0	1.2	0	0	0	0	0//0	0/0/			0/0/	Other continuous casting slab with a thickness of less than 0.25% with a thickness greater than 400MM
	0/0/0	0	1.2	0	0	0	0	0//0	0/0/			0/0/	Other billets with less than 0.25% carbon content
													-Containing by weight 0.25% or more of carbon
	0/0/0	0	0	0	0	0	0	0//0	0/0/			0/0/	With the continuous casting round billet (wheel diameter is 380MM and 450MM, tolerance of + 1.2%, the carbon content of manganese content:: 0.38%-0.85%, 0.68%-1.2%, P = 0.012%, total oxide content is less than 0.0012%)
	0/0/0	0	0	0	0	0	0	0//0	0/0/			0/0/	Other billets with a carbon content of less than 0.25%
													Flat-rolled products of iron or non-alloy steel, of a width of 600mm or more, hot-rolled, not clad, plated or coated:
	0/0/0	0	2	0	0	0	0	0//0	0/0/			0/0/0	-In coils, not further worked than hot-rolled, with patterns in relief
													-Other, in coils, not further worked than hot-rolled, pickled:
	0/0/0	0		0	0	0	0	0//0	0/0/			0/0/0	--Of a thickness of 4.75mm or more
													--Of a thickness of 3mm or more but less than 4.75mm:
	0/0/0	0		0	0	0	0	0//0	0/0/			0/0/0	---Of a yield strength exceeding 355N/mm²
	0/0/0	0		0	0	0	0	0//0	0/0/			0/0/0	---Other
													--Of a thickness of less than 3mm:
	0/0/0	0	3	0	0	0	0	0//0	0/0/			0/0/0	---Of a thickness of less than 1.5mm
	0/0/0	0		0	0	0	0	0//0	0/0/0			0/0/0	---Other
													-Other, in coils, not further worked than hot-rolled:
	0/0/0	0	2.4	0	0	0	0	0//0	0/0/			0/0/0	--Of a thickness exceeding 10mm
	0/0/0	0	2	0	0	0	0	0//0	0/0/			0/0/0	--Of a thickness of 4.75mm or more but not exceeding 10mm
													--Of a thickness of 3mm or more but less than 4.75mm:
	0/0/0	0	2	0	0	0	0	0//0	0/0/			0/0/0	---Of a yield strength exceeding 355N/mm²
	0/0/0	0	2	0	0	0	0	0//0	0/0/0			0/0/0	---Other

税则号列	货品名称〔CIQ 扩展编码及品名－T2 表示见附表 2〕	最惠(%)	暂定税率	普通	增值/消费	出口退税	计量单位	监管条件	检验检疫	特殊证件对美关税
	--厚度小于 3 毫米：									
7208.3910	---厚度小于 1.5 毫米〔999〕	3		14	13/	0	千克			/28
7208.3990	---其他〔999〕	3		14	13/	0	千克			/28
7208.4000	-已轧压花纹的非卷材，除热轧外未经进一步加工〔999〕	6		17	13/	0	千克			/26
	-其他非卷材，除热轧外未经进一步加工：									
	--厚度超过 10 毫米：									
7208.5110	---厚度超过 50 毫米〔999〕	6		17	13/	0	千克			/31
7208.5120	---厚度在 20 毫米以上，但不超过 50 毫米〔999〕	6		17	13/	0	千克			/31
7208.5190	---其他〔999〕	6		17	13/	0	千克			/31
7208.5200	--厚度在 4.75 毫米及以上，但不超过 10 毫米〔999〕	6		17	13/	0	千克			/31
	--厚度在 3 毫米及以上，但小于 4.75 毫米：									
7208.5310	---屈服强度大于 355 牛顿/平方毫米〔999〕	6		17	13/	0	千克			/
7208.5390	---其他〔999〕	6		17	13/	0	千克			/16
	--厚度小于 3 毫米：									
7208.5410	---厚度小于 1.5 毫米〔999〕	6		17	13/	0	千克			/31
7208.5490	---其他〔999〕	6		17	13/	0	千克			/31
7208.9000	-其他〔999〕	6		17	13/	0	千克			/31
72.09	**宽度在 600 毫米及以上的铁或非合金钢平板轧材，经冷轧，但未经包覆、镀层或涂层：**									
	-卷材，除冷轧外未经进一步加工：									
	--厚度在 3 毫米及以上：									
7209.1510	---屈服强度大于 355 牛顿/平方毫米〔999〕	6		17	13/	13	千克			/
7209.1590	---其他〔999〕	6		17	13/	13	千克			/31
	--厚度超过 1 毫米，但小于 3 毫米：									
7209.1610	---屈服强度大于 275 牛顿/平方毫米〔999〕	6		17	13/	13	千克	A	M	/31
7209.1690	---其他〔999〕	6		17	13/	13	千克			/31
	--厚度在 0.5 毫米及以上，但不超过 1 毫米：									
7209.1710	---屈服强度大于 275 牛顿/平方毫米〔999〕	3		17	13/	13	千克	A	M	/28
7209.1790	---其他〔999〕	3		17	13/	13	千克			/28
	--厚度小于 0.5 毫米：									
7209.1810	---厚度小于 0.3 毫米〔999〕	6	4	17	13/	13	千克			/
7209.1890	---其他〔999〕	6		17	13/	13	千克			/31
	-非卷材，除冷轧外未经进一步加工：									
7209.2500	--厚度在 3 毫米及以上〔999〕	6		17	13/	13	千克			/16
7209.2600	--厚度超过 1 毫米，但小于 3 毫米〔999〕	6		17	13/	13	千克			/26
7209.2700	--厚度在 0.5 毫米及以上，但不超过 1 毫米〔999〕	6		17	13/	13	千克			/31
7209.2800	--厚度小于 0.5 毫米〔999〕	6		17	13/	13	千克			/31
7209.9000	-其他〔999〕	6		17	13/	13	千克			/31
72.10	**宽度在 600 毫米及以上的铁或非合金钢平板轧材，经包覆、镀层或涂层：**									
	-镀或涂锡的：									
7210.1100	--厚度在 0.5 毫米及以上〔999〕	9		20	13/	13	千克			/
7210.1200	--厚度小于 0.5 毫米〔999〕	5		20	13/	13	千克			/
7210.2000	-镀或涂铅的，包括镀铅锡钢板〔999〕	4		20	13/	13	千克			/
7210.3000	-电镀锌的〔999〕	8		20	13/	13	千克			/33
	-用其他方法镀或涂锌的：									
7210.4100	--瓦楞形〔999〕	8		20	13/	13	千克			/
7210.4900	--其他〔999〕	4		20	13/	13	千克			/29
7210.5000	-镀或涂氧化铬或铬及氧化铬的〔999〕	8		20	13/	13	千克			/33
	-镀或涂铝的：									
7210.6100	--镀或涂铝锌合金的〔999〕	8		20	13/	13	千克			/33
7210.6900	--其他〔999〕	8		20	13/	13	千克			/33
	-涂漆或涂塑的：									
7210.7010	---厚度小于 1.5 毫米〔999〕	4		20	13/	13	千克			/29
7210.7090	---其他〔999〕	4		20	13/	13	千克			/29
7210.9000	-其他〔999〕	8		20	13/	13	千克			/18
72.11	**宽度小于 600 毫米的铁或非合金钢平板轧材，但未经包覆、镀层或涂层：**									
	-除热轧外未经进一步加工：									
7211.1300	--经四面轧制或在闭合匣内轧制的非卷材，宽度超过 150 毫米，厚度不小于 4 毫米，未轧压花纹〔999〕	6		30	13/	0	千克			/16
7211.1400	--其他，厚度在 4.75 毫米及以上〔999〕	6		30	13/	0	千克			/16

协定税率 %										特惠税率 %			Article Description
亚太5国	东/冰/格	巴基斯坦	韩国	瑞士	哥达	秘鲁	澳大利亚	新西/坡/智	港/澳/台	亚太2国	老/柬/缅	36/3/1	
													--Of a thickness of less than 3mm：
	0/0/0	0	1.2	0	0	0	0	0//0	0/0/			0/0/0	---Of a thickness of less than 1. 5mm
	0/0/0	0	1.2	0	0	0	0	0//0	0/0/0			0/0/0	---Other
	0/0/0	0	2.4	0	0	0	0	0//0	0/0/			0/0/0	-Not in coils, not further worked than hot-rolled, with patterns in relief
													-Other, not in coils, not further worked than hot-rolled：
													--Of a thickness exceeding 10mm：
	0/0/0	0	3.6	0	0	0	0	0//0	0/0/			0/0/0	---Of a thickness exceeding 50mm
	0/0/0	0	3.6	0	0	0	0	0//0	0/0/			0/0/0	---Of a thickness exceeding 20mm but not exceeding 50mm
	0/0/0	0	2.4	0	0	0	0	0//0	0/0/			0/0/0	---Other
	0/0/0	0	2.4	0	0	0	0	0//0	0/0/			0/0/0	--Of a thickness of 4. 75mm or more but not exceeding 10mm
													--Of a thickness of 3mm or more but less than 4. 75mm：
5.1	0/0/0	0	2.4	0	0	0	0	0//0	0/0/			0/0/0	---Of a yield strength exceeding 355N/mm^2
5.1	0/0/0	0	2.4	0	0	0	0	0//0	0/0/			0/0/0	---Other
													--Of a thickness of less than 3mm：
5.1	0/0/0	0	0	0	0	0	0	0//0	0/0/			0/0/0	---Of a thickness of less than1. 5mm：
5.1	0/0/0	0	3.6	0	0	0	0	0//0	0/0/			0/0/0	---Other
	0/0/0	0		0	0	0	0	0//0	0/0/			0/0/0	-Other
													Flat-rolled products of iron or non-alloy steel, of a width of 600mm or more, cold-rolled (cold-reduced), not clad, plated or coated：
													-In coils, not further worked than cold-rolled (cold-reduced)：
													--Of a thickness of 3mm or more：
	0/0/0	0	2.4	0	0	0	0	0//0	0/0/			0/0/0	---Of a yield strength exceeding 355N/mm^2
	0/0/0	0	2.4	0	0	0	0	0//0	0/0/			0/0/0	---Other
													--Of a thickness exceeding 1mm but less than 3mm：
4.2	0/0/0	0	2.4	0	0	0	0	0//0	0/0/			0/0/0	---Of a yield strength exceeding 275N/mm^2
4.2	0/0/0	0	4.2	0	0	0	0	0//0	0/0/0			0/0/0	---Other
													--Of a thickness of 0. 5mm or more but not exceeding 1mm：
2.1	0/0/0	0	1.8	0	0	0	0	0//0	0/0/			0/0/0	---Of a yield strength exceeding 275N/mm^2
2.1	0/0/0	0	1.2	0	0	0	0	0//0	0/0/0			0/0/0	---Other
													--Of a thickness of less than 0. 5mm：
4.2	0/0/0	0	4.2	0	0	0	0	0//0	0/0/			0/0/0	---Of a thickness less than 0. 3mm
4.2	0/0/0	0	4.2	0	0	0	0	0//0	0/0/0			0/0/0	---Other
													-Not in coils, not further worked than cold-rolled (cold-reduced)：
	0/0/0	0	2.4	0	0	0	0	0//0	0/0/			0/0/0	--Of a thickness of 3mm or more
	0/0/0	0		0	0	0	0	0//0	0/0/			0/0/0	--Of a thickness exceeding 1mm but less than 3mm
4.2	0/0/0	0	4.2	0	0	0	0	0//0	0/0/			0/0/0	--Of a thickness of 0. 5mm or more but not exceeding 1mm
	0/0/0	0		0	0	0	0	0//0	0/0/			0/0/0	--Of a thickness of less than 0. 5mm
4.2	0/0/0	0	2.4	0	0	0	0	0//0	0/0/			0/0/0	-Other
													Flat-rolled products of iron or non-alloy steel, of a width of 600mm or more, clad, plated or coated：
													-Plated or coated with tin：
	0/0/0	4	4	0	0	0	0	0/0/0	0/0/			0/0/0	--Of a thickness of 0. 5mm or more
	0/0/0	0		0	0	0	0	0//0	0/0/			0/0/0	--Of a thickness of less than 0. 5mm
	0/0/0	0	0	0	0	0	0	0//0	0/0/			0/0/0	-Plated or coated with lead, including terneplate
	0/0/0	4		0	0	0	0	0//0	0/0/0			0/0/0	-Electrolytically plated or coated with zinc
													-Otherwise plated or coated with zinc：
	0/0/0	4	0	0	0	0	0	0//0	0/0/			0/0/0	--Corrugated
	0/0/0	0		0	0	0	0	0//0	0/0/0			0/0/0	--Other
	0/0/0	4	3.2	0	0	0	0	0//0	0/0/			0/0/0	-Plated or coated with chromium oxides or with chromium and chromium oxides
													-Plated or coated with aluminium：
	0/0/0	4		0	0	0	0	0//0	0/0/			0/0/0	--Plated or coated with aluminium-zinc alloys
	0/0/0	4		0	0	0	0	0//0	0/0/			0/0/0	--Other
													-Painted, varnished or coated with plastics：
	0/0/0	0	2.4	0	0	0	0	0//0	0/0/			0/0/0	---Of a thickness of less than 1.5mm
	0/0/0	0	2.4	0	0	0	0	0//0	0/0/			0/0/0	---Other
	0/0/0	4	4.8	0	0	0	0	0//0	0/0/			0/0/0	-Other
													Flat-rolled products of iron or non-alloy steel, of a width of less than 600mm, not clad, plated or coated：
													-Not further worked than hot-rolled：
	0/0/0	0	2.4	0	0	0	0	0//0	0/0/			0/0/0	--Rolled on four faces or in a closed box pass, of a width exceeding 150mm and a thickness of not less than 4mm, not in coils and without patterns in relief
	0/0/0	0	2.4	0	0	0	0	0//0	0/0/			0/0/0	--Other, of a thickness of 4. 75mm or more

税则号列	货品名称〔CIQ扩展编码及品名—T2表示见附表2〕	最惠(%)	暂定税率	普通	增值/消费	出口退税	计量单位	监管条件	检验检疫	特殊证件对美关税
7211.1900	--其他〔999〕	6		30	13/	0	千克			/16
	-除冷轧外未经进一步加工：									
7211.2300	--按重量计含碳量低于0.25%〔999〕	6		30	13/	0	千克	A	M	/26
7211.2900	--其他〔999〕	6		30	13/	0	千克			/31
7211.9000	-其他〔999〕	6		30	13/	0	千克			/26
72.12	**宽度小于600毫米的铁或非合金钢平板轧材，经包覆、镀层或涂层：**									
7212.1000	-镀或涂锡的〔999〕	5		20	13/	0	千克			/25
7212.2000	-电镀锌的〔999〕	8		20	13/	0	千克			/28
7212.3000	-用其他方法镀或涂锌的〔999〕	8		20	13/	0	千克			/28
7212.4000	-涂漆或涂塑的〔999〕	4		20	13/	10	千克			/24
7212.5000	-镀或涂其他材料的〔999〕	8		20	13/	0	千克			/18
7212.6000	-经包覆的〔999〕	8		20	13/	0	千克			/28
72.13	**不规则盘卷的铁及非合金钢的热轧条、杆：**									
7213.1000	-带有轧制过程中产生的凹痕、凸缘、槽沟及其他变形的〔999〕	3		20	13/	0	千克			/
7213.2000	-其他，易切削钢制〔999〕	3		20	13/	0	千克			/
	-其他：									
7213.9100	--直径小于14毫米圆形截面的〔999〕	5		20	13/	0	千克			/
7213.9900	--其他〔999〕	5		20	13/	0	千克			/
72.14	**铁或非合金钢的其他条、杆，除锻造、热轧、热拉拔或热挤压外未经进一步加工，包括轧制后扭曲的：**									
7214.1000	-锻造的〔999〕	7		10	13/	10	千克			/
7214.2000	-带有轧制过程中产生的凹痕、凸缘、槽沟或其他变形以及轧制后扭曲的〔101 螺纹钢，102 其他型钢〕	3		20	13/	0	千克	A	M	/28
7214.3000	-其他，易切削钢制〔999〕	7		20	13/	0	千克	A	M	/32
	-其他：									
7214.9100	--矩形(正方形除外)截面的〔999〕	3		20	13/	0	千克			/23
7214.9900	--其他〔101 螺纹钢，102 其他型钢〕	3		20	13/	0	千克	A	M	/28
72.15	**铁及非合金钢的其他条、杆：**									
7215.1000	-易切削钢制，除冷成形或冷加工外未经进一步加工〔999〕	7		20	13/	0	千克			/32
7215.5000	-其他，除冷成形或冷加工外未经进一步加工〔101 螺纹钢，102 其他型钢〕	7		20	13/	0	千克			/32
7215.9000	-其他〔999〕	3		20	13/	0	千克			/28
72.16	**铁或非合金钢的角材、型材及异型材：**									
	-槽钢、工字钢及H型钢，除热轧、热拉拔或热挤压外未经进一步加工，截面高度低于80毫米：									
7216.1010	---H型钢〔999〕	3		14	13/	0	千克	A	M	/13
7216.1020	---工字钢〔999〕	3		14	13/	0	千克	A	M	/13
7216.1090	---其他〔999〕	3		14	13/	0	千克	A	M	/28
	-角钢及丁字钢，除热轧、热拉拔或热挤压外未经进一步加工，截面高度低于80毫米：									
7216.2100	--角钢〔999〕	6		17	13/	0	千克	A	M	/31
7216.2200	--丁字钢〔999〕	6		14	13/	0	千克	A	M	/31
	-槽钢、工字钢及H型钢，除热轧、热拉拔或热挤压外未经进一步加工，截面高度在80毫米及以上：									
7216.3100	--槽钢〔999〕	6		14	13/	0	千克	A	M	/31
	--工字钢：									
7216.3210	---截面高度在200毫米以上〔999〕	6		14	13/	0	千克	A	M	/31
7216.3290	---其他〔999〕	6		14	13/	0	千克	A	M	/31
	--H型钢：									
	---截面高度在200毫米以上：									
7216.3311	----截面高度在800毫米以上〔999〕	6		14	13/	0	千克	A	M	/16
7216.3319	----其他〔999〕	6		14	13/	0	千克	A	M	/31
7216.3390	---其他〔999〕	6		14	13/	0	千克	A	M	/31
	-角钢及丁字钢，除热轧、热拉拔或热挤压外未经进一步加工，截面高度在80毫米及以上：									
7216.4010	---角钢〔999〕	3		17	13/	0	千克	A	M	/28
7216.4020	---丁字钢〔999〕	3		14	13/	0	千克	A	M	/13
	-其他角材、型材及异型材，除热轧、热拉拔或热挤压外未经进一步加工：									
7216.5010	---乙字钢〔999〕	6		14	13/	0	千克			/

协定税率 %										特惠税率 %			Article Description
亚太5国	东/冰/格	巴基斯坦	韩国	瑞士	哥达	秘鲁	澳大利亚	新西/坡/智	港/澳/台	亚太2国	老/柬/缅	36/3/1	
	0/0/0	0	3.6	0	0	0	0	0//0	0/0/			0/0/0	--Other
													-Not further worked than cold-rolled (cold-reduced):
	0/0/0	0	3.6	0	0	0	0	0//0	0/0/			0/0/0	--Containing by weight less than 0.25% of carbon
	0/0/0	0	3.6	0	0	0	0	0//0	0/0/			0/0/0	--Other
	0/0/0	0	2.4	0	0	0	0	0//0	0/0/			0/0/0	-Other
													Flat-rolled products of iron or non-alloy steel, of a width of less than 600mm, clad, plated or coated:
	0/0/0	0	2	0	0	0	0	0//0	0/0/			0/0/0	-Plated or coated with tin
	0/0/0	4	4.8	0	0	0	0	0//0	0/0/			0/0/0	-Electrolytically plated or coated with zinc
	0/0/0	4	3.2	0	0	0	0	0//0	0/0/			0/0/0	-Otherwise plated or coated with zinc
	0/0/0	0	2.4	0	0	0	0	0//0	0/0/			0/0/0	-Painted, varnished or coated with plastics
	0/0/0	4	4.8	0	0	0	0	0//0	0/0/			0/0/0	-Otherwise plated or coated
	0/0/0	4	3.2	0	0	0	0	0//0	0/0/			0/0/0	-Clad
													Bars and rods, hot-rolled, in irregularly wound coils, of iron or non-alloy steel:
	0/0/0	0	0	0	0	0	0	0//0	0/0/			0/0/0	-Containing indentations, ribs, grooves or other deformations produced during the rolling process
	0/0/0	0	1.8	0	0	0	0	0//0	0/0/			0/0/0	-Other, of free-cutting steel
													-Other:
4.3	0/0/0	0	2	0	0	0	0	0//0	0/0/			0/0/0	--Of circular cross-section measuring less than 14mm in diameter
	0/0/0	0	3	0	0	0	0	0//0	0/0/			0/0/0	--Other
													Other bars and rods of iron or non-alloy steel, not further worked than forged, hot-rolled, hot-drawn or hot-extruded, but including those twisted after rolling:
	0/0/0	4	2.8	0	0	0	0	0//0	0/0/			0/0/0	-Forged
0	0/0/0	0	0	0	0	0	0	0//0	0/0/			0/0/0	-Containing indentations, ribs, grooves or other deformations produced during the rolling process or twisted after rolling
	0/0/0	4	2.8	0	0	0	0	0//0	0/0/			0/0/0	-Other, of free-cutting steel
													-Other:
	0/0/0	0	0	0	0	0	0	0//0	0/0/			0/0/0	--Of rectangular cross section (other than square)
	0/0/0	0	0	0	0	0	0	0//0	0/0/			0/0/0	--Other
													Other bars and rods of iron or non-alloy steel:
	0/0/0	4	2.8	2.1	0	0	0	0//0	0/0/			0/0/0	-Of free-cutting steel, not further worked than cold-formed or cold-finished
	0/0/0	4	4.2	0	0	0	0	0//0	0/0/			0/0/0	-Other, not further worked than cold-formed or cold-finished
	0/0/0	0	0	0	0	0	0	0//0	0/0/			0/0/0	-Other
													Angles, shapes and sections of iron or non-alloy steel:
													-U, I or H sections, not further worked than hot-rolled, hot-drawn or extruded, of a height of less than 80mm:
	0/0/0	0	0	0	0	0	0	0//0	0/0/			0/0/0	---H sections
	0/0/0	0	0	0	0	0	0	0//0	0/0/			0/0/0	---I sections
	0/0/0	0	0	0	0	0	0	0//0	0/0/			0/0/0	---Other
													-L or T sections, not further worked than hot-rolled, hot-drawn or extruded, of a height of less than 80mm:
	0/0/0	0	2.4	0	0	0	0	0//0	0/0/			0/0/0	--L sections
	0/0/0	0	0	0	0	0	0	0//0	0/0/			0/0/0	--T sections
													-U, I or H sections, not further worked than hot-rolled, hot-drawn or extruded of a height of 80mm or more:
	0/0/0	0	2.4	0	0	0	0	0//0	0/0/			0/0/0	--U sections
													--I sections:
	0/0/0	0	2.4	0	0	0	0	0//0	0/0/			0/0/0	---Of a height exceeding 200mm
	0/0/0	0	2.4	0	0	0	0	0//0	0/0/			0/0/0	---Other
													--H sections:
													---Of a height exceeding 200mm:
	0/0/0	0	0	0	0	0	0	0//0	0/0/			0/0/0	----Of a height exceeding 800mm
	0/0/0	0	3.6	0	0	0	0	0//0	0/0/			0/0/0	----Other
	0/0/0	0	2.4	0	0	0	0	0//0	0/0/			0/0/0	---Other
													-L or T sections, not further worked than hot-rolled, hot-drawn or extruded, of a height of 80mm or more:
	0/0/0	0	0	0	0	0	0	0//0	0/0/			0/0/0	---L sections
	0/0/0	0	0	0	0	0	0	0//0	0/0/			0/0/0	---T sections
													-Other angles, shapes and sections, not further worked than hot-rolled, hot-drawn or extruded:
	0/0/0	0	0	0	0	0	0	0//0	0/0/			0/0/0	---Z sections

税则号列	货品名称〔CIQ 扩展编码及品名—T2 表示见附表 2〕	最惠(%)	暂定税率	普通	增值/消费	出口退税	计量单位	监管条件	检验检疫	特殊证件对美关税
7216.5020	---球扁钢〔999〕	3		20	13/	0	千克			/13
7216.5090	---其他〔101 方钢,102 其他型钢,103 其他异型钢〕	3		20	13/	0	千克			/28
	-角材、型材及异型材,除冷成形或冷加工外未经进一步加工:									
7216.6100	--平板轧材制的〔101 方钢,102 其他型钢,103 其他异型钢〕	3		20	13/	0	千克			/13
7216.6900	--其他〔101 方钢,102 其他型钢,103 其他异型钢〕	3		20	13/	0	千克			/28
	-其他:									
7216.9100	--平板轧材经冷成形或冷加工制的〔101 方钢,102 其他型钢,103 其他异型钢〕	3		20	13/	0	千克			/28
7216.9900	--其他〔101 方钢,102 其他型钢,103 其他异型钢〕	3		20	13/	0	千克			/23
72.17	**铁丝或非合金钢丝:**									
7217.1000	-未经镀或涂层,不论是否抛光〔999〕	8		40	13/	0	千克			/33
7217.2000	-镀或涂锌的〔999〕	8		40	13/	10	千克			/33
	-镀或涂其他贱金属的:									
7217.3010	---镀或涂铜的〔999〕	8		40	13/	10	千克			/33
7217.3090	---其他〔999〕	8		40	13/	13	千克			/33
7217.9000	-其他〔101 表面有镀层铁丝或钢丝,102 其他线材〕	8		40	13/	0	千克			/28
	第三分章　不锈钢									
72.18	**不锈钢,锭状或其他初级形状;不锈钢半制成品:**									
7218.1000	-锭状及其他初级形状〔999〕	2		11	13/	0	千克			/32
	-其他:									
7218.9100	--矩形(正方形除外)截面的〔999〕	2		11	13/	0	千克			/27
7218.9900	--其他〔999〕	2		11	13/	0	千克			/27
7218.9900 10	正方形截面的不锈钢半制成品〔999〕	2		11	13/	0	千克			/27
7218.9900 90	其他不锈钢半制成品〔999〕	2		11	13/	0	千克			/27
72.19	**不锈钢平板轧材,宽度在 600 毫米及以上:**									
	-除热轧外未经进一步加工的卷材:									
7219.1100	--厚度超过 10 毫米〔999〕	4		14	13/	13	千克			/29
7219.1200	--厚度在 4.75 毫米及以上,但不超过 10 毫米〔999〕	4		14	13/	13	千克			/29
	--厚度在 3 毫米及以上,但小于 4.75 毫米:									
	---未经酸洗的:									
7219.1312	----按重量计含锰量在 5.5%及以上铬锰系不锈钢〔999〕	4		14	13/	0	千克			/14
7219.1319	----其他〔999〕	4		14	13/	13	千克			/29
	---经酸洗的:									
7219.1322	----按重量计含锰量在 5.5%及以上铬锰系不锈钢〔999〕	4		14	13/	0	千克			/14
7219.1329	----其他〔999〕	4		14	13/	13	千克			/29
	--厚度小于 3 毫米:									
	---未经酸洗的:									
7219.1412	----按重量计含锰量在 5.5%及以上铬锰系不锈钢〔999〕	4		14	13/	0	千克			/14
7219.1419	----其他〔999〕	4		14	13/	13	千克			/29
	---经酸洗的:									
7219.1422	----按重量计含锰量在 5.5%及以上铬锰系不锈钢〔999〕	4		14	13/	0	千克			/14
7219.1429	----其他〔999〕	4		14	13/	13	千克			/14
	-除热轧外未经进一步加工的非卷材:									
7219.2100	--厚度超过 10 毫米〔999〕	6		40	13/	13	千克			/16
7219.2200	--厚度在 4.75 毫米及以上,但不超过 10 毫米〔999〕	6		40	13/	13	千克			/31
7219.2300	--厚度在 3 毫米及以上,但小于 4.75 毫米〔999〕	6		40	13/	13	千克			/31
	--厚度小于 3 毫米:									
7219.2410	---厚度超过 1 毫米但小于 3 毫米〔999〕	6		40	13/	13	千克			/26
7219.2420	---厚度在 0.5 毫米及以上,但不超过 1 毫米〔999〕	6		40	13/	13	千克			/16
7219.2430	---厚度小于 0.5 毫米〔999〕	6		40	13/	13	千克			/31
	-除冷轧外未经进一步加工:									
7219.3100	--厚度在 4.75 毫米及以上〔999〕	6		40	13/	13	千克			/26
7219.3200	--厚度在 3 毫米及以上,但小于 4.75 毫米〔999〕	6		40	13/	13	千克			/31
	--厚度超过 1 毫米,但小于 3 毫米:									
7219.3310	---按重量计含锰量在 5.5%及以上的铬锰系不锈钢〔101 硅锰铁,102 冷轧不锈钢板〕	6		40	13/	13	千克			/16
7219.3390	---其他〔999〕	6		40	13/	13	千克			/31
7219.3400	--厚度在 0.5 毫米及以上,但不超过 1 毫米〔999〕	6		40	13/	13	千克			/31
7219.3500	--厚度小于 0.5 毫米〔999〕	6		40	13/	13	千克			/26

协定税率 %										特惠税率 %			
亚太5国	东/冰/格	巴基斯坦	韩国	瑞士	哥达	秘鲁	澳大利亚	新西/坡/智	港/澳/台	亚太2国	老/柬/缅	36/3/1	Article Description
	0/0/0	0	0	0	0	0	0	0//0	0/0/			0/0/0	---Bulb flat steel
	0/0/0	0	0	0	0	0	0	0//0	0/0/			0/0/0	---Other
													-Angles, shapes and sections, not further worked than cold-formed or cold-finished:
	0/0/0	0	0	0	0	0	0	0//0	0/0/			0/0/0	--Obtained from flat-rolled products
	0/0/0	0	0	0	0	0	0	0//0	0/0/			0/0/0	--Other
													-Other:
	0/0/0	0	0	0	0	0	0	0//0	0/0/			0/0/0	--Cold-formed or cold-finished from flat-rolled products
	0/0/0	0	0	0	0	0	0	0//0	0/0/			0/0/0	--Other
													Wire of iron or non-alloy steel:
	0/0/0	4		0	0	0	0	0//0	0/0/0			0/0/0	-Not plated or coated, whether or not polished
	0/0/0	4	3.2	0	0	0	0	0//0	0/0/			0/0/0	-Plated or coated with zinc
													-Plated or coated with other base metals
6.4	0/0/0	4	6.4	0	0	0	0	0//0	0/0/			0/0/0	---Plated or coated with copper
6.4	0/0/0	4	4.8	0	0	0	0	0//0	0/0/			0/0/0	---Other
	0/0/0	4	3.2	0	0	0	0	0//0	0/0/			0/0/0	-Other
													Ⅲ. STAINLESS STEEL
													Stainless steel in ingots or other primary forms; semi-finished products of stainless steel:
	0/0/0	0	0	0	0	0	0	0//0	0/0/			0/0/0	-Ingots and other primary forms
													-Other:
	0/0/0	0	0	0	0	0	0	0//0	0/0/			0/0/0	--Of rectangular (other than square) cross-section
	0/0/0	0	0	0	0	0	0	0//0	0/0/			0/0/0	--Other
	0/0/0	0	0	0	0	0	0	0//0	0/0/		//	0/0/0	Stainless steel semi—finished products with square section
	0/0/0	0	0	0	0	0	0	0//0	0/0/		//	0/0/0	Other semi—finished stainless steel products
													Flat-rolled products of stainless steel, of a width of 600mm or more:
													-Not further worked than hot-rolled, in coils:
	0/0/0	0	0	0	0	0	0	0//0	0/0/			0/0/0	--Of a thickness exceeding 10mm
	0/0/0	0	1.6	0	0	0	0	0//0	0/0/0			0/0/0	--Of a thickness of 4.75mm or more but not exceeding 10mm
													--Of a thickness of 3mm or more but less than 4.75mm:
													---Not acid pickled:
	0/0/0	0	0	0	0	0	0	0//0	0/0/			0/0/0	----Containing more than 5.5% by weight of manganese of Ferro-chromium-manganese steel
	0/0/0	0	1.6	0	0	0	0	0//0	0/0/0			0/0/0	----Other
													---Acid pickled:
	0/0/0	0	0	0	0	0	0	0//0	0/0/			0/0/0	----Containing more than 5.5% by weight of manganese of Ferro-chromiam-manganese steel
	0/0/0	0	1.6	0	0	0	0	0//0	0/0/0			0/0/0	----Other
													--Of a thickness of less than 3mm:
													---Not acid pickled:
	0/0/0	0	0	0	0	0	0	0//0	0/0/			0/0/0	----Containing more than 5.5% by weight of manganese of Ferro-chromium-marganese steel
	0/0/0	0	0	0	0	0	0	0//0	0/0/			0/0/0	----Other
													---Acid Pickled:
	0/0/0	0	0	0	0	0	0	0//0	0/0/			0/0/0	----Containing more than 5.5% by weight of manganese of ferro chromium-manganese steel
	0/0/0	0	0	0	0	0	0	0//0	0/0/			0/0/0	----Other
													-Not further worked than hot-rolled, not in coils:
5.6	0/0/0	4	6	0	0	0	0	0/0/0	0/0/			0/0/	--Of a thickness exceeding 10mm
5.6	0/0/0	4	7	0	0	0	0	0/0/0	0/0/			0/0/	--Of a thickness of 4.75mm or more but not exceeding 10mm
5.6	0/0/0	4	6	0	0	0	0	0/0/0	0/0/0			0/0/	—Of a thickness of 3mm or more but less than 4.75mm
													—Of a thickness of less than 3mm:
5.6	0/0/0	4	6	0	0	0	0	0/0/0	0/0/0			0/0/	—Of a thickness exceeding 1mm, but less than 3mm
5.6	0/0/0	4	7	0	0	0	0	0/0/0	0/0/			0/0/	—Of a thickness of 0.5mm or more but not exceeding 1mm
5.6	0/0/0	4	6	0	0	0	0	0/0/0	0/0/			0/0/	—Of a thickness of less than 0.5mm
													-Not further worked than cold-rolled (cold-reduced):
	0/0/0	4	4	0	0	0	0	0/0/0	0/0/0			0/0/	—Of a thickness of 4.75mm or more
	0/0/0	4	4	0	0	0	0	0/0/0	0/0/0			0/0/	—Of a thickness of 3mm or more but less than 4.75mm
													—Of a thickness exceeding 1mm but less than 3mm:
	0/0/0	4	4	0	0	0	0	0/0/0	0/0/0			0/0/	—Containing more than 5.5% by weight of manganese of ferro chromium-manganese steel
	0/0/0	4.5	6	0	0	0	0	0/0/0	0/0/0			0/0/	—Other
	0/0/0	4	7	0	0	0	0	0/0/0	0/0/0			0/0/	—Of a thickness of 0.5mm or more but not exceeding 1mm
	0/0/0	4	7	0	0	0	0	0/0/0	0/0/0			0/0/	—Of a thickness of less than 0.5mm

税则号列	货品名称〔CIQ 扩展编码及品名—T2 表示见附表 2〕	最惠(%)	暂定税率	普通	增值/消费	出口退税	计量单位	监管条件	检验检疫	特殊证件对美关税
7219.9000	-其他〔999〕	6		40	13/	13	千克			/16
72.20	**不锈钢平板轧材,宽度小于 600 毫米:**									
	-除热轧外未经进一步加工:									
7220.1100	--厚度在 4.75 毫米及以上〔999〕	6		20	13/	10	千克			/31
7220.1200	--厚度小于 4.75 毫米〔999〕	6		20	13/	10	千克			/16
	-除冷轧外未经进一步加工:									
7220.2020	---厚度在 0.35 毫米及以下〔999〕	6		20	13/	10	千克			/31
7220.2030	---厚度在 0.35 毫米及以上但小于 3 毫米〔999〕	6		20	13/	10	千克			/26
7220.2040	---厚度在 3 毫米及以上〔999〕	6		20	13/	10	千克			/31
7220.9000	-其他〔101 冷轧不锈钢板,102 热轧不锈钢板〕	6		20	13/	10	千克			/16
72.21	**不规则盘卷的不锈钢热轧条、杆:**									
7221.0000	不规则盘卷的不锈钢热轧条、杆〔999〕	6		20	13/	13	千克			/31
72.22	**不锈钢其他条、杆;不锈钢角材、型材及异型材:**									
	-条、杆,除热轧、热拉拔或热挤压外未经进一步加工:									
7222.1100	--圆形截面的〔999〕	6		40	13/	10	千克			/26
7222.1900	--其他〔999〕	6		40	13/	10	千克			/31
7222.2000	-条、杆,除冷成形或冷加工外未经进一步加工〔999〕	6		40	13/	10	千克			/16
7222.3000	-其他条、杆〔999〕	6		40	13/	10	千克			/26
7222.4000	-角材、型材及异型材〔101 其他型钢,102 其他异型钢〕	6		17	13/	10	千克	A	M	/26
72.23	**不锈钢丝:**									
7223.0000	不锈钢丝〔102〕	6		20	13/	10	千克			/31
	第四分章　其他合金钢;合金钢或非合金钢制的空心钻钢									
72.24	**其他合金钢,锭状或其他初级形状;其他合金钢制的半制成品:**									
7224.1000	-锭状及其他初级形状〔999〕	2		11	13/	0	千克			/27
	-其他:									
7224.9010	---单件重量在 10 吨及以上的粗铸锻件坯〔999〕	2		11	13/	0	千克			/
7224.9090	---其他									
7224.9090 10	其他合金钢圆坯,直径≥700mm(其他合金钢锭及其他初级形态的)〔999〕	2		11	13/	0	千克			/27
7224.9090 90	其他合金钢坯,直径≥700mm 的合金钢圆坯除外(其他合金钢锭及其他初级形态的)〔999〕	2		11	13/	0	千克			/27
72.25	**其他合金钢平板轧材,宽度在 600 毫米及以上:**									
	-硅电钢制:									
7225.1100	--取向性硅电钢〔999〕	3		20	13/	13	千克	A7	M	/28
7225.1900	--其他〔999〕	6		20	13/	13	千克			/31
7225.3000	-其他卷材,除热轧外未经进一步加工〔999〕	3		14	13/	10	千克			/28
	-其他非卷材,除热轧外未经进一步加工:									
7225.4010	---工具钢〔999〕	3		17	13/	13	千克	A	M	/28
	---其他:									
7225.4091	----含硼合金钢〔999〕	3		17	13/	0	千克	A	M	/28
7225.4099	----其他〔999〕	3		17	13/	13	千克			/23
7225.5000	-其他,除冷轧外未经进一步加工〔999〕	3		17	13/	13	千克			/28
	-其他:									
7225.9100	--电镀或涂锌的〔999〕	7		17	13/	10	千克			/32
7225.9200	--用其他方法镀或涂锌的〔999〕	7		17	13/	10	千克			/32
	--其他:									
7225.9910	---高速钢制〔999〕	3		17	13/	10	千克	A	M	/
7225.9990	---其他〔999〕	7		17	13/	10	千克			/32
72.26	**其他合金钢平板轧材,宽度小于 600 毫米:**									
	-硅电钢制:									
7226.1100	--取向性硅电钢〔999〕	3		20	13/	13	千克	A	M	/13
7226.1900	--其他〔999〕	3		20	13/	13	千克			/23
7226.2000	-高速钢制〔999〕	3		20	13/	10	千克	A	M	/28
	-其他:									
	--除热轧外未经进一步加工:									
7226.9110	---工具钢〔999〕	3		20	13/	10	千克	A	M	/28
	---其他:									
7226.9191	----含硼合金钢〔999〕	3		20	13/	0	千克	A	M	/28
7226.9199	----其他									
7226.9199 10	宽度<600 毫米的铁基非晶合金带材(除热轧外未经进一步加工)〔999〕	3		20	13/	10	千克			/28

协定税率 %										特惠税率 %			Article Description
亚太5国	东/冰/格	巴基斯坦	韩国	瑞士	哥达	秘鲁	澳大利亚	新西/坡/智	港/澳/台	亚太2国	老/柬/缅	36/3/1	
	0/0/0	4	4	0	0	0	0	0/0/0	0/0/0			0/0/	-Other
													Flat-rolled products stainless steel, of a width of less than 600mm:
													-Not further worked than hot-rolled:
	0/0/0	4		0	0	0	0	0/0/0	0/0/			0/0/	--Of a thickness of 4.75mm or more
	0/0/0	4	4	0	0	0	0	0/0/0	0/0/			0/0/	--Of a thickness of less than 4.75mm
													-Not further worked than cold-rolled (cold-reduced):
	0/0/0	4	6	0	0	0	0	0/0/0	0/0/			0/0/	---Of a thickness of 0.35mm orless
	0/0/0	4	6	0	0	0	0	0/0/0	0/0/			0/0/	---Of a thickness of more than 0.35mm but less than 3mm
	0/0/0	4	4	0	0	0	0	0/0/0	0/0/			0/0/	---Of a thickness of 3mm or more
	0/0/0	4	4	0	0	0	0	0/0/0	0/0/0			0/0/	-Other
													Bars and rods, hot-rolled, in irregularly wound coils, of stainless steel:
4.8	0/0/0	4.5	8	0	0	0	0	0/0/0	0/0/			0/0/	Bars and rods, hot-rolled, in irregularly wound coils, of stainless steel
													Other bars and rods of stainless steel; angles, shapes and sections of stainless steel:
													-Bars and rods, not further worked than hot-rolled, hot-drawn or extruded:
5.4	0/0/0	4	9	0	0	0	0	0/0/0	0/0/			0/0/	--Of circular cross-section
5.4	0/0/0	4	9	0	0	0	0	0/0/0	0/0/			0/0/	--Other
	0/0/0	4.5		0	0	0	0	0/0/0	0/0/			0/0/	-Bars and rods, not further worked than cold-formed or cold-finished
5.3	0/0/0	4	9	0	0	0	0	0/0/0	0/0/			0/0/	-Other bars and rods
	0/0/0	4		0	0	0	0	0/0/0	0/0/			0/0/	-Angles, shapes and sections
													Wire of stainless steel:
	0/0/0	4.5		0	0	0	0	0/0/0	0/0/			0/0/0	Wire of stainless steel
													Ⅳ. OTHER ALLOY STEEL; HOLLOW DRILL BARS AND RODS, OF ALLOY OR NON-ALLOY STEEL
													Other alloy steel in ingots or other primary forms; semi-finished products of other alloy steel:
	0/0/0	0	0	0	0	0	0	0//0	0/0/			0/0/0	-Ingots and other primary forms
													-Other:
	0/0/0	0	0	0	0	0	0	0//0	0/0/			0/0/0	---Raw casting forging stocks, individual piece weight of 10t or more
													---Other
	0/0/0	0	0	0	0	0	0	0//0	0/0/			0/0/0	Other alloy steel round billet, larger than 700mm in diameter (other alloy ingots and other primary forms)
	0/0/0	0	0	0	0	0	0	0//0	0/0/			0/0/0	Other alloy steel billet, except alloy steel round billet, with a diameter larger than 700mm (other alloy ingots and other primary forms)
													Flat-rolled products of other alloy steel, of a width of 600mm or more:
													-Of silicon-electrical steel:
2.1	0/0/0	0	2.1	0	0	0	0	0//0	0/0/			0/0/0	--Grain-oriented
	0/0/0	0		0	0	0	0	0//0	0/0/0			0/0/0	--Other
	0/0/0	0		0	0	0	0	0//0	0/0/			0/0/0	-Other, not further worked than hot-rolled, in coils
													-Other, not further worked than hot-rolled, not in coils
	0/0/0	0	0	0	0	0	0	0//0	0/0/			0/0/0	---Tool steel
													---Other:
	0/0/0	0	0	0	0	0	0	0//0	0/0/			0/0/0	----Alloy steel containing boron
	0/0/0	0	0	0	0	0	0	0//0	0/0/			0/0/0	----Other
	0/0/0	0		0	0	0	0	0//0	0/0/			0/0/0	-Other, not further worked than cold-rolled (cold-reduced)
													-Other:
	0/0/0	4	2.8	0	0	0	0	0//0	0/0/			0/0/0	--Electrolytically plated or coated with zinc
	0/0/0	4	4.2	0	0	0	0	0//0	0/0/			0/0/0	--Otherwise plated or coated with zinc
													--Other:
	0/0/0	0	0	0	0	0	0	0//0	0/0/			0/0/0	---Of high speed steel
	0/0/0	4	2.8	0	0	0	0	0//0	0/0/			0/0/0	---Other
													Flat-rolled products of other alloy steel, of a width of less than 600mm:
													-Of silicon-electrical steel:
	0/0/0	0		0	0	0	0	0//0	0/0/			0/0/0	--Grain-oriented
	0/0/0	0		0	0	0	0	0//0	0/0/			0/0/0	--Other
	0/0/0	0	1.2	0	0	0	0	0//0	0/0/			0/0/0	-Of high speed steel
													-Other:
													--Not further worked than hot-rolled:
	0/0/0	0	1.2	0	0	0	0	0//0	0/0/			0/0/0	---Tool steel
													---Other:
	0/0/0	0	1.2	0	0	0	0	0//0	0/0/			0/0/0	----Alloy steel containing boron
													----Other
	0/0/0	0	1.2	0	0	0	0	0//0	0/0/			0/0/0	Amorphous alloy strip, with a width less than 600 mm (in hot rolled without further processing)

税则号列	货品名称〔CIQ扩展编码及品名－T2表示见附表2〕	最惠(%)	暂定税率	普通	增值/消费	出口退税	计量单位	监管条件	检验检疫	特殊证件对美关税
7226.9199　90	宽度＜600毫米热轧其他合金钢板材(除热轧外未经进一步加工)〔999〕	3		20	13/	10	千克			/28
7226.9200	--除冷轧外未经进一步加工〔999〕	3		20	13/	10	千克			/23
	--其他：									
7226.9910	---电镀锌的〔999〕	7		20	13/	10	千克			/32
7226.9920	---用其他方法镀或涂锌的〔101 镀锌板，102 涂层板〕	7		20	13/	10	千克			/27
7226.9990	---其他									
7226.9990　01	铁镍合金带材(生产集成电路框架用)(宽度＜600mm)〔999〕	7	4	20	13/	10	千克			/24
7226.9990　90	其他合金板材(宽度＜600mm)〔999〕	7		20	13/	10	千克			/27
72.27	**不规则盘卷的其他合金钢热轧条、杆：**									
7227.1000	-高速钢制〔999〕	3		20	13/	10	千克	A	M	/
7227.2000	-硅锰钢制〔999〕	6		20	13/	10	千克	A	M	/
	-其他：									
7227.9010	---含硼合金钢制〔999〕	3		20	13/	0	千克	A	M	/28
7227.9090	---其他〔999〕	3		20	13/	10	千克			/
72.28	**其他合金钢条、杆；其他合金钢角材、型材及异型材；合金钢或非合金钢制的空心钻钢：**									
7228.1000	-高速钢条、杆〔999〕	3		20	13/	13	千克	A	M	/28
7228.2000	-硅锰钢条、杆〔999〕	6		20	13/	0	千克	A	M	/31
	-其他条、杆，除热轧、热拉拔或热挤压外未经进一步加工：									
7228.3010	---含硼合金钢制〔999〕	3		20	13/	0	千克	A	M	/28
7228.3090	---其他〔999〕	3		20	13/	13	千克			/28
7228.4000	-其他条、杆，除锻造外未经进一步加工〔999〕	3		20	13/	13	千克			/28
7228.5000	-其他条、杆，除冷成形或冷加工外未经进一步加工〔999〕	3		20	13/	13	千克			/28
7228.6000	-其他条、杆〔999〕	3		20	13/	10	千克			/28
	-角材、型材及异型材：									
7228.7010	---履带板型钢〔999〕	6		17	13/	10	千克	A	M	/
7228.7090	---其他〔999〕	5		17	13/	10	千克	A	M	/30
7228.8000	-空心钻钢〔999〕	7		35	13/	13	千克	A	M	/
72.29	**其他合金钢丝：**									
7229.2000	-硅锰钢丝〔999〕	7		20	13/	10	千克			/32
	-其他：									
7229.9010	---高速钢丝〔999〕	3		20	13/	13	千克			/
7229.9090	---其他〔999〕	7		20	13/	10	千克			/32

协定税率 %										特惠税率 %			Article Description
亚太5国	东/冰/格	巴基斯坦	韩国	瑞士	哥达	秘鲁	澳大利亚	新西/坡/智	港/澳/台	亚太2国	老/柬/缅	36/3/1	
	0/0/0	0	1.2	0	0	0	0	0//0	0/0/			0/0/0	Other alloy steel plates ,with a width of 600 mm (other than hot rolling without further processing)
	0/0/0	0	1.8	0	0	0	0	0//0	0/0/			0/0/0	--Not further worked than cold-rolled (cold-reduced)
													--Other:
	0/0/0	4	2.8	0	0	0	0	0//0	0/0/			0/0/0	---Electrolytically plated or coated with zinc
	0/0/0	4	2.8	0	0	0	0	0//0	0/0/			0/0/0	---Otherwise plated or coated with zinc
													---Other
	0/0/0	4	2.8	0	0	0	0	0//0	0/0/			0/0/0	Other flat-rolled products of other alloy steel, Fe-Ni alloys strip, width<600mm (production of the frame for electronic integrated circuits)
	0/0/0	4	2.8	0	0	0	0	0//0	0/0/			0/0/0	Other flat-rolled products of other alloy steel, width<600mm
													Bars and rods, hot-rolled, in irregularly wound coils, of other alloy steel:
	0/0/0	0	0	0	0	0	0	0//0	0/0/			0/0/0	-Of high speed steel
	0/0/0	0	3.6	0	0	0	0	0//0	0/0/			0/0/0	-Of silico-manganese steel
													-Other:
	0/0/0	0	0	0	0	0	0	0//0	0/0/			0/0/0	---Of containing boron alloy steel
	0/0/0	0	0	0	0	0	0	0//0	0/0/			0/0/0	---Other
													Other bars and rods of other alloy steel; angles, shapes and sections, of other alloy steel; hollow drill bars and rods, of alloy or non-alloy steel:
	0/0/0	0	1.2	0	0	0	0	0//0	0/0/			0/0/0	-Bars and rods, of high speed steel
	0/0/0	0	2.4	0	0	0	0	0//0	0/0/			0/0/0	-Bars and rods, of silico-manganese steel
													-Other bars and rods, not further worked than hot-crolled, hot-drawn or extruded:
	0/0/0	0	1.2	0	0	0	0	0//0	0/0/			0/0/0	---Of containing boron alloy steel
	0/0/0	0	1.2	0	0	0	0	0//0	0/0/			0/0/0	---Other
	0/0/0	0	1.2	0	0	0	0	0//0	0/0/			0/0/0	-Other bars and rods, not further worked than forged
	0/0/0	0	1.2	0	0	0	0	0//0	0/0/			0/0/0	-Other bars and rods, not further worked than cold-formed of cold-finished
	0/0/0	0	1.2	0	0	0	0	0//0	0/0/			0/0/0	-Other bars and rods
													-Angles, shapes and sections:
	0/0/0	0	0	0	0	0	0	0//0	0/0/			0/0/0	---Shapes of crawler tread
	0/0/0	0	2.4	0	0	0	0	0//0	0/0/			0/0/0	---Other
	0/0/0	4	0	0	0	0	0	0//0	0/0/			0/0/0	-Hollow drill bars and rods
													Wire of other alloy steel:
	0/0/0	4	4.2	0	0	0	0	0//0	0/0/			0/0/	-Of silico-manganese steel
													-Other:
	0/0/0	0	1.2	0	0	0	0	0//0	0/0/			0/0/	---Of high speed steel
	0/0/0	4		0	0	0	0	0//0	0/0/			0/0/	---Other

第七十三章
钢铁制品

注释：

一、本章所称"铸铁"，适用于经铸造而得的产品，按重量计其铁元素含量超过其他元素单项含量并与第七十二章注释一（四）所述的钢的化学成分不同。

二、本章所称"丝"，是指热或冷成形的任何截面形状的产品，但其截面尺寸均不超过16毫米。

税则号列	货品名称〔CIQ扩展编码及品名—T2表示见附表2〕	最惠(%)	暂定税率	普通	增值/消费	出口退税	计量单位	监管条件	检验检疫	特殊证件对美关税
73.01	**钢铁板桩，不论是否钻孔、打眼或组装；焊接的钢铁角材、型材及异型材：**									
7301.1000	-钢铁板桩〔999〕	7		20	13/	13	千克			/32
7301.2000	-角材、型材及异型材〔999〕	7		30	13/	13	千克			/32
73.02	**铁道及电车道铺轨用钢铁材料（钢轨、护轨、齿轨、道岔尖轨、辙叉、尖轨拉杆及其他岔道段体、轨枕、鱼尾板、轨座、轨座楔、钢轨垫板、钢轨夹、底板、固定板及其他专门用于连接或加固路轨的材料）：**									
7302.1000	-钢轨〔999〕	6		14	13/	13	千克	A	M	/31
7302.3000	-道岔尖轨、辙叉、尖轨拉杆及其他岔道段体〔999〕	8		17	13/	13	千克	A	M	/
7302.4000	-鱼尾板及钢轨垫板〔999〕	7		17	13/	13	千克	A	M	/
	-其他：									
7302.9010	---轨枕〔999〕	6		14	13/	13	千克	A	M	/
7302.9090	---其他〔999〕	7		17	13/	13	千克	A	M	/32
73.03	**铸铁管及空心异型材：**									
7303.0010	---内径在500毫米及以上的圆形截面管〔101〕	4		40	13/	13	千克			/
7303.0090	---其他〔101〕	4		40	13/	13	千克			/29
73.04	**无缝钢铁管及空心异型材（铸铁的除外）：**									
	-石油或天然气管道管：									
	--不锈钢制：									
7304.1110	---外径大于等于215.9毫米，但不超过406.4毫米〔101无缝钢管压力管道，102无缝钢管〕	5		17	13/	13	千克	A	M	/30
7304.1120	---外径超过114.3毫米，但小于215.9毫米〔101无缝钢管压力管道，102无缝钢管〕	5		17	13/	13	千克	A	M	/30
7304.1130	---外径不超过114.3毫米〔101无缝钢管压力管道，102无缝钢管〕	5		17	13/	13	千克	A	M	/30
7304.1190	---其他〔101无缝钢管压力管道，102无缝钢管〕	5		17	13/	13	千克	A	M	/30
	--其他：									
7304.1910	---外径大于等于215.9毫米，但不超过406.4毫米〔101无缝钢管压力管道，102无缝钢管〕	5		17	13/	13	千克	A	M	/45
7304.1920	---外径超过114.3毫米，但小于215.9毫米〔101无缝钢管压力管道，102无缝钢管〕	5		17	13/	13	千克	A	M	/20
7304.1930	---外径不超过114.3毫米〔101无缝钢管压力管道，102无缝钢管〕	5		17	13/	13	千克	A	M	/45
7304.1990	---其他〔101无缝钢管压力管道，102无缝钢管〕	5		17	13/	13	千克	A	M	/45
	-钻探石油及天然气用的套管、导管及钻管：									
	--不锈钢钻管：									
7304.2210	---外径不超过168.3毫米〔101无缝钢管压力管道，102无缝钢管〕	4		17	13/	13	千克	A	M	/19
7304.2290	---其他〔101无缝钢管压力管道，102无缝钢管〕	4		17	13/	13	千克	A	M	/19
	--其他钻管：									
7304.2310	---外径不超过168.3毫米〔101无缝钢管压力管道，102无缝钢管〕	4		17	13/	13	千克	A	M	/29
7304.2390	---其他〔101无缝钢管压力管道，102无缝钢管〕	4		17	13/	13	千克	A	M	/19
7304.2400	--其他不锈钢管〔101无缝钢管压力管道，102无缝钢管〕	4		17	13/	13	千克	A	M	/44
	--其他：									
7304.2910	---屈服强度小于552兆帕的〔101无缝钢管压力管道，102无缝钢管〕	4		17	13/	13	千克	A	M	/44
7304.2920	---屈服强度大于等于552兆帕，但小于758兆帕的〔101无缝钢管压力管道，102无缝钢管〕	4		17	13/	13	千克	A	M	/19
7304.2930	---屈服强度大于等于758兆帕的〔101无缝钢管压力管道，102无缝钢管〕	4		17	13/	13	千克	A	M	/19
	-铁或非合金钢的其他圆形截面管：									

Chapter 73
Articles of iron or steel

Notes:

1. In this Chapter the expression "cast iron" applies to products obtained by casting in which iron predominates by weight over each of the other elements and which do not comply with the chemical composition of steel as defined in Note 1 (d) to Chapter 72.
2. In this Chapter the word "wire" means hot or cold-formed products of any cross-sectional shape, of which no cross-sectional dimension exceeds 16mm.

协定税率 %										特惠税率 %			
亚太5国	东/冰/格	巴基斯坦	韩国	瑞士	哥达	秘鲁	澳大利亚	新西/坡/智	港/澳/台	亚太2国	老/柬/缅	36/3/1	Article Description
													Sheet piling of iron or steel, whether or not drilled, punched or made from assembled elements; welded angles, shapes and sections, of iron or steel:
6.3	0/0/0	4	2.8	0	0	0	0	0//0	0/0/			0/0/0	-Sheet piling
	0/0/0	4	2.8	0	0	0	0	0//0	0/0/			0/0/0	-Angles, shapes and sections
													Railway or tramway track construction material of iron or steel, the following: rails, check-rails and rack rails, switch blades, crossing frogs, point rods and other crossing pieces, sleepers (cross-ties), fish-plates, chairs, chair wedges, sole plates (base plates), rail clips, bed-plates, ties and other material specialized for jointing or fixing rails:
	0/0/0	0	2.4	0	0	0	0	0//0	0/0/			0/0/0	-Rails
	0/0/0	4	0	0	0	0	0	0//0	0/0/			0/0/0	-Switch blades, crossing frogs, point rods and other crossing pieces
	0/0/0	4	2.8	0	0	0	0	0//0	0/0/			0/0/0	-Fish-plates and sole plates
													-Other:
5.1	0/0/0	0	0	0	0	0	0	0//0	0/0/			0/0/0	---Sleepers(cross-ties)
6	0/0/0	4	0	2.1	0	0	0	0//0	0/0/			0/0/0	---Other
													Tubes, pipes and hollow profiles, of cast iron:
	0/0/0	0	0	0	0	0	0	0//0	0/0/			0/0/0	---Tubes and pipes of circular cross-section, of the internal diameter of 500mm or more
	0/0/0	0	0	0	0	0	0	0//0	0/0/			0/0/0	---Other
													Tubes, pipes and hollow profiles, seamless, of iron (other than cast iron) or steel:
													-Line pipe of a kind used for oil or gas pipelines:
													--Of stainless steel:
	0/0/0	0	2	0	0	0	0	0//0	0/0/			0/0/0	---Having an outside diameter of 215.9mm or more but not exceeding 406.4mm
	0/0/0	0	2	0	0	0	0	0//0	0/0/			0/0/0	---Having an outside diameter exceeding 114.3mm but less than 215.9mm
	0/0/0	0	2	0	0	0	0	0//0	0/0/			0/0/0	---Having an outside diameter≤114.3mm
	0/0/0	0	0	0	0	0	0	0//0	0/0/			0/0/0	---Other
													--Other:
	0/0/0	0	2	0	0	0	0	0//0	0/0/			0/0/0	---Having an outside diameter of 215.9mm or more but not exceeding 406.4mm
	0/0/0	0	2	0	0	0	0	0//0	0/0/			0/0/0	---Having an outside diameter exceeding 114.3mm but less than 215.9mm
	0/0/0	0	2	0	0	0	0	0//0	0/0/			0/0/0	---Having an outside diameter not exceeding 114.3mm
	0/0/0	0	0	0	0	0	0	0//0	0/0/			0/0/0	---Other
													-Casing, tubing and drill pipe, of a kind used in drilling for oil or gas:
													--Drill pipe, of stainless steel:
	0/0/0	0	0	0	0	0	0	0//0	0/0/			0/0/0	---Having an outside diameter≤168.3mm
	0/0/0	0	0	0	0	0	0	0//0	0/0/			0/0/0	---Other
													--Other drill pipe:
	0/0/0	0	0	0	0	0	0	0//0	0/0/			0/0/0	---Having an outside diameter ≤168.3mm
	0/0/0	0	0	0	0	0	0	0//0	0/0/			0/0/0	---Other
2	0/0/0	0	0	0	0	0	0	0//0	0/0/			0/0/0	--Other pipe, of stainless steel
													--Other:
2	0/0/0	0	0	0	0	0	0	0//0	0/0/			0/0/0	---Yield strength<552MPa
2	0/0/0	0	0	0	0	0	0	0//0	0/0/			0/0/0	---552MPa≤Yield strength<758MPa
2	0/0/0	0	0	0	0	0	0	0//0	0/0/			0/0/0	---Yield strength≥758MPa
													-Other, of circular cross-section, of iron or non-alloy steel:

税则号列	货品名称〔CIQ扩展编码及品名－T2表示见附表2〕	最惠(%)	暂定税率	普通	增值/消费	出口退税	计量单位	监管条件	检验检疫	特殊证件对美关税
	--冷拔或冷轧的：									
7304.3110	---锅炉管〔101 无缝钢管压力管道,102 无缝钢管〕	4		17	13/	13	千克	A	M	/44
7304.3120	---地质钻管、套管〔101 无缝钢管压力管道,102 无缝钢管〕	8		17	13/	13	千克	A	M	/23
7304.3190	---其他〔101 无缝钢管压力管道,102 无缝钢管〕	4		17	13/	10	千克	A	M	/29
	--其他：									
7304.3910	---锅炉管〔101 无缝钢管压力管道,102 无缝钢管〕	4		17	13/	10	千克	A	M	/44
7304.3920	---地质钻管、套管〔101 无缝钢管压力管道,102 无缝钢管〕	5		17	13/	10	千克	A	M	/20
7304.3990	---其他〔101 无缝钢管压力管道,102 无缝钢管〕	4		17	13/	10	千克	A	M	/29
	-不锈钢的其他圆形截面管：									
	--冷拔或冷轧的：									
7304.4110	---锅炉管〔101 无缝钢管压力管道,102 无缝钢管〕	8		17	13/	10	千克	A	M	/48
7304.4190	---其他〔101 无缝钢管压力管道,102 无缝钢管〕	8		40	13/	13	千克	A	M	/43
	--其他：									
7304.4910	---锅炉管〔101 无缝钢管压力管道,102 无缝钢管〕	8		17	13/	13	千克	A	M	/43
7304.4990	---其他〔101 无缝钢管压力管道,102 无缝钢管〕	8		40	13/	10	千克	A	M	/48
	-其他合金钢的其他圆形截面管：									
	--冷拔或冷轧的：									
7304.5110	---锅炉管									
7304.5110 01	高温承压用合金钢无缝钢管(抗拉强度≥620MPa、屈服强度≥440MPa)(外径在127mm以上(含127mm),化学成分(wt%)中碳(C)的含量≥0.07且≤0.13、铬(Cr)的含量≥8.5且≤9.5、钼(Mo)的含量≥0.3且≤0.6、钨(W)的含量≥1.5且≤2.0、抗拉强度≥620Mpa、屈服强度≥440Mpa)	4		17	13/	10	千克	A	M	/19
7304.5110 90	冷轧的其他合金钢无缝锅炉管(冷拔或冷轧的,包括内螺纹)〔101 无缝钢管压力管道,102 无缝钢管〕	4		17	13/	10	千克	A	M	/19
7304.5120	---地质钻管、套管〔101 无缝钢管压力管道,102 无缝钢管〕	4		17	13/	10	千克	A	M	/19
7304.5190	---其他									
7304.5190 01	高温承压用合金钢无缝钢管(抗拉强度≥620MPa、屈服强度≥440MPa)(外径在127mm以上(含127mm),化学成分(wt%)中碳(C)的含量≥0.07且≤0.13、铬(Cr)的含量≥8.5且≤9.5、钼(Mo)的含量≥0.3且≤0.6、钨(W)的含量≥1.5且≤2.0、抗拉强度≥620Mpa、屈服强度≥440Mpa)〔101 无缝钢管压力管道,102 无缝钢管〕	4		17	13/	10	千克	A	M	/44
7304.5190 90	冷轧的其他合金钢制其他无缝管(冷拔或冷轧的)〔101 无缝钢管压力管道,102 无缝钢管〕	4		17	13/	10	千克	A	M	/44
	--其他：									
7304.5910	---锅炉管									
7304.5910 01	高温承压用合金钢无缝钢管(抗拉强度≥620MPa、屈服强度≥440MPa)(外径在127mm以上(含127mm),化学成分(wt%)中碳(C)的含量≥0.07且≤0.13、铬(Cr)的含量≥8.5且≤9.5、钼(Mo)的含量≥0.3且≤0.6、钨(W)的含量≥1.5且≤2.0、抗拉强度≥620Mpa、屈服强度≥440Mpa)〔101 无缝钢管压力管道,102 无缝钢管〕	4		17	13/	10	千克	A	M	/29
7304.5910 90	非冷轧其他合金钢无缝锅炉管(非冷拔或冷轧的)〔101 无缝钢管压力管道,102 无缝钢管〕	4		17	13/	10	千克	A	M	/29
7304.5920	---地质钻管、套管〔101 无缝钢管压力管道,102 无缝钢管〕	4		17	13/	10	千克	A	M	/19
7304.5990	---其他									
7304.5990 01	高温承压用合金钢无缝钢管(抗拉强度≥620MPa、屈服强度≥440MPa)(外径在127mm以上(含127mm),化学成分(wt%)中碳(C)的含量≥0.07且≤0.13、铬(Cr)的含量≥8.5且≤9.5、钼(Mo)的含量≥0.3且≤0.6、钨(W)的含量≥1.5且≤2.0、抗拉强度≥620Mpa、屈服强度≥440Mpa)〔101 无缝钢管压力管道,102 无缝钢管〕	4		17	13/	10	千克	A	M	/44
7304.5990 90	非冷轧其他合金钢制无缝圆形截面管(非冷拔或冷轧的)〔101 无缝钢管压力管道,102 无缝钢管〕	4		17	13/	10	千克	A	M	/44
7304.9000	-其他〔101 无缝钢管压力管道,102 无缝钢管〕	4		17	13/	10	千克	A	M	/39
73.05	**其他圆形截面钢铁管(例如,焊、铆及用类似方法接合的管),外径超过406.4毫米：**									
	-石油或天然气管道管：									
7305.1100	--纵向埋弧焊接的〔101 焊接钢管压力管道,102 焊接钢管〕	7		17	13/	13	千克	A	M	/32
7305.1200	--其他纵向焊接的〔101 焊接钢管压力管道,102 焊接钢管〕	3		17	13/	13	千克	A	M	/
7305.1900	--其他〔101 焊接钢管压力管道,102 焊接钢管〕	7		17	13/	13	千克	A	M	/

协定税率 %										特惠税率 %			
亚太5国	东/冰/格	巴基斯坦	韩国	瑞士	哥达	秘鲁	澳大利亚	新西/坡/智	港/澳/台	亚太2国	老/柬/缅	36/3/1	Article Description
													--Cold-drawn or cold-rolled (cold-reduced):
	0/0/0	0	0	0	0	0	0	0//0	0/0/			0/0/0	---Boiler tubes and pipes
	0/0/0	4	0	0	0	0	0	0//0	0/0/			0/0/0	---Geological casing and drill pipes
	0/0/0	0	0	0	0	0	0	0//0	0/0/			0/0/0	---Other
													--Other:
	0/0/0	0	0	0	0	0	0	0//0	0/0/			0/0/0	---Boiler tubes and pipes
	0/0/0	0	0	0	0	0	0	0//0	0/0/			0/0/0	---Geological casing and drill pipes
	0/0/0	0	1.6	0	0	0	0	0//0	0/0/			0/0/0	---Other
													-Other, of circular cross-section, of stainless steel:
													--Cold-drawn or cold-rolled (cold-reduced):
	0/0/0	4	4	0	0	0	0	0/0/0	0/0/			0/0/	---Boiler tubes and pipes
	0/0/0	4	7	0	0	0	0	0/0/0	0/0/			0/0/	---Other
													--Other:
	0/0/0	4	4	0	0	0	0	0/0/0	0/0/			0/0/	---Boiler tubes and pipes
	0/0/0	4	4	0	0	0	0	0/0/0	0/0/			0/0/	---Other
													-Other, of circular cross-section, of other alloy steel:
													--Cold-drawn or cold-rolled (cold-reduced):
													---Boiler tubes and pipes
	0/0/0	0	0	0	0	0	0	0//0	0/0/			0/0/0	Alloy steel seamless steel tubes for pressure and high temperature (tensile strength, yield strength ⩾ 620MPa ⩾ 440MPa ⩾ 127mm) (boiler tube, the chemical composition (wt%) 0.07 ⩽ C ⩽ 0.13, 8.5 ⩽ Cr ⩽ 9.5, 0.3 ⩽ Mo ⩽ 0.6, 1.5 ⩽ W ⩽ 2, cold drawn or cold rolled, whether or not after further processing, including the internal thread)
	0/0/0	0	0	0	0	0	0	0//0	0/0/			0/0/0	Other alloy steel seamless boiler tubes (cold cold drawn or cold rolled, including internal thread)
	0/0/0	0	0	0	0	0	0	0//0	0/0/			0/0/0	---Geological casing and drill pipes
													---Other
	0/0/0	0	0	0	0	0	0	0//0	0/0/			0/0/0	Alloy steel seamless steel tubes for pressure and high temperature (⩾ 620MPa, tensile strength, yield strength ⩾ 440MPa) (chemical composition diameter ⩾ 127mm, (wt%) 0.07 ⩽ C ⩽ 0.13, 8.5 ⩽ Cr ⩽ 9.5, 0.3 ⩽ Mo ⩽ 0.6, 1.5 ⩽ W ⩽ 2, cold drawn or cold rolled, whether or not after further processing)
	0/0/0	0	0	0	0	0	0	0//0	0/0/			0/0/0	Other alloy steel cold rolling for other seamless tubes (cold drawn or cold-rolled)
													--Other:
													---Boiler tubes and pipes
	0/0/0	0	0	0	0	0	0	0//0	0/0/			0/0/0	Alloy steel seamless steel tubes for pressure and high temperature (tensile strength, yield strength ⩾ 620MPa ⩾ 440MPa ⩾ 127mm) (boiler tube, the chemical composition (wt%) 0.07 ⩽ C ⩽ 0.13, 8.5 ⩽ Cr ⩽ 9.5, 0.3 ⩽ Mo ⩽ 0.6, 1.5 ⩽ W ⩽ 2, non cold drawn or cold rolled, whether or not the further engineering)
	0/0/0	0	0	0	0	0	0	0//0	0/0/			0/0/0	Other non rolled alloy steel seamless boiler tubes (non cold drawn or cold)
	0/0/0	0	0	0	0	0	0	0//0	0/0/			0/0/0	---Geological casing and drill pipes
													---Other
	0/0/0	0	0	0	0	0	0	0//0	0/0/			0/0/0	Alloy steel seamless steel tubes for pressure and high temperature (⩾ 620MPa, tensile strength, yield strength ⩾ 440MPa) (chemical composition diameter ⩾ 127mm, (wt%) 0.07 ⩽ C ⩽ 0.13, 8.5 ⩽ Cr ⩽ 9.5, 0.3 ⩽ Mo ⩽ 0.6, 1.5 ⩽ W ⩽ 2, non cold drawn or cold-rolled, whether or not after further processing)
	0/0/0	0	0	0	0	0	0	0//0	0/0/			0/0/0	Other non rolled alloy steel seamless pipe (non circular cross section of cold drawn or cold rolled)
	0/0/0	0	0	0	0	0	0	0//0	0/0/			0/0/0	-Other
													Other tubes and pipes (for example, welded, riveted or similarly closed), having circular cross-sections, the external diameter of which exceeds 406.4mm, of iron or steel:
													-Line pipe of a kind used for oil or gas pipelines:
	0/0/0	4	4.2	0	0	0	0	0//0	0/0/			0/0/0	—Longitudinally submerged arc welded
	0/0/0	0	0	0	0	0	0	0//0	0/0/			0/0/0	—Other, longitudinally welded
	0/0/0	4	0	0	0	0	0	0//0	0/0/			0/0/0	—Other

税则号列	货品名称〔CIQ 扩展编码及品名—T2 表示见附表 2〕	最惠(%)	暂定税率	普通	增值/消费	出口退税	计量单位	监管条件	检验检疫	特殊证件对美关税
7305.2000	-钻探石油或天然气用套管〔101 焊接钢管压力管道,102 焊接钢管〕	7		17	13/	13	千克	A	M	/
	-其他焊接的:									
7305.3100	--纵向焊接的〔101 焊接钢管压力管道,102 焊接钢管〕	6		30	13/	10	千克	A	M	/31
7305.3900	--其他〔101 焊接钢管压力管道,102 焊接钢管〕	6		30	13/	10	千克	A	M	/26
7305.9000	-其他〔101 焊接钢管压力管道,102 焊接钢管〕	6		30	13/	10	千克	A	M	/
73.06	**其他钢铁管及空心异型材(例如,辊缝、焊、铆及类似方法接合的):**									
	-石油及天然气管道管:									
7306.1100	--不锈钢焊缝管〔101 焊接钢管压力管道,102 焊接钢管〕	7		17	13/	13	千克	A	M	/
7306.1900	--其他〔101 焊接钢管压力管道,102 焊接钢管〕	7		17	13/	13	千克	A	M	/32
	-钻探石油及天然气用的套管及导管:									
7306.2100	--不锈钢焊缝管〔101 焊接钢管压力管道,102 焊接钢管〕	3		17	13/	13	千克	A	M	/23
7306.2900	--其他〔101 无缝钢管压力管道,102 焊接钢管压力管道,103 无缝钢管,104 焊接钢管〕	3		17	13/	13	千克	A	M	/23
	-铁或非合金钢的其他圆形截面焊缝管:									
	---外径不超 10 毫米的:									
7306.3011	----壁厚在 0.7 毫米及以下〔101〕	3		30	13/	13	千克			/28
7306.3019	----其他〔101〕	3		30	13/	10	千克			/23
7306.3090	---其他〔101〕	3		30	13/	10	千克			/28
7306.4000	-不锈钢的其他圆形截面细焊缝管〔101〕	6		30	13/	10	千克			/16
7306.5000	-其他合金钢的圆形截面细焊缝管〔101〕	3		30	13/	10	千克			/28
	-非圆形截面的其他焊缝管:									
7306.6100	--矩形或正方形截面的〔101 焊接钢管压力管道,102 铸铁管压力管道,103 其它铸铁管压力管道〕	3		30	13/	10	千克			/23
7306.6900	--其他非圆形截面的〔101 焊接钢管压力管道,102 铸铁管压力管道〕	3		30	13/	10	千克			/23
7306.9000	-其他									
7306.9000 10	多壁式管道(直接与化学品接触表面由特殊耐腐蚀材料制成)〔101 无缝钢管压力管道,102 焊接钢管压力管道,103 铸铁管压力管道,104 无缝钢管,105 焊接钢管,106 铸铁管,107 其他钢铁及制品〕	6		30	13/	10	千克/个	3A	M	/26
7306.9000 90	未列名其他钢铁管及空心异型材〔101 无缝钢管压力管道,102 焊接钢管压力管道,103 铸铁管压力管道,104 无缝钢管,105 焊接钢管,106 铸铁管,107 其他钢铁及制品〕	6		30	13/	10	千克/个	A	M	/26
73.07	**钢铁管子附件(例如,接头、肘管、管套):**									
	-铸件:									
7307.1100	--无可锻性铸铁制〔101 其它金属制法兰及管件压力管件,102 其它金属制法兰及管件〕	5		20	13/	13	千克			/15
7307.1900	--其他〔101 其它金属制法兰及管件压力管件,102 其它金属制法兰及管件,103 其他金属及制品〕	8		20	13/	13	千克			/18
	-其他,不锈钢制:									
7307.2100	--法兰〔999〕	8		20	13/	13	千克			/18
7307.2200	--螺纹肘管、弯管及管套〔101 不锈钢制螺纹管子附件压力管件,102 不锈钢制其它管子附件〕	8		20	13/	13	千克			/18
7307.2300	--对焊件〔101 不锈钢制对焊件管子附件压力管件,102 不锈钢制其它管子附件〕	8		20	13/	13	千克			/18
7307.2900	--其他〔101 不锈钢制对焊件管子附件压力管件,102 不锈钢制其它管子附件〕	8		20	13/	13	千克			/18
	-其他:									
7307.9100	--法兰〔101 其它金属制法兰及管件压力管件,102 其它金属制法兰及管件〕	7		20	13/	13	千克			/27
7307.9200	--螺纹肘管、弯管及管套〔101 其它金属制法兰及管件压力管件,102 其它金属制法兰及管件,103 其他金属及制品〕	4		20	13/	13	千克			/24
7307.9300	--对焊件〔101 其它金属制法兰及管件压力管件,102 其它金属制法兰及管件〕	7		20	13/	13	千克			/32
7307.9900	--其他〔101 其它金属制法兰及管件压力管件,102 其它金属制法兰及管件〕	4		20	13/	13	千克			/14
73.08	**钢铁结构体(税目 94.06 的活动房屋除外)及其部件(例如,桥梁及桥梁体段、闸门、塔楼、格构杆、屋顶、屋顶框架、门窗及其框架、门槛、百叶窗、栏杆、支柱及立柱);上述结构体用的已加工钢铁板、杆、角材、型材、异型材、管子及类似品:**									
7308.1000	-桥梁及桥梁体段〔999〕	8		30	13/	13	千克			/

协定税率 %										特惠税率 %			
亚太5国	东/冰/格	巴基斯坦	韩国	瑞士	哥达	秘鲁	澳大利亚	新西/坡/智	港/澳/台	亚太2国	老/柬/缅	36/3/1	Article Description
	0/0/0	4	0	0	0	0	0	0//0	0/0/			0/0/C	-Casing of a kind used in drilling for oil or gas
													-Other, welded:
	0/0/0	0	3.6	0	0	0	0	0//0	0/0/			0/0/C	--Longitudinally welded
	0/0/0	0	3.6	0	0	0	0	0//0	0/0/			0/0/0	--Other
	0/0/0	0	0	0	0	0	0	0//0	0/0/			0/0/0	-Other
													Other tubes, pipes and hollow profiles (for example, open seam or welded, riveted or similarly closed), of iron or steel:
													-Line pipe of a kind used for oil or gas pipelines:
	0/0/0	4	2.8	0	0	0	0	0//0	0/0/			0/0/0	--Welded, of stainless steel
	0/0/0	4	4.2	0	0	0	0	0//0	0/0/			0/0/0	--other
													-Casing and tubing of a kind used in drilling for oil or gas:
	0/0/0	0	0	0	0	0	0	0//0	0/0/			0/0/0	--Welded of stainless steel
	0/0/0	0	0	0	0	0	0	0//0	0/0/			0/0/0	--Welded other
													-Other, welded, of circular cross-section, of iron or non-alloy steel:
													---Having an Outeside diameter not exceedins 10mm:
	0/0/0	0	0	0	0	0	0	0//0	0/0/			0/0/0	----Having a wall thickness of 0.7mm or less
	0/0/0	0	1.8	0	0	0	0	0//0	0/0/			0/0/0	----Other
	0/0/0	0	1.8	0	0	0	0	0//0	0/0/			0/0/0	---Other
	0/0/0	0		0	0	0	0	0//0	0/0/			0/0/0	-Other, welded, of circular cross-section, of stainless steel
	0/0/0	0	1.8	0	0	0	0	0//0	0/0/			0/0/0	-Other, welded, of circular cross-section, of other alloy steel
													-Other, welded, of non-circular cross-section:
	0/0/0	0	0	0	0	0	0	0//0	0/0/			0/0/0	--Of square or rectangular cross-section
	0/0/0	0	1.8	0	0	0	0	0//0	0/0/			0/0/0	--Of other non-circular cross section
													-Other
	0/0/0	0		0	0	0	0	0//0	0/0/			0/0/0	Multiple-wall channel (produced by special erosionproof materials)
	0/0/0	0		0	0	0	0	0//0	0/0/			0/0/0	Other tubes, pipes and hollow profiles, not elsewhere specified or included
													Tube or pipe fittings (for example, couplings, elbows, sleeves), of iron or steel:
													-Cast fittings:
	0/0/0	0	0	0	0	0	0	0//0	0/0/			0/0/0	--Of non-malleable cast iron
	0/0/0	4	0	2.4	0	0	0	0//0	0/0/			0/0/0	--Other
													-Other, of stainless steel:
6.4	0/0/0	4	0	0	0	0	0	0//0	0/0/			0/0/0	--Flanges
	0/0/0	4	0	0	0	0	0	0//0	0/0/			0/0/0	--Threaded elbows, bends and sleeves
	0/0/0	4	0	0	0	0	0	0//0	0/0/			0/0/0	--Butt welding fittings
	0/0/0	4		2.5	0	0	0	0//0	0/0/			0/0/0	--Other
													-Other:
	0/0/0	4	4.2	0	0	0	0	0//0	0/0/			0/0/0	--Flanges
	0/0/0	0	0	0	0	0	0	0//0	0/0/			0/0/0	--Threaded elbows, bends and sleeves
	0/0/0	4	0	0	0	0	0	0//0	0/0/			0/0/0	--Butt welding fittings
	0/0/0	0	0	0	0	0	0	0//0	0/0/			0/0/0	--Other
													Structures (excluding prefabricated buildings of heading No. 94.06) and parts of structures (for example, bridges and bridge-sections, lock-gates, towers, lattice masts, roofs, roofing frameworks, doors and windows and their frames and thresholds for doors, shutters, balustrades, pillars and columns), of iron or steel; plates, rods, angles, shapes, sections, tubes and the like, prepared for use in structures, of iron or steel:
	0/0/0	0	0	0	0	0	0	0//0	0/0/			0/0/0	-Bridges and bridge-sections

税则号列	货品名称〔CIQ扩展编码及品名—T2表示见附表2〕	最惠(%)	暂定税率	普通	增值/消费	出口退税	计量单位	监管条件	检验检疫	特殊证件对美关税
7308.2000	-塔楼及格构杆〔999〕	8		30	13/	13	千克			/28
7308.3000	-门窗及其框架、门槛〔999〕	8		50	13/	13	千克		L	/33
7308.4000	-脚手架、模板或坑道支撑用的支柱及类似设备〔999〕	8		30	13/	13	千克			/28
7308.9000	-其他〔999〕	4		30	13/	13	千克			/29
73.09	**盛装物料用的钢铁囤、柜、罐、桶及类似容器(装压缩气体或液化气体的除外),容积超过300升,不论是否衬里或隔热,但无机械或热力装置:**									
7309.0000	盛装物料用的钢铁囤、柜、罐、桶及类似容器(装压缩气体或液化气体的除外),容积超过300升,不论是否衬里或隔热,但无机械或热力装置〔999〕	8		35	13/	10	千克			/28
73.10	**盛装物料用的钢铁柜、桶、罐、听、盒及类似容器(装压缩气体或液化气体的除外),容积不超过300升,不论是否衬里或隔热,但无机械或热力装置:**									
7310.1000	-容积在50升及以上									
7310.1000 10	总容积大于100升不超过300升的容器(与所处理或盛放的化学品接触表面由特殊耐腐蚀材料制成)〔999〕	8		40	13/	10	千克/个	3		/33
7310.1000 90	50L≤容积≤300L的其他钢铁制盛物容器(钢铁柜、桶、罐、听及类似容器)〔999〕	8		40	13/	10	千克/个			/33
	-容积在50升以下:									
	--焊边或卷边接合的罐:									
7310.2110	---易拉罐及罐体〔999〕	8		70	13/	10	千克	A	R	/33
7310.2190	---其他〔999〕	8		70	13/	10	千克			/18
	--其他:									
7310.2910	---易拉罐及罐体〔999〕	8		70	13/	10	千克	A	R	/28
7310.2990	---其他〔999〕	8		70	13/	13	千克	A	R	/18
73.11	**装压缩气体或液化气体用的钢铁容器:**									
7311.0010	---零售包装用〔999〕	8		70	13/	10	千克	6A	M	/18
7311.0090	---其他〔999〕	8		17	13/	13	千克	6A	M	/18
73.12	**非绝缘的钢铁绞股线、绳、缆、编带、吊索及类似品:**									
7312.1000	-绞股线、绳、缆〔101 其他深加工金属制品,102 钢丝绳,103 其他钢铁及制品〕	4		20	13/	10	千克	A	M	/29
7312.9000	-其他〔101〕	4		20	13/	10	千克			/14
73.13	**带刺钢铁丝;围篱用的钢铁绞带或单股扁丝(不论是否带刺)及松绞的双股丝:**									
7313.0000	带刺钢铁丝;围篱用的钢铁绞带或单股扁丝(不论是否带刺)及松绞的双股丝〔101〕	7		70	13/	10	千克			/17
73.14	**钢铁丝制的布(包括环形带)、网、篱、格栅;网眼钢铁板:**									
	-机织品:									
7314.1200	--不锈钢制的机器用环形带〔101〕	8		20	13/	10	千克			/28
7314.1400	--不锈钢制的其他机织品〔101〕	8		20	13/	10	千克			/33
7314.1900	--其他〔101〕	7		20	13/	10	千克			/27
7314.2000	-交点焊接的网、篱及格栅,其丝的最大截面尺寸在3毫米及以上,网眼尺寸在100平方厘米及以上〔101〕	7		70	13/	10	千克			/27
	-其他交点焊接的网、篱及格栅:									
7314.3100	--镀或涂锌的〔101〕	7		70	13/	10	千克			/32
7314.3900	--其他〔101〕	7		70	13/	10	千克			/17
	-其他网、篱及格栅:									
7314.4100	--镀或涂锌的〔101〕	8		20	13/	10	千克			/18
7314.4200	--涂塑的〔101〕	8		20	13/	10	千克			/18
7314.4900	--其他〔101〕	8		20	13/	10	千克			/33
7314.5000	-网眼钢铁板〔101〕	8		70	13/	10	千克			/33
73.15	**钢铁链及其零件:**									
	-铰接链及其零件:									
	--滚子链:									
7315.1110	---自行车用〔999〕	8		80	13/	13	千克			/
7315.1120	---摩托车用〔101 其他车辆零部件,102 滚子链〕	8		80	13/	13	千克			/

协定税率 %										特惠税率 %			
亚太5国	东/冰/格	巴基斯坦	韩国	瑞士	哥达	秘鲁	澳大利亚	新西/坡/智	港/澳/台	亚太2国	老/柬/缅	36/3/1	Article Description
	0/0/0	0	3.3	0	0	0	0	0//0	0/0/			0/0/0	-Towers and lattice masts
	0/0/0	0	4	0	0	0	0	0/0/0	0/0/			0/0/0	-Doors, windows and their frames and thresholds for doors
	0/0/0	0	0	0	0	0	0	0//0	0/0/			0/0/0	-Equipment for scaffolding, shuttering, propping or pit-propping
	0/0/0	0	0	0	0	0	0	0//0	0/0/			0/0/0	-Other
													Reservoirs, tanks, vats and similar containers for any material (other than compressed or liquefied gas), of iron or steel, of a capacity exceeding 300 L, whether or not lined or heat-insulated, but not fitted with mechanical or thermal equipment:
	0/0/0	4.5	4.2	3.2	0	0	0	0/0/0	0/0/			0/0/0	Reservoirs, tanks, vats and similar containers for any material (other than compressed or liquefied gas), of iron or steel, of a capacity exceeding 300L whether or not lined or heat-insulated, but not fitted with mechanical or thermal equipment
													Tanks, casks, drums, cans, boxes and similar containers, for any material (other than compressed or liquefied gas), of iron or steel, of a capacity not exceeding 300L whether or not lined or heat-insulated, but not fitted with mechanical or thermal equipment:
													-Of a capacity of 50L or more
	0/0/0	4.5	7.3	3.2	0	0	0	0/0/0	0/0/			0/0/0	Containers, 100L<capacity≤300L (surface in contact with chemicals treated or contained is made of special corrosion-resistant materials)
	0/0/0	4.5	7.3	3.2	0	0	0	0/0/0	0/0/			0/0/0	Tanks, casks, drums, cans, boxes and similar containers, 50L≤capacity≤300L, of iron or steel
													-Of a capacity of less than 50L:
													--Cans which are to be closed by soldering or crimping:
	0/0/0	14	7	5.3	0	0	0	0/0/0	0/0/			0/0/	---Cans and tank
	0/0/0	14	7	5.3	0	0	0	0/0/0	0/0/			0/0/	---Other
													--Other:
	0/0/0	14	7	7.3	0	0	0	0/0/0	0/0/			0/0/0	---Pop can and tank
	0/0/0	14	7	7.3	0	0	0	0/0/0	0/0/			0/0/0	---Other
													Containers for compressed or liquefied gas, of iron or steel:
	0/0/0	14	7	5.3	0	0	0	0/0/0	0/0/			0/0/	---For retail packing
	0/0/0	4	4.8	0	0	0	0	0//0	0/0/			0/0/	---Other
													Stranded wire, ropes, cables, plaited bands, slings and the like, of iron or steel, not electrically insulated:
	0/0/0	0	0	0	0	0	0	0//0	0/0/			0/0/	-Stranded wire, ropes and cables
	0/0/0	0	0	0	0	0	0	0//0	0/0/			0/0/0	-Other
													Barbed wire of iron or steel; twisted hoop or single flat wire, barbed or not, and loosely twisted double wire, of a kind used for fencing, of iron or steel:
6.3	0/0/0	4	0	0	0	0	0	0//0	0/0/			0/0/0	Barbed wire of iron or steel; twisted hoop or single flat wire, barbed or not, and loosely twisted double wire, of a kind used for fencing, of iron or steel
													Cloth (including endless bands), grill, netting and fencing, of iron or steel wire; expanded metal of iron or steel:
													-Woven cloth:
	0/0/0	5.4	4.8	6.2	0	0	0	0/0/0	0/0/			0/0/0	--Endless bands for machinery, of stainless steel
	0/0/0	5.4	4.8	0	0	0	0	0/0/0	0/0/			0/0/0	--Other woven cloth, of stainless steel
	0/0/0	3.2	0		0	0	0	0//0	0/0/			0/0/0	--Other
	0/0/0	4	0	0	0	0	0	0//0	0/0/			0/0/0	-Grill, netting and fencing, welded at the intersection, of wire with a maximum cross-sectional dimension of 3mm or more and having a mesh size of $100cm^2$ or more
													-Other grill, netting and fencing, welded at the intersection:
	0/0/0	4	0	0	0	0	0	0//0	0/0/			0/0/0	--Plated or coated with zinc
	0/0/0	4	2.8	0	0	0	0	0//0	0/0/			0/0/0	--Other
													-Other grill, netting and fencing:
6	0/0/0	4	0	0	0	0	0	0//0	0/0/			0/0/0	--Plated or coated with zinc
	0/0/0	4	3.2	2.4	0	0	0	0//0	0/0/			0/0/0	--Coated whith plastics
	0/0/0	4	0	2.4	0	0	0	0//0	0/0/			0/0/0	--Other
	0/0/0	4	0	0	0	0	0	0//0	0/0/			0/0/0	-Expanded metal
													Chain and parts thereof, of iron or steel:
													-Articulated link chain and parts thereof:
													--Roller chain:
	0/0/0	4.8	4.8	3.6	0	0	0	0/0/0	0/0/			0/0/	---For bicycles
	0/0/0	5.4	7.2	3.6	0	0	0	0/0/0	0/0/			0/0/	---For motorcycles

税则号列		货品名称〔CIQ扩展编码及品名－T2表示见附表2〕	最惠(%)	暂定税率	普通	增值/消费	出口退税	计量单位	监管条件	检验检疫	特殊证件对美关税
7315.1190		---其他〔999〕	8		80	13/	13	千克			/33
7315.1200		--其他链〔999〕	8		80	13/	13	千克			/18
7315.1900		--零件〔999〕	8		80	13/	13	千克			/28
7315.2000		-防滑链〔999〕	8		80	13/	13	千克			/28
		-其他链：									
7315.8100		--日字环节链〔999〕	8		80	13/	13	千克			/33
7315.8200		--其他焊接链〔999〕	8		80	13/	13	千克			/33
7315.8900		--其他〔999〕	8		80	13/	13	千克			/33
7315.9000		-其他零件〔999〕	8		80	13/	13	千克			/33
73.16		**钢铁锚、多爪锚及其零件：**									
7316.0000		钢铁锚、多爪锚及其零件〔999〕	8		40	13/	13	千克			/28
73.17		**钢铁制的钉、平头钉、图钉、波纹钉、U形钉(税目83.05的货品除外)及类似品，不论钉头是否用其他材料制成，但不包括铜头钉：**									
7317.0000		钢铁制的钉、平头钉、图钉、波纹钉、U形钉(税目83.05的货品除外)及类似品，不论钉头是否用其他材料制成，但不包括铜头钉〔999〕	8		80	13/	10	千克			/18
73.18		**钢铁制的螺钉、螺栓、螺母、方头螺钉、钩头螺钉、铆钉、销、开尾销、垫圈(包括弹簧垫圈)及类似品：**									
		-螺纹制品：									
7318.1100		--方头螺钉〔999〕	8		80	13/	10	千克			/18
7318.1200		--其他木螺钉									
7318.1200	01	非用于民用航空器维护和修理的其他木螺钉(不包括不锈钢紧固件)〔999〕	8		80	13/	10	千克			/33
7318.1200	90	其他木螺钉〔999〕	8		80	13/	10	千克			/33
7318.1300		--钩头螺钉及环头螺钉〔999〕	8		80	13/	10	千克			/18
7318.1400		--自攻螺钉									
7318.1400	01	非用于民用航空器维护和修理的自攻螺钉(不包括不锈钢紧固件)〔999〕	8		80	13/	10	千克			/28
7318.1400	90	其他自攻螺钉〔999〕	8		80	13/	10	千克			/28
		--其他螺钉及螺栓，不论是否带有螺母或垫圈：									
7318.1510		---抗拉强度≥800兆帕的									
7318.1510	01	抗拉强度≥800兆帕，杆径＞6mm的其他螺钉及螺栓(不包括不锈钢紧固件)(不论是否带有螺母或垫圈，非用于民用航空器维护和修理的)〔999〕	8		80	13/	10	千克			/18
7318.1510	90	其他抗拉强度≥800兆帕的螺钉及螺栓(不论是否带有螺母或垫圈)〔999〕	8		80	13/	10	千克			/18
7318.1590		---其他									
7318.1590	01	杆径＞6mm的其他螺钉及螺栓(不包括不锈钢紧固件)(不论是否带有螺母或垫圈，非用于民用航空器维护和修理的)〔101螺钉，102螺栓〕	8		80	13/	10	千克			/28
7318.1590	90	其他螺钉及螺栓(不论是否带有螺母或垫圈)〔101螺钉，102螺栓〕	8		80	13/	10	千克			/28
7318.1600		--螺母〔999〕	8		80	13/	10	千克			/18
7318.1900		--其他〔999〕	5		80	13/	10	千克			/15
		-无螺纹制品：									
7318.2100		--弹簧垫圈及其他防松垫圈									
7318.2100	01	弹簧垫圈及其他防松垫圈(不包括不锈钢紧固件)(非用于民用航空器维护和修理的)〔999〕	8		80	13/	10	千克			/28
7318.2100	90	其他弹簧垫圈及其他防松垫圈〔999〕	8		80	13/	10	千克			/28
7318.2200		--其他垫圈									
7318.2200	01	其他垫圈(不包括不锈钢紧固件)(非用于民用航空器维护和修理的)〔999〕	8		80	13/	10	千克			/18
7318.2200	90	其他垫圈〔999〕	8		80	13/	10	千克			/18
7318.2300		--铆钉〔999〕	8		80	13/	10	千克			/28
7318.2400		--销及开尾销〔999〕	8		80	13/	10	千克			/18
7318.2900		--其他〔999〕	8		80	13/	10	千克			/18
73.19		**钢铁制的手工缝针、编织针、引针、钩针、刺绣穿孔锥及类似制品；其他税目未列名的钢铁制安全别针及其他别针：**									

协定税率 %										特惠税率 %			
亚太5国	东/冰/格	巴基斯坦	韩国	瑞士	哥达	秘鲁	澳大利亚	新西/坡/智	港/澳/台	亚太2国	老/柬/缅	36/3/1	Article Description
	0/0/0	5.4	4.8	3.6	0	0	0	0/0/0	0/0/			0/0/	---Other
	0/0/0	5.4	8.4	3.6	0	0	0	0/0/0	0/0/			0/0/	--Other chain
	0/0/0	5.4	4.8	3.6	0	0	0	0/0/0	0/0/			0/0/	--Parts
	0/0/0	5.4	4.8	3.6	0	0	0	0/0/0	0/0/			0/0/	-Skid chain
													-Other chain:
	0/0/0	5.4	4.8	3.6	0	0	0	0/0/0	0/0/			0/0/	--Stud-link
	0/0/0	5.4	4.8	3.6	0	0	0	0/0/0	0/0/			0/0/0	--Other, welded link
	0/0/0	5.4	4.8	3.6	0	0	0	0/0/0	0/0/			0/0/	--Other
	0/0/0	4	4	0	0	0	0	0//0	0/0/			0/0/	-Other parts
													Anchors, grapnels and parts thereof, of iron or steel:
	0/0/0	4	4	0	0	0	0	0//0	0/0/			0/0/	Anchors, grapnels and parts thereof, of iron or steel
													Nails, tacks, drawing pins, corrugated nails, staples (other than those of heading No. 83.05) and similar articles, of iron or steel, whether or not with heads of other material, but excluding such articles with heads of copper:
	0/0/0	4.5	4	0	0	0	0	0//0	0/0/			0/0/	Nails, tacks, drawing pins, corrugated nails, staples (other than those of heading No. 83.05) and similar articles, of iron or steel, whether or not with heads of other material, but excluding such articles with heads of copper
													Screws, bolts, nuts, coach screws, screw hooks, rivets, cotters, cotter-pins, washers (including spring washers) and similar articles, of iron of steel:
													-Threaded articles:
	0/0/0	4		0	0	0	0	0//0	0/0/			0/0/	--Coach screws
													--Other wood screws
	0/0/0	4	4	0	0	0	0	0//0	0/0/			0/0/	Other wood screws, not used for the maintenance and repair of Civil Aircraft (excluding stainless steel fasteners)
	0/0/0	4	4	0	0	0	0	0//0	0/0/			0/0/	Other screws of wood
	0/0/0	4		0	0	0	0	0//0	0/0/			0/0/	--Screw hooks and screw rings
													--Self-tapping screws
	0/0/0	4		3	0	0	0	0/0/0	0/0/			0/0/	Self-tapping screws, not used for the maintenance and repair of Civil Aircraft (excluding stainless steel fasteners)
	0/0/0	4		3	0	0	0	0/0/0	0/0/			0/0/	Other self-tapping screws
													--Other screws and bolts, whether or not with their nuts or washers:
													---Tensile strength≥800MPa
4	0/0/0	0	4.8	2.4	0	0	0	0//0	0/0/			0/0/0	Other screws and bolts, with tensile strength 800MPa or more, stem diameters exceeding 6mm (whether or not with their nuts or washers, not used for the maintenance and repair of Civil Aircraft) (excluding stainless steel fasteners)
4	0/0/0	0	4.8	2.4	0	0	0	0//0	0/0/			0/0/0	Other screws and bolts, tensile strength≥800MPa (whether or not with their nuts or washers)
													---Other
4	0/0/0	0	4.8	2.4	0	0	0	0//0	0/0/			0/0/0	Other screws and bolts, stem diameter more than 6mm (whether or not with their nuts or washers, not used for the maintenance and repair of Civil Aircraft) (excluding stainless steel fasteners)
4	0/0/0	0	4.8	2.4	0	0	0	0//0	0/0/			0/0/0	Other screws and bolts, (whether or not with their nuts or washers)
	0/0/0	4		2.4	0	0	0	0//0	0/0/			0/0/0	--Nuts
	0/0/0	0	0	0	0	0	0	0//0	0/0/			0/0/0	--Other
													-Non-threaded articles:
													--Spring washers and other lock washers
	0/0/0	4		0	0	0	0	0/0/0	0/0/			0/0/0	Spring washers and other lock washers (not used for the maintenance and repair of Civil Aircraft) (excluding stainless steel fasteners)
	0/0/0	4		0	0	0	0	0/0/0	0/0/			0/0/0	Other spring washers and other lock washers
													--Other washers
	0/0/4	4.5		0	0	0	0	0/0/0	0/0/			0/0/0	Other washers (not used for the maintenance and repair of Civil Aircraft) (excluding stainless steel fasteners)
	0/0/4	4.5		0	0	0	0	0/0/0	0/0/			0/0/0	Other washers
	0/0/0	4		0	0	0	0	0/0/0	0/0/			0/0/0	--Rivets
	0/0/4	4.5	7	3	0	0	0	0/0/0	0/0/			0/0/0	--Cotters and cotter-pins
	0/0/0	4.5		0	0	0	0	0/0/0	0/0/			0/0/0	--Other
													Sewing needles, knitting needles, bodkins, crochet hooks, embroidery stilettos and similar articles, for use in the hand, of iron or steel; safety pins and other pins of iron or steel, not elsewhere specified or included:

税则号列	货品名称〔CIQ 扩展编码及品名—T2 表示见附表 2〕	最惠(%)	暂定税率	普通	增值/消费	出口退税	计量单位	监管条件	检验检疫	特殊证件对美关税
	-安全别针及其他别针：									
7319.4010	---安全别针〔999〕	7		90	13/	10	千克			/27
7319.4090	---其他〔999〕	7		90	13/	10	千克			/32
7319.9000	-其他〔999〕	7		80	13/	10	千克			/27
73.20	**钢铁制弹簧及弹簧片：**									
	-片簧及簧片：									
7320.1010	---铁道车辆用〔999〕	6		14	13/	10	千克			/31
7320.1020	---汽车用〔999〕	8		14	13/	10	千克			/
7320.1090	---其他〔999〕	8		50	13/	10	千克			/28
	-螺旋弹簧：									
7320.2010	---铁道车辆用〔999〕	6		14	13/	10	千克			/26
7320.2090	---其他〔999〕	8		50	13/	10	千克			/18
	-其他：									
7320.9010	---铁道车辆用〔999〕	6		14	13/	10	千克			/31
7320.9090	---其他〔999〕	8		50	13/	10	千克			/28
73.21	**非电热的钢铁制家用炉、灶(包括附有集中供暖用的热水锅的炉)、烤肉架、烤炉、煤气灶、加热板和类似非电热的家用器具及其零件：**									
	-炊事器具及加热板：									
7321.1100	--使用气体燃料或可使用气体燃料及其他燃料的〔999〕	7		80	13/	13	千克/个	6		/32
	--使用液体燃料的：									
7321.1210	---煤油炉〔999〕	7		80	13/	10	千克/个			/
7321.1290	---其他〔999〕	7		80	13/	13	千克/个			/
7321.1900	--其他，包括使用固体燃料的〔999〕	7		80	13/	13	千克/个			/17
	-其他器具：									
7321.8100	--使用气体燃料或可使用气体燃料及其他燃料的〔999〕	7		80	13/	10	千克/个	6		/27
7321.8200	--使用液体燃料的〔999〕	7		80	13/	10	千克/个			/17
7321.8900	--其他，包括使用固体燃料的〔999〕	7		80	13/	13	千克/个			/32
7321.9000	-零件〔999〕	8		80	13/	13	千克			/33
73.22	**非电热的钢铁制集中供暖用散热器及其零件；非电热的钢铁制空气加热器、暖气分布器(包括可分布新鲜空气或调节空气的)及其零件，装有电动风扇或鼓风机：**									
	-散热器及其零件：									
7322.1100	--铸铁制〔999〕	8		80	13/	10	千克			/
7322.1900	--其他〔999〕	8		80	13/	10	千克			/33
7322.9000	-其他〔999〕	8		80	13/	10	千克			/18
73.23	**餐桌、厨房或其他家用钢铁器具及其零件；钢铁丝绒；钢铁制擦锅器、洗刷擦光用的块垫、手套及类似品：**									
7323.1000	-钢铁丝绒；擦锅器及洗刷擦光用的块垫、手套及类似品〔999〕	7		80	13/	10	千克	A	R	/27
	-其他：									
7323.9100	--铸铁制，未搪瓷〔101 食品接触铸铁产品，102 食品用铸铁包装〕	7		80	13/	10	千克	A	R	/27
7323.9200	--铸铁制，已搪瓷〔101 食品接触铸铁产品，102 食品用铸铁包装〕	7		100	13/	13	千克	A	R	/32
7323.9300	--不锈钢制〔101 食品接触不锈钢产品，102 食品用不锈钢包装〕	7		80	13/	13	千克	A	R	/32
	--钢铁(铸铁除外)制，已搪瓷：									
7323.9410	---面盆〔101 食品接触搪瓷产品，102 食品用搪瓷包装〕	7		100	13/	13	千克	A	R	/
7323.9420	---烧锅〔999〕	7		100	13/	13	千克	A	R	/
7323.9490	---其他〔101 食品接触搪瓷产品，102 食品用搪瓷包装〕	7		100	13/	13	千克	A	R	/32
7323.9900	--其他〔101 食品接触铁产品，102 食品用铁包装〕	7		80	13/	13	千克	A	R	/32
73.24	**钢铁制卫生器具及其零件：**									
7324.1000	-不锈钢制洗涤槽及脸盆〔999〕	7		80	13/	13	千克			/27
	-浴缸：									
7324.2100	--铸铁制，不论是否搪瓷〔999〕	7		100	13/	13	千克			/32
7324.2900	--其他〔999〕	7		100	13/	13	千克			/32
7324.9000	-其他，包括零件〔999〕	7		100	13/	13	千克			/17
73.25	**其他钢铁铸造制品：**									
	-无可锻性铸铁制：									
7325.1010	---工业用〔999〕	7		40	13/	10	千克			/27
7325.1090	---其他〔999〕	8		90	13/	10	千克			/33
	-其他：									
7325.9100	--研磨机用的研磨球及类似品〔999〕	8		40	13/	10	千克			/

协定税率 %										特惠税率 %			
亚太5国	东/冰/格	巴基斯坦	韩国	瑞士	哥达	秘鲁	澳大利亚	新西/坡/智	港/澳/台	亚太2国	老/柬/缅	36/3/1	Article Description
													-Safety pins and other pins:
	0/0/0	4	4	0	0	0	0	0//0	0/0/			0/0/0	---Safety pins
	0/0/0	4	4	0	0	0	0	0//0	0/0/			0/0/	---Other
	0/0/0	4		3	0	0	0	0//0	0/0/			0/0/0	-Other
													Springs and leaves for springs, of iron or steel:
													-Leaf-springs and leaves thereof:
	0/0/0	0	0	0	0	0	0	0//0	0/0/			0/0/0	---For railway locomotives and rollingstock
	0/0/0	4	7	0	0	0	0	0//0	0/0/			0/0/0	---For motor vehicles
	0/0/0	4		3	0	0	0	0/0/0	0/0/			0/0/0	---Other
													-Helical springs:
	0/0/0	0	0	0	0	0	0	0//0	0/0/			0/0/0	---For railway locomotives and rollingstock
6.8	0/0/4	4	7	3	0	0	0	0/0/0	0/0/			0/0/0	---Other
													-Other:
	0/0/0	0	0	0	0	0	0	0//0	0/0/			0/0/0	---For railway locomotives and rollingstock
	0/0/0	4.8		3.6	0	0	0	0/0/0	0/0/			0/0/0	---Other
													Stoves, ranges, grates, cookers (including those with subsidiary boilers for central heating), barbecues, braziers, gas-rings, plate warmers and similar non-electric domestic appliances, and parts thereof, of iron or steel:
													-Cooking appliances and plate warmers:
	0/0/0	10.8	6	4.5	0	0	0	0/0/0	0/0/			0/0/	--For gas fuel or for both gas and other fuels
													--For liquid fuel:
	0/0/0		14.7	6.3	0	0	0	0/0/0	0/0/			0/0/	---Kerosene cooking stoves
	0/0/0		14.7	6.3	0	0	0	0/0/0	0/0/			0/0/	---Other
	0/0/0		14.7	6.3	0	0	0	0/0/0	0/0/			0/0/	--Other including appliances for solid fuel
													-Other appliances:
4.2	0/0/0	10.4	16.1	6.9	0	0	0	0/0/0	0/0/			0/0/	--For gas fuel or for both gas and other fuels
	0/0/0		14.7	6.3	0	0	0	0/0/0	0/0/			0/0/	--For liquid fuel
	0/0/0		14.7	6.3	0	0	0	0/0/0	0/0/			0/0/	--Other induding appliances for solid fuel
6.4	0/0/0	4.5	4.8	3.6	0	0	0	0/0/0	0/0/			0/0/0	-Parts
													Radiators for central heating, not electrically heated, and parts thereof, of iron or steel; air heaters and hot air distributors (including distributors which can also distribute fresh or conditioned air), not electrically heated, incorporating a motor-dirven fan or blower, and parts thereof, of iron or steel:
													-Radiators and parts thereof:
	0/0/0		14.7	6.3	0	0	0	0/0/0	0/0/			0/0/	--Of cast iron
	0/0/0		14.7	6.3	0	0	0	0/0/0	0/0/			0/0/	--Other
	0/0/0		12	6	0	0	0	0/0/0	0/0/			0/0/0	-Other
													Table, kitchen or other household articles and parts thereof, of iron or steel; iron or steel wool; pot scourers and scouring or polishing pads, gloves and the like, of iron or steel:
	0/0/0	10.1	5.6	4.2	0	0	0	0/0/0	0/0/			0/0/	-Iron or steel wool; pot scourers and scouring or polishing pads, gloves and the like
													-Other:
	0/0/0		12	6	0	0	0	0/0/0	0/0/			0/0/	--Of cast iron, not enamelled
	0/0/0		12	6	0	0	0	0/0/0	0/0/			0/0/	--Of cast iron, enamelled
4.9	0/0/0	4.5	4.8	3.6	0	0	0	0/0/0	0/0/			0/0/0	--Of stainless steel
													--Of iron (other than cast iron) or steel, enamelled:
	0/0/0		12	6	0	0	0	0/0/0	0/0/			0/0/	---Basin
	0/0/0		12	6	0	0	0	0/0/0	0/0/			0/0/	---Casserole
	0/0/0		12	6	0	0	0	0/0/0	0/0/			0/0/	---Other
	0/0/0		12	6	0	0	0	0/0/0	0/0/			0/0/	--Other
													Sanitary ware and parts thereof, of iron or steel:
	0/0/0		7.2	5.4	0	0	0	0/0/0	0/0/			0/0/0	-Sinks and wash basins, of stainless steel
													-Baths:
	0/0/0	4	4	0	0	0	0	0/0/0	0/0/			0/0/	--Of cast iron, whether or not enamelled
	0/0/0		21	7	0	0	0	0/0/0	0/0/			0/0/	--Other
	0/0/0		17.5	7	0	0	0	0/0/0	0/0/			0/0/	-Other, including parts
													Other cast articles of iron or steel:
													-Of non-malleable cast iron:
	0//0	4	4.2	0	0	0	0	0//0	0/0/			0/0/0	---For technical use
	0/0/0		12	6	0	0	0	0/0/0	0/0/			0/0/	---Other
													-Other:
	0/0/0	4.5	4.2	3.2	0	0	0	0/0/0	0/0/			0/0/	--Grinding balls and similar articles for mills

税则号列	货品名称〔CIQ扩展编码及品名－T2表示见附表2〕	最惠(%)	暂定税率	普通	增值/消费	出口退税	计量单位	监管条件	检验检疫	特殊证件对美关税
	--其他：									
7325.9910	---工业用〔999〕	8		40	13/	10	千克			/18
7325.9990	---其他〔999〕	8		90	13/	10	千克			/33
73.26	**其他钢铁制品：**									
	-经锻造或冲压，但未经进一步加工：									
7326.1100	--研磨机用的研磨球及类似品〔999〕	8		40	13/	13	千克			/18
	--其他：									
7326.1910	---工业用〔999〕	8		40	13/	10	千克			/18
7326.1990	---其他〔999〕	8		90	13/	10	千克			/28
	-钢铁丝制品：									
7326.2010	---工业用〔999〕	8		40	13/	10	千克			/18
7326.2090	---其他〔999〕	8		90	13/	13	千克			/28
	-其他：									
	---工业用：									
7326.9011	----钢铁纤维及其制品〔999〕	8		40	13/	10	千克			/18
7326.9019	----其他〔999〕	8		40	13/	10	千克			/33
7326.9090	---其他〔999〕	8		90	13/	10	千克			/33

协定税率 %										特惠税率 %			Article Description
亚太5国	东/冰/格	巴基斯坦	韩国	瑞士	哥达	秘鲁	澳大利亚	新西/坡/智	港/澳/台	亚太2国	老/柬/缅	36/3/1	
													--Other:
6.8	0/0/0	4.5	4.2	3.2	0	0	0	0/0/0	0/0/			0/0/	---For technical use
4.8	0/0/0	9	12	6	0	0	0	0/0/0	0/0/			0/0/	---Other
													Other articles of iron or steel:
													-Forged or stamped, but not further worked:
	0/0/0	4.5	4.2	3.2	0	0	0	0/0/0	0/0/			0/0/	--Grinding balls and similar articles for mills
													--Other:
	0/0/0	0		3.2	0	0	0	0/0/0	0/0/			0/0/	---For technical use
	0/0/0	0	8	6	0	0	0	0/0/0	0/0/			0/0/	---Other
													-Articles of iron or steel wire:
4	0/0/0	4	4	0	0	0	0	0//0	0/0/			0/0/	---For technical use
5.6	0/0/0	8.1	7.2	5.4	0	0	0	0/0/0	0/0/			0/0/	---Other
													-Other:
													--For technical use:
6.8	0/0/0	0	4.2	3.2	0	0	0	0/0/0	0/0/			0/0/0	----Steel fiber and its products
6.8	0/0/0	0	4.2	3.2	0	0	0	0/0/0	0/0/			0/0/0	----Other
6.8	0/0/0	0	0	2.4	0	0	0	0/0/0	0/0/			0/0/0	--Other

第七十四章
铜及其制品

注释：

本章所用有关名词解释如下：

一、精炼铜

按重量计含铜量至少为99.85%的金属；或按重量计含铜量至少为97.5%，但其他各种元素的含量不超过下表中规定的限量的金属：

其他元素表

元　素		所含重量百分比
Ag	银	0.25
As	砷	0.5
Cd	镉	1.3
Cr	铬	1.4
Mg	镁	0.8
Pb	铅	1.5
S	硫	0.7
Sn	锡	0.8
Te	碲	0.8
Zn	锌	1
Zr	锆	0.3
其他元素*，每种		0.3

*其他元素，例如，铝、铍、钴、铁、锰、镍、硅。

二、铜合金

除未精炼铜以外的金属物质，按重量计含铜量大于其他元素单项含量，但：

(一)按重量计至少有一种其他元素的含量超过上表中规定的限量；

(二)按重量计其他元素的总含量超过2.5%。

三、铜母合金

含有其他元素，但按重量计含铜量超过10%的合金，该合金无实用可锻性，通常用作生产其他合金的添加剂或用作冶炼有色金属的脱氧剂、脱硫剂及类似用途。但按重量计含磷量超过15%的磷化铜(磷铜)归入税目28.53。

四、条、杆

轧、挤、拔或锻制的实心产品，非成卷的，其全长截面均为圆形、椭圆形、矩形(包括正方形)、等边三角形或规则外凸多边形(包括相对两边为弧拱形，另外两边为等长平行直线的“扁圆形”及“变形矩形”)。对于矩形(包括正方形)、三角形或多边形截面的产品，其全长边角可经磨圆。矩形(包括“变形矩形”)截面的产品，其厚度应大于宽度的十分之一。所述条、杆也包括同样形状及尺寸的铸造或烧结产品。该产品在铸造或烧结后再经加工(简单剪修或去氧化皮的除外)，但不具有其他税目所列制品或产品的特征。

线锭及坯段已具锥形尾端或经其他简单加工以便送入机器制成盘条或管子等的，仍应作为未锻轧铜归入税目74.03。

五、型材及异型材

轧、挤、拔、锻制的产品或其他成型产品，不论是否成卷，其全长截面相同，但与条、杆、丝、板、片、带、箔、管的定义不相符合。同时也包括同样形状的铸造或烧结产品。该产品在铸造或烧结后再经加工(简单剪修或去氧化皮的除外)，但不具有其他税目所列制品或产品的特征。

六、丝

盘卷的轧、挤或拔制实心产品，其全长截面均为圆形、椭圆形、矩形(包括正方形)、等边三角形或规则外凸多边形(包括相对两边为弧拱形，另外两边为等长平行直线的“扁圆形”及“变形矩形”)。对于矩形(包括正方形)、三角形或多边形截面的产品，其全长边角可经磨圆。矩形(包括“变形矩形”)截面的产品，其厚度应大于宽度的十分之一。

七、板、片、带、箔

成卷或非成卷的平面产品(税目74.03的未锻轧产品除外)，截面均为厚度相同的实心矩形(不包括正方形)，不论边角是否磨圆(包括相对两边为弧拱形，另外两边为等长平行直线的“变形矩形”)，并且符合以下规格：

(一)矩形(包括正方形)的，厚度不超过宽度的十分之一；

(二)矩形或正方形以外形状的，任何尺寸，但不具有其他税目所列制品或产品的特征。

Chapter 74
Copper and articles thereof

Notes:

In this Chapter the following expressions have the meanings hereby assigned to them:

1. Refined copper

Metal containing at least 99.85% by weight of copper; or metal containing at least 97.5% by weight of copper, provided that the content by weight of any other element does not exceed the limit specified in the following table:

TABLE - Other elements

Element		Limiting content % by weight
Ag	Silver	0.25
As	Arsenic	0.5
Cd	Cadmium	1.3
Cr	Chromium	1.4
Mg	Magnesium	0.8
Pb	Lead	1.5
S	Sulphur	0.7
Sn	Tin	0.8
Te	Tellurium	0.8
Zn	Zinc	1
Zr	Zirconium	0.3
Other elements*, each		0.3

* Other elements are, for example, Al, Be, Co, Fe, Mn, Ni, Si.

2. Copper alloys

Metallic substances other than unrefined copper in which copper predominates by weight over each of the other elements, provided that:

(a) the content by weight of at least one of the other elements is greater than the limit specified in the foregoing table; or

(b) the total content by weight of such other elements exceeds 2.5%.

3. Master alloys

Alloys containing with other elements more than 10% by weight of copper, not usefully malleable and commonly used as an additive in the manufacture of other alloys or as de-oxidants, de-sulphurizing agents or for similar uses in the metallurgy of non-ferrous metals. However, copper phosphide (phosphor copper) containing more than 15% by weight of phosphorus falls in heading No.28.53.

4. Bars and rods

Rolled, extruded, drawn or forged products, not in coils, which have a uniform solid cross-section along their whole length in the shape of circles, ovals, rectangles (including squares), equilateral triangles or regular convex polygons (including "flattened circles" and "modified rectangles", of which two opposite sides are convex arcs, the other two sides being straight, of equal length and parallel). Products, with a rectangular (including square), triangular or polygonal cross-section may have corners rounded along their whole length. The thickness of such products which have a rectangular (including "modified rectangular") cross-section exceeds one-tenth of the width. The expression also covers cast or sintered products, of the same forms and dimensions, which have been subsequently worked after production (otherwise than by simple trimming or de-scaling), provided that they have not thereby assumed the character of articles or products of other headings.

Wire-bars and billets with their ends tapered or otherwise worked simply to facilitate their entry into machines for converting them into, for example, drawing stock (wire-rod) or tubes, are however to be taken to be unwrought copper of heading No.74.03.

5. Profiles

Rolled, extruded, drawn, forged or formed pruducts, coiled or not, of a uniform cross-section along their whole length, which do not conform to any of the definitions of bars, rods, wire, plates, sheets, strip, foil, tubes or pipes. The expression also covers cast or sintered products, of the same forms, which have been subsequently worked after production (otherwise than by simple trimming or de-scaling), provided that they have not thereby assumed the character of articles or products of other headings.

6. Wire

Rolled, extruded or drawn products, in coils, which have a uniform solid cross-section along their whole length in the shape of circles, ovals, rectangles (including squares), equilateral triangles or regular convex polygons (including "flattened circles" and "modified rectangles", of which two opposite sides are convex arcs, the other two sides being straight, of equal length and parallel). Products with a rectangular (including square), triangular or polygonal cross-section may have corners rounded along their whole length. The thickness of such products which have a rectangular (including "modified rectangular") cross-section exceeds one-tenth of the width.

7. Plates, sheets, strip and foil

Flat-surfaced products (other than the unwrought products of heading No.74.03), coiled or not, of soild rectangular (other than square) cross-section with or without rounded corners (including " modified rectangles" of which two opposite sides are convex arcs, the other two sides being straight, of equal length and parallel) of a uniform thickness, which are:

(a) of rectanglular (including square) shape with a thickness not exceeding one-tenth of the width,

(b) of a shape other than rectangular or square, of any size, provided that they do not assume the character of articles or products of other headings.

税目 74.09 及 74.10 还适用于具有花样(例如,凹槽、肋条形、格槽、珠粒及菱形)的板、片、带、箔以及穿孔、抛光、涂层或制成瓦楞形的这类产品,但不具有其他税目所列制品或产品的特征。

八、管

全长截面及管壁厚度相同并只有一个闭合空间的空心产品,成卷或非成卷的,其截面为圆形、椭圆形、矩形(包括正方形)、等边三角形或规则外凸多边形。对于截面为矩形(包括正方形)、等边三角形或规则外凸多边形的产品,不论全长边角是否磨圆,只要其内外截面为同一圆心并为同样形状及同一轴向,也可视为管子。上述截面的管子可经抛光、涂层、弯曲、攻丝、钻孔、缩腰、胀口、成锥形或装法兰、颈圈或套环。

子目注释:

本章所用有关名词解释如下:

一、铜锌合金(黄铜)

铜与锌的合金,不论是否含有其他元素。含有其他元素时:

(一)按重量计含锌量应大于其他各种元素的单项含量;

(二)按重量计含镍量应低于 5%[参见铜镍锌合金(德银)];

(三)按重量计含锡量应低于 3%[参见铜锡合金(青铜)]。

二、铜锡合金(青铜)

铜与锡的合金,不论是否含有其他元素。含有其他元素时,按重量计含锡量应大于其他各种元素的单项含量。当按重量计含锡量在 3%及以上时,锌的含量可大于锡的含量,但必须小于 10%。

三、铜镍锌合金(德银)

铜、镍、锌的合金,不论是否含有其他元素,按重量计含镍量在 5%及以上[参见铜锌合金(黄铜)]。

四、铜镍合金

铜与镍的合金,不论是否含有其他元素,但按重量计含锌量不得大于 1%。含有其他元素时,按重量计含镍量应大于其他各种元素的单项含量。

税则号列	货品名称〔CIQ 扩展编码及品名—T2 表示见附表 2〕	最惠(%)	暂定税率	普通	增值/消费	出口退税	计量单位	监管条件	检验检疫	特殊证件对美关税
74.01	**铜锍;沉积铜(泥铜):**									
7401.0000	铜锍,沉积铜(泥铜)									
7401.0000 10	沉积铜(泥铜)〔999〕	2		11	13/	0	千克	9A	M	/
7401.0000 90	铜锍〔999〕	2	0	11	13/	0	千克			/
74.02	**未精炼铜;电解精炼用的铜阳极:**									
7402.0000	未精炼铜;电解精炼用的铜阳极									
7402.0000 01	未精炼铜、电解精炼用铜阳极(含黄金价值部分)〔101 粗铜,102 电解铜〕	2	0	11	0/	0	千克			/25
7402.0000 90	未精炼铜、电解精炼用铜阳极(非黄金价值部分)〔101 粗铜,102 电解铜〕	2	0	11	13/	0	千克			/25
74.03	**未锻轧的精炼铜及铜合金:**									
	-精炼铜:									
	--阴极及阴极型材:									
	---阴极:									
7403.1111	----按重量计铜含量超过 99.9935%的									
7403.1111 01	高纯阴极铜(99.9999%>铜含量>99.9935%)(未锻轧的)〔999〕	2	0	11	13/	0	千克			/25
7403.1111 90	高纯阴极铜(铜含量≥99.9999%)未锻轧的〔999〕	2	0	11	13/	0	千克			/25
7403.1119	----其他〔999〕	2	0	11	13/	0	千克			/25
7403.1190	---阴极型材〔999〕	2	0	11	13/	0	千克			/
7403.1200	--线锭〔999〕	2	0	11	13/	0	千克			/
7403.1300	--坯段〔999〕	2	0	11	13/	0	千克			/25
7403.1900	--其他〔999〕	2	0	11	13/	0	千克			/30
	-铜合金:									
7403.2100	--铜锌合金(黄铜)〔999〕	1	1	14	13/	0	千克			/26
7403.2200	--铜锡合金(青铜)〔999〕	1	1	17	13/	0	千克			/31
7403.2900	--其他铜合金(税目 74.05 的铜母合金除外)〔999〕	1	1	17	13/	0	千克			/31
74.04	**铜废碎料:**									
7404.0000	铜废碎料									
7404.0000 10	以回收铜为主的废电机等(包括废电机、电线、电缆、五金电器)〔999〕	1.5	1.5	11	13/	0	千克	9A	M	/26.5
7404.0000 90	其他铜废碎料〔999〕	1.5	0	11	13/	0	千克	AP	M	/25
74.05	**铜母合金:**									

Headings Nos.74. 09 and 74. 10 apply, *inter alia*, to plates, sheets, strip and foil with patterns (for example, grooves, ribs, chequers, tears, buttons, lozenges) and to such products which have been perforated, corrugated, polished or coated, provided that they do not thereby assume the character of articles or products of other headings.

8. Tubes and pipes

Hollow products, coiled or not, which have a uniform cross-section with only one enclosed void along their whole length in the shape of circles, ovals, rectangles (including squares), equilateral triangles or regularconvex polygons, and which have a uniform wall thickness. Products with a rectangular (including square), equilateral triangular or regular convex polygonal cross-section, which may have corners rounded along their whole length, are also to be taken to be tubes and pipes provided the inner and outer cross-sections are concentric and have the same form and orientation. Tubes and pipes of the foregoing cross-sections may be polished, coated, bent, threaded, drilled, waisted, expanded, cone-shaped or fitted with flanges, collars or rings.

Subheading Note:

In this Chapter the following expressions have the meanings hereby assigned to them:

1. Copper-zinc base alloys (brasses)

Alloys of copper and zinc, with or without other elements. When other elments are present:

(a) zinc predominates by weight over each of such other elements;

(b) any nickel content by weight is less than 5% (see copper-nickel-zinc alloys (nickel silvers)); and

(c) any tin content by weight is less than 3% (see copper-tin alloys (bronzes)).

2. Copper-tin base alloys (bronzes)

Alloys of copper and tin, with or without other elements When other elements are present, tin predominates by weight over each of such other elements, except that when the tin content is 3% or more the zinc content by weight may exceed that of tin but must be less than 10%.

3. Copper-nickel-zinc base alloys (nickel silvers)

Alloys of copper, nickel and zinc, with or without other elements. The nickel content is 5% or more by weight (see copper-zinc alloys (brasses)).

4. Copper-nickel base alloys

Alloys of copper and nickel, with or without other elements but in any case containing by weight not more than 1% of zinc. When other elements are present, nickel predominates by weight over each of such other elements.

协定税率 %										特惠税率 %			
亚太5国	东/冰/格	巴基斯坦	韩国	瑞士	哥达	秘鲁	澳大利亚	新西/坡/智	港/澳/台	亚太2国	老/柬/缅	36/3/1	Article Description
													Copper mattes; cement copper (precipitated copper):
													Copper mattes; cement copper (precipitated copped)
	0/0/0	0	0	0	0	0	0	0//0	0/0/		0//	0/0/0	cement copper (precipitated copped)
	0/0/0	0	0	0	0	0	0	0//0	0/0/		0//	0/0/0	Copper mattes
													Unrefined copper; copper anodes for electrolytic refining:
													Unrefined copper; copper anodes for electrolytic refining
	0/0/0.8	0	0	0	0		0	0//0	0/0/			0/0/0	Unrefined copper, copper anodes for electrolytic refining (containing gold value part)
	0/0/0.8	0	0	0	0		0	0//0	0/0/			0/0/0	Unrefined copper, copper anodes for electrolytic refining (not containing gold value part)
													Refined copper and copper alloys, unwrought:
													-Refined copper:
													--Cathodes and sections of cathodes:
													---Cathodes:
													----Containing at least 99. 9935% by weight of copper
1	0/0/0	0	0	0	0	0	0	0//0	0/0/			0/0/0	Higher purity copper cathode (99. 9999% > copper content > 99. 9935%)
1	0/0/0	0	0	0	0	0	0	0//0	0/0/			0/0/0	Higher purity copper cathode (copper content ≥ 99. 9999%), unwrought
	0/0/0	0	0	0	0	0	0	0//0	0/0/			0/0/0	----Other
	0/0/0	0	0	0	0	0	0	0//0	0/0/			0/0/0	---Sections of cathodes
	0/0/0	0	0	0.6	0	0	0	0//0	0/0/			0/0/0	--Wire-bars
	0/0/0.8	0	0	0	0	0	0	0//0	0/0/			0/0/0	--Billets
	0/0/0.8	0	0	0	0	0	0	0//0	0/0/			0/0/0	--Other
													-Copper alloys:
0.5	0/0/0.4	0	0	0	0	0	0	0//0	0/0/			0/0/0	--Copper-zinc base alloys (brass)
	0/0/0	0	0	0	0	0	0	0//0	0/0/			0/0/0	--Copper-tin base alloys (bronze)
	0/0/0	0	0	0	0	0	0	0//0	0/0/			0/0/0	--Other copper alloys (other than master alloys of heading No. 74. 05)
													Copper waste and scrap:
													Copper waste and scrap
0.8	0/0/0.6	0	0	0	0		0	0//0	0/0/		0//	0/0/0	Waste electric machines, waste wires, cables, mainly for recoverying copper
0.8	0/0/0.6	0	0	0	0		0	0//0	0/0/		0//	0/0/0	Other copper waste and scrap
													Master alloys of copper:

税则号列	货品名称〔CIQ扩展编码及品名—T2表示见附表2〕	最惠(%)	暂定税率	普通	增值/消费	出口退税	计量单位	监管条件	检验检疫	特殊证件对美关税
7405.0000	铜母合金〔999〕	4		17	13/	0	千克			/29
74.06	**铜粉及片状粉末：**									
	-非片状粉末：									
7406.1010	---精炼铜制〔999〕	3		14	13/	0	千克			/13
7406.1020	---铜镍合金(白铜)或铜镍锌合金(德银)制〔999〕	6		40	13/	0	千克			/16
7406.1030	---铜锌合金(黄铜)制〔999〕	6		30	13/	0	千克			/16
7406.1040	---铜锡合金(青铜)制〔999〕	6		30	13/	0	千克			/16
7406.1090	---其他铜合金制〔999〕	6		30	13/	0	千克			/16
	-片状粉末：									
7406.2010	---精炼铜制〔999〕	4		14	13/	0	千克			/14
7406.2020	---铜镍合金(白铜)或铜镍锌合金(德银)制〔999〕	6		40	13/	0	千克			/
7406.2090	---其他铜合金制〔999〕	6		30	13/	0	千克			/31
74.07	**铜条、杆、型材及异型材：**									
	-精炼铜制：									
7407.1010	---铬锆铜制〔999〕	4	4	14	13/	13	千克			/
7407.1090	---其他〔999〕	4	4	14	13/	0	千克			/29
	-铜合金制：									
	--铜锌合金(黄铜)									
	---铜条、杆：									
7407.2111	----直线度≤0.5毫米/米〔999〕	7	7	20	13/	13	千克			/32
7407.2119	----其他〔999〕	7	7	20	13/	13	千克			/32
7407.2190	---其他〔999〕	7	7	20	13/	13	千克			/32
7407.2900	--其他〔999〕	7	7	20	13/	13	千克			/17
74.08	**铜丝：**									
	-精炼铜制：									
7408.1100	--最大截面尺寸超过6毫米〔999〕	4	4	14	13/	13	千克			/29
7408.1900	--其他									
7408.1900 01	其他含氧量＜5PPM的精炼铜丝(截面尺寸≤6mm)〔999〕	4	2	14	13/	13	千克			/27
7408.1900 90	其他截面尺寸≤6mm的精炼铜丝〔999〕	4	4	14	13/	13	千克			/29
	-铜合金制：									
7408.2100	--铜锌合金(黄铜)〔999〕	7	7	20	13/	13	千克			/27
	--铜镍合金(白铜)或铜镍锌合金(德银)：									
7408.2210	---铜镍锌铅合金(加铅德银)丝〔999〕	8	8	40	13/	13	千克			/33
7408.2290	---其他〔999〕	8	8	40	13/	0	千克			/18
7408.2900	--其他〔999〕	7	7	20	13/	13	千克			/17
74.09	**铜板、片及带，厚度超过0.15毫米：**									
	-精炼铜制：									
	--盘卷的：									
7409.1110	---含氧量不超过10PPM的〔999〕	4	4	14	13/	13	千克			/14
7409.1190	---其他〔999〕	4	4	14	13/	13	千克			/29
7409.1900	--其他〔999〕	4	4	14	13/	13	千克			/29
	-铜锌合金(黄铜)制：									
7409.2100	--盘卷的〔999〕	7	7	20	13/	13	千克			/32
7409.2900	--其他〔999〕	7	7	20	13/	13	千克			/32
	-铜锡合金(青铜)制：									
7409.3100	--盘卷的〔999〕	7	7	20	13/	13	千克			/32
7409.3900	--其他〔999〕	7	7	20	13/	13	千克			/32
7409.4000	-铜镍合金(白铜)或铜镍锌合金(德银)制〔999〕	7	7	40	13/	13	千克			/32
7409.9000	-其他铜合金制〔999〕	7	7	20	13/	13	千克			/27
74.10	**铜箔(不论是否印花或用纸、纸板、塑料或类似材料衬背)，厚度(衬背除外)不超过0.15毫米：**									
	-无衬背：									
7410.1100	--精炼铜制〔999〕	4		14	13/	13	千克			/29
	--铜合金制：									
7410.1210	---铜镍合金(白铜)或铜镍锌合金(德银)〔999〕	7		40	13/	13	千克			/27
7410.1290	---其他〔999〕	7		20	13/	13	千克			/27
	-有衬背：									
	--精炼铜制：									

协定税率 %										特惠税率 %			Article Description
亚太5国	东/冰/格	巴基斯坦	韩国	瑞士	哥达	秘鲁	澳大利亚	新西/坡/智	港/澳/台	亚太2国	老/柬/缅	36/3/1	
	0/0/0	0	0	0	0	0	0	0//C	0/0/			0/0/	Master alloys of copper
													Copper powders and flakes:
													-Powders of non-lamellar structure:
	0/0/0	0	0	0	0	0	0	0//0	0/0/			0/0/0	---Of refined copper
4.2	0/0/0	0	0	0	0	0	0	0//0	0/0/			0/0/0	---Of copper-nickel base alloys (cupronickel) or copper-nickel-zinc base alloys (nickel silver)
	0/0/0	0	2.4	0	0	0	0	0//0	0/0/			0/0/0	---Of copper-zinc base alloys (brass)
	0/0/0	0	0	0	0	0	0	0//0	0/0/			0/0/0	---Of copper-tin base alloys (bronze)
	0/0/0	0	0	0	0	0	0	0//0	0/0/			0/0/0	---Other
													-Powders of lamellar structure; flakes:
	0/0/0	0	0	0	0	0	0	0//0	0/0/			0/0/0	---Of refined copper
4.2	0/0/0	0	0	0	0	0	0	0//0	0/0/			0/0/0	---Of copper-nickel base alloys (cupronick el) or copper-nickel-zinc base alloys (nickel silver)
4.2	0/0/0	0	0	0	0	0	0	0//0	0/0/			0/0/0	---Other
													Copper bars, rods and profiles:
													-Of refined copper:
	0/0/0	0	0	0	0	0	0	0//0	0/0/0			0/0/0	---Chrome-zircorium-copper
	0/0/0	0	0	0	0	0	0	0//0	0/0/0			0/0/0	---Other
													-Of copper alloys:
													--Of copper-zinc base alloys (brass):
													---Of copper bars, rods:
	0/0/0	4		2.1	0	0	0	0//0	0/0/0			0/0/0	----Linearity≤0.5mm/m
	0/0/0	4		2.1	0	0	0	0//0	0/0/0			0/0/0	----Other
	0/0/0	4		2.1	0	0	0	0//0	0/0/0			0/0/0	---Other
	0/0/0	4	0	2.1	0	0	0	0//0	0/C/0			0/0/0	--Other
													Copper wire:
													-Of refined copper:
2.6	0/0/0	0	0	0	0	0	0	0//0	0/0/0			0/0/0	--Of which the maximum cross-sectional dimension exceeds 6mm
													--Other
2.6	0/0/0	0	0	0	0	0	0	0//0	0/0/0			0/0/0	Other refined copper wire, containing oxygen less than 5PPM (cross-sectional dimension≤6mmm)
2.6	0/0/0	0	0	0	0	0	0	0//0	0/0/0			0/0/0	Other refined copper wire, cross-sectional dimension ≤6mm
													-Of copper alloys:
	0/0/0	4	4.2	0	0	0	0	0//0	0/0/0			0/0/0	--Of copper-zinc base alloys (brass)
													--Of copper-nickel base alloys (cupronickel) or copper-nickel-zinc base alloys (nickel silver):
	0/0/0	4	0	0	0	0	0	0//0	0/0/			0/0/0	---Wire of nickel copper zinc lead base alloy
	0/0/0	4	0	0	0	0	0	0//0	0/0/			0/0/0	---Other
	0/0/0	4	2.8	0	0	0	0	0//0	0/0/			0/0/0	--Other
													Copper plates, sheets and strip, of a thickness exceeding 0.15mm:
													-Of refined copper:
													--In coils:
	0/0/0	0	0	0	0	0	0	0//0	0/0/			0/0/0	---Containing oxygen not exceeding 10ppm
	0/0/0	0	0	0	0	0	0	0//0	0/0/			0/0/0	---Other
	0/0/0	0	0	0	0	0	0	0//0	0/0/0			0/0/0	--Other
													-Of copper-zinc base alloys (brass):
	0/0/0	4	4.2	2.1	0	0	0	0//0	0/0/0			0/0/0	--In coils
	0/0/0	4	4.2	0	0	0	0	0//0	0/0/0			0/0/0	--Other
													-Of copper-tin base alloys (bronze):
	0/0/0	4	2.8	0	0	0	0	0//0	0/0/0			0/0/0	--In coils
	0/0/0	4	0	0	0	0	0	0//0	0/0/0			0/0/0	--Other
	0/0/0	4	0	0	0	0	0	0//0	0/0/0			0/0/0	-Of copper-nickel base alloys (cupro-nickel) or copper-nickel-zinc base alloys (nickel silver)
	0/0/0	4	2.8	0	0	0	0	0//0	0/0/0			0/0/0	-Of other copper alloys
													Copper foil (whether or not printed or backed with paper, paperboard, plastics or similar backing materials) of a thickness (excluding any backing) not exceeding 0.15mm:
													-Not backed:
2.6	0/0/0	0	0	0	0	0	0	0//0	0/0/0			0/0/	--Of refined copper
													--Of copper alloys:
	0/0/0	4	0	0	0	0	0	0//0	0/0/0			0/0/	---Of copper-nickel base alloys (cupronickel) or copper-nickel-zinc base alloys (nickel silver)
	0/0/0	4	0	0	0	0	0	0//0	0/0/0			0/0/	---Other
													-Backed:
													--Of refined copper:

税则号列	货品名称〔CIQ扩展编码及品名—T2表示见附表2〕	最惠(%)	暂定税率	普通	增值/消费	出口退税	计量单位	监管条件	检验检疫	特殊证件对美关税
7410.2110	---印制电路用覆铜板〔999〕	4		14	13/	13	千克			/29
7410.2190	---其他〔999〕	4		14	13/	13	千克			/29
	--铜合金制：									
7410.2210	---铜镍合金(白铜)或铜镍锌合金(德银)〔999〕	7		40	13/	13	千克			/32
7410.2290	---其他〔999〕	7		20	13/	13	千克			/32
74.11	**铜管：**									
	-精炼铜制：									
	---外径不超过25毫米的：									
7411.1011	----带有螺纹或翅片的〔101〕	4		14	13/	13	千克			/29
7411.1019	----其他									
7411.1019 01	其他含氧量＜5PPM，外径≤25mm的精炼铜管〔101〕	4	2	14	13/	13	千克			/27
7411.1019 90	外径≤25mm的其他精炼铜管〔101〕	4		14	13/	13	千克			/29
7411.1020	---外径超过70毫米的〔101〕	4		14	13/	13	千克			/29
7411.1090	---其他〔101〕	4		14	13/	13	千克			/24
	-铜合金制：									
	--铜锌合金(黄铜)：									
7411.2110	---盘卷的〔101〕	7		20	13/	13	千克			/32
7411.2190	---其他〔101〕	7		20	13/	13	千克			/32
7411.2200	--铜镍合金(白铜)或铜镍锌合金(德银)〔101〕	7		40	13/	13	千克			/17
7411.2900	--其他〔101〕	7		20	13/	13	千克			/27
74.12	**铜制管子附件(例如，接头、肘管、管套)：**									
7412.1000	-精炼铜制〔101其它金属制法兰及管件压力管件，102其它金属制法兰及管件〕	4		14	13/	0	千克			/24
	-铜合金制：									
7412.2010	--铜镍合金(白铜)或铜镍锌合金(德银)〔101其它金属制法兰及管件压力管件，102其它金属制法兰及管件〕	7		40	13/	0	千克			/32
7412.2090	---其他〔101其它金属制法兰及管件压力管件，102其它金属制法兰及管件〕	7		20	13/	0	千克			/27
74.13	**非绝缘的铜丝绞股线、缆、编带及类似品：**									
7413.0000	非绝缘的铜丝绞股线、缆、编带及类似品〔999〕	5		14	13/	0	千克			/30
74.15	**铜制或钢铁制带铜头的钉、平头钉、图钉、U形钉(税目83.05的货品除外)及类似品；铜制螺钉、螺栓、螺母、钩头螺钉、铆钉、销、开尾销、垫圈(包括弹簧垫圈)及类似品：**									
7415.1000	-钉、平头钉、图钉、U形钉及类似品〔999〕	8		80	13/	0	千克			/18
	-其他无螺纹制品：									
7415.2100	--垫圈(包括弹簧垫圈)〔999〕	8		80	13/	0	千克			/28
7415.2900	--其他〔999〕	8		80	13/	0	千克			/28
	-其他螺纹制品：									
	--螺钉；螺栓及螺母：									
7415.3310	---木螺钉〔999〕	8		80	13/	0	千克			/
7415.3390	---其他〔101螺钉，102螺栓，103螺母〕	8		80	13/	0	千克			/28
7415.3900	--其他〔999〕	8		80	13/	0	千克			/18
74.18	**餐桌、厨房或其他家用铜制器具及其零件；铜制擦锅器、洗刷擦光用的块垫、手套及类似品；铜制卫生器具及其零件：**									
	-餐桌、厨房或其他家用器具及其零件；擦锅器及洗刷擦光用的块垫、手套及类似品：									
7418.1010	---擦锅器及洗刷擦光用的块垫、手套及类似品〔999〕	7		80	13/	10	千克	A	R	/17
7418.1020	---非电热的铜制家用烹饪器具及其零件〔101食品接触铜产品，102食品用铜包装〕	7		80	13/	10	千克	A	R	/
7418.1090	---其他〔101食品接触铜产品，102食品用铜包装〕	7		80	13/	10	千克	A	R	/32
7418.2000	-卫生器具及其零件〔999〕	9		80	13/	10	千克			/34
74.19	**其他铜制品：**									
7419.1000	-链条及其零件〔999〕	9		80	13/	0	千克			/34
	-其他：									
	--铸造、模压、冲压或锻造，但未经进一步加工的：									
7419.9110	---工业用〔999〕	9		40	13/	0	千克			/29
7419.9190	---其他〔999〕	9		80	13/	10	千克			/19
	--其他：									

协定税率 %										特惠税率 %			Article Description
亚太5国	东/冰/格	巴基斯坦	韩国	瑞士	哥达	秘鲁	澳大利亚	新西/坡/智	港/澳/台	亚太2国	老/柬/缅	36/3/1	
2.6	0/0/0	0	0	0	0	0	0	0//0	0/0/0			0/0/	---Copper-clad board used to print circuit
2.6	0/0/0	0	0	0	0	0	0	0//0	0/0/0			0/0/	---Other
													--Of copper alloys:
	0/0/0	4	0	0	0	0	0	0//0	0/0/			0/0/	---Of copper-nickel base alloys (cupronickel) or copper-nickel-zinc base alloys (nickel silver)
	0/0/0	4	0	0	0	0	0	0//0	0/0/			0/0/	---Other
													Copper tubes and pipes:
													-Of refined copper:
													---Having an outside diameter not exceeding 25mm:
2.6	0/0/0	0	0	0	0	0	0	0//0	0/0/			0/0/0	----Threaded or with fins
													----Other
2.6	0/0/0	0	0	0	0	0	0	0//0	0/0/			0/0/0	Other refined copper wire, containing oxygen less than 5PPM, having an outside diameter not exceeding 25mm
2.6	0/0/0	0	0	0	0	0	0	0//0	0/0/			0/0/0	Refined copper tubing, outer diameter≤25mm
2.6	0/0/0	0	0	0	0	0	0	0//0	0/0/			0/0/0	---Having an outside diameter exceeding 70mm
2.6	0/0/0	0	0	1.2	0	0	0	0//0	0/0/			0/0/0	---Other
													-Of copper alloys:
													--Of copper-zinc base alloys(brass):
6.3	0/0/0	4	0	0	0	0	0	0//0	0/0/			0/0/0	---In coils
	0/0/0	4	4.2	0	0	0	0	0//0	0/0/			0/0/0	---Other
	0/0/0	4	0	0	0	0	0	0//0	0/0/			0/0/0	--Of copper-nickel base alloys (cupronickel) or copper-nickel-zinc base alloys (nickel silver)
	0/0/0	4	0	0	0	0	0	0//0	0/0/			0/0/0	--Other
													Copper tube or pipe fittings (for example, couplings, elbows, sleeves):
	0/0/0	0	0	1.2	0	0	0	0//0	0/0/			0/0/0	-Of refined copper
													-Of copper alloys:
4.6	0/0/2.8	4	0	2.1	0	0	0	0//0	0/0/			0/0/0	---Of copper-nickel base alloys (cupronickel) or copper-nickel-zinc base alloys (nickel silver)
4.6	0/0/0	4	0	0	0	0	0	0//0	0/0/			0/0/0	---Other
													Stranded wire, cables, plaited bands and the like, of copper, not electrically insulated:
	0/0/0	0	3	0	0	0	0	0//0	0/0/			0/0/0	Stranded wire, cables, plaited bands and the like, of copper, not electrically insulated
													Nails, tacks, drawing pins, staples (other than those of heading No. 83.05) and similar articles, of copper or of iron or steel with heads of copper; screws, bolts, nuts, screw hooks, rivets, cotters, cotter-pins, washers (including spring washers) and similar articles, of copper:
	0/0/0	4	0	0	0	0	0	0//0	0/0/			0/0/0	-Nails and tacks, drawing pins, staples and similar articles
													-Other articles, not threaded:
	0/0/0	4	4	0	0	0	0	0/0/0	0/0/			0/0/0	--Washers (including spring washers)
	0/0/0	4	4	0	0	0	0	0/0/0	0/0/			0/0/0	--Other
													-Other threaded articles:
													--Screws; bolts and nuts:
6.4	0/0/0	4	0	0	0	0	0	0//0	0/0/			0/0/0	---Screws for wood
	0/0/0	4	0	0	0	0	0	0//0	0/0/			0/0/0	---Other
	0/0/0	4	4	0	0	0	0	0//0	0/0/			0/0/0	--Other
													Table, kitchen or other household articles and parts thereof, of copper; pot scourers and scouring or polishing pads, gloves and the like, of copper; sanitary ware and parts thereof, of copper:
													-Table, kitchen or other household articles and parts thereof; pot scourers and scouring or polishing pads, gloves and the like:
	0/0/0	13	7.2	5.4	0	0	0	0/0/0	0/0/			0/0/0	---Pot scourers and scouring or polishing pads, gloves and the like
	0/0/0		12	6	0	0	0	0/0/0	0/0/			0/0/	---Cooking apparatus of a kind used for domestic purposes, non-electric, and parts thereof, of copper
	0/0/0	13	7.2	5.4	0	0	0	0/0/0	0/0/			0/0/0	---Other
	0/0/0	0	7.2	5.4	0	0	0	0/0/0	0/0/			0/0/0	-Sanitary ware and parts thereof
													Other articles of copper:
	0/0/0	10.1	5.6	4.2	0	0	0	0/0/0	0/0/			0/0/	-Chain and parts thereof
													-Other:
													--Cast, moulded, stamped or forged, but not further worked:
	0/0/0	4	0	0	0	0	0	0/0/0	0/0/			0/0/0	---For technical use
	0/0/0	20	12	6	0	0	0	0/0/0	0/0/			0/0/	---Other
													--Other:

税则号列	货品名称〔CIQ 扩展编码及品名—T2 表示见附表 2〕	最惠(%)	暂定税率	普通	增值/消费	出口退税	计量单位	监管条件	检验检疫	特殊证件对美关税
7419.9920	---铜弹簧〔101〕	9		40	13/	10	千克			/34
7419.9930	---铜丝制的布(包括环形带)〔101〕	7		20	13/	10	千克			/32
7419.9940	---铜丝制的网、格栅、网眼铜板〔101〕	8		20	13/	10	千克			/18
7419.9950	---非电热的铜制家用供暖器具及其零件〔101 其它装压缩或液化气的容器及其零件,102 深加工铜制品〕	9		80	13/	10	千克			/
	---其他:									
7419.9991	----工业用〔101 其它装压缩或液化气的容器及其零件,102 深加工铜制品〕	9		40	13/	0	千克			/29
7419.9999	----其他〔101 其它装压缩或液化气的容器及其零件,102 深加工铜制品〕	9		80	13/	10	千克			/29

协定税率 %										特惠税率 %			Article Description
亚太5国	东/冰/格	巴基斯坦	韩国	瑞士	哥达	秘鲁	澳大利亚	新西/坡/智	港/澳/台	亚太2国	老/柬/缅	36/3/1	
	0/0/0	4.5	4	3	0	0	0	0//C	0/0/			0/0/	---Copper springs
	0/0/0	5	0	0	0	0	0	0//C	0/0/			0/0/0	---Cloth (cincluding endless bands), of copper wire
	0/0/0	5.8	3.2	0	0	0	0	0//0	0/0/			0/0/0	---Grill and netting、of copper wire expanded metal of copper
6.3	0/0/0	20	12	6	0	0	0	0/0/C	0/0/			0/0/	---Heating apparatus of a kind used for dimestic purposes, non-electric, and parts thereof, of copper
													---Other:
5.9	0//0	4.5	0	3	0	0	0	0/0/0	0/0/			0/0/0	----For technical use
5.9	0/0/0	16	14	6	0	0	0	0/0/0	0/0/			0/0/0	----Other

第七十五章
镍及其制品

注释：

本章所用有关名词解释如下：

一、条、杆

轧、挤、拔或锻制的实心产品，非成卷的，其全长截面均为圆形、椭圆形、矩形（包括正方形）、等边三角形或规则外凸多边形（包括相对两边为弧拱形，另外两边为等长平行直线的"扁圆形"及"变形矩形"）。对于矩形（包括正方形）、三角形或多边形截面的产品，其全长边角可经磨圆。矩形（包括"变形矩形"）截面的产品，其厚度应大于宽度的十分之一。所述条、杆也包括同样形状及尺寸的铸造或烧结产品。该产品在铸造或烧结后再经加工（简单剪修或去氧化皮的除外），但不具有其他税目所列制品或产品的特征。

二、型材及异型材

轧、挤、拔、锻制的产品或其他成型产品，不论是否成卷，其全长截面相同，但与条、杆、丝、板、片、带、箔、管的定义不相符合。同时也包括同样形状的铸造或烧结产品。该产品在铸造或烧结后再经加工（简单剪修或去氧化皮的除外），但不具有其他税目所列制品或产品的特征。

三、丝

盘卷的轧、挤或拔制实心产品，其全长截面均为圆形、椭圆形、矩形（包括正方形）、等边三角形或规则外凸多边形（包括相对两边为弧拱形，另外两边为等长平行直线的"扁圆形"及"变形矩形"）。对于矩形（包括正方形）、三角形或多边形截面的产品，其全长边角可经磨圆。矩形（包括"变形矩形"）截面的产品，其厚度应大于宽度的十分之一。

四、板、片、带、箔

成卷或非成卷的平面产品（税目75.02的未锻轧产品除外），截面均为厚度相同的实心矩形（不包括正方形），不论边角是否磨圆（包括相对两边为弧拱形，另外两边为等长平行直线的"变形矩形"），并且符合以下规格：

（一）矩形（包括正方形）的，厚度不超过宽度的十分之一；
（二）矩形或正方形以外形状的，任何尺寸，但不具有其他税目所列制品或产品的特征。

税目75.06还适用于具有花样（例如，凹槽、肋条形、格槽、珠粒及菱形）的板、片、带、箔以及穿孔、抛光、涂层或制成瓦楞形的这类产品，但不具有其他税目所列制品或产品的特征。

五、管

全长截面及管壁厚度相同并只有一个闭合空间的空心产品，成卷或非成卷的，其截面为圆形、椭圆形、矩形（包括正方形）、等边三角形或规则外凸多边形。对于截面为矩形（包括正方形）、等边三角形或规则外凸多边形的产品，不论全长边角是否磨圆，只要其内外截面为同一圆心并为同样形状及同一轴向，也可视为管子。上述截面的管子可经抛光、涂层、弯曲、攻丝、钻孔、缩腰、胀口、成锥形或装法兰、颈圈或套环。

子目注释：

一、本章所用有关名词解释如下：

（一）非合金镍

按重量计镍及钴的含量至少为99%的金属，但：

1. 按重量计含钴量不超过1.5%；
2. 按重量计其他各种元素的含量不超过下表中规定的限量：

其他元素表

元　　素		所含重量百分比
Fe	铁	0.5
O	氧	0.4
其他元素，每种		0.3

（二）镍合金

按重量计含镍量大于其他元素单项含量的金属物质，但：

1. 按重量计含钴量超过1.5%；
2. 按重量计至少有一种其他元素的含量超过上表中规定的限量；
3. 除镍及钴以外，按重量计其他元素的总含量超过1%。

二、子目号7508.10所称"丝"，不受本章注释三的限制，仅适用于截面尺寸不超过6毫米的任何截面形状的产品，不论是否盘卷。

Chapter 75
Nickel and articles thereof

Notes:

In this Chapter the following expressions have the meanings hereby assigned to them:

1. Bars and rods

Rolled, extruded, drawn or forged products, not in coils, which have a uniform soild cross-section along their whole length in the shape of circles, ovals, rectangles (including squares), equilateral triangles or regular convex polygons (including "flattened circles" and "modified rectangles", of which two opposite sides are convex arcs, the other two sides being straight, of equal length and parallel). Products with a rectangular (including square), triangular or polygonal cross-section may have corners rounded along their whole length. The thickness of such products which have a rectangular (including "modified rectangular") cross-section exceeds one-tenth of the width. The expression also covers cast or sintered products, of the same forms and dimensions, which have been subsequently worked after production (otherwise than by simple trimming or de-scaling), provided that they have not thereby assumed the character of articles or products of other headings.

2. Profiles

Rolled, extruded, drawn, forged or formed products, coiled or not, of a uniform cross-section along their whole length, which do not conform to any of the definitions of bars, rods, wire, plates, sheets, strip, foil, tubes or pipes. The expression also covers cast or sintered products, of the same forms, which have been subsequently worked after production (otherwise than by simple trimming or de-scaling), provided that they have not thereby assumed the character of articles or products of other headings.

3. Wire

Rolled, extruded or drawn products, in coils, which have a uniform soild cross-section along their whole length in the shape of circles, ovals, rectangles (in cluding squares), equilateral triangles or regular convexpolygons (including "flattened circles" and "modified rectangles", of which two opposite sides are convex arcs, the other two sides being straight, of equal length and parallel). Products with a rectangular (including square), triangular or polygonal cross-section may have corners rounded along their whole length. The thickness of such products which have a rectangular (including "modified rectangular") cross-section exceeds one-tenth of the width.

4. Plates, sheets, strip and foil

Flat-surfaced products (other than the unwrought products of heading 75.02), coiled or not, of soild rectangular (other than square) cross-section with or without rounded corners (including " modified rectangles" of which two opposite sides are convex arcs, the other two sides being straight, of equal length and parallel) of a uniform thickness, which are:

(a) of rectanglular (including square) shape with a thickness not exceeding one-tenth of the width,

(b) of a shape other than rectangular or square, of any size, provided that they do not assume the character of articles or products of other headings.

Heading 75.06 applies, *inter alia*, to plates, sheets, strip and foil with patterns (for example, grooves, ribs, chequers, tears, buttons, lozenges) and to such products which have been perforated, corrugated, polished or coated, provided that they do not thereby assume the character of articles or products of other headings.

5. Tubes and pipes

Hollow products, coiled or not, which have a uniform cross-section with only one enclosed void along their whole length in the shape of circles, ovals, rectangles (including squares), equilateral triangles of regular convex polygons, and which have a uniform wall thickness. Products with a rectangular (including square), equilateral triangular, or regular convex polygonal cross-section, which may have corners rounded along their whole length, are also to be considered as tubes and pipes provided the inner and outer cross-sections are concentric and have the same form and orientation. Tubes and pipes of the foregoing crosssections may be polished, coated, bent, threaded, drilled, waisted, expanded, cone-shaped or fitted with flanges, collars or rings.

Subheading Notes:

1. In this Chapter the following expressions have the meanings hereby assigned to them:

(a) Nickel, not alloyed

Metal containing by weight at least 99% of nickel plus cobalt, provided that:

(i) the cobalt content by weight does not exceed 1.5%, and

(ii) the content by weight of any other element does not exceed the limit specified in the following table:

TABLE - Other elements

Element	Limiting content % by weight
Fe Iron	0.5
O Oxygen	0.4
Other elements, each	0.3

(b) Nickel alloys

Metallic substances in which nickel predominates by weight over each of the other elements provided that:

(i) the content by weight of cobalt exceeds 1.5%,

(ii) the content by weight of at least one of the other elements is greater than the limit specified in the foregoing table, or

(iii) the total content by weight of elements other than nickel plus cobalt exceeds 1%.

2. Notwithstanding the provisions of Chapter Note 3, for the purposes of subheading No.7508.10 the term "wire" applies only to products, whether or not in coils, of any cross-sectional shape, of which no cross-sectional dimension exceeds 6mm.

税则号列	货品名称〔CIQ扩展编码及品名—T2表示见附表2〕	最惠(%)	暂定税率	普通	增值/消费	出口退税	计量单位	监管条件	检验检疫	特殊证件对美关税
75.01	**镍锍、氧化镍烧结物及镍冶炼的其他中间产品：**									
7501.1000	-镍锍〔999〕	3	0	11	13/	0	千克	4xy		/
	-氧化镍烧结物及镍冶炼的其他中间产品：									
7501.2010	---镍湿法冶炼中间品〔999〕	3	0	11	13/	0	千克	4xy		/
7501.2090	---其他〔999〕	3	0	11	13/	0	千克	4xy		/25
75.02	**未锻轧镍：**									
	-非合金镍：									
7502.1010	---按重量计镍、钴总量在99.99%及以上的，但钴含量不超过0.005%〔999〕	3	1	11	13/	0	千克	4xy		/26
7502.1090	---其他〔999〕	3	2	11	13/	0	千克	4xy		/27
7502.2000	-镍合金〔999〕	3	3	11	13/	0	千克	4xy		/
75.03	**镍废碎料：**									
7503.0000	镍废碎料〔999〕	1.5	1	11	13/	0	千克	4Axy	M	/26
75.04	**镍粉及片状粉末：**									
7504.0010	---非合金镍粉及片状粉末〔999〕	4		17	13/	10	千克	3		/29
7504.0020	---合金镍粉及片状粉末〔999〕	4		17	13/	10	千克			/14
75.05	**镍条、杆、型材及异型材或丝：**									
	-条、杆、型材及异型材：									
7505.1100	--非合金镍制〔999〕	6		14	13/	10	千克			/16
7505.1200	--镍合金制〔999〕	6		14	13/	13	千克			/16
	-丝：									
7505.2100	--非合金镍制〔999〕	6		17	13/	10	千克			/26
7505.2200	--镍合金制〔999〕	6		17	13/	13	千克			/16
75.06	**镍板、片、带、箔：**									
7506.1000	-非合金镍制〔999〕	6		14	13/	10	千克			/26
7506.2000	-镍合金制〔999〕	6		14	13/	0	千克			/16
75.07	**镍管及管子附件(例如，接头、肘管、管套)：**									
	-镍管：									
7507.1100	--非合金镍制〔101〕	6		17	13/	0	千克			/
7507.1200	--镍合金制〔101〕	6		17	13/	13	千克			/16
7507.2000	-管子附件〔101 镍管压力管道，102 其它金属制法兰及管件〕	6		17	13/	0	千克			/16
75.08	**其他镍制品：**									
	-镍丝布、网及格栅：									
7508.1010	---镍丝布〔101〕	6		20	13/	0	千克			/31
7508.1080	---其他工业用镍制品〔101〕	6		40	13/	0	千克			/31
7508.1090	---其他〔101〕	6		70	13/	0	千克			/16
	-其他：									
7508.9010	---电镀用镍阳极〔101〕	4	4	14	13/	0	千克			/29
7508.9080	---其他工业用镍制品〔101〕	6		40	13/	0	千克			/16
7508.9090	---其他〔101〕	6		70	13/	0	千克			/16

协定税率 %										特惠税率 %			Article Description
亚太5国	东/冰/格	巴基斯坦	韩国	瑞士	哥达	秘鲁	澳大利亚	新西/坡/智	港/澳/台	亚太2国	老/柬/缅	36/3/1	
													Nickel mattes, nickel oxide sinters and other intermediate products of nickel metallurgy
	0/0/0	0	0	0	0	0	0	0//0	0/0/			0/0/0	-Nickel mattes
													-Nickel oxide sinters and other intermediate products of nickel metallurgy:
	0/0/0	0	0	0	0	0	0	0//0	0/0/			0/0/0	---Intermediate products of nickel metallurgy by wet process
	0/0/0	0	0	0	0	0	0	0//0	0/0/			0/0/0	---Other
													Unwrought nickel:
													-Nickel, not alloyed:
	0/0/0	0	0	0	0	0	0	0//0	0/0/			0/0/0	---Containing 99.99% or more than by total weight of nickel and cobalt, but containing cobalt not exceeding 0.005%
	0/0/0	0	0	0	0	0	0	0//0	0/0/			0/0/0	---Other
	0/0/0	0	0	0	0	0	0	0//0	0/0/			0/0/0	-Nickel, alloys
													Nickel waste and scrap:
	0/0/0	0	0	0	0	0	0	0//0	0/0/			0/0/0	Nickel waste and scrap
													Nickel powders and flakes:
	0/0/0	0	0	0	0	0	0	0//0	0/0/			0/0/	---Nickel powders and flakes, not alloyed
	0/0/0	0	0	0	0	0	0	0//0	0/0/			0/0/	---Nickel powders and flakes, alloys
													Nickel bars, rods, profiles and wire:
													-Bars, rods and profiles:
	0/0/0	0	2.4	0	0	0	0	0//0	0/0/			0/0/0	--Of nickel, not alloyed
	0/0/0	0	2.4	0	0	0	0	0//0	0/0/			0/0/0	--Of nickel alloys
													-Wire:
	0/0/0	0	0	1.8	0	0	0	0//0	0/0/			0/0/0	--Of nickel, not alloyed
	0/0/0	0	0	0	0	0	0	0//0	0/0/			0/0/0	--Of nickel alloys
													Nickel plates, sheets, strip and foil:
	0/0/0	0	2.4	0	0	0	0	0//0	0/0/			0/0/	-Of nickel, not alloyed
	0/0/0	0	0	0	0	0	0	0//0	0/0/			0/0/	-Of nickel alloys
													Nickel tubes, pipes and tube or pipe fittings (for example, couplings, elbows, sleeves):
													-Tubes and pipes:
	0/0/0	0	0	3.1	0	0	0	0//0	0/0/			0/0/	--Of nickel, not alloyed
	0/0/0	0	2.4	0	0	0	0	0//0	0/0/			0/0/	--Of nickel alloys
	0/0/0	0	0	0	0	0	0	0//0	0/0/			0/0/	-Tube or pipe fittings
													Other articles of nickel:
													-Cloth, grill and netting, of nickel wire:
	0/0/0	0	0	0	0	0	0	0//0	0/0/			0/0/	---Wire cloth
	0/0/0	0	0	0	0	0	0	0//0	0/0/			0/0/	---Other articles of nickel, for technical use
	0/0/0	0	0	0	0	0	0	0//0	0/0/			0/0/	---Other
													-Other:
	0/0/0	0	0	0	0	0	0	0//0	0/0/			0/0/	---Electroplating anodes
	0/0/0	0	0	0	0	0	0	0//0	0/0/			0/0/	---Other articles of nickel, for technical use
	0/0/0	4	0	0	0	0	0	0//0	0/0/			0/0/	---Other

第七十六章
铝及其制品

注释：

本章所用有关名词解释如下：

一、条、杆

轧、挤、拔或锻制的实心产品，非成卷的，其全长截面均为圆形、椭圆形、矩形（包括正方形）、等边三角形或规则外凸多边形（包括相对两边为弧拱形，另外两边为等长平行直线的"扁圆形"及"变形矩形"）。对于矩形（包括正方形）、三角形或多边形截面的产品，其全长边角可经磨圆。矩形（包括"变形矩形"）截面的产品其厚度应大于宽度的十分之一。所述条、杆也包括同样形状及尺寸的铸造或烧结产品。该产品在铸造或烧结后再经加工（简单剪修或去氧化皮的除外），但不具有其他税目所列制品或产品的特征。

二、型材及异型材

轧、挤、拔、锻制的产品或其他成型产品，不论是否成卷，其全长截面相同，但与条、杆、丝、板、片、带、箔、管的定义不相符合。同时也包括同样形状的铸造或烧结产品。该产品在铸造或烧结后再经加工（简单剪修或去氧化皮的除外），但不具有其他税目所列制品或产品的特征。

三、丝

盘卷的轧、挤或拔制实心产品，其全长截面均为圆形、椭圆形、矩形（包括正方形）等边三角形或规则外凸多边形（包括相对两边为弧拱形，另外两边为等长平行直线的"扁圆形"及"变形矩形"）。对于矩形（包括正方形）、三角形或多边形截面的产品，其全长边角可经磨圆。矩形（包括"变形矩形"）截面的产品，其厚度应大于宽度的十分之一。

四、板、片、带、箔

成卷或非成卷的平面产品（税目76.01的未锻轧产品除外），截面均为厚度相同的实心矩形（不包括正方形），不论边角是否磨圆（包括相对两边为弧拱形，另外两边为等长平行直线的"变形矩形"），并且符合以下规格：

（一）矩形（包括正方形）的，厚度不超过宽度的十分之一；

（二）矩形或正方形以外形状的，任何尺寸，但不具有其他税目所列制品或产品的特征。

税目76.06和76.07还适用于具有花样（例如，凹槽、肋条形、格槽、珠粒及菱形）的板、片、带、箔以及穿孔、抛光、涂层或制成瓦楞形的这类产品，但不具有其他税目所列制品或产品的特征。

五、管

全长截面及管壁厚度相同并只有一个闭合空间的空心产品，成卷或非成卷的，其截面为圆形、椭圆形、矩形（包括正方形）、等边三角形或规则外凸多边形。对于截面为矩形（包括正方形）、等边三角形或规则外凸多边形的产品，不论全长边角是否磨圆，只要其内外截面为同一圆心并为同样形状及同一轴向，也可视为管子。上述截面的管子可经抛光、涂层、弯曲、攻丝、钻孔、缩腰、胀口、成锥形或装法兰、颈圈或套环。

子目注释：

一、本章所用有关名词解释如下：

（一）非合金铝

按重量计含铝量至少为99%的金属，但其他各种元素的含量不超过下表中规定的限量：

其他元素表

元　　素	所含重量百分比
Fe＋Si（铁＋硅）	1
其他元素[①]，每种	0.1[②]

①其他元素，例如，铬、铜、镁、锰、镍、锌。

②含铜成分可大于0.1%，但不得大于0.2%，且铬和锰的含量均不得超过0.05%。

（二）铝合金

按重量计含铝量大于其他元素单项含量的金属物质，但：

1. 按重量计至少有一种其他元素或铁加硅的含量大于上表中规定的限量；

2. 按重量计其他元素的总含量超过1%。

二、子目7616.91所称"丝"，不受本章注释三的限制，仅适用于截面尺寸不超过6毫米的任何截面形状产品，不论是否盘卷。

Chapter 76
Aluminium and articles thereof

Notes:

In this Chapter the following expressions have the meanings hereby assigned to them:

1. Bars and rods

Rolled, extruded, drawn or forged products, not in coils, which have a uniform solid cross-section along their whole length in the shape of circles, ovals, rectangles (including squares), equilateral triangles or regular convex polygons (including "flattened circles" and "modified rectangles", of which two opposite sides are convex arcs, the other two sides being straight, of equal length and parallel). Products with a rectangular (including square), triangular or polygonal cross-section may have corners rounded along their whole length. The thickness of such products which have a rectangular (including "modified rectangular") cross-section exceeds one-tenth of the width. The expression also covers cast or sintered products, of the same forms and dimensions, which have been subsequently worked after production (otherwise than by simple trimming or de-scaling), provided that they have not thereby assumed the character of articles or products of other headings.

2. Profiles

Rolled, extruded, drawn, forged or formed products, coiled or not, of a uniform cross-section along their whole length, which do not conform to any of the definitions of bars, rods, wire, plates, sheets, strip, foil, tubes or pipes. The expression also covers cast or sintered products, of the same forms, which havebeen subsequently worked after production (otherwise than by simple trimming or descaling), provided that they have not thereby assumed the character of articles or products of other headings.

3. Wire

Rolled, extruded or drawn products, in coils, which have a uniform soild cross-section along their whole length in the shape of circles, ovals, rectangles (including squares), equilateral triangles or regular convex polygons (including "flattened circles" and "modified rectangles", of which two opposite sides are convex arcs, the other two sides being straight, of equal length and parallel). Products with a rectangular (including square), triangular or polygonal cross-section may have corners rounded along their whole length. The thickness of such products which have a rectangular (including "modified rectangular") cross-section exceeds one-tenth of the width.

4. Plates, sheets, strip and foil

Flat-surfaced products (other than the unwrought products of heading No.76.01), coiled or not, of solid rectangular (other than square) cross-section with or without rounded corners (including " modified rectangles" of which two opposite sides are convex arcs, the other two sides being straight, of equal length and parallel) of a uniform thickness, which are:

(a) of rectanglular (including square) shape with a thickness not exceeding one-tenth of the width,

(b) of a shape other than rectangular or square, of any size, provided that they do not assume the character of articles or products of other headings.

Headings No.76.06 and 76.07 apply, *inter alia*, to plates, sheets, strip and foil with patterns (for example, grooves, ribs, chequers, tears, buttons, lozenges) and to such products which have been perforated, corrugated, polished or coated, provided that they do not thereby assume the character of articles or products of other headings.

5. Tubes and pipes

Hollow products, coiled or not, which have a uniform cross-section with only one enclosed void along their whole length in the shape of circles, ovals, rectangles (including squares), equilateral triangles or regular convex polygons, and which have a uniform wall thickness. Products with a rectangular (including square), equilateral triangular or regular convex polygonal cross-section, which may have corners rounded along their whole length, are also to be considered as tubes and pipes provided the inner and outer cross-sections are concentric and have the same form and orientation. Tubes and pipes of the foregoing cross-sections may be polished, coated, bent, threaded, drilled, waisted, expanded, cone-shaped or fitted with flanges, collars or rings.

Subheading Notes:

1. In this Chapter the following expressions have the meanings hereby assigned to them:

(a) Aluminium, not alloyed

Metal containing by weight at least 99% of aluminium, provided that the content by weight of any other element does not exceed the limit specified in the following table:

TABLE - Other elements

Element	Limiting content % by weight
Fe+Si(iron plus silicon)	1
Other elements ①, each	0.1②

①Other elements are, for example, Cr, Cu, Mg, Mn, Ni, Zn.

②Copper is permitted in a proportion greater than 0.1% but not more than 0.2%, provided that neither the chromium nor manganese content exceeds 0.05%.

(b) Aluminium alloys

Metallic substances in which aluminium predominates by weight over each of the other elements, provided that:

(ⅰ) the content by weight of at least one of the other elements or of iron plus silicon taken together is greater than the limit specified in the foregoing table;

(ⅱ) the total content by weight of such other elements exceeds 1%.

2. Notwithstanding the provisions of Chapter Note 1 (c), for the purposes of subheading No.7616.91 the term "wire" applies only to products, whether or not in coils, of any cross-sectional shape, of which no cross-sectional dimension exceeds 6mm.

税则号列		货品名称〔CIQ 扩展编码及品名—T2 表示见附表 2〕	最惠(%)	暂定税率	普通	增值/消费	出口退税	计量单位	监管条件	检验检疫	特殊证件对美关税
76.01		**未锻轧铝：**									
		-非合金铝：									
7601.1010		---按重量计含铝量在 99.95%及以上〔999〕	5	5	14	13/	0	千克			/30
7601.1090		---其他〔999〕	5	0	14	13/	0	千克			/25
7601.2000		-铝合金									
7601.2000	10	碱金属含量(钠＋钾＋钙)＜10ppm，氢含量＜0.12 毫升/100 克铝的低碱精炼铝合金〔999〕	7	7	14	13/	0	千克			/32
7601.2000	90	其他未锻轧铝合金〔999〕	7	7	14	13/	0	千克			/32
76.02		**铝废碎料：**									
7602.0000		铝废碎料									
7602.0000	10	以回收铝为主的废电线等(包括废电线、电缆、五金电器)〔999〕	1.5	1.5	14	13/	0	千克	9A	M	/51.5
7602.0000	90	其他铝废碎料〔999〕	1.5	0	14	13/	0	千克	AP	M	/50
76.03		**铝粉及片状粉末：**									
7603.1000		-非片状粉末									
7603.1000	10	颗粒＜500μm 的微细球形铝粉(颗粒均匀，铝含量≥97%)〔101 其他铝及制品，301 属于危险化学品的金属〕	6		30	13/	0	千克	3A	M	/16
7603.1000	90	其他非片状铝粉〔999，301 属于危险化学品的金属，302 低风险金属材料〕	6		30	13/	0	千克	AB	MN	/16
7603.2000		-片状铝粉末〔999〕	7		30	13/	0	千克			/32
76.04		**铝条、杆、型材及异型材：**									
		-非合金铝制：									
7604.1010		---铝条、杆〔999〕	5	5	30	13/	0	千克			/25
7604.1090		---其他〔999〕	5	5	30	13/	0	千克			/30
		-铝合金制：									
7604.2100		--空心异型材〔999〕	5	5	30	13/	13	千克	A	M	/15
		--其他：									
7604.2910		---铝合金条、杆									
7604.2910	10	柱形实心体铝合金(在 293K(20 摄氏度)时的极限抗拉强度能达到 460 兆帕(0.46×10^{9} 牛顿/平方米)或更大)〔999〕	5	5	30	13/	13	千克	3		/15
7604.2910	90	其他铝合金制条、杆〔101 铝条，102 其他铝及制品〕	5	5	30	13/	0	千克			/15
7604.2990		---其他〔999〕	5	5	30	13/	13	千克	A	M	/25
76.05		**铝丝：**									
		-非合金铝制：									
7605.1100		--最大截面尺寸超过 7 毫米〔999〕	8	8	17	13/	0	千克			/33
7605.1900		--其他〔999〕	8	8	17	13/	0	千克			/33
		-铝合金制：									
7605.2100		--最大截面尺寸超过 7 毫米〔999〕	8	8	17	13/	0	千克			/18
7605.2900		--其他〔999〕	8	8	17	13/	0	千克			/18
76.06		**铝板、片及带，厚度超过 0.2 毫米：**									
		-矩形(包括正方形)：									
		--非合金铝制：									
		---厚度在 0.30 毫米及以上，但不超过 0.36 毫米：									
7606.1121		----铝塑复合的〔101 铝板，102 其他铝及制品〕	6	6	50	13/	13	千克			/31
7606.1129		----其他〔999〕	6	4	50	13/	13	千克			/29
		---其他：									
7606.1191		----铝塑复合的〔101 铝板，102 其他铝及制品〕	6	6	30	13/	13	千克			/16
7606.1199		----其他〔999〕	6	6	30	13/	13	千克			/31
		--铝合金制：									
7606.1220		---厚度小于 0.28 毫米〔999〕	6	6	30	13/	13	千克			/31
7606.1230		---厚度在 0.28 毫米及以上，但不超过 0.35 毫米〔999〕	6	6	30	13/	13	千克			/26
		---厚度在超过 0.35 毫米以上，但不超过 4 毫米：									
7606.1251		----铝塑复合的〔101 铝板，102 其他铝及制品〕	6	6	50	13/	13	千克			/31
7606.1259		----其他〔999〕	6	6	50	13/	13	千克			/31
7606.1290		---其他〔999〕	6	6	50	13/	13	千克			/16
		-其他：									
7606.9100		--非合金铝制〔999〕	6	6	30	13/	13	千克			/31
7606.9200		--铝合金制〔999〕	8	8	30	13/	13	千克			/28
76.07		**铝箔(不论是否印花或用纸、纸板、塑料或类似材料衬背)，厚度(衬背除外)不超过 0.2 毫米：**									
		-无衬背：									
		--轧制后未经进一步加工的：									

协定税率 %										特惠税率 %			
亚太5国	东/冰/格	巴基斯坦	韩国	瑞士	哥达	秘鲁	澳大利亚	新西/坡/智	港/澳/台	亚太2国	老/柬/缅	36/3/1	Article Description
													Unwrought aluminium:
													-Aluminium, not alloyed:
	0/0/0	0	2	0	0	0	0	0//0	0/0/			0/0/0	---Containing by weight 99.95% or more of aluminium
2.5	0/0/0	0	0	0	0	0	0	0//0	0/0/			0/0/0	---Other
													-Aluminium alloys
4.6	0/0/0	0	0	0	0	0	0	0//0	0/0/			0/0/0	The content of alkali metals (Na + K + calcium) < 10ppm, low alkali hydrogen content of < 0.12 ml/100 grams of aluminum in the refining process of aluminum alloy
4.6	0/0/0	0	0	0	0	0	0	0//0	0/0/			0/0/0	Other unwrought aluminum alloy
													Aluminium waste and scrap:
													Aluminium waste and scrap
	0/0/0.6	0	0	0	0		0	0//0	0/0/			0/0/0	Aluminium waste wires, cables, hardware and electric appliance, mainly for recoverying aluminium
	0/0/0.6	0	0	0	0		0	0//0	0/0/			0/0/0	Aluminium waste and scrap
													Aluminium powders and flakes:
													-Powders of non-lamellar structure
	0/0/0	0	0	0	0	0	0	0//0	0/0/			0/0/0	Microspherical aluminum powder, granularity < 500μm, containing ≥ 97% by weight of aluminium
	0/0/0	0	0	0	0	0	0	0//0	0/0/			0/0/0	Other powders of non-lamellar structure, of aluminium
	0/0/0	4	0	0	0	0	0	0//0	0/0/			0/0/0	-Powders of lamellar structure; flakes
													Aluminium bars, rods and profiles:
													-Of aluminium, not alloyed:
	0/0/0	0	0	0	0	0	0	0//0	0/0/			0/0/0	---Bars and rods
	0/0/0	0	3	0	0	0	0	0//0	0/0/			0/0/0	---Other
													-Of aluminium alloys:
	0/0/0	0	3	0	0	0	0	0//0	0/0/			0/0/0	--Hollow profiles
													--Other:
													---Bars and rods
3.3	0/0/0	0	3	0	0	0	0	0//0	0/0/			0/0/0	Aluminum alloy bar and rod [tensile strength reaches at least 460 Mpa ($0.46\times10^9 N/m^2$) at 293k (20℃)]
3.3	0/0/0	0	3	0	0	0	0	0//0	0/0/			0/0/0	Other aluminum alloy bar and rod, cross-section perimeter ≤ 210mm
3.3	0/0/0	0	0	0	0	0	0	0//0	0/0/			0/0/0	---Other
													Aluminium wire:
													-Of aluminium, not alloyed:
	0/0/0	4	0	0	0	0	0	0//0	0/0/			0/0/	--Of which the maximum cross-sectional dimension exceeding 7mm
5.2	0/0/0	4	0	0	0	0	0	0//0	0/0/			0/0/	--Other
													-Of aluminium alloys:
	0/0/0	4	0	0	0	0	0	0//0	0/0/			0/0/	--Of which the maximum cross-sectional dimension exceeding 7mm
	0/0/0	4	0	0	0	0	0	0//0	0/0/			0/0/	--Other
													Aluminium plates, sheets and strip, of a thickness exceeding 0.2mm:
													-Rectangular (including square):
													--Of aluminium, not alloyed:
													---Of a thickness of 0.30mm or more but not exceeding 0.36mm:
4.2	0/0/0	0	0	0	0	0	0	0//0	0/0/			0/0/0	----Aluminum-plastic composite
4.2	0/0/0	0	3.6	0	0	0	0	0//0	0/0/			0/0/0	----Other
													---Other:
3.9	0/0/0	0	0	0	0	0	0	0//0	0/0/0			0/0/0	----Aluminum-plastic composite
3.9	0/0/0	0	2.4	0	0	0	0	0//0	0/0/0			0/0/0	----Other
													--Of aluminium alloys:
4.2	0/0/0	0	3.6	0	0	0	0	0//0	0/0/0			0/0/0	---Of a thickness less than 0.28mm
4.2	0/0/0	0	3.6	0	0	0	0	0//0	0/0/0			0/0/0	---Of a thickness of 0.28mm or more but not exceeding 0.35mm
													---Of a thickness more than 0.35mm but not exceeding 4mm:
3.9	0/0/0	0	2.4	1.8	0	0	0	0//0	0/0/			0/0/0	----Aluminum-plastic composite
3.9	0/0/0	0	3.6	1.8	0	0	0	0//0	0/0/			0/0/0	----Other
3.9	0/0/0	0	0	1.8	0	0	0	0//0	0/0/			0/0/0	---Other
													-Other:
	0/0/0	0	3.6	0	0	0	0	0//0	0/0/0			0/0/0	--Of aluminium, not alloyed
	0/0/0	4	6	0	0	0	0	0/0/0	0/0/0			0/0/0	--Of aluminium alloys
													Aluminium foil (whether or not printed or backed with paper, paperboard, plastics or similar backing materials) of a thickness (excluding any backing) not exceeding 0.2mm:
													-Not backed:
													--Rolled but not further worked:

税则号列	货品名称〔CIQ 扩展编码及品名－T2 表示见附表 2〕	最惠(%)	暂定税率	普通	增值/消费	出口退税	计量单位	监管条件	检验检疫	特殊证件对美关税
7607.1110	---厚度不超过 0.007 毫米〔999〕	6		35	13/	13	千克			/31
7607.1120	---厚度大于 0.007 毫米，但不超过 0.01 毫米〔999〕	6		35	13/	13	千克			/16
7607.1190	---其他〔999〕	6		35	13/	13	千克			/31
7607.1900	--其他									
7607.1900 01	化成箔(厚度≤0.2mm)〔999〕	6	3	35	13/	13	千克			/28
7607.1900 90	其他无衬背铝箔(厚度≤0.2mm)〔999〕	6		35	13/	13	千克			/31
7607.2000	-有衬背〔999〕	6		35	13/	13	千克			/26
76.08	**铝管：**									
7608.1000	-非合金铝制〔101〕	8		30	13/	13	千克			/33
	-铝合金制：									
7608.2010	---外径不超过 10 厘米的									
7608.2010 10	外径≤10 厘米的管状铝合金[在 293K(20 摄氏度)时的极限抗拉强度能达到 460 兆帕(0.46×10^9 牛顿/平方米)或更大]〔101 铝管压力管道，102 铝管〕	8		30	13/	13	千克	3A	M	/33
7608.2010 90	外径≤10 厘米的其他合金制铝管〔101 铝管压力管道，102 铝管〕	8		30	13/	13	千克	A	M	/33
	---其他：									
7608.2091	----壁厚不超过 25 毫米									
7608.2091 10	外径＞10 厘米，壁厚≤25 毫米的管状铝合金[在 293K(20 摄氏度)时的极限抗拉强度能达到 460 兆帕(0.46×10^9 牛顿/平方米)或更大]〔101 铝管压力管道，102 铝管〕	8		30	13/	13	千克	3A	M	/33
7608.2091 90	外径＞10 厘米，壁厚≤25 毫米的其他合金制铝管〔101 铝管压力管道，102 铝管〕	8		30	13/	13	千克	A	M	/33
7608.2099	----其他									
7608.2099 10	外径＞10 厘米，其他管状铝合金[在 293K(20 摄氏度)时的极限抗拉强度能达到 460 兆帕(0.46×10^9 牛顿/平方米)或更大]〔101 铝管压力管道，102 铝管〕	8		30	13/	13	千克	3A	M	/18
7608.2099 90	外径＞10 厘米，其他合金制铝管〔101 铝管压力管道，102 铝管〕	8		30	13/	13	千克	A	M	/18
76.09	**铝制管子附件(例如，接头、肘管、管套)：**									
7609.0000	铝制管子附件(例如，接头、肘管、管套)〔101 其它金属制法兰及管件压力管件，102 深加工铝制品压力管件，103 其它金属制法兰及管件，104 深加工铝制品〕	8		35	13/	13	千克			/18
76.10	**铝制结构体(税目 94.06 的活动房屋除外)及其部件(例如，桥梁及桥梁体段、塔、格构杆、屋顶、屋顶框架、门窗及其框架、门槛、栏杆、支柱及立柱)；上述结构体用的已加工铝板、杆、型材、异型材、管子及类似品：**									
7610.1000	-门窗及其框架、门槛〔999〕	9		80	13/	13	千克		L	/29
7610.9000	-其他〔999〕	6		50	13/	13	千克			/26
76.11	**盛装物料用的铝制囤、柜、罐、桶及类似容器(装压缩气体或液化气体的除外)，容积超过 300 升，不论是否衬里或隔热，但无机械或热力装置：**									
7611.0000	盛装物料用的铝制囤、柜、罐、桶及类似容器(装压缩气体或液化气体的除外)，容积超过 300 升，不论是否衬里或隔热，但无机械或热力装置〔999〕	9		35	13/	13	千克			/19
76.12	**盛装物料用的铝制桶、罐、听、盒及类似容器，包括软管容器及硬管容器(装压缩气体或液化气体的除外)，容积不超过 300 升，不论是否衬里或隔热，但无机械或热力装置：**									
7612.1000	-软管容器〔999〕	9		50	13/	13	千克			/34
	-其他：									
7612.9010	---易拉罐及罐体〔101 深加工铝制品，102 食品用铝包装〕	9		100	13/	13	千克	A	R	/34
7612.9090	---其他〔999〕	9		70	13/	13	千克			/19
76.13	**装压缩气体或液化气体用的铝制容器：**									
7613.0010	---零售包装用〔101 装压缩或液化气的铝容器，102 深加工铝制品〕	9		70	13/	13	千克			/19
7613.0090	---其他〔101 装压缩或液化气的铝容器，102 深加工铝制品〕	6		17	13/	13	千克	6		/16
76.14	**非绝缘的铝制绞股线、缆、编带及类似品：**									
7614.1000	-带钢芯的〔999〕	6		20	13/	13	千克	A	M	/16
7614.9000	-其他〔999〕	6		20	13/	13	千克			/26

协定税率 %										特惠税率 %			Article Description
亚太5国	东/冰/格	巴基斯坦	韩国	瑞士	哥达	秘鲁	澳大利亚	新西/坡/智	港/澳/台	亚太2国	老/柬/缅	36/3/1	
3.9	0/0/0	0	3.6	1.8	0	0	0	0//0	0/0/			0/0/	---Of a thickness not exceeding 0.007mm
3.9	0/0/0	0	0	0	0	0	0	0//0	0/0/			0/0/	---Of a thickness exceeding 0.007mm, but not exceeding 0.01mm
3.9	0//0	0	0	0	0	0	0	0//0	0/0/0			0/0/	---Other
													--Other
3.9	0//0	0	2.4	0	0	0	0	0//0	0/0/0			0/0/	Formed foils(thickness≤0.2mm)
3.9	0//0	0	2.4	0	0	0	0	0//0	0/0/0			0/0/	Other aluminum foils without lining back(thickness≤0.2mm)
	0//0	0	3.6	1.8	0	0	0	0//0	0/0/0			0/0/	-Backed
													Aluminium tubes and pipes:
	0/0/0	4	4.8	0	0	0	0	0//0	0/0/			0/0/0	-Of aluminium, not alloyed
													-Of aluminium alloys:
													---Having an outside diameter not exceeding locm
	0/0/0	4	4.8	0	0	0	0	0//0	0/0/			0/0/0	Tube aluminum alloy, outer diameter≤10cm, can reach at least 460 MPa-Pa(0.46×10^9 N/m²) at 293K(20℃)
	0/0/0	4	4.8	0	0	0	0	0//0	0/0/			0/0/0	Other alloy aluminum pipes, outer diameter≤10 cm
													---Other:
													----Having a wall thickness not exceeding 25mm
	0/0/0	4	0	0	0	0	0	0//0	0/0/			0/0/0	Tubular aluminum alloy, outer diameter>10 cm, wall thickness ≤ 25mm, can reach at least 460 MPa(0.46×10^9N/m²) at 293K (20℃)
	0/0/0	4	0	0	0	0	0	0//0	0/0/			0/0/0	Other alloy aluminum pipes, outer diameter>10 cm, wall thickness ≤25mm
													----Ohter
	0/0/0	4	0	0	0	0	0	0//0	0/0/			0/0/0	The tensile strength of tube aluminum alloy can reach at least 460 MPa(0.46×10^9N/m²) at 293K (20℃)
	0/0/0	4	0	0	0	0	0	0//0	0/0/			0/0/0	Other aluminium tubes and pipes, alloys
													Aluminium tube or pipe fittings (for example, couplings, elbows, sleeves):
	0/0/0	4	3.2	0	0	0	0	0//0	0/0/			0/0/0	Aluminium tube or pipe fittings (for example, couplings, elbows, sleeves)
													Aluminium structures (excluding prefabricated buildings of heading 94.06) and parts of structures (for example, bridges and bridge-sections, towers, lattice masts, roofs, roofing frameworks, doors and windows and their frames and thresholds for doors, balustrades, pillars and columns); aluminium plates, rods, profiles, tubes and the like, prepared for use in structures:
	0/0/0	25	17.5	7.5	0	0	0	0/0/0	0/0/			0/0/	-Doors, windows and their frames and thresholds for doors
	0/0/0	0	0	0	0	0	0	0//0	0/0/			0/0/0	-Other
													Aluminium reservoirs, tanks, vats and similar containers, for any material (other than compressed or liquefied gas), of a capacity exceeding 300L, whether or not lined or heat-insulated, but not fitted with mechanical or thermal equipment:
	0/0/0	5.4	4.8	3.6	0	0	0	0/0/0	0/0/			0/0/	Aluminium reservoirs, tanks, vats and similar containers, for any material (other than compressed or liquefied gas), of a capacity exceeding 300L whether or not lined or heat-insulated, but not fitted with mechanical or thermal equipment
													Aluminium casks, drums, cans, boxes and similar containers (including rigid or collapsible tubular containers), for any material (other than compressed or liquefied gas), of a capacity not exceeding 300 l, whether or not lined or heat-insulated, but not fitted with mechanical or thermal equipment:
	0/0/0	4.8	4.8	3.6	0	0	0	0/0/0	0/0/			0/0/0	-Collapsible tubular containers
													-Other:
	0/0/0	30		9	0	0	0	0/0/0	0/0/			0/0/	---Tear tab ends and bodies thereof
	0/0/0	5.4	4.8	3.6	0	0	0	0/0/0	0/0/			0/0/0	---Other
													Aluminium containers for compressed or liquefied gas:
7.2	0/0/0	5.4	4.8	6.2	0	0	0	0/0/0	0/0/			0/0/	---For retail packing
	0/0/0	0	0	0	0	0	0	0//0	0/0/			0/0/	---Other
													Stranded wire, cables, plaited bands and the like, of aluminium, not electrically insulated:
	0/0/0	0	0	0	0	0	0	0//0	0/0/			0/0/0	-With steel core
4.8	0/0/0	0	0	0	0	0	0	0//0	0/0/			0/0/0	-Other

税则号列	货品名称〔CIQ 扩展编码及品名－T2 表示见附表 2〕	最惠(%)	暂定税率	普通	增值/消费	出口退税	计量单位	监管条件	检验检疫	特殊证件对美关税
76.15	**餐桌、厨房或其他家用铝制器具及其零件；铝制擦锅器、洗刷擦光用的块垫、手套及类似品；铝制卫生器具及其零件：**									
	-餐桌、厨房或其他家用器具及其零件；擦锅器及洗刷擦光用的块垫、手套及类似品：									
7615.1010	---擦锅器、洗刷、擦光用的块垫、手套及类似品〔999〕	7		90	13/	13	千克	A	R	/
7615.1090	---其他									
7615.1090 10	铝制高压锅〔101 深加工铝制品，102 食品接触铝产品〕	7		90	13/	13	千克	A	R	/32
7615.1090 90	其他餐桌厨房等家用铝制器具及其零件〔101 深加工铝制品，102 食品接触铝产品，103 食品用铝包装〕	7		90	13/	13	千克	A	R	/32
7615.2000	-卫生器具及其零件〔101 深加工铝制品，102 食品接触铝产品，103 食品用铝包装〕	8		90	13/	13	千克			/18
76.16	**其他铝制品：**									
7616.1000	-钉、平头钉、U 形钉(税目 83.05 的货品除外)、螺钉、螺栓、螺母、钩头螺钉、铆钉、销、开尾销、垫圈及类似品〔101 螺钉，102 螺栓，103 螺母，104 垫圈，105 其它紧固件，106 深加工铝制品〕	8		40	13/	13	千克			/18
	-其他：									
7616.9100	--铝丝制的布、网、篱及格栅〔101〕	8		40	13/	13	千克			/18
	--其他：									
7616.9910	---工业用									
7616.9910 10	高度小于直径的柱形实心体铝合金[在 293K(20 摄氏度)时的极限抗拉强度能达到 460 兆帕(0.46×10^9 牛顿/平方米)或更大]〔101〕	8		40	13/	13	千克	3		/18
7616.9910 90	其他工业用铝制品(不包括铝丝布、网、格栅及栅栏)〔101〕	8		40	13/	13	千克			/18
7616.9990	---其他〔101〕	8		80	13/	13	千克			/18

协定税率 %										特惠税率 %			
亚太5国	东/冰/格	巴基斯坦	韩国	瑞士	哥达	秘鲁	澳大利亚	新西/坡/智	港/澳/台	亚太2国	老/柬/缅	36/3/1	Article Description
													Table, kitchen or other household articles and parts thereof, of aluminium; pot scourers and scouring or polishing pads, gloves and the like, of aluminium; sanitary ware and parts thereof, of aluminium:
													-Table, kitchen or other household articles and parts thereof; pot scourers and scouring or polishing pads, gloves and the like:
	0/0/0	13	7.2	5.4	0	0	0	0/0/0	0/0/			0/0/0	---Pot scourers and scouring or polishing pads, gloves and the like
													---Other
	0/0/0	10.8	10.5	4.5	0	0	0	0/0/0	0/0/			0/0/0	Aluminum pressure cooker
	0/0/0	10.8	10.5	4.5	0	0	0	0/0/0	0/0/			0/0/0	Other household aluminum utensils used on dining tables and in kitchens and parts thereof
	0/0/0	13	7.2	5.4	0	0	0	0/0/0	0/0/			0/0/	-Sanitary ware and parts thereof
													Other articles of aluminium:
5.2	0/0/0	4	4	0	0	0	0	0/0/0	0/0/			0/0/0	-Nails, tacks, staples (other than those of heading 83.05), screws, bolts, nuts, screw hooks, rivets, cotters, cotter-pins, washers and similar articles
													-Other:
3	0/0/0	8	4	0	0	0	0	0/0/0	0/0/			0/0/0	--Cloth, grill, netting and fencing, of aluminium wire
													--Other:
													---For technical use
5.2	0/0/0	4.5	7	3	0	0	0	0/0/0	0/0/			0/0/0	Aluminum of cylinder shape with height less than diameter[tensile strengh can reach 460 MPa (0.46 × 10^9 N/m^2) or more at 293k (20℃)]
5.2	0/0/0	4.5	7	3	0	0	0	0/0/0	0/0/			0/0/0	Other articles of alumnum for thechnical use(other than cloth, grill, netting and fencing, of aluminum wire)
5.2	0/0/0	6	6	4.5	0	0	0	0/0/0	0/0/			0/0/0	---Other

第七十八章
铅及其制品

注释：

本章所用有关名词解释如下：

一、条、杆

轧、挤、拔或锻制的实心产品，非成卷的，其全长截面均为圆形、椭圆形、矩形（包括正方形）、等边三角形或规则外凸多边形（包括相对两边为弧拱形，另外两边为等长平行直线的“扁圆形”及“变形矩形”）。对于矩形（包括正方形）、三角形或多边形截面的产品，其全长边角可经磨圆。矩形（包括“变形矩形”）截面的产品，其厚度应大于宽度的十分之一。所述条、杆也包括同样形状及尺寸的铸造或烧结产品。该产品在铸造或烧结后再经加工（简单剪修或去氧化皮的除外），但不具有其他税目所列制品或产品的特征。

二、型材及异型材

轧、挤、拔、锻制的产品或其他成型产品，不论是否成卷，其全长截面相同，但与条、杆、丝、板、片、带、箔、管的定义不相符合。同时也包括同样形状的铸造或烧结产品。该产品在铸造或烧结后再结加工（简单剪修或去氧化皮的除外），但不具有其他税目所列制品或产品的特征。

三、丝

盘卷的轧、挤或拔制实心产品，其全长截面均为圆形、椭圆形、矩形（包括正方形）、等边三角形或规则外凸多边形（包括相对两边为弧拱形，另外两边为等长平行直线的“扁圆形”及“变形矩形”）。对于矩形（包括正方形）、三角形或多边形截面的产品，其全长边角可经磨圆。矩形（包括“变形矩形”）截面的产品，其厚度应大于宽度的十分之一。

四、板、片、带、箔

成卷或非成卷的平面产品（税目78.01的未锻轧产品除外），截面均为厚度相同的实心矩形（不包括正方形），不论边角是否磨圆（包括相对两边为弧拱形，另外两边为等长平行直线的“变形矩形”），并且符合以下规格：

（一）矩形（包括正方形）的，厚度不超过宽度的十分之一，

（二）矩形或正方形以外形状的，任何尺寸，但不具有其他税目所列制品或产品的特征。

税目78.04还适用于具有花样（例如，凹槽、肋条形、格槽、珠粒及菱形）的板、片、带、箔以及穿孔、抛光、涂层或制成瓦楞形的这类产品，但不具有其他税目所列制品或产品的特征。

五、管

全长截面及管壁厚度相同并只有一个闭合空间的实心产品，成卷或非成卷的，其截面为圆形、椭圆形、矩形（包括正方形）、等边三角形或规则外凸多边形。对于截面为矩形（包括正方形）、等边三角形或规则外凸多边形的产品，不论全长边角是否磨圆，只要其内外截面为同一圆心并为同样形状及同一轴向，也可视为管子。上述截面的管子可经抛光、涂层、弯曲、攻丝、钻孔、缩腰、胀口、成锥形或装法兰、颈圈或套环。

子目注释：

本章所称“精炼铅”，是指：

按重量计含铅量至少为99.9%的金属，但其他各种元素的含量不超过下表中规定的限量：

其他元素表

元　素		所含重量百分比
Ag	银	0.02
As	砷	0.005
Bi	铋	0.05
Ca	钙	0.002
Cd	镉	0.002
Cu	铜	0.08
Fe	铁	0.002
S	硫	0.002
Sb	锑	0.005
Sn	锡	0.005
Zn	锌	0.002
其他（例如碲），每种		0.001

Chapter 78
Lead and articles thereof

Notes:

In this Chapter the following expressions have the meanings hereby assigned to them:

1. Bars and rods

Rolled, extruded, drawn or forged products, not in coils, which have a uniform solid cross-section along their whole length in the shape of circles, ovals, rectangles (including squares), equilateral triangles or regular convex polygons (including "flattened circles" and "modified rectangles", of which two opposite sides are convex arcs, the other two sides being straight, of equal length and parallel). Products with a rectangular (including square), triangular or polygonal cross-section may have corners rounded along their whole length. The thickness of such products which have a rectangular (including "modified rectangular") cross-section exceeds one-tenth of the width. The expression also covers cast or sintered products, of the same forms and dimensions, which have been subsequently worked after production (otherwise than by simple trimming or de-scaling), provided that they have not thereby assumed the character of articles or products of other headings.

2. Profiles

Rolled, extruded, drawn, forged or formed products, coiled or not, of a uniform cross-section along their whole length, which do not conform to any of the definitions of bars, rods, wire, plates, sheets, strip, foil, tubes or pipes. The expression also covers cast or sintered products, of the same forms, which have been subsequently worked after production (otherwise than by simple trimming or de-scaling), provided that they have not thereby assumed the character of articles or products of other headings.

3. Wire

Rolled, extruded or drawn products, in coils, which have a uniform solid cross-section along their whole length in the shape of circles, ovals, rectangles (including squares), equilateral triangles or regular convex polygons (including "flattened circles" and "modified rectangles", of which two opposite sides are convex arcs, the other two sides being straight, of equal length and parallel). Products with a rectangular (including square), triangular or polygonal cross-section may have corners rounded along their whole length. The thickness of such products which have a rectangular (including "modified rectangular") cross-section exceeds one-tenth of the width.

4. Plates, sheets, strip and foil

Flat-surfaced products (other than the unwrought products of heading No.78. 01), coiled or not, of solid rectangular (other than square) cross-section with or without rounded corners (including "modified rectangles" of which two opposite sides are convex arcs, the other two sides being straight, of equal length and parallel) of a uniform thickness, which are:

(a) of rectangular (including square) shape with a thickness not exceeding one-tenth of the width,

(b) of a shape other than rectangular or square, of any size, proviede that they do not assume the character of articles or products of other headings.

Heading No.78. 04 applies, *inter alia*, to plates, sheets, strip and foil with patterns (for example, grooves, ribs, chequers, tears, buttons, lozenges) and to such products which have been perforated, corrugated, polished or coated, provided that they do not thereby assume the character of articles or products of other headings.

5. Tubes and pipes

Hollow products, coiled or not, which have a uniform cross-section with only one enclosed void along their whole langth in the shape of circles, ovals, rectangles (including squares), equilateral triangles or regular convex polygons, and which have a uniform wall thickness. Products with a rectangular (including square), equilateral triangular or regular convex polygonal cross-section, which may have corners rounded along their whole length, are also to be considered as tubes and pipes provided the inner and outer cross-sections are concentric and have the same form and orientation. Tubes and pipes of the foregoing cross-sections may be polished, coated, bent, threaded, drilled, waisted, expanded, cone-shaped or fitted with flanges, collars or rings.

Subheading Note:

In this Chapter the expression "refined lead" means:

Metal containing by weight at least 99.9% of lead, provided that the content by weight of any other element does not exceed the limit specified in the following table:

TABLE — Other elements

Element		Limiting centen% by weight
Ag	Silver	0.02
As	Arsenic	0.005
Bi	Bismuth	0.05
Ca	Calcium	0.002
Cd	Cadmium	0.002
Cu	Copper	0.08
Fe	Iron	0.002
S	Sulphur	0.002
Sb	Antimony	0.005
Sn	Tin	0.005
Zn	Zinc	0.002
Other(for example Te), each		0.001

税则号列	货品名称〔CIQ 扩展编码及品名－T2 表示见附表 2〕	最惠(%)	暂定税率	普通	增值/消费	出口退税	计量单位	监管条件	检验检疫	特殊证件对美关税
78.01	**未锻轧铅：**									
7801.1000	-精炼铅〔999〕	3		20	13/	0	千克			/
	-其他：									
7801.9100	--按重量计所含其他元素是以锑为主的〔999〕	3		20	13/	0	千克			/28
7801.9900	--其他〔999〕	3		20	13/	0	千克			/28
78.02	**铅废碎料：**									
7802.0000	铅废碎料〔999〕	1.5		10	13/	0	千克	9		/
78.04	**铅板、片、带、箔；铅粉及片状粉末：**									
	-板、片、带、箔：									
7804.1100	--片、带及厚度(衬背除外)不超过 0.2 毫米的箔〔999〕	6		30	13/	10	千克			/16
7804.1900	--其他〔999〕	6		30	13/	0	千克			/31
7804.2000	-粉末及片状粉末〔999〕	6		35	13/	0	千克			/16
78.06	**其他铅制品：**									
7806.0010	---铅条、杆、型材及异型材或丝〔101〕	6		30	13/	0	千克			/16
7806.0090	---其他〔101 其它装压缩或液化气的容器及其零件，102 深加工铅制品〕	6		40	13/	0	千克			/16

协定税率 %										特惠税率 %			Article Description
亚太5国	东/冰/格	巴基斯坦	韩国	瑞士	哥达	秘鲁	澳大利亚	新西/坡/智	港/澳/台	亚太2国	老/柬/缅	36/3/1	
													Unwrought lead:
	0/0/0	0	0	0	0	0	0	0//0	0/0/			0/0/0	-Refined lead
													-Other:
	0/0/1.2	0	0	0	0	0	0	0//0	0/0/			0/0/0	--Containing by weight antimony as the principal other element
2.7	0/0/0	0	0	0	0	0	0	0//0	0/0/			0/0/0	--Other
													Lead waste and scrap:
	0/0/0	0	0	0	0	0	0	0//0	0/0/			0/0/	Lead waste and scrap
													Lead plates sheets, strip and foil; lead powders and flakes:
													-Plates, sheets, strip and foil:
	0/0/0	0	0	0	0	0	0	0//0	0/0/			0/0/0	--Sheets, strip and foil of a thickness (excluding any backing) not exceeding 0.2mm
	0/0/0	0	0	0	0	0	0	0//0	0/0/			0/0/0	--Other
	0/0/0	0	0	0	0	0	0	0//0	0/0/			0/0/0	-Powders and flakes
													Other articles of lead:
	0/0/0	0	2.4	0	0	0	0	0//0	0/0/			0/0/0	---Lead bars, rods, profiles and wire
	0/0/0	4.5	0	0	0	0	0	0//0	0/0/			0/0/0	---Other

第七十九章
锌及其制品

注释：

本章所用名词解释如下：

一、条、杆

轧、挤、拔或锻制的实心产品，非成卷的，其全长截面均为圆形、椭圆形、矩形(包括正方形)、等边三角形或规则外凸多边形(包括相对两边为弧拱形，另外两边为等长平行直线的“扁圆形”及“变形矩形”)。对于矩形(包括正方形)、三角形或多边形截面的产品，其全长边角可经磨圆。矩形(包括“变形矩形”)截面的产品，其厚度应大于宽度的十分之一。所述条、杆也包括同样形状及尺寸的铸造或烧结产品。该产品在铸造烧结后再经加工(简单剪修或去氧化皮的除外)，但不具有其他税目所列制品或产品的特征。

二、型材及异型材

轧、挤拔、锻制的产品或其他成型产品，不论是否成卷，其全长截面相同，但与条、杆、丝、板、片、带、箔、管的定义不相符合。同时也包括同样形状的铸造或烧结产品。该产品在铸造或烧结后再经加工(简单剪修或去氧化皮的除外)，但不具有其他税目所列制品或产品的特征。

三、丝

盘卷的轧、挤或拔制实心产品，其全长截面均为圆形、椭圆形、矩形(包括正方形)、等边三角形或规则外凸多边形(包括相对两边为弧拱形，另外两边为等长平行直线的“扁圆形”及“变形矩形”)。对于矩形(包括正方形)、三角形或多边形截面的产品，其全长边角可经磨圆。矩形(包括“变形矩形”)截面的产品，其厚度应大于宽度的十分之一。

四、板、片、带、箔

成卷或非成卷的平面产品(税目79.01的未锻轧产品除外)，截面均为厚度相同的实心矩形(不包括正方形)，不论边角是否磨圆(包括相对两边为弧拱形，另外两边为等长平行直线的“变形矩形”)，并且符合以下规格：

(一)矩形(包括正方形)的，厚度不超过宽度的十分之一；

(二)矩形或正方形以外形状的，任何尺寸，但不具有其他税目所列制品或产品的特征。

税目79.05还适用于具有花样(例如，凹槽、肋条形、格槽、珠粒及菱形)的板、片、带、箔以及穿孔、抛光、涂层或制成瓦楞形的这类产品，但不具有其他税目所列制品或产品的特征。

五、管

全长截面及管壁厚度相同并只有一个闭合空间的空心产品，成卷或非成卷的，其截面为圆形、椭圆形、矩形(包括正方形)、等边三角形或规则外凸多边形。对于截面为矩形(包括正方形)、等边三角形或规则外凸多边形的产品，不论全长边角是否磨圆，只要其内外截面为同一圆心并为同样形状及同一轴向，也可视为管子。上述截面的管子可经抛光、涂层、弯曲、攻丝、钻孔、缩腰、胀口、成锥形或装法兰、颈圈或套环。

子目注释：

本章所用有关名词解释如下：

一、非合金锌

按重量计含锌量至少为97.5%的金属。

二、锌合金

按重量计含锌量大于其他元素单项含量的金属物质，但按重量计其他元素的总含量超过2.5%。

三、锌末

冷凝锌雾所得的锌末。该产品由球形微粒组成，比锌粉更为精细，按重量计至少80%的微粒可以通过孔径为63微米的筛子，而且必须含有按重量计至少为85%的金属锌。

Chapter 79
Zinc and articles thereof

Notes:

In this Chapter the following expressions have the meanings hereby assigned to them:

1. Bars and rods

Rolled, extruded, drawn or forged products, not in coils, which have a uniform solid cross-section along their whole length in the shape of circles, ovals, rectangle (including squares), equilateral triangles or regular convex polygons (including "flattened circles" and "modified rectangles", of which two opposite sides are convex arcs, the other two sides being straight, of equal length and parallel). Products with a rectangular (including square), triangular or polygonal cross-section may have corners rounded along their whole length. The thickness of such products which have a rectangular (including "modified rectangular") cross-section exceeds one-tenth of the width. The expression also covers cast or sintered products, of the same forms and dimensions, which have been subsequently worked after production (otherwise than by simple trimming or de-scaling), provided that they have not thereby assumed the character of articles or products of other headings.

2. Profiles

Rolled, extruded, drawn, forged or formed products, coiled or not, of a uniform cross-section along their whole length, which do not conform to any of the definitions of bars, rods, wire, plates, sheets, strip, foil, tubes or pipes. The expression also covers cast or sintered products, of the same forms, which have been subsequently worked after production (otherwise than by simple trimming or de-scaling), provided that they have not thereby assumed the character of articles or products of other headings.

3. Wire

Rolled, extruded or drawn products, in coils, which have a uniform solid cross-section along their whole length in the shape of circles, ovals, rectangles (including squares), equilateral triangles or regular convex polygons (including "flattened circles" and "modified rectangles", of which two opposite sides are convex arcs, the other two sides being straight, of equal length and parallel). Products with a rectangular (including square), triangular or polygonal cross-section may have corners rounded along their whole length. The thickness of such products which have a rectangular (including "modified rectangular") cross-section exceeds one-tenth of the width

4. Plates, sheets, strip and foil

Flat-surfaced products (other than the unwrought products of heading No.79.01), coiled or not, of solid rectangular (other than square) cross-section with or without rounded corners (including "modified rectangles" of which two opposite sides are convex arcs, the other two sides being straight, of equal length and parallel) of a uniform thickness, which are:

(a) of rectangular (including square) shape with a thickness not exceeding one-tenth of the width,

(b) of a shape other than rectangular or square, of any size, provided that they do not assume the character of articles or products of other headings.

Heading No.79.05 applies, *inter alia*, to plates, sheets strip and foil with patterns (for example, grooves, ribs chequers, tears, buttons, lozenges) and to such products which have been perforated, corrugated, polished or coated, provided that they do not thereby assume the character of articles or products of other headings.

5. Tubes and pipes

Hollow products, coiled or not, which have a uniform cross-section with only one enclosed void along their whole length in the shape of circles, ovals, rectangles (including squares), equilateral triangles or regular convex polygons, and which have a uniform wall thickness. Products with a rectangular (including square), equilateral triangular or regular convex polygonal cross-section, which may have corners rounded along their whole length, are also to be considered as tubes and pipes provided the inner and outer cross-sections are concentric and have the same form and orientation. Tubes and pipes of the foregoing cross-sections may be polished, coated, bent, threaded, drilled, waisted, expanded, cone-shaped or fitted with flanges, collars or rings.

Subheading Note:

In this Chapter the following expressions have the meanings hereby assigned to them:

1. Zinc, not alloyed

Metal containing by weight at least 97.5% of zinc.

2. Zinc alloys

Metallic substances in which zinc predominates by weight over each of the other elements, provided that the total content by weight of such other elements exceeds 2.5%.

3. Zinc dust

Dust obtained by condensation of zinc vapour, consisting of spherical particles which are finer than zinc powders. At least 80% by weight of the particles pass through a sieve with 63 micrometres (microns) mesh. It must contain at least 85% by weight of metallic zinc.

税则号列		货品名称〔CIQ 扩展编码及品名—T2 表示见附表 2〕	最惠(%)	暂定税率	普通	增值/消费	出口退税	计量单位	监管条件	检验检疫	特殊证件对美关税
79.01		**未锻轧锌:**									
		-非合金锌:									
		--按重量计含锌量在 99.99%及以上:									
7901.1110		---按重量计含锌量在 99.995%及以上〔999〕	3	1	20	13/	0	千克			/26
7901.1190		---其他〔999〕	3	1	20	13/	0	千克			/
7901.1200		--按重量计含锌量低于 99.99%〔999〕	3	1	20	13/	0	千克			/21
7901.2000		-锌合金〔999〕	3	1	20	13/	0	千克			/26
79.02		**锌废碎料:**									
7902.0000		锌废碎料〔999〕	1.5	1	20	13/	0	千克	A	M	/26
79.03		**锌末、锌粉及片状粉末:**									
7903.1000		-锌末〔999 包括锌合金,301 属于危险化学品的金属〕	6		20	13/	0	千克	A	M	/31
7903.9000		-其他									
7903.9000	10	颗粒＜500μm 的锌及其合金(含量≥97%,不论球形、椭球体、雾化、片状、研碎金属燃料)〔999:含量≥97%,不论球形,椭球体,雾化,片状,研碎金属燃料,301 属于危险化学品的金属,302 低风险金属材料〕	6		20	13/	0	千克	3A	M	/16
7903.9000	90	其他锌粉及片状粉末〔101 其他锌及制品,301 属于危险化学品的金属〕	6		20	13/	0	千克	AB	MN	/16
79.04		**锌条、杆、型材及异型材或丝:**									
7904.0000		锌条、杆、型材及异型材或丝〔999〕	6		30	13/	0	千克			/31
79.05		**锌板、片、带、箔:**									
7905.0000		锌板、片、带、箔〔999〕	6		30	13/	0	千克			/16
79.07		**其他锌制品:**									
7907.0020		---锌管及锌制管子附件(例如,接头、肘管、管套)〔101 其它装压缩或液化气的容器及其零件,102 深加工锌制品〕	6		30	13/	0	千克			/16
7907.0030		---电池壳体坯料(锌饼)〔101〕	6		40	13/	0	千克			/
7907.0090		---其他〔101 其它装压缩或液化气的容器及其零件,102 深加工锌制品〕	6		40	13/	0	千克			/31

协定税率 %										特惠税率 %			Article Description
亚太5国	东/冰/格	巴基斯坦	韩国	瑞士	哥达	秘鲁	澳大利亚	新西/坡/智	港/澳/台	亚太2国	老/柬/缅	36/3/1	
													Unwrought zinc:
													-Zinc, not alloyed:
													--Containing by weight 99.99% or more of zinc:
	0/0/0	0	0	0	0	0	0	0//0	0/0/			0/0/0	---Containing by weight 99.995% or more of zinc
	0/0/0	0	0	0	0	0	0	0//0	0/0/			0/0/0	---Other
	0/0/0	0	0	0	0	0	0	0//0	0/0/			0/0/0	--Containing by weight less than 99.99% of zinc
	0/0/0	0	0	0	0	0	0	0//0	0/0/			0/0/0	-Zinc alloys
													Zinc waste and scrap:
	0/0/0	0	0	0	0	0	0	0//0	0/0/			0/0/0	Zinc waste and scrap
													Zinc dust, powders and flakes:
	0/0/0	0	2.4	0	0	0	0	0//0	0/0/			0/0/0	-Zinc dust
													-Other
	0/0/0	0	2.4	1.8	0	0	0	0//0	0/0/			0/0/0	Zinc and its alloys, granularity＜500μm (containing zinc≥97%, whether spheroid, ellipsoid, atomized, flake formed, ground metallic fuels)
	0/0/0	0	2.4	1.8	0	0	0	0//0	0/0/			0/0/0	Other zine powders and flakes
													Zinc bars, rods, profiles and wire:
	0/0/0	0	3.6	0	0	0	0	0//0	0/0/			0/0/	Zinc bars, rods, profiles and wire
													Zinc plates, sheets, strip and foil:
	0/0/0	0	0	0	0	0	0	0//0	0/0/			0/0/0	Zinc plates, sheets, strip and foil
													Other articles of zinc:
	0/0/0	0	0	0	0	0	0	0//0	0/0/			0/0/0	---Zinc tubes pipes and tube or pipe fittings (for example, couplings, elbows, sleeves)
4.2	0/0/0	0	0	0	0	2.1	0	0//0	0/0/			0/0/0	---Cellpacking blanks(zinc biscuits)
	0/0/0	0	0	0	0	0	0	0//0	0/0/			0/0/0	---Other

第八十章
锡及其制品

注释：

本章所用有关名词解释如下：

一、条、杆

轧、挤、拔或锻制的实心产品，非成卷的，其全长截面均为圆形、椭圆形、矩形（包括正方形）、等边三角形或规则外凸多边形（包括相对两边为弧拱形，另外两边为等长平行直线的“扁圆形”及“变形矩形”）。对于矩形（包括正方形）、三角形或多边形截面的产品，其全长边角可经磨圆。矩形（包括“变形矩形”）截面的产品，其厚度应大于宽度的十分之一。所述条、杆也包括同样形状及尺寸的铸造或烧结产品。该产品在造铸或烧结后再经加工（简单剪修或去氧化皮的除外），但不具有其他税目所列制品或产品的特征。

二、型材及异型材

轧、挤、拔、锻制的产品或其他成型产品，不论是否成卷，其全长截面相同，但与条、杆、丝、板、片、带、箔、管的定义不相符合。同时也包括同样形状的铸造或烧结产品。该产品在铸造或烧结后再经加工（简单剪修或去氧化皮的除外），但不具有其他税目所列制品或产品的特征。

三、丝

盘卷的轧、挤或拔制实心产品，其全长截面均为圆形、椭圆形、矩形（包括正方形）、等边三角形或规则外凸多边形（包括相对两边为弧拱形，另外两边为等长平行直线的“扁圆形”及“变形矩形”）。对于矩形（包括正方形）、三角形或多边形截面的产品，其全长边角可经磨圆。矩形（包括“变形矩形”）截面的产品，其厚度应大于宽度的十分之一。

四、板、片、带、箔

成卷或非成卷的平面产品（税目 80.01 的未锻轧产品除外），截面均为厚度相同的实心矩形（不包括正方形），不论边角是否磨圆（包括相对两边为弧拱形，另外两边为等长平行直线的“变形矩形”），并且符合以下规格：

（一）矩形（包括正方形）的，厚度不超过宽度的十分之一；

（二）矩形或正方形以外形状的，任何尺寸，但不具有其他税目所列制品或产品的特征。

五、管

全长截面及管壁厚度相同并只有一个闭合空间的实心产品，成卷或非成卷的，其截面为圆形、椭圆形、矩形（包括正方形）、等边三角形或规则外凸多边形。对于截面为矩形（包括正方形）、等边三角形或规则外凸多边形的产品，不论全长边角是否磨圆，只要其内外截面为同一圆心并为同样形状及同一轴向，也可视为管子。上述截面的管子可经抛光、涂层、弯曲、攻丝、钻孔、缩腰、胀口、成锥形或装法兰、颈圈或套环。

子目注释：

本章所用有关名词解释如下：

一、非合金锡

按重量计含锡量至少为 99% 的金属，但含铋量或含铜量不超过下表中规定的限量：

其他元素表

元　素	所含重量百分比
Bi　铋	0.1
Cu　铜	0.4

二、锡合金

按重量计含锡量大于其他元素单项含量的金属物质，但：

（一）按重量计其他元素的总含量超过 1%；或

（二）按重量计含铋量或含铜量应等于或大于上表中规定的限量。

Chapter 80
Tin and articles thereof

Notes:

In this Chapter the following expressions have the meanings hereby assigned to them:

1. Bars and rods

Rolled, extruded, drawn or forged products, not in coils, which have a uniform solid cross-section along their whole length in the shape of circles, ovals, rectangles (including squares), equilateral triangles or regular convex polygons (including "flattened circles" and "modified rectangles", of which two opposite sides are convex arcs, the other two sides being straight, of equal length and parallel). Products with a rectangular (including square), triangular or polygonal cross-section may have corners rounded along their whole length. The thickness of such products which have a rectangular (including "modified rectangular") cross-section exceeds one-tenth of the width. The expression also covers cast or sintered products, of the same forms and dimensions, which have been subsequently worked after production (otherwise than by simple trimming or de-scaling), provided that they have not thereby assumed the character of articles or products of other headings.

2. Profiles

Rolled, extruded, drawn, forged or formed products, coiled or not, of a uniform cross-section along their whole length, which do not conform to any of the definitions of bars, rods, wire, plates, sheets, strip, foil, tubes or pipes. The expression also covers cast or sintered products, of the same forms, which have been subsequently worked after production (otherwise than by simple trimming or de-scaling), provided that they have not thereby assumed the character of articles or products of other headings.

3. Wire

Rolled, extruded or drawn products, in coils, which have a uniform solid cross-section along their whole length in the shape of circles, ovals, rectangles (including squares), equilateral triangles or regular convex polygons (including "flattened circles" and "modified rectangles", of which two opposite sides are convex arcs, the other two sides being straight, of equal length and parallel). Products with a rectangular (including square), triangular or polygonal cross-section may have corners rounded along their whole length. The thickness of such products which have a rectangular (including "modified rectangular") cross-section exceeds one-tenth of the width.

4. Plates, sheets, strip and foil

Flat-surfaced products (other than the unwrought products of heading No.80.01), coiled or not, of solid rectangular (other than square) cross-section with or without rounded corners (including "modified rectangles" of which two opposite sides are convex arcs, the other two sides being straight, of equal length and parallel) of a uniform thickness, which are:

(a) of rectangular (including square) shape with a thickness not exceeding one-tenth of the width,

(b) of a shape other than rectangular or square, of any size, proviede that they do not assume the character of articles or products of other headings.

5. Tubes and pipes

Hollow products, coiled or not, which have a uniform cross-section with only one enclosed void along their whole length in the shape of circles, ovals, rectangles (including squares), equilateral triangles or regular convex polygons, and which have a uniform wall thickness. Products with a rectangular (including square), equilateral triangular or regular convex polygonal cross-section, which may have corners rounded along their whole length, are also to be considered as tubes and pipes provided the inner and outer cross-sections are concentric and have the same form and orientation. Tubes and pipes of the foregoing cross-sections may be polished, coated, bent, threaded, drilled, waisted, expanded, cone-shaped or fitted with flanges, collars or rings.

Subheading Note:

In this Chapter the following expressions have the meanings hereby assigned to them:

1. Tin, not alloyed.

Metal containing by weight at least 99% of tin, provided that the content by weight of any bismuth or copper is less than the limit specified in the following table:

TABLE — Other elements

Element		Limiting content % by weight
Bi	Bismuth	0.1
Cu	Copper	0.4

2. **Tin alloys**

Metallic substances in which tin predominates by weight over each of the other elements, provided that:

(a) the total content by weight of such other elements exceeds 1%; or

(b) the content by weight of either bismuth or copper is equal to or greater than the limit specified in the foregoing table.

税则号列	货品名称〔CIQ扩展编码及品名－T2表示见附表2〕	最惠(%)	暂定税率	普通	增值/消费	出口退税	计量单位	监管条件	检验检疫	特殊证件对美关税
80.01	未锻轧锡：									
8001.1000	-非合金锡〔999〕	3		20	13/	0	千克	4xy		/28
	-锡合金：									
8001.2010	---锡基巴毕脱合金〔999〕	3		20	13/	0	千克	4xy		/13
	---焊锡：									
8001.2021	----按重量计含铅量在0.1%以下的〔101焊锡，102锡合金〕	3		30	13/	0	千克	4xy		/28
8001.2029	----其他〔101焊锡，102锡合金〕	3		30	13/	0	千克	4xy		/28
8001.2090	---其他〔999〕	3		30	13/	0	千克	4xy		/33
80.02	锡废碎料：									
8002.0000	锡废碎料〔999〕	1.5		30	13/	0	千克	4Axy	M	/26.5
80.03	锡条、杆、型材及异型材或丝：									
8003.0000	锡条、杆、型材及异型材或丝〔999〕	8		40	13/	0	千克	4xy		/33
80.07	其他锡制品：									
8007.0020	---锡板、片及带，厚度超过0.2毫米〔101〕	8		40	13/	0	千克	4xy		/33
8007.0030	---锡箔(不论是否印花或用纸、纸板、塑料或类似材料衬背)，厚度(衬背除外)不超过0.2毫米；锡粉及片状粉末〔101〕	8		40	13/	10	千克			/28
8007.0040	---锡管及管子附件(例如，接头、肘管、管套)〔101其它装压缩或液化气的容器及其零件，102深加工锡制品〕	8		45	13/	0	千克	4xy		/18
8007.0090	---其他〔101其它装压缩或液化气的容器及其零件，102深加工锡制品〕	8		80	13/	0	千克			/33

协定税率 %										特惠税率 %			Article Description
亚太5国	东/冰/格	巴基斯坦	韩国	瑞士	哥达	秘鲁	澳大利亚	新西/坡/智	港/澳/台	亚太2国	老/柬/缅	36/3/1	
													Unwrought tin:
	0/0/0	0	0	0	0	0	0	0//0	0/0/			0/0/0	-Tin, not alloyed
													-Tin alloys:
2.4	0/0/0	0	0	0	0	0	0	0//0	0/0/			0/0/0	---Babbitt metal
													---solder:
	0/0/0	0	0	0	0	0	0	0//0	0/0/			0/0/0	----Containing by weight less than 0.1% of lead
	0/0/0	0	0	0	0	0	0	0//0	0/0/			0/0/0	----Other
	0/0/0	0	0	0	0	0	0	0//0	0/0/			0/0/0	---Other
													Tin waste and scrap:
	0/0/0	0	0	0	0	0	0	0//0	0/0/			0/0/	Tin waste and scrap
													Tin bars, rods, profiles and wire:
	0/0/0	4	3.2	0	0	0	0	0//0	0/0/			0/0/0	Tin bars, rods, profiles and wire
													Other articles of tin:
	0/0/0	4	0	0	0	0	0	0//0	0/0/			0/0/	---Tin plates, sheets and strip, of a thickness exceeding 0.2mm
	0/0/0	4	0	0	0	0	0	0//0	0/0/			0/0/	---Tin foil(whether or not printed or backed with paper, paperboard, plastics or similar backing materials), of a thickness(excluding and backing) not exceeding 0.2mm; tin powders and flakes
6.4	0/0/0	4	0	2.4	0	0	0	0//0	0/0/			0/0/	---Tin tubes, pipes and tube or pipe fittings(for example, couplings, elbows, sleeves)
	0/0/0	5.1	4.8	0	0	0	0	0//0	0/0/			0/0/	---Other

第八十一章
其他贱金属、金属陶瓷及其制品

子目注释：

第七十四章注释中有关"条、杆"、"型材及异型材"、"丝"及"板、片、带、箔"的规定也适用于本章。

税则号列		货品名称〔CIQ 扩展编码及品名－T2 表示见附表 2〕	最惠(%)	暂定税率	普通	增值/消费	出口退税	计量单位	监管条件	检验检疫	特殊证件对美关税
81.01		**钨及其制品，包括废碎料：**									
8101.1000		-粉末									
8101.1000	10	颗粒＜500μm 的钨及其合金（含量≥97%，不论球形、椭球体、雾化、片状、研碎金属燃料）〔999〕	6		20	13/	0	千克	3		/26
8101.1000	90	其他钨粉末〔999〕	6		20	13/	0	千克	4xy		/26
		-其他：									
8101.9400		--未锻轧钨，包括简单烧结而成的条、杆〔999〕	3		20	13/	0	千克	4xy		/23
8101.9600		--丝〔999〕	8		20	13/	10	千克			/28
8101.9700		--废碎料〔999〕	3		20	13/	0	千克	49Axy	M	/28
		--其他：									
8101.9910		---条、杆，但简单烧结而成的除外；型材及异型材、板、片、带、箔〔999〕	5		30	13/	0	千克			/15
8101.9990		---其他〔999〕	8		70	13/	0	千克			/18
81.02		**钼及其制品，包括废碎料：**									
8102.1000		-粉末〔999〕	6		20	13/	0	千克	4xy		/16
		-其他：									
8102.9400		--未锻轧钼，包括简单烧结而成的条、杆〔999〕	3		20	13/	0	千克	4xy		/28
8102.9500		--条、杆，但简单烧结而成的除外；型材及异型材、板、片、带、箔〔101〕	8		30	13/	0	千克			/33
8102.9600		--丝〔101〕	8		20	13/	10	千克			/33
8102.9700		--废碎料〔999〕	3		20	13/	0	千克	49xy		/
8102.9900		--其他〔101 其他深加工金属制品，103 二硫化钼润滑膜〕	8		70	13/	0	千克	4xy		/18
81.03		**钽及其制品，包括废碎料：**									
		-未锻轧钽，包括简单烧结而成的条、杆；粉末：									
		---钽粉：									
8103.2011		----松装密度小于 2.2g/cm^3 的〔999〕	6		14	13/	13	千克	4xy		/31
8103.2019		----其他〔999〕	6		14	13/	0	千克	4xy		/16
8103.2090		---其他〔999〕	6		14	13/	0	千克	4xy		/26
8103.3000		-废碎料〔999〕	6	0	14	13/	0	千克	4Axy	M	/25
		-其他：									
		---钽丝：									
8103.9011		----直径小于 0.5mm〔101 其他深加工金属制品〕	8		30	13/	13	千克	4xy		/
8103.9019		----其他〔101 其他深加工金属制品〕	8		30	13/	13	千克	4xy		/18
8103.9090		---其他									
8103.9090	10	钽坩锅（容积在 50ml 至 2L 之间、钽纯度≥98%）〔101 其他深加工金属制品〕	8		30	13/	0	千克	3		/18
8103.9090	90	其他锻轧钽及其制品〔101：其他深加工金属制品〕	8		30	13/	13	千克	4xy		/18
81.04		**镁及其制品，包括废碎料：**									
		-未锻轧镁：									
8104.1100		--按重量计含镁量至少为 99.8%〔999〕	6		20	13/	0	千克			/31
8104.1900		--其他〔301〕	6		20	13/	0	千克			/16
8104.2000		-废碎料〔999〕	1.5		20	13/	0	千克	9A	M	/26.5
8104.3000		-锉屑、车屑及颗粒，已按规格分级的；粉末									
8104.3000	10	颗粒＜500μm 的镁及其合金（含量≥97%，不论球形、椭球体、雾化、片状、研碎金属燃料）〔301 属于危险化学品的金属〕	8		30	13/	0	千克	3		/33
8104.3000	90	其他已分级的镁锉屑，车屑，颗粒；粉末〔301 属于危险化学品的金属〕	8		30	13/	0	千克			/33
		-其他：									
8104.9010		---锻轧镁〔101 其他深加工金属制品，103 片状、带状或条状〕	8		30	13/	0	千克			/18
8104.9020		---镁制品									

Chapter 81
Other base metals; cermets; artiles thereof

Subheading Note:

Notes 1 to Chapter 74, defining "bars and rods", "profiles", "wire" and "plates, sheets, strip and foil" applies, *mutatis mutandis*, to this Chapter.

协定税率 %										特惠税率 %			
亚太5国	东/冰/格	巴基斯坦	韩国	瑞士	哥达	秘鲁	澳大利亚	新西/坡/智	港/澳/台	亚太2国	老/柬/缅	36/3/1	Article Description
													Tungsten (wolfram) and articles thereof, including waste and scrap:
													-Powders
	0/0/0	0	0	0	0	0	0	0//0	0/0/			0/0/	Tungesten and tungsten alloys, granularity < 500μm, (containing tungsten≥97%, whether in the form of spheroid, elipsoid, flakes, atomized or pulverized metallic fuel)
	0/0/0	0	0	0	0	0	0	0//0	0/0/			0/0/	Other tungsten powders
													-Other:
	0/0/0	0	0	0.9	0	0	0	0//0	0/0/			0/0/	--Unwrought tungsten, including bars and rods obtained simply by sintering
	0/0/0	4	0	0	0	0	0	0//0	0/0/			0/0/	--Wire
	0/0/0	0	0	0	0	0	0	0//0	0/0/			0/0/	--Waste and scrap
													--Other:
	0/0/0	0	0	0	0	0	0	0//0	0/0/			0/0/	---Bars and rods, other than those obtained simply by sintering, profiles, plates, sheets, strip and foil
	0/0/0	4	0	0	0	0	0	0//0	0/0/			0/0/	---Other
													Molybdenum and articles thereof, including waste and scrap:
	0/0/0	0	0	0	0	0	0	0//0	0/0/			0/0/	-Powders
													-Other:
	0/0/0	0	0	0	0	0	0	0//0	0/0/			0/0/	--Unwrought molybdenum, including bars and rods obtained simply by sintering
	0/0/0	4	3.2	0	0	0	0	0//0	0/0/			0/0/	--Bars and rods, other than those obtained simply by sintering, profiles, plates, sheets, strip and foil
	0/0/0	4	0	0	0	0	0	0//0	0/0/			0/0/	--Wire
	0/0/0	0	0	0	0	0	0	0//0	0/0/			0/0/	--Waste and scrap
	0/0/0	4	0	0	0	0	0	0//0	0/0/			0/0/	--Other
													Tantalum and articles thereof, including waste and scrap:
													-Unwrought tantalum, including bars and rods obtained simply by sinteing; powders:
													---Powders:
4.2	0/0/0	0	0	0	0	0	0	0//0	0/0/			0/0/	----Loose density less than 2.2g/cm^3
	0/0/0	0	0	0	0	0	0	0//0	0/0/			0/0/	----Other
	0/0/0	0	0	0	0	0	0	0//0	0/0/			0/0/	---Other
	0/0/0	0	0	0	0	0	0	0//0	0/0/			0/0/	-Waste and scrap
													-Other:
													---Wire of tantalum:
5.6	0/0/0	4	0	0	0	0	0	0//0	0/0/			0/0/	----Diameter less than 0.5mm
5.6	0/0/0	4	0	0	0	0	0	0//0	0/0/			0/0/	----Other
													---Other
7.2	0/0/0	4	0	0	0	0	0	0//0	0/0/			0/0/	Tantalum crucible, of a volune between 50 milliliter and 2 litre, tantaium≥98%
7.2	0/0/0	4	0	0	0	0	0	0//0	0/0/			0/0/	Other wrought tantalum and articles thereof
													Magnesium and articles thereof, including waste and scrap:
													-Unwrought magnesium:
3	0/0/0	0	0	0	0	0	0	0//0	0/0/			0/0/	--Containing at least 99.8% by weight of magnesium
	0/0/0	0	0	0	0	0	0	0//0	0/0/			0/0/	--Other
	0/0/0	0	0	0	0	0	0	0//0	0/0/			0/0/	-Waste and scrap
													-Raspings, turnings and granules, graded according to size; powders
	0/0/0	4	0	0	0	0	0	0//0	0/0/			0/0/	Magnesium and magnesium alloys, granularity<500μm (containing magnesium≥97%, whether spheroid, ellipsoid, atomized, flake formed, ground metallic fuels)
	0/0/0	4	0	0	0	0	0	0//0	0/0/			0/0/	Other magnesium raspings, turnings and granules, graded according to size; powders
													-Other:
	0/0/0	4	0	0	0	0	0	0//0	0/0/			0/0/	---Wrought magnesium
													---Magnesium articles

税则号列	货品名称〔CIQ扩展编码及品名—T2表示见附表2〕	最惠(%)	暂定税率	普通	增值/消费	出口退税	计量单位	监管条件	检验检疫	特殊证件对美关税
8104.9020 10	镁金属基复合材料(包括各种结构件和制品、各种预成形件,其中增强材料的比拉伸强度大于7.62×10⁴m和比模量大于3.18×10⁶m)〔101其他深加工金属制品〕	8		70	13/	10	千克	3		/33
8104.9020 90	其他镁制品〔101其他深加工金属制品〕	8		70	13/	0	千克			/33
81.05	**钴锍及其他冶炼钴时所得的中间产品;钴及其制品,包括废碎料:**									
	-钴锍及其他冶炼钴时所得的中间产品;未锻轧钴;粉末:									
8105.2010	---钴湿法冶炼中间品〔999〕	4	0	14	13/	0	千克	4xy		/
8105.2020	---未锻轧钴〔999〕	4		14	13/	0	千克	4xy		/
8105.2090	---其他									
8105.2090 01	钴锍及其他冶炼钴时所得中间产品〔999〕	4	0	14	13/	0	千克	4xy		/25
8105.2090 10	钴≥99.5%的超细钴粉(费氏粒度0.8-1.5μm,松装密度0.4-0.8g/cm³)〔999〕	4		14	13/	0	千克			/29
8105.2090 90	其他钴锍、粉末〔999〕	4		14	13/	0	千克	4xy		/29
8105.3000	-废碎料〔999〕	4		14	13/	0	千克	49xy		/
8105.9000	-其他〔101〕	8		30	13/	0	千克	4xy		/18
81.06	**铋及其制品,包括废碎料:**									
8106.0010	---未锻轧铋;废碎料;粉末									
8106.0010 11	高纯度未锻轧的铋(纯度≥99.99%,含银量低于十万分之一)〔999〕	3	1	20	13/	0	千克	3		/26
8106.0010 19	高纯度未锻轧的铋废料、粉末(纯度≥99.99%,含银量低于十万分之一)〔999〕	3		20	13/	0	千克	3		/28
8106.0010 91	其他未锻轧铋〔999〕	3	1	20	13/	0	千克	4xy		/26
8106.0010 92	其他未锻轧铋废碎料〔999〕	3		20	13/	0	千克	49Axy	M	/28
8106.0010 99	其他未锻轧铋粉末〔999〕	3		20	13/	0	千克	4xy		/28
8106.0090	---其他									
8106.0090 10	高纯度铋及铋制品(纯度≥99.99%,含银量低于十万分之一)〔999〕	8		30	13/	10	千克	3		/18
8106.0090 90	其他铋及铋制品〔999〕	8		30	13/	0	千克	4xy		/18
81.07	**镉及其制品,包括废碎料:**									
8107.2000	-未锻轧镉;粉末〔999〕	3		14	13/	0	千克			/28
8107.3000	-废碎料〔999〕	3		14	13/	0	千克	9		/
8107.9000	-其他〔101〕	8		30	13/	0	千克			/18
81.08	**钛及其制品,包括废碎料:**									
	-未锻轧钛;粉末:									
	---未锻轧钛:									
8108.2021	----未锻轧海绵钛(金属钛粒)〔999〕	3		14	13/	0	千克	4xy		/28
8108.2029	----其他									
8108.2029 10	颗粒<500μm的钛及其合金(含量≥97%,不论球形、椭球体、雾化、片状、研碎金属燃料)〔301属于危险化学品的金属,302低风险金属材料〕	3		14	13/	0	千克	3A	M	/13
8108.2029 90	其他未锻轧钛〔999〕	3		14	13/	0	千克	4xy		/13
8108.2030	---粉末〔101其他有色金属及其制品,301属于危险化学品的金属〕	3		14	13/	0	千克	A4xy	M	/33
8108.3000	-废碎料〔999〕	3		14	13/	0	千克	49Axy	M	/28
	-其他:									
8108.9010	---条、杆、型材及异型材									
8108.9010 10	钛合金,实心圆柱体,包括锻件(20℃下极限抗拉强度≥900兆帕,外径超过75mm)〔999〕	8		30	13/	13	千克	3		/18
8108.9010 20	钛金属基复合材料的条、杆、型材及异型材(其中增强材料的比拉伸强度大于7.62×10⁶米和比模量大于3.18×10⁷米)〔999〕	8		30	13/	13	千克	3		/18
8108.9010 90	其他钛条、杆、型材及异型材〔999〕	8		30	13/	13	千克			/18
8108.9020	---丝〔101其他深加工金属制品〕	8		30	13/	13	千克			/18
	---板、片、带、箔:									
8108.9031	----厚度不超过0.8毫米〔101其他深加工金属制品〕	8	4	30	13/	13	千克			/24
8108.9032	----厚度超过0.8毫米									
8108.9032 10	钛金属基复合材料的板、片、带、箔(其中增强材料的比拉伸强度大于7.62×10⁴米和比模量大于3.18×10⁷米,厚度大于0.8毫米)〔101其他深加工金属制品〕	8	4	30	13/	13	千克	3		/14
8108.9032 90	其他厚度>0.8毫米的钛板、片、带、箔〔101其他深加工金属制品〕	8	4	30	13/	13	千克			/14
8108.9040	---管									

协定税率 %										特惠税率 %			Article Description
亚太5国	东/冰/格	巴基斯坦	韩国	瑞士	哥达	秘鲁	澳大利亚	新西/坡/智	港/澳/台	亚太2国	老/柬/缅	36/3/1	
	0/0/0	4	0	0	0	0	0	0//0	0/0/			0/0/	Masnesium composite materials (including various structural parts and products, various prefabricated parts and their specific tensile strength is bigger than 7.62×10^4 m and specific modulus bigger than 3.18×10^6 m)
	0/0/0	4	0	0	0	0	0	0//0	0/0/			0/0/	Other magnesium articlec
													Cobalt mattes and other intermediate products of cobalt matallurgy; cobalt and articles thereof, including waste and scrap:
													-Cobalt mattes and other intermediate products of cobalt matallurgy; unwrought cobalt; powders:
	0/0/0	0	0	0	0	0	0	0//0	0/0/			0/0/0	---Intermediate products of cobalt metallurgy by wet process
	0/0/0	0	0	0	0	0	0	0//0	0/0/			0/0/0	---Unwrought cobalt
													---Other
	0/0/0	0	0	0	0	0	0	0//0	0/0/			0/0/0	Mid-product smelted with cobalt and sulfur and others
	0/0/0	0	0	0	0	0	0	0//0	0/0/			0/0/0	Supper-fine cobalt powders, containing ≥99.5% by weight of cobalt (fischer granularinty 0.8～1.5μm. bulk package density 0.4～0.8g/cm^3)
	0/0/0	0	0	0	0	0	0	0//0	0/0/			0/0/0	Other cobalt mattes; powders
	0/0/0	0	0	0	0	0	0	0//0	0/0/			0/0/0	-Waste and scrap
	0/0/0	4	3.2	0	0	0	0	0//0	0/0/			0/0/0	-Other
													Bismuth and articles thereof, including waste and scrap:
													---Unwroght bismuth; waste and scrap; powders
	0/0/0	0	0	0	0	0	0	0//0	0/0/			0/0/	Highlypure unwroght bismuth, purity≥99.99% (containing silver quality<1.0×10^{-6})
	0/0/0	0	0	0	0	0	0	0//0	0/0/			0/0/	Highlypure unwroght bismuth, waste and scrap, powders, purity≥99.99% (containing silver quality<1.0×10^{-6})
	0/0/0	0	0	0	0	0	0	0//0	0/0/			0/0/	Other unwroght bismuth
	0/0/0	0	0	0	0	0	0	0//0	0/0/			0/0/	Other unwroght bismuth waste and scap
	0/0/0	0	0	0	0	0	0	0//0	0/0/			0/0/	Other unwroght bismuth powders
													---Other
	0/0/0	4	3.2	0	0	0	0	0//0	0/0/			0/0/	Highly-pure unwrought bismuth and aricles thereof (Purity≥99.99%, purity containing silver quantity is lower than 1/100000)
	0/0/0	4	3.2	0	0	0	0	0//0	0/0/			0/0/	Other bismuth and articles thereof
													Cadmium and articles thereof, including waste and scrap:
	0/0/0	0	0	0	0	0	0	0//0	0/0/			0/0/	-Unwrought cadmium; powders
	0/0/0	0	0	0	0	0	0	0//0	0/0/			0/0/	-Waste and scrap
5.6	0/0/0	4	0	0	0	0	0	0//0	0/0/			0/0/	-Other
													Titanium and articles thereof, including waste and scrap:
													-Unwrought titanium; powders:
													---Unwrousht titanium:
	0/0/0	0	0	0	0	0	0	0//0	0/0/			0/0/	----Sponge titanium
													----Other
	0/0/0	0	0	0	0	0	0	0//0	0/0/			0/0/	Titanium and its alloy with the particles <500μm (containing ≥97%, whether in balls, atomized, in sheet or in pulverized metal fuel)
	0/0/0	0	0	0	0	0	0	0//0	0/0/			0/0/	Other unwrought titanium; powders
	0/0/0	0	0	0	0	0	0	0//0	0/0/			0/0/	---Powders
	0/0/0	0	0	0	0	0	0	0//0	0/0/			0/0/	-Waste and scrap
													-Other:
													---Bars, rods, shapes and sections
	0/0/0	4	3.2	0	0	0	0	0//0	0/0/			0/0/	Titanium alloys, solid cylinder, including castings (ultimate tensile strength≥900MPa at 20℃, outer diameter>75mm)
	0/0/0	4	3.2	0	0	0	0	0//0	0/0/			0/0/	Bars, rods, shaps and sections, made of composite material with titanium metal (the degree of streangth of intensity waterial >7.62×10^6 m, and specific modulus >3.18×10^7 m)
	0/0/0	4	3.2	0	0	0	0	0//0	0/0/			0/0/	Other bars, rods, shapes and sections, of titanium
6.4	0/0/0	4	0	0	0	0	0	0//0	0/0/			0/0/	---Wire
													---Plates, sheets, strap, foil:
	0/0/0	4	0	0	0	0	0	0//0	0/0/			0/0/	----Of a thickness not more than 0.8mm
													----Of a thickness more than 0.8mm
	0/0/0	4	0	0	0	0	0	0//0	0/0/			0/0/	Plates.sheets, strip and foil made of conyosite material with titanium metal (the degree of strength of intensity material>7.62×10^4 m, and specific mondulus>3.18×10^7 mm, thickness>0.8mm)
	0/0/0	4	0	0	0	0	0	0//0	0/0/			0/0/	Other plates, sheets, strap, foil of titanium thickness>0.8mm
													---Tubes or pipes

税则号列	货品名称〔CIQ 扩展编码及品名－T2 表示见附表 2〕	最惠(%)	暂定税率	普通	增值/消费	出口退税	计量单位	监管条件	检验检疫	特殊证件对美关税
8108.9040 10	钛合金管(20℃下极限抗拉强度≥900MPa,外径>75mm)〔999〕	8		30	13/	13	千克	3		/28
8108.9040 90	其他钛管〔999〕	8		30	13/	13	千克			/28
8108.9090	---其他〔101〕	8		30	13/	13	千克			/18
81.09	**锆及其制品,包括废碎料:**									
8109.2000	-未锻轧锆;粉末									
8109.2000 10	颗粒<500μm 的锆及其合金(含量≥97%,不论球形、椭球体、雾化、片状、研碎金属燃料)〔301 属于危险化学品的金属,302 低风险金属材料〕	3		20	13/	0	千克	3A	M	/33
8109.2000 90	其他未锻轧锆;粉末〔101 其他有色金属及其制品,301 属于危险化学品的金属〕	3		20	13/	0	千克	3A	M	/33
8109.3000	-废碎料〔999〕	3		20	13/	0	千克	39A	M	/28
8109.9000	-其他									
8109.9000 10	锆管(铪与锆重量比低于 1:500 的锆金属和合金的管或组件)〔999〕	8		30	13/	10	千克	3		/18
8109.9000 90	其他锻轧锆及锆制品〔102 金属锆片,103 金属锆条,104 金属锆丝,105 干的,碎屑〕	8		30	13/	0	千克	3		/18
81.10	**锑及其制品,包括废碎料:**									
	-未锻轧锑;粉末:									
8110.1010	---未锻轧锑〔101 高铅锑,102 锑合金,103 其他锑及其制品〕	3	1	30	13/	0	千克	4xy		/26
8110.1020	---粉末〔101 高铅锑,102 锑合金,103 其他锑及其制品,301 属于危险化学品的金属〕	3		30	13/	0	千克	4Axy	M	/28
8110.2000	-废碎料〔999〕	3		30	13/	0	千克	49xy		/
8110.9000	-其他〔101 锑合金,102 其他锑及其制品〕	8		40	13/	0	千克	4xy		/18
81.11	**锰及其制品,包括废碎料:**									
8111.0010	---未锻轧锰;废碎料;粉末									
8111.0010 10	锰废碎料〔999〕	3		20	13/	0	千克	49xy		/28
8111.0010 90	未锻轧锰;粉末〔101 锰粉,102 锰片,103 锰锭,104 未锻轧锰桃、锰球、锰块,301 属于危险化学品的金属〕	3		20	13/	0	千克	4Axy	M	/28
8111.0090	---其他〔101〕	8		30	13/	0	千克	4xy		/18
81.12	**铍、铬、锗、钒、镓、铪、铟、铼、铌、铊及其制品,包括废碎料:**									
	-铍:									
8112.1200	--未锻轧铍;粉末〔301 其他有色金属及其制品,302 属于危险化学品的金属〕	3		30	13/	0	千克	3A	M	/28
8112.1300	--废碎料〔999〕	3		30	13/	0	千克	39		/
8112.1900	--其他〔101〕	8		30	13/	0	千克	3		/18
	-铬:									
8112.2100	--未锻轧铬;粉末〔999〕	3		20	13/	0	千克	4xy		/13
8112.2200	--废碎料〔999〕	3		20	13/	0	千克	49xy		/
8112.2900	--其他〔999〕	3		20	13/	0	千克	4xy		/23
	-铊:									
8112.5100	--未锻轧铊;粉末〔301 其他有色金属及其制品,302 属于危险化学品的金属〕	3		20	13/	0	千克	AB	MN	/
8112.5200	--废碎料〔999〕	3		20	13/	0	千克	9		/
8112.5900	--其他〔999〕	8		30	13/	0	千克			/18
	-其他:									
	--未锻轧的;废碎料;粉末:									
8112.9210	---锗									
8112.9210 10	未锻轧锗废碎料〔999〕	3		20	13/	0	千克	49Axy	M	/28
8112.9210 90	未锻轧的锗;锗粉末〔999〕	3		20	13/	0	千克	4xy		/28
8112.9220	---钒									
8112.9220 01	未锻轧、废碎料或粉末状的钒氮合金〔102〕	3	0	20	13/	0	千克	4xy		/25
8112.9220 10	未锻轧的钒废碎料〔999〕	3		20	13/	0	千克	49Axy	M	/28
8112.9220 90	未锻轧的钒;钒粉末〔999〕	3		20	13/	0	千克	4xy		/28
8112.9230	---铟									
8112.9230 10	未锻轧的铟及铟粉末〔999〕	3		20	13/	0	千克	4xy		/28
8112.9230 90	未锻轧的铟废碎料〔999〕	3		20	13/	0	千克	49xy		/28
8112.9240	---铌									
8112.9240 10	铌废碎料〔999〕	3		20	13/	0	千克	49Axy	M	/28
8112.9240 90	未锻轧的铌;铌粉末〔999〕	3	1	20	13/	0	千克	4xy		/26
8112.9290	---其他									
8112.9290 11	未锻轧的铪废碎料〔999〕	3		20	13/	0	千克	39A	M	/28
8112.9290 19	未锻轧的铪;粉末〔301〕	3		20	13/	0	千克	3A	M	/28

协定税率 %										特惠税率 %			Article Description
亚太5国	东/冰/格	巴基斯坦	韩国	瑞士	哥达	秘鲁	澳大利亚	新西/坡/智	港/澳/台	亚太2国	老/柬/缅	36/3/1	
	0/0/0	4	3.2	0	0	0	0	0//0	0/0/			0/0/	Tubes or pipes of titanium (ultimate tensile strength≥900MPa at 20℃, outer diameter>75mm)
	0/0/0	4	3.2	0	0	0	0	0//0	0/0/			0/0/	Other titanium tubes or pipes
	0/0/3.2	4	0	0	0	0	0	0//0	0/0/			0/0/	---Other
													Zirconium and articles thereof, including waste and scrap:
													-Unwrought zirconium; powders
	0/0/0	0	0	0	0	0	0	0//0	0/0/			0/0/	Zirconium and alloys, granularity<500μm (containing zirconium≥97%, whether spheroid, ellipsoid, atomized, flake formed, ground metallic fuels)
	0/0/0	0	0	0	0	0	0	0//0	0/0/			0/0/	Other unwrought zirconium; powders
	0/0/0	0	0	0	0	0	0	0//0	0/0/			0/0/	-Waste and scrap
													-Other
	0/0/0	4	3.2	0	0	0	0	0//0	0/0/			0/0/	Tubes or pipes of zirconium and its alloys (ratio of hafnium and zirconium<1 500 by weight)
	0/0/0	4	3.2	0	0	0	0	0//0	0/0/			0/0/	Other wrought zirconium and articles thereof
													Antimony and articles thereof, including waste and scrap:
													-Unwrought antimony; powders:
	0/0/0	0	0	0	0	0	0	0//0	0/0/			0/0/	---Unwrought antimony
	0/0/0	0	0	0	0	0	0	0//0	0/0/			0/0/	---Powders
	0/0/0	0	0	0	0	0	0	0//0	0/0/			0/0/	-Antimony waste and scrap
	0/0/0	4	0	0	0	0	0	0//0	0/0/			0/0/	-Other
													Manganese and articles thereof, including waste and scrap:
													---Unwrought manganese; waste and scrap; powders
	0/0/0	0	0	0	0	0	0	0//0	0/0/			0/0/0	Unwrought manganese waste and scraps
	0/0/0	0	0	0	0	0	0	0//0	0/0/			0/0/0	Unwrought manganese powders
	0/0/0	4	0	0	0	0	0	0//0	0/0/			0/0/0	---Other
													Beryllium, chromium, germanium, vanadium, gallium, hafnium, indium, niobium (columbium), rhenium and thallium, and articles of these metals, including waste and scrap:
													-Beryllium:
	0/0/0	0	0	0	0	0	0	0//0	0/0/			0/0/0	--Unwrought; powders
	0/0/0	0	0	0	0	0	0	0//0	0/0/			0/0/0	--Waste and scrap
	0/0/0	4	0	0	0	0	0	0//0	0/0/			0/0/0	--Other
													-Chromium:
	0/0/0	0	0	0	0	0	0	0//0	0/0/			0/0/0	--Unwrought; powders
	0/0/0	0	0	0	0	0	0	0//0	0/0/			0/0/0	--Waste and scrap
	0/0/1.2	0	0	0	0	0	0	0//0	0/0/			0/0/0	--Other
													-Thallium:
	0/0/0	0	0	0	0	0	0	0//0	0/0/			0/0/0	--Unwrought; powders
	0/0/0	0	0	0	0	0	0	0//0	0/0/			0/0/0	--Waste and scrap
	0/0/0	4	0	0	0	0	0	0//0	0/0/			0/0/0	--Other
													-Other:
													--Unwrought; waste and scrap; powders:
													---Germanium
	0/0/0	0	0	0	0	0	0	0//0	0/0/			0/0/0	Unwrought germanium waste and scraps
	0/0/0	0	0	0	0	0	0	0//0	0/0/			0/0/0	Unwrought germanium; powders
													---Vanadium
	0/0/0	0	0	0	0	0	0	0//0	0/0/			0/0/0	Unwrought, waste and scrap, powders, vanadium-nitrogen alloys
	0/0/0	0	0	0	0	0	0	0//0	0/0/			0/0/0	Unwrought, vanadium waste and scraps
	0/0/0	0	0	0	0	0	0	0//0	0/0/			0/0/0	Unwrought vanadium; Powders
													---Indium
	0/0/0	0	0	0	0	0	0	0//0	0/0/			0/0/0	Indium and indium powder not forged
	0/0/0	0	0	0	0	0	0	0//0	0/0/			0/0/0	Unwrought indium waste and scrap
													---Niobium
	0/0/0	0	0	0	0	0	0	0//0	0/0/			0/0/0	Unwrought niobium waste and scrap
	0/0/0	0	0	0	0	0	0	0//0	0/0/			0/0/0	Unwrought niobium; powders
													---Other
2.7	0/0/0	0	0	0	0	0	0	0//0	0/0/			0/0/0	Unwrought hafnium waste and scrap
2.7	0/0/0	0	0	0	0	0	0	0//0	0/0/			0/0/0	Unwrought hafnium; powders

税则号列	货品名称〔CIQ 扩展编码及品名—T2 表示见附表 2〕	最惠(%)	暂定税率	普通	增值/消费	出口退税	计量单位	监管条件	检验检疫	特殊证件对美关税
8112.9290 91	未锻轧的镓、铼废碎料〔999,301 属于危险化学品的金属〕	3		20	13/	0	千克	49Axy	M	/28
8112.9290 99	未锻轧的镓、铼;粉末〔999,301 属于危险化学品的金属〕	3		20	13/	0	千克	4xyA	M	/28
	--其他:									
8112.9910	---锗〔101〕	3		20	13/	10	千克	4xy		/28
8112.9920	---钒									
8112.9920 01	其他钒氮合金〔101〕	3	0	20	13/	0	千克	4xy		/25
8112.9920 90	其他钒及其制品〔101〕	3		20	13/	0	千克	4xy		/28
8112.9930	---铟〔101〕	8		20	13/	0	千克	4xy		/18
8112.9940	---铌〔101〕	8		20	13/	0	千克	4xy		/18
8112.9990	---其他									
8112.9990 10	锻轧的铪及其制品〔101〕	8		30	13/	0	千克	3		/18
8112.9990 90	锻轧的镓、铼及其制品〔101〕	8		30	13/	0	千克	4xy		/18
81.13	**金属陶瓷及其制品,包括废碎料:**									
	金属陶瓷及其制品包括废碎料:									
8113.0010	---颗粒;粉末									
8113.0010 10	颗粒或粉末状碳化钨废碎料〔999〕	8		30	13/	0	千克	9A	M	/33
8113.0010 90	颗粒或粉末状其他金属陶瓷及其制品〔999〕	8		30	13/	0	千克			/33
8113.0090	---其他									
8113.0090 10	其他碳化钨废碎料,颗粒或粉末除外〔999〕	8		30	13/	0	千克	9A	M	/33
8113.0090 90	其他金属陶瓷及其制品,颗粒或粉末除外(包括废料)〔999〕	8		30	13/	0	千克			/33

协定税率 %										特惠税率 %			
亚太5国	东/冰/格	巴基斯坦	韩国	瑞士	哥达	秘鲁	澳大利亚	新西/坡/智	港/澳/台	亚太2国	老/柬/缅	36/3/1	Article Description
2.7	0/0/0	0	0	0	0	0	0	0//0	0/0/			0/0/0	Unwrought gallium, rhenium sawte and scraps
2.7	0/0/0	0	0	0	0	0	0	0//0	0/0/			0/0/0	Unwrought gallium, rhenium; powders
													--Other:
	0/0/0	0	0	0	0	0	0	0//0	0/0/			0/0/C	---Germanium
													---Vanadiurn
	0/0/0	0	0	0	0	0	0	0//0	0/0/			0/0/0	Other vanadium-nitrogen alloys
	0/0/0	0	0	0	0	0	0	0//0	0/0/			0/0/0	Other vanadium and articles thereof
	0/0/0	4	0	0	0	0	0	0//0	0/0/			0/0/0	---Indium
	0/0/0	4	0	0	0	0	0	0//0	0/0/			0/0/0	---Niobium
													---Other
5.6	0/0/0	0	0	0	0	0	0	0//0	0/0/			0/0/0	Wrought hafnium and articles thereof
5.6	0/0/0	0	0	0	0	0	0	0//0	0/0/			0/0/0	Other wrought gallium, rhenium and articles therof
													Cermets and articles thereof, including waste and scrap:
													Cermets and articles thereof, including waste and scrap:
													---Granules, powder
	0/0/0	4		0	0	0	0	0//0	0/0/0			0/0/	Waster and scrap of tungsten carbide, granules or powders
	0/0/0	4		0	0	0	0	0//0	0/0/0			0/0/	Other metal cermets and articles thereof, granules or powders
													---Other
	0/0/0	4		0	0	0	0	0//0	0/0/0			0/0/	Other tungsten carbide waste and scrap, other than granules or powders
	0/0/0	4		0	0	0	0	0//0	0/0/0			0/0/	Cther metal cermets and articles thereof, other than grainor powders (including waster and scrap)

第八十二章
贱金属工具、器具、利口器、餐匙、餐叉及其零件

注释：

一、除喷灯、轻便锻炉、带支架的砂轮、修指甲和修脚用器具及税目82.09的货品外，本章仅包括带有用下列材料制成的刀片、工作刃、工作面或其他工作部件的物品：

(一)贱金属；

(二)硬质合金或金属陶瓷；

(三)装于贱金属、硬质合金或金属陶瓷底座上的宝石或半宝石(天然、合成或再造)；

(四)附于贱金属底座上的磨料，当附上磨料后，所具有的切齿、沟、槽或类似结构仍保持其特性及功能。

二、本章所列物品的贱金属零件，应与该制品归入同一税号，但具体列名的零件及手工工具的工具夹具(税目84.66)除外。第十五类注释二所述的通用零件，均不归入本章。电动剃须刀及电动毛发推剪的刀头、刀片应归入税目85.10。

三、由税目82.11的一把或多把刀具与税号82.15至少数量相同的物品构成的成套货品应归入税目82.15。

税则号列		货品名称〔CIQ扩展编码及品名—T2表示见附表2〕	最惠(%)	暂定税率	普通	增值/消费	出口退税	计量单位	监管条件	检验检疫	特殊证件对美关税
82.01		**锹、铲、镐、锄、叉及耙；斧子、钩刀及类似砍伐工具；各种修枝用剪刀；镰刀、秣刀、树篱剪、伐木楔子及其他农业、园艺或林业用手工工具：**									
8201.1000		-锹及铲									
8201.1000	10	含植物性材料的锹及铲〔101其他木制品，102农用手工具〕	8		50	9/	9,10	千克/把	AB	PQ	/28
8201.1000	90	其他锹及铲〔999〕	8		50	9/	9,10	千克/把			/28
8201.3000		-镐、锄及耙									
8201.3000	10	含植物性材料的镐、锄、耙〔101其他木制品，102农用手工具〕	8		50	9/	9,10	千克/把	AB	PQ	/33
8201.3000	90	其他镐、锄、耙〔999〕	8		50	9/	9,10	千克/把			/33
8201.4000		-斧子、钩刀及类似砍伐工具									
8201.4000	10	含植物性材料的砍伐工具(包括斧子、钩刀及类似砍伐工具)〔101其他木制品，102农用手工具〕	8		50	9/	9,10	千克/把	AB	PQ	/18
8201.4000	90	其他斧子、钩刀及类似砍伐工具〔999〕	8		50	9/	9,10	千克/把			/18
8201.5000		-修枝剪及类似的单手操作剪刀(包括家禽剪)									
8201.5000	10	含植物性材料的单手操作农用剪(包括家禽剪)〔101其他木制品，102农用手工具〕	8		50	9/	9,10	千克/把	AB	PQ	/33
8201.5000	90	其他修枝剪等单手操作农用剪(包括家禽剪)〔999〕	8		50	9/	9,10	千克/把			/33
8201.6000		-树篱剪、双手修枝剪及类似的双手操作剪刀									
8201.6000	10	含植物性材料的双手操作农用剪〔101其他木制品，102农用手工具〕	8		50	9/	9	千克/把	AB	PQ	/33
8201.6000	90	其他修枝等双手操作农用剪〔999〕	8		50	9/	9	千克/把			/33
		-用于农业、园艺或林业的其他手工工具：									
8201.9010		---叉									
8201.9010	10	含植物性材料的农业、园艺、林业用叉〔101其他木制品，102农用手工具〕	8		50	9/	9	千克/把	AB	PQ	/18
8201.9010	90	其他农业、园艺、林业用叉〔999〕	8		50	9/	9	千克/把			/18
8201.9090		---其他									
8201.9090	10	含植物性材料的农林、园艺、林业用手工工具〔101其他木制品，102农用手工具〕	8		50	9/	9,10	千克/把	AB	PQ	/18
8201.9090	90	其他农业、园艺、林业用手工工具〔999〕	8		50	9/	9,10	千克/把			/18
82.02		**手工锯；各种锯的锯片(包括切条、切槽或无齿锯片)：**									
8202.1000		-手工锯〔999〕	8		50	13/	9,10	千克/把			/33
		-带锯片：									

Chapter 82
Tools, implements, cutlery, spoons and forks, parts thereof of base metal

Notes:

1. Apart from blow lamps, portable forges, grinding wheels with frameworks, manicure or pedicure sets, and goods of heading No. 82.09, this Chapter covers only articles with a blade, working No. edge, working surface or other working part of :
   (a) Base metal;
   (b) Metal carbides or cermets;
   (c) Precious or semi-precious stones (natural, synthetic or reconstructed) on a support of base metal, metal carbide or cermet; or
   (d) Abrasive materials on a support of base metal, provided that the articles have cutting teeth, flutes, grooves, or the like, of base metal, which retain their identity and function after the application of the abrasive.
2. Parts of base metal of the articles of this Chapter are to be classified with the articles of which they are parts, except parts separately specified as such and tool-holders for hand tools (heading No.84. 66). However, parts of general use as defined in Note 2 to Section XV are in all cases excluded from this Chapter. Heads, blades and cutting plates for electric shavers and electric hair clippers are to be classified in heading No.85. 10.
3. Sets consisting of one or more knives of heading No.82. 11 and at least an equal number of articles of heading No.82. 15 are to be classified in heading No.82. 15.

协定税率 %										特惠税率 %			
亚太5国	东/冰/格	巴基斯坦	韩国	瑞士	哥达	秘鲁	澳大利亚	新西/坡/智	港/澳/台	亚太2国	老/柬/缅	36/3/1	Article Description
													Hand tools, the following: spades, shovels, mattocks, picks, hoes, forks and rakes; axes, bill hooks and similar hewing tools; secateurs and prundrs of any kind; scythes, hay knives, hedge shears, timber wedges and other tools of a kind used in agriculture, horticulture or forestry:
													-Spades and shovels
	0/0/0	4	0	0	0	0	0	0//0	0/0/			0/0/0	Spades and shovels with vegetable materials
	0/0/0	4	0	0	0	0	0	0//0	0/0/			0/0/0	Other spades and shovels
													-Mattocks, picks, hoes and rakes
	0/0/0	4	0	0	0	0	0	0//0	0/0/			0/0/0	Mattocks, picks, hoes and rakes with vegetable materials
	0/0/0	4	0	0	0	0	0	0//0	0/0/			0/0/0	Other mattocks, picks, hoes and rakes
													-Axes, bill hooks and similar hewing tools
	0/0/0	4	0	0	0	0	0	0//0	0/0/			0/0/0	Hewing tools with vegetable materials(including axes, bill hooks and similar hewing tools)
	0/0/0	4	0	0	0	0	0	0//0	0/0/			0/0/0	Other axes, bill hooks and similar hewing tools
													-Secateurs and similar one-handed pruners and shears (including poultry shears)
	0/0/0	4	0	0	0	0	0	0//0	0/0/			0/0/0	Secateurs and similar one-handed pruners and shears (including poultry shears), with vegetable materials, of a kind used in agriculture
	0/0/0	4	0	0	0	0	0	0//0	0/0/			0/0/0	Other secateurs and similar one-handed pruners and shears (including poultry shears), of a kind used in agriculture
													-Hedge shears, two-handed pruning shears and similar two-handed shears
	0/0/0	4	0	0	0	0	0	0//0	0/0/			0/0/0	Hedge shears, two-handed pruning shears and similar two-handed shears, with vegetable materials, of a kind used in agriculture
	0/0/0	4	0	0	0	0	0	0//0	0/0/			0/0/0	Other hedge shears, two-handed pruning shears and similar two-handed shears, of a kind used in agriculture
													-Other hand tools of a kind used in agriculture, horticulture or forestry:
													---Forks
	0/0/0	4	0	0	0	0	0	0//0	0/0/			0/0/0	Forks of a kind used in agriculture, horticulture or forestry, with vegetable materials
	0/0/0	4	0	0	0	0	0	0//0	0/0/			0/0/0	Other forks of a kind used in agriculture, horticulture or forestry
													---Other
	0/0/0	4	3.2	0	0	0	0	0//0	0/0/			0/0/0	Hand tools of a kind used in agriculture, horticulture or forestry, with vegetable materials
	0/0/0	4	3.2	0	0	0	0	0//0	0/0/			0/0/0	Other hand tools of a kind used in agriculture, horticulture or forestry
													Hand saws; blades for saws of all kinds (including slitting, slotting or toothless saw blades):
	0/0/0	4	3.3	0	0	0	0	0//0	0/0/			0/0/0	-Hand saws
													-Band saw blades:

税则号列	货品名称〔CIQ扩展编码及品名－T2表示见附表2〕	最惠(%)	暂定税率	普通	增值/消费	出口退税	计量单位	监管条件	检验检疫	特殊证件对美关税
8202.2010	---双金属带锯条〔999〕	8		20	13/	13	千克			/28
8202.2090	---其他〔999〕	8		20	13/	13	千克			/28
	-圆锯片(包括切条或切槽锯片)：									
8202.3100	--带有钢制工作部件〔999〕	8		20	13/	13	千克			/33
	--其他，包括部件：									
8202.3910	---带有天然或合成金刚石、立方氮化硼制的工作部件〔999〕	8		20	13/	13	千克			/33
8202.3990	---其他〔999〕	8		20	13/	13	千克			/33
8202.4000	-链锯片〔999〕	8		20	13/	13	千克			/18
	-其他锯片：									
	--直锯片，加工金属用：									
8202.9110	---机械锯用〔999〕	8		20	13/	13	千克			/18
8202.9190	---其他〔999〕	8		50	13/	13	千克			/18
	--其他：									
8202.9910	---机械锯用〔999〕	8		20	13/	13	千克			/28
8202.9990	---其他〔999〕	8		50	13/	13	千克			/18
82.03	**钢锉、木锉、钳子(包括剪钳)、镊子、白铁剪、切管器、螺栓切头器、打孔冲子及类似手工工具：**									
8203.1000	-钢锉、木锉及类似工具〔999〕	8		50	13/	13	千克/把			/33
8203.2000	-钳子(包括剪钳)、镊子及类似工具〔999〕	8		50	13/	13	千克/把			/28
8203.3000	-白铁剪及类似工具〔999〕	8		50	13/	13	千克/把			/28
8203.4000	-切管器、螺栓切头器、打孔冲子及类似工具〔999〕	8		50	13/	13	千克/把			/18
82.04	**手动扳手及扳钳(包括转矩扳手，但不包括丝锥扳手)；可互换的扳手套筒，不论是否带手柄：**									
	-手动扳手及扳钳：									
8204.1100	--固定的〔999〕	8		50	13/	13	千克/把			/28
8204.1200	--可调的〔999〕	8		50	13/	13	千克/把			/18
8204.2000	-可互换的扳手套筒，不论是否带手柄〔999〕	8		50	13/	13	千克/套			/33
82.05	**其他税号未列名的手工工具(包括玻璃刀)；喷灯；台钳、夹钳及类似品，但作为机床或水射流切割机附件或零件的除外；砧；轻便锻炉；带支架的手摇或脚踏砂轮：**									
8205.1000	-钻孔或攻丝工具〔999〕	8		50	13/	13	千克/个			/18
8205.2000	-锤子〔999〕	8		50	13/	13	千克/个			/28
8205.3000	-木工用刨子、凿子及类似切削工具〔999〕	8		50	13/	13	千克/个			/28
8205.4000	-螺丝刀〔999〕	8		50	13/	13	千克/个			/28
	-其他手工工具(包括玻璃刀)：									
8205.5100	--家用工具〔999〕	7		50	13/	13	千克/个			/27
8205.5900	--其他〔999〕	8		50	13/	13	千克/个			/18
8205.6000	-喷灯〔999〕	8		50	13/	13	千克/个			/28
8205.7000	-台钳、夹钳及类似品〔101台钳、夹钳及类似品，102其它五金工具〕	8		50	13/	13	千克/个			/28
8205.9000	-其他，包括由本税目项下两个或多个子目所列物品组成的成套货品〔999〕	8		50	13/	13	千克			/18
82.06	**由税目82.02至82.05中两个或多个税号所列工具组成的零售包装成套货品：**									
8206.0000	由税目82.02至82.05中两个或多个税号所列工具组成的零售包装成套货品〔999〕	8		50	13/	13	千克			/18
82.07	**手工工具(不论是否有动力装置)及机床(例如，锻压、冲压、攻丝、钻孔、镗孔、铰孔及铣削、车削或上螺丝用的机器)的可互换工具，包括金属拉拔或挤压用模以及凿岩或钻探工具：**									
	-凿岩或钻探工具：									
8207.1300	--带有金属陶瓷制的工作部件〔999〕	8		20	13/	13	千克			/28
	--其他，包括部件：									
8207.1910	---带有天然或合成金钢石、立方氮化硼制的工作部件〔999〕	8		20	13/	13	千克			/18
8207.1990	---其他〔999〕	8		20	13/	13	千克			/18
	-金属拉拔或挤压用模：									
8207.2010	---带有天然或合成金刚石、立方氮化硼制的工作部件〔999〕	8		20	13/	13	千克/套			/33

协定税率 %										特惠税率 %			Article Description
亚太5国	东/冰/格	巴基斯坦	韩国	瑞士	哥达	秘鲁	澳大利亚	新西/坡/智	港/澳/台	亚太2国	老/柬/缅	36/3/1	
	0/0/0	4	3.2	2.4	0	0	0	0//0	0/0/			0/0/0	---Double metal band saw blade
	0/0/0	4	3.2	2.4	0	0	0	0//0	0/0/			0/0/0	---Other
													-Circular saw blades (including slitting or slotting saw blades):
	0/0/0	4	3.2	0	0	0	0	0//0	0/0/			0/0/0	--With working part of steel
													--Other, including parts:
	0/0/0	4	0	0	0	0	0	0//0	0/0/			0/0/0	---with working part of natural or synthetic diamond, cubic boron nitride
	0/0/0	4	0	0	0	0	0	0//0	0/0/			0/0/0	---Other
	0/0/0	4	0	2.4	0	0	0	0//0	0/0/			0/0/0	-Chain saw blades
													-Other saw blades:
													--Straight saw blades, for working metal:
5.2	0/0/0	4	3.2	2.4	0	0	0	0//0	0/0/			0/0/0	---For sawing machines
	0/0/0	4	0	2.4	0	0	0	0//0	0/0/			0/0/0	---Other
													--Other:
	0/0/0	4	3.3	2.5	0	0	0	0//0	0/0/			0/0/0	---For sawing machines
	0/0/0	4.5	4.2	3.2	0	0	0	0/0/0	0/0/			0/0/	---Other
													Files, rasps, pliers (including cutting pliers), pincers, tweezers, metal cutting shears, pipe-cutters, bolt croppers, perforating punches and similar hand tools:
	0/0/0	4	4.2	3.2	0	0	0	0/0/0	0/0/			0/0/0	-Files, rasps and similar tools
	0/0/0		4.2	3.2	0	0	0	0/0/0	0/0/0			0/0/	-Pliers (including cutting pliers), pincers, tweezers and similar tools
	0/0/0	4	4.2	3.2	0	0	0	0/0/0	0/0/			0/0/	-Meta. cutting shears and similar tools
	0/0/0	4.5	4.2	3.2	0	0	0	0/0/0	0/0/			0/0/	-Pipe-cutters, bolt croppers, perforating punches and similar tools
													Hand-operated spanners and wrenches (including torque meter wrenches but not including tap wrenches); interchangeable spanner sockets, with or without handles:
													-Hand-operated spanners and wrenches:
	0/0/0	4.5	4.2	3.2	0	0	0	0/0/0	0/0/			0/0/0	--Non-adjustable
	0/0/0	4	4	0	0	0	0	0//0	0/0/0			0/0/0	--Adjustable
	0/0/0	4	4	0	0	0	0	0//0	0/0/			0/0/	-Interchangeable spanner sockets, with or without handles
													Hand tools (including glaziers' diamonds), not elsewhere specified or included; blow lamps; vices, clamps and the like, other than accessories for and parts of, machine tools or water jet cutting machine; anvils; portable forges; hand or pedal operated grinding wheels with frame works:
	0/0/0	4	4	0	0	0	0	0//0	0/0/			0/0/	-Drilling, threading or tapping tools
	0/0/0	4.5	4	0	0	0	0	0//0	0/0/0			0/0/0	-Hammers and sledge hammers
	0/0/0	4	4.2	3.2	0	0	0	0/0/0	0/0/			0/0/	-Planes, chisels, gouges and similar cutting tools for working wood
	0/0/0	4.5	4.2	3.2	0	0	0	0/0/0	0/0/0			0/0/0	-Screwdrivers
													-Other hand tools (including glaziers' diamonds):
	0/0/0	4	4.2	3.2	0	0	0	0/0/0	0/0/			0/0/	--Household tools
5.2	0/0/0	0	4	3	0	0	0	0//0	0/0/0			0/0/	--Other
	0/0/0	4	4	3	0	0	0	0//0	0/0/			0/0/	-Blow lamps
	0/0/0	4	4.2	5.5	0	0	0	0/0/0	0/0/			0/0/	-Vices, clamps and the like
	0/0/0	4	4.2	3.2	0	0	0	0/0/0	0/0/			0/0/	-Other, including sets of articles of two or more the foregoing subheadings
													Tools of two or more of the headings Nos.82.02 to 82.05, put up in sets for retail sale:
	0/0/0	4	4.2	4.4	0	0	0	0/0/0	0/0/			0/0/	Tools of two or more of the headings Nos.82.02 to 82.05, put up in sets for retail sale
													Interchangeable tools for hand tools, whether or not power-operated, or for machine-tools (for example, for pressing, stamping, punching, tapping, threading, drilling, boring, broaching, milling, turning or screw driving), including dies for drawing or extruding metal, and rock drilling or earth boring tools:
													-Rock drilling or earth boring tools:
	0/0/0	4	0	0	0	0	0	0//0	0/0/			0/0/0	--With working part of cermets
													--Other, including parts:
	0/0/0	4	0	0	0	0	0	0//0	0/0/			0/0/0	---With working part of natural or synthetic diamonds or cubic boronnitride
	0/0/0	4	3.2	0	0	0	0	0//0	0/0/			0/0/0	---Other
													-Dies for drawing or extruding metal:
	0/0/0	4	0	0	0	0	0	0//0	0/0/0			0/0/0	---With working part of natural or synthetic diamonds or cubic boronnitride

税则号列	货品名称〔CIQ 扩展编码及品名—T2 表示见附表 2〕	最惠(%)	暂定税率	普通	增值/消费	出口退税	计量单位	监管条件	检验检疫	特殊证件对美关税
8207.2090	---其他〔999〕	8		20	13/	13	千克/套			/33
8207.3000	-锻压或冲压工具									
8207.3000 10	加工税号 87.03 所列车辆车身冲压件用的 4 种关键模具(侧围外板、翼子板、拼接整体侧围内板、拼焊整体侧围加强板用模具)〔999〕	8	6	20	13/	13	千克			/31
8207.3000 20	加工税号 87.03 所列车辆车身冲压件用的 4 种特种模具(σb≥980N/mm^2 的冷冲压、热成型、内高压成型和铝板用模具)〔999〕	8	6	20	13/	13	千克			/31
8207.3000 90	其他锻压或冲压工具〔999〕	8		20	13/	13	千克			/33
8207.4000	-攻丝工具〔999〕	8		20	13/	13	千克/件			/33
	-钻孔工具,但凿岩及钻探用的除外:									
8207.5010	---带有天然或合成金刚石、立方氮化硼制的工作部件〔999〕	8		20	13/	13	千克/件			/28
8207.5090	---其他〔999〕	8		20	13/	13	千克/件			/33
	-镗孔或铰孔工具:									
8207.6010	---带有天然或合成金刚石、立方氮化硼制的工作部件〔999〕	8		20	13/	13	千克/件			/33
8207.6090	---其他〔999〕	8		20	13/	13	千克/件			/33
	-铣削工具:									
8207.7010	---带有天然或合成金刚石、立方氮化硼制的工作部件〔999〕	8		20	13/	13	千克/件			/33
8207.7090	---其他〔999〕	8		20	13/	13	千克/件			/33
	-车削工具:									
8207.8010	---带有天然或合成金刚石、立方氮化硼制的工作部件〔999〕	8		20	13/	13	千克/件			/18
8207.8090	---其他〔999〕	8		20	13/	13	千克/件			/28
	-其他可互换工具:									
8207.9010	---带有天然或合成金刚石、立方氮化硼制的工作部件〔999〕	8		20	13/	13	千克/件			/18
8207.9090	---其他〔999〕	8		20	13/	13	千克/件			/28
82.08	**机器或机械器具的刀及刀片:**									
	-金属加工用:									
	---硬质合金制的:									
8208.1011	----经镀或涂层的〔999〕	8		20	13/	13	千克			/28
8208.1019	----其他〔999〕	8		20	13/	13	千克			/33
8208.1090	---其他〔999〕	8		20	13/	13	千克			/28
8208.2000	-木器加工用〔999〕	8		20	13/	13	千克			/33
8208.3000	-厨房器具或食品工业机器用〔999〕	8		20	13/	13	千克	A	R	/18
8208.4000	-农业、园艺或林业机器用〔999〕	8		20	9/	9,10	千克			/18
8208.9000	-其他〔999〕	8		20	13/	13	千克			/33
82.09	**未装配的工具用金属陶瓷板、杆、刀头及类似品:**									
8209.0010	---板〔999〕	8		20	13/	13	千克			/33
	---条、杆:									
8209.0021	----晶粒度<0.8 微米〔999〕	8		20	13/	13	千克			/33
8209.0029	----其他〔999〕	8		20	13/	13	千克			/33
8209.0030	---刀头〔999〕	8		20	13/	13	千克			/33
8209.0090	---其他〔999〕	8		20	13/	13	千克			/18
82.10	**用于加工或调制食品或饮料的手动机械器具,重量不超过 10 千克:**									
8210.0000	用于加工或调制食品或饮料的手动机械器具,重量不超过 10 千克〔999〕	8		80	13/	13	千克/台	A	R	/28
82.11	**有刃口的刀及其刀片,不论是否有锯齿(包括整枝刀),但税目 82.08 的刀除外:**									
8211.1000	-成套货品〔999〕	8		80	13/	10	千克/套			/33
	-其他:									
8211.9100	--刃面固定的餐刀〔101 餐桌用具,102 食品接触不锈钢产品,103 食品接触铁产品,104 食品接触铝产品,105 食品接触其他金属产品〕	7		80	13/	10	千克/把	A	R	/32
8211.9200	--刃面固定的其他刀〔101 其它食品加工机器及其零件,102 食品接触不锈钢产品,103 食品接触铁产品,104 食品接触铝产品,105 食品接触其他金属产品〕	7		80	13/	10	千克/把			/27
8211.9300	--刃面不固定的刀〔101 其它食品加工机器及其零件,102 食品接触不锈钢产品,103 食品接触铝产品,104 食品接触其他金属产品,105 食品接触铁产品〕	7		80	13/	13	千克/把			/32

协定税率 %										特惠税率 %			Article Description
亚太5国	东/冰/格	巴基斯坦	韩国	瑞士	哥达	秘鲁	澳大利亚	新西/坡/智	港/澳/台	亚太2国	老/柬/缅	36/3/1	
	0/0/0	4	0	2.4	0	0	0	0//0	0/0/0			0/0/0	---Other
													-Tools for pressing, stamping or punching
6.8	0/0/0	4	4.8	0	0	0	0	0//0	0/0/0			0/0/0	Processing of car body stamping parts with four key mold(side wall outer panel, fender, integral joint side wall inner plate, fight the whole welding of side wall reinforcing plate mold)
6.8	0/0/0	4	4.8	0	0	0	0	0//0	0/0/0			0/0/0	Processing of car body stamping parts with four special mould(cold stamping of sigma B is more than or equal to 980N/mm^2, thermoforming, in high-pressure molding and aluminum plate with mold)
6.8	0/0/0	4	4.8	0	0	0	0	0//0	0/0/0			0/0/0	Other tools for pressing, stamping or punching
	0/0/0	4		0	0	0	0	0//0	0/0/0			0/0/0	-Tools for tapping or threading
													-Tools for drilling, other than for rock drilling:
	0/0/0	4		0	0	0	0	0//0	0/0/0			0/0/0	---With working part of natural or synthetic diamonds or cubic boronnitride
	0/0/0	4		0	0	0	0	0//0	0/0/0			0/0/0	---Other
													-Tools for boring or broaching:
	0/0/0	4		0	0	0	0	0//0	0/0/0			0/0/0	---With working part of natural or synthetic diamonds or cubic boronnitride
	0/0/0	4	4.8	0	0	0	0	0//0	0/0/			0/0/0	---Other
													-Tools for milling:
	0/0/0	4		0	0	0	0	0//0	0/0/0			0/0/0	---With working part of natural or synthetic diamonds or cubic boronnitride
	0/0/0	4		0	0	0	0	0//0	0/0/0			0/0/0	---Other
													-Tools for turning:
5.2	0/0/0	4	5.2	0	0	0	0	0//0	0/0/0			0/0/0	---With working part of natural or synthetic diamonds or cubic boronnitride
5.2	0/0/0	4	5.2	0	0	0	0	0//0	0/0/0			0/0/0	---Other
													-Other interchangeable tools:
5.2	0/0/0	4	5.2	0	0	0	0	0//0	0/0/0			0/0/0	---With working part of natural or synthetic diamonds or cubic boronnitride
5.2	0/0/0	4	5.2	2.4	0	0	0	0//0	0/0/0			0/0/0	---Other
													Knives and cutting blades, for machines or for mechanical appliances:
													-For metal working:
													---Of metal carbides:
	0/0/0	4	4.8	2.4	0	0	0	0//0	0/0/			0/0/	----Plated or coated
	0/0/0	4	4.8	2.4	0	0	0	0//0	0/0/			0/0/	----Other
	0/0/0	4	4.8	2.4	0	0	0	0//0	0/0/			0/0/	---Other
	0/0/0	4	0	0	0	0	0	0//0	0/0/0			0/0/0	-For wood working
	0/0/0	4	3.2	0	0	0	0	0//0	0/0/			0/0/0	-For kitchen appliances or for machines used by the food industry
	0/0/0	4	0	2.4	0	0	0	0//0	0/0/0			0/0/	-For agricultural, horticultural or forestry machines
5.2	0/0/0	0	0	2.4	0	0	0	0//0	0/0/0			0/0/	-Other
													Plates, sticks, tips and the like for tools, unmounted, of cermets:
5.2	0/0/0	4	3.2	0	0	0	0	0//0	0/0/			0/0/0	---plates
													---Bar, rod:
5.2	0/0/0	4	0	2.4	0	0	0	0//0	0/0/			0/0/0	----Grain size <0.8μm
5.2	0/0/0	4	0	2.4	0	0	0	0//0	0/0/			0/0/0	----Other
5.2	0/0/0	4	4.8	0	0	0	0	0//0	0/0/			0/0/0	---Tips
5.2	0/0/0	4	0	0	0	0	0	0//0	0/0/			0/0/0	---Other
													Hand-operated mechanical appliances, weighing 10g or less, used in the preparation, conditioning or serving of food or drink:
5.2	0/0/0	13	7.2	5.4	0	0	0	0/0/0	0/0/			0/0/	Hand-operated mechanical appliances, weighing 10kg or less, used in the preparation, conditioning or serving of food or drink
													Knives with cutting blades, serrated or not (including pruning knives), other than knives of heading No.82.08, and blades therefor:
	0/0/0	0	7.2	5.4	0	0	0	0/0/0	0/0/			0/0/	-Sets of assorted articles
													-Other:
	0/0/0	0	7.2	5.4	0	0	0	0/0/0	0/0/			0/0/	--Table knives having fixed blades
	0/0/0	0	4.8	5	0	0	0	0/0/0	0/0/			0/0/0	--Other knives having fixed blades
	0/0/0	0	7.2	0	0	0	0	0/0/0	0/0/			0/0/	--Knives having other than fixed blades

税则号列	货品名称〔CIQ 扩展编码及品名—T2 表示见附表 2〕	最惠(%)	暂定税率	普通	增值/消费	出口退税	计量单位	监管条件	检验检疫	特殊证件对美关税
8211.9400	--刀片〔101 其它食品加工机器及其零件,102 食品接触不锈钢产品,103 食品接触铁产品,104 食品接触铝产品,105 食品接触其他金属产品〕	7		80	13/	13	千克			/27
8211.9500	--贱金属制的刀柄〔101 其它食品加工机器及其零件,102 食品接触其他金属产品〕	7		80	13/	13	千克			/32
82.12	**剃刀及其刀片(包括未分开的刀片条):**									
8212.1000	-剃刀〔999〕	7		80	13/	10	千克/把			/27
8212.2000	-安全刀片,包括未分开的刀片条〔999〕	7		80	13/	10	千克/片			/17
8212.9000	-其他零件〔999〕	7		80	13/	10	千克			/27
82.13	**剪刀、裁缝剪刀及类似品、剪刀片:**									
8213.0000	剪刀、裁缝剪刀及类似品、剪刀片〔101 其它机电产品及其零件,103 其他金属及制品〕	7		80	13/	10	千克			/32
82.14	**其他利口器(例如,理发推剪、屠刀、砍骨刀、切肉刀、切菜刀、裁纸刀);修指甲及修脚用具(包括指甲锉):**									
8214.1000	-裁纸刀、开信刀、改错刀、铅笔刀及其刀片〔999〕	7		80	13/	10	千克			/27
8214.2000	-修指甲及修脚用具(包括指甲锉)〔999〕	7		90	13/	10	千克			/32
8214.9000	-其他									
8214.9000　10	切菜刀等厨房用利口器〔101 厨房用具,102 食品接触不锈钢产品,103 食品接触铁产品,104 食品接触铝产品,105 食品接触其他金属产品〕	7		80	13/	10	千克	A	R	/32
8214.9000　90	理发推子等其他利口器〔999〕	7		80	13/	10	千克			/32
82.15	**餐匙、餐叉、长柄勺、漏勺、糕点夹、鱼刀、黄油刀、糖块夹及类似的厨房或餐桌用具:**									
8215.1000	-成套货品,至少其中一件物品是镀贵金属的〔101 厨房用具,102 餐桌用具,103 食品接触其他金属产品,104 食品用其他金属包装〕	7		80	13/	10	千克	A	R	/32
8215.2000	-其他成套货品〔101 厨房用具,102 餐桌用具,103 食品接触其他金属产品,104 食品用其他金属包装〕	7		80	13/	10	千克	A	R	/27
	-其他:									
8215.9100	--镀贵金属的〔101 厨房用具,102 餐桌用具,103 食品接触其他金属产品,104 食品用其他金属包装〕	7		80	13/	10	千克	A	R	/32
8215.9900	--其他〔101 厨房用具,102 餐桌用具,103 食品接触其他金属产品,104 食品用其他金属包装〕	7		80	13/	13	千克	A	R	/32

协定税率 %										特惠税率 %			Article Description
亚太5国	东/冰/格	巴基斯坦	韩国	瑞士	哥达	秘鲁	澳大利亚	新西/坡/智	港/澳/台	亚太2国	老/柬/缅	36/3/1	
	0/0/0	0	5.6	4.2	0	0	0	0/0/0	0/0/			0/0/	--Blades
	0/0/0	0	4.8	6.2	0	0	0	0/0/0	0/0/			0/0/0	--Handles of base metal
													Razors and razor blades (including razor blade blanks in strips):
	0/0/0	0	4.8	3.6	0	0	0	0/0/0	0/0/			0/0/0	-Razors
	0/0/0	0	5.6	4.2	0	0	0	0/0/0	0/0/			0/0/	-Safety razor blades, including razor blade blanks in strips
	0/0/0	0	4.8	3.6	0	0	0	0/0/0	0/0/			0/0/0	-Other parts
													Scissors, tailors' shears and similar shears, and blades therefor:
4.6	0/0/0	0	4.8	3.6	0	0	0	0/0/0	0/0/			0/0/0	Scissors, tailors' shears and similar shears, and blades therefor
													Other articles of cutlery (for example, hair clippers, butchers' or kitchen cleavers, choppers and mincing knives, paper knives); manicure or pedicure sets and instruments (including nail files):
4.6	0/0/0	4.5	4.8	3.6	0	0	0	0/0/0	0/0/			0/0/0	-Paper knives, letter openers, erasing knives, pencil sharpeners and blades therefor
4.6	0/0/0	0	7.2	5.4	0	0	0	0/0/0	0/0/			0/0/0	-Manicure or pedicure sets and instruments (including nail files)
													-Other
	0/0/0		7.2	5.4	0	0	0	0/0/0	0/0/			0/0/	Kitchen cleavers, choppers mincing knives and other articles of cutlery
	0/0/0		7.2	5.4	0	0	0	0/0/0	0/0/			0/0/	Hair clippers and other articles of cutlery
													Spoons, forks, ladles, skimmers, cakeservers, fish-knives, butter-knives, sugar tongs and similar kitchen or tableware:
	0/0/0	0	7.2	5.4	0	0	0	0/0/0	0/0/			0/0/	-Sets of assorted articles containing at least one article plated with precious metal
	0/0/0	0	7.2	5.4	0	0	0	0/0/0	0/0/			0/0/	-Other sets of assorted articles
													-Other:
	0/0/0	0	7.2	5.4	0	0	0	0/0/0	0/0/			0/0/	--Plated with precious metal
	0/0/0	0	7.2	5.4	0	0	0	0/0/0	0/0/			0/0/0	--Other

第八十三章
贱金属杂项制品

注释：

一、在本章，贱金属零件应与制品一同归类。但税目 73.12、73.15、73.17、73.18 及 73.20 的钢铁制品或其他贱金属(第七十四章至第七十六章及第七十八章至第八十一章)制的类似物品不应视为本章制品的零件。

二、税目 83.02 所称"脚轮"，是指直径(对于有胎的，连胎计算在内，下同)不超过 75 毫米的或直径虽超过 75 毫米，但所装轮或胎的宽度必须小于 30 毫米的脚轮。

税则号列	货品名称〔CIQ 扩展编码及品名—T2 表示见附表 2〕	最惠(%)	暂定税率	普通	增值/消费	出口退税	计量单位	监管条件	检验检疫	特殊证件对美关税
83.01	**贱金属制的锁(钥匙锁、数码锁及电动锁)；贱金属制带锁的扣环及扣环框架；上述锁的贱金属制钥匙：**									
8301.1000	-挂锁〔999〕	7		80	13/	10	千克/把			/27
	-机动车用锁：									
8301.2010	---中央控制门锁〔101 其他车辆零部件，102 机动车锁〕	9		80	13/	13	千克/套		L	/19
8301.2090	---其他〔101 其他车辆零部件，102 机动车锁〕	9		80	13/	13	千克/套		L	/19
8301.3000	-家具用锁〔999〕	7		80	13/	10	千克/个			/27
8301.4000	-其他锁〔999〕	9		80	13/	10	千克/个			/19
8301.5000	-带锁的扣环及扣环框架〔999〕	9		80	13/	10	千克			/19
8301.6000	-零件〔999〕	9		80	13/	10	千克			/29
8301.7000	-钥匙〔999〕	7		80	13/	10	千克			/32
83.02	**用于家具、门窗、楼梯、百叶窗、车厢、鞍具、衣箱、盒子及类似品的贱金属附件及架座；贱金属制帽架、帽钩、托架及类似品；用贱金属做支架的小脚轮；贱金属制的自动闭门器：**									
8302.1000	-铰链(折叶)〔101 其他车辆零部件，102 其他深加工金属制品〕	9		80	13/	13	千克		L	/34
8302.2000	-小脚轮〔999〕	9		80	13/	13	千克			/34
8302.3000	-机动车辆用的其他附件及架座〔101 其他车辆零部件，102 其他深加工金属制品〕	9		80	13/	13	千克		L	/19
	-其他附件及架座：									
8302.4100	--建筑用〔999〕	9		80	13/	13	千克			/34
8302.4200	--其他，家具用〔999〕	9		80	13/	10	千克			/34
8302.4900	--其他〔999〕	9		80	13/	13	千克			/19
8302.5000	-帽架、帽钩、托架及类似品〔999〕	7		80	13/	13	千克			/27
8302.6000	-自动闭门器〔999〕	9		80	13/	13	千克/个			/34
83.03	**装甲或加强的贱金属制保险箱、保险柜及保险库的门和带锁保险储存橱、钱箱、契约箱及类似品：**									
8303.0000	装甲或加强的贱金属制保险箱、保险柜及保险库的门和带锁保险储存橱、钱箱、契约箱及类似品〔999〕	9		50	13/	13	千克/个		L	/34
83.04	**贱金属制的档案柜、卡片索引柜、文件盘、文件篮、笔盘、公章架及类似的办公用具，但税目 94.03 的办公室家具除外：**									
8304.0000	贱金属制的档案柜、卡片索引柜、文件盘、文件篮、笔盘、公章架及类似的办公用具，但税目 94.03 的办公室家具除外〔999〕	9		80	13/	10	千克			/29
83.05	**活页夹、卷宗夹的贱金属附件，贱金属制的信夹、信角、文件夹、索引标签及类似的办公用品；贱金属制的成条订书钉(例如，供办公室、室内装饰或包装用)：**									
8305.1000	-活页夹或宗卷夹的附件〔999〕	9		80	13/	10	千克			/
8305.2000	-成条订书钉〔999〕	7		80	13/	10	千克			/32
8305.9000	-其他，包括零件〔999〕	7		80	13/	10	千克			/27
83.06	**非电动的贱金属铃、钟、锣及类似品；贱金属雕塑像及其他装饰品；贱金属相框或画框及类似框架；贱金属镜子：**									
8306.1000	-铃、钟、锣及类似品〔999〕	8		80	13/	10	千克			/
	-雕塑像及其他装饰品：									
8306.2100	--镀贵金属的〔999〕	7		100	13/	10	千克			/32
	--其他：									

Chapter 83
Miscellaneous articles of base metal

Notes:

1. For the purposes of this Chapter, parts of base metal are to be classified with their parent artcles. However, articles of iron or steel of heading Nos.73. 12, 73. 15, 73. 17, 73. 18 or 73. 20, or similar articles of other base metal (Chapters 74 to 76 and 78 to 81) are not to be taken as parts of articles of this Chapter.
2. For the purposes of heading No.83. 02 the word "castors" means those having a diameter (including, where appropriate, tyres) not exceeding 75mm, or those having a diameter (including, where appropriate, tyres) exceeding 75mm provided that the width of the wheel or tyre fitted thereto is less than 30mm.

协定税率 %										特惠税率 %			
亚太5国	东/冰/格	巴基斯坦	韩国	瑞士	哥达	秘鲁	澳大利亚	新西/坡/智	港/澳/台	亚太2国	老/柬/缅	36/3/1	Article Description
													Padlocks and locks (key, combination or electrically operated), of base metal; clasps and frames with clasps, incorporating locks, of base metal; keys for any of the foregoing articles, of base metal:
	0/0/0	10.1	5.6	4.2	0	0	0	0/0/0	0/0/			0/0/	-Padlocks
													-Locks of a kind used for motor vehicles:
	5/0/0	8	7	0	0	0	0	0//0	0/0/			0/0/0	---Central controll door lock
	5/0/0	8	7	0	0	0	0	0//0	0/0/			0/0/0	---Other
	0/0/0	10.1	5.6	4.2	0	0	0	0/0/0	0/0/			0/0/0	-Locks of a kind used for furniture
	0/0/0	9	5.6	4.2	0	0	0	0/0/0	0/0/			0/0/0	-Other locks
	0/0/0	10.1	5.6	4.2	0	0	0	0/0/0	0/0/			0/0/	-Clasps and frames with clasps, incorporating locks
	0/0/0	5.4	4.8	3.6	0	0	0	0/0/0	0/0/			0/0/0	-Parts of locks
	0/0/0	4	6	0	0	0	0	0//0	0/0/			0/0/0	-Keys presented separately
													Base metal mountings, fittings and similar articles suitable for furniture, doors, staircases, windows, blinds, coachwork, saddlery, trunks, chests, caskets, or the like; base metal hat-racks, hat-pegs, brackets and similar fixtures; castors with mountings of base metal; automatic door closers of base metal:
	0/0/0	4.5	0	0	0	0	0	0//0	0/0/			0/0/0	-Hinges
	0/0/0	5.4	4.8	3.6	0	0	0	0/0/0	0/0/			0/0/0	-Castors
	0/0/0	4	6	0	0	0	0	0//0	0/0/			0/0/0	-Other mountings, fittings and similar articles suitable for motor vehicles
													-Other mountings, fittings and similar articles:
	0/0/0	10.1	5.6	4.2	0	0	0	0/0/0	0/0/			0/0/	--Suitable for buildings
	0/0/0	5.4	4.8	3.6	0	0	0	0/0/0	0/0/			0/0/0	--Other, suitable for furniture
	0/0/0	5.4	4.8	3.6	0	0	0	0/0/0	0/0/			0/0/0	--Other
	0/0/0	10.1	5.6	4.2	0	0	0	0/0/0	0/0/			0/0/	-Hat-racks, hat-pegs, brackets and similar fixtures
	0/0/0	5.4	4.8	3.6	0	0	0	0/0/0	0/0/			0/0/0	-Automatic door closers
													Armoured or reinforced safes, strong-boxes and doors and safe deposit lockers for strong-rooms, cash or deed boxes and the like, of base metal:
	0/0/0	10.1	5.6	4.2	0	0	0	0/0/0	0/0/			0/0/	Armoured or reinforced safes, strong-boxes and doors and safe deposit lockers for strong-rooms, cash or deed boxes and the like, of base metal
													Filing cabinets, card-index cabinets, paper trays, paper rests, pen trays, office-stamp stands and similar office or desk equipment, of base metal, other than office furniture of heading No.94. 03:
	0/0/0	4.5	4.2	3.2	0	0	0	0/0/0	0/0/			0/0/0	Filing cabinets, card-index cabinets, paper trays, paper rests, pen trays, office-stamp stands and similar office or desk equipment, of base metal, other than office furniture of heading No.94. 03
													Fittings for loose-leaf binders or files, letter clips, letter corners, paper clips, indexing tags and similar office articles, of base metal; staples in strips (for example, for offices, upholstery, packaging), of base metal:
	0/0/0	4.5	4.2	3.2	0	0	0	0/0/0	0/0/			0/0/0	-Fittings for loose-leaf binders of files
	0/0/0	4.5	4.2	3.2	0	0	0	0/0/0	0/0/			0/0/0	-Staples in strips
	0/0/0	4.5	4.2	3.2	0	0	0	0/0/0	0/0/			0/0/0	-Other, including parts
													Bells, gongs and the like, non-electric, of base metal; statuettes and other ornaments, of base metal; photograph, picture or similar frames, of base metal; mirrors of base metal:
	0/0/0	4	3.2	0	0	0	0	0//0	0/0/			0/0/0	-Bells, gongs and the like
													-Statuettes and other ornaments:
	0/0/0	4	0	0	0	0	0	0//0	0/0/			0/0/0	--Plated with precious metal
													--Other:

税则号列	货品名称〔CIQ 扩展编码及品名－T2 表示见附表 2〕	最惠(%)	暂定税率	普通	增值/消费	出口退税	计量单位	监管条件	检验检疫	特殊证件对美关税
8306.2910	---景泰蓝的〔999〕	7		100	13/	13	千克			/
8306.2990	---其他〔999〕	7		100	13/	13	千克			/27
8306.3000	-相框、画框及类似框架、镜子〔999〕	7		100	13/	13	千克			/32
83.07	**贱金属软管,不论是否有附件:**									
8307.1000	-钢铁制〔999〕	8		35	13/	13	千克			/18
8307.9000	-其他贱金属制〔999〕	8		35	13/	13	千克			/18
83.08	**贱金属制的扣、钩、环、眼及类似品,用于衣着或衣着附件、鞋靴、珠宝首饰、手表、书籍、天篷、皮革制品、旅行用品或马具或其他制成品;贱金属制的管形铆钉及开口铆钉;贱金属制的珠子及亮晶片:**									
8308.1000	-钩、环及眼〔999〕	9		80	13/	13	千克			/29
8308.2000	-管形铆钉及开口铆钉〔999〕	9		80	13/	13	千克			/19
8308.9000	-其他,包括零件〔999〕	9		80	13/	13	千克			/29
83.09	**贱金属制的塞子、盖子(包括冠形瓶塞、螺口盖及倒水塞)、瓶帽、螺口塞、塞子帽、封志及其他包装用附件:**									
8309.1000	-冠形瓶塞〔999〕	9		90	13/	13	千克			/29
8309.9000	-其他〔999〕	9		80	13/	13	千克			/19
83.10	**贱金属制的标志牌、铭牌、地名牌及类似品、号码、字母及类似标志,但税目 94.05 的货品除外:**									
8310.0000	贱金属制的标志牌、铭牌、地名牌及类似品、号码、字母及类似标志,但税目 94.05 的货品除外〔999〕	9		80	13/	13	千克			/29
83.11	**贱金属或硬质合金制的丝、条、管、板、电极及类似品,以焊剂涂面或以焊剂为芯,用于焊接或沉积金属、硬质合金;贱金属粉粘聚而成的丝或条,供金属喷镀用:**									
8311.1000	-以焊剂涂面的贱金属制电极,电弧焊用〔999〕	8		30	13/	13	千克			/18
8311.2000	-以焊剂为芯的贱金属制焊丝,电弧焊用〔999〕	8		30	13/	13	千克			/28
8311.3000	-以焊剂涂面或以焊剂为芯的贱金属条或丝,钎焊或气焊用〔999〕	8		30	13/	13	千克			/18
8311.9000	-其他〔999〕	8		30	13/	13	千克			/18

协定税率 %										特惠税率 %			
亚太5国	东/冰/格	巴基斯坦	韩国	瑞士	哥达	秘鲁	澳大利亚	新西/坡/智	港/澳/台	亚太2国	老/柬/缅	36/3/1	Article Description
	0/0/0	4	0	0	0	0	0	0//0	0/0/			0/0/0	---Cloisonne
	0/0/0	4	3.2	0	0	0	0	0/0/0	0/0/			0/0/0	---Other
	0/0/0	4	3.2	0	0	0	0	0//0	0/0/			0/0/0	-Photograph, picture or similar frames; mirrors
													Flexible tubing of base metal, with or without fittings:
	0/0/0	4	3.3	2.5	0	0	0	0//0	0/0/			0/0/0	-Of iron or steel
	0/0/0	4	3.3	0	0	0	0	0//0	0/0/			0/0/0	-Of other base metal
													Clasps, frames with clasps, buckles, buckle-clasps, hooks, eyes, eyelets and the like, of base metal, of a kind used for clothing, clothing allessories footwear, jewelry, watches, books, awnings, leather, travel goods or harness or other made up articles; tubular or bifurcated rivets, of base metal; beads and spangles, of base metal:
	0/0/0	0	7.3	3.2	0	0	0	0/0/0	0/0/			0/0/0	-Hooks, eyes and eyelets
	0/0/0	4.5	4.2	3.2	0	0	0	0/0/0	0/0/			0/0/0	-Tubular or bifurcated rivets
	0/0/0	4.5	7.3	3.2	0	0	0	0/0/0	0/0/			0/0/0	-Other, including parts
													Stoppers, caps and lids (including crown corks, screw caps and pouring stoppers), capsules for bottles, threaded bungs, bung covers, seals and other packing accessories, of base metal:
	0/0/0	11.5	7.2	5.4	0	0	0	0/0/0	0/0/			0/0/	-Crown corks
	0/0/0	4.8	4.8	3.6	0	0	0	0/0/0	0/0/			0/0/0	-Other
													Sign-plates, name-plates, address-plates and similar plates, numbers, letters and other symbols, of base metal, excluding those of heading No.94. 05:
	0/0/0		7.2	5.4	0	0	0	0/0/0	0/0/			0/0/	Sign-plates, name-plates, address-plates and similar plates, numbers, letters and other symbols, of base metal, excluding those of heading No.94. 05
													Wire, rods, tubes, plates, electrodes and similar products, of base metal or of metal carbides, coated or cored with flux material, of a kind used for soldering, brazing, welding or deposition of metal or of metal carbides; wire and rods, of agglomerated base metal powder, used for metal spraying:
	0/0/0	4	0	0	0	0	0	0//0	0/0/			0/0/0	-Coated electrodes of base metal, for electric arc-welding
	0/0/0	4	4.8	0	0	0	0	0//0	0/0/			0/0/0	-Cored wire of base metal, for electric arc-welding
	0/0/0	4		0	0	0	0	0//0	0/0/			0/0/0	-Coated rods and cored wire, of base metal, for soldering, brazing or welding by flame
5.2	0/0/0	4	0	0	0	0	0	0//0	0/0/			0/0/0	-Other

第十六类
机器、机械器具、电气设备及其零件；录音机及放声机、电视图像、声音的录制和重放设备及其零件、附件

注释：

一、本类不包括：

(一)第三十九章的塑料或税目40.10的硫化橡胶制的传动带、输送带；除硬质橡胶以外的硫化橡胶制的机器、机械器具、电气器具或其他专门技术用途的物品(税目40.16)；

(二)机器、机械器具或其他专门技术用途的皮革、再生皮革(税目42.05)或毛皮（税目43.03)的制品；

(三)各种材料（例如，第三十九章、第四十章、第四十四章、第四十八章及第十五类的材料）制的筒管、卷轴、纡子、锥形筒管、芯子、线轴及类似品；

(四)提花机及类似机器用的穿孔卡片（例如，归入第三十九章、第四十八章或第十五类的）；

(五)纺织材料制的传动带、输送带或带料(税目59.10)或专门技术用途的其他纺织材料制品(税目59.11)；

(六)税目71.02至71.04的宝石或半宝石(天然、合成或再造）或税目71.16的完全以宝石或半宝石制成的物品，但已加工未装配的唱针用蓝宝石和钻石除外（税目85.22)；

(七)第十五类注释二所规定的贱金属制通用零件(第十五类)及塑料制的类似品(第三十九章)；

(八)钻管(税目73.04)；

(九)金属丝、带制的环形带(第十五类)；

(十)第八十二章或第八十三章的物品；

(十一)第十七类的物品；

(十二)第九十章的物品；

(十三)第九十一章的钟、表及其他物品；

(十四)税目82.07的可互换工具及作为机器零件的刷子(税目96.03)；类似的可互换工具应按其构成工作部件的材料归类（例如，归入第四十章、第四十二章、第四十三章、第四十五章、第五十九章或税目68.04、69.09)；

(十五)第九十五章的物品；

(十六)打字机色带或类似色带，不论是否装轴或装盒(应按其材料属性归类；如已上油或经其他方法处理能着色的，应归入税目96.12)，或税号96.20的独脚架、双脚架、三脚架及类似品。

二、除本类注释一、第八十四章注释一及第八十五章注释一另有规定的以外，机器零件（不属于税目84.84、85.44、85.45、85.46或85.47所列物品的零件）应按下列规定归类：

(一)凡在第八十四章、第八十五章的税目(税目84.09、84.31、84.48、84.66、84.73、84.87、85.03、85.22、85.29、85.38及85.48除外)列名的货品，均应归入该两章的相应税目；

(二)专用于或主要用于某一种机器或同一税目的多种机器（包括税目84.79或85.43的机器）的零件，应与该种机器一并归类，或酌情归入税目84.09、84.31、84.48、84.66、84.73、85.03、85.22、85.29或85.38。但能同时主要用于税目85.17和85.25至85.28所列机器的零件，应归入税目85.17；

(三)所有其他零件应酌情归入税目84.09、84.31、84.48、84.66、84.73、85.03、85.22、85.29或85.38，如不能归入上述税目，则应归入税目84.87或85.48。

三、由两部及两部以上机器装配在一起形成的组合式机器，或具有两种及两种以上互补或交替功能的机器，除条文另有规定的以外，应按具有主要功能的机器归类。

四、由不同独立部件(不论是否分开或由管道、传动装置、电缆或其他装置连接)组成的机器(包括机组)，如果组合后明显具有一种第八十四章或第八十五章某个税号所列功能，则全部机器应按其功能归入有关税目。

五、上述各注释所称“机器”，是指第八十四章或第八十五章各税目所列的各种机器、设备、装置及器具。

第八十四章
核反应堆、锅炉、机器、机械器具及其零件

注释：

一、本章不包括：

(一)第六十八章的石磨、石碾及其他物品；

(二)陶瓷材料制的机器或器具(例如泵)及供任何材料制的机器或器具用的陶瓷零件(第六十九章)；

(三)实验室用玻璃器(税目70.17)；玻璃制的机器、器具或其他专门技术用途的物品及其零件(税目70.19或70.20)；

(四)税目73.21或73.22的物品或其他贱金属制的类似物品（第七十四章至第七十六章或第七十八章至第八十一章)；

(五)税目85.08的真空吸尘器；

(六)税目85.09的家用电动器具；税目85.25的数字照相机；

(七)第十七类物品用的散热器；或

SECTION XVI
MACHINERY AND MECHANICAL APPLIANCES; ELECTRICAL EQUIPMENT; PARTS THEREOF; SOUND RECORDERS AND REPRODUCERS, TELEVISION IMAGE AND SOUND RECORDERS AND REPRODUCERS, AND PARTS AND ACCESSORIES OF SUCH ARTICLES

Notes:

1. This Section does not cover:
   (a) Transmission or conveyor belts or belting, of plastics of Chapter 39, or of vulcanized rubber (heading No.40. 10); or other articles of a kind used in machinery or mechanical or electrical appliances or for other technical uses, of vulcanized rubber other than hard rubber (heading No.40. 16);
   (b) Articles of leather or of composition leather (heading No.42. 05) or of furskin (heading No.43. 03), of a kind used in machinery or mechanical appliances or for other technical uses;
   (c) Bobbins, spools, cops, cones, cores, reels or similar supports of any material (for example, Chapter 39, 40, 44 or 48 or Section XV);
   (d) Perforated cards for Jacquard or similar machines (for example, Chapter 39 or 48 Section XV);
   (e) Transmission or conveyor belts or belting of textile material (heading No.59. 10) or other articles of textile material for technical uses (heading No.59. 11);
   (f) Precious or semi-precious stones (natural, synthetic or reconstructed) of headings Nos.71. 02 to 71. 04, or articles wholly of such stones of heading 71. 16, except unmounted worked sapphires and diamonds for styli (heading No.85. 22);
   (g) Parts of general use, as defined in Note 2 to Section XV, of base metal (Section XV), or similar goods of plastics (Chapter 39);
   (h) Drill pipe (heading No.73. 04);
   (ij) Endless belts of metal wire or strip (Section XV);
   (k) Articles of Chapter 82 or 83;
   (l) Articles of Section XVII;
   (m) Articles of Chapter 90;
   (n) Clocks, watches or other articles of Chapter 91;
   (o) Interchangeable tools of headingNo.82. 07 or brushes of a kind used as parts of machines (heading No. 96. 03), similar interchangable tools are to be classified according to constituent material of their working part (for example in Chapter 40, 42, 43, 45, 59 or heading No. 68.04, or 69. 09);
   (p) Articles of Chapter 95; or
   (q) Typewriter or similar ribbons, whether or not on spools or in cartridges(classified according to their constituent material, or in heading No. 96.12 if inked or otherwise prepared for giving impressions) or unipod, bipod, tripod or the like of heading No.96.20.
2. Subject to Note 1 to this Section, Note 1 to Chapter 84 and Note 1 to Chapter 85, parts of machines (not being parts of the articles of heading No.84. 84, 85. 44, 85. 45, 85. 46 or 85. 47) are to be classified according to the following rules:
   (a) Parts which are goods included in any of the headings of Chapter 84 or 85 (other than headingsNo.84. 09, 84. 31, 84. 48, 84. 66, 84. 73, 84. 87, 85. 03, 85. 22, 85. 29, 85. 38, and 85. 48) are in all cases to be classified in their respective headings;
   (b) Other parts, if suitable for use solely or principally with a particular kind of machine, or with a number of machines of the same heading (including a machine of heading No.84. 79 or 85. 43) are to be classified with the machines of that kind or in heading No. 84. 09, 84. 31, 84. 48, 84. 66, 84. 73, 85. 03, 85. 22, 85. 29 or 85. 38 as appropriate. However, parts which are equally suitable for use principally with the goods of headings No.85. 17 and 85. 25 to 85. 28 are to be classified in headingNo.85. 17;
   (c) All other parts are to be classified in heading No.84. 09, 84. 31, 84. 48, 84 66, 84. 73, 85. 03, 85. 22, 85. 29 or 85. 38 as appropriate or, failing that, in heading No.84. 87 or 85. 48.

3. Unless the context otherwise requires, composite machines consisting of two or more machines fitted together to form a whole and other machines adapted for the purpose of performing two or more complementary or alternative functions are to be classified as if consisting only of that component or as being that machine which performs the principal function.
4. Where a machine (including a combination of machines) consists of individual components (whether separate or interconnected by piping, by transmission devices, by electric cables or by other devices) intended to contribute together to a clearly defined function covered by one of the headings in Chapter 84 or Chapter 85, then the whole falls to be classified in the heading appropriate to that function.
5. For the purposes of these Notes, the expression "machine" means any machine, machinery, plant, equipment, apparatus or appliance cited in the headings of Chapter 84 or 85.

Chapter 84
Nuclear reactors, boilers, machinery and mechanical appliances; parts thereof

Notes:

1. This Chapter does not cover:
   (a) Millstones, grindstones and other articles of Chapter 68;
   (b) Machinery or appliances (for example, pumps) of ceramic material and ceramic parts of machinery or appliances of any material (Chapter 69);
   (c) Laboratory glassware (heading No.70. 17); machinery, appliances or other articles for technical uses or parts thereof, of glass (heading No.70. 19 or 70. 20);
   (d) Articles of heading No.73. 21 or 73. 22 or similar articles of other base metals (Chapters 74 to 76 or 78 to 81);
   (e) Vacuum cleaners of heading No.85.08
   (f) Electro-mechanical domestic appliances of heading No.85.09; digital cameras of heading No.85.25; or
   (g) Seltion XVII items with radiator;

(八)非机动的手工操作地板清扫器(税目96.03)。

二、除第十六类注释三及本章注释九另有规定的以外,如果某种机器或器具既符合税目84.01至84.24或税目84.46中一个或几个税目的规定,又符合税目84.25至84.80中一个或几个税目的规定,则应酌情归入税目84.01至84.24或税目84.86中的相应税目,而不归入税目84.25至84.80中的有关税目。

但税目84.19不包括:

(一)催芽装置、孵卵器或育雏器(税目84.36);

(二)谷物调湿机(税目84.37);

(三)萃取糖汁的浸提装置(税目84.38);

(四)纱线、织物及纺织制品的热处理机器(税目84.51);

(五)温度变化(即使必不可少)仅作为辅助功能的机器、设备或实验室设备。

税目84.22不包括:

(一)缝合袋子或类似品用的缝纫机;

(二)税目84.72的办公室用机器。

税目84.24不包括:

(一)喷墨印刷(打印)机器(税目84.43)。

(二)水射流切割机(税目84.56)。

三、如果用于加工各种材料的某种机床既符合税目84.56的规定,又符合税目84.57、84.58、84.59、84.60、84.61、84.64或84.65的规定,则应归入税目84.56。

四、税目84.57仅适用于可以完成下列不同形式机械操作的金属加工机床,但车床(包括车削中心)除外:

(一)按照机械加工程序从刀具库中自动更换刀具(加工中心);

(二)同时或顺序地自动使用不同的动力头对固定不动的工件进行加工(单工位组合机床);

(三)自动将工件送向不同的动力头(多工位组合机床)。

五、(一)税目84.71所称"自动数据处理设备",是指具有如下功能的机器:

1. 存储处理程序和执行程序直接需要的起码的数据;
2. 按照用户的要求随意编辑程序;
3. 按照用户指令进行算术计算;以及
4. 在运行过程中,可不需人为干预而通过逻辑判断,执行一个处理程序,这个处理程序可改变计算机指令的执行。

(二)自动数据处理设备可以是一套由若干单独部件所组成的系统。

(三)除本条注释(四)及(五)另有规定以外,一个部件如果符合下列所有规定,即可视为自动数据处理系统的一部分:

1. 专用于或主要用于自动数据处理系统;
2. 可以直接或通过一个或几个其他部件同中央处理机相连接;
3. 能够以本系统所使用的方式(代码或信号)接收或传送数据。

自动数据处理设备的部件如果单独报验,应归入税目84.71。

但是,键盘、X—Y坐标输入装置及盘(片)式存储部件,只要符合上述注释(三)2及(三)3所列的规定,应一律作为税目84.71的部件归类。

(四)税目84.71不包括单独报验的下述设备,即使该设备符合上述注释五(三)的所有规定:

1. 打印机、复印机、传真机,不论是否组合式;
2. 发送或接收声音、图像或其他数据的设备,包括有线或无线网络(例如局域网或广域网)通信设备;
3. 扬声器及传声器(麦克风);
4. 电视摄相机、数字照相机及视频摄录一体机;
5. 监视器及投影机,未装有电视接收装置。

(五)装有自动数据处理设备或与自动数据处理设备连接使用,但却从事数据处理以外的某项专门功能的机器,应按其功能归入相应的税目,对于无法按功能归类的,应归入未列名税目。

六、税目84.82还包括最大直径及最小直径与标称直径相差均不超过1%或0.05毫米(以相差数值较小的为准)的抛光钢珠,其他钢珠归入税目73.26。

七、具有一种以上用途的机器在归类时,其主要用途可作为唯一的用途对待。除本章注释二、第十六类注释三另有规定的以外,凡任何税目都未列明其主要用途的机器,以及没有哪一种用途是主要用途的机器,均应归入税目84.79。税目84.79还包括将金属丝、纺织纱线或其他各种材料以及它们的混合材料制成绳、缆的机器(例如,捻股机、绞扭机、制缆机)。

八、税目84.70所称"袖珍式",仅适用于外形尺寸不超过170毫米×100毫米×45毫米的机器。

九、(一)第八十五章注释九(一)及(二)也同样适用于本条注释及品目84.86中所称的"半导体器件"及"集成电器"。但本条注释及品目84.86所称"半导体器件",也包括光敏半导体器件及发光二极管(LED)。

(二)本条注释和税目84.86所称"平板显示器的制造",包括将各层基片制造成平板,但不包括玻璃的制造或将印刷电路板或其他电子元件装配在平板上。所称"平板显示"不包括阴极射线管技术。

(三)税目84.86也包括专用于或主要用于下列用途的机器及装置:

1. 制造或修补掩膜版及刻线;

(h)Hand-operated mechanical floor sweepers, not motorized (heading No. 96. 03).

2. Subject to the operation of Note 3 to Section XVI and subject to Note9 to this chapter, a machine or appliance which answers to a description in one or more of the headings No.84. 01 to 84. 24 or heading 84.46 and at the same time to a description in one or other of the headings Nos.84. 25 to 84. 80 is to be classified under the appropriate headings of the former group or under heading 84. 86, as the case may be, and not the latter.

HeadingNo.84. 19 does not, however, cover:

(a)Germination plant, incubators or brooders (headingNo.84. 36);

(b)Grain dampening machines (heading No.84. 37);

(c)Diffusing apparatus for sugar juice extraction (headingNo.84. 38);

(d)Machinery for the heat-treatment of textile yarns, fabrics or made up textile articles (heading No.84. 51); or

(e)Machinery or plant, designed for mechanical operation or la boratorg equipment, in which a change of temperature, even if necessary, is subsidiary.

Heading No.84. 22 does not cover:

(a)Sewing machines for closing bags or similar containers ;

(b)Office machinery of heading No.84. 72.

Heading No.84. 24 does not cover:

(a)Ink-jet printing machines (heading No.84. 43).

(b)Water-jet cutting machines(heading No.84. 56).

3. A machine-tool for working any material which answers to a description in heading No.84. 56 and at the same time to a description in heading Nos.84. 57, 84. 58, 84. 59, 84. 60, 84. 61, 84. 64 or 84. 65 is to be classified in heading No.84. 56.

4. Heading No.84. 57 applies only to machine-tools for working metal other than lathes (including turning centres), which can carry out different types of machining operations either:

(a)by automatic tool change from a magazine or the like in conformity with a machining programme (machining centres),

(b)by the automatic use, simultaneously or sequentially, of different unit heads working on a fixed position workpiece (unit construction machines, single station), or

(c)by the automatic transfer of the workpiece to different unit heads (multi-station transfer machines).

5. (a)For the purposes of heading No.84. 71, the expression "automatic data processing machines" means machines capable of:

(ⅰ)Storing the processing program or programs and at least the data immediately necessary for the execution of the program;

(ⅱ)being freely programmed in accordance with the requirements of the user;

(ⅲ)performing arthmetical computations specified by the user; and,

(ⅳ)executing, without human intervention, a processing program which requires them to modify their execution, by logical decision during the processing run;

(b)Automatic data processing machines may be in the form of systems consisting of a variable number of separate units.

(c)Subject to paragraph(d)and(e)below, a unit is to be rgearded as being a part of an automatic data processing system if it meets all of the following condition

(ⅰ)It is of a kind solehy or praincipally used in an automatic data processing system;

(ⅱ)It is connectable to the central processing unit either directly or through one or more other units; and

(ⅲ)It is able to accept or delirer data in afrom(codes or signals), which can be used by the system.

Separatly presented units of an automatic data processing malhine are to be classified heading 84.71.

However keybards X—Y co-ordinate input devices and disk storage units which satisfy the cond it ions of paragraphs (c)(ⅱ)and(c)(ⅲ)above are in all cases to be dassified as anits of heading No.84.71.

(d)Heading 84. 71 does not cover the following when prestented separateby eren if they meet all of conditions set forth in Notes (c)above:

(ⅰ)printers copying machines facsimile machines whether or not combined.

(ⅱ)Apparats for the transmission or reception of voice images or other data including apparatus for communication in a wired or wireless network (Such as alocal or wide area netaork)

(ⅲ)Loud speakers and microphones

(ⅳ)Television camera, digital cemera and video camera recorders

(ⅴ)Monitors and projectors not incorp orating television reception apparatus recezvers.

(e)Machines performing a specific function other than data processing and incorporating or working in conjunction with an automatic data processing machine are to be classified in the headings appropriate to their respective functions or, failing that, in residual headings.

6. Heading No.84. 82 applies, *inter alia*, to polished steel balls, the maximum and minimum diameters of which do not differ from the nominal diameter by more than 1% or by more than 0. 05mm, whichever is less. Other steel balls are to be classified in heading No. 73. 26.

7. A machine which is used for more than one purpose is, for the purposes of classification, to be treated as if its principal purpose were its sole purpose. Subject to Note 2 to this Chapter and Note 3 to Section XVI, a machine, the principal purpose of which is not described in any heading or for which no one purpose is the principal purpose, unless the context otherwise requires, is to be classified in heading No.84. 79. Heading No.84. 79 also covers machines for making rope or cable (for example, stranding, twisting or cabling machines) from metal wire, textile yarn or any other material or from a combination of such materials.

8. For the purposes of headingNo.84. 70, the term "pocket-size" applies only to machines the dimensions of which do not exceed 170mm ×100mm×45mm.

9. (a)Notes 8(a) and 8(b) to chapter 85 also apply with respect to the expressions "semicoiductor devices and electonic integrated circuits" respectively, as used in this Note and in heading 84. 86. However for the parposes of this Note and of heading 84. 86. the expression semicondutor devices also covers photo sensitive semicondactor devices and light emitting diodes(LED).

(b)For the purposes of this Note and of heading 84.86 the expression "manufacture of flat pane displays" covers the fabrication of substrtes into aftat panel. It does not cover the manufacture of glass or the assembly of plinted circuit boards or other electronie components onto the flat panel The expression "flat panel display" does not cover calhoderay tube technology.

(c)Heading No.84.86 also includesmachines apparatus solely or principally of a kind used for

(ⅰ)The manafactre or rapair of masks and retides

2. 组装半导体器件或集成电路；

3. 升降、搬运、装卸单晶柱、圆片、半导体器件、集成电路及平板显示器。

（四）除十六类注释一及第八十四章注释一另有规定的以外，符合税目 84.86 规定的机器及装置，应归入该税目而不归入本协调制度的其他税目。

子目注释：

一、子目 8465.20 所称"加工中心"，仅适用于加工木材、软木、骨、硬质橡胶、硬质塑料或类似硬质材料的加工机床。这些设备可根据机械加工程序，从刀具库或类似装置中自动更换刀具，以完成不同形式的机械加工。

二、子目 8471.49 所称"系统"，是指各部件符合第八十四章注释五（三）所列条件，并且至少由一个中央处理部件、一个输入部件（例如，键盘或扫描仪）及一个输出部件（例如，视频显示器或打印机）组成的自动数据处理设备。

三、子目 8481.20 所称"油压或气压传动阀"，是指在液压或气压系统中专用于传递"流体动力"的阀门，其能源以加压流体（液体或气体）的形式供给。这些阀门可以具有各种形式（例如，减压阀、止回阀）。子目 8481.20 优先于税目 84.81 的所有其他子目。

四、子目 8482.40 仅包括滚柱直径相同，最大不超过 5 毫米，且长度至少是直径三倍的圆滚柱轴承，滚柱的两端可以磨圆。

税则号列	货品名称〔CIQ 扩展编码及品名－T2 表示见附表 2〕	最惠(%)	暂定税率	普通	增值/消费	出口退税	计量单位	监管条件	检验检疫	特殊证件对美关税
84.01	**核反应堆；核反应堆的未辐照燃料元件（释热元件）；同位素分离机器及装置：**									
8401.1000	-核反应堆〔999〕	2		8	13/	13	千克/台	3		/
8401.2000	-同位素分离机器、装置及其零件〔999〕	1		8	13/	13	个/千克	3		/
	-未辐照燃料元件（释热元件）：									
8401.3010	---未辐照燃料元件〔999〕	2		8	13/	13	千克			/
8401.3090	---未辐照燃料元件的零件〔999〕	1		8	13/	13	千克			/
	-核反应堆零件：									
8401.4010	---未辐照相关组件〔999〕	1		8	13/	13	千克/台			/
8401.4020	---堆内构件〔999〕	1		8	13/	13	千克/台	3		/
8401.4090	---其他									
8401.4090 10	核反应堆压力容器（包括其顶板）（专门设计或制造来用于容纳核反应堆的堆芯）〔999〕	1		8	13/	13	千克/台	3		/
8401.4090 20	核反应堆控制棒和设备（专用于核反应堆裂变控制棒、支承结构或悬吊结构等）〔999〕	1		8	13/	13	千克/台	3		/
8401.4090 30	核反应堆压力管（专用于容纳核燃料元件和一次冷却剂的，压力＞5.1MPa）〔999〕	1		8	13/	13	千克/台	3		/
8401.4090 90	其他核反应堆零件〔999〕	1		8	13/	13	千克/台			/
84.02	**蒸汽锅炉（能产生低压水蒸气的集中供暖用的热水锅炉除外）；过热水锅炉：**									
	-蒸汽锅炉：									
	--蒸发量超过 45 吨/时的水管锅炉：									
8402.1110	---蒸发量在 900 吨/时及以上的发电用锅炉〔999〕	3		11	13/	13	台/千克	6A	M	/
8402.1190	---其他〔999〕	10		35	13/	13	台/千克	6A	M	/
8402.1200	--蒸发量不超过 45 吨/时的水管锅炉									
8402.1200 10	纸浆厂废料锅炉（蒸发量≤45 吨/时蒸汽水管锅炉）〔999〕	5		35	13/	13	台/千克	6A	M	/
8402.1200 90	其他蒸发量未超 45 吨/时水管锅炉〔999〕	5		35	13/	13	台/千克	6A	M	/
8402.1900	--其他蒸汽锅炉，包括混合式锅炉〔999〕	5		35	13/	13	台/千克	6A	M	/30
8402.2000	-过热水锅炉〔999〕	10		35	13/	13	台/千克	6A	M	/20
8402.9000	-零件〔999〕	2		11	13/	13	千克			/27
84.03	**集中供暖用的热水锅炉，但税目 84.02 的货品除外：**									
	-锅炉：									
8403.1010	---家用型〔999〕	8		80	13/	13	台/千克	6A	M	/33
8403.1090	---其他〔101 承压热水锅炉，102 沼气锅炉〕	8		80	13/	13	台/千克	6A	M	/18
8403.9000	-零件〔999〕	6		80	13/	13	千克			/16
84.04	**税目 84.02 或 84.03 所列锅炉的辅助设备（例如，节热器、过热器、除灰器、气体回收器）；水蒸气或其他蒸汽动力装置的冷凝器：**									
	-税目 84.02 或 84.03 所列锅炉的辅助设备：									
8404.1010	---税目 84.02 所列锅炉的辅助设备									
8404.1010 10	使用（可再生）生物质燃料的非水管蒸汽锅炉的辅助设备（例如，节热器、过热器、除灰器、气体回收器）〔999〕	7	5	35	13/	13	千克	6		/
8404.1010 90	其他蒸汽锅炉、过热水锅炉的辅助设备（例如，节热器、过热器、除灰器、气体回收器）〔999〕	7		35	13/	13	千克	6		/

(ⅱ)Assemb semiconductordevices or electronic;integrated circuits;and

(ⅲ)Lifting handing loadingor unlading of boules, wafers, semicondu ctor devices electonic integrated circuits and flat panel displays.

(d)Subject to Notel to section XVI and Note 1 to chapter 84.machines and apparatus answring to the description in heading 84.86 are to be classfied in that heading and in no other heading of the Nomenclature.

Subheading Notes:

1. Subheading No. 8465.20 called "machining center", processing machine is only suitable for the processing of wood, cork, bone, hard rubber, hard plastics or similar hard materials. These devices can automatically replace the tool from the tool library or similar device according to the machining procedure to complete different forms of machining.
2. For the purposes of subheading No.8471. 49, the term "systems" means automatic data processing machines whose units satisfy the conditions laid down in Note 5 (b) to Chapter 84 and which comprise at least a central processing unit, one input unit (for example: a keyboard or a scanner), and one output unit (for example: a visual display unit or a printer).
3. Subheading No.8481.20 called "hydraulic or pneumatic valve" refers to the transfer of "fluid power valve in hydraulic or pneumatic system secondary energy in a pressurized fluid (liquid or gas) in the form of supply. These valves can have various forms (e.g., pressure relief valves, check valves).Subheading No. 8481.20 priority to all other Subheading of Heading No. 84.81
4. Subheading No.8482. 40 applies only to bearings with cylindrical rollers of a uniform diameter not exceeding 5mm and having a length which is at least three times the diameter. The ends of the rollers may be rounded.

协定税率 %										特惠税率 %			
亚太5国	东/冰/格	巴基斯坦	韩国	瑞士	哥达	秘鲁	澳大利亚	新西/坡/智	港/澳/台	亚太2国	老/柬/缅	36/3/1	Article Description
													Nuclear reactors; fuel elements (cartridges), non-irradiated, for nuclear reactors; machinery and apparatus for isotopic separation:
	0/0/0	0	0	0	0	0	0	0//0	0/0/			0/0/	-Nuclear reactors
	0/0/0	0	0	0	0	0	0	0//0	0/0/			0/0/	-Machinery and apparatus for isotopic separation, and parts thereof
													-Fuel elements (cartridges), non-irradiated:
	0/0/0	0	0	0	0	0	0	0//0	0/0/			0/0/	---Fuel elements, non-irrdadiated
	0/0/0	0	0	0	0	0	0	0//0	0/0/			0/0/	---Parts for fuel elements non-irradiated
													-Parts of nuclear reactors:
	0/0/0	0	0	0	0	0	0	0//0	0/0/			0/0/	---Non-irradiated Associated Assembly
	0/0/0	0	0	0	0	0	0	0//0	0/0/			0/0/	---Reactor internals
													---Other
	0/0/0	0	0	0	0	0	0	0//0	0/0/			0/0/	Pressure vessels for nuclear reactors(including top slabs) specially designed or produced to hold the reactor core of the nuclear reactors
	0/0/0	0	0	0	0	0	0	0//0	0/0/			0/0/	Control rods and devices of nuclear reactors (fission control rod and support and suspension structures thereof, specified for nuclear reactors)
	0/0/0	0	0	0	0	0	0	0//0	0/0/			0/0/	Pressure tubes of nuclear reactors (specified for holding fuel elements or primary coolants, pressure>5.1MPa)
	0/0/0	0	0	0	0	0	0	0//0	0/0/			0/0/	Other parts of nuclear reactors
													Steam or other vapour generating boilers (other than central heating hot water boilers capable also of producting low pressure steam); super-heated water boilers:
													-Steam or other vapour generating boilers:
													--Watertube boilers with a steam production exceeding 45t per hour:
2	0/0/0	0	0	0	0	0	0	0//0	0/0/			0/0/	---Boilers for generating electricity with a steam production 900t or more per hour
6.5	0/0/0	6.3	5.6	4.2	0	0	0	0/0/0	0/0/			0/0/	---Other
													--Watertube boilers with a steam production not exceeding 45t per hour
3.3	0/0/0	0	3	0	0	0	0	0//0	0/0/			0/0/	Waster material boiler of pulp mill(steam water tube boilers with their evaporation≤45tons/hour)
3.3	0/0/0	0	3	0	0	0	0	0//0	0/0/			0/0/	Other wate tube boilers with the evaporation ≤45tons/hour
	0/0/0	0	3	0	0	0	0	0//0	0/0/			0/0/	--Other vapour generating boilers, including hybrid boilers
	0/0/0	11.5	6.4	4.8	0	0	0	0/0/0	0/0/			0/0/	-Super-heated water boilers
	0/0/0	0	0	0	0	0	0	0//0	0/0/			0/0/	-Parts
													Central heating boilers other than those of headingNo.84. 02:
													-Boilers:
5.2	0/0/0	4.5	4	0	0	0	0	0//0	0/0/			0/0/	---Household type
5.2	0/0/0	4	4	0	0	0	0	0//0	0/0/			0/0/	---Other
	0/0/0	0	2.4	0	0	0	0	0//0	0/0/			0/0/	-Parts
													Auxiliary plant for use with boilers of headingNo.84. 02 or 84. 03 (for example, economizers, super-heaters, soot removers, gas recoverers); condensers for steam or other vapour power units:
													-Auxiliary plant for use with boilers of headingNo.84. 02 or 84. 03:
													---For use with boilers of headingNo.84. 02
3.5	0/0/0	0	0	2.1	0	0	0	0//0	0/0/			0/0/	Use (renewable) of biomass fuel pipe steam boiler auxiliary equipment (for example, heat exchanger, superheater, ash separator and gas collector)
3.5	0/0/0	0	0	2.1	0	0	0	0//0	0/0/			0/0/	Other steam boiler, hot water boiler auxiliary equipment(e.g., economizer, superheater, soot removers, gas recovery device)

税则号列	货品名称〔CIQ 扩展编码及品名－T2 表示见附表 2〕	最惠(%)	暂定税率	普通	增值/消费	出口退税	计量单位	监管条件	检验检疫	特殊证件对美关税
8404.1020	---税目 84.03 所列锅炉的辅助设备〔999〕	8	5	80	13/	13	千克	6		/
8404.2000	-水蒸气或其他蒸汽动力装置的冷凝器〔999〕	8	5	35	13/	13	千克	6		/30
	-零件：									
8404.9010	---子目 8404.1020 所列设备的零件〔999〕	7	5	80	13/	13	千克			/30
8404.9090	---其他									
8404.9090 10	使用(可再生)生物质燃料的非水管蒸汽锅炉的辅助设备的零件；水蒸气或其他蒸汽动力装置的冷凝器的零件(编号 84041010、84042000 所列辅助设备的)〔999〕	7	5	35	13/	13	千克			/30
8404.9090 90	其他辅助设备用零件(编号 84041010、84042000 所列辅助设备的)〔999〕	7		35	13/	13	千克			/32
84.05	**煤气发生器，不论有无净化器；乙炔发生器及类似的水解气体发生器，不论有无净化器：**									
8405.1000	-煤气发生器，不论有无净化器；乙炔发生器及类似的水解气体发生器，不论有无净化器〔999〕	10		30	13/	13	千克	A	M	/20
8405.9000	-零件〔999〕	6		30	13/	13	千克			/26
84.06	**汽轮机：**									
8406.1000	-船舶动力用汽轮机〔999〕	5		35	13/	13	台/千克			/
	-其他汽轮机：									
	--输出功率超过 40 兆瓦的：									
8406.8110	---输出功率不超过 100 兆瓦的〔999〕	5		35	13/	13	台/千克			/30
8406.8120	---输出功率超过 100 兆瓦，但不超过 350 兆瓦的〔999〕	5		35	13/	13	台/千克			/
8406.8130	---输出功率超过 350 兆瓦的〔999〕	6		11	13/	13	台/千克			/
8406.8200	--输出功率不超过 40 兆瓦的〔999〕	5		35	13/	13	台/千克			/15
8406.9000	-零件〔999〕	2		11	13/	13	千克			/27
84.07	**点燃往复式或旋转式活塞内燃发动机：**									
	-航空器发动机：									
8407.1010	---输出功率不超过 298 千瓦〔999〕	2		11	13/	13	台/千克			/12
8407.1020	---输出功率超过 298 千瓦							6		
8407.1020 10	输出功率＞298kw 无人驾驶航空飞行器、无人驾驶飞艇用高效率内燃引擎，设计或改型后用于在 15420 米(50000 英尺)以上高空飞行的吸气活塞式或转子式内燃发动机〔999〕	2		11	13/	13	台/千克	3		/
8407.1020 90	其他输出功率＞298kw 航空器内燃引擎(指点燃往复式或旋转式)〔999〕	2		11	13/	13	台/千克			/
	-船舶发动机：									
8407.2100	--舷外发动机〔999〕	8		35	13/	13	台/千克			/18
8407.2900	--其他〔999〕	8		20	13/	13	台/千克			/13
	-用于第八十七章所列车辆的往复式活塞发动机：									
8407.3100	--气缸容量(排气量)不超过 50 毫升〔101 其他车辆零部件，102 汽油发动机〕	10		35	13/	13	台/千克	y4xA6	LM	/
8407.3200	--气缸容量(排气量)超过 50 毫升，但不超过 250 毫升〔101 其他车辆零部件，102 汽油发动机〕	10		35	13/	13	台/千克	y4xA6	LM	/
8407.3300	--气缸容量(排气量)超过 250 毫升，但不超过 1000 毫升〔101 其他车辆零部件，102 汽油发动机〕	10		70	13/	13	台/千克	A6	LM	/
	--气缸容量(排气量)超过 1000 毫升：									
8407.3410	---气缸容量(排气量)超过 1000 毫升，但不超过 3000 毫升〔101 其他车辆零部件，102 汽油发动机〕	10		70	13/	13	台/千克	A6	LM	/
8407.3420	---气缸容量(排气量)超过 3000 毫升									
8407.3420 10	排气量≥5.9 升的天然气发动机(第八十七章所列车辆用的点燃往复式活塞发动机)〔101 其他车辆零部件，102 汽油发动机〕	10		35	13/	13	台/千克	6		/
8407.3420 90	其他排气量＞3000cc 车用往复式活塞引擎(第八十七章所列车辆用的点燃往复式活塞发动机)〔101 其他车辆零部件，102 汽油发动机〕	10		35	13/	13	台/千克	6		/
	-其他发动机：									
8407.9010	---沼气发动机〔999〕	10		35	13/	13	台/千克			/
8407.9090	---其他									
8407.9090 10	转速＜3600r/min 汽油发动机(发电机用)〔999〕	18		35	13/	13	台/千克			/23

协定税率 %										特惠税率 %			Article Description
亚太5国	东/冰/格	巴基斯坦	韩国	瑞士	哥达	秘鲁	澳大利亚	新西/坡/智	港/澳/台	亚太2国	老/柬/缅	36/3/1	
4	0/0/0	4	4	0	0	0	0	0//0	0/0/			0/0/	---For use with boilers of headingNo.84. 03
	0/0/0	10.1	5.6	4.2	0	0	0	0/0/0	0/0/			0/0/	-Condensers for steam or other vapour power units
													-Parts:
0	0/0/0	0	0	0	0	0	0	0//0	0/0/			0/0/	---Of the auxiliary plant of subheading No. 8404. 1020
													---Other
0	0/0/0	0	0	0	0	0	0	0//0	0/0/			0/0/	Use (renewable) of biomass fuel pipe steam boiler auxiliary equipment parts; Water vapor or other steam condenser of power plant parts (no. 84041010, 84042000, auxiliary equipment listed)
0	0/0/0	0	0	0	0	0	0	0//0	0/0/			0/0/	Other auxiliary equipment with parts listed (no. 84041010, 84042000, auxiliary equipment)
													Producer gas or water gas generators, with or without their purifiers; acetylene gas generators and similar water process gas generators, with or without their purifiers:
	0/0/0	10.1	9.8	4.2	0	0	0	0/0/0	0/0/			0/0/	-Producer gas or water gas generators, with or without their purifiers; acetylene gas generators and similar water process gas generators, with or without their purifiers
	0/0/0	4	0	0	0	0	0	0//0	0/0/			0/0/	-Parts
													Steam turbines and other vapour turbines:
3.5	0/0/0	0	2	0	0	0	0	0//0	0/0/			0/0/0	-Turbines for marine propulsion
													-Other turbines:
													--Of an output exceeding 40 MW:
	0/0/0	0	0	0	0	0	0	0//0	0/0/			0/0/0	---Of an output not exceeding 100 MW
3.5	0/0/0	0	0	0	0	0	0	0//0	0/0/			0/0/0	---Of an output exceeding 100 MW but not exceeding 350 MW
4.2	0/0/0	0	0	0	0	0	0	0//0	0/0/			0/0/0	---Of an output exceeding 350 MW
3.5	0/0/0	0	0	2.6	0	0	0	0//0	0/0/			0/0/0	--Of an output not exceeding 40 MW
	0/0/0	0	0	0.6	0	0	0	0//0	0/0/			0/0/0	-Parts
													Spark-ignition reciprocating or rotary internal combustion piston engines:
													-Aircraft engines:
	0/0/0	0	0	0	0	0	0	0//0	0/0/			0/0/	---Of an output not exceeding 298kW
													---Of an output exceeding 298kW
	0/0/0	0	0	0	0	0	0	0//0	0/0/			0/0/	Spark-ignition reciprocating or rotary internal combustion piston aircraft engines , of an output exceeding 298kW
	0/0/0	0	0	0	0	0	0	0//0	0/0/			0/0/	Spark-ignition reciprocating or rotary internal combustion piston aircraft engines , of an output exceeding 298kW
													-Marine propulsion engines:
	0/0/0	4		0	0	0	0	0//0	0/0/			0/0/	--Outboard motors
	0/0/0	4		0	0	0	0	0//0	0/0/			0/0/	--Other
													-Reciprocating piston engines of a kind used for the propulsion of vehicles of Chapter 87:
	0/0/0	4	7	0	0	0	0	0//0	0/0/			0/0/	--Of a cylinder capacity not exceeding 50cc
	0/0/0	4	7	0	0	0	0	0//0	0/0/			0/0/	--Of a cylinder capacity exceeding 50cc but not exceeding 250cc
	0/0/0	7.2	7	0	0	0	0	0/0/0	0/0/			0/0/	--Of a cylinder capacity exceeding 250cc but not exceeding 1000cc
													--Of a cylinder capacity exceeding 1000cc:
6.5	5/0/0	7	7	0	0		0	0//0	0/0/				---Of a cylinder capacity exceeding 1000cc but not exceeding 3000cc
													---Of a cylinder capacity exceeding 3000cc
6.5	5/0/0	7	7	0	0		0	0//0	0/0/			0//	Natural gas engines with displacement≥5.9L(spark-ignition reciprocating piston engines for the vehicles listed in Chapter 87)
6.5	5/0/0	7	7	0	0		0	0//0	0/0/			0//	Other vehicle use reciprocating piston engines with displacement>3000cc(spark-ignition reciprocating piston engines for the vehicles listed in Chapter 87)
													-Other engines:
7	0/0/0	5.4	4.8	3.6	0	0	0	0/0/0	0/0/			0/0/	---Friedamp engines
													---Other
	0/0/0		10.8	5.4	0	0	0	0/0/0	0/0/			0/0/	Speed < 3600r/min gasoline engine (generator)

税则号列	货品名称〔CIQ 扩展编码及品名—T2 表示见附表 2〕	最惠(%)	暂定税率	普通	增值/消费	出口退税	计量单位	监管条件	检验检疫	特殊证件对美关税
8407.9090 20	转速＜4650r/min 汽油发动机(品目 8426、84288430 所列机械用，立式输出轴汽油发动机除外)〔999〕	18		35	13/	13	台/千克			/23
8407.9090 31	叉车用汽油发动机(800 转/分≤转速≤3400 转/分)(立式输出轴汽油发动机除外)〔999〕	18	9	35	13/	13	台/千克			/14
8407.9090 39	其他转速＜4650 转/分汽油发动机(税目 84.27 所列机械用，立式输出轴汽油发动机除外)〔999〕	18		35	13/	13	台/千克			/23
8407.9090 40	立式输出轴汽油发动机(非第八十七章所列车辆用其他往复式活塞发动机)〔999〕	18	9	35	13/	13	台/千克			/14
8407.9090 90	其他往复或旋转式活塞内燃引擎(非第八十七章所列车辆用其他点燃往复式或旋转式活塞发动机)〔999〕	18		35	13/	13	台/千克			/23
84.08	**压燃式活塞内燃发动机(柴油或半柴油发动机)：**									
8408.1000	-船舶发动机〔999〕	5		11	13/	13	台/千克			/35
	-用于第八十七章所列车辆的发动机：									
8408.2010	---输出功率在 132.39 千瓦(180 马力)及以上									
8408.2010 01	输出功率在 441 千瓦及以上的柴油发动机(600 马力)〔101 其他车辆零部件，102 柴油发动机〕	9	4	14	13/	13	台/千克	6		/
8408.2010 10	功率≥132.39kW 拖拉机用柴油机〔101 其他车辆零部件，102 柴油发动机〕	9		14	9/	13	台/千克	6		/
8408.2010 90	功率≥132.39kW 其他用柴油机[指 87 章车辆用压燃式活塞内燃发动机(132.39kW＝180 马力)]〔101 其他车辆零部件，102 柴油发动机〕	9		14	13/	13	台/千克	6		/
8408.2090	---其他									
8408.2090 10	功率＜132.39 千瓦拖拉机用柴油机〔101 其他车辆零部件，102 柴油发动机〕	25		35	9/	9,13	台/千克	6		/
8408.2090 20	升功率≥50 千瓦，输出功率＜132.39 千瓦的轿车用柴油发动机〔101 其他车辆零部件，102 柴油发动机〕	25	20	35	13/	13	台/千克	6		/
8408.2090 90	功率＜132.39 千瓦其他用柴油机(指第 87 章车辆用压燃式活塞内燃发动机)〔101 其他车辆零部件，102 柴油发动机〕	25		35	13/	13	台/千克	6		/
	-其他发动机：									
8408.9010	---机车发动机〔101 其他车辆零部件，102 柴油发动机〕	6		11	13/	13	台/千克			/11
	---其他：									
8408.9091	----输出功率不超过 14 千瓦									
8408.9091 11	功率≤14 千瓦农业用单缸柴油机[非 87 章车辆用压燃式活塞内燃发动机(14kW＝19.05 马力)]〔999〕	5		35	9/	9	台/千克			/15
8408.9091 19	功率≤14 千瓦农业用柴油发动机[非 87 章车辆用压燃式活塞内燃发动机(14 千瓦＝19.05 马力)]〔999〕	5		35	9/	9	台/千克			/15
8408.9091 91	功率≤14 千瓦其他用单缸柴油机[非 87 章车辆用压燃式活塞内燃发动机(14 千瓦＝19.05 马力)]〔999〕	5		35	13/	9	台/千克			/15
8408.9091 99	功率≤14 千瓦其他用柴油发动机[非 87 章车辆用压燃式活塞内燃发动机(14 千瓦＝19.05 马力)]〔999〕	5		35	13/	9	台/千克			/15
8408.9092	----输出功率超过 14 千瓦，但小于 132.39 千瓦(180 马力)									
8408.9092 10	转速＜4650r/min 柴油发动机，14 千瓦＜功率＜132.39 千瓦(税目 84.26-84.30 所列工程机械用)〔999〕	8		35	13/	13	台/千克			/33
8408.9092 20	14 千瓦＜功率＜132.39 千瓦的农业用柴油机[非 87 章车辆用压燃式活塞内燃发动机(1 千瓦＝1.36 马力)]〔999〕	8		35	9/	9,13	台/千克			/33
8408.9092 90	14 千瓦＜功率＜132.39 千瓦的其他用柴油机[非 87 章车辆用压燃式活塞内燃发动机(1 千瓦＝1.36 马力)]〔999〕	8		35	13/	13	台/千克			/33
8408.9093	----输出功率在 132.39 千瓦(180 马力)及以上									
8408.9093 10	功率≥132.39 千瓦的农业用柴油机[非 87 章用压燃式活塞内燃发动机(132.39 千瓦＝180 马力)]〔999〕	5		14	9/	13	台/千克			/10
8408.9093 90	功率≥132.39 千瓦其他用柴油发动机[非 87 章用压燃式活塞内燃发动机(132.39 千瓦＝180 马力)]〔999〕	5		14	13/	13	台/千克			/10

协定税率 %										特惠税率 %			
亚太5国	东/冰/格	巴基斯坦	韩国	瑞士	哥达	秘鲁	澳大利亚	新西/坡/智	港/澳/台	亚太2国	老/柬/缅	36/3/1	Article Description
	0/0/0		10.8	5.4	0	0	0	0/0/0	0/0/			0/0/	Speed < 4650r/min gasoline engine (heading 84.26, 84.28-84.30 listed machinery)
	0/0/0		10.8	5.4	0	0	0	0/0/0	0/0/			0/0/	Gasoline engine forklift (800 rpm is less than or equal to the speed below 3400r/min) (except for vertical output shaft of the gasoline engine)
	0/0/0		10.8	5.4	0	0	0	0/0/0	0/0/			0/0/	Other speed <4650 r/min gasoline engine (heading 84.27 column machinery, vertical output shaft of the gasoline engine except)
	0/0/0		10.8	5.4	0	0	0	0/0/0	0/0/			0/0/	Vertical output shaft of the gasoline engine (the eighty-seventh chapter car trainnon other reciprocating piston engines)
	0/0/0		10.8	5.4	0	0	0	0/0/0	0/0/			0/0/	Other reciprocating or rotary internal combustion piston engines (spark-ignition reciprocating or rotary piston engines for the vehicles not listed in Chapter 87)
													Compression-ignition internal combustion piston engines (diesel or semi-diesel engines):
2.5	0/0/0	0	2.5	0	0	0	0	0/0/0	0/0/			0/0/	-Marine propulsion engines
													-Engines of a kind used for the propulsion of vehicles of Chapter 87:
													---Of an output of 132.39kW (180HP) or more
6.3	5/0/0	6.3	5.4	0	0	0	0	0//0	0/0/			0/0/	Diesel genines, output power≥441kW(600HP)
6.3	5/0/0	6.3	5.4	0	0	0	0	0//0	0/0/			0/0/	Diesel engines for tractors, output power≥132.39kW
6.3	5/0/0	6.3	5.4	0	0	0	0	0//0	0/0/			0/0/	Other diesel engines, output power≥132.39kW (refers to compression-ignition internal combustion piston engines for the vehicles listed in Chaper 87)
													---Other
17.5	5/0/0	17.5	17.5		0		0	0//0	0/0/			0//	Diesel engines for tractors, output power<132.39kW
17.5	5/0/0	17.5	17.5		0		0	0//0	0/0/			0//	L power more than 50 kilowatts, diesel engine power output of132.39 kilowatts of car "
17.5	5/0/0	17.5	17.5		0		0	0//0	0/0/			0//	Other diesel engines, output power<132.39kw (refers to compression-ignition internal combustion piston engines for the vehicles listed in Chapter 87)
													-Other engines:
3.9	0/0/0	0	0	0	0	0	0	0//0	0/0/			0/0/	---Locomotive engines
													---Other:
													----Of an output not exceeding 14kW
3.3	0/0/0	0	3	0	0	0	0	0//0	0/0/			0/0/	Single-cylinder diesel engines for agricultural use, output power≤14kW (19.05HP) (other than compression-ignition internal combustion piston engines for the vehicles of chapter 87)
3.3	0/0/0	0	3	0	0	0	0	0//0	0/0/			0/0/	Diesel engines for agricultural use, output power ≤ 14kW (19.05HP) (other than compression-ignition internal combustion piston engines for the vehicles of chapter 87)
3.3	0/0/0	0	3	0	0	0	0	0//0	0/0/			0/0/	Single-cyclinder diesel engines for other use, output power≤14kW (19.05HP), (other than compression-ignition internal combustion piston engines for the vehicles of chapter 87)
3.3	0/0/0	0	3	0	0	0	0	0//0	0/0/			0/0/	Other diesel engines, output power≤14kW (19.05HP) (other than compression-ignition internal combustion piston engines for the vehicles of chapter 87)
													----Of an output exceeding 14kW but not exceeding 132.39kW (180HP)
7.2	0/0/0	4	5	0	0	0	0	0//0	0/0/			0/0/	Diesel engines, rotational speed<4650 r/min, 14kW<output power <132.39 kW (for engineering machinery listed in heading No. 8426 to 8430)
7.2	0/0/0	4	5	0	0	0	0	0//0	0/0/			0/0/	Diesel engines for agricutural use, 14kW < output powder < 132.39kW (compression-ignition internal combustion piston engines for the vehicles not listed in Chapter87) (1kW=1.36HP)
7.2	0/0/0	4	5	0	0	0	0	0//0	0/0/			0/0/	Diesel engine for other use, 14kW < output powder < 132.39kW (compression-ignition internal combustion piston engines for the vehicles not listed in Chapter87) (1kW=1.36HP)
													----Of an output of 132.39KW (180HP) or more
3.3	0/0/0	0	3	0	0	0	0	0//0	0/0/			0/0/	Diesel engines for agricultural use, output powder ≥ 132.39kW (180HP) (compression-ignition internal combustion piston engines for the vehicles not listed in Chapter 87)
3.3	0/0/0	0	3	0	0	0	0	0//0	0/0/			0/0/	Diesel engine for other use, output powder≥132.39kW (180HP) (compression-ignition internal combustion piston engines for the vehicles not listed in Chapter 87)

税则号列		货品名称〔CIQ扩展编码及品名—T2表示见附表2〕	最惠(%)	暂定税率	普通	增值/消费	出口退税	计量单位	监管条件	检验检疫	特殊证件对美关税
84.09		**专用于或主要用于税目84.07或84.08所列发动机的零件：**									
8409.1000		-航空器发动机用〔999〕	2		11	13/	13	千克			/
		-其他：									
		--专用于或主要用于点燃式活塞内燃发动机的：									
8409.9110		---船舶发动机用〔999〕	6		17	13/	13	千克			/16
		---其他：									
8409.9191		----电控燃油喷射装置〔101其他车辆零部件，102其它动力设备及其零部件〕	5		35	13/	13	千克/套			/
8409.9199		----其他									
8409.9199	20	废气再循环(EGR)装置(专用或主要用于内燃发动机)〔101其他车辆零部件，102其它动力设备及其零部件〕	5		35	13/	13	千克			/
8409.9199	30	连杆(专用或主要用于内燃发动机)〔101其他车辆零部件，102其它动力设备及其零部件〕	5		35	13/	13	千克			/
8409.9199	40	喷嘴(专用或主要用于内燃发动机)〔101其他车辆零部件，102其它动力设备及其零部件〕	5		35	13/	13	千克			/
8409.9199	50	气门摇臂(专用或主要用于内燃发动机)〔101其他车辆零部件，102其它动力设备及其零部件〕	5		35	13/	13	千克			/
8409.9199	90	其他点燃式活塞内燃发动机用零件〔101其他车辆零部件，102其它动力设备及其零部件〕	5		35	13/	13	千克			/
		--其他：									
8409.9910		---船舶发动机用〔999〕	5		11	13/	13	千克			/30
8409.9920		---机车发动机用〔101其他车辆零部件，102其它动力设备及其零部件〕	2		11	13/	13	千克			/7
		---其他：									
8409.9991		----输出功率在132.39千瓦(180马力)及以上的发动机用〔101其他车辆零部件，102其它动力设备及其零部件〕	2		11	13/	13	千克			/
8409.9999		----其他									
8409.9999	10	电控柴油喷射装置及其零件(指品目8408所列的其他发动机用)〔101其他车辆零部件，102其它动力设备及其零部件〕	8	5	35	13/	13	千克			/
8409.9999	90	其他发动机的专用零件(指税目84.07或84.08所列的其他发动机)〔101其他车辆零部件，102其它动力设备及其零部件〕	8		35	13/	13	千克			/
84.10		**水轮机、水轮及其调节器：**									
		-水轮机及水轮：									
8410.1100		--功率不超过1000千瓦〔999〕	8		35	13/	13	台/千克			/33
8410.1200		--功率超过1000千瓦，但不超过10000千瓦〔999〕	8		35	13/	13	台/千克			/
		--功率超过10000千瓦：									
8410.1310		---功率超过30000千瓦的冲击式水轮机及水轮〔999〕	8		35	13/	13	台/千克			/
8410.1320		---功率超过35000千瓦的贯流式水轮机及水轮〔999〕	8		35	13/	13	台/千克			/
8410.1330		---功率超过200000千瓦的水泵水轮机及水轮〔999〕	8		35	13/	13	台/千克			/
8410.1390		---其他〔999〕	8		35	13/	13	台/千克			/
		-零件，包括调节器：									
8410.9010		---调节器〔999〕	6		35	13/	13	千克/套			/
8410.9090		---其他〔999〕	6		35	13/	13	千克			/
84.11		**涡轮喷气发动机，涡轮螺桨发动机及其他燃气轮机：**									
		-涡轮喷气发动机：									
		--推力不超过25千牛顿：									
8411.1110		---涡轮风扇发动机〔999〕	1		11	13/	13	台/千克	3		/
8411.1190		---其他〔999〕	1		11	13/	13	台/千克			/
		--推力超过25千牛顿：									
8411.1210		---涡轮风扇发动机〔999〕	1		11	13/	13	台/千克	3		/
8411.1290		---其他									
8411.1290	10	小型燃烧率高轻型涡轮喷气发动机(推力大于或等于90千牛顿的涡轮喷气发动机)〔999〕	1		11	13/	13	台/千克	3		/
8411.1290	90	其他涡轮喷气发动机(推力超过25kN)〔999〕	1		11	13/	13	台/千克			/
		-涡轮螺桨发动机：									
8411.2100		--功率不超过1100千瓦〔999〕	2		11	13/	13	台/千克			/
		--功率超过1100千瓦：									
8411.2210		---功率超过1100千瓦，但不超过2238千瓦〔999〕	2		11	13/	13	台/千克			/
8411.2220		---功率超过2238千瓦，但不超过3730千瓦〔999〕	2		11	13/	13	台/千克			/
8411.2230		---功率超过3730千瓦〔999〕	2		11	13/	13	台/千克			/

协定税率 %										特惠税率 %			
亚太5国	东/冰/格	巴基斯坦	韩国	瑞士	哥达	秘鲁	澳大利亚	新西/坡/智	港/澳/台	亚太2国	老/柬/缅	36/3/1	Article Description
													Parts suitable for use solely or principally with the engines of heading No.84. 07 or 84. 08:
	0/0/0	0	0	0	0	0	0	0//0	0/0/			0/0/0	-For aircraft engines
													-Other:
													--Suitable for use solely or principally with spark-ignition internal combustion piston engines:
3.9	0/0/0	0	3.9	0	0	0	0	0//0	0/0/			0/0/0	---For marine propulsion engines
													---Other:
3.3	0/0/0	0	3	0	0	0	0	0/0/0	0/0/			0/0/0	----Electric fuel injection devices
													----Other
3.3	0/0/0	0	2	1.5	0	0	0	0/0/0	0/0/			0/0/0	Exhaust gas recycling apparatuses (EGR)(suitable for use solely or principally with combustion piston engines)
3.3	0/0/0	0	2	1.5	0	0	0	0/0/0	0/0/			0/0/0	Links (connecting rods)(suitable for use solely or principally with combustion piston engines)
3.3	0/0/0	0	2	1.5	0	0	0	0/0/0	0/0/			0/0/0	Nozzles(suitable for use solely or principally with combustion piston engines)
3.3	0/0/0	0	2	1.5	0	0	0	0/0/0	0/0/			0/0/0	Valve rockers arms(suitable for use solely or principally with combustion piston engines)
3.3	0/0/0	0	2	1.5	0	0	0	0/0/0	0/0/			0/0/0	Other parts of spark-ignition internal combustion piston engines
													--Other:
3.3	0/0/0	0	3	1.5	0	0	0	0/0/0	0/0/			0/0/0	---For marine propulsion engines
1.3	0/0/0.8	0	0	0	0	0	0	0//0	0/0/			0/0/0	---For locomotive engines
													---Other:
1.3	0/0/0	0	0.8	0	0	0	0	0//0	0/0/			0/0/0	----For engines with an output of 132. 39kW (180HP) or more
													----Other
5.2	0/0/0	4	5	0	0	0	0	0/0/0	0/0/			0/0/0	Electronically controlled diesel fuel injection device and its parts(refer to other items listed in the 8408 engine use)
5.2	0/0/0	4	5	0	0	0	0	0/0/0	0/0/			0/0/0	Special parts for other engines(other engines listed in Heding No.84. 07 or 84.08)
													Hydraulic turbines, water wheels, and regulators therefor:
													-Hydraulic turbines and water wheels:
	0/0/0	4	4	0	0	0	0	0//0	0/0/			0/0/	--Of a power not exceeding 1000kW
	0/0/0	4	4	0	0	0	0	0/0/0	0/0/			0/0/	--Of a power exceeding 1000KW but not exceeding 10000kW
													--Of a power exceeding 10000kW:
5.6	0/0/0	4	4	0	0	0	0	0/0/0	0/0/			0/0/	---Impulse hydraulic turbines and water wheels of a power exceeding 30000 kW
5.6	0/0/0	4	4	0	0	0	0	0/0/0	0/0/			0/0/	---Radial hydraulic turbines and water wheels of a power exceeding 35000 kW
5.6	0/0/0	4	4	0	0	0	0	0//0	0/0/			0/0/	---Pumping hydraulic turbines and water wheels of a power exceeding 200000kW
5.6	0/0/0	4	4	0	0	0	0	0//0	0/0/			0/0/	---Other
													-Parts, including regulators:
4.2	0/0/0	0	0	0	0	0	0	0//0	0/0/			0/0/	---Regulators
	0/0/0	0	2.4	0	0	0	0	0//0	0/0/			0/0/	---Other
													Turbo-jets, turbo-propellers and other gas turbines:
													-Turbo-jets:
													--Of a thrust not exceeding 25kN:
	0/0/0	0	0	0	0	0	0	0//0	0/0/			0/0/0	---Turbofan engines
	0/0/0	0	0	0	0	0	0	0//0	0/0/			0/0/0	---Other
													--Of a thrust exceeding 25kN:
0	0/0/0	0	0	0	0	0	0	0//0	0/0/			0/0/0	---Turbofan engines
													---Other
0.5	0/0/0	0	0	0	0	0	0	0//0	0/0/			0/0/0	Minitype turbo-jets with high combustion rate(turo-jets with propulsive force≥90kN)
0.5	0/0/0	0	0	0	0	0	0	0//0	0/0/			0/0/0	Other turbo-jets(propulsive force>25kN)
													-Turbo-propellers:
	0/0/0	0	0	0	0	0	0	0//0	0/0/			0/0/0	--Of a power not exceeding 1100kW
													--Of a power exceeding 1100kW:
1.4	0/0/0	0	0	0	0	0	0	0//0	0/0/			0/0/0	---Of a power exceeding 1100kW but not exceeding 2238kW
1.4	0/0/0	0	0	0	0	0	0	0//0	0/0/			0/0/0	---Of a power exceeding 2238kW but not exceeding 3730kW
1.4	0/0/0	0	0	0	0	0	0	0//0	0/0/			0/0/0	---Of a power exceeding 3730kW

税则号列	货品名称〔CIQ 扩展编码及品名－T2 表示见附表 2〕	最惠(%)	暂定税率	普通	增值/消费	出口退税	计量单位	监管条件	检验检疫	特殊证件对美关税
	-其他燃气轮机：									
8411.8100	--功率不超过 5000 千瓦									
8411.8100 01	涡轮轴航空发动机(功率≤5000kW)〔999〕	15	1	35	13/	13	台/千克			/
8411.8100 90	功率≤5000kW 的其他燃气轮机〔999〕	15		35	13/	13	台/千克			/
8411.8200	--功率超过 5000 千瓦〔999〕	3		35	13/	13	台/千克			/
	-零件：									
8411.9100	--涡轮喷气发动机或涡轮螺桨发动机用〔999〕	1		11	13/	13	千克			/
	--其他：									
8411.9910	---涡轮轴发动机用									
8411.9910 10	涡轮轴航空发动机用零件〔999〕	5	1	35	13/	13	千克			/
8411.9910 90	其他涡轮轴发动机用零件〔999〕	5		35	13/	13	千克			/
8411.9990	---其他〔999〕	5		35	13/	13	千克			/
84.12	**其他发动机及动力装置：**									
	-喷气发动机，但涡轮喷气发动机除外：									
8412.1010	---航空器及航天器用									
8412.1010 10	冲压喷气发动机(包括超燃冲压喷气发动机)〔999〕	3		11	13/	13	台/千克	3		/
8412.1010 20	脉冲喷气发动机〔999〕	3		11	13/	13	台/千克	3		/
8412.1010 30	组合循环发动机〔999〕	3		11	13/	13	台/千克	3		/
8412.1010 90	其他航空、航天器用喷气发动机(涡轮喷气发动机除外)〔999〕	3		11	13/	13	台/千克			/
8412.1090	---其他〔999〕	10		35	13/	13	台/千克			/15
	-液压动力装置：									
8412.2100	--直线作用(液压缸)的〔999〕	12		35	13/	13	台/千克			/22
	--其他：									
8412.2910	---液压马达〔999〕	10		35	13/	13	台/千克			/30
8412.2990	---其他									
8412.2990 10	抓桩器(抱桩器)〔999〕	14	7	35	13/	13	台/千克			/17
8412.2990 20	压力值在 20mpa 以上的飞机用液压作动器〔999〕	14	1	35	13/	13	台/千克			/11
8412.2990 90	其他液压动力装置〔999〕	14		35	13/	13	台/千克			/24
8412.3100	--直线作用(气压缸)的									
	气压动力装置：									
8412.3100 01	三坐标测量机用平衡气缸〔999〕	14	7	35	13/	13	台/千克			/27
8412.3100 90	其他直线作用的气压动力装置(气压缸)〔999〕	14		35	13/	13	台/千克			/34
8412.3900	--其他〔999〕	14		35	13/	13	台/千克			/24
8412.8000	-其他									
8412.8000 10	液体火箭发动机(推力大于或等于 90 千牛顿可贮存推进剂的)〔999〕	10		35	13/	13	台/千克	3		/20
8412.8000 20	固体火箭发动机(总冲大于或等于 1100 千牛顿每秒的)〔999〕	10		35	13/	13	台/千克	3		/20
8412.8000 90	其他发动机及动力装置〔999〕	10		35	13/	13	台/千克			/20
	-零件：									
8412.9010	---子目 8412.1010 所列机器的零件									
8412.9010 10	燃烧调节装置(冲压或脉冲喷气发动机的)〔999〕	2		11	13/	13	千克	3		/
8412.9010 20	火箭发动机的壳体〔999〕	2		11	13/	13	千克	3		/
8412.9010 90	航空、航天器用喷气发动机的零件(涡轮喷气发动机的零件，编号 8412.9010 10 除外)〔999〕	2		11	13/	13	千克			/
8412.9090	---其他									
8412.9090 10	风力发动机零件〔999〕	8	5	35	13/	13	千克			/
8412.9090 90	其他发动机及动力装置的零件〔999〕	8		35	13/	13	千克			/
84.13	**液体泵，不论是否装有计量装置；液体提升机：**									
	-装有或可装计量装置的泵：									
8413.1100	--分装燃料或润滑油的泵，用于加油站或车库〔999〕	10	6	30	13/	13	台/千克			/26
8413.1900	--其他〔999〕	10	6	30	13/	13	台/千克			/16
8413.2000	-手泵，但子目 8413.11 或 8413.19 的货品除外〔999〕	10		30	13/	13	台/千克			/30
	-活塞式内燃发动机用的燃油泵、润滑油泵或冷却剂泵：									
	---燃油泵：									
8413.3021	----输出功率在 132.39 千瓦(180 马力)及以上的发动机用燃油泵〔101 其他车辆零部件，102 燃油泵〕	3		30	13/	13	台/千克			/23
8413.3029	----其他〔101 其他车辆零部件，102 燃油泵〕	3		30	13/	13	台/千克			/23
8413.3030	---润滑油泵〔101 其他车辆零部件，102 燃油泵〕	3		30	13/	13	台/千克			/23
8413.3090	---其他〔101 其他车辆零部件，102 燃油泵〕	3		30	13/	13	台/千克			/23
8413.4000	-混凝土泵〔999〕	8		30	13/	13	台/千克			/33
	-其他往复式排液泵：									

协定税率 %										特惠税率 %			Article Description
亚太5国	东/冰/格	巴基斯坦	韩国	瑞士	哥达	秘鲁	澳大利亚	新西/坡/智	港/澳/台	亚太2国	老/柬/缅	36/3/1	
													-Other gas turbines:
													--Of a power not exceeding 5000kW
	0/0/0	10.8	6	4.5	0	0	0	0/0/0	0/0/			0/0/	Turbine shaft aeroengine(power≤5000kW)
	0/0/0	10.8	6	4.5	0	0	0	0/0/0	0/0/			0/0/	Other gas turbines, Power≤5000kW
2.1	0/0/0	0	0	0	0	0	0	0//0	0/0/			0/0/0	--Of a power exceeding 5000kW
													-Parts:
	0/0/0	0	0	0	0	0	0	0//0	0/0/			0/0/0	--Of turbo-jets or turbo-propellers
													--Other:
													---Of turbine shaft engines
3.5	0/0/0	0	0	0	0	0	0	0//0	0/0/			0/0/0	The turbine shaft Aeroengine Parts
3.5	0/0/0	0	0	0	0	0	0	0//0	0/0/			0/0/0	Other part of turbine shaft engines
	0/0/0	0	2	0	0	0	0	0//0	0/0/			0/0/0	---Other
													Other engines and motors:
													-Jet engines other than turbo-jets:
													---For aircraft or spacecraft
	0/0/0	0	0	0	0	0	0	0//0	0/0/			0/0/0	Ramjet engines(including scramjet engines)
	0/0/0	0	0	0	0	0	0	0//0	0/0/			0/0/0	Pulse jet engines
	0/0/0	0	0	0	0	0	0	0//0	0/0/			0/0/0	Combined cycle engines
	0/0/0	0	0	0	0	0	0	0//0	0/0/			0/0/0	Other jet engines (other than turbo-jets) for aircraft or spacecraft
	0/0/0	4	4	0	0	0	0	0//0	0/0/			0/0/	---Other
													-Hydraulic power engines and motors:
	0/0/0	5.4	8.4	3.6	0	0	0	0/0/0	0/0/0			0/0/	--Linear acting (cylinders)
													--Other:
	0/0/0	4.5	7	3	0	0	0	0/0/0	0/0/			0/0/	---Hydraulic motors
													---Other
	0/0/0	10.1	8.4	4.2	0	0	0	0/0/0	0/0/			0/0/	Pile gripper
	0/0/0	10.1	8.4	4.2	0	0	0	0/0/0	0/0/			0/0/	Hydraulic actuator for aircraft, with pressure above 20MPa
	0/0/0	10.1	8.4	4.2	0	0	0	0/0/0	0/0/			0/0/	Other hydrulic power engines and motors
													--Linear acting (cylinders)
													-Pneumatic power engines and motors:
9.1	0/0/0	6.3	0	0	0	0	0	0/0/0	0/0/0			0/0/	Balance cylinder for three-dimensional measuring machine
9.1	0/0/0	6.3	0	0	0	0	0	0/0/0	0/0/0			0/0/	Other pneumatic power engines and motors of straightening(cylinders)
	0/0/0	10.1	5.6	0	0	0	0	0/0/0	0/0/			0/0/	--Other
													-Other
	0/0/0	4	4	0	0	0	0	0//0	0/0/			0/0/	Liquid-propellant rocket engines (thrust≥90kN, capable of storing propellant)
	0/0/0	4	4	0	0	0	0	0//0	0/0/			0/0/	Solid-propellant rocket engine (of a total impulse≥1100kN)
	0/0/0	4	4	0	0	0	0	0//0	0/0/			0/0/	Other engines and motors
													-Parts:
													---For machines of subheading No.8412. 1010
	0/0/0	0	0	0	0	0	0	0//0	0/0/			0/0/0	Combustion control devices (for ramjet engine or pulse jet engines)
	0/0/0	0	0	0	0	0	0	0//0	0/0/			0/0/0	Shells of rocket engines
	0/0/0	0	0	0	0	0	0	0//0	0/0/			0/0/0	Parts of jet engines for aircraft or spacecraft, (other than parts of turbo-jets engines and parts of subheading No.8412. 9010 10)
													---Other
	0/0/0	4	4.8	0	0	0	0	0//0	0/0/			0/0/0	Wind power engine parts
	0/0/0	4	4.8	0	0	0	0	0//0	0/0/			0/0/0	Other parts for engines and motors
													Pumps for liquids, whether or not fitted with a measuring device; liquid elevators:
													-Pumps fitted or designed to be fitted with a measuring device:
	0/0/0	4	4	0	0	0	0	0/0/0	0/0/			0/0/0	--Pumps for dispensing fuel or lubricants, of the type used in filling-stations or in garages
	0/0/0	4.5	7	3	0	0	0	0/0/0	0/0/			0/0/0	--Other
	0/0/0	4	4	0	0	0	0	0/0/0	0/0/			0/0/0	-Hand pumps, other than those of subheadingNo. 8413.11 or 8413.19
													-Fuel, lubricating or cooling medium pumps for internal combustion piston engines:
													---Fuel pumps:
2	0/0/0	0	0	0	0	0	0	0//0	0/0/			0/0/0	----Fuel pumps for engines of an output of 132.39kW (180HP) or more
	0/0/0	0	0	0	0	0	0	0//0	0/0/			0/0/0	----Other
	0/0/0	0	0	0	0	0	0	0//0	0/0/			0/0/0	---Lubricating oil pumps
2	0/0/0	0	0	0	0	0	0	0//0	0/0/			0/0/0	---Other
	0/0/0	4	3.2	0	0	0	0	0//0	0/0/			0/0/0	-Concrete pumps
													-Other reciprocating positive displacement pumps:

税则号列		货品名称〔CIQ 扩展编码及品名－T2 表示见附表 2〕	最惠(%)	暂定税率	普通	增值/消费	出口退税	计量单位	监管条件	检验检疫	特殊证件对美关税
8413.5010		---气动式									
8413.5010	10	农业用气动往复式排液泵〔999〕	10	6	40	9/	9	台/千克			/11
8413.5010	20	气动式耐腐蚀波纹或隔膜泵(流量大于 0.6m³/h,接触表面由特殊耐腐蚀材料制成)〔999〕	10	6	40	13/	13	台/千克	3		/11
8413.5010	90	其他非农业用气动往复式排液泵〔999〕	10	6	40	13/	13	台/千克			/11
8413.5020		---电动式									
8413.5020	10	农业用电动往复式排液泵〔999〕	10	6	40	9/	9	台/千克			/26
8413.5020	20	电动式耐腐蚀波纹或隔膜泵(流量大于 0.6m³/h,接触表面由特殊耐腐蚀材料制成)〔999〕	10	6	40	13/	13	台/千克	3		/26
8413.5020	30	电动往复式排液多重密封泵(两用物项管制)〔999〕	10	6	40	13/	13	台/千克	3		/26
8413.5020	90	其他非农业用电动往复式排液泵〔999〕	10	6	40	13/	13	台/千克			/26
		---液压式:									
8413.5031		----柱塞泵									
8413.5031	01	农业用柱塞泵〔999〕	10	6	40	9/	9	台/千克			/16
8413.5031	90	其他非农业用柱塞泵〔999〕	10	6	40	13/	13	台/千克			/16
8413.5039		----其他									
8413.5039	01	其他农业用液压往复式排液泵〔999〕	10	6	40	9/	9	台/千克			/26
8413.5039	20	液压式耐腐蚀波纹或隔膜泵(流量大于 0.6m³/h,接触表面由特殊耐腐蚀材料制成)〔999〕	10	6	40	13/	13	台/千克	3		/26
8413.5039	90	其他非农业用液压往复式排液泵〔999〕	10	6	40	13/	13	台/千克			/26
8413.5090		---其他									
8413.5090	10	其他农用往复式排液泵〔999〕	10	6	40	9/	9	台/千克			/31
8413.5090	20	其他耐腐蚀波纹或隔膜泵(流量大于 0.6m³/h,接触表面由特殊耐腐蚀材料制成)〔999〕	10	6	40	13/	13	台/千克	3		/31
8413.5090	90	其他非农用往复式排液泵〔999〕	10	6	40	13/	13	台/千克			/31
		-其他回转式排液泵:									
		---齿轮泵									
8413.6021		----电动式									
8413.6021	01	农业用电动齿轮泵(回转式排液泵)〔999〕	10	6	40	9/	9	台/千克			/11
8413.6021	10	电动齿轮多重密封泵(非农业用回转式排液泵)〔999〕	10	6	40	13/	13	台/千克	3		/11
8413.6021	90	其他非农业用电动齿轮泵(回转式排液泵,多重密封泵除外)〔999〕	10	6	40	13/	13	台/千克			/11
8413.6022		----液压式									
8413.6022	01	农业用回转式液压油泵(输入转速＞2000r/min,输入功率＞190kW,最大流量＞2×280L/min)〔999〕	10	3	40	9/	9	台/千克			/23
8413.6022	02	非农业用回转式液压油泵(输入转速＞2000r/min,输入功率＞190kW,最大流量＞2×280L/min)〔999〕	10	3	40	13/	13	台/千克			/23
8413.6022	10	其他农业用液压齿轮泵(回转式排液泵)〔999〕	10	6	40	9/	9	台/千克			/26
8413.6022	20	液压齿轮多重密封泵(非农业用回转式排液泵)〔999〕	10	6	40	13/	13	台/千克	3		/26
8413.6022	90	其他非农业用液压齿轮泵(回转式排液泵,多重密封泵除外)〔999〕	10	6	40	13/	13	台/千克			/26
8413.6029		----其他									
8413.6029	01	其他农业用齿轮泵(回转式排液泵)〔999〕	10	6	40	9/	9	台/千克			/31
8413.6029	90	其他非农业用齿轮泵(回转式排液泵)〔999〕	10	6	40	13/	13	台/千克			/31
		---叶片泵:									
8413.6031		----电动式									

协定税率 %										特惠税率 %			
亚太5国	东/冰/格	巴基斯坦	韩国	瑞士	哥达	秘鲁	澳大利亚	新西/坡/智	港/澳/台	亚太2国	老/柬/缅	36/3/1	Article Description
													---Pneumatic
	0/0/0	4	6	0	0	0	0	0/0/0	0/0/			0/0/0	Pneumatic reciprocating positive displacement pumps for agricultural use
	0/0/0	4	6	0	0	0	0	0/0/0	0/0/			0/0/0	Pneumatic corrosion-resisting bellows or diaphragm pumps (flow capacity>0. 6m³/h, with a contact surface of special corrosion-resisting material)
	0/0/0	4	6	0	0	0	0	0/0/0	0/0/			0/0/0	Pneumatic reciprocating positive displacement pumps for non-argricultural use
													---Electric
	0/0/0	4.5	4	4.2	0	0	0	0/0/0	0/0/			0/0/0	Electric reciprocating positive displacement pumps for agricutlural use
	0/0/0	4.5	4	4.2	0	0	0	0/0/0	0/0/			0/0/0	Electric corrosion-resisting bellows diaphragm pumps (flow capacity >0. 6m³/h with a contact-surface of special corrosion-resisting materials)
	0/0/0	4.5	4	4.2	0	0	0	0/0/0	0/0/			0/0/0	Electric reciprocating multiple-sealed positive displacement pumps for non-argricultural use
	0/0/0	4.5	4	4.2	0	0	0	0/0/0	0/0/			0/0/0	Other electric reciprocating positive displacement pumps for non-argricultlral use
													---Hydraulic:
													----Plunger pumps
	0/0/0	4.5	7	0	0	0	0	0/0/0	0/0/			0/0/0	Plunger pumps for agriculture use
	0/0/0	4.5	7	0	0	0	0	0/0/0	0/0/			0/0/0	Other plunger pumps for non-agriculture use
													----Other
	0/0/0	0	6	0	0	0	0	0/0/0	0/0/			0/0/0	Other hydraulic reciprocating positive displacement pumps for agricultural use
	0/0/0	0	6	0	0	0	0	0/0/0	0/0/			0/0/0	Hydraulic corrosion-resisting bellows or diaphragm pumps(flow capacity>0. 6m³/h with a contact-surface of special corrosion-resisting materials)
	0/0/0	0	6	0	0	0	0	0/0/0	0/0/			0/0/0	Other hydraulic reciprocating positive displacement pumps for non-argricultural use
													---Other
	0/0/0	4.5	7	0	0	0	0	0/0/0	0/0/			0/0/0	Other reciprocating positive displacement pumps for agricutural use
	0/0/0	4.5	7	0	0	0	0	0/0/0	0/0/			0/0/0	Other corrosion-resisting bellows or diaphragm pumps(flow capacity >0. 6m³/h with a contact-surface of special corrosion-resisting materials)
	0/0/0	4.5	7	0	0	0	0	0/0/0	0/0/			0/0/0	Other reciprocating positive displacement pumps for non-argricultural use
													-Other rotary positive displacement pumps:
													---Gear pumps
													----Electric
	0//4	4.5	7	0	0	0	0	0/0/0	0/0/			0/0/0	Electric gear pumps for agricultural use(rotary positive displacement pumps)
	0//4	4.5	7	0	0	0	0	0/0/0	0/0/			0/0/0	Electric multiple-sealed gear pumps (rotary positive displacement pumps for non-agricultural use)
	0//4	4.5	7	0	0	0	0	0/0/0	0/0/			0/0/0	Other electric gear pumps for non-agricultural use(rotary positive displacement pumps for non-agricultural use)
													----Hydraulic
	0/0/0	4	6	0	0	0	0	0//0	0/0/			0/0/0	Rotary hydraulic oil pumps for agricultural use (input speed>2000 r/min, input power>190 kW, maximum flow quantity>2×280L/min)
	0/0/0	4	6	0	0	0	0	0//0	0/0/			0/0/0	Rotary hydraulic oil pumps for non-agricultural use (input speed>2000 r/min, input power>190 kW, maximum flow quantity>2×280L/min)
	0/0/0	4	6	0	0	0	0	0//0	0/0/			0/0/0	Other hydraulic gear pumps for agricultural use (rotary positive displacement pumps)
	0/0/0	4	6	0	0	0	0	0//0	0/0/			0/0/0	Hydraulic gear multiple-sealed pumps (rotary positive discharging hydraulic pump for non-agricultural use)
	0/0/0	4	6	0	0	0	0	0//0	0/0/			0/0/0	Other hydraulic gear pumps for non-agricultural use(except rotary positive displacement pumps, multiple-sealed pumps)
													----Other
	0/0/0	4.5	4	0	0	0	0	0//0	0/0/			0/0/0	Other gear pumps for agricultural use(rotary positive displacement pumps)
	0/0/0	4.5	4	0	0	0	0	0//0	0/0/			0/0/0	Other gear pumps for non-agricultural use(rotary positive displacement pumps)
													---Vane pumps:
													----Electric

税则号列	货品名称〔CIQ扩展编码及品名－T2表示见附表2〕	最惠(%)	暂定税率	普通	增值/消费	出口退税	计量单位	监管条件	检验检疫	特殊证件对美关税
8413.6031 01	农业用电动叶片泵(回转式排液泵)〔999〕	10	6	40	9/	9	台/千克			/26
8413.6031 10	电动叶片多重密封泵(非农业用回转式排液泵)〔999〕	10	6	40	13/	13	台/千克	3		/26
8413.6031 90	其他非农业用电动叶片泵(回转式排液泵,多重密封泵除外)〔999〕	10	6	40	13/	13	台/千克			/26
8413.6032	----液压式									
8413.6032 01	农业用液压叶片泵(回转式排液泵)〔999〕	10	6	40	9/	9	台/千克			/26
8413.6032 10	液压叶片多重密封泵(非农业用回转式排液泵)〔999〕	10	6	40	13/	13	台/千克	3		/26
8413.6032 90	其他非农业用液压叶片泵(回转式排液泵,多重密封泵除外)〔999〕	10	6	40	13/	13	台/千克			/26
8413.6039	----其他									
8413.6039 01	其他农业用叶片泵(回转式排液泵)〔999〕	10	6	40	9/	9	台/千克			/31
8413.6039 90	其他非农业用叶片泵(回转式排液泵)〔999〕	10	6	40	13/	13	台/千克			/31
8413.6040	---螺杆泵									
8413.6040 01	农业用螺杆泵(回转式排液泵)〔999〕	10	6	40	9/	9	台/千克			/16
8413.6040 10	螺杆多重密封泵(非农业用回转式排液泵)〔999〕	10	6	40	13/	13	台/千克	3		/16
8413.6040 90	其他非农业用螺杆泵(回转式排液泵,多重密封泵除外)〔999〕	10	6	40	13/	13	台/千克			/16
8413.6050	---径向柱塞泵									
8413.6050 01	农业用径向柱塞泵(回转式排液泵)〔999〕	10	6	40	9/	9	台/千克			/31
8413.6050 90	其他非农业用径向柱塞泵(回转式排液泵)〔999〕	10	6	40	13/	13	台/千克			/31
8413.6060	---轴向柱塞泵									
8413.6060 01	农业用轴向柱塞泵(回转式排液泵)〔999〕	10	6	40	9/	9	台/千克			/31
8413.6060 90	其他非农业用轴向柱塞泵(回转式排液泵)〔999〕	10	6	40	13/	13	台/千克			/31
8413.6090	---其他									
8413.6090 10	农业用其他回转式排液泵〔999〕	10	8	40	9/	9	台/千克			/13
8413.6090 90	其他回转式排液泵〔999〕	10	8	40	13/	13	台/千克			/13
	-其他离心泵:									
8413.7010	---转速在10000转/分及以上									
8413.7010 10	农业用其他离心泵(转速在10000转/分及以上)〔999〕	8		40	9/	9	台/千克			/13
8413.7010 20	液体推进剂用泵(转速≥10000转/分,出口压力≥7000千帕的)〔999〕	8		40	13/	13	台/千克	3		/13
8413.7010 30	离心泵多重密封泵(两用物项管制)〔999〕	8		40	13/	13	台/千克	3		/13
8413.7010 90	其他非农用离心泵(转速在10000转/分及以上)〔999〕	8		40	13/	13	台/千克			/13
	---其他:									
8413.7091	----电动潜油泵及潜水电泵									
8413.7091 10	农业用电动潜油泵及潜水电泵(转速在10000转/分以下)〔999〕	8		40	9/	9	台/千克			/28
8413.7091 90	其他非农业用电动潜油泵及潜水电泵(转速在10000转/分以下)〔999〕	8		40	13/	13	台/千克			/28
8413.7099	----其他									
8413.7099 10	其他农业用离心泵(转速在10000转/分以下)〔999〕	8		40	9/	9	台/千克			/13
8413.7099 20	一次冷却剂泵(全密封驱动泵,有惯性质量系统的泵,及鉴定为NC－1泵等)〔999〕	8		40	13/	13	台/千克	3		/13
8413.7099 30	转速小于10000转/分的离心式屏蔽泵(流量大于0.6m^3/h,接触表面由特殊耐腐蚀材料制成)〔999〕	8		40	13/	13	台/千克	3		/13
8413.7099 40	转速小于10000转/分的离心式磁力泵(流量大于0.6m^3/h,接触表面由特殊耐腐蚀材料制成)〔999〕	8		40	13/	13	台/千克	3		/13

协定税率 %										特惠税率 %			
亚太5国	东/冰/格	巴基斯坦	韩国	瑞士	哥达	秘鲁	澳大利亚	新西/坡/智	港/澳/台	亚太2国	老/柬/缅	36/3/1	Article Description
	0/0/0	4	4	0	0	0	0	0//0	0/0/			0/0/0	Electric vane pumps for agricultural use(rotary positive displacement pumps)
	0/0/0	4	4	0	0	0	0	0//0	0/0/			0/0/0	Electric multiple-sealed vane pumps (rotary positive displacement pumps for non-agricultural use)
	0/0/0	4	4	0	0	0	0	0//0	0/0/			0/0/0	Other electric vane pumps for non-agricultural use(except rotary positive displacement pumps, multiple-sealed pumps)
													----Hydraulic
	0/0/0	4	7	0	0	0	0	0//0	0/0/			0/0/0	Hydraulic vane pumps for agricultural use(rotary positive displacement pumps)
	0/0/0	4	7	0	0	0	0	0//0	0/0/			0/0/0	Hydraulic vane multiple-sealed pumps(rotary positive displacement pumps for non-agricultural use)
	0/0/0	4	7	0	0	0	0	0//0	0/0/			0/0/0	Other hydraulic vane pumps for non-agricultural use(except rotary positive displacement pumps, multiple-sealed pumps)
													----Other
	0/0/0	4	7	0	0	0	0	0//0	0/0/			0/0/0	Other vane pumps for agricultural use(rotary positive displacement pumps)
	0/0/0	4	7	0	0	0	0	0//0	0/0/			0/0/0	Other vane pumps for non-agricultural use(rotary positive displacement pumps)
													---Screw pumps
	0/0/0	4	7	0	0	0	0	0//0	0/0/			0/0/0	Screw pumps for agricultural use (rotary positive displacement pumps)
	0/0/0	4	7	0	0	0	0	0//0	0/0/			0/0/0	Screw pumps (rotary positive multiple-sealed displacement pumps for non-agricultural use.)
	0/0/0	4	7	0	0	0	0	0//0	0/0/			0/0/0	Other screw pumps for non-agricultural use(except rotary positive displacement pumps, multiple-sealed pumps)
													---Radial plunger pumps
	0/0/0	4	7	0	0	0	0	0//0	0/0/			0/0/0	Radial plunger pumps for agricultural use(rotary positive displacement pumps)
	0/0/0	4	7	0	0	0	0	0//0	0/0/			0/0/0	Other radial plunger pumps for non-agricultural use(rotary positive displacement pumps)
													---Axial plunger pumps
	0/0/0	4.5	6	0	0	0	0	0//0	0/0/			0/0/0	Axial plunger pumps for agricultural use(rotary positive displacement pumps)
	0/0/0	4.5	6	0	0	0	0	0//0	0/0/			0/0/0	Other axial plunger pumps for non-agricultural use(rotary positive displacement pumps)
													---Other
	0/0/0	4.5	6	3	0	0	0	0/0/0	0/0/			0/0/0	Other rotary positive displacement pumps for agricutural use
	0/0/0	4.5	6	3	0	0	0	0/0/0	0/0/			0/0/0	Other rotary positive displacement pumps
													-Other centrifugal pumps:
													---Rotational speed no less than 10000r/min
5.2	0/0/0	4	0	0	0	0	0	0//0	0/0/			0/0/0	Other centrifugal pumps for agricultural use, rotational speed ≥ 10000r/min
5.2	0/0/0	4	0	0	0	0	0	0//0	0/0/			0/0/0	Liquid-propellant pumps, rotational speed ≥ 10000r/min, outlet pressure≥7000kPa
5.2	0/0/0	4	0	0	0	0	0	0//0	0/0/			0/0/0	centrifugal Multiple sealedg pumps(subject to regulation of sensitive items)
5.2	0/0/0	4	0	0	0	0	0	0//0	0/0/			0/0/0	Other centrifugal pumps, for non-argricultural use rotational speed≥ 10000r/min,
													---Other:
													----Electric submersible oil pumps and electric submrsible pumps
	0/0/0	4	4	0	0	0	0	0/0/0	0/0/			0/0/0	Electric submersible oil pumps and electric submrsible pumps for agricultural use(rotational speed≥10000r/min)
	0/0/0	4	4	0	0	0	0	0/0/0	0/0/			0/0/0	Other electric submersible oil pumps and electric submrsible pumps for non-agricultural use (rotational speed≥10000r/min)
													----Other
5.2	0/0/0	4	0	2.4	0	0	0	0//0	0/0/			0/0/0	Other centrifugal pumps for agricultural use (rotational speed < 10000r/min)
5.2	0/0/0	4	0	2.4	0	0	0	0//0	0/0/			0/0/0	Primary coolant pumps (completely-sealed driving pumps, pumps with inertia mass system, approved NC-1pumps)
5.2	0/0/0	4	0	2.4	0	0	0	0//0	0/0/			0/0/0	Canned centrifugal pumps, rotational speed<10000r/min (flow capacity>0. 6m^3/h with a contact-surface of special corrosion-resisting materials)
5.2	0/0/0	4	0	2.4	0	0	0	0//0	0/0/			0/0/0	Magnetically-driven centrifugal pumps, rotational speed < 10000r/min (flow capacity>0. 6m^3/h with a contact-surface of special corrosion-resisting materials)

税则号列		货品名称〔CIQ 扩展编码及品名—T2 表示见附表 2〕	最惠(%)	暂定税率	普通	增值/消费	出口退税	计量单位	监管条件	检验检疫	特殊证件对美关税
8413.7099	50	液体推进剂用泵(8000 转/分＜转速＜10000 转/分,出口压力≥7000kPa 的)〔999〕	8		40	13/	13	台/千克	3		/13
8413.7099	60	其他离心泵多重密封泵(两用物项管制)〔999〕	8		40	13/	13	台/千克	3		/13
8413.7099	90	其他非农业用离心泵(转速在 10000 转/分以下)〔999〕	8		40	13/	13	台/千克			/13
		-其他泵;液体提升机:									
8413.8100		--泵									
8413.8100	10	农业用其他液体泵〔999〕	8		40	9/	9	台/千克			/28
8413.8100	20	生产重水用多级泵(专门为利用氨—氢交换法生产重水而设计或制造的多级泵)〔999〕	8		40	13/	13	台/千克	3		/28
8413.8100	90	其他非农用液体泵〔999〕	8		40	13/	13	台/千克			/28
8413.8200		--液体提升机〔999〕	8		30	13/	13	台/千克			/28
		-零件:									
8413.9100		--泵用〔999〕	5		30	13/	13	千克			/15
8413.9200		--液体提升机用〔999〕	6	4	30	13/	13	千克			/24
84.14		**空气泵或真空泵、空气及其他气体压缩机、风机、风扇;装有风扇的通风罩或循环气罩,不论是否装有过滤器:**									
8414.1000		-真空泵									
8414.1000	10	耐腐蚀真空泵(流量大于 5m³/h,接触表面由特殊耐腐蚀材料制成)〔101 其它空气压缩机(站)及零件 I 类器具,102 其它空气压缩机(站)及零件 II 类器具,103 其它空气压缩机(站)及零件 III 类器具,104 其它空气压缩机(站)及零件 0I 类器具,105 其它空气压缩机(站)及零件 0 类器具〕	8	5	30	13/	13	台/千克	3		/30
8414.1000	20	真空泵(抽气口≥38 厘米,速度≥15m³/秒,产生＜10^{-4} 托极限真空度〔999〕	8	5	30	13/	13	台/千克	3		/30
8414.1000	30	能在含 UF6 气氛中使用的真空泵(用耐 UF6 腐蚀的材料制成或保护。这些泵可以是旋转式或正压式,可有排代式密封和碳氟化合物密封并且可以有特殊工作流体存在)〔999〕	8	5	30	13/	13	台/千克	3		/30
8414.1000	40	专门设计或制造的抽气能力≥5m³/min 的真空泵(专用于同位素气体扩散浓缩)〔999〕	8	5	30	13/	13	台/千克	3		/30
8414.1000	50	能在含 UF_6 气氛中使用的真空泵(耐 UF_6 腐蚀的,也可用氟碳密封和特殊工作流体)〔999〕	8	5	30	13/	13	台/千克	3		/30
8414.1000	60	专门或主要用于半导体晶圆或平板显示屏制造的真空泵〔999〕	2.7/1.3		30	13/	13	台/千克			/27.7,26.3
8414.1000	90	其他真空泵〔999〕	8	5	30	13/	13	台/千克			/30
8414.2000		-手动或脚踏式空气泵〔999〕	8		30	13/	13	台/千克			/28
		-用于制冷设备的压缩机:									
		---电动机驱动的压缩机:									
8414.3011		----冷藏箱或冷冻箱用,电动机额定功率不超过 0.4 千瓦〔999〕	8		80	13/	13	台/千克	A	LM	/33
8414.3012		----冷藏箱或冷冻箱用,电动机额定功率超过 0.4 千瓦,但不超过 5 千瓦〔999〕	8		80	13/	13	台/千克	A	LM	/33
8414.3013		----空气调节器用,电动机额定功率超过 0.4 千瓦,但不超过 5 千瓦〔999〕	8		80	13/	13	台/千克	A	LM	/33
8414.3014		----空气调节器用,电动机额定功率超过 5 千瓦〔999〕	8		80	13/	13	台/千克			/18
8414.3015		----冷冻或冷藏设备用,电动机额定功率超过 5 千瓦〔999〕	8		30	13/	13	台/千克			/28
8414.3019		----其他〔999〕	8		30	13/	13	台/千克	A	LM	/28
8414.3090		---非电动机驱动的压缩机〔102 其他车辆零部件,101 其它制冷设备用压缩机及其零件〕	8		80	13/	13	台/千克			/33
8414.4000		-装在拖车底盘上的空气压缩机〔999〕	8		30	13/	13	台/千克			/28
		-风机、风扇:									
		--台扇、落地扇、壁扇、换气扇或吊扇,包括风机,本身装有一个输出功率不超过 125 瓦的电动机:									
8414.5110		---吊扇〔101 吊扇 I 类器具,102 吊扇 II 类器具,103 吊扇 III 类器具,104 吊扇 0I 类器具,105 吊扇 0 类器具〕	6		130	13/	13	台/千克	A	LM	/16
8414.5120		---换气扇[T2]	6		130	13/	13	台/千克	A	LM	/31
8414.5130		---具有旋转导风轮的风扇[T2]	6		130	13/	13	台/千克	A	L	/31
		---其他:									
8414.5191		----台扇〔101 台扇 I 类器具,102 台扇 II 类器具,103 台扇 III 类器具,104 台扇 0I 类器具,105 台扇 0 类器具〕	6		130	13/	13	台/千克	A	LM	/

协定税率 %										特惠税率 %			Article Description
亚太5国	东/冰/格	巴基斯坦	韩国	瑞士	哥达	秘鲁	澳大利亚	新西/坡/智	港/澳/台	亚太2国	老/柬/缅	36/3/1	
5.2	0/0/0	4	0	2.4	0	0	0	0//0	0/0/			0/0/0	Liquid-propellant pumps (8000r/min < rotational speed < 10000r/min, outlet pressure≥7000kPa)
5.2	0/0/0	4	0	2.4	0	0	0	0//0	0/0/			0/0/0	Other centrifugal pumps and multiple-sealed pumps(subject to regulation of sensitive items)
5.2	0/0/0	4	0	2.4	0	0	0	0//0	0/0/			0/0/0	Other centrifugal pumps for non-argricultural use, rotational speed <10000r/min
													-Other pumps; liquid elevators:
													--Pumps
4	0/0/0	0	0	2.4	0	0	0	0//0	0/0/0			0/0/0	Other liquid pumps for agricultural use
4	0/0/0	0	0	2.4	0	0	0	0//0	0/0/0			0/0/0	Multiple-staged pumps specified for heavy water (specially designed or manufactured for heavy water production with ammonia-hydrogen exchange)
4	0/0/0	0	0	2.4	0	0	0	0//0	0/0/0			0/0/0	Other liquid pump for non-argricultural use
	0/0/0	4	3.2	4.2	0	0	0	0//0	0/0/			0/0/0	--Liquid elevators
													-Parts:
2.5	0/0/0	0	0	1.5	0	0	0	0//0	0/0/0			0/0/0	--Of pumps
	0/0/0	0	0	0	0	0	0	0//0	0/0/			0/0/0	--Of liquid elevators
													Air or vacuum pumps, air or other gas compressors and fans; ventilating or recycling hoods incorporating a fan, whether or not fitted with filters:
													-Vacuum pumps
	0/0/0	4	3.2	2.4	0	0	0	0//0	0/0/0			0/0/	Corrosion-resisting vacuum pumps (flow capacity>5m^3/h, with a contact-surface of special corrosion-resisting materials)
	0/0/0	4	3.2	2.4	0	0	0	0//0	0/0/0			0/0/	Vacucm pumps (aspirating hole≥38cm, speed≥15kl/s, capacity< 10^{-4} absolute vaccum degree
	0/0/0	4	3.2	2.4	0	0	0	0//0	0/0/0			0/0/	Vacuum pumps, suitable to be used in UF_6 atmosphere (made of or lined with aluminum, nickel or alloys containing more than 60% nickel)
	0/0/0	4	3.2	2.4	0	0	0	0//0	0/0/0			0/0/	Vacuum pump whose specially designed or produced air-exhausting capacity≥5m^3/min (especially used for the diffusion and concentration of isotope gas)
	0/0/0	4	3.2	2.4	0	0	0	0//0	0/0/0			0/0/	Vacuum pumps, suitable to be used in UF_6 atmosphere (can be sealed with fluorine-carbon or can be used with other special working fluid)
	0/0/0	4	3.2	2.4	0	0	0	0//0	0/0/0			0/0/	Vacuum pump, specially or primary semiconductor wafer or flat panel display
	0/0/0	4	3.2	2.4	0	0	0	0//0	0/0/0			0/0/	Other vacuum pumps
	0/0/0	4	0	0	0	0	0	0//0	0/0/			0/0/	-Handor footoperated pumps
													-Compressors of a kind used in refrigerating equipment:
													---Driven by a motor:
5.2	0/0/0	4	4.8	0	0	0	0	0/0/0	0/0/			0/0/0	----For refrigerators or freezers, of a motor power not exceeding 0.4kW
5.2	0/0/0	4	7	0	0	0	0	0/0/0	0/0/			0/0/0	----For refrigerators or freezers, of a motor power exceeding 0.4kW but not exceeding 5kW
5.2	0/0/0	4	0	0	0	0	0	0/0/0	0/0/0			0/0/0	----For air conditioning machines, of a motor power exceeding, 0.4kW but not exceeding 5kW
5.2	0/0/0	4	4	0	0	0	0	0/0/0	0/0/0			0/0/0	----For air conditioning machines, motor power>5kW
5.2	0/0/0	4	4	0	0	0	0	0//0	0/0/			0/0/0	----For refrigerators or freezers, motor power>5kW
5.2	0/0/0	4	7	0	0	0	0	0/0/0	0/0/			0/0/0	----Other
5.2	0/0/3.6	4	5.4	0	0	0	0	0/0/0	0/0/			0/0/0	---Comptessor by a non-motor
	0/0/0	4	3.2	0	0	0	0	0//0	0/0/			0/0/	-Air compressors mounted on a wheeled chassis for towing
													-Fans:
													--Table, floor, wall, window, ceiling or roof fans, with a self-contained electric motor of an output not exceeding 125W:
4.2	0/0/0	20	12	6	0	0	0	0/0/0	0/0/		0//	0/0/0	---Ceiling or roof fans
4.8	0/0/0	0	12	6	0	0	0	0/0/0	0/0/0		0//	0/0/0	---Window fans
	0/0/0	5.4	4.8	3.6	0	0	0	0/0/0	0/0/		0//	0/0/0	---Repeating front louver fan
													---Other:
4.2	0/0/0	4	4	0	0	0	0	0//0	0/0/		0//	0/0/0	----Table fans

税则号列		货品名称〔CIQ 扩展编码及品名－T2 表示见附表 2〕	最惠(%)	暂定税率	普通	增值/消费	出口退税	计量单位	监管条件	检验检疫	特殊证件对美关税
8414.5192		----落地扇〔101 落地扇 I 类器具,102 落地扇 II 类器具,103 落地扇 III 类器具,104 落地扇 0I 类器具,105 落地扇 0 类器具〕	6		130	13/	13	台/千克	A	LM	/
8414.5193		----壁扇〔101 壁扇 I 类器具,102 壁扇 II 类器具,103 壁扇 III 类器具,104 壁扇 0I 类器具,105 壁扇 0 类器具〕	6		130	13/	13	台/千克	A	LM	/31
8414.5199		----其他[T2]	6		130	13/	13	台/千克		L	/31
		--其他：									
8414.5910		---吊扇[T2]	8		30	13/	13	台/千克	A	LM	/33
8414.5920		---换气扇[T2]	8		30	13/	13	台/千克	A	LM	/33
8414.5930		---离心通风机〔999〕	8		30	13/	13	台/千克			/33
8414.5990		---其他									
8414.5990	10	罗茨式鼓风机〔999〕	8		30	13/	13	台/千克	A	M	/33
8414.5990	20	吸气≥1m^3UF6/min 的耐 UF6 腐蚀的鼓风机(出口压力高达 500 千帕,设计成在 UF6 环境中长期运行。这种鼓风机的压力比为 10:1 或更低,用耐 UF6 的材料制成或用这种材料进行保护)〔999〕	8		30	13/	13	台/千克	3A	M	/33
8414.5990	30	吸气≥2m³/min 的耐 UF_6 腐蚀鼓风机(轴向离心式或正排量鼓风机,压力比在 1.2∶1 和 6∶1 之间)〔999〕	8		30	13/	13	台/千克	3A	M	/33
8414.5990	40	吸气≥56m³/s 的鼓风机(用于循环硫化氢气体的单级、低压头离心式鼓风机)〔999〕	8		30	13/	13	台/千克	3A	M	/33
8414.5990	50	电子产品散热用轴流风扇〔101 换气扇 I 类器具,102 换气扇 II 类器具,103 换气扇 III 类器具,104 换气扇 0I 类器具,105 换气扇 0 类器具〕	8		30	13/	13	台/千克			/33
8414.5990	60	专门或主要用于微处理器、电信设备、自动数据处理设备或装置的散热扇〔101 换气扇 I 类器具,102 换气扇 II 类器具,103 换气扇 III 类器具,104 换气扇 0I 类器具,105 换气扇 0 类器具〕	2.7/1.3		30	13/	13	台/千克			/27.7,26.3
8414.5990	91	其他台扇、落地扇、壁扇(电动机输出功率超过 125 瓦的)[T2]	8		30	13/	13	台/千克	A	M	/33
8414.5990	99	其他风机、风扇[T2]	8		30	13/	13	台/千克		L	/33
		-罩的平面最大边长不超过 120 厘米的通风罩或循环气罩：									
8414.6010		---抽油烟机〔999〕	8	6	130	13/	13	台/千克		L	/31
8414.6090		---其他									
8414.6090	11	生物安全柜(符合世界卫生组织规定的生物安全水平三级标准,罩的最大边长≤120 厘米)〔101 非家用过滤及净化装置,102 气体纯化过滤、净化机器及装置〕	8		130	13/	13	台/千克	3		/33
8414.6090	12	活动(柔软的)隔离装置;手套箱(具有与三级生物安全柜类似标准,罩的最大边长≤120 厘米)〔101 非家用过滤及净化装置,102 气体纯化过滤、净化机器及装置〕	8		130	13/	13	台/千克	3		/33
8414.6090	13	层流罩(柜)(垂直流密闭通风柜,具有三级生物安全柜类似标准,罩的最大边长≤120厘米)〔101 非家用过滤及净化装置,102 气体纯化过滤、净化机器及装置〕	8		130	13/	13	台/千克	3		/33
8414.6090	14	吸收塔(两用物项管制,罩的最大边长≤120 厘米)〔101 非家用过滤及净化装置,102 气体纯化过滤、净化机器及装置〕	8		130	13/	13	台/千克	3		/33
8414.6090	15	带有风扇的高效空气粒子过滤单元的封闭洁净设备(高效空气粒子过滤单元(HEPA),罩的最大边长≤120 厘米)〔101 非家用过滤及净化装置,102 气体纯化过滤、净化机器及装置〕	8		130	13/	13	台/千克	3		/33
8414.6090	16	厌氧微生物柜(具有与三级生物安全柜类似标准,罩的最大边长≤120 厘米)〔999〕	8		130	13/	13	台/千克	3		/33
8414.6090	90	其他≤120 厘米的通风罩或循环气罩(指罩的平面最大边长不超过 120 厘米,装有风扇的)〔999〕	8		130	13/	13	台/千克			/33
		-其他：									
8414.8010		---燃气轮机用的自由活塞式发生器〔999〕	8		50	13/	13	台/千克			/
8414.8020		---二氧化碳压缩机〔999〕	7		30	13/	13	台/千克			/27
8414.8030		---发动机用增压器									
8414.8030	01	乘用车机械增压器〔999〕	7	5	30	13/	13	台/千克			/30
8414.8030	90	发动机用增压器〔101 其他车辆零部件,102 其它风机及其零件,103 其它空气压缩机(站)及零件〕	7		30	13/	13	台/千克			/32
8414.8040		---空气及其他气体压缩机									
8414.8040	10	吸气≥1m^3UF6/min 的耐 UF6 腐蚀压缩机(出口压力高达 500 千帕,设计成在 UF6 环境中长期运行。这种压缩机的压力比为 10:1 或更低,用耐 UF6 的材料制成或用这种材料进行保护)〔999〕	7		30	13/	13	台/千克	3		/12
8414.8040	20	MLIS 用 UF6/载气压缩机(能在 UF6 环境中长期操作 UF6/载气混合气压缩机)〔999〕	7		30	13/	13	台/千克	3		/12
8414.8040	30	吸气≥56 立方米/秒的压缩机(用于循环硫化氢气体的单级、低压头离心式压缩机)〔999〕	7		30	13/	13	台/千克	3		/12

协定税率 %										特惠税率 %			Article Description
亚太5国	东/冰/格	巴基斯坦	韩国	瑞士	哥达	秘鲁	澳大利亚	新西/坡/智	港/澳/台	亚太2国	老/柬/缅	36/3/1	
4.2	0/0/0	4	4	0	0	0	0	0//0	0/0/		0//	0/0/0	----Floor fans
4.8	0/0/0	4	4	0	0	0	0	0//0	0/0/		0//	0/0/0	----Wall fans
	0/0/0	0	4	0	0	0	0	0/0/0	0/0/0		0//	0/0/0	----Other
													--Other:
5.2	0/0/0	4	0	0	0	0	0	0//0	0/0/			0/0/	---Ceiling or roof fans
5.2	0/0/0	4	0	0	0	0	0	0//0	0/0/			0/0/	---Window fans
5.2	0/0/0	4.5	0	0	0	0	0	0/0/0	0/0/			0/0/	---Centrifugal ventilation fans
													---Other
5.2	0/0/0	4	0	2.4	0	0	0	0//0	0/0/0			0/0/0	Root's blower
5.2	0/0/0	4	0	2.4	0	0	0	0//0	0/0/0			0/0/0	Blower, suitable to be used in UF_6 atmosphere, extraction capability ≥1m³/min (axial centrifugal fans or positive-discharge fans, pressure ratio between 2 :1～6 :1)
5.2	0/0/0	4	0	2.4	0	0	0	0//0	0/0/0			0/0/0	Blower, suitable to be used in UF_6 atmosphere, extraction capability ≥2m³/min (axial centrifugal fans or positive-discharge fans, pressure ratio between 1. 2 :1 and 6 :1)
5.2	0/0/0	4	0	2.4	0	0	0	0//0	0/0/0			0/0/0	Blower, extraction capability≥56m³/s (one-stage, low-pressure centrifugal blowers used for cycling hydrogen sulphide gas)
5.2	0/0/0	4	0	2.4	0	0	0	0//0	0/0/0			0/0/0	Axial flow fans for heat elimination of electronic products
5.2	0/0/0	4	0	2.4	0	0	0	0//0	0/0/0			0/0/0	Radiating fan, specially or primary for microprocessor, telecommunication equipment, automatic data processing equipment or device
5.2	0/0/0	4	0	2.4	0	0	0	0//0	0/0/0			0/0/0	Other desk fans, floor-standing fans and wall-mounted fans (electric output power>125W)
5.2	0/0/0	4	0	2.4	0	0	0	0//0	0/0/0			0/0/0	Other fans
													-Hoods having a maximum horizontal side not exceeding 120cm:
	0/0/0	4	4	0	0	0	0	0//0	0/0/		0//	0/0/0	---Range hoods
													---Other
	0/0/0	4	4	0	0	0	0	0/0/0	0/0/		0//	0/0/0	Biological safety cabinets (conform to the biological safety criterion of level-III as stipulated by WHO, the longest sides covered ≤120 cm)
	0/0/0	4	4	0	0	0	0	0/0/0	0/0/		0//	0/0/0	Active (soft) isolating device, glove boxes (up to standards similar to biological safety criterion of level-III, the longest sides covered ≤ 120 cm)
	0/0/0	4	4	0	0	0	0	0/0/0	0/0/		0//	0/0/0	Laminar flow hoods (vertical closed ventilation hoods, up to standards similar to biological safety criterion of level-III, the longest sides covered ≤120 cm)
	0/0/0	4	4	0	0	0	0	0/0/0	0/0/		0//	0/0/0	Absorbing tower (subject to regulation of sensitive items, the longest sides covered ≤120 cm)
	0/0/0	4	4	0	0	0	0	0/0/0	0/0/		0//	0/0/0	HEPA closed cleaning equipment with fans (HEPA referring high efficiency particulate air filter, the longest sides covered ≤120cm)
	0/0/0	4	4	0	0	0	0	0/0/0	0/0/		0//	0/0/0	Anaerobe Cabinet (conform to the biological safety criterion of level-Ⅲ, hoods having a maximum horizontal side not exceeding 120cm)
	0/0/0	4	4	0	0	0	0	0/0/0	0/0/		0//	0/0/0	Other ventilating or recycling hoods with the side length≤120cm (meaning the maximum side length≤120cm, fitted with a fan)
													-Other:
5.2	0/0/0	4	0	0	0	0	0	0//0	0/0/			0/0/	---Free piston generators for gas turbines
4.6	0/0/0	0	2.8	0	0	0	0	0//0	0/0/			0/0/	---CO_2 compressors
													---Supercharger for engines
4.6	0/0/0	0	4.2		0		0	0//0	0/0/			0//	Passenger car mechanical supercharger
4.6	0/0/0	0	4.2		0		0	0//0	0/0/			0//	Supercharger for engine
													---Air and other gases compressors
4.6	0/0/0	0	0	3.6	0	0	0	0//0	0/0/0			0/0/	Aspirated > 1 cubic meters/ min of corrosion resistance to UF6 (axial compressorcentrifugal or positive displacement compressor, pressure than in 2 :1 and 6 :1)
4.6	0/0/0	0	0	3.6	0	0	0	0//0	0/0/0			0/0/	The carrier gas compressor with UF6/ MLIS (long-term operation of UF6/ carrier gas mixed gas compressor in the UF6 environment)
4.6	0/0/0	0	0	3.6	0	0	0	0//0	0/0/0			0/0/	The compressor suction is more than 56 m3/ S (for single level, low headcentrifugal compressor cycle of hydrogen sulfide gas)

税则号列		货品名称〔CIQ扩展编码及品名－T2表示见附表2〕	最惠(%)	暂定税率	普通	增值/消费	出口退税	计量单位	监管条件	检验检疫	特殊证件对美关税
8414.8040	40	吸气≥2m3/min的耐UF6腐蚀压缩机(轴向离心式或正排量压缩机,压力比在1.2:1和6:1之间)〔999〕	7		30	13/	13	台/千克	3		/12
8414.8040	90	其他空气及气体压缩机〔999〕	7		30	13/	13	台/千克			/12
8414.8090		---其他									
8414.8090	51	其他生物安全柜(符合世界卫生组织规定的生物安全水平三级标准)〔101 非家用过滤及净化装置,102 气体纯化过滤、净化机器及装置〕	7		30	13/	13	台/千克	3		/27
8414.8090	52	其他活动(柔软的)隔离装置与其他手套箱(具有与三级生物安全柜类似标准)〔101 非家用过滤及净化装置,102 气体纯化过滤、净化机器及装置〕	7		30	13/	13	台/千克	3		/27
8414.8090	53	其他层流罩(柜)(垂直流密闭通风柜,具有与三级生物安全柜类似标准)〔101 非家用过滤及净化装置,102 气体纯化过滤、净化机器及装置〕	7		30	13/	13	台/千克	3		/27
8414.8090	54	其他吸收塔(两用物项管制)〔999〕	7		30	13/	13	台/千克	3		/27
8414.8090	55	其他带有风扇的高效空气粒子过滤单元的封闭洁净设备[高效空气粒子过滤单元(HEPA)]〔101 非家用过滤及净化装置,102 气体纯化过滤、净化机器及装置〕	7		30	13/	13	台/千克	3		/27
8414.8090	56	其他厌氧微生物柜(具有与三级生物安全柜类似标准)〔999〕	7		30	13/	13	台/千克	3		/27
8414.8090	90	其他空气泵及通风罩(通风罩指装有风扇的通风罩或循环气罩,平面边长＞120cm)〔101 其它风机及其零件,102 站及零件〕	7		30	13/	13	台/千克			/27
		-零件:									
		---子目8414.3011至8414.3014及8414.3090所列机器的零件:									
8414.9011		----压缩机进、排气阀片〔999〕	8	5	80	13/	13	千克			/25
8414.9019		----其他〔999〕	8	5	80	13/	13	千克			/15
8414.9020		---子目8414.5110至8414.5199及8414.6000所列机器的零件〔101 其它风机及其零件,102 其它电扇及其零件〕	7	6	130	13/	13	千克			/26
8414.9090		---其他									
8414.9090	10	分子泵(气体离心机的静态部件,专门设计或制造的内部有已加工或挤压的螺纹槽和已加工的腔的泵体)[T2]	7	4	30	13/	13	千克	3		/24
8414.9090	90	税目84.14其他未列名零件〔101 其它风机及其零件,102 其它电扇及其零件,103 其它空气压缩机(站)及零件〕	7	4	30	13/	13	千克			/24
84.15		**空气调节器,装有电扇及调温、调湿装置,包括不能单独调湿的空调器:**									
		-窗式、壁式、置于天花板或地板上的,独立的或分体的:									
8415.1010		---独立式〔999〕	8		130	13/	13	台/千克	A	LM	/28
		---分体式:									
8415.1021		----制冷量不超过4000大卡/时〔999〕	8		130	13/	13	台/千克	A	LM	/28
8415.1022		----制冷量超过4000大卡/时									
8415.1022	10	4000大卡/时＜制冷量≤12046大卡/时(14000W)分体式空调,窗式、壁式、置于天花板或地板上的(装有电扇及调温、调湿装置,包括不能单独调湿的空调器)〔999〕	8		90	13/	13	台/千克	A	LM	/28
8415.1022	90	其他制冷量＞12046大卡/时(14000W)分体式空调,窗式、壁式、置于天花板或地板上的(装有电扇及调温、调湿装置,包括不能单独调湿的空调器)〔999〕	8		90	13/	13	台/千克	A	LM	/28
8415.2000		-机动车辆上供人使用的[T2]	10		110	13/	13	台/千克			/30
		-其他:									
		--装有制冷装置及一个冷热循环换向阀的(可逆式热泵):									
8415.8110		---制冷量不超过4000大卡/时[T2]	8		130	13/	13	台/千克	A	LM	/28
8415.8120		---制冷量超过4000大卡/时									
8415.8120	01	4000大卡/时＜制冷量≤12046大卡/时(14000W)热泵式空调器(装有制冷装置及一个冷热循环换向阀的)[T2]	10		90	13/	13	台/千克	A	LM	/30

协定税率 %										特惠税率 %			Article Description
亚太5国	东/冰/格	巴基斯坦	韩国	瑞士	哥达	秘鲁	澳大利亚	新西/坡/智	港/澳/台	亚太2国	老/柬/缅	36/3/1	
4.6	0/0/0	0	0	3.6	0	0	0	0//0	0/0/0			0/0/	UF6 corrosion resistance than the compressor suction of 2 cubic meters/ min (axial centrifugal or positive displacement compressor, pressure ratio in 1.2 and 6 between)
4.6	0/0/0	0	0	3.6	0	0	0	0//0	0/0/0			0/0/	Other air and gas compressors
													---Other
4.6	0/0/2.8	0	0	3.6	0	0	0	0//0	0/0/0			0/0/	Other biological safety cabinet (conform to the biological safety criterion of level-III as stipulated by WHO)
4.6	0/0/2.8	0	0	3.6	0	0	0	0//0	0/0/0			0/0/	Other active (soft) isolating device and other glove boxes (up to standard similar to biological safety cabinet of level-Ⅲ)
4.6	0/0/2.8	0	0	3.6	0	0	0	0//0	0/0/0			0/0/	Other Laminar flow hoods (vertical closed ventilation hoods, up to standards similar to biological safety criterion of level-III)
4.6	0/0/2.8	0	0	3.6	0	0	0	0//0	0/0/0			0/0/	Absorbing tower (subject to regulation of sensitive items)
4.6	0/0/2.8	0	0	3.6	0	0	0	0//0	0/0/0			0/0/	Other HEPA closed cleaning equipment with fans (HEPA referring high efficiency particulate air filter.)
4.6	0/0/2.8	0	0	3.6	0	0	0	0//0	0/0/0			0/0/	Other anaerobe Cabinet (conform to the biological safety criterion of level-Ⅲ)
4.6	0/0/2.8	0	0	3.6	0	0	0	0//0	0/0/0			0/0/	Other air pumps, air compressors and ventilating hoods (ventilating or recycling hoods incorporating fan, having a maximum horizontal side>120cm)
													-Parts:
													---Of the machines of subheadings No. 8414. 3011 to 8414. 3014 and 8414. 3090:
5.6	0/0/0	4	0	0	0	0	0	0//0	0/0/		0//	0/0/0	----In take valve leaf or discharge valve leaf
5.6	0/0/0	4	0	2.4	0	0	0	0//0	0/0/0			0/0/	----Other
4.6	0/0/0	5.4	4.8	3.6	0	0	0	0/0/0	0/0/0			0/0/	---Of the machines of subheadings No.8414. 5110 to 8414. 5199 and 8414. 6000
													---Other
4.6	0/0/0	4.5	0	3.6	0	0	0	0//0	0/0/0			0/0/	Molec ular pumpcstatic component of gas centrifuge, Specialized design and manufacture, interior has been processing extrusion screw groove and processing chamber of the pump body
4.6	0/0/0	4.5	0	3.6	0	0	0	0//0	0/0/0			0/0/	Other parts ont listed in Heading No.84. 14
													Air conditioning machines, comprising a motor-driven fan and elements for changing the temperature and humidity, including those machines in which the humidity cannot be separately regulated:
													-Window, wall types, on the ceiling or floor, self-contained or "split-system":
5.2	0/0/0	0	6	4.5	0	0	0	0/0/0	0/0/			0/0/	---Self-contained
													---Split-system:
5.2	0/0/0	0	6	4.5	0	0	0	0/0/0	0/0/			0/0/	----Of a refirigerating effect not exceeding 4000 Cal per hour
													----Of a refrigerating effect exceeding 4000 Cal per hour
5.2	0/0/0	0	6	4.5	0	0	0	0/0/0	0/0/			0/0/	Air conditioning machines, comprising a motor-driven fan and elements for changing the temperature and humidity, including those machines in which the humidity cannot be separately regulated , split-system ,window or wall types, of a refrigerating effect exceeding 4000 Cal per hour, but not exceeding 12046 Cal(14000W) per hour
5.2	0/0/0	0	6	4.5	0	0	0	0/0/0	0/0/			0/0/	Other air conditioning machines, including those machines in which the humidity cannot be separately regulated , split-system ,window, wall types and On the ceiling or floor, of a refrigerating effect exceeding 12046 Cal per hour
	5/0/0		14	6	0		0	0//0	0/0/			0//	-Of a kind used for persons, in motor vehicles
													-Other:
													--Incorporating a refrigerating unit and a valve for reversal of the cooling/heat cycle(reversible heat pumps):
	0/0/0	10.8	6	4.5	0	0	0	0/0/0	0/0/			0/0/	---Of a refrigerating effect not exceeding 4000 Cal per hour
													---Of a refrigerating effect exceeding 4000 Cal per hour
	0/0/0		14	6	0	0	0	0/0/0	0/0/			0/0/	Heat pump type air conditioner, 4000Cal/hour<refrigerating effect ≤12046Cal/hour(incorporating a refrigerating unit and a valve for reversal of the cooling/heat cycle)

税则号列	货品名称〔CIQ扩展编码及品名—T2表示见附表2〕	最惠(%)	暂定税率	普通	增值/消费	出口退税	计量单位	监管条件	检验检疫	特殊证件对美关税
8415.8120 90	其他制冷量＞12046大卡/时(14000W)热泵式空调器(装有制冷装置及一个冷热循环换向阀的)[T2]	10		90	13/	13	台/千克	A	LM	/30
	--其他,装有制冷装置的:									
8415.8210	---制冷量不超过4000大卡/时[T2]	8		130	13/	13	台/千克	A	LM	/28
8415.8220	---制冷量超过4000大卡/时									
8415.8220 01	4000大卡/时＜制冷量≤12046大卡/时(14000W)的其他空调(仅装有制冷装置,而无冷热循环装置的)[T2]	10		90	13/	13	台/千克	A	LM	/30
8415.8220 90	其他制冷量＞12046大卡/时(14000W)的其他空调(仅装有制冷装置,而无冷热循环装置的)[T2]	10		90	13/	13	台/千克	A	LM	/30
8415.8300	--未装有制冷装置的[T2]	8		90	13/	13	台/千克			/28
	-零件:									
8415.9010	---子目8415.1010、8415.1021、8415.8110及8415.8210所列设备的零件〔999〕	8	6	130	13/	13	千克			/31
8415.9090	---其他〔999〕	8	6	90	13/	13	千克			/26
84.16	**使用液体燃料、粉状固体燃料或气体燃料的炉用燃烧器;机械加煤机,包括其机械炉箅、机械出灰器及类似装置:**									
8416.1000	-使用液体燃料的炉用燃烧器〔999〕	10		35	13/	13	千克	6		/30
	-其他炉用燃烧器,包括复式燃烧器:									
	---气体的:									
8416.2011	----使用天然气的									
8416.2011 01	溴化锂空调用天然气燃烧机〔999〕	10	5	35	13/	13	千克	6		/25
8416.2011 90	其他使用天然气的炉用燃烧器〔999〕	10		35	13/	13	千克	6		/30
8416.2019	----其他〔999〕	10		35	13/	13	千克	6		/35
8416.2090	---其他							6		
8416.2090 01	溴化锂空调用复式燃烧机〔999〕	10	5	35	13/	13	千克	6		/30
8416.2090 90	其他使用粉状固体燃料炉用燃烧器(包括其他复式燃烧器)〔999〕	10		35	13/	13	千克	6		/35
8416.3000	-机械加煤机,包括其机械炉箅、机械出灰器及类似装置〔101煤炭行业成套设备,102其他行业成套设备〕	8		35	13/	13	千克	6		/
8416.9000	-零件〔999〕	6		35	13/	13	千克			/16
84.17	**非电热的工业或实验室用炉及烘箱,包括焚烧炉:**									
8417.1000	-矿砂、黄铁矿或金属的焙烧、熔化或其他热处理用炉及烘箱〔999〕	10		35	13/	13	台/千克	6A	M	/30
8417.2000	-面包房用烤炉及烘箱,包括做饼干用的〔999〕	10		35	13/	13	台/千克	A	R	/20
	-其他:									
8417.8010	---炼焦炉〔999〕	10		35	13/	13	台/千克	6A	M	/
8417.8020	---放射性废物焚烧炉〔999〕	5		35	13/	13	台/千克	6A	M	/
8417.8030	---水泥回转窑〔999〕	10		35	13/	13	台/千克	A	M	/
8417.8040	---石灰石分解炉〔999〕	10		35	13/	13	台/千克	A	M	/
8417.8050	---垃圾焚烧炉〔999〕	10	5	35	13/	13	台/千克	6A	M	/
8417.8090	---其他									
8417.8090 10	平均温度＞1000℃的耐腐蚀焚烧炉(为销毁管制化学品或化学弹药用)〔999〕	10		35	13/	13	台/千克	36A	M	/35
8417.8090 20	热裂解炉〔999〕	10	5	35	13/	13	台/千克	6A	M	/30
8417.8090 90	其他非电热的工业用炉及烘箱(包括实验室用炉、烘箱和焚烧炉)〔999〕	10		35	13/	13	台/千克	6A	M	/35
	-零件:									
8417.9010	---海绵铁回转窑用〔999〕	7		35	13/	13	千克			/
8417.9020	---炼焦炉用〔999〕	7		35	13/	13	千克			/
8417.9090	---其他									
8417.9090 10	垃圾焚烧炉和放射性废物焚烧炉的零件〔999〕	7	5	35	13/	13	千克			/25
8417.9090 90	其他非电热工业用炉及烘箱的零件(包括实验室用炉及烘箱的零件和焚烧炉零件)〔999〕	7		35	13/	13	千克			/27
84.18	**电气或非电气的冷藏箱、冷冻箱及其他制冷设备;热泵,但税目84.15的空气调节器除外:**									
	-冷藏-冷冻组合机,各自装有单独外门的:									
8418.1010	---容积超过500升[T2]	9		100	13/	13	台/千克	A		/34
8418.1020	---容积超过200升,但不超过500升[T2]	8		130	13/	13	台/千克	A	LM	/33
8418.1030	---容积不超过200升[T2]	8		130	13/	13	台/千克	A	LM	/18
	-家用型冷藏箱:									
	--压缩式:									

协定税率 %										特惠税率 %			Article Description
亚太5国	东/冰/格	巴基斯坦	韩国	瑞士	哥达	秘鲁	澳大利亚	新西/坡/智	港/澳/台	亚太2国	老/柬/缅	36/3/1	
	0/0/0		14	6	0	0	0	0/0/0	0/0/			0/0/	Other heat pump type air conditioner, refirigerating effect ＞ 12046Cal/hour(incorporating a refrigerating unit and a valve for reversal of the cooling/beat cycle)
													--Other, incorporating a refrigerating unit:
	0/0/0	10.8		4.5	0	0	0	0/0/0	0/0/			0/0/	---Of a refrigerating effect not exceeding 4000 Cal per hour
													---Of a refrigerating effect exceeding 4000 Cal per hour
	0/0/0			6	0	0	0	0/0/0	0/0/			0/0/	Other air conditioner, 4000Cal/hour ＜ refirigerating effect ≤ 12046Cal/hour, incorporating a refrigerating unit, No thermal cycling device
	0/0/0			6	0	0	0	0/0/0	0/0/			0/0/	Other air conditioner, refirigerating effect＞12046Cal/hour, incorporating a refrigerating unit, No thermal cycling device
	0/0/0	4	4	0	0	0	0	0/0/0	0/0/			0/0/0	--Not incorporating a refrigerating unit
													-Parts:
5.2	0/0/0	4	4	0	0	0	0	0/0/0	0/0/			0/0/0	---Of the machines of subheading No. 8415. 1010, 8415. 1021, 8415. 8110 and 8415. 8210
5.2	0/0/0	4	4	0	0	0	0	0/0/0	0/0/0			0/0/0	---Other
													Furnace burners for liquid fuel, for pulverzied solid fuel or for gas; mechanical stokers, including their mechanical grates, mechanical ash dischargers and similar appliances:
6.5	0/0/0	4	4	0	0	0	0	0/0/0	0/0/			0/0/	-Furnace burners for liquid fuel
													-Other furnace burners, including combination burners:
													---For gas:
													----Of using natural gas
	0/0/0	4.5	4.2	3.2	0	0	0	0/0/0	0/0/			0/0/	Natural gas burners for lithium bromide air conditioners
	0/0/0	4.5	4.2	3.2	0	0	0	0/0/0	0/0/			0/0/	Other natural gas furnace burners
	0/0/0	4.5	4.2	3.2	0	0	0	0/0/0	0/0/			0/0/	----Other
													---Other
	0/0/0	4.5	4.2	0	0	0	0	0/0/0	0/0/			0/0/	Combination burners for lithium bromide air conditioner
	0/0/0	4.5	4.2	0	0	0	0	0/0/0	0/0/			0/0/	Other furnace burners for pulverzied solid fuel(including other combination burners)
	0/0/0	4	0	0	0	0	0	0//0	0/0/			0/0/	-Mechanical stokers, including their mechanical grates, mechanical ash dischargers and similar appliances
	0/0/0	0	0	0	0	0	0	0//0	0/0/			0/0/	-Parts
													Industrial or laboratory furnaces and ovens, including incinerators, non-electric:
	0/0/0	4	4	0	0	0	0	0/0/0	0/0/			0/0/	-Furnaces and ovens for the roasting, melting or other heat-treatment of ores, pyrites or of metals
	0/0/0	4	4	0	0	0	0	0//0	0/0/			0/0/	-Bakery ovens, including biscuit ovens
													-Other:
	0/0/0	4	4	0	0	0	0	0//0	0/0/			0/0/	---Coke ovens
3.5	0/0/0	0	0	0	0	0	0	0//0	0/0/			0/0/	---Burn furnaces for radioactive waste
7	0/0/0	4	4	0	0	0	0	0/0/0	0/0/			0/0/	---Cement rotary kilns
	0/0/0	4	4	0	0	0	0	0//0	0/0/			0/0/	---Limestone decomposition furnace
	0/0/0	4	7	4.2	0	0	0	0/0/0	0/0/0			0/0/	---Refuse incinerator
													---Other
	0/0/0	4.5	7	4.2	0	0	0	0/0/0	0/0/0			0/0/	Corrosion-resisting incinerators, average temperature＞1000℃ (for incinerating controlled chemicals or chemical ammunitions)
	0/0/0	4.5	7	4.2	0	0	0	0/0/0	0/0/0			0/0/	Thermal cracking furnace
	0/0/0	4.5	7	4.2	0	0	0	0/0/0	0/0/0			0/0/	Other non-electric industrial furnaces and ovens(including laboratory furnaces, ovens and incinerators)
													-Parts:
4.9	0/0/0	4	0	0	0	0	0	0//0	0/0/			0/0/	---For sponge iron rotary kiln
4.9	0/0/0	4	0	0	0	0	0	0//0	0/0/			0/0/	---For coke ovens
													---Other
	0/0/0	4	0	2.1	0	0	0	0//0	0/0/			0/0/	Furnace and radioactive waste incinerator waste incineration parts
	0/0/0	4	0	2.1	0	0	0	0//0	0/0/			0/0/	Other electric industrial stove and oven parts (including laboratory parts and incinerator parts) from the stove and oven
													Refrigerators, freezers and other refrigerating or freezing equipment, electric or other; heat pumps other than air conditioning machines of headingNo.84. 15:
													-Combined refrigerator-freezers, fitted with separate external doors:
	0/0/0	0	7	0	0	0	0	0/0/0	0/0/			0/0/0	---Of a capacity exceeding 500 L
	0/0/0	0	6	4.5	0	0	0	0/0/0	0/0/			0/0/	---Of a capacity exceeding 200 L, not exceeding 500 L
	0/0/0	0		4.5	0	0	0	0/0/0	0/0/			0/0/	---Of a capacity not exceeding 200 L
													-Refrigerators, household type:
													--Compression-type:

税则号列	货品名称〔CIQ 扩展编码及品名—T2 表示见附表 2〕	最惠(%)	暂定税率	普通	增值/消费	出口退税	计量单位	监管条件	检验检疫	特殊证件对美关税
8418.2110	---容积超过 150 升[T2]	8		130	13/	13	台/千克	A	LMR	/33
8418.2120	---容积超过 50 升,但不超过 150 升[T2]	8		130	13/	13	台/千克	A	LMR	/33
8418.2130	---容积不超过 50 升[T2]	8		130	13/	13	台/千克	A	LMR	/18
	--其他:									
8418.2910	---半导体制冷式〔999〕	8		130	13/	13	台/千克	A	LMR	/
8418.2920	---电气吸收式[T2]	8		130	13/	13	台/千克	A	LR	/18
8418.2990	---其他〔999〕	8		130	13/	13	台/千克	A	LMR	/
	-柜式冷冻箱,容积不超过 800 升:									
8418.3010	---制冷温度在-40℃及以下〔999〕	9		50	13/	13	台/千克	A	M	/14
	---制冷温度在-40℃以上:									
8418.3021	----容积超过 500 升〔999〕	9		100	13/	13	台/千克	A		/29
8418.3029	----其他〔999〕	8		130	13/	13	台/千克	A	LM	/28
	-立式冷冻箱,容积不超过 900 升:									
8418.4010	---制冷温度在-40℃及以下〔999〕	9		50	13/	13	台/千克	A	M	/14
	---制冷温度在-40℃以上:									
8418.4021	----容积超过 500 升〔999〕	9		100	13/	13	台/千克	A		/14
8418.4029	----其他〔999〕	8		130	13/	13	台/千克	A	LM	/28
8418.5000	-装有冷藏或冷冻装置的其他设备(柜、箱、展示台、陈列箱及类似品)用于存储及展示[T2]	9		100	13/	13	台/千克	A	LM	/19
	-其他制冷设备;热泵:									
	--热泵,税目 84.15 的空气调节器除外:									
8418.6120	---压缩式									
8418.6120 10	压缩式制冷机组的热泵(介质为氢、氦的可冷却到≤23K 且排热>150W)〔999〕	9		90	13/	13	台/千克	3		/34
8418.6120 90	其他压缩式热泵,税目 84.15 的空气调节器除外〔999〕	9		90	13/	13	台/千克			/34
8418.6190	---其他〔999〕	9		130	13/	13	台/千克			/34
	--其他:									
8418.6920	---制冷机组									
8418.6920 10	其他压缩式制冷设备(介质为氦或氢,可冷却到≤23K 且排热>150W)〔999〕	9		90	13/	13	台/千克	3		/34
8418.6920 90	其他制冷机组〔999〕	9		90	13/	13	台/千克			/34
8418.6990	---其他									
8418.6990 10	带制冷装置的发酵罐(不发散气溶胶,且容积大于 20 升)〔999〕	9		130	13/	13	台/千克	3		/14
8418.6990 20	制冰机、冰激凌机[T2]	9		130	13/	13	台/千克	A		/14
8418.6990 90	其他制冷设备〔999〕	9		130	13/	13	台/千克			/14
	-零件:									
8418.9100	--冷藏或冷冻设备专用的特制家具〔999〕	9		130	13/	13	千克			/34
	--其他:									
8418.9910	---制冷机组及热泵用〔999〕	9	6	90	13/	13	千克			/16
	---其他:									
8418.9991	----制冷温度在-40℃及以下的冷冻设备用〔999〕	9	6	50	13/	13	千克			/11
8418.9992	----制冷温度在-40℃以上,但容积超过 500 升的冷藏或冷冻设备用〔999〕	9	6	100	13/	13	千克			/31
8418.9999	----其他									
8418.9999 10	耐腐蚀冷凝器(20 平方米>换热面积>0.15 平方米)〔999〕	9	6	130	13/	13	千克	3		/11
8418.9999 90	税目 84.18 其他制冷设备用零件〔999〕	9	6	130	13/	13	千克			/11
84.19	**利用温度变化处理材料的机器、装置及类似的实验室设备,例如,加热、烹煮、烘炒、蒸馏、精馏、消毒、灭菌、汽蒸、干燥、蒸发、气化、冷凝、冷却的机器设备,不论是否电热的(不包括税目 85.14 的炉,烘箱及其他设备),但家用的除外;非电热的快速热水器或贮备式热水器:**									
	-非电热的快速热水器或贮备式热水器:									
8419.1100	--燃气快速热水器〔999〕	8		100	13/	13	台/千克	A	M	/33
	--其他:									
8419.1910	---太阳能热水器〔999〕	8	5	100	13/	13	台/千克	A	M	/10
8419.1990	---其他〔101 燃气热水器,102 其他非电热热水器及其零件〕	8		100	13/	13	台/千克	A	M	/13

协定税率 %										特惠税率 %			Article Description
亚太5国	东/冰/格	巴基斯坦	韩国	瑞士	哥达	秘鲁	澳大利亚	新西/坡/智	港/澳/台	亚太2国	老/柬/缅	36/3/1	
	0/0/0	0	4	0	0	0	0	0/0/0	0/0/			0/0/0	---Of a capacity exceeding 150 L
5.2	0/0/0	0	4	0	0	0	0	0/0/0	0/0/			0/0/0	---Of a capacity exceeding 50 L, not exceeding 150 L
5.2	0/0/0	0	4	0	0	0	0	0/0/0	0/0/			0/0/0	---Of a capacity not exceeding 50 L
													--Other:
	0/0/0			8	0	0	0	0/0/0	0/0/			0/0/	---Semiconductor freezing type
	0/0/0	10.8	6	4.5	0	0	0	0/0/0	0/0/			0/0/	---Absorption-type, electrical
	0/0/0			8	0	0	0	0/0/0	0/0/			0/0/	---Other
													-Freezers of the chest type, not exceeding 800L capacity:
	0/0/0	4		0	0	0	0	0//0	0/0/			0/0/0	---Of a refrigerating temperature of -40℃ or lower
													---Of a refrigerating temperature higher than -40℃:
	0/0/0	23	16.1	6.9	0	0	0	0/0/0	0/0/			0/0/	----Of a capacity exceeding 500 L
	0/0/0			8	0	0	0	0/0/0	0/0/			0/0/	----Other
													-Freezers of the upright type, not exceeding 900L capacity:
	0/0/0	4		0	0	0	0	0//0	0/0/			0/0/0	---Of a refrigerating temperature of -40℃ or lower
													---Of a refrigerating temperature higher than -40℃:
6.3	0/0/0	10.8		4.5	0	0	0	0/0/0	0/0/			0/0/	----Of a capacity exceeding 500 L
	0/0/0	0		0	0	0	0	0/0/0	0/0/			0/0/	----Other
	0/0/0	4	4	0	0	0	0	0/0/0	0/0/			0/0/0	-Other furniture (chests, cabinets, display counters, show cases and the like) for storage and display, incorporating refrigerating or freezing equipment
													-Other refrigerating or freezing equipment; heat pumps:
													--Heat pumps other than air conditioning madimes of heading 84.15:
													---Compression-type
5.9	0/0/0	4	4	0	0	0	0	0/0/0	0/0/			0/0/0	Hot pump for compression-type refrigerating units (medium being hydrogen or helium, and can be cooled to temperature ≤23K, and remove heat >150W)
5.9	0/0/0	4	4	0	0	0	0	0/0/0	0/0/			0/0/0	Other compression-type hot pumps, excluding air conditioning machines listed in heading No. 84.15
4.5	0/0/0	6.3	6	4.5	0	0	0	0/0/0	0/0/			0/0/	---Other
													--Other:
													---Refigerating units
5.9	0/0/0	4.5	4	0	0	0	0	0/0/0	0/0/			0/0/0	Other compression-type refrigerating equipment (medium being hydrogen or helium, and can be cooled to temperature ≤23K, and remove heat >150W)
5.9	0/0/0	4.5	4	0	0	0	0	0/0/0	0/0/			0/0/0	Other refrigerating units
													---Other
5.9	0/0/0	4	4	3	0	0	0	0/0/0	0/0/			0/0/0	Fermenters with refrigeration appliances (not divergent aerosol, capacity>20L)
5.9	0/0/0	4	4	3	0	0	0	0/0/0	0/0/			0/0/0	Ice-making machine, ice cream machine
5.9	0/0/0	4	4	3	0	0	0	0/0/0	0/0/			0/0/0	Other refrigrating equipments
													-Parts:
5.9	0/0/0	14.4	7.2	5.4	0	0	0	0/0/0	0/0/			0/0/	--Furniture designed to receive refrigerating or freezing equipment
													--Other:
	0/0/0	4	4	0	0	0	0	0/0/0	0/0/			0/0/0	---Of refrigerating units and heat pumps
													---Other:
	0/0/0	4	0	0	0	0	0	0//0	0/0/			0/0/0	----Of freezing equipment of a refrigerating temperature of -40℃ or lower
	0/0/0	4	4	0	0	0	0	0//0	0/0/			0/0/0	----Of refrigerating or freezing equipment of a refrigerating temperature higher than-40℃ and a capacity exceeding 500 L
													----Other
	0/0/0	4	4	0	0	0	0	0/0/0	0/0/			0/0/0	Corrosion-resisting condensers (20m² > area of heat-exchange > 0.15m²)
	0/0/0	4	4	0	0	0	0	0/0/0	0/0/			0/0/0	Parts of other refrigerating equipment of heading No.84.18
													Machinery, plant or laboratory equipment, whether or not electrically heated (excluding furnaces, ovens and other equipment of heading No. 85.14), for the treatment of materials by a process involving a change of temperature such as heating, cooking, roasting, distilling, rectifying, sterilizing, pasteurizing, steaming, drying, evaporating, vaporizing, condensing or cooling, other than machinery or plant of a kind used for domestic purposes; instantaneous or storage water heaters, non-electric:
													-Instantaneous or storage water heaters, non-electric:
	0/0/0	35	24.5	8	0	0	0	0/0/0	0/0/			0/0/	--Instantaneous gas water heaters
													--Other:
6.4	0/0/0	35		8	0	0	0	0/0/0	0/0/0			0/0/	---Solar water heater
	0/0/0			8	0	0	0	0/0/0	0/0/0			0/0/	---Other

税则号列		货品名称〔CIQ扩展编码及品名—T2表示见附表2〕	最惠(%)	暂定税率	普通	增值/消费	出口退税	计量单位	监管条件	检验检疫	特殊证件对美关税
8419.2000		-医用或实验室用消毒器具〔999〕	4		30	13/	13	台/千克	A	M	/24
		-干燥器:									
8419.3100		--农产品干燥用〔999〕	8		30	9/	9	台/千克	A	M	/33
8419.3200		--木材、纸浆、纸或纸板干燥用〔999〕	9		30	13/	13	台/千克	A	M	/34
		--其他:									
8419.3910		---微空气流动陶瓷坯件干燥器〔999〕	9		30	13/	13	台/千克	A	M	/
8419.3990		---其他									
8419.3990	10	冻干设备(10千克≤24小时凝冰量≤1000千克,并可蒸汽消毒)〔999〕	9		30	13/	13	台/千克	3A	M	/29
8419.3990	20	烟丝烘干机〔999〕	9		30	13/	13	台/千克	AO	M	/29
8419.3990	30	干燥箱(具有与三级生物安全柜类似标准)〔999〕	9		30	13/	13	台/千克	3A	M	/29
8419.3990	40	生产奶粉用干燥器〔999〕	9	4	30	13/	13	台/千克	A	M	/24
8419.3990	50	污泥干燥机〔999〕	9	5	30	13/	13	台/千克	A	M	/25
8419.3990	90	其他用途的干燥器〔999〕	9		30	13/	13	台/千克	A	M	/29
		-蒸馏或精馏设备:									
8419.4010		---提净塔〔999〕	10		30	13/	13	台/千克	A	MR	/35
8419.4020		---精馏塔〔999〕	10		30	13/	13	台/千克	A	MR	/35
8419.4090		---其他									
8419.4090	10	氢—低温蒸馏塔(温度≤—238℃,压力为0.5-5兆帕,内径≥1米等条件)〔999〕	10		30	13/	13	台/千克	3A	M	/35
8419.4090	20	耐腐蚀蒸馏塔(内径大于0.1米,接触表面由特殊耐腐蚀材料制成)〔999〕	10		30	13/	13	台/千克	3A	M	/35
8419.4090	90	其他蒸馏或精馏设备〔999〕	10		30	13/	13	台/千克	A	M	3/35
8419.5000		-热交换装置									
8419.5000	10	热交换器(专用于核反应堆的一次冷却剂回路的)〔101螺旋板式交换器,102其它热交换装置〕	10		30	13/	13	台/千克	3		/20
8419.5000	20	蒸汽发生器(专用于核反应堆内生成的热量输送到进水以产生蒸汽的)〔999〕	10		30	13/	13	台/千克	3		/20
8419.5000	30	冷却UF6的热交换器(专门设计或制造的用耐UF6材料制成或保护的热交换器,在压差为100kPa下渗透压力变化率小于10Pa/h)〔999〕	10		30	13/	13	台/千克	3A	M	/20
8419.5000	40	冷却气体用热交换器(用耐UF_6腐蚀材料制成或加以保护的)〔999〕	10		30	13/	13	台/千克	3A	M	/20
8419.5000	50	耐腐蚀热交换器(0.15平方米<换热面积<20平方米)〔999〕	10		30	13/	13	台/千克	3A	M	/20
8419.5000	60	用氟聚合物制造的、入口管和出口管内径不超过3厘米的热交换装置〔999〕	3.3/1.7		30	13/	13	台/千克	A	M	/13.3,11.7
8419.5000	90	其他热交换装置〔101废热锅炉,102螺旋板式交换器,103其它热交换装置〕	10		30	13/	13	台/千克	A	M	/20
		-液化空气或其他气体的机器:									
		---制氧机:									
8419.6011		----制氧量在15000立方米/小时及以上〔999〕	12		30	13/	13	台/千克	A	M	/
8419.6019		----其他〔999〕	13		30	13/	13	台/千克	A	M	/18
8419.6090		---其他									
8419.6090	10	液化器(将来自级联的UF_6气体压缩并冷凝成液态UF_6)〔999〕	10		30	13/	13	台/千克	3A	M	3/15
8419.6090	20	通过冷凝分离和去除污染物的气体液化设备〔101其它液化空气或其它气体用的机器,102其它液化空气或气体用的机器及其零件〕	10	5	30	13/	13	台/千克	A	M	/10
8419.6090	90	其他液化空气或其他气体用的机器〔101其它液化空气或其它气体用的机器,102其它液化空气或气体用的机器及其零件〕	10		30	13/	13	台/千克	A	M	/15
		-其他机器设备:									
8419.8100		--加工热饮料或烹调、加热食品用〔999〕	10	6	30	13/	13	台/千克	A	LMR	3/16
		--其他:									
8419.8910		---加氢反应器〔999〕	0		30	13/	13	台/千克	A	M	/5
8419.8990		---其他									
8419.8990	10	带加热装置的发酵罐(不发散气溶胶,且容积大于20升)〔999〕	0		30	13/	13	台/千克	3A	M	/20
8419.8990	21	凝华器(或冷阱)(从扩散级联中取出UF_6并可再蒸发转移)〔101氨气提法二氧化碳气提塔等,102其它利用温度变化处理材料的机器〕	0		30	13/	13	台/千克	3A	M	/20
8419.8990	22	低温制冷设备(能承受-120℃或更低的温度)〔101氨气提法二氧化碳气提塔等,102其它利用温度变化处理材料的机器〕	0		30	13/	13	台/千克	3A	M	/20
8419.8990	23	UF6冷阱(能冻结分离出UF6的冷阱)〔101氨气提法二氧化碳气提塔等,102其它利用温度变化处理材料的机器〕	0		30	13/	13	台/千克	3A	M	/20

协定税率 %										特惠税率 %			
亚太5国	东/冰/格	巴基斯坦	韩国	瑞士	哥达	秘鲁	澳大利亚	新西/坡/智	港/澳/台	亚太2国	老/柬/缅	36/3/1	Article Description
	0/0/0	0	0	0	0	0	0	0//0	0/0/			0/0/	-Medical, surgical or laboratory sterilizers
													-Dryers:
	0/0/0	4	3.2	0	0	0	0	0//0	0/0/		0//	0/0/0	--For agricultural products
	0/0/0	4	0	0	0	0	0	0//0	0/0/0		0//	0/0/0	--For wood,paper pulp, paper or paperboard
													--Other:
4.5	0/0/0	3.6	0	0	0	0	0	0//0	0/0/			0/0/	---Breeze pottery blanks dryers
													---Other
4.5	0/0/3.6	3.6	3.6	0	0	0	0	0//0	0/0/0			0/0/	Freezer-dryers (10kg/24h≤volume of icing ≤1000kg/24h, capable of be sterilized by steam)
4.5	0/0/3.6	3.6	3.6	0	0	0	0	0//0	0/0/0			0/0/	Tobacco dryer
4.5	0/0/3.6	3.6	3.6	0	0	0	0	0//0	0/0/0			0/0/	Drying tunnel(conform to the biological safety criterion of level-Ⅲ)
4.5	0/0/3.6	3.6	3.6	0	0	0	0	0//0	0/0/0			0/0/	The production of milk powder with dryer
4.5	0/0/3.6	3.6	3.6	0	0	0	0	0//0	0/0/0			0/0/	The sludge drying machine
4.5	0/0/3.6	3.6	3.6	0	0	0	0	0//0	0/0/0			0/0/	Dryers for other use
													-Distilling or rectifying plant:
	0/0/0	4	4	0	0	0	0	0/0/0	0/0/			0/0/	---Stripping towers
	0/0/0	4	4	0	0	0	0	0/0/0	0/0/			0/0/	---Rectifying towers
													---Other
	0/0/0	4	4	0	0	0	0	0/0/0	0/0/			0/0/	Hydrogen-low temperature distilling towers (temperature≤-238℃, pressure=0.5MPa~5MPa, inside diameter≥1m)
	0/0/0	4	4	0	0	0	0	0/0/0	0/0/			0/0/	Corrosion-resisten distilling towers (inside diameter>0.1m, with a contact surface of special corrosion-resisten materials)
	0/0/0	4	4	0	0	0	0	0/0/0	0/0/			0/0/	Other distillation or rectification equipment
													-Heat exchange units
6.5	0/0/0	0	0	4.2	0	0	0	0/0/0	0/0/0		0//	0/0/0	Heat exchanger(used exclusively for nuclear reactor primary coolant loop)
6.5	0/0/0	0	0	4.2	0	0	0	0/0/0	0/0/0		0//	0/0/0	Steam generators (used exclusively to transmit the heat generated within nuclear reactors to the inlet to produce vapors)
6.5	0/0/0	0	0	4.2	0	0	0	0/0/0	0/0/0		0//	0/0/0	Heat exchangers for cooling UF_6 (rate of change of osmotic pressure change rate < 10Pa/h under differential pressure of less than 100kPa)
6.5	0/0/0	0	0	4.2	0	0	0	0/0/0	0/0/0		0//	0/0/0	Heat exchangers for cooling gases (made of or protected with UF_6-resistant materials)
6.5	0/0/0	0	0	4.2	0	0	0	0/0/0	0/0/0		0//	0/0/0	Corrosion-resisting heat exchangers ($20m^2$ > area of heat-exchange area>$0.15m^2$)
6.5	0/0/0	0	0	4.2	0	0	0	0/0/0	0/0/0		0//	0/0/0	Heat exchange device, made of fluoropolymer, inlet pipe and outlet pipe inner diameter not exceeding 3 cm
6.5	0/0/0	0	0	4.2	0	0	0	0/0/0	0/0/0		0//	0/0/0	Other heat exchange devices
													-Machinery for liquefying air or other gases:
													---Oxygen producers:
	0/0/0	5.4	4.8	3.6	0	0	0	0/0/0	0/0/			0/0/	----Oxygen preparation volume no less than $15000m^3/h$
	0/0/0	5.9	5.2	3.9	0	0	0	0/0/0	0/0/			0/0/	----Other
													---Other
	0/0/0	4	4	0	0	0	0	0/0/0	0/0/			0/0/	Liquefiers (to compress and condense gaseous UF_6 from cascade into liquefied UF_6)
	0/0/0	4	4	0	0	0	0	0/0/0	0/0/			0/0/	Through the gas condensate separation and pollutants removal of liquefaction equipment
	0/0/0	4	4	0	0	0	0	0/0/0	0/0/			0/0/	Other machinery for liquefying air or other gases
													-Other machinery, plant and equipment:
	0/0/0	4.5	4	0	0	0	0	0/0/0	0/0/		0//	0/0/0	--For making hot drinks of for cooking or heating food
													--Other:
											0//	0/0/0	---Hydroformer vessels
													---Other
											0//	0/0/0	Fermenter fitted with heat devices(not diverging aerosol, volume>20L)
											0//	0/0/0	Sublimator (or cold trap) (take out UF_6 diffusion cascade and can transfer by evaporation)
											0//	0/0/0	Low-temperature refrigeration equipment (bearing -120℃ or evem lower temperature)
											0//	0/0/0	UF_6 cold traps(bearing-120℃ or even lower tem perature)

税则号列	货品名称〔CIQ扩展编码及品名—T2表示见附表2〕	最惠(%)	暂定税率	普通	增值/消费	出口退税	计量单位	监管条件	检验检疫	特殊证件对美关税
8419.8990 90	其他利用温度变化处理材料的机器(包括类似的实验室设备)〔101 氨气提法二氧化碳气提塔等,102 其它利用温度变化处理材料的机器,103 非压力容器产品〕	0		30	13/	13	台/千克	A	M	/20
	-零件:									
8419.9010	---热水器用〔999〕	0		100	13/	13	千克			/25
8419.9090	---其他〔999〕	4		30	13/	13	千克			/24
84.20	**研光机或其他滚压机器及其滚筒,但加工金属或玻璃用的除外:**									
8420.1000	-研光机或其他滚压机器									
8420.1000 01	织物轧光机〔999〕	8	6	30	13/	13	台/千克			/31
8420.1000 20	专门或主要用于印刷电路板基板或印刷电路制造的滚压机(加工金属或玻璃用的除外)〔999〕	0		30	13/	13	台/千克			/25
8420.1000 90	其他研光机或滚压机器(加工金属或玻璃用的除外)〔101 纺织行业成套设备,102 轻工行业成套设备,103 印刷行业成套设备,104 其他行业成套设备〕	8		30	13/	13	台/千克			/33
	-零件:									
8420.9100	--滚筒〔101 纺织行业成套设备,102 轻工行业成套设备,103 印刷行业成套设备,104 其他行业成套设备〕	8		30	13/	13	个/千克			/33
8420.9900	--其他〔999〕	8		30	13/	13	千克			/28
84.21	**离心机,包括离心干燥机;液体或气体的过滤、净化机器及装置:**									
	-离心机,包括离心干燥机:									
8421.1100	--奶油分离器〔999〕	8		30	13/	13	台/千克	A	R	/
	--干衣机:									
8421.1210	---干衣量不超过10千克〔101 干衣机I类器具,102 干衣机II类器具,103 干衣机III类器具,104 干衣机0I类器具,105 干衣机0类器具〕	7		70	13/	13	台/千克		L	/32
8421.1290	---其他〔101 干衣机I类器具,102 干衣机II类器具,103 干衣机III类器具,104 干衣机0I类器具,105 干衣机0类器具〕	8		30	13/	13	台/千克			/28
	--其他:									
8421.1910	---脱水机〔999〕	10	6	30	13/	13	台/千克		L	/31
8421.1920	---固液分离机〔999〕	10		30	13/	13	台/千克			/35
8421.1990	---其他									
8421.1990 20	液-液离心接触器(为化学交换过程的铀浓缩而专门设计或制造的)〔999〕	10		30	13/	13	台/千克	3		/20
8421.1990 30	离心分离器,包括倾析器(不发散气溶胶、可对致病性微生物进行连续分离的)〔999〕	10		30	13/	13	台/千克	3		/20
8421.1990 90	其他离心机及离心干燥机〔101 其它干燥器及其零件,102 其他离心机及类似装置及其零件〕	10		30	13/	13	台/千克			/20
	-液体的过滤、净化机器及装置:									
	--过滤或净化水用:									
8421.2110	---家用型[T2]	7	5	63	13/	13	台/千克	A	R	/25
	---其他:									
8421.2191	----船舶压载水处理设备〔999〕	5		50	13/	13	台/千克			/30
8421.2199	----其他									
8421.2199 10	喷灌设备用叠式净水过滤器〔999〕	5	1	50	13/	13	台/千克			/21
8421.2199 20	船舶压载水处理设备用过滤器〔999〕	5	2	50	13/	13	台/千克			/22
8421.2199 90	其他非家用型过滤或净化水的装置〔999〕	5		50	13/	13	台/千克			/25
8421.2200	--过滤或净化饮料(水除外)用[T2]	8		40	13/	13	台/千克	A	R	3/28
8421.2300	--内燃发动机的滤油器〔101 其他车辆零部件,102 动力设备零部件,103 非家用过滤及净化装置〕	8		40	13/	13	个/千克			/18
	--其他:									
8421.2910	---压滤机							O		
8421.2910 10	用氟聚合物制造的厚度不超过140微米的过滤膜或净化膜的压滤机〔999〕	1.7/0.8		40	13/	13	个/千克			/26.7,25.8
8421.2910 90	其他压滤机〔999〕	5		40	13/	13	个/千克			/30
8421.2990	---其他									
8421.2990 10	用氟聚合物制造的厚度不超过140微米的过滤膜或净化膜的其他液体过滤或净化机器及装置〔999〕	1.7/0.8		40	13/	13	个/千克			/11.7,10.8
8421.2990 40	液体截流过滤设备(可连续分离致病性微生物、毒素和细胞培养物)〔999〕	5		40	13/	13	个/千克	3		/15
8421.2990 90	其他液体的过滤、净化机器及装置[T2]	5		40	13/	13	个/千克			/15
	-气体的过滤、净化机器及装置:									
8421.3100	--内燃发动机的进气过滤器〔101 其他车辆零部件,102 动力设备零部件,103 非家用过滤及净化装置,104 其他离心机及类似装置及其零件〕	10		40	13/	13	个/千克			/15

协定税率 %										特惠税率 %			Article Description
亚太5国	东/冰/格	巴基斯坦	韩国	瑞士	哥达	秘鲁	澳大利亚	新西/坡/智	港/澳/台	亚太2国	老/柬/缅	36/3/1	
											0//	0/0/0	Other machinery for the treatment of materials by a process involving a change of temperature (including similar laboratory equipment)
													-Parts:
												0/0/0	---Of water heaters
	0/0/0	0	0	0	0	0	0	0//0	0/0/0			0/0/	---Other
													Calendering or other rolling machines, other than for metals or glass, and cylinders therefor:
													-Calendering or other rolling machines
	0/0/0	4	0	0	0	0	0	0//0	0/0/0			0/0/0	Textile calenders
	0/0/0	4	0	0	0	0	0	0//0	0/0/0			0/0/0	Rolling machine, especially for the manufacture of printed circuit board or printed circuit (except for processing metal or glass)
	0/0/0	4	0	0	0	0	0	0//0	0/0/0			0/0/0	Other calendar or rolling machines (excluding those for processing metals or glass)
													-Parts:
	0/0/0	4	0	0	0	0	0	0//0	0/0/			0/0/0	--Cylinders
	0/0/0	4	0	0	0	0	0	0//0	0/0/			0/0/0	--Other
													Centrifuges, including centrifugal dryers; filtering or purifying machinery and apparatus, for liquids or gases:
													-Centrifuges, including centrifugal dryers:
	0/0/0	4	0	0	0	0	0	0//0	0/0/			0/0/	--Cream separators
													--Clothes-dryers:
	0/0/0	12.6	7	5.3	0	0	0	0/0/0	0/0/			0/0/	---Of a dry linen capacity not exceeding 10kg
	0/0/0	4	3.2	0	0	0	0	0//0	0/0/			0/0/	---Other
													--Other:
	0/0/0	4	4	0	0	0	0	0//0	0/0/			0/0/	---Dewaterers
	0/0/0	4.5	4	0	0	0	0	0/0/0	0/0/			0/0/	---Solid-liquor separators
													---Other
	0/0/0	4.5	4	3	0	0	0	0/0/0	0/0/			0/0/	Liquid-liquid centrifugal contactors (specially designed or manufactured for uranium concentration in chemical exchange process)
	0/0/0	4.5	4	3	0	0	0	0/0/0	0/0/			0/0/	Centrifugal separator including decanters (not diverging aerosol, capable of continuously separating disease microorganism)
	0/0/0	4.5	4	3	0	0	0	0/0/0	0/0/			0/0/	Other centrifuges and centrifugal dryers
													-Filtering or purifying machinery and apparatus for liquids:
													--For filtering or purifying water:
4.6	0/0/0	17.5	17.5	7	0	0	0	0/0/0	0/0/			0/0/	---Of the household type
													---Other:
3.3	0/0/0	0	3	0	0	0	0	0//0	0/0/0			0/0/	----Ship ballast water treatment equipment
													----Other
3.3	0/0/0	0	3	0	0	0	0	0//0	0/0/0			0/0/	Stack type water purifying filter for irrigation equipment
3.3	0/0/0	0	3	0	0	0	0	0//0	0/0/0			0/0/	Ballast water treatment equipment with a filter
3.3	0/0/0	0	3	0	0	0	0	0//0	0/0/0			0/0/	Other non-household filtering or purifying water equipment
	0/0/4.8	5.4	4.8	0	0	0	0	0/0/0	0/0/			0/0/	--For filtering or purifying beverages other than water
	0/0/0	4.5	4	0	0	0	0	0/0/0	0/0/			0/0/	--Oil or petrol-filters for internal combustion engines
													--Other:
													---Press filters
3.3	0/0/0	0	2	0	0	0	0	0//0	0/0/			0/0/	Press filters, with a filter membrane or purification film with a thickness of not more than 140 microns, made of a fluoropolymer
3.3	0/0/0	0	2	0	0	0	0	0//0	0/0/			0/0/	Other press filters
													---Other
3.3	0/0/0	0	0	1.5	0	0	0	0//0	0/0/0			0/0/0	Other liquid filtration or purification machines and devices made of fluoropolymer films with a thickness of not more than 140 microns
3.3	0/0/0	0	0	1.5	0	0	0	0//0	0/0/0			0/0/0	Liquid closure filtration equipment (which can continuously separate pathogenic microorganisms, toxins and cell culture)
3.3	0/0/0	0	0	1.5	0	0	0	0//0	0/0/0			0/0/0	Other filtering, purifying machinery and apparatuses for other liquids
													-Filtering or purifying machinery and apparatus for gases:
	0/0/0	4	7	0	0	0	0	0//0	0/0/			0/0/	--Intake air filters for internal combustion engines

税则号列		货品名称〔CIQ 扩展编码及品名—T2 表示见附表 2〕	最惠(%)	暂定税率	普通	增值/消费	出口退税	计量单位	监管条件	检验检疫	特殊证件对美关税
		--其他：									
8421.3910		---家用型[T2]	7	5	100	13/	13	个/千克			/30
		---工业用除尘器：									
8421.3921		----静电除尘器									
8421.3921	10	装备不锈钢外壳、入口管和出口管内径不超过 1.3 厘米的工业用静电除尘器〔999〕	1.7/0.8		40	13/	13	个/千克			/21.7,20.8
8421.3921	90	其他工业用静电除尘器〔999〕	5		40	13/	13	个/千克			/25
8421.3922		----袋式除尘器									
8421.3922	10	装备不锈钢外壳、入口管和出口管内径不超过 1.3 厘米的工业用袋式除尘器〔999〕	1.7/0.8		40	13/	13	个/千克			/21.7,20.8
8421.3922	90	其他工业用袋式除尘器〔999〕	5		40	13/	13	个/千克			/25
8421.3923		----旋风式除尘器									
8421.3923	10	装备不锈钢外壳、入口管和出口管内径不超过 1.3 厘米的工业用旋风式除尘器〔999〕	1.7/0.8		40	13/	13	个/千克			/11.7,10.8
8421.3923	90	其他工业用旋风式除尘器〔999〕	5		40	13/	13	个/千克			/15
8421.3924		----电袋复合除尘器									
8421.3924	10	装备不锈钢外壳、入口管和出口管内径不超过 1.3 厘米的电袋复合除尘器〔999〕	1.7/0.8		40	13/	13	个/千克			/26.7,25.8
8421.3924	90	其他电袋复合除尘器〔999〕	5		40	13/	13	个/千克			/30
8421.3929		----其他									
8421.3929	10	装备不锈钢外壳、入口管和出口管内径不超过 1.3 厘米的其他工业用除尘器〔999〕	1.7/0.8		40	13/	13	个/千克			/26.7,25.8
8421.3929	90	其他工业用除尘器〔999〕	5		40	13/	13	个/千克			/30
8421.3930		---内燃发动机排气过滤及净化装置									
8421.3930	01	摩托车发动机排气过滤及净化装置〔101 其他车辆零部件，102 非家用过滤及净化装置，103 气体纯化过滤、净化机器及装置〕	5	3	40	13/	13	个/千克			/13
8421.3930	20	装备不锈钢外壳、入口管和出口管内径不超过 1.3 厘米的其他内燃发动机排气过滤及净化装置〔999〕	1.7/0.8		40	13/	13	个/千克			/11.7,10.8
8421.3930	90	其他内燃发动机排气过滤及净化装置〔101 其他车辆零部件，102 非家用过滤及净化装置，103 气体纯化过滤、净化机器及装置〕	5		40	13/	13	个/千克			/15
8421.3940		---烟气脱硫装置									
8421.3940	10	装备不锈钢外壳、入口管和出口管内径不超过 1.3 厘米的烟气脱硫装置〔999〕	1.7/0.8		40	13/	13	个/千克			/26.7,25.8
8421.3940	90	其他烟气脱硫装置〔101 非家用过滤及净化装置，102 气体纯化过滤、净化机器及装置〕	5		40	13/	13	个/千克			/30
8421.3950		---烟气脱硝装置									
8421.3950	10	装备不锈钢外壳、入口管和出口管内径不超过 1.3 厘米的烟气脱硝装置〔999〕	1.7/0.8		40	13/	13	个/千克			/11.7,10.8
8421.3950	90	其他烟气脱硝装置〔101 非家用过滤及净化装置，102 气体纯化过滤、净化机器及装置〕	5		40	13/	13	个/千克			/15
8421.3990		---其他									
8421.3990	10	装备不锈钢外壳、入口管和出口管内径不超过 1.3 厘米的其他气体过滤或净化机器及装置〔999〕	1.7/0.8		40	13/	13	个/千克			/11.7,10.8
8421.3990	90	其他气体过滤、净化机器及装置〔101 非家用过滤及净化装置，102 气体纯化过滤、净化机器及装置〕	5		40	13/	13	个/千克			/15
		-零件：									
		--离心机用，包括离心干燥机用：									
8421.9110		---干衣量不超过 10 千克的干衣机用〔999〕	0		70	13/	13	千克			/5
8421.9190		---其他									
8421.9190	11	离心机壳/收集器（容纳气体离心机的转筒组件的耐 UF_6 部件）〔999〕	0		30	13/	13	千克	3		/20
8421.9190	12	收集器（由内径不同的同心管组成用于供取 UF_6 气体的管件）〔999〕	0		30	13/	13	千克	3		/20
8421.9190	13	气体扩散膜（由耐 UF_6 材料制成的多细孔过滤薄膜）〔999〕	0		30	13/	13	千克	3		/20
8421.9190	14	扩散室（专门设计或制造的密闭式容器，用于容纳气体扩散膜，由耐 UF6 的材料制成或用这种材料进行保护）〔999〕	0		30	13/	13	千克	3		/20
8421.9190	90	其他离心机用零件〔999〕	0		30	13/	13	千克			/20
		--其他：									
8421.9910		---家用型过滤、净化装置用〔999〕	7	5	100	13/	13	千克			/10
8421.9990		---其他									

协定税率 %										特惠税率 %			Article Description
亚太5国	东/冰/格	巴基斯坦	韩国	瑞士	哥达	秘鲁	澳大利亚	新西/坡/智	港/澳/台	亚太2国	老/柬/缅	36/3/1	
													--Other:
4.6	0/0/0	6.8	9.7	4.5	0	0	0	0/0/0	0/0/0			0/0/	---Of the household type
													---Dust collectors for industry uses:
													----Electrostatic
3.3	0/0/0	0	0	0	0	0	0	0//0	0/0/0			0/0/	Industrial electrostatic precipitator with stainless steel casing, inlet pipe and outlet pipe inner diameter not exceeding 1.3 cm
3.3	0/0/0	0	0	0	0	0	0	0//0	0/0/0			0/0/	Other industrial electrostatic precipitators
													----Baghoused
3.3	0/0/0	0	0	0	0	0	0	0//0	0/0/			0/0/	Industrial bag type dust collector equipped with stainless steel shell, inlet pipe and outlet pipe inner diameter not exceeding 1.3 cm
3.3	0/0/0	0	0	0	0	0	0	0//0	0/0/			0/0/	Other industrial bag type dust collector
													---Cyclone
3.3	0/0/0	0	0	0	0	0	0	0//0	0/0/0			0/0/	Industrial cyclone dust collector with stainless steel casing, inlet pipe and outlet pipe inner diameter not exceeding 1.3 cm
3.3	0/0/0	0	0	0	0	0	0	0//0	0/0/0			0/0/	Other industrial cyclone dust collector
													----Electric bag composite dust collector
3.3	0/0/0	0	3	0	0	0	0	0//0	0/0/0			0/0/	Electric bag composite dust remover with stainless steel casing, inlet pipe and outlet pipe inner diameter less than 1.3 cm
3.3	0/0/0	0	3	0	0	0	0	0//0	0/0/0			0/0/	Other electric bag composite dust collector
													----Other
3.3	0/0/0	0	3	0	0	0	0	0//0	0/0/0			0/0/	Other industrial dust remover with stainless steel casing, inlet pipe and outlet pipe diameter not exceeding 1.3 cm
3.3	0/0/0	0	3	0	0	0	0	0//0	0/0/0			0/0/	Other industrial dust collector
													---Exhaust air filtering or purifyirg apparatus for internal combustion engines
3.3	0/0/0	0	3	0	0	0	0	0//0	0/0/			0/0/0	Exthaust air filtering or purifying apparatus for motorcycle engine
3.3	0/0/0	0	3	0	0	0	0	0//0	0/0/			0/0/0	Internal combustion engine exhaust filtering and purifying device, equipped with stainless steel shell, entrance pipe and the outlet pipe diameter of not more than 1.3 cm
3.3	0/0/0	0	3	0	0	0	0	0//0	0/0/			0/0/0	Other exhast air filtering or purifying appratus internal combustion engines
													---Flue gas desulpharisation apparatus
3.3	0/0/0	0	0	0	0	0	0	0//0	0/0/0			0/0/0	Flue gas desulfurization device equipped with stainless steel casing, inlet pipe and outlet pipe diameter less than 1.3 cm
3.3	0/0/0	0	0	0	0	0	0	0//0	0/0/0			0/0/0	Other flue gas desulfurization device
													---Flue gas denitration apparatus
3.3	0/0/0	0	0	0	0	0	0	0//0	0/0/0			0/0/0	Flue gas denitration device equipped with stainless steel casing, inlet pipe and outlet pipe diameter less than 1.3 cm
3.3	0/0/0	0	0	0	0	0	0	0//0	0/0/0			0/0/0	Other flue gas denitrification device
													---Other
3.3	0/0/0	0	2	0	0	0	0	0//0	0/0/0			0/0/0	Other gas filtration or purification equipment and devices equipped with stainless steel casing, inlet pipe and outlet pipe inner diameter not exceeding 1.3 cm
3.3	0/0/0	0	2	0	0	0	0	0//0	0/0/0			0/0/0	Other filtering or purifying machinery and apparatus, for gases
													-Parts:
													--Of centrifuges, including centrifugal dryers:
												0/0/0	---Of clothes-dryers of a dry linen capacity not exceeding 10kg
													---Other
												0/0/0	Centrifugal cover/collectors (accommodate gas centrifuge rotor components to UF_6 resistance)
												0/0/0	Collectors (parts of tube used for providing air of UF_6, made up of concentric tubes with different radiuses)
												0/0/0	Air diffusion membrances(multiple stoma filtration membrane made of UF_6 resistance materials)
												0/0/0	Diffusion rooms(a closed spectacle that accommodate other diffusion membrances, with one inlet pipe and two outlet pipes)
												0/0/0	Other parts of centrifuge machines
													-Other:
4.6	0/0/0	0	4	0	0	0	0	0/0/0	0/0/			0/0/	---Of household-type filtering or purifying machines
													---Other

税则号列	货品名称〔CIQ 扩展编码及品名—T2 表示见附表 2〕	最惠(%)	暂定税率	普通	增值/消费	出口退税	计量单位	监管条件	检验检疫	特殊证件对美关税
8421.9990 10	用氟聚合物制造的厚度不超过 140 微米的过滤膜或净化膜的液体过滤或净化机器及装置的零件;装备不锈钢外壳、入口管和出口管内径不超过 1.3 厘米的气体过滤或净化机器及装置的零件〔999〕	1.7/0.8		40	13/	13	千克			/6.7,5.8
8421.9990 90	其他过滤、净化装置用零件〔101 其它工业用旋除尘器及其零件,102 非家用过滤及净化装置,103 气体纯化过滤、净化机器及装置,104 其它过滤及其喷射装置及其零件〕	5		40	13/	13	千克			/10
84.22	**洗碟机;瓶子及其他容器的洗涤或干燥机器;瓶、罐、箱、袋或其他容器装填、封口、密封、贴标签的机器;瓶、罐、管、筒或类似容器的包封机器;其他包装或打包机器(包括热缩包装机器);饮料充气机:**									
	-洗碟机:									
8422.1100	--家用型[T2]	8	6	90	13/	13	台/千克			/31
8422.1900	--其他[T2]	8		90	13/	13	台/千克			/33
8422.2000	-瓶子或其他容器的洗涤或干燥机器[T2]	8		35	13/	13	台/千克			/28
	-瓶、罐、箱、袋或其他容器的装填、封口、密封、贴标签的机器;瓶、罐、管、筒或类似容器的包封机器;饮料充气机:									
8422.3010	---饮料及液体食品灌装设备									
8422.3010 10	乳品加工用自动化灌装设备〔999〕	12	10	45	13/	13	台/千克	A	R	3/35
8422.3010 90	其他饮料及液体食品灌装设备〔999〕	12		45	13/	13	台/千克	A	R	3/37
	---水泥包装机:									
8422.3021	----全自动灌包机〔999〕	8		45	13/	13	台/千克			/
8422.3029	----其他〔999〕	8		45	13/	13	台/千克			/13
8422.3030	---其他包装机									
8422.3030 01	全自动无菌灌装生产线用包装机(加工速度≥20000 只/小时)〔999〕	8	6	35	13/	13	台/千克	A	R	/31
8422.3030 90	其他包装机〔999〕	8		35	13/	13	台/千克	A	R	/33
8422.3090	---其他									
8422.3090 01	全自动无菌灌装生产线用贴吸管机(加工速度≥22000 只/小时)〔999〕	8	6	35	13/	13	台/千克	A	R	/31
8422.3090 10	充装设备(两用物项管制)〔999〕	8		35	13/	13	台/千克	3		/33
8422.3090 90	其他瓶、罐、箱、袋或其他容器的装填、封口、密封、贴标签的机器;其他瓶、罐、管、筒或类似容器的包封机器;饮料充气机〔999〕	8		35	13/	13	台/千克	A	R	/33
8422.4000	-其他包装或打包机器(包括热缩包装机器)〔999〕	8		35	13/	13,9	台/千克			/33
8422.4000 10	半导体检测分选编带机〔999〕	8	5	35	13/	13	台/千克			/30
8422.4000 90	其他包装或打包机器(包括热缩包装机器)	8		35	13/	13	台/千克			/33
	-零件:									
8422.9010	---洗碟机用〔999〕	8	6	90	13/	13	千克			/31
8422.9020	---饮料及液体食品灌装设备用〔999〕	8.5		45	13/	13	千克			/33.5
8422.9090	---其他〔101 建材行业成套设备,102 包装行业成套设备,103 其它餐具清洗机及其零件〕	8.5		35	13/	13	千克			/33.5
84.23	**衡器(感量为 50 毫克或更精密的天平除外),包括计数或检验用的衡器;衡器用的各种砝码、秤砣:**									
8423.1000	-体重计,包括婴儿秤;家用秤〔101 电子衡器,102 机械衡器〕	6		80	13/	13	台/千克			/31
	-输送带上连续称货的秤:									
8423.2010	---电子皮带秤〔999〕	0		80	13/	13	台/千克			/25
8423.2090	---其他〔999〕	10		80	13/	13	台/千克			/35
	-恒定秤、物料定量装袋或装容器用的秤,包括库秤:									
8423.3010	---定量包装秤									
8423.3010 10	以电子方式称重的定量包装秤〔999〕	0		80	13/	13	台/千克			/25
8423.3010 90	其他定量包装秤〔999〕	10		80	13/	13	台/千克			/35
8423.3020	---定量分选秤〔101 电子衡器,102 机械衡器〕	10		80	13/	13	台/千克			/35
8423.3030	---配料秤									
8423.3030 10	以电子方式称重的配料秤〔999〕	0		80	13/	13	台/千克			/25

协定税率 %										特惠税率 %			Article Description
亚太5国	东/冰/格	巴基斯坦	韩国	瑞士	哥达	秘鲁	澳大利亚	新西/坡/智	港/澳/台	亚太2国	老/柬/缅	36/3/1	
3.3	0/0/0	0	0	0	0	0	0	0//0	0/0/0			0/0/0	Parts of liquid membrane filtration or purification device and machine, made of fluorine polymer thickness less than 140 microns filtration or purification ; gas filter equipment stainless steel shell, entrance pipe and the outlet pipe diameter not exceeding 1.3 cm or purification machines and apparatus parts
3.3	0/0/0	0	0	0	0	0	0	0//0	0/0/0			0/0/0	Other parts of filtering and purifying machines and apparatuses
													Dish washing machines; machinery for cleaning or drying bottles or other containers; machinery for filling, closing, sealing or labelling bottles, cans, boxes, bags or other containers; machinery for capsuling bottles, jars, tubes and similar containers other packing or wrapping machinery (including heat-shrink wrapping machinery); machinery for aerating beverages:
													-Dish washing machines:
	0/0/0	4		0	0	0	0	0//0	0/0/			0/0/0	--Of the household type
	0/0/0	10.1	5.6	0	0	0	0	0/0/0	0/0/			0/0/	--Other
	0/0/0	4	4	0	0	0	0	0/0/0	0/0/			0/0/0	-Machinery for cleaning or drying bottles or other containers
													-Machinery for filling, closing, sealing, or labelling bottles, cans, boxes, bags or other containers; machinery for capsuling bottles, jars, tubes and similar containers; machinery for aerating beverages:
													---Bottling or canning machinery for beverages or liquid food
7.8	0/0/0	4.5	4.8	3.6	0	0	0	0/0/0	0/0/			0/0/0	With the automatic filling equipment in dairy processing
7.8	0/0/0	4.5	4.8	3.6	0	0	0	0/0/0	0/0/			0/0/0	Other botting or canning machinery for beverages or liquid food
													---Machinery for packing cement:
5.2	0/0/0	4.5	4.8	3.6	0	0	0	0/0/0	0/0/			0/0/0	----Automatic filling and sacking machines
5.2	0/0/0	4.5	4.8	3.6	0	0	0	0/0/0	0/0/			0/0/0	----Other
													---Other packing machines
5.2	0/0/0	4.5	0	0	0	0	0	0/0/0	0/0/			0/0/0	Packing machines for fully automatic aseptic filling production lines (processing speed≥2000 bottles/hour)
5.2	0/0/0	4.5	0	0	0	0	0	0/0/0	0/0/			0/0/0	Other packing machines
													---Other
5.2	0/0/0	4.5	0	0	0	0	0	0/0/0	0/0/			0/0/0	Pipette machines for fully automatic filling production lines (processing speed ≥2000 bottles/hour)
5.2	0/0/0	4.5	0	0	0	0	0	0/0/0	0/0/			0/0/0	Filling equipment(Subject to regulation of sensitive items)
5.2	0/0/0	4.5	0	0	0	0	0	0/0/0	0/0/			0/0/0	Machines for the filling, sealing, sealing, labeling of other bottles, cans, boxes, bags or other containers, and other packaging machines for bottles, cans, tubes, tubes, or similar containers; machinery for aerating beverages
5.2	0/0/0	5	5	0	0	0	0	0/0/0	0/0/			0/0/0	-Other packing or wrapping machinery (including heat-shrink wrapping machinery)
5.2	0/0/0	4	4	0	0	0	0	0/0/0	0/0/		//	0/0/0	Semiconductor testing, sorting and taping machine
5.2	0/0/0	4	4	0	0	0	0	0/0/0	0/0/		//	0/0/0	Other packaging or packaging machines (including heat shrinkable packaging machines)
													-Parts:
	0/0/0	4.5	4.2	3.2	0	0	0	0/0/0	0/0/			0/0/0	---Of dish washing machines
	0/0/3.4	4	3.4	0	0	0	0	0//0	0/0/			0/0/0	---Of bottling or canning machinery for beverages or liquid food
	0//0	4	0	2.6	0	0	0	0//0	0/0/			0/0/0	---Other
													Weighing machinery (excluding balances of a sensitivity of 50 mg or better), including weight operated counting or checking machines; weighing machine weights of all kinds:
	0/0/0	4.5	4.2	3.2	0	0	0	0/0/0	0/0/			0/0/0	-Personal weighing machines, including baby scales; household scales
													-Scales for continuous weighing of goods on conveyors:
	0//	4	4					//	0/0/			0/0/0	---Electronic belt weighing machines
	0/0/0	4	4	0	0	0	0	0//0	0/0/			0/0/0	---Other
													-Constant weight scales and scales for discharging a predetermined weight of material into a bag or container, including hopper scales:
													---Rationed packing scales
	0/0/0	4.5	4.2	3.2	0	0	0	0/0/0	0/0/			0/0/0	Electronic rationed packing scales
	0/0/0	4.5	4.2	3.2	0	0	0	0/0/0	0/0/			0/0/0	Other rationed packing scales
	0/0/0	4.5	4.2	3.2	0	0	0	0/0/0	0/0/			0/0/0	---Rationed sorting scales
													---Proporating scales
	0/0/0	4.5	4.2	3.2	0	0	0	0/0/0	0/0/			0/0/0	Ecletronic proporating scales

税则号列		货品名称〔CIQ 扩展编码及品名－T2 表示见附表 2〕	最惠(%)	暂定税率	普通	增值/消费	出口退税	计量单位	监管条件	检验检疫	特殊证件对美关税
8423.3030	90	其他配料秤〔999〕	10		80	13/	13	台/千克			/35
8423.3090		---其他									
8423.3090	10	以电子方式称重的恒定秤，库秤及其他包装秤，分选秤〔999〕	0		80	13/	13	台/千克			/25
8423.3090	90	其他恒定秤，库秤及其他包装秤，分选秤〔999〕	10		80	13/	13	台/千克			/35
		-其他衡器：									
		--最大称量不超过 30 千克：									
8423.8110		---计价秤〔101 电子衡器，102 机械衡器〕	0		80	13/	13	台/千克			/25
8423.8120		---弹簧秤〔999〕	10		80	13/	13	台/千克			/35
8423.8190		---其他									
8423.8190	10	其他以电子方式称重的衡器，最大称量不超过 30 千克〔999〕	0		80	13/	13	台/千克			/20
8423.8190	90	最大称量≤30 千克的其他衡器〔999〕	10		80	13/	13	台/千克			/30
		--最大称量超过 30 千克，但不超过 5000 千克：									
8423.8210		---地中衡									
8423.8210	10	其他以电子方式称重的地中衡，最大称量大于 30 千克但不超过 5000 千克，但对车辆称重的衡器除外〔999〕	0		80	13/	13	台/千克			/20
8423.8210	90	30＜最大称量≤5000kg 的其他地中衡〔999〕	10		80	13/	13	台/千克			/30
8423.8290		---其他									
8423.8290	10	其他以电子方式称重的衡器，最大称量大于 30 千克但不超过 5000 千克，但对车辆称重的衡器除外〔999〕	0		80	13/	13	台/千克			/20
8423.8290	90	30＜最大称量≤5000kg 的其他衡器〔999〕	10		80	13/	13	台/千克			/30
		--其他：									
8423.8910		---地中衡									
8423.8910	10	其他以电子方式称重的地中衡，最大称量超过 5000 千克，但对车辆称重的衡器除外〔999〕	0		80	13/	13	台/千克			/25
8423.8910	90	最大秤量＞5000KG 的其他地中衡〔999〕	10		80	13/	13	台/千克			/35
8423.8920		---轨道衡									
8423.8920	10	其他以电子方式称重的轨道衡，最大称量超过 5000 千克，但对车辆称重的衡器除外〔999〕	0		80	13/	13	台/千克			/25
8423.8920	90	最大秤量＞5000KG 的其他轨道衡〔999〕	10		80	13/	13	台/千克			/35
8423.8930		---吊秤									
8423.8930	10	其他以电子方式称重的吊秤，最大称量超过 5000 千克，但对车辆称重的衡器除外〔999〕	0		80	13/	13	台/千克			/10
8423.8930	90	最大秤量＞5000KG 的其他吊秤〔999〕	10		80	13/	13	台/千克			/20
8423.8990		---其他									
8423.8990	10	其他以电子方式称重的衡器，最大称量超过 5000 千克，但对车辆称重的衡器除外〔999〕	0		80	13/	13	台/千克			/10
8423.8990	90	最大秤量＞5000KG 的其他衡器〔999〕	10		80	13/	13	台/千克			/20
8423.9000		-衡器用的各种砝码、秤砣；衡器的零件									
8423.9000	10	以电子方式称重的衡器的零件，但对车辆称重的衡器零件除外〔999〕	0		80	13/	13	千克/台			/20
8423.9000	90	其他衡器用的各种砝码、秤砣及其零件〔999〕	8		80	13/	13	千克/台			/28
84.24		**液体或粉末的喷射、散布或喷雾的机械器具(不论是否手工操作)；灭火器，不论是否装药；喷枪及类似器具；喷汽机、喷砂机及类似的喷射机器：**									
8424.1000		-灭火器，不论是否装药〔999〕	8		70	13/	13	个/千克	A	LM	/18
8424.2000		-喷枪及类似器具〔999〕	8		40	13/	13	个/千克			/13
8424.3000		-喷气机、喷砂机及类似的喷射机器〔999〕	8		40	13/	13	台/千克			/28
		-农业或园艺用喷雾器：									
8424.4100		--便携式喷雾器〔999〕	8		30	9/	9	台/千克		L	/33
8424.4900		--其他〔999〕	8		30	9/	9	台/千克		L	/13
		-其他器具：									

协定税率 %										特惠税率 %			
亚太5国	东/冰/格	巴基斯坦	韩国	瑞士	哥达	秘鲁	澳大利亚	新西/坡/智	港/澳/台	亚太2国	老/柬/缅	36/3/1	Article Description
	0/0/0	4.5	4.2	3.2	0	0	0	0/0/0	0/0/			0/0/0	Other proporating scales
													---Other
	0/0/0	4.5	4.2	3.2	0	0	0	0/0/0	0/0/			0/0/0	Constant weight scales , hopper scales and other packing scales ,soting scales,in ecletronic
	0/0/0	4.5	4.2	3.2	0	0	0	0/0/0	0/0/			0/0/0	Other constant weight scales , hopper scales and other packing scales ,soting scales
													-Other weighing machinery:
													--Having a maximum weighing capacity not exceeding 30kg:
	0//	4.5	4.2					//	0/0/			0/0/0	---Account balances
	0/0/0	4.5	4.2	3.2	0	0	0	0/0/0	0/0/			0/0/0	---Spring balances
													---Other
	0/0/0	4.5	4.2	6.1	0	0	0	0/0/0	0/0/			0/0/0	Other electronic weighing scales,having a maximum weighing capacity not exceeding 30KG
	0/0/0	4.5	4.2	6.1	0	0	0	0/0/0	0/0/			0/0/0	Other weighing scales,having a maximum weighing capacity not exceeding 30KG
													--Having a maximum weighing capacity exceeding 30kg but not exceeding 5000kg:
													---Weighbridges
	0/0/0	4.5	4.2	3.2	0	0	0	0/0/0	0/0/			0/0/0	Other electronic weighbridges,having a maximum weighing capacity exceeding 30KG but not exceeding 5000KG,but the vehicle weighing scales except
	0/0/0	4.5	4.2	3.2	0	0	0	0/0/0	0/0/			0/0/0	Other weighbridges , having a maximum weighing capacity exceeding 30KG but not exceeding 5000KG
													---Other
	0/0/0	4.5	4.2	0	0	0	0	0/0/0	0/0/			0/0/0	Other electronic weighing machinery, aving a maximum weighing capacity exceeding 30KG but not exceeding 5000KG,but the vehicle weighing scales except
	0/0/0	4.5	4.2	0	0	0	0	0/0/0	0/0/			0/0/0	Other weighing machinery ,having a maximum weighing capacity exceeding 30KG but not exceeding 5000KG
													--Other:
													---Weighbridges
	0/0/0	4	4	0	0	0	0	0//0	0/0/			0/0/0	Other electronic weighbridges, having a maximum weighing capacity exceeding 5000KG,but the vehicle weighing scales except
	0/0/0	4	4	0	0	0	0	0//0	0/0/			0/0/0	Other weighbridges , having a maximum weighing capacity exceeding 5000KG
													---Track scales
	0/0/0	4	4	0	0	0	0	0//0	0/0/			0/0/0	Other electronic track scales , having a maximum weighing capacity exceeding 5000KG
	0/0/0	4	4	0	0	0	0	0//0	0/0/			0/0/0	Other track scales , having a maximum weighing capacity exceeding 5000KG
													---Hanging scales
	0/0/0	4	4	0	0	0	0	0//0	0/0/			0/0/0	Other electronic Hanging scales, having a maximum weighing capacity exceeding 5000KG
	0/0/0	4	4	0	0	0	0	0//0	0/0/			0/0/0	Hanging scales, having a maximum weighing capacity exceeding 5000KG
													---Other
	0/0/0	4	4	0	0	0	0	0//0	0/0/			0/0/0	Other electronic weighing machinery ,having a maximum weighing capacity exceeding 5000KG,but the vehicle weighing scales except
	0/0/0	4	4	0	0	0	0	0//0	0/0/			0/0/0	Other weighing machinery ,having a maximum weighing capacity exceeding 5000KG,but the vehicle weighing scales except
													-Weighing machine weights of all kinds; parts of weighing machinery
	0/0/0	4	4	3	0	0	0	0/0/0	0/0/			0/0/0	Electronic weighing instrument parts, but the parts of vehicle weighing scales except
	0/0/0	4	4	3	0	0	0	0/0/0	0/0/			0/0/0	kinds of weight, weight and other parts of the weighing machine
													Mechanical appliances (whether or not hand-operated) for projecting, dispersing or spraying liquids or powders; fire extinguishers, whether or not charged; spray guns and similar appliances; steam or sand blasting machines and similar jet projecting machines:
	0/0/0	4	5	0	0	0	0	0//0	0/0/			0/0/	-Fire extinguishers, whether or not charged
5.2	0/0/0	4	0	0	0	0	0	0//0	0/0/			0/0/	-Spray guns and similar appliances
	0/0/0	4	3.3	2.5	0	0	0	0//0	0/0/0			0/0/	-Steam or sand blasting machines and similar jet projecting machines
													-Agricultural or horticultural sprayers:
5.2	0/0/0	4	0	0	0	0	0	0//0	0/0/			0/0/	-Portable sprayers
5.2	0/0/0	4	0	0	0	0	0	0//0	0/0/			0/0/	--Other
													-Other appliances:

税则号列	货品名称〔CIQ扩展编码及品名—T2表示见附表2〕	最惠(%)	暂定税率	普通	增值/消费	出口退税	计量单位	监管条件	检验检疫	特殊证件对美关税
8424.8200	--农业或园艺用〔999〕	8		30	9/	9	台/千克		L	/28
	--其他:									
8424.8910	---家用型[T2]	0		80	13/	13	台/千克			/10
8424.8920	---喷涂机器人〔999〕	0		80	13/	13	台/千克			/10
	---其他:									
8424.8991	----船用洗舱机〔999〕	0		30	13/	13	台/千克			/25
8424.8999	----其他									
8424.8999 10	分离喷嘴(由狭缝状、曲率半径极小的弯曲通道组成,内有分离楔尖)[T2]	0		30	13/	13	台/千克	3	L	/10
8424.8999 90	其他用途的喷射、喷雾机械器具[T2]	0		30	13/	13	台/千克		L	/10
	-零件:									
8424.9010	---子目8424.1000所列器具的零件〔999〕	0		70	13/	13	千克			/5
8424.9020	---子目8424.8910所列器具的零件〔101蒸脸器,102家用型喷射、喷雾机械器具〕	0		80	13/	13	千克		L	/5
8424.9090	---其他〔999〕	0		30	13/	9,13	千克			/10
84.25	滑车及提升机,但倒卸式提升机除外;卷扬机及绞盘;千斤顶:									
	-滑车及提升机,但倒卸式提升机及提升车辆用的提升机除外:									
8425.1100	--电动的〔999〕	6		30	13/	13	台/千克			/16
8425.1900	--其他〔999〕	5		30	13/	13	台/千克			/15
	-卷扬机;绞盘:									
	--电动的:									
8425.3110	---矿井口卷扬装置;专为井下使用设计的卷扬机〔999〕	10		30	13/	13	台/千克			/
8425.3190	---其他〔999〕	5		30	13/	13	台/千克			/25
	--其他:									
8425.3910	---矿井口卷扬装置;专为井下使用设计的卷扬机〔999〕	10		30	13/	13	台/千克			/30
8425.3990	---其他〔999〕	5		30	13/	13	台/千克			/30
	-千斤顶;提升车辆用的提升机:									
8425.4100	--车库中使用的固定千斤顶系统〔999〕	3		30	13/	13	台/千克			/23
	--其他液压千斤顶及提升机:									
8425.4210	---液压千斤顶〔999〕	3		30	13/	13	台/千克			/13
8425.4290	---其他〔999〕	5		30	13/	13	台/千克			/30
	--其他:									
8425.4910	---其他千斤顶〔999〕	5		30	13/	13	台/千克			/15
8425.4990	---其他〔999〕	10		30	13/	13	台/千克			/30
84.26	船用桅杆式起重机;起重机,包括缆式起重机;移动式吊运架、跨运车及装有起重机的工作车:									
	-高架移动式起重机、桁架桥式起重机、龙门起重机、桥式起重机、移动式吊运架及跨运车:									
	--固定支架的高架移动式起重机:									
8426.1120	---通用桥式起重机〔999〕	8		30	13/	13	台/千克			/33
8426.1190	---其他〔999〕	8		30	13/	13	台/千克			/28
8426.1200	--带胶轮的移动式吊运架及跨运车〔999〕	6		30	13/	13	台/千克			/26
	--其他:									
8426.1910	---装船机〔999〕	5		30	13/	13	台/千克			/
	---卸船机:									
8426.1921	----抓斗式〔999〕	5		30	13/	13	台/千克			/
8426.1929	----其他〔999〕	5		30	13/	13	台/千克	O		/
8426.1930	---龙门式起重机〔999〕	10		30	13/	13	台/千克			3/35
	---装卸桥:									
8426.1941	----门式装卸桥〔999〕	10		30	13/	13	台/千克			3/
8426.1942	----集装箱装卸桥〔999〕	10		30	13/	13	台/千克			3/
8426.1943	----其他动臂式装卸桥〔999〕	10		30	13/	13	台/千克			/
8426.1949	----其他〔999〕	10		30	13/	13	台/千克			/
8426.1990	---其他〔999〕	10		30	13/	13	台/千克			/
8426.2000	-塔式起重机〔999〕	10		30	13/	13	台/千克	O		3/
8426.3000	-门座式起重机及座式旋臂起重机〔999〕	6		30	13/	13	台/千克			/31
	-其他自推进机械:									
	--带胶轮的:									
8426.4110	---轮胎式起重机〔999〕	5		30	13/	13	台/千克	O		3/
8426.4190	---其他〔999〕	5		30	13/	13	台/千克			3/35
	--其他:									
8426.4910	---履带式起重机〔999〕	8		30	13/	13	台/千克	O		3/33

协定税率 %										特惠税率 %			Article Description
亚太5国	东/冰/格	巴基斯坦	韩国	瑞士	哥达	秘鲁	澳大利亚	新西/坡/智	港/澳/台	亚太2国	老/柬/缅	36/3/1	
5.2	0/0/0	4	0	0	0	0	0	0//0	0/0/			0/0/	-Agricultural or horticultural
													--Other:
												0/0/0	---Of the household type
												0/0/0	---Spraying robot
													---Other:
												0/0/0	----Marine cabinet washer
													----Other
												0/0/0	Separating nozzles(composed of slik-like curved and channels of very small curvature radius, with separation of wedge tip)
												0/0/0	Mechanical appliances for projecting, or spraying for other use
													-Parts:
												0/0/0	---Of the apparatus of subheading No.8424.1000
												0/0/0	---Of the apparatus of subheading No.8424.8910
												0/0/0	---Other
													Pulley tackle and hoists other than skip hoists; winches and capstans; jacks:
													-Pulley tackle and hoists other than skip hoists or hoists of a kind used for raising vehicles:
	0/0/0	0	3.6	0	0	0	0	0//0	0/0/			0/0/0	--Powered by electric motor
	0/0/0	0	2	0	0	0	0	0//0	0/0/			0/0/0	--Other
													-Winches; capstans:
													--Powered by electric motor:
7	0/0/0	4	4	0	0	0	0	0//0	0/0/			0/0/0	---Pit-head winding gear; winches specially designed for use underground
	0/0/0	0	3	0	0	0	0	0//0	0/0/			0/0/0	---Other
													--Other:
7	0/0/0	4	4	0	0	0	0	0//0	0/0/			0/0/0	---Pit-head winding gear; winches specially designed for use underground
	0/0/0	0	3	0	0	0	0	0//0	0/0/			0/0/0	---Other
													-Jacks; hoists of a kind used for raising vehicles:
2	0/0/0	0	0	0	0	0	0	0//0	0/0/			0/0/0	--Built-in jacking systems of a type used in garages
													--Other jacks and hoists, hydraulic:
	0/0/0	0	0	0	0	0	0	0//0	0/0/			0/0/0	---Hydraulic jacks
	0/0/0	0	3	0	0	0	0	0//0	0/0/			0/0/0	---Other
													--Other:
	0/0/0	0	2	0	0	0	0	0//0	0/0/			0/0/0	---Other jacks
	0/0/0	4	4	0	0	0	0	0//0	0/0/			0/0/0	---Other
													Ships derricks; cranes, including cable cranes; mobile lifting frames, straddle carriers and works trucks fitted with a crane:
													-Overhead travelling cranes, transporter cranes, gantry cranes, bridge cranes, mobile lifting frames and straddle carriers:
													--Overhead travelling cranes on fixed support:
	0/0/0	4	4.8	0	0	0	0	0//0	0/0/			0/0/0	---Bridge cranes, all-purpose
	0/0/0	4	4.8	0	0	0	0	0//0	0/0/			0/0/0	---Other
	0/0/0	0	3.6	0	0	0	0	0//0	0/0/			0/0/0	--Mobile lifting frames on tyres and straddle carriers
													--Other:
2.5	0/0/0	0	3	0	0	0	0	0//0	0/0/			0/0/0	---Ship loading cranes
													---Ship unloading cranes:
3.3	0/0/0	0	3	0	0	0	0	0//0	0/0/			0/0/0	----Grab ship unloading cranes
3.3	0/0/0	0	3	0	0	0	0	0//0	0/0/			0/0/0	----Other
6.5	0/0/0	4	6	0	0	0	0	0//0	0/0/			0/0/0	---Gantry cranes
													---Loading and unlcading bridges:
6.5	0/0/0	4	6	0	0	0	0	0//0	0/0/			0/0/0	----Frame loading and unloading bridges
6.5	0/0/0	4	6	0	0	0	0	0//0	0/0/			0/0/0	----Container loading and unloading bridges
6.5	0/0/0	4	7	0	0	0	0	0//0	0/0/			0/0/0	----Derrick loading and unloading bridges
6.5	0/0/0	4	6	0	0	0	0	0//0	0/0/			0/0/0	----Other
6.5	0/0/0	4	7	0	0	0	0	0/0/0	0/0/			0/0/0	---Other
	0/0/0	4	7	0	0	0	0	0//0	0/0/			0/0/0	-Tower cranes
	0/0/0	0	3.6	0	0	0	0	0//0	0/0/			0/0/0	-Portal or pedestal jib cranes
													-Other machinery, self-propelled:
													--On tyres:
3.5	0/0/0	0	3	0	0	0	0	0//0	0/0/			0/0/0	---Wheel-mounted cranes
	0/0/0	0	3	0	0	0	0	0//0	0/0/			0/0/0	---Other
													--Other:
5.6	0/0/0	4	4.8	0	0	0	0	0//0	0/0/			0/0/0	---Crawler cranes

税则号列	货品名称〔CIQ 扩展编码及品名－T2 表示见附表 2〕	最惠(%)	暂定税率	普通	增值/消费	出口退税	计量单位	监管条件	检验检疫	特殊证件对美关税
8426.4990	---其他〔999〕	8		30	13/	13	台/千克			3/
	-其他机械：									
8426.9100	--供装于公路车辆的〔999〕	8		30	13/	13	台/千克			/
8426.9900	--其他〔999〕	6		30	13/	13	台/千克			3/31
84.27	**叉车；其他装有升降或搬运装置的工作车：**									
	-电动机推进的机动车：									
8427.1010	---有轨巷道堆垛机〔999〕	9		30	13/	13	台/千克	A	M	3/
8427.1020	---无轨巷道堆垛机〔999〕	9		30	13/	13	台/千克	A	M	3/29
8427.1090	---其他〔999〕	9		30	13/	13	台/千克	A	M	/19
	-其他机动车：									
8427.2010	---集装箱叉车〔999〕	9		30	13/	13	台/千克	A	M	/
8427.2090	---其他〔999〕	9		30	13/	13	台/千克	A	M	3/19
8427.9000	-其他车〔999〕	9		30	13/	13	台/千克	A	M	3/19
84.28	**其他升降、搬运、装卸机械(例如，升降机、自动梯、输送机、缆车)：**									
	-升降机及倒卸式起重机：									
8428.1010	---载客电梯									
8428.1010 01	无障碍升降机〔999〕	8	4	30	13/	13	台/千克	A	M	/
8428.1010 90	其他载客电梯〔999〕	8		30	13/	13	台/千克	A	M	/
8428.1090	---其他〔101 载货电梯、升降机，102 起重机，103 机械式停车设备及其它装卸、储运设备及其零件，104 集装箱装卸桥，105 其他装卸桥、提升、起重设备及零件〕	6		30	13/	13	台/千克	A	M	3/31
8428.2000	-气压升降机及输送机〔101 载货电梯、升降机，102 其他装卸桥、提升、起重设备及零件〕	5		30	13/	13	台/千克			/15
	-其他用于连续运送货物或材料的升降机及输送机：									
8428.3100	--地下专用的〔101 载货电梯、升降机，102 其他装卸桥、提升、起重设备及零件〕	5		30	13/	13	台/千克			/
8428.3200	--其他，斗式〔101 载货电梯、升降机，102 其他装卸桥、提升、起重设备及零件〕	5		30	13/	13	台/千克			/15
8428.3300	--其他，带式〔101 载货电梯、升降机，102 其他装卸桥、提升、起重设备及零件〕	5		30	13/	13	台/千克			/30
	--其他：									
8428.3910	---链式〔101 载货电梯、升降机，102 其他装卸桥、提升、起重设备及零件〕	5		30	13/	13	台/千克			/25
8428.3920	---辊式〔101 载货电梯、升降机，102 其他装卸桥、提升、起重设备及零件〕	5		30	13/	13	台/千克			/30
8428.3990	---其他[T2]	5		30	13/	13	台/千克			/25
8428.4000	-自动梯及自动人行道〔999〕	5		30	13/	13	台/千克	A	M	/
	-缆车、座式升降机、滑雪拉索、索道用牵引装置：									
8428.6010	---货运架空索道〔999〕	8		30	13/	13	台/千克			/
	---客运架空索道：									
8428.6021	----单线循环式〔999〕	8		30	13/	13	台/千克			3/
8428.6029	----其他〔999〕	8		30	13/	13	台/千克			/
8428.6090	---其他〔101 载货电梯、升降机，102 客货运缆车〕	8		30	13/	13	台/千克			/
	-其他机械：									
8428.9010	---矿车推动机、铁道机车或货车的转车台、货车倾卸装置及类似的铁道货车搬运装置〔999〕	10		30	13/	13	台/千克			/
8428.9020	---机械式停车设备〔999〕	5		30	13/	13	台/千克			/
	---其他装卸机械：									
8428.9031	----堆取料机械〔999〕	5		30	13/	13	台/千克			/30
8428.9039	----其他装卸机械〔999〕	5		30	13/	13	台/千克			/30
8428.9040	---搬运机器人〔999〕	5		30	13/	13	台/千克			/30
8428.9090	---其他									
8428.9090 10	放化分离作业和热室用遥控机械手(能贯穿 0.6 米以上热室壁或壁厚为 0.6 米以上热室顶)〔999〕	5		30	13/	13	台/千克	3		/25
8428.9090 20	核反应堆燃料装卸机(用于在核反应堆中插入或取出燃料的操作设备)〔999〕	5		30	13/	13	台/千克	3		/25
8428.9090 90	其他升降、搬运、装卸机械〔999〕	5		30	13/	13	台/千克			/25
84.29	**机动推土机、侧铲推土机、筑路机、平地机、铲运机、机械铲、挖掘机、机铲装载机、捣固机械及压路机：**									
	-推土机及侧铲推土机：									

协定税率 %										特惠税率 %			
亚太5国	东/冰/格	巴基斯坦	韩国	瑞士	哥达	秘鲁	澳大利亚	新西/坡/智	港/澳/台	亚太2国	老/柬/缅	36/3/1	Article Description
5.6	0/0/0	5.9	7.8	3.9	0	0	0	0/0/0	0/0/			0/0/	---Other
													-Other machinery:
	0/0/0	4	7	0	0	0	0	0//0	0/0/			0/0/0	--Designed for mounting on road vehicles
	0/0/0	0	3.6	0	0	0	0	0//0	0/0/			0/0/0	--Other
													Fork-lift trucks; other works trucks fitted with lifting or handling equipment:
													-Self-propelled trucks powered by an electric motor:
	0/0/0	4	0	0	0	0	0	0//0	0/0/			0/0/0	---Track alleyway stackers
	0/0/0	4	5.4	0	0	0	0	0//0	0/0/			0/0/0	---Trackless alleyway stackers
	0/0/0	4	0	0	0	0	0	0//0	0/0/			0/0/0	---Other
													-Other self-propelled trucks:
5.9	0/0/0	4	0	0	0	0	0	0//0	0/0/			0/0/0	---Fork-lift trucks cranes
5.9	0/0/0	4	0	0	0	0	0	0//0	0/0/			0/0/0	---Other
	0/0/0	4	0	0	0	0	0	0//0	0/0/			0/0/0	-Other trucks
													Other lifting, handling, loading or unloading machinery (for example, lifts, escalators, conveyors, teleferics):
													-Lifts and skip hoists:
													---Designed for the transport of persons
5.2	0/0/0	4	3.2	2.4	0	0	0	0/0/0	0/0/			0/0/0	Accessibility lifts
5.2	0/0/0	4	3.2	2.4	0	0	0	0/0/0	0/0/			0/0/0	Other passenger elevators
3.9	0/0/0	0	0	0	0	0	0	0//0	0/0/0			0/0/0	---Other
	0/0/0	0	3	0	0	0	0	0//0	0/0/			0/0/0	-Pneumatic elevators and conveyors
													-Other continuous-action elevators and conveyors, for goods or materials:
	0/0/0	0	0	0	0	0	0	0//0	0/0/			0/0/0	--Specially designed for underground use
	0/0/0	0	2		0	0	0	0//0	0/0/			0/0/0	--Other, bucket type
3.3	0/0/0	0	3	0	0	0	0	0//0	0/0/0			0/0/0	—Other, belt type
													—Other:
3.3	0/0/0	0	3	0	0	0	0	0//0	0/0/0			0/0/0	---Chain type
3.3	0/0/0	0	2	0	0	0	0	0//0	0/0/0			0/0/0	---Roller type
3.3	0/0/0	0	0	2.6	0	0	0	0//0	0/0/0			0/0/0	---Other
	0/0/0	0	0	0	0	0	0	0//0	0/0/			0/0/0	-Ξscalators and moving walkways
													-Teleferics, chair-lifts, ski-draglines; traction mechanisms for funiculars:
5.6	0/0/0	4	0	0	0	0	0	0//0	0/0/			0/0/0	—Cargo aerial cableways
													—Passanger aerial cableways:
5.6	0/0/0	4	0	0	0	0	0	0//0	0/0/			0/0/0	----Monocable endless
5.6	0/0/0	4	0	0	0	0	0	0//0	0/0/			0/0/0	----Other
	0/0/0	4	3.2	0	0	0	0	0//0	0/0/			0/0/0	---Other
													-Other machinery:
	0/0/0	4.5	4	0	0	0	0	0//0	0/0/			0/0/0	---Mine wagon pushers, locmotive or wagon traversers, wagon tippers and similar railway wagon handling equipment
	0/0/0	0	2	0	0	0	0	0//0	0/0/			0/0/0	---Machinery parking equipment
													---Unloading machinery:
	0/0/0	0	3	1.5	0	0	0	0//0	0/0/0			0/0/0	----Stacker reclaimers machinery
	0/0/0	0	3	1.5	0	0	0	0//0	0/0/0			0/0/0	----Other unloading machinery
	0/0/0	0	3	1.5	0	0	0	0//0	0/0/0			0/0/0	---Handling robot
													---Other
	0/0/0	0	3	1.5	0	0	0	0//0	0/0/0			0/0/0	Remote manipulators for radioactive chemical separating operation and hot cell (capable of penetrating wall of hot cell thickness>0. 6m or top of hot cell thickness>0. 6m)
	0/0/0	0	3	1.5	0	0	0	0//0	0/0/0			0/0/0	nuclear reactor fuel loader and unloader (operational appliances used for putting inor taking out the fuels in nuclear reactor)
	0/0/0	0	3	1.5	0	0	0	0//0	0/0/0			0/0/0	Other lifting, carrying, loading or unloading machinery
													Self-propelled bulldozers, angledozers, graders, levellers, scrapers, mechanical shovels, excavators, shovel loaders, tamping machines and road rollers:
													-Bulldozers and angledozers:

税则号列	货品名称〔CIQ扩展编码及品名－T2表示见附表2〕	最惠(%)	暂定税率	普通	增值/消费	出口退税	计量单位	监管条件	检验检疫	特殊证件对美关税
	--履带式：									
8429.1110	---发动机输出功率超过235.36千瓦(320马力)的〔999〕	7		17	13/	13	台/千克	A	M	/27
8429.1190	---其他〔999〕	7		30	13/	13	台/千克	A	M	/32
	--其他：									
8429.1910	---发动机输出功率超过235.36千瓦(320马力)的〔999〕	7		17	13/	13	台/千克	A	M	/
8429.1990	---其他〔999〕	7		30	13/	13	台/千克	A	M	/
	-筑路机及平地机：									
8429.2010	---发动机输出功率超过235.36千瓦(320马力)的〔999〕	5		17	13/	9,13	台/千克	A	M	/
8429.2090	---其他〔999〕	5		30	13/	9,13	台/千克	A	M	/15
	-铲运机：									
8429.3010	---斗容量超过10立方米的〔999〕	3		17	13/	13	台/千克	A	M	/
8429.3090	---其他〔999〕	5		30	13/	13	台/千克	A	M	/
	-捣固机械及压路机：									
	---机动压路机：									
8429.4011	----机重18吨及以上的振动压路机〔999〕	7		20	13/	13	台/千克	OA	M	/
8429.4019	----其他〔999〕	8		40	13/	13	台/千克	OA	M	/33
8429.4090	---其他〔101压路机，102捣固机〕	6		30	13/	13	台/千克	A	M	/
	-机械铲、挖掘机及机铲装载机：									
8429.5100	--前铲装载机〔999〕	5		30	13/	13	台/千克	A	M	/10
	--上部结构可旋转360度的机械：									
	---挖掘机：									
8429.5211	----轮胎式〔999〕	8		30	13/	13	台/千克	OA	M	/
8429.5212	----履带式〔999〕	8		30	13/	13	台/千克	OA	M	/33
8429.5219	----其他〔999〕	8		30	13/	13	台/千克	OA	M	/
8429.5290	---其他〔999〕	8		30	13/	13	台/千克	OA	M	/
8429.5900	--其他〔999〕	8		30	13/	13	台	OA	M	/28
84.30	**泥土、矿物或矿石的运送、平整、铲运、挖掘、捣固、压实、开采或钻探机械；打桩机及拔桩机；扫雪机及吹雪机：**									
8430.1000	-打桩机及拔桩机〔999〕	10		30	13/	13	台/千克			/15
8430.2000	-扫雪机及吹雪机〔999〕	10		30	13/	13	台/千克			/15
	-采(截)煤机、凿岩机及隧道掘进机：									
	--自推进的：									
8430.3110	---采(截)煤机〔999〕	10		30	13/	13	台/千克	O		/30
8430.3120	---凿岩机〔999〕	10		30	13/	13	台/千克	O		/
8430.3130	---隧道掘进机〔999〕	10		30	13/	13	台/千克	O		/
8430.3900	--其他〔999〕	6		30	13/	13	台/千克			/26
	-其他钻探或凿井机械：									
	--自推进的：									
	---石油及天然气钻探机：									
8430.4111	----钻探深度在6000米及以上的〔999〕	5		11	13/	13	台/千克			/15
8430.4119	----其他〔999〕	5		17	13/	13	台/千克			/25
	---其他钻探机：									
8430.4121	----钻探深度在6000米及以上的〔999〕	5		11	13/	13	台/千克			/15
8430.4122	----钻探深度在6000米以下的履带式自推进钻机〔999〕	5		17	13/	13	台/千克			/15
8430.4129	----钻探深度在6000米以下的其他钻探机〔999〕	5		17	13/	13	台/千克			/25
8430.4190	---其他〔999〕	5		30	13/	13	台/千克			/15
8430.4900	--其他〔999〕	5		30	13/	13	台/千克			/30
	-其他自推进机械：									
8430.5010	---其他采油机械〔999〕	3		17	13/	13	台/千克			/13
8430.5020	---矿用电铲〔999〕	7		30	13/	13	台/千克			/
	---采矿钻机：									
8430.5031	----牙轮直径380毫米及以上〔999〕	5		30	13/	13	台/千克			/15
8430.5039	----其他〔999〕	5		30	13/	13	台/千克			/15
8430.5090	---其他〔999〕	5		30	13/	13	台/千克			/30
	-其他非自推进机械：									
8430.6100	--捣固或压实机械〔999〕	6		30	13/	13	台			/
	--其他：									
	---工程钻机：									
8430.6911	----钻筒直径在3米及以上〔999〕	6		30	13/	13	台/千克			/
8430.6919	----其他〔999〕	6		30	13/	13	台/千克			/31
8430.6920	---铲运机〔101铲运机，102其它工程机械及其零件，103建筑工业行业成套设备〕	6		30	13/	13	台/千克			/26
8430.6990	---其他〔999〕	6		30	13/	13	台/千克			/26
84.31	**专用于或主要用于税目84.25至84.30所列机械的零件：**									

协定税率 %										特惠税率 %			
亚太5国	东/冰/格	巴基斯坦	韩国	瑞士	哥达	秘鲁	澳大利亚	新西/坡/智	港/澳/台	亚太2国	老/柬/缅	36/3/1	Article Description
													--Track laying:
4.9	0/0/0	4	0	0	0	0	0	0//0	0/0/			0/0/0	---With an engine of an output exceeding 235.36kW (320HP)
4.9	0/0/0	4	0	0	0	0	0	0//0	0/0/			0/0/0	---Other
													--Other:
	0/0/0	4	0	0	0	0	0	0//0	0/0/			0/0/0	---With an engine of an output exceeding 235.36kW (320HP)
	0/0/0	4	0	0	0	0	0	0//0	0/0/			0/0/0	---Other
													-Graders and levellers:
3.5	0/0/0	0	0	0	0	0	0	0//0	0/0/			0/0/0	---With an engine of an output exceeding 235.36kW (320HP)
3.5	0/0/0	0	0	0	0	0	0	0//0	0/0/			0/0/0	---Other
													-Scrapers:
2.1	0/0/0	0	0	0	0	0	0	0//0	0/0/			0/0/0	---Having a capacity of shovel exceeding $10m^3$
3.5	0/0/0	0	0	0	0	0	0	0//0	0/0/			0/0/0	---Other
													-Tamping machines and road rollers:
													---Self-propelled road rollers:
4.9	0/0/0	4	0	0	0	0	0	0//0	0/0/			0/0/0	----Vibration type, of a deadweight of 18t or more
5.6	0/0/0	4	0	0	0	0	0	0//0	0/0/			0/0/0	----Other
4.2	0/0/0	0	0	0	0	0	0	0//0	0/0/			0/0/0	---Other
													-Mechanical shovels, excavators and shovel loaders:
	0/0/0	0	2	0	0	0	0	0//0	0/0/			0/0/0	--Front-end shovel loaders
													--Machinery with a 360° revolving super-structure:
													---Excavators:
7.2	0/0/0	4	7.2	0	0	0	0	0//0	0/0/			0/0/0	----Tyre-mounted
	0/0/0	4		0	0	0	0	0//0	0/0/			0/0/0	----Track-mounted
5.2	0/0/0	4	5.2	0	0	0	0	0//0	0/0/			0/0/0	----Other
5.2	0/0/0	4	5.2	0	0	0	0	0//0	0/0/			0/0/0	---Other
	0/0/0	4	0	0	0	0	0	0//0	0/0/			0/0/0	--Other
													Other moving, grading, levelling, scraping, excavating, tamping, compacting, extracting or boring machinery, for earth, minerals or ores; pile-drivers and pile-extractors; snow-ploughs and snow-blowers:
	0/0/0	4	4	0	0	0	0	0//0	0/0/			0/0/0	-Pile-drivers and pile-extranctors
	0/0/0	4	4	0	0	0	0	0//0	0/0/			0/0/0	-Snow-ploughs and snow-blowers
													-Coal or rock cutters and tunnelling machinery:
													--Self-propelle:
	0/0/0	4	4	0	0	0	0	0/0/0	0/0/			0/0/0	---Mining (cutting) coal machine
	0/0/0	4	4	0	0	0	0	0/0/0	0/0/			0/0/0	---Rock drilling machine
	0/0/0	4	4	0	0	0	0	0/0/0	0/0/			0/0/0	---Tunnel boring machine
	0/0/0	0	2.4	0	0	0	0	0//0	0/0/			0/0/0	--Other
													-Other boring or sinking machinery:
													--Self-propelled:
													---Oil and natural gas drilling machinery:
3.5	0/0/0	0	0	0	0	0	0	0//0	0/0/			0/0/0	----Of drilling depth of 6000m or more
3.5	0/0/0	0	0	0	0	0	0	0//0	0/0/			0/0/0	----Other
													---Other drilling machinery:
3.5	0/0/0	0	0	0	0	0	0	0//0	0/0/			0/0/0	----Of drilling depth of 6000m or more
	0/0/0	0	2	0	0	0	0	0//0	0/0/			0/0/0	----Crawler boring machinery of drilling depth not exceeding 6000 m
	0/0/0	0	0	0	0	0	0	0//0	0/0/			0/0/0	----Other boring machinery of drilling depth exceeding 6000 m
	0/0/0	0	0	0	0	0	0	0//0	0/0/			0/0/0	---Other
	0/0/0	0	2	0	0	0	0	0//0	0/0/			0/0/0	--Other
													-Other machinery, self-propelled:
2.1	0/0/0	0	0	0	0	0	0	0//0	0/0/			0/0/0	---For oil production
	0/0/0	4	0	0	0	0	0	0//0	0/0/			0/0/0	---Mining power shovels
													---Mining drills:
3.5	0/0/0	0	0	0	0	0	0	0//0	0/0/			0/0/0	----Gear wheel diameter more than 380mm
3.5	0/0/0	0	0	0	0	0	0	0//0	0/0/			0/0/0	----Other
	0/0/0	0	3	0	0	0	0	0//0	0/0/			0/0/0	---Other
													-Other machinery, not self-propelled:
	0/0/0	0	0	0	0	0	0	0//0	0/0/			0/0/0	--Tamping or compacting machinery
													--Other:
													---Engineering drills:
4.2	0/0/0	0	0	0	0	0	0	0//0	0/0/			0/0/0	----Boring casing diameter more than 3m
	0/0/0	0	2.4	0	0	0	0	0//0	0/0/			0/0/0	----Other
4.2	0/0/0	0	0	0	0	0	0	0//0	0/0/			0/0/0	---Serapers
	0/0/0	0	0	0	0	0	0	0//0	0/0/			0/0/0	---Other
													Parts suitable for use solely or principally with the machinery of headings No.84. 25 to 84. 30:

税则号列	货品名称〔CIQ 扩展编码及品名－T2 表示见附表 2〕	最惠(%)	暂定税率	普通	增值/消费	出口退税	计量单位	监管条件	检验检疫	特殊证件对美关税
8431.1000	-税目 84.25 所列机械的零件〔999〕	3		30	13/	13	千克			/13
	-税目 84.27 所列机械的零件：									
8431.2010	---装有差速器的驱动桥及其零件，不论是否装有传动部件〔999〕	6		30	13/	13	千克/个			/31
8431.2090	---其他〔999〕	6	3	30	13/	13	千克			/23
	-税目 84.28 所列机械的零件：									
8431.3100	--升降机、倒卸式起重机或自动梯的零件									
8431.3100 01	无障碍升降机的零件〔999〕	3	1	30	13/	13	千克			/21
8431.3100 90	其他升降机、倒卸式起重机零件(包括自动梯零件)〔999〕	3		30	13/	13	千克			/23
8431.3900	--其他〔999〕	5		30	13/	13	千克			/25
	-税目 84.26、84.29 或 84.30 所列机械的零件：									
8431.4100	--戽斗、铲斗、抓斗、及夹斗〔101 其它工程机械及其零件，102 其他装卸桥、提升、起重设备及零件〕	6		17	13/	13	千克/个			/31
8431.4200	--推土机或侧铲推土机用铲〔999〕	6		17	13/	13	千克/个			/26
	--子目 8430.41 或 8430.49 所列钻探或凿井机械的零件：									
8431.4310	---石油或天然气钻探机用〔999〕	4		11	13/	13	千克			/9
8431.4320	---其他钻探机用〔999〕	4		11	13/	13	千克			/14
8431.4390	---其他〔999〕	5		17	13/	13	千克			/30
	--其他：									
8431.4920	---装有差速器的驱动桥及其零件，不论是否装有传动部件〔999〕	5		17	13/	13	千克/个			/30
	---其他：									
8431.4991	----矿用电铲用〔101 其它工程机械及其零件，102 其他装卸桥、提升、起重设备及零件〕	5		17	13/	13	千克			/25
8431.4999	----其他〔101 其它工程机械及其零件，102 其他装卸桥、提升、起重设备及零件〕	5		17	13/	13	千克			/25
84.32	**农业、园艺及林业用整地或耕作机械；草坪及运动场地滚压机：**									
8432.1000	-犁〔999〕	5		30	9/	9	台/千克			/
	-耙、松土机、中耕机、除草机及耕耘机：									
8432.2100	--圆盘耙〔999〕	5		30	9/	9	台/千克			/25
8432.2900	--其他〔101 耕作机，102 其它农牧业机械及其零件〕	4		30	9/	9	台/千克			/24
	-播种机、种植机及移植机：									
	--免耕直接播种机、种植机及移植机：									
	---免耕直接播种机：									
8432.3111	----谷物播种机〔999〕	4		30	9/	9	台/千克			/24
8432.3119	----其他〔999〕	4		30	9/	9	台/千克			/24
	---免耕直接种植机：									
8432.3121	----马铃薯种植机〔999〕	4		30	9/	9	台/千克			/
8432.3129	----其他〔999〕	4		30	9/	9	台/千克			/29
	---免耕直接移植机(栽植机)：									
8432.3131	----水稻插秧机〔999〕	4		30	9/	9	台/千克			3/
8432.3139	----其他〔999〕	4		30	9/	9	台/千克			/29
	--其他：									
	---播种机：									
8432.3911	----谷物播种机〔999〕	4		30	9/	9	台/千克			/24
8432.3919	----其他〔999〕	4		30	9/	9	台/千克			/24
	---种植机：									
8432.3921	----马铃薯种植机〔999〕	4		30	9/	9	台/千克			/
8432.3929	----其他〔999〕	4		30	9/	9	台/千克			/
	---移植机(栽植机)：									
8432.3931	----水稻插秧机〔999〕	4		30	9/	9	台/千克			3/
8432.3939	----其他〔999〕	4		30	9/	9	台/千克			/
	-施肥机：									
8432.4100	--粪肥施肥机〔999〕	4		30	9/	9	台/千克			/14
8432.4200	--化肥施肥机〔999〕	4		30	9/	9	台/千克			/29
	-其他机械：									
8432.8010	---草坪及运动场地滚压机〔999〕	7		40	13/	13	台/千克			/27
8432.8090	---其他〔999〕	4		30	9/	9,13	台/千克			/14
8432.9000	-零件〔999〕	4		17	13/	13	千克			/29
84.33	**收割机、脱粒机，包括草料打包机；割草机；蛋类、水果或其他农产品的清洁、分选、分级机器，但税目 84.37 的机器除外：**									

协定税率 %										特惠税率 %			Article Description
亚太5国	东/冰/格	巴基斯坦	韩国	瑞士	哥达	秘鲁	澳大利亚	新西/坡/智	港/澳/台	亚太2国	老/柬/缅	36/3/1	
	0/0/0	0	0	0	0	0	0	0//0	0/0/			0/0/0	-Of machinery of heading No. 84. 25
													-Of machinery of heading No. 84. 27:
3.9	0/0/0	0	3.6	0	0	0	0	0//0	0/0/			0/0/0	---Drive-axle with differential and parts thereof, whether or not provided transmussion components
3.9	0/0/0	0	3.6	0	0	0	0	0//0	0/0/			0/0/0	---Other
													-Of machinery of heading No. 84. 28:
													--Of lifts, skip hoists or escalators
	0/0/0	0	0	0	0	0	0	0//0	0/0/			0/0/0	Parts of accessibility lifts
	0/0/0	0	0	0	0	0	0	0//0	0/0/			0/0/0	Other lifters, unloading crane parts (including automatic elevator parts)
2.5	0/0/0	0	3	0	0	0	0	0//0	0/0/			0/0/0	--Other
													-Of machinery of headingNo.84. 26, 84. 29 or 84. 30:
3.9	0/0/0	0	2.4	0	0	0	0	0//0	0/0/			0/0/0	--Buckets, shovels, grabs and grips
	0/0/0	0	0	0	0	0	0	0//0	0/0/			0/0/0	--Bulldozer or angledozer blades
													--Parts of boring or sinking machinery of subheading No.8430. 41 or 8430. 49:
2.6	0/0/0	0	0	0	0	0	0	0//0	0/0/			0/0/0	---Of oil and natural gas drilling machinery
2.6	0/0/0	0	0	0	0	0	0	0//0	0/0/			0/0/0	---Of other drilling machinery
3.3	0/0/0	0	2	0	0	0	0	0//0	0/0/			0/0/0	---Other
													--Other
3.3	0/0/0	0	3	0	0	0	0	0//0	0/0/			0/0/0	---Drive-axle with differential and parts thereof, whether or not provided transmussion components
													---Other:
3.3	0/0/0	0	2	0	0	0	0	0//0	0/0/			0/0/0	----For electrical shovels for mining
3.3	0/0/0	0	3	0	0	0	0	0//0	0/0/			0/0/0	----Other
													Agricultural, horticultural or forestry machinery for soil preparation or cultivation; lawn or sports-ground rollers:
	0/0/0	0	2	0	0	0	0	0//0	0/0/			0/0/0	-Ploughs
													-Harrows, scarifiers, cultivators, weeders and hoes:
	0/0/0	0	0	0	0	0	0	0//0	0/0/			0/0/0	--Disc harrows
	0/0/0	0	0	0	0	0	0	0//0	0/0/			0/0/	--Other
													-Seeders, planters and transplanters:
													--No—till direct seeders,planters and transplanters:
													---No—till direct seeders:
2.6	0/0/0	0	0	0	0	0	0	新0//0	0/0/			0/0/	----Seeders for grain
2.6	0/0/0	0	1.6	0	0	0	0	0//0	0/0/			3/1	---Other
													--No—till direct seeders
2.6	0/0/0	0	0	0	0	0	0	0//0	0/0/			0/0/	----Planters for potato
2.6	0/0/0	0	0	0	0	0	0	0//0	0/0/			0/0/	----Other
													--No—till direct transplanters:
2.6	0/0/0	0	0	0	0	0	0	0//0	0/0/			0/0/	---Tansplanters for rice
2.6	0/0/0	0	2.4	0	0	0	0	0//0	0/0/			0/0/	----other
													—Other:
													—Seeders:
2.6	0/0/0	0	0	0	0	0	0	0//0	0/0/			0/0/	—Seeders for grain
2.6	0/0/0	0	1.6	0	0	0	0	0//0	0/0/			0/0/	—other
													—planters:
2.6	0/0/0	0	0	0	0	0	0	0//0	0/0/			0/0/	----Planters for potato
2.6	0/0/0	0	0	0	0	0	0	0//0	0/0/			0/0/	----Other
													—transplanters:
2.6	0/0/0	0	0	0	0	0	0	0//0	0/0/			0/0/	----Tansplanters for rice
2.6	0/0/0	0	2.4	0	0	0	0	0//0	0/0/			0/0/	----Other
													-Manure spreaders and fertilizer distributors
	0/0/0	0	0	0	0	0	0	0//0	0/0/			0/0/	--Manure spreaders
	0/0/0	0	0	0	0	0	0	0//0	0/0/			0/0/	--Fertfllzer dmtrl butors
													-Other machinery:
5.6	0/0/0	4	4.2	0	0	0	0	0//0	0/0/			0/0/	—Lawn or sports-ground rollers
	0/0/0	0	0	0	0	0	0	0//0	0/0/			0/0/	—Other
	0/0/0	0	0	0	0	0	0	0//0	0/0/			0/0/	-Parts
													Harvesting or threshing machinery, including straw or fodder balers; grass or hay mowers; machines for cleaning, sorting or grading eggs, fruit or other agricultural produce, other than machinery of heading No.84. 37:

税则号列		货品名称〔CIQ扩展编码及品名－T2表示见附表2〕	最惠(%)	暂定税率	普通	增值/消费	出口退税	计量单位	监管条件	检验检疫	特殊证件对美关税
		-草坪、公园或运动场地用的割草机：									
8433.1100		--机动的，切割装置在同一水平面上旋转的〔999〕	6		30	9/	9,13	台/千克			/11
8433.1900		--其他〔999〕	6		30	13/	13	台/千克			/11
8433.2000		-其他割草机，包括牵引装置用的刀具杆〔999〕	4		30	9/	9	台/千克			/14
8433.3000		-其他干草切割、翻晒机器〔999〕	5		30	9/	9	台/千克			/25
8433.4000		-草料打包机，包括收集打包机〔999〕	5		30	9/	9	台/千克			/15
		-其他收割机；脱粒机：									
8433.5100		--联合收割机									
8433.5100	01	功率≥160马力的联合收割机〔999〕	8	5	17	9/	9	台/千克			3/25
8433.5100	90	功率<160马力的联合收割机〔999〕	8		17	9/	9	台/千克			3/28
8433.5200		--其他脱粒机〔999〕	8		30	9/	9	台/千克			/
8433.5300		--根茎或块茎收获机									
8433.5300	01	功率≥160马力的土豆、甜菜收获机〔999〕	8	4	30	9/	9	台/千克			3/24
8433.5300	90	其他根茎或块茎收获机〔999〕	8		30	9/	9	台/千克			/28
		--其他：									
8433.5910		---甘蔗收获机									
8433.5910	01	功率≥160马力的甘蔗收获机〔999〕	8	4	30	9/	9	台/千克			3/9
8433.5910	90	其他甘蔗收获机〔999〕	8		30	9/	9	台/千克			/13
8433.5920		---棉花采摘机〔999〕	8	5	30	9/	9	台/千克	A	M	3/10
8433.5990		---其他									
8433.5990	01	自走式青储饲料收获机〔999〕	8	5	30	9/	9	台/千克			3/30
8433.5990	02	茶叶采摘机〔999〕	8	4	30	9/	9	台/千克			/29
8433.5990	90	其他收割机及脱粒机〔101收割机，102脱粒机〕	8		30	9/	9	台/千克			3/33
		-蛋类、水果或其他农产品的清洁、分选、分级机器：									
8433.6010		---蛋类清洁、分级、分选机器〔999〕	5		30	9/	9	台/千克			/
8433.6090		---其他〔999〕	5		30	9/	9,13	台/千克			/25
		-零件：									
8433.9010		---联合收割机用〔999〕	5		11	13/	13	千克			/25
8433.9090		---其他〔999〕	3		17	13/	13	千克			/8
84.34		**挤奶机及乳品加工机器：**									
8434.1000		-挤奶机〔999〕	8		20	9/	9	台/千克			/13
8434.2000		-乳品加工机器〔999〕	6	2	30	13/	13	台/千克	A	R	3/27
8434.9000		-零件〔999〕	5		17	13/	13	千克			/10
84.35		**制酒、制果汁或制类似饮料用的压榨机、轧碎机及类似机器：**									
8435.1000		-机器〔999〕	8		30	13/	13	台/千克	A	R	/28
8435.9000		-零件〔999〕	6		30	13/	13	千克			/26
84.36		**农业、园艺、林业、家禽饲养业或养蜂业用的其他机器，包括装有机械或热力装置的催芽设备；家禽孵卵器及育雏器：**									
8436.1000		-动物饲料配制机〔999〕	7		30	9/	9	台/千克			/27
		-家禽饲养用的机器；家禽孵卵器及育雏器：									
8436.2100		--家禽孵卵器及育雏器〔999〕	5		30	9/	9	台/千克			/15
8436.2900		--其他〔999〕	8		30	9/	9	台/千克			/28
8436.8000		-其他机器									
8436.8000	01	青储饲料切割上料机〔999〕	8	3	30	9/	13,9	台/千克			/8
8436.8000	02	自走式饲料搅拌投喂车〔999〕	8	5	30	9/	13,9	台/千克			/10
8436.8000	90	农、林业、园艺等用的其他机器(包括装有机械或热力装置的催芽设备)〔999〕	8		30	9/	9,13	台/千克			/13
		-零件：									
8436.9100		--家禽饲养用机器的零件或家禽孵卵器及育雏器的零件〔999〕	6		17	13/	13	千克			/16
8436.9900		--其他〔999〕	6		17	13/	13	千克			/16
84.37		**种子、谷物或干豆的清洁、分选或分级机器；谷物磨粉业加工机器或谷物、干豆加工机器，但农业用机器除外：**									
		-种子、谷物或干豆的清洁、分选或分级机器：									
8437.1010		---光学色差颗粒选别机(色选机)〔999〕	8		30	9/	9,13	台/千克			/
8437.1090		---其他〔999〕	8		30	9/	9	台/千克			/13
8437.8000		-其他机器〔999〕	8		30	13/	9	台/千克	A	R	/28
8437.9000		-零件〔999〕	6		30	13/	13	千克			/26

协定税率 %										特惠税率 %			Article Description
亚太5国	东/冰/格	巴基斯坦	韩国	瑞士	哥达	秘鲁	澳大利亚	新西/坡/智	港/澳/台	亚太2国	老/柬/缅	36/3/1	
													-Mowers for lawns, parks or sports grounds:
	0/0/0	0	0	0	0	0	0	0//0	0/0/			0/0/	--Powered, with the cutting device rotating in a horizontal plane
	0/0/0	0	0	0	0	0	0	0//0	0/0/			0/0/	--Other
	0/0/0	0	0	0	0	0	0	0//0	0/0/			0/0/	-Other mowers, including cutter bars for tractor mounting
	0/0/0	0	0	0	0	0	0	0//0	0/0/			0/0/	-Other haymaking machinery
	0/0/0	0	3	0	0	0	0	0//0	0/0/			0/0/	-Straw or fodder balers, including pick-up balers
													-Other harvesting machinery; threshing machinery:
													--Combine harvester-threshers
5.2	0/0/0	4	4.8	0	0	0	0	0//0	0/0/			0/0/	Combine harvester-threshers, power≥160HP
5.2	0/0/0	4	4.8	0	0	0	0	0//0	0/0/			0/0/	Combine harvester-threshers, power<160HP
	0/0/0	4	0	0	0	0	0	0//0	0/0/			0/0/	--Other threshing machinery
													--Root or tuber harvesting machines
	0/0/0	4	3.2	0	0	0	0	0//0	0/0/			0/0/	Potatoes, beets harvesting machines, power ≥160HP
	0/0/0	4	3.2	0	0	0	0	0//0	0/0/			0/0/	Other root or tuber harvesting machines
													--Other:
													---Sugarcane harvesters
5.6	0/0/0	4	0	0	0	0	0	0//0	0/0/			0/0/	Sugarcane harvesting machines, power ≥160HP
5.6	0/0/0	4	0	0	0	0	0	0//0	0/0/			0/0/	Other sugarcane harvesters
5.6	0/0/0	4	0	0	0	0	0	0//0	0/0/			0/0/	---Cotton picker
													---Other
	0/0/0	4	0	0	0	0	0	0//0	0/0/			0/0/	Self-propelled silage harvester
	0/0/0	4	0	0	0	0	0	0//0	0/0/			0/0/	Tea picker
	0/0/0	4	0	0	0	0	0	0//0	0/0/			0/0/	Other harvesers and threshers
													-Machines for cleaning, sorting or grading eggs, fruit or other agricultural produce:
	0/0/0	0	2	0	0	0	0	0//0	0/0/				---Machine for cleaning, Sorting or grading eggs
	0/0/0	0	2	0	0	0	0	0//0	0/0/				---Other
													-Parts:
	0/0/0	0	3	0	0	0	0	0//0	0/0/			0/0/	---Of combine harvester-threshers
	0/0/0	0	0	0	0	0	0	0//0	0/0/			0/0/0	---Other
													Milking machines and dairy machinery:
	0/0/0	4	4	0	0		0	0//0	0/0/			0/0/	-Milking machines
4.2	0/0/0	0	0	0	0	0	0	0//0	0/0/			0/0/	-Dairy machinery
	0/0/0	0	0	0	0	0	0	0//0	0/0/			0/0/	-Parts
													Presses, crushers and similar machinery used in the manufacture of wine, cider, fruit juices or similar beverages:
	0/0/0	4	4	0	0	0	0	0//0	0/0/			0/0/	-Machinery
	0/0/0	0	0	0	0	0	0	0//0	0/0/			0/0/	-Parts
													Other agricultural, horticultural, forestry, poultry-keeping or bee-keeping machinery, including germination plant fitted with mechanical or thermal equipment; poultry incubators and brooders:
	0/0/0	4	4.2	3.6	0	0	0	0//0	0/0/			0/0/	-Machinery for preparing animal feeding stuffs
													-Poultry-keeping machinery; poultry incubators and brooders:
	0/0/0	0	3	0	0	0	0	0//0	0/0/			0/0/	--Poultry incubators and brooders
	0/0/0	4	7	0	0	0	0	0//0	0/0/			0/0/	--Other
													-Other machinery
	0/0/0	4	4	0	0	0	0	0//0	0/0/			0/0/	Silage cutting feeders
	0/0/0	4	4	0	0	0	0	0//0	0/0/			0/0/	self-propelled type feed mixing and feeding vehicle
	0/0/0	4	4	0	0	0	0	0//0	0/0/			0/0/	Other machines for agricultural, horticultural, forestry (lincluding germination equipments fitted with mechanical or thermal equipment)
													-Parts:
	0/0/0	0	3.6	0	0	0	0	0//0	0/0/			0/0/	--Of poultry-keeping machinery or poultry incubators and brooders
	0/0/0	0	2.4	3.1	0	0	0	0//0	0/0/			0/0/	--Other
													Machines for cleaning, sorting or grading seed, grain or dried leguminous vegetables; machinery used in the milling industry or for the working of cereals or dried leguminous vegetables, other than farm-type machi-nery:
													-Machines for cleaning, sorting or grading seed, grain or dried leguminous vegetables:
	0/0/0	4	4	0	0	0	0	0//0	0/0/			0/0/	---Optical color granule sorter(color sorter)
	0/0/0	4	7	0	0	0	0	0//0	0/0/			0/0/	---Other
5.2	0/0/0	4	7	0	0	0	0	0//0	0/0/			3/0/	-Other machinery
	0/0/0	0	2.4	1.8	0	0	0	0//0	0/0/			0/0/	-Parts

税则号列		货品名称〔CIQ扩展编码及品名－T2 表示见附表 2〕	最惠(%)	暂定税率	普通	增值/消费	出口退税	计量单位	监管条件	检验检疫	特殊证件对美关税
84.38		**本章其他税目未列名的食品、饮料工业用的生产或加工机器，但提取、加工动物油脂或植物固定油脂的机器除外：**									
8438.1000		-糕点加工机器及生产通心粉、面条或类似产品的机器									
8438.1000	10	糕点生产线〔999〕	7		30	13/	13	台/千克	A	R	3/27
8438.1000	90	通心粉，面条的生产加工机器(包括类似产品的加工机)〔999〕	7		30	13/	13	台/千克	A	R	/27
8438.2000		-生产糖果、可可粉、巧克力的机器〔999〕	8		30	13/	13	台/千克	A	R	/33
8438.3000		-制糖机器〔999〕	8		30	13/	13	台/千克	A	R	/33
8438.4000		-酿酒机器〔999〕	7		30	13/	13	台/千克	A	R	/32
8438.5000		-肉类或家禽加工机器〔999〕	7		30	13/	13	台/千克	A	R	/27
8438.6000		-水果、坚果或蔬菜加工机器〔999〕	8		30	13/	13	台/千克	A	R	/18
8438.8000		-其他机器〔999〕	8		30	13/	9,13	台/千克	A	R	/28
8438.9000		-零件〔999〕	5		30	13/	13	千克			/25
84.39		**纤维素纸浆、纸及纸板的制造或整理机器：**									
8439.1000		-制造纤维素纸浆的机器〔999〕	8		30	13/	13	台/千克			3/33
8439.2000		-纸或纸板的抄造机器〔999〕	8		30	13/	13	台/千克			3/
8439.3000		-纸或纸板的整理机器〔999〕	8		30	13/	13	台/千克			3/33
		-零件：									
8439.9100		--制造纤维素纸浆的机器用〔999〕	6		30	13/	13	千克			/11
8439.9900		--其他〔999〕	6		30	13/	13	千克			/31
84.40		**书本装订机器，包括锁线订书机：**									
		-机器：									
8440.1010		---锁线装订机〔999〕	10		35	13/	13	台/千克			/35
8440.1020		---胶订机〔999〕	12		35	13/	13	台/千克			3/
8440.1090		---其他〔999〕	12		35	13/	13	台/千克			/37
8440.9000		-零件〔999〕	8		35	13/	13	千克			/33
84.41		**其他制造纸浆制品、纸制品或纸板制品的机器，包括各种切纸机：**									
8441.1000		-切纸机〔999〕	12		50	13/	13	台/千克			/37
8441.2000		-制造包、袋或信封的机器〔999〕	12		30	13/	13	台/千克			/
		-制造箱、盒、管、桶或类似容器的机器，但模制成型机器除外：									
8441.3010		---制造纸塑铝复合罐的生产设备〔999〕	12		30	13/	13	台/千克			/
8441.3090		---其他〔999〕	12		30	13/	13	台/千克			/17
8441.4000		-纸浆、纸或纸板制品模制成型机器〔999〕	12		30	13/	13	台/千克			/37
		-其他机器：									
8441.8010		---制造纸塑铝软包装的生产设备〔999〕	12		30	13/	13	台/千克			/22
8441.8090		---其他〔999〕	12		30	13/	13	台/千克			/37
		-零件：									
8441.9010		---切纸机用									
8441.9010	01	切纸机用弧形辊〔999〕	8	4	50	13/	13	千克			/24
8441.9010	02	切纸机用横切刀单元〔999〕	8	3	50	13/	13	千克			/23
8441.9010	90	其他切纸机零件〔999〕	8		50	13/	13	千克			/28
8441.9090		---其他〔999〕	8		30	13/	13	千克			/28
84.42		**制印刷版(片)、滚筒及其他印刷部件用的机器、器具及设备(税目84.56至84.65的机器除外)；印刷用版(片)、滚筒及其他印刷部件；制成供印刷用(例如，刨平、压纹或抛光)的板(片)、滚筒及石板：**									
		-机器、器具及设备：									
8442.3010		---铸字机〔999〕	0		35	13/	13	台/千克			/20
		---制版机器、器具及设备：									
8442.3021		----计算机直接制版设备									
8442.3021	10	凹版式计算机直接制版设备(CTP)〔999〕	0		35	13/	13	台/千克			/25
8442.3021	90	除凹版式以外的其他计算机直接制版设备(CTP)〔999〕	0		35	13/	13	台/千克			/25
8442.3029		----其他〔999〕	0		35	13/	13	台/千克			/25
8442.3090		---其他〔999〕	0		35	13/	13	台/千克			/25
8442.4000		-上述机器、器具及设备的零件									
8442.4000	10	计算机直接制版机器用零件〔999〕	0		20	13/	13	千克			/25

协定税率 %									特惠税率 %				Article Description
亚太5国	东/冰/格	巴基斯坦	韩国	瑞士	哥达	秘鲁	澳大利亚	新西/坡/智	港/澳/台	亚太2国	老/柬/缅	36/3/1	
													Machinery, not specified or included else-where in this Chapter, for the industrial preparation or manufacture of food or drink, other than machinery for the extraction or preparation of animal or fixed vegetable fats or oils:
													-Bakery machinery and machinery for the manufacture of macaroni, spaghetti or similar products
	0/0/0	4	4.2	2.1	0	0	0	0//0	0/0/			0/0/0	Bakery production lines
	0/0/0	4	4.2	2.1	0	0	0	0//0	0/0/			0/0/0	Machines for producing and processing macaroni and noodles (including processing machine of similar products)
	0/0/0	4	0	0	0	0	0	0//0	0/0/			0/0/0	-Machinery for the manufacture of confectionery, cocoa or chocolate
	0/0/0	4	4		0	0	0	0//0	0/0/			0/0/0	-Machinery for sugar manufacture
	0/0/0	4	2.8	0	0	0	0	0//0	0/0/			0/0/0	-Brewery machinery
	0/0/0	4	2.8	0	0	0	0	0//0	0/0/			0/0/0	-Machinery for the preparation of meat or poultry
	0/0/0	4	4	0	0	0	0	0/0/0	0/0/			0/0/0	-Machinery for the preparation of fruits, nuts or vegetables
5.2	0/0/0	4	0	2.6	0	0	0	0//0	0/0/0			0/0/0	-Other machinery
	0/0/0	0	0	0	0	0	0	0//0	0/0/			0/0/0	-Parts
													Machinery for making pulp of fibrous cellulosic material or for making or finishing paper or paperboard:
	0/0/0	4	3.3	0	0	0	0	0//0	0/0/			0/0/0	-Machinery for making pulp of fibrous cellulosic material
5.6	0/0/0	4	0	2.5	0	0	0	0//0	0/0/0			0/0/0	-Machinery for making paper or paper board
	0/0/0	4	0	0	0	0	0	0//0	0/0/0			0/0/0	-Machinery for finishing paper or paper board
													-Parts:
	0/0/0	0	3.6	0	0	0	0	0//0	0/0/			0/0/0	--Of machinery for making pulp of fibrous cellulosic material
3	0/0/0	0	3.6	1.8	0	0	0	0//0	0/0/			0/0/0	--Other
													Book-binding machinery, including book-sewing machines:
													-Machinery:
7	0/0/0	4	4	0	0	0	0	0//0	0/0/			0/0/	---Sewing bookbinders
	0/0/0	5.4	4.8	0	0	0	0	0/0/0	0/0/			0/0/	---Glueing bookbinders
	0/0/0	5.4	4.8	0	0	0	0	0/0/0	0/0/			0/0/	---Other
	0/0/0	4	0	2.4	0	0	0	0//0	0/0/			0/0/	-Parts
													Other machinery for making up paper pulp, paper or paperboard, including cutting machines of all kinds:
	0/0/0	5.4	4.8		0	0	0	0/0/0	0/0/0			0/0/0	-Cutting machines
7.8	0/0/0	5.4	4.8	3.6	0	0	0	0/0/0	0/0/			0/0/0	-Machines for making bags, sacks or envelopes
													-Machines for making cartons, boxes, cases, tubes, drums or similar containers, other than by moulding:
7.8	0/0/0	6.1	5.4	4.1	0	0	0	0/0/0	0/0/			0/0/	---Machines for paper, plastic and aluminium composite can manufacture
7.8	0/0/0	6.1	9.4	4.1	0	0	0	0/0/0	0/0/			0/0/	---Other
	0/0/0	5.4	8.4	3.6	0	0	0	0/0/0	0/0/			0/0/0	-Machines for moulding articles in paper pulp, paper or paperboard
													-Other machinery:
7.8	0/0/0	5.4	4.8	3.6	0	0	0	0/0/0	0/0/			0/0/0	---Machines for paper plastic and aluminium flexible packaging manufacture
7.8	0/0/0	5.4	4.8	3.6	0	0	0	0/0/0	0/0/0			0/0/0	---Other
													-Parts:
													---Of cutting machines
	0/0/0	4	3.2	0	0	0	0	0//0	0/0/			0/0/0	Bowed roll, of a kind used in paper cutter
	0/0/0	4	3.2	0	0	0	0	0//0	0/0/			0/0/0	Crosscut knife unit, of a kind used in paper cutter
	0/0/0	4	3.2	0	0	0	0	0//0	0/0/			0/0/0	Other parts of paper cutter
	0/0/0	4	0		0	0	0	0//0	0/0/			0/0/0	---Other
													Machinery, apparatus and equipment (other than the machinetools of headings 84.56 to 84.65) for preparing or making platescylinders or other printing components; plates, cylinders andother printing components; plates, cylinders and lithographicstones, prepared for printing purposes (for example, planed, grained or polished):
													-Machinery, apparatus and equipment:
	0//	4						//	0/0/			0/0/0	---Type casters
													---Other machinery, apparatus and equipment for typesetting:
													----Machines for preparing CTP plates
	0//	4						//	0/0/			0/0/0	Concave layout of computer direct plate making equipment(CTP)
	0//	4						//	0/0/			0/0/0	Other computer direct plate making equipment in addition to outside the concaveformat (CTP)
	0//	4	5.4					//	0/0/			0/0/0	----Other
	0//	4	5.4					//	0/0/			0/0/0	---Other
													-Parts of the foregoing machinery, apparatus or equipment
	0//	4						//	0/0/			0/0/0	Computer to plate machine parts

税则号列	货品名称〔CIQ扩展编码及品名—T2表示见附表2〕	最惠(%)	暂定税率	普通	增值/消费	出口退税	计量单位	监管条件	检验检疫	特殊证件对美关税
8442.4000 90	其他铸字、排字、制版机器的零件〔999〕	0		20	13/	13	千克			/25
8442.5000	-印刷用版、滚筒及其他印刷部件;制成供印刷用(例如,刨平、压纹或抛光)的板、滚筒及石板〔999〕	0		35	13/	13	千克			/25
84.43	**用税目84.42的印刷用版(片)、滚筒及其他印刷部件进行印刷的机器;其他打印机、复印机及传真机,不论是否组合式;上述机器的零件及附件:**									
	-用税目84.42的印刷用版(片)、滚筒及其他印刷部件进行印刷的机器:									
8443.1100	--卷取进料式胶印机〔999〕	10		35	13/	13	台/千克			/
8443.1200	--办公室用片取进料式胶印机(片尺寸一边长不超过22cm,另一边长不超过36cm)〔999〕	10		35	13/	13	台/千克			3/
	--其他胶印机:									
	---平张纸进料式:									
8443.1311	----单色机〔999〕	10		35	13/	13	台/千克			/
8443.1312	----双色机〔999〕	10		35	13/	13	台/千克			/
8443.1313	----四色机									
8443.1313 01	四色平张纸胶印机(对开单张单面印刷速度≥17000张/小时)〔999〕	10	7	35	13/	13	台/千克			/
8443.1313 02	四色平张纸胶印机(对开单张双面印刷速度≥13000张/小时)〔999〕	10	7	35	13/	13	台/千克			/
8443.1313 03	四色平张纸胶印机(全张或超全张单张单面印刷速度≥13000张/小时)〔999〕	10	7	35	13/	13	台/千克			/
8443.1313 90	其他四色平张纸胶印机(用税目84.42项下商品进行印刷的机器)〔999〕	10		35	13/	13	台/千克			/
8443.1319	----其他									
8443.1319 01	五色及以上平张纸胶印机(对开单张单面印刷速度≥17000张/小时)〔999〕	10	7	35	13/	13	台/千克			/
8443.1319 02	五色及以上平张纸胶印机(对开单张双面印刷速度≥13000张/小时)〔999〕	10	7	35	13/	13	台/千克			/
8443.1319 03	五色及以上平张纸胶印机(全张或超全张单张单面印刷速度≥13000张/小时)〔999〕	10	7	35	13/	13	台/千克			/
8443.1319 90	其他平张纸进料式胶印机(用税目84.42项下商品进行印刷的机器)〔999〕	10		35	13/	13	台/千克			/
8443.1390	---其他〔999〕	10		35	13/	13	台/千克			/15
8443.1400	--卷取进料式凸版印刷机,但不包括苯胺印刷机〔999〕	10		35	13/	13	台/千克			3/15
8443.1500	--除卷取进料式以外的凸版印刷机,但不包括苯胺印刷机〔999〕	10		35	13/	13	台/千克			3/15
8443.1600	--苯胺印刷机									
8443.1600 01	苯胺印刷机,线速度≥350米/分钟,幅宽≥800毫米(柔性版印刷机,用税目84.42项下商品进行印刷的机器)〔999〕	10	3	35	13/	13	台/千克			3/23
8443.1600 02	机组式柔性版印刷机,线速度≥160m/min,250mm≤幅宽<800mm(具有烫印或全息或丝网印刷功能单元的)〔999〕	10	5	35	13/	13	台/千克			3/25
8443.1600 90	其他苯胺印刷机(柔性版印刷机,用税目84.42项下商品进行印刷的机器)〔999〕	10		35	13/	13	台/千克			3/30
8443.1700	--凹版印刷机									
8443.1700 01	凹版印刷机,印刷速度≥350米/分钟(用税目84.42项下商品进行印刷的机器)〔999〕	10	9	35	13/	13	台/千克			/34
8443.1700 90	其他凹版印刷机(用税目84.42项下商品进行印刷的机器)〔999〕	10		35	13/	13	台/千克			/35
	--其他:									
	---网式印刷机:									
8443.1921	----圆网印刷机									
8443.1921 01	纺织用圆网印花机〔999〕	10	6	35	13/	13	台/千克			/31
8443.1921 90	其他圆网印刷机(用税目84.42项下商品进行印刷的机器)〔999〕	10		35	13/	13	台/千克			/35
8443.1922	----平网印刷机									
8443.1922 01	纺织用平网印花机〔999〕	10	6	35	13/	13	台/千克			/31
8443.1922 10	用于光盘生产的盘面印刷机(用税目84.42项下商品进行印刷的机器)〔999〕	10		35	13/	13	台/千克			/35

协定税率 %										特惠税率 %			Article Description
亚太5国	东/冰/格	巴基斯坦	韩国	瑞士	哥达	秘鲁	澳大利亚	新西/坡/智	港/澳/台	亚太2国	老/柬/缅	36/3/1	
	0//	4						//	0/0/			0/0/0	Other components of typecasting, typesetting and platemaking machines
	0//	4						//	0/0/			0/0/0	-Plates, cylinders and other printing components; plates, cylinders and lithographic stones, prepared for printing purposes (for example, planed, grained or polished)
													Printing machinery used for printing, cylinders and other printing components of heading84. 42;other printers Copying mechines and facsimile machines, whether or not combined; Part and accessories there of:
													-Printing machinery used for printing by means of plates, cylinders and other printing components of heading No.84. 42:
7	0/0/0	4	4	0	0	0	0	0//0	0/0/			0/0/0	--Offset printing machinery reel-fed
	0/0/0	5.4	4.8	3.6	0	0	0	0/0/0	0/0/			0/0/0	--Offset printhg machinery sheet-fed, office type(using sheets with one side not exceeding 22cm and the other side not exceedig 36cm in the unfoldool state)
													--Other offset printing machinery:
													---Sheet fed:
7	0/0/0	4	4	0	0	0	0	0//0	0/0/			0/0/0	----Single color
7	0/0/0	4	4	0	0	0	0	0//0	0/0/			0/0/0	----Double colors
													----Four colors
7	0/0/0	4.5	4	0	0	0	0	0//0	0/0/			0/0/0	Four-color sheet fed offset printing presses(single folio double side printing speed≥17000pcs/hr)
7	0/0/0	4.5	4	0	0	0	0	0//0	0/0/			0/0/0	Four-color sheet fed offset printing press(single folio double sides printing speed≥13000pcs/hr)
7	0/0/0	4.5	4	0	0	0	0	0//0	0/0/			0/0/0	Four-color sheet fed offset printing press(sheetwise or full-sheet one piece single side printing speed≥13000pcs/hr)
7	0/0/0	4.5	4	0	0	0	0	0//0	0/0/			0/0/0	Other four-color sheet fed offset printing press (machines printing with commodities in Duty item 84.42)
													----Other
7	0/0/0	4.5	4	0	0	0	0	0//0	0/0/			0/0/0	Five (or higher)-color sheet fed offset printing press (speed ≥ 16000pcs/hr)
7	0/0/0	4.5	4	0	0	0	0	0//0	0/0/			0/0/0	Five(or higher)-color sheet fed offset printing press(single folio double sides printing speed≥13000pcs/hr)
7	0/0/0	4.5	4	0	0	0	0	0//0	0/0/			0/0/0	Five(or higher)-color sheet fed offset printins press(sheetwise or full-sheet one piece single side printing speed≥13000pcs/hr)
7	0/0/0	4.5	4	0	0	0	0	0//0	0/0/			0/0/0	Other sheet fed offset printing press (machines printing with commodities under heading No. 84. 42)
7	0/0/0	4	4	0	0	0	0	0//0	0/0/			0/0/0	---Other
	0/0/0	5.4		3.6	0	0	0	0/0/0	0/0/			0/0/0	--Letterpress printing machinery, reelfed, excluding flexographic printing
	0/0/0	5.4		3.6	0	0	0	0/0/0	0/0/			0/0/0	--Letterpress printing machinery other than reelfed, excluding flexographic printing
													--Flexographic printing machinery
	0/0/0	4		0	0	0	0	0//0	0/0/			0/0/0	Flexographic pringting machinery, linear speed ≥350m/min, Wide≥800mm flexographic persses, using good in heading No. 84. 42 to printing
	0/0/0	4		0	0	0	0	0//0	0/0/			0/0/0	Flexographic press, unit-Type, linear speed≥160m/min, 250mm≤width<800mm(with function of stamping or holography or screen printing)
	0/0/0	4		0	0	0	0	0//0	0/0/			0/0/0	Other flexographic printing machinery(flexographic press and machines printing with commodities under heading No. 84.42)
													--Gravure printing machinery
6.5	0/0/0	11.5	11.7	5.4	0	0	0	0/0/0	0/0/			0/0/	Gravure printing machinery, linear speed≥350m/min, using goods in heading No. 84. 42 to printing
6.5	0/0/0	11.5	11.7	5.4	0	0	0	0/0/0	0/0/			0/0/	Other gravure printing machinery, using goods in heading No. 84. 42 to printing
													--Other:
													---Screen printing machinery:
													----Cylinder screen press
6.5	0/0/0	4	4	0	0	0	0	0//0	0/0/			0/0/0	Rotary screen printing machines for textile
6.5	0/0/0	4	4	0	0	0	0	0//0	0/0/			0/0/0	Other rotary screen printing machines(printing machinery using the commodities under heading No.84.42)
													----Platen screen press
9	0/0/0	4.5	6	3	0	0	0	0//0	0/0/0			0/0/0	Flat screen printing machines for textile
9	0/0/0	4.5	6	3	0	0	0	0//0	0/0/0			0/0/0	Disk presser for producing compact disks(machines using the commodities under heading No. 84. 42 for printing)

税则号列		货品名称〔CIQ 扩展编码及品名—T2 表示见附表 2〕	最惠(%)	暂定税率	普通	增值/消费	出口退税	计量单位	监管条件	检验检疫	特殊证件对美关税
8443.1922	90	其他平网印刷机(用税目 84.42 项下商品进行印刷的机器)〔999〕	10		35	13/	13	台/千克			/35
8443.1929		----其他〔999〕	10		35	13/	13	台/千克			/
8443.1980		---其他〔999〕	8		35	13/	13	台/千克	O		3/18
		-其他印刷(打印)机、复印机及传真机,不论是否组合式:									
		--具有打印、复印或传真中两种及以上功能的机器,可与自动数据处理设备或网络连接:									
8443.3110		---静电感光式									
8443.3110	10	静电感光式多功能一体加密传真机(可与自动数据处理设备或网络连接)〔101 多功能一体打印机,102 打印机,103 复印机,104 电话机,105 传真机,106 电传打字机〕	3.3/1.7	①	70	13/	13	台/千克	M	L	/28
8443.3110	90	其他静电感光式多功能一体机(可与自动数据处理设备或网络连接)〔101 多功能一体打印机,102 打印机,103 复印机,104 电话机,105 传真机,106 电传打字机〕	3.3/1.7	①	70	13/	13	台/千克		L	/28
8443.3190		---其他								L	
8443.3190	10	其他具有打印和复印两种功能的机器(可与自动数据处理设备或网络连接)〔101 多功能一体打印机,102 打印机,103 复印机,104 电话机,105 传真机,106 电传打字机〕	0		17	13/	13	台/千克	A	L	/25
8443.3190	20	其他多功能一体加密传真机(兼有打印、复印中一种及以上功能的机器)〔101 多功能一体打印机,102 打印机,103 复印机,104 电话机,105 传真机,106 电传打字机〕	0		17	13/	13	台/千克	AM	LM	/25
8443.3190	90	其他具有打印、复印或传真中两种及以上功能的机器(具有打印和复印两种功能的机器除外,可与自动数据处理设备或网络连接)〔101 打印机,102 复印机,103 电话机,104 传真机,105 电传打字机〕	0		17	13/	13	台/千克	A	LM	/25
		--其他,可与自动数据处理设备或网络连接:									
		---专用于税目 84.71 所列设备的打印机:									
8443.3211		----针式打印机〔999〕	0		14	13/	13	台/千克	A	L	/25
8443.3212		----激光打印机〔999〕	0		14	13/	13	台/千克	A	L	/25
8443.3213		----喷墨打印机〔999〕	0		14	13/	13	台/千克	A	L	/25
8443.3214		----热敏打印机〔999〕	0		14	13/	13	台/千克	A	L	/20
8443.3219		----其他〔999〕	0		14	13/	13	台/千克	A	L	/20
		---数字式印刷设备:									
8443.3221		----喷墨印刷机〔999〕	2.7/1.3		30	13/	13	台/千克			/22.7,21.3
8443.3222		----静电照相印刷机(激光印刷机)〔999〕	2.7/1.3		35	13/	13	台/千克			/22.7,21.3
8443.3229		----其他〔999〕	2.7/1.3		30	13/	13	台/千克			/27.7,26.3
8443.3290		---其他									
8443.3290	10	其他加密传真机(可与自动数据处理设备或网络连接)〔999〕	0		17	13/	13	台/千克	AM	LM	/25
8443.3290	90	其他印刷(打印)机、复印机、传真机和电传打字机(可与自动数据处理设备或网络连接)〔101 打印机,102 油印机,103 复印机,104 电话机,105 电传打字机〕	0		17	13/	13	台/千克	A	LM	/25
		--其他:									
		---静电感光复印设备:									
8443.3911		----将原件直接复印的(直接法)〔101 印刷行业成套设备,102 打印机,103 复印机〕	0		70	13/	13	台/千克		L	/
8443.3912		----将原件通过中间体转印的(间接法)〔101 印刷行业成套设备,102 打印机,103 复印机〕	5/3.8		70	13/	13	台/千克		L	/
		---其他感光复印设备:									
8443.3921		----带有光学系统的〔101 印刷行业成套设备,102 打印机,103 复印机〕	0		70	13/	13	台/千克		L	/
8443.3922		----接触式的〔101 印刷行业成套设备,102 打印机,103 复印机〕	11/8.3		70	13/	13	台/千克		L	/
8443.3923		----热敏复印设备〔999〕	11/8.3		70	13/	13	台/千克		L	/21,18.3
8443.3924		----热升华复印设备〔101 印刷行业成套设备,102 打印机,103 复印机〕	11/8.3		70	13/	13	台/千克		L	/
		---数字式印刷设备:									
8443.3931		----喷墨印刷机〔999〕	4/3		30	13/	13	台/千克			/14,13
8443.3932		----静电照相印刷机(激光印刷机)〔999〕	4/3		35	13/	13	台/千克			/

① 1—6 月:3%。

协定税率 %										特惠税率 %			
亚太5国	东/冰/格	巴基斯坦	韩国	瑞士	哥达	秘鲁	澳大利亚	新西/坡/智	港/澳/台	亚太2国	老/柬/缅	36/3/1	Article Description
9	0/0/0	4.5	6	3	0	0	0	0//0	0/0/0			0/0/0	Other platen screen presses(printing machinery using the commodities under heading No. 84. 42)
6.5	0/0/0	4	4	0	0	0	0	0/0/0	0/0/0			0/0/0	----Other
5.2	0/0/0	4	0	0	0	0	0	0//0	0/0/0			0/0/0	---Other
													-Other printers, copying machines and facsimile machines, whether or not combined:
													--Machines which perform two or more of the functions of printing, copying or facsimile transmission, capable of connecting to an automatic data processing machine or to a network:
													---Electrostatic photosensitive-type
	0/0/0	4.5		0	0	0	0	0/0/0	0/0/			0/0/0	Electrostatic-sensitive multifunctional integrated encrypting facsimile machines (capable of connecting to an automatic data processing machine or to a network)
	0/0/0	4.5		0	0	0	0	0/0/0	C/0/			0/0/0	Other electrostatic-sensitive multifunctional integrated machines (capable of cconnecting to an automatic data processing machine or to a network)
													---Other
												0/0/0	Other machines which perform two of the function of printing, copying(capable of connecting to an automatic data processing machine or to a network)
												0/0/0	Other multifunctional integrated encrypting facsimile machines (machines with the function of printing, copying or both)
												0/0/0	Other machines which perform two or more of the function of printing, copying, facsimile transmission(other than machines which perform two of the function of printing, copying, capable of connecting to an automatic data processing machine or to a network)
													--Other, capable of connecting to an automatic data processing machine or to a net work:
													---Printer of a kind solely used in the machines of heading No.84. 71:
												0/0/0	----Stylus printers
												0/0/0	----Laser printers
												0/0/0	----Ink-jet-printers
												0/0/0	----Thermal printers
												0/0/0	----Other
													---Digital printing machines:
	0/0/0	4	3.2	0	0	0	0	0/0/0	0/0/			0/0/0	----Ink-jet printing machines
1.8/0.8	0/0/0	4	4.8	0	0	0	0	0//0	0/0/			0/0/0	----Electrostatic photographic printing machines (laser printing machines)
1.8/0.8	0/0/0	4	3.2	0	0	0	0	0//0	0/0/			0/0/0	----Other
													---Other
												0/0/0	Other encryption facsimile machine (capable commecting to an automatic data processing machine or to a network)
												0/0/0	Other presses(pinters), copying machine, facsimile machine, and teleprinters (capable of connecting to an automatic data processing machine or to a network)
													--Other:
													---Electrostatic photo-copying appcocrtus:
												0/0/0	----Operating by reproducing the original image directly onto the capy(direct process)
	0/0/0	4		0	0	0	0	0/0/0	0/0/			0/0/0	----Operating by reproducing the original image via an intermediate onto the copy (indirect process)
													---Other photocopying apparatus:
												0/0/0	----Incorporoting an optical system
	0/0/0		0	6	0	0	0	0/0/0	0/0/			0/0/	----Of the contact type
	0/0/0		0	6	0	0	0	0/0/0	0/0/			0/0/	----Thermo copying apparatus
	0/0/0		0	6	0	0	0	0/0/0	0/0/			0/0/	----Thermo-sublime copying apparatus
													---Digital printing machines:
	0/0/0	4	0	0	0	0	0	0/0/0	0/0/			0/0/0	----Ink-jet printing machines
2.6/2	0/0/0	4	0	0	0	0	0	0//0	0/0/			0/0/0	----Electrostatic photographic printing machine (Laser printing machines)

税则号列	货品名称〔CIQ 扩展编码及品名－T2 表示见附表 2〕	最惠(%)	暂定税率	普通	增值/消费	出口退税	计量单位	监管条件	检验检疫	特殊证件对美关税
8443.3939	----其他〔999〕	4/3		30	13/	13	台/千克			/24,23
8443.3990	---其他〔999〕	0		30	13/	13	台/千克		L	/25
	-零件及附件：									
	--用税目 84.42 的印刷版、滚筒及其他印刷部件进行印刷的机器零件及附件：									
	---印刷用辅助机器：									
8443.9111	----卷筒料给料机								L	
8443.9111 10	卷筒料自动给料机，给料线速度≥12m/s〔999〕	4/2		35	13/	13	千克/台	O		/9,7
8443.9111 90	其他卷筒料给料机〔999〕	4/2		35	13/	13	千克/台	O		/9,7
8443.9119	----其他〔999〕	4/2		35	13/	13	千克/台	O		/24,22
8443.9190	---其他									
8443.9190 10	胶印机用墨量遥控装置(包括墨色控制装置，墨量调节装置、墨斗体等组成部分)〔999〕	2/1	①	20	13/	13	千克/个	O		/26
8443.9190 90	传统印刷机用零件及附件(胶印机用墨量遥控装置除外)〔999〕	2/1		20	13/	13	千克/个			/27,26
	--其他：									
8443.9910	---数字印刷设备用辅助机器〔999〕	4/2		35	13/	13	千克/台	O		/29,27
	---数字印刷设备的零件：									
8443.9921	----热敏打印头〔999〕	2/1		20	13/	13	千克/个			/27,26
8443.9929	----其他									
8443.9929 10	压电式喷墨头(非用品目 84.42 项下商品进行印刷的机器零件)〔999〕	2/1		20	13/	13	千克			/7,6
8443.9929 90	其他数字印刷设备的零件(非用税目 84.42 项下商品进行印刷的机器零件)〔999〕	2/1		20	13/	13	千克			/7,6
8443.9990	---其他									
8443.9990 10	其他印刷(打印)机、复印机及传真机的感光鼓和含感光鼓的碳粉盒〔999〕	0		35	13/	13	千克			3/25
8443.9990 90	其他印刷(打印)机、复印机及传真机的零件和附件〔999〕	0		35	13/	13	千克			/25
84.44	**化学纺织纤维挤压、拉伸、变形或切割机器：**									
8444.0010	---合成纤维长丝纺丝机〔999〕	8		30	13/	13	台/千克			/
8444.0020	---合成纤维短丝纺丝机〔999〕	8		30	13/	13	台/千克			/
8444.0030	---人造纤维纺丝机〔999〕	8		30	13/	13	台/千克			/
8444.0040	---化学纤维变形机〔999〕	8		30	13/	13	台/千克			/33
8444.0050	---化学纤维切断机〔999〕	8		30	13/	13	台/千克			/33
8444.0090	---其他〔999〕	8		30	13/	13	台/千克			/33
84.45	**纺织纤维的预处理机器；纺纱机、并线机、加捻机及其他生产纺织纱线的机器；摇纱机、络纱机(包括卷纬机)及处理税目 84.46 或 84.47 所列机器用的纺织纱线的机器：**									
	-纺织纤维的预处理机器：									
	--梳理机：									
	---棉纤维型：									
8445.1111	----清梳联合机〔999〕	8		30	13/	13	台/千克			/
8445.1112	----自动抓棉机〔999〕	8		30	13/	13	台/千克			/
8445.1113	----梳棉机〔999〕	8		30	13/	13	台/千克			/
8445.1119	----其他〔999〕	8		30	13/	13	台/千克			/
8445.1120	---毛纤维型〔999〕	8		30	13/	13	台/千克			/28
8445.1190	---其他									
8445.1190 01	宽幅非织造布梳理机(工作幅宽>3.5 米，工作速度>120 米/分钟)〔999〕	8	6	30	13/	13	台/千克			/31
8445.1190 90	其他纺织纤维梳理机〔999〕	8		30	13/	13	台/千克			/33
	--精梳机：									
8445.1210	---棉精梳机〔999〕	8		30	13/	13	台/千克			/
8445.1220	---毛精梳机〔999〕	8		30	13/	13	台/千克			/
8445.1290	---其他〔999〕	8		30	13/	13	台/千克			/
	--拉伸机或粗纱机：									
8445.1310	---拉伸机〔999〕	8		30	13/	13	台/千克			/

① 1—6月：1%。

协定税率 %										特惠税率 %			Article Description
亚太5国	东/冰/格	巴基斯坦	韩国	瑞士	哥达	秘鲁	澳大利亚	新西/坡/智	港/澳/台	亚太2国	老/柬/缅	36/3/1	
2.6/2	0/0/0	4	3.2	0	0	0	0	0/0/0	0/0/			0/0/0	----Other
												0/0/0	---Other
													-Parts and accessories:
													--Parts and accessories of printing machinery used for printing by means of plates, cylinders and other printing components of heading 84.42:
													---Machines for uses ancillary to printing:
													----Roll material feeder
	0/0/0	5.4	4.8	3.6/2	0	0	0	0/0/0	0/0/			0/0/0	Automatic rolling materials feeder, Feeding linear velocity≥12m/s
	0/0/0	5.4	4.8	3.6/2	0	0	0	0/0/0	0/0/			0/0/0	Other roll material feeder
	0/0/0	5.4	4.8	0	0	0	0	0/0/0	0/0/			0/0/0	----Other
													---Other
	0/0/0	0	2.4	1.8/1	0	0	0	0//0	0/0/			0/0/0	Ink remote control device for offset printing machine(including ink ink quantity control device, adjusting device, etc. the ink fountain body part)
	0/0/0	0	2.4	1.8/1	0	0	0	0//0	0/0/			0/0/0	Traditional printing machine with spare parts and accessories (except for offset printing ink quantity remote control device)
													--Other:
3.2/1.6	0/0/0	5.4	4.8	0	0	0	0	0/0/0	0/0/			0/0/0	---Machines for uses ancillary to digital printing machines
													---Parts of digital printing machines:
	0/0/0	0	2.4	0	0	0	0	0//0	0/0/			0/0/0	----Thermal print heads
													----Other
	0/0/0	0	3	0	0	0	0	0//0	0/0/			0/0/0	Piezoelectric ink gun (printing machine parts unlisted under item 84. 42)
	0/0/0	0	3	0	0	0	0	0//0	0/0/			0/0/0	Other parts of digital printing machine(other than parts and accessories of machinery using the commodities under heading No.84. 22 for printing)
													---Other
												0/0/0	Silicon drum? of other presses (printers), copying machines and facsimile machines
												0/0/0	Spare parts and accessories of other presses (printers), copying machines and facsimile machines
													Machines for extruding, drawing, texturing or cutting man-made textile materials:
5.6	0/0/0	4.5	0		0	0	0	0//0	0/0/0			0/0/	---Synthetic filaments spinning jets
5.2	0/0/0	4.5	4	0	0	0	0	0//0	0/0/			0/0/	---Synthetic staple fibres spinning jets
5.2	0/0/0	4.5	4	0	0	0	0	0//0	0/0/			0/0/	---Artificial fibres spinning jets
5.2	0/0/0	4.5	4	3	0	0	0	0//0	0/0/			0/0/	---Man-made filaments crimping machinery
5.2	0/0/0	4.5	4	3	0	0	0	0//0	0/0/			0/0/	---Man-made filaments cutting machinery
5.2	0/0/0	4.5	4	3	0	0	0	0//0	0/0/			0/0/	---Other
													Machines for preparing textile fibres; spinning, doubling or twisting machines and other machinery for producing textile yarns; textile reeling or winding (including weft-winding) machines and machines for preparing textile yarns for use on the machines of headingNo.84. 46 or 84. 47:
													-Machines for preparing textile fibres:
													--Carding machines:
													---For cotton type fibres:
5.2	0/0/0	4	4	0	0	0	0	0//0	0/0/			0/0/0	----Blowing-carding-Machinery
5.2	0/0/0	4	4		0	0	0	0//0	0/0/			0/0/0	----Bale Pucker
5.2	0/0/0	4.5	4	3	0	0	0	0//0	0/0/			0/0/0	----Card or carding Machine
5.2	0/0/0	4	4	0	0	0	0	0//0	0/0/			0/0/0	----Other
5.2	0/0/0	4.5	4	0	0	0	0	0//0	0/0/			0/0/0	---For wool type fibres
													---Other
5.2	0/0/0	4.5		0	0	0	0	0//0	0/0/			0/0/0	Extra-width non-woven cloth carding machine (working width > 3. 5m, working speed >120m/min)
5.2	0/0/0	4.5		0	0	0	0	0//0	0/0/			0/0/0	Other carding machines for textile fibres
													--Combing Machines:
5.6	0/0/0	4	4		0	0	0	0//0	0/0/			0/0/0	---Cotton Comber
5.6	0/0/0	4	4	0	0	0	0	0//0	0/0/			0/0/0	---Worsted Comber
5.6	0/0/0	4	4	0	0	0	0	0//0	0/0/			0/0/0	---Other
													--Drawing or roving machines:
	0/0/0	4	4	0	0	0	0	0//0	0/0/			0/0/0	---Drawing machines

税则号列	货品名称〔CIQ扩展编码及品名—T2表示见附表2〕	最惠(%)	暂定税率	普通	增值/消费	出口退税	计量单位	监管条件	检验检疫	特殊证件对美关税
	---粗纱机：									
8445.1321	----棉纺粗纱机〔999〕	8		30	13/	13	台/千克			/
8445.1322	----毛纺粗纱机〔999〕	8		30	13/	13	台/千克			/
8445.1329	----其他〔999〕	8		30	13/	13	台/千克			/
8445.1900	--其他〔999〕	8		30	13/	13	台/千克			/28
	-纺纱机：									
	---自由端纺纱机：									
8445.2031	----转杯纺纱机									
8445.2031　01	全自动转杯纺纱机〔999〕	8	5	30	13/	13	台/千克			/
8445.2031　90	其他自由端转杯纺纱机〔999〕	8		30	13/	13	台/千克			/
8445.2032	----喷气纺纱机〔999〕	8		30	13/	13	台/千克			/
8445.2039	----其他〔999〕	8		30	13/	13	台/千克			/
	---环锭细纱机：									
8445.2041	----棉细纱机〔999〕	8		40	13/	13	台/千克			/
8445.2042	----毛细纱机〔999〕	8		40	13/	13	台/千克			/
8445.2049	----其他〔999〕	8		40	13/	13	台/千克			/
8445.2090	---其他〔999〕	8		30	13/	13	台/千克			/
8445.3000	-并线机或加捻机〔999〕	8		30	13/	13	台/千克			/33
	-络纱机(包括卷纬机)或摇纱机：									
8445.4010	---自动络筒机〔999〕	8		30	13/	13	台/千克	O		/33
8445.4090	---其他〔101自动络筒机,102卷纬机及遥纱机,103其它纺织机械及其零件〕	8		30	13/	13	台/千克			/33
	-其他：									
8445.9010	---整经机〔999〕	8		30	13/	13	台/千克			/
8445.9020	---浆纱机〔999〕	8		30	13/	13	台/千克			/
8445.9090	---其他〔999〕	8		30	13/	13	台/千克			/
84.46	**织机：**									
8446.1000	-所织织物宽度不超过30厘米的织机〔999〕	8		30	13/	13	台/千克			/33
	-所织织物宽度超过30厘米的梭织机：									
	--动力织机：									
8446.2110	---地毯织机〔999〕	8		35	13/	13	台/千克			/
8446.2190	---其他〔999〕	8		30	13/	13	台/千克			/
8446.2900	--其他〔999〕	8		30	13/	13	台/千克			/
	-所织织物宽度超过30厘米的无梭织机：									
8446.3020	---剑杆织机〔999〕	8		30	13/	13	台/千克			/
8446.3030	---片梭织机〔999〕	8		30	13/	13	台/千克			/
8446.3040	---喷水织机〔999〕	8		30	13/	13	台/千克	O		/
8446.3050	---喷气织机〔999〕	8	3	30	13/	13	台/千克	O		/28
8446.3090	---其他〔999〕	8		30	13/	13	台/千克			/
84.47	**针织机、缝编机及制粗松螺旋花线、网眼薄纱、花边、刺绣品、装饰带、编织带或网的机器及簇绒机：**									
	-圆型针织机：									
8447.1100	--圆筒直径不超过165毫米〔999〕	8		30	13/	13	台/千克			/33
8447.1200	--圆筒直径超过165毫米〔999〕	8		30	13/	13	台/千克			/33
	-平型针织机;缝编机：									
	---经编机：									
8447.2011	----特里科经编机〔999〕	8		30	13/	13	台/千克			/
8447.2012	----拉舍尔经编机〔999〕	8		30	13/	13	台/千克			/
8447.2019	----其他〔999〕	8		30	13/	13	台/千克			/
8447.2020	---平型纬编机〔999〕	8		30	13/	13	台/千克			/33
8447.2030	---缝编机〔999〕	8		30	13/	13	台/千克			/18
	-其他：									
	---簇绒机：									
8447.9011	----地毯织机〔999〕	7		35	13/	13	台/千克			/12
8447.9019	----其他〔999〕	8		30	13/	13	台/千克			/13
8447.9020	---绣花机〔999〕	8		30	13/	13	台/千克			/
8447.9090	---其他〔101采棉机,102清花机,103其它纺织机械及其零件〕	8		30	13/	13	台/千克			/28
84.48	**税目84.44、84.45、84.46或84.47所列机器的辅助机器(例如,多臂机、提花机、自停装置及换梭装置);专用于或主要用于税目84.44、84.45、84.46或84.47所列机器的零件、附件(例如,锭子、锭壳、钢丝针布、梳、喷丝头、梭子、综丝、综框、针织机用针)：**									

协定税率 %										特惠税率 %			
亚太5国	东/冰/格	巴基斯坦	韩国	瑞士	哥达	秘鲁	澳大利亚	新西/坡/智	港/澳/台	亚太2国	老/柬/缅	36/3/1	Article Description
													---Roving machines:
5.6	0/0/0	4	4		0	0	0	0//C	0/0/			0/0/0	----Cotton Roving Frames
5.6	0/0/0	4	4	0	0	0	0	0//C	0/0/			0/0/0	----Worsted Roving Machines
5.6	0/0/0	4	4	0	0	0	0	0//C	0/0/			0/0/0	----Other
5.2	0/0/0	4			0	0	0	0//C	0/0/			0/0/0	--Other
													-Textile spinning machines:
													---Open-end spinner:
													----Rotor spinning machine
5.2	0/0/0	4	4	0	0	0	0	0//0	0/0/			0/0/0	Fully automatic rotor spinning machines
5.2	0/0/0	4	4	0	0	0	0	0//0	0/0/			0/0/0	Other open-end spinner machine
5.6	0/0/0	4	4		0	0	0	0//0	0/0/			0/0/0	----Jet spinner
5.6	0/0/0	4	4	0	0	0	0	0//0	0/0/			0/0/0	----Other
													---Ring spining frames:
7.2	0/0/0	4.5	4.2	3.2	0	0	0	0/0/C	0/0/			0/0/0	----Cotton Ring Spinning Frame
	0/0/0	4	4	0	0	0	0	0//0	0/0/			0/0/0	----Worsted Ring Spinning Frame
	0/0/0	4	4	0	0	0	0	0//0	0/0/			0/0/0	----Other
5.2	0/0/0	4	4		0	0	0	0//0	0/0/			0/0/0	----Other
5.2	0/0/0	4	4	0	0	0	0	0//0	0/0/			0/0/0	-Textile doubling or twisting machines
													-Textile winding (including weft-winding) or reeling machines:
7.2	0/0/0	4.5	7	0	0	0	0	0//0	0/0/			0/0/0	---Automatic bobbin winders
5.2	0/0/0	4	6.5	0	0	0	0	0//0	0/0/			0/0/0	---Other
													-Other:
5.2	0/0/0	4	4		0	0	0	0//0	0/0/			0/0/0	---Warping machines
5.2	0/0/0	4	4		0	0	0	0//0	0/0/			0/0/0	---Sizing machines
5.2	0/0/0	4	6.5	3	0	0	0	0//0	0/0/			0/0/0	---Other
													Weaving machines(looms):
5.2	0/0/0	4	3.2	2.4	0	0	0	0//0	0/0/			0/0/	-For weaving fabrics of a width not exceeding 30cm
													-For weaving fabrics of width exceeding 30cm, shuttle type:
													—Power looms:
5.2	0/0/0	4.5	4.8	3.6	0	0	0	0/0/0	0/0/			0/0/	—-For making carpets or rugs
5.2	0/0/0	4	4		0	0	0	0/0/0	0/0/			0/0/	—-Other
	0/0/0	4	4	0	0	0	0	0//0	0/0/			0/0/	—Other
													-For weaving fabrics of a width exceeding 30cm, shuttleless type:
5.2	0/0/0	4	3.2	2.4	0	0	0	0//0	0/0/			0/0/	---Rapier looms
5.2	0/0/0	4	0		0	0	0	0//0	0/0/			0/0/	---Carrier looms
5.2	0/0/0	4	0	0	0	0	0	0//0	0/0/0			0/0/	---Water jet looms
6.8	0/0/0	4	4.8	0	0	0	0	0//0	0/0/			0/0/	---Air jet looms
5.2	0/0/0	4	0	0	0	0	0	0//0	0/0/			0/0/	---Other
													Knitting machines, stitch-bonding machines and machines for making gimped yarn, tulle lace, embroidery, trimmings, braid or net and machines for tufting:
													-Circular knitting machines:
7	0/0/0	4	0	0	0	0	0	0//0	C/0/0			0/0/0	--With cylinder diameter not exceeding 165mm
	0/0/0	4	0	0	0	0	0	0//0	C/0/0			0/0/0	--With cylinder diameter exceeding 165mm
													-Flat knitting machines; stitch-bonding machines:
													—-Warp knitting machines:
5.2	0/0/0	4	0	0	0	0	0	0//0	0/0/			0/0/0	—--Tricot machines
5.2	0/0/0	4	3.2	0	0	0	0	0//0	0/0/			0/0/0	—--Raschel machines
5.2	0/0/0	4	3.2	0	0	0	0	0//0	0/0/			0/0/0	—--Other
5.2	0/0/0	4	0	2.4	0	0	0	0//0	0/0/0			0/0/0	---Flat weft rnitting machimes
5.2	0/0/0	4	0	0	0	0	0	0//0	0/0/			0/0/0	---Stitch-bonding machines
													-Other:
													---Tufting machines:
4.6	0/0/0	0	0	0	0	0	0	0//0	C/0/			0/0/0	----For making carpets or rugs
5.2	0/0/0	4	0	0	0	0	0	0//0	C/0/			0/0/0	----Other
5.2	0/0/0	4	3.2		0	0	0	0//0	C/0/			0/0/0	---Embroidery machines
4	0/0/0	4	5		0	0	0	0//0	C/0/			0/0/0	---Other
													Auxiliary machinery for use with machines of headingNos. 84. 44, 84. 45, 84. 46 or 84. 47(for example, dobbies, Jacquards, automatic stop motions, shuttle changing mechanisms); parts and accessories suitable for use solely or principally with the machines of this heading or of headingNos.84. 44, 84. 45, 84. 46 or 84. 47(for example, spindles and spindle flyers, card clothing, combs, extruding nipples, shuttles, healds and heald-frames, hosiery needles):

税则号列		货品名称〔CIQ扩展编码及品名－T2表示见附表2〕	最惠(%)	暂定税率	普通	增值/消费	出口退税	计量单位	监管条件	检验检疫	特殊证件对美关税
		-税目84.44、84.45、84.46或84.47所列机器的辅助机器：									
8448.1100		--多臂机或提花机及其所用的卡片缩小、复制、穿孔或汇编机器									
8448.1100	01	多臂机或提花机(转速指标500转/分以上)〔999〕	8	3	20	13/	13	千克			/
8448.1100	90	多臂机或提花机所用卡片缩小、复制、穿孔或汇编机器(包括其所用的卡片缩小、复制、穿孔或汇编机器)〔999〕	8		20	13/	13	千克			/
8448.1900		--其他〔999〕	8		20	13/	13	千克			/33
		-税目84.44所列机器及其辅助机器的零件、附件：									
8448.2020		---喷丝头或喷丝板〔999〕	6		14	13/	13	个/千克			/31
8448.2090		---其他〔999〕	6		17	13/	13	千克			/31
		-税目84.45所列机器及其辅助机器的零件、附件：									
8448.3100		--钢丝针布〔999〕	6		17	13/	13	千克			/31
8448.3200		--纺织纤维预处理机器的零件、附件，但钢丝针布除外〔999〕	6		17	13/	13	千克			/31
		--锭子、锭壳、纺丝环、钢丝圈：									
8448.3310		---络筒锭〔999〕	6		17	13/	13	个/千克			/
8448.3390		---其他〔999〕	6		17	13/	13	千克			/26
		--其他：									
8448.3910		---气流杯〔999〕	6		14	13/	13	个/千克			/
8448.3920		---电子清纱器〔999〕	6	3	17	13/	13	个/千克			/
8448.3930		---空气捻接器〔999〕	6	3	17	13/	13	个/千克			/28
8448.3940		---环锭细纱机紧密纺装置〔101 细纱机，102 其它纺织机械及其零件〕	6		17	13/	13	个/千克			/
8448.3990		---其他〔999〕	6	3	17	13/	13	千克			/28
		-织机及其辅助机器的零件、附件：									
8448.4200		--织机用筘、综丝及综框〔999〕	6		50	13/	13	千克			/31
		--其他：									
8448.4910		---接、投梭箱〔999〕	6		17	13/	13	个/千克			/
8448.4920		---引纬、送经装置〔999〕	6	3	17	13/	13	个/千克			/
8448.4930		---梭子〔999〕	6		50	13/	13	个/千克			/26
8448.4990		---其他〔999〕	6	3	17	13/	13	千克			/28
		-税目84.47所列机器及其辅助机器的零件、附件：									
		--沉降片、织针及其他成圈机件：									
8448.5120		---针织机用28号以下的弹簧针、钩针及复合针〔999〕	6		50	13/	13	千克			/31
8448.5190		---其他〔999〕	6		17	13/	13	千克			/31
8448.5900		--其他〔999〕	6	3	17	13/	13	千克			/28
84.49		**成匹、成形的毡呢或无纺织物制造或整理机器，包括制毡呢帽机器；帽模：**									
8449.0010		---针刺机									
8449.0010	01	高速针刺机，针刺频率＞2000次/分钟〔999〕	8	6	30	13/	13	台/千克			/31
8449.0010	90	其他针刺机〔999〕	8		30	13/	13	台/千克			/33
8449.0020		---水刺设备									
8449.0020	01	高速宽幅水刺设备(工作幅宽＞3.5米，工作速度＞250米/分钟，水刺压力≥400帕)〔999〕	8	6	30	13/	13	台/千克			/
8449.0020	90	其他水刺设备〔999〕	8		30	13/	13	台/千克			/
8449.0090		---其他〔999〕	8		30	13/	13	千克			/28
84.50		**家用型或洗衣房用洗衣机，包括洗涤干燥两用机：**									
		-干衣量不超过10千克的洗衣机：									
		--全自动的：									
8450.1110		---波轮式〔101 洗衣机Ⅰ类器具，102 洗衣机Ⅱ类器具，103 洗衣机Ⅲ类器具，104 洗衣机0Ⅰ类器具，105 洗衣机0类器具〕	7		130	13/	13	台/千克	A	LM	/32
8450.1120		---滚筒式〔101 洗衣机Ⅰ类器具，102 洗衣机Ⅱ类器具，103 洗衣机Ⅲ类器具，104 洗衣机0Ⅰ类器具，105 洗衣机0类器具〕	7		130	13/	13	台/千克	A	LM	/32
8450.1190		---其他〔101 洗衣机Ⅰ类器具，102 洗衣机Ⅱ类器具，103 洗衣机Ⅲ类器具，104 洗衣机0Ⅰ类器具，105 洗衣机0类器具〕	7		130	13/	13	台/千克	A	LM	/32

协定税率 %										特惠税率 %			Article Description
亚太5国	东/冰/格	巴基斯坦	韩国	瑞士	哥达	秘鲁	澳大利亚	新西/坡/智	港/澳/台	亚太2国	老/柬/缅	36/3/1	
													-Auxiliary machinery for machines of heading No. 84. 44, 84. 45, 84. 46 or 84. 47:
													--Dobbies and Jacquards; card reducing, copying, punching or assembling machines for use there with
	0/0/0	4	3.2	0	0	0	0	0//0	0/0/			0/0/0	Dobbies or jacquards (index of revolution speed>500r/min)
	0/0/0	4	3.2	0	0	0	0	0//0	0/0/			0/0/0	Card narrowing ,copying, perforation, or compilation machines used by dobbies or jacquards (including the use of card narrowing, copying, perforation or compilation machines)
	0/0/0	4	3.2	2.4	0	0	0	0//0	0/0/			0/0/0	--Other
													-Parts and accessories of machines of heading No. 84. 44 or of their auxiliary machinery:
	0/0/0	0	2.4	1.8	0	0	0	0//0	0/0/			0/0/0	---Extruding nipples or spinnerets
	0/0/0	0	3.6	1.8	0	0	0	0//0	0/0/			0/0/0	---Other
													-Parts and accessories of machines of headingNo. 84. 45 or of their auxiliary machinery:
	0/0/0	0	2.4	3.2	0	0	0	0//0	0/0/			0/0/0	--Card clothing
	0/0/0	0	3.6	1.8	0	0	0	0//0	0/0/			0/0/0	--Of machines for preparing textile fibres, other than card clothing
													--Spindles, spindle flyers, spinning rings and ring travellers:
4.8	0/0/0	0	0	0	0	0	0	0//0	0/0/			0/0/0	---Winding spindle
	0/0/0	0	2.4	1.8	0	0	0	0//0	0/0/			0/0/0	---Other
													--Other:
4.2	0/0/0	0	0	0	0	0	0	0//0	0/0/			0/0/0	---Open-end rotors
	0/0/0	0	0	3.2	0	0	0	0//0	0/0/			0/0/0	---Electronic yarn clearers
	0/0/0	0	0	0	0	0	0	0//0	0/0/			0/0/0	---Air twisting devices
4.8	0/0/0	0	0	3.1	0	0	0	0//0	0/0/			0/0/0	---Compact set of ring spinning frames
	0/0/0	0	3.6	3.2	0	0	0	0//0	0/0/			0/0/0	---Other
													-Parts and accessories of weaving machines (looms) or of their auxiliary machinery:
	0/0/0	0	3.6	1.8	0	0	0	0//0	0/0/			0/0/0	--Reeds for looms, healds and heald-frames
													--Other:
4.2	0/0/0	0	0	1.8	0	0	0	0//0	0/0/			0/0/0	---Catching and throwing shuttle boxes
	0/0/0	0	2.4	1.8	0	0	0	0//0	0/0/			0/0/0	---Weft insertion and let-off motions
	0/0/0	0	0	0	0	0	0	0//0	0/0/			0/0/0	---Shuttles
	0/0/0	0	3.6	1.8	0	0	0	0//0	0/0/			0/0/0	---Other
													-Parts and accessories of machines of heading No.84. 47 or of their auxiliary machinery:
													--Sinkers, needles and other articles used in forming stitches:
	0/0/0	0	2.4	0	0	0	0	0//0	0/0/			0/0/0	---Barbered needles, crotchet hooks and complex needles for knitting machines, smaler than gauge No. 28
	0/0/0	0	3.6	0	0	0	0	0//0	0/0/			0/0/0	---Other
	0/0/0	4	0	1.8	0	0	0	0//0	0/0/0			0/0/0	--Other
													Machinery for the manufacture or finishing of felt or nonwovens in the piece or in shapes, including machinery for making felt hats; blocks for making hats:
													---Machinery for stitch
	0/0/0	4	3.2	0	0	0	0	0//0	0/0/			0/0/	High-speed needle-punching machines, stroke frequency>2000time/min
	0/0/0	4	3.2	0	0	0	0	0//0	0/0/			0/0/	Other needle-punching machines
													---Spunlaced Equipment
	0/0/0	4	0	0	0	0	0	0//0	0/0/			0/0/	High-speed width spun-laced equipment (working width > 3. 5m, working speed >250m/min, spun-laced pressure ⩾400 Pa)
	0/0/0	4	0	0	0	0	0	0//0	0/0/			0/0/	Other spun-laced equipment
	0/0/0	4	4.8	0	0	0	0	0//0	0/0/			0/0/	---Other
													Household or laundry-type washing machines, including machines which both wash and dry:
													-Machines, each of a dry linen capacity not exceeding 10kg:
													--Fully-automatic machines:
4.6	0/0/0	4	4	0	0	0	0	0/0/0	0/0/			0/0/0	---Of the continuously rotating impeller
4.6	0/0/0	4	6.5	0	0	0	0	0/0/0	0/0/			0/0/0	---Of the drum type
4.6	0/0/0	4		0	0	0	0	0/0/0	0/0/			0/0/0	---Other

税则号列	货品名称〔CIQ扩展编码及品名－T2表示见附表2〕	最惠(%)	暂定税率	普通	增值/消费	出口退税	计量单位	监管条件	检验检疫	特殊证件对美关税
8450.1200	--其他机器，装有离心甩干机〔101 洗衣机 I 类器具，102 洗衣机 II 类器具，103 洗衣机 III 类器具，104 洗衣机 0I 类器具，105 洗衣机 0 类器具〕	7		130	13/	13	台/千克	A	LM	/
8450.1900	--其他〔101 洗衣机 I 类器具，102 洗衣机 II 类器具，103 洗衣机 III 类器具，104 洗衣机 0I 类器具，105 洗衣机 0 类器具〕	7		130	13/	13	台/千克	A	LM	/
	-干衣量超过 10 千克的洗衣机：						台			
	---全自动的：									
8450.2011	----波轮式[T2]	10		80	13/	13	台/千克			/20
8450.2012	----滚筒式[T2]	10		80	13/	13	台/千克			/30
8450.2019	----其他〔101 洗衣机 I 类器具，102 洗衣机 II 类器具，103 洗衣机 III 类器具，104 洗衣机 0I 类器具，105 洗衣机 0 类器具〕	10		80	13/	13	台/千克			/15
8450.2090	---其他〔101 洗衣机 I 类器具，102 洗衣机 II 类器具，103 洗衣机 III 类器具，104 洗衣机 0I 类器具，105 洗衣机 0 类器具〕	10		80	13/	13	台/千克			/30
	-零件：									
8450.9010	---干衣量不超过 10 千克的洗衣机用〔999〕	5		130	13/	13	千克			/30
8450.9090	---其他〔999〕	8	5	80	13/	13	千克			/15
84.51	**纱线、织物及纺织制品的洗涤、清洁、绞拧、干燥、熨烫、挤压、(包括熔压)、漂白、染色、上浆、整理、涂布或浸渍机器(税目 84.50 的机器除外)；列诺伦(亚麻油地毡)及类似铺地制品的布基或其他底布的浆料涂布机器；纺织物的卷绕、退绕、折叠、剪切或剪齿边机器：**									
8451.1000	-干洗机〔101 干洗机 I 类器具，102 干洗机 II 类器具，103 干洗机 III 类器具，104 干洗机 0I 类器具，105 干洗机 0 类器具〕	10		80	13/	13	台/千克			/35
	-干燥机：									
8451.2100	--干衣量不超过 10 千克〔101 干衣机 I 类器具，102 干衣机 II 类器具，103 干衣机 III 类器具，104 干衣机 0I 类器具，105 干衣机 0 类器具〕	8		80	13/	13	台/千克			/33
8451.2900	--其他〔101 干衣机 I 类器具，102 干衣机 II 类器具，103 干衣机 III 类器具，104 干衣机 0I 类器具，105 干衣机 0 类器具〕	8		30	13/	13	台/千克			/18
8451.3000	-熨烫机及挤压机(包括熔压机)[T2]	8		30	13/	13	台/千克			/33
8451.4000	-洗涤、漂白或染色机器〔101 染色机，102 其它印染机械及其零件，103 纺织行业成套设备〕	8		20	13/	13	台/千克			/33
8451.5000	-纺织物的卷绕、退绕、折叠、剪切或剪齿边机器〔999〕	8		20	13/	13	台/千克			/18
8451.8000	-其他机器									
8451.8000 01	服装定型焙烘炉；服装液氨整理机；预缩机；罐蒸机[T2]	8		30	13/	13	台/千克			/28
8451.8000 02	剪绒，洗缩联合机；剪毛联合机；柔软整理机[T2]	8		30	13/	13	台/千克			/28
8451.8000 03	定型机；精练机；丝光机；磨毛机[T2]	8		30	13/	13	台/千克			/28
8451.8000 04	涂层机〔999〕	8		30	13/	13	台/千克			/28
8451.8000 90	税目 84.51 未列名的其他机器[T2]	8		30	13/	13	台/千克			/28
8451.9000	-零件〔101 其它印染机械及其零件，102 纺织行业成套设备，103 其它衣物处理设备及其零件〕	8		20	13/	13	千克			/28
84.52	**缝纫机，但税目 84.40 的锁线订书机除外；缝纫机专用的特制家具、底座及罩盖；缝纫机针：**									
	-家用型缝纫机：									
8452.1010	---多功能型〔999〕	9		80	13/	13	台/千克			/34
	---其他：									
8452.1091	----手动式〔999〕	9		80	13/	13	台/千克			/34
8452.1099	----其他〔101 电动家用缝纫机，102 机械家用缝纫机〕	9		80	13/	13	台/千克			/
	-其他缝纫机：									
	--自动的：									
8452.2110	---平缝机〔101 电动工业用缝纫机，102 机械工业用缝纫机〕	9		40	13/	13	台/千克			/34
8452.2120	---包缝机〔101 电动工业用缝纫机，102 机械工业用缝纫机〕	9		40	13/	13	台/千克			/34
8452.2130	---绷缝机〔101 电动工业用缝纫机，102 机械工业用缝纫机〕	9		40	13/	13	台/千克			/34
8452.2190	---其他〔101 电动工业用缝纫机，102 机械工业用缝纫机，103 其它缝纫机〕	9		40	13/	13	台/千克			/34
8452.2900	--其他〔101 电动工业用缝纫机，102 机械工业用缝纫机，103 其它缝纫机〕	9		40	13/	13	台/千克			/34

协定税率 %										特惠税率 %			
亚太5国	东/冰/格	巴基斯坦	韩国	瑞士	哥达	秘鲁	澳大利亚	新西/坡/智	港/澳/台	亚太2国	老/柬/缅	36/3/1	Article Description
4.6	0/0/0	0		7	0	0	0	0/0/0	0/0/			0/0/	--Other machines, with built-in centrifugal drier
	0/0/0	0		7	0	0	0	0/0/0	0/0/			0/0/	--Other
													-Machines, each of a dry linen capacity exceeding 10kg:
													---Full automatic :
	0/0/0	4		0	0	0	0	0//0	0/0/			0/0/0	----wave-wheel type
	0/0/0	4		0	0	0	0	0//0	0/0/			0/0/0	----Drum-type
	0/0/0	4		0	0	0	0	0//0	0/0/			0/0/0	----Other
	0/0/0	4		0	0	0	0	0//0	0/0/			0/0/0	---Other
													-Parts:
3.3	0/0/0	0	3	0	0	0	0	0//0	0/0/			0/0/0	---Of the machines, each of a dry linen capacity not exceeding 10kg
5.2	0/0/6.4	11.5	6.4	4.8	0	0	0	0/0/0	0/0/			0/0/	---Other
													Machinery (other than machines of headingNo. 84. 50) for washing, cleaning, wringing, drying, ironing, pressing (including fusing presses), bleaching, dyeing, dressing, finishing, coating or impregnating textile yarns, fabrics or made up textile articles and machines for applying the paste to the base fabric or other support used in the manufacture of floor coverings such as linoleum; machines for reeling, unreeling, folding, cutting or pinking textile fabrics:
6.5	0/0/0	14.4	12.6	6.3	0	0	0	0/0/0	0/0/			0/0/	-Dry-cleaning machines
													-Drying machines:
5.2	0/0/0	6.8	6	4.5	0	0	0	0/0/0	0/0/			0/0/	--Each of a dry linen capacity not exceeding 10kg
5.2	0/0/0	4	3.2	0	0	0	0	0//0	0/0/			0/0/0	--Other
5.2	0/0/0	4	3.2	0	0	0	0	0/0/0	0/0/			0/0/0	-Ironing machines and presses (including fusing presses)
5.2	0/0/0	4	0	0	0	0	0	0//0	0/0/0			0/0/0	-Washing, bleaching or dyeing machines
5.2	0/0/0	4	0	0	0	0	0	0//0	0/0/0			0/0/0	-Machines for reeling, unreeling, folding, cutting or pinking textile fabrics
													-Other machinery
7.2	0/0/0	4.5	8.4		0	0	0	0/0/0	0/0/0			0/0/0	Baking furnaces for finalizing the design of clothes; machine with liquid ammonia for finishing clothes; pre-shrinkage machine; tank vapor
7.2	0/0/0	4.5	8.4		0	0	0	0/0/0	0/0/0			0/0/0	Pile shearing and shrinking combine, potting steamer, sheepshearing combination machine, supple finishing machine
7.2	0/0/0	4.5	8.4		0	0	0	0/0/0	0/0/0			0/0/0	Boarding machine; refining machine; mercerizing range; napping grinder
7.2	0/0/0	4.5	8.4		0	0	0	0/0/0	0/0/0			0/0/0	Coating machine
7.2	0/0/0	4.5	8.4		0	0	0	0/0/0	0/0/0			0/0/0	Other machinery of heading No.8451, not elsewhere specified or included
5.2	0/0/0	4	3.2	0	0	0	0	0//0	0/0/			0/0/0	-Parts
													Sewing machines, other than book-sewing machines of heading No. 84. 40; furniture, bases and covers specially designed for sewing machines; sewing machine needles:
													-Sewing machines of household type:
5.9	0/0/0	16.8	12.6	6.3	0	0	0	0/0/0	0/0/			0/0/	---Multifuncitonal
													---Other:
5.9	0/0/0	16.8	12.6	6.3	0	0	0	0/0/0	0/0/			0/0/	----Hand ooperated
5.9	0/0/0	16.8	12.6	6.3	0	0	0	0/0/0	0/0/			0/0/	----Other
													-Other sewing machines:
													--Automatic units:
5.9	0/0/0	4.5	4.8	3.6	0	0	0	0/0/0	0/0/			0/0/0	---Flatseam
5.9	0/0/0	4.5	4.8	3.6	0	0	0	0/0/0	0/0/0			0/0/0	---Overlock machine
5.9	0/0/0	4.5	4.8	3.6	0	0	0	0/0/0	0/0/0			0/0/0	---Interlock machine
5.9	0/0/0	4.5	4.8	3.6	0	0	0	0/0/0	0/0/0			0/0/0	---Other
5.9	0/0/0	4.5	4.8	3.6	0	0	0	0/0/0	0/0/			0/0/0	--Other

税则号列	货品名称〔CIQ 扩展编码及品名—T2 表示见附表 2〕	最惠(%)	暂定税率	普通	增值/消费	出口退税	计量单位	监管条件	检验检疫	特殊证件对美关税
8452.3000	-缝纫机针〔999〕	9		100	13/	13	千克			/34
	-缝纫机专用的特制家具、底座和罩盖及其零件;缝纫机的其他零件:									
	---家用型缝纫机用:									
8452.9011	----旋梭〔999〕	8		80	13/	13	千克			/
8452.9019	----其他〔999〕	8		80	13/	13	千克			/33
	---其他:									
8452.9091	----旋梭〔999〕	8		80	13/	13	千克			/
8452.9092	----缝纫机专用的特制家具、底座和罩盖及其零件〔999〕	8		100	13/	13	千克			/18
8452.9099	----其他〔999〕	8		80	13/	13	千克			/33
84.53	**生皮、皮革的处理、鞣制或加工机器,鞋靴、毛皮及其他皮革制品的制作或修理机器,但缝纫机除外:**									
8453.1000	-生皮、皮革的处理、鞣制或加工机器〔999〕	8		30	13/	13	台/千克			3/33
8453.2000	-鞋靴制作或修理机器〔999〕	8		30	13/	13	台/千克			/33
8453.8000	-其他机器〔999〕	8		30	13/	13	台/千克			/
8453.9000	-零件〔999〕	8		30	13/	13	千克			/33
84.54	**金属冶炼及铸造用的转炉、浇包、锭模及铸造机:**									
8454.1000	-转炉〔999〕	8		35	13/	13	台/千克			/28
	-锭模及浇包:									
8454.2010	---炉外精炼设备									
8454.2010 10	VOD 炉(真空脱气炉)〔999〕	8		35	13/	13	台/千克	O		/28
8454.2010 90	其他炉外精炼设备〔999〕	8		35	13/	13	台/千克	O		/28
8454.2090	---其他〔999〕	8		35	13/	13	台/千克			/33
	-铸造机:									
8454.3010	---冷室压铸机〔999〕	12		35	13/	13	台/千克	O		/
	---钢坯连铸机:									
8454.3021	----方坯连铸机〔999〕	10		35	13/	13	台/千克			/
8454.3022	----板坯连铸机〔999〕	12		35	13/	13	台/千克	O		/
8454.3029	----其他〔999〕	12		35	13/	13	台/千克	O		/
8454.3090	---其他〔999〕	12		35	13/	13	台/千克			3/17
	-零件:									
8454.9010	---炉外精炼设备用〔999〕	8		20	13/	13	千克			/28
	---钢坯连铸机用:									
8454.9021	----结晶器〔999〕	8		20	13/	13	千克			/
8454.9022	----振动装置〔999〕	8		20	13/	13	千克			/
8454.9029	----其他〔999〕	8		20	13/	13	千克			/33
8454.9090	---其他〔999〕	8		20	13/	13	千克			/28
84.55	**金属轧机及其轧辊:**									
	-轧管机:									
8455.1010	---热轧管机〔999〕	12		35	13/	13	台/千克			/
8455.1020	---冷轧管机〔999〕	12		35	13/	13	台/千克	O		/32
8455.1030	---定减径轧管机〔999〕	12		35	13/	13	台/千克	O		/
8455.1090	---其他〔999〕	12		35	13/	13	台/千克	O		/
	-其他轧机:									
	--热轧机或冷热联合轧机:									
8455.2110	---板材热轧机〔999〕	15		35	13/	13	台/千克			/
8455.2120	---型钢轧机〔999〕	15		35	13/	13	台/千克	O		/
8455.2130	---线材轧机〔999〕	15		35	13/	13	台/千克	O		/20
8455.2190	---其他〔999〕	15		35	13/	13	台/千克	O		/
	--冷轧机:									
8455.2210	---板材冷轧机〔999〕	10		35	13/	13	台/千克	O		/30
8455.2290	---其他									
8455.2290 10	铝箔粗轧机〔999〕	15		35	13/	13	台/千克			/35
8455.2290 90	其他金属冷轧机〔999〕	15		35	13/	13	台/千克			/35
8455.3000	-轧机用轧辊〔999〕	8		20	13/	13	个/千克			/18
8455.9000	-其他零件〔999〕	8		20	13/	13	千克			/28
84.56	**用激光、其他光、光子束、超声波、放电、电化学法、电子束、离子束或等离子弧处理各种材料的加工机床;水射流切割机:**									
	-用激光、其他光或光子束处理的:									
8456.1100	--用激光处理的									

协定税率 %										特惠税率 %			
亚太5国	东/冰/格	巴基斯坦	韩国	瑞士	哥达	秘鲁	澳大利亚	新西/坡/智	港/澳/台	亚太2国	老/柬/缅	36/3/1	Article Description
5.9	0/0/0	6.3	5.6	4.2	0	0	0	0/0/0	0/0/			0/0/	-Sewing machine needles
													-Furniture, bases and covers for sewing machines and parts thereof; other parts of sewing machines:
													---Of sewing machines of the household type:
5.2	0/0/0	6.3	5.6	4.2	0	0	0	0/0/0	0/0/			0/0/	----Rotating shuttles
5.2	0/0/0	5.6	5.6	4.2	0	0	0	0/0/0	0/0/			0/0/	----Other
													---Other:
5.6	0/0/0	6.3	5.6	4.2	0	0	0	0/0/0	0/0/			0/0/0	----Rotating shuttles
	0/0/0	10.1	5.6	4.2	0	0	0	0/0/0	0/0/			0/0/	---Furniture, bases and covers for sewing machines and parts thereof
5.2	0/0/0	6.3	5.6	4.2	0	0	0	0/0/0	0/0/0			0/0/0	----Other
													Machinery for preparing, tanning or working hides, skins or leather or for making or repairing footwear or other articles of hides, skins or leather, other than sewing machines:
5.2	0/0/0	4	3.3	0	0	0	0	0//0	0/0/			0/0/	-Machinery for preparing, tanning or working hides, skins or leather
5.2	0/0/0	4	3.3	0	0	0	0	0//0	0/0/			0/0/	-Machinery for making or repairing footwear
	0/0/0	4	3.3	0	0	0	0	0//0	0/0/			0/0/	-Other machinery
	0/0/0	4.5	3.2	0	0	0	0	0//0	0/0/			0/0/	-Parts
													Converters, ladles, ingot moulds and casting machines, of a kind used in metallurgy or in metal foundries:
	0/0/0	4	0	0	0	0	0	0//0	0/0/			0/0/0	-Converters
													-Ingot moulds and ladles:
													---Fining equipments, outside of converters
	0/0/0	4	0	0	0	0	0	0//0	0/0/			0/0/0	VOD furnaces(vacuum degassing furnaces)
	0/0/0	4	0	0	0	0	0	0//0	0/0/			0/0/0	Other secondary refining equipments
	0/0/0	4	3.3		0	0	0	0//0	0/0/			0/0/0	---Other
													-Casting machines:
7.8	0/0/0	5.4	4.8	3.6	0	0	0	0/0/0	0/0/			0/0/0	---Cold chamber die-casting machines
													---Ingot continuous casting machines:
6.5	0/0/0	4	4	3	0	0	0	0//0	0/0/			0/0/0	----Ingot block
7.8	0/0/0	5.4	4.8	3.6	0	0	0	0/0/0	0/0/			0/0/0	----Ingot slab
7.8	0/0/0	5.4	4.8	3.6	0	0	0	0/0/0	0/0/			0/0/0	----Other
7.8	0/0/0	5.4	8.4	3.6	0	0	0	0/0/0	0/0/			0/0/0	---Other
													-Parts:
	0/0/0	4	3.2	0	0	0	0	0//0	0/0/			0/0/0	---For the fining equipments outside of converters
													---For ingot continuous casting machines:
	0/0/0	4	0	0	0	0	0	0//0	0/0/			0/0/0	----Crystallizers
	0/0/0	4	0	0	0	0	0	0//0	0/0/			0/0/0	----Vibrating devices
	0/0/0	4	3.2	2.4	0	0	0	0//0	0/0/			0/0/0	----Other
	0/0/0	4	0	2.4	0	0	0	0//0	0/0/			0/0/0	---Other
													Metal-rolling mills and rolls therefof:
													-Tube mills:
7.8	0/0/0	4.5	4.8	3.6	0	0	0	0/0/0	0/0/			0/0/0	---Tube mills, for hot-rolled
7.8	0/0/0	4.5	4.8	3.6	0	0	0	0/0/0	0/0/			0/0/0	---Tube mills for cold-rolled
7.8	0/0/0	4.5	4.8	3.6	0	0	0	0/0/0	0/0/			0/0/0	---Fixed and reduced tube mills
7.8	0/0/0	4.5	4.8	3.6	0	0	0	0/0/0	0/0/			0/0/0	---Other
													-Other rolling mills:
													--Hot or combination hot and cold:
9.8	0/0/0	6.8	6	4.5	0	0	0	0/0/0	0/0/			0/0/	---Sheet mills, hot-rolled
9.8	0/0/0	6.8	6	4.5	0	0	0	0/0/0	0/0/			0/0/	---Rolled-steel section mills
9.8	0/0/0	6.8	6	4.5	0	0	0	0/0/0	0/0/			0/0/	---Wire mills
10.5	0/0/0	6.8	6	4.5	0	0	0	0/0/0	0/0/			0/0/	---Other
													--Cold mills:
	0/0/0	4	4	0	0	0	0	0//0	0/0/			0/0/	---Sheet mills
													---Other
	0/0/0	10.8	6	4.5	0	0	0	0/0/0	0/0/			0/0/	Aluminium foil roughing mills
	0/0/0	10.8	6	4.5	0	0	0	0/0/0	0/0/			0/0/	Other cold rolling mills of metal
	0/0/0	4	0	0	0	0	0	0//0	0/0/			0/0/0	-Rolls for rolling mills
4	0/0/0	0	0	0	0	0	0	0//0	0/0/			0/0/0	-Other parts
													Machine-tools for working any material by removal of material, by laser or other light or photon beam, ultrasonic, electro-discharge, electro-chemical, electron beam, ionic-beam or plasma arc processes; water-jet cutting machines
													-Operated by laser or other light or photon beam processes
													--Operated by laser processes

税则号列	货品名称〔CIQ扩展编码及品名－T2表示见附表2〕	最惠(%)	暂定税率	普通	增值/消费	出口退税	计量单位	监管条件	检验检疫	特殊证件对美关税
8456.1100 10	辐照元件激光切割机(切割燃料包壳以使辐照核材料能溶解,含遥控设备)〔999〕	0		30	13/	13	台/千克	3A	M	/25
8456.1100 90	其他用激光处理的机床〔999〕	0		30	13/	13	台/千克	A	M	/25
8456.1200	--用其他光或光子束处理的〔999〕	0		30	13/	13	台/千克	A	M	/
8456.2000	-用超声波处理的〔999〕	10		30	13/	13	台/千克	A	M	/35
	-用放电处理的:									
8456.3010	---数控的									
8456.3010 10	数控放电加工机床(2轴或多轴成形控制的无线型放电加工机床)〔999〕	9		30	13/	13	台/千克	3AO	M	/34
8456.3010 90	其他数控的放电处理加工机床〔999〕	9		30	13/	13	台/千克	AO	M	/34
8456.3090	---其他									
8456.3090 10	非数控放电加工机床(2轴或多轴成形控制的无线型放电加工机床)〔999〕	10		30	13/	13	台/千克	3A	M	/20
8456.3090 90	-其他非数控的放电处理加工机床〔999〕	10		30	13/	13	台/千克	A	M	/20
	-用等离子弧处理的:									
8456.4010	---等离子切割机〔999〕	0		30	13/	13	台/千克	A	LM	/5
8456.4090	---其他〔999〕	0		30	13/	13	台/千克	A	M	/
8456.5000	-水射流切割机〔999〕	0		30	13/	13	台/千克	A	M	/5
8456.9000	-其他[T2]	0		30	13/	13	台/千克	A	M	/20
84.57	**加工金属的加工中心、单工位组合机床及多工位组合机床:**									
	-加工中心:									
8457.1010	---立式〔999〕	9		20	13/	13	台/千克	AO	M	/34
8457.1020	---卧式〔999〕	9		20	13/	13	台/千克	AO	M	/34
8457.1030	---龙门式〔999〕	9		20	13/	13	台/千克	AO	M	/34
	---其他:									
8457.1091	----铣车复合〔999〕	9		20	13/	13	台/千克	AO	M	/34
8457.1099	----其他〔999〕	9		20	13/	13	台/千克	AO	M	/
8457.2000	-单工位组合机床〔999〕	8		20	13/	13	台/千克	OA	M	/33
8457.3000	-多工位组合机床〔999〕	5		20	13/	13	台/千克	OA	M	/30
84.58	**切削金属的车床(包括车削中心):**									
	-卧式车床:									
8458.1100	--数控的									
8458.1100 10	两用物项管制的切削金属的卧式数控车床(包括车削中心)〔999〕	9		20	13/	13	台/千克	3O		/34
8458.1100 90	其他切削金属的卧式数控车床(包括车削中心)〔999〕	9		20	13/	13	台/千克	AO	M	/34
8458.1900	--其他〔999〕	9		50	13/	13	台/千克	A	M	/29
	-其他车床:									
	--数控的:									
8458.9110	---立式									
8458.9110 10	两用物项管制的切削金属立式数控车床(包括车削中心)〔999〕	5		20	13/	13	台/千克	3O		/30
8458.9110 90	其他切削金属的立式数控车床(包括车削中心)〔999〕	5		20	13/	13	台/千克	AO	M	/30
8458.9120	---其他									
8458.9120 10	其他两用物项管制的切削金属数控车床(包括车削中心)〔999〕	5		20	13/	13	台/千克	3O		/30
8458.9120 90	其他切削金属的数控车床(包括车削中心)〔999〕	5		20	13/	13	台/千克	AO	M	/30
8458.9900	--其他〔999〕	9		50	13/	13	台/千克	A	M	/34
84.59	**切削金属的钻床、镗床、铣床、攻丝机床(包括直线移动式动力头机床),但税目84.58的车床(包括车削中心)除外:**									
8459.1000	-直线移动式动力头机床〔999〕	9		50	13/	13	台/千克	A	M	/19
	-其他钻床:									
8459.2100	--数控的〔999〕	9		20	13/	13	台/千克	AO	M	/34
8459.2900	--其他〔999〕	9		50	13/	13	台/千克	A	M	/34
	-其他镗铣机床:									
8459.3100	--数控的〔999〕	9		20	13/	13	台/千克	OA	M	/
8459.3900	--其他〔999〕	9		50	13/	13	台/千克	A	M	/
	-其他镗床:									
8459.4100	--数控的〔999〕	9		20	13/	13	台/千克	OA	M	/34
8459.4900	--其他〔999〕	9		50	13/	13	台/千克	A	M	/34
	-升降台式铣床:									
8459.5100	--数控的〔999〕	9		20	13/	13	台/千克	OA	M	/

协定税率 %										特惠税率 %			
亚太5国	东/冰/格	巴基斯坦	韩国	瑞士	哥达	秘鲁	澳大利亚	新西/坡/智	港/澳/台	亚太2国	老/柬/缅	36/3/1	Article Description
												0/0/0	Irradiated-component laser cutting machines (cutting the fuel claddings to make the irradiated nuclear materials to melt down, with a remote control)
												0/0/0	Other laser processing machine tools
												0/0/0	--Operated by other light or photon beam processes
	0/0/4	4			0	0	0	0/0/0	0/0/			0/0/	-Operated by ultrasonic processes
													-Operated by electro-discharge processes:
													---Numerically controlled
	0/0/	4			0	0	0	0//0	0/0/			0/0/	CNC EDM machne tools (wireless-type EDM machine tools controlled by 2-axis or multi-axis contours)
	0/0/	4			0	0	0	0//0	0/0/			0/0/	Other CNC processing machine tools
													---Other
	0/0/4	4		0	0	0	0	0/0/0	0/0/			0/0/	Non-CNC EDM machine tools (wireless-type EDM machine tools controlled by 2-axis or multi-axis contours)
	0/0/4	4		0	0	0	0	0/0/0	0/0/			0/0/	-Other non-CNC EDM machine Tools
													-Operated by plasma arc processes:
												0/0/0	---Cutting machines of plasmaarc
												0/0/0	---Other
												0/0/0	-Water-jet cutting machines
												0/0/0	-Other
													Machining centres, unit construction machines (single station) and multi-station transfer machines, for working metal:
													-Machining centres:
6.3	0/0/	4	6.7		0	0	0	0//0	0/0/			0/0/	---Vertical
6.3	0/0/	4	6.7		0	0	0	0//0	0/0/			0/0/	---Horizontal
6.3	0/0/	4	6.7	0	0	0	0	0//0	0/0/			0/0/	---Plano
													---Other:
6.3	0/0/	4	6.7		0	0	0	0//0	0/0/			0/0/	----Milling and turning composite
6.3	0/0/	4	6.7		0	0	0	0//0	0/0/			0/0/	----Other
	0/0/	4	5.6	0	0	0	0	0//0	0/0/			0/0/	-Unit construction machines (single station)
	0/0/	0			0	0	0	0//0	0/0/			0/0/	-Multi-station transfer machines
													Lathes (including turning centres) for removing metal:
													-Horizontal lathes:
													—Numerically controlled
	0/0/3.9	4		5	0	0	0	0//0	0/0/0			0/0/0	Lathes for removing metal, fual-use items control, horizontal lathes, numerically controlled(including turning centres)
	0/0/3.9	4		5	0	0	0	0//0	0/0/0			0/0/0	Other lathes for removing metal, horizontal lathes, numerically controlled(including turning centres)
	0/0/4.8	5.4	8.4	3.6	0	0	0	0/0/0	0/0/			0/0/0	--Other
													-Other lathes:
													--Numerically controlled:
													---Vertical
	0/0/0	0		0	0	0	0	0//0	0/0/0			0/0/0	Lathes for removing metal, fual-use items control, vertical, numerically controlled(including turning centres)
	0/0/0	0		0	0	0	0	0//0	0/0/0			0/0/0	Lathes for removing metal, numerically controlled(including turning centres)
													—Other
	0/0/0	0		0	0	0	0	0//0	0/0/0			0/0/0	Other lathes for removing metal, fual-use items control, (including turning centres)
	0/0/0	0		0	0	0	0	0//0	0/0/0			0/0/0	Other lathes for removing metal(including turning centres)
	0/0/4.8	5.4	8.4	3.6	0	0	0	0/0/0	0/0/			0/0/0	--Other
													Machine-tools (including way-type unit head machines) for drilling, boring, milling, threading or tapping by removing metal, other than lathes (including turning centres) of heading No.84.58:
	0/0/6	10.8	10.5	4.5	0	0	0	0/0/0	0/0/			0/0/	-Way-type unit head machines
													-Other drilling machines:
	0/0/3.9	4		0	0	0	0	0//0	0/0/0			0/0/0	--Numerically controlled
	0/0/6	10.8	10.5	4.5	0	0	0	0/0/0	0/0/			0/0/	--Other
													-Other boring-milling machines:
	0/0/	4		2.9	0	0	0	0//0	0/0/			0/0/0	--Numerically controlled
	0/0/	4		0	0	0	0	0//0	0/0/			0/0/0	--Other
													-Other boring machines:
	0/0/	4		0	0	0	0	0//0	0/0/			0/0/0	--Numerically xontrolled
	0/0/6	10.8		4.5	0	0	0	0/0/0	0/0/			0/0/	-- Other
													-Milling machines, knee-type:
	0/0/	4			0	0	0	0//0	0/0/			0/0/0	--Numerically controlled

税则号列	货品名称〔CIQ 扩展编码及品名—T2 表示见附表 2〕	最惠(%)	暂定税率	普通	增值/消费	出口退税	计量单位	监管条件	检验检疫	特殊证件对美关税
8459.5900	--其他〔999〕	9		50	13/	13	台/千克	A	M	/19
	-其他铣床：									
	--数控的：									
8459.6110	---龙门铣床〔999〕	5		20	13/	13	台/千克	OA	M	/
8459.6190	---其他〔999〕	5		20	13/	13	台/千克	OA	M	/30
	--其他：									
8459.6910	---龙门铣床〔999〕	9		50	13/	13	台/千克	A	M	/
8459.6990	---其他〔999〕	9		50	13/	13	台/千克	A	M	/29
8459.7000	-其他攻丝机床〔999〕	9		50	13/	13	台/千克	A	M	/29
84.60	**用磨石、磨料或抛光材料对金属或金属陶瓷进行去毛刺、刃磨、磨削、珩磨、研磨、抛光或其他精加工的机床，但税目 84.61 的切齿机、齿轮磨床或齿轮精加工机床除外：**									
	-平面磨床：									
	--数控的：									
8460.1210	---在任一坐标的定位精度至少是 0.01 毫米〔999〕	9		20	13/	13	台/千克	OA	M	/34
8460.1290	---其他〔999〕	9		50	13/	13	台/千克			/
	--其他：									
8460.1910	---在任一坐标的定位精度至少是 0.01 毫米〔999〕	9		50	13/	13	台/千克			/34
8460.1990	---其他〔999〕	9		50	13/	13	台/千克	A	M	/19
	-其他磨床：									
	--数控无心磨床：									
8460.2210	---在任一坐标的定位精度至少是 0.01 毫米〔999〕	9		20	13/	13	台/千克	OA	M	/34
8460.2290	---其他〔999〕	9		50	13/	13	台/千克	A	M	/19
	--数控外圆磨床：									
	---在任一坐标的定位精度至少是 0.01 毫米：									
8460.2311	----曲轴磨床〔999〕	9		20	13/	13	台/千克	OA	M	/34
8460.2319	----其他〔999〕	9		20	13/	13	台/千克	OA	M	/34
8460.2390	---其他〔999〕	9		50	13/	13	台/千克	A	M	/
	--其他，数控的：									
	---在任一坐标的定位精度至少是 0.01 毫米：									
8460.2411	----内圆磨床〔999〕	9		20	13/	13	台/千克	OA	M	/34
8460.2419	----其他〔999〕	9		20	13/	13	台/千克	OA	M	/34
8460.2490	---其他〔999〕	9		50	13/	13	台/千克	A	M	/
	--其他：									
	---在任一坐标的定位精度至少是 0.01 毫米：									
8460.2911	----外圆磨床〔999〕	12		50	13/	13	台/千克	A	M	/
8460.2912	----内圆磨床〔999〕	9		50	13/	13	台/千克	A	M	/
8460.2913	----轧辊磨床〔999〕	9		50	13/	13	台/千克			/19
8460.2919	----其他〔999〕	12		50	13/	13	台/千克	A	M	/
8460.2990	---其他〔999〕	9		50	13/	13	台/千克	A	M	/
	-刃磨(工具或刀具)机床：									
8460.3100	--数控的〔999〕	9		20	13/	13	台/千克	A	M	/34
8460.3900	--其他〔999〕	12		50	13/	13	台/千克	A	M	/37
	-珩磨或研磨机床：									
8460.4010	---珩磨〔999〕	12		50	13/	13	台/千克	A	M	/22
8460.4020	---研磨〔999〕	12		50	13/	13	台/千克	A	M	/37
	-其他：									
8460.9010	---砂轮机〔101 磨床，102 砂磨工具〕	12		50	13/	13	台/千克			/37
8460.9020	---抛光机床〔999〕	12		50	13/	13	台/千克	A	M	/22
8460.9090	---其他〔999〕	12		50	13/	13	台/千克	A	M	/37
84.61	**切削金属或金属陶瓷的刨床、牛头刨床、插床、拉床、切齿机、齿轮磨床或齿轮精加工机床、锯床、切断机及其他税目未列名的切削机床：**									
	-牛头刨床或插床：									
8461.2010	---牛头刨床〔999〕	12		50	13/	13	台/千克			/
8461.2020	---插床〔999〕	12		50	13/	13	台/千克			/
8461.3000	-拉床〔999〕	12		50	13/	13	台/千克			/37
	-切齿机、齿轮磨床或齿轮精加工机床：									

协定税率 %										特惠税率 %			
亚太5国	东/冰/格	巴基斯坦	韩国	瑞士	哥达	秘鲁	澳大利亚	新西/坡/智	港/澳/台	亚太2国	老/柬/缅	36/3/1	Article Description
	0/0/6	10.8		4.5	0	0	0	0/0/0	0/0/			0/0/	--Other
													-Other milling machines:
													--Numerically controlled:
	0/0/	0		0	0	0	0	0//0	0/0/			0/0/0	---Planomilling machines
	0/0/	0		0	0	0	0	0//0	0/0/			0/0/0	---Other
													--Other:
7.5	0/0/4.8	4.5		3.6	0	0	0	0/0/0	0/0/			0/0/0	---Planomilling machines
8.3	0/0/4.8	5.4	11	3.6	0	0	0	0/0/0	0/0/			0/0/0	---Other
	0/0/4.8	5.4			0	0	0	0/0/0	0/0/			0/0/0	-Other threading or tapping machines
													Machine-tools for deburring, sharpening, grinding, honing, lapping, polishing or otherwise finishing metal or cermets by means of grinding stones, abrasives or polishing products, other than gear cutting, gear grinding or gear finishing machines of heading No.84. 61:
													-Flat-surface grinding machines:
													--Numerically controlled:
	0/0/	4		0	0	0	0	0//0	0/0/0			0/0/0	--The positioning in any one axis can be set up to an accuracy of at least 0.01mm
	0/0/6	10.8	10.5	4.5	0	0	0	0/0/0	0/0/			0/0/	---Other
													--Other
	0/0/6	10.8		4.5	0	0	0	0/0/0	0/0/			0/0/	--The positioning in anY 0ne axis can be set up to an accuracy of at least 0.01mm
	0/0/6	10.8	10.5	4.5	0	0	0	0/0/0	0/0/			0/0/	---Other
													-Other grinding machines:
													--Centreless grinding machines, numerically controlled:
	0/0/	4		5	0	0	0	0//0	0/0/			0/0/0	--The positioning in any one axis can be set up to an accuracy of at least 0.01mm:
	0/0/6	10.8	10.5	4.5	0	0	0	0/0/0	0/0/			0/0/	---Other
													--Other cylindrical grinding Inachines, numerically controlled:
													---The Positioning in any one axis can be set up to an accuracy of at least 0.01mm:
	0/0/	4			0	0	0	0//0	0/0/			0/0/0	---Crank shaft grinding machines
	0/0/	4			0	0	0	0//0	0/0/			0/0/0	----Other
	0/0/6	10.8	10.5	4.5	0	0	0	0/0/0	0/0/			0/0/	---Other
													--Other, numerically controlled:
													---The posltlomng in any one axis can be set up to an accuracy of at least 0.01mm:
	0/0/	4			0	0	0	0//0	0/0/			0/0/0	---Internal grinding machines
	0/0/	4		5	0	0	0	0//0	0/0/			0/0/0	----Other
	0/0/6	10.8	10.5	4.5	0	0	0	0/0/0	0/0/			0/0/	---Other
													--Other:
													--The posmomng in anY 0ne axis can be set up to an accuracy of at least 0.01mm:
	0/0/	10.8		4.5	0	0	0	0/0/0	0/0/			0/0/	----Cylindrical grinding mflchines
	0/0/	10.8		4.5	0	0	0	0/0/0	0/0/			0/0/	----Internal grinding machrues
	0/0/5.2	5.9		3.9	0	0	0	0/0/0	0/0/			0/0/	----Grinding machines of roll
	0/0/	5.9			0	0	0	0/0/0	0/0/			0/0/	----Other
	0/0/	5.9	10.5		0	0	0	0/0/0	0/0/			0/0/	---Other
													-Sharpening (tool or cutter grinding) machines:
	0/0/	4			0	0	0	0//0	0/0/			0/0/0	--Numerically controlled
	0/0/6	10.8			0	0	0	0/0/0	0/0/			0/0/	--Other
													-Honing or lapping machines:
	0/0/5.2	5.9		3.9	0	0	0	0/0/0	0/0/			0/0/	---Honing
	0/0/0	5.9		3.9	0	0	0	0/0/0	0/0/0			0/0/	---Lapping
													-Other:
	0/0/0	10.8	6	4.5	0	0	0	0/0/0	0/0/0			0/0/	---Grinding wheel machines
	0/0/0	10.8	0	4.5	0	0	0	0/0/0	0/0/0			0/0/	---Polishing machines
	0/0/6	10.8	10.5	4.5	0	0	0	0/0/0	0/0/			0/0/	---Other
													Machine-tools for planing, shaping, slotting, broaching, gear cutting, gear grinding or gear finishing, sawing, cutting-off and other machine-tools working by removing metal or cermets, not elsewhere specified or included:
													-Shaping or slotting machines:
	0/0/0	10.8	6	4.5	0	0	0	0/0/0	0/0/			0/0/	---Shaping machines
	0/0/0	10.8	6	4.5	0	0	0	0/0/0	0/0/0			0/0/	---Slotting machines
	0/0/0	5.4	4.8	3.6	0	0	0	0/0/0	0/0/0			0/0/	-Broaching machines
													-Gear cutting, gear grinding or gear finishing machines:

税则号列	货品名称〔CIQ 扩展编码及品名－T2 表示见附表 2〕	最惠(%)	暂定税率	普通	增值/消费	出口退税	计量单位	监管条件	检验检疫	特殊证件对美关税
	---数控的：									
8461.4011	----齿轮磨床〔999〕	9		20	13/	13	台/千克	OA	M	/34
8461.4019	----其他〔999〕	9		20	13/	13	台/千克	OA	M	/34
8461.4090	---其他〔999〕	9		50	13/	13	台/千克	A	M	/34
8461.5000	-锯床或切断机									
8461.5000 10	辐照元件刀具切割机［切割燃料包壳以使辐照核材料能溶解(含遥控设备)］〔999〕	12		50	13/	13	台/千克	3		/37
8461.5000 90	其他锯床或切断机〔999〕	12		50	13/	13	台/千克			/37
	-其他：									
	--刨床：									
8461.9011	---龙门刨床〔999〕	12		50	13/	13	台/千克			/
8461.9019	---其他〔999〕	12		50	13/	13	台/千克			/
8461.9090	---其他〔999〕	12		50	13/	13	台/千克			/37
84.62	**加工金属的锻造(包括模锻)或冲压机床;加工金属的弯曲、折叠、矫直、矫平、剪切、冲孔或开槽机床;其他加工金属或硬质合金的压力机：**									
	-锻造(包括模锻)或冲压机床及锻锤：									
8462.1010	---数控的〔101 锻造机床,102 冲压机床〕	9		20	13/	13	台/千克			/34
8462.1090	---其他〔101 锻造机床,102 冲压机床〕	9		50	13/	13	台/千克			/34
	-弯曲、折叠、矫直或矫平机床：									
	--数控的：									
8462.2110	---矫直机〔999〕	9		20	13/	13	台/千克			/34
8462.2190	---其他〔101 折叠机,102 矫直机或矫平机,103 折弯机〕	9		20	13/	13	台/千克			/34
	--其他：									
8462.2910	---矫直机〔999〕	9		50	13/	13	台/千克			/29
8462.2990	---其他〔101 折叠机,102 矫直机或矫平机,103 折弯机〕	9		50	13/	13	台/千克			/34
	-剪切机床,但冲剪两用机除外：									
	--数控的：									
8462.3110	---板带纵剪机〔999〕	7		20	13/	13	台/千克			/
8462.3120	---板带横剪机〔999〕	7		20	13/	13	台/千克			/
8462.3190	---其他〔999〕	7		20	13/	13	台/千克			/32
	--其他：									
8462.3910	---板带纵剪机〔999〕	9		50	13/	13	台/千克			/
8462.3920	---板带横剪机〔999〕	9		50	13/	13	台/千克			/34
8462.3990	---其他〔999〕	9		50	13/	13	台/千克			/19
	-冲孔或开槽机床,包括冲剪两用机：									
	--数控的：									
	---冲床：									
8462.4111	----自动模式数控步冲压力机〔101 冲压机床,102 开槽机,103 冲孔机,104 组合机床〕	9		20	13/	13	台/千克			/34
8462.4119	----其他〔101 冲压机床,102 组合机床〕	9		20	13/	13	台/千克			/34
8462.4190	---其他〔101 开槽机,102 冲孔机,103 组合机床〕	9		20	13/	13	台/千克			/34
8462.4900	--其他〔101 开槽机,102 冲孔机,103 组合机床〕	9		50	13/	13	台/千克			/34
	-其他：									
	--液压压力机：									
8462.9110	---金属型材挤压机〔999〕	9		50	13/	13	台/千克			/34
8462.9190	---其他〔101 冲压机床,102 挤压机,103 其它锻压或成型机床〕	9		50	13/	13	台/千克			/34
	--其他：									
8462.9910	---机械压力机〔101 冲压机床,102 挤压机,103 其它锻压或成型机床〕	9		50	13/	13	台/千克			/34
8462.9990	---其他〔999〕	9		50	13/	13	台/千克			/34
84.63	**金属或金属陶瓷的其他非切削加工机床：**									
	-杆、管、型材、异型材、丝及类似品的拉拔机：									
	---冷拔管机：									
8463.1011	----拉拔力为 300 吨及以下〔999〕	9		50	13/	13	台/千克			/
8463.1019	----其他〔999〕	9		50	13/	13	台/千克			/
8463.1020	---拔丝机〔999〕	9		50	13/	13	台/千克			/34
8463.1090	---其他〔999〕	9		50	13/	13	台/千克			/19

协定税率 %										特惠税率 %			
亚太5国	东/冰/格	巴基斯坦	韩国	瑞士	哥达	秘鲁	澳大利亚	新西/坡/智	港/澳/台	亚太2国	老/柬/缅	36/3/1	Article Description
													---Numerically controlled:
	0/0/	4			0	0	0	0/0/0	0/0/			0/0/0	----Gear grinder
	0/0/	4			0	0	0	0/0/0	0/0/			0/0/0	----Other
	0/0/6	10.8			0	0	0	0/0/0	0/0/			0/0/	---Other
													-Sawing or cutting-off machines
	0/0/0	5.4		3.6	0	0	0	0/0/0	0/0/0			0/0/	Irradiated-component cutting machine toole[cutting the fuel claddings to make the irradiated nuclear materials to melt down(including remote control)]
	0/0/0	5.4		3.6	0	0	0	0/0/0	0/0/0			0/0/	Other sawing or cutting-off
													-Other:
													---Planing machines:
	0/0/0	10.8	6	4.5	0	0	0	0/0/0	0/0/0			0/0/	----Double-column (open-side) planing machines
	0/0/0	10.8	6	0	0	0	0	0/0/0	0/0/0			0/0/	----Other
	0/0/4.8	5.4	8.4	3.6	0	0	0	0/0/0	0/0/			0/0/	---Other
													Machine-tools (including presses) for working metal by forging, hammering or die-stamping; machine-tools (including presses) for working metal by bending, folding, straightening, flattening, shearing, punching or notching; presses for working metal or metal carbides, not specified above:
													-Forging or die-stamping machines (including presses) and hammers:
6.3	0/0/	4	6.7	2.9	0	0	0	0/0/0	0/0/0			0/0/0	---Numerically controlled
6.3	0/0/0	4.5	8.4	3.6	0	0	0	0/0/0	0/0/0			0/0/0	---Other
													-Bending, folding, straightening or flattening machines (including presses):
													--Numerically controlled:
	0/0/	4		2.9	0	0	0	0/0/0	0/0/			0/0/0	---Straightening machines
	0/0/	4		2.9	0	0	0	0/0/0	0/0/			0/0/0	---Other
													--Other:
	0/0/4	4		5.2	0	0	0	0/0/0	0/0/			0/0/0	---Straightening machines
	0/0/4	4		0	0	0	0	0/0/0	0/0/			0/0/0	---Other
													-Shearing machines (including presses), other than combined punching and shearing machines:
													--Numerically controlled:
	0/0/	4		0	0	0	0	0/0/0	0/0/			0/0/0	---Shearing lengthwise
	0/0/	4		0	0	0	0	0/0/0	0/0/			0/0/0	---Shearing transverse
	0/0/	4		0	0	0	0	0/0/0	0/0/			0/0/0	---Other
													--Other:
8.6	0/0/4	4		0	0	0	0	0/0/0	0/0/			0/0/0	---Shearing lengthwise
8.6	0/0/4	4		0	0	0	0	0/0/0	0/0/			0/0/0	---Shearing transverse
8.6	0/0/0	4		0	0	0	0	0/0/0	0/0/			0/0/0	---Other
													-Punching or notching machines (including presses), including combined punching and shearing machines:
													--Numerically controlled:
													---Punch press:
	0/0/	4		2.9	0	0	0	0/0/0	0/0/			0/0/0	----CNC automatic tool change punch press
	0/0/	4		0	0	0	0	0/0/0	0/0/			0/0/0	----Other
	0/0/	4		0	0	0	0	0/0/0	0/0/			0/0/0	---Other
	0/0/0	4		0	0	0	0	0/0/0	0/0/0			0/0/0	--Other
													-Other:
													--Hydraulic presses:
8.3	0/0/4	4	9.2	0	0	0	0	0/0/0	0/0/			0/0/0	---Metal section squeezing machine
8.3	0/0/4	4	9.2	3	0	0	0	0/0/0	0/0/			0/0/0	---Other
													--Other:
8.6	0/0/0	4	9.2	0	0	0	0	0/0/0	0/0/0			0/0/0	---Mechanical presses
8.6	0/0/4	4	9.2	0	0	0	0	0/0/0	0/0/			0/0/0	---Other
													Other machine-tools for working metal or cermets, without removing material:
													-Draw-benches for bars, tubes, profiles, wire or the like:
													---Cold-drawing tube benches:
	0/0/4	4	7	0	0	0	0	0/0/0	0/0/			0/0/	----With 300t or less
	0/0/0	4		0	0	0	0	0/0/0	0/0/0			0/0/	----Other
	0/0/4	4		0	0	0	0	0/0/0	0/0/			0/0/	---Wiredrawing machines
	0/0/4	4		0	0	0	0	0/0/0	0/0/			0/0/	---Other

税则号列		货品名称〔CIQ 扩展编码及品名－T2 表示见附表 2〕	最惠(%)	暂定税率	普通	增值/消费	出口退税	计量单位	监管条件	检验检疫	特殊证件对美关税
8463.2000		-螺纹滚轧机〔999〕	9		50	13/	13	台/千克			/34
8463.3000		-金属丝加工机〔999〕	9		50	13/	13	台/千克			/34
8463.9000		-其他									
8463.9000	10	滚压成形机床(数控,装 3 个以上压辊)〔999〕	9		50	13/	13	台/千克	3		/29
8463.9000	20	具有滚压功能的旋压成形机床(数控,装 3 个以上压辊)〔999〕	9		50	13/	13	台/千克	3		/29
8463.9000	90	其他非切削加工机床(是指加工金属或金属陶瓷的)〔999〕	9		50	13/	13	台/千克			/29
84.64		石料、陶瓷、混凝土、石棉水泥或类似矿物材料的加工机床、玻璃冷加工机床:									
		-锯床:									
8464.1010		---圆盘锯〔999〕	0		30	13/	13	台/千克			/10
8464.1020		---钢丝锯〔999〕	0		30	13/	13	台/千克			/25
8464.1090		---其他〔999〕	0		30	13/	13	台/千克			/25
		-研磨或抛光机床:									
8464.2010		---玻璃研磨或抛光机床〔999〕	0		30	13/	13	台/千克			/25
8464.2090		---其他〔999〕	0		30	13/	13	台/千克			/25
		-其他:									
		---玻璃的其他冷加工机床:									
8464.9011		----切割机〔999〕	0		30	13/	13	台/千克			/25
8464.9012		----刻花机〔999〕	0		30	13/	13	台/千克			/25
8464.9019		----其他〔999〕	0		30	13/	13	台/千克			/25
8464.9090		---其他〔999〕	0		30	13/	13	台/千克			/25
84.65		木材、软木、骨、硬质橡胶、硬质塑料或类似硬质材料的加工机床(包括用打钉或打 U 形钉、胶粘或其他方法组合前述材料的机器):									
8465.1000		-不需更换工具即可进行不同机械加工的机器〔999〕	9		30	13/	13	台/千克			/34
8465.2000		-加工中心〔999〕	9		30	13/	13	台/千克			/
		-其他:									
8465.9100		--锯床〔999〕	9		30	13/	13	台/千克			/34
8465.9200		--刨、铣或切削成形机器〔999〕	9		30	13/	13	台/千克			/34
8465.9300		--研磨、砂磨或抛光机器〔101 研磨或抛光机器,102 加工木材等材料的其它机床〕	9		30	13/	13	台/千克			/19
8465.9400		--弯曲或装配机器〔999〕	9		30	13/	13	台/千克			/34
8465.9500		--钻孔或凿榫机器〔999〕	9		30	13/	13	台/千克			/34
8465.9600		--剖开、切片或刮削机器〔999〕	9		30	13/	13	台/千克			/34
8465.9900		--其他〔999〕	9		30	13/	13	台/千克			/34
84.66		专用于或主要用于税目 **84.56** 至 **84.65** 所列机器的零件、附件,包括工件或工具的夹具、自启板牙切头、分度头及其他专用于机器的附件;各种手提工具的工具夹具:									
8466.1000		-工具夹具及自启板牙切头〔999〕	7		17	13/	13	千克			/32
8466.2000		-工件夹具〔999〕	7		17	13/	13	千克			/32
8466.3000		-分度头及其他专用于机器的附件〔999〕	7		17	13/	13	千克			/32
		-其他:									
8466.9100		--税目 84.64 所列机器用〔101 机床附件,102 机床零件〕	0		17	13/	13	千克			/20
8466.9200		--税目 84.65 所列机器用〔101 机床附件,102 机床零件〕	6		17	13/	13	千克			/31
		--税目 84.56 至 84.61 所列机器用:									
8466.9310		---刀库及自动换刀装置〔101 机床附件,102 机床零件〕	0		17	13/	13	千克			/25
8466.9390		---其他〔101 机床附件,102 机床零件〕	0		17	13/	13	千克			/20
8466.9400		--税目 84.62 或 84.63 所列机器用									
8466.9400	10	滚压成形机床用芯轴(转筒成形用的芯轴,内径在 75 毫米至 400 毫米之间)〔999〕	6		17	13/	13	千克	3		/26
8466.9400	20	有滚压功能的旋压成形机用芯轴(转筒成形用的芯轴,内径在 75 毫米至 400 毫米之间)〔999〕	6		17	13/	13	千克	3		/26
8466.9400	90	税目 84.62－84.63 机器用其他零件〔101 机床附件,102 机床零件〕	6		17	13/	13	千克			/26
84.67		手提式风动或液压工具及本身装有电动或非电动动力装置的手提式工具:									
		-风动的:									
8467.1100		--旋转式(包括旋转冲击式的)〔999〕	8		30	13/	13	台/千克			/18
8467.1900		--其他〔999〕	8		30	13/	13	台/千克			/18
		-本身装有电动动力装置的:									
8467.2100		--各种钻〔999〕	8		30	13/	13	台/千克	A	L	/33

协定税率 %										特惠税率 %			Article Description
亚太5国	东/冰/格	巴基斯坦	韩国	瑞士	哥达	秘鲁	澳大利亚	新西/坡/智	港/澳/台	亚太2国	老/柬/缅	36/3/1	
	0/0/6	10.8		4.5	0	0	0	0/0/0	0/0/			0/0/	-Thread rolling machines
	0/0/4	4		0	0	0	0	0//0	0/0/			0/0/	-Machines for working wire
													-Other
	0/0/4	4		3	0	0	0	0//0	0/0/			0/0/	Roll forming machine tools(CNC with three or more rollers)
	0/0/4	4		3	0	0	0	0//0	0/0/			0/0/	Spin forming machines with roll forming function(CNC with three or more rollers)
	0/0/4	4		3	0	0	0	0//0	0/0/			0/0/	Other non-cutting machine tools(for processing metals or metal ceramics)
													Machine-tools for working stone, ceramics, concrete, asbestos-cement or like mineral materials or for cold working glass:
													-Sawing machines:
												0/0/0	---Of disk saw
												0/0/0	---Of scroll saw
												0/0/0	---Other
													-Grinding or polishing machines:
												0/0/0	---Machines for grinding or polishing glass or glassware
												0/0/0	---Other
													-Other:
													---Other machines for cold-working glass or glassware:
												0/0/0	----Cutting-off machines
												0/0/0	----Carving machines
												0/0/0	----Other
												0/0/0	---Other
													Machine-tools (including machines for nailing, stapling, glueing or otherwise assembling) for working wood, cork, bone, hard rubber, hard plastics or similar hard materials:
	0/0/0	4	7	0	0	0	0	0/0/0	0/0/			0/0/	-Machines which can carry out different types of machining operations without tool change between such operations
	0/0/0	4	7	0	0	0	0	0/0/0	0/0/			0/0/	-Machining centres
													-Other:
	0/0/0	4	7	0	0	0	0	0//0	0/0/			0/0/	--Sawing machines
	0/0/0	4	7	0	0	0	0	0/0/0	0/0/			0/0/	--Planing, milling or moulding (by cutting) machines
	0/0/0	4	7	0	0	0	0	0//0	0/0/			0/0/	--Grinding, sanding or polishing machines
	0/0/0	4	7	0	0	0	0	0/0/0	0/0/			0/0/	--Bending or assembling machines
	0/0/0	4	7	3	0	0	0	0/0/0	0/0/			0/0/	--Drilling or mortising machines
	0/0/0	4	7	0	0	0	0	0/0/0	0/0/			0/0/	--Splitting, slicing or paring machines
	0/0/0	4	7	0	0	0	0	0/0/0	0/0/			0/0/	--Other
													Parts and accessories suitable for use solely or principally with the machines of headings No.84.56 to 84.65, including work or tool holders, self-opening dieheads, dividing heads and other special attachments for machine-tools; tool holders for any type of tool for working in the hand:
	0/0/0	4	4.2	2.1	0	0	0	0//0	0/0/			0/0/0	-Tool holders and self-opening dieheads
4.9	0/0/0	0	2.8	2.1	0	0	0	0//0	0/0/0			0/0/0	-Work holders
	0/0/0	4	4.2	2.1	0	0	0	0//0	0/0/			0/0/0	-Dividing heads and other special attachments for machine-tools
													-Other:
												0/0/0	--For machines of heading No.84.64
	0/0/0	0	3.6	0	0	0	0	0//0	0/0/			0/0/0	--For machines of heading No.84.65
													--For machines of headings No.84.56 to 84.61:
												0/0/0	---Tool storage ond automatic tool change machine
												0/0/0	---Other
													--For machines of heading No.84.62 or 84.63
	0/0/0	0	0	1.8	0	0	0	0//0	0/0/0			0/0/0	Mandrels for roll forming machines tools(mandrel for forming of revolving drum, inner diameter 75mm～400mm)
	0/0/0	0	0	1.8	0	0	0	0//0	0/0/0			0/0/0	Mandrels for spin forming machines with roll forming functions (spindles for forming of revolving drum, inner diameter 75mm～400mm)
	0/0/0	0	0	1.8	0	0	0	0//0	0/0/0			0/0/0	Other parts for machines of heading No.84.62 ～ 84.63
													Tools for working in the hand, pneumatic and hydraulic and with self-contained electric or non-electric motor:
													-Pneumatic:
	0/0/0	4	4.8	0	0	0	0	0//0	0/0/			0/0/0	--Rotary type (including combined rotary-percussion)
	0/0/0	4	0	0	0	0	0	0//0	0/0/			0/0/0	--Other
													-With self-contained electric motor:
5.2	0/0/0	4	4	0	0	0	0	0/0/0	0/0/			0/0/0	--Drills of all kinds

税则号列	货品名称〔CIQ 扩展编码及品名—T2 表示见附表 2〕	最惠(%)	暂定税率	普通	增值/消费	出口退税	计量单位	监管条件	检验检疫	特殊证件对美关税
	--锯：									
8467.2210	---链锯〔999〕	8		30	13/	13	台/千克	A	L	/13
8467.2290	---其他〔999〕	8		30	13/	13	台/千克	A	L	/33
	--其他：									
8467.2910	---砂磨工具(包括磨光机、砂光机、砂轮机等)〔999〕	8		30	13/	13	台/千克	A	L	/33
8467.2920	---电刨〔999〕	8		30	13/	13	台/千克	A	L	/
8467.2990	---其他〔999〕	8		30	13/	13	台/千克	A	L	/28
	-其他工具：									
8467.8100	--链锯〔999〕	8		30	13/	13	台/千克			/28
8467.8900	--其他〔101 手提式液压工具,102 其他手提式动力工具及其零件〕	8		30	13/	13	台/千克			/13
	-零件：									
	--链锯用：									
8467.9110	---电动的〔999〕	6		30	13/	13	千克			/16
8467.9190	---其他〔999〕	6		30	13/	13	千克			/16
8467.9200	--风动工具用〔999〕	6		30	13/	13	千克			/16
	--其他：									
8467.9910	---电动工具用〔999〕	8		30	13/	13	千克			/33
8467.9990	---其他〔999〕	6		30	13/	13	千克			/16
84.68	**焊接机器及装置,不论是否兼有切割功能,但税目 85.15 的货品除外;气体加温表面回火机器及装置：**									
8468.1000	-手提喷焊器〔999〕	9		30	13/	13	台/千克			/29
8468.2000	-其他气体焊接或表面回火机器及装置									
8468.2000 10	自动焊接机[将端塞焊接于燃料细棒(或棒)的自动焊接机]〔999〕	9		30	13/	13	台/千克	3		/29
8468.2000 90	其他气体焊接或表面回火机器及装置〔999〕	9		30	13/	13	台/千克			/29
8468.8000	-其他机器及装置〔101 波峰焊设备,102 其它焊接设备及其零件〕	9		30	13/	13	台/千克			/34
8468.9000	-零件〔999〕	7	3	30	13/	13	千克			/23
84.70	**计算机器及具有计算功能的袖珍式数据记录、重现及显示机器;装有计算装置的会计计算机、邮资盖戳机、售票机及类似机器;现金出纳机：**									
8470.1000	-不需外接电源的电子计算器及具有计算功能的袖珍式数据记录、重现及显示机器〔999〕	0		80	13/	13	台/千克			/25
	-其他电子计算器：									
8470.2100	--装有打印装置的〔999〕	0		80	13/	13	台/千克			/
8470.2900	--其他〔999〕	0		80	13/	13	台/千克			/25
8470.3000	-其他计算机器〔999〕	0		40	13/	13	台/千克			/5
	-现金出纳机：									
8470.5010	---销售点终端出纳机〔999〕	0		40	13/	13	台/千克		L	/25
8470.5090	---其他〔999〕	0		40	13/	13	台/千克		L	/10
8470.9000	-其他〔999〕	0		40	13/	13	台/千克			/25
84.71	**自动数据处理设备及其部件;其他税目未列名的磁性或光学阅读机、将数据以代码形式转录到数据记录媒体的机器及处理这些数据的机器：**									
	-重量不超过 10 千克的便携自动数据处理设备,至少由一个中央处理部件、一个键盘及一个显示器组成：									
8471.3010	---平板电脑〔101 便携数字自动数据处理机,102 掌上电脑〕	0		70	13/	13	台/千克	A	L	/25
8471.3090	---其他〔101 便携数字自动数据处理机,102 掌上电脑〕	0		70	13/	13	台/千克	A	L	/25
	-其他自动数据处理设备：									
	--同一机壳内至少有一个中央处理部件及一个输入和输出部件,不论是否组合式：									
8471.4110	---巨型机、大型机及中型机									
8471.4110 10	高性能数字计算机(高性能数字计算机是指调整后峰值性能(APP)大于 8.0 加权每秒万亿次浮点运算的数字计算机)〔999〕	0		14	13/	13	台/千克	3		/20
8471.4110 90	其他巨、大、中型自动数据处理设备〔999〕	0		14	13/	13	台/千克			/20
8471.4120	---小型机〔999〕	0		14	13/	13	台/千克		L	/5
8471.4140	---微型机〔999〕	0		70	13/	13	台/千克	A	L	/5
8471.4190	---其他〔999〕	0		70	13/	13	台/千克		L	/10
	--其他,以系统形式进口或出口的：									
8471.4910	---巨型机、大型机及中型机									

协定税率 %										特惠税率 %			Article Description
亚太5国	东/冰/格	巴基斯坦	韩国	瑞士	哥达	秘鲁	澳大利亚	新西/坡/智	港/澳/台	亚太2国	老/柬/缅	36/3/1	
													--Saws:
5.2	0/0/0	4	4	0	0	0	0	0//0	0/0/			0/0/0	---Chain saws
5.2	0/0/0	4	4	0	0	0	0	0/0/0	0/0/			0/0/0	---Other
													--Other:
5.2	0/0/0	4	4	5.2	0	0	0	0/0/0	0/0/			0/0/0	---Grinding tools(including burnisher, belt sander, wheel-sander)
5.2	0/0/0	4	4	0	0	0	0	0//0	0/0/			0/0/0	---Planings
5.2	0/0/0	4	4	0	0	0	0	0/0/0	0/0/			0/0/0	---Other
													-Other tools:
	0/0/0	4	0	0	0	0	0	0//0	0/0/			0/0/0	--Chain saws
	0/0/0	4	4.8	0	0	0	0	0//0	0/0/			0/0/0	--Other
													-Parts:
													--Of chain saws:
3.9	0/0/0	0	0	0	0	0	0	0//0	0/0/			0/0/0	---With self-contained electric motor
4.2	0/0/0	0	0	1.8	0	0	0	0//0	0/0/			0/0/0	---Other
	0//0	0	0	0	0	0	0	0//0	0/0/			0/0/0	--Of pneumatic tools
													--Other:
5.2	0/0/0	4.5	4	3	0	0	0	0/0/0	0/0/			0/0/0	---With self-contained elecric motor
	0/0/0	0	2.4	0	0	0	0	0//0	0/0/			0/0/0	---Other
													Machinery and apparatus for soldering, brazing or welding, whether or not capable of cutting, other than those of headingNo.85. 15; gas-operated surface tempering machines and appliances:
	0/0/0	5.4	4.8	3.6	0	0	0	0/0/0	0/0/			0/0/0	-Hand-held blow pipes
													-Other gas-operated machinery and apparatus
	0/0/0	5.4	4.8	0	0	0	0	0/0/0	0/0/			0/0/0	Automatic welding machine [the automatic welder machine that joint the end plug with the fuel thin-stick (or stick)]
	0/0/0	5.4	4.8	0	0	0	0	0/0/0	0/0/			0/0/0	Other gas welding or surface tempering machines and equipments
	0/0/0	5.4		3.6	0	0	0	0/0/0	0/0/			0/0/0	-Other machinery and apparatus
	0/0/0	4	0	0	0	0	0	0//0	0/0/			0/0/0	-Parts
													Calculating machines and pocket-size data recording, reproducing and displaying machines with calculating functions; accounting machines, postage-franking machines, ticket-issuing machines and similar machines, incorporating a calculating device; cash registers:
												0/0/0	-Electronic calculators capable of operation without an external source of electric power and pocket-size data recording, reproducing and displaying machines with caluclating functions
													-Other electronic calculating machines:
												0/0/0	--Incorporating a printing device
												0/0/0	--Other
												0/0/0	-Other calculating machines
													-Cash registers:
												0/0/0	---Terminal registers for market
												0/0/0	---Other
												0/0/0	-Other
													Automatic data processing machines and units thereof; magnetic or optical readers, machines for transcribing data onto data media in coded form and machines for processing such data, not elsewhere specified or included:
													-Portable automatic data processing machines, weighing not more than 10kg, consisting of at least a central processing unit, a keyboard and a display:
												0/0/0	---Panel computer
												0/0/0	---Other
													-Other automatic data processing machines:
													--Comprising in the same housing at least a central processing unit and an input and output unit, whether or not combined:
													---mainframes
												0/0/0	Automatic data processing machines, mainframes
												0/0/0	Other automatic data processing machines, mainframes
												0/0/0	---Mini-computers
												0/0/0	---Microprocessings
												0/0/0	---Other
													--Other, presented in the form of systems:
													---Mainframes

税则号列		货品名称〔CIQ 扩展编码及品名－T2 表示见附表 2〕	最惠(%)	暂定税率	普通	增值/消费	出口退税	计量单位	监管条件	检验检疫	特殊证件对美关税
8471.4910	10	系统形式报验的高性能数字计算机(计算机指自动数据处理设备，高性能数字计算机是指调整后峰值性能(APP)大于 8.0 加权每秒万亿次浮点运算的数字计算机)〔999〕	0		29	13/	13	台/千克	3		/5
8471.4910	90	其他系统形式报验的巨、大、中型机，计算机指自动数据处理设备〔999〕	0		29	13/	13	台/千克			/5
8471.4920		---小型机〔999〕	0		29	13/	13	台/千克		L	/20
8471.4940		---微型机〔999〕	0		70	13/	13	台/千克		L	/20
		---其他：									
8471.4991		----分散型工业过程控制设备〔999〕	0		70	13/	13	台/千克			/20
8471.4999		----其他〔999〕	0		70	13/	13	台/千克		L	/10
		-子目号 8471.41 或 8471.49 所列以外的处理部件，不论是否在同一机壳内有一个或两个下列部件：存储部件、输入部件、输出部件：									
8471.5010		---巨型机、大型机及中型机的									
8471.5010	10	高性能数字计算机处理部件(不论是否在同一机壳内有一或两个存储，输入或输出部件，高性能数字计算机是指调整后峰值性能(APP)大于 8.0 加权每秒万亿次浮点运算的数字计算机)〔999〕	0		14	13/	13	台/千克	3		/10
8471.5010	90	其他巨，大，中型机处理部件(不论是否在同一机壳内有一或两个存储，输入或输出部件)〔999〕	0		14	13/	13	台/千克			/10
8471.5020		---小型机的〔999〕	0		14	13/	13	台/千克			/10
8471.5040		---微型机的									
8471.5040	01	含显示器和主机的微型机(不论是否在同一机壳内有一或两个存储，输入或输出部件)〔999〕	0		70	13/	13	台/千克		L	/20
8471.5040	90	其他的微型机的处理部件(不论是否在同一机壳内有一或两个存储，输入或输出部件)〔999〕	0		70	13/	13	台/千克			/20
8471.5090		---其他〔999〕	0		70	13/	13	台/千克			/10
		-输入或输出部件，不论是否在同一机壳内有存储部件：									
8471.6040		---巨型机、大型机、中型机及小型机用终端〔999〕	0		14	13/	13	台/千克			/25
8471.6050		---扫描仪〔999〕	0		14	13/	13	台/千克		L	/25
8471.6060		---数字化仪〔999〕	0		14	13/	13	台/千克			/10
		---键盘、鼠标器：									
8471.6071		----键盘〔999〕	0		40	13/	13	个/千克			/25
8471.6072		----鼠标器〔999〕	0		40	13/	13	个/千克			/25
8471.6090		---其他〔999〕	0		14	13/	13	台/千克			/25
		-存储部件：									
8471.7010		---硬盘驱动器〔999〕	0		14	13/	13	台/千克			/25
8471.7020		---软盘驱动器〔999〕	0		14	13/	13	台/千克			/5
8471.7030		---光盘驱动器〔999〕	0		14	13/	13	台/千克			/25
8471.7090		---其他〔999〕	0		14	13/	13	台/千克			/20
8471.8000		-自动数据处理设备的其他部件〔999〕	0		40	13/	13	台/千克			/25
8471.9000		-其他									
8471.9000	10	专用于复制的光盘刻录机(也称光盘复读机)〔999〕	0		40	13/	13	台/千克			/20
8471.9000	90	未列名的磁性或光学阅读器(包括将数据以代码形式转录的机器及处理这些数据的机器)〔999〕	0		40	13/	13	台/千克		L	/20
84.72		**其他办公室用机器(例如，胶版复印机、油印机、地址印写机、自动付钞机、硬币分类、计数及包装机、削铅笔机、打洞机或订书机)：**									
8472.1000		-胶版复印机、油印机〔999〕	0		40	13/	13	台/千克		L	/
		-信件分类或折叠机或信件装封机、信件开封或闭封机、粘贴或盖销邮票机：									
8472.3010		---邮政信件分拣及封装设备〔999〕	8		40	13/	13	台/千克			/28
8472.3090		---其他〔999〕	8		40	13/	13	台/千克			/
		-其他：									
8472.9010		---自动柜员机〔999〕	0		40	13/	13	台/千克		L	/25
		---装订用机器：									

协定税率 %										特惠税率 %			
亚太5国	东/冰/格	巴基斯坦	韩国	瑞士	哥达	秘鲁	澳大利亚	新西/坡/智	港/澳/台	亚太2国	老/柬/缅	36/3/1	Article Description
												0/0/0	Mainframes(automatic data processing machines) presented in the form of systems
												0/0/0	Mainframes(automatic data processing machines) presented in the form of systems
												0/0/0	---Mini-computers
												0/0/0	---Microprocessings
													---Other:
												0/0/0	----Processing machines for the distributed control system
												0/0/0	----Other
													-Processing units other than those of subheading No. 8471.41 or 8471.49, whether or not containing in the same housing one or two of the following types of unit: storage units, input units, output units:
													---Mainframes
												0/0/0	High-performance digital computer parts, whether or not in the same case with one or two storage, input or output component, the processor after polymerization way can make aggregation "adjusted peak performance (APP) is greater than 8.0 Weighted one trillion floating point operations per second (Weighted TeraFLOPS) specially designed or modified electronic components
												0/0/0	processing units of Mainframes (whether or not containing in the same housing one or two storage units, input units, output units)
												0/0/0	---Mini-computers
													---Microprocessings
												0/0/0	Microprocessings, with display and host(whether or not containing in the same housing one or two ofstorage nuits, input or output units)
												0/0/0	Other processing unit of microprocessings(whether or not containing in the same housing one or two ofstorage nuits, input or output units)
												0/0/0	---Other
													-Input or output units, whether or not containing storage units in the same housing:
												0/0/0	---Terminating machines for the huge computers, mainframes and mini-computers
												0/0/0	---Scanner
												0/0/0	---Digitizer
													---Keyboards, mouses:
												0/0/0	----Keyboards
												0/0/0	----Mouses
												0/0/0	---Other
													-Storage units:
												0/0/0	---Rigid disk drivers
												0/0/0	---Floppy disk drivers
												0/0/0	---CD drivers
												0/0/0	---Other
												0/0/0	-Other units of automatic data processing machines
													-Other
												0/0/0	CD-R machines used exclusively for copying(also called CD repeaters)
												0/0/0	Magnetic or optical readers, not elsewhere specified or included(including machines for transcribing data onto data media in coded form and machines for processing such data)
													Other office machines (for example, hectograph or stencil duplicating machines, addressing machines, automatic banknote dispensers, coin-sorting machines, coin-counting or wrapping machines, pencil-sharpening machines, perforating or stapling machines):
	0//	10.1	5.6					//	0/0/			0/0/	-Duplicating machines
													-Machines for sorting or folding mail or for inserting mail in envelopes or bands, machines for opening, closing or sealing mail and machines for affixing or cancelling postage stamps:
	0/0/0	4	4		0	0	0	0//0	0/0/			0/0/0	---Machines for sorting or banding mail
	0/0/0	6.3	5.6	0	0	0	0	0/0/0	0/0/			0/0/	---Other
													-Other:
												0/0/0	---Automated teller
													---Stapling machines:

税则号列	货品名称〔CIQ 扩展编码及品名－T2 表示见附表 2〕	最惠(%)	暂定税率	普通	增值/消费	出口退税	计量单位	监管条件	检验检疫	特殊证件对美关税
8472.9021	----打洞机〔999〕	0		40	13/	13	台/千克			/25
8472.9022	----订书机〔999〕	0		40	13/	13	台/千克			/25
8472.9029	----其他〔999〕	0		40	13/	13	台/千克			/5
8472.9030	---碎纸机〔999〕	0		40	13/	13	台/千克			/20
8472.9040	---地址印写机及地址铭牌压印机〔999〕	0		40	13/	13	台/千克			/
8472.9050	---文字处理机〔101 打印机，102 打字机〕	0		40	13/	13	台/千克			/5
8472.9060	---打字机，但税目 84.43 的打印机除外〔101 打印机，102 打字机〕	8		40	13/	13	台/千克			/13
8472.9090	---其他〔999〕	0		40	13/	13	台/千克			/25
84.73	**专用于或主要用于税目 84.70 至 84.72 所列机器的零件、附件（罩套、提箱及类似品除外）：**									
	-税目 84.70 所列机器的零件、附件：									
8473.2100	--子目 8470.10、8470.21 或 8470.29 所列电子计算器的零件、附件〔999〕	0		50	13/	13	千克			/25
8473.2900	--其他〔999〕	0		35	13/	13	千克			/25
	-税目 84.71 所列机器的零件、附件：									
8473.3010	---子目 8471.4110、8471.4120、8471.4910、8471. 4920、8471. 5010、8471. 5020、8471. 6090、8471. 7010、8471. 7020、8471. 7030 及 8471. 7090 所列机器及装置的零件、附件〔999〕	0		14	13/	13	千克			/25
8473.3090	---其他〔999〕	0		40	13/	13	千克			/25
	-税目 84.72 所列机器的零件、附件：									
8473.4010	---自动柜员机用出钞器和循环出钞器〔999〕	0		35	13/	13	千克			/25
8473.4020	---税目 8472.9050、8472.9060 所列机器的零件、附件〔999〕	0		35	13/	13	千克			/25
8473.4090	---其他									
8473.4090 10	钞票清分机零附件〔999〕	0		35	13/	13	千克			/25
8473.4090 90	其他办公室用机器零件附件〔999〕	0		35	13/	13	千克			/25
8473.5000	-同样适用于税目 84.70 至 84.72 中两个或两个以上税号所列机器的零件、附件〔101 其它计算机、辅助设备及其零件，102 其它办公机器及其零件〕	0		35	13/	13	千克			/25
84.74	**泥土、石料、矿石或其他固体（包括粉状、浆状）矿物质的分类、筛选、分离、洗涤、破碎、磨粉、混合或搅拌机器；固体矿物燃料、陶瓷坯泥、未硬化水泥、石膏材料或其他粉状、浆状矿产品的粘聚或成型机器；铸造用砂模的成形机器：**									
8474.1000	-分类、筛选、分离或洗涤机器〔101 其它工程机械及其零件，102 建筑工业行业成套设备〕	5		30	13/	13	台/千克			/25
	-破碎或磨粉机器：									
8474.2010	---齿辊式[T2]	5		30	13/	13	台/千克			/25
8474.2020	---球磨式[T2]	5		30	13/	13	台/千克			/30
8474.2090	---其他[T2]	5		30	13/	13	台/千克			/30
	-混合或搅拌机器：									
8474.3100	--混凝土或砂浆混合机器〔101 其它工程机械及其零件，102 建筑工业行业成套设备〕	7		30	13/	13	台/千克			/32
8474.3200	--矿物与沥青的混合机器〔101 其它工程机械及其零件，102 建筑工业行业成套设备〕	7		30	13/	13	台/千克			/12
8474.3900	--其他〔101 其它工程机械及其零件，102 建筑工业行业成套设备〕	5		30	13/	13	台/千克			/25
	-其他机器：									
8474.8010	---辊压成型机〔101 其它工程机械及其零件，102 建筑工业行业成套设备〕	5		30	13/	13	台/千克			/30
8474.8020	---模压成型机[T2]	5		30	13/	13	台/千克			/25
8474.8090	---其他									
8474.8090 10	纸面角线石膏板搅拌成型机〔101 其它工程机械及其零件，102 建筑工业行业成套设备〕	5		30	13/	13	台/千克			/25
8474.8090 90	税目 84.74 未列名的其他机器（如矿产品的粘聚或成型机器及铸造用砂模的成型机器）[T2]	5		30	13/	13	台/千克			/25
8474.9000	-零件〔101 其它工程机械及其零件，102 建筑工业行业成套设备〕	5		30	13/	13	千克			/25
84.75	**白炽灯泡、灯管、放电灯管、电子管、闪光灯泡及类似品的封装机器；玻璃或玻璃制品的制造或热加工机器：**									
8475.1000	-白炽灯泡、灯管、放电灯管、电子管、闪光灯泡及类似品的封装机器〔999〕	8		30	13/	13	台/千克			/
	-玻璃或玻璃制品的制造或热加工机器：									
8475.2100	--制造光导纤维及其预制棒的机器〔999〕	5/3.8		30	13/	13	台/千克			1/30,28.8
	--其他：									

协定税率 %										特惠税率 %			
亚太5国	东/冰/格	巴基斯坦	韩国	瑞士	哥达	秘鲁	澳大利亚	新西/坡/智	港/澳/台	亚太2国	老/柬/缅	36/3/1	Article Description
												0/0/0	----Perforator
												0/0/0	----Stapler
												0/0/0	----Other
												0/0/0	---Paper shrudders
	0//	10.1	5.6					//	0/0/			0/0/	---Addressing machines and address plate embossing machines
												0/0/0	---Word—processing machines
	0/0/0	5.4		3.6	0	0	0	0/0/0	0/0/			0/0/	---Typewnters other than priners of heading No.84.43
												0/0/0	---Other
													Parts and accessories (other than covers, carrying cases and the like) suitable for use solely or principally with machines of headings No. 84.70 to 84.72:
													-Parts and accessories of the machines of heading No.84.70:
												0/0/0	--Of the electronic calculating machines of subheading No.8470.10, 8470.21 or 8470.29
												0/0/0	--Other
													-Parts and accessories of the machines of heading No.84.71:
												0/0/0	--Of the machines of subheading 8471.4110, 8471.4120, 8471.4910, 8471.4920, 8471.5010, 8471.5020, 8471.6090, 8471.7010, 8471.7020, 8471.7030 and 8471.7090
												0/0/0	---Other
													-Parts and accessories of the machines of heading No.84.72:
	0//	4.5	7.3					//	0/0/			0/0/0	---Banknote dispenser of automated teller and recycle banknote
	0//	4	4.8					//	0/0/			0/0/0	---Parts and accessories of the subheadings No.8472.9050、8472.9060
													---Other
	0//	4.5	4.2					//	0/0/			0/0/0	Parts and accessories of banknote sorters
	0//	4.5	4.2					//	0/0/			0/0/0	Parts and accessories of other office machines
												0/0/0	-Parts and accessories equally suitable for use with machines of two or more of the heading No.84.70 to 84.72
													Machinery for sorting, screening, separating, washing, crushing, grinding, mixing or kneading earth, stone, ores or other mineral substances, in solid (including powder or paste) form; machinery for agglomerating, shaping or moulding solid mineral fuels, ceramic paste unhardned cements plastering materials or other mineral products in powder or paste form, machines for forming foundry moulds of sand
	0/0/0	0	2	0	0	0	0	0//0	0/0/			0/0/0	-Sorting, screening, separating or washing machines
													-Crushing or grinding machines:
	0/0/0	0	2	0	0	0	0	0//0	0/0/			0/0/0	---Toothing roller type
	0/0/0	0	3	0	0	0	0	0//0	0/0/			0/0/0	---Em-Peters type
	0/0/0	0	2	0	0	0	0	0//0	0/0/			0/0/0	---Other
													-Mixing or kneading machines:
	0/0/0	4	2.8	0	0	0	0	0//0	0/0/			0/0/0	--Concrete or mortar mixers
	0/0/0	4	2.8		0	0	0	0//0	0/0/			0/0/0	--Machines for mixing mineral substances with bitumen
	0/0/0	0	2	2.6	0	0	0	0//0	0/0/			0/0/0	--Other
													-Other machinery:
3.3	0/0/0	0	2	0	0	0	0	0//0	0/0/			0/0/0	---Rolling forming machines
3.3	0/0/0	0	3	0	0	0	0	0//0	0/0/			0/0/0	---Molud pressing machines
													---Other
3.3	0/0/0	0	2	0	0	0	0	0//0	0/0/			0/0/0	Paper faced angle line gypsum board mixing machines
3.3	0/0/0	0	2	0	0	0	0	0//0	0/0/			0/0/0	Other machines, not elsewhere specified or included of heading No. 84.74 (for example, machinery for agglomerating, shaping or moulding or machines for forming foundry moulds of sand)
	0/0/0	0	2	1.5	0	0	0	0//0	0/0/			0/0/0	-Parts
													Machines for assembling electric or electronic lamps, tubes or valves or flash-bulbs, in glass envelopes; machines for manufacturing or hot working glass or glassware:
	0/0/0	4	3.2	0	0	0	0	0//0	0/0/			0/0/0	-Machines for assembling electric or electronic lamps, tubes or valves or flashbulbs, in glass envelopes
													-Machines for manufacturing or hot working glass or glassware:
	0/0/0	4	4	0	0	0	0	0/0/0	0/0/			0/0/0	--Machines for making optical fibres and preforms thereof
													--Other:

税则号列	货品名称〔CIQ 扩展编码及品名－T2 表示见附表 2〕	最惠(%)	暂定税率	普通	增值/消费	出口退税	计量单位	监管条件	检验检疫	特殊证件对美关税
	---玻璃的热加工设备：									
8475.2911	----连续式玻璃热弯炉〔999〕	8		30	13/	13	台/千克			/33
8475.2912	----玻璃纤维拉丝机(光纤拉丝机除外)〔999〕	8		30	13/	13	台/千克			/33
8475.2919	----其他〔999〕	8		30	13/	13	台/千克			/33
8475.2990	---其他〔999〕	8		30	13/	13	台/千克			/33
8475.9000	-零件									
8475.9000 10	税号 8475.21 所列机器的零件〔999〕	2.7/1.3		30	13/	13	千克			/12.7,11.3
8475.9000 90	其他品目 84.75 所列机器的零件(灯泡等封装机及玻璃等制造机器的零件)〔999〕	8		30	13/	13	千克			/18
84.76	**自动售货机(例如，出售邮票、香烟、食品或饮料的机器)，包括钱币兑换机：**									
	-饮料自动销售机：									
8476.2100	--装有加热或制冷装置的〔999〕	11		50	13/	13	台/千克	A	R	/36
8476.2900	--其他〔999〕	12		50	13/	13	台/千克	A	R	/
	-其他机器：									
8476.8100	--装有加热或制冷装置的〔999〕	11		50	13/	13	台/千克			/16
8476.8900	--其他									
8476.8900 10	钱币兑换机〔999〕	0		50	13/	13	台/千克			/5
8476.8900 90	其他无加热或制冷装置的自动售货机〔999〕	12		50	13/	13	台			/17
8476.9000	-零件									
8476.9000 10	钱币兑换机的零件〔999〕	0		50	13/	13	千克			/25
8476.9000 90	其他品目 84.76 所列机器的零件〔999〕	8		50	13/	13	千克			/33
84.77	**本章其他税目未列名的橡胶或塑料及其产品的加工机器：**									
	-注射机：									
8477.1010	---注塑机									
8477.1010 10	用于光盘生产的精密注塑机(加工塑料的)〔999〕	0		45	13/	13	台/千克			/25
8477.1010 90	其他注塑机〔101 电子行业成套设备，102 化工行业成套设备，103 轻工行业成套设备〕	0		45	13/	13	台/千克			/25
8477.1090	---其他〔101 电子行业成套设备，102 化工行业成套设备，103 轻工行业成套设备〕	0		30	13/	13	台/千克			/25
	-挤出机：									
8477.2010	---塑料造粒机〔101 电子行业成套设备，102 化工行业成套设备，103 轻工行业成套设备〕	5		30	13/	13	台/千克			/30
8477.2090	---其他〔101 电子行业成套设备，102 化工行业成套设备，103 轻工行业成套设备〕	5		30	13/	13	台/千克			/25
	-吹塑机：									
8477.3010	---挤出吹塑机〔101 电子行业成套设备，102 化工行业成套设备，103 轻工行业成套设备〕	5		30	13/	13	台/千克			/25
8477.3020	---注射吹塑机〔101 电子行业成套设备，102 化工行业成套设备，103 轻工行业成套设备〕	5		30	13/	13	台/千克			/
8477.3090	---其他〔101 电子行业成套设备，102 化工行业成套设备，103 轻工行业成套设备〕	5		30	13/	13	台/千克			/25
	-真空模塑机器及其他热成型机器：									
8477.4010	---塑料中空成型机〔101 电子行业成套设备，102 化工行业成套设备，103 轻工行业成套设备〕	5		30	13/	13	台/千克			/30
8477.4020	---塑料压延成型机〔101 电子行业成套设备，102 化工行业成套设备，103 轻工行业成套设备〕	5		30	13/	13	台/千克			/30
8477.4090	---其他〔101 电子行业成套设备，102 化工行业成套设备，103 轻工行业成套设备〕	5		30	13/	13	台/千克			/30
	-其他模塑或成型机器：									
8477.5100	--用于充气轮胎模塑或翻新的机器及内胎模塑或用其他方法成型的机器〔999〕	5		30	13/	13	台/千克			/30
	--其他：									
8477.5910	---三维打印机(3D 打印机)〔999〕	5		30	13/	13	台/千克			/10
8477.5990	---其他〔101 电子行业成套设备，102 化工行业成套设备，103 轻工行业成套设备〕	5		30	13/	13	台/千克			/30
8477.8000	-其他机器〔101 电子行业成套设备，102 化工行业成套设备，103 轻工行业成套设备〕	5		30	13/	13	台/千克			/30
8477.9000	-零件〔101 电子行业成套设备，102 化工行业成套设备，103 轻工行业成套设备〕	0		30	13/	13	千克			/20

协定税率 %										特惠税率 %			Article Description
亚太5国	东/冰/格	巴基斯坦	韩国	瑞士	哥达	秘鲁	澳大利亚	新西/坡/智	港/澳/台	亚太2国	老/柬/缅	36/3/1	
													---Equipments for hot working glass or glasswares:
5.2	0/0/0	4	4	0	0	0	0	0//0	0/0/			0/0/0	----Continuous hot bending furnaces
5.2	0/0/0	4	4	0	0	0	0	0//0	0/0/			0/0/0	----Fiber glass winder(excluding opticae fiber winder)
	0/0/0	4	4	0	0	0	0	0/0/0	0/0/			0/0/0	----Other
	0/0/0	4	4	0	0	0	0	0//0	0/0/			0/0/0	---Other
													-Parts
	0/0/0	4	3.2	0	0	0	0	0//0	0/0/			0/0/0	Parts of machines of heading No.8475.21
	0/0/0	4	3.2	0	0	0	0	0//0	0/0/			0/0/0	Parts of machines of heading No.84.75(parts of machines for assembling lamps in glass envelopes or; parts of machines for manufacturing or hot working glass or glassware)
													Automatic goods-vending machines (for example, postage stamp, cigarette, food or beverage machines), including money-changing machines:
													-Automatic beverage-vending machines:
	0/0/0	10.1	5.6	4.2	0	0	0	0/0/0	0/0/			0/0/	--Incorporating heating or refrigerating devices
	0/0/0	10.8	6	4.5	0	0	0	0/0/0	0/0/			0/0/	--Other
													-Other machines:
	0/0/0	6.3	5.6	4.2	0	0	0	0/0/0	0/0/			0/0/	--Incorporating heating or refrigerating devices
													--Other
	0/0/0	10.8	6	0	0	0	0	0/0/0	0/0/			0/0/	Money-changing machines
	0/0/0	10.8	6	0	0	0	0	0/0/0	0/0/			0/0/	Other automatic goods-vending machines not incorporating heating or refrigerating devices
													-Parts
	0/0/0	4	4	0	0	0	0	0//0	0/0/			0/0/0	parts of money-changing machines
	0/0/0	4	4	0	0	0	0	0//0	0/0/			0/0/0	Parts of machines of heading No.84.76
													Machinery for working rubber or plastics or for the manufacture of products from these materials, not specified or included elsewhere in this Chapter:
													-Injection-moulding machines:
													---For working plastics
												0/0/0	Precision injection-moulders for disks production (for working plastics)
												0/0/0	Other working plastics machines
												0/0/0	---Other
													-Extruders:
3.3	0/0/0	0	0	0	0	0	0	0//0	0/0/0			0/0/0	---Plastic pelletizers
3.3	0/0/0	0	0	2.6	0	0	0	0//0	0/0/0			0/0/0	---Other
													-Blow moulding machines:
	0/0/0	0	2	0	0	0	0	0//0	0/0/			0/0/0	---Extruders blow moulding machines
	0/0/0	0	0	0	0	0	0	0//0	0/0/			0/0/0	---Injection blow moulding machines
	0/0/0	0	2	0	0	0	0	0//0	0/0/			0/0/0	---Other
													-Vacuum moulding machines and other thermoforming machines:
3.3	0/0/0	0	0		0	0	0	0//0	0/0/0			0/0/0	—Plastics brideg-die-forming machines
3.3	0/0/0	0	0	1.5	0	0	0	0//0	0/0/0			0/0/0	—Plastics calender-forming machines
3.3	0/0/0	0	0	2.6	0	0	0	0//0	0/0/0			0/0/0	—Other
													-Other machinery for moulding or otherwise forming:
	0/0/0	0	2	0	0	0	0	0//0	0/0/			0/0/0	--For moulding or retreading pneumatic tyres or for moulding or otherwise forming inner tubes
													--Other:
3.3	0/0/0	0	3	0	0	0	0	0//0	0/0/0			0/0/0	---3D printing
3.3	0/0/0	0	3	0	0	0	0	0//0	0/0/0			0/0/0	---Other
3.3	0/0/0	0	0	2.6	0	0	0	0//0	0/0/0			0/0/0	-Other machinery
												0/0/0	-Parts

税则号列	货品名称〔CIQ扩展编码及品名—T2表示见附表2〕	最惠(%)	暂定税率	普通	增值/消费	出口退税	计量单位	监管条件	检验检疫	特殊证件对美关税
84.78	**本章其他税目未列名的烟草加工及制作机器：**									
8478.1000	-机器〔999〕	5		30	13/	13	台/千克	O		/25
8478.9000	-零件〔999〕	8	5	30	13/	13	千克	O		/
84.79	**本章其他税目未列名的具有独立功能的机器及机械器具：**									
	-公共工程用机器：									
	---摊铺机：									
8479.1021	----沥青混凝土摊铺机〔999〕	8		30	13/	13	台/千克	O		/33
8479.1022	----稳定土摊铺机〔999〕	8		30	13/	13	台/千克			/
8479.1029	----其他〔999〕	8		30	13/	13	台/千克	O		/
8479.1090	---其他〔999〕	8		30	13/	13	台/千克			/18
8479.2000	-提取、加工动物油脂或植物固定油脂的机器〔999〕	8		30	13/	13	台/千克	A	R	/33
8479.3000	-木碎料板或木纤维板的挤压机及其他木材或软木处理机〔999〕	8		30	13/	13	台/千克			/
8479.4000	-绳或缆的制造机器〔999〕	7	5	30	13/	13	台/千克			/30
	-未列名工业机器人：									
8479.5010	---多功能工业机器人〔101 电子行业成套设备，102 其他行业成套设备〕	0		20	13/	13	台/千克			/25
8479.5090	---其他									
8479.5090 10	机器人，末端操纵装置[能处理高能炸药或能抗大于 5×10^4 戈瑞(硅)辐射的]〔999〕	0		30	13/	13	台/千克	3		/20
8479.5090 90	其他工业机器人(多功能工业机器人除外)〔101 电子行业成套设备，102 其他行业成套设备〕	0		30	13/	13	台/千克			/20
8479.6000	-蒸发式空气冷却器[T2]	8		30	13/	13	台/千克	A	M	/28
	-旅客登机(船)桥：									
8479.7100	--用于机场的〔999〕	0		30	13/	13	台/千克	A	M	/
8479.7900	--其他〔999〕	0		30	13/	13	台/千克	A	M	/25
	-其他机器及机械器具：									
	--处理金属的机械，包括线圈绕线机：									
8479.8110	---绕线机〔101 机械行业成套设备，102 电子行业成套设备〕	9		30	13/	13	台/千克			/34
8479.8190	---其他〔101 机械行业成套设备，102 电子行业成套设备〕	9		30	13/	13	台/千克			/29
8479.8200	--混合、搅拌、轧碎、研磨、筛选、均化或乳化机器									
8479.8200 10	两用物项管制搅拌器(耐腐蚀热交换器、搅拌器用，带搅拌的发酵罐)〔101 轻工行业成套设备，102 其他行业成套设备〕	7		30	13/	13	台/千克	3		/17
8479.8200 20	用于废物和废水处理的混合、搅拌、轧碎、研磨、筛选、均化或乳化机器〔101 轻工行业成套设备，102 其他行业成套设备〕	7	5	30	13/	13	台/千克			/15
8479.8200 90	其他混合、搅拌、轧碎、研磨机器(包括筛选、均化、乳化机器)〔101 轻工行业成套设备，102 其他行业成套设备〕	7		30	13/	13	台/千克			/17
	--其他：									
8479.8910	---船舶用舵机及陀螺稳定器〔101 船舶用零部件，102 船舶行业成套设备〕	0		14	13/	13	台/千克			/25
8479.8920	---空气增湿器及减湿器[T2]	0		70	13/	13	台/千克		L	/10
8479.8940	---邮政用包裹、印刷品分拣设备〔999〕	0		30	13/	13	台/千克			/10
8479.8950	---放射性废物压实机〔999〕	0		30	13/	13	台/千克			/
	---在印刷电路电路板上装配元器件的机器：									
8479.8961	----自动插件机〔999〕	0		30	13/	13	台/千克	A	M	/25
8479.8962	----自动贴片机〔999〕	0		30	13/	13	台/千克	A	M	/25
8479.8969	----其他〔999〕	0		30	13/	13	台/千克	A	M	/20
	---其他：									
8479.8992	----自动化立体仓储设备[T2]	0		30	13/	13	台/千克	A	M	/25
8479.8999	----其他									
8479.8999 10	用于光盘生产的金属母盘生产设备(具有独立功能的)〔999〕	0		30	13/	13	台/千克	A	M	/20
8479.8999 20	用于光盘生产的粘合机(具有独立功能的)〔999〕	0		30	13/	13	台/千克	A	M	/20
8479.8999 30	用于光盘生产的真空金属溅镀机(具有独立功能的)〔999〕	0		30	13/	13	台/千克	A	M	/20
8479.8999 40	保护胶涂覆机及染料层旋涂机(光盘生产用，具有独立功能的)〔999〕	0		30	13/	13	台/千克	A	M	/20
8479.8999 51	等静压压力机(两用物项管制机器及机械器具)〔999〕	0		30	13/	13	台/千克	3		/20
8479.8999 52	生物反应器(两用物项管制机器及机械器具)〔999〕	0		30	13/	13	台/千克	3		/20

协定税率 %										特惠税率 %			Article Description
亚太5国	东/冰/格	巴基斯坦	韩国	瑞士	哥达	秘鲁	澳大利亚	新西/坡/智	港/澳/台	亚太2国	老/柬/缅	36/3/1	
													Machinery for preparing or making up tobacco, not specified or included elsewhere in this Chapter:
2.5	0/0/	0		0	0	0		0/ /0	0/0/			0/0/	-Machinery
	0/0/	4		0	0	0		0/ /0	0/0/			0/0/	-Parts
													Machines and mechanical appliances having individual functions, not specified or included elsewhere in this Chapter:
													-Machinery for public works, building or the like:
													---Spreading machines:
5.2	0/0/0	4	0	0	0	0	0	0/ /0	0/0/			0/0/0	----Machines for spreading bituminous concrete
5.2	0/0/0	4	0	0	0	0	0	0/ /0	0/0/			0/0/0	----Stabilizer spreading machines
5.2	0/0/0	4	0	0	0	0	0	0/ /0	0/0/			0/0/0	----Other
5.2	0/0/0	4	3.2	0	0	0	0	0/ /0	0/0/			0/0/0	---Other
	0/0/0	4	4	0	0	0	0	0/0/0	0/0/			0/0/0	-Machinery for the extraction or preparation of animal or fixed vegetable fats or oils
	0/0/0	4	4	0	0	0	0	0/ /0	0/0/			0/0/0	-Presses for the manufacture of particle board or fibre building board or wood or other ligneous materials and other machinery for treating wood or cork
	0/0/0	4	0	0	0	0	0	0/ /0	0/0/			0/0/0	-Rope or cable-making machines
													-Industrial robots, not elsewhere specified or included:
												0/0/0	---Industrial robots for multiple uses
													---Other
												0/0/0	Robots, end-control devices (capable of handling high-energy explosives or resisting radiance > 5×10^4 Gy (Si))
												0/0/0	Other industrial robots (other than multiple-functional industrial robots)
5.2	0/0/0	4	4	0	0	0	0	0/ /0	0/0/			0/0/0	-Evaporative air coolers
													-Passenger boarding (boats) bridge use at airport:
												0/0/0	--Of a kind used in airports
												0/0/0	--Other
													-Other machines and mechanical appliances:
													--For treating metal, including electric wire coil-winders:
6.3	0/0/0	4	3.8	2.9	0	0	0	0/ /0	0/0/0			0/0/0	---Filament winding machines
5.9	0/0/0	4	3.8	2.9	0	0	0	0/ /0	0/0/0			0/0/0	---Other
													--Mixing, kneading, crushing, grinding, screening, sifting, homogenizing, emulsifying or stirring machines
4.6	0/0/0	0	0		0	0	0	0/ /0	0/0/0			0/0/0	Beaters subject to regulations of sensitive item (Rotproof heat exchanger and ferment jar for use of beater)
4.6	0/0/0	0	0		0	0	0	0/ /0	0/0/0			0/0/0	For mixed waste and wastewater treatment, mixing, crushing, grinding, screening, homogenizing or emulsifying machine
4.6	0/0/0	0	0		0	0	0	0/ /0	0/0/0			0/0/0	Other mixing, kneading, crushing, grinding, screening, sifting, homogenizing, emulsifying or stirring machines
													--Other:
												0/0/0	---Steering and rudder equipment or gyroscopic stabilizers for ships
												0/0/0	---Air humidifiers or dehumidifiers
												0/0/0	---Bundle and printed matter sorting machines used in post offices
												0/0/0	---Presses for radioactive waste material
													---Machines for assemblying elements on printed circuit boards:
												0/0/0	----Automatic plug-in machines
												0/0/0	----Automatic coreslice adhering machines
												0/0/0	----Other
													---Other:
												0/0/0	----Three-dimensional automatic warehouse equipmentt
													----Other
												0/0/0	Metal master production equipment for CD production (having independent functions)
												0/0/0	Fusing machine for CD production (having independent functions)
												0/0/0	Vacuum metal-splashers for CD production (having independent functions)
												0/0/0	Protective rubber-coating machine and dye-layer spin-coating machine (for CD production, having independent functions)
												0/0/0	Isostatic press (Dual-use items control machines and mechanical appliances)
												0/0/0	Biological reactor (Dual-use items control machines and mechanical appliances)

税则号列	货品名称〔CIQ扩展编码及品名—T2表示见附表2〕	最惠(%)	暂定税率	普通	增值/消费	出口退税	计量单位	监管条件	检验检疫	特殊证件对美关税
8479.8999 53	恒化器(两用物项管制机器及机械器具)〔999〕	0		30	13/	13	台/千克	3		/20
8479.8999 54	连续灌流系统(两用物项管制机器及机械器具)〔999〕	0		30	13/	13	台/千克	3		/20
8479.8999 55	三坐标或多坐标联动和程控的纤维缠绕机(两用物项管制机器及机械器具)〔999〕	0		30	13/	13	台/千克	3		/20
8479.8999 59	其他两用物项管制机器及机械器具〔999〕	0		30	13/	13	台/千克	3		/20
8479.8999 60	绕线机(能卷绕直径在75mm至400mm、长度为600mm或更长的)〔999〕	0		30	13/	13	台/千克	3A	M	/20
8479.8999 90	本章其他未列名机器及机械器具(具有独立功能的)[T2]	0		30	13/	13	台/千克	A	M	/20
	-零件:									
8479.9010	---船舶用舵机及陀螺稳定器用[T2]	0		14	13/	13	千克			/20
8479.9020	---空气增湿器及减湿器用〔999〕	0		70	13/	13	千克			/5
8479.9090	---其他									
8479.9090 10	绕线机的精密芯轴(专用于编号8479899060绕线机的精密芯轴)[T2]	0		20	13/	13	千克	3		/20
8479.9090 90	税目84.79所列机器的其他零件[T2]	0		20	13/	13	千克			/20
84.80	**金属铸造用型箱;型模底板;阳模;金属用型模(锭模除外)、硬质合金、玻璃、矿物材料、橡胶或塑料用型模:**									
8480.1000	-金属铸造用型箱〔999〕	8		20	13/	13	千克			/33
8480.2000	-型模底板〔999〕	8		20	13/	13	千克			/33
8480.3000	-阳模〔999〕	8		20	13/	13	千克			/28
	-金属、硬质合金用型模:									
	--注模或压模:									
8480.4110	---压铸模[T2]	8		20	13/	13	千克			/33
8480.4120	---粉末冶金用压模[T2]	8		20	13/	13	千克			/33
8480.4190	---其他[T2]	8		20	13/	13	千克			/28
8480.4900	--其他[T2]	8		20	13/	13	千克			/18
8480.5000	-玻璃用型模[T2]	8		20	13/	13	套/千克			/13
8480.6000	-矿物材料用型模〔999〕	8		20	13/	13	套/千克			/13
	-塑料或橡胶用型模:									
	--注模或压模:									
8480.7110	---硫化轮胎用囊式型模〔999〕	0		20	13/	13	套/千克			/25
8480.7190	---其他									
8480.7190 10	用于光盘生产的专用模具(注模或压模)〔999〕	0		20	13/	13	套/千克			/25
8480.7190 90	其他塑料或橡胶用注模或压模〔101机械行业成套设备,102电子行业成套设备,103轻工行业成套设备〕	0		20	13/	13	套/千克			/25
8480.7900	--其他									
8480.7900 10	农用双壁波纹管生产线用其他模具〔999〕	5		20	13/	13	套/千克			/35
8480.7900 90	塑料或橡胶用其他型模[T2]	5		20	13/	13	套/千克			/35
84.81	**用于管道、锅炉、罐、桶或类似品的龙头、旋塞、阀门及类似装置,包括减压阀及恒温控制阀:**									
8481.1000	-减压阀									
8481.1000 01	喷灌设备用减压阀(用于管道、锅炉、罐、桶或类似品的)〔101安全附件,102减压阀〕	5	2	30	13/	13	套/千克			/12
8481.1000 90	其他减压阀(用于管道、锅炉、罐、桶或类似品的)〔101安全附件,102减压阀〕	5		30	13/	13	套/千克			/15
	-油压或气压传动阀:									
8481.2010	---油压的〔101安全附件,102传动阀〕	5		30	13/	13	套/千克			/15
8481.2020	---气压的〔101安全附件,102传动阀〕	5		30	13/	13	套/千克			/25
8481.3000	-止回阀〔101安全附件,102止回阀〕	5		30	13/	13	套/千克			/15
8481.4000	-安全阀或溢流阀〔101安全附件,102安全阀或溢流阀〕	5		30	13/	13	套/千克			/10
	-其他器具:									
	---换向阀:									
8481.8021	----电磁式									
8481.8021 10	两用物项管制的电磁式换向阀[T2]	7		30	13/	13	套/千克	3		/27
8481.8021 90	其他电磁式换向阀(用于管道、锅炉、罐、桶或类似品的)〔101安全附件,102其它阀门及类似品〕	7		30	13/	13	套/千克			/27
8481.8029	----其他									
8481.8029 10	两用物项管制的其他换向阀[T2]	7		30	13/	13	套/千克	3		/17

协定税率 %										特惠税率 %			Article Description
亚太5国	东/冰/格	巴基斯坦	韩国	瑞士	哥达	秘鲁	澳大利亚	新西/坡/智	港/澳/台	亚太2国	老/柬/缅	36/3/1	
												0/0/0	Chemostat(Dual-use items control machines and mechanical appliances)
												0/0/0	Continuous langendorff (Dual-use items control machines and mechanical appliances)
												0/0/0	Filament winding Machines coordinated and programmed in three or more axes,(Dual-use items control machines and mechanical appliances)
												0/0/0	Other dual-use items control machines and mechanical appliances
												0/0/0	winding machines (capable of winding wire diameter 75mm～400mm, length≥600mm)
												0/0/0	Machines and mechanical appliances having independent functions, not specified or included elsewhere in this Chapter
													-Parts:
												0/0/0	---Of the machines of subheading No.8479. 8910
												0/0/0	---Of the machines of subheading No.8479. 8920
													---Other
												0/0/0	Precision mandrels for winding machines (precision mandrels used exclusively for No.84798990.60 winding machines)
												0/0/0	Other parts of machiners of heading No.84. 79
													Moulding boxes for metal foundry; mould bases; moulding patterns; moulds for metal (other than ingot moulds), metal carbides, glass, mineral materials, rubber or plastics:
	0/0/0	4	4	0	0	0	0	0//0	0/0/			0/0/0	-Moulding boxes for metal foundry
	0/0/0	4	3.2	0	0	0	0	0//0	0/0/			0/0/0	-Mould bases
	0/0/0	4	4	0	0	0	0	0/0/0	0/0/			0/0/0	-Moulding patterns
													-Moulds for metal or metal carbides:
													--Injection or compression types:
5.2	0/0/0	4	4.8	0	0	0	0	0//0	0/0/0			0/0/0	---Die-casting mould
5.2	0/0/0	4	4.8	0	0	0	0	0//0	0/0/0			0/0/0	---Die-casting mould use for powder metallurgy
5.2	0/0/0	4	4.8	0	0	0	0	0//0	0/0/0			0/0/0	---Other
5.2	0/0/0	4	4.8	0	0	0	0	0//0	0/0/			0/0/0	--Other
	0/0/0	4	5	0	0	0	0	0//0	0/0/			0/0/0	-Moulds for glass
	0/0/0	4	3.3	0	0	0	0	0//0	0/0/			0/0/0	-Moulds for mineral materials
													-Moulds for rubber or plastics:
													--Other:
												0/0/0	---Tyre vulcanizing mould for capsule type(injection or compression types)
													---Other
												0/0/0	Injection molds for CD production(injection or compression types)
												0/0/0	Other injection or compression types for rubber or plastics
													--Other
3.3	0//0	0	0	0	0	0	0	0//0	0/0/0			0/0/0	Other molds for agricultural double-wall corrugated pipe production lines
3.3	0//0	0	0	0	0	0	0	0//0	0/0/0			0/0/0	Other moulds for rubber plastics
													Taps, cocks, valves and similar appliances for pipes, boiler shells, tanks, vats or the like, including pressure-reducing valves and thermostatically controlled valves:
													-Pressure-reducing valves
	0/0/0	0	3	1.5	0	0	0	0//0	0/0/			0/0/0	Pressure-reducing valves for spray irrigation equipment (used in pipes, boiler shells, tanks, vats or similar products)
	0/0/0	0	3	1.5	0	0	0	0//0	0/0/			0/0/0	Other pressure-reducing valves(used in pipes, boiler shells, thanks, vats or similar products)
													-Valves for oleohydraulic or pneumatic transmissions:
	0/0/0	0	3	1.5	0	0	0	0//0	0/0/0			0/0/0	---For oleohydraulic transmissions
	0/0/2	0	3	1.5	0	0	0	0//0	0/0/			0/0/0	---For pneumatic transmissions
	0/0/0	0	3	1.5	0	0	0	0//0	0/0/0			0/0/0	-Check (nonreturn) valves
	0/0/0	0	3	0	0	0	0	0//0	0/0/0			0/0/0	-Safety or relief valves
													-Other appliances:
													---Directional valve:
													----Electromagnetic
4.6	0/0/2.8	0	4.2	2.1	0	0	0	0//0	0/0/0			0/0/0	Electromagnetic directional valve of dual-use items control
4.6	0/0/2.8	0	4.2	2.1	0	0	0	0//0	0/0/0			0/0/0	Other electromagnetic selector valve(used for tubing, boilers, Cans, barrels or similar products)
													----Other
4.6	0/0/0	0	4.2	2.1	0	0	0	0//0	0/0/0			0/0/0	Other selector valve of dual-use items control

税则号列		货品名称〔CIQ扩展编码及品名—T2表示见附表2〕	最惠(%)	暂定税率	普通	增值/消费	出口退税	计量单位	监管条件	检验检疫	特殊证件对美关税
8481.8029	90	其他换向阀(用于管道、锅炉、罐、桶或类似品的)〔101安全附件,102其它阀门及类似品〕	7		30	13/	13	套/千克			/17
		---流量阀:									
8481.8031		----电子膨胀阀									
8481.8031	10	两用物项管制的电子膨胀流量阀〔101安全附件,102其它阀门及类似品〕	7		30	13/	13	套/千克	3		/32
8481.8031	90	其他电子膨胀流量阀(用于管道、锅炉、罐、桶或类似品的)〔101安全附件,102其它阀门及类似品〕	7		30	13/	13	套/千克			/32
8481.8039		----其他									
8481.8039	10	两用物项管制的其他流量阀〔101安全附件,102其它阀门及类似品〕	7		30	13/	13	套/千克	3		/17
8481.8039	90	其他流量阀(用于管道、锅炉、罐、桶或类似品的)〔101安全附件,102其它阀门及类似品〕	7		30	13/	13	套/千克			/17
8481.8040		---其他阀门									
8481.8040	10	两用物项管制的其他阀门[T2]	7	5	30	13/	13	套/千克	3		/15
8481.8040	20	高压涡轮间隙控制阀门(用于管道、锅炉、罐、桶或类似品的)	7	1	30	13/	13	套/千克			/11
8481.8040	90	其他阀门(用于管道、锅炉、罐、桶或类似品的)[T2]	7	5	30	13/	13	套/千克		L	/15
8481.8090		---其他〔101安全附件,102其它阀门及类似品〕	5		50	13/	13	套/千克			/15
		-零件:									
8481.9010		---阀门用〔101安全附件,102其它阀门及类似品零件〕	8	4	30	13/	13	千克		L	/14
8481.9090		---其他〔101安全附件,102其它阀门及类似品零件〕	8		50	13/	13	千克			/28
84.82		**滚动轴承:**									
		-滚珠轴承:									
8482.1010		---调心球轴承〔999〕	8		20	13/	13	套/千克			/18
8482.1020		---深沟球轴承〔999〕	8		20	13/	13	套/千克			/33
8482.1030		---角接触轴承〔999〕	8		20	13/	13	套/千克			/33
8482.1040		---推力球轴承									
8482.1040	10	飞机发动机用外径30CM的推力球轴承(滚珠轴承)〔999〕	8	1	20	13/	13	套/千克			/21
8482.1040	90	其他推力球轴承(滚珠轴承)〔999〕	8		20	13/	13	套/千克			/28
8482.1090		---其他〔999〕	8		20	13/	13	套/千克			/28
8482.2000		-锥形滚子轴承,包括锥形滚子组件〔999〕	8		20	13/	13	套/千克			/28
8482.3000		-鼓形滚子轴承〔999〕	8	6	20	13/	13	套/千克			/26
8482.4000		-滚针轴承〔999〕	8	6	20	13/	13	套/千克			/16
8482.5000		-其他圆柱形滚子轴承									
8482.5000	10	三环、二环偏心滚动轴承〔999〕	8	4	20	13/	13	套/千克			/24
8482.5000	90	其他圆柱形滚子轴承〔999〕	8		20	13/	13	套/千克			/28
8482.8000		-其他,包括球、柱混合轴承〔999〕	8		20	13/	13	套/千克			/28
		-零件:									
8482.9100		--滚珠、滚针及滚柱〔999〕	8	6	20	13/	13	千克			/26
8482.9900		--其他〔999〕	6	3	20	13/	13	千克			/23
84.83		**传动轴(包括凸轮轴及曲柄轴)及曲柄;轴承座及滑动轴承;齿轮及齿轮传动装置;滚珠或滚子螺杆传动装置;齿轮箱及其他变速装置,包括扭矩变换器;飞轮及滑轮,包括滑轮组;离合器及联轴器(包括万向节):**									
		-传动轴(包括凸轮轴及曲柄轴)及曲柄:									
		---船舶用传动轴:									
8483.1011		----柴油机曲轴〔999〕	6		14	13/	13	个/千克			/31
8483.1019		----其他〔999〕	6		14	13/	13	个/千克			/16
8483.1090		---其他〔999〕	6		30	13/	13	个/千克			/26
8483.2000		-装有滚珠或滚子轴承的轴承座〔999〕	6		30	13/	13	个/千克			/16
8483.3000		-未装滚珠或滚子轴承的轴承座;滑动轴承									
8483.3000	10	磁悬浮轴承(轴承组合件,由悬浮在充满阻尼介质的环形磁铁组成)〔999〕	6	4	30	13/	13	个/千克	3		/24
8483.3000	20	轴承/阻尼器(安装在阻尼器上的具有枢轴/盖的轴承)〔999〕	6	4	30	13/	13	个/千克	3		/24
8483.3000	90	其他未装有滚珠或滚子轴承的轴承座;其他滑动轴承〔999〕	6	4	30	13/	13	个/千克			/24

协定税率 %										特惠税率 %			Article Description
亚太5国	东/冰/格	巴基斯坦	韩国	瑞士	哥达	秘鲁	澳大利亚	新西/坡/智	港/澳/台	亚太2国	老/柬/缅	36/3/1	
4.6	0/0/0	0	4.2	2.1	0	0	0	0//0	0/0/0			0/0/0	Other selector valve(used for tubing, boilers, Cans, barrels or similar products)
													---Flow control valves:
													----Electronic expansion valves
4.6	0/0/0	0	4.2	0	0	0	0	0//0	0/0/0			0/0/0	Electronic expansion flow valve of dual-use items control
4.6	0/0/0	0	4.2	0	0	0	0	0//0	0/0/0			0/0/0	Other electronic expansion flow valve(used for tubing, boilers, Cans, barrels or similar products)
													----Other
4.6	0/0/0	0	4.2	2.1	0	0	0	0//0	0/0/0			0/0/0	Other flow control valve of sensitive items control
4.6	0/0/0	0	4.2	2.1	0	0	0	0//0	0/0/0			0/0/0	Other flow control valve(used for tubing, boilers, Cans, barrels or similar products)
													---Other valve
4.6	0/0/0	0	0	2.1	0	0	0	0//0	0/0/0			0/0/0	Other valve of sensitive items control
4.6	0/0/0	0	0	2.1	0	0	0	0//0	0/0/0		//	0/0/0	HP Turbine clearance control valve (for pipes, boilers, tanks, barrels or similar)
4.6	0/0/0	0	0	2.1	0	0	0	0//0	0/0/0			0/0/0	Other valve(used for tubing, boilers, Cans, barrels or similar products)
	0/0/0	0	0	0	0	0	0	0//0	0/0/			0/0/0	---Other
													-Parts:
	0/0/0	4	0	2.4	0	0	0	0//0	0/0/0			0/0/0	---Of valves
	0/0/0	4	0	0	0	0	0	0//0	0/0/0			0/0/0	---Other
													Ball or roller bearings:
													-Ball bearings:
5.2	0/0/3.2	4	0	0	0	0	0	0/0/0	0/0/			0/0/0	---Self-aliging ball bearing
5.2	0/0/0	4	0	0	0	0	0	0/0/0	0/0/			0/0/0	---Deep groove ball bearing
5.2	0/0/0	4	0	0	0	0	0	0/0/0	0/0/			0/0/0	---Angular contact ball bearing
													---Thrust ball bearing
5.2	0/0/0	4	0	0	0	0	0	0/0/0	0/0/			0/0/0	Thrust ball bearing for airplane engine, external diameter =30cm
5.2	0/0/0	4	0	0	0	0	0	0/0/0	0/0/			0/0/0	Other thrust ball bearing
5.2	0/0/0	4	0	2.4	0	0	0	0/0/0	0/0/			0/0/0	---Other
	0/0/0	4	0	0	0	0	0	0//0	0/0/			0/0/0	-Tapered roller bearings, including cone and tapered roller assemblies
	0/0/0	4	0	0	0	0	0	0//0	0/0/			0/0/0	-Spherical roller bearings
	0//0	4	0	0	0	0	0	0//0	0/0/0			0/0/0	-Needle roller bearings
													-Other cylindrical roller bearings
	0/0/0	4	4.8	2.4	0	0	0	0/0/0	0/0/			0/0/0	Tricyclic or bicyclic eccentric rolling bearing
	0/0/0	4	4.8	2.4	0	0	0	0/0/0	0/0/			0/0/0	Other cylindrical roller bearings
5.2	0/0/0	4	4.8	2.4	0	0	0	0//0	0/0/			0/0/0	-Other, including combined ball/roller bearings
													-Parts:
	0/0/0	4	0	0	0	0	0	0//0	0/0/			0/0/0	--Balls, needles and rollers
	0/0/0	0	0	1.8	0	0	0	0//0	0/0/0			0/0/0	--Other
													Transmission shafts (including cam shafts and crank shafts) and cranks; bearing housings and plain shaft bearings; gears and gearing ball or roller screws; gear boxes and other speed changers, including torque converters; flywheels and pulleys, including pulley blocks; clutches and shaft couplings (including universal joints):
													-Transmission shafts (including cam shafts and crank shafts) and cranks:
													---Transmission shafts for ships:
3.9	0/0/0	0	3.9	0	0	0	0	0//0	0/0/			0/0/0	----Crank shaft for diesel engine
3.9	0/0/0	4	3.6	0	0	0	0	0//0	0/0/			0/0/0	----Other
3.9	0/0/0	4	3.6	1.8	0	0	0	0//0	0/0/			0/0/0	---Other
	0/0/0	0	0	1.8	0	0	0	0//0	0/0/			0/0/0	-Bearing housings, incorporating ball or roller bearings
													-Bearing housings, not incorporating ball or roller bearings; plain shaft bearings
	0/0/0	0	0	1.8	0	0	0	0//0	0/0/			0/0/0	Magnetic suspension bearing (assembly of bearing, compased of circular magnets of supending in filled with damping mediun)
	0/0/0	0	0	1.8	0	0	0	0//0	0/0/			0/0/0	Bearings dampers (installed on the bearing with a pivot lid on the damper)
	0/0/0	0	0	1.8	0	0	0	0//0	0/0/			0/0/0	Other bearing housing not incorporalins ball or rouer bearings; other plain shaft bearins

税则号列	货品名称〔CIQ 扩展编码及品名－T2 表示见附表 2〕	最惠(%)	暂定税率	普通	增值/消费	出口退税	计量单位	监管条件	检验检疫	特殊证件对美关税
	-齿轮及齿轮传动装置，但单独进口或出口的带齿的轮、链轮及其他传动元件除外；滚珠或滚子螺杆传动装置；齿轮箱及其他变速装置，包括扭矩变换器：									
8483.4010	---滚子螺杆传动装置〔999〕	8		30	13/	13	个/千克			/28
8483.4020	---行星齿轮减速器〔999〕	8		30	13/	13	个/千克			/33
8483.4090	---其他〔999〕	8		30	13/	13	个/千克			/28
8483.5000	-飞轮及滑轮，包括滑轮组〔999〕	8		30	13/	13	个/千克			/33
8483.6000	-离合器及联轴器（包括万向节）									
8483.6000 01	压力机用组合式湿式离合/制动器（离合扭矩为 60kNM-300kNM，制动扭矩为 30kNM-100kNM）〔999〕	8	4	30	13/	13	个/千克			/24
8483.6000 90	离合器及联轴器（包括万向节）〔999〕	8		30	13/	13	个/千克			/28
8483.9000	-单独报验的带齿的轮、链轮及其他传动元件；零件									
8483.9000 10	车用凸轮轴相位调节器（汽车发动机用）〔999〕	8	4	30	13/	13	千克			/24
8483.9000 90	税目 84.83 所列货品用其他零件（包括单独报验的带齿的轮、链轮及其他传动元件）〔999〕	8		30	13/	13	千克			/28
84.84	**密封垫或类似接合衬垫，用金属片与其他材料制成或用双层或多层金属片制成；成套或各种不同材料的密封垫或类似接合衬垫，装于袋、套或类似包装内；机械密封件：**									
8484.1000	-密封垫或类似接合衬垫（用金属片与其他材料制成或用双层或多层金属片制成）〔999〕	8	5	30	13/	13	千克			/15
8484.2000	-机械密封件									
8484.2000 10	耐 UF_6 腐蚀的转动轴封（专门设计的真空密封装置，缓冲气体泄漏率 $1000cm^3/min$）〔999〕	8	5	30	13/	13	千克	3		/25
8484.2000 20	转动轴封（专门设计的带有密封式进气口和出气口的转动轴封）〔999〕	8	5	30	13/	13	千克	3		/25
8484.2000 30	MLIS 用转动轴封（专门设计的带密封进气口和出气口的转动轴封）〔999〕	8	5	30	13/	13	千克	3		/25
8484.2000 90	其他机械密封件〔999〕	8	5	30	13/	13	千克			/25
8484.9000	-其他〔999〕	8	5	30	13/	13	千克			/10
84.86	**专用于或主要用于制造半导体单晶柱或晶圆、半导体器件、集成电路或平板显示器的机器及装置；本章注释九（三）规定的机器及装置，零件及附件：**									
	-制造单晶柱或晶圆用的机器及装置：									
8486.1010	---利用温度变化处理单晶硅的机器及装置〔999〕	0		30	13/	13	台/千克			/
8486.1020	---研磨设备〔999〕	0		30	13/	13	台/千克			/
8486.1030	---切割设备〔999〕	0		30	13/	13	台/千克			/
8486.1040	---化学机械抛光设备（CMP）〔999〕	0		30	13/	13	台/千克			/
8486.1090	---其他〔999〕	0		30	13/	13	台/千克			/
	-制造半导体器件或集成电路用的机器及装置：									
8486.2010	---氧化、扩散、退火及其他热处理设备〔999〕	0		30	13/	13	台/千克			/
	---薄膜沉积设备：									
8486.2021	----化学气相沉积装置（CVD）〔999〕	0		30	13/	13	台/千克			/
8486.2022	----物理气相沉积装置（PVD）〔999〕	0		30	13/	13	台/千克			/
8486.2029	----其他〔999〕	0		30	13/	13	台/千克			/
	---将电路图投影或绘制到感光半导体材料上的装置：									
8486.2031	----分步重复光刻机（步进光刻机）〔999〕	0		100	13/	13	台/千克			/
8486.2039	----其他〔101 其它机床，102 电子行业成套设备〕	0		100	13/	13	台/千克			/
	---刻蚀及剥离设备：									
8486.2041	----等离子体干法刻蚀机[T2〕	0		30	13/	13	台/千克			/
8486.2049	----其他〔101 其它机床，102 电子行业成套设备〕	0		30	13/	13	台/千克			/
8486.2050	---离子注入机〔999〕	0		11	13/	13	台/千克			/
8486.2090	---其他〔101 其它机床，102 电子行业成套设备〕	0		30	13/	13	台/千克			/
	-制造平板显示器用的机器及装置：									
8486.3010	---扩散、氧化、退火及其他热处理设备〔999〕	0		30	13/	13	台/千克			/
	---薄膜沉积设备：									
8486.3021	----化学气相沉积设备（CVD）〔999〕	0		30	13/	13	台/千克			/

协定税率 %										特惠税率 %			Article Description
亚太5国	东/冰/格	巴基斯坦	韩国	瑞士	哥达	秘鲁	澳大利亚	新西/坡/智	港/澳/台	亚太2国	老/柬/缅	36/3/1	
													-Gears and gearing, other than toothed wheels, chain sprockets and other transmission elements presented separately; ball or roller screws; gear boxes and other speed changers, including torque converters:
5.2	0/0/0	4	0	2.4	0	0	0	0//0	0/0/0			0/0/0	---Roller Screws
5.2	0/0/0	4	5.2	2.4	0	0	0	0//0	0/0/			0/0/0	---Planet decelerators
5.2	0/0/3.2	4	4.8	2.4	0	0	0	0//0	0/0/0			0/0/0	---Other
	0/0/0	4	3.2	2.4	0	0	0	0//0	0/0/			0/0/0	-Flywheels and pulleys, including pulley blocks
													-Clutches and shaft couplings (including universal joints)
	0/0/0	4	4.8	2.4	0	0	0	0//0	0/0/			0/0/0	Combined wet clutches/ brakes for presses (the on-off torque is 60KNM~300KNM and the braking torque is 30KNM~100KNM)
	0/0/0	4	4.8	2.4	0	0	0	0//0	0/0/			0/0/0	Clutches and shaft couplings(including universal joints)
													-Toothed wheels, chain sprockets and other transmission elements presented separately; parts
	0/0/0	4	0	2.4	0	0	0	0//0	0/0/0			0/0/0	Car camshaft phase regulator (car engine)
	0/0/0	4	0	2.4	0	0	0	0//0	0/0/0			0/0/0	Other components for goods of heading 84.83 goods (toothed wheels, chain sprockets and other transmission components including separately presented)
													Gaskets and similar joints of metal sheeting combined with other material or of two or more layers of metal; sets or assortments of gaskets and similar joints, dissimilar in composition, put up in pouches, envelopes or similar packings mechanical seals:
	0/0/0	4	4.8	2.4	0	0	0	0//0	0/0/0			0/0/0	-Gaskets and similar joints of metal sheeting combined with other material or of two or more layers of metal
													-Mechanical seals
	0/0/0	4	4.8	2.4	0	0	0	0//0	0/0/			0/0/0	UF_6 resisting rotary shaft seals(specially designed vacuum airtight devices, rate of leakage of buffer gas $1000cm^3/min$)
	0/0/0	4	4.8	2.4	0	0	0	0//0	0/0/			0/0/0	Rotary shalt seals (specially designed shaft seals with an airtight inlet and outlet)
	0/0/0	4	4.8	2.4	0	0	0	0//0	0/0/			0/0/0	Rotary shalt seals for MLIS(specially designed, shaft seals an airtight inlet and outlet)
	0/0/0	4	4.8	2.4	0	0	0	0//0	0/0/			0/0/0	Other mechanical seals
	0/0/0	4	4.8	0	0	0	0	0//0	0/0/			0/0/0	-Other
													Machines and apparatus of a kind used soldy or principally for the manufacture of semiconduc tor boules or wafors, semiconductor devices, electronic integrated circuits or flat panel displays; machines and apparatus specified in Note 9(C) to this chapter; Parts and accessories
													-Machines and apparatus for the manvifacture of boules or wafers:
											0//	0/0/0	---Machines and apparatus for the treatment of monocrystalline sillicon by aprocess involving a change of temperature
												0/0/0	---Grinding machines
												0/0/0	---Sawing machines
												0/0/0	---Chemical mechanical polishers (CMP)
												0/0/0	---other
													-Machines and apparatus for the manufacture of semiconductor devices or of electronic integrated circuis:
											0//	0/0/0	---Diffusion, oxidatation annealing and other heat treatment equipment
													---Film deposition oquipment:
												0/0/0	----Chemical Vapor Deposition (CVD) equipment
												0/0/0	----Physical Vapour Deposition (PVD) equipment
												0/0/0	----Other
													---Apparatus for the projection or drawing of circuit patterns on sensitized semiconductor materials:
												0/0/0	----step and repeat alignersw
												0/0/0	----Other
													---Etching and stripoing equipment:
												0/0/0	----Dry plasma etching
												0/0/0	----Other
												0/0/0	---Ion Implanters
												0/0/0	---Other
													-Machines and apparatus for the manufacture of flat panel displays:
											0//	0/0/0	---Oxidatation diffusinon annealing and other heat treatment equipment
													---Film deposition equipment:
												0/0/0	---- Chemical vapour deposition (CVD) equipment

税则号列	货品名称〔CIQ 扩展编码及品名－T2 表示见附表 2〕	最惠(%)	暂定税率	普通	增值/消费	出口退税	计量单位	监管条件	检验检疫	特殊证件对美关税
8486.3022	----物理气相沉积设备(PVD)〔999〕	0		30	13/	13	台/千克			/
8486.3029	----其他〔999〕	0		30	13/	13	台/千克			/
	---将电路图投影或绘制到感光半导体材料上的装置：									
8486.3031	----分布重复光刻机〔999〕	0		100	13/	13	台/千克			/
8486.3039	----其他〔101 其它机床,102 电子行业成套设备〕	0		100	13/	13	台/千克			/
	---湿法蚀刻、显影、剥离、清洗装置：									
8486.3041	----超声波清洗装置[T2]	3.3/1.7		30	13/	13	台/千克			/
8486.3049	----其他[T2]	0		30	13/	13	台/千克			/
8486.3090	---其他〔101 其它机床,102 电子行业成套设备〕	0		30	13/	13	台/千克			/
	-本章注释九(三)规定的机器及装置：									
8486.4010	---主要用于或专用于制作和修复掩膜版(mask)或投影掩膜版(reticle)的装置〔999〕	0		70	13/	13	台/千克			/
	---主要用于或专有于装配与封装半导体器件或集成电路的设备：									
8486.4021	----塑封机〔999〕	1.7/0.8		30	13/	13	台/千克			/
8486.4022	----引线键合装置〔999〕	2.7/1.3		30	13/	13	台/千克			/
8486.4029	----其他〔999〕	0		17	13/	13	台/千克			/
	---主要用于或专用于升降、装卸、搬运单晶柱、晶圆、半导体器件、集成电路或平板显示器的装置：									
8486.4031	----集成电路工厂专用的自动搬运机器人[T2]	0		20	13/	13	台/千克			/
8486.4039	----其他[T2]	1.7/0.8		30	13/	13	台/千克			/
	-零件及附件：									
8486.9010	---升降、搬运、装卸机器用(自动搬运设备用除外)[T2]	0		30	13/	13	千克			/
8486.9020	---引线键合装置用〔999〕	0		30	13/	13	千克			/
	---其他：									
8486.9091	----带背板的溅射靶材组件〔999〕	0		17	13/	13	千克			/
8486.9099	----其他〔999〕	0		17	13/	13	千克			/
84.87	**本章其他税目未列名的机器零件,不具有电气接插件、绝缘体,线圈、触点或其他电气器材特征的：**									
8487.1000	-船用推进器及桨叶〔999〕	6		14	13/	13	千克			/26
8487.9000	-其他〔999〕	8		30	13/	13	千克			/28

协定税率 %										特惠税率 %			Article Description
亚太5国	东/冰/格	巴基斯坦	韩国	瑞士	哥达	秘鲁	澳大利亚	新西/坡/智	港/澳/台	亚太2国	老/柬/缅	36/3/1	
												0/0/0	----Physical Vapour Deposition (PVD) equipment
												0/0/0	----Other
													---Apparatus for the projection or drawing of circuit patterns on sensitized stmiconductor materials:
												0/0/0	----Step and repeat alignersw
												0/0/0	----Other
													---Apparatus for wet-etching developing stripping or cleaning:
	0/0/0	4		0	0	0	0	0/0/0	0/0/			0/0/0	----Ultrasonic apparatus for cleaning
												0/0/0	----Other
												0/0/0	---Other
													-Machines and apparatus specified in Note 9 (c) to this chapter:
												0/0/0	---Apparatus solely or principally of a kind used for the manufacture or repair of masks and reticles
													---Machines solely or principally of a kind used for assembling or encapsulating semiconductor devices or electronic integrated circuits:
1.5/0.7	0/0/0	0	4.5	0	0	0	0	0//0	0/0/			0/0/0	----Plastics encapsulating machines
2.6/1.2	0/0/0	4		2.4/1.3	0	0	0	0//0	0/0/			0/0/0	----Wire bonders
												0/0/0	----Other
													---Apparatus solely or principally of a kind used for lifting, handling, loading or unloading of boules, wafers, semiconductor devices, electronic integrated circuits and flat panel displays:
												0/0/0	----Automated material handling machines solely or principally of a kind used in the electronic integrated circuits factories
1.2/0.6	0/0/0	0	3.5	0	0	0	0	0//0	0/0/			0/0/0	----Other
													-Parts and accessories:
	0//							//	0/0/			0/0/0	---Of machines for lifting, handling, loading or unloading (other than automated material handling machines)
	0//							//	0/0/			0/0/0	---Of wire bonders
													---Other:
												0/0/0	With the backplane of the sputtering target assembly
												0/0/0	----Other〔999〕
													Machinery parts, not containing electrical connectors insulators, coils, contacts or other eledrical features, not specified or included cleswhere in this chopter:
	0/0/0	0	3.6	0	0	0	0	0//0	0/0/			0/0/0	-Ships'or boats'propellers and blades therefor
	0/0/0	4	3.2	2.4	0	0	0	0//0	0/0/0			0/0/0	-Other

第八十五章
电机、电气设备及其零件;录音机及放声机、电视图像、声音的录制和重放设备及其零件、附件

注释:

一、本章不包括:

(一)电暖的毯子、褥子、足套及类似品,电暖的衣服 、靴、鞋、耳套或其他供人穿戴的电暖物品;

(二)税目70.11的玻璃制品;

(三)税目84.86的机器及装置;

(四)用于医疗、外科、牙科或兽医的真空设备(税目90.18)

(五)第九十四章的电热家具。

二、税目85.01至85.04不适用于税目85.11、85.12、85.40、85.41或85.42的货品,但金属槽汞弧整流器仍归入税目85.04。

三、税号85.07所称"蓄电池",包括与其一同报验的辅助元件,这些辅助元件具有储电、供电功能,或保护蓄电池免遭损坏,例如,电路连接器、温控装置(例如,热敏电阻)及电路保护装置,也可包括蓄电池的部分保护外壳。

四、税目85.09仅包括通常供家用的下列电动器具:

(一)任何重量的地板打蜡机、食品研磨机及食品搅拌器、水果或蔬菜的榨汁机;

(二)重量不超过20千克的其他机器。

但该税目不适用于风机、风扇或装有风扇的通风罩及循环气罩(不论是否装有过滤器)(税目84.14)、离心干衣机(税目84.21)、洗碟机(税目84.22)、家用洗衣机(税目84.50)、滚筒式或其他形式的熨烫机器(税目84.20或84.51)、缝纫机(税目84.52)、电剪子(税目84.67)或电热器具(税目85.16)。

五、税目85.23所称:

(一)"固态、非易决性存储器件"(例如,"闪存卡"或"电子闪存卡",是指带有接口的存储器件,共在同一壳体内包含一块或多块闪存(FLASH E^2 PROM),以集成电路的形式装配在一块印刷电路板上。它们可以包括一个集成电路形式的控制器及分立无源元件,例如,电容器及电阻器;

(二)所称"智能卡"是指装有一块或多块集成电路微处理器、随机存取存储器(RAM)或只读存储器(ROM)芯片的卡。这些卡可带有触点、磁条或嵌入式天线,但不包含任何其他有源或无源电路元件。

六、税目85.34所称"印刷电路",是指采用各种印制方法(例如,压印、覆镀、腐蚀)或采用"膜电路"工艺,将导线、接点或其他印制元件(例如,电感器、电阻器、电容器)按预定的图形单独或互相连接地印制在绝缘基片上的电路,但能够产生、整流、调制或放大电信号的元件(例如,半导体元件)除外。

所称"印刷电路",不包括装有非印制元件的电路,也不包括单个的分立式电阻器、电容器及电感器,但印刷电路可配有非经印刷的连接元件。

用同样工艺制得的无源元件及有源元件组成的薄膜电路或厚膜电路应归入税目85.42。

七、税目85.36所称"光导纤维、光导纤维束或光缆用连接器",是指在有线数字通讯设备中,简单机械地把光纤端部相连成一线的连接器。它们不具备请如对信号进行放大、再生或修正等其他功能。

八、税目85.37不包括电视接收机或其他电气设备用的无绳红外遥控器(税目85.43)

九、税目85.41及85.42所称:

(一)"二极管、晶体管及类似的半导体器件",是指那些依靠外加电场引起电阻率的变化而进行工作的半导体器件。

(二)"集成电路",是指:

1. 单片集成电路,即电路元件(二极管、晶体管、电阻器、电容器、电感器等)主要整体制作在一片半导体材料或化合物半导体材料(例如掺杂硅砷化镓、硅锗或磷化铟)基片的表面,并不可分割地连接在一起的电路。

本注释所述物品在归类时,即使本协调制度其他税号涉及上述物品,尤其是物品的功能,仍应优先考虑归入税目85.41及85.42,但涉及税目85.23的情况除外。

2. 混合集成电路,即通过薄膜或厚膜工艺制得的无源元件(电阻器、电容器、电感器等)和通过半导体工艺制得的有源元件(二极管、晶体管、单片集成电路等)用互连或连接线不可分割地组合在同一绝缘基片(玻璃、陶瓷等)上的电路。这种电路也可包括分立元件。

Chapter 85
Electrical machinery and equipment and parts thereof; sound recorders and reproducers, television image and sound recorders and reproducers, and parts and accessories of such articles

Notes:

1. This Chapter does not cover:
   (a) Electrically warmed blankets, bed pads, foot-muffs or the like; electrically warmed clothing, footwear or ear pads or other electrically warmed articles worn on or about the person;
   (b) Articles of glass of heading No. 70. 11.
   (c) Machines and apparaatus of heading 84. 86;
   (d) Vacuum apparatus of a kind used in medical, surgical, dencal or veterinary purposes (Heading No. 90. 18);
   (e) Electrically heated furniture of Chapter 94.
2. HeadingsNo. 85. 01 to 85. 04 do not apply to goods described in headingNo. 85. 11, 85. 12, 85. 40, 85. 41 or 85. 42. However, metal tank mercury arc rectifiers remain classified in headingNo. 85. 04.
3. Heading 85.07 called "battery", including auxiliary components together with its inspection, the auxiliary components has a power storage and power supply function, or protect the battery from damage, for example, circuit connector, temperature control device (e. g., thermistor) and circuit protection device, May also include a battery partial protection housing.
4. HeadingNo. 85. 09 covers only the following electro-mechanical machines of the kind commonly used for domestic purposes:
   (a) Floor polishers, food grinders and mixers, and fruit or vegetable juice extractors, of any weight;
   (b) Other machines provided the weight of such machines does not exceed 20 kg.
   The heading does not, however, apply to fans or ventilating or recycling hoods incorporating a fan, whether or not fitted with filters (headingNo. 84. 14), centrifugal clothes-dryers (headingNo. 84. 21), dish washing machines (headingNo. 84. 22), household washing machines (headingNo. 84. 50), roller or other ironing machines (headingNo. 84. 20 or 84. 51), sewing machines (headingNo. 84. 52), electric scissors (headingNo. 84. 67) or to electro-thermic appliances (headingNo. 85. 16).
5. For the purposes of heading 85. 23:
   (a) "Solid-state non-volatile storage devices" (for example, "flash memory cards" or "flash electronic storage cards") are storage devices with a connecting socket, comprising in the same housing one or more flash memories (for example, "FLASH E^2 PROM") in the form of integrated circuits mounted on a printed circuit board. They may include a controller in the form of an integrated circuit and discrete passive components, such as capacitors and resistors;
   (b) The term "smart cards" means cards which have embedded in them one or more electronic integrated circuits (a microprocessor, random access memory (RAM) or readonly memory (ROM)) in the form of chips. These cards may contain contacts, a magnetic stripe or an embedded antenna but do not contain any other active or passive circuit elements.
6. For the purposes of headingNo. 85. 34 "printed circuits" are circuits obtained by forming on an insulating base, by any printing process (for example, embossing, plating-up, etching) or by the "film circuit" technique, conductor elements, contacts or other printed components (for example, inductances, resistors, capacitors) alone or interconnected according to a pre-established pattern, other than elements which can produce, rectify, modulate or amplify an electrical signal (for example, semiconductor elements).
   The expression "printed circuits" does not cover circuits combined with elements other than those obtained during the printing process, nor does it cover individual, discrete resistors, capacitors or inductances.
   Thinor thick-film circuits comprising passive and active elements obtained during the same technological process are to be classified in heading No. 85. 42.
7. For the purpose of heading 85. 36. "connectors for opticalfl bres, optical fibre bundles or cables" means connectors that simply mechanically align optical fibres end to end in a ligital line system. They perform on other function, such as the am plification, regeneration or modification of a signal.
8. Heading 85. 37 does not include cordless infrared devices for the remote control of television receivers or other elctrical quipment (heading 85. 43).
9. For the purposes of headings No. 85. 41 and 85. 42:
   (a) "Diodes, transistors and similar semiconductor devices" are semiconductor devices the operation of which depends on variations in resistivity on the application of an electric field;
   (b) "Electronic integrated circuits" are:
      (i) Monolithic integrated circuits in which the circuit elements (diodes, transistors resistors capacitors, interconnections, etc) are created in the mass (essentially) and on the surface of a semiconductor or compound semiconductor materical (for example, doped silicon, gallium arsenide silicon, gemanium indium phospide) and are inseparably associated;
   For the classification of the articles defined in this Note, headings 85.41 and 85.42 shall thke precedence over any other headings in the Nomenclature, except in the case of heading 85.23, which might cover them by reference to, in paricular, their function.
      (ii) Hybrid integrated circuits in which passive elements (resistors, capacitors, inductances, etc), obtained by thin-or thick-film technology, and active elements (diodes, transistors, monolithic integrated circuits, etc.), obtained by semiconductor technology, are combined to all intents and purposes indivisibly, by interconne cltions or interconnecting cables on a single insulating substrate (glass, ceramic, etc.). These circuits may also include discrete components;

3. 多芯片集成电路是由两个或多个单片集成电路不可分割地组合在一片或多片的绝缘基片上构成的电路,不论是否带有引线框架,但不带有其他有源或无源的电路元件。

4. 多元件集成电路(MCOs):由一个或多个单片、混合或多芯片集成电路以及下列至少一个元件组成:硅基传感器、执行器、振荡器、谐振器或其组件所构成的组合体,或者具有税目 85.32、85.33、85.41 所列商品功能的元件,或税目 85.04 的电感器。其像集成电路一样实际上不可分割地组合成一体,作为一种元件,通过引脚、引线、焊球、底面触点、凸点或导电压点进行连接,组装到印刷电路板(PCB)或其他载体上。

在本定义中:

(1)"元件"可以是分立的,独立制造后组装到多元件(MCO)的其余部分上,或者集成到其他元件内。

(2)"硅基"是指在硅基片上制造,或由硅材料制造而成,或者制造在集成电路裸片上。

(3)①硅基传感器是由在半导体材料内部或表面制作的微电子或机械结构组成,具有探测物理量和化学量并将其转换成电信号(因电特性变化或机械结构位移而产生)的功能。"物理量或化学量"与现实世界的现象相关,例如,压力、声波、加速度、振动、运动、方向、张力、磁场强度、电场强度、光、放射性、湿度、流量和化学浓度等。

②硅基执行器是由在半导体材料内部或表面制作的微电子或机械结构组成,具有将电信号转换成物理运动的功能。

③硅基谐振器是由在半导体材料内部或表面制作的微电子或机械结构组成,具有按预先设定的频率产生机械或电振荡的功能,频率取决于响应外部输入的结构的物理参数。

④硅基振荡器是有缘器件,由在半导体材料内部或表面制作的微电子或机械结构组成,具有按预先设定的频率产生机械或电振荡的功能,频率取决于这些结构的物理参数。

本注释所述物品在归类时,即使本目录其他税目涉及上述物品,尤其是物品的功能,仍应优先考虑归入税目 85.41 及 85.42,但涉及税目 85.23 的情况除外。

十、税目 85.48 所称"废原电池、废原电池组及废蓄电池",是指因破损、拆解、耗尽或其他原因而不能再使用,也不能再充电的电池。

子目注释:

子目号 8 527.12 仅包括有内置放大器但无内置扬声器的盒式磁带放声机,它不需外接电源即能工作,且外形尺寸不超过 170 毫米×100 毫米×45 毫米。

税则号列		货品名称〔CIQ 扩展编码及品名－T2 表示见附表 2〕	最惠(%)	暂定税率	普通	增值/消费	出口退税	计量单位	监管条件	检验检疫	特殊证件对美关税
85.01		**电动机及发电机(不包括发电机组):**									
		-输出功率不超过 37.5 瓦的电动机:									
8501.1010		---玩具用〔999〕	12		80	13/	13	台/千克			/
		---其他:									
8501.1091		----微电机,机座尺寸在 20 毫米及以上,但不超过 39 毫米									
8501.1091	01	激光视盘机机芯精密微型电机(1 瓦≤功率<18 瓦,20mm≤直径≤30mm)〔999〕	9	5	70	13/	13	台/千克			/30
8501.1091	02	摄像机、摄录一体机用精密微型电机(0.5 瓦≤功率≤10 瓦),20mm≤直径≤39mm)〔999〕	9	5	70	13/	13	台/千克			/30
8501.1091	90	其他机座最大尺寸在 20mm 至 39mm 微电机(输出功率不超过 37.5 瓦)〔999〕	9		70	13/	13	台/千克			/34
8501.1099		----其他									
8501.1099	01	功率≤0.5W 非用于激光视盘机机芯的微型电机(圆柱形直径≤6mm,高≤25mm;扁圆型直径≤15mm,厚≤5mm)〔999〕	9	5	35	13/	13	台/千克			/30
8501.1099	02	激光视盘机机芯用精密微型电机(0.5 瓦≤功率≤2 瓦),5mm≤直径≤20mm〔999〕	9	5	35	13/	13	台/千克			/30
8501.1099	03	摄像机、摄录一体机用精密微型电机(0.5 瓦≤功率≤10 瓦,5mm≤直径<20mm 或 39mm<直径≤40mm)〔999〕	9	5	35	13/	13	台/千克			/30
8501.1099	90	其他微电机(输出功率不超过 37.5 瓦)〔101 玩具电机,102 微电机〕	9		35	13/	13	台/千克			/34
8501.2000		-交直流两用电动机,输出功率超过 37.5 瓦〔999〕	12		35	13/	13	台/千克		L	/32
		-其他直流电动机;直流发电机:									
8501.3100		--输出功率不超过 750 瓦〔101 微电机,102 直流电动机,103 其它发电机(组)及其零件〕	12		35	13/	13	台/千克		L	/32
8501.3200		--输出功率超过 750 瓦,但不超过 75 千瓦〔101 直流电动机,102 其它发电机(组)及其零件〕	10		35	13/	13	台/千克		L	/30
8501.3300		--输出功率超过 75 千瓦,但不超过 375 千瓦〔101 直流电动机,102 其它发电机(组)及其零件〕	5		35	13/	13	台/千克			/25

(iii) Multichip integrated circuits consisting of two or more interconnected monolithic integrated circuits combined to all intents and purposes indivisibly, whether or not on one or more insulating substrates, with or without leadframes, but with no other active or passive circuit elements.

(iv) Multi element integrated circuit (MCOs) is composed of one or more single, mixed or multi chip integrated circuit and at least containing one of the following components: the combination of silicon sensor, actuator, oscillator, resonator or its components, or with heading No.85.32, 85.33, 85.41 items of commodities listed in the function components. Inductor of heading 85.04. In fact, the same is inseparably integrated like integrated circuits, as an components, through the pin, lead wire, solder ball, bottom contact, bump or conductive pressure points are connected to the printed circuit board assembly (PCB) or other carrier, through the connecting of pins, eads, balls, lands, bumps, or pads.

For the purpose ot this definition:

(i) "Components" may be discrete, manu factured independently then assembled onto the rest of the MCO, or integrated into other components.

(ij) "Silicon based" means built on a silicon substrate, or made of silicon materials, or manufactured onto integrated circuit die.

(iii) a) "Silicon based sensors" consist of microelectronic or meehanical strue tures that are created in the nlass or on the surface of a semiconductor and that have the function of detecting physical or chemical quantities and transducing these into electric signals, caused by resulting variations in electric properties or displacement 0f a mechanical structure. "Physical or chemical quan tities" relates tO real world phenomena, such as pressure, acoustic waves, acceleration, vibration, movement, orientation, strain, magnetic field strength, electric field strength, light, radioaclivity, humidity, flow, ehemi eals concentration, etc.

b) "Silicon based actuators" consist of microelectronic and mechanical structures that are created in the mass or on the surface of a semiconductor and that have the function of converting e lectrical signals into physical movement.

c) "Silicon based resonators" are components that consist of microelec tronic or mechanical structures that are created in the mass or on the surface of a semiconductor and have the function of generating a mechanical or electrical oscillation of a predefined frequency that depends on the physical geometry of these structures in re sponse to an external input.

d) "Silicon based oscillators" are active components that consist of micro electronic or mechanical structures that are created in the mass or on the surface of a semieond uctor and that have the function of generating a mechanical or electrical oscillation of a predefined frequency that depends on the physical geometry of these structures.

For the classification of the articles defined in this Note, headingsNo. 85. 41 and 85. 42 shall take precedence over any other heading in the Nomenclature which might cover them by reference to, in particular, their function.

10. For the purposes of headingNo. 85. 48, spent primary cells, "spent primary batteries and spent electric accumulators" are those which are neither usable as such because of breakage, cutting-up, wear or other reasons, nor capable of being recharged.

Subheading Notes:

Subheadings 8527. 12 cover only cassetteplayers with built-in amplifier, without built-in loudspeaker, capable of operating without an external source of electric power and the dimensions of which do not exceed 170mm×100mm×45mm.

协定税率 %										特惠税率 %			Article Description
亚太5国	东/冰/格	巴基斯坦	韩国	瑞士	哥达	秘鲁	澳大利亚	新西/坡/智	港/澳/台	亚太2国	老/柬/缅	36/3/1	
													Electric motors and generators (excluding generating sets):
													-Motors of an output not exceeding 37. 5W:
7.8	0/0/0	23.3	17.1	7.4	0	0	0	0/0/0	0/0/0			0/0/	---For use in toys
													---Other:
													----Micromotors with a housing size of 20mm or more but not exceeding 39mm
5.9	0/0/0	4	5.4	2.7	0	0	0	0/0/0	0/0/			0/0/0	Precision micromotors for the movement of laser disc players(1W≤power≤18W, 20mm≤diameter≤30mm)
5.9	0/0/0	4	5.4	2.7	0	0	0	0/0/0	0/0/			0/0/0	Micro motor with a video camera, camcorder (0.5W≤ power ≤ 10W), 20mm ≤ diameter ≤ 39mm)
5.9	0/0/0	4	5.4	2.7	0	0	0	0/0/0	0/0/			0/0/0	Other micromotors with a housing size of 20mm or more but not exceeding 39mm (output≤37. 5W)
													----Other
5.9	0/0/0	4.5	5.4	2.7	0	0	0	0/0/0	0/0/0			0/0/0	Micromotors, power≤0. 5W, not for movements of laser disc players(cylindricd diameter≤6mm, high≤25mm; oblate diameter≤15mm, thick≤5mm)
5.9	0/0/0	4.5	5.4	2.7	0	0	0	0/0/0	0/0/0			0/0/0	Precision micro motor with laser videodisc (0.5≤power ≤ 2W), 5mm ≤ diameter ≤ 20mm
5.9	0/0/0	4.5	5.4	2.7	0	0	0	0/0/0	0/0/0			0/0/0	Precision micromotors for video camera, camcorder, movement of laser discplayers(0.5W≤power≤2W, 5mm≤Diameter<20mm Or 39 mm< diameter≤ 40 mm)
5.9	0/0/0	4.5	5.4	2.7	0	0	0	0/0/0	0/0/0			0/0/0	Other micromotors(output power≤37. 5W)
	0/0/0	5.4	4.8	3.6	0	0	0	0/0/0	0/0/			0/0/0	-Universal AC/DC motors of an output exceeding 37. 5 W
													-Other DC motors; DC generators:
7.8	0/0/0	4.8	7.8	0	0	0	0	0/0/0	0/0/0			0/0/0	--Of an output not exceeding 750 W
	0/0/0	4	4	0	0	0	0	0/0/0	0/0/			0/0/0	--Of an output exceeding 750 W but not exceeding 75 kW
	0/0/0	0	0	0	0	0	0	0//0	0/0/			0/0/0	--Of an output exceeding 75 kW but not exceeding 375 kW

税则号列		货品名称〔CIQ扩展编码及品名－T2表示见附表2〕	最惠(%)	暂定税率	普通	增值/消费	出口退税	计量单位	监管条件	检验检疫	特殊证件对美关税
8501.3400		--输出功率超过375千瓦〔101直流电动机,102其它发电机(组)及其零件〕	10		35	13/	13	台/千克			/30
8501.4000		-其他单相交流电动机〔999〕	10		35	13/	13	台/千克		L	/30
		-其他多相交流电动机:									
8501.5100		--输出功率不超过750瓦									
8501.5100	10	发电机(功率≥40瓦特,频率600至2000赫兹,谐波畸变低于10%等)〔999〕	5		35	13/	13	台/千克	3		/30
8501.5100	90	其他输出功率≤750W多相交流电动机〔999〕	5		35	13/	13	台/千克		L	/30
8501.5200		--输出功率超过750瓦,但不超过75千瓦〔999〕	10		35	13/	13	台/千克		L	/35
8501.5300		--输出功率超过75千瓦									
8501.5300	10	高速(200km/h及以上)电力机车的交流异步牵引电动机〔999〕	10	3	35	13/	13	台/千克			/23
8501.5300	90	其他功率＞75kW多相交流电动机〔999〕	10		35	13/	13	台/千克			/30
		-交流发电机:									
8501.6100		--输出功率不超过75千伏安〔999〕	5		30	13/	13	台/千克			/25
8501.6200		--输出功率超过75千伏安,但不超过375千伏安〔999〕	10		30	13/	13	台/千克			/15
8501.6300		--输出功率超过375千伏安,但不超过750千伏安〔999〕	10		30	13/	13	台/千克			/30
		--输出功率超过750千伏安:									
8501.6410		---输出功率超过750千伏安,但不超过350兆伏安									
8501.6410	10	由使用可再生燃料锅炉和涡轮机组驱动的交流发电机,750KVA＜输出功率≤350MVA〔999〕	10	5	30	13/	13	台/千克	O		/25
8501.6410	90	其他750KVA＜输出功率≤350MVA的交流发电机〔999〕	10		30	13/	13	台/千克	O		3/30
8501.6420		---输出功率超过350兆伏安,但不超过665兆伏安									
8501.6420	10	由使用可再生燃料锅炉和涡轮机组驱动的交流发电机,350MVA＜输出功率≤665MVA〔999〕	5.5	5	14	13/	13	台/千克			3/
8501.6420	90	其他350MVA＜输出功率≤665MVA交流发电机〔999〕	5.5		14	13/	13	台/千克	O		3/
8501.6430		---输出功率超过665兆伏安									
8501.6430	10	由使用可再生燃料锅炉和涡轮机组驱动的交流发电机,输出功率＞665MVA〔999〕	6	5	11	13/	13	台/千克			3/15
8501.6430	90	其他输出功率＞665MVA交流发电机〔999〕	6		11	13/	13	台/千克			3/16
85.02		**发电机组及旋转式变流机:**									
		-装有压燃式活塞内燃发动机(柴油或半柴油发动机)的发电机组:									
8502.1100		--输出功率不超过75千伏安〔999〕	10		45	13/	13	台/千克			/15
8502.1200		--输出功率超过75千伏安,但不超过375千伏安〔999〕	10		45	13/	13	台/千克	O		3/30
		--输出功率超过375千伏安:									
8502.1310		---输出功率超过375千伏安,但不超过2兆伏安〔999〕	10		45	13/	13	台/千克	O		3/30
8502.1320		---输出功率超过2兆伏安〔999〕	10		30	13/	13	台/千克	O		3/30
8502.2000		-装有点燃式活塞内燃发动机的发电机组〔999〕	10		45	13/	13	台/千克			3/35
		-其他发电机组:									
8502.3100		--风力驱动的〔999〕	8	5	30	13/	13	台/千克			/30
8502.3900		--其他									
8502.3900	10	依靠可再生能源(太阳能、小水电、潮汐、沼气、地热能、生物质/余热驱动的汽轮机)生产电力的发电机组〔999〕	10	5	30	13/	13	台/千克			3/10
8502.3900	90	其他发电机组(风力驱动除外)〔999〕	10		30	13/	13	台/千克			/15
8502.4000		-旋转式变流机〔999〕	10		30	13/	13	台/千克			/
85.03		**专用于或主要用于税目85.01或85.02所列机器的零件:**									
8503.0010		---子目8501.1010及8501.1091所列电动机用〔999〕	8		70	13/	13	千克			/33
8503.0020		---子目8501.6420及8501.6430所列发电机用〔999〕	3		11	13/	13	千克			/28
8503.0030		---子目8502.3100所列发电机组用〔999〕	3	1	30	13/	13	千克			/26
8503.0090		---其他									
8503.0090	10	电动机定子(用于真空中频率600－2000Hz、功率50－1000VA条件下)〔999〕	8		30	13/	13	千克	3		/33
8503.0090	20	由使用可再生燃料锅炉和涡轮机组驱动的输出功率超过750千伏安不超过350兆伏安的交流发电机的零件〔999〕	8	5	30	13/	13	千克			/30
8503.0090	30	靠可再生能源(太阳能、小水电、潮汐、沼气、地热能、生物质/余热驱动的汽轮机)生产电力发电机组的零件〔999〕	8	5	30	13/	13	千克			/30
8503.0090	90	其他电动机、发电机(组)零件〔999〕	8		30	13/	13	千克			/33

协定税率 %										特惠税率 %			Article Description
亚太5国	东/冰/格	巴基斯坦	韩国	瑞士	哥达	秘鲁	澳大利亚	新西/坡/智	港/澳/台	亚太2国	老/柬/缅	36/3/1	
	0/0/0	5.4	8.4	3.6	0	0	0	0/0/0	0/0/			0/0/0	--Of an output exceeding 375 kW
	0/0/0	5.4	7.2	3.6	0	0	0	0/0/0	0/0/			0/0/0	-Other AC motors, single-phase
													-Other AC motors, multi-phase:
													--Of an output not exceeding 750 W
	0/0/2	0		0	0	0	0	0//0	0/0/			0/0/0	Generators(power≥40W, frequency=600～2000Hz, harmonic distortion<10%)
	0/0/2	0		0	0	0	0	0//0	0/0/			0/0/0	Other AC motors, multi-phase, output power≤750W
	0/0/0	4.5	7	3	0	0	0	0/0/0	0/0/			0/0/0	--Of an output exceeding 750 W but not exceeding 75 kW
													--Of an output exceeding 75 kW
6.5	0/0/0	5.4	7.2	3.6	0	0	0	0/0/0	0/0/			0/0/0	High speed(200km/h and above)AC electric locomotive traction motor
6.5	0/0/0	5.4	7.2	3.6	0	0	0	0/0/0	0/0/			0/0/0	Other AC electric motors, multi-phase, output power>75kW
													-AC generators (alternators):
	0/0/0	0	2	0	0	0	0	0//0	0/0/			0/0/0	--Of an output not exceeding 75 kVA
	0/0/0	5.4	8.4	3.6	0	0	0	0/0/0	0/0/			0/0/0	--Of an output exceeding 75 KVA but not exceeding 375 kVA
	0/0/0	5.4	8.4	3.6	0	0	0	0/0/0	0/0/			0/0/0	--Of an output exceeding 375 KVA but not exceeding 750 kVA
													--Of an output exceeding 750 kVA:
													---Of an output exceeding 750 kVA but not exceeding 350 MVA
	0/0/0	4	7	0	0	0	0	0/0/0	0/0/			0/0/0	By the use of renewable fuel boiler and turbine drive the alternator, <750 kva power output of 350 mva or less
	0/0/0	4	7	0	0	0	0	0/0/0	0/0/			0/0/0	Other<750 kva power output of 350 mva or less of the alternator
													---Of an output exceeding 350 MVA but not exceeding 665 MVA
3.6	0/0/0	0	0	0	0	0	0	0//0	0/0/			0/0/0	By the use of renewable fuel boiler and turbine drive the alternator, 350 mva power output of 665 mva or less
3.6	0/0/0	0	0	0	0	0	0	0//0	0/0/			0/0/0	The other 350MVA<output power 665MVA AC generator
													---Of an output exceeding 665 MVA
3.9	0/0/0	0	0	0	0	0	0	0//0	0/0/			0/0/0	By the use of renewable fuel boiler and turbine drive the alternator, output>665 mva
3.9	0/0/0	0	0	0	0	0	0	0//0	0/0/			0/0/0	Other output power > 665MVA AC generator
													Electric generating sets and rotary converters:
													-Generating sets with compression-ignition internal combustion piston engines (diesel or semi-diesel engines):
	0/0/0	4	4	0	0	0	0	0/0/0	0/0/			0/0/0	--Of an output not exceeding 75 kVA
	0/0/0	4	6	0	0	0	0	0/0/0	0/0/			0/0/0	--Of an output exceeding 75 kVA but not exceeding 375 kVA
													--Of an output exceeding 375 kVA:
6.5	0/0/0	4	7	0	0	0	0	0/0/0	0/0/			0/0/0	---Of an output exceeding 375 kVA but not exceeding 2 MVA
7	0/0/0	4	7	0	0	0	0	0/0/0	0/0/			0/0/0	---Of an output exceeding 2 MVA
	0/0/0	4.5	4	0	0	0	0	0/0/0	0/0/			0/0/0	-Generating sets with spark-ignition internal combustion piston engines
													-Other generating sets:
	0/0/0	4	4.8	0	0	0	0	0//0	0/0/			0/0/0	--Wind-powered
													--Other
	0/0/0	4	6	0	0	0	0	0//0	0/0/			0/0/0	Rely on renewable energy (solar, small hydropower, tidal, methane gas, geothermal energy, biomass/waste heat driven turbine) in the production of electric power generating set
	0/0/0	4	6	0	0	0	0	0//0	0/0/			0/0/0	Other units(except wind driven)
	0/0/0	4	4	0	0	0	0	0//0	0/0/			0/0/0	-Electric rotary converters
													Parts suitable for use solely or principally with the machines of headingNo. 85. 01 or 85. 02:
5.2	0/0/0	5.4	7.8	3.6	0	0	0	0/0/0	0/0/0			0/0/0	---Of the motors of subheading No. 8501. 1010 and 8501. 1091
2	0/0/0	0	0	0.9	0	0	0	0//0	0/0/			0/0/0	---Of the generators of subheading No. 8501. 6420 and 8501. 6430
2.5	0/0/0	0	0	0	0	0	0	0//0	0/0/			0/0/0	---Of the generating sets of subheading No. 8502. 3100
													---Other
5.2	0//0	4.5	0	2.4	0	0	0	0//0	0/0/0			0/0/0	Motor stator (used under vacuum conditions, frequency range = 600Hz～2000Hz, power=50VA～1000VA)
5.2	0//0	4.5	0	2.4	0	0	0	0//0	0/0/0			0/0/0	The alternator output power is driven by the use of renewable fuel boiler and turbine unit more than 750 thousand ampere of not more than 350 MVA parts
5.2	0//0	4.5	0	2.4	0	0	0	0//0	0/0/0			0/0/0	Rely on renewable energy (solar, small hydropower, tidal, methane gas, geothermal energy, biomass/waste heat driven turbine) production power generating sets of parts
5.2	0//0	4.5	0	2.4	0	0	0	0//0	0/0/0			0/0/0	Other parts of electric motors, generators and generating sets

税则号列		货品名称〔CIQ 扩展编码及品名－T2 表示见附表 2〕	最惠(%)	暂定税率	普通	增值/消费	出口退税	计量单位	监管条件	检验检疫	特殊证件对美关税
85.04		**变压器、静止式变流器(例如整流器)及电感器：**									
		-放电灯或放电管用镇流器：									
8504.1010		---电子镇流器〔999〕	10		35	13/	13	个/千克		L	/30
8504.1090		---其他〔101 电子镇流器,102 其它镇流器及其零件〕	10		35	13/	13	个/千克		L	/30
		-液体介质变压器：									
8504.2100		--额定容量不超过 650 千伏安〔999〕	10		50	13/	13	个/千克			/30
8504.2200		--额定容量超过 650 千伏安,但不超过 10 兆伏安〔999〕	10		50	13/	13	个/千克			/35
		--额定容量超过 10 兆伏安：									
		---额定容量超过 10 兆伏安,但小于 400 兆伏安：									
8504.2311		----额定容量超过 10 兆伏安,但小于 220 兆伏安〔999〕	10		50	13/	13	个/千克			/35
8504.2312		----额定容量在 220 兆伏安及以上,但小于 330 兆伏安〔999〕	10		50	13/	13	个/千克			/
8504.2313		----额定容量在 330 兆伏安及以上,但小于 400 兆伏安〔999〕	10		50	13/	13	个/千克			/
		---额定容量在 400 兆伏安及以上：									
8504.2321		----额定容量在 400 兆伏安及以上,但小于 500 兆伏安〔999〕	6		11	13/	13	个/千克			/
8504.2329		----其他〔999〕	6		11	13/	13	个/千克			/31
		-其他变压器：									
		--额定容量不超过 1 千伏安：									
8504.3110		---互感器〔999〕	5		50	13/	13	个/千克			/25
8504.3190		---其他〔999〕	5		50	13/	13	个/千克			/30
		--额定容量超过 1 千伏安,但不超过 16 千伏安：									
8504.3210		---互感器〔999〕	5		50	13/	13	个/千克			/25
8504.3290		---其他〔999〕	5		50	13/	13	个/千克			/35
		--额定容量超过 16 千伏安,但不超过 500 千伏安：									
8504.3310		---互感器〔999〕	5		50	13/	13	个/千克			/25
8504.3390		---其他〔999〕	5		50	13/	13	个/千克			/15
		--额定容量超过 500 千伏安：									
8504.3410		---互感器〔999〕	10		50	13/	13	个/千克			/
8504.3490		---其他〔999〕	10		50	13/	13	个/千克			/30
		-静止式变流器：									
		---稳压电源：									
8504.4013		----税目 84.71 所列机器用[T2]	0		40	13/	13	个/千克	A	L	/25
8504.4014		----其他直流稳压电源,功率小于 1 千瓦,精度低于万分之一[T2]	2.3/1.2		80	13/	13	个/千克			/22.3,21.2
8504.4015		----其他交流稳压电源,功率小于 10 千瓦,精度低于千分之一[T2]	0		80	13/	13	个/千克			/10
8504.4019		----其他									
8504.4019	10	同位素电磁分离器离子源磁体电源(高功率直流型)〔101:Ⅰ类稳压电源,102:Ⅱ类稳压电源,103:Ⅲ类稳压电源〕	0		50	13/	13	个/千克	3		/20
8504.4019	20	直流高功率电源(能 8 小时连续产生 100V,500A 电流,稳定度优于 0.1%)[T2]	0		50	13/	13	个/千克	3		/20
8504.4019	30	高压直流电源(能 8 小时连续产生 20kV,1A 电流,稳定度优于 0.2%)[T2]	0		50	13/	13	个/千克	3		/20
8504.4019	40	同位素电磁分离器离子源高压电源[T2]	0		50	13/	13	个/千克	3		/20
8504.4019	90	其他稳压电源[T2]	0		50	13/	13	个/千克		L	/20
8504.4020		---不间断供电电源(UPS)〔999〕	3.3/1.7		50	13/	13	台/千克			/23.3,21.7
8504.4030		---逆变器									
8504.4030	10	两用物项管制的逆变器(功率≥40 瓦特,频率 600 至 2000 赫兹,谐波畸变低于 10%等)〔999〕	3.3/1.7		30	13/	13	个/千克	3		/28.3,26.7
8504.4030	20	纯电动或混合动力汽车用逆变器模块,功率密度≥8 千瓦/升〔999〕	3.3/1.7		30	13/	13	个/千克			/28.3,26.7
8504.4030	90	其他逆变器〔999〕	3.3/1.7		30	13/	13	个/千克			/28.3,26.7
		---其他：									
8504.4091		----具有变流功能的半导体模块									

协定税率 %										特惠税率 %			Article Description
亚太5国	东/冰/格	巴基斯坦	韩国	瑞士	哥达	秘鲁	澳大利亚	新西/坡/智	港/澳/台	亚太2国	老/柬/缅	36/3/1	
													Electrical transformers, static converters (for example, rectifiers) and inductors:
													-Ballasts for discharge lamps or tubes:
	0/0/0	4	4	0	0	0	0	0/0/0	0/0/			0/0/0	---Electronic ballats
	0/0/0	4	4	0	0	0	0	0//0	0/0/			0/0/0	---Other
													-Liquid dielectric transformers:
	0/0/0	4.5	4.2	3.2	0	0	0	0/0/0	0/0/			0/0/0	--Having a power handling capacity not exceeding 650 kVA
	0/0/0	5.7	5	3.8	0	0	0	0/0/0	0/0/			0/0/0	--Having a power handling capacity exceeding 650 kVA but not exceeding 10 MVA
													--Having a power handling capacity exceeding 10 MVA:
													---Having a power handling capacity exceeding 10MVA but less than 400MVA:
6.5	0/0/0	4	6	0	0	0	0	0//0	0/0/			0/0/0	----Having a power handling capacity exceding 10MVA but less than 220MVA
6.5	0/0/0	4	4	0	0	0	0	0//0	0/0/			0/0/0	----Having a power handling capacity exceding 220MVA but less than 330MVA
6.5	0/0/0	4	4	0	0	0	0	0//0	0/0/			0/0/0	----Having a power handling capacity exceding 330MVA but less than 400MVA
													---Having a power handling capacity of 400 MVA or more:
3.9	0/0/0	0	0	0	0	0	0	0//0	0/0/			0/0/0	----Having a power handling capacity exceding 400MVA but less than 500MVA
3.9	0/0/0	0	0	0	0	0	0	0//0	0/0/			0/0/0	----Other
													-Other transformers:
													--Having a power handling capacity not exceeding 1 kVA:
3.3	0/0/0	0	0	0	0	0	0	0//0	0/0/0			0/0/0	---Mutual inductor
3.3	0/0/0	0	0	0	0	0	0	0/0/0	0/0/0			0/0/0	---Other
													--Having a power handling capacity exceeding 1kVA but not exceeding 16kVA:
	0/0/0	0	3	0	0	0	0	0//0	0/0/			0/0/0	---Mutual inductor
	0/0/0	0	0	0	0	0	0	0//0	0/0/			0/0/0	---Other
													--Having a power handling capacity exceeding 16 kVA but not exceeding 500 kVA:
	0/0/0	0	3	0	0	0	0	0//0	0/0/			0/0/0	---Mutual inductor
	0/0/0	0	3	0	0	0	0	0//0	0/0/			0/0/0	---Other
													--Having a power handling capacity exceeding 500 kVA:
	0/0/0	11.2	8.4	0	0	0	0	0/0/0	0/0/			0/0/	---Mutual inductor
	0/0/0	10.1	8.4	0	0	0	0	0/0/0	0/0/			0/0/	---Other
													-Static converters:
													---Voltage-stabilized suppliers:
												0/0/0	----Of the machines of heading No. 84. 71
1.5/0.8	0/0/0	4	4.2	2.1/1.2	0	0	0	0//0	0/0/			0/0/0	----Other DC voltage-stabilized suppliers, of a power of less than 1 kW and an accuracy of not better than 0. 0001
												0/0/0	----Other AC voltage-stabilized suppliers, of a power of less than 10 kW and an accuracy of not better than 0. 001
													----Other
												0/0/0	Ion source magnetic power suppliers of isotopioes electromagnetic separators (high-power, DC type)
												0/0/0	High-power DC power suppliers (capable of generating 100V, 500A current uninterrupted in 8 hours, stability better than 0. 1%)
												0/0/0	High-voltage DC power suppliers (capable of generating 20KV, 1A current uninterrupted in 8 hours, stability better than 0. 2%)
												0/0/0	Ion source high-voltage power suppliers of isotopies electromagnetic separators
												0/0/0	Other voltage-stabilized suppliers
2.1/1.1	0/0/0	4.5	6		0	0	0	0/0/0	0/0/			0/0/0	---Uninterrupted power suppliers
													---Inverter
	0/0/0	4.5	6	3/1.7	0	0	0	0/0/0	0/0/			0/0/0	Inverter of sensitive items control(power≥40W, frequency=600Hz ~2000Hz, harmonic distortion<10%)
	0/0/0	4.5	6	3/1.7	0	0	0	0/0/0	0/0/			0/0/0	Pure electric or hybrid cars use inverter module, power density or 8kw/l
	0/0/0	4.5	6	3/1.7	0	0	0	0/0/0	0/0/			0/0/0	Other inverter
													---Other:
													----Semiconductor modules with a converting function

税则号列		货品名称〔CIQ扩展编码及品名－T2表示见附表2〕	最惠(%)	暂定税率	普通	增值/消费	出口退税	计量单位	监管条件	检验检疫	特殊证件对美关税
8504.4091	10	具有变流功能的半导体模块(自动数据处理设备机器及组件、电讯设备用的)〔999〕	0		30	13/	13	个/千克			/25
8504.4091	90	其他具有变流功能的半导体模块〔999〕	3.3/1.7		30	13/	13	个/千克			/28.3,26.7
8504.4099		----其他									
8504.4099	10	静止式变流器(自动数据处理设备机器及组件、电讯设备用)〔999〕	0		30	13/	13	个/千克			/20
8504.4099	20	ITA产品用的印刷电路组件(包括外接组件,如符合PCMCIA标准的卡)〔999〕	0		30	13/	13	个/千克			/20
8504.4099	30	专用85030090.10电动机定子的频率变换器(1.多相输出600Hz或更高;2.高稳定性(频率控制优于0.2%))〔999〕	3.3/1.7		30	13/	13	个/千克	3		/23.3,21.7
8504.4099	40	两用物项管制的频率变换器(功率≥40瓦特,频率600至2000赫兹,谐波畸变低于10%等)〔999〕	3.3/1.7		30	13/	13	个/千克	3		/23.3,21.7
8504.4099	50	电源(真空或受控环境感应炉用电源,额定输出功率≥5千瓦)〔999〕	3.3/1.7		30	13/	13	个/千克	3		/23.3,21.7
8504.4099	60	模块式电脉冲发生器(在15ms内输出电流＞100A,密封在防尘罩内,温宽范围大)〔999〕	3.3/1.7		30	13/	13	个/千克	3		/23.3,21.7
8504.4099	70	高速(200km/h及以上)电力机车的牵引变流器〔999〕	3.3/1.7	①	30	13/	13	个/千克			/23
8504.4099	80	汽车冲压线用压力机变频调速装置〔999〕	3.3/1.7		30	13/	13	个/千克			/23.3,21.7
8504.4099	92	纯电动汽车或插电式混合动力汽车用车载充电机〔999〕	3.3/1.7		30	13/	13	个/千克			/23.3,21.7
8504.4099	99	其他未列名静止式变流器〔999〕	3.3/1.7		30	13/	13	个/千克			/23.3,21.7
8504.5000		-其他电感器〔999〕	0		35	13/	13	个/千克			/25
		-零件:									
		---变压器用:									
8504.9011		----子目号8504.2321,8504.2329所列变压器用〔999〕	1.7/0.8		11	13/	13	千克			/26.7,25.8
8504.9019		----其他〔999〕	2.7/1.3		50	13/	13	千克			/27.7,26.3
8504.9020		---稳压电源及不间断供电电源用〔999〕	2.7/1.3		50	13/	13	千克			/22.7,21.3
8504.9090		---其他									
8504.9090	10	用于将可再生能源发电机组输出的直流电转换成交流电的逆变器的零件〔999〕	2.7/1.3		30	13/	13	千克			/27.7,26.3
8504.9090	90	其他静止式变流器及电感器零件〔999〕	2.7/1.3		30	13/	13	千克			/27.7,26.3
85.05		**电磁铁;永磁铁及磁化后准备制永磁铁的物品;电磁铁或永磁铁卡盘、夹具及类似的工件夹具;电磁联轴节、离合器及制动器;电磁起重吸盘:**									
		-永磁铁及磁化后准备制永磁铁的物品:									
		--金属的:									
8505.1110		---稀土的〔999〕	7		20	13/	13	千克			/32
8505.1190		---其他〔999〕	7		20	13/	13	千克			/27
8505.1900		--其他									
8505.1900	10	磁极块(直径大于2m,用在同位素电磁分离器内)〔999〕	7		20	13/	13	千克	3		/32
8505.1900	90	其他非金属永磁铁及永磁体〔999〕	7		20	13/	13	千克			/32
8505.2000		-电磁联轴节、离合器及制动器〔999〕	8		20	13/	13	千克			/33
		-其他,包括零件:									
8505.9010		---电磁起重吸盘〔999〕	8		20	13/	13	个/千克			/28
8505.9090		---其他									
8505.9090	10	超导螺线电磁体(产生超过2个泰斯拉磁场,长径比≥2mm,内径≥300mm等)〔999〕	8		20	13/	13	个/千克	3		/33
8505.9090	20	专门或主要用于核磁共振成像装置的电磁体,但税号90.18所列其他电磁铁除外〔999〕	0		20	13/	13	个/千克			/25
8505.9090	90	其他电磁铁;电磁铁或永磁铁卡盘、夹具及类似的工件夹具;编号8505的零件〔999〕	8		20	13/	13	个/千克			/33
85.06		原电池及原电池组:									
		-二氧化锰的:									

① 暂定税率1－6月:3%

协定税率 %										特惠税率 %			Article Description
亚太5国	东/冰/格	巴基斯坦	韩国	瑞士	哥达	秘鲁	澳大利亚	新西/坡/智	港/澳/台	亚太2国	老/柬/缅	36/3/1	
	0/0/4	4.5	0	3/1.7	0	0	0	0/0/0	0/0/			0/0/0	Semi-conductor modules with converting function (for automatic data-processing machines and units as well as telecommunication equipments)
	0/0/4	4.5	0	3/1.7	0	0	0	0/0/0	0/0/			0/0/0	Other Semi-conductor modules with converting function
													----Other
	0/0/0	4.5	6	3/1.7	0	0	0	0/0/0	0/0/			0/0/0	Static converters (for automatic data processing machines and units thereof and telecommunication apparatus)
	0/0/0	4.5	6	3/1.7	0	0	0	0/0/0	0/0/			0/0/0	Printed circuit assemblies for products falling within the ITA (including external assemblies, for example, cards in accordance with PCMCIA)
	0/0/0	4.5	6	3/1.7	0	0	0	0/0/0	0/0/			0/0/0	Frequency converters, specially, for stators of heading 8503. 009010
	0/0/0	4.5	6	3/1.7	0	0	0	0/0/0	0/0/			0/0/0	Frequency converters (power≥40W, frequency＝600Hz～2000Hz, harmonic distortion<10％)
	0/0/0	4.5	6	3/1.7	0	0	0	0/0/0	0/0/			0/0/0	Power suppliers (for vacuum or atmosphere-controlled induction furnace, rated output power≥5kW)
	0/0/0	4.5	6	3/1.7	0	0	0	0/0/0	0/0/			0/0/0	Module-type electric pulse generator (output electric current>100A in 15ms and greater in temperature span when sealed in dustproof cover)
	0/0/0	4.5	6	3/1.7	0	0	0	0/0/0	0/0/			0/0/0	High speed electric locomotive traction converter (for (200 km/ h) electric locomotive)
	0/0/0	4.5	6	3/1.7	0	0	0	0/0/0	0/0/			0/0/0	Press of variable frequency speed regulating device in automobile press line
	0/0/0	4.5	6	3/1.7	0	0	0	0/0/0	0/0/			0/0/0	Pure electric vehicle or a plug in hybrid electric vehicle on-board charger
	0/0/0	4.5	6	3/1.7	0	0	0	0/0/0	0/0/			0/0/0	Other static converters, not elsewhere specified or included
												0/0/0	-Other inductors
													-Parts:
													---Of transformers:
1.1/0.5	0/0/0	0	3	1.5/0.8	0	0	0	0//0	0/0/			0/0/0	----Of the transformers of subheading No. 8504. 2321, 8504. 2329
1.5/0.7	0/0/0	3.6	4.8	2.4/1.3	0	0	0	0//0	0/0/0			0/0/0	----Other
1.8/0.8	0/0/3.2	4	4.8	2.4/1.3	0	0	0	0//0	0/0/0			0/0/0	---Of voltage-stabilized suppliers and uninterrupted power suppliers
													---Other
1.8/0.8	0/0/0	4	4.8	2.4/1.3	0	0	0	0//0	0/0/0			0/0/0	For the output of renewable energy power generation unit of DC to AC inverter components
1.8/0.8	0/0/0	4	4.8	2.4/1.3	0	0	0	0//0	0/0/0			0/0/0	Static converters and other parts of the inductor
													Electro-magnets; permanent magnets and articles intended to become permanent magnets after magnetization; electro-magnetic or permanent magnet chucks, clamps and similar holding devices; electro-magnetic couplings, clutches and brakes; electro-magnetic lifting heads:
													-Permanent magnets and articles intended to become permanent magnets after magnetization:
													--Of metal:
	0/0/2.8	4	0	0	0	0	0	0//0	0/0/0			0/0/0	---Of rare-earth
	0/0/0	4	0	0	0	0	0	0//0	0/0/0			0/0/0	---Other
													--Other
4.6	0/0/0	4	2.8	0	0	0	0	0//0	0/0/			0/0/0	Magnet pole pieces (diameter>2m, used for electromagnetic isotope separator)
4.6	0/0/0	4	2.8	0	0	0	0	0//0	0/0/			0/0/0	Non-metal permanent magnets
5.2	0/0/0	4	4.8	0	0	0	0	0//0	0/0/			0/0/0	-Electro-magnetic couplings, clutches and brakes
													-Other, including parts:
	0/0/0	4	0	0	0	0	0	0//0	0/0/			0/0/0	---Electro-magnetic lifting heads
													---Other
5.6	0/0/0	4	0	2.4	0	0	0	0//0	0/0/			0/0/0	Superconduction spiral electro magnets (capable of generating more than two Tesla magnetic fields, L/D≥2, inside diameter≥300mm)
5.6	0/0/0	4	0	2.4	0	0	0	0//0	0/0/			0/0/0	Solely or primarily for the electromagnet magnetic resonance imaging device, but excludingelectromagnet of heading No.90.18
5.6	0/0/0	4	0	2.4	0	0	0	0//0	0/0/			0/0/0	Other electromagnets; electromagnet or permanent magnet chuck, fixture and similar workpiece fixture; parts of heading No.85.05
													Primary cells and primary batteries:
													-Manganese dioxide:

税则号列	货品名称〔CIQ 扩展编码及品名－T2 表示见附表 2〕	最惠(%)	暂定税率	普通	增值/消费	出口退税	计量单位	监管条件	检验检疫	特殊证件对美关税
	---碱性锌锰的:									
8506.1011	----扣式									
8506.1011 10	扣式碱性锌锰的原电池及原电池组,汞含量<电池重量的 0.0005%[T2]	8		80	13/	13	个/千克	A	M	/28
8506.1011 90	扣式碱性锌锰的原电池及原电池组,汞含量≥电池重量的 0.0005%[T2]	8		80	13/4	0	个/千克	A	M	/28
8506.1012	----圆柱形									
8506.1012 10	圆柱形无汞碱性锌锰的原电池及原电池组,汞含量<电池重量的 0.0001%[T2]	8		80	13/	13	个/千克	A	M	/28
8506.1012 90	圆柱形含汞碱性锌锰的原电池及原电池组,汞含量≥电池重量的 0.0001%[T2]	8		80	13/4	0	个/千克	A	M	/28
8506.1019	----其他									
8506.1019 10	其他无汞碱性锌锰的原电池及原电池组,汞含量<电池重量的 0.0001%[T2]	8		80	13/	13	个/千克	A	M	/33
8506.1019 90	其他碱性锌锰的原电池及原电池组,汞含量≥电池重量的 0.0001%[T2]	8		80	13/4	13	个/千克	A	M	/33
8506.1090	---其他									
8506.1090 10	其他二氧化锰的原电池及原电池组,汞含量<电池重量的 0.0001%,扣式电池的汞含量<电池重量的 0.0005%〔101 锌－锰原电池及原电池组,102 碱性锌－锰原电池及原电池组,103 其他二氧化锰的原电池及原电池组〕	8		80	13/	13	个/千克	A	M	/33
8506.1090 90	其他二氧化锰的原电池及原电池组,汞含量≥电池重量的 0.0001%,扣式电池的汞含量≥电池重量的 0.0005%〔101 锌－锰原电池及原电池组,102 碱性锌－锰原电池及原电池组,103 其他二氧化锰的原电池及原电池组〕	8		80	13/4	13	个/千克	A	M	/33
8506.3000	-氧化汞的〔999〕	8		40	13/4	0	个/千克	A	M	/
8506.4000	-氧化银的									
8506.4000 10	氧化银的原电池及原电池组(无汞),汞含量<电池重量的 0.0001%,扣式电池的汞含量<电池重量的 0.0005%〔101 锌银扣式电池,102 锌银其他电池,103 其他氧化银的原电池及原电池组〕	8		40	13/	13	个/千克	A	M	/33
8506.4000 90	氧化银的原电池及原电池组(含汞),汞含量≥电池重量的 0.0001%,扣式电池的汞含量≥电池重量的 0.0005%〔101 锌银扣式电池,102 锌银其他电池,103 其他氧化银的原电池及原电池组〕	8		40	13/4	13	个/千克	A	M	/33
8506.5000	-锂的〔101 锂－二氧化锰扣式电池,102 锂－二氧化锰其他电池,103 其他锂的原电池及原电池组〕	8		40	13/	13	个/千克	A	M	/33
8506.6000	-锌空气的									
8506.6000 10	锌空气的原电池及原电池组(无汞),汞含量<电池重量的 0.0001%,扣式电池的汞含量<电池重量的 0.0005%〔999〕	8		40	13/	13	个/千克	A	M	/33
8506.6000 90	锌空气的原电池及原电池组(含汞),汞含量≥电池重量的 0.0001%,扣式电池的汞含量≥电池重量的 0.0005%〔999〕	8		40	13/4	13	个/千克	A	M	/33
8506.8000	-其他原电池及原电池组									
8506.8000 11	无汞燃料电池,汞含量<电池重量的 0.0001%,扣式电池的汞含量<电池重量的 0.0005%〔999〕	8		40	13/	13	个/千克	A	M	/28
8506.8000 19	其他无汞原电池及原电池组,汞含量<电池重量的 0.0001%,扣式电池的汞含量<电池重量的 0.0005%〔999〕	8		40	13/	13	个/千克	A	M	/28
8506.8000 91	含汞燃料电池,汞含量≥电池重量的 0.0001%,扣式电池的汞含量≥电池重量的 0.0005%〔999〕	8		40	13/4	13	个/千克	A	M	/28
8506.8000 99	其他原电池及原电池组,汞含量≥电池重量的 0.0001%,扣式电池的汞含量≥电池重量的 0.0005%〔999〕	8		40	13/4	13	个/千克	A	M	/28
	-零件:									
8506.9010	---子目 8506.1000 所列电池用〔999〕	8		80	13/	13	千克			/28
8506.9090	---其他〔999〕	8		40	13/	13	千克			/28
85.07	**蓄电池,包括隔板,不论是否矩形(包括正方形):**									
8507.1000	-铅酸蓄电池,用于启动活塞式发动机[T2]	10		90	13/4	0	个/千克	A	M	/35
8507.2000	-其他铅酸蓄电池[T2]	10		90	13/4	0	个/千克	A	M	/30
8507.3000	-镍镉蓄电池[T2]	10		40	13/4	0	个/千克	A	M	/15
8507.4000	-镍铁蓄电池〔999〕	10		40	13/4	13	个/千克	A	M	/30
8507.5000	-镍氢蓄电池[T2]	10		40	13/	13	个/千克	A	M	/35
8507.6000	-锂离子蓄电池									

协定税率 %										特惠税率 %			Article Description
亚太5国	东/冰/格	巴基斯坦	韩国	瑞士	哥达	秘鲁	澳大利亚	新西/坡/智	港/澳/台	亚太2国	老/柬/缅	36/3/1	
													---Alkaline zinc-manganese dioxide:
													----Button shape
	0/0/0	20	14	6	0	0	0	0/0/0	0/0/			0/0/	Button type alkaline zinc manganese battery and battery pack, mercury content < 0.0005% by weight of the battery
	0/0/0	20	14	6	0	0	0	0/0/0	0/0/			0/0/	Button type alkaline zinc manganese battery and battery pack, mercury content of 0.0005% by weight of the battery or higher
													----Cycinder shape
	0/0/0	20	14	6	0	0	0	0/0/0	0/0/			0/0/	Cylindrical mercury-free alkaline zinc manganese battery and original battery mercury content < 0.0001% by weight of the battery
	0/0/0	20	14	6	0	0	0	0/0/0	0/0/			0/0/	Cylindrical mercury alkaline zinc manganese battery and the mercury content of 0.0001% by weight of the battery or the battery pack
													----Other
	0/0/0	20		6	0	0	0	0/0/0	0/0/			0/0/	Other mercury-free alkaline zinc manganese battery and battery pack, mercury content < 0.0001% by weight of the battery
	0/0/0	20		6	0	0	0	0/0/0	0/0/			0/0/	Other alkaline zinc manganese battery and battery pack, mercury content of 0.0001% by weight of the battery or higher
													---Other
	0/0/0	20	14	6	0	0	0	0/0/0	0/0/			0/0/	Other manganese dioxide, primary cells and primary batteries, mercury content < 0.0001% by weight of the battery, button cell of mercury content < 0.0005% by weight of the battery
	0/0/0	20	14	6	0	0	0	0/0/0	0/0/			0/0/	Other manganese dioxide, primary cells and primary batteries, the mercury content of 0.0001% by weight of the battery, or the mercury content of the button cell battery or 0.0005% of the weight
	0/0/0	10.1	5.6	4.2	0	0	0	0/0/0	0/0/			0/0/	-Mercuric oxide
													-Silver oxide
5.2	0/0/0	10.1	5.6	4.2	0	0	0	0/0/0	0/0/			0/0/	Silver oxide battery and the battery pack (mercury), mercury content < 0.0001% by weight of the battery, button cell of mercury content < 0.0005% by weight of the battery
5.2	0/0/0	10.1	5.6	4.2	0	0	0	0/0/0	0/0/			0/0/	Primary cells and primary batteries, silver oxide(mercury), mercury content of 0.0001% by weight of the battery, or the mercury content of the button cell battery weight of 0.0005% or higher
	0/0/0	10.1		4.2	0	0	0	0/0/0	0/0/			0/0/	-Lithium
													-Air-zinc
	0/0/0	10.1	5.6		0	0	0	0/0/0	0/0/			0/0/	Primary cells and primary batteries, air-zinc(No mercury), mercury content < 0.0001% by weight of the battery, button cell of mercury content < 0.0005% by weight of the battery
	0/0/0	10.1	5.6		0	0	0	0/0/0	0/0/			0/0/	Primary cells and primary batteries, air-zinc(mercury), mercury content of 0.0001% by weight of the battery, or the mercury content of the button cell battery weight of 0.0005% or higher
													-Other primary cells and primary batteries
	0/0/0	10.1	5.6	4.2	0	0	0	0/0/0	0/0/			0/0/0	Mercury-free fuel cell, mercury content < 0.0001% by weight of the battery, button cell mercury content < 0.0005% by weight of the battery
	0/0/0	10.1	5.6	4.2	0	0	0	0/0/0	0/0/			0/0/0	mercury content < 0.0001% by weight of the battery, button cell of mercury content < 0.0005% by weight of the battery
	0/0/0	10.1	5.6	4.2	0	0	0	0/0/0	0/0/			0/0/0	Mercury fuel cell, a mercury content of 0.0001% by weight of the battery, or the mercury content of the button cell battery or 0.0005% of the weight
	0/0/0	10.1	5.6	4.2	0	0	0	0/0/0	0/0/			0/0/0	the mercury content of 0.0001% by weight of the battery, or the mercury content of the button cell battery or 0.0005% of the weight
													-Parts:
5.2	0/0/0	10.1		4.2	0	0	0	0/0/0	0/0/			0/0/	---Of the cells of subheading No. 8506.1000
	0/0/0	4	7	0	0	0	0	0/0/0	0/0/			0/0/	---Other
													Electric accumulators, including separators therefor, whether or not rectangular(including square):
6.5	0/0/0	0	7	0	0	0	0	0/0/0	0/0/			0/0/	-Lead-acid, of a kind used for starting piston engines
6.5	0/0/0	0	4	0	0	0	0	0/0/0	0/0/			0/0/	-Other lead-acid accumulators
6.5	0/0/0	4	4	0	0	0	0	0/0/0	0/0/			0/0/	-Nickel-cadmium
6.5	0/0/0	4.5	4.8	3.6	0	0	0	0/0/0	0/0/			0/0/	-Nickel-iron
6.5	0/0/0	4.5	4.8	3.6	0	0	0	0/0/0	0/0/			0/0/	-Nickel-metal hydride
													-Lithium ion

税则号列	货品名称〔CIQ扩展编码及品名—T2表示见附表2〕	最惠(%)	暂定税率	普通	增值/消费	出口退税	计量单位	监管条件	检验检疫	特殊证件对美关税
8507.6000 10	纯电动汽车或插电式混合动力汽车用锂离子蓄电池单体(容量≥10Ah,比能量≥110Wh/kg)〔999〕	10		40	13/	13	个/千克	A	M	/35
8507.6000 20	纯电动汽车或插电式混合动力汽车用锂离子蓄电池系统(包含蓄电池模块、容器、盖、冷却系统、管理系统等,比能量≥80Wh/kg)〔999〕	10		40	13/	13	个/千克	A	M	/35
8507.6000 90	其他锂离子蓄电池[T2]	10		40	13/	13	个/千克	A	M	/35
	-其他蓄电池:									
8507.8030	---全钒液流电池〔999〕	10		40	13/	13	个/千克	A	M	/
8507.8090	---其他									
8507.8090 10	燃料电池[T2]	10		40	13/	13	个/千克	A	M	/30
8507.8090 90	其他蓄电池[T2]	10		40	13/4	13	个/千克	A	M	/30
	-零件:									
8507.9010	---铅酸蓄电池用									
8507.9010 01	铅酸蓄电池电极〔999〕	10	5	90	13/	0	千克			/25
8507.9010 90	其他铅酸蓄电池零件〔999〕	10		90	13/	0	千克			/30
8507.9090	---其他〔999〕	8	5	40	13/	13	千克			/30
85.08	**真空吸尘器:**									
	-电动的:									
8508.1100	--功率不超过1500瓦,且带有容积不超过20升的集尘袋或其他集尘容积器[T2]	8		130	13/	13	台/千克			/33
8508.1900	--其他[T2]	0		30	13/	13	台/千克			/25
8508.6000	-其他真空吸尘器[T2]	0		30	13/	13	台/千克			/25
	-零件:									
8508.7010	---子目8508.1100所列吸尘器用〔999〕	6		100	13/	13	千克			/31
8508.7090	---其他〔999〕	0		20	13/	13	千克			/5
85.09	**家用电动器具,税目85.08的真空吸尘器除外:**									
	-食品研磨机及搅拌器;水果或蔬菜的榨汁机:									
8509.4010	---水果或蔬菜的榨汁机[T2]	7	6	100	13/	13	台/千克	A	LR	/31
8509.4090	---其他[T2]	7	6	100	13/	13	台/千克	A	LR	/11
	-其他器具:									
8509.8010	---地板打蜡机[T2]	8		100	13/	13	台/千克			/
8509.8020	---厨房废物处理器[T2]	8		100	13/	13	台/千克			/33
8509.8090	---其他	8		100	13/	13	台/千克	A		/33
8509.9000	-零件[T2]	6		100	13/	13	千克			/31
85.10	**电动剃须刀、电动毛发推剪及电动脱毛器:**									
8510.1000	-剃须刀[T2]	8		100	13/	13	个/千克			/33
8510.2000	-毛发推剪[T2]	8		100	13/	13	个/千克			/33
8510.3000	-脱毛器[T2]	8		100	13/	13	个/千克			/33
8510.9000	-零件〔999〕	8		100	13/	13	千克			/33
85.11	**点燃式或压燃式内燃发动机用的电点火及电启动装置(例如,点火磁电机、永磁直流发电机、点火线圈、火花塞、电热塞及启动电机);附属于上述内燃发动机的发电机(例如,直流发电机、交流发电机)及断流器:**									
8511.1000	-火花塞〔101其他车辆零部件,102动力设备零部件〕	8		30	13/	13	个/千克			/18
	-点火磁电机;永磁直流发电机;磁飞轮:									
8511.2010	---机车、航空器及船舶用[T2]	5		11	13/	13	个/千克			/10
8511.2090	---其他〔999〕	8		30	13/	13	个/千克			/33
	--分电器;点火线圈:									
8511.3010	---机车、航空器及船舶用[T2]	5		11	13/	13	个/千克			/10
8511.3090	---其他〔101其他车辆零部件,102其它发电机(组)及其零件〕	8		30	13/	13	个/千克			/13
	-启动电机及两用启动发电机:									
8511.4010	---机车、航空器及船舶用[T2]	5		11	13/	13	个/千克			/10
	---其他:									
8511.4091	----输出功率在132.39千瓦(180马力)及以上的发动机用启动电机〔999〕	8		30	13/	13	个/千克			/33
8511.4099	----其他〔999〕	8		30	13/	13	个/千克			/33
	-其他发电机:									
8511.5010	---机车、航空器及船舶用〔999〕	5		11	13/	13	个/千克			/10
8511.5090	---其他〔999〕	8		30	13/	13	个/千克			/33

协定税率 %										特惠税率 %			Article Description
亚太5国	东/冰/格	巴基斯坦	韩国	瑞士	哥达	秘鲁	澳大利亚	新西/坡/智	港/澳/台	亚太2国	老/柬/缅	36/3/1	
8	0/0/0	5	9.6	3.6	0	0	0	0/0/0	0/0/0			0/0/	Pure electric vehicle or a plug in hybrid electric vehicle lithium ion batterymonomer (capacity is greater than or equal to 10Ah, ratio of energy is higher than or equal to 110Wh/kg)
8	0/0/0	5	9.6	3.6	0	0	0	0/0/0	0/0/0			0/0/	Pure electric vehicles and plug-in hybrid vehicle lithium ion battery (includedbattery module, container, cover, cooling system, management system, specific energy is greater than or equal to 80Wh/kg)
8	0/0/0	5	9.6	3.6	0	0	0	0/0/0	0/0/0			0/0/	Other lithium ion
													-Other accumulators
6.5	0/0/0	4.5	4.8	3.6	0	0	0	0/0/0	0/0/			0/0/	---Vanadium redox flow battery
													---Other
6.5	0/0/0	4.5	4.8	3.6	0	0	0	0/0/0	0/0/			0/0/	fuel cell
6.5	0/0/0	4.5	4.8	3.6	0	0	0	0/0/0	0/0/			0/0/	Other accumulators
													-Parts:
													---Of lead-acid accumulators
	0/0/0	4	4	0	0	0	0	0//0	0/0/	5		0/0/	Electrode of lead-acid battery
	0/0/0	4	4	0	0	0	0	0//0	0/0/	5		0/0/	Other lead-acid battery parts
	0/0/0	4	4.8	0	0	0	0	0//0	0/0/	4		0/0/0	---Other
													Vacuum cleaners:
													-With self-contained electric-motor:
5.2	0/0/0	4	4	0	0	0	0	0/0/0	0/0/0			0/0/0	--Of a power not exceeding 1500W and hawing a dust bag or other receptade capaeity not excecding 20L
												0/0/0	--Other
												0/0/0	-Other vacuum cleaners
													-Parts:
	0/0/0	5.4	4.8	3.6	0	0	0	0/0/0	0/0/			0/0/	---Of the deamers of subheading No. 8508. 1100
												0/0/0	---Other
													Electro-mechanical domestic appliances, with self-contained electric motor, other than vacuum cleaners of heading No. 85. 08:
													-Food grinders and mixers; fruit or vegetable juice extractors:
	0/0/0	4	7	0	0	0	0	0/0/0	0/0/			0/0/	---Fruit or vegetable juice extractors
	0/0/0	4	4	0	0	0	0	0/0/0	0/0/0			0/0/	---Other
													-Other appliances:
	0/0/0	30		8	0	0	0	0/0/0	0/0/			0/0/	---Floor polishers
	0/0/0	20	14	6	0	0	0	0/0/0	0/0/			0/0/	---Kitchen waste disposers
	0/0/0	30			0	0	0	0/0/0	0/0/			0/0/	---Other
	0/0/0	5.4	4.8	3.6	0	0	0	0/0/0	0/0/			0/0/	-Parts
													Shavers, hair clippers and hair-removing appliances, with self-contained electric motor:
	0//0	30		8	0	0	0	0/0/0	0/0/			0/0/	-Shavers
	0/0/0	30		8	0	0	0	0/0/0	0/0/			0/0/	-Hair clippers
	0/0/0	20	12	6	0	0	0	0/0/0	0/0/			0/0/	-Hair-removing appliances
	0/0/0	24.5	17.1	7.4	0	0	0	0/0/0	0/0/			0/0/	-Parts
													Electrical ignition or starting equipment of a kind used for spark-ignition or compression-ignition internal combustion engines (for example, ignition magnetos, magneto-dynamos, ignition coils, sparking plugs and glow plugs, starter motors); generators (for example, dynamos, alternators) and cut-outs of a kind used in conjunction with such engines:
	0/0/0	4.5	4	0	0	0	0	0/0/0	0/0/			0/0/	-Sparking plugs
													-Ignition magnetos; magneto-dynamos; magnetic flywheels:
	0/0/0	0	0	0	0	0	0	0//0	0/0/			0/0/0	---For locomotives, aircraft or ships
	0/0/0	4	4	0	0	0	0	0//0	0/0/			0/0/0	---Other
													--Distributors; ignition coils:
	0/0/0	0	0	0	0	0	0	0//0	0/0/			0/0/0	---For locomotives, aircraft or ships
	0/0/0	4	5	0	0	0	0	0//0	0/0/			0/0/0	---Other
													-Starter motors and dual purpose starter-generators:
	0/0/0	0	2	0	0	0	0	0//0	0/0/			0/0/0	---For locomotives, aircraft or ships
													---Other:
	0/0/0	4	3.3	0	0	0	0	0//0	0/0/			0/0/0	----Starter motors for engines of an output of 132. 39kW(180HP) or more
	0/0/0	4	5	0	0	0	0	0//0	0/0/			0/0/0	----Other
													-Other generators:
	0/0/0	0	2	0	0	0	0	0//0	0/0/			0/0/0	---For locomotives, aircraft or ships
	0/0/0	4		0	0	0	0	0//0	0/0/			0/0/0	---Other

税则号列	货品名称〔CIQ 扩展编码及品名－T2 表示见附表 2〕	最惠(%)	暂定税率	普通	增值/消费	出口退税	计量单位	监管条件	检验检疫	特殊证件对美关税
8511.8000	-其他装置〔999〕	8		30	13/	13	个/千克			/13
	-零件：									
8511.9010	---税目 85.11 所列供机车、航空器及船舶用的各种装置的零件〔101 航空器用零部件，102 船舶用零部件，103 铁道机车用零部件〕	4.5		11	13/	13	千克			/9.5
8511.9090	---其他〔999〕	5		30	13/	13	千克			/30
85.12	**自行车或机动车辆用的电气照明或信号装置(税目 85.39 的物品除外)、风挡刮水器、除霜器及去雾器：**									
8512.1000	-自行车用照明或视觉信号装置〔999〕	10		45	13/	13	个/千克			/35
	-其他照明或视觉信号装置：									
8512.2010	---机动车辆用照明装置〔999〕	10		45	13/	13	个/千克		L	/15
8512.2090	---其他〔999〕	10		45	13/	13	个/千克		L	/15
	-音响信号装置：									
	---机动车辆用：									
8512.3011	----喇叭、蜂鸣器〔999〕	10		45	13/	13	个/千克		L	/15
8512.3012	----防盗报警器〔999〕	10		40	13/	13	个/千克		L	/15
8512.3019	----其他〔999〕	10		45	13/	13	个/千克			/15
8512.3090	----其他〔999〕	10		45	13/	13	个/千克			/20
8512.4000	-风挡刮水器、除霜器及去雾器〔999〕	10		45	13/	13	个/千克			/15
8512.9000	-零件〔999〕	8		45	13/	13	千克			/13
85.13	**自供能源(例如，使用干电池、蓄电池、永磁发电机)的手提式电灯，但税目 85.12 的照明装置除外：**									
	-灯：									
8513.1010	---手电筒〔999〕	5		100	13/	13	个/千克			/15
8513.1090	---其他〔999〕	6		70	13/	13	个/千克			/31
	-零件：									
8513.9010	---手电筒用〔999〕	5		100	13/	13	千克			/30
8513.9090	---其他〔999〕	5		70	13/	13	千克			/30
85.14	**工业或实验室用电炉及电烘箱(包括通过感应或介质损耗工作的)；工业或实验室用其他通过感应或介质损耗对材料进行热处理的设备：**									
	-电阻加热的炉及烘箱：									
8514.1010	---可控气氛热处理炉〔999〕	0		30	13/	13	台/千克			/30
8514.1090	---其他〔999〕	0		30	13/	13	台/千克			/10
8514.2000	-通过感应或介质损耗工作的炉及烘箱									
8514.2000 10	真空感应炉或受控环境感应炉(工作温度＞850℃，感应线圈直径≤600mm，功率≥5 千瓦)〔999〕	0		30	13/	13	台/千克	3		/10
8514.2000 90	其他感应或介质损耗工作炉及烘箱(包括实验室用)〔999〕	0		30	13/	13	台/千克			/10
8514.3000	-其他炉及烘箱									
8514.3000 20	电弧重熔炉、电弧熔炉和电弧融化铸造炉(容量 1 千～2 万立方厘米，使用自耗电极，工作温度 1700℃以上)〔999〕	0		30	13/	13	台/千克	3		/10
8514.3000 30	电子束熔化炉(功率≥50 千瓦，能在＞1200℃的熔化温度工作)〔999〕	0		30	13/	13	台/千克	3		/10
8514.3000 40	等离子体雾化和熔化炉(功率≥50 千瓦，能在＞1200℃的熔化温度工作)〔999〕	0		30	13/	13	台/千克	3		/10
8514.3000 90	工业用其他电炉及电烘箱(包括实验室用)〔999〕	0		30	13/	13	台/千克			/10
8514.4000	-其他通过感应或介质损耗对材料进行热处理的设备									
8514.4000 01	焊缝中频退火装置〔999〕	10	7	30	13/	13	台/千克			/27
8514.4000 90	其他感应或介质损耗的加热设备(包括实验室用)〔999〕	10		30	13/	13	台/千克			/30
	-零件：									
8514.9010	---炼钢电炉用〔999〕	8		30	13/	13	千克			/33
8514.9090	---其他〔999〕	0		30	13/	13	千克			/10
85.15	**电气(包括电热气体)、激光、其他光、光子束、超声波、电子束、磁脉冲或等离子弧焊接机器及装置，不论是否兼有切割功能；用于热喷金属或金属陶瓷的电气机器及装置：**									

协定税率 %										特惠税率 %			Article Description
亚太5国	东/冰/格	巴基斯坦	韩国	瑞士	哥达	秘鲁	澳大利亚	新西/坡/智	港/澳/台	亚太2国	老/柬/缅	36/3/1	
	0/0/0	4	3.3	0	0	0	0	0//0	0/0/			0/0/0	-Other equipment
													-Parts:
	0/0/0	0		0	0	0	0	0//0	0/0/			0/0/0	---Of the equipment of headingNo. 85. 11 used for locomotives, aircraft or ships
	0/0/0	0	2	0	0	0	0	0//0	0/0/			0/0/0	---Other
													Electrical lighting or signalling equipment (excluding articles of headingNo.85. 39), windscreen wipers, defrosters and demisters, of a kind used for cycles or motor vehicles:
	0/0/0	4.5	4.2	3.2	0	0	0	0/0/0	0/0/			0/0/0	-Lighting or visual signalling equipment of a kind used on bicycles
													-Other lighting or visual signalling equipment:
	5/0/0	8	7	0	0	0	0	0//0	0/0/0			0/0/0	---Lighting equipment of a kind used for motor vehicles
	5/0/0	8	7	0	0	0	0	0//0	0/0/			0/0/0	---Other
													-Sound signalling equipment:
													---For motor vehicles:
6.5	5/0/0	7.7	6	0	0	0	0	0//0	0/0/			0/0/0	----Loudspeaker, buzzers
6.5	0/0/0	4	6	0	0	0	0	0//0	0/0/			0/0/0	----Burglay alarm
6.5	5/0/0	7.7	6	0	0	0	0	0//0	0/0/			0/0/0	----Other
6.5	5/0/0	7.7		0	0	0	0	0//0	0/0/			0/0/0	---Other
	5/0/0	8		0	0	0	0	0//0	0/0/			0/0/0	-Windscreen wipers, defrosters and demisters
	0/0/0	4	3.2	0	0	0	0	0//0	0/0/0			0/0/0	-Parts
													Portable electric lamps designed to function by their own source of energy (for example, dry batteries, accumulators, magnetos), other than lighting equipment of headingNo. 85. 12:
													-Lamps:
3.3	0/0/0	6	6	4.5	0	0	0	0/0/0	0/0/			0/0/0	---Portable electric torches designed to function by dry batteries
	0/0/0	12.6	7	5.3	0	0	0	0/0/0	0/0/			0/0/	---Other
													-Parts:
	0/0/0	10.1	5.6	4.2	0	0	0	0/0/0	0/0/			0/0/0	---Of the torches of subheading No. 8513. 1010
	0/0/0	10.1	5.6	4.2	0	0	0	0/0/0	0/0/			0/0/	---Other
													Industrial or laboratory electric furnaces and ovens (including those functioning by induction or dielectric loss); other industrial or laboratory equipment for the heat treatment of materials by induction or dielectric loss:
													-Resistance heated furnaces and ovens:
												0/0/0	---Furnaces for heat treatment, atmosphere controllable
												0/0/0	---Other
													-Furnaces and ovens functioning by induction or dielectric loss
												0/0/0	Vacuum induction furnaces or controlled atmosphere induction furnaces (rated output power≥5kW, diameter of induction coil≤600mm, working temperature>850℃)
												0/0/0	Other furnaces and ovens functioning by induction or dielectric loss (including laboratory)
													-Other furnaces and ovens
												0/0/0	Arc remelting furnaces and casting furnaces (capacity＝1000～20000cm³, with consumable electrode, working temperature>1700℃)
												0/0/0	Electron-beam melting furnaces (power≥50kW, capable of working at smelting temperature>1200℃)
												0/0/0	Plasma atomization and melting furnaces (power≥50kW, capable of working at smelting temperature>1200℃)
												0/0/0	Other industrial or laboratory electric furnaces and ovens
													-Other equipment for the heat treatment of materials by induction or dielectric loss
	0/0/0	4.5	0	0	0	0	0	0/0/0	0/0/			0/0/0	Welding seam intermediate frequency annealing device
	0/0/0	4.5	0	0	0	0	0	0/0/0	0/0/			0/0/0	Other equipment for the heat treatment of materials by induction or dielectric loss
													-Parts:
	0/0/0	4	0	0	0	0	0	0//0	0/0/			0/0/0	---Of steel making electric furnaces
												0/0/0	---Other
													Electric (including electrically heated gas), laser or other light or photon beam, ultrasonic, electron beam, magnetic pulse or plasma arc soldering, brazing or welding machines and apparatus, whether or not capable of cutting; electric machines and apparatus for hot spraying of metals or cermets:

税则号列		货品名称〔CIQ扩展编码及品名—T2表示见附表2〕	最惠(%)	暂定税率	普通	增值/消费	出口退税	计量单位	监管条件	检验检疫	特殊证件对美关税
		-钎焊机器及装置:									
8515.1100		--烙铁及焊枪〔101 钎焊机器及装置,102 钎焊烙铁及焊枪〕	10		30	13/	13	个/千克			/30
8515.1900		--其他									
8515.1900	10	专门或主要用于印刷电路组件制造的其他波峰焊接机器〔999〕	3.3/1.7		30	13/	13	台/千克			/28.3,26.7
8515.1900	90	其他钎焊机器及装置〔999〕	10		30	13/	13	台/千克			/35
		-电阻焊接机器及装置:									
		--全自动或半自动的:									
8515.2120		---机器人									
8515.2120	01	汽车生产线电阻焊接机器人〔999〕	10	5	30	13/	13	台/千克	AO	L	/30
8515.2120	90	其他电阻焊接机器人〔999〕	10		30	13/	13	台/千克	AO	L	/35
		---其他:									
8515.2191		----直缝焊管机〔999〕	10		30	13/	13	台/千克			/30
8515.2199		----其他〔999〕	10		30	13/	13	台/千克	AO	L	/30
8515.2900		--其他〔999〕	10		30	13/	13	台/千克	A	L	/35
		-电弧(包括等离子弧)焊接机器及装置:									
		--全自动或半自动的:									
8515.3120		---机器人〔999〕	10		30	13/	13	台/千克	AO	L	/35
		---其他:									
8515.3191		----螺旋焊管机〔999〕	10		30	13/	13	台/千克			3/35
8515.3199		----其他〔999〕	10		30	13/	13	台/千克	AO	L	3/30
8515.3900		--其他〔999〕	10		30	13/	13	台/千克	A	L	3/30
		-其他机器及装置:									
8515.8010		---激光焊接机器人									
8515.8010	01	汽车生产线激光焊接机器人〔999〕	8	5	30	13/	13	台/千克			/30
8515.8010	90	其他激光焊接机器人〔999〕	8		30	13/	13	台/千克			/33
8515.8090		----其他									
8515.8090	10	电子束、激光自动焊接机(将端塞焊接于燃料细棒(或棒)的自动焊接机)〔101 波峰焊设备,102 其它焊接设备及其零件〕	8		30	13/	13	台/千克	3		3/28
8515.8090	90	其他焊接机器及装置[T2]	8		30	13/	13	台/千克		L	3/28
8515.9000		-零件									
8515.9000	10	专门或主要用于印刷电路组件制造的其他波峰焊接机器的零件〔999〕	2/1		30	13/	13	千克		L	/22,21
8515.9000	90	其他电气等焊接机器及装置零件(包括激光,其他光,光子束,超声波,电子束磁脉冲等)〔999〕	6	3	30	13/	13	千克		L	/23
85.16		**电热的快速热水器、储存式热水器、浸入式液体加热器;电气空间加热器及土壤加热器;电热的理发器具(例如,电吹风机、电卷发器、电热发钳)及干手器;电熨斗;其他家用电热器具;加热电阻器,但税目85.45的货品除外:**									
		-电热的快速热水器、储存式热水器、浸入式液体加热器:									
8516.1010		---储存式电热水器[T2]	7		100	13/	13	个/千克	A	L	/27
8516.1020		---即热式电热水器[T2]	7		100	13/	13	个/千克	A	L	/12
8516.1090		---其他[T2]	7		100	13/	13	个/千克	A	L	/12
		-电气空间加热器及土壤加热器:									
8516.2100		--储存式散热器[T2]	7		100	13/	13	个/千克			/32
		--其他:									
8516.2910		---土壤加热器[T2]	7		40	13/	13	个/千克			/17
8516.2920		---辐射式空间加热器[T2]	7		100	13/	13	个/千克		L	/32
		---对流式空间加热器:									
8516.2931		----风扇式[T2]	7		100	13/	13	个/千克		L	/32
8516.2932		----充液式[T2]	7		100	13/	13	个/千克		L	/32
8516.2939		----其他[T2]	7		100	13/	13	个/千克		L	/27
8516.2990		---其他[T2]	7		100	13/	13	个/千克		L	/32
		-电热的理发器具及干手器:									
8516.3100		--吹风机[T2]	7		100	13/	13	个/千克	A	LM	/32
8516.3200		--其他理发器具[T2]	7		100	13/	13	个/千克	A	LM	/
8516.3300		--干手器[T2]	7		100	13/	13	个/千克	A	LM	/
8516.4000		-电熨斗[T2]	7		100	13/	13	个/千克	A	LM	/
8516.5000		-微波炉[T2]	7		130	13/	13	个/千克	A	LMR	/32

协定税率 %										特惠税率 %			Article Description
亚太5国	东/冰/格	巴基斯坦	韩国	瑞士	哥达	秘鲁	澳大利亚	新西/坡/智	港/澳/台	亚太2国	老/柬/缅	36/3/1	
													-Brazing or soldering machines and apparatus:
	0/0/0	4	4	0	0	0	0	0/0/0	0/0/			0/0/0	--Soldering irons and guns
													--Other
	0/0/0	4		5.3	0	0	0	0/0/0	0/0/			0/0/0	Other wave soldering machines, especially for the manufacture of printed circuit assemblies
	0/0/0	4		5.3	0	0	0	0/0/0	0/0/			0/0/0	Other soldering machines and devices
													-Machines and apparatus for resistance welding of metals:
													--Fully or partly automatic:
													---Robot
	0/0/0	4.5	7		0	0	0	0/0/0	0/0/			0/0/0	Resistance of automotive production line welding robot
	0/0/0	4.5	7		0	0	0	0/0/0	0/0/			0/0/0	Other resistance welding robot
													---Other:
	0/0/0	4	7	0	0	0	0	0//0	0/0/			0/0/0	----Straight seam pipemill
	0/0/0	4.5	7		0	0	0	0/0/0	0/0/			0/0/0	----Other:
6.5	0/0/0	4	7	0	0	0	0	0/0/0	0/0/			0/0/0	--Other
													-Machines and apparatus for arc (including plasma arc) welding of metals:
													--Fully or partly automatic:
	5/0/0	8	7	0	0	0	0	0//0	0/0/			0/0/0	---Robot
													---Other:
	0/0/0	4	4	0	0	0	0	0//0	0/0/			0/0/0	----Spiral weld pipe mill
	/0/0	8	7	0	0	0	0	0//0	0/0/			0/0/0	----Other
	0/0/0	4	4	0	0	0	0	0//0	0/0/			0/0/0	--Other
													-Other machines and apparatus:
													---Laser welding robot
5.2	0/0/0	4	0	4.3	0	0	0	0//0	0/0/0			0/0/0	Laser welding robot used for auto production line
5.2	0/0/0	4	0	4.3	0	0	0	0//0	0/0/0			0/0/0	Other laser wdlding robot
													---Other
5.2	0/0/0	4	0	4.3	0	0	0	0//0	0/0/0			0/0/0	Automatic electron beam, laser wdlding machine(automatic welding machine for welding end plug onto fuelpins or rods)
5.2	0/0/0	4	0	4.3	0	0	0	0//0	0/0/0			0/0/0	Other welding machines and devices
													-Parts
3.9	0/0/0	0	0	1.8	0	0	0	0//0	0/0/			0/0/0	Parts of other wave soldering machines, especially for the manufacture of printed circuit assemblies
3.9	0/0/0	0	0	1.8	0	0	0	0//0	0/0/			0/0/0	Parts of other electric brazing or welding machines and apparatus(including laser or other light or photon beam, ultrasonic, electron beam, magnetic pulse)
													Electric instantaneous or storage water heaters and immersion heaters; electric space heating apparatus and soil heating apparatus; electro-thermic hair-dressing apparatus (for example, hair dryers, hair curlers, curling tong heaters) and hand dryers; electric smoothing irons; other electro-thermic appliances of a kind used for domestic purposes; electric heating resistors, other than those of headingNo. 85. 45:
													-Electric instantaneous or storage water heaters and immersion heaters:
	0/0/0	4	4	0	0	0	0	0/0/0	0/0/			0/0/0	---Electric storage water heaters
	0/0/0	4	4	0	0	0	0	0/0/0	0/0/			0/0/0	---Electric instantaneous water heaters
	0/0/0	4		0	0	0	0	0/0/0	0/0/			0/0/0	---Other
													-Electric space heating apparatus and electric soil heating apparatus:
	0/0/0			7	0	0	0	0/0/0	0/0/0			0/0/	--Storage heating radiators
													--Other:
5.6	0/0/0	4	4	0	0	0	0	0//0	0/0/			0/0/0	---Electric soil heating apparatus
	0/0/0	4	4	0	0	0	0	0/0/0	0/0/			0/0/0	---Radiat space heating apparatus
													---Convectiom space heating apparatus:
	0/0/0	4	4	0	0	0	0	0/0/0	0/0/			0/0/0	---Fan type
	0/0/0	4	4	0	0	0	0	0/0/0	0/0/			0/0/0	---Oil-filled type
	0/0/0	4	4	0	0	0	0	0/0/0	0/0/			0/0/0	---Other
	0/0/0	4	4	0	0	0	0	0/0/0	0/0/			0/0/0	---Other
													-Electro-thermic hair-dressing or hand-drying apparatus:
	0/0/0	4	4	3	0	0	0	0/0/0	0/0/			0/0/0	--Hair dryers
	0/0/0	35	24.5	7	0	0	0	0/0/0	0/0/			0/0/	--Other hair-dressing apparatus
	0/0/0	35		7	0	0	0	0/0/0	0/0/			0/0/	--Hand-drying apparatus
	0/0/0	35		7	0	0	0	0/0/0	0/0/0			0/0/	-Electric smoothing irons
4.6	0/0/0	6.8	6	4.5	0	0	0	0/0/0	0/0/			0/0/	-Microwave ovens

税则号列	货品名称〔CIQ 扩展编码及品名—T2 表示见附表 2〕	最惠(%)	暂定税率	普通	增值/消费	出口退税	计量单位	监管条件	检验检疫	特殊证件对美关税
	-其他炉；电锅、电热板、加热环、烧烤炉及烘烤器：									
8516.6010	---电磁炉［T2］	7		130	13/	13	个/千克	A	L	/32
8516.6030	---电饭锅［T2］	7		130	13/	13	个/千克	A	LR	/
8516.6040	---电炒锅［T2］	7		130	13/	13	个/千克	A	R	/
8516.6050	---电烤箱［T2］	7		130	13/	13	个/千克	A	LM	/32
8516.6090	---其他［T2］	7		130	13/	13	个/千克	A	LM	/32
	-其他电热器具：									
	--咖啡壶或茶壶：									
8516.7110	---滴液式咖啡机［T2］	7		130	13/	13	个/千克	A	LR	/32
8516.7120	---蒸馏渗滤式咖啡机［T2］	7		130	13/	13	个/千克	A	LR	/32
8516.7130	---泵压式咖啡机［T2］	7		130	13/	13	个/千克	A	LR	/32
8516.7190	---其他［T2］	7		130	13/	13	个/千克	A	LR	/17
	--烤面包器：									
8516.7210	---家用自动面包机［T2］	7		130	13/	13	个/千克	A	LMR	/
8516.7220	---片式烤面包机(多士炉)［T2］	7		130	13/	13	个/千克	A	LMR	/32
8516.7290	---其他［T2］	7		130	13/	13	个/千克	A	LMR	/32
	--其他：									
8516.7910	---电热饮水机［T2］	7		100	13/	13	台/千克	A	L	/32
8516.7990	---其他	7		100	13/	13	个/千克	A		/32
8516.8000	-加热电阻器［T2］	7		40	13/	13	个/千克			/17
	-零件：									
8516.9010	---土壤加热器及加热电阻器用〔999〕	6		40	13/	13	千克			/16
8516.9090	---其他〔999〕	6		100	13/	13	千克			/31
85.17	**电话机，包括用于蜂窝网络或其他无线网络的电话机；其他发送或接收声音、图像或其他数据用的设备，包括有线或无线网络(例如，局域网或广域网)的通信设备，税目 84.43、85.25、85.27 或 85.28 的发送或接收设备除外：**									
	-电话机，包括蜂窝网络或其他无线网络用电话机：									
8517.1100	--无绳电话机									
8517.1100 10	无绳加密电话机〔999〕	0		30	13/	13	台/千克	AM	LM	/25
8517.1100 90	其他无绳电话机〔999〕	0		30	13/	13	台/千克	A	LM	/25
	--用于蜂窝网络或其他无线网络的电话机：									
8517.1210	---手持(包括车载)式无线电话机									
8517.1210 11	GSM 数字式手持无线电话整套散件［T2］	0		20	13/	13	台/千克			/25
8517.1210 19	其他 GSM 数字式手持无线电话机［T2］	0		20	13/	13	台/千克	A	LM	/25
8517.1210 21	CDMA 数字式手持无线电话整套散件［T2］	0		20	13/	13	台/千克			/25
8517.1210 29	其他 CDMA 数字式手持无线电话机［T2］	0		20	13/	13	台/千克	A	LM	/25
8517.1210 90	其他手持式无线电话机(包括车载式无线电话机)［T2］	0		20	13/	13	台/千克	A	LM	/25
8517.1220	---对讲机〔101 对讲机，102 其它通讯设备及其零件〕	0		17	13/	13	台/千克			/25
8517.1290	---其他［T2］	0		14	13/	13	台/千克		L	/25
8517.1800	--其他									
8517.1800 10	其他加密电话机〔999〕	0		30	13/	13	台/千克	AM	LM	/30
8517.1800 90	其他电话机〔999〕	0		30	13/	13	台/千克	A	LM	/30
	-其他发送或接收声音、图像或其他数据用的设备，包括有线或无线网络(例如，局域网或广域网)的通信设备：									
	--基站：									
8517.6110	---移动通信基站									
8517.6110 10	GSM 式移动通信基地站〔999〕	0		14	13/	13	台/千克	O		/25
8517.6110 20	CDMA 式移动通信基地站〔999〕	0		14	13/	13	台/千克	O		/25
8517.6110 30	TACS 式移动通信基地站〔999〕	0		14	13/	13	台/千克			/25
8517.6110 90	其他移动通信基地站〔999〕	0		14	13/	13	台/千克	O		/25
8517.6190	---其他［T2］	0		14	13/	13	台/千克	O		/20
	--接收、转换并且发送或再生声音、图像或其他数据用的设备，包括交换及路由设备：									
	---数字式程控电话或电报交换机：									
8517.6211	----局用电话交换机；长途电话交换机；电报交换机〔101 电话交换机，102 网络交换机，103 其它通讯设备及其零件〕	0		17	13/	13	台/千克		L	/10

协定税率 %										特惠税率 %			
亚太5国	东/冰/格	巴基斯坦	韩国	瑞士	哥达	秘鲁	澳大利亚	新西/坡/智	港/澳/台	亚太2国	老/柬/缅	36/3/1	Article Description
													-Other ovens; cookers, cooking plates, boiling rings, grillers and roasters:
5.6	0/0/0	10.8	6	4.5	0	0	0	0/0/0	0/0/			0/0/	---Electromagnetic ovens
	0/0/0	10.8	6	4.5	0	0	0	0/0/0	0/0/0			0/0/	---Electric rice cookers
	0/0/0	10.8	6	4.5	0	0	0	0/0/0	0/0/			0/0/	---Electric frying pans
	0/0/0	10.8	6	4.5	0	0	0	0//0	0/0/0			0/0/	---Roaster oven
	0/0/0	10.8	6	4.5	0	0	0	0/0/0	0/0/			0/0/	---Other
													-Other electro-thermic appliances:
													--Coffee or tea makers:
	0//0	32		0	0	0	0	0/0/0	0/0/			0/0/	---Drip coffee maker
	0//0	32		0	0	0	0	0/0/0	0/0/			0/0/	---Steam espresso makers
	0/0/0	32		0	0	0	0	0/0/0	0/0/			0/0/	---Pump-espresso makers
	0/0/0	32		0	0	0	0	0/0/0	0/0/			0/0/	---Other
													--Toasters:
	0//0	32		7	0	0	0	0/0/0	0/0/0			0/0/	---Household automated bread makers
	0//0	32		7	0	0	0	0/0/0	0/0/			0/0/	---Slice pop-up toasters
	0//0	32		7	0	0	0	0/0/0	0/0/			0/0/	---Other
													--Other:
	0//0	32		7	0	0	0	0/0/0	0/0/			0/0/	---Electro-thermic water dispensers
	0//0				0	0	0	0/0/0	0/0/			0/0/	---Other
	0/0/0	4	4	3	0	0	0	0/0/0	0/0/			0/0/0	-Electric heating resistors
													-Parts:
	0/0/0	4	3.2	0	0	0	0	0//0	0/0/			0/0/0	---For electric soil heating apparatus or electric heating resistors
	0/0/0	5.4	4.8	0	0	0	0	0/0/0	0/0/			0/0/0	---Other
													Telephone sets, including telephones for cellular networks or for other wireless networks; other apparatus for the transmission or reception of voice, images or other data, including apparatus for communication in a wired or wireless network(such as a local or wide are network), other than transmission or reception apparatus of heading 84.43, 85.25, 85.27 or 85.28:
													-Telephone sets, including telephones for cellular networks or for other wireless networks:
													--Line telephone sets with cordless handsets
												0/0/0	Cordless encrypting telephones
												0/0/0	Other cordless telephones
													--Telephones for cellular net works or for other wireless networks:
													---Wirelrss telephone handsets (including vehicle installed)
												0/0/0	Full set of parts of GSM digital wireless telephones handheld
												0/0/0	Other GSM digital wireless telephones handsets
												0/0/0	Full set of parts of CDMA digital wireless phones handheld
												0/0/0	Other CDMA wirelesst elephones handheld
												0/0/0	Other wireless telephones handsets(including vehicle installed)
												0/0/0	---Walkie-talkie
												0/0/0	---Other
													--Other
												0/0/0	Other encrypting telephones
												0/0/0	Other telephones
													-Other apparatus for tromsmission or reception of voice, images or other data including apparatus for communication in a wired or wireless network (such as a local or wide area network):
													--Base stations:
													---Mobile communication base station
												0/0/0	GSM mobile communication base station
												0/0/0	CDMA mobile communication base station
												0/0/0	TACS mobile communication base station
												0/0/0	Other mobile communication base station
												0/0/0	---Other
													--Machines for the reception, conversion and transmission or regeneration of voice images or other data, induding switchig and routing apparatus:
													---Digital program-controlled telephonic or telephooic switching apparatus:
												0/0/0	----Public telephonic switching apparatus, toll telephonic switching apparatus telegrapbic switching apparatus

税则号列		货品名称〔CIQ扩展编码及品名－T2表示见附表2〕	最惠(%)	暂定税率	普通	增值/消费	出口退税	计量单位	监管条件	检验检疫	特殊证件对美关税
8517.6212		----移动通信交换机[T2]	0		40	13/	13	台/千克	O		/5
8517.6219		----其他电话交换机〔999〕	0		40	13/	13	台/千克	A	L	/20
		---光通讯设备：									
8517.6221		----光端机及脉冲编码调制设备(PCM)〔101调制解调器，102光通信数字同步设备，103其它通讯设备及其零件〕	0		17	13/	13	台/千克	O	L	/20
8517.6222		----波分复用光传输设备〔999〕	0		30	13/	13	台/千克	O	L	/25
8517.6229		----其他									
8517.6229	10	光通迅加密路由器[T2]	0		30	13/	13	台/千克	AMO	LM	/5
8517.6229	90	其他光通讯设备[T2]	0		30	13/	13	台/千克	A	LM	/5
		---其他有线数字通信设备：									
8517.6231		----通信网络时钟同步设备〔999〕	0		30	13/	13	台/千克		L	/5
8517.6232		----以太网络交换机									
8517.6232	10	非光通讯加密以太网络交换机〔999〕	0		30	13/	13	台/千克	M	L	/20
8517.6232	90	其他非光通讯以太网络交换机〔999〕	0		30	13/	13	台/千克		L	/20
8517.6233		----IP电话信号转换设备〔999〕	0		30	13/	13	台/千克	A	L	/25
8517.6234		----调制解调器〔999〕	0		30	13/	13	台/千克	A	L	/5
8517.6235		----集线器〔999〕	0		40	13/	13	台/千克	A	L	/20
8517.6236		----路由器									
8517.6236	10	非光通讯加密路由器〔999〕	0		40	13/	13	台/千克	M	L	/25
8517.6236	90	其他路由器〔999〕	0		40	13/	13	台/千克		L	/25
8517.6237		----有线网络接口卡									
8517.6237	10	为聚合高性能数字计算机性能而专门设计的有线网络接口卡，单链路单向通信速率超过2.0GB/s，高性能数字计算机是指调整后峰值性能(APP)大于8.0加权每秒万亿次浮点运算的数字计算机〔999〕	0		30	13/	13	台/千克	3		/25
8517.6237	90	其他有线网络接口卡〔999〕	0		30	13/	13	台/千克		L	/25
8517.6239		----其他									
8517.6239	10	为聚合高性能数字计算机性能而专门设计的交换机，单链路单向通信速率超过2.0GB/s，自定义通信协议。高性能数字计算机是指调整后峰值性能(APP)大于8.0加权每秒万亿次浮点运算的数字计算机〔999〕	0		30	13/	13	台/千克	3O		/10
8517.6239	90	其他有线数字通信设备〔999〕	0		30	13/	13	台/千克		L	/10
		---其他：									
8517.6292		----无线网络接口卡〔999〕	0		14	13/	13	台/千克		L	/25
8517.6293		----无线接入固定台〔999〕	0		14	13/	13	台/千克		L	/25
8517.6294		----无线耳机[T2]	0		14	13/	13	个/千克			/25
8517.6299		----其他〔999〕	0		14	13/	13	台/千克		L	/25
		--其他：									
8517.6910		---其他无线设备									
8517.6910	01	用于呼叫、提示和寻呼的便携式接收器[T2]	0		14	13/	13	台/千克	A	M	/10
8517.6910	90	其他无线通信设备[T2]	3/1.5		14	13/	13	台/千克	A	LM	/13,11.5
8517.6990		---其他有线设备[T2]	0		30	13/	13	台/千克		L	/10
		-零件：									
8517.7010		---数字式程控电话或电报交换机用〔999〕	0		14	13/	13	千克			/25
8517.7020		---光端机及脉冲编码调制设备(PCM)用〔999〕	0		14	13/	13	千克			/30
8517.7030		---手持式无线电话机用(天线除外)〔999〕	0		17	13/	13	千克			/25
8517.7040		---对讲机用(天线除外)[T2]	0		20	13/	13	千克			/25
8517.7060		---光通信设备的激光收发模块〔999〕	0		30	13/	13	千克			/20
8517.7070		---税目85.17所列设备用天线及其零件									
8517.7070	01	无线电话电报装置的天线〔999〕	0		20	13/	13	千克			/25
8517.7070	90	税目85.17所列设备用其他天线及其零件〔999〕	0		20	13/	13	千克			/25
8517.7090		---其他〔999〕	0		20	13/	13	千克			/25

协定税率 %										特惠税率 %			Article Description
亚太5国	东/冰/格	巴基斯坦	韩国	瑞士	哥达	秘鲁	澳大利亚	新西/坡/智	港/澳/台	亚太2国	老/柬/缅	36/3/1	
												0/0/0	----Mobile communication switching system
												0/0/0	----Other telephonic switching appatatus
													---Optical communication equipments:
												0/0/0	----Optical line terminal equipments and pulse code modulation e-quipments
												0/0/0	----Optical transmission equipments for wave-division multiplexing
													----Other
												0/0/0	Optical communication encrypting routers
												0/0/0	Other optical communication equipment
													---Other telecommunication apparatus for digit line system:
												0/0/0	----Communication network synchronization equipments
													----Ethernet exchangers
												0/0/0	Non-optical communication encypting ethernet exchangers
												0/0/0	Other non-optical communication ethernet exchangers
												0/0/0	----IP telephone signal converters
												0/0/0	----Modem
												0/0/0	----Hubs
													----Routers
												0/0/0	Non-optical communication encrypting routers
												0/0/0	Other routers
													----Wired network interface card
												0/0/0	Specially designed for the polymerization of high-performance digital computer performance cable network interface card, single link one-way communication rate of more than 2.0 GB/s, high-performance digital computer is adjusted peak performance (APP) is greater than 8.0 digital computer weighted one trillion floating point operations per second
												0/0/0	Wired network interface cards
													----Other
												0/0/0	Specially designed for the polymerization of high-performance digital computer performance switches, one-way communication rate of more than 2.0 GB/s single link, the custom communication protocol. High performance digital computer is adjusted peak performance (APP) is greater than 8.0 weighted one trillion floating point operations per second, a digital computer
												0/0/0	Other telecommunication apparatus for digital line system
													---Other:
												0/0/0	----Wireless network interface cards
												0/0/0	----Fixed wireless access station
												0/0/0	----Wireless headset
												0/0/0	----Other
													--Other:
													---Other equipments in a wireless network
	0/0/0	0	0	0	0	0	0	0//0	0/0/			0/0/0	Portable receivers for calling ,promoting and paging
	0/0/0	0	0	0	0	0	0	0//0	0/0/			0/0/0	Other wireless communication equipments
												0/0/0	---Other equipments in a wired network
													-Parts:
												0/0/0	---Of digital program-controlled telephonic or telegraphic switching appootus
												0/0/0	---Of optical line terminal equipments and pulse code modulation e-quipments
												0/0/0	---Of wireless tevephone handsets(other than aerials)
	0//	4	3.2					//	0/0/			0/0/0	---of walkle-talkie(other than aerials)
												0/0/0	---Laser receiving and transmitting unit of optical communication e-quipments
													---Antenna and parts thereof of heading No. 85. 17
	0//							//	0/0/			0/0/0	Antenna for wireless telephones and telegrams
	0//							//	0/0/			0/0/0	Other antenna and parts thereof of heading No. 85. 17
												0/0/0	---Other

税则号列	货品名称〔CIQ扩展编码及品名—T2表示见附表2〕	最惠(%)	暂定税率	普通	增值/消费	出口退税	计量单位	监管条件	检验检疫	特殊证件对美关税
85.18	**传声器(麦克风)及其座架;扬声器,不论是否装成音箱;耳机、耳塞机,不论是否装有传声器,由传声器及一个或多个扬声器组成的组合机,音频扩大器;电气扩音机组:**									
8518.1000	-传声器(麦克风)及其座架									
8518.1000 01	电讯用频率在300～3400Hz麦克风(直径不超过10mm,高不超过3mm)[T2]	0		40	13/	13	个/千克			/25
8518.1000 90	其他传声器(麦克风)及其座架[T2]	0		40	13/	13	个/千克			/25
	-扬声器,不论是否装成音箱:									
8518.2100	--单喇叭音箱[T2]	0		40	13/	13	个/千克			/25
8518.2200	--多喇叭音箱[T2]	0		40	13/	13	个/千克			/20
8518.2900	--其他[T2]	0		40	13/	13	个/千克			/25
8518.3000	-耳机、耳塞机,不论是否装有传声器,以及由传声器及一个或多个扬声器组成的组合机[T2]	0		40	13/	13	个/千克			/25
8518.4000	-音频扩大器									
8518.4000 01	电器扩音器(列入ITA的有线电话重复器用的)[T2]	0		40	13/	13	台/千克			/20
8518.4000 90	其他音频扩大器[T2]	0		40	13/	13	台/千克			/20
8518.5000	-电气扩音机组[T2]	0		40	13/	13	套/千克		L	/20
8518.9000	-零件									
8518.9000 01	税目8518.400001所列货品的零件(列入ITA的有线电话重复器用的)[T2]	0		40	13/	13	千克			/25
8518.9000 90	税目85.18所列货品的其他零件[T2]	0		40	13/	13	千克			/25
85.19	**声音录制或重放设备:**									
8519.2000	-用硬币、钞票、银行卡、代币或其他支付方式使其工作的设备									
8519.2000 10	以特定支付方式使其工作的激光唱机(用硬币、钞票、银行卡、代币或其他支付方式使其工作)〔101:Ⅰ类激光唱机,102:Ⅱ类激光唱机,103:Ⅲ类激光唱机〕	12		80	13/	13	台			/17
8519.2000 90	其他以特定支付方式使其工作的声音录制或重放设备(用硬币、钞票、银行卡、代币或其他支付方式使其工作)[T2]	12		80	13/	13	台		L	/17
8519.3000	-转盘(唱机唱盘)[T2]	7		130	13/	13	台			/32
8519.5000	-电话应答机[T2]	0		80	13/	13	台		L	/5
	-其他设备:									
	--使用磁性、光学或半导体媒体:									
	---使用磁性媒体的:									
8519.8111	----未装有声音录制装置的盒式磁带型声音重放装置,编辑节目用放声机除外[T2]	0		130	13/	13	台	A	LM	/5
8519.8112	----装有声音重放装置的盒式磁带录音机[T2]	0		130	13/	13	台	A	LM	/25
8519.8119	----其他 [T2]	0		80	13/	13	台	6A	LM	/
	---使用光学媒体的:									
8519.8121	----激光唱机,未装有声音录制装置[T2]	0		80	13/	13	台	A	LM	/25
8519.8129	----其他									
8519.8129 10	具有录音功能的激光唱机[T2]	0		80	13/	13	台	6A	LM	/20
8519.8129 90	其他使用光学媒体的声音录制或重放设备[T2]	0		80	13/	13	台	A	LM	/20
	---使用半导体媒体:									
8519.8131	----装有声音重放装置的闪速存储器型声音录制设备〔101电子行业成套设备,102Ⅰ类录音机,103Ⅱ类录音机,104Ⅲ类录音机〕	0		80	13/	13	台	6A	LM	/25
8519.8139	----其他[T2]	0		80	13/	13	台	6A	LM	/5
	--其他:									
8519.8910	---不带录制装置的其他唱机,不论是否带有扬声器[T2]	0		130	13/	13	台	A	L	/25
8519.8990	---其他声音录制或重放设备[T2]	0		80	13/	13	台	6A	LM	/20
85.21	**视频信号录制或重放设备,不论是否装有高频调谐器:**									
	-磁带型:									
	---录像机:									

协定税率 %										特惠税率 %			Article Description
亚太5国	东/冰/格	巴基斯坦	韩国	瑞士	哥达	秘鲁	澳大利亚	新西/坡/智	港/澳/台	亚太2国	老/柬/缅	36/3/1	
													Microphones and stands therefor; loudspeakers, whether or not mounted in their enclosures; headphones earphones, whether or not combined with a microphone, and sets consisting of a microphone and one or more loudspeakers; audio-frequency electric amplifiers; electric sound amplifier sets:
													-Microphones and stands therefor
	0//	4.5						//	0/0/0			0/0/0	Microphones, telecommunication use, frequency between 300Hz～3400Hz(with a diameter≤10mm and a height≤3mm)
	0//	4.5						//	0/0/0			0/0/0	Other microphones and stands therefor
													-Loudspeakers, whether or not mounted in their enclosures:
	0//	4	4					//	0/0/			0/0/0	--Single loudspeakers, mounted in their enclosures
	0//	4	4					//	0/0/			0/0/0	--Multiple loudspeakers, mounted in the same enclosure
												0/0/0	--Other
												0/0/0	-Headphones and earphones, whether or not combined with a microphone, and sets consisting of a microphone and one or more loudspeakers
													-Audio-frequency electric amplifiers
	0//	5.4	4.8					//	0/0/0			0/0/0	Amplifiers for electric equipment(on ITA cable phone repeatedly used)
	0//	5.4	4.8					//	0/0/0			0/0/0	Other audio-frequency electric amplifiers
	0//	4	7					//	0/0/			0/0/0	-Electric sound amplifier sets
													-Parts
	0//4.2	4	8.4					//	0/0/0			0/0/0	Parts for goods of heading No. 8518. 400001(for telephone repeaters falling within ITA)
	0//4.2	4	8.4					//	0/0/0			0/0/0	Other parts of goods of heading No. 85. 18
													Sound recording or reproducing apparatus:
													-Apparatus oporated by coins barknotes, bank cards tokens or by other means of payment
7.8	0/0/0	14.8	12	6	0	0	0	0/0/0	0/0/			0/0/	Laser phonographs that work by special means of payment (coins, notes, bank card, token coins or other means of payment are used to make it work)
7.8	0/0/0	14.8	12	6	0	0	0	0/0/0	0/0/			0/0/	Other sound recording or reproducing apparatus that work by special means of payment (coins, notes, bank card, token coins or other means of payment are used to make it work)
	0/0/0	30		7	0	0	0	0/0/0	0/0/			0/0/	-Tuntables(record-decks)
												0/0/0	-Telephone answering machines
													-Other apparatus:
													--Using magnetic, optical or semiconductor media:
													---Using magnetic media:
	0//	12.2	6.8					//	0/0/			0/0/	----Cassette-type sound reproducing apparatus not incorporating a sound recording device, other than transchibing machines
	0//	30	21					//	0/0/			0/0/	----Cassette-type magnetic tape recorders in corporating sound reproducing apparatus
	0//	14.8	12					//	0/0/			0/0/	----Other
													---Using optical media:
	0//	26	21					//	0/0/			0/0/	----Compact disc players, not in corporating a sound recondig devices
													----Other
	0//	14.4	12					//	0/0/			0/0/	Recordable laser phonographs
	0//	14.4	12					//	0/0/			0/0/	Other sound recording or reproducing apparontus using optics media
													---Using semiconductor media:
	0//	20	14					//	0/0/			0/0/	----Flash memory type recorders incorporating sound reproducing apparatus
	0//	14.8	12					//	0/0/			0/0/	----Other
													--Other:
	0//	30	21					//	0/0/			0/0/	---Other record-players, not incorporating a sound recording device with or without loudspeaker
	0//	14.4	12					//	0/0/			0/0/	---Other sound recording or reproducing apparatus
													Video recording or reproducing apparatus, whether or not incorporating a video tuner:
													-Magnetic tape-type:
													---Video tape recorders:

税则号列	货品名称〔CIQ 扩展编码及品名—T2 表示见附表 2〕	最惠(%)	暂定税率	普通	增值/消费	出口退税	计量单位	监管条件	检验检疫	特殊证件对美关税
8521.1011	----广播级[T2]	T3		T3	13/	13	台/千克			/
8521.1019	----其他[T2]	T3		T3	13/	13	台/千克			/
8521.1020	---放像机[T2]	T3		T3	13/	13	台/千克			/5
	-其他：									
	---激光视盘机：									
8521.9011	----视频高密光盘(VCD)播放机									
8521.9011 10	具有录制功能的视频高密光盘(VCD)播放机(不论是否装有高频调谐放大器)[T2]	0		130	13/	13	台/千克	A	LM	/
8521.9011 90	其他视频高密光盘(VCD)播放机(不论是否装有高频调谐放大器)[T2]	0		130	13/	13	台/千克	A	LM	/
8521.9012	----数字化视频光盘(DVD)播放机									
8521.9012 10	具有录制功能的数字化视频光盘(DVD)播放机(不论是否装有高频调谐放大器)[T2]	0		130	13/	13	台/千克	A	LM	/25
8521.9012 90	其他数字化视频光盘(DVD)播放机(不论是否装有高频调谐放大器)[T2]	0		130	13/	13	台/千克	A	LM	/25
8521.9019	----其他									
8521.9019 10	具有录制功能的其他激光视盘播放机(不论是否装有高频调谐放大器)[T2]	0		130	13/	13	台/千克	A	LM	/25
8521.9019 90	其他激光视盘播放机(不论是否装有高频调谐放大器)[T2]	0		130	13/	13	台/千克	A	LM	/25
8521.9090	---其他									
8521.9090 10	用于光盘生产的金属母盘生产设备(不论是否装有高频调谐放大器)〔999〕	0		130	13/	13	台/千克	A	M	/20
8521.9090 20	光盘型广播级录像机〔999〕	0		130	13/	13	台/千克	6A	M	/20
8521.9090 90	其他视频信号录制或重放设备(不论是否装有高频调谐放大器)[T2]	0		130	13/	13	台/千克	6A	LM	/20
85.22	**专用于或主要用于税目 85.19 或 85.21 所列设备的零件、附件：**									
8522.1000	-拾音头[T2]	12		130	13/	13	个/千克			/
	-其他：									
8522.9010	---转盘或唱机用[T2]	12.5/9.4		130	13/	13	千克			/37.5,34.4
	---盒式磁带录音机或放声机用：									
8522.9021	----走带机构(机芯)，不论是否装有磁头[T2]	12.5/9.4		100	13/	13	千克			/
8522.9022	----磁头[T2]	12.5/9.4		100	13/	13	个/千克			/37.5,34.4
8522.9023	----磁头零件[T2]	10/7.5		100	13/	13	千克			/20,17.5
8522.9029	----其他[T2]	15/11.3		100	13/	13	千克			/
	---视频信号录制或重放设备用：									
8522.9031	----激光视盘机的机芯									
8522.9031 10	车载导航仪视频播放机机芯〔999〕	15/11.3		100	13/	13	千克			/40,36.3
8522.9031 90	其他激光视盘机的机芯[T2]	15/11.3		100	13/	13	千克			/40,36.3
8522.9039	----其他〔999〕	15/11.3		100	13/	13	千克			/40,36.3
	---其他：									
8522.9091	----车载音频转播器或发射器[T2]	10/7.5		80	13/	13	台/千克			/15,12.5
8522.9099	----其他[T2]	10/7.5		80	13/	13	千克			/35,27.5
85.23	**录制声音或其他信息用的圆盘、磁带、固态非易失性数据存储器件、"智能卡"及其他媒体，不论是否已录制，包括供复制圆盘用的母片及母带，但不包括第三十七章的产品：**									
	-磁性媒体：									
	--磁条卡：									
8523.2110	---未录制〔999〕	0		70	13/	13	个/千克			/20
8523.2120	---已录制〔999〕	0		130	9/	13,9	个/千克			/20
	--其他：									

① 完税价格 不高于 2000 美元/台：14.4%；完税价格 高于 2000 美元/台：3.0%，加 1844.2 元

② 价格≤ 2000 美元/台：21%；价 格＞2000 美元/台：2.1%＋3061.8 元/ 台

③ 完税价格 不高于 2000 美元/台：22.1%；完税价格 高于 2000 美元/台：3.0%，加 3094.2 元

④ 完税价格 不高于 2000 美元/台：16.2%；完税价格 高于 2000 美元/台：3.0%，加 2138.4 元

协定税率 %										特惠税率 %			Article Description
亚太5国	东/冰/格	巴基斯坦	韩国	瑞士	哥达	秘鲁	澳大利亚	新西/坡/智	港/澳/台	亚太2国	老/柬/缅	36/3/1	
	0//	①	②					//	0/0/			0/0/	----Broadcast quality
	0//	③	②					//	0/0/		//	0/0/	----Other
	0//	④	②					//	0/0/		//	0/0/	---Video tape reproducers
													-Other:
													---Laser video compact disk player:
													----Video Compact Disc player
	0//	14.4	12					//	0/0/			0/0/	Recordable video compact Disc(VCD)player(whether or not incorporating with a high-frequency amplifier tuner)
	0//	14.4	12					//	0/0/			0/0/	Other video compact disc(VCD) player(whether or not incorporating with ahigh-frequency ammelifer tuner)
													----Digital Video Disc player
	0//	14.4	14					//	0/0/			0/0/	Recordable Digital video Disc(DVD)player(whether or not in corporating with a high-frequency tuner)
	0//	14.4	14					//	0/0/			0/0/	Other Digital video Disc(DVD) player(whether or not incorporating with a high-frequency tuned amplifier)
													----Other
	0//	14.4	12					//	0/0/			0/0/	Laser video compact disk (VCD) player with CD-R drivers(whether or not incorporating with a high - frequency tuned amplifier)
	0//	14.4	12					//	0/0/			0/0/	Other laser video compact disk (VCD) player(whether or not incorporating with a high - frequency tuned amplifier)
													---Other
	0//	14.4	14					//	0/0/			0/0/	Metal master disc production equipments for CD production(whether or not incorporating with a high - frequency tuned amplifier)
	0//	14.4	14					//	0/0/			0/0/	Disc-type broadcast-quality video recorders
	0//	14.4	14					//	0/0/			0/0/	Other video recording or reproducing apparatus, whether or not incorporating with a high-frequency tuner amlifier
													Parts and accessories suitable for use solely or principally with the apparatus of headings No. 85. 19 or 85. 21:
	0/0/0	35		12	0	0	0	0/0/0	0/0/			0/0/	-Pick-up cartridges
													-Other:
8.1/6.1	0/0/0	18	15	12.5/9.4	0	0	0	0/0/0	0/0/			0/0/	---Of turntables (record decks) or record-players
													---Of cassette magnetic tape recorders or reproducers:
8.1/6.1	0/0/0	22.5	15	12.5/9.4	0	0	0	0/0/0	0/0/			0/0/	----Transport mechanisms, whether or not incorporating a magnetic head
8.1/6.1	0/0/0	22.5	16.2	12.5/9.4	0	0	0	0/0/0	0/0/			0/0/	----Magnetic heads
6.5/4.9	0/0/0	16.2	12	6	0	0	0	0/0/0	0/0/			0/0/	----Farts of magnetic heads
9.8/7.3	0/0/0	27	19.5	15/11.3	0	0	0	0/0/0	0/0/			0/0/	----Other
													---Of video recording or reproducing apparatus:
													----Movements for laser video compact disk player
9.8/7.3	0/0/0	18.9	19.5	15/11.3	0	0	0	0/0/0	0/0/			0/0/	Car navigator video player core
9.8/7.3	0/0/0	18.9	19.5	15/11.3	0	0	0	0/0/0	0/0/			0/0/	Other movements for laser video compact disk player
9.8/7.3	0/0/0	18.9	19.5		0	0	0	0/0/0	0/0/			0/0/	----Other
													---Other:
6.5/4.9	0/0/0	14.4	12	6	0	0	0	0/0/0	0/0/			0/0/0	----Tone converters or transmission apparatus of a kind used for vehices
6.5/4.9	0/0/0	14.4	12	6	0	0	0	0/0/0	0/0/			0/0/0	----Other
													Discs, tapes, solid-state nonvolatile storage devices, "smart cards" and other media for the recording of sound or of other phenomena whether or not recorded including matrices and masters for the production of discs, but excluding products of chapter 37:
													-Magnetic media:
													--Cads incorporating a magnetic stripe:
	0//	12.6	7					//	0/0/			0/0/	---Unrecorded
	0//	10.8	6					//	0/0/			0/0/	---Recorded
													--Other:

税则号列	货品名称〔CIQ 扩展编码及品名—T2 表示见附表 2〕	最惠(%)	暂定税率	普通	增值/消费	出口退税	计量单位	监管条件	检验检疫	特殊证件对美关税
	---磁盘：									
8523.2911	----未录制〔999〕	0		14	13/	13	个/千克			/25
8523.2919	----其他〔999〕	0		14	9/	9,13	个/千克			/5
	---磁带：									
8523.2921	----未录制的宽度不超过 4 毫米磁带〔999〕	0		130	13/	13	盘/千克			/
8523.2922	----未录制的宽度超过 4 毫米，但不超过 6.5 毫米的磁带〔999〕	0		130	13/	13	盘/千克			/
8523.2923	----未录制的宽度超过 6.5 毫米的磁带〔999〕	0		20	13/	13	盘/千克			/25
8523.2928	----重放声音或图像信息的磁带〔999〕									
8523.2928 10	含人类遗传资源信息资料的重放声音或图像信息的磁带〔999〕	0		130	9/	13,9	盘/千克	V		/20
8523.2928 20	录有广播电影电视节目的重放声音或图像信息的磁带〔999〕	0		130	9/	13,9	盘/千克	b		/20
8523.2928 90	其他重放声音或图像信息的磁带〔999〕	0		130	9/	13,9	盘/千克	f		/20
8523.2929	----已录制的其他磁带〔999〕									
8523.2929 10	其他含人类遗传资源信息资料的磁带〔999〕	0		14	13/	9,13	盘/千克	V		/
8523.2929 20	录有广播电影电视节目的其他磁带〔999〕	0		14	13/	9,13	盘/千克	b		/
8523.2929 90	已录制的其他磁带〔999〕	0		14	13/	9,13	盘/千克	f		/
8523.2990	---其他〔999〕									
8523.2990 10	其他含人类遗传资源信息资料的磁性媒体〔999〕	0		14	13/	9,13	盘/千克	V		/30
8523.2990 20	其他录有广播电影电视节目的磁性媒体〔999〕	0		14	13/	9,13	盘/千克	b		/30
8523.2990 90	其他磁性媒体〔999〕	0		14	13/	9,13	盘/千克	f		/30
	-光学媒体：									
8523.4100	--未录制〔999〕	0		14	13/	13	张/千克			/25
	--其他：									
8523.4910	---仅用于重放声音信息的〔999〕									
8523.4910 10	含人类遗传资源信息资料的仅用于重放声音信息的光学媒体〔999〕	0		130	9/	13,9	张/千克	V		/20
8523.4910 20	录有广播电影电视节目的仅用于重放声音信息的光学媒体〔999〕	0		130	9/	13,9	张/千克	b		/20
8523.4910 90	其他仅用于重放声音信息的已录制光学媒体〔999〕	0		130	9/	13,9	张/千克	f		/20
8523.4920	---用于重放声音、图像以外信息的，税目 84.71 所列机器用〔999〕									
8523.4920 10	含人类遗传资源信息资料的用于重放声音、图像以外信息的光学媒体〔999〕	0		14	9/	9,13	张/千克	V		/5
8523.4920 90	其他用于重放声音、图像以外信息的光学媒体(品目 8471 所列机器用，已录制)〔999〕	0		14	9/	9,13	张/千克			/5
8523.4990	---其他〔999〕									
8523.4990 10	其他含人类遗传资源信息资料的光学媒体〔999〕	0		14	13/	9,13	张/千克	V		/5
8523.4990 20	其他录有广播电影电视节目的光学媒体〔999〕	0		14	13/	9,13	张/千克	b		/5
8523.4990 30	其他赴境外加工并返回境内的已录制光盘〔999〕	0		14	13/	9,13	张/千克	Z		/5
8523.4990 90	其他已录制光学媒体〔999〕	0		14	13/	9,13	张/千克	f		/5
	-半导体媒体：									
	--固态非易失性存储器件(闪速存储器)：									
8523.5110	---未录制[T2]	0		70	13/	13	个/千克			/25
8523.5120	---已录制[T2]	0		14	10/	10,16	个/千克			

协定税率 %										特惠税率 %			Article Description
亚太5国	东/冰/格	巴基斯坦	韩国	瑞士	哥达	秘鲁	澳大利亚	新西/坡/智	港/澳/台	亚太2国	老/柬/缅	36/3/1	
													--Magnetic discs:
												0/0/0	----Unrecorded
												0/0/0	----Other
													--Magnetic tapes:
												0/0/0	----Of a width not exceedig 4mm unrecorded
												0/0/0	----Of a width excecdig 4mm, but not exceedig 6.5mm unrecorded
												0/0/0	----Of a width exceeding 6.5mm unrecorded
													----For reproducing sound or image phencomena
	0//	4	6					//	0/0/		//	0/0/0	Tape containing information about human genetic resources that reproduces sound or image information
	0//	4	6					//	0/0/		//	0/0/0	Tape recording sound or image information reproduced from radio, film and television programs
	0//	4	6					//	0/0/		//	0/0/0	Other tapes that reproduce sound or image information
													----Other recorded magnetic tapes
	//							//	//		//	0/0/0	Other tapes containing information on human genetic resources
	//							//	//		//	0/0/0	Other tapes recording radio, film and television programs
	//							//	//		//	0/0/0	Other tapes recorded
													--Other
	//							//	//		//	0/0/0	Other magnetic media containing information on human genetic resources
	//							//	//		//	0/0/0	Other magnetic media recording radio, film and television programs
	//							//	//		//	0/0/0	Other magnetic media
													-Optical media:
												0/0/0	--Unrecorded
													--Other
													---For reproducing sound
	0//	4.5	4					//	0/0/		//	0/0/	Optical media containing information about human genetic resources for reproducing sound information only
	0//	4.5	4					//	0/0/		//	0/0/	Optical media recording radio, film and television programs for reproducing sound information only
	0//	4.5	4					//	0/0/		//	0/0/	Other recorded optical media for reproducing sound information only
													---Forreproducing phenomena other than sound or image for the machines of heading 84.71
	//							//	//		//	0/0/0	Optical media containing information of human genetic resources for reproducing information other than sound and image
	//							//	//		//	0/0/0	Other optical media for reproducing information other than sound and image
													---Other
	//							//	//		//	0/0/0	Other Optical Media Containing Information on Human Genetic Resources
	//							//	//		//	0/0/0	Other Optical Media Containing Radio, Film and Television Programs
	//							//	//		//	0/0/0	Other recorded CD—ROMs processed abroad and returned to China
	//							//	//		//	0/0/0	Other recorded optical media
													-Semiconductor media:
													--Solid-state non-volatile storage devices(flash memorizer):
												0/0/0	---Unrecorded
												0/0/0	---Recorded

税则号列	货品名称〔CIQ 扩展编码及品名—T2 表示见附表 2〕	最惠(%)	暂定税率	普通	增值/消费	出口退税	计量单位	监管条件	检验检疫	特殊证件对美关税
8523.5120 10	含人类遗传资源信息资料的固态非易失性存储器件(闪速存储器)〔999〕	0		14	9/	9,13	个/千克	V		/10
8523.5120 20	录有广播电影电视节目的固态非易失性存储器件(闪速存储器)〔999〕	0		14	9/	9,13	个/千克	b		/10
8523.5120 30	赴境外加工并返回境内的已录制的固态非易失性存储器件(闪速存储器)〔999〕	0		14	9/	9	个/千克	Z		/10
8523.5120 90	其他已录制的固态非易失性存储器件(闪速存储器)〔999〕	0		14	9/	9,13	个/千克			/10
	--"智能卡":									
8523.5210	---未录制[T2]	0		21	9/	13	个/千克			/25
8523.5290	---其他[T2]	0		21	9/	9,13	个/千克			/20
	--其他:									
8523.5910	---未录制〔999〕	0		70	13/	13	个/千克			/25
8523.5920	---已录制〔999〕									
8523.5920 10	其他含人类遗传资源信息资料的半导体媒体〔999〕	0		14	9/	9,13	个/千克	V		/10
8523.5920 20	其他录有广播电影电视节目的半导体媒体〔999〕	0		14	9/	9,13	个/千克	b		/10
8523.5920 30	其他赴境外加工并返回境内的已录制的半导体媒体〔999〕	0		14	9/	9	个/千克	Z		/10
8523.5920 90	其他已录制的半导体媒体〔999〕	0		14	9/	9,13	个/千克			/10
	-其他:									
	---唱片:									
8523.8011	----已录制〔101 磁带、磁盘,102 其它视听设备及其零件〕									
8523.8011 10	录有广播电影电视节目的唱片	0		130	9/	13,9	张/千克	b		/20
8523.8011 20	赴境外加工并返回境内的已录制唱片	0		130	9/	13,9	张/千克	Z		/20
8523.8011 90	其他已录制唱片	0		130	9/	13,9	张/千克	f		/20
8523.8019	----其他〔101 磁带、磁盘,102 其它视听设备及其零件〕	0		70	13/	9,13	张/千克			/5
	---税目 84.71 所列机器用:									
8523.8021	----未录制〔101 软、硬、光盘驱动器,102 磁带、磁盘〕	0		14	13/	13	张/千克			/20
8523.8029	----其他〔101 软、硬、光盘驱动器,102 磁带、磁盘〕									
8523.8029 10	其他含人类遗传资源信息资料的品目 8471 所列机器用其他媒体〔999〕	0		14	13/	9,13	张/千克	V		/5
8523.8029 90	其他品目 8471 所列机器用其他媒体(磁性、光学或半导体媒体除外)〔999〕	0		14	13/	9,13	张/千克			/5
	---其他:									
8523.8091	----未录制〔101 软、硬、光盘驱动器,102 磁带、磁盘〕	0		14	9/	13	张/千克			/5
8523.8099	----其他〔101 软、硬、光盘驱动器,102 磁带、磁盘〕									
8523.8099 10	其他含人类遗传资源信息资料的媒体〔999〕	0		14	9/	9,13	张/千克	V		/
8523.8099 20	其他录有广播电影电视节目的媒体〔999〕	0		14	9/	9,13	张/千克	b		/
8523.8099 90	其他媒体(磁性、光学或半导体媒体除外)〔999〕	0		14	9/	9,13	张/千克	f		/
85.25	**无线电广播、电视发送设备,不论是否装有接收装置或声音的录制、重放装置;电视摄像机、数字照相机及视频摄录一体机:**									
8525.5000	-发送设备[T2]	0		30	13/	13	台/千克	O		/5
	-装有接收装置的发送设备:									
8525.6010	---卫星地面站设备[T2]	0		14	13/	13	台/千克	O		/20
8525.6090	---其他[T2]	0		30	13/	13	台/千克			/5
	-电视摄像机、数字照相机及视频摄录一体机:									
	---电视摄像机:									
8525.8011	----特种用途的									
8525.8011 10	抗辐射电视摄像机[能抗 5×10⁴ 戈瑞(硅)以上辐射而又不会降低使用质量][T2]	3.3/1.7		17	13/	13	台/千克	3A	M	/8.3,6.7
8525.8011 90	其他特种用途电视摄像机[T2]	3.3/1.7		17	13/	13	台/千克	A	M	/8.3,6.7
8525.8012	----非特种用途的广播级[T2]	T3		T3	13/	13	台/千克	A	M	/36.7
8525.8013	----非特种用途的其他类型									

① 完税价格不高于 5000 美元/台:26.8%;完税价格高于 5000 美元/台:3.0%,加 9639.0 元。

协定税率 %										特惠税率 %			Article Description
亚太5国	东/冰/格	巴基斯坦	韩国	瑞士	哥达	秘鲁	澳大利亚	新西/坡/智	港/澳/台	亚太2国	老/柬/缅	36/3/1	
	//							//	//		//	0/0/0	Solid State Nonvolatile Memory Device (Flash Memory) Containing Human Genetic Resources Information
	//							//	//		//	0/0/0	Solid State Nonvolatile Memory Device (Flash Memory) for Recording Radio, Film and Television Programs
	//							//	//		//	0/0/0	Recorded solid state nonvolatile memory devices (flash memory) processed abroad and returned to China
	//							//	//		//	0/0/0	Other recorded solid－state non－volatile memory devices (flash memory)
													--"Smart cards":
												0/0/0	---Unrecorded
												0/0/0	---Other
													--Other:
												0/0/0	---Unrecorded
													---Recorded
	//							//	//		//	0/0/0	Other Semiconductor Media Containing Information on Human Genetic Resources
	//							//	//		//	0/0/0	Other Semiconductor Media with Radio, Film and Television Programs
	//							//	//		//	0/0/0	Other recorded semiconductor media processed overseas and returned to China
	//							//	//		//	0/0/0	Cther recorded semiconductor media
													-Other:
													---Gramophone recorols:
													----Recorded
	0//	10.8	6					//	0/0/		//	0/0/	Record recording of radio, film and television programs
	0//	10.8	6					//	0/0/		//	0/0/	Recorded Records Processed Overseas and Returned to China
	0//	10.8	6					//	0/0/		//	0/0/	Other recorded records
												0/0/0	---Other
													---For the machines of heading No. 84. 71:
												0/0/0	----Unrecorded
													----Other
	//							//	//		//	0/0/0	Other media used by other machines listed in heading 8471 containing information on human genetic resources
	//							//	//		//	0/0/0	Other media used by other machines listed in headings 8471
													---Other:
												0/0/0	----Unrecorded
													----Other
	//							//	//		//	0/0/0	Other media containing information on human genetic resources
	//							//	//		//	0/0/0	Other Media Recording Radio, Film and Television Programs
	//							//	//		//	0/0/0	Other media
													Transmission apparatus for radio-broadcasting or television, whether or not incorporating reception apparatus or sound recording or reproducing apparatus; television cameras; digital cameras and video camera recorders;
												0/0/0	-Transmission apparatus
													-Transmission apparatus incorporating reception apparatus:
												0/0/0	---Satellite earth station
												0/0/0	---Other
													-Television cameras、digital cameras and video camera recorders:
													---Telvision cameras:
													----For special purposes
2.1/1.1	0/0/0	4		0	0	0	0	0/0/0	0/0/			0/0/	Radiation－resistant telvision cameras (capable of resisting fradiance $>5\times10^4$ GY(Si) and not lowering operation quality)
2.1/1.1	0/0/0	4		0	0	0	0	0/0/0	0/0/			0/0/	Other telveision cameras for special use
7.6/3.8	0/0/0	①		11.7/5.8	0	0	0	0/0/0	0/0/		//	0/0/	----Broodcast quality not for special purposes
													----Other not for special purposes

税则号列		货品名称〔CIQ 扩展编码及品名—T2 表示见附表 2〕	最惠(%)	暂定税率	普通	增值/消费	出口退税	计量单位	监管条件	检验检疫	特殊证件对美关税
8525.8013	01	手机用摄像组件(由镜头+CCD/CMOS+数字信号处理电路三部分构成)[T2]	T3	4	T3	13/	13	台/千克			/29
8525.8013	02	高清摄像头(必须满足以下三个条件:1. 镜头元件必须使用5层玻璃镜头;2. 使用USB2.0高速接口;3. 硬件传感器像素达到130万及以上)[T2]	T3	③	T3	13/	13	台/千克			/35
8525.8013	90	其他非特种用途电视摄像机及其他摄像组件(其他摄像组件由非广播级镜头+CCD/CMOS+数字信号处理电路构成)〔101:Ⅰ类电视摄像机,102:Ⅱ类电视摄像机,103:Ⅲ类电视摄像机〕	T3		T3	13/	13	台/千克			/36.7
		---数字照相机:									
8525.8021		----特种用途的〔999〕	0		17	13/	13	台/千克			/5
8525.8022		----非特种用途的,单镜头反光型〔999〕	T3		T3	13/	13	台/千克			/25
8525.8025		----非特种用途其他可换镜头数字照相机〔999〕	T3		T3	13/	13	台/千克			/25
8525.8029		----非特种用途的其他类型									
8525.8029	10	非特种用途的航拍照相无人机(单镜头反光型除外)〔999〕	T3		T3	13/	13	台/千克			/25
8525.8029	90	其他非特种用途的其他数字照相机(单镜头反光型除外)〔999〕	T3		T3	13/	13	台/千克			/25
		---视频摄录一体机:									
8525.8031		----特种用途[T2]	0		17	13/	13	台/千克	A	M	/10
8525.8032		----非特种用途的广播级〔101:Ⅰ类电视摄像机,102:Ⅱ类电视摄像机,103:Ⅲ类电视摄像机〕	T3		T3	13/	13	台/千克	A	M	/25
8525.8033		----非特种用途的家用型〔101:Ⅰ类家用型摄录一体机,102:Ⅱ类家用型摄录一体机,103:Ⅲ类家用型摄录一体机〕	0		130	13/	13	台/千克	A	M	/25
8525.8039		----非特种用途的其他类型									
8525.8039	10	非特种用途的航拍摄录一体无人机(非广播级、非多用途)〔301:Ⅰ类电视摄像机,302:Ⅱ类电视摄像机,303:Ⅲ类电视摄像机〕	T3		T3	13/	13	台/千克	A	M	/25
8525.8039	90	非特种用途的其他视频摄录一体机(非广播级、非多用途)〔301:Ⅰ类电视摄像机,302:Ⅱ类电视摄像机,303:Ⅲ类电视摄像机〕	T3		T3	13/	13	台/千克	A	M	/25
85.26		**雷达设备、无线电导航设备及无线电遥控设备:**									
		-雷达设备:									
8526.1010		---导航用									
8526.1010	10	用于导弹、火箭等的导航雷达设备(用于弹道导弹、运载火箭、探空火箭、巡航导弹、无人驾驶航空飞行器的目标探测)〔999〕	0		8	13/	13	台/千克	3		/20
8526.1010	90	其他导航用雷达设备〔999〕	0		8	13/	13	台/千克			/20
8526.1090		---其他									
8526.1090	10	飞机机载雷达(包括气象雷达,地形雷达和空中交通管制应答系统)〔999〕	0		14	13/	13	台/千克			/5
8526.1090	20	雷达生命探测仪〔999〕	0		14	13/	13	台/千克	O		/5
8526.1090	30	用于导弹、火箭等的机载雷达设备(用于弹道导弹、运载火箭、探空火箭、巡航导弹、无人驾驶航空飞行器的目标探测)〔999〕	0		14	13/	13	台/千克	3		/5
8526.1090	40	用于导弹、火箭等的其他雷达设备(用于弹道导弹、运载火箭、探空火箭、巡航导弹、无人驾驶航空飞行器的目标探测)〔999〕	0		14	13/	13	台/千克	3		/5
8526.1090	90	其他雷达设备〔999〕	0		14	13/	13	台/千克			/5
		-其他:									
		--无线电导航设备:									
8526.9110		---机动车辆用〔999〕	0		8	13/	13	台/千克			/5
8526.9190		---其他									
8526.9190	10	制导装置(使300km射程导弹达到≤10km圆公算偏差)〔999〕	0		8	13/	13	台/千克	3		/5
8526.9190	90	其他无线电导航设备〔999〕	0		8	13/	13	台/千克			/5
8526.9200		--无线电遥控设备〔999〕	1.7/0.8		14	13/	13	台/千克	O		/21.7,20.8
85.27		**无线电广播接收设备,不论是否与声音的录制、重放装置或时钟组合在同一机壳内:**									

① 完税价格不高于5000美元/台,26.8%;完税价格高于5000美元/台:3.0%,加9639.0元

② 价格≤5000美元/台:24.5%;价格>5000美元/台:2.1%+9072元/台

③ 1—6月:10%。

协定税率 %										特惠税率 %			Article Description
亚太5国	东/冰/格	巴基斯坦	韩国	瑞士	哥达	秘鲁	澳大利亚	新西/坡/智	港/澳/台	亚太2国	老/柬/缅	36/3/1	
7.6/3.8	0/0/0	①	②	11.7/5.8	0	0	0	0/0/0	0/0/0		//	0/0/	Camera components for cellphones(including lens＋CCD/CMOS ＋ digital signal processing electric circuit)
7.6/3.8	0/0/0	①	②	11.7/5.8	0	0	0	0/0/0	0/0/0			0/0/	High definition cameras(Must meet the following three conditions: 1. lens element must used Five floors Glass lenses; 2. used USB2.0 high speed interface; 3. hardware sensor pixel ≥130W)
7.6/3.8	0/0/0	①	②	11.7/5.8	0	0	0	0/0/0	0/0/0			0/0/	Other telecameras not for special use and other camera components (the latter is composed of non-broadcast-quality lens＋ CCD/CMOS ＋digital signal processing electric circuit)
													---Digital cameras:
												0/0/0	----For special purposes
												0/0/0	
												0/0/0	----Not special purpose other interchangeable lens digital camera
													----Other not for special purposes
												0/0/0	Unmanned aerial photography UAV (except for single lens reflex)
												0/0/0	Unmanned aerial photography and unmanned aerial vehicles (non radio, non multipurpose)
													---Video camera recorders:
												0/0/0	----For special puposes
												0/0/0	----Broadcast quality not for special purposes
												0/0/0	----Householdtype not for special purposes
													----Other not for special purposes
												0/0/0	Unmanned aerial photography and unmanned aerial vehicles (non racio, non multipurpose)
												0/0/0	Non specific use of other video recording integrated machines (non radio, non multipurpose)
													Radar apparatus, radio navigational aid apparatus and radio remote control apparatus:
													-Radar apparatus:
													---For navigational aid
	0//		1.2					//	0/0/			0/0/	Navigational radar equipments for missiles or rockets (for target detection of ballistic missiles, carrier rockets, sounding rockets)
	0//		1.2					//	0/0/			0/0/	Other radar apparatus for navigational aid
													---Other
	0//		3					//	0/0/			0/0/	Airborne radars (including meteorological radars, terrain following radars and air traffic control response system)
	0//		3					//	0/0/			0/0/	Radar life detecting instrument
	0//		3					//	0/0/			0/0/	Airborne radars for missiles and rockets (for ballistic missiles, carrier rockets and sounding rockets, etc. to detect targets)
	0//		3					//	0/0/			0/0/	Other radars for missiles and rockets (for ballistic missiles, carrier rockets and sounding rockets, etc. to detect targets)
	0//		3					//	0/0/			0/0/	Other radars
													-Other:
													--Radio navigational aid apparatus:
	0//							//	0/0/			0/0/	---For motor vehicles
													---Other
	0//		0.8					//	0/0/			0/0/	Guidance devices (making 300km-range misslies, circle probability or estimated chances deviation≤10km)
	0//		0.8					//	0/0/			0/0/	Other radio navigational aid apparatus
	0/0/0	0	2	0	0	0	0	0//0	0/0/			0/0/	--Radio remote control apparatus
													Reception apparatus for radio-broadcasting, whether or not combined, in the same housing, with sound recording or reproducing apparatus or a clock:

税则号列		货品名称〔CIQ扩展编码及品名－T2表示见附表2〕	最惠(%)	暂定税率	普通	增值/消费	出口退税	计量单位	监管条件	检验检疫	特殊证件对美关税
		-不需外接电源的无线电收音机：									
8527.1200		--袖珍盒式磁带收放机[T2]	0		130	13/	13	台/千克			/
8527.1300		--其他收录(放)音组合机〔101Ⅰ类收录(放)音组合机；102：Ⅱ类收录(放)音组合机；103：Ⅲ类收录(放)音组合机〕	0		130	13/	13	台/千克			/
8527.1900		--其他〔101：Ⅰ类收音机，102：Ⅱ类收音机，103：Ⅲ类收音机〕	0		130	13/	13	台/千克			/20
		-需外接电源的汽车用无线电收音机：									
8527.2100		--收录(放)音组合机									
8527.2100	10	具备接收和转换数字广播数据系统信号功能需外接电源的汽车用收录(放)音组合机〔101：Ⅰ类收录(放)音组合机；102：Ⅱ类收录(放)音组合机；103：Ⅲ类收录(放)音组合机〕	0		130	13/	13	台/千克			/5
8527.2100	90	其他需外接电源汽车收录(放)音组合机[T2]	15		130	13/	13	台/千克			/20
8527.2900		--其他〔101：Ⅰ类收音机，102：Ⅱ类收音机，103：Ⅲ类收音机〕	0		130	13/	13	台/千克			/5
		-其他：									
8527.9100		--收录(放)音组合机[T2]	0		130	13/	13	台/千克			/25
8527.9200		--带时钟的收音机[T2]	0		130	13/	13	台/千克		L	/25
8527.9900		--其他〔101：Ⅰ类收音机，102：Ⅱ类收音机，103：Ⅲ类收音机〕	0		130	13/	13	台/千克			/25
85.28		**监视器及投影机，未装电视接收装置；电视接收装置，不论是否装有无线电收音装置或声音、图像的录制或重放装置：**									
		-阴极射线管监视器：									
8528.4200		--可直接连接且设计用于税目84.71的自动数据处理设备的[T2]	0		40	13/	13	台/千克	6		/20
		--其他：									
8528.4910		---彩色的[T2]	0		130	13/	13	台/千克	6		/5
8528.4990		---单色的[T2]	0		100	13/	13	台/千克	6		/5
		-其他监视器：									
		--可直接连接且设计用于税目84.71的自动数据处理设备的：									
		---液晶的：									
8528.5211		----专用于或主要用于税目84.71的自动数据处理设备的〔999〕	0		40	13/	13	台/千克			/10
8528.5212		----其他，彩色的〔999〕	15		130	13/	13	台/千克	6		/40
8528.5219		----其他，单色的〔999〕	10		100	13/	13	台/千克	6		/20
		---其他：									
8528.5291		----专用于或主要用于税目84.71的自动数据处理设备的，彩色的〔999〕	0		40	13/	13	台/千克			/25
8528.5292		----其他，彩色的〔999〕	15		130	13/	13	台/千克	6		/25
8528.5299		----其他，单色的〔999〕	10		100	13/	13	台/千克	6		/
		--其他：									
8528.5910		---彩色的									
8528.5910	10	专用于车载导航仪的液晶监视器〔999〕	20	15	130	13/	13	台/千克	6		/35
8528.5910	90	其他彩色的监视器[T2]	20		130	13/	13	台/千克	6		/40
8528.5990		---单色的[T2]	10		100	13/	13	台/千克	6		/35
		-投影机：									
		--可直接连接且设计用于税目84.71的自动数据处理设备的：									
8528.6210		---专用于或主要用于税目84.71的自动数据处理设备的									
8528.6210	10	专用或主要用于品目84.71商品的彩色投影机〔999〕	0		14	13/	13	台/千克			/20
8528.6210	90	其他专用或主要用于品目8471商品的投影机〔999〕	0		14	13/	13	台/千克			/20
8528.6220		---其他，彩色的〔999〕	15		130	13/	13	台/千克	6		/40
8528.6290		---其他，单色的〔999〕	10		100	13/	13	台/千克			/
		--其他：									
8528.6910		---彩色的[T2]	15		130	13/	13	台/千克	6		/40
8528.6990		---单色的[T2]	10		100	13/	13	台/千克			/15
		-电视接收装置，不论是否装有无线电收音装置或声音、图像的录制或重放装置：									
		--在设计上不带有视频显示器或屏幕的：									

协定税率 %										特惠税率 %			Article Description
亚太5国	东/冰/格	巴基斯坦	韩国	瑞士	哥达	秘鲁	澳大利亚	新西/坡/智	港/澳/台	亚太2国	老/柬/缅	36/3/1	
													-Radio-broadcast receivers capable of operating without an external source of power:
	0//	20	12					//	0/0/			0/0/	--Pocket-size radio cassette-players
	0//	10.8	6					//	0/0/			0/0/	--Other apparatus combined with sound recording or reproducing apparatus
	0//	10.8	9					//	0/0/			0/0/	--Other
													-Radio-broadcast receivers not capable of operating without an external source of power, of a kind used in motor vehicles:
													--Combined with sound recording or reproducing apparatus
	0/0/0	10.8	9	4.5	0	0	0	0/0/0	0/0/			0/0/	Vehicle mounted (released) sound combination machine for receiving and converting digital broadcast data system signal function requiring external power supply
	0/0/0	10.8	9	4.5	0	0	0	0/0/0	0/0/			0/0/	
	0//	10.8	9					//	0/0/			0/0/	--Other
													-Other:
	0//	10.8	6					//	0/0/			0/0/	--Combined with sound recording or reproducing apparatus
	0//	10.8	6					//	0/0/			0/0/	--Not combined with sound recording or reproducing apparatus but combined with a clock
	0//	27	18.9					//	0/0/			0/0/	--Other
													Monitors and projectors, not incorporatig television reception apparatus; reception apparatus for tele vision, whether or not incorporating radiobroad cast receivers or sound or video recordig or reproducing apparatus:
													-Cathode-ray tube monitors:
												0/0/0	--Capable of directly connecting to and designed for use with an auto matic data processing machine of heading 84.71
													--Other:
	0//	26	21					//	0/0/			0/0/	---Colour
	0//	13.7	7.6					//	0/0/			0/0/	---monochrone
													-Other monitors:
													--Capable of directly connecting tO and designed for use with an automatic data processing machine of heading 84.71:
													---0f LCD:
												0/0/0	----Of a kind solely or principally used in an automatic data processing system of heading 84.71
9.8	0/0/0	23.4	19.5			0	0	0/0/0	0/0/			0/0/	----Other, colour
6.5	0/0/0	13.7		5.7	0	0	0	0/0/0	0/0/			0/0/	----Other, monochrome
													---Other:
												0/0/0	----Of a kind solely or principally used in an automatic data processing system of heading 84.71, colour
9.8	0/0/0	23.4	19.5			0	0	0/0/0	0/0/			0/0/	----Other, colour
6.5	0/0/0	13.7		5.7	0	0	0	0/0/0	0/0/			0/0/	----Other, monochrome
													--Other:
													---Colour
13	0/0/0	23.4	19.5			0	0	0/0/0	0/0/			0/0/	LCD Monitors, specially used for Vehicle Navigator
13	0/0/0	23.4	19.5			0	0	0/0/0	0/0/			0/0/	Cther colors monitors
6.5	0/0/0	13.7		5.7	0	0	0	0/0/0	0/0/			0/0/	---monochrome
													-Projectors:
													--Capable of directly connecting tO and designed for use with an automatic data processing machine of heading 84.71:
													----Of a kind solely or principally used in an auto matic data processing system of heading 84.71
												0/0/0	Specially used or mainly used for color projector of heading No.84.71
												0/0/0	Other used or mainly used for projector of heading No.84.71
9.8	0/0/0	23	19.5		0	0	0	0/0/0	0/0/			0/0/	---Other, colour
	0/0/0	10.8		4.5	0	0	0	0/0/0	0/0/			0/0/	---Other, monochrome
													--Other:
9.8	0/0/0	23	19.5		0	0	0	0/0/0	0/0/			0/0/	---Colour
	0/0/0	10.8		4.5	0	0	0	0/0/0	0/0/			0/0/	---Monochrome
													-Reception apparatus for television, whether or not incorporating radio-broadcast receivers or sound or video recording or reproducing apparatus:
													--Not designed to incorporate a video display or screen:

税则号列		货品名称〔CIQ扩展编码及品名—T2表示见附表2〕	最惠(%)	暂定税率	普通	增值/消费	出口退税	计量单位	监管条件	检验检疫	特殊证件对美关税
8528.7110		---彩色卫星电视接收机[T2]	10/5		130	13/	13	台/千克	O		/30,25
8528.7180		---其他彩色的[T2]	10/5		130	13/	13	台/千克			/35;30
8528.7190		---单色的[T2]	5/2.5		100	13/	13	台/千克			/
		--其他,彩色的:									
		---阴极射线显像管的:									
8528.7211		----模拟电视接收机[T2]	10		130	13/	13	台/千克	6		/
8528.7212		----数字电视接收机[T2]	10		130	13/	13	台/千克	6		/
8528.7219		----其他[T2]	10		130	13/	13	台/千克	6		/
		---液晶显示器的:									
8528.7221		----模拟电视接收机[T2]	15		130	13/	13	台/千克			/40
8528.7222		----数字电视接收机[T2]	15		130	13/	13	台/千克			/40
8528.7229		----其他[T2]	15		130	13/	13	台/千克			/30
		---等离子显示器的:									
8528.7231		----模拟电视接收机[T2]	10		130	13/	13	台/千克			/
8528.7232		----数字电视接收机[T2]	15		130	13/	13	台/千克			/30
8528.7239		----其他[T2]	15		130	13/	13	台/千克			/
		---其他:									
8528.7291		----模拟电视接收机[T2]	10		130	13/	13	台/千克			/
8528.7292		----数字电视接收机[T2]	15		130	13/	13	台/千克			/40
8528.7299		----其他[T2]	15		130	13/	13	台/千克			/
8528.7300		--其他,单色的[T2]	7		100	13/	13	台/千克	6		/
85.29		**专用于或主要用于税目85.25至85.28所列装置或设备的零件:**									
		-各种天线或天线反射器及其零件:									
8529.1010		---雷达设备及无线电导航设备用〔999〕	0		8	13/	13	千克			/5
8529.1020		---无线电收音机及其组合机、电视接收机用[T2]	0		90	13/	13	千克		L	/25
8529.1090		---其他									
8529.1090	21	卫星电视接收用天线[T2]	0		20	13/	13	千克/个	O		/20
8529.1090	29	其他无线广播电视用天线(税目85.25至85.28所列其他装置或设备的,包括天线反射器)[T2]	0		20	13/	13	千克/个	O		/20
8529.1090	90	其他无线电设备天线及其零件(税目85.25至85.28所列其他装置或设备的,包括天线反射器)[T2]	0		20	13/	13	千克/个		L	/20
		-其他:									
8529.9010		---电视发送、差转设备及卫星电视地面接收转播设备用									
8529.9010	11	卫星电视接收用解码器[T2]	0		30	13/	13	千克/个	O	L	/20
8529.9010	12	卫星电视接收用收视卡[T2]	0		30	13/	13	千克/个	O		/20
8529.9010	13	卫星电视接收用器件板卡[T2]	0		30	13/	13	千克/个	O		/20
8529.9010	14	卫星电视接收用专用零件[T2]	0		30	13/	13	千克/个	O		/20
8529.9010	90	其他电视发送,差转等设备零件(包括其他卫星电视地面接收转播设备零件)[T2]	0		30	13/	13	千克/个			/20
		---电视摄像机、静像视频摄像机及其他视频摄录一体机、数字照相机用:									
8529.9041		----特种用途的[T2]	5.3/4		17	13/	13	千克			/10.3,9
8529.9042		----非特种用途的取像模块									
8529.9042	10	电视摄像机、摄录一体机、数码相机用取像模块[T2]	8/6	3	100	13/	13	千克			/28
8529.9042	20	手机、平板电脑用取像模块〔999〕	8/6	4	100	13/	13	千克			/29
8529.9042	90	其他非特种用途的取像模块[T2]	8/6		100	13/	13	千克			/33,31
8529.9049		----其他[T2]	8/6	2	100	13/	13	千克			/27
8529.9050		---雷达设备及无线电导航设备用〔999〕	1/0.8		8	13/	13	千克			/26,25.8
8529.9060		---无线电收音机及其组合机用[T2]	10/7.5	7	130	13/	13	千克			/32
		---电视接收机用(高频调谐器除外):									
8529.9081		----彩色电视接收机用(等离子显像组件及其零件、有机发光显示屏除外)[T2]	10/7.5	6	80	13/	13	千克			/31
8529.9082		----等离子显像组件及其零件[T2]	10/7.5	5	80	13/	13	千克			/30
8529.9083		----有机发光二极管显示屏〔999〕	15	5	50	13/	13	千克/个			/30
8529.9089		----其他[T2]	0		50	13/	13	千克			/10
8529.9090		---其他									
8529.9090	11	卫星电视接收用高频调谐器[T2]	0		57	13/	13	千克/个	O		/25

协定税率 %										特惠税率 %			Article Description
亚太5国	东/冰/格	巴基斯坦	韩国	瑞士	哥达	秘鲁	澳大利亚	新西/坡/智	港/澳/台	亚太2国	老/柬/缅	36/3/1	
8/4	/0/0	21.6			0		0	0//0	0/0/			0//	---Colour satellite television receivers
7/3.5	0/0/	18.9			0		0	0/0,0	0/0/			0//	---Other colour
	0/0/0	10.8	6	4.5/2.5	0	0	0	0/0,0	0/0/			0/0/	---monochrome
													--Other, colour:
													---Of cathode-ray tube monitors:
6.5	/0/	18.9		10	0		0	0//0	0/0/			0//	----Analogue
6.5	/0/	18.9		10	0		18	0//0	0/0/			0//	----Digital
6.5	/0/	18.9		10	0		0	0//0	0/0/			0//	----Other
													---Of LCD:
10.5	5/0/	21					0	0//0	0/0/			0//	----Analogue
10.5	5/0/	21	21				18	0//C	0/0/			0//	----Digital
10.5	5/0/	21					0	0//C	0/0/			0//	----Other
													---Of plasma:
7	5/0/	18.9					0	0//C	0/0/			0//	----Analogue
10.5	5/0/	18.9					18	0//0	0/0/			0//	----Digital
10.5	5/0/	18.9	21				0	0//0	0/0/			0//	----Other
													---Other:
7	5/0/	18.9			0	0	0	0//0	0/0/			0/0/	----Analogue
10.5	5/0/	18.9					18	0//0	0/0/			0//	----Digital
10.5	5/0/	18.9			0		0	0//0	0/0/			0//	----Other
	0/0/0	10.8	6	4.5	0	0	0	0/0/C	0/0/			0/0/	--Other, monchrome
													Parts suitable for use solely or principally with the apparatus of headingsNo. 85. 25 to 85. 28:
													-Aerials and aerial reflectors of all kinds; parts suitable for use therewith:
	0//		0.6					//	0/0/			0/0/	---For radar apparatus and radio navigational aid apparatus
												0/0/0	---For radio-broadcast receivers and their combinations, television receivers
													---Other
	0//							//	0/0/			0/0/	Satellite TV receiving antenna
	0//							//	0/0/			0/0/	Other radio broadcasting and television antenna (suitable for use solely or principally with the apparatus of heading No. 85. 25 to 85. 28, including antenna reflectors)
	0//							//	0/0/			0/0/	Other radio antennas and parts(suitable for use solely or principally with the apparatus of heading No. 85. 25 to 85. 28, including antenna reflectors)
													-Other:
													---Of television transmission or translation apparatus, satellite television ground receiving and relaying apparatus
												0/0/0	Decoders for statellite TV recervers
												0/0/0	CA card for receiving satellite television
												0/0/0	CRD cards for receiving statellite TV
												0/0/0	Parts exclusive for receiving statellite TV signals
												0/0/0	Parts of other television tronsmission or translation apparatus (including parts of satellite television ground receiving and relaying apparatus)
													---Of television cameras、still image rideo cameras other video camera recorders and igital cameras:
3.4/2.6	0/0/0	4	5.2	0	0	0	0	0//0	C/0/			0/0/	----Of special purpose
													----Cameera modules without special pnrpose
5.2/3.9	0/0/0	4.5	4.8	3.6	0	0	0	0/0/0	0/0/0			0/0/	V deo camera recorders, digital camera, with image capture module
5.2/3.9	0/0/0	4.5	4.8	3.6	0	0	0	0/0/0	0/0/0			0/0/	Mobile phone, tablet computer with image capture module
5.2/3.9	0/0/0	4.5	4.8	3.6	0	0	0	0/0/0	0/0/0			0/0/	O-her cameera modules not for special purpose
7.2/5.4	0/0/0	4.5	7.2	3.6	0	0	0	0/0/0	0/0/0			0/0/	----Other
0.7/0.5	0/0/0	0	0.6	0	0	0	0	0//0	0/0/			0/0/	---Of radar apparatus and radio navigational aid apparatus
6.5/4.9	0/0/0	6.8	6	4.5	0	0	0	0/0/0	0/0/			0/0/0	---Of radio-broadcast receivers and their combinations
													---Of television receivers (Other than H. F tuners):
9.8	0/0/	6.8		4.5		0	0	0/0/0	0/0/			0/0/	----Of colour television receivers (other than plasma display modules or parts thereof, organic light emitting diode display screen)
8/6	0/0/0	6.8	12	4.5			0	0//0	0/0/				----Plasma display modules and parts thereof
9.8	0/0/	6.8		4.5		0		0/0/0	0/0/			0/0/	----Organic light emitting diode display screen
												0/0/0	----Other
													---Other
												0/0/0	High-frequency tuners for satellite television

税则号列	货品名称〔CIQ 扩展编码及品名－T2 表示见附表 2〕	最惠(%)	暂定税率	普通	增值/消费	出口退税	计量单位	监管条件	检验检疫	特殊证件对美关税
8529.9090　90	税目 85.25 至 85.28 所列装置或设备其他零件〔999〕	0		57	13/	13	千克/个			/25
85.30	**铁道、电车道、道路或内河航道、停车场、港口或机场用的电气信号、安全或交通管理设备(税目 86.08 的货品除外)：**									
8530.1000	-铁道或电车道用的设备〔999〕	8		20	13/	13	个/千克			/
8530.8000	-其他设备〔999〕	8		20	13/	13	个/千克			/28
8530.9000	-零件〔999〕	6		20	13/	13	千克			/26
85.31	**电气音响或视觉信号装置(例如，电铃、电笛、显示板、防盗或防火报警器)，但税目 85.12 或 85.30 的货品除外：**									
8531.1000	-防盗或防火报警器及类似装置[T2]	10		40	13/	13	个/千克	A	LM	/20
8531.2000	-装有液晶装置(LCD)或发光二极管(LED)的显示板〔999〕	0		70	13/	13	个/千克			/25
	-其他装置：									
8531.8010	---蜂鸣器									
8531.8010　01	音量不超过 110db 的小型蜂鸣器〔999〕	10	7.5	70	13/	13	个/千克			/32.5
8531.8010　90	其他蜂鸣器〔999〕	10		70	13/	13	个/千克			/35
8531.8090	---其他[T2]	5/3.8		70	13/	13	个/千克			/15,13.8
	-零件：									
8531.9010	---防盗或防火报警器及类似装置用〔999〕	0		40	13/	13	千克			/10
8531.9090	---其他[T2]	0		70	13/	13	千克			/20
85.32	**固定、可变或可调(微调)电容器：**									
8532.1000	-固定电容器，用于 50/60 赫兹电路，其额定无功功率不低于 0.5 千瓦(电力电容器)〔999〕	0		20	13/	13	千克/千个			/25
	-其他固定电容器：									
	--钽电容器：									
8532.2110	---片式〔999〕	0		35	13/	13	千克/千个			/25
8532.2190	---其他〔999〕	0		35	13/	13	千克/千个			/30
	--铝电介电容器：									
8532.2210	---片式〔999〕	0		35	13/	13	千克/千个			/25
8532.2290	---其他〔999〕	0		35	13/	13	千克/千个			/25
8532.2300	--单层瓷介电容器〔999〕	0		35	13/	13	千克/千个			/25
	--多层瓷介电容器：									
8532.2410	---片式〔999〕	0		35	13/	13	千克/千个			/25
8532.2490	---其他〔999〕	0		35	13/	13	千克/千个			/30
	--纸介质或塑料介质电容器：									
8532.2510	---片式〔999〕	0		35	13/	13	千克/千个			/30
8532.2590	---其他〔999〕	0		35	13/	13	千克/千个			/25
8532.2900	--其他〔999〕	0		35	13/	13	千克/千个			/25
8532.3000	-可变或可调(微调)电容器〔999〕	0		35	13/	13	千克/千个			/25
	-零件：									
8532.9010	---子目号 8532.1000 所列电容器用〔999〕	0		20	13/	13	千克			/10
8532.9090	---其他〔999〕	0		35	13/	13	千克			/10
85.33	**电阻器(包括变阻器及电位器)，但加热电阻器除外：**									
8533.1000	-固定碳质电阻器，合成或薄膜式〔999〕	0		50	13/	13	千克/千个			/25
	-其他固定电阻器：									
	--额定功率不超过 20 瓦：									
8533.2110	---片式〔999〕	0		50	13/	13	千克/千个			/25
8533.2190	---其他〔999〕	0		50	13/	13	千克/千个			/30
8533.2900	--其他〔999〕	0		50	13/	13	千克/千个			/20
	-线绕可变电阻器，包括变阻器及电位器：									
8533.3100	--额定功率不超过 20 瓦〔999〕	0		50	13/	13	千克/千个			/30
8533.3900	--其他〔999〕	0		50	13/	13	千克/千个			/25
8533.4000	-其他可变电阻器，包括变阻器及电位器〔999〕	0		50	13/	13	千克/千个			/25
8533.9000	-零件〔999〕	0		50	13/	13	千克			/25
85.34	**印刷电路：**									
8534.0010	---4 层以上的〔999〕	0		35	13/	13	块/千克			/25
8534.0090	---其他〔999〕	0		50	13/	13	块/千克			/25

协定税率 %										特惠税率 %			
亚太5国	东/冰/格	巴基斯坦	韩国	瑞士	哥达	秘鲁	澳大利亚	新西/坡/智	港/澳/台	亚太2国	老/柬/缅	36/3/1	Article Description
												0/0/0	Other parts of apparatus of headings No. 85. 25 ～ 85. 28
													Electrical signalling, safety or traffic control equipment for railways, tramways, roads, inland waterways, parking facilities, port installations or airfields (other than those of heading No. 86. 08):
5.2	0/0/0	4	4	0	0	0	0	0//0	0/0/			0/0/	-Equipment for railways or tramways
	0/0/0	4	3.2	0	0	0	0	0//0	0/0/			0/0/0	-Other equipment
	0/0/0	4	3.2	0	0	0	0	0//0	0/0/			0/0/0	-Parts
													Electric sound or visual signalling apparatus (for example, bells, sirens, indicator panels, burglar or fire alarms), other than those of headingNos. 85. 12 or 85. 30:
	0/0/0	4	4	0	0	0	0	0/0/0	0/0/			0/0/0	-Burglar or fire alarms and similar apparatus
												0/0/0	-Indicator panels incorporating liquid crystal devices (LCD) or light emitting diodes (LED)
													-Other apparatus:
													---Buzzers
	0/0/0	10.8	7.5	4.5	0	0	0	0/0/0	0/0/			0/0/	Small buzzers, volue<110dB
	0/0/0	10.8	7.5	4.5	0	0	0	0/0/0	0/0/			0/0/	Other buzzers
	0/0/0	4	4	0	0	0	0	0/0/0	0/0/			0/0/	---Other
													-Parts:
												0/0/0	---Of burglar or fire alarms and similar apparatus
												0/0/0	---Other
													Electrical capacitors, fixed, variable or adjustable (preset):
												0/0/0	-Fixed capacitors designed for use in 50/60 Hz circuits and having a reactive power handling capacity of not less than 0. 5 kV (power capacitors)
													-Other fixed capacitors:
													--Tantalum:
												0/0/0	---Laminate
												0/0/0	---Other
													--Aluminium electrolytic:
												0/0/0	---Laminate
												0/0/0	---Other
												0/0/0	--Ceramic dielectric, single layer
													--Ceramic dielectric, multilayer:
												0/0/0	---Laminate
												0/0/0	---Other
													--Dielectric of paper or plastics:
												0/0/0	---Laminate
												0/0/0	---Other
												0/0/0	--Other
												0/0/0	-Variable or adjustable (pre-set) capacitors
													-Parts:
												0/0/0	---Of the capacitors of subheadingNo. 8532. 1000
												0/0/0	---Other
													Electrical resistors (including rheostats and potentiometers), other than heating resistors:
												0/0/0	-Fixed carbon resistors, composition or film types
													-Other fixed resistors:
													--For a power handling capacity not exceeding 20W:
												0/0/0	---Laminate
												0/0/0	---Other
												0/0/0	--Other
													-Wirewound variable resistors, including rheostats and potentiometers:
												0/0/0	--For a power handling capacity not exceeding 20 W
												0/0/0	--Other
												0/0/0	-Other variable resistors, including rheostats and potentiometers
												0/0/0	-Parts
													Printed circuits:
												0/0/0	---Of more than 4 layers
												0/0/0	---Other

税则号列		货品名称〔CIQ 扩展编码及品名－T2 表示见附表 2〕	最惠(%)	暂定税率	普通	增值/消费	出口退税	计量单位	监管条件	检验检疫	特殊证件对美关税
85.35		**电路的开关、保护或连接用的电气装置(例如,开关、熔断器、避雷器、电压限幅器、电涌抑制器、插头及其他连接器、接线盒),用于电压超过 1000 伏的线路:**									
8535.1000		-熔断器〔999〕	10		50	13/	13	个/千克	A	L	/35
		-自动断路器:									
8535.2100		--用于电压低于 72.5 千伏的线路:〔999〕	10		50	13/	13	个/千克	A	L	/35
		--其他:									
8535.2910		---用于 72.5 千伏≤电压≤220 千伏的线路〔999〕	10		50	13/	13	个/千克			/35
8535.2920		---用于 220 千伏<电压≤750 千伏的线路〔999〕	10		50	13/	13	个/千克			/35
8535.2990		---其他〔999〕	10		50	13/	13	个/千克			/
		-隔离开关及断续开关:									
8535.3010		---用于 72.5 千伏≤电压≤220 千伏的〔999〕	10		50	13/	13	个/千克			/
8535.3020		---用于 220 千伏<电压≤750 千伏的〔999〕	10		50	13/	13	个/千克			/
8535.3090		---其他〔999〕	10		50	13/	13	个/千克	A	L	/35
8535.4000		-避雷器、电压限幅器及电涌抑制器〔999〕	10		50	13/	13	个/千克			/35
8535.9000		-其他									
8535.9000	10	触发式火花隙(阳极延迟时间≤15ms,阳极峰值额定电流≥500A)〔101 高压开关装置,102 其它高压电器及其零件〕	10		50	13/	13	千克	3		/30
8535.9000	20	具有快速开关功能的模件或组件(阳极峰值电压≥2kV;电流≥500A;接通时间为 1 微秒或更短)〔101 高压开关装置,102 其它高压电器及其零件〕	10		50	13/	13	千克	3		/30
8535.9000	90	其他电压>1000 伏电路开关等电气装置〔101 高压开关装置,102 其它高压电器及其零件〕	10		50	13/	13	千克		L	/30
85.36		**电路的开关、保护或连接用的电器装置(例如,开关、继电器、熔断器、电涌抑制器、插头、插座、灯座及其他连接器、接线盒),用于电压不超过 1000 伏的线路;光导纤维、光导纤维束或光缆用连接器:**									
8536.1000		-熔断器〔999〕	10		50	13/	13	个/千克	A	L	/35
8536.2000		-自动断路器〔101 断路器,102 其它低压电器及其零件〕	9		50	13/	13	个/千克	A	L	/34
8536.3000		-其他电路保护装置〔999〕	3/1.5		50	13/	13	个/千克	A	L	/28,26.5
		-继电器:									
		--用于电压不超过 60 伏的线路:									
8536.4110		---用于电压不超过 36 伏的线路〔999〕	10		50	13/	13	个/千克			/35
8536.4190		---其他〔999〕	10		50	13/	13	个/千克	A	L	/35
8536.4900		--其他〔999〕	10		50	13/	13	个/千克	A	L	/35
8536.5000		-其他开关〔999〕	0		50	13/	13	个/千克	A	L	/25
		-灯座、插头及插座:									
8536.6100		--灯座〔999〕	10		50	13/	13	个/千克			/30
8536.6900		--其他〔101 插头,102 插座,103 转换器〕	0		50	13/	13	个/千克		L	/25
8536.7000		-光导纤维、光导纤维束或光缆用连接器〔101 其它低压电器及其零件,102 路由器,103 光缆,104 光通信数字同步设备〕	8		30	13/	13	千克		L	/28
		-其他装置:									
		---接插件:									
8536.9011		----工作电压不超过 36 伏的〔999〕	0		50	13/	13	千克			/25
8536.9019		----其他〔999〕	0		50	13/	13	千克	A	L	/25
8536.9090		---其他〔999〕	0		50	13/	13	千克	A	L	/20
85.37		**用于电气控制或电力分配的盘、板、台、柜及其他基座,装有两个或多个税目 85.35 或 85.36 所列的装置,包括装有第九十章所列的仪器或装置,以及数控装置,但税目 85.17 的交换机除外:**									
		-用于电压不超过 1000 伏的线路:									
		---数控装置:									
8537.1011		----可编程序控制器									
8537.1011	01	机床用可编程序控制器(PLC)〔101 低压电器及其零件,102 集成电路,103 其它电子元器件〕	5	3	14	13/	13	个/千克			/23
8537.1011	10	调节和编程控制器(8479.899960 绕线机用)〔101 集成电路,102 其它电子元器件〕	5		14	13/	13	个/千克	3		/25
8537.1011	90	其他可编程控制器(用于电压不超过 1000 伏的线路)〔999〕	5		14	13/	13	个/千克			/25

协定税率 %										特惠税率 %			Article Description
亚太5国	东/冰/格	巴基斯坦	韩国	瑞士	哥达	秘鲁	澳大利亚	新西/坡/智	港/澳/台	亚太2国	老/柬/缅	36/3/1	
													Electrical apparatus for switching or protecting electrical circuits, or for making connections to or in electrical circuits (for example, switches, fuses, lightning arresters, voltage limiters, surge suppressors, plugs and other conneltors, junction boxes), for a voltage exceeding 1000 volts:
	0/0/0	10.1	5.6	4.2	0	0	0	0/0/0	0/0/			0/0/	-Fuses
													-Automatic circuit breakers:
	0/0/0	10.1	5.6	0	0	0	0	0/0/0	0/0/			0/0/	--For a voltage of less than 72.5 kV
													--Other:
	0/0/0	4.5	5.6	0	0	0	0	0//0	0/0/			0/0/0	---For 72.5kV≤Voltage≤220kV
	0/0/0	4.5	5.6	0	0	0	0	0//0	0/0/			0/0/0	---For 220kV≤Voltage≤750kV
	0/0/0	4	4	0	0	0	0	0//0	0/0/			0/0/0	---For Voltage>750kV
													-Isolating switches and make-and-break switches:
8	0/0/0	4	4	4.2	0	0	0	0//0	0/0/			0/0/0	---For 72.5kV≤Voltage≤220kV
	0/0/0	4	4	4.2	0	0	0	0//0	0/0/			0/0/0	---For 220kV≤Voltage≤750kV
	0/0/0	4	4	4.2	0	0	0	0//0	0/0/			0/0/0	---Other
	0/0/0	18	7.2	5.4	0	0	0	0/0/0	0/0/			0/0/	-Lightning arresters, voltage limiters and surge suppressors
													-Other
6.5	0/0/0	4.5	7	3	0	0	0	0/0/0	0/0/			0/0/0	Triggered spark gap(time for delay of anode≤15ms, rating current of anode's peak value≥500A)
6.5	0/0/0	4.5	7	3	0	0	0	0/0/0	0/0/			0/0/0	Module or groupware that can be speedily switched on or off (peak voltage value of anode≥2kV, current≥500A, time for switching on 1 ms)
6.5	0/0/0	4.5	7	3	0	0	0	0/0/0	0/0/			0/0/0	Other electrical apparatuses for switching or protecting electrical circuits, or for making connections to or in electrical circuits, for a voltage exceeding 1000 V)
													Electrical apparatus for switching or protecting electrical circuits, or for making connections to or in electricalcircuits (for example, switches, relays, fuses, surge suppressors, plugs, sockets, lamp-holders, and other connecltors junction boxes), for a voltage not exceeding 1000 volts; connectors for optical fibres. optical fibre bundles or cables:
	0/0/0	4.5		3	0	0	0	0/0/0	0/0/0			0/0/0	-Fuses
	0/0/0	4	0	2.7	0	0	0	0//0	0/0/			0/0/0	-Automatic circuit breakers
	0/0/0	4	5.4	0	0	0	0	0//0	0/0/			0/0/0	-Other apparatus for protecting electrical circuits
													-Relays:
													--For a voltage not exceeding 60 V:
	0/0/4	4.5	6	0	0	0	0	0/0/0	0/0/			0/0/0	---For a voltage not exceeding 36V
	0/0/0	4	7	0	0	0	0	0/0/0	0/0/			0/0/0	---Other
	0/0/0	4.5	6	0	0	0	0	0/0/0	0/0/			0/0/0	--Other
												0/0/0	-Other switches
													-Lamp-holders, plugs and sockets:
	0/0/0	4	6	0	0	0	0	0/0/0	0/0/			0/0/0	--Lamp-holders
												0/0/0	--Other
	0/0/0	4		2.4	0	0	0	0//0	0/0/			0/0/0	-Connectors for optical fibres, optical fibre bundles or cables
													-Other apparatus:
													---Connector:
												0/0/0	----Working voltage not exceeding 36 V
												0/0/0	----Other
												0/0/0	---Other
													Boards, panels, consoles, desks, cabinets and other bases, equipped with two or more apparatus of headingNo. 85.35 or 85.36, for electric control or the distribution of electricity, including those incorporating instruments or apparatus of Chapter 90, and numerical control apparatus, other than switching apparatus of headingNo. 85.17:
													-For a voltage not exceeding 1000 V:
													---Numerical control panels:
													----Programmable logic controuers(PLC)
2.5	0/0/0	0	2.5	1.5	0	0	0	0//0	0/0/0			0/0/0	Programmable logic controuers for machine tools
2.5	0/0/0	0	2.5	1.5	0	0	0	0//0	0/0/0			0/0/0	Adiusting and programming controllers for winding machine of subbeading No. 8479.899060
2.5	0/0/0	0	2.5	1.5	0	0	0	0//0	0/0/0			0/0/0	Other programming logic controllers (for the circuit with its voltage ≤1000V)

税则号列		货品名称〔CIQ 扩展编码及品名—T2 表示见附表 2〕	最惠(%)	暂定税率	普通	增值/消费	出口退税	计量单位	监管条件	检验检疫	特殊证件对美关税
8537.1019		---其他									
8537.1019	01	机床用其他数控单元(包括单独进口的 CNC 操作单元)〔999〕	5	3	14	13/	13	个/千克			/28
8537.1019	90	其他非机床用数控装置(用于电压不超过 1000 伏的线路)〔999〕	5		14	13/	13	个/千克			/30
8537.1090		---其他									
8537.1090	01	电梯用控制柜及控制柜专用印刷电路板(用于电压不超过 1000 伏的线路)〔999〕	8	4	50	13/	13	个/千克			/24
8537.1090	21	控制器[用于机器人或末端操纵装置(详见核两用清单)]〔999〕	8		50	13/	13	个/千克	3		/28
8537.1090	22	数字控制器(专用于税目 8479.899959 电动式振动试验系统)〔999〕	8		50	13/	13	个/千克	3		/28
8537.1090	90	其他电力控制或分配的装置(电压不超过 1000 伏的线路)〔999〕	8		50	13/	13	个/千克	A	L	/28
		-用于电压超过 1000 伏的线路:									
8537.2010		---全封闭组合式高压开关装置,用于电压在 500 千伏及以上的线路〔101 高压开关装置,102 其它高压电器及其零件〕	8		30	13/	13	台/千克			/33
8537.2090		---其他〔999〕	8		50	13/	13	千克			/28
85.38		**专用于或主要用于税号 85.35、85.36 或 85.37 所列装置的零件:**									
		-税目 85.37 所列货品用的盘、板、台、柜及其他基座,但未装有关装置:									
8538.1010		---税目 8537.2010 所列货品用〔999〕	2.8/1.4		50	13/	13	千克			/27.8,26.4
8538.1090		---其他〔999〕	2.3/1.2		50	13/	13	千克			/22.3,21.2
8538.9000		-其他〔101 高压电器及其零件,102 低压电器及其零件〕	7		50	13/	13	千克			/32
85.39		**白炽灯泡、放电灯管,包括封闭式聚光灯及紫外线灯管或红外线灯泡;弧光灯;发光二极管(LED)灯泡(管):**									
8539.1000		-封闭式聚光灯〔999〕	8		45	13/	13	只/千克			/13
		-其他白炽灯泡,但不包括紫外线灯管或红外线灯泡:									
		--卤钨灯:									
8539.2110		---科研、医疗专用〔999〕	8		20	13/	13	只/千克			/33
8539.2120		---火车、航空器及船舶用〔999〕	8		20	13/	13	只/千克			/13
8539.2130		---机动车辆用〔999〕	8		45	13/	13	只/千克			/13
8539.2190		---其他〔999〕	6		70	13/	13	只/千克			/16
		--其他灯,功率不超过 200 瓦,但额定电压超过 100 伏:									
8539.2210		---科研、医疗专用〔999〕	5		20	13/	13	只/千克			/10
8539.2290		---其他〔999〕	5		70	13/	13	只/千克			/30
		--其他:									
8539.2910		---科研、医疗专用〔999〕	5		20	13/	13	只/千克			/25
8539.2920		---火车、航空器及船舶用〔999〕	5		20	13/	13	只/千克			/10
8539.2930		---机动车辆用〔999〕	5		45	13/	13	只/千克			/10
		---其他:									
8539.2991		----12 伏及以下的〔999〕	6		70	13/	13	只/千克			/31
8539.2999		----其他〔999〕	6		70	13/	13	只/千克			/16
		-放电灯管,但紫外线灯管除外:									
		--热阴极荧光灯:									
8539.3110		---科研、医疗专用〔999〕	8		20	13/	13	只/千克			/18
8539.3120		---火车、航空器及船舶用〔999〕	8		20	13/	13	只/千克			/13
		---其他:									
8539.3191		----紧凑型〔999〕	8		70	13/	13	只/千克			/28
8539.3199		----其他〔999〕	8		70	13/	13	只/千克			/28
		--汞或钠蒸汽灯;金属卤化物灯:									
8539.3230		---钠蒸气灯〔999〕	8		20	13/	13	只/千克			/33
8539.3240		---汞蒸气灯									
8539.3240	01	彩色投影机用的照明光源(汞蒸汽灯)〔999〕	8	3	20	13/	13	只/千克			/28
8539.3240	90	其他汞蒸汽灯〔999〕	8		20	13/	13	只/千克			/33
8539.3290		---其他〔999〕	8		70	13/	13	只/千克			/33
		--其他:									
8539.3910		---科研、医疗专用〔999〕	8		20	13/	13	只/千克			/18
8539.3920		---火车、航空器及船舶用〔999〕	8		20	13/	13	只/千克			/13
8539.3990		---其他									
8539.3990	10	用于平板显示器背光源的冷阴极管荧光灯〔999〕	0		70	13/	13	只/千克			/25
8539.3990	90	其他用途的其他放电灯管〔999〕	8		70	13/	13	只/千克			/33

协定税率 %										特惠税率 %			Article Description
亚太5国	东/冰/格	巴基斯坦	韩国	瑞士	哥达	秘鲁	澳大利亚	新西/坡/智	港/澳/台	亚太2国	老/柬/缅	36/3/1	
													----Other
2.5	0/0/0	0	2.5	2.6	0	0	0	0//0	0/0/0			0/0/0	Other digital control units for machine tool (CNC operating unit with separate import)
2.5	0/0/0	0	2.5	2.6	0	0	0	0//0	0/0/0			0/0/0	Other digital controller not for machine tool(for a voltage≤1000V)
													---Other
4	0/0/0	0	5	4.4	0	0	0	0//0	0/0/			0/0/0	Control cabinet (electric cabinet) for elevators and circuit board for control cabinet(for the circuit with its voltage≤1000V)
4	0/0/0	0	5	4.4	0	0	0	0//0	0/0/			0/0/0	Controllers(use for roloots or end - operation devices, see the dual - purpose nuclear goods list for details)
4	0/0/0	0	5	4.4	0	0	0	0//0	0/0/			0/0/0	Digital controllers (only use of electric vibration test system subweading No. 8479. 899959)
4	0/0/0	0	5	4.4	0	0	0	0//0	0/0/			0/0/0	Other power contorl or distribution devices (for the circuit with its voltage≤1000V)
													-For a voltage exceeding 1000 V:
4	0/0/0	0	5	3.5	0	0	0	0//0	0/0/			0/0/0	---Gas insulated switchgear, for a voltage of 500 kV or more
4	0/0/0	0	5	0	0	0	0	0//0	0/0/			0/0/0	---Other
													Parts suitable for use solely or principally with the apparatus of headingNo. 85. 35, 85. 36 or 85. 37:
													-Boards, panels, consoles, desks, cabinets and other bases for the goods of headingNo. 85. 37, not equipped with their apparatus:
1.4/0.7	0/0/0	0	3.3	0	0	0	0	0//0	0/0/			0/0/0	---For the goods of headingNo. 8537. 2010
1.2/0.6	0/0/0	0	3.5	2.1/1.2	0	0	0	0//0	0/0/			0/0/0	---Other
	0/0/0	4	0	3.7	0	0	0	0//0	0/0/0			0/0/0	-Other
													Electric filament or discharge lamps, including sealed beam lamp units and ultra-violet or infra-red lamps; arc-lamps; Light—emitting diode (LED) Lamps:
	0/0/0	4	4	0	0	0	0	0//0	0/0/			0/0/0	-Sealed beam lamp units
													-Other filament lamps, excluding ultra-violet or infra-red lamps:
													--Tungsten halogen:
	0/0/0	4	0	0	0	0	0	0//0	0/0/			0/0/0	---For scientific or medical uses only
	0/0/0	4	3.2	0	0	0	0	0//0	0/0/			0/0/0	---For locomotives and rolling-stock, aircraft or ships
	0/0/0	4.5	7	0	0	0	0	0//0	0/0/			0/0/0	---For motor vehicles
	0/0/0	8.4	4.2	3.2	0	0	0	0/0/0	0/0/			0/0/0	---Other
													--Other, of a power not exceeding 200 W and for a voltage exceeding 100 V:
	0/0/0	4.5		3.2	0	0	0	0/0/0	0/0/			0/0/0	---For scientific or medical uses only
	0/0/0	0	0	0	0	0	0	0//0	0/0/			0/0/0	---Other
													--Other:
4	0/0/0	0	0	0	0	0	0	0//0	0/0/			0/0/0	---For scientific or medical uses only
	0/0/0	4.5	4.2	3.2	0	0	0	0/0/0	0/0/			0/0/0	---For locomotives and rolling-stock, aircraft or ships
	0/0/0	0	3	0	0	0	0	0//0	0/0/			0/0/0	---For motor vehicles
													---Other:
	0/0/0	5.4	4.8	3.6	0	0	0	0/0/0	0/0/			0/0/0	----Of a voltage 12 V or less
	0/0/0	5.4	4.8	3.6	0	0	0	0/0/0	0/0/			0/0/0	----Other
													-Discharge lamps, other than ultra-violet lamps:
													--Fluorescent, hot cathode:
6.4	0/0/0	4		0	0	0	0	0//0	0/0/			0/0/0	---For scientific or medical uses only
	0/0/0	4		0	0	0	0	0//0	0/0/			0/0/0	---For locomotives and rolling-stock, aircraft or ships
													---Other:
	0/0/0	4	0	0	0	0	0	0//0	0/0/			0/0/0	----Compact type
	0/0/0	4	0	0	0	0	0	0//0	0/0/			0/0/0	----Other
													--Mercury or sodium vapour lamps; metal halide lamps:
	0/0/0	4	3.2	0	0	0	0	0//0	0/0/			0/0/0	---Sodium vapour lamps
													---Mercury vapour lamps
	0/0/0	4	3.2	0	0	0	0	0//0	0/0/			0/0/0	Mercury vapor light for color LCD projectors
	0/0/0	4	3.2	0	0	0	0	0//0	0/0/			0/0/0	Other mercury vapor light
	0/0/0	4	0	0	0	0	0	0//0	0/0/			0/0/0	---Other
													--Other:
6.4	0/0/0	4		0	0	0	0	0//0	0/0/			0/0/0	---For scientific or medical uses only
	0/0/0	4		0	0	0	0	0//0	0/0/			0/0/0	---For locomotives and rolling-stock, aircraft or ships
													---Other
	0/0/0	4	4.8	0	0	0	0	0//0	0/0/0			0/0/0	Cold cathode fluorescent lamp for flat panel display backlight source
	0/0/0	4	4.8	0	0	0	0	0//0	0/0/0			0/0/0	Other discharge lamps for other purposes

税则号列	货品名称〔CIQ 扩展编码及品名—T2 表示见附表 2〕	最惠(%)	暂定税率	普通	增值/消费	出口退税	计量单位	监管条件	检验检疫	特殊证件对美关税
	-紫外线灯管或红外线灯泡;弧光灯:									
8539.4100	--弧光灯〔999〕	8		20	13/	13	只/千克			/28
8539.4900	--其他〔999〕	8		20	13/	13	只/千克			/18
8539.5000	-发光二极管(LED)灯泡(管)〔999〕	8		80	13/	13	只/千克			/33
8539.9000	-零件〔999〕	8		20	13/	13	千克			/33
85.40	**热电子管、冷阴极管或光阴极管(例如,真空管或充气管、汞弧整流管、阴极射线管、电视摄像管):**									
	-阴极射线电视显像管,包括视频监视器用阴极射线管:									
8540.1100	--彩色的〔999〕	8		40	13/	13	只/千克	6		/
8540.1200	--单色的〔999〕	8		40	13/	13	只/千克	6		/13
	-电视摄像管;变像管及图像增强管;其他光阴极管:									
8540.2010	---电视摄像管〔999〕	8		35	13/	13	只/千克			/
8540.2090	---其他									
8540.2090 10	电子条纹相机的条纹显像管(专用于编号 9006.5900 40 的条纹显像管)〔999〕	8		17	13/	13	只/千克			/33
8540.2090 90	其他电视摄像管;其他变像管及图像增强管;其他光阴极管〔999〕	8		17	13/	13	只/千克			/33
	-单色的数据/图形显示管;彩色的数据/图形显示管,屏幕荧光点间距小于 0.4 毫米:									
8540.4010	---彩色的数据/图形显示管,屏幕荧光点间距小于 0.4 毫米〔999〕	8		17	13/	13	只/千克	6	L	/
8540.4020	---单色的数据/图形显示管〔999〕	8		17	13/	13	只/千克	6	L	/18
	-其他阴极射线管:									
8540.6010	---雷达显示管〔999〕	6		14	13/	13	只/千克			/
8540.6090	---其他〔999〕	8		17	13/	13	只/千克	6	L	/28
	-微波管(例如,磁控管、速调管、行波管、返波管),但不包括栅控管:									
8540.7100	--磁控管〔999〕	8		17	13/	13	只/千克			/33
	--其他:									
8540.7910	---速调管〔999〕	8		17	13/	13	只/千克			/13
8540.7990	---其他〔999〕	8		17	13/	13	只/千克			/18
	-其他管:									
8540.8100	--接收管或放大管〔999〕	8		17	13/	13	只/千克			/28
8540.8900	--其他									
8540.8900 10	光电倍增管(光电阴极面积大于 20 平方厘米,并且阳极脉冲上升时间小于 1 纳秒)〔999〕	8		17	13/	13	只/千克	3		/33
8540.8900 90	其他电子管(包括光阴极管或汞弧整流管〔999〕	8		17	13/	13	只/千克			/33
	-零件:									
	--阴极射线管用:									
8540.9110	---电视显像管用〔999〕	6		40	13/	13	千克			/
8540.9120	---雷达显示管用〔999〕	5		14	13/	13	千克			/
8540.9190	---其他〔999〕	8	4	17	13/	13	千克			/9
	--其他:									
8540.9910	---电视摄像管用〔999〕	8		35	13/	13	千克			/
8540.9990	---其他〔999〕	8		17	13/	13	千克			/33
85.41	**二极管、晶体管及类似的半导体器件;光敏半导体器件,包括不论是否装在组件内或组装成块的光电池;发光二极管;已装配的压电晶体:**									
8541.1000	-二极管,但光敏二极管或发光二极管除外〔999〕	0		30	13/	13	个/千克			/25
	-晶体管,但光敏晶体管除外:									
8541.2100	--耗散功率小于 1 瓦的〔999〕	0		30	13/	13	个/千克			/25
8541.2900	--其他〔999〕	0		30	13/	13	个/千克			/25
8541.3000	-半导体开关元件、两端交流开关元件及三端双向可控硅开关元件,但光敏器件除外〔999〕	0		30	13/	13	个/千克			/25
	-光敏半导体器件,包括不论是否装在组件内或组装成块的光电池;发光二极管:									
8541.4010	---发光二极管〔999〕	0		30	13/	13	个/千克			/25

协定税率 %										特惠税率 %			Article Description
亚太5国	东/冰/格	巴基斯坦	韩国	瑞士	哥达	秘鲁	澳大利亚	新西/坡/智	港/澳/台	亚太2国	老/柬/缅	36/3/1	
													-Ultraviolet or infrared lamps; arc-lamps:
	0/0/0	4		0	0	0	0	0//0	0/0/			0/0/0	--Arc-lamps
	0/0/0	4		0	0	0	0	0//0	0/0/			0/0/0	--Other
	0/0/0	0	0	0	0	0	0	0/0/0	0/0/			0/0/0	-Light-emitting diode(LED)lamps
	0/0/0	4		0	0	0	0	0//0	0/0/0			0/0/0	-Parts
													Thermionic, cold cathode or photo-cathode valves and tubes (for example, vacuum or vapour or gas filled valves and tubes, mercury arc rectifying valves and tubes, cathode-ray tubes, television camera tubes):
													-Cathode-ray television picture tubes, including video monitor cathode-ray tubes:
	0/0/0	5.4	7.2	3.6	0	0	0	0/0/0	0/0/			0/0/	--Colour
	0/0/0	10.8	6	4.5	0	0	0	0/0/0	0/0/			0/0/	--Monochrome
													-Television camera tubes; image converters and intensifiers; other photo-cathode tubes:
	0/0/0	5.4	4.8	3.6	0	0	0	0/0/0	0/0/			0/0/	---Television camera tubes
													---Other
	0/0/0	4	0	0	0	0	0	0//0	0/0/			0/0/0	Stripe kinescope of electronic stripe camera (striation kinescope tube specially used for Serial Number 9006.5900 40)
	0/0/0	4	0	0	0	0	0	0//0	0/0/			0/0/0	Other television camera tubes, other image converter tube and image intensifier tubes, other photo cathode tubes
													-Data/graphic display tubes, monochrome; data/graphic display-tubes, colour, with a phosphor dot screen pitch smaller than 0.4mm
	0/0/0	4	0	0	0	0	0	0//0	0/0/			0/0/0	---Data/graphic displaytubes, colour, with a phosphor dot screen pitch smaller than 4mm
	0/0/0	4	0	0	0	0	0	0//0	0/0/			0/0/0	---Data/graphic display tubes, monochrome
													-Other cathode-ray tubes:
3.9	0/0/0	0	0	0	0	0	0	0//0	0/0/			0/0/0	---Radar display tubes
	0/0/0	4	0	0	0	0	0	0//0	0/0/			0/0/0	---Other
													-Microwave tubes (for example, magnetrons, klystrons, travelling wave tubes, carcinotrons), excluding grid-controlled tubes:
	0/0/0	4	4.8	0	0	0	0	0//0	0/0/			0/0/0	--Magnetrons
													--Other:
	0/0/0	4	0	0	0	0	0	0//0	0/0/			0/0/0	---Klystrons
	0/0/0	4	0	0	0	0	0	0//0	0/0/			0/0/0	---Other
													-Other valves and tubes:
	0/0/0	4		0	0	0	0	0//0	0/0/			0/0/0	--Receiver or amplifier valves and tubes
													--Other
	0/0/0	4	0	0	0	0	0	0//0	0/0/0			0/0/0	Electron-multiplier phototube (Photoelectric cathode area greater than 20 square centimeters, and the anode pulse rise time less than 1ns)
	0/0/0	4	0	0	0	0	0	0//0	0/0/0			0/0/0	Other electron tube(including photo-cathode valves and mercury arc rectifying valves and tubes)
													-Parts:
													--Of cathode-ray tubes:
	0/0/0	0	0	0	0	0	0	0//0	0/0/			0/0/0	---Of television picture tubes
3.3	0/0/0	0	0	0	0	0	0	0//0	0/0/			0/0/0	---Of radar display tubes
	0/0/0	4		0	0	0	0	0//0	0/0/			0/0/0	---Other
													--Other:
5.2	0/0/0	4	0	0	0	0	0	0//0	0/0/			0/0/0	---Of television camera tubes
	0/0/0	4		0	0	0	0	0//0	0/0/			0/0/0	---Other
													Diodes, transistors and similar semi-conductor devices; photosensitive semi-conductor devices, including photovoltaic cells whether or not assembled in modules or made up into panels; light emitting diodes; mounted piezo-electric crystals:
												0/0/0	-Diodes, other than photosensitive or light emitting diodes
													-Transistors, other than photosensitive transistors:
												0/0/0	--With a dissipation rate of less than 1 W
												0/0/0	--Other
												0/0/0	-Thyristors, diacs and triacs, other than photosensitive devices
													-Photosensitive semiconductor devices, including photovoltaic cells whether or not assembled in modules or made up into panels; light emitting diodes:
												0/0/0	---Light emitting diodes

税则号列	货品名称〔CIQ扩展编码及品名－T2表示见附表2〕	最惠(%)	暂定税率	普通	增值/消费	出口退税	计量单位	监管条件	检验检疫	特殊证件对美关税
8541.4020	---太阳能电池〔999〕	0		30	13/	13	个/千克			/25
8541.4090	---其他〔999〕	0		30	13/	13	个/千克			/25
8541.5000	-其他半导体器件〔999〕	0		30	13/	13	个/千克			/20
8541.6000	-已装配的压电晶体〔999〕	0		30	13/	13	个/千克			/25
8541.9000	-零件〔999〕	0		30	13/	13	千克			/20
85.42	集成电路：									
	-集成电路：									
	--处理器及控制器，不论是否带有存储器、转换器、逻辑电路、放大器、时钟及时序电路或其他电路：									
	---多元件集成电路：									
8542.3111	----具有变流功能的半导体模块									
8542.3111 10	多元件集成电路中的自动数据处理设备机器及组件、电讯设备用的具有变流动能的半导体模块〔999〕	0		30	13/	13	个/千克			/
8542.3111 90	多元件集成电路中的其他具有变流功能的半导体模块〔999〕	3.3/1.7		30	13/	13	个/千克			/
8542.3119	----其他〔999〕	1.3/0.6		46	13/	13	个/千克			/
8542.3190	---其他〔999〕	0		24	13/	13	个/千克			/
	--存储器：									
8542.3210	---多元件集成电路〔999〕	1.4/0.7	0	45	13/	13	个/千克			/
8542.3290	---其他〔999〕	0		24	13/	13	个/千克			/
	--放大器：									
8542.3310	---多元件集成电路〔999〕	1.4/0.7		45	13/	13	个/千克			/
8542.3390	---其他〔999〕	0		24	13/	13	个/千克			/
	--其他：									
8542.3910	---多元件集成电路〔999〕	1.4/0.7		45	13/	13	个/千克			/
8542.3990	---其他〔999〕	0		24	13/	13	个/千克			/
8542.9000	-零件〔999〕	0		30	13/	13	千克			/
85.43	**本章其他税目未列名的具有独立功能的电气设备及装置：**									
8543.1000	-粒子加速器									
8543.1000 10	脉冲电子加速器(峰值能量为500千电子伏或更高)〔999〕	5		11	13/	13	台/千克	3		/35
8543.1000 20	中子发生器系统，包括中子管(真空下，利用静电加速来诱发氚-氘核反应)〔999〕	5		11	13/	13	台/千克	3		/35
8543.1000 90	其他粒子加速器〔999〕	5		11	13/	13	台/千克			/35
	-信号发生器：									
8543.2010	---输出信号频率在1500兆赫兹以下的通用信号发生器〔999〕	7.5/5.6		80	13/	13	台/千克			/17.5,15.6
8543.2090	---其他									
8543.2090 10	高速脉冲发生器(脉冲上升时间小于500ps)〔999〕	4/3		20	13/	13	台/千克	3		/24,23
8543.2090 90	其他输出信号频率≥1500MHz的通用信号发生器〔999〕	4/3		20	13/	13	台/千克			/24,23
8543.3000	-电镀、电解或电泳设备及装置									
8543.3000 10	电化学还原槽；锂汞齐电解槽(电化学还原槽为化学交换过程的铀浓缩设计的)〔999〕	0		35	13/	13	台/千克	3		/10
8543.3000 20	产氟电解槽(每小时产250克以上)〔999〕	0		35	13/	13	台/千克	3		/10
8543.3000 90	其他电镀、电解或电泳设备及装置〔999〕	0		35	13/	13	台/千克			/10
	-其他设备及装置：									
8543.7091	----金属、矿藏探测器〔101机电产品及其零件，102电子测量分析设备及其零件〕	0		17	13/	13	台/千克			/20
8543.7092	----高、中频放大器〔999〕	0		17	13/	13	台/千克		L	/5
8543.7093	----电篱网激发器〔999〕	8		35	13/	13	台/千克			/13
8543.7099	----其他									
8543.7099 10	飞行数据记录器、报告器〔101机电产品及其零件，102电子测量分析设备及其零件〕	0		35	13/	13	台/千克			/10
8543.7099 20	无线广播电视用激励器(具有独立功能)〔101机电产品及其零件，102电视接收、发送装置及其零件〕	0		35	13/	13	台/千克	O		/10
8543.7099 30	模/数转换器(能设计或改进成军用、或设计成抗辐射的)〔101机电产品及其零件，102调制解调器〕	0		35	13/	13	台/千克	3		/10

协定税率 %										特惠税率 %			
亚太5国	东/冰/格	巴基斯坦	韩国	瑞士	哥达	秘鲁	澳大利亚	新西/坡/智	港/澳/台	亚太2国	老/柬/缅	36/3/1	Article Description
												0/0/ɔ	---Solar cells
												0/0/ɔ	---Other
												0/0/0	-Other semiconductor devices
												0/0/0	-Mounted piezo-electric crystals
												0/0/0	-Parts
													Electronic integrated circuits:
													-Electronic integrated circuits:
													--Proceosors and controuers, whether or not combined with memories, converter, logic circuit, amplifier, clock and timing circuit or other circuit
													---Multi—component integrated circuits:
													----Semiconductor modules with converting function
	0/0/4	4.5	0	3/1.7	0	0	0	0/0/0	0/0/			0/0/0	Automatic data processing equipment machine and assembly in multi element integrated circuit, semiconductor module with variable kinetic energy for telecommunication equipment
	0/0/4	4.5	0	3/1.7	0	0	0	0/0/C	0/0/			0/0/0	Semiconductor module with variable current function in multi element integrated circuit
0.8/0.4	0/0/0	0	4	0	0	0	0	0/0/C	0/0/			0/0/0	----Other
												0/0/0	---Other
													--Memories
0.9/0.5	0/0/0	0	4	0	0	0	0	0/0/0	0/0/			0/0/0	---Multi-component integrated circuits
												0/0/0	---other
													--Amplifier
0.9/0.5	0/0/0	0	4	0	0	0	0	0/0/0	0/0/			0/0/0	---Multi-component integrated circuits
												0/0/0	---other
													--Other:
0.9/0.5	0/0/0	0	4	0	0	0	0	0/0/0	0/0/			0/0/0	—-Multi-component integrated circuits
												0/0/0	—-other
												0/0/0	-Parts
													Electrical machines and apparatus, having individual functions, not specified or included elsewhere in this Chapter:
													-Particle accelerators
	0/0/0	0	2	0	0	0	0	0//0	ɔ/0/			0/0/0	Fulsed electron accelerators(peak value power≥500kEV)
	0/0/0	0	2	0	0	0	0	0//0	ɔ/0/			0/0/0	Neutron generator systems, including neutron tubes(in vacuum condition, induce the tritium-deuteron reaction through acceleration of static)
	0/0/0	0	2	0	0	0	0	0//0	0/0/			0/0/0	Cther particle accelerator
													-Signal generators:
	0/0/0	10.8		4.5	0	0	0	0/0/0	0/0/0			0/0/	---Universal signal generators, with a frequency range of less than 1500 MHz
													---Other
	0/0/0	4	0	0	0	0	0	0//0	0/0/0			0/0/0	High - speed pulse generator(risetime of pulse <500ps)
	0/0/0	4	0	0	0	0	0	0//0	0/0/0			0/0/0	Other versatile signal generators with the ouput signal frequency≥1500MHz
													-Machines and apparatus for electro-plating, electrolysis or electrophoresis
												0/0/0	Electrochemical lithium amalgam electrolysis cells reduction cells (specially designed for uranium concentration in chemical exchange process)
												0/0/0	Fluorine generating electrolytic cells(produce more than 250 g/h)
												0/0/0	Other machines and equipment for electro-plating, electrolysis or electrophoresis
													-Other machines and apparatus:
												0/0/0	----Metal or mine detectors
												0/0/0	----High or intermediate frequency amplifiers
	0/0/0	4	4	0	0	0	0	0/0/0	0/0/0			0/0/0	----Electric fence energizers
													----Other
												0/0/0	Flying data recorders and reporters
												0/0/0	Exciters for wireless television broadcasting (having independently functions)
												0/0/0	Analog/digital converters(capable of being designed or improved for military uses or being designed to resist radiation)

税则号列	货品名称〔CIQ 扩展编码及品名－T2 表示见附表 2〕	最惠(%)	暂定税率	普通	增值/消费	出口退税	计量单位	监管条件	检验检疫	特殊证件对美关税
8543.7099 40	质谱仪用的离子源(原子质量单位≥230,分辨率＞2/230)〔999〕	0		35	13/	13	台/千克	3		/10
8543.7099 50	密码机、密码卡(不包括数字电视智能卡、蓝牙模块、用于知识产权保护的加密狗)〔101 电话密码机,102 传真密码机,103 其他密码机,104 密码卡〕	0		35	13/	13	台/千克	M		/10
8543.7099 90	其他未列名的具有独立功能的电气设备及装置〔999〕	0		35	13/	13	台/千克			/10
	-零件:									
8543.9010	---粒子加速器用〔999〕	0		11	13/	13	千克			/5
	---信号发生器用:									
8543.9021	----输出信号频率在 1500 兆赫兹以下的通用信号发生器用〔999〕	0		80	13/	13	千克			/10
8543.9029	----其他〔999〕	0		20	13/	13	千克			/10
8543.9030	---金属、矿藏探测器用〔999〕	0		17	13/	13	千克			/25
8543.9040	---高、中频放大器用〔999〕	0		17	13/	13	千克			/10
8543.9090	---其他〔999〕	0		35	13/	13	千克			/25
85.44	**绝缘(包括漆包或阳极化处理)电线、电缆(包括同轴电缆)及其他绝缘电导体,不论是否有接头;由每根被覆光纤组成的光缆,不论是否与电导体装配或装有接头:**									
	-绕组电线:									
8544.1100	--铜制〔999〕	10	6	70	13/	13	千克/米			/26
8544.1900	--其他〔101 电线,102 其它电线电缆〕	10		70	13/	13	千克/米			/30
8544.2000	-同轴电缆及其他同轴电导体[T2]	10		20	13/	13	千克			/20
	-车辆、航空器、船舶用点火布线组及其他布线组:									
8544.3020	---机动车辆用									
8544.3020 01	车辆用电控柴油机的线束〔999〕	10	5	20	13/	13	千克			/10
8544.3020 90	机动车辆用其他点火布线组及其他布线组〔999〕	10		20	13/	13	千克			/15
8544.3090	---其他〔101 绞股线,102 电线,103 电缆,104 其它电线电缆〕	5		70	13/	13	千克			/15
	-其他电导体,额定电压不超过 1000 伏:									
	--有接头:									
	---额定电压不超过 80 伏:									
8544.4211	----电缆[T2]	0		20	13/	13	千克/米			/25
8544.4219	----其他[T2]	0		70	13/	13	千克			/25
	---额定电压超过 80 伏,但不超过 1000 伏:									
8544.4221	----电缆〔101 电线,102 电缆,103 其它电线电缆〕	0		20	13/	13	千克/米	A	LM	/20
8544.4229	----其他〔101 绞股线,102 电线,103 其它电线电缆〕	0		70	13/	13	千克	A	LM	/25
	--其他:									
	---额定电压不超过 80 伏:									
8544.4911	----电缆[T2]	0		20	13/	13	千克/米			/20
8544.4919	----其他[T2]	0		70	13/	13	千克			/30
	---额定电压超过 80 伏,但不超过 1000 伏:									
8544.4921	----电缆〔101 电缆,102 其它电线电缆〕	6		20	13/	13	千克/米	A	LM	/26
8544.4929	----其他〔101 绞股线,102 电线,103 其它电线电缆〕	8		70	13/	13	千克			/18
	-其他电导体,额定电压超过 1000 伏:									
	---电缆:									
8544.6012	----额定电压不超过 35 千伏〔999〕	8		50	13/	13	千克/米	A	LM	/18
8544.6013	----额定电压超过 35 千伏,但不超过 110 千伏〔999〕	8		20	13/	13	千克/米			/33
8544.6014	----额定电压超过 110 千伏,但不超过 220 千伏〔999〕	8		20	13/	13	千克/米			/28
8544.6019	----其他〔101 电缆,102 其它电线电缆〕	8		20	13/	13	千克/米			/33
8544.6090	---其他									
8544.6090 01	额定电压≥500 千伏的气体绝缘金属封闭输电线[T2]	15	10	70	13/	13	千克			/30
8544.6090 90	额定电压＞1 千伏的其他电导线[T2]	15		70	13/	13	千克			/35
8544.7000	-光缆〔999〕	0		20	13/	13	千克/米			/20
85.45	**碳电极、碳刷、灯碳棒、电池碳棒及电气设备用的其他石墨或碳精制品,不论是否带金属:**									
	-碳电极:									
8545.1100	--炉用〔999〕	8		35	13/	0	千克	3		/33
8545.1900	--其他〔999〕	10		35	13/	0	千克	3		/15
8545.2000	-碳刷〔999〕	10		35	13/	13	千克			/35
8545.9000	-其他〔999〕	10		35	13/	13	千克	3		/20
85.46	**各种材料制的绝缘子:**									

协定税率 %										特惠税率 %			Article Description
亚太5国	东/冰/格	巴基斯坦	韩国	瑞士	哥达	秘鲁	澳大利亚	新西/坡/智	港/澳/台	亚太2国	老/柬/缅	36/3/1	
												0/0/0	Ion source for mass spectrograph (atomic quality unit≥230, exculpation>2/230)
												0/0/0	Cipher, cipher card (not including the intelligent digital TV card, Bluetooth module, for intellectual property protection dongle)
												0/0/0	Other unisted electrical equipment and devices, having independently functions
													-Parts:
												0/0/0	---Of particle accelerators
													---Of signal generators:
												0/0/0	----Of the generators of subheading No. 8543. 2010
												0/0/0	----Other
												0/0/0	---Of metal or mine detectors
												0/0/0	---Of high or intermediate frequency amplifiers
												0/0/0	---Other
													Insulated (including enamelled or anodized) wire, cable (including co-axial cable) and other insulated electric conductors, whether or not ritted with connectors; optical fibre cables, made up of individually sheathed fibres, whether or not assembled with electric conductors or fitted with connectors:
													-Winding wire:
6.5	0/0/0	4	6	3	0	0	0	0/0/0	0/0/0			0/0/0	--Of copper
	0/0/0	20	14	6	0	0	0	0/0/0	0/0/			0/0/	--Other
6.5	0/0/0	0	4	5.3	0	0	0	0/0/0	0/0/0			0/0/0	-Co-axial cable and other co-axial electric conductors
													-Ignition wiring sets and other wiring sets of a kind used in vehicles, aircraft or ships:
													---For motor vehicles
	5/0/0	8	6	0	0	0	0	0//0	0/0/			0/0/0	Wiring harness for electronic control diesel engines of vehicles
	5/0/0	8	6	0	0	0	0	0//0	0/0/			0/0/0	Other ignition wiring sets and other wiring sets of a king used for motor vehicles
	/0/0	4	3	0	0	0	0	0//0	0/0/			0/0/0	---Other
													-Other electric conductors, for a voltage not exceeding 1000 V:
													--Fitted with connectors:
													---For a voltage not exceeding 80 V:
												0/0/0	----Electric cable
												0/0/0	----Other
													---for a voltage exceeding 80V but not exceeding 1000 V:
												0/0/0	----Electric cable
												0/0/0	----Other
													--Other:
													---For a voltage not exceeding 80 V:
												0/0/0	----Electric cable
												0/0/0	----Other
													---For a voltage exceeding 80 V but not exceeding 1000 V:
3.9	0/0/0	0	3.9	1.8	0	0	0	0//0	0/0/			0/0/0	----Electric cable
5.2	0/0/0	0	0	3.6	0	0	0	0/0/0	0/0/0			0/0/0	----Other
													-Other electric conductors, for a voltage exceeding 1000 V:
													---Electric cable:
5.2	0/0/0	0	4	3	0	0	0	0/0/0	0/0/			0/0/0	----For a voltage not execedding 35 kV
5.2	0/0/0	4	3.3	0	0	0	0	0//0	0/0/			0/0/0	----For a voltage execedding 35 kV, but not execedding 110 kV
5.2	0/0/0	4	0	0	0	0	0	0//0	0/0/			0/0/0	----For a voltage execedding 110 kV, but not execedding 220 kV
5.2	0/0/0	4	5.4		0	0	0	0//0	0/0/			0/0/0	----Other
													---Other
9.8	0/0/0	18	14.7	0	0	0	0	0/0/0	0/0/			0/0/	Gas-insulated transmission electric wire, rated voltage≥500kV
9.8	0/0/0	18	14.7	0	0	0	0	0/0/0	0/0/			0/0/	Other electric conductor with a rated voltage>1kV
												0/0/0	-Optical fibre cables
													Carbon electrodes, carbon brushes, lamp carbons, battery carbons and other articles of graphite or other carbon, with or without metal, of a kind used for electrical purposes:
													-Carbon Electrodes:
	0/0/0	4	3.2	0	0	0	0	0//0	0/0/			0/0/0	--Of a kind used for furnaces
	0/0/0	4.5	4.2	3.2	0	0	0	0/0/0	0/0/			0/0/0	--Other
	0/0/0	4.5	4.2	3.2	0	0	0	0/0/0	0/0/			0/0/0	-Brushes
	0/0/0	4.5	4.2	3.2	0	0	0	0/0/0	0/0/			0/0/0	-Other
													Electrical insulators of any material:

税则号列		货品名称〔CIQ扩展编码及品名—T2表示见附表2〕	最惠(%)	暂定税率	普通	增值/消费	出口退税	计量单位	监管条件	检验检疫	特殊证件对美关税
8546.1000		-玻璃制〔999〕	10		35	13/	13	千克			/35
		-陶瓷制：									
8546.2010		---输变电线路绝缘瓷套管〔999〕	6		35	13/	13	千克			/31
8546.2090		---其他									
8546.2090	01	输变电架空线路用长棒形瓷绝缘子瓷件(单支长度为1～2米,实芯)〔999〕	12	3	35	13/	13	千克			/13
8546.2090	90	其他陶瓷制绝缘子(包括非输变电线路绝缘瓷套管)〔999〕	12		35	13/	13	千克			/22
8546.9000		-其他〔999〕	10		35	13/	13	千克			/35
85.47		**电气机器、器具或设备用的绝缘零件,除了为装配需要而在模制时装入的小金属零件(例如螺纹孔)以外,全部用绝缘材料制成,但税目85.46的绝缘子除外;内衬绝缘材料的贱金属制线路导管及其接头:**									
8547.1000		-陶瓷制绝缘零件〔999〕	7		35	13/	13	千克			/17
8547.2000		-塑料制绝缘零件〔999〕	7		35	13/	13	千克			/27
		-其他：									
8547.9010		---内衬绝缘材料的贱金属制线路导管及其接头〔999〕	7		50	13/	13	千克			/12
8547.9090		---其他〔999〕	7		35	13/	13	千克			/32
85.48		**原电池、原电池组及蓄电池的废碎料;废原电池、废原电池组及废蓄电池;机器或设备的本章其他税目未列名的电气零件:**									
8548.1000		-原电池、原电池组及蓄电池的废碎料;废原电池、废原电池组及废蓄电池〔999〕	8		36	13/	13	千克	9		/
8548.9000		-其他									
8548.9000	01	电磁干扰滤波器〔101其它机电产品及其零件,102集成电路,103其它电子元器件〕	8	3	40	13/	13	千克			/28
8548.9000	02	非电磁干挠滤波器〔999〕	8	6	40	13/	13	千克			/31
8548.9000	10	可调脉冲单模染料振荡器(平均输出功率＞1 W,重复率＞1 kHz,脉宽＜100ns可见光范围)〔999〕	8		40	13/	13	千克	3		/33
8548.9000	20	可调脉冲染料激光放大器和振荡器(不包括单模振荡器)(平均输出功率＞30 W,重复率＞1kHZ,脉宽＜100ns可见光范围)〔999〕	8		40	13/	13	千克	3		/33
8548.9000	30	触摸感应数据输入装置(即触摸屏)无显示的性能,安装于有显示屏的设备中,通过检测显示区域内触摸动作的发生及位置进行工作。触摸感应可通过电阻、静电电容、声学脉冲识别、红外光或其他触摸感应技术来获得〔999〕	4/2		40	13/	13	千克			/29,27
8548.9000	90	第85章其他编号未列名的电气零件〔999〕	8		40	13/	13	千克			/33

协定税率 %										特惠税率 %			Article Description
亚太5国	东/冰/格	巴基斯坦	韩国	瑞士	哥达	秘鲁	澳大利亚	新西/坡/智	港/澳/台	亚太2国	老/柬/缅	36/3/1	
	0/0/0	4.5	4.2	3.2	0	0	0	0/0/0	0/0/			0/0/0	-Of glass
													-Of ceramics:
	0/0/0	0	2.4	1.8	0	0	0	0//0	0/0/			0/0/0	---Power transmission and converting ceramic bushings
													---Other
	0/0/0	5.4	4.8	3.6	0	0	0	0/0/0	0/0/			0/0/0	Porcelain parts of long - rod porcelain insulators for electric transmission and transformation overhead lines (length of a single rod: 1 ~2m, solid)
	0/0/0	5.4	4.8	3.6	0	0	0	0/0/0	0/0/			0/0/0	Other electrical insulators of ceramics (including not power transmission and transformation and converting ceramic bushings)
	0/0/0	4.5	4	3	0	0	0	0/0/0	0/0/			0/0/0	-Other
													Insulating fittings for electrical machines, appliances or equipment, being fittings wholly of insulating material apart from any minor components of metal (for example, threaded sockets) incorporated during moulding solely for purposes of assembly, other than insulators of headingNo. 85. 46; electrical conduit tubing and joints therefor, of base metal lined with insulating material:
	0/0/0	4	4.8	2.4	0	0	0	0//0	0/0/			0/0/0	-Insulating fittings of ceramics
	0/0/3.2	4	4.8	2.4	0	0	0	0//0	0/0/			0/0/0	-Insulating fittings of plastics
													-Other:
	0/0/0	4	4	0	0	0	0	0/0/0	0/0/			0/0/0	---Electrical conduit tubing and joints therefor, of base metal lined with insulating material
	0/0/0	4	0	0	0	0	0	0//0	0/0/			0/0/0	---Other
													Waste and scrap of primary cells, primary batteries and electric accumulators; spent primary cells, spent primary batteries and spent electric accumulators; electrical parts of machinery or apparatus, not specified or included elsewhere in this Chapter:
	0/0/0	4	0	0	0	0	0	0//0	0/0/	4		0/0/	-Waste and scrap of primary cells, primary batteries and electric accumulators; spent primary cells, spent primary batteries and spent electric accumulators
													-Other
	0/0/0	5.4	8.4	3.6	0	0	0	0/0/0	0/0/			0/0/	Patch filters
	0/0/0	5.4	8.4	3.6	0	0	0	0/0/0	0/0/			0/0/	Non electromagnetic interference filter
	0/0/0	5.4	8.4	3.6	0	0	0	0/0/0	0/0/			0/0/	Ingle - mode tunable pulsed dye oscillators (average output power > 1w, repetition rate > 1khz, pulse width < 100ns of wavelength range of visible light)
	0/0/0	5.4	8.4	3.6	0	0	0	0/0/0	0/0/			0/0/	Single - mode tunable pulsed dye amplifiers and oscillators (average output power > 30W, repetition rate > 1kHz, pulse width < 100ns of wavelength range of visible light, excluding single transverse - mode oscillators)
	0/0/0	5.4	8.4	3.6	0	0	0	0/0/0	0/0/			0/0/	
	0/0/0	5.4	8.4	3.6	0	0	0	0/0/0	0/0/			0/0/	Other electrical parts, not specified or included elsewhere in the Chapter 85

第十七类
车辆、航空器、船舶
及有关运输设备

注释：

一、本类不包括税目 95.03 或 95.08 的物品以及税目 95.06 的长雪橇、平底雪橇及类似品。

二、本类所称"零件"及"零件、附件",不适用于下列货品,不论其是否确定为供本类货品使用：

(一)各种材料制的接头、垫圈或类似品(按其构成材料归类或归入税目 84.84)或硫化橡胶(硬质橡胶除外)的其他制品(税目 40.16)；

(二)第十五类注释二所规定的贱金属制通用零件(第十五类)或塑料制的类似品(第三十九章)；

(三)第八十二章的物品(工具)；

(四)税目 83.06 的物品；

(五)税目 84.01 至 84.79 的机器或装置及其零件,但供本类所列货品使用的散热器除外；税目 84.81 或 84.82 的物品及税目84.83的物品(这些物品是构成发动机或其他动力装置所必需的)；

(六)电机或电气设备(第八十五章)；

(七)第九十章的物品；

(八)第九十一章的物品；

(九)武器(第九十三章)；

(十)税目 94.05 的灯具或照明装置；

(十一)作为车辆零件的刷子(税目 96.03)。

三、第八十六章至第八十八章所称"零件"或"附件",不适用于那些非专用于或非主要用于这几章所列物品的零件、附件。同时符合这几章内两个或两个以上税目规定的零件、附件,应按其主要用途归入相应的税目。

四、在本类中：

(一)既可在道路上,又可在轨道上行驶的特殊构造的车辆,应归入第八十七章的相应税目；

(二)水陆两用的机动车辆,应归入第八十七章的相应税目；

(三)可兼作地面车辆使用的特殊构造的航空器,应归入第八十八章的相应税目。

五、气垫运输工具应按本类最相似的运输工具归类,其规定如下：

(一)在导轨上运行的(气垫火车),归入第八十六章；

(二)在陆地行驶或水陆两用的,归入第八十七章；

(三)在水上航行的,不论能否在海滩或浮码头登陆及能否在冰上行驶,一律归入第八十九章。

气垫运输工具的零件、附件,应按照上述规定,与最相类似的运输工具的零件、附件一并归类。

气垫火车的导轨固定装置及附件应与铁道轨道固定装置及附件一并归类。气垫火车运行系统的信号、安全或交通管理设备应与铁路的信号、安全或交通管理设备一并归类。

第八十六章
铁道及电车道机车、车辆及其零件;铁道及电车道轨道固定装置及其零件、附件;各种机械(包括电动机械)交通信号设备

注释：

一、本章不包括：

(一)木制或混凝土制的铁道或电车道轨枕及气垫火车用的混凝土导轨(税目 44.06 或 68.10)；

(二)税目 73.02 的铁道及电车道辅轨用钢铁材料；

(三)税目 85.30 的电气信号、安全或交通管理设备。

二、税目 86.07 主要适用于：

(一)轴、轮、行走机构、金属轮箍、轮圈、毂及轮子的其他零件；

(二)车架、底架、转向架；

(三)轴箱；制动装置；

(四)车辆缓冲器；钩或其他联结器及车厢走廊联结装置；

(五)车身。

三、除上述注释一另有规定的以外,税目 86.08 包括：

(一)已装配的轨道、转车台、站台缓冲器、量载规；

(二)铁道及电车道、道路、内河航道、停车场、港口或机场用的臂板信号机、机械信号盘、平交道口控制器、信号及道岔控制器及其他机械(包括电动机械)信号、安全或交通管理设备,不论是否装有电力照明装置。

SECTION XVII
VEHICLES, AIRCRAFT, VESSELS AND ASSOCIATED TRANSPORT EQUIPMENT

Notes:

1. This Section does not cover articles of headingNo. 95.03 or 95.08, or bobsleighs, toboggans or the like of heading. 95.06.
2. The expressions "parts" and "parts and accessories" do not apply to the following articles, whether or not they are identifiable as for the goods of this Section:
   (a) Joints, washers or the like of any material (classified according to their constituent material or in headingNo. 84.84) or other articles of vulcanized rubber other than hard rubber (heading. 40.16);
   (b) Parts of general use, as defined in Note 2 to Section XV, of base metal (Section XV), or similar goods of plastics (Chapter 39);
   (c) Articles of Chapter 82 (tools);
   (d) Articles of headingNo. 83.06;
   (e) Machines or apparatus of headings No. 84.01 to 84.79, or parts thereof but except for goods listed in this kind of radiator; articles of heading. 84.81 or 84.82 or, provided they constitute integral parts of engines or motors, articles of headingNo. 84.83;
   (f) Electrical machinery or equipment (Chapter 85);
   (g) Articles of Chapter 90;
   (h) Articles of Chapter 91;
   (ij) Arms (Chapter 93);
   (k) Lamps or lighting fittings of headingNo. 94.05;
   (e) Brushes of a kind used as parts of vehicles (headingNo. 96.03).
3. References in Chapters 86 to 88 to "parts" or "accessories" do not apply to parts or accessories which are not suitable for use solely or principally with the articles of those Chapters. A part or accessory which answers to a description in two or more of the headings of those Chapters is to be classified under that heading which corresponds to the principal use of that part or accessory.
4. For the purposes of this Section:
   (a) Vehicles specially constructed to travel on both road and rail are classified under the appropriate heading of Chapter 87;
   (b) Amphibious motor vehicles are classified under the appropriate heading of Chapter 87;
   (c) Aircraft specially constructed so that they can also be used as road vehicles are classified under the appropriate heading of Chapter 88.
5. Air-cushion vehicles are to be classified within this Section with the vehicles to which they are most akin as follows:
   (a) In Chapter 86 if designed to travel on a guide-track (hovertrains);
   (b) In Chapter 87 if designed to travel over land or over both land and water;
   (c) In Chapter 89 if designed to travel over water, whether or not able to land on beaches or landingstages or also able to travel over ice.

   Parts and accessories of air-cushion vehicles are to be classified in the same way as those of vehicles of the heading in which the air-cushion vehicles are classified under the above provisions.

   Hovertrain track fixtures and fittings are to be classified as railway track fixtures and fittings, and signalling, safety or traffic control equipment for hovertrain transport systems as signalling, safety or traffic control equipment for railways.

Chapter 86
Railway or tramway locomotives, rolling-stock and parts thereof; railway or tramway track fixtures and fittings and parts thereof; mechanical (including electro-mechanical) traffic signalling equipment of all kinds

Notes:

1. This Chapter does not cover:
   (a) Railway or tramway sleepers of wood or of concrete, or concrete guide-track sections for hovertrain (heading No. 44.06 or 68.10);
   (b) Railway or tramway track construction material of iron or steel of heading No. 73.02;
   (c) Electrical signalling, safety of traffic control equipment of heading No. 85.30.
2. Heading No. 86.07 applies, *inter alia*, to:
   (a) Axles, wheels, wheel sets (running gear), metal tyres, hoops and hubs and other parts of wheels;
   (b) Frames, underframes, bogies and bissel-bogies;
   (c) Axle boxes; brake gear;
   (d) Buffers for rolling-stock; hooks and other coupling gear and corridor connections;
   (e) Coachwork.
3. Subject to the provisions of Note 1 above, headingNo. 86.08 applies, *inter alia*, to:
   (a) Assembled track, turntables, platform buffers, loading gauges;
   (b) Semaphores, mechanical signal discs, level crossing control gear, signal and point controls, and other mechanical (including electro-mechanical) signalling, safety or traffic control equipment, whether or not fitted with electric lighting, for railways, tramways, roads, inland waterways, parking facilities, port installations or airfields.

税则号列	货品名称〔CIQ 扩展编码及品名—T2 表示见附表 2〕	最惠(%)	暂定税率	普通	增值/消费	出口退税	计量单位	监管条件	检验检疫	特殊证件对美关税
86.01	铁道电力机车,由外部电力或蓄电池驱动:									
	-由外部电力驱动:									
	---直流电机驱动的:									
8601.1011	----微型机控制的〔999〕	3		11	13/	13	辆/千克			/
8601.1019	----其他〔999〕	3		11	13/	13	辆/千克			/
8601.1020	---交流电机驱动的〔999〕	3		11	13/	13	辆/千克			/
8601.1090	---其他〔999〕	3		11	13/	13	辆/千克			/
8601.2000	-由蓄电池驱动〔999〕	3		11	13/	13	辆/千克			/
86.02	其他铁道机车;机车煤水车:									
	-柴油电力机车:									
8602.1010	---微型机控制的〔999〕	3		11	13/	13	辆/千克			/
8602.1090	---其他〔999〕	3		11	13/	13	辆/千克			/8
8602.9000	-其他〔999〕	3		11	13/	13	辆/千克			/
86.03	铁道及电车道用的机动客车、货车、敞车,但税目 **86.04** 的货品除外:									
8603.1000	-由外部电力驱动〔999〕	3		11	13/	13	辆/千克			/
8603.9000	-其他〔999〕	3		11	13/	13	辆/千克			/
86.04	铁道及电车道用的维修或服务车,不论是否机动(例如,工场车、起重机车、道碴捣固车、轨道校正车、检验车及查道车):									
	---检验车及查道车:									
8604.0011	----隧道限界检查车〔999〕	3		14	13/	13	辆/千克			/
8604.0012	----钢轨在线打磨列车〔999〕	3		14	13/	13	辆/千克			/8
8604.0019	----其他〔999〕	5		14	13/	13	辆/千克			/
	---其他:									
8604.0091	----电气化接触网架线机(轨行式)〔999〕	5		20	13/	13	辆/千克			/
8604.0099	----其他〔999〕	5		20	13/	13	辆/千克			/
86.05	铁道及电车道用的非机动客车;行李车、邮政车和其他铁道及电车道用的非机动特殊用途车辆(税目 **86.04** 的货品除外):									
8605.0010	---铁道客车〔999〕	5		14	13/	13	辆/千克			/
8605.0090	---其他〔999〕	5		14	13/	13	辆/千克			/
86.06	铁道及电车道用的非机动有篷及无篷货车:									
8606.1000	-油罐货车及类似车〔999〕	5		14	13/	13	辆/千克			/
8606.3000	-自卸货车,但子目号 8606.1000 的货品除外〔999〕	5		14	13/	13	辆/千克			/
	-其他:									
8606.9100	--带篷及封闭的〔999〕	5		14	13/	13	辆/千克			/
8606.9200	--敞篷的,厢壁固定且高度超过 60 厘米〔999〕	5		14	13/	13	辆/千克			/
8606.9900	--其他〔999〕	5		14	13/	13	辆/千克			/
86.07	铁道及电车道机车或其他车辆的零件:									
	-转向架、轴、轮及其零件:									
8607.1100	--驾驶转向架〔999〕	3		11	13/	13	套/千克			/
8607.1200	--其他转向架〔999〕	3		11	13/	13	套/千克			/28
	--其他,包括零件:									
8607.1910	---轴〔999〕	3		11	13/	13	根/千克			/28
8607.1990	---其他〔999〕	3		11	13/	13	千克			/28
	-制动装置及其零件:									
8607.2100	--空气制动器及其零件〔999〕	3		11	13/	13	千克			/28
8607.2900	--其他〔999〕	3		11	13/	13	千克			/13
8607.3000	-钩、其他联结器、缓冲器及其零件〔999〕	3		11	13/	13	千克			/28
	-其他:									
8607.9100	--机车用〔999〕	3		11	13/	13	千克			/28
8607.9900	--其他〔999〕	3		11	13/	13	千克			/23
86.08	铁道及电车道轨道固定装置及附件;供铁道、电车道、道路、内河航道、停车场、港口或机场用的机械(包括电动机械)信号、安全或交通管理设备;上述货品的零件:									
8608.0010	---轨道自动计轴设备〔999〕	3		20	13/	13	千克/台			/
8608.0090	---其他〔999〕	4		20	13/	13	千克			/29
86.09	集装箱(包括运输液体的集装箱),经特殊设计、装备适用于各种运输方式:									
	---20 英尺的:									

协定税率 %										特惠税率 %			Article Description
亚太5国	东/冰/格	巴基斯坦	韩国	瑞士	哥达	秘鲁	澳大利亚	新西/坡/智	港/澳/台	亚太2国	老/柬/缅	36/3/1	
													Rail locomotives powered from an external source of electricity or by electric accumulators:
													-Powered from an external source of electricity:
													---Drived by DC motors:
2	0/0/0	0	0	0	0	0	0	0//0	0/0/			0/0/0	----Controlled by microprocessings
2	0/0/0	0	0	0	0	0	0	0//0	0/0/			0/0/0	----Other
2	0/0/0	0	0	0	0	0	0	0//0	0/0/			0/0/0	---Drived by AC motors
2	0/0/0	0	0	0	0	0	0	0//0	0/0/			0/0/0	---Other
	0/0/0	0	0	0	0	0	0	0//0	0/0/			0/0/0	-Powered by electric accumulators
													Other rail locomotives; locomotive tenders:
													-Diesel-electric locomotives:
2	0/0/0	0	0	0	0	0	0	0//0	0/0/			0/0/0	---Controled by microprocessings
2	0/0/0	0	0	0	0	0	0	0//0	0/0/			0/0/0	---Other
	0/0/0	0	0	0	0	0	0	0//0	0/0/			0/0/0	-Other
													Self-propelled railway or tramway coaches, vans and trucks, other than those of headingNo. 86. 04:
2	0/0/0	0	0	0	0	0	0	0//0	0/0/			0/0/0	-Powered from an external source of electricity:
	0/0/0	0	0	0	0	0	0	0//0	0/0/			0/0/0	-Other
													Railway or tramway maintenance or service vehicles, whether or not self-propelled (for example, workshops, cranes, ballast tampers, trackliners, testing coaches and track inspection vehicles):
													---Testing coaches and track inspection vehicles:
2	0/0/0	0	0	0	0	0	0	0//0	0/0/			0/0/0	----Inspection vehicles for tunnel clearance
2	0/0/0	0	0	0	0	0	0	0//0	0/0/			0/0/0	----Sanding vehicles for on-line rails
3.3	0/0/0	0	0	0	0	0	0	0//0	0/0/			0/0/0	----Other
													---Other:
3.3	0/0/0	0	0	0	0	0	0	0//0	0/0/			0/0/0	----Installing vehicles for suspension of contact wire (running on rails)
	0/0/0	4	0	0	0	0	0	0//0	0/0/			0/0/0	----Other
													Railway or tramway passenger coaches, not self-propelled; luggage vans, post office coaches and other special purpose railway or tramway coaches, not self-propelled (excluding those of headingNo. 86. 04):
	0/0/0	0	0	0	0	0	0	0//0	0/0/			0/0/0	---Railway passenger coaches
	0/0/0	0	0	0	0	0	0	0//0	0/0/			0/0/0	---Other
													Railway or tramway goods vans and wagons, not self-propelled:
	0/0/0	0	0	0	0	0	0	0//0	0/0/			0/0/0	-Tank wagons and the like
	0/0/0	0	0	0	0	0	0	0//0	0/0/			0/0/0	-Self-discharging vans and wagons, other than those of subheadingNo. 8606. 1000
													-Other:
	0/0/0	0	0	0	0	0	0	0//0	0/0/			0/0/0	--Covered and closed
	0/0/0	0	0	0	0	0	0	0//0	0/0/			0/0/0	--Open, with non-removable sides of a hight exceeding 60 cm
	0/0/0	0	0	0	0	0	0	0//0	0/0/			0/0/0	--Other
													Parts of railway or tramway locomotives or rolling-stock:
													-Bogies, bissel-bogies, axles and wheels, and parts thereof:
	0/0/0	0	0	0	0	0	0	0//0	0/0/			0/0/0	--Driving bogies and bissel-bogies
2	0/0/0	0	0	0	0	0	0	0//0	0/0/			0/0/0	--Other bogies and bissel-bogies
													--Other, including parts:
	0/0/0	0	0	0	0	0	0	0//0	0/0/			0/0/0	---Axles
	0/0/0	0	0	0	0	0	0	0//0	0/0/			0/0/0	---Other
													-Brakes and parts thereof:
	0/0/0	0	0	0	0	0	0	0//0	0/0/			0/0/0	--Air brakes and parts thereof
	0/0/0	0	0	0	0	0	0	0//0	0/0/			0/0/0	--Other
	0/0/0	0	0	0	0	0	0	0//0	0/0/			0/0/0	-Hooks and other coupling devices, buffers, and parts thereof
													-Other:
	0/0/0	0	0	0	0	0	0	0//0	0/0/			0/0/0	--Of locomotives
	0/0/0	0	0	0.9	0	0	0	0//0	0/0/			0/0/0	--Other
													Railway or tramway track fixtures and fittings; mechanical (including electro-mechanical) signalling, safety or traffic control equipment for railways, tramways, roads, inland waterways, parking facilities, port installations or airfields; parts of the foregoing:
2	0/0/0	0	0	0	0	0	0	0//0	0/0/			0/0/0	---Rail automatic axle counting equipments
	0/0/0	0	0	0	0	0	0	0//0	0/0/			0/0/0	---Other
													Containers (including containers for the transport of fluids) specially designed and equipped for carriage by one or more modes of transport:
													---Of 20 feet:

税则号列	货品名称〔CIQ扩展编码及品名—T2表示见附表2〕	最惠(%)	暂定税率	普通	增值/消费	出口退税	计量单位	监管条件	检验检疫	特殊证件对美关税
8609.0011	----保温式〔999〕	10		35	13/	13	个/千克	AB	PQ	/
8609.0012	----罐式〔999〕	10		35	13/	13	个/千克	AB	PQ	/20
8609.0019	----其他〔999〕	10		35	13/	13	个/千克	AB	PQ	/35
	---40英尺的：									
8609.0021	----保温式的〔999〕	10		35	13/	13	个/千克	AB	PQ	/
8609.0022	----罐式〔999〕	10		35	13/	13	个/千克	AB	PQ	/
8609.0029	----其他〔999〕	10		35	13/	13	个/千克	AB	PQ	/
8609.0030	---45、48、53英尺的〔999〕	10		35	13/	13	个/千克	AB	PQ	/
8609.0090	---其他〔999〕	10		35	13/	13	个/千克	AB	PQ	/35

协定税率 %										特惠税率 %			
亚太5国	东/冰/格	巴基斯坦	韩国	瑞士	哥达	秘鲁	澳大利亚	新西/坡/智	港/澳/台	亚太2国	老/柬/缅	36/3/1	Article Description
	0/0/0	4.5	4.2	3.2	0	0	0	0/0/0	0/0/			0/0/0	----Insulated
6.5	0/0/0	4.5	4.2	3.2	0	0	0	0/0/0	0/0/			0/0/0	----Tank type
6.5	0/0/0	4.5	4.2	3.2	0	0	0	0/0/0	0/0/			0/0/0	----Other
													---Of 40 feet:
	0/0/0	4.5	4.2	3.2	0	0	0	0/0/0	0/0/			0/0/0	----Insulated
	0/0/0	4.5	4.2	3.2	0	0	0	0/0/0	0/0/			0/0/0	----Tank type
	0/0/0	4.5	4.2	3.2	0	0	0	0/0/0	0/0/			0/0/0	----Other
	0/0/0	4.5	4.2	3.2	0	0	0	0/0/0	0/0/			0/0/0	---Of 45,48,53 feet
	0/0/0	4.5	4.2	3.2	0	0	0	0/0/0	0/0/			0/0/0	---Other

第八十七章
车辆及其零件、附件，但铁道及电车道车辆除外

注释：

一、本章不包括仅可在钢轨上运行的铁道及电车道车辆。

二、本章所称"牵引车、拖拉机"，是指主要为牵引或推动其他车辆、器具或重物的车辆。除了上述主要用途以外，不论其是否还具有装运工具、种子、肥料或其他货品的辅助装置。

用于安装在税目 87.01 的牵引车、拖拉机上，作为可替换设备的机器或作业工具，即使与牵引车、拖拉机一同进口或出口，不论是否已安装在车(机)上，仍应归入其各自相应的税目。

三、装有驾驶室的机动车辆底盘，应归入税目 87.02 至 87.04，而不归入税目 87.06。

四、税目 87.12 包括所有儿童两轮车，其他儿童脚踏车归入税目 95.03。

税则号列	货品名称〔CIQ 扩展编码及品名－T2 表示见附表 2〕	最惠(%)	暂定税率	普通	增值/消费	出口退税	计量单位	监管条件	检验检疫	特殊证件对美关税
87.01	**牵引车、拖拉机(税目 87.09 的牵引车除外)：**									
8701.1000	-单轴拖拉机〔999〕	9		20	9/	9	辆/千克	6		/14
8701.2000	-半挂车用的公路牵引车〔999〕	6		20	13/	13	辆/千克	46Axy	ML	/31
8701.3000	-履带式牵引车、拖拉机									
8701.3000 10	履带式拖拉机〔999〕	6		20	9/	9,13	辆/千克	A6	M	/31
8701.3000 90	履带式牵引车〔999〕	6		20	13/	9,13	辆/千克	A6	M	/31
	-其他，其发动机功率：									
	--不超过 18 千瓦：									
8701.9110	---拖拉机〔999〕	8		20	13/	9,13	辆/千克	6A	LM	/13
8701.9190	---其他〔999〕	8		20	13/	9,13	辆/千克	6A	LM	/33
	--超过 18 千瓦，但不超过 37 千瓦：									
8701.9210	---拖拉机〔999〕	8		20	13/	9,13	辆/千克	6A	LM	/13
8701.9290	---其他〔999〕	8		20	13/	9,13	辆/千克	6A	LM	/33
	--超过 37 千瓦，但不超过 75 千瓦：									
8701.9310	---拖拉机〔999〕	8		20	13/	9,13	辆/千克	6A	M	/13
8701.9390	---其他〔999〕	8		20	13/	9,13	辆/千克	6A	LM	/33
	--超过 75 千瓦，但不超过 130 千瓦：									
8701.9410	---拖拉机									
8701.9410 10	发动机功率超过 110 千瓦但不超过 130 千瓦的轮式拖拉机〔999〕	8	5	20	13/	13,9	辆/千克	6A	M	/10
	--超过 75 千瓦，但不超过 130 千瓦：									
8701.9410 90	发动机功率超过 75 千瓦但不超过 130 千瓦的其他拖拉机〔999〕	8		20	13/	9,13	辆/千克	6A	M	/13
8701.9490	---其他〔999〕	8		20	13/	9,13	辆/千克	6A	LM	/33
	--超过 130 千瓦：									
8701.9510	---拖拉机									
8701.9510 10	发动机功率超过 130 千瓦的轮式拖拉机〔999〕	8	5	20	13/	13,9	辆/千克	6A	M	/10
8701.9510 90	发动机功率超过 130 千瓦的其他拖拉机〔999〕	8		20	13/	9,13	辆/千克	6A	M	/13
8701.9590	---其他〔999〕	8		20	13/	9,13	辆/千克	6A	LM	/33
87.02	**客运机动车辆，10 座及以上(包括驾驶座)：**									
	-仅装有压燃式活塞内燃发动机(柴油或半柴油发动机)的车辆：									
8702.1020	---机坪客车〔999〕	4		90	13/	13	辆/千克	6AO	M	/
	---其他：									
8702.1091	----30 座及以上(大型客车)〔999〕	15		90	13/	13	辆/千克	46AOxy	LM	/
8702.1092	----20 座及以上，但不超过 29 座									
8702.1092 10	20≤座≤23 仅装有压燃式活塞内燃发动机(柴油或半柴油发动机)的客车〔999〕	15		230	13/5	13	辆/千克	46AOxy	LM	/
8702.1092 90	24≤座≤29 仅装有压燃式活塞内燃发动机(柴油或半柴油发动机)的客车〔999〕	15		230	13/	13	辆/千克	46AOxy	LM	/
8702.1093	----10 座及以上，但不超过 19 座〔999〕	15		230	13/5	13	辆/千克	46AOxy	LM	/
	-同时装有压燃式活塞内燃发动机(柴油或半柴油发动机)及驱动电动机的车辆：									
8702.2010	---机坪客车〔999〕	4		90	13/	13	辆/千克	6AO	M	/
	---其他：									
8702.2091	----30 座及以上(大型客车)〔999〕	15		90	13/	13	辆/千克	46AOxy	LM	/
8702.2092	----20 座及以上，但不超过 29 座									

Chapter 87
Vehicles other than railway or tramway rolling-stock, and parts and accessories thereof

Notes:

1. This Chapter does not cover railway or tramway rolling-stock designed solely for running on rails.
2. For the purposes of this Chapter, "tractors" means vehicles constructed essentially for hauling or pushing another vehicle, appliance or load, whether or not they contain subsidiary provision for the transport, in connection with the main use of the tractor, of tools, seeds, fertilizers or other goods.
   Machines and working tools designed for fitting to tractors of headingNo. 87. 01 as interchangeable equipment remain classified in their respective headings even if presented with the tractor, and whether or not mounted on it.
3. Motor chassis fitted with cabs fall in headings No. 87. 02 to 87. 04, and not in headingNo. 87. 06.
4. HeadingNo. 87. 12 includes all children's bicycles. Other children's cycles fall in headingNo. 95. 03.

协定税率 %										特惠税率 %			Article Description
亚太5国	东/冰/格	巴基斯坦	韩国	瑞士	哥达	秘鲁	澳大利亚	新西/坡/智	港/澳/台	亚太2国	老/柬/缅	36/3/1	
													Tractors (other than tractors of h eading No. 87. 09):
	0/0/0	4	3.6	0	0	0	0	0//0	0/0/			0/0/	-Pedestrian controlled tractors
	5/0/0	4.8	3.6	0	0		0	0//0	0/0/			0//	-Road tractors for semi-trailers
													-Track-laying tractors
	0/0/0	0	0	0	0	0	0	0//0	0/0/			0/0/	Track-laying tractors
	0/0/0	0	0	0	0	0	0	0//0	0/0/			0/0/	Track-laying tractors
													-Other, of an engine power:
													--Not exceeding 18kW:
	0/0/0	0	0	0	0	0	0	0//0	0/0/			0/0/	---Tractors
	0/0/0	4	0	0	0	0	0	0//0	0/0/			0/0/	---other
													--Exceeding 18kW, but not exceeding 37kW:
	0/0/0	0	0	0	0	0	0	0//0	0/0/			0/0/	---Tractors
	0/0/0	4	0	0	0	0	0	0//0	0/0/			0/0/	---Other
													--Exceeding 37kW, but not exceeding 75kW:
	0/0/0	0	0	0	0	0	0	0//0	0/0/			0/0/	---Tractors
	0/0/0	4	0	0	0	0	0	0//0	0/0/			0/0/	---Other
													--Exceeding 75kW, but not exceeding 130kW:
													---Tractors
	0/0/0	0	0	0	0	0	0	0//0	0/0/			0/0/	Wheeled tractors, Engine power exceeding 110 kW but not exceeding 130 kw
													--Exceeding 75kW, but not exceeding 130kW:
	0/0/0	0	0	0	0	0	0	0//0	0/0/			0/0/	Other tractors, Engine power exceeding 75 kW but not exceeding 130 kw
	0/0/0	4	0	0	0	0	0	0//0	0/0/			0/0/	---Other
													--Exceeding 130kw:
													---Tractors
	0/0/0	0	0	0	0	0	0	0//0	0/0/			0/0/	Wheeled tractors, Engine power exceeding 130 kw
	0/0/0	0	0	0	0	0	0	0//0	0/0/			0/0/	Wheeled tractors, Engine power exceeding 130 kw
	0/0/0	4	0	0	0	0	0	0//0	0/0/			0/0/	---Other
													Motor vehicles for the transport of ten or more persons, including the driver:
													-With only compression-ignition internal combustion piston engine (diesel or semidiesel):
	0/0/0	0	2.4	0	0	0	0	0//0	0/0/			0/0/	---Buses for transport passengers at airport
													---Other:
	/0/0		17.5		0		0	0//0	0/0/			0//	----With 30 seats or more
													----With 20 seats or more, but not exceeding 29 seats
	/0/0		17.5		0		0	0//0	0/0/			0//	Passenger buses, 20-23 seats, with compression- ignition internal combustion piston engine(with diesel or semidiesel engine)
	/0/0		17.5		0		0	0//0	0/0/			0//	Passenger buses, 24-29 seats, with compression- ignition internal combustion piston engine(diesel or semi-diesel)
	/0/0		17.5		0		0	0//0	0/0/			0//	----With 10 Seats or more, but not exceeding 19 seats
													--With both compression—ignition internal combustion piston engine (diesel or semi—diesel) and electric motor as motors for propulsion:
	0/0/0	0	2.4	0	0	0	0	0//0	0/0/			0/0/	---Buses for transport passengers at airport
													---Other:
	/0/0		17.5		0		0	0//0	0/0/			0//	----With 30 seats or more
													----With 20 seats or more, but not exceeding 29 seats

税则号列		货品名称〔CIQ扩展编码及品名—T2表示见附表2〕	最惠(%)	暂定税率	普通	增值/消费	出口退税	计量单位	监管条件	检验检疫	特殊证件对美关税
8702.2092	10	20≤座≤23同时装有压燃式活塞内燃发动机(柴油或半柴油发动机)及驱动电动机的客车〔999〕	15		230	13/5	13	辆/千克	46AOxy	LM	/
8702.2092	90	24≤座≤29同时装有压燃式活塞内燃发动机(柴油或半柴油发动机)及驱动电动机的客车〔999〕	15		230	13/5	13	辆/千克	46AOxy	LM	/
8702.2093		----10座及以上,但不超过19座〔999〕	15		230	13/5	13	辆/千克	46AOxy	LM	/
		-同时装有点燃往复式活塞内燃发动机及驱动电动机的车辆:									
8702.3010		---30座及以上(大型客车)〔999〕	15		90	13/	13	辆/千克	46AOxy	LM	/
8702.3020		---20座及以上,但不超过29座									
8702.3020	10	20≤座≤23同时装有点燃往复式活塞内燃发动机及驱动电动机的客车〔999〕	15		230	13/5	13	辆/千克	46AOxy	LM	/
8702.3020	90	24≤座≤29同时装有点燃往复式活塞内燃发动机及驱动电动机的客车〔999〕	15		230	13/5	13	辆/千克	46AOxy	LM	/
8702.3030		---10座及以上,但不超过19座〔999〕	15		230	13/5	13	辆/千克	46AOxy	LM	/
		-仅装有驱动电动机的车辆:									
8702.4010		---30座及以上(大型客车)〔999〕	15		90	13/	13	辆/千克	46AOxy	LM	/
8702.4020		---20座及以上,但不超过29座									
8702.4020	10	20≤座≤23仅装有驱动电动机的客车〔999〕	15		230	13/5	13	辆/千克	46AOxy	LM	/
8702.4020	90	24≤座≤29仅装有驱动电动机的客车〔999〕	15		230	13/5	13	辆/千克	46AOxy	LM	/
8702.4030		---10座及以上,但不超过19座〔999〕	15		230	13/5	13	辆/千克	46AOxy	LM	/
		-其他:									
8702.9010		---30座及以上(大型客车)〔999〕	15		90	13/	13	辆/千克	46AOxy	LM	/
8702.9020		---20座及以上,但不超过29座									
8702.9020	01	20≤座≤23装有非压燃式活塞内燃发动机的客车〔999〕	15		230	13/5	13	辆/千克	46AOxy	LM	/
8702.9020	90	24≤座≤29装有非压燃式活塞内燃发动机的客车〔999〕	15		230	13/	13	辆/千克	46AOxy	LM	/
8702.9030		---10座及以上,但不超过19座〔999〕	15		230	13/5	13	辆/千克	46AOxy	LM	/
87.03		**主要用于载人的机动车辆(税目87.02的货品除外),包括旅行小客车及赛车:**									
		-雪地行走专用车;高尔夫球车及类似车辆:									
		---高尔夫球车及类似车辆:									
8703.1011		----全地形车〔101电动全地形车,102内燃机动全地形车,103混合动力全地形车,104其他能源全地形车〕	15		150	13/	13	辆/千克	46xy		/
8703.1019		----其他〔999〕	15		150	13/	13	辆/千克	6		/
8703.1090		---其他〔999〕	15		150	13/	13	辆/千克	6		/
		-仅装有点燃往复式活塞内燃发动机的其他车辆:									
		--气缸容量(排气量)不超过1000毫升:									
8703.2130		---小轿车									
8703.2130	10	仅装有排量≤1升的点燃往复式活塞内燃发动机的小轿车〔999〕	15		230	13/1	13	辆/千克	46AOxy	LM	/
8703.2130	90	仅装有排量≤1升的点燃往复式活塞内燃发动机小轿车的成套散件〔999〕	15		230	13/	13	辆/千克	46Oxy		/
8703.2140		---越野生(4轮驱动)									
8703.2140	10	仅装有排量≤1升的点燃往复式活塞内燃发动机的越野车(4轮驱动)〔999〕	15		230	13/1	13	辆/千克	46AOxy	LM	/
8703.2140	90	仅装有排量≤1升的点燃往复式活塞内燃发动机的越野车(4轮驱动)的成套散件〔999〕	15		230	13/	13	辆/千克	46Oxy		/
8703.2150		---9座及以下的小客车									
8703.2150	10	仅装有排量≤1升的点燃往复式活塞内燃发动机的小客车(9座及以下)〔999〕	15		230	13/1	13	辆/千克	46AOxy	LM	/
8703.2150	90	仅装有排量≤1升的点燃往复式活塞内燃发动机的小客车的成套散件(9座及以下)〔999〕	15		230	13/	13	辆/千克	46Oxy		/
8703.2190		---其他									
8703.2190	10	仅装有排量≤1升的点燃往复式活塞内燃发动机的其他载人车辆〔999〕	15		230	13/1	13	辆/千克	46AOxy	LM	/
8703.2190	90	仅装有排量≤1升的点燃往复式活塞内燃发动机的其他载人车辆的成套散件〔999〕	15		230	13/	13	辆/千克	46Oxy		/

协定税率 %										特惠税率 %			
亚太5国	东/冰/格	巴基斯坦	韩国	瑞士	哥达	秘鲁	澳大利亚	新西/坡/智	港/澳/台	亚太2国	老/柬/缅	36/3/1	Article Description
	/0/0		17.5		0		0	0//0	0/0/			0//	Passenger buses, 20-23 seats, with compression- ignition internal combustion piston engine(with diesel or semidiesel engine, with drive motor)
	/0/0		17.5		0		0	0//0	0/0/			0//	
	/0/0		17.5		0		0	0//0	0/0/				----With 10 seats or more.but not exceeding 19 seats
													-With both spark－ignition internal combustion reciprocating piston engine and electric motor as motors for propulsion:
	5/0/0		17.5		0		0	0//0	0/0/			0//	---With 30 seats or more
													---With 20 seats or more.but not exceeding 29 seats
	5/0/0		17.5		0		0	0//0	0/0/			0//	Passenger buses, 20-23 seats, with spark-ignition internal combustion reciprocating piston engine, with drive motor
	5/0/0		17.5		0		0	0//0	0/0/			0//	Passenger buses, 24-29 seats, with spark-ignition internal combustion reciprocating piston engine, with drive motor
	5/0/0		17.5		0	0	0	0//0	0/0/			0/0/	---With 10 seats or more, but not exceeding 19 seats
													-With only electric motor for propulsion:
	5/0/0		17.5		0		0	0//0	0/0/			0//	---With 30 seats or more
													---With 20 seats or more, but not exceeding 29 seats
	5/0/0		17.5		0		0	0//0	0/0/			0//	Passenger buses, 20-23 seats, with drive motor
	5/0/0		17.5		0		0	0//0	0/0/			0//	Passenger buses, 24-29 seats, with drive motor
	5/0/0		17.5		0	0	0	0//0	0/0/			0/0/	---With 10 seats or more, but not exceeding 19 seats
													-Other:
	5/0/0		17.5		0		0	0//0	0/0/			0//	---With 30 seats or more
													---With 20 seats or more, but not exceeding 29 seats
	5/0/0		17.5		0		0	0//0	0/0/			0//	Buses for transport passengers, with non-compression-ignition internal combustion piston engine, with 20～23 seats
	5/0/0		17.5		0		0	0//0	0/0/			0//	Buses for transport passengers, with non-compression-ignition internal combustion piston engine, with 24～29 seats
	5/0/0		17.5		0	0	0	0//0	0/0/			0/0/	---With 10 seats or more, but not exceeding 19 seats
													Motor cars and other motor vehicles principally designed for the transport of persons (other than those of headingNo. 87. 02), including station wagons and racing cars:
													-Vehicles specially designed for travelling on snow; golf cars and similar vehicles:
													---Golf cars and similar vehicles
	0/0/0		17.5		0	0	0	0/0/0	0/0/			0/0/	---All terrain vehicle
	0/0/0	25			0	0	0	0/0/0	0/0/			0/0/	----Other
	0/0/0				0	0	0	0/0/0	0/0/			0/0/	---Other
													-Other vehicles, with spark-ignition internal combustion reciprocating piston engine:
													--Of a cylinder capacity not exceeding 1000 cc:
													---Saloon cars
13.5	/0/	22.5			0		0	0//0	0/0/				Saloon cars of cylinder capacity not exceeding 1L, with spark-ignition internal combustion eciprocating piston engine
13.5	/0/	22.5			0		0	0//0	0/0/				Complete parts of saloon cars with spark-ignition internal combustion reciprocating piston engine, cylinder capacity≤1L
													---Gross-country cars (4WD)
13.5	/0/	22.5			0		0	0//0	0/0/				Off-road vehicles(4WD) of cylinder capacity not exceeding 1L, with spark-ignition internal combustion eciprocating piston engine
13.5	/0/	22.5			0		0	0//0	0/0/				Complete parts of gross-country cars (4WD) with spark-ignition internal combustion reciprocating piston engine, cylinger capacity≤1L
													---Station wagons (with 9 seats or less)
13.5	/0/	22.5			0		0	0//0	0/0/				Station wagons(9 seats or less), of a cylinder capacity exceeding 1L, with spark-ignition internal combustion reciprocating piston engine
13.5	/0/	22.5			0		0	0//0	0/0/				Complete parts of station wagons (with 9 seats or less) with spark-ignition internal combustion reciprocating piston engine, cylinder capacity≤1L
													---Other
13.5	/0/	22.5			0		0	0//0	0/0/				Other passenger vehicles of a cylinder capacity exceeding 1L with spark-ignition internal combustion reciprocating piston engine
13.5	/0/	22.5			0		0	0//0	0/0/				Complete parts of other vehicles with spark-ignition internal combustion reciprocating piston engine, cylinder capacity≤1L

税则号列		货品名称〔CIQ扩展编码及品名－T2表示见附表2〕	最惠(%)	暂定税率	普通	增值/消费	出口退税	计量单位	监管条件	检验检疫	特殊证件对美关税
		--气缸容量(排气量)超过1000毫升,但不超过1500毫升:									
8703.2230		---小轿车									
8703.2230	10	仅装有1<排量≤1.5升点燃往复式活塞内燃发动机小轿车〔999〕	15		230	13/3	13	辆/千克	46AOxy	LM	/
8703.2230	90	仅装有1<排量≤1.5升点燃往复式活塞内燃发动机小轿车的成套散件〔999〕	15		230	13/	13	辆/千克	46Oxy		/
8703.2240		---越野车(4轮驱动)									
8703.2240	10	仅装有1<排量≤1.5升点燃往复活塞内燃发动机四轮驱动越野车〔999〕	15		230	13/3	13	辆/千克	46AOxy	LM	/
8703.2240	90	仅装有1<排量≤1.5升点燃往复活塞内燃发动机四轮驱动越野车的成套散件〔999〕	15		230	13/	13	辆/千克	46Oxy		/
8703.2250		---9座及以下的小客车									
8703.2250	10	仅装有1<排量≤1.5升点燃往复式活塞内燃发动机小客车(≤9座)〔999〕	15		230	13/3	13	辆/千克	46AOxy	LM	/
8703.2250	90	仅装有1<排量≤1.5升点燃往复式活塞内燃发动机小客车的成套散件(≤9座)〔999〕	15		230	13/	13	辆/千克	46Oxy		/
8703.2290		---其他									
8703.2290	10	仅装有1<排量≤1.5升点燃往复式活塞内燃发动机其他载人车辆〔999〕	15		230	13/3	13	辆/千克	46AOxy	LM	/
8703.2290	90	仅装有1<排量≤1.5升点燃往复式活塞内燃发动机其他载人车的成套散件〔999〕	15		230	13/	13	辆/千克	46Oxy		/
		--气缸容量(排气量)超过1500毫升,但不超过3000毫升:									
		---气缸容量(排气量)超过1500毫升,但不超过2000毫升:									
8703.2341		----小轿车									
8703.2341	10	仅装有1.5<排量≤2升的点燃往复式活塞内燃发动机小轿车〔999〕	15		230	13/5	13	辆/千克	46AOxy	LM	/
8703.2341	90	仅装有1.5<排量≤2升的点燃往复式活塞内燃发动机小轿车的成套散件〔999〕	15		230	13/	13	辆/千克	46Oxy		/
8703.2342		----越野车(4轮驱动)									
8703.2342	10	仅装有1.5<排量≤2升的点燃往复式活塞内燃发动机越野车(4轮驱动)〔999〕	15		230	13/5	13	辆/千克	46AOxy	LM	/
8703.2342	90	仅装有1.5<排量≤2升的点燃往复式活塞内燃发动机越野车的成套散件(4轮驱动)〔999〕	15		230	13/	13	辆/千克	46Oxy		/
8703.2343		----9座及以下的小客车									
8703.2343	10	仅装有1.5<排量≤2升的点燃往复式活塞内燃发动机小客车(9座及以下的)〔999〕	15		230	13/5	13	辆/千克	46AOxy	LM	/
8703.2343	90	仅装有1.5<排量≤2升的点燃往复式活塞内燃发动机小客车的成套散件(9座及以下的)〔999〕	15		230	13/	13	辆/千克	46Oxy		/
8703.2349		----其他									
8703.2349	10	仅装有1.5<排量≤2升的点燃往复式活塞内燃发动机的其他载人车辆〔999〕	15		230	13/5	13	辆/千克	46AOxy	LM	/
8703.2349	90	仅装有1.5<排量≤2升的点燃往复式活塞内燃发动机的其他载人车辆的成套散件〔999〕	15		230	13/	13	辆/千克	46Oxy		/
		---气缸容量(排气量)超过2000毫升,但不超过2500毫升:									
8703.2351		----小轿车									
8703.2351	10	仅装有2<排量≤2.5升的点燃往复式活塞内燃发动机小轿车〔999〕	15		230	13/9	13	辆/千克	46AOxy	LM	/
8703.2351	90	仅装有2<排量≤2.5升的点燃往复式活塞内燃发动机小轿车的成套散件〔999〕	15		230	13/	13	辆/千克	46Oxy		/
8703.2352		----越野车(4轮驱动)									

协定税率 %										特惠税率 %			
亚太5国	东/冰/格	巴基斯坦	韩国	瑞士	哥达	秘鲁	澳大利亚	新西/坡/智	港/澳/台	亚太2国	老/柬/缅	36/3/1	Article Description
													--Of a cylinder capacity exceeding 1000ccc but not exceeding 1500cc:
													---Saloon cars
13.5	/0/	22.5	22.5		0		0	0//0	0/0/				Saloon cars of cylinder capacity exceeding 1L but not exceeding 1. 5L, with spark-ignition internal combustion eciprocating piston engine
13.5	/0/	22.5	22.5		0		0	0//0	0/0/				Complete parts of saloon car with spark-igition internal combustion reciprocating piston engine, 1L<cylinder capacity≤1. 5L
													---Cross-country cars (4WD)
13.5	/0/	22.5			0		0	0//0	0/0/				Off-road vehicles(4WD) of cylinder capacity exceeding 1L but not exceeding 1.5L, with spark-ignition internal combustion eciprocating piston engine
13.5	/0/	22.5			0		0	0//0	0/0/				Complete parts of cross-country cars(4WD) with spark-ignition inernal combustion reciprocating piston engine, 1L<cylinder capacity≤1. 5L
													---Station wagons (with 9 seats or less)
13.5	/0/	22.5			0		0	0//0	0/0/				Station wagons(9 seats or less) of cylinder capacity exceeding 1L but not exceeding 1.5L, with spark-ignition internal combustion eciprocating piston engine
13.5	/0/	22.5			0		0	0//0	0/0/				Complete parts of station wagons(with 9seats or less) with spark-ignition internal combustion reciprocating piston engine, 1L<cylinder capacity≤1. 5L
													---Other
13.5	/0/	22.5			0		0	0//0	0/0/				Other passenger vehicles of cylinder capacity exceeding 1L but not exceeding 1.5L, with spark-ignition internal combustion eciprocating piston engine
13.5	/0/	22.5			0		0	0//0	0/0/				Complete parts of other vehicles with spark-ingition internal combustion reciprocating piston engine, 1L<cylinder capacity≤1. 5L
													--Of a cylinder capacity exceeding 1500cc but not exceeding 3000cc:
													---Of a cylinder capacity exceeding 1500cc but not exceeding 2000cc:
													----Saloon cars
13.5	/0/	22.5	22.5		0		10	0//0	0/0/				Saloon cars of cylinder capacity exceeding 1.5L but not exceeding 2L, with spark-ignition internal combustion eciprocating piston engine
13.5	/0/	22.5	22.5		0		10	0//0	0/0/				Complete parts of saloon cars with spark-ignition internal cmbustion reciprocating piston engine, 1. 5L<cylinder capacity≤2L
													----Cross-country cars (4WD)
13.5	/0/	22.5	22.5		0		10	0//0	0/0/				Off-road vehicles(4WD) of cylinder capacity exceeding 1.5L but not exceeding 2L, with spark-ignition internal combustion eciprocating piston engine
13.5	/0/	22.5	22.5		0		10	0//0	0/0/				Complete parts of cross-country cars (4WD) with spark-ignition internal combustion reciprocating piston engine, 1. 5L<cylinder capacity≤2L
													----Station wagons (with 9 seats or less)
13.5	/0/	22.5	22.5		0		10	0//0	0/0/				Station wagons(9 seats or less) of cylinder capacity exceeding 1.5L but not exceeding 2L, with spark-ignition internal combustion eciprocating piston engine
13.5	/0/	22.5	22.5		0		10	0//0	0/0/				Complete parts of station wagons(with 9 seats or less) with spark-ignition internal combustion reciprocating piston engine, 1. 5L<cylinder capacity≤2L
													----Other
13.5	/0/	22.5			0		10	0//0	0/0/				Other passenger vehicles of cylinder capacity exceeding 1.5L but not exceeding 2L, with spark-ignition internal combustion eciprocating piston engine
13.5	/0/	22.5			0		10	0//0	0/0/				Complete parts of other motor vehicles principally designed for the transport of person's with spark-ignition internal combustion reciprocating piston engine, 1. 5L<cylinder capacity≤2L
													---Of a culinder capacity exceeding 2000cc but not exceeding 2500cc:
													----Saloon cars
13.5	/0/	22.5	22.5		0		10	0//0	0/0/				Saloon cars of cylinder capacity exceeding 2L but not exceeding 2. 5L, with spark-ignition internal combustion eciprocating piston engine
13.5	/0/	22.5	22.5		0		10	0//0	0/0/				Complete parts of saloon cars with spark-ignition internal combustion reciprocating piston engine, 2L<cylinder capacity≤2. 5L
													----Cross-country cars (4WD)

税则号列	货品名称〔CIQ扩展编码及品名—T2表示见附表2〕	最惠(%)	暂定税率	普通	增值/消费	出口退税	计量单位	监管条件	检验检疫	特殊证件对美关税
8703.2352 10	仅装有2<排量≤2.5升的点燃往复式活塞内燃发动机越野车(4轮驱动)〔999〕	15		230	13/9	13	辆/千克	46AOxy	LM	/
8703.2352 90	仅装有2<排量≤2.5升的点燃往复式活塞内燃发动机越野车的成套散件(4轮驱动)〔999〕	15		230	13/	13	辆/千克	46Oxy		/
8703.2353	----9座及以下的小客车									
8703.2353 10	仅装有2<排量≤2.5升的点燃往复式活塞内燃发动机小客车(9座及以下的)〔999〕	15		230	13/9	13	辆/千克	46AOxy	LM	/
8703.2353 90	仅装有2<排量≤2.5升的点燃往复式活塞内燃发动机的小客车的成套散件(9座及以下的)〔999〕	15		230	13/	13	辆/千克	46Oxy		/
8703.2359	----其他									
8703.2359 10	仅装有2<排量≤2.5升的点燃往复式活塞内燃发动机的其他载人车辆〔999〕	15		230	13/9	13	辆/千克	46AOxy	LM	/
8703.2359 90	仅装有2<排量≤2.5升的点燃往复式活塞内燃发动机的其他载人车辆的成套散件〔999〕	15		230	13/	13	辆/千克	46Oxy		/
	---气缸容量(排气量)超过2500毫升,但不超过3000毫升:									
8703.2361	----小轿车									
8703.2361 10	仅装有2.5<排量≤3升的点燃往复式活塞内燃发动机小轿车〔999〕	15		270	13/12	13	辆/千克	46AOxy	ML	/
8703.2361 90	仅装有2.5<排量≤3升的点燃往复式活塞内燃发动机小轿车的成套散件〔999〕	15		270	13/	13	辆/千克	46Oxy		/
8703.2362	----越野车(4轮驱动)									
8703.2362 10	仅装有2.5<排量≤3升的点燃往复式活塞内燃发动机越野车(4轮驱动)〔999〕	15		270	13/12	13	辆/千克	46AOxy	ML	/
8703.2362 90	仅装有2.5<排量≤3升的点燃往复式活塞内燃发动机越野车的成套散件(4轮驱动)〔999〕	15		270	13/	13	辆/千克	46Oxy		/
8703.2363	----9座及以下的小客车									
8703.2363 10	仅装有2.5<排量≤3升的点燃往复式活塞内燃发动机小客车(9座及以下的)〔999〕	15		270	13/12	13	辆/千克	46AOxy	ML	/
8703.2363 90	仅装有2.5<排量≤3升的点燃往复式活塞内燃发动机小客车的成套散件(9座及以下的)〔999〕	15		270	13/	13	辆/千克	46Oxy		/
8703.2369	----其他									
8703.2369 10	仅装有2.5<排量≤3升的点燃往复式活塞内燃发动机的其他载人车辆〔999〕	15		270	13/12	13	辆/千克	46AOxy	ML	/
8703.2369 90	仅装有2.5<排量≤3升的点燃往复式活塞内燃发动机的其他载人车辆的成套散件〔999〕	15		270	13/12	13	辆/千克	46Oxy		/
	--气缸容量(排气量)超过3000毫升:									
	---气缸容量(排气量)超过3000毫升,但不超过4000毫升:									
8703.2411	----小轿车									
8703.2411 10	仅装有3<排量≤4升的点燃往复式活塞内燃发动机小轿车〔999〕	15		270	13/25	13	辆/千克	46AOxy	LM	/
8703.2411 90	仅装有3<排量≤4升的点燃往复式活塞内燃发动机小轿车的成套散件〔999〕	15		270	13/	13	辆/千克	46Oxy		/
8703.2412	----越野车(4轮驱动)									
8703.2412 10	仅装有3<排量≤4升的点燃往复式活塞内燃发动机越野车(4轮驱动)〔999〕	15		270	13/25	13	辆/千克	46AOxy	LM	/
8703.2412 90	仅装有3<排量≤4升的点燃往复式活塞内燃发动机越野车的成套散件(4轮驱动)〔999〕	15		270	13/	13	辆/千克	46Oxy		/
8703.2413	----9座及以下的小客车									

协定税率 %										特惠税率 %			
亚太5国	东/冰/格	巴基斯坦	韩国	瑞士	哥达	秘鲁	澳大利亚	新西/坡/智	港/澳/台	亚太2国	老/柬/缅	36/3/1	Article Description
13.5	/0/	22.5	22.5		0		10	0//0	0/0/				Off-road vehicles(4WD) of cylinder capacity exceeding 2L but not exceeding 2.5L, with spark-ignition internal combustion eciprocating piston engine
13.5	/0/	22.5	22.5		0		10	0//0	0/0/				Complete parts of crass-country cars(4WD) with spark-ignition internal combustion reciprocating piston engine, 2L< cylinder capacity ≤ 2. 5L
													----Station wagons (with 9 seats or less)
13.5	/0/	22.5	22.5		0		10	0//0	0/0/				Station wagons(9 seats or less) of cylinder capacity exceeding 2L but not exceeding 2.5L, with spark-ignition internal combustion eciprocating piston engine
13.5	/0/	22.5	22.5		0		10	0//0	0/0/				Complete parts of station wagons(with 9 seats or less) with spark-ignition internal combustion reciprocating piston engine, 2L< cylinder capacity ≤ 2. 5L
													----Other
13.5	/0/	22.5			0		10	0//0	0/0/				Other passenger vehicles of cylinder capacity exceeding 2L but not exceeding 2.5L, with spark-ignition internal combustion eciprocating piston engine
13.5	/0/	22.5			0		10	0//0	0/0/				Complete parts of other motor vehicles(with 9 seats or less) designed for transport of person's, with spark-ignition internal combustion reciprocating piston engine, 2L< cylinder capacity ≤ 2. 5L
													--Of a cylinder capacity exceeding 2500cc but not exceeding 3000cc:
													----Saloon cars
13.5	/0/	22.5	22.5		0		10	0//0	0/0/				Saloon cars of cylinder capacity exceeding 2.5L but not exceeding 3L, with spark-ignition internal combustion eciprocating piston engine
13.5	/0/	22.5	22.5		0		10	0//0	0/0/				Complete parts of saloon cars with spark-ignition internal combustion reciprocating piston engine, 2. 5L< cylinder capacity ≤ 3L
													----Cross-country cars (4WD)
13.5	0/0/	22.5			0		10	0/0/0	0/0/				Off-road vehicles(4WD) of cylinder capacity exceeding 2.5L but not exceeding 3L, with spark-ignition internal combustion eciprocating piston engine
13.5	0/0/	22.5			0		10	0/0/0	0/0/				Complete parts of cross-country cars (4WD) with spark-ignition internal combustion reciprocating piston engine, 2. 5L< cylinder capacity ≤ 3L
													----Station wagons (with 9 seats or less)
13.5	0/0/	22.5	22.5		0		10	0/0/0	0/0/				Station wagons(9 seats or less) of cylinder capacity exceeding 2.5L but not exceeding 3L, with spark-ignition internal combustion eciprocating piston engine
13.5	0/0/	22.5	22.5		0		10	0/0/0	0/0/				Complete parts of station wagons(with 9 seats or less) with spark-ignition internal combustion reciporcating piston engine, 2. 5L< cylinder capacity ≤ 3L
													----Other
13.5	0/0/	22.5			0		10	0/0/0	0/0/				Other passenger vehicles of cylinder capacity exceeding 2.5L but not exceeding 3L, with spark-ignition internal combustion eciprocating piston engine
13.5	0/0/	22.5			0		10	0/0/0	0/0/				Complete parts of other passenger vehicles of a cylinder capacity exceeding 2.5L but not exceeding 3L, with spark-ignition internal combustion reciprocating piston engine
													--Of a cylinder capacity exceeding 3000cc:
													---Of a cylinder capacity exceeding 3000cc but not exceeding 4000cc:
													----Saloon cars
13.5	/0/	22.5	22.5		0		10	0//0	0/0/			0//	Saloon cars of cylinder capacity exceeding 3L but not exceeding 4L, with spark-ignition internal combustion eciprocating piston engine
13.5	/0/	22.5	22.5		0		10	0//0	0/0/			0//	Complete parts of saloon cars with spark-ignition internal combustion reciprocating piston engine, 3L< cylinder capacity ≤ 4L
													----Cross-country cars (4WD)
13.5	/0/	22.5	22.5		0		10	0//0	0/0/			0//	Off-road vehicles(4WD) of cylinder capacity exceeding 3L but not exceeding 4L, with spark-ignition internal combustion eciprocating piston engine
13.5	/0/	22.5	22.5		0		10	0//0	0/0/			0//	Complete parts of crass-country cars(4WD) with spark-ignition internal combustion reciprocating piston engine, 3L< cylinder capacity ≤ 4L
													----Station wagons (with 9 seats or less)

税则号列	货品名称〔CIQ 扩展编码及品名—T2 表示见附表 2〕	最惠(%)	暂定税率	普通	增值/消费	出口退税	计量单位	监管条件	检验检疫	特殊证件对美关税
8703.2413 10	仅装有 3<排量≤4 升的点燃往复式活塞内燃发动机的小客车(9 座及以下的)〔999〕	15		270	13/25	13	辆/千克	46AOxy	LM	/
8703.2413 90	仅装有 3<排量≤4 升的点燃往复式活塞内燃发动机的小客车的成套散件(9 座及以下的)〔999〕	15		270	13/	13	辆/千克	46Oxy		/
8703.2419	----其他									
8703.2419 10	仅装有 3<排量≤4 升的点燃往复式活塞内燃发动机的其他载人车辆〔999,101 福特 F150 猛禽〕	15		270	13/25	13	辆/千克	46AOxy	LM	/
8703.2419 90	仅装有 3<排量≤4 升的点燃往复式活塞内燃发动机的其他载人车辆的成套散件〔999〕	15		270	13/25	13	辆/千克	46Oxy		/
	---气缸容量(排气量)超过 4000 毫升:									
8703.2421	----小轿车									
8703.2421 10	仅装有排气量>4 升的点燃往复式活塞内燃发动机小轿车〔999〕	15		270	13/40	13	辆/千克	46AOxy	LM	/
8703.2421 90	仅装有排气量>4 升的点燃往复式活塞内燃发动机小轿车的成套散件〔999〕	15		270	13/	13	辆/千克	46Oxy		/
8703.2422	----越野车(4 轮驱动)									
8703.2422 10	仅装有排气量>4 升的点燃往复式活塞内燃发动机越野车(4 轮驱动)〔999〕	15		270	13/40	13	辆/千克	46AOxy	LM	/
8703.2422 90	仅装有排气量>4 升的点燃往复式活塞内燃发动机越野车的成套散件(4 轮驱动)〔999〕	15		270	13/	13	辆/千克	46Oxy		/
8703.2423	----9 座及以下的小客车									
8703.2423 10	仅装有排气量>4 升的点燃往复式活塞内燃发动机的小客车(9 座及以下的)〔999〕	15		270	13/40	13	辆/千克	46AOxy	LM	/
8703.2423 90	仅装有排气量>4 升的点燃往复式活塞内燃发动机的小客车的成套散件(9 座及以下的)〔999〕	15		270	13/	13	辆/千克	46Oxy		/
8703.2429	----其他									
8703.2429 10	仅装有排气量>4 升的点燃往复式活塞内燃发动机的其他载人车辆〔999〕	15		270	13/40	13	辆/千克	46AOxy	LM	/
8703.2429 90	仅装有排气量>4 升的点燃往复式活塞内燃发动机的其他载人车辆的成套散件〔999〕	15		270	13/40	13	辆/千克	46Oxy		/
	-仅装有压燃式活塞内燃发动机(柴油或半柴油发动机)的其他车辆:									
	--气缸容量(排气量)不超过 1500 毫升:									
	---气缸容量(排气量)不超过 1000 毫升:									
8703.3111	----小轿车									
8703.3111 10	仅装有排气量≤1 升的压燃式活塞内燃发动机小轿车〔999〕	15		230	13/1	13	辆/千克	46AOxy	LM	/
8703.3111 90	仅装有排气量≤1 升的压燃式活塞内燃发动机小轿车的成套散件〔999〕	15		230	13/	13	辆/千克	46Oxy		/
8703.3119	----其他									
8703.3119 10	仅装有排气量≤1 升的压燃式活塞内燃发动机的其他载人车辆〔999〕	15		230	13/1	13	辆/千克	46AOxy	LM	/
8703.3119 90	仅装有排气量≤1 升的压燃式活塞内燃发动机的其他载人车辆的成套散件〔999〕	15		230	13/	13	辆/千克	46Oxy		/
	---气缸容量(排气量)超过 1000 毫升,但不超过 1500 毫升:									
8703.3121	----小轿车									
8703.3121 10	仅装有 1 升<排气量≤1.5 升的压燃式活塞内燃发动机小轿车〔999〕	15		230	13/3	13	辆/千克	46AOxy	LM	/
8703.3121 90	仅装有 1 升<排气量≤1.5 升的压燃式活塞内燃发动机小轿车的成套散件〔999〕	15		230	13/	13	辆/千克	46Oxy		/
8703.3122	----越野车(4 轮驱动)									
8703.3122 10	仅装有 1 升<排气量≤1.5 升的压燃式活塞内燃发动机越野车(4 轮驱动)〔999〕	15		230	13/3	13	辆/千克	46AOxy	LM	/
8703.3122 90	仅装有 1 升<排气量≤1.5 升的压燃式活塞内燃发动机越野车的成套散件(4 轮驱动)〔999〕	15		230	13/	13	辆/千克	46Oxy		/

协定税率 %										特惠税率 %			
亚太5国	东/冰/格	巴基斯坦	韩国	瑞士	哥达	秘鲁	澳大利亚	新西/坡/智	港/澳/台	亚太2国	老/柬/缅	36/3/1	Article Description
13.5	/0/	22.5			0		10	0//0	0/0/			0//	Station wagons(9 seats or less) of cylinder capacity exceeding 3L but not exceeding 4L, with spark-ignition internal combustion eciprocating piston engine
13.5	/0/	22.5			0		10	0//0	0/0/			0//	Complete parts of station wagons(with 9 seats or less)with spark-ignition internal combustion reciprocating piston engine, 3＜cylinder capacity≤4L
													----Other
13.5	/0/	22.5			0		10	0//0	0/0/			0//	Other passenger vehicles of cylinder capacity exceeding 3L but not exceeding 4L, with spark-ignition internal combustion eciprocating piston engine
13.5	/0/	22.5			0		10	0//0	0/0/			0//	Complete parts of other passenger vehicles of a cylinder capacity exceeding 3L but not exceeding 4L, with spark-ignition internal combustion reciprocating piston engine
													---Of a cylinder capacity exceeding 4000cc:
													----Saloon cars
13.5	/0/	22.5	22.5		0		10	0//0	0/0/			0//	Saloon cars of cylinder capacity exceeding 4L, with spark-ignition internal combustion eciprocating piston engine
13.5	/0/	22.5	22.5		0		10	0//0	0/0/			0//	Complete parts of saloon cars with spork-ignition internal combustion reciprocating piston engine, cylinder capacity＞4L
													----Cross-country cars (4WD)
13.5	/0/	22.5			0		10	0//0	0/0/			0//	Off-road vehicles(4WD) of cylinder capacity exceeding 4L, with spark-ignition internal combustion eciprocating piston engine
13.5	/0/	22.5			0		10	0//0	0/0/			0//	Complete parts of cross-country cars with spark-ignition internal combustion reciprocating piston engine, cylinder capacity＞4L
													----Station wagons (with 9 seats or less)
13.5	/0/	22.5			0		10	0//0	0/0/			0//	Station wagons(9 seats or less) of cylinder capacity exceeding 4L, with spark-ignition internal combustion eciprocating piston engine
13.5	/0/	22.5			0		10	0//0	0/0/			0//	Complete parts of station wagons with spark-ignition internal combustion reciporcating piston engine, cylinder capacity＞4L(with 9 seats or less)
													----Other
13.5	/0/	22.5			0		10	0//0	0/0/			0//	Other passenger vehicles of cylinder capacity exceeding 4L, with spark-ignition internal combustion eciprocating piston engine
13.5	/0/	22.5			0		10	0//0	0/0/			0//	Complete parts of other passenger vehicles of a cylinder capacity exceeding 4L, with spark-ignition internal combustion reciprocating piston engine
													-Other vehicles, with compression-ignition internal combustion piston engine(diesel or semi-diesel):
													--Of a cylinder capacity not exceedlirg 1500cc:
													---Of a cylinder capacity not exceeding 1000 cc:
													----Saloon cars
	/0/0				0		10	0//0	0/0/			0//	Saloon cars of a cylinder capacity not exceeding 1L, with compression-ignition internal combustion reciprocating piston engine
	/0/0				0		10	0//0	0/0/			0//	Complete parts of saloon cars with compression-ignition internal combustion piston engine, cylinder capacity≤1L
													----Other
	0/0/0				0	0	10	0/0/0	0/0/			0/0/	Other passenger cars of a cylinder capacity not exceeding 1L, with compression-ignition internal combustion reciprocating piston engine
	0/0/0				0	0	10	0/0/0	0/0/			0/0/	Complete parts of other moter vehicles designed for transport of person's with compression-ignition internal cmobustion piston engine, cylinder capaeity≤1L
													---Of a cylinder capacity exceeding 1000cc but not exceeding 1500cc:
													----Saloon cars
	/0/0				0		10	0//0	0/0/				Saloon cars of a cylinder capacity exceeding 1L but not exceeding 1.5L, with compression-ignition internal combustion reciprocating piston engine
	/0/0				0		10	0//0	0/0/				Complete parts of salotn cars with compression-ignition internal combustion piston engine, 1L＜cylinder capacity≤1.5L
													----Cross-country cars (4WD)
	/0/0				0		10	0//0	0/0/				Off-road vehicles(4WD) of cylinder capacity exceeding 1L but not exceeding 1.5L, with compression-ignition internal combustion reciprocating piston engine
	/0/0				0		10	0//0	0/0/				Complete parts of cross-country cars(4WD) with compression-ignition internal combustion piston engine, 1L＜cylinder≤1.5L

税则号列	货品名称〔CIQ扩展编码及品名—T2表示见附表2〕	最惠(%)	暂定税率	普通	增值/消费	出口退税	计量单位	监管条件	检验检疫	特殊证件对美关税
8703.3123	----9座及以下的小客车									
8703.3123 10	仅装有1升<排气量≤1.5升的压燃式活塞内燃发动机小客车(9座及以下的)〔999〕	15		230	13/3	13	辆/千克	46AOxy	LM	/
8703.3123 90	仅装有1升<排气量≤1.5升的压燃式活塞内燃发动机小客车的成套散件(9座及以下的)〔999〕	15		230	13/	13	辆/千克	46Oxy		/
8703.3129	----其他									
8703.3129 10	仅装有1升<排气量≤1.5升的压燃式活塞内燃发动机的其他载人车辆〔999〕	15		230	13/3	13	辆/千克	46AOxy	LM	/
8703.3129 90	仅装有1升<排气量≤1.5升的装压燃式活塞内燃发动机的其他载人车辆的成套散件〔999〕	15		230	13/	13	辆/千克	46Oxy		/
	--气缸容量(排气量)超过1500毫升,但不超过2500毫升:									
	---气缸容量(排气量)超过1500毫升,但不超过2000毫升:									
8703.3211	----小轿车									
8703.3211 10	仅装有1.5<排量≤2升的压燃式活塞内燃发动机小轿车〔999〕	15		230	13/5	13	辆/千克	46AOxy	LM	/
8703.3211 90	仅装有1.5<排量≤2升的压燃式活塞内燃发动机小轿车的成套散件〔999〕	15		230	13/	13	辆/千克	46Oxy		/
8703.3212	----越野车(4轮驱动)									
8703.3212 10	仅装有1.5<排量≤2升的压燃式活塞内燃发动机越野车(4轮驱动)〔999〕	15		230	13/5	13	辆/千克	46AOxy	LM	/
8703.3212 90	仅装有1.5<排量≤2升的压燃式活塞内燃发动机越野车的成套散件(4轮驱动)〔999〕	15		230	13/	13	辆/千克	46Oxy		/
8703.3213	----9座及以下的小客车									
8703.3213 10	仅装有1.5<排量≤2升的装压燃式活塞内燃发动机小客车(9座及以下的)〔999〕	15		230	13/5	13	辆/千克	46AOxy	LM	/
8703.3213 90	仅装有1.5<排量≤2升的压燃式活塞内燃发动机小客车的成套散件(9座及以下的)〔999〕	15		230	13/	13	辆/千克	46Oxy		/
8703.3219	----其他									
8703.3219 10	仅装有1.5<排量≤2升的压燃式活塞内燃发动机的其他载人车辆〔999〕	15		230	13/5	13	辆/千克	46AOxy	LM	/
8703.3219 90	仅装有1.5<排量≤2升的压燃式活塞内燃发动机的其他载人车辆的成套散件〔999〕	15		230	13/	13	辆/千克	46Oxy		/
	---气缸容量(排气量)超过2000毫升,但不超过2500毫升:									
8703.3221	----小轿车									
8703.3221 10	仅装有2<排量≤2.5升的压燃式活塞内燃发动机小轿车〔999〕	15		230	13/9	13	辆/千克	46AOxy	LM	/
8703.3221 90	仅装有2<排量≤2.5升的燃式活塞内燃发动机小轿车的成套散件〔999〕	15		230	13/	13	辆/千克	46Oxy		/
8703.3222	----越野车(4轮驱动)									
8703.3222 10	仅装有2<排量≤2.5升的燃式活塞内燃发动机越野车(4轮驱动)〔999〕	15		230	13/9	13	辆/千克	46AOxy	LM	/
8703.3222 90	仅装有2<排量≤2.5升的燃式活塞内燃发动机越野车的成套散件(4轮驱动)〔999〕	15		230	13/	13	辆/千克	46Oxy		/
8703.3223	----9座及以下的小客车									
8703.3223 10	仅装有2<排量≤2.5升的燃式活塞内燃发动机小客车(9座及以下的)〔999〕	15		230	13/9	13	辆/千克	46AOxy	LM	/
8703.3223 90	仅装有2<排量≤2.5升的压燃式活塞内燃发动机小客车的成套散件(9座及以下的)〔999〕	15		230	13/	13	辆/千克	46Oxy		/
8703.3229	----其他									

协定税率 %										特惠税率 %			Article Description
亚太5国	东/冰/格	巴基斯坦	韩国	瑞士	哥达	秘鲁	澳大利亚	新西/坡/智	港/澳/台	亚太2国	老/柬/缅	36/3/1	
													----Station wagons (with 9 seats or less)
	/0/0				0		10	0//0	0/0/				Station wagons(9 seats or less) of cylinder capacity exceeding 1L but not exceeding 1.5L, with compression-ignition internal combustion reciprocating piston engine
	/0/0				0		10	0//0	0/0/				Complate parts of station wagons (with 9 seats or less) with compression-ignition internal combustion piston engine, 1L<cylinder capacity≤1. 5L
													----Other
	0/0/0				0	0	10	0/0/0	0/0/			0/0/	Other passenger vehicles of cylinder capacity exceeding 1L but not exceeding 1.5L, with compression-ignition internal combustion reciprocating piston engine
	0/0/0				0	0	10	0/0/0	0/0/			0/0/	Complete parts of other motor vehicles designed for the transport of person's with comperssion-ignition internal combustion piston engine, 1L<cylinder capacity≤1. 5L
													--Of a cylinder capaity exceeding 1500cc, but not exceeding 2500cc:
													---Of a cylinder capacity exceeding 1500cc, but not exceeding 2000cc:
													----Saloon cars
13.5	/0/0	22.5			0		10	0//0	0/0/				Saloon cars of a cylinder capacity exceeding 1.5L but not exceeding 2L, with compression-ignition internal combustion reciprocating piston engine
13.5	/0/0	22.5			0		10	0//0	0/0/				Complete parts of saloon cars with compression-ignition internal combustion piston engine, 1. 5L<cylinder capacity≤2L
													----Cross-country cars (4WD)
13.5	/0/0	22.5	22.5		0		10	0//0	0/0/				Off-road vehicles(4WD) of cylinder capacity exceeding 1.5L but not exceeding 2L, with compression-ignition internal combustion reciprocating piston engine
13.5	/0/0	22.5	22.5		0		10	0//0	0/0/				Complete parts of cross-country cars(4WD) with compression-ignition internal combustion piston engine, 1. 5L<cylinder capcity≤2L
													----Station wagons (with 9 seats or less)
13.5	/0/0	22.5	22.5		0		10	0//0	0/0/				Station wagons(9 seats or less) of cylinder capacity exceeding 1.5L but not exceeding 2L, with compression-ignition internal combustion reciprocating piston engine
13.5	/0/0	22.5	22.5		0		10	0//0	0/0/				Complete parts of station wagons with compression-ignition internel combustion piston engine, 1. 5L<cylinder capacity≤2L(with 9 seats or less)
													----Other
13.5	/0/0	22.5			0		10	0//0	0/0/				Other passenger vehicles of cylinder capacity exceeding 1.5L but not exceeding 2L, with compression-ignition internal combustion reciprocating piston engine
13.5	/0/0	22.5			0		10	0//0	0/0/				Complete parts of other motor vehicles principally designed for the transport of persons with compression-ignition internal combustion piston engine, 1. 5L<cylinder capacity ≤2L
													---Of a cylinder capacity exceeding 2000cc, but not exceeding 2500cc:
													----Saloon cars
13.5	/0/0	22.5			0		10	0//0	0/0/				Saloon cars of a cylinder capacity exceeding 2L but not exceeding 2. 5L, with compression-ignition internal combustion reciprocating piston engine
13.5	/0/0	22.5			0		10	0//0	0/0/				Complete parts of saloon cars with compression -ignition internal combustion piston engine, 2L<cylinder capacity ≤2. 5L
													----Cross-country cars (4WD)
13.5	/0/0	22.5			0		10	0//0	0/0/				Off-road vehicles(4WD) of cylinder capacity exceeding 2L but not exceeding 2.5L, with compression-ignition internal combustion reciprocating piston engine
13.5	/0/0	22.5			0		10	0//0	0/0/				Complete parts of cross-country cars(4WD) with compression-ignition internal combustion piston engine, 2L<cylinder capcity≤2. 5L
													----Station wagons (with 9 seats or less)
13.5	/0/0	22.5	22.5		0		10	0//0	0/0/				Station wagons(9 seats or less) of cylinder capacity exceeding 2L but not exceeding 2.5L, with compression-ignition internal combustion reciprocating piston engine
13.5	/0/0	22.5	22.5		0		10	0//0	0/0/				Complete parts of station wagons with compression-ignition internel combustion piston engine, 2L<cylinder capacity≤2. 5L(with 9 seats or less)
													----Other

税则号列	货品名称〔CIQ扩展编码及品名－T2表示见附表2〕	最惠(%)	暂定税率	普通	增值/消费	出口退税	计量单位	监管条件	检验检疫	特殊证件对美关税
8703.3229 10	仅装有2＜排量≤2.5升的压燃式活塞内燃发动机的其他载人车辆〔999〕	15		230	13/9	13	辆/千克	46AOxy	LM	/
8703.3229 90	仅装有2＜排量≤2.5升的压燃式活塞内燃发动机的其他载人车辆的成套散件〔999〕	15		230	13/	13	辆/千克	46Oxy		/
	--气缸容量(排气量)超过2500毫升:									
	---气缸容量(排气量)超过2500毫升,但不超过3000毫升:									
8703.3311	----小轿车									
8703.3311 10	仅装有2.5＜排量≤3升的压燃式活塞内燃发动机小轿车〔999〕	15		270	13/12	13	辆/千克	46AOxy	LM	/
8703.3311 90	仅装有2.5＜排量≤3升的压燃式活塞内燃发动机小轿车的成套散件〔999〕	15		270	13/	13	辆/千克	46Oxy		/
8703.3312	----越野车(4轮驱动)									
8703.3312 10	仅装有2.5＜排量≤3升的压燃式活塞内燃发动机越野车(4轮驱动)〔999〕	15		270	13/12	13	辆/千克	46AOxy	LM	/
8703.3312 90	仅装有2.5＜排量≤3升的压燃式活塞内燃发动机越野车的成套散件(4轮驱动)〔999〕	15		270	13/	13	辆/千克	46Oxy		/
8703.3313	----9座及以下的小客车									
8703.3313 10	仅装有2.5＜排量≤3升的压燃式活塞内燃发动机小客车(9座及以下的)〔999〕	15		270	13/12	13	辆/千克	46AOxy	LM	/
8703.3313 90	仅装有2.5＜排量≤3升的压燃式活塞内燃发动机小客车的成套散件(9座及以下的)〔999〕	15		270	13/	13	辆/千克	46Oxy		/
8703.3319	----其他									
8703.3319 10	仅装有2.5＜排量≤3升的压燃式活塞内燃发动机的其他载人车辆〔999〕	15		270	13/12	13	辆/千克	46AOxy	LM	/
8703.3319 90	仅装有2.5＜排量≤3升的压燃式活塞内燃发动机的其他载人车辆的成套散件〔999〕	15		270	13/12	13	辆/千克	46Oxy		/
	---气缸容量(排气量)超过3000毫升,但不超过4000毫升:									
8703.3321	----小轿车									
8703.3321 10	仅装有3＜排量≤4升的压燃式活塞内燃发动机小轿车〔999〕	15		270	13/25	13	辆/千克	46AOxy	LM	/
8703.3321 90	仅装有3＜排量≤4升的压燃式活塞内燃发动机小轿车的成套散件〔999〕	15		270	13/	13	辆/千克	46Oxy		/
8703.3322	----越野车(4轮驱动)									
8703.3322 10	仅装有3＜排量≤4升的压燃式活塞内燃发动机越野车(4轮驱动)〔999〕	15		270	13/25	13	辆/千克	46AOxy	LM	/
8703.3322 90	仅装有3＜排量≤4升的压燃式活塞内燃发动机越野车的成套散件(4轮驱动)〔999〕	15		270	13/	13	辆/千克	46Oxy		/
8703.3323	----9座及以下的小客车									
8703.3323 10	仅装有3＜排量≤4升的压燃式活塞内燃发动机小客车(9座及以下的)〔999〕	15		270	13/25	13	辆/千克	46AOxy	LM	/
8703.3323 90	仅装有3＜排量≤4升的压燃式活塞内燃发动机小客车的成套散件(9座及以下的)〔999〕	15		270	13/	13	辆/千克	46Oxy		/
8703.3329	----其他									
8703.3329 10	仅装有3＜排量≤4升的压燃式活塞内燃发动机的其他载人车辆〔999〕	15		270	13/25	13	辆/千克	46AOxy	LM	/
8703.3329 90	仅装有3＜排量≤4升的压燃式活塞内燃发动机的其他载人车辆的成套散件〔999〕	15		270	13/25	13	辆/千克	46Oxy		/
	---气缸容量(排气量)超过4000毫升:									
8703.3361	----小轿车									

协定税率 %										特惠税率 %			Article Description
亚太5国	东/冰/格	巴基斯坦	韩国	瑞士	哥达	秘鲁	澳大利亚	新西/坡/智	港/澳/台	亚太2国	老/柬/缅	36/3/1	
13.5	/0/0	22.5			0		10	0/0/0	0/0/				Other passenger vehicles of cylinder capacity exceeding 2L but not exceeding 2.5L, with compression-ignition internal combustion reciprocating piston engine
13.5	/0/0	22.5			0		10	0/0/0	0/0/				Complete parts of other motor vehicles designed for the transport of person's with compression-ignition internal combustion piston engine, 2L<cylinder capacity ≤2.5L
													--Of a cyhinder capacity exceeding 2500cc:
													---Of a cylinder capacity exceeding 2500cc, but not exceeding 3000cc:
													----Saloon cars
13.5	0/0/0	22.5			0		10	0/0/0	0/0/				Saloon cars of a cylinder capacity exceeding 2,5L but not exceeding 3L, with compression-ignition internal combustion reciprocating piston engine
13.5	0/0/0	22.5			0		10	0/0/0	0/0/				Complete parts of saloon cars with compression -ignition internal combustion piston engine, 2.5L<cylinder capacity ≤3L
													----Gross-country cars(4wd)
13.5	0/0/0	22.5	22.5		0		10	0/0/0	0/0/				Off-road vehicles(4WD) of cylinder capacity exceeding 2,5L but not exceeding 3L, with compression-ignition internal combustion reciprocating piston engine
13.5	0/0/0	22.5	22.5		0		10	0/0/0	0/0/				Complete parts of cross-country cars(4WD) with compression-ignition internal combustion piston engine, 2.5L<cylinder capacity≤3L
													----Station wagons (with 9 seats or less)
13.5	0/0/0	22.5			0		10	0/0/0	0/0/				Station wagons(9 seats or less) of cylinder capacity exceeding 2.5L but not exceeding 3L, with compression-ignition internal combustion reciprocating piston engine
13.5	0/0/0	22.5			0		10	0/0/0	0/0/				Complate parts of station wagon(with 9 seats or less) with compression-ignition internal combustion piston engine, 2.5L<cylinder capacity≤3L
													----Other
13.5	0/0/0	22.5			0		10	0/0/0	0/0/				Other passenger vehicles of cylinder capacity exceeding 2.5L but not exceeding 3L, with compression-ignition internal combustion reciprocating piston engine
13.5	0/0/0	22.5			0		10	0/0/0	0/0/				Complete parts of other passenger vehicles of a cylinder capacity exceeding 2.5L but not exceeding 3L, with compression-ignition internal combustion reciprocating piston engine
													---Of a cylinder capacity exceeding 3000cc, but not exceeding 4000cc:
													----Saloon cars
13.5	0/0/0	22.5			0		10	0/0/0	0/0/			0//	Saloon cars of a cylinder capacity exceeding 3L but not exceeding 4L, with compression-ignition internal combustion reciprocating piston engine
13.5	0/0/0	22.5			0		10	0/0/0	0/0/			0//	Complate parts of station saloon cars with compression-ignition internal combustion piston egnine, 3L<cylinder capacity≤4L
													----Cross-country cars (4WD)
13.5	0/0/0	22.5			0		10	0/0/0	0/0/			0//	Off-road vehicles(4WD) of cylinder capacity exceeding 3L but not exceeding 4L, with compression-ignition internal combustion reciprocating piston engine
13.5	0/0/0	22.5			0		10	0/0/0	0/0/			0//	Complete parts of cross-country cars(4WD) with compression-ignition internal combustion piston engine, 3L<cylinder capacity≤4L
													----Station wagons (with 9 seats or less)
13.5	0/0/0	22.5			0		10	0/0/0	0/0/			0//	Station wagons(9 seats or less) of cylinder capacity exceeding 3L but not exceeding 4L, with compression-ignition internal combustion reciprocating piston engine
13.5	0/0/0	22.5			0		10	0/0/0	0/0/			0//	Complate parts of station wagons(with 9 seats or less) with compression-ignition internal combustion piston engine, 3L<cylinder capacity≤4L
													----Other
13.5	0/0/0	22.5			0		10	0/0/0	0/0/			0//	Other passenger vehicles of cylinder capacity exceeding 3L but not exceeding 4L, with compression-ignition internal combustion reciprocating piston engine
13.5	0/0/0	22.5			0		10	0/0/0	0/0/			0//	Complete parts of other passenger vehicles of a cylinder capacity exceeding 3L but not exceeding 4L, with compression-ignition internal combustion reciprocating piston engine
													---Of a cylinder capacity exceeding 4000cc:
													----Saloon cars

税则号列	货品名称〔CIQ 扩展编码及品名－T2 表示见附表 2〕	最惠(%)	暂定税率	普通	增值/消费	出口退税	计量单位	监管条件	检验检疫	特殊证件对美关税
8703.3361 10	仅装有排量＞4 升的压燃式活塞内燃发动机小轿车〔999〕	15		270	13/40	13	辆/千克	46AOxy	LM	/
8703.3361 90	仅装有排量＞4 升的压燃式活塞内燃发动机小轿车的成套散件〔999〕	15		270	13/	13	辆/千克	46Oxy		/
8703.3362	----越野车(4 轮驱动)									
8703.3362 10	仅装有排量＞4 升的压燃式活塞内燃发动机越野车(4 轮驱动)〔999〕	15		270	13/40	13	辆/千克	46AOxy	LM	/
8703.3362 90	仅装有排量＞4 升的压燃式活塞内燃发动机越野车的成套散件(4 轮驱动)〔999〕	15		270	13/	13	辆/千克	46Oxy		/
8703.3363	----9 座及以下的小客车									
8703.3363 10	仅装有排量＞4 升的压燃式活塞内燃发动机小客车(9 座及以下的)〔999〕	15		270	13/40	13	辆/千克	46AOxy	LM	/
8703.3363 90	仅装有排量＞4 升的压燃式活塞内燃发动机小客车的成套散件(9 座及以下的)〔999〕	15		270	13/	13	辆/千克	46Oxy		/
8703.3369	----其他									
8703.3369 10	仅装有排量＞4 升的压燃式活塞内燃发动机其他载人车辆〔999〕	15		270	13/40	13	辆/千克	46AOxy	LM	/
8703.3369 90	仅装有排量＞4 升的压燃式活塞内燃发动机其他载人车辆的成套散件〔999〕	15		270	13/40	13	辆/千克	46Oxy		/
	-同时装有点燃往复式活塞内燃发动机及驱动电动机的其他车辆，可通过接插外部电源进行充电的除外：									
	---气缸容量(排气量)不超过 1000 毫升：									
8703.4011	----小轿车									
8703.4011 10	同时装有点燃往复式活塞内燃发动机(排量≤1 升)及驱动电动机的小轿车(可通过接插外部电源进行充电的除外)〔999〕	15		230	13/1	13	辆/千克	46AOxy	LM	/
8703.4011 90	同时装有点燃往复式活塞内燃发动机(排量≤1 升)及驱动电动机的小轿车的成套散件(可通过接插外部电源进行充电的除外)〔999〕	15		230	13/	13	辆/千克	46Oxy		/
8703.4012	----越野车(4 轮驱动)									
8703.4012 10	同时装有点燃往复式活塞内燃发动机(排量≤1 升)及驱动电动机的越野车(4 轮驱动)(可通过接插外部电源进行充电的除外)〔999〕	15		230	13/1	13	辆/千克	46AOxy	LM	/
8703.4012 90	同时装有点燃往复式活塞内燃发动机(排量≤1 升)及驱动电动机的越野车(4 轮驱动)的成套散件(可通过接插外部电源进行充电的除外)〔999〕	15		230	13/	13	辆/千克	46Oxy		/
8703.4013	----9 座及以下的小客车									
8703.4013 10	同时装有点燃往复式活塞内燃发动机(排量≤1 升)及驱动电动机的小客车(9 座及以下，可通过接插外部电源进行充电的除外)〔999〕	15		230	13/1	13	辆/千克	46AOxy	LM	/
8703.4013 90	同时装有点燃往复式活塞内燃发动机(排量≤1 升)及驱动电动机的小客车的成套散件(9 座及以下，可通过接插外部电源进行充电的除外)〔999〕	15		230	13/1	13	辆/千克	46Oxy		/
8703.4019	----其他									
8703.4019 10	同时装有点燃往复式活塞内燃发动机(排量≤1 升)及驱动电动机的其他载人车辆(可通过接插外部电源进行充电的除外)〔999〕	15		230	13/1	13	辆/千克	46AOxy	LM	/
8703.4019 90	同时装有点燃往复式活塞内燃发动机(排量≤1 升)及驱动电动机的其他载人车辆的成套散件(可通过接插外部电源进行充电的除外)〔999〕	15		230	13/1	13	辆/千克	46Oxy		/
	---气缸容量(排气量)超过 1000 毫升，但不超过 1500 毫升：									
8703.4021	----小轿车									
8703.4021 10	同时装有点燃往复式活塞内燃发动机(1＜排量≤1.5 升)及驱动电动机的小轿车(可通过接插外部电源进行充电的除外)〔999〕	15		230	13/3	13	辆/千克	46AOxy	LM	/

协定税率 %										特惠税率 %			Article Description
亚太5国	东/冰/格	巴基斯坦	韩国	瑞士	哥达	秘鲁	澳大利亚	新西/坡/智	港/澳/台	亚太2国	老/柬/缅	36/3/1	
13.5	0/0/0	22.5			0		0	0/0/0	0/0/			0//	Saloon cars of a cylinder capacity exceeding 4L, with compression-ignition internal combustion reciprocating piston engine
13.5	0/0/0	22.5			0		0	0/0/0	0/0/			0//	Complete parts of saloon cars with compression -ignition internal combustion piston engine, cylinder capacity >4L
													----Cross-country cars (4WD)
13.5	0/0/0	22.5			0		0	0/0/0	0/0/			0//	Off-road vehicles (4WD) of cylinder capacity exceeding 4L, with compression-ignition internal combustion reciprocating piston engine
13.5	0/0/0	22.5			0		0	0/0/0	0/0/			0//	Complete parts of cross-country cars(4WD) with compression-ignition internal combustion piston engine, cylinder capacity>4L
													----Station wagons (with 9 seats or less)
13.5	0/0/0	22.5			0		0	0/0/0	0/0/			0//	Station wagons(9 seats or less) of cylinder capacity exceeding 4L, with compression-ignition internal combustion reciprocating piston engine
13.5	0/0/0	22.5			0		0	0/0/0	0/0/			0//	Complete parts of station wagons(with 9 seats or less) with compression-ignition internal combustion piston engine, cylinder capacity> 4L
													----Other
13.5	0/0/0	22.5			0		0	0/0/0	0/0/			0//	Other passenger vehicles of cylinder capacity exceeding 4L, with compression-ignition internal combustion reciprocating piston engine
13.5	0/0/0	22.5			0		0	0/0/0	0/0/			0//	Complete parts of other passenger vehicles of a cylinder capacity exceeding 4L, with compression-ignition internal combustion reciprocating piston engine
													-Other vehicles, with only compression—ignition internal combustion piston engine(diesel or semi—diesel):
													---Of a cylinder capacity exceeding 1000cc:
													----Saloon cars
13.5	/0/	22.5			0		0	0//0	0/0/				Saloon cars of cylinder capacity not exceeding 1L, with spark-ignition internal combustion eciprocating piston engine, with drive motor (Except for charging by external power supply)
13.5	/0/	22.5			0		0	0//0	0/0/				Complete parts of saloon cars of cylinder capacity not exceeding 1L, with spark-ignition internal combustion eciprocating piston engine, with drive motor (Except for charging by external
													----Cross-country cars(4WD)
13.5	/0/	22.5			0		0	0//0	0/0/				Off-road vehicles(4WD) of cylinder capacity not exceeding 1L, with spark-ignition internal combustion eciprocating piston engine, with drive motor (Except for charging by external power supply)
13.5	/0/	22.5			0		0	0//0	0/0/				Complete parts of off-road vehicles(4WD) of cylinder capacity not exceeding 1L, with spark-ignition internal combustion eciprocating piston engine, with drive motor (Except for charging by external
													----Station wagons(with 9 seats or less)
13.5	/0/	22.5			0		0	0//0	0/0/				Station wagons(9 seats or less) of cylinder capacity not exceeding 1L, with spark-ignition internal combustion eciprocating piston engine, with drive motor (Except for charging by external power supply)
13.5	/0/	22.5			0		0	0//0	0/0/				Complete parts of station wagons(9 seats or less) of cylinder capacity not exceeding 1L, with spark-ignition internal combustion eciprocating piston engine, with drive motor (Except for charging by external
													----Other
13.5	/0/	22.5			0		0	0//0	0/0/				Other passenger vehicles of cylinder capacity not exceeding 1L, with spark-ignition internal combustion eciprocating piston engine, with drive motor (Except for charging by external power supply)
13.5	/0/	22.5			0		0	0//0	0/0/				Complete parts of Other passenger vehicles of cylinder capacity not exceeding 1L, with spark-ignition internal combustion eciprocating piston engine, with drive motor (Except for charging by external
													---Of a cylinder capacity exceeding 1000cc, but not exceeding 1500cc:
													----Saloon cars
13.5	/0/	22.5	22.5		0		0	0//0	0/0/				Saloon cars of cylinder capacity exceeding 1L but not exceeding 1.5L, with spark-ignition internal combustion eciprocating piston engine, with drive motor (Except for charging by external power supply)

税则号列		货品名称〔CIQ 扩展编码及品名－T2 表示见附表 2〕	最惠(%)	暂定税率	普通	增值/消费	出口退税	计量单位	监管条件	检验检疫	特殊证件对美关税
8703.4021	90	同时装有点燃往复式活塞内燃发动机(1＜排量≤1.5 升)及驱动电动机的小轿车的成套散件(可通过接插外部电源进行充电的除外)〔999〕	15		230	13/3	13	辆/千克	46Oxy		/
8703.4022		----越野车(4 轮驱动)									
8703.4022	10	同时装有点燃往复式活塞内燃发动机(1＜排量≤1.5 升)及驱动电动机的四轮驱动越野车(可通过接插外部电源进行充电的除外)〔999〕	15		230	13/3	13	辆/千克	46AOxy	LM	/
8703.4022	90	同时装有点燃往复式活塞内燃发动机(1＜排量≤1.5 升)及驱动电动机的四轮驱动越野车的成套散件(可通过接插外部电源进行充电的除外)〔999〕	15		230	13/3	13	辆/千克	46Oxy		/
8703.4023		----9 座及以下的小客车									
8703.4023	10	同时装有点燃往复式活塞内燃发动机(1＜排量≤1.5 升)及驱动电动机的小客车(9 座及以下,可通过接插外部电源进行充电的除外)〔999〕	15		230	13/3	13	辆/千克	46AOxy	LM	/
8703.4023	90	同时装有点燃往复式活塞内燃发动机(1＜排量≤1.5 升)及驱动电动机的小客车的成套散件(9 座及以下,可通过接插外部电源进行充电的除外)〔999〕	15		230	13/3	13	辆/千克	46Oxy		/
8703.4029		----其他									
8703.4029	10	同时装有点燃往复式活塞内燃发动机(1＜排量≤1.5 升)及驱动电动机的其他载人车辆(可通过接插外部电源进行充电的除外)〔999〕	15		230	13/3	13	辆/千克	46AOxy	LM	/
8703.4029	90	同时装有点燃往复式活塞内燃发动机(1＜排量≤1.5 升)及驱动电动机的其他载人车辆的成套散件(可通过接插外部电源进行充电的除外)〔999〕	15		230	13/3	13	辆/千克	46Oxy		/
		---气缸容量(排气量)超过 1500 毫升,但不超过 2000 毫升:									
8703.4031		----小轿车									
8703.4031	10	同时装有点燃往复式活塞内燃发动机(1.5＜排量≤2 升)及驱动电动机的小轿车(可通过接插外部电源进行充电的除外)〔999〕	15		230	13/5	13	辆/千克	46AOxy	LM	/
8703.4031	90	同时装有点燃往复式活塞内燃发动机(1.5＜排量≤2 升)及驱动电动机的小轿车的成套散件(可通过接插外部电源进行充电的除外)〔999〕	15		230	13/5	13	辆/千克	46Oxy		/
8703.4032		----越野车(4 轮驱动)									
8703.4032	10	同时装有点燃往复式活塞内燃发动机(1.5＜排量≤2 升)及驱动电动机的四轮驱动越野车(可通过接插外部电源进行充电的除外)〔999〕	15		230	13/5	13	辆/千克	46AOxy	LM	/
8703.4032	90	同时装有点燃往复式活塞内燃发动机(1.5＜排量≤2 升)及驱动电动机的四轮驱动越野车的成套散件(可通过接插外部电源进行充电的除外)〔999〕	15		230	13/5	13	辆/千克	46Oxy		/
8703.4033		----9 座及以下的小客车									
8703.4033	10	同时装有点燃往复式活塞内燃发动机(1.5＜排量≤2 升)及驱动电动机的小客车(9 座及以下,可通过接插外部电源进行充电的除外)〔999〕	15		230	13/5	13	辆/千克	46AOxy	LM	/
8703.4033	90	同时装有点燃往复式活塞内燃发动机(1.5＜排量≤2 升)及驱动电动机的小客车的成套散件(9 座及以下,可通过接插外部电源进行充电的除外)〔999〕	15		230	13/5	13	辆/千克	46Oxy		/
8703.4039		----其他									

协定税率 %										特惠税率 %			Article Description
亚太5国	东/冰/格	巴基斯坦	韩国	瑞士	哥达	秘鲁	澳大利亚	新西/坡/智	港/澳/台	亚太2国	老/柬/缅	36/3/1	
13.5	/0/	22.5	22.5		0		0	0//0	0/0/				Complete parts of saloon cars of cylinder capacity exceeding 1L but not exceeding 1.5L, with spark-ignition internal combustion eciprocating piston engine, with drive motor (Except for charging by external
													----Cross-country cars(4WD)
13.5	/0/	22.5			0		0	0//0	0/0/				Off-road vehicles(4WD) of cylinder capacity exceeding 1L but not exceeding 1.5L, with spark-ignition internal combustion eciprocating piston engine, with drive motor (Except for charging by external power supply)
13.5	/0/	22.5			0		0	0//0	0/0/				Complete parts of Off-road vehicles(4WD) of cylinder capacity exceeding 1L but not exceeding 1.5L, with spark-ignition internal combustion eciprocating piston engine, with drive motor (Except for charging by external
													----Station wagons(with 9 seats or less)
13.5	/0/	22.5			0		0	0//0	0/0/				Station wagons(9 seats or less) of cylinder capacity exceeding 1L but not exceeding 1.5L, with spark-ignition internal combustion eciprocating piston engine, with drive motor (Except for charging by external power supply)
13.5	/0/	22.5			0		0	0//0	0/0/				Complete parts of Station wagons(9 seats or less) of cylinder capacity exceeding 1L but not exceeding 1.5L, with spark-ignition internal combustion eciprocating piston engine, with drive motor (Except for charging by external
													----Other
13.5	/0/	22.5			0		0	0//0	0/0/				Other passenger vehicles of cylinder capacity exceeding 1L but not exceeding 1.5L, with spark-ignition internal combustion eciprocating piston engine, with drive motor (Except for charging by external power supply)
13.5	/0/	22.5			0		0	0//0	0/0/				Complete parts of Other passenger vehicles of cylinder capacity exceeding 1L but not exceeding 1.5L, with spark-ignition internal combustion eciprocating piston engine, with drive motor (Except for charging by external
													---Of a cylinder capacity exceeding 1500cc, but not exceeding 2000cc:
													----Saloon cars
13.5	/0/	22.5	22.5		0		10	0//0	0/0/				Saloon cars of cylinder capacity exceeding 1.5L but not exceeding 2L, with spark-ignition internal combustion eciprocating piston engine, with drive motor (Except for charging by external power supply)
13.5	/0/	22.5	22.5		0		10	0//0	0/0/				Complete parts of saloon cars of cylinder capacity exceeding 1L but not exceeding 1.5L, with spark-ignition internal combustion eciprocating piston engine, with drive motor (Except for charging by external
													----Cross-country cars(4WD)
13.5	/0/	22.5	22.5		0		10	0//0	0/0/				Off-road vehicles(4WD) of cylinder capacity exceeding 1.5L but not exceeding 2L, with spark-ignition internal combustion eciprocating piston engine, with drive motor (Except for charging by external power supply)
13.5	/0/	22.5	22.5		0		10	0//0	0/0/				Complete parts of Off-road vehicles(4WD) of cylinder capacity exceeding 1L but not exceeding 1.5L, with spark-ignition internal combustion eciprocating piston engine, with drive motor (Except for charging by external
													----Station wagons(with 9 seats or less)
13.5	/0/	22.5	22.5		0		10	0//0	0/0/				Station wagons(9 seats or less) of cylinder capacity exceeding 1.5L but not exceeding 2L, with spark-ignition internal combustion eciprocating piston engine, with drive motor (Except for charging by external power supply)
13.5	/0/	22.5	22.5		0		10	0//0	0/0/				Complete parts of Station wagons(9 seats or less) of cylinder capacity exceeding 1L but not exceeding 1.5L, with spark-ignition internal combustion eciprocating piston engine, with drive motor (Except for charging by external
													----Other

税则号列		货品名称〔CIQ 扩展编码及品名—T2 表示见附表 2〕	最惠(%)	暂定税率	普通	增值/消费	出口退税	计量单位	监管条件	检验检疫	特殊证件对美关税
8703.4039	10	同时装有点燃往复式活塞内燃发动机(1.5<排量≤2 升)及驱动电动机的其他载人车辆(可通过接插外部电源进行充电的除外)〔999〕	15		230	13/5	13	辆/千克	46AOxy	LM	/
8703.4039	90	同时装有点燃往复式活塞内燃发动机(1.5<排量≤2 升)及驱动电动机的其他载人车辆的成套散件(可通过接插外部电源进行充电的除外)〔999〕	15		230	13/5	13	辆/千克	46Oxy		/
		---气缸容量(排气量)超过 2000 毫升,但不超过 2500 毫升:									
8703.4041		----小轿车									
8703.4041	10	同时装有点燃往复式活塞内燃发动机(2<排量≤2.5 升)及驱动电动机的小轿车(可通过接插外部电源进行充电的除外)〔999〕	15		230	13/9	13	辆/千克	46AOxy	LM	/
8703.4041	90	同时装有点燃往复式活塞内燃发动机(2<排量≤2.5 升)及驱动电动机的小轿车的成套散件(可通过接插外部电源进行充电的除外)〔999〕	15		230	13/9	13	辆/千克	46Oxy		/
8703.4042		----越野车(4 轮驱动)									
8703.4042	10	同时装有点燃往复式活塞内燃发动机(2<排量≤2.5 升)及驱动电动机的四轮驱动越野车(可通过接插外部电源进行充电的除外)〔999〕	15		230	13/9	13	辆/千克	46AOxy	LM	/
8703.4042	90	同时装有点燃往复式活塞内燃发动机(2<排量≤2.5 升)及驱动电动机的四轮驱动越野车的成套散件(可通过接插外部电源进行充电的除外)〔999〕	15		230	13/9	13	辆/千克	46Oxy		/
8703.4043		----9 座及以下的小客车									
8703.4043	10	同时装有点燃往复式活塞内燃发动机(2<排量≤2.5 升)及驱动电动机的小客车(9 座及以下,可通过接插外部电源进行充电的除外)〔999〕	15		230	13/9	13	辆/千克	46AOxy	LM	/
8703.4043	90	同时装有点燃往复式活塞内燃发动机(2<排量≤2.5 升)及驱动电动机的小客车的成套散件(9 座及以下,可通过接插外部电源进行充电的除外)〔999〕	15		230	13/9	13	辆/千克	46Oxy		/
8703.4049		----其他									
8703.4049	10	同时装有点燃往复式活塞内燃发动机(2<排量≤2.5 升)及驱动电动机的其他载人车辆(可通过接插外部电源进行充电的除外)〔999〕	15		230	13/9	13	辆/千克	46AOxy	LM	/
8703.4049	90	同时装有点燃往复式活塞内燃发动机(2<排量≤2.5 升)及驱动电动机的其他载人车辆的成套散件(可通过接插外部电源进行充电的除外)〔999〕	15		230	13/9	13	辆/千克	46Oxy		/
		---气缸容量(排气量)超过 2500 毫升,但不超过 3000 毫升:									
8703.4051		----小轿车									
8703.4051	10	同时装有点燃往复式活塞内燃发动机(2.5<排量≤3 升)及驱动电动机的小轿车(可通过接插外部电源进行充电的除外)〔999〕	15		270	13/12	13	辆/千克	46AOxy	ML	/
8703.4051	90	同时装有点燃往复式活塞内燃发动机(2.5<排量≤3 升)及驱动电动机的小轿车的成套散件(可通过接插外部电源进行充电的除外)〔999〕	15		270	13/12	13	辆/千克	46Oxy		/
8703.4052		----越野车(4 轮驱动)									
8703.4052	10	同时装有点燃往复式活塞内燃发动机(2.5<排量≤3 升)及驱动电动机的四轮驱动越野车(可通过接插外部电源进行充电的除外)〔999〕	15		270	13/12	13	辆/千克	46AOxy	ML	/

协定税率 %										特惠税率 %			Article Description
亚太5国	东/冰/格	巴基斯坦	韩国	瑞士	哥达	秘鲁	澳大利亚	新西/坡/智	港/澳/台	亚太2国	老/柬/缅	36/3/	
13.5	/0/	22.5			0		10	0//0	0/0/				Other passenger vehicles of cylinder capacity exceeding 1.5L but not exceeding 2L, with spark-ignition internal combustion eciprocating piston engine, with drive motor (Except for charging by external power supply)
13.5	/0/	22.5			0		10	0//0	0/0/				Complete parts of Other passenger vehicles of cylinder capacity exceeding 1,5L but not exceeding 2L, with spark-ignition internal combustion eciprocating piston engine, with drive motor (Except for charging by external
													---Of a cylinder capacity exceeding 2000cc, but not exceeding 2500cc:
													----Saloon cars
13.5	/0/	22.5	22.5		0		10	0//0	0/0/				Saloon cars of cylinder capacity exceeding 2L but not exceeding 2.5L, with spark-ignition internal combustion eciprocating piston engine, with drive motor (Except for charging by external power supply)
13.5	/0/	22.5	22.5		0		10	0//0	0/0/				Complete parts of saloon cars of cylinder capacity exceeding 1L but not exceeding 1.5L, with spark-ignition internal combustion eciprocating piston engine, with drive motor (Except for charging by external
													----Cross-country cars(4WD)
13.5	/0/	22.5	22.5		0		10	0//0	0/0/				Off-road vehicles(4WD) of cylinder capacity exceeding 2L but not exceeding 2.5L, with spark-ignition internal combustion eciprocating piston engine, with drive motor (Except for charging by external power supply)
13.5	/0/	22.5	22.5		0		10	0//0	0/0/				Complete parts of Off-road vehicles(4WD) of cylinder capacity exceeding 1L but not exceeding 1.5L, with spark-ignition internal combustion eciprocating piston engine, with drive motor (Except for charging by external
													---Station wagons(with 9 seats or less)
13.5	/0/	22.5	22.5		0		10	0//0	0/0/				Station wagons(9 seats or less) of cylinder capacity exceeding 2L but not exceeding 2.5L, with spark-ignition internal combustion eciprocating piston engine, with drive motor (Except for charging by external power supply)
13.5	/0/	22.5	22.5		0		10	0//0	0/0/				Complete parts of Station wagons(9 seats or less) of cylinder capacity exceeding 1L but not exceeding 1.5L, with spark-ignition internal combustion eciprocating piston engine, with drive motor (Except for charging by external
													----Other
13.5	/0/	22.5			0		10	0//0	0/0/				Other passenger vehicles of cylinder capacity exceeding 2L but not exceeding 2.5L, with spark-ignition internal combustion eciprocating piston engine, with drive motor (Except for charging by external power supply)
13.5	/0/	22.5			0		10	0//0	0/0/				Complete parts of Other passenger vehicles of cylinder capacity exceeding 2L but not exceeding 2.5L, with spark-ignition internal combustion eciprocating piston engine, with drive motor (Except for charging by external
													---Of a cylinder capacity exceeding 2500cc, but not exceeding32000cc:
													----Saloon cars
13.5	/0/	22.5	22.5		0		10	0//0	0/0/				Saloon cars of cylinder capacity exceeding 2.5L but not exceeding 3L, with spark-ignition internal combustion eciprocating piston engine, with drive motor (Except for charging by external power supply)
13.5	/0/	22.5	22.5		0		10	0//0	0/0/				Complete parts of saloon cars of cylinder capacity exceeding 1L but not exceeding 1.5L, with spark-ignition internal combustion eciprocating piston engine, with drive motor (Except for charging by external
													----Cross-country cars(4WD)
13.5	0/0/	22.5			0		10	0/0/0	0/0/				Off-road vehicles(4WD) of cylinder capacity exceeding 2.5L but not exceeding 3L, with spark-ignition internal combustion eciprocating piston engine, with drive motor (Except for charging by external power supply)

税则号列		货品名称〔CIQ扩展编码及品名－T2表示见附表2〕	最惠(%)	暂定税率	普通	增值/消费	出口退税	计量单位	监管条件	检验检疫	特殊证件对美关税
8703.4052	90	同时装有点燃往复式活塞内燃发动机(2.5＜排量≤3升)及驱动电动机的四轮驱动越野车的成套散件(可通过接插外部电源进行充电的除外)〔999〕	15		270	13/12	13	辆/千克	46Oxy		/
8703.4053		----9座及以下的小客车									
8703.4053	10	同时装有点燃往复式活塞内燃发动机(2.5＜排量≤3升)及驱动电动机的小客车(9座及以下,可通过接插外部电源进行充电的除外)〔999〕	15		270	13/12	13	辆/千克	46AOxy	ML	/
8703.4053	90	同时装有点燃往复式活塞内燃发动机(2.5＜排量≤3升)及驱动电动机的小客车的成套散件(9座及以下,可通过接插外部电源进行充电的除外)〔999〕	15		270	13/12	13	辆/千克	46Oxy		/
8703.4059		----其他									
8703.4059	10	同时装有点燃往复式活塞内燃发动机(2.5＜排量≤3升)及驱动电动机的其他载人车辆(可通过接插外部电源进行充电的除外)〔999〕	15		270	13/12	13	辆/千克	46AOxy	ML	/
8703.4059	90	同时装有点燃往复式活塞内燃发动机(2.5＜排量≤3升)及驱动电动机的其他载人车辆的成套散件(可通过接插外部电源进行充电的除外)〔999〕	15		270	13/12	13	辆/千克	46Oxy		/
		---气缸容量(排气量)超过3000毫升,但不超过4000毫升:									
8703.4061		----小轿车									
8703.4061	10	同时装有点燃往复式活塞内燃发动机(3＜排量≤4升)及驱动电动机的小轿车(可通过接插外部电源进行充电的除外)〔999〕	15		270	13/25	13	辆/千克	46AOxy	LM	/
8703.4061	90	同时装有点燃往复式活塞内燃发动机(3＜排量≤4升)及驱动电动机的小轿车的成套散件(可通过接插外部电源进行充电的除外)〔999〕	15		270	13/25	13	辆/千克	46Oxy		/
8703.4062		----越野车(4轮驱动)									
8703.4062	10	同时装有点燃往复式活塞内燃发动机(3＜排量≤4升)及驱动电动机的四轮驱动越野车(可通过接插外部电源进行充电的除外)〔999〕	15		270	13/25	13	辆/千克	46AOxy	LM	/
8703.4062	90	同时装有点燃往复式活塞内燃发动机(3＜排量≤4升)及驱动电动机的四轮驱动越野车的成套散件(可通过接插外部电源进行充电的除外)〔999〕	15		270	13/25	13	辆/千克	46Oxy		/
8703.4063		----9座及以下的小客车									
8703.4063	10	同时装有点燃往复式活塞内燃发动机(3＜排量≤4升)及驱动电动机的小客车(9座及以下,可通过接插外部电源进行充电的除外)〔999〕	15		270	13/25	13	辆/千克	46AOxy	LM	/
8703.4063	90	同时装有点燃往复式活塞内燃发动机(3＜排量≤4升)及驱动电动机的小客车的成套散件(9座及以下,可通过接插外部电源进行充电的除外)〔999〕	15		270	13/25	13	辆/千克	46Oxy		/
8703.4069		----其他									
8703.4069	10	同时装有点燃往复式活塞内燃发动机(3＜排量≤4升)及驱动电动机的其他载人车辆(可通过接插外部电源进行充电的除外)〔999〕	15		270	13/25	13	辆/千克	46AOxy	LM	/
8703.4069	90	同时装有点燃往复式活塞内燃发动机(3＜排量≤4升)及驱动电动机的其他载人车辆的成套散件(可通过接插外部电源进行充电的除外)〔999〕	15		270	13/25	13	辆/千克	46Oxy		/
		---气缸容量(排气量)超过4000毫升:									
8703.4071		----小轿车									
8703.4071	10	同时装有点燃往复式活塞内燃发动机(排量＞4升)及驱动电动机的小轿车(可通过接插外部电源进行充电的除外)〔999〕	15		270	13/40	13	辆/千克	46AOxy	LM	/

协定税率 %										特惠税率 %			
亚太5国	东/冰/格	巴基斯坦	韩国	瑞士	哥达	秘鲁	澳大利亚	新西/坡/智	港/澳/台	亚太2国	老/柬/缅	36/3/1	Article Description
13.5	0/0/	22.5			0		10	0/0/0	0/0/				Complete parts of Off-road vehicles(4WD) of cylinder capacity exceeding 1L but not exceeding 1.5L, with spark-ignition internal combustion eciprocating piston engine, with drive motor (Except for charging by external
													----Station wagons(with 9 seats or less)
13.5	0/0/	22.5	22.5		0		10	0/0/0	0/0/				Station wagons(9 seats or less) of cylinder capacity exceeding 2.5L but not exceeding 3L, with spark-ignition internal combustion eciprocating piston engine, with drive motor (Except for charging by external power supply)
13.5	0/0/	22.5	22.5		0		10	0/0/0	0/0/				Complete parts of Station wagons(9 seats or less) of cylinder capacity exceeding 1L but not exceeding 1.5L, with spark-ignition internal combustion eciprocating piston engine, with drive motor (Except for charging by external
													----Other
13.5	0/0/	22.5			0		10	0/0/0	0/0/				Other passenger vehicles of cylinder capacity exceeding 2.5L but not exceeding 3L, with spark-ignition internal combustion eciprocating piston engine, with drive motor (Except for charging by external power supply)
13.5	0/0/	22.5			0		10	0/0/0	0/0/				Complete parts of Other passenger vehicles of cylinder capacity exceeding 2.5L but not exceeding 3L, with spark-ignition internal combustion eciprocating piston engine, with drive motor (Except for charging by external
													---Of a cylinder capacity exceeding 3000cc, but not exceeding 4000cc:
													----Saloon cars
13.5	/0/	22.5	22.5		0		10	0//0	0/0/			0//	Saloon cars of cylinder capacity exceeding 3L but not exceeding 4L, with spark-ignition internal combustion eciprocating piston engine, with drive motor (Except for charging by external power supply)
13.5	/0/	22.5	22.5		0		10	0//0	0/0/			0//	Complete parts of saloon cars of cylinder capacity exceeding 1L but not exceeding 1.5L, with spark-ignition internal combustion eciprocating piston engine, with drive motor (Except for charging by external
													----Cross-country cars(4WD)
13.5	/0/	22.5	22.5		0		10	0//0	0/0/			0//	Off-road vehicles(4WD) of cylinder capacity exceeding 3L but not exceeding 4L, with spark-ignition internal combustion eciprocating piston engine, with drive motor (Except for charging by external power supply)
13.5	/0/	22.5	22.5		0		10	0//0	0/0/			0//	Complete parts of Off-road vehicles(4WD) of cylinder capacity exceeding 1L but not exceeding 1.5L, with spark-ignition internal combustion eciprocating piston engine, with drive motor (Except for charging by external
													----Station wagons(with 9 seats or less)
13.5	/0/	22.5			0		10	0//0	0/0/			0//	Station wagons(9 seats or less) of cylinder capacity exceeding 3L but not exceeding 4L, with spark-ignition internal combustion eciprocating piston engine, with drive motor (Except for charging by external power supply)
13.5	/0/	22.5			0		10	0//0	0/0/			0//	Complete parts of Station wagons(9 seats or less) of cylinder capacity exceeding 1L but not exceeding 1.5L, with spark-ignition internal combustion eciprocating piston engine, with drive motor (Except for charging by external
													----Other
13.5	/0/	22.5			0		10	0//0	0/0/			0//	Other passenger vehicles of cylinder capacity exceeding 3L but not exceeding 4L, with spark-ignition internal combustion eciprocating piston engine, with drive motor (Except for charging by external power supply)
13.5	/0/	22.5			0		10	0//0	0/0/			0//	Complete parts of Other passenger vehicles of cylinder capacity exceeding 3L but not exceeding 4L, with spark-ignition internal combustion eciprocating piston engine, with drive motor (Except for charging by external
													---Of a cylinder capacity exceeding 4000cc:
													----Saloon cars
13.5	/0/	22.5	22.5		0		10	0//0	0/0/			0//	Saloon cars of cylinder capacity exceeding 4L, with spark-ignition internal combustion eciprocating piston engine, with drive motor (Except for charging by external power supply)

税则号列		货品名称〔CIQ 扩展编码及品名－T2 表示见附表 2〕	最惠(%)	暂定税率	普通	增值/消费	出口退税	计量单位	监管条件	检验检疫	特殊证件对美关税
8703.4071	90	同时装有点燃往复式活塞内燃发动机(排量＞4 升)及驱动电动机的小轿车的成套散件(可通过接插外部电源进行充电的除外)〔999〕	15		270	13/40	13	辆/千克	46Oxy		/
8703.4072		----越野车(4 轮驱动)									
8703.4072	10	同时装有点燃往复式活塞内燃发动机(排量＞4 升)及驱动电动机的四轮驱动越野车(可通过接插外部电源进行充电的除外)〔999〕	15		270	13/40	13	辆/千克	46AOxy	LM	/
8703.4072	90	同时装有点燃往复式活塞内燃发动机(排量＞4 升)及驱动电动机的四轮驱动越野车的成套散件(可通过接插外部电源进行充电的除外)〔999〕	15		270	13/40	13	辆/千克	46Oxy		/
8703.4073		----9 座及以下的小客车									
8703.4073	10	同时装有点燃往复式活塞内燃发动机(排量＞4 升)及驱动电动机的小客车(9 座及以下,可通过接插外部电源进行充电的除外)〔999〕	15		270	13/40	13	辆/千克	46AOxy	LM	/
8703.4073	90	同时装有点燃往复式活塞内燃发动机(排量＞4 升)及驱动电动机的小客车的成套散件(9 座及以下,可通过接插外部电源进行充电的除外)〔999〕	15		270	13/40	13	辆/千克	46Oxy		/
8703.4079		----其他									
8703.4079	10	同时装有点燃往复式活塞内燃发动机(排量＞4 升)及驱动电动机的其他载人车辆(可通过接插外部电源进行充电的除外)〔999〕	15		270	13/40	13	辆/千克	46AOxy	LM	/
8703.4079	90	同时装有点燃往复式活塞内燃发动机(排量＞4 升)及驱动电动机的其他载人车辆的成套散件(可通过接插外部电源进行充电的除外)〔999〕	15		270	13/40	13	辆/千克	46Oxy		/
8703.4090		---其他									
8703.4090	10	其他同时装有点燃往复式活塞内燃发动机及驱动电动机的载人车辆(可通过接插外部电源进行充电的除外)〔999〕	15		270	13/	13	辆/千克	46AOxy	LM	/
8703.4090	90	其他同时装有点燃往复式活塞内燃发动机及驱动电动机的载人车辆的成套散件(可通过接插外部电源进行充电的除外)〔999〕	15		270	13/	13	辆/千克	46Oxy		/
		-同时装有压燃式活塞内燃发动机(柴油或半柴油发动机)及驱动电动机的其他车辆,可通过接插外部电源进行充电的除外:									
		---气缸容量(排气量)不超过 1000 毫升:									
8703.5011		----小轿车									
8703.5011	10	同时装有压燃式活塞内燃发动机(柴油或半柴油发动机,排量≤1 升)及驱动电动机的小轿车(可通过接插外部电源进行充电的除外)〔999〕	15		230	13/1	13	辆/千克	46AOxy	LM	/
8703.5011	90	同时装有压燃式活塞内燃发动机(柴油或半柴油发动机,排量≤1 升)及驱动电动机的小轿车的成套散件(可通过接插外部电源进行充电的除外)〔999〕	15		230	13/1	13	辆/千克	46Oxy		/
8703.5019		----其他									
8703.5019	10	同时装有压燃式活塞内燃发动机(柴油或半柴油发动机,排量≤1 升)及驱动电动机的其他载人车辆(可通过接插外部电源进行充电的除外)〔999〕	15		230	13/1	13	辆/千克	46AOxy	LM	/
8703.5019	90	同时装有压燃式活塞内燃发动机(柴油或半柴油发动机,排量≤1 升)及驱动电动机的其他载人车辆的成套散件(可通过接插外部电源进行充电的除外)〔999〕	15		230	13/1	13	辆/千克	46Oxy		/
		---气缸容量(排气量)超过 1000 毫升,但不超过 1500 毫升:									
8703.5021		----小轿车									
8703.5021	10	同时装有压燃式活塞内燃发动机(柴油或半柴油发动机,1 升＜排量≤1.5 升)及驱动电动机的小轿车(可通过接插外部电源进行充电的除外)〔999〕	15		230	13/3	13	辆/千克	46AOxy	LM	/

协定税率 %										特惠税率 %			Article Description
亚太5国	东/冰/格	巴基斯坦	韩国	瑞士	哥达	秘鲁	澳大利亚	新西/坡/智	港/澳/台	亚太2国	老/柬/缅	36/3/1	
13.5	/0/	22.5	22.5		0		10	0//0	0/0/			0//	Complete parts of saloon cars of cylinder capacity exceeding 1L but not exceeding 1.5L, with spark-ignition internal combustion eciprocating piston engine, with drive motor (Except for charging by external
													----Cross-country cars(4WD)
13.5	/0/	22.5			0		10	0//0	0/0/			0//	Off-road vehicles (4WD) of cylinder capacity exceeding 4L, with spark-ignition internal combustion eciprocating piston engine, with drive motor (Except for charging by external power supply)
13.5	/0/	22.5			0		10	0//0	0/0/			0//	Complete parts of Off-road vehicles(4WD) of cylinder capacity exceeding 1L but not exceeding 1.5L, with spark-ignition internal combustion eciprocating piston engine, with drive motor (Except for charging by external
													----Station wagons(with 9 seats or less)
13.5	/0/	22.5			0		10	0//0	0/0/			0//	Station wagons(9 seats or less) of cylinder capacity exceeding 4L, with spark-ignition internal combustion eciprocating piston engine, with drive motor (Except for charging by external power supply)
13.5	/0/	22.5			0		10	0//0	0/0/			0//	Complete parts of Station wagons(9 seats or less) of cylinder capacity exceeding 1L but not exceeding 1.5L, with spark-ignition internal combustion eciprocating piston engine, with drive motor (Except for charging by external
													----Other
13.5	/0/	22.5			0		10	0//0	0/0/			0//	Other passenger vehicles of cylinder capacity exceeding 4L, with spark-ignition internal combustion eciprocating piston engine, with drive motor (Except for charging by external power supply)
13.5	/0/	22.5			0		10	0//0	0/0/			0//	Complete parts of other passenger vehicles of cylinder capacity exceeding 4L, with spark-ignition internal combustion eciprocating piston engine, with drive motor (Except for charging by external
													---Other
13.5	0/0/10	22.5	22.5		0	0	0	0/0/0	0/0/			0/0/	Passenger vehicles of other cylinder capacity exceeding 4L, with spark-ignition internal combustion eciprocating piston engine, with drive motor (Except for charging by external power supply)
13.5	0/0/10	22.5	22.5		0	0	0	0/0/0	0/0/			0/0/	Complete parts of passenger vehicles of ohter cylinder capacity exceeding 4L, with spark-ignition internal combustion eciprocating piston engine, with drive motor (Except for charging by external
													-Other vehicles, with both compression—ignition internal combustion piston engine(diesel or semi—diesel) and electric motor as motors for propulsion, other than those capable of being charged by plugging to external source ot electric power:
													---Of fl cylinder capacity not exceeding 1000cc:
													----Saloon cars
	/0/0				0		10	0//0	0/0/			0//	Saloon cars of cylinder capacity cylinder not exceeding 1L, with compression-ignition internal combustion reciprocating piston engine (with diesel or semidiesel engine), with drive motor (Except for charging by external power supply)
	/0/0				0		10	0//0	0/0/			0//	Complete parts of saloon cars of cylinder capacity cylinder not exceeding 1L, with compression-ignition internal combustion reciprocating piston engine (with diesel or semidiesel engine), with drive motor (Except for charging by external power supply)
													----other
	0/0/0				0	0	10	0/0/0	0/0/			0/0/	Other passenger vehicles of cylinder capacity cylinder not exceeding 1L, with compression-ignition internal combustion reciprocating piston engine(with diesel or semidiesel engine), with drive motor (Except for charging by external power supply)
	0/0/0				0	0	10	0/0/0	0/0/			0/0/	Complete parts ofOther passenger vehicles of cylinder capacity cylinder not exceeding 1L, with compression-ignition internal combustion reciprocating piston engine(with diesel or semidiesel engine), with drive motor (Except for charging by external power supply)
													---Of a cylinder capacity exceeding 1000cc, but not exceeding 1500cc:
													----Saloon cars
	/0/0				0		10	0//0	0/0/				Saloon cars of cylinder capacity cylinder exceeding 1L but not exceeding 1.5L, with compression-ignition internal combustion reciprocating piston engine(with diesel or semidiesel engine), with drive motor (Except for charging by external power supply)

税则号列		货品名称〔CIQ扩展编码及品名－T2表示见附表2〕	最惠(%)	暂定税率	普通	增值/消费	出口退税	计量单位	监管条件	检验检疫	特殊证件对美关税
8703.5021	90	同时装有压燃式活塞内燃发动机(柴油或半柴油发动机,1升＜排量≤1.5升)及驱动电动机的小轿车的成套散件(可通过接插外部电源进行充电的除外)〔999〕	15		230	13/3	13	辆/千克	46Oxy		/
8703.5022		----越野车(4轮驱动)									
8703.5022	10	同时装有压燃式活塞内燃发动机(柴油或半柴油发动机,1升＜排量≤1.5升)及驱动电动机的四轮驱动越野车(可通过接插外部电源进行充电的除外)〔999〕	15		230	13/3	13	辆/千克	46AOxy	LM	/
8703.5022	90	同时装有压燃式活塞内燃发动机(柴油或半柴油发动机,1升＜排量≤1.5升)及驱动电动机的四轮驱动越野车的成套散件(可通过接插外部电源进行充电的除外)〔999〕	15		230	13/3	13	辆/千克	46Oxy		/
8703.5023		----9座及以下的小客车									
8703.5023	10	同时装有压燃式活塞内燃发动机(柴油或半柴油发动机,1升＜排量≤1.5升)及驱动电动机的小客车(9座及以下,可通过接插外部电源进行充电的除外)〔999〕	15		230	13/3	13	辆/千克	46AOxy	LM	/
8703.5023	90	同时装有压燃式活塞内燃发动机(柴油或半柴油发动机,1升＜排量≤1.5升)及驱动电动机的小客车的成套散件(9座及以下,可通过接插外部电源进行充电的除外)〔999〕	15		230	13/3	13	辆/千克	46Oxy		/
8703.5029		----其他									
8703.5029	10	同时装有压燃式活塞内燃发动机(柴油或半柴油发动机,1升＜排量≤1.5升)及驱动电动机的其他载人车辆(可通过接插外部电源进行充电的除外)〔999〕	15		230	13/3	13	辆/千克	46AOxy	LM	/
8703.5029	90	同时装有压燃式活塞内燃发动机(柴油或半柴油发动机,1升＜排量≤1.5升)及驱动电动机的其他载人车辆的成套散件(可通过接插外部电源进行充电的除外)〔999〕	15		230	13/3	13	辆/千克	46Oxy		/
		---气缸容量(排气量)超过1500毫升,但不超过2000毫升:									
8703.5031		----小轿车									
8703.5031	10	同时装有压燃式活塞内燃发动机(柴油或半柴油发动机,1.5升＜排量≤2升)及驱动电动机的小轿车(可通过接插外部电源进行充电的除外)〔999〕	15		230	13/5	13	辆/千克	46AOxy	LM	/
8703.5031	90	同时装有压燃式活塞内燃发动机(柴油或半柴油发动机,1.5升＜排量≤2升)及驱动电动机的小轿车的成套散件(可通过接插外部电源进行充电的除外)〔999〕	15		230	13/5	13	辆/千克	46Oxy		/
8703.5032		----越野车(4轮驱动)									
8703.5032	10	同时装有压燃式活塞内燃发动机(柴油或半柴油发动机,1.5升＜排量≤2升)及驱动电动机的四轮驱动越野车(可通过接插外部电源进行充电的除外)〔999〕	15		230	13/5	13	辆/千克	46AOxy	LM	/
8703.5032	90	同时装有压燃式活塞内燃发动机(柴油或半柴油发动机,1.5升＜排量≤2升)及驱动电动机的四轮驱动越野车的成套散件(可通过接插外部电源进行充电的除外)〔999〕	15		230	13/5	13	辆/千克	46Oxy		/
8703.5033		----9座及以下的小客车									
8703.5033	10	同时装有压燃式活塞内燃发动机(柴油或半柴油发动机,1.5升＜排量≤2升)及驱动电动机的小客车(9座及以下,可通过接插外部电源进行充电的除外)〔999〕	15		230	13/5	13	辆/千克	46AOxy	LM	/

协定税率 %										特惠税率 %			Article Description
亚太5国	东/冰/格	巴基斯坦	韩国	瑞士	哥达	秘鲁	澳大利亚	新西/坡/智	港/澳/台	亚太2国	老/柬/缅	36/3/1	
	/0/0				0		10	0//0	0/0/				Complete parts of saloon cars of cylinder capacity cylinder exceeding 1L but not exceeding 1.5L, with compression-ignition internal combustion reciprocating piston engine (with diesel or semidiesel engine), with drive motor (Except for charging by external power supply)
													----Cross-country cars (4WD)
	/0/0				0		10	0//0	0/0/				Off-road vehicles (4WD) of cylinder capacity cylinder exceeding 1L but not exceeding 1.5L, with compression-ignition internal combustion reciprocating piston engine (with diesel or semidiesel engine), with drive motor (Except for charging by external power supply)
	/0/0				0		10	0//0	0/0/				Complete parts of off-road vehicles (4WD) of cylinder capacity cylinder exceeding 1L but not exceeding 1.5L, with compression-ignition internal combustion reciprocating piston engine (with diesel or semidiesel engine), with drive motor (Except for charging by external power supply)
													----Station wagcms (with 9 seats or less)
	/0/0				0		10	0//0	0/0/				Station wagons (9 seats or less) of cylinder capacity cylinder exceeding 1L but not exceeding 1.5L, with compression-ignition internal combustion reciprocating piston engine (with diesel or semidiesel engine), with drive motor (Except for charging by external power supply)
	/0/0				0		10	0//0	0/0/				Complete parts of station wagons (9 seats or less) of cylinder capacity cylinder exceeding 1L but not exceeding 1.5L, with compression-ignition internal combustion reciprocating piston engine (with diesel or semidiesel engine), with drive motor (Except for charging by external power supply)
													----Other
	0/0/0				0	0	10	0/0/0	0/0/			0/0/	Other passenger vehicles of cylinder capacity cylinder exceeding 1L but not exceeding 1.5L, with compression-ignition internal combustion reciprocating piston engine (with diesel or semidiesel engine), with drive motor (Except for charging by external power supply)
	0/0/0				0	0	10	0/0/0	0/0/			0/0/	Complete parts of other passenger vehicles of cylinder capacity cylinder exceeding 1L but not exceeding 1.5L, with compression-ignition internal combustion reciprocating piston engine (with diesel or semidiesel engine), with drive motor (Except for charging by external power supply)
													---Of a cylinder capacity exceeding 1500cc, but not exceeding 2000cc:
													----Saloon cars
13.5	/0/0	22.5			0		10	0//0	0/0/				Saloon cars of cylinder capacity cylinder exceeding 1.5L but not exceeding 2L, with compression-ignition internal combustion reciprocating piston engine (with diesel or semidiesel engine), with drive motor (Except for charging by external power supply)
13.5	/0/0	22.5			0		10	0//0	0/0/				Complete parts of saloon cars of cylinder capacity cylinder exceeding 1L but not exceeding 1.5L, with compression-ignition internal combustion reciprocating piston engine (with diesel or semidiesel engine), with drive motor (Except for charging by external power supply)
													----Cross-country cars (4WD)
13.5	/0/0	22.5	22.5		0		10	0//0	0/0/				Off-road vehicles (4WD) of cylinder capacity cylinder exceeding 1.5L but not exceeding 2L, with compression-ignition internal combustion reciprocating piston engine (with diesel or semidiesel engine), with drive motor (Except for charging by external power supply)
13.5	/0/0	22.5	22.5		0		10	0//0	0/0/				Complete parts of off-road vehicles (4WD) of cylinder capacity cylinder exceeding 1L but not exceeding 1.5L, with compression-ignition internal combustion reciprocating piston engine (with diesel or semidiesel engine), with drive motor (Except for charging by external power supply)
													----Station wagcms (with 9 seats or less)
13.5	/0/0	22.5	22.5		0		10	0//0	0/0/				Station wagons (9 seats or less) of cylinder capacity cylinder exceeding 1.5L but not exceeding 2L, with compression-ignition internal combustion reciprocating piston engine (with diesel or semidiesel engine), with drive motor (Except for charging by external power supply)

税则号列		货品名称〔CIQ扩展编码及品名－T2表示见附表2〕	最惠(%)	暂定税率	普通	增值/消费	出口退税	计量单位	监管条件	检验检疫	特殊证件对美关税
8703.5033	90	同时装有压燃式活塞内燃发动机(柴油或半柴油发动机,1.5升＜排量≤2升)及驱动电动机的小客车的成套散件(9座及以下,可通过接插外部电源进行充电的除外)〔999〕	15		230	13/5	13	辆/千克	46Oxy		/
8703.5039		----其他									
8703.5039	10	同时装有压燃式活塞内燃发动机(柴油或半柴油发动机,1.5升＜排量≤2升)及驱动电动机的其他载人车辆(可通过接插外部电源进行充电的除外)〔999〕	15		230	13/5	13	辆/千克	46AOxy	LM	/
8703.5039	90	同时装有压燃式活塞内燃发动机(柴油或半柴油发动机,1.5升＜排量≤2升)及驱动电动机的其他载人车辆的成套散件(可通过接插外部电源进行充电的除外)〔999〕	15		230	13/5	13	辆/千克	46Oxy		/
		---气缸容量(排气量)超过2000毫升,但不超过2500毫升:									
8703.5041		----小轿车									
8703.5041	10	同时装有压燃式活塞内燃发动机(柴油或半柴油发动机,2升＜排量≤2.5升)及驱动电动机的小轿车(可通过接插外部电源进行充电的除外)〔999〕	15		230	13/9	13	辆/千克	46AOxy	LM	/
8703.5041	90	同时装有压燃式活塞内燃发动机(柴油或半柴油发动机,2升＜排量≤2.5升)及驱动电动机的小轿车的成套散件(可通过接插外部电源进行充电的除外)〔999〕	15		230	13/9	13	辆/千克	46Oxy		/
8703.5042		----越野车(4轮驱动)									
8703.5042	10	同时装有压燃式活塞内燃发动机(柴油或半柴油发动机,2升＜排量≤2.5升)及驱动电动机的四轮驱动越野车(可通过接插外部电源进行充电的除外)〔999〕	15		230	13/9	13	辆/千克	46AOxy	LM	/
8703.5042	90	同时装有压燃式活塞内燃发动机(柴油或半柴油发动机,2升＜排量≤2.5升)及驱动电动机的四轮驱动越野车的成套散件(可通过接插外部电源进行充电的除外)〔999〕	15		230	13/9	13	辆/千克	46Oxy		/
8703.5043		----9座及以下的小客车									
8703.5043	10	同时装有压燃式活塞内燃发动机(柴油或半柴油发动机,2升＜排量≤2.5升)及驱动电动机的小客车(9座及以下,可通过接插外部电源进行充电的除外)〔999〕	15		230	13/9	13	辆/千克	46AOxy	LM	/
8703.5043	90	同时装有压燃式活塞内燃发动机(柴油或半柴油发动机,2升＜排量≤2.5升)及驱动电动机的小客车的成套散件(9座及以下,可通过接插外部电源进行充电的除外)〔999〕	15		230	13/9	13	辆/千克	46Oxy		/
8703.5049		----其他									
8703.5049	10	同时装有压燃式活塞内燃发动机(柴油或半柴油发动机,2升＜排量≤2.5升)及驱动电动机的其他载人车辆(可通过接插外部电源进行充电的除外)〔999〕	15		230	13/9	13	辆/千克	46AOxy	LM	/
8703.5049	90	同时装有压燃式活塞内燃发动机(柴油或半柴油发动机,2升＜排量≤2.5升)及驱动电动机的其他载人车辆的成套散件(可通过接插外部电源进行充电的除外)〔999〕	15		230	13/9	13	辆/千克	46Oxy		/
		---气缸容量(排气量)超过2500毫升,但不超过3000毫升:									
8703.5051		----小轿车									
8703.5051	10	同时装有压燃式活塞内燃发动机(柴油或半柴油发动机,2.5升＜排量≤3升)及驱动电动机的小轿车(可通过接插外部电源进行充电的除外)〔999〕	15		270	13/12	13	辆/千克	46AOxy	LM	/

协定税率 %										特惠税率 %			Article Description
亚太5国	东/冰/格	巴基斯坦	韩国	瑞士	哥达	秘鲁	澳大利亚	新西/坡/智	港/澳/台	亚太2国	老/柬/缅	36/3/1	
13.5	/0/0	22.5	22.5		0		10	0//0	0/0/				Complete parts of station wagons(9 seats or less) of cylinder capacity cylinder exceeding 1L but not exceeding 1.5L, with compression-ignition internal combustion reciprocating piston engine (with diesel or semidiesel engine), with drive motor (Except for charging by external power supply)
													----Other
13.5	/0/0	22.5			0		10	0//0	0/0/				Other passenger vehicles of cylinder capacity cylinder exceeding 1.5L but not exceeding 2L, with compression-ignition internal combustion reciprocating piston engine (with diesel or semidiesel engine), with drive motor (Except for charging by external power supply)
13.5	/0/0	22.5			0		10	0//0	0/0/				Complete parts of other passenger vehicles of cylinder capacity cylinder exceeding 1.5L but not exceeding 2L, with compression-ignition internal combustion reciprocating piston engine (with diesel or semidiesel engine), with drive motor (Except for charging by external power supply)
													--Of a cylinder capacity exceeding 2000cc, but not exceeding 2500cc:
													----Saloon cars
13.5	/0/0	22.5			0		10	0//0	0/0/				Saloon cars of cylinder capacity cylinder exceeding 2L but not exceeding 2.5L, with compression-ignition internal combustion reciprocating piston engine (with diesel or semidiesel engine), with drive motor (Except for charging by external power supply)
13.5	/0/0	22.5			0		10	0//0	0/0/				Complete parts of saloon cars of cylinder capacity cylinder exceeding 1L but not exceeding 1.5L, with compression-ignition internal combustion reciprocating piston engine (with diesel or semidiesel engine), with drive motor (Except for charging by external power supply)
													----Cross-country cars (4WD)
13.5	/0/0	22.5			0		10	0//0	0/0/				Off-road vehicles (4WD) of cylinder capacity cylinder exceeding 2L but not exceeding 2.5L, with compression-ignition internal combustion reciprocating piston engine (with diesel or semidiesel engine), with drive motor (Except for charging by external power supply)
13.5	/0/0	22.5			0		10	0//0	0/0/				Complete parts of off-road vehicles (4WD) of cylinder capacity cylinder exceeding 1L but not exceeding 1.5L, with compression-ignition internal combustion reciprocating piston engine (with diesel or semidiesel engine), with drive motor (Except for charging by external power supply)
													----Station wagons (with 9 seats or less)
13.5	/0/0	22.5	22.5		0		10	0//0	0/0/				Station wagons (9 seats or less) of cylinder capacity cylinder exceeding 2L but not exceeding 2.5L, with compression-ignition internal combustion reciprocating piston engine (with diesel or semidiesel engine), with drive motor (Except for charging by external power supply)
13.5	/0/0	22.5	22.5		0		10	0//0	0/0/				Complete parts of station wagons (9 seats or less) of cylinder capacity cylinder exceeding 2L but not exceeding 2.5L, with compression-ignition internal combustion reciprocating piston engine (with diesel or semidiesel engine), with drive motor (Except for charging by external power supply)
													----Other
13.5	/0/0	22.5			0		10	0//0	0/0/				Other passenger vehicles of cylinder capacity cylinder exceeding 2L but not exceeding 2.5L, with compression-ignition internal combustion reciprocating piston engine (with diesel or semidiesel engine), with drive motor (Except for charging by external power supply)
13.5	/0/0	22.5			0		10	0//0	0/0/				Complete parts of other passenger vehicles of cylinder capacity cylinder exceeding 2L but not exceeding 2.5L, with compression-ignition internal combustion reciprocating piston engine (with diesel or semidiesel engine), with drive motor (Except for charging by external power supply)
													---Of a cylinder capacity exceeding 2500cc, but not exceeding 3000cc:
													----Saloon cars
13.5	0/0/0	22.5			0		10	0/0/0	0/0/				Saloon cars of cylinder capacity cylinder exceeding 2.5L but not exceeding 3L, with compression-ignition internal combustion reciprocating piston engine (with diesel or semidiesel engine), with drive motor (Except for charging by external power supply)

税则号列		货品名称〔CIQ扩展编码及品名—T2表示见附表2〕	最惠(%)	暂定税率	普通	增值/消费	出口退税	计量单位	监管条件	检验检疫	特殊证件对美关税
8703.5051	90	同时装有压燃式活塞内燃发动机(柴油或半柴油发动机,2.5升<排量≤3升)及驱动电动机的小轿车的成套散件(可通过接插外部电源进行充电的除外)〔999〕	15		270	13/12	13	辆/千克	46Oxy		/
8703.5052		----越野车(4轮驱动)									
8703.5052	10	同时装有压燃式活塞内燃发动机(柴油或半柴油发动机,2.5升<排量≤3升)及驱动电动机的四轮驱动越野车(可通过接插外部电源进行充电的除外)〔999〕	15		270	13/12	13	辆/千克	46AOxy	LM	/
8703.5052	90	同时装有压燃式活塞内燃发动机(柴油或半柴油发动机,2.5升<排量≤3升)及驱动电动机的四轮驱动越野车的成套散件(可通过接插外部电源进行充电的除外)〔999〕	15		270	13/12	13	辆/千克	46Oxy		/
8703.5053		----9座及以下的小客车									
8703.5053	10	同时装有压燃式活塞内燃发动机(柴油或半柴油发动机,2.5升<排量≤3升)及驱动电动机的小客车(9座及以下,可通过接插外部电源进行充电的除外)〔999〕	15		270	13/12	13	辆/千克	46AOxy	LM	/
8703.5053	90	同时装有压燃式活塞内燃发动机(柴油或半柴油发动机,2.5升<排量≤3升)及驱动电动机的小客车的成套散件(9座及以下,可通过接插外部电源进行充电的除外)〔999〕	15		270	13/12	13	辆/千克	46Oxy		/
8703.5059		----其他									
8703.5059	10	同时装有压燃式活塞内燃发动机(柴油或半柴油发动机,2.5升<排量≤3升)及驱动电动机的其他载人车辆(可通过接插外部电源进行充电的除外)〔999〕	15		270	13/12	13	辆/千克	46AOxy	LM	/
8703.5059	90	同时装有压燃式活塞内燃发动机(柴油或半柴油发动机,2.5升<排量≤3升)及驱动电动机的其他载人车辆的成套散件(可通过接插外部电源进行充电的除外)〔999〕	15		270	13/12	13	辆/千克	46Oxy		/
		---气缸容量(排气量)超过3000毫升,但不超过4000毫升:									
8703.5061		----小轿车									
8703.5061	10	同时装有压燃式活塞内燃发动机(柴油或半柴油发动机,3升<排量≤4升)及驱动电动机的小轿车(可通过接插外部电源进行充电的除外)〔999〕	15		270	13/25	13	辆/千克	46AOxy	LM	/
8703.5061	90	同时装有压燃式活塞内燃发动机(柴油或半柴油发动机,3升<排量≤4升)及驱动电动机的小轿车的成套散件(可通过接插外部电源进行充电的除外)〔999〕	15		270	13/25	13	辆/千克	46Oxy		/
8703.5062		----越野车(4轮驱动)									
8703.5062	10	同时装有压燃式活塞内燃发动机(柴油或半柴油发动机,3升<排量≤4升)及驱动电动机的四轮驱动越野车(可通过接插外部电源进行充电的除外)〔999〕	15		270	13/25	13	辆/千克	46AOxy	LM	/
8703.5062	90	同时装有压燃式活塞内燃发动机(柴油或半柴油发动机,3升<排量≤4升)及驱动电动机的四轮驱动越野车的成套散件(可通过接插外部电源进行充电的除外)〔999〕	15		270	13/25	13	辆/千克	46Oxy		/
8703.5063		----9座及以下的小客车									
8703.5063	10	同时装有压燃式活塞内燃发动机(柴油或半柴油发动机,3升<排量≤4升)及驱动电动机的小客车(9座及以下,可通过接插外部电源进行充电的除外)〔999〕	15		270	13/25	13	辆/千克	46AOxy	LM	/

协定税率 %										特惠税率 %			Article Description
亚太5国	东/冰/格	巴基斯坦	韩国	瑞士	哥达	秘鲁	澳大利亚	新西/坡/智	港/澳/台	亚太2国	老/柬/缅	36/3/1	
13.5	0/0/0	22.5			0		10	0/0/0	0/0/				Complete parts of saloon cars of cylinder capacity cylinder exceeding 2.5L but not exceeding 3L, with compression-ignition internal combustion reciprocating piston engine (with diesel or semidiesel engine), with drive motor (Except for charging by external power supply)
													----Cross-country cars (4WD)
13.5	0/0/0	22.5	22.5		0		10	0/0/0	0/0/				Off-road vehicles(4WD) of cylinder capacity cylinder exceeding 2.5L but not exceeding 3L, with compression-ignition internal combustion reciprocating piston engine (with diesel or semidiesel engine), with drive motor (Except for charging by external power supply)
13.5	0/0/0	22.5	22.5		0		10	0/0/0	0/0/				Complete parts of off-road vehicles(4WD) of cylinder capacity cylinder exceeding 2.5L but not exceeding 3L, with compression-ignition internal combustion reciprocating piston engine(with diesel or semidiesel engine), with drive motor (Except for charging by external power supply)
													----Station wagcms(with 9 seats or less)
13.5	0/0/0	22.5			0		10	0/0/0	0/0/				Station wagons(9 seats or less) of cylinder capacity cylinder exceeding 2.5L but not exceeding 3L, with compression-ignition internal combustion reciprocating piston engine(with diesel or semidiesel engine), with drive motor (Except for charging by external power supply)
13.5	0/0/0	22.5			0		10	0/0/0	0/0/				Complete parts of station wagons(9 seats or less) of cylinder capacity cylinder exceeding 2.5L but not exceeding 3L, with compression-ignition internal combustion reciprocating piston engine (with diesel or semidiesel engine), with drive motor (Except for charging by external power supply)
													----Other
13.5	0/0/0	22.5			0		10	0/0/0	0/0/				Other passenger vehicles of cylinder capacity cylinder exceeding 2.5L but not exceeding 3L, with compression-ignition internal combustion reciprocating piston engine (with diesel or semidiesel engine), with drive motor (Except for charging by external power supply)
13.5	0/0/0	22.5			0		10	0/0/0	0/0/				Complete parts of other passenger vehicles of cylinder capacity cylinder exceeding 2.5L but not exceeding 3L, with compression-ignition internal combustion reciprocating piston engine(with diesel or semidiesel engine), with drive motor (Except for charging by external power supply)
													---Of a cylinder capacity exceeding 3000cc, but not exceeding 4000cc:
													----Saloon cars
13.5	0/0/0	22.5			0		10	0/0/0	0/0/			0//	Saloon cars of cylinder capacity cylinder exceeding 3L but not exceeding 4L, with compression-ignition internal combustion reciprocating piston engine (with diesel or semidiesel engine), with drive motor (Except for charging by external power supply)
13.5	0/0/0	22.5			0		10	0/0/0	0/0/			0//	Complete parts of saloon cars of cylinder capacity cylinder exceeding 3L but not exceeding 4L, with compression-ignition internal combustion reciprocating piston engine (with diesel or semidiesel engine), with drive motor (Except for charging by external power supply)
													----Cross-country cars (4WD)
13.5	0/0/0	22.5			0		10	0/0/0	0/0/			0//	Off-road vehicles (4WD) of cylinder capacity cylinder exceeding 3L but not exceeding 4L, with compression-ignition internal combustion reciprocating piston engine (with diesel or semidiesel engine), with drive motor (Except for charging by external power supply)
13.5	0/0/0	22.5			0		10	0/0/0	0/0/			0//	Complete parts of off-road vehicles(4WD) of cylinder capacity cylinder exceeding 3L but not exceeding 4L, with compression-ignition internal combustion reciprocating piston engine(with diesel or semidiesel engine), with drive motor (Except for charging by external power supply)
													----Station wagcms(with 9 seats or less)
13.5	0/0/0	22.5			0		10	0/0/0	0/0/			0//	Station wagons(9 seats or less) of cylinder capacity cylinder exceeding 3L but not exceeding 4L, with compression-ignition internal combustion reciprocating piston engine(with diesel or semidiesel engine), with drive motor (Except for charging by external power supply)

税则号列		货品名称〔CIQ扩展编码及品名－T2表示见附表2〕	最惠(%)	暂定税率	普通	增值/消费	出口退税	计量单位	监管条件	检验检疫	特殊证件对美关税
8703.5063	90	同时装有压燃式活塞内燃发动机(柴油或半柴油发动机,3升＜排量≤4升)及驱动电动机的小客车的成套散件(9座及以下,可通过接插外部电源进行充电的除外)〔999〕	15		270	13/25	13	辆/千克	46Oxy		/
8703.5069		----其他									
8703.5069	10	同时装有压燃式活塞内燃发动机(柴油或半柴油发动机,3升＜排量≤4升)及驱动电动机的其他载人车辆(可通过接插外部电源进行充电的除外)〔999〕	15		270	13/25	13	辆/千克	46AOxy	LM	/
8703.5069	90	同时装有压燃式活塞内燃发动机(柴油或半柴油发动机,3升＜排量≤4升)及驱动电动机的其他载人车辆的成套散件(可通过接插外部电源进行充电的除外)〔999〕	15		270	13/25	13	辆/千克	46Oxy		/
		---气缸容量(排气量)超过4000毫升:									
8703.5071		----小轿车									
8703.5071	10	同时装有压燃式活塞内燃发动机(柴油或半柴油发动机,排量＞4升)及驱动电动机的小轿车(可通过接插外部电源进行充电的除外)〔999〕	15		270	13/40	13	辆/千克	46AOxy	LM	/
8703.5071	90	同时装有压燃式活塞内燃发动机(柴油或半柴油发动机,排量＞4升)及驱动电动机的小轿车的成套散件(可通过接插外部电源进行充电的除外)〔999〕	15		270	13/40	13	辆/千克	46Oxy		/
8703.5072		----越野车(4轮驱动)									
8703.5072	10	同时装有压燃式活塞内燃发动机(柴油或半柴油发动机,排量＞4升)及驱动电动机的四轮驱动越野车(可通过接插外部电源进行充电的除外)〔999〕	15		270	13/40	13	辆/千克	46AOxy	LM	/
8703.5072	90	同时装有压燃式活塞内燃发动机(柴油或半柴油发动机,排量＞4升)及驱动电动机的四轮驱动越野车的成套散件(可通过接插外部电源进行充电的除外)〔999〕	15		270	13/40	13	辆/千克	46Oxy		/
8703.5073		----9座及以下的小客车									
8703.5073	10	同时装有压燃式活塞内燃发动机(柴油或半柴油发动机,排量＞4升)及驱动电动机的的小客车(9座及以下,可通过接插外部电源进行充电的除外)〔999〕	15		270	13/40	13	辆/千克	46AOxy	LM	/
8703.5073	90	同时装有压燃式活塞内燃发动机(柴油或半柴油发动机,排量＞4升)及驱动电动机的小客车的成套散件(9座及以下,可通过接插外部电源进行充电的除外)〔999〕	15		270	13/40	13	辆/千克	46Oxy		/
8703.5079		----其他									
8703.5079	10	同时装有压燃式活塞内燃发动机(柴油或半柴油发动机,排量＞4升)及驱动电动机的的其他载人车辆(可通过接插外部电源进行充电的除外)〔999〕	15		270	13/40	13	辆/千克	46AOxy	LM	/
8703.5079	90	同时装有压燃式活塞内燃发动机(柴油或半柴油发动机,排量＞4升)及驱动电动机的的其他载人车辆的成套散件(可通过接插外部电源进行充电的除外)〔999〕	15		270	13/40	13	辆/千克	46Oxy		/
8703.5090		---其他									
8703.5090	10	其他同时装有压燃式活塞内燃发动机(柴油或半柴油发动机)及驱动电动机的载人车辆(可通过接插外部电源进行充电的除外)〔999〕	15		270	13/	13	辆/千克	46AOxy	LM	/
8703.5090	90	其他同时装有压燃式活塞内燃发动机(柴油或半柴油发动机)及驱动电动机的载人车辆的成套散件(可通过接插外部电源进行充电的除外)〔999〕	15		270	13/	13	辆/千克	46Oxy		/

协定税率 %										特惠税率 %			
亚太5国	东/冰/格	巴基斯坦	韩国	瑞士	哥达	秘鲁	澳大利亚	新西/坡/智	港/澳/台	亚太2国	老/柬/缅	36/3/1	Article Description
13.5	0/0/0	22.5			0		10	0/0/0	0/0/			0//	Complete parts of station wagons(9 seats or less) of cylinder capacity cylinder exceeding 3L but not exceeding 4L, with compression-ignition internal combustion reciprocating piston engine(with diesel or semidiesel engine), with drive motor (Except for charging by external power supply)
													----Other
13.5	0/0/0	22.5			0		10	0/0/0	0/0/			0//	Other passenger vehicles of cylinder capacity cylinder exceeding 3L but not exceeding 4L, with compression-ignition internal combustion reciprocating piston engine(with diesel or semidiesel engine), with drive motor (Except for charging by external power supply)
13.5	0/0/0	22.5			0		10	0/0/0	0/0/			0//	Complete parts of other passenger vehicles of cylinder capacity cylinder exceeding 3L but not exceeding 4L, with compression-ignition internal combustion reciprocating piston engine(with diesel or semidiesel engine), with drive motor (Except for charging by external power supply)
													---Of a cylinder capacity exceeding4000cc:
													----Saloon cars
13.5	0/0/0	22.5			0		0	0/0/0	0/0/			0//	Saloon cars of cylinder capacity cylinder exceeding 4L, with compression-ignition internal combustion reciprocating piston engine (with diesel or semidiesel engine), with drive motor (Except for charging by external power supply)
13.5	0/0/0	22.5			0		0	0/0/0	0/0/			0//	Complete parts of saloon cars of cylinder capacity cylinder exceeding 3L but not exceeding 4L, with compression-ignition internal combustion reciprocating piston engine(with diesel or semidiesel engine), with drive motor (Except for charging by external power supply)
													----Cross-country cars (4WD)
13.5	0/0/0	22.5			0		0	0/0/0	0/0/			0//	Off-road vehicles(4WD) of cylinder capacity cylinder exceeding 4L, with compression-ignition internal combustion reciprocating piston engine(with diesel or semidiesel engine), with drive motor (Except for charging by external power supply)
13.5	0/0/0	22.5			0		0	0/0/0	0/0/			0//	Complete parts of off-road vehicles(4WD) of cylinder capacity cylinder exceeding 4L, with compression-ignition internal combustion reciprocating piston engine(with diesel or semidiesel engine), with drive motor (Except for charging by external power supply)
													----Station wagcms(with 9 seats or less)
13.5	0/0/0	22.5			0		0	0/0/0	0/0/			0//	Station wagons(9 seats or less) of cylinder capacity cylinder exceeding 4L, with compression-ignition internal combustion reciprocating piston engine(with diesel or semidiesel engine), with drive motor (Except for charging by external power supply)
13.5	0/0/0	22.5			0		0	0/0/0	0/0/			0//	Complete parts of station wagons(9 seats or less) of cylinder capacity cylinder exceeding 4L, with compression-ignition internal combustion reciprocating piston engine(with diesel or semidiesel engine), with drive motor (Except for charging by external power supply)
													----Other
13.5	0/0/0	22.5			0		0	0/0/0	0/0/			0//	Other passenger vehicles of cylinder capacity cylinder exceeding 3L but not exceeding 4L, with compression-ignition internal combustion reciprocating piston engine(with diesel or semidiesel engine), with drive motor (Except for charging by external power supply)
13.5	0/0/0	22.5			0		0	0/0/0	0/0/			0//	Complete parts of other passenger vehicles of cylinder capacity cylinder exceeding 4L, with compression-ignition internal combustion reciprocating piston engine(with diesel or semidiesel engine), with drive motor (Except for charging by external power supply)
													---Other
13.5	0/0/10	22.5	22.5		0	0	0	0/0/0	0/0/			0/0/	Passenger vehicles of other cylinder capacity cylinder exceeding 3L but not exceeding 4L, with compression-ignition internal combustion reciprocating piston engine(with diesel or semidiesel engine), with drive motor (Except for charging by external power supply)
13.5	0/0/10	22.5	22.5		0	0	0	0/0/0	0/0/			0/0/	Complete parts of passenger vehicles of other cylinder capacity cylinder exceeding 4L, with compression-ignition internal combustion reciprocating piston engine(with diesel or semidiesel engine), with drive motor (Except for charging by external power supply)

税则号列		货品名称〔CIQ扩展编码及品名－T2表示见附表2〕	最惠(%)	暂定税率	普通	增值/消费	出口退税	计量单位	监管条件	检验检疫	特殊证件对美关税
8703.6000		-同时装有点燃往复式活塞内燃发动机及驱动电动机、可通过接插外部电源进行充电的其他车辆〔999〕	15		270	13/	13	辆/千克	46AO	LM	/
8703.7000		-同时装有压燃活塞内燃发动机(柴油或半柴油发动机)及驱动电动机、可通过接插外部电源进行充电的其他车辆〔999〕	15		270	13/	13	辆/千克	46AO	LM	/
8703.8000		-仅装有驱动电动机的其他车辆〔999〕	15		270	13/	13	辆/千克	6AO	LM	/
8703.9000		-其他									
8703.9000	21	其他型排气量≤1升的其他载人车辆〔999〕	15		270	13/1	13	辆/千克	46AOxy	LM	/
8703.9000	22	其他型1升＜排气量≤1.5升的其他载人车辆〔999〕	15		270	13/3	13	辆/千克	46AOxy	LM	/
8703.9000	23	其他型1.5升＜排气量≤2升的其他载人车辆〔999〕	15		270	13/5	13	辆/千克	46AOxy	LM	/
8703.9000	24	其他型2升＜排气量≤2.5升的其他载人车辆〔999〕	15		270	13/9	13	辆/千克	46AOxy	LM	/
8703.9000	25	其他型2.5升＜排气量≤3升的其他载人车辆〔999〕	15		270	13/12	13	辆/千克	46AOxy	LM	/
8703.9000	26	其他型3升＜排气量≤4升的其他载人车辆〔999〕	15		270	13/25	13	辆/千克	46AOxy	LM	/
8703.9000	27	其他型排气量＞4升的其他载人车辆〔999〕	15		270	13/40	13	辆/千克	46AOxy	LM	/
8703.9000	29	其他无法区分排气量的载人车辆〔999〕	15		270	13/	13	辆/千克	6AO	LM	/
8703.9000	90	8703.9000所列车辆的成套散件〔999〕	15		270	13/	13	辆/千克	6O		/
87.04		**货运机动车辆：**									
		-非公路用自卸车：									
8704.1030		---电动轮货运自卸车〔999〕	6		20	13/	13	辆/千克	6A	M	/
8704.1090		---其他〔999〕	6		20	13/	13	辆/千克	6A	M	/
		-装有压燃式活塞内燃发动机(柴油或半柴油发动机)的其他货车：									
8704.2100		--车辆总重量不超过5吨〔999〕	15		70	13/	9,13	辆/千克	46AOxy	LM	/
		--车辆总重量超过5吨，但不超过20吨：									
8704.2230		---车辆总重量超过5吨，但小于14吨〔999〕	15		70	13/	13	辆/千克	46Axy	LM	/
8704.2240		---车辆总重量在14吨及以上，但不超过20吨〔999〕	15		40	13/	13	辆/千克	46Axy	LM	/
8704.2300		--车辆总重量超过20吨									
8704.2300	10	固井水泥车、压裂车、混砂车、连续油管车、液氮泵车用底盘(车辆总重量＞35吨，装驾驶室)〔999〕	15	10	40	13/	13	辆/千克	46AOxy	LM	/
8704.2300	20	起重≥55吨汽车起重机用底盘(装有压燃式活塞内燃发动机)〔999〕	15	8	40	13/	13	辆/千克	46AOxy	LM	/
8704.2300	30	车辆总重量≥31吨清障车专用底盘〔999〕	15	10	40	13/	13	辆/千克	46AOxy	LM	/
8704.2300	90	柴油型的其他超重型货车(装有压燃式活塞内燃发动机，超重型指车辆总重量＞20吨)〔999〕	15		40	13/	13	辆/千克	46AOxy	LM	/
		-装有点燃式活塞内燃发动机的其他货车：									
8704.3100		--车辆总重量不超过5吨〔999〕	15		70	13/	13	辆/千克	46AOxy	LM	/
		--车辆总重量超过5吨：									
8704.3230		---车辆总重量超过5吨，但不超过8吨〔999〕	15		70	13/	13	辆/千克	46Axy	LM	/
8704.3240		---车辆总重量超过8吨〔999〕	15		70	13/	13	辆/千克	46Axy	LM	/
8704.9000		-其他〔101电动汽车，102内燃机汽车，103混合动力汽车，104其他能源汽车〕	15		70	13/	13	辆/千克	46Axy	LM	/
87.05		**特殊用途的机动车辆(例如，抢修车、起重车、救火车、混凝土搅拌车、道路清洁车、喷洒车、流动工场车及流动放射线检查车)，但主要用于载人或运货的车辆除外：**									
		-起重车：									
		---全路面起重车：									
8705.1021		----最大起重重量不超过50吨〔101起重车，102汽车起重机〕	15		30	13/	13	辆/千克	6A	ML	/40
8705.1022		----最大起重重量超过50吨，但不超过100吨〔101起重车，102汽车起重机〕	10		30	13/	13	辆/千克	6A	ML	/35
8705.1023		----最大起重重量超过100吨〔101起重车，102汽车起重机〕	10		30	13/	13	辆/千克	6A	ML	/35
		---其他：									
8705.1091		----最大起重重量不超过50吨〔101起重车，102汽车起重机〕	15		30	13/	13	辆/千克	6A	ML	/40

协定税率 %										特惠税率 %			Article Description
亚太5国	东/冰/格	巴基斯坦	韩国	瑞士	哥达	秘鲁	澳大利亚	新西/坡/智	港/澳/台	亚太2国	老/柬/缅	36/3/1	
13.5	/0/	22.5			0		0	0//0	0/0/				-Other vehicles, with both cornpression-ignition internal combustion piston engine (diesel or semi-diesel) and electric motor as motors for propulsion, capable of being charged by plugging to external source of electric power
13.5	0/0/10		22.5		0	0	0	0/0/0	0/0/			0/0/	-Other vehicles, with only electric motor for propulsion
13.5	0/0/10	22.5	22.5		0	0	0	0/0/0	0/0/			0/0/	-With electric motor for propulSlon
													-Other
13.5	0/0/10	22.5	22.5		0	0	0	0/0/0	0/0/			0/0/	Other motor vehicles designed for transport of person's, cylinder capacity ≤1L
13.5	0/0/10	22.5	22.5		0	0	0	0/0/0	0/0/			0/0/	Other motor vehicles designed for transport of person's, 1.5L<cylinder capacity ≤2L
13.5	0/0/10	22.5	22.5		0	0	0	0/0/0	0/0/			0/0/	Other motor vehicles designed for transport of person's, 2L<cylinder capacity ≤2.5L
13.5	0/0/10	22.5	22.5		0	0	0	0/0/0	0/0/			0/0/	Other motor vehicles designed for transport of person's, 2.5L<cylinder capacity ≤3L
13.5	0/0/10	22.5	22.5		0	0	0	0/0/0	0/0/			0/0/	Other motor vehicles designed for transport of person's, 3L<cylinder capacity ≤4L
13.5	0/0/10	22.5	22.5		0	0	0	0/0/0	0/0/			0/0/	Other motor vehicles designed for transport of person's, cylinder capacity >4L
13.5	0/0/10	22.5	22.5		0	0	0	0/0/0	0/0/			0/0/	Other motor vehicles designed for transport of person's, 1L<cylinder capacity ≤1.5L
13.5	0/0/10	22.5	22.5		0	0	0	0/0/0	0/0/			0/0/	Electronic vehicles and other passenger vehicles which can not distingguished cylinder capacity
13.5	0/0/10	22.5	22.5		0	0	0	0/0/0	0/0/			0/0/	Complete parts of passenger vehicles of subheading No.8703.9000
													Motor vehicles for the transport of goods:
													-Dumpers designed for off-highway use:
	0/0/0	0	0	0	0	0	0	0//0	0/0/			0/0/0	---Electromobile dumpers for the transport of goods
	0/0/0	0	0	0	0	0	0	0//0	0/0/			0/0/0	---Other
													-Other, with compression-ignition internal combustion piston engine (diesel or semidiesesl):
	/0/0		17.5		0		0	0//0	0/0/			0//	—G. v. w. not exceeding 5 tons
													—G. v. w. exceeding 5 tons, but not exceeding 20 tons:
13.5	5/0/0	18	12	6	0	0	0	0//0	0/0/			0/0/	---G. v. w. exceeding 5 tons, but notexceeding 14 tons
13.5	5/0/0	18	12	6	0	0	0	0//0	0/0/			0/0/	---G. v. w. of 14 tons or more, but not exceeding 20 tons
													--G. v. w. exceeding 20 tons
	5/0/0		9	4.5	0		0	0//0	0/0/			0//	Cementing truck, car, fracturing sand mixing truck, coiled tubing unit, liquid nitrogen pump vehicle chassis (gross vehicle weight > 35 tons, installed cab)
	5/0/0		9	4.5	0		0	0//0	0/0/			0//	Chassis for crane lorries, lifting capacity≥55tons, with compression-ignition internal combustion piston engine
	5/0/0		9	4.5	0		0	0//0	0/0/			0//	Special chassis for wreckers truck with total vehicle G. v. w≥31 tons
	5/0/0		9	4.5	0		0	0//0	0/0/			0//	Other overweight truck, with compression-ignition internal combustion piston engine (diesel or semi-diesel, G. v. w>20 tons)
													-Other, with spark-ignition internal combustion piston engine:
	5/0/0		17.5		0		0	0//0	0/0/			0//	--G. v. w. not exceeding 5 tons
													--G. v. w. exceeding 5 tons:
	5/0/0		12	6	0	0	0	0//0	0/0/			0/0/	---G. v. w. exceeding 5 tons, but not exceeding 8 tons
	5/0/0		12	6	0	0	0	0//0	0/0/			0/0/	---G. v. w. exceeding 8 tons
	0/0/0		17.5		0	0	0	0/0/0	0/0/			0/0/	-Other
													Special purpose motor vehicles, other than those principally designed for the transport of persons or goods (for example, breakdown lorries, crane lorries, fire fighting vehicles, concrete-mixer lorries, road sweeper lorries, spraying lorries, mobile workshops, mobile radiological units):
													-Crane lorries:
													---All-road crane lorries:
	0/0/0	10.8	9	4.5	0	0	0	0/0/0	0/0/			0/0/	----Of a maxium lifting capacity not more than 50tons
	0/0/0	4	6	0	0	0	0	0/0/0	0/0/			0/0/0	----Of a maxium lifting capacity exceeding 50tons, but not exceeding 100tons
	0/0/0	4	6	0	0	0	0	0/0/0	0/0/			0/0/0	----Of a maxium lifting capacity exceeding 100tons
													---Other:
	0/0/0	10.8	9	4.5	0	0	0	0/0/0	0/0/			0/0/	----Of a maxium lifting capacity not more than 50tons

税则号列	货品名称〔CIQ扩展编码及品名－T2表示见附表2〕	最惠(%)	暂定税率	普通	增值/消费	出口退税	计量单位	监管条件	检验检疫	特殊证件对美关税
8705.1092	----最大起重重量超过50吨，但不超过100吨〔101起重车，102汽车起重机〕	10		30	13/	13	辆/千克	6A	ML	/35
8705.1093	----最大起重重量超过100吨〔101起重车，102汽车起重机〕	10		30	13/	13	辆/千克	6A	ML	/35
8705.2000	-钻探车〔999〕	12		17	13/	13	辆/千克	6A	ML	/17
	-救火车：									
8705.3010	---装有云梯的救火车〔999〕	3		8	13/	13	辆/千克	A6	LM	/8
8705.3090	---其他〔999〕	3		8	13/	13	辆/千克	A6	LM	/8
8705.4000	-混凝土搅拌车〔999〕	15		35	13/	13	辆/千克	A6	LM	/20
	-其他：									
8705.9010	---无线电通信车〔999〕	9		35	13/	13	辆/千克	A6	LM	/14
8705.9020	---放射线检查车〔999〕	9		14	13/	13	辆/千克	6A	ML	/14
8705.9030	---环境监测车〔999〕	12		20	13/	13	辆/千克	6A	ML	/17
8705.9040	---医疗车〔999〕	12		30	13/	13	辆/千克	6A	ML	/17
	---电源车：									
8705.9051	----航空电源车(频率为400赫兹)〔999〕	12		30	13/	13	辆/千克	6		/17
8705.9059	----其他〔999〕	12		30	13/	13	辆/千克	6A	ML	/17
8705.9060	---飞机加油车、调温车、除冰车〔999〕	12		35	13/	13	辆/千克	A6	M	/17
8705.9070	---道路(包括跑道)扫雪车〔999〕	12		35	13/	13	辆/千克	A6	LM	/17
8705.9080	---石油测井车、压裂车、混沙车〔999〕	12		35	13/	13	辆/千克	A6	LM	/17
	---其他：									
8705.9091	----混凝土泵车〔999〕	12		35	13/	13	辆/千克	A6	LM	/17
8705.9099	----其他									
8705.9099 01	跑道除冰车〔999〕	12	10	35	13/	13	辆/千克	A6	M	/15
8705.9099 30	用于导弹、火箭等的车辆(为弹道导弹、运载火箭等运输、装卸和发射而设计的)〔999〕	12		35	13/	13	辆/千克	36		/17
8705.9099 90	其他特殊用途的机动车辆(主要用于载人或运货的车辆除外)〔999〕	12		35	13/	13	辆/千克	A6	LM	/17
87.06	**装有发动机的机动车辆底盘，税目87.01至87.05所列车辆用：**									
8706.0010	---非公路用自卸车底盘〔999〕	6		14	13/	13	台/千克	6		/
	---货车底盘：									
8706.0021	----车辆总重量在14吨及以上的〔999〕	6		30	13/	13	台/千克	46AOxy	ML	/
8706.0022	----车辆总重量在14吨以下的〔999〕	6		45	13/	13	台/千克	46AOxy	ML	/
8706.0030	---大型客车底盘〔999〕	6		70	13/	13	台/千克	46Oxy		/
8706.0040	---汽车起重机底盘〔999〕	6		100	13/	13	台/千克	6AO	ML	/
8706.0090	---其他〔999〕	6		100	13/	13	台/千克	46AOxy	ML	/
87.07	**机动车辆的车身(包括驾驶室)，税目87.01至87.05所列车辆用：**									
8707.1000	-税目87.03所列车辆用〔999〕	6		100	13/	13	台/千克	6		/31
	-其他：									
8707.9010	---税号8702.1092、8702.1093、8702.9020及8702.9030所列车辆用〔999〕	6		70	13/	13	台/千克	6		/31
8707.9090	---其他〔999〕	6		70	13/	13	台/千克	6		/31
87.08	**机动车辆的零件、附件，税目87.01至87.05所列车辆用：**									
8708.1000	-缓冲器(保险杠)及其零件〔999〕	6		100	13/	13	千克	6		/
	-车身(包括驾驶室)的其他零件、附件：									
8708.2100	--坐椅安全带〔999〕	6		100	13/	13	千克	6A	LM	/
	--其他：									
8708.2930	---车窗玻璃升降器〔999〕	6		100	13/	13	千克	6		/
	---天窗：									
8708.2941	----电动的〔999〕	6		100	13/	13	千克/套	6	L	/
8708.2942	----手动的〔999〕	6		100	13/	13	千克/套	6	L	/
	---其他车身覆盖件：									
8708.2951	----侧围〔999〕	6		100	13/	13	千克	6		/
8708.2952	----车门〔999〕	6		100	13/	13	千克/个	6		/
8708.2953	----发动机罩盖〔999〕	6		100	13/	13	千克	6		/
8708.2954	----前围〔999〕	6		100	13/	13	千克	6		/
8708.2955	----行李箱盖(或背门)〔999〕	6		100	13/	13	千克	6		/
8708.2956	----后围〔999〕	6		100	13/	13	千克	6		/
8708.2957	----翼子板(或叶子板)〔999〕	6		100	13/	13	千克	6		/
8708.2959	----其他〔999〕	6		100	13/	13	千克	6		/

协定税率 %										特惠税率 %			Article Description
亚太5国	东/冰/格	巴基斯坦	韩国	瑞士	哥达	秘鲁	澳大利亚	新西/坡/智	港/澳/台	亚太2国	老/柬/缅	36/3/1	
	0/0/0	4	6	0	0	0	0	0/0/0	0/0/			0/0/0	----Of a maxium lifting capacity exceeding 50tons, but not exceeding 100 tons
	0/0/0	4	6	0	0	0	0	0/0/0	0/0/			0/0/0	----Of a maxium lifting capacity exceeding 100 tons
	0/0/0	5.4	7.2	3.6	0	0	0	0/0/0	0/0/			0/0/0	-Mobile drilling derricks
													-Fire fighting vehicles:
	0/0/0	0	1.8	0	0	0	0	0//0	0/0/			0/0/0	---Mounted with scaling ladder
	0/0/0	0	1.8	0	0	0	0	0//0	0/0/			0/0/0	---Other
13.5	0/0/0	6.8	9	4.5	0	0	0	0/0/0	0/0/			0/0/	-Concrete-mixer lorries
													-Other:
8.1	0/0/0	4	5.4	0	0	0	0	0/0/0	0/0/			0/0/0	---Radio communication vans
8.1	0/0/0	4	5.4	0	0	0	0	0//0	0/0/			0/0/0	---Mobile radiological units
10.8	0/0/0	4.5	7.2	3.6	0	0	0	0/0/0	0/0/			0/0/	---Mobile environmental monitoring units
10.8	0/0/0	4.5	8.4	3.6	0	0	0	0/0/0	0/0/			0/0/	---Mobile clinics
													---Mobile electric generator sets:
10.8	0/0/0	4.5	7.2	3.6	0	0	0	0/0/0	0/0/			0/0/	----Airplane charging vehicles (frequency 400Hz)
10.8	0/0/0	4.5	7.2	3.6	0	0	0	0/0/0	0/0/			0/0/	----Other
10.8	0/0/0	4.5	7.2	3.6	0	0	0	0/0/0	0/0/			0/0/	---Mobile vehicles for aircraft refuelling, air-conditioning or deicing
10.8	0/0/0	4.5	7.2	3.6	0	0	0	0/0/0	0/0/			0/0/	---Snow sweep vehicles for cleansing streets or airfield runways
10.8	0/0/0	4.5	7.2	3.6	0	0	0	0/0/0	0/0/			0/0/	---Petrolcum well logging trucks, fracturing unit trucks and mixing sand trucks
													---Other:
10.8	0/0/0	4.5	7.2	3.6	0	0	0	0/0/0	0/0/			0/0/	----Truck mounted concrete pump
													----Other
10.8	0/0/0	4.5	7.2	3.6	0	0	0	0/0/0	0/0/			0/0/	Runway deicing vehicle
10.8	0/0/0	4.5	7.2	3.6	0	0	0	0/0/0	0/0/			0/0/	Vehicles for carrying missiles or rockets (specially designed for transporting, handling and launching of ballistic missiles or carrier rockets)
10.8	0/0/0	4.5	7.2	3.6	0	0	0	0/0/0	0/0/			0/0/	Other special purpose motor vehicles (other than those principally designed for the transport of person's or goods)
													Chassis fitted with engines, for the motor vehicles of headings No. 87. 01 to 87. 05:
	0/0/0	4	4.8	0	0	0	0	0//0	0/0/			0/0/	---Chassis fitted of off-highway dumpers
													---Chassis fitted of trucks:
	5/0/0		6	0	0		0	0//0	0/0/			0//	----For vehicles g. v. w of 14tons or more
	5/0/0		6	0	0	0	0	0//0	0/0/			0/0/	----For vehicles g. v. w less than 14 tons
	0/0/0		12	6	0		0	0/0/0	0/0/			0//	---For passenger motor vehicles with 30 seats or more
	0/0/0		12	6	0	0	0	0/0/0	0/0/			0/0/	---For crane lorries
	0/0/0		6	0	0	0	0	0/0/0	0/0/			0/0/	---Other
													Bodies (including cabs), for the motor vehicles of headings No. 87. 01 to 87. 05:
	0/0/0		6	0	0	0	0	0/0/0	0/0/			0/0/	-For the vehicles of headingNo. 87. 03
													-Other:
5.4	0/0/0	4.5	6	0	0	0	0	0/0/0	0/0/			0/0/	---For the vehicles of subheadingNo. 8702. 1092、8702. 1093、8702. 9020 or 8702. 9030
5.4	0/0/0	4.5	6	0	0	0	0	0/0/0	0/0/			0/0/	---Other
													Parts and accessories of the motor vehicles of headings No. 87. 01 to 87. 05:
5.8	0/0/0	0	7	0	0	0	0	0/0/0	0/0/0			0/0/0	-Bumpers and parts thereof
													-Other parts and accessories of bodies (including cabs):
	0/0/0	4.5	6	0	0	0	0	0/0/0	0/0/			0/0/0	--Safety seat belts
													--Other:
5.4	5/0/4	8.1	6	0	0	0	0	0//0	0/0/0			0/0/0	---Windowpane raiser
													---Sunroofs:
5.4	0/0/0	4	9	0	0	0	0	0/0/0	0/0/0			0/0/0	----Electric
5.4	0/0/0	4	6	0	0	0	0	0/0/0	0/0/0			0/0/0	----Hand-operated
													---Other covered parts of bodies:
5.4	0/0/0	4	7	0	0	0	0	0/0/0	0/0/0			0/0/0	----Side appearance of bodies
5.4	0/0/0	4	7	0	0	0	0	0/0/0	0/0/0			0/0/0	----doors
5.4	0/0/0	4	7	0	0	0	0	0/0/0	0/0/0			0/0/0	----Bonnets
5.4	0/0/0	4	7	0	0	0	0	0/0/0	0/0/0			0/0/0	----Frontal appearance of bodies
5.4	0/0/0	4	7	0	0	0	0	0/0/0	0/0/0			0/0/0	----Rear compartment covers (or rear door)
5.4	0/0/0	4	7	0	0	0	0	0/0/0	0/0/0			0/0/0	----Rear appearance of bodies
5.4	0/0/0	4	7	0	0	0	0	0/0/0	0/0/0			0/0/0	----Running-boards
5.4	0/0/0	4	7	0	0	0	0	0/0/0	0/0/0			0/0/0	----Other

税则号列	货品名称〔CIQ扩展编码及品名—T2表示见附表2〕	最惠(%)	暂定税率	普通	增值/消费	出口退税	计量单位	监管条件	检验检疫	特殊证件对美关税
8708.2990	---其他〔999〕	6		100	13/	13	千克	6	L	/
	-制动器、助力制动器及其零件:									
8708.3010	---装在蹄片上的制动摩擦片〔999〕	6		100	13/	13	千克	6		/
	---防抱死制动系统(ABS):									
8708.3021	----子目号87.01、8704.1030及8704.1090所列车辆用〔999〕	6		11	13/	13	千克	6		/11
8708.3029	----其他〔999〕	6		100	13/	13	千克	6		/
	---其他:									
8708.3091	----税目87.01所列车辆用〔999〕	6		14	13/	13	千克	6	L	/
8708.3092	----子目号8702.1091及8702.9010所列车辆用〔999〕	6		70	13/	13	千克	6	L	/
8708.3093	----子目号8704.1030及8704.1090所列车辆用〔999〕	6		11	13/	13	千克	6		/
8708.3094	----子目号8704.2100、8704.2230、8704.3100及8704.3230所列车辆用〔999〕	6		45	13/	13	千克	6	L	/
8708.3095	----子目号8704.2240、8704.2300及8704.3240所列车辆用〔999〕	6		30	13/	13	千克	6	L	/
8708.3096	----税目87.05所列车辆用〔999〕	6		100	13/	13	千克	6	L	/
8708.3099	----其他车辆用									
8708.3099 11	纯电动或混合动力汽车用电动制动器(由制动器电子控制单元、踏板行程模拟器、制动执行器等组成)〔999〕	6	5	100	13/	13	千克/个	6		/
8708.3099 19	其他机动车辆用制动器(包括助力制动器)〔999〕	6		100	13/	13	千克/个	6		/
8708.3099 90	其他机动车辆用制动器(包括助力制动器)的零件〔999〕	6		100	13/	13	千克/个	6	L	/
	-变速箱及其零件:									
8708.4010	---税目87.01所列车辆用									
8708.4010 10	发动机功率65千瓦及以上的动力换挡拖拉机用变速箱〔999〕	6	3	14	13/	13	个/千克	6		/
8708.4010 90	其他牵引车、拖拉机用变速箱及其零件〔999〕	6		14	13/	13	个/千克	6		/
8708.4020	---子目号8702.1091及8702.9010所列车辆用〔999〕	6		70	13/	13	个/千克	6		/
8708.4030	---子目号8704.1030及8704.1090所列车辆用									
8708.4030 01	扭矩＞1500Nm非公路自卸车用变速箱〔999〕	6	3	11	13/	13	个/千克	6		/
8708.4030 90	其他非公路自卸车用变速箱及其零件〔999〕	6		11	13/	13	个/千克	6		/
8708.4040	---子目号8704.2100、8704.2230、8704.3100及8704.3230所列车辆用〔999〕	6		45	13/	13	个/千克	6		/
8708.4050	---子目号8704.2240、8704.2300及8704.3240所列车辆用〔999〕	6		30	13/	13	个/千克	6		/
8708.4060	---税目87.05所列车辆用〔999〕	6		100	13/	13	个/千克	6		/
	---其他:									
8708.4091	----小轿车用自动换挡变速箱及其零件									
8708.4091 10	小轿车自动变速箱用液力变矩器	6	3	100	13/	13	个/千克	6		/
8708.4091 20	小轿车自动变速箱用铝阀芯	6	3	100	13/	13	个/千克	6		/
8708.4091 91	其他小轿车用自动换挡变速箱〔999〕	6		100	13/	13	个/千克	6		/
8708.4091 99	其他小轿车用自动换挡变速箱的零件〔999〕	6		100	13/	13	个/千克	6		/
8708.4099	----其他									
8708.4099 10	其他未列名机动车辆用变速箱〔999〕	6		100	13/	13	个/千克	6		/
8708.4099 20	其他未列名机动车辆自动变速箱用液力变矩器	6	3	100	13/	13	个/千克	6		/
8708.4099 30	其他未列名机动车辆自动变速箱用铝阀芯	6	3	100	13/	13	个/千克	6		/
8708.4099 90	其他未列名机动车辆用变速箱的零件〔999〕	6		100	13/	13	个/千克	6		/
	-装有差速器的驱动桥及其零件,不论是否装有其他传动部件;非驱动桥及其零件:									
	---装有差速器的驱动桥及其零件,不论是否装有其他传动部件:									
8708.5071	----税目87.01所列车辆用									
8708.5071 10	发动机功率65千瓦及以上的动力换挡拖拉机用驱动桥(装有差速器的,不论是否装有其他传动件)〔999〕	6	3	14	13/	13	个/千克	6		/
8708.5071 90	其他牵引车、拖拉机用驱动桥及其零件(装有差速器的,不论是否装有其他传动件)〔999〕	6		14	13/	13	个/千克	6		/
8708.5072	----子目号8702.1091及8702.9010所列车辆用									
8708.5072 01	轴荷≥10吨的中后驱动桥的零件〔999〕	6		70	13/	13	个/千克	6		/
8708.5072 91	其他大型客车用驱动桥(装有差速器的,不论是否装有其他传动件)〔999〕	6		70	13/	13	个/千克	6		/
8708.5072 99	其他大型客车用驱动桥的零件(装有差速器的,不论是否装有其他传动件)〔999〕	6		70	13/	13	个/千克	6		/

协定税率 %										特惠税率 %			Article Description
亚太5国	东/冰/格	巴基斯坦	韩国	瑞士	哥达	秘鲁	澳大利亚	新西/坡/智	港/澳/台	亚太2国	老/柬/缅	36/3/1	
5.4	0/0/0	4.5	9	3	0	0	0	0/0/0	0/0/0			0/0/0	---Other
													-Brakes and servo-brakes and parts thereof:
	0/0/0	4.5	4	0	0	0	0	0/0/0	0/0/			0/0/0	---Mounted brake linings
													---Anti-skid brake system:
5.4	0/0/0	0	3.6	0	0	0	0	0//0	0/0/			0/0/0	----Of the rehicles of heading 87.01,8704.1030 and 8704.1090
5.4	5/0/0	8.1	9	0	0	0	0	0//0	0/0/			0/0/0	----Other
													---Other:
5.4	0/0/0	0	3.6	0	0	0	0	0//0	0/0/			0/0/0	----Of the vehicles of heading No. 87.01
5.4	5/0/0	8.1	7	0	0	0	0	0//0	0/0/			0/0/0	----Of the vehicles of subheading No. 8702.1091 and 8702.9010
5.4	0/0/0	0	3.6	0	0	0	0	0//0	0/0/			0/0/0	----Of the vehicles of subheading No. 8704.1030 and 8704.1090
5.4	5/0/0	8.1	7	0	0	0	0	0//0	0/0/			0/0/0	----Of the vehicles of subheading No. 8704.2100, 8704.2230, 8704.3100 and 8704.3230
5.4	0/0/0	4	4	0	0	0	0	0/0/0	0/0/			0/0/0	----Of the vehicles of subheading No. 8704.2240, 8704.2300 and 8704.3240
5.4	0/0/0	4	6	0	0	0	0	0/0/0	0/0/			0/0/0	----Of the vehicles of heading No. 87.05
													----Other
5.4	5/0/0	9	7	3	0	0	0	0//0	0/0/			0/0/0	Electric brake for pure electric or hybrid vehicles (electronic control unit, composed of a brake pedal travel simulator, the brake actuator etc.)
5.4	5/0/0	9	7	3	0	0	0	0//0	0/0/			0/0/0	Brakes of other vehicles (including booster brake)
5.4	5/0/0	9	7	3	0	0	0	0//0	0/0/			0/0/0	Parts of brakes for other motor vehicles (including servo-brakes)
													-Gear boxes and parts thereof:
													---Of the vehicles of heading of No. 87.01
	0/0/0	0		0	0	0	0	0//0	0/0/0			0/0/0	Transmission gear box of engine power 65 kW and above for shift tractor
	0/0/0	0		0	0	0	0	0//0	0/0/0			0/0/0	Transmission and other parts for drive-axles
	5/0/0			0	0		0	0//0	0/0/0			0//	---Of the vehicles of subheading No. 8702.1091 and 8702.9010
													---Of the vehicles of subheading No. 8704.1030 and 8704.1090
	0/0/0	0	4.8	0	0		0	0//0	0/0/0			0//	Gear boxes for off-highway dumpers use, troque>1500Nm
	0/0/0	0	4.8	0	0		0	0//0	0/0/0			0//	Other gear boxes and parts for off-highway dumpers use
	5/0/0			0	0		0	0//0	0/0/0			0//	---Of the vehicles of subheading No. 8704.2100, 8704.2230, 8704.3100 and 8704.3230
	5/0/0			0	0		0	0//0	0/0/0			0//	---Of the vehicles of subheading No. 8704.2240, 8704.2300 and 8704.3240
	0/0/0	4.5		0	0	0	0	0/0/0	0/0/0			0/0/0	---Of the vehicles of heading No. 87.05
													---Other:
													----Automatic gearshift for saloon cars and parts ththereof
	5/0/0		8	0	0		0	0//0	0/0/		//	0//	Torque converter for automatic transmission of car
	5/0/0		8	0	0		0	0//0	0/0/		//	0//	Aluminum valve element for automatic transmission of car
	5/0/0		8	0	0		0	0//0	0/0/			0//	Cther automatic gearshift for saloon cars
	5/0/0		8	0	0		0	0//0	0/0/			0//	Parts of automatic gearshift for saloon cars
													----Other
	0/0/0	0		0	0		0	0/0/0	0/0/0			0//	Other gearboxes for other not else where specified vehicles
	0/0/0	0		0	0		0	0/0/0	0/0/0		//	0//	Torque converter for automatic transmission of other motor vehicles not listed
	0/0/0	0		0	0		0	0/0/0	0/0/0		//	0//	Aluminum valve element for automatic transmission of other motor vehicles not listed
	0/0/0	0		0	0		0	0/0/0	0/0/0			0//	Spare parts for gearboxes for other not elsewhere specified vehicles
													-Drive-axles with differential, whether or not provided with other transmission components and non-driving axles and parts thereof:
													---Drive-axles with differential and part thereof, whether or not provided with other transmission components:
													----Of the vehicles of heading No. 87.01
5.4	0/0/0	0	3.6	0	0	0	0	0//0	0/0/			0/0/0	Differential of engine power 65 kW and above for shift tractor
5.4	0/0/0	0	3.6	0	0	0	0	0//0	0/0/			0/0/0	Drive-axles with differential and parts there of the vehicles of heading No. 87.01, whether or not provided with other transmission components.
													----Of the vehicles of subheading No. 8702.1091 and 8702.9010
5.4	5/0/0	9	9	0	0	0	0	0//0	0/0/			0/0/0	Parts of middle and rear drive-axles and parts thereof, axle loading capacity≥10t
5.4	5/0/0	9	9	0	0	0	0	0//0	0/0/			0/0/0	Other drive-axles for other buses (with differential, whether or not provided with other transmission components)
5.4	5/0/0	9	9	0	0	0	0	0//0	0/0/			0/0/0	Parts of drive-axles with differential for other large buses (whether or not provided with other transmission components)

税则号列	货品名称〔CIQ 扩展编码及品名－T2 表示见附表 2〕	最惠(%)	暂定税率	普通	增值/消费	出口退税	计量单位	监管条件	检验检疫	特殊证件对美关税
8708.5073	----子目号 8704.1030 及 8704.1090 所列车辆用〔999〕	6		11	13/	13	个/千克	6		/
8708.5074	----子目号 8704.2100.8704.2230.8704.3100 及 8704.3230 所列车辆用									
8708.5074　10	柴、汽油型轻型货车用驱动桥(8704.2100.2230.3100.3230 所列总重量≤14 吨车辆用，装差速器)〔999〕	6		45	13/	13	个/千克	6		/
8708.5074　90	柴、汽油型轻型货车用驱动桥的零件(8704.2100.2230.3100.3230 所列总重量≤14 吨车辆用，装差速器)〔999〕	6		45	13/	13	个/千克	6		/
8708.5075	----子目号 8704.2240、8704.2300 及 8704.3240 所列车辆用									
8708.5075　10	其他柴、汽油型重型货车用驱动桥(指编号 8704.2240，8704.2300 及 8704.3240 所列车辆用)〔999〕	6		30	13/	13	个/千克	6		/
8708.5075　90	其他柴、汽油型重型货车用驱动桥的零件(指编号 8704.2240，8704.2300 及 87043.240 所列车辆用)〔999〕	6		30	13/	13	个/千克	6		/
8708.5076	----税目 87.05 所列车辆用									
8708.5076　10	特种车用驱动桥(指 8705 所列车辆用，装有差速器，不论是否装有其他传动件)〔999〕	6		100	13/	13	个/千克	6		/
8708.5076　90	特种车用驱动桥的零件(指 87.05 所列车辆用，装有差速器，不论是否装有其他传动件)〔999〕	6		100	13/	13	个/千克	6		/
8708.5079	----其他									
8708.5079　10	未列名机动车辆用驱动桥(装有差速器的，不论是否装有其他传动件)〔999〕	6		100	13/	13	个/千克	6		/
8708.5079　90	未列名机动车辆用驱动桥的零件(装有差速器的，不论是否装有其他传动件)〔999〕	6		100	13/	13	个/千克	6		/
	---非驱动桥及其零件：									
8708.5081	----税目 87.01 所列车辆用〔999〕	6		14	13/	13	千克	6		/
8708.5082	----子目号 8702.1091 及 8702.9010 所列车辆用〔999〕	6		70	13/	13	千克	6		/
8708.5083	----子目号 8704.1030 及 8704.1090 所列车辆用〔999〕	6		11	13/	13	千克	6		/
8708.5084	----子目号 8704.2100、8704.2230、8704.3100 及 8704.3230 所列车辆用〔999〕	6		45	13/	13	千克	6		/
8708.5085	----子目号 8704.2240、8704.2300 及 8704.3240 所列车辆用〔999〕	6		30	13/	13	千克	6		/
8708.5086	----税目 87.05 所列车辆用〔999〕	6		100	13/	13	千克	6		/11
8708.5089	----其他									
8708.5089　10	未列名机动车辆用非驱动桥〔999〕	6		100	13/	13	千克/个	6		/
8708.5089　90	未列名机动车辆用非驱动桥的零件〔999〕	6		100	13/	13	千克/个	6		/
	-车轮及其零件、附件：									
8708.7010	---税目 87.01 所列车辆用〔999〕	6		14	13/	13	千克	6		/
8708.7020	---子目号 8702.1091 及 8702.9010 所列车辆用〔999〕	6		70	13/	13	千克	6		/
8708.7030	---子目 8704.1030 及 8704.1090 所列车辆用〔999〕	6		11	13/	13	千克	6		/
8708.7040	---子目 8704.2100、8704.2230、8704.3100 及 8704.3230 所列车辆用〔999〕	6		45	13/	13	千克	6		/
8708.7050	---子目 8704.2240、8704.2300 及 8704.3240 所列车辆用〔999〕	6		30	13/	13	千克	6		/
8708.7060	---税目 87.05 所列车辆用〔999〕	6		100	13/	13	千克	6		/
	---其他：									
8708.7091	----铝合金制的〔999〕	6		100	13/	13	千克	6A	M	/
8708.7099	----其他〔999〕	6		100	13/	13	千克	6		/
	-悬挂系统及其零件(包括减振器)：									
8708.8010	---税目 87.03 所列车辆用〔999〕	6		100	13/	13	千克	6		/
8708.8090	---其他〔999〕	6		100	13/	13	千克	6		/
	-其他零件、附件：									
	--散热器及其零件：									
8708.9110	---水箱散热器〔999〕	6		100	13/	13	个/千克	6		/
8708.9120	---机油冷却器〔999〕	6		100	13/	13	个/千克	6		/
8708.9190	---其他〔999〕	6		100	13/	13	个/千克	6		/
8708.9200	--消声器(消音器)排气管及零件〔999〕	6		100	13/	13	千克	6		/
	--离合器及其零件：									
8708.9310	---税目 87.01 所列车辆用							6		

协定税率 %										特惠税率 %			
亚太5国	东/冰/格	巴基斯坦	韩国	瑞士	哥达	秘鲁	澳大利亚	新西/坡/智	港/澳/台	亚太2国	老/柬/缅	36/3/1	Article Description
5.4	0/0/0	0	3.6	0	0	0	0	0//0	0/0/			0/0/0	----Of the vehicles of subheading No. 8704. 1030 and 8704. 1090
													----Of the vehicles of subheading No. 8704. 2100, 8704. 2230, 8704. 3100 and 8704. 3230
5.4	5/0/0	9	7	0	0	0	0	0//0	0/0/			0/0/0	Drive-axles for diesel oil and gasoline light trucks(used by ≤14 ton vehicles listed in 8707. 2100,2300,3100 and 3230 and with differential gears)
5.4	5/0/0	9	7	0	0	0	0	0//0	0/0/			0/0/C	Parts of drive-axles for diesel oil and gasoline light trucks(used by ≤14 tons vehicles of subheading No. 8707. 2100,2300,3100 and 3230 and with differential)
													----Of the vehicles of subheading No. 8704. 2240, 8704. 2300 and 8704. 3240
5.4	5/0/0	9	7	0	0	0	0	0//0	0/0/			0/0/0	Drive-axles for other diesel oil and gasoline heavy trucks (referring to vehicles subheading No. 8704. 2240,8704. 2300 and 8704. 3240)
5.4	5/0/0	9	7	0	0	0	0	0//0	0/0/			0/0/0	Parts of drive-axles bridges for other diesel oil and gasoline heavy trucks (referring to vehicles subheading No. 8704. 2240,8704. 2300 and 8704. 3240)
													----Of the vehicles of heading No. 87. 05
5.4	0/0/0	4	6	0	0	0	0	0/0/0	0/0/			0/0/0	Drive-axles for special vehicles (referring to vehicles of heading No. 8705, with differential, whether or not provided transmussion components)
5.4	0/0/0	4	6	0	0	0	0	0/0/0	0/0/			0/0/0	Parts of drive-axles for special vehicles(referring to vehicles of heading No. 87. 05, with differential, whether or not provided transmussion components)
													---Other
5.4	5/0/0	9	9	5.3	0	0	0	0//0	0/0/			0/0/0	Drive-axles for unlisted motor vehicles(with differential, whether or not provided transmussion components)
5.4	5/0/0	9	9	5.3	0	0	0	0//0	0/0/			0/0/0	Parts of drive-axles of unlisted motor vehicles (with differential, whether or not provided transmussion components)
													---Non-driving axles and parts thereof:
	0/0/0	5	3.6	0	0	0	0	0//0	0/0/			0/0/0	----Of the vehicles of heading No. 87. 01
	0/0/0	8.7	10.5	4.5	0	0	0	0/0/0	0/0/			0/0/	----Of the vehicles of subheading No. 8702. 1091 and 8702. 9010
	0/0/0	5	3.6	0	0	0	0	0//0	0/0/			0/0/0	----Of the vehicles of subheading No. 8704. 1030 and 8704. 1090
	0/0/0	4.5	6	0	0	0	0	0/0/0	0/0/			0/0/0	----Of the vehicles of subheading No. 8704. 2100, 8704. 2230, 8704. 3100 and 8704. 3230
	0/0/0	4	6	0	0	0	0	0/0/0	0/0/			0/0/0	----Of the vehicles of subheading No. 8704. 2240, 8704. 2300 and 8704. 3240
	0/0/0	4	6	0	0	0	0	0/0/0	0/0/			0/0/0	----Of the vehicles of heading No. 87. 05
													----Other
	0/0/0	4.5		0	0	0	0	0/0/0	0/0/			0/0/0	Non-drive-axles for not specified motor vehicles
	0/0/0	4.5		0	0	0	0	0/0/0	0/0/			0/0/0	Parts of non-drive-axles for not specified motor vehicles
													-Road wheels and parts and accessories thereof:
	0/0/0	5	3.6	0	0	0	0	0//0	0/0/0			0/0/0	---Of the vehicles of heading No. 87. 01
	0/0/0	4.5	6	0	0	0	0	0/0/0	0/0/0			0/0/0	---Of the vehicles of subheadings No. 8702. 1091 and 8702. 9010
	0/0/0	5	3.6	0	0	0	0	0//0	0/0/0			0/0/0	---Of the vehicles of subheadings No. 8704. 1030 and 8704. 1090
	0/0/0	4.5	4	0	0	0	0	0/0/0	0/0/0			0/0/0	---Of the vehicles of subheadings No. 8704. 2100, 8704. 2230, 8704. 3100 and 8704. 3230
	0/0/0	4	6	0	0	0	0	0/0/0	0/0/0			0/0/0	---Of the vehicles of subheadings No. 8704. 2240, 8704. 2300 and 8704. 3240
	0/0/0	4	6	0	0	0	0	0/0/0	0/0/0			0/0/0	---Of the vehicles of heading No. 87. 05
													---Other:
	0/0/0	0		0	0	0	0	0/0/0	0/0/0			0/0/0	----Of aluminium alloy
	0/0/0	4.5		0	0	0	0	0/0/0	0/0/0			0/0/0	----Other
													-Suspension systems and parts there of (in-cluding shock-absorbers):
5.4	0/0/0	0	4	0	0	0	0	0/0/0	0/0/			0/0/0	---Of the vehicles of heading No. 87. 03
5.4	0/0/0	4.5	4	0	0	0	0	0/0/0	0/0/			0/0/0	---Other
													-Other parts and accessories:
													--Radiators and parts therof:
	0/0/0	0	6	0	0	0	0	0/0/0	0/0/			0/0/0	---Water tank radiators
	0/0/0	0	6	0	0	0	0	0/0/0	0/0/			0/0/0	---Oil coolers
	0/0/0	0	6	0	0	0	0	0/0/0	0/0/			0/0/0	---Other
	0/0/0	0		0	0	0	0	0/0/0	0/0/			0/0/0	--Silencers (mufflers) and exhaust pipes, parts therof
													--Clutches and parts thereof:
													---Of the vehicles of heading No. 87. 01

税则号列	货品名称〔CIQ扩展编码及品名－T2表示见附表2〕	最惠(%)	暂定税率	普通	增值/消费	出口退税	计量单位	监管条件	检验检疫	特殊证件对美关税
8708.9310 10	发动机功率65千瓦及以上的动力换挡拖拉机用离合器〔999〕	6	3	14	13/	13	千克	6		/
8708.9310 90	其他牵引车、拖拉机用离合器及其零件〔999〕	6		14	13/	13	千克	6		/
8708.9320	---子目8702.1091及8702.9010所列车辆用〔999〕	6		70	13/	13	千克	6		/
8708.9330	---子目号8704.1030及8704.1090所列车辆用〔999〕	6		11	13/	13	千克	6		/
8708.9340	---子目8704.-2100、8704.-2230、8704.3100及8704.3230所列车辆用〔999〕	6		45	13/	13	千克	6		/
8708.9350	---子目号8704.2240、8704.2300及8704.3240所列车辆用〔999〕	6		30	13/	13	千克	6		/
8708.9360	---税目87.05所列车辆用〔999〕	6		100	13/	13	千克	6		/
8708.9390	---其他〔999〕	6		100	13/	13	千克	6		/
	--转向盘、转向柱及转向器及其零件：									
8708.9410	---税目87.01所列车辆用〔999〕	6		14	13/	13	千克	6		/
8708.9420	---子目8702.1091及8702.9010所列车辆用									
8708.9420 01	座位≥30位的客车用转向器零件〔999〕	6		70	13/	13	千克	6		/
8708.9420 90	大型客车用其他转向盘、转向柱及其零件(包括转向器)〔999〕	6		70	13/	13	千克	6		/
8708.9430	---子目号8704.1030及8704.1090所列车辆用〔999〕	6		11	13/	13	千克	6		/
8708.9440	---子目号8704.2100、8704.2230、8704.3100及8704.3230所列车辆用〔999〕	6		45	13/	13	千克	6		/
8708.9450	---子目号8704.2240、8704.2300及8708.3240所列车辆用									
8708.9450 01	总重≥14吨柴油型货车转向器的零件〔999〕	6		30	13/	13	千克	6		/
8708.9450 90	其他重型货车用转向盘、转向柱、转向器及其零件(指编号8704.2240、8704.2300及8704.3240所列车辆用)〔999〕	6		30	13/	13	千克	6		/
8708.9460	---税目87.05所列车辆用转向器〔999〕	6		100	13/	13	千克	6		/
8708.9490	---其他									
8708.9490 01	采用电动转向系统的转向盘、转向柱、转向器及其零件〔999〕	6		100	13/	13	千克	6		/
8708.9490 90	其他未列名机动车辆用转向盘、转向柱及其零件(包括转向器)〔999〕	6		100	13/	13	千克	6		/
8708.9500	--带充气系统的安全气囊及其零件〔999〕	6		100	13/	13	千克	6		/
	--其他：									
8708.9910	---税目87.01所列车辆用〔999〕	6		14	13/	13	千克	6		/
	---子目号8702.1091及8702.9010所列车辆用：									
8708.9921	----车架〔999〕	6		70	13/	13	千克	6		/
8708.9929	----其他〔999〕	6		70	13/	13	千克	6		/
	---子目8704.1030及8704.1090所列车辆用：									
8708.9931	----车架〔999〕	6		11	13/	13	千克	6		/
8708.9939	----其他〔999〕	6	3	11	13/	13	千克	6		/
	---子目8704.2100、8704.2230、8704.3100及8704.3230所列车辆用：									
8708.9941	----车架〔999〕	6		45	13/	13	千克	6		/
8708.9949	----其他〔999〕	6		45	13/	13	千克	6		/
	---子目8704.2240、8704.2300及8704.3240所列车辆用：									
8708.9951	----车架〔999〕	6		30	13/	13	千克	6		/
8708.9959	----其他〔999〕	6		30	13/	13	千克	6	L	/
8708.9960	---税目87.05所列车辆用〔999〕	6		100	13/	13	千克	6		/
	---其他：									
8708.9991	----车架〔999〕	6		100	13/	13	千克/个	6		/
8708.9992	----传动轴〔999〕	6		100	13/	13	千克	6		/
8708.9999	----其他									
8708.9999 10	混合动力汽车动力传动装置及其零件(由发电机、电动机和动力分配装置等组成,税目87.01至87.04所列车辆用)〔999〕	6		100	13/	13	千克	6		/
8708.9999 90	机动车辆用未列名零件、附件(税目87.01至87.04所列车辆用)〔999〕	6		100	13/	13	千克	6		/

协定税率 %										特惠税率 %			Article Description
亚太5国	东/冰/格	巴基斯坦	韩国	瑞士	哥达	秘鲁	澳大利亚	新西/坡/智	港/澳/台	亚太2国	老/柬/缅	36/3/1	
	0/0/0	5	3.6	0	0	0	0	0//0	0/0/			0/0/0	Clutch of engine power 65 kW and above for shift tractor
	0/0/0	5	3.6	0	0	0	0	0//0	0/0/			0/0/0	Drive-axles with Clutch and parts there of the vehicles of heading No. 87.01, whether or not provided with other transmission components.
	0/0/0	4.5	7	0	0	0	0	0/0/0	0/0/			0/0/0	---Of the vehicles of subheadings No. 8702. 1091 and 8702. 9010
	0/0/0	5	3.6	0	0	0	0	0//0	0/0/			0/0/0	---Of the vehicles of subheadings No. 8704. 1030 and 8704. 1090
	0/0/0	4.5	6	0	0	0	0	0/0/0	0/0/			0/0/0	---Of the vehicles of subheadings No. 8704. 2100, 8704. 2230, 8704. 3100 and 8704. 3230
	0/0/0	4	7	0	0	0	0	0/0/0	0/0/			0/0/0	---Of the vehicles of subheadings No. 8704. 2240, 8704. 2300 and 8704. 3240
	0/0/0	4	7	0	0	0	0	0/0/0	0/0/			0/0/0	---Of the vehicles of heading No. 87. 05
	0/0/0	5		0	0	0	0	0/0/0	0/0/			0/0/0	---Other
													--Steering wheels, steering columns and steering boxes parts thereof:
	0/0/0	0	3.6	0	0	0	0	0//0	0/0/			0/0/0	---Of the vehicles of heading No. 87. 01
													---Of the vehicles of subheadings No. 8702. 1091 and 8702. 9010
	0/0/0	4.5	6	0	0	0	0	0/0/0	0/0/			0/0/0	Parts of steering boxes for the buses with 30 seats or more
	0/0/0	4.5	6	0	0	0	0	0/0/0	0/0/			0/0/0	Other steering wheels, steering columns and parts thereof for large buses
	0/0/0	0	3.6	0	0	0	0	0//0	0/0/			0/0/0	---Of the vehicles of subheadings No. 8704. 1030 and 8704. 1090
	0/0/0	4.5	6	0	0	0	0	0/0/0	0/0/			0/0/0	---Of the vehicles of subheadings No. 8704. 2100, 8704. 2230, 8704. 3100 and 8704. 3230
													---Of the vehicles of subheadings No. 8704. 2240, 8704. 2300 and 8704. 3240
	0/0/0	4.5	6	0	0	0	0	0/0/0	0/0/			0/0/0	Redirector components of diesel oil trucks whose weight≥14 tons
	0/0/0	4.5	6	0	0	0	0	0/0/0	0/0/			0/0/0	Steering wheels, steering columns, steering boxes and parts thereof for the vehicles of subheading No. 8704. 2240, 8704. 2300 and 8704. 3240
	0/0/0	4.5	6	0	0	0	0	0/0/0	0/0/			0/0/0	---Of the vehicles of heading No. 87. 05
													---Other
	0/0/0	4.5		5.3	0	0	0	0/0/0	0/0/			0/0/0	Steering wheels, steering columns, steering boxes and thereof parts, with electric power steering system
	0/0/0	4.5		5.3	0	0	0	0/0/0	0/0/			0/0/0	Steering wheels, steering columns, steering gears and thereof parts for other unlisted motor vehicles
5.4	5/0/0	9	9	0	0		0	0//0	0/0/			0//	--Safety air-bags with inflater system; parts thereof
													--Other:
	0/0/0	0	2.4	0	0	0	0	0//0	0/0/			0/0/0	---Of the vehicles of heading No. 87. 01
													---Of the vehicles of subheadings No. 8702. 1091 and 8702. 9010:
	0/0/0	25	17.5		0	0	0	0/0/0	0/0/			0/0/	----Frames
	0/0/0	25	17.5		0	0	0	0/0/0	0/0/			0/0/	----Other
													---Of the vehicles of subheading No. 8704. 1030 and 8704. 1090:
	0/0/0	0	3.6	0	0	0	0	0//0	0/0/			0/0/0	----Frames
	0/0/0	0	3.6	0	0	0	0	0//0	0/0/			0/0/0	----Other
													---Of the vehicles of subheadings No. 87 04. 2100, 8704. 2230, 8704. 3100 and 8704. 3230:
	0/0/0		17.5		0	0	0	0/0/0	0/0/			0/0/	----Frames
	0/0/0	0	17.5		0	0	0	0/0/0	0/0/			0/0/	----Other
													---Of the vehicles of subheadings No. 87 04. 2240, 8704. 2300 and 8704. 3240:
	0/0/0	4	6	0	0	0	0	0/0/0	0/0/			0/0/0	----Frames
	0/0/0	4.5	6	0	0	0	0	0/0/0	0/0/			0/0/0	----Other
	0/0/0	10.8	6	4.5	0	0	0	0/0/0	0/0/			0/0/	---Of the vehicles of heading No. 87. 05
													---Other:
	0/0/0	4.5	6	0	0	0	0	0/0/0	0/0/0			0/0/0	----Frames
	0/0/0	4.5	6	0	0	0	0	0/0/0	0/0/0			0/0/0	----Transmission shafts
													----Other
	0/0/0	0	6	0	0	0	0	0/0/0	0/0/0			0/0/0	Transmission device of hybrid electric vehicle and part (made of generators, motor and power spilt device, of vehicles of subheading No. 87. 01 to 87. 04)
	0/0/0	0	6	0	0	0	0	0/0/0	0/0/0			0/0/0	Parts and accessories of motor vehicles, not elsewhere specified or included (of the vehicles of subheading No. 87. 01 to 87. 04)

税则号列		货品名称〔CIQ扩展编码及品名－T2表示见附表2〕	最惠(%)	暂定税率	普通	增值/消费	出口退税	计量单位	监管条件	检验检疫	特殊证件对美关税
87.09		**短距离运输货物的机动车辆，未装有提升或搬运设备，用于工厂、仓库、码头或机场；火车站台上用的牵引车；上述车辆的零件：**									
		-车辆：									
		--电动的：									
8709.1110		---牵引车〔999〕	10		30	13/	13	辆/千克	6		/35
8709.1190		---其他〔999〕	10		30	13/	13	辆/千克	6		/35
		--其他：									
8709.1910		---牵引车〔999〕	10		30	13/	13	辆/千克	6		/35
8709.1990		---其他〔999〕	10		30	13/	13	辆/千克	6		/35
8709.9000		-零件〔999〕	8		17	13/	13	千克	6		/33
87.10		**坦克及其他机动装甲战斗车辆，不论是否装有武器；上述车辆的零件：**									
8710.0010		---整车〔999〕	15		100	13/	0	辆/千克	6		/
8710.0090		---零件〔999〕	15		100	13/	0	千克	6		/
87.11		**摩托车（包括机器脚踏两用车）及装有辅助发动机的脚踏车，不论有无边车；边车：**									
8711.1000		-装有往复式活塞内燃发动机，气缸容量（排气量）不超过50毫升									
8711.1000	10	微马力摩托车及脚踏两用车（装有往复式活塞发动机，微马力指排气量＝50cc）〔999〕	45		150	13/	13	辆/千克	y4xA6	LM	/70
8711.1000	90	微马力摩托车及脚踏两用车（装有往复式活塞发动机，微马力指排气量＜50cc）〔999〕	45		150	13/	13	辆/千克	6A	LM	/70
		-装有往复式活塞内燃发动机，气缸容量（排气量）超过50毫升，但不超过250毫升									
8711.2010		---气缸容量超过50毫升，但不超过100毫升〔999〕	45		150	13/	13	辆/千克	y4xA6	LM	/70
8711.2020		---气缸容量超过100毫升，但不超过125毫升〔999〕	45		150	13/	13	辆	y4xA6	LM	/70
8711.2030		---气缸容量超过125毫升，但不超过150毫升〔999〕	45		150	13/	13	辆/千克	y4xA6	LM	/70
8711.2040		---气缸容量超过150毫升，但不超过200毫升〔999〕	45		150	13/	13	辆/千克	y4xA6	LM	/70
8711.2050		---气缸容量超过200毫升，但不超过250毫升									
8711.2050	10	200＜排气量＜250毫升装往复式活塞内燃发动机摩托车及脚踏两用车〔999〕	45		150	13/	13	辆/千克	46Axy	LM	/70
8711.2050	90	排气量＝250毫升装往复式活塞内燃发动机摩托车及脚踏两用车〔101自行车零配件，102其它非机动脚踏车零配件，103摩托车〕	45		150	13/3	13	辆/千克	46Axy	LM	/70
		-装有往复式活塞内燃发动机，气缸容量（排气量）超过250毫升，但不超过500毫升：									
8711.3010		---气缸容量超过250毫升，但不超过400毫升〔999〕	45		150	13/10	13	辆/千克	46Axy	LM	/70
8711.3020		---气缸容量超过400毫升，但不超过500毫升〔999〕	45		150	13/10	13	辆/千克	46Axy	LM	/70
8711.4000		-装有往复式活塞内燃发动机，气缸容量（排气量）超过500毫升，但不超过800毫升〔999〕	40		150	13/10	13	辆/千克	46Axy	LM	/65
8711.5000		-装有往复式活塞内燃发动机，气缸容量（排气量）超过800毫升〔999〕	30		150	13/10	13	辆/千克	46Axy	LM	/55
8711.6000		-装有驱动电动机的									
8711.6000	10	电动自行车（包括机器脚踏两用车；脚踏车）〔999〕	45		150	13/	13	辆/千克	6A	M	/70
8711.6000	90	其他装有电驱动电动机的摩托车〔999〕	45		150	13/	13	辆/千克	6A	LM	/70
8711.9000		-其他									
8711.9000	10	其他排气量≤250毫升摩托车及脚踏两用车〔999〕	45		150	13/3	13	辆/千克	6A	LM	/70
8711.9000	20	其他排气量＞250毫升摩托车及脚踏两用车〔999〕	45		150	13/10	13	辆/千克	6A	LM	/70
8711.9000	30	其他无法区分排气量的摩托车及脚踏两用车〔999〕	45		150	13/3	13	辆/千克	6A	LM	/70
8711.9000	90	装有其他辅助发动机的脚踏车，边车〔999〕	45		150	13/	13	辆/千克	6A	LM	/70
		-其他：									
87.12		**自行车及其他非机动脚踏车（包括运货三轮脚踏车）：**									
8712.0020		---竞赛型自行车〔999〕	7		130	13/	13	辆/千克	6		/32
8712.0030		---山地自行车〔999〕	7		130	13/	13	辆/千克	6		/32
		---越野自行车：									
8712.0041		----16、18、20英寸〔10116、18英寸越野自行车，10220英寸越野自行车，103其他越野自行车〕	7		130	13/	13	辆/千克	6		/32
8712.0049		----其他〔101:16、18英寸越野自行车，102:20英寸越野自行车，103:其他越野自行车，104:货运三轮脚踏车〕	7		130	13/	13	辆/千克	6		/32
		---其他自行车：									

协定税率 %										特惠税率 %			
亚太5国	东/冰/格	巴基斯坦	韩国	瑞士	哥达	秘鲁	澳大利亚	新西/坡/智	港/澳/台	亚太2国	老/柬/缅	36/3/1	Article Description
													Works trucks, self-propelled, not fitted with lifting or handling equipment, of the type used in factories, warehouses, dock areas or airports for short distance transport of goods; tractors of the type used on railway station platforms; parts of the foregoing vehicles:
													-Vehicles:
													--Electrical:
	0/0/0	4	4	0	0	0	0	0/0/0	0/0/			0/0/0	---Tractors
	0/0/0	4	4	0	0	0	0	0/0/0	0/0/			0/0/0	---Other
													--Other:
	0/0/0	4.5	6.3	3.2	0	0	0	0/0/0	0/0/			0/0/0	---Tractors
	0/0/0	4.5	6.3	3.2	0	0	0	0/0/0	0/0/			0/0/0	---Other
	0/0/0	4	3.3	0	0	0	0	0//0	0/0/			0/0/0	-Parts
													Tanks and other armoured fighting vehicles, motorized, whether or not fitted with weapons, and parts of such vehicles:
	0/0/0	10.8	6	4.5	0	0	0	0/0/0	0/0/			0/0/	---Assembled
	0/0/0	10.8	6	4.5	0	0	0	0/0/0	0/0/			0/0/	---Parts and accessories
													Motorcycles (including mopeds) and cycles fitted with an auxiliary motor, with or without side-cars; side-cars:
													-With reciprocating internal combustion piston engine of a cylinder capacity not exceeding 50 cc
	0/0/0	45	31.5	23.4	0	0	0	0/0/0	0/0/			0/0/	Micro horsepower motorcycles and mopeds(with reciprocating internal combustion piston engine, micro horsep ower cylinder capacity=50cc)
	0/0/0	45	31.5	23.4	0	0	0	0/0/0	0/0/			0/0/	Micro horsepower motorcycles and mopeds(with reciprocating internal combustion piston engine, micro horsepower cylinder capacity<50cc)
													-With reciprocating internal combustion piston engine of a cylinder capacity exceeding 50 cc, but not exceeding 250cc
	0/0/0		31.5	23.4	0	0	0	0/0/0	0/0/			0/0/	---Of a cylinder capacity exceeding 50cc, but not exceeding 100cc
	0/0/0		31.5	23.4	0	0	0	0/0/0	0/0/			0/0/	---Of a cylinder capacity exceeding 100cc but not exceeding 125cc
	0/0/0		31.5	23.4	0	0	0	0/0/0	0/0/			0/0/	---Of a cylinder capacity exceeding 125cc but not exceeding 150cc
	0/0/0		31.5	23.4	0		0	0/0/0	0/0/			0//	—Of a cylinder capacity exceeding 150cc, but not exceeding 200cc
													—Of a cylinder capacity exceeding 200cc< but not exceeding 250cc
	0/0/0		31.5	23.4	0		0	0/0/0	0/0/			0//	200cc<displocement< 250cc loaded exhaust volume of reciprocating piston internal combustion engine for motorcycles and mopeds
	0/0/0		31.5	23.4	0		0	0/0/0	0/0/			0//	Displacement =250cc with reciprocating internal combustion piston engine for motorcycles and mopeds
													-With reciprocating internal combustion piston engine of a cylinder capacity exceeding 250cc, but not exceeding 500cc:
32.9	0/0/0	32.8	31.5		0		0	0/0/0	0/0/			0//	—Of a cylinder capacity exceeding 250cc, but not exceeding 400cc
32.9	0/0/0	32.8	31.5		0		0	0/0/0	0/0/			0//	—Of a cylinder capacity exceeding 400cc, but not exceeding 500cc
	0/0/0		28		0		0	0/0/0	0/0/			0//	-With reciprocating internal combustion piston engine of a cylinder capacity exceeding 500 cc, but not exceeding 800 cc
	0/0/0		21		0		0	0/0/0	0/0/			0//	-With reciprocating internal combustion piston engine of a cylinder capacity exceeding 800 cc
													-With electric motor for propulSlon
	0/0/0				0		0	0/0/0	0/0/			0//	Electric bicycle and side-cars, and mopeds
	0/0/0				0		0	0/0/0	0/0/			0//	Other motorcycle with electric drive motor
													-Other
	0/0/0				0		0	0/0/0	0/0/			0//	Motorcycles and mopedes, of a cylinder capacity not exceeding 250m
	0/0/0				0		0	0/0/0	0/0/			0//	Motorcycles and mopedes, of a cylinder capacity exceeding 250m
	0/0/0				0		0	0/0/0	0/0/			0//	Motorcycles and mopedes, a cylinder capacity of its engine can not be distinguished
	0/0/0				0		0	0/0/0	0/0/			0//	Mopeds and side-cars, fitted with an auxiliary motor
													-Other:
													Bicycles and other cycles (including delivery tricycles), not motorized:
4.9	0/0/0	4.5	5.2	3.9	0	0	0	0/0/0	0/0/0			0/0/	---Racing bicycle
4.9	0/0/0	4.5	5.2	3.9	0	0	0	0/0/0	0/0/0			0/0/	---Mountain bicycle
													---Cross-country bicycles:
4.9	0/0/0	4.5	5.2	3.9	0	0	0	0/0/0	0/0/0			0/0/0	----16inchs, 18inchs and 20inchs
4.9	0/0/0	4.5	5.2	3.9	0	0	0	0/0/0	0/0/0			0/0/	----Other
													---Other cycles:

税则号列	货品名称〔CIQ扩展编码及品名－T2表示见附表2〕	最惠(%)	暂定税率	普通	增值/消费	出口退税	计量单位	监管条件	检验检疫	特殊证件对美关税
8712.0081	----16英寸及以下									
8712.0081 10	12～16英寸的未列名自行车〔999〕	5		130	13/	13	辆/千克	6	L	/30
8712.0081 90	11英寸及以下的未列名自行车〔999〕	5		130	13/	13	辆/千克	6	L	/30
8712.0089	----其他〔10112－16英寸其它自行车,10211英寸及以下其它自行车,103其它自行车〕	5		130	13/	13	辆/千克	6	L	/30
8712.0090	---其他〔101:12－16英寸其它自行车,102:11英寸及以下其它自行车,103:其它自行车,104:货运三轮脚踏车,105:其他脚踏车〕	5		130	13/	13	辆/千克	6	L	/30
87.13	**残疾人用车,不论是否机动或其他机械驱动:**									
8713.1000	-非机械驱动〔999〕	5		20	0/	13	辆/千克	6		/
8713.9000	-其他〔999〕	4		20	0/	13	辆/千克	6		/
87.14	**零件、附件,税目87.11至87.13所列车辆用:**									
8714.1000	-摩托车(包括机器脚踏两用车)用									
8714.1000 01	星型轮及碟刹件〔999〕	15	10	100	13/	13	千克	6		/35
8714.1000 10	摩托车架〔999〕	15		100	13/	13	千克	46xy		/40
8714.1000 90	摩托车其他零件,附件(包括机动脚踏两用车的零件、附件)〔999〕	15		100	13/	13	千克	6		/40
8714.2000	-残疾人车辆用〔101其他车辆零部件,102其它非机动脚踏车零配件〕	5		17	13/	13	千克	6		/30
	-其他:									
8714.9100	--车架、轮叉及其零件〔101自行车零配件,102其它非机动脚踏车零配件〕	5		80	13/	13	千克	6		/30
	--轮圈及辐条:									
8714.9210	---轮圈〔101自行车零配件,102其它非机动脚踏车零配件〕	5		80	13/	13	千克	6		/30
8714.9290	---辐条〔101自行车零配件,102其它非机动脚踏车零配件〕	5		80	13/	13	千克	6		/30
	--轮毂(倒轮制动毂及毂闸除外);飞轮、链轮:									
8714.9310	---轮毂〔101自行车零配件,102其它非机动脚踏车零配件〕	5		80	13/	13	千克	6		/30
8714.9320	---飞轮〔101自行车零配件,102其它非机动脚踏车零配件〕	5		80	13/	13	千克	6		/30
8714.9390	---其他〔101自行车零配件,102其它非机动脚踏车零配件〕	5		80	13/	13	千克	6		/30
8714.9400	--制动器(包括倒轮制动毂及毂闸)及其零件〔101自行车零配件,102其它非机动脚踏车零配件〕	5		80	13/	13	千克	6		/30
8714.9500	--鞍座〔101自行车零配件,102其它非机动脚踏车零配件〕	5		80	13/	13	千克/个	6		/30
	--脚蹬、曲柄链轮及其零件:									
8714.9610	---脚蹬及其零件〔101自行车零配件,102其它非机动脚踏车零配件〕	5		80	13/	13	千克	6		/30
8714.9620	---曲柄链轮及其零件〔101自行车零配件,102其它非机动脚踏车零配件〕	5		80	13/	13	千克	6		/30
8714.9900	--其他〔101自行车零配件,102其它非机动脚踏车零配件〕	5		80	13/	13	千克	6		/30
87.15	**婴孩车及其零件:**									
8715.0000	婴孩车及其零件									
8715.0000 10	婴孩车〔101婴儿推车,102学步车〕	6		80	13/	13	千克	6A	LM	/31
8715.0000 90	婴孩车零件〔999〕	6		80	13/	13	千克	6A	LM	/31
87.16	**挂车及半挂车或其他非机械驱动车辆及其零件:**									
8716.1000	-供居住或野营用厢式挂车及半挂车〔999〕	10		35	13/	13	辆/千克	6A	LM	/35
8716.2000	-农用自装或自卸式挂车及半挂车〔999〕	10		35	13/	9,13	辆/千克	6		/35
	-其他货运挂车及半挂车:									
	--罐式挂车及半挂车:									
8716.3110	---油罐挂车及半挂车〔999〕	10		20	13/	13	辆/千克	6A	ML	/35
8716.3190	---其他〔999〕	10		35	13/	13	辆/千克	6A	ML	/35
	--其他:									
8716.3910	---货柜挂车及半挂车〔999〕	10		20	13/	13	辆/千克	6A	ML	/35
8716.3990	---其他〔999〕	10		35	13/	13	辆	6A	ML	/35
8716.4000	-其他挂车及半挂车〔999〕	10		35	13/	13	辆/千克	6A	ML	/35
8716.8000	-其他车辆〔999〕	10		80	13/	13	辆/千克	6		/35
8716.9000	-零件〔999〕	10		35	13/	13	千克	6		/15

协定税率 %										特惠税率 %			Article Description
亚太5国	东/冰/格	巴基斯坦	韩国	瑞士	哥达	秘鲁	澳大利亚	新西/坡/智	港/澳/台	亚太2国	老/柬/缅	36/3/1	
													----Not larger than 16inchs
3.5	0/0/0	4.5	5.2	3.9	0	0	0	0/0/0	0/0/0			0/0/	Bicycles，12inches～16inches，not elsewhere specified or included
3.5	0/0/0	4.5	5.2	3.9	0	0	0	0/0/0	0/0/0			0/0/	Bicycles，11inchs or less，not elsewhere specified or included
3.5	0/0/0	4.5	5.2	3.9	0	0	0	0/0/0	0/0/0			0/0/	----Other
3.5	0/0/0	14.5		5	0	0	0	0/0/0	0/0/0			0/0/	---Other
													Carriages for disabled persons，whether or not motorised or otherwise mechanically propelled：
	0/0/0	5	0	0	0	0	0	0//0	0/0/			0/0/	-Not mechanically propelled
	0/0/0	0	1.6	0	0	0	0	0//0	0/0/			0/0/	-Other
													Parts and accessories of vehicles of headings No. 87. 11 to 87. 13：
													-Of motorcycles (including mopeds)
	0/0/0	0	21		0	0	0	0/0/0	0/0/			0/0/	Star-shaped wheels and disc brakes
	0/0/0	0	21		0	0	0	0/0/0	0/0/			0/0/	Frams of motorcycles
	0/0/0	0	21		0	0	0	0/0/0	0/0/			0/0/	Other parts and accessories thereof，of motorcycles and mopeds
	0/0/0	0	0	0	0	0	0	0//0	0/0/			0/0/C	-Of carriages for disabled persons
													-Other：
	0/0/0	5.4	4.8	3.6	0	0	0	0/0/0	0/0/0			0/0/	--Frames and forks，and parts thereof
													--Wheel rims and spokes：
	0/0/0	4.8	4.8	3.6	0	0	0	0/0/0	0/0/0			0/0/	---Wheel rims
	0/0/0	5.4	4.8	3.6	0	0	0	0/0/0	0/0/0			0/0/	---Spokes
													--Hubs，other than coaster braking hubs and hub brakes，and free-wheel，sprocket wheels：
	0/0/0	5.4	4.8	3.6	0	0	0	0/0/0	0/0/0			0/0/	---Hubs
	0/0/0	5.4	4.8	3.6	0	0	0	0/0/0	0/0/0			0/0/	---Free-wheel
	0/0/0	5.4	4.8	3.6	0	0	0	0/0/0	0/0/0			0/0/	---Other
	0/0/0	4.8	4.8	3.6	0	0	0	0/0/0	0/0/0			0/0/	--Brakes，including coaster braking hubs and hub brakes，and parts thereof
	0/0/0	5.4	4.8	3.6	0	0	0	0/0/0	0/0/0			0/0/	--Saddles
													--Pedals and crank-gear，and parts thereof：
	0/0/0	5.4	4.8	3.6	0	0	0	0/0/0	0/0/0			0/0/	---Pedals and parts thereof
	0/0/0	4.8	4.8	3.6	0	0	0	0/0/0	0/0/0			0/0/	---Crank-gear and parts thereof
3.5	0/0/0	0	4.8	3.6	0	0	0	0/0/0	0/0/0			0/0/	--Other
													Baby carriages and parts thereof：
													Baby carriages and parts thereof
	0/0/0	20	12	6	0	0	0	0/0/0	0/0/			0/0/	Baby carriages
	0/0/0	20	12	6	0	0	0	0/0/0	0/0/			0/0/	Baby car parts
													Trailers and semi-trailers；other vehicles，not mechanically propelled；parts thereof：
	0/0/0	4	6	0	0	0	0	0/0/0	0/0/			0/0/	-Trailers and semi-trailers of the caravan type，for housing or camping
	0/0/0	4	6	0	0	0	0	0//0	0/0/			0/0/	-Self-loading or self-unloading trailers and semi-trailers for agricultural purposes
													-Other trailers and semi-trailers for the transport of goods：
													--Tanker trailers and tanker semi-trailers：
	0/0/0	4	6	0	0	0	0	0/0/0	0/0/			0/0/	---Oil tanker trailers and semi-trailers
	0/0/0	4	4	0	0	0	0	0//0	0/0/			0/0/	---Other
													--Other：
	0/0/0	4	4	0	0	0	0	0//0	0/0/			0/0/	---Van trailers and semi-trailers
	0/0/0	4	4	0	0	0	0	0//0	0/0/			0/0/	---Other
	0/0/0	4	4	0	0	0	0	0//0	0/0/			0/0/	-Other trailers and semi-trailers
	0/0/0	4.5	4	0	0	0	0	0/0/0	0/0/			0/0/	-Other vehicles
	0/0/0	4	4	0	0	0	0	0/0/0	0/0/			0/0/0	-Parts

第八十八章
航空器、航天器及其零件

子目注释：

子目 8802.11 至 8802.40 所称“空载重量”，是指航空器在正常飞行状态下，除去机组人员、燃料及非永久性安装设备后的重量。

税则号列	货品名称〔CIQ 扩展编码及品名—T2 表示见附表 2〕	最惠(%)	暂定税率	普通	增值/消费	出口退税	计量单位	监管条件	检验检疫	特殊证件对美关税
88.01	**气球及飞艇；滑翔机、悬挂滑翔机及其他无动力航空器：**									
8801.0010	---滑翔机、及悬挂滑翔机：〔999〕	3		11	13/	13	架/千克			/23
8801.0090	---其他									
8801.0090 10	自然视距以外可控飞行的无人驾驶飞艇（在 30 分钟≤最大续航时间＜1 小时，阵风≥46.3 千米/小时条件下具有起飞和稳定飞行能力；或者最大续航时间≥1 小时。）〔999〕	3		11	13/	13	架/千克	3		/23
8801.0090 90	气球、其他飞艇及无动力航空器（滑翔机除外）〔999〕	3		11	13/	13	架/千克			/23
88.02	**其他航空器（例如，直升机、飞机）；航天器（包括卫星）及其运载工具、亚轨道运载工具：**									
	-直升机：									
8802.1100	--空载重量不超过 2000 千克									
8802.1100 10	空载重量不超过 2 吨的无人驾驶直升机（两用物项和技术出口管制的）〔999〕	2		11	13/	13	架/千克	3O		/7
8802.1100 90	其他空载重量不超过 2 吨的直升机〔999〕	2		11	13/	13	架/千克	O		/7
	--空载重量超过 2000 千克：									
8802.1210	---空载重量超过 2000 千克，但不超过 7000 千克〔999〕	2		11	13/	13	架	O		/12
8802.1220	---空载重量超过 7000 千克〔999〕	2		11	13/	13	架/千克	O		/
8802.2000	-飞机及其他航空器，空载重量不超过 2000 千克									
8802.2000 11	空载重量小于等于 2 吨的无人驾驶航空飞行器（两用物项出口管制的）〔101 飞机，102 航天器〕	5		11	13/	13	架/千克	3O		/10
8802.2000 19	其他无人驾驶航空飞行器（空载重量小于等于 2 吨）〔101 飞机，102 航天器〕	5		11	13/	13	架/千克	3O		/10
8802.2000 90	其他小型飞机及其他航空器（小型指空载重量不超过 2000 千克的）〔101 飞机，102 航天器〕	5		11	13/	13	架/千克			/10
8802.3000	-飞机及其他航空器，空载重量超过 2000 千克，但不超过 15000 千克〔101 飞机，102 航天器〕	4		11	13/	13	架/千克	O		/9
	-飞机及其他航空器，空载重量超过 15000 千克：									
8802.4010	---空载重量超过 15000 千克，但不超过 45000 千克〔101 飞机，102 航天器〕	5		11	13/	13	架/千克	O		/
8802.4020	---空载重量超过 45000 千克〔999〕	1		11	13/	13	架/千克	O		/
8802.6000	-航天器（包括卫星）及其运载工具、亚轨道运载工具									
8802.6000 10	通信卫星〔999〕	0		11	13/	13	架/千克			/
8802.6000 90	航天器（包括卫星，但通信卫星除外）及其运载工具（包括亚轨道运载工具）〔101 航天器，102 其它航空器〕	2		11	13/	13	架/千克			/
88.03	**税目 88.01 或 88.02 所列货品的零件：**									
8803.1000	-推进器、水平旋翼及其零件〔999〕	1		11	13/	13	千克			/
8803.2000	-起落架及其零件〔999〕	1		11	13/	13	千克			/
8803.3000	-飞机及直升机的其他零件〔999〕	1		11	13/	13	千克			/
8803.9000	-其他									
8803.9000 10	两用物项管制的火箭及其零部件〔999〕	0		11	13/	13	千克	3		/5
8803.9000 90	其他未列名的航空器、航天器零件（指税目 88.01 或 88.02 所列货品用的）〔999〕	0		11	13/	13	千克			/5
88.04	**降落伞（包括可操纵降落伞及滑翔伞）、旋翼降落伞及其零件、附件：**									
8804.0000	降落伞（包括可操纵降落伞及滑翔伞）、旋翼降落伞及其零件、附件〔999〕	2		11	13/	13	千克			/7
88.05	**航空器的发射装置、甲板停机装置或类似装置和地面飞行训练器及其零件：**									
8805.1000	-航空器的发射装置及其零件；甲板停机装置或类似装置及其零件〔999〕	1.5		11	13/	13	千克			/6.5
	-地面飞行训练器及其零件：									
8805.2100	--空战模拟器及其零件〔999〕	0		11	13/	13	千克			/
8805.2900	--其他〔999〕	0		11	13/	13	千克	O		/

Chapter 88
Aircraft, spacecraft, and parts thereof

Subheading Note:

For the purposes of subheadings Nos. 8802. 11 to Nos. 8802. 40, the expression "unladen weight" means the weight of the machine in normal flying order, excluding the weight of the crew and of fuel and equipment other than permanently fitted items of equipment.

协定税率 %										特惠税率 %			Article Description
亚太5国	东/冰/格	巴基斯坦	韩国	瑞士	哥达	秘鲁	澳大利亚	新西/坡/智	港/澳/台	亚太2国	老/柬/缅	36/3/1	
													Balloons and dirigibles; gliders, hang gliders and other non-powered aircraft:
	0/0/0	0	0	0	0	0	0	0//0	0/0/			0/0/0	---Cliders and hang gliders
													---Other
	0/0/0	0	0	0	0	0	0	0//0	0/0/			0/0/0	Natural sights outside of controlled flight of unmanned airship, in 30 minutes or less maximum duration < 1 hour, under the condition of wind acuity ≥46.3 kilometers per hour and stable flight take-off ability; Or a maximum duration for≥1 hour or more
	0/0/0	0	0	0	0	0	0	0//0	0/0/			0/0/0	Balloons and dirigibles; and other non-powered aircraft (excluding gliders)
													Other aircraft (for example, helicopters, aeroplanes); spacecraft (including satellites) and suborbital and spacecraft launch vehicles:
													-Helicopters:
													--Of an unladen weight not exceeding 2000kg
1.3	0/0/0	0	0	0	0	0	0	0//0	0/0/			0/0/0	Light weight less than 2 tons of unmanned helicopter
1.3	0/0/0	0	0	0	0	0	0	0//0	0/0/			0/0/0	Other helicopters Of an unladen weight not exceeding 2000kg
													--Of an unladen weight exceeding 2000kg:
1.3	0/0/0	0	0	0	0	0	0	0//0	0/0/			0/0/0	---Of an unladen weight exceeding 2000kg, but not exceeding 7000kg
1.3	0/0/0	0	0	0	0	0	0	0//0	0/0/			0/0/0	---Of an unladen weight exceeding 7000kg
													-Aeroplanes and other aircraft, of an unladen weight not exceeding 2000kg
	0/0/0	0	2	0	0	0	0	0//0	0/0/			0/0/0	Dual-use items export control of unmanned air vehicle
	0/0/0	0	2	0	0	0	0	0//0	0/0/			0/0/0	Other unmanned air vehicle
	0/0/0	0	2	0	0	0	0	0//0	0/0/			0/0/0	Other small planes and other aircrafts(unladen weight≤2000kg)
	0/0/0	0	0	0	0	0	0	0//0	0/0/			0/0/0	-Aeroplanes and other aircraft, of an unladen weight exceeding 2000kg, but not exceeding 15000kg
													-Aeroplanes and other aircraft, of an unladen weight exceeding 15000kg:
3.5	0/0/0	0	0	0	0	0	0	0//0	0/0/			0/0/0	---Of an unladen weight exceeding 15000kg, but not exceeding 45000kg
0.7	0/0/0	0	0	0	0	0	0	0//0	0/0/			0/0/0	---Of an unladen weight exceeding 45000kg
													-Spacecraft (including satellites) and suborbital and spacecraft launch vehicles
	0/0/0	0	0	0	0	0	0	0//0	0/0/			0/0/0	Communication satellite
	0/0/0	0	0	0	0	0	0	0//0	0/0/			0/0/0	Spacecraft(including satellites) and suborbital and spacecraft launch vehicles
													Parts of goods of heading No. 88. 01 or 88. 02:
	0/0/0	0	0	0	0	0	0	0//0	0/0/			0/0/0	-Propellers and rotors and parts thereof
	0/0/0	0	0	0	0	0	0	0//0	0/0/			0/0/0	-Under-carriages and parts thereof
	0/0/0	0	0	0	0	0	0	0//0	0/0/			0/0/	-Other parts of aeroplanes or helicopters
													-Other
												0/0/0	Missile and parts and accessories thereof, of sensitive items control
												0/0/0	Parts of other aircraft, sfacecraft, not elsewhere specified or included (parts of goods of heading No. 88. 01 or 88. 02)
													Parachutes (including dirigible parachutes and paragliders) and rotochutes; parts thereof and accessories thereto:
	0/0/0	0	0	0	0	0	0	0//0	0/0/			0/0/0	Parachutes (including dirigible parachutes and paragliders) and rotochutes; parts thereof and accessories thereto
													Aircraft launching gear; deck-arrestor or similar gear; ground flying trainers; parts of the foregoing articles:
	0/0/0	0	0	0	0	0	0	0//0	0/0/			0/0/0	-Aircraft launching gear and parts thereof; deck-arrestor or similar gear and parts thereof
													-Ground flying trainers and parts thereof:
	0//							//	0/0/			0/0/	--Air combat simulators and parts thereof
	0//							//	0/0/			0/0/0	--Other

第八十九章
船舶及浮动结构体

注释：

已装配、未装配或已拆卸的船体、未完工或不完整的船舶以及未装配或已拆卸的完整船舶，如果不具有某种船舶的基本特征，应归入税目89.06。

税则号列	货品名称〔CIQ扩展编码及品名－T2表示见附表2〕	最惠(%)	暂定税率	普通	增值/消费	出口退税	计量单位	监管条件	检验检疫	特殊证件对美关税
89.01	**巡航船、游览船、渡船、货船、驳船及类似的客运或货运船舶：**									
	-巡航船、游览船及主要用于客运的类似船舶；各式渡船：									
8901.1010	---机动船舶									
8901.1010 10	高速客船(包括主要用于客运的类似船舶)〔999〕	5		14	13/	13	艘/千克	O		3/
8901.1010 90	其他机动巡航船游览船及各式渡船(包括主要用于客运的类似船舶)〔999〕	5		14	13/	13	艘/千克	O		3/
8901.1090	---非机动船舶〔999〕	8		30	13/	13	艘/千克			3/
	-液货船：									
	---成品油船：									
8901.2011	----载重量不超过10万吨〔999〕	9		14	13/	13	艘/千克	O		/
8901.2012	----载重量超过10万吨，但不超过30万吨〔999〕	9		14	13/	13	艘/千克			/
8901.2013	----载重量超过30万吨〔999〕	6		14	13/	13	艘/千克			/
	---原油船：									
8901.2021	----载重量不超过15万吨〔999〕	9		14	13/	13	艘/千克	O		/
8901.2022	----载重量超过15万吨，但不超过30万吨〔999〕	9		14	13/	13	艘/千克			/
8901.2023	----载重量超过30万吨〔999〕	6		14	13/	13	艘/千克			/
	---液化石油气船：									
8901.2031	----容积在20000立方米及以下〔999〕	9		14	13/	13	艘/千克	O		/
8901.2032	----容积在20000立方米以上〔999〕	6		14	13/	13	艘/千克			/
	---液化天然气船：									
8901.2041	----容积在20000立方米及以下〔999〕	9		14	13/	13	艘/千克			/
8901.2042	----容积在20000立方米以上〔999〕	6		14	13/	13	艘/千克			/
8901.2090	---其他〔999〕	9		14	13/	13	艘/千克	O		/
8901.3000	-冷藏船，但子目8901.20的船舶除外〔999〕	9		14	13/	13	艘/千克			/
	-其他货运船舶及其他客货兼运船舶：									
	---机动集装箱船：									
8901.9021	----可载标准集装箱在6000箱及以下〔999〕	9		14	13/	13	艘/千克	O		/
8901.9022	----可载标准集装箱在6000箱以上〔999〕	6		14	13/	13	艘/千克			/
	---机动滚装船：									
8901.9031	----载重量在2万吨及以下〔999〕	9		14	13/	13	艘/千克	O		/
8901.9032	----载重量在2万吨以上的〔999〕	6		14	13/	13	艘/千克			/
	---机动散货船：									
8901.9041	----载重量不超过15万吨〔999〕	9		14	13/	13	艘/千克	3O		/
8901.9041 10	特殊民用物项管制的自航自卸式泥驳(具体商品描述详见相关公告)〔999〕	9		14	13/	13	艘/千克	3O		/
8901.9041 90	其他载重量不超过15万吨散货船〔999〕	9		14	13/	13	艘/千克	O		/
8901.9042	----载重量超过15万吨，但不超过30万吨〔999〕	9		14	13/	13	艘/千克			/
8901.9043	----载重量超过30万吨〔999〕	9		14	13/	13	艘/千克			/
8901.9050	---机动多用途船〔999〕	9		14	13/	13	艘/千克			/
8901.9080	---其他机动船舶〔999〕	9		14	13/	13	艘/千克	O		/
8901.9090	---非机动船舶〔999〕	8		30	13/	13	艘/千克	O		3/
89.02	**捕鱼船；加工船及其他加工保藏鱼类产品的船舶：**									
8902.0010	---机动船舶〔999〕	7		14	13/	13	艘/千克	O		/
8902.0090	---非机动船舶〔999〕	8		30	13/	9,13	艘/千克			/
89.03	**娱乐或运动用快艇及其他船舶；划艇及轻舟：**									
8903.1000	-充气的〔999〕	10		30	13/	13	艘/千克			/15
	-其他：									
8903.9100	--帆船，不论是否装有辅助发动机									
8903.9100 01	8米＜长度＜90米的机动帆船〔101客运船舶，102货运船舶，103客、货两用船舶〕	8		30	13/10	13	艘/千克			/33
8903.9100 90	其他帆船(不论是否装有辅助发动机)〔101客运船舶，102货运船舶，103客、货两用船舶〕	8		30	13/	13	艘/千克			/33

Chapter 89
Ships, boats and floating structures

Note:

A hull, an unfinished or incomplete vessel, assembled, unassembled or disassembled, or a complete vessel unassembled or disassembled, is to be classified in heading No. 89. 06 if it does not have the essential character of a vessel of a particular kind.

协定税率 %										特惠税率 %			Article Description
亚太5国	东/冰/格	巴基斯坦	韩国	瑞士	哥达	秘鲁	澳大利亚	新西/坡/智	港/澳/台	亚太2国	老/柬/缅	36/3/1	
													Cruise ships, excursion boats, ferry-boats, cargo ships, barges and similar vessels for the transport of persons or goods:
													-Cruise ships, excursion boats and similar vessels principally designed for the transport of persons; ferry-boats of all kinds:
													---Motor vessels
	0/0/0	0	3	0	0	0	0	0/0/0	0/0/			0/0/	High-speed passenger vessels (similar vessels principally designed for the transport of persons)
	0/0/0	0	3	0	0	0	0	0/0/0	0/0/			0/0/	Other cruise ships, excursion boats ferry-boats of all kinds (similar vessels principally designed for the transport of persons)
	0/0/0	4	4.8	0	0	0	0	0//0	0/0/			0/0/	---Other
													-Tankers:
													---Finished oil tankers:
	5/0/0		5.4	0	0	0	0	0//0	0/0/			0/0/	----Loading not exceeding 100000t
	5/0/0		5.4	0	0	0	0	0//0	0/0/			0/0/	----Loading exceeding 100000t, but not exceeding 300000t
	5/0/0		3.6	0	0	0	0	0//0	0/0/			0/0/	----Loading exceeding 300000t
													---Crude oil tankers:
	5/0/0		5.4	0	0	0	0	0//0	0/0/			0/0/	----Loading not exceeding 150000t
	5/0/0		5.4	0	0	0	0	0//0	0/0/			0/0/	----Loading exceeding 150000t, but not exceeding 300000t
	5/0/0		3.6	0	0	0	0	0//0	0/0/			0/0/	----Loading exceeding 300000t
													---Liquified petroleum gas carriers:
	5/0/0		5.4	0	0	0	0	0//0	0/0/			0/0/	----Volume with 20000m^3 or less
	5/0/0		3.6	0	0	0	0	0//0	0/0/			0/0/	----Volume more than 20000m^3
													---Liquified natural gas carriers:
	5/0/0		5.4	0	0	0	0	0//0	0/0/			0/0/	----Volume with 20000m^3 or less
	5/0/0		3.6	0	0	0	0	0//0	0/0/			0/0/	----Volume more than 20000m^3
	5/0/0		5.4	0	0	0	0	0//0	0/0/			0/0/	---Other
	0/0/0	4	5.4	0	0	0	0	0/0/0	0/0/			0/0/	-Refrigerated vessels, other than those of subheading No. 8901. 20
													-Other vessels for the transport of goods and other vessels for the transport of both persons and goods:
													---Motor container vessels:
	5/0/0		5.4	0	0	0	0	0//0	0/0/			0/0/	----Capable loading standard containers with 6000 or less
	5/0/0		3.6	0	0	0	0	0//0	0/0/			0/0/	----Capable loading standard containers more than 6000
													---Motor Ro-Ro carriers:
	5/0/0		5.4	0	0	0	0	0//0	0/0/			0/0/	----Loading with 20000t or less
	5/0/0		3.6	0	0	0	0	0//0	0/0/			0/0/	----Loading more than 20000t
													---Motor bulk carriers:
	5/0/0		6	0	0	0	0	0//0	0/0/			0/0/	----Loading not exceeding 150000t
	5/0/0		5.4	0	0	0	0	0//0	0/0/		//	0/0/	Self propelled dump barge for special civil items control (see relevant announcement for specific commodity description)
	5/0/0		5.4	0	0	0	0	0//0	0/0/		//	0/0/	Other bulk carriers with a capacity of no more than 150000 tons
	5/0/0		5.4	0	0	0	0	0//0	0/0/			0/0/	----Loading exceeding 150000t, not exceeding 300000t
	5/0/0		5.4	0	0	0	0	0//0	0/0/			0/0/	----Loading exceeding 300000t
	5/0/0		5.4	0	0	0	0	0//0	0/0/			0/0/	---Multi-purposes motor vessels
	0/0/0	4	5.4	0	0	0	0	0/0/0	0/0/			0/0/	---Other motor vessels
	0/0/0	4	4.8	0	0	0	0	0/0/0	0/0/			0/0/	---Other non-motor vessels
													Fishing vessels; factory ships and other vessels for processing or preserving fishery products:
	0/0/0	4	4.2	0	0	0	0	0/0/0	0/0/			0/0/	---Motor vessels
	0/0/0	4	4.8	0	0	0	0	0//0	0/0/			0/0/	---Other
													Yachts and other vessels for pleasure or sports; rowing boats and canoes:
	0/0/0	4	6	0	0	0	0	0//0	0/0/			0/0/0	-Inflatable
													-Other:
													--Sailboats, with or without auxiliary motor
	0/0/0	4	4.8	0	0	0	0	0//0	0/0/			0/0/0	Motor vessels, 8m<length<90m
	0/0/0	4	4.8	0	0	0	0	0//0	0/0/			0/0/0	Other sailboats(with or without auxiliary motor)

税则号列	货品名称〔CIQ 扩展编码及品名—T2 表示见附表 2〕	最惠(%)	暂定税率	普通	增值/消费	出口退税	计量单位	监管条件	检验检疫	特殊证件对美关税
8903.9200	--汽艇,但装有舷外发动机的除外									
8903.9200 01	8 米＜长度＜90 米的汽艇(装有舷外发动机的除外)〔101 客运船舶,102 货运船舶,103 客、货两用船舶〕	10		30	13/10	13	艘/千克			3/20
8903.9200 90	其他汽艇(装有舷外发动机的除外)〔101 客运船舶,102 货运船舶,103 客、货两用船舶〕	10		30	13/	13	艘/千克			3/20
8903.9900	--其他									
8903.9900 01	8 米＜长度＜90 米的娱乐或运动用其他机动船舶或快艇〔101 客运船舶,102 其它船舶〕	10		30	13/10	13	艘/千克			3/35
8903.9900 90	娱乐或运动用其他船舶或快艇(包括划艇及轻舟)〔999〕	10		30	13/	13	艘/千克			/35
89.04	**拖轮及顶推船:**									
8904.0000	拖轮及顶推船〔999〕	9		14	13/	13	艘/千克			/
89.05	**灯船、消防船、挖泥船、起重船及其他不以航行为主要功能的船舶;浮船坞;浮动或潜水式钻探或生产平台:**									
8905.1000	-挖泥船〔999〕	3		11	13/	13	艘/千克	3		/
8905.1000 10	耙吸式挖泥船、绞吸式挖泥船、斗式挖泥船、吸沙船	3		11	13/	13	艘/千克	3		/
8905.1000 90	其他挖泥船	3		11	13/	13	艘/千克			/
8905.2000	-浮动或潜水式钻探或生产平台〔999〕	6		11	13/	13	座/千克			/31
	-其他:									
8905.9010	---浮船坞〔999〕	8		30	13/	13	个/千克			/
8905.9090	---其他〔999〕	3		11	13/	13	个/千克			/28
89.06	**其他船舶,包括军舰及救生船,但划艇除外:**									
8906.1000	-军舰〔999〕	5		14	13/	13	艘/千克			/
	-其他:									
8906.9010	---机动船舶〔999〕	5		14	13/	13	艘/千克			/30
8906.9020	---非机动船舶〔999〕	8		30	13/	0	艘/千克			/33
8906.9030	---未制成或不完整的船舶,包括船舶分段〔999〕	8		30	13/	0	艘/千克			/33
89.07	**其他浮动结构体(例如,筏、柜、潜水箱、浮码头、浮筒及航标):**									
8907.1000	-充气筏〔999〕	8		30	13/	13	艘/千克			/18
8907.9000	-其他〔999〕	8		30	13/	13	个/千克			/28
89.08	**供拆卸的船舶及其他浮动结构体:**									
8908.0000	供拆卸的船舶及其他浮动结构体〔999〕	3		11	13/	13	艘/千克	9AB	MPQ	/28

协定税率 %										特惠税率 %			Article Description
亚太5国	东/冰/格	巴基斯坦	韩国	瑞士	哥达	秘鲁	澳大利亚	新西/坡/智	港/澳/台	亚太2国	老/柬/缅	36/3/1	
													--Motorboats, other than outboard motorboats
	0/0/0	4.5	6.3	3.2	0	0	0	0/0/0	0/0/			0/0/0	Motorboats, 8m＜length＜90m(other than outboard motorboats)
	0/0/0	4.5	6.3	3.2	0	0	0	0/0/0	0/0/			0/0/0	Other motorboats(other than outboard motorboats)
													--Other
	0/0/0	4		0	0	0	0	0//0	0/0/			0/0/0	Yachts and other vessels for pleasure or sports, 8m＜length＜90m
	0/0/0	4		0	0	0	0	0//0	0/0/			0/0/0	Other yachts and other vessels for pleasure or sports(including rowing boats and canoes)
													Tugs and pusher craft:
	0/0/0	4	5.4	0	0	0	0	0/0/0	0/0/			0/0/0	Tugs and pusher craft
													Light-vessels, fire-floats, dredgers, floating cranes, and other vessels the navigability of which is subsidiary to their main function; floating docks; floating or submersible drilling or roduction platforms:
	0/0/0	0	2	0	0	0	0	0//0	0/0/			0/0/0	-Dredgers
	0/0/0	0	1.8	0	0	0	0	0//0	0/0/		//	0/0/0	Drag suction dredger, cutter suction dredger, bucket dredger, sand suction dredger
	0/0/0	0	1.8	0	0	0	0	0//0	0/0/		//	0/0/0	Other dredgers
	0/0/0	0	3.6	0	0	0	0	0//0	0/0/			0/0/0	-Floating or submersible drilling or production platforms
													-Other:
	5/0/0		4.8	0	0	0	0	0//0	0/0/			0/0/0	---Floating docks
	0/0/0	0	1.8	0	0	0	0	0//0	0/0/			0/0/0	---Other
													Other vessels, including warships and lifeboats other than rowing boats:
	0/0/0	0	3	0	0	0	0	0//0	0/0/			0/0/	-Warships
													-Other:
	0/0/0	0		0	0	0	0	0//0	0/0/			0/0/0	---Motor vessels
	0/0/0	4	4.8	0	0	0	0	0//0	0/0/			0/0/0	---Not-motorized vessels
	0/0/0	4	4.8	0	0	0	0	0//0	0/0/			0/0/0	---Unfinished or incomplete vessels, including subsections of vessels
													Other floating structures (for example, rafts, tanks, coffer-dams, landing-stages, buoys and beacons):
	0/0/0	4	4.8	0	0	0	0	0//0	0/0/			0/0/0	-Inflatable rafts
	0/0/0	4	4.8	0	0	0	0	0//0	0/0/			0/0/0	-Other
													Vessels and other floating structures for breaking up:
	0/0/0	0	1.8	0	0	0	0	0//0	0/0/			0/0/0	Vessels and other floating structures for breaking up

第十八类
光学、照相、电影、计量、检验、医疗或外科用仪器及设备、精密仪器及设备;钟表;乐器;上述物品的零件、附件

第九十章
光学、照相、电影、计量、检验、医疗或外科用仪器及设备、精密仪器及设备;上述物品的零件、附件

注释:

一、本章不包括:

(一)机器、设备或其他专门技术用途的硫化橡胶(硬质橡胶除外)制品(税目40.16)、皮革或再生皮革制品(税目42.04)或纺织材料制品(税目59.11);

(二)纺织材料制的承托带及其他承托物品,其承托器官的作用仅依靠自身的弹性(例如,孕妇用的承托带,用于胸部、腹部、关节或肌肉的承托绷带)(第十一类);

(三)税目69.03的耐火材料制品;税目69.09的实验室、化学或其他专门技术用途的陶瓷器;

(四)税目70.09的未经光学加工的玻璃镜及税目83.06或第七十一章的非光学元件的贱金属或贵金属制的镜子;

(五)税目70.07、70.08、70.11、70.14、70.15或70.17的货品;

(六)第十五类注释二所规定的贱金属制通用零件(第十五类)或塑料制的类似品(第三十九章);

(七)税目84.13的装有计量装置的泵;计数和检验用的衡器或单独报验的天平砝码(税目84.23);升降、起重及搬运机械(税目84.25至84.28);纸张或纸板的各种切割机器(税目84.41);税目84.66的用于机床或水射流切割机上调整工件或工具的附件,包括具有读度用的光学装置的附件(例如,"光学"分度头),但其本身主要是光学仪器的除外(例如,校直望远镜);计算机器(税目84.70);税目84.81的阀门及其他装置;税目84.86的机器及装置(包括将电路图投影或绘制到感光半导体材料上的装置);

(八)自行车或机动车辆用探照灯或聚光灯(税目85.12);税目85.13的手提式电灯;电影录音机、还音机及转录机(税目85.19);拾音头或录音头(税目85.22);电视摄像机、及数字照相机视频摄录一体机(税目85.25);雷达设备、无线电导航设备或无线电遥控设备(税目85.26);光导纤维、光导纤维束或光缆用连接器(税目85.36);税目85.37的数控制装置;税目85.39的封闭式聚光灯;税目85.44的光缆;

(九)税目94.05的探照灯及聚光灯;

(十)第九十五章的物品;

(十一)税目96.20的独脚架、双脚架、三脚架及类似品;

(十二)容量的计量器具(按其构成的材料归类);

(十三)卷轴、线轴及类似芯子(按其构成材料归类,例如,归入税目39.23或第十五类)。

二、除上述注释一另有规定的以外,本章各税目所列机器、设备、仪器或器具的零件、附件,应按下列规定归类:

(一)凡零件、附件本身已构成本章或第八十四章、第八十五章或第九十一章各税目(税目84.87、85.48或90.33除外)所包括的货品,应一律归入其相应的税目;

(二)其他零件、附件,如果专用于或主要用于某种或同一税目项下的多种机器、仪器或器具(包括税目90.10、90.13或90.31的机器、仪器或器具),应归入相应机器、仪器或器具的税目;

(三)所有其他零件、附件均应归入税目90.33。

三、第十六类注释三、四也适用于本章。

四、税目90.05不包括武器用望远镜瞄准具、潜艇或坦克上的潜望镜式望远镜及本章或第十六类的机器、设备、仪器或器具用的望远镜;这类望远镜瞄准具及望远镜应归入税目90.13。

五、计量或检验用的光学仪器、器具或机器,如果既可归入税目90.13,又可归入税目90.31,则应归入税目90.31。

六、税目90.21所称"矫形器具",是指下列用途的器具:

预防或矫正人体畸变;

生病、手术或受伤后人体部位的支撑或固定;

矫形器具包括用于矫正畸形的鞋及特种鞋垫,但需符合下列任一条件:

(一)定制的;

(二)成批生产的、单独报验、且不成双的、设计为左右两脚同样适用。

七、税目90.32仅适用于:

(一)液体或气体的流量、液位、压力或其他变化量的自动控制仪器及装置或温度自动控制装置,不论其是否依靠要被自控的因素所发生的电现象来进行工作,这些仪器或装置将被自控因素调到并保持在一设定值上,通过持续或定期测量实际值来保持稳定,修正偏差;

(二)电量自动调节器及自动控制非电量的仪器或装置,依靠要被控制的因素所发生的电现象来进行工作,这些仪器或装置将被控制的因素调到并保持在一设定值上,通过持续或定期测量实际值来保持稳定,修正任何偏差。

SECTION XVIII

OPTICAL, PHOTOGRAPHIC, CINEMATOGRAPHIC, MEASURING, CHECKING, PRECISION, MEDICALOR SURGICAL INSTRUMENTS AND APPARATUS; CLOCKS AND WATCHES; MUSICAL INSTRUMENTS; PARTS AND ACCESSORIES THEREOF

Chapter 90

Optical, photographic, cinematographic, measuring, checking, precision, medical or surgical instruments and apparatus; parts and accessories thereof

Notes:

1. This Chapter does not cover:

(a) Articles of a kind used in machines, appliances or for other technical uses, of vulcanized rubber other than hard rubber (heading No. 40.16), of leather or of composition leather (heading No. 42.05) or of textile material (heading No. 59.11);

(b) Supporting belts or other support articles of textile material, whose intended effect on the organ to be supported or held derives solely from their elasticity (for example, maternity belts, thoracic support bandages, abdominal support bandages, supports for joints or muscles) (Section XI);

(c) Refractory goods of heading No. 69.03; ceramic wares for laboratory, chemical or other technical uses, of heading No. 69.09;

(d) Glass mirrors, not optically worked, of heading No. 70.09, or mirrors of base metal or of precious metal, not being optical elements (heading No. 83.06 or Chapter 71);

(e) Goods of heading No. 70.07, 70.08, 70.11, 70.14, 70.15 or 70.17;

(f) Parts of general use, as defined in Note 2 to Section XV, of base metal (Section XV) or similar goods of plastics (Chapter 39);

(g) Pumps incorporating measuring devices, of heading No. 84.13; weight-operated counting or checking machinery, or separately presented weights for balances (heading No. 84.23); lifting or handling machinery (headings No. 84.25 to 84.28); paper or paperboard cutting machines of all kinds (heading No. 84.41); fittings for adjusting work or tools on machine-tools or water iet iutting machine, of heading No. 84.66, including fittings with optical devices for reading the scale (for example, "optical" dividing heads) but not those which are in themselves essentially optical instruments (for example, alignment telescopes); calculating machines (heading No. 84.70); valves or other appliances of heading 84.81; machines and apparats (including opparatus for the projection or dralving of circuit pattern on sensitized semiconductor materials) of heading 84.86.

(h) Searchlights or spotlights of a kind used for cycles or motor vehicles (heading No. 85.12); portable electric lamps of heading 85.13; cinematographic sound recording, reproducing or re-recording apparatus (heading No. 85.19); sound-heads (heading No. 85.22); television cameras digital cameras and video camera retorders(heading No. 85.25) radar apparatus, radio navigational aid apparatus or radio remote control apparatus(heading No. 85.26); conneltors for optical fibres optical fibre bundles or cables (heading 85.36); numerical control apparatus of heading No. 85.37; sealed beam lamp units of heading No. 85.39; optical fibre cables of heading No. 85.44;

(ij) Searchlights or spotlights of heading No. 94.05;

(k) Articles of Chapter 95;

(l) unipod, bipod, tripod or the like of heading No.96.20;

(m) Capacity measures, which are to be classified according to their constituent material;

(n) Spools, reels or similar supports (which are to be classified according to their constituent material, for example, in heading No. 39.23 or Section XV).

2. Subject to Note 1 above, parts and accessories for machines, apparatus, instruments or articles of this Chapter are to be classified according to the following rules:

(a) Parts and accessories which are goods included in any of the headings of this Chapter or of Chapter 84, 85 or 91 (other than heading No. 84.87, 87.48 or 90.33) are in all cases to be classified in their respective headings;

(b) Other parts and accessories, if suitable for use solely or principally with a particular kind of machine, instrument or apparatus, or with a number of machines, instruments or apparatus of the same heading (including a machine, instrument or apparatus of heading No. 90.10, 90.13 or 90.31) are to be classified with the machines, instruments or apparatus of that kind;

(c) All other parts and accessories are to be classified in heading No. 90.33.

3. The provisions of Notes 3 and 4 to Section XVI or XVI apply also to this Chapter.

4. Heading No. 90.05 does not apply to telescopic sights for fitting to arms, periscopic telescopes for fitting to submarines or tanks, or to telescopes for machines, appliances, instruments or apparatus of this Chapter of Section XVI; such telescopic sights and telescopes are to be classified in heading No. 90.13.

5. Measuring or checking optical instruments, appliances or machines which, but for this Note, could be classified both in heading No. 90.13 and in heading No. 90.31 are to be classified in heading No. 90.31.

6. For the purposes of heading No. 90.21, the expression "orthopaedic appliances" means appliances for:

Preventing or correcting bodily deformities;

Supporting or holding parts of the body following an illness, operation or injury.

Orthopaedic appliances include footwear and special insoles designed to correct orthopaedic conditions, provided that they are either:

(a) made to measure or

(b) mass-produced, presented singly. and not in pairs and designed to fit either foot equally

7. Heading No. 90.32 applies only to:

(a) Instruments and apparatus for automatically controlling the flow, level, pressure or other variables of liquids or gases, or for automatically controlling temperature, whether or not their operation depends on an electrical phenomenon which varies according to the factor to be automatically controlled; which are designed to bring this factor to, and maintain it at, a desired value, stabilised against disturbances, by constantly or periodically measuring its actual value;

(b) Automatic regulators of electrical quantities, and instruments or apparatus for automatically controlling non-electrical quantities the operation of which depends on an electrical phenomenon varying according to the factor to be controlled, which are designed to bring this factor to, and maintain it at, a desired value, stabilised against disturbances, by constantly or periodically measuring its actual value.

税则号列		货品名称〔CIQ扩展编码及品名－T2表示见附表2〕	最惠(%)	暂定税率	普通	增值/消费	出口退税	计量单位	监管条件	检验检疫	特殊证件对美关税
90.01		**光导纤维及光导纤维束;光缆,但税目85.44的货品除外;偏振材料制的片及板;未装配的各种材料制透镜(包括隐形眼镜片)、棱镜、反射镜及其他光学元件,但未经光学加工的玻璃制上述元件除外:**									
9001.1000		-光导纤维、光导纤维束及光缆									
9001.1000	01	非色散位移单模光纤(G.652,包括G652A、G652B、G652C、G652D等)〔999〕	5		20	13/	13	千克			/30
9001.1000	02	其他单模光纤〔999〕	5		20	13/	13	千克			/30
9001.1000	90	光导纤维束、光缆及其他光导纤维(但品目8544的货品除外)〔999〕	5		20	13/	13	千克			/30
9001.2000		-偏振材料制的片及板									
9001.2000	10	液晶投影仪用偏光板〔999〕	2.7/1.3		20	13/	13	千克			/27.7,26.3
9001.2000	20	数字电影放映机用偏光板〔999〕	2.7/1.3		20	13/	13	千克			/27.7,26.3
9001.2000	90	其他偏振材料制的片及板〔999〕	2.7/1.3		20	13/	13	千克			/27.7,26.3
9001.3000		-隐形眼镜片〔999〕	7	6	70	13/	13	片/千克			/26
		-玻璃制眼镜片:									
9001.4010		---变色镜片〔999〕	7		90	13/	13	片/千克			/
		---其他:									
9001.4091		----太阳镜片〔999〕	7		90	13/	13	片/千克			/
9001.4099		----其他〔999〕	7		70	13/	13	片/千克			/32
		-其他材料制眼镜片:									
9001.5010		---变色镜片〔999〕	7		90	13/	13	片/千克			/27
		---其他:									
9001.5091		----太阳镜片〔999〕	7		90	13/	13	片/千克			/32
9001.5099		----其他〔999〕	7		70	13/	13	片/千克			/32
		-其他:									
9001.9010		---彩色滤光片〔999〕	4/3		20	13/	13	千克			/24,23
9001.9090		---其他									
9001.9090	10	光通信用微光组件的光学元件(包括波长800-1700nm薄膜滤光片、自聚焦透镜、法拉第旋转片)〔999〕	4/3	1	20	13/	13	千克			/21
9001.9090	20	微型镜片(激光视盘机激光收发装置用)〔999〕	4/3	①	20	13/	13	千克			/23
9001.9090	30	非涅耳透镜投影屏(屏幕对角线≥80英寸,投射比≤0.26,增益比≥0.8,镜头间距≤100微米)〔999〕	4/3		20	13/	13	千克			/24,23
9001.9090	40	液晶显示屏背光模组的光学元件(包括导光板、反射板、扩散片、增亮片)〔101计算机、辅助设备及其零件,102视听设备及其零件〕	4/3	2	20	13/	13	千克			/22
9001.9090	50	液晶投影仪用偏光元件〔999〕	4/3		20	13/	13	千克			/24,23
9001.9090	60	数字电影放映机用偏光元件〔999〕	4/3		20	13/	13	千克			/24,23
9001.9090	90	税目90.01未列名的其他光学元件(未经光学加工的玻璃制元件除外)〔999〕	4/3		20	13/	13	千克			/24,23
90.02		**已装配的各种材料制透镜、棱镜、反射镜及其他光学元件,作为仪器或装置的零件、配件,但未经光学加工的玻璃制上述元件除外:**									
		-物镜:									
		--照相机、投影仪、照片放大机及缩片机用:									
9002.1110		---子目号9006.3000、9006.5921、9006.5929所列照相机用〔999〕	6		14	13/	13	千克/个			/
9002.1120		---缩微阅读机用〔999〕	6		14	13/	13	千克/个			/
		---其他照相机用:									
9002.1131		----单反相机镜头									
9002.1131	10	单反相机镜头(整机)〔999〕	6	3	80	13/	13	千克/个			/28
9002.1131	90	单反相机镜头的零件及附件〔999〕	6	3	80	13/	13	千克/个			/28
9002.1139		----其他〔999〕	6	3	80	13/	13	千克/个			/28
9002.1190		---其他									
9002.1190	10	彩色投影机和数字光处理器的镜头及镜头组件〔999〕	10	3	80	13/	13	千克/个			/28
9002.1190	90	其他照相机,投影仪等用物镜(包括照片放大机用物镜)〔999〕	10		80	13/	13	千克/个			/35
		--其他:									
9002.1910		---摄影机或放映机用〔999〕	7.5/5.6		40	13/	13	千克/个			/32.5,30.6

① 1—6月:3%。

协定税率 %										特惠税率 %			Article Description
亚太5国	东/冰/格	巴基斯坦	韩国	瑞士	哥达	秘鲁	澳大利亚	新西/坡/智	港/澳/台	亚太2国	老/柬/缅	36/3/1	
													Optical fibres and optical fibre bundles; optical fibre cables, other than those of heading No 85.44; sheets and plates of polarizing material; lenses (including contact lenses), prisms, mirrors and other optical elements, of any material, unmounted, other than such elements of glass not optically worked:
													-Optical fibres, optical fibre bundles and cables
4.5	0/0/0	0	4.5	0	0	0	0	0//0	0/0/			0/0/0	Dispersion-unshifted single-mode fibers (G. 652 including G652A、G652B、G652C、G652D)
4.5	0/0/0	0	4.5	0	0	0	0	0//0	0/0/			0/0/0	Other single-mode fibers
4.5	0/0/0	0	4.5	0	0	0	0	0//0	0/0/			0/0/0	Optical fiber bundles, cables and other optical fibres (excluding the items under Heading No.85.44)
													-Sheets and plates of polarizing material
2.6/1.2	0/0/	4	3.2	0	0	0	0	0//0	0/0/			0/0/0	Polarizer for LCD rojector
2.6/1.2	0/0/	4	3.2	0	0	0	0	0//0	0/0/			0/0/0	Polarizer for digit film projector
2.6/1.2	0/0/	4	3.2	0	0	0	0	0//0	0/0/			0/0/0	Other sheets and plates of polarizing material
	0/0/0	4	7	0	0	0	0	0/0/0	0/0/			0/0/0	-Contact lenses
													-Spectacle lenses of glass:
	0/0/0	20	12	6	0	0	0	0/0/0	0/0/			0/0/	---Photochromic
													---Other:
	0/0/0	20	12	6	0	0	0	0/0/0	0/0/			0/0/	----For sunglasses
	0/0/0	20	12	6	0	0	0	0/0/0	0/0/			0/0/	----Other
													-Spectacle lenses of other materials:
	0/0/0	20	12	6	0	0	0	0/0/0	0/0/			0/0/	---Photochromic
													---Other:
	0/0/0	20	12	6	0	0	0	0/0/0	0/0/			0/0/	----For sunglasses
	0/0/0	20	8	6	0	0	0	0/0/0	0/0/			0/0/	----Other
													-Other:
2.6/2	0/0/0	4	4.8	0	0	0	0	0//0	0/0/			0/0/0	---Color filter
													---Other
2.6/2	0/0/0	4	3.2	2.4	0	0	0	0//0	0/0/			0/0/0	Optical element optical components (including light wavelength of 800-1700nm thin film filter, self focusing lens, Faraday rotation piece)
2.6/2	0/0/0	4	3.2	2.4	0	0	0	0//0	0/0/			0/0/0	Micro lenses(VCD and laser transceiver device)
2.6/2	0/0/0	4	3.2	2.4	0	0	0	0//0	0/0/			0/0/0	The Fresnel lens projection screen (screen diagonal 80 inches or more, projection than 0.26 or less, gain more than 0.8 or higher, lens distance 100 microns or less)
2.6/2	0/0/0	4	3.2	2.4	0	0	0	0//0	0/0/			0/0/0	Optical element of LCD backlight module (including light guide plate, a reflecting plate, a diffusion piece, brightening sheet)
2.6/2	0/0/0	4	3.2	2.4	0	0	0	0//0	0/0/			0/0/0	LCD projector with polarized components
2.6/2	0/0/0	4	3.2	2.4	0	0	0	0//0	0/0/			0/0/0	Digital movie projector with polarized components
2.6/2	0/0/0	4	3.2	2.4	0	0	0	0//0	0/0/			0/0/0	Other optical elements, not specified or included elsewhere in the heading No. 9001 (other than of glass made elements not optically processed)
													Lenses, prisms, mirrors and other optical elements, of any material, mounted, being parts of or fittings for instruments or apparatus, other than such elements of glass not optically worked:
													-Objective lenses:
													--For cameras, projectors or photographic enlargers or reducers:
4.8	0/0/0	4	0	0	0	0	0	0//0	0/0/			0/0/0	---For the photographic cameras of subheadings No. 9006.3000、9006.5921、9006.5929
3.9	0/0/0	4	0	0	0	0	0	0//0	0/0/			0/0/0	---For microfilm, microfiche or other microform readers
													---For other cameras:
													----Lens for single lens reftex cameras
	0/0/0	10.8		4.5	0	0	0	0/0/0	0/0/			0/0/	SLR camera lens (machine)
	0/0/0	10.8		4.5	0	0	0	0/0/0	0/0/			0/0/	Parts and accessories of SLR camera lens
	0/0/0	10.8	6	4.5	0	0	0	0/0/0	0/0/			0/0/0	----Other
													---Other
	0/0/0	10.8	9	4.5	0	0	0	0/0/0	0/0/0			0/0/0	Lenses and lens components for colour crystal projector and digital light processor
	0/0/0	10.8	9	4.5	0	0	0	0/0/0	0/0/0			0/0/0	Other objective lenses for cameras, projectors (including lenses for photographic enlargers)
													--Other:
	0/0/0	10.8	6	4.5	0	0	0	0/0/0	0/0/			0/0/	---For cinematographic cameras or projectors

税则号列	货品名称〔CIQ 扩展编码及品名－T2 表示见附表 2〕	最惠(%)	暂定税率	普通	增值/消费	出口退税	计量单位	监管条件	检验检疫	特殊证件对美关税
9002.1990	---其他									
9002.1990 10	摄像机、摄录一体机的镜头〔999〕	7.5/5.6	3	50	13/	13	千克/个			/28
9002.1990 20	手机、平板电脑用物镜(800 万像素及以上)〔999〕	7.5/5.6		50	13/	13	千克/个			/32.5,30.6
9002.1990 90	税目 90.02 未列名的其他物镜〔999〕	7.5/5.6		50	13/	13	千克/个			/32.5,30.6
	-滤色镜：									
9002.2010	---照相机用〔999〕	7.5/5.6		80	13/	13	千克/个			/32.5,30.6
9002.2090	---其他〔999〕	7.5/5.6		40	13/	13	千克/个			/17.5,15.6
	-其他：									
9002.9010	---照相机用									
9002.9010 10	照相机用带屈光度调节装置的目镜(但物镜，滤色镜除外)〔999〕	7.5/5.6		80	13/	13	千克			/27.5,25.6
9002.9010 90	其他照相机用未列名光学元件(但物镜、滤色镜除外)〔999〕	7.5/5.6		80	13/	13	千克			/27.5,25.6
9002.9090	---其他									
9002.9090 10	抗辐射镜头[能抗 5×10^4 戈瑞(硅)以上辐射而又不会降低使用质量]〔999〕	7.5/5.6		40	13/	13	千克	3		/27.5,25.6
9002.9090 20	其他带屈光度调节装置的目镜〔999〕	7.5/5.6		40	13/	13	千克			/27.5,25.6
9002.9090 30	掩模版〔999〕	7.5/5.6		40	13/	13	千克			/27.5,25.6
9002.9090 90	其他光学仪器用未列名光学元件(但物镜，滤色镜除外)〔999〕	7.5/5.6		40	13/	13	千克			/27.5,25.6
90.03	**眼镜架及其零件：**									
	-眼镜架：									
9003.1100	--塑料制〔999〕	7		70	13/	13	千克/副			/32
	--其他材料制：									
9003.1910	---金属材料制〔999〕	7	6	70	13/	13	千克/副			/31
9003.1920	---天然材料制									
9003.1920 10	濒危动植物产品制眼镜架〔999〕	7		70	13/	0	千克/副	FE		/
9003.1920 90	其他天然材料制眼镜架〔999〕	7		70	13/	13	千克/副			/
9003.1990	---其他〔999〕	7		70	13/	13	千克/副			/
9003.9000	-零件〔999〕	6		70	13/	13	千克			/31
90.04	**矫正视力、保护眼睛或其他用途的眼镜、挡风镜及类似品：**									
9004.1000	-太阳镜〔999〕	7	6	100	13/	13	千克/副			/16
	-其他：									
9004.9010	---变色镜〔999〕	7		100	13/	13	千克/副			/27
9004.9090	---其他〔999〕	7		90	13/	13	千克/副			/32
90.05	**双筒望远镜、单筒望远镜、其他光学望远镜及其座架；其他天文仪器及其座架，但不包括射电天文仪器：**									
9005.1000	-双筒望远镜〔999〕	10		50	13/	13	个/千克			/35
	-其他仪器：									
9005.8010	---天文望远镜及其他天文仪器〔999〕	3		8	13/	13	台/千克			/13
9005.8090	---其他〔999〕	10		50	13/	13	台/千克			/30
	-零件、附件(包括座架)：									
9005.9010	---天文望远镜及其他天文仪器用〔999〕	2		8	13/	13	千克			/7
9005.9090	---其他〔999〕	6		30	13/	13	千克			/31
90.06	**照相机(电影摄影机除外)；照相闪光灯装置及闪光灯泡，但税目 85.39 的放电灯泡除外：**									
9006.3000	-水下、航空测量或体内器官检查用的特种照相机；法庭或犯罪学用的比较照相机〔999〕	9		17	13/	13	台/千克			/34
9006.4000	-一次成像照相机〔999〕	5		70	13/	13	台/千克			/30
	-其他照相机：									
9006.5100	--通过镜头取景(单镜头反光式(SLR))，使用胶片宽度不超过 35mm〔999〕	9		100	13/	13	架/千克			/
	--其他，使用胶片宽度小于 35mm									
9006.5210	---缩微照相机，使用缩微胶卷、胶片或其他缩微品的〔999〕	9		17	13/	13	架/千克			/14
9006.5290	---其他〔999〕	9		100	13/	13	架/千克			/14
9006.5300	--其他，使用胶片宽度为 35mm〔999〕	9		100	13/	13	架/千克			/34
	--其他：									
9006.5910	---激光照相排版设备〔999〕	9		35	13/	13	台/千克			/
	---制版照相机：									
9006.5921	----电子分色机〔999〕	9		20	13/	13	台/千克			/

协定税率 %										特惠税率 %			
亚太5国	东/冰/格	巴基斯坦	韩国	瑞士	哥达	秘鲁	澳大利亚	新西/坡/智	港/澳/台	亚太2国	老/柬/缅	36/3/1	Article Description
													---Other
	0/0/0	10.8	9	4.5	0	0	0	0/0/0	0/0/0			0/0/0	Lenses for vidicon and amcorder
	0/0/0	10.8	9	4.5	0	0	0	0/0/0	0/0/0			0/0/0	Mobile phone, tablet computer in an objective lens (8000000 pixels and above)
	0/0/0	10.8	9	4.5	0	0	0	0/0/0	0/0/0			0/0/0	Other objective lenses not specified or included
													-Filters:
4.9/3.6	0/0/0	10.8	9	4.5	0	0	0	0/0/0	0/0/			0/0/	---For cameras
4.9/3.6	0/0/0	10.8	9	4.5	0	0	0	0/0/0	0/0/			0/0/	---Other
													-Other:
													---For cameras
	0/0/0	10.8	9	4.5	0	0	0	0/0/0	0/0/0			0/0/	Eyepiece with diopter adjustment device for camera(excluding objective lenses and filters)
	0/0/0	10.8	9	4.5	0	0	0	0/0/0	0/0/0			0/0/	Other optical elements for cameras (other than objective, filters)
													---Other
	0/0/0	10.8	9	4.5	0	0	0	0/0/0	0/0/0			0/0/0	Radiation resistance lenses (capable of resisting radiance>5×10^4 Gy (Si) and not lowering operation quality)
	0/0/0	10.8	9	4.5	0	0	0	0/0/0	0/0/0			0/0/0	Other eyepiece with diopter adjustment device
	0/0/0	10.8	9	4.5	0	0	0	0/0/0	0/0/0			0/0/0	Photomask
	0/0/0	10.8	9	4.5	0	0	0	0/0/0	0/0/0			0/0/0	Other unlisted optial elements for optial instruments (other than objective lenses and filters)
													Frames and mountings for spectacles, goggles or the like, and parts thereof:
													-Frames and mountings:
	0/0/0	18	7.2	5.4	0	0	0	0/0/0	0/0/			0/0/	--Of plastics
													--Of other materials:
	0/0/0	4	4	0	0	0	0	0//0	0/0/			0/0/	---Of metal materials
													---Of natural materials
	0/0/0	4	4	0	0	0	0	0//0	0/0/			0/0/	Frames and mountings of product of endangered animals and plants
	0/0/0	4	4	0	0	0	0	0//0	0/0/			0/0/	Frames and mountings of other natural materials
	0/0/0	4	4	0	0	0	0	0//0	0/0/			0/0/	---Other
	0/0/0	4	4	0	0	0	0	0//0	0/0/			0/0/	-Parts
													Spectacles, goggles and the like, corrective, protective or other:
	0/0/0	20	12	6	0	0	0	0/0/0	0/0/			0/0/	-Sunglasses
													-Other:
	0/0/0	11.5	6.4	4.8	0	0	0	0/0/0	0/0/			0/0/	---Photochromic spectacles
	0/0/0		8	6	0	0	0	0/0/0	0/0/			0/0/	---Other
													Binoculars, monoculars, other optical telescopes, and mountings therefor; other astronomical instruments and mountings therefor, but not including instruments for radio-astronomy:
	0/0/0	10.8	6	4.5	0	0	0	0/0/0	0/0/			0/0/	-Binoculars
													-Other instruments:
	0/0/0	0	0	0	0	0	0	0//0	0/0/			0/0/0	---Astronomical telescopes and other astronomical instruments
	0/0/0	5.4	4.8	3.6	0	0	0	0/0/0	0/0/			0/0/0	---Other
													-Parts and accessories (including mountings):
1.6	0/0/0	0	0	0	0	0	0	0//0	0/0/			0/0/0	---For astronomical telescopes and other astronomica instruments
	0/0/0	4	0	0	0	0	0	0//0	0/0/			0/0/0	---Other
													Photographic (other than cinematographic) cameras; photographic flashlight apparatus and flashbulbs, other than discharge lamps of heading No. 85.39:
	0/0/0	4		0	0	0	0	0//0	0/0/			0/0/0	-Cameras specially designed for underwater use, for aerial survey or for medical or surgical examination of internal organs; comparison cameras for forensic or criminological purposes
	0/0/0	0	2	0	0	0	0	0//0	0/0/			0/0/0	-Instant print cameras
													-Other cameras:
	0/0/0		17.5	9	0		0	0/0/0	0/0/			0//	--With a through-the-lens viewfinder (single lens reflex (SLR)), for roll film of a width not exceeding 35 mm
													--Other, for roll film of a width less than 35 mm
	0/0/0	4	0	0	0	0	0	0//0	0/0/			0/0/0	---Cameras of a kind used for recording documents on microfilm, microfiche or other microforms
	0//0		17.5	9	0		0	0/0/0	0/0/			0//	---Other
	0/0/0		12	6	0	0	0	0/0/0	0/0/			0/0/	--Other, for roll film of a width of 35mm
													--Other:
	0/0/0	4	5.4	0	0	0	0	0/0/0	0/0/			0/0/0	---Laser photo typesetting equipment
													---Cameras of a kind used for preparing printing plates or cylinders:
	0/0/0	5.4	4.8	3.6	0	0	0	0/0/0	0/0/			0/0/0	----Electronic colour scanners

税则号列	货品名称〔CIQ扩展编码及品名—T2表示见附表2〕	最惠(%)	暂定税率	普通	增值/消费	出口退税	计量单位	监管条件	检验检疫	特殊证件对美关税
9006.5929	----其他〔999〕	9		20	13/	13	台/千克			/
9006.5990	---其他									
9006.5990 10	分幅相机(记录速率超过每秒225000帧)〔999〕	9		100	13/	13	架/千克	3		/
9006.5990 20	分幅相机(帧曝光时间为50纳秒或更短)〔999〕	9		100	13/	13	架/千克	3		/
9006.5990 90	使用胶片宽＞35mm的其他照相机〔999〕	9		100	13/	13	架/千克			/
	-照相闪光灯装置及闪光灯泡:									
9006.6100	--放电式(电子式)闪光灯装置									
9006.6100 01	照相手机用闪光灯组件〔999〕	9	4	80	13/	13	个/千克			/29
9006.6100 02	照相机外置式电子闪光灯(闪光指数GN≥30,具有无线闪光功能,支持自动变焦)〔999〕	9		80	13/	13	个/千克			/34
9006.6100 90	其他放电式(电子式)闪光灯装置〔999〕	9		80	13/	13	个/千克			/34
	--其他:									
9006.6910	---闪光灯泡〔101其它电光源及其零件,102其他电子式光学仪器零件〕	9		80	13/	13	个/千克			/34
9006.6990	---其他〔999〕	9		80	13/	13	个/千克			/29
	-零件、附件:									
	--照相机用:									
9006.9110	---税号9006.3000、9006.5921、9006.5929所列照相机用〔999〕	8		17	13/	13	千克			/18
9006.9120	---一次成像照相机用〔999〕	5		100	13/	13	千克			/30
	---其他:									
9006.9191	----自动调焦组件〔999〕	8	6	100	13/	13	千克/套			/31
9006.9192	----快门组件〔999〕	8	6	100	13/	13	千克/套			/31
9006.9199	----其他〔999〕	8	6	100	13/	13	千克			/26
9006.9900	--其他〔999〕	8		80	13/	13	千克			/33
90.07	**电影摄影机、放映机,不论是否带有声音的录制或重放装置:**									
	-摄影机:									
9007.1010	---高速摄影机〔999〕	12		40	13/	13	台/千克			/
9007.1090	---其他〔999〕	12		40	13/	13	台/千克			/
	-放映机:									
9007.2010	---数字式									
9007.2010 01	2K及以上分辨率的硬盘式数字电影放映机〔999〕	8		40	13/	13	台/千克			/
9007.2010 90	其他数字式放映机〔999〕	8		40	13/	13	台/千克			/
9007.2090	---其他〔999〕	8		40	13/	13	台/千克			/33
	-零件、附件:									
9007.9100	-摄影机用〔999〕	8	5	40	13/	13	千克			/15
9007.9200	-放映机用									
9007.9200 10	2K及以上分辨率的硬盘式数字电影放映机用零附件〔999〕	8	3	40	13/	13	千克			/13
9007.9200 90	电影放映机(不包括2K及以上分辨率的硬盘式)用零附件〔999〕	8	5	40	13/	13	千克			/15
90.08	**影像投影仪,但电影用除外;照片(电影片除外)放大机及缩片机:**									
	-投影仪、放大机及缩片机:									
9008.5010	---幻灯机〔999〕	10		40	13/	13	台/千克			/
9008.5020	---缩微胶卷、缩微胶片或其他缩微品的阅读机,不论是否可以进行复制〔101:Ⅰ类设备,102:Ⅱ类设备,103:其他类缩微阅读机设备〕	10		17	13/	13	台/千克			/15
	---其他影像投影仪:									
9008.5031	----正射投影仪〔101:Ⅰ类设备,102:Ⅱ类设备,103:其他类正射投影仪设备〕	12		40	13/	13	台/千克			/17
9008.5039	----其他〔101:有源式,Ⅰ类设备,102:有源式,Ⅱ类设备,103:有源式,其他类影像投影仪设备,104:机械式〕	12		40	13/	13	台/千克			/22
9008.5040	---照片(电影片除外)放大机及缩片机〔101:有源式,Ⅰ类设备,102:有源式,Ⅱ类设备,103:有源式,其他类照片(电影片除外)放大机及缩片机设备,104:机械式〕	12		80	13/	13	台/千克			/22
	-零件、附件:									
9008.9010	---缩微阅读机用〔999〕	8		17	13/	13	千克			/
9008.9020	---照片放大机及缩片机用〔999〕	8		80	13/	13	千克			/
9008.9090	--其他〔999〕	8		40	13/	13	千克			/28
90.10	**本章其他税目未列名的照相(包括电影)洗印用装置及设备;负片显示器;银幕及其他投影屏幕:**									

协定税率 %										特惠税率 %			Article Description
亚太5国	东/冰/格	巴基斯坦	韩国	瑞士	哥达	秘鲁	澳大利亚	新西/坡/智	港/澳/台	亚太2国	老/柬/缅	36/3/1	
	0/0/0	4	4	0	0	0	0	0//0	0/0/			0/0/0	----Other
													---Other
5.9	0/0/0		17.5		0		0	0/0/0	0/0/			0//	Frame cameras (rate of recording>225000 frame/sec)
5.9	0/0/0		17.5		0		0	0/0/0	0/0/			0//	Electromc (or electromc shutter) framing cameras (frane exposure time≤51 nanoseconds)
5.9	0/0/0		17.5		0		0	0/0/0	0/0/			0//	Other cameras, for roll film of a width>35mm
													-Photographic flashlight apparatus and flashbulbs:
													--Discharge lamp ("electronic") flashlight apparatus
	0/0/0		7.2	5.4	0	0	0	0/0/0	0/0/			0/0/	Flashlight component for camera mobile phone
	0/0/0		7.2	5.4	0	0	0	0/0/0	0/0/			0/0/	Camera external electronic flash (flash index GN ≥ 30, with wireless flash function, support auto zoom)
	0/0/0		7.2	5.4	0	0	0	0/0/0	0/0/			0/0/	Other discharge lamp("electronic") flashlight apparatus
													--Other:
	0/0/0	13	12.6	5.4	0	0	0	0/0/0	0/0/			0/0/	---Flasbbulbs
	0/0/0	13	7.2	5.4	0	0	0	0/0/0	0/0/			0/0/	---Other
													-Parts and accessories:
													--For cameras:
5.2	0/0/0	4	3.2	0	0	0	0	0//0	0/0/	0		0/0/0	---For cameras of subheadings No.9006.3000, 9006.5921 and 9006.5929
3.3	0/0/0	0	0	0	0	0	0	0//0	0/0/	0		0/0/0	---For instant print cameras
													---Other:
5.2	0/0/0	4	4	0	0	0	0	0/0/0	0/0/	0		0/0/0	----Automatic focal setting units
5.2	0/0/0	4	4	0	0	0	0	0/0/0	0/0/	0		0/0/0	----Shutter units
5.2	0/0/0	4	4	0	0	0	0	0/0/0	0/0/	0		0/0/0	----Other
	0/0/0	5.4	4.8	3.6	0	0	0	0/0/0	0/0/			0/0/0	--Other
													Cinematographic cameras and projectors, whether or not incorporating sound recording or reproducing apparatus:
													-Cameras:
	0/0/0	6.3	5.6	4.2	0	0	0	0/0/0	0/0/			0/0/	---High speed cameras
	0/0/0	10.1	5.6	4.2	0	0	0	0/0/0	0/0/			0/0/	---Other
													-Projectors:
													---Digital
	0/0/0	10.1	5.6	4.2	0	0	0	0/0/0	0/0/			0/0/	Digital film projector, resolution ≥2K, disk type
	0/0/0	10.1	5.6	4.2	0	0	0	0/0/0	0/0/			0/0/	Other digital projectors
5.2	0/0/0	10.1	5.6	4.2	0	0	0	0/0/0	0/0/			0/0/	---Other
													-Parts and accessories:
	0/0/0	4	3.3	0	0	0	0	0//0	0/0/			0/0/	--For cameras
													--For projectors
	0/0/0	4	0	0	0	0	0	0//0	0/0/			0/0/	Parts and accessories of hard disk digit film projector with a resolution ratio of 2k or above
	0/0/0	4	0	0	0	0	0	0//0	0/0/			0/0/	Parts and accessories of film projector, excluding of a hard disk digit with a resolution ratio of 2k or above
													Image projectors, other than cinematographic; photographic (other than cinematographic) enlargers and reducers:
													-Image projectors, enlargers and reducers:
	0/0/0	6.3	5.6	4.2	0	0	0	0/0/0	0/0/			0/0/	---Slide projectors
	0/0/0	4	4	0	0	0	0	0//0	0/0/			0/0/	---Microfilm, microfiche or other microform readers, whether or not capable of producing copies
													---Other image projectors:
	0/0/0			5.4	0	0	0	0/0/0	0/0/			0/0/	----Orthographical projectors
	0/0/0			5.4	0	0	0	0/0/0	0/0/			0/0/	----Other
	0/0/0		12	6	0	0	0	0/0/0	0/0/			0/0/	---Photographic(other than cinematographic) enlargers and reducers
													-Parts and accessories:
5.2	0/0/0	4	0	0	0	0	0	0//0	0/0/			0/0/	---Of microfilm, microfiche or other microform readers
5.2	0/0/0	6.3	5.6	4.2	0	0	0	0/0/0	0/0/			0/0/	---Of photographic enlargers and reducers
	0/0/0	10.1	5.6	4.2	0	0	0	0/0/0	0/0/			0/0/	---Other
													Apparatus and equipment for photographic (including cinematographic) laboratories, not specified or included elsewhere in this Chapter; negatoscopes; projection screens:

税则号列	货品名称〔CIQ 扩展编码及品名—T2 表示见附表 2〕	最惠(%)	暂定税率	普通	增值/消费	出口退税	计量单位	监管条件	检验检疫	特殊证件对美关税
	-照相(包括电影)胶卷或成卷感光纸的自动显影装置及设备或将已冲洗胶卷自动曝光到成卷感光纸上的装置及设备：									
9010.1010	---电影用〔999〕	12		40	13/	13	台/千克			/
9010.1020	---特种照相用〔999〕	8		20	13/	13	台/千克			/33
	---其他：									
9010.1091	----彩色胶卷用〔999〕	12		100	13/	13	台/千克			/
9010.1099	----其他〔999〕	12		100	13/	13	台/千克			/37
	-照相(包括电影)洗印用其他装置及设备；负片显示器：									
9010.5010	---负片显示器〔999〕	0		50	13/	13	台/千克			/5
	---其他：									
9010.5021	----电影用〔999〕	0		40	13/	13	台/千克			/
9010.5022	----特种照相用〔999〕	0		20	13/	13	台/千克			/25
9010.5029	----其他〔999〕	0		100	13/	13	台/千克			/25
9010.6000	-银幕及其他投影屏幕〔999〕	4.7/2.3		50	13/	13	个/千克			/9.7,7.3
	-零件、附件：									
9010.9010	---电影用〔999〕	0		40	13/	13	千克			/
9010.9020	---特种照相用〔999〕	0		20	13/	13	千克			/25
9010.9090	---其他〔999〕	0		100	13/	13	千克			/10
90.11	**复式光学显微镜，包括用于显微照相、显微电影摄影及显微投影的：**									
9011.1000	-立体显微镜〔999〕	0		14	13/	13	台/千克			/25
9011.2000	-显微照相、显微电影摄影及显微投影用的其他显微镜〔999〕	0		14	13/	13	台/千克			/20
9011.8000	-其他显微镜									
9011.8000 10	高倍测量显微镜，放大倍数≥1000 倍，分辨率≤0.08 微米〔999〕	2.3/1.2		14	13/	13	台/千克			/22.3，21.2
9011.8000 90	其他显微镜〔999〕	2.3/1.2		14	13/	13	台/千克			/22.3，21.2
9011.9000	-零件、附件〔999〕	0		14	13/	13	千克			/20
90.12	**显微镜，但光学显微镜除外；衍射设备：**									
9012.1000	-显微镜，但光学显微镜除外；衍射设备〔999〕	0		14	13/	13	台/千克			/20
9012.9000	-零件、附件〔999〕	0		14	13/	13	千克			/5
90.13	**其他税目未列名的液晶装置；激光器，但激光二极管除外；本章其他税目未列名的光学仪器及器具：**									
9013.1000	-武器用望远镜瞄准具；潜望镜式望远镜；作为本章或第十六类的机器、设备、仪器或器具部件的望远镜									
9013.1000 10	设计用为本章或第十六类的机器、设备、仪器或器具部件的望远镜〔999〕	0		14	13/	13	个/千克			/25
9013.1000 90	武器用望远镜瞄准具及潜望镜式望远镜〔999〕	8		14	13/	13	个/千克			/33
9013.2000	-激光器，但激光二极管除外									
9013.2000 10	激光切割机用气体激光发生器、切割功率≥2 千瓦〔999〕	2/1		11	13/	13	个/千克			/12，11
9013.2000 20	AVLIS、MLIS 和 CRISLA 激光系统〔999〕	2/1		11	13/	13	个/千克	3		/12，11
9013.2000 30	氩离子激光器(平均输出功率≥40瓦特、工作波长 400～515 纳米)〔999〕	2/1		11	13/	13	个/千克	3		/12，11
9013.2000 40	紫翠玉激光器(带宽≤0.005 纳米，重复率>125 赫兹，功率>30 瓦特等)〔999〕	2/1		11	13/	13	个/千克	3		/12，11
9013.2000 50	脉冲二氧化碳激光器(重复率>250 赫兹，功率>500 瓦，脉冲宽度<200 纳秒等)〔999〕	2/1		11	13/	13	个/千克	3		/12，11
9013.2000 60	脉冲受激准分子激光器(XeF、XeCl、KrF 型，重复率>250赫兹，功率>500 瓦等)〔999〕	2/1		11	13/	13	个/千克	3		/12，11
9013.2000 70	铜蒸汽激光器(平均输出功率≥40 瓦特、工作波长 500～600 纳米)〔999〕	2/1		11	13/	13	个/千克	3		/12，11
9013.2000 80	掺钕激光器(非玻璃激光器，两用物项管制商品)〔999〕	2/1		11	13/	13	个/千克	3		/12，11
9013.2000 91	用于 2.5GB/S 及以上 SDH、波分复用光传输设备的 980 纳米、1480 纳米的泵浦激光器〔999〕	2/1		11	13/	13	个/千克			/12，11

协定税率 %										特惠税率 %			Article Description
亚太5国	东/冰/格	巴基斯坦	韩国	瑞士	哥达	秘鲁	澳大利亚	新西/坡/智	港/澳/台	亚太2国	老/柬/缅	36/3/1	
													-Apparatus and equipment for automatically developing photographic (including cinematographic) film or paper in rolls or for automatically exposing developed film to rolls of photographic paper:
7.8	0/0/0	6.3	5.6	4.2	0	0	0	0/0/0	0/0/			0/0/	---Of a kind used in cinematographic film
5.2	0/0/0	4	0	0	0	0	0	0//0	0/0/			0/0/0	---Of a kind used in special photographic film or paper
													---Other:
	0/0/0		17.5	12	0	0	0	0/0/0	0/0/			0/0/	----For the colour photographic film in rolls
	0/0/0	10.8	10.5	4.5	0	0	0	0/0/0	0/0/			0/0/	----Other
													-Other apparatus and equipment for photographic (including cinematographic) laboratories; negatoscope:
	0//	6.3	5.6					//	0/0/			0/0/	---Negatoscopes
													---Other:
	0//	10.1	5.6					//	0/0/			0/0/	----Of a kind used in cinematographic film
	0//	4	3.3					//	0/0/			0/0/0	----Of a kind used in special photographic film or paper
	0//	12.2	6.8					//	0/0/			0/0/	----Other
	0/0/0	10.1	5.6	4.2/2.3	0	0	0	0/0/0	0/0/			0/0/	-Projection screens
													-Parts and accessories:
												0/0/0	---Of a kind used in cinematographic film
												0/0/0	---Of a kind used in special photographic film or paper
												0/0/0	---Other
													Compound optical microscopes, including those for photomicrography, cinephotomi-crography or microprojection:
												0/0/0	-Stereoscopic microscopes
												0/0/0	-Other microscopes, for photomicrography, cinephotomicrography or microprojection
													-Other microscopes
	0/0/0	4	2.8	2.1/1.2	0	0	0	0//0	0/0/			0/0/	High expansion measuring microscopes, magnification factor ≥ 1000, resolution ratio≤0.08μ
	0/0/0	4	2.8	2.1/1.2	0	0	0	0//0	0/0/			0/0/	Other microscopes
												0/0/0	-Parts and accessories
													Microscopes other than optical microscopes; diffraction apparatus:
												0/0/0	-Microscopes other than optical microscopes and diffraction apparatus
												0/0/0	-Parts and accessories
													Liquid crystal devices not constituting articles provided for more specifically in other headings; lasers, other than laser diodes; other optical appliances and instruments, not specified or included elsewhere in this Chapter:
													-Telescopic sights for fitting to arms; periscopes; telescopes designed to form parts of machines, appliances, instruments or apparatus of this Chapter or Section XVI
	0/0/0	4	0	0	0	0	0	0//0	0/0/			0/0/	Telescopes designed to form parts of machines, appliances, instruments or apparatus of this Chapter or Section XVI
	0/0/0	4	0	0	0	0	0	0//0	0/0/			0/0/	Parts and accessories of telescopic sights for fitting to arms, periscopes, telescopes
													-Lasers, other than laser diodes
	0/0/0	0	2.4	1.8/1	0	0	0	0//0	0/0/			0/0/	Gas laser generators for laser cutting machines, cutting power ≥ 2 kW
	0/0/0	0	2.4	1.8/1	0	0	0	0//0	0/0/			0/0/	AVLIS, MLIS, CRISLA laser systems
	0/0/0	0	2.4	1.8/1	0	0	0	0//0	0/0/			0/0/	Argon ion lasers (average output power≥40W, working wavelength =400nm～515nm)
	0/0/0	0	2.4	1.8/1	0	0	0	0//0	0/0/			0/0/	Alexandrite lasers (bandwidth≤0.005nm, repetition rate>125Hz, power>30W)
	0/0/0	0	2.4	1.8/1	0	0	0	0//0	0/0/			0/0/	Pulsed carbon dioxide lasers (repetition rate > 250Hz, power > 500W, pules width<200ns)
	0/0/0	0	2.4	1.8/1	0	0	0	0//0	0/0/			0/0/	Pulsed excimer lasers (XeF、XeCl or KrF type, recurrent rate > 250Hz, power>500W)
	0/0/0	0	2.4	1.8/1	0	0	0	0//0	0/0/			0/0/	Copper vapor lasers(average output power≥40W, working wavelength=500nm～600nm)
	0/0/0	0	2.4	1.8/1	0	0	0	0//0	0/0/			0/0/	Neodymium doped laser (not glass laser)(Dual-use items controlled commodity)
	0/0/0	0	2.4	1.8/1	0	0	0	0//0	0/0/			0/0/	980nm, 1480nm pump laser of SDH≥2.5GB/s, optical transmission equipment for wave-divison multicomplexing

税则号列		货品名称〔CIQ扩展编码及品名—T2表示见附表2〕	最惠(%)	暂定税率	普通	增值/消费	出口退税	计量单位	监管条件	检验检疫	特殊证件对美关税
9013.2000	92	用于2.5GB/S及以上光通信设备的850纳米、1260～1625纳米，且功率≤200毫瓦的激光器(泵浦激光机除外)〔999〕	2/1		11	13/	13	个/千克			/12,11
9013.2000	99	其他激光器，但激光二极管除外〔999〕	2/1		11	13/	13	个/千克			/12,11
		-其他装置、仪器及器具：									
9013.8010		---放大镜〔999〕	12		50	13/	13	个/千克			/37
9013.8020		---光学门眼〔999〕	12		50	13/	13	个/千克			/22
9013.8030		---液晶显示板									
9013.8030	10	10.1英寸及以下的液晶显示板〔999〕	5		50	13/	13	个/千克			/30
9013.8030	20	10.1英寸＜尺寸≤32英寸的液晶显示板〔999〕	5		50	13/	13	个/千克			/30
9013.8030	90	其他液晶显示板〔999〕	5		50	13/	13	个/千克			/30
9013.8090		---其他〔999〕	5		17	13/	13	个/千克			/30
		-零件、附件：									
9013.9010		---子目9013.1000及9013.2000所列货品用									
9013.9010	10	武器用望远镜瞄准器具或潜望镜式望远镜用零件及附件〔999〕	6		11	13/	13	千克			/16
9013.9010	90	激光器以及作为本章或第十六类的机器、设备、仪器或器具部件的望远镜用的零件及附件(武器用望远镜瞄准器具或潜望镜式望远镜用零件及附件除外)〔999〕	0		11	13/	13	千克			/10
9013.9020		---子目9013.8030所列货品用〔999〕	0		17	13/	13	千克			/25
9013.9090		---其他									
9013.9090	10	太阳能定日镜的零件〔999〕	0		17	13/	13	千克			/25
9013.9090	90	品目90.13所列其他货品的零附件〔999〕	0		17	13/	13	千克			/25
90.14		**定向罗盘；其他导航仪器及装置：**									
9014.1000		-定向罗盘〔999〕	0		8	13/	13	个/千克			/20
		-航空或航天导航仪器及装置(罗盘除外)：									
9014.2010		---自动驾驶仪									
9014.2010	10	无人航空飞行器的自动驾驶仪〔999〕	0		8	13/	13	个/千克	3		/
9014.2010	90	其他自动驾驶仪〔999〕	0		8	13/	13	个/千克			/
9014.2090		---其他									
9014.2090	11	航空惯性导航仪〔999〕	0		8	13/	13	个/千克	3		/
9014.2090	12	其他航天惯性导航仪(天文陀螺盘及其他利用天体或卫星进行导航的装置)〔999〕	0		8	13/	13	个/千克	3		/
9014.2090	13	陀螺稳定平台〔999〕	0		8	13/	13	个/千克	3		/
9014.2090	15	陀螺仪(额定漂移率小于0.5度/小时的陀螺仪)〔999〕	0		8	13/	13	个/千克	3		/
9014.2090	16	专门设计的导航信息处理机(用于弹道导弹、运载火箭、探空火箭等的目标探测)〔999〕	0		8	13/	13	个/千克	3		/
9014.2090	17	地形等高线绘制设备(用于弹道导弹、运载火箭、探空火箭、巡航导弹、无人驾驶航空飞行器的目标探测)〔999〕	0		8	13/	13	个/千克	3		/
9014.2090	18	场景绘图及相关设备(用于弹道导弹、运载火箭、探空火箭等的目标探测)〔999〕	0		8	13/	13	个/千克	3		/
9014.2090	90	其他航空或航天导航仪器及装置(但罗盘除外)〔999〕	0		8	13/	13	个/千克			/
9014.8000		-其他仪器及装置									
9014.8000	10	比例误差小于0.25%的加速度表〔101电子，102机械〕	0		8	13/	13	个/千克	3		/10
9014.8000	20	高度表(用于弹道导弹、运载火箭、探空火箭、巡航导弹、无人驾驶航空飞行器的目标探测)〔999〕	0		8	13/	13	个/千克	3		/10
9014.8000	90	其他导航仪器及装置〔999〕	0		8	13/	13	个/千克			/10
		-零件、附件：									
9014.9010		---自动驾驶仪用〔999〕	0		8	13/	13	千克			/5
9014.9090		---其他〔999〕	0		8	13/	13	千克			/5
90.15		**大地测量(包括摄影测量)、水道测量、海洋、水文、气象或地球物理用仪器及装置，不包括罗盘；测距仪：**									
9015.1000		-测距仪〔101电子，102机械〕	3/1.5		14	13/	13	台/千克			/13,11.5
9015.2000		-经纬仪及视距仪〔999〕	3/1.5		14	13/	13	台/千克			/13,11.5
9015.3000		-水平仪〔999〕	9		14	13/	13	台/千克			/34
9015.4000		-摄影测量用仪器及装置〔999〕	3/1.5		14	13/	13	千克			/28,26.5
9015.8000		-其他仪器及装置									
9015.8000	10	机载或舰载重力仪(精度为1毫伽或更好、稳态记录时间至多为2分钟的)〔999〕	1.7/0.8		14	13/	13	台/千克	3		/6.7,5.8

协定税率 %										特惠税率 %			Article Description
亚太5国	东/冰/格	巴基斯坦	韩国	瑞士	哥达	秘鲁	澳大利亚	新西/坡/智	港/澳/台	亚太2国	老/柬/缅	36/3/1	
	0/0/0	0	2.4	1.8/1	0	0	0	0//0	0/0/			0/0/	For the 850 nm, 1260～1625 nm and above 2.5GB/S optical communicationdevice, and the laser power less than 200 mW (excluding pumped laser machine)
	0/0/0	0	2.4	1.8/1	0	0	0	0//0	0/0/			0/0/	Other lasers, other than laser diodes
													-Other devices, appliances and instruments:
7.8	0/0/0	4.5	4.8	3.6	0	0	0	0/0/0	0/0/			0/0/	---Hand magnifying glasses
7.8	0/0/0	4.5	4.8	3.6	0	0	0	0/0/0	0/0/			0/0/	---Door eyes
													---Liquid crystal display panel
	0/0/	0	5				3	0//0	0/0/				size ≤ 10.1 inch liquid crystal display panel
	0/0/	0	5				3	0//0	0/0/				10.1 inch < size ≤ 32 inch liquid crystal display panel
	0/0/	0	5				3	0//0	0/0/				Other liquid crystal display panel(chapter 90 not else where specified or included)
	0/0/	0		0	0	0	0	0//0	0/0/			0/0/	---Other
													-Parts and accessories:
													---For goods of subhedding No. 9013.1000 and 9013.2000
	0/0/0	0	2.4	0	0	0	0	0//0	0/0/			0/0/	Parts and accessories of telescopic sights for fitting to arms, periscopes, telescopes designed to form parts of machines
	0/0/0	0	2.4	0	0	0	0	0//0	0/0/			0/0/	Parts and accessories of laser machines, equipment, instruments or apparatus components with the telescope, as well as this chapter or Section 16 (weapon with a telescope aimed at periscope telescope equipment or parts and accessories except)
	0//	4	4.8					//	0/0/			0/0/	---For goods of subhedding No. 9013.8030
													---Other
	0//	4	8					//	0/0/			0/0/	Solar heliostat parts
	0//	4	8					//	0/0/			0/0/	The 90.13 items listed parts and accessories of other goods
													Direction finding compasses; other navigational instruments and appliances:
	0//		1.2					//	0/0/			0/0/0	-Direction finding compasses
													-Instruments and appliances for aeronautical or space navigation (other than compasses):
													---Automatic pilot
	0//		1.2					//	0/0/			0/0/0	Automatic piolt for unmanned aircrafts
	0//		1.2					//	0/0/			0/0/0	Other navigatioral automatic pilot
													---Other
	0//							//	0/0/			0/0/0	Inertial navigation instruments for airplanes
	0//							//	0/0/			0/0/0	Other space inertial navigational instument(astronomical gyrocompass and astronomical or satellite navigational devices thereof)
	0//							//	0/0/			0/0/0	Gyro stabilized platforms
	0//							//	0/0/			0/0/0	Gyroscopes (rated drift rate<0.5 degree/h)
	0//							//	0/0/			0/0/0	Specially-designed navigation information processors (for target detection of ballistic missiles, carrier rockets or sounding rockets)
	0//							//	0/0/			0/0/0	Terrain contour mapping equipments for target detection of ballistic missiles, carrier rockets or sounding rockets
	0//							//	0/0/			0/0/0	Scene mapping equipments and relative equipments (for target detection of ballistic missiles, carrier rockets or sounding rockets)
	0//							//	0/0/			0/0/0	Other instruments and appliances for aeronautical or space navigation (other than compasses)
													-Other instruments and appliances
	0//							//	0/0/			0/0/0	Accelerometers, proportion error<0.25%
	0//							//	0/0/			0/0/0	Altimeters (for target detection of ballistic missiles, carrier rockets or sounding rockets)
	0//							//	0/0/			0/0/0	Other navigational instruments and appliances
													-Parts and accessories:
	0//							//	0/0/			0/0/0	---For automatic pilot
	0//							//	0/0/			0/0/	---Other
													Surveying (including photogrammetrical surveying), hydrographic, oceanographic, hydrological, meteorological or geophysical instruments and appliances, excluding compasses; rangefinders:
	0/0/0	4	3.6	3/1.5	0	0	0	0//0	0/0/			0/0/0	-Rangefinders
	0/0/0	4	0	0	0	0	0	0//0	0/0/			0/0/0	-Theodolites and tachymeters(tacheometers)
	0/0/0	4	3.6	0	0	0	0	0//0	0/0/			0/0/0	-Levels
	0/0/0	4	0	0	0	0	0	0//0	0/0/			0/0/0	-Photogrammetrical surveying instruments and appliances
													-Other instruments and appliances
1.1/0.5	0/0/0	0	2		0	0	0	0//0	0/0/			0/0/0	Air-borne or ship-borne gravimeters (accuracy 1 milligamma or more better, duration of static recording≤2 min)

税则号列	货品名称〔CIQ 扩展编码及品名－T2 表示见附表 2〕	最惠(%)	暂定税率	普通	增值/消费	出口退税	计量单位	监管条件	检验检疫	特殊证件对美关税
9015.8000 20	机载或舰载重力梯度仪(精度为 1 毫伽或更好、稳态记录时间至多为 2 分钟的)〔999〕	1.7/0.8		14	13/	13	台/千克	3		/6.7,5.8
9015.8000 90	其他测量仪器及装置〔101 电子,102 机械〕	1.7/0.8		14	13/	13	台/千克			/6.7,5.8
9015.9000	-零件、附件									
9015.9000 10	用于机、舰载重力仪和重力梯度仪的部件〔999〕	1.7/0.8		14	13/	13	千克	3		/11.7,10.8
9015.9000 90	其他税目 90.15 所列仪器及装置的零、附件〔101 电子,102 机械〕	1.7/0.8		14	13/	13	千克			/11.7,10.8
90.16	**感量为 50 毫克或更精密的天平,不论是否带有砝码:**									
9016.0010	---感量为 0.1 毫克或更精密的天平〔101 电子衡器,102 机械量具〕	9		14	13/	13	台/千克			/29
9016.0090	---其他〔101 电子衡器,102 机械量具〕	9		30	13/	13	台/千克			/34
90.17	**绘图、划线或数学计算仪器及器具(例如,绘图机、比例缩放仪、分度规、绘图工具、计算尺及盘式计算器);本章其他税目未列名的手用测量长度的器具(例如,量尺、量带、千分尺及卡尺):**									
9017.1000	-绘图台及绘图机,不论是否自动〔101 电子衡器,102 机械量具〕	8		20	13/	13	台/千克			/18
9017.2000	-其他绘图、划线或数学计算器具〔999〕	0		70	13/	13	个/千克			/20
9017.3000	-千分尺、卡尺及量规〔999〕	8		20	13/	13	个/千克			/18
9017.8000	-其他仪器及器具〔999〕	8		20	13/	13	个/千克			/28
9017.9000	-零件、附件〔999〕	0		20	13/	13	千克			/25
90.18	**医疗、外科、牙科或兽医用仪器及器具,包括闪烁扫描装置、其他电气医疗装置及视力检查仪器:**									
	-电气诊断装置(包括功能检查或生理参数检查用装置):									
9018.1100	--心电图记录仪〔999〕	0		17	13/	13	台/千克	6O		/5
	--超声波扫描装置:									
9018.1210	---B 型超声波诊断仪〔999〕	3.5/2.6		35	13/	13	台/千克	6OA	M	/8.5,7.6
	---其他:									
9018.1291	----彩色超声波诊断仪									
9018.1291 10	彩色超声波诊断仪(整机)〔999〕	2.5/1.9		17	13/	13	台/千克	6OA	M	/7.5,6.9
9018.1291 90	彩色超声波诊断仪的零件及附件〔999〕	2.5/1.9		17	13/	13	台/千克	6		/7.5,6.9
9018.1299	----其他〔999〕	2.5/1.9		17	13/	13	台/千克	6A	M	/7.5,6.9
	--核磁共振成像装置:									
9018.1310	---成套装置〔999〕	3.2/2.4		17	13/	13	套/千克	6OA	M	/28.2,27.4
9018.1390	---零件〔999〕	3.2/2.4		17	13/	13	个/千克	6		/8.2,7.4
9018.1400	--闪烁摄影装置〔999〕	5		17	13/	13	台/千克	6A	M	/10
	--其他:									
9018.1930	---病员监护仪									
9018.1930 10	病员监护仪(整机)〔999〕	1.3/0.7		17	13/	13	台/千克	6A	M	/26.3,25.7
9018.1930 90	病员监护仪的零件及附件〔999〕	1.3/0.7		17	13/	13	台/千克	6		/26.3,25.7
	---听力诊断装置:									
9018.1941	----听力计〔999〕	1.3/0.7		17	13/	13	台/千克	6A	M	/21.3,20.7
9018.1949	----其他〔999〕	1.3/0.7		17	13/	13	台/千克	6A	M	/11.3,10.7
9018.1990	---其他〔999〕	1.3/0.7		17	13/	13	台/千克	6A	M	/6.3,5.7
9018.2000	-紫外线及红外线装置〔101 诊断仪器及零部件,102 治疗仪器及零部件〕	0		17	13/	13	台/千克	6A	M	/10
	-注射器、针、导管、插管及类似品:									
9018.3100	--注射器,不论是否装有针头[T2]	8		50	13/	13	个/千克	6A	M	/13
	--管状金属针头及缝合用针:									
9018.3210	---管状金属针头[T2]	8		50	13/	13	千克	6A	M	/33
9018.3220	---缝合用针〔999〕	4		17	13/	13	千克	6A	M	/9
9018.3900	--其他〔999〕	4		17	13/	13	个/千克	6A	M	/9
	-牙科用其他仪器及器具:									
9018.4100	--牙钻机,不论是否与其他牙科设备组装在同一底座上〔999〕	4		17	13/	13	台/千克	6A	M	/29
	--其他:									
9018.4910	---装有牙科设备的牙科用椅〔999〕	4		17	13/	13	台/千克	6A	M	/9
9018.4990	---其他〔999〕	4		17	13/	13	台/千克	6A	M	/14
9018.5000	-眼科用其他仪器及器具〔101 诊断仪器及零部件,102 治疗仪器及零部件〕	1.3/0.7		17	13/	13	千克	6A	M	/26.3,25.7
	-其他仪器及器具:									
9018.9010	---听诊器〔999〕	4		17	13/	13	个/千克	6		/9
9018.9020	---血压测量仪器及器具									
9018.9020 10	电血压测量仪器及器具〔999〕	1.3/0.7		17	13/	13	个/千克	6A	M	/21.3,20.7

协定税率 %										特惠税率 %			Article Description
亚太5国	东/冰/格	巴基斯坦	韩国	瑞士	哥达	秘鲁	澳大利亚	新西/坡/智	港/澳/台	亚太2国	老/柬/缅	36/3/1	
1.1/0.5	0/0/0	0	2		0	0	0	0//0	0/0/			0/0/0	Air-borne or ship-borne gravity gradiometers (accuracy 1 milligamma or more better, duration of static recording≤2 min)
1.1/0.5	0/0/0	0	2		0	0	0	0//0	0/0/			0/0/0	Other instruments and appliances
													-Parts and accessories
	0/0/0	0	2	0	0	0	0	0//0	0/0/			0/0/0	Parts and components of other geodetic measuring instruments and devices
	0/0/0	0	2	0	0	0	0	0//0	0/0/			0/0/0	Other parts and accessoried of heading No.90.15
													Balances of a sensitivity of 50 mg or better, with or without weights:
	0/0/0	4	3.6		0	0	0	0//0	0/0/			0/0/0	---Of a sensitivity of 0.1 mg or better
	0/0/0	4.5	4.2	0	0	0	0	0/0/0	0/0/			0/0/0	---Other
													Drawing, marking-out or mathematical-calculating instruments (for example, drafting machines, pantographs, protractors, drawing sets, slide rules, disc calculators); instruments for measuring length, for use in the hand (for example, measuring rods and tapes, micrometers, callipers), not specified or included elsewhere in this Chapter:
	0/0/0	4	3.2	0	0	0	0	0//0	0/0/			0/0/0	-Drafting tables and machines, whether or not automatic
												0/0/0	-Other drawing, marking-out or mathematical calculating instruments
	0/0/0	4	3.2	2.4	0	0	0	0//0	0/0/			0/0/0	-Micrometers, callipers and gauges
	0/0/0	4	0	2.4	0	0	0	0//0	0/0/			0/0/0	-Other instruments
												0/0/0	-Parts and accessories
													Instruments and appliances used in medical, surgical, dental or veterinary sciences, including scintigraphic apparatus, other electro-medical apparatus and sight-testing instruments:
													-Electro-diagnostic apparatus (including apparatus for functional exploratory examination or for checking physiological parameters):
	0//							//	0/0/			0/0/0	--Electro-cardiographs
													--Ultrasonic scanning apparatus:
3/2.2	0/0/0	0	4.2	0	0	0	0	0//0	0/0/			0/0/0	---B-ultrasonic diagnostic equipment
													---Other:
													----Chromoscope ultrasonic diagnostice-quipment
2.3/1.7	0/0/0	0	4.5	0	0	0	0	0//0	0/0/			0/0/0	Color ultrasonic diagnostic apparatus (machine)
2.3/1.7	0/0/0	0	4.5	0	0	0	0	0//0	0/0/			0/0/0	Parts and accessories of color ultrasonic diagnostic instrument
2.3/1.7	0/0/0	0	4.5	0	0	0	0	0//0	0/0/			0/0/0	----Other
													--Magnetic resonance imaging apparatus:
	0/0/0	0	2.4	0	0	0	0	0//0	0/0/			0/0/0	---Complete sets
	0/0/0	0	2.4	0	0	0	0	0//0	0/0/			0/0/0	---Parts
	0/0/0	0	3	0	0	0	0	0//0	0/0/			0/0/0	--Scintigraphic apparatus
													--Other:
													---Patient moniturs
0.8/0.5	0/0/0	0	0	0	0	0	0	0//0	0/0/			0/0/0	The patient monitor (machine)
0.8/0.5	0/0/0	0	0	0	0	0	0	0//0	0/0/			0/0/0	Parts and accessories of patient monitor
													---Hearing diagnostic apparatas:
0.8/0.5	0/0/0	0	0	0	0	0	0	0//0	0/0/			0/0/0	----Audiometer
0.8/0.5	0/0/0	0		0	0	0	0	0//0	0/0/			0/0/0	----Other
0.8/0.5	0/0/0	0	0	0	0	0	0	0//0	0/0/			0/0/0	---Other
	0//							//	0/0/			0/0/0	-Ultra-violet or infra-red ray apparatus
													-Syringes, needles, catheters, cannulae and the like:
5.2	0/0/0	0	3.2	2.4	0	0	0	0//0	0/0/			0/0/0	--Syringes, with or without needles
													--Tubular metal needles and needles for sutures:
5.2	0/0/3.2	0	3.2	0	0	0	0	0//0	0/0/			0/0/0	---Tubular metal needles
2.6	0/0/0	0	0	0	0	0	0	0//0	0/0/			0/0/0	---Needles for sutures
	0/0/0	0	0	1.2	0	0	0	0//0	0/0/			0/0/0	--Other
													-Other instruments and appliances, used in dental sciences:
	0/0/0	0	0	0	0	0	0	0//0	0/0/			0/0/0	--Dental drill engines, whether or not combined on a single base with other dental equipment
													--Other:
	0/0/0	0	1.6	1.2	0	0	0	0//0	0/0/			0/0/0	---Dentists' chairs incorporating dental equipment
	0/0/0	0	0	1.2	0	0	0	0//0	0/0/			0/0/0	---Other
0.8/0.5	0/0/0	0	2.6	1.2/0.7	0	0	0	0//0	0/0/			0/0/0	-Other ophthalmic instruments and appliances
													-Other instruments and appliances:
2.6	0/0/0	0	0	0	0	0	0	0//0	0/0/			0/0/0	---Stethoscopes
													---Sphygmomanometers and appliances
2.6	0/0/0	0	0	0	0	0	0	0//0	0/0/			0/0/0	Electronic Sphygmomanometers and appliances

税则号列		货品名称〔CIQ 扩展编码及品名－T2 表示见附表 2〕	最惠(%)	暂定税率	普通	增值/消费	出口退税	计量单位	监管条件	检验检疫	特殊证件对美关税
9018.9020	90	其他血压测量仪器及器具〔999〕	4		17	13/	13	个/千克	6A	M	/24
9018.9030		---内窥镜									
9018.9030	10	内窥镜(整机)〔999〕	1.3/0.7		17	13/	13	台/千克	6A	M	/11.3,10.7
9018.9030	90	内窥镜的零件及附件〔999〕	1.3/0.7		17	13/	13	台/千克	6		/11.3,10.7
9018.9040		---肾脏透析设备(人工肾)〔999〕	1.3/0.7		17	13/	13	台/千克	6A	M	/6.3,5.7
9018.9050		---透热疗法设备〔999〕	1.3/0.7		17	13/	13	台/千克	6A	M	/6.3,5.7
9018.9060		---输血设备〔101 一次性使用输血器,102 血液透析、过滤设备,103 一次性使用血路产品,104 血泵,105 其他输血设备〕	1.3/0.7		17	13/	13	台/千克	6A	M	/6.3,5.7
9018.9070		---麻醉设备									
9018.9070	10	电麻醉设备〔999〕	1.3/0.7		17	13/	13	台/千克	6A	M	/6.3,5.7
9018.9070	90	其他麻醉设备〔999〕	4		17	13/	13	台/千克	6A	M	/9
9018.9099		---其他:									
9018.9091		----宫内节育器〔999〕	4		17	0/	0	个/千克	6A	M	/9
9018.9099		----其他									
9018.9099	11	电子的其他医疗、外科用仪器器具(整机)[T2]	1.3/0.7		17	13/	13	台/千克	6A	M	/26.3,25.7
9018.9099	19	其他医疗、外科或兽医用仪器器具(整机)[T2]	4		17	13/	13	台/千克	6A	M	/29
9018.9099	91	电子的其他医疗、外科用仪器器具的零件及附件[T2]	1.3/0.7		17	13/	13	台/千克	6A	M	/26.3,25.7
9018.9099	99	其他医疗、外科或兽医用仪器器具的零件及附件[T2]	4		17	13/	13	台/千克	6		/29
90.19		**机械疗法器具;按摩器具;心理功能测验装置;臭氧治疗器;氧气治疗器、喷雾治疗器、人工呼吸器及其他治疗用呼吸器具:**									
		-机械疗法器具;按摩器具;心理功能测验装置:									
9019.1010		---按摩器具[T2]	10		40	13/	13	台/千克	A	M	/35
9019.1090		---其他[T2]	4		30	13/	13	台/千克			/14
9019.2000		-臭氧治疗器、氧气治疗器、喷雾治疗器、人工呼吸器及其他治疗用呼吸器具〔999〕	4		17	13/	13	台/千克	A	M	/14
90.20		**其他呼吸器具及防毒面具,但不包括既无机械零件又无可互换过滤器的防护面具:**									
9020.0000		其他呼吸器具及防毒面具(但不包括既无机械零件又无可互换过滤器的防护面具)〔999〕	8	4	30	13/	13	千克		L	/9
90.21		**矫形器具,包括支具、外科手术带、疝气带;夹板及其他骨折用具;人造的人体部分;助听器及为弥补生理缺陷或残疾而穿戴、携带或植入人体内的其他器具:**									
9021.1000		-矫形或骨折用器具〔101 与人体接触的进入式医疗器具,102 与人体接触的非进入式医疗器具〕	4		17	13/	13	千克			/9
		-假牙及牙齿固定件:									
9021.2100		--假牙〔999〕	4		17	13/	13	千克			/9
9021.2900		--其他〔999〕	4	2	17	13/	13	千克			/
		-其他人造的人体部分:									
9021.3100		--人造关节〔999〕	4		17	13/	13	千克/套			/
9021.3900		--其他〔999〕	4		17	13/	13	千克			/9
9021.4000		-助听器,不包括零件、附件〔999〕	4		17	13/	13	个/千克			/
9021.5000		-心脏起搏器,不包括零件、附件〔999〕	1.3/0.7		17	13/	13	个/千克	A	M	/
		-其他:									
		---支架:									
9021.9011		----血管支架〔999〕	1.3/0.7		17	13/	13	千克/个			/
9021.9019		----其他〔999〕	1.3/0.7		17	13/	13	千克/个			/
9021.9090		---其他									
9021.9090	10	人工耳蜗植入装置〔999〕	1.3/0.7	0	17	13/	13	千克			/
9021.9090	90	其他弥补生理缺陷、残疾用器具等(包括穿戴、携带或植入人体内的器具及零件)〔101 与人体接触的进入式医疗器具,102 与人体接触的非进入式医疗器具,103 其他医疗器具〕	1.3/0.7		17	13/	13	千克			/
90.22		**X 射线或 α 射线、β 射线、γ 射线的应用设备,不论是否用于医疗、外科、牙科或兽医,包括射线照相及射线治疗设备,X 射线管及其他 X 射线发生器、高压发生器、控制板及控制台、荧光屏、检查或治疗用的桌、椅及类似品:**									

协定税率 %										特惠税率 %			
亚太5国	东/冰/格	巴基斯坦	韩国	瑞士	哥达	秘鲁	澳大利亚	新西/坡/智	港/澳/台	亚太2国	老/柬/缅	36/3/1	Article Description
2.6	0/0/0	0	0	0	0	0	0	0//0	0/0/			0/0/0	Other Sphygmomanometers and appliances
													---Endoscopes
0.8/0.5	0/0/0	0	0	0	0	0	0	0//0	0/0/			0/0/0	Endoscope (machine)
0.8/0.5	0/0/0	0	0	0	0	0	0	0//0	0/0/			0/0/0	Parts and accessories of endoscope mirror
0.8/0.5	0/0/0	0	0	0	0	0	0	0//0	0/0/			0/0/0	---Artificial kidney (dialysis) apparatus
0.8/0.5	0/0/0	0	0	0	0	0	0	0//0	0/0/			0/0/0	---Diathermy apparatus
0.8/0.5	0/0/0	0	0	1.2/0.7	0	0	0	0//0	0/0/			0/0/0	---Blood transfusion apparatus
													---Anaesthetic apparatus and instruments
2.6	0/0/0	0	0	0	0	0	0	0//0	0/0/			0/0/0	Electronic anaesthetic apparatus and instruments
2.6	0/0/0	0	0	0	0	0	0	0//0	0/0/			0/0/0	Other anaesthetic apparatus and instruments
													---Other:
2	0/0/0	0	0	0	0	0	0	0//0	0/0/			0/0/0	----Intrauterine device
													----Other
2.6	0/0/0	0	0	1.2	0	0	0	0//0	0/0/			0/0/0	Other medical and surgical instruments for electronic surgery (whole machine)
2.6	0/0/0	0	0	1.2	0	0	0	0//0	0/0/			0/0/0	Other instruments for medical, surgical, or veterinary medicine (whole machine)
2.6	0/0/0	0	0	1.2	0	0	0	0//0	0/0/			0/0/0	Parts and accessories of the other medical and surgical instruments of the electronics
2.6	0/0/0	0	0	1.2	0	0	0	0//0	0/0/			0/0/0	Other parts and accessories for medical, surgical or veterinary instruments
													Mechano-therapy appliances; massage apparatus; psychological aptitude-testing apparatus; ozone therapy, oxygen therapy, aerosol therapy, artificial respiration or other therapeutic respiration apparatus:
													-Mechano-therapy appliances; massage apparatus; psychological aptitude-testing apparatus:
	0/0/0	10.8	6	4.5	0	0	0	0/0/0	0/0/			0/0/	---Massage apparatus
	0/0/0	0	0	1.2	0	0	0	0//0	0/0/			0/0/0	---Other
	0/0/0	0	2.4	1.2	0	0	0	0//0	0/0/			0/0/0	-Ozone therapy, oxygen therapy, aerosol therapy, artificial respiration or other therapeutic respiration apparatus
													Other breathing appliances and gas masks, excluding protective masks having neither mechanical parts nor replaceable filters:
	0/0/0	4	3.2	0	0	0	0	0//0	0/0/			0/0/0	Other breathing appliances and gas masks, excluding protective masks having neither mechanical parts nor replaceable filters
													Orthopaedic appliances, including crutches, surgical belts and trusses; splints and other fracture appliances; artificial parts of the body; hearing aids and other appliances which are worn or carried, or implanted in the body, to compensate for a defect or disability:
	0/0/0	0	2.4	2.1	0	0	0	0//0	0/0/			0/0/0	-Orthopaedic or fracture appliances
													-Artificial teeth and dental fittings:
	0/0/0	0	0	0	0	0	0	0//0	0/0/			0/0/0	--Artificial teeth
	0/0/0	0	0	1.2	0	0	0	0//0	0/0/			0/0/0	--Other
													-Other artificial parts of the body:
	0/0/0	0	0	1.2	0	0	0	0//0	0/0/0			0/0/0	--Artificial joints
	0/0/0	0	1.6	0	0	0	0	0//0	0/0/			0/0/0	--Other
	0/0/0	0	0	1.2	0	0	0	0//0	0/0/			0/0/0	-Hearing aids, excluding parts and accessories
0.8/0.5	0/0/0	0	0	1.2/0.7	0	0	0	0//0	0/0/			0/0/0	-Pacemakers for stimulating heart muscles, excluding parts and accessories
													-Other:
													---Brace:
	0/0/0	0	0	1.2/0.7	0	0	0	0//0	0/0/			0/0/0	----Intravascular stents
	0/0/0	0	1.6	1.2/0.7	0	0	0	0//0	0/0/			0/0/0	----Other bracket
													---Other
	0/0/0	0	0	1.2/0.7	0	0	0	0//0	0/0/			0/0/0	Cochlear implant devices
	0/0/0	0	0	1.2/0.7	0	0	0	0//0	0/0/			0/0/0	Other appliances to compensate for a defect or disability (including appliances and parts which are worn or carried, or implanted in the body)
													Apparatus based on the use of X-rays or of alpha, beta or gamma radiations, whether or not for medical, surgical, dental or veterinary uses, including radiography or radiotherapy apparatus, X-ray tubes and other X-ray generators, high tension generators, control panels and desks, screens, examination or treatment tables, chairs and the like:

税则号列	货品名称〔CIQ 扩展编码及品名—T2 表示见附表 2〕	最惠(%)	暂定税率	普通	增值/消费	出口退税	计量单位	监管条件	检验检疫	特殊证件对美关税
	-X 射线的应用设备,不论是否用于医疗、外科、牙科或兽医,包括射线照相或射线治疗设备:									
9022.1200	--X 射线断层检查仪〔T2〕	2.7/2		11	13/	13	台/千克	6OA	M	/7.7,7
9022.1300	--其他,牙科用〔999〕	0		11	13/	13	台/千克	6OA	M	/20
9022.1400	--其他,医疗、外科或兽医用									
9022.1400 10	医用直线加速器〔999〕	1.3/0.7		11	13/	13	台/千克	6OA	M	/
9022.1400 90	其他医疗或兽医用 X 射线应用设备〔999〕	1.3/0.7		11	13/	13	台/千克	6OA	M	/26.3,25.7
	--其他:									
9022.1910	---低剂量 X 射线安全检查设备									
9022.1910 10	采用 X 光机技术或 X 射线加速器技术的 X 射线安全检查设备(能量大于 100 千电子伏,不包括采用 X 射线交替双能加速器技术的第二代 X 射线安全检查设备)〔999〕	1.3/0.7		11	13/	13	台/千克	A	M	/6.3,5.7
9022.1910 90	其他低剂量 X 射线安全检查设备〔999〕	1.3/0.7		11	13/	13	台/千克	A	M	/6.3,5.7
9022.1920	---X 射线无损探伤检测仪〔999〕	1.3/0.7		11	13/	13	台/千克	A	M	/21.3,20.7
9022.1990	---其他									
9022.1990 10	X 射线全自动燃料芯块检查台(专门设计或制造用于检验燃料芯块的最终尺寸和表面缺陷)〔999〕	1.3/0.7		11	13/	13	台/千克	3A	M	/11.3,10.7
9022.1990 20	X 射线晶圆制造厚度测量设备	1.3/0.7		11	13/	13	台/千克	A	M	/11.3,10.7
9022.1990 90	其他 X 射线应用设备〔999〕	1.3/0.7		11	13/	13	台/千克	6A	M	/11.3,10.7
	-α 射线、β 射线、γ 射线的应用设备,不论是否用于医疗、外科、牙科或兽医,包括射线照相或射线治疗设备:									
9022.2100	--医疗、外科、牙科或兽医用〔101 诊断仪器及零部件,102 治疗仪器及零部件〕	0		11	13/	13	台/千克	6A	M	/10
	--其他:									
9022.2910	---γ 射线无损探伤检测仪〔999〕	2/1		11	13/	13	台/千克	A	M	/
9022.2990	---其他									
9022.2990 10	γ 射线全自动燃料芯块检查台(专门设计或制造用于检验燃料芯块的最终尺寸和表面缺陷)〔999〕	2/1		11	13/	13	台/千克	3A	M	/7,6
9022.2990 90	其他非医疗用 α、β、γ 射线设备〔999〕	2/1		11	13/	13	台/千克	A	M	/7,6
9022.3000	-X 射线管〔999〕	0.7/0.3		11	13/	13	个/千克	A	M	3/5.7,5.3
	-其他,包括零件、附件:									
9022.9010	---X 射线影像增强器〔999〕	0		11	13/	13	个/千克	AO	M	/
9022.9090	---其他									
9022.9090 01	射线发生器的零部件〔999〕	5	1	11	13/	13	个/千克			/26
9022.9090 20	闪光 X 射线发生器(峰值能量≥500 千电子伏)〔999〕	5		11	13/	13	个/千克	3O		/30
9022.9090 30	X 射线断层检查仪专用探测器〔999〕	5		11	13/	13	个/千克	O		/30
9022.9090 40	数字化 X 射线摄影系统平板探测器〔999〕	5	3	11	13/	13	个/千克			/28
9022.9090 90	税目 90.22 所列其他设备及零件(包括高压发生器、控制板及控制台、荧光屏等)〔999〕	5		11	13/	13	个/千克			/30
90.23	**专供示范(例如,教学或展览)而无其他用途的仪器、装置及模型:**									
9023.0010	---教习头〔999〕	0		20	13/	13	千克			/25
9023.0090	---其他〔999〕	0		20	13/	13	千克			/5
90.24	**各种材料(例如,金属、木材、纺织材料、纸张、塑料)的硬度、强度、压缩性、弹性或其他机械性能的试验机器及器具:**									
	-金属材料的试验用机器及器具:									
9024.1010	---电子万能试验机〔999〕	2.3/1.2		20	13/	13	台/千克			/12.3,11.2
9024.1020	---硬度计〔999〕	2.3/1.2		20	13/	13	台/千克			/12.3,11.2
9024.1090	---其他〔999〕	2.3/1.2		20	13/	13	台/千克			/7.3,6.2
9024.8000	-其他机器及器具〔999〕	2.5/1.9		20	13/	13	台/千克			/7.5,6.9
9024.9000	-零件、附件〔999〕	2/1		20	13/	13	千克			/7,6
90.25	**记录式或非记录式的液体比重计及类似的浮子式仪器、温度计、高温计、气压计、湿度计、干湿球湿度计及其组合装置:**									
	-温度计及高温计,未与其他仪器组合:									
9025.1100	--液体温度计,可直接读数〔999〕	4		40	13/	13	个/千克			/24

协定税率 %										特惠税率 %			
亚太5国	东/冰/格	巴基斯坦	韩国	瑞士	哥达	秘鲁	澳大利亚	新西/坡/智	港/澳/台	亚太2国	老/柬/缅	36/3/1	Article Description
													-Apparatus based on the use of X-rays, whether or not for medical, surgical, dental or veterinary uses, including radiography or radiotherapy apparatus:
1.9/1.4	0/0/0	0	2.4	0	0	0	0	0//0	0/0/			0/0/0	--Computed tomography apparatus
	0//							//	0/0/			0/0/0	--Other, for dental uses
													--Other, for medical, surgical or veterinary uses
	0/0/0	0	0	0	0	0	0	0//0	0/0/			0/0/0	Linear accelerators for medical use
	0/0/0	0	0	0	0	0	0	0//0	0/0/			0/0/0	Other apparatus based on the use of X-rays, for medical or veterinary uses
													-For other uses:
													--Low dosage X-ray security inspecting equipment
	0/0/0	0	2.4	0	0	0	0	0//0	0/0/			0/0/0	x-ray security inspection equipments adopting the technology of x-ray apparatuses or x-ray accelerat- ors (with energy higher than 100 kilo electron volt, excluding the second generation security inspection equipments adopting the technology of alternating dual-energy x-ray accelerators)
	0/0/0	0	2.4	0	0	0	0	0//0	0/0/			0/0/0	Other low dosage X-ray security inspecting equipment
	0/0/0	0		1.2/0.7	0	0	0	0//0	0/0/			0/0/0	---X-ray non-destructive testing appliances
													---Other
	0/0/0	0		1.2/0.7	0	0	0	0//0	0/0/			0/0/0	X-ray fully-automatic fuel core exouiwins table(Specially designed or made to inspect final dimensions and superficial defects of fuel core)
	0/0/0	0		1.2/0.7	0	0	0	0//0	0/0/		//	0/0/0	X—ray wafer thickness measuring equipment
	0/0/0	0		1.2/0.7	0	0	0	0//0	0/0/			0/0/0	Other apparatus based on the use of X-rays
													-Apparatus based on the use of alpha, beta or gamma radiations, whether or not for medical, surgical, dental or veterinary uses, including radiography or radiothe rapy apparatus:
	0//							//	0/0/			0/0/0	--For medical, surgical, dental or veterinary uses
													--Other:
	0/0/0	4	0	0	0	0	0	0//0	0/0/			0/0/0	---γ-Ray non-destructivetesting appliances
													---Other
	0/0/0	4	0	0	0	0	0	0//0	0/0/			0/0/0	γ-Ray fully-autornatic fuel core examiwins table(specially designed or made to inspect final dimensions and superficial defects of fuel core)
	0/0/0	4	0	0	0	0	0	0//0	0/0/			0/0/0	Other α-rays、β-rays、γ-rays, not for medical uses
	0/0/0	0	0.8	0	0	0	0	0//0	0/0/			0/0/0	-X-ray tubes
													-Other, including parts and accessories:
	0//		3.6					//	0/0/			0/0/0	---X-ray intensifiers
													---Other
	0/0/0	0	3.6	1.8	0	0	0	0//0	0/0/			0/0/0	Parts and components of radiation generators
	0/0/0	0	3.6	1.8	0	0	0	0//0	0/0/			0/0/0	Flash X-ray generators (peak value power≥500keV)
	0/0/0	0	3.6	1.8	0	0	0	0//0	0/0/			0/0/0	Detectors specified for X-ray tomography instruments
	0/0/0	0	3.6	1.8	0	0	0	0//0	0/0/			0/0/0	Digital X ray photogrammetry system plate detector
	0/0/0	0	3.6	1.8	0	0	0	0//0	0/0/			0/0/0	Other apparatus and its parts of heading 90.22, (including high voltage generators, control panels and console, screens)
													Instruments, apparatus and models, designed for demonstrational purposes (for example, in education or exhibitions), unsuitable for other uses:
	0//	4						//	0/0/			0/0/0	---Training head
	0//	4						//	0/0/			0/0/0	---Other
													Machines and appliances for testing the hardness, strength, compressibility, elasticity or other mechanical properties of materials (for example, metals, wood, textiles, paper, plastics):
													-Machines and appliances for testing metals:
1.5/0.8	0/0/0	4	2.8	0	0	0	0	0//0	0/0/			0/0/0	---Electric multitesting machines
1.5/0.8	0/0/0	4	2.8	2.1/1.2	0	0	0	0//0	0/0/			0/0/0	---Machiness and applinances for testing hardness
1.5/0.8	0/0/0	4	4.5	0	0	0	0	0//0	0/0/			0/0/0	---Other
	0/0/0	0	3	0	0	0	0	0//0	0/0/			0/0/0	-Other machines and appliances
	0/0/0	0		1.8/1	0	0	0	0//0	0/0/			0/0/0	-Parts and accessories
													Hydrometers and similar floating instruments, thermometers and pyrometers, barometers, hygrometers and psychrometers, recording or not, and any combination of these instruments:
													-Thermometers and pyrometers, not combined with other instruments:
	0/0/0	0	0	0	0	0	0	0//0	0/0/			0/0/0	--Liquid-filled, for direct reading

税则号列	货品名称〔CIQ 扩展编码及品名－T2 表示见附表 2〕	最惠(%)	暂定税率	普通	增值/消费	出口退税	计量单位	监管条件	检验检疫	特殊证件对美关税
	--其他：									
9025.1910	---工业用〔101 电子温度计，102 温度计〕	2.8/1.4		20	13/	13	个/千克			/12.8,11.4
9025.1990	---其他									
9025.1990 10	红外线人体测温仪〔999〕	2.8/1.4		80	13/	13	个/千克			/12.8,11.4
9025.1990 90	非液体的其他温度计，高温计〔101 电子温度计，102 温度计〕	2.8/1.4		80	13/	13	个/千克			/12.8,11.4
9025.8000	-其他仪器〔101 温度计，102 比重计，103 湿度计，104 其他机械式仪表及其零件〕	11		30	13/	13	个/千克			/31
9025.9000	-零件、附件									
9025.9000 10	红外线测温仪传感器元件〔999〕	2.7/1.3		20	13/	13	千克/个			/12.7,11.3
9025.9000 90	其他比重计、温度计等类似仪器的零件〔101 温度计零件，102 比重计零件，103 其他机械式仪表及其零件〕	2.7/1.3		20	13/	13	千克/个			/12.7,11.3
90.26	**液体或气体的流量、液位、压力或其他变化量的测量或检验仪器及装置（例如，流量计、液位计、压力表、热量计），但不包括税目 90.14、90.15、90.28 或 90.32 的仪器及装置：**									
9026.1000	-测量、检验液体流量或液位的仪器及装置〔101 电子测量仪，102 机械测量仪〕	0		17	13/	13	个/千克			/10
	-测量、检验压力的仪器及装置：									
9026.2010	---压力/差压变送器									
9026.2010 10	锰铜压力计（压力超过 10GPa）〔999〕	0		17	13/	13	个/千克	3		/10
9026.2010 20	镱制成的压力计，流体动力学实验专用仪器仪表，测量压力超过 10GPa 的〔101 电子分析仪，102 机械分析仪〕	0		17	13/	13	个/千克	3		/10
9026.2010 30	聚偏二氟乙烯/聚二氟乙烯制成的压力计（流体动力学实验专用仪器仪表，测量压力超过 10GPa 的）〔101 电子分析仪，102 机械分析仪〕	0		17	13/	13	个/千克	3		/10
9026.2010 90	其他压力，差压变送器〔101 电子分析仪，102 机械分析仪〕	0		17	13/	13	个/千克			/10
9026.2090	---其他									
9026.2090 10	压力传感器（两用物项管制商品）〔101 电子分析仪，102 机械分析仪〕	0		17	13/	13	个/千克	3		/10
9026.2090 90	其他测量、检验压力的仪器及装置〔101 电子分析仪，102 机械分析仪〕	0		17	13/	13	个/千克			/10
	-其他仪器及装置：									
9026.8010	---测量气体流量的仪器及装置〔101 电子分析仪，102 机械分析仪〕	0		17	13/	13	个/千克			/10
9026.8090	---其他〔101 电子分析仪，102 机械分析仪〕	0		17	13/	13	个/千克			/10
9026.9000	-零件、附件〔101 电子分析仪，102 机械分析仪〕	0		17	13/	13	千克			/10
90.27	**理化分析仪器及装置（例如，偏振仪、折光仪、分光仪、气体或烟雾分析仪）；测量或检验黏性、多孔性、膨胀性、表面张力及类似性能的仪器及装置；测量或检验热量、声量或光量的仪器及装置（包括曝光表）；检镜切片机：**									
9027.1000	-气体或烟雾分析仪									
9027.1000 10	用于连续操作的气体检测器[可用于出口管制的化学品或有机化合物（含有磷、硫、氟或氯，其浓度低于 0.3mg/m^3）的检测，或为检测受抑制的胆碱酯酶的活性而设计]〔101 电子分析仪，102 机械分析仪〕	3.5/2.6		17	13/	13	台/千克	3		/8.5,7.6
9027.1000 90	其他气体或烟雾分析仪〔101 电子分析仪，102 机械分析仪〕	3.5/2.6		17	13/	13	台/千克			/8.5,7.6
	-色谱仪及电泳仪：									
	---色谱仪：									
9027.2011	----气相色谱仪〔999〕	0		17	13/	13	台/千克			/5
9027.2012	----液相色谱仪〔999〕	0		17	13/	13	台/千克			/5
9027.2019	----其他〔999〕	0		17	13/	13	台/千克			/5
9027.2020	---电泳仪〔999〕	0		17	13/	13	台/千克			/5
9027.3000	-使用光学射线（紫外线、可见光、红外线）的分光仪、分光光度计及摄谱仪〔101 电子分析仪，102 机械分析仪〕	0		17	13/	13	台/千克			/10
9027.5000	-使用光学射线（紫外线、可见光、红外线）的其他仪器及装置〔101 电子分析仪，102 机械分析仪〕	0		17	13/	13	台/千克	6		/5
	-其他仪器及装置：									
	---质谱仪：									
9027.8011	----集成电路生产用氦质谱检漏台〔999〕	0		17	13/	13	台/千克			/
9027.8012	----质谱联用仪〔999〕	0		17	13/	13	台/千克			/5
9027.8019	----其他									
9027.8019 10	两用物项管制的 UF6 质谱仪/离子源〔999〕	0		17	13/	13	台/千克	3		/5
9027.8019 20	测大于 230 质量单位离子质谱仪（分辨率高于 2/230）〔999〕	0		17	13/	13	台/千克	3		/5

协定税率 %										特惠税率 %			Article Description
亚太5国	东/冰/格	巴基斯坦	韩国	瑞士	哥达	秘鲁	澳大利亚	新西/坡/智	港/澳/台	亚太2国	老/柬/缅	36/3/1	
													--Other:
1.8/0.9	0/0/0	4	0	0	0	0	0	0//0	0/0/			0/0/0	---For technical use
													---Other
1.8/0.9	0/0/0	4	0	0	0	0	0	0//0	0/0/			0/0/0	Infrared body thermometer
1.8/0.9	0/0/0	4	0	0	0	0	0	0//0	0/0/			0/0/0	Other thermometers and pyrometers, non-liquid
	0/0/0	4.5	7.7	3.3	0	0	0	0/0/0	0/0/			0/0/	-Other instruments
													-Parts and accessories
1.8/0.8	0/0/0	4	0	2.4/1.3	0	0	0	0//0	0/0/			0/0/0	Sensor capacitor element of infrared thermo-meter
1.8/0.8	0/0/0	4	0	2.4/1.3	0	0	0	0//0	0/0/			0/0/0	Parts of other hydrometers, thermometers and similar instruments
													Instruments and apparatus for measuring or checking the flow, level, pressure or other variables of liquids or gases (for example, flow meters, level gauges, manometers, heat meters), excluding instruments and apparatus of heading No. 90. 14, 90. 15, 90. 28 or 90. 32:
												0/0/0	-For measuring or checking the flow or level of liquids
													-For measuring or checking pressure:
													---Pressure/differential pressure transducers
												0/0/0	Manganese-copper pressure gauges (pressure>10GPa)
												0/0/0	Made of ytterbium gauge(pressure>10GPa)
												0/0/0	Made of polyvinylidene fluoride pressure gauge(pressure>10GPa)
												0/0/0	Other pressure, differential pressure transducers
													---Other
												0/0/0	Pressure sensor(not glass laser)(Dual-use items controlled commodity)
												0/0/0	Other instruments and equipment for measuring or checking pressure
													-Other instruments or apparatus:
												0/0/0	---Measurement of gas flowapparatus and device
												0/0/0	---Other
												0/0/0	-Parts and accessories
													Instruments and apparatus for physical or chemical analysis (for example, polarimeters, refractometers, spectrometers, gas or smoke analysis apparatus); instruments and apparatus for measuring or checking viscosity, porosity, expansion, surface tension or the like; instruments and apparatus for measuring or checking quantities of heat, sound or light (including exposure meters); microtomes:
													-Gas or smoke analysis apparatus
	0/0/0	4	4.2	2.1	0	0	0	0//0	0/0/			0/0/0	Used in continuously operating gas tester [for testing chemicals or organic compounds under export control (containing phosphor, sulfur, fluorine or chlorine with concentration lower than 0. 3mg/m^3) or for testing the activity of cholinesterase under control]
	0/0/0	4	4.2	2.1	0	0	0	0//0	0/0/			0/0/0	Other gas or smoke analysis apparatus
													-Chromatographs and electrophoresis instruments:
													---Chromatographs instruments:
												0/0/0	----Gas chromatographs instruments
												0/0/0	----Liquid chromatosraphs instruments
												0/0/0	----Other
												0/0/0	---Electrophoresis instruments
												0/0/0	-Spectrometers, spectrophotometers and spectrographs using optical radiations (UV, visible, IR)
												0/0/0	-Other instruments and apparatus using optical radiations (UV, visible, IR)
													-Other instruments and apparatus:
													---Mass spectrograph:
												0/0/0	----Integrated circuit belium spectra leak detectors
												0/0/0	----Mass spectrometer
													----Other
												0/0/0	UF_6 mass spectrographs/ion sources (capable of on-line taking samples of charging gas, product gas or tail gas from UF_6 flow)
												0/0/0	Ion mass spectrographs (resolution>2/230)

税则号列	货品名称〔CIQ 扩展编码及品名—T2 表示见附表 2〕	最惠(%)	暂定税率	普通	增值/消费	出口退税	计量单位	监管条件	检验检疫	特殊证件对美关税
9027.8019　90	其他质谱仪〔999〕	0		17	13/	13	台/千克			/5
	---其他：									
9027.8091	----曝光表〔999〕	4.7/2.3		70	13/	13	个/千克			/9.7,7.3
9027.8099	----其他〔101 电子测量仪，102 电子分析仪，103 机械测量仪，104 机械分析仪〕	0		17	13/	13	台/千克	6		/5
9027.9000	-检镜切片机；零件、附件〔999〕	0		17	13/	13	千克			/5
90.28	**生产或供应气体、液体及电力用的计量仪表，包括它们的校准仪表：**									
	-气量计：									
9028.1010	---煤气表〔999〕	10		30	13/	13	个/千克			/35
9028.1090	---其他〔999〕	10		30	13/	13	个/千克			/15
	-液量计：									
9028.2010	---水表〔999〕	10		30	13/	13	个/千克			/35
9028.2090	---其他〔999〕	10		30	13/	13	个/千克			/15
	-电量计：									
	---电度表：									
9028.3011	----单相感应式〔999〕	0		30	13/	13	个/千克			/
9028.3012	----三相感应式〔999〕	0		30	13/	13	个/千克			/
9028.3013	----单相电子式(静止式)〔999〕	0		30	13/	13	个/千克			/25
9028.3014	----三相电子式(静止式)〔999〕	0		30	13/	13	个/千克			/25
9028.3019	----其他〔999〕	0		30	13/	13	个/千克			/
9028.3090	---其他〔999〕	0		30	13/	13	个/千克			/20
	-零件、附件：									
9028.9010	---工业用〔101 其他电子仪表，102 其他机械式仪表及其零件〕	0		30	13/	13	千克			/25
9028.9090	---其他〔101 其他电子仪表，102 其他机械式仪表及其零件〕	0		50	13/	13	千克			/20
90.29	**转数计、产量计数器、车费计、里程计、步数计及类似仪表；速度计及转速表，税目 90.14 及 90.15 的仪表除外；频闪观测仪：**									
	-转数计、产量计数器、车费计、里程计、步数计及类似仪表：									
9029.1010	---转数计〔999〕	12		50	13/	13	个/千克			/37
9029.1020	---车费计、里程计〔101 其他车辆零部件，102 其他电子仪表〕	12		35	13/	13	个/千克			/32
9029.1090	---其他〔999〕	12		35	13/	13	个/千克			/32
	-速度计及转速表，频闪观测仪：									
9029.2010	---车辆用速度计〔999〕	10		35	13/	13	个/千克			/15
9029.2090	---其他〔999〕	10		35	13/	13	个/千克			/30
9029.9000	-零件、附件〔999〕	6		35	13/	13	千克			/26
90.30	**示波器、频谱分析仪及其他用于电量测量或检验的仪器和装置，但不包括税目 90.28 的各种仪表；α 射线、β 射线、γ 射线、X 射线、宇宙射线或其他离子射线的测量或检验仪器及装置：**									
9030.1000	-离子射线的测量或检验仪器及装置〔999〕	1.7/0.8		20	13/	13	台/千克			/
	-示波器：									
9030.2010	---测试频率在 300 兆赫兹以下的通用示波器〔999〕	0		80	13/	13	台/千克			/20
9030.2090	---其他〔999〕	0		20	13/	13	台/千克			/10
	-检测电压、电流、电阻或功率的其他仪器及装置：									
	--万用表，不带记录装置：									
9030.3110	---量程在五位半及以下的数字万用表〔999〕	0		130	13/	13	台/千克			/5
9030.3190	---其他〔999〕	0		20	13/	13	台/千克			/10
9030.3200	--万用表，带记录装置〔999〕	2.7/1.3		20	13/	13	台/千克			/12.7,11.3
	--其他，不带记录装置：									
9030.3310	---量程在五位半及以下的数字电流表、电压表〔999〕	7.5/5.6		130	13/	13	台/千克			/27.5,25.6
9030.3320	---电阻测试仪〔101 电子测量仪，102 机械测量仪〕	10		80	13/	13	台/千克			/20
9030.3390	---其他〔999〕	4.5/3.4		20	13/	13	台/千克			/24.5,23.4
9030.3900	--其他，带记录装置〔999〕	2.7/1.3		20	13/	13	台/千克			/12.7,11.3
	-通讯专用的其他仪器及装置(例如，串音测试器、增益测量仪、失真度表、噪声计)：									
9030.4010	---测试频率在 12.4 千兆赫兹以下的数字式频率计〔999〕	0		80	13/	13	台/千克			/10
9030.4090	---其他〔101 其他行业成套设备，102 电子测量仪〕	0		20	13/	13	台/千克			/5
	-其他仪器及装置：									
9030.8200	--测试或检验半导体晶片或器件用〔999〕	0		20	13/	13	台/千克			/
	--其他，带有记录装置：									

协定税率 %										特惠税率 %			
亚太5国	东/冰/格	巴基斯坦	韩国	瑞士	哥达	秘鲁	澳大利亚	新西/坡/智	港/澳/台	亚太2国	老/柬/缅	36/3/1	Article Description
												0/0/0	Other mass spectrograph
													---Other:
	0/0/0	10.1	5.6	42/23	0	0	0	0/0/0	0/0/			0/0/	----Exposure meters
												0/0/0	----Other
												0/0/0	-Microtomes; parts and accessories
													Gas, liquid or electricity supply or production meters, including calibrating meters therefor:
													-Gas meters:
	0/0/0	4	4	0	0	0	0	0//0	0/0/			0/0/	---Coal gas meters
	0/0/0	4	4	0	0	0	0	0/0/0	0/0/			0/0/	---Other
													-Liquid meters:
	0/0/0	4	4	0	0	0	0	0/0/0	0/0/			0/0/	---Water meters
	0/0/0	4		0	0	0	0	0/0/0	0/0/			0/0/	---Other
													-Electricity meters:
													---Watt-hour meter:
	0//	4	4					//	0/0/			0/0/	----Single- phase inductions type
	0//	4	4					//	0/0/			0/0/	----Threephase inductions type
	0//	4	4					//	0/0/			0/0/	----Single-phase induction type(motionless type)
	0//	4	4					//	0/0/			0/0/	----Three-phase induction type(motionless type)
	0//	4	7					//	0/0/			0/0/	----Other
	0//	4	4					//	0/0/			0/0/	---Other
													-Parts and accessories:
	0//	4	3.3					//	0/0/			0/0/0	---For technical use
	0//	4						//	0/0/			0/0/0	---Other
													Revolution counters, production counters, taximeters, mileometers, pedometers and the like; speed indicators and tachometers, other than those of heading No. 90. 14 or 90. 15; stroboscopes:
													-Revolution counters, production counters, taximeters, mileometers, pedometers and the like:
	0/0/0	10.8	6	8	0	0	0	0/0/0	0/0/			0/0/	---Revolution counters
	0/0/0	10.8		4.5	0	0	0	0/0/0	0/0/			0/0/	---Taximeters and mileometers
	0/0/0	10.8		4.5	0	0	0	0/0/0	0/0/			0/0/	---Other
													-Speed indicators and tachometers; stroboscopes:
	0/0/0	4	7	0	0	0	0	0//0	0/0/			0/0/	--Speed indicators for motor vehicles
	0/0/0	4.5	4	0	0	0	0	0//0	0/0/			0/0/	--Other
	0/0/0	0		1.8	0	0	0	0//0	0/0/			0/0/0	-Parts and accessories
													Oscilloscopes, spectrum analysers and other instruments and apparatus for measuring or checking electrical quantities, excluding meters of heading No. 90. 28; instruments and apparatus for measuring or detecting alpha, beta, gamma, X-ray, cosmic or other ionizing radiations:
	0/0/0	0		0	0	0	0	0//0	0/0/			0/0/0	-Instruments and apparatus for measuring or detecting ionizing radiations
													-Oscilloscopes and oscillographs:
	0//	4	3.2					//	0/0/			0/0/0	---For general use, of test frequency less than 300 MHz
	0//		2					//	0/0/			0/0/0	---Other
													-Other instruments and apparatus, for measuring or checking voltage, current, resistance or power:
													--Multimeters without a recording device:
	0//	10.8	6					//	0/0/			0/0/	---Digital, of measuring range of 5. 5 or less
	0//		3					//	0/0/			0/0/0	---Other
	0/0/0	4	3.2	0	0	0	0	0//0	0/0/			0/0/0	--Multimeters with a recording device
													--other without a recording device:
	0/0/0	10.8	6	4.5	0	0	0	0/0/0	0/0/			0/0/	---Digital ammeters or voltmeters. of measuing rang of 5. 5or less
	0/0/0	9		4.2	0	0	0	0/0/0	0/0/			0/0/	---Resistnace measaring instruments
	0/0/0	4		2.7	0	0	0	0//0	0/0/			0/0/0	---Other
	0/0/0	4		24/13	0	0	0	0//0	0/0/			0/0/0	--Other with a recordins device
													-Other instruments and apparatus, specially designed for telecommunications (for example, cross-talk meters, gain measuring instruments, distortion factor meters, psophometers):
												0/0/0	---Digital frequency meters, of test frequency less than 12. 4 GHz
												0/0/0	---Other
													-Other instruments and apparatus:
												0/0/0	--For measuring or checking semiconductor wafers or devices
													--Other, with a recording device:

税则号列	货品名称〔CIQ 扩展编码及品名－T2 表示见附表 2〕	最惠(%)	暂定税率	普通	增值/消费	出口退税	计量单位	监管条件	检验检疫	特殊证件对美关税
9030.8410	---电感及电容测试仪〔999〕	3.3/1.7		80	13/	13	台/千克			/28.3,26.7
9030.8490	---其他〔999〕	2.7/1.3		20	13/	13	台/千克			/12.7,11.3
	--其他：									
9030.8910	---电感及电容测试仪〔999〕	4.7/2.3		80	13/	13	台/千克			/14.7,12.3
9030.8990	---其他									
9030.8990 10	中子探测和测量仪表(专用于测定核反应堆堆芯内中子通量的)〔999〕	2.7/1.3		20	13/	13	台/千克	3		/12.7,11.3
9030.8990 90	其他电量的测量或检验仪器及装置(未装有记录装置的)〔999〕	2.7/1.3		20	13/	13	台/千克			/12.7,11.3
9030.9000	-零件、附件									
9030.9000 01	检测半导体晶片及器件的仪器零件(包括附件)〔999〕	0		17	13/	13	千克			/10
9030.9000 02	ITA 产品用的印刷电路组件(包括外接组件，如符合 PCMCIA 标准的卡)〔999〕	0		17	13/	13	千克			/10
9030.9000 90	税目 90.30 所属货品的零件及附件〔999〕	2.3/1.2		17	13/	13	千克			/12.3,11.2
90.31	**本章其他税目未列名的测量或检验仪器、器具及机器；轮廓投影仪：**									
9031.1000	-机械零件平衡试验机									
9031.1000 10	陀螺动态平衡测试仪〔999〕	2.3/1.2		17	13/	13	台/千克	3		/22.3,21.2
9031.1000 90	其他机械零件平衡试验机〔999〕	2.3/1.2		17	13/	13	台/千克			/22.3,21.2
9031.2000	-试验台									
9031.2000 10	陀螺/马达运转试验台〔999〕	7		17	13/	13	台/千克	3		/
9031.2000 20	加速度表测试台〔999〕	7		17	13/	13	台/千克	3		/
9031.2000 30	试车台(能试推力＞90kN 火箭发动机的或同时测量三个推力分量的)〔999〕	7		17	13/	13	台/千克	3		/
9031.2000 40	惯性平台测试台(测试平台包括高精度离心机和转台)〔999〕	7		17	13/	13	台/千克	3		/
9031.2000 90	其他试验台〔999〕	7		17	13/	13	台/千克			/
	-其他光学仪器及器具：									
9031.4100	--制造半导体器件时检验半导体晶片、器件或检测光掩模或光栅用〔999〕	0		17	13/	13	台/千克			/
	--其他：									
9031.4910	---轮廓投影仪〔999〕	3.3/1.7		20	13/	13	台/千克			/28.3,26.7
9031.4920	---光栅测量装置〔999〕	0		17	13/	13	台/千克			/25
9031.4990	---其他									
9031.4990 10	光盘质量在线检测仪及离线检测仪〔999〕	0		17	13/	13	台/千克			/20
9031.4990 90	其他光学测量或检验仪器和器具(第九十章其他编号未列名的)〔999〕	0		17	13/	13	台/千克			/20
	-其他仪器、器具及机器：									
9031.8010	---光纤通信及光纤性能测试仪〔999〕	4/3		17	13/	13	台/千克			/
9031.8020	---坐标测量仪〔999〕	4/3		17	13/	13	台/千克			/14,13
	---无损探伤检测仪器(射线探伤仪除外)：									
9031.8031	----超声波探伤检测仪〔999〕	4/3		17	13/	13	台/千克			/14,13
9031.8032	----磁粉探伤检测仪〔999〕	4/3		17	13/	13	台/千克			/14,13
9031.8033	----涡流探伤检测仪〔999〕	4/3	①	17	13/	13	台/千克			/13
9031.8039	----其他〔999〕	4/3		17	13/	13	台/千克			/14,13
9031.8090	---其他									
9031.8090 10	惯性测量单元测试仪〔999〕	4/3		17	13/	13	台/千克	3		/
9031.8090 20	陀螺调谐测试仪〔999〕	4/3		17	13/	13	台/千克	3		/
9031.8090 30	跑道摩擦系数测试仪〔999〕	4/3	①	17	13/	13	台/千克			/
9031.8090 40	音频生命探测仪〔999〕	4/3	2	17	13/	13	台/千克			/
9031.8090 50	音视频生命探测仪〔999〕	4/3	2	17	13/	13	台/千克			/
9031.8090 60	集成电路测试分选设备〔999〕	4/3	2	17	13/	13	台/千克			/
9031.8090 90	其他测量，检验仪器，器具及机器(指第 90 章其他编号未列名的)〔101 电子测量仪，102 机械测量仪〕	4/3		17	13/	13	台/千克			/
9031.9000	-零件、附件									

① 1—6 月：3%。

协定税率 %										特惠税率 %			Article Description
亚太5国	东/冰/格	巴基斯坦	韩国	瑞士	哥达	秘鲁	澳大利亚	新西/坡/智	港/澳/台	亚太2国	老/柬/缅	36/3/1	
	0/0/0	4		0	0	0	0	0/0/0	0/0/			0/0/	---For measuring inductances or capacitances
	0/0/0	4	4.8	2.4/1.3	0	0	0	0//0	0/0/			0/0/0	---Other
													--Other:
	0/0/0	10.1		4.2/2.3	0	0	0	0/0/0	0/0/			0/0/	---For measuring inductances or capacitances
													---Other
	0/0/3.2	4		0	0	0	0	0//0	0/0/			0/0/0	Neutron detection and measurement instruments (used exclusively to measure the neutron flux of the reactor cores)
	0/0/3.2	4		0	0	0	0	0//0	0/0/			0/0/0	Other instruments and apparatus for measuring or checking electrical quantities (without a recording device)
													-Parts and accessories
	0/0/0	4	2.8	2.1/1.2	0	0	0	0//0	0/0/			0/0/0	Parts of instruments for measuring or checking semiconductor wafers or devices
	0/0/0	4	2.8	2.1/1.2	0	0	0	0//0	0/0/			0/0/0	Printed circuit components for products falling within the ITA(including such components for external connections such as cards that conform to the PCMCLA standard)
	0/0/0	4	2.8	2.1/1.2	0	0	0	0//0	0/0/			0/0/0	Parts and accessories of goods of heading 90. 30
													Measuring or checking instruments, appliances and machines, not specified or included elsewhere in this Chapter; profile projectors:
													-Machines for balancing mechanical parts
1.5/0.8	0/0/0	4	0	0	0	0	0	0//0	0/0/			0/0/0	Gyro dynamic balancing testers
1.5/0.8	0/0/0	4	0	0	0	0	0	0//0	0/0/			0/0/0	Other machines for balancing mechanical parts
													-Test benches
	0/0/0	4	4.2	3.6	0	0	0	0//0	0/0/			0/0/0	Gyro/motor running test-benches
	0/0/0	4	4.2	3.6	0	0	0	0//0	0/0/			0/0/0	Accelerometer test-benches
	0/0/0	4	4.2	3.6	0	0	0	0//0	0/0/			0/0/0	Testbed (capable of testing rocket engine with a thrust >90kN or testing three individual thrust forces at the same time)
	0/0/0	4	4.2	3.6	0	0	0	0//0	0/0/			0/0/0	Inertial platform test-benches (including high-precision centrifuge and turntable)
	0/0/0	4	4.2	3.6	0	0	0	0//0	0/0/			0/0/0	Other test benches
													-Other optical instruments and appliances:
												0/0/0	--For inspecting semiconductor wafers or devices or for inspecting photomasks or reticles used in manufacturing semiconductor devices:
													--Other:
	0/0/0	4	6	0	0	0	0	0//0	0/0/			0/0/0	---Profile proiecters
												0/0/0	---Measuring grating device
													---Other
												0/0/0	Automatic inspection detectors (AID) for CD production
												0/0/0	Other measuring or checking optical instruments and appliances, not elsewhere specified or included in chapter 90
													-Other instruments, appliances and machines:
2.6/2	0/0/0	0	3	0	0	0	0	0//0	0/0/			0/0/0	--Optical telecommunication and optical fibre performance testing instruments
	0/0/0	0	3	0	0	0	0	0//0	0/0/			0/0/0	--Coordinate measuring machine
													--Apparatus for exaninations, without damaging structure (other than apparatus for radiological examinations):
2.6/2	0/0/0	0	3.2	0	0	0	0	0//0	0/0/			0/0/0	----Apparatus for ultrasonic examinations
2.6/2	0/0/0	0	3.2	0	0	0	0	0//0	0/0/			0/0/0	----Apparatus for magnetic examinations
2.6/2	0/0/0	0	3.2	0	0	0	0	0//0	0/0/			0/0/0	----Apparatus for eddy examinations
2.6/2	0/0/0	0		0	0	0	0	0//0	0/0/			0/0/0	----Other
													---Other
2.6/2	0//2	0	2	2.6	0	0	0	0//0	0/0/0			0/0/0	Inertial measurement unit testers
2.6/2	0//2	0	2	2.6	0	0	0	0//0	0/0/0			0/0/0	Gyro tuning testers
2.6/2	0//2	0	2	2.6	0	0	0	0//0	0/0/0			0/0/0	Runway friction coefficient testers
2.6/2	0//2	0	2	2.6	0	0	0	0//0	0/0/0			0/0/0	Audio life detection instrument
2.6/2	0//2	0	2	2.6	0	0	0	0//0	0/0/0			0/0/0	Audio and video life detection instrument
2.6/2	0//2	0	2	2.6	0	0	0	0//0	0/0/0			0/0/0	Integrated circuit testing and sorting equipment
2.6/2	0//2	0	2	2.6	0	0	0	0//0	0/0/0			0/0/0	Other measuring or checking instruments, appliances and machines (not elsewhere specified or included in Chapter 90)
													-Parts and accessories

税则号列	货品名称〔CIQ 扩展编码及品名—T2 表示见附表 2〕	最惠(%)	暂定税率	普通	增值/消费	出口退税	计量单位	监管条件	检验检疫	特殊证件对美关税
9031.9000 20	惯性测量单元稳定元件加工夹具〔999〕	0		17	13/	13	千克	3		/10
9031.9000 30	惯性平台平衡夹具〔999〕	0		17	13/	13	千克	3		/10
9031.9000 90	编号 9031 的仪器及器具的其他零件(第 90 章其他编号未列名的)〔999〕	0		17	13/	13	千克			/10
90.32	**自动调节或控制仪器及装置:**									
9032.1000	-恒温器〔101 其它电子测量分析设备及其零件,102 其它机械测量分析设备及其零件〕	7		17	13/	13	台/千克			/27
9032.2000	-恒压器〔101 其它电子测量分析设备及其零件,102 其它机械测量分析设备及其零件〕	2.3/1.2		17	13/	13	台/千克			/12.3,11.2
	-其他仪器及装置:									
9032.8100	--液压或气压的〔999〕	2.3/1.2		17	13/	13	台/千克			/12.3,11.2
	--其他:									
	---列车自动控制系统(ATC)车载设备:									
9032.8911	----列车自动防护系统(ATP)车载设备〔999〕	7		17	13/	13	台/千克			/12
9032.8912	----列车自动运行系统(ATO)车载设备〔999〕	7		17	13/	13	台/千克			/
9032.8919	----其他〔999〕	7		17	13/	13	台/千克			/12
9032.8990	---其他									
9032.8990 10	具有可再生能源和智能电网应用的自动电压和电流调节器;非液压或气压的自动调控流量、液位和湿度的仪器(自动控制、调节装置)〔999〕	7	5	17	13/	13	台/千克			/
9032.8990 20	组合喷气发动机的燃烧调节装置(自动控制、调节装置)〔999〕	7		17	13/	13	台/千克	3		/
9032.8990 30	三坐标测量机用自动控制柜〔999〕	7	3	17	13/	13	台/千克			/
9032.8990 40	飞机自动驾驶系统(包括自动驾驶、电子控制飞行、自动故障分析、警告系统配平系统及推力监控设备及其相关仪表)〔999〕	7	1	17	13/	13	台/千克			/
9032.8990 50	机床用成套数控伺服装置(包括 CNC 操作单元,带有配套的伺服放大器和伺服电机)〔999〕	7	3	17	13/	13	台/千克			/
9032.8990 60	电喷点火程序控制单元(自动控制、调节装置)〔999〕	7	3	17	13/	13	台/千克			/
9032.8990 70	印刷机用成套数控伺服传动装置(包括运动控制器或可编程序自动控制器、人机界面单元,带有配套的伺服驱动器和伺服电机)〔999〕	7	3	17	13/	13	台/千克			/
9032.8990 80	纯电动或混合动力汽车用电机控制器总成(自动控制、调节装置)〔999〕	7	4	17	13/	13	台/千克			/
9032.8990 90	其他自动调节或控制仪器及装置〔999〕	7		17	13/	13	台/千克			/
9032.9000	-零件、附件									
9032.9000 01	飞机自动驾驶系统的零件(包括自动驾驶、电子控制飞行、自动故障分析、警告系统配平系统及推力监控设备及其相关仪表的零件)〔999〕	5	1	17	13/	13	千克			/11
9032.9000 90	其他自动调节或控制仪器零件、附件〔999〕	5		17	13/	13	千克			/15
90.33	**第九十章所列机器、器具、仪器或装置用的本章其他税目未列名的零件、附件:**									
9033.0000	第九十章所列机器、器具、仪器或装置用的本章其他税目未列名的零件、附件									
9033.0000 10	用于 90 章环境产品的其他税目未列名的零件、附件:(太阳能定日镜、9015.80 的商品,90.26 的商品,90.27 的商品(9027.8011 和 9027.8091 除外),9031.49 的商品,测振仪,手振动仪,可再生能源和智能电网应用的自动电压和电流调节器,自动调控流量、液位和湿度的仪器)〔101 其它电子测量分析设备及其零件,102 其它机械测量分析设备及其零件〕	6	5	17	13/	13	千克			/25
9033.0000 90	第 90 章其他编号未列名零、附件(指第 90 章所列机器、器具、仪器或装置用)〔101 其它电子测量分析设备及其零件,102 其它机械测量分析设备及其零件〕	6		17	13/	13	千克			/26

协定税率 %										特惠税率 %			Article Description
亚太5国	东/冰/格	巴基斯坦	韩国	瑞士	哥达	秘鲁	澳大利亚	新西/坡/智	港/澳/台	亚太2国	老/柬/缅	36/3/1	
												0/0/0	Processing clamps for stabling element of inertial measurement unit
												0/0/0	Inertial platform balancing clamps
												0/0/0	Other parts of instruments, appliances and machines of heading No. 90. 31, not elsewhere specified or included in chapter 90
													Automatic regulating or controlling instruments and apparatus:
	0/0/0	4	0	2.1	0	0	0	0//0	0/0/			0/0/0	-Thermostats
	0/0/0	4	2.8	0	0	0	0	0//0	0/0/			0/0/0	-Manostats
													-Other instruments and apparatus:
15/0.8	0/0/0	4	4.5	21/12	0	0	0	0//0	0/0/			0/0/0	--Hydraulic or pneumatic
													--Other:
													---Automatic control systems(ATC) for train apparatus:
	0/0/0	4	4.2		0	0	0	0//0	0/0/			0/0/0	----Automatic protective systems(ATP) for train apparatus
	0/0/0	4	4.2		0	0	0	0//0	0/0/			0/0/0	----Automatic motion systems(ATO) for train apparatus
	0/0/0	4	4.2		0	0	0	0//0	0/0/			0/0/0	----Other
													---Other
	0/0/0	4	4.2		0	0	0	0//0	0/0/			0/0/0	With renewable energy and smart grid application of the automatic voltage and current regulator; instrument non hydraulic or pneumatic automatic control flow, liquid level and humidity(automatic control device)
	0/0/0	4	4.2		0	0	0	0//0	0/0/			0/0/0	Combustion adjusting device for combined jet engine(automatic control and regulating devices)
	0/0/0	4	4.2		0	0	0	0//0	0/0/			0/0/0	Automatic control cabinet with three coordinate measuring machine
	0/0/0	4	4.2		0	0	0	0//0	0/0/			0/0/0	The aircraft autopilot system(including automatic driving, electronic control flight, automatic fault analysis and warning system trim system and thrust monitoring equipment and instrumentation)
	0/0/0	4	4.2		0	0	0	0//0	0/0/			0/0/0	With complete sets of CNC servo device for machine tools(including CNC operating unit, with supporting servo amplifier and servo motor)
	0/0/0	4	4.2		0	0	0	0//0	0/0/			0/0/0	EFI ignition program control unit(automatic control and regulation device)
	0/0/0	4	4.2		0	0	0	0//0	0/0/			0/0/0	Printing machine with complete sets of numerical control servo drive device (including motion controller or automatic programmable controller, man-machine interface unit, servo drive and servo motor) that contains form a complete set
	0/0/0	4	4.2		0	0	0	0//0	0/0/			0/0/0	Pure electric or hybrid cars with motor controller assembly, automatic control, adjusting device)
	0/0/0	4	4.2		0	0	0	0//0	0/0/			0/0/0	Other automatic regulating or controlling instruments and devices
													-Parts and accessories
	0/0/0	0	3	1.5	0	0	0	0//0	0/0/			0/0/0	Parts of automatic pilotting systems for aircraft(including instruments of automatic pilotting, electronic flight control, automatic failure analysis, warning systems balancing system and thrust monitoring equipment and in struments and meters)
	0/0/0	0	3	1.5	0	0	0	0//0	0/0/			0/0/0	Other parts and acessories of automatic regulating or controlling instruments
													Parts and accessories (not specified or included elsewhere in this Chapter) for machines, appliances, instruments or apparatus of Chapter 90:
													Parts and accessories (not specified or included elsewhere in this Chapter) for machines, appliances, instruments or apparatus of Chapter 90
	0/0/0	4	0	1.8	0	0	0	0//0	0/0/			0/0/0	Chapter 90 environmental products used for the other items not listed parts, accessories: (solar heliostat, 9015. 80, 90. 26 of goods, the goods 90. 27 (except 9027. 8011 and 9027. 8091), 9031. 49 goods, vibration, hand vibration meter, renewable energy and smart grid applications of automatic voltage and current regulator, automatic regulation and control flow, liquid level instruments and humidity)
	0/0/0	4	0	1.8	0	0	0	0//0	0/0/			0/0/0	Chapter 90 other number their zero, attachment (refer to chapter 90 listed machines, apparatus, instruments and devices)

第九十一章
钟表及其零件

注释:

一、本章不包括:

(一)钟表玻璃及钟锤(按其构成材料归类);

(二)表链(根据不同情况,归入税目71.13或71.17);

(三)第十五类注释二所规定的贱金属制通用零件(第十五类)、塑料制的类似品(第三十九章)及贵金属或包贵金属制的类似品(一般归入税目71.15);但钟、表发条则应作为钟、表的零件归类(税目91.14);

(四)轴承滚珠(根据不同情况,归入税目73.26或84.82);

(五)税目84.12的物品,不需擒纵器可以工作的;

(六)滚珠轴承(税目84.82);

(七)第八十五章的物品,本身未组装在或未与其他零件组装在钟、表机芯内,也未组装成专用于或主要用于钟、表机芯零件的(第八十五章)。

二、税目91.01仅包括表壳完全以贵金属或包贵金属制的表,以及用贵金属或包贵金属与税目71.01至71.04的天然、养殖珍珠或宝石、半宝石(天然、合成或再造)合制的表。用贱金属上镶嵌贵金属制成表壳的表应归入税目91.02。

三、本章所称"表芯",是指由摆轮及游丝、石英晶体或其他能确定时间间隔的装置来进行调节的机构,并带有显示器或可装机械指示器的系统。表芯的厚度不超过12毫米,长、宽或直径不超过50毫米。

四、除注释一另有规定的以外,钟、表的机芯及其他零件,既适用于钟或表,又适用于其他物品(例如精密仪器)的,均应归入本章。

税则号列	货品名称(CIQ扩展编码及品名—T2表示见附表2)	最惠(%)	暂定税率	普通	增值/消费	出口退税	计量单位	监管条件	检验检疫	特殊证件对美关税
91.01	**手表、怀表及其他表,包括秒表,表壳用贵金属或包贵金属制成的:**									
	-电力驱动的手表,不论是否附有秒表装置:									
9101.1100	--仅有机械指示器的〔999〕	8		100	13/①	13	只/千克			/
	--其他:									
9101.1910	---仅有光电显示器的〔999〕	8		100	13/①	13	只/千克			/
9101.1990	---其他〔999〕	8		100	13/①	13	只/千克			/
	-其他手表,不论是否附有秒表装置:									
9101.2100	--自动上弦的									
9101.2100　10	含濒危动物皮自动上弦贵金属机械手表(表壳用贵金属或包贵金属制成的)〔999〕	8		80	13/①	0	只/千克	EF		/
9101.2100　90	其他自动上弦贵金属机械手表(表壳用贵金属或包贵金属制成的)〔999〕	8		80	13/①	13	只/千克			/
9101.2900	--其他									
9101.2900　10	含濒危动物皮非自动上弦贵金属机械手表(表壳用贵金属或包贵金属制成的)〔999〕	8		80	13/①	0	只/千克	EF		/
9101.2900　90	其他非自动上弦贵金属机械手表(表壳用贵金属或包贵金属制成的)〔999〕	8		80	13/①	13	只/千克			/
	-其他:									
9101.9100	--电力驱动的〔999〕	8		100	13/	13	只/千克			/
9101.9900	--其他〔999〕	15		80	13/	13	只/千克			/
91.02	**手表、怀表及其他表,包括秒表,但税目91.01的货品除外:**									
	-电力驱动的手表,不论是否附有秒表装置:									
9102.1100	--仅有机械指示器的〔999〕	10		100	13/①	13	只/千克			/35
9102.1200	--仅有光电显示器的〔999〕	15		100	13/①	13	只/千克			/40
9102.1900	--其他〔999〕	8		100	13/①	13	只/千克			/33
	-其他手表,不论是否装有秒表装置:									
9102.2100	--自动上弦的									

① 进口关税完税价格在10000元人民币及以上时,税率为20%。

Chapter 91
Clocks and watches and parts thereof

Notes:

1. This Chapter does not cover:
   (a) Clock or watch glasses or weights (classified according to their constituent material);
   (b) Watch chains (heading No. 71. 13 or 71. 17, as the case may be);
   (c) Parts of general use defined in Note 2 to Section XV, of base metal (Section XV), or similar goods of plastics (Chapter 39) or of precious metal or metal clad with precious metal (generally heading No. 71. 15); clock or watch springs are, however, to be classified as clock or watch parts (heading No. 91. 14);
   (d) Bearing balls (heading No. 73. 26 or 84. 82, as the case may be);
   (e) Articles of heading No. 84. 12 constructed to work without an escapement;
   (f) Ball bearings (heading No. 84. 82);
   (g) Articles of Chapter 85, not yet assembled together or with other components into watch or clock movements or into articles suitable for use solely or principally as parts of such movements (Chapter 85).
2. Heading 91. 01 covers only watches with case wholly of precious metal or of metal clad with precious metal, or of the same materials combined with natural or cultured pearls, or precious or semiprecious stones (natural, synthetic or reconstructed) of headings 71. 01 to 71. 04. Watches with case of base metal inlaid with precious metal fall in heading 91. 02.
3. For the purposes of this Chapter, the expression "watch movements" means devices regulated by a balance-wheel and hairspring, quartz crystal or any other system capable of determining intervals of time, with a display or a system to which a mechanical display can be incorporated. Such watch movements shall not exceed 12 mm in thickness and 50 mm in width, length or diameter.
4. Except as provided in Note 1, movements and other parts suitable for use both in clocks or watches and in other articles (for example, precision instruments) are to be classified in this Chapter.

协定税率 %										特惠税率 %			
亚太5国	东/冰/格	巴基斯坦	韩国	瑞士	哥达	秘鲁	澳大利亚	新西/坡/智	港/澳/台	亚太2国	老/柬/缅	36/3/1	Article Description
													Wrist-watches, pocket-watches and other watches, including stop-watches, with case of precious metal or of metal clad with precious metal:
													-Wrist-watches, electrically operated whether or not incorporating a stop-watch facility:
5.2	0/0/0	4.5	4.4	5.7	0	0	0	0/0/0	0/0/		//	0/0/	--With mechanical display only
													--Other:
	0/0/0	11.5	6.4	4.8	0	0	0	0/0/0	0/0/			0/0/	---With optoelectronic display only
	0/0/0	10.8	6	7.8	0	0	0	0/0/0	0/0/			0/0/	---Other
													-Other wrist-watches, whether or not incorporating a stop-watch facility:
													--Automatic winding
5.2	0/0/0	4.5	4.4	5.7	0	0	0	0/0/0	0/0/			0/0/	Mechanical-watches of precious metal, containing endangered animals skins, automatic winding (with case of precious metal or of metal clad with precious metal)
5.2	0/0/0	4.5	4.4	5.7	0	0	0	0/0/0	0/0/			0/0/	Other mechanical-watches of precious metal, automatic winding (with case of precious metal or of metal clad with precious metal)
													--Other
5.2	0/0/0	10.8	6	7.8	0	0	0	0/0/0	0/0/			0/0/	Mechanical-watches of precious metal, containing endangered animals skins, non-automatic winding, (with case of precious metal or of metal clad with precious metal)
5.2	0/0/0	10.8	6	7.8	0	0	0	0/0/0	0/0/			0/0/	Other mechanical-watches of precious metal, non-automatic winding, (with case of precious metal or metalclad with precious meta)
													-Other:
	0/0/0	10.8	6	4.5	0	0	0	0/0/0	0/0/			0/0/	--Electrically operated
	0/0/0		12	10.4	0	0	0	0/0/0	0/0/			0/0/	--Other
													Wrist-watches, pocket-watches and other watches, including stop-watches, other than those of heading No. 91. 01:
													-Wrist-watches, electrically operated, whether or not incorporating a stop-watch facility:
6.5	0/0/0	5.6	5	6.5	0	0	0	0/0/0	0/0/			0/0/	--With mechanical display only
	0/0/0		16.1	6.9	0	0	0	0/0/0	0/0/			0/0/	--With optoelectronic clisplay only
	0/0/0	10.8	6	4.5	0	0	0	0/0/0	0/0/			0/0/	--Other
													-Other wrist-watches, whether or not incorporating a stop-watch facility:
													--Automatic winding

税则号列		货品名称〔CIQ 扩展编码及品名－T2 表示见附表 2〕	最惠(%)	暂定税率	普通	增值/消费	出口退税	计量单位	监管条件	检验检疫	特殊证件对美关税
9102.2100	10	含濒危动物皮其他自动上弦的机械手表(用贵金属或包贵金属制壳的除外)〔999〕	11		80	13/①	0	只/千克	EF		/36
9102.2100	90	其他自动上弦的机械手表(用贵金属或包贵金属制壳的除外)〔999〕	11		80	13/①	13	只/千克			/36
9102.2900		--其他									
9102.2900	10	含濒危动物皮其他非自动上弦机械手表(用贵金属或包贵金属制壳的除外)〔999〕	10		80	13/①	0	只/千克	EF		/35
9102.2900	90	其他非自动上弦的机械手表(用贵金属或包贵金属制壳的除外)〔999〕	10		80	13/①	13	只/千克			/35
		-其他:									
9102.9100		--电力驱动的〔999〕	10		100	13/	13	只/千克			/35
9102.9900		--其他〔999〕	15		80	13/	13	只/千克			/
91.03		**以表芯装成的钟,但不包括税目 91.04 的钟:**									
9103.1000		-电力驱动的〔999〕	15		100	13/	13	只/千克			/25
9103.9000		-其他〔999〕	15		100	13/	13	只/千克			/40
91.04		**仪表板钟及车辆、航空器、航天器或船舶用的类似钟:**									
9104.0000		仪表板钟及车辆、航空器、航天器或船舶用的类似钟〔999〕	10		100	13/	13	只/千克			/35
91.05		**其他钟:**									
		-闹钟:									
9105.1100		--电力驱动的〔999〕	15		100	13/	13	只/千克			/40
9105.1900		--其他〔999〕	10		100	13/	13	只/千克			/
		-挂钟:									
9105.2100		--电力驱动的〔999〕	15		100	13/	13	只/千克			/40
9105.2900		--其他〔999〕	10		100	13/	13	只/千克			/35
		-其他:									
		--电力驱动的:									
9105.9110		---天文钟〔999〕	2		8	13/	13	只/千克			/
9105.9190		---其他〔999〕	15		100	13/	13	只/千克			/40
9105.9900		--其他〔999〕	10		100	13/	13	只/千克			/30
91.06		**时间记录器以及测量、记录或指示时间间隔的装置,装有钟、表机芯或同步电动机的(例如,考勤钟、时刻记录器):**									
9106.1000		-考勤钟、时刻记录器〔999〕	10		50	13/	13	只/千克			/20
9106.9000		-其他〔101 其他车辆零部件,102 其他钟表、计时器及零件〕	10		50	13/	13	只/千克		L	/20
91.07		**装有钟、表机芯或同步电动机的定时开关:**									
9107.0000		装有钟、表机芯或同步电动机的定时开关〔999〕	8		50	13/	13	个/千克			/28
91.08		**已组装的完整表芯:**									
		-电力驱动的:									
9108.1100		--仅有机械指示器或有可装机械指示器的装置的〔999〕	16	10	80	13/	13	只/千克			/
9108.1200		--仅有光电显示器的〔999〕	16		80	13/	13	只/千克			/
9108.1900		--其他〔999〕	16		80	13/	13	只/千克			/
9108.2000		-自动上弦的〔999〕	16		80	13/	13	只/千克			/
		-其他:									
9108.9010		---表面尺寸在 33.8 毫米及以下〔999〕	16		80	13/	13	只/千克			/
9108.9090		---其他〔999〕	16		80	13/	13	只/千克			/
91.09		**已组装的完整钟芯:**									
9109.1000		-电力驱动的〔999〕	16		100	13/	13	只/千克			/41
9109.9000		-其他〔999〕	16		100	13/	13	只/千克			/
91.10		**未组装或部分组装的完整钟、表机芯(机芯套装件);已组装的不完整钟、表机芯;未组装的不完整钟、表机芯:**									
		-表的:									
9110.1100		--未组装或部分组装的完整机芯(机芯套装件)〔999〕	16		80	13/	13	只/千克			/

① 进口关税完税价格在 10000 元人民币及以上时,税率为 20%。

协定税率 %										特惠税率 %			Article Description
亚太5国	东/冰/格	巴基斯坦	韩国	瑞士	哥达	秘鲁	澳大利亚	新西/坡/智	港/澳/台	亚太2国	老/柬/缅	36/3/1	
	0/0/0	4.5	4.4	5.7	0	0	0	0/0/0	0/0/			0/0/	Mechanical-watches, containing endangered animals skins, automatic winding(other than with case of precious metal or metal clad with precious metal)
	0/0/0	4.5	4.4	5.7	0	0	0	0/0/0	0/0/			0/0/	Other mechanical-watches, automatic winding(other than with case of precious metal or of metal clad with precious metal)
													--Other
	0/0/0	10.8	6	7.8	0	0	0	0/0/0	0/0/			0/0/	Othe mechanical-watches, containing endangered animals skins, non-automatic winding(other than with case of precious metal or of metal clad with precious metal)
	0/0/0	10.8	6	7.8	0	0	0	0/0/0	0/0/			0/0/	Other mechanical - watches, non-automatic winding, (other than with case of precious metal or metalclad with precious metal)
													-Other:
	0/0/0	10.8	6	7.8	0	0	0	0/0/0	0/0/			0/0/	--Electrically operated
	0/0/0		12	10.4	0	0	0	0/0/0	0/0/			0/0/	--Other
													Clocks with watch movements, excluding clocks of heading No. 91. 04:
	0/0/0		16.1	12	0	0	0	0/0/0	0/0/			0/0/	-Electrically operated
	0/0/0		12	10.4	0	0	0	0/0/0	0/0/			0/0/	-Other
													Instrument panel clocks and clocks of a similar type for vehicles, aircraft, spacecraft or vessels:
	0/0/0	4	4	0	0	0	0	0//0	0/0/			0/0/	Instrument panel clocks and clocks of a similar type for vehicles, aircraft, spacecraft or vessels
													Other clocks:
													-Alarm clocks:
	0/0/0	23	16.1	12	0	0	0	0/0/0	0/0/			0/0/0	--Electrically operated
	0/0/0	20	12	6	0	0	0	0/0/0	0/0/			0/0/	--Other
													-Wall clocks:
	0/0/0	23	16.1	6.9	0	0	0	0/0/0	0/0/			0/0/	--Electrically operated
	0/0/0		12	6	0	0	0	0/0/0	0/0/			0/0/	--Other
													-Other:
													--Electrically operated:
	0/0/0	0	0	0.9	0	0	0	0//0	0/0/			0/0/0	---Astronomical chronometer
	0/0/0		16.1	6.9	0	0	0	0/0/0	0/0/			0/0/	---Other
	0/0/0	11.5	6.4	8.3	0	0	0	0/0/0	0/0/			0/0/	--Other
													Time of day recording apparatus and apparatus for measuring, recording or otherwise indicating intervals of time, with clock or watch movement or with synchronous motor (for example, time-registers, time-recorders):
	0/0/0	11.5	6.4	4.8	0	0	0	0/0/0	0/0/			0/0/	-Time-registers; time-recorders
	0/0/0	11.5	6.4	8.3	0	0	0	0/0/0	0/0/			0/0/	-Other
													Time switches with clock or watch movement or with synchronous motor:
	0/0/4.8	5.4	4.8	3.6	0	0	0	0/0/0	0/0/			0/0/	Time switches with clock or watch movement or with synchronous motor
													Watch movements, complete and assembled:
													-Electrically operated:
	0/0/0	11.5	6.4	4.8	0	0	0	0/0/0	0/0/			0/0/	--With mechanical display only or with a device to which a mechanical display can be incorporated
	0/0/0	11.5	6.4	8.3	0	0	0	0/0/0	0/0/			0/0/	--With optoelectronic display only
10.4	0/0/0	7.2	6.4	8.3	0	0	0	0/0/0	0/0/			0/0/	--Other
10.4	0/0/0	11.5	6.4	8.3	0	0	0	0/0/0	0/0/			0/0/	-Automatic winding
													-Other:
	0/0/0	11.5	6.4	8.3	0	0	0	0/0/0	0/0/			0/0/	---Measuring 33. 8mm or less
	0/0/0	11.5	6.4	8.3	0	0	0	0/0/0	0/0/			0/0/	---Other
													Clock movements, complete and assembled:
	0/0/0	11.5	6.4	4.8	0	0	0	0/0/0	0/0/			0/0/	-Eletrically operated
	0/0/0	11.5	6.4	4.8	0	0	0	0/0/0	0/0/			0/0/	-Other
													Complete watch or clock movements, unassembled or partly assembled (movement sets); incomplete watch or clock movements, assembled; rough watch or clock movements:
													-Of watches:
	0/0/0	11.5	6.4	8.3	0	0	0	0/0/0	0/0/			0/0/	--Complete movements, unassembled or partly assembled (movement sets)

税则号列	货品名称〔CIQ扩展编码及品名一T2表示见附表2〕	最惠(%)	暂定税率	普通	增值/消费	出口退税	计量单位	监管条件	检验检疫	特殊证件对美关税
9110.1200	--已组装的不完整表机芯〔999〕	16		70	13/	13	千克			/
9110.1900	--未组装的不完整表机芯〔999〕	16		70	13/	13	千克			/
	-其他：									
9110.9010	---未组装或部分组装的完整钟芯〔999〕	16		100	13/	13	千克/只			/
9110.9090	---其他〔999〕	16		80	13/	13	千克			/
91.11	**表壳及其零件：**									
9111.1000	-贵金属表壳或包贵金属表壳									
9111.1000 10	按重量计含金量在80%及以上的黄金表壳〔999〕	14		80	13/	0	只/千克	J		/
9111.1000 90	其他贵金属或包贵金属制的表壳〔999〕	14		80	13/	0,13	只/千克			/
9111.2000	-贱金属表壳，不论是否镀金或镀银〔999〕	14		80	13/	13	只/千克			/
9111.8000	-其他表壳〔999〕	14		80	13/	13	只/千克			/
9111.9000	-零件〔999〕	14		80	13/	0,13	千克			/
91.12	**钟壳和本章所列其他货品的类似外壳及其零件：**									
9112.2000	-壳〔999〕	14		80	13/	13	只/千克			/39
9112.9000	-零件〔999〕	12		80	13/	13	千克			/
91.13	**表带及其零件：**									
9113.1000	-贵金属或包贵金属制									
9113.1000 10	按重量计含金量在80%及以上的黄金表带〔999〕	20		130	13/	0	千克	J		/
9113.1000 90	其他贵金属或包贵金属制的表带及零件〔999〕	20		130	13/	0,13	千克			/
9113.2000	-贱金属制，不论是否镀金或镀银〔999〕	14		100	13/	13	千克			/39
9113.9000	-其他									
9113.9000 10	濒危动物皮制的表带及其零件〔999〕	14		100	13/	0	千克	FE		/39
9113.9000 90	其他非金属制的表带及其零件〔999〕	14		100	13/	13	千克			/39
91.14	**钟、表的其他零件：**									
9114.1000	-发条，包括游丝〔999〕	14		50	13/	13	千克			/
9114.3000	-钟面或表面〔999〕	14		50	13/	13	千克			/
9114.4000	-夹板及横担(过桥)〔999〕	14		50	13/	13	千克			/
	-其他：									
9114.9010	---宝石轴承〔999〕	14		50	13/	13	千克			/
9114.9090	---其他〔999〕	14		70	13/	13	千克			/39

协定税率 %										特惠税率 %			Article Description
亚太5国	东/冰/格	巴基斯坦	韩国	瑞士	哥达	秘鲁	澳大利亚	新西/坡/智	港/澳/台	亚太2国	老/柬/缅	36/3/1	
	0/0/0	11.5	6.4	4.8	0	0	0	0/0/0	0/0/			0/0/	--Incomplete movements，assembled
	0/0/0	11.5	6.4	4.8	0	0	0	0/0/0	0/0/			0/0/	--Rough movements
													-Other：
	0/0/0	11.5	6.4	4.8	0	0	0	0/0/0	0/0/			0/0/	---Complete movements，unassembled or partly assembled
	0/0/0	11.5	6.4	4.8	0	0	0	0/0/0	0/0/			0/0/	---Other
													Watch cases and parts thereof：
													-Cases of precious metal or of metal clad with precious metal
	0/0/0	10.1	5.6	7.3	0	0	0	0/0/0	0/0/			0/0/	Watch-cases of gold，containing 80% or more by weight of gold
	0/0/0	10.1	5.6	7.3	0	0	0	0/0/0	0/0/			0/0/	Other watch-cases of precious metal or of metal clad with precious metal
9.1	0/0/0	6.3	5.6	4.2	0	0	0	0/0/0	0/0/			0/0/	-Cases of base metal，whether or not gold-plated silver-plated
	0/0/0	10.1	5.6	4.2	0	0	0	0/0/0	0/0/			0/0/	-Other cases
	0/0/0	10.1	5.6	4.2	0	0	0	0/0/0	0/0/			0/0/	-Parts
													Clock cases and cases of a similar type for other goods of this Chapter, and parts thereof：
	0/0/0	10.1	5.6	4.2	0	0	0	0/0/0	0/0/			0/0/	-Cases
	0/0/0	5.4	4.8	3.6	0	0	0	0/0/0	0/0/			0/0/	-Parts
													Watch straps，watch bands and watch bracelets，and parts thereof：
													-Of precious metal or of metal clad with pecious metal
	0/0/0	20	12		0	0	0	0/0/0	0/0/			0/0/	Gold watch straps，containing 80% or more of gold by weight of gold
	0/0/0	20	12		0	0	0	0/0/0	0/0/			0/0/	Other watch straps and parts thereof of precious metals or of metal clad with precious metal
	0/0/0	10.1	5.6	4.2	0	0	0	0/0/0	0/0/			0/0/	-Of base metal，whether or not gold- plated or silver-plated
													-Other
	0/0/0	10.1	5.6	4.2	0	0	0	0/0/0	0/0/			0/0/0	Watch straps，watch bands and watch bracelets，and parts thereof，of endangered animals skins
	0/0/0	10.1	5.6	4.2	0	0	0	0/0/0	0/0/			0/0/0	Other watch straps，watch bands and watch bracelets and parts thereof，of non-metal
													Other clock or watch parts：
	0/0/0	6.3	5.6	4.2	0	0	0	0/0/0	0/0/			0/0/	-Springs，including hair-springs
	0/0/0	10.1	5.6	7.3	0	0	0	0/0/0	0/0/			0/0/	-Dials
9.1	0/0/0	10.1	5.6	4.2	0	0	0	0/0/0	0/0/			0/0/	-Plates and bridges
													-Other：
	0/0/0	6.3	5.6	4.2	0	0	0	0/0/0	0/0/			0/0/	---Jewel bearings
	0/0/0	10.1	5.6	7.3	0	0	0	0/0/0	0/0/			0/0/	---Other

第九十二章
乐器及其零件、附件

注释：

一、本章不包括：

(一)第十五类注释二所规定的贱金属制通用零件(第十五类)或塑料制的类似品(第三十九章)；

(二)第八十五章或第九十章的传声器、扩大器、扬声器、耳机、开关、频闪观测仪及其他附属仪器、器具或设备，虽用于本章物品但未与该物品组成一体或安装在同一机壳内；

(三)玩具乐器或器具(税目 95.03)；

(四)清洁乐器用的刷子(税目 96.03)，或独脚架、双脚架、三脚架及类似品(税目 96.20)；或

(五)收藏品或古物(税目 97.05 或 97.06)。

二、用于演奏税目 92.02、92.06 所列乐器的弓、槌及类似品，如果与该乐器一同进口或出口，数量合理，用途明确，应归入有关乐器的相应税目。

税目 92.09 的卡片、盘或卷，即使与乐器一同进口或出口，也不视为该乐器的组成部分，而应作为单独进口或出口的物品对待。

税则号列	货品名称〔CIQ 扩展编码及品名－T2 表示见附表 2〕	最惠(%)	暂定税率	普通	增值/消费	出口退税	计量单位	监管条件	检验检疫	特殊证件对美关税
92.01	**钢琴，包括自动钢琴、拨弦古钢琴及其他键盘弦乐器：**									
9201.1000	-竖式钢琴〔999〕	10		70	13/	13	台/千克			/35
9201.2000	-大钢琴									
9201.2000 01	完税价格≥5 万美元的大钢琴〔999〕	10	1	70	13/	13	台/千克			/21
9201.2000 90	其他大钢琴〔999〕	10		70	13/	13	台/千克			/30
9201.9000	-其他〔999〕	10		70	13/	13	台/千克			/20
92.02	**其他弦乐器(例如，吉他、小提琴、竖琴)：**									
9202.1000	-弓弦乐器									
9202.1000 11	完税价格≥1.5 万美元的含濒危动物皮及濒危木的弓弦乐器〔999〕	10	1	70	13/	0	只/千克	FE		/26
9202.1000 19	其他含濒危动物皮及濒危木的弓弦乐器〔999〕	10		70	13/	0	只/千克	FE		/35
9202.1000 91	完税价格≥1.5 万美元的不含野生动物皮弓弦乐器〔999〕	10	1	70	13/	13	只/千克			/26
9202.1000 99	其他弓弦乐器〔999〕	10		70	13/	13	只/千克			/35
9202.9000	-其他									
9202.9000 10	含濒危物种成分的其他弦乐器〔101 吉他，102 小提琴，103 大提琴，104 竖琴，105 二胡，106 其他弓弦乐器〕	10		70	13/	0	只/千克	FE		/20
9202.9000 90	其他弦乐器〔101 吉他，102 小提琴，103 大提琴，104 竖琴，105 二胡，106 其他弓弦乐器〕	10		70	13/	13	只/千克			/20
92.05	**管乐器(例如，键盘管风琴、手风琴、单簧管、小号、风笛)，但游艺场风琴及手摇风琴除外：**									
9205.1000	-铜管乐器									
9205.1000 01	完税价格≥2000 美元的铜管乐器〔999〕	10	1	70	13/	13	只/千克			/11
9205.1000 90	其他铜管乐器〔999〕	10		70	13/	13	只/千克			/20
	-其他：									
9205.9010	---键盘管风琴、簧风琴及类似乐器(包括游离金属簧片键盘乐器)〔999〕	10		80	13/	13	只/千克			/35
9205.9020	---手风琴及类似乐器〔999〕	10		80	13/	13	只/千克			/30
9205.9030	---口琴〔999〕	10		80	13/	13	只/千克			/35
9205.9090	---其他									
9205.9090 01	完税价格≥1 万美元的其他管乐器(但游艺场风琴及手摇风琴除外)〔999〕	10	1	70	13/	13	只/千克			/26
9205.9090 91	其他含濒危物种成分的管乐器(但游艺场风琴及手摇风琴除外)〔999〕	10		70	13/	0	只/千克	EF		/35
9205.9090 99	其他管乐器(但游艺场风琴及手摇风琴除外)〔999〕	10		70	13/	13	只/千克			/35
92.06	**打击乐器(例如，鼓、木琴、钹、响板、响葫芦)：**									
9206.0000	打击乐器(例如，鼓、木琴、铙、钹、响板、响葫芦)									

Chapter 92
Musical instruments; parts and accessories of such articles

Notes:

1. This Chapter does not cover:
   (a) Parts of general use, as defined in Note 2 to Section XV, of base metal (Section XV), or similar goods of plastics (Chapter 39);
   (b) Microphones, amplifiers, loudspeakers, headphones, switches, stroboscopes or other accessory instruments, apparatus or equipment of Chapter 85 or 90, for use with but not incorporated in or housed in the same cabinet as instruments of this Chapter;
   (c) Toy instruments or apparatus (heading No. 95.03);
   (d) Brushes for cleaning musical instruments (heading No. 96.03); or
   (e) Collectors' pieces or antiques (heading No. 97.05 or 97.06).
2. Bows and sticks and similar devices used in playing the musical instruments of headings No. 92.02 and 92.06 presented with such instruments in numbers normal thereto and clearly intended for use therewith, are to be classified in the same heading as the relative instruments.
   Cards, discs and rolls of heading No. 92.09 presented with an instrument are to be treated as separate articles and not as forming a part of such instrument.

协定税率 %										特惠税率 %			
亚太5国	东/冰/格	巴基斯坦	韩国	瑞士	哥达	秘鲁	澳大利亚	新西/坡/智	港/澳/台	亚太2国	老/柬/缅	36/3/1	Article Description
													Pianos, including automatic pianos; harpsichords and other keyboard stringed instruments:
	0/0/0	12.6	7	5.3	0	0	0	0/0/0	0/0/			0/0/	-Upright pianos
													-Grand pianos
	0/0/0	12.6	7	5.3	0	0	0	0/0/0	0/0/			0/0/	Grand pianos, duty-paid price≥USD 50000/set
	0/0/0	12.6	7	5.3	0	0	0	0/0/0	0/0/			0/0/	Other grand pianos
	0/0/0	12.6	7	5.3	0	0	0	0/0/0	0/0/			0/0/	-Other
													Other string musical instruments (for example, guitars, violins, harps):
													-Played with a bow
	0/0/0	12.6	0	5.3	0	0	0	0/0/0	0/0/			0/0/0	Played with a bow, duty-paid price≥USD 15000/set, containing endangered animals skins and endangered wood
	0/0/0	12.6	0	5.3	0	0	0	0/0/0	0/0/			0/0/0	Other played with a bow, containing endangered animals skins and endangered wood
	0/0/0	12.6	0	5.3	0	0	0	0/0/0	0/0/			0/0/0	Played with a bow, duty-paid price≥USD 15000/set, other than endangered animals skins
	0/0/0	12.6	0	5.3	0	0	0	0/0/0	0/0/			0/0/0	Other played with a bow
													-Other
	0/0/0	11.2	7	5.3	0	0	0	0/0/0	0/0/			0/0/0	Other played with a bow, containing endangered species composition
	0/0/0	11.2	7	5.3	0	0	0	0/0/0	0/0/			0/0/0	Other string musical instruments
													Wind musical instruments(for example keyboard pipe organs、accordions、clarinets、trumpets、bag pipes) other than fairground or gans and mechanical street organs:
													-Brass-wind instruments
	0/0/0	12.6	0	5.3	0	0	0	0/0/0	0/0/			0/0/0	Brass-wind instruments, duty-paid price≥USD 2000/set
	0/0/0	12.6	0	5.3	0	0	0	0/0/0	0/0/			0/0/0	Other brass-wind instruments
													-Other:
	0/0/0	20	12	6	0	0	0	0/0/0	0/0/			0/0/	---Keyboard pipe organs; harmoniums and similar keyboard instruments with free metal reeds
	0/0/0	21	12.6	6.3	0	0	0	0/0/0	0/0/			0/0/	---Accordions and similar instruments
	0/0/0	21	12.6	6.3	0	0	0	0/0/0	0/0/			0/0/	---mouth organs
													---Other
	0/0/0	12.6	0	5.3	0	0	0	0/0/0	0/0/			0/0/	Other brass-wind instruments, duty-paid price ≥USD 10000/set
	0/0/0	12.6	0	5.3	0	0	0	0/0/0	0/0/			0/0/	Other wind musical instruments, containing components of endangered animals, other than fairground organs and mechanical street organs:
	0/0/0	12.6	0	5.3	0	0	0	0/0/0	0/0/			0/0/	Other wind musical instruments, other than fairground organs and mechanical street organs:
													Percussion musical instruments (for example, drums, xylophones, cymbals, castanets, maracas):
													Percussion musical instruments (for example, drums, xylophones, cymbals, castanets, maracas)

税则号列	货品名称〔CIQ 扩展编码及品名—T2 表示见附表 2〕	最惠(%)	暂定税率	普通	增值/消费	出口退税	计量单位	监管条件	检验检疫	特殊证件对美关税
9206.0000 10	含濒危动物皮及濒危木的打击乐器(例如,鼓、木琴、钹、响板)〔101 鼓,102 钹,103 锣,104 木琴,105 其他打击乐器〕	10		70	13/	0	只/千克	EF		/20
9206.0000 90	其他打击乐器(例如,鼓、木琴、钹、响板)〔101 鼓,102 钹,103 锣,104 木琴,105 其他打击乐器〕	10		70	13/	13	只/千克			/20
92.07	**通过电产生或扩大声音的乐器(例如,电风琴、电吉他、电手风琴):**									
9207.1000	-键盘乐器,但手风琴除外〔101 电子琴,102 电风琴,103 其他电声乐器〕	12		100	13/	13	只/千克		L	/37
9207.9000	-其他									
9207.9000 10	其他通过电产生或扩大声音的含濒危物种成分的乐器〔301 电吉他,302 其他电声乐器〕	12		100	13/	0	个/千克	EF		/22
9207.9000 90	其他通过电产生或扩大声音的乐器〔301 电吉他,302 其他电声乐器〕	12		100	13/	13	个/千克			/22
92.08	**百音盒、游艺场风琴、手摇风琴、机械鸣禽、乐锯及本章其他税目未列名的其他乐器;各种媒诱音响器、哨子、号角、口吹音响信号器:**									
9208.1000	-百音盒〔999〕	10		80	13/	13	个/千克			/30
9208.9000	-其他〔999〕	10		80	13/	13	个/千克			/35
92.09	**乐器的零件(例如百音盒的机械装置)、附件(例如,机械乐器用的卡片、盘及带卷);节拍器、音叉及各种定音管:**									
9209.3000	-乐器用的弦〔999〕	10		70	13/	13	千克			/20
	-其他:									
9209.9100	--钢琴的零件、附件									
9209.9100 10	钢琴含濒危物种成分的零件、附件〔301〕	10		70	13/	0	千克	EF		/35
9209.9100 90	钢琴的其他零件、附件〔301〕	10		70	13/	13	千克			/35
9209.9200	--税目 92.02 所列乐器的零件、附件									
9209.9200 10	品目 92.02 所列乐器含濒危物种成分的零件、附件〔301〕	10		70	13/	0	千克	EF		/20
9209.9200 90	品目 92.02 所列乐器的其他零件、附件〔301〕	10		70	13/	13	千克			/20
9209.9400	--税目 92.07 所列乐器的零件、附件〔999〕									
9209.9400 10	品目 92.07 所列乐器含濒危物种成分的零件、附件〔301〕	10		70	13/	0	千克	EF		/35
9209.9400 90	品目 92.07 所列乐器的其他零件、附件〔301〕	10		70	13/	13	千克			/35
	--其他:									
9209.9910	---节拍器、音叉及定音管〔999〕	10		70	13/	13	千克			/35
9209.9920	---百音盒的机械装置〔999〕	10		70	13/	13	千克			/35
9209.9990	---其他〔999〕									
9209.9990 10	本章其他编号未列名的含濒危物种成分的乐器零件〔301〕	10		70	13/	0	千克	EF		/30
9209.9990 90	本章其他编号未列名的其他乐器零件〔301〕	10		70	13/	13	千克			/30

协定税率 %										特惠税率 %			
亚太5国	东/冰/格	巴基斯坦	韩国	瑞士	哥达	秘鲁	澳大利亚	新西/坡/智	港/澳/台	亚太2国	老/柬/缅	36/3/1	Article Description
	0/0/0	11.2	7	5.3	0	0	0	0/0/0	0/0/			0/0/0	Percussion musical instruments (for example, drums, xylophones, cymbals, castanets, maracas) containing endangered animal skins and endangered wood
	0/0/0	11.2	7	5.3	0	0	0	0/0/0	0/0/			0/0/0	Other percussion musical instruments (for example, drums, xylophones, cymbals, castanets, maracas)
													Musical instruments, the sound of which is produced or must be amplified electrically (for example, organs, guitars, accordions):
	0/0/0	30		12	0	0	0	0/0/0	0/0/			0/0/	-Keyboard instruments, other than accordions
													-Other
	0/0/0	30		12	0	0	0	0/0/0	0/0/			0/0/	Other musical instruments, the sound of which is produced or must be amplified electrically, containing components of endangered animals
	0/0/0	30		12	0	0	0	0/0/0	0/0/			0/0/	Other musical instruments, the sound of which is produced or must be amplified electrically
													Musical boxes, fairground organs, mechanical street organs, mechanical singing birds, musical saws and other musical instruments not falling within any other heading of this Chapter; decoy calls of all kinds; whistles, call horns and other mouth-blown sound signalling instruments:
	0/0/0	22	15.4	6.6	0	0	0	0/0/0	0/0/			0/0/	-Musical boxes
	0/0/0		15.4	6.6	0	0	0	0/0/0	0/0/			0/0/	-Other
													Parts (for example, mechanisms for musical boxes) and accessories (for example, cards, discs and rolls for mechanical instruments) of musical instruments; metronomes, tuning forks and pitch pipes of all kinds:
	0/0/0	12.6	7	5.3	0	0	0	0/0/0	0/0/			0/0/	-Musical instrument strings
													-Other:
													--Parts and accessories for pianos
	0/0/0	12.6	7	5.3	0	0	0	0/0/0	0/0/			0/0/	Piano Parts, Accessories with Endangered Species Components
	0/0/0	12.6	7	5.3	0	0	0	0/0/0	0/0/			0/0/	Other parts and accessories for piano
													--Parts and accessories for the musical instruments of heading No. 92. 02
	0/0/0	12.6	7	5.3	0	0	0	0/0/0	0/0/			0/0/0	Items listed in heading 92.02 contain parts and accessories containing endangered species
	0/0/0	12.6	7	5.3	0	0	0	0/0/0	0/0/			0/0/0	Other parts and accessories of musical instruments listed in heading 92.02
													--Parts and accessories for the musical instruments of heading No. 92. 07
	0/0/0	12.6	10.5	5.3	0	0	0	0/0/0	0/0/			0/0/	Items listed in heading 92.07 contain parts and accessories containing endangered species
	0/0/0	12.6	10.5	5.3	0	0	0	0/0/0	0/0/			0/0/	Other parts and accessories of musical instruments listed in heading 92.07
													--Other:
	0/0/0	12.6	7	5.3	0	0	0	0/0/0	0/0/			0/0/	---Metsonomes tuning froks and pitch pipes
6.5	0/0/0	12.6	7	5.3	0	0	0	0/0/0	0/0/			0/0/	---Mechanisms for musicol boxes
													---Other
	0/0/0	12.6	7	5.3	0	0	0	0/0/0	0/0/			0/0/0	Unlisted musical instrument parts containing endangered species in this Chapter
	0/0/0	12.6	7	5.3	0	0	0	0/0/0	0/0/			0/0/0	Other musical instrument parts not numbered in this chapter

第十九类
武器、弹药及其零件、附件

第九十三章
武器、弹药及其零件、附件

注释：

一、本章不包括：

（一）第三十六章的货品（例如，火帽、雷管、信号弹）；

（二）第十五类注释二所规定的贱金属制通用零件（第十五类）或塑料制的类似品（第三十九章）；

（三）装甲战斗车辆（税目 87.10）；

（四）武器用的望远镜瞄准具及其他光学装置（第九十章），但安装在武器上或与武器一同进口或出口以备安装在该武器上的除外；

（五）弓、箭、钝头击剑或玩具（第九十五章）；

（六）收藏品及古物（税目 97.05 或 97.06）。

二、税目 93.06 所称"零件"，不包括税目 85.26 的无线电设备及雷达设备。

税则号列	货品名称〔CIQ 扩展编码及品名—T2 表示见附表 2〕	最惠(%)	暂定税率	普通	增值/消费	出口退税	计量单位	监管条件	检验检疫	特殊证件对美关税
93.01	**军用武器，但左轮手枪、其他手枪及税目 93.07 的兵器除外：**									
	-火炮武器（例如，榴弹炮及迫击炮）：									
9301.1010	--自推进的〔999〕	13		80	13/	0	座/千克			/
9301.1090	--其他〔999〕	13		80	13/	0	座/千克			/
9301.2000	-火箭发射装置；火焰喷射器；手榴弹发射器；鱼雷发射管及类似发射装置自推进的〔999〕	13		80	13/	0	个/千克			/
9301.9000	-其他〔999〕	13		80	13/	0	支/千克			/
93.02	**左轮手枪及其他手枪，但税目 93.03 或 93.04 的货品除外：**									
9302.0000	左轮手枪及其他手枪，但税目 93.03 或 93.04 的货品除外〔999〕	13		80	13/	0	支/千克			/
93.03	**靠爆炸药发射的其他火器及类似装置（例如，运动用猎枪及步枪、前装枪、维利式信号枪及其他专为发射信号弹的装置、发射空包弹的左轮手枪和其他手枪、弩枪式无痛捕杀器、抛缆枪）：**									
9303.1000	-前装枪〔999〕	13		80	13/	13	支/千克			/
9303.2000	-其他运动、狩猎或打靶用猎枪，包括组合式滑膛来复枪〔999〕	13		80	13/	13	支/千克			/
9303.3000	-其他运动、狩猎或打靶用步枪〔999〕	13		80	13/	13	支/千克			/
9303.9000	-其他〔999〕									
9303.9000 10	复核射孔器（已装配）	13		80	13/	13	支/千克	k		/33
9303.9000 90	其他火器及类似装置	13		80	13/	13	支/千克			/33
93.04	**其他武器（例如，弹簧枪、气枪、气手枪、警棍），但不包括税目 93.07 的货品：**									
9304.0000	其他武器（例如，弹簧枪、气枪、警棍），但不包括税目 93.07 的货品〔999〕	13		80	13/	13	支/千克			/23
93.05	**税目 93.01 至 93.04 所列物品的零件、附件：**									
9305.1000	-左轮手枪或其他手枪用〔999〕	13		80	13/	0,13	千克			/
9305.2000	-税目 93.03 的猎枪或步枪用〔999〕	13		80	13/	0,13	千克			/
	-其他：									
9305.9100	--税目 93.01 的军用武器用〔999〕	13		80	13/	0	千克			/
9305.9900	--其他〔999〕	13		80	13/	0,13	千克			/23
93.06	**炸弹、手榴弹、鱼雷、地雷、水雷、导弹及类似武器及其零件；子弹、其他弹药和射弹及其零件，包括弹丸及弹垫：**									
	-猎枪子弹及其零件；气枪弹丸：									
9306.2100	--猎枪子弹〔999〕	13		80	13/	13	千克			/
9306.2900	--其他〔999〕	13		80	13/	13	千克			/23
	-其他子弹及其零件：									
9306.3080	---铆接机或类似工具用及弩枪式无痛捕杀器用子弹及其零件〔999〕	13		80	13/	0,13	千克			/
9306.3090	---其他〔999〕	13		80	13/	0,13	千克			/
9306.9000	-其他									

SECTION XIX
ARMS AND AMMUNITION; PARTS AND ACCESSORIES THEREOF

Chapter 93
Arms and ammunition; parts and accessories thereof

Notes:

1. This Chapter does not cover:
   (a) Goods of Chapter 36 (for example, percussion caps, detonators, signalling flares);
   (b) Parts of general use, as defined in Note 2 to Section XV, of base metal (Section XV), or similar goods of plastics (Chapter 39);
   (c) Armoured fighting vehicles (heading No. 87.10);
   (d) Telescopic sights and other optical devices suitable for use with arms, unless mounted on a firearm or presented with the firearm on which they are designed to be mounted (Chapter 90);
   (e) Bows, arrows, fencing foils or toys (Chapter 95);
   (f) Collectors' pieces or antiques (heading No. 97.05 or 97.06).
2. In heading No. 93.06, the reference to "parts thereof" does not include radio or radar apparatus of heading No. 85.26.

协定税率 %										特惠税率 %			Article Description
亚太5国	东/冰/格	巴基斯坦	韩国	瑞士	哥达	秘鲁	澳大利亚	新西/坡/智	港/澳/台	亚太2国	老/柬/缅	36/3/1	
													Military weapons, other than revolvers, pistols and the arms of heading No. 93.07:
													-Artillery weapons (for example, guns, howitzers and mortars):
	0/0/0	5.9	5.2	3.9	0	0	0	0/0/0	0/0/			0/0/	---Self-propelled
	0/0/0	5.9	5.2	3.9	0	0	0	0/0/0	0/0/			0/0/	---Other
	0/0/0	5.9	5.2	3.9	0	0	0	0/0/0	0/0/			0/0/	-Rocket launchers; flame-throwers; grenade launchers; torpedo tubes and similar projectors
	0/0/0	5.9	5.2	3.9	0	0	0	0/0/0	0/0/			0/0/	-Other
													Revolvers and pistols, other than those of heading 93.03 or 93.04:
	0/0/0	5.9	5.2	3.9	0	0	0	0/0/0	0/0/			0/0/	Revolvers and pistols, other than those of heading No. 93.03 or 93.04
													Other firearms and similar devices which operate by the firing of an explosive charge (for example, sporting shotguns and rifles, muzzle-loading firearms, Very pistols and other devices designed to project only signal flares, pistols and revolvers for firing blank ammunition, captive-bolt humane killers, linethrowing guns):
	0/0/0	5.9	5.2	3.9	0	0	0	0/0/0	0/0/			0/0/	-Muzzle-loading firearms
	0/0/0	5.9	5.2	6.8	0	0	0	0/0/0	0/0/			0/0/	-Other sporting, hunting or target shooting shotguns, including combination shotgunrifles
	0/0/0	5.9	5.2	3.9	0	0	0	0/0/0	0/0/			0/0/	-Other sporting, hunting or target shooting rifles
													-Other
	0/0/0	5.9	5.2	3.9	0	0	0	0/0/0	0/0/		//	0/0/	Review perforator (assembled)
	0/0/0	5.9	5.2	3.9	0	0	0	0/0/0	0/0/		//	0/0/	Other firearms and similar devices
													Other arms (for example, spring, air or gas guns and pistols, truncheons), excluding those of heading No. 93.07:
	0/0/0	5.9	5.2		0	0	0	0/0/0	0/0/			0/0/	Other arms (for example, spring, air or gas guns and pistols, truncheons), excluding those of heading No. 93.07
													Parts and accessories of articles of headings No. 93.01 to 93.04:
	0/0/0	5.9	5.2	3.9	0	0	0	0/0/0	0/0/			0/0/	-Of revolvers or pistols
	0/0/0	5.9	5.2	3.9	0	0	0	0/0/0	0/0/			0/0/	-Of shotguns or rifles of heading No. 93.03
													-Other:
	0/0/0	5.9	5.2	3.9	0	0	0	0/0/0	0/0/			0/0/	--Of military weapons of heading No. 93.01
	0/0/0	5.9	5.2	3.9	0	0	0	0/0/0	0/0/			0/0/	--Other
													Bombs, grenades, torpedoes, mines, missiles, and similar munitions of war and parts thereof; cartridges and other ammunition and projectiles and parts thereof, including shot and cartridge wads:
													-Shotgun cartridges and parts thereof; air gun pellets:
	0/0/0	5.9	5.2	3.9	0	0	0	0/0/0	0/0/			0/0/	--Cartridges
	0/0/0	5.9	5.2	3.9	0	0	0	0/0/0	0/0/			0/0/	--Other
													-Other cartridges and parts thereof:
	0/0/0	5.9	5.2	3.9	0	0	0	0/0/0	0/0/			0/0/	---Cartridges for riveting or similar tools or for captivebolt humane killers and parts thereof
	0/0/0	5.9	5.2	3.9	0	0	0	0/0/0	0/0/			0/0/	---Other
													-Other

税则号列		货品名称〔CIQ 扩展编码及品名—T2 表示见附表 2〕	最惠(%)	暂定税率	普通	增值/消费	出口退税	计量单位	监管条件	检验检疫	特殊证件对美关税
9306.9000	10	两用物项管制的导弹及其零件(能把 500 千克以上有效载荷投掷到 300 千米以上的)〔999〕	13		80	13/	0	千克	3		/
9306.9000	20	运载火箭(能把 500 千克以上有效载荷投掷到 300 千米以上的)〔999〕	13		80	13/	0	千克	3		/
9306.9000	30	探空火箭(能把 500 千克以上有效载荷投掷到 300 千米以上的)〔999〕	13		80	13/	0	千克	3		/
9306.9000	40	巡航导弹(能把 500 千克以上有效载荷投掷到 300 千米以上的)〔999〕	13		80	13/	0	千克	3		/
9306.9000	50	聚能射孔弹、聚能切割弹、高能气体压裂弹等油气井用射弹	13		80	13/	13	千克	k		/
9306.9000	90	其他弹药和射弹及其零件(包括炸弹、手榴弹、鱼雷、地雷、水雷、导弹等)〔999〕	13		80	13/	0,13	千克			/
93.07		**剑、短弯刀、刺刀、长矛和类似的武器及其零件;刀鞘、剑鞘:**									
9307.0010		---军用									
9307.0010	10	军用刀鞘、剑鞘、濒危动物制〔999〕	13		80	13/	0	千克/件	FE		/23
9307.0010	90	其他军用剑、刀、长矛和类似的武器及其零件(包括刀鞘、剑鞘)〔999〕	13		80	13/	0	千克/件			/23
9307.0090		---其他									
9307.0090	10	其他濒危动物制的刀鞘、剑鞘〔999〕	13		80	13/	13	千克/件	FE		/23
9307.0090	90	其他剑、刀、长矛和类似的武器及其零件(包括刀鞘、剑鞘)〔999〕	13		80	13/	13	千克/件			/23

协定税率 %										特惠税率 %			Article Description
亚太5国	东/冰/格	巴基斯坦	韩国	瑞士	哥达	秘鲁	澳大利亚	新西/坡/智	港/澳/台	亚太2国	老/柬/缅	36/3/1	
	0/0/0	5.9	5.2	3.9	0	0	0	0/0/0	0/0/			0/0/	Missiles and parts thereof under contorol of sensitive item(capable of throwing an available load over 500kg beyond 300km)
	0/0/0	5.9	5.2	3.9	0	0	0	0/0/0	0/0/			0/0/	Carrier rockets (capable of throwing an available load over 500kg beyond 300km)
	0/0/0	5.9	5.2	3.9	0	0	0	0/0/0	0/0/			0/0/	Sounding rockets (capable of throwing an available load over 500kg beyond 300km)
	0/0/0	5.9	5.2	3.9	0	0	0	0/0/0	0/0/			0/0/	Cruise missiles (capable of throwing an available load over 500kg beyond 300km)
	0/0/0	5.9	5.2	3.9	0	0	0	0/0/0	0/0/		//	0/0/	Charge for oil and gas wells, such as shaped charge, shaped charge, high energy gas fracturing projectile, etc.
	0/0/0	5.9	5.2	3.9	0	0	0	0/0/0	0/0/			0/0/	Other ammunition and projectiles and parts thereof (including bombs, grenades, torpedoes, mines, missiles)
													Swords, cutlasses, bayonets, lances and similar arms and parts thereof and scabbards and sheaths therefor:
													---For military
	0/0/0	5.9	5.2	3.9	0	0	0	0/0/0	0/0/			0/0/0	Scabbards and sheaths of endangered animals, for military
	0/0/0	5.9	5.2	3.9	0	0	0	0/0/0	0/0/			0/0/0	Other swords, cutlasses, lances and similar arms and parts thereof (including scabbards and sheaths), for military
													---Other
	0/0/0	5.9	5.2	3.9	0	0	0	0/0/0	0/0/			0/0/0	Scabbards and sheaths of endangered animals
	0/0/0	5.9	5.2	3.9	0	0	0	0/0/0	0/0/			0/0/0	Other swords, cutlasses, lances and similar arms and parts thereof (including scabbards and sheaths)

第二十类
杂 项 制 品

第九十四章

家具;寝具、褥垫、弹簧床垫、软坐垫及类似的填充制品;未列名灯具及照明装置;发光标志、发光铭牌及类似品;活动房屋

注释:

一、本章不包括:

(一)第三十九章、第四十章或第六十三章的充气或充水的褥垫、枕头及坐垫;

(二)落地镜〔例如税目 70.09 的试衣镜(旋转镜)〕;

(三)第七十一章的物品;

(四)第十五类注释二所规定的贱金属制通用零件(第十五类)、塑料制的类似品(第三十九章)或税目 83.03 的保险箱;

(五)冷藏或冷冻设备专用的特制家具(税目 84.18);缝纫机专用的特制家具(税目 84.52);

(六)第八十五章的灯具及照明装置;

(七)税目 85.18、85.19、85.21 或税目 85.25 至 85.28 所列装置专用的特制家具(应分别归入税目 85.18、85.22 或 85.29);

(八)税目 87.14 的物品;

(九)装有税目 90.18 所列牙科用器具或漱口盂的牙科用椅(税目 90.18);

(十)第九十一章的物品(例如,钟及钟壳);

(十一)玩具家具、玩具灯或玩具照明装置(税目 95.03)、台球桌或其他供游戏用的特制家具(税目 95.04)、魔术用的特制家具或中国灯笼及类似的装饰品(电气彩灯串除外)(税目 95.05)。

(十二)独脚架、双脚架、三脚架及类似品(税目 96.20)

二、税目 94.01 至 94.03 的物品(零件除外),只适用于落地式的物品。

对下列物品,即使是悬挂的、固定在墙壁上的或叠摞的,仍归入上述各税目:

(一)碗橱、书柜、其他架式家具(包括与将其固定于墙上的支撑物一同报验的单层搁架)及组合家具。

(二)坐具及床。

三、(一)税目 94.01 至 94.03 所列货品的零件,不包括玻璃(包括镜子)、大理石或其他石料以及第六十八章及第六十九章所列任何其他材料的片、块(不论是否切割成形,但未与其他零件组装);

(二)税目 94.04 的货品,如果单独进口或出口,不能作为税目 94.01、94.02 或 94.03 所列货品的零件归类。

四、税目 94.06 所称"活动房屋",是指在工厂制成成品或制成部件并一同进口或出口,供以后在有关地点上组装的房屋,例如,工地用房、办公室、学校、店铺、工作棚、车房或类似的建筑物。

税则号列		货品名称〔CIQ 扩展编码及品名—T2 表示见附表 2〕	最惠(%)	暂定税率	普通	增值/消费	出口退税	计量单位	监管条件	检验检疫	特殊证件对美关税
94.01		**坐具(包括能作床用的两用椅,但税目 94.02 的货品除外)及其零件:**									
9401.1000		-飞机用坐具〔999〕	0		100	13/	13	个/千克			/20
		-机动车辆用坐具:									
9401.2010		---皮革或再生皮革面的[T2]	6		100	13/	13	个/千克		L	/11
9401.2090		---其他〔101 其他车辆零部件,102 其他家具,103 靠垫〕	6		100	13/	13	个/千克		L	/11
9401.3000		-可调高度的转动坐具〔999〕	0		100	13/	13	个/千克			/10
		-能做床用的两用椅,但庭园坐具或野营设备除外:									
9401.4010		---皮革或再生皮革面的〔999〕	0		100	13/	13	个/千克		L	/25
9401.4090		---其他〔999〕	0		100	13/	13	个/千克		L	/25
		-藤、柳条、竹及类似材料制的坐具:									
9401.5200		--竹制的〔999〕	0		100	13/	13	个/千克	AB	PQ	/25
9401.5300		--藤制的〔999〕	0		100	13/	13	个/千克	AB	PQ	/25
9401.5900		--其他〔101 柳及柳制品,102 柳条及类似材料制的家具〕	0		100	13/	13	个/千克	AB	PQ	/
		-木框架的其他坐具:									
		--装软垫的:									
9401.6110		---皮革或再生皮革面的〔101 其他木制品,102 软体家具〕	0		100	13/	13	个/千克	AB	PQ	/25
9401.6190		---其他〔101 其他木制品,102 软体家具〕	0		100	13/	13	个/千克	AB	PQ	/10
9401.6900		--其他									
9401.6900	10	其他濒危木框架的坐具〔101 其他木制品,102 其他家具〕	0		100	13/	0	个/千克	ABEF	PQ	/25
9401.6900	90	其他木框架的坐具(不包括税目 9401.1000～9401.5000 的坐具)〔101 其他木制品,102 其他家具〕	0		100	13/	13	个/千克	AB	PQ	/25

SECTION XX
MISCELLANEOUS MANUFACTURED ARTICLES
Chapter 94
Furniture; bedding, mattresses, mattress supports, cushions and similar stuffed furnishings; lamps and lighting fittings, not elsewhere specified or included; illuminated signs, illuminated name-plates and the like; prefabricated buildings

Notes:

1. This Chapter does not cover:
   (a) Pneumatic or water mattresses, pillows or cushions, of Chapter 39, 40 or 63;
   (b) Mirrors designed for placing on the floor or ground (for example, cheval-glasses (swing-mirrors) of heading No. 70.09);
   (c) Articles of Chapter 71;
   (d) Parts of general use as defined in Note 2 to Section XV, of base metal (Section XV), or similar goods of plastics (Chapter 39), or safes of heading NO. 83.03;
   (e) Furniture specially designed as parts of refrigerating or freezing equipment of heading 84.18; furniture specially designed for sewing machines (heading NO. 84.52);
   (f) Lamps or lighting fittings of Chapter 85;
   (g) Furniture specially designed as parts of apparatus of heading No. 85.18 (heading No. 85.18), of headings No. 85.19 to 85.21 (heading 85.22) or of headings Nos. 85.25 to 85.28 (heading No. 85.29);
   (h) Articles of heading No. 87.14;
   (ij) Dentists' chairs incorporating dental appliances of heading 90.18 or dentists' spittoons (heading No. 90.18);
   (k) Articles of Chapter 91 (for example, clocks and clock cases);
   (l) Toy furniture or toy lamps or lighting fittings (heading No. 95.03), billiard tables or other furniture specially constructed for games (heading No. 95.04), furniture for conjuring tricks or decorations (other than electric garlands) such as Chinese lanterns (heading No. 95.05).
2. The articles (other than parts) referred to in headings No. 94.01 to 94.03 are to be classified in those headings only if they are designed for placing on the floor or ground.
   The following are, however, to be classified in the above-mentioned headings even if they are designed to be hung, to be fixed to the wall or to stand one on the other:
   (a) Cupboards, bookcases, other shelved furniture (including single shelves presented with supports for fixing them to the wall) and unit furniture
   (b) Seats and beds.
3. (a) In headings No. 94.01 to 94.03 references to parts of goods do not include references to sheets or slabs (whether or not cut to shape but not combined with other parts) of glass (including mirrors), marble or other stone or of any other material referred to in Chapter 68 and 69.
   (b) Goods described in heading No. 94.04, presented separately, are not to be classified in heading No. 94.01, 94.02 or 94.03 as parts of goods.
4. For the purposes of heading No. 94.06, the expression "prefabricated buildings" means buildings which are finished in the factory or put up as elements, presented together, to be assembled on site, such as housing or worksite accommodation, offices, schools, shops, sheds, garages or similar buildings.

协定税率 %										特惠税率 %			Article Description
亚太5国	东/冰/格	巴基斯坦	韩国	瑞士	哥达	秘鲁	澳大利亚	新西/坡/智	港/澳/台	亚太2国	老/柬/缅	36/3/1	
													Seats (other than those of heading No. 94.02), whether or not convertible into beds, and parts thereof:
												0/0/0	-Seats of a kind used for aircraft
													-Seats of a kind used for motor vehicles:
	5/0/0	8	7	0	0	0	0	0//0	0/0/			0/0/	---With outer surface of leather or composition leather
	5/0/0	8	6	0	0	0	0	0//0	0/0/			0/0/	---Other
												0/0/0	-Swivel seats with variable height adjustment
													-Seats other than garden seats or camping equipment, convertible into beds:
												0/0/0	---With outer surface of leather or composition leather
												0/0/0	---Other
													-Seats of cane, osier, bamboo or similar materials:
											0//	0/0/0	--Of bamboo
											0//	0/0/0	--Of rattan
											0//	0/0/0	--Other
													-Other seats, with wooden frames:
													--Upholstered:
												0/0/0	---With outer surface of leather or composition leather
												0/0/0	---Other
													--Other
												0/0/0	Other seats, with endangered wood frames
												0/0/0	Other seats, with wood frames (other than seats of No. 94011000～94015000)

税则号列	货品名称〔CIQ扩展编码及品名—T2表示见附表2〕	最惠(%)	暂定税率	普通	增值/消费	出口退税	计量单位	监管条件	检验检疫	特殊证件对美关税
	-金属框架的其他坐具：									
	--装软垫的：									
9401.7110	---皮革或再生皮革面的〔999〕	0		100	13/	13	个/千克			/25
9401.7190	---其他〔999〕	0		100	13/	13	个/千克			/20
9401.7900	--其他〔101 其他家具，102 其他体育竞技运动器具〕	0		100	13/	13	个/千克			/20
	-其他坐具：									
9401.8010	---石制的〔999〕	0		100	13/	13	个/千克			/25
9401.8090	---其他									
9401.8090 10	其他濒危木制坐具［T2］	0		100	13/	0	个/千克	EF		/5
9401.8090 91	儿童用汽车安全坐椅〔999〕	0		100	13/	13	个/千克	A	LM	/5
9401.8090 99	其他坐具〔101 其他家具，102 靠垫，103 其他日用纺织制品〕	0		100	13/	13	个/千克		L	/5
	-零件：									
	---机动车辆用：									
9401.9011	----坐椅调角器〔101 其他车辆零部件，102 其他家具〕	6		100	13/	13	套/千克			/11
9401.9019	----其他〔101 其他车辆零部件，102 家具零件〕	0		100	13/	13	千克		L	/5
9401.9090	---其他									
9401.9090 10	其他座具的濒危木制零件〔999〕	0		100	13/	0	千克	EF		/10
9401.9090 90	其他座具的零件〔301 家具零件，302 其他金属及制品〕	0		100	13/	13	千克			/10
94.02	**医疗、外科、牙科或兽医用家具(例如，手术台、检查台、带机械装置的病床、牙科用椅)；有旋转、倾斜、升降装置的理发用椅及类似椅；上述物品的零件：**									
	-牙科、理发及类似用途的椅及其零件：									
9402.1010	---理发用椅及其零件〔999〕	0		100	13/	13	个/千克			/
9402.1090	---其他〔999〕	0		30	13/	13	个/千克			/10
9402.9000	-其他〔999〕	0		30	13/	13	件/千克			/10
94.03	**其他家具及其零件：**									
9403.1000	-办公室用金属家具〔999〕	0		100	13/	13	件/千克			/20
9403.2000	-其他金属家具〔999〕	0		100	13/	13	件/千克			/20
9403.3000	-办公室用木家具									
9403.3000 10	濒危木制办公室用木家具〔101 其他木制品，102 木家具〕	0		100	13/	0	件/千克	ABFE	PQ	/20
9403.3000 90	其他办公室用木家具〔101 其他木制品，102 木家具〕	0		100	13/	13	件/千克	AB	MPQ	/20
9403.4000	-厨房用木家具									
9403.4000 10	濒危木制厨房用木家具〔101 其他木制品，102 木家具〕	0		100	13/	0	件/千克	ABFE	PQ	/25
9403.4000 90	其他厨房用木家具〔101 其他木制品，102 木家具〕	0		100	13/	13	件/千克	AB	MPQ	/25
	-卧室用木家具：									
9403.5010	---红木制									
9403.5010 10	卧室用濒危红木制家具〔101 其他木制品，102 木家具〕	0		100	13/	0	件/千克	ABFE	PQ	/
9403.5010 90	其他卧室用红木制家具〔101 其他木制品，102 木家具〕	0		100	13/	13	件/千克	AB	PQ	/
	---其他：									
9403.5091	----天然漆(大漆)漆木家具［T2］	0		100	13/	13	件/千克	AB	MPQ	/20
9403.5099	----其他									
9403.5099 10	卧室用其他濒危木家具〔101 其他木制品，102 木家具〕	0		100	13/	0	件/千克	ABFE	PQ	/25
9403.5099 90	卧室用其他木家具［T2］	0		100	13/	13	件/千克	AB	MPQ	/25
	-其他木家具：									
9403.6010	---红木制									
9403.6010 10	濒危红木制其他家具(非卧室用)〔101 其他木制品，102 木家具〕	0		100	13/	0	件/千克	ABFE	PQ	/25
9403.6010 90	其他红木制家具(非卧室用)〔101 其他木制品，102 木家具〕	0		100	13/	13	件/千克	AB	PQ	/25
	---其他：									
9403.6091	----天然漆(大漆)漆木家具［T2］	0		100	13/	13	件/千克	AB	MPQ	/25
9403.6099	----其他									
9403.6099 10	濒危木制其他家具(非卧室用)［T2］	0		100	13/	0	件/千克	ABFE	PQ	/25
9403.6099 90	其他木家具(非卧室用)〔101 其他木制品，102 木家具〕	0		100	13/	13	件/千克	AB	PQ	/25
9403.7000	-塑料家具〔999〕	0		100	13/	13	件/千克			/20
	-其他材料制的家具，包括藤、柳条、竹或类似材料制的：									
9403.8200	--竹制的〔999 竹制或藤制家具，998 其他竹及竹制品〕	0		100	13/	13	件/千克	AB	PQ	/
9403.8300	--藤制的〔999 竹制或藤制家具，998 藤及藤制品〕	0		100	13/	13	件/千克	AB	PQ	/
	--其他：									
9403.8910	---柳条及类似材料制的［T2］	0		100	13/	13	件/千克	AB	PQ	/
9403.8920	---石制的〔999〕	0		100	13/	13	件/千克			/25
9403.8990	---其他〔999〕	0		100	13/	13	件/千克			/25
9403.9000	-零件									

协定税率 %										特惠税率 %			
亚太5国	东/冰/格	巴基斯坦	韩国	瑞士	哥达	秘鲁	澳大利亚	新西/坡/智	港/澳/台	亚太2国	老/柬/缅	36/3/1	Article Description
													-Other seats, with metal frames:
													--Upholstered:
												0/0/0	---With outer surface of leather or composition leather
												0/0/0	---Other
												0/0/0	--Other
													-Other seats:
												0/0/0	---Of stone
													---Other
												0/0/0	Other seats of endangered wood
												0/0/0	Automobile safety seat for children
												0/0/0	Other seats
													-Parts:
													---Of the motor Vehicles:
	5/0/0	8		0	0	0	0	0//0	0/0/			0/0/0	----Seat angle requlating devices
												0/0/0	----Other
													---Other
												0/0/0	other parts of seats of endangered wood
												0/0/0	other parts of seats
													Medical, surgical, dental or veterinary furniture (for example, operating tables, examination tables, hospital beds with mechanical fittings, dentists' chairs); barbers' chairs and similar chairs, having rotating as well as both reclining and elevating movements; parts of the foregoing articles:
													-Dentists', barbers' or similar chairs and parts thereof:
												0/0/0	--Barbers chairs and parts thereof
												0/0/0	---Other
												0/0/0	-Other
													Other furniture and parts thereof:
												0/0/0	-Metal furniture of a kind used in offices
												0/0/0	-Other metal furniture
													-Wooden furniture of a kind used in offices
											0/0/	0/0/0	Furniture of endangered wood, of a kind used in offices
											0/0/	0/0/0	Other wooden furniture of a kind used in offices
													-Wooden furniture of a kind used in the kitchen
											/0/	0/0/0	Furniture of endangered wood, of a kind used in the kitchen
											/0/	0/0/0	Other wooden furniture of a kind used in the kitchen
													-Wooden furniture of a kind used in the bedroom:
													---Of rose wood
											/0/	0/0/0	Furniture of endangered rose wood, of a kind used in the bedroom
											/0/	0/0/0	Other furniture of rose wood, of a kind used in the bedroom
													---Other:
											/0/	0/0/0	----Lacquer, lacquer wood furniture
													----Other
											/0/	0/0/0	Furniture of other endangered wood, of a kind used in the bedroom
											/0/	0/0/0	Furniture of other wood, of a kind used in the bedroom
													-Other wooden furniture:
													---Of rose wood
											/0/	0/0/0	Other furniture of rose endangered wood (other than use in the bedroom)
											/0/	0/0/0	Other furniture of rose wood (use in the bedroom)
													---Other:
											/0/	0/0/0	----Lacquer, lacquer wood furniture
													----Other
											/0/	0/0/0	Other furniture of endangered wood(other than use in the bedroom)
											/0/	0/0/0	Other furniture of wood(other than use in the bedroom)
												0/0/0	-Furniture of plastics
													-Furniture of other materials, including cane, osier, bamboo or similar materials:
											/0/	0/0/0	--Of bamboo
											/0/	0/0/0	--Of rattan
													---Other:
											/0/	0/0/0	---Of osier or similar materials
												0/0/0	---Of stone
												0/0/0	---Other
													-Parts

税则号列		货品名称〔CIQ扩展编码及品名－T2表示见附表2〕	最惠(%)	暂定税率	普通	增值/消费	出口退税	计量单位	监管条件	检验检疫	特殊证件对美关税
9403.9000	91	其他品目94.03所列物品的濒危木制零件〔999〕	0		100	13/	0	千克	EF		/25
9403.9000	99	其他品目94.03所列物品零件〔999〕	0		100	13/	13	千克			/25
94.04		**弹簧床垫;寝具及类似用品,装有弹簧、内部用任何材料填充、衬垫或用海绵橡胶、泡沫塑料制成,不论是否包面(例如,褥垫、棉被、羽绒被、靠垫、坐垫及枕头):**									
9404.1000		-弹簧床垫〔999〕	10		100	13/	13	个/千克			/20
		-褥垫:									
9404.2100		--海绵橡胶或泡沫塑料制,不论是否包面									
9404.2100	10	蔺草包面的垫子(单件面积大于1平方米,无论是否包边)〔101蔺草及其制品,102褥垫,103靠垫〕	10		100	13/	13	个/千克	4ABxy	PQ	/30
9404.2100	90	海绵橡胶或泡沫塑料制褥垫(不论是否包面)〔101褥垫,102靠垫〕	10		100	13/	13	个/千克			/30
9404.2900		--其他材料制〔999〕	10		100	13/	13	个/千克			/35
		-睡袋:									
9404.3010		---羽毛或羽绒填充的									
9404.3010	10	濒危野禽羽毛或羽绒填充的睡袋〔999〕	10		130	13/	0	个/千克	FE		/
9404.3010	90	其他羽毛或羽绒填充的睡袋〔999〕	10		130	13/	13	个/千克			/
9404.3090		---其他〔999〕	10		100	13/	13	个/千克			/35
		-其他:									
9404.9010		---羽毛或羽绒填充的									
9404.9010	10	濒危野禽羽绒和羽毛填充其他寝具(含类似品)〔101褥垫,102靠垫〕	10		130	13/	0	千克	EF		/35
9404.9010	90	其他羽绒和羽毛填充的其他寝具(含类似品)〔101褥垫,102靠垫〕	10		130	13/	13	千克			/35
9404.9020		---兽毛填充的									
9404.9020	10	濒危兽毛填充的寝具(用野生兽毛填充的,含盖被及类似品)〔999〕	10		130	13/	0	千克	EF		/35
9404.9020	90	其他兽毛填充的其他寝具(含类似品)〔999〕	10		130	13/	13	千克			/35
9404.9030		---丝棉填充的〔999〕	10		130	13/	13	千克			/35
9404.9040		---化学纤维棉填充的〔T2〕	10		130	13/	13	千克			/30
9404.9090		---其他〔101靠垫,102其他日用纺织制品〕	10		130	13/	13	千克			/30
94.05		**其他税目未列名的灯具及照明装置,包括探照灯、聚光灯及其零件;装有固定光源的发光标志、发光铭牌及类似品,以及其他税目未列名的这些货品的零件:**									
9405.1000		-枝形吊灯及天花板或墙壁上的其他电气照明装置,但不包括公共露天场所或街道上的电气照明装置〔T2〕	5		80	13/	13	个/千克		L	/25
9405.2000		-电气的台灯、床头灯或落地灯									
9405.2000	10	含濒危物种成分的电气台灯、床头灯、落地灯〔T2〕	10		80	13/	0	台/千克	EF	L	/35
9405.2000	90	其他电气台灯、床头灯、落地灯〔T2〕	10		80	13/	13	台/千克		L	/35
9405.3000		-圣诞树用的成套灯具〔T2〕	8		100	13/	13	套/千克			/33
		-其他电灯及照明装置:									
9405.4010		---探照灯〔T2〕	10		70	13/	13	台/千克			/30
9405.4020		---聚光灯〔T2〕	10		70	13/	13	台/千克			/30
9405.4090		---其他〔T2〕	6		80	13/	13	千克			/16
9405.5000		-非电气的灯具及照明装置〔999〕	10		80	13/	13	千克			/35
9405.6000		-发光标志、发光铭牌及类似品〔999〕	10		80	13/	13	千克		L	/30
		-零件:									
9405.9100		--玻璃制〔999〕	8		70	13/	13	千克			/18
9405.9200		--塑料制〔999〕	8		70	13/	13	千克			/28
9405.9900		--其他〔999〕	8		70	13/	13	千克			/28
94.06		**活动房屋:**									
9406.1000		-木制的〔999〕	8		70	13/	13	千克	AB	PQ	/28
9406.9000		-其他									
9406.9000	10	用动植物材料制作的活动房屋(木制的除外)〔999〕	8		70	13/	13	千克	AB	PQ	/33
9406.9000	20	带有风扇的高效空气粒子过滤单元(HEPA)的封闭洁净室〔999〕	8		70	13/	13	千克	3		/33
9406.9000	90	其他活动房屋〔999〕	8		70	13/	13	千克			/33

协定税率 %										特惠税率 %			Article Description
亚太5国	东/冰/格	巴基斯坦	韩国	瑞士	哥达	秘鲁	澳大利亚	新西/坡/智	港/澳/台	亚太2国	老/柬/缅	36/3/1	
												0/0/0	Parts of the articles of heading No. 94.03 of endangered wood
												0/0/0	Parts of the articles of heading No. 94.03
													Mattress supports; articles of bedding and similar furnishing (for example, mattresses, quilts, eiderdowns, cushions, pouffes and pillows) fitted with springs or stuffed or internally fitted with any material or of cellular rubber or plastics, whether or not covered:
	0/0/0	20	12	6	0	0	0	0/0/0	0/0/			0/0/	-Mattress supports
													-Mattresses:
													--Of cellular rubber or plastics, whether or not covered
	0/0/0	20	12	6	0	0	0	0/0/0	0/0/			0/0/0	Mattresses covered with rush (area of single piece>1m², whether or not edged)
	0/0/0	20	12	6	0	0	0	0/0/0	0/0/			0/0/0	Mattresses of foam rubber or foamed plastics (whether or not covered)
6.5	0/0/0	0	12	6	0	0	0	0/0/0	0/0/			0/0/0	--Of other materials
													-Sleeping bags:
													---Stunffed with feathers or down
	0/0/0	20	12	6	0	0	0	0/0/0	0/0/			0/0/0	Sleeping bags stuffed with feathers or down of endang ered wild birds
	0/0/0	20	12	6	0	0	0	0/0/0	0/0/			0/0/0	Sleeping bags, stuffed with other feathers or down
	0/0/0		12	6	0	0	0	0/0/0	0/0/			0/0/0	---Other
													-Other:
													---Stuffed with feathers or down
	0//0	0	12	6	0	0	0	0/0/0	0/0/			0/0/0	Other articles of bedding and similar furnishing, stuffed with feathers of down of endangered wild birds
	0//0	0	12	6	0	0	0	0/0/0	0/0/			0/0/0	Other articles of bedding and similar furnishing, stuffed with pther feathers of down
													---Stuffed with animal hair
	0/0/0	0	12	6	0	0	0	0/0/0	0/0/			0/0/0	Articles of bedding, stuffed with endangered wild animal hair(including quilt and similar furnishing)
	0/0/0	0	12	6	0	0	0	0/0/0	0/0/			0/0/0	Articles of bedding and similar furnishing, stuffed with other animal hair
	0/0/0	0	12	6	0	0	0	0/0/0	0/0/			0/0/0	---Stuffed with silk wadding
	0/0/0	0	12	6	0	0	0	0/0/0	0/0/			0/0/0	---Stuffed with man-made fibres
	0/0/0	0	12	6	0	0	0	0/0/0	0/0/			0/0/0	---Other
													Lamps and lighting fittings including searchlights and spotlights and parts thereof, not elsewhere specified or included; illuminated signs, illuminated name-plates and the like, having apermanently fixed light source, andparts thereof not elsewhere specified or included:
	0/0/0	4	4	0	0	0	0	0//0	0/0/			0/0/0	-Chandeliers and other electric ceiling or wall lighting fittings, excluding those of a kind used for lighting public open spaces or thorough-fares
													-Electric table, desk, bedeside or floor-standing lamps
	0/0/0	20	14	6	0	0	0	0/0/0	0/0/			0/0/0	Encangered species composition containing electric lamp, bedside lamp, floor lamp
	0/0/0	20	14	6	0	0	0	0/0/0	0/0/			0/0/0	Other electric lamp, bedside lamp, floor lamp
	0/0/0	11.5	6.4	4.8	0	0	0	0/0/0	0/0/			0/0/0	-Lighting sets of a kind used for Christmas trees
													-Other electric lamps and lighting fittings:
	0/0/0	12.6	7	5.3	0	0	0	0/0/0	0/0/			0/0/0	---Searchlights
	0/0/0	12.6	7	5.3	0	0	0	0/0/0	0/0/			0/0/0	---Spotlights
	0/0/0	0	0	0	0	0	0	0/0/0	0/0/			0/0/0	---Other
	0/0/0		14	6	0	0	0	0/0/0	0/0/			0/0/	-Non-electrical lamps and lighting fittings
	0/0/0	20	12	6	0	0	0	0/0/0	0/0/			0/0/	-Illuminated signs, illuminated name plates and the like
													-Parts:
	0/0/0	20	14	6	0	0	0	0/0/0	0/0/			0/0/	--Of glass
	0/0/0	20	12	6	0	0	0	0/0/0	0/0/			0/0/	--Of plastics
	0/0/0		12	6	0	0	0	0/0/0	0/0/			0/0/0	--Other
													Prefabricated buildings:
5.2	0/0/0	4	4	0	0	0	0	0/0/0	0/0/			0/0/0	-Of wood
													-Other
5.2	0/0/0	4	4	0	0	0	0	0/0/0	0/0/			0/0/0	Prefabricated buildings of materials of animal or vegetable, excuding of wood
5.2	0/0/0	4	4	0	0	0	0	0/0/0	0/0/			0/0/0	Sealec clean room with fan, for filtering unit of high efficiency particulate air(HEPA)
5.2	0/0/0	4	4	0	0	0	0	0/0/0	0/0/			0/0/0	Other prefabricated buildings

第九十五章
玩具、游戏品、运动用品及其零件、附件

注释：

一、本章不包括：

(一)蜡烛(税目34.06)；

(二)税目36.04的烟花、爆竹或其他烟火制品；

(三)已切成一定长度但未制成钓鱼线的纱线、单丝、绳、肠线及类似品(第三十九章、税目42.06或第十一类)；

(四)税目42.02、43.03或43.04的运动用袋或其他容器；

(五)第六十一章或第六十二章的纺织品制的化妆舞会服装；第六十一章或第六十二章的纺织品制的运动服装或特殊衣着(例如，击剑服或足球守门员球衣)，无论是否附带保护配件，例如，肘部、膝部或腹股沟部位的保护垫或填充物；

(六)第六十三章的纺织品制的旗帜及帆板或滑行车用帆；

(七)第六十四章的运动鞋靴(装有冰刀或滑轮的溜冰鞋除外)或第六十五章的运动用帽；

(八)手杖、鞭子、马鞭或类似品(税目66.02)及其零件(税目66.03)；

(九)税目70.18的未装配的玩偶或其他玩具用的玻璃假眼；

(十)第十五类注释二所规定的贱金属制通用零件(第十五类)或塑料制的类似货品(第三十九章)；

(十一)税目83.06的铃、钟、锣及类似品；

(十二)液体泵(税目84.13)、液体或气体的过滤净化机器及装置(税目84.21)、电动机(税目85.01)、变压器(税目84.04)；录制声音或其他信息用的圆盘、磁带、固态非易失性数据存储器件、"智能卡"及其他媒体，不论是否已录制(税目85.23)；无线电遥控设备(税目85.26)或无绳红外线遥控器件(85.43)；

(十三)第十七类的运动用车辆(长雪橇、平底雪橇及类似品除外)；

(十四)儿童两轮车(税目87.12)；

(十五)运动用船艇，例如，轻舟、赛艇(第八十九章)及其桨、橹和类似品(木制的归入第四十四章)；

(十六)运动及户外游戏用的眼镜、护目镜及类似品(税目90.04)；

(十七)媒诱音响器及哨子(税目92.08)；

(十八)第九十三章的武器及其他物品；

(十九)各种电气彩灯串(税目94.05)；

(二十)独脚架、双脚架、三脚架及类似品(税目96.20)；

(二十一)球拍线、帐篷或类似的野营用品、手套、棒球手套和露指手套(按其构成材料归类)；或

(二十二)餐具、厨房用具、盥洗用品、地毯及纺织材料制的其他铺地制品、服装、床上及餐桌用织物制品、盥洗及厨房用织物制品及具有实用功能的类似货品(按其构成材料归类)。

二、本章包括天然或养殖珍珠、宝石或半宝石(天然、合成或再造)、贵金属或包贵金属只作为小零件的物品。

三、除上述注释一另有规定的以外，凡专用于或主要用于本章各税目所列物品的零件、附件，应与有关物品一并归类。

四、除上述注释一另有规定的以外，税目95.03主要适用于该税号所列的物品与一项或多项其他货品组合而成的物品，只要这些物品为零售包装，且组合后具有玩具的基本特征。这些组合物品不能视为归类总规则三(二)所指的成套货品，如果单独报验，应归入其他税号。

五、税目95.03不包括因其设计、形状或构成材料可确认为专供动物使用的物品，例如"宠物玩具"归入其相应的税目。

子目注释：

一、子目9504.50包括：

(一)在电视机、监视器或其他外部屏幕或表面上重放图像的视频游戏控制器；

(二)自带显示屏的视频游戏设备，不论是否便携式。

本子目不包括用硬币、钞票、银行卡、代币或任何其他支付方式使其工作的视频游戏控制器或设备(子目9504.30)

税则号列	货品名称〔CIQ扩展编码及品名—T2表示见附表2〕	最惠(%)	暂定税率	普通	增值/消费	出口退税	计量单位	监管条件	检验检疫	特殊证件对美关税
95.03	**三轮车、踏板车、踏板汽车和类似的带轮玩具：玩偶车；玩偶；其他玩具；缩小(按比例缩小)的模型及类似的娱乐用模型，不论是否活动；各种智力玩具：**									
9503.0010	---供儿童乘骑的带轮玩具〔101儿童三轮车，102儿童推车，103最大鞍座高度435mm—635mm范围内的儿童自行车，104儿童踏板车，105儿童玩偶车，106其他童车〕	0		80	13/	13	辆/千克		L	/20
	---玩偶，不论是否着装；玩具动物：									

Chapter 95
Toys, games and sports requisites; parts and accessories thereof

Notes:

1. This Chapter does not cover:
   (a) Candles (heading No. 34.06);
   (b) Fireworks or other pyrotechnic articles of heading No. 36.04;
   (c) Yarns, monofilament, cords or gut or the like for fishing, cut to length but not made up into fishing lines, of Chapter 39, heading No. 42.06 or Section Ⅺ;
   (d) Sports bags or other containers of heading No. 42.02, 43.03 or 43.04;
   (e) Fancy dress of textiles, of Chapter 61 or 62; sports clothing and special articles of apparel of textiles, of Chapter 61 or 62, whether or not in corporating incidentally protective components such as pads or padding in the elbow, knee or groin areas (for example, fencing clothing or soccer goalkeeper jerseys);
   (f) Textile flags or bunting, or sails for boats, sailboards or land craft, of Chapter 63;
   (g) Sports footwear (other than skating boots with ice or roller skates attached) of Chapter 64, or sports headgear of Chapter 65;
   (h) Walking-sticks, whips, riding-crops or the like (heading No. 66.02), or parts thereof (heading No. 66.03);
   (ij) Unmounted glass eyes for dolls or other toys, of heading No. 70.18;
   (k) Parts of general use, as defined in Note 2 to Section ⅩⅤ, of base metal (Section ⅩⅤ), or similar goods of plastics (Chapter 39);
   (l) Bells, gongs or the like of heading No. 83 06;
   (m) Pumps for liquids (heading No. 84.13), filtering or purifying machinery and apparatus for liquids or gases (heading No. 84.21), electric motors (heading No. 85.01), electric transformers (heading No. 85.04); discs, tapes, solid-state non-volatile storage devices, "smart cards" and other media for the recording of sound or of other phenomena, wheter or not recorded (heading 85.23), radio remote control appratus (heading85.26) or cordless infrared remote control devices (heading85.43)
   (n) Sports vehicles (other than bobsleighs, toboggans and the like) of Section ⅩⅦ;
   (o) Children's bicycles (heading No. 87.12);
   (p) Sports craft such as canoes and skiffs (Chapter 89), or their means of propulsion (Chapter 44 for such articles made of wood);
   (q) Spectacles, goggles or the like, for sports or outdoor games (heading No. 90.04);
   (r) Decoy calls or whistles (heading No. 92.08);
   (s) Arms or other articles of Chapter 93;
   (t) Electric garlands of all kinds (heading No. 94.05);
   (u) unipod, bipod, tripod or the like (heading No.96.20);
   (v) Racket strings, tents or other camping goods, or gloves, mittens and mitts (classified according to their constituent material). or
   (w) Tableware, kitchenware, toilet articles, carpetsand other textile floor coverings, apparel, bed linen, table linen, toilet linen, kitchen linen and similar articles having a utilitarian function (classified according to their constituent material).

2. This Chapter includes articles in which natural or cultured pearls, precious or semi-precious stones (natural, synthetic or reconstructed), precious metal or metal clad with precious metal constitute only minor consistuents.
3. Subject to Note 1 above, parts and accessories which are suitable for use solely or principally with articles of this Chapter are to be classified with those articles.
4. Subject to the provisions of Note 1 above, heading 95.03 applies, inter alia, to articles of this heading combined with one or more items, which cannot be considered as sets under the terms of Ceneral Interpretative Rule 3 (b), and which, if presented separately, would be classified in other headings, provided the articles are put together for retail sale and the combinations have the essential character of toys.
5. Heading 95.03 does not cover articles which, on account of their design, shape or constituent material, are identifiable as intended exclusively for animals, for example, "pet toys" (classification in their own appropriate heading).

Subheading Note:

1. Subheading 9504.50 covers:
   (a) Video game consoles from which the image is reproduced on a television receiver, a monitor or other external screen or surface;
   (b) Video game machines having a self-contained video screen, whether or not portable.
   This subheading does not cover video game consoles or machines operated by coins, banknotes, bank cards, tokens or by any other means of payment (subheading9504.30)

协定税率 %										特惠税率 %			Article Description
亚太5国	东/冰/格	巴基斯坦	韩国	瑞士	哥达	秘鲁	澳大利亚	新西/坡/智	港/澳/台	亚太2国	老/柬/缅	36/3/1	
													Tricycles, scooters, pedal cars and similar wheeled toys; dals carriages; dolls; Other toys; re duced-size ("scale") models and similar recreational models working or not; puzzles of all kinds;
												0/0/0	---Tricycles, scooters, pedal cars and similar wheeled toys; doll's carriage
													---Dolls, whether or not dressed; toy representing animals or non-human creatures:

税则号列	货品名称〔CIQ 扩展编码及品名—T2 表示见附表 2〕	最惠(%)	暂定税率	普通	增值/消费	出口退税	计量单位	监管条件	检验检疫	特殊证件对美关税
9503.0021	----动物〔101 布绒玩具,102 竹木玩具,103 塑胶玩具,104 电玩具,105 软体造型玩具,106 弹射玩具,107 金属玩具〕	0		80	13/	13	个/千克	A	LM	/25
9503.0029	----其他〔101 布绒玩具,102 竹木玩具,103 塑胶玩具,104 电玩具,105 纸制玩具,106 软体造型玩具,107 弹射玩具,108 金属玩具,109 玩具收藏品〕	0		80	13/	13	个/千克	A	LM	/25
9503.0060	---智力玩具[101 布绒玩具,102 竹木玩具,103 塑胶玩具,104 电玩具,105 纸制玩具,106 类似文具玩具,107 软体造型玩具,108 金属玩具,109 玩具收藏品]	0		80	13/	13	套/千克	A	LM	/25
	---其他玩具:									
9503.0083	----带动力装置的玩具及模型									
9503.0083 10	玩具无人机〔999〕	0		80	13/	13	套/千克	A	LM	/25
9503.0083 90	带动力装置的玩具及模型〔301 布绒玩具,302 竹木玩具,303 塑胶玩具,304 电玩具,305 弹射玩具,306 金属玩具,307 其他未列名玩具,308 玩具收藏品〕	0		80	13/	13	套/千克	A	LM	/25
9503.0089	----其他〔101 乘骑玩具,102 其他未列名玩具,103 玩具收藏品〕	0		80	13/	13	个/千克	A	LM	/25
9503.0090	----零件、附件〔999〕	0		80	13/	13	千克	A	LM	/25
95.04	**视频游戏控制器及设备、游艺场所、桌上或室内游戏用品,包括弹球机、台球、娱乐专用桌及保龄球自动球道设备:**									
9504.2000	-各种台球用品及附件									
9504.2000 10	濒危木制的台球用品及附件〔999〕	0		80	13/	0	千克	EF		/20
9504.2000 90	其他台球用品及附件〔999〕	0		80	13/	13	千克			/20
	-用硬币、钞票、银行卡、代币及任何其他支付方式使其工作的其他游戏用品,但保龄球自动球道设备除外:									
9504.3010	---电子游戏机〔999〕	0		130	13/	13	台/千克			/10
9504.3090	---其他〔999〕	0		80	13/	13	台/千克			/
9504.4000	-扑克牌〔999〕	0		80	13/	13	副/千克			/10
	-视频游戏控制器及设备,但子目 9504.30 的货品除外:									
	---与电视接收机配套使用的:									
9504.5011	----零件及附件〔999〕	0		130	13/	13	个/千克			/25
9504.5019	----其他〔999〕	0		130	13/	13	台/千克		L	/
	---其他:									
9504.5091	----零件〔999〕	0		130	13/	13	个/千克			/
9504.5099	----其他〔999〕	0		130	13/	13	台/千克		L	/20
	-其他:									
9504.9010	---其他电子游戏机〔999〕	0		130	13/	13	台/千克		L	/
	---保龄球自动球道设备及器具:									
9504.9021	----保龄球自动分瓶机〔999〕	0		80	13/	13	台/千克			/10
9504.9022	----保龄球〔999〕	0		80	13/	13	个/千克			/10
9504.9023	----保龄球瓶〔999〕	0		80	13/	13	个/千克			/20
9504.9029	----其他〔999〕	0		80	13/	13	台/千克			/10
9504.9030	---中国象棋、国际象棋、跳棋等棋类用品〔999〕	0		80	13/	13	副/千克			/25
9504.9040	---麻将及类似桌上游戏用品〔101 麻将,102 除麻将外〕	0		80	13/	13	副/千克			/25
9504.9090	---其他〔101 其它游戏机,102 游乐设备零件,103 其他游戏器具〕	0		80	13/	13	台/千克			/20
95.05	**节日(包括狂欢节)用品或其他娱乐用品,包括魔术道具及嬉戏品:**									
9505.1000	-圣诞节用品									
9505.1000 10	含动植物性材料的圣诞用品(不包括成套圣诞节灯具)〔101 木制工艺品,102 其他木制品,103 其他草及草制品,104 其他竹藤柳草类,105 含动物产品类〕	0		100	13/	13	千克	AB	PQ	/25
9505.1000 90	其他圣诞节用品(不包括成套圣诞节灯具)〔101 含木制品,102 不含木制品〕	0		100	13/	13	千克			/25
9505.9000	-其他〔101 含木制品,102 不含木制品〕	0		100	13/	13	千克			/10
95.06	**一般的体育活动、体操、竞技及其他运动(包括乒乓球运动)或户外游戏用的本章其他税目未列名用品及设备;游泳池或戏水池:**									
	-滑雪屐及其他滑雪用具:									
9506.1100	--滑雪屐〔999〕	6		50	13/	13	双/千克			/26
9506.1200	--滑雪屐扣件(滑雪屐带)〔999〕	6		50	13/	13	千克			/26
9506.1900	--其他〔999〕	6		50	13/	13	千克			/26

协定税率 %										特惠税率 %			Article Description
亚太5国	东/冰/格	巴基斯坦	韩国	瑞士	哥达	秘鲁	澳大利亚	新西/坡/智	港/澳/台	亚太2国	老/柬/缅	36/3/1	
												0/0/0	----Animals
												0/0/0	----Other
												0/0/0	---Puzzles
													---Other toys:
													----Toys and models with power devices
												0/0/0	Toy UAV
												0/0/0	Toys and models with power devices
												0/0/0	----Other
												0/0/0	---Parts and accessories
													Vide game controller、Articles for funfair, table or parlour games, including pintables, billiards, special tables for casino games and automatic bowling alley equipment:
													-Articles and accessories for billiards of all kinds
												0/0/0	Articles and accessories for billiards of endangered wood
												0/0/0	Other articles and accessories for billiards of au kinds
													-Other games, operated by coins, banknotes bank cords, tokens or by other means of payment, other than automatic bowing alley equipment:
												0/0/0	---Video games
												0/0/0	---Other
												0/0/0	-Playing cards
													-Video game consoles or machines operated, other than heading 9504.30:
													---Video games of a kind used with a television receiver:
												0/0/0	----Parts and accessories
												0/0/0	----Other
													---Other:
												0/0/0	----Parts
												0/0/0	----Other
													-Other:
												0/0/0	---Other video games
													---Automatic bowling alley equipments and appliances:
												0/0/0	----Automatic bowling pin distributing machines
												0/0/0	----Bowling balls
												0/0/0	----Bowling pins
												0/0/0	----Other
												0/0/0	---Chess and other board games, including Chinese chess, international chess, Chinese cherkers and draughts
												0/0/0	---Mahjong and similiar table games
												0/0/0	---Other
													Festive, carnival or other entertainment articles, including conjuring tricks and novelty jokes:
													-Articles for Christmas festivities
												0/0/0	Articles for Christmas festivities containing animals or vegetable materials (other than lighting sets of a kind used for Christmas)
												0/0/0	Other articles for Christmas festivities (other than lighting sets of a kind used for Christmas)
												0/0/0	-Other
													Articles and equipment for general physical exercise, gymnastics, athletics, other sports (including table-tennis) or out door games, not specified or included elsewhere in this Chapter; swimming pools and paddling pools:
													-Snow-skis and other snow-ski equipment:
	0//0	0	5.6	4.2	0	0	0	0/0/0	0/0/			0/0/	--Skis
	0/0/0	0	5.6	4.2	0	0	0	0/0/0	0/0/			0/0/	--Ski-fastenings (ski-bindings)
	0/0/0	0	5.6	4.2	0	0	0	0/0/0	0/0/			0/0/	--Other

税则号列	货品名称〔CIQ扩展编码及品名－T2表示见附表2〕	最惠(%)	暂定税率	普通	增值/消费	出口退税	计量单位	监管条件	检验检疫	特殊证件对美关税
	-滑水板、冲浪板、帆板及其他水上运动用具：									
9506.2100	--帆板〔999〕	6		50	13/	13	个/千克			/31
9506.2900	--其他〔999〕	6		50	13/	13	个/千克			/16
	-高尔夫球棍及其他高尔夫球用具：									
9506.3100	--棍，全套〔999〕	6		50	13/10	13	根/千克			/26
9506.3200	--球〔999〕	6		50	13/10	13	个/千克			/26
9506.3900	--其他〔999〕	6		50	13/	13	千克			/31
	-乒乓球运动用品及器械：									
9506.4010	---乒乓球〔999〕	6		50	13/	13	百个/千克			/31
9506.4090	---其他〔999〕	6		50	13/	13	千克			/
	-网球拍、羽毛球拍或类似的球拍，不论是否装弦：									
9506.5100	--草地网球拍，不论是否装弦〔999〕	6		50	13/	13	支/千克			/
9506.5900	--其他〔999〕	6		50	13/	13	支/千克			/31
	-球，但高尔夫球及乒乓球除外：									
9506.6100	--草地网球〔999〕	6		50	13/	13	个/千克			/
	--可充气的球：									
9506.6210	---篮球、足球、排球〔999〕	6		50	13/	13	个/千克			/31
9506.6290	---其他〔999〕	6		50	13/	13	个/千克			/16
9506.6900	--其他〔999〕	6		50	13/	13	个/千克			/31
	-溜冰鞋及旱冰鞋，包括装有冰刀的溜冰靴：									
9506.7010	---溜冰鞋〔999〕	6		50	13/	13	双/千克			/26
9506.7020	---旱冰鞋〔999〕	6		50	13/	13	双/千克			/26
	-其他：									
	--一般的体育活动、体操或竞技用品及设备：									
	---健身及康复器械：									
9506.9111	----跑步机									
9506.9111 10	跑步机(整机)〔101 电动跑步机，102 其他跑步机〕	6		50	13/	13	台/千克			/16
9506.9111 90	跑步机的零件及附件〔101 电动跑步机，102 其他跑步机〕	6		50	13/	13	台/千克			/16
9506.9119	----其他〔101 力量型训练器材，102 力量型训练长凳，103 曲柄踏板类训练器材，104 划船机，105 踏步机、台阶机和登山机，106 椭圆训练机，107 带固定飞轮和不带自由飞轮的练习自行车，108 其他健身器材〕	6		50	13/	13	千克			/16
9506.9120	---滑板〔999〕	6		50	13/	13	个/千克			/16
9506.9190	---其他〔999〕	6		50	13/	13	千克			/16
9506.9900	--其他〔101 康复健身器械及其零件，102 其他体育竞技运动器具〕	6		50	13/	13	个/千克			/16
95.07	**钓鱼竿、钓鱼钩及其他钓鱼用品；捞鱼网、捕蝶网及类似网；囮子"鸟"(税目92.08或97.05的货品除外)以及类似的狩猎用品：**									
9507.1000	-钓鱼竿									
9507.1000 10	用植物性材料制作的钓鱼竿〔101 其他木制品，102 其他竹藤柳草类，103 钓鱼器具〕	6		80	13/	13	副/千克	AB	PQ	/31
9507.1000 90	其他钓鱼竿〔999〕	6		80	13/	13	副/千克			/31
9507.2000	-钓鱼钩，不论有无系钩丝〔999〕	6		80	13/	13	千克			/26
9507.3000	-钓线轮〔999〕	6		80	13/	13	个/千克			/31
9507.9000	-其他〔999〕	6		80	13/	13	千克			/16
95.08	**旋转木马、秋千、射击用靶及其他游乐场的娱乐设备；流动马戏团及流动动物园；流动剧团：**									
9508.1000	-流动马戏团及流动动物园									
9508.1000 10	有濒危动物的流动马戏团(包括流动动物园)〔999〕	6		100	13/	0	千克	FEAB	PQ	/
9508.1000 90	其他流动马戏团及流动动物园〔999〕	6		100	13/	13	千克	AB	PQ	/
9508.9000	-其他〔101 大型游乐设施，102 其他游戏器具〕	6		100	13/	13	千克	AB	PQ	/16

协定税率 %										特惠税率 %			Article Description
亚太5国	东/冰/格	巴基斯坦	韩国	瑞士	哥达	秘鲁	澳大利亚	新西/坡/智	港/澳/台	亚太2国	老/柬/缅	36/3/1	
													-Water-skis, surf-boards, sailboards and other water-sport equipment:
	0/0/0	0	4.8	3.6	0	0	0	0/0/0	0/0/			0/0/	--Sailboards
	0/0/0	0	5.6	4.2	0	0	0	0/0/0	0/0/			0/0/	--Other
													-Golf clubs and other golf equipment:
	0//0	0	5.6	4.2	0	0	0	0/0/0	0/0/			0/0/0	--Clubs, complete
	0/0/0	0	4.8	3.6	0	0	0	0/0/0	0/0/			0/0/	--Balls
	0//0	0	5.6	4.2	0	0	0	0/0/0	0/0/0			0/0/0	--Other
													-Articles and equipment for table-tennis:
	0/0/0	0	4.8	3.6	0	0	0	0/0/0	0/0/			0/0/	---Table-tennis balls
	0/0/0	0	5.6	4.2	0	0	0	0/0/0	0/0/			0/0/	---Other
													-Tennis, badminton or similar rackets, whether or not strung:
	0/0/0	0	5.6	4.2	0	0	0	0/0/0	0/0/			0/0/	--Lawn-tennis rackets, whether or not strung
	0/0/0	0	5.6	4.2	0	0	0	0/0/0	0/0/			0/0/	—Other
													-Balls, other than golf balls and tabletennis balls:
	0/0/0	0	4.8	3.6	0	0	0	0/0/0	0/0/			0/0/	--Lawn-tennis balls
													--Inflatable:
	0/0/0	0	4.8	3.6	0	0	0	0/0/0	0/0/			0/0/	---Basketballs, footballs or volleyballs
	0/0/0	0	4.8	3.6	0	0	0	0/0/0	0/0/			0/0/	---Other
	0/0/0	0	4.8	3.6	0	0	0	0/0/0	0/0/			0/0/	--Other
													-Ice skates and roller skates, including skating boots with skates attached:
3.9	0/0/0	0	5.6	4.2	0	0	0	0/0/0	0/0/			0/0/	---Ice skates
3.9	0/0/0	0	5.6	4.2	0	0	0	0/0/0	0/0/			0/0/	---Roller skates
													-Other:
													--Articles and equipment for general physical exercise, gymnastics or athletics:
													---Equipment for exercise and recovery:
													----Runing machines
	0/0/0	0	4.8	3.6	0	0	0	0/0/0	0/0/0			0/0/	The treadmill (machine)
	0/0/0	0	4.8	3.6	0	0	0	0/0/0	0/0/0			0/0/	Parts and accessories of treadmill
	0/0/0	0	4.8	3.6	0	0	0	0/0/0	0/0/0			0/0/	----Other
	0/0/0	0	4.8	3.6	0	0	0	0/0/0	0/0/			0/0/	---Skateboards
	0/0/0	0	4.8	3.6	0	0	0	0/0/0	0/0/			0/0/0	---Other
	0/0/0	0	4.8	0	0	0	0	0/0/0	0/0/			0/0/	--Other
													Fishing rods, fish-hooks and other line fishing tackle; fish landing nets, butterfly nets and similar nets; decoy "birds" (other than those of heading 92. 08 or 97. 05) and similar hunting or shooting requisites:
													-Fishing rods
	0//0	21		6	0	0	0	0/0/0	0/0/			0/0/	Fishing rods of vegetable materials
	0//0	21		6	0	0	0	0/0/0	0/0/			0/0/	Other fishing rods
	0//0	21	14.7	6	0	0	0	0/0/0	0/0/			0/0/0	-Fish-hooks, whether or not snelled
	0//0	21	14.7	6	0	0	0	0/0/0	0/0/			0/0/	-Fishing reels
3.9	0/0/0	18.9	14.7	6	0	0	0	0/0/0	0/0/			0/0/	-Other
													Roundabouts, swings, shooting galleries and other fairground amusements; travelling circuses and travelling menageries; travelling theatres:
													-Travelling circuses and travelling menageries
	0/0/0	10.8	6	4.5	0	0	0	0/0/0	0/0/			0/0/	Travelling circuses and travelling menageries, having endangered animals
	0/0/0	10.8	6	4.5	0	0	0	0/0/0	0/0/			0/0/	Other travelling circuses and travelling menageries
	0/0/0	9.6	6	4.5	0	0	0	0/0/0	0/0/			0/0/	-Other

第九十六章
杂 项 制 品

注释：

一、本章不包括：

(一)化妆盥洗用笔(第三十三章)；

(二)第六十六章的制品(例如，伞或手杖的零件)；

(三)仿首饰(税目 71.17)；

(四)第十五类注释二所规定的贱金属制通用零件(第十五类)或塑料制的类似品(第三十九章)；

(五)第八十二章的利口器及其他物品，其柄或其他零件是雕刻或模塑材料制的；但税目 96.01 或 96.02 适用于单独进口或出口的上述物品的柄或其他零件；

(六)第九十章的物品，例如，眼镜架(税目 90.03)、数学绘图笔(税目 90.17)、各种牙科、医疗、外科或兽医专用刷子(税目 90.18)；

(七)第九十一章的物品(例如，钟壳或表壳)；

(八)乐器及其零件、附件(第九十二章)；

(九)第九十三章的物品(武器及其零件)；

(十)第九十四章的物品(例如，家具、灯具及照明装置)；

(十一)第九十五章的物品(玩具、游戏品、运动用品)；

(十二)艺术品、收藏品及古物(第九十七章)。

二、税目 96.02 所称"植物质或矿物质雕刻材料"，是指：

(一)用于雕刻的硬种子、硬果核、硬果壳、坚果及类似植物材料(例如，象牙果及棕榈子)；

(二)琥珀、海泡石、粘聚琥珀、粘聚海泡石、黑玉及其矿物代用品。

三、税目 96.03 所称"制帚、制刷用成束、成簇的材料"，仅指未装配的成束、成簇的兽毛、植物纤维或其他材料。这些成束、成簇的材料无需分开即可安装在帚、刷之上，或只需经过简单加工(例如将顶端修剪成形)即可安装的。

四、除税目 96.01 至 96.06 或 96.15 的货品以外，本章的物品还包括全部或部分用贵金属、包贵金属、天然或养殖珍珠、宝石或半宝石(天然、合成或再造)制成的物品。而且，税目 96.01 至 96.06 及 96.15 包括天然或养殖珍珠、宝石或半宝石(天然、合成或再造)、贵金属或包贵金属只作为小零件的物品。

税则号列		货品名称〔CIQ 扩展编码及品名－T2 表示见附表 2〕	最惠(%)	暂定税率	普通	增值/消费	出口退税	计量单位	监管条件	检验检疫	特殊证件对美关税
96.01		**已加工的兽牙、骨、玳瑁壳、角、鹿角、珊瑚、珍珠母及其他动物质雕刻材料及其制品(包括塑模制品)：**									
9601.1000		-已加工的兽牙及其制品									
9601.1000	10	已加工的濒危兽牙及其制品[T2]	20		100	13/	0	千克	AFEB	PQ	/
9601.1000	90	其他已加工的兽牙及其制品[T2]	20		100	13/	13	千克	AB	PQ	/
9601.9000		-其他									
9601.9000	10	其他已加工濒危动物质雕刻料(包括其制品)〔101 含木制品的工艺品，102 不含木制品的工艺品〕	20		100	13/	0	千克	AFEB	PQ	/45
9601.9000	20	牛角纽扣坯圆片(濒危动物制除外)	20	6	100	13/	13	千克	AB	PQ	/31
9601.9000	90	其他已加工动物质雕刻料及其制品〔101 含木制品的工艺品，102 不含木制品的工艺品〕	20		100	13/	13	千克	AB	PQ	/45
96.02		**已加工的植物质或矿物质雕刻材料及其制品；蜡、硬脂、天然树胶、天然树脂或塑型膏制成的模塑或雕刻制品以及其他税目未列名的模塑或雕刻制品；已加工的未硬化明胶(税目 35.03 的明胶除外)及未硬化明胶制品：**									
9602.0010		---装药用胶囊〔999〕	5		40	13/	13	千克			/15
9602.0090		---其他[T2]	12		100	13/	13	千克	AB	PQ	/
96.03		**帚、刷(包括作为机器、器具、车辆零件的刷)、非机动的手工操作地板清扫器、拖把及毛掸；供制帚、刷用的成束或成簇的材料；油漆块垫及滚筒；橡皮扫帚(橡皮辊除外)：**									
9603.1000		-用枝条或其他植物材料捆扎而成的帚及刷，不论是否有把〔101 其他竹及竹制品，102 棕及棕制品，103 扫帚〕	12		100	13/	13	把/千克	AB	PQ	/32
		-牙刷、剃须刷、发刷、指甲刷、睫毛刷及其他人体化妆用刷，包括作为器具零件的上述刷：									
9603.2100		--牙刷，包括齿板刷〔101 牙刷，102 齿板刷〕	8		100	13/	13	把/千克	A	M	/28

Chapter 96
Miscellaneous manufactured articles

Notes:

1. This Chapter does not cover:
   (a) Pencils for cosmetic or toilet uses (Chapter 33);
   (b) Articles of Chapter 66 (for example, parts of umbrellas or walking-sticks);
   (c) Imitation jewellery (heading No. 71.17);
   (d) Parts of general use, as defined in Note 2 to Section XV, of base metal (Section XV), or similar goods of plastics (Chapter 39);
   (e) Cutlery or other articles of Chapter 82 with handles or other parts of carving or moulding materials; heading No. 96.01 or 96.02 applies, however, to separately pressented handles or other parts of such articles;
   (f) Articles of Chapter 90 (for exampple, spectacle frames (heading No. 90.03), mathematical drawing pens (heading No. 90.17), brushes of a kind specialized for use in dentistry or for medical, surgical or veterinary purposes (heading No. 90.18);
   (g) Articles of Chapter 91 (for example, clock or watch cases);
   (h) Musical instruments or parts or accessories thereof (Chapter 92);
   (ij) Articles of Chapter 93 (arms and parts thereof);
   (k) Articles of Chapter 94 (for example, furniture, lamps and lighting fittings);
   (l) Articles of Chapter 95 (toys, games, sports requisites);
   (m) Works of art, collectors' pieces or antiques (Chapter 97).
2. In heading No. 96.02 the expression "vegetable or mineral carving material" means:
   (a) Hard seeds, pips, hulls and nuts and similar vegetable materials of a kind used for carving (for example, corozo and dom);
   (b) Amber, meerschaum, agglomerated amber and agglomerated meerschaum, jet and mineral substitutes for jet.
3. In heading No. 96.03 the expression "prepared knots and tufts for broom or brush making" applies only to unmounted knots and tufts of animal hair, vegetable fibre or other material, which are ready for incorporation without division in brooms or brushes, or which require only such further minor processes as trimming to shape at the top, to render them ready for such incorporation.
4. Articles of this Chapter, other than those of headings No. 96.01 to 96.06 or 96.15, remain classified in the Chapter whether or not composed wholly or partly of precious metal or metal clad with precious metal, of natural or cultured pearls, or precious or semiprecious stones (natural, synthetic or reconstructed). However, headings No. 96.01 to 96.06 and 96.15 include articles in which natural or cultured pearls, precious or semi-precious stones (natural, synthetic or reconstructed), precious metal or metal clad with precious metal constitute only minor constituents.

协定税率 %										特惠税率 %			Article Description
亚太5国	东/冰/格	巴基斯坦	韩国	瑞士	哥达	秘鲁	澳大利亚	新西/坡/智	港/澳/台	亚太2国	老/柬/缅	36/3/1	
													Worked ivory, bone, tortoise-shell, horn, antlers, coral, mother-of-pearl and other animal carving material and articles of these materials (including articles obtained by moulding):
													-Worked ivory and articles of ivory
	0/0/0	20	12	6	0	0	0	0/0/0	0/0/			0/0/	Worked ivory and articles of ivory, of endangered animals
	0/0/0	20	12	6	0	0	0	0/0/0	0/0/			0/0/	Other worked ivory and articles of ivory
													-Other
	0/0/0	20	12	6	0	0	0	0/0/0	0/0/			0/0/0	Other worked carving material and articles of these materials of endangered animals
	0/0/0	20	12	6	0	0	0	0/0/0	0/0/		//	0/0/0	Fillet of horn button (except for endangered animals)
	0/0/0	20	12	6	0	0	0	0/0/0	0/0/			0/0/0	Other worked animal carving material and articles of these materials
													Worked vegetable or mineral carving material and articles of these materials; moulded or carved articles of wax, of stearin, of natural gums or natural resins or of modelling pastes, and other moulded or carved articles, not elsewhere specified or included; worked, unhardened gelatin (except gelatin of heading No35.03) and articles of unhardened gelatin:
	0/0/0	4.5	4.2	3.2	0	0	0	0/0/0	0/0/			0/0/	---Pharmaceutical capsules
	0/0/0	25	17.5	7.5	0	0	0	0/0/0	0/0/			0/0/0	---Other
													Brooms, brushes (including brushes constituting parts of machines, appliances or vehicles), hand-operated mechanical floor sweepers, not motorized, mops and feather dusters; prepared knots and tufts for broom or brush making; paint pads and rollers; squeegees (other than roller squeegees):
	0/0/0	25	17.5	7.5	0	0	0	0/0/0	0/0/			0/0/	-Brooms and brushes, consisting of twigs or other vegetable materials bound together, with or without handles
													-Tooth brushes, shaving brushes, hair brushes, nail brushes, eyelash brushes and other toilet brushes for use on the person, including such brushes constituting parts of appliances:
	0/0/0	25	17.5	7.5	0	0	0	0/0/0	0/0/			0/0/	--Tooth brushes, including dental-plate brushes

税则号列		货品名称〔CIQ扩展编码及品名－T2表示见附表2〕	最惠(%)	暂定税率	普通	增值/消费	出口退税	计量单位	监管条件	检验检疫	特殊证件对美关税
9603.2900		--其他									
9603.2900	10	濒危野生动物毛制剃须刷、发刷(包括睫毛刷等人体化妆刷)〔101 含木制品,102 不含木制品〕	6		100	13/	0	支/千克	FE		/26
9603.2900	90	剃须刷,发刷,睫毛刷等人体化妆刷(包括作为器具零件的编号960329所属的刷)〔101 含木制品,102 不含木制品〕	6		100	13/	13	支/千克			/26
		-画笔、毛笔及化妆用的类似笔:									
9603.3010		---画笔									
9603.3010	10	濒危动物毛制的画笔〔999〕	8		100	13/	0	支/千克	FE		/28
9603.3010	90	其他画笔〔999〕	8		100	13/	13	支/千克			/28
9603.3020		---毛笔									
9603.3020	10	濒危动物毛制的毛笔〔999〕	8		100	13/	0	支/千克	FE		/28
9603.3020	90	其他毛笔〔999〕	8		100	13/	13	支/千克			/28
9603.3090		---其他									
9603.3090	10	濒危动物毛制化妆用的类似笔〔999〕	6		100	13/	0	支/千克	FE		/26
9603.3090	90	其他化妆用的类似笔〔999〕	6		100	13/	13	支/千克			/26
		-油漆刷、涂料刷、清漆刷及类似的刷(子目号9603.30的货品除外);油漆块垫及滚筒:									
		---漆刷及类似刷:									
9603.4011		----猪鬃制〔101 含木制品,102 不含木制品〕	6		100	13/	13	把/千克			/26
9603.4019		----其他〔101 含木制品,102 不含木制品〕	6		100	13/	13	把/千克			/16
9603.4020		---油漆块垫及滚筒〔101 含木制品,102 不含木制品〕	6		100	13/	13	个/千克			/16
		-作为机器、器具、车辆零件的刷:									
		---金属丝刷:									
9603.5011		----作为机器、器具零件的刷[T2]	8		50	13/	13	个/千克			/28
9603.5019		----其他[T2]	8		100	13/	13	个/千克			/33
		---其他:									
9603.5091		----作为机器、器具零件的刷									
9603.5091	10	濒危动物毛制作为机器零件其他刷(包括器具零件的其他刷)〔101 含木制品,102 不含木制品〕	8		50	13/	0	个/千克	FE		/28
9603.5091	90	其他作为机器、器具零件的其他刷[T2]	8		50	13/	13	个/千克			/28
9603.5099		----其他									
9603.5099	10	濒危动物毛制作为车辆零件的其他刷〔101 其他车辆零部件,102 含木制品,103 不含木制品〕	8		100	13/	0	个/千克	FE		/28
9603.5099	90	其他作为车辆零件的其他刷[T2]	8		100	13/	13	个/千克			/28
		-其他:									
9603.9010		---羽毛掸									
9603.9010	10	濒危野禽羽毛掸〔999〕	6		130	13/	0	个/千克	AFEB	PQ	/
9603.9010	90	其他羽毛掸〔999〕	6		130	13/	13	个/千克	AB	PQ	/
9603.9090		---其他									
9603.9090	10	濒危动物毛、鬃、尾制其他帚,刷(包括拖把及其他毛掸)〔101 含木制品,102 不含木制品〕	6		100	13/	0	个/千克	AFEB	PQ	/26
9603.9090	20	其他动植物材料制帚,刷,拖把等(包括动植物材料制非机动的手工操作地板清扫器、毛掸)〔101 其他木制品,102 其他竹及竹制品,103 棕及棕制品,104 扫帚,105 藁杆,106 其他竹藤柳草类〕	6		100	13/	13	个/千克	AB	PQ	/26
9603.9090	90	其他材料制帚,刷,拖把及毛掸(包括其他材料制非机动的手工操作地板清扫器等)〔101 含木制品,102 不含木制品〕	6		100	13/	13	个/千克			/26
96.04		**手用粗筛、细筛:**									
9604.0000		手用粗筛、细筛〔101 含木制品,102 不含木制品〕	6		100	13/	13	个/千克	AB	PQ	/16
96.05		**个人梳妆、缝纫或清洁鞋靴、衣服用的成套旅行用具:**									
9605.0000		个人梳妆、缝纫或清洁鞋靴、衣服用的成套旅行用具〔101 含木制品,102 不含木制品〕	6		100	13/	13	套/千克			/26
96.06		**纽扣、揿扣、纽扣芯及纽扣和揿扣的其他零件;纽扣坯:**									
9606.1000		-揿扣及其零件〔101 含木制品,102 不含木制品〕	6		100	13/	13	千克			/31
		-纽扣:									
9606.2100		--塑料制,未用纺织材料包裹[T2]	6		100	13/	13	千克			/31
9606.2200		--贱金属制,未用纺织材料包裹[T2]	6		100	13/	13	千克			/31
9606.2900		--其他									
9606.2900	10	含濒危动物成分的其他纽扣[T2]	6		100	13/	0	千克	FE		/31
9606.2900	90	其他纽扣	6		100	13/	13	千克			/31
9606.3000		-纽扣芯及纽扣的其他零件;纽扣坯[T2]	6		100	13/	13	千克			/31

协定税率 %										特惠税率 %			Article Description
亚太5国	东/冰/格	巴基斯坦	韩国	瑞士	哥达	秘鲁	澳大利亚	新西/坡/智	港/澳/台	亚太2国	老/柬/缅	36/3/1	
													--Other
3.9	0/0/0	6.8	6	4.5	0	0	0	0/0/0	0/0/			0/0/0	Shaving brushes, hair brushes(including eyelash brushes and other toilet brushes for use on the person) of wild animal hair
3.9	0/0/0	6.8	6	4.5	0	0	0	0/0/0	0/0/			0/0/0	Shaving brushes, hair brushes, eyelash brushes and other toilet brushes for use on the person(including parts and appliances of subheading No. 960329)
													-Artists' brushes, writing brushes and similar brushes for the application of cosmetics:
													---Artists' brushes
4.8	0/0/0	13.5	17.5	7.5	0	0	0	0/0/0	0/0/			0/0/	Artists' brushes of endangered animal hair
4.8	0/0/0	13.5	17.5	7.5	0	0	0	0/0/0	0/0/			0/0/	Other artists' brushes
													---Writing brushes
5.2	0/0/0	16.2	12	6	0	0	0	0/0/0	0/0/			0/0/	Writing brushes of endangered animal hair
5.2	0/0/0	16.2	12	6	0	0	0	0/0/0	0/0/			0/0/	Other writing brushes
													---Other
3.9	0/0/0	20.3	17.5	6	0	0	0	0/0/0	0/0/			0/0/	Similar brushes for the application of cosmetics, of endangered animal hair
3.9	0/0/0	20.3	17.5	6	0	0	0	0/0/0	0/0/			0/0/	Other similar brushes for the application of cosmeties
													-Paint, distemper, varnish or similar brushes (other than brushes of subheading No. 9603. 30); paint pads and rollers:
													---Paint, distemper, varnish or similar brushes:
	0/0/0	20	12	6	0	0	0	0/0/0	0/0/			0/0/	----Of pigs', hogs' or boars' bristle
	0/0/0	23	16.1	6	0	0	0	0/0/0	0/0/			0/0/	----Other
	0/0/0	23	16.1	6	0	0	0	0/0/0	0/0/			0/0/	---Paint pads and rollers
													-Other brushes constituting parts of machines, appliances or vehicles:
													---Brushes of metal wire:
	0/0/0	10.1	5.6	4.2	0	0	0	0/0/0	0/0/			0/0/	----Constituting parts of machines or appliances
	0/0/0	6.3	5.6	7.3	0	0	0	0/0/0	0/0/			0/0/	----Other
													---Other:
													----Constituting parts of machines or appliances
	0/0/0	10.1	5.6	4.2	0	0	0	0/0/0	0/0/			0/0/	Other brushes constituting parts of machines or appliances, of endangered animal hair
	0/0/0	10.1	5.6	4.2	0	0	0	0/0/0	0/0/			0/0/	Other brushes constituting parts of machines or appliances
													----Other
	0/0/0	6.3	5.6	4.2	0	0	0	0/0/0	0/0/			0/0/	Other brushes constituting parts of vehicles, of endangered animal hair
	0/0/0	6.3	5.6	4.2	0	0	0	0/0/0	0/0/			0/0/	Other brushes constituting parts of vehicles
													-Other:
													---Feather dusters
3.9	0/0/0	17	12.6	6	0	0	0	0/0/0	0/0/			0/0/	Feather dusters of endangered wild birds
3.9	0/0/0	17	12.6	6	0	0	0	0/0/0	0/0/			0/0/	Other feather dusters
													---Other
	0/0/0	12	6	4.5	0	0	0	0/0/0	0/0/			0/0/	Other brooms, brushes (including mops, feather dusters), of hair, bristles or tails, of endangered animals
	0/0/0	12	6	4.5	0	0	0	0/0/0	0/0/			0/0/	Brooms, brushes, mops (including feather dusters, hand-operated mechanical floor sweepers, not motorized) of other animal or vegetable materials
	0/0/0	12	6	4.5	0	0	0	0/0/0	0/0/			0/0/	Brooms, brushes, mops and feather dusters(incleuling hand-operated mechanical floor sweepers, not motorized, of other materials)
													Hand sieves and hand riddles:
	0/0/0	21	14.7	6	0	0	0	0/0/0	0/0/			0/0/	Hand sieves and hand riddles
													Travel sets for personal toilet, sewing or shoe or clothes cleaning:
	0/0/0	10.8	6	4.5	0	0	0	0/0/0	0/0/			0/0/	Travel sets for personal toilet, sewing or shoe or clothes cleaning
													Buttons, press-fasteners, snap-fasteners and press-studs, button moulds and other parts of these articles; button blanks:
	0/0/0	21	14.7	6	0	0	0	0/0/0	0/0/			0/0/	-Press-fasteners, snap-fasteners and press-studs and parts thereof
													-Buttons:
	0/0/0	21	14.7	6	0	0	0	0/0/0	0/0/0			0/0/0	--Of plastics, not covered with textile material
	0/0/0	10.8	6	4.5	0	0	0	0/0/0	0/0/0			0/0/0	--Of base metal, not covered with textile material
													--Other
	0/0/0	10.8	6	4.5	0	0	0	0/0/0	0/0/			0/0/0	Other buttons containing materials of endangered animals
	0/0/0	10.8	6	4.5	0	0	0	0/0/0	0/0/			0/0/0	Other buttons
	0/0/0	10.8	6	4.5	0	0	0	0/0/0	0/0/			0/0/0	-Button moulds and other parts of buttons; button blanks

税则号列	货品名称〔CIQ扩展编码及品名—T2表示见附表2〕	最惠(%)	暂定税率	普通	增值/消费	出口退税	计量单位	监管条件	检验检疫	特殊证件对美关税
96.07	拉链及其零件：									
	-拉链：									
9607.1100	--装有贱金属制啮牙齿的〔101 含木制品，102 不含木制品〕	6		130	13/	13	米/千克			/31
9607.1900	--其他〔101 含木制品，102 不含木制品〕	6		130	13/	13	米/千克			/31
9607.2000	-零件〔101 含木制品，102 不含木制品〕	6		130	13/	13	千克			/31
96.08	**圆珠笔；毡尖和其他渗水式笔尖笔及唛头笔；自来水笔、铁笔型自来水笔及其他钢笔；蜡纸铁笔；活动铅笔；钢笔杆、铅笔套及类似的笔套；上述物品的零件(包括帽、夹)，但税目96.09的货品除外：**									
9608.1000	-圆珠笔〔999〕	8		80	13/	13	支/千克			/28
9608.2000	-毡尖和其他渗水式笔尖笔及唛头笔〔101 彩笔，102 其他笔〕	12		80	13/	13	支/千克			/32
	-自来水笔、铁笔型自来水笔及其他钢笔：									
9608.3010	---墨汁画笔〔101 毛笔，102 其他笔〕	12		80	13/	13	支/千克			/32
9608.3020	---自来水笔〔999〕	12		80	13/	13	支/千克			/32
9608.3090	---其他〔999〕	12		80	13/	13	支/千克			/32
9608.4000	-活动铅笔〔999〕	12		80	13/	13	支/千克			/32
9608.5000	-由上述两个或多个子目所列物品组成的成套货品〔999〕	12		80	13/	13	套/千克			/32
9608.6000	-圆珠笔芯，由圆珠笔头和墨芯构成〔999〕	12		80	13/	13	支/千克			/32
	-其他：									
9608.9100	--钢笔头及笔尖粒〔999〕	8		70	13/	13	支/千克			/28
	--其他：									
9608.9910	---机器、仪器用笔〔999〕	8		40	13/	13	支/千克			/18
9608.9920	---蜡纸铁笔；钢笔杆、铅笔杆及类似的笔杆〔101 蜡纸铁笔，102 笔杆等〕	12		80	13/	13	支/千克			/32
9608.9990	---其他〔999〕	10		80	13/	13	千克			/30
96.09	**铅笔(税目96.08的铅笔除外)、颜色铅笔、铅笔芯、蜡笔、图画碳笔、书写或绘画用粉笔及裁缝划粉：**									
	-铅笔及颜色铅笔：									
9609.1010	---铅笔〔999〕	12		80	13/	13	千克/百支			/32
9609.1020	---颜色铅笔〔999〕	12		80	13/	13	千克			/32
9609.2000	-铅笔芯，黑的或其他颜色的〔999〕	12		80	13/	13	千克			/32
9609.9000	-其他〔101 蜡笔，102 碳笔，103 粉笔〕	6		80	13/	13	千克			/26
96.10	**具有书写或绘画面的石板、黑板及类似板，不论是否镶框：**									
9610.0000	具有书写或绘画面的石板、黑板及类似板，不论是否镶框〔999〕	6		80	13/	13	千克			/26
96.11	**手用日期戳、封缄戳、编号戳及类似印戳(包括标签压印器)；手工操作的排字盘及带有排字盘的手印器：**									
9611.0000	手用日期戳、封缄戳、编号戳及类似印戳(包括标签压印器)；手工操作的排字盘及带有排字盘的手印器									
9611.0000 10	含濒危动物成分的手用日期戳(包括封缄戳及类似印戳)〔101 含木制品，102 不含木制品〕	8		80	13/	0	千克	FE		/33
9611.0000 90	手用日期戳、封缄戳及类似印戳(包括编号戳、标签压印器；手工排字盘及带有字盘的手印器)〔101 含木制品，102 不含木制品〕	8		80	13/	13	千克			/33
96.12	**打字机色带或类似色带，已上油或经其他方法处理能着色的，不论是否装轴或装盒；印台，不论是否已加印油或带盒子：**									
9612.1000	-色带〔999〕	8		35	13/	13	个/千克			/18
9612.2000	-印台〔101 含木制品，102 不含木制品〕	10		100	13/	13	个/千克			/20
96.13	**香烟打火机和其他打火器(不论是机械的，还是电气的)及其零件，但打火石及打火机芯除外：**									
9613.1000	-袖珍气体打火机，一次性的〔999〕	10		130	13/	13	个/千克	B	N	/
9613.2000	-袖珍气体打火机，可充气的〔999〕	10		130	13/	13	个/千克	B	N	/35
9613.8000	-其他打火器〔101 台式打火机，102 器及其零件〕	10		130	13/	13	个/千克	B	N	/20
9613.9000	-零件〔999〕	10		130	13/	13	千克			/20

协定税率 %										特惠税率 %			Article Description
亚太5国	东/冰/格	巴基斯坦	韩国	瑞士	哥达	秘鲁	澳大利亚	新西/坡/智	港/澳/台	亚太2国	老/柬/缅	36/3/1	
													Slide fasteners and parts thereof:
													-Slide fasteners:
	0/0/0	21	14.7	6	0	0	0	0/0/0	0/0/			0/0/0	--Fitted with chain scoops of base metal
3.9	0/0/0	13.2	14.7	6	0	0	0	0/0/0	0/0/			0/0/	--Other
	0/0/0	21	14.7	6	0	0	0	0/0/0	0/0/			0/0/	-Parts
													Ball point pens; felt tipped and other porous-tipped pens and markers; fountain pens, stylograph pens and other pens; duplicating stylos; propelling or sliding pencils; pen-holders, pencil-holders and similar holders; parts (including caps and clips) of the foregoing articles, other than those of heading No. 96.09:
5.2	0/0/0	6.8	6	4.5	0	0	0	0/0/0	0/0/			0/0/0	-Ball point pens
	0/0/0	21	14.7	6.3	0	0	0	0/0/0	0/0/			0/0/	-Felt tipped and other porous-tipped pens and markers
													-Fountain pens, stylograph pens and other pens:
	0/0/0	21	12.6	6.3	0	0	0	0/0/0	0/0/			0/0/	---Indian ink drawing pens
	0/0/0	21	14.7	6.3	0	0	0	0/0/0	0/0/			0/0/0	---Fountain pens
	0/0/0	21	14.7	6.3	0	0	0	0/0/0	0/0/			0/0/0	---Other
	0/0/0	21	14.7	6.3	0	0	0	0/0/0	0/0/			0/0/	-Propelling or sliding pencils
	0/0/0	21	14.7	6.3	0	0	0	0/0/0	0/0/			0/0/	-Sets of articles from two or more of the foregoing subheadings
	0/0/0	21	14.7	6.3	0	0	0	0/0/0	0/0/			0/0/	-Refills for ball point pens, comprising the ball point and ink-reservoir
													-Other:
	0/0/0	5.4	4.8	3.6	0	0	0	0/0/0	0/0/			0/0/	--Pen nibs and nib points
													--Other:
	0/0/0	12.6	7	5.3	0	0	0	0/0/0	0/0/			0/0/	---Of a kind used on machines or instruments
	0/0/0	21	14.7	6.3	0	0	0	0/0/0	0/0/			0/0/	---Duplicating stylos; pen-holders, pencil-holders and similar holders
	0/0/0	21	14.7	0	0	0	0	0/0/0	0/0/			0/0/	---Other
													Pencils (other than pencils of heading No. 96.08), crayons, pencil leads, pastels, drawing charcoals, writing or drawing chalks and tailors' chalks:
													-Pencils and crayons, with leads encased in a rigid sheath:
	0/0/0	21	14.7	6.3	0	0	0	0/0/0	0/0/			0/0/0	---Pencils
	0/0/0	21	14.7	6.3	0	0	0	0/0/0	0/0/			0/0/	---Crayons
	0/0/0	21	14.7	6.3	0	0	0	0/0/0	0/0/			0/0/	-Pencil leads, black or coloured
	0/0/0	10.8	6	4.5	0	0	0	0/0/0	0/0/			0/0/	-Other
													Slates and boards, with writing or drawing surfaces, whether or not framed:
	0/0/0	10.8	6	4.5	0	0	0	0/0/0	0/0/			0/0/	Slates and boards, with writing or drawing surfaces, whether or not framed
													Date, sealing or numbering stamps, and the like (including devices for printing or embossing labels), designed for operating in the hand; hand-operated composing sticks and hand printing sets incorporating such composing sticks:
													Date, sealing or numbering stamps, and the like (including devices for printing or embossing labels), designed for operating in the hand; hand-operated composing sticks and hand printing sets incorporating such composing sticks
	0/0/0	21	14.7	6.3	0	0	0	0/0/0	0/0/			0/0/	Date, sealing, and the like, designed for operating in the hand, containing materials of endangered animals
	0/0/0	21	14.7	6.3	0	0	0	0/0/0	0/0/			0/0/	Other date, sealing or numbering stamps, and the like (including devices for printing or embossing labels), designed for operating in the hand; hand-operated composing sticks and hand printing sets incorporating such composing sticks
													Typewriter or similar ribbons, inked or otherwise prepared for giving impressions, whether or not on spools or in cartridges; ink-pads, whether or not inked, with or without boxes:
	0/0/0	4.5	6.3	3.2	0	0	0	0/0/0	0/0/			0/0/0	-Inked ribbons
	0/0/0	25	17.5	7.5	0	0	0	0/0/0	0/0/			0/0/	-Ink-pads
													Cigarette lighters and other lighters, whether or not mechanical or electrical, and parts thereof other than flints and wicks:
	0/0/0	25	17.5	7.5	0	0	0	0/0/0	0/0/			0/0/	-Pocket lighters, gas fuelled, non refillable
	0/0/0	25	17.5	7.5	0	0	0	0/0/0	0/0/			0/0/	-Pocket lighters, gas fuelled, refillable
	0/0/0	25	17.5	7.5	0	0	0	0/0/0	0/0/			0/0/	-Other lighters
	0/0/0	25	17.5	7.5	0	0	0	0/0/0	0/0/			0/0/	-Parts

税则号列	货品名称〔CIQ 扩展编码及品名—T2 表示见附表 2〕	最惠(%)	暂定税率	普通	增值/消费	出口退税	计量单位	监管条件	检验检疫	特殊证件对美关税
96.14	**烟斗(包括烟斗头)和烟嘴及其零件：**									
9614.0010	---烟斗及烟斗头									
9614.0010 10	含濒危动物成分的烟斗及烟斗头(仅指野生哺乳类牙齿制产品)〔101 含木制品,102 不含木制品〕	10		130	13/	0	个/千克	ABFE	PQ	/35
9614.0010 20	用植物性材料制作的烟斗及烟斗头〔101 其他木制品,102 含木制品,103 不含木制品〕	10		130	13/	13	个/千克	AB	PQ	/35
9614.0010 90	其他烟斗及烟斗头〔101 含木制品,102 不含木制品〕	10		130	13/	13	个/千克			/35
9614.0090	---其他									
9614.0090 10	含濒危野生动物成分的烟嘴及其零件(仅指野生哺乳类牙齿制产品)〔101 含木制品,102 不含木制品〕	10		130	13/	0	千克	FE		/35
9614.0090 90	其他烟嘴及其零件〔101 含木制品,102 不含木制品〕	10		130	13/	13	千克			/35
96.15	**梳子、发夹及类似品；发卡、卷发夹、卷发器或类似品及其零件，但税目 85.16 的货品除外：**									
	-梳子、发夹及类似品：									
9615.1100	--硬质橡胶或塑料制〔999〕	6		130	13/	13	千克			/26
9615.1900	--其他									
9615.1900 10	含濒危动物成分的其他材料制梳子(包括角质发夹等,金属、塑料及家畜来源的产品除外)〔101 含木制品,102 不含木制品〕	6		130	13/	0	千克	FE		/26
9615.1900 90	其他材料制梳子、发夹及类似品(硬质橡胶、塑料制的除外)〔101 含木制品,102 不含木制品〕	6		130	13/	13	千克			/26
9615.9000	-其他〔101 含木制品,102 不含木制品〕	6		130	13/	13	千克			/26
96.16	**香水喷雾器或类似的化妆用喷雾器及其座架、喷头；粉扑及粉拍，施敷脂粉或化妆品用：**									
9616.1000	-香水喷雾器或类似的化妆用喷雾器及其座架、喷头〔101 含木制品,102 不含木制品〕	6		130	13/	13	千克			/26
9616.2000	-粉扑及粉拍,施敷脂粉或化妆品用〔101 含木制品,102 不含木制品〕	6		130	13/	13	千克			/26
96.17	**带壳的保温瓶和其他真空容器及其零件，但玻璃瓶胆除外：**									
	---保温瓶：									
9617.0011	----玻璃内胆制〔999〕	8		130	13/	13	个/千克			/28
9617.0019	----其他保温瓶(玻璃胆除外)〔999〕	8		130	13/	13	个/千克			/28
9617.0090	---其他〔999〕	8		130	13/	13	千克			/28
96.18	**裁缝用人体模型及其他人体活动模型；橱窗装饰用的自动模型及其他活动陈列品：**									
9618.0000	裁缝用人体模型及其他人体活动模型;橱窗装饰用的自动模型及其他活动陈列品									
9618.0000 10	用植物性材料制作的人体模型〔999〕	10		80	13/	13	千克	AB	PQ	/30
9618.0000 90	裁缝用其他人体模型(包括橱窗装饰用的自动模型及其他活动陈列品)〔101 含木制品,102 不含木制品〕	10		80	13/	13	千克			/30
96.19	**任何材料制的卫生巾(护垫)及止血塞、婴儿尿布及尿布衬里和类似品：**									
	---尿裤及尿布：									
9619.0011	----供婴儿使用的〔999〕	4	0	80	13/	13	千克	A	M	/10
9619.0019	----其他〔999〕	4	0	80	13/	13	千克	A	M	/10
9619.0020	---卫生巾(护垫)及止血塞〔999〕	4		80	13/	13	千克	A	M	/14
9619.0090	---其他〔999〕	6		80	13/	13	千克	A	M	/16
96.20	**独脚架、双脚架、三脚架及类似品：**									
9620.0000	独脚架、双脚架、三脚架及类似品〔999〕	8		80	13/	0,6,13	千克			/33

协定税率 %										特惠税率 %			
亚太5国	东/冰/格	巴基斯坦	韩国	瑞士	哥达	秘鲁	澳大利亚	新西/坡/智	港/澳/台	亚太2国	老/柬/缅	36/3/1	Article Description
													Smoking pipes (including pipe bowls) and cigar or cigarette holders, and parts thereof:
													---Pipes and pipe bowls
	0/0/0	25		7.5	0	0	0	0/0/0	0/0/			0/0/	Smoking pipes (including pipe bowls) containing materials of endangered animals(only referring to products made of ivory of wild mammals)
	0/0/0	25		7.5	0	0	0	0/0/0	0/0/			0/0/	Smoking pipes and pipe bowls, of vegetable materials
	0/0/0	25		7.5	0	0	0	0/0/0	0/0/			0/0/	Other smoking pipes and pipe bowls
													---Other
	0/0/0	25		7.5	0	0	0	0/0/0	0/0/			0/0/	Cigar or cigarette holders, and parts thereof, containing endangered wild animal materials (only referring to products made of ivory of wild mammals)
	0/0/0	25		7.5	0	0	0	0/0/0	0/0/			0/0/	Other cigar or cigarette holders, and parts thereof
													Combs, hair-slides and the like; hairpins, curling pins, curling grips, hair-curlers and the like, other than those of heading No. 85.16, and parts thereof:
													-Combs, hair-slides and the like:
3.9	0/0/0	13	7.2	5.4	0	0	0	0/0/0	0/0/			0/0/0	--Of hard rubber or plastics
													--Other
	0/0/0	18	7.2	5.4	0	0	0	0/0/0	0/0/			0/0/0	Combs containing endangered animals materials (including hair-slides made of horns, but not including products made of metal, plastic or material of domestic animals)
	0/0/0	18	7.2	5.4	0	0	0	0/0/0	0/0/			0/0/0	Combs, hair-slides and the like, of other materials(other than hard rubber or plastics materials)
3.9	0/0/0	13	7.2	5.4	0	0	0	0/0/0	0/0/			0/0/0	-Other
													Scent sprays and similar toilet sprays, and mounts and heads therefor; powderpuffs and pads for the application of cosmetics or toilet preparations:
3.9	0/0/0	13	7.2	5.4	0	0	0	0/0/0	0/0/			0/0/	-Scent sprays and similar toilet sprays, and mounts and heads therefor
3.9	0/0/0	13	7.2	5.4	0	0	0	0/0/0	0/0/			0/0/	-Powder-puffs and pads for the application of cosmetics or toilet preparations
													Vacuum flasks and other vacuum vessels, complete with cases; parts thereof, other than glass inners:
													---Vacuum flasks:
	0/0/0	24	16.8	7.2	0	0	0	0/0/0	0/0/			0/0/	----Glass bottle
	0/0/0	24	16.8	7.2	0	0	0	0/0/0	0/0/			0/0/	----Other vacuum flask (except glass bile)
	0/0/0	18	7.2	5.4	0	0	0	0/0/0	0/0/			0/0/	---Other
													Tailors' dummies and other lay figures; automata and other animated displays used for shop window dressing:
													Tailors' dummies and other lay figures; automata and other animated displays used for shop window dressing
	0/0/0	21	14.7	6.3	0	0	0	0/0/0	0/0/			0/0/	Dummies of vegetable materials
	0/0/0	21	14.7	6.3	0	0	0	0/0/0	0/0/			0/0/	Tailors' other dummies (including automaton and other animated displays used for shop window dressing)
													Sanitary towels(Pads) and tampons, napkins and napkin liners for babies and similar articles, of any material:
													---Diaper and napkin
	0//0	0					0	0//0	0/0/0			0/0/0	----Forbabies
	0//0	0					0	0//0	0/0/0			0/0/0	----Other
	0/0/0	6.8	4	0	0	0	0	0//0	0/0/0			0/0/0	---Sanitary towels(Pads)and tampons
3.9	0/0/0	6.8	5.6	4.2	0	0	0	0/0/0	0/0/0			0/0/0	---Other
													Monopods, bipods, tripods and similar articles:
	/0/0	0	0	0	0	0	0		0/0/			0/0/0	Monopods, bipods, tripods and similar articles

第二十一类
艺术品、收藏品及古物

第九十七章
艺术品、收藏品及古物

注释：

一、本章不包括：

（一）品目 49.07 的未经使用的邮票、印花税票、邮政信笺（印有邮票的纸品）及类似的票证

（二）作舞台、摄影的布景及类似用途的已绘制画布（税目 59.07），但可归入税目 97.06 的除外；

（三）天然或养殖珍珠、宝石或半宝石（税目 71.01 至 71.03）。

二、税目 97.02 所称“雕版画、印制画、石印画的原本”，是指以艺术家完全手工制作的单块或数块印版直接印制出来的黑白或彩色原本，不论艺术家使用何种方法或材料，但不包括使用机器或照相制版方法制作的。

三、税目 97.03 不适用于成批生产的复制品及具有商业性质的传统手工艺品，即使这些物品是艺术家设计或创造的。

四、（一）除上述注释一至三另有规定的以外，可归入本章各税目的物品，均应归入本章的相应税目而不归入本目录的其他税目；

（二）税目 97.06 不适用于可以归入本章其他各税目的物品。

五、已装框的油画、粉画及其他绘画、版画、拼贴画及类似装饰板，如果框架的种类及价值与作品相称，应与作品一并归类。如果框架的种类及价值与作品不相称，应分别归类。

税则号列	货品名称〔CIQ 扩展编码及品名—T2 表示见附表 2〕	最惠(%)	暂定税率	普通	增值/消费	出口退税	计量单位	监管条件	检验检疫	特殊证件对美关税
97.01	**油画、粉画及其他手绘画，但带有手工绘制及手工描饰的制品或税目 49.06 的图纸除外；拼贴画及类似装饰板：**									
	-油画、粉画及其他手绘画：									
	---原件：									
9701.1011	----唐卡〔999〕	6		50	13/	0	幅/千克			/
9701.1019	----其他〔999〕	1		50	13/	0	幅/千克			/21
9701.1020	---复制品〔999〕	6		50	13/	0	幅/千克			/16
9701.9000	-其他									
9701.9000 10	含濒危动物成分的拼贴画（包括类似装饰板，指一切源自濒危动物的产品）〔999〕	6		50	13/	0	千克	ABFE	PQ	/16
9701.9000 20	用其他动植物材料制作的拼贴画（包括类似装饰板，指一切源自野生动物的产品）〔999〕	6		50	13/	0	千克	AB	PQ	/16
9701.9000 90	其他拼贴画及类似装饰板〔999〕	6		50	13/	0	千克			/16
97.02	**雕版画、印制画、石印画的原本：**									
9702.0000	雕版画、印制画、石印画的原本〔999〕	1		50	13/	0	幅/千克			/11
97.03	**各种材料制的雕塑品原件：**									
9703.0000	各种材料制的雕塑品原件									
9703.0000 10	濒危动植物材料制的雕塑品原件（指一切源自濒危动植物的产品）〔999〕	1		50	13/	0	幅/千克	FE		/21
9703.0000 90	其他各种材料制的雕塑品原件〔999〕	1		50	13/	0	幅/千克			/21
97.04	**使用过或未使用过的邮票、印花税票、邮戳印记、首日封、邮政信笺（印有邮票的纸品）及类似品，但税目 49.07 的货品除外：**									
9704.0010	---邮票〔999〕	4		50	13/	0	千克			/29
9704.0090	---其他〔999〕	6		50	13/	0	千克			/
97.05	**具有动物学、植物学、矿物学、解剖学、历史学、考古学、古生物学、人种学或钱币学意义的收集品及珍藏品：**									

SECTION XXI
WORKS OF ART, COLLECTORS' PIECES AND ANTIQUES

Chapter 97
Works of art, collectors' pieces and antiques

Notes:

1. This Chapter does not cover:
   (a) Unused postage or revenue stamps, postal stationery (stamped paper) or the like, of heading 49.07;
   (b) Theatrical scenery, studio back-cloths or the like, of painted canvas (heading No. 59.07) except if they may be classified in heading No. 97.06;
   (c) Pearls, natural or cultured, or precious or semi-precious stones (headings No. 71.01 to 71.03).
2. For the purposes of heading No. 97.02, the expression "original engravings, prints and lithographs" means impressions produced directly, in black and white or in colour, of one or of several plates wholly executed by hand by the artist, irrespective of the process or of the material employed by him, but not including any mechanical or photomechanical process.
3. Heading No. 97.03 does not apply to mass-produced reproductions or works of conventional craftsmanship of a commercial character, even if these articles are designed or created by artists.
4. (a) Subject to Notes 1 to 3 above, articles of this Chapter are to be classified in this Chapter and not in any other Chapter of the Nomenclature.
   (b) heading No. 97.06 does not apply to articles of the preceding headings of this Chapter.
5. Frames around paintings, drawings, pastels, collages or similar decorative plaques, engravings, prints or lithographs are to be classified with those articles, provided they are of a kind and of a value normal to those articles. Frames which are not of a kind or of a value normal to the articles referred to in this Note are to be classified separately.

协定税率 %										特惠税率 %			Article Description
亚太5国	东/冰/格	巴基斯坦	韩国	瑞士	哥达	秘鲁	澳大利亚	新西/坡/智	港/澳/台	亚太2国	老/柬/缅	36/3/1	
													Paintings, drawings and pastels, executed entirely by hand, other than drawings of heading No. 49.06 and other than hand-painted or hand-decorated manufactured articles; collages and similar decorative plaques:
													-Paintings, drawings and pastels:
													---The originals:
	0/0/0	5.4	4.8	3.6	0	0	0	0/0/0	0/0/			0/0/0	----Thangka
	0/0/0	5.4	4.8	1	0	0	0	0/0/0	0/0/			0/0/0	----Other
	0/0/0	10.1	5.6	4.2	0	0	0	0/0/0	0/0/			0/0/0	---Reproductions
													-Other
	0/0/0	10.1	5.6	4.2	0	0	0	0/0/0	0/0/			0/0/0	Collages and similar decorative plaques, containing materials of endangered animals (referring to collages of materials of all kinds of endangered animals)
	0/0/0	10.1	5.6	4.2	0	0	0	0/0/0	0/0/			0/0/0	Collages and similar decorative plaques of other animal or vegetable materials (referring to collages of materials of all kinds of wild animals)
	0/0/0	10.1	5.6	4.2	0	0	0	0/0/0	0/0/			0/0/0	Other collages and similar decorative plaques
													Original engravings, prints and lithographs:
	0/0/0	5.4	4.8	1	0	0	0	0/0/0	0/0/			0/0/	Original engravings, prints and lithographs
													Original sculptures and statuary, in any material:
													Original sculptures and statuary, in any material
	0/0/0	4.8	4.8	1	0	0	0	0/0/0	0/0/			0/0/0	Original sculptures and statuary, in endangered animals and vegetable material (referring to articles from endangered animals and vegetable)
	0/0/0	4.8	4.8	1	0	0	0	0/0/0	0/0/			0/0/0	Other original sculptures and statuary, in any materials
													Used or unused postage or revenue stamps, stamp-postmarks, first-day covers, postal stationery (stamped paper), and the like, other than those of heading No. 49.07:
	0/0/0	4	0	0	0	0	0	0//0	0/0/			0/0/0	---Postage
	0/0/5.6	6.3	5.6	4.2	0	0	0	0/0/0	0/0/			0/0/	---Other
													Collections and collectors pieces of zoological, botanical, mineralogical, anatomical, historical, archaeological, palaeontological, ethnographic or numismatic interest:

税则号列		货品名称〔CIQ扩展编码及品名－T2表示见附表2〕	最惠(%)	暂定税率	普通	增值/消费	出口退税	计量单位	监管条件	检验检疫	特殊证件对美关税
9705.0000		具有动物学、植物学、矿物学、解剖学、历史学、考古学、古生物学、人种学或钱币学意义的收集品及珍藏品									
9705.0000	10	含濒危动植物的收藏品（具有动植物学意义的）〔101 植物标本，999 具有动植物学意义的〕	0		0	13/	0	千克	ABFE	PQ	/10
9705.0000	20	古生物化石	0		0	13/	0	千克	ABz	PQ	/10
9705.0000	30	有矿物学研究价值、可供收集和珍藏的钟乳石	0		0	13/	0	千克	ABu	PQ	/10
9705.0000	40	含有人类遗传资源的组织标本、手术样本	0		0	13/	0	千克	ABV	VW	/10
9705.0000	90	具有动、植、矿物学意义的收藏品（还包括具有解剖、历史、考古、古生物学意义的收藏品）〔101 植物标本，999 还包括具有解剖、历史、考古、古生物学意义的收藏品〕	0		0	13/	0	千克	AB	PQ	/10
97.06		**超过 100 年的古物：**									
9706.0000		超过 100 年的古物									
9706.0000	10	超过 100 年的濒危野生动植古物（具收藏或文史价值的）〔101 植物标本，999 具收藏或文史价值的〕	0		0	13/	0	千克	ABFE	PQ	/20
9706.0000	90	其他超过 100 年的古物〔999〕	0		0	13/	0	千克			/20

协定税率 %										特惠税率 %			Article Description
亚太5国	东/冰/格	巴基斯坦	韩国	瑞士	哥达	秘鲁	澳大利亚	新西/坡/智	港/澳/台	亚太2国	老/柬/缅	36/3/1	
													Collections and collectors' pieces of zoological, botanical, mineralogical, anatomical, historical, archaeological, palaeontological, ethnographic or numismatic interest
												0/0/0	Collections and collectors' pieces, containing endangered plants or animal (with zoological and botanical interest)
	//							//	//		//	0/0/0	Paleontological fossils
	//							//	//		//	0/0/0	Stalactites of mineralogical value for collection and collection
	//							//	//		//	0/0/0	Tissue specimens and surgical specimens containing human genetic resources
												0/0/0	Collections and collectors' pieces (with zoological, botanical, mineralogical, anatomical, historical, archaeological, palaeontological, ethnographic or numismatic interest)
													Antiques of an age exceeding one hundred years:
													Antiques of an age exceeding one hundred years
												0/0/0	Antiques of an age exceeding one hundred years of endangered wild animal or vegetable(having literary or historical collection value)
												0/0/0	Other antiques of an age exceeding one hundred years

第二十二类
特殊交易品及未分类商品

第九十八章
特殊交易品及未分类商品

税则号列	货品名称〔CIQ 扩展编码及品名一T2 表示见附表 2〕	最惠(%)	暂定税率	普通	增值/消费	出口退税	计量单位	监管条件	检验检疫	特殊证件对美关税
98.01	未分类商品									
9801.0010	人民币 2000 元及以下的非税、非证进口商品〔999〕	0		0	0/	0	千克			/
9801.0090	其他未分类商品〔101 植物真菌，102 植物线虫，103 其他植物病原体，104 杂草，105 螨类，106 多足虫类动物，107 其他植物有害生物，108 土壤，109 科研用试剂和其它材料，110 其他植物检疫类特殊物品，单项记录价值≤2000RMB 的非税、证进口商品〕	0		0	0/	9,13	千克			/
9801.3010	流通中的人民币现钞(包括纸币及硬币)〔999〕	0		0	0/		千克	m		/
9801.3090	流通中的外币现钞(包括纸币及硬币)〔999〕	0		0	0/		千克			/
98.03	出口计算机软件(仅用于出口，不包括与产品固化或集成为一体的软件)									
9803.0010	定制型系统软件〔999〕	0		0	0/	0	套			/
9803.0020	定制型支撑软件〔999〕	0		0	0/	0	套			/
9803.0030	定制型应用软件〔999〕	0		0	0/	0	套			/
9803.0090	其他定制型软件〔999〕	0		0	0/	0	套			/

SECTION XXII
ARTICLES OF SPECIAL TRADE AND GOOD UNCLASSIFIED

Chapter 98
Articles of Special Trade and Good Unclassified

协定税率 %										特惠税率 %			Article Description
亚太5国	东/冰/格	巴基斯坦	韩国	瑞士	哥达	秘鲁	澳大利亚	新西/坡/智	港/澳/台	亚太2国	老/柬/缅	36/3/1	
													Good unclassified
													Import goods exempted from the levy of customs duties and not subject to license control, value≤2000RMB
													Other unclassified commodities
	//							//	//		//	//	RMB cash in circulation (including notes and coins)
	//							//	//		//	//	Foreign currency notes in circulation (including notes and coins)
													Computer software, not including software hardwired or integrated in products
													System software
													Support software
													Application software
													Other software

2

进出口商品规范申报目录

Index Catalogue on Essential Standard Data Required by China Customs for the Declaration of Import and Export Goods

中华人民共和国海关进出口商品规范申报目录

使 用 说 明

进出口品货物收货人或其代理人在填报海关进出品货物报关单的“商品名称、规格型号”栏目时，应按照本《申报目录》中所申报要素的内容填报。为方便《申报目录》的使用，特作说明如下：

一、《申报目录》采用了与《中华人民共和国海关进出品税则》（以下简称《税则》）一致的结构，所列商品按照类、章层次排列。除了《税则》中已有的类注释、章注释外，为了准确理解对商品规范申报的要求，在相关章前对应该章的共性问题用“注解”加以说明。在使用《申报目录》时，首先应阅读各章的注解，再查阅具体商品对应的规范申报内容。

二、《申报目录》正文由“商品编码”、“商品要素”、“备注详解\举例说明”栏组成。

三、《申报目录》的“商品描述”栏所列的全部编码与《税则》中“税则号列”栏所列全部编码保持一致；《申报目录》的“商品描述”与《税则》中“货品名称”内容相同。

四、《申报目录》对不同商品设置了特定的申报要素内容。报关单中的“商品名称、规格型号”栏应当按照《申报目录》中相应商品所列“申报要素”、“备注详解\举例说明”的各项内容填写。

五、《申报目录》属于结构性目录，其中所列商品按照不同位数编码所代表的层次进行排列，当某一层次编码商品所要求的申报要素与上一层次编码商品的申报要素相同时，则该商品的“商品编码”就不列示在书中，但表示该层次“商品编码”对应的商品使用上一层次编码商品所列的“申报要素”。例如：

（一）4 位编码对应商品有“申报要素”的如下所示：

商品编码器	商品描述	申报要素/备注详解/举例说明
01.01	马、驴、骡：	1.品名；2.是否野生；3.是否改良种用举例；改良种用野马
	~~马~~	
~~0101.2100~~	~~改良种用~~	
~~0101.2900~~	~~其他~~	

“01.01”下面所属的“商品编码”所对应的商品的“申报要素”都与“01.01”一致，所以“01.01”下面所属的“商品编码”都省略，读者如有压根可参考《税则》。

（二）一级子目对应商品有“申报要素”的如下列示：

商品编码器	商品描述	申报要素/备注详解/举例说明
84.79	本章其他税目未列名的具有独立功能的机器及机器器具	
8479.1	-公共工程用机器：	1.品名；2.用途；3.功能
	~~--摊铺机：~~	
~~8479.1021~~	~~---沥青混凝土摊铺机~~	
~~8479.1022~~	~~---稳定土摊铺机~~	
~~8479.1029~~	~~---其他~~	
~~8479.1090~~	~~--其他~~	

“-公共工程用机器：”下面所属的“商品编码”所对应的商品的“申报要素”都与“-公共工程用机器：”一致，所以“-公共工程用机器：”下面所属的“商品编码”都省略列示，读者如有需要可参考《税则》。

依此类推二级子目、三有子目、四级子目都如上述列示。在《申报目录》中如低级子目有对应“申报要素”的，其上层子目对应的“申报要素”栏为空，但其上层子目的“商品编码”会一一列示。

为了更方便读者使用本“申报目录”，书中列示出 5 位、6 位、7 位编码，这样更加明确了商品归类的查询，更加专业的说明商品归类原则，以便读者对进出口商品进行正确归类。

进出口商品规范申报目录

商品编码	申报要素
0101	1.品牌类型 2.出口享惠情况 3.是否改良种用 4.品种
0102	1.品牌类型 2.出口享惠情况 3.是否改良种用
01031	1.品牌类型 2.出口享惠情况 3.是否改良种用
01039	1.品牌类型 2.出口享惠情况 3.个体重量
0104	1.品牌类型 2.出口享惠情况 3.是否改良种用
0105	1.品牌类型 2.出口享惠情况 3.是否改良种用 4.个体重量
01061	1.品牌类型 2.出口享惠情况 3.是否改良种用
0106201	1.品牌类型 2.出口享惠情况 3.是否改良种用
0106202	1.品牌类型 2.出口享惠情况 3.用途(食用)
0106209	1.品牌类型 2.出口享惠情况
010631	1.品牌类型 2.出口享惠情况 3.是否改良种用
010632	1.品牌类型 2.出口享惠情况 3.是否改良种用
010633	1.品牌类型 2.出口享惠情况 3.是否改良种用
0106391	1.品牌类型 2.出口享惠情况 3.是否改良种用 4.如为信鸽请注明足环号
0106392	1.品牌类型 2.出口享惠情况 3.用途(食用)
0106399	1.品牌类型 2.出口享惠情况 3.如为信鸽请注明足环号
01064	1.品牌类型 2.出口享惠情况 3.是否改良种用
01069	1.品牌类型 2.出口享惠情况 3.是否改良种用
0201	1.品牌类型 2.出口享惠情况 3.制作或保存方法(鲜、冷)4.加工方法(整头及半头、带骨或去骨等)5.牛肉部位(如眼肉、腱子肉等)6.包装规格 7.英文品名 8.品牌 9.厂号(名称或号码)10.牛种(安格斯牛、和牛等)11.牛龄 12.级别(A级、B级等)13.饲养方式(草饲、谷饲等)14.签约日期 15.加工程度(精修、粗修等)
0202	1.品牌类型 2.出口享惠情况 3.制作或保存方法(冻)4.加工方法(整头及半头、带骨或去骨等)5.牛肉部位(如眼肉、腱子肉等)6.包装规格 7.英文品名 8.品牌 9.厂号(名称或号码)10.牛种(安格斯牛、和牛等)11.牛龄 12.级别(A级、B级等)13.饲养方式(草饲、谷饲等)14.签约日期 15.加工程度(精修、粗修等)
0203	1.品牌类型 2.出口享惠情况 3.制作或保存方法(鲜、冷、冻)4.加工方法(整头及半头、带骨或去骨等)5.包装规格 6.厂号(名称或号码)
0204	1.品牌类型 2.出口享惠情况 3.制作或保存方法(鲜、冷、冻)4.加工方法(整头及半头、带骨或去骨等)5.包装规格 6.厂号(名称或号码)
0205	1.品牌类型 2.出口享惠情况 3.制作或保存方法(鲜、冷、冻)4.包装规格 5.厂号(名称或号码)
0206	1.品牌类型 2.出口享惠情况 3.制作或保存方法(鲜、冷、冻)4.种类(舌、肝、心管、板筋等)5.包装规格 6.厂号(名称或号码)
020711	1.品牌类型 2.出口享惠情况 3.制作或保存方法(鲜、冷)4.加工方法(整只、带骨或去骨等)5.厂号(名称或号码)6.品牌
020712	1.品牌类型 2.出口享惠情况 3.制作或保存方法(冻)4.加工方法(整只、带骨或去骨等)5.厂号(名称或号码)6.品牌
020713	1.品牌类型 2.出口享惠情况 3.制作或保存方法(鲜、冷)4.加工方法(整只、带骨或去骨等)5.厂号(名称或号码)6.品牌
0207141	1.品牌类型 2.出口享惠情况 3.制作或保存方法(冻)4.加工方法(整只、带骨或去骨等)5.厂号(名称或号码)6.品牌
02071421	1.品牌类型 2.出口享惠情况 3.制作或保存方法(冻)4.加工方法(整只、带骨或去骨等)5.厂号(名称或号码)6.品牌
02071422	1.品牌类型 2.出口享惠情况 3.制作或保存方法(冻)4.加工方法(整只、带骨或去骨等)5.厂号(名称或号码)6.品牌 7.规格(个体重量)
02071429	1.品牌类型 2.出口享惠情况 3.制作或保存方法(冻)4.加工方法(整只、带骨或去骨等)5.种类(心、肝等)6.厂号(名称或号码)7.品牌
020724	1.品牌类型 2.出口享惠情况 3.制作或保存方法(鲜、冷)4.加工方法(整只、带骨或去骨等)
020725	1.品牌类型 2.出口享惠情况 3.制作或保存方法(冻)4.加工方法(整只、带骨或去骨等)
020726	1.品牌类型 2.出口享惠情况 3.制作或保存方法(鲜、冷)4.加工方法(整只、带骨或去骨等)5.杂碎请列明具体种类
020727	1.品牌类型 2.出口享惠情况 3.制作或保存方法(冻)4.加工方法(整只、带骨或去骨等)5.杂碎请列明具体种类 6.厂号(名称或号码)7.品牌 8.英文品名
020741	1.品牌类型 2.出口享惠情况 3.制作或保存方法(鲜、冷)4.加工方法(整只)
020742	1.品牌类型 2.出口享惠情况 3.制作或保存方法(冻)4.加工方法(整只)
020743	1.品牌类型 2.出口享惠情况 3.制作或保存方法(鲜、冷)
020744	1.品牌类型 2.出口享惠情况 3.制作或保存方法(鲜、冷)4.加工方法(带骨或去骨等)5.杂碎请列明具体种类
020745	1.品牌类型 2.出口享惠情况 3.制作或保存方法(冻)4.加工方法(带骨或去骨等)5.杂碎请列明具体种类
020751	1.品牌类型 2.出口享惠情况 3.制作或保存方法(鲜、冷)4.加工方法(整只)
020752	1.品牌类型 2.出口享惠情况 3.制作或保存方法(冻)4.加工方法(整只)
020753	1.品牌类型 2.出口享惠情况 3.制作或保存方法(鲜、冷)
020754	1.品牌类型 2.出口享惠情况 3.制作或保存方法(鲜、冷)4.加工方法(带骨或去骨等)5.杂碎请列明具体种类
020755	1.品牌类型 2.出口享惠情况 3.制作或保存方法(冻)4.加工方法(带骨或去骨等)5.杂碎请列明具体种类
02076	1.品牌类型 2.出口享惠情况 3.制作或保存方法(鲜、冷、冻)4.加工方法(整只、带骨或去骨等)5.杂碎请列明具体种类
0208101	1.品牌类型 2.出口享惠情况 3.制作或保存方法(鲜、冷)4.包装规格
0208102	1.品牌类型 2.出口享惠情况 3.制作或保存方法(冻)4.包装规格
0208109	1.品牌类型 2.出口享惠情况 3.制作或保存方法(鲜、冷、冻)4.杂碎请列明具体种类及用途 5.包装规格
02083	1.品牌类型 2.出口享惠情况 3.制作或保存方法(鲜、冷、冻)4.杂碎请列明具体种类及用途 5.包装规格
02084	1.品牌类型 2.出口享惠情况 3.制作或保存方法(鲜、冷、冻)4.杂碎请列明具体种类及用途 5.包装规格
02085	1.品牌类型 2.出口享惠情况 3.制作或保存方法(鲜、冷、冻)4.杂碎请列明具体种类及用途 5.包装规格
02086	1.品牌类型 2.出口享惠情况 3.制作或保存方法(鲜、冷、冻)4.杂碎请列明具体种类及用途 5.包装规格
02089	1.品牌类型 2.出口享惠情况 3.制作或保存方法(鲜、冷、冻)4.杂碎请列明具体种类及用途 5.包装规格
0209	1.品牌类型 2.出口享惠情况 3.制作或保存方法(未炼制、未提取脂肪、干、熏、盐腌、盐渍等)
02101	1.品牌类型 2.出口享惠情况 3.部位(腿肉、腹肉等),是否带骨 4.制作或保存方法(干、熏、盐腌、盐渍等)
02102	1.品牌类型 2.出口享惠情况 3.制作或保存方法(干、熏、盐腌、盐渍等)
02109	1.品牌类型 2.出口享惠情况 3.用途 4.制作或保存方法(干、熏、盐腌、盐渍等)5.杂碎请列明具体种类
03011	1.品牌类型 2.出口享惠情况 3.用途(观赏用)4.状态(活)5.拉丁名称
0301911	1.品牌类型 2.出口享惠情况 3.状态(活)4.是否为鱼苗 5.拉丁名称
0301919	1.品牌类型 2.出口享惠情况 3.状态(活)4.拉丁名称
0301921	1.品牌类型 2.出口享惠情况 3.状态(活)4.是否为鱼苗 5.拉丁名称
0301929	1.品牌类型 2.出口享惠情况 3.状态(活)4.拉丁名称
0301931	1.品牌类型 2.出口享惠情况 3.状态(活)4.是否为鱼苗 5.拉丁名称
0301939	1.品牌类型 2.出口享惠情况 3.状态(活)4.拉丁名称
0301941	1.品牌类型 2.出口享惠情况 3.状态(活)4.是否为鱼苗 5.拉丁名称
0301949	1.品牌类型 2.出口享惠情况 3.状态(活)4.拉丁名称
0301951	1.品牌类型 2.出口享惠情况 3.状态(活)4.是否为鱼苗 5.拉丁名称
0301959	1.品牌类型 2.出口享惠情况 3.状态(活)4.拉丁名称
0301991	1.品牌类型 2.出口享惠情况 3.状态(活)4.是否为鱼苗 5.拉丁名称
0301999	1.品牌类型 2.出口享惠情况 3.状态(活)4.拉丁名称
03021	1.品牌类型 2.出口享惠情况 3.制作或保存方法(鲜、冷)4.拉丁名称 5.个体重量[如1000－2000克/条(块)等]
03022	1.品牌类型 2.出口享惠情况 3.制作或保存方法(鲜、冷)4.拉丁名称 5.个体重量[如1000－2000克/条(块)等]
03023	1.品牌类型 2.出口享惠情况 3.制作或保存方法(鲜、冷)4.拉丁名称 5.个体重量[如1000－2000克/条(块)等]
03024	1.品牌类型 2.出口享惠情况 3.制作或保存方法(鲜、冷)4.拉丁名称 5.个体重量[如1000－2000克/条(块)等]
03025	1.品牌类型 2.出口享惠情况 3.制作或保存方法(鲜、冷)4.拉丁名称 5.个体重量[如1000－2000克/条(块)等]
03027	1.品牌类型 2.出口享惠情况 3.制作或保存方法(鲜、冷)4.拉丁名称 5.个体重量[如1000－2000克/条(块)等]
03028	1.品牌类型 2.出口享惠情况 3.制作或保存方法(鲜、冷)4.拉丁名称 5.个体重量[如1000－2000克/条(块)等]
03029	1.品牌类型 2.出口享惠情况 3.制作或保存方法(鲜、冷)4.拉丁名称
03031	1.品牌类型 2.出口享惠情况 3.制作或保存方法(冻)4.拉丁名称 5.个体重量[如1000－2000克/条(块)等]
03032	1.品牌类型 2.出口享惠情况 3.制作或保存方法(冻)4.拉丁名称 5.个体重量[如1000－2000克/条(块)等]
03033	1.品牌类型 2.出口享惠情况 3.制作或保存方法(冻)4.拉丁名称 5.个体重量[如1000－2000克/条(块)等]
03034	1.品牌类型 2.出口享惠情况 3.制作或保存方法(冻)4.拉丁名称 5.个体重量[如1000－2000克/条(块)等]
03035	1.品牌类型 2.出口享惠情况 3.制作或保存方法(冻)4.拉丁名称 5.个体重量[如1000－2000克/条(块)等]
03036	1.品牌类型 2.出口享惠情况 3.制作或保存方法(冻)4.拉丁名称 5.个体重量[如1000－2000克/条(块)等]
03038	1.品牌类型 2.出口享惠情况 3.制作或保存方法(冻)4.拉丁名称 5.个体重量[如1000－2000克/条(块)等]

商品编码	申报要素
03039	1.品牌类型 2.出口享惠情况 3.制作或保存方法(冻)4.拉丁名称
03043	1.品牌类型 2.出口享惠情况 3.制作或保存方法(鲜、冷)4.拉丁名称 5.规格[克重/片(块)等]
03044	1.品牌类型 2.出口享惠情况 3.制作或保存方法(鲜、冷)4.拉丁名称 5.规格[克重/片(块)等]
03045	1.品牌类型 2.出口享惠情况 3.制作或保存方法(鲜、冷)4.拉丁名称 5.规格[克重/片(块)等]
030461	1.品牌类型 2.出口享惠情况 3.制作或保存方法(冻)4.拉丁名称 5.规格[克重/片(块)等]
0304621	1.品牌类型 2.出口享惠情况 3.制作或保存方法(冻)4.拉丁名称 5.规格[克重/片(块)等]
0304629	1.品牌类型 2.出口享惠情况 3.制作或保存方法(冻)4.拉丁名称 5.规格[克重/片(块)等]6.是否带皮、刺、鳞、鳍
030463	1.品牌类型 2.出口享惠情况 3.制作或保存方法(冻)4.拉丁名称 5.规格[克重/片(块)等]6.是否带皮、刺、鳞、鳍
030469	1.品牌类型 2.出口享惠情况 3.制作或保存方法(冻)4.拉丁名称 5.规格[克重/片(块)等]6.是否带皮、刺、鳞、鳍
03047	1.品牌类型 2.出口享惠情况 3.制作或保存方法(冻)4.拉丁名称 5.规格[克重/片(块)等]6.是否带皮、刺、鳞、鳍
030481	1.品牌类型 2.出口享惠情况 3.制作或保存方法(冻)4.拉丁名称 5.规格[克重/片(块)等]6.是否带皮、刺、鳞、鳍
030482	1.品牌类型 2.出口享惠情况 3.制作或保存方法(冻)4.拉丁名称 5.规格[克重/片(块)等]6.是否带皮、刺、鳞、鳍
030483	1.品牌类型 2.出口享惠情况 3.制作或保存方法(冻)4.拉丁名称 5.规格[克重/片(块)等]6.是否带皮、刺、鳞、鳍
030484	1.品牌类型 2.出口享惠情况 3.制作或保存方法(冻)4.拉丁名称 5.规格[克重/片(块)等]
030485	1.品牌类型 2.出口享惠情况 3.制作或保存方法(冻)4.拉丁名称 5.规格[克重/片(块)等]
030486	1.品牌类型 2.出口享惠情况 3.制作或保存方法(冻)4.拉丁名称 5.规格[克重/片(块)等]6.是否带皮、刺、鳞、鳍
030487	1.品牌类型 2.出口享惠情况 3.制作或保存方法(冻)4.拉丁名称 5.规格[克重/片(块)等]6.是否带皮、刺、鳞、鳍
030488	1.品牌类型 2.出口享惠情况 3.制作或保存方法(冻)4.拉丁名称 5.规格[克重/片(块)等]
030489	1.品牌类型 2.出口享惠情况 3.制作或保存方法(冻)4.拉丁名称 5.规格[克重/片(块)等]6.是否带皮、刺、鳞、鳍
03049	1.品牌类型 2.出口享惠情况 3.制作或保存方法(冻)4.拉丁名称 5.规格[克重/片(块)等]
03051	1.品牌类型 2.出口享惠情况 3.用途 4.拉丁名称
03052	1.品牌类型 2.出口享惠情况 3.制作或保存方法(干、熏、盐腌、盐渍)4.拉丁名称
03053	1.品牌类型 2.出口享惠情况 3.制作或保存方法(干、盐腌、盐渍)4.拉丁名称
03054	1.品牌类型 2.出口享惠情况 3.制作或保存方法(熏)4.拉丁名称
03055	1.品牌类型 2.出口享惠情况 3.制作或保存方法(干)4.拉丁名称
03056	1.品牌类型 2.出口享惠情况 3.制作或保存方法(盐腌、盐渍)4.拉丁名称
03057	1.品牌类型 2.出口享惠情况 3.用途 4.拉丁名称
030611	1.品牌类型 2.出口享惠情况 3.制作或保存方法(冻)4.状态(带壳、去壳)5.拉丁名称 6.个体重量 7.包装规格
030612	1.品牌类型 2.出口享惠情况 3.制作或保存方法(冻)4.状态(带壳、去壳)5.拉丁名称 6.个体重量 7.包装规格
030614	1.品牌类型 2.出口享惠情况 3.制作或保存方法(冻)4.状态(带壳、去壳)5.拉丁名称 6.个体重量 7.包装规格
030615	1.品牌类型 2.出口享惠情况 3.制作或保存方法(冻)4.状态(带壳、去壳)5.拉丁名称 6.个体重量 7.包装规格
030616	1.品牌类型 2.出口享惠情况 3.制作或保存方法(冻)4.状态(带壳、去壳)5.拉丁名称 6.规格(如41～50个/磅)7.包装规格
030617	1.品牌类型 2.出口享惠情况 3.制作或保存方法(冻)4.状态(带壳、去壳)5.拉丁名称 6.规格(如41～50个/磅)7.包装规格 8.品牌
030619	1.品牌类型 2.出口享惠情况 3.制作或保存方法(冻)
0306311	1.品牌类型 2.出口享惠情况 3.是否为种苗 4.拉丁名称
0306319	1.品牌类型 2.出口享惠情况 3.制作或保存方法(活、鲜、冷等)4.状态(带壳、去壳)5.拉丁名称 6.个体重量 7.包装规格
0306321	1.品牌类型 2.出口享惠情况 3.是否为种苗 4.拉丁名称
0306329	1.品牌类型 2.出口享惠情况 3.制作或保存方法(活、鲜、冷等)4.状态(带壳、去壳)5.拉丁名称 6.个体重量 7.包装规格
0306331	1.品牌类型 2.出口享惠情况 3.是否为种苗 4.拉丁名称
0306339	1.品牌类型 2.出口享惠情况 3.制作或保存方法(活、鲜、冷等)4.状态(带壳、去壳)5.拉丁名称 6.个体重量 7.包装规格
0306341	1.品牌类型 2.出口享惠情况 3.是否为种苗 4.拉丁名称
0306349	1.品牌类型 2.出口享惠情况 3.制作或保存方法(活、鲜、冷等)4.状态(带壳、去壳)5.拉丁名称 6.个体重量 7.包装规格
0306351	1.品牌类型 2.出口享惠情况 3.是否为种苗 4.拉丁名称
0306352	1.品牌类型 2.出口享惠情况 3.制作或保存方法(鲜、冷等)4.状态(带壳、去壳)5.拉丁名称 6.个体重量 7.包装规格
0306359	1.品牌类型 2.出口享惠情况 3.制作或保存方法(活、鲜、冷等)4.状态(带壳、去壳)5.拉丁名称 6.个体重量 7.包装规格
0306361	1.品牌类型 2.出口享惠情况 3.是否为种苗 4.拉丁名称
0306362	1.品牌类型 2.出口享惠情况 3.制作或保存方法(鲜、冷等)4.状态(带壳、去壳)5.拉丁名称 6.个体重量 7.包装规格
0306369	1.品牌类型 2.出口享惠情况 3.制作或保存方法(活、鲜、冷等)4.拉丁名称 5.状态(是否全虾、去头、去肠线,去尾、带壳、去壳、裹面粉等)6.个体重量 7.包装规格
0306391	1.品牌类型 2.出口享惠情况 3.是否为种苗
0306399	1.品牌类型 2.出口享惠情况 3.制作或保存方法(活、鲜、冷等)
030691	1.品牌类型 2.出口享惠情况 3.制作或保存方法(干、盐腌、盐渍等)4.状态(带壳、去壳)5.拉丁名称 6.个体重量 7.包装规格
030692	1.品牌类型 2.出口享惠情况 3.制作或保存方法(干、盐腌、盐渍等)4.状态(带壳、去壳)5.拉丁名称
030693	1.品牌类型 2.出口享惠情况 3.制作或保存方法(干、盐腌、盐渍等)4.状态(带壳、去壳)5.拉丁名称 6.个体重量 7.包装规格
030694	1.品牌类型 2.出口享惠情况 3.制作或保存方法(干、盐腌、盐渍等)4.状态(带壳、去壳)5.拉丁名称 6.个体重量 7.包装规格
030695	1.品牌类型 2.出口享惠情况 3.制作或保存方法(干、盐腌、盐渍等)4.状态(带壳、去壳)5.拉丁名称 6.个体重量 7.包装规格
030699	1.品牌类型 2.出口享惠情况 3.制作或保存方法(干、盐腌、盐渍等)
0307111	1.品牌类型 2.出口享惠情况 3.是否为种苗 4.拉丁名称
0307119	1.品牌类型 2.出口享惠情况 3.制作或保存方法(活、鲜、冷)4.状态(带壳、去壳)5.拉丁名称 6.个体重量 7.包装规格
030712	1.品牌类型 2.出口享惠情况 3.制作或保存方法(冻)4.状态(带壳、去壳)5.拉丁名称 6.个体重量 7.包装规格
030719	1.品牌类型 2.出口享惠情况 3.制作或保存方法(干、盐腌、盐渍等)4.状态(带壳、去壳)5.拉丁名称 6.个体重量 7.包装规格
0307211	1.品牌类型 2.出口享惠情况 3.是否为种苗 4.拉丁名称
0307219	1.品牌类型 2.出口享惠情况 3.制作或保存方法(活、鲜、冷)4.状态(带壳、去壳)5.拉丁名称 6.个体重量 7.包装规格
030722	1.品牌类型 2.出口享惠情况 3.制作或保存方法(冻)4.状态(带壳、去壳)5.拉丁名称 6.个体重量 7.包装规格
030729	1.品牌类型 2.出口享惠情况 3.制作或保存方法(干、盐腌、盐渍等)4.状态(带壳、去壳)5.拉丁名称 6.个体重量 7.包装规格
0307311	1.品牌类型 2.出口享惠情况 3.是否为种苗 4.拉丁名称
0307319	1.品牌类型 2.出口享惠情况 3.制作或保存方法(活、鲜、冷)4.状态(带壳、去壳)5.拉丁名称 6.个体重量 7.包装规格
030732	1.品牌类型 2.出口享惠情况 3.制作或保存方法(冻)4.状态(带壳、去壳)5.拉丁名称 6.个体重量 7.包装规格
030739	1.品牌类型 2.出口享惠情况 3.制作或保存方法(干、盐腌、盐渍等)4.状态(带壳、去壳)5.拉丁名称 6.个体重量 7.包装规格
0307421	1.品牌类型 2.出口享惠情况 3.是否为种苗 4.拉丁名称
03074291	1.品牌类型 2.出口享惠情况 3.制作或保存方法(活、鲜、冷)4.拉丁名称 5.个体重量 6.包装规格
03074299	1.品牌类型 2.出口享惠情况 3.制作或保存方法(活、鲜、冷)4.拉丁名称
0307431	1.品牌类型 2.出口享惠情况 3.制作或保存方法(冻)4.拉丁名称(规范到属)5.个体重量 6.包装规格
0307439	1.品牌类型 2.出口享惠情况 3.制作或保存方法(冻)4.拉丁名称
0307491	1.品牌类型 2.出口享惠情况 3.制作或保存方法(干、盐腌、盐渍等)4.拉丁名称 5.个体重量 6.包装规格
0307499	1.品牌类型 2.出口享惠情况 3.制作或保存方法(干、盐腌、盐渍等)4.拉丁名称
030751	1.品牌类型 2.出口享惠情况 3.制作或保存方法(活、鲜、冷)4.拉丁名称 5.个体重量 6.包装规格
030752	1.品牌类型 2.出口享惠情况 3.制作或保存方法(冻)4.拉丁名称 5.个体重量 6.包装规格
030759	1.品牌类型 2.出口享惠情况 3.制作或保存方法(干、盐腌、盐渍等)4.拉丁名称 5.个体重量 6.包装规格
0307601	1.品牌类型 2.出口享惠情况 3.是否为种苗 4.拉丁名称
0307609	1.品牌类型 2.出口享惠情况 3.制作或保存方法(活、鲜、冷、冻、干、盐腌、盐渍等)4.拉丁名称 5.个体重量 6.包装规格
0307711	1.品牌类型 2.出口享惠情况 3.是否为种苗 4.拉丁名称
0307719	1.品牌类型 2.出口享惠情况 3.制作或保存方法(活、鲜、冷)4.拉丁名称
030772	1.品牌类型 2.出口享惠情况 3.制作或保存方法(冻)4.拉丁名称
030779	1.品牌类型 2.出口享惠情况 3.制作或保存方法(干、盐腌、盐渍等)4.拉丁名称
0307811	1.品牌类型 2.出口享惠情况 3.是否为种苗 4.拉丁名称
0307819	1.品牌类型 2.出口享惠情况 3.制作或保存方法(活、鲜、冷)4.拉丁名称
0307821	1.品牌类型 2.出口享惠情况 3.是否为种苗 4.拉丁名称
0307829	1.品牌类型 2.出口享惠情况 3.制作或保存方法(活、鲜、冷)4.拉丁名称
030783	1.品牌类型 2.出口享惠情况 3.制作或保存方法(冻)4.拉丁名称
030784	1.品牌类型 2.出口享惠情况 3.制作或保存方法(冻)4.拉丁名称
030787	1.品牌类型 2.出口享惠情况 3.制作或保存方法(干、盐腌、盐渍等)4.拉丁名称
030788	1.品牌类型 2.出口享惠情况 3.制作或保存方法(干、盐腌、盐渍等)4.拉丁名称
0307911	1.品牌类型 2.出口享惠情况 3.是否为种苗 4.拉丁名称

商品编码	申报要素
0307919	1.品牌类型 2.出口享惠情况 3.制作或保存方法(活、鲜、冷)4.拉丁名称
030792	1.品牌类型 2.出口享惠情况 3.制作或保存方法(冻)4.拉丁名称
030799	1.品牌类型 2.出口享惠情况 3.制作或保存方法(干、盐腌、盐渍等)4.拉丁名称
0308111	1.品牌类型 2.出口享惠情况 3.种苗请注明个体长度、尾数/千克等
0308119	1.品牌类型 2.出口享惠情况 3.制作或保存方法(活、鲜、冷)
030812	1.品牌类型 2.出口享惠情况 3.制作或保存方法(冻)4.是否经水煮 5.包装规格
030819	1.品牌类型 2.出口享惠情况 3.制作或保存方法(干、盐腌、盐渍等)4.是否经水煮 5.包装规格
0308211	1.品牌类型 2.出口享惠情况 3.种苗请注明个体长度、尾数/千克等
0308219	1.品牌类型 2.出口享惠情况 3.制作或保存方法(活、鲜、冷)
030822	1.品牌类型 2.出口享惠情况 3.制作或保存方法(冻)4.包装规格
030829	1.品牌类型 2.出口享惠情况 3.制作或保存方法(干、盐腌、盐渍等)4.包装规格
03083011	1.品牌类型 2.出口享惠情况 3.种苗请注明个体长度、尾数/千克等
03083019	1.品牌类型 2.出口享惠情况 3.制作或保存方法(活、鲜、冷)
0308309	1.品牌类型 2.出口享惠情况 3.制作或保存方法(冻、干、盐腌、盐渍等)4.包装规格
03089011	1.品牌类型 2.出口享惠情况 3.种苗请注明个体长度、尾数/千克等
03089012	1.品牌类型 2.出口享惠情况 3.制作或保存方法(活、鲜、冷)
03089019	1.品牌类型 2.出口享惠情况 3.制作或保存方法(活、鲜、冷)
0308909	1.品牌类型 2.出口享惠情况 3.制作或保存方法(冻、干、盐腌、盐渍等)4.包装规格
0401	1.品牌类型 2.出口享惠情况 3.制作或保存方法(未浓缩及未加糖或其他甜物质)4.脂肪含量(按重量计)5.成分含量 6.包装规格(如 1 升/盒)7.品牌
0402	1.品牌类型 2.出口享惠情况 3.制作或保存方法(浓缩及加糖或其他甜物质)4.外观(粉状、粒状等)5.脂肪含量(按重量计)6.成分含量 7.包装规格(如 25 公斤/包)8.品牌
0403	1.品牌类型 2.出口享惠情况 3.制作或保存方法(发酵、酸化、浓缩、加糖及其他甜物质)4.成分含量 5.包装规格 6.品牌
04041	1.品牌类型 2.出口享惠情况 3.制作或保存方法(浓缩、加糖及其他甜物质)4.成分含量 5.品牌
04049	1.品牌类型 2.出口享惠情况 3.成分含量
04051	1.品牌类型 2.出口享惠情况 3.成分含量(乳脂、乳的无脂固形物、水及其他成分含量)4.包装规格 5.品牌 6.如添加乳化剂,请注明
04052	1.品牌类型 2.出口享惠情况 3.成分含量 4.包装规格 5.品牌
04059	1.品牌类型 2.出口享惠情况 3.成分含量 4.包装规格 5.品牌
04061	1.品牌类型 2.出口享惠情况 3.制作或保存方法(未熟化、未固化等)4.成分含量 5.包装规格 6.品牌
04062	1.品牌类型 2.出口享惠情况 3.制作方法(磨碎、粉化等)4.乳脂含量 5.包装规格 6.品牌
04063	1.品牌类型 2.出口享惠情况 3.制作或保存方法(未熟化、未固化等)4.成分含量 5.包装规格 6.品牌
04064	1.品牌类型 2.出口享惠情况 3.制作或保存方法(熟化、固化、磨碎或粉化等)4.成分含量 5.是否带蓝纹或娄地青霉生产的带有纹理 6.包装规格 7.品牌
04069	1.品牌类型 2.出口享惠情况 3.制作或保存方法(熟化、固化、磨碎或粉化等)4.成分含量 5.包装规格 6.品牌
04071	1.品牌类型 2.出口享惠情况 3.是否孵化用受精禽蛋
04072	1.品牌类型 2.出口享惠情况 3.制作或保存方法(鲜、带壳)
04079	1.品牌类型 2.出口享惠情况 3.制作或保存方法(鲜、带壳、腌制、煮过)
0408	1.品牌类型 2.出口享惠情况 3.制作或保存方法(鲜、冻、干、去壳、蒸、水煮、制成型等)
0409	1.品牌类型 2.出口享惠情况 3.来源(天然)4.品牌 5.包装规格
0410001	1.品牌类型 2.出口享惠情况 3.品种(燕子的品种)4.外形(燕盏或燕碎,燕条等)5.含水量
04100041	1.品牌类型 2.出口享惠情况 3.制作或保存方法(鲜)4.品牌
04100042	1.品牌类型 2.出口享惠情况 3.制作或保存方法(鲜)4.外观(粉)5.品牌
04100043	1.品牌类型 2.出口享惠情况 3.外观(粉)4.品牌
04100049	1.品牌类型 2.出口享惠情况 3.品牌
0410009	1.品牌类型 2.出口享惠情况 3.用途(食用)
0501	1.品牌类型 2.出口享惠情况 3.是否经加工
05021	1.品牌类型 2.出口享惠情况
05029	1.品牌类型 2.出口享惠情况 3.用途(制刷用)
0504001	1.品牌类型 2.出口享惠情况 3.制作或保存方法(鲜、冷、冻、干、熏、盐腌、盐渍)
05040021	1.品牌类型 2.出口享惠情况 3.制作或保存方法(冷、冻)4.品牌
05040029	1.品牌类型 2.出口享惠情况 3.制作或保存方法(鲜、冷、冻、干、熏、盐腌、盐渍)
0504009	1.品牌类型 2.出口享惠情况 3.制作或保存方法(鲜、冷、冻、干、熏、盐腌、盐渍)
05051	1.品牌类型 2.出口享惠情况 3.用途 4.制作或保存方法(仅经洗涤、消毒或为了保藏而做过处理)5.含绒量(包含绒子和绒丝含量)6.羽毛长度
05059	1.品牌类型 2.出口享惠情况 3.用途 4.制作或保存方法(仅经洗涤、消毒或为了保藏而做过处理)
05061	1.品牌类型 2.出口享惠情况 3.处理方法(经酸处理等)
05069011	1.品牌类型 2.出口享惠情况 3.成分 4.处理方法(未经加工或经脱脂等)5.外观(粉末)6.是否废料
05069019	1.品牌类型 2.出口享惠情况 3.处理方法(未经加工或经脱脂等)
0506909	1.品牌类型 2.出口享惠情况 3.处理方法(未经加工、经脱脂、脱胶等)
0507	1.品牌类型 2.出口享惠情况 3.处理方法(未经加工或经脱脂等)4.是否为粉末及废料
0508	1.品牌类型 2.出口享惠情况 3.处理方法(未经加工或经脱脂等)4.是否为粉末及废料
0510	1.品牌类型 2.出口享惠情况 3.制作或保存方法(鲜、冷、冻、干或用其他方法暂时保藏)
05111	1.品牌类型 2.出口享惠情况
05119111	1.品牌类型 2.出口享惠情况
05119119	1.品牌类型 2.出口享惠情况 3.用途
0511919	1.品牌类型 2.出口享惠情况 3.用途
0511991	1.品牌类型 2.出口享惠情况
0511992	1.品牌类型 2.出口享惠情况
0511993	1.品牌类型 2.出口享惠情况
0511994	1.品牌类型 2.出口享惠情况
0511999	1.品牌类型 2.出口享惠情况 3.用途
0601	1.品牌类型 2.出口享惠情况 3.状态(休眠、生长、开花)4.种类(球茎、块茎、鳞茎、块根等)5.是否种用
06021	1.品牌类型 2.出口享惠情况 3.栽培方法(无根插枝、接穗等)
0602201	1.品牌类型 2.出口享惠情况 3.是否种用
0602209	1.品牌类型 2.出口享惠情况
0602301	1.品牌类型 2.出口享惠情况 3.是否种用
0602309	1.品牌类型 2.出口享惠情况
0602401	1.品牌类型 2.出口享惠情况 3.是否种用
0602409	1.品牌类型 2.出口享惠情况
0602901	1.品牌类型 2.出口享惠情况
06029091	1.品牌类型 2.出口享惠情况 3.是否种用
06029092	1.品牌类型 2.出口享惠情况
06029093	1.品牌类型 2.出口享惠情况
06029094	1.品牌类型 2.出口享惠情况
06029095	1.品牌类型 2.出口享惠情况
06029099	1.品牌类型 2.出口享惠情况 3.直径、高度(整株植物从根部到树杈顶部的高度范围)
0603	1.品牌类型 2.出口享惠情况 3.用途(制花束或装饰用)4.制作或保存方法(鲜、干、染色、漂白、浸渍等)
0604	1.品牌类型 2.出口享惠情况 3.用途(制花束或装饰用)4.是否带花及花蕾 5.制作或保存方法(鲜、干、染色、漂白、浸渍等)
0701	1.品牌类型 2.出口享惠情况 3.制作或保存方法(鲜、冷)4.是否种用
0702	1.品牌类型 2.出口享惠情况 3.制作或保存方法(鲜、冷)
0703	1.品牌类型 2.出口享惠情况 3.制作或保存方法(鲜、冷)
0704	1.品牌类型 2.出口享惠情况 3.制作或保存方法(鲜、冷)
0705	1.品牌类型 2.出口享惠情况 3.制作或保存方法(鲜、冷)
0706	1.品牌类型 2.出口享惠情况 3.制作或保存方法(鲜、冷)
0707	1.品牌类型 2.出口享惠情况 3.制作或保存方法(鲜、冷)
0708	1.品牌类型 2.出口享惠情况 3.制作或保存方法(鲜、冷)
0709	1.品牌类型 2.出口享惠情况 3.制作或保存方法(鲜、冷)
07101	1.品牌类型 2.出口享惠情况 3.制作或保存方法(冻)
07102	1.品牌类型 2.出口享惠情况 3.制作或保存方法(冻)
07103	1.品牌类型 2.出口享惠情况 3.制作或保存方法(冻)
07104	1.品牌类型 2.出口享惠情况 3.制作或保存方法(冻)
07108	1.品牌类型 2.出口享惠情况 3.制作或保存方法(冻)
07109	1.品牌类型 2.出口享惠情况 3.制作或保存方法(冻)
0711	1.品牌类型 2.出口享惠情况 3.用途(不适于直接食用)4.制作或保存方法(用盐水、二氧化硫气体、亚硫酸水或其他防腐液)
0712	1.品牌类型 2.出口享惠情况 3.制作或保存方法(干制,包括脱水、蒸干或冻干)
0713101	1.品牌类型 2.出口享惠情况 3.制作或保存方法(干制且脱荚)4.是否种用
0713109	1.品牌类型 2.出口享惠情况 3.制作或保存方法(干制且脱荚)4.品种(黄豌豆、青豌豆、白豌豆等)
07132	1.品牌类型 2.出口享惠情况 3.制作或保存方法(干制且脱荚)4.是否种用
07133	1.品牌类型 2.出口享惠情况 3.制作或保存方法(干制且脱荚)4.是否种用
07134	1.品牌类型 2.出口享惠情况 3.制作或保存方法(干制且脱荚)4.是否种用
07135	1.品牌类型 2.出口享惠情况 3.制作或保存方法(干制且脱荚)4.是否种用
07136	1.品牌类型 2.出口享惠情况 3.制作或保存方法(干制且脱荚)4.是否种用

商品编码	申报要素
07139	1.品牌类型 2.出口享惠情况 3.制作或保存方法(干制且脱荚)4.是否种用
0714	1.品牌类型 2.出口享惠情况 3.制作或保存方法(鲜、冷、冻、干)4.是否种用
08011	1.品牌类型 2.出口享惠情况 3.制作或保存方法 4.加工方法(去壳或未去壳)5.是否种用 6.种类
08012	1.品牌类型 2.出口享惠情况 3.制作或保存方法 4.加工方法(去壳或未去壳)
080131	1.品牌类型 2.出口享惠情况 3.制作或保存方法 4.加工方法(去壳或未去壳)
080132	1.品牌类型 2.出口享惠情况 3.制作或保存方法 4.加工方法(去壳或未去壳)5.等级
08021	1.品牌类型 2.出口享惠情况 3.制作或保存方法 4.加工方法(去壳或未去壳)
08022	1.品牌类型 2.出口享惠情况 3.制作或保存方法 4.加工方法(去壳或未去壳)5.品种
08023	1.品牌类型 2.出口享惠情况 3.制作或保存方法 4.加工方法(去壳或未去壳)5.品种
08024	1.品牌类型 2.出口享惠情况 3.制作或保存方法 4.加工方法(去壳或未去壳)
08025	1.品牌类型 2.出口享惠情况 3.制作或保存方法 4.加工方法(去壳或未去壳)
08026	1.品牌类型 2.出口享惠情况 3.制作或保存方法 4.加工方法(去壳或未去壳)5.是否种用 6.签约日期
08027	1.品牌类型 2.出口享惠情况 3.制作或保存方法 4.加工方法(去壳或未去壳)
08028	1.品牌类型 2.出口享惠情况 3.制作或保存方法 4.加工方法(去壳或未去壳)
08029	1.品牌类型 2.出口享惠情况 3.制作或保存方法 4.加工方法(去壳或未去壳)
0803	1.品牌类型 2.出口享惠情况 3.制作或保存方法(鲜、干)4.干制方法(脱水、蒸干或冻干)5.种类(大香蕉、蕉仔、皇帝蕉等)6.等级(A级、B级、C级等)7.品牌
08041	1.品牌类型 2.出口享惠情况 3.制作或保存方法(鲜、干)4.等级
08042	1.品牌类型 2.出口享惠情况 3.制作或保存方法(鲜、干)4.等级
08043	1.品牌类型 2.出口享惠情况 3.制作或保存方法(鲜、干)4.种类(如青菠萝、金菠萝等)5.等级 6.去除果冠请注明
08044	1.品牌类型 2.出口享惠情况 3.制作或保存方法(鲜、干)4.等级
08045	1.品牌类型 2.出口享惠情况 3.制作或保存方法(鲜、干)4.等级
08051	1.品牌类型 2.出口享惠情况 3.制作或保存方法(鲜、干)4.种类(如脐橙、夏橙等)5.等级 6.品牌
08052	1.品牌类型 2.出口享惠情况 3.制作或保存方法(鲜、干)4.等级
08054	1.品牌类型 2.出口享惠情况 3.制作或保存方法(鲜、干)4.等级
08055	1.品牌类型 2.出口享惠情况 3.制作或保存方法(鲜、干)4.等级 5.品牌
08059	1.品牌类型 2.出口享惠情况 3.制作或保存方法(鲜、干)4.等级
08061	1.品牌类型 2.出口享惠情况 3.制作或保存方法(鲜)4.种类 5.规格 6.品牌
08062	1.品牌类型 2.出口享惠情况 3.制作或保存方法(干)4.等级 5.品牌
080711	1.品牌类型 2.出口享惠情况 3.制作或保存方法(鲜)4.等级 5.品牌
080719	1.品牌类型 2.出口享惠情况 3.制作或保存方法(鲜)4.等级
08072	1.品牌类型 2.出口享惠情况 3.制作或保存方法(鲜)4.等级 5.品牌
08081	1.品牌类型 2.出口享惠情况 3.制作或保存方法(鲜)4.种类(蛇果、加纳果、青苹果、富士等)5.等级 6.品牌
08083	1.品牌类型 2.出口享惠情况 3.制作或保存方法(鲜)4.等级
08084	1.品牌类型 2.出口享惠情况 3.制作或保存方法(鲜)4.等级
08091	1.品牌类型 2.出口享惠情况 3.制作或保存方法(鲜)4.等级
080921	1.品牌类型 2.出口享惠情况 3.制作或保存方法(鲜)4.等级
080929	1.品牌类型 2.出口享惠情况 3.制作或保存方法(鲜)4.等级 5.品种(如 Bing，lambert，Van，Tulare，Chelan，Tieton，Skeena 等)6.品牌(厂商)7.尺寸(按果径最大处以毫米为单位计算)
08093	1.品牌类型 2.出口享惠情况 3.制作或保存方法(鲜)4.等级
08094	1.品牌类型 2.出口享惠情况 3.制作或保存方法(鲜)4.等级
08101	1.品牌类型 2.出口享惠情况 3.制作或保存方法(鲜)4.等级
08102	1.品牌类型 2.出口享惠情况 3.制作或保存方法(鲜)4.等级
08103	1.品牌类型 2.出口享惠情况 3.制作或保存方法(鲜)4.等级
08104	1.品牌类型 2.出口享惠情况 3.制作或保存方法(鲜)4.等级 5.品牌
08105	1.品牌类型 2.出口享惠情况 3.制作或保存方法(鲜)4.种类(Hayward，Hort16A，SunGold，Jintao，Sorelli，kiwiberry 等)5.等级
08106	1.品牌类型 2.出口享惠情况 3.制作或保存方法(鲜)4.等级 5.种类 6.品牌
08107	1.品牌类型 2.出口享惠情况 3.制作或保存方法(鲜)4.等级
0810901	1.品牌类型 2.出口享惠情况 3.制作或保存方法(鲜)4.等级
0810903	1.品牌类型 2.出口享惠情况 3.制作或保存方法(鲜)4.等级
0810904	1.品牌类型 2.出口享惠情况 3.制作或保存方法(鲜)4.等级
0810905	1.品牌类型 2.出口享惠情况 3.制作或保存方法(鲜)4.等级
0810906	1.品牌类型 2.出口享惠情况 3.制作或保存方法(鲜)4.等级
0810907	1.品牌类型 2.出口享惠情况 3.制作或保存方法(鲜)4.等级
0810908	1.品牌类型 2.出口享惠情况 3.制作或保存方法(鲜)4.等级 5.种类
0810909	1.品牌类型 2.出口享惠情况 3.制作或保存方法(鲜)4.等级
08111	1.品牌类型 2.出口享惠情况 3.制作或保存方法(冻)
08112	1.品牌类型 2.出口享惠情况 3.制作或保存方法(冻)
0811901	1.品牌类型 2.出口享惠情况 3.制作或保存方法(冻,未去壳)
0811909	1.品牌类型 2.出口享惠情况 3.制作或保存方法(冻)
0812	1.品牌类型 2.出口享惠情况 3.是否适于直接食用 4.制作或保存方法(用盐水、二氧化硫气体、亚硫酸水或其他防腐液)
08131	1.品牌类型 2.出口享惠情况 3.制作或保存方法(干)
08132	1.品牌类型 2.出口享惠情况 3.制作或保存方法(干)
08133	1.品牌类型 2.出口享惠情况 3.制作或保存方法(干)
0813401	1.品牌类型 2.出口享惠情况 3.制作或保存方法(干)4.等级
0813402	1.品牌类型 2.出口享惠情况 3.制作或保存方法(干)
0813403	1.品牌类型 2.出口享惠情况 3.制作或保存方法(干)
0813404	1.品牌类型 2.出口享惠情况 3.制作或保存方法(干)4.加工程度(去壳、未去壳)
0813409	1.品牌类型 2.出口享惠情况 3.制作或保存方法(干)
08135	1.品牌类型 2.出口享惠情况 3.制作或保存方法(干)4.种类
0814	1.品牌类型 2.出口享惠情况 3.制作或保存方法(鲜、冻、干，用盐水、亚硫酸水或其他防腐液暂时保藏的)
090111	1.品牌类型 2.出口享惠情况 3.制作或保存方法(豆、粉等、未焙炒且未浸除咖啡碱)4.品种 5.产区
090112	1.品牌类型 2.出口享惠情况 3.制作或保存方法(豆、粉等、未焙炒且已浸除咖啡碱)4.品种 5.产区
090121	1.品牌类型 2.出口享惠情况 3.制作或保存方法(豆、粉等、已焙炒且未浸除咖啡碱)4.品种 5.产区
090122	1.品牌类型 2.出口享惠情况 3.制作或保存方法(豆、粉等、已焙炒且已浸除咖啡碱)4.品种 5.产区
0901901	1.品牌类型 2.出口享惠情况 3.种类(咖啡豆荚或豆皮)4.品种 5.产区
0901902	1.品牌类型 2.出口享惠情况 3.成分 4.品种 5.产区
0902	1.品牌类型 2.出口享惠情况 3.制作或保存方法(未发酵、半发酵、发酵)4.内包装每件净重 5.品牌
0903	1.品牌类型 2.出口享惠情况
0904	1.品牌类型 2.出口享惠情况 3.制作或保存方法(未磨、已磨、干、粉)
0905	1.品牌类型 2.出口享惠情况 3.加工方法(未磨、已磨)
0906	1.品牌类型 2.出口享惠情况 3.加工方法(未磨、已磨)
0907	1.品牌类型 2.出口享惠情况 3.加工方法(未磨、已磨)
0908	1.品牌类型 2.出口享惠情况 3.加工方法(未磨、已磨)
0909	1.品牌类型 2.出口享惠情况 3.加工方法(未磨、已磨)
09101	1.品牌类型 2.出口享惠情况 3.加工方法(未磨、已磨)
09102	1.品牌类型 2.出口享惠情况
09103	1.品牌类型 2.出口享惠情况
09109	1.品牌类型 2.出口享惠情况 3.成分含量
1001	1.品牌类型 2.出口享惠情况 3.是否种用 4.是否硬粒 5.种类(白麦、红麦、冬麦、春麦)
1002	1.品牌类型 2.出口享惠情况 3.是否种用
1003	1.品牌类型 2.出口享惠情况 3.是否种用
1004	1.品牌类型 2.出口享惠情况 3.是否种用
1005	1.品牌类型 2.出口享惠情况 3.是否种用
10061021	1.品牌类型 2.出口享惠情况 3.种类 4.加工方法(去壳、未去壳)5.是否种用 6.粒长 7.长宽比 8.包装规格
10061029	1.品牌类型 2.出口享惠情况 3.种类 4.加工方法(去壳、未去壳)5.是否种用 6.粒长 7.长宽比 8.包装规格
10061081	1.品牌类型 2.出口享惠情况 3.种类 4.加工方法(去壳、未去壳)5.粒长 6.长宽比 7.包装规格
10061089	1.品牌类型 2.出口享惠情况 3.种类 4.加工方法(去壳、未去壳)5.粒长 6.长宽比 7.包装规格
1006202	1.品牌类型 2.出口享惠情况 3.种类 4.加工方法(去壳、未去壳)5.制作或保存方法(糙米)6.粒长 7.长宽比 8.包装规格
1006208	1.品牌类型 2.出口享惠情况 3.种类 4.加工方法(去壳、未去壳)5.是否种用 6.粒长 7.长宽比 8.包装规格
1006302	1.品牌类型 2.出口享惠情况 3.种类 4.加工方法(去壳、未去壳)5.粒长 6.长宽比 7.包装规格
1006308	1.品牌类型 2.出口享惠情况 3.种类 4.加工方法(去壳、未去壳)5.粒长 6.长宽比 7.包装规格
1006402	1.品牌类型 2.出口享惠情况 3.种类 4.加工方法(去壳、未去壳)5.包装规格
1006408	1.品牌类型 2.出口享惠情况 3.种类 4.加工方法(去壳、未去壳)5.包装规格
1007	1.品牌类型 2.出口享惠情况 3.用途(食用)4.是否种用 5.包装规格
1008	1.品牌类型 2.出口享惠情况 3.是否种用 4.包装规格
1101	1.品牌类型 2.出口享惠情况 3.状态(细粉)
1102	1.品牌类型 2.出口享惠情况 3.种类(玉米、籼米等)4.状态(细粉)
1103	1.品牌类型 2.出口享惠情况 3.种类(小麦、玉米、燕麦等)4.状态(粗粒、粗粉、团粒等)
1104	1.品牌类型 2.出口享惠情况 3.种类(燕麦、大麦、小麦等)4.制作或保存方法(去壳、滚压、制片等)

商品编码	申报要素
1105	1.品牌类型 2.出口享惠情况 3.状态(细粉、粗粉、粉末、粉片、颗粒及团粒)
1106	1.品牌类型 2.出口享惠情况 3.种类(豌豆、鹰嘴豆等)4.状态(细粉、粗粉、粉末)
1107	1.品牌类型 2.出口享惠情况 3.制作或保存方法(未焙制、已焙制)
110811	1.品牌类型 2.出口享惠情况 3.种类(小麦淀粉)
110812	1.品牌类型 2.出口享惠情况 3.种类(玉米淀粉)
110813	1.品牌类型 2.出口享惠情况 3.种类(马铃薯淀粉)
110814	1.品牌类型 2.出口享惠情况 3.种类(木薯淀粉)
110819	1.品牌类型 2.出口享惠情况 3.种类(大米淀粉、竹芋淀粉等)
11082	1.品牌类型 2.出口享惠情况
1109	1.品牌类型 2.出口享惠情况
12011	1.品牌类型 2.出口享惠情况 3.种类(黄大豆、黑大豆、青大豆等)4.是否种用 5.转(非转)基因请注明
1201901	1.品牌类型 2.出口享惠情况 3.种类(黄大豆)4.蛋白含量 5.油含量 6.升贴水 7.转(非转)基因请注明
1201902	1.品牌类型 2.出口享惠情况 3.种类(黑大豆)4.转(非转)基因请注明
1201903	1.品牌类型 2.出口享惠情况 3.种类(青大豆)4.转(非转)基因请注明
1201909	1.品牌类型 2.出口享惠情况 3.种类 4.转(非转)基因请注明
1202	1.品牌类型 2.出口享惠情况 3.制作或保存方法(未去壳、去壳、未焙炒、未烹煮)4.是否种用
1203	1.品牌类型 2.出口享惠情况 3.用途(榨油用)
1204	1.品牌类型 2.出口享惠情况
12051	1.品牌类型 2.出口享惠情况 3.是否种用 4.芥子酸含量及所得固体成分每克葡萄糖苷酸(酯)含量
12059	1.品牌类型 2.出口享惠情况 3.是否种用
1206001	1.品牌类型 2.出口享惠情况 3.是否种用
1206009	1.品牌类型 2.出口享惠情况
1207	1.品牌类型 2.出口享惠情况 3.是否种用
1208	1.品牌类型 2.出口享惠情况 3.状态(细粉、粗粉)
1209	1.品牌类型 2.出口享惠情况 3.用途(种植用)
1210	1.品牌类型 2.出口享惠情况 3.制作或保存方法(鲜、干、未研磨、研磨、未制成团粒等)
1211	1.品牌类型 2.出口享惠情况 3.用途(作香料、药料、杀虫、杀菌等类似用途)4.制作或保存方法(鲜、干等)
12122	1.品牌类型 2.出口享惠情况 3.制作或保存方法(鲜、冷、冻、干等)4.拉丁名称
121291	1.品牌类型 2.出口享惠情况 3.制作或保存方法(鲜、冷、冻等)
121292	1.品牌类型 2.出口享惠情况 3.制作或保存方法(鲜、冷、冻等)
121293	1.品牌类型 2.出口享惠情况 3.制作或保存方法(鲜、冷、冻等)
121294	1.品牌类型 2.出口享惠情况 3.制作或保存方法(鲜、冷、冻等)
121299	1.品牌类型 2.出口享惠情况 3.用途(主要供人食用)
1213	1.品牌类型 2.出口享惠情况 3.制作或保存方法(切碎、碾磨、挤压等)4.加工程度(未经处理)
12141	1.品牌类型 2.出口享惠情况 3.状态(粗粉及团粒等)
12149	1.品牌类型 2.出口享惠情况
13012	1.品牌类型 2.出口享惠情况 3.用途(食品、饮料、制药等)
13019	1.品牌类型 2.出口享惠情况
130211	1.品牌类型 2.出口享惠情况 3.制作或保存方法(液汁、浸膏、粉末)
130212	1.品牌类型 2.出口享惠情况 3.制作或保存方法(液汁、浸膏、粉末)
130213	1.品牌类型 2.出口享惠情况 3.制作或保存方法(液汁、浸膏、粉末)4.请注明有效成分含量(α 酸等)
130214	1.品牌类型 2.出口享惠情况 3.制作或保存方法(液汁、浸膏、粉末)
130219	1.品牌类型 2.出口享惠情况 3.制作或保存方法(液汁、浸膏、粉末)
13022	1.品牌类型 2.出口享惠情况 3.用途(食品用、医药用)
130231	1.品牌类型 2.出口享惠情况 3.等级(食品级、医药级等)
130232	1.品牌类型 2.出口享惠情况 3.来源 4.黏度 5.级别(食用级、工业级)
13023911	1.品牌类型 2.出口享惠情况 3.种类(卡帕胶、阿欧塔胶、莱姆达胶等)4.用途(乳品、肉类、水、糖果、果冻、甜品)
13023912	1.品牌类型 2.出口享惠情况 3.用途
13023919	1.品牌类型 2.出口享惠情况 3.用途
1302399	1.品牌类型 2.出口享惠情况 3.来源 4.用途
14011	1.品牌类型 2.出口享惠情况 3.用途(主要作编结用)
14012	1.品牌类型 2.出口享惠情况 3.用途(主要作编结用)4.种类 5.请注明加工程度(去皮或未去皮)6.直径 7.长度
14019	1.品牌类型 2.出口享惠情况 3.用途(主要作编结用)
14042	1.品牌类型 2.出口享惠情况 3.纤维长度
1404901	1.品牌类型 2.出口享惠情况 3.用途(主要供染料或鞣料用)
1404909	1.品牌类型 2.出口享惠情况
1501	1.品牌类型 2.出口享惠情况
1502	1.品牌类型 2.出口享惠情况 3.加工方法 4.是否含瘦肉
1503	1.品牌类型 2.出口享惠情况 3.加工程度(未经乳化、混合或其他方法制作)
15041	1.品牌类型 2.出口享惠情况 3.成分含量 4.加工程度(未经化学改性)5.饲料用的鱼油、脂及其分离品请注明是否精炼 6.保健用鱼油请注明 DHA＋EPA 浓度 7.品牌(中文及外文名称,无品牌请申报厂商)
15042	1.品牌类型 2.出口享惠情况 3.成分含量 4.加工程度(未经化学改性)5.饲料用的鱼油、脂及其分离品请注明是否精炼 6.保健用鱼油请注明 DHA＋EPA 浓度 7.品牌(中文及外文名称,无品牌请申报厂商)
15043	1.品牌类型 2.出口享惠情况 3.成分含量 4.加工程度(未经化学改性)5.品牌(中文及外文名称,无品牌请申报厂商)
1505	1.品牌类型 2.出口享惠情况
1506	1.品牌类型 2.出口享惠情况 3.加工程度(未经化学改性)
1507	1.品牌类型 2.出口享惠情况 3.加工方法(初榨、非初榨)4.加工程度(未经化学改性)
1508	1.品牌类型 2.出口享惠情况 3.加工方法(初榨、非初榨)4.加工程度(未经化学改性)
1509	1.品牌类型 2.出口享惠情况 3.加工方法(初榨、非初榨)4.加工程度(未经化学改性)5.用途 6.包装规格 7.品牌 8.酸度 9.产区
1510	1.品牌类型 2.出口享惠情况 3.加工程度(未经化学改性)4.包装规格 5.品牌
15111	1.品牌类型 2.出口享惠情况 3.加工方法(初榨)4.加工程度(未经化学改性)
15119	1.品牌类型 2.出口享惠情况 3.加工方法(初榨、非初榨)4.加工程度(未经化学改性)5.包装规格
1512	1.品牌类型 2.出口享惠情况 3.加工方法(初榨、非初榨)4.加工程度(未经化学改性)
1513	1.品牌类型 2.出口享惠情况 3.加工方法(初榨、非初榨)4.加工程度(未经化学改性)
151411	1.品牌类型 2.出口享惠情况 3.加工方法(初榨)4.加工程度(未经化学改性)5.芥子酸含量
151419	1.品牌类型 2.出口享惠情况 3.加工方法(精制)4.加工程度(未经化学改性)5.芥子酸含量及所得固体成分每克葡萄糖苷酸(酯)含量
15149	1.品牌类型 2.出口享惠情况 3.加工方法(初榨、非初榨)4.加工程度(未经化学改性)
15151	1.品牌类型 2.出口享惠情况 3.加工方法(初榨、非初榨)4.加工程度(未经化学改性)
15152	1.品牌类型 2.出口享惠情况 3.加工方法(初榨、非初榨)4.加工程度(未经化学改性)
15153	1.品牌类型 2.出口享惠情况 3.加工方法(初榨、非初榨)4.加工程度(未经化学改性)
15155	1.品牌类型 2.出口享惠情况 3.加工方法(初榨、非初榨)4.加工程度(未经化学改性)5.包装规格
15159	1.品牌类型 2.出口享惠情况 3.加工方法(初榨、非初榨)4.加工程度(未经化学改性)
1516	1.品牌类型 2.出口享惠情况 3.加工方法(全部或部分氢化、相互酯化、再酯化或反油酸)
15171	1.品牌类型 2.出口享惠情况 3.加工方法 4.加工原料(动物油脂、植物油脂)5.品牌
1517901	1.品牌类型 2.出口享惠情况 3.成分含量 4.加工原料(豆油、菜子油、棕榈油等)5.品牌
1517909	1.品牌类型 2.出口享惠情况 3.成分含量 4.加工原料(动物油脂、植物油脂)5.品牌
1518	1.品牌类型 2.出口享惠情况 3.成分含量 4.加工方法(经熟炼、氧化、脱水、硫化、吹制等)
1520	1.品牌类型 2.出口享惠情况 3.甘油含量
15211	1.品牌类型 2.出口享惠情况 3.成分
15219	1.品牌类型 2.出口享惠情况
1522	1.品牌类型 2.出口享惠情况 3.来源
1601001	1.品牌类型 2.出口享惠情况 3.是否用天然肠衣做外包装 4.成分含量 5.包装规格 6.品牌(中文及外文名称)
1601002	1.品牌类型 2.出口享惠情况 3.成分含量 4.包装规格 5.品牌(中文及外文名称)
1601003	1.品牌类型 2.出口享惠情况 3.成分含量 4.包装规格 5.品牌(中文及外文名称)
16021	1.品牌类型 2.出口享惠情况 3.成分含量 4.包装规格 5.品牌(中文及外文名称)
16022	1.品牌类型 2.出口享惠情况 3.制作或保存方法(煮、蒸、烤、煎、炸、炒等)4.成分含量 5.包装规格 6.品牌(中文及外文名称)
160231	1.品牌类型 2.出口享惠情况 3.制作或保存方法(煮、蒸、烤、煎、炸、炒等)4.成分含量 5.包装规格 6.品牌(中文及外文名称)
1602321	1.品牌类型 2.出口享惠情况 3.制作或保存方法(煮、蒸、烤、煎、炸、炒等)4.成分含量 5.包装规格 6.品牌(中文及外文名称)
1602329	1.品牌类型 2.出口享惠情况 3.制作或保存方法(煮、蒸、烤、煎、炸、炒等)4.成分含量 5.包装规格 6.品牌(中文及外文名称)
1602391	1.品牌类型 2.出口享惠情况 3.制作或保存方法(煮、蒸、烤、煎、炸、炒等)4.成分含量 5.包装规格 6.品牌(中文及外文名称)
1602399	1.品牌类型 2.出口享惠情况 3.制作或保存方法(煮、蒸、烤、煎、炸、炒等)4.成分含量 5.包装规格 6.品牌(中文及外文名称)

商品编码	申报要素
160241	1.品牌类型 2.出口享惠情况 3.制作或保存方法(煮、蒸、烤、煎、炸、炒等)4.成分含量 5.包装规格 6.品牌(中文及外文名称)
160242	1.品牌类型 2.出口享惠情况 3.制作或保存方法(煮、蒸、烤、煎、炸、炒等)4.成分含量 5.包装规格 6.品牌(中文及外文名称)
1602491	1.品牌类型 2.出口享惠情况 3.制作或保存方法(煮、蒸、烤、煎、炸、炒等)4.成分含量 5.包装规格 6.品牌(中文及外文名称)
1602499	1.品牌类型 2.出口享惠情况 3.制作或保存方法(煮、蒸、烤、煎、炸、炒等)4.成分含量 5.包装规格 6.品牌(中文及外文名称)
1602501	1.品牌类型 2.出口享惠情况 3.制作或保存方法(煮、蒸、烤、煎、炸、炒等)4.成分含量 5.包装规格 6.品牌(中文及外文名称)
1602509	1.品牌类型 2.出口享惠情况 3.制作或保存方法(煮、蒸、烤、煎、炸、炒等)4.成分含量 5.包装规格 6.品牌(中文及外文名称)
1602901	1.品牌类型 2.出口享惠情况 3.制作或保存方法(煮、蒸、烤、煎、炸、炒等)4.成分含量 5.包装规格 6.品牌(中文及外文名称)
1602909	1.品牌类型 2.出口享惠情况 3.制作或保存方法(煮、蒸、烤、煎、炸、炒等)4.成分含量 5.包装规格 6.品牌(中文及外文名称)
1603	1.品牌类型 2.出口享惠情况 3.制作或保存方法(精、汁)4.包装规格
16041	1.品牌类型 2.出口享惠情况 3.制作或保存方法(整条或切块、非整条或切块、烤、煎、炸等)4.包装规格
16042	1.品牌类型 2.出口享惠情况 3.制作或保存方法(整条或切块、非整条或切块、烤、煎、炸等)4.包装规格
16043	1.品牌类型 2.出口享惠情况 3.包装规格 4.品牌
16051	1.品牌类型 2.出口享惠情况 3.制作或保存方法(烤、煎、炸等)4.包装规格
16052	1.品牌类型 2.出口享惠情况 3.制作或保存方法(烤、煎、炸等)4.是否非密封包装 5.包装规格
16053	1.品牌类型 2.出口享惠情况 3.制作或保存方法(烤、煎、炸等)4.包装规格
16054	1.品牌类型 2.出口享惠情况 3.制作或保存方法(烤、煎、炸等)4.包装规格
16055	1.品牌类型 2.出口享惠情况 3.制作或保存方法(烤、煎、炸等)4.包装规格
16056	1.品牌类型 2.出口享惠情况 3.制作或保存方法(烤、煎、炸等)4.包装规格
17011	1.品牌类型 2.出口享惠情况 3.加工方法(未加香料或着色剂)4.按重量计干燥状态的糖含量对应的旋光度 5.品牌(中文及外文名称,无品牌请申报厂商)
170191	1.品牌类型 2.出口享惠情况 3.加工方法(加香料或着色剂)4.品牌(中文及外文名称,无品牌请申报厂商)
170199	1.品牌类型 2.出口享惠情况 3.成分含量 4.品牌(中文及外文名称,无品牌请申报厂商)
17021	1.品牌类型 2.出口享惠情况 3.按重量计干燥无水乳糖的含量 4.品牌(中文及外文名称,无品牌请申报厂商)
17022	1.品牌类型 2.出口享惠情况 3.品牌(中文及外文名称,无品牌请申报厂商)
17023	1.品牌类型 2.出口享惠情况 3.按重量计干燥状态的果糖含量 4.用途(食用、医用)5.品牌(中文及外文名称,无品牌请申报厂商)
17024	1.品牌类型 2.出口享惠情况 3.按重量计干燥状态的果糖含量 4.品牌(中文及外文名称,无品牌请申报厂商)
17025	1.品牌类型 2.出口享惠情况 3.按重量计干燥状态的果糖含量 4.品牌(中文及外文名称,无品牌请申报厂商)
17026	1.品牌类型 2.出口享惠情况 3.种类(高果糖浆、高果糖晶体、低聚酯果糖等)4.按重量计干燥状态的果糖含量 5.用途(食用、医用)6.品牌(中文及外文名称,无品牌请申报厂商)
17029	1.品牌类型 2.出口享惠情况 3.成分含量 4.品牌(中文及外文名称,无品牌请申报厂商)
1703	1.品牌类型 2.出口享惠情况 3.原料 4.成分含量 5.品牌(中文及外文名称,无品牌请申报厂商)
1704	1.品牌类型 2.出口享惠情况 3.成分含量 4.包装规格 5.品牌 6.品牌(中文及外文名称,无品牌请申报厂商)
1801	1.品牌类型 2.出口享惠情况 3.制作或保存方法(整颗或破碎的、生的或焙炒的)
1802	1.品牌类型 2.出口享惠情况
1803	1.品牌类型 2.出口享惠情况 3.是否脱脂(未脱脂、全部脱脂或部分脱脂)
1804	1.品牌类型 2.出口享惠情况
1805	1.品牌类型 2.出口享惠情况 3.制作或保存方法(粉末状、未加糖或其他甜物质)4.可可脂含量 5.包装规格
18061	1.品牌类型 2.出口享惠情况 3.制作或保存方法(粉末状、加糖或其他甜物质)4.容器包装或内包装每件净重 5.成分含量 6.品牌(中文及外文名称)
18062	1.品牌类型 2.出口享惠情况 3.成分含量 4.形状(条状、块状等)5.容器包装或内包装每件净重 6.品牌
18063	1.品牌类型 2.出口享惠情况 3.成分含量 4.形状(条状、块状等)5.容器包装或内包装每件净重 6.是否夹心 7.品牌
18069	1.品牌类型 2.出口享惠情况 3.成分含量 4.容器包装或内包装每件净重 5.品牌
19011	1.品牌类型 2.出口享惠情况 3.成分含量 4.用途(供婴幼儿食用/适用的年龄阶段)5.包装规格 6.品牌(中文及外文名称)
19012	1.品牌类型 2.出口享惠情况 3.成分含量 4.用途(供烘焙面包、糕饼等用)5.包装规格
19019	1.品牌类型 2.出口享惠情况 3.成分含量 4.包装规格 5.品牌(中文及外文名称)
19021	1.品牌类型 2.出口享惠情况 3.成分含量 4.制作或保存方法(生的、未包馅或未经其他方法加工)5.是否速冻请注明
19022	1.品牌类型 2.出口享惠情况 3.成分含量 4.制作或保存方法(包馅或经其他方法加工)
1902301	1.品牌类型 2.出口享惠情况 3.成分含量
1902302	1.品牌类型 2.出口享惠情况 3.成分含量
1902303	1.品牌类型 2.出口享惠情况 3.种类(即食面条、快熟面条)4.成分含量 5.包装规格 6.品牌
1902309	1.品牌类型 2.出口享惠情况 3.成分含量 4.包装规格 5.品牌
19024	1.品牌类型 2.出口享惠情况 3.成分含量
1903	1.品牌类型 2.出口享惠情况 3.成分含量 4.包装规格
19041	1.品牌类型 2.出口享惠情况 3.制作或保存方法(膨化或烘炒)4.成分含量 5.包装规格 6.品牌(中文及外文名称)
19042	1.品牌类型 2.出口享惠情况 3.制作或保存方法(未烘炒、未烘炒与烘炒或膨化混合)4.成分含量 5.包装规格 6.品牌(中文及外文名称)
19043	1.品牌类型 2.出口享惠情况 3.制作或保存方法(干、碾碎)4.成分含量 5.包装规格 6.品牌(中文及外文名称)
19049	1.品牌类型 2.出口享惠情况 3.制作或保存方法(经过预煮或经其他方法制作)4.成分含量 5.包装规格 6.品牌(中文及外文名称)
19051	1.品牌类型 2.出口享惠情况 3.成分含量 4.包装规格 5.品牌
19052	1.品牌类型 2.出口享惠情况 3.成分含量 4.包装规格 5.品牌
19053	1.品牌类型 2.出口享惠情况 3.成分含量 4.包装规格 5.品牌
19054	1.品牌类型 2.出口享惠情况 3.成分含量 4.包装规格 5.品牌
19059	1.品牌类型 2.出口享惠情况 3.成分含量 4.制作或保存方法(烘焙等)5.包装规格 6.品牌
2001	1.品牌类型 2.出口享惠情况 3.制作方法(用醋或醋酸制作或保藏)4.包装规格 5.品牌(中文及外文名称)
2002101	1.品牌类型 2.出口享惠情况 3.制作或保存方法(整个、切片等)4.包装规格 5.品牌
2002109	1.品牌类型 2.出口享惠情况 3.制作或保存方法(整个、切片等)4.包装规格
2002901	1.品牌类型 2.出口享惠情况 3.包装规格(重量/罐)4.品牌
2002909	1.品牌类型 2.出口享惠情况 3.制作或保存方法(绞碎等)4.包装规格
2003	1.品牌类型 2.出口享惠情况 3.制作方法 4.包装规格 5.品牌
2004	1.品牌类型 2.出口享惠情况 3.制作或保存方法(冻等)4.包装规格
20051	1.品牌类型 2.出口享惠情况 3.制作或保存方法(未冷冻等)4.包装规格
20052	1.品牌类型 2.出口享惠情况 3.制作或保存方法(未冷冻等)4.包装规格
20054	1.品牌类型 2.出口享惠情况 3.制作或保存方法(未冷冻等)4.包装规格
200551	1.品牌类型 2.出口享惠情况 3.制作或保存方法(未冷冻等)4.是否脱荚 5.包装规格
200559	1.品牌类型 2.出口享惠情况 3.制作或保存方法(未冷冻等)4.包装规格 5.品牌
20056	1.品牌类型 2.出口享惠情况 3.制作或保存方法(未冷冻等)4.包装规格 5.品牌
20057	1.品牌类型 2.出口享惠情况 3.制作或保存方法(未冷冻等)4.包装规格
20058	1.品牌类型 2.出口享惠情况 3.制作或保存方法(未冷冻等)4.包装规格
2005911	1.品牌类型 2.出口享惠情况 3.制作或保存方法(未冷冻等)4.包装规格 5.品牌
2005919	1.品牌类型 2.出口享惠情况 3.制作或保存方法(未冷冻等)4.包装规格
2005992	1.品牌类型 2.出口享惠情况 3.制作或保存方法(未冷冻等)4.包装规格 5.品牌
2005994	1.品牌类型 2.出口享惠情况 3.制作或保存方法(未冷冻等)4.包装规格
2005995	1.品牌类型 2.出口享惠情况 3.制作或保存方法(未冷冻等)4.包装规格
2005996	1.品牌类型 2.出口享惠情况 3.制作或保存方法(未冷冻等)4.包装规格
2005999	1.品牌类型 2.出口享惠情况 3.制作或保存方法(未冷冻等)4.包装规格
2006	1.品牌类型 2.出口享惠情况 3.制作或保存方法(沥干、糖渍、裹糖)4.包装规格
2007	1.品牌类型 2.出口享惠情况 3.制作或保存方法(烹煮)4.包装规格 5.品牌

商品编码	申报要素
2008	1.品牌类型 2.出口享惠情况 3.制作或保存方法 4.包装规格 5.品牌
2009	1.品牌类型 2.出口享惠情况 3.成分含量 4.白利糖度值 5.浓缩果汁请注明浓缩倍数 6.加工方法(是否发酵、加酒精、冷冻、混合等)7.保存方法(储藏温度)8.包装规格 9.品牌
2101	1.品牌类型 2.出口享惠情况 3.成分含量 4.包装规格 5.品牌
21021	1.品牌类型 2.出口享惠情况 3.是否活性酵母 4.包装规格 5.品牌
21022	1.品牌类型 2.出口享惠情况 3.是否活性酵母 4.是否已死的单细胞微生物 5.包装规格 6.品牌
21023	1.品牌类型 2.出口享惠情况 3.包装规格 4.品牌
21031	1.品牌类型 2.出口享惠情况 3.成分 4.包装规格 5.品牌
21032	1.品牌类型 2.出口享惠情况 3.成分 4.包装规格 5.品牌
21033	1.品牌类型 2.出口享惠情况 3.成分 4.包装规格 5.品牌
2103901	1.品牌类型 2.出口享惠情况 3.成分 4.包装规格 5.品牌
2103902	1.品牌类型 2.出口享惠情况 3.成分含量(酒精含量、香料和各种配料含量及糖含量等)4.包装规格 5.品牌
2103909	1.品牌类型 2.出口享惠情况 3.成分 4.包装规格 5.品牌
2104	1.品牌类型 2.出口享惠情况 3.成分含量 4.包装规格 5.品牌
2105	1.品牌类型 2.出口享惠情况 3.包装规格 4.品牌
21061	1.品牌类型 2.出口享惠情况 3.成分含量 4.包装规格 5.品牌
2106901	1.品牌类型 2.出口享惠情况 3.成分含量 4.包装规格 5.品牌
2106902	1.品牌类型 2.出口享惠情况 3.成分含量 4.包装规格 5.品牌
2106903	1.品牌类型 2.出口享惠情况 3.成分含量 4.包装规格 5.品牌
2106904	1.品牌类型 2.出口享惠情况 3.成分含量 4.是否可直接饮用 5.包装规格 6.品牌
2106905	1.品牌类型 2.出口享惠情况 3.成分含量 4.包装规格 5.品牌
2106909	1.品牌类型 2.出口享惠情况 3.成分含量 4.包装规格 5.品牌
22011	1.品牌类型 2.出口享惠情况 3.包装规格 4.品牌
2201901	1.品牌类型 2.出口享惠情况 3.加工方法(未加糖或其他甜物质及未加味)4.来源(天然)5.包装规格 6.品牌
2201909	1.品牌类型 2.出口享惠情况 3.加工方法(未加糖或其他甜物质及未加味)4.包装规格 5.品牌
22021	1.品牌类型 2.出口享惠情况 3.加工方法(加糖、加味或其他甜物质)4.包装规格 5.品牌
220291	1.品牌类型 2.出口享惠情况 3.成分含量(酒精浓度等)4.包装规格 5.品牌
220299	1.品牌类型 2.出口享惠情况 3.成分 4.包装规格 5.品牌
2203	1.品牌类型 2.出口享惠情况 3.品名(中文及外文名称)4.是否麦芽酿造 5.酒精含量 6.麦芽浓度 7.包装规格 8.品牌(中文及外文名称)9.生产日期
22041	1.品牌类型 2.出口享惠情况 3.品名(中文及外文名称)4.种类(汽酒)5.加工方法(鲜葡萄酿造)6.酒精含量 7.级别 8.年份(没有年份的申报无年份)9.产区(中文及外文名称)10.酒庄名(中文及外文名称)11.葡萄品种(中文及外文名称)12.包装规格
22042	1.品牌类型 2.出口享惠情况 3.品名(中文及外文名称)4.加工方法(鲜葡萄酿造)5.酒精浓度 6.级别 7.年份(没有年份的申报无年份)8.产区(中文及外文名称)9.酒庄名(中文及外文名称)10.葡萄品种(中文及外文名称)11.包装规格(单位包装规格 * 每箱单位数)
22043	1.品牌类型 2.出口享惠情况 3.品名(中文及外文名称)4.种类(酿酒葡萄汁)5.包装规格 6.品牌(中文及外文名称)
2205	1.品牌类型 2.出口享惠情况 3.品名(中文及外文名称)4.加工方法(鲜葡萄酿造、加植物或香料)5.包装规格 6.品牌(中文及外文名称)
2206001	1.品牌类型 2.出口享惠情况 3.品名(中文及外文名称)4.加工方法(发酵、混合)5.包装规格 6.品牌(中文及外文名称)
2206009	1.品牌类型 2.出口享惠情况 3.品名(中文及外文名称)4.成分含量 5.加工方法(发酵、混合)6.酒精浓度 7.包装规格 8.品牌(中文及外文名称)9.年份 10.等级
2207	1.品牌类型 2.出口享惠情况 3.品名(中文及外文名称)4.加工方法(未改性、改性)5.酒精浓度 6.品牌(中文及外文名称)
22082	1.品牌类型 2.出口享惠情况 3.品名(中文及外文名称)4.原料 5.酒精浓度 6.包装规格 7.品牌(中文及外文名称)8.级别 9.产地
22083	1.品牌类型 2.出口享惠情况 3.品名(中文及外文名称)4.原料 5.酒精浓度 6.包装规格 7.品牌(中文及外文名称)8.产地
22084	1.品牌类型 2.出口享惠情况 3.品名(中文及外文名称)4.原料 5.酒精浓度 6.包装规格 7.品牌(中文及外文名称)
22085	1.品牌类型 2.出口享惠情况 3.品名(中文及外文名称)4.原料 5.酒精浓度 6.包装规格 7.品牌(中文及外文名称)
22086	1.品牌类型 2.出口享惠情况 3.品名(中文及外文名称)4.原料 5.酒精浓度 6.包装规格 7.品牌(中文及外文名称)
22087	1.品牌类型 2.出口享惠情况 3.品名(中文及外文名称)4.原料 5.酒精浓度 6.包装规格 7.品牌(中文及外文名称)
2208901	1.品牌类型 2.出口享惠情况 3.品名(中文及外文名称)4.原料 5.酒精浓度 6.包装规格 7.品牌(中文及外文名称)
2208902	1.品牌类型 2.出口享惠情况 3.原料 4.酒精浓度 5.包装规格 6.品牌
2208909	1.品牌类型 2.出口享惠情况 3.品名(中文及外文名称)4.原料 5.酒精浓度 6.包装规格 7.品牌(中文及外文名称)
2209	1.品牌类型 2.出口享惠情况 3.品名(中文及外文名称)4.醋酸浓度 5.包装规格 6.品牌(中文及外文名称)
23011	1.品牌类型 2.出口享惠情况 3.用途(不适合供人食用)4.状态(渣粉、团粒)
2301201	1.品牌类型 2.出口享惠情况 3.用途(不适合供人食用)4.状态(渣粉、团粒)5.成分含量(蛋白质含量等)6.种类(红、白鱼粉)
2301209	1.品牌类型 2.出口享惠情况 3.用途(不适合供人食用)4.状态(渣粉、团粒)
2302	1.品牌类型 2.出口享惠情况 3.种类(玉米的、小麦的等)
2303	1.品牌类型 2.出口享惠情况 3.种类 4.是否配制
2304	1.品牌类型 2.出口享惠情况 3.原料
2305	1.品牌类型 2.出口享惠情况 3.原料
2306	1.品牌类型 2.出口享惠情况 3.原料
2307	1.品牌类型 2.出口享惠情况
2308	1.品牌类型 2.出口享惠情况 3.用途(饲料用等)
23091	1.品牌类型 2.出口享惠情况 3.成分含量 4.用途(狗食、猫食等)5.加工方法(配制的)6.包装规格 7.品牌(中文及外文名称)
2309901	1.品牌类型 2.出口享惠情况 3.成分含量(须分别标明载体及活性物质)4.加工方法(配制的)5.包装规格 6.品牌(中文及外文名称)
2309909	1.品牌类型 2.出口享惠情况 3.成分含量 4.加工方法(配制的)5.包装规格 6.品牌(中文及外文名称)
24011	1.品牌类型 2.出口享惠情况 3.加工方法(未去梗)
24012	1.品牌类型 2.出口享惠情况 3.加工方法(去梗、部分去梗)
24013	1.品牌类型 2.出口享惠情况 3.是否废料
2402	1.品牌类型 2.出口享惠情况 3.种类(卷烟、雪茄烟)4.来源(烟草制或烟草代用品制)5.品牌 6.型号或系列名称
24031	1.品牌类型 2.出口享惠情况 3.用途(吸用等)
240391	1.品牌类型 2.出口享惠情况 3.加工方法(均化或再造)
240399	1.品牌类型 2.出口享惠情况 3.是否烟草精汁
2501	1.品牌类型 2.出口享惠情况 3.成分含量 4.外观(颜色、形状)5.包装 6.是否食用盐
2502	1.品牌类型 2.出口享惠情况 3.加工方法(焙烧、未焙烧)
2503	1.品牌类型 2.出口享惠情况 3.包装 4.加工工艺 5.状态(液态、固态、粉状、块状)6.成分含量 7.定价方式(公式定价、现货价等)8.需要二次结算、无需二次结算 9.计价日期
2504	1.品牌类型 2.出口享惠情况 3.用途 4.外观(粉末、鳞片、块等)5.来源(是否天然)6.是否球化加工 7.石墨含量 8.细度指标(细度、鳞片大小)
2505	1.品牌类型 2.出口享惠情况 3.用途 4.来源(如海砂、湖砂或河砂等)
2506	1.品牌类型 2.出口享惠情况 3.加工方法(天然状态、粗加修整、简单切割等)4.外观(颜色、形状)5.规格
2507	1.品牌类型 2.出口享惠情况 3.成分 4.活化、未活化请注明 5.用途 6.外观 7.加工方法(是否煅烧)8.白度 9.细度
25081	1.品牌类型 2.出口享惠情况 3.种类 4.外观(颜色、形状)5.活化、未活化请注明 6.用途 7.蒙脱石含量
25083	1.品牌类型 2.出口享惠情况 3.外观(颜色、形状)4.活化、未活化请注明 5.氧化铝含量 6.级别 7.是否含有添加剂或改性
25084	1.品牌类型 2.出口享惠情况 3.外观(颜色、形状)4.活化、未活化请注明 5.氧化铝含量 6.级别 7.是否含有添加剂或改性
25085	1.品牌类型 2.出口享惠情况 3.种类 4.外观(颜色、形状)5.是否活化 6.用途
25086	1.品牌类型 2.出口享惠情况 3.种类 4.外观(颜色、形状)5.是否活化 6.用途
25087	1.品牌类型 2.出口享惠情况 3.种类 4.外观(颜色、形状)5.是否活化 6.用途
2509	1.品牌类型 2.出口享惠情况
2510101	1.品牌类型 2.出口享惠情况 3.加工方法(是否碾磨及其他进一步加工)4.成分(磷灰石、天然磷酸钙、天然磷酸铝钙及磷酸盐白垩)5.来源 6.注明五氧化二磷含量
2510109	1.品牌类型 2.出口享惠情况 3.加工方法(是否碾磨及其他进一步加工)4.成分(磷灰石、天然磷酸钙、天然磷酸铝钙及磷酸盐白垩)5.注明五氧化二磷含量
2510201	1.品牌类型 2.出口享惠情况 3.加工方法(是否碾磨及其他进一步加工)4.成分(磷灰石、天然磷酸钙、天然磷酸铝钙及磷酸盐白垩)5.来源 6.注明五氧化二磷含量
2510209	1.品牌类型 2.出口享惠情况 3.加工方法(是否碾磨及其他进一步加工)4.成分(磷灰石、天然磷酸钙、天然磷酸铝钙及磷酸盐白垩)5.注明五氧化二磷含量
25111	1.品牌类型 2.出口享惠情况 3.加工方法 4.级别(钻井级、化工级、涂料级等)5.细度(目数)
25112	1.品牌类型 2.出口享惠情况 3.加工方法
2512	1.品牌类型 2.出口享惠情况 3.用途 4.外观(颜色、形状)5.是否活化 6.表观比重 7.品牌 8.种类 9.是否改性 10.二氧化硅含量
25131	1.品牌类型 2.出口享惠情况 3.加工方法(如天然原状、破碎)4.外观(颜色、形状)5.用途
25132	1.品牌类型 2.出口享惠情况 3.种类(刚玉岩、天然刚玉砂、天然石榴石、天然磨料等)

商品编码	申报要素
2514	1.品牌类型 2.出口享惠情况 3.用途 4.加工方法(天然原状、粗加修整、锯、割等)5.外观(颜色、形状)
25151	1.品牌类型 2.出口享惠情况 3.加工方法(天然原状、粗加修整、锯、割等)4.外观(颜色、形状)5.表观比重 6.体积或面积数量(立方米数或平方米数)7.花色品种的中英文名称 8.规格(长宽高)9.矿区名称
25152	1.品牌类型 2.出口享惠情况 3.加工方法(天然原状、粗加修整、锯、割等)4.外观(颜色、形状)5.除蜡石外要注明表观比重
25161	1.品牌类型 2.出口享惠情况 3.加工方法(天然原状、粗加修整、锯、割等)4.外观(颜色、形状)5.体积或面积数量(立方米数或平方米数)6.花色的中英文名称(如埃及金线米黄等)7.规格(长宽高)8.矿区名称
25162	1.品牌类型 2.出口享惠情况 3.加工方法(天然原状、粗加修整、锯、割等)4.外观(颜色、形状)5.体积或面积数量(立方米数或平方米数)6.花色的中英文名称(如埃及金线米黄等)7.规格(长宽高)
25169	1.品牌类型 2.出口享惠情况 3.用途 4.加工方法(天然原状、粗加修整、锯、割等)5.外观(颜色、形状)
25171	1.品牌类型 2.出口享惠情况 3.用途 4.外观(颜色、形状)
25172	1.品牌类型 2.出口享惠情况 3.用途 4.外观(颜色、形状)5.来源(是否矿渣、浮渣、残渣等)
25173	1.品牌类型 2.出口享惠情况 3.用途 4.外观(颜色、形状)
25174	1.品牌类型 2.出口享惠情况 3.外观(颜色、形状)
2518	1.品牌类型 2.出口享惠情况 3.加工方法(夯混、是否煅烧或烧结、粗加修整、锯、割等)4.外观(颜色、形状)
2519	1.品牌类型 2.出口享惠情况 3.加工方法 4.成分含量 5.外观(粉末、粒状、块状等)6.粉状请注明细度,粒状请注明直径
2520	1.品牌类型 2.出口享惠情况 3.用途(是否牙科用或其他用途)4.来源
2521	1.品牌类型 2.出口享惠情况 3.用途
2522	1.品牌类型 2.出口享惠情况
2523	1.品牌类型 2.出口享惠情况 3.用途 4.品牌或厂家名称
2524	1.品牌类型 2.出口享惠情况 3.外观(颜色、形状)4.是否青石棉 5.是否长纤维 6.型号
2525	1.品牌类型 2.出口享惠情况 3.用途 4.外观(颜色、形状)
25261	1.品牌类型 2.出口享惠情况 3.加工方法(天然原状、粗加修整、简单切割、是否破碎)
2526201	1.品牌类型 2.出口享惠情况 3.加工方法(天然原状、粗加修整、简单切割、是否破碎)
2526202	1.品牌类型 2.出口享惠情况 3.加工方法(天然原状、粗加修整、简单切割、是否破碎)4.白度
2528001	1.品牌类型 2.出口享惠情况
2528009	1.品牌类型 2.出口享惠情况 3.成分含量
25291	1.品牌类型 2.出口享惠情况 3.用途 4.外观(颜色、形状)
25292	1.品牌类型 2.出口享惠情况 3.用途 4.外观(颜色、形状)5.氟化钙含量
25293	1.品牌类型 2.出口享惠情况 3.用途 4.外观(颜色、形状)
2530101	1.品牌类型 2.出口享惠情况 3.用途 4.加工方法(天然开采、简单破碎、磨粉、未膨胀等)5.外观(颜色、形状)6.成分含量 7.白度
2530102	1.品牌类型 2.出口享惠情况 3.用途 4.加工方法(天然开采、简单破碎、磨粉、未膨胀等)5.外观(颜色、形状)6.成分含量
25302	1.品牌类型 2.出口享惠情况 3.用途 4.加工方法(天然开采、简单破碎、磨粉、未膨胀等)5.外观(颜色、形状)6.成分含量
2530901	1.品牌类型 2.出口享惠情况 3.用途 4.加工方法(天然开采、简单破碎、磨粉、未膨胀等)5.外观(颜色、形状)6.成分含量
2530902	1.品牌类型 2.出口享惠情况 3.用途 4.加工方法(天然开采、简单破碎、磨粉、未膨胀等)5.外观(颜色、形状)6.成分含量 7.稀土元素的重量百分比,以[A]表示
2530909	1.品牌类型 2.出口享惠情况 3.用途 4.加工方法(天然开采、简单破碎、磨粉、未膨胀等)5.外观(颜色、形状)6.成分含量
260111	1.品牌类型 2.出口享惠情况 3.加工方法 4.外观(颜色、形状)5.成分含量 6.平均粒度 7.来源(矿区名称)8.签约日期 9.定价方式(公式定价、现货价等)10.需要二次结算、无需二次结算 11.计价日期 12.有滞期费请注明
260112	1.品牌类型 2.出口享惠情况 3.加工方法 4.外观(颜色、形状)5.成分含量 6.来源(矿区名称)7.签约日期 8.定价方式(公式定价、现货价等)9.需要二次结算、无需二次结算 10.计价日期 11.有滞期费请注明
26012	1.品牌类型 2.出口享惠情况 3.加工方法 4.外观(颜色、形状)5.成分含量 6.来源(矿区名称)7.签约日期 8.定价方式(公式定价、现货价)9.需要二次结算、无需二次结算 10.计价日期 11.有滞期费请注明
2602	1.品牌类型 2.出口享惠情况 3.用途 4.加工方法 5.外观(颜色、形状)6.成分含量 7.来源(矿区名称)8.签约日期 9.定价方式(公式定价、现货价等)10.需要二次结算、无需二次结算 11.计价日期 12.有滞期费请注明
2603	1.品牌类型 2.出口享惠情况 3.加工方法 4.外观(颜色、形状)5.成分含量 6.含水率 7.来源(矿区名称)8.签约日期 9.定价方式(公式定价、现货价等)10.需要二次结算、无需二次结算 11.计价日期 12.有滞期费请注明
2604	1.品牌类型 2.出口享惠情况 3.加工方法 4.外观(颜色、形状)5.成分含量 6.来源(矿区名称)7.签约日期 8.定价方式(公式定价、现货价等)9.需要二次结算、无需二次结算 10.计价日期 11.有滞期费请注明
2605	1.品牌类型 2.出口享惠情况 3.加工方法 4.外观(颜色、形状)5.主要伴生矿物元素含量 6.用途 7.来源(矿区名称)8.签约日期 9.定价方式(公式定价、现货价等)10.需要二次结算、无需二次结算 11.计价日期 12.有滞期费请注明
2606	1.品牌类型 2.出口享惠情况 3.加工方法 4.外观(颜色、形状)5.成分含量 6.来源(矿区名称)7.签约日期 8.定价方式(公式定价、现货价等)9.需要二次结算、无需二次结算 10.计价日期 11.有滞期费请注明
2607	1.品牌类型 2.出口享惠情况 3.加工方法 4.外观(颜色、形状)5.成分含量 6.来源(矿区名称)7.签约日期 8.定价方式(公式定价、现货价等)9.需要二次结算、无需二次结算 10.计价日期 11.有滞期费请注明
2608	1.品牌类型 2.出口享惠情况 3.加工方法 4.外观(颜色、形状)5.成分含量 6.来源(矿区名称)7.签约日期 8.定价方式(公式定价、现货价等)9.需要二次结算、无需二次结算 10.计价日期 11.有滞期费请注明
2609	1.品牌类型 2.出口享惠情况 3.加工方法 4.外观(颜色、形状)5.成分含量 6.来源(矿区名称)7.签约日期 8.定价方式(公式定价、现货价等)9.需要二次结算、无需二次结算 10.计价日期 11.有滞期费请注明
2610	1.品牌类型 2.出口享惠情况 3.加工方法 4.外观(颜色、形状)5.成分含量 6.来源(矿区名称)7.签约日期 8.定价方式(公式定价、现货价等)9.需要二次结算、无需二次结算 10.计价日期 11.有滞期费请注明
2611	1.品牌类型 2.出口享惠情况 3.加工方法 4.外观(颜色、形状)5.成分含量 6.来源(矿区名称)7.签约日期
26121	1.品牌类型 2.出口享惠情况 3.加工方法 4.外观(颜色、形状)5.成分含量 6.种类(独居矿、钍石等)7.来源(矿区名称)8.签约日期 9.定价方式(公式定价、现货价等)10.需要二次结算、无需二次结算 11.计价日期 12.有滞期费请注明
26122	1.品牌类型 2.出口享惠情况 3.加工方法 4.外观(颜色、形状)5.成分含量 6.种类(独居矿、钍石等)7.来源(矿区名称)8.签约日期 9.定价方式(公式定价、现货价等)10.需要二次结算、无需二次结算 11.计价日期 12.有滞期费请注明 13.稀土元素的重量百分比,以[A]表示
2613	1.品牌类型 2.出口享惠情况 3.加工方法 4.外观(颜色、形状)5.成分含量 6.来源(矿区名称)7.签约日期 8.定价方式(公式定价、现货价等)9.需要二次结算、无需二次结算 10.计价日期 11.有滞期费请注明
2614	1.品牌类型 2.出口享惠情况 3.加工方法 4.外观(颜色、形状)5.成分含量 6.来源(矿区名称)7.签约日期 8.定价方式(公式定价、现货价等)9.需要二次结算、无需二次结算 10.计价日期 11.有滞期费请注明
26151	1.品牌类型 2.出口享惠情况 3.加工方法 4.外观(颜色、形状)5.成分含量 6.粒度 7.来源(矿区名称)8.签约日期 9.定价方式(公式定价、现货价等)10.需要二次结算、无需二次结算 11.计价日期 12.有滞期费请注明
26159	1.品牌类型 2.出口享惠情况 3.加工方法 4.外观(颜色、形状)5.成分含量 6.来源(矿区名称)7.签约日期 8.定价方式(公式定价、现货价等)9.需要二次结算、无需二次结算 10.计价日期 11.有滞期费请注明
26161	1.品牌类型 2.出口享惠情况 3.加工方法 4.外观(颜色、形状)5.成分含量 6.来源(矿区名称)7.签约日期 8.定价方式(公式定价、现货价等)9.需要二次结算、无需二次结算 10.计价日期 11.有滞期费请注明
26169	1.品牌类型 2.出口享惠情况 3.加工方法 4.外观(颜色、形状)5.成分含量 6.黄金矿砂请申报粒度(货物通过 74 微米(或 200 目)标准筛的筛下物的量比)7.来源(矿区名称)8.签约日期 9.定价方式(公式定价、现货价等)10.需要二次结算、无需二次结算 11.计价日期 12.有滞期费请注明
2617	1.品牌类型 2.出口享惠情况 3.加工方法 4.外观(颜色、形状)5.成分含量 6.来源(矿区名称)7.签约日期 8.定价方式(公式定价、现货价等)9.需要二次结算、无需二次结算 10.计价日期 11.有滞期费请注明
2618	1.品牌类型 2.出口享惠情况 3.用途 4.加工方法 5.外观(颜色、形状)6.成分含量 7.来源

商品编码	申报要素
2619	1.品牌类型 2.出口享惠情况 3.用途 4.加工方法 5.外观(颜色、形状)6.成分含量 7.来源 8.定价方式(公式定价、现货价等)9.需要二次结算、无需二次结算 10.计价日期 11.有滞期费请注明
2620	1.品牌类型 2.出口享惠情况 3.用途 4.加工方法 5.外观(颜色、形状)6.成分含量 7.来源
2621	1.品牌类型 2.出口享惠情况 3.用途 4.加工方法 5.外观(颜色、形状)6.来源
270111	1.品牌类型 2.出口享惠情况 3.挥发物含量(以干燥、无矿物质计)4.热值(以潮湿、无矿物质计以及收到基)5.灰分 6.含硫量 7.含水量 8.定价方式(公式定价、现货价等)9.需要二次结算、无需二次结算 10.签约日期 11.有滞期费请注明 12.计价日期
2701121	1.品牌类型 2.出口享惠情况 3.挥发物含量(以干燥、无矿物质计)4.热值(以潮湿、无矿物质计以及收到基)5.胶质层最大厚度 6.粘结指数 7.灰分 8.含硫量 9.含水量 10.定价方式(公式定价、现货价等)11.需要二次结算、无需二次结算 12.签约日期 13.计价日期 14.有滞期费请注明 15.品种(按检验证明上的描述申报)
2701129	1.品牌类型 2.出口享惠情况 3.挥发物含量(以干燥、无矿物质计)4.热值(以潮湿、无矿物质计以及收到基)5.粘结指数 6.灰分 7.含硫量 8.含水量 9.定价方式(公式定价、现货价等)10.需要二次结算、无需二次结算 11.签约日期 12.计价日期 13.有滞期费请注明
270119	1.品牌类型 2.出口享惠情况 3.挥发物含量(以干燥、无矿物质计)4.热值(包括以潮湿无矿物质计以及收到基)5.灰分 6.含硫量 7.含水量 8.透光率 9.定价方式(公式定价、现货价等)10.需要二次结算、无需二次结算 11.签约日期 12.计价日期 13.有滞期费请注明
27012	1.品牌类型 2.出口享惠情况 3.外观 4.挥发物含量(以干燥、无矿物质计)5.等级 6.热值(包括以潮湿无矿物质计以及收到基)7.灰分 8.含硫量 9.含水量 10.定价方式(公式定价、现货价等)11.需要二次结算、无需二次结算 12.签约日期 13.计价日期 14.有滞期费请注明
27021	1.品牌类型 2.出口享惠情况 3.外观 4.是否黑玉 5.挥发物含量(以干燥、无灰基计)6.热值(包括以潮湿无矿物质计以及收到基)7.透光率 8.含水量 9.定价方式(公式定价、现货价等)10.需要二次结算、无需二次结算 11.签约日期 12.计价日期 13.有滞期费请注明
27022	1.品牌类型 2.出口享惠情况 3.外观 4.是否黑玉 5.挥发物含量(以干燥、无灰基计)6.热值(包括以潮湿无矿物质计以及收到基)7.透光率 8.含水量 9.定价方式(公式定价、现货价等)10.需要二次结算、无需二次结算 11.签约日期 12.计价日期 13.有滞期费请注明
2703	1.品牌类型 2.出口享惠情况 3.外观 4.来源 5.签约日期 6.计价日期
2704001	1.品牌类型 2.出口享惠情况 3.用途 4.来源 5.挥发物含量(以干燥、无矿物质计)6.气孔率 7.含磷量 8.灰分 9.粒度 10.含水量 11.含硫量 12.签约日期 13.计价日期
2704009	1.品牌类型 2.出口享惠情况 3.用途 4.来源 5.签约日期 6.计价日期
2705	1.品牌类型 2.出口享惠情况 3.来源 4.签约日期 5.计价日期
2706	1.品牌类型 2.出口享惠情况 3.外观 4.来源 5.成分含量 6.签约日期 7.计价日期
27071	1.品牌类型 2.出口享惠情况 3.成分含量 4.定价方式(公式定价、现货价等)5.需要二次结算、无需二次结算 6.签约日期 7.计价日期 8.有滞期费请注明
27072	1.品牌类型 2.出口享惠情况 3.成分含量 4.定价方式(公式定价、现货价等)5.需要二次结算、无需二次结算 6.签约日期 7.计价日期 8.有滞期费请注明
27073	1.品牌类型 2.出口享惠情况 3.成分含量 4.定价方式(公式定价、现货价等)5.需要二次结算、无需二次结算 6.签约日期 7.计价日期 8.有滞期费请注明
27074	1.品牌类型 2.出口享惠情况 3.成分含量(以美国标准实验方法 D86 为准,250℃时)4.结晶点 5.外观 6.定价方式(公式定价、现货价等)7.需要二次结算、无需二次结算 8.签约日期 9.计价日期 10.有滞期费请注明
27075	1.品牌类型 2.出口享惠情况 3.成分含量(需用 HS/T50 方法测得芳烃含量)4.250℃蒸馏出芳烃体积含量 5.馏程 6.定价方式(公式定价、现货价等)7.需要二次结算、无需二次结算 8.签约日期 9.计价日期 10.有滞期费请注明
27079	1.品牌类型 2.出口享惠情况 3.成分含量(需用 HS/T50 方法测得芳烃含量)4.定价方式(公式定价、现货价等)5.需要二次结算、无需二次结算 6.签约日期 7.计价日期 8.有滞期费请注明
2708	1.品牌类型 2.出口享惠情况 3.外观 4.来源 5.签约日期 6.计价日期
2709	1.品牌类型 2.出口享惠情况 3.种类 4.密度或 API 度 5.若为凝析油需注明 6.定价方式(公式定价、现货价等)7.需要二次结算、无需二次结算 8.签约日期 9.计价日期 10.有滞期费请注明
2710121	1.品牌类型 2.出口享惠情况 3.馏程 4.硫成分含量 5.定价方式(公式定价、现货价等)6.需要二次结算、无需二次结算 7.签约日期 8.计价日期 9.有滞期费请注明
2710122	1.品牌类型 2.出口享惠情况 3.馏程 4.定价方式(公式定价、现货价等)5.需要二次结算、无需二次结算 6.签约日期 7.计价日期 8.有滞期费请注明
2710123	1.品牌类型 2.出口享惠情况 3.馏程 4.用途 5.品牌 6.型号 7.包装规格 8.定价方式(公式定价、现货价等)9.需要二次结算、无需二次结算 10.签约日期 11.计价日期 12.有滞期费请注明
27101291	1.品牌类型 2.出口享惠情况 3.成分含量 4.定价方式(公式定价、现货价等)5.需要二次结算、无需二次结算 6.签约日期 7.计价日期 8.有滞期费请注明
27101299	1.品牌类型 2.出口享惠情况 3.馏程 4.成分含量 5.定价方式(公式定价、现货价等)6.需要二次结算、无需二次结算 7.签约日期 8.计价日期 9.有滞期费请注明
2710191	1.品牌类型 2.出口享惠情况 3.馏程 4.定价方式(公式定价、现货价等)5.需要二次结算、无需二次结算 6.签约日期 7.计价日期 8.有滞期费请注明
27101922	1.品牌类型 2.出口享惠情况 3.馏程 4.运动粘度指标(100℃)5.硫含量 6.水和沉淀物含量 7.闪点(7 号燃料油注明开口闪点,其它注明闭口闪点)8.灰分含量 9.定价方式(公式定价、现货价等)10.需要二次结算、无需二次结算 11.签约日期 12.计价日期 13.有滞期费请注明
27101923	1.品牌类型 2.出口享惠情况 3.馏程 4.硫含量 5.定价方式(公式定价、现货价等)6.需要二次结算、无需二次结算 7.签约日期 8.计价日期 9.有滞期费请注明
27101929	1.品牌类型 2.出口享惠情况 3.馏程 4.定价方式(公式定价、现货价等)5.需要二次结算、无需二次结算 6.签约日期 7.计价日期 8.有滞期费请注明
27101991	1.品牌类型 2.出口享惠情况 3.用途 4.从石油或沥青提取矿物油类的百分比含量 5.品牌 6.型号 7.包装规格 8.定价方式(公式定价、现货价等)9.需要二次结算、无需二次结算 10.签约日期 11.计价日期 12.有滞期费请注明
27101992	1.品牌类型 2.出口享惠情况 3.用途 4.从石油或沥青提取矿物油类的百分比含量 5.品牌 6.型号 7.包装规格 8.定价方式(公式定价、现货价等)9.需要二次结算、无需二次结算 10.签约日期 11.计价日期 12.有滞期费请注明
27101993	1.品牌类型 2.出口享惠情况 3.用途 4.品牌 5.型号 6.包装规格 7.定价方式(公式定价、现货价等)8.需要二次结算、无需二次结算 9.签约日期 10.计价日期 11.有滞期费请注明
27101994	1.品牌类型 2.出口享惠情况 3.初馏点 4.98%馏出温度 5.正构烷烃含量 6.芳烃含量 7.包装规格 8.定价方式(公式定价、现货价等)9.需要二次结算、无需二次结算 10.签约日期 11.计价日期 12.有滞期费请注明
27101999	1.品牌类型 2.出口享惠情况 3.成分含量 4.包装规格 5.定价方式(公式定价、现货价等)6.需要二次结算、无需二次结算 7.签约日期 8.计价日期 9.有滞期费请注明
27102	1.品牌类型 2.出口享惠情况 3.用途 4.成分 5.从石油或沥青提取矿物油类的百分比含量 6.定价方式(公式定价、现货价等)7.需要二次结算、无需二次结算 8.签约日期 9.计价日期 10.有滞期费请注明
27109	1.品牌类型 2.出口享惠情况 3.来源 4.定价方式(公式定价、现货价等)5.需要二次结算、无需二次结算 6.签约日期 7.计价日期 8.有滞期费请注明
271111	1.品牌类型 2.出口享惠情况 3.状态(液化或气态)4.成分含量 5.加工方法(压力货、冷冻货等)6.定价方式(公式定价、现货价等)7.需要二次结算、无需二次结算 8.签约日期 9.计价日期 10.有滞期费请注明 11.百万英热值(MMBtu)
271112	1.品牌类型 2.出口享惠情况 3.状态(液化或气态)4.成分含量 5.加工方法(压力货、冷冻货等)6.定价方式(公式定价、现货价等)7.需要二次结算、无需二次结算 8.签约日期 9.计价日期 10.有滞期费请注明
2711131	1.品牌类型 2.出口享惠情况 3.状态(液化或气态)4.成分含量 5.包装容器容积 6.加工方法(压力货、冷冻货等)7.定价方式(公式定价、现货价等)8.需要二次结算、无需二次结算 9.签约日期 10.计价日期 11.有滞期费请注明
2711139	1.品牌类型 2.出口享惠情况 3.状态(液化或气态)4.成分含量 5.加工方法(压力货、冷冻货等)6.定价方式(公式定价、现货价等)7.需要二次结算、无需二次结算 8.签约日期 9.计价日期 10.有滞期费请注明
271114	1.品牌类型 2.出口享惠情况 3.状态(液化或气态)4.成分含量 5.加工方法(压力货、冷冻货等)6.定价方式(公式定价、现货价等)7.需要二次结算、无需二次结算 8.签约日期 9.计价日期 10.有滞期费请注明

商品编码	申报要素
2711191	1.品牌类型 2.出口享惠情况 3.状态(液化或气态)4.成分含量 5.包装容器容积 6.加工方法(压力货、冷冻货等)7.定价方式(公式定价、现货价等)8.需要二次结算、无需二次结算 9.签约日期 10.计价日期 11.有滞期费请注明
2711199	1.品牌类型 2.出口享惠情况 3.状态(液化或气态)4.成分含量 5.加工方法(压力货、冷冻货等)6.定价方式(公式定价、现货价等)7.需要二次结算、无需二次结算 8.签约日期 9.计价日期 10.有滞期费请注明
271121	1.品牌类型 2.出口享惠情况 3.状态(液化或气态)4.成分含量 5.加工方法(压力货、冷冻货等)6.定价方式(公式定价、现货价等)7.需要二次结算、无需二次结算 8.签约日期 9.计价日期 10.有滞期费请注明 11.百万英热值(MMBtu)
271129	1.品牌类型 2.出口享惠情况 3.状态(液化或气态)4.成分含量 5.加工方法(压力货、冷冻货等)6.定价方式(公式定价、现货价等)7.需要二次结算、无需二次结算 8.签约日期 9.计价日期 10.有滞期费请注明
27121	1.品牌类型 2.出口享惠情况 3.用途 4.是否零售包装
27122	1.品牌类型 2.出口享惠情况 3.加工方法 4.外观 5.含油量
27129	1.品牌类型 2.出口享惠情况 3.成分
27131	1.品牌类型 2.出口享惠情况 3.用途 4.加工方法(是否煅烧)5.外观 6.含硫量 7.定价方式(公式定价、现货价等)8.需要二次结算、无需二次结算 9.签约日期 10.计价日期 11.有滞期费请注明
27132	1.品牌类型 2.出口享惠情况 3.针入度 4.用途 5.加工方法(是否煅烧)6.外观 7.品牌 8.包装规格 9.含蜡量 10.定价方式(公式定价、现货价等)11.需要二次结算、无需二次结算 12.签约日期 13.计价日期 14.有滞期费请注明
27139	1.品牌类型 2.出口享惠情况 3.用途 4.加工方法(是否煅烧)5.外观 6.定价方式(公式定价、现货价等)7.需要二次结算、无需二次结算 8.签约日期 9.计价日期 10.有滞期费请注明
2714	1.品牌类型 2.出口享惠情况 3.用途 4.加工方法 5.外观 6.成分含量(沥青、水)7.定价方式(公式定价、现货价等)8.需要二次结算、无需二次结算 9.签约日期 10.计价日期 11.有滞期费请注明
2715	1.品牌类型 2.出口享惠情况 3.用途 4.加工方法 5.外观 6.成分含量 7.定价方式(公式定价、现货价等)8.需要二次结算、无需二次结算 9.签约日期 10.计价日期 11.有滞期费请注明
2716	1.品牌类型 2.出口享惠情况
2801	1.品牌类型 2.出口享惠情况 3.成分含量 4.包装 5.品牌 6.型号
2802	1.品牌类型 2.出口享惠情况 3.成分含量 4.包装
2803	1.品牌类型 2.出口享惠情况 3.来源 4.有无活性 5.成分含量 6.包装 7.型号 8.品牌
28041	1.品牌类型 2.出口享惠情况 3.成分含量
28042	1.品牌类型 2.出口享惠情况 3.成分含量
28043	1.品牌类型 2.出口享惠情况 3.成分含量
28044	1.品牌类型 2.出口享惠情况 3.成分含量
28045	1.品牌类型 2.出口享惠情况 3.成分含量
2804611	1.品牌类型 2.出口享惠情况 3.用途(用于电子工业等)4.加工方法(经掺杂等)5.成分含量 6.直径
2804612	1.品牌类型 2.出口享惠情况 3.用途(用于电子工业等)4.加工方法(经掺杂等)5.成分含量 6.直径
2804619	1.品牌类型 2.出口享惠情况 3.用途 4.加工方法(西门子法、硅烷热分解法等经掺杂 P 型、经掺杂 N 型,未经掺杂)5.成分含量 6.外观(多晶硅碎料、块料或锅底料、头尾料等)7.电阻率 8.是否需清洗 9.品牌 10.型号
280469	1.品牌类型 2.出口享惠情况 3.用途 4.加工方法(经掺杂等)5.成分含量 6.牌号 9.1
28047	1.品牌类型 2.出口享惠情况 3.成分含量
28048	1.品牌类型 2.出口享惠情况 3.成分含量
28049	1.品牌类型 2.出口享惠情况 3.用途(用于电子工业等)4.加工方法(经掺杂等)5.成分含量 6.包装
28051	1.品牌类型 2.出口享惠情况 3.成分含量 4.包装
28053	1.品牌类型 2.出口享惠情况 3.混合稀土应注明各组分含量 4.是否电池级的稀土金属、钪及钇 5.包装 6.稀土元素的重量百分比,以[A]表示
28054	1.品牌类型 2.出口享惠情况 3.成分含量 4.包装 7.1
2806	1.品牌类型 2.出口享惠情况 3.成分含量 6.1
2807	1.品牌类型 2.出口享惠情况 3.成分含量 4.加工工艺(如回收硫酸硫磺硫酸硫矿硫酸)
2808	1.品牌类型 2.出口享惠情况 3.成分含量
2809	1.品牌类型 2.出口享惠情况 3.成分含量
2810	1.品牌类型 2.出口享惠情况 3.成分含量
281111	1.品牌类型 2.出口享惠情况 3.成分含量 4.包装(槽罐集装箱、塑料桶等)
281112	1.品牌类型 2.出口享惠情况 3.成分含量
281119	1.品牌类型 2.出口享惠情况 3.成分含量
281121	1.品牌类型 2.出口享惠情况 3.成分含量
281122	1.品牌类型 2.出口享惠情况 3.成分含量 4.是否经过表面处理 5.品牌 6.外观 7.加工工艺 8.细度 9.型号
281129	1.品牌类型 2.出口享惠情况 3.成分含量
2812	1.品牌类型 2.出口享惠情况 3.成分含量
2813	1.品牌类型 2.出口享惠情况 3.成分含量
2814	1.品牌类型 2.出口享惠情况 3.氨含量
2815	1.品牌类型 2.出口享惠情况 3.成分含量 4.用途 5.外观
2816	1.品牌类型 2.出口享惠情况 3.成分含量
2817	1.品牌类型 2.出口享惠情况 3.用途 4.天然的请注明 5.成分含量
2818101	1.品牌类型 2.出口享惠情况 3.成分含量 4.外观 5.晶型 6.6.莫氏硬度
2818109	1.品牌类型 2.出口享惠情况 3.成分含量 4.外观 5.晶型
28182	1.品牌类型 2.出口享惠情况 3.外观 4.成分含量 5.用途(冶金用或非冶金用)
28183	1.品牌类型 2.出口享惠情况 3.成分含量
28191	1.品牌类型 2.出口享惠情况 3.成分含量
28199	1.品牌类型 2.出口享惠情况 3.成分含量
2820	1.品牌类型 2.出口享惠情况 3.成分含量
28211	1.品牌类型 2.出口享惠情况 3.成分含量
28212	1.品牌类型 2.出口享惠情况 3.铁按三氧化二铁计含量
2822	1.品牌类型 2.出口享惠情况 3.成分含量
2823	1.品牌类型 2.出口享惠情况 3.成分含量,是否与其他物质混合 4.是否经表面处理
2824	1.品牌类型 2.出口享惠情况 3.成分含量
2825101	1.品牌类型 2.出口享惠情况 3.水合肼的含量
2825102	1.品牌类型 2.出口享惠情况 3.成分含量
2825109	1.品牌类型 2.出口享惠情况 3.成分含量
28252	1.品牌类型 2.出口享惠情况 3.成分含量
28253	1.品牌类型 2.出口享惠情况 3.成分含量
28254	1.品牌类型 2.出口享惠情况 3.成分含量
28255	1.品牌类型 2.出口享惠情况 3.成分含量
28256	1.品牌类型 2.出口享惠情况 3.成分含量
28257	1.品牌类型 2.出口享惠情况 3.成分含量
28258	1.品牌类型 2.出口享惠情况 3.成分含量
28259011	1.品牌类型 2.出口享惠情况 3.成分含量
28259012	1.品牌类型 2.出口享惠情况 3.状态(粉末)4.外观(淡黄色)5.粒度 6.成分含量
28259019	1.品牌类型 2.出口享惠情况 3.成分含量
2825902	1.品牌类型 2.出口享惠情况 3.成分含量
2825903	1.品牌类型 2.出口享惠情况 3.成分含量
2825904	1.品牌类型 2.出口享惠情况 3.成分含量
2825909	1.品牌类型 2.出口享惠情况 3.成分含量
2826121	1.品牌类型 2.出口享惠情况 3.氟质量分数 4.铝质量分数 5.烧碱量 6.松装密度 7.成分含量
2826129	1.品牌类型 2.出口享惠情况 3.成分含量
282619	1.品牌类型 2.出口享惠情况 3.成分含量
28263	1.品牌类型 2.出口享惠情况 3.成分含量
28269	1.品牌类型 2.出口享惠情况 3.成分含量
28271	1.品牌类型 2.出口享惠情况 3.肥料用请注明 4.成分含量 5.外观(粉状、颗粒)
28272	1.品牌类型 2.出口享惠情况 3.成分含量
28273	1.品牌类型 2.出口享惠情况 3.成分含量
28274	1.品牌类型 2.出口享惠情况 3.成分含量
28275	1.品牌类型 2.出口享惠情况 3.成分含量
28276	1.品牌类型 2.出口享惠情况 3.成分含量
2828	1.品牌类型 2.出口享惠情况 3.成分含量
28291	1.品牌类型 2.出口享惠情况 3.成分含量
28299	1.品牌类型 2.出口享惠情况 3.成分含量 4.如为高氯酸铵请注明粒度
2830	1.品牌类型 2.出口享惠情况 3.成分含量
2831	1.品牌类型 2.出口享惠情况 3.成分含量
2832	1.品牌类型 2.出口享惠情况 3.成分含量
2833	1.品牌类型 2.出口享惠情况 3.成分含量
28341	1.品牌类型 2.出口享惠情况 3.成分含量
283421	1.品牌类型 2.出口享惠情况 3.肥料用请注明 4.成分含量
283429	1.品牌类型 2.出口享惠情况 3.成分含量
28351	1.品牌类型 2.出口享惠情况 3.成分含量
283522	1.品牌类型 2.出口享惠情况 3.成分含量
283524	1.品牌类型 2.出口享惠情况 3.成分含量
283525	1.品牌类型 2.出口享惠情况 3.正磷酸氢钙请注明氟含量 4.用途(饲料、食品等)5.成分含量
283526	1.品牌类型 2.出口享惠情况 3.成分含量
283529	1.品牌类型 2.出口享惠情况 3.成分含量
28353	1.品牌类型 2.出口享惠情况 3.用途(饲料、食品等)4.成分含量
28362	1.品牌类型 2.出口享惠情况 3.成分含量
28363	1.品牌类型 2.出口享惠情况 3.成分含量
28364	1.品牌类型 2.出口享惠情况 3.成分含量
28365	1.品牌类型 2.出口享惠情况 3.成分含量 4.用途 5.品牌
28366	1.品牌类型 2.出口享惠情况 3.成分含量
28369	1.品牌类型 2.出口享惠情况 3.成分含量
2837	1.品牌类型 2.出口享惠情况 3.成分含量 4.包装
2839	1.品牌类型 2.出口享惠情况 3.成分含量
2840	1.品牌类型 2.出口享惠情况 3.成分含量

商品编码	申报要素
28413	1.品牌类型 2.出口享惠情况 3.成分含量
28415	1.品牌类型 2.出口享惠情况 3.成分含量
28416	1.品牌类型 2.出口享惠情况 3.成分含量
28417	1.品牌类型 2.出口享惠情况 3.成分含量
2841801	1.品牌类型 2.出口享惠情况 3.成分含量 4.含量(WO3 含量)
2841802	1.品牌类型 2.出口享惠情况 3.成分含量
2841803	1.品牌类型 2.出口享惠情况 3.成分含量
2841804	1.品牌类型 2.出口享惠情况 3.成分含量 4.含量(WO3 含量)
2841809	1.品牌类型 2.出口享惠情况 3.成分含量
28419	1.品牌类型 2.出口享惠情况 3.成分含量
2842	1.品牌类型 2.出口享惠情况 3.成分含量 4.包装
2843	1.品牌类型 2.出口享惠情况 3.成分含量 4.包装
2844	1.品牌类型 2.出口享惠情况 3.成分含量
2845	1.品牌类型 2.出口享惠情况 3.成分含量
28461	1.品牌类型 2.出口享惠情况 3.成分含量 4.稀土元素的重量百分比,以[A]表示
2846901	1.品牌类型 2.出口享惠情况 3.成分含量 4.稀土元素的重量百分比,以[A]表示
2846902	1.品牌类型 2.出口享惠情况 3.成分含量 4.稀土元素的重量百分比,以[A]表示
2846903	1.品牌类型 2.出口享惠情况 3.成分含量 4.稀土元素的重量百分比,以[A]表示
2846904	1.品牌类型 2.出口享惠情况 3.成分含量 4.稀土元素的重量百分比,以[A]表示
2846909	1.品牌类型 2.出口享惠情况 3.成分含量 4.稀土元素的重量百分比,以[A]表示
2847	1.品牌类型 2.出口享惠情况 3.成分含量 4.包装
2849	1.品牌类型 2.出口享惠情况 3.成分含量 4.品牌 5.型号 6.外观 7.用途 8.碳化钨请注明粒度
2850	1.品牌类型 2.出口享惠情况 3.成分含量
2852	1.品牌类型 2.出口享惠情况 3.成分含量
28531	1.品牌类型 2.出口享惠情况 3.成分含量 4.包装规格
2853901	1.品牌类型 2.出口享惠情况 3.是否饮用 4.成分含量 5.包装规格
2853903	1.品牌类型 2.出口享惠情况 3.成分含量
2853904	1.品牌类型 2.出口享惠情况 3.铜母合金请注明磷的重量百分比
2853905	1.品牌类型 2.出口享惠情况 3.成分含量
2853909	1.品牌类型 2.出口享惠情况 3.成分含量
29011	1.品牌类型 2.出口享惠情况 3.成分含量 4.用途 5.用作气体燃料的应报明包装容器容积 6.散装货物应报明
290121	1.品牌类型 2.出口享惠情况 3.成分含量 4.用途 5.用作气体燃料的应报明包装容器容积 6.散装货物应报明
290122	1.品牌类型 2.出口享惠情况 3.成分含量 4.用途 5.用作气体燃料的应报明包装容器容积 6.散装货物应报明 7.签约日期 8.定价方式(公式定价、现货价等)9.需要二次结算、无需二次结算 10.计价日期
2901231	1.品牌类型 2.出口享惠情况 3.成分含量 4.用途 5.用作气体燃料的应报明包装容器容积 6.散装货物应报明 7.签约日期 8.定价方式(公式定价、现货价等)9.需要二次结算、无需二次结算 10.计价日期
2901232	1.品牌类型 2.出口享惠情况 3.成分含量 4.用途 5.用作气体燃料的应报明包装容器容积 6.散装货物应报明
2901233	1.品牌类型 2.出口享惠情况 3.成分含量 4.用途 5.用作气体燃料的应报明包装容器容积 6.散装货物应报明
290124	1.品牌类型 2.出口享惠情况 3.成分含量 4.用途 5.用作气体燃料的应报明包装容器容积 6.散装货物应报明 7.签约日期 8.定价方式(公式定价、现货价等)9.需要二次结算、无需二次结算 10.计价日期
290129	1.品牌类型 2.出口享惠情况 3.成分含量 4.用途 5.用作气体燃料的应报明包装容器容积 6.散装货物应报明
290211	1.品牌类型 2.出口享惠情况 3.成分含量 4.用途 5.签约日期 6.定价方式(公式定价、现货价等)7.需要二次结算、无需二次结算 8.计价日期
290219	1.品牌类型 2.出口享惠情况 3.成分含量 4.用途
29022	1.品牌类型 2.出口享惠情况 3.成分含量 4.签约日期 5.定价方式(公式定价、现货价等)6.需要二次结算、无需二次结算 7.计价日期
29023	1.品牌类型 2.出口享惠情况 3.成分含量 4.签约日期 5.定价方式(公式定价、现货价等)6.需要二次结算、无需二次结算 7.计价日期
29024	1.品牌类型 2.出口享惠情况 3.成分含量 4.签约日期 5.定价方式(公式定价、现货价等)6.需要二次结算、无需二次结算 7.计价日期
29025	1.品牌类型 2.出口享惠情况 3.成分含量 4.签约日期 5.定价方式(公式定价、现货价等)6.需要二次结算、无需二次结算 7.计价日期
29026	1.品牌类型 2.出口享惠情况 3.成分含量 4.签约日期 5.定价方式(公式定价、现货价等)6.需要二次结算、无需二次结算 7.计价日期

商品编码	申报要素
29027	1.品牌类型 2.出口享惠情况 3.成分含量 4.签约日期 5.定价方式(公式定价、现货价等)6.需要二次结算、无需二次结算 7.计价日期
2902901	1.品牌类型 2.出口享惠情况 3.成分含量
2902902	1.品牌类型 2.出口享惠情况 3.成分含量 4.结晶温度
2902903	1.品牌类型 2.出口享惠情况 3.成分含量
2902904	1.品牌类型 2.出口享惠情况 3.成分含量
2902905	1.品牌类型 2.出口享惠情况 3.成分含量
2902909	1.品牌类型 2.出口享惠情况 3.成分含量
29031	1.品牌类型 2.出口享惠情况 3.成分含量 4.用途
290321	1.品牌类型 2.出口享惠情况 3.成分含量 4.用途 5.签约日期 6.定价方式(公式定价、现货价等)7.需要二次结算、无需二次结算 8.计价日期
290322	1.品牌类型 2.出口享惠情况 3.成分含量 4.用途
290323	1.品牌类型 2.出口享惠情况 3.成分含量 4.用途
290329	1.品牌类型 2.出口享惠情况 3.成分含量 4.用途
29033	1.品牌类型 2.出口享惠情况 3.成分含量 4.用途
29037	1.品牌类型 2.出口享惠情况 3.成分含量 4.用途
29038	1.品牌类型 2.出口享惠情况 3.成分含量 4.用途
29039	1.品牌类型 2.出口享惠情况 3.成分含量 4.用途
2904	1.品牌类型 2.出口享惠情况 3.成分含量 4.用途
290511	1.品牌类型 2.出口享惠情况 3.成分含量 4.用途 5.包装规格 6.签约日期 7.定价方式(公式定价、现货价等)8.需要二次结算、无需二次结算 9.计价日期
290512	1.品牌类型 2.出口享惠情况 3.成分含量 4.用途 5.包装规格 6.签约日期 7.定价方式(公式定价、现货价等)8.需要二次结算、无需二次结算 9.计价日期
290513	1.品牌类型 2.出口享惠情况 3.成分含量 4.用途 5.包装规格 6.签约日期 7.定价方式(公式定价、现货价等)8.需要二次结算、无需二次结算 9.计价日期
2905141	1.品牌类型 2.出口享惠情况 3.成分含量 4.用途 5.包装规格 6.签约日期 7.定价方式(公式定价、现货价等)8.需要二次结算、无需二次结算 9.计价日期
2905142	1.品牌类型 2.出口享惠情况 3.成分含量 4.用途 5.包装规格
2905143	1.品牌类型 2.出口享惠情况 3.成分含量 4.用途 5.包装规格
2905161	1.品牌类型 2.出口享惠情况 3.成分含量 4.用途 5.包装规格
2905169	1.品牌类型 2.出口享惠情况 3.成分含量 4.用途 5.包装规格 6.签约日期 7.定价方式(公式定价、现货价等)8.需要二次结算、无需二次结算 9.计价日期
290517	1.品牌类型 2.出口享惠情况 3.成分含量 4.用途 5.包装规格
2905191	1.品牌类型 2.出口享惠情况 3.成分含量 4.用途 5.包装规格
2905199	1.品牌类型 2.出口享惠情况 3.成分含量 4.用途 5.包装规格 6.签约日期 7.定价方式(公式定价、现货价等)8.需要二次结算、无需二次结算 9.计价日期
29052	1.品牌类型 2.出口享惠情况 3.成分含量 4.用途 5.包装规格
290531	1.品牌类型 2.出口享惠情况 3.成分含量 4.用途 5.包装规格 6.签约日期 7.定价方式(公式定价、现货价等)8.需要二次结算、无需二次结算 9.计价日期
290532	1.品牌类型 2.出口享惠情况 3.成分含量 4.用途 5.包装规格 6.签约日期 7.定价方式(公式定价、现货价等)8.需要二次结算、无需二次结算 9.计价日期
290539	1.品牌类型 2.出口享惠情况 3.成分含量 4.用途 5.包装规格
290541	1.品牌类型 2.出口享惠情况 3.成分含量 4.用途 5.包装规格
290542	1.品牌类型 2.出口享惠情况 3.成分含量 4.用途 5.包装规格
290543	1.品牌类型 2.出口享惠情况 3.成分含量 4.用途 5.包装规格
290544	1.品牌类型 2.出口享惠情况 3.成分含量 4.用途 5.包装规格
290545	1.品牌类型 2.出口享惠情况 3.成分含量 4.用途 5.包装规格 6.签约日期 7.定价方式(公式定价、现货价等)8.需要二次结算、无需二次结算 9.计价日期 10.丙三醇(甘油)请报明颜色及外观状态
290549	1.品牌类型 2.出口享惠情况 3.成分含量 4.用途 5.包装规格
29055	1.品牌类型 2.出口享惠情况 3.成分含量 4.用途 5.包装规格
2906	1.品牌类型 2.出口享惠情况 3.成分含量 4.用途
2907111	1.品牌类型 2.出口享惠情况 3.成分含量 4.用途 5.签约日期 6.定价方式(公式定价、现货价等)7.需要二次结算、无需二次结算 8.计价日期
2907119	1.品牌类型 2.出口享惠情况 3.成分含量 4.用途
290712	1.品牌类型 2.出口享惠情况 3.成分含量 4.用途
290713	1.品牌类型 2.出口享惠情况 3.成分含量 4.用途
290715	1.品牌类型 2.出口享惠情况 3.成分含量 4.用途
290719	1.品牌类型 2.出口享惠情况 3.成分含量 4.用途
290721	1.品牌类型 2.出口享惠情况 3.成分含量 4.用途
290722	1.品牌类型 2.出口享惠情况 3.成分含量 4.用途
290723	1 品牌类型 2.出口享惠情况 3.成分含量 4.用途 5.签约日期 6.定价方式(公式定价、现货价等)7.需要二次结算、无需二次结算 8.计价日期
290729	1.品牌类型 2.出口享惠情况 3.成分含量 4.用途
2908	1.品牌类型 2.出口享惠情况 3.成分含量 4.用途
290911	1.品牌类型 2.出口享惠情况 3.成分含量 4.用途

商品编码	申报要素
2909191	1.品牌类型 2.出口享惠情况 3.成分含量 4.用途
2909199	1.品牌类型 2.出口享惠情况 3.成分含量 4.用途 5.签约日期 6.定价方式(公式定价、现货价等)7.需要二次结算、无需二次结算 8.计价日期
29092	1.品牌类型 2.出口享惠情况 3.成分含量 4.用途
29093	1.品牌类型 2.出口享惠情况 3.成分含量 4.用途
290941	1.品牌类型 2.出口享惠情况 3.成分含量 4.用途 5.签约日期 6.定价方式(公式定价、现货价等)7.需要二次结算、无需二次结算 8.计价日期
290943	1.品牌类型 2.出口享惠情况 3.成分含量 4.用途 5.签约日期 6.定价方式(公式定价、现货价等)7.需要二次结算、无需二次结算 8.计价日期
290944	1.品牌类型 2.出口享惠情况 3.成分含量 4.用途
290949	1.品牌类型 2.出口享惠情况 3.成分含量 4.用途
29095	1.品牌类型 2.出口享惠情况 3.成分含量 4.用途
29096	1.品牌类型 2.出口享惠情况 3.成分含量 4.用途
29101	1.品牌类型 2.出口享惠情况 3.成分含量 4.用途
29102	1.品牌类型 2.出口享惠情况 3.成分含量 4.用途 5.签约日期 6.定价方式(公式定价、现货价等)7.需要二次结算、无需二次结算 8.计价日期
29103	1.品牌类型 2.出口享惠情况 3.成分含量 4.用途
29104	1.品牌类型 2.出口享惠情况 3.成分含量 4.用途
29105	1.品牌类型 2.出口享惠情况 3.成分含量 4.用途
29109	1.品牌类型 2.出口享惠情况 3.成分含量 4.用途
2911	1.品牌类型 2.出口享惠情况 3.成分含量 4.用途
2912	1.品牌类型 2.出口享惠情况 3.成分含量 4.用途 5.四聚甲醛报明外观
2913	1.品牌类型 2.出口享惠情况 3.成分含量 4.用途
291411	1.品牌类型 2.出口享惠情况 3.成分含量 4.用途 5.丙酮报明包装 6.签约日期 7.定价方式(公式定价、现货价等)8.需要二次结算、无需二次结算 9.计价日期
291412	1.品牌类型 2.出口享惠情况 3.成分含量 4.用途
291413	1.品牌类型 2.出口享惠情况 3.成分含量 4.用途
291419	1.品牌类型 2.出口享惠情况 3.成分含量 4.用途
291422	1.品牌类型 2.出口享惠情况 3.成分含量 4.用途 5.签约日期 6.定价方式(公式定价、现货价等)7.需要二次结算、无需二次结算 8.计价日期
291423	1.品牌类型 2.出口享惠情况 3.成分含量 4.用途
291429	1.品牌类型 2.出口享惠情况 3.成分含量 4.用途
29143	1.品牌类型 2.出口享惠情况 3.成分含量 4.用途
29144	1.品牌类型 2.出口享惠情况 3.成分含量 4.用途
29145	1.品牌类型 2.出口享惠情况 3.成分含量 4.用途
29146	1.品牌类型 2.出口享惠情况 3.成分含量 4.用途
29147	1.品牌类型 2.出口享惠情况 3.成分含量 4.用途
29149	1.品牌类型 2.出口享惠情况 3.成分含量 4.用途
29151	1.品牌类型 2.出口享惠情况 3.成分含量 4.用途 5.外观(颜色、形状)
29152111	1.品牌类型 2.出口享惠情况 3.成分含量 4.用途 5.外观(颜色、形状)6.需要二次结算、无需二次结算 7.计价日期
29152119	1.品牌类型 2.出口享惠情况 3.成分含量 4.用途 5.外观(颜色、形状)6.签约日期 7.定价方式(公式定价、现货价等)8.需要二次结算、无需二次结算 9.计价日期
29152190	1.品牌类型 2.出口享惠情况 3.成分含量 4.用途 5.外观(颜色、形状)
291524	1.品牌类型 2.出口享惠情况 3.成分含量 4.用途 5.外观(颜色、形状)
291529	1.品牌类型 2.出口享惠情况 3.成分含量 4.用途 5.外观(颜色、形状)
29153	1.品牌类型 2.出口享惠情况 3.成分含量 4.用途 5.外观(颜色、形状)
29154	1.品牌类型 2.出口享惠情况 3.成分含量 4.用途 5.外观(颜色、形状)
29155	1.品牌类型 2.出口享惠情况 3.成分含量 4.用途 5.外观(颜色、形状)
29156	1.品牌类型 2.出口享惠情况 3.成分含量 4.用途 5.外观(颜色、形状)
29157	1.品牌类型 2.出口享惠情况 3.成分含量 4.用途 5.外观(颜色、形状)
29159	1.品牌类型 2.出口享惠情况 3.成分含量 4.用途 5.外观(颜色、形状)
291611	1.品牌类型 2.出口享惠情况 3.成分含量 4.用途 5.外观(颜色、形状)
2916121	1.品牌类型 2.出口享惠情况 3.成分含量 4.用途 5.外观(颜色、形状)
2916122	1.品牌类型 2.出口享惠情况 3.成分含量 4.用途 5.外观(颜色、形状)
2916123	1.品牌类型 2.出口享惠情况 3.成分含量 4.用途 5.外观(颜色、形状)

商品编码	申报要素
2916124	1.品牌类型 2.出口享惠情况 3.成分含量 4.用途 5.外观(颜色、形状)6.签约日期 7.定价方式(公式定价、现货价等)8.需要二次结算、无需二次结算 9.计价日期
2916129	1.品牌类型 2.出口享惠情况 3.成分含量 4.用途 5.外观(颜色、形状)
291613	1.品牌类型 2.出口享惠情况 3.成分含量 4.用途 5.外观(颜色、形状)
291614	1.品牌类型 2.出口享惠情况 3.成分含量 4.用途 5.外观(颜色、形状)6.签约日期 7.定价方式(公式定价、现货价等)8.需要二次结算、无需二次结算 9.计价日期
291615	1.品牌类型 2.出口享惠情况 3.成分含量 4.用途 5.外观(颜色、形状)
291616	1.品牌类型 2.出口享惠情况 3.成分含量 4.用途 5.外观(颜色、形状)
291619	1.品牌类型 2.出口享惠情况 3.成分含量 4.用途 5.外观(颜色、形状)
29162	1.品牌类型 2.出口享惠情况 3.成分含量 4.用途 5.外观(颜色、形状)
29163	1.品牌类型 2.出口享惠情况 3.成分含量 4.用途 5.外观(颜色、形状)
29171	1.品牌类型 2.出口享惠情况 3.成分含量 4.用途
29172	1.品牌类型 2.出口享惠情况 3.成分含量 4.用途
291732	1.品牌类型 2.出口享惠情况 3.成分含量 4.用途
291733	1.品牌类型 2.出口享惠情况 3.成分含量 4.用途
291734	1.品牌类型 2.出口享惠情况 3.成分含量 4.用途
291735	1.品牌类型 2.出口享惠情况 3.成分含量 4.用途
29173611	1.品牌类型 2.出口享惠情况 3.成分含量 4.用途 5.对苯二甲酸请注明 4－CBA 值 6.对苯二甲酸请注明 P－TL 酸值 7.对苯二甲酸请注明色度 8.对苯二甲酸请注明水分 9.签约日期 10.定价方式(公式定价、现货价等)11.需要二次结算、无需二次结算 12.计价日期
29173619	1.品牌类型 2.出口享惠情况 3.成分含量 4.用途 5.对苯二甲酸请注明 4－CBA 值 6.对苯二甲酸请注明 P－TL 酸值 7.对苯二甲酸请注明色度 8.对苯二甲酸请注明水分
2917369	1.品牌类型 2.出口享惠情况 3.成分含量 4.用途 5.对苯二甲酸请注明 4－CBA 值 6.对苯二甲酸请注明 P－TL 酸值 7.对苯二甲酸请注明色度 8.对苯二甲酸请注明水分
291737	1.品牌类型 2.出口享惠情况 3.成分含量 4.用途
2917391	1.品牌类型 2.出口享惠情况 3.成分含量 4.用途 5.签约日期 6.定价方式(公式定价、现货价等)7.需要二次结算、无需二次结算 8.计价日期
2917399	1.品牌类型 2.出口享惠情况 3.成分含量 4.用途
2918	1.品牌类型 2.出口享惠情况 3.成分含量 4.用途
2919	1.品牌类型 2.出口享惠情况 3.成分含量 4.用途
2920	1.品牌类型 2.出口享惠情况 3.成分含量 4.用途
2921	1.品牌类型 2.出口享惠情况 3.成分含量 4.用途
2922	1.品牌类型 2.出口享惠情况 3.成分含量 4.用途 5.乙醇胺及其盐应报明色度 6.乙醇胺及其盐应报明包装
2923	1.品牌类型 2.出口享惠情况 3.成分含量 4.用途
2924	1.品牌类型 2.出口享惠情况 3.成分含量 4.用途 5.包装规格
2925	1.品牌类型 2.出口享惠情况 3.成分含量 4.用途
29261	1.品牌类型 2.出口享惠情况 3.成分含量 4.用途 5.签约日期 6.定价方式(公式定价、现货价等)7.需要二次结算、无需二次结算 8.计价日期
29262	1.品牌类型 2.出口享惠情况 3.成分含量 4.用途
29263	1.品牌类型 2.出口享惠情况 3.成分含量 4.用途
29264	1.品牌类型 2.出口享惠情况 3.成分含量 4.用途
29269	1.品牌类型 2.出口享惠情况 3.成分含量 4.用途
2927	1.品牌类型 2.出口享惠情况 3.成分含量 4.用途
2928	1.品牌类型 2.出口享惠情况 3.成分含量 4.用途
29291	1.品牌类型 2.出口享惠情况 3.成分含量 4.用途 5.型号
29299	1.品牌类型 2.出口享惠情况 3.成分含量 4.用途
2930	1.品牌类型 2.出口享惠情况 3.成分含量 4.用途
2931	1.品牌类型 2.出口享惠情况 3.成分含量 4.用途
2932	1.品牌类型 2.出口享惠情况 3.成分含量(对于成分较复杂，字节较长商品可用 CAS 号代替)4.用途
2933	1.品牌类型 2.出口享惠情况 3.成分含量 4.用途 5.乌洛托品请注明外观 6.6－己内酰胺请注明外观 7.签约日期
2934	1.品牌类型 2.出口享惠情况 3.成分含量 4.用途
2935	1.品牌类型 2.出口享惠情况 3.成分含量 4.用途
2936	1.品牌类型 2.出口享惠情况 3.成分含量 4.用途 5.包装
2937	1.品牌类型 2.出口享惠情况 3.成分含量 4.用途 5.包装
2938	1.品牌类型 2.出口享惠情况 3.成分含量 4.用途 5.来源(天然、合成再制)
2939	1.品牌类型 2.出口享惠情况 3.成分含量 4.用途 5.来源(天然、合成再制)
2940	1.品牌类型 2.出口享惠情况 3.成分含量 4.用途

商品编码	申报要素
2941	1.品牌类型 2.出口享惠情况 3.包装 4.用途(用于制口服、注射还是外用药)
2942	1.品牌类型 2.出口享惠情况 3.成分含量 4.用途
3001	1.品牌类型 2.出口享惠情况 3.用途 4.加工工艺 5.品牌(英文) 6.型号
3002	1.品牌类型 2.出口享惠情况 3.用途 4.加工工艺 5.是否配定剂量 6.是否零售包装 7.是否为检定参照物 8.品牌 9.型号 10.包装规格
3003	1.品牌类型 2.出口享惠情况 3.用途 4.成分 5.是否配定剂量或零售包装 6.品牌 7.型号 8.包装规格
3004	1.品牌类型 2.出口享惠情况 3.用途 4.成分 5.是否配定剂量或零售包装 6.品牌 7.包装规格
3005	1.品牌类型 2.出口享惠情况 3.用途 4.成分 5.是否经过药物浸涂或制成零售包装 6.品牌 7.型号 8.包装规格
30061	1.品牌类型 2.出口享惠情况 3.用途 4.品牌 5.型号 6.包装规格
30062	1.品牌类型 2.出口享惠情况 3.用途 4.成分 5.品牌 6.型号 7.包装规格
30063	1.品牌类型 2.出口享惠情况 3.用途 4.成分 5.品牌 6.型号 7.包装规格
30064	1.品牌类型 2.出口享惠情况 3.用途 4.成分 5.品牌 6.型号 7.包装规格
30065	1.品牌类型 2.出口享惠情况 3.组成(指箱或包中的药品、器具等) 4.品牌 5.型号
30066	1.品牌类型 2.出口享惠情况 3.用途 4.成分 5.品牌 6.型号 7.包装规格
30067	1.品牌类型 2.出口享惠情况 3.用途 4.成分 5.品牌 6.型号 7.包装规格
300691	1.品牌类型 2.出口享惠情况 3.用途 4.品牌 5.型号
300692	1.品牌类型 2.出口享惠情况
3101	1.品牌类型 2.出口享惠情况 3.用途 4.加工工艺 5.外观 6.每包重量 7.是否经过化学处理或与化学肥料混合 8.品牌
3102	1.品牌类型 2.出口享惠情况 3.每包重量 4.总氮含量 5.品牌 6.型号 7.成分含量
3103	1.品牌类型 2.出口享惠情况 3.每包重量 4.总磷含量 5.品牌 6.型号
31042	1.品牌类型 2.出口享惠情况 3.每包重量 4.按照重量计氯化钾含量 5.总钾含量(以氧化物计) 6.品牌 7.型号
31043	1.品牌类型 2.出口享惠情况 3.每包重量 4.总钾含量(以氧化物计) 5.品牌 6.型号
31049	1.品牌类型 2.出口享惠情况 3.每包重量 4.总钾含量(以氧化物计) 5.品牌 6.型号
3105	1.品牌类型 2.出口享惠情况 3.成分含量 4.包装件重 5.总氮含量、总磷含量、总钾(以氧化物计)含量 6.品牌 7.型号
3201	1.品牌类型 2.出口享惠情况 3.用途 4.加工工艺 5.品牌 6.型号
3202	1.品牌类型 2.出口享惠情况 3.成分含量 4.型号 5.是否为无铬鞣料 6.品牌 7.包装规格
3203	1.品牌类型 2.出口享惠情况 3.用途 4.加工工艺 5.包装 6.品牌 7.型号 8.成分含量
3204	1.品牌类型 2.出口享惠情况 3.成分含量 4.用途 5.染料须报明种类 6.包装规格 7.品牌 8.型号
3205	1.品牌类型 2.出口享惠情况 3.成分 4.包装 5.品牌 6.型号
3206111	1.品牌类型 2.出口享惠情况 3.成分含量 4.用途 5.包装 6.型号 7.品牌 8.如果加入放射性盐,请注明放射性比度 9.级别 10.签约日期
3206119	1.品牌类型 2.出口享惠情况 3.成分含量 4.用途 5.包装规格 6.型号 7.品牌 8.如果加入放射性盐,请注明放射性比度
320619	1.品牌类型 2.出口享惠情况 3.成分含量 4.用途 5.包装规格 6.型号 7.品牌 8.如果加入放射性盐,请注明放射性比度
32062	1.品牌类型 2.出口享惠情况 3.成分含量 4.用途 5.包装规格 6.型号 7.品牌 8.如果加入放射性盐,请注明放射性比度
32064	1.品牌类型 2.出口享惠情况 3.成分含量 4.用途 5.包装规格 6.型号 7.品牌 8.如果加入放射性盐,请注明放射性比度
32065	1.品牌类型 2.出口享惠情况 3.成分含量 4.用途 5.包装规格 6.型号 7.品牌 8.如果加入放射性盐,请注明放射性比度 9.稀土元素的重量百分比,以[A]表示
3207	1.品牌类型 2.出口享惠情况 3.用途 4.外观 5.成分含量 6.包装 7.品牌 8.型号
3208	1.品牌类型 2.出口享惠情况 3.成分含量 4.用途 5.是否分散于或溶于非水介质 6.施工状态下挥发性有机物含量 7.包装 8.品牌 9.型号
3209	1.品牌类型 2.出口享惠情况 3.成分含量 4.用途 5.是否分散于或溶于非水介质 6.施工状态下挥发性有机物含量 7.包装 8.品牌 9.型号
3210	1.品牌类型 2.出口享惠情况 3.成分含量 4.用途 5.施工状态下挥发性有机物含量 6.包装 7.品牌 8.型号
3211	1.品牌类型 2.出口享惠情况 3.成分含量 4.用途 5.品牌 6.型号
32121	1.品牌类型 2.出口享惠情况 3.成分含量 4.用途 5.包装 6.外观 7.品牌 8.规格 9.加工工艺
32129	1.品牌类型 2.出口享惠情况 3.成分含量 4.用途 5.包装 6.外观 7.品牌
3213	1.品牌类型 2.出口享惠情况 3.用途 4.包装 5.品牌 6.型号 7.是否成套
3214	1.品牌类型 2.出口享惠情况 3.成分含量 4.用途 5.施工状态下挥发性有机物含量 6.包装 7.品牌 8.型号
32151	1.品牌类型 2.出口享惠情况 3.用途(如子目 8443.31、8443.32 或 8443.39 所列设备用等) 4.包装 5.颜色 6.成分含量 7.是否具有曝光显影功能 8.若为工程形态需注明 9.是否为固体
32159	1.品牌类型 2.出口享惠情况 3.用途 4.包装 5.成份含量
3301	1.品牌类型 2.出口享惠情况 3.用途 4.加工工艺 5.包装规格 6.品牌 7.型号 8.成份含量
33021	1.品牌类型 2.出口享惠情况 3.成分 4.用途 5.酒精含量 6.品牌 7.型号 8.包装规格
33029	1.品牌类型 2.出口享惠情况 3.成分 4.用途 5.品牌 6.型号 7.包装规格
3303	1.品牌类型 2.出口享惠情况 3.包装规格 4.品牌
3304	1.品牌类型 2.出口享惠情况 3.用途 4.包装规格 5.品牌
3305	1.品牌类型 2.出口享惠情况 3.用途 4.包装规格 5.品牌 6.型号(货号)
3306	1.品牌类型 2.出口享惠情况 3.包装规格 4.品牌 5.型号(货号)
3307	1.品牌类型 2.出口享惠情况 3.用途 4.包装规格 5.品牌 6.型号(货号)
340111	1.品牌类型 2.出口享惠情况 3.成分含量 4.外观 5.包装规格 6.品牌 7.型号(货号)
3401191	1.品牌类型 2.出口享惠情况 3.成分含量 4.外观 5.包装规格 6.品牌 7.型号(货号)
3401199	1.品牌类型 2.出口享惠情况 3.成分含量 4.外观 5.包装规格 6.浸渍物的成分 7.品牌 8.型号(货号)
34012	1.品牌类型 2.出口享惠情况 3.成分含量 4.外观 5.包装规格 6.品牌 7.型号(货号)
34013	1.品牌类型 2.出口享惠情况 3.成分含量 4.外观 5.包装规格 6.品牌 7.型号(货号)
34021	1.品牌类型 2.出口享惠情况 3.种类(阳离子、阴离子、非离子、两性等) 4.成分 5.品牌 6.型号
34022	1.品牌类型 2.出口享惠情况 3.用途 4.是否零售包装 5.成分 6.品牌 7.型号
34029	1.品牌类型 2.出口享惠情况 3.用途 4.是否零售包装 5.成分 6.品牌 7.型号
3403	1.品牌类型 2.出口享惠情况 3.用途 4.成分含量 5.从石油或沥青提取矿物油类的百分比含量 6.包装规格 7.品牌 8.型号
3404	1.品牌类型 2.出口享惠情况 3.用途 4.外观 5.成分 6.品牌 7.型号
3405	1.品牌类型 2.出口享惠情况 3.用途 4.成分 5.品牌 6.型号
3406	1.品牌类型 2.出口享惠情况 3.成分 4.品牌
3407	1.品牌类型 2.出口享惠情况 3.用途 4.外观 5.包装 6.成分含量 7.品牌 8.型号
3501	1.品牌类型 2.出口享惠情况 3.包装 4.品牌 5.型号 6.用途
3502	1.品牌类型 2.出口享惠情况 3.用途 4.外观 5.成分含量
3503	1.品牌类型 2.出口享惠情况 3.用途 4.外观 5.包装
3504	1.品牌类型 2.出口享惠情况 3.用途 4.来源 5.包装 6.蛋白质含量
3505	1.品牌类型 2.出口享惠情况 3.用途 4.还原糖含量 5.包装 6.品牌 7.型号
35061	1.品牌类型 2.出口享惠情况 3.用途 4.包装 5.成分含量 6.品牌 7.型号
3506911	1.品牌类型 2.出口享惠情况 3.用途 4.包装 5.成分含量 6.品牌 7.型号
3506912	1.品牌类型 2.出口享惠情况 3.用途 4.包装 5.成分含量 6.品牌 7.型号
3506919	1.品牌类型 2.出口享惠情况 3.光学透明膜黏合剂和光固化液体黏合剂需注明英文品名 4.用途(如显示屏或触摸屏制造用等) 5.包装 6.遮光包装需注明 7.成分含量 8.光学透明膜黏合剂和光固化液体黏合剂需注明透光率 9.光学透明膜黏合剂需注明断差吸收能力 10.品牌 11.型号
350699	1.品牌类型 2.出口享惠情况 3.用途 4.包装 5.成分含量 6.品牌 7.型号
3507	1.品牌类型 2.出口享惠情况 3.用途 4.种类
3601	1.品牌类型 2.出口享惠情况 3.成分
3602	1.品牌类型 2.出口享惠情况 3.成分
3603	1.品牌类型 2.出口享惠情况
3604	1.品牌类型 2.出口享惠情况
3605	1.品牌类型 2.出口享惠情况
36061	1.品牌类型 2.出口享惠情况 3.用途 4.包装容器的容积
3606901	1.品牌类型 2.出口享惠情况 3.用途 4.外观 5.稀土元素的重量百分比,以[A]表示

商品编码	申报要素
3606909	1.品牌类型 2.出口享惠情况 3.用途 4.外观
3701	1.品牌类型 2.出口享惠情况 3.用途 4.材质 5.是否成卷 6.是否一次成像 7.规格尺寸(长×宽×厚度)8.品牌 9.型号 10.进口总面积(平方米)11.包装规格(张/盒)
3702	1.品牌类型 2.出口享惠情况 3.用途 4.材质 5.是否成卷 6.是否一次成像 7.规格尺寸(长×宽×厚度)8.品牌 9.型号 10.进口总面积(平方米),包括涂布和白边面积之和 11.包装规格(张/盒或平方米/卷)
3703	1.品牌类型 2.出口享惠情况 3.用途 4.是否成卷 5.规格尺寸 6.品牌 7.型号
3704	1.品牌类型 2.出口享惠情况 3.用途 4.规格尺寸 5.品牌
3705	1.品牌类型 2.出口享惠情况 3.用途 4.规格尺寸 5.品牌
3706	1.品牌类型 2.出口享惠情况 3.用途 4.规格尺寸 5.品牌
37071	1.品牌类型 2.出口享惠情况 3.用途 4.包装 5.成分 6.是否含银 7.是否有感光作用 8.品牌 9.型号
37079	1.品牌类型 2.出口享惠情况 3.用途 4.包装 5.成分 6.是否含银 7.品牌 8.型号
3801	1.品牌类型 2.出口享惠情况 3.用途 4.状态 5.加工工艺 6.成分含量 7.品牌 8.型号
3802101	1.品牌类型 2.出口享惠情况 3.用途 4.来源 5.包装规格 6.干品填充密度
3802109	1.品牌类型 2.出口享惠情况 3.用途 4.来源 5.包装规格
38029	1.品牌类型 2.出口享惠情况 3.用途 4.来源 5.包装规格
3803	1.品牌类型 2.出口享惠情况 3.用途
3804	1.品牌类型 2.出口享惠情况
3805	1.品牌类型 2.出口享惠情况 3.用途 4.成分 5.二聚戊烯、萜烯烃、萜品醇及水合萜品请注明含量
3806	1.品牌类型 2.出口享惠情况 3.来源
3807	1.品牌类型 2.出口享惠情况 3.用途
3808	1.品牌类型 2.出口享惠情况 3.用途 4.成分含量 5.包装规格(净重),是否零售包装 6.品牌 7.型号
3809	1.品牌类型 2.出口享惠情况 3.用途 4.成分 5.品牌 6.型号
3810	1.品牌类型 2.出口享惠情况 3.用途 4.成分 5.品牌 6.型号
3811	1.品牌类型 2.出口享惠情况 3.包装 4.用途 5.成分 6.品牌 7.型号
3812	1.品牌类型 2.出口享惠情况 3.用途 4.成分 5.品牌 6.型号
3813	1.品牌类型 2.出口享惠情况 3.用途 4.成分
3814	1.品牌类型 2.出口享惠情况 3.用途 4.成分含量 5.品牌 6.型号
3815	1.品牌类型 2.出口享惠情况 3.用途(如促进某某聚合物的聚合等)4.成分含量
3816	1.品牌类型 2.出口享惠情况 3.用途 4.成分
3817	1.品牌类型 2.出口享惠情况 3.用途 4.成分
3818001	1.品牌类型 2.出口享惠情况 3.用途 4.外观 5.成分 6.直径 7.加工程度
3818009	1.品牌类型 2.出口享惠情况 3.用途 4.外观 5.成分 6.加工程度
3819	1.品牌类型 2.出口享惠情况 3.用途 4.成分 5.从石油或沥青提取矿物油类的百分比含量 6.品牌 7.型号
3820	1.品牌类型 2.出口享惠情况 3.用途 4.成分 5.品牌 6.型号
3821	1.品牌类型 2.出口享惠情况 3.用途 4.成分
3822	1.品牌类型 2.出口享惠情况 3.用途 4.包装 5.成分 6.是否血源筛查用诊断试剂 7.是否有衬背
3823	1.品牌类型 2.出口享惠情况 3.成分含量 4.来源(动植物油脂等)5.加工程度(是否经过皂化、是否经过水解)6.品牌 7.型号
38241	1.品牌类型 2.出口享惠情况 3.用途 4.成分含量 5.品牌 6.型号
38243	1.品牌类型 2.出口享惠情况 3.用途 4.成分含量 5.品牌 6.型号
38244	1.品牌类型 2.出口享惠情况 3.用途 4.成分含量 5.品牌 6.型号
38245	1.品牌类型 2.出口享惠情况 3.用途 4.成分含量 5.品牌 6.型号
38246	1.品牌类型 2.出口享惠情况 3.用途 4.外观 5.来源 6.成分含量 7.品牌 8.型号
38247	1.品牌类型 2.出口享惠情况 3.用途 4.成分含量 5.品牌 6.型号
38248	1.品牌类型 2.出口享惠情况 3.用途 4.成分含量 5.品牌 6.型号
382491	1.品牌类型 2.出口享惠情况 3.用途 4.成分含量 5.包装规格 6.品牌 7.型号
3824991	1.品牌类型 2.出口享惠情况 3.用途 4.成分含量 5.包装规格 6.品牌 7.型号
3824992	1.品牌类型 2.出口享惠情况 3.用途 4.成分含量 5.包装规格 6.品牌 7.型号
3824993	1.品牌类型 2.出口享惠情况 3.用途 4.成分含量 5.包装规格 6.品牌 7.型号
38249991	1.品牌类型 2.出口享惠情况 3.用途 4.成分含量 5.包装规格 6.品牌 7.型号
38249992	1.品牌类型 2.出口享惠情况 3.用途 4.成分含量 5.包装规格 6.品牌 7.型号
38249993	1.品牌类型 2.出口享惠情况 3.用途 4.成分含量 5.包装规格 6.品牌 7.型号
38249999	1.品牌类型 2.出口享惠情况 3.用途 4.成分含量 5.包装规格 6.品牌 7.型号
3825	1.品牌类型 2.出口享惠情况 3.用途 4.来源
3826	1.品牌类型 2.出口享惠情况 3.用途 4.成分含量 5.从石油或沥青提取矿物油类的百分比含量
39011	1.品牌类型 2.出口享惠情况 3.外观(形状、颜色等)4.成分含量 5.单体单元的种类和比例 6.比重 7.底料来源 8.级别 9.品牌 10.型号 11.签约日期 12.用途
39012	1.品牌类型 2.出口享惠情况 3.外观(形状、颜色等)4.成分含量 5.单体单元的种类和比例 6.比重 7.底料来源 8.级别 9.品牌 10.型号 11.签约日期 12.用途
39013	1.品牌类型 2.出口享惠情况 3.外观(形状、颜色等)4.成分含量 5.单体单元的种类和比例 6.底料来源 7.级别 8.品牌 9.牌号或型号 10.签约日期 11.生产厂商 12.用途
39014	1.品牌类型 2.出口享惠情况 3.外观(形状、颜色等)4.成分含量 5.单体单元的种类和比例 6.比重 7.底料来源 8.级别 9.品牌 10.型号 11.签约日期 12.用途
3901901	1.品牌类型 2.出口享惠情况 3.外观(形状、颜色等)4.成分含量 5.单体单元的种类和比例 6.比重 7.底料来源 8.级别 9.品牌 10.型号 11.签约日期 12.用途
3901909	1.品牌类型 2.出口享惠情况 3.外观(形状、颜色等)4.成分含量 5.单体单元的种类和比例 6.底料来源 7.级别 8.品牌 9.型号 10.签约日期 11.用途
3902	1.品牌类型 2.出口享惠情况 3.外观(形状、颜色等)4.成分含量 5.单体单元的种类和比例 6.底料来源 7.级别 8.品牌 9.型号 10.签约日期 11.用途
39031	1.品牌类型 2.出口享惠情况 3.外观(形状、颜色等)4.是否可发性,是否改性 5.成分含量 6.单体单元的种类和比例 7.底料来源 8.级别 9.品牌 10.型号 11.签约日期 12.用途
39032	1.品牌类型 2.出口享惠情况 3.外观(形状、颜色等)4.成分含量 5.单体单元的种类和比例 6.底料来源 7.品牌 8.型号 9.签约日期 10.用途
39033	1.品牌类型 2.出口享惠情况 3.外观(形状、颜色等)4.成分含量 5.单体单元的种类和比例 6.是否改性 7.底料来源 8.级别 9.品牌 10.型号 11.签约日期 12.用途
39039	1.品牌类型 2.出口享惠情况 3.外观(形状、颜色等)4.成分含量 5.单体单元的种类和比例 6.底料来源 7.品牌 8.型号 9.签约日期 10.用途
39041	1.品牌类型 2.出口享惠情况 3.外观(形状、颜色等)4.是否掺杂其他物质 5.成分含量 6.单体单元的种类和比例 7.底料来源 8.品牌 9.型号 10.签约日期 11.用途
39042	1.品牌类型 2.出口享惠情况 3.外观(形状、颜色等)4.是否塑化 5.成分含量 6.单体单元的种类和比例 7.底料来源 8.品牌 9.型号 10.签约日期 11.用途
39043	1.品牌类型 2.出口享惠情况 3.外观(形状、颜色等)4.成分含量 5.单体单元的种类和比例 6.底料来源 7.品牌 8.型号 9.签约日期 10.用途
39044	1.品牌类型 2.出口享惠情况 3.外观(形状、颜色等)4.成分含量 5.单体单元的种类和比例 6.底料来源 7.品牌 8.型号 9.签约日期 10.用途
39045	1.品牌类型 2.出口享惠情况 3.外观(形状、颜色等)4.成分含量 5.单体单元的种类和比例 6.底料来源 7.品牌 8.型号 9.签约日期 10.用途
39046	1.品牌类型 2.出口享惠情况 3.外观(形状、颜色等)4.成分含量 5.单体单元的种类和比例 6.底料来源 7.品牌 8.型号 9.签约日期 10.用途
39049	1.品牌类型 2.出口享惠情况 3.外观(形状、颜色等)4.成分含量 5.单体单元的种类和比例 6.底料来源 7.品牌 8.型号 9.签约日期 10.用途
3905	1.品牌类型 2.出口享惠情况 3.外观(形状、颜色等)4.成分含量 5.单体单元的种类和比例 6.底料来源 7.品牌 8.型号 9.签约日期 10.用途
3906	1.品牌类型 2.出口享惠情况 3.外观(形状、颜色等)4.成分含量 5.单体单元的种类和比例 6.底料来源 7.品牌 8.型号 9.签约日期 10.用途
3907101	1.品牌类型 2.出口享惠情况 3.外观(形状、颜色等)4.成分含量 5.单体单元的种类和比例 6.底料来源 7.品牌 8.型号 9.签约日期 10.用途
3907109	1.品牌类型 2.出口享惠情况 3.外观(形状、颜色等)4.成分含量 5.单体单元的种类和比例 6.底料来源 7.品牌 8.型号 9.签约日期 10.用途
39072	1.品牌类型 2.出口享惠情况 3.外观(形状、颜色等)4.成分含量 5.单体单元的种类和比例 6.底料来源 7.品牌 8.型号 9.签约日期
39073	1.品牌类型 2.出口享惠情况 3.外观(形状、颜色等)4.成分含量及溴含量 5.底料来源 6.品牌 7.型号 8.签约日期
39074	1.品牌类型 2.出口享惠情况 3.外观(形状、颜色等)4.成分含量 5.底料来源 6.品牌 7.型号 8.签约日期
39075	1.品牌类型 2.出口享惠情况 3.外观(形状、颜色等)4.成分含量 5.单体单元的种类和比例 6.底料来源 7.品牌 8.型号 9.用途

商品编码	申报要素
39076	1.品牌类型 2.出口享惠情况 3.外观(形状、颜色等)4.是否切片 5.成分含量 6.单体单元的种类和比例 7.粘数 8.底料来源 9.级别 10.品牌 11.型号 12.签约日期
39077	1.品牌类型 2.出口享惠情况 3.外观(形状、颜色等)4.成分含量 5.单体单元的种类和比例 6.底料来源 7.品牌 8.型号 9.签约日期 10.用途
390791	1.品牌类型 2.出口享惠情况 3.外观(形状、颜色等)4.是否饱和 5.成分含量 6.单体单元的种类和比例 7.底料来源 8.品牌 9.型号 10.签约日期
3907991	1.品牌类型 2.出口享惠情况 3.外观(形状、颜色等)4.是否饱和 5.成分含量 6.单体单元的种类和比例 7.底料来源 8.品牌 9.型号 10.签约日期
3907999	1.品牌类型 2.出口享惠情况 3.外观(形状、颜色等)4.是否饱和 5.成分含量 6.单体单元的种类和比例 7.若为热塑性液晶需注明 8.底料来源 9.品牌 10.型号 11.签约日期
3908	1.品牌类型 2.出口享惠情况 3.外观(形状、颜色等)4.是否切片 5.成分含量 6.单体单元的种类和比例 7.底料来源 8.级别 9.品牌 10.型号 11.签约日期 12.用途
3909	1.品牌类型 2.出口享惠情况 3.外观(形状、颜色等)4.成分含量 5.单体单元的种类和比例 6.底料来源 7.品牌 8.型号 9.签约日期 10.用途
3910	1.品牌类型 2.出口享惠情况 3.外观(形状、颜色等)4.用途 5.是否溶于水 6.成分含量 7.底料来源 8.品牌 9.型号 10.签约日期
39111	1.品牌类型 2.出口享惠情况 3.外观(形状、颜色等)4.成分含量 5.底料来源 6.品牌 7.型号 8.签约日期 9.用途
39119	1.品牌类型 2.出口享惠情况 3.外观(形状、颜色等)4.成分含量 5.单体单元的种类和比例 6.底料来源 7.品牌 8.型号 9.签约日期 10.用途
39121	1.品牌类型 2.出口享惠情况 3.外观(形状、颜色等)4.是否塑化 5.成分含量 6.底料来源 7.品牌 8.型号 9.签约日期 10.用途
39122	1.品牌类型 2.出口享惠情况 3.外观(形状、颜色等)4.成分含量 5.底料来源 6.品牌 7.型号 8.签约日期 9.用途
39123	1.品牌类型 2.出口享惠情况 3.外观(形状、颜色等)4.成分含量 5.底料来源 6.品牌 7.型号 8.签约日期 9.用途
39129	1.品牌类型 2.出口享惠情况 3.外观(形状、颜色等)4.成分含量 5.底料来源 6.品牌 7.型号 8.签约日期 9.用途
3913	1.品牌类型 2.出口享惠情况 3.外观(形状、颜色等)4.成分含量 5.底料来源 6.品牌 7.型号 8.签约日期 9.用途
3914	1.品牌类型 2.出口享惠情况 3.用途 4.外观(形状、颜色等)5.成分 6.底料来源 7.品牌 8.型号 9.签约日期 10.级别 11.阴离子还是阳离子还是两性
39151	1.品牌类型 2.出口享惠情况 3.外观(颜色、尺寸)4.来源 5.成分 6.是否已经破坏性处理 7.如为铝塑复合膜需注明 8.如为成卷,需注明是否带有轴心
39152	1.品牌类型 2.出口享惠情况 3.外观(颜色、尺寸)4.来源 5.成分 6.是否已经破坏性处理 7.如为成卷,需注明是否带有轴心
39153	1.品牌类型 2.出口享惠情况 3.外观(颜色、尺寸)4.来源 5.成分 6.是否已经破坏性处理 7.如为成卷,需注明是否带有轴心
3915901	1.品牌类型 2.出口享惠情况 3.外观(颜色、尺寸)4.来源 5.成分 6.是否已经破坏性处理 7.如为 PET 瓶(砖)需注明 8.如为成卷,需注明是否带有轴心
3915909	1.品牌类型 2.出口享惠情况 3.外观(颜色、尺寸)4.来源 5.成分 6.是否已经破坏性处理 7.如为废光盘破碎料请注明 8.如为成卷,需注明是否带有轴心
3916	1.品牌类型 2.出口享惠情况 3.外观 4.成分 5.单丝请注明截面直径 6.品牌 7.型号 8.用途
39171	1.品牌类型 2.出口享惠情况 3.成分 4.用途 5.品牌 6.型号
39172	1.品牌类型 2.出口享惠情况 3.成分(乙烯聚合物、丙烯聚合物、氯乙烯聚合物等)4.品牌 5.型号 6.用途
39173	1.品牌类型 2.出口享惠情况 3.成分 4.是否装有附件 5.爆破压力 6.是否经加强或与其他材料合制 7.种类(硬管、半硬管或软管)8.品牌 9.型号 10.用途
39174	1.品牌类型 2.出口享惠情况 3.材质
3918	1.品牌类型 2.出口享惠情况 3.材质 4.品牌 5.型号 6.用途
39191	1.品牌类型 2.出口享惠情况 3.用途 4.外观(板、片、膜、箔、带、扁条)5.是否成卷 6.是否单面自粘 7.成分含量 8.规格尺寸 9.品牌 10.型号
3919901	1.品牌类型 2.出口享惠情况 3.用途 4.外观(板、片、膜、箔、带、扁条)5.是否成卷 6.是否单面自粘 7.成分含量 8.规格尺寸 9.品牌 10.型号
3919909	1.品牌类型 2.出口享惠情况 3.用途(如半导体晶圆制造用等)4.外观(板、片、膜、箔、带、扁条)5.是否成卷 6.是否单面自粘 7.成分含量 8.规格尺寸 9.若为半导体晶圆制造用需注明形状(如圆形等)10.品牌 11.型号
39201	1.品牌类型 2.出口享惠情况 3.用途 4.外观 5.是否与其他材料合制 6.成分 7.规格尺寸 8.是否非泡沫 9.品牌(中文及外文名称,无品牌请申报厂商)10.型号 11.适用电池种类
39202	1.品牌类型 2.出口享惠情况 3.用途 4.外观 5.是否与其他材料合制 6.成分 7.规格尺寸 8.是否非泡沫 9.品牌(中文及外文名称,无品牌请申报厂商)10.型号 11.适用电池种类
39203	1.品牌类型 2.出口享惠情况 3.用途 4.外观 5.是否与其他材料合制 6.成分 7.规格尺寸 8.是否非泡沫 9.品牌 10.型号
39204	1.品牌类型 2.出口享惠情况 3.用途 4.外观 5.是否与其他材料合制 6.成分 7.规格尺寸 8.PVC 制品请注明增塑剂含量 9.是否非泡沫 10.品牌 11.型号
39205	1.品牌类型 2.出口享惠情况 3.用途 4.外观 5.是否与其他材料合制 6.成分 7.规格尺寸 8.是否非泡沫 9.品牌 10.型号
39206	1.品牌类型 2.出口享惠情况 3.用途 4.外观(包括颜色、形状等)5.是否与其他材料合制 6.成分 7.规格尺寸 8.是否非泡沫 9.品牌 10.型号
39207	1.品牌类型 2.出口享惠情况 3.用途 4.外观 5.是否与其他材料合制 6.成分 7.规格尺寸 8.是否非泡沫 9.品牌 10.型号
39209	1.品牌类型 2.出口享惠情况 3.用途 4.外观 5.是否与其他材料合制 6.成分 7.规格尺寸 8.是否非泡沫 9.品牌 10.型号
3921	1.品牌类型 2.出口享惠情况 3.成分 4.外观 5.是否与其他材料合制 6.泡沫塑料请注明 7.用途 8.规格尺寸 9.品牌 10.型号
3922	1.品牌类型 2.出口享惠情况 3.用途 4.材质 5.品牌 6.型号
39231	1.品牌类型 2.出口享惠情况 3.用途(如半导体晶圆、掩模或光罩用等)4.材质 5.半导体晶圆、掩模或光罩用需报是否具有特定形状或装置 6.半导体晶圆、掩模或光罩用需注明是否有 ROHS 认证 7.品牌 8.规格或型号
39232	1.品牌类型 2.出口享惠情况 3.用途 4.材质 5.品牌 6.规格或型号
39233	1.品牌类型 2.出口享惠情况 3.用途 4.材质 5.品牌 6.规格或型号
39234	1.品牌类型 2.出口享惠情况 3.用途 4.材质 5.品牌 6.规格或型号
39235	1.品牌类型 2.出口享惠情况 3.用途 4.材质 5.品牌 6.规格或型号
39239	1.品牌类型 2.出口享惠情况 3.用途 4.材质 5.品牌 6.规格或型号
3924	1.品牌类型 2.出口享惠情况 3.用途 4.材质 5.品牌 6.规格或型号
3925	1.品牌类型 2.出口享惠情况 3.用途 4.塑料制囤、柜、罐、桶及类似容器请注明容积 5.材质 6.品牌
3926	1.品牌类型 2.出口享惠情况 3.用途 4.材质 5.品牌 6.规格和型号
40011	1.品牌类型 2.出口享惠情况 3.外观 4.包装 5.签约日期 6.干胶含量
400121	1.品牌类型 2.出口享惠情况 3.外观 4.型号 5.包装 6.签约日期
400122	1.品牌类型 2.出口享惠情况 3.外观 4.型号 5.包装规格 6.是否随附生产国主管当局出具的检验证书,并列明橡胶的等级、规格及检验结果 7.签约日期
400129	1.品牌类型 2.出口享惠情况 3.外观 4.型号 5.包装 6.签约日期
40013	1.品牌类型 2.出口享惠情况 3.外观 4.型号 5.包装 6.签约日期
400211	1.品牌类型 2.出口享惠情况 3.用途 4.外观 5.成分含量 6.签约日期 7.品牌 8.型号
400219	1.品牌类型 2.出口享惠情况 3.用途 4.外观 5.丁苯橡胶请注明是否充油、热塑 6.成分含量 7.签约日期 8.品牌 9.型号
40022	1.品牌类型 2.出口享惠情况 3.外观 4.成分含量 5.签约日期 6.品牌 7.型号
40023	1.品牌类型 2.出口享惠情况 3.外观 4.成分含量 5.签约日期 6.品牌 7.型号
40024	1.品牌类型 2.出口享惠情况 3.外观 4.成分含量 5.签约日期 6.品牌 7.型号
40025	1.品牌类型 2.出口享惠情况 3.外观 4.成分含量 5.签约日期 6.品牌 7.型号
40026	1.品牌类型 2.出口享惠情况 3.外观 4.成分含量 5.签约日期 6.品牌 7.型号
40027	1.品牌类型 2.出口享惠情况 3.外观 4.成分含量 5.签约日期 6.品牌 7.型号
40028	1.品牌类型 2.出口享惠情况 3.外观 4.成分含量 5.签约日期 6.品牌 7.型号 8.混合过程加工方式
40029	1.品牌类型 2.出口享惠情况 3.外观 4.成分含量 5.签约日期 6.品牌 7.型号
4003	1.品牌类型 2.出口享惠情况 3.外观 4.来源
4004	1.品牌类型 2.出口享惠情况 3.外观 4.来源 5.水分 6.杂质 7.干胶含量
4005	1.品牌类型 2.出口享惠情况 3.外观 4.成分 5.签约日期 6.品牌 7.型号
4006	1.品牌类型 2.出口享惠情况 3.用途 4.外观 5.材质 6.品牌 7.型号
4007	1.品牌类型 2.出口享惠情况 3.外观 4.截面尺寸 5.材质 6.品牌 7.型号
4008	1.品牌类型 2.出口享惠情况 3.外观 4.是否海绵橡胶 5.规格尺寸 6.材质 7.品牌 8.型号

商品编码	申报要素
4009	1.品牌类型 2.出口享惠情况 3.用途 4.外观 5.材质构成(是否加强或与其他材料合制)6.是否装有附件 7.品牌 8.型号
40101	1.品牌类型 2.出口享惠情况 3.用途 4.外观 5.材质构成(有加强材料的也要注明其材质)6.规格尺寸 7.品牌 8.型号
401031	1.品牌类型 2.出口享惠情况 3.用途 4.外观 5.材质 6.规格尺寸(外周长)7.截面形状 8.品牌
401032	1.品牌类型 2.出口享惠情况 3.用途 4.外观 5.材质 6.规格尺寸(外周长)7.截面形状 8.品牌
401033	1.品牌类型 2.出口享惠情况 3.用途 4.外观 5.材质 6.规格尺寸(外周长)7.截面形状 8.品牌
401034	1.品牌类型 2.出口享惠情况 3.用途 4.外观 5.材质 6.规格尺寸(外周长)7.截面形状 8.品牌
401035	1.品牌类型 2.出口享惠情况 3.用途 4.外观 5.材质 6.规格尺寸(外周长)7.品牌
401036	1.品牌类型 2.出口享惠情况 3.用途 4.外观 5.材质 6.规格尺寸(外周长)7.品牌
401039	1.品牌类型 2.出口享惠情况 3.用途 4.外观 5.材质 6.规格尺寸(外周长)7.截面形状 8.品牌
40111	1.品牌类型 2.出口享惠情况 3.用途 4.型号 5.辋圈尺寸 6.断面宽度 7.胎面花纹 8.品牌 9.速度等级
40112	1.品牌类型 2.出口享惠情况 3.用途 4.型号 5.辋圈尺寸 6.断面宽度 7.胎面花纹 8.品牌
40113	1.品牌类型 2.出口享惠情况 3.用途 4.型号 5.辋圈尺寸 6.断面宽度 7.胎面花纹 8.品牌
40114	1.品牌类型 2.出口享惠情况 3.用途 4.型号 5.辋圈尺寸 6.断面宽度 7.胎面花纹 8.品牌
40115	1.品牌类型 2.出口享惠情况 3.用途 4.型号 5.辋圈尺寸 6.断面宽度 7.胎面花纹 8.品牌
40117	1.品牌类型 2.出口享惠情况 3.用途 4.型号 5.辋圈尺寸 6.胎面花纹(人字型胎面或类似胎面等)7.断面宽度 8.品牌
40118	1.品牌类型 2.出口享惠情况 3.用途 4.型号 5.辋圈尺寸 6.胎面花纹(人字型胎面或类似胎面等)7.断面宽度 8.品牌
40119	1.品牌类型 2.出口享惠情况 3.用途 4.型号 5.辋圈尺寸 6.胎面花纹(人字型胎面或类似胎面等)7.断面宽度 8.品牌
4012	1.品牌类型 2.出口享惠情况 3.用途 4.是否实心 5.充气轮胎请注明翻新或旧的 6.品牌 7.型号
4013	1.品牌类型 2.出口享惠情况 3.用途 4.品牌
4014	1.品牌类型 2.出口享惠情况 3.用途 4.品牌
401511	1.品牌类型 2.出口享惠情况 3.用途 4.品牌
401519	1.品牌类型 2.出口享惠情况 3.用途 4.品牌 5.成分(含胶率)6.规格型号(S、M、XL 等)
40159	1.品牌类型 2.出口享惠情况 3.用途 4.品牌
4016	1.品牌类型 2.出口享惠情况 3.用途 4.材质(海绵橡胶、非海绵橡胶)5.是否机器及仪器用 6.品牌 7.型号
4017	1.品牌类型 2.出口享惠情况 3.外观 4.成分
4101	1.品牌类型 2.出口享惠情况 3.制作或保存方法(鲜、干、盐渍、石灰浸渍、浸酸、未鞣制、退鞣处理)4.状态(整张/半张,是否去肉修边等)5.平均每张重量 6.种类(公牛、未育/已育母牛、奶牛、阉牛、小牛、马)7.产区(如澳大利亚维多利亚、新南威尔士等)
4102	1.品牌类型 2.出口享惠情况 3.制作或保存方法(鲜、干、盐渍、石灰浸渍、浸酸、未鞣制、退鞣处理)4.种类(羔羊、绵羊)5.状态(带毛、不带毛)6.规格(毛长)7.请注明平方英尺数/张 8.等级 9.用途(毛革一体、制革)
4103	1.品牌类型 2.出口享惠情况 3.制作或保存方法(鲜、干、盐渍、石灰浸渍、浸酸、未鞣制、退鞣处理)4.种类(山羊、猪、爬行动物等)5.是否源于野生动物 6.规格(长/宽或面积)
4104	1.品牌类型 2.出口享惠情况 3.制作或保存方法(干、鞣制无毛、表面是否涂覆、涂覆何种物质)4.状态(湿,如蓝湿,整张/半张/背皮/头颈等)5.种类(公牛、母牛、奶牛、阉牛、马)6.是否源于野生动物 7.规格(厚度、平均尺寸及平均重量)8.品种 9.用途 10.级别(头层皮 TR1/2/3,二层皮 A/B/C/D 级)
4105	1.品牌类型 2.出口享惠情况 3.制作或保存方法(干、鞣制无毛)4.种类(羔羊、绵羊)5.状态(湿,如蓝湿)6.是否源于野生动物 7.规格(厚度、张幅)
4106	1.品牌类型 2.出口享惠情况 3.制作或保存方法(干、鞣制无毛)4.种类(如爬行动物、小山羊)5.状态(湿)6.是否源于野生动物 7.规格(厚度、张幅、张数)
410711	1.品牌类型 2.出口享惠情况 3.制作或保存方法(表面是否涂覆、涂覆何种物质)4.种类(牛、马)5.状态(是否整张、无毛全粒面未剖层或无毛粒面剖层、牛皮层数)6.规格(厚度、平均面积)7.颜色 8.用途(鞋面、箱包、鞋底、家具、汽车座椅、皮带等)
410712	1.品牌类型 2.出口享惠情况 3.制作或保存方法(表面是否涂覆、涂覆何种物质)4.种类(牛、马)5.状态(是否整张、无毛全粒面未剖层或无毛粒面剖层、牛皮层数)6.规格(厚度、平均面积)7.颜色 8.用途(鞋面、箱包、鞋底、家具、汽车座椅、皮带等)
4107191	1.品牌类型 2.出口享惠情况 3.制作或保存方法(表面是否涂覆、涂覆何种物质)4.种类(牛、马)5.状态(是否整张、无毛全粒面未剖层或无毛粒面剖层、牛皮层数)6.用途(机器带用)7.规格(厚度、平均面积)8.颜色
4107199	1.品牌类型 2.出口享惠情况 3.制作或保存方法(表面是否涂覆、涂覆何种物质)4.种类(牛、马)5.状态(是否整张、无毛全粒面未剖层或无毛粒面剖层、牛皮层数)6.规格(厚度、平均面积)7.颜色 8.用途(鞋面、箱包、鞋底、家具、汽车座椅、皮带等)
410791	1.品牌类型 2.出口享惠情况 3.制作或保存方法(表面是否涂覆、涂覆何种物质)4.种类(牛、马)5.状态(是否整张、无毛全粒面未剖层或无毛粒面剖层、牛皮层数)6.规格(厚度、平均面积)7.颜色 8.用途(鞋面、箱包、鞋底、家具、汽车座椅、皮带等)
410792	1.品牌类型 2.出口享惠情况 3.制作或保存方法(表面是否涂覆、涂覆何种物质)4.种类(牛、马)5.状态(是否整张、无毛全粒面未剖层或无毛粒面剖层、牛皮层数)6.规格(厚度、平均面积)7.颜色 8.用途(鞋面、箱包、鞋底、家具、汽车座椅、皮带等)
4107991	1.品牌类型 2.出口享惠情况 3.制作或保存方法(表面是否涂覆、涂覆何种物质)4.种类(牛、马)5.状态(是否整张、无毛全粒面未剖层或无毛粒面剖层、牛皮层数)6.用途(机器带用)7.规格(厚度、平均面积)8.颜色
4107999	1.品牌类型 2.出口享惠情况 3.制作或保存方法(表面是否涂覆、涂覆何种物质)4.种类(牛、马)5.状态(是否整张、无毛全粒面未剖层或无毛粒面剖层、牛皮层数)6.规格(厚度、平均面积)7.颜色 8.用途(鞋面、箱包、鞋底、家具、汽车座椅、皮带等)
4112	1.品牌类型 2.出口享惠情况 3.种类 4.状态(无毛全粒面或无毛羊皮纸化等)5.规格(厚度及面积)6.颜色
4113	1.品牌类型 2.出口享惠情况 3.制作或保存方法 4.状态(无毛全粒面等)5.规格(长/宽或面积)6.整张/背皮/腹皮等
4114	1.品牌类型 2.出口享惠情况 3.制作或保存方法(漆皮、镀金属)4.规格(厚度)5.请注明平方英尺数/张
41151	1.品牌类型 2.出口享惠情况 3.制作或保存方法(再生)4.状态(块、张、条卷、边角料、粉末)5.规格(厚度)
41152	1.品牌类型 2.出口享惠情况 3.状态(块、张、条、卷、边角料、粉末)4.用途 5.是否经过筛选
4201	1.品牌类型 2.出口享惠情况 3.材质 4.用途
420211	1.品牌类型 2.出口享惠情况 3.种类(衣箱、提箱、小手袋等)4.表面材质(皮革、再生皮革等)5.品牌及款号
420212	1.品牌类型 2.出口享惠情况 3.种类(衣箱、提箱、小手袋等)4.表面材质(塑料、纺织物等)5.品牌及款号
420219	1.品牌类型 2.出口享惠情况 3.种类(衣箱、提箱、小手袋等)4.表面材质(塑料、纺织物等)5.品牌及款号
42022	1.品牌类型 2.出口享惠情况 3.种类 4.表面材质(皮革、再生皮革、塑料、纺织物等)5.品牌及款号
42023	1.品牌类型 2.出口享惠情况 3.种类(钱夹、钱包、手机套等适放在口袋、手提袋内)4.表面材质(皮革、再生皮革、塑料、纺织物等)5.品牌及款号
42029	1.品牌类型 2.出口享惠情况 3.种类 4.表面材质(塑料、纺织物等)5.品牌及款号
42031	1.品牌类型 2.出口享惠情况 3.材质(皮革或再生皮革)4.衣服种类 5.是否源于野生动物 6.品牌及款号
42032	1.品牌类型 2.出口享惠情况 3.用途(专供运动用、劳保用等)4.材质(皮革或再生皮革)
42033	1.品牌类型 2.出口享惠情况 3.材质(皮革或再生皮革)4.品牌(中文及外文品牌)5.款号
42034	1.品牌类型 2.出口享惠情况 3.材质(皮革或再生皮革)
4205001	1.品牌类型 2.出口享惠情况 3.材质(皮革或再生皮革)
4205002	1.品牌类型 2.出口享惠情况 3.用途(机械、技术用等)4.材质(皮革或再生皮革)
4205009	1.品牌类型 2.出口享惠情况 3.用途 4.材质(皮革或再生皮革)5.品牌
4206	1.品牌类型 2.出口享惠情况
43011	1.品牌类型 2.出口享惠情况 3.状态(生毛皮)4.外观(整张、带头、尾、爪等)5.重量、张数 6.品种(深棕、黑十字等)7.性别(公、母)8.尺寸(50 号、40 号等)9.颜色 10.等级(以各拍卖会等级体系为准、残次皮需明确种类及等级)(中英文)11.是否来自拍卖会及拍卖日期、把号
43013	1.品牌类型 2.出口享惠情况 3.种类(中国羔羊、波斯羔羊、狐皮、兔皮等)4.状态(生毛皮)5.外观(整张、头、尾、爪等)
43016	1.品牌类型 2.出口享惠情况 3.种类(中国羔羊、波斯羔羊、狐皮、兔皮等)4.状态(生毛皮)5.外观(整张、头、尾、爪等)6.品种(蓝狐、蓝霜狐皮等)7.尺寸(50 号、40 号等)8.颜色(深、浅)9.质量(世家皇冠、世家级)10.是否来自拍卖会及拍卖会日期
4301801	1.品牌类型 2.出口享惠情况 3.种类(中国羔羊、波斯羔羊、狐皮、兔皮等)4.状态(生毛皮)5.外观(整张、头、尾、爪等)6.颜色(白色、黑色等)

商品编码	申报要素
4301809	1.品牌类型 2.出口享惠情况 3.种类(中国羔羊、波斯羔羊、狐皮、兔皮等)4.状态(生毛皮)5.外观(整张、头、尾、爪等)
43019	1.品牌类型 2.出口享惠情况 3.种类(中国羔羊、波斯羔羊、狐皮、兔皮等)4.状态(生毛皮)5.外观(整张、头、尾、爪等)
430211	1.品牌类型 2.出口享惠情况 3.制作或保存方法(鞣制未缝制或已缝制毛皮)4.外观(整张、带头、尾、爪等)5.重量、张数 6.品种(深棕、黑十字等)7.性别(公、母)8.尺寸(50 号、40 号等)9.颜色 10.等级(以各拍卖会等级体系为准、残次皮需明确种类及等级)(中英文)11.是否来自拍卖会及拍卖日期、把号
4302191	1.品牌类型 2.出口享惠情况 3.种类(中国羔羊、波斯羔羊、狐皮、兔皮等)4.制作或保存方法(鞣制未缝制或已缝制毛皮)5.外观(整张、头、尾、爪等)6.品种(蓝狐、蓝霜狐皮等 7.尺寸(50 号、40 号等)8.颜色(深、浅)9.质量(世家皇冠、世家级)10.是否来自拍卖会及拍卖会日期
4302192	1.品牌类型 2.出口享惠情况 3.种类(中国羔羊、波斯羔羊、狐皮、兔皮等)4.制作或保存方法(鞣制未缝制或已缝制毛皮)5.外观(整张、头、尾、爪等)6.规格
4302193	1.品牌类型 2.出口享惠情况 3.种类(中国羔羊、波斯羔羊、狐皮、兔皮等)4.制作或保存方法(鞣制未缝制或已缝制毛皮)5.外观(整张、头、尾、爪等)6.规格
4302199	1.品牌类型 2.出口享惠情况 3.种类(中国羔羊、波斯羔羊、狐皮、兔皮等)4.制作或保存方法(鞣制未缝制或已缝制毛皮)5.外观(整张、头、尾、爪等)6.规格
43022	1.品牌类型 2.出口享惠情况 3.种类(中国羔羊、波斯羔羊、狐皮、兔皮等)4.制作或保存方法(鞣制未缝制或已缝制毛皮)5.外观(整张、头、尾、爪等)
43023	1.品牌类型 2.出口享惠情况 3.种类(中国羔羊、波斯羔羊、狐皮、兔皮等)4.制作或保存方法(鞣制未缝制或已缝制毛皮)5.外观(整张、头、尾、爪等)6.规格
4303	1.品牌类型 2.出口享惠情况 3.材质(里、外)4.衣服种类
4304	1.品牌类型 2.出口享惠情况 3.材质(人造毛皮)
44011	1.品牌类型 2.出口享惠情况 3.种类(中文、拉丁文属名、拉丁文种名)4.外观(圆木段、块、枝、成捆或类似形状等)
44012	1.品牌类型 2.出口享惠情况 3.种类(中文、拉丁文属名、拉丁文种名)4.规格 5.用途
440131	1.品牌类型 2.出口享惠情况 3.外观(棒)4.规格(直径×长度)
440139	1.品牌类型 2.出口享惠情况 3.外观(块、片或类似形状等)
44014	1.品牌类型 2.出口享惠情况 3.外观(末、废料、碎片等)
44021	1.品牌类型 2.出口享惠情况 3.材质 4.是否活化
44029	1.品牌类型 2.出口享惠情况 3.材质 4.是否活化 5.碳含量 6.挥发份
44031	1.品牌类型 2.出口享惠情况 3.种类(中文、拉丁文属名、拉丁文种名)4.加工方法(用油漆、着色剂等防腐剂处理等,是否经纵锯、纵切、刨切或旋切)5.截面尺寸(圆木直径或方木宽度 * 厚度)6.长度 7.蓝变、未蓝变 8.烘干、未烘干 9.签约日期
44032	1.品牌类型 2.出口享惠情况 3.种类(中文、拉丁文属名、拉丁文种名)4.加工方法(是否经纵锯、纵切、刨切或旋切)5.截面尺寸(圆木直径或方木宽度 * 厚度)6.长度 7.级别(锯材级、切片级等)8.蓝变、未蓝变 9.烘干、未烘干 10.签约日期
44034	1.品牌类型 2.出口享惠情况 3.种类(中文、拉丁文属名、拉丁文种名)4.加工方法(是否经纵锯、纵切、刨切或旋切)5.截面尺寸(圆木直径或方木宽度 * 厚度)6.长度 7.级别(锯材级、切片级等)8.蓝变、未蓝变 9.烘干、未烘干 10.签约日期
44039	1.品牌类型 2.出口享惠情况 3.种类(中文、拉丁文属名、拉丁文种名)4.加工方法(是否经纵锯、纵切、刨切或旋切)5.截面尺寸(圆木直径或方木宽度 * 厚度)6.长度 7.级别(锯材级、切片级等)8.蓝变、未蓝变 9.烘干、未烘干 10.签约日期
4404	1.品牌类型 2.出口享惠情况 3.种类(中文、拉丁文属名、拉丁文种名)4.外观(棒状、条状等)
4405	1.品牌类型 2.出口享惠情况
4406	1.品牌类型 2.出口享惠情况 3.加工方法(是否浸渍)4.规格(长×宽×高)5.种类(中文、拉丁文属名、拉丁文种名)
44071	1.品牌类型 2.出口享惠情况 3.种类(中文、拉丁文属名、拉丁文种名)4.规格(厚度 * 宽度 * 长度)5.加工方法(是否经纵锯、纵切、刨切或旋切)6.等级 7.蓝变、未蓝变 8.带边皮、不带边皮 9.烘干、未烘干 10.签约日期
44072	1.品牌类型 2.出口享惠情况 3.种类(中文及拉丁学名)4.规格(厚度 * 宽度 * 长度)5.等级
440791	1.品牌类型 2.出口享惠情况 3.种类(中文及拉丁学名)4.规格(厚度 * 宽度 * 长度)5.等级
440792	1.品牌类型 2.出口享惠情况 3.种类(中文及拉丁学名)4.规格(厚度 * 宽度 * 长度)5.等级 6.毛边板或直边板请注明
440793	1.品牌类型 2.出口享惠情况 3.种类(中文及拉丁学名)4.规格(厚度 * 宽度 * 长度)5.等级
440794	1.品牌类型 2.出口享惠情况 3.种类(中文及拉丁学名)4.规格(厚度 * 宽度 * 长度)5.等级
440795	1.品牌类型 2.出口享惠情况 3.种类(中文及拉丁学名)4.规格(厚度 * 宽度 * 长度)5.等级
440796	1.品牌类型 2.出口享惠情况 3.种类(中文及拉丁学名)4.规格(厚度 * 宽度 * 长度)5.等级
440797	1.品牌类型 2.出口享惠情况 3.种类(中文及拉丁学名)4.规格(厚度 * 宽度 * 长度)5.等级
440799	1.品牌类型 2.出口享惠情况 3.种类(中文及拉丁学名)4.规格(厚度 * 宽度 * 长度)5.等级
4408	1.品牌类型 2.出口享惠情况 3.用途(饰面用等)4.种类(中文、拉丁文属名、拉丁文种名)5.规格(厚度×宽度×长度)6.加工工艺(纵锯、刨切、旋切等)7.请注明立方米数或平方米数
4409	1.品牌类型 2.出口享惠情况 3.种类(中文、拉丁文属名、拉丁文种名)4.外观(舌榫、槽榫、半槽榫等)5.规格(厚度×宽度×长度)6.加工工艺
4410	1.品牌类型 2.出口享惠情况 3.材质(木质或类似木质材料)4.请注明立方米数或平方米数
44111	1.品牌类型 2.出口享惠情况 3.加工方法(是否经机械加工或盖面、干法、湿法等)4.密度 5.厚度 6.请注明是否辐射松制 7.请注明立方米数或平方米数
44119	1.品牌类型 2.出口享惠情况 3.加工方法(是否经机械加工或盖面、干法、湿法等)4.密度 5.请注明是否辐射松制 6.请注明立方米数或平方米数
4412	1.品牌类型 2.出口享惠情况 3.每层材质及树种名称 4.最大单层厚度 5.规格(厚度×宽度×长度)6.加工工艺 7.请注明立方米数或平方米数
4413	1.品牌类型 2.出口享惠情况 3.加工方法(压缩、浸渍等)4.外观(块、板、条、异型)
4414	1.品牌类型 2.出口享惠情况 3.材质(木制)4.种类(如是单一材质申报中文、拉丁文属名、拉丁文种名)
4415	1.品牌类型 2.出口享惠情况 3.材质(木制)4.种类(中文、拉丁文属名、拉丁文种名)5.用途
4416	1.品牌类型 2.出口享惠情况 3.材质(木制)4.种类(如是单一材质申报中文、拉丁文属名、拉丁文种名)
4417	1.品牌类型 2.出口享惠情况 3.材质(木制)4.种类(如是单一材质申报中文、拉丁文属名、拉丁文种名)
44181	1.品牌类型 2.出口享惠情况 3.用途(建筑用)4.材质(木制)5.种类(中文、拉丁文属名、拉丁文种名)
44182	1.品牌类型 2.出口享惠情况 3.用途(建筑用)4.材质(木制)5.种类(中文、拉丁文属名、拉丁文种名)6.规格
44184	1.品牌类型 2.出口享惠情况 3.用途(建筑用)4.材质(木制)5.种类(中文、拉丁文属名、拉丁文种名)6.规格
44185	1.品牌类型 2.出口享惠情况 3.用途(建筑用)4.材质(木制)5.种类(中文、拉丁文属名、拉丁文种名)6.规格
44186	1.品牌类型 2.出口享惠情况 3.材质(木制)4.种类(中文、拉丁文属名、拉丁文种名)5.类型(柱、梁)6.规格
44187	1.品牌类型 2.出口享惠情况 3.加工方法(已装拼)4.材质(木制等)5.种类(中文、拉丁文属名、拉丁文种名)6.类型(马赛克地板、多层地板等)7.规格
44189	1.品牌类型 2.出口享惠情况 3.用途(建筑用)4.材质(木制等)5.种类(中文及拉丁学名)
44191	1.品牌类型 2.出口享惠情况 3.材质(竹制、木制等)4.是否是一次性产品 5.种类(如是单一材质申报中文、拉丁文属名、拉丁文种名)
4419901	1.品牌类型 2.出口享惠情况 3.材质(竹制、木制等)4.是否是一次性产品 5.种类(如是单一材质申报中文、拉丁文属名、拉丁文种名)6.小包装类别(塑料、纸制等)7.包含附件请注明附件名称
4419909	1.品牌类型 2.出口享惠情况 3.材质(竹制、木制等)4.是否是一次性产品 5.种类(如是单一材质申报中文、拉丁文属名、拉丁文种名)
4420	1.品牌类型 2.出口享惠情况 3.材质(木制)4.种类(如是单一材质申报中文、拉丁文属名、拉丁文种名)5.用途
44211	1.品牌类型 2.出口享惠情况 3.材质(竹制、木制等)4.种类(如是单一材质申报中文、拉丁文属名、拉丁文种名)
4421911	1.品牌类型 2.出口享惠情况 3.材质(竹制)4.种类(如是单一材质申报中文、拉丁文属名、拉丁文种名)5.是否是一次性产品 6.尺寸(长、宽、厚、直径等)
4421919	1.品牌类型 2.出口享惠情况 3.材质(竹制)4.种类(如是单一材质申报中文、拉丁文属名、拉丁文种名)
4421991	1.品牌类型 2.出口享惠情况 3.材质(木制等)4.种类(如是单一材质申报中文、拉丁文属名、拉丁文种名)5.是否是一次性产品 6.尺寸(长、宽、厚、直径等)
4421999	1.品牌类型 2.出口享惠情况 3.材质(木制等)4.种类(如是单一材质申报中文、拉丁文属名、拉丁文种名)
45011	1.品牌类型 2.出口享惠情况 3.加工程度(未加工、简单加工等)
45019	1.品牌类型 2.出口享惠情况 3.状态(碎的、粒状的或粉状的)4.是否是废料

商品编码	申报要素
4502	1.品牌类型 2.出口享惠情况 3.加工方法(经除去表皮或粗切成方形等加工)4.外观(块、板、片或条状等)
4503	1.品牌类型 2.出口享惠情况 3.规格 4.等级
4504	1.品牌类型 2.出口享惠情况 3.外观(块、板、片等形状)
460121	1.品牌类型 2.出口享惠情况 3.材质(竹、藤、稻草等)4.用途
460122	1.品牌类型 2.出口享惠情况 3.材质(竹、藤、稻草等)
46012911	1.品牌类型 2.出口享惠情况 3.材质(竹、藤、稻草等)4.单位面积
46012919	1.品牌类型 2.出口享惠情况 3.材质(竹、藤、稻草等)
4601292	1.品牌类型 2.出口享惠情况 3.材质(竹、藤、稻草等)
4601299	1.品牌类型 2.出口享惠情况 3.材质(竹、藤、稻草等)
46019	1.品牌类型 2.出口享惠情况 3.材质(竹、藤、稻草等)
4602	1.品牌类型 2.出口享惠情况 3.材质(竹、藤、草、玉米皮、柳条等)4.植物材料制请注明 5.品牌
4701	1.品牌类型 2.出口享惠情况 3.品名(机械木浆)4.品牌 5.签约日期
4702	1.品牌类型 2.出口享惠情况 3.品名(溶解级化学木浆)4.品牌 5.签约日期 6.黏度 7.α 纤维素含量 8.灰分
4703	1.品牌类型 2.出口享惠情况 3.材质(针叶木、非针叶木)4.加工方法(漂白、未漂白、半漂白)5.水分含量 6.品牌 7.签约日期 8.形状(卷筒或平板)
4704	1.品牌类型 2.出口享惠情况 3.材质(针叶木、非针叶木)4.加工方法(漂白、未漂白、半漂白)5.水分含量 6.品牌
4705	1.品牌类型 2.出口享惠情况 3.加工方法(用机械和化学联合制浆法)4.水分含量 5.品牌
47061	1.品牌类型 2.出口享惠情况 3.种类(棉短绒)4.用途(造纸或生产粘胶纤维等)5.粘度(具体数值或范围区间,单位为分升/克)6.α 纤维素含量(不溶级分,以 R18、硫酸盐法或亚硫酸盐法计)7.725℃时灰分(申报具体百分比数值或范围区间)
47062	1.品牌类型 2.出口享惠情况 3.来源(从回收纸或纸板提取的)4.原料种类(如美废 13 号)
47063	1.品牌类型 2.出口享惠情况 3.来源(从回收纸或纸板提取的)4.用途(造纸或生产粘胶纤维等)5.粘度(具体数值或范围区间,单位为分升/克)6.α 纤维素含量(不溶级分,以 R18、硫酸盐法或亚硫酸盐法计)7.725℃时灰分(申报具体百分比数值或范围区间)
47069	1.品牌类型 2.出口享惠情况 3.材质(草浆等)4.加工方法(机械、化学、半化学)
47071	1.品牌类型 2.出口享惠情况 3.种类(未漂白废牛皮纸、废瓦楞纸)4.状态(废碎)5.产地标准及标号(美废、欧废、港废等)6.签约日期
47072	1.品牌类型 2.出口享惠情况 3.种类(漂白废牛皮纸、废报纸等)4.状态(废碎)5.产地标准及标号(美废、欧废、港废等)6.签约日期
47073	1.品牌类型 2.出口享惠情况 3.种类(未漂白废牛皮纸、废报纸等)4.状态(废碎)5.产地标准及标号(美废、欧废、港废等)6.签约日期
47079	1.品牌类型 2.出口享惠情况 3.种类(未漂白废牛皮纸、废报纸等)4.产地标准及标号(美废、欧废、港废等)5.签约日期
4801	1.品牌类型 2.出口享惠情况 3.用途(书写、印刷等用)4.加工程度(未涂布、未染面等)5.规格(成条、成卷的宽度或成张的边长、每平方米克重)6.机械或化学—机械法制得的纤维含量 7.粗糙度 8.签约日期 9.品牌或厂商(中文或者英文)
48021	1.品牌类型 2.出口享惠情况 3.用途 4.种类 5.加工程度(未涂布、未染面等)6.规格(成条、成卷的宽度或成张的边长、每平方米克重)7.签约日期 8.品牌或厂商(中文或者英文)
48022	1.品牌类型 2.出口享惠情况 3.用途 4.种类 5.加工程度(未涂布、未染面等)6.规格(成条、成卷的宽度或成张的边长、每平方米克重)7.签约日期 8.品牌或厂商(中文或者英文)
48024	1.品牌类型 2.出口享惠情况 3.用途 4.种类 5.加工程度(未涂布、未染面等)6.规格(成条、成卷的宽度或成张的边长、每平方米克重)7.签约日期 8.品牌或厂商(中文或者英文)
48025	1.品牌类型 2.出口享惠情况 3.用途(书写、印刷等用)4.种类 5.加工程度(未涂布、未染面等)6.规格(成条、成卷的宽度或成张的边长、每平方米克重)7.纤维种类和含量 8.签约日期 9.品牌或厂商(中文或者英文)
48026	1.品牌类型 2.出口享惠情况 3.用途(书写、印刷等用)4.种类 5.加工程度(未涂布、未染面等)6.规格(成条、成卷的宽度或成张的边长、每平方米克重)7.纤维种类和含量 8.签约日期 9.品牌或厂商(中文或者英文)
4803	1.品牌类型 2.出口享惠情况 3.种类(卫生纸、面巾纸等类似纸)4.规格(成条、成卷的宽度或成张的边长)5.签约日期 6.品牌或厂商(中文或者英文)
48041	1.品牌类型 2.出口享惠情况 3.种类(牛皮挂面纸)4.加工程度(未漂白、漂白、未涂布)5.规格(成条、成卷的宽度或成张的边长、每平方米克重)6.纤维种类和含量 7.请注明耐破度、紧度、横向环压指数、横向耐折度 8.品牌 9.签约日期 10.厂商
48042	1.品牌类型 2.出口享惠情况 3.种类(袋用牛皮纸)4.加工程度(未漂白、漂白、未涂布)5.规格(成条、成卷的宽度或成张的边长、每平方米克重)6.纤维种类和含量 7.请注明缪伦耐破度、横向伸长率、纵向伸长率 8.是否机器上光 9.品牌 10.签约日期
480431	1.品牌类型 2.出口享惠情况 3.种类 4.加工程度(未漂白、漂白、未涂布)5.规格(成条、成卷的宽度或成张的边长、每平方米克重)6.纤维种类和含量 7.请注明耐破度、紧度、横向环压指数、横向耐折度 8.品牌 9.签约日期
480439	1.品牌类型 2.出口享惠情况 3.种类(耐磨纸原纸等)4.加工程度(未漂白、漂白、未涂布)5.规格(成条、成卷的宽度或成张的边长、每平方米克重)6.纤维种类和含量 7.品牌 8.签约日期
480441	1.品牌类型 2.出口享惠情况 3.种类 4.加工程度(未漂白、漂白、未涂布)5.规格(成条、成卷的宽度或成张的边长、每平方米克重)6.纤维种类和含量 7.请注明耐破度、紧度、横向环压指数、横向耐折度 8.品牌 9.签约日期
480442	1.品牌类型 2.出口享惠情况 3.种类 4.加工程度(未漂白、漂白、水体均匀漂白、未涂布)5.规格(成条、成卷的宽度或成张的边长、每平方米克重)6.纤维种类和含量 7.请注明耐破度、紧度、横向环压指数、横向耐折度 8.品牌 9.签约日期
480449	1.品牌类型 2.出口享惠情况 3.种类 4.加工程度(未漂白、漂白、未涂布)5.规格(成条、成卷的宽度或成张的边长、每平方米克重)6.纤维种类和含量 7.请注明耐破度、紧度、横向环压指数、横向耐折度 8.品牌 9.签约日期
480451	1.品牌类型 2.出口享惠情况 3.种类 4.加工程度(未漂白、漂白、未涂布)5.规格(成条、成卷的宽度或成张的边长、每平方米克重)6.纤维种类和含量 7.请注明耐破度、紧度、横向环压指数、横向耐折度 8.品牌 9.签约日期
480452	1.品牌类型 2.出口享惠情况 3.种类 4.加工程度(未漂白、漂白、水体均匀漂白、未涂布)5.规格(成条、成卷的宽度或成张的边长、每平方米克重)6.纤维种类和含量 7.请注明耐破度、紧度、横向环压指数、横向耐折度 8.品牌 9.签约日期
480459	1.品牌类型 2.出口享惠情况 3.种类 4.加工程度(未漂白、漂白、未涂布)5.规格(成条、成卷的宽度或成张的边长、每平方米克重)6.纤维种类和含量 7.请注明耐破度、紧度、横向环压指数、横向耐折度 8.品牌 9.签约日期
48051	1.品牌类型 2.出口享惠情况 3.种类 4.加工程度(未涂布)5.规格(成条、成卷的宽度或成张的边长、每平方米克重)6.纤维种类和含量 7.签约日期 8.品牌或厂商(中文或者英文)
48052	1.品牌类型 2.出口享惠情况 3.种类 4.加工程度(未涂布)5.规格(成条、成卷的宽度或成张的边长、每平方米克重)6.原料 7.强度(缪伦耐破指数)8.签约日期 9.品牌或厂商(中文或者英文)
48053	1.品牌类型 2.出口享惠情况 3.种类 4.加工程度(未涂布)5.规格(成条、成卷的宽度或成张的边长、每平方米克重)6.灰分含量 7.强度(缪伦耐破指数)8.签约日期 9.品牌或厂商(中文或者英文)
48054	1.品牌类型 2.出口享惠情况 3.种类 4.加工程度(未涂布)5.规格(成条、成卷的宽度或成张的边长、每平方米克重)6.签约日期 7.品牌或厂商(中文或者英文)
48055	1.品牌类型 2.出口享惠情况 3.种类 4.加工程度(未涂布)5.规格(成条、成卷的宽度或成张的边长、每平方米克重)6.签约日期 7.品牌或厂商(中文或者英文)
4805911	1.品牌类型 2.出口享惠情况 3.种类 4.加工程度(未涂布)5.规格(成条、成卷的宽度或成张的边长、每平方米克重)6.签约日期 7.型号 8.品牌或厂商(中文或者英文)
4805919	1.品牌类型 2.出口享惠情况 3.种类 4.加工程度(未涂布)5.规格(成条、成卷的宽度或成张的边长、每平方米克重)6.签约日期 7.品牌或厂商(中文或者英文)
480592	1.品牌类型 2.出口享惠情况 3.种类 4.加工程度(未涂布)5.规格(成条、成卷的宽度或成张的边长、每平方米克重)6.签约日期 7.品牌或厂商(中文或者英文)
480593	1.品牌类型 2.出口享惠情况 3.种类 4.加工程度(未涂布)5.规格(成条、成卷的宽度或成张的边长、每平方米克重)6.签约日期 7.品牌或厂商(中文或者英文)
48061	1.品牌类型 2.出口享惠情况 3.种类 4.规格(成条、成卷的宽度或成张的边长)5.签约日期 6.品牌或厂商(中文或者英文)
48062	1.品牌类型 2.出口享惠情况 3.种类 4.规格(成条、成卷的宽度或成张的边长)5.签约日期 6.品牌或厂商(中文或者英文)
48063	1.品牌类型 2.出口享惠情况 3.种类 4.规格(成条、成卷的宽度或成张的边长)5.签约日期 6.品牌或厂商(中文或者英文)
48064	1.品牌类型 2.出口享惠情况 3.种类 4.规格(成卷的宽度或成张的边长)5.签约日期 6.品牌或厂商(中文或者英文)
4807	1.品牌类型 2.出口享惠情况 3.加工方法(黏合多层)4.加工程度(未经表面涂布或未浸渍)5.规格(成条、成卷的宽度或成张的边长)6.签约日期 7.品牌或厂商(中文或者英文)
48081	1.品牌类型 2.出口享惠情况 3.种类(瓦楞纸、皱纹牛皮纸等)4.规格(成条、成卷的宽度或成张的边长)5.签约日期 6.品牌或厂商(中文或者英文)

商品编码	申报要素
48084	1.品牌类型 2.出口享惠情况 3.用途 4.种类 5.规格(成条、成卷的宽度或成张的边长)6.签约日期 7.品牌或厂商(中文或者英文)
48089	1.品牌类型 2.出口享惠情况 3.用途 4.种类 5.规格(成条、成卷的宽度或成张的边长)6.签约日期 7.品牌(中文及外文名称,无品牌请申报厂商)
48092	1.品牌类型 2.出口享惠情况 3.种类(自印复写纸)4.加工程度(涂布或浸渍)5.规格(成条、成卷的宽度或成张的边长)6.签约日期 7.品牌或厂商(中文或者英文)
48099	1.品牌类型 2.出口享惠情况 3.种类(复写纸、拷贝纸等)4.加工程度(涂布或浸渍)5.规格(成条、成卷的宽度或成张的边长)6.签约日期 7.品牌或厂商(中文或者英文)
48101	1.品牌类型 2.出口享惠情况 3.用途(书写、印刷等)4.种类(牛皮纸、白板纸、铜版纸等)5.状态(成卷或张等)6.加工程度(单面或双面涂布无机物、漂白)7.规格(宽度或边长、每平方米克重)8.纤维种类和含量 9.签约日期 10.品牌或厂商(中文或者英文)
48102	1.品牌类型 2.出口享惠情况 3.用途(书写、印刷等)4.种类(牛皮纸、白板纸、铜版纸等)5.状态(成卷或张等)6.加工程度(单面或双面涂布无机物、漂白)7.规格(宽度或边长、每平方米克重)8.纤维种类和含量 9.签约日期 10.品牌或厂商(中文或者英文)
48103	1.品牌类型 2.出口享惠情况 3.用途(包装等)4.种类(牛皮纸、白板纸、铜版纸等)5.状态(成卷或张等)6.加工程度(单面或双面涂布无机物、漂白)7.规格(宽度或边长、每平方米克重)8.纤维种类和含量 9.签约日期 10.品牌或厂商(中文或者英文)
48109	1.品牌类型 2.出口享惠情况 3.用途(书写、印刷等)4.种类(牛皮纸、白板纸、铜版纸等)5.状态(成卷或张等)6.加工程度(单面或双面涂布无机物、漂白)7.规格(宽度或边长、每平方米克重、各纤维含量)8.签约日期 9.品牌或厂商(中文或者英文)
4811	1.品牌类型 2.出口享惠情况 3.种类 4.加工程度(涂布、浸渍、饰面、漂白等)5.规格(外观形状,如成条等)6. 每平方米克重 7.品牌 8.型号
4812	1.品牌类型 2.出口享惠情况 3.材质(纸浆制)4.外观(块、板、片)5.品牌或厂商(中文或者英文)
48131	1.品牌类型 2.出口享惠情况 3.规格(如成小本或管状、宽度)4.品牌或厂商(中文或者英文)
48132	1.品牌类型 2.出口享惠情况 3.规格(成卷、宽度)4.品牌或厂商(中文或者英文)
48139	1.品牌类型 2.出口享惠情况 3.规格(宽度等)4.品牌或厂商(中文或者英文)
48142	1.品牌类型 2.出口享惠情况 3.加工程度(用木粒或草粒、塑料、编结材料等饰面、涂面)4.品牌或厂商(中文或者英文)5.规格尺寸 6.签约日期
48149	1.品牌类型 2.出口享惠情况 3.加工程度(用木粒或草粒、塑料、编结材料等饰面、涂面)4.是否为窗用透明纸 5.品牌或厂商(中文或者英文)6.规格尺寸 7.签约日期
48162	1.品牌类型 2.出口享惠情况 3.种类(自印复写纸、热敏转印纸等)4.规格(成条、成卷的宽度或成张的边长)5.品牌或厂商(中文或者英文)
4816901	1.品牌类型 2.出口享惠情况 3.种类(自印复写纸、热敏转印纸等)4.规格(成条、成卷的宽度或成张的边长)5.品牌或厂商(中文或者英文)
4816909	1.品牌类型 2.出口享惠情况 3.种类(复写纸、拷贝纸、转印纸、油印蜡纸、胶版纸等)4.规格(成条、成卷的宽度或成张的边长)5.品牌或厂商(中文或者英文)
4817	1.品牌类型 2.出口享惠情况 3.材质(纸制)
4818	1.品牌类型 2.出口享惠情况 3.用途(家庭、卫生、医院用等)4.材质(纸制)5.种类(卫生纸、纸台布等)6.规格(成条、成卷的宽度或成张的边长)
48191	1.品牌类型 2.出口享惠情况 3.材质(瓦楞纸或纸板制)4.规格
48192	1.品牌类型 2.出口享惠情况 3.材质 4.规格
48193	1.品牌类型 2.出口享惠情况 3.材质 4.规格 5.底宽长度
48194	1.品牌类型 2.出口享惠情况 3.材质 4.规格 5.底宽长度
48195	1.品牌类型 2.出口享惠情况 3.材质 4.规格
48196	1.品牌类型 2.出口享惠情况 3.材质 4.规格
4820	1.品牌类型 2.出口享惠情况 3.材质
4821	1.品牌类型 2.出口享惠情况 3.材质 4.加工程度(印制、非印制)
48221	1.品牌类型 2.出口享惠情况 3.用途(纺织纱线用等)4.材质(纸制)
48229	1.品牌类型 2.出口享惠情况 3.用途 4.材质(纸制)
48232	1.品牌类型 2.出口享惠情况 3.材质(纸制)4.规格(切成一定尺寸或形状、边长、宽度)
48234	1.品牌类型 2.出口享惠情况 3.用途(已印制的自动记录器用等)4.材质(纸制)5.规格(切成一定尺寸或形状、边长、宽度)
482361	1.品牌类型 2.出口享惠情况 3.材质(竹浆纸制)4.种类(盘、碟、盆、杯等)5.规格
482369	1.品牌类型 2.出口享惠情况 3.材质 4.种类(盘、碟、盆、杯等)5.规格
48237	1.品牌类型 2.出口享惠情况 3.加工方法(压制、模制)4.材质(纸浆制)5.规格(切成一定尺寸或形状、边长、宽度)
4823901	1.品牌类型 2.出口享惠情况 3.用途 4.材质(以纸或纸板为底制成)5.规格
4823902	1.品牌类型 2.出口享惠情况 3.材质(纸制)4.规格(切成一定尺寸或形状、边长、宽度)
4823903	1.品牌类型 2.出口享惠情况 3.材质(纸制)4.规格(切成一定尺寸或形状、边长、宽度)
4823909	1.品牌类型 2.出口享惠情况 3.材质(纸制)4.规格(切成何种的形状边长、宽度等)
4901	1.品牌类型 2.出口享惠情况 3.种类(字典、百科全书等)4.状态(成册、单张)
4902	1.品牌类型 2.出口享惠情况 3.出版周期(日刊、周刊等)
4903	1.品牌类型 2.出口享惠情况 3.用途(儿童用)4.种类(图画书、绘画或涂色书)
4904	1.品牌类型 2.出口享惠情况 3.种类(原稿或印本等)
49051	1.品牌类型 2.出口享惠情况
49059	1.品牌类型 2.出口享惠情况 3.状态(成册、非成册)
4906	1.品牌类型 2.出口享惠情况 3.品名(设计图纸原稿或手稿及其复制件)
4907001	1.品牌类型 2.出口享惠情况 3.外观(新的)4.种类(小型张、四方联等)
4907002	1.品牌类型 2.出口享惠情况 3.外观(新的)
4907003	1.品牌类型 2.出口享惠情况 3.种类(证券、特许权等)
4907009	1.品牌类型 2.出口享惠情况 3.种类(证券、特许权等)4.信息内容物种类(如软件、数据、互联网内容物或服务等)5.给予信息内容物使用权的种类(如存取、复制或密钥等)
4908	1.品牌类型 2.出口享惠情况 3.加工方法(釉转印等)
4909	1.品牌类型 2.出口享惠情况 3.加工方法(印刷或有图画等)
4910	1.品牌类型 2.出口享惠情况
49111	1.品牌类型 2.出口享惠情况 3.用途(有商业价值、无商业价值)
491191	1.品牌类型 2.出口享惠情况 3.用途(有商业价值、无商业价值等)
491199	1.品牌类型 2.出口享惠情况 3.材质 4.用途(有商业价值、无商业价值等)5.信息内容物种类(如软件、数据、互联网内容物或服务等)6.给予信息内容物使用权的种类(如存取、复制或密钥等)7.印刷内容
5001	1.品牌类型 2.出口享惠情况 3.用途(用于缫丝)4.种类
50020011	1.品牌类型 2.出口享惠情况 3.种类(桑蚕厂丝)4.是否加捻
50020012	1.品牌类型 2.出口享惠情况 3.种类(桑蚕土丝)4.是否加捻
50020013	1.品牌类型 2.出口享惠情况 3.种类(桑蚕双宫丝)4.是否加捻
50020019	1.品牌类型 2.出口享惠情况 3.种类 4.是否加捻
50020020	1.品牌类型 2.出口享惠情况 3.种类(柞蚕丝)4.是否加捻
50020090	1.品牌类型 2.出口享惠情况 3.种类 4.是否加捻
5003	1.品牌类型 2.出口享惠情况 3.是否梳理
5004	1.品牌类型 2.出口享惠情况 3.是否供零售用
5005	1.品牌类型 2.出口享惠情况 3.种类(绢纺纱线等)4.是否供零售用 5.成分含量
5006	1.品牌类型 2.出口享惠情况 3.种类(绢纺纱线、蚕胶丝、丝纱线、绸纱线)4.包装(供零售用)5.成分含量
5007	1.品牌类型 2.出口享惠情况 3.种类(绸丝、桑蚕丝、绢丝、柞蚕丝等)4.织造方法(机织物)5.染整方法(漂白、未漂白、色织)6.成分含量 7.幅宽
510111	1.品牌类型 2.出口享惠情况 3.加工程度(含脂、脱脂、碳化等)4.剪羊毛请注明细度(微米数)5.剪羊毛请注明长度 6.剪羊毛请注明草杂含量
510119	1.品牌类型 2.出口享惠情况 3.加工程度(未梳、含脂、脱脂、碳化等)
510121	1.品牌类型 2.出口享惠情况 3.加工程度(未梳、含脂、脱脂、碳化等)4.剪羊毛请注明细度(微米数)5.剪羊毛请注明长度 6.剪羊毛请注明草杂含量
510129	1.品牌类型 2.出口享惠情况 3.加工程度(未梳、含脂、脱脂、碳化等)
51013	1.品牌类型 2.出口享惠情况 3.加工程度(未梳、含脂、脱脂、碳化等)
510211	1.品牌类型 2.出口享惠情况 3.种类(未梳理的兔毛、喀什米尔山羊毛、山羊绒、骆驼毛)
5102191	1.品牌类型 2.出口享惠情况 3.种类(未梳理的兔毛、喀什米尔山羊毛、山羊绒、骆驼毛)
5102192	1.品牌类型 2.出口享惠情况 3.种类(未梳理的兔毛、喀什米尔山羊毛、山羊绒、骆驼毛)4.颜色 5.纤维长度 6.净绒率
5102193	1.品牌类型 2.出口享惠情况 3.种类(未梳理的兔毛、喀什米尔山羊毛、山羊绒、骆驼毛)
5102199	1.品牌类型 2.出口享惠情况 3.种类(未梳理的兔毛、喀什米尔山兰毛、山羊绒、骆驼毛)
51022	1.品牌类型 2.出口享惠情况 3.种类(未梳理的兔毛、喀什米尔山羊毛、山羊绒、骆驼毛)

商品编码	申报要素
5103	1.品牌类型 2.出口享惠情况 3.种类(羊毛落毛、动物细毛或粗毛废料)
5104	1.品牌类型 2.出口享惠情况 3.种类(源于羊毛、动物粗、细毛等的回收纤维)
51051	1.品牌类型 2.出口享惠情况 3.种类(羊毛条、羊毛片毛、兔毛、喀什米尔山羊毛)4.梳理方法(粗梳或精梳)
510521	1.品牌类型 2.出口享惠情况 3.种类(羊毛条、羊毛片毛、兔毛、喀什米尔山羊毛)4.梳理方法(粗梳或精梳)
510529	1.品牌类型 2.出口享惠情况 3.种类(羊毛条、羊毛片毛、兔毛、喀什米尔山羊毛)4.梳理方法(粗梳或精梳)5.其他精梳羊毛请注明支数 6.其他精梳羊毛请注明细度
51053	1.品牌类型 2.出口享惠情况 3.种类(羊毛条、羊毛片毛、兔毛、喀什米尔山羊毛)4.梳理方法(粗梳或精梳)
51054	1.品牌类型 2.出口享惠情况 3.种类(羊毛条、羊毛片毛、兔毛、喀什米尔山羊毛)4.梳理方法(粗梳或精梳)
5106	1.品牌类型 2.出口享惠情况 3.梳理方法(粗疏)4.是否供零售用 5.成分含量
5107	1.品牌类型 2.出口享惠情况 3.梳理方法(精梳羊毛纱线)4.是否供零售用 5.成分含量
5108	1.品牌类型 2.出口享惠情况 3.梳理方法(精梳羊毛纱线)4.是否供零售用 5.成分含量
5109	1.品牌类型 2.出口享惠情况 3.种类(羊毛等)4.是否供零售用 5.成分含量
5110	1.品牌类型 2.出口享惠情况 3.种类(马毛等粗毛纱线)4.成分含量
5111	1.品牌类型 2.出口享惠情况 3.种类(羊毛、驼马毛、美洲驼毛等)4.织造方法(机织)5.梳理方法(粗梳)6.成分含量 7.幅宽 8.每平方米克重
5112	1.品牌类型 2.出口享惠情况 3.种类(羊毛、驼马毛、美洲驼毛等)4.织造方法(机织)5.梳理方法(精梳)6.成分含量 7.幅宽 8.每平米克重
5113	1.品牌类型 2.出口享惠情况 3.种类(马毛等)4.织造方法(机织)5.成分含量 6.幅宽 7.每平方米克重
5201	1.品牌类型 2.出口享惠情况 3.是否梳理 4.纤维长度 5.品级
52021	1.品牌类型 2.出口享惠情况 3.来源(废棉线、回收纤维等)4.成分含量 5.颜色
520291	1.品牌类型 2.出口享惠情况 3.来源(废棉线、回收纤维等)4.成分含量
520299	1.品牌类型 2.出口享惠情况 3.来源(废棉线、回收纤维等)4.成分含量 5.棉种类(包括精落、抄斩、车肚、统破籽、回丝等)
5203	1.品牌类型 2.出口享惠情况 3.是否梳理 4.纤维长度
5204	1.品牌类型 2.出口享惠情况 3.是否供零售用 4.成分含量 5.纱线细度 6.每只重量 7.是否上浆 8.终捻捻向
5205	1.品牌类型 2.出口享惠情况 3.梳理方法(粗梳、精梳)4.纱线形态(单纱、股线或缆线)5.是否供零售用 6.成分含量 7.纱线细度 8.品牌 9.加工工艺(环锭纺、气流纺、赛络纺等)
5206	1.品牌类型 2.出口享惠情况 3.梳理方法(粗梳、精梳)4.纱线形态(单纱、股线或缆线)5.是否供零售用 6.成分含量 7.纱线细度 8.品牌或厂商名称
5207	1.品牌类型 2.出口享惠情况 3.是否供零售用 4.成分含量
5208	1.品牌类型 2.出口享惠情况 3.织造方法(机织物)4.染整方法(漂白、未漂白、色织、染色、印花等)5.组织结构(平纹、三线或四线斜纹、四线双面斜纹或十字斜纹、其他斜纹)6.成分含量 7.每平方米克重 8.品牌
5209	1.品牌类型 2.出口享惠情况 3.织造方法(机织物)4.染整方法(漂白、未漂白、色织、染色、印花等)5.组织结构(平纹、粗斜纹、其他三线或四线斜纹、其他斜纹等)6.成分含量 7.幅宽 8.每平方米克重 9.品牌
5210	1.品牌类型 2.出口享惠情况 3.织造方法(机织物)4.染整方法(漂白、未漂白、色织、染色、印花等)5.组织结构(平纹、三线或四线斜纹、四线双面斜纹或十字斜纹、其他斜纹等)6.注明与其混纺的化纤是长丝还是短纤 7.成分含量 8.幅宽 9.每平方米克重 10.品牌
5211	1.品牌类型 2.出口享惠情况 3.织造方法(机织物)4.染整方法(漂白、未漂白、色织、染色、印花等)5.组织结构(平纹、粗斜纹、其他三线或四线斜纹、其他斜纹等)6.注明与其混纺的化纤是长丝还是短纤 7.成分含量 8.幅宽 9.每平方米克重 10.品牌
5212	1.品牌类型 2.出口享惠情况 3.织造方法(机织物)4.染整方法(漂白、未漂白、色织、染色、印花等)5.组织结构(平纹、斜纹等)6.成分含量 7.幅宽 8.每平方米克重 9.品牌
53011	1.品牌类型 2.出口享惠情况 3.加工程度(生的、经沤制、破开或打成栉梳、回收等)
530121	1.品牌类型 2.出口享惠情况 3.加工程度(生的、经沤制、破开或打成栉梳、回收等)4.可纺支数 5.长度
530129	1.品牌类型 2.出口享惠情况 3.加工程度(生的、经沤制、破开或打成栉梳、回收等)

商品编码	申报要素
53013	1.品牌类型 2.出口享惠情况 3.加工程度(生的、经沤制、破开或打成栉梳、回收等)4.是否为短纤或废麻 5.种类(二粗、机械短麻、落麻)
53021	1.品牌类型 2.出口享惠情况 3.加工程度(生的、沤制的)
53029	1.品牌类型 2.出口享惠情况 3.加工程度(生的、沤制的)4.是否为短纤或废麻
53031	1.品牌类型 2.出口享惠情况 3.种类(黄麻、洋麻、菽麻等)4.加工程度(未纺制的、生或沤制的)
53039	1.品牌类型 2.出口享惠情况 3.种类(黄麻、洋麻、菽麻等)4.加工程度(未纺制的、生或沤制的)5.是否为短纤或废麻
53050011	1.品牌类型 2.出口享惠情况 3.种类(椰壳纤维、蕉麻、苎麻等)4.加工程度(生的或经加工但未纺制的)
53050012	1.品牌类型 2.出口享惠情况 3.种类(椰壳纤维、蕉麻、苎麻等)4.加工程度(生的或经加工但未纺制的)
53050013	1.品牌类型 2.出口享惠情况 3.种类(椰壳纤维、蕉麻、苎麻等)4.加工程度(生的或经加工但未纺制的)5.是否为短纤或废麻
53050019	1.品牌类型 2.出口享惠情况 3.种类(椰壳纤维、蕉麻、苎麻等)4.加工程度(生的或经加工但未纺制的)
5305002	1.品牌类型 2.出口享惠情况 3.种类(椰壳纤维、蕉麻、苎麻等)4.加工程度(生的或经加工但未纺制的)
5305009	1.品牌类型 2.出口享惠情况 3.种类(椰壳纤维、蕉麻、苎麻等)4.是否为短纤或废麻 5.加工程度及工艺(生的或经加工但未纺制的、是否梳理、是否机卷及是否制成椰绳)6.等级及用途
5306	1.品牌类型 2.出口享惠情况 3.纱线形态(单纱、股线或缆线)4.细度
5307	1.品牌类型 2.出口享惠情况 3.种类(黄麻、洋麻、菽麻等)4.纱线形态(单纱、股线或缆线)5.细度
53081	1.品牌类型 2.出口享惠情况 3.种类(椰壳纤维纱线、大麻纱线、苎麻纱线、纸纱线等)4.成分含量 5.细度
53082	1.品牌类型 2.出口享惠情况 3.种类(椰壳纤维纱线、大麻纱线、苎麻纱线、纸纱线等)4.成分含量 5.细度
5308901	1.品牌类型 2.出口享惠情况 3.种类(椰壳纤维纱线、大麻纱线、苎麻纱线、纸纱线等)4.染整方法(漂白、未漂白、色织)5.成分含量 6.细度
5308909	1.品牌类型 2.出口享惠情况 3.种类(椰壳纤维纱线、大麻纱线、苎麻纱线、纸纱线等)4.成分含量 5.细度
5309	1.品牌类型 2.出口享惠情况 3.织造方法(机织)4.染整方法(漂白、未漂白、色织)5.成分含量 6.幅宽 7.每平方米克重
5310	1.品牌类型 2.出口享惠情况 3.种类(黄麻、洋麻、菽麻等)4.织造方法(机织)5.染整工艺(漂白、未漂白、色织)6.成分含量 7.幅宽 8.每平方米克重
5311	1.品牌类型 2.出口享惠情况 3.种类(黄麻、洋麻、菽麻等)4.织造方法(机织)5.染整方法(漂白、未漂白、色织)6.成分含量 7.幅宽 8.每平方米克重
5401	1.品牌类型 2.出口享惠情况 3.是否供零售用 4.纤维成分(聚酯等)5.每只重量 6.是否上浆 7.终捻捻向
54021	1.品牌类型 2.出口享惠情况 3.种类(高强力纱或变形纱线等)4.纱线形态(单纱、股线或缆线)5.是否供零售用 6.纤维成分(聚酰胺等)7.纱线细度
54022	1.品牌类型 2.出口享惠情况 3.种类(高强力纱或变形纱线等)4.纱线形态(单纱、股线或缆线)5.是否供零售用 6.纤维成分(聚酯等)7.纱线细度
54023	1.品牌类型 2.出口享惠情况 3.种类(高强力纱或变形纱线等)4.纱线形态(单纱、股线或缆线)5.是否供零售用 6.纤维成分(聚酯等)7.纱线细度
540244	1.品牌类型 2.出口享惠情况 3.种类(高强力纱或变形纱线等)4.纱线形态(单纱、股线或缆线)5.高强纱请注明用途 6.是否供零售用 7.纤维成分(聚酯等)8.纱线细度 9.是否加捻(如加捻请注明捻度)
540245	1.品牌类型 2.出口享惠情况 3.种类(高强力纱或变形纱线等)4.纱线形态(单纱、股线或缆线)5.高强纱请注明用途 6.是否供零售用 7.纤维成分(聚酰胺等)8.纱线细度 9.是否加捻(如加捻请注明捻度)
540246	1.品牌类型 2.出口享惠情况 3.种类(高强力纱或变形纱线等)4.纱线形态(单纱、股线或缆线)5.高强纱请注明用途 6.是否供零售用 7.纤维成分(聚酯等)8.纱线细度 9.是否加捻(如加捻请注明捻度)
540247	1.品牌类型 2.出口享惠情况 3.种类(高强力纱或变形纱线等)4.纱线形态(单纱、股线或缆线)5.高强纱请注明用途 6.是否供零售用 7.纤维成分(聚酯等)8.纱线细度 9.是否加捻(如加捻请注明捻度)
540248	1.品牌类型 2.出口享惠情况 3.种类(高强力纱或变形纱线等)4.纱线形态(单纱、股线或缆线)5.高强纱请注明用途 6.是否供零售用 7.纤维成分(聚丙烯等)8.纱线细度 9.是否加捻(如加捻请注明捻度)

商品编码	申报要素
5402491	1.品牌类型 2.出口享惠情况 3.种类(高强力纱或变形纱线等)4.纱线形态(单纱、股线或缆线)5.高强纱请注明用途 6.是否供零售用 7.纤维成分(聚酯等)8.纱线细度 9.是否加捻(如加捻请注明捻度)10.断裂强度
5402499	1.品牌类型 2.出口享惠情况 3.种类(高强力纱或变形纱线等)4.纱线形态(单纱、股线或缆线)5.高强纱请注明用途 6.是否供零售用 7.纤维成分(聚酯等)8.纱线细度 9.是否加捻(如加捻请注明捻度)
540251	1.品牌类型 2.出口享惠情况 3.种类(高强力纱或变形纱线等)4.纱线形态(单纱、股线或缆线)5.是否供零售用 6.纤维成分(聚酰胺等)7.纱线细度 8.是否加捻(如加捻请注明捻度)
540252	1.品牌类型 2.出口享惠情况 3.种类(高强力纱或变形纱线等)4.纱线形态(单纱、股线或缆线)5.是否供零售用 6.纤维成分(聚酯等)7.纱线细度 8.是否加捻(如加捻请注明捻度)
540253	1.品牌类型 2.出口享惠情况 3.种类(高强力纱或变形纱线等)4.纱线形态(单纱、股线或缆线)5.是否供零售用 6.纤维成分(聚丙烯)7.纱线细度 8.是否加捻(如加捻请注明捻度)
5402592	1.品牌类型 2.出口享惠情况 3.种类(高强力纱或变形纱线等)4.纱线形态(单纱、股线或缆线)5.是否供零售用 6.纤维成分(聚乙烯)7.纱线细度 8.是否加捻(如加捻请注明捻度)9.断裂强度
5402599	1.品牌类型 2.出口享惠情况 3.种类(高强力纱或变形纱线等)4.纱线形态(单纱、股线或缆线)5.是否供零售用 6.纤维成分(聚酯等)7.纱线细度 8.是否加捻(如加捻请注明捻度)
54026	1.品牌类型 2.出口享惠情况 3.种类(高强力纱或变形纱线等)4.纱线形态(单纱、股线或缆线)5.是否供零售用 6.纤维成分(聚酯等)7.纱线细度
5403	1.品牌类型 2.出口享惠情况 3.种类(高强力纱或变形纱线等)4.纱线形态(单纱、股线或缆线)5.是否供零售用 6.纤维成分(如粘胶等)7.纱线细度 8.纱线捻度 9.高强力纱需注明断裂强度(单位:厘牛顿/特克斯)10.股数
5404	1.品牌类型 2.出口享惠情况 3.种类(单丝、扁条等)4.纤维成分 5.单丝细度或扁条表观宽度
5405	1.品牌类型 2.出口享惠情况 3.种类(单丝、扁条等)4.纤维成分 5.单丝细度或扁条表观宽度
5406	1.品牌类型 2.出口享惠情况 3.包装(供零售用)4.纤维成分
54071	1.品牌类型 2.出口享惠情况 3.织造方法(机织、平行纱层叠黏合)4.染整方法(漂白、色织、染色等)5.组织结构(平纹、斜纹、缎纹等)6.成分含量 7.尺寸 8.每平方米克重 9.是否为高强力纱 10.品牌
54072	1.品牌类型 2.出口享惠情况 3.织造方法(机织、平行纱层叠黏合)4.染整方法(漂白、色织、染色等)5.组织结构(平纹、斜纹、缎纹等)6.成分含量 7.尺寸 8.每平方米克重 9.品牌
54073	1.品牌类型 2.出口享惠情况 3.织造方法(机织、平行纱层叠黏合)4.染整方法(漂白、色织、染色等)5.组织结构(平纹、斜纹、缎纹等)6.成分含量 7.尺寸 8.每平方米克重 9.品牌
54074	1.品牌类型 2.出口享惠情况 3.织造方法(机织、平行纱层叠黏合)4.染整方法(漂白、色织、染色等)5.组织结构(平纹、斜纹、缎纹等)6.成分含量 7.尺寸 8.每平方米克重 9.品牌
54075	1.品牌类型 2.出口享惠情况 3.织造方法(机织、平行纱层叠黏合)4.染整方法(漂白、色织、染色等)5.组织结构(平纹、斜纹、缎纹等)6.成分含量(聚酯变形长丝等成分及含量)7.尺寸 8.每平方米克重 9.品牌
54076	1.品牌类型 2.出口享惠情况 3.织造方法(机织、平行纱层叠黏合)4.染整方法(漂白、色织、染色等)5.组织结构(平纹、斜纹、缎纹等)6.成分含量(聚酯非变形长丝等成分及含量)7.尺寸 8.每平方米克重 9.品牌
54077	1.品牌类型 2.出口享惠情况 3.织造方法(机织、平行纱层叠黏合)4.染整方法(漂白、色织、染色等)5.组织结构(平纹、斜纹、缎纹等)6.合成纤维种类(长丝、短纤)7.成分含量 8.尺寸 9.每平方米克重 10.品牌
54078	1.品牌类型 2.出口享惠情况 3.织造方法(机织、平行纱层叠黏合)4.染整方法(漂白、色织、染色等)5.组织结构(平纹、斜纹、缎纹等)6.成分含量 7.尺寸 8.每平方米克重 9.品牌
54079	1.品牌类型 2.出口享惠情况 3.织造方法(机织、平行纱层叠黏合)4.染整方法(漂白、色织、染色等)5.组织结构(平纹、斜纹、缎纹等)6.成分含量 7.尺寸 8.每平方米克重 9.品牌
5408	1.品牌类型 2.出口享惠情况 3.织造方法(机织、平行纱层叠黏合)4.染整方法(漂白、色织、染色等)5.组织结构(平纹、斜纹、缎纹等)6.成分含量 7.尺寸 8.每平方米克重 9.品牌
5501	1.品牌类型 2.出口享惠情况 3.纤维成分 4.单丝细度 5.丝束长度 6.是否加捻(如加捻请注明捻度)7.丝束总细度
5502	1.品牌类型 2.出口享惠情况 3.纤维成分 4.单丝细度 5.丝束长度 6.是否加捻(如加捻请注明捻度)7.丝束总细度
5503	1.品牌类型 2.出口享惠情况 3.加工程度(未梳、未经纺前加工)4.纤维成分 5.长度 6.细度
5504	1.品牌类型 2.出口享惠情况 3.加工程度(未梳、未经纺前加工)4.人造纤维种类 5.细度 6.长度
5505	1.品牌类型 2.出口享惠情况 3.来源(落绵、废纱、回收纤维)4.纤维成分 5.颜色(白色、杂色等)
5506	1.品牌类型 2.出口享惠情况 3.加工程度(已梳、经纺前加工)4.纤维成分
5507	1.品牌类型 2.出口享惠情况 3.加工程度(已梳、经纺前加工)4.纤维成分
5508	1.品牌类型 2.出口享惠情况 3.成分含量 4.纱线细度 5.每只重量 6.是否上浆 7.终捻捻向 8.是否供零售用
5509	1.品牌类型 2.出口享惠情况 3.种类(单纱、股线、缆线)4.是否供零售用 5.成分含量 6.纱线细度 7.股线注明股数
5510	1.品牌类型 2.出口享惠情况 3.种类(单纱、股线、缆线)4.是否供零售用 5.成分含量 6.纱线细度 7.股线注明股数
5511	1.品牌类型 2.出口享惠情况 3.种类(单纱、股线、缆线)4.是否供零售用 5.成分含量 6.纱线细度
5512	1.品牌类型 2.出口享惠情况 3.织造方法(机织)4.染整方法(漂白、未漂白、色织、染色等)5.组织结构(平纹、斜纹、缎纹等)6.合成纤维种类(长丝、短纤)7.成分含量 8.幅宽 9.每平方米克重 10.品牌
5513	1.品牌类型 2.出口享惠情况 3.种类(单纱、股线、缆线)4.织造方法(机织)5.染整方法(漂白、未漂白、色织、染色等)6.组织结构(平纹、三线或四线斜纹、四线双面斜纹或十字斜纹、其他斜纹等)7.成分含量 8.幅宽 9.每平方米克重 10.品牌
5514	1.品牌类型 2.出口享惠情况 3.织造方法(机织)4.染整方法(漂白、未漂白、色织、染色等)5.组织结构(平纹、三线或四线斜纹、四线双面斜纹或十字斜纹、其他斜纹等)6.成分含量 7.幅宽 8.每平方米克重 9.品牌
5515	1.品牌类型 2.出口享惠情况 3.织造方法(机织)4.染整方法(漂白、未漂白、色织、染色等)5.组织结构(平纹、斜纹、缎纹等)6.成分含量 7.幅宽 8.每平方米克重 9.品牌
5516	1.品牌类型 2.出口享惠情况 3.织造方法(机织)4.染整方法(漂白、未漂白、色织、染色等)5.组织结构(平纹、斜纹、缎纹等)6.成分含量 7.幅宽 8.每平方米克重 9.品牌
56012	1.品牌类型 2.出口享惠情况 3.纤维成分(如棉制)
56013	1.品牌类型 2.出口享惠情况 3.状态(纤维屑、球结)
5602	1.品牌类型 2.出口享惠情况 3.加工方法(针刺缝编、涂布、浸渍、层压、包覆等)4.纤维成分含量
560311	1.品牌类型 2.出口享惠情况 3.加工方法(涂布、浸渍、层压、包覆等)4.是否化学纤维长丝制 5.每平方米克重 6.成分含量 7.用途
560312	1.品牌类型 2.出口享惠情况 3.加工方法(涂布、浸渍、层压、包覆等)4.是否化学纤维长丝制 5.每平方米克重 6.成分含量 7.用途
560313	1.品牌类型 2.出口享惠情况 3.加工方法(涂布、浸渍、层压、包覆等)4.是否化学纤维长丝制 5.每平方米克重 6.成分含量 7.用途
5603141	1.品牌类型 2.出口享惠情况 3.加工方法(涂布、浸渍、层压、包覆等)4.是否化学纤维长丝制 5.每平方米克重 6.成分含量 7.用途
5603149	1.品牌类型 2.出口享惠情况 3.加工方法 4.化学纤维长丝制应注明 5.每平方米克重 6.成分含量 7.用途
5603911	1.品牌类型 2.出口享惠情况 3.加工方法(涂布、浸渍、层压、包覆等)4.每平方米克重 5.成分含量 6.用途
5603919	1.品牌类型 2.出口享惠情况 3.加工方法 4.每平方米克重 5.成分含量 6.用途
5603921	1.品牌类型 2.出口享惠情况 3.加工方法(涂布、浸渍、层压、包覆等)4.每平方米克重 5.成分含量 6.用途
5603929	1.品牌类型 2.出口享惠情况 3.加工方法 4.每平方米克重 5.成分含量 6.用途
5603931	1.品牌类型 2.出口享惠情况 3.加工方法(涂布、浸渍、层压、包覆等)4.每平方米克重 5.成分含量 6.用途
5603939	1.品牌类型 2.出口享惠情况 3.加工方法 4.每平方米克重 5.成分含量 6.用途
5603941	1.品牌类型 2.出口享惠情况 3.加工方法(涂布、浸渍、层压、包覆等)4.每平方米克重 5.成分含量 6.用途
5603949	1.品牌类型 2.出口享惠情况 3.加工方法 4.每平方米克重 5.成分含量 6.用途
5604	1.品牌类型 2.出口享惠情况 3.加工方法(浸渍、涂布或包覆等)4.内层材质 5.外层材质
5605	1.品牌类型 2.出口享惠情况 3.含金属纱线 4.成分含量
5606	1.品牌类型 2.出口享惠情况 3.种类(绳绒及粗松花线、纵行起圈纱线等)
560721	1.品牌类型 2.出口享惠情况 3.用途(包扎用等)4.纤维成分
560729	1.品牌类型 2.出口享惠情况 3.纤维成分
560741	1.品牌类型 2.出口享惠情况 3.用途(包扎用等)4.纤维成分
560749	1.品牌类型 2.出口享惠情况 3.纤维成分
56075	1.品牌类型 2.出口享惠情况 3.纤维成分 4.是否编织
56079	1.品牌类型 2.出口享惠情况 3.纤维成分

商品编码	申报要素
560811	1.品牌类型 2.出口享惠情况 3.用途(渔网、购物网等)4.纤维成分 5.成网方式(结制)
560819	1.品牌类型 2.出口享惠情况 3.用途(渔网、购物网等)4.纤维成分
56089	1.品牌类型 2.出口享惠情况 3.用途(渔网、购物网等)4.纤维成分
5609	1.品牌类型 2.出口享惠情况 3.用途 4.纤维成分
5701	1.品牌类型 2.出口享惠情况 3.织造方法(栽绒、手织等)4.纤维成分 5.规格尺寸
57021	1.品牌类型 2.出口享惠情况 3.织造方法(机织、手织等)4.纤维成分 5.规格尺寸
57022	1.品牌类型 2.出口享惠情况 3.织造方法(栽绒、手织等)4.纤维成分 5.规格尺寸
57023	1.品牌类型 2.出口享惠情况 3.织造方法(栽绒、手织等)4.纤维成分 5.规格尺寸
57024	1.品牌类型 2.出口享惠情况 3.织造方法(栽绒、手织等)4.纤维成分 5.规格尺寸
57025	1.品牌类型 2.出口享惠情况 3.织造方法(栽绒、手织等)4.纤维成分 5.规格尺寸
57029	1.品牌类型 2.出口享惠情况 3.织造方法(栽绒、手织等)4.纤维成分 5.规格尺寸
5703	1.品牌类型 2.出口享惠情况 3.织造方法(簇绒)4.纤维成分 5.固定方式(施胶、绒头固定方法等)6.规格尺寸
5704	1.品牌类型 2.出口享惠情况 3.织造方法(毡呢)4.纤维成分 5.规格尺寸(最大表面面积)
5705	1.品牌类型 2.出口享惠情况 3.纤维成分 4.是否含有膨润土 5.规格尺寸 6.织造方法(无纺、粘绒、植绒、针织等)7.固定方式(施胶、涂层粘合等)
58011	1.品牌类型 2.出口享惠情况 3.织造方法(机织)4.幅宽 5.纤维成分
580121	1.品牌类型 2.出口享惠情况 3.织造方法(机织)4.起绒方式(经起绒、纬起绒或绳绒)5.幅宽 6.纤维成分
580122	1.品牌类型 2.出口享惠情况 3.织造方法(机织)4.割绒请注明 5.幅宽 6.纤维成分
580123	1.品牌类型 2.出口享惠情况 3.织造方法(机织)4.起绒方式(经起绒、纬起绒或绳绒)5.幅宽 6.纤维成分
580126	1.品牌类型 2.出口享惠情况 3.织造方法(机织)4.起绒方式(经起绒、纬起绒或绳绒)5.幅宽 6.纤维成分
5801271	1.品牌类型 2.出口享惠情况 3.织造方法(机织)4.起绒方式(经起绒、纬起绒或绳绒)5.幅宽 6.纤维成分
5801272	1.品牌类型 2.出口享惠情况 3.织造方法(机织)4.起绒方式(经起绒、纬起绒或绳绒)5.是否为割绒 6.幅宽 7.纤维成分
580131	1.品牌类型 2.出口享惠情况 3.织造方法(机织)4.起绒方式(经起绒、纬起绒或绳绒)5.幅宽 6.纤维成分
580132	1.品牌类型 2.出口享惠情况 3.织造方法(机织)4.起绒方式(经起绒、纬起绒或绳绒)5.是否为割绒 6.幅宽 7.纤维成分
580133	1.品牌类型 2.出口享惠情况 3.织造方法(机织)4.起绒方式(经起绒、纬起绒或绳绒)5.幅宽 6.纤维成分
580136	1.品牌类型 2.出口享惠情况 3.织造方法(机织)4.起绒方式(经起绒、纬起绒或绳绒)5.幅宽 6.纤维成分
5801371	1.品牌类型 2.出口享惠情况 3.织造方法(机织)4.起绒方式(经起绒、纬起绒或绳绒)5.幅宽 6.纤维成分
5801372	1.品牌类型 2.出口享惠情况 3.织造方法(机织)4.起绒方式(经起绒、纬起绒或绳绒)5.是否为割绒 6.幅宽 7.纤维成分
5801901	1.品牌类型 2.出口享惠情况 3.织造方法(机织)4.幅宽 5.纤维成分
5801909	1.品牌类型 2.出口享惠情况 3.织造方法(机织)4.起绒方式(经起绒、纬起绒或绳绒)5.幅宽 6.纤维成分
580211	1.品牌类型 2.出口享惠情况 3.织造方法(机织)4.起绒方式(簇绒或毛圈)5.是否漂白 6.幅宽 7.纤维成分
580219	1.品牌类型 2.出口享惠情况 3.织造方法(机织)4.起绒方式(簇绒或毛圈)5.幅宽 6.纤维成分
58022	1.品牌类型 2.出口享惠情况 3.织造方法(机织)4.起绒方式(簇绒或毛圈)5.幅宽 6.纤维成分
58023	1.品牌类型 2.出口享惠情况 3.织造方法(机织)4.起绒方式(簇绒或毛圈)5.幅宽 6.纤维成分
5803	1.品牌类型 2.出口享惠情况 3.组织结构(纱罗)4.幅宽 5.纤维成分
5804	1.品牌类型 2.出口享惠情况 3.种类(网眼、花边)4.织造方法(机制、手工制)5.幅宽 6.纤维成分
5805	1.品牌类型 2.出口享惠情况 3.用途(装饰用)4.种类(手工针绣嵌花装饰毯等)5.幅宽 6.纤维成分
58061	1.品牌类型 2.出口享惠情况 3.织造方法(机织)4.起绒方式(毛巾、绳绒等)5.成分含量 6.幅宽
58062	1.品牌类型 2.出口享惠情况 3.织造方法(机织)4.成分含量 5.幅宽
58063	1.品牌类型 2.出口享惠情况 3.织造方法(机织)4.成分含量 5.幅宽
58064	1.品牌类型 2.出口享惠情况 3.织造方法(机织)4.成分含量 5.幅宽
5807	1.品牌类型 2.出口享惠情况 3.织造方法(机织、针织等)4.成分含量 5.幅宽 6.刺绣请注明
5808	1.品牌类型 2.出口享惠情况 3.规格(成匹)4.幅宽 5.成分含量
5809	1.品牌类型 2.出口享惠情况 3.用途(衣着、装饰等)4.织造方法(金属线或含金属纱线机织)5.幅宽 6.成分含量
5810	1.品牌类型 2.出口享惠情况 3.织造方法(刺绣)4.是否见底布 5.成分含量
5811	1.品牌类型 2.出口享惠情况 3.表面成分含量 4.胎料材质
5901	1.品牌类型 2.出口享惠情况 3.用途 4.处理材质 5.成分含量 6.处理工艺(涂布、浸渍、层压)
5902	1.品牌类型 2.出口享惠情况 3.成分含量 4.是否高强力纱制
5903	1.品牌类型 2.出口享惠情况 3.处理材质 4.成分含量 5.处理工艺(涂布、浸渍、层压)6.是否双面涂层或包覆
5904	1.品牌类型 2.出口享惠情况
5905	1.品牌类型 2.出口享惠情况 3.是否糊墙用 4.是否为纸衬背 5.表面层纤维成分含量 6.幅宽
59061	1.品牌类型 2.出口享惠情况 3.织造方法(机织、针织、钩编等)4.处理材料(橡胶)5.是否是胶粘带、绝缘带 6.幅宽
590691	1.品牌类型 2.出口享惠情况 3.织造方法(机织、针织、钩编等)4.处理材料(橡胶)5.幅宽
5906991	1.品牌类型 2.出口享惠情况 3.织造方法(机织、针织、钩编等)4.处理材料(橡胶)5.是否是胶粘带、绝缘带 6.幅宽
5906999	1.品牌类型 2.出口享惠情况 3.织造方法(机织、针织、钩编等)4.处理材料(橡胶)5.幅宽
5907001	1.品牌类型 2.出口享惠情况 3.处理材料 4.是否为绝缘带
5907002	1.品牌类型 2.出口享惠情况 3.是否为已绘制画布 4.处理材料
5907009	1.品牌类型 2.出口享惠情况 3.处理材料
5908	1.品牌类型 2.出口享惠情况 3.用途
5909	1.品牌类型 2.出口享惠情况 3.纤维成分
5910	1.品牌类型 2.出口享惠情况 3.纤维成分 4.厚度
59111	1.品牌类型 2.出口享惠情况 3.用途 4.成分含量
59112	1.品牌类型 2.出口享惠情况 3.成分含量
59113	1.品牌类型 2.出口享惠情况 3.用途 4.是否为环状或有联接装置的纺织物或毡呢 5.每平方米克重 6.成分含量
59114	1.品牌类型 2.出口享惠情况 3.用途 4.成分含量
59119	1.品牌类型 2.出口享惠情况 3.用途(如半导体晶圆制造用等)4.若为半导体晶圆制造用需注明是否为自粘式和是否为圆形 5.成分含量
60011	1.品牌类型 2.出口享惠情况 3.织造方法(针织或钩编)4.起绒方法(毛圈或长毛绒)5.幅宽 6.纤维成分含量
60012	1.品牌类型 2.出口享惠情况 3.织造方法(针织或钩编)4.起绒方法(毛圈或长毛绒)5.幅宽 6.纤维成分含量
60019	1.品牌类型 2.出口享惠情况 3.织造方法(针织或钩编)4.幅宽 5.纤维成分含量
6002	1.品牌类型 2.出口享惠情况 3.织造方法(针织或钩编)4.是否含橡胶线 5.成分含量 6.幅宽
6003	1.品牌类型 2.出口享惠情况 3.织造方法(针织或钩编)4.成分含量 5.幅宽
6004	1.品牌类型 2.出口享惠情况 3.织造方法(针织或钩编)4.是否含橡胶线 5.成分含量 6.幅宽
6005	1.品牌类型 2.出口享惠情况 3.织造方法(针织、经编)4.染整方法(色织、染色、漂白等)5.成分含量 6.幅宽
6006	1.品牌类型 2.出口享惠情况 3.织造方法(针织或钩编)4.染整方法(色织、染色、漂白等)5.成分含量 6.幅宽
6101	1.品牌类型 2.出口享惠情况 3.织造方法(针织或钩编)4.种类(防风大衣、短大衣、斗篷等)5.类别(男式)6.成分含量 7.品牌(中文及外文名称)8.货号
6102	1.品牌类型 2.出口享惠情况 3.织造方法(针织或钩编)4.种类(防风大衣、短大衣、斗篷等)5.类别(女式)6.成分含量 7.品牌(中文及外文名称)8.货号
61031	1.品牌类型 2.出口享惠情况 3.织造方法(针织或钩编)4.种类(西服、便服套装、上衣、长裤、马裤、工装裤等)5.类别(男式)6.成分含量 7.品牌(中文及外文名称)8.货号 9.套装组成及数量
61032	1.品牌类型 2.出口享惠情况 3.织造方法(针织或钩编)4.种类(西服、便服套装、上衣、长裤、马裤、工装裤等)5.类别(男式)6.成分含量 7.品牌(中文及外文名称)8.货号 9.套装组成及数量
61033	1.品牌类型 2.出口享惠情况 3.织造方法(针织或钩编)4.种类(西服、便服套装、上衣、长裤、马裤、工装裤等)5.类别(男式)6.成分含量 7.是否全开襟 8.是否有扣 9.是否有拉链 10.品牌(中文及外文名称)11.货号

商品编码	申报要素
61034	1.品牌类型 2.出口享惠情况 3.织造方法(针织或钩编)4.种类(西服、便服套装、上衣、长裤、马裤、工装裤等)5.类别(男式)6.成分含量 7.品牌(中文及外文名称)8.货号
61041	1.品牌类型 2.出口享惠情况 3.织造方法(针织或钩编)4.种类(西服、便服套装、上衣、长裤、马裤、工装裤等)5.类别(女式)6.成分含量 7.品牌(中文及外文名称)8.货号 9.套装组成及数量
61042	1.品牌类型 2.出口享惠情况 3.织造方法(针织或钩编)4.种类(西服、便服套装、上衣、长裤、马裤、工装裤等)5.类别(女式)6.成分含量 7.品牌(中文及外文名称)8.货号 9.套装组成及数量
610431	1.品牌类型 2.出口享惠情况 3.织造方法(针织或钩编)4.种类(西服、便服套装、上衣、长裤、马裤、工装裤等)5.类别(女式)6.成分含量 7.是否开襟 8.是否有扣 9.是否有拉链 10.品牌(中文及外文名称)11.货号
610432	1.品牌类型 2.出口享惠情况 3.织造方法(针织或钩编)4.种类(西服、便服套装、上衣、长裤、马裤、工装裤等)5.类别(女式)6.成分含量 7.是否开襟 8.是否有扣 9.是否有拉链 10.品牌(中文及外文名称)11.货号
610433	1.品牌类型 2.出口享惠情况 3.织造方法(针织或钩编)4.种类(西服、便服套装、上衣、长裤、马裤、工装裤等)5.类别(女式)6.成分含量 7.是否开襟 8.是否有扣 9.是否有拉链 10.品牌(中文及外文名称)11.货号
610439	1.品牌类型 2.出口享惠情况 3.织造方法(针织或钩编)4.种类(西服、便服套装、上衣、长裤、马裤、工装裤等)5.类别(女式)6.成分含量 7.是否开襟 8.是否有扣 9.是否有拉链 10.品牌(中文及外文名称)11.货号
61044	1.品牌类型 2.出口享惠情况 3.织造方法(针织或钩编)4.种类(西服、便服套装、上衣、长裤、马裤、工装裤等)5.类别(女式)6.成分含量 7.品牌(中文及外文名称)8.货号
61045	1.品牌类型 2.出口享惠情况 3.织造方法(针织或钩编)4.种类(西服、便服套装、上衣、长裤、马裤、工装裤等)5.类别(女式)6.成分含量 7.品牌(中文及外文名称)8.货号
61046	1.品牌类型 2.出口享惠情况 3.织造方法(针织或钩编)4.种类(西服、便服套装、上衣、长裤、马裤、工装裤等)5.类别(女式)6.成分含量 7.品牌(中文及外文名称)8.货号
6105	1.品牌类型 2.出口享惠情况 3.织造方法(针织或钩编)4.种类(衬衫、POLO 衫等)5.类别(男式)6.成分含量 7.品牌(中文及外文名称)8.货号
6106	1.品牌类型 2.出口享惠情况 3.织造方法(针织或钩编)4.种类(衬衫、POLO 衫等)5.类别(女式)6.成分含量 7.品牌(中文及外文名称)8.货号
6107	1.品牌类型 2.出口享惠情况 3.织造方法(针织或钩编)4.种类(内衣、内裤等)5.类别(男式)6.成分含量 7.品牌(中文及外文名称)8.货号
6108	1.品牌类型 2.出口享惠情况 3.织造方法(针织或钩编)4.种类(内衣、内裤等)5.类别(女式)6.成分含量 7.品牌(中文及外文名称)8.货号
6109	1.品牌类型 2.出口享惠情况 3.织造方法(针织或钩编)4.种类(T 恤衫、汗衫等)5.如为 T 恤衫,请申报是否有领、是否有扣、是否有拉链 6.成分含量 7.品牌(中文及外文名称)8.货号
6110	1.品牌类型 2.出口享惠情况 3.织造方法(针织、钩编,是否为起绒)4.种类(套头衫、开襟衫、背心等)5.成分含量 6.品牌(中文及外文名称)7.货号
6111	1.品牌类型 2.出口享惠情况 3.织造方法(针织或钩编)4.种类(外衣、雨衣等)5.类别(婴儿)6.成分含量 7.尺寸(衣长及裤长)8.品牌(中文及外文名称)9.货号
6112	1.品牌类型 2.出口享惠情况 3.织造方法(针织或钩编)4.种类(运动套装、运动装、滑雪服、游泳服)5.类别(男式、女式)6.成分含量 7.品牌(中文及外文名称)8.货号 9.套装组成及数
6113	1.品牌类型 2.出口享惠情况 3.织造方法(针织或钩编)4.处理材料(塑料、橡胶)5.品牌(中文及外文名称)6.货号
6114	1.品牌类型 2.出口享惠情况 3.织造方法(针织或钩编)4.种类(连身衣、夏服、水洗服、无袖罩衫等)5.类别(男式、女式、儿童)6.成分含量 7.品牌(中文及外文名称)8.货号
61151	1.品牌类型 2.出口享惠情况 3.织造方法(针织或钩编)4.用途 5.品牌(中文及外文名称)6.货号
611521	1.品牌类型 2.出口享惠情况 3.织造方法(针织或钩编)4.种类(连裤袜、统袜、矫正袜)5.成分含量 6.单丝细度 7.品牌(中文及外文名称)8.货号
611522	1.品牌类型 2.出口享惠情况 3.织造方法(针织或钩编)4.种类(连裤袜、统袜、矫正袜)5.成分含量 6.单丝细度 7.品牌(中文及外文名称)8.货号
611529	1.品牌类型 2.出口享惠情况 3.织造方法(针织或钩编)4.种类(连裤袜、统袜、矫正袜)5.成分含量 6.品牌(中文及外文名称)7.货号
61153	1.品牌类型 2.出口享惠情况 3.织造方法(针织或钩编)4.种类(连裤袜、统袜、矫正袜)5.类别(女式)6.是否为女士统袜 7.成分含量 8.单丝细度 9.品牌(中文及外文名称)10.货号
611594	1.品牌类型 2.出口享惠情况 3.织造方法(针织或钩编)4.种类(连裤袜、统袜、矫正袜)5.成分含量 6.单丝细度 7.品牌(中文及外文名称)8.货号
611595	1.品牌类型 2.出口享惠情况 3.织造方法(针织或钩编)4.种类(连裤袜、统袜、矫正袜)5.成分含量 6.单丝细度 7.品牌(中文及外文名称)8.货号
611596	1.品牌类型 2.出口享惠情况 3.织造方法(针织或钩编)4.种类(连裤袜、统袜、矫正袜)5.类别(男式、女式)6.是否为女士统袜 7.成分含量 8.单丝细度 9.品牌(中文及外文名称)10.货号
611599	1.品牌类型 2.出口享惠情况 3.织造方法(针织或钩编)4.种类(连裤袜、统袜、矫正袜)5.类别(男式、女式)6.是否为女士统袜 7.成分含量 8.单丝细度 9.品牌(中文及外文名称)10.货号
61161	1.品牌类型 2.出口享惠情况 3.织造方法(针织或钩编)4.处理材料(塑料、橡胶)5.成分含量 6.品牌(中文及外文名称)7.货号
61169	1.品牌类型 2.出口享惠情况 3.织造方法(针织或钩编)4.成分含量 5.品牌(中文及外文名称)6.货号
61171	1.品牌类型 2.出口享惠情况 3.织造方法(针织或钩编)4.成分含量 5.品牌(中文及外文名称)6.货号
61178	1.品牌类型 2.出口享惠情况 3.织造方法(针织或钩编)4.成分含量 5.品牌(中文及外文名称)
61179	1.品牌类型 2.出口享惠情况 3.织造方法(针织或钩编)4.成分含量
62011	1.品牌类型 2.出口享惠情况 3.织造方法(机织等)4.种类(大衣、雨衣、短大衣、斗篷、短斗篷及类似品)5.类别(男式)6.面料成分含量 7.填充物成分含量 8.品牌(中文及外文名称)9.货号
62019	1.品牌类型 2.出口享惠情况 3.织造方法(机织等)4.种类(带风帽的防寒短上衣(包括滑雪短上衣)、防风衣、防风短上衣及类似品)5.类别(男式)6.面料成分含量 7.填充物成分含量 8.品牌(中文及外文名称)9.货号
62021	1.品牌类型 2.出口享惠情况 3.织造方法(机织等)4.种类(大衣、雨衣、短大衣、斗篷、短斗篷及类似品)5.类别(女式)6.面料成分含量 7.填充物成分含量 8.品牌(中文及外文名称)9.货号
62029	1.品牌类型 2.出口享惠情况 3.织造方法(机织等)4.种类(带风帽的防寒短上衣(包括滑雪短上衣)、防风衣、防风短上衣及类似品)5.类别(女式)6.面料成分含量 7.填充物成分含量 8.品牌(中文及外文名称)9.货号
62031	1.品牌类型 2.出口享惠情况 3.织造方法(机织等)4.种类(西服、便服套装、上衣、长裤、马裤、工装裤等)5.类别(男式)6.成分含量 7.品牌(中文及外文名称)8.货号 9.套装组成及数
62032	1.品牌类型 2.出口享惠情况 3.织造方法(机织等)4.种类(西服、便服套装、上衣、长裤、马裤、工装裤等)5.类别(男式)6.成分含量 7.品牌(中文及外文名称)8.货号 9.套装组成及数
620331	1.品牌类型 2.出口享惠情况 3.织造方法(机织等)4.种类(西服、便服套装、上衣、长裤、马裤、工装裤等)5.类别(男式)6.成分含量 7.是否开襟 8.是否有扣 9.是否有拉链 10.品牌(中文及外文名称)11.货号
620332	1.品牌类型 2.出口享惠情况 3.织造方法(机织等)4.种类(西服、便服套装、上衣、长裤、马裤、工装裤等)5.类别(男式)6.成分含量 7.是否开襟 8.是否有扣 9.是否有拉链 10.品牌(中文及外文名称)11.货号
620333	1.品牌类型 2.出口享惠情况 3.织造方法(机织等)4.种类(西服、便服套装、上衣、长裤、马裤、工装裤等)5.类别(男式)6.成分含量 7.是否开襟 8.是否有扣 9.是否有拉链 10.品牌(中文及外文名称)11.货号
620339	1.品牌类型 2.出口享惠情况 3.织造方法(机织等)4.种类(西服、便服套装、上衣、长裤、马裤、工装裤等)5.类别(男式)6.成分含量 7.是否开襟 8.是否有扣 9.是否有拉链 10.品牌(中文及外文名称)11.货号
62034	1.品牌类型 2.出口享惠情况 3.织造方法(机织等)4.种类(西服、便服套装、上衣、长裤、马裤、工装裤等)5.类别(男式)6.成分含量 7.品牌(中文及外文名称)8.货号
62041	1.品牌类型 2.出口享惠情况 3.织造方法(机织等)4.种类(西服、便服套装、上衣、长裤、马裤、工装裤等)5.类别(女式)6.成分含量 7.品牌(中文及外文名称)8.货号 9.套装组成及数量
62042	1.品牌类型 2.出口享惠情况 3.织造方法(机织等)4.种类(西服、便服套装、上衣、长裤、马裤、工装裤等)5.类别(女式)6.成分含量 7.品牌(中文及外文名称)8.货号 9.套装组成及数量
62043	1.品牌类型 2.出口享惠情况 3.织造方法(机织等)4.种类(西服、便服套装、上衣、长裤、马裤、工装裤等)5.类别(女式)6.成分含量 7.是否全开襟 8.是否有扣 9.是否有拉链 10.品牌(中文及外文名称)11.货号

商品编码	申报要素
62044	1.品牌类型 2.出口享惠情况 3.织造方法(机织等)4.种类(西服、便服套装、上衣、长裤、马裤、工装裤等)5.类别(女式)6.成分含量 7.品牌(中文及外文名称)8.货号
62045	1.品牌类型 2.出口享惠情况 3.织造方法(机织等)4.种类(西服、便服套装、上衣、长裤、马裤、工装裤等)5.类别(女式)6.成分含量 7.品牌(中文及外文名称)8.货号
62046	1.品牌类型 2.出口享惠情况 3.织造方法(机织等)4.种类(西服、便服套装、上衣、长裤、马裤、工装裤等)5.类别(女式)6.成分含量 7.品牌(中文及外文名称)8.货号
6205	1.品牌类型 2.出口享惠情况 3.织造方法(机织等)4.种类(衬衫、POLO衫等)5.类别(男式)6.成分含量 7.如为T恤衫,请申报是否有领、是否有扣、是否有拉链 8.品牌(中文及外文名称)9.货号
6206	1.品牌类型 2.出口享惠情况 3.织造方法(机织等)4.种类(衬衫、POLO衫等)5.类别(女式)6.成分含量 7.如为T恤衫,请申报是否有领、是否有扣、是否有拉链 8.品牌(中文及外文名称)9.货号
6207	1.品牌类型 2.出口享惠情况 3.织造方法(机织等)4.种类(内衣、内裤等)5.类别(男式)6.成分含量 7.品牌(中文及外文名称)8.货号
6208	1.品牌类型 2.出口享惠情况 3.织造方法(机织等)4.种类(内衣、内裤等)5.类别(女式)6.成分含量 7.品牌(中文及外文名称)8.货号
6209	1.品牌类型 2.出口享惠情况 3.织造方法(机织等)4.种类(外衣、雨衣等)5.类别(婴儿)6.成分含量 7.尺寸(衣长及裤长)8.品牌(中文及外文名称)9.货号
62101	1.品牌类型 2.出口享惠情况 3.织造方法(机织等)4.种类(上衣、长裤、短裤等)5.类别(男式、女式)6.成分含量 7.品牌(中文及外文名称)8.货号
62102	1.品牌类型 2.出口享惠情况 3.织造方法(机织等)4.种类(上衣、长裤、短裤等)5.类别(男式、女式)6.处理材料(塑料、橡胶)7.成分含量 8.品牌(中文及外文名称)9.货号
62103	1.品牌类型 2.出口享惠情况 3.织造方法(机织等)4.种类(上衣、长裤、短裤等)5.类别(男式、女式)6.处理材料(塑料、橡胶)7.成分含量 8.品牌(中文及外文名称)9.货号
62104	1.品牌类型 2.出口享惠情况 3.织造方法(机织等)4.种类(上衣、长裤、短裤等)5.类别(男式)6.处理材料(塑料、橡胶)7.成分含量 8.品牌(中文及外文名称)9.货号
62105	1.品牌类型 2.出口享惠情况 3.织造方法(机织等)4.种类(上衣、长裤、短裤等)5.类别(女式)6.处理材料(塑料、橡胶)7.成分含量 8.品牌(中文及外文名称)9.货号
6211	1.品牌类型 2.出口享惠情况 3.织造方法(机织等)4.种类(连身衣、夏服、水洗服、无袖罩衫等)5.类别(男式、女式、儿童)6.成分含量 7.品牌(中文及外文名称)8.货号 9.若为套装申报组成及数量
6212	1.品牌类型 2.出口享惠情况 3.种类(胸罩、腹带、束腰胸衣、吊袜带、吊裤带等)4.成分含量 5.品牌(中文及外文名称)6.货号
6213	1.品牌类型 2.出口享惠情况 3.织造方法(机织、刺绣、非刺绣)4.成分含量 5.尺寸 6.品牌(中文及外文名称)7.货号
6214	1.品牌类型 2.出口享惠情况 3.织造方法(机织等)4.成分含量 5.品牌(中文及外文名称)6.货号
6215	1.品牌类型 2.出口享惠情况 3.织造方法(机织等)4.成分含量 5.品牌(中文及外文名称)6.货号
6216	1.品牌类型 2.出口享惠情况 3.织造方法(机织等)4.是否浸渍(塑料或橡胶)5.是否为运动手套 6.成分含量 7.品牌(中文及外文名称)8.货号
6217	1.品牌类型 2.出口享惠情况 3.成分含量 4.织造方法 5.品牌(中文及外文名称)6.货号
6301	1.品牌类型 2.出口享惠情况 3.种类(毯子、旅行毯、电暖毯)4.成分含量
6302	1.品牌类型 2.出口享惠情况 3.用途(床上用品、餐桌用、盥洗用、厨房用)4.织造方法(针织、钩编、机织是否印花、刺绣、毛圈等,针织或钩编需说明是否手工制)5.成分含量
6303	1.品牌类型 2.出口享惠情况 3.种类(窗帘、帘帷、帐幔、床帷)4.织造方法(针织、钩编、机织等)5.成分含量
63041	1.品牌类型 2.出口享惠情况 3.织造方法(针织、钩编、机织、手工、刺绣等)4.成分含量
63042	1.品牌类型 2.出口享惠情况 3.是否装饰用 4.织造方法(针织、钩编、机织、手工、刺绣等)5.成分含量 6.是否以以下物质浸渍或涂层【a一氯氰菊酯(ISO),虫螨腈(ISO),溴氰菊酯(INN,ISO),高效氯氟氰菊酯(ISO),除虫菊酯(ISO),甲基嘧啶磷(ISO)】
63049	1.品牌类型 2.出口享惠情况 3.是否装饰用 4.织造方法(针织、钩编、机织、手工、刺绣等)5.成分含量
6305	1.品牌类型 2.出口享惠情况 3.用途(储运袋、茶包等)4.成分含量
6306	1.品牌类型 2.出口享惠情况 3.种类(油苫布、天蓬、遮阳蓬、风帆、野营用品)4.成分含量
63071	1.品牌类型 2.出口享惠情况 3.成分含量 4.是否清洁剂浸渍、涂布或包覆 5.功能用途
63072	1.品牌类型 2.出口享惠情况 3.成分含量
63079	1.品牌类型 2.出口享惠情况 3.成分含量
6308	1.品牌类型 2.出口享惠情况 3.是否为零售包装 4.是否为制成品(制成品,非制成品)
6309	1.品牌类型 2.出口享惠情况 3.是否为旧
6310	1.品牌类型 2.出口享惠情况 3.是否经分拣 4.成分含量 5.颜色(如白色或杂色)
64011	1.品牌类型 2.出口享惠情况 3.款式(高统、装金属护头等)4.鞋面材料 5.鞋底材料 6.品牌(中文及外文名称)7.货号
64019	1.品牌类型 2.出口享惠情况 3.款式(未过踝、过膝、过踝但未到膝)4.鞋面材料 5.鞋底材料 6.品牌(中文及外文名称)7.货号
64021	1.品牌类型 2.出口享惠情况 3.款式(是否过踝)4.鞋面材料 5.鞋底材料 6.品牌(中文及外文名称)7.货号
64022	1.品牌类型 2.出口享惠情况 3.款式(人字拖等)4.鞋面材料 5.鞋底材料 6.请注明是否栓塞制 7.品牌(中文及外文名称)8.货号
64029	1.品牌类型 2.出口享惠情况 3.款式(是否过踝)4.鞋面材料 5.鞋底材料 6.品牌(中文及外文名称)7.货号
64031	1.品牌类型 2.出口享惠情况 3.款式(滑冰靴、滑雪靴、拳击靴等)4.鞋面材料 5.鞋底材料 6.品牌(中文及外文名称)7.货号
64032	1.品牌类型 2.出口享惠情况 3.款式 4.鞋面材料 5.鞋底材料 6.品牌(中文及外文名称)7.货号
64034	1.品牌类型 2.出口享惠情况 3.款式(装金属护头等)4.鞋面材料 5.鞋底材料 6.品牌(中文及外文名称)7.货号
64035	1.品牌类型 2.出口享惠情况 3.款式(是否过踝或过小腿)4.鞋面材料 5.鞋底材料 6.内底长度 7.品牌(中文及外文名称)8.货号
64039	1.品牌类型 2.出口享惠情况 3.款式(未过踝、过膝、过踝但未过膝)4.鞋面材料 5.鞋底材料 6.内底长度 7.品牌(中文及外文名称)8.货号
6404	1.品牌类型 2.出口享惠情况 3.款式 4.鞋面材料 5.鞋底材料 6.品牌(中文及外文名称)7.货号
6405	1.品牌类型 2.出口享惠情况 3.款式 4.鞋面材料 5.鞋底材料 6.品牌(中文及外文名称)7.货号
6406	1.品牌类型 2.出口享惠情况 3.材质 4.加工程度(是否已成型)5.用途
6501	1.品牌类型 2.出口享惠情况 3.材质(毡呢)4.品牌(中文及外文名称)
6502	1.品牌类型 2.出口享惠情况 3.材质 4.制作工艺(编结、拼制)5.品牌(中文及外文名称)
6504	1.品牌类型 2.出口享惠情况 3.制作工艺(编结、拼制)4.品牌(中文及外文名称)
6505001	1.品牌类型 2.出口享惠情况 3.品牌
6505002	1.品牌类型 2.出口享惠情况 3.制作工艺(是否钩编)4.品牌(中文及外文名称)
65050091	1.品牌类型 2.出口享惠情况 3.材质(毡呢)4.品牌(中文及外文名称)
65050099	1.品牌类型 2.出口享惠情况 3.制作工艺(针织、机织等)4.品牌(中文及外文名称)
65061	1.品牌类型 2.出口享惠情况 3.材质 4.用途 5.是否带有能滤除生物因子滤器的面罩 6.品牌(中文及外文名称)
65069	1.品牌类型 2.出口享惠情况 3.材质 4.品牌(中文及外文名称)
6507	1.品牌类型 2.出口享惠情况 3.材质
6601	1.品牌类型 2.出口享惠情况 3.种类或用途 4.品牌(中文及外文名称)
6602	1.品牌类型 2.出口享惠情况 3.材质 4.品牌(中文及外文名称)
6603	1.品牌类型 2.出口享惠情况 3.材质
6701	1.品牌类型 2.出口享惠情况 3.是否濒危物种
6702	1.品牌类型 2.出口享惠情况 3.制作材料(塑料丝等)
6703	1.品牌类型 2.出口享惠情况 3.加工程度(经梳理、脱色等)4.制作材料 5.长度(英寸)
6704	1.品牌类型 2.出口享惠情况 3.制作材料 4.如为人发制请申报长度(英寸)
6801	1.品牌类型 2.出口享惠情况 3.种类(长方砌石、扁平石、路缘石)4.材质
6802	1.品牌类型 2.出口享惠情况 3.用途(用于建筑可直接使用)4.材质(大理石、花岗岩)5.加工程度(切、锯、抛光及是否石刻等)6.尺寸(最大表面积的最大边长)7.花色品种的中英文名称
6803	1.品牌类型 2.出口享惠情况 3.加工程度 4.材质
68041	1.品牌类型 2.出口享惠情况 3.用途(碾磨或磨浆、磨光用等)4.材质(石料、粘聚合成料等)5.是否装支架
68042	1.品牌类型 2.出口享惠情况 3.用途(碾磨或磨浆、磨光用等)4.材质(石料、粘聚合成料等)5.是否装支架 6.品牌
6804301	1.品牌类型 2.出口享惠情况 3.用途(碾磨或磨浆、磨光用等)4.材质(石料、粘聚合成料等)5.是否装支架
6804309	1.品牌类型 2.出口享惠情况 3.用途(碾磨或磨浆、磨光用等)4.材质(石料、粘聚合成料等)5.是否装支架

商品编码	申报要素
6805	1.品牌类型 2.出口享惠情况 3.基底材质 4.砂粒材质 5.是否有涂层（如有，请申报材质）6.品牌 7.型号 8.尺寸
68061	1.品牌类型 2.出口享惠情况 3.材质（矿物纤维等）4.形状 5.含有石棉纤维的要注明其含量
68062	1.品牌类型 2.出口享惠情况 3.材质（页状蛭石、膨胀黏土、泡沫矿渣等）4.形状 5.含有石棉纤维的要注明其含量
68069	1.品牌类型 2.出口享惠情况 3.材质 4.形状 5.含有石棉纤维的要注明其含量
6807	1.品牌类型 2.出口享惠情况 3.形状
6808	1.品牌类型 2.出口享惠情况 3.种类（镶板、平板瓦、砖等）4.原料（稻草、刨花等）5.粘料（水泥、石膏等矿物性黏合材料）
6809	1.品牌类型 2.出口享惠情况 3.加工方法（是否装饰、经贴面或加强等）4.是否未经装饰，仅用纸或纸板贴面或加强的 5.成分含量
6810	1.品牌类型 2.出口享惠情况 3.用途（铁道用等）4.种类（砖、瓦、管及建筑构件钢筋混凝土板等）5.材料（水泥、混凝土、人造石）
6811	1.品牌类型 2.出口享惠情况 3.种类（砖、瓦、管、板等）4.材料（石棉水泥、纤维素水泥等）
6812	1.品牌类型 2.出口享惠情况 3.种类（纱线、机织物、服装、鞋帽、衬垫等）4.材料（青石棉、其他石棉、石棉纤维）
6813	1.品牌类型 2.出口享惠情况 3.材质 4.种类（片、卷、带、闸衬、闸垫、扇形等）
6814	1.品牌类型 2.出口享惠情况 3.材质（云母）4.形状（板、片、带等）5.是否粘聚或复制的
68151	1.品牌类型 2.出口享惠情况 3.材质 4.用途
68152	1.品牌类型 2.出口享惠情况 3.材质
681591	1.品牌类型 2.出口享惠情况 3.材质
6815992	1.品牌类型 2.出口享惠情况 3.材质
68159931	1.品牌类型 2.出口享惠情况 3.材质
68159932	1.品牌类型 2.出口享惠情况 3.材质
68159939	1.品牌类型 2.出口享惠情况 3.材质 4.碳纤维纱线请注明碳含量、比模量和比极限抗拉强度
6815994	1.品牌类型 2.出口享惠情况 3.材质
6815999	1.品牌类型 2.出口享惠情况 3.材质
6901	1.品牌类型 2.出口享惠情况 3.材质（硅质化石粉、硅藻土或类似硅土等）4.种类（砖、瓦等）
6902	1.品牌类型 2.出口享惠情况 3.种类（耐火砖、瓦、块等）4.成分含量 5.耐火温度
6903	1.品牌类型 2.出口享惠情况 3.种类（坩埚、支架、马弗罩等）4.成分含量 5.耐火温度
6904	1.品牌类型 2.出口享惠情况 3.种类（建筑用砖、地面砖等）4.品牌
6905	1.品牌类型 2.出口享惠情况 3.种类（屋顶瓦、烟囱罩等）
6906	1.品牌类型 2.出口享惠情况 3.种类（套管、导管、槽管等）
6907	1.品牌类型 2.出口享惠情况 3.种类（贴面砖、铺面砖、马赛克等）4.尺寸（最大表面积的最大边长）5.按重量计吸水率 6.品牌 7.颜色
6909	1.品牌类型 2.出口享惠情况 3.用途（实验室用、化学、农业用等）4.种类（瓷制、陶制）5.莫氏硬度
6910	1.品牌类型 2.出口享惠情况 3.材质（瓷制、陶制）4.品牌 5.规格型号
6911101	1.品牌类型 2.出口享惠情况 3.材质（瓷制、陶制）4.种类（餐具、厨房器具等）5.是否为骨瓷 6.品牌
6911102	1.品牌类型 2.出口享惠情况 3.材质（瓷制、陶制）4.种类（餐具、厨房器具等）5.品牌
69119	1.品牌类型 2.出口享惠情况 3.材质（瓷制、陶制）4.种类（餐具、厨房器具等）5.品牌
6912	1.品牌类型 2.出口享惠情况 3.材质（瓷制、陶制）4.种类（餐具、厨房器具等）5.品牌
6913	1.品牌类型 2.出口享惠情况 3.材质（瓷制、陶制）4.用途
6914	1.品牌类型 2.出口享惠情况 3.材质（瓷制、陶制）4.用途
7001	1.品牌类型 2.出口享惠情况 3.用途 4.状态（废、碎、块料）
70021	1.品牌类型 2.出口享惠情况 3.用途 4.直径
7002201	1.品牌类型 2.出口享惠情况 3.用途（光导纤维预制棒等）4.直径 5.品牌 6.进口状态（芯棒或成品预制棒）7.种类（单模、多模、特种预制棒等）
7002209	1.品牌类型 2.出口享惠情况 3.用途
700231	1.品牌类型 2.出口享惠情况 3.用途（光导纤维用、光通信用等）4.材质（熔融石英、熔融硅石等）5.级别（波导级）6.外径
700232	1.品牌类型 2.出口享惠情况 3.用途（光导纤维用、光通信用等）4.材质（熔融石英、熔融硅石等）5.线膨胀系数 6.级别（波导级）7.外径
700239	1.品牌类型 2.出口享惠情况 3.用途（光导纤维用、光通信用等）4.材质（熔融石英、熔融硅石等）5.线膨胀系数 6.级别（波导级）7.外径
700312	1.品牌类型 2.出口享惠情况 3.用途 4.加工方法（整块着色、具有吸收层等）5.状态（是否夹丝）6.形状（板、片、型材、异型材）7.工艺（铸制或轧制）8.品牌（生产厂家）9.型号 10.规格尺寸（长×宽×厚）
700319	1.品牌类型 2.出口享惠情况 3.用途 4.状态（是否夹丝）5.形状（板、片、型材、异型材）6.工艺（铸制或轧制）7.品牌（生产厂家）8.型号 9.规格尺寸（长×宽×厚）
70032	1.品牌类型 2.出口享惠情况 3.用途 4.状态（是否夹丝）5.形状（板、片、型材、异型材）6.工艺（铸制或轧制）7.品牌（生产厂家）8.型号 9.规格尺寸（长×宽×厚）
70033	1.品牌类型 2.出口享惠情况 3.用途 4.状态（是否夹丝）5.形状（板、片、型材、异型材）6.工艺（铸制或轧制）7.品牌（生产厂家）8.型号 9.规格尺寸（长×宽×厚）
70042	1.品牌类型 2.出口享惠情况 3.用途 4.加工方法（整块着色、具有吸收层等）5.状态（是否经过表面加工）6.形状（板、片）7.工艺（拉制或吹制）
70049	1.品牌类型 2.出口享惠情况 3.用途 4.状态（是否经过表面加工）5.形状（板、片）6.工艺（拉制或吹制）
70051	1.品牌类型 2.出口享惠情况 3.用途 4.加工方法（具有吸收、反射或非反射层的）5.状态（是否夹丝）6.形状（板、片）7.工艺（浮法、表面研磨、抛光）
700521	1.品牌类型 2.出口享惠情况 3.用途 4.加工方法（整块着色、不透明、镶色等）5.状态（是否夹丝）6.形状（板、片）7.工艺（浮法、表面研磨、抛光）
700529	1.品牌类型 2.出口享惠情况 3.用途 4.状态（是否夹丝）5.形状（板、片）6.工艺（浮法、表面研磨、抛光）
70053	1.品牌类型 2.出口享惠情况 3.用途 4.状态（是否夹丝）5.形状（板、片）6.工艺（浮法、表面研磨、抛光）
7006	1.品牌类型 2.出口享惠情况 3.用途 4.加工方法（经弯曲、磨边、镂刻、钻孔、涂珐琅等）5.状态（未用其他材料镶框或装配）6.形状（板、片、型材、异型材）7.如为液晶玻璃基板，需申报第几代 8.品牌（生产厂家）9.型号 10.规格尺寸（长×宽×厚）
7007	1.品牌类型 2.出口享惠情况 3.用途（车辆、航空器、航天器、船舶等）4.加工方法（钢化、层压）5.品牌
7008	1.品牌类型 2.出口享惠情况 3.用途（隔温、隔音）4.类型（中空、真空等）5.层数 6.品牌
70091	1.品牌类型 2.出口享惠情况 3.用途（车辆后视用等）4.加工方法（未经光学加工）
70099	1.品牌类型 2.出口享惠情况 3.用途（车辆后视用等）4.加工方法（未经光学加工）5.是否镶框
70101	1.品牌类型 2.出口享惠情况 3.用途（用于运输或盛装货物）4.容积
70102	1.品牌类型 2.出口享惠情况 3.用途（用于运输或盛装货物）
70109	1.品牌类型 2.出口享惠情况 3.用途（用于运输或盛装货物）4.容积
7011	1.品牌类型 2.出口享惠情况 3.用途（制灯泡、阴极射线管等）4.加工方法（用荧光物质衬里、未封口无配件等）
70131	1.品牌类型 2.出口享惠情况 3.用途（供餐桌、厨房、盥洗室、办公室、室内装饰用）4.材质（是否玻璃陶瓷制）5.器皿种类（杯等）6.工艺流程（手工、机械、半手工）
70132	1.品牌类型 2.出口享惠情况 3.用途（供餐桌、厨房、盥洗室、办公室、室内装饰用）4.是否铅晶质玻璃 5.器皿种类（杯等）6.平脚还是高脚杯 7.规格 8.型号 9.品牌 10.工艺流程（手工、机械、半手工）
70133	1.品牌类型 2.出口享惠情况 3.用途（供餐桌、厨房、盥洗室、办公室、室内装饰用）4.是否铅晶质玻璃 5.器皿种类（杯等）6.平脚还是高脚杯 7.规格 8.型号 9.品牌 10.工艺流程（手工、机械、半手工）
70134	1.品牌类型 2.出口享惠情况 3.用途（供餐桌、厨房、盥洗室、办公室、室内装饰用）4.是否铅晶质玻璃 5.器皿种类（杯等）6.线膨胀系数 7.工艺流程（手工、机械、半手工）
70139	1.品牌类型 2.出口享惠情况 3.用途（供餐桌、厨房、盥洗室、办公室、室内装饰用）4.是否铅晶质玻璃 5.器皿种类（杯等）6.工艺流程（手工、机械、半手工）
7014001	1.品牌类型 2.出口享惠情况 3.用途（具体列明用于光学仪器名称）4.形状、尺寸及外观 5.是否经光学加工
7014009	1.品牌类型 2.出口享惠情况 3.用途（是否用于光学仪器）4.形状、尺寸及外观 5.是否经光学加工
7015101	1.品牌类型 2.出口享惠情况 3.用途（用于制造眼镜等）4.加工方法（未经光学加工）5.形状（弧面、弯曲、凹形、扇形等）6.元件种类（视力矫正玻璃毛坯等）7.特殊功能（变色等）
7015109	1.品牌类型 2.出口享惠情况 3.用途（用于制造眼镜等）4.加工方法（未经光学加工）5.形状（弧面、弯曲、凹形、扇形等）6.元件种类（视力矫正玻璃毛坯等）
7015901	1.品牌类型 2.出口享惠情况 3.用途（用于制造钟表等）4.加工方法（未经光学加工）5.形状（弧面、弯曲、凹形、扇形等）6.元件种类（视力矫正玻璃毛坯等）
7015902	1.品牌类型 2.出口享惠情况 3.用途（用于制造眼镜等）4.加工方法（未经光学加工）5.形状（弧面、弯曲、凹形、扇形等）6.元件种类（视力矫正玻璃毛坯等）7.特殊功能（变色等）

商品编码	申报要素
7015909	1.品牌类型 2.出口享惠情况 3.用途(用于制造眼镜等)4.加工方法(未经光学加工)5.形状(弧面、弯曲、凹形、扇形等)6.元件种类(视力矫正玻璃毛坯等)
7016	1.品牌类型 2.出口享惠情况 3.用途(建筑铺面用)4.加工方法(压制、模制等)5.制品种类(马赛克、花饰铅条窗玻璃、铺面砖、块、片等)
7017	1.品牌类型 2.出口享惠情况 3.用途(实验室、卫生、配药用)4.材质(熔融石英、熔融硅石)5.器皿种类(量筒等)6.线膨胀系数
7018	1.品牌类型 2.出口享惠情况 3.用途(装饰用等)4.加工方法(灯工方法等)5.玻璃球的直径 6.材质(钙钠玻璃、铅晶玻璃等)7.品牌 8.型号
70191	1.品牌类型 2.出口享惠情况 3.材质(玻璃纤维制)4.种类(梳条、粗纱、纱线、短纤)5.长度
70193	1.品牌类型 2.出口享惠情况 3.材质(玻璃纤维制)4.种类(席、薄片、纤维网、垫、板等)
70194	1.品牌类型 2.出口享惠情况 3.材质(玻璃纤维制)4.织造方法(机织)5.纱线类型(粗纱)
701951	1.品牌类型 2.出口享惠情况 3.材质(玻璃纤维制)4.织造方法(机织)5.纱线类型(细纱等)6.幅宽
701952	1.品牌类型 2.出口享惠情况 3.材质(玻璃纤维制)4.织造方法(机织)5.纱线类型(细纱等)6.幅宽 7.每平方米克重 8.单纱细度 9.标称厚度
701959	1.品牌类型 2.出口享惠情况 3.材质(玻璃纤维制)4.织造方法(机织)5.纱线类型(细纱等)6.幅宽 7.每平方米克重 8.单纱细度
7019901	1.品牌类型 2.出口享惠情况 3.用途 4.材质(玻璃棉制)
7019902	1.品牌类型 2.出口享惠情况 3.用途 4.材质(玻璃纤维布浸胶)5.每平方米重量
7019909	1.品牌类型 2.出口享惠情况 3.用途 4.材质(玻璃纤维制)
70200011	1.品牌类型 2.出口享惠情况 3.用途 4.材质(玻璃制)5.导电层材质、电阻值
70200012	1.品牌类型 2.出口享惠情况 3.用途 4.材质(玻璃制)
70200013	1.品牌类型 2.出口享惠情况 3.用途 4.材质(熔融石英或其他熔融硅石制)
70200019	1.品牌类型 2.出口享惠情况 3.用途 4.材质(玻璃制)
7020009	1.品牌类型 2.出口享惠情况 3.用途 4.材质(玻璃制)
7101	1.品牌类型 2.出口享惠情况 3.种类(黑珍珠等)4.加工程度(打孔、未加工等)5.状态(未成串、未镶嵌等)6.来源(天然、养殖)7.等级
7102	1.品牌类型 2.出口享惠情况 3.用途 4.加工程度(未加工、经简单锯开、劈开、粗磨等)5.来源(天然)
71031	1.品牌类型 2.出口享惠情况 3.种类(红宝石、蓝宝石、祖母绿、翡翠等)4.加工程度(未加工,经简单锯开、粗制成形)5.状态(未成串、未镶嵌等)6.来源(天然)7.等级 8.矿物学名及英文名称 9.规格 10.化学成分 11.缅甸公盘成交需申报玉石编号、件数、重量 12.颜色
710391	1.品牌类型 2.出口享惠情况 3.种类(水晶/紫晶、软玉/和田玉等)4.加工程度(未加工,经简单锯开、粗制成形、钻孔、打磨、热处理、充填等)5.状态(未成串、未镶嵌等)6.来源(天然)7.等级 8.矿物学名 9.规格 10.化学成分 11.颜色
7103991	1.品牌类型 2.出口享惠情况 3.种类(水晶/紫晶、软玉/和田玉等)4.加工程度(未加工,经简单锯开、粗制成形、钻孔、打磨、热处理、充填等)5.状态(未成串、未镶嵌等)6.来源(天然)7.等级 8.矿物学名 9.规格 10.化学成分 11.颜色
7103992	1.品牌类型 2.出口享惠情况 3.种类(水晶/紫晶、软玉/和田玉等)4.加工程度(未加工,经简单锯开、粗制成形、钻孔、打磨、热处理、充填等)5.状态(未成串、未镶嵌等)6.来源(天然)7.等级 8.矿物学名 9.规格 10.化学成分 11.颜色
7103993	1.品牌类型 2.出口享惠情况 3.种类(水晶/紫晶、软玉/和田玉等)4.加工程度(未加工,经简单锯开、粗制成形、钻孔、打磨、热处理、充填等)5.状态(未成串、未镶嵌等)6.来源(天然)7.等级 8.矿物学名 9.规格 10.化学成分 11.颜色
7103994	1.品牌类型 2.出口享惠情况 3.种类(水晶/紫晶、软玉/和田玉等)4.加工程度(未加工,经简单锯开、粗制成形、钻孔、打磨、热处理、充填等)5.状态(未成串、未镶嵌等)6.来源(天然)7.等级 8.矿物学名 9.规格 10.化学成分 11.颜色
7103999	1.品牌类型 2.出口享惠情况 3.种类(红宝石、蓝宝石、祖母绿、翡翠等)4.加工程度(未加工,经简单锯开、粗制成形)5.状态(未成串、未镶嵌等)6.来源(天然)7.等级 8.矿物学名 9.规格 10.化学成分 11.颜色
7104	1.品牌类型 2.出口享惠情况 3.用途 4.种类(压电石英等)5.加工程度(经简单锯开、粗制成形)6.状态(未成串、未镶嵌等)7.来源(合成、再造)
7105	1.品牌类型 2.出口享惠情况 3.种类(压电石英等)4.状态(未成串、未镶嵌等)5.来源(天然、合成、再造)
71061	1.品牌类型 2.出口享惠情况 3.形状(粉末)4.材质(纯银、银合金、镀金、镀铂)5.加工程度(未锻造、半制成)6.纯度 7.平均粒径
71069	1.品牌类型 2.出口享惠情况 3.形状(粉末)4.材质(纯银、银合金、镀金、镀铂)5.加工程度(未锻造、半制成)6.纯度
7107	1.品牌类型 2.出口享惠情况 3.基底材质(铜等)
7108	1.品牌类型 2.出口享惠情况 3.形状(粉末)4.材质(纯金、金合金、镀铂)5.纯度 6.加工程度(未锻造、半制成)7.货币用请注明用途
7109	1.品牌类型 2.出口享惠情况 3.基底材质(铜、银等)
7110	1.品牌类型 2.出口享惠情况 3.形状(粉末等)4.材质(铂、钯、铑、铱、锇、钌)5.加工程度(未锻造、板、片等)6.贵金属成分含量
7111	1.品牌类型 2.出口享惠情况 3.基底材质(铜、银、金等)
7112	1.品牌类型 2.出口享惠情况 3.状态(废碎料、灰)4.来源(由破碎含有贵金属的电路板而得等)5.贵金属的成分含量
7113	1.品牌类型 2.出口享惠情况 3.材质(铂、金、银等)4.加工方法(镶嵌宝石、包金、包银等)5.首饰种类(戒指等)6.贵金属成分含量
7114	1.品牌类型 2.出口享惠情况 3.种类(餐具等)4.材质(铂、金、银等)5.加工方法(包金、镀金等)6.贵金属成分含量
7115	1.品牌类型 2.出口享惠情况 3.用途(工业用、实验室用等)4.种类(坩埚等)5.形状(格栅形状等)6.材质(铂等)7.贵金属成分含量
7116	1.品牌类型 2.出口享惠情况 3.种类(手镯等)4.材质(养殖珍珠、天然珍珠、宝石、半宝石)
7117	1.品牌类型 2.出口享惠情况 3.种类(袖扣、饰扣、手镯等)4.材质 5.品牌 6.是否镀贵金属
7118	1.品牌类型 2.出口享惠情况 3.用途(法定货币、非法定货币)4.材质(铜制等)5.成分含量
7201	1.品牌类型 2.出口享惠情况 3.形状(锭、块等)4.材质(生铁、镜铁)5.成分含量(铁、碳、铬、锰、磷、硅的含量)
72021	1.品牌类型 2.出口享惠情况 3.材质(锰铁、硅铁、铬铁、镍铁等)4.成分含量(铁含量及合金元素的含量)5.碳含量
72022	1.品牌类型 2.出口享惠情况 3.材质(锰铁、硅铁、铬铁、镍铁等)4.成分含量(铁含量及合金元素的含量)
72023	1.品牌类型 2.出口享惠情况 3.材质(锰铁、硅铁、铬铁、镍铁等)4.成分含量(铁含量及合金元素的含量)
72024	1.品牌类型 2.出口享惠情况 3.材质(锰铁、硅铁、铬铁、镍铁等)4.成分含量(铁含量及合金元素的含量)5.定价方式(公式定价、现货价等)6.需要二次结算、无需二次结算 7.计价日期 8.签约日期
72025	1.品牌类型 2.出口享惠情况 3.材质(锰铁、硅铁、铬铁、镍铁等)4.成分含量(铁含量及合金元素的含量)
72026	1.品牌类型 2.出口享惠情况 3.材质(锰铁、硅铁、铬铁、镍铁等)4.成分含量(铁含量及合金元素的含量)5.定价方式(公式定价、现货价等)6.需要二次结算、无需二次结算 7.计价日期 8.签约日期
72027	1.品牌类型 2.出口享惠情况 3.材质(锰铁、硅铁、铬铁、镍铁等)4.成分含量(铁含量及合金元素的含量)
72028	1.品牌类型 2.出口享惠情况 3.材质(锰铁、硅铁、铬铁、镍铁等)4.成分含量(铁含量及合金元素的含量)
720291	1.品牌类型 2.出口享惠情况 3.材质(锰铁、硅铁、铬铁、镍铁等)4.成分含量(铁含量及合金元素的含量)
720292	1.品牌类型 2.出口享惠情况 3.材质(锰铁、硅铁、铬铁、镍铁等)4.成分含量(铁含量及合金元素的含量)
720293	1.品牌类型 2.出口享惠情况 3.材质(锰铁、硅铁、铬铁、镍铁等)4.成分含量(铁含量及合金元素的含量)
720299	1.品牌类型 2.出口享惠情况 3.材质(锰铁、硅铁、铬铁、镍铁等)4.成分含量(铁含量及合金元素的含量)5.稀土元素的重量百分比,以[A]表示
7203	1.品牌类型 2.出口享惠情况 3.形状(块、团、团粒等)4.来源(是直接从铁矿还原所得还是海锦铁产品)5.成分含量(铁、碳、合金元素、非合金元素的含量)
72041	1.品牌类型 2.出口享惠情况 3.用途(供再熔炼钢用)4.形状(废碎、切割、压缩成包或板、条状等)5.材质(铸铁、合金钢、不锈钢等)6.来源(机械加工产生、由破碎何种钢铁制品而得)7.是否汽车压件、废五金电器 8.成分含量(所含金属总含量和各种金属名称及含量)
720421	1.品牌类型 2.出口享惠情况 3.用途(供再熔炼钢用)4.形状(废碎、切割、压缩成包或板、条状等)5.材质(铸铁、合金钢、不锈钢等)6.来源(机械加工产生、由破碎何种钢铁制品而得)7.是否汽车压件、废五金电器 8.钢号 9.成分含量(所含金属总含量和各种金属名称及含量)
720429	1.品牌类型 2.出口享惠情况 3.用途(供再熔炼钢用)4.形状(废碎、切割、压缩成包或板、条状等)5.材质(铸铁、合金钢、不锈钢等)6.来源(机械加工产生、由破碎何种钢铁制品而得)7.是否汽车压件、废五金电器 8.成分含量(所含金属总含量和各种金属名称及含量)
72043	1.品牌类型 2.出口享惠情况 3.用途(供再熔炼钢用)4.形状(废碎、切割、压缩成包或板、条状等)5.材质(铸铁、合金钢、不锈钢等)6.来源(机械加工产生、由破碎何种钢铁制品而得)7.是否汽车压件、废五金电器 8.成分含量(所含金属总含量和各种金属名称及含量)

商品编码	申报要素
720441	1.品牌类型 2.出口享惠情况 3.用途(供再熔炼钢用)4.形状(废碎、切割、压缩成包或板、条状等)5.材质(铸铁、合金钢、不锈钢等)6.来源(机械加工产生、由废碎何种钢铁制品而得)7.是否汽车压件、废五金电器 8.成分含量(所含金属总含量和各种金属名称及含量)
720449	1.品牌类型 2.出口享惠情况 3.用途(供再熔炼钢用)4.形状(废碎、切割、压缩成包或板、条状等)5.材质(铸铁、合金钢、不锈钢等)6.来源(机械加工产生、由废碎何种钢铁制品而得)7.是否汽车压件、废五金电器 8.稀土元素的重量百分比,以[A]表示 9.成分含量(所含金属总含量和各种金属名称及含量)
72045	1.品牌类型 2.出口享惠情况 3.用途(供再熔炼钢用)4.形状(废碎、切割、压缩成包或板、条状等)5.材质(铸铁、合金钢、不锈钢等)6.来源(机械加工产生、由废碎何种钢铁制品而得)7.是否汽车压件、废五金电器 8.成分含量(所含金属总含量和各种金属名称及含量)
72051	1.品牌类型 2.出口享惠情况 3.形状(颗粒、粉末)4.材质(生铁、镜铁、合金钢等)5.成分含量(铁、碳、合金元素、非合金元素的含量)6.粒度 7.稀土元素的重量百分比,以[A]表示
720521	1.品牌类型 2.出口享惠情况 3.形状(颗粒、粉末)4.材质(生铁、镜铁、合金钢等)5.成分含量(铁、碳、合金元素、非合金元素的含量)6.粒度 7.稀土元素的重量百分比,以[A]表示
720529	1.品牌类型 2.出口享惠情况 3.形状(颗粒、粉末)4.材质(生铁、镜铁、合金钢等)5.成分含量(铁、碳、合金元素、非合金元素的含量)6.粒度
7206	1.品牌类型 2.出口享惠情况 3.形状(方锭、其他初级形状等)4.材质(铁、非合金钢)5.成分含量(铁、碳、合金元素、非合金元素的含量)
720711	1.品牌类型 2.出口享惠情况 3.形状(大方坯、小方坯等)4.材质(铁、非合金钢)5.加工方法(初轧、粗锻等)6.成分含量(铁、碳、合金元素、非合金元素的含量)7.截面形状(正方形等)8.截面尺寸
720712	1.品牌类型 2.出口享惠情况 3.形状(大方坯、小方坯等)4.材质(铁、非合金钢)5.加工方法(初轧、粗锻等)6.成分含量(铁、碳、合金元素、非合金元素的含量)7.截面形状(正方形等)8.截面尺寸
720719	1.品牌类型 2.出口享惠情况 3.形状(大方坯、小方坯等)4.材质(铁、非合金钢)5.加工方法(初轧、粗锻等)6.成分含量(铁、碳、合金元素、非合金元素的含量)7.截面形状(正方形等)8.定价方式(公式定价、现货价等)9.需要二次结算、无需二次结算 10.计价日期 11.签约日期
72072	1.品牌类型 2.出口享惠情况 3.形状(大方坯、小方坯等)4.材质(铁、非合金钢)5.加工方法(初轧、粗锻等)6.成分含量(铁、碳、合金元素、非合金元素的含量)7.截面形状(正方形等)
7208	1.品牌类型 2.出口享惠情况 3.形状(平板、卷板)4.材质(铁、非合金钢)5.加工方法(热轧等)6.加工程度(是否酸洗、是否轧有花纹、是否包覆及镀层、涂层等)7.成分含量(铁、碳、合金元素、非合金元素的含量)8.规格(板材的厚度、宽度)9.技术参数(屈服强度)10.钢号
7209	1.品牌类型 2.出口享惠情况 3.形状(平板、卷板)4.材质(铁、非合金钢)5.加工方法(冷轧)6.加工程度(未包覆、未镀层、未涂层等)7.成分含量(铁、碳、合金元素、非合金元素的含量)8.规格(板材的厚度、宽度)9.技术参数(屈服强度)10.钢号
7210	1.品牌类型 2.出口享惠情况 3.形状(平板、卷板)4.材质(铁、非合金钢)5.加工方法(经包覆、经镀层、经涂层)6.成分含量(铁、碳、合金元素、非合金元素的含量)7.规格(板材的厚度、宽度)8.涂层种类(锡、铅、电镀锌、涂锌等)9.钢号
7211	1.品牌类型 2.出口享惠情况 3.形状(平板、卷板)4.材质(铁、非合金钢)5.加工方法(热轧、冷轧、未包覆、未镀层、未涂层等)6.成分含量(铁、碳、合金元素、非合金元素的含量)7.规格(板材的厚度、宽度)8.钢号
7212	1.品牌类型 2.出口享惠情况 3.形状(平板、卷板)4.材质(铁、非合金钢)5.加工方法(热轧、冷轧、经包覆、经镀层、经涂层)6.成分含量(铁、碳、合金元素、非合金元素的含量)7.规格(板材的厚度、宽度)8.涂层种类(锡、铅、电镀锌、涂锌等)
72131	1.品牌类型 2.出口享惠情况 3.形状(条、杆)4.材质(铁、非合金钢)5.加工方法(热轧)6.状态(不规则盘卷、带有凹痕、凸缘等)7.成分含量(合金元素、非合金元素的含量)8.规格(条、杆的直径)
72132	1.品牌类型 2.出口享惠情况 3.形状(条、杆)4.材质(易切削钢)5.加工方法(热轧)6.状态(不规则盘卷、不带有凹痕、凸缘等)7.成分含量(合金元素、非合金元素的含量)8.规格(条、杆的直径)
72139	1.品牌类型 2.出口享惠情况 3.形状(条、杆)4.材质(铁、非合金钢)5.加工方法(热轧)6.状态(不规则盘卷)7.成分含量(合金元素、非合金元素的含量)8.截面形状 9.规格(圆形截面需报条、杆的直径)
72141	1.品牌类型 2.出口享惠情况 3.形状(条、杆)4.材质(铁、非合金钢)5.加工方法(锻造)6.成分含量(合金元素、非合金元素的含量)7.规格(条、杆的直径)

商品编码	申报要素
72142	1.品牌类型 2.出口享惠情况 3.形状(条、杆)4.材质(铁、非合金钢)5.加工方法(热轧、热拉拔、热挤压)6.状态(带有轧制产生的变形或轧制后扭曲的)7.成分含量(合金元素、非合金元素的含量)8.规格(条、杆的直径)9.钢号
72143	1.品牌类型 2.出口享惠情况 3.形状(条、杆)4.材质(易切削钢)5.加工方法(热轧、热拉拔、热挤压)6.成分含量(合金元素、非合金元素的含量)7.状态(不带有轧制产生的变形或轧制后扭曲的)8.规格(条、杆的直径)
72149	1.品牌类型 2.出口享惠情况 3.形状(条、杆)4.材质(铁、非合金钢)5.加工方法(热轧、热拉拔、热挤压)6.成分含量(合金元素、非合金元素的含量)7.状态(不带有轧制产生的变形或轧制后扭曲的)8.规格(条、杆的直径)9.截面形状(正方形等)
7215	1.品牌类型 2.出口享惠情况 3.形状(条、杆)4.材质(铁、非合金钢)5.加工方法(热加工、冷加工)6.加工程度 7.成分含量(铁、碳、合金元素、非合金元素的含量)8.规格(条、杆的直径)9.易切削钢请注明
7216	1.品牌类型 2.出口享惠情况 3.形状(槽钢、角钢、工字钢、H 型钢等)4.材质(铁、非合金钢)5.加工方法(热轧、热拉拔、热挤压、冷加工、冷成形等)6.加工程度(例如,打孔、冲孔、扭绞、涂层等)7.成分含量(合金元素、非合金元素的含量)8.规格(型材的截面高度)
7217	1.品牌类型 2.出口享惠情况 3.形状(丝)4.材质(铁、非合金钢)5.加工方法(镀层、涂层)6.成分含量(铁、碳、合金元素、非合金元素的含量)7.涂层种类(锌、铜等)8.直径 9.状态(盘卷等)
7218	1.品牌类型 2.出口享惠情况 3.形状(方锭等)4.材质(不锈钢)5.截面形状(正方形等)6.钢号
72191	1.品牌类型 2.出口享惠情况 3.形状(卷板、平板等)4.材质(不锈钢)5.加工方法(热轧、冷轧)6.加工程度(是否经酸洗)7.成分含量 8.规格(板材的厚度、宽度)9.钢号
72192	1.品牌类型 2.出口享惠情况 3.形状(卷板、平板等)4.材质(不锈钢)5.加工方法(热轧、冷轧)6.加工程度 7.成分含量 8.规格(板材的厚度、宽度)9.钢号
72193	1.品牌类型 2.出口享惠情况 3.形状(卷板、平板等)4.材质(不锈钢)5.加工方法(热轧、冷轧)6.加工程度 7.成分含量 8.规格(板材的厚度、宽度)9.钢号
72199	1.品牌类型 2.出口享惠情况 3.形状(卷板、平板等)4.材质(不锈钢)5.加工方法(热轧、冷轧)6.加工程度 7.成分含量 8.规格(板材的厚度、宽度)9.钢号
7220	1.品牌类型 2.出口享惠情况 3.形状(卷板、平板等)4.材质(不锈钢)5.加工方法(热轧、冷轧)6.加工程度 7.成分含量(铁、碳、铬及合金元素、非合金元素的含量)8.规格(板材的厚度、宽度)9.钢号
7221	1.品牌类型 2.出口享惠情况 3.形状(条、杆)4.材质(不锈钢)5.加工方法(热轧)6.状态(不规则盘卷)7.成分含量(铁、碳、铬及合金元素、非合金元素的含量)8.钢号 9.直径
7222	1.品牌类型 2.出口享惠情况 3.形状(条、杆、角材、型材、异型材)4.材质(不锈钢)5.加工方法(热轧、热拉拔、热挤压、冷成形、冷加工)6.成分含量(铁、碳、铬及合金元素、非合金元素的含量)7.截面形状(圆形、方形等)8.钢号
7223	1.品牌类型 2.出口享惠情况 3.形状(丝)4.材质(不锈钢)5.加工方法(镀层、涂层)6.成分含量(铁、碳、铬及合金元素、非合金元素的含量)7.截面尺寸(圆形填直径,矩形填宽度厚度 8.钢号
72241	1.品牌类型 2.出口享惠情况 3.形状(方锭等)4.材质(硅锰钢等)5.成分含量(铁、碳及合金元素、非合金元素的含量)6.钢号
72249	1.品牌类型 2.出口享惠情况 3.形状(方锭等)4.材质(硅锰钢等)5.成分含量(铁、碳及合金元素、非合金元素的含量)6.粗铸锻件坯请注明单件重量 7.钢号
72251	1.品牌类型 2.出口享惠情况 3.形状(平板、卷材)4.材质(硅电钢、高速钢等,取向性硅电钢请注明)5.加工方法(热轧、冷轧、镀层、涂层种类)6.成分含量(铁、碳、合金元素、非合金元素的含量)7.规格(板材的厚度、宽度)8.牌号 9.厂家名称
72253	1.品牌类型 2.出口享惠情况 3.形状(平板、卷材)4.材质(硅电钢、高速钢等,取向性硅电钢请注明)5.加工方法(冷轧或热轧、是否镀层及涂层)6.成分含量(铁、碳、合金元素、非合金元素的含量)7.规格(板材的厚度、宽度)8.钢号
72254	1.品牌类型 2.出口享惠情况 3.形状(平板、卷材)4.材质(硅电钢、高速钢等,取向性硅电钢请注明)5.加工方法(冷轧或热轧、是否镀层及涂层)6.成分含量(铁、碳、合金元素、非合金元素的含量)7.规格(板材的厚度、宽度)8.钢号
72255	1.品牌类型 2.出口享惠情况 3.形状(平板、卷材)4.材质(硅电钢、高速钢等,取向性硅电钢请注明)5.加工方法(冷轧或热轧、是否镀层及涂层)6.成分含量(铁、碳、合金元素、非合金元素的含量)7.规格(板材的厚度、宽度)8.钢号

商品编码	申报要素
72259	1.品牌类型 2.出口享惠情况 3.形状(平板、卷材)4.材质(硅电钢、高速钢等,取向性硅电钢请注明)5.加工方法(冷轧或热轧、是否镀层及涂层)6.成分含量(铁、碳、合金元素、非合金元素的含量)7.规格(板材的厚度、宽度)8.涂层种类(电镀锌、涂锌等)9.钢号
72261	1.品牌类型 2.出口享惠情况 3.形状(平板、卷材)4.材质(硅电钢、高速钢等,取向性硅电钢请注明)5.加工方法(热轧、冷轧、镀层、涂层种类)6.成分含量(铁、碳、合金元素、非合金元素的含量)7.规格(板材的厚度、宽度)8.牌号 9.厂家名称
72262	1.品牌类型 2.出口享惠情况 3.形状(平板、卷材)4.材质(硅电钢、高速钢等,取向性硅电钢请注明)5.加工方法(热轧、冷轧、镀层、涂层)6.成分含量(铁、碳、合金元素、非合金元素的含量)7.规格(板材的厚度、宽度)8.钢号
72269	1.品牌类型 2.出口享惠情况 3.形状(平板、卷材)4.材质(硅电钢、高速钢等,取向性硅电钢请注明)5.加工方法(热轧、冷轧、镀层、涂层)6.成分含量(铁、碳、合金元素、非合金元素的含量)7.规格(板材的厚度、宽度)8.涂层种类(电镀锌、涂锌等)9.钢号
7227	1.品牌类型 2.出口享惠情况 3.形状(条、杆)4.材质(高速钢、硅锰钢等)5.加工方法(热轧)6.状态(不规则盘卷)7.成分含量(铁、碳、合金元素、非合金元素的含量)8.钢号
72281	1.品牌类型 2.出口享惠情况 3.用途(适用场所或下游产品)4.形状(条、杆、角材、型材、异型材)5.材质(高速钢、硅锰钢等)6.加工方法(热轧、热拉拔、热挤压、冷成形、冷加工)7.成分含量(铁、碳、合金元素、非合金元素的含量)8.钢号
72282	1.品牌类型 2.出口享惠情况 3.用途(适用场所或下游产品)4.形状(条、杆、角材、型材、异型材)5.材质(高速钢、硅锰钢等)6.加工方法(热轧、热拉拔、热挤压、冷成形、冷加工)7.成分含量(铁、碳、合金元素、非合金元素的含量)8.钢号
72283	1.品牌类型 2.出口享惠情况 3.用途(适用场所或下游产品)4.形状(条、杆、角材、型材、异型材)5.材质(高速钢、硅锰钢等)6.加工方法(热轧、热拉拔、热挤压、冷成形、冷加工)7.成分含量(铁、碳、合金元素、非合金元素的含量)8.钢号
72284	1.品牌类型 2.出口享惠情况 3.用途(适用场所或下游产品)4.形状(条、杆、角材、型材、异型材)5.材质(高速钢、硅锰钢等)6.加工方法(热轧、热拉拔、热挤压、冷成形、冷加工)7.成分含量(铁、碳、合金元素、非合金元素的含量)8.钢号
72285	1.品牌类型 2.出口享惠情况 3.用途(适用场所或下游产品)4.形状(条、杆、角材、型材、异型材)5.材质(高速钢、硅锰钢等)6.加工方法(热轧、热拉拔、热挤压、冷成形、冷加工)7.成分含量(铁、碳、合金元素、非合金元素的含量)8.钢号
72286	1.品牌类型 2.出口享惠情况 3.用途(适用场所或下游产品)4.形状(条、杆、角材、型材、异型材)5.材质(高速钢、硅锰钢等)6.加工方法(热轧、热拉拔、热挤压、冷成形、冷加工)7.成分含量(铁、碳、合金元素、非合金元素的含量)8.钢号
7228701	1.品牌类型 2.出口享惠情况 3.用途(适用场所或下游产品)4.形状(条、杆、角材、型材、异型材)5.材质(高速钢、硅锰钢等)6.加工方法(热轧、热拉拔、热挤压、冷成形、冷加工)7.成分含量(铁、碳、合金元素、非合金元素的含量)8.空心钻钢需额外申报最大外形尺寸和最大内孔尺寸 9.钢号
7228709	1.品牌类型 2.出口享惠情况 3.用途(适用场所或下游产品)4.形状(条、杆、角材、型材、异型材)5.材质(高速钢、硅锰钢等)6.加工方法(热轧、热拉拔、热挤压、冷成形、冷加工)7.成分含量(铁、碳、合金元素、非合金元素的含量)8.钢号
72288	1.品牌类型 2.出口享惠情况 3.用途(适用场所或下游产品)4.形状(条、杆、角材、型材、异型材)5.材质(高速钢、硅锰钢等)6.加工方法(热轧、热拉拔、热挤压、冷成形、冷加工)7.成分含量(铁、碳、合金元素、非合金元素的含量)8.空心钻钢需额外申报最大外形尺寸和最大内孔尺寸 9.钢号
7229	1.品牌类型 2.出口享惠情况 3.形状(丝)4.材质(高速钢、硅锰钢等)5.加工方法(镀层、涂层)6.成分含量(铁、碳、合金元素、非合金元素的含量)7.用途 8.钢号
7301	1.品牌类型 2.出口享惠情况 3.形状(板桩、焊接的角材、型材、异型材)4.材质(铁、非合金钢、不锈钢、合金钢)5.加工方法(冷轧、热轧等)6.规格(截面尺寸)
7302	1.品牌类型 2.出口享惠情况 3.用途(铁道及电车道铺轨用等)4.材质(铁、非合金钢、不锈钢、合金钢)5.制品种类(钢轨、轨枕、岔道段体等)
7303	1.品牌类型 2.出口享惠情况 3.规格(管的内径)4.形状(圆形截面管、空心异型材)5.材质(铸铁)
73041	1.品牌类型 2.出口享惠情况 3.规格(管的外径)4.用途(锅炉用、石油或天然气钻探用等)5.形状(管、空心异型材)6.材质(铁、非合金钢、不锈钢、合金钢)7.加工方法(冷拔、冷轧、热轧等)8.种类(无缝管)
730422	1.品牌类型 2.出口享惠情况 3.规格(管的外径)4.用途(锅炉用、石油或天然气钻探用等)5.形状(管、空心异型材)6.材质(铁、非合金钢、不锈钢、合金钢)7.加工方法(冷拔、冷轧、热轧等)8.种类(无缝管)
730423	1.品牌类型 2.出口享惠情况 3.规格(管的外径)4.用途(锅炉用、石油或天然气钻探用等)5.形状(管、空心异型材)6.材质(铁、非合金钢、不锈钢、合金钢)7.加工方法(冷拔、冷轧、热轧等)8.种类(无缝管)
730424	1.品牌类型 2.出口享惠情况 3.规格(管的外径)4.用途(锅炉用、石油或天然气钻探用等)5.形状(管、空心异型材)6.材质(铁、非合金钢、不锈钢、合金钢)7.加工方法(冷拔、冷轧、热轧等)8.种类(无缝管)
730429	1.品牌类型 2.出口享惠情况 3.规格(管的外径)4.用途(锅炉用、石油或天然气钻探用等)5.形状(管、空心异型材)6.材质(铁、非合金钢、不锈钢、合金钢)7.加工方法(冷拔、冷轧、热轧等)8.种类(无缝管)9.屈服强度
73043	1.品牌类型 2.出口享惠情况 3.规格(管的外径)4.用途(锅炉用、石油或天然气钻探用等)5.形状(管、空心异型材)6.材质(铁、非合金钢、不锈钢、合金钢)7.加工方法(冷拔、冷轧、热轧等)8.种类(无缝管)
73044	1.品牌类型 2.出口享惠情况 3.规格(管的外径)4.用途(锅炉用、石油或天然气钻探用等)5.形状(管、空心异型材)6.材质(铁、非合金钢、不锈钢、合金钢)7.加工方法(冷拔、冷轧、热轧等)8.种类(无缝管)
73045	1.品牌类型 2.出口享惠情况 3.规格(管的外径)4.用途(锅炉用、石油或天然气钻探用等)5.形状(管、空心异型材)6.材质(铁、非合金钢、不锈钢、合金钢)7.加工方法(冷拔、冷轧、热轧等)8.种类(无缝管)
73049	1.品牌类型 2.出口享惠情况 3.规格(管的外径)4.用途(锅炉用、石油或天然气钻探用等)5.形状(管、空心异型材)6.材质(铁、非合金钢、不锈钢、合金钢)7.加工方法(冷拔、冷轧、热轧等)8.种类(无缝管)
7305	1.品牌类型 2.出口享惠情况 3.规格(管的外径)4.用途(石油或天然气管道用等)5.材质(铁、非合金钢、不锈钢、合金钢)6.种类(焊接管)7.加工方法(铆、纵向焊、埋弧焊)8.截面形状(圆形)
7306	1.品牌类型 2.出口享惠情况 3.规格(圆管的外径、壁厚)4.用途(石油或天然气管道用等)5.材质(铁、非合金钢、不锈钢、合金钢)6.种类(焊接管)7.加工方法(铆、纵向焊、埋弧焊)8.截面形状(圆形、方形或椭圆形等)
7307	1.品牌类型 2.出口享惠情况 3.用途(用于管子之间连通)4.材质(无可锻性铸铁、不锈钢、其他钢铁)5.种类(法兰、管套、十字接头、对焊件等)6.加工方法(铸造、锻造等)
7308	1.品牌类型 2.出口享惠情况 3.用途(支撑用等)4.材质(钢铁)5.种类(门窗、立柱、塔楼、脚手架、桥梁体段等)
7309	1.品牌类型 2.出口享惠情况 3.用途(盛装液体用等)4.材质(钢铁)5.种类(罐、桶等)6.规格(容积)7.是否装有机械或热力装置
7310	1.品牌类型 2.出口享惠情况 3.用途(盛装液体用等)4.材质(钢铁)5.种类(罐、桶等)6.加工方法(焊边接合、卷边接合等)7.规格(容积)8.是否装有机械或热力装置
7311	1.品牌类型 2.出口享惠情况 3.用途(压缩气体或液化气体用、零售包装用等)4.材质(钢铁)5.种类(罐、桶等)
7312	1.品牌类型 2.出口享惠情况 3.材质(钢铁)4.制品种类(绞股线、吊索、绳等)5.注明"非绝缘"
7313	1.品牌类型 2.出口享惠情况 3.用途(围篱用)4.材质(钢铁)5.种类(带刺钢铁丝、绞带、单股扁丝、松绞的双股丝)6.截面尺寸
7314	1.品牌类型 2.出口享惠情况 3.用途(工业用等)4.材质(铁、非合金钢、不锈钢、合金钢)5.种类(网、篱、格栅等)6.加工方法(镀锌、涂锌、涂塑等)7.规格(网眼尺寸、丝的截面尺寸)
7315	1.品牌类型 2.出口享惠情况 3.用途(自行车用、摩托车用等)4.材质(钢铁)5.种类(铰接链、滚子链、日字环节链等)
7316	1.品牌类型 2.出口享惠情况 3.材质(钢铁)4.种类(钢铁锚、多爪锚等)
7317	1.品牌类型 2.出口享惠情况 3.材质(钢铁)4.种类(图钉、U形钉、平头钉、波纹钉等)
731811	1.品牌类型 2.出口享惠情况 3.材质 4.螺钉种类(方头)5.品牌 6.型号
731812	1.品牌类型 2.出口享惠情况 3.材质 4.品牌 5.型号
731813	1.品牌类型 2.出口享惠情况 3.材质 4.品牌 5.型号
731814	1.品牌类型 2.出口享惠情况 3.材质 4.品牌 5.型号
7318151	1.品牌类型 2.出口享惠情况 3.材质 4.抗拉强度 5.品牌 6.规格型号
7318159	1.品牌类型 2.出口享惠情况 3.材质 4.种类(螺钉、螺母、垫圈、铆钉、销等)5.抗拉强度 6.品牌 7.规格型号
731816	1.品牌类型 2.出口享惠情况 3.材质 4.品牌 5.型号
731819	1.品牌类型 2.出口享惠情况 3.材质 4.种类(螺钉、螺母、垫圈、铆钉、销等)5.品牌 6.型号

商品编码	申报要素
73182	1.品牌类型 2.出口享惠情况 3.材质 4.品牌 5.型号
7319	1.品牌类型 2.出口享惠情况 3.材质(钢铁)4.种类(缝针、织补针、刺绣针、别针等)
7320	1.品牌类型 2.出口享惠情况 3.用途(汽车用、铁道车辆用等)4.材质(钢铁)5.种类(片簧、螺旋弹簧等)
7321	1.品牌类型 2.出口享惠情况 3.材质(钢铁)4.种类(煤油炉、煤气灶、烤肉架、烤炉等)5.原理(非电热)6.燃料种类(液体、固体、气体燃料)7.品牌 8.型号
7322	1.品牌类型 2.出口享惠情况 3.用途(集中供暖用等)4.材质(钢铁)5.种类(散热器、空气加热器、暖气分布器等)6.原理(非电热)7.是否装有电动风扇或鼓风机
7323	1.品牌类型 2.出口享惠情况 3.用途(厨房用、餐桌用等)4.材质(铁、非合金钢、不锈钢、合金钢)5.种类(水壶、煎锅等)6.加工方法(已搪瓷、未搪瓷)7.品牌
7324	1.品牌类型 2.出口享惠情况 3.用途(卫生间用等)4.材质(铁、非合金钢、不锈钢、合金钢)5.种类(脸盆、浴缸等)6.加工方法(已搪瓷、未搪瓷)7.品牌
7325	1.品牌类型 2.出口享惠情况 3.用途(工业用、非工业用、研磨机用等)4.材质(无可锻性铸铁等)5.种类(井盖、研磨球等)
7326	1.品牌类型 2.出口享惠情况 3.用途(工业用、非工业用)4.材质(钢铁)5.种类(捕鼠器、香烟盒等)6.加工方法(锻造、冲压等,是否经进一步加工)
7401	1.品牌类型 2.出口享惠情况 3.材质(铜锍、沉积铜)4.成分含量(铜化合物的含量)
7402	1.品牌类型 2.出口享惠情况 3.成分含量(铜的含量及黄金含量)4.形状(块状、粉末等)5.材质(未精炼铜)6.用途(电解精炼用等)7.定价方式(公式定价、现货价等)8.需要二次结算、无需二次结算 9.计价日期 10.签约日期
740311	1.品牌类型 2.出口享惠情况 3.形状(型材、线锭、坯段等)4.材质(精炼铜、黄铜、青铜、白铜等)5.加工方法(未锻轧等)6.成分含量(铜及合金元素的含量)7.定价日期 8.签约日期 9.定价方式
740312	1.品牌类型 2.出口享惠情况 3.形状(型材、线锭、坯段等)4.材质(精炼铜、黄铜、青铜、白铜等)5.加工方法(未锻轧等)6.成分含量(铜及合金元素的含量)
740313	1.品牌类型 2.出口享惠情况 3.形状(型材、线锭、坯段等)4.材质(精炼铜、黄铜、青铜、白铜等)5.加工方法(未锻轧等)6.成分含量(铜及合金元素的含量)
740319	1.品牌类型 2.出口享惠情况 3.形状(型材、线锭、坯段等)4.材质(精炼铜、黄铜、青铜、白铜等)5.加工方法(未锻轧等)6.成分含量(铜及合金元素的含量)
74032	1.品牌类型 2.出口享惠情况 3.形状(型材、线锭、坯段等)4.材质(精炼铜、黄铜、青铜、白铜等)5.加工方法(未锻轧等)6.成分含量(铜及合金元素的含量)
7404	1.品牌类型 2.出口享惠情况 3.用途(供回收铜用)4.材质(铜)5.状态(废、碎、管、板、线、棒、边角料等)6.来源(废的电机、电线、电缆、五金等)7.成分含量(回收金属的含量)
7405	1.品牌类型 2.出口享惠情况 3.用途(用作炼铜的添加剂)4.成分含量(铜、磷的含量)
7406	1.品牌类型 2.出口享惠情况 3.用途(用作电镀基底、金属颜料等)4.形状(片状粉末、非片状粉末)5.材质(精炼铜、黄铜、青铜、白铜等)6.成分含量(铜及合金元素的含量)7.粒度 8.牌号或型号
74071	1.品牌类型 2.出口享惠情况 3.形状(条、杆、型材、异型材)4.材质(精炼铜、黄铜、青铜、白铜等)5.成分含量(铜及合金元素的含量)
74072111	1.品牌类型 2.出口享惠情况 3.形状(条、杆、型材、异型材)4.材质(精炼铜、黄铜、青铜、白铜等)5.成分含量(铜及合金元素的含量)6.直线度
74072119	1.品牌类型 2.出口享惠情况 3.形状(条、杆、型材、异型材)4.材质(精炼铜、黄铜、青铜、白铜等)5.成分含量(铜及合金元素的含量)
7407219	1.品牌类型 2.出口享惠情况 3.形状(条、杆、型材、异型材)4.材质(精炼铜、黄铜、青铜、白铜等)5.成分含量(铜及合金元素的含量)
740729	1.品牌类型 2.出口享惠情况 3.形状(条、杆、型材、异型材)4.材质(精炼铜、黄铜、青铜、白铜等)5.成分含量(铜及合金元素的含量)
7408	1.品牌类型 2.出口享惠情况 3.形状(丝)4.材质(精炼铜、黄铜、青铜、白铜等)5.成分含量(铜及合金元素的含量)6.规格(丝的最大截面尺寸)7.牌号或型号
7409	1.品牌类型 2.出口享惠情况 3.形状(板、片、带)4.材质(精炼铜、黄铜、青铜、白铜等)5.状态(盘卷、平板等)6.成分含量(铜及合金元素的含量)7.规格(长×宽×厚)8.品牌或厂商名称 9.牌号或型号

商品编码	申报要素
7410	1.品牌类型 2.出口享惠情况 3.形状(箔)4.材质(精炼铜、黄铜、青铜、白铜等)5.状态(有无衬背)6.成分含量(铜及合金元素的各自含量)7.规格(整体厚度、铜箔厚度、长度、宽度)8.用途 9.品牌 10.牌号 11.种类(压延铜箔、电解铜箔,刚性覆铜板、柔性覆铜板)12.覆铜板的铜箔层数 13.基材材质(纸基、玻璃布基、复合基、环保型基等)14.生产厂商
7411	1.品牌类型 2.出口享惠情况 3.材质(精炼铜、黄铜、青铜、白铜等)4.成分含量(铜及合金元素的含量)5.外径 6.有无螺纹或翅片 7.用途 8.品牌 9.型号或牌号
7412	1.品牌类型 2.出口享惠情况 3.用途(用于管子之间连通)4.材质(精炼铜、黄铜、青铜、白铜等)5.种类(接头、肘管、管套)6.成分含量(铜及合金元素的含量)7.品牌 8.型号或牌号
7413	1.品牌类型 2.出口享惠情况 3.材质(铜)4.种类(绞股线、缆、编带等)5.注明“非绝缘”6.品牌 7.型号或牌号
7415	1.品牌类型 2.出口享惠情况 3.材质(铜)4.种类(图钉、U形钉、螺钉、螺母、垫圈、铆钉等)5.型号或品牌
7418101	1.品牌类型 2.出口享惠情况 3.用途(厨房用、餐桌用、卫生用等)4.材质(铜)5.种类(水壶、煎锅等)6.品牌 7.型号
7418102	1.品牌类型 2.出口享惠情况 3.材质(铜)4.种类(煤油炉、煤气灶等)5.原理(非电热)6.品牌 7.型号
7418109	1.品牌类型 2.出口享惠情况 3.用途(厨房用、餐桌用、卫生用等)4.材质(铜)5.种类(水壶、煎锅等)6.品牌 7.型号
74182	1.品牌类型 2.出口享惠情况 3.用途(厨房用、餐桌用、卫生用等)4.材质(铜)5.种类(水壶、煎锅等)6.品牌 7.型号
74191	1.品牌类型 2.出口享惠情况 3.用途(工业用、非工业用)4.材质(铜)5.种类(链条、容器等)6.加工方法(锻造、冲压等)7.型号
741991	1.品牌类型 2.出口享惠情况 3.用途(工业用、非工业用)4.材质(铜)5.种类(链条、容器等)6.加工方法(锻造、冲压等)7.型号
7419992	1.品牌类型 2.出口享惠情况 3.材质(铜)4.品牌 5.型号 6.用途
7419993	1.品牌类型 2.出口享惠情况 3.材质(铜)4.种类 5.品牌 6.型号 7.用途
7419994	1.品牌类型 2.出口享惠情况 3.材质(铜)4.种类(网、格栅、网眼铜板等)5.品牌 6.型号 7.用途
7419995	1.品牌类型 2.出口享惠情况 3.材质(铜)4.种类 5.原理(非电热)6.品牌 7.型号 8.用途
7419999	1.品牌类型 2.出口享惠情况 3.用途(工业用、非工业用)4.材质(铜)5.种类(链条、容器等)6.加工方法(锻造、冲压等)
75011	1.品牌类型 2.出口享惠情况 3.材质(镍锍、氧化镍烧结物等)4.来源 5.成分含量(镍化合物的含量)
75012	1.品牌类型 2.出口享惠情况 3.材质(镍锍、氧化镍烧结物等)4.来源 5.成分含量(镍化合物的含量)6.定价方式(公式定价、现货价等)7.申报价格是否为最终结算价格 8.定价日期
75021	1.品牌类型 2.出口享惠情况 3.形状(锭、块等)4.材质(非合金镍、镍合金)5.加工方法(未锻轧)6.成分含量(例如未锻轧非合金镍锭,含镍 99.986%,含钴 0.004%)7.定价方式(公式定价、现货价等)8.需要二次结算、无需二次结算 9.计价日期 10.签约日期
75022	1.品牌类型 2.出口享惠情况 3.形状(锭、块等)4.材质(非合金镍、镍合金)5.加工方法(未锻轧)6.成分含量(例如未锻轧非合金镍锭,含镍 99.986%,含钴 0.004%)
7503	1.品牌类型 2.出口享惠情况 3.用途(供回收镍用)4.状态(废、碎)5.来源(非合金镍、镍合金的废碎料)6.成分含量(镍及合金元素的含量)
7504001	1.品牌类型 2.出口享惠情况 3.形状(片状粉末、非片状粉末)4.材质(非合金镍、镍合金)5.成分含量(镍及合金元素的含量)6.粒度 7.定价方式(公式定价、现货价等)8.需要二次结算、无需二次结算 9.计价日期 10.签约日期
7504002	1.品牌类型 2.出口享惠情况 3.形状(片状粉末、非片状粉末)4.材质(非合金镍、镍合金)5.成分含量(镍及合金元素的含量)6.粒度
75051	1.品牌类型 2.出口享惠情况 3.形状(条、杆、型材、异型材、丝)4.材质(非合金镍、镍合金)5.成分含量(镍及合金元素的含量)
75052	1.品牌类型 2.出口享惠情况 3.形状(条、杆、型材、异型材、丝)4.材质(非合金镍、镍合金)5.成分含量(镍及合金元素的含量)6.丝的直径
7506	1.品牌类型 2.出口享惠情况 3.形状(板、片、带、箔)4.材质(非合金镍、镍合金)5.成分含量(镍及合金元素的含量)6.规格(长×宽×厚)
7507	1.品牌类型 2.出口享惠情况 3.材质(非合金镍、镍合金)4.种类(管、接头、肘管、管套等)5.成分含量(镍及合金元素的含量)
7508	1.品牌类型 2.出口享惠情况 3.用途(电镀用、工业用、非工业用)4.材质(非合金镍、镍合金)5.种类(网、篱、格栅等)6.品牌 7.型号
7601	1.品牌类型 2.出口享惠情况 3.形状(锭、块)4.材质(非合金铝、铝合金)5.加工方法(未锻轧或铸造、烧结等)6.成分含量(铝及合金元素的含量)7.定价方式(公式定价、现货价等)8.需要二次结算、无需二次结算 9.计价日期 10.签约日期

商品编码	申报要素
7602	1.品牌类型 2.出口享惠情况 3.用途(供回收铝用)4.状态(废、碎、板、管、线、边角料等)5.来源(废电线、废电缆、废五金电器等)6.成分含量(回收金属的含量)7.包装形式(散装、集装箱)
7603	1.品牌类型 2.出口享惠情况 3.形状(片状粉末、非片状粉末)4.材质(非合金铝、铝合金)5.成分含量(铝的含量)6.粒度 7.用途
7604	1.品牌类型 2.出口享惠情况 3.形状(条、杆、型材、异型材)4.材质(非合金铝、铝合金)5.成分含量(铝及合金元素的含量)6.型材、异型材请注明是否空心 7.铝合金条、杆请注明截面周长 8.柱形实心体铝合金请注明 20℃时的极限抗拉强度 9.牌号
7605	1.品牌类型 2.出口享惠情况 3.形状(丝)4.材质(非合金铝、铝合金)5.成分含量(铝及合金元素的含量)6.规格(丝的最大截面尺寸)
7606	1.品牌类型 2.出口享惠情况 3.形状(矩形等)4.材质(非合金铝、铝合金)5.状态(板、片、带)6.成分含量(铝及合金元素的含量)7.规格(长×宽×厚)8.品牌(中英文)9.用途 10.牌号
7607	1.品牌类型 2.出口享惠情况 3.形状(箔)4.材质(铝)5.状态(有无衬背、衬背材料)6.规格(长×宽×厚)7.加工方法(轧制等)8.加工程度(是否进一步加工)
7608	1.品牌类型 2.出口享惠情况 3.材质(非合金铝、铝合金)4.种类(管)5.成分含量(铝及合金元素的含量)6.管壁厚度、管壁外径、孔眼直径、管材长度
7609	1.品牌类型 2.出口享惠情况 3.用途 4.材质(非合金铝、铝合金)5.种类(接头、肘管、管套)
7610	1.品牌类型 2.出口享惠情况 3.材质(铝)4.种类(门窗、门槛、塔楼、桥梁体段等)5.加工方法(铆接、栓接、钻孔、弯曲等)
7611	1.品牌类型 2.出口享惠情况 3.用途(盛装液体用等)4.材质(铝)5.种类(罐、桶等)6.规格(容积)7.品牌
7612	1.品牌类型 2.出口享惠情况 3.用途(盛装液体用等)4.材质(铝)5.种类(罐、桶等)6.规格(容积)7.品牌
7613	1.品牌类型 2.出口享惠情况 3.用途(盛装液体用等)4.材质(铝)5.种类(罐、桶等)6.规格(容积)7.品牌
7614	1.品牌类型 2.出口享惠情况 3.材质(铝)4.种类(绞股线、缆、编带等)5.状态(非绝缘)6.带钢芯请注明
7615	1.品牌类型 2.出口享惠情况 3.用途(厨房用、餐桌用、卫生用等)4.材质(铝)5.种类(水壶、煎锅等)
7616	1.品牌类型 2.出口享惠情况 3.用途(工业用、非工业用)4.材质(铝)5.种类(图钉、螺钉、布、网、篱等)
7801	1.品牌类型 2.出口享惠情况 3.形状(锭、块)4.材质(精炼铅、铅合金)5.加工方法(未锻轧)6.成分含量(铅及合金元素的含量)7.定价方式(公式定价、现货价等)8.需要二次结算、无需二次结算 9.计价日期 10.签约日期
7802	1.品牌类型 2.出口享惠情况 3.用途(供回收铅用)4.材质(铅)5.状态(废、碎)6.来源(精炼铅、铅合金的废碎料)7.成分含量(铅的含量)
7804	1.品牌类型 2.出口享惠情况 3.形状(板、片、带、箔、粉末及片状粉末)4.材质(铅)5.规格(板、箔的厚度)6.粒度
7806001	1.品牌类型 2.出口享惠情况 3.形状(条、杆、型材、异型材、丝)4.材质(铅)
7806009	1.品牌类型 2.出口享惠情况 3.用途(工业用、非工业用)4.材质(铅)5.种类(容器、铅坠等)
790111	1.品牌类型 2.出口享惠情况 3.形状(锭、块)4.材质(非合金锌、锌合金)5.加工方法(未锻轧)6.成分含量(锌及合金元素的含量)7.定价方式(公式定价、现货价等)8.需要二次结算、无需二次结算 9.计价日期 10.签约日期
790112	1.品牌类型 2.出口享惠情况 3.形状(锭、块)4.材质(非合金锌、锌合金)5.加工方法(未锻轧)6.成分含量(锌及合金元素的含量)
790120	1.品牌类型 2.出口享惠情况 3.形状(锭、块)4.材质(非合金锌、锌合金)5.加工方法(未锻轧)6.成分含量(锌及合金元素的含量)
7902	1.品牌类型 2.出口享惠情况 3.用途(供回收锌用)4.状态(废、碎)5.来源(精炼锌、锌合金的废碎料)6.成分含量(锌的含量)
7903	1.品牌类型 2.出口享惠情况 3.用途(用作硬质合金的黏合剂)4.形状(片状粉末、非片状粉末)5.材质(锌)6.成分含量(锌的含量)7.粒度
7904	1.品牌类型 2.出口享惠情况 3.形状(条、杆、型材、异型材、丝)4.材质(锌)
7905	1.品牌类型 2.出口享惠情况 3.形状(矩形等)4.材质(锌等)5.状态(板、片、带)6.成分含量(锌及合金元素的含量)7.规格(长×宽×厚)8.品牌(中英文)9.用途 10.加工程度(是否经表面处理剂处理方法和所用材料)
7907	1.品牌类型 2.出口享惠情况 3.用途 4.材质(锌)5.种类(管、接头、肘管、管套等)
8001	1.品牌类型 2.出口享惠情况 3.形状(锭、块、粒)4.材质(非合金锡、锡合金)5.加工方法(未锻轧)6.成分含量(锡及合金元素的含量)
8002	1.品牌类型 2.出口享惠情况 3.用途(供回收锡用)4.状态(废、碎)5.来源(非合金锡、锡合金的废碎料)6.成分含量(锡的含量)
8003	1.品牌类型 2.出口享惠情况 3.形状(条、杆、型材、异型材、丝)4.材质(锡)5.状态(是否带焊剂)
8007002	1.品牌类型 2.出口享惠情况 3.形状(板、片、带)4.规格(长、宽、厚)5.材质(锡)6.状态(有无衬背、衬背材料)
8007003	1.品牌类型 2.出口享惠情况 3.形状(箔、粉末)4.材质(锡)5.状态(有无衬背、衬背材料)6.规格(锡箔长×宽×厚、粉末粒度)
8007004	1.品牌类型 2.出口享惠情况 3.材质(锡)4.种类(接头、肘管、管套等)
8007009	1.品牌类型 2.出口享惠情况 3.材质(锡)4.种类
81011	1.品牌类型 2.出口享惠情况 3.形状(粉末)4.材质(钨)5.成分含量(钨的含量)6.粒度
810194	1.品牌类型 2.出口享惠情况 3.形状(条、杆等)4.材质(钨)5.加工方法(未锻轧、简单烧结等)
810196	1.品牌类型 2.出口享惠情况 3.形状(丝)4.材质(钨)
810197	1.品牌类型 2.出口享惠情况 3.用途(供回收钨用)4.材质(钨)5.状态(废、碎)6.来源
810199	1.品牌类型 2.出口享惠情况 3.形状(条、杆、型材、异型材、板、片、带、箔)4.材质(钨、钨合金)5.加工方法(锻轧)6.用途 7.成分含量 8.每个重量 9.圆柱形请注明是否空心、内径
81021	1.品牌类型 2.出口享惠情况 3.形状(粉末)4.材质(钼)5.粉末请注明细度
810294	1.品牌类型 2.出口享惠情况 3.形状(条、杆)4.材质(钼)5.加工方法(未锻轧、简单烧结等)
810295	1.品牌类型 2.出口享惠情况 3.形状(条、杆、型材、异型材、板、片、带、箔)4.材质(钼、钼合金)5.加工方法(锻轧)
810296	1.品牌类型 2.出口享惠情况 3.形状(丝)4.材质(钼)
810297	1.品牌类型 2.出口享惠情况 3.用途(供回收钼用)4.材质(钼)5.来源
810299	1.品牌类型 2.出口享惠情况 3.材质(钼)4.种类
81032	1.品牌类型 2.出口享惠情况 3.形状(粉末、条、杆、型材、异型材、板、片、带、箔)4.材质(钽、钽合金)5.加工方法(锻轧、未锻轧、简单烧结等)6.状态(废、碎)7.成分含量(钽的含量)8.粉末需申报松装密度
81033	1.品牌类型 2.出口享惠情况 3.形状(粉末、条、杆、型材、异型材、板、片、带、箔)4.材质(钽、钽合金)5.加工方法(锻轧、未锻轧、简单烧结等)6.状态(废、碎)7.成分含量(钽的含量)
81039	1.品牌类型 2.出口享惠情况 3.形状(粉末、条、杆、型材、异型材、板、片、带、箔)4.材质(钽、钽合金)5.加工方法(锻轧、未锻轧、简单烧结等)6.状态(废、碎)7.成分含量(钽的含量)8.丝需申报直径
81041	1.品牌类型 2.出口享惠情况 3.材质(镁)4.加工方法(未锻轧)5.成分含量(镁的含量)6.粉末粒度
81042	1.品牌类型 2.出口享惠情况 3.用途(供回收镁用)4.状态(废、碎)5.来源
81043	1.品牌类型 2.出口享惠情况 3.形状(粉末等)4.材质(镁)5.来源(锉屑、车屑等)6.成分含量(镁的含量)7.粒度
81049	1.品牌类型 2.出口享惠情况 3.材质(镁)4.加工方法(锻轧等)
8105201	1.品牌类型 2.出口享惠情况 3.形状(粉末、条、杆、型材、异型材、板、片、带、箔)4.材质(钴、钴合金、钴锍)5.加工方法(锻轧、未锻轧)6.状态(废、碎)7.成分含量(以干基钴为标准)8.粉末粒度 9.定价方式(公式定价、现货价等)10.需要二次结算、无需二次结算 11.计价日期 12.签约日期
8105202	1.品牌类型 2.出口享惠情况 3.形状(粉末、条、杆、型材、异型材、板、片、带、箔)4.材质(钴、钴合金、钴锍)5.加工方法(锻轧、未锻轧)6.状态(废、碎)7.成分含量(以干基钴为标准)8.粉末粒度
8105209	1.品牌类型 2.出口享惠情况 3.形状(粉末、条、杆、型材、异型材、板、片、带、箔)4.材质(钴、钴合金、钴锍)5.加工方法(锻轧、未锻轧)6.状态(废、碎)7.成分含量(以干基钴为标准)8.粉末粒度
81053	1.品牌类型 2.出口享惠情况 3.形状(粉末、条、杆、型材、异型材、板、片、带、箔)4.材质(钴、钴合金、钴锍)5.加工方法(锻轧、未锻轧)6.状态(废、碎)7.成分含量(以干基钴为标准)8.粉末粒度
81059	1.品牌类型 2.出口享惠情况 3.形状(粉末、条、杆、型材、异型材、板、片、带、箔)4.材质(钴、钴合金、钴锍)5.加工方法(锻轧、未锻轧)6.状态(废、碎)7.成分含量(以干基钴为标准)8.粉末粒度
8106	1.品牌类型 2.出口享惠情况 3.形状(粉末、条、杆、型材、异型材、板、片、带、箔)4.材质(铋、铋合金)5.加工方法(锻轧、未锻轧)6.状态(废、碎)7.成分含量(铋的含量)
8107	1.品牌类型 2.出口享惠情况 3.形状(粉末、条、杆、型材、异型材、板、片、带、箔)4.材质(镉、镉合金)5.加工方法(锻轧、未锻轧)6.状态(废、碎)
81082	1.品牌类型 2.出口享惠情况 3.形状(粉末、杆等)4.材质(钛)5.加工方法(未锻轧)6.成分含量(钛的含量)7.粉末粒度
81083	1.品牌类型 2.出口享惠情况 3.用途(供回收钛用)4.状态(废、碎)5.来源
81089	1.品牌类型 2.出口享惠情况 3.形状(条、杆、型材、异型材、板、片、带、箔等)4.材质(钛)5.种类 6.加工方法 7.板、片、带、箔的厚度

商品编码	申报要素
8109	1.品牌类型 2.出口享惠情况 3.形状(粉末、条、杆、型材、异型材、板、片、带、箔)4.材质(锆、锆合金)5.加工方法(未锻轧等)6.状态(废、碎)7.成分含量(锆的含量)8.粉末粒度
8110	1.品牌类型 2.出口享惠情况 3.形状(粉末、条、杆、型材、异型材、板、片、带、箔)4.材质(锑、锑合金)5.加二方法(未锻轧等)6.状态(废、碎)7.成分含量(锑的含量)8.粉末粒度
8111	1.品牌类型 2.出口享惠情况 3.形状(粉末、条、杆、型材、异型材、板、片、带、箔)4.材质(锰、锰合金)5.加工方法(未锻轧、锻压、模压等)6.状态(废、碎)7.成分含量(锰的含量)8.粉末粒度
8112	1.品牌类型 2.出口享惠情况 3.形状(粉末、条、杆、型材、异型材、板、片、带、箔)4.材质(铍、铬等贱金属及其合金)5.加工方法(未锻轧等)6.状态(废、碎)7.成分含量 8.粉末粒度
8113	1.品牌类型 2.出口享惠情况 3.材质(金属陶瓷)4.状态(废、碎)
8201	1.品牌类型 2.出口享惠情况 3.用途(砍伐用、修枝用等)4.材质(合金钢制等)5.种类(锹、铲、剪等)6.式样(单手操作等)7.品牌
8202	1.品牌类型 2.出口享惠情况 3.用途(加工金属用等)4.材质(合金钢制等)5.种类(手工锯、带锯片、圆锯片、直锯片等)6.圆锯片带有钢制、金刚石制、氮化硼制工作部件请注明 7.品牌
8203	1.品牌类型 2.出口享惠情况 3.用途(锉木材用等)4.材质(合金钢制等)5.种类(锉、钳子、镊子等)6.品牌
82041	1.品牌类型 2.出口享惠情况 3.材质(合金钢制等)4.种类(扳手、扳钳、扳手套筒等)5.式样(固定的、可调的)6.品牌
82042	1.品牌类型 2.出口享惠情况 3.材质(合金钢制等)4.种类(扳手、扳钳、扳手套筒等)5.品牌
8205	1.品牌类型 2.出口享惠情况 3.用途(家用等)4.材质(合金钢制等)5.种类(锤子、螺丝刀等)6.是否成套 7.品牌
8206	1.品牌类型 2.出口享惠情况 3.材质(合金钢制等)4.包含的种类(扳手、钳子、螺丝刀等)5.是否零售包装成套 6.品牌
8207	1.品牌类型 2.出口享惠情况 3.用途(钻探、铣削、锻压、镗孔用等)4.材质(合金钢制等)5.种类(锻模、铣刀等)6.是否带工作部件,若带有请注明材质(金属陶瓷、金刚石等)7.品牌 8.型号
8208	1.品牌类型 2.出口享惠情况 3.用途(金属加工用、木器加工用等)4.材质(不锈钢制等)5.种类(机器用刀片等)6.金属加工用的需要申报是否经镀层或涂层 7.品牌
8209001	1.品牌类型 2.出口享惠情况 3.用途(工具用)4.材质(金属陶瓷制)5.种类(板、杆、刀头等)6.是否装配 7.品牌
82090021	1.品牌类型 2.出口享惠情况 3.用途(工具用)4.材质(金属陶瓷制)5.种类(板、杆、刀头等)6.是否装配 7.晶粒度 8.品牌
82090029	1.品牌类型 2.出口享惠情况 3.用途(工具用)4.材质(金属陶瓷制)5.种类(板、杆、刀头等)6.是否装配 7.品牌
8209003	1.品牌类型 2.出口享惠情况 3.用途(工具用)4.材质(金属陶瓷制)5.种类(板、杆、刀头等)6.是否装配 7.品牌
8209009	1.品牌类型 2.出口享惠情况 3.用途(工具用)4.材质(金属陶瓷制)5.种类(板、杆、刀头等)6.是否装配 7.品牌
8210	1.品牌类型 2.出口享惠情况 3.用途(加工食品用等)4.材质(不锈钢制等)5.种类(绞肉机、榨汁机等)6.原理(手动)7.单件重量 8.品牌
8211	1.品牌类型 2.出口享惠情况 3.材质(不锈钢制等)4.种类(餐刀、折叠刀等)5.式样(刃面固定、可换刃面)6.是否成套 7.品牌
8212	1.品牌类型 2.出口享惠情况 3.材质(不锈钢制等)4.种类(剃刀、安全刀片等)5.品牌
8213	1.品牌类型 2.出口享惠情况 3.用途(裁缝用等)4.材质(不锈钢制等)5.种类(剪刀、剪刀片等)6.品牌
8214	1.品牌类型 2.出口享惠情况 3.材质(不锈钢制等)4.种类(裁纸刀、指甲锉、手动理发推剪、切菜刀等)5.品牌
8215	1.品牌类型 2.出口享惠情况 3.用途(餐桌、厨房用)4.材质(不锈钢制等)5.种类(餐叉、漏勺等)6.是否镀贵金属 7.是否成套 8.品牌
8301	1.品牌类型 2.出口享惠情况 3.用途(机动车用、家具用等)4.材质(不锈钢制等)5.种类(钥匙锁、数码锁、电动锁、钥匙等)6.品牌
83021	1.品牌类型 2.出口享惠情况 3.用途(机动车用、家具用等)4.材质(不锈钢制等)5.品牌
83022	1.品牌类型 2.出口享惠情况 3.用途(机动车用、家具用等)4.材质(不锈钢制等)5.直径 6.所装轮或胎的宽度 7.品牌
83023	1.品牌类型 2.出口享惠情况 3.用途(机动车用、家具用等)4.材质(不锈钢制等)5.品牌
83024	1.品牌类型 2.出口享惠情况 3.用途(机动车用、家具用等)4.材质(不锈钢制等)5.品牌
83025	1.品牌类型 2.出口享惠情况 3.用途(机动车用、家具用等)4.材质(不锈钢制等)5.品牌
83026	1.品牌类型 2.出口享惠情况 3.用途(机动车用、家具用等)4.材质(不锈钢制等)5.品牌
8303	1.品牌类型 2.出口享惠情况 3.材质(不锈钢制等)4.种类(保险箱、保险柜、保险库的门等)5.品牌
8304	1.品牌类型 2.出口享惠情况 3.用途(办公室用)4.材质(不锈钢制等)5.种类(档案柜、卡片索引柜、文件盘等)6.式样(非落地)7.品牌
8305	1.品牌类型 2.出口享惠情况 3.用途(办公室用、室内装饰或包装用)4.材质(不锈钢制等)5.种类(活页夹、宗卷夹、成条钉书钉等)6.品牌
8306	1.品牌类型 2.出口享惠情况 3.材质(不锈钢制等)4.种类(铃、钟、锣、雕塑像、相框、画框等)5.是否镀贵金属 6.铃、钟、锣请注明非电动 7.品牌
8307	1.品牌类型 2.出口享惠情况 3.材质(钢铁制、其他贱金属制)4.种类(软管)5.品牌
8308	1.品牌类型 2.出口享惠情况 3.用途(用于衣服、提包上等)4.材质(不锈钢制等)5.种类(扣、钩、环、铆钉等)6.品牌
8309	1.品牌类型 2.出口享惠情况 3.形状(冠形、圆形等)4.材质(不锈钢制等)5.种类(塞子、盖子等)6.品牌
8310	1.品牌类型 2.出口享惠情况 3.用途(汽车用等)4.材质(不锈钢制、贱金属种类等)5.种类(标志、铭牌等)6.品牌
8311	1.品牌类型 2.出口享惠情况 3.用途(电弧焊用、气焊用、钎焊用等)4.材质(贱金属、硬质合金制)5.种类(电极、焊条、焊丝等)6.状态(以焊剂涂面、以焊剂为芯)7.品牌
84011	1.品牌类型 2.出口享惠情况 3.用途 4.品牌 5.型号
84012	1.品牌类型 2.出口享惠情况 3.用途 4.品牌 5.型号
84013	1.品牌类型 2.出口享惠情况 3.用途 4.品牌 5.型号
84014	1.品牌类型 2.出口享惠情况 3.用途(适用于 XX 品牌 XX 机或通用于 XX 机等)4.品牌 5.型号
84021	1.品牌类型 2.出口享惠情况 3.用途 4.构造方式 5.蒸发量 6.品牌 7.型号
84022	1.品牌类型 2.出口享惠情况 3.用途 4.温度 5.品牌 6.型号
84029	1.品牌类型 2.出口享惠情况 3.用途 4.品牌 5.型号
8403101	1.品牌类型 2.出口享惠情况 3.用途 4.品牌 5.型号 6.是否装有循环装置 7.功率 8.温度
8403109	1.品牌类型 2.出口享惠情况 3.用途 4.品牌 5.型号 6.温度
84039	1.品牌类型 2.出口享惠情况 3.用途(适用于 XX 品牌 XX 机或通用于 XX 机等)4.品牌 5.型号
84041	1.品牌类型 2.出口享惠情况 3.用途 4.品牌
84042	1.品牌类型 2.出口享惠情况 3.用途 4.品牌
84049	1.品牌类型 2.出口享惠情况 3.用途(适用于 XX 品牌 XX 机或通用于 XX 机等)4.品牌 5.型号
84051	1.品牌类型 2.出口享惠情况 3.品牌 4.型号
84059	1.品牌类型 2.出口享惠情况 3.用途(适用于 XX 品牌 XX 机或通用于 XX 机等)4.品牌 5.型号
84061	1.品牌类型 2.出口享惠情况 3.用途 4.品牌 5.型号 6.输出功率
84068	1.品牌类型 2.出口享惠情况 3.用途 4.输出功率 5.品牌 6.型号
84069	1.品牌类型 2.出口享惠情况 3.用途(适用于 XX 品牌 XX 机或通用于 XX 机等)4.品牌 5.型号
84071	1.品牌类型 2.出口享惠情况 3.用途 4.输出功率 5.品牌 6.型号 7.燃料类型
840721	1.品牌类型 2.出口享惠情况 3.用途 4.发动机安装位置(舷外或舷内)5.品牌 6.型号 7.燃料类型 8.功率
840729	1.品牌类型 2.出口享惠情况 3.用途 4.发动机安装位置(舷外或舷内)5.品牌 6.型号 7.燃料类型 8.是否提供主动力 9.功率
84073	1.品牌类型 2.出口享惠情况 3.用途 4.排气量 5.成套散件或毛坯请注明 6.燃料类型 7.状态(成品、半成品、成套散件)8.生产件的通用零件编号后加注"/TY"9.成套散件装配后完整品的零部件的编号 10.品牌 11.型号 12.零部件完整编号并在前加注"S/"、"W/"或"WF/"之一(生产件填报"S/",品牌和适用的整车厂牌一致的维修件填报"W/",品牌和适用的整车厂牌不一致的维修件的填报"WF/")
84079	1.品牌类型 2.出口享惠情况 3.用途 4.燃料类型 5.品牌 6.型号 7.转速
84081	1.品牌类型 2.出口享惠情况 3.用途 4.品牌 5.型号 6.输出功率
84082	1.品牌类型 2.出口享惠情况 3.用途 4.输出功率 5.成套散件或毛坯请注明 6.生产件的通用零件编号后加注"/TY"7.成套散件装配后完整品的零部件的编号 8.品牌 9.型号 10.零部件完整编号并在前加注"S/"、"W/"或"WF/"之一(生产件填报"S/",品牌和适用的整车厂牌一致的维修件填报"W/",品牌和适用的整车厂牌不一致的维修件的填报"WF/")
84089	1.品牌类型 2.出口享惠情况 3.用途 4.输出功率 5.品牌 6.型号 7.转速
84091	1.品牌类型 2.出口享惠情况 3.适用何种用途发动机(如飞机用、船舶用等)4.适用发动机的类型(点燃式/压燃式)5.品牌 6.零件号
840991	1.品牌类型 2.出口享惠情况 3.适用何种用途发动机(如飞机用、船舶用等)4.适用发动机的类型(点燃式/压燃式)5.品牌 6.零件号

商品编码	申报要素
840999	1.品牌类型 2.出口享惠情况 3.适用何种用途发动机(如飞机用、船舶用等)4.适用发动机的类型(点燃式/压燃式)5.发动机输出功率 6.品牌 7.零件号
841011	1.品牌类型 2.出口享惠情况 3.功率 4.品牌 5.型号
841012	1.品牌类型 2.出口享惠情况 3.功率 4.品牌 5.型号
841013	1.品牌类型 2.出口享惠情况 3.功率 4.工作方式 5.品牌 6.型号
8410901	1.品牌类型 2.出口享惠情况 3.品牌 4.原理 5.型号
8410909	1.品牌类型 2.出口享惠情况 3.品牌 4.型号
84111	1.品牌类型 2.出口享惠情况 3.原理 4.推力 5.品牌 6.型号
84112	1.品牌类型 2.出口享惠情况 3.原理 4.功率 5.品牌 6.型号
84118	1.品牌类型 2.出口享惠情况 3.原理 4.功率 5.品牌 6.型号
84119	1.品牌类型 2.出口享惠情况 3.用途(适用于 XX 品牌 XX 机或通用于 XX 机等)4.品牌 5.型号
84121	1.品牌类型 2.出口享惠情况 3.用途 4.原理 5.品牌 6.型号
84122	1.品牌类型 2.出口享惠情况 3.原理 4.用途 5.品牌 6.型号
84123	1.品牌类型 2.出口享惠情况 3.原理 4.用途 5.品牌 6.型号
84128	1.品牌类型 2.出口享惠情况 3.原理 4.用途 5.品牌 6.型号
84129	1.品牌类型 2.出口享惠情况 3.用途 4.品牌 5.型号
84131	1.品牌类型 2.出口享惠情况 3.用途 4.是否装有或可装计量装置 5.品牌 6.型号
84132	1.品牌类型 2.出口享惠情况 3.是否手动 4.品牌 5.型号
84133	1.品牌类型 2.出口享惠情况 3.用途(是否为活塞式内燃发动机用)4.适用发动机的输出功率 5.品牌 6.型号
84134	1.品牌类型 2.出口享惠情况 3.用途 4.品牌 5.型号
84135	1.品牌类型 2.出口享惠情况 3.驱动方式(气动、电动、液压等)4.原理(往复式、回转式、离心式等)5.用途 6.品牌 7.型号
84136	1.品牌类型 2.出口享惠情况 3.驱动方式(气动、电动、液压等)4.原理(往复式、回转式、离心式等)5.用途 6.品牌 7.型号
84137	1.品牌类型 2.出口享惠情况 3.驱动方式(气动、电动、液压等)4.原理(往复式、回转式、离心式等)5.转速 6.用途 7.品牌 8.型号
84138	1.品牌类型 2.出口享惠情况 3.用途 4.品牌 5.型号 6.原理(柱塞式、齿轮式、螺杆式等)
84139	1.品牌类型 2.出口享惠情况 3.用途(适用于 XX 品牌 XX 机或通用于 XX 机等)4.品牌 5.型号
84141	1.品牌类型 2.出口享惠情况 3.用途(如半导体晶圆或平板显示屏制造用等)4.品牌 5.型号 6.性能(抽气能力)
84142	1.品牌类型 2.出口享惠情况 3.是否手动或脚踏 4.品牌 5.型号
84143	1.品牌类型 2.出口享惠情况 3.用途 4.驱动方式 5.额定功率 6.品牌 7.型号
84144	1.品牌类型 2.出口享惠情况 3.用途 4.品牌 5.型号
841451	1.品牌类型 2.出口享惠情况 3.类型(如吊扇、落地扇、壁扇等)4.输出功率 5.品牌 6.型号
8414591	1.品牌类型 2.出口享惠情况 3.类型(如吊扇、落地扇、壁扇等)4.输出功率 5.品牌 6.型号
8414592	1.品牌类型 2.出口享惠情况 3.类型(如吊扇、落地扇、壁扇等)4.输出功率 5.品牌 6.型号
8414593	1.品牌类型 2.出口享惠情况 3.类型(如吊扇、落地扇、壁扇等)4.输出功率 5.品牌 6.型号
8414599	1.品牌类型 2.出口享惠情况 3.用途(如微处理器、电信设备、自动数据处理设备或装置用等)4.类型(如吊扇、落地扇、壁扇等)5.输出功率 6.品牌 7.型号
84146	1.品牌类型 2.出口享惠情况 3.罩的平面最大边长 4.品牌 5.型号
8414801	1.品牌类型 2.出口享惠情况 3.用途 4.品牌 5.型号
8414802	1.品牌类型 2.出口享惠情况 3.用途 4.品牌 5.型号
8414803	1.品牌类型 2.出口享惠情况 3.用途 4.品牌 5.型号 6.压力比
8414804	1.品牌类型 2.出口享惠情况 3.用途 4.品牌 5.型号
8414809	1.品牌类型 2.出口享惠情况 3.用途 4.品牌 5.型号
84149	1.品牌类型 2.出口享惠情况 3.用途(适用于 XX 品牌 XX 机或通用于 XX 机等)4.品牌 5.型号 6.材质
8415101	1.品牌类型 2.出口享惠情况 3.是否窗式或壁式安装 4.是否为独立式或分体式 5.品牌 6.型号
8415102	1.品牌类型 2.出口享惠情况 3.是否窗式或壁式安装 4.是否为独立式或分体式 5.制冷量 6.品牌 7.型号
84152	1.品牌类型 2.出口享惠情况 3.用途 4.品牌 5.型号
841581	1.品牌类型 2.出口享惠情况 3.是否装有制冷装置 4.是否装有冷热换向阀 5.制冷量 6.品牌 7.型号
841582	1.品牌类型 2.出口享惠情况 3.是否装有制冷装置 4.是否装有冷热换向阀 5.制冷量 6.品牌 7.型号
841583	1.品牌类型 2.出口享惠情况 3.品牌 4.结构 5.型号
84159	1.品牌类型 2.出口享惠情况 3.用途(适用于 XX 品牌 XX 机或通用于 XX 机等)4.若为多元件集成电路需注明结构组成 5.适用机型制冷量(以"大卡/时"计)6.品牌 7.型号
84161	1.品牌类型 2.出口享惠情况 3.用途 4.燃料类型 5.品牌 6.型号
84162	1.品牌类型 2.出口享惠情况 3.用途 4.燃料类型 5.品牌 6.型号
84163	1.品牌类型 2.出口享惠情况 3.用途 4.品牌
84169	1.品牌类型 2.出口享惠情况 3.用途(适用于 XX 品牌 XX 机或通用于 XX 机等)4.品牌 5.型号

商品编码	申报要素
84171	1.品牌类型 2.出口享惠情况 3.用途 4.加热方式 5.品牌 6.型号
84172	1.品牌类型 2.出口享惠情况 3.用途 4.加热方式 5.品牌 6.型号
84178	1.品牌类型 2.出口享惠情况 3.用途 4.加热方式 5.品牌 6.型号
84179	1.品牌类型 2.出口享惠情况 3.用途(适用于 XX 品牌 XX 机或通用于 XX 机等)4.品牌 5.型号
84181	1.品牌类型 2.出口享惠情况 3.结构[冷藏－冷冻组合机(各自装有单独外门的)]4.容积 5.品牌 6.型号
84182	1.品牌类型 2.出口享惠情况 3.用途(是否家用)4.原理 5.容积 6.品牌 7.型号
84183	1.品牌类型 2.出口享惠情况 3.容积 4.最低制冷温度 5.是否柜式 6.品牌 7.型号
84184	1.品牌类型 2.出口享惠情况 3.结构(是否为立式)4.容积 5.最低制冷温度 6.品牌 7.型号
84185	1.品牌类型 2.出口享惠情况 3.用途 4.品牌 5.型号 6.容积 7.最低制冷温度
84186	1.品牌类型 2.出口享惠情况 3.原理(是否为压缩式)4.品牌 5.型号
84189	1.品牌类型 2.出口享惠情况 3.用途(适用于 XX 品牌 XX 机或通用于 XX 机等)4.适用机型的制冷温度和容积 5.品牌 6.型号
84191	1.品牌类型 2.出口享惠情况 3.原理 4.加热方式 5.用途 6.品牌 7.型号
84192	1.品牌类型 2.出口享惠情况 3.用途 4.品牌 5.型号
84193	1.品牌类型 2.出口享惠情况 3.用途 4.干燥材质 5.品牌 6.型号
84194	1.品牌类型 2.出口享惠情况 3.用途 4.品牌 5.型号 6.原理
84195	1.品牌类型 2.出口享惠情况 3.若为用氟聚合物制造的需注明 4.若为用氟聚合物制造的需注明入口管和出口管内径尺寸 5.用途 6.品牌 7.型号
8419601	1.品牌类型 2.出口享惠情况 3.用途 4.制氧量 5.品牌 6.型号
8419609	1.品牌类型 2.出口享惠情况 3.用途 4.品牌 5.型号
84198	1.品牌类型 2.出口享惠情况 3.用途 4.品牌 5.型号
84199	1.品牌类型 2.出口享惠情况 3.用途(适用于 XX 品牌 XX 机或通用于 XX 机等)4.品牌 5.型号
84201	1.品牌类型 2.出口享惠情况 3.用途(如印刷电路板基板或印刷电路制造用等)4.品牌 5.型号
84209	1.品牌类型 2.出口享惠情况 3.用途(适用于 XX 品牌 XX 机或通用于 XX 机等)4.品牌 5.型号
842111	1.品牌类型 2.出口享惠情况 3.用途 4.原理 5.品牌 6.型号
842112	1.品牌类型 2.出口享惠情况 3.用途 4.原理 5.干衣量 6.品牌 7.型号
842119	1.品牌类型 2.出口享惠情况 3.用途 4.原理 5.品牌 6.型号
842121	1.品牌类型 2.出口享惠情况 3.用途 4.品牌 5.型号 6.原理 7.单位时间水处理量
842122	1.品牌类型 2.出口享惠情况 3.用途 4.原理 5.品牌 6.型号
842123	1.品牌类型 2.出口享惠情况 3.用途 4.原理 5.品牌 6.型号
842129	1.品牌类型 2.出口享惠情况 3.用途 4.原理 5.若为用氟聚合物制造的需注明 6.氟聚合物制的需报过滤或净化介质的外观(膜等)及厚度 7.品牌 8.型号
842131	1.品牌类型 2.出口享惠情况 3.用途 4.原理 5.品牌 6.型号
8421391	1.品牌类型 2.出口享惠情况 3.用途 4.原理 5.品牌 6.型号 7.额定功率(非电动的不需注明额定功率)
8421392	1.品牌类型 2.出口享惠情况 3.用途 4.若为装备不锈钢外壳需注明 5.若为装备不锈钢外壳需注明入口管和出口管内径尺寸 6.原理 7.品牌 8.型号 9.额定功率(非电动的不需注明额定功率)
8421393	1.品牌类型 2.出口享惠情况 3.用途 4.若为装备不锈钢外壳需注明 5.若为装备不锈钢外壳需注明入口管和出口管内径尺寸 6.原理 7.品牌 8.型号 9.额定功率(非电动的不需注明额定功率)
8421394	1.品牌类型 2.出口享惠情况 3.用途 4.若为装备不锈钢外壳需注明 5.若为装备不锈钢外壳需注明入口管和出口管内径尺寸 6.原理 7.品牌 8.型号 9.额定功率(非电动的不需注明额定功率)
8421395	1.品牌类型 2.出口享惠情况 3.用途 4.若为装备不锈钢外壳需注明 5.若为装备不锈钢外壳需注明入口管和出口管内径尺寸 6.原理 7.品牌 8.型号 9.额定功率(非电动的不需注明额定功率)
8421399	1.品牌类型 2.出口享惠情况 3.用途 4.若为装备不锈钢外壳需注明 5.若为装备不锈钢外壳需注明入口管和出口管内径尺寸 6.原理 7.品牌 8.型号 9.额定功率(非电动的不需注明额定功率)
842191	1.品牌类型 2.出口享惠情况 3.用途(适用于 XX 品牌 XX 机或通用于 XX 机等)4.品牌 5.型号
8421991	1.品牌类型 2.出口享惠情况 3.用途(适用于 XX 品牌 XX 机或通用于 XX 机等)4.品牌 5.型号
8421999	1.品牌类型 2.出口享惠情况 3.用途(适用于 XX 品牌 XX 机或通用于 XX 机等)4.氟聚合物制的液体过滤或净化用需报介质外观及厚度 5.装备不锈钢外壳的气体过滤净化用需报入、出口管内径尺寸 6.品牌 7.型号
84221	1.品牌类型 2.出口享惠情况 3.品牌 4.型号
84222	1.品牌类型 2.出口享惠情况 3.用途 4.品牌 5.型号
84223	1.品牌类型 2.出口享惠情况 3.用途 4.品牌 5.型号

商品编码	申报要素
84224	1.品牌类型 2.出口享惠情况 3.用途 4.品牌 5.型号
84229	1.品牌类型 2.出口享惠情况 3.用途(适用于 XX 品牌 XX 机或通用于 XX 机等)4.品牌 5.型号
84231	1.品牌类型 2.出口享惠情况 3.用途 4.品牌 5.型号
84232	1.品牌类型 2.出口享惠情况 3.用途 4.原理 5.品牌 6.型号
8423301	1.品牌类型 2.出口享惠情况 3.用途 4.原理(如电子式称重等)5.品牌 6.型号
8423302	1.品牌类型 2.出口享惠情况 3.用途 4.品牌 5.型号
8423303	1.品牌类型 2.出口享惠情况 3.用途 4.原理(如电子式称重等)5.品牌 6.型号
8423309	1.品牌类型 2.出口享惠情况 3.用途 4.原理(如电子式称重等)5.品牌 6.型号
8423811	1.品牌类型 2.出口享惠情况 3.用途 4.原理 5.最大称量 6.品牌 7.型号
8423812	1.品牌类型 2.出口享惠情况 3.用途 4.原理 5.最大称量 6.品牌 7.型号
8423819	1.品牌类型 2.出口享惠情况 3.用途 4.原理(如电子式称重等)5.最大称量 6.品牌 7.型号
842382	1.品牌类型 2.出口享惠情况 3.用途 4.原理(如电子式称重等)5.最大称量 6.品牌 7.型号
842389	1.品牌类型 2.出口享惠情况 3.用途 4.原理(如电子式称重等)5.最大称量 6.品牌 7.型号
84239	1.品牌类型 2.出口享惠情况 3.用途(适用机型,如电子式称重衡器用等)4.品牌 5.型号
84241	1.品牌类型 2.出口享惠情况 3.用途 4.品牌 5.型号
84242	1.品牌类型 2.出口享惠情况 3.用途 4.品牌 5.喷射材料 6.型号
84243	1.品牌类型 2.出口享惠情况 3.喷射材料 4.用途 5.品牌 6.型号
84244	1.品牌类型 2.出口享惠情况 3.用途 4.品牌 5.喷射材料 6.型号
84248	1.品牌类型 2.出口享惠情况 3.用途 4.品牌 5.喷射材料 6.型号
84249	1.品牌类型 2.出口享惠情况 3.用途(适用于 XX 品牌 XX 机或通用于 XX 机等)4.品牌 5.型号
8425	1.品牌类型 2.出口享惠情况 3.用途 4.驱动方式 5.品牌 6.型号 7.最大提升高度(距离)8.最大提升重量
8426	1.品牌类型 2.出口享惠情况 3.用途 4.结构类型 5.品牌 6.型号
8427	1.品牌类型 2.出口享惠情况 3.用途 4.推进方式 5.品牌 6.型号 7.最大提升高度(距离)8.最大提升重量
8428101	1.品牌类型 2.出口享惠情况 3.用途 4.品牌 5.型号 6.提升速度 7.停层数 8.载重量
8428109	1.品牌类型 2.出口享惠情况 3.用途 4.品牌 5.型号
84282	1.品牌类型 2.出口享惠情况 3.驱动方式 4.品牌 5.型号
84283	1.品牌类型 2.出口享惠情况 3.用途 4.运送方式 5.工作构件类型(斗式、带式等)6.品牌 7.型号
84284	1.品牌类型 2.出口享惠情况 3.品牌 4.型号
84286	1.品牌类型 2.出口享惠情况 3.用途 4.原理 5.结构类型 6.品牌 7.型号
84289	1.品牌类型 2.出口享惠情况 3.用途 4.品牌 5.型号
84291	1.品牌类型 2.出口享惠情况 3.行走装置类型(轮胎式、履带式等)4.发动机输出功率 5.品牌 6.是否自推进 7.型号 8.机械重量
84292	1.品牌类型 2.出口享惠情况 3.是否自推进 4.发动机输出功率 5.品牌 6.型号
84293	1.品牌类型 2.出口享惠情况 3.是否自推进 4.斗容量 5.品牌 6.型号
84294	1.品牌类型 2.出口享惠情况 3.原理 4.是否自推进 5.机重 6.品牌 7.型号
842951	1.品牌类型 2.出口享惠情况 3.是否自推进 4.品牌 5.行走装置类型(轮胎式、履带式等)6.型号
8429521	1.品牌类型 2.出口享惠情况 3.行走装置类型(轮胎式、履带式等)4.是否自推进 5.是否上部结构可旋转 360 度 6.品牌 7.型号 8.斗容量 9.功率 10.机重
8429529	1.品牌类型 2.出口享惠情况 3.是否自推进 4.是否上部结构可旋转 360 度 5.品牌 6.行走装置类型(轮胎式、履带式等)7.型号
842959	1.品牌类型 2.出口享惠情况 3.是否自推进 4.品牌 5.行走装置类型(轮胎式、履带式等)6.型号 7.斗容量 8.功率 9.机重
84301	1.品牌类型 2.出口享惠情况 3.品牌 4.型号
84302	1.品牌类型 2.出口享惠情况 3.品牌 4.型号 5.是否自推进
84303	1.品牌类型 2.出口享惠情况 3.是否自推进 4.品牌 5.型号
8430411	1.品牌类型 2.出口享惠情况 3.用途 4.是否自推进 5.钻探深度 6.品牌 7.型号
84304121	1.品牌类型 2.出口享惠情况 3.用途 4.是否自推进 5.钻探深度 6.品牌 7.型号
84304122	1.品牌类型 2.出口享惠情况 3.用途 4.是否自推进 5.钻探深度 6.品牌 7.型号 8.机身号 9.钻头直径 10.机身重量
84304129	1.品牌类型 2.出口享惠情况 3.用途 4.是否自推进 5.钻探深度 6.品牌 7.型号
8430419	1.品牌类型 2.出口享惠情况 3.用途 4.是否自推进 5.钻探深度 6.品牌 7.型号
843049	1.品牌类型 2.出口享惠情况 3.用途 4.是否自推进 5.钻探深度 6.品牌 7.型号
84305	1.品牌类型 2.出口享惠情况 3.用途 4.是否自推进 5.牙轮直径 6.品牌 7.型号
84306	1.品牌类型 2.出口享惠情况 3.用途 4.是否自推进 5.钻筒直径 6.品牌 7.型号
8431	1.品牌类型 2.出口享惠情况 3.用途(适用于 XX 品牌 XX 机或通用于 XX 机等)4.如为破碎锤注明是否带有钎杆 5.品牌 6.型号
84321	1.品牌类型 2.出口享惠情况 3.用途 4.品牌 5.型号
84322	1.品牌类型 2.出口享惠情况 3.用途 4.品牌 5.型号
84323	1.品牌类型 2.出口享惠情况 3.用途 4.品牌 5.型号
84324	1.品牌类型 2.出口享惠情况 3.用途 4.品牌 5.型号
84328	1.品牌类型 2.出口享惠情况 3.用途 4.品牌 5.型号
84329	1.品牌类型 2.出口享惠情况 3.用途(适用于 XX 品牌 XX 机或通用于 XX 机等)4.品牌 5.型号
84331	1.品牌类型 2.出口享惠情况 3.用途 4.驱动方式 5.切割装置的旋转类型 6.品牌 7.型号
84332	1.品牌类型 2.出口享惠情况 3.用途 4.品牌 5.型号
84333	1.品牌类型 2.出口享惠情况 3.品牌 4.型号
84334	1.品牌类型 2.出口享惠情况 3.品牌 4.型号
843351	1.品牌类型 2.出口享惠情况 3.用途 4.品牌 5.型号 6.功率
843352	1.品牌类型 2.出口享惠情况 3.用途 4.品牌 5.型号
843353	1.品牌类型 2.出口享惠情况 3.用途 4.品牌 5.型号 6.功率
843359	1.品牌类型 2.出口享惠情况 3.用途 4.品牌 5.型号 6.功率
84336	1.品牌类型 2.出口享惠情况 3.用途 4.品牌 5.型号
84339	1.品牌类型 2.出口享惠情况 3.用途(适用于 XX 品牌 XX 机或通用于 XX 机等)4.品牌 5.型号
84341	1.品牌类型 2.出口享惠情况 3.用途 4.品牌 5.型号
84342	1.品牌类型 2.出口享惠情况 3.用途 4.品牌 5.型号
84349	1.品牌类型 2.出口享惠情况 3.用途(适用于 XX 品牌 XX 机或通用于 XX 机等)4.品牌 5.型号
84351	1.品牌类型 2.出口享惠情况 3.用途 4.品牌 5.型号
84359	1.品牌类型 2.出口享惠情况 3.用途(适用于 XX 品牌 XX 机或通用于 XX 机等)4.品牌 5.型号
84361	1.品牌类型 2.出口享惠情况 3.用途 4.品牌 5.型号
84362	1.品牌类型 2.出口享惠情况 3.用途 4.品牌 5.型号
84368	1.品牌类型 2.出口享惠情况 3.用途 4.品牌 5.型号
84369	1.品牌类型 2.出口享惠情况 3.用途(适用于 XX 品牌 XX 机或通用于 XX 机等)4.品牌 5.型号
84371	1.品牌类型 2.出口享惠情况 3.用途 4.品牌 5.型号
84378	1.品牌类型 2.出口享惠情况 3.用途 4.品牌 5.型号
84379	1.品牌类型 2.出口享惠情况 3.用途(适用于 XX 品牌 XX 机或通用于 XX 机等)4.品牌 5.型号
84381	1.品牌类型 2.出口享惠情况 3.用途 4.品牌 5.型号
84382	1.品牌类型 2.出口享惠情况 3.用途 4.品牌 5.型号
84383	1.品牌类型 2.出口享惠情况 3.用途 4.品牌 5.型号
84384	1.品牌类型 2.出口享惠情况 3.用途 4.品牌 5.型号
84385	1.品牌类型 2.出口享惠情况 3.用途 4.品牌 5.型号
84386	1.品牌类型 2.出口享惠情况 3.用途 4.品牌 5.型号
84388	1.品牌类型 2.出口享惠情况 3.用途 4.品牌 5.型号
84389	1.品牌类型 2.出口享惠情况 3.用途(适用于 XX 品牌 XX 机或通用于 XX 机等)4.品牌 5.型号
84391	1.品牌类型 2.出口享惠情况 3.用途 4.品牌 5.型号
84392	1.品牌类型 2.出口享惠情况 3.用途 4.品牌 5.型号
84393	1.品牌类型 2.出口享惠情况 3.用途 4.品牌 5.型号
84399	1.品牌类型 2.出口享惠情况 3.用途(适用于 XX 品牌 XX 机或通用于 XX 机等)4.品牌 5.型号
84401	1.品牌类型 2.出口享惠情况 3.用途 4.品牌 5.型号
84409	1.品牌类型 2.出口享惠情况 3.用途(适用于 XX 品牌 XX 机或通用于 XX 机等)4.品牌 5.型号
84411	1.品牌类型 2.出口享惠情况 3.用途 4.品牌 5.型号
84412	1.品牌类型 2.出口享惠情况 3.用途 4.品牌 5.型号
84413	1.品牌类型 2.出口享惠情况 3.用途 4.品牌 5.型号
84414	1.品牌类型 2.出口享惠情况 3.用途 4.品牌 5.型号
84418	1.品牌类型 2.出口享惠情况 3.用途 4.品牌 5.型号
84419	1.品牌类型 2.出口享惠情况 3.用途(适用于 XX 品牌 XX 机或通用于 XX 机等)4.品牌 5.型号
84423	1.品牌类型 2.出口享惠情况 3.用途 4.原理 5.品牌 6.型号
84424	1.品牌类型 2.出口享惠情况 3.用途(适用于 XX 品牌 XX 机或通用于 XX 机等)4.品牌 5.型号
84425	1.品牌类型 2.出口享惠情况 3.用途 4.原理 5.品牌 6.型号
844311	1.品牌类型 2.出口享惠情况 3.用途 4.原理 5.进料方式 6.品牌 7.型号
844312	1.品牌类型 2.出口享惠情况 3.用途 4.原理 5.进料方式 6.品牌 7.型号
844313	1.品牌类型 2.出口享惠情况 3.用途 4.原理 5.进料方式 6.品牌 7.型号 8.印刷速度 9.印刷方式

商品编码	申报要素
844314	1.品牌类型 2.出口享惠情况 3.用途 4.原理 5.进料方式 6.品牌 7.型号
844315	1.品牌类型 2.出口享惠情况 3.用途 4.原理 5.进料方式 6.品牌 7.型号
844316	1.品牌类型 2.出口享惠情况 3.用途 4.原理 5.进料方式 6.品牌 7.型号 8.线速度 9.幅宽
844317	1.品牌类型 2.出口享惠情况 3.用途 4.原理 5.进料方式 6.印刷速度 7.品牌 8.型号
844319	1.品牌类型 2.出口享惠情况 3.用途 4.原理 5.进料方式 6.品牌 7.型号
844331	1.品牌类型 2.出口享惠情况 3.原理 4.功能 5.品牌 6.型号
8443321	1.品牌类型 2.出口享惠情况 3.用途(是否专用于税目 84.71 所列设备)4.原理 5.品牌 6.型号 7.打印幅宽 8.打印速度
8443322	1.品牌类型 2.出口享惠情况 3.用途 4.原理 5.品牌 6.型号
8443329	1.品牌类型 2.出口享惠情况 3.用途 4.原理 5.品牌 6.型号
844339	1.品牌类型 2.出口享惠情况 3.用途(是否专用于税目 84.71 所列设备)4.原理 5.品牌 6.型号
84439	1.品牌类型 2.出口享惠情况 3.用途(适用于 XX 品牌 XX 机或通用于 XX 机等)4.品牌 5.型号
8444	1.品牌类型 2.出口享惠情况 3.用途 4.品牌 5.型号
8445	1.品牌类型 2.出口享惠情况 3.用途 4.原理 5.品牌 6.型号
8446	1.品牌类型 2.出口享惠情况 3.用途 4.原理 5.织物宽度 6.品牌 7.型号
84471	1.品牌类型 2.出口享惠情况 3.圆筒直径 4.品牌 5.型号
84472	1.品牌类型 2.出口享惠情况 3.原理 4.品牌 5.型号 6.幅宽
84479	1.品牌类型 2.出口享惠情况 3.原理 4.品牌 5.型号
8448	1.品牌类型 2.出口享惠情况 3.用途(适用于 XX 品牌 XX 机或通用于 XX 机等)4.品牌 5.型号
8449	1.品牌类型 2.出口享惠情况 3.原理 4.品牌 5.型号
84501	1.品牌类型 2.出口享惠情况 3.原理 4.是否全自动 5.干衣量 6.品牌 7.型号
84502	1.品牌类型 2.出口享惠情况 3.原理 4.是否全自动 5.干衣量 6.品牌 7.型号
84509	1.品牌类型 2.出口享惠情况 3.用途(适用于 XX 品牌 XX 机或通用于 XX 机等)4.品牌 5.型号
84511	1.品牌类型 2.出口享惠情况 3.用途 4.品牌 5.型号 6.衣容量(千克)
84512	1.品牌类型 2.出口享惠情况 3.用途 4.干衣量 5.品牌 6.型号
84513	1.品牌类型 2.出口享惠情况 3.用途 4.品牌 5.型号
84514	1.品牌类型 2.出口享惠情况 3.用途 4.品牌 5.型号
84515	1.品牌类型 2.出口享惠情况 3.用途 4.品牌 5.型号
84518	1.品牌类型 2.出口享惠情况 3.用途 4.品牌 5.型号
84519	1.品牌类型 2.出口享惠情况 3.用途(适用于 XX 品牌 XX 机或通用于 XX 机等)4.品牌 5.型号
84521	1.品牌类型 2.出口享惠情况 3.用途 4.是否手动 5.品牌 6.型号
84522	1.品牌类型 2.出口享惠情况 3.用途 4.是否自动 5.品牌 6.型号
84523	1.品牌类型 2.出口享惠情况 3.用途 4.品牌 5.型号
84529	1.品牌类型 2.出口享惠情况 3.用途(适用于 XX 品牌 XX 机或通用于 XX 机等)4.品牌 5.型号
84531	1.品牌类型 2.出口享惠情况 3.用途 4.品牌 5.型号
84532	1.品牌类型 2.出口享惠情况 3.用途 4.品牌 5.型号
84538	1.品牌类型 2.出口享惠情况 3.用途 4.品牌 5.型号
84539	1.品牌类型 2.出口享惠情况 3.用途(适用于 XX 品牌 XX 机或通用于 XX 机等)4.品牌 5.型号
84541	1.品牌类型 2.出口享惠情况 3.用途 4.品牌 5.型号
84542	1.品牌类型 2.出口享惠情况 3.用途 4.品牌 5.型号
84543	1.品牌类型 2.出口享惠情况 3.用途 4.品牌 5.型号
84549	1.品牌类型 2.出口享惠情况 3.用途(适用于 XX 品牌 XX 机或通用于 XX 机等)4.品牌 5.型号
84551	1.品牌类型 2.出口享惠情况 3.用途 4.加工方式 5.品牌 6.型号
84552	1.品牌类型 2.出口享惠情况 3.用途 4.加工方式 5.品牌 6.型号
84553	1.品牌类型 2.出口享惠情况 3.用途(适用于 XX 品牌 XX 机或通用于 XX 机等)4.品牌 5.型号 6.规格(轧辊长度、辊身直径、辊颈直径)
84559	1.品牌类型 2.出口享惠情况 3.用途(适用于 XX 品牌 XX 机或通用于 XX 机等)4.品牌 5.型号
84561	1.品牌类型 2.出口享惠情况 3.功能 4.加工方式 5.品牌 6.型号
84562	1.品牌类型 2.出口享惠情况 3.功能 4.加工方式 5.品牌 6.型号
8456301	1.品牌类型 2.出口享惠情况 3.控制方式 4.功能 5.加工方式 6.品牌 7.型号 8.功率 9.加工精度
8456309	1.品牌类型 2.出口享惠情况 3.控制方式 4.功能 5.加工方式 6.品牌 7.型号 8.功率
84564	1.品牌类型 2.出口享惠情况 3.功能 4.加工方式 5.品牌 6.型号
84565	1.品牌类型 2.出口享惠情况 3.功能 4.加工方式 5.品牌 6.型号
84569	1.品牌类型 2.出口享惠情况 3.功能 4.加工方式 5.品牌 6.型号
84571	1.品牌类型 2.出口享惠情况 3.用途 4.功能(如金属钻、镗、铣等)5.可加装刀库注明刀库容量及选配件 6.是否可自动换刀 7.品牌 8.型号 9.中韩自贸协定项下进口数控机床请注明所用数控装置品牌、型号及原产地
84572	1.品牌类型 2.出口享惠情况 3.用途 4.功能(如金属钻、镗、铣等)5.加工工位数 6.动力头个数 7.品牌 8.型号 9.中韩自贸协定项下进口数控机床请注明所用数控装置品牌、型号及原产地
84573	1.品牌类型 2.出口享惠情况 3.用途 4.功能(如金属钻、镗、铣等)5.加工工位数 6.动力头个数 7.品牌 8.型号 9.中韩自贸协定项下进口数控机床请注明所用数控装置品牌、型号及原产地
8458	1.品牌类型 2.出口享惠情况 3.用途 4.控制方式 5.主轴方向(垂直或水平)6.品牌 7.型号 8.ECFA 和中韩自贸协定项下进口数控机床请注明所用数控装置品牌、型号及原产地
84591	1.品牌类型 2.出口享惠情况 3.用途 4.功能 5.动力头移动方式 6.品牌 7.控制方式 8.型号 9.可加装刀库注明刀库容量及选配件
84592	1.品牌类型 2.出口享惠情况 3.用途 4.功能 5.控制方式 6.品牌 7.型号 8.ECFA 和中韩自贸协定项下进口数控机床请注明所用数控装置品牌、型号及原产地
84593	1.品牌类型 2.出口享惠情况 3.用途 4.功能 5.控制方式 6.品牌 7.型号 8.中韩自贸协定项下进口数控机床请注明所用数控装置品牌、型号及原产地
84594	1.品牌类型 2.出口享惠情况 3.用途 4.功能 5.控制方式 6.品牌 7.型号 8.中韩自贸协定项下进口数控机床请注明所用数控装置品牌、型号及原产地
84595	1.品牌类型 2.出口享惠情况 3.用途 4.功能 5.控制方式 6.是否为升降台式 7.品牌 8.中韩自贸协定项下进口数控机床请注明所用数控装置品牌、型号及原产地 9.型号
84596	1.品牌类型 2.出口享惠情况 3.用途 4.功能 5.控制方式 6.是否为龙门式 7.品牌 8.中韩自贸协定项下进口数控机床请注明所用数控装置品牌、型号及原产地 9.型号
84597	1.品牌类型 2.出口享惠情况 3.用途 4.功能 5.品牌 6.控制方式 7.型号 8.中韩自贸协定项下进口数控机床请注明所用数控装置品牌、型号及原产地
84601	1.品牌类型 2.出口享惠情况 3.用途 4.控制方式 5.坐标定位精度 6.品牌 7.型号 8. ECFA 和中韩自贸协定项下进口数控机床请注明所用数控装置品牌、型号及原产地
84602	1.品牌类型 2.出口享惠情况 3.用途 4.控制方式 5.坐标定位精度 6.结构类型(内圆、外圆等)7.品牌 8.型号 9.中韩自贸协定项下进口数控机床请注明所用数控装置品牌、型号及原产地
84603	1.品牌类型 2.出口享惠情况 3.用途 4.控制方式 5.品牌 6.型号 7.中韩自贸协定项下进口数控机床请注明所用数控装置品牌、型号及原产地
84604	1.品牌类型 2.出口享惠情况 3.用途 4.品牌 5.型号 6.ECFA 和中韩自贸协定项下进口数控机床请注明所用数控装置品牌、型号及原产地
84609	1.品牌类型 2.出口享惠情况 3.用途 4.品牌 5.型号
84612	1.品牌类型 2.出口享惠情况 3.用途 4.功能 5.结构类型 6.品牌 7.型号
84613	1.品牌类型 2.出口享惠情况 3.用途 4.功能 5.结构类型 6.品牌 7.型号
84614	1.品牌类型 2.出口享惠情况 3.用途 4.控制方式 5.功能 6.品牌 7.型号 8.中韩自贸协定项下进口数控机床请注明所用数控装置品牌、型号及原产地
84615	1.品牌类型 2.出口享惠情况 3.用途 4.功能 5.品牌 6.型号 7.ECFA 和中韩自贸协定项下进口数控机床请注明所用数控装置品牌、型号及原产地
84619	1.品牌类型 2.出口享惠情况 3.用途 4.功能 5.结构类型 6.品牌 7.型号
84621	1.品牌类型 2.出口享惠情况 3.用途 4.功能 5.控制方式 6.品牌 7.型号 8. ECFA 和中韩自贸协定项下进口数控机床请注明所用数控装置品牌、型号及原产地
84622	1.品牌类型 2.出口享惠情况 3.用途 4.功能 5.控制方式 6.品牌 7.型号 8.中韩自贸协定项下进口数控机床请注明所用数控装置品牌、型号及原产地
84623	1.品牌类型 2.出口享惠情况 3.用途 4.功能 5.控制方式 6.品牌 7.型号 8.中韩自贸协定项下进口数控机床请注明所用数控装置品牌、型号及原产地
84624	1.品牌类型 2.出口享惠情况 3.用途 4.功能 5.控制方式 6.品牌 7.型号 8.中韩自贸协定项下进口数控机床请注明所用数控装置品牌、型号及原产地
846291	1.品牌类型 2.出口享惠情况 3.用途 4.功能 5.品牌 6.型号 7.中韩自贸协定项下进口数控机床请注明所用数控装置品牌、型号及原产地
846299	1.品牌类型 2.出口享惠情况 3.用途 4.功能 5.品牌 6.型号 7.ECFA 和中韩自贸协定项下进口数控机床请注明所用数控装置品牌、型号及原产地

商品编码	申报要素
8463	1.品牌类型 2.出口享惠情况 3.用途 4.功能 5.品牌 6.型号
8464	1.品牌类型 2.出口享惠情况 3.用途 4.功能 5.加工材料 6.品牌 7.型号
8465	1.品牌类型 2.出口享惠情况 3.用途 4.功能 5.加工材料 6.品牌 7.型号
8466	1.品牌类型 2.出口享惠情况 3.用途(适用于 XX 品牌 XX 机或通用于 XX 机等)4.品牌 5.型号
84671	1.品牌类型 2.出口享惠情况 3.驱动方式 4.是否为手提式 5.品牌 6.型号
84672	1.品牌类型 2.出口享惠情况 3.驱动方式 4.是否为手提式 5.品牌 6.型号
84678	1.品牌类型 2.出口享惠情况 3.驱动方式 4.是否为手提式 5.品牌 6.型号
84679	1.品牌类型 2.出口享惠情况 3.用途(适用于 XX 品牌 XX 机或通用于 XX 机等)4.品牌 5.型号
84681	1.品牌类型 2.出口享惠情况 3.原理 4.是否为手提式 5.品牌 6.型号
84682	1.品牌类型 2.出口享惠情况 3.原理 4.是否为手提式 5.品牌 6.型号
84688	1.品牌类型 2.出口享惠情况 3.原理 4.是否为手提式 5.品牌 6.型号
84689	1.品牌类型 2.出口享惠情况 3.用途(适用于 XX 品牌 XX 机或通用于 XX 机等)4.品牌 5.型号
84701	1.品牌类型 2.出口享惠情况 3.是否需外接电源 4.品牌 5.型号
84702	1.品牌类型 2.出口享惠情况 3.是否有打印装置 4.品牌 5.型号
84703	1.品牌类型 2.出口享惠情况 3.品牌 4.型号
84705	1.品牌类型 2.出口享惠情况 3.用途 4.品牌 5.型号
84709	1.品牌类型 2.出口享惠情况 3.用途 4.品牌 5.型号
84713	1.品牌类型 2.出口享惠情况 3.机型 4.配置(系统组成部件)5.品牌 6.型号
847141	1.品牌类型 2.出口享惠情况 3.机型 4.配置(系统组成部件)5.品牌 6.型号 7.操作系统
8471491	1.品牌类型 2.出口享惠情况 3.机型 4.配置(系统组成部件)5.是否以系统形式报验 6.品牌 7.型号 8.操作系统
8471492	1.品牌类型 2.出口享惠情况 3.机型 4.配置(系统组成部件)5.是否以系统形式报验 6.品牌 7.型号 8.操作系统
8471494	1.品牌类型 2.出口享惠情况 3.机型 4.配置(系统组成部件)5.是否以系统形式报验 6.品牌 7.型号 8.操作系统
84714991	1.品牌类型 2.出口享惠情况 3.机型 4.配置(列如:包括现场控制站、操作员站以及工程师站等)5.是否以系统形式报验 6.品牌 7.型号 8.操作系统
84714999	1.品牌类型 2.出口享惠情况 3.机型 4.配置(系统组成部件)5.是否以系统形式报验 6.品牌 7.型号 8.操作系统
84715	1.品牌类型 2.出口享惠情况 3.机型 4.配置(系统组成部件)5.品牌 6.型号 7.操作系统 8.用途
8471604	1.品牌类型 2.出口享惠情况 3.品牌 4.型号
8471605	1.品牌类型 2.出口享惠情况 3.品牌 4.型号
8471606	1.品牌类型 2.出口享惠情况 3.品牌 4.型号
84716071	1.品牌类型 2.出口享惠情况 3.品牌 4.型号 5.连接方式(有线、无线)
84716072	1.品牌类型 2.出口享惠情况 3.品牌 4.型号 5.连接方式(有线、无线)6.DPI(分辨率)7.CPI(鼠标精度)
8471609	1.品牌类型 2.出口享惠情况 3.品牌 4.型号
8471701	1.品牌类型 2.出口享惠情况 3.品牌 4.型号 5.硬盘容量及缓存容量 6.转速
8471702	1.品牌类型 2.出口享惠情况 3.品牌 4.型号
8471703	1.品牌类型 2.出口享惠情况 3.品牌 4.型号 5.是否带有刻录功能 6.刻录速度
8471709	1.品牌类型 2.出口享惠情况 3.品牌 4.型号
84718	1.品牌类型 2.出口享惠情况 3.品牌 4.型号
84719	1.品牌类型 2.出口享惠情况 3.品牌 4.型号
84721	1.品牌类型 2.出口享惠情况 3.用途 4.品牌 5.型号
84723	1.品牌类型 2.出口享惠情况 3.用途 4.品牌 5.型号
8472901	1.品牌类型 2.出口享惠情况 3.用途(存款、取款、存取款一体机等)4.品牌 5.型号 6.配置 7.安装方式(穿墙式等)
8472902	1.品牌类型 2.出口享惠情况 3.用途 4.品牌 5.型号
8472903	1.品牌类型 2.出口享惠情况 3.用途 4.品牌 5.型号
8472904	1.品牌类型 2.出口享惠情况 3.用途 4.品牌 5.型号
8472905	1.品牌类型 2.出口享惠情况 3.用途 4.品牌 5.型号
8472906	1.品牌类型 2.出口享惠情况 3.用途 4.品牌 5.型号
8472909	1.品牌类型 2.出口享惠情况 3.用途 4.品牌 5.型号
84732	1.品牌类型 2.出口享惠情况 3.用途(适用于 XX 品牌 XX 机或通用于 XX 机等)4.品牌 5.型号
8473301	1.品牌类型 2.出口享惠情况 3.用途(适用于 XX 品牌 XX 机或通用于 XX 机等)4.品牌 5.型号
8473309	1.品牌类型 2.出口享惠情况 3.用途(适用于 XX 品牌 XX 机或通用于 XX 机等)4.品牌 5.型号 6.如为内存条需申报容量

商品编码	申报要素
84734	1.品牌类型 2.出口享惠情况 3.用途(适用于 XX 品牌 XX 机或通用于 XX 机等)4.品牌 5.型号
84735	1.品牌类型 2.出口享惠情况 3.用途(适用于 XX 品牌 XX 机或通用于 XX 机等)4.品牌 5.型号
84741	1.品牌类型 2.出口享惠情况 3.用途 4.品牌 5.型号
84742	1.品牌类型 2.出口享惠情况 3.用途 4.原理 5.品牌 6.型号
84743	1.品牌类型 2.出口享惠情况 3.用途 4.品牌 5.型号
84748	1.品牌类型 2.出口享惠情况 3.用途 4.原理 5.品牌 6.型号
84749	1.品牌类型 2.出口享惠情况 3.用途(适用于 XX 品牌 XX 机或通用于 XX 机等)4.品牌 5.型号
84751	1.品牌类型 2.出口享惠情况 3.用途 4.品牌 5.型号
84752	1.品牌类型 2.出口享惠情况 3.用途 4.品牌 5.型号
84759	1.品牌类型 2.出口享惠情况 3.用途(适用于 XX 品牌 XX 机或通用于 XX 机等)4.品牌 5.型号
84762	1.品牌类型 2.出口享惠情况 3.供应商品种类 4.是否装有加热或制冷装置 5.品牌 6.型号
84768	1.品牌类型 2.出口享惠情况 3.供应商品种类 4.是否装有加热或制冷装置 5.品牌 6.型号
84769	1.品牌类型 2.出口享惠情况 3.用途(适用于 XX 品牌 XX 机或通用于 XX 机等)4.品牌 5.型号
8477101	1.品牌类型 2.出口享惠情况 3.用途 4.功能 5.品牌 6.型号 7.合模力 8.螺杆直径 9.注射容量 10.射出速度
8477109	1.品牌类型 2.出口享惠情况 3.用途 4.功能 5.品牌 6.型号 7.合模力
84772	1.品牌类型 2.出口享惠情况 3.用途 4.功能 5.品牌 6.型号
84773	1.品牌类型 2.出口享惠情况 3.用途 4.功能 5.品牌 6.型号
84774	1.品牌类型 2.出口享惠情况 3.用途 4.功能 5.品牌 6.型号
84775	1.品牌类型 2.出口享惠情况 3.用途 4.功能 5.品牌 6.型号
84778	1.品牌类型 2.出口享惠情况 3.用途 4.品牌 5.型号
84779	1.品牌类型 2.出口享惠情况 3.用途(适用于 XX 品牌 XX 机或通用于 XX 机等)4.品牌 5.型号
84781	1.品牌类型 2.出口享惠情况 3.用途 4.品牌 5.型号
84789	1.品牌类型 2.出口享惠情况 3.用途(适用于 XX 品牌 XX 机或通用于 XX 机等)4.品牌 5.型号
84791	1.品牌类型 2.出口享惠情况 3.用途 4.功能 5.品牌 6.型号
84792	1.品牌类型 2.出口享惠情况 3.用途 4.功能 5.品牌 6.型号
84793	1.品牌类型 2.出口享惠情况 3.用途 4.功能 5.品牌 6.型号
84794	1.品牌类型 2.出口享惠情况 3.用途 4.品牌 5.型号
84795	1.品牌类型 2.出口享惠情况 3.用途 4.功能 5.品牌 6.型号
84796	1.品牌类型 2.出口享惠情况 3.用途 4.功能 5.品牌 6.型号
84797	1.品牌类型 2.出口享惠情况 3.用途 4.品牌 5.型号
84798	1.品牌类型 2.出口享惠情况 3.用途 4.功能 5.品牌 6.型号
84799	1.品牌类型 2.出口享惠情况 3.用途(适用于 XX 品牌 XX 机或通用于 XX 机等)4.品牌 5.型号
84801	1.品牌类型 2.出口享惠情况 3.用途 4.适用材料 5.品牌 6.型号
84802	1.品牌类型 2.出口享惠情况 3.用途 4.适用材料 5.品牌 6.型号
84803	1.品牌类型 2.出口享惠情况 3.用途 4.适用材料 5.品牌 6.型号
84804	1.品牌类型 2.出口享惠情况 3.用途 4.适用材料 5.品牌 6.型号 7.原理
84805	1.品牌类型 2.出口享惠情况 3.用途 4.适用材料 5.品牌 6.型号
84806	1.品牌类型 2.出口享惠情况 3.用途 4.适用材料 5.品牌 6.型号
84807	1.品牌类型 2.出口享惠情况 3.用途 4.适用材料 5.品牌 6.型号 7.原理
84811	1.品牌类型 2.出口享惠情况 3.用途 4.品牌 5.型号
84812	1.品牌类型 2.出口享惠情况 3.用途 4.品牌 5.型号
84813	1.品牌类型 2.出口享惠情况 3.用途 4.品牌 5.型号
84814	1.品牌类型 2.出口享惠情况 3.用途 4.品牌 5.型号
8481802	1.品牌类型 2.出口享惠情况 3.用途 4.是否电磁式 5.品牌 6.型号
8481803	1.品牌类型 2.出口享惠情况 3.用途 4.品牌 5.型号
8481804	1.品牌类型 2.出口享惠情况 3.用途 4.品牌 5.型号
8481809	1.品牌类型 2.出口享惠情况 3.用途 4.品牌 5.型号
84819	1.品牌类型 2.出口享惠情况 3.用途(适用于 XX 品牌 XX 机或通用于 XX 机等)4.品牌 5.型号
84821	1.品牌类型 2.出口享惠情况 3.结构类型 4.品牌 5.型号
84822	1.品牌类型 2.出口享惠情况 3.结构类型 4.品牌 5.型号
84823	1.品牌类型 2.出口享惠情况 3.结构类型 4.品牌 5.型号
84824	1.品牌类型 2.出口享惠情况 3.结构类型 4.滚柱直径、长度 5.品牌 6.型号
84825	1.品牌类型 2.出口享惠情况 3.结构类型 4.品牌 5.型号
84828	1.品牌类型 2.出口享惠情况 3.结构类型 4.品牌 5.型号
848291	1.品牌类型 2.出口享惠情况 3.用途(适用于 XX 品牌 XX 机或通用于 XX 机等)4.如是滚珠请申报最大、最小及标称直径 5.品牌 6.型号
848299	1.品牌类型 2.出口享惠情况 3.用途(适用于 XX 品牌 XX 机或通用于 XX 机等)4.品牌 5.型号

商品编码	申报要素
84831	1.品牌类型 2.出口享惠情况 3.用途 4.品牌 5.型号
84832	1.品牌类型 2.出口享惠情况 3.注明是否装有滚珠或滚子轴承 4.用途 5.品牌 6.型号
84833	1.品牌类型 2.出口享惠情况 3.如为轴承座需注明是否带有滚珠或滚子轴承 4.用途 5.品牌 6.型号
84834	1.品牌类型 2.出口享惠情况 3.原理 4.用途 5.品牌 6.型号
84835	1.品牌类型 2.出口享惠情况 3.用途 4.品牌 5.型号
84836	1.品牌类型 2.出口享惠情况 3.用途 4.品牌 5.型号
84839	1.品牌类型 2.出口享惠情况 3.用途 4.品牌 5.型号
84841	1.品牌类型 2.出口享惠情况 3.组成材料 4.品牌 5.型号
84842	1.品牌类型 2.出口享惠情况 3.结构 4.品牌 5.型号
84849	1.品牌类型 2.出口享惠情况 3.各自构成材料 4.是否成套包装 5.品牌 6.型号
84861	1.品牌类型 2.出口享惠情况 3.用途 4.功能 5.品牌 6.型号
84862	1.品牌类型 2.出口享惠情况 3.用途 4.功能 5.品牌 6.型号
84863	1.品牌类型 2.出口享惠情况 3.用途 4.功能 5.品牌 6.型号
84864	1.品牌类型 2.出口享惠情况 3.用途 4.功能 5.品牌 6.型号
84869	1.品牌类型 2.出口享惠情况 3.用途(适用于 XX 品牌 XX 机或通用于 XX 机等)4.品牌 5.型号
8487	1.品牌类型 2.出口享惠情况 3.用途(适用于 XX 品牌 XX 机或通用于 XX 机等)4.品牌 5.型号
8501101	1.品牌类型 2.出口享惠情况 3.用途 4.输出功率 5.品牌 6.型号
8501109	1.品牌类型 2.出口享惠情况 3.用途 4.输出功率 5.机座尺寸 6.品牌 7.型号
85012	1.品牌类型 2.出口享惠情况 3.用途 4.是否交直流两用 5.输出功率 6.品牌 7.型号
85013	1.品牌类型 2.出口享惠情况 3.是否为直流 4.输出功率 5.品牌 6.型号
85014	1.品牌类型 2.出口享惠情况 3.是否为单相交流 4.输出功率 5.品牌 6.型号
85015	1.品牌类型 2.出口享惠情况 3.输出功率 4.品牌 5.型号
85016	1.品牌类型 2.出口享惠情况 3.用途 4.是否为交流 5.输出功率 6.品牌 7.型号
8502	1.品牌类型 2.出口享惠情况 3.组成原动机类型 4.输出功率 5.品牌 6.型号
8503001	1.品牌类型 2.出口享惠情况 3.用途(适用于 XX 品牌 XX 机或通用于 XX 机等)4.品牌 5.型号
8503002	1.品牌类型 2.出口享惠情况 3.用途(所适用整机的类型及输出功率)4.品牌 5.型号
8503003	1.品牌类型 2.出口享惠情况 3.用途(适用于 XX 品牌 XX 机或通用于 XX 机等)4.品牌 5.型号
8503009	1.品牌类型 2.出口享惠情况 3.用途(所适用整机的类型及输出功率)4.品牌 5.型号
85041	1.品牌类型 2.出口享惠情况 3.用途 4.品牌 5.型号
85042	1.品牌类型 2.出口享惠情况 3.额定容量 4.是否为液体介质 5.品牌 6.型号
85043	1.品牌类型 2.出口享惠情况 3.额定容量 4.是否为液体介质 5.品牌 6.型号
8504401	1.品牌类型 2.出口享惠情况 3.用途 4.类型(交流稳压电源或直流稳压电源)5.额定输出功率 6.精度 7.品牌 8.型号
8504402	1.品牌类型 2.出口享惠情况 3.功率 4.品牌 5.型号
8504403	1.品牌类型 2.出口享惠情况 3.功率 4.品牌 5.型号
85044091	1.品牌类型 2.出口享惠情况 3.用途 4.是否封装 5.品牌 6.型号
85044099	1.品牌类型 2.出口享惠情况 3.用途 4.功率 5.品牌 6.型号
85045	1.品牌类型 2.出口享惠情况 3.用途 4.品牌 5.型号
85049	1.品牌类型 2.出口享惠情况 3.用途(适用于 XX 品牌 XX 机或通用于 XX 机等)4.品牌 5.型号
8505111	1.品牌类型 2.出口享惠情况 3.材质 4.品牌 5.型号 6.稀土元素的重量百分比,以[A]表示
8505119	1.品牌类型 2.出口享惠情况 3.材质 4.品牌 5.型号
850519	1.品牌类型 2.出口享惠情况 3.材质 4.品牌 5.型号
85052	1.品牌类型 2.出口享惠情况 3.用途 4.品牌 5.型号
8505901	1.品牌类型 2.出口享惠情况 3.用途 4.原理 5.品牌 6.型号
8505909	1.品牌类型 2.出口享惠情况 3.用途(如核磁共振成像装置用等)4.原理 5.品牌 6.型号
85061011	1.品牌类型 2.出口享惠情况 3.用途 4.材质 5.形状 6.品牌 7.型号 8.容量 9.是否含汞
85061012	1.品牌类型 2.出口享惠情况 3.用途 4.材质 5.形状 6.品牌 7.型号 8.容量 9.是否含汞
85061019	1.品牌类型 2.出口享惠情况 3.用途 4.材质 5.品牌 6.型号 7.容量 8.是否含汞
8506109	1.品牌类型 2.出口享惠情况 3.用途 4.材质 5.品牌 6.型号 7.容量 8.是否含汞
85063	1.品牌类型 2.出口享惠情况 3.用途 4.材质 5.品牌 6.型号 7.容量 8.是否含汞

商品编码	申报要素
85064	1.品牌类型 2.出口享惠情况 3.用途 4.材质 5.品牌 6.型号 7.容量 8.是否含汞
85065	1.品牌类型 2.出口享惠情况 3.用途 4.材质 5.品牌 6.型号 7.容量 8.是否含汞
85066	1.品牌类型 2.出口享惠情况 3.用途 4.材质 5.品牌 6.型号 7.容量 8.是否含汞
85068	1.品牌类型 2.出口享惠情况 3.用途 4.材质 5.品牌 6.型号 7.容量 8.是否含汞
85069	1.品牌类型 2.出口享惠情况 3.用途(适用原电池或原电池组类型)4.品牌 5.型号
85071	1.品牌类型 2.出口享惠情况 3.用途 4.材质 5.品牌 6.型号 7.容量 8.是否含汞 9.额定电压
85072	1.品牌类型 2.出口享惠情况 3.用途 4.材质 5.品牌 6.型号 7.容量 8.是否含汞 9.额定电压
85073	1.品牌类型 2.出口享惠情况 3.用途 4.材质 5.品牌 6.型号 7.容量 8.是否含汞 9.额定电压
85074	1.品牌类型 2.出口享惠情况 3.用途 4.材质 5.品牌 6.型号 7.容量 8.是否含汞 9.额定电压
85075	1.品牌类型 2.出口享惠情况 3.用途 4.材质 5.品牌 6.型号 7.容量 8.是否含汞 9.额定电压
85076	1.品牌类型 2.出口享惠情况 3.用途 4.材质 5.品牌 6.型号 7.容量 8.是否含汞 9.额定电压
85078	1.品牌类型 2.出口享惠情况 3.用途 4.材质 5.品牌 6.型号 7.容量 8.是否含汞 9.额定电压
85079	1.品牌类型 2.出口享惠情况 3.用途(适用于 XX 品牌 XX 机或通用于 XX 机等)4.品牌 5.型号
85081	1.品牌类型 2.出口享惠情况 3.驱动方式 4.集尘器容积 5.品牌 6.型号 7.功率
85086	1.品牌类型 2.出口享惠情况 3.驱动方式 4.品牌 5.型号
85087	1.品牌类型 2.出口享惠情况 3.用途(适用于 XX 品牌 XX 机或通用于 XX 机等)4.品牌 5.型号
85094	1.品牌类型 2.出口享惠情况 3.用途 4.机重 5.功率 6.品牌 7.型号
85098	1.品牌类型 2.出口享惠情况 3.用途 4.机重 5.功率 6.品牌 7.型号
85099	1.品牌类型 2.出口享惠情况 3.用途(适用于 XX 品牌 XX 机或通用于 XX 机等)4.品牌 5.型号
85101	1.品牌类型 2.出口享惠情况 3.品牌 4.型号
85102	1.品牌类型 2.出口享惠情况 3.品牌 4.型号
85103	1.品牌类型 2.出口享惠情况 3.品牌 4.型号
85109	1.品牌类型 2.出口享惠情况 3.用途(适用于 XX 品牌 XX 机或通用于 XX 机等)4.品牌 5.型号
85111	1.品牌类型 2.出口享惠情况 3.用途 4.功能 5.生产件的通用零件编号后加注"/TY"6.成套散件装配后完整品的零部件的编号 7.品牌 8.型号 9.零部件完整编号并在前加注"S/"、"W/"或"WF/"之一(生产件填报"S/",品牌和适用的整车厂牌一致的维修件填报"W/",品牌和适用的整车厂牌不一致的维修件的填报"WF/")
85112	1.品牌类型 2.出口享惠情况 3.用途 4.功能 5.品牌 6.型号
85113	1.品牌类型 2.出口享惠情况 3.用途 4.功能 5.品牌 6.型号
8511401	1.品牌类型 2.出口享惠情况 3.用途 4.功能 5.品牌 6.型号
8511409	1.品牌类型 2.出口享惠情况 3.用途 4.功能 5.适用发动机的输出功率 6.品牌 7.型号
85115	1.品牌类型 2.出口享惠情况 3.用途 4.功能 5.品牌 6.型号
85118	1.品牌类型 2.出口享惠情况 3.用途 4.功能 5.品牌 6.型号
85119	1.品牌类型 2.出口享惠情况 3.用途(适用于 XX 品牌 XX 机或通用于 XX 机等)4.品牌 5.型号
85121	1.品牌类型 2.出口享惠情况 3.用途 4.功能 5.品牌 6.型号
8512201	1.品牌类型 2.出口享惠情况 3.用途 4.功能 5.生产件的通用零件编号后加注"/TY"6.成套散件装配后完整品的零部件的编号 7.品牌 8.型号 9.零部件完整编号并在前加注"S/"、"W/"或"WF/"之一(生产件填报"S/",品牌和适用的整车厂牌一致的维修件填报"W/",品牌和适用的整车厂牌不一致的维修件的填报"WF/")
8512209	1.品牌类型 2.出口享惠情况 3.用途 4.功能 5.生产件的通用零件编号后加注"/TY"6.成套散件装配后完整品的零部件的编号 7.品牌 8.型号 9.零部件完整编号并在前加注"S/"、"W/"或"WF/"之一(生产件填报"S/",品牌和适用的整车厂牌一致的维修件填报"W/",品牌和适用的整车厂牌不一致的维修件的填报"WF/")
85123	1.品牌类型 2.出口享惠情况 3.用途 4.功能 5.生产件的通用零件编号后加注"/TY"6.成套散件装配后完整品的零部件的编号 7.品牌 8.型号 9.零部件完整编号并在前加注"S/"、"W/"或"WF/"之一(生产件填报"S/",品牌和适用的整车厂牌一致的维修件填报"W/",品牌和适用的整车厂牌不一致的维修件的填报"WF/")

商品编码	申报要素
85124	1.品牌类型 2.出口享惠情况 3.用途 4.功能 5.生产件的通用零件编号后加注“/TY”6.成套散件装配后完整品的零部件的编号 7.品牌 8.型号 9.零部件完整编号并在前加注“S/”、“W/”或“WF/”之一(生产件填报“S/”,品牌和适用的整车厂牌一致的维修件填报“W/”,品牌和适用的整车厂牌不一致的维修件的填报“WF/”)
85129	1.品牌类型 2.出口享惠情况 3.用途(适用于 XX 品牌 XX 机或通用于 XX 机等)4.功能 5.生产件的通用零件编号后加注“/TY”6.成套散件装配后完整品的零部件的编号 7.品牌 8.型号 9.零部件完整编号并在前加注“S/”、“W/”或“WF/”之一(生产件填报“S/”,品牌和适用的整车厂牌一致的维修件填报“W/”,品牌和适用的整车厂牌不一致的维修件的填报“WF/”)
85131	1.品牌类型 2.出口享惠情况 3.是否手提式 4.品牌 5.型号
85139	1.品牌类型 2.出口享惠情况 3.用途(适用于 XX 品牌 XX 机或通用于 XX 机等)4.品牌 5.型号
85141	1.品牌类型 2.出口享惠情况 3.用途(工业用,实验室用)4.加热原理 5.品牌 6.型号
85142	1.品牌类型 2.出口享惠情况 3.用途(工业用,实验室用)4.加热原理 5.品牌 6.型号
85143	1.品牌类型 2.出口享惠情况 3.用途(工业用,实验室用)4.加热原理 5.品牌 6.型号
85144	1.品牌类型 2.出口享惠情况 3.用途(工业用,实验室用)4.加热原理 5.品牌 6.型号
85149	1.品牌类型 2.出口享惠情况 3.用途(适用于 XX 品牌 XX 机或通用于 XX 机等)4.品牌 5.型号
851511	1.品牌类型 2.出口享惠情况 3.原理 4.焊接过程中是否使用钎料 5.品牌 6.型号
851519	1.品牌类型 2.出口享惠情况 3.原理 4.若为印刷电路组件制造用需注明 5.焊接过程中是否使用钎料 6.品牌 7.型号
85152	1.品牌类型 2.出口享惠情况 3.原理 4.是否为全自动或半自动 5.品牌 6.型号
85153	1.品牌类型 2.出口享惠情况 3.原理 4.是否为全自动或半自动 5.品牌 6.型号
85158	1.品牌类型 2.出口享惠情况 3.原理 4.品牌 5.型号
85159	1.品牌类型 2.出口享惠情况 3.用途(适用于 XX 品牌 XX 机或通用于 XX 机等)4.若为印刷电路组件制造用需注明 5.品牌 6.型号
8516101	1.品牌类型 2.出口享惠情况 3.工作方式(储存式、即热式、浸入式等)4.加热原理 5.品牌 6.型号 7.容量
8516102	1.品牌类型 2.出口享惠情况 3.工作方式(储存式、即热式、浸入式等)4.加热原理 5.品牌 6.型号
8516109	1.品牌类型 2.出口享惠情况 3.工作方式(储存式、即热式、浸入式等)4.加热原理 5.品牌 6.型号
85162	1.品牌类型 2.出口享惠情况 3.用途 4.工作方式(储存式、辐射式、对流式等)5.品牌 6.型号
85163	1.品牌类型 2.出口享惠情况 3.用途 4.加热原理 5.品牌 6.型号
85164	1.品牌类型 2.出口享惠情况 3.用途 4.加热原理 5.品牌 6.型号
85165	1.品牌类型 2.出口享惠情况 3.用途 4.加热原理 5.品牌 6.型号
85166	1.品牌类型 2.出口享惠情况 3.用途 4.加热原理 5.品牌 6.型号
85167	1.品牌类型 2.出口享惠情况 3.用途 4.加热原理 5 品牌 6.型号
85168	1.品牌类型 2.出口享惠情况 3.用途 4.品牌 5.型号
85169	1.品牌类型 2.出口享惠情况 3.用途(适用于 XX 品牌 XX 机或通用于 XX 机等)4.品牌 5.型号
85171	1.品牌类型 2.出口享惠情况 3.用途 4.适用网络种类(蜂窝网络、无线网络、有线网络、以太网等)5.品牌 6.型号 7.是否加密
851761	1.品牌类型 2.出口享惠情况 3.用途 4.品牌 5.型号 6.是否加密
8517621	1.品牌类型 2.出口享惠情况 3.用途 4.控制方式 5.处理信号的类型 6.型号
8517622	1.品牌类型 2.出口享惠情况 3.用途 4.通讯方式 5.品牌 6.型号 7.是否加密
8517623	1.品牌类型 2.出口享惠情况 3.用途 4.通讯方式 5.适用网络种类(蜂窝网络、有线网络、以太网等)6.品牌 7.型号
8517629	1.品牌类型 2.出口享惠情况 3.用途 4.功能 5.适用网络种类(蜂窝网络、有线网络、以太网等)6.品牌 7.型号
851769	1.品牌类型 2.出口享惠情况 3.用途 4.品牌 5.型号
8517701	1.品牌类型 2.出口享惠情况 3.用途(适用于 XX 品牌 XX 机或通用于 XX 机等)4.品牌 5.型号
8517702	1.品牌类型 2.出口享惠情况 3.用途(适用于 XX 品牌 XX 机或通用于 XX 机等)4.品牌 5.型号
8517703	1.品牌类型 2.出口享惠情况 3.用途(适用于 XX 品牌 XX 机或通用于 XX 机等)4.显示屏或显示模块请申报尺寸(英寸)5.显示屏或显示模块请申报种类(如 LED、OLED 等)6.显示屏或显示模块请申报是否需要二次加工 7.品牌 8.型号
8517704	1.品牌类型 2.出口享惠情况 3.用途(适用于 XX 品牌 XX 机或通用于 XX 机等)4.品牌 5.型号
8517706	1.品牌类型 2.出口享惠情况 3.用途(适用于 XX 品牌 XX 机或通用于 XX 机等)4.品牌 5.型号
8517707	1.品牌类型 2.出口享惠情况 3.用途(适用于 XX 品牌 XX 机或通用于 XX 机等)4.品牌 5.型号
8517709	1.品牌类型 2.出口享惠情况 3.用途(适用于 XX 品牌 XX 机或通用于 XX 机等)4.品牌 5.型号
85181	1.品牌类型 2.出口享惠情况 3.品牌 4.型号
851821	1.品牌类型 2.出口享惠情况 3.结构类型(是否有箱体)4.用途 5.品牌 6.型号
851822	1.品牌类型 2.出口享惠情况 3.结构类型(是否有箱体)4.用途 5.品牌 6.型号 7.喇叭数量和尺寸
851829	1.品牌类型 2.出口享惠情况 3.结构类型(是否有箱体)4.用途 5.品牌 6.型号 7.喇叭尺寸
85183	1.品牌类型 2.出口享惠情况 3.品牌 4.型号
85184	1.品牌类型 2.出口享惠情况 3.品牌 4.型号
85185	1.品牌类型 2.出口享惠情况 3.组成部件 4.品牌 5.型号
85189	1.品牌类型 2.出口享惠情况 3.用途(适用于 XX 品牌 XX 机或通用于 XX 机等)4.品牌 5.型号
85192	1.品牌类型 2.出口享惠情况 3.支付方式 4.品牌 5.型号
85193	1.品牌类型 2.出口享惠情况 3.品牌 4.型号
85195	1.品牌类型 2.出口享惠情况 3.品牌 4.型号
85198	1.品牌类型 2.出口享惠情况 3.使用媒介 4.品牌 5.型号
85211	1.品牌类型 2.出口享惠情况 3.用途 4.使用媒介 5.品牌 6.型号
85219	1.品牌类型 2.出口享惠情况 3.使用媒介 4.类型 5.品牌 6.型号
8522	1.品牌类型 2.出口享惠情况 3.用途(适用于 XX 品牌 XX 机或通用于 XX 机等)4.品牌 5.型号
852321	1.品牌类型 2.出口享惠情况 3.用途 4.是否录制 5.品牌 6.型号 7.录制内容类型
8523291	1.品牌类型 2.出口享惠情况 3.用途 4.是否录制 5.品牌 6.型号 7.录制内容类型
8523292	1.品牌类型 2.出口享惠情况 3.用途 4.是否录制 5.磁带宽度 6.品牌 7.型号 8.录制内容类型
8523299	1.品牌类型 2.出口享惠情况 3.用途 4.是否录制 5.品牌 6.型号 7.录制内容类型
85234	1.品牌类型 2.出口享惠情况 3.用途 4.是否录制 5.录制内容类型 6.品牌 7.型号 8.存储容量 9.读取速度
852351	1.品牌类型 2.出口享惠情况 3.用途 4.是否录制 5.品牌 6.型号 7.容量
852352	1.品牌类型 2.出口享惠情况 3.用途 4.是否录制 5.品牌 6.型号 7.是否加密 8.存储容量
852359	1.品牌类型 2.出口享惠情况 3.用途 4.是否录制 5.品牌 6.型号
85238	1.品牌类型 2.出口享惠情况 3.用途 4.是否录制 5.品牌 6.型号
85255	1.品牌类型 2.出口享惠情况 3.用途 4.品牌 5.型号
85256	1.品牌类型 2.出口享惠情况 3.用途 4.结构组成 5.品牌 6.型号
85258011	1.品牌类型 2.出口享惠情况 3.用途 4.是否可装内置存储装置 5.品牌 6.型号
85258012	1.品牌类型 2.出口享惠情况 3.用途 4.是否可装内置存储装置 5.品牌 6.型号
85258013	1.品牌类型 2.出口享惠情况 3.用途 4.高清摄像头报玻璃镜头层数 5.高清摄像头报接口类型(是否 USB2.0 以上接口)6.高清摄像头报硬件传感器像素 7.是否可装内置存储装置 8.品牌 9.型号
85258021	1.品牌类型 2.出口享惠情况 3.用途 4.是否可装内置存储装置 5.品牌 6.型号
85258022	1.品牌类型 2.出口享惠情况 3.用途 4.是否可装内置存储装置 5.品牌 6.型号
85258025	1.品牌类型 2.出口享惠情况 3.用途 4.是否可装内置存储装置 5.品牌 6.型号
85258029	1.品牌类型 2.出口享惠情况 3.用途 4.是否可装内置存储装置 5.品牌 6.型号 7.像素
8525803	1.品牌类型 2.出口享惠情况 3.用途 4.是否可装内置存储装置 5.品牌 6.型号
85261	1.品牌类型 2.出口享惠情况 3.用途 4.品牌 5.型号
852691	1.品牌类型 2.出口享惠情况 3.用途 4.品牌 5.型号
852692	1.品牌类型 2.出口享惠情况 3.用途 4.品牌 5.型号 6.控制距离
85271	1.品牌类型 2.出口享惠情况 3.使用媒介(是否为盒式磁带)4.是否需外接电源 5.品牌 6.型号 7.外形尺寸
852721	1.品牌类型 2.出口享惠情况 3.用途 4.结构组成 5.具备接收和转换数字广播数据系统信号功能的需注明 6.品牌 7.型号
852729	1.品牌类型 2.出口享惠情况 3.用途 4.结构组成 5.品牌 6.型号
85279	1.品牌类型 2.出口享惠情况 3.用途 4.品牌 5.型号
852842	1.品牌类型 2.出口享惠情况 3.用途 4.显示原理 5.显示屏幕尺寸 6.接口类型(包括接口电路)7.品牌 8.型号
852849	1.品牌类型 2.出口享惠情况 3.用途 4.显示原理 5.显示屏幕尺寸 6.品牌 7.型号

商品编码	申报要素
8528521	1.品牌类型 2.出口享惠情况 3.用途 4.显示原理 5.显示屏幕尺寸 6.接口类型(包括接口电路)7.构成(是否带标记板、解码板或高频头板等信号处理板)8.品牌 9.型号
8528529	1.品牌类型 2.出口享惠情况 3.用途 4.显示原理 5.显示屏幕尺寸 6.接口类型(包括接口电路)7.品牌 8.型号
8528591	1.品牌类型 2.出口享惠情况 3.用途 4.显示原理 5.显示屏幕尺寸 6.品牌 7.型号 8.最高分辨率
8528599	1.品牌类型 2.出口享惠情况 3.用途 4.显示原理 5.显示屏幕尺寸 6.品牌 7.型号
85286	1.品牌类型 2.出口享惠情况 3.用途 4.显示原理 5.接口类型(包括接口电路)6.品牌 7.型号 8.亮度
852871	1.品牌类型 2.出口享惠情况 3.用途 4.是否带显示屏 5.品牌 6.型号
852872	1.品牌类型 2.出口享惠情况 3.用途 4.显示原理 5.显示屏幕尺寸 6.品牌 7.型号
852873	1.品牌类型 2.出口享惠情况 3.用途 4.显示原理 5.显示屏幕尺寸 6.品牌 7.型号
85291	1.品牌类型 2.出口享惠情况 3.用途(适用于 XX 品牌 XX 机或通用于 XX 机等)4.品牌 5.型号
8529901	1.品牌类型 2.出口享惠情况 3.用途(适用于 XX 品牌 XX 机或通用于 XX 机等)4.品牌 5.型号
85299041	1.品牌类型 2.出口享惠情况 3.用途(适用于 XX 品牌 XX 机或通用于 XX 机等)4.品牌 5.型号
85299042	1.品牌类型 2.出口享惠情况 3.用途(适用于 XX 品牌 XX 机或通用于 XX 机等)4.是否带有数字信号处理电路 5.品牌 6.型号
85299049	1.品牌类型 2.出口享惠情况 3.用途(适用于 XX 品牌 XX 机或通用于 XX 机等)4.品牌 5.型号
8529905	1.品牌类型 2.出口享惠情况 3.用途(适用于 XX 品牌 XX 机或通用于 XX 机等)4.品牌 5.型号
8529906	1.品牌类型 2.出口享惠情况 3.用途(适用于 XX 品牌 XX 机或通用于 XX 机等)4.品牌 5.型号
8529908	1.品牌类型 2.出口享惠情况 3.用途(适用于 XX 品牌 XX 机或通用于 XX 机等)4.品牌 5.型号
8529909	1.品牌类型 2.出口享惠情况 3.用途(适用于 XX 品牌 XX 机或通用于 XX 机等)4.品牌 5.型号
85301	1.品牌类型 2.出口享惠情况 3.用途 4.品牌 5.型号
85308	1.品牌类型 2.出口享惠情况 3.用途 4.品牌 5.型号
85309	1.品牌类型 2.出口享惠情况 3.用途(适用于 XX 品牌 XX 机或通用于 XX 机等)4.品牌 5.型号
85311	1.品牌类型 2.出口享惠情况 3.用途 4.品牌 5.型号 6.工作原理
85312	1.品牌类型 2.出口享惠情况 3.用途 4.显示原理 5.品牌 6.型号 7.规格尺寸
8531801	1.品牌类型 2.出口享惠情况 3.用途 4.音量 5.品牌 6.型号
8531809	1.品牌类型 2.出口享惠情况 3.用途 4.品牌 5.型号
85319	1.品牌类型 2.出口享惠情况 3.用途(适用于 XX 品牌 XX 机或通用于 XX 机等)4.品牌 5.型号
85321	1.品牌类型 2.出口享惠情况 3.用途 4.额定无功功率 5.适用频率 6.品牌 7.型号
85322	1.品牌类型 2.出口享惠情况 3.结构类型(单层、多层等和片式、非片式)4.介质类型 5.品牌 6.型号
85323	1.品牌类型 2.出口享惠情况 3.是否可变、可调 4.品牌 5.型号
85329	1.品牌类型 2.出口享惠情况 3.用途(适用于 XX 品牌 XX 机或通用于 XX 机等)4.品牌 5.型号
85331	1.品牌类型 2.出口享惠情况 3.结构类型 4.介质 5.品牌 6.型号
85332	1.品牌类型 2.出口享惠情况 3.额定功率 4.结构类型(片式、线绕式等)5.品牌 6.型号
85333	1.品牌类型 2.出口享惠情况 3.额定功率 4.结构类型(片式、线绕式等)5.品牌 6.型号
85334	1.品牌类型 2.出口享惠情况 3.品牌 4.型号
85339	1.品牌类型 2.出口享惠情况 3.用途(适用于 XX 品牌 XX 机或通用于 XX 机等)4.品牌 5.型号
8534	1.品牌类型 2.出口享惠情况 3.电路层数 4.是否装有机械元件或电气元件 5.品牌 6.型号
8535	1.品牌类型 2.出口享惠情况 3.用途 4.电压 5.品牌 6.型号
85361	1.品牌类型 2.出口享惠情况 3.用途 4.电压 5.品牌 6.型号
85362	1.品牌类型 2.出口享惠情况 3.用途 4.电压 5.品牌 6.型号
85363	1.品牌类型 2.出口享惠情况 3.用途 4.电压 5.品牌 6.型号
85364	1.品牌类型 2.出口享惠情况 3.用途 4.电压 5.品牌 6.型号
85365	1.品牌类型 2.出口享惠情况 3.用途 4.电压 5.品牌 6.型号
85366	1.品牌类型 2.出口享惠情况 3.用途 4.电压 5.品牌 6.型号
85367	1.品牌类型 2.出口享惠情况 3.用途 4.品牌 5.型号
85369	1.品牌类型 2.出口享惠情况 3.用途 4.电压 5.品牌 6.型号
8537	1.品牌类型 2.出口享惠情况 3.用途 4.原理 5.电压 6.品牌 7.型号
8538	1.品牌类型 2.出口享惠情况 3.用途(适用于 XX 品牌 XX 机或通用于 XX 机等)4.品牌 5.型号
85391	1.品牌类型 2.出口享惠情况 3.用途 4.类型 5.品牌 6.型号
853921	1.品牌类型 2.出口享惠情况 3.用途 4.类型 5.品牌 6.型号
853922	1.品牌类型 2.出口享惠情况 3.用途 4.类型 5.功率 6.额定电压 7.品牌 8.型号
853929	1.品牌类型 2.出口享惠情况 3.用途 4.类型 5.功率 6.额定电压 7.品牌 8.型号
853931	1.品牌类型 2.出口享惠情况 3.类型 4.品牌 5.型号
853932	1.品牌类型 2.出口享惠情况 3.类型 4.品牌 5.型号
8539391	1.品牌类型 2.出口享惠情况 3.类型 4.品牌 5.型号
8539392	1.品牌类型 2.出口享惠情况 3.类型 4.品牌 5.型号
8539399	1.品牌类型 2.出口享惠情况 3.类型 4.品牌 5.型号
85394	1.品牌类型 2.出口享惠情况 3.类型 4.品牌 5.型号
85395	1.品牌类型 2.出口享惠情况 3.类型 4.品牌 5.型号
85399	1.品牌类型 2.出口享惠情况 3.用途(适用于 XX 品牌 XX 机或通用于 XX 机等)4.品牌 5.型号
85401	1.品牌类型 2.出口享惠情况 3.原理 4.品牌 5.型号
85402	1.品牌类型 2.出口享惠情况 3.用途 4.品牌 5.型号
8540401	1.品牌类型 2.出口享惠情况 3.是否彩色 4.荧光点距 5.品牌 6.型号
8540402	1.品牌类型 2.出口享惠情况 3.是否单色 4.荧光点距 5.品牌 6.型号
85406	1.品牌类型 2.出口享惠情况 3.用途 4.类型 5.品牌 6.型号
85407	1.品牌类型 2.出口享惠情况 3.用途 4.类型 5.品牌 6.型号
85408	1.品牌类型 2.出口享惠情况 3.用途 4.类型 5.品牌 6.型号
85409	1.品牌类型 2.出口享惠情况 3.用途(适用于 XX 品牌 XX 机或通用于 XX 机等)4.品牌 5.型号
85411	1.品牌类型 2.出口享惠情况 3.品牌 4.型号
85412	1.品牌类型 2.出口享惠情况 3.耗散功率 4.品牌 5.型号
85413	1.品牌类型 2.出口享惠情况 3.类型 4.是否由多个半导体元件构成 5.品牌 6.型号
8541401	1.品牌类型 2.出口享惠情况 3.品牌 4.型号
8541402	1.品牌类型 2.出口享惠情况 3.额定功率 4.品牌 5.型号 6.转换效率
8541409	1.品牌类型 2.出口享惠情况 3.品牌 4.型号
85415	1.品牌类型 2.出口享惠情况 3.类型 4.是否由多个半导体元件构成 5.品牌 6.型号
85416	1.品牌类型 2.出口享惠情况 3.是否已装配 4.品牌 5.型号
85419	1.品牌类型 2.出口享惠情况 3.用途(适用于 XX 品牌 XX 机或通用于 XX 机等)4.品牌 5.型号
854231	1.品牌类型 2.出口享惠情况 3.用途 4.功能 5.是否封装 6.品牌 7.型号 8.是否为已蚀刻且未切割、未封装的集成电路原片请注明 9.是否量产(量产或非量产)
854232	1.品牌类型 2.出口享惠情况 3.用途 4.功能 5.是否封装 6.品牌 7.型号 8.是否为已蚀刻且未切割、未封装的集成电路原片请注明 9.是否量产(量产或非量产)10.容量
854233	1.品牌类型 2.出口享惠情况 3.用途 4.功能 5.是否封装 6.品牌 7.型号 8.是否为已蚀刻且未切割、未封装的集成电路原片请注明 9.是否量产(量产或非量产)
854239	1.品牌类型 2.出口享惠情况 3.用途 4.功能 5.是否封装 6.品牌 7.型号 8.是否为已蚀刻且未切割、未封装的集成电路原片请注明 9.是否量产(量产或非量产)
85429	1.品牌类型 2.出口享惠情况 3.用途(适用于 XX 品牌 XX 机或通用于 XX 机等)4.品牌 5.型号
85431	1.品牌类型 2.出口享惠情况 3.用途 4.功能 5.品牌 6.型号
85432	1.品牌类型 2.出口享惠情况 3.用途 4.功能 5.输出信号频率范围 6.品牌 7.型号
85433	1.品牌类型 2.出口享惠情况 3.用途 4.功能 5.品牌 6.型号
85437	1.品牌类型 2.出口享惠情况 3.用途 4.功能 5.品牌 6.型号
85439	1.品牌类型 2.出口享惠情况 3.用途(适用于 XX 品牌 XX 机或通用于 XX 机等)4.品牌 5.型号
85441	1.品牌类型 2.出口享惠情况 3.用途 4.材质 5.品牌 6.型号
85442	1.品牌类型 2.出口享惠情况 3.用途 4.结构类型(同轴、有接头等)5.品牌 6.型号
8544302	1.品牌类型 2.出口享惠情况 3.用途 4.品牌 5.型号 6.额定电压
8544309	1.品牌类型 2.出口享惠情况 3.用途 4.结构类型(有接头等)5.品牌 6.型号 7.额定电压
85444211	1.品牌类型 2.出口享惠情况 3.用途 4.结构类型(是否有接头是否同轴电缆)5.品牌 6.型号 7.额定电压
85444219	1.品牌类型 2.出口享惠情况 3.用途 4.结构类型(是否有接头是否同轴导体)5.品牌 6.型号 7.额定电压
85444221	1.品牌类型 2.出口享惠情况 3.用途 4.结构类型(是否有接头是否同轴电缆)5.品牌 6.型号 7.额定电压

商品编码	申报要素
85444229	1.品牌类型 2.出口享惠情况 3.用途 4.结构类型(是否有接头是否同轴导体)5.品牌 6.型号 7.额定电压
85444911	1.品牌类型 2.出口享惠情况 3.用途 4.结构类型(是否有接头是否同轴电缆)5.品牌 6.型号 7.额定电压
85444919	1.品牌类型 2.出口享惠情况 3.用途 4.结构类型(是否有接头是否同轴导体)5.品牌 6.型号 7.额定电压
85444921	1.品牌类型 2.出口享惠情况 3.用途 4.结构类型(是否有接头是否同轴电缆)5.品牌 6.型号 7.额定电压
85444929	1.品牌类型 2.出口享惠情况 3.用途 4.结构类型(是否有接头是否同轴导体)5.品牌 6.型号 7.额定电压
85446	1.品牌类型 2.出口享惠情况 3.用途 4.结构类型(有接头等)5.品牌 6.型号 7.额定电压
85447	1.品牌类型 2.出口享惠情况 3.是否每根光纤被覆 4.品牌 5.型号
8545	1.品牌类型 2.出口享惠情况 3.用途 4.材质 5.品牌 6.型号
8546	1.品牌类型 2.出口享惠情况 3.用途 4.材质 5.品牌 6.型号
8547	1.品牌类型 2.出口享惠情况 3.用途 4.材质 5.品牌 6.型号
85481	1.品牌类型 2.出口享惠情况 3.用途 4.品牌 5.型号
85489	1.品牌类型 2.出口享惠情况 3.用途 4.若为触摸屏需注明结构(是否有显示屏)5.品牌 6.型号
8601	1.品牌类型 2.出口享惠情况 3.用途 4.驱动装置类型 5.控制装置类型 6.品牌 7.型号
86021	1.品牌类型 2.出口享惠情况 3.用途 4.驱动装置类型 5.控制装置类型 6.品牌 7.型号
86029	1.品牌类型 2.出口享惠情况 3.用途 4.驱动装置类型 5.品牌 6.型号
8603	1.品牌类型 2.出口享惠情况 3.用途 4.驱动装置类型 5.品牌 6.型号
8604	1.品牌类型 2.出口享惠情况 3.用途 4.类型 5.品牌 6.型号
8605	1.品牌类型 2.出口享惠情况 3.用途 4.类型 5.品牌 6.型号
8606	1.品牌类型 2.出口享惠情况 3.用途 4.类型 5.结构 6.品牌 7.型号
8607	1.品牌类型 2.出口享惠情况 3.用途(适用于 XX 品牌 XX 车或通用于 XX 机等)4.品牌 5.型号
8608	1.品牌类型 2.出口享惠情况 3.用途 4.品牌 5.型号
8609	1.品牌类型 2.出口享惠情况 3.类型(公路等)4 规格尺寸 5.品牌
87011	1.品牌类型 2.出口享惠情况 3.品牌 4.型号
87012	1.品牌类型 2.出口享惠情况 3.用途 4.品牌 5.型号
87013	1.品牌类型 2.出口享惠情况 3.品牌 4.结构类型 5.型号
87019	1.品牌类型 2.出口享惠情况 3.结构类型 4.功率 5.用途 6.品牌 7.型号
8702102	1.品牌类型 2.出口享惠情况 3.发动机类型(柴油、半柴油、汽油等)4.成套散件请注明 5.厂牌(如与签注名称相同可省略)6.签注名称 7.排气量(毫升)8.规格型号
8702109	1.品牌类型 2.出口享惠情况 3.发动机类型(柴油、半柴油、汽油等)4.成套散件请注明 5.座位数 6.厂牌(如与签注名称相同可省略)7.签注名称 8.排气量(毫升)9.规格型号
8702201	1.品牌类型 2.出口享惠情况 3.发动机类型(柴油及驱动电动机等)4.成套散件请注明 5.厂牌(如与签注名称相同可省略)6.签注名称 7.排气量(毫升)8.规格型号
8702209	1.品牌类型 2.出口享惠情况 3.发动机类型(柴油及驱动电动机等)4.成套散件请注明 5.座位数 6.厂牌(如与签注名称相同可省略)7.签注名称 8.排气量(毫升)9.规格型号
87023	1.品牌类型 2.出口享惠情况 3.发动机类型(汽油及驱动电动机等)4.成套散件请注明 5.座位数 6.厂牌(如与签注名称相同可省略)7.签注名称 8.排气量(毫升)9.规格型号
87024	1.品牌类型 2.出口享惠情况 3.发动机类型(电动等)4.成套散件请注明 5.座位数 6.厂牌(如与签注名称相同可省略)7.签注名称 8.功率(千瓦)9.规格型号
87029	1.品牌类型 2.出口享惠情况 3.发动机类型(柴油、半柴油、汽油等)4.成套散件请注明 5.座位数 6.厂牌(如与签注名称相同可省略)7.签注名称 8.排气量(毫升)9.规格型号
87031011	1.品牌类型 2.出口享惠情况 3.发动机类型(柴油、半柴油、汽油等)4.成套散件请注明 5.座位数 6.厂牌(如与签注名称相同可省略)7.签注名称 8.排气量(毫升)9.型号
87031019	1.品牌类型 2.出口享惠情况 3.发动机类型(柴油、半柴油、汽油等)4.成套散件请注明 5.排气量(毫升)6.厂牌(如与签注名称相同可省略)7.签注名称 8.型号
8703109	1.品牌类型 2.出口享惠情况 3.发动机类型(柴油、半柴油、汽油等)4.成套散件请注明 5.排气量(毫升)6.厂牌(如与签注名称相同可省略)7.签注名称 8.型号
87032	1.品牌类型 2.出口享惠情况 3.发动机类型(柴油、半柴油、汽油等)4.成套散件请注明 5.座位数 6.厂牌(如与签注名称相同可省略)7.签注名称 8.排气量(毫升)9.型号 10.是否中规车请注明(中规车、非中规车)11.非中规车请注明原销售目的国车版、型(美规、欧规、加规、中东规等)

商品编码	申报要素
87033	1.品牌类型 2.出口享惠情况 3.发动机类型(柴油、半柴油、汽油等)4.成套散件请注明 5.座位数 6.厂牌(如与签注名称相同可省略)7.签注名称 8.排气量(毫升)9.型号 10.是否中规车请注明(中规车、非中规车)11.非中规车请注明原销售目的国车版、型(美规、欧规、加规、中东规等)
87034	1.品牌类型 2.出口享惠情况 3.发动机类型(汽油及驱动电动机等)4.成套散件请注明 5.座位数 6.是否可通过接插外部电源进行充电 7.厂牌(如与签注名称相同可省略)8.签注名称 9.排气量(毫升)10.型号 11.是否中规车请注明(中规车、非中规车)12.非中规车请注明原销售目的国车版、型(美规、欧规、加规、中东规等)
87035	1.品牌类型 2.出口享惠情况 3.发动机类型(柴油及驱动电动机等)4.成套散件请注明 5.座位数 6.是否可通过接插外部电源进行充电 7.厂牌(如与签注名称相同可省略)8.签注名称 9.排气量(毫升)10.型号 11.是否中规车请注明(中规车、非中规车)12.非中规车请注明原销售目的国车版、型(美规、欧规、加规、中东规等)
87036	1.品牌类型 2.出口享惠情况 3.发动机类型(汽油及驱动电动机等)4.成套散件请注明 5.座位数 6.是否可通过接插外部电源进行充电 7.厂牌(如与签注名称相同可省略)8.签注名称 9.排气量(毫升)10.型号 11.是否中规车请注明(中规车、非中规车)12.非中规车请注明原销售目的国车版、型(美规、欧规、加规、中东规等)
87037	1.品牌类型 2.出口享惠情况 3.发动机类型(柴油及驱动电动机等 4.成套散件请注明 5.座位数 6.是否可通过接插外部电源进行充电 7.厂牌(如与签注名称相同可省略)8.签注名称 9.排气量(毫升)10.型号 11.是否中规车请注明(中规车、非中规车)12.非中规车请注明原销售目的国车版、型(美规、欧规、加规、中东规等)
87038	1.品牌类型 2.出口享惠情况 3.发动机类型(电动等)4.成套散件请注明 5.座位数 6.厂牌(如与签注名称相同可省略)7.签注名称 8.功率(千瓦)9.型号 10.是否中规车请注明(中规车、非中规车)11.非中规车请注明原销售目的国车版、型(美规、欧规、加规、中东规等)
87039	1.品牌类型 2.出口享惠情况 3.发动机类型(柴油、半柴油、汽油等)4.成套散件请注明 5.座位数 6.厂牌(如与签注名称相同可省略)7.签注名称 8.排气量(毫升)9.型号 10.是否中规车请注明(中规车、非中规车)11.非中规车请注明原销售目的国车版、型(美规、欧规、加规、中东规等)
8704103	1.品牌类型 2.出口享惠情况 3.用途 4.是否为电动轮 5.品牌(厂牌)6.型号
8704109	1.品牌类型 2.出口享惠情况 3.用途 4.是否为电动轮 5.发动机类型(柴油、半柴油、汽油等)6.车体长、宽、高(空载状态)7.汽车总重量 8.品牌(厂牌)9.型号
870421	1.品牌类型 2.出口享惠情况 3.发动机类型(柴油、半柴油、汽油等)4.车辆总重 5.整备质量 6.驾驶室座位排数 7.驾驶室座位数 8.载货重量 9.品牌(厂牌)10.型号 11.是否中规车请注明(中规车、非中规车)12.非中规车请注明原销售目的国车版、型(美规、欧规、加规、中东规等)
870422	1.品牌类型 2.出口享惠情况 3.发动机类型(柴油、半柴油、汽油等)4.车辆总重 5.品牌(厂牌)6.型号
870423	1.品牌类型 2.出口享惠情况 3.发动机类型(柴油、半柴油、汽油等)4.车辆总重 5.品牌(厂牌)6.型号
870431	1.品牌类型 2.出口享惠情况 3.发动机类型(柴油、半柴油、汽油等)4.车辆总重 5.整备质量 6.驾驶室座位排数 7.驾驶室座位数 8.载货重量 9.品牌(厂牌)10.型号 11.是否中规车请注明(中规车、非中规车)12.非中规车请注明原销售目的国车版、型(美规、欧规、加规、中东规等)
870432	1.品牌类型 2.出口享惠情况 3.发动机类型(柴油、半柴油、汽油等)4.车辆总重 5.品牌(厂牌)6.型号
87049	1.品牌类型 2.出口享惠情况 3.发动机类型(柴油、半柴油、汽油等)4.车辆总重 5.品牌(厂牌)6.型号 7.是否中规车请注明(中规车、非中规车)8.非中规车请注明原销售目的国车版、型(美规、欧规、加规、中东规等)
87051	1.品牌类型 2.出口享惠情况 3.作业范围(全路面等)4.最大起重重量 5.品牌(厂牌)6.型号
87052	1.品牌类型 2.出口享惠情况 3.用途 4.品牌 5.型号
87053	1.品牌类型 2.出口享惠情况 3.固定安装配置 4.品牌 5.型号
87054	1.品牌类型 2.出口享惠情况 3.固定安装配置 4.品牌 5.型号
87059	1.品牌类型 2.出口享惠情况 3.用途 4.固定安装配置 5.品牌(厂牌)6.型号
8706001	1.品牌类型 2.出口享惠情况 3.适用车型 4.品牌 5.型号
8706002	1.品牌类型 2.出口享惠情况 3.适用车型 4.车辆总重量 5.是否带驾驶室 6.品牌 7.型号

商品编码	申报要素
8706003	1.品牌类型 2.出口享惠情况 3.适用车型 4.是否带驾驶室 5.品牌 6.型号
8706004	1.品牌类型 2.出口享惠情况 3.适用车型 4.是否带驾驶室 5.品牌 6.型号
8706009	1.品牌类型 2.出口享惠情况 3.适用车型 4.品牌 5.型号
8707	1.品牌类型 2.出口享惠情况 3.适用车型 4.品牌 5.型号
87081	1.品牌类型 2.出口享惠情况 3.成套散件或毛坯请注明 4.生产件的通用零件编号后加注“/TY”5.成套散件装配后完整品的零部件的编号 6.品牌 7.适用车型 8.型号 9.零部件完整编号并在前加注“S/”、“W/”或“WF/”之一(生产件填报“S/”,品牌和适用的整车厂牌一致的维修件填报“W/”,品牌和适用的整车厂牌不一致的维修件的填报“WF/”)
870821	1.品牌类型 2.出口享惠情况 3.成套散件或毛坯请注明 4.生产件的通用零件编号后加注“/TY”5.成套散件装配后完整品的零部件的编号 6.品牌 7.适用车型 8.型号 9.零部件完整编号并在前加注“S/”、“W/”或“WF/”之一(生产件填报“S/”,品牌和适用的整车厂牌一致的维修件填报“W/”,品牌和适用的整车厂牌不一致的维修件的填报“WF/”)
8708293	1.品牌类型 2.出口享惠情况 3.成套散件或毛坯请注明 4.生产件的通用零件编号后加注“/TY”5.成套散件装配后完整品的零部件的编号 6.品牌 7.适用车型 8.型号 9.零部件完整编号并在前加注“S/”、“W/”或“WF/”之一(生产件填报“S/”,品牌和适用的整车厂牌一致的维修件填报“W/”,品牌和适用的整车厂牌不一致的维修件的填报“WF/”)
87082941	1.品牌类型 2.出口享惠情况 3.成套散件或毛坯请注明 4.生产件的通用零件编号后加注“/TY”5.成套散件装配后完整品的零部件的编号 6.品牌 7.适用车型 8.型号 9.零部件完整编号并在前加注“S/”、“W/”或“WF/”之一(生产件填报“S/”,品牌和适用的整车厂牌一致的维修件填报“W/”,品牌和适用的整车厂牌不一致的维修件的填报“WF/”)
87082942	1.品牌类型 2.出口享惠情况 3.品牌 4.适用车型 5.型号
8708295	1.品牌类型 2.出口享惠情况 3.品牌 4.适用车型 5.型号
8708299	1.品牌类型 2.出口享惠情况 3.品牌 4.适用车型 5.型号
87083	1.品牌类型 2.出口享惠情况 3.适用车型 4.成套散件或毛坯请注明 5.生产件的通用零件编号后加注“/TY”6.成套散件装配后完整品的零部件的编号 7.品牌 8.型号 9.零部件完整编号并在前加注“S/”、“W/”或“WF/”之一(生产件填报“S/”,品牌和适用的整车厂牌一致的维修件填报“W/”,品牌和适用的整车厂牌不一致的维修件的填报“WF/”
8708401	1.品牌类型 2.出口享惠情况 3.适用车型 4.成套散件或毛坯请注明 5.生产件的通用零件编号后加注“/TY”6.成套散件装配后完整品的零部件的编号 7.品牌 8.型号 9.零部件完整编号并在前加注“S/”、“W/”或“WF/”之一(生产件填报“S/”,品牌和适用的整车厂牌一致的维修件填报“W/”,品牌和适用的整车厂牌不一致的维修件的填报“WF/”)
8708402	1.品牌类型 2.出口享惠情况 3.适用车型 4.成套散件或毛坯请注明 5.生产件的通用零件编号后加注“/TY”6.成套散件装配后完整品的零部件的编号 7.品牌 8.型号 9.零部件完整编号并在前加注“S/”、“W/”或“WF/”之一(生产件填报“S/”,品牌和适用的整车厂牌一致的维修件填报“W/”,品牌和适用的整车厂牌不一致的维修件的填报“WF/”)10.座位数
8708403	1.品牌类型 2.出口享惠情况 3.适用车型 4.成套散件或毛坯请注明 5.生产件的通用零件编号后加注“/TY”6.成套散件装配后完整品的零部件的编号 7.品牌 8.扭矩 9.型号 10.零部件完整编号并在前加注“S/”、“W/”或“WF/”之一(生产件填报“S/”,品牌和适用的整车厂牌一致的维修件填报“W/”,品牌和适用的整车厂牌不一致的维修件的填报“WF/”)
8708404	1.品牌类型 2.出口享惠情况 3.适用车型 4.成套散件或毛坯请注明 5.生产件的通用零件编号后加注“/TY”6.成套散件装配后完整品的零部件的编号 7.品牌 8.扭矩 9.型号 10.零部件完整编号并在前加注“S/”、“W/”或“WF/”之一(生产件填报“S/”,品牌和适用的整车厂牌一致的维修件填报“W/”,品牌和适用的整车厂牌不一致的维修件的填报“WF/”)
8708405	1.品牌类型 2.出口享惠情况 3.适用车型 4.成套散件或毛坯请注明 5.生产件的通用零件编号后加注“/TY”6.成套散件装配后完整品的零部件的编号 7.品牌 8.扭矩 9.型号 10.零部件完整编号并在前加注“S/”、“W/”或“WF/”之一(生产件填报“S/”,品牌和适用的整车厂牌一致的维修件填报“W/”,品牌和适用的整车厂牌不一致的维修件的填报“WF/”)
8708406	1.品牌类型 2.出口享惠情况 3.适用车型 4.成套散件或毛坯请注明 5.生产件的通用零件编号后加注“/TY”6.成套散件装配后完整品的零部件的编号 7.品牌 8.扭矩 9.型号 10.零部件完整编号并在前加注“S/”、“W/”或“WF/”之一(生产件填报“S/”,品牌和适用的整车厂牌一致的维修件填报“W/”,品牌和适用的整车厂牌不一致的维修件的填报“WF/”)
8708409	1.品牌类型 2.出口享惠情况 3.适用车型 4.原理(是否为 6 档及 6 档以上)5.成套散件或毛坯请注明 6.生产件的通用零件编号后加注“/TY”7.成套散件装配后完整品的零部件的编号 8.品牌 9.扭矩 10.型号 11.零部件完整编号并在前加注“S/”、“W/”或“WF/”之一(生产件填报“S/”,品牌和适用的整车厂牌一致的维修件填报“W/”,品牌和适用的整车厂牌不一致的维修件的填报“WF/”)
87085071	1.品牌类型 2.出口享惠情况 3.适用车型 4.驱动位置 5.轴荷 6.成套散件或毛坯请注明 7.生产件的通用零件编号后加注“/TY”8.成套散件装配后完整品的零部件的编号 9.品牌 10.型号 11.零部件完整编号并在前加注“S/”、“W/”或“WF/”之一(生产件填报“S/”,品牌和适用的整车厂牌一致的维修件填报“W/”,品牌和适用的整车厂牌不一致的维修件的填报“WF/”)
87085072	1.品牌类型 2.出口享惠情况 3.适用车型 4.驱动位置 5.轴荷 6.成套散件或毛坯请注明 7.生产件的通用零件编号后加注“/TY”8.成套散件装配后完整品的零部件的编号 9.品牌 10.型号 11.零部件完整编号并在前加注“S/”、“W/”或“WF/”之一(生产件填报“S/”,品牌和适用的整车厂牌一致的维修件填报“W/”,品牌和适用的整车厂牌不一致的维修件的填报“WF/”)
87085073	1.品牌类型 2.出口享惠情况 3.适用车型 4.驱动位置 5.轴荷 6.成套散件或毛坯请注明 7.生产件的通用零件编号后加注“/TY”8.成套散件装配后完整品的零部件的编号 9.品牌 10.型号 11.零部件完整编号并在前加注“S/”、“W/”或“WF/”之一(生产件填报“S/”,品牌和适用的整车厂牌一致的维修件填报“W/”,品牌和适用的整车厂牌不一致的维修件的填报“WF/”)
87085074	1.品牌类型 2.出口享惠情况 3.适用车型 4.驱动位置 5.成套散件或毛坯请注明 6.生产件的通用零件编号后加注“/TY”7.成套散件装配后完整品的零部件的编号 8.品牌 9.型号 10.零部件完整编号并在前加注“S/”、“W/”或“WF/”之一(生产件填报“S/”,品牌和适用的整车厂牌一致的维修件填报“W/”,品牌和适用的整车厂牌不一致的维修件的填报“WF/”)
87085075	1.品牌类型 2.出口享惠情况 3.适用车型 4.驱动位置 5.成套散件或毛坯请注明 6.生产件的通用零件编号后加注“/TY”7.成套散件装配后完整品的零部件的编号 8.品牌 9.型号 10.零部件完整编号并在前加注“S/”、“W/”或“WF/”之一(生产件填报“S/”,品牌和适用的整车厂牌一致的维修件填报“W/”,品牌和适用的整车厂牌不一致的维修件的填报“WF/”)
87085076	1.品牌类型 2.出口享惠情况 3.适用车型 4.驱动位置 5.成套散件或毛坯请注明 6.生产件的通用零件编号后加注“/TY”7.成套散件装配后完整品的零部件的编号 8.品牌 9.型号 10.零部件完整编号并在前加注“S/”、“W/”或“WF/”之一(生产件填报“S/”,品牌和适用的整车厂牌一致的维修件填报“W/”,品牌和适用的整车厂牌不一致的维修件的填报“WF/”)
87085079	1.品牌类型 2.出口享惠情况 3.适用车型 4.成套散件或毛坯请注明 5.生产件的通用零件编号后加注“/TY”6.成套散件装配后完整品的零部件的编号 7.品牌 8.型号 9.零部件完整编号并在前加注“S/”、“W/”或“WF/”之一(生产件填报“S/”,品牌和适用的整车厂牌一致的维修件填报“W/”,品牌和适用的整车厂牌不一致的维修件的填报“WF/”)
8708508	1.品牌类型 2.出口享惠情况 3.适用车型 4.成套散件或毛坯请注明 5.生产件的通用零件编号后加注“/TY”6.成套散件装配后完整品的零部件的编号 7.品牌 8.型号 9.零部件完整编号并在前加注“S/”、“W/”或“WF/”之一(生产件填报“S/”,品牌和适用的整车厂牌一致的维修件填报“W/”,品牌和适用的整车厂牌不一致的维修件的填报“WF/”)
87087	1.品牌类型 2.出口享惠情况 3.材质 4.适用车型 5.成套散件或毛坯请注明 6.生产件的通用零件编号后加注“/TY”7.成套散件装配后完整品的零部件的编号 8.车轮尺寸 9.品牌 10.型号 11.零部件完整编号并在前加注“S/”、“W/”或“WF/”之一(生产件填报“S/”,品牌和适用的整车厂牌一致的维修件填报“W/”,品牌和适用的整车厂牌不一致的维修件的填报“WF/”)
87088	1.品牌类型 2.出口享惠情况 3.适用车型 4.成套散件或毛坯请注明 5.生产件的通用零件编号后加注“/TY”6.成套散件装配后完整品的零部件的编号 7.品牌 8.型号 9.零部件完整编号并在前加注“S/”、“W/”或“WF/”之一(生产件填报“S/”,品牌和适用的整车厂牌一致的维修件填报“W/”,品牌和适用的整车厂牌不一致的维修件的填报“WF/”)
870891	1.品牌类型 2.出口享惠情况 3.适用车型 4.成套散件或毛坯请注明 5.生产件的通用零件编号后加注“/TY”6.成套散件装配后完整品的零部件的编号 7.品牌 8.型号 9.零部件完整编号并在前加注“S/”、“W/”或“WF/”之一(生产件填报“S/”,品牌和适用的整车厂牌一致的维修件填报“W/”,品牌和适用的整车厂牌不一致的维修件的填报“WF/”)

商品编码	申报要素
870892	1.品牌类型 2.出口享惠情况 3.适用车型 4.成套散件或毛坯请注明 5.生产件的通用零件编号后加注"/TY"6.成套散件装配后完整品的零部件的编号 7.品牌 8.型号 9.零部件完整编号并在前加注"S/"、"W/"或"WF/"之一(生产件填报"S/",品牌和适用的整车厂牌一致的维修件填报"W/",品牌和适用的整车厂牌不一致的维修件的填报"WF/")
870893	1.品牌类型 2.出口享惠情况 3.适用车型 4.成套散件或毛坯请注明 5.生产件的通用零件编号后加注"/TY"6.成套散件装配后完整品的零部件的编号 7.品牌 8.型号 9.零部件完整编号并在前加注"S/"、"W/"或"WF/"之一(生产件填报"S/",品牌和适用的整车厂牌一致的维修件填报"W/",品牌和适用的整车厂牌不一致的维修件的填报"WF/")
8708941	1.品牌类型 2.出口享惠情况 3.适用车型 4 成套散件或毛坯请注明 5.生产件的通用零件编号后加注"/TY"6.成套散件装配后完整品的零部件的编号 7.品牌 8.型号 9.零部件完整编号并在前加注"S/"、"W/"或"WF/"之一(生产件填报"S/",品牌和适用的整车厂牌一致的维修件填报"W/",品牌和适用的整车厂牌不一致的维修件的填报"WF/")
8708942	1.品牌类型 2.出口享惠情况 3.适用车型 4.成套散件或毛坯请注明 5.生产件的通用零件编号后加注"/TY"6.成套散件装配后完整品的零部件的编号 7.座位数 8.品牌 9.型号 10.零部件完整编号并在前加注"S/"、"W/"或"WF/"之一(生产件填报"S/",品牌和适用的整车厂牌一致的维修件填报"W/",品牌和适用的整车厂牌不一致的维修件的填报"WF/")
8708943	1.品牌类型 2.出口享惠情况 3.适用车型 4.成套散件或毛坯请注明 5.生产件的通用零件编号后加注"/TY"6.成套散件装配后完整品的零部件的编号 7.品牌 8.型号 9.零部件完整编号并在前加注"S/"、"W/"或"WF/"之一(生产件填报"S/",品牌和适用的整车厂牌一致的维修件填报"W/",品牌和适用的整车厂牌不一致的维修件的填报"WF/")
8708944	1.品牌类型 2.出口享惠情况 3.适用车型 4.成套散件或毛坯请注明 5.生产件的通用零件编号后加注"/TY"6.成套散件装配后完整品的零部件的编号 7.品牌 8.型号 9.零部件完整编号并在前加注"S/"、"W/"或"WF/"之一(生产件填报"S/",品牌和适用的整车厂牌一致的维修件填报"W/",品牌和适用的整车厂牌不一致的维修件的填报"WF/")
8708945	1.品牌类型 2.出口享惠情况 3.适用车型 4.成套散件或毛坯请注明 5.生产件的通用零件编号后加注"/TY"6.成套散件装配后完整品的零部件的编号 7.品牌 8.型号 9.零部件完整编号并在前加注"S/"、"W/"或"WF/"之一(生产件填报"S/",品牌和适用的整车厂牌一致的维修件填报"W/",品牌和适用的整车厂牌不一致的维修件的填报"WF/")
8708946	1.品牌类型 2.出口享惠情况 3.适用车型 4.成套散件或毛坯请注明 5.生产件的通用零件编号后加注"/TY"6.成套散件装配后完整品的零部件的编号 7.品牌 8.型号 9.零部件完整编号并在前加注"S/"、"W/"或"WF/"之一(生产件填报"S/",品牌和适用的整车厂牌一致的维修件填报"W/",品牌和适用的整车厂牌不一致的维修件的填报"WF/")
8708949	1.品牌类型 2.出口享惠情况 3.适用车型 4.成套散件或毛坯请注明 5.生产件的通用零件编号后加注"/TY"6.成套散件装配后完整品的零部件的编号 7.品牌 8.型号 9.零部件完整编号并在前加注"S/"、"W/"或"WF/"之一(生产件填报"S/",品牌和适用的整车厂牌一致的维修件填报"W/",品牌和适用的整车厂牌不一致的维修件的填报"WF/")
870895	1.品牌类型 2.出口享惠情况 3.适用车型 4.成套散件或毛坯请注明 5.生产件的通用零件编号后加注"/TY"6.成套散件装配后完整品的零部件的编号 7.品牌 8.型号 9.零部件完整编号并在前加注"S/"、"W/"或"WF/"之一(生产件填报"S/",品牌和适用的整车厂牌一致的维修件填报"W/",品牌和适用的整车厂牌不一致的维修件的填报"WF/")
8708991	1.品牌类型 2.出口享惠情况 3.适用车型 4.品牌 5.型号
87089921	1.品牌类型 2.出口享惠情况 3.适用车型 4.成套散件或毛坯请注明 5.生产件的通用零件编号后加注"/TY"6.成套散件装配后完整品的零部件的编号 7.品牌 8.型号 9.零部件完整编号并在前加注"S/"、"W/"或"WF/"之一(生产件填报"S/",品牌和适用的整车厂牌一致的维修件填报"W/",品牌和适用的整车厂牌不一致的维修件的填报"WF/")
87089929	1.品牌类型 2.出口享惠情况 3.适用车型 4.座位数 5.品牌 6.型号
87089931	1.品牌类型 2.出口享惠情况 3.适用车型 4.成套散件或毛坯请注明 5.生产件的通用零件编号后加注"/TY"6.成套散件装配后完整品的零部件的编号 7.品牌 8.型号 9.零部件完整编号并在前加注"S/"、"W/"或"WF/"之一(生产件填报"S/",品牌和适用的整车厂牌一致的维修件填报"W/",品牌和适用的整车厂牌不一致的维修件的填报"WF/")
87089939	1.品牌类型 2.出口享惠情况 3.适用车型 4.品牌 5.型号
87089941	1.品牌类型 2.出口享惠情况 3.适用车型 4.成套散件或毛坯请注明 5.生产件的通用零件编号后加注"/TY"6.成套散件装配后完整品的零部件的编号 7.品牌 8.型号 9.零部件完整编号并在前加注"S/"、"W/"或"WF/"之一(生产件填报"S/",品牌和适用的整车厂牌一致的维修件填报"W/",品牌和适用的整车厂牌不一致的维修件的填报"WF/")
87089949	1.品牌类型 2.出口享惠情况 3.适用车型 4.品牌 5.型号
87089951	1.品牌类型 2.出口享惠情况 3.适用车型 4.成套散件或毛坯请注明 5.生产件的通用零件编号后加注"/TY"6.成套散件装配后完整品的零部件的编号 7.品牌 8.型号 9.零部件完整编号并在前加注"S/"、"W/"或"WF/"之一(生产件填报"S/",品牌和适用的整车厂牌一致的维修件填报"W/",品牌和适用的整车厂牌不一致的维修件的填报"WF/")
87089959	1.品牌类型 2.出口享惠情况 3.适用车型 4.品牌 5.型号
8708996	1.品牌类型 2.出口享惠情况 3.适用车型 4.品牌 5.型号
87089991	1.品牌类型 2.出口享惠情况 3.适用车型 4.成套散件或毛坯请注明 5.生产件的通用零件编号后加注"/TY"6.成套散件装配后完整品的零部件的编号 7.品牌 8.型号 9.零部件完整编号并在前加注"S/"、"W/"或"WF/"之一(生产件填报"S/",品牌和适用的整车厂牌一致的维修件填报"W/",品牌和适用的整车厂牌不一致的维修件的填报"WF/")
87089992	1.品牌类型 2.出口享惠情况 3.适用车型 4.品牌 5.型号
87089999	1.品牌类型 2.出口享惠情况 3.适用车型 4.品牌 5.型号
87091	1.品牌类型 2.出口享惠情况 3.发动机类型 4.适用场所 5.品牌 6.型号 7.技术参数(最高时速、转弯半径等)
87099	1.品牌类型 2.出口享惠情况 3.用途(适用于 XX 品牌 XX 车或通用于 XX 机等)4.品牌 5.型号
8710	1.品牌类型 2.出口享惠情况 3.品牌 4.型号
87111	1.品牌类型 2.出口享惠情况 3.发动机类型 4.排气量 5.品牌 6.型号
87112	1.品牌类型 2.出口享惠情况 3.发动机类型 4.排气量 5.品牌 6.型号
87113	1.品牌类型 2.出口享惠情况 3.发动机类型 4.排气量 5.品牌 6.型号
87114	1.品牌类型 2.出口享惠情况 3.发动机类型 4.排气量 5.品牌 6.型号
87115	1.品牌类型 2.出口享惠情况 3.发动机类型 4.排气量 5.品牌 6.型号
87116	1.品牌类型 2.出口享惠情况 3.发动机类型 4.品牌 5.型号
87119	1.品牌类型 2.出口享惠情况 3.发动机类型 4.排气量 5.品牌 6.型号
8712	1.品牌类型 2.出口享惠情况 3.用途(竞赛型、山地型、越野型等)4.轮径 5.品牌 6.型号
8713	1.品牌类型 2.出口享惠情况 3.用途 4.驱动方式 5.品牌 6.型号
8714	1.品牌类型 2.出口享惠情况 3.用途(适用于 XX 品牌 XX 车或通用于 XX 机等)4.品牌 5.型号
8715	1.品牌类型 2.出口享惠情况 3.若为零件请注明适用车型 4.品牌
87161	1.品牌类型 2.出口享惠情况 3.用途 4.类型 5.品牌 6.型号
87162	1.品牌类型 2.出口享惠情况 3.用途 4.类型 5.品牌 6.型号
87163	1.品牌类型 2.出口享惠情况 3.用途 4.类型 5.品牌 6.型号
87164	1.品牌类型 2.出口享惠情况 3.品牌 4.型号
87168	1.品牌类型 2.出口享惠情况 3.品牌 4.型号
87169	1.品牌类型 2.出口享惠情况 3.用途(适用于 XX 品牌 XX 车或通用于 XX 机等)4.品牌 5.型号
8801	1.品牌类型 2.出口享惠情况 3.用途 4.品牌 5.型号
88021	1.品牌类型 2.出口享惠情况 3.用途 4.类型 5.空载重量 6.品牌 7.型号
88022	1.品牌类型 2.出口享惠情况 3.用途 4.类型 5.空载重量 6.品牌 7.型号 8.公务机请注明 9.民航局注册号、飞机出厂序列号(S/ N,即 SERIAL NUMBER)10.旧飞机请注明并申报飞机原生产日期
88023	1.品牌类型 2.出口享惠情况 3.用途 4.类型 5.空载重量 6.品牌 7.型号 8.公务机请注明 9.民航局注册号、飞机出厂序列号(S/ N,即 SERIAL NUMBER)10.旧飞机请注明并申报飞机原生产日期
88024	1.品牌类型 2.出口享惠情况 3.用途 4.类型 5.空载重量 6.品牌 7.型号 8.公务机请注明 9.民航局注册号、飞机出厂序列号(S/ N,即 SERIAL NUMBER)10.旧飞机请注明并申报飞机原生产日期
88026	1.品牌类型 2.出口享惠情况 3.若为通信用需注明 4.品牌 5.型号
8803	1.品牌类型 2.出口享惠情况 3.用途(适用于 XX 品牌 XX 机或通用于 XX 机等)4.品牌 5.型号
8804	1.品牌类型 2.出口享惠情况 3.用途(适用于 XX 品牌 XX 机或通用于 XX 机等)4.品牌 5.型号
8805	1.品牌类型 2.出口享惠情况 3.用途(适用于 XX 品牌 XX 机或通用于 XX 机等)4.品牌 5.型号
89011	1.品牌类型 2.出口享惠情况 3.驱动方式 4.品牌 5.型号 6.最高时速
8901201	1.品牌类型 2.出口享惠情况 3.用途 4.载重量 5.品牌 6.型号

商品编码	申报要素
8901202	1.品牌类型 2.出口享惠情况 3.用途 4.载重量 5.品牌 6.型号
8901203	1.品牌类型 2.出口享惠情况 3.用途 4.容积 5.品牌 6.型号
8901204	1.品牌类型 2.出口享惠情况 3.用途 4.容积 5.品牌 6.型号
8901209	1.品牌类型 2.出口享惠情况 3.用途 4.载重量 5.品牌 6.型号
89013	1.品牌类型 2.出口享惠情况 3.品牌 4.型号
8901902	1.品牌类型 2.出口享惠情况 3.用途 4.可载标准集装箱数 5.品牌 6.型号
8901903	1.品牌类型 2.出口享惠情况 3.用途 4.载重量 5.品牌 6.型号
8901904	1.品牌类型 2.出口享惠情况 3.用途 4.载重量 5.品牌 6.型号
8901905	1.品牌类型 2.出口享惠情况 3.用途 4.品牌 5.型号
8901908	1.品牌类型 2.出口享惠情况 3.用途 4.品牌 5.型号
8901909	1.品牌类型 2.出口享惠情况 3.用途 4.品牌 5.型号
8902	1.品牌类型 2.出口享惠情况 3.用途 4.驱动方式 5.品牌 6.型号
89031	1.品牌类型 2.出口享惠情况 3.用途 4.类型 5.发动机安装方式 6.船体长度 7.固定安装配置 8.品牌 9.型号
890391	1.品牌类型 2.出口享惠情况 3.用途 4.类型 5.发动机安装方式 6.船体长度 7.品牌 8.型号 9.发动机品牌、型号 10.发动机功率
890392	1.品牌类型 2.出口享惠情况 3.用途 4.类型 5.发动机安装方式 6.船体长度 7.品牌 8.型号 9.发动机品牌、型号 10.发动机功率
890399	1.品牌类型 2.出口享惠情况 3.用途 4.类型 5.船体长度 6.固定安装配置 7.品牌 8.型号 9.发动机品牌、型号 10.发动机功率
8904	1.品牌类型 2.出口享惠情况 3.功能 4.品牌 5.型号
89051	1.品牌类型 2.出口享惠情况 3.用途 4.品牌 5.型号
89052	1.品牌类型 2.出口享惠情况 3.用途 4.品牌 5.型号
89059	1.品牌类型 2.出口享惠情况 3.用途 4.结构 5.品牌 6.型号
8906	1.品牌类型 2.出口享惠情况 3.用途 4.驱动方式 5.品牌 6.型号
8907	1.品牌类型 2.出口享惠情况 3.材质 4.品牌 5.型号
8908	1.品牌类型 2.出口享惠情况 3.轻吨数(不包括非金属固定压载在内的空船重量)4.船型(如油轮、客船、驳船、集装箱船等)
90011	1.品牌类型 2.出口享惠情况 3.结构 4.用途 5.品牌 6.型号
90012	1.品牌类型 2.出口享惠情况 3.用途 4.材质 5.规格尺寸 6.品牌 7.型号
90013	1.品牌类型 2.出口享惠情况 3.品牌 4.型号 5.材质 6.种类(软片或硬片)7.颜色 8.直径 9.使用周期(日抛、月抛等)10.度数(近视或远视度数,是否带散光度数)
90014	1.品牌类型 2.出口享惠情况 3.材质 4.类型(变色等)5.品牌 6.型号
90015	1.品牌类型 2.出口享惠情况 3.材质 4.类型(变色等)5.品牌 6.型号
9001901	1.品牌类型 2.出口享惠情况 3.用途(适用于 XX 品牌 XX 机或通用于 XX 机等)4.材质 5.品牌 6.型号
9001909	1.品牌类型 2.出口享惠情况 3.用途(适用于 XX 品牌 XX 机或通用于 XX 机等)4.材质 5.如为薄膜滤光片请申报波长 6.品牌 7.型号
9002	1.品牌类型 2.出口享惠情况 3.用途(适用于 XX 品牌 XX 机或通用于 XX 机等)4.是否已装配 5.品牌 6.型号
9003	1.品牌类型 2.出口享惠情况 3.材质 4.品牌 5.型号
9004	1.品牌类型 2.出口享惠情况 3.用途 4.类型(变色等)5.品牌 6.型号
90051	1.品牌类型 2.出口享惠情况 3.用途 4.是否双筒 5.品牌 6.型号
90058	1.品牌类型 2.出口享惠情况 3.用途 4.品牌 5.型号
90059	1.品牌类型 2.出口享惠情况 3.用途(适用于 XX 品牌 XX 机或通用于 XX 机等)4.品牌 5.型号
90063	1.品牌类型 2.出口享惠情况 3.用途 4.原理 5.品牌 6.型号
90064	1.品牌类型 2.出口享惠情况 3.用途 4.原理 5.品牌 6.型号
900651	1.品牌类型 2.出口享惠情况 3.用途 4.原理 5.胶片宽度 6.品牌 7.型号
900652	1.品牌类型 2.出口享惠情况 3.用途 4.原理 5.胶片宽度 6.品牌 7.型号
900653	1.品牌类型 2.出口享惠情况 3.用途 4.原理 5.胶片宽度 6.品牌 7.型号
900659	1.品牌类型 2.出口享惠情况 3.用途 4.原理 5.品牌 6.型号
90066	1.品牌类型 2.出口享惠情况 3.用途 4.原理 5.品牌 6.型号
90069	1.品牌类型 2.出口享惠情况 3.用途(适用于 XX 品牌 XX 机或通用于 XX 机等)4.品牌 5.型号
90071	1.品牌类型 2.出口享惠情况 3.用途 4.原理 5.胶片宽度 6.摄影速度 7.品牌 8.型号
90072	1.品牌类型 2.出口享惠情况 3.用途 4.原理 5.品牌 6.型号
90079	1.品牌类型 2.出口享惠情况 3.用途(适用于 XX 品牌 XX 机或通用于 XX 机等)4.品牌 5.型号
9008501	1.品牌类型 2.出口享惠情况 3.用途 4.品牌 5.型号
9008502	1.品牌类型 2.出口享惠情况 3.用途 4.品牌 5.型号
9008503	1.品牌类型 2.出口享惠情况 3.用途 4.原理 5.品牌 6.型号
9008504	1.品牌类型 2.出口享惠情况 3.用途 4.品牌 5.型号
90089	1.品牌类型 2.出口享惠情况 3.用途(适用于 XX 品牌 XX 机或通用于 XX 机等)4.品牌 5.型号
90101	1.品牌类型 2.出口享惠情况 3.用途 4.原理 5.品牌 6.型号
90105	1.品牌类型 2.出口享惠情况 3.用途 4.原理 5.品牌 6.型号
90106	1.品牌类型 2.出口享惠情况 3.用途 4.品牌 5.型号
90109	1.品牌类型 2.出口享惠情况 3.用途(适用于 XX 品牌 XX 机或通用于 XX 机等)4.品牌 5.型号
90111	1.品牌类型 2.出口享惠情况 3.用途 4.原理 5.品牌 6.型号 7.倍数
90112	1.品牌类型 2.出口享惠情况 3.用途 4.原理 5.品牌 6.型号 7.倍数
90118	1.品牌类型 2.出口享惠情况 3.用途 4.原理 5.品牌 6.型号 7.倍数
90119	1.品牌类型 2.出口享惠情况 3.用途(适用于 XX 品牌 XX 机或通用于 XX 机等)4.品牌 5.型号
90121	1.品牌类型 2.出口享惠情况 3.用途 4.原理 5.品牌 6.型号
90129	1.品牌类型 2.出口享惠情况 3.用途(适用于 XX 品牌 XX 机或通用于 XX 机等)4.品牌 5.型号
90131	1.品牌类型 2.出口享惠情况 3.用途 4.品牌 5.型号
90132	1.品牌类型 2.出口享惠情况 3.用途 4.原理 5.品牌 6.型号
9013801	1.品牌类型 2.出口享惠情况 3.原理 4.品牌 5.型号
9013802	1.品牌类型 2.出口享惠情况 3.原理 4.品牌 5.型号
9013803	1.品牌类型 2.出口享惠情况 3.用途 4.原理(是否为液晶)5.尺寸 6.品牌 7.型号 8.配置(请注明配置显示驱动板、HDMI 接口、标记板、解码板、高频头、视频接口、触摸功能等)
9013809	1.品牌类型 2.出口享惠情况 3.用途 4.原理 5.品牌 6.型号
90139	1.品牌类型 2.出口享惠情况 3.用途(适用于 XX 品牌 XX 机或通用于 XX 机等)4.品牌 5.型号
90141	1.品牌类型 2.出口享惠情况 3.用途 4.原理 5.品牌 6.型号
90142	1.品牌类型 2.出口享惠情况 3.用途 4.品牌 5.型号
90148	1.品牌类型 2.出口享惠情况 3.用途 4.原理 5.品牌 6.型号
90149	1.品牌类型 2.出口享惠情况 3.用途(适用于 XX 品牌 XX 机或通用于 XX 机等)4.品牌 5.型号
90151	1.品牌类型 2.出口享惠情况 3.用途 4.原理 5.品牌 6.型号
90152	1.品牌类型 2.出口享惠情况 3.用途 4.原理 5.品牌 6.型号
90153	1.品牌类型 2.出口享惠情况 3.用途 4.原理 5.品牌 6.型号
90154	1.品牌类型 2.出口享惠情况 3.用途 4.原理 5.品牌 6.型号
90158	1.品牌类型 2.出口享惠情况 3.用途 4.原理 5.品牌 6.型号
90159	1.品牌类型 2.出口享惠情况 3.用途(适用于 XX 品牌 XX 机或通用于 XX 机等)4.品牌 5.型号
9016	1.品牌类型 2.出口享惠情况 3.感量 4.品牌 5.型号
90171	1.品牌类型 2.出口享惠情况 3.用途 4.功能 5.品牌 6.型号
90172	1.品牌类型 2.出口享惠情况 3.用途 4.功能 5.是否手用 6.品牌 7.型号
90173	1.品牌类型 2.出口享惠情况 3.用途 4.功能 5.是否手用 6.品牌 7.型号
90178	1.品牌类型 2.出口享惠情况 3.用途 4.功能 5.品牌 6.型号
90179	1.品牌类型 2.出口享惠情况 3.用途(适用于 XX 品牌 XX 机或通用于 XX 机等)4.品牌 5.型号
90181	1.品牌类型 2.出口享惠情况 3.用途 4.如为整机,请申报原理 5.品牌 6.型号 7.探头数量
90182	1.品牌类型 2.出口享惠情况 3.用途 4.原理 5.品牌 6.型号
901831	1.品牌类型 2.出口享惠情况 3.用途 4.品牌 5.型号
901832	1.品牌类型 2.出口享惠情况 3.用途 4.品牌 5.型号
901839	1.品牌类型 2.出口享惠情况 3.用途 4.材质 5.品牌 6.型号
901841	1.品牌类型 2.出口享惠情况 3.用途 4.品牌 5.型号
9018491	1.品牌类型 2.出口享惠情况 3.用途 4.品牌 5.型号
9018499	1.品牌类型 2.出口享惠情况 3.用途 4.原理 5.品牌 6.型号
90185	1.品牌类型 2.出口享惠情况 3.用途 4.原理 5.品牌 6.型号
9018901	1.品牌类型 2.出口享惠情况 3.用途 4.品牌 5.型号
9018902	1.品牌类型 2.出口享惠情况 3.用途 4.原理(如电子式等)5.品牌 6.型号
9018903	1.品牌类型 2.出口享惠情况 3.用途 4.品牌 5.型号 6.配置(如含三晶片摄像系统、监视器、冷光源等)
9018904	1.品牌类型 2.出口享惠情况 3.用途 4.原理 5.品牌
9018905	1.品牌类型 2.出口享惠情况 3.用途 4.原理 5.品牌
9018906	1.品牌类型 2.出口享惠情况 3.用途 4.品牌 5.型号
9018907	1.品牌类型 2.出口享惠情况 3.用途 4.原理(如电子式等)5.品牌 6.型号
9018909	1.品牌类型 2.出口享惠情况 3.用途 4.原理(如电子式等)5.品牌 6.型号
9019101	1.品牌类型 2.出口享惠情况 3.用途 4.功能 5.品牌 6.型号
9019109	1.品牌类型 2.出口享惠情况 3.用途 4.功能 5.原理 6.品牌 7.型号
90192	1.品牌类型 2.出口享惠情况 3.用途 4.功能 5.品牌 6.型号
9020	1.品牌类型 2.出口享惠情况 3.用途 4.构成 5.有无机械零件或可互换过滤装置 6.品牌 7.型号
90211	1.品牌类型 2.出口享惠情况 3.用途 4.品牌 5.材质 6.型号 7.技术参数
90212	1.品牌类型 2.出口享惠情况 3.品牌 4.材质 5.型号
902131	1.品牌类型 2.出口享惠情况 3.用途 4.人造关节部位 5.品牌 6.材质 7.型号
902139	1.品牌类型 2.出口享惠情况 3.用途 4.品牌 5.材质 6.型号
90214	1.品牌类型 2.出口享惠情况

商品编码	申报要素
90215	1.品牌类型 2.出口享惠情况 3.材质
90219	1.品牌类型 2.出口享惠情况 3.用途 4.原理 5.品牌 6.型号
902212	1.品牌类型 2.出口享惠情况 3.用途 4.原理 5.品牌 6.型号 7.排数
902213	1.品牌类型 2.出口享惠情况 3.用途 4.原理 5.品牌 6.型号
902214	1.品牌类型 2.出口享惠情况 3.用途 4.原理 5.品牌 6.型号
902219	1.品牌类型 2.出口享惠情况 3.用途 4.原理 5.品牌 6.型号
90222	1.品牌类型 2.出口享惠情况 3.用途 4.原理 5.品牌 6.型号
90223	1.品牌类型 2.出口享惠情况 3.用途 4.原理 5.品牌 6.型号
90229	1.品牌类型 2.出口享惠情况 3.用途 4.原理 5.品牌 6.型号
9023	1.品牌类型 2.出口享惠情况 3.用途 4.品牌 5.型号
90241	1.品牌类型 2.出口享惠情况 3.功能 4.试验材料类型 5.品牌 6.型号
90248	1.品牌类型 2.出口享惠情况 3.功能 4.试验材料类型 5.品牌 6.型号
90249	1.品牌类型 2.出口享惠情况 3.用途(适用于 XX 品牌 XX 机或通用于 XX 机等)4.品牌 5.型号
90251	1.品牌类型 2.出口享惠情况 3.原理 4.是否可直接读数 5.品牌 6.型号
90258	1.品牌类型 2.出口享惠情况 3.原理 4.品牌 5.型号
90259	1.品牌类型 2.出口享惠情况 3.用途(适用于 XX 品牌 XX 机或通用于 XX 机等)4.品牌 5.型号
90261	1.品牌类型 2.出口享惠情况 3.功能 4.检测对象 5.品牌 6.型号
90262	1.品牌类型 2.出口享惠情况 3.功能 4.检测对象 5.品牌 6.型号
90268	1.品牌类型 2.出口享惠情况 3.功能 4.检测对象 5.品牌 6.型号
90269	1.品牌类型 2.出口享惠情况 3.用途(适用于 XX 品牌 XX 机或通用于 XX 机等)4.品牌 5.型号
90271	1.品牌类型 2.出口享惠情况 3.原理 4.功能 5.检测对象 6.品牌 7.型号
90272	1.品牌类型 2.出口享惠情况 3.原理 4.功能 5.检测对象 6.品牌 7.型号
90273	1.品牌类型 2.出口享惠情况 3.原理 4.功能 5.检测对象 6.品牌 7.型号
90275	1.品牌类型 2.出口享惠情况 3.原理 4.功能 5.检测对象 6.品牌 7.型号
90278	1.品牌类型 2.出口享惠情况 3.原理 4.功能 5.检测对象 6.品牌 7.型号
90279	1.品牌类型 2.出口享惠情况 3.用途(适用于 XX 品牌 XX 机或通用于 XX 机等)4.品牌 5.型号
90281	1.品牌类型 2.出口享惠情况 3.用途 4.品牌 5.型号
90282	1.品牌类型 2.出口享惠情况 3.用途 4.品牌 5.型号
90283	1.品牌类型 2.出口享惠情况 3.用途 4.原理 5.品牌 6.型号
90289	1.品牌类型 2.出口享惠情况 3.用途(适用于 XX 品牌 XX 机或通用于 XX 机等)4.品牌 5.型号
90291	1.品牌类型 2.出口享惠情况 3.用途 4.品牌 5.型号
90292	1.品牌类型 2.出口享惠情况 3.用途 4.品牌 5.型号
90299	1.品牌类型 2.出口享惠情况 3.用途(适用于 XX 品牌 XX 机或通用于 XX 机等)4.品牌 5.型号
90301	1.品牌类型 2.出口享惠情况 3.用途 4.功能 5.品牌 6.型号
90302	1.品牌类型 2.出口享惠情况 3.用途 4.功能 5.频率 6.品牌 7.型号
903031	1.品牌类型 2.出口享惠情况 3.用途 4.功能 5.量程 6.是否带记录装置 7.品牌 8.型号
903032	1.品牌类型 2.出口享惠情况 3.用途 4.功能 5.量程 6.是否带记录装置 7.品牌 8.型号
9030331	1.品牌类型 2.出口享惠情况 3.用途 4.功能 5.量程 6.是否带记录装置 7.品牌 8.型号
9030332	1.品牌类型 2.出口享惠情况 3.用途 4.功能 5.是否带记录装置 6.品牌 7.型号
9030339	1.品牌类型 2.出口享惠情况 3.用途 4.功能 5.是否带记录装置 6.品牌 7.型号
903039	1.品牌类型 2.出口享惠情况 3.用途 4.功能 5.是否带记录装置 6.品牌 7.型号
90304	1.品牌类型 2.出口享惠情况 3.用途 4.功能 5.测试频率 6.品牌 7.型号
903082	1.品牌类型 2.出口享惠情况 3.用途 4.功能 5.是否带记录装置 6.品牌 7.型号 8.测试结果显示内容(例如,电压值、电流值等)
903084	1.品牌类型 2.出口享惠情况 3.用途 4.功能 5.是否带记录装置 6.品牌 7.型号
903089	1.品牌类型 2.出口享惠情况 3.用途 4.功能 5.是否带记录装置 6.品牌 7.型号
90309	1.品牌类型 2.出口享惠情况 3.用途(适用于 XX 品牌 XX 机或通用于 XX 机等)4.品牌 5.型号
90311	1.品牌类型 2.出口享惠情况 3.用途 4.功能 5.品牌 6.型号
90312	1.品牌类型 2.出口享惠情况 3.用途 4.功能 5.品牌 6.型号
90314	1.品牌类型 2.出口享惠情况 3.用途 4.功能 5.品牌 6.型号
90318	1.品牌类型 2.出口享惠情况 3.用途 4.原理 5.功能 6.品牌 7.型号
90319	1.品牌类型 2.出口享惠情况 3.用途(适用于 XX 品牌 XX 机或通用于 XX 机等)4.品牌 5.型号
90321	1.品牌类型 2.出口享惠情况 3.用途 4.原理 5.功能 6.品牌 7.型号
90322	1.品牌类型 2.出口享惠情况 3.用途 4.原理 5.功能 6.品牌 7.型号
90328	1.品牌类型 2.出口享惠情况 3.用途 4.原理 5.功能 6.品牌 7.型号
90329	1.品牌类型 2.出口享惠情况 3.用途(适用于 XX 品牌 XX 机或通用于 XX 机等)4.品牌 5.型号
9033	1.品牌类型 2.出口享惠情况 3.用途(适用于 XX 品牌 XX 机或通用于 XX 机等)4.品牌 5.型号
9101	1.品牌类型 2.出口享惠情况 3.外壳材质(贵金属或包贵金属制)4.驱动方式(电子、机械、自动、非自动)5.指示方式(指针、光电)6.品牌 7.型号
9102	1.品牌类型 2.出口享惠情况 3.外壳材质(金属制等)4.驱动方式(电子、机械、自动、非自动)5.指示方式(指针、光电)6.品牌 7.型号
9103	1.品牌类型 2.出口享惠情况 3.驱动方式(电子、机械、自动、非自动)4.品牌 5.型号
9104	1.品牌类型 2.出口享惠情况 3.驱动方式(电子、机械、自动、非自动)4.品牌 5.型号
91051	1.品牌类型 2.出口享惠情况 3.驱动方式(电子、机械、自动、非自动)4.品牌 5.型号
91052	1.品牌类型 2.出口享惠情况 3.驱动方式(电子、机械、自动、非自动)4.品牌 5.型号
9105911	1.品牌类型 2.出口享惠情况 3.用途(车辆、船舶等用)4.品牌 5.型号
9105919	1.品牌类型 2.出口享惠情况 3.用途(闹钟、天文钟等)4.驱动方式(电子、机械)5.品牌 6.型号
910599	1.品牌类型 2.出口享惠情况 3.用途(闹钟、天文钟等)4.驱动方式(电子、机械)5.品牌 6.型号
9106	1.品牌类型 2.出口享惠情况 3.用途(闹钟、天文钟等)4.驱动方式(电子、机械)5.品牌 6.型号
9107	1.品牌类型 2.出口享惠情况 3.用途(闹钟、天文钟等)4.驱动方式(电子、机械)5.品牌 6.型号
91081	1.品牌类型 2.出口享惠情况 3.用途(闹钟、天文钟等)4.驱动方式(电子、机械)5.表面尺寸 6.指示方式 7.品牌
91082	1.品牌类型 2.出口享惠情况 3.用途(闹钟、天文钟等)4.驱动方式(电子、机械)5.表面尺寸 6.指示方式 7.品牌
9108901	1.品牌类型 2.出口享惠情况 3.用途(考勤钟、停车记时表等)4.驱动方式(电子、机械)5.表芯的表面尺寸 6.品牌
9108909	1.品牌类型 2.出口享惠情况 3.表面尺寸
9109	1.品牌类型 2.出口享惠情况 3.驱动方式(电子、机械、自动、非自动)
91101	1.品牌类型 2.出口享惠情况 3.驱动方式(电子、机械、自动、非自动)
91109	1.品牌类型 2.出口享惠情况 3.用途
91111	1.品牌类型 2.出口享惠情况 3.材质 4.贵金属含量
91112	1.品牌类型 2.出口享惠情况 3.材质
91118	1.品牌类型 2.出口享惠情况 3.材质
91119	1.品牌类型 2.出口享惠情况 3.材质
9112	1.品牌类型 2.出口享惠情况 3.用途
91131	1.品牌类型 2.出口享惠情况 3.材质(贵金属、贱金属等)4.贵金属含量
91132	1.品牌类型 2.出口享惠情况 3.材质(贵金属、贱金属等)
91139	1.品牌类型 2.出口享惠情况 3.材质(贵金属、贱金属等)4.是否野生动物皮制
91141	1.品牌类型 2.出口享惠情况 3.用途 4.材质
91143	1.品牌类型 2.出口享惠情况 3.材质(贵金属、贱金属等)
91144	1.品牌类型 2.出口享惠情况 3.材质(贵金属、贱金属等)
9114901	1.品牌类型 2.出口享惠情况 3.用途 4.材质
9114909	1.品牌类型 2.出口享惠情况 3.材质(贵金属、贱金属等)
9201	1.品牌类型 2.出口享惠情况 3.产品编码 4.材质(象牙琴键、贵金属、贱金属等)5.种类(新旧、竖卧式、是否数码)6.品牌 7.型号 8.旧钢琴请申报生产年份
9202	1.品牌类型 2.出口享惠情况 3.是否为野生动物皮制 4.用途 5.型号 6.品牌
9205	1.品牌类型 2.出口享惠情况 3.种类 4.品牌 5.型号
9206	1.品牌类型 2.出口享惠情况 3.是否为野生动物皮制 4.用途 5.品牌 6.型号
9207	1.品牌类型 2.出口享惠情况 3.种类 4.品牌 5.型号

商品编码	申报要素
92081	1.品牌类型 2.出口享惠情况 3.种类 4.品牌
92089	1.品牌类型 2.出口享惠情况 3.品牌
92093	1.品牌类型 2.出口享惠情况 3.用途(适用乐器类型)4.品牌 5.材质 6.型号
92099	1.品牌类型 2.出口享惠情况 3.用途
9301	1.品牌类型 2.出口享惠情况 3.驱动方式 4.型号
9302	1.品牌类型 2.出口享惠情况 3.型号
9303	1.品牌类型 2.出口享惠情况 3.型号
9304	1.品牌类型 2.出口享惠情况 3.型号
9305	1.品牌类型 2.出口享惠情况 3.型号
9306	1.品牌类型 2.出口享惠情况 3.型号
9307	1.品牌类型 2.出口享惠情况 3.用途
94011	1.品牌类型 2.出口享惠情况 3.用途 4.品牌
94012	1.品牌类型 2.出口享惠情况 3.用途(适用车型)4.材质(骨架及覆面)5.品牌(中文及外文名称,无品牌请申报厂商)
94013	1.品牌类型 2.出口享惠情况 3.用途 4.材质 5.是否可调节、可转动 6.品牌
94014	1.品牌类型 2.出口享惠情况 3.用途 4.材质 5.是否可作床用 6.品牌
94015	1.品牌类型 2.出口享惠情况 3.用途 4.材质 5.品牌
9401611	1.品牌类型 2.出口享惠情况 3.用途 4.座面的表面材质 5.框架材质 6.是否装软垫 7.品牌
9401619	1.品牌类型 2.出口享惠情况 3.用途 4.表面材质 5.框架材质 6.是否装软垫 7.品牌
940169	1.品牌类型 2.出口享惠情况 3.用途 4.座面的表面材质 5.框架材质 6.是否装软垫 7.品牌
94017	1.品牌类型 2.出口享惠情况 3.用途 4.座面的表面材质 5.框架材质 6.是否装软垫 7.品牌
94018	1.品牌类型 2.出口享惠情况 3.用途 4.材质 5.品牌
9401901	1.品牌类型 2.出口享惠情况 3.用途(适用车型)4.材质
9401909	1.品牌类型 2.出口享惠情况 3.用途 4.材质
9402101	1.品牌类型 2.出口享惠情况 3.用途 4.材质 5.品牌
9402109	1.品牌类型 2.出口享惠情况 3.用途 4.配置附属装置 5.是否带医疗用具 6.品牌
94029	1.品牌类型 2.出口享惠情况 3.用途 4.配置附属装置 5.是否带医疗用具 6.品牌
94031	1.品牌类型 2.出口享惠情况 3.材质 4.是否办公室用 5.品牌 6.规格
94032	1.品牌类型 2.出口享惠情况 3.用途 4.材质 5.品牌 6.规格
94033	1.品牌类型 2.出口享惠情况 3.材质 4.是否办公室用 5.品牌 6.规格
94034	1.品牌类型 2.出口享惠情况 3.材质 4.是否厨房用 5.品牌 6.规格
94035	1.品牌类型 2.出口享惠情况 3.材质 4.是否卧室用 5.品牌 6.规格
94036	1.品牌类型 2.出口享惠情况 3.用途 4.材质 5.品牌 6.规格
94037	1.品牌类型 2.出口享惠情况 3.用途 4.材质 5.品牌 6.规格
94038	1.品牌类型 2.出口享惠情况 3.用途 4.材质 5.品牌 6.规格
94039	1.品牌类型 2.出口享惠情况 3.用途 4.材质 5.规格
94041	1.品牌类型 2.出口享惠情况 3.品牌 4.规格
94042	1.品牌类型 2.出口享惠情况 3.材质 4.品牌 5.规格
94043	1.品牌类型 2.出口享惠情况 3.材质(填充物)4.品牌 5.规格
94049	1.品牌类型 2.出口享惠情况 3.材质(填充物)4.品牌 5.规格
94051	1.品牌类型 2.出口享惠情况 3.用途 4.品牌
94052	1.品牌类型 2.出口享惠情况 3.材质 4.用途 5.品牌
94053	1.品牌类型 2.出口享惠情况 3.材质 4.用途 5.品牌
94054	1.品牌类型 2.出口享惠情况 3.用途 4.品牌
94055	1.品牌类型 2.出口享惠情况 3.材质 4.用途 5.品牌
94056	1.品牌类型 2.出口享惠情况 3.材质 4.用途 5.品牌
94059	1.品牌类型 2.出口享惠情况 3.材质 4.用途
9406	1.品牌类型 2.出口享惠情况 3.材质 4.内部配置 5.规格(尺寸)
9503001	1.品牌类型 2.出口享惠情况 3.用途 4.种类 5.品牌
9503002	1.品牌类型 2.出口享惠情况 3.用途 4.种类 5.品牌
9503006	1.品牌类型 2.出口享惠情况 3.用途 4.种类 5.品牌
95030083	1.品牌类型 2.出口享惠情况 3.用途 4.种类 5.是否带有动力装置 6.品牌
95030089	1.品牌类型 2.出口享惠情况 3.用途 4.种类 5.品牌
9503009	1.品牌类型 2.出口享惠情况 3.用途 4.种类 5.品牌
95042	1.品牌类型 2.出口享惠情况 3.用途 4.品牌
9504301	1.品牌类型 2.出口享惠情况 3.用途 4.种类 5.品牌
9504309	1.品牌类型 2.出口享惠情况 3.用途 4.品牌
95044	1.品牌类型 2.出口享惠情况 3.用途 4.品牌
95045	1.品牌类型 2.出口享惠情况 3.用途 4.种类 5.是否与电视接收机配套使用 6.品牌
9504901	1.品牌类型 2.出口享惠情况 3.种类 4.品牌

商品编码	申报要素
9504902	1.品牌类型 2.出口享惠情况 3.种类 4.品牌
9504903	1.品牌类型 2.出口享惠情况 3.种类 4.品牌
9504904	1.品牌类型 2.出口享惠情况 3.种类 4.品牌
9504909	1.品牌类型 2.出口享惠情况 3.材质 4.品牌
95051	1.品牌类型 2.出口享惠情况 3.用途 4.品牌
95059	1.品牌类型 2.出口享惠情况 3.用途 4.品牌
95061	1.品牌类型 2.出口享惠情况 3.种类 4.品牌 5.型号
95062	1.品牌类型 2.出口享惠情况 3.种类 4.品牌 5.型号
95063	1.品牌类型 2.出口享惠情况 3.品牌 4.型号
95064	1.品牌类型 2.出口享惠情况 3.品牌 4.型号
95065	1.品牌类型 2.出口享惠情况 3.种类 4.品牌 5.型号
95066	1.品牌类型 2.出口享惠情况 3.种类 4.品牌 5.型号
95067	1.品牌类型 2.出口享惠情况 3.种类 4.品牌 5.型号
950691	1.品牌类型 2.出口享惠情况 3.用途 4.种类 5.品牌 6.型号
950699	1.品牌类型 2.出口享惠情况 3.材质 4.品牌 5.型号
95071	1.品牌类型 2.出口享惠情况 3.材质 4.品牌 5.型号
95072	1.品牌类型 2.出口享惠情况 3.品牌 4.型号
95073	1.品牌类型 2.出口享惠情况 3.品牌 4.型号
95079	1.品牌类型 2.出口享惠情况 3.用途 4.品牌 5.型号
9508	1.品牌类型 2.出口享惠情况
96011	1.品牌类型 2.出口享惠情况 3.是否野生动物产品
96019	1.品牌类型 2.出口享惠情况 3.材质 4.加工工艺
9602001	1.品牌类型 2.出口享惠情况
9602009	1.品牌类型 2.出口享惠情况 3.材质 4.加工工艺
96031	1.品牌类型 2.出口享惠情况 3.用途 4.材质
96032	1.品牌类型 2.出口享惠情况 3.用途 4.材质
96033	1.品牌类型 2.出口享惠情况 3.用途 4.材质
96034	1.品牌类型 2.出口享惠情况 3.用途 4.材质
96035	1.品牌类型 2.出口享惠情况 3.用途(具体作为何种机器、器具零件,作用)4.材质
96039	1.品牌类型 2.出口享惠情况 3.用途 4.材质
9604	1.品牌类型 2.出口享惠情况
9605	1.品牌类型 2.出口享惠情况 3.组成(内装货品)
96061	1.品牌类型 2.出口享惠情况 3.材质 4.种类 5.是否用纺织材料包裹
96062	1.品牌类型 2.出口享惠情况 3.材质 4.纺织材料包裹\非纺织材料包裹 5.种类(是否袖口、饰扣)
96063	1.品牌类型 2.出口享惠情况 3.种类
9607	1.品牌类型 2.出口享惠情况 3.材质 4.品牌
9608	1.品牌类型 2.出口享惠情况 3.种类 4.品牌 5.型号
9609	1.品牌类型 2.出口享惠情况 3.种类 4.品牌 5.型号
9610	1.品牌类型 2.出口享惠情况 3.种类 4.品牌
9611	1.品牌类型 2.出口享惠情况 3.用途
9612	1.品牌类型 2.出口享惠情况 3.材质 4.品牌 5.型号
9613	1.品牌类型 2.出口享惠情况 3.种类 4.型号 5.品牌
9614001	1.品牌类型 2.出口享惠情况 3.材质 4.品牌 5.型号
9614009	1.品牌类型 2.出口享惠情况 3.材质 4.品牌
9615	1.品牌类型 2.出口享惠情况 3.材质 4.品牌(中文及外文名称)
96161	1.品牌类型 2.出口享惠情况 3.用途
96162	1.品牌类型 2.出口享惠情况 3.用途 4.材质
9617	1.品牌类型 2.出口享惠情况 3.是否带外壳的保温瓶 4.内胆材质 5.品牌(中文及外文名称)6.型号
9618	1.品牌类型 2.出口享惠情况 3.用途 4.材质
9619001	1.品牌类型 2.出口享惠情况 3.用途(婴儿用、成人用等)4.品牌(包括中英文品牌名称)5.系列 6.码数(型号)7.包装规格(每包所含片数)8.个体重量(每包重量)
9619002	1.品牌类型 2.出口享惠情况 3.品牌(中文及外文品牌名称)4.系列 5.包装规格(每包所含片数)6.每包重量(kg)
9619009	1.品牌类型 2.出口享惠情况 3.品牌(中文及外文品牌名称)4.系列 5.包装规格(每包所含片数)6.每包重量(kg)
9620	1.品牌类型 2.出口享惠情况 3.品牌 4.用途
97011011	1.品牌类型 2.出口享惠情况 3.是否野生动物产品 4.尺寸大小
97011019	1.品牌类型 2.出口享惠情况 3.是否野生动物产品 4.尺寸大小 5.作者 6.作品名称
9701102	1.品牌类型 2.出口享惠情况 3.是否野生动物产品 4.尺寸大小
97019	1.品牌类型 2.出口享惠情况 3.是否野生动物产品 4.尺寸大小
9702	1.品牌类型 2.出口享惠情况 3.尺寸大小 4.原作者姓名 5.创作年份 6.作品名称
9703	1.品牌类型 2.出口享惠情况 3.材质(是否濒危动植物制)4.尺寸大小 5.作者 6.作品名称
9704	1.品牌类型 2.出口享惠情况 3.种类 4.指运国(地区)
9705	1.品牌类型 2.出口享惠情况 3.种类 4.年代 5.是否野生动物产品
9706	1.品牌类型 2.出口享惠情况 3.年代 4.是否野生动物产品

3

常用代码表

Common Codes List

监管方式代码表

监管方式代码	监管方式简称	监管方式全称
0110	一般贸易	一般贸易
0130	易货贸易	易货贸易
0139	旅游购物商品	用于旅游者5万美元以下的出口小批量订货
0200	料件销毁	加工贸易料件、残次品(折料)销毁
0214	来料加工	来料加工装配贸易进口料件及加工出口货物
0245	来料料件内销	来料加工料件转内销
0255	来料深加工	来料深加工结转货物
0258	来料余料结转	来料加工余料结转
0265	来料料件复出	来料加工复运出境的原进口料件
0300	来料料件退换	来料加工料件退换
0314	加工专用油	国营贸易企业代理来料加工企业进口柴油
0320	不作价设备	加工贸易外商提供的不作价进口设备
0345	来料成品减免	来料加工成品凭征免税证明转减免税
0400	边角料销毁	加工贸易边角料、副产品(按状态)销毁
0420	加工贸易设备	加工贸易项下外商提供的进口设备
0444	保区进料成品	按成品征税的保税区进料加工成品转内销货物
0445	保区来料成品	按成品征税的保税区来料加工成品转内销货物
0446	加工设备内销	加工贸易免税进口设备转内销
0456	加工设备结转	加工贸易免税进口设备结转
0466	加工设备退运	加工贸易免税进口设备退运出境
0500	减免设备结转	用于监管年限内减免税设备的结转
0513	补偿贸易	补偿贸易
0544	保区进料料件	按料件征税的保税区进料加工成品转内销货物
0545	保区来料料件	按料件征税的保税区来料加工成品转内销货物
0615	进料对口	进料加工(对口合同)
0642	进料以产顶进	进料加工成品以产顶进
0644	进料料件内销	进料加工料件转内销
0654	进料深加工	进料深加工结转货物
0657	进料余料结转	进料加工余料结转
0664	进料料件复出	进料加工复运出境的原进口料件
0700	进料料件退换	进料加工料件退换
0715	进料非对口	进料加工(非对口合同)
0744	进料成品减免	进料加工成品凭征免税证明转减免税
0815	低值辅料	低值辅料
0844	进料边角料内销	进料加工项下边角料转内销
0845	来料边角料内销	来料加工项下边角料内销
0864	进料边角料复出	进料加工项下边角料复出口
0865	来料边角料复出	来料加工项下边角料复出口
1039	市场采购	市场采购
1139	国轮油物料	中国籍运输工具境内添加的保税油料、物料
1200	保税间货物	海关保税场所及保税区域之间往来的货物
1210	网购保税	跨境电子商务网购保税
1215	保税工厂	保税工厂
1233	保税仓库货物	保税仓库进出境货物
1234	保税区仓储转口	保税区进出境仓储转口货物
1239	网购保税 A	跨境电子商务网购保税 A
1300	修理物品	进出境修理物品
1371	保税维修	保税维修
1427	出料加工	出料加工
1500	租赁不满1年	租期不满1年的租赁贸易货物
1523	租赁贸易	租期在1年及以上的租赁贸易货物
1616	寄售代销	寄售、代销贸易
1741	免税品	免税品
1831	外汇商品	免税外汇商品
2025	合资合作设备	合资合作企业作为投资进口设备物品
2210	对外投资	对外投资
2225	外资设备物品	外资企业作为投资进口的设备物品
2439	常驻机构公用	外国常驻机构进口办公用品
2600	暂时进出货物	暂时进出口货物
2700	展览品	进出境展览品
2939	陈列样品	驻华商业机构不复运出口的进口陈列样品
3010	货样广告品	进出口的货样广告品
3039	无	无
3100	无代价抵偿	无代价抵偿进出口货物
3239	零售电商	跨境电子商务零售
3339	其他进出口免费	其他进出口免费提供货物
3410	承包工程进口	对外承包工程进口物资
3422	对外承包出口	对外承包工程出口物资
3511	援助物资	国家和国际组织无偿援助物资
3611	无偿军援	无偿军援
3612	捐赠物资	进出口捐赠物资
3910	军事装备	军事装备
4019	边境小额	边境小额贸易(边民互市贸易除外)

监管方式代码	监管方式简称	监管方式全称
4039	对台小额	对台小额贸易
4139	对台小额商品交易市场	进入对台小额商品交易专用市场的货物
4200	驻外机构运回	我驻外机构运回旧公用物品
4239	驻外机构购进	我驻外机构境外购买运回国的公务用品
4400	来料成品退换	来料加工成品退换
4500	直接退运	直接退运
4539	进口溢误卸	进口溢卸、误卸货物
4561	退运货物	因质量不符、延误交货等原因退运进出境货物
4600	进料成品退换	进料成品退换
5000	料件进出区	料件进出海关特殊监管区域
5010	特殊区域研发货物	海关特殊监管区域与境外之间进出的研发货物
5014	区内来料加工	海关特殊监管区域与境外之间进出的来料加工货物
5015	区内进料加工货物	海关特殊监管区域与境外之间进出的进料加工货物
5033	区内仓储货物	加工区内仓储企业从境外进口的货物
5034	区内物流货物	海关特殊监管区域与境外之间进出的物流货物
5100	成品进出区	成品进出海关特殊监管区域
5200	区内边角调出	用于区内外非实际进出境货物
5300	设备进出区	设备及物资进出海关特殊监管区域
5335	境外设备进区	海关特殊监管区域从境外进口的设备及物资
5361	区内设备退运	海关特殊监管区域设备及物资退运境外
6033	物流中心进出境货物	保税物流中心与境外之间进出仓储货物
9600	内贸货物跨境运输	内贸货物跨境运输
9610	电子商务	跨境贸易电子商务
9639	海关处理货物	海关变卖处理的超期未报货物、走私违规货物
9700	后续补税	无原始报关单的后续补税
9739	其他贸易	其他贸易
9800	租赁征税	租赁期1年及以上的租赁贸易货物的租金
9839	留赠转卖物品	外交机构转售境内或国际活动留赠放弃特批货物
9900	其他	其他

征免性质代码表

征免性质代码	征免性质简称	征免性质全称
101	一般征税	一般征税进出口货物
118	整车征税	构成整车特征的汽车零部件纳税
119	零部件征税	不构成整车特征的汽车零部件纳税
201	无偿援助	无偿援助进出口物资
299	其他法定	其他法定减免税进出口货物
301	特定区域	特定区域进口自用物资及出口货物
307	保税区	保税区进口自用物资
399	其他地区	其他执行特殊政策地区出口货物
401	科教用品	大专院校及科研机构进口科教用品
402	示范平台用品	
403	技术改造	企业技术改造进口货物
405	科技开发用品	科学研究、技术开发机构进口科技开发用品
406	重大项目	国家重大项目进口货物
407	动漫用品	动漫开发生产用品
408	重大技术装备	生产重大技术装备进口关键零部件及原材料
409	科技重大专项	科技重大专项进口关键设备、零部件和原材料
412	基础设施	通信、港口、铁路、公路、机场建设进口设备
413	残疾人	残疾人组织和企业进出口货物
417	远洋渔业	远洋渔业自捕水产品
418	国产化	国家定点生产小轿车和摄录机企业进口散件
419	整车特征	构成整车特征的汽车零部件进口
420	远洋船舶	远洋船舶及设备部件
421	内销设备	内销远洋船用设备及关键部件
422	集成电路	集成电路生产企业进口货物
423	新型显示器件	新型显示器件生产企业进口物资
499	**ITA** 产品	非全税号信息技术产品
501	加工设备	加工贸易外商提供的不作价进口设备
502	来料加工	来料加工装配和补偿贸易进口料件及出口成品
503	进料加工	进料加工贸易进口料件及出口成品
506	边境小额	边境小额贸易进口货物
510	港澳 **OPA**	港澳在内地加工的纺织品获证出口
601	中外合资	中外合资经营企业进出口货物
602	中外合作	中外合作经营企业进出口货物
603	外资企业	外商独资企业进出口货物
605	勘探开发煤层气	勘探开发煤层气
606	海洋石油	勘探、开发海洋石油进口货物
608	陆上石油	勘探、开发陆上石油进口货物

征免性质代码	征免性质简称	征免性质全称
609	贷款项目	利用贷款进口货物
611	贷款中标	国际金融组织贷款、外国政府贷款中标机电设备零部件
698	公益收藏	国有公益性收藏单位进口藏品
704	花卉种子	花卉种子
705	科普影视	科普影视
707	博览会留购展品	博览会留购展品
710	民用卫星	民用卫星
711	救助船舶设备	救助船舶设备
789	鼓励项目	国家鼓励发展的内外资项目进口设备
799	自有资金	外商投资额度外利用自有资金进口设备、备件、配件
801	救灾捐赠	救灾捐赠进口物资
802	慈善捐赠	境外捐赠人无偿向我境内受赠人捐赠的直接用于慈善事业的免税进口物资
803	抗艾滋病药物	进口抗艾滋病病毒药物
811	种子种源	进口种子(苗)、种畜(禽)、鱼种(苗)和种用野生动植物种源
818	中央储备粮油	中央储备粮油免征进口环节增值税政策
819	科教图书	进口科研教学用图书资料
888	航材减免	经核准的航空公司进口维修用航空器材
898	国批减免	国务院特准减免税的进出口货物
899	选择征税	选择征税
901	科研院所	科研院所进口科学研究、科技开发和教学用品
902	高等学校	高等学校进口科学研究、科技开发和教学用品
903	工程研究中心	国家工程研究中心进口科学研究、科技开发和教学用品
904	国家企业技术中心	国家企业技术中心进口科学研究、科技开发和教学用品
905	转制科研机构	转制科研机构进口科学研究、科技开发和教学用品
906	重点实验室	国家重点实验室及企业国家重点实验室进口科学研究、科技开发和教学用品
907	国家工程技术研究中心	国家工程技术研究中心进口科学研究、科技开发和教学用品
908	科技民非单位	科技类民办非企业单位进口科学研究、科技开发和教学用品
909	示范平台	国家中小企业公共服务示范平台(技术类)进口科学研究、科技开发和教学用品
910	外资研发中心	外资研发中心进口科学研究、科技开发和教学用品
911	科教图书	出版物进口单位进口用于科研、教学的图书、文献、报刊及其他资料
921	大型客机研制物资	大型客机、大型客机发动机研制进口物资
922	进博会留购展品	进博会留购展品
997	自贸协定	
998	内部暂定	享受内部暂定税率的进出口货物
999	例外减免	例外减免税进出口货物

征减免税方式代码表

征减免税方式代码	征减免税方式名称
1	照章征税
2	折半征税
3	全免
4	特案
5	随征免性质
6	保证金
7	保函
8	折半补税
9	全额退税

运输方式代码表

运输方式代码	运输方式名称
0	非保税区
1	监管仓库
2	水路运输
3	铁路运输
4	公路运输
5	航空运输
6	邮件运输
7	保税区
8	保税仓库
9	其他方式运输
H	边境特殊海关作业区
T	综合实验区
W	物流中心
X	物流园区
Y	保税港区
Z	出口加工区
L	旅客携带
G	固定设施运输

关区代码表

关区代码	关区简称
0000	**海关总署**
0100	**北京关区**
0101	京机场关
0102	京监管处
0103	京关展览
0104	京西城关
0105	京会展关
0106	大兴机场
0107	机场库区
0108	京综合处
0109	机场旅检
0110	平谷海关
0111	京车站关
0112	京邮局关
0113	京中关村
0114	海淀海关
0115	京东城关
0116	大兴旅检
0117	亦庄海关
0118	京朝阳关
0119	通州海关
0121	京稽查处
0123	机场调技
0124	北京站
0125	西客站
0126	丰台海关
0127	京快件
0128	顺义海关
0129	天竺海关
0130	亦庄物流
0200	**天津海关**
0201	津南开关
0202	新港海关
0203	塘沽海关
0204	东港海关
0205	津塘沽办
0206	津邮局关
0207	津机场办
0208	津保税区
0209	津蓟州关
0210	武清海关
0211	津加工区
0212	津物流园
0213	天津东疆
0214	津滨综保
0215	津机快件
0216	津开物流
0217	东疆港区
0218	静海海关
0219	津北辰关
0220	津关税处
0221	津宁河关
0222	津大港关
0223	津临港关
0224	津南疆关
0225	津西青关
0226	津北塘关
0227	津河西关
0228	津东丽关
0229	津蓟物流
0400	**石家庄区**
0401	鹿泉海关
0402	秦皇岛关
0403	唐山海关
0404	廊坊海关
0405	保定海关
0406	邯郸海关
0407	秦加工区
0408	沧州海关
0409	廊坊综保
0410	石机场关
0411	张家口关
0412	曹妃甸关
0413	邢台海关
0414	曹综保区
0415	衡水海关
0416	石关快件
0417	承德海关
0418	石综保区
0419	武安物流
0420	京唐物流
0421	正定海关
0422	京唐港关
0423	雄安海关
0424	黄骅港关
0425	辛集物流
0426	北戴河关
0500	**太原关区**
0501	晋阳海关
0502	并机场关
0503	大同海关
0504	临汾海关
0505	方略物流
0506	太原综保
0507	运城海关
0508	晋城海关
0509	兰花物流
0510	太原邮件
0511	武宿海关
0512	长治海关
0513	阳泉海关
0514	朔州海关
0600	**满洲里关**
0601	海拉尔关
0602	额尔古纳
0603	满十八里
0604	赤峰海关
0605	通辽海关
0606	满哈沙特
0607	满室韦
0608	满互贸区
0609	满铁路
0610	满市区
0611	满机场
0612	阿尔山关
0613	赤峰物流
0614	额布都格
0615	满综保区
0616	满关邮办
0700	**呼特关区**
0701	赛罕海关
0702	二关铁路
0703	包头海关
0704	呼关邮办
0705	二关公路
0706	包头箱站
0707	额济纳关
0708	乌拉特关
0709	满达口岸
0710	东乌海关
0711	机场海关
0712	呼加工区
0713	鄂尔多斯
0714	集宁海关
0715	乌海海关
0716	鄂综保区
0717	包头保 B
0718	巴市保 B
0719	二关公直
0800	**沈阳关区**
0801	浑南海关
0802	锦州海关
0803	沈邮局关
0804	抚顺海关
0805	铁西海关
0806	辽阳海关
0807	沈机场关
0808	辽中海关
0809	沈快件
0810	葫芦岛关
0811	辽宁朝阳
0812	沈抚新区
0813	铁岭海关
0814	铁保(B 型)
0815	阜新海关
0900	**大连海关**
0901	大连港湾
0902	大连机场
0903	连开发区
0904	连加工区
0905	北良港关
0906	连保税区
0907	连物流园
0908	连大窑湾
0909	连邮局关
0910	连保税港
0911	长兴岛关
0912	大连快件
0915	庄河海关
0916	七贤岭关
0917	旅顺海关
0919	金石滩关
0930	丹东海关
0931	本溪海关
0932	丹太平湾
0940	营口海关
0941	盘锦海关
0942	盘港物流
0943	营口综保
0950	鲅鱼圈关
0951	营港物流
0953	仙人岛办
0960	大东港关
0980	鞍山海关
1500	**长春关区**
1501	绿园海关
1502	兴隆海关
1503	长白海关
1504	临江口岸
1505	图们海关
1506	通化海关
1507	珲春海关
1508	吉林海关
1509	延吉海关
1510	长春综保
1511	龙嘉机场
1512	松原海关
1513	白城海关
1514	白山海关
1515	图们车办
1516	通海关村
1517	珲长岭子
1518	吉关车办
1519	图们三合
1521	一汽场站
1522	长白山海关
1523	四平海关
1524	辽源海关
1525	图们桥办
1526	通集青石
1527	珲春圈河
1528	吉林物流

关区代码	关区简称	关区代码	关区简称	关区代码	关区简称	关区代码	关区简称
1529	延吉南坪	2207	洋山海关	2309	盐城海关	2364	武进出加
1531	兴隆铁路	2208	宝山海关	2310	扬州海关	2365	张保税港
1536	通集铁路	2209	龙吴海关	2311	徐州海关	2366	宿迁海关
1537	珲沙坨子	2210	浦东海关	2312	江阴海关	2367	泰出加区
1539	图开山屯	2211	卢湾监管	2313	张保税区	2368	苏高综保
1546	通集公路	2212	奉贤海关	2314	苏工业区	2369	昆山综保
1547	珲综保区	2213	莘庄海关	2315	淮安海关	2370	连关物流
1549	延古城里	2214	漕河泾发	2316	泰州海关	2371	盐机场办
1557	珲春车办	2215	西北物流	2317	禄口机场	2372	盐城综保
1559	延吉邮办	2216	浦机综保	2318	金陵江北	2373	淮安综保
1569	延吉机办	2217	嘉定海关	2319	如皋海关	2374	锡高综保
1579	延关快件	2218	外高桥关	2320	锡关机办	2375	靖江海关
1591	长邮海关	2219	沪杨浦关	2321	常溧阳办	2376	南通综保
1593	长白邮办	2220	金山海关	2322	镇丹阳办	2377	龙潭综保
1595	图们邮办	2221	松江海关	2323	金陵海关	2378	江宁综保
1596	通集邮办	2222	青浦海关	2324	常熟海关	2379	苏相城办
1900	**哈尔滨区**	2223	沪科创关	2325	昆山海关	2380	太仓综保
1901	哈尔滨关	2224	崇明海关	2326	吴江海关	2381	苏园贸易
1902	绥关铁路	2225	外港海关	2327	太仓海关	2382	盐东台办
1903	黑河海关	2226	贸易网点	2328	苏吴中办	2383	如东海关
1904	同江海关	2227	普陀区站	2329	启东海关	2384	如皋物流
1905	佳木斯海关	2228	沪会展关	2330	泰泰兴办	2385	泰州综保
1906	牡丹江关	2229	航交办	2331	宜兴海关	2386	镇江综保
1907	东宁海关	2230	沪徐汇关	2332	锡锡山办	2387	常州综保
1908	逊克海关	2231	洋山市内	2333	南通关办	2388	武进综保
1909	齐齐哈尔	2232	嘉定出口	2334	新沂保 B	2389	常熟综保
1910	大庆海关	2233	浦东机场	2335	昆山加工	2390	吴江综保
1911	密山海关	2234	沪钻交所	2336	苏园加工	2391	徐州物流
1912	虎林海关	2235	松江综 A	2337	徐州综保	2392	通海门办
1913	同江富锦	2236	洋山芦潮	2338	苏关邮办	2393	通海安办
1914	抚远海关	2237	松江综 B	2339	南通加工	2394	吴中综保
1915	漠河海关	2238	青浦综保	2340	无锡加工	2395	大丰物流
1916	萝北海关	2239	奉贤综保	2341	连关加工	2396	海安物流
1917	嘉荫海关	2240	漕河泾综	2342	连赣榆办	2397	江阴综保
1918	饶河海关	2241	沪黄浦关	2343	宁南加工	2398	扬州综保
1919	冰城香办	2242	沪业二处	2344	苏高加工	**2900**	**杭州关区**
1920	哈开发区	2243	沪虹口关	2345	镇江加工	2901	钱综三处
1921	绥综保区	2244	上海快件	2346	苏园物流	2902	钱江海关
1922	冰城邮办	2245	金桥加工	2347	苏园 B 区	2903	温州海关
1923	哈关车办	2246	保税物流	2348	金港海关	2904	舟山海关
1924	哈机场关	2247	沪化工区	2349	金陵邮办	2905	台州海关
1925	绥关公路	2248	洋山港区	2350	苏高物流	2906	绍兴海关
1926	哈综保区	2249	洋山保税	2351	金陵江宁	2907	湖州海关
1927	哈综口岸	2250	沪空港办	2352	龙潭物流	2908	嘉兴海关
1928	绥综口岸	2251	沪金桥办	2353	常关出加	2909	钱关下沙
1929	牡保 B 型	2252	虹桥 B 保	2354	扬关出加	2910	杭州机场
1930	冰城海关	**2300**	**南京海关**	2355	常熟出加	2911	钱关邮办
1931	鹤岗海关	2301	连云港关	2356	吴江出加	2912	钱关萧办
2200	**上海海关**	2302	南通海关	2357	常关武办	2915	丽水海关
2201	浦江海关	2303	苏州海关	2358	苏园保税	2916	杭州快件
2202	吴淞海关	2304	无锡海关	2359	吴中出加	2917	衢州海关
2203	虹桥机场	2305	张家港关	2360	盐关港办	2918	钱关余办
2204	闵开发区	2306	常州海关	2361	淮关出加	2919	钱关富办
2205	车站海关	2307	镇江海关	2362	澄关物流	2920	金华海关
2206	邮局海关	2308	新生圩关	2363	太仓物流	2921	义乌海关

关区代码	关区简称
2922	金关永办
2923	义乌物流
2924	金义综保
2927	义关机办
2928	杭关电商
2929	钱关建办
2931	温关邮办
2932	温经开关
2933	温关机办
2934	温关鳌办
2935	温关瑞办
2936	温关乐办
2937	温州物流
2941	嵊泗海关
2942	舟关金塘
2943	舟关综保
2951	台关临办
2952	台关温办
2953	台关玉办
2961	绍关虞办
2962	绍关诸办
2963	绍关新办
2971	湖关安办
2972	湖关德办
2981	嘉关乍办
2982	嘉关善办
2983	嘉兴综保
2984	嘉关宁办
2985	嘉兴桐办
2986	嘉综 B 区
2991	杭州综保
2992	杭州物流
3100	**宁波关区**
3101	海曙海关
3102	镇海海关
3103	甬北城办
3104	北仑海关
3105	甬保税区
3106	大榭海关
3107	余姚海关
3108	慈溪海关
3109	甬机场关
3110	象山海关
3111	甬加工区
3112	甬物流区
3113	慈加工区
3114	鄞州海关
3115	栎社海关
3116	梅山港区
3117	梅山保税
3118	宁波快件
3119	甬邮局关
3120	镇海物流
3121	甬北港办
3122	甬北穿办

关区代码	关区简称
3123	甬江海关
3124	奉化海关
3125	宁海海关
3126	甬新区关
3300	**合肥海关**
3301	芜湖海关
3302	安庆海关
3303	马鞍山关
3304	黄山海关
3305	蚌埠海关
3306	铜陵海关
3307	阜阳海关
3308	池州海关
3309	滁州海关
3310	庐州海关
3311	新桥机场
3312	芜湖综保
3313	合关加办
3315	宣城海关
3316	蚌埠物流
3317	合肥综保
3318	淮南海关
3319	宿州海关
3320	合关快件
3321	安庆物流
3322	宣城物流
3323	空港物流
3324	马综保区
3325	六安海关
3326	淮北海关
3327	亳州海关
3500	**福州关区**
3501	马尾海关
3502	榕福清办
3503	宁德海关
3504	三明海关
3505	榕罗源办
3506	莆田海关
3507	机场海关
3508	福州新港
3509	榕邮局办
3510	南平海关
3511	武夷山关
3512	黄岐监管
3513	榕快安办
3515	平潭港区
3516	平潭海关
3520	福州加工
3521	翔福保 B
3522	福物流园
3523	福保税港
3700	**厦门关区**
3701	厦门海关
3702	泉刺桐办
3703	漳州海关

关区代码	关区简称
3704	东山海关
3705	泉石狮办
3706	龙岩海关
3707	泉泉港办
3708	海沧港区
3709	海沧保税
3710	高崎海关
3711	东渡海关
3712	海沧海关
3713	邮局海关
3714	象屿保税
3715	机场海关
3716	集同海关
3717	厦物流园
3718	泉综保区
3719	厦门加工
3720	厦门物流
3722	大嶝监管
3723	泉晋江办
3724	邮轮海关
3725	翔安海关
3726	泉陆地港
3727	古雷海关
3728	泉安溪办
3729	泉南安办
3730	厦五通办
3731	漳招银办
3732	泉州海关
3777	厦稽查处
3788	厦侦查局
4000	**南昌关区**
4001	赣江海关
4002	九江海关
4003	赣州海关
4004	景德镇关
4005	吉安海关
4006	昌北机场
4007	青山湖关
4008	龙南海关
4009	新余海关
4010	浔关区办
4011	洪关区办
4012	虔关区办
4013	上饶海关
4014	南昌物流
4015	吉井加工
4016	鹰潭海关
4017	赣州综保
4018	宜春海关
4019	南昌综保
4020	龙南物流
4021	萍乡海关
4022	抚州海关
4023	九江综保
4024	南昌快件

关区代码	关区简称
4025	南昌邮件
4200	**青岛海关**
4201	烟台海关
4202	日照海关
4203	龙口海关
4204	威海海关
4205	济南海关
4206	潍坊海关
4207	淄博海关
4208	烟加 B 区
4209	荣成海关
4210	青保税区
4211	济宁海关
4212	泰安海关
4213	临沂海关
4214	青前湾港
4215	菏泽海关
4216	东营海关
4217	枣庄海关
4218	青开发区
4219	蓬莱海关
4220	青机场关
4221	烟机场办
4222	莱州海关
4223	青岛邮关
4224	烟关长办
4225	威海港办
4226	青聊城办
4227	青岛大港
4228	烟关快件
4229	德州海关
4230	前湾保税
4231	烟开发区
4232	日岚山办
4233	济机场办
4234	济加工区
4235	济邮局办
4236	荣龙眼办
4237	现场业务
4238	威邮局办
4239	潍诸城办
4240	青关快件
4241	烟加工区
4242	威综保北
4243	济曲阜办
4244	青滨州办
4245	烟台邮办
4246	青加工区
4247	威机场办
4248	青莱芜办
4249	潍加工区
4250	青西加区
4251	淄博物流
4253	日照物流
4254	青岛物流

关区代码	关区简称
4255	潍寿光办
4256	威港快件
4257	临综保区
4258	前湾口岸
4259	黄关快件
4260	青港快件
4261	烟港快件
4262	威综保南
4263	海阳海关
4264	烟莱阳办
4265	胶州海关
4266	即墨海关
4267	烟招远办
4268	青董港关
4269	石港快件
4270	威文登办
4271	日照综保
4272	大港快件
4277	青西保 B
4300	**济南海关**
4301	泉城海关
4302	济机场关
4303	济综保区
4305	济邮局关
4310	潍坊海关
4311	潍诸城办
4312	潍综保区
4313	潍寿光办
4315	诸城物流
4320	淄博海关
4321	淄博物流
4330	泰安海关
4341	济机快件
4342	济邮快件
4350	东营海关
4351	东营综保
4360	聊城海关
4370	德州海关
4380	滨州海关
4381	滨州物流
4390	莱芜海关
4600	**郑州关区**
4601	金水海关
4602	洛阳海关
4603	南阳海关
4604	郑机场关
4605	郑邮局关
4606	郑车站关
4607	安阳海关
4608	新区海关
4609	商丘海关
4610	周口海关
4611	河南物流
4612	新郑海关
4613	郑州空港
4614	焦作海关
4615	三门峡关
4616	新乡海关
4617	信阳海关
4618	鹤壁海关
4619	德众物流
4620	郑航空港
4621	许昌海关
4622	南阳综保
4623	商丘物流
4624	漯河海关
4625	濮阳海关
4626	民权办
4700	**武汉海关**
4701	宜昌海关
4702	荆州海关
4703	襄阳海关
4704	黄石海关
4705	汉阳海关
4706	宜三峡办
4707	鄂加工区
4708	现场一处
4709	武江物流
4710	武关货管
4711	武关快件
4712	武关机场
4713	邮局海关
4714	新港海关
4715	汉口海关
4716	十堰海关
4718	武昌海关
4719	东湖综保
4720	黄石物流
4721	仙桃海关
4722	东湖陆港
4723	宜昌物流
4724	襄阳物流
4725	空港综保
4726	新港综保
4727	荆门海关
4728	鄂州海关
4729	随州海关
4730	恩施海关
4731	经开综保
4732	仙桃物流
4733	荆门保 B
4900	**长沙关区**
4901	衡阳海关
4902	岳阳海关
4903	郴州海关
4904	常德海关
4905	星关霞办
4906	株洲海关
4907	韶山海关
4908	湘机场关
4909	株关醴办
4910	郴州综保
4911	永州海关
4913	金霞物流
4914	张家界关
4915	衡阳综保
4916	星沙海关
4917	湘潭综保
4918	星关浏办
4919	岳阳综保
4920	湘郴海关
4921	黄花综保
4922	株洲物流
4923	邵阳海关
4924	益阳海关
4925	怀化海关
4926	湘西海关
5000	**广东分署**
5100	**广州海关**
5101	内港新风
5102	越秀海关
5103	清远海关
5104	清远英德
5105	天河保税
5106	南沙散货
5107	肇庆大旺
5108	肇庆德庆
5109	海珠滘心
5110	南海海关
5111	南海官窑
5112	南海九江
5113	南海北村
5114	南海平洲
5115	荔湾海关
5116	南海业务
5117	桂江车场
5118	平洲旅检
5119	南海三山
5120	海珠海关
5121	内港芳村
5122	内港洲嘴
5123	内港四仓
5124	双东车场
5125	从化海关
5126	内港赤航
5130	广州萝岗
5131	花都海关
5132	花都码头
5133	穗知识城
5134	穗保税处
5135	天河海关
5136	穗统计处
5137	穗价格处
5138	高明食出
5139	穗监管处
5140	穗关税处
5141	广州机场
5142	民航快件
5143	广州车站
5144	穗机综保
5145	广州邮办
5146	穗关会展
5147	穗邮办监
5148	穗大郎站
5149	大铲海关
5150	顺德海关
5151	顺德保税
5152	顺德食出
5153	顺德车场
5154	北窖车场
5155	顺德旅检
5157	陈村车场
5158	顺德勒流
5160	番禺海关
5161	沙湾车场
5162	番禺旅检
5163	番禺货柜
5164	番禺船舶
5165	南沙保税
5166	南沙新港
5167	南沙货港
5168	南沙汽车
5169	南沙海关
5170	肇庆海关
5171	肇庆高要
5172	肇庆车场
5173	肇庆新港
5174	肇庆旅检
5175	肇庆码头
5176	肇庆四会
5177	肇庆三榕
5178	云浮海关
5179	罗定海关
5180	佛山海关
5181	高明海关
5182	佛山澜石
5183	三水码头
5184	佛山窖口
5185	佛山快件
5186	佛山保税
5187	佛山车场
5188	佛山火车
5189	佛山新港
5190	韶关海关
5191	韶关乐昌
5192	三水海关
5193	三水车场
5194	三水港
5195	审单中心
5196	云浮新港

关区代码	关区简称
5197	白云电商
5198	穗河源关
5199	穗技术处
5200	**黄埔关区**
5201	埔老港关
5202	埔新港关
5203	增城海关
5204	东莞海关
5205	太平海关
5206	惠州海关
5207	凤岗海关
5208	穗东海关
5209	埔东海关
5210	埔红海办
5211	河源海关
5212	新沙海关
5213	埔长安关
5214	常平海关
5216	沙田海关
5217	寮步车场
5218	江龙车场
5219	埔物流园
5220	东莞物流
5221	埔荔城办
5222	清溪物流
5223	东莞邮办
5224	萝岗海关
5225	虎门综保
5300	**深圳海关**
5301	皇岗海关
5302	罗湖海关
5303	沙头角关
5304	蛇口海关
5305	福强海关
5306	笋岗海关
5307	南头海关
5308	龙岗海关
5309	布吉海关
5310	淡水办
5311	深关车站
5312	深监管处
5313	深调查局
5314	深关邮局
5315	惠东海关
5316	大鹏海关
5317	深机场关
5318	梅林海关
5319	同乐海关
5320	文锦渡关
5321	福田海关
5322	沙保税关
5323	深审单处
5324	深审价办
5325	深关税处
5326	深数统处

关区代码	关区简称
5327	深法规处
5328	深规范处
5329	深保税处
5330	盐保税关
5331	三门岛办
5332	深财务处
5333	深侦查局
5334	深稽查处
5335	深技术处
5336	深办公室
5337	大亚湾核
5338	惠州港关
5339	坪山海关
5340	沙湾海关
5341	深惠州关
5342	深红海办
5343	深盐物流
5344	惠石化办
5345	深圳湾关
5346	深机快件
5348	深关大铲
5349	前海港区
5350	大运通关
5351	前海保税
5352	梅沙海关
5353	西九龙关
5354	莲塘海关
5355	福中海关
5356	前海海关
5357	观澜海关
5358	西沥海关
5700	**拱北关区**
5701	拱稽查处
5710	闸口海关
5720	中山海关
5721	中山港
5724	中石岐办
5725	坦洲货场
5726	中山物流
5727	小榄港
5728	神湾港
5729	中山快件
5730	香洲海关
5740	湾仔海关
5741	湾仔船舶
5750	九洲海关
5760	拱白石办
5770	斗门海关
5771	斗井岸办
5772	斗平沙办
5780	高栏海关
5788	大桥海关
5790	拱监管处
5791	拱跨工区
5792	拱保税区

关区代码	关区简称
5793	万山海关
5794	桂山中途
5795	横琴海关
5796	澳大校区
5798	拱关邮检
5799	南屏快件
6000	**汕头海关**
6001	汕关货一
6002	汕关货二
6003	汕关行邮
6004	潮汕机场
6006	汕关保税
6007	汕关业务
6008	濠江海关
6009	汕关邮包
6010	汕保物流
6011	揭阳海关
6012	普宁海关
6013	澄海海关
6014	广澳海关
6015	南澳海关
6016	濠江现场
6018	揭关惠来
6019	龙湖海关
6020	汕港海关
6021	潮州海关
6022	饶平海关
6023	饶平快件
6028	潮阳海关
6031	汕尾海关
6032	海城海关
6033	尾关陆丰
6038	汕关快件
6041	梅州海关
6042	梅州兴宁
6400	**海口关区**
6401	海口港
6402	三亚海关
6403	八所海关
6404	洋浦区关
6405	海保税区
6406	文昌海关
6407	美兰机场
6408	洋浦港
6409	海口综保
6410	马村港
6411	椰城海关
6412	三沙海关
6700	**湛江关区**
6701	湛江海关
6702	茂名海关
6703	徐闻海关
6704	海东海关
6705	茂名水东
6706	湛江吴川

关区代码	关区简称
6707	廉江海关
6708	茂名高州
6709	茂名信宜
6710	东海岛关
6711	霞山海关
6712	霞海海关
6713	湛江机场
6714	湛江博贺
6715	湛江快件
6716	湛江物流
6717	湛江调顺
6718	湛江遂溪
6800	**江门关区**
6810	江门海关
6811	高沙海关
6812	外海海关
6813	江门旅检
6815	外海电商
6816	江门车场
6817	江门保税
6820	新会海关
6821	新会港
6827	新会稽查
6830	台山海关
6831	台公益港
6837	台山稽查
6840	开平海关
6841	开平码头
6847	开平电商
6850	恩平海关
6851	恩平港
6857	恩平稽查
6860	鹤山海关
6861	鹤山码头
6866	南方电商
6867	鹤松电商
6870	阳江海关
6871	阳江港
6872	阳江车场
6877	阳江稽查
7200	**南宁关区**
7201	邕州海关
7202	北海海关
7203	梧州海关
7204	桂林海关
7205	柳州海关
7206	防城海关
7207	东兴海关
7208	凭祥海关
7209	贵港海关
7210	水口海关
7211	龙邦海关
7212	钦州海关
7213	桂林机办
7214	北海综保

关区代码	关区简称
7215	南关钦保
7216	南宁综保
7217	钦州港关
7218	玉林海关
7219	南凭综保
7220	友谊关
7221	邕机场关
7222	邕邮局关
7223	贺州海关
7224	河池海关
7225	爱店海关
7227	防港保 B
7900	**成都关区**
7901	蓉青关
7902	蓉机双流
7903	蓉乐关
7904	蓉攀关
7905	蓉绵关
7906	蓉邮关
7907	蓉盐关
7908	蓉内关
7909	公路场站
7910	蓉机快件
7911	蓉泸关
7912	蓉戎关
7913	蓉南关
7914	蓉绵加工
7915	蓉锦关
7916	蓉锦西区
7917	蓉遂关
7918	蓉旌关
7919	蓉通关
7920	蓉机保 B
7921	蓉泸保 B
7922	蓉锦双流
7923	蓉戎保 B
7924	蓉青保 B
7925	蓉新关
7926	蓉利关
7927	蓉新物流
8000	**重庆关区**
8001	重庆海关
8002	两江海关
8003	重庆机场
8004	重庆邮局
8005	万州海关
8006	渝州海关
8007	重庆水港
8008	渝加工区
8009	涪陵海关
8010	寸滩水港
8011	渝关快件
8012	两寸海关
8013	西永综保
8014	西永海关
8015	渝贸园区
8016	渝铁物流
8017	渝公物流
8018	黔江海关
8019	江津综保
8020	永川海关
8021	涪陵综保
8022	果园保 B
8300	**贵阳海关**
8301	筑城海关
8302	黔机场关
8303	遵义海关
8304	贵阳综保
8305	贵阳现场
8306	贵安综保
8307	贵安海关
8308	六盘水关
8309	遵义综保
8310	凯里海关
8311	毕节海关
8312	兴义海关
8313	铜仁海关
8600	**昆明关区**
8601	滇中海关
8602	畹町海关
8603	瑞丽海关
8604	章凤海关
8605	盈江海关
8606	孟连海关
8607	南伞海关
8608	孟定海关
8609	打洛海关
8610	腾冲海关
8611	沧源海关
8612	勐腊海关
8613	河口海关
8614	金水河关
8615	天保海关
8616	田蓬海关
8617	大理海关
8618	芒市海关
8619	腾驻隆阳
8620	昆明机场
8621	邮局海关
8622	西双版纳
8623	丽江海关
8624	思茅海关
8625	河口山腰
8626	怒江海关
8627	昆明高新
8628	昆明加工
8629	香格里拉
8631	勐康海关
8632	昆明快件
8633	红河综保
8634	昆明综保
8635	昆综口岸
8636	高新物流
8637	红综口岸
8638	磨憨快件
8639	机场电商
8640	腾俊物流
8641	都龙海关
8642	瑞驻姐告
8643	瑞驻弄岛
8644	孟驻临翔
8645	西驻关累
8646	蒙自海关
8647	曲靖海关
8648	玉溪海关
8800	**拉萨海关**
8801	聂拉木关
8802	日喀则关
8803	狮泉河关
8804	机场海关
8805	八廓海关
8806	普兰海关
8807	亚东海关
8808	吉隆海关
8809	林芝海关
9000	**西安关区**
9001	关中海关
9002	咸阳机场
9003	宝鸡海关
9004	邮局海关
9005	陕加工 A
9006	陕加工 B
9007	西安综保
9008	高新综保
9009	车站海关
9010	延安海关
9011	渭南海关
9012	榆林海关
9013	西咸物流
9014	汉中海关
9015	商洛海关
9016	航空综保
9400	**乌关区**
9401	乌昌公路
9402	霍尔果斯
9403	吐尔尕特
9404	阿拉山口
9405	塔城海关
9406	伊宁海关
9407	吉木乃关
9408	喀什海关
9409	红其拉甫
9410	阿勒泰关
9411	塔克什肯
9412	乌拉斯太
9413	哈密关
9414	红山嘴
9415	伊尔克什
9416	库尔勒关
9417	乌机场关
9418	乌加工区
9419	都拉塔关
9420	乌昌关
9421	霍中心 A
9422	石河子关
9423	山口综保
9424	喀什综保
9425	卡拉苏关
9426	奎屯物流
9427	中哈合作中心配套区
9428	乌邮局关
9429	乌综保区
9430	阿克苏关
9500	**兰州关区**
9501	金城海关
9502	酒泉海关
9503	中川机场
9504	武威物流
9505	天水海关
9506	金昌海关
9507	兰州综保
9508	敦煌机场
9509	平凉海关
9600	**银川海关**
9601	兴庆海关
9602	河东机场
9603	石嘴山关
9604	银川综保
9605	银关快件
9606	石嘴山物流
9607	中卫海关
9700	**西宁关区**
9701	西海海关
9702	青海物流
9703	西宁机场
9704	格尔木海关
9900	**政法司**

检验检疫机构代码调整

机构代码	检验检疫机构名称
110000	北京海关本部
115100	首都机场海关本部
115101	首都机场海关快件处
115200	税管局(京津)
115300	大兴机场海关本部
115400	车站海关本部
115500	邮局海关本部
115600	中关村海关本部
115700	东城海关本部
115800	西城海关本部
115900	丰台海关本部
116000	海淀海关本部
116100	通州海关本部
116200	顺义海关本部
116300	亦庄海关本部
116301	亦庄保税物流中心
116400	天竺海关本部
116500	朝阳海关本部
116600	平谷海关本部
116700	会展海关本部
116800	北京风控分局
120000	天津海关本部
125200	塘沽海关本部
125400	静海海关本部
125500	蓟州海关本部
125700	宁河海关本部
125800	天津临港海关本部
126000	天津南疆海关本部
126200	北辰海关本部
126300	武清海关本部
126500	天津东疆海关本部
126700	天津滨海机场海关本部
126800	天津邮局海关本部
126900	天津大港海关本部
127000	北塘海关本部
127100	天津新港海关本部
127200	西青海关本部
127300	东丽海关(筹)
127400	南开海关(筹)
127500	天津河西海关(筹)
127600	天津保税区海关本部
127700	天津海关风险防控分局
130000	石家庄海关本部
135100	秦皇岛海关本部
135200	唐山海关本部
135300	邯郸海关本部
135400	承德海关本部
135500	张家口海关本部
135600	沧州海关本部
135700	廊坊海关本部
135800	邢台海关本部
135900	保定海关本部
136000	衡水海关本部
136100	黄骅港海关本部
136200	石家庄机场海关本部
136300	鹿泉海关本部
136400	正定海关本部
136500	北戴河海关本部
136600	曹妃甸海关本部
136700	京唐港海关本部
136800	雄安海关本部
136900	石家庄海关风险防控分局
140000	太原海关本部
145100	大同海关本部
145200	阳泉海关本部
145300	长治海关本部
145400	临汾海关本部
145500	太原机场海关本部
145600	运城海关本部
145700	朔州海关本部
145800	晋阳海关本部
145900	武宿海关本部
146000	晋城海关本部
146100	忻州海关本部
150000	呼和浩特海关本部
155200	二连海关本部
155210	二连海关驻铁路口岸办事处
155220	二连海关驻公路口岸办事处
155400	包头海关本部
155900	额济纳海关本部
156000	东乌海关本部
156100	乌拉特海关本部
156300	集宁海关本部
156400	乌海海关本部
156500	阿拉善海关本部
156600	赛罕海关本部
156700	呼和浩特白塔机场海关本部
156800	鄂尔多斯海关本部
156900	呼和浩特海关风险防控分局
160000	满洲里海关本部
165100	满洲里机场海关本部
165200	满洲里车站海关本部
165300	满洲里十八里海关本部
165400	海拉尔海关本部
165500	额尔古纳海关本部
165600	额布都格海关本部
165700	阿日哈沙特海关本部
165800	阿尔山海关本部
165900	通辽海关本部
166000	赤峰海关本部
166100	满洲里海关风险防控分局
210000	大连海关本部
215100	大窑湾海关本部
215200	大连周水子机场海关本部
215300	北良港海关(筹)本部
215400	大连邮局海关本部
215500	七贤岭海关本部
215600	金普海关本部
215700	金石滩海关本部
215800	大连港湾海关本部
215810	大连港湾海关驻和尚岛办事处
215900	旅顺海关本部
216000	庄河海关本部
216100	大连长兴岛海关本部
216200	营口海关本部
216300	鲅鱼圈海关本部
216310	鲅鱼圈海关驻仙人岛办事处
216400	盘锦海关本部
216500	鞍山海关本部
216600	大东港海关本部
216700	丹东海关本部
216800	本溪海关本部
216900	大连海关风险防控分局本部

机构代码	检验检疫机构名称	机构代码	检验检疫机构名称	机构代码	检验检疫机构名称
220000	长春海关本部	236500	鹤岗海关本部	316600	嘉定海关本部
225100	延吉海关本部	236600	萝北海关本部	316700	金山海关本部
225120	延吉海关驻机场办事处	236700	黑河海关本部	316800	松江海关本部
225200	珲春海关本部	236710	黑河海关大黑河岛办事处	316900	青浦海关本部
225220	珲春海关驻长岭办事处	236800	逊克海关本部	317000	奉贤海关本部
225230	珲春海关驻圈河办事处	236900	绥化海关本部	317100	崇明海关本部
225300	白城海关本部	237000	漠河海关本部	317200	会展海关本部
225400	通化海关本部	237100	哈尔滨海关风险防控分局	317300	吴淞海关本部
225410	通化海关驻集安办事处	240000	沈阳海关本部	317400	龙吴海关本部
225600	长白海关本部	245100	浑南海关本部	317500	保税区海关本部
225700	吉林海关本部	245200	锦州海关本部	317600	科创海关本部
225800	长春龙嘉机场海关本部	245210	锦州海关驻港口办事处	317700	钻交所海关本部
225900	图们海关本部	245300	沈阳邮局海关本部	317800	上海风控分局
226000	长春绿园海关本部	245400	抚顺海关本部	320000	南京海关本部
226100	长春兴隆海关本部	245500	铁西海关本部	322220	动植物检疫处
226200	长春邮局海关本部	245600	辽阳海关本部	325100	金陵海关机关本部
226300	松原海关本部	245700	沈阳桃仙机场海关本部	325110	金陵海关驻邮局办事处
226400	四平海关本部(筹)	245800	辽中海关本部	325120	金陵海关驻江宁办事处
226500	辽源海关本部	245900	阜新海关本部	325130	金陵海关驻江北办事处
226600	白山海关本部(筹)	246000	葫芦岛海关本部	325200	苏州海关机关本部
226700	长白山海关本部(筹)	246100	辽宁朝阳海关本部	325210	苏州海关驻邮局办事处
226800	长春海关风险防控分局	246200	沈抚新区海关本部	325220	苏州海关驻虎丘办事处
230000	哈尔滨海关本部	246300	沈阳海关风险防控分局	325230	苏州海关驻吴中办事处
235100	冰城海关本部	246400	铁岭海关本部	325240	苏州海关驻相城办事处
235110	冰城海关香坊办事处	310000	上海海关本部	325300	苏州工业园区海关机关本部
235120	冰城海关驻邮局办事处	315100	浦东机场海关本部	325310	苏州工业园区海关驻唯亭办事处
235200	哈关机办	315110	上海空港办	325320	苏州工业园区海关驻娄葑办事处
235300	齐齐哈尔本部	315200	浦东海关本部	325400	无锡海关机关本部
235400	牡丹江关本部	315210	浦东金桥办	325410	无锡海关驻机场办事处
235500	绥芬河关本部	315300	风控局(上海)	325420	无锡海关驻锡山办事处
235510	绥关公路	315400	虹桥机场海关本部	325430	无锡海关驻新吴办事处
235600	东宁海关本部	315500	浦江海关本部	325500	南京禄口机场海关机关本部
235700	佳木斯关本部	315600	外港海关本部	325600	新生圩海关机关本部
235800	抚远海关本部	315700	宝山海关本部	325700	江阴海关机关本部
235900	同江海关本部	315800	洋山海关本部	325800	连云港海关机关本部
235910	同江海关东港办事处	315900	车站海关本部	325810	连云港海关驻港区办事处
236000	大庆海关本部	316000	邮局海关本部	325820	连云港海关驻赣榆办事处
236100	密山海关本部	316100	黄浦海关本部	325900	南通海关机关本部
236200	虎林海关本部	316200	徐汇海关本部	325910	南通海关驻海门办事处
236300	饶河海关本部	316300	虹口海关本部	325920	南通海关驻海安办事处
236400	嘉荫海关本部	316400	杨浦海关本部	326000	张家港海关机关本部
236410	嘉荫海关伊春机场办事处	316500	莘庄海关本部	326100	金港海关机关本部

机构代码	检验检疫机构名称
326200	镇江海关机关本部
326210	镇江海关驻丹阳办事处
326300	常州海关机关本部
326310	常州海关驻溧阳办事处
326320	常州海关驻武进办事处
326400	徐州海关机关本部
326410	徐州海关驻机场办事处
326500	盐城海关机关本部
326510	盐城海关驻机场办事处
326520	盐城海关驻大丰办事处
326600	淮安海关机关本部
326700	扬州海关机关本部
326710	扬州海关机关驻扬州港办事处
326800	泰州海关机关本部
326810	泰州海关驻泰兴办事处
326900	如皋海关机关本部
327000	宿迁海关机关本部
327100	靖江海关机关本部
327200	如东海关机关本部
327300	启东海关机关本部
327400	太仓海关机关本部
327500	常熟海关机关本部
327600	昆山海关机关本部
327700	吴江海关机关本部
327800	宜兴海关机关本部
329000	南京海关风险防控分局
330000	杭州海关本部
335100	温州海关
335120	温关乐办
335150	温关瑞办
335200	金华海关
335220	金关永办
335300	舟山海关
335330	舟关定办
335400	嵊泗海关
335500	台州海关
335510	台关临办
335530	台关玉办
335600	绍兴海关
335620	绍关诸办
335630	绍关新办
335700	嘉兴海关
335710	嘉关乍办
335720	嘉关嘉办
335800	湖州海关
335810	湖关德办
335830	湖关安办
335900	衢州海关
336000	丽水海关
336200	义乌海关
336210	驻机场办事处
336300	杭州机场
336400	杭关风控
338300	钱江海关
338310	钱关邮办
338320	钱关下沙
338330	钱关余办
338340	钱关建办
338350	钱关萧办
338360	钱关富办
340000	合肥海关本部
345100	芜湖海关本部
345200	安庆海关本部
345300	铜陵海关本部
345400	马鞍山海关本部
345500	蚌埠海关本部
345600	阜阳海关本部
345700	黄山海关本部
345800	池州海关本部
345900	滁州海关本部
346000	宣城海关本部
346100	庐州海关本部
346110	庐州海关驻邮局办事处
346200	淮北海关本部
346300	宿州海关本部
346400	六安海关本部
346500	合肥新桥机场海关本部
346600	亳州海关本部
346700	淮南海关本部
346800	合肥海关风控分局
350000	福州海关本部
355100	榕城关本部
355110	榕城关邮局办
355120	榕城关快安办
355130	榕城关福清办
355140	榕城关罗源湾办
355200	长乐机场关本部
355300	马尾关本部
355400	宁德关本部
355410	宁德关漳湾办
355500	三明关本部
355600	莆田关本部
355610	莆田关秀屿办
355700	南平关本部
355710	南平关邵武办
355800	平潭关本部
355810	平潭关金井办
355900	武夷山关本部
356000	福州关风控分局
360000	南昌海关本部
365100	九江海关本部
365200	景德镇海关本部
365300	赣州海关本部
365400	上饶海关本部
365500	宜春海关本部
365600	吉安海关本部
365700	机场海关本部
365800	新余海关本部
365900	青山湖海关本部
366000	赣江新区海关本部
366100	萍乡海关本部
366200	抚州海关本部
366300	鹰潭海关本部
366400	龙南海关本部
370000	青岛海关本部
375100	青岛大港海关本部
375200	黄岛海关本部
375300	烟台海关本部
375310	烟台海关机场办事处
375330	烟台海关招远办事处
375340	烟台海关港口办事处
375350	烟台海关芝罘办事处
375380	烟台海关莱阳办事处
375390	烟台海关邮局办事处
375400	荣成海关本部
375410	荣成海关龙眼港办事处

机构代码	检验检疫机构名称
375420	荣成海关石岛港办事处
375500	龙口海关本部
375600	莱州海关本部
375800	济宁海关本部
375810	济宁海关曲阜办事处
376000	日照海关本部
376010	日照海关岚山港办事处
376200	威海海关本部
376210	威海海关文登办事处
376220	威海海关机场办事处
376240	威海海关邮局办事处
376250	威海海关海港办事处
376400	菏泽海关本部
376700	枣庄海关本部
376800	临沂海关本部
377300	青岛流亭机场海关本部
377400	蓬莱海关本部
377500	海阳海关本部
377600	董家口港海关本部
377700	风险防控局(青岛)
377800	青岛邮局海关本部
377900	即墨海关本部
378000	胶州海关本部
378100	青岛风险防控分局
380000	宁波海关本部
385100	宁波机场海关本部
385200	宁波邮局海关本部
385300	镇海海关本部
385400	北仑海关本部
385410	北仑海关驻甬城办事处
385420	北仑海关驻临港办事处
385430	北仑海关驻穿山办事处
385500	大榭海关本部
385600	梅山海关本部
385700	象山海关本部
385800	甬江海关本部
385900	鄞州海关本部
386000	奉化海关本部
386100	宁海海关本部
386200	慈溪海关本部
386300	余姚海关本部
386400	海曙海关本部
386500	宁波保税区海关本部
386600	栎社海关本部
386700	杭州湾新区海关本部
386800	宁波海关风险防控分局
390000	厦门海关本部
395100	海沧海关本部
395200	机场海关本部
395300	漳州海关本部
395301	漳州角美科
395310	漳州招银办
395400	泉州海关本部
395410	泉港办
395420	泉州安溪办
395421	泉州永春科
	395421 泉州德化科
395422	泉州德化科
	395422 泉州刺桐办
395430	泉州刺桐办
395440	泉州晋江办
395441	泉州陆地港科
	395441 泉州综保区科
395442	泉州综保区科
	395442 泉州石狮办
395450	泉州石狮办
395460	泉州南安办
395500	厦门邮轮海关本部
395510	厦门五通办
395600	厦门邮局海关本部
395700	高崎海关本部
395800	集同海关本部
395900	翔安海关本部
395901	翔安大嶝科
396000	东渡海关本部
396100	古雷海关本部
396101	古雷漳浦科
396102	古雷查验
396200	东山海关本部
396201	东山诏安科
396202	东山云霄科
396300	龙岩海关本部
396400	厦门海关风控分局
400000	济南海关本部
405100	济南机场海关本部
405200	济南邮局海关本部
405300	泉城海关本部
405400	淄博海关本部
405500	潍坊海关本部
405510	潍坊海关驻寿光办事处
405520	潍坊海关驻诸城办事处
405600	泰安海关本部
405700	东营海关本部
405800	德州海关本部
405900	滨州海关本部
406000	聊城海关本部
406100	莱芜海关本部
406200	济南海关风险防控分局
410000	郑州海关本部
415100	洛阳海关本部
415200	焦作海关本部
415300	安阳海关本部
415400	商丘海关本部
415410	商丘海关驻民权办事处
415500	漯河海关本部
415600	南阳海关本部
415700	信阳海关本部
415800	三门峡海关本部
415900	新郑海关本部
416000	许昌海关本部
416100	新乡海关本部
416200	鹤壁海关本部
416300	郑州机场海关本部
416400	郑州车站海关本部
416500	郑州邮局海关本部
416600	金水海关本部
416700	郑州新区海关本部
416800	周口海关本部
416900	平顶山海关本部
417000	濮阳海关本部
417100	开封海关本部
417200	驻马店海关本部
417300	济源海关本部
417400	郑州海关风险防控分局
420000	武汉海关本部
425100	武汉天河机场海关本部

机构代码	检验检疫机构名称	机构代码	检验检疫机构名称	机构代码	检验检疫机构名称
425200	武汉新港海关本部	445630	佛山机关南海办事处	456500	邕州海关本部
425300	武汉邮局海关本部	445640	佛山海关三水办事处	456600	贺州海关本部
425400	汉阳海关本部	445650	佛山海关高明办事处	456700	平孟海关本部
425500	武昌海关本部	446200	肇庆海关本部	456800	硕龙海关本部
425600	汉口海关本部	446600	河源海关本部	456900	南宁邮局海关本部
425700	襄阳海关本部	446800	清远海关本部	457000	峒中海关本部
425800	宜昌海关本部	447200	广州车站海关本部	457100	爱店海关本部
425900	黄石海关本部	447300	白云机场海关本部	457200	友谊关海关本部
426000	十堰海关本部	447310	广州机场关跨境电商监管办	457300	南宁海关风控分局
426100	荆州海关本部	447400	番禺海关本部	460000	海口海关本部
426200	荆门海关本部	447500	花都海关本部	465100	三亚海关本部
426300	鄂州海关本部	447700	从化海关本部	465110	三亚海关驻凤凰机场办
426400	随州海关本部	447710	从化海关马场办事处	465120	三亚海关驻三亚国际邮轮港办
426500	恩施海关本部	448300	云浮海关本部	465200	八所海关本部
426600	仙桃海关本部	448400	南沙海关本部	465300	洋浦经济开发区海关本部
426700	武汉海关风险防控分局	448500	广州邮局海关本部	465400	文昌海关本部
430000	长沙海关本部	448600	广州会展中心海关本部	465500	海口美兰机场海关本部
435100	张家界海关本部	448700	越秀海关本部	465600	海口港海关本部
435200	长沙黄花机场海关本部	448800	海珠海关本部	465700	椰城海关本部
435300	永州海关本部	448900	荔湾海关本部	465800	洋浦港海关本部
435400	益阳海关本部	449000	大铲海关本部	465900	博鳌机场海关本部
435500	邵阳海关本部	449100	罗定海关本部	466000	马村港海关本部
435600	岳阳海关本部	449200	广州海关风控分局	466100	三沙海关本部
435700	常德海关本部	450000	南宁海关本部	466200	海口海关风控分局
435800	怀化海关本部	455000	南宁吴圩机场海关本部	470000	深圳海关本部
435900	衡阳海关本部	455100	梧州海关本部	475100	蛇口海关本部
436000	郴州海关本部	455200	北海海关本部	475200	皇岗海关本部
436100	株洲海关本部	455220	北海海关铁山港办	475300	罗湖海关本部
436110	株洲海关驻醴陵办事处	455300	防城港海关本部	475400	文锦渡海关本部
436200	星沙海关本部	455310	防城港海关企沙港办	475500	沙头角海关本部
436210	星沙海关驻浏阳办事处	455400	凭祥海关本部	475600	大鹏海关本部
436300	长沙邮局海关本部	455500	水口海关本部	475700	龙岗海关本部
436400	韶山海关本部	455600	东兴海关本部	475800	同乐海关本部
436500	湘西海关本部	455700	钦州海关本部	475900	笋岗海关本部
436600	娄底海关本部	455800	桂林海关本部	476000	深圳宝安机场海关本部
436700	长沙风险防控分局	455810	桂林海关机场办	476100	福田海关本部
440000	广州海关本部	455900	柳州海关本部	476200	深圳邮局海关本部
445100	天河海关本部	456000	玉林海关本部	476300	坪山海关本部
445200	韶关海关本部	456100	贵港海关本部	476400	深圳湾海关本部
445600	佛山海关本部	456200	龙邦海关本部	476500	观澜海关本部
445610	佛山海关禅城办事处	456300	钦州港海关本部	476600	大铲湾海关本部
445620	佛山海关顺德办事处	456400	河池海关本部	476700	西沥海关本部

机构代码	检验检疫机构名称
476800	前海海关本部
476900	梅沙海关本部
477000	西九龙站海关本部
477100	莲塘海关本部
477200	三门岛海关本部
477300	梅林海关本部
477400	福强海关本部
477500	沙湾海关本部
477600	南头海关本部
477700	福中海关本部
477800	布吉海关本部
477900	惠州海关本部
477910	惠州海关驻淡水办事处
477920	惠州海关驻博罗办事处
478000	惠州港海关本部
478100	惠东海关本部
478200	深圳海关风险防控分局
480000	拱北海关本部
485100	斗门海关本部
485200	高栏海关本部
485300	万山海关本部
485400	横琴海关本部
485500	港珠澳大桥海关本部
485600	闸口海关本部
485700	九洲海关本部
485800	湾仔海关本部
485900	香洲海关本部
486000	中山海关本部
486010	中山海关驻石岐办事处
486020	中山海关驻民众办事处
486100	中山港海关本部
486200	青茂海关本部
486300	拱北海关风险防控分局
500000	重庆海关本部
505100	万州海关本部
505200	重庆港海关本部
505300	涪陵海关本部
505400	两路寸滩海关本部
505500	西永海关本部
505600	重庆江北机场海关本部
505700	黔江海关本部
505800	重庆邮局海关本部
505900	渝州海关本部
506000	永川海关本部
506100	两江海关本部
506200	风控分局机关本部
510000	成都海关本部
515100	成都双流机场海关本部
515200	成都邮局海关本部
515300	青白江海关本部
515400	锦城海关本部
515500	天府新区海关本部
515600	绵阳海关本部
515700	自贡海关本部
515800	攀枝花海关本部
515900	泸州海关本部
516000	德阳海关本部
516100	广元海关本部
516200	遂宁海关本部
516300	内江海关本部
516400	乐山海关本部
516500	宜宾海关本部
516600	南充海关本部
516700	达州海关本部
516800	广安海关本部
516900	成都海关风险防控分局
520000	贵阳海关本部
525100	遵义海关本部
525200	兴义海关本部
525300	贵阳机场海关本部
525400	筑城海关本部
525500	贵安新区海关本部
525600	六盘水海关本部
525700	凯里海关本部
525800	毕节海关本部
525900	铜仁海关本部
530000	昆明海关本部
535100	昆明长水机场海关本部
535200	昆明邮局海关本部
535300	滇中海关本部
535400	瑞丽海关本部
535410	瑞丽海关姐告办
535420	瑞丽海关弄岛办
535500	畹町海关本部
535600	芒市海关本部
535700	盈江海关本部
535800	章凤海关本部
535900	腾冲海关本部
535910	腾冲海关隆阳办
536000	大理海关本部
536100	怒江海关本部
536200	丽江海关本部
536300	香格里拉海关本部
536400	孟定海关本部
536410	孟定海关临翔办
536500	南伞海关本部
536600	沧源海关本部
536700	西双版纳海关本部
536710	西双版纳海关关累办
536800	打洛海关本部
536900	勐腊海关本部
536910	勐腊海关磨憨办
537000	思茅海关本部
537100	勐康海关本部
537200	孟连海关本部
537300	河口海关本部
537310	河口海关山腰办
537400	蒙自海关本部
537500	金水河海关本部
537600	天保海关本部
537700	都龙海关本部
537800	田蓬海关本部
537900	曲靖海关本部
538000	玉溪海关本部
538100	昆明风险防控分局
540000	拉萨海关本部
545100	拉萨贡嘎机场海关本部
545200	八廓海关本部
545300	聂拉木海关本部
545400	吉隆海关本部
545500	普兰海关本部
545600	亚东海关本部
545700	日喀则海关本部
545800	狮泉河海关本部

机构代码	检验检疫机构名称
545900	林芝海关本部
546000	拉萨海关风险防控分局
560000	黄埔海关本部
565100	黄埔老港海关本部
565110	黄埔老港船舶监管办事处
565200	黄埔新港海关本部
565300	增城海关本部
565310	增城荔城办
565400	东莞海关本部
565410	东莞驻邮办
565500	太平海关本部
565700	凤岗海关本部
565800	穗东海关本部
565900	东江口海关本部
566200	新沙海关本部
566300	东莞长安海关本部
566400	常平海关本部
566600	沙田海关本部
567400	萝岗海关本部
567500	风险防控局(黄埔)
567600	黄埔海关风险防控分局
570000	汕头海关本部
575100	潮汕机场海关本部
575200	汕头港海关本部
575300	广澳海关本部
575400	澄海海关本部
575500	龙湖海关本部
575600	濠江海关本部
575700	潮阳海关本部
575800	梅州海关本部
575900	汕尾海关本部
575910	汕尾海关驻陆丰办
576000	潮州海关本部
576100	揭阳海关本部
576110	揭阳海关驻惠来办
576200	饶平海关本部
576300	海城海关本部
576400	普宁海关本部
576500	汕头海关风控分局
580000	湛江海关本部
585100	湛江机场
585200	湛江霞山
585300	湛江东海岛
585400	湛江海东新区
585500	湛江徐闻
585600	湛江霞海
585700	湛江廉江
585800	湛江茂名
585810	湛江水东
585900	湛江风险
590000	江门海关本部
595100	外海海关本部
595200	高沙海关本部
595300	新会海关本部
595310	新会港办
595400	鹤山海关本部
595500	开平海关本部
595600	台山海关本部
595700	恩平海关本部
595800	阳江海关本部
595810	阳江港办
595900	江门海关风险防控分局
610000	西安海关本部
615100	榆林海关本部
615200	宝鸡海关本部
615300	汉中海关本部
615400	西安咸阳机场海关本部
615500	延安海关本部
615600	渭南海关本部
615700	西安车站海关本部
615800	关中海关本部
615900	西安邮局海关本部
616000	商洛海关本部
616100	西安风险防控分局
620000	兰州海关本部
625100	酒泉海关本部
625200	天水海关本部
625300	平凉海关本部
625400	金昌海关本部
625500	敦煌机场海关本部
625600	金城海关本部
625601	金城海关综保区工作点
625700	兰州机场海关本部
630000	西宁海关本部
635100	西宁曹家堡机场海关本部
635200	西海海关本部
635300	格尔木海关本部
640000	银川海关本部
645100	银川机场海关本部
645200	兴庆海关本部
645300	石嘴山海关本部
645400	中卫海关本部
650000	乌鲁木齐海关本部
655100	阿勒泰海关本部
655110	塔克什肯办事处
655200	塔城海关本部
655300	阿拉山口海关本部
655400	伊宁海关本部
655500	霍尔果斯海关本部
655600	阿克苏海关本部
655700	库尔勒海关本部
655800	喀什海关本部
655810	喀什海关驻机场办事处(筹)
655900	吐尔尕特海关本部
656000	吉木乃海关本部
656100	卡拉苏海关本部
656200	石河子海关本部
656300	霍尔果斯国际边境合作中心海关本部
656400	哈密海关本部
656500	乌昌海关本部
656600	乌鲁木齐地窝堡机场海关本部
656700	乌鲁木齐邮局海关本部
656800	红其拉甫海关本部
656900	伊尔克什坦海关本部
657000	都拉塔海关本部
657100	和田海关本部(筹)
657200	乌鲁木齐海关风险防控分局
910000	中国检验认证集团本部
920000	中国检验有限公司本部

国内地区代码表

地区代码	地区名称
11013	中关村国家自主创新示范区(东城园)
11019	东城区
11023	中关村国家自主创新示范区(西城园)
11029	西城区
11039	崇文区
11049	宣武区
11053	中关村国家自主创新示范区(朝阳园)
11059	朝阳区
11063	中关村国家自主创新示范区(丰台园)
11069	丰台区
11073	中关村国家自主创新示范区(石景山园)
11079	石景山
11083	中关村国家自主创新示范区(海淀园)
11089	海淀区其他
11093	中关村国家自主创新示范区(门头沟园)
11099	门头沟
11103	中关村国家自主创新示范区(房山园)
11109	房山
11113	中关村国家自主创新示范区(顺义园)
11115	北京天竺出口加工区
11116	北京天竺综合保税区
11119	顺义
11123	中关村国家自主创新示范区(昌平园)
11129	昌平
11132	北京经济技术开发区
11133	中关村国家自主创新示范区(大兴一亦庄园)
11139	大兴其他
1113W	北京亦庄保税物流中心
11143	中关村国家自主创新示范区(通州园)
11149	通县
11153	中关村国家自主创新示范区(怀柔园)
11159	怀柔
11163	中关村国家自主创新示范区(平谷园)
11169	平谷
11173	中关村国家自主创新示范区(延庆园)
11179	延庆
11183	中关村国家自主创新示范区(密云园)
11189	密云
11909	北京其他
12019	和平区
12029	河东区
12039	河西区
12043	天津新技术产业园区
12049	南开区其他
12059	河北区
12069	红桥区
12072	天津经济技术开发区
12074	天津港保税区
12075	天津出口加工区
12076	天津东疆保税港区
12077	天津保税物流园
12079	滨海新区(塘沽其他)
1207W	天津经济技术开发区保税物流中心
12089	滨海新区(汉沽)
12099	滨海新区(大港)
12106	天津滨海新区综合保税区
12109	东丽区
12119	西青区
12129	津南区
12139	北辰区
12149	宁河县
12159	武清县
12169	静海县
12179	宝坻县
12189	蓟县
12909	天津其他
13013	石家庄高新技术产业开发实验区
13016	石家庄综合保税区
13019	石家庄其他
13022	曹妃甸经济技术开发区
13026	曹妃甸综合保税区
13029	唐山
1302W	唐山港京唐港区保税物流中心(B型)
13032	秦皇岛经济技术开发区
13035	河北秦皇岛出口加工区
13039	秦皇岛其他
13049	邯郸
13059	邢台
13063	保定高新技术产业开发区
13069	保定其他
13079	张家口
13089	承德
13099	沧州
13105	河北廊坊出口加工区
13109	廊坊
13119	衡水
13129	武安
1312W	河北武安保税物流中心(B型)
13909	河北其他
14012	山西太原经济技术开发区
14013	太原高新技术产业开发区
14016	太原武宿综合保税区
14019	太原其他
14022	大同经济技术开发区
14029	大同
14039	阳泉
14049	长治
14059	晋城
1405W	山西兰花保税物流中心(B型)
14069	朔州
14079	雁北
14089	忻州
14099	吕梁
14102	晋中经济技术开发区
14109	晋中
14119	临汾
1411W	山西方略保税物流中心
14129	运城
14139	古交
14909	山西其他
15015	内蒙古呼和浩特出口加工区
15019	呼和浩特
15023	包头高新技术产业开发区
15029	包头其他
15039	乌海
15049	赤峰
1504W	赤峰保税物流中心
15059	二连
15066	满洲里综合保税区
15069	满洲里
15079	呼伦贝尔盟
15089	哲里木盟
15099	兴安盟
15109	乌兰察布盟
15119	巴彦淖尔市
15129	伊克昭盟
15139	阿拉善盟
15149	锡林郭勒盟
15909	内蒙古其他
21012	沈阳经济技术开发区
21013	沈阳南湖科技开发区
21015	辽宁沈阳、张士出口加工区
21016	沈阳综合保税区
21019	沈阳其他
21022	大连经济技术开发区
21023	大连高新技术产业园区
21024	大连大窑湾保税区
21025	辽宁大连出口加工区
21026	大窑湾保税港区
21027	大连保税物流园区
21029	大连其他
21033	鞍山高新技术产业开发区
21039	鞍山其他
21049	抚顺
21059	本溪
21069	丹东
21079	锦州
21089	营口
2108W	营口港保税物流中心
21099	阜新
21109	辽阳
21119	盘锦
2111W	盘锦港保税物流中心(B型)
21129	铁岭
2112W	铁岭保税物流中心(B型)
21139	朝阳
21149	葫芦岛市
21159	瓦房店
21169	海城
21179	兴城
21189	铁法

地区代码	地区名称
21199	北票
21209	开源
21909	辽宁其他
22012	长春经济技术开发区
22013	长春南湖一南岭新技术产业园区
22016	长春兴隆综合保税区
22019	长春其他
22023	吉林高新技术产业开发区
22029	吉林其他
2202W	吉林市保税物流中心(B型)
22039	四平
22049	辽源
22059	通化
22069	白山
22075	吉林珲春出口加工区
22079	珲春
22089	图们
22099	白城
22109	延边
22119	公主岭
22129	梅河口
22139	集安
22149	桦甸
22159	九台
22169	蛟河
22179	松原
22189	延吉市
22909	吉林其他
23012	哈尔滨经济技术开发区
23013	哈尔滨高技术开发区
23016	哈尔滨综合保税区
23019	哈尔滨其他
23029	齐齐哈尔
23039	鸡西
23049	鹤岗
23059	双鸭山
23063	大庆高新技术产业开发区
23069	大庆其他
23079	伊春
23089	佳木斯
23099	七台河
23109	牡丹江
23119	黑河
23126	绥芬河综合保税区
23129	绥芬河
23139	松花江
23149	绥化
23159	大兴安岭
23169	阿城
23179	同江
23189	富锦
23199	铁力
23209	密山
23909	黑龙江其他
31019	黄浦

地区代码	地区名称
31029	南市
31039	卢湾
31043	上海漕河泾新技术开发区
31049	徐汇其他
31052	上海经济技术开发区
31059	长宁
31069	静安
31079	普陀
3107W	上海西北物流园区保税物流中心
31089	闸北
31099	虹口
31109	杨浦
31112	上海闵行经济技术开发区
31113	上海浦江高科技园区
31115	上海漕河泾出口加工区
31119	闵行其他
31129	宝山
31145	上海嘉定出口加工区
31149	嘉定
31159	川沙
31162	上海闵行经济技术开发区(临港新城)
31166	洋山保税港区
31169	南汇
31175	上海闵行出口加工区
31179	奉贤
31185	上海松江出口加工区
31189	松江
31199	金山
31205	上海青浦出口加工区
31209	青浦
31219	崇明
31222	上海浦东新区
31224	上海外高桥保税区
31225	上海金桥出口加工区南区
31226	上海浦东机场综合保税区
31227	上海保税物流园区
31229	浦东其他
31909	上海其他
32013	南京浦口高新技术外向型开发区
32015	江苏南京出口加工区
32016	南京综合保税区
32019	南京其他
3201W	南京龙潭港保税物流中心
32023	无锡高新技术产业开发区
32025	江苏无锡出口加工区
32026	无锡高新区综合保税区
32029	无锡其他
32039	徐州
3203W	徐州保税物流中心(B型)
32043	常州高新技术产业开发区
32045	江苏常州出口加工区
32046	常州综合保税区
32049	常州其他
32052	苏州工业园区

地区代码	地区名称
32053	苏州高新技术产业开发区
32055	江苏苏州工业园区加工区
32056	苏州工业园综合保税区、苏州高新综保区
32059	苏州其他
32062	南通经济技术开发区
32065	江苏南通出口加工区
32066	南通综合保税区
32069	南通其他
3206W	如皋港保税物流中心(B型)
32072	连云港经济技术开发区
32075	江苏连云港出口加工区
32079	连云港其他
3207W	连云港保税物流中心
32085	江苏省淮安出口加工区
32086	淮安综合保税区
32089	淮安市
32096	盐城综合保税区
32099	盐城
3209W	大丰港保税物流中心(B型)
32105	江苏扬州出口加工区
32106	扬州综合保税区
32109	扬州
32115	江苏镇江出口加工区
32116	镇江综合保税区
32119	镇江
32125	江苏泰州出口加工区
32126	泰州综合保税区
32129	泰州
32139	仪征
32145	江苏常熟出口加工区
32146	常熟综合保税区
32149	常熟
32154	江苏张家港保税区
32156	张家港保税港区
32157	张家港保税物流园
32159	张家港其他
32166	江阴综合保税区
32169	江阴
3216W	江阴保税物流中心
32179	宿迁
32189	丹阳
32199	东台
32209	兴化
32229	宜兴
32235	江苏昆山出口加工区
32236	昆山综合保税区
32239	昆山
32249	启东
32255	江苏吴江出口加工区
32256	吴江综合保税区
32259	吴江市
32266	太仓港综合保税区
32269	太仓市
3226W	太仓保税物流中心

地区代码	地区名称
32546	武进综合保税区
3256W	江苏海安保税物流中心(B型)
32909	江苏其他
33012	杭州经济技术开发区
33013	杭州高新技术产业开发区
33015	浙江杭州出口加工区
33019	杭州其他
33022	宁波经济技术开发区
33023	宁波高新技术产业开发区
33024	宁波北仑港保税区
33025	浙江宁波出口加工区
33026	宁波梅山保税港区
33027	宁波保税物流园
33029	宁波其他
3302W	宁波栎社保税物流中心
33032	温州经济技术开发区
33039	温州其他
3303W	温州保税物流中心(B型)
33045	浙江嘉兴出口加工区
33046	嘉兴综合保税区
33049	嘉兴
33059	湖州
33069	绍兴
33072	金华经济技术开发区
33076	金义综合保税区(一期)
33079	金华
33089	衢州
33096	舟山港综合保税区
33099	舟山
33109	丽水
33119	台州
33129	余姚
33139	海宁
33149	兰溪
33159	瑞安
33169	萧山
3316W	杭州保税物流中心
33179	江山
33189	义乌
3318W	义乌保税物流中心
33199	东阳
33202	宁波杭州湾经济技术开发区
33205	浙江慈溪出口加工区
33209	慈溪
33219	奉化
33229	诸暨
33239	黄岩
3352W	宁波镇海保税物流中心(B型)
33909	浙江其他
34012	合肥经济技术开发区
34013	合肥科技工业园区
34015	安徽合肥出口加工区
34016	合肥综合保税区
34019	合肥其他
3401W	合肥空港保税物流中心(B型)
34022	芜湖经济技术开发区
34023	芜湖高新技术产业开发区
34025	安徽芜湖出口加工区
34026	芜湖综合保税区
34029	芜湖其他
34033	蚌埠高新技术产业开发区
34039	蚌埠
3403W	蚌埠(皖北)保税物流中心
34042	安徽淮南经济技术开发区
34043	淮南高新技术产业开发区
34049	淮南
34052	马鞍山经济技术开发区
34053	马鞍山慈湖高新技术产业开发区
34056	马鞍山综合保税区
34059	马鞍山
34069	淮北
34072	铜陵经济技术开发区
34079	铜陵
34082	安庆桐城经济技术开发区
34089	安庆
3408W	安庆(皖西南)保税物流中心(B型)
34099	黄山
34109	阜阳
34119	宿州
34122	滁州经济技术开发区
34129	滁州
34132	安徽六安经济技术开发区
34139	六安
34142	宣城宁国经济技术开发区
34149	宣城
3414W	安徽皖东南保税物流中心(B型)
34159	巢湖
34162	池州经济技术开发区
34169	池州
34179	亳州
34909	安徽其他
35012	福州经济技术开发区
35013	福州科技园区
35014	福建马尾保税区
35015	福建福州、福清出口加工区
35016	福州保税港区
35017	福州保税物流园区
35019	福州其他
35021	厦门特区
35023	厦门火炬高技术产业开发区
35024	厦门象屿保税区
35025	福建厦门出口加工区
35026	厦门海沧保税港区
35027	厦门象屿保税物流园
35029	厦门其他
3502W	厦门火炬(翔安)保税物流中心
35039	莆田
35049	三明
35055	福建泉州出口加工区
35056	泉州综合保税区
35059	泉州
35069	漳州
35079	南平
35089	宁德
35099	龙岩
35109	永安
35119	石狮
35128	平潭综合试验区
35129	平潭
35909	福建其他
36012	南昌经济技术开发区
36013	南昌高新技术产业开发区
36015	江西南昌出口加工区
36016	南昌综合保税区
36019	南昌其他
3601W	南昌保税物流中心
36023	景德镇高新技术产业开发区
36029	景德镇
36032	萍乡经济技术开发区
36039	萍乡
36042	九江经济技术开发区
36045	江西九江出口加工区
36049	九江
36053	新余高新技术产业开发区
36059	新余
36063	鹰潭高新技术产业开发区
36069	鹰潭
36072	赣州经济技术开发区
36075	江西赣州出口加工区
36076	赣州综合保税区
36079	赣州
3607W	龙南保税物流中心(B型)
36082	宜春经济技术开发区
36089	宜春
36092	上饶经济技术开发区
36099	上饶
36102	井冈山经济技术开发区
36105	井冈山出口加工区
36109	吉安
36119	抚州
36129	瑞昌
36909	江西其他
37013	济南高技术产业开发区
37015	山东济南出口加工区
37016	济南综合保税区
37019	济南其他
37022	青岛经济技术开发区
37023	青岛高新技术产业开发区
37024	青岛保税区
37025	山东青岛出口加工区
37026	青岛前湾保税港区
37027	青岛保税物流园
37029	青岛其他
3702W	青岛保税物流中心

地区代码	地区名称
37033	淄博高新技术产业开发区
37039	淄博
3703W	淄博保税物流中心
37049	枣庄
37056	东营综合保税区
37059	东营
37062	烟台经济技术开发区
37065	山东烟台出口加工区
37069	烟台其他
37073	潍坊高新技术产业开发区
37075	山东潍坊出口加工区
37076	潍坊综合保税区
37079	潍坊其他
37089	济宁
37099	泰安
37103	威海火炬高技术产业开发区
37105	山东威海出口加工区
37106	威海综合保税区北区
37109	威海其他
37119	日照
3711W	日照保税物流中心
37129	山东省滨州其他
3712W	鲁中运达保税物流中心
37139	德州
37149	聊城
37156	临沂综合保税区
37159	临沂
37169	菏泽
37179	青州
37189	龙口
37199	曲阜
37209	莱芜
37219	新泰
37229	胶州
37239	诸城
3723W	青岛保税港区诸城功能区保税物流中心(B型)
37249	莱阳
37259	滕州
37266	威海综合保税区南区
37269	文登
37279	荣城
37289	即墨
37299	平度
37909	山东其他
41012	郑州经济技术开发区
41013	郑州高新技术开发区
41015	河南郑州出口加工区
41016	新郑综合保税区
41018	郑州航空港经济综合实验区
41019	郑州其他
4101W	河南保税物流中心
41029	开封
41033	洛阳高新技术产业开发区
41039	洛阳其他
41049	平顶山
41059	安阳
41069	鹤壁
41079	新乡
41089	焦作
4108W	河南德众保税物流中心
41099	濮阳
41109	许昌
41119	漯河
41129	三门峡
41139	商丘
4113W	河南商丘保税物流中心(B型)
41149	周口
41159	驻马店
41166	南阳卧龙综合保税区
41169	南阳
41179	信阳
41189	义马
41199	汝州
41209	济源
41219	禹州
41229	卫辉
41239	辉县
41249	泌阳
41909	河南其他
42012	武汉经济技术开发区
42013	武汉东湖新技术开发区
42015	湖北武汉出口加工区
42016	武汉东湖综合保税区
42019	武汉其他
4201W	武汉东西湖保税物流中心
42022	黄石经济技术开发区
42029	黄石
4202W	黄石棋盘洲保税物流中心
42039	十堰
42049	沙市
42059	宜昌
4205W	宜昌三峡保税物流中心(B型)
42062	襄阳经济技术开发区
42063	襄阳高新技术产业开发区
42069	襄阳其他
4206W	襄阳保税物流中心(B型)
42079	鄂州
42089	荆门
42099	黄冈
42109	孝感
42119	咸宁
42122	荆州经济技术开发区
42129	荆州
42139	郧阳
42149	鄂西
42159	随州
42169	老河口
42179	枣阳
42189	神农架
42506	武汉新港空港
42909	湖北其他
43012	长沙经济技术开发区
43013	长沙科技开发区
43016	长沙黄花综合保税区
43019	长沙其他
4301W	长沙金霞保税物流中心
43023	株州高新技术产业开发区
43029	株州其他
4302W	株洲铜塘湾保税物流中心(B型)
43032	湘潭经济技术开发区
43033	湘潭高新技术产业开发区
43036	湘潭综合保税区
43039	湘潭
43043	衡阳高新技术产业开发区
43046	衡阳综合保税区
43049	衡阳
43059	邵阳
43066	岳阳城陵矶综合保税区
43069	岳阳
43072	常德经济技术开发区
43073	常德高新技术产业开发区
43079	常德
43089	张家界
43093	益阳高新技术产业开发区
43099	益阳
43109	娄底
43115	湖南郴州出口加工区
43116	郴州综合保税区
43119	郴州
43129	永州
43139	怀化
43149	湘西
43159	醴陵
43169	湘乡
43179	耒阳
43189	汨罗
43199	津市
43202	浏阳经济技术开发区
43209	浏阳其他
43909	湖南其他
44012	广州经济技术开发区
44013	广州天河高新技术产业开发区
44014	广州保税区
44015	广东广州出口加工区
44016	广州白云机场综合保税区
44017	广州保税物流园区
44019	广州其他
44029	韶关
44031	深圳特区
44033	深圳科技工业园
44034	福田盐田沙头角保税区
44035	广东深圳出口加工区
44036	深圳前海湾保税港区
44037	深圳盐田保税物流园

地区代码	地区名称
44039	深圳其他
4403W	深圳机场保税物流中心
44041	珠海特区
44043	珠海高新技术产业开发区
44044	珠海保税区
44045	珠澳跨境工业区珠海园区
44048	珠海横琴新区
44049	珠海其他
44051	汕头特区
44054	汕头保税区
44059	汕头其他
4405W	汕头保税物流中心(B型)
44063	佛山高新技术产业开发区
44069	佛山其他
44079	江门
44082	湛江经济技术开发区
44089	湛江其他
4408W	湛江保税物流中心(B型)
44099	茂名
44129	肇庆
44133	惠州高新技术产业开发区
44139	惠州其他
44149	梅州
44159	汕尾
44169	河源
44179	阳江
44189	清远
44193	东莞松山湖高新技术产业开发区
44199	东莞
4419W	东莞保税物流中心
44203	中山火炬高技术产业开发区
44209	中山其他
4420W	中山保税物流中心
44219	潮州
44229	顺德
4422W	佛山国通保税物流中心(B型)
44235	广东南沙出口加工区
44236	广州南沙保税港区
44239	番禺
44249	揭阳
44289	南海
44299	云浮市
44306	广州南沙保税港区
44309	南沙其他
44536	深圳盐田综合保税区(一期)
4469W	东莞清溪保税物流中心(B型)
44909	广东其他
45013	南宁高新技术产业开发区
45016	南宁综合保税区
45019	南宁其他
4501W	南宁保税物流中心
45029	柳州
45033	桂林高新技术产业开发区
45039	桂林其他
45049	梧州

地区代码	地区名称
45055	广西北海出口加工区
45059	北海
45069	玉林
45079	百色
45089	河池
45096	广西钦州保税港区
45099	钦州
45106	广西凭祥综合保税区
45109	凭祥
45119	东兴
45129	防城港市
45139	贵港市
45149	崇左
45159	来宾
45169	贺州
45909	广西其他
46011	海口
46013	海南国际科技园区
46014	海南海口保税区
46016	海口综合保税区
46021	三亚
46031	三沙
46041	五指山
46051	琼海
46061	儋州
46062	洋浦经济开发区
46066	洋浦保税港区
46071	文昌
46081	万宁
46091	东方
46101	定安
46111	屯昌
46121	澄迈
46131	临高
46141	白沙
46151	昌江
46161	乐东
46171	陵水
46181	保亭
46191	琼中
46901	海南其他
46902	海南洋浦经济技术开发区
46906	海南洋浦保税港区
4724W	襄阳保税物流中心(B型)
50012	万州经济技术开发区
50019	万州区
50029	涪陵区
50039	渝中区
50049	大渡口区
50052	重庆两江新区江北区
50056	重庆两路寸滩保税港区(水港)
50059	江北区
50066	重庆西永综合保税区
50069	沙坪坝区
5006W	重庆铁路保税物流中心

地区代码	地区名称
50073	重庆高新技术产业开发区
50079	九龙坡区
50082	重庆经济技术开发区
50089	南岸区
50092	重庆两江新区北碚区
50099	北碚区
50109	万盛区
50119	双桥区
50122	重庆两江新区渝北区
50125	重庆出口加工区
50126	重庆两路寸滩保税港区(空港)
50129	渝北区
50139	巴南区
5013W	重庆南彭公路保税物流中心(B型)
50212	长寿经济技术开发区
50219	长寿县
50229	綦江区
50239	潼南县
50249	重庆市铜梁区
50259	大足区
50269	荣昌县
50279	重庆市璧山区
50289	梁平县
50299	城口县
50309	丰都县
50319	垫江县
50329	武隆县
50339	忠县
50349	开县
50359	云阳县
50369	奉节县
50379	巫山县
50389	巫溪县
50399	黔江
50409	石柱土家族自治县
50419	秀山土家族苗族自治县
50429	酉阳土家族苗族自治县
50439	彭水苗族土家族自治县
50816	重庆江津综合保税区
50819	江津区
50829	合川区
50839	永川区
50849	南川区
51012	成都经济技术开发区
51013	成都高新技术产业开发区
51015	四川成都出口加工区
51016	成都高新综合保税区
51019	成都其他
5101W	成都空港保税物流中心
51039	自贡
51049	攀枝花
51053	泸州高新技术产业开发区
51059	泸州
5105W	泸州港保税物流中心(B型)

地区代码	地区名称
51069	德阳
51072	绵阳经济技术开发区
51073	绵阳高新技术产业开发区
51075	四川绵阳出口加工区
51079	绵阳其他
51082	广元经济技术开发区
51089	广元
51099	遂宁
51109	内江
51113	乐山高新技术产业开发区
51119	乐山
51142	宜宾临港经济开发区
51149	宜宾
5114W	宜宾港保税物流中心(B型)
51159	南充
51169	达县
51179	雅安
51189	阿坝
51199	甘孜
51209	凉山
51229	广汉
51239	江油
51249	都江堰
51259	峨眉山
51269	资阳
51279	眉山
51289	广安
51299	巴中
5151W	成都铁路保税物流中心(B型)
51909	四川其他
52013	贵阳高新技术产业开发区
52016	贵阳综合保税区
52019	贵阳其他
52029	六盘水
52036	遵义综合保税区
52039	遵义
52049	铜仁
52059	黔西南
52069	毕节
52079	安顺
52089	黔东南
52099	黔南
52502	贵阳贵安新区
52506	贵安综合保税区
52909	贵州其他
53012	昆明经济技术开发区
53013	昆明高新技术产业开发区
53015	云南昆明出口加工区
53016	昆明综合保税区
53019	昆明其他
5301W	昆明高新保税物流中心(B型)
53029	东川
53039	昭通
53042	曲靖经济技术开发区
53049	曲靖
53059	楚雄
53069	玉溪

地区代码	地区名称
53072	云南省蒙自经济技术开发区
53076	云南红河综合保税区
53079	红河
53089	文山
53099	普洱
53109	西双版纳
53119	大理
53129	保山
53139	德宏
53149	丽江
53159	怒江
53169	迪庆
53179	临沧
53189	畹町
53199	瑞丽
53209	河口
5351W	腾俊国际陆港保税物流中心(B型)
53909	云南其他
54012	拉萨经济技术开发区
54019	拉萨
54029	昌都
54039	山南
54049	日喀则
54059	那曲
54069	阿里
54079	林芝
54909	西藏其他
61012	陕西航天经济技术开发区
61013	西安新技术产业开发区
61015	陕西西安出口加工区
61016	西安综合保税区和西安高新综合保税区
61019	西安其他
61029	铜川
61033	宝鸡高新技术产业开发区
61039	宝鸡其他
61049	咸阳
6104W	陕西西咸保税物流中心
61059	渭南
61062	汉中经济技术开发区
61069	汉中
61079	安康
61089	商洛
61099	延安
61109	榆林
61909	陕西其他
62013	兰州宁卧庄新技术产业开发区
62016	兰州新区综合保税区
62019	兰州其他
62029	嘉峪关
62039	金昌
62049	白银
62059	天水
62069	酒泉
62079	张掖
62089	武威

地区代码	地区名称
6208W	武威保税物流中心
62099	定西
62109	陇南
62119	平凉
62129	庆阳
62139	临夏
62149	甘南
62909	甘肃其他
63012	西宁经济技术开发区
63013	青海高新技术产业开发区
63019	西宁
63029	海东
6302W	青海曹家堡保税物流中心(B型)
63039	海北
63049	黄南
63059	海南
63069	果洛
63079	玉树
63089	海西
63909	青海其他
64012	银川经济技术开发区
64016	银川综合保税区
64019	银川
64029	石嘴山
6402W	石嘴山保税物流中心(B型)
64039	吴中
64049	固原
64059	中卫
64909	宁夏其他
65012	乌鲁木齐经济技术开发区
65013	乌鲁木齐高新技术产业开发区
65015	新疆乌鲁木齐出口加工区
65016	乌鲁木齐综合保税区
65019	乌鲁木齐其他
65029	克拉玛依
65036	阿拉山口综合保税区
65039	博乐
65049	巴音
65059	阿克苏
65069	克孜
65076	喀什综合保税区
65079	喀什
65089	和田
65095	中哈霍尔果斯国际边境合作中心中方配套区(一期)
65099	伊宁
6509A	中哈霍尔果斯国际边境合作中心中方配套区(一期)
6509W	奎屯保税物流中心
65109	塔城
65119	阿勒泰
65122	石河子经济技术开发区
65129	石河子
65219	吐鲁番
65229	哈密
65239	昌吉回族自治州
65909	新疆其他

监管证件名称代码表

许可证或批文代码	许可证或批文名称	许可证或批文代码	许可证或批文名称
1	进口许可证	V	人类遗传资源材料出口、出境证明
2	两用物项和技术进口许可证	X	有毒化学品进出口环境管理放行通知单
3	两用物项和技术出口许可证	Y	原产地证明
4	出口许可证	Z	赴境外加工光盘进口备案证明
5	纺织品临时出口许可证	b	进口广播电影电视节目带(片)提取单
6	旧机电产品禁止进口	c	内销征税联系单
7	自动进口许可证	d	援外项目任务通知函
8	禁止出口商品	e	关税配额外优惠税率进口棉花配额证
9	禁止进口商品	f	音像制品(成品)进口批准单
A	入境检验检疫	g	技术出口合同登记证
B	出境检验检疫(电子底账)	h	核增核扣表
D	毛坯钻石进出境检验	i	技术出口许可证
E	濒危物种允许出口证明书	k	民用爆炸物品进出口审批单
F	濒危物种允许进口证明书	m	银行调运人民币现钞进出境证明
G	两用物项和技术出口许可证(定向)	n	音像制品(版权引进)批准单
I	麻醉药品精神药物进(出)口准许证	q	国别关税配额证明
H	港澳 OPA 纺织品证明	r	预归类标志
J	黄金及黄金制品进出口准许证	s	适用 ITA 税率的商品用途认定证明
K	深加工结转申请表	t	关税配额证明
L	药品进出口准许证	v	自动进口许可证(加工贸易)
M	密码产品和设备进口许可证	x	出口许可证(加工贸易)
O	自动进口许可证(新旧机电产品)	y	出口许可证(边境小额贸易)
P	固体废物进口许可证	u	钟乳石出口批件
Q	进口药品通关单	z	古生物化石出境批件
R	进口兽药通关单		
S	农药进出口登记管理放行通知单		
T	银行调运外币现钞进出境证明文件		
U	合法捕捞产品通关证明		

检验检疫证件代码表

证件代码	证件名称	证件代码	证件名称
L	民用商品入境验证	R	进口食品卫生监督检验
M	进口商品检验	S	出口食品卫生监督检验
N	出口商品检验	V	进境卫生检疫
P	进境动植物、动植物产品检疫	W	出境卫生检疫
Q	出境动植物、动植物产品检疫		

特殊证件代码表

特殊监管证件代码	特殊监管证件说明	具体要求或发布单位
1	含甲苯、丙酮、丁酮、硫酸4种易制毒化学品之一且比例高于40%的货物应当办理《两用物项和技术进出口许可证》	海关总署关于明确易制毒化学品监管有关问题的通知 主要内容:为进一步规范易制毒化学品进出口监管,经研究并商商务部,现就易制毒化学品进出口许可证件管理有关要求明确如下:一、根据商务部公告2007年第23号,含甲苯、丙酮、丁酮、硫酸4种易制毒化学品之一且比例高于40%的货物应当办理《两用物项和技术进出口许可证》(以下简称"两用物项许可证")。含甲苯、丙酮、丁酮、硫酸4种易制毒化学品之一且比例高于40%的货物是指:(一)上述4种物项的单一成份含量超过40%的混合物;(二)上述4种物项的单一成份含量不超过40,但其总含量超过40%的混合物。上述易制毒化学品混合物进出口时,商务发证机构按照含量占比最高的物项核发两用物项许可证,许可证"商品名称"和"海关商品编号"栏目均按该物项填报,"规格型号"栏目则填报不同成份的品名简称及其含量。例如,含甲苯20%、丙酮30%、丁酮20%和硫酸10%的混合物办理两用物项许可证时,许可证商品名称栏目填写"丙酮",海关商品编号栏目填写"2914110000",规格型号栏目填写"丙30甲20丁20硫10"。海关在办理易制毒化学品混合物通关手续时,应要求进出口经营者按照货物实际商品名称及相应海关商品编号申报,验核两用物项许可证,并人工核扣许可证进出口数量。二、因加工贸易方式在境内产生的副产品属于易制毒化学品的货物,企业办理其内销手续时无须申领《两用物项和技术进口许可证》。三、含易制毒化学品的混合物办理深加工结转手续时,转入方企业无须提交《两用物项和技术进口许可证》。 施行时间:2012年8月6日。
2	其第二法定计量数量(计量单位为升)应统一按附件中给定公式,由第一法定数量(计量单位为千克)换算后向海关申报	中华人民共和国海关总署公告 2013年第10号 自2009年1月1日起,国家按照升(第二法定数量)对成品油计征进口环节消费税。海关总署陆续发布了2008年第99号公告、2009年第15号公告(已废止)和2010年第46号公告,对应税成品油商品的第二法定数量进行了规范。为确保海关统计数据的准确性,便于企业在办理各类海关手续中遵循统一标准,经研究,现就成品油的法定数量申报要求补充规定如下:一、进出口货物的收发货人及其代理人在向海关申报《中华人民共和国进出口税则》和《中华人民共和国海关统计商品目录》中商品品目"2710"项下商品时,其第二法定计量数量(计量单位为升)应统一按附件中给定公式,由第一法定数量(计量单位为千克)换算后向海关申报。二.第一法定数量未在合同等报关单随附单证及其他相关单证中直接列明的,应先按照实际密度及体积计算并申报第一法定数量,再换算第二法定数量。零售包装的成品油,其第一法定数量应为扣除零售包装后的液体部分重量。按照商业惯例成品油通常会含有一定数量的水份,申报第一法定数量时不应扣除含水量。三、本公告适用于进出口货物报关单、进出境货物备案清单等各类具有第二法定计量单位和法定数量栏目的海关单证的申报及修改。四、本公告内容自2013年4月1日起执行。 特此公告。 2013年3月8日
3	重点旧机电产品目录	商务部
4	消耗臭氧层物质目录	商务部

企业产品许可类别代码表

类别代码	类别名称	强制级别	证书类别
000	企业产品许可类别		
100	通关司类		
101	检疫处理单位审批	D	98
102	实施绿色通道制度申请	D	99
103	直通放行申请		98,99
104	检疫处理人员审批		98,99
200	卫生司类		
203	出入境特殊物品卫生检疫审批	A	19,20
300	动植司类		
301	出境水果包装厂注册登记	B	21
302	出境水果果园注册登记	B	99
303	进境水果境外果园/包装厂注册登记	C	21
304	出境水生动物养殖场/包转场检验检疫注册登记	A	99
305	出口饲料和饲料添加剂生产、加工、存放企业注册登记	C	99
306	进口饲料和饲料添加剂生产企业注册登记	C	98
307	进境非食用动物产品生产、加工、存放企业注册登记	C	98
308	出境货物木质包装除害处理标识加施资格申请	B	99
309	出境种苗花卉生产经营企业注册登记	B	99
310	出境竹木草制品生产企业注册登记	C	99
311	出口植物产品生产、加工、存放企业注册登记	C	99
312	进境植物繁殖材料隔离检疫圃申请	C	98
315	供港澳陆生动物饲养场、中转场检验检疫注册	C	12
317	进出境动物指定隔离检疫场使用申请	C	98,99
318	出境动物及其非食用动物产品生产、加工、存放企业注册登记	C	99
319	进境栽培介质使用单位注册	C	98
320	进境动物遗传物质进口代理及使用单位备案	A	98
321	进境动物及动物产品国外生产单位注册	C	98
322	饲料进口企业备案	B	98
323	饲料出口企业备案	C	99
324	出境货物木质包装除害处理合格凭证	C	99
325	进境动植物检疫许可证	A	17
326	进境粮食加工储存单位注册	C	98
400	检验司类		
401	进出口商品免验	A	98,99
402	进口旧机电产品备案	C	39
404	出口产品型式试验	B	32
408	汽车预审备案	C	98
409	免于强制性认证特殊用途进口汽车检测处理程序车辆	C	98
410	免于办理强制性产品认证	C	40
411	强制性产品(CCC)认证	C	40
412	进口涂料备案	C	98
413	进口可用作原料的固体废物国内收货人注册登记	D	98
414	进口可用作原料的固体废物国外供货商注册登记	D	98
415	进出境集装箱场站登记	C	98,99
416	进口棉花境外供货商登记注册	B	98
417	出口玩具质量许可(注册登记)	A	11
418	对出口食品包装生产企业和进口食品包装的进口商实行备案	B	21
419	输美日用陶瓷生产厂认证	A	99
421	进出口商品检验鉴定机构许可	B	98,99
422	进口废物原料装运前检验证书	C	33
423	进口旧机电产品装运前检验证书	C	27
500	食品局类		
501	出口肉类产品养殖场备案	A	99
502	出口蛋禽养殖场备案	B	99
503	出口蜂产品养蜂基地备案	C	99
504	出口食品原料种植场备案	C	99
505	供港澳蔬菜生产加工企业备案	C	99
506	供港澳蔬菜种植基地备案	C	99
507	出口粮谷豆类生产加工企业注册登记	C	99
508	进口食品境外出口商代理商备案	C	98
509	进口食品进口商备案	C	98
510	进口肉类收货人备案	C	98
511	进口肉类存储冷库备案	C	98
512	出口加工用水产养殖场备案	A	99
513	进口水产品存储冷库备案	C	98
514	出口化妆品生产企业备案	C	99
515	进口化妆品收货人备案	C	98
516	进口化妆品产品备案	A	98
517	进口预包装食品标签备案	A	25
518	出口食品生产企业备案	A	15
519	进口食品境外生产企业注册	A	16
520	出口食品生产企业境外注册	A	14
522	水果冻肉预检验证书	C	98
523	进口化妆品产品套装备案	A	25
600	综合类		18
601	进口其他证书	D	98
602	出口其他证书	A	99
700	认监委类		
800	准入肉类名单		17
900	进口肉类名录		17

包装种类代码表

种类代码	种类名称
00	散装
01	裸装
22	纸制或纤维板制盒/箱
23	木制或竹藤等植物性材料制盒/箱
29	其他材料制盒/箱
32	纸制或纤维板制桶
33	木制或竹藤等植物性材料制桶
39	其他材料制桶
04	球状罐类
06	包/袋
92	再生木托
93	天然木托
98	植物性铺垫材料
99	其他包装

关联理由代码表

关联理由代码	关联理由名称
1	通关单超过有效期
2	换证凭单/条超过有效期
3	进口复出口
4	出口复进口
5	出境预检
6	登检换证
7	与其它报检批拼箱
8	保税出库
9	进口车辆换证
10	拼单

结汇方式代码表

结汇方式代码	结汇方式名称	结汇方式代码	结汇方式名称
1	信汇	6	信用证
2	电汇	7	先出后结
3	票汇	8	先结后出
4	付款交单	9	其他
5	承兑交单		

用途代码表

用途代码	用途名称	用途代码	用途名称
11	种用或繁殖	23	食品容器
12	食用	24	食品洗涤剂
13	奶用	25	食品消毒剂
14	观赏或演艺	26	仅工业用途
15	伴侣	27	化妆品
16	实验	28	化妆品原料
17	药用	29	肥料
18	饲用	30	保健品
19	食品包装材料	31	治疗、预防、诊断
20	食品加工设备	32	科研
21	食品添加剂	33	展览展示
22	介质土	99	其他

货物属性代码表

属性代码	属性名称	属性代码	属性名称
11	3C 目录内	21	旧品
12	3C 目录外	22	成套设备
13	无需办理 3C 认证	23	带皮木材/板材
14	预包装	24	不带皮木材/板材
15	非预包装	25	A 级特殊物品
16	转基因产品	26	B 级特殊物品
17	非转基因产品	27	C 级特殊物品
18	首次进出口	28	D 级特殊物品

属性代码	属性名称
19	正常
20	废品
29	V/W 非特殊物品
30	市场采购

危包规格代码表

规格代码	规格名称	规格简称
1A1	钢制不可拆装桶顶圆桶	闭口钢桶
1A2	钢制可拆装桶顶圆桶	开口钢桶
1B1	铝制不可拆装桶顶圆桶	闭口铝桶
1B2	铝制可拆装桶顶圆桶	开口铝桶
1D	胶合板圆桶	胶板圆桶
1G	纤维圆桶	纤维圆桶
1H1	塑料不可拆装桶顶圆桶	闭口塑料圆桶
1H2	塑料可拆装桶顶圆桶	开口塑料圆桶
2C1	塞式木琵琶桶	木琵琶桶
2C2	非水密型木琵琶桶	木琵琶桶
3A1	钢制不可拆装罐顶罐	闭口钢罐
3A2	钢制可拆装罐顶罐	开口钢罐
3B1	铝制不可拆装罐顶罐	闭口铝罐
3B2	铝制可拆装罐顶罐	开口铝罐
3H1	塑料制不可拆装罐顶罐	闭口塑料罐
3H2	塑料制可拆装罐顶罐	开口塑料罐
4A	钢箱	钢箱
4B	铝箱	铝箱
4C1	大木箱	大木箱
4C2	箱壁防撒漏木箱	防漏木箱
4D	胶合板箱	胶合板箱
4F	再生木木箱	再生木木箱
4G	纤维板箱	纤维板箱
4H1	膨胀的塑料箱	塑料箱
4H2	硬质的塑料箱	塑料箱
5H	塑料编织袋	塑料编织袋
5H1	塑料编织无内衬或涂层的袋	塑料编织袋
5H2	塑料编织防撒漏的袋	塑料编织袋
5H3	塑料编织防水的袋	塑料编织袋
5H4	塑料薄膜袋	塑料薄膜袋
5L1	无内衬或涂层的纺织品编织袋	纺织品编织袋
5L2	纺织品防撒漏的纺织品编织袋	纺织品编织袋
5L3	纺织品防水的纺织品编织袋	纺织品编织袋
5M1	多层的纸袋	纸袋
5M2	多层防水纸袋	纸袋
6HA1	塑料容器在钢桶内复合包装	钢桶塑料复包
6HA2	塑料容器在钢条或钢皮箱内复合包装	钢皮箱塑料复包
6HB	塑料容器在铝桶内复合包装	铝桶塑料复包
5M1	多层的纸袋	纸袋
6HB2	塑料容器在铝条或铝皮箱内复合包装	铝皮箱塑料复包
6HC	塑料容器在木箱内复合包装	木箱塑料复包
6HD1	塑料容器在胶合板桶内复合包装	胶板桶塑料复包
6HD2	塑料容器在胶合板箱内复合包装	胶板箱塑料复包
6HG1	塑料容器在纤维桶内复合包装	纤维桶塑料复包
6HG2	塑料容器在纤维板箱内复合包装	纤维板箱塑料复包
6HH1	塑料容器在塑料桶内复合包装	塑料桶塑料复包
6HH2	塑料容器在硬塑料箱内复合包装	硬塑料箱复包
6PA1	玻璃、陶瓷、粗陶器在钢桶内复合包装	玻璃钢桶复包
6PA2	玻璃、陶瓷、粗陶器在钢条或钢皮箱内复合包装	玻璃陶瓷钢皮箱复包
6PB1	玻璃、陶瓷、粗陶器在铝桶内复合包装	玻璃陶瓷铝桶复包
6PB2	玻璃、陶瓷、粗陶器在铝条或铝皮箱内复合包装	玻璃陶瓷铝皮箱复包
6PC	玻璃、陶瓷、粗陶器在木箱内复合包装	玻璃陶瓷木箱复包
6PD1	玻璃、陶瓷、粗陶器在胶合板内复合包装	玻璃陶瓷胶板复包
6PD2	玻璃、陶瓷、粗陶器在柳条筐内复合包装	玻璃陶瓷柳条筐复包
6PG1	玻璃、陶瓷、粗陶器在纤维桶内复合包装	玻璃陶瓷纤维桶复包
6PG2	玻璃、陶瓷、粗陶器在纤维板箱内复合包装	玻璃陶瓷纤维板复包
6PH1	玻璃、陶瓷、粗陶器在膨胀塑料包装内复合包	玻璃陶瓷膨塑复包
6PH2	玻璃、陶瓷、粗陶器在硬塑料包装内复合包装	玻璃陶瓷硬塑复包

集装箱规格代码表

规格代码	规格名称
11	普通 2 * 标准箱(L)
12	冷藏 2 * 标准箱(L)
13	罐式 2 * 标准箱(L)
21	普通标准箱(S)
22	冷藏标准箱(S)
23	罐式标准箱(S)
31	其他标准箱(S)
32	其他 2 * 标准箱(L)
N	无

货币代码表

代码	中文名称	英文名称
HKD	港币	Hong Kong Dollar
IDR	印度尼西亚卢比	Rupiah
JPY	日本元	Yen
MOP	澳门元	Pataca
MYR	马来西亚林吉特	Malaysian Ringgit
EUR	欧元	Euro
DKK	丹麦克朗	Danish Krone
GBP	英镑	Pound Sterling
NOK	挪威克朗	Norwegian Krone
SEK	瑞典克朗	Swedish Krona

代码	中文名称	英文名称	代码	中文名称	英文名称
PHP	菲律宾比索	Philippine Piso	CHF	瑞士法郎	Swiss Franc
SGD	新加坡元	Singapore Dollar	RUB	俄罗斯卢布	Russian Ruble
KRW	韩国圆	Won	CAD	加拿大元	Canadian Dollar
THB	泰国铢	Baht	USD	美元	US Dollar
CNY	人民币	Yuan Renminbi	AUD	澳大利亚元	Australian Dollar
TWD	新台币	New Taiwan Dollar	NZD	新西兰元	New Zealand Dollar

计量单位代码表

计量单位代码	计量单位名称	计量单位代码	计量单位名称	计量单位代码	计量单位名称
001	台	043	百个	096	毫升
002	座	044	百片	097	英加仑
003	辆	045	刀	098	美加仑
004	艘	046	疋	099	立方英尺
005	架	047	公担	101	立方尺
006	套	048	扇	110	平方码
007	个	049	百枝	111	平方英尺
008	只	050	千只	112	平方尺
009	头	051	千块	115	英制马力
010	张	052	千盒	116	公制马力
011	件	053	千枝	118	令
012	支	054	千个	120	箱
013	枝	055	亿支	121	批
014	根	056	亿个	122	罐
015	条	057	万套	123	桶
016	把	058	千张	124	扎
017	块	059	万张	125	包
018	卷	060	千伏安	126	箩
019	副	061	千瓦	127	打
020	片	062	千瓦时	128	筐
021	组	063	千升	129	罗
022	份	067	英尺	130	匹
023	幅	070	吨	131	册
025	双	071	长吨	132	本
026	对	072	短吨	133	发
027	棵	073	司马担	134	枚
028	株	074	司马斤	135	捆
029	井	075	斤	136	袋
030	米	076	磅	139	粒
031	盘	077	担	140	盒
032	平方米	078	英担	141	合
033	立方米	079	短担	142	瓶
034	筒	080	两	143	千支
035	千克	081	市担	144	万双
036	克	083	盎司	145	万粒
037	盆	084	克拉	146	千粒
038	万个	085	市尺	147	千米
039	具	086	码	148	千英尺
040	百副	088	英寸	149	百万贝可
041	百支	089	寸	163	部
042	百把	095	升	164	亿株

成交方式代码表

成交方式代码	成交方式名称
1	CIF
2	C&F
3	FOB
4	C&I
5	市场价
6	垫仓
7	EXW

国别(地区)代码表

别码	中文国别符号	国际标准英文简称	英文国别名称	优惠/普通税率标记	船舶吨税优/普标记
101	阿富汗	AFG	Afghanistan	L	H
102	巴林	BHR	Bahrian	L	H
103	孟加拉国	BGD	Bangladesh	L	L
104	不丹	BTN	Bhutan	H	H
105	文莱	BRN	Brunei	L	H
106	缅甸	MMR	Myanmar	L	H
107	柬埔寨	KHM	Cambodia	L	H
108	塞浦路斯	CYP	Cyprus	L	L
109	朝鲜	PRK	Korea,DPR	L	L
110	香港	HKG	Hong Kong	L	L
111	印度	IND	India	L	L
112	印度尼西亚	IDN	Indonesia	L	L
113	伊朗	IRN	Iran	L	L
114	伊拉克	IRQ	Iraq	L	H
115	以色列	ISR	Israel	L	L
116	日本	JPN	Japan	L	L
117	约旦	JOR	Jordan	L	H
118	科威特	KWT	Kuwait	L	H
119	老挝	LAO	LaoPDR	L	H
120	黎巴嫩	LBN	Lebanon	L	L
121	澳门	MAC	Macau	L	L
122	马来西亚	MYS	Malaysia	L	L
123	马尔代夫	MDV	Maldives	L	H
124	蒙古	MNG	Mongolia	L	L
125	尼泊尔联邦民主共和国	NPL	Nepal,FDR	L	H
126	阿曼	OMN	Oman	L	L
127	巴基斯坦	PAK	Pakistan	L	L
128	巴勒斯坦	PSE	Palestine	H	H
129	菲律宾	PHL	Philippines	L	L
130	卡塔尔	QAT	Qatar	L	H
131	沙特阿拉伯	SAU	Saudi Arabia	L	H
132	新加坡	SGP	Singapore	L	L
133	韩国	KOR	Korea,Rep.	L	L
134	斯里兰卡	LKA	Sri Lanka	L	L
135	叙利亚	SYR	Syrian Arab Republic	L	H
136	泰国	THA	Thailand	L	L
137	土耳其	TUR	Turkey	L	L
138	阿联酋	ARE	United Arab Emirates	L	H
139	也门	YEM	Yemen	L	L
141	越南	NVM	Viet Nam	L	L
142	中国	CHN	China	L	L
143	台澎金马关税区	TWN	Taiwan,Prov.of China	L	H
144	东帝汶	TLS	Timor—Leste	L	H
145	哈萨克斯坦	KAZ	Kazakhstan	L	H
146	吉尔吉斯斯坦	KGZ	Kyrgyzstan	L	H
147	塔吉克斯坦	TJK	Tajikistan	L	H
148	土库曼斯坦	TKM	Turkmenistan	L	H
149	乌兹别克斯坦	UZB	Uzbekistan	L	H
199	亚洲其他国家(地区)		Oth. Asia nes		H
201	阿尔及利亚	DZA	Algeria	L	L
202	安哥拉	AGO	Angola	L	H
203	贝宁	BEN	Benin	L	H
204	博茨瓦纳	BWA	Botswana	L	H
205	布隆迪	BDI	Burundi	L	H
206	喀麦隆	CMR	Cameroon	L	H
207	加那利群岛		Canary Islands	H	H
208	佛得角	CPV	Cape Vrde	L	H
209	中非	CAF	Central African Republic	L	H
210	塞卜泰(休达)		Ceuta	H	H
211	乍得	TCD	Chad	L	H
212	科摩罗	COM	Comoros	H	H
213	刚果(布)	COG	Congo	L	L
214	吉布提	DJI	Djibouti	L	H
215	埃及	EGY	Egypt	L	L
216	赤道几内亚	GNQ	Equatorial Guinea	L	H
217	埃塞俄比亚	ETH	Ethiopia	L	L
218	加蓬	GAB	Gabon	L	H
219	冈比亚	GMB	Gambia	L	H
220	加纳	GHA	Ghana	L	L
221	几内亚	GIN	Guinea	L	H
222	几内亚比绍	GNB	Guinea-Bissau	L	H
223	科特迪瓦	CIV	Cote d'lvoire	L	H
224	肯尼亚	KEN	Kenya	L	L
225	利比里亚	LBR	Liberia	L	L
226	利比亚	LBY	Libyan Arab Jamahiriya	L	H
227	马达加斯加	MDG	Madagascar	L	H
228	马拉维	MWI	Malawi	L	H
229	马里	MLI	Mali	L	H
230	毛里塔尼亚	MRT	Mauritania	L	H
231	毛里求斯	MUS	Mauritius	L	H
232	摩洛哥	MAR	Morocco	L	L
233	莫桑比克	MOZ	Mozambique	L	H
234	纳米比亚	NAM	Namibia	L	H
235	尼日尔	NER	Niger	L	H
236	尼日利亚	NGA	Nigeria	L	H
237	留尼汪	REU	Reunion	H	H
238	卢旺达	RWA	Rwanda	L	H
239	圣多美和普林西比	STP	Sao Tome and Principe	H	H
240	塞内加尔	SEN	Senegal	L	H
241	塞舌尔	SYC	Seychelles	H	H
242	塞拉利昂	SLE	Sierra Leone	L	H
243	索马里	SOM	Somalia	L	H
244	南非	ZAF	South Africa	L	L

别码	中文国别符号	国际标准英文简称	英文国别名称	优惠/普通税率标记	船舶吨税优/普标记
245	西撒哈拉	ESH	Western Sahara	H	H
246	苏丹	SDN	Sudan	L	L
247	坦桑尼亚	TZA	Tanzania	L	H
248	多哥	TGO	Togo	L	H
249	突尼斯	TUN	Tunisia	L	L
250	乌干达	UGA	Uganda	L	H
251	布基纳法索	BFA	Burkina Faso	L	H
252	刚果(金)	COD	Congo,DR	L	L
253	赞比亚	ZMB	Zambia	L	H
254	津巴布韦	ZWE	Zimbabwe	L	H
255	莱索托	LSO	Lesotho	L	H
256	梅利利亚		Melilla	H	H
257	斯威士兰	SWZ	Swaziland	L	H
258	厄立特里亚	ERI	Eritrea	L	H
259	马约特	MYT	Mayotte	L	H
260	南苏丹共和国		Republic of South Sudan	L	H
299	非洲其他国家(地区)		Oth. Afr. nes		H
301	比利时	BEL	Belgium	L	L
302	丹麦	DNK	Denmark	L	L
303	英国	GBR	United Kingdom	L	L
304	德国	DEU	Germany	L	L
305	法国	FRA	France	L	L
306	爱尔兰	IRL	Ireland	L	L
307	意大利	ITA	Italy	L	L
308	卢森堡	LUX	Luxembourg	L	L
309	荷兰	NLD	Netherlands	L	L
310	希腊	GRC	Greece	L	L
311	葡萄牙	PRT	Portugal	L	L
312	西班牙	ESP	Spain	L	L
313	阿尔巴尼亚	ALB	Albania	L	L
314	安道尔	AND	Andorra	H	H
315	奥地利	AUT	Austria	L	L
316	保加利亚	BGR	Bulgaria	L	L
318	芬兰	FIN	Finland	L	L
320	直布罗陀	GIB	Gibraltar	H	L
321	匈牙利	HUN	Hungary	L	L
322	冰岛	ISL	Iceland	L	H
323	列支敦士登	LIE	Liechtenstein	L	H
324	马耳他	MLT	Malta	L	L
325	摩纳哥	MCO	Monaco	L	H
326	挪威	NOR	Norway	L	L
327	波兰	POL	Poland	L	L
328	罗马尼亚	ROM	Romania	L	L
329	圣马力诺	SMR	San Marino	L	H
330	瑞典	SWE	Sweden	L	L
331	瑞士	CHE	Switzerland	L	H
334	爱沙尼亚	EST	Estonia	L	L
335	拉脱维亚	LVA	Latvia	L	L
336	立陶宛	LTU	Lithuania	L	L
337	格鲁吉亚	GEO	Georgia	L	L
338	亚美尼亚	ARM	Armenia	L	H
339	阿塞拜疆	AZE	Azerbai jan	L	H
340	白俄罗斯	BLR	Belarus	L	H
343	摩尔多瓦	MDA	Moldova	L	H
344	俄罗斯联邦	RUS	Russian Federation	L	L
347	乌克兰	UKR	Ukraine	L	L
349	塞尔维亚和黑山			H	H
350	斯洛文尼亚	SVN	Slovenia	L	L
351	克罗地亚	HRV	Croatia	L	L
352	捷克	CZE	Czech Republic	L	L
353	斯洛伐克	SVK	Slovakia	L	L
354	前南马其顿	MKD	Macedonia,FYR	L	H
355	波黑	BIH	Bosnia and Hercegovina	L	H
356	梵蒂冈城国	VAT	Vatican City State	H	H
357	法罗群岛	FRO	Faroe Islangds	L	H
358	塞尔维亚	SRB	Serbia	L	H
359	黑山	MNE	Montenegro	L	H
399	欧洲其他国家(地区)		Oth. Eur. nes		H
401	安提瓜和巴布达	ATG	Antigua & Barbuda	L	H
402	阿根廷	ARG	Argentina	L	L
403	阿鲁巴	ABW	Aruba	H	H
404	巴哈马	BHS	Bahamas	H	L
405	巴巴多斯	BRB	Barbados	L	H
406	伯利兹	BLZ	Belize	L	H
408	多民族玻利维亚国	BOL	Estado Plurinacional de Bolivia	L	H
409	博内尔		Bonaire	H	H
410	巴西	BRA	Brazil	L	L
411	开曼群岛	CYM	Cayman Islands	H	L
412	智利	CHL	Chile	L	L
413	哥伦比亚	COL	Colombia	L	H
414	多米尼克	DMA	Dominica	L	H
415	哥斯达黎加	CRI	Costa Rica	L	H
416	古巴	CUB	Cuba	L	L
417	库腊索岛		Curacao	H	H
418	多米尼加共和国	DOM	Dominican Republic	L	H
419	厄瓜多尔	ECU	Ecuador	L	H
420	法属圭亚那	GUF	French Guiana	H	H
421	格林纳达	GRD	Grenada	L	H
422	瓜德罗普	GLP	Guadeloupe	H	H
423	危地马拉	GTM	Guatemala	L	H
424	圭亚那	GUY	Guyana	L	H
425	海地	HTI	Haiti	L	H
426	洪都拉斯	HND	Honduras	L	H
427	牙买加	JAM	Jamaica	L	H
428	马提尼克	MTQ	Martinique	H	H
429	墨西哥	MEX	Mexico	L	L
430	蒙特塞拉特	MSR	Montserrat	H	H
431	尼加拉瓜	NIC	Nicaragua	L	H
432	巴拿马	PAN	Panama	L	L
433	巴拉圭	PRY	Paraguay	L	H
434	秘鲁	PER	Peru	L	L
435	波多黎各	PRI	Puerto Rico	L	H
436	萨巴		Saba	H	H
437	圣卢西亚	LCA	Saint Lucia	L	H
438	圣马丁岛		Saint Martin Islands	H	H
439	圣文森特和格林纳丁斯	VCT	Saint Vincent and Grenadines	L	H
440	萨尔瓦多	SLV	El Salvador	L	H
441	苏里南	SUR	Suriname	L	H
442	特立尼达和多巴哥	TTO	Trinidad and Tobago	L	H
443	特克斯和凯科斯群岛	TCA	Turks and Caicos Islands	H	H
444	乌拉圭	URY	Uruguay	L	H
445	委内瑞拉	VEN	Venezuela	L	H
446	英属维尔京群岛	VGB	Virgin Islands, British	H	H
447	圣其茨和尼维斯	KNA	Saint Kitts and Nevis	L	H

别码	中文国别符号	国际标准英文简称	英文国别名称	优惠/普通税率标记	船舶吨税优/普标记
448	圣皮埃尔和密克隆	SPM	Saint Pierre and Miquelon	L	H
449	荷属安地列斯	ANT	Netherlands Antilles	H	H
499	拉丁美洲其他国家(地区)		Oth. L.Amer. nes		H
501	加拿大	CAN	Canada	L	L
502	美国	USA	United States	L	L
503	格陵兰	GRL	Greenland	L	H
504	百慕大	BMU	Bermuda	H	L
599	北美洲其他国家(地区)		Oth. N.Amer. nes		H
601	澳大利亚	AUS	Australia	L	H
602	库克群岛	COK	Cook Islands	L	H
603	斐济	FJI	Fiji	L	H
604	盖比群岛		Gambier Islands	H	H
605	马克萨斯群岛		Marquesas Islands	H	H
606	瑙鲁	NRU	Nauru	H	H
607	新喀里多尼亚	NCL	New Caledonia	L	H
608	瓦努阿图	VUT	Vanuatu	L	H
609	新西兰	NZL	New Zealand	L	L
610	诺福克岛	NFK	Norfolk Island	H	H
611	巴布亚新几内亚	PNG	Papua New Guinea	L	H
612	社会群岛		Society Islands	H	H
613	所罗门群岛	SLB	Solomon Islands	L	H
614	汤加	TON	Tonga	L	H
615	土阿莫土群岛		Tuamotu Islands	H	H
616	土布艾群岛		Tubai Islands	H	H
617	萨摩亚	WSM	Samoa	L	H
618	基里巴斯	KIR	Kiribati	H	H
619	图瓦卢	TUV	Tuvalu	H	H
620	密克罗尼西亚联邦	FSM	Micronesia,Fs	L	H
621	马绍尔群岛	MHL	Marshall Islands	H	H
622	帕劳	PLW	Palau	H	H
623	法属波利尼西亚	PYF	French Polynesia	L	H
625	瓦利斯和浮图纳	WLF	Wallis and Futuna	L	H
699	大洋洲其他国家(地区)		Oth. Ocean. nes		H
701	国(地)别不详		Countries (reg.) unknown	H	H
702	联合国及机构和国际组织		UN and oth.int'lorg		
999	中性包装原产国别		Conutries of Neutral Package	H	H

地区性质代码表

地区性质代码	地区性质名称
1	经济特区
2	沿海开放城市
3	经济技术开发区
4	经济开放区
5	海南省
6	西藏自治区
7	广东省
8	福建省
9	北京市、新疆
A	保税工业区
B	新技术开发园区

企业性质代码表

企业性质代码	企业性质名称
1	国有
2	合作
3	合资
4	独资
5	集体
6	私营
7	个体工商户
8	报关
9	其他

4

中华人民共和国海关进口关税税率附表

（2020 年 1 月 1 日起实施）

Import tariff attached table

（Enforced from January 1，2020）

附表 1：

Attached table 1：

2020 年关税配额商品税目、税率表

（2020 年 1 月 1 日起实施）

In-Quota Interim Duty Rate on Imported Goods，2020

（Enforced from January 1，2020）

说明：2020 年在国家规定配额内的进口货物，按下表配额内的税率执行；超过配额数量的进口货物，执行税则当中的法定关税税率，即配额外税率。

Explanation： During 2020，according to the state regulations，goods imported within quota，will be processed using the In-Quota Duty Rate Schedule below；goods imported exceeding the quota amount，will be processed using Statutory Tariff Rate in the Tariff Schedule，that is，Out-Quota Tariff Rate.

序号 No.	货品名称 Description of Goods	税则号列 Tariff No.	2020 年进口税率(%) Import Duty Rate(%)				
			配额外税率 Out-Quota Duty Rate		配额内税率 In-Quota Duty Rate	国别关税配额税率	
			普通税率 Gen.	最惠国税率 M. F. N.		新西兰 (%)	澳大利亚 (%)
1	小麦	10011100	180	65	1		
		10011900	180	65	1		
		10019100	180	65	1		
		10019900	180	65	1		
		11010000	130	65	6		
		11031100	130	65	9		
		11032010	180	65	10		
2	玉米	10051000	180	20	1		
		10059000	180	65	1		
		11022000	130	40	9		
		11031300	130	65	9		
		11042300	180	65	10		
3	稻谷和大米	10061021	180	65	1		
		10061029	180	65	1		
		10061081	180	65	1		
		10061089	180	65	1		
		10062020	180	65	1		
		10062080	180	65	1		
		10063020	180	65	1		
		10063080	180	65	1		
		10064020	180	10	1		
		10064080	180	10	1		
		11029021	130	40	9		
		11029029	130	40	9		
		11031931	70	10	9		
		11031939	70	10	9		
4	糖	17011200	125	50	15		
		17011300	125	50	15		
		17011400	125	50	15		
		17019100	125	50	15		
		17019910	125	50	15		

序号 No.	货品名称 Description of Goods	税则号列 Tariff No.	2020年进口税率(%) Import Duty Rate(%)				
			配额外税率 Out-Quota Duty Rate		配额内税率 In-Quota Duty Rate	国别关税配额税率	
			普通税率 Gen.	最惠国税率 M. F. N.		新西兰 (%)	澳大利亚 (%)
		17019920	125	50	15		
		17019990	125	50	15		
5	羊毛	51011100	50	38	1	0	0
		51011900	50	38	1	0	0
		51012100	50	38	1	0	0
		51012900	50	38	1	0	0
		51013000	50	38	1	0	0
		51031010	50	38	1	0	0
6	毛条	51051000	50	38	3	0	
		51052100	50	38	3	0	
		51052900	50	38	3	0	
7	棉花	52010000	125	40[注1]	1		
		52030000	125	40	1		
8	化肥	31021000	150	50	4[注2]		
		31052000	150	50	4[注3]		
		31053000	150	50	4[注4]		

[注1]:对配额外进口的一定数量棉花,适用滑准税形式暂定关税,具体方式如下:

1.当进口棉花完税价格高于或等于15.000元/千克时,按0.300元/千克计征从量税;

2.当进口棉花完税价格低于15.000元/千克时,暂定从价税率按下式计算:Ri=9.45/Pi +2.6%×Pi -1对上式计算结果四舍五入保留3位小数。其中Ri为暂定从价税率,当按上式计算值高于40%时,Ri取值40%;Pi为关税完税价格,单位为元/千克。

[注2、3、4]:暂定税率为1%。

附表2: CIQ扩展编码及品名

HS编码	CIQ扩展品名
0106191010	(1)斑马,(2)犀,(3)貘,(4)其他野生奇蹄动物,(5)鹿,(6)长颈鹿,(7)黄羊,(8)河马,(9)羚牛,(10)羚羊,(11)青羊(斑羚),(12)叉角羚,(13)骆马,(14)美洲驼,(15)角马,(16)梅花鹿,(17)马鹿,(18)其他野生偶蹄动物,(19)狐狸,(20)貂,(21)大熊猫,(22)小熊猫,(23)熊,(24)水獭,(25)果子狸,(26)狮,(27)虎,(28)豹,(29)貉,(30)豺,(31)狼,(32)大灵猫,(33)小灵猫,(34)野狗,(35)其他野生食肉动物,(36)旱獭,(37)松鼠,(38)花鼠,(39)麝鼠,(40)海狸鼠,(41)河狸,(42)地鼠,(43)豪猪,(44)其他野生啮齿动物,(45)猩猩,(46)狒狒,(47)山魈,(48)其他野生灵长动物,(49)象,(50)刺猬,(51)穿山甲,(52)袋鼠,(53)蝙蝠,(54)其他野生哺乳动物
0106191090	(1)其他饲养奇蹄动物,(2)其他饲养偶蹄动物,(3)伴侣犬,(4)工作犬,(5)其他用途犬,(6)伴侣猫,(7)其他用途猫,(8)其他饲养食肉动物,(9)大鼠,(10)小鼠,(11)豚鼠,(12)其他饲养啮齿动物,(13)其他饲养兔形目动物,(14)其他饲养哺乳动物
0106199010	(1)斑马,(2)犀,(3)貘,(4)其他野生奇蹄动物,(5)鹿,(6)长颈鹿,(7)黄羊,(8)河马,(9)羚牛,(10)羚羊,(11)青羊(斑羚),(12)叉角羚,(13)骆马,(14)美洲驼,(15)角马,(16)梅花鹿,(17)马鹿,(18)其他野生偶蹄动物,(19)狐狸,(20)貂,(21)大熊猫,(22)小熊猫,(23)熊,(24)水獭,(25)果子狸,(26)狮,(27)虎,(28)豹,(29)貉,(30)豺,(31)狼,(32)大灵猫,(33)小灵猫,(34)野狗,(35)其他野生食肉动物,(36)旱獭,(37)松鼠,(38)花鼠,(39)麝鼠,(40)海狸鼠,(41)河狸,(42)地鼠,(43)豪猪,(44)其他野生啮齿动物,(45)猩猩,(46)狒狒,(47)山魈,(48)其他野生灵长动物,(49)象,(50)刺猬,(51)穿山甲,(52)袋鼠,(53)蝙蝠,(54)其他野生哺乳动物
0106199090	(1)其他饲养奇蹄动物,(2)其他饲养偶蹄动物,(3)伴侣犬,(4)工作犬,(5)其他用途犬,(6)伴侣猫,(7)其他用途猫,(8)其他饲养食肉动物,(9)大鼠,(10)小鼠,(11)豚鼠,(12)其他饲养啮齿动物,(13)其他饲养兔形目动物,(14)其他饲养哺乳动物
0106201900	(1)乌龟,(2)草龟,(3)绿毛龟,(4)鳖(甲鱼、团鱼),(5)玳瑁,(6)鳄龟,(7)其他龟鳖,(8)蛇,(9)蜥蜴,(10)鳄,(11)壁虎,(12)巨蜥,(13)蟒,(14)其他爬行动物
0106209090	(1)乌龟,(2)草龟,(3)绿毛龟,(4)鳖(甲鱼、团鱼),(5)玳瑁,(6)鳄龟,(7)其他龟鳖,(8)蛇,(9)蜥蜴,(10)鳄,(11)壁虎,(12)巨蜥,(13)蟒,(14)其他爬行动物
0106391010	(1)鹌鹑,(2)鹧鸪,(3)孔雀,(4)竹鸡,(5)松鸡,(6)锦鸡,(7)雉(山鸡),(8)乌骨鸡,(9)鸬鹚,(10)鹈鹕,(11)其他野生鸡形目禽鸟,(12)天鹅,(13)鸳鸯,(14)野鸭,(15)大雁,(16)其他野生雁形目禽鸟,(17)画眉,(18)杜鹃(野生禽鸟),(19)百灵,(20)金丝鸟,(21)相思鸟,(22)鹤,(23)鸵鸟,(24)鹂鹋,(25)朱鹮,(26)火烈鸟,(27)巨嘴鸟,(28)厚嘴妥空,(29)其他野生禽鸟
0106399010	(1)鹌鹑,(2)鹧鸪,(3)孔雀,(4)竹鸡,(5)松鸡,(6)锦鸡,(7)雉(山鸡),(8)乌骨鸡,(9)鸬鹚,(10)鹈鹕,(11)其他野生鸡形目禽鸟,(12)天鹅,(13)鸳鸯,(14)野鸭,(15)大雁,(16)其他野生雁形目禽鸟,(17)画眉,(18)杜鹃(野生禽鸟),(19)百灵,(20)金丝鸟,(21)相思鸟,(22)鹤,(23)鸵鸟,(24)鹂鹋,(25)朱鹮,(26)火烈鸟,(27)鹰,(28)巨嘴鸟,(29)厚嘴妥空,(30)其他野生禽鸟

HS 编码	CIQ 扩展品名
0106901910	(1)斑马,(2)犀,(3)貘,(4)其他野生奇蹄动物,(5)鹿,(6)长颈鹿,(7)黄羊,(8)河马,(9)羚牛,(10)羚羊,(11)青羊斑羚,(12)叉角羚,(13)骆马,(14)美洲驼,(15)角马,(16)梅花鹿,(17)马鹿,(18)其他野生偶蹄动物,(19)狐狸,(20)貂,(21)大熊猫,(22)小熊猫,(23)熊,(24)水獭,(25)果子狸,(26)狮,(27)虎,(28)豹,(29)貉,(30)豺,(31)狼,(32)大灵猫,(33)小灵猫,(34)野狗,(35)其他野生食肉动物,(36)旱獭,(37)松鼠,(38)花鼠,(39)麝鼠,(40)海狸鼠,(41)河狸,(42)地鼠,(43)豪猪,(44)其他野生啮齿动物,(45)其他野生灵长动物,(46)象,(47)刺猬,(48)穿山甲,(49)袋鼠,(50)蝙蝠,(51)其他野生哺乳动物
0106901990	(1)其他饲养奇蹄动物,(2)其他饲养偶蹄动物,(3)其他用途犬,(4)其他用途猫,(5)其他饲养食肉动物,(6)大鼠,(7)小鼠,(8)豚鼠,(9)其他饲养啮齿动物,(10)其他饲养兔形目动物,(11)其他饲养哺乳动物
0106909010	(1)其他饲养奇蹄动物,(2)其他饲养偶蹄动物,(3)其他用途犬,(4)其他用途猫,(5)其他饲养食肉动物,(6)大鼠,(7)小鼠,(8)豚鼠,(9)其他饲养啮齿动物,(10)其他饲养兔形目动物,(11)其他饲养哺乳动物,(12)斑马,(13)犀,(14)貘,(15)其他野生奇蹄动物,(16)鹿,(17)长颈鹿,(18)黄羊,(19)河马,(20)羚牛,(21)羚羊,(22)青羊(斑羚),(23)叉角羚,(24)骆马,(25)美洲驼,(26)角马,(27)梅花鹿,(28)马鹿,(29)其他野生偶蹄动物,(30)狐狸,(31)貂,(32)大熊猫,(33)小熊猫,(34)熊,(35)水獭,(36)果子狸,(37)狮,(38)虎,(39)豹,(40)貉,(41)豺,(42)狼,(43)大灵猫,(44)小灵猫,(45)野狗,(46)其他野生食肉动物,(47)旱獭,(48)松鼠,(49)花鼠,(50)麝鼠,(51)海狸鼠,(52)河狸,(53)地鼠,(54)豪猪,(55)其他野生啮齿动物,(56)其他野生灵长动物,(57)象,(58)刺猬,(59)穿山甲,(60)袋鼠,(61)蝙蝠,(62)其他野生哺乳动物,(63)牛蛙,(64)青蛙,(65)金线蛙,(66)棘胸蛙,(67)其他蛙,(68)大鲵娃娃鱼,(69)小鲵,(70)蟾蜍,(71)蝾螈,(72)鱼螈,(73)其他两栖动物,(74)蚕,(75)蟋蟀,(76)蚱蜢,(77)蝉,(78)蝴蝶,(79)其他昆虫其他动物,(80)禾虫,(81)蜈蚣其他动物,(82)蝎其他动物,(83)蚯蚓其他动物,(84)其他本章动物
0106909090	(1)其他饲养奇蹄动物,(2)其他饲养偶蹄动物,(3)伴侣犬,(4)工作犬,(5)其他用途犬,(6)伴侣猫,(7)其他用途猫,(8)其他饲养食肉动物,(9)大鼠,(10)小鼠,(11)豚鼠,(12)其他饲养啮齿动物,(13)其他饲养兔形目动物,(14)其他饲养哺乳动物,(15)牛蛙,(16)青蛙,(17)金线蛙,(18)棘胸蛙,(19)其他蛙,(20)娃娃鱼,(21)小鲵,(22)蟾蜍,(23)蝾螈,(24)鱼螈,(25)其他两栖动物,(26)蚕,(27)蟋蟀,(28)蚱蜢,(29)蝉,(30)蝴蝶,(31)其他昆虫(其他动物),(32)禾虫,(33)蜈蚣(其他动物),34 蝎(其他动物),35 蚯蚓(其他动物),(36)其他本章动物
204500000	(1)鲜的去骨山羊肉,(2)鲜的带骨山羊肉,(3)鲜的整头及半头山羊肉,(4)冷藏去骨山羊肉,(5)冷藏带骨山羊肉,(6)冷藏整头及半头山羊肉,(7)冻藏去骨山羊肉,(8)冻藏带骨山羊肉,(9)冻藏整头及半头山羊肉,(10)鲜的去骨野羊肉,(11)鲜的带骨野羊肉,(12)鲜的整头及半头野羊肉,(13)冷藏去骨野羊肉,(14)冷藏带骨野羊肉,(15)冻藏整头及半头野羊肉,(16)冻藏去骨野羊肉,(17)冻藏带骨野羊肉,(18)冷藏整头及半头野羊肉,(19)冷藏去骨山羊肉,6 月龄以下,(20)冷藏带骨山羊肉,6 月龄以下,(21)冷藏整头及半头山羊肉,6 月龄以下,(22)冻藏去骨山羊肉,6 月龄以下,(23)冻藏带骨山羊肉,6 月龄以下,(24)冻藏整头及半头山羊肉,6 月龄以下
0205000010	(1)鲜的去骨野马肉,(2)鲜的带骨野马肉,(3)鲜的整头及半头野马肉,(4)冷藏去骨野马肉,(5)冷藏带骨野马肉,(6)冷藏整头及半头野马肉,(7)冻藏去骨野马肉,(8)冻藏带骨野马肉,(9)冻藏整头及半头野马肉,(10)鲜的去骨野驴肉,(11)鲜的带骨野驴肉,(12)鲜的整头及半头野驴肉,(13)冷藏去骨野驴肉,(14)冷藏带骨野驴肉,(15)冷藏整头及半头野驴肉,(16)冻藏去骨野驴肉,(17)冻藏带骨野驴肉,(18)冻藏整头及半头野驴肉
0205000090	(1)鲜的去骨马肉,(2)鲜的带骨马肉,(3)鲜的整头及半头马肉,(4)冷藏去骨马肉,(5)冷藏带骨马肉,(6)冷藏整头及半头马肉,(7)冻藏去骨马肉,(8)冻藏带骨马肉,(9)冻藏整头及半头马肉,(10)鲜的去骨驴肉,(11)鲜的带骨驴肉,(12)鲜的整头及半头驴肉,(13)冻藏去骨驴肉,(14)冷藏带骨驴肉,(15)冷藏整头及半头驴肉,(16)冷藏去骨驴肉,(17)冻藏带骨驴肉,(18)冻藏整头及半头驴肉,(19)鲜的去骨骡肉,(20)鲜的带骨骡肉,(21)鲜的整头及半头骡肉,(22)冷藏去骨骡肉,(23)冷藏带骨骡肉,(24)冷藏整头及半头骡肉,(25)冻藏去骨骡肉,(26)冻藏带骨骡肉,(27)冻藏整头及半头骡肉
0206100000	(1)鲜的牛心,(2)冷藏牛心,(3)鲜的牛鞭,(4)冷藏牛鞭,(5)鲜的牛舌,(6)冷藏牛舌,(7)鲜的牛尾,(8)冷藏牛尾,(9)鲜的牛肝,(10)冷藏牛肝,(11)鲜的牛筋,(12)冷藏牛筋,(13)鲜的牛横膈膜,(14)冷藏牛横膈膜,(15)鲜的牛头及头块,(16)冷藏牛头及头块,(17)鲜的牛食用皮,(18)冷藏牛食用皮,(19)鲜的牛肾,(20)冷藏牛肾,(21)鲜的牛脚,(22)冷藏牛脚,(23)鲜的其他牛杂碎,(24)冷藏其他牛杂碎,(25)鲜的野牛心,(26)冷藏野牛心,(27)鲜的野牛舌,(28)冷藏野牛舌,(29)鲜的野牛尾,(30)冷藏野牛尾,(31)鲜的野牛肝,(32)冷藏野牛肝,(33)鲜的野牛筋,(34)冷藏野牛筋,(35)鲜的野牛横膈膜,(36)冷藏野牛横膈膜,(37)鲜的野牛头及头块,(38)冷藏野牛头及头块,(39)鲜的野牛食用皮,(40)冷藏野牛食用皮,(41)鲜的野牛肾,(42)冷藏野牛肾,(43)鲜的野牛脚,(44)冷藏野牛脚,(45)鲜的其他野牛杂碎,(46)冷藏其他野牛杂碎,(47)冷藏牛心 30 月龄以下,(48)冷藏牛舌 30 月龄以下,(49)冷藏牛尾 30 月龄以下,(50)冷藏牛肝 30 月龄以下,(51)冷藏牛筋 30 月龄以下,(52)冷藏牛横膈膜 30 月龄以下,(53)冷藏牛头及头块冰鲜牛头 30 月龄以下,(54)冷藏牛头及头块冰鲜牛唇 30 月龄以下,(55)冷藏牛肾 30 月龄以下,(56)冷藏牛脚冰鲜牛蹄 30 月龄以下,(57)冷藏其他牛杂碎冰鲜牛骨 30 月龄以下
0206290000	(1)牛心,(2)冻牛鞭,(3)冻牛尾,(4)冻牛筋,(5)牛横膈膜,(6)牛头及头块,(7)牛食用皮,(8)牛肾,(9)牛脚,(10)其他牛杂碎,(11)野牛心,(12)野牛尾,(13)野牛筋,(14)野牛横膈膜,(15)野牛头及头块,(16)野牛食用皮,(17)野牛肾,(18)野牛脚,(19)其他野牛杂碎,(20)牛心 30 月龄以下,(21)冻牛尾 30 月龄以下,(22)冻牛筋 30 月龄以下,(23)牛横膈膜 30 月龄以下,(24)牛头及头块冷冻牛头肉 30 月龄以下,(25)牛头及头块冷冻牛头肉,(26)牛头及头块冷冻牛唇,(27)牛头及头块冷冻牛唇 30 月龄以下,(28)牛肾 30 月龄以下,(29)牛脚去除蹄匣,(30)其他牛杂碎冷冻牛骨,(31)其他牛杂碎冷冻牛骨 30 月龄以下,(32)其他牛杂碎冷冻牛动脉管,(33)其他牛杂碎冷冻牛心管,(34)其他牛杂碎冷冻牛睾丸,(35)其他牛杂碎冷冻牛食管,(36)其他牛杂碎冷冻牛骨髓,(37)其他牛杂碎冷冻牛软骨,(38)其他牛杂碎冷冻牛软骨不含喉软骨
0206300000	(1)鲜的猪心,(2)冷藏猪心,(3)鲜的猪肝,(4)冷藏猪肝,(5)鲜的猪肺,(6)冷藏猪肺,(7)鲜的猪肾,(8)冷藏猪肾,(9)鲜的猪舌,(10)冷藏猪舌,(11)鲜的猪尾,(12)冷藏猪尾,(13)鲜的猪耳,(14)冷藏猪耳,(15)鲜的猪蹄,(16)冷藏猪蹄,(17)鲜的猪睾丸,(18)冷藏猪睾丸,(19)鲜的猪食用皮,(20)冷藏猪食用皮,(21)鲜的猪头及头块,(22)冷藏猪头及头块,(23)鲜的猪横膈膜,(24)冷藏猪横膈膜,(25)鲜的其他猪杂碎,(26)冷藏其他猪杂碎,(27)鲜的野猪心,(28)冷藏野猪心,(29)鲜的野猪肝,(30)冷藏野猪肝,(31)鲜的野猪肺,(32)冷藏野猪肺,(33)鲜的野猪肾,(34)冷藏野猪肾,(35)鲜的野猪舌,(36)冷藏野猪舌,(37)鲜的野猪尾,(38)冷藏野猪尾,(39)鲜的野猪耳,(40)冷藏野猪耳,(41)鲜的野猪蹄,(42)冷藏野猪蹄,(43)鲜的野猪全蹄,(44)冷藏野猪全蹄,(45)鲜的野猪睾丸,(46)冷藏野猪睾丸,(47)鲜的野猪食用皮,(48)冷藏野猪食用皮,(49)鲜的野猪头及头块,(50)冷藏野猪头及头块,(51)鲜的野猪横膈膜,(52)冷藏野猪横膈膜,(53)鲜的其他野猪杂碎,(54)冷藏其他野猪杂碎

HS编码	CIQ扩展品名
0206490000	(1)猪心,(2)猪肺,(3)猪肾,(4)猪舌,(5)猪尾,(6)猪耳,(7)猪蹄,(8)猪睾丸,(9)猪食用皮,(10)猪头及头块,(11)猪横膈膜,(12)其他猪杂碎,(13)野猪心,(14)野猪肺,(15)野猪肾,(16)野猪舌,(17)野猪尾,(18)野猪耳,(19)野猪蹄,(20)野猪全蹄,(21)野猪睾丸,(22)野猪食用皮,(23)野猪头及头块,(24)野猪横膈膜,(25)其他野猪杂碎,(26)猪耳不包括内耳,(27)猪耳冷冻猪耳根,(28)猪蹄全蹄,(29)猪蹄冷冻猪脚圈,(30)猪蹄冷冻猪脚趾,(31)猪头及头块冷冻猪脸,(32)猪头及头块冷冻猪头,(33)猪头及头块不包括内耳,(34)猪头及头块冷冻猪下颚,(35)猪头及头块冷冻猪鼻,(36)猪头及头块冷冻猪唇,(37)其他猪杂碎冷冻猪鞭,(38)其他猪杂碎冷冻猪喉骨,(39)其他猪杂碎冷冻猪气管,(40)其他猪杂碎冷冻猪脑,(41)其他猪杂碎冷冻猪食管,(42)其他猪杂碎冷冻猪心管,(43)其他猪杂碎冷冻猪软骨,(44)其他猪杂碎冷冻猪骨
0206800010	(1)饲料用绵羊肠,(2)饲料用绵羊真胃绵羊肚,(3)饲料用绵羊瓣胃绵羊百叶,(4)饲料用绵羊网胃,(5)饲料用绵羊瘤胃,(6)饲料用绵羊心,(7)饲料用绵羊肝,(8)饲料用绵羊肺,(9)饲料用绵羊肾,(10)饲料用其他绵羊杂碎,(11)饲料用山羊肠,(12)饲料用山羊真胃山羊肚,(13)饲料用山羊瓣胃山羊百叶,(14)饲料用山羊网胃,(15)饲料用山羊瘤胃,(16)饲料用山羊心,(17)饲料用山羊肝,(18)饲料用山羊肺,(19)饲料用山羊肾,(20)饲料用其他山羊杂碎,(21)鲜的绵羊心,(22)冷藏绵羊心,(23)鲜的绵羊肝,(24)冷藏绵羊肝,(25)鲜的绵羊肺,(26)冷藏绵羊肺,(27)鲜的绵羊肾,(28)冷藏绵羊肾,(29)鲜的绵羊舌,(30)冷藏绵羊舌,(31)鲜的绵羊睾丸,(32)冷藏绵羊睾丸,(33)鲜的绵羊蹄,(34)冷藏绵羊蹄,(35)鲜的绵羊头及头块,(36)冷藏绵羊头及头块,(37)鲜的其他绵羊杂碎,(38)冷藏其他绵羊杂碎,(39)鲜的山羊心,(40)冷藏山羊心,(41)鲜的山羊肝,(42)冷藏山羊肝,(43)鲜的山羊肺,(44)冷藏山羊肺,(45)鲜的山羊肾,(46)冷藏山羊肾,(47)鲜的山羊舌,(48)冷藏山羊舌,(49)鲜的山羊睾丸,(50)冷藏山羊睾丸,(51)鲜的山羊蹄,(52)冷藏山羊蹄,(53)鲜的山羊头及头块,(54)冷藏山羊头及头块,(55)鲜的其他山羊杂碎,(56)冷藏其他山羊杂碎,(57)鲜的野山羊心,(58)冷藏野山羊心,(59)鲜的野山羊肝,(60)冷藏野山羊肝,(61)鲜的野山羊肺,(62)冷藏野山羊肺,(63)鲜的野山羊肾,(64)冷藏野山羊肾,(65)鲜的野山羊舌,(66)冷藏野山羊舌,(67)鲜的野山羊睾丸,(67)冷藏野山羊睾丸,(68)鲜的野山羊脚,(69)冷藏野山羊脚,(70)鲜的野山羊头及头块,(71)冷藏野山羊头及头块,(72)鲜的其他野山羊杂碎,(73)冷藏其他野山羊杂碎
0206800090	(1)鲜的马心,(2)冷藏马心,(3)鲜的马肝,(4)冷藏马肝,(5)鲜的马肺,(6)冷藏马肺,(7)鲜的马肾,(8)冷藏马肾,(9)鲜的马舌,(10)冷藏马舌,(11)鲜的马睾丸,(12)冷藏马睾丸,(13)鲜的马脚,(14)冷藏马脚,(15)鲜的马头及头块,(16)冷藏马头及头块,(17)鲜的其他马杂碎,(18)冷藏其他马杂碎,(19)鲜的野马心,(20)冷藏野马心,(21)鲜的野马肝,(22)冷藏野马肝,(23)鲜的野马肺,(24)冷藏野马肺,(25)鲜的野马肾,(26)冷藏野马肾,(27)鲜的野马舌,(28)冷藏野马舌,(29)鲜的野马睾丸,(30)冷藏野马睾丸,(31)鲜的野马脚,(32)冷藏野马脚,(33)鲜的野马头及头块,(34)冷藏野马头及头块,(35)鲜的其他野马杂碎,(36)冷藏其他野马杂碎,(37)鲜的驴心,(38)冷藏驴心,(39)鲜的驴肝,(40)冷藏驴肝,(41)鲜的驴肺,(42)冷藏驴肺,(43)鲜的驴肾,(44)冷藏驴肾,(45)鲜的驴舌,(46)冷藏驴舌,(47)鲜的驴睾丸,(48)冷藏驴睾丸,(49)鲜的驴脚,(50)冷藏驴脚,(51)鲜的驴头及头块,(52)冷藏驴头及头块,(53)鲜的其他驴杂碎,(54)冷藏其他驴杂碎,(55)鲜的野驴心,(56)冷藏野驴心,(57)鲜的野驴肝,(58)冷藏野驴肝,(59)鲜的野驴肺,(60)冷藏野驴肺,(61)鲜的野驴肾,(62)冷藏野驴肾,(63)鲜的野驴舌,(64)冷藏野驴舌,(65)鲜的野驴睾丸,(66)冷藏野驴睾丸,(67)鲜的野驴脚,(68)冷藏野驴脚,(69)鲜的野驴头及头块,(70)冷藏野驴头及头块,(71)鲜的其他野驴杂碎,(72)冷藏其他野驴杂碎,(73)鲜的骡心,(74)冷藏骡心,(75)鲜的骡肝,(76)冷藏骡肝,(77)鲜的骡肺,(78)冷藏骡肺,(79)鲜的骡肾,(80)冷藏骡肾,(81)鲜的骡舌,(82)冷藏骡舌,(83)鲜的骡睾丸,(84)冷藏骡睾丸,(85)鲜的骡脚,(86)冷藏骡脚,(87)鲜的骡头及头块,(88)冷藏骡头及头块,(89)鲜的其他骡杂碎,(90)冷藏其他骡杂碎
0206900010	(1)饲料用绵羊肠,(2)饲料用绵羊真胃绵羊肚,(3)饲料用绵羊瓣胃绵羊百叶,(4)饲料用绵羊网胃,(5)饲料用绵羊瘤胃,(6)饲料用绵羊心,(7)饲料用绵羊肝,(8)饲料用绵羊肺,(9)饲料用绵羊肾,(10)饲料用其他绵羊杂碎,(11)饲料用山羊肠,(12)饲料用山羊真胃山羊肚,(13)饲料用山羊瓣胃山羊百叶,(14)饲料用山羊网胃,(15)饲料用山羊瘤胃,(16)饲料用山羊心,(17)饲料用山羊肝,(18)饲料用山羊肺,(19)饲料用山羊肾,(20)饲料用其他山羊杂碎,(21)绵羊心,(22)绵羊肝,(23)绵羊肺,(24)绵羊肾,(25)绵羊舌,(26)绵羊睾丸,(27)绵羊蹄,(28)绵羊头及头块,(29)其他绵羊杂碎,(30)山羊心,(31)山羊肝,(32)山羊肺,(33)山羊肾,(34)山羊舌,(35)山羊睾丸,(36)山羊蹄,(37)山羊头及头块,(38)其他山羊杂碎,(39)野羊心,(40)野羊肝,(41)野羊肺,(42)野羊肾,(43)野羊舌,(44)野羊睾丸,(45)野羊蹄,(46)野羊头及头块,(47)其他野羊杂碎,(48)绵羊蹄去除蹄匣,(49)绵羊头及头块冷冻绵羊脸颊肉,(50)其他绵羊杂碎冷冻绵羊鞭,(51)其他绵羊杂碎冷冻绵羊横膈膜,(52)其他绵羊杂碎,冷冻绵羊筋不包括蹄筋,(53)其他绵羊杂碎冷冻绵羊筋,(54)其他绵羊杂碎冷冻绵羊板筋,(55)其他绵羊杂碎冷冻绵羊尾,(56)其他绵羊杂碎冷冻绵羊软骨不含喉/声带软骨,(57)其他绵羊杂碎冷冻绵羊食管,(58)其他绵羊杂碎冷冻绵羊动脉管,(59)其他绵羊杂碎冷冻绵羊心管,(60)其他绵羊杂碎冷冻绵羊骨,(61)其他绵羊杂碎冷冻绵羊骨髓,(62)山羊蹄去除蹄匣,(63)山羊头及头块冷冻山羊脸颊肉,(64)其他山羊杂碎冷冻山羊鞭,(65)其他山羊杂碎冷冻山羊横膈膜,(66)其他山羊杂碎冷冻山羊筋不包括蹄筋,(67)其他山羊杂碎冷冻山羊筋,(68)其他山羊杂碎冷冻山羊板筋,(69)其他山羊杂碎冷冻山羊尾,(70)其他山羊杂碎冷冻山羊软骨不含喉/声带软骨,(71)其他山羊杂碎冷冻山羊食管,(72)其他山羊杂碎冷冻山羊动脉管,(73)其他山羊杂碎冷冻山羊心管,(74)其他山羊杂碎冷冻山羊骨,(75)其他山羊杂碎冷冻山羊骨髓
0206900090	(1)马心,(2)马肝,(3)马肺,(4)马肾,(5)马舌,(6)马睾丸,(7)马脚,(8)马头及头块,(9)其他马杂碎,(10)野马心,(11)野马肝,(12)野马肺,(13)野马肾,(14)野马舌,(15)野马睾丸,(16)野马脚,(17)野马头及头块,(18)其他野马杂碎,(19)驴心,(20)驴肝,(21)驴肺,(22)驴肾,(23)驴舌,(24)驴睾丸,(25)驴脚,(26)驴头及头块,(27)其他驴杂碎,(28)野驴心,(29)野驴肝,(30)野驴肺,(31)野驴肾,(32)野驴舌,(33)野驴睾丸,(34)野驴脚,(35)野驴头及头块,(36)其他野驴杂碎,(37)骡心,(38)骡肝,(39)骡肺,(40)骡肾,(41)骡舌,(42)骡睾丸,(43)骡脚,(44)骡头及头块,(45)其他骡杂碎,(46)其他驴杂碎,驴皮
0207260000	(1)鲜的带骨火鸡肉,不包括火鸡胸、火鸡腿,(2)冷藏带骨火鸡肉,不包括火鸡胸、火鸡腿,(3)鲜的其他火鸡肉,不包括火鸡胸、火鸡腿,(4)冷藏其他火鸡肉,不包括火鸡胸、火鸡腿,(5)鲜的的火鸡胸、火鸡腿,(6)冷藏的火鸡胸、火鸡腿,(7)鲜的火鸡爪,(8)冷藏火鸡爪,(9)鲜的火鸡肫、胃,(10)冷藏火鸡肫、胃,(11)鲜的火鸡翼,不包括翼尖,(12)冷藏火鸡翼,不包括翼尖,(13)鲜的火鸡翼,包括翼尖,(14)冷藏火鸡翼,包括翼尖,(15)鲜的火鸡颈,(16)冷藏火鸡颈,(17)其他鲜的火鸡杂碎,(18)其他冷藏火鸡杂碎
0207270000	(1)火鸡胸、火鸡腿,(2)火鸡肫、火鸡胃,(3)火鸡翼,不包括翼尖,(4)火鸡爪,(5)火鸡翼,包括翼尖,(6)火鸡颈,(7)其他火鸡肉,不包括火鸡胸、火鸡腿,(8)带骨火鸡肉,不包括火鸡胸、火鸡腿,(9)其他冻火鸡杂碎,(10)其他冻火鸡杂碎冷冻火鸡肾
0207440000	(1)鲜的鸭肉,(2)冷藏鸭肉,(3)鲜的鸭胸,(4)冷藏鸭胸,(5)鲜的鸭爪,(6)冷藏鸭爪,(7)鲜的鸭翼,不包括翼尖,(8)冷藏鸭翼,不包括翼尖,(9)鲜的鸭翼,包括翼尖,(10)冷藏鸭翼,包括翼尖,(11)鲜的鸭翼翼尖,(12)冷藏鸭翼翼尖,(13)鲜的鸭翼尖,(14)冷藏鸭翼尖,(15)鲜的鸭腿,(16)冷藏鸭腿,(17)鲜的鸭颈,(18)冷藏鸭颈.(19)鲜的鸭肫、胃,(20)冷藏鸭肫、胃,(21)鲜的其他鸭肉及杂碎,(22)冷藏其他鸭肉及杂碎

HS 编码	CIQ 扩展品名
0207450000	(1)鸭肉,(2)鸭胸,(3)鸭爪,(4)鸭翼,不包括翼尖,(5)鸭翼,包括翼尖,(6)鸭翼翼尖,(7)鸭翼尖,(8)鸭腿,(9)鸭肝,(10)鸭颈,(11)鸭肫、胃,(12)其他鸭肉及杂碎
0207540000	(1)鲜的鹅肉,(2)冷藏鹅肉,(3)鲜的鹅胸,(4)冷藏鹅胸,(5)鲜的鹅爪,(6)冷藏鹅爪,(7)鲜的鹅翼,不包括翼尖,(8)冷藏鹅翼,不包括翼尖,(9)鲜的鹅翼,包括翼尖,(10)冷藏鹅翼,包括翼尖,(11)鲜的鹅翼翼尖,(12)冷藏鹅翼翼尖,(13)鲜的鹅腿,(14)冷藏鹅腿,(15)鲜的鹅颈,(16)冷藏鹅颈,(17)鲜的其他鹅肉及杂碎,(18)冷藏其他鹅肉及杂碎
0207550000	(1)冻藏鹅肉,(2)冻藏鹅胸,(3)冻藏鹅爪,(4)冻藏鹅翼,不包括翼尖,(5)冻藏鹅鹅翼,包括翼尖,(6)冻藏鹅翼翼尖,(7)冻藏鹅腿,(8)冻藏鹅肝,(9)冻藏鹅颈,(10)冻藏其它鹅肉及杂碎
0208500000	(1)鲜的蛇肉,(2)冷藏蛇肉,(3)冻藏蛇肉,(4)鲜的鳄鱼肉,(5)冷藏鳄鱼肉,(6)冻藏鳄鱼肉,(7)鲜的龟肉,(8)冷藏龟肉,(9)冻藏龟肉,(10)鲜的甲鱼肉,(11)冷藏甲鱼肉,(12)冻藏甲鱼肉,(13)鲜的其他饲养爬行动物肉及食用杂碎,(14)冷藏其他饲养爬行动物肉及食用杂碎,(15)冻藏其他饲养爬行动物肉及食用杂碎,(16)鲜的其他野生爬行动物肉及食用杂碎,(17)冷藏其他野生爬行动物肉及食用杂碎,(18)冻藏其他野生爬行动物肉及食用杂碎
0208909010	(1)未列出的鲜的野生奇蹄动物肉,(2)未列出的冷藏野生奇蹄动物肉,(3)未列出的冻藏野生奇蹄动物肉,(4)鲜的野鹿肉,(5)冷藏野鹿肉,(6)冻藏野鹿肉,(7)鲜的骆驼肉,(8)冷藏骆驼肉,(9)冻藏骆驼肉,(10)未列出的鲜的野生偶蹄动物肉,(11)未列出的冷藏野生偶蹄动物肉,(12)未列出的冻藏野生偶蹄动物肉,(13)鲜的山鸡肉,(14)冷藏山鸡肉,(15)冻藏山鸡肉,(16)鲜的珍珠鸡肉,(17)冷藏珍珠鸡肉,(18)冻藏珍珠鸡肉,(19)鲜的竹鸡肉,(20)冷藏竹鸡肉,(21)冻藏竹鸡肉,(22)鲜的松鸡肉,(23)冷藏松鸡肉,(24)冻藏松鸡肉,(25)鲜的沙鸡肉,(26)冷藏沙鸡肉,(27)冻藏沙鸡肉,(28)鲜的石鸡肉,(29)冷藏石鸡肉,(30)冻藏石鸡肉,(31)鲜的榛鸡肉,(32)冷藏榛鸡肉,(33)冻藏榛鸡肉,(34)鲜的野鸭肉,(35)冷藏野鸭肉,(36)冻藏野鸭肉,(37)鲜的野鹅肉,(38)冷藏野鹅肉,(39)冻藏野鹅肉,(40)鲜的野鸽肉,(41)冷藏野鸽肉,(42)冻藏野鸽肉,(43)鲜的鹌鹑肉,(44)冷藏鹌鹑肉,(45)冻藏鹌鹑肉,(46)鲜的鹧鸪肉,(47)冷藏鹧鸪肉,(48)冻藏鹧鸪肉,(49)鲜的麻雀肉,(50)冷藏麻雀肉,(51)冻藏麻雀肉,(52)鲜的野生鸵鸟肉,(53)冷藏野生鸵鸟肉,(54)冻藏野生鸵鸟肉,(55)未列出的鲜的野生禽鸟肉,(56)未列出的冷藏野生禽鸟肉,(57)未列出的冻藏野生禽鸟肉,(58)鲜的熊肉,(59)冷藏熊肉,(60)冻藏熊肉,(61)鲜的袋鼠肉,(62)冷藏袋鼠肉,(63)冻藏袋鼠肉,(64)未列出其他的鲜的野生动物肉,(65)未列出其他的冷藏野生动物肉,(66)未列出其他的冻藏野生动物肉,(67)鲜、冷的两栖类,(68)冻的两栖类 ,(69)鲜、冷的爬行类 野,(70)冻的爬行类,(71)鲜、冷的海洋哺乳动物,(72)冻的海洋哺乳动物
0208909090	(1)未列出的鲜的饲养奇蹄动物肉,(2)未列出的冻藏饲养奇蹄动物肉,(3)未列出的鲜的饲养奇蹄动物杂碎,(4)未列出的冻藏饲养奇蹄动物杂碎,(5)鲜的鹿肉,(6)冷藏鹿肉,(7)冻藏鹿肉,(8)鲜的鹿心,(9)冷藏鹿心,(10)冻藏鹿心,(11)鲜的鹿肝,(12)冷藏鹿肝,(13)冻藏鹿肝,(14)鲜的鹿肺,(15)冷藏鹿肺,(16)冻藏鹿肺,(17)鲜的鹿肾,(18)冷藏鹿肾,(19)冻藏鹿肾,(20)鲜的鹿舌,(21)冷藏鹿舌,(22)冻藏鹿舌,(23)鲜的鹿鞭,(24)冷藏鹿鞭,(25)冻藏鹿鞭,(26)鲜的鹿睾丸,(27)冷藏鹿睾丸,(28)冻藏鹿睾丸,(29)鲜的其他鹿杂碎,(30)冷藏其他鹿杂碎,(31)冻藏其他鹿杂碎,(32)鲜的骆驼肉,(33)冷藏骆驼肉,(34)冻藏骆驼肉,(35)鲜的骆驼杂碎,(36)冷藏骆驼杂碎,(37)冻藏骆驼杂碎,(38)未列出的鲜的饲养偶蹄动物肉,(39)未列出的冷藏饲养偶蹄动物肉,(40)未列出的冻藏饲养偶蹄动物肉,(41)未列出的鲜的饲养偶蹄动物杂碎,(42)未列出的冷藏饲养偶蹄动物杂碎,(43)未列出的冻藏饲养偶蹄动物杂碎,(44)鲜的饲养鸵鸟肉,(45)冷藏饲养鸵鸟肉,(46)冻藏饲养鸵鸟肉,(47)鲜的饲养鸵鸟杂碎,(48)冷藏饲养鸵鸟杂碎,(49)冻藏饲养鸵鸟杂碎,(50)未列出的鲜的饲养禽鸟肉,(51)未列出的冷藏饲养禽鸟肉,(52)未列出的冻藏饲养禽鸟肉,(53)未列出的鲜的饲养禽鸟杂碎,(54)未列出的冷藏饲养禽鸟杂碎,(55)未列出的冻藏饲养禽鸟杂碎,(56)鲜的犬肉,(57)冷藏犬肉,(58)冻藏犬肉,(59)鲜的犬杂碎,(60)冷藏犬杂碎,(61)冻藏犬杂碎,(62)鲜的袋鼠肉,(63)冷藏袋鼠肉,(64)冻藏袋鼠肉,(65)鲜的袋鼠杂碎,(66)冷藏袋鼠杂碎,(67)冻藏袋鼠杂碎,(68)未列出的鲜的饲养动物肉,(69)未列出的冻藏饲养动物肉,(70)未列出的冷藏饲养动物肉,(71)未列出的鲜的饲养动物杂碎,(72)未列出的冷藏饲养动物杂碎,(73)未列出的冻藏饲养动物杂碎,(74)鲜的饲养牛蛙肉及食用杂碎,(75)冷藏饲养牛蛙肉及食用杂碎,(76)冻藏饲养牛蛙肉及食用杂碎,(77)鲜的其他饲养两栖动物肉及杂碎,(78)冷藏其他饲养两栖动物肉及杂碎,(79)冻藏其他饲养两栖动物肉及杂碎,(80)鲜的其他野生两栖动物肉及杂碎,(81)冷藏其他野生两栖动物肉及杂碎,(82)冻藏其他野生两栖动物肉及杂碎,(83)未列出的鲜的饲养爬行动物肉及杂碎,(84)未列出的冷藏饲养爬行动物肉及杂碎,(85)未列出的冻藏饲养爬行动物肉及杂碎,(86)未列出的鲜的野生爬行动物肉及杂碎,(87)未列出的冷藏野生爬行动物肉及杂碎,(88)未列出的冻藏野生爬行动物肉及杂碎,(89)未列出的鲜的饲养海洋哺乳动物肉及杂碎,(90)未列出的冷藏饲养海洋哺乳动物肉及杂碎,(91)未列出的冻藏饲养海洋哺乳动物肉及杂碎,(92)未列出的鲜的野生海洋哺乳动物肉及杂碎,(93)未列出的冷藏野生海洋哺乳动物肉及杂碎,(94)未列出的冻藏野生海洋哺乳动物肉及杂碎,(95)冻藏其他鹿杂碎冷冻鹿尾,(96)冻藏其他鹿杂碎冷冻鹿筋,不包括鹿蹄筋,(97)冻藏其他鹿杂碎冷冻鹿肌腱
0209100000	(1)工业用肥猪肉(不带瘦肉),(2)工业用猪油脂,(3)饲料用肥猪肉(不带瘦肉),(4)饲料用猪油脂,(5)饲料用野生猪、牛、羊油脂,(6)未炼制的鲜的食用纯肥猪肉,(7)未炼制的冷藏食用纯肥猪肉,(8)未炼制的冻藏食用纯肥猪肉,(9)未炼制的干制食用纯肥猪肉,(10)未炼制的熏制食用纯肥猪肉,(11)未炼制的盐制食用纯肥猪肉,(12)未炼制的鲜的食用猪脂肪,(13)未炼制的冷藏食用猪脂肪,(14)未炼制的冻藏食用猪脂肪,(15)未炼制的干制食用猪脂肪,(16)未炼制的熏制食用猪脂肪,(17)未炼制的盐制食用猪脂肪,(18)用其他方法提取的鲜的食用纯肥猪肉,(19)用其他方法提取的冷藏食用纯肥猪肉,(20)用其他方法提取的冻藏食用纯肥猪肉,(21)用其他方法提取的干制食用纯肥猪肉,(22)用其他方法提取的熏制食用纯肥猪肉,(23)用其他方法提取的盐制食用纯肥猪肉,(24)用其他方法提取的鲜的食用猪脂肪,(25)用其他方法提取的冷藏食用猪脂肪,(26)用其他方法提取的冻藏食用猪脂肪,(27)用其他方法提取的干制食用猪脂肪,(28)用其他方法提取的熏制食用猪脂肪,(29)用其他方法提取的盐制食用猪脂肪,(30)冰鲜未炼制猪脂肪(食用,不包括内脏脂肪),(31)冷冻未炼制猪脂肪(食用,不包括内脏脂肪)
0209900000	(1)工业用禽油脂,(2)饲料用禽油脂,(3)未炼制的鲜的食用家禽脂肪,(4)未炼制的冷藏食用家禽脂肪,(5)未炼制的冻藏食用家禽脂肪,(6)未炼制的干制食用家禽脂肪,(7)未炼制的熏制食用家禽脂肪,(8)未炼制的盐制食用家禽脂肪,(9)包括鲜、冷、冻、干、熏、盐制的用其他方法提取的鲜的食用家禽脂肪,(10)包括鲜、冷、冻、干、熏、盐制的用其他方法提取的冷藏食用家禽脂肪,(11)包括鲜、冷、冻、干、熏、盐制的用其他方法提取的冻藏食用家禽脂肪,(12)用其他方法提取的干制食用家禽脂肪,(13)包括鲜、冷、冻、干、熏、盐制的用其他方法提取的熏制食用家禽脂肪,(14)用其他方法提取的盐制食用家禽脂肪,(15)冷冻未炼制鸡脂肪(食用,不包括内脏脂肪)
0301991990	(1)草鱼,(2)鳙鱼(胖头鱼),(3)鲢鱼,(4)青鱼,(5)鲶鱼(鲇鱼),(6)武昌鱼,(7)大马哈鱼,(8)黄鳝,(9)泥鳅,(10)鲫鱼,(11)牛头鲴鱼,(12)斑点叉尾鮰鱼,(13)黄蜡鲳鱼(狮鼻鲳鱼参),(14)多瑙哲罗鱼,(15)其他淡水鱼,(16)海鳗,(17)鲽鱼,(18)红鱼(似石首鱼),(19)牙鲆鱼,(20)石斑鱼,(21)大鲮鲆鱼,(22)带鱼,(23)鲳鱼,(24)鲑鱼,(25)金枪鱼,(26)鲱鱼,(27)鲣鱼,(28)沙丁鱼,(29)黄鱼,(30)鲨鱼,(31)鲭鱼,(32)鳀鱼,(33)鳕鱼,(34)鲳鱼,(35)卡拉白鱼,(36)其他海水鱼,(37)金鱼,(38)锦鲤,(39)其他鱼,(40)其他受精卵

HS 编码	CIQ 扩展品名
0301999990	(1)草鱼,(2)鳙鱼(胖头鱼),(3)鲢鱼,(4)青鱼,(5)淡水鲈鱼,(6)鲶鱼(鲇鱼),(7)武昌鱼,(8)大马哈鱼,(9)黄鳝,(10)泥鳅,(11)鲫鱼,(12)鲟鱼,(13)牛头鲖鱼,(14)斑点叉尾鲖鱼,(15)黄蜡鲳鱼(狮鼻鲳鱼参),(16)罗非鱼,(17)多瑙哲罗鱼,(18)其他淡水鱼,(19)海鳗,(20)鲽鱼,(21)红鱼(似石首鱼),(22)牙鲆鱼,(23)石斑鱼,(24)大鲮鲆鱼,(25)海水鲈鱼,(26)带鱼,(27)鳎鱼,(28)鲑鱼,(29)金枪鱼,(30)鲱鱼,(31)鲣鱼,(32)沙丁鱼,(33)黄鱼,(34)鲨鱼,(35)鲭鱼,(36)鳀鱼,(37)鳕鱼,(38)鲳鱼,(39)卡拉白鱼,(40)其他海水鱼,(41)金鱼,(42)锦鲤,(43)其他鱼
0302110000	(1)养殖河鳟,(2)养殖虹鳟,(3)野生河鳟,(4)野生虹鳟,(5)克拉克大麻哈鱼,(6)阿瓜大麻哈鱼,(7)吉雨大麻哈鱼,(8)亚利桑那大麻哈鱼,(9)金腹大麻哈鱼
0302130000	(1)养殖红大麻哈鱼,(2)养殖细磷大麻哈鱼,(3)养殖大麻哈鱼,(4)养殖大鳞大麻哈鱼,(5)养殖银大麻哈鱼,(6)养殖马苏大麻哈鱼,(7)养殖玫瑰大麻哈鱼,(8)野生红大麻哈鱼,(9)野生细磷大麻哈鱼,(10)野生大麻哈鱼,(11)野生大鳞大麻哈鱼,(12)野生银大麻哈鱼,(13)野生马苏大麻哈鱼,(14)野生玫瑰大麻哈鱼
0302430000	(1)饲料用沙丁鱼、黍鲱鱼,(2)沙丁鱼、沙瑙鱼属,(3)养殖小沙丁鱼属,(4)养殖黍鲱,(5)养殖西鲱,(6)沙丁鱼、沙瑙鱼属,(7)野生小沙丁鱼属,(8)野生黍鲱,(9)野生西鲱
0302490000	(1)羽鳃鲐属,(2)马鲛属,(3)鲹属,(4)鲳属,(5)鲜或冷秋刀鱼,(6)圆鲹属,(7)毛鳞鱼,(8)鲜或冷鲔鱼,(9)狐鲣属,(10)鲜或冷枪鱼,(11)鲜或冷旗鱼,(12)旗鱼科
0302590000	(1)饲料用其他海水鱼,(2)犀鳕科,(3)多丝真鳕科,(4)鳕科,(5)长尾鳕科,(6)黑鳕科,(7)无须鳕科,(8)深海鳕科,(9)南极鳕科
0302730000	(1)饲料用其他海水鱼,(2)养殖鲤属,(3)养殖鲫属,(4)养殖草鱼,(5)养殖鲢属,(6)养殖鲮属,(7)养殖青鱼,(8)卡特拉鲃、野鲮属、哈氏纹唇鱼、何氏细须鲃、鲂属,(9)野生鲤属,(10)野生鲫属,(11)野生草鱼,(12)野生鲢属,(13)野生鲮属,(14)野生青鱼,(15)卡特拉鲃、野鲮属、哈氏纹唇鱼、何氏细须鲃、鲂属
0302899090	(1)饲料用马面鱼,(2)饲料用其他海水鱼,(3)养殖石斑鱼,(4)养殖鲥鱼,(5)养殖鲷科,菱羊鲷除外(非生食),(6)养殖鲷科,菱羊鲷除外(可能用于生食),(7)养殖安康鱼(非生食),(8)养殖安康鱼(可能用于生食),(9)养殖海鲂,(10)养殖鲆鱼,(11)养殖鲽鱼,(12)其他养殖鱼(非生食),(13)其他养殖鱼(可能用于生食),(14)黄狮鱼(非生食),(15)黄狮鱼(可能用于生食),(16)养殖海鲈鱼(非生食),(17)养殖海鲈鱼(可能用于生食),(18)野生石斑鱼,(19)野生鲥鱼,(20)野生鲷科,菱羊鲷除外,(21)野生安康鱼,(22)野生海鲂,(23)野生鲆鱼,(24)野生鲽鱼,(25)海鲫鱼,(26)金线鱼,(27)马面鱼,(28)马鲛鱼,(29)野生海鲈鱼(非生食),(30)野生海鲈鱼(可能用于生食),(31)其他野生鱼(非生食),(32)其他野生鱼(可能用于生食)
0302910010	(1)鲜或冷养殖濒危鱼鱼肝,(2)鲜或冷野生濒危鱼鱼肝,(3)鲜或冷养殖濒危鱼鱼卵,(4)鲜或冷野生濒危鱼鱼卵,(5)鲜或冷养殖濒危鱼鱼精,(6)鲜或冷野生濒危鱼鱼精
0302910090	(1)其他鲜或冷养殖鱼鱼肝,(2)其他鲜或冷野生鱼鱼肝,(3)其他鲜或冷养殖鱼鱼卵,(4)其他鲜或冷野生鱼鱼卵,(5)其他鲜或冷养殖鱼鱼精,(6)其他鲜或冷野生鱼鱼精
0303120000	(1)养殖细磷大麻哈鱼,(2)养殖大麻哈鱼,(3)养殖大鳞大麻哈鱼,(4)养殖银大麻哈鱼,(5)养殖马苏大麻哈鱼,(6)养殖玫瑰大麻哈鱼,(7)野生细磷大麻哈鱼,(8)野生大麻哈鱼,(9)野生大鳞大麻哈鱼,(10)野生银大麻哈鱼,(11)野生马苏大麻哈鱼,(12)野生玫瑰大麻哈鱼
0303140000	(1)养殖河鳟,(2)养殖虹鳟,(3)野生河鳟,(4)野生虹鳟,(5)克拉克大麻哈鱼,(6)阿瓜大麻哈鱼,(7)吉雨大麻哈鱼,(8)亚利桑那大麻哈鱼,(9)金腹大麻哈鱼
0303240000	(1)饲料用其他海水鱼,(2)养殖(鱼芒)鲶属,(3)养殖胡鲶属,(4)养殖真鲖属,(5)野生(鱼芒)鲶属,(6)野生胡鲶属,(7)野生真鲖属
0303250000	(1)饲料用其他海水鱼,(2)养殖鲤属,(3)养殖鲫属,(4)养殖草鱼,(15)卡特拉鲃、野鲮属、哈氏纹唇鱼、何氏细须鲃、鲂属,(14)野生青鱼,(5)养殖鲢属,(6)养殖鲮属,(7)养殖青鱼,(8)卡特拉鲃、野鲮属、哈氏纹唇鱼、何氏细须鲃、鲂属,(9)野生鲤属,(10)野生鲫属,(11)野生草鱼,(12)野生鲢属,(13)野生鲮属
0303390090	(1)养殖鲽科,(2)养殖鲆科,(3)养殖舌鳎科,(4)养殖鳎科,(5)养殖菱鲆科,(6)养殖刺鲆科,(7)野生鲽科,(8)野生鲆科,(9)野生舌鳎科,(10)野生鳎科,(11)野生菱鲆科,(12)野生刺鲆科
0303530000	(1)但子目 0303.91 至 0303.99 的可食用鱼杂碎除外饲料用沙丁鱼、黍鲱鱼,(2)沙丁鱼、沙瑙鱼属,(3)养殖小沙丁鱼属,(4)养殖黍鲱,(5)养殖西鲱,(6)沙丁鱼、沙瑙鱼属,(7)野生小沙丁鱼属,(8)野生黍鲱,(9)野生西鲱
0303550000	(1)饲料用其他海水鱼,(2)养殖对称竹荚鱼,(3)养殖新西兰竹荚鱼及竹荚鱼(竹荚鱼属),(4)野生对称竹荚鱼,(5)野生新西兰竹荚鱼及竹荚鱼(竹荚鱼属)
0303590090	(1)鳀属,(2)羽鳃鲐属,(3)马鲛属,(4)鲹属,(5)鲳属,(6)冻的秋刀鱼,(7)圆鲹属,(8)毛鳞鱼,(9)冻的鲔鱼,(10)狐鲣属,(11)冻的枪鱼,(12)冻的旗鱼,(13)旗鱼科
0303899090	(1)饲料用马面鱼,(2)饲料用其他海水鱼,(3)养殖石斑鱼,(4)养殖鲥鱼,(5)养殖鲷科,(6)养殖安康鱼,(7)养殖海鲂,(8)养殖鲆鱼,(9)养殖鲽鱼,(10)养殖红鱼,(11)其他养殖鱼,(12)野生石斑鱼,(13)野生鲥鱼,(14)野生鲷科,(15)野生安康鱼,(16)野生海鲂,(17)野生鲆鱼,(18)野生鲽鱼,(19)野生红鱼,(20)海鲫鱼,(21)金线鱼,(22)马面鱼,(23)马鲛鱼,(24)蓝圆鲹,(25)其他野生鱼
0303910010	(1)养殖冷冻鱼鱼肝,(2)野生冷冻鱼鱼肝,(3)养殖冷冻鱼鱼卵,(4)野生冷冻鱼鱼卵,(5)养殖冷冻鱼鱼精,(6)野生冷冻鱼鱼精
0303910090	(1)养殖冷冻鱼鱼肝,(2)野生冷冻鱼鱼肝,(3)养殖冷冻鱼鱼卵,(4)野生冷冻鱼鱼卵,(5)养殖冷冻鱼鱼精,(6)野生冷冻鱼鱼精
0304390090	(1)养殖西鲤,(2)养殖黑鲫,(3)养殖草鱼,(4)养殖鲢属,(5)养殖鲮属,(6)养殖青鱼,(7)鳗鲡属,(8)养殖黑鱼(鳢属),(9)野生西鲤,(10)野生黑鲫,(11)野生草鱼,(12)野生鲢属,(13)野生鲮属,(14)野生青鱼,(15)其他野生鳗鱼(鳗鲡属),(16)野生黑鱼(鳢属)
0304430000	(1)养殖鲽科,(2)养殖鲆科,(3)养殖舌鳎科,(4)养殖鳎科,(5)养殖菱鲆科,(6)养殖刺鲆科,(7)野生鲽科,(8)野生鲆科,(9)野生舌鳎科,(10)野生鳎科,(11)野生菱鲆科,(12)野生刺鲆科
0304510090	(1)养殖罗非鱼(口孵非鲫属),(2)养殖鲶鱼(鱼芒)鲶属,(3)养殖胡鲶属,(4)养殖真鲖属,(5)养殖鲤属,(6)养殖鲫属,(7)养殖草鱼,(8)养殖鲢属,(9)养殖鲮属,(10)养殖青鱼,(11)养殖其他鳗鱼(鳗鲡属),(12)养殖尼罗河鲈鱼(尼罗尖吻鲈),(13)养殖黑鱼(鳢属),(14)野生罗非鱼(口孵非鲫属),(15)野生鲶鱼(鱼芒)鲶属,(16)野生胡鲶属,(17)野生真鲖属,(18)野生鲤属,(19)野生鲫属,(20)野生草鱼,(21)野生鲢属,(22)野生鲮属,(23)野生青鱼,(24)野生其他鳗鱼(鳗鲡属),(25)野生尼罗河鲈鱼(尼罗尖吻鲈),(26)野生黑鱼(鳢属),(27)养殖鲶属,(28)养殖其他鲤科鱼(卡特拉鲃、野鲮属、哈氏纹唇鱼、何氏细须鲃、鲂属),(29)野生鲶属,(30)野生其他鲤科鱼(卡特拉鲃、野鲮属、哈氏纹唇鱼、何氏细须鲃、鲂属)

HS编码	CIQ扩展品名
0304530000	(1)犀鳕科,(2)多丝真鳕科,(3)鳕科,(4)长尾鳕科,(5)黑鳕科,(6)无须鳕科,(7)深海鳕科,(8)南极鳕科
0304590090	(1)养殖石斑鱼,(2)养殖鲥鱼,(3)养殖鲷科(非生食),(4)养殖鲷科(可能用于生食),(5)养殖安康鱼,(6)养殖海鲂,(7)养殖鲆鱼,(8)养殖其他鱼,(9)野生鲷科(非生食),(10)野生鲷科(可能用于生食),(11)野生石斑鱼,(12)野生鲥鱼,(13)野生安康鱼,(14)野生海鲂,(15)野生鲆鱼,(16)野生鲽鱼,(17)海鲫鱼,(18)金线鱼,(19)马面鱼,(20)马鲛鱼,(21)野生其他鱼
0304629000	(1)养殖(鱼芒)鲶属,(2)养殖胡鲶属,(3)养殖真鮰属,(4)野生(鱼芒)鲶属,(5)野生胡鲶属,(6)野生真鮰属,(7)养殖鲶属,(8)野生鲶属
0304690090	(1)冻的养殖鲤属,(2)冻的养殖鲫属,(3)冻的养殖草鱼,(4)冻的养殖鲢属,(5)冻的养殖鲮属,(6)冻的养殖青鱼,(7)养殖其他鳗鱼(鳗鲡属),(8)养殖黑鱼(鳢属),(9)冻的野生鲤属,(10)冻的野生鲫属,(11)冻的野生草鱼,(12)冻的野生鲢属,(13)冻的野生鲮属,(14)冻的野生青鱼,(15)野生其他鳗鱼(鳗鲡属),(16)野生黑鱼(鳢属),(17)养殖其他鲤科鱼(卡特拉鲃、野鲮属、哈氏纹唇鱼、何氏细须鲃、鲂属),(18)野生其他鲤科鱼(卡特拉鲃、野鲮属、哈氏纹唇鱼、何氏细须鲃、鲂属)
0304810000	(1)养殖大西洋鲑鱼(非生食),(2)养殖大西洋鲑鱼(可能用于生食),(3)养殖红大麻哈鱼,(4)养殖细磷大麻哈鱼,(5)养殖大麻哈鱼,(6)养殖大鳞大麻哈鱼,(7)养殖银大麻哈鱼,(8)养殖马苏大麻哈鱼,(9)养殖玫瑰大麻哈鱼,(10)野生大西洋鲑鱼(非生食),(11)野生大西洋鲑鱼(可能用于生食),(12)野生红大麻哈鱼,(13)野生细磷大麻哈鱼,(14)野生大麻哈鱼,(15)野生大鳞大麻哈鱼,(16)野生银大麻哈鱼,(17)野生马苏大麻哈鱼,(18)野生玫瑰大麻哈鱼,(19)多瑙哲罗鱼
0304820000	(1)养殖河鳟,(2)养殖虹鳟,(3)野生河鳟,(4)野生虹鳟,(5)克拉克大麻哈鱼,(6)阿瓜大麻哈鱼,(7)吉雨大麻哈鱼鱼,(8)亚利桑那大麻哈鱼,(9)金腹大麻哈鱼
0304830000	(1)养殖鲽科,(2)养殖鲆科,(3)养殖舌鳎科,(4)养殖鳎科,(5)养殖菱鲆科,(6)养殖刺鲆科,(7)野生鲽科,(8)野生鲆科,(9)野生舌鳎科,(10)野生鳎科,(11)野生菱鲆科,(12)野生刺鲆科
0304930090	(1)冻的养殖罗非鱼(口孵非鲫属),(2)冻的养殖(鱼芒)鲶属,(3)冻的养殖胡鲶属,(4)冻的养殖真鮰属,(5)冻的养殖鲤属,(6)冻的养殖鲫属,(7)冻的养殖草鱼,(8)冻的养殖鲢属,(9)冻的养殖鲮属,(10)冻的养殖青鱼(鲤科鱼),(11)冻的养殖其他鳗鱼(鳗鲡属),(12)冻的养殖尼罗河鲈鱼(尼罗尖吻鲈),(13)冻的养殖黑鱼(鳢属),(14)冻的野生罗非鱼(口孵非鲫属)),(15)冻的野生(鱼芒)鲶属,(16)冻的野生胡鲶属,(17)冻的野生真鮰属,(18)冻的野生鲤属,(19)冻的野生鲫属,(20)冻的野生草鱼,(21)冻的野生鲢属,(22)冻的野生鲮属,(23)冻的野生青鱼,(24)冻的野生其他鳗鱼(鳗鲡属),(25)冻的野生尼罗河鲈鱼(尼罗尖吻鲈),(26)冻的野生黑鱼(鳢属),(27)冻的养殖鲶属,(28)冻的养殖其他鲤科鱼(卡特拉鲃、野鲮属、哈氏纹唇鱼、何氏细须鲃、鲂属),(29)冻的野生鲶属,(30)冻的野生其他鲤科鱼(卡特拉鲃、野鲮属、哈氏纹唇鱼、何氏细须鲃、鲂属)
0304990090	(1)养殖石斑鱼,(2)养殖鲥鱼,(3)养殖鲷科,(4)养殖安康鱼,(5)养殖海鲂,(6)养殖鲆鱼,(7)养殖鲽鱼,(8)养殖红鱼,(9)养殖其他鱼,(10)野生石斑鱼,(11)野生鲥鱼,(12)野生鲷科,(13)野生安康鱼,(14)野生海鲂,(15)野生鲆鱼,(16)野生鲽鱼,(17)野生红鱼,(18)海鲫鱼,(19)金线鱼,(20)马面鱼,(21)马鲛鱼,(22)野生其他鱼
0305200010	(1)干制的养殖濒危鱼鱼肝,(2)干制的野生濒危鱼鱼肝,(3)干制的养殖濒危鱼鱼卵,(4)干制的野生濒危鱼鱼卵,(5)干制的养殖濒危鱼鱼精,(6)干制的野生濒危鱼鱼精,(7)熏制的养殖濒危鱼鱼肝,(8)熏制的野生濒危鱼鱼肝,(9)熏制的养殖濒危鱼鱼卵,(10)熏制的野生濒危鱼鱼卵,(11)熏制的养殖濒危鱼鱼精,(12)熏制的野生濒危鱼鱼精,(13)盐制的养殖濒危鱼鱼肝,(14)盐制的野生濒危鱼鱼肝,(15)盐制的养殖濒危鱼鱼卵,(16)盐制的野生濒危鱼鱼卵,(17)盐制的养殖濒危鱼鱼精,(18)盐制的野生濒危鱼鱼精
0305200090	(1)其他干制的养殖鱼鱼肝,(2)其他干制的野生鱼鱼肝,(3)其他干制的养殖鱼鱼卵,(4)其他干制的野生鱼鱼卵,(5)其他干制的养殖鱼鱼精,(6)其他干制的野生鱼鱼精,(7)其他熏制的养殖鱼鱼肝,(8)其他熏制的野生鱼鱼肝,(9)其他熏制的养殖鱼鱼卵,(10)其他熏制的野生鱼鱼卵,(11)其他熏制的养殖鱼鱼精,(12)其他熏制的野生鱼鱼精,(13)其他盐制的养殖鱼鱼肝,(14)其他盐制的野生鱼鱼肝,(15)其他盐制的养殖鱼鱼卵,(16)其他盐制的野生鱼鱼卵,(17)其他盐制的养殖鱼鱼精,(18)其他盐制的野生鱼鱼精
0305320000	(1)干制的犀鳕科,(2)干制的多丝真鳕科,(3)干制的鳕科,(4)干制的长尾鳕科,(5)干制的黑鳕科,(6)干制的无须鳕科,(7)干制的深海鳕科,(8)干制的南极鳕科,(9)盐腌或盐渍的犀鳕科,(10)盐腌或盐渍的多丝真鳕科,(11)盐腌或盐渍的鳕科,(12)盐腌或盐渍的长尾鳕科,(13)盐腌或盐渍的黑鳕科,(14)盐腌或盐渍的无须鳕科,(15)盐腌或盐渍的深海鳕科,(16)盐腌或盐渍的南极鳕科
0305390090	(1)干制的养殖石斑鱼,(2)干制的养殖鲥鱼,(3)干制的养殖鲷科,(4)干制的养殖安康鱼,(5)干制的养殖海鲂,(6)干制的养殖鲆鱼,(7)干制的养殖鲽鱼,(8)干制的养殖红鱼,(9)干制的养殖杂鱼,(10)盐腌或盐渍的养殖石斑鱼,(11)盐腌或盐渍的养殖鲥鱼,(12)盐腌或盐渍的养殖鲷科,(13)盐腌或盐渍的养殖安康鱼,(14)盐腌或盐渍的养殖海鲂,(15)盐腌或盐渍的养殖鲆鱼,(16)盐腌或盐渍的养殖鲽鱼,(17)盐腌或盐渍的养殖红鱼,(18)盐腌或盐渍的养殖杂鱼,(19)干制的野生石斑鱼,(20)干制的野生鲥鱼,(21)干制的野生鲷科,(22)干制的野生安康鱼,(23)干制的野生海鲂,(24)干制的野生鲆鱼,(25)干制的野生鲽鱼,(26)干制的野生红鱼,(27)干制的海鲫鱼,(28)干制的金线鱼,(29)干制的马面鱼,(30)干制的马鲛鱼,(31)干制的野生杂鱼,(32)盐腌或盐渍的野生石斑鱼,(33)盐腌或盐渍的野生鲥鱼,(34)盐腌或盐渍的野生鲷科,(35)盐腌或盐渍的野生安康鱼,(36)盐腌或盐渍的野生海鲂,(37)盐腌或盐渍的野生鲆鱼,(38)盐腌或盐渍的野生鲽鱼,(39)盐腌或盐渍的野生红鱼,(40)盐腌或盐渍的海鲫鱼,(41)盐腌或盐渍的金线鱼,(42)盐腌或盐渍的马面鱼,(43)盐腌或盐渍的马鲛鱼,(44)盐腌或盐渍的野生杂鱼
0305420000	(1)养殖大西洋鲱鱼,(2)养殖太平洋鲱鱼,(3)野生大西洋鲱鱼,(4)野生太平洋鲱鱼
0305430000	(1)养殖河鳟,(2)养殖虹鳟,(3)野生河鳟,(4)野生虹鳟,(5)克拉克大麻哈鱼,(6)阿瓜大麻哈鱼,(7)吉雨大麻哈鱼,(8)亚利桑那大麻哈鱼,(9)金腹大麻哈鱼
0305490090	(1)熏制的养殖石斑鱼,(2)熏制的养殖鲥鱼,(3)熏制的养殖鲷科,(4)熏制的养殖安康鱼,(5)熏制的养殖海鲂,(6)熏制的养殖鲆鱼,(7)熏制的养殖鲽鱼,(8)熏制的养殖红鱼,(9)熏制的其他养殖鱼,(10)熏制的野生石斑鱼,(11)熏制的野生鲥鱼,(12)熏制的野生鲷科,(13)熏制的野生安康鱼,(14)熏制的野生海鲂,(15)熏制的野生鲆鱼,(16)熏制的野生鲽鱼,(17)熏制的野生红鱼,(18)熏制的海鲫鱼,(19)熏制的金线鱼,(20)熏制的马面鱼,(21)熏制的马鲛鱼,(22)熏制的其他野生鱼
0305599090	(1)干制的养殖石斑鱼,(2)干制的养殖鲥鱼,(3)干制的养殖鲷科,(4)干制的养殖安康鱼,(5)干制的养殖海鲂,(6)干制的养殖鲆鱼,(7)干制的养殖鲽鱼,(8)干制的养殖红鱼,(9)干制的养殖其他鱼,(10)干制的野生石斑鱼,(11)干制的野生鲥鱼,(12)干制的野生鲷科,(13)干制的野生安康鱼,(14)干制的野生海鲂,(15)干制的野生鲆鱼,(16)干制的野生鲽鱼,(17)干制的野生红鱼,(18)干制的海鲫鱼,(19)干制的金线鱼,(20)干制的马面鱼,(21)干制的马鲛鱼,(22)干制的野生其他鱼

HS编码	CIQ扩展品名
0305699090	(1)盐腌或盐渍的养殖石斑鱼,(2)盐腌或盐渍的养殖鲥鱼,(3)盐腌或盐渍的养殖鲷科鱼,(4)盐腌或盐渍的养殖安康鱼,(5)盐腌或盐渍的养殖海鲂,(6)盐腌或盐渍的养殖鲆鱼,(7)盐腌或盐渍的养殖鲽鱼,(8)盐腌或盐渍的养殖红鱼,(9)盐腌或盐渍的养殖其他鱼,(10)盐腌或盐渍的野生石斑鱼,(11)盐腌或盐渍的野生鲥鱼,(12)盐腌或盐渍的野生鲷科鱼,(13)盐腌或盐渍的野生安康鱼,(14)盐腌或盐渍的野生海鲂,(15)盐腌或盐渍的野生鲆鱼,(16)盐腌或盐渍的野生鲽鱼,(17)盐腌或盐渍的野生红鱼,(18)盐腌或盐渍的海鲫鱼,(19)盐腌或盐渍的金线鱼,(20)盐腌或盐渍的马面鱼,(21)盐腌或盐渍的马鲛鱼,(22)盐腌或盐渍的其他野生其他鱼
0306149019	(1)冻的养殖毛蟹,(2)仿岩蟹,(3)冻的养殖堪察加拟石蟹,(4)冻的养殖短足拟石蟹,(5)冻的养殖扁足拟石蟹,(6)冻的养殖雪蟹,(7)冻的养殖日本雪蟹,(8)冻的野生毛蟹,(9)冻的野生仿石蟹(仿岩蟹),(10)冻的野生堪察加拟石蟹,(11)冻的野生短足拟石蟹,(12)冻的野生扁足拟石蟹,(13)冻的野生雪蟹,(14)冻的野生日本雪蟹
0306149090	(1)饲料用青蟹,(2)饲料用其他海水蟹,(3)饲料用淡水蟹,(4)养殖花蟹,(5)养殖软壳蟹,(6)养殖老虎蟹,(7)养殖青蟹,(8)养殖中华绒螯蟹,(9)养殖其他蟹,(10)野生花蟹,(11)野生软壳蟹,(12)野生老虎蟹,(13)野生青蟹,(14)帝王蟹,(15)雪蟹,(16)毛蟹,(17)面包蟹,(18)棕蟹,(19)蜘蛛蟹,(20)野生其他蟹
0306171100	(1)养殖河虾,(2)养殖罗氏沼虾,(3)养殖其他小虾,(4)野生河虾,(5)野生红虾,(6)野生罗氏沼虾,(7)野生其他小虾
0306171900	(1)养殖河虾,(2)养殖罗氏沼虾,(3)养殖其他小虾,(4)野生河虾,(5)野生红虾,(6)野生罗氏沼虾,(7)野生其他小虾
0306319000	(1)活龙虾,(2)鲜或冷的带壳或去壳养殖岩礁虾,(3)鲜或冷的带壳或去壳野生岩礁虾,(4)鲜或冷的带壳或去壳养殖其他龙虾(真龙虾属、龙虾属、岩龙虾属),(5)鲜或冷的带壳或去壳野生其他龙虾(真龙虾属、龙虾属、岩龙虾属)
0306339919	(1)其他海水虾蟹,(2)鲜或冷的养殖毛蟹,(3)鲜或冷的养殖仿石蟹(仿岩蟹),(4)鲜或冷的养殖堪察加拟石蟹,(5)鲜或冷的养殖短足拟石蟹,(6)鲜或冷的养殖扁足拟石蟹,(7)鲜或冷的养殖雪蟹,(8)鲜或冷的养殖日本雪蟹,(9)鲜或冷的养殖金霸王蟹(帝王蟹),(10)鲜或冷的野生毛蟹,(11)鲜或冷的野生仿石蟹(仿岩蟹),(12)鲜或冷的野生堪察加拟石蟹,(13)鲜或冷的野生短足拟石蟹,(14)鲜或冷的野生扁足拟石蟹,(15)鲜或冷的野生雪蟹,(16)鲜或冷的野生日本雪蟹,(17)鲜或冷的野生金霸王蟹(帝王蟹)
0306339990	(1)活的青蟹,(2)活的其他海水虾蟹,(5)饲料用淡水蟹,(4)饲料用其他海水蟹,(3)饲料用青蟹,(6)鲜或冷的养殖青蟹,(7)鲜或冷的野生青蟹,(8)其他鲜或冷的带壳或去壳养殖蟹,(9)其他鲜或冷的带壳或去壳野生蟹
0306359090	(1)活的南美白对虾,(2)活的斑节对虾,(3)活的其他对虾,(4)活的其他海水虾蟹,(5)青虾,(6)马来沼虾,(7)活的其他淡水虾蟹,(8)活的虾蛄,(9)活的糠虾,(10)活的其他甲壳动物
0306369090	(1)活的南美白对虾,(2)活的斑节对虾,(3)活的其他对虾,(4)活的其他海水虾蟹,(5)青虾,(6)马来沼虾,(7)活的其他淡水虾蟹,(8)活的虾蛄,(9)活的糠虾,(10)活的其他甲壳动物
0306391000	(1)其他海水虾蟹,(2)青虾,(3)马来沼虾,(4)中华小长臂虾,(5)其他淡水虾蟹,(6)虾蛄,(7)糠虾,(8)其他甲壳动物,(9)鳖卵,(10)龟卵
0306931000	(1)养殖干制蟹类制品,(2)野生干制蟹类制品,(3)养殖盐腌及盐渍蟹类制品,(4)野生盐腌及盐渍蟹类制品
0306932000	(1)养殖干制蟹类制品,(2)野生干制蟹类制品,(3)养殖盐腌及盐渍蟹类制品,(4)野生盐腌及盐渍蟹类制品
0306940000	(1)养殖干制虾类制品,(2)野生干制虾类制品,(3)养殖盐腌及盐渍虾类制品,(4)野生盐腌及盐渍虾类制品
0306959000	(1)养殖干制虾类制品,(2)野生干制虾类制品,(5)养殖盐腌及盐渍虾类制品,(6)野生盐腌及盐渍虾类制品
0306990000	(1)活的其他淡水虾蟹,(2)未列出的饲料用其他淡水产品,(3)鲜、冷的其他养殖甲壳动物,(4)鲜、冷的其他野生甲壳动物,(5)干制的其他养殖甲壳动物,(6)干制的其他野生甲壳动物,(7)盐腌或盐渍的其他养殖甲壳动物,(8)盐腌或盐渍的其他野生甲壳动物
0307219090	(1)活的扇贝,(2)非生食的鲜、冷的养殖扇贝,(3)可用于生食的鲜、冷的养殖扇贝,(4)非生食的鲜、冷的野生扇贝,(5)可用于生食的鲜、冷的野生扇贝
0307429100	(1)活的乌贼(墨鱼),(2)活的鱿鱼,(3)饲料用乌贼,(4)饲料用鱿鱼,(5)其他鲜、冷的养殖墨鱼(乌贼属、巨粒僧头乌贼、耳乌贼属),(6)其他鲜、冷的野生墨鱼(乌贼属、巨粒僧头乌贼、耳乌贼属),(7)其他鲜、冷的养殖鱿鱼(柔鱼属、枪乌贼属、双柔鱼属、拟乌贼属),(8)其他鲜、冷的野生鱿鱼(柔鱼属、枪乌贼属、双柔鱼属、拟乌贼属)
0307429900	(1)活的乌贼(墨鱼),(2)活的鱿鱼,(3)饲料用乌贼,(4)饲料用鱿鱼,(5)其他鲜、冷的养殖墨鱼,(6)其他鲜、冷的野生墨鱼,(7)其他鲜、冷的养殖鱿鱼,(8)其他鲜、冷的野生鱿鱼
0307431000	(1)冻的养殖墨鱼(乌贼属、巨粒僧头乌贼、耳乌贼属),(2)冻的野生墨鱼(乌贼属、巨粒僧头乌贼、耳乌贼属),(3)冻的养殖鱿鱼(柔鱼属、枪乌贼属、双柔鱼属、拟乌贼属),(4)冻的野生鱿鱼(柔鱼属、枪乌贼属、双柔鱼属、拟乌贼属)
0307491000	(1)干制的养殖墨鱼(乌贼属、巨粒僧头乌贼、耳乌贼属),(2)干制的野生墨鱼(乌贼属、巨粒僧头乌贼、耳乌贼属),(3)干制的养殖鱿鱼(柔鱼属、枪乌贼属、双柔鱼属、拟乌贼属),(4)干制的野生鱿鱼(柔鱼属、枪乌贼属、双柔鱼属、拟乌贼属),(5)盐制的养殖墨鱼(乌贼属、巨粒僧头乌贼、耳乌贼属),(6)盐制的野生墨鱼(乌贼属、巨粒僧头乌贼、耳乌贼属),(7)盐制的养殖鱿鱼(柔鱼属、枪乌贼属、双柔鱼属、拟乌贼属),(8)盐制的野生鱿鱼(柔鱼属、枪乌贼属、双柔鱼属、拟乌贼属)
0307499000	(1)其他干制的养殖墨鱼,(2)其他干制的野生墨鱼,(3)其他干制的养殖鱿鱼,(4)其他干制的野生鱿鱼,(5)其他盐制的养殖墨鱼,(6)其他盐制的野生墨鱼,(7)其他盐制的养殖鱿鱼,(8)其他盐制的野生鱿鱼
0307609090	(1)活的田螺,(2)活的蜗牛,(3)鲜、冷的养殖蜗牛及螺,(4)鲜、冷的野生蜗牛及螺,(5)冻的养殖蜗牛及螺,(6)冻的野生蜗牛及螺,(7)干的养殖蜗牛及螺,(8)干的野生蜗牛及螺,(9)盐腌或盐渍的养殖蜗牛及螺,(10)盐腌或盐渍的野生蜗牛及螺
0307719100	(1)活的其他海水贝,(2)活的其他淡水贝,(3)活的其他软体及其他水生无脊椎动物,(4)鲜、冷的养殖蛤,(5)鲜、冷的野生蛤
0307719990	(1)鲜、冷的鸟蛤,(2)鲜、冷的舟贝,(3)非生食的鲜、冷的赤贝,(4)可用于生食的鲜、冷的赤贝,(5)鲜、冷的养殖缢蛏,(6)活的文蛤,(7)活的食用杂色蛤,(8)活的紫石房蛤,(9)赤贝,(10)活的泥蚶,(11)活的缢蛏,(12)活的其他鸟蛤及舟贝
0307720090	(1)冻的其他养殖蛤,(2)冻的其他野生蛤,(3)冻的养殖鸟蛤,(4)冻的野生鸟蛤,(5)冻的养殖舟贝,(6)冻的野生舟贝,(7)冻的养殖缢蛏,(8)冻的养殖扇贝,(9)冻的野生扇贝,(10)冻的野生北极贝,(11)冻的养殖杂色蛤
0307790090	(1)干制的其他养殖蛤,(2)干制的其他野生蛤,(3)干制的其他养殖鸟蛤,(4)干制的其他野生鸟蛤,(5)干制的其他养殖舟贝,(6)干制的其他野生舟贝,(7)盐制的其他养殖蛤,(8)盐制的其他野生蛤,(9)盐制的其他养殖鸟蛤,(10)盐制的其他野生鸟蛤,(11)盐制的其他养殖舟贝,(12)盐制的其他野生舟贝

HS 编码	CIQ 扩展品名
0307911090	(1)毛蚶(赤贝),(2)泥蚶,(3)文蛤,(4)杂色蛤苗,(5)大竹蛏,(6)缢蛏,(7)紫石房蛤,(8)海螺,(9)象拔蚌,(10)其他海水贝,(11)河蚌,(12)河蚬,(13)其他淡水贝,(14)其他软体及其他水生无脊椎动物
0307919090	(1)活的软体动物,(2)非生食的养殖北极贝,(3)可用于生食的养殖北极贝,(4)非生食的野生北极贝,(5)可用于生食的野生北极贝,(6)鲜、冷的其他养殖双壳贝类,(7)鲜、冷的其他野生双壳贝类,(8)鲜、冷的其他养殖单壳贝类,(9)鲜、冷的其他野生单壳贝类,(10)鲜、冷的养殖头足类,(11)鲜、冷的其他野生头足类,(12)鲜、冷的其他养殖软体动物,(13)鲜、冷的其他野生软体动物,(14)活的有害软体动物,(15)活的海螺
0308901990	(1)饲料用红赤虫,(2)饲料用丰年虫,(3)鲜或冷,(4)鲜或冷的其他养殖棘皮类,(5)鲜或冷的其他野生棘皮类,(6)活的珊瑚虫,(7)活的海鞘,(8)活的食用海肠,(9)活的饲料用海肠,(10)活的其他食用水生无脊椎动物,(11)活的其他饲料用水生无脊椎动物,(12)活的其他种用观赏水生无脊椎动物
0308909010	(1)其他冻的养殖濒危水生无脊椎动物,(2)其他冻的野生濒危水生无脊椎动物,(3)其他干制的养殖濒危水生无脊椎动物,(4)其他干制的野生濒危水生无脊椎动物,(5)其他盐制的养殖濒危水生无脊椎动物,(6)其他盐制的野生濒危水生无脊椎动物
0308909090	(1)其他冷冻的养殖棘皮类,(2)其他冷冻的野生棘皮类,(3)其他冻的养殖水生无脊椎动物,(4)其他冻的野生水生无脊椎动物,(5)其他干制的养殖水生无脊椎动物,(6)其他干制的野生水生无脊椎动物,(7)其他盐制的养殖水生无脊椎动物,(8)其他盐制的野生水生无脊椎动物
0401200000	(1)巴氏杀菌乳,(2)超高温灭菌乳,(3)保持灭菌乳,(4)巴氏杀菌工艺调制乳,(5)生乳,(6)其他乳与乳制品,(7)其他调制乳,(8)灭菌工艺调制乳
0401400000	(1)稀奶油,(2)淡炼乳,(3)加糖炼乳,(4)调制淡炼乳,(5)其他乳与乳制品
0401500000	(1)稀奶油,(2)奶油,(3)无水奶油,(4)淡炼乳,(5)加糖炼乳,(6)调制淡炼乳,(7)其他乳与乳制品
0402210000	(1)全脂乳粉,(3)部分脱脂乳粉,(4)儿童调制乳粉,(5)其他乳与乳制品,(6)孕产妇调制乳粉,(7)其他调制乳粉
0402910000	(1)巴氏杀菌工艺调制乳,(2)稀奶油,(3)奶油,(4)无水奶油,(5)其他奶油,(6)淡炼乳,(7)调制淡炼乳,(8)其他炼乳,(9)其他乳与乳制品,(10)灭菌工艺调制乳,(11)其他调制乳
0402990000	(1)巴氏杀菌工艺调制乳,(2)稀奶油,(3)奶油,(4)无水奶油,(5)其他奶油,(6)加糖炼乳,(7)调制加糖炼乳,(8)其他炼乳,(9)其他乳与乳制品,(10)灭菌工艺调制乳,(11)其他调制乳
0407290090	(1)食用鸭蛋,(2)食用鹅蛋,(3)食用鸽蛋,(4)食用鹌鹑蛋,(5)食用鹧鸪蛋,(6)食用火鸡蛋,(7)食用鸵鸟蛋,(8)食用
0408990000	(1)即食蛋沙律,(2)其他食用蛋制品,(3)全蛋液,(4)蛋黄液,(5)蛋白液,(6)冰全蛋,(7)冰蛋黄,(8)冰蛋白
0410009090	(1)食用龟蛋,(2)食用鳖蛋,(3)其他两栖类动物食用蛋品,(4)其他爬行类动物食用蛋品,(5)批准为新食品原料,(6)其他未列出的动物源性食品
0502901910	(1)野猪毛(鬃),(2)野牛毛(绒),(3)野羊毛(绒),(4)獾毛,(5)其他饲养奇蹄动物鬃毛,(6)其他野生奇蹄动物鬃毛,(7)其他饲养偶蹄动物鬃毛,(8)其他野生偶蹄动物鬃毛,(9)未列出的其他动物鬃毛
0502901990	(1)牛毛,(2)牦牛毛,(3)水牛毛,(4)绵羊毛,(5)山羊毛,(6)野猪毛(鬃),(7)野牛毛(绒),(8)野羊毛(绒),(9)獾毛,(10)其他饲养奇蹄动物鬃毛,(11)其他野生奇蹄动物鬃毛,(12)其他饲养偶蹄动物鬃毛,(13)其他野生偶蹄动物鬃毛,(14)未列出的其他动物鬃毛
0502902010	(1)獾毛,(2)其他饲养奇蹄动物鬃毛,(3)其他野生奇蹄动物鬃毛,(4)其他饲养偶蹄动物鬃毛,(5)其他野生偶蹄动物鬃毛,(6)未列出的其他动物鬃毛
0502902090	(1)獾毛,(2)其他饲养奇蹄动物鬃毛,(3)其他野生奇蹄动物鬃毛,(4)其他饲养偶蹄动物鬃毛,(5)其他野生偶蹄动物鬃毛,(6)未列出的其他动物鬃毛
0504001900	(1)鲜、冷、冻猪肠衣,(2)干、熏的猪肠衣,(3)鲜、冷、冻牛肠衣,(4)干、熏、盐腌或腌渍的牛肠衣,(5)鲜、冷、冻绵羊肠衣,(6)干、熏的绵羊肠衣,(7)鲜、冷、冻山羊肠衣,(8)干、熏的山羊肠衣,(9)鲜、冷、冻鹿肠衣,(10)干、熏、盐腌或腌渍的鹿肠衣,(11)鲜、冷、冻其他动物肠衣,(12)干、熏、盐腌或腌渍的其他动物肠衣,(13)(干、熏、盐腌或腌渍的牛肠衣)(牛肠衣(盐渍),(14)鲜、冷、冻山羊肠衣)(山羊肠衣(冷冻),(15)(鲜、冷、冻猪肠衣)(猪肠衣(冷冻),(16)(鲜、冷、冻绵羊肠衣)(绵羊肠衣(冷冻)
0504002900	(1)鲜、冷、冻的猪胃、猪肚,(2)干、熏、盐腌或盐渍的猪胃、猪肚,(3)鲜、冷、冻的牛真胃,(4)鲜、冷、冻的牛瓣胃、牛百叶,(5)鲜、冷、冻的牛网胃,(6)鲜、冷、冻的牛瘤胃,(7)干、熏、盐腌或盐渍的牛真胃,(8)干、熏、盐腌或盐渍的牛瓣胃、牛百叶,(9)干、熏、盐腌或盐渍的牛网胃,(10)干、熏、盐腌或盐渍的牛瘤胃,(11)鲜、冷、冻的绵羊真胃,(12)鲜、冷、冻的绵羊瓣胃、绵羊百叶,(13)鲜、冷、冻的绵羊网胃,(14)鲜、冷、冻的绵羊瘤胃,(15)干、熏、盐腌或盐渍的绵羊真胃,(16)干、熏、盐腌或盐渍的绵羊瓣胃、绵羊百叶,(17)干、熏、盐腌或盐渍的绵羊网胃,(18)干、熏、盐腌或盐渍的绵羊瘤胃,(19)鲜、冷、冻的山羊真胃,(20)鲜、冷、冻的山羊瓣胃、山羊百叶,(21)鲜、冷、冻的山羊网胃,(22)鲜、冷、冻的山羊瘤胃,(23)干、熏、盐腌或盐渍的山羊真胃,(24)干、熏、盐腌或盐渍的山羊瓣胃、山羊百叶,(25)干、熏、盐腌或盐渍的山羊网胃,(26)干、熏、盐腌或盐渍的山羊瘤胃,(27)鲜、冷、冻的鹿真胃,(28)鲜、冷、冻的鹿瓣胃、鹿百叶,(29)鲜、冷、冻的鹿网胃,(30)鲜、冷、冻的鹿瘤胃,(31)干、熏、盐腌或盐渍的鹿真胃,(32)干、熏、盐腌或盐渍的鹿瓣胃、鹿百叶,(33)干、熏、盐腌或盐渍的鹿网胃,(34)干、熏、盐腌或盐渍的鹿瘤胃,(35)鲜、冷、冻的其他动物的胃,(36)干、熏、盐腌或盐渍的其他动物的胃,(37)鲜、冷、冻的猪胃、猪肚冷冻猪胃,(38)鲜、冷、冻的牛真胃冷冻牛真胃,(39)鲜、冷、冻的牛瓣胃、牛百叶冰鲜牛瓣胃 30 月龄以下,(40)鲜、冷、冻的牛瓣胃、牛百叶冷冻牛瓣胃,(41)鲜、冷、冻的牛瓣胃、牛百叶冷冻牛瓣胃 30 月龄以下,(42)鲜、冷、冻的牛网胃冷冻牛网胃,(43)鲜、冷、冻的牛瘤胃冷冻牛瘤胃,(44)鲜、冷、冻的绵羊真胃冷冻绵羊真胃,(45)鲜、冷、冻的绵羊瓣胃、绵羊百叶冷冻绵羊瓣胃,(46)鲜、冷、冻的绵羊网胃冷冻绵羊网胃,(47)鲜、冷、冻的绵羊瘤胃冷冻绵羊瘤胃,(48)鲜、冷、冻的山羊真胃冷冻山羊真胃,(49)鲜、冷、冻的山羊瓣胃、山羊百叶冷冻山羊瓣胃,(50)鲜、冷、冻的山羊网胃冷冻山羊网胃,(51)鲜、冷、冻的山羊瘤胃冷冻山羊瘤胃
0504009000	(1)鲜、冷、冻的猪肠,(2)干、熏、盐腌或盐渍的猪肠,(3)鲜、冷、冻的猪膀胱,(4)干、熏、盐腌或盐渍的猪膀胱,(5)鲜、冷、冻的牛肠,(6)干、熏、盐腌或盐渍的牛肠,(7)鲜、冷、冻的牛膀胱,(8)干、熏、盐腌或盐渍的牛膀胱,(9)鲜、冷、冻的绵羊肠,(10)干、熏、盐腌或盐渍的绵羊肠,(11)鲜、冷、冻的绵羊膀胱,(12)干、熏、盐腌或盐渍的绵羊膀胱,(13)鲜、冷、冻的山羊肠,(14)干、熏、盐腌或盐渍的山羊肠,(15)鲜、冷、冻的山羊膀胱,(16)干、熏、盐腌或盐渍的山羊膀胱,(17)鲜、冷、冻的鹿肠,(18)干、熏、盐腌或盐渍的鹿肠,(19)鲜、冷、冻的鹿膀胱,(20)干、熏、盐腌或盐渍的鹿膀胱,(21)鲜、冷、冻的其他动物肠,(22)干、熏、盐腌或盐渍的其他动物肠,(23)鲜、冷、冻的其他动物膀胱,(24)干、熏、盐腌或盐渍的其他动物膀胱
0505901000	(1)鸡毛,(2)鸭毛,(3)鸭绒,(4)鹅毛,(5)鹅绒,(6)火鸡毛,(7)其他禽鸟羽毛

HS 编码	CIQ 扩展品名
0505909090	(1)鸡毛,(2)鸭毛,(3)鸭绒,(4)鹅毛,(5)鹅绒,(6)火鸡毛,(7)其他禽鸟羽毛
0506100000	(1)猪骨,(2)猪蹄壳,(3)牛骨,(4)牛蹄壳,(5)含饲养偶蹄动物的杂骨、骨块、骨粒(工业用牛骨粒、羊骨粒、猪骨粒除外),(6)其他饲养偶蹄动物骨、蹄、角,(7)未列出的其他动物骨、蹄、角
0506901190	(1)饲料用牛骨粉(骨成分67%以上),(2)饲料用羊骨粉(骨成分67%以上),(3)饲料用混合型饲养偶蹄动物骨粉
0506901990	(1)饲料用猪骨粉(骨成分67%以上),(2)饲料用混合型饲养偶蹄动物骨粉,(3)饲料用其他饲养偶蹄动物粉,(4)饲料用野生偶蹄猪、牛、羊骨粉(骨成分67%以上),(5)饲料用其他动物骨粉(骨成份67%以上),(6)饲料用其他动物蹄粉,(7)饲料用其他动物角粉,(8)未列出的饲料用其他动物粉
0507100030	(1)含饲养偶蹄动物的杂骨、骨块、骨粒,(2)其他饲养偶蹄动物骨、蹄、角,(3)其他野生偶蹄动物骨、蹄、角,(4)象牙,(5)未列出的其他动物骨、蹄、角,(6)河马牙
0507100090	(1)含饲养偶蹄动物的杂骨、骨块、骨粒(工业用牛骨粒、羊骨粒、猪骨粒除外),(2)其他饲养偶蹄动物骨、蹄、角,(3)其他野生偶蹄动物骨、蹄、角,(4)未列出的其他动物骨、蹄、角,(5)工业用牛骨粒,(6)工业用羊骨粒,(7)工业用猪骨粒
0507902000	(1)饲养鹿的鹿茸,(2)非饲养鹿的鹿茸,(3)药用鹿茸,(4)药用马鹿茸
0507909010	(1)饲养鹿的鹿角(工业用烘干鹿角除外),(2)含饲养偶蹄动物的杂骨、骨块、骨粒,(3)其他饲养偶蹄动物骨、蹄、角,(4)非饲养鹿的鹿角(工业用烘干鹿角除外),(5)其他野生偶蹄动物骨、蹄、角,(6)未列出的其他动物骨、蹄、角,(7)工业用烘干鹿角,(8)药用水牛角,(9)药用龟甲,(10)药用鳖甲,(11)药用鹿角
0507909090	(1)猪蹄壳,(2)牛蹄壳,(3)牛角(工业用烘干牛角除外),(4)饲养鹿的鹿角(工业用烘干鹿角除外),(5)含饲养偶蹄动物的杂骨、骨块、骨粒(工业用牛骨粒、羊骨粒、猪骨粒除外),(6)其他饲养偶蹄动物骨、蹄、角,(7)非饲养鹿的鹿角(工业用烘干鹿角除外),(8)其他野生偶蹄动物骨、蹄、角,(9)未列出的其他动物骨、蹄、角,(10)工业用牛骨粒,(11)工业用羊骨粒,(12)工业用猪骨粒,(13)包括蹄,甲,爪及喙及其粉末和废料,(14)工业用烘干牛角,(15)药用水牛角,(16)药用龟甲,(17)药用鳖甲,(18)药用鹿角
0508001090	(1)药用瓦楞子,(2)药用海螵蛸,(3)药用蛤壳,(4)药用石决明,(5)药用牡蛎(壳),(6)药用珍珠母,(7)未列出的饲料用其他动物粉,(8)未经加工虾蟹壳
0510001010	(1)药用牛黄,(2)药用人工牛黄,(3)药用体外培育牛黄
0510009090	(1)药用九香虫,(2)药用虫白蜡,(3)药用土鳖虫,(4)药用蝉蜕,(5)药用僵蚕,(6)药用桑螵蛸,(7)药用地龙,(8)药用蜈蚣,(9)药用全蝎,(10)药用鸡内金,(11)药用猪胆粉,(12)药用哈蟆油,(13)药用蛇蜕,(14)药用水蛭,(18)其他药用动物源性中药材
0511911190	(1)鲈鱼卵,(2)鲑鱼卵,(3)鲟鱼卵,(4)牙鲆鱼卵,(5)虹鳟鱼卵,(6)河鲀鱼卵,(7)大鲮鲆鱼卵,(8)其他受精卵
0511991090	(1)猪精液,(2)绵羊精液,(3)山羊精液,(4)马精液,(5)其他精液
0511992090	(1)牛胚胎,(2)猪胚胎,(3)马胚胎,(4)绵羊胚胎,(5)山羊胚胎,(6)其他胚胎
0511994010	(1)马鬃毛(含马尾毛)(未经加工马(鬃)尾毛除外),(2)其他饲养奇蹄动物鬃毛,(3)野马鬃毛(含尾毛)(未经加工马(鬃)尾毛除外),(4)其他野生奇蹄动物鬃毛,(5)未经加工马(鬃)尾毛
0511994090	(1)马鬃毛(含马尾毛)(未经加工马(鬃)尾毛除外),(2)其他饲养奇蹄动物鬃毛,(3)野马鬃毛(含尾毛),(4)其他野生奇蹄动物鬃毛,(5)未经加工马(鬃)尾毛
0511999010	(1)其他动物卵细胞,(2)其他动物繁殖材料,(3)其他野生奇蹄动物鬃毛,(4)其他野生偶蹄动物鬃毛,(5)偶蹄动物标本,(6)奇蹄动物标本,(7)禽鸟标本,(8)爬行动物标本,(9)其他动物标本,(10)动物尸体,(11)未经加工马属动物(鬃)尾毛,(12)未经加工鹿毛,(13)未经加工负鼠毛
0511999090	(1)鳖卵,(2)龟卵,(3)蚕卵,(4)牛卵细胞,(5)猪卵细胞,(6)绵羊卵细胞,(7)山羊卵细胞,(8)其他动物卵细胞,(9)其他动物繁殖材料,(10)其他昆虫(其他动物),(11)其他饲养奇蹄动物鬃毛,(12)其他饲养偶蹄动物鬃毛,(13)其他禽鸟羽毛,(14)蚕茧(未经加工的蚕茧除外),(15)蚕蛹(未经加工的蚕蛹除外),(16)其他蚕产品(不包含蚕丝等纺织原料),(17)偶蹄动物标本,(18)奇蹄动物标本,(19)禽鸟标本,(20)爬行动物标本,(21)其他动物标本,(22)动物尸体,(23)药用穿山甲(鳞片)),(24)药用蛤蚧,(25)药用蟾酥,(26)药用金钱白花蛇,(27)药用蕲蛇,(28)药用乌梢蛇,(29)宠物食品加工用动物副产品,(30)未经加工的蚕茧,(31)未经加工的蚕蛹,(32)未经加工的长吐,滞头,(33)未经加工的蜂巢,(34)未经加工的蜂胶,(35)未经加工马属动物(鬃)尾毛,(36)未经加工鹿毛,(37)未经加工负鼠毛
0601109199	(1)球根海棠,(2)其他观赏花木,(3)洋葱(鳞球块根茎),(4)蒜(种用),(5)芋艿(种用),(6)郁金香球茎,(7)朱顶兰球茎,(8)睡莲块根,(9)水仙花球茎,(10)其他鳞球块根茎
0601200099	(1)洋葱(鳞球块根茎),(2)蒜(种用),(3)芋艿(种用)),(4)甘薯块茎,(5)百合球茎,(6)郁金香球茎,(7)朱顶兰球茎,(8)睡莲块根,(9)水仙花球茎,(10)其他鳞球块根茎
0602201000	(1)芭蕉苗木,(2)番石榴苗木,(3)柑桔苗木,(4)海棠苗木,(5)胡桃苗木,(6)梨苗木,(7)李苗木,(8)荔枝苗木,(9)芒果苗木,(10)葡萄苗木,(11)苹果苗木,(12)木瓜苗木,(13)山核桃苗木,(14)山楂苗木,(15)柿苗木,(16)香蕉苗木,(17)杏苗木,(18)椰子苗木,(19)枇杷苗木,(20)橄榄苗木,(21)桃苗木,(22)草莓苗木,(23)樱桃苗木,(24)甘蔗苗木,(25)木莓苗木,(26)其他果树苗木,(27)其他组培苗
0602909110	(1)春兰,(2)君子兰,(3)蝴蝶兰,(4)惠兰,(5)石槲兰,(6)卡特利亚兰,(7)舞女兰,(8)兰花,(9)其他组培苗,(10)营养体
0602909191	(1)其他林木苗木,(2)其他观赏花木,(3)其他组培苗,(4)营养体
0602909199	(1)白腊槭苗木,(2)长叶松苗木,(3)岛松苗木,(4)其他松属苗木,(5)黄檀苗木,(6)柳苗木,(7)榆苗木,(8)杉属苗木,(9)梧桐苗木,(10)棕榈苗木,(11)栎树苗木,(12)槟榔苗木,(13)其他林木苗木,(14)牡丹,(15)安祖花,(16)其他观赏花木,(17)其他组培苗,(18)营养体
0602909991	(1)其他观赏花木,(2)其他盆景,(3)组培苗,(4)营养体

HS 编码	CIQ 扩展品名
0602909999	(1)长春花,(2)复盆子,(3)龙舌兰,(4)水仙,(5)黄杨,(6)郁金香,(7)茶花,(8)春兰,(9)君子兰,(10)芦荟,(11)含笑花,(12)仙客来,(13)万年青,(14)牡丹,(15)月季,(16)惠兰,(17)洋桔梗,(18)天竺葵,(19)唐菖蒲,(20)一品红,(21)非洲菊,(22)满天星,(23)安祖花,(24)球根海棠,(25)马蹄莲,(26)石槲兰,(27)卡特利亚兰,(28)舞女兰,(29)海枣,(30)富贵竹,(31)散尾葵,(32)万寿菊,(33)绿藤,(34)姜花,(35)年桔,(36)草皮,(37)其他观赏花木,(38)三角枫盆景,(39)五角枫盆景,(40)鸡爪槭盆景,(41)山茶花盆景,(42)翠竹盆景,(43)白花杜鹃盆景,(44)金豆盆景,(45)腊梅盆景,(46)榕盆景,(47)榆盆景,(48)五针松盆景,(49)罗汉松盆景,(50)金钱松盆景,(51)福建茶盆景,(52)乌头叶蛇葡萄盆景,(53)朱砂根盆景,(54)紫金牛盆景,(55)凌宵盆景,(56)花孝顺竹盆景,(57)凤尾竹盆景,(58)黄杨盆景,(59)锦鸡儿盆景,(60)雪松属盆景,(61)朴盆景,(62)木桃盆景,(63)代代盆景,(64)佛手盆景,(65)金桔盆,(66)其他盆景,(67)花卉组培苗,(68)马铃薯组培苗,(69)葡萄苗组培苗,(70)甘薯组培苗,(71)苹果组培苗,(72)水稻组培苗,(73)其他组培苗,(74)营养体,(75)杜鹃切花,(76)山茶花切花,(77)月季切花,(78)芍药切花,(79)满天星切花,(80)美人蕉切花,(81)木兰花切花,(82)樱花切花,(83)牡丹切花,(84)郁金香切花,(85)杂草
0604901000	(1)苔藓及地衣,(2)苔藓(栽培介质),(3)泥炭藓(栽培介质)
0709999090	(1)魔芋,(2)其他薯类,(3)大白菜,(4)小松菜(5)青梗菜,(6)油菜,(7)菜心,(8)芥蓝,(9)其他十字花科蔬菜,(10)牛蒡,(11)苦苣,(12)茼蒿,(13)其他菊科蔬菜,(14)韭菜,(15)荞头,(16)百合,(17)金针菜,(18)其他百合科蔬菜,(19)芫荽,(20)结球茴香,(21)其他伞形科蔬菜,(22)其他茄科蔬菜,(23)冬瓜,(24)其他葫芦科蔬菜,(25)黄秋葵,(26)生姜,(27)芡实,(28)茭白,(29)玉米笋,(30)香椿芽,(31)鱼腥草,(32)食用大黄,(33)马齿苋,(34)苋菜,(35)番杏,(36)落葵,(37)蕨菜,(38)紫苏,(39)薄荷,(40)保鲜其他未列出蔬菜,(41)欧芹,(42)芜菁,(43)茼蒿,(44)西葫芦,(45)苏子叶
0710809090	(1)冷冻魔芋,(2)冷冻其他薯类,(3)冷冻萝卜,(4)冷冻芜菁,(5)冷冻山葵,(6)冷冻大白菜,(7)冷冻甘蓝,(8)冷冻抱子甘蓝,(9)冷冻羽衣甘蓝,(10)冷冻小松菜,(11)冷冻青梗菜,(12)冷冻小白菜,(13)冷冻油菜,(14)冷冻菜心,(15)冷冻芥蓝,(16)冷冻青江菜,(17)冷冻芥菜,(18)冷冻花椰菜,(19)冷冻西兰花,(20)冷冻其他十字花科蔬菜,(21)冷冻牛蒡,(22)冷冻洋蓟,(23)冷冻苦苣,(24)冷冻菊苣,(25)冷冻茼蒿,(26)冷冻莴苣,(27)冷冻生菜,(28)冷冻其他菊科蔬菜,(29)冷冻洋葱,(30)冷冻大葱,(31)冷冻青葱,(32)冷冻韭葱,(33)冷冻韭菜,(34)冷冻荞头,(35)冷冻百合,(36)冷冻金针菜,(37)冷冻芦笋,(38)冷冻其他百合科蔬菜,(39)冷冻胡萝卜,(40)冷冻芹菜,(41)冷冻芫荽,(42)冷冻结球茴香,(43)冷冻其他伞形科蔬菜,(44)冷冻茄子,(45)冷冻辣椒、甜椒,(46)冷冻其他茄科蔬菜,(47)冷冻黄瓜,(48)冷冻南瓜,(49)冷冻西葫芦,(50)冷冻瓠瓜,(51)冷冻苦瓜,(52)冷冻冬瓜,(53)冷冻丝瓜,(54)冷冻其他葫芦科蔬菜,(55)冷冻蚕豆,(56)冷冻毛豆,(57)冷冻四棱豆,(58)冷冻豆苗,(59)冷冻豆芽,(60)冷冻银耳,(61)冷冻木耳,(62)冷冻蘑菇,(63)冷冻金针菇,(64)冷冻杏鲍菇,(65)冷冻草菇,(66)冷冻猴头菇,(67)冷冻姬菇,(68)冷冻平菇,(69)冷冻秀珍菇,(70)冷冻口蘑,(71)冷冻其他块菌,(72)冷冻其他食用菌,(73)冷冻黄秋葵,(74)冷冻生姜,(75)冷冻芡实,(76)冷冻茭白,(77)冷冻玉米笋,(78)冷冻竹笋,(79)冷冻香椿芽,(80)冷冻鱼腥草,(81)冷冻食用大黄,(82)冷冻马齿苋,(83)冷冻苋菜,(84)冷冻番杏,(85)冷冻落葵,(86)冷冻蕨菜,(87)冷冻紫苏,(88)冷冻薄荷,(89)冷冻油橄榄,(90)冷冻其他未列出蔬菜
0711903900	(1)腌渍萝卜,(2)腌渍芜菁(包括大头菜),(3)腌渍甘蓝(包菜、卷心菜),(4)腌渍芥菜,(5)腌渍洋葱,(6)腌渍荞头,(7)腌渍胡萝卜,(8)腌渍茄子,(9)腌渍豇豆,(10)腌渍菜豆,(11)腌渍其他豆科蔬菜,(12)腌渍生姜,(13)腌渍蕨菜,(14)腌渍紫苏,(15)腌渍其他包叶菜类蔬菜,(16)腌渍其他小叶菜类蔬菜,(17)腌渍其他根菜类蔬菜,(18)腌渍其他果菜类蔬菜,(19)不适于直接食用的盐渍其他瓜菜类蔬菜,(20)腌渍其他未列出蔬菜
0711909000	(1)腌渍萝卜,(2)腌渍芜菁(包括大头菜),(3)腌渍甘蓝(包菜、卷心菜),(4)腌渍芥菜,(5)腌渍洋葱,(6)腌渍荞头,(7)腌渍胡萝卜,(8)腌渍茄子,(9)腌渍豇豆,(10)腌渍菜豆,(11)腌渍其他豆科蔬菜,(12)腌渍生姜,(13)腌渍鱼腥草,(14)腌渍食用大黄,(15)腌渍马齿苋,(16)腌渍蕨菜,(17)腌渍紫苏,(18)腌渍薄荷,(19)腌渍其他未列出蔬菜
0712909990	(1)脱水魔芋,(2)脱水其他薯类,(3)脱水萝卜,(4)脱水甘蓝(包菜、卷心菜),(5)脱水芥菜,(6)脱水花椰菜(白花菜),(7)脱水西兰花(绿花菜),(8)脱水其他十字花科蔬菜,(9)脱水牛蒡,(10)脱水青葱,(11)脱水芦笋,(12)脱水胡萝卜,(13)脱水芹菜,(14)干甜椒,(15)脱水南瓜,(16)脱水西葫芦(笋瓜),(17)脱水瓠瓜,(18)脱水苦瓜,(19)脱水甜玉米,(20)脱水鱼腥草,(21)脱水食用大黄,(22)脱水马齿苋,(23)脱水菠菜,(24)脱水紫苏 ,(25)脱水薄荷 ,(26)脱水山野菜,(27)脱水其他未列出蔬菜,(28)马蹄叶,(29)刺嫩芽,(30)地瓜梗,(31)蓖麻叶,(32)甜墨角兰,(33)莳萝的粉
0811909090	(1)冷冻荔枝,(2)冷冻菠萝,(3)冷冻桃,(4)冷冻草莓,(5)冷冻苹果,(6)冷冻梨,(7)冷冻西瓜,(8)冷冻樱桃,(9)冷冻猕猴桃,(10)冷冻龙眼,(11)冷冻葡萄,(12)冷冻榴莲,(13)冷冻菠萝蜜,(15)其他未列名冷冻坚果,(16)冷冻蔓越莓,(17)冷冻无花果,(18)冷冻越橘,(19)冷冻黑莓,(20)冷冻木莓,(21)冷冻穗醋栗,(22)冷冻香蕉,(23)冷冻柠檬,(24)冷冻蓝莓,(25)冷冻芒果,(26)冷冻鳄梨,(27)其它冷冻植物产品
1207999900	(1)未去壳油用花生,(2)其他籽仁为皮或衣等包被的油籽,(3)油用茶籽,(4)油用大麻籽,(5)油橄榄,(6)油桐籽,(7)油用橡子仁,(8)葡萄籽,(9)其他籽仁为坚硬外壳包被的油籽,(10)去壳油用花生,(11)油棕果、油棕仁,(12)西豆,(13)黑加仑籽,(14)琉璃苣籽,(15)苏籽,(16)月见草籽,(17)水飞蓟籽,(18)奇亚籽
1209299000	(1)鸭茅属种子,(2)苜蓿属种子,紫苜蓿种子除外,(3)车轴草属种子,(4)杂高粱种子,(5)苏丹草种子,(6)草苇芦属种子,(7)狼尾草属种子,(8)梯牧草子
1209910000	(1)菜豆种子,(2)番茄种子,(3)葱种子,(4)莴苣种子,(5)萝卜种子,(6)黄瓜种子,(7)辣椒种子,(8)白菜种子,(9)菠菜种子,(10)南瓜种子,(11)茄子种子,(12)西葫芦种子,(13)甜菜种子,(14)牛蒡种子,(15)黄秋葵种子,(16)芦笋种子,(17)空心菜种子,(18)苦瓜种子,(19)韭菜种子,(20)花椰菜种子,(21)芹属种子,(22)蕹菜种子,(23)生菜种子,(24)青瓜种子,(25)非种用芥菜种子,(26)芥兰种子,(27)甘蓝种子,(28)刺葵种子,(29)豆薯种子,(30)丝瓜种子,(31)芫荽种子,(32)刀豆种子,(33)其他蔬菜种子
1209990090	(1)其他花卉种子,(2)乔荆相思种子,(3)银荆相思种子,(4)红槭种子,(5)糖槭种子,(6)雪松种子,(7)崖柏种子,(8)珙桐种子,(9)赤桉种子,(10)黑核桃种子,(11)班克松种子,(12)黄花松种子,(13)晚松种子,(14)火炬松种子,(15)西蒙得木种子,(16)湿地松种子,(17)黑木相思种子,(18)其他林木种子,(19)剪股颖属种子,(20)早熟禾属种子,(21)黍属种子,(22)臂形草属种子,(23)狗尾草属种子,(24)笔花豆属种子,(25)雀稗属种子,(26)狗牙根种子,(27)其他牧草种子,(28)大麻种子,(29)烟草种子,(30)药用植物种子,(31)糖类植物种子,(32)种用甜菜,(33)罂粟子,(34)其他经济类植物种子,(35)洋香瓜种子,(36)梅子种子,(37)其他瓜果种子

HS 编码	CIQ 扩展品名
1211903999	(1)药用玉竹,(2)药用白芷,(3)药用桔梗,(4)药用高良姜,(5)药用黄精,(6)药用葛根,(7)药用白茅根,(8)药用芦根,(9)药用薤白,(10)药用白及,(11)药用板蓝根,(12)药用苍术,(13)药用柴胡,(14)药用赤芍,(15)药用刺五加,(16)药用丹参,(17)药用地骨皮,(18)药用地榆,(19)药用独活,(20)药用莪术,(21)药用防风,(22)药用附子,(23)药用钩藤,(24)药用骨碎补,(25)药用何首乌,(26)药用红景天,(27)药用厚朴,(28)药用麦冬麦门冬,(29)药用牡丹皮,(30)药用木通,(31)药用牛膝,(32)药用前胡,(33)药用羌活,(34)药用秦艽,(35)药用青风藤,(36)药用桑白皮,(37)药用升麻,(38)药用石菖蒲,(39)药用太子参,(40)药用天冬天门冬,(41)药用土茯苓,(42)药用威灵仙,(43)药用五加皮,(44)药用细辛,(45)药用香附,(46)药用续断川断,(47)药用玄参,(48)药用延胡索元胡,(49)药用远志,(50)药用泽泻,(51)药用知母,(52)药用竹茹,(53)药用茜草,(54)药用巴戟天,(55)药用木贼,(56)药用首乌藤,(57)药用桑枝,(58)药用金银花,(59)药用桑叶,(60)药用荷叶,(61)药用淡竹叶,(62)药用紫苏,(63)药用山银花,(64)药用艾叶,(65)药用杜仲叶,(66)药用番泻叶,(67)药用红花,(68)药用厚朴花,(69)药用芦荟,(70)药用玫瑰花,(71)药用木棉花,(72)药用枇杷叶,(73)药用蒲黄,(74)药用辛夷,(75)药用淫羊藿,(76)药用银杏叶,(77)药用佩兰,(78)药用侧柏叶,(79)药用泽兰,(80)药用罗布麻,(81)药用金荞麦,(82)药用刀豆,(83)药用山楂,(84)药用木瓜,(85)药用火麻仁,(86)药用决明子,(87)药用余甘子,(88)药用佛手,(89)药用沙棘,(90)药用罗汉果,(91)药用青果,(92)药用栀子,(93)药用砂仁,(94)药用香橼,(95)药用桑椹,(96)药用橘红,(97)药用橘皮或陈皮,(98)药用莱菔子,(99)药用紫苏子,(100)药用酸枣仁,(101)药用覆盆子,(102)药用柏子仁,(103)药用补骨脂,(104)药用瓜蒌,(105)药用诃子,(106)药用芥子,(107)药用连翘,(108)药用牛蒡子,(109)药用青皮,(110)药用山茱萸,(111)药用菟丝子,(112)药用吴茱萸,(113)药用五味子,(114)药用夏枯草球,(115)药用亚麻子,(116)药用郁李仁,(117)药用枳壳,(118)药用枳实,(119)药用韭菜子,(120)药用沙苑子,(121)药用槐角,(122)药用蒺藜,(123)药用金樱子,(124)药用女贞子,(125)药用益智,(126)药用灵芝,(127)药用猪苓,(128)药用薄荷,(129)药用藿香,(130)药用大蓟,(131)药用墨旱莲,(132)药用益母草,(133)药用茵陈,(134)药用马齿苋,(135)药用小蓟,(136)药用鱼腥草,(137)药用香薷,(138)药用蒲公英,(139)药用车前草,(140)药用鸡骨草,(141)药用积雪草,(142)药用金钱草,(143)药用荆芥,(144)药用片姜黄,(145)药用车前子,(146)食用橘红,(147)食用藿香,(148)食用香薷,(149)食用蒲公英,(150)食用夏枯草球,(151)其他药用根和根茎类中药材,(152)其他食用根和根茎类中药材,(153)其他药用茎、皮类中药材,(154)其他食用茎、皮类中药材,(155)其他药用叶、花类中药材,(156)其他食用叶、花类中药材,(157)其他药用果实类中药材,(158)其他食用果实类中药材,(159)其他药用种子类中药材,(160)其他食用种子类中药材,(161)其他药用全草类中药材,(162)其他食用全草类中药材,(163)其他药用未列明类别中药材,(164)其他食用未列明类别中药材,(165)食用凉粉草,(166)白头翁 PULSATILLAE RADIX,(167)北豆根 MENISPERMI RHIZOMA,(168)槟榔 ARECAE SEMEN,(169)草豆蔻草寇 ALPINIAE KATSUMADAI SEMEN,(170)穿山龙 DIOSCOREAE NIPPONICAE ,(171)大腹皮茯毛 ARECAE PERICARPIUM,(172)防己 STEPHANIAE TETRANDRAE RADIX,(173)黄藤 FIBRAUREAE CAULIS,(174)鸡血藤 SPATHOLOB CAULIS,(175)老鹳草玄草 ERODII HERBA GERANII HERBA,(176)莲须 NELUMBINIS STAMEN,(177)马钱子 STRYCHNI SEMEN,(178)马钱子粉 STRYCHNI SEMEN PULVERATUM,(179)蔓荆子 VITICIS FRUCTUS,(180)猫爪草 RANUNCULI TERNATI RADIX,(181)山豆根 SOPHORAE TONKINENSIS RADIX ET RHIZOMA,(182)水飞蓟 SILYBI FRUCTUS,(183)松花粉 PINI POLLEN,(184)天仙子 HYOSCYAMI SEMEN,(185)西青果 CHEBULAE FRUCTUS IMMATURUS,(186)仙茅 CURCULIGINIS RHIZOMA,(187)郁金 CURCUMAE RADIX,(188)重楼 PARIDIS RHIZOMA,(189)紫草 ARNEBIAE RADIX,(190)胡芦巴葫芦巴 TRIGONELLAE SEMEN,(191)药用吐根,(192)药用白鲜皮,
1302199099	(1)供工业用的植物及植物提取物,(2)供制食品或医药用的植物提取物,(3)批准为新食品原料,301 属于危险化学品的食品添加剂,302 斑蝥素,毒性物质,需申报仅用于工业用途不用于食品添加剂有检疫要求,303 一般化学品,需申报仅用于工业用途不用于食品添加剂有检疫要求,304 易燃液体,需申报仅用于工业用途不用于食品添加剂有检疫要求,305 有检疫要求食品添加剂
1502900000	(1)工业用牛油脂,(2)工业用羊油脂,(3)工业用野生猪、牛、羊油脂,(4)饲料用牛油脂,(5)饲料用羊油脂,(6)饲料用野生猪、牛、羊油脂,(7)未炼制的食用牛脂肪,(8)未炼制的食用羊脂肪,(9)已炼制的食用牛油(脂),(10)已炼制的食用羊油(脂)
1506000090	(1)工业用其他饲养偶蹄动物油脂,(2)工业用野生猪、牛、羊油脂,(3)工业用其他野生偶蹄动物油脂,(4)工业用马油脂,(5)未列出的工业用其他动物油脂,(6)饲料用其他饲养偶蹄动物油脂,(7)饲料用其他野生偶蹄动物油脂,(8)饲料用马油脂,(9)未列出的饲料用其他动物油脂,(10)未炼制的其他食用动物油(脂),(11)已炼制的其他食用动物油(脂),(13)野生虾虾油,(14)其他养殖水产动物油脂,(15)其他野生水产动物油脂
1515909090	(1)饲料添加剂,(2)其他初榨植物食用油,(3)食用茶油,(4)其他食用植物油,301 属于危险化学品的食品添加剂,302 一般化学品,需申报仅用于工业用途不用于食品添加剂有检疫要求,303 易燃液体,需申报仅用于工业用途不用于食品添加剂有检疫要求,304 有检疫要求食品添加剂
1601001090	(1)动物肉及杂碎,(2)其他熟制禽肉制品,(3)其他熟制畜肉制品
1601002090	(1)动物肉及杂碎,(2)其他熟制禽肉制品,(3)其他熟制畜肉制品,(4)其他养殖制作及保藏水产制品,(5)其他野生制作及保藏水产制品
1602200010	(1)动物肉及杂碎,(2)其他熟制禽肉制品,(3)其他熟制畜肉制品
1602200090	(1)动物肉及杂碎,(2)其他熟制禽肉制品,(3)其他熟制畜肉制品
1602310000	(1)火鸡肉及杂碎,(2)热处理火鸡肉,(3)其他热处理火鸡肉
1602329100	(1)非热处理鸡肉,(2)热处理鸡肉,(3)其他热处理鸡肉
1602329200	(1)非热处理鸡肉,(2)热处理鸡肉,(3)其他热处理鸡肉
1602329900	(1)非热处理其他禽肉,(2)热处理鸡肉,(3)其他热处理鸡肉
1602391000	(1)鸭肉罐头,(2)鹅肉罐头,(3)其他家禽肉及杂碎的罐头
1602399100	(1)非热处理其他禽肉,(2)热处理鸭肉,(3)其他热处理鸭肉
1602399900	(1)非热处理其他禽肉,(2)热处理鹅肉,(3)其他热处理鹅肉,(4)其他熟制禽肉制品
1602420090	(1)猪蹄,(2)去骨熟制猪肉制品,(3)带骨熟制猪肉制品
1602909090	(1)其他动物肉脏及杂碎,(2)去骨熟制羊肉制品,(3)带骨熟制羊肉制品,(4)去骨熟制鹿肉制品,(5)带骨熟制鹿肉制品,(6)去骨熟制马肉制品,(7)带骨熟制马肉制品,(8)其他熟制禽肉制品,(9)其他去骨熟制畜肉制品,(10)其他带骨熟制畜肉制品
1604111000	(1)养殖水产制品,(2)野生水产制品,(3)养殖鱼类罐头,(4)野生鱼类罐头

HS 编码	CIQ 扩展品名
1604130000	(1)沙丁鱼水产制品,(2)小沙丁鱼属水产制品,(3)黍鲱水产制品,(4)西鲱水产制品,(5)沙丁鱼罐头,(6)小沙丁鱼属罐头,(7)黍鲱罐头,(8)西鲱罐头
1604140000	(1)金枪鱼水产制品,(2)鲣鱼水产制品,(3)狐鲣属水产制品,(4)金枪鱼罐头,(5)鲣鱼罐头,(6)狐鲣属罐头
1604170010	(1)养殖鱼类罐头,(2)野生鱼类罐头,(3)养殖花鳗鲡制成的烤鳗,(4)野生花鳗鲡制成的烤鳗,(5)养殖花鳗鲡制成的其他水产制品,(6)野生花鳗鲡制成的其他水产制品
1604170020	(1)养殖鱼类罐头,(2)野生鱼类罐头,(3)养殖欧洲鳗鲡制成的烤鳗,(4)野生欧洲鳗鲡制成的烤鳗,(5)养殖欧洲鳗鲡制成的其他水产制品,(6)野生欧洲鳗鲡制成的其他水产制品
1604170090	(1)养殖鱼类罐头,(2)野生鱼类罐头,(3)养殖日本鳗鲡制成的烤鳗,(4)野生日本鳗鲡制成的烤鳗,(5)养殖日本鳗鲡制成的其他水产制品,(6)野生日本鳗鲡制成的其他水产制品,(9)其他养殖鳗鲡制成的烤鳗,(10)其他野生鳗鲡制成的烤鳗,(11)其他养殖鳗鲡制成的其他水产制品,(12)其他野生鳗鲡制成的其他水产制品
1604199090	(1)养殖石斑鱼,(2)养殖鲥鱼,(3)养殖鲷科,(4)养殖安康鱼,(5)养殖海鲂,(6)养殖鲆鱼,(7)养殖鲽鱼,(8)养殖红鱼,(9)养殖鲈鱼,(10)养殖黄鱼,(11)养殖鲮鱼,(12)其他养殖鱼,(13)野生石斑鱼,(14)野生鲥鱼,(15)野生鲷科,(16)野生安康鱼,(17)野生海鲂,(18)野生鲆鱼,(19)野生鲽鱼,(20)野生红鱼,(21)海鲫鱼,(22)金线鱼,(23)马面鱼,(24)野生鲮鱼,(25)野生鲈鱼,(26)野生黄鱼,(27)马鲛鱼,(28)带鱼,(29)其他野生鱼,(30)养殖石斑鱼罐头,(31)养殖鲥鱼罐头,(32)养殖鲷科罐头,(33)养殖安康鱼罐头,(34)养殖海鲂罐头,(35)养殖鲆鱼罐头,(36)养殖鲽鱼罐头,(37)养殖红鱼罐头,(38)其他养殖鱼罐头,(39)野生石斑鱼罐头,(40)野生鲥鱼罐头,(41)野生鲷科罐头,(42)野生安康鱼罐头,(43)野生海鲂罐头,(44)野生鲆鱼罐头,(45)野生鲽鱼罐头,(46)野生红鱼罐头,(47)海鲫鱼罐头,(48)金线鱼罐头,(49)马面鱼罐头,(50)马鲛鱼罐头,(51)其他野生鱼罐头
1604201990	(1)养殖石斑鱼,(2)养殖鲥鱼,(3)养殖鲷科,(4)养殖安康鱼,(5)养殖海鲂,(6)养殖鲆鱼,(7)养殖鲽鱼,(8)养殖红鱼,(9)其他养殖鱼,(10)野生石斑鱼,(11)野生鲥鱼,(12)野生鲷科,(13)野生安康鱼,(14)野生海鲂,(15)野生鲆鱼,(16)野生鲽鱼,(17)野生红鱼,(18)海鲫鱼,(19)金线鱼,(20)马面鱼,(21)马鲛鱼,(22)其他野生鱼
1604209990	(1)养殖石斑鱼,(2)养殖鲥鱼,(3)养殖鲷科,(4)养殖安康鱼,(5)养殖海鲂,(6)养殖鲆鱼,(7)养殖鲽鱼,(8)养殖红鱼,(9)其他养殖鱼,(10)野生石斑鱼,(11)野生鲥鱼,(12)野生鲷科,(13)野生安康鱼,(14)野生海鲂,(15)野生鲆鱼,(16)野生鲽鱼,(17)野生红鱼,(18)海鲫鱼,(19)金线鱼,(20)马面鱼,(21)马鲛鱼,(22)其他野生鱼
1605401100	(1)养殖水产制品,(2)野生水产制品,(3)养殖甲壳类罐头,(4)野生甲壳类罐头
1605401900	(1)养殖水产制品,(2)野生水产制品,(3)养殖甲壳类罐头,(4)野生甲壳类罐头
1605409000	(1)养殖水产制品,(2)野生水产制品,(3)养殖甲壳类罐头,(4)野生甲壳类罐头
1605580010	(1)野生水产制品,(2)野生水产罐头
1605580090	(1)野生水产制品,(2)野生水产罐头
1605630000	(1)养殖水产制品,(2)野生水产制品,(3)养殖水产罐头,(4)野生水产罐头
1605690010	(1)野生水产制品,(2)野生水产罐头
1605690090	(1)养殖水产制品,(2)野生水产制品,(3)养殖水产罐头,(4)野生水产罐头
1901900000	(1)其他冷冻饮品,(2)纯麦片,(3)发酵豆制品,(4)方便米、粉,(5)通心粉,(6)米粉,(7)速食粮食产品,(8)其他粮食制品,(9)其他含肉速冻粮食制品,(10)其他不含肉速冻粮食制品,(11)其他不含馅速冻粮食制品,(12)非发酵豆制品,(13)婴幼儿谷类辅助食品,(14)婴幼儿罐装辅助食品,(15)特殊医学用途配方食品,(16)灭菌工艺调制乳,(17)其他调制乳,(18)儿童调制乳粉,(19)孕产妇调制乳粉,(20)其他调制乳粉,(21)淡炼乳,(22)加糖炼乳,(23)调制淡炼乳,(24)调制加糖炼乳,(25)其他炼乳,(26)乳基婴儿配方乳粉基粉,(27)乳基较大婴儿和幼儿配方乳粉基粉,(28)其他乳与乳制品,(29)巴氏杀菌工艺调制乳,(30)其他纯谷物的冲调谷物制品,(31)含其他原料的谷物类冲调谷物制品,(32)淀粉质类冲调谷物制品,(33)其他食糖
1904900000	(1)食用,(2)膨化食品,(3)其他糕点饼干,(4)纯麦片,(5)方便米、粉,(6)速食粮食产品,(7)其他粮食制品,(8)其他含肉速冻粮食制品,(9)其他不含肉速冻粮食制品,(10)其他不含馅速冻粮食制品,(11)其他纯谷物的冲调谷物制品,(12)含其他原料的谷物类冲调谷物制品,(13)淀粉质类冲调谷物制品
2005999100	(1)荞头罐头,(2)其他鳞茎类罐头,(3)红焖大头菜罐头,(4)其他芸苔属类罐头,(5)香菜心罐头,(6)雪菜罐头,(7)橄榄菜罐头,(8)其他叶菜类罐头,(9)其他茄果类罐头,(10)美味黄瓜罐头,(11)苦瓜罐头,(12)其他瓜类罐头,(13)青刀豆罐头,(14)芸豆罐头,(15)红豆罐头,(16)发酵豆类罐头,(17)其他豆类罐头,(18)其他茎类罐头,(19)胡萝卜罐头,(20)姜罐头,(21)地瓜罐头,(22)其他根茎类和薯芋类罐头,(23)莲藕罐头,(24)清水莲子罐头,(25)其他水生类罐头,(26)绿豆芽罐头,(27)黄豆芽罐头,(28)其他芽菜类罐头,(29)其他多年生蔬菜罐头,(30)玉米笋罐头,(31)四鲜烤夫罐头,(32)什锦蔬菜罐头,(33)其他蔬菜罐头
2008999000	(1)苹果罐头,(2)葡萄罐头,(3)海棠罐头,(4)干装苹果罐头,(5)什锦水果罐头,(6)马口铁什锦水果罐头,(7)玻璃瓶什锦水果罐头,(8)复合塑料袋什锦水果罐头,(9)橄榄罐头,(10)芒果罐头,(11)双色罐头,(12)枇杷罐头,(13)杨梅罐头,(14)猕猴桃罐头,(15)番石榴罐头,(16)番荔枝罐头,(17)山楂罐头,(18)李子罐头,(19)榴莲罐头,(20)其他瓜果类罐头,(21)其他浆果和小型水果类罐头,(22)其他核果类水果罐头,(23)其他热带和亚热带水果罐头,(24)其他未列名水果罐头,(25)熟制葵花子,(26)未列出的其他熟制坚果炒货,(27)果脯,(28)其他蜜饯,冷冻油炸甘薯
2103909000	(1)食用茶油,(2)食用芝麻油,(3)食用植物调和油,(4)海鲜酱,(5)即食沙律酱,(6)冰梅酱,(7)柱侯酱,(8)排骨酱,(9)沙茶酱,(10)沙爹酱,(11)豆瓣酱,(12)甜酸酱,(13)黄豆酱,(14)其他酱,(15)酿造食醋,(16)配制食醋,(17)白米醋,(18)添丁甜醋,(19)苹果醋,(20)大红浙醋,(21)其他食醋,(22)调味剂,(23)鸡精,(24)鲜味粉,(25)鲜味膏,(26)其他鲜味剂,(27)混合调味品,(28)豆豉,(29)姜豉,(30)沙姜粉,(31)五香粉,(32)调味汁,(33)未列出的其他调味品,(34)红豆馅,(35)芝麻酱,(36)榛子酱,(37)扁桃仁酱,(38)其他坚果及籽类的泥(酱),(39)水产调味品
2106100000	(1)蛋白型固体饮料,(2)具有保健食品批准文号,(3)大豆蛋白,(4)豌豆蛋白,(5)特殊医学用途配方食品,(6)蚕豆蛋白,(7)其他豆类蛋白,(8)小麦蛋白,(9)燕麦蛋白,(10)大米蛋白,(11)玉米蛋白,(12)其他谷类蛋白,(13)花生蛋白,(14)其他坚果及籽类蛋白,(15)马铃薯蛋白,(16)其他薯类蛋白,(17)其他未列明植物蛋白,(18)过瘤蛋白

HS 编码	CIQ 扩展品名
2106909090	(1)其他食用植物调和油,(2)其他食用植物油,(3)代用茶,(4)其他茶叶及制品,(5)其他乳与乳制品,(6)即食坚果沙律,(7)熟制坚果炒货,(8)含乳饮料,(9)植物蛋白饮料,(10)蛋白型固体饮料,(11)果香型固体饮料如菊花精、柠檬茶、果珍,(12)果冻,(13)未列出的其他饮料、冷冻饮品、咖啡、果冻,(14)其他原酒,(15)未列出的其他酒,(16)冰片糖,(17)糖浆,(18)糖霜,(19)胶基糖果,(20)其他食糖,(21)其他糖果,(22)其他糖与糖果,巧克力与可可制品,(23)发酵豆制品,(24)红豆馅,(25)即食通粉沙律,(26)湿粉,(27)湿面,(28)速食粮食产品,(29)其他粮食制品,(30)含肉饺子,(31)不含肉饺子,(32)其他不含馅速冻粮食制品,(33)其他蜜饯,(34)具有保健食品批准文号,(35)母乳营养补充剂,(36)婴幼儿谷类辅助食品,(37)婴幼儿罐装辅助食品,(38)特殊医学用途配方食品,(39)食用其他加工油脂,(40)其他未列出的加工食品,(41)燕窝制品,以燕窝为主要原料的食品,(42)运动营养食品,(43)孕产妇营养补充品,(44)辅食营养补充品,(45)非发酵豆制品,(46)其他蛋白饮料,(47)其他特殊用途饮料,(48)植物饮料,(49)其他酿酒原料,(50)酵母制品食品加工用酵母制品活性酵母,(51)酵母制品酵母制品食品加工用酵母制品非活性酵母,(52)酵母制品酵母衍生制品食品加工用酵母衍生制品,(53)酵母制品食品加工用其他酵母产品,(54)酵母制品食品加工用乳酸菌,(55)食品加工用乳酸菌产品,(56)酵母制品其他食品加工用菌种及其产品,(57)酵母制品乳酸菌饮料,(58)大豆蛋白,(59)豌豆蛋白,(60)蚕豆蛋白,(61)其他豆类蛋白,(62)小麦蛋白,(63)燕麦蛋白,(64)大米蛋白,(65)玉米蛋白,(66)其他谷类蛋白,(67)花生蛋白,(68)其他坚果及籽类蛋白,(69)马铃薯蛋白,(70)其他薯类蛋白,(71)其他植物蛋白,(72)纯麦片,(73)其他纯谷物的冲调谷物制品,(74)含其他原料的谷物类冲调谷物制品,(75)淀粉质类冲调谷物制品,(76)无检疫要求食品添加剂
2202990011	(1)碳酸饮料,(2)含乳饮料,(3)植物蛋白饮料,(4)茶饮料,(5)运动饮料,(6)其他软饮料,(7)未列出的其他饮料、冷冻饮品、咖啡、果冻,(8)具有保健食品批准文号,(9)植物饮料,(10)乳酸菌饮料
2202990019	(1)碳酸饮料,(2)含乳饮料,(3)植物蛋白饮料,(4)茶饮料,(5)运动饮料,(6)其他软饮料,(7)未列出的其他饮料、冷冻饮品、咖啡、果冻,(8)植物饮料,(9)乳酸菌饮料,(10)保健食品
2202990099	(1)碳酸饮料,(2)含乳饮料,(3)植物蛋白饮料,(4)茶饮料,(5)运动饮料,(6)其他软饮料,(7)蛋白型固体饮料,(8)其他咖啡,(9)未列出的其他饮料、冷冻饮品、咖啡、果冻,(10)燕窝制品,以燕窝主要原料制成的饮料,(11)乳酸菌饮料,112 植物饮料
2301101900	(1)饲料用猪肉粉(肉成分 67%以上),(2)饲料用猪肉骨粉,(3)饲料用猪血粉,(4)饲料用鹿肉骨粉,(5)饲料用鹿血粉,(6)饲料用混合型饲养偶蹄动物肉骨粉,(7)饲料用其他饲养偶蹄动物粉,(8)饲料用野生偶蹄猪、牛、羊肉粉(肉成分 67%以上),(9)饲料用其他野生偶蹄动物粉,(10)饲料用禽肉骨粉,(11)饲料用禽血粉,(12)饲料用其他动物肉粉(肉成份 67%以上),(13)饲料用其他动物肉骨粉,(14)饲料用其他动物血粉
2308000000	(1)饲用苜蓿草,(2)饲用燕麦草,(3)其他饲草,(4)饲用其他淀粉,(5)饲用青贮,(6)饲用植物颗粒和植物粉,(7)其他未列明植物饲料,(8)辣椒粕,(9)橄榄粕,(10)榴莲粕,(11)扁桃仁粕
2309909000	(1)饲料用乳粉、蛋粉、乳清粉,(2)未列出的饲料用其他动物粉,(3)添加剂预混合饲料,(4)浓缩饲料,(5)全价配合饲料,(6)精料补充料,(7)其他配制的动物饲料,(8)其他宠物食品,(9)饲用蛋粉
2501001900	(1)饲料添加剂,(2)矿盐,(3)海盐,(4)除海盐、矿盐外
2503000000	(1)属于危险化学品的食品添加剂,(2)易燃固体,需申报仅用于工业用途不用于食品添加剂无检疫要求
2506100000	(1)石英砂,(2)石英粉,(3)熔融石英砂,(4)熔融石英粉,(5)其他石英
2519909100	(1)矿物源性饲料添加剂,(2)氧化镁(包括轻质和重质)(无检疫要求食品添加剂)),(3)氧化镁
2524901010	(1)栽培介质,(2)毒害品,(3)长纤维石棉,301 杂项物质
2524901090	(1)栽培介质,(2)长纤维石棉,301 杂项物质
2530102000	(1)蛭石(栽培介质),(2)珍珠岩(栽培介质),(3)石材
2805199000	(1)碱金属、碱土金属,(2)钡合金,(3)金属钾,(4)钾合金,(5)钾钠合金,(6)金属铷,(7)金属铯,(8)金属锶,(9)金属钡,(10)其他二级有机钡化合物,301 易于自燃的物质,302 遇水放出易燃气体的物质
2806100000	301 腐蚀性物质,需申报仅用于工业用途不用于食品添加剂无检疫要求,302 属于危险化学品的食品添加剂,303 毒性气体,需申报仅用于工业用途不用于食品添加剂无检疫要求
2811199090	301 其他危险化学品,需申报仅用于工业用途不用于食品添加剂无检疫要求,302 无检疫要求食品添加剂,303 一般化学品,需申报仅用于工业用途不用于食品添加剂无检疫要求,304 属于危险化学品的食品添加剂
2811210000	(1)二氧化碳和氧气混合物,301 二氧化碳和环氧乙烷混合物,302 非易燃无毒气体,需申报仅用于工业用途不用于食品添加剂无检疫要求,303 需申报仅用于工业用途不用于食品添加剂无检疫要求的化学品,304 属于危险化学品的食品添加剂
2825909000	301 其他危险化学品,需申报仅用于工业用途不用于食品添加剂无检疫要求,302 煅烧钙(无检疫要求食品添加剂),303 氢氧化钙(无检疫要求食品添加剂),304 无检疫要求食品添加剂,305 一般化学品,需申报仅用于工业用途不用于食品添加剂无检疫要求,306 属于危险化学品的食品添加剂
2827399000	(1)矿物源性饲料添加剂,301 其他危险化学品,需申报仅用于工业用途不用于食品添加剂无检疫要求,302 无检疫要求食品添加剂,303 一般化学品,需申报仅用于工业用途不用于食品添加剂无检疫要求,304 属于危险化学品的食品添加剂
2827600000	(1)矿物源性饲料添加剂,301 其他危险化学品,需申报仅用于工业用途不用于食品添加剂无检疫要求,302 无检疫要求食品添加剂,303 一般化学品,需申报仅用于工业用途不用于食品添加剂无检疫要求,304 属于危险化学品的食品添加剂
2828900000	301 其他危险化学品,需申报仅用于工业用途不用于食品添加剂无检疫要求,302 无检疫要求食品添加剂,303 一般化学品,需申报仅用于工业用途不用于食品添加剂无检疫要求,304 属于危险化学品的食品添加剂
2831101000	301 其他危险化学品,需申报仅用于工业用途不用于食品添加剂无检疫要求,302 无检疫要求食品添加剂,303 一般化学品,需申报仅用于工业用途不用于食品添加剂无检疫要求,304 属于危险化学品的食品添加剂
2832200000	301 其他危险化学品,需申报仅用于工业用途不用于食品添加剂无检疫要求,302 无检疫要求食品添加剂,303 一般化学品,需申报仅用于工业用途不用于食品添加剂无检疫要求,304 属于危险化学品的食品添加剂
2833299090	(1)矿物源性饲料添加剂,301 其他危险化学品,需申报仅用于工业用途不用于食品添加剂无检疫要求,302 无检疫要求食品添加剂,303 需申报仅用于工业用途不用于食品添加剂无检疫要求的化学品,304 属于危险化学品的食品添加剂

HS 编码	CIQ 扩展品名
2834100000	301 其他危险化学品,需申报仅用于工业用途不用于食品添加剂无检疫要求,302 无检疫要求食品添加剂,303 一般化学品,需申报仅用于工业用途不用于食品添加剂无检疫要求,304 属于危险化学品的食品添加剂
2835299000	(1)矿物源性饲料添加剂,(2)碳酸钙(包括轻质和重质碳酸钙)(无检疫要求食品添加剂),(3)生物碳酸钙(无检疫要求食品添加剂),(4)活性钙(无检疫要求食品添加剂),(5)需申报仅用于工业用途不用于食品添加剂无检疫要求的化学品
2836500000	(1)矿物源性饲料添加剂,(2)无检疫要求食品添加剂,(3)无检疫要求食品添加剂,(4)无检疫要求食品添加剂,301 需申报仅用于工业用途不用于食品添加剂无检疫要求的化学品
2836999000	(1)矿物源性饲料添加剂,301 氧化性物质,需申报仅用于工业用途不用于食品添加剂无检疫要求,302 其他危险化学品,需申报仅用于工业用途不用于食品添加剂无检疫要求,303 无检疫要求食品添加剂,304 一般化学品,需申报仅用于工业用途不用于食品添加剂无检疫要求,305 属于危险化学品的食品添加剂,306 高锰酸钾(属于危险化学品的食品添加剂)
2842100000	(1)矿物源性饲料添加剂,301 其他危险化学品,需申报仅用于工业用途不用于食品添加剂无检疫要求,302 无检疫要求食品添加剂,303 一般化学品,需申报仅用于工业用途不用于食品添加剂无检疫要求,304 属于危险化学品的食品添加剂
2842905000	301 其他危险化学品,需申报仅用于工业用途不用于食品添加剂无检疫要求,302 无检疫要求食品添加剂,303 一般化学品,需申报仅用于工业用途不用于食品添加剂无检疫要求,304 属于危险化学品的食品添加剂
2842909090	(1)矿物源性饲料添加剂,301 其他危险化学品,需申报仅用于工业用途不用于食品添加剂无检疫要求,302 无检疫要求食品添加剂,303 一般化学品,需申报仅用于工业用途不用于食品添加剂无检疫要求,304 属于危险化学品的食品添加剂
2853909090	301 遇水放出易燃气体的物质,302 毒性物质和感染性物质,303 杂项物质,304 其他危险化学品,305 其他化工产品
2903399090	301 易燃气体,302 非易燃无毒气体,303 易燃液体,305 毒性物质和感染性物质,306 腐蚀性物质,307 杂项物质,308 其他危险化学品,309 其他化工产品
2903799090	(1)三氟氯乙烯(抑制了的),(2)三氟溴乙烯,(3)氯溴甲烷,(4)(1－氯－2－溴乙烷),(5)(1－氯－1－溴丙烷),(6)(1－氯－2－溴丙烷),(7)(1－氯－3－溴丙烷),(8)(2－氯－1－溴丙烷),(9)(2－氯－2－溴丙烷)
2903820010	(1)艾氏剂(含量＞75%),(2)异艾氏剂(含量＞10%),(3)狄氏剂,(4)艾氏剂乳剂(含量＞75%),(5)异艾氏剂乳剂(含量＞10%),(6)异狄氏剂乳剂(含量＞5%),(7)其他一级有机氯液态农药,(8)艾氏剂可湿性粉剂(含量 7%～75%),(9)七氯(含量＞8%),(10)艾氏剂乳剂(含量 2%～75%),(11)七氯乳剂(含量 2%～80%),(12)七氯
2905290000	(1)环丙基甲醇,(2)丙炔醇,(3)1－丁炔－3－醇,(4)2－甲基－3－丁炔－2－醇,(5)3－甲基－1－戊炔－3－醇,(6)3－甲基－2－戊烯－4－炔醇
2905499000	(1)2－苯乙硫醇,(2)赤藓糖醇,(3)2,5－二甲基－3－呋喃硫醇,(4)2－丙硫醇,(5)2－甲基－1－丁硫醇,(6)2－戊基硫醇,(7)3－甲基－2－丁硫醇,(8)3－甲基丁基硫醇,(9)4－甲氧基－2－甲基－2－丁硫醇
2907121900	301 其他危险化学品,需申报仅用于工业用途不用于食品添加剂无检疫要求,302 无检疫要求食品添加剂,303 一般化学品,需申报仅用于工业用途不用于食品添加剂无检疫要求,304 属于危险化学品的食品添加剂
2907159000	301 其他危险化学品,需申报仅用于工业用途不用于食品添加剂无检疫要求,302 无检疫要求食品添加剂,303 一般化学品,需申报仅用于工业用途不用于食品添加剂无检疫要求,304 属于危险化学品的食品添加剂
2907299090	301 其他危险化学品,需申报仅用于工业用途不用于食品添加剂无检疫要求,302 无检疫要求食品添加剂,303 一般化学品,需申报仅用于工业用途不用于食品添加剂无检疫要求,304 属于危险化学品的食品添加剂
2912190090	(1)异丁醛(危险化学品),(2)正丁醛,(3)正戊醛,(4)3－甲基丁醛,(5)2－乙基丁醛,(6)3,3－二乙氧基丙烯,(7)2－丁烯醛(抑制了的),(8)α－甲基丙烯醛,(9)丙醛(危险化学品),(10)正己醛,(11)2－甲基戊醛(危险化学品),(12)正庚醛,(13)2,3－二甲基戊醛,(14)其他辛醛,(15)乙基己醛,(16)3－羟(基)丁醛,(17)2－羟基苯甲醛,(18)2－甲基戊醛(属于危险化学品的食品添加剂),(19)异丁醛(属于危险化学品的食品添加剂),(20)丙醛(属于危险化学品的食品添加剂),(21)易燃液体,(22)毒性物质和感染性物质,(23)其他化工产品
2915130000	(1)甲酸甲酯,(2)甲酸乙酯(危险化学品),(3)甲酸正丙酯,(4)甲酸异丙酯,(5)甲酸正丁酯,(6)甲酸异丁酯,(7)原甲酸(三)甲酯,(8)甲酸烯丙酯,(9)氯甲酸甲酯,(10)氯甲酸乙酯,(11)氯甲酸异丙酯,(12)其他甲酸酯类化合物,(13)甲酸正戊酯,(14)甲酸异戊酯(危险化学品),(15)甲酸正己酯,(16)原甲酸(三)乙酯,(17)甲酸环己酯,(18)甲酸异戊酯(属于危险化学品的食品添加剂),(19)甲酸乙酯(属于危险化学品的食品添加剂),(20)易燃液体,(21)毒性物质和感染性物质),(22)其他化工产品
2915219090	301 腐蚀性物质,需申报仅用于工业用途不用于食品添加剂无检疫要求,302 无检疫要求食品添加剂,303 需申报仅用于工业用途不用于食品添加剂无检疫要求的化学品,304 属于危险化学品的食品添加剂
2915299090	(1)饲料添加剂,301 其他危险化学品,需申报仅用于工业用途不用于食品添加剂无检疫要求,302 无检疫要求食品添加剂,303 一般化学品,需申报仅用于工业用途不用于食品添加剂无检疫要求,304 属于危险化学品的食品添加剂
2915390090	301 其他危险化学品,需申报仅用于工业用途不用于食品添加剂无检疫要求,302 无检疫要求食品添加剂,303 一般化学品,需申报仅用于工业用途不用于食品添加剂无检疫要求,304 属于危险化学品的食品添加剂
2915509000	(1)饲料添加剂,301 其他危险化学品,需申报仅用于工业用途不用于食品添加剂无检疫要求,302 无检疫要求食品添加剂,303 一般化学品,需申报仅用于工业用途不用于食品添加剂无检疫要求,304 属于危险化学品的食品添加剂
2915900090	301 其他危险化学品,需申报仅用于工业用途不用于食品添加剂无检疫要求,302 无检疫要求食品添加剂,303 一般化学品,需申报仅用于工业用途不用于食品添加剂无检疫要求,304 属于危险化学品的食品添加剂
2916190090	(1)饲料添加剂,301 其他危险化学品,302 无检疫要求的食品添加剂,303 需申报仅用于工业用途不用于食品添加剂无检疫要求的化学品,304 属于危险化学品的食品添加剂
2916209090	301 其他危险化学品,需申报仅用于工业用途不用于食品添加剂无检疫要求,302 无检疫要求食品添加剂,303 一般化学品,需申报仅用于工业用途不用于食品添加剂无检疫要求,304 属于危险化学品的食品添加剂
2916310000	(1)饲料添加剂,301 其他危险化学品,需申报仅用于工业用途不用于食品添加剂无检疫要求,302 无检疫要求食品添加剂,303 一般化学品,需申报仅用于工业用途不用于食品添加剂无检疫要求,304 属于危险化学品的食品添加剂

HS 编码	CIQ 扩展品名
2916399090	(1)可得然胶,(2)硫酸钙(石膏),(3) 4-茴香酸,(4)肉桂酸,(5)肉桂酸-3-苯丙酯,(6)肉桂酸苯乙酯,(7)肉桂酸苄酯,(8)肉桂酸芳樟酯,(9)肉桂酸甲酯,(10)肉桂酸肉桂酯,(11)肉桂酸烯丙酯,(12)肉桂酸乙酯,(13)肉桂酸异丁酯,(14)肉桂酸异戊酯,(15)薪草提取物
2917209090	301 其他危险化学品,需申报仅用于工业用途不用于食品添加剂无检疫要求,302 无检疫要求食品添加剂,303 一般化学品,需申报仅用于工业用途不用于食品添加剂无检疫要求,304 属于危险化学品的食品添加剂
2918110000	(1)饲料添加剂,301 其他危险化学品,需申报仅用于工业用途不用于食品添加剂无检疫要求,302 无检疫要求食品添加剂,303 一般化学品,需申报仅用于工业用途不用于食品添加剂无检疫要求,304 属于危险化学品的食品添加剂
2918300090	(1)乙酰丙酸,(2)乙酰丙酸乙酯,(3)乙酰乙酸乙酯,(4)乙酰化双淀粉己二酸酯,(5)丙酮酸,(6)丙酮酸顺式-3-己烯酯(丙酮酸叶醇酯),(7)丙酮酸叶醇酯(丙酮酸顺式-3-己烯酯),(8)丙酮酸乙酯,(9)丙酮酸异戊酯,(10)茉莉酮酸甲酯
2919900090	301 毒性物质和感染性物质,需申报仅用于工业用途不用于食品添加剂无检疫要求,302 无检疫要求食品添加剂,303 一般化学品,需申报仅用于工业用途不用于食品添加剂无检疫要求,304 属于危险化学品的食品添加剂
2920900090	301 爆炸品,302 易燃气体,303 易燃液体,304 有机过氧化物,305 毒性物质和感染性物质,306 腐蚀性物质,307 杂项物质,308 其他化工产品
2922110001	3011-氨基乙醇,无检疫要求食品添加剂,3021-氨基乙醇,一般化学品,需申报仅用于工业用途不用于食品添加剂无检疫要求,303N,N-二甲基乙醇胺,易燃液体,需申报仅用于工业用途不用于食品添加剂无检疫要求,3042-氨基乙醇,腐蚀性物质,需申报仅用于工业用途不用于食品添加剂无检疫要求,305 属于危险化学品的食品添加剂
2922491990	(1)饲料添加剂,(2)天门冬氨酸钙(有检疫要求食品添加剂),(3)L-丝氨酸(有检疫要求食品添加剂),(4)10-十一烯酸烯丙酯(有检疫要求食品添加剂),(5)dL-缬氨酸(有检疫要求食品添加剂),(6)L-精氨酸(有检疫要求食品添加剂),(7)l-组氨酸(有检疫要求食品添加剂),(8)甘氨酸(有检疫要求食品添加剂),(9)牛磺酸(2-氨基乙基磺酸)(有检疫要求食品添加剂),(10)L-酪氨酸(有检疫要求食品添加剂),301 需申报仅用于工业用途不用于食品添加剂有检疫要求的化学品
2922499990	(1)饲料添加剂,301 有检疫要求食品添加剂,302 需申报仅用于工业用途不用于食品添加剂无检疫要求的化学品,303 需申报仅用于工业用途不用于食品添加剂有检疫要求的化学品,304 毒性物质和感染性物质
2923200000	(1)饲料添加剂,(2)具有保健食品批准文号,301 改性大豆磷脂(无检疫要求食品添加剂),302 酶解大豆磷脂(无检疫要求食品添加剂),303 需申报仅用于工业用途不用于食品添加剂无检疫要求的化学品
2927000090	301 爆炸品,302 易燃气体,303 易燃液体,304 易燃固体,305 自反应物质和混合物,306 易于自燃的物质,307 毒性物质和感染性物质,308 其他化工产品
2928000090	301 爆炸品,302 易燃液体,303 易燃固体,304 自反应物质和混合物,305 易于自燃的物质,306 毒性物质和感染性物质,307 杂项物质,308 其他危险化学品,309 其他化工产品
2930909099	301 其他化工产品,302 爆炸品,303 易燃气体,304 毒性气体,305 易燃液体,306 易于自燃的物质,307 毒性物质和感染性物质,308 腐蚀性物质,309 杂项物质,310 其他危险化学品
2931399090	301 需申报仅用于工业用途不用于食品添加剂无检疫要求的化学品,302 其他危险化学品,303 无检疫要求的食品添加剂,304 属于危险化学品的食品添加剂,305 毒性物质和感染性物质
2936240000	(1)饲料添加剂,301 维生素 D2(无检疫要求食品添加剂),302 烟酸(无检疫要求食品添加剂),303 烟酰胺(无检疫要求食品添加剂),304 泛酸(无检疫要求食品添加剂),305 泛酸钙(无检疫要求食品添加剂),306 需申报仅用于工业用途不用于食品添加剂无检疫要求的化学品
2936270020	(1)化工产品,301 抗坏血酸钙(无检疫要求食品添加剂),302 抗坏血酸钠(无检疫要求食品添加剂),303 需申报仅用于工业用途不用于食品添加剂无检疫要求的化学品
2936270030	301 无检疫要求食品添加剂,302 需申报仅用于工业用途不用于食品添加剂无检疫要求的化学品,303 其他化工产品
2936270090	(1)饲料添加剂,(2)化工产品,301 无检疫要求食品添加剂,302 需申报仅用于工业用途不用于食品添加剂无检疫要求的化学品
2936280000	(1)饲料添加剂,(2)具有保健食品批准文号 .301 生育酚(无检疫要求食品添加剂),302 维生素 E(无检疫要求食品添加剂),303 天然维生素 E(无检疫要求食品添加剂),304d-α 醋酸生育酚(无检疫要求食品添加剂),305 需申报仅用于工业用途不用于食品添加剂无检疫要求的化学品
2936290090	(1)饲料添加剂,301 生物素(无检疫要求食品添加剂),302 维生素 D(无检疫要求食品添加剂),303 维生素 B 族(无检疫要求食品添加剂),304 维生素 k(植物甲萘醌)(无检疫要求食品添加剂),305 需申报仅用于工业用途不用于食品添加剂无检疫要求的化学品)
2939799091	301 无检疫要求食品添加剂,302 需申报仅用于工业用途不用于食品添加剂无检疫要求的化学品
2940001000	(1)饲料添加剂,(2)蔗糖脂肪酸酯(无检疫要求食品添加剂),(3)乙酰磺胺酸钾(安赛蜜)(无检疫要求食品添加剂),(4)蔗糖聚丙烯醚(无检疫要求食品添加剂),(5)麦芽糖醇液(无检疫要求食品添加剂),(6)d-核糖(无检疫要求食品添加剂),(7)d-木糖(无检疫要求食品添加剂),(8)L-阿戊糖(无检疫要求食品添加剂),(9)L-鼠李糖(无检疫要求食品添加剂),(10)八乙酸蔗糖酯(无检疫要求食品添加剂)
2940009000	(1)饲料添加剂,(2)合成糖,(3)蔗糖脂肪酸酯(无检疫要求食品添加剂),(4)乙酰磺胺酸钾(安赛蜜)(无检疫要求食品添加剂),(5)蔗糖聚丙烯醚(无检疫要求食品添加剂),(6)麦芽糖醇液(无检疫要求食品添加剂),(7)d-核糖(无检疫要求食品添加剂),(8)d-木糖(无检疫要求食品添加剂),(9)L-阿戊糖(无检疫要求食品添加剂),(10)L-鼠李糖(无检疫要求食品添加剂),(11)八乙酸蔗糖酯(无检疫要求食品添加剂),(12)需申报仅用于工业用途不用于食品添加剂无检疫要求的化学品
2942000000	(1)饲料添加剂,301 爆炸品,302 易燃气体,303 非易燃无毒气体,304 毒性气体,305 易燃液体,306 易燃固体,307 易于自燃的物质,308 遇水放出易燃气体的物质,309 氧化性物质,310 有机过氧化物,311 毒性物质和感染性物质,312 腐蚀性物质,313 杂项物质,314 其他危险化学品
3001200090	(1)动物白蛋白,(2)动物球蛋白,(3)动物纤维蛋白原,(4)其他动物血清蛋白,(5)动物培养器官,(6)动物培养细胞,(7)动物微生物培养培养基,(8)其他动物器官、细胞、培养基,(9)未列出的其他动物产品,(10)其他化工产品,(11)医用动物细胞系,(12)其他医用生物制品,(13)工业用牛胰腺,(14)工业用猪胰腺,(15)牛胆汁,(16)牛胆粉、牛胆膏

HS 编码	CIQ 扩展品名
3002190090	(1)猪全血,(2)马全血,(3)兔全血,(4)狗全血,(5)其他动物全血,(6)猪血浆,(7)马血浆,(8)兔血浆,(9)狗血浆,(10)其他动物血浆,(11)胎牛血清,(12)小(犊)牛血清,(13)猪血清,(14)马血清,(15)兔血清,(16)小鼠血清,(17)其他动物血清,(18)动检抗原,(19)动检抗体,(20)动检抗血清,(21)动检补体,(22)动检溶血素,(23)动物球蛋白,(24)动物纤维蛋白原,(25)其他动物血清蛋白,(26)其他动物性血液制品,(27)动物微生物培养培养基,(28)诊断用试剂及试剂盒,301 其他化工产品,401 医用诊断试剂,402 医用检测试剂,403 医用抗体,404 医用抗毒素,405 医用抗原,406 医用变态反应原,407 生长因子之外医用细胞因子,408 其他医用蛋白,409 其他医用生物制品
3002903010	(1)动检细菌,(2)动检病毒,(3)动检真菌,(4)动检放线菌,(5)动检螺旋体,(6)动检立克次氏体,(7)动检支原体,(8)动检衣原体,(9)动检菌种,(10)动检毒种,(11)其他动检微生物,(12)动检寄生虫,(13)植物细菌,(14)植物病毒,(15)医用细菌,(16)医用病毒,(17)其他医用微生物
3002903090	(1)动检细菌,(2)动检病毒,(3)动检真菌,(4)动检放线菌,(5)动检螺旋体,(6)动检立克次氏体,(7)动检支原体,(8)动检衣原体,(9)动检菌种,(10)动检毒种,(11)其他动检微生物,(12)动检寄生虫,(13)植物细菌,(14)植物病毒,(15)医用细菌,(16)医用病毒,(17)医用真菌,(18)除细菌、真菌、病毒以外的其他医用微生物,(19)环保微生物,(20)人体寄生虫,(21)医用微生态制剂,(31)食品加工用酵母制品(活性酵母),(32)品加工用酵母制品(非活性酵母),(33)食品加工用酵母衍生制品,(34)食品加工用其他酵母产品,(35)食品加工用乳酸菌,(36)食品加工用乳酸菌产品,(37)其他食品加工用菌种及其产品
3002904010	(1)动检细菌,(2)动检病毒,(3)动检真菌,(4)动检放线菌,(5)动检螺旋体,(6)动检立克次氏体,(7)动检支原体,(8)动检衣原体,(9)动检菌种,(10)动检毒种,(11)其他动检微生物,(12)动检寄生虫,(13)其他化工产品,(14)医用核酸及其制品,(15)其他医用生物制品
3002904090	(1)动检细菌,(2)动检病毒,(3)动检真菌,(4)动检放线菌,(5)动检螺旋体,(6)动检立克次氏体,(7)动检支原体,(8)动检衣原体,(9)动检菌种,(10)动检毒种,(11)其他动检微生物,(12)动检寄生虫,(13)医用核酸及其制品,(14)其他医用生物制品
3002909011	(1)猪全血,(2)马全血,(3)兔全血,(4)狗全血,(5)其他动物全血,(6)猪血浆,(7)马血浆,(8)兔血浆,(9)狗血浆,(10)其他动物血浆,(11)胎牛血清,(12)小(犊)牛血清,(13)猪血清,(14)马血清,(15)兔血清,(16)小鼠血清,(17)其他动物血清,(18)动检抗原,(19)动检抗体,(20)动检抗血清,(21)动检补体,(22)动检溶血素,(23)动物球蛋白,(24)动物纤维蛋白原,(25)其他动物血清蛋白,(26)其他动物性血液制品,(27)动物微生物培养培养基,(28)诊断用试剂及试剂盒,(29)其他化工产品,(30)牛血清成品,(31)牛血蛋白,(32)牛血清白蛋白
3002909019	(1)猪全血,(2)马全血,(3)兔全血,(4)狗全血,(5)其他动物全血,(6)猪血浆,(7)马血浆,(8)兔血浆,(9)狗血浆,(10)其他动物血浆,(11)胎牛血清,(12)小(犊)牛血清,(13)猪血清,(14)马血清,(15)兔血清,(16)小鼠血清,(17)其他动物血清,(18)动检抗原,(19)动检抗体,(20)动检抗血清,(21)动检补体,(22)动检溶血素,(23)动物球蛋白,(24)动物纤维蛋白原,(25)其他动物血清蛋白,(26)其他动物性血液制品,(27)动物微生物培养培养基,(28)诊断用试剂及试剂盒,(29)医用抗体,(30)医用抗原,(31)其他医用生物制品,(32)人源血浆,(33)人源血清,(34)血细胞(人源血细胞(红细胞、白细胞、血小板)),(35)血浆蛋白(人血浆蛋白(白蛋白、球蛋白、纤维蛋白原)),(36)人血液因子制剂,(37)其他人血制品
3002909091	(1)动检细菌,(2)动检病毒,(3)动检真菌,(4)动检放线菌,(5)动检螺旋体,(6)动检立克次氏体,(7)动检支原体,(8)动检衣原体,(9)其他动检微生物,(10)动检寄生虫,(11)猪全血,(12)马全血,(13)兔全血,(14)狗全血,(15)其他动物全血,(16)猪血浆,(17)马血浆,(18)兔血浆,(19)狗血浆,(20)其他动物血浆,(21)胎牛血清,(22)犊牛血清,(23)猪血清,(24)马血清,(25)兔血清,(26)小鼠血清,(27)其他动物血清,(28)动检抗原,(29)动检抗体,(30)动检抗血清,(31)动检补体,(32)动检溶血素,(33)动物球蛋白,(34)动物纤维蛋白原,(35)其他动物血清蛋白,(36)其他动物性血液制品,(37)动物微生物培养培养基,(38)诊断用试剂及试剂盒,(39)其他化工产品,(40)毒素,(41)牛血清成品,(42)牛血蛋白,(43)牛血清白蛋白
3002909099	(1)动检细菌,(2)动检病毒,(3)动检真菌,(4)动检放线菌,(5)动检螺旋体,(6)动检立克次氏体,(7)动检支原体,(8)动检衣原体,(9)其他动检微生物,(10)动检寄生虫,(11)猪全血,(12)小(犊)牛血清,(13)兔全血,(14)狗全血,(15)其他动物全血,(16)猪血浆,(17)马血浆,(18)兔血浆,(19)狗血浆,(20)其他动物血浆,(21)胎牛血清,(22)犊牛血清,(23)猪血清,(24)马血清,(25)兔血清,(26)小鼠血清,(27)其他动物血清,(28)动检抗原,(29)动检抗体,(30)动检抗血清,(31)动检补体,(32)动检溶血素,(33)动物白蛋白,(34)动物球蛋白,(35)动物纤维蛋白原,(36)其他动物血清蛋白,(37)其他动物性血液制品,(38)动物微生物培养培养基,(39)不包括酵母及类似产品诊断用试剂及试剂盒,(40)医用抗体,(41)医用抗原,(42)毒素,(43)其他医用生物制品,(44)人源全血,(45)人源血浆,(46)人源血清,(47)红细胞、白细胞、血小板,(48)脐带血,(49)其他人血制品,(50)环保微生物,(51)牛血清成品,(52)牛血蛋白,(53)牛血清白蛋白
3203002000	301 其他危险化学品,需申报仅用于工业用途不用于食品添加剂无检疫要求,302 无检疫要求食品添加剂,303 一般化学品,需申报仅用于工业用途不用于食品添加剂无检疫要求,304 属于危险化学品的食品添加剂
3204110000	301 其他危险化学品,需申报仅用于工业用途不用于食品添加剂无检疫要求,302 无检疫要求食品添加剂,303 需申报仅用于工业用途不用于食品添加剂无检疫要求的化学品,304 一般化学品,需申报仅用于工业用途不用于食品添加剂无检疫要求,305 属于危险化学品的食品添加剂
3204120000	301 其他危险化学品,需申报仅用于工业用途不用于食品添加剂无检疫要求,302 无检疫要求食品添加剂,303 一般化学品,需申报仅用于工业用途不用于食品添加剂无检疫要求,304 属于危险化学品的食品添加剂
3204130000	301 其他危险化学品,需申报仅用于工业用途不用于食品添加剂无检疫要求,302 无检疫要求食品添加剂,303 需申报仅用于工业用途不用于食品添加剂无检疫要求的化学品,304 一般化学品,需申报仅用于工业用途不用于食品添加剂无检疫要求,305 属于危险化学品的食品添加剂
3204140000	301 其他危险化学品,需申报仅用于工业用途不用于食品添加剂无检疫要求,302 无检疫要求食品添加剂,303 一般化学品,需申报仅用于工业用途不用于食品添加剂无检疫要求,304 属于危险化学品的食品添加剂
3204199000	(1)饲料添加剂,301 其他危险化学品,需申报仅用于工业用途不用于食品添加剂无检疫要求,302 无检疫要求食品添加剂,303 一般化学品,需申报仅用于工业用途不用于食品添加剂无检疫要求,304 属于危险化学品的食品添加剂

HS 编码	CIQ 扩展品名
3208909010	(1)属于危险化学品的涂料,(2)银幕白漆,(3)聚酯树脂清漆,(4)红丹油性防锈漆,(5)远红外线辐射涂料,(6)硼钡酚醛防锈漆,(7)互感器环氧酯磁漆,(8)环氧防腐漆,(9)环氧绝缘烘漆,(10)环氧绝缘漆,(11)环氧烘漆,(12)环氧清漆,(13)环氧磁漆,(14)环氧醇酸清烘漆,(15)环氧酚醛防腐烘漆,(16)环氧腻子,(17)环氧富锌底漆,(18)环氧聚氯酯耐水漆,(19)环烷酸铜防虫漆,(20)松香防污漆,(21)氨基透明烘漆,(22)氨基清烘漆,(23)氨基静电清烘漆,(24)氨基醇酸绝缘漆,(25)酚醛绝缘漆,(26)酚醛烘漆,(27)酚醛清漆,(28)酚醛漆包线漆,(29)酚醛透明漆,(30)酚醛硅钢片漆,(31)铝红酚醛防锈漆,(32)铝粉酚醛磁漆,(33)铝粉缩醛磁漆,(34)铝粉醇酸磁漆,(35)银灰氨基锤纹漆,(36)银灰酚醛磁漆,(37)聚酰亚胺漆包线漆,(38)醇酸绝缘漆,(39)醇酸烘漆,(40)醇酸清漆,(41)醇酸漆包线漆
3210000091	(1)染皮鞋水,(2)再生胶沥青涂料,(3)银灰三防锤纹漆,(4)有机硅耐高温漆,(5)沥青半导体漆,(6)沥青防污漆,(7)沥青底漆,(8)沥青绝缘漆,(9)沥青清烘漆,(10)沥青清漆,(11)沥青耐酸漆,(12)沥青锅炉漆,(13)沥青磁漆,(14)沥青醇酸氨基烘漆,(15)鱼油沥青涂料,(16)油封清漆,(17)油基硅钢片漆,(18)玻璃管绝缘漆,(19)贴花快燥清漆,(20)钙酯清漆,(21)铝粉有机硅耐热漆,(22)铝粉环氧沥青耐油底漆,(23)铝粉氯化橡胶底漆,(24)黑色氯丁橡胶可剥漆,(25)酯胶清烘漆,(26)酯胶清漆,(27)煤焦沥青清漆,(28)聚合清油,(29)硝化纤维漆布,(30)硝化纤维漆纸,(31)硝化纤维漆片
3210000099	(1)染皮鞋水,(2)再生胶沥青涂料,(3)银灰三防锤纹漆,(4)有机硅耐高温漆,(5)沥青半导体漆,(6)沥青防污漆,(7)沥青底漆,(8)沥青绝缘漆,(9)沥青清烘漆,(10)沥青清漆,(11)沥青耐酸漆,(12)沥青锅炉漆,(13)沥青磁漆,(14)沥青醇酸氨基烘漆,(15)鱼油沥青涂料,(16)油封清漆,(17)油基硅钢片漆,(18)玻璃管绝缘漆,(19)贴花快燥清漆,(20)钙酯清漆,(21)铝粉有机硅耐热漆,(22)铝粉环氧沥青耐油底漆,(23)铝粉氯化橡胶底漆,(24)黑色氯丁橡胶可剥漆,(25)酯胶清烘漆,(26)酯胶清漆,(27)煤焦沥青清漆,(28)聚合清油,(29)硝化纤维漆布,(30)硝化纤维漆纸,(31)硝化纤维漆片
3301120000	(1)面部香精油,(2)发用香精精油,(3)体用香精精油,(4)易燃液体,(5)无检疫要求食品添加剂,(6)无检疫要求的食品添加剂,(7)属于危险化学品的食品添加剂
3301130000	(1)面部香精油,(2)发用香精精油,(3)体用香精精油,(4)易燃液体,(5)无检疫要求食品添加剂,(6)无检疫要求的食品添加剂,(7)属于危险化学品的食品添加剂
3301191000	(1)面部香精油,(2)发用香精精油,(3)体用香精精油,(4)易燃液体,(5)无检疫要求食品添加剂,(6)无检疫要求的食品添加剂,(7)属于危险化学品的食品添加剂
3301250000	(1)面部香精油,(2)发用香精精油,(3)体用香精精油,(4)无检疫要求食品添加剂,(5)需申报仅用于工业用途不用于食品添加剂无检疫要求的化学品
3301291000	(1)面部香精油,(2)发用香精精油,(3)体用香精精油,(4)易燃液体,(5)无检疫要求食品添加剂,(6)无检疫要求的食品添加剂,(7)属于危险化学品的食品添加剂
3301309090	(1)吐鲁香膏,(2)晚香玉浸膏,(3)香榧子壳浸膏,(4)秘鲁香膏油,(5)秘鲁香脂
3301901090	301 易燃液体,302 无检疫要求食品添加剂,303 属于危险化学品的食品添加剂
3302109001	301 易燃液体,302 无检疫要求食品添加剂,303 无检疫要求的食品添加剂,304 属于危险化学品的食品添加剂
3302109090	501 其他危险化学品,502 无检疫要求食品添加剂,503 无检疫要求的食品添加剂,504 属于危险化学品的食品添加剂
3303000010	(1)液体香水、香氛,(2)固体香膏(粉)),(3)花露水、去痱水
3303000020	(1)液体香水、香氛,(2)固体香膏(粉)),(3)花露水、去痱水
3304100011	(1)防晒化妆品,(2)婴幼儿驻留类肤用化妆品,(3)成人口唇驻留类化妆品,(4)成人口唇淋洗类化妆品,(5)成人口唇膜类化妆品,(6)成人口唇美容化妆品
3304100012	(1)防晒化妆品,(2)婴幼儿驻留类肤用化妆品,(3)成人口唇驻留类化妆品,(4)成人口唇淋洗类化妆品,(5)成人口唇膜类化妆品,(6)成人口唇美容化妆品
3304100091	(1)防晒化妆品,(2)婴幼儿驻留类肤用化妆品,(3)成人口唇驻留类化妆品,(4)成人口唇淋洗类化妆品,(5)成人口唇膜类化妆品,(6)成人口唇美容化妆品
3304100092	(1)防晒化妆品,(2)婴幼儿驻留类肤用化妆品,(3)成人口唇驻留类化妆品,(4)成人口唇淋洗类化妆品,(5)成人口唇膜类化妆品,(6)成人口唇美容化妆品
3304200011	(1)美白化妆品,(2)防晒化妆品,(3)婴幼儿驻留类肤用化妆品,(4)成人眼部驻留类化妆品,(5)成人眼部淋洗类化妆品,(6)成人眼部膜类化妆品,(7)成人眼部美容化妆品
3304200012	(1)美白化妆品,(2)防晒化妆品,(3)婴幼儿驻留类肤用化妆品,(4)成人眼部驻留类化妆品,(5)成人眼部淋洗类化妆品,(6)成人眼部膜类化妆品,(7)成人眼部美容化妆品
3304200091	(1)美白化妆品,(2)防晒化妆品,(3)婴幼儿驻留类肤用化妆品,(4)成人眼部驻留类化妆品,(5)成人眼部淋洗类化妆品,(6)成人眼部膜类化妆品,(7)成人眼部美容化妆品
3304200092	(1)美白化妆品,(2)防晒化妆品,(3)婴幼儿驻留类肤用化妆品,(4)成人眼部驻留类化妆品,(5)成人眼部淋洗类化妆品,(6)成人眼部膜类化妆品,(7)成人眼部美容化妆品
3304200093	(1)成人眼部膜类化妆品
3304300001	(1)成人指(趾)甲护理化妆品,(2)成人指(趾)甲美容化妆品,(3)婴幼儿指(趾)甲化妆品
3304300002	(1)成人指(趾)甲护理化妆品,(2)成人指(趾)甲美容化妆品,(3)婴幼儿指(趾)甲化妆品
3304300003	(1)成人指(趾)甲护理化妆品,(2)成人指(趾)甲美容化妆品,(3)婴幼儿指(趾)甲化妆品
3304910000	(1)成人爽身粉,(2)成人面部用美容化妆品,(3)成人体用美容化妆品,(4)婴幼儿美容化妆品,(5)固体香膏(粉),(6)美白化妆品,(7)防晒化妆品,(8)婴幼儿爽身粉,(9)婴幼儿驻留类肤用化妆品,(10)婴幼儿淋洗类肤用化妆品,(11)成人面部驻留类化妆品,(12)成人面部淋洗类化妆品,(13)婴幼儿淋洗类发用化妆品,(14)成人淋洗类毛发月化妆品,(15)成人驻留类毛发用化妆品,(16)成人眼部美容化妆品,(17)成人眉用美容化妆品

HS 编码	CIQ 扩展品名
3304990021	(201)婴幼儿驻留类肤用化妆品,202 婴幼儿淋洗类肤用化妆品,203 成人面部驻留类化妆品,204 成人面部淋洗类化妆品,205 成人面部膜类化妆品,206 成人眼部驻留类化妆品,207 成人口唇驻留类化妆品,208 成人眼部淋洗类化妆品,209 成人口唇淋洗类化妆品,210 成人体用驻留类化妆品,211 成人体用淋洗类化妆品,212 成人体用膜类化妆品,213 成人面部用美容化妆品,214 成人体用美容化妆品,215 成人睫毛用美容化妆品,216 成人眉用美容化妆品,217 婴幼儿美容化妆品,218 面部香精油,219 发用香精精油,220 体用香精精油,221 美白化妆品,222 防晒化妆品,223 美乳化妆品,224 健美化妆品,225 脱毛化妆品
3304990029	(201)婴幼儿驻留类肤用化妆品,202 婴幼儿淋洗类肤用化妆品,203 成人面部驻留类化妆品,204 成人面部淋洗类化妆品,205 成人面部膜类化妆品,206 成人眼部驻留类化妆品,207 成人口唇驻留类化妆品,208 成人眼部淋洗类化妆品,209 成人口唇淋洗类化妆品,210 成人体用驻留类化妆品,211 成人体用淋洗类化妆品,212 成人体用膜类化妆品,213 成人面部用美容化妆品,214 成人体用美容化妆品,215 成人睫毛用美容化妆品,216 成人眉用美容化妆品,217 婴幼儿美容化妆品,218 面部香精油,219 发用香精精油,220 体用香精精油,221 美白化妆品,222 防晒化妆品,223 美乳化妆品,224 健美化妆品,225 脱毛化妆品
3304990031	(201)婴幼儿驻留类肤用化妆品,202 婴幼儿淋洗类肤用化妆品,203 成人面部驻留类化妆品,204 成人面部淋洗类化妆品,205 成人面部膜类化妆品,206 成人眼部驻留类化妆品,207 成人口唇驻留类化妆品,208 成人眼部淋洗类化妆品,209 成人口唇淋洗类化妆品,210 成人体用驻留类化妆品,211 成人体用淋洗类化妆品,212 成人体用膜类化妆品,213 成人面部用美容化妆品,214 成人体用美容化妆品,215 成人睫毛用美容化妆品,216 成人眉用美容化妆品,217 婴幼儿美容化妆品,218 面部香精油,219 发用香精精油,220 体用香精精油,221 美白化妆品,222 防晒化妆品,223 美乳化妆品,224 健美化妆品,225 脱毛化妆品
3304990039	(201)婴幼儿驻留类肤用化妆品,202 婴幼儿淋洗类肤用化妆品,203 成人面部驻留类化妆品,204 成人面部淋洗类化妆品,205 成人面部膜类化妆品,206 成人眼部驻留类化妆品,207 成人口唇驻留类化妆品,208 成人眼部淋洗类化妆品,209 成人口唇淋洗类化妆品,210 成人体用驻留类化妆品,211 成人体用淋洗类化妆品,212 成人体用膜类化妆品,213 成人面部用美容化妆品,214 成人体用美容化妆品,215 成人睫毛用美容化妆品,216 成人眉用美容化妆品,217 婴幼儿美容化妆品,218 面部香精油,219 发用香精精油,220 体用香精精油,221 美白化妆品,222 防晒化妆品,223 美乳化妆品,224 健美化妆品,225 脱毛化妆品
3304990091	(1)婴幼儿驻留类肤用化妆品,(3)成人面部驻留类化妆品,(4)成人体用驻留类化妆品,(5)婴幼儿淋洗类肤用化妆品,(6)成人面部淋洗类化妆品,(7)成人口唇淋洗类化妆品,(8)成人体用淋洗类化妆品,(12)防晒化妆品,(20)成人面部膜类化妆品,(21)成人眼部驻留类化妆品,(22)成人口唇驻留类化妆品,(23)成人眼部淋洗类化妆品,(24)成人体用膜类化妆品,(25)面部香精油,(26)发用香精精油,(27)体用香精精油,(28)美白化妆品
3304990099	(1)婴幼儿驻留类肤用化妆品,(3)成人面部驻留类化妆品,(4)成人体用驻留类化妆品,(5)婴幼儿淋洗类肤用化妆品,(6)成人面部淋洗类化妆品,(7)成人口唇淋洗类化妆品,(8)成人体用淋洗类化妆品,(12)防晒化妆品,(20)成人面部膜类化妆品,(21)成人眼部驻留类化妆品,(22)成人口唇驻留类化妆品,(23)成人眼部淋洗类化妆品,(24)成人体用膜类化妆品,(25)面部香精油,(26)发用香精精油,(27)体用香精精油,(28)美白化妆品
3305900000	(1)染发化妆品,(2)育发化妆品,(3)婴幼儿淋洗类发用化妆品,(4)婴幼儿驻留类发用化妆品,(5)成人淋洗类毛发用化妆品,(6)成人驻留类毛发用化妆品,(7)其他危险化学品
3504009000	(1)具有保健食品批准文号,(2)乳铁蛋白无检疫要求食品添加剂,(3)需申报仅用于工业用途不用于食品添加剂无检疫要求的化学品,(4)其他医用蛋白,(5)大豆蛋白,(6)豌豆蛋白,(7)蚕豆蛋白,(8)其他豆类蛋白,(9)小麦蛋白,(10)燕麦蛋白,(11)大米蛋白,(12)玉米蛋白,(13)其他谷类蛋白,(14)花生蛋白,(15)其他坚果及籽类蛋白,(16)马铃薯蛋白,(17)其他薯类蛋白,(18)其他植物蛋白,浓缩牛奶蛋白
3506919090	(1)丙烯酸酯胶粘剂,(2)氯丁酚醛胶粘剂,(3)聚氨基甲酸酯胶粘剂,(4)202 胶粘剂,(5)传真纸粘合剂,(6)聚氨酯粘合剂,(7)嫌气性密封粘合剂,(8)酚醛·丁腈粘合剂,(9)酚醛·缩醛有机硅粘合剂,(10)酚醛·缩醛粘合剂,(11)聚乙烯醇缩醛胶,(12)聚硅氧橡胶基印模膏,(13)过氯乙烯胶,(14)体患除凝胶,(15)汽车门窗胶,(16)橡胶金属胶,(17)液体密封胶,(18)聚氨酯涂层胶,(19)黑醇酸隔热胶,(20)橡胶水,(21)蜡纸胶水,(22)氟橡胶胶浆,(23)硝基胶液,(24)缩醛胶液,(25)缩醛烘干胶液,(26)硅酸苯悬浮液,(27)聚氨酯化学灌浆材料,(28)伏栏,(29)电子束光刻胶
3604100000	(1)喷花类玩具烟花爆竹,(2)旋转类玩具烟花爆竹,(3)旋转升空类玩具烟花爆竹,(4)火箭类玩具烟花爆竹,(5)吐珠类玩具烟花爆竹,(6)线香类玩具烟花爆竹,(7)摩擦炮类玩具烟花爆竹,(8)造型玩具类玩具烟花爆竹,(9)地面礼花类玩具烟花爆竹,(10)烟雾类玩具烟花爆竹,(11)礼花弹类玩具烟花爆竹,(12)玩具烟花爆竹组合,(13)爆竹,(14)喷花类大型烟花,(15)旋转类大型烟花,(16)火箭类大型烟花,(17)吐珠类大型烟花,(18)地面礼花类大型烟花,(19)礼花弹类大型烟花,(20)大型烟花组合
3814000000	(1)脱漆剂,(2)有机硅漆稀释剂,(3)过氯乙烯锤纹漆稀释剂,(4)过氯乙烯漆稀释剂,(5)沥青漆稀释剂,(6)环氧漆稀释剂,(7)氨基漆稀释剂,(8)氨基静电漆稀释剂,(9)酚醛皱纹漆稀释剂,(10)硝基铝箔漆稀释剂,(11)硝基漆稀释剂,(12)聚氨酯漆稀释剂,(13)聚酯漆包线漆稀释剂,(14)聚酯漆稀释剂,(15)缩醛漆稀释剂,(16)醇酸漆稀释剂
3909200000	(1)−18℃≤闪点<23℃,三聚氰胺甲醛树酯,(2)−18℃≤闪点<23℃,三聚氰胺树酯,(3)−18℃≤闪点<23℃,甲醇改性三羟甲基三聚氰胺甲醛树脂,(4)−18℃≤闪点<23℃,苯代三聚氰胺甲醛树脂,(5)其他
3924100000	(1)食品接触聚苯乙烯产品,(2)食品接触聚乙烯产品,(3)食品接触聚丙烯产品,(4)食品接触聚氯乙烯产品,(5)食品接触三聚氰胺−甲醛产品,(6)食品接触丙烯腈−丁二烯−苯乙烯产品,(7)食品接触丙烯腈−苯乙烯产品,(8)食品接触不饱和聚酯树脂及其玻璃钢产品,(9)食品接触对苯二甲酸乙二醇酯产品,(10)食品接触尼龙产品,(11)食品接触聚碳酸酯产品,(12)食品接触聚偏二氯乙烯产品,(13)食品接触聚甲基丙烯酸甲酯产品,(14)食品接触聚甲基戊烯产品,(15)食品接触复合塑料(仅指多种塑料材质复合)产品,(16)食品接触其他塑料产品,(17)食品用聚苯乙烯包装,(18)食品用聚乙烯包装,(19)食品用聚丙烯包装,(20)食品用聚氯乙烯瓶盖垫片,(21)食品用其他聚氯乙烯包装,(22)食品用三聚氰胺−甲醛包装,(23)食品用丙烯腈−丁二烯−苯乙烯包装,(24)食品用丙烯腈−苯乙烯包装,(25)食品用不饱和聚酯树脂及其玻璃钢包装,(26)食品用对苯二甲酸乙二醇酯包装,(27)食品用尼龙包装),(28)食品用聚碳酸酯包装,(29)食品用聚偏二氯乙烯包装,(30)食品用聚甲基丙烯酸甲酯包装,(31)食品用聚甲基戊烯包装,(32)食品用复合塑料(仅指多种塑料材质复合)包装,(33)食品用其他塑料包装,(34)非食品用塑料容器用具
4301809010	〔(1)斑马皮,(2)野驴皮,(3)其他野生奇蹄动物皮张,(4)野猪皮,(5)野羊皮,(6)野骆驼皮,(7)野鹿皮,(8)其他野生偶蹄动物皮张,(9)其他禽鸟皮,(10)象皮,(11)袋鼠皮,(12)海豹皮,(13)鳄鱼皮,(14)蜥蜴皮,(15)蛇皮,(16)蟒蛇皮,(17)未列出的其他动物皮张,(18)艾鼬皮,(19)臭鼬皮,(20)短尾猫皮,(21)负鼠皮,(22)海狸皮,(23)旱獭皮,(24)貉子皮,(25)浣熊皮,(26)灰鼠皮,(27)狼皮,(28)猞猁皮,(29)麝鼠皮,(30)水獭皮,(31)松鼠皮〕
4301809090	〔(1)驴皮,(2)骡皮,(3)其他饲养奇蹄动物皮张,(4)猪皮,(5)绵羊皮,(6)山羊皮,(7)骆驼皮,(8)鹿皮,(9)其他饲养偶蹄动物皮张,(10)鸡、鸭、鹅皮,(11)兔皮,(12)未列出的其他动物皮张,(13)艾鼬皮,(14)臭鼬皮,(15)短尾猫皮,(16)负鼠皮,(17)海狸皮,(18)旱獭皮,(19)貉子皮,(20)浣熊皮,(21)灰鼠皮,(22)狼皮,(23)猞猁皮,(24)麝鼠皮,(25)水獭皮,(26)松鼠皮〕
4403499090	(1)针叶原木,(2)白柳桉原木及其他柳桉原木,(3)羯布罗香木等原木,(4)安哥拉香桃花心木等原木,(5)其他非针叶原木
4407299099	(1)其他热带木木材,(2)加蓬榄木、非洲白梧桐等木厚板材,(3)橡胶木方
4408391990	(1)针叶木薄板,(2)非针叶木薄板

HS 编码	CIQ 扩展品名
4408901911	(1)针叶木薄板,(2)非针叶木薄板
4408901919	(1)针叶木薄板,(2)非针叶木薄板
4408901991	(1)针叶木薄板,(2)非针叶木薄板
4408901999	(1)针叶木薄板,(2)非针叶木薄板
4410909000	(1)其他厚度超过 6 毫米的板材、方材、垫木,(2)其他厚度小于或等于 6 毫米的薄板
4411121900	(1)针叶木纤维板,(2)非针叶木纤维板,(3)其他纤维板
4411122900	(1)针叶木纤维板,(2)非针叶木纤维板,(3)其他纤维板
4411129100	(1)针叶木纤维板,(2)非针叶木纤维板,(3)其他纤维板
4411131100	(1)针叶木纤维板,(2)非针叶木纤维板,(3)其他纤维板
4411131900	(1)针叶木纤维板,(2)非针叶木纤维板,(3)其他纤维板
4411132900	(1)针叶木纤维板,(2)非针叶木纤维板,(3)其他纤维板
4411139100	(1)针叶木纤维板,(2)非针叶木纤维板,(3)其他纤维板
4411139900	(1)针叶木纤维板,(2)非针叶木纤维板,(3)其他纤维板
4411142900	(1)针叶木纤维板,(2)非针叶木纤维板,(3)其他纤维板
4411149900	(1)针叶木纤维板,(2)非针叶木纤维板,(3)其他纤维板
4411921000	(1)针叶木纤维板,(2)非针叶木纤维板,(3)其他纤维板
4411939000	(1)针叶木纤维板,(2)非针叶木纤维板,(3)其他纤维板
4411942100	(1)针叶木纤维板,(2)非针叶木纤维板,(3)其他纤维板
4415100020	(1)针叶木木质包装,(2)非针叶木木质包装
4415100090	(1)针叶木木质包装,(2)非针叶木木质包装,(3)其他木质包装
4415209090	(1)针叶木木质包装,(2)非针叶木木质包装,(3)其他木质包装
4416009090	(1)其他木制品,(2)针叶木木质包装,(3)非针叶木木质包装
4419901000	(1)木质餐具及厨房用具,(2)食品接触木制产品
4823909000	(1)其它纸及纸制品,(2)食品接触原纸产品,(3)食品接触复合纸产品(纸和塑料膜等其他材料复合),(4)食品接触上蜡纸产品,(5)食品接触其他纸产品,(6)食品用原纸包装,(7)食品用复合纸包装(纸和塑料膜等其他材料复合),(8)食品用上蜡纸包装,(9)食品用其他纸包装
5102199010	(1)未洗净其他野生奇蹄动物鬃毛,(2)未洗净野牛毛(绒),(3)未洗净其他野生偶蹄动物鬃毛,(4)未洗净兔绒,(5)未洗净未列出的其他动物鬃毛,(6)洗净未列出的野生奇蹄动物鬃毛,(7)洗净野牛毛(绒),(8)洗净未列出的野生偶蹄动物鬃毛,(9)洗净兔绒,(10)洗净其他动物毛
5102199090	(1)未洗净其他饲养奇蹄动物鬃毛,(2)未洗净其他野生奇蹄动物鬃毛,(3)未洗净牦牛绒,(4)未洗净其他饲养偶蹄动物鬃毛,(5)未洗净其他野生偶蹄动物鬃毛,(6)未洗净兔绒,(7)未洗净未列出的其他动物鬃毛,(8)洗净未列出的饲养奇蹄动物鬃毛,(9)洗净未列出的野生奇蹄动物鬃毛,(10)洗净牦牛绒,(11)洗净未列出的饲养偶蹄动物鬃毛,(12)洗净未列出的野生偶蹄动物鬃毛,(13)洗净兔绒,(14)洗净其他动物毛
5102200010	(1)未洗净其他野生奇蹄动物鬃毛,(2)未洗净野牛毛(绒),(3)未洗净其他野生偶蹄动物鬃毛,(4)未洗净未列出的其他动物鬃毛,(5)洗净未列出的野生奇蹄动物鬃毛,(6)洗净未列出的野生偶蹄动物鬃毛,(7)洗净未列出的其他动物鬃毛
5102200090	(1)未洗净其他饲养奇蹄动物鬃毛,(2)未洗净其他野生奇蹄动物鬃毛,(3)未洗净其他饲养偶蹄动物鬃毛,(4)未洗净野牛毛(绒),(5)未洗净其他野生偶蹄动物鬃毛,(6)未洗净未列出的其他动物鬃毛,(7)洗净未列出的其他动物鬃毛
5103109010	(1)未洗净其他野生奇蹄动物鬃毛,(2)未洗净野牛毛(绒),(3)未洗净其他野生偶蹄动物鬃毛,(4)未洗净兔绒,(5)未洗净未列出的其他动物鬃毛,(6)洗净濒危野生动物细毛
8414512000	(1)换气扇 I 类器具,(2)换气扇 II 类器具,(3)换气扇 III 类器具,(4)换气扇 0I 类器具,(5)换气扇 0 类器具,(6)其它电扇及其零件 I 类器具,(7)其它电扇及其零件 II 类器具,(8)其它电扇及其零件 III 类器具,(9)其它电扇及其零件 0I 类器具,(10)其它电扇及其零件 0 类器具
8414513000	(1)有旋转导风轮的风扇 I 类器具,(2)有旋转导风轮的风扇 II 类器具,(3)有旋转导风轮的风扇 III 类器具,(4)有旋转导风轮的风扇 0I 类器具,(5)有旋转导风轮的风扇 0 类器具
8414519900	(1)其它电扇及其零件 I 类器具,(2)其它电扇及其零件 II 类器具,(3)其它电扇及其零件 III 类器具,(4)其它电扇及其零件 0I 类器具,(5)其它电扇及其零件 0 类器具
8414591000	(1)吊扇 I 类器具,(2)吊扇 II 类器具,(3)吊扇 III 类器具,(4)吊扇 0I 类器具,(5)吊扇 0 类器具,(6)其它电扇及其零件 I 类器具,(7)其它电扇及其零件 II 类器具,(8)其它电扇及其零件 III 类器具,(9)其它电扇及其零件 0I 类器具,(10)其它电扇及其零件 0 类器具
8414592000	(1)换气扇 I 类器具,(2)换气扇 II 类器具,(3)换气扇 III 类器具,(4)换气扇 0I 类器具,(5)换气扇 0 类器具,(6)其它电扇及其零件 I 类器具,(7)其它电扇及其零件 II 类器具,(8)其它电扇及其零件 III 类器具,(9)其它电扇及其零件 0I 类器具,(10)其它电扇及其零件 0 类器具
8414599091	(1)台扇 I 类器具,(2)台扇 II 类器具,(3)台扇 III 类器具,(4)台扇 0I 类器具,(5)台扇 0 类器具,(6)落地扇 I 类器具,(7)落地扇 II 类器具,(8)落地扇 III 类器具,(9)落地扇 0I 类器具,(10)落地扇 0 类器具,(11)壁扇 I 类器具,(12)壁扇 II 类器具,(13)壁扇 III 类器具,(14)壁扇 0I 类器具,(15)壁扇 0 类器具,(16)其它电扇及其零件 I 类器具,(17)其它电扇及其零件 II 类器具,(18)其它电扇及其零件 III 类器具,(19)其它电扇及其零件 0I 类器具,(20)其它电扇及其零件 0 类器具
8414599099	(1)其它电扇及其零件 I 类器具,(2)其它电扇及其零件 II 类器具,(3)其它电扇及其零件 III 类器具,(4)其它电扇及其零件 0I 类器具,(5)其它电扇及其零件 0 类器具
8414909010	(1)其它风机及其零件,(2)其它电扇及其零件 I 类器具,(3)其它电扇及其零件 II 类器具,(4)其它电扇及其零件 III 类器具,(5)其它电扇及其零件 0I 类器具,(6)其它电扇及其零件 0 类器具,(7)带有迷宫式密封装置往复式压缩机,(8)其它空气压缩机(站)及零件,(9)其它制冷设备用压缩机及其零件

HS编码	CIQ扩展品名
8415200000	(1)车用空气调节器I类器具,(2)车用空气调节器II类器具,(3)车用空气调节器III类器具,(4)车用空气调节器0I类器具,(5)车用空气调节器0类器具
8415811000	(1)独立窗式空调调节器I类器具,(2)独立窗式空调调节器II类器具,(3)独立窗式空调调节器III类器具,(4)独立窗式空调调节器0I类器具,(5)独立窗式空调调节器0类器具,(6)分体空调调节器I类器具,(7)分体空调调节器II类器具,(8)分体空调调节器III类器具,(9)分体空调调节器0I类器具,(10)分体空调调节器0类器具,(11)其它空气调节装置及其零件I类器具,(12)其它空气调节装置及其零件II类器具,(13)其它空气调节装置及其零件III类器具,(14)其它空气调节装置及其零件0I类器具,(15)其它空气调节装置及其零件0类器具
8415812001	(1)独立窗式空调调节器I类器具,(2)独立窗式空调调节器II类器具,(3)独立窗式空调调节器III类器具,(4)独立窗式空调调节器0I类器具,(5)独立窗式空调调节器0类器具,(6)分体空调调节器I类器具,(7)分体空调调节器II类器具,(8)分体空调调节器III类器具,(9)分体空调调节器0I类器具,(10)分体空调调节器0类器具,(11)其它空气调节装置及其零件I类器具,(12)其它空气调节装置及其零件II类器具,(14)其它空气调节装置及其零件0I类器具,(15)其它空气调节装置及其零件0类器具,(13)其它空气调节装置及其零件III类器具
8415812090	(1)独立窗式空调调节器I类器具,(2)独立窗式空调调节器II类器具,(3)独立窗式空调调节器III类器具,(4)独立窗式空调调节器0I类器具,(5)独立窗式空调调节器0类器具,(6)分体空调调节器I类器具,(7)分体空调调节器II类器具,(8)分体空调调节器III类器具,(9)分体空调调节器0I类器具,(10)分体空调调节器0类器具,(11)其它空气调节装置及其零件I类器具,(12)其它空气调节装置及其零件II类器具,(13)其它空气调节装置及其零件III类器具,(14)其它空气调节装置及其零件0I类器具,(15)其它空气调节装置及其零件0类器具
8415821000	(1)独立窗式空调调节器I类器具,(2)独立窗式空调调节器II类器具,(3)独立窗式空调调节器III类器具,(4)独立窗式空调调节器0I类器具,(5)独立窗式空调调节器0类器具,(6)分体空调调节器I类器具,(7)分体空调调节器II类器具,(8)分体空调调节器III类器具,(9)分体空调调节器0I类器具,(10)分体空调调节器0类器具,(11)其它空气调节装置及其零件I类器具,(12)其它空气调节装置及其零件II类器具,(13)其它空气调节装置及其零件III类器具,(14)其它空气调节装置及其零件0I类器具,(15)其它空气调节装置及其零件0类器具
8415822001	(1)独立窗式空调调节器I类器具,(2)独立窗式空调调节器II类器具,(3)独立窗式空调调节器III类器具,(4)独立窗式空调调节器0I类器具,(5)独立窗式空调调节器0类器具,(6)分体空调调节器I类器具,(7)分体空调调节器II类器具,(8)分体空调调节器III类器具,(9)分体空调调节器0I类器具,(10)分体空调调节器0类器具,(11)其它空气调节装置及其零件I类器具,(12)其它空气调节装置及其零件II类器具,(13)其它空气调节装置及其零件III类器具,(14)其它空气调节装置及其零件0I类器具,(15)其它空气调节装置及其零件0类器具
8415822090	(1)独立窗式空调调节器I类器具,(2)独立窗式空调调节器II类器具,(3)独立窗式空调调节器III类器具,(4)独立窗式空调调节器0I类器具,(5)独立窗式空调调节器0类器具,(6)分体空调调节器I类器具,(7)分体空调调节器II类器具,(8)分体空调调节器III类器具,(9)分体空调调节器0I类器具,(10)分体空调调节器0类器具,(11)其它空气调节装置及其零件I类器具,(12)其它空气调节装置及其零件II类器具,(13)其它空气调节装置及其零件III类器具,(14)其它空气调节装置及其零件0I类器具,(15)其它空气调节装置及其零件0类器具
8415830000	(1)未装有制冷装置的空调器I类器具,(2)未装有制冷装置的空调器II类器具,(3)未装有制冷装置的空调器III类器具,(4)未装有制冷装置的空调器0I类器具,(5)未装有制冷装置的空调器0类器具
8418101000	(1)冷藏冷冻组合机I类器具,(2)冷藏冷冻组合机II类器具,(3)冷藏冷冻组合机III类器具,(4)冷藏冷冻组合机0I类器具,(5)冷藏冷冻组合机0类器具
8418102000	(1)冷藏冷冻组合机I类器具,(2)冷藏冷冻组合机II类器具,(3)冷藏冷冻组合机III类器具,(4)冷藏冷冻组合机0I类器具,(5)冷藏冷冻组合机0类器具
8418103000	(1)冷藏冷冻组合机I类器具,(2)冷藏冷冻组合机II类器具,(3)冷藏冷冻组合机III类器具,(4)冷藏冷冻组合机0I类器具,(5)冷藏冷冻组合机0类器具
8418211000	(1)压缩式家用型冷藏箱I类器具,(2)压缩式家用型冷藏箱II类器具,(3)压缩式家用型冷藏箱III类器具,(4)压缩式家用型冷藏箱0I类器具,(5)压缩式家用型冷藏箱0类器具
8418212000	(1)压缩式家用型冷藏箱I类器具,(2)压缩式家用型冷藏箱II类器具,(3)压缩式家用型冷藏箱III类器具,(4)压缩式家用型冷藏箱0I类器具,(5)压缩式家用型冷藏箱0类器具
8418213000	(1)压缩式家用型冷藏箱I类器具,(2)压缩式家用型冷藏箱II类器具,(3)压缩式家用型冷藏箱III类器具,(4)压缩式家用型冷藏箱0I类器具,(5)压缩式家用型冷藏箱0类器具
8418292000	(1)电气吸收式家用型冷藏箱I类器具,(2)电气吸收式家用型冷藏箱II类器具,(3)电气吸收式家用型冷藏箱III类器具,(4)电气吸收式家用型冷藏箱0I类器具,(5)电气吸收式家用型冷藏箱0类器具
8418500000	(1)制冰机I类器具,(2)制冰机II类器具,(3)制冰机III类器具,(4)制冰机0I类器具,(5)制冰机0类器具,(6)其它冷藏冷冻柜设备及其零件
8418699020	(1)制冰机I类器具,(2)制冰机II类器具,(3)制冰机III类器具,(4)制冰机0类器具,(5)制冰机0I类器具,(6)冰激凌机I类器具,(7)冰激凌机II类器具,(8)冰激凌机III类器具,(9)冰激凌机0类器具,(10)冰激凌机0I类器具
8421211000	(1)非家用过滤及净化装置,(2)家用型过滤或净化水的机器及装置I类器具,(3)家用型过滤或净化水的机器及装置II类器具,(4)家用型过滤或净化水的机器及装置III类器具,(5)家用型过滤或净化水的机器及装置0I类器具,(6)家用型过滤或净化水的机器及装置0类器具
8421220000	(1)非家用过滤及净化装置,(2)其它过滤及其喷射装置及其零件I类器具,(3)其它过滤及其喷射装置及其零件II类器具,(4)其它过滤及其喷射装置及其零件III类器具,(5)其它过滤及其喷射装置及其零件0I类器具,(6)其它过滤及其喷射装置及其零件0类器具
8421299090	(1)非家用过滤及净化装置,(2)其它过滤及其喷射装置及其零件I类器具,(3)其他离心机及类似装置及其零件,(4)其它过滤及其喷射装置及其零件II类器具,(5)其它过滤及其喷射装置及其零件III类器具,(6)其它过滤及其喷射装置及其零件0I类器具,(7)其它过滤及其喷射装置及其零件0类器具
8421391000	(1)其他离心机及类似装置及其零件,(2)家用型气体过滤、净化机器及装置I类器具,(3)家用型气体过滤、净化机器及装置II类器具,(4)家用型气体过滤、净化机器及装置III类器具,(5)家用型气体过滤、净化机器及装置0I类器具,(6)家用型气体过滤、净化机器及装置0类器具
8422110000	(1)洗碟机及其零件I类器具,(2)洗碟机及其零件II类器具,(3)洗碟机及其零件III类器具,(4)洗碟机及其零件0I类器具,(5)洗碟机及其零件0类器具

HS 编码	CIQ 扩展品名
8422190000	(1)洗碟机及其零件 I 类器具,(2)洗碟机及其零件 II 类器具,(3)洗碟机及其零件 III 类器具,(4)洗碟机及其零件 0I 类器具,(5)洗碟机及其零件 0 类器具
8422200000	(1)其它食品加工机器及其零件,(2)其它餐具清洗机及其零件 I 类器具,(3)其它餐具清洗机及其零件 II 类器具,(4)其它餐具清洗机及其零件 III 类器具,(5)其它餐具清洗机及其零件 0I 类器具,(6)其它餐具清洗机及其零件 0 类器具,(7)其它大型家用及其类似用途电器及其零件 I 类器具,(8)其它大型家用及其类似用途电器及其零件 II 类器具,(9)其它大型家用及其类似用途电器及其零件 III 类器具,(10)其它大型家用及其类似用途电器及其零件 0I 类器具,(11)其它大型家用及其类似用途电器及其零件 0 类器具
8424891000	(1)家用型喷射、喷雾机械器具 I 类器具,(2)家用型喷射、喷雾机械器具 II 类器具,(3)家用型喷射、喷雾机械器具 III 类器具,(4)家用型喷射、喷雾机械器具 0I 类器具,(5)家用型喷射、喷雾机械器具 0 类器具
8424899910	(1)其它过滤及其喷射装置及其零件 I 类器具,(2)其它过滤及其喷射装置及其零件 II 类器具,(3)其它过滤及其喷射装置及其零件 III 类器具,(4)其它过滤及其喷射装置及其零件 0I 类器具,(5)其它过滤及其喷射装置及其零件 0 类器具
8424899990	(1)其它过滤及其喷射装置及其零件 I 类器具,(2)其它过滤及其喷射装置及其零件 II 类器具,(3)其它过滤及其喷射装置及其零件 III 类器具,(4)其它过滤及其喷射装置及其零件 0I 类器具,(5)其它过滤及其喷射装置及其零件 0 类器具
8428399000	(1)载货电梯、升降机,(2)机械式停车设备及其它装卸、储运设备及其零件,(3)其他装卸桥、提升、起重设备及零件
8450201100	(1)洗衣机 I 类器具,(2)洗衣机 II 类器具,(3)洗衣机 III 类器具,(4)洗衣机 0I 类器具,(5)洗衣机 0 类器具
8450201200	(1)洗衣机 I 类器具,(2)洗衣机 II 类器具,(3)洗衣机 III 类器具,(4)洗衣机 0I 类器具,(5)洗衣机 0 类器具
8451300000	(1)印花机,(2)纺织行业成套设备,(3)熨烫机 I 类器具,(4)熨烫机 II 类器具,(5)熨烫机 III 类器具,(6)熨烫机 0I 类器具,(7)熨烫机 0 类器具
8451800001	(1)其它印染机械及其零件,(2)纺织行业成套设备,(3)其它衣物处理设备及其零件 I 类器具,(4)其它衣物处理设备及其零件 II 类器具,(5)其它衣物处理设备及其零件 III 类器具,(6)其它衣物处理设备及其零件 0I 类器具,(7)其它衣物处理设备及其零件 0 类器具,(8)其它大型家用及其类似用途电器及其零件 I 类器具,(9)其它大型家用及其类似用途电器及其零件 II 类器具,(10)其它大型家用及其类似用途电器及其零件 III 类器具,(11)其它大型家用及其类似用途电器及其零件 0I 类器具,(12)其它大型家用及其类似用途电器及其零件 0 类器具
8451800002	(1)其它印染机械及其零件,(2)纺织行业成套设备,(3)其它衣物处理设备及其零件 I 类器具,(4)其它衣物处理设备及其零件 II 类器具,(5)其它衣物处理设备及其零件 III 类器具,(6)其它衣物处理设备及其零件 0I 类器具,(7)其它衣物处理设备及其零件 0 类器具,(8)其它大型家用及其类似用途电器及其零件 I 类器具,(9)其它大型家用及其类似用途电器及其零件 II 类器具,(10)其它大型家用及其类似用途电器及其零件 III 类器具,(11)其它大型家用及其类似用途电器及其零件 0I 类器具,(12)其它大型家用及其类似用途电器及其零件 0 类器具
8451800003	(1)其它印染机械及其零件,(2)纺织行业成套设备,(3)其它衣物处理设备及其零件 I 类器具,(4)其它衣物处理设备及其零件 II 类器具,(5)其它衣物处理设备及其零件 III 类器具,(6)其它衣物处理设备及其零件 0I 类器具,(7)其它衣物处理设备及其零件 0 类器具,(8)其它大型家用及其类似用途电器及其零件 I 类器具,(9)其它大型家用及其类似用途电器及其零件 II 类器具,(10)其它大型家用及其类似用途电器及其零件 III 类器具,(11)其它大型家用及其类似用途电器及其零件 0I 类器具,(12)其它大型家用及其类似用途电器及其零件 0 类器具
8451800090	(1)印花机,(2)染色机,(3)其它印染机械及其零件,(4)纺织行业成套设备,(5)其它衣物处理设备及其零件 I 类器具,(6)其它衣物处理设备及其零件 II 类器具,(7)其它衣物处理设备及其零件 III 类器具,(8)其它衣物处理设备及其零件 0I 类器具,(9)其它衣物处理设备及其零件 0 类器具,(10)其它大型家用及其类似用途电器及其零件 I 类器具,(11)其它大型家用及其类似用途电器及其零件 II 类器具,(12)其它大型家用及其类似用途电器及其零件 III 类器具,(13)其它大型家用及其类似用途电器及其零件 0I 类器具,(14)其它大型家用及其类似用途电器及其零件 0 类器具
8456900000	(1)电化学处理加工机床,(2)火焰切割机,(3)其它特种加工机床
8474201000	(1)其它工程机械及其零件,(2)建筑工业行业成套设备
8474202000	(1)其它工程机械及其零件,(2)建筑工业行业成套设备
8474209000	(1)其它工程机械及其零件,(2)建筑工业行业成套设备
8474802000	(1)其它工程机械及其零件,(2)建材行业成套设备,(3)建筑工业行业成套设备,(4)其他行业成套设备
8474809090	(1)其它工程机械及其零件,(2)建材行业成套设备,(3)建筑工业行业成套设备,(4)其他行业成套设备
8479600000	(1)蒸发式空气冷却器 I 类器具,(2)蒸发式空气冷却器 II 类器具,(3)蒸发式空气冷却器 III 类器具,(4)蒸发式空气冷却器 0I 类器具,(5)蒸发式空气冷却器 0 类器具
8479892000	(1)空气增湿器及减湿器 I 类器具,(2)空气增湿器及减湿器 II 类器具,(3)空气增湿器及减湿器 III 类器具,(4)空气增湿器及减湿器 0I 类器具,(5)空气增湿器及减湿器 0 类器具
8479899200	(1)机械行业成套设备,(2)石油化工行业成套设备,(3)铁路运输行业成套设备,(4)交通行业成套设备,(5)电子行业成套设备,(6)通讯行业成套设备,(7)电力行业成套设备,(8)化工行业成套设备,(9)石油天然气行业成套设备,(10)冶金行业成套设备,(11)纺织行业成套设备,(12)轻工行业成套设备,(13)建材行业成套设备,(14)水利行业成套设备,(15)兵工民品行业成套设备,(16)劳动和劳动安全行业成套设备,(17)公共安全行业成套设备,(18)广播电影电视行业成套设备,(19)船舶行业成套设备,(20)环保行业成套设备,(21)包装行业成套设备,(22)煤炭行业成套设备,(23)建筑工业行业成套设备,(24)海洋行业成套设备,(25)地质矿产行业成套设备,(26)地震行业成套设备,(27)印刷行业成套设备,(28)其他行业成套设备
8479899990	(1)机械行业成套设备,(2)石油化工行业成套设备,(3)铁路运输行业成套设备,(4)交通行业成套设备,(5)电子行业成套设备,(6)通讯行业成套设备,(7)电力行业成套设备,(8)化工行业成套设备,(9)石油天然气行业成套设备,(10)冶金行业成套设备,(11)纺织行业成套设备,(12)轻工行业成套设备,(13)建材行业成套设备,(14)水利行业成套设备,(15)兵工民品行业成套设备,(16)劳动和劳动安全行业成套设备,(17)公共安全行业成套设备,(18)广播电影电视行业成套设备,(19)船舶行业成套设备,(20)环保行业成套设备,(21)包装行业成套设备,(22)煤炭行业成套设备,(23)建筑工业行业成套设备,(24)海洋行业成套设备,(25)地质矿产行业成套设备,(26)地震行业成套设备,(27)印刷行业成套设备,(28)其他行业成套设备
8479901000	(1)船舶用零部件,(2)船舶行业成套设备
8479909010	(1)船舶用零部件,(2)机械行业成套设备,(3)电子行业成套设备,(4)船舶行业成套设备,(5)其他行业成套设备,(6)其它过滤及其喷射装置及其零件 I 类器具,(7)其它过滤及其喷射装置及其零件 II 类器具,(8)其它过滤及其喷射装置及其零件 III 类器具,(9)其它过滤及其喷射装置及其零件 0I 类器具,(10)其它过滤及其喷射装置及其零件 0 类器具
8479909090	(1)船舶用零部件,(2)机械行业成套设备,(3)电子行业成套设备,(4)船舶行业成套设备,(5)其他行业成套设备,(6)其它过滤及其喷射装置及其零件

HS 编码	CIQ 扩展品名
8480411000	(1)机械行业成套设备,(2)电子行业成套设备,(3)轻工行业成套设备
8480412000	(1)机械行业成套设备,(2)电子行业成套设备,(3)轻工行业成套设备
8480419000	(1)机械行业成套设备,(2)电子行业成套设备,(3)轻工行业成套设备
8480490000	(1)机械行业成套设备,(2)电子行业成套设备,(3)轻工行业成套设备
8480500000	(1)轻工行业成套设备,(2)其他行业成套设备
8480790090	(1)机械行业成套设备,(2)电子行业成套设备,(3)轻工行业成套设备
8481802110	(1)安全附件,(2)其它阀门及类似品
8481802910	(1)安全附件,(2)其它阀门及类似品
8481804010	(1)安全附件,(2)其它阀门及类似品
8481804090	(1)安全附件,(2)其它阀门及类似品
8486204100	(1)其它机床,(2)电子行业成套设备
8486304100	(1)电子行业成套设备,(2)非家用过滤及净化装置
8486304900	(1)其它机床,(2)电子行业成套设备,(3)非家用过滤及净化装置
8486403100	(1)电子行业成套设备,(2)机械式停车设备及其它装卸、储运设备及其零件
8486403900	(1)起重机,(2)机械式停车设备及其它装卸、储运设备及其零件,(3)升降机,(4)其他装卸桥、提升、起重设备及零件
8486901000	(1)机械式停车设备及其它装卸、储运设备及其零件,(2)其他装卸桥、提升、起重设备及零件
8504401300	(1)Ⅰ类稳压电源,(2)Ⅱ类稳压电源,(3)Ⅲ类稳压电源
8504401400	(1)Ⅰ类稳压电源,(2)Ⅱ类稳压电源,(3)Ⅲ类稳压电源
8504401500	(1)Ⅰ类稳压电源,(2)Ⅱ类稳压电源,(3)Ⅲ类稳压电源
8504401920	(1)Ⅰ类稳压电源,(2)Ⅱ类稳压电源,(3)Ⅲ类稳压电源
8504401930	(1)Ⅰ类稳压电源,(2)Ⅱ类稳压电源,(3)Ⅲ类稳压电源
8504401990	(1)Ⅰ类稳压电源,(2)Ⅱ类稳压电源,(3)Ⅲ类稳压电源
8506101110	(1)锌－锰原电池及原电池组,(2)碱性锌－锰原电池及原电池组,(3)其他二氧化锰的原电池及原电池组
8506101190	(1)锌－锰原电池及原电池组,(2)碱性锌－锰原电池及原电池组,(3)其他二氧化锰的原电池及原电池组
8506101210	(1)锌－锰原电池及原电池组,(2)碱性锌－锰原电池及原电池组,(3)其他二氧化锰的原电池及原电池组
8506101290	(1)锌－锰原电池及原电池组,(2)碱性锌－锰原电池及原电池组,(3)其他二氧化锰的原电池及原电池组
8506101910	(1)锌－锰原电池及原电池组,(2)碱性锌－锰原电池及原电池组,(3)其他二氧化锰的原电池及原电池组,(4)碱性的腐蚀性物质
8506101990	(1)锌－锰原电池及原电池组,(2)碱性锌－锰原电池及原电池组,(3)其他二氧化锰的原电池及原电池组,(4)碱性的腐蚀性物质
8507100000	(1)起动用铅酸蓄电池,(2)牵引用铅酸蓄电池,(3)摩托车用铅酸蓄电池,(4)固定型防酸式铅酸蓄电池,(5)内燃机车用铅酸蓄电池,(6)其他铅酸蓄电池,(7)注有酸液
8507200000	(1)起动用铅酸蓄电池,(2)牵引用铅酸蓄电池,(3)摩托车用铅酸蓄电池,(4)固定型防酸式铅酸蓄电池,(5)内燃机车用铅酸蓄电池,(6)其他铅酸蓄电池
8507300000	(1)圆柱镍镉电池,(2)方形开口镉镍单体蓄电池,(3)其他镍镉电池
8507500000	(1)密封金属氢化物镍可充单体电池,(2)其他镍氢蓄电池
8507600090	(1)蜂窝电话用锂离子蓄电池,(2)其他锂离子蓄电池
8507809010	(1)其它蓄电池及其零件,(2)注有碱液的,(3)含氢氧化钾固体
8507809090	(1)其它蓄电池及其零件,(2)注有碱液的,(3)含氢氧化钾固体
8508110000	(1)真空吸尘器 I 类器具,(2)真空吸尘器 II 类器具,(3)真空吸尘器 III 类器具,(4)真空吸尘器 0I 类器具,(5)真空吸尘器 0 类器具
8508190000	(1)真空吸尘器 I 类器具,(2)真空吸尘器 II 类器具,(3)真空吸尘器 III 类器具,(4)真空吸尘器 0I 类器具,(5)真空吸尘器 0 类器具
8508600000	(1)真空吸尘器 I 类器具,(2)真空吸尘器 II 类器具,(3)真空吸尘器 III 类器具,(4)真空吸尘器 0I 类器具,(5)真空吸尘器 0 类器具
8509401000	(1)食品研磨机,搅拌机及果、菜榨汁器 I 类器具,(2)食品研磨机,搅拌机及果、菜榨汁器 II 类器具,(3)食品研磨机,搅拌机及果、菜榨汁器 III 类器具,(4)食品研磨机,搅拌机及果、菜榨汁器 0I 类器具,(5)食品研磨机,搅拌机及果、菜榨汁器 0 类器具,(6)豆浆机 I 类器具,(7)豆浆机 II 类器具,(8)豆浆机 III 类器具,(9)豆浆机 0I 类器具,(10)豆浆机 0 类器具
8509409000	(1)食品研磨机,搅拌机及果、菜榨汁器 I 类器具,(2)食品研磨机,搅拌机及果、菜榨汁器 II 类器具,(3)食品研磨机,搅拌机及果、菜榨汁器 III 类器具,(4)食品研磨机,搅拌机及果、菜榨汁器 0I 类器具,(5)食品研磨机,搅拌机及果、菜榨汁器 0 类器具
8509801000	(1)地板打蜡机 I 类器具,(2)地板打蜡机 II 类器具,(3)地板打蜡机 III 类器具,(4)地板打蜡机 0I 类器具,(5)地板打蜡机 0 类器具
8509802000	(1)厨房废物处理器 I 类器具,(2)厨房废物处理器 II 类器具,(3)厨房废物处理器 III 类器具,(4)厨房废物处理器 0I 类器具,(5)厨房废物处理器 0 类器具
8509809090	(1)其它电动器具及其零件 I 类器具,(2)其它电动器具及其零件 II 类器具,(3)其它电动器具及其零件 III 类器具,(4)其它电动器具及其零件 0I 类器具,(5)其它电动器具及其零件 0 类器具,(6)其它小型家用及类似用途电器及其零件 I 类器具,(7)其它小型家用及类似用途电器及其零件 II 类器具,(8)其它小型家用及类似用途电器及其零件 III 类器具,(9)其它小型家用及类似用途电器及其零件 0I 类器具,(10)其它小型家用及类似用途电器及其零件 0 类器具
8509900000	(1)其它电动器具及其零件,(2)其它小型家用及类似用途电器及其零件
8510100000	(1)电动剃须刀 I 类器具,(2)电动剃须刀 II 类器具,(3)电动剃须刀 III 类器具,(4)电动剃须刀 0I 类器具,(5)电动剃须刀 0 类器具
8510200000	(1)电动毛发推剪 I 类器具,(2)电动毛发推剪 II 类器具,(3)电动毛发推剪 III 类器具,(4)电动毛发推剪 0I 类器具,(5)电动毛发推剪 0 类器具
8510300000	(1)电动脱毛机 I 类器具,(2)电动脱毛机 II 类器具,(3)电动脱毛机 III 类器具,(4)电动脱毛机 0I 类器具,(5)电动脱毛机 0 类器具
8511201000	(1)航空器用零部件,(2)船舶用零部件,(3)铁道机车用零部件,(4)组及其零件

HS 编码	CIQ 扩展品名
8511301000	(1)航空器用零部件,(2)船舶用零部件,(3)铁道机车用零部件
8511401000	(1)其它电动机及其零件,(2)其它发电机(组)及其零件
8515809090	(1)波峰焊设备,(2)其它焊接设备及其零件
8516101000	(1)电热水器 I 类器具,(2)电热水器 II 类器具,(3)电热水器 III 类器具,(4)电热水器 0I 类器具,(5)电热水器 0 类器具
8516102000	(1)电热水器 I 类器具,(2)电热水器 II 类器具,(3)电热水器 III 类器具,(4)电热水器 0I 类器具,(5)电热水器 0 类器具
8516109000	(1)电热水器 I 类器具,(2)电热水器 II 类器具,(3)电热水器 III 类器具,(4)电热水器 0I 类器具,(5)电热水器 0 类器具
8516210000	(1)电气储存式散热器 I 类器具,(2)电气储存式散热器 II 类器具,(3)电气储存式散热器 III 类器具,(4)电气储存式散热器 0I 类器具,(5)电气储存式散热器 0 类器具
8516291000	(1)其它电热器具及其零件 I 类器具,(2)其它电热器具及其零件 II 类器具,(3)其它电热器具及其零件 III 类器具,(4)其它电热器具及其零件 0I 类器具,(5)其它电热器具及其零件 0 类器具
8516292000	(1)其它电热器具及其零件 I 类器具,(2)其它电热器具及其零件 II 类器具,(3)其它电热器具及其零件 III 类器具,(4)其它电热器具及其零件 0I 类器具,(5)其它电热器具及其零件 0 类器具,(6)其它小型家用及类似用途电器及其零件 I 类器具,(7)其它小型家用及类似用途电器及其零件 II 类器具,(8)其它小型家用及类似用途电器及其零件 III 类器具,(9)其它小型家用及类似用途电器及其零件 0I 类器具,(10)其它小型家用及类似用途电器及其零件 0 类器具
8516293100	(1)其它电热器具及其零件 I 类器具,(2)其它电热器具及其零件 II 类器具,(3)其它电热器具及其零件 III 类器具,(4)其它电热器具及其零件 0I 类器具,(5)其它电热器具及其零件 0 类器具,(6)其它小型家用及类似用途电器及其零件 I 类器具,(7)其它小型家用及类似用途电器及其零件 II 类器具,(8)其它小型家用及类似用途电器及其零件 III 类器具,(9)其它小型家用及类似用途电器及其零件 0I 类器具,(10)其它小型家用及类似用途电器及其零件 0 类器具
8516293200	(1)其它电热器具及其零件 I 类器具,(2)其它电热器具及其零件 II 类器具,(3)其它电热器具及其零件 III 类器具,(4)其它电热器具及其零件 0I 类器具,(5)其它电热器具及其零件 0 类器具,(6)其它小型家用及类似用途电器及其零件 I 类器具,(7)其它小型家用及类似用途电器及其零件 II 类器具,(8)其它小型家用及类似用途电器及其零件 III 类器具,(9)其它小型家用及类似用途电器及其零件 0I 类器具,(10)其它小型家用及类似用途电器及其零件 0 类器具
8516293900	(1)其它电热器具及其零件 I 类器具,(2)其它电热器具及其零件 II 类器具,(3)其它电热器具及其零件 III 类器具,(4)其它电热器具及其零件 0I 类器具,(5)其它电热器具及其零件 0 类器具,(6)其它小型家用及类似用途电器及其零件 I 类器具,(7)其它小型家用及类似用途电器及其零件 II 类器具,(8)其它小型家用及类似用途电器及其零件 III 类器具,(9)其它小型家用及类似用途电器及其零件 0I 类器具,(10)其它小型家用及类似用途电器及其零件 0 类器具
8516299000	(1)电气空间加热器 I 类器具,(2)电气空间加热器 II 类器具,(3)电气空间加热器 III 类器具,(4)电气空间加热器 0I 类器具,(5)电气空间加热器 0 类器具
8516310000	(1)电吹风机 I 类器具,(2)电吹风机 II 类器具,(3)电吹风机 III 类器具,(4)电吹风机 0I 类器具,(5)电吹风机 0 类器具
8516320000	(1)电热理发器具 I 类器具,(2)电热理发器具 II 类器具,(3)电热理发器具 III 类器具,(4)电热理发器具 0I 类器具,(5)电热理发器具 0 类器具,(6)焗油机 I 类器具,(7)焗油机 II 类器具,(8)焗油机 III 类器具,(9)焗油机 0I 类器具,(10)焗油机 0 类器具
8516330000	(1)电热干手器 I 类器具,(2)电热干手器 II 类器具,(3)电热干手器 III 类器具,(4)电热干手器 0I 类器具,(5)电热干手器 0 类器具
8516400000	(1)电熨斗 I 类器具,(2)电熨斗 II 类器具,(3)电熨斗 III 类器具,(4)电熨斗 0I 类器具,(5)电熨斗 0 类器具
8516500000	(1)微波炉 I 类器具,(2)微波炉 II 类器具,(3)微波炉 III 类器具,(4)微波炉 0I 类器具,(5)微波炉 0 类器具
8516601000	(1)电磁炉 I 类器具,(2)电磁炉 II 类器具,(3)电磁炉 III 类器具,(4)电磁炉 0I 类器具,(5)电磁炉 0 类器具
8516603000	(1)电饭锅 I 类器具,(2)电饭锅 II 类器具,(3)电饭锅 III 类器具,(4)电饭锅 0I 类器具,(5)电饭锅 0 类器具
8516604000	(1)电炒锅 I 类器具,(2)电炒锅 II 类器具,(3)电炒锅 III 类器具,(4)电炒锅 0I 类器具,(5)电炒锅 0 类器具
8516605000	(1)电热炉 I 类器具,(2)电热炉 II 类器具,(3)电热炉 III 类器具,(4)电热炉 0I 类器具,(5)电热炉 0 类器具
8516609000	(1)电热炉 I 类器具,(2)电热炉 II 类器具,(3)电热炉 III 类器具,(4)电热炉 0I 类器具,(5)电热炉 0 类器具,(6)光波炉 I 类器具,(7)光波炉 II 类器具,(8)光波炉 III 类器具,(9)光波炉 0I 类器具,(10)光波炉 0 类器具,(11)油炸锅 I 类器具,(12)油炸锅 II 类器具,(13)油炸锅 III 类器具,(14)油炸锅 0I 类器具,(15)油炸锅 0 类器具
8516711000	(1)电热咖啡壶或茶壶 I 类器具,(2)电热咖啡壶或茶壶 II 类器具,(3)电热咖啡壶或茶壶 III 类器具,(4)电热咖啡壶或茶壶 0I 类器具,(5)电热咖啡壶或茶壶 0 类器具
8516712000	(1)电热咖啡壶或茶壶 I 类器具,(2)电热咖啡壶或茶壶 II 类器具,(3)电热咖啡壶或茶壶 III 类器具,(4)电热咖啡壶或茶壶 0I 类器具,(5)电热咖啡壶或茶壶 0 类器具
8516713000	(1)电热咖啡壶或茶壶 I 类器具,(2)电热咖啡壶或茶壶 II 类器具,(3)电热咖啡壶或茶壶 III 类器具,(4)电热咖啡壶或茶壶 0I 类器具,(5)电热咖啡壶或茶壶 0 类器具
8516719000	(1)电热咖啡壶或茶壶 I 类器具,(2)电热咖啡壶或茶壶 II 类器具,(3)电热咖啡壶或茶壶 III 类器具,(4)电热咖啡壶或茶壶 0I 类器具,(5)电热咖啡壶或茶壶 0 类器具,(6)电热水壶 I 类器具,(7)电热水壶 II 类器具,(8)电热水壶 III 类器具,(9)电热水壶 0I 类器具,(10)电热水壶 0 类器具
8516721000	(1)电热烤面包器 I 类器具,(2)电热烤面包器 II 类器具,(3)电热烤面包器 III 类器具,(4)电热烤面包器 0I 类器具,(5)电热烤面包器 0 类器具
8516722000	(1)电热烤面包器 I 类器具,(2)电热烤面包器 II 类器具,(3)电热烤面包器 III 类器具,(4)电热烤面包器 0I 类器具,(5)电热烤面包器 0 类器具
8516729000	(1)电热烤面包器 I 类器具,(2)电热烤面包器 II 类器具,(3)电热烤面包器 III 类器具,(4)电热烤面包器 0I 类器具,(5)电热烤面包器 0 类器具
8516791000	(1)其它电热器具及其零件 I 类器具,(2)其它电热器具及其零件 II 类器具,(3)其它电热器具及其零件 III 类器具,(4)其它电热器具及其零件 0I 类器具,(5)其它电热器具及其零件 0 类器具,(6)其它小型家用及类似用途电器及其零件 I 类器具,(7)其它小型家用及类似用途电器及其零件 II 类器具,(8)其它小型家用及类似用途电器及其零件 III 类器具,(9)其它小型家用及类似用途电器及其零件 0I 类器具,(10)其它小型家用及类似用途电器及其零件 0 类器具

HS编码	CIQ扩展品名
8516799090	(1)电蒸炉Ⅰ类器具,(2)电蒸炉Ⅱ类器具,(3)电蒸炉Ⅲ类器具,(4)电蒸炉0Ⅰ类器具,(5)电蒸炉0类器具,(6)电子炖盅Ⅰ类器具,(7)电子炖盅Ⅱ类器具,(8)电子炖盅Ⅲ类器具,(9)电子炖盅0Ⅰ类器具,(10)电子炖盅0类器具,(11)其它电热器具及其零件Ⅰ类器具,(12)其它电热器具及其零件Ⅱ类器具,(13)其它电热器具及其零件Ⅲ类器具,(14)其它电热器具及其零件0Ⅰ类器具,(15)其它电热器具及其零件0类器具,(16)其它小型家用及类似用途电器及其零件Ⅰ类器具,(17)其它小型家用及类似用途电器及其零件Ⅱ类器具,(18)其它小型家用及类似用途电器及其零件Ⅲ类器具,(19)其它小型家用及类似用途电器及其零件0Ⅰ类器具,(20)其它小型家用及类似用途电器及其零件0类器具
8516800000	(1)其它电热器具及其零件Ⅰ类器具,(2)其它电热器具及其零件Ⅱ类器具,(3)其它电热器具及其零件Ⅲ类器具,(4)其它电热器具及其零件0Ⅰ类器具,(5)其它电热器具及其零件0类器具
8517121011	(1)不带附件及包装,(2)包含附件及包装
8517121019	(1)不带附件及包装,(2)包含附件及包装
8517121021	(1)不带附件及包装,(2)包含附件及包装
8517121029	(1)不带附件及包装,(2)包含附件及包装
8517121090	(1)不带附件及包装,(2)包含附件及包装
8517129000	(1)不带附件及包装,(2)包含附件及包装,(3)其它通讯设备及其零件
8517619000	(1)不带附件及包装,(2)包含附件及包装,(3)其它通讯设备及其零件
8517621200	(1)网络交换机,(2)其它通讯设备及其零件
8517622910	(1)光通信数字同步设备,(2)其它通讯设备及其零件
8517622990	(1)光通信数字同步设备,(2)其它通讯设备及其零件
8517629400	(1)Ⅰ类其它扬声器及其零件,(2)Ⅱ类其它扬声器及其零件,(3)Ⅲ类其它扬声器及其零件
8517691001	(1)无线接收装置,(2)无线寻呼机,(3)其它通讯设备及其零件
8517691090	(1)不带附件及包装,(2)包含附件及包装
8517699000	(1)其它办公机器及其零件,(2)其它通讯设备及其零件
8517704000	(1)移动通讯设备,(2)其它通讯设备及其零件
8518100001	(1)Ⅰ类其它扬声器及其零件,(2)Ⅱ类其它扬声器及其零件,(3)Ⅲ类其它扬声器及其零件
8518100090	(1)Ⅰ类其它扬声器及其零件,(2)Ⅱ类其它扬声器及其零件,(3)Ⅲ类其它扬声器及其零件
8518210000	(1)Ⅰ类单喇叭音箱,(2)Ⅱ类单喇叭音箱,(3)Ⅲ类单喇叭音箱
8518220000	(1)Ⅰ类多喇叭音箱,(2)Ⅱ类多喇叭音箱,(3)Ⅲ类多喇叭音箱
8518290000	(1)Ⅰ类其它扬声器及其零件,(2)Ⅱ类其它扬声器及其零件,(3)Ⅲ类其它扬声器及其零件
8518300000	(1)Ⅰ类其它扬声器及其零件,(2)Ⅱ类其它扬声器及其零件,(3)Ⅲ类其它扬声器及其零件
8518400001	(1)Ⅰ类音频功率放大器,(2)Ⅱ类音频功率放大器,(3)Ⅲ类音频功率放大器
8518400090	(1)Ⅰ类音频功率放大器,(2)Ⅱ类音频功率放大器,(3)Ⅲ类音频功率放大器
8518500000	(1)Ⅰ类电气扩音机组,(2)Ⅱ类电气扩音机组,(3)Ⅲ类电气扩音机组
8518900001	(1)Ⅰ类其它扬声器及其零件,(2)Ⅱ类其它扬声器及其零件,(3)Ⅲ类其它扬声器及其零件,(4)Ⅰ类其它收录放音装置及其零件,(5)Ⅱ类其它收录放音装置及其零件,(6)Ⅲ类其它收录放音装置及其零件
8518900090	(1)Ⅰ类其它扬声器及其零件,(2)Ⅱ类其它扬声器及其零件,(3)Ⅲ类其它扬声器及其零件,(4)Ⅰ类其它收录放音装置及其零件,(5)Ⅱ类其它收录放音装置及其零件,(6)Ⅲ类其它收录放音装置及其零件
8519200090	(1)Ⅰ类录音机走带机构,(2)Ⅱ类录音机走带机构,(3)Ⅲ类录音机走带机构类,(4)Ⅰ类收音机,(5)Ⅱ类收音机,(6)Ⅲ类收音机,(7)Ⅰ类收录(放)音组合机,(8)Ⅱ类收录(放)音组合机,(9)Ⅲ类收录(放)音组合机,(10)Ⅰ类其它收录放音装置及其零件,(11)Ⅱ类其它收录放音装置及其零件,(12)Ⅲ类其它收录放音装置及其零件
8519300000	(1)Ⅰ类放音机,(2)Ⅱ类放音机,(3)Ⅲ类放音机,(4)Ⅰ类激光唱机,(5)Ⅱ类激光唱机,(6)Ⅲ类激光唱机
8519500000	Ⅰ类收录(放)音组合机;(2)Ⅱ类收录(放)音组合机;(3)Ⅲ类收录(放)音组合机
8519811100	(1)Ⅰ类放音机,(2)Ⅱ类放音机,(3)Ⅲ类放音机
8519811900	(1)Ⅰ类录音机,(2)Ⅱ类录音机,(3)Ⅲ类录音机
8519812100	(1)Ⅰ类激光唱机,(2)Ⅱ类激光唱机,(3)Ⅲ类激光唱机
8519812910	(1)Ⅰ类录音机,(2)Ⅱ类录音机,(3)Ⅲ类录音机
8519812990	(1)Ⅰ类录音机,(2)Ⅱ类录音机,(3)Ⅲ类录音机
8519813900	(1)Ⅰ类录音机,(2)Ⅱ类录音机,(3)Ⅲ类录音机
8519891000	(1)Ⅰ类放音机,(2)Ⅱ类放音机,(3)Ⅲ类放音机
8519899000	(1)Ⅰ类录音机,(2)Ⅱ类录音机,(3)Ⅲ类录音机
8521101100	(1)Ⅰ类磁带录放像机,(2)Ⅱ类磁带录放像机,(3)Ⅲ类磁带录放像机
8521101900	(1)Ⅰ类磁带录放像机,(2)Ⅱ类磁带录放像机,(3)Ⅲ类磁带录放像机
8521102000	(1)Ⅰ类磁带录放像机,(2)Ⅱ类磁带录放像机,(3)Ⅲ类磁带录放像机
8521901110	(1)Ⅰ类激光视盘放像机,(2)Ⅱ类激光视盘放像机,(3)Ⅲ类激光视盘放像机
8521901190	(1)Ⅰ类激光视盘放像机,(2)Ⅱ类激光视盘放像机,(3)Ⅲ类激光视盘放像机
8521901210	(1)Ⅰ类激光视盘放像机,(2)Ⅱ类激光视盘放像机,(3)Ⅲ类激光视盘放像机
8521901290	(1)Ⅰ类激光视盘放像机,(2)Ⅱ类激光视盘放像机,(3)Ⅲ类激光视盘放像机
8521901910	(1)Ⅰ类激光视盘放像机,(2)Ⅱ类激光视盘放像机,(3)Ⅲ类激光视盘放像机
8521901990	(1)Ⅰ类激光视盘放像机,(2)Ⅱ类激光视盘放像机,(3)Ⅲ类激光视盘放像机

HS 编码	CIQ 扩展品名
8521909090	(1)Ⅰ类其它摄录放像装置及其零件,(2)Ⅱ类其它摄录放像装置及其零件,(3)Ⅲ类其它摄录放像装置及其零件
8522100000	(1)Ⅰ类其它收录放音装置及其零件,(2)Ⅱ类其它收录放音装置及其零件,(3)Ⅲ类其它收录放音装置及其零件
8522901000	(1)Ⅰ类其它收录放音装置及其零件,(2)Ⅱ类其它收录放音装置及其零件,(3)Ⅲ类其它收录放音装置及其零件
8522902100	(1)Ⅰ类录音机走带机构,(2)Ⅱ类录音机走带机构,(3)Ⅲ类录音机走带机构
8522902200	(1)Ⅰ类其它收录放音装置及其零件,(2)Ⅱ类其它收录放音装置及其零件,(3)Ⅲ类其它收录放音装置及其零件
8522902300	(1)Ⅰ类其它收录放音装置及其零件,(2)Ⅱ类其它收录放音装置及其零件,(3)Ⅲ类其它收录放音装置及其零件
8522902900	(1)Ⅰ类其它收录放音装置及其零件,(2)Ⅱ类其它收录放音装置及其零件,(3)Ⅲ类其它收录放音装置及其零件
8522903190	(1)Ⅰ类其它收录放音装置及其零件,(2)Ⅱ类其它收录放音装置及其零件,(3)Ⅲ类其它收录放音装置及其零件
8522909100	(1)Ⅰ类其它收录放音装置及其零件,(2)Ⅱ类其它收录放音装置及其零件,(3)Ⅲ类其它收录放音装置及其零件
8522909900	(1)Ⅰ类其它收录放音装置及其零件,(2)Ⅱ类其它收录放音装置及其零件,(3)Ⅲ类其它收录放音装置及其零件
8523511000	(1)其它计算机、辅助设备及其零件,(2)磁带、磁盘
8523512000	(1)其它计算机、辅助设备及其零件,(2)磁带、磁盘
8523521000	(1)软、硬、光盘驱动器,(2)其它计算机、辅助设备及其零件,(3)磁带、磁盘
8523529000	(1)软、硬、光盘驱动器,(2)其它计算机、辅助设备及其零件,(3)磁带、磁盘
8525500000	(1)Ⅰ类其它电视接收、发送装置及其零件,(2)Ⅱ类其它电视接收、发送装置及其零件,(3)Ⅲ类其它电视接收、发送装置及其零件
8525601000	(1)Ⅰ类卫星电视接收机,(2)Ⅱ类卫星电视接收机,(3)Ⅲ类卫星电视接收机
8525609000	(1)Ⅰ类其它电视接收、发送装置及其零件,(2)Ⅱ类其它电视接收、发送装置及其零件,(3)Ⅲ类其它电视接收、发送装置及其零件
8525801110	(1)Ⅰ类电视摄像机,(2)Ⅱ类电视摄像机,(3)Ⅲ类电视摄像机
8525801190	(1)Ⅰ类电视摄像机,(2)Ⅱ类电视摄像机,(3)Ⅲ类电视摄像机
8525801200	(1)Ⅰ类电视摄像机,(2)Ⅱ类电视摄像机,(3)Ⅲ类电视摄像机
8525801301	(1)Ⅰ类电视摄像机,(2)Ⅱ类电视摄像机(3)Ⅲ类电视摄像机
8525801302	(1)Ⅰ类电视摄像机,(2)Ⅱ类电视摄像机,(3)Ⅲ类电视摄像机
8525803100	(1)Ⅰ类电视摄像机,(2)Ⅱ类电视摄像机,(3)Ⅲ类电视摄像机,(4)Ⅰ类家用型摄录一体机,(5)Ⅱ类家用型摄录一体机,(6)Ⅲ类家用型摄录一体机
8527120000	(1)Ⅰ类放音机,(2)Ⅱ类放音机,(3)Ⅲ类放音机
8527210090	Ⅰ类收录(放)音组合机;(2)Ⅱ类收录(放)音组合机;(3)Ⅲ类收录(放)音组合机
8527910000	Ⅰ类收录(放)音组合机;(2)Ⅱ类收录(放)音组合机;(3)Ⅲ类收录(放)音组合机
8527920000	(1)Ⅰ类其它收录放音装置及其零件,(2)Ⅱ类其它收录放音装置及其零件,(3)Ⅲ类其它收录放音装置及其零件,(4)其它收录放音装置及其零件
8528420000	(1)彩色视频监视器,(2)黑白或其它单色视频监视器
8528491000	(1)Ⅰ类彩色视频监视器,(2)Ⅱ类彩色视频监视器,(3)Ⅲ类彩色视频监视器
8528499000	(1)Ⅰ类黑白或其它单色视频监视器,(2)Ⅱ类黑白或其它单色视频监视器,(3)Ⅲ类黑白或其它单色视频监视器
8528591090	(1)Ⅰ类彩色视频监视器,(2)Ⅱ类彩色视频监视器,(3)Ⅲ类彩色视频监视器
8528599000	(1)Ⅰ类黑白或其它单色视频监视器,(2)Ⅱ类黑白或其它单色视频监视器,(3)Ⅲ类黑白或其它单色视频监视器
8528691000	(1)Ⅰ类视频投影机,(2)Ⅱ类视频投影机,(3)Ⅲ类视频投影机
8528699000	(1)Ⅰ类视频投影机,(2)Ⅱ类视频投影机,(3)Ⅲ类视频投影机
8528711000	(1)Ⅰ类卫星电视接收机,(2)Ⅱ类卫星电视接收机,(3)Ⅲ类卫星电视接收机
8528718000	(1)Ⅰ类彩色电视机,(2)Ⅱ类彩色电视机,(3)Ⅲ类彩色电视机
8528719000	(1)Ⅰ类单色电视机,(2)Ⅱ类单色电视机,(3)Ⅱ类单色电视机
8528721100	(1)Ⅰ类彩色电视机,(2)Ⅱ类彩色电视机,(3)Ⅲ类彩色电视机
8528721200	(1)Ⅰ类彩色电视机,(2)Ⅱ类彩色电视机,(3)Ⅱ类彩色电视机
8528721900	(1)Ⅰ类彩色电视机,(2)Ⅱ类彩色电视机,(3)Ⅲ类彩色电视机
8528722100	(1)Ⅰ类彩色电视机,(2)Ⅱ类彩色电视机,(3)Ⅱ类彩色电视机
8528722200	(1)Ⅰ类彩色电视机,(2)Ⅱ类彩色电视机,(3)Ⅲ类彩色电视机
8528722900	(1)Ⅰ类彩色电视机,(2)Ⅱ类彩色电视机,(3)Ⅲ类彩色电视机
8528723100	(1)Ⅰ类彩色电视机,(2)Ⅱ类彩色电视机,(3)Ⅲ类彩色电视机
8528723200	(1)Ⅰ类彩色电视机,(2)Ⅱ类彩色电视机,(3)Ⅲ类彩色电视机
8528723900	(1)Ⅰ类彩色电视机,(2)Ⅱ类彩色电视机,(3)Ⅲ类彩色电视机
8528729100	(1)Ⅰ类彩色电视机,(2)Ⅱ类彩色电视机,(3)Ⅲ类彩色电视机
8528729200	(1)Ⅰ类彩色电视机,(2)Ⅱ类彩色电视机,(3)Ⅲ类彩色电视机
8528729900	(1)Ⅰ类彩色电视机,(2)Ⅱ类彩色电视机,(3)Ⅲ类彩色电视机
8528730000	(1)Ⅰ类单色电视机,(2)Ⅱ类单色电视机,(3)Ⅲ类单色电视机
8529102000	(1)Ⅰ类其它收录放音装置及其零件,(2)Ⅱ类其它收录放音装置及其零件,(3)Ⅲ类其它收录放音装置及其零件,(4)Ⅰ类其它电视接收、发送装置及其零件,(5)Ⅱ类其它电视接收、发送装置及其零件,(6)Ⅲ类其它电视接收、发送装置及其零件
8529109021	(1)Ⅰ类其它电视接收、发送装置及其零件,(2)Ⅱ类其它电视接收、发送装置及其零件,(3)Ⅲ类其它电视接收、发送装置及其零件

HS 编码	CIQ 扩展品名
8529109029	(1)Ⅰ类其它收录放音装置及其零件,(2)Ⅱ类其它收录放音装置及其零件,(3)Ⅲ类其它收录放音装置及其零件,(4)Ⅰ类其它电视接收、发送装置及其零件,(5)Ⅱ类其它电视接收、发送装置及其零件,(6)Ⅲ类其它电视接收、发送装置及其零件
8529109090	(1)Ⅰ类其它收录放音装置及其零件,(2)Ⅱ类其它收录放音装置及其零件,(3)Ⅲ类其它收录放音装置及其零件,(4)Ⅰ类其它电视接收、发送装置及其零件,(5)Ⅱ类其它电视接收、发送装置及其零件,(6)Ⅲ类其它电视接收、发送装置及其零件
8529901011	(1)Ⅰ类其它电视接收、发送装置及其零件,(2)Ⅱ类其它电视接收、发送装置及其零件,(3)Ⅲ类其它电视接收、发送装置及其零件
8529901012	(1)Ⅰ类其它电视接收、发送装置及其零件,(2)Ⅱ类其它电视接收、发送装置及其零件,(3)Ⅲ类其它电视接收、发送装置及其零件
8529901013	(1)Ⅰ类其它电视接收、发送装置及其零件,(2)Ⅱ类其它电视接收、发送装置及其零件,(3)Ⅲ类其它电视接收、发送装置及其零件
8529901014	(1)Ⅰ类其它电视接收、发送装置及其零件,(2)Ⅱ类其它电视接收、发送装置及其零件,(3)Ⅲ类其它电视接收、发送装置及其零件
8529901090	(1)Ⅰ类其它电视接收、发送装置及其零件,(2)Ⅱ类其它电视接收、发送装置及其零件,(3)Ⅲ类其它电视接收、发送装置及其零件
8529904100	(1)Ⅰ类其它摄录放像装置及其零件,(2)Ⅱ类其它摄录放像装置及其零件,(3)Ⅲ类其它摄录放像装置及其零件
8529904210	(1)Ⅰ类家用型摄录一体机,(2)Ⅱ类家用型摄录一体机,(3)Ⅲ类家用型摄录一体机,(4)Ⅰ类其它摄录放像装置及其零件,(5)Ⅱ类其它摄录放像装置及其零件,(6)Ⅲ类其它摄录放像装置及其零件
8529904290	(1)Ⅰ类其它摄录放像装置及其零件,(2)Ⅱ类其它摄录放像装置及其零件,(3)Ⅲ类其它摄录放像装置及其零件
8529904900	(1)Ⅰ类家用型摄录一体机,(2)Ⅱ类家用型摄录一体机,(3)Ⅲ类家用型摄录一体机,(4)Ⅰ类其它摄录放像装置及其零件,(5)Ⅱ类其它摄录放像装置及其零件,(6)Ⅲ类其它摄录放像装置及其零件
8529906000	(1)Ⅰ类其它收录放音装置及其零件,(2)Ⅱ类其它收录放音装置及其零件,(3)Ⅲ类其它收录放音装置及其零件
8529908100	(1)Ⅰ类其它电视接收、发送装置及其零件,(2)Ⅱ类其它电视接收、发送装置及其零件,(3)Ⅲ类其它电视接收、发送装置及其零件
8529908200	(1)Ⅰ类其它电视接收、发送装置及其零件,(2)Ⅱ类其它电视接收、发送装置及其零件,(3)Ⅲ类其它电视接收、发送装置及其零件
8529908900	(1)Ⅰ类其它电视接收、发送装置及其零件,(2)Ⅱ类其它电视接收、发送装置及其零件,(3)Ⅲ类其它电视接收、发送装置及其零件
8529909011	(1)Ⅰ类其它电视接收、发送装置及其零件,(2)Ⅱ类其它电视接收、发送装置及其零件,(3)Ⅲ类其它电视接收、发送装置及其零件
8531100000	(1)防盗报警装置,(2)防火报警装置
8531809000	(1)可燃气体报警器,(2)有毒气体报警器,(3)其它视听设备及其零件
8531909000	(1)可燃气体报警器,(2)有毒气体报警器,(3)其它视听设备及其零件
8544200000	(1)绞股线,(2)电缆,(3)同轴电缆,(4)其它电线电缆
8544421100	(1)电缆,(2)电脑连接线,(3)游戏机线,(4)其它电线电缆
8544421900	(1)绞股线,(2)电线,(3)电脑连接线,(4)游戏机线,(5)其它电线电缆
8544491100	(1)电缆,(2)电脑连接线,(3)游戏机线,(4)其它电线电缆
8544491900	(1)绞股线,(2)电线,(3)电脑连接线,(4)游戏机线,(5)其它电线电缆
8544609001	(1)绞股线,(2)电线,(3)其它电线电缆
8544609090	(1)绞股线,(2)电线,(3)其它电线电缆
9018310000	(1)一次性使用无菌注射器,(2)玻璃注射器,(3)预填充药剂及与药液配套的注射器,(4)胰岛素注射器,(5)兽医金属注射器,(6)兽医塑钢连续注射器,(7)一次性使用精密过滤输液器,(8)滴定管式输液器,(9)一次性使用避光输液器,(10)一次性使用压力输液设备用输液器,(11)一次性使用吊瓶式和袋式输液器,(12)一次性使用流量设定微调式输液器,(13)其他注射器、输液器
9018321000	(1)一次性使用无菌注射针,(2)不锈钢注射针管,(3)一次性使用静脉输液针,(4)金属骨髓内针,(5)泪道探针,(6)一次性使用无菌牙科注射针,(7)一次性使用麻醉穿刺针,(8)其他管状金属针头
9018909911	(1)诊断仪器及零部件,(2)治疗仪器及零部件,(3)其他医疗仪器及零部件,(4)与人体接触的进入式医疗器具,(5)与人体接触的非进入式医疗器具,(6)其他医疗器具
9018909919	(1)诊断仪器及零部件,(2)治疗仪器及零部件,(3)其他医疗仪器及零部件,(4)与人体接触的进入式医疗器具,(5)与人体接触的非进入式医疗器具,(6)其他医疗器具
9018909991	(1)诊断仪器及零部件,(2)治疗仪器及零部件,(3)其他医疗仪器及零部件,(4)与人体接触的进入式医疗器具,(5)与人体接触的非进入式医疗器具,(6)其他医疗器具
9018909999	(1)诊断仪器及零部件,(2)治疗仪器及零部件,(3)其他医疗仪器及零部件,(4)与人体接触的进入式医疗器具,(5)与人体接触的非进入式医疗器具,(6)其他医疗器具
9019101000	(1)按摩垫I类器具,(2)按摩垫II类器具,(3)按摩垫III类器具,(4)按摩垫0I类器具,(5)按摩垫0类器具,(6)按摩椅I类器具,(7)按摩椅II类器具,(8)按摩椅III类器具,(9)按摩椅0I类器具,(10)按摩椅0类器具,(11)按摩床I类器具,(12)按摩床II类器具,(13)按摩床III类器具,(14)按摩床0I类器具,(15)按摩床0类器具,(16)其它按摩器具及其零件I类器具,(17)其它按摩器具及其零件II类器具,(18)其它按摩器具及其零件III类器具,(19)其它按摩器具及其零件0I类器具,(20)其它按摩器具及其零件0类器具
9019109000	(1)心理功能测验装置,(2)与人体接触的机械疗法器具,(3)其他机械疗法器具,(4)按摩垫I类器具,(5)按摩垫II类器具,(6)按摩垫III类器具,(7)按摩垫0I类器具,(8)按摩垫0类器具,(9)按摩椅I类器具,(10)按摩椅II类器具,(11)按摩椅III类器具,(12)按摩椅0I类器具,(13)按摩椅0类器具,(14)按摩床I类器具,(15)按摩床II类器具,(16)按摩床III类器具,(17)按摩床0I类器具,(18)按摩床0类器具,(19)其它按摩器具及其零件I类器具,(20)其它按摩器具及其零件II类器具,(21)其它按摩器具及其零件III类器具,(22)其它按摩器具及其零件0I类器具,(23)其它按摩器具及其零件0类器具
9022120000	(1)医用X射线诊断放射设备,(2)X射线计算机体层摄影设备,(3)X射线断层扫描高频发生设备,(4)X射线断层扫描附属设备,(5)乳腺X射线机,(6)其他X射线断层检查设备
9401201000	(1)其他车辆零部件,(2)软体家具
9401809010	(1)其他家具,(2)靠垫,(3)其他日用纺织制品
9403509100	(1)其他木制品,(2)木家具,(3)儿童用
9403509990	(1)其他木制品,(2)木家具,(3)儿童用
9403609100	(1)其他木制品,(2)木家具,(3)儿童用
9403609910	(1)其他木制品,(2)木家具

HS 编码	CIQ 扩展品名
9403891000	(1)柳及柳制品,(2)柳条及类似材料制的家具
9404904000	(1)褥垫,(2)靠垫,(3)其他日用纺织制品,(4)其他纺织制品
9405100000	(1)0 类吊灯,(2)I 类吊灯,(3)II 类吊灯,(4)III 类吊灯,(5)0 类壁灯,(6)I 类壁灯,(7)II 类壁灯,(8)0 类吸顶灯,(9)I 类吸顶灯,(10)II 类吸顶灯,(11)III 类吸顶灯,(12)光管支架,(13)0 类射灯,(14)I 类射灯,(15)II 类射灯,(16)III 类射灯,(17)0 类筒灯,(18)I 类筒灯,(19)II 类筒灯,(20)III 类筒灯,(21)0 类嵌灯,(22)I 类嵌灯,(23)II 类嵌灯,(24)III 类嵌灯,(25)灯盘
9405200010	(1)0 类台灯,(2)I 类台灯,(3)II 类台灯,(4)III 类台灯,(5)0 类落地灯,(6)I 类落地灯,(7)II 类落地灯,(8)III 类落地灯,(9)0 类吸顶灯,(10)I 类吸顶灯,(11)II 类吸顶灯,(12)III 类吸顶灯,(13)光管支架,(14)0 类射灯,(15)I 类射灯,(16)II 类射灯,(17)III 类射灯,(18)0 类筒灯,(19)I 类筒灯,(20)II 类筒灯,(21)III 类筒灯,(22)0 类嵌灯,(23)I 类嵌灯,(24)II 类嵌灯,(25)III 类嵌灯,(26)灯盘,(27)0 类夹灯,(28)I 类夹灯,(29)II 类夹灯,(30)III 类夹灯
9405200090	(1)0 类台灯,(2)I 类台灯,(3)II 类台灯,(4)III 类台灯,(5)0 类落地灯,(6)I 类落地灯,(7)II 类落地灯,(8)III 类落地灯,(9)0 类吸顶灯,(10)I 类吸顶灯,(11)II 类吸顶灯,(12)III 类吸顶灯,(13)光管支架,(14)0 类射灯,(15)I 类射灯,(16)II 类射灯,(17)III 类射灯,(18)0 类筒灯,(19)I 类筒灯,(20)II 类筒灯,(21)III 类筒灯,(22)0 类嵌灯,(23)I 类嵌灯,(24)II 类嵌灯,(25)III 类嵌灯,(26)灯盘,(27)0 类夹灯,(28)I 类夹灯,(29)II 类夹灯,(30)III 类夹灯
9405300000	(1)II 类圣诞树用成套灯具,(2)III 类圣诞树用成套灯具
9405401000	(1)O 类探照灯,(2)I 类探照灯,(3)II 类探照灯,(4)III 类探照灯
9405402000	(1)0 类聚光灯具,(2)I 类聚光灯具,(3)II 类聚光灯具,(4)III 类聚光灯具
9405409000	(1)0 类路灯,(2)I 类路灯,(3)II 类路灯,(4)III 类路灯,(5)0 类庭院灯,(6)I 类庭院灯,(7)II 类庭院灯,(8)III 类庭院灯,(9)0 类草地灯,(10)I 类草地灯,(11)II 类草地灯,(12)III 类草地灯,(13)0 类手提灯,(14)I 类手提灯,(15)II 类手提灯,(16)III 类手提灯,(17)0 类儿童感兴趣灯,(18)II 类儿童感兴趣灯,(19)III 类儿童感兴趣灯,(20)0 类水族箱用灯,(21)I 类水族箱用灯,(22)II 类水族箱用灯,(23)III 类水族箱用灯,(24)0 类夜灯,(25)I 类夜灯,(26)II 类夜灯,(27)III 类夜灯,(28)0 类地埋灯,(29)I 类地埋灯,(30)II 类地埋灯,(31)III 类地埋灯,(32)0 类舞台、电视、电影及摄影场所室内外用灯具,(33)I 类舞台、电视、电影及摄影场所室内外用灯具,(34)II 类舞台、电视、电影及摄影场所室内外用灯具,(35)III 类舞台、电视、电影及摄影场所室内外用灯具,(36)0 类游泳池和类似场所用灯具,(37)I 类游泳池和类似场所用灯具,(38)II 类游泳池和类似场所用灯具,(39)III 类游泳池和类似场所用灯具,(40)0 类通风式灯,(41)I 类通风式灯,(42)II 类通风式灯,(43)III 类通风式灯,(44)0 类应急照明灯,(45)I 类应急照明灯,(46)II 类应急照明灯,(47)III 类应急照明灯,(48)0 类限制表面温度灯具,(49)I 类限制表面温度灯具,(50)II 类限制表面温度灯具,(51)III 类限制表面温度灯具,(52)0 类医院、康复和诊所用灯具,(53)I 类医院、康复和诊所用灯,(54)II 类医院、康复和诊所用灯具,(55)III 类医院、康复和诊所用灯具,(56)0 类非专业用照相和电影用灯具,(57)I 类非专业用照相和电影用灯具,(58)II 类非专业用照相和电影用灯具,(59)III 类非专业用照相和电影用灯具,(60)LED 灯,(61)LED 灯管,(62)LED 模块,(63)其它灯具及其零件
9601100010	(1)未列出的其他动物骨、蹄、角,(2)含木制品的工艺品,(3)不含木制品的工艺品
9601100090	(1)未列出的其他动物骨、蹄、角,(2)含木制品的工艺品,(3)不含木制品的工艺品
9603501100	(1)含木制品,(2)不含木制品
9603501900	(1)其他车辆零部件,(2)含木制品,(3)不含木制品
9603509190	(1)含木制品,(2)不含木制品
9603509990	(1)其他车辆零部件,(2)含木制品,(3)不含木制品
9606210000	(1)含木制品,(2)不含木制品
9606220000	(1)含木制品,(2)不含木制品
9606290010	(1)含木制品,(2)不含木制品
9606300000	(1)含木制品,(2)不含木制品

附表 3: 2020 年进口商品从量、复合税税率表

税则号列	货品名称(简称)	2020 年最惠国税率	普通税率
02071200	整只,冻的鸡	1.3 元/千克	5.6 元/千克
02071411	冻的的带骨鸡块	0.6 元/千克	4.2 元/千克
02071419	冻的其他鸡块	0.7 元/千克	9.5 元/千克
02071421	冻的鸡翼(不包括翼尖)	0.8 元/千克	8.1 元/千克
02071422	鲜、冷、冻鸡爪	1 元/千克	3.2 元/千克
02071429	冻的其他鸡杂碎	0.5 元/千克	3.2 元/千克
05040021	冷和冻的鸡肫	1.3 元/千克	7.7 元/千克
22030000	麦芽酿造的啤酒	0	7.5 元/升
27090000	石油原油及从沥青矿物提取的原油	0	85 元/吨
37023190	彩色摄影用未曝光无齿孔彩色胶卷,宽度≤105 mm,用纸、纸板及纺织物以外任何材料制成	56 元/平方米	433 元/平方米
37023220	照相制版用未曝光涂卤化银液无齿孔胶卷,宽度≤105 mm,用纸、纸板及纺织物以外任何材料制成	4.5 元/平方米	104 元/平方米
37023290	其他未曝光涂乳液无齿孔胶卷,宽度≤105 mm,用纸、纸板及纺织物以外任何材料制成	21 元/平方米	202 元/平方米
37023920	照相制版用未曝光未涂卤化银无齿孔感光胶卷,宽度≤105 mm,用纸、纸板及纺织物以外任何材料制成	12 元/平方米	104 元/平方米
37023990	其他未曝光未涂卤化银无齿孔感光胶卷,宽度≤105 m,用纸、纸板及纺织物以外任何材料制成	24 元/平方米	202 元/平方米

税则号列	货品名称(简称)	2020年最惠国税率	普通税率
37024100	彩色摄影用未曝光无齿孔彩色胶卷,宽度＞610 mm,长度＞200m,用纸、纸板及纺织物以外任何材料制成	7.1元/平方米	202元/平方米
37024221	印刷电路板制造用未曝光光致抗蚀干膜,宽度＞610 mm,长度＞200m,用纸、纸板及纺织物以外任何材料制成	0.6元/平方米	110元/平方米
37024229	照相制版用其他未曝光无齿孔胶卷,宽度＞610 mm,长度＞200m,用纸、纸板及纺织物以外任何材料制成	1.6元/平方米	110元/平方米
37024292	红色或红外激光胶片	2.4元/平方米	213元/平方米
37024299	其他未曝光无齿孔宽长胶卷	7元/平方米	213元/平方米
37024321	照相制版用未曝光无齿孔激光照排片,宽度＞610 mm,长度≤200m,用纸、纸板及纺织物以外任何材料制成	0	104元/平方米
37024329	其他照相制版用未曝光无齿孔胶卷,宽度＞610 mm,长度≤200m,用纸、纸板及纺织物以外任何材料制成	3.7元/平方米	104元/平方米
37024390	其他用未曝光无齿孔胶卷,宽度 610 mm,长度≤200m,用纸、纸板及纺织物以外任何材料制成	17元/平方米	202元/平方米
37024421	照相制版用无齿孔未曝光激光照排片,105mm＜宽度≤610mm,用纸、纸板及纺织物以外任何材料制成	2.0元/平方米	115元/平方米
37024422	印刷电路板制造用未曝光光致抗蚀干膜,105mm＜宽度≤610mm,用纸、纸板及纺织物以外任何材料制成	5元/平方米	115元/平方米
37024429	其他照相制版用无齿孔未曝光胶卷,105mm＜宽度≤610mm,用纸、纸板及纺织物以外任何材料制成	2.9元/平方米	115元/平方米
37024490	其他用无齿孔未曝光胶卷,105mm＜宽度≤610mm,用纸、纸板及纺织物以外任何材料制成	27元/平方米	202元/平方米
37025200	彩色摄影用未曝光彩色胶卷,宽度≤16 mm	95元/平方米	433元/平方米
37025300	幻灯片用未曝光彩色摄影胶卷,16 mm＜宽度≤35 mm,长度＜30m,用纸、纸板及纺织物以外任何材料制成	128元/平方米	433元/平方米
37025410	非幻灯片用未曝光彩色胶卷,宽度35mm,长度≤2 m,用纸、纸板及纺织物以外任何材料制成	18元/平方米	433元/平方米
37025490	非幻灯片用彩色摄影用未曝光彩色胶卷,16 mm＜宽度＜35 mm,2 m＜长度≤30m,用纸、纸板及纺织物以外任何材料制成	24元/平方米	433元/平方米
37025520	未曝光的彩色电影胶片,16mm＜ 宽度≤35mm,长度＞30m,用纸、纸板及纺织物以外任何材料制成	9元/平方米	232元/平方米
37025590	未曝光彩色摄影用胶卷,16mm＜ 宽度≤35mm,长度＞30m,用纸、纸板及纺织物以外任何材料制成,电影胶片除外	27元/平方米	433元/平方米
37025620	未曝光的彩色电影胶片,宽度＞35mm,用纸、纸板及纺织物以外任何材料制成	13元/平方米	232元/平方米
37025690	未曝光的彩色摄影用胶卷,宽度＞35mm,用纸、纸板及纺织物以外任何材料制成,电影胶片除外	74元/平方米	433元/平方米
37029600	未曝光非彩色胶卷,宽度≤35mm,长度≤30m,用纸、纸板及纺织物以外任何材料制成	21元/平方米	210元/平方米
37029700	未曝光的非彩色胶卷,宽度≤35mm,长度＞30m,用纸、纸板及纺织物以外任何材料制成	9元/平方米	210元/平方米
37029800	未曝光的非彩色胶卷,宽度＞35mm,用纸、纸板及纺织物以外任何材料制成	10元/平方米	210元/平方米
85211011	广播级录像机	①	②
85211019	其他磁带录像机	①	②
85211020	磁带放像机	①	②
85258012	非特种用途的广播级电视摄像机	③	④
85258013	非特种用途的其他电视摄像机	③	④
85258022	非特种用途的单反数字照相机	0	④
85258025	非特种用途的,其他可换镜头的数字照相机	0	④
85258029	非特种用途的其他数字照相机	0	④
85258032	非特种用途的广播级视频摄录一体机	0	④
85258039	非特种用途的其他视频摄录一体机	0	④

注:①从量复合税:完税价格不高于2000美元/台:30%,完税价格高于2000美元/台:3%,加3283元。

②完税价格不高于2000美元/台:130%,完税价格高于2000美元/台:6%,加20600元

③1—6月:11.7%与从量复合税(完税价格不高于5000美元/台:35%;完税价格高于5000美元/台:3%,加9728元,从低执行。7—12月:5.8%与从量复合税(完税价格不高于5000美元/台:35%;完税价格高于5000美元/台:3%,加9728元)从低执行。

④完税价格不高于5000美元/台:130%;完税价格高于5000美元/台:6%,加51500元。

附表 4:

Attached table 4:

进口反倾销、反补贴税清单

Import Antidumping and Countervailing Tariffs List

2019 年反倾销反补贴

HS 编码	商品名称	原产国名称	厂商中文名称	厂商英文名称	反倾销税率	反倾销开始时间	反倾销结束日期
0207110000	鲜或冷藏的整只鸡(CIQ 码:101:鲜的整只鸡,102:冷藏整只鸡)	巴西		SEARA ALIMENTOS LTDA	17.80%	2019 年 2 月 17 日	2024 年 2 月 16 日
		巴西		JBS AVES LTDA	17.80%	2019 年 2 月 17 日	2024 年 2 月 16 日
		巴西		SEARA COMERCIO DE ALIMENTOS LTDA	17.80%	2019 年 2 月 17 日	2024 年 2 月 16 日
		巴西		AGRICOLA JANDELLE S/A	17.80%	2019 年 2 月 17 日	2024 年 2 月 16 日
		巴西		BRF S.A.	25.80%	2019 年 2 月 17 日	2024 年 2 月 16 日
		巴西		C. Vale — Cooperativa Agroindustrial	32.40%	2019 年 2 月 17 日	2024 年 2 月 16 日
		巴西		Cooperativa Central Aurora Alimentos	20.20%	2019 年 2 月 17 日	2024 年 2 月 16 日
		巴西		LAR COOPERATIVA AGROINDUSTRIAL	20.20%	2019 年 2 月 17 日	2024 年 2 月 16 日
		巴西		Copacol — Cooperativa Agroindustrial Consolata	20.20%	2019 年 2 月 17 日	2024 年 2 月 16 日
		巴西		COOPAVEL COOPERATIVA AGROINDUSTRIAL	20.20%	2019 年 2 月 17 日	2024 年 2 月 16 日
		巴西		São Salvador Alimentos S/A	20.20%	2019 年 2 月 17 日	2024 年 2 月 16 日
		巴西		RIVELLI ALIMENTOS S/A	20.20%	2019 年 2 月 17 日	2024 年 2 月 16 日
		巴西		GONCALVES & TORTOLA S/A	20.20%	2019 年 2 月 17 日	2024 年 2 月 16 日
		巴西		COOPERATIVA AGROINDUSTRIAL COPAGRIL	20.20%	2019 年 2 月 17 日	2024 年 2 月 16 日
		巴西		VIBRA AGROINDUSTRIAL S/A	20.20%	2019 年 2 月 17 日	2024 年 2 月 16 日
		巴西		AGROSUL AGROAVICOLA INDUSTRIAL, S. A	20.20%	2019 年 2 月 17 日	2024 年 2 月 16 日
		巴西		KAEFER AGRO INDUSTRIAL LTDA	20.20%	2019 年 2 月 17 日	2024 年 2 月 16 日
		巴西		VOSSKO DO BRASIL ALIMENTOS CONGELADOS LTDA	20.20%	2019 年 2 月 17 日	2024 年 2 月 16 日
		巴西		AVENORTE AVICOLA CIANORTE LTDA.	20.20%	2019 年 2 月 17 日	2024 年 2 月 16 日
		巴西		ADORO S/A	20.20%	2019 年 2 月 17 日	2024 年 2 月 16 日
		巴西		BONASA ALIMENTOS SA	20.20%	2019 年 2 月 17 日	2024 年 2 月 16 日
		巴西		FLAMBOIÃ ALIMENTOS LTDA	20.20%	2019 年 2 月 17 日	2024 年 2 月 16 日
		巴西		FRIGORIFICO NOVA ARAÇÁ LTDA	20.20%	2019 年 2 月 17 日	2024 年 2 月 16 日
		巴西		RIO BRANCO ALIMENTOS S.A.	20.20%	2019 年 2 月 17 日	2024 年 2 月 16 日
		巴西		ZANCHETTA ALIMENTOS LTDA	20.20%	2019 年 2 月 17 日	2024 年 2 月 16 日
		巴西		AGRODANIELI INDÚSTRIA E COMÉRCIO LTDA.	20.20%	2019 年 2 月 17 日	2024 年 2 月 16 日
		巴西		BELLO ALIMENTOS LTDA.	20.20%	2019 年 2 月 17 日	2024 年 2 月 16 日
		巴西		COASUL COOPERATIVA AGROINDUSTRIAL	20.20%	2019 年 2 月 17 日	2024 年 2 月 16 日
		巴西		COOPERATIVA LANGUIRU LTDA	20.20%	2019 年 2 月 17 日	2024 年 2 月 16 日

HS编码	商品名称	原产国名称	厂商中文名称	厂商英文名称	反倾销税率	反倾销开始时间	反倾销结束日期
207110000	鲜或冷藏的整只鸡(CIQ码:101:鲜的整只鸡,102:冷藏整只鸡)	巴西		All Others	32.40%	2019年2月17日	2024年2月16日
		国(地)别不详的	国(地)别不详的	国(地)别不详的	32.40%	2019年2月17日	2024年2月16日
		巴西		SHB COMERCIO E INDUSTRIA DE ALIMENTOS S.A.	25.80%	2019年2月17日	2024年2月16日
		巴西		COMPANHIA MINUANO DE ALIMENTOS	25.80%	2019年2月17日	2024年2月16日
0207120000	冻的整只鸡(CIQ码:999)	巴西		SEARA ALIMENTOS LTDA	17.80%	2019年2月17日	2024年2月16日
		巴西		JBS AVES LTDA	17.80%	2019年2月17日	2024年2月16日
		巴西		SEARA COMERCIO DE ALIMENTOS LTDA	17.80%	2019年2月17日	2024年2月16日
		巴西		AGRICOLA JANDELLE S/A	17.80%	2019年2月17日	2024年2月16日
		巴西		BRF S.A.	25.80%	2019年2月17日	2024年2月16日
		巴西		C. Vale — Cooperativa Agroindustrial	32.40%	2019年2月17日	2024年2月16日
		巴西		Cooperativa Central Aurora Alimentos	20.20%	2019年2月17日	2024年2月16日
		巴西		LAR COOPERATIVA AGROINDUSTRIAL	20.20%	2019年2月17日	2024年2月16日
		巴西		Copacol — Cooperativa Agroindustrial Consolata	20.20%	2019年2月17日	2024年2月16日
		巴西		COOPAVEL COOPERATIVA AGROINDUSTRIAL	20.20%	2019年2月17日	2024年2月16日
		巴西		São Salvador Alimentos S/A	20.20%	2019年2月17日	2024年2月16日
		巴西		RIVELLI ALIMENTOS S/A	20.20%	2019年2月17日	2024年2月16日
		巴西		GONCALVES & TORTOLA S/A	20.20%	2019年2月17日	2024年2月16日
		巴西		COOPERATIVA AGROINDUSTRIAL COPAGRIL	20.20%	2019年2月17日	2024年2月16日
		巴西		VIBRA AGROINDUSTRIAL S/A	20.20%	2019年2月17日	2024年2月16日
		巴西		AGROSUL AGROAVICOLA INDUSTRIAL, S. A	20.20%	2019年2月17日	2024年2月16日
		巴西		KAEFER AGRO INDUSTRIAL LTDA	20.20%	2019年2月17日	2024年2月16日
		巴西		VOSSKO DO BRASIL ALIMENTOS CONGELADOS LTDA	20.20%	2019年2月17日	2024年2月16日
		巴西		AVENORTE AVICOLA CIANORTE LTDA.	20.20%	2019年2月17日	2024年2月16日
		巴西		ADORO S/A	20.20%	2019年2月17日	2024年2月16日
		巴西		BONASA ALIMENTOS SA	20.20%	2019年2月17日	2024年2月16日
		巴西		FLAMBOIÃ ALIMENTOS LTDA	20.20%	2019年2月17日	2024年2月16日
		巴西		FRIGORIFICO NOVA ARAÇÁ LTDA	20.20%	2019年2月17日	2024年2月16日
		巴西		RIO BRANCO ALIMENTOS S.A.	20.20%	2019年2月17日	2024年2月16日
		巴西		ZANCHETTA ALIMENTOS LTDA	20.20%	2019年2月17日	2024年2月16日
		巴西		AGRODANIELI INDÜSTRIA E COMÉRCIO LTDA.	20.20%	2019年2月17日	2024年2月16日
		巴西		BELLO ALIMENTOS LTDA.	20.20%	2019年2月17日	2024年2月16日
		巴西		COASUL COOPERATIVA AGROINDUSTRIAL	20.20%	2019年2月17日	2024年2月16日

HS编码	商品名称	原产国名称	厂商中文名称	厂商英文名称	反倾销税率	反倾销开始时间	反倾销结束日期
207120000	冻的整只鸡（CIQ码:999）	巴西		COOPERATIVA LANGUIRU LTDA	20.20%	2019年2月17日	2024年2月16日
		巴西		All Others	32.40%	2019年2月17日	2024年2月16日
		国（地）别不详的	国(地)别不详的	国(地)别不详的	32.40%	2019年2月17日	2024年2月16日
		巴西		SHB COMERCIO E INDUSTRIA DE ALIMENTOS S.A.	25.80%	2019年2月17日	2024年2月16日
		巴西		COMPANHIA MINUANO DE ALIMENTOS	25.80%	2019年2月17日	2024年2月16日
207131100	鲜或冷的带骨的鸡块（CIQ码:101:鲜的带骨的鸡块,102:冷藏带骨的鸡块）	巴西		SEARA ALIMENTOS LTDA	17.80%	2019年2月17日	2024年2月16日
		巴西		JBS AVES LTDA	17.80%	2019年2月17日	2024年2月16日
		巴西		SEARA COMERCIO DE ALIMENTOS LTDA	17.80%	2019年2月17日	2024年2月16日
		巴西		AGRICOLA JANDELLE S/A	17.80%	2019年2月17日	2024年2月16日
		巴西		BRF S.A.	25.80%	2019年2月17日	2024年2月16日
		巴西		C. Vale — Cooperativa Agroindustrial	32.40%	2019年2月17日	2024年2月16日
		巴西		Cooperativa Central Aurora Alimentos	20.20%	2019年2月17日	2024年2月16日
		巴西		LAR COOPERATIVA AGROINDUSTRIAL	20.20%	2019年2月17日	2024年2月16日
		巴西		Copacol — Cooperativa Agroindustrial Consolata	20.20%	2019年2月17日	2024年2月16日
		巴西		COOPAVEL COOPERATIVA AGROINDUSTRIAL	20.20%	2019年2月17日	2024年2月16日
		巴西		São Salvador Alimentos S/A	20.20%	2019年2月17日	2024年2月16日
		巴西		RIVELLI ALIMENTOS S/A	20.20%	2019年2月17日	2024年2月16日
		巴西		GONCALVES & TORTOLA S/A	20.20%	2019年2月17日	2024年2月16日
		巴西		COOPERATIVA AGROINDUSTRIAL COPAGRIL	20.20%	2019年2月17日	2024年2月16日
		巴西		VIBRA AGROINDUSTRIAL S/A	20.20%	2019年2月17日	2024年2月16日
		巴西		AGROSUL AGROAVICOLA INDUSTRIAL, S. A	20.20%	2019年2月17日	2024年2月16日
		巴西		KAEFER AGRO INDUSTRIAL LTDA	20.20%	2019年2月17日	2024年2月16日
		巴西		VOSSKO DO BRASIL ALIMENTOS CONGELADOS LTDA	20.20%	2019年2月17日	2024年2月16日
		巴西		AVENORTE AVICOLA CIANORTE LTDA.	20.20%	2019年2月17日	2024年2月16日
		巴西		ADORO S/A	20.20%	2019年2月17日	2024年2月16日
		巴西		BONASA ALIMENTOS SA	20.20%	2019年2月17日	2024年2月16日
		巴西		FLAMBOIÃ ALIMENTOS LTDA	20.20%	2019年2月17日	2024年2月16日
		巴西		FRIGORIFICO NOVA ARAÇÁ LTDA	20.20%	2019年2月17日	2024年2月16日
		巴西		RIO BRANCO ALIMENTOS S.A.	20.20%	2019年2月17日	2024年2月16日
		巴西		ZANCHETTA ALIMENTOS LTDA	20.20%	2019年2月17日	2024年2月16日
		巴西		AGRODANIELI INDÚSTRIA E COMÉRCIO LTDA.	20.20%	2019年2月17日	2024年2月16日
		巴西		BELLO ALIMENTOS LTDA.	20.20%	2019年2月17日	2024年2月16日
		巴西		COASUL COOPERATIVA AGROINDUSTRIAL	20.20%	2019年2月17日	2024年2月16日
		巴西		COOPERATIVA LANGUIRU LTDA	20.20%	2019年2月17日	2024年2月16日

HS编码	商品名称	原产国名称	厂商中文名称	厂商英文名称	反倾销税率	反倾销开始时间	反倾销结束日期
207131100	鲜或冷的带骨的鸡块（CIQ码：101：鲜的带骨的鸡块，102：冷藏带骨的鸡块）	巴西		All Others	32.40%	2019年2月17日	2024年2月16日
		国（地）别不详的	国(地)别不详的	国(地)别不详的	32.40%	2019年2月17日	2024年2月16日
		巴西		SHB COMERCIO E INDUSTRIA DE ALIMENTOS S.A.	25.80%	2019年2月17日	2024年2月16日
		巴西		COMPANHIA MINUANO DE ALIMENTOS	25.80%	2019年2月17日	2024年2月16日
207131900	其他鲜或冷的鸡块（CIQ码：101：其他鲜的鸡块，102：其他冷藏鸡块）	巴西		SEARA ALIMENTOS LTDA	17.80%	2019年2月17日	2024年2月16日
		巴西		JBS AVES LTDA	17.80%	2019年2月17日	2024年2月16日
		巴西		SEARA COMERCIO DE ALIMENTOS LTDA	17.80%	2019年2月17日	2024年2月16日
		巴西		AGRICOLA JANDELLE S/A	17.80%	2019年2月17日	2024年2月16日
		巴西		BRF S.A.	25.80%	2019年2月17日	2024年2月16日
		巴西		C. Vale — Cooperativa Agroindustrial	32.40%	2019年2月17日	2024年2月16日
		巴西		Cooperativa Central Aurora Alimentos	20.20%	2019年2月17日	2024年2月16日
		巴西		LAR COOPERATIVA AGROINDUSTRIAL	20.20%	2019年2月17日	2024年2月16日
		巴西		Copacol — Cooperativa Agroindustrial Consolata	20.20%	2019年2月17日	2024年2月16日
		巴西		COOPAVEL COOPERATIVA AGROINDUSTRIAL	20.20%	2019年2月17日	2024年2月16日
		巴西		São Salvador Alimentos S/A	20.20%	2019年2月17日	2024年2月16日
		巴西		RIVELLI ALIMENTOS S/A	20.20%	2019年2月17日	2024年2月16日
		巴西		GONCALVES & TORTOLA S/A	20.20%	2019年2月17日	2024年2月16日
		巴西		COOPERATIVA AGROINDUSTRIAL COPAGRIL	20.20%	2019年2月17日	2024年2月16日
		巴西		VIBRA AGROINDUSTRIAL S/A	20.20%	2019年2月17日	2024年2月16日
		巴西		AGROSUL AGROAVICOLA INDUSTRIAL, S. A	20.20%	2019年2月17日	2024年2月16日
		巴西		KAEFER AGRO INDUSTRIAL LTDA	20.20%	2019年2月17日	2024年2月16日
		巴西		VOSSKO DO BRASIL ALIMENTOS CONGELADOS LTDA	20.20%	2019年2月17日	2024年2月16日
		巴西		AVENORTE AVICOLA CIANORTE LTDA.	20.20%	2019年2月17日	2024年2月16日
		巴西		ADORO S/A	20.20%	2019年2月17日	2024年2月16日
		巴西		BONASA ALIMENTOS SA	20.20%	2019年2月17日	2024年2月16日
		巴西		FLAMBOIÃ ALIMENTOS LTDA	20.20%	2019年2月17日	2024年2月16日
		巴西		FRIGORIFICO NOVA ARAÇÁ LTDA	20.20%	2019年2月17日	2024年2月16日
		巴西		RIO BRANCO ALIMENTOS S.A.	20.20%	2019年2月17日	2024年2月16日
		巴西		ZANCHETTA ALIMENTOS LTDA	20.20%	2019年2月17日	2024年2月16日
		巴西		AGRODANIELI INDÜSTRIA E COMÉRCIO LTDA.	20.20%	2019年2月17日	2024年2月16日
		巴西		BELLO ALIMENTOS LTDA.	20.20%	2019年2月17日	2024年2月16日
		巴西		COASUL COOPERATIVA AGROINDUSTRIAL	20.20%	2019年2月17日	2024年2月16日
		巴西		COOPERATIVA LANGUIRU LTDA	20.20%	2019年2月17日	2024年2月16日
		巴西		All Others	32.40%	2019年2月17日	2024年2月16日

HS编码	商品名称	原产国名称	厂商中文名称	厂商英文名称	反倾销税率	反倾销开始时间	反倾销结束日期
207131900	其他鲜或冷的鸡块（CIQ码：101：其他鲜的鸡块，102：其他冷藏鸡块）	国（地）别不详的	国(地)别不详的	国(地)别不详的	32.40%	2019年2月17日	2024年2月16日
		巴西		SHB COMERCIO E INDUSTRIA DE ALIMENTOS S.A.	25.80%	2019年2月17日	2024年2月16日
		巴西		COMPANHIA MINUANO DE ALIMENTOS	25.80%	2019年2月17日	2024年2月16日
207132101	鲜或冷的整翅（翼）（CIQ码：101：鲜的整翅，102：冷藏的整翅）	巴西		SEARA ALIMENTOS LTDA	17.80%	2019年2月17日	2024年2月16日
		巴西		JBS AVES LTDA	17.80%	2019年2月17日	2024年2月16日
		巴西		SEARA COMERCIO DE ALIMENTOS LTDA	17.80%	2019年2月17日	2024年2月16日
		巴西		AGRICOLA JANDELLE S/A	17.80%	2019年2月17日	2024年2月16日
		巴西		BRF S.A.	25.80%	2019年2月17日	2024年2月16日
		巴西		C. Vale — Cooperativa Agroindustrial	32.40%	2019年2月17日	2024年2月16日
		巴西		Cooperativa Central Aurora Alimentos	20.20%	2019年2月17日	2024年2月16日
		巴西		LAR COOPERATIVA AGROINDUSTRIAL	20.20%	2019年2月17日	2024年2月16日
		巴西		Copacol — Cooperativa Agroindustrial Consolata	20.20%	2019年2月17日	2024年2月16日
		巴西		COOPAVEL COOPERATIVA AGROINDUSTRIAL	20.20%	2019年2月17日	2024年2月16日
		巴西		Säo Salvador Alimentos S/A	20.20%	2019年2月17日	2024年2月16日
		巴西		RIVELLI ALIMENTOS S/A	20.20%	2019年2月17日	2024年2月16日
		巴西		GONCALVES & TORTOLA S/A	20.20%	2019年2月17日	2024年2月16日
		巴西		COOPERATIVA AGROINDUSTRIAL COPAGRIL	20.20%	2019年2月17日	2024年2月16日
		巴西		VIBRA AGROINDUSTRIAL S/A	20.20%	2019年2月17日	2024年2月16日
		巴西		AGROSUL AGROAVICOLA INDUSTRIAL, S. A	20.20%	2019年2月17日	2024年2月16日
		巴西		KAEFER AGRO INDUSTRIAL LTDA	20.20%	2019年2月17日	2024年2月16日
		巴西		VOSSKO DO BRASIL ALIMENTOS CONGELADOS LTDA	20.20%	2019年2月17日	2024年2月16日
		巴西		AVENORTE AVICOLA CIANORTE LTDA.	20.20%	2019年2月17日	2024年2月16日
		巴西		ADORO S/A	20.20%	2019年2月17日	2024年2月16日
		巴西		BONASA ALIMENTOS SA	20.20%	2019年2月17日	2024年2月16日
		巴西		FLAMBOIÃ ALIMENTOS LTDA	20.20%	2019年2月17日	2024年2月16日
		巴西		FRIGORIFICO NOVA ARAÇÁ LTDA	20.20%	2019年2月17日	2024年2月16日
		巴西		RIO BRANCO ALIMENTOS S.A.	20.20%	2019年2月17日	2024年2月16日
		巴西		ZANCHETTA ALIMENTOS LTDA	20.20%	2019年2月17日	2024年2月16日
		巴西		AGRODANIELI INDÜSTRIA E COMÉRCIO LTDA.	20.20%	2019年2月17日	2024年2月16日
		巴西		BELLO ALIMENTOS LTDA.	20.20%	2019年2月17日	2024年2月16日
		巴西		COASUL COOPERATIVA AGROINDUSTRIAL	20.20%	2019年2月17日	2024年2月16日
		巴西		COOPERATIVA LANGUIRU LTDA	20.20%	2019年2月17日	2024年2月16日
		巴西		All Others	32.40%	2019年2月17日	2024年2月16日

HS编码	商品名称	原产国名称	厂商中文名称	厂商英文名称	反倾销税率	反倾销开始时间	反倾销结束日期
207132101	鲜或冷的整翅(翼)(CIQ码:101:鲜的整翅,102:冷藏的整翅)	国(地)别不详的	国(地)别不详的	国(地)别不详的	32.40%	2019年2月17日	2024年2月16日
		巴西		SHB COMERCIO E INDUSTRIA DE ALIMENTOS S.A.	25.80%	2019年2月17日	2024年2月16日
		巴西		COMPANHIA MINUANO DE ALIMENTOS	25.80%	2019年2月17日	2024年2月16日
207132102	鲜或冷的翅(翼)根(CIQ码:101:鲜的翼根,102:冷藏翼根)	巴西		SEARA ALIMENTOS LTDA	17.80%	2019年2月17日	2024年2月16日
		巴西		JBS AVES LTDA	17.80%	2019年2月17日	2024年2月16日
		巴西		SEARA COMERCIO DE ALIMENTOS LTDA	17.80%	2019年2月17日	2024年2月16日
		巴西		AGRICOLA JANDELLE S/A	17.80%	2019年2月17日	2024年2月16日
		巴西		BRF S.A.	25.80%	2019年2月17日	2024年2月16日
		巴西		C. Vale — Cooperativa Agroindustrial	32.40%	2019年2月17日	2024年2月16日
		巴西		Cooperativa Central Aurora Alimentos	20.20%	2019年2月17日	2024年2月16日
		巴西		LAR COOPERATIVA AGROINDUSTRIAL	20.20%	2019年2月17日	2024年2月16日
		巴西		Copacol — Cooperativa Agroindustrial Consolata	20.20%	2019年2月17日	2024年2月16日
		巴西		COOPAVEL COOPERATIVA AGROINDUSTRIAL	20.20%	2019年2月17日	2024年2月16日
		巴西		São Salvador Alimentos S/A	20.20%	2019年2月17日	2024年2月16日
		巴西		RIVELLI ALIMENTOS S/A	20.20%	2019年2月17日	2024年2月16日
		巴西		GONCALVES & TORTOLA S/A	20.20%	2019年2月17日	2024年2月16日
		巴西		COOPERATIVA AGROINDUSTRIAL COPAGRIL	20.20%	2019年2月17日	2024年2月16日
		巴西		VIBRA AGROINDUSTRIAL S/A	20.20%	2019年2月17日	2024年2月16日
		巴西		AGROSUL AGROAVICOLA INDUSTRIAL, S. A	20.20%	2019年2月17日	2024年2月16日
		巴西		KAEFER AGRO INDUSTRIAL LTDA	20.20%	2019年2月17日	2024年2月16日
		巴西		VOSSKO DO BRASIL ALIMENTOS CONGELADOS LTDA	20.20%	2019年2月17日	2024年2月16日
		巴西		AVENORTE AVICOLA CIANORTE LTDA.	20.20%	2019年2月17日	2024年2月16日
		巴西		ADORO S/A	20.20%	2019年2月17日	2024年2月16日
		巴西		BONASA ALIMENTOS SA	20.20%	2019年2月17日	2024年2月16日
		巴西		FLAMBOIÃ ALIMENTOS LTDA	20.20%	2019年2月17日	2024年2月16日
		巴西		FRIGORIFICO NOVA ARAÇÁ LTDA	20.20%	2019年2月17日	2024年2月16日
		巴西		RIO BRANCO ALIMENTOS S.A.	20.20%	2019年2月17日	2024年2月16日
		巴西		ZANCHETTA ALIMENTOS LTDA	20.20%	2019年2月17日	2024年2月16日
		巴西		AGRODANIELI INDÜSTRIA E COMÉRCIO LTDA.	20.20%	2019年2月17日	2024年2月16日
		巴西		BELLO ALIMENTOS LTDA.	20.20%	2019年2月17日	2024年2月16日
		巴西		COASUL COOPERATIVA AGROINDUSTRIAL	20.20%	2019年2月17日	2024年2月16日
		巴西		COOPERATIVA LANGUIRU LTDA	20.20%	2019年2月17日	2024年2月16日
		巴西		All Others	32.40%	2019年2月17日	2024年2月16日

HS编码	商品名称	原产国名称	厂商中文名称	厂商英文名称	反倾销税率	反倾销开始时间	反倾销结束日期
207132102	鲜或冷的翅(翼)根(CIQ码:101:鲜的翼根,102:冷藏翼根)	国(地)别不详的	国(地)别不详的	国(地)别不详的	32.40%	2019年2月17日	2024年2月16日
		巴西		SHB COMERCIO E INDUSTRIA DE ALIMENTOS S.A.	25.80%	2019年2月17日	2024年2月16日
		巴西		COMPANHIA MINUANO DE ALIMENTOS	25.80%	2019年2月17日	2024年2月16日
207132103	(鲜或冷的翅(翼)中(CIQ码:101:鲜的翼中,102:冷藏翼中))	巴西		SEARA ALIMENTOS LTDA	17.80%	2019年2月17日	2024年2月16日
		巴西		JBS AVES LTDA	17.80%	2019年2月17日	2024年2月16日
		巴西		SEARA COMERCIO DE ALIMENTOS LTDA	17.80%	2019年2月17日	2024年2月16日
		巴西		AGRICOLA JANDELLE S/A	17.80%	2019年2月17日	2024年2月16日
		巴西		BRF S.A.	25.80%	2019年2月17日	2024年2月16日
		巴西		C. Vale — Cooperativa Agroindustrial	32.40%	2019年2月17日	2024年2月16日
		巴西		Cooperativa Central Aurora Alimentos	20.20%	2019年2月17日	2024年2月16日
		巴西		LAR COOPERATIVA AGROINDUSTRIAL	20.20%	2019年2月17日	2024年2月16日
		巴西		Copacol — Cooperativa Agroindustrial Consolata	20.20%	2019年2月17日	2024年2月16日
		巴西		COOPAVEL COOPERATIVA AGROINDUSTRIAL	20.20%	2019年2月17日	2024年2月16日
		巴西		Säo Salvador Alimentos S/A	20.20%	2019年2月17日	2024年2月16日
		巴西		RIVELLI ALIMENTOS S/A	20.20%	2019年2月17日	2024年2月16日
		巴西		GONCALVES & TORTOLA S/A	20.20%	2019年2月17日	2024年2月16日
		巴西		COOPERATIVA AGROINDUSTRIAL COPAGRIL	20.20%	2019年2月17日	2024年2月16日
		巴西		VIBRA AGROINDUSTRIAL S/A	20.20%	2019年2月17日	2024年2月16日
		巴西		AGROSUL AGROAVICOLA INDUSTRIAL, S. A	20.20%	2019年2月17日	2024年2月16日
		巴西		KAEFER AGRO INDUSTRIAL LTDA	20.20%	2019年2月17日	2024年2月16日
		巴西		VOSSKO DO BRASIL ALIMENTOS CONGELADOS LTDA	20.20%	2019年2月17日	2024年2月16日
		巴西		AVENORTE AVICOLA CIANORTE LTDA.	20.20%	2019年2月17日	2024年2月16日
		巴西		ADORO S/A	20.20%	2019年2月17日	2024年2月16日
		巴西		BONASA ALIMENTOS SA	20.20%	2019年2月17日	2024年2月16日
		巴西		FLAMBOIÃ ALIMENTOS LTDA	20.20%	2019年2月17日	2024年2月16日
		巴西		FRIGORIFICO NOVA ARAÇÁ LTDA	20.20%	2019年2月17日	2024年2月16日
		巴西		RIO BRANCO ALIMENTOS S. A.	20.20%	2019年2月17日	2024年2月16日
		巴西		ZANCHETTA ALIMENTOS LTDA	20.20%	2019年2月17日	2024年2月16日
		巴西		AGRODANIELI INDÜSTRIA E COMÉRCIO LTDA.	20.20%	2019年2月17日	2024年2月16日
		巴西		BELLO ALIMENTOS LTDA.	20.20%	2019年2月17日	2024年2月16日
		巴西		COASUL COOPERATIVA AGROINDUSTRIAL	20.20%	2019年2月17日	2024年2月16日
		巴西		COOPERATIVA LANGUIRU LTDA	20.20%	2019年2月17日	2024年2月16日
		巴西		All Others	32.40%	2019年2月17日	2024年2月16日

HS编码	商品名称	原产国名称	厂商中文名称	厂商英文名称	反倾销税率	反倾销开始时间	反倾销结束日期
0207132103	(鲜或冷的翅(翼)中(CIQ码:101:鲜的翼中,102:冷藏翼中))	国(地)别不详的	国(地)别不详的	国(地)别不详的	32.40%	2019年2月17日	2024年2月16日
		巴西		SHB COMERCIO E INDUSTRIA DE ALIMENTOS S.A.	25.80%	2019年2月17日	2024年2月16日
		巴西		COMPANHIA MINUANO DE ALIMENTOS	25.80%	2019年2月17日	2024年2月16日
207132104	鲜或冷的两节翅(翼)(CIQ码:101:鲜的两节翼,102:冷藏两节翼)	巴西		SEARA ALIMENTOS LTDA	17.80%	2019年2月17日	2024年2月16日
		巴西		JBS AVES LTDA	17.80%	2019年2月17日	2024年2月16日
		巴西		SEARA COMERCIO DE ALIMENTOS LTDA	17.80%	2019年2月17日	2024年2月16日
		巴西		AGRICOLA JANDELLE S/A	17.80%	2019年2月17日	2024年2月16日
		巴西		BRF S.A.	25.80%	2019年2月17日	2024年2月16日
		巴西		C. Vale — Cooperativa Agroindustrial	32.40%	2019年2月17日	2024年2月16日
		巴西		Cooperativa Central Aurora Alimentos	20.20%	2019年2月17日	2024年2月16日
		巴西		LAR COOPERATIVA AGROINDUSTRIAL	20.20%	2019年2月17日	2024年2月16日
		巴西		Copacol — Cooperativa Agroindustrial Consolata	20.20%	2019年2月17日	2024年2月16日
		巴西		COOPAVEL COOPERATIVA AGROINDUSTRIAL	20.20%	2019年2月17日	2024年2月16日
		巴西		São Salvador Alimentos S/A	20.20%	2019年2月17日	2024年2月16日
		巴西		RIVELLI ALIMENTOS S/A	20.20%	2019年2月17日	2024年2月16日
		巴西		GONCALVES & TORTOLA S/A	20.20%	2019年2月17日	2024年2月16日
		巴西		COOPERATIVA AGROINDUSTRIAL COPAGRIL	20.20%	2019年2月17日	2024年2月16日
		巴西		VIBRA AGROINDUSTRIAL S/A	20.20%	2019年2月17日	2024年2月16日
		巴西		AGROSUL AGROAVICOLA INDUSTRIAL, S. A	20.20%	2019年2月17日	2024年2月16日
		巴西		KAEFER AGRO INDUSTRIAL LTDA	20.20%	2019年2月17日	2024年2月16日
		巴西		VOSSKO DO BRASIL ALIMENTOS CONGELADOS LTDA	20.20%	2019年2月17日	2024年2月16日
		巴西		AVENORTE AVICOLA CIANORTE LTDA.	20.20%	2019年2月17日	2024年2月16日
		巴西		ADORO S/A	20.20%	2019年2月17日	2024年2月16日
		巴西		BONASA ALIMENTOS SA	20.20%	2019年2月17日	2024年2月16日
		巴西		FLAMBOIÃ ALIMENTOS LTDA	20.20%	2019年2月17日	2024年2月16日
		巴西		FRIGORIFICO NOVA ARAÇÁ LTDA	20.20%	2019年2月17日	2024年2月16日
		巴西		RIO BRANCO ALIMENTOS S.A.	20.20%	2019年2月17日	2024年2月16日
		巴西		ZANCHETTA ALIMENTOS LTDA	20.20%	2019年2月17日	2024年2月16日
		巴西		AGRODANIELI INDÙSTRIA E COMÉRCIO LTDA.	20.20%	2019年2月17日	2024年2月16日
		巴西		BELLO ALIMENTOS LTDA.	20.20%	2019年2月17日	2024年2月16日
		巴西		COASUL COOPERATIVA AGROINDUSTRIAL	20.20%	2019年2月17日	2024年2月16日
		巴西		COOPERATIVA LANGUIRU LTDA	20.20%	2019年2月17日	2024年2月16日
		巴西		All Others	32.40%	2019年2月17日	2024年2月16日

HS编码	商品名称	原产国名称	厂商中文名称	厂商英文名称	反倾销税率	反倾销开始时间	反倾销结束日期
0207132104	鲜或冷的两节翅(翼)(CIQ码:101:鲜的两节翼,102:冷藏两节翼)	国(地)别不详的	国(地)别不详的	国(地)别不详的	32.40%	2019年2月17日	2024年2月16日
		巴西		SHB COMERCIO E INDUSTRIA DE ALIMENTOS S.A.	25.80%	2019年2月17日	2024年2月16日
		巴西		COMPANHIA MINUANO DE ALIMENTOS	25.80%	2019年2月17日	2024年2月16日
207132901	鲜或冷的鸡翅(翼)尖(CIQ码:101:鲜的翼尖;102:冷藏翼尖)	巴西		SEARA ALIMENTOS LTDA	17.80%	2019年2月17日	2024年2月16日
		巴西		JBS AVES LTDA	17.80%	2019年2月17日	2024年2月16日
		巴西		SEARA COMERCIO DE ALIMENTOS LTDA	17.80%	2019年2月17日	2024年2月16日
		巴西		AGRICOLA JANDELLE S/A	17.80%	2019年2月17日	2024年2月16日
		巴西		BRF S.A.	25.80%	2019年2月17日	2024年2月16日
		巴西		C. Vale — Cooperativa Agroindustrial	32.40%	2019年2月17日	2024年2月16日
		巴西		Cooperativa Central Aurora Alimentos	20.20%	2019年2月17日	2024年2月16日
		巴西		LAR COOPERATIVA AGROINDUSTRIAL	20.20%	2019年2月17日	2024年2月16日
		巴西		Copacol — Cocperativa Agroindustrial Consolata	20.20%	2019年2月17日	2024年2月16日
		巴西		COOPAVEL COOPERATIVA AGROINDUSTRIAL	20.20%	2019年2月17日	2024年2月16日
		巴西		Säo Salvador Alimentos S/A	20.20%	2019年2月17日	2024年2月16日
		巴西		RIVELLI ALIMENTOS S/A	20.20%	2019年2月17日	2024年2月16日
		巴西		GONCALVES & TORTOLA S/A	20.20%	2019年2月17日	2024年2月16日
		巴西		COOPERATIVA AGROINDUSTRIAL COPAGRIL	20.20%	2019年2月17日	2024年2月16日
		巴西		VIBRA AGROINDUSTRIAL S/A	20.20%	2019年2月17日	2024年2月16日
		巴西		AGROSUL AGROAVICOLA INDUSTRIAL, S. A	20.20%	2019年2月17日	2024年2月16日
		巴西		KAEFER AGRO INDUSTRIAL LTDA	20.20%	2019年2月17日	2024年2月16日
		巴西		VOSSKO DO BRASIL ALIMENTOS CONGELADOS LTDA	20.20%	2019年2月17日	2024年2月16日
		巴西		AVENORTE AVICOLA CIANORTE LTDA.	20.20%	2019年2月17日	2024年2月16日
		巴西		ADORO S/A	20.20%	2019年2月17日	2024年2月16日
		巴西		BONASA ALIMENTOS SA	20.20%	2019年2月17日	2024年2月16日
		巴西		FLAMBOIÃ ALIMENTOS LTDA	20.20%	2019年2月17日	2024年2月16日
		巴西		FRIGORIFICO NOVA ARAÇÁ LTDA	20.20%	2019年2月17日	2024年2月16日
		巴西		RIO BRANCO ALIMENTOS S.A.	20.20%	2019年2月17日	2024年2月16日
		巴西		ZANCHETTA ALIMENTOS LTDA	20.20%	2019年2月17日	2024年2月16日
		巴西		AGRODANIELI INDŪSTRIA E COMÉRCIO LTDA.	20.20%	2019年2月17日	2024年2月16日
		巴西		BELLO ALIMENTOS LTDA.	20.20%	2019年2月17日	2024年2月16日
		巴西		COASUL COOPERATIVA AGROINDUSTRIAL	20.20%	2019年2月17日	2024年2月16日
		巴西		COOPERATIVA LANGUIRU LTDA	20.20%	2019年2月17日	2024年2月16日
		巴西		All Others	32.40%	2019年2月17日	2024年2月16日

HS编码	商品名称	原产国名称	厂商中文名称	厂商英文名称	反倾销税率	反倾销开始时间	反倾销结束日期
207132901	鲜或冷的鸡翅（翼）尖（CIQ码：101：鲜的翼尖；102：冷藏翼尖）	国（地）别不详的	国(地)别不详的	国(地)别不详的	32.40%	2019年2月17日	2024年2月16日
		巴西		SHB COMERCIO E INDUSTRIA DE ALIMENTOS S.A.	25.80%	2019年2月17日	2024年2月16日
		巴西		COMPANHIA MINUANO DE ALIMENTOS	25.80%	2019年2月17日	2024年2月16日
207132902	鲜或冷的鸡膝软骨（CIQ码：101：鲜的鸡膝软骨，102：冷藏鸡膝软骨）	巴西		SEARA ALIMENTOS LTDA	17.80%	2019年2月17日	2024年2月16日
		巴西		JBS AVES LTDA	17.80%	2019年2月17日	2024年2月16日
		巴西		SEARA COMERCIO DE ALIMENTOS LTDA	17.80%	2019年2月17日	2024年2月16日
		巴西		AGRICOLA JANDELLE S/A	17.80%	2019年2月17日	2024年2月16日
		巴西		BRF S.A.	25.80%	2019年2月17日	2024年2月16日
		巴西		C. Vale — Cooperativa Agroindustrial	32.40%	2019年2月17日	2024年2月16日
		巴西		Cooperativa Central Aurora Alimentos	20.20%	2019年2月17日	2024年2月16日
		巴西		LAR COOPERATIVA AGROINDUSTRIAL	20.20%	2019年2月17日	2024年2月16日
		巴西		Copacol — Cooperativa Agroindustrial Consolata	20.20%	2019年2月17日	2024年2月16日
		巴西		COOPAVEL COOPERATIVA AGROINDUSTRIAL	20.20%	2019年2月17日	2024年2月16日
		巴西		São Salvador Alimentos S/A	20.20%	2019年2月17日	2024年2月16日
		巴西		RIVELLI ALIMENTOS S/A	20.20%	2019年2月17日	2024年2月16日
		巴西		GONCALVES & TORTOLA S/A	20.20%	2019年2月17日	2024年2月16日
		巴西		COOPERATIVA AGROINDUSTRIAL COPAGRIL	20.20%	2019年2月17日	2024年2月16日
		巴西		VIBRA AGROINDUSTRIAL S/A	20.20%	2019年2月17日	2024年2月16日
		巴西		AGROSUL AGROAVICOLA INDUSTRIAL, S. A	20.20%	2019年2月17日	2024年2月16日
		巴西		KAEFER AGRO INDUSTRIAL LTDA	20.20%	2019年2月17日	2024年2月16日
		巴西		VOSSKO DO BRASIL ALIMENTOS CONGELADOS LTDA	20.20%	2019年2月17日	2024年2月16日
		巴西		AVENORTE AVICOLA CIANORTE LTDA.	20.20%	2019年2月17日	2024年2月16日
		巴西		ADORO S/A	20.20%	2019年2月17日	2024年2月16日
		巴西		BONASA ALIMENTOS SA	20.20%	2019年2月17日	2024年2月16日
		巴西		FLAMBOIÃ ALIMENTOS LTDA	20.20%	2019年2月17日	2024年2月16日
		巴西		FRIGORIFICO NOVA ARAÇÁ LTDA	20.20%	2019年2月17日	2024年2月16日
		巴西		RIO BRANCO ALIMENTOS S.A.	20.20%	2019年2月17日	2024年2月16日
		巴西		ZANCHETTA ALIMENTOS LTDA	20.20%	2019年2月17日	2024年2月16日
		巴西		AGRODANIELI INDÜSTRIA E COMÉRCIO LTDA.	20.20%	2019年2月17日	2024年2月16日
		巴西		BELLO ALIMENTOS LTDA.	20.20%	2019年2月17日	2024年2月16日
		巴西		COASUL COOPERATIVA AGROINDUSTRIAL	20.20%	2019年2月17日	2024年2月16日
		巴西		COOPERATIVA LANGUIRU LTDA	20.20%	2019年2月17日	2024年2月16日
		巴西		All Others	32.40%	2019年2月17日	2024年2月16日

HS编码	商品名称	原产国名称	厂商中文名称	厂商英文名称	反倾销税率	反倾销开始时间	反倾销结束日期
207132902	鲜或冷的鸡膝软骨（CIQ码：101：鲜的鸡膝软骨，102：冷藏鸡膝软骨）	国（地）别不详的	国(地)别不详的	国(地)别不详的	32.40%	2019年2月17日	2024年2月16日
		巴西		SHB COMERCIO E INDUSTRIA DE ALIMENTOS S.A.	25.80%	2019年2月17日	2024年2月16日
		巴西		COMPANHIA MINUANO DE ALIMENTOS	25.80%	2019年2月17日	2024年2月16日
207132990	其他鲜或冷的鸡杂碎（CIQ码：101：鲜的鸡胸、鸡腿，102：冷藏的鸡胸、鸡腿，103：鲜的鸡翼，包括翼尖，104：冷藏鸡翼，包括翼尖，105：鲜的鸡翼翼尖，106：冷藏鸡翼翼尖，107：鲜的鸡爪，108：冷藏鸡爪，109：鲜的鸡肫、胃，110：冷藏鸡肫、胃，111：其他鲜的鸡杂碎，112：其他冷藏鸡杂碎）	巴西		SEARA ALIMENTOS LTDA	17.80%	2019年2月17日	2024年2月16日
		巴西		JBS AVES LTDA	17.80%	2019年2月17日	2024年2月16日
		巴西		SEARA COMERCIO DE ALIMENTOS LTDA	17.80%	2019年2月17日	2024年2月16日
		巴西		AGRICOLA JANDELLE S/A	17.80%	2019年2月17日	2024年2月16日
		巴西		BRF S.A.	25.80%	2019年2月17日	2024年2月16日
		巴西		C. Vale — Cooperativa Agroindustrial	32.40%	2019年2月17日	2024年2月16日
		巴西		Cooperativa Central Aurora Alimentos	20.20%	2019年2月17日	2024年2月16日
		巴西		LAR COOPERATIVA AGROINDUSTRIAL	20.20%	2019年2月17日	2024年2月16日
		巴西		Copacol — Cooperativa Agroindustrial Consolata	20.20%	2019年2月17日	2024年2月16日
		巴西		COOPAVEL COOPERATIVA AGROINDUSTRIAL	20.20%	2019年2月17日	2024年2月16日
		巴西		São Salvador Alimentos S/A	20.20%	2019年2月17日	2024年2月16日
		巴西		RIVELLI ALIMENTOS S/A	20.20%	2019年2月17日	2024年2月16日
		巴西		GONCALVES & TORTOLA S/A	20.20%	2019年2月17日	2024年2月16日
		巴西		COOPERATIVA AGROINDUSTRIAL COPAGRIL	20.20%	2019年2月17日	2024年2月16日
		巴西		VIBRA AGROINDUSTRIAL S/A	20.20%	2019年2月17日	2024年2月16日
		巴西		AGROSUL AGROAVICOLA INDUSTRIAL, S. A	20.20%	2019年2月17日	2024年2月16日
		巴西		KAEFER AGRO INDUSTRIAL LTDA	20.20%	2019年2月17日	2024年2月16日
		巴西		VOSSKO DO BRASIL ALIMENTOS CONGELADOS LTDA	20.20%	2019年2月17日	2024年2月16日
		巴西		AVENORTE AVICOLA CIANORTE LTDA.	20.20%	2019年2月17日	2024年2月16日
		巴西		ADORO S/A	20.20%	2019年2月17日	2024年2月16日
		巴西		BONASA ALIMENTOS SA	20.20%	2019年2月17日	2024年2月16日
		巴西		FLAMBOIÃ ALIMENTOS LTDA	20.20%	2019年2月17日	2024年2月16日
		巴西		FRIGORIFICO NOVA ARAÇÁ LTDA	20.20%	2019年2月17日	2024年2月16日
		巴西		RIO BRANCO ALIMENTOS S.A.	20.20%	2019年2月17日	2024年2月16日
		巴西		ZANCHETTA ALIMENTOS LTDA	20.20%	2019年2月17日	2024年2月16日
		巴西		AGRODANIELI INDÚSTRIA E COMÉRCIO LTDA.	20.20%	2019年2月17日	2024年2月16日
		巴西		BELLO ALIMENTOS LTDA.	20.20%	2019年2月17日	2024年2月16日
		巴西		COASUL COOPERATIVA AGROINDUSTRIAL	20.20%	2019年2月17日	2024年2月16日
		巴西		COOPERATIVA LANGUIRU LTDA	20.20%	2019年2月17日	2024年2月16日
		巴西		All Others	32.40%	2019年2月17日	2024年2月16日

HS编码	商品名称	原产国名称	厂商中文名称	厂商英文名称	反倾销税率	反倾销开始时间	反倾销结束日期
		国（地）别不详的	国(地)别不详的	国(地)别不详的	32.40%	2019年2月17日	2024年2月16日
		巴西		SHB COMERCIO E INDUSTRIA DE ALIMENTOS S.A.	25.80%	2019年2月17日	2024年2月16日
		巴西		COMPANHIA MINUANO DE ALIMENTOS	25.80%	2019年2月17日	2024年2月16日
207141100	冻的带骨鸡块(包括鸡胸脯、鸡大腿等)(CIQ码：101：冷冻带骨鸡肉，除鸡胸、鸡腿，102：鸡胸、鸡腿)	巴西		SEARA ALIMENTOS LTDA	17.80%	2019年2月17日	2024年2月16日
		巴西		JBS AVES LTDA	17.80%	2019年2月17日	2024年2月16日
		巴西		SEARA COMERCIO DE ALIMENTOS LTDA	17.80%	2019年2月17日	2024年2月16日
		巴西		AGRICOLA JANDELLE S/A	17.80%	2019年2月17日	2024年2月16日
		巴西		BRF S.A.	25.80%	2019年2月17日	2024年2月16日
		巴西		C. Vale — Cooperativa Agroindustrial	32.40%	2019年2月17日	2024年2月16日
		巴西		Cooperativa Central Aurora Alimentos	20.20%	2019年2月17日	2024年2月16日
		巴西		LAR COOPERATIVA AGROINDUSTRIAL	20.20%	2019年2月17日	2024年2月16日
		巴西		Copacol — Cooperativa Agroindustrial Consolata	20.20%	2019年2月17日	2024年2月16日
		巴西		COOPAVEL COOPERATIVA AGROINDUSTRIAL	20.20%	2019年2月17日	2024年2月16日
		巴西		Säo Salvador Alimentos S/A	20.20%	2019年2月17日	2024年2月16日
		巴西		RIVELLI ALIMENTOS S/A	20.20%	2019年2月17日	2024年2月16日
		巴西		GONCALVES & TORTOLA S/A	20.20%	2019年2月17日	2024年2月16日
		巴西		COOPERATIVA AGROINDUSTRIAL COPAGRIL	20.20%	2019年2月17日	2024年2月16日
		巴西		VIBRA AGROINDUSTRIAL S/A	20.20%	2019年2月17日	2024年2月16日
		巴西		AGROSUL AGROAVICOLA INDUSTRIAL, S. A	20.20%	2019年2月17日	2024年2月16日
		巴西		KAEFER AGRO INDUSTRIAL LTDA	20.20%	2019年2月17日	2024年2月16日
		巴西		VOSSKO DO BRASIL ALIMENTOS CONGELADOS LTDA	20.20%	2019年2月17日	2024年2月16日
		巴西		AVENORTE AVICOLA CIANORTE LTDA.	20.20%	2019年2月17日	2024年2月16日
		巴西		ADORO S/A	20.20%	2019年2月17日	2024年2月16日
		巴西		BONASA ALIMENTOS SA	20.20%	2019年2月17日	2024年2月16日
		巴西		FLAMBOIÃ ALIMENTOS LTDA	20.20%	2019年2月17日	2024年2月16日
		巴西		FRIGORIFICO NOVA ARAÇÁ LTDA	20.20%	2019年2月17日	2024年2月16日
		巴西		RIO BRANCO ALIMENTOS S.A.	20.20%	2019年2月17日	2024年2月16日
		巴西		ZANCHETTA ALIMENTOS LTDA	20.20%	2019年2月17日	2024年2月16日
		巴西		AGRODANIELI INDÜSTRIA E COMÉRCIO LTDA.	20.20%	2019年2月17日	2024年2月16日
		巴西		BELLO ALIMENTOS LTDA.	20.20%	2019年2月17日	2024年2月16日
		巴西		COASUL COOPERATIVA AGROINDUSTRIAL	20.20%	2019年2月17日	2024年2月16日
		巴西		COOPERATIVA LANGUIRU LTDA	20.20%	2019年2月17日	2024年2月16日
		巴西		All Others	32.40%	2019年2月17日	2024年2月16日

HS编码	商品名称	原产国名称	厂商中文名称	厂商英文名称	反倾销税率	反倾销开始时间	反倾销结束日期
207141100	冻的带骨鸡块(包括鸡胸脯、鸡大腿等)(CIQ码:101:冷冻带骨鸡肉,除鸡胸、鸡腿,102:鸡胸、鸡腿)	国(地)别不详的	国(地)别不详的	国(地)别不详的	32.40%	2019年2月17日	2024年2月16日
		巴西		SHB COMERCIO E INDUSTRIA DE ALIMENTOS S.A.	25.80%	2019年2月17日	2024年2月16日
		巴西		COMPANHIA MINUANO DE ALIMENTOS	25.80%	2019年2月17日	2024年2月16日
207141900	冻的不带骨鸡块(包括鸡胸脯、鸡大腿等)(CIQ码:101:冷冻不带骨鸡肉,除鸡胸、鸡腿,102:鸡胸、鸡腿)	巴西		SEARA ALIMENTOS LTDA	17.80%	2019年2月17日	2024年2月16日
		巴西		JBS AVES LTDA	17.80%	2019年2月17日	2024年2月16日
		巴西		SEARA COMERCIO DE ALIMENTOS LTDA	17.80%	2019年2月17日	2024年2月16日
		巴西		AGRICOLA JANDELLE S/A	17.80%	2019年2月17日	2024年2月16日
		巴西		BRF S.A.	25.80%	2019年2月17日	2024年2月16日
		巴西		C. Vale — Cooperativa Agroindustrial	32.40%	2019年2月17日	2024年2月16日
		巴西		Cooperativa Central Aurora Alimentos	20.20%	2019年2月17日	2024年2月16日
		巴西		LAR COOPERATIVA AGROINDUSTRIAL	20.20%	2019年2月17日	2024年2月16日
		巴西		Copacol — Cooperativa Agroindustrial Consolata	20.20%	2019年2月17日	2024年2月16日
		巴西		COOPAVEL COOPERATIVA AGROINDUSTRIAL	20.20%	2019年2月17日	2024年2月16日
		巴西		São Salvador Alimentos S/A	20.20%	2019年2月17日	2024年2月16日
		巴西		RIVELLI ALIMENTOS S/A	20.20%	2019年2月17日	2024年2月16日
		巴西		GONCALVES & TORTOLA S/A	20.20%	2019年2月17日	2024年2月16日
		巴西		COOPERATIVA AGROINDUSTRIAL COPAGRIL	20.20%	2019年2月17日	2024年2月16日
		巴西		VIBRA AGROINDUSTRIAL S/A	20.20%	2019年2月17日	2024年2月16日
		巴西		AGROSUL AGROAVICOLA INDUSTRIAL, S. A	20.20%	2019年2月17日	2024年2月16日
		巴西		KAEFER AGRO INDUSTRIAL LTDA	20.20%	2019年2月17日	2024年2月16日
		巴西		VOSSKO DO BRASIL ALIMENTOS CONGELADOS LTDA	20.20%	2019年2月17日	2024年2月16日
		巴西		AVENORTE AVICOLA CIANORTE LTDA.	20.20%	2019年2月17日	2024年2月16日
		巴西		ADORO S/A	20.20%	2019年2月17日	2024年2月16日
		巴西		BONASA ALIMENTOS SA	20.20%	2019年2月17日	2024年2月16日
		巴西		FLAMBOIÃ ALIMENTOS LTDA	20.20%	2019年2月17日	2024年2月16日
		巴西		FRIGORIFICO NOVA ARAÇÁ LTDA	20.20%	2019年2月17日	2024年2月16日
		巴西		RIO BRANCO ALIMENTOS S.A.	20.20%	2019年2月17日	2024年2月16日
		巴西		ZANCHETTA ALIMENTOS LTDA	20.20%	2019年2月17日	2024年2月16日
		巴西		AGRODANIELI INDÚSTRIA E COMÉRCIO LTDA.	20.20%	2019年2月17日	2024年2月16日
		巴西		BELLO ALIMENTOS LTDA.	20.20%	2019年2月17日	2024年2月16日
		巴西		COASUL COOPERATIVA AGROINDUSTRIAL	20.20%	2019年2月17日	2024年2月16日
		巴西		COOPERATIVA LANGUIRU LTDA	20.20%	2019年2月17日	2024年2月16日
		巴西		All Others	32.40%	2019年2月17日	2024年2月16日

HS 编码	商品名称	原产国名称	厂商中文名称	厂商英文名称	反倾销税率	反倾销开始时间	反倾销结束日期
207141900	冻的不带骨鸡块(包括鸡胸脯、鸡大腿等)(CIQ 码:101:冷冻不带骨鸡肉,除鸡胸、鸡腿,102:鸡胸、鸡腿)	国(地)别不详的	国(地)别不详的	国(地)别不详的	32.40%	2019 年 2 月 17 日	2024 年 2 月 16 日
		巴西		SHB COMERCIO E INDUSTRIA DE ALIMENTOS S.A.	25.80%	2019 年 2 月 17 日	2024 年 2 月 16 日
		巴西		COMPANHIA MINUANO DE ALIMENTOS	25.80%	2019 年 2 月 17 日	2024 年 2 月 16 日
207142101		巴西		SEARA ALIMENTOS LTDA	17.80%	2019 年 2 月 17 日	2024 年 2 月 16 日
		巴西		JBS AVES LTDA	17.80%	2019 年 2 月 17 日	2024 年 2 月 16 日
		巴西		SEARA COMERCIO DE ALIMENTOS LTDA	17.80%	2019 年 2 月 17 日	2024 年 2 月 16 日
		巴西		AGRICOLA JANDELLE S/A	17.80%	2019 年 2 月 17 日	2024 年 2 月 16 日
		巴西		BRF S.A.	25.80%	2019 年 2 月 17 日	2024 年 2 月 16 日
		巴西		C. Vale — Cooperativa Agroindustrial	32.40%	2019 年 2 月 17 日	2024 年 2 月 16 日
		巴西		Cooperativa Central Aurora Alimentos	20.20%	2019 年 2 月 17 日	2024 年 2 月 16 日
		巴西		LAR COOPERATIVA AGROINDUSTRIAL	20.20%	2019 年 2 月 17 日	2024 年 2 月 16 日
		巴西		Copacol — Cooperativa Agroindustrial Consolata	20.20%	2019 年 2 月 17 日	2024 年 2 月 16 日
		巴西		COOPAVEL COOPERATIVA AGROINDUSTRIAL	20.20%	2019 年 2 月 17 日	2024 年 2 月 16 日
		巴西		São Salvador Alimentos S/A	20.20%	2019 年 2 月 17 日	2024 年 2 月 16 日
		巴西		RIVELLI ALIMENTOS S/A	20.20%	2019 年 2 月 17 日	2024 年 2 月 16 日
		巴西		GONCALVES & TORTOLA S/A	20.20%	2019 年 2 月 17 日	2024 年 2 月 16 日
		巴西		COOPERATIVA AGROINDUSTRIAL COPAGRIL	20.20%	2019 年 2 月 17 日	2024 年 2 月 16 日
		巴西		VIBRA AGROINDUSTRIAL S/A	20.20%	2019 年 2 月 17 日	2024 年 2 月 16 日
		巴西		AGROSUL AGROAVICOLA INDUSTRIAL, S. A	20.20%	2019 年 2 月 17 日	2024 年 2 月 16 日
		巴西		KAEFER AGRO INDUSTRIAL LTDA	20.20%	2019 年 2 月 17 日	2024 年 2 月 16 日
		巴西		VOSSKO DO BRASIL ALIMENTOS CONGELADOS LTDA	20.20%	2019 年 2 月 17 日	2024 年 2 月 16 日
		巴西		AVENORTE AVICOLA CIANORTE LTDA.	20.20%	2019 年 2 月 17 日	2024 年 2 月 16 日
		巴西		ADORO S/A	20.20%	2019 年 2 月 17 日	2024 年 2 月 16 日
		巴西		BONASA ALIMENTOS SA	20.20%	2019 年 2 月 17 日	2024 年 2 月 16 日
		巴西		FLAMBOIÃ ALIMENTOS LTDA	20.20%	2019 年 2 月 17 日	2024 年 2 月 16 日
		巴西		FRIGORIFICO NOVA ARAÇÁ LTDA	20.20%	2019 年 2 月 17 日	2024 年 2 月 16 日
		巴西		RIO BRANCO ALIMENTOS S. A.	20.20%	2019 年 2 月 17 日	2024 年 2 月 16 日
		巴西		ZANCHETTA ALIMENTOS LTDA	20.20%	2019 年 2 月 17 日	2024 年 2 月 16 日
		巴西		AGRODANIELI INDÜSTRIA E COMÉRCIO LTDA.	20.20%	2019 年 2 月 17 日	2024 年 2 月 16 日
		巴西		BELLO ALIMENTOS LTDA.	20.20%	2019 年 2 月 17 日	2024 年 2 月 16 日
		巴西		COASUL COOPERATIVA AGROINDUSTRIAL	20.20%	2019 年 2 月 17 日	2024 年 2 月 16 日
		巴西		COOPERATIVA LANGUIRU LTDA	20.20%	2019 年 2 月 17 日	2024 年 2 月 16 日
		巴西		All Others	32.40%	2019 年 2 月 17 日	2024 年 2 月 16 日

HS编码	商品名称	原产国名称	厂商中文名称	厂商英文名称	反倾销税率	反倾销开始时间	反倾销结束日期
207142101		国（地）别不详的	国(地)别不详的	国(地)别不详的	32.40%	2019年2月17日	2024年2月16日
		巴西		SHB COMERCIO E INDUSTRIA DE ALIMENTOS S.A.	25.80%	2019年2月17日	2024年2月16日
		巴西		COMPANHIA MINUANO DE ALIMENTCS	25.80%	2019年2月17日	2024年2月16日
207142102	冻的翅（翼）根（CIQ码：999）	巴西		SEARA ALIMENTOS LTDA	17.80%	2019年2月17日	2024年2月15日
		巴西		JBS AVES LTDA	17.80%	2019年2月17日	2024年2月16日
		巴西		SEARA COMERCIO DE ALIMENTOS LTDA	17.80%	2019年2月17日	2024年2月16日
		巴西		AGRICOLA JANDELLE S/A	17.80%	2019年2月17日	2024年2月16日
		巴西		BRF S.A.	25.80%	2019年2月17日	2024年2月16日
		巴西		C. Vale — Cooperativa Agroindustrial	32.40%	2019年2月17日	2024年2月16日
		巴西		Cooperativa Central Aurora Alimentos	20.20%	2019年2月17日	2024年2月16日
		巴西		LAR COOPERATIVA AGROINDUSTRIAL	20.20%	2019年2月17日	2024年2月16日
		巴西		Copacol — Cooperativa Agroindustrial Consolata	20.20%	2019年2月17日	2024年2月16日
		巴西		COOPAVEL COOPERATIVA AGROINDUSTRIAL	20.20%	2019年2月17日	2024年2月16日
		巴西		São Salvador Alimentos S/A	20.20%	2019年2月17日	2024年2月16日
		巴西		RIVELLI ALIMENTOS S/A	20.20%	2019年2月17日	2024年2月16日
		巴西		GONCALVES & TORTOLA S/A	20.20%	2019年2月17日	2024年2月16日
		巴西		COOPERATIVA AGROINDUSTRIAL COPAGRIL	20.20%	2019年2月17日	2024年2月16日
		巴西		VIBRA AGROINDUSTRIAL S/A	20.20%	2019年2月17日	2024年2月16日
		巴西		AGROSUL AGROAVICOLA INDUSTRIAL，S. A	20.20%	2019年2月17日	2024年2月16日
		巴西		KAEFER AGRO INDUSTRIAL LTDA	20.20%	2019年2月17日	2024年2月16日
		巴西		VOSSKO DO BRASIL ALIMENTOS CONGELADOS LTDA	20.20%	2019年2月17日	2024年2月16日
		巴西		AVENORTE AVICOLA CIANORTE LTDA.	20.20%	2019年2月17日	2024年2月16日
		巴西		ADORO S/A	20.20%	2019年2月17日	2024年2月16日
		巴西		BONASA ALIMENTOS SA	20.20%	2019年2月17日	2024年2月16日
		巴西		FLAMBOIÃ ALIMENTOS LTDA	20.20%	2019年2月17日	2024年2月16日
		巴西		FRIGORIFICO NOVA ARAÇÁ LTDA	20.20%	2019年2月17日	2024年2月16日
		巴西		RIO BRANCO ALIMENTOS S. A.	20.20%	2019年2月17日	2024年2月16日
		巴西		ZANCHETTA ALIMENTOS LTDA	20.20%	2019年2月17日	2024年2月16日
		巴西		AGRODANIELI INDÜSTRIA E COMÉRCIO LTDA.	20.20%	2019年2月17日	2024年2月16日
		巴西		BELLO ALIMENTOS LTDA.	20.20%	2019年2月17日	2024年2月16日
		巴西		COASUL COOPERATIVA AGROINDUSTRIAL	20.20%	2019年2月17日	2024年2月16日
		巴西		COOPERATIVA LANGUIRU LTDA	20.20%	2019年2月17日	2024年2月16日
		巴西		All Others	32.40%	2019年2月17日	2024年2月16日

HS编码	商品名称	原产国名称	厂商中文名称	厂商英文名称	反倾销税率	反倾销开始时间	反倾销结束日期
207142102	冻的翅(翼)根(CIQ码:999)	国(地)别不详的	国(地)别不详的	国(地)别不详的	32.40%	2019年2月17日	2024年2月16日
		巴西		SHB COMERCIO E INDUSTRIA DE ALIMENTOS S.A.	25.80%	2019年2月17日	2024年2月16日
		巴西		COMPANHIA MINUANO DE ALIMENTOS	25.80%	2019年2月17日	2024年2月16日
207142103	冻的翅(翼)中＜‘span＞(CIQ码:999)	巴西		SEARA ALIMENTOS LTDA	17.80%	2019年2月17日	2024年2月16日
		巴西		JBS AVES LTDA	17.80%	2019年2月17日	2024年2月16日
		巴西		SEARA COMERCIO DE ALIMENTOS LTDA	17.80%	2019年2月17日	2024年2月16日
		巴西		AGRICOLA JANDELLE S/A	17.80%	2019年2月17日	2024年2月16日
		巴西		BRF S.A.	25.80%	2019年2月17日	2024年2月16日
		巴西		C. Vale — Cooperativa Agroindustrial	32.40%	2019年2月17日	2024年2月16日
		巴西		Cooperativa Central Aurora Alimentos	20.20%	2019年2月17日	2024年2月16日
		巴西		LAR COOPERATIVA AGROINDUSTRIAL	20.20%	2019年2月17日	2024年2月16日
		巴西		Copacol — Cooperativa Agroindustrial Consolata	20.20%	2019年2月17日	2024年2月16日
		巴西		COOPAVEL COOPERATIVA AGROINDUSTRIAL	20.20%	2019年2月17日	2024年2月16日
		巴西		São Salvador Alimentos S/A	20.20%	2019年2月17日	2024年2月16日
		巴西		RIVELLI ALIMENTOS S/A	20.20%	2019年2月17日	2024年2月16日
		巴西		GONCALVES & TORTOLA S/A	20.20%	2019年2月17日	2024年2月16日
		巴西		COOPERATIVA AGROINDUSTRIAL COPAGRIL	20.20%	2019年2月17日	2024年2月16日
		巴西		VIBRA AGROINDUSTRIAL S/A	20.20%	2019年2月17日	2024年2月16日
		巴西		AGROSUL AGROAVICOLA INDUSTRIAL, S. A	20.20%	2019年2月17日	2024年2月16日
		巴西		KAEFER AGRO INDUSTRIAL LTDA	20.20%	2019年2月17日	2024年2月16日
		巴西		VOSSKO DO BRASIL ALIMENTOS CONGELADOS LTDA	20.20%	2019年2月17日	2024年2月16日
		巴西		AVENORTE AVICOLA CIANORTE LTDA.	20.20%	2019年2月17日	2024年2月16日
		巴西		ADORO S/A	20.20%	2019年2月17日	2024年2月16日
		巴西		BONASA ALIMENTOS SA	20.20%	2019年2月17日	2024年2月16日
		巴西		FLAMBOIÃ ALIMENTOS LTDA	20.20%	2019年2月17日	2024年2月16日
		巴西		FRIGORIFICO NOVA ARAÇÁ LTDA	20.20%	2019年2月17日	2024年2月16日
		巴西		RIO BRANCO ALIMENTOS S.A.	20.20%	2019年2月17日	2024年2月16日
		巴西		ZANCHETTA ALIMENTOS LTDA	20.20%	2019年2月17日	2024年2月16日
		巴西		AGRODANIELI INDÜSTRIA E COMÉRCIO LTDA.	20.20%	2019年2月17日	2024年2月16日
		巴西		BELLO ALIMENTOS LTDA.	20.20%	2019年2月17日	2024年2月16日
		巴西		COASUL COOPERATIVA AGROINDUSTRIAL	20.20%	2019年2月17日	2024年2月16日
		巴西		COOPERATIVA LANGUIRU LTDA	20.20%	2019年2月17日	2024年2月16日
		巴西		All Others	32.40%	2019年2月17日	2024年2月16日

HS 编码	商品名称	原产国名称	厂商中文名称	厂商英文名称	反倾销税率	反倾销开始时间	反倾销结束日期
207142103	冻的翅（翼）中＜‘span＞（CIQ 码：999）	国（地）别不详的	国(地)别不详的	国(地)别不详的	32.40%	2019 年 2 月 17 日	2024 年 2 月 16 日
		巴西		SHB COMERCIO E INDUSTRIA DE ALIMENTOS S.A.	25.80%	2019 年 2 月 17 日	2024 年 2 月 16 日
		巴西		COMPANHIA MINUANO DE ALIMENTOS	25.80%	2019 年 2 月 17 日	2024 年 2 月 16 日
207142104	冻的两节翅（翼）（CIQ 码：999）	巴西		SEARA ALIMENTOS LTDA	17.80%	2019 年 2 月 17 日	2024 年 2 月 16 日
		巴西		JBS AVES LTDA	17.80%	2019 年 2 月 17 日	2024 年 2 月 16 日
		巴西		SEARA COMERCIO DE ALIMENTOS LTDA	17.80%	2019 年 2 月 17 日	2024 年 2 月 16 日
		巴西		AGRICOLA JANDELLE S/A	17.80%	2019 年 2 月 17 日	2024 年 2 月 16 日
		巴西		BRF S.A.	25.80%	2019 年 2 月 17 日	2024 年 2 月 16 日
		巴西		C. Vale — Ccoperativa Agroindustrial	32.40%	2019 年 2 月 17 日	2024 年 2 月 16 日
		巴西		Cooperativa Central Aurora Alimentos	20.20%	2019 年 2 月 17 日	2024 年 2 月 16 日
		巴西		LAR COOPERATIVA AGROINDUSTRIAL	20.20%	2019 年 2 月 17 日	2024 年 2 月 16 日
		巴西		Copacol — Cooperativa Agroindustrial Consolata	20.20%	2019 年 2 月 17 日	2024 年 2 月 16 日
		巴西		COOPAVEL COOPERATIVA AGROINDUSTRIAL	20.20%	2019 年 2 月 17 日	2024 年 2 月 16 日
		巴西		São Salvador Alimentos S/A	20.20%	2019 年 2 月 17 日	2024 年 2 月 16 日
		巴西		RIVELLI ALIMENTOS S/A	20.20%	2019 年 2 月 17 日	2024 年 2 月 16 日
		巴西		GONCALVES & TORTOLA S/A	20.20%	2019 年 2 月 17 日	2024 年 2 月 16 日
		巴西		COOPERATIVA AGROINDUSTRIAL COPAGRIL	20.20%	2019 年 2 月 17 日	2024 年 2 月 16 日
		巴西		VIBRA AGROINDUSTRIAL S/A	20.20%	2019 年 2 月 17 日	2024 年 2 月 16 日
		巴西		AGROSUL AGROAVICOLA INDUSTRIAL，S. A	20.20%	2019 年 2 月 17 日	2024 年 2 月 16 日
		巴西		KAEFER AGRO INDUSTRIAL LTDA	20.20%	2019 年 2 月 17 日	2024 年 2 月 16 日
		巴西		VOSSKO DO BRASIL ALIMENTOS CONGELADOS LTDA	20.20%	2019 年 2 月 17 日	2024 年 2 月 16 日
		巴西		AVENORTE AVICOLA CIANORTE LTDA.	20.20%	2019 年 2 月 17 日	2024 年 2 月 16 日
		巴西		ADORO S/A	20.20%	2019 年 2 月 17 日	2024 年 2 月 16 日
		巴西		BONASA ALIMENTOS SA	20.20%	2019 年 2 月 17 日	2024 年 2 月 16 日
		巴西		FLAMBOIÃ ALIMENTOS LTDA	20.20%	2019 年 2 月 17 日	2024 年 2 月 16 日
		巴西		FRIGORIFICO NOVA ARAÇÁ LTDA	20.20%	2019 年 2 月 17 日	2024 年 2 月 16 日
		巴西		RIO BRANCO ALIMENTOS S.A.	20.20%	2019 年 2 月 17 日	2024 年 2 月 16 日
		巴西		ZANCHETTA ALIMENTOS LTDA	20.20%	2019 年 2 月 17 日	2024 年 2 月 16 日
		巴西		AGRODANIELI INDÚSTRIA E COMÉRCIO LTDA.	20.20%	2019 年 2 月 17 日	2024 年 2 月 16 日
		巴西		BELLO ALIMENTOS LTDA.	20.20%	2019 年 2 月 17 日	2024 年 2 月 16 日
		巴西		COASUL COOPERATIVA AGROINDUSTRIAL	20.20%	2019 年 2 月 17 日	2024 年 2 月 16 日
		巴西		COOPERATIVA LANGUIRU LTDA	20.20%	2019 年 2 月 17 日	2024 年 2 月 16 日
		巴西		All Others	32.40%	2019 年 2 月 17 日	2024 年 2 月 16 日

HS 编码	商品名称	原产国名称	厂商中文名称	厂商英文名称	反倾销税率	反倾销开始时间	反倾销结束日期
207142104	冻的两节翅（翼）（CIQ 码：999）	国（地）别不详的	国(地)别不详的	国(地)别不详的	32.40%	2019 年 2 月 17 日	2024 年 2 月 16 日
		巴西		SHB COMERCIO E INDUSTRIA DE ALIMENTOS S.A.	25.80%	2019 年 2 月 17 日	2024 年 2 月 16 日
		巴西		COMPANHIA MINUANO DE ALIMENTOS	25.80%	2019 年 2 月 17 日	2024 年 2 月 16 日
207142200	冻的鸡爪（CIQ 码：999）	巴西		SEARA ALIMENTOS LTDA	17.80%	2019 年 2 月 17 日	2024 年 2 月 16 日
		巴西		JBS AVES LTDA	17.80%	2019 年 2 月 17 日	2024 年 2 月 16 日
		巴西		SEARA COMERCIO DE ALIMENTOS LTDA	17.80%	2019 年 2 月 17 日	2024 年 2 月 16 日
		巴西		AGRICOLA JANDELLE S/A	17.80%	2019 年 2 月 17 日	2024 年 2 月 16 日
		巴西		BRF S.A.	25.80%	2019 年 2 月 17 日	2024 年 2 月 16 日
		巴西		C. Vale — Cooperativa Agroindustrial	32.40%	2019 年 2 月 17 日	2024 年 2 月 16 日
		巴西		Cooperativa Central Aurora Alimentos	20.20%	2019 年 2 月 17 日	2024 年 2 月 16 日
		巴西		LAR COOPERATIVA AGROINDUSTRIAL	20.20%	2019 年 2 月 17 日	2024 年 2 月 16 日
		巴西		Copacol — Cooperativa Agroindustrial Consolata	20.20%	2019 年 2 月 17 日	2024 年 2 月 16 日
		巴西		COOPAVEL COOPERATIVA AGROINDUSTRIAL	20.20%	2019 年 2 月 17 日	2024 年 2 月 16 日
		巴西		São Salvador Alimentos S/A	20.20%	2019 年 2 月 17 日	2024 年 2 月 16 日
		巴西		RIVELLI ALIMENTOS S/A	20.20%	2019 年 2 月 17 日	2024 年 2 月 16 日
		巴西		GONCALVES & TORTOLA S/A	20.20%	2019 年 2 月 17 日	2024 年 2 月 16 日
		巴西		COOPERATIVA AGROINDUSTRIAL COPAGRIL	20.20%	2019 年 2 月 17 日	2024 年 2 月 16 日
		巴西		VIBRA AGROINDUSTRIAL S/A	20.20%	2019 年 2 月 17 日	2024 年 2 月 16 日
		巴西		AGROSUL AGROAVICOLA INDUSTRIAL, S. A	20.20%	2019 年 2 月 17 日	2024 年 2 月 16 日
		巴西		KAEFER AGRO INDUSTRIAL LTDA	20.20%	2019 年 2 月 17 日	2024 年 2 月 16 日
		巴西		VOSSKO DO BRASIL ALIMENTOS CONGELADOS LTDA	20.20%	2019 年 2 月 17 日	2024 年 2 月 16 日
		巴西		AVENORTE AVICOLA CIANORTE LTDA.	20.20%	2019 年 2 月 17 日	2024 年 2 月 16 日
		巴西		ADORO S/A	20.20%	2019 年 2 月 17 日	2024 年 2 月 16 日
		巴西		BONASA ALIMENTOS SA	20.20%	2019 年 2 月 17 日	2024 年 2 月 16 日
		巴西		FLAMBOIÃ ALIMENTOS LTDA	20.20%	2019 年 2 月 17 日	2024 年 2 月 16 日
		巴西		FRIGORIFICO NOVA ARAÇÁ LTDA	20.20%	2019 年 2 月 17 日	2024 年 2 月 16 日
		巴西		RIO BRANCO ALIMENTOS S.A.	20.20%	2019 年 2 月 17 日	2024 年 2 月 16 日
		巴西		ZANCHETTA ALIMENTOS LTDA	20.20%	2019 年 2 月 17 日	2024 年 2 月 16 日
		巴西		AGRODANIELI INDÜSTRIA E COMÉRCIO LTDA.	20.20%	2019 年 2 月 17 日	2024 年 2 月 16 日
		巴西		BELLO ALIMENTOS LTDA.	20.20%	2019 年 2 月 17 日	2024 年 2 月 16 日
		巴西		COASUL COOPERATIVA AGROINDUSTRIAL	20.20%	2019 年 2 月 17 日	2024 年 2 月 16 日
		巴西		COOPERATIVA LANGUIRU LTDA	20.20%	2019 年 2 月 17 日	2024 年 2 月 16 日
		巴西		All Others	32.40%	2019 年 2 月 17 日	2024 年 2 月 16 日

HS编码	商品名称	原产国名称	厂商中文名称	厂商英文名称	反倾销税率	反倾销开始时间	反倾销结束日期
207142200	冻的鸡爪(CIQ码:999)	国(地)别不详的	国(地)别不详的	国(地)别不详的	32.40%	2019年2月17日	2024年2月16日
		巴西		SHB COMERCIO E INDUSTRIA DE ALIMENTOS S.A.	25.80%	2019年2月17日	2024年2月16日
		巴西		COMPANHIA MINUANO DE ALIMENTOS	25.80%	2019年2月17日	2024年2月16日
207142901	冻的翅(翼)尖(CIQ码:999)	巴西		SEARA ALIMENTOS LTDA	17.80%	2019年2月17日	2024年2月16日
		巴西		JBS AVES LTDA	17.80%	2019年2月17日	2024年2月16日
		巴西		SEARA COMERCIO DE ALIMENTOS LTDA	17.80%	2019年2月17日	2024年2月16日
		巴西		AGRICOLA JANDELLE S/A	17.80%	2019年2月17日	2024年2月16日
		巴西		BRF S.A.	25.80%	2019年2月17日	2024年2月16日
		巴西		C. Vale — Cooperativa Agroindustrial	32.40%	2019年2月17日	2024年2月16日
		巴西		Cooperativa Central Aurora Alimentos	20.20%	2019年2月17日	2024年2月16日
		巴西		LAR COOPERATIVA AGROINDUSTRIAL	20.20%	2019年2月17日	2024年2月16日
		巴西		Copacol — Cooperativa Agroindustrial Consolata	20.20%	2019年2月17日	2024年2月16日
		巴西		COOPAVEL COOPERATIVA AGROINDUSTRIAL	20.20%	2019年2月17日	2024年2月16日
		巴西		São Salvador Alimentos S/A	20.20%	2019年2月17日	2024年2月16日
		巴西		RIVELLI ALIMENTOS S/A	20.20%	2019年2月17日	2024年2月16日
		巴西		GONCALVES & TORTOLA S/A	20.20%	2019年2月17日	2024年2月16日
		巴西		COOPERATIVA AGROINDUSTRIAL COPAGRIL	20.20%	2019年2月17日	2024年2月16日
		巴西		VIBRA AGROINDUSTRIAL S/A	20.20%	2019年2月17日	2024年2月16日
		巴西		AGROSUL AGROAVICOLA INDUSTRIAL, S. A	20.20%	2019年2月17日	2024年2月16日
		巴西		KAEFER AGRO INDUSTRIAL LTDA	20.20%	2019年2月17日	2024年2月16日
		巴西		VOSSKO DO BRASIL ALIMENTOS CONGELADOS LTDA	20.20%	2019年2月17日	2024年2月16日
		巴西		AVENORTE AVICOLA CIANORTE LTDA.	20.20%	2019年2月17日	2024年2月16日
		巴西		ADORO S/A	20.20%	2019年2月17日	2024年2月16日
		巴西		BONASA ALIMENTOS SA	20.20%	2019年2月17日	2024年2月16日
		巴西		FLAMBOIÃ ALIMENTOS LTDA	20.20%	2019年2月17日	2024年2月16日
		巴西		FRIGORIFICO NOVA ARAÇÁ LTDA	20.20%	2019年2月17日	2024年2月16日
		巴西		RIO BRANCO ALIMENTOS S.A.	20.20%	2019年2月17日	2024年2月16日
		巴西		ZANCHETTA ALIMENTOS LTDA	20.20%	2019年2月17日	2024年2月16日
		巴西		AGRODANIELI INDÚSTRIA E COMÉRCIO LTDA.	20.20%	2019年2月17日	2024年2月16日
		巴西		BELLO ALIMENTOS LTDA.	20.20%	2019年2月17日	2024年2月16日
		巴西		COASUL COOPERATIVA AGROINDUSTRIAL	20.20%	2019年2月17日	2024年2月16日
		巴西		COOPERATIVA LANGUIRU LTDA	20.20%	2019年2月17日	2024年2月16日
		巴西		All Others	32.40%	2019年2月17日	2024年2月16日

HS编码	商品名称	原产国名称	厂商中文名称	厂商英文名称	反倾销税率	反倾销开始时间	反倾销结束日期
207142901	冻的翅（翼）尖（CIQ码：999）	国（地）别不详的	国(地)别不详的	国(地)别不详的	32.40%	2019年2月17日	2024年2月16日
		巴西		SHB COMERCIO E INDUSTRIA DE ALIMENTOS S.A.	25.80%	2019年2月17日	2024年2月16日
		巴西		COMPANHIA MINUANO DE ALIMENTOS	25.80%	2019年2月17日	2024年2月16日
207142902	冻的鸡膝软骨（CIQ码:999）	巴西		SEARA ALIMENTOS LTDA	17.80%	2019年2月17日	2024年2月16日
		巴西		JBS AVES LTDA	17.80%	2019年2月17日	2024年2月16日
		巴西		SEARA COMERCIO DE ALIMENTOS LTDA	17.80%	2019年2月17日	2024年2月16日
		巴西		AGRICOLA JANDELLE S/A	17.80%	2019年2月17日	2024年2月16日
		巴西		BRF S.A.	25.80%	2019年2月17日	2024年2月16日
		巴西		C. Vale — Cooperativa Agroindustrial	32.40%	2019年2月17日	2024年2月16日
		巴西		Cooperativa Central Aurora Alimentos	20.20%	2019年2月17日	2024年2月16日
		巴西		LAR COOPERATIVA AGROINDUSTRIAL	20.20%	2019年2月17日	2024年2月16日
		巴西		Copacol — Cooperativa Agroindustrial Consolata	20.20%	2019年2月17日	2024年2月16日
		巴西		COOPAVEL COOPERATIVA AGROINDUSTRIAL	20.20%	2019年2月17日	2024年2月16日
		巴西		São Salvador Alimentos S/A	20.20%	2019年2月17日	2024年2月16日
		巴西		RIVELLI ALIMENTOS S/A	20.20%	2019年2月17日	2024年2月16日
		巴西		GONCALVES & TORTOLA S/A	20.20%	2019年2月17日	2024年2月16日
		巴西		COOPERATIVA AGROINDUSTRIAL COPAGRIL	20.20%	2019年2月17日	2024年2月16日
		巴西		VIBRA AGROINDUSTRIAL S/A	20.20%	2019年2月17日	2024年2月16日
		巴西		AGROSUL AGROAVICOLA INDUSTRIAL, S. A	20.20%	2019年2月17日	2024年2月16日
		巴西		KAEFER AGRO INDUSTRIAL LTDA	20.20%	2019年2月17日	2024年2月16日
		巴西		VOSSKO DO BRASIL ALIMENTOS CONGELADOS LTDA	20.20%	2019年2月17日	2024年2月16日
		巴西		AVENORTE AVICOLA CIANORTE LTDA.	20.20%	2019年2月17日	2024年2月16日
		巴西		ADORO S/A	20.20%	2019年2月17日	2024年2月16日
		巴西		BONASA ALIMENTOS SA	20.20%	2019年2月17日	2024年2月16日
		巴西		FLAMBOIÃ ALIMENTOS LTDA	20.20%	2019年2月17日	2024年2月16日
		巴西		FRIGORIFICO NOVA ARAÇÁ LTDA	20.20%	2019年2月17日	2024年2月16日
		巴西		RIO BRANCO ALIMENTOS S.A.	20.20%	2019年2月17日	2024年2月16日
		巴西		ZANCHETTA ALIMENTOS LTDA	20.20%	2019年2月17日	2024年2月16日
		巴西		AGRODANIELI INDÜSTRIA E COMÉRCIO LTDA.	20.20%	2019年2月17日	2024年2月16日
		巴西		BELLO ALIMENTOS LTDA.	20.20%	2019年2月17日	2024年2月16日
		巴西		COASUL COOPERATIVA AGROINDUSTRIAL	20.20%	2019年2月17日	2024年2月16日
		巴西		COOPERATIVA LANGUIRU LTDA	20.20%	2019年2月17日	2024年2月16日
		巴西		All Others	32.40%	2019年2月17日	2024年2月16日

HS编码	商品名称	原产国名称	厂商中文名称	厂商英文名称	反倾销税率	反倾销开始时间	反倾销结束日期
207142902	冻的鸡膝软骨(CIQ码:999)	国(地)别不详的	国(地)别不详的	国(地)别不详的	32.40%	2019年2月17日	2024年2月16日
		巴西		SHB COMERCIO E INDUSTRIA DE ALIMENTOS S.A.	25.80%	2019年2月17日	2024年2月16日
207142990	其他冻的食用杂碎(CIQ码:101:鸡翼,包括翼尖,102:鸡翼翼尖,103:鸡肝,104:其他鸡杂碎)	巴西		COMPANHIA MINUANO DE ALIMENTOS	25.80%	2019年2月17日	2024年2月16日
		巴西		SEARA ALIMENTOS LTDA	17.80%	2019年2月17日	2024年2月16日
		巴西		JBS AVES LTDA	17.80%	2019年2月17日	2024年2月16日
		巴西		SEARA COMERCIO DE ALIMENTOS LTDA	17.80%	2019年2月17日	2024年2月16日
		巴西		AGRICOLA JANDELLE S/A	17.80%	2019年2月17日	2024年2月16日
		巴西		BRF S.A.	25.80%	2019年2月17日	2024年2月16日
		巴西		C. Vale — Cooperativa Agroindustrial	32.40%	2019年2月17日	2024年2月16日
		巴西		Cooperativa Central Aurora Alimentos	20.20%	2019年2月17日	2024年2月16日
		巴西		LAR COOPERATIVA AGROINDUSTRIAL	20.20%	2019年2月17日	2024年2月16日
		巴西		Copacol — Cooperativa Agroindustrial Consolata	20.20%	2019年2月17日	2024年2月16日
		巴西		COOPAVEL COOPERATIVA AGROINDUSTRIAL	20.20%	2019年2月17日	2024年2月16日
		巴西		São Salvador Alimentos S/A	20.20%	2019年2月17日	2024年2月16日
		巴西		RIVELLI ALIMENTOS S/A	20.20%	2019年2月17日	2024年2月16日
		巴西		GONCALVES & TORTOLA S/A	20.20%	2019年2月17日	2024年2月16日
		巴西		COOPERATIVA AGROINDUSTRIAL COPAGRIL	20.20%	2019年2月17日	2024年2月16日
		巴西		VIBRA AGROINDUSTRIAL S/A	20.20%	2019年2月17日	2024年2月16日
		巴西		AGROSUL AGROAVICOLA INDUSTRIAL, S. A	20.20%	2019年2月17日	2024年2月16日
		巴西		KAEFER AGRO INDUSTRIAL LTDA	20.20%	2019年2月17日	2024年2月16日
		巴西		VOSSKO DO BRASIL ALIMENTOS CONGELADOS LTDA	20.20%	2019年2月17日	2024年2月16日
		巴西		AVENORTE AVICOLA CIANORTE LTDA.	20.20%	2019年2月17日	2024年2月16日
		巴西		ADORO S/A	20.20%	2019年2月17日	2024年2月16日
		巴西		BONASA ALIMENTOS SA	20.20%	2019年2月17日	2024年2月16日
		巴西		FLAMBOIÃ ALIMENTOS LTDA	20.20%	2019年2月17日	2024年2月16日
		巴西		FRIGORIFICO NOVA ARAÇÁ LTDA	20.20%	2019年2月17日	2024年2月16日
		巴西		RIO BRANCO ALIMENTOS S.A.	20.20%	2019年2月17日	2024年2月16日
		巴西		ZANCHETTA ALIMENTOS LTDA	20.20%	2019年2月17日	2024年2月16日
		巴西		AGRODANIELI INDÜSTRIA E COMÉRCIO LTDA.	20.20%	2019年2月17日	2024年2月16日
		巴西		BELLO ALIMENTOS LTDA.	20.20%	2019年2月17日	2024年2月16日
		巴西		COASUL COOPERATIVA AGROINDUSTRIAL	20.20%	2019年2月17日	2024年2月16日
		巴西		COOPERATIVA LANGUIRU LTDA	20.20%	2019年2月17日	2024年2月16日
		巴西		All Others	32.40%	2019年2月17日	2024年2月16日

HS 编码	商品名称	原产国名称	厂商中文名称	厂商英文名称	反倾销税率	反倾销开始时间	反倾销结束日期
207142990	其他冻的食用杂碎(CIQ 码:101:鸡翼,包括翼尖,102:鸡翼翼尖,103:鸡肝,104:其他鸡杂碎)	国(地)别不详的	国(地)别不详的	国(地)别不详的	32.40%	2019 年 2 月 17 日	2024 年 2 月 16 日
		巴西		SHB COMERCIO E INDUSTRIA DE ALIMENTOS S.A.	25.80%	2019 年 2 月 17 日	2024 年 2 月 16 日
		巴西		COMPANHIA MINUANO DE ALIMENTOS	25.80%	2019 年 2 月 17 日	2024 年 2 月 16 日
504002100	冷,冻的鸡胗(即鸡胃)(CIQ 码:101:冷藏的鸡胗、胃,102:冻藏的鸡胗、胃)	巴西		SEARA ALIMENTOS LTDA	17.80%	2019 年 2 月 17 日	2024 年 2 月 16 日
		巴西		JBS AVES LTDA	17.80%	2019 年 2 月 17 日	2024 年 2 月 16 日
		巴西		SEARA COMERCIO DE ALIMENTOS LTDA	17.80%	2019 年 2 月 17 日	2024 年 2 月 16 日
		巴西		AGRICOLA JANDELLE S/A	17.80%	2019 年 2 月 17 日	2024 年 2 月 16 日
		巴西		BRF S.A.	25.80%	2019 年 2 月 17 日	2024 年 2 月 16 日
		巴西		C. Vale — Cooperativa Agroindustrial	32.40%	2019 年 2 月 17 日	2024 年 2 月 16 日
		巴西		Cooperativa Central Aurora Alimentos	20.20%	2019 年 2 月 17 日	2024 年 2 月 16 日
		巴西		LAR COOPERATIVA AGROINDUSTRIAL	20.20%	2019 年 2 月 17 日	2024 年 2 月 16 日
		巴西		Copacol — Cooperativa Agroindustrial Consolata	20.20%	2019 年 2 月 17 日	2024 年 2 月 16 日
		巴西		COOPAVEL COOPERATIVA AGROINDUSTRIAL	20.20%	2019 年 2 月 17 日	2024 年 2 月 16 日
		巴西		Säo Salvador Alimentos S/A	20.20%	2019 年 2 月 17 日	2024 年 2 月 16 日
		巴西		RIVELLI ALIMENTOS S/A	20.20%	2019 年 2 月 17 日	2024 年 2 月 16 日
		巴西		GONCALVES & TORTOLA S/A	20.20%	2019 年 2 月 17 日	2024 年 2 月 16 日
		巴西		COOPERATIVA AGROINDUSTRIAL COPAGRIL	20.20%	2019 年 2 月 17 日	2024 年 2 月 16 日
		巴西		VIBRA AGROINDUSTRIAL S/A	20.20%	2019 年 2 月 17 日	2024 年 2 月 16 日
		巴西		AGROSUL AGROAVICOLA INDUSTRIAL, S. A	20.20%	2019 年 2 月 17 日	2024 年 2 月 16 日
		巴西		KAEFER AGRO INDUSTRIAL LTDA	20.20%	2019 年 2 月 17 日	2024 年 2 月 16 日
		巴西		VOSSKO DO BRASIL ALIMENTOS CONGELADOS LTDA	20.20%	2019 年 2 月 17 日	2024 年 2 月 16 日
		巴西		AVENORTE AVICOLA CIANORTE LTDA.	20.20%	2019 年 2 月 17 日	2024 年 2 月 16 日
		巴西		ADORO S/A	20.20%	2019 年 2 月 17 日	2024 年 2 月 16 日
		巴西		BONASA ALIMENTOS SA	20.20%	2019 年 2 月 17 日	2024 年 2 月 16 日
		巴西		FLAMBOIÃ ALIMENTOS LTDA	20.20%	2019 年 2 月 17 日	2024 年 2 月 16 日
		巴西		FRIGORIFICO NOVA ARAÇÁ LTDA	20.20%	2019 年 2 月 17 日	2024 年 2 月 16 日
		巴西		RIO BRANCO ALIMENTOS S. A.	20.20%	2019 年 2 月 17 日	2024 年 2 月 16 日
		巴西		ZANCHETTA ALIMENTOS LTDA	20.20%	2019 年 2 月 17 日	2024 年 2 月 16 日
		巴西		AGRODANIELI INDÜSTRIA E COMÉRCIO LTDA.	20.20%	2019 年 2 月 17 日	2024 年 2 月 16 日
		巴西		BELLO ALIMENTOS LTDA.	20.20%	2019 年 2 月 17 日	2024 年 2 月 16 日
		巴西		COASUL COOPERATIVA AGROINDUSTRIAL	20.20%	2019 年 2 月 17 日	2024 年 2 月 16 日
		巴西		COOPERATIVA LANGUIRU LTDA	20.20%	2019 年 2 月 17 日	2024 年 2 月 16 日
		巴西		All Others	32.40%	2019 年 2 月 17 日	2024 年 2 月 16 日

HS编码	商品名称	原产国名称	厂商中文名称	厂商英文名称	反倾销税率	反倾销开始时间	反倾销结束日期
504002100	冷,冻的鸡胗(即鸡胃)(CIQ码:101:冷藏的鸡胗、胃,102:冻藏的鸡胗、胃)	国(地)别不详的	国(地)别不详的	国(地)别不详的	32.40%	2019年2月17日	2024年2月16日
		巴西		SHB COMERCIO E INDUSTRIA DE ALIMENTOS S.A.	25.80%	2019年2月17日	2024年2月16日
		巴西		COMPANHIA MINUANO DE ALIMENTOS	25.80%	2019年2月17日	2024年2月16日
1108130000	马铃薯淀粉(CIQ码:999)	欧盟	德国艾维贝马铃薯淀粉工厂	Avebe Kartoffelstarkefabrik Prignitz/Wendland GmbH	12.6%	2019年2月6日	2024年2月5日
		欧盟	法国罗盖特公司	ROQUETTE FRERES	56.7%	2019年2月6日	2024年2月5日
		欧盟	荷兰艾维贝公司	AVEBE U.A.	56.7%	2019年2月6日	2024年2月5日
		欧盟	其他欧盟公司	All Others	56.7%	2019年2月6日	2024年2月5日
		欧盟	艾维贝合作社公司	COOPERATIE AVEBE U.A.	12.6%	2019年2月6日	2024年2月5日
		国(地)别不详	国(地)别不详	国(地)别不详	56.7%	2019年2月6日	2024年2月5日
2303300011	干玉米酒糟(CIQ码:999)	美国	博伊特研究中心公司	POET RESEARCH CENTER, INC.	50%	2017年1月12日	2022年1月11日
		美国	博伊特生物精炼-福斯托里亚有限责任公司	POET BIOREFINING - FOSTORIA, LLC	50%	2017年1月12日	2022年1月11日
		美国	北极光乙醇有限责任公司	NORTHERN LIGHTS ETHANOL, LLC	50%	2017年1月12日	2022年1月11日
		美国	大平原乙醇有限责任公司	GREAT PLAINS ETHANOL, LLC	50%	2017年1月12日	2022年1月11日
		美国	詹姆斯谷乙醇有限责任公司	JAMES VALLEY ETHANOL, LLC	50%	2017年1月12日	2022年1月11日
		美国	苏河乙醇有限责任公司	SIOUX RIVER ETHANOL, LLC	50%	2017年1月12日	2022年1月11日
		美国	博伊特生物精炼-利普西克有限责任公司	POET BIOREFINING - LEIPSIC, LLC	50%	2017年1月12日	2022年1月11日
		美国	博伊特生物精炼-马里昂有限责任公司	POET BIOREFINING - MARION, LLC	50%	2017年1月12日	2022年1月11日
		美国	大草原乙醇有限责任公司	PRAIRIE ETHANOL, LLC	50%	2017年1月12日	2022年1月11日
		美国	博伊特生物精炼-亚历山德里亚有限责任公司	POET BIOREFINING - ALEXANDRIA, LLC	50%	2017年1月12日	2022年1月11日
		美国	博伊特生物精炼-北曼彻斯特有限责任公司	POET BIOREFINING - NORTH MANCHESTER, LLC	50%	2017年1月12日	2022年1月11日
		美国	博伊特生物精炼-波特兰有限责任公司	POET BIOREFINING - PORTLAND, LLC	50%	2017年1月12日	2022年1月11日
		美国	乙醇2000有限责任合伙	ETHANOL2000 LIMITED LIABILITY PARTNERSHIP	50%	2017年1月12日	2022年1月11日
		美国	北极星乙醇有限责任公司	NORTHSTAR ETHANOL, LLC	50%	2017年1月12日	2022年1月11日
		美国	领先-玉米有限责任公司	PRO-CORN, LLC	50%	2017年1月12日	2022年1月11日
		美国	阿格拉资源有限责任公司	AGRA RESOURCES, LLC	50%	2017年1月12日	2022年1月11日
		美国	密苏里东北粮食有限责任公司	NORTHEAST MISSOURI GRAIN, LLC	50%	2017年1月12日	2022年1月11日
		美国	密苏里乙醇有限责任公司	MISSOURI ETHANOL, LLC	50%	2017年1月12日	2022年1月11日
		美国	密歇根乙醇有限责任公司	MICHIGAN ETHANOL, LLC	50%	2017年1月12日	2022年1月11日
		美国	TCE有限责任公司	TCE, LLC	50%	2017年1月12日	2022年1月11日
		美国	地平线乙醇有限责任公司	HORIZON ETHANOL, LLC	50%	2017年1月12日	2022年1月11日
		美国	爱荷华乙醇有限责任公司	IOWA ETHANOL, LLC	50%	2017年1月12日	2022年1月11日
		美国	前沿乙醇有限责任公司	FRONTIER ETHANOL, LLC	50%	2017年1月12日	2022年1月11日
		美国	高峰乙醇有限责任公司	PINNACLE ETHANOL, LLC	50%	2017年1月12日	2022年1月11日
		美国	水獭溪乙醇有限责任公司	OTTER CREEK ETHANOL, LLC	50%	2017年1月12日	2022年1月11日
		美国	航行者乙醇有限责任公司	VOYAGER ETHANOL, LLC	50%	2017年1月12日	2022年1月11日
		美国	博伊特生物精炼-克洛弗代尔有限责任公司	POET BIOREFINING - CLOVERDALE, LLC	50%	2017年1月12日	2022年1月11日
		美国	大河资源有限责任公司	Big River Resources, LLC	53.7%	2017年1月12日	2022年1月11日

HS 编码	商品名称	原产国名称	厂商中文名称	厂商英文名称	反倾销税率	反倾销开始时间	反倾销结束日期
2303300011	干玉米酒糟（CIQ码:999）	美国	马奎斯能源有限责任公司	Marquis Energy LLC	42.2%	2017 年 1 月 12 日	2022 年 1 月 11 日
		美国	马奎斯能源(威斯康星)有限责任公司	Marquis Energy — Wisconsin, LLC	42.2%	2017 年 1 月 12 日	2022 年 1 月 11 日
		美国	卓越能源有限责任公司	Absolute Energy, LLC	49.8%	2017 年 1 月 12 日	2022 年 1 月 11 日
		美国	恩思乙醇有限责任公司	Ace Ethanol, LLC	49.8%	2017 年 1 月 12 日	2022 年 1 月 11 日
		美国	阿奇尔丹尼斯米德兰公司	Archer — Daniels — Midland Company	49.8%	2017 年 1 月 12 日	2022 年 1 月 11 日
		美国	埃尔克霍恩谷乙醇有限责任公司	Elkhorn Valley Ethanol, Limited Liability Company	49.8%	2017 年 1 月 12 日	2022 年 1 月 11 日
		美国	弗林特希尔斯资源有限合伙	Flint Hills Resources, LP	49.8%	2017 年 1 月 12 日	2022 年 1 月 11 日
		美国	金谷能源有限责任公司	Golden Grain Energy, LLC	49.8%	2017 年 1 月 12 日	2022 年 1 月 11 日
		美国	伊利诺斯河能源公司	Illinois River Energy, LLC	49.8%	2017 年 1 月 12 日	2022 年 1 月 11 日
		美国	路易达孚大章克申有限公司	Louis Dreyfus Commodities Grand Junction LLC	49.8%	2017 年 1 月 12 日	2022 年 1 月 11 日
		美国	爱国者可再生燃料有限责任公司	Patriot Renewable Fuels, LLC	49.8%	2017 年 1 月 12 日	2022 年 1 月 11 日
		美国	安德森阿尔比恩乙醇公司	The Andersons Albion Ethanol LLC	49.8%	2017 年 1 月 12 日	2022 年 1 月 11 日
		美国	安德森克里默思乙醇公司	The Andersons Clymers Ethanol LLC	49.8%	2017 年 1 月 12 日	2022 年 1 月 11 日
		美国	安德森丹尼森乙醇公司	The Andersons Denison Ethanol LLC	49.8%	2017 年 1 月 12 日	2022 年 1 月 11 日
		美国	安德森马拉松乙醇公司	The Andersons Marathon Ethanol LLC	49.8%	2017 年 1 月 12 日	2022 年 1 月 11 日
		美国	瓦莱罗可再生燃料有限责任公司	Valero Renewable Fuels Company, LLC	49.8%	2017 年 1 月 12 日	2022 年 1 月 11 日
		美国	其他美国公司	All Others	53.7%	2017 年 1 月 12 日	2022 年 1 月 11 日
		国(地)别不详	国(地)别不详	国(地)别不详	53.7%	2017 年 1 月 12 日	2022 年 1 月 11 日
2804619012	含硅量＞99.9999999%的太阳能级多晶硅（CIQ码:999）	美国	REC 太阳能级硅有限责任公司	REC Solar Grade Silicon LLC	57%	2019 年 1 月 20 日	2020 年 1 月 19 日
		美国	REC 先进硅材料有限责任公司	REC Advanced Silicon Materials LLC	57%	2019 年 1 月 20 日	2020 年 1 月 19 日
		美国	赫姆洛克半导体公司	Hemlock Semiconductor Corporation	53.3%	2019 年 1 月 20 日	2020 年 1 月 19 日
		美国	MEMC 帕萨迪纳有限公司	MEMC Pasadena, Inc.	53.6%	2019 年 1 月 20 日	2020 年 1 月 19 日
		美国		AE Polysilicon Corporation	57%	2019 年 1 月 20 日	2020 年 1 月 19 日
		美国	其他美国公司	All Others	57%	2019 年 1 月 20 日	2020 年 1 月 19 日
		韩国	熊津多晶硅有限公司	Woongjin Polysilicon Co., Ltd.	113.8%	2019 年 1 月 20 日	2020 年 1 月 19 日
		韩国	OCI 株式会社	OCI Company Ltd.	4.4%	2019 年 1 月 20 日	2020 年 1 月 19 日
		韩国	韩国硅业株式会社	Hankook Silicon Co., Ltd.	9.5%	2019 年 1 月 20 日	2020 年 1 月 19 日
		韩国		KCC Corp. and Korean advanced materials KAM Corp.	113.8%	2019 年 1 月 20 日	2020 年 1 月 19 日
		韩国		Innovation Silicon Co., Ltd.	113.8%	2019 年 1 月 20 日	2020 年 1 月 19 日
		韩国	其他韩国公司	All Others	88.7%	2019 年 1 月 20 日	2020 年 1 月 19 日
		国(地)别不详	国(地)别不详	国(地)别不详	113.8	2019 年 1 月 20 日	2020 年 1 月 19 日
		韩国	韩华化学株式会社	HanwhaChemicalCorporation	8.9%	2019 年 1 月 20 日	2020 年 1 月 19 日
		韩国	SMP 株式会社	SMPLtd.	88.7%	2019 年 1 月 20 日	2020 年 1 月 19 日
2804619013	含硅量＞99.9999999%的太阳能级多晶硅废碎料（CIQ码:999）	美国	REC 太阳能级硅有限责任公司	REC Solar Grade Silicon LLC	57%	2019 年 1 月 20 日	2020 年 1 月 19 日
		美国	REC 先进硅材料有限责任公司	REC Advanced Silicon Materials LLC	57%	2019 年 1 月 20 日	2020 年 1 月 19 日
		美国	赫姆洛克半导体公司	Hemlock Semiconductor Corporation	53.3%	2019 年 1 月 20 日	2020 年 1 月 19 日
		美国	MEMC 帕萨迪纳有限公司	MEMC Pasadena, Inc.	53.6%	2019 年 1 月 20 日	2020 年 1 月 19 日
		美国		AE Polysilicon Corporation	57%	2019 年 1 月 20 日	2020 年 1 月 19 日
		美国	其他美国公司	All Others	57%	2019 年 1 月 20 日	2020 年 1 月 19 日
		韩国	熊津多晶硅有限公司	Woongjin Polysilicon Co., Ltd.	113.8	2019 年 1 月 20 日	2020 年 1 月 19 日

HS编码	商品名称	原产国名称	厂商中文名称	厂商英文名称	反倾销税率	反倾销开始时间	反倾销结束日期
2804619013	含硅量>99.9999999%的太阳能级多晶硅废碎料(CIQ码:999)	韩国	OCI株式会社	OCI Company Ltd.	4.4%	2019年1月20日	2020年1月19日
		韩国	韩国硅业株式会社	Hankook Silicon Co.,Ltd.	9.5%	2019年1月20日	2020年1月19日
		韩国	KCC Corp. and Korean Advanced Materials	KAM Corp.	113.8%	2019年1月20日	2020年1月19日
		韩国	Innovation Silicon Co.,Ltd.	Innovation Silicon Co.,Ltd.	113.8%	2019年1月20日	2020年1月19日
		韩国	其他韩国公司	All Others	88.7%	2019年1月20日	2020年1月19日
		国(地)别不详	国(地)别不详	国(地)别不详	113.8%	2019年1月20日	2020年1月19日
		韩国	韩华化学株式会社	HanwhaChemicalCorporation	8.9%	2019年1月20日	2020年1月19日
		韩国	SMP株式会社	SMPLtd.	88.7%	2019年1月20日	2020年1月19日
2804619092	含硅量≥99.99%的太阳能级多晶硅(CIQ码:999)	美国	REC太阳能级硅有限责任公司	REC Solar Grade Silicon LLC	57%	2019年1月20日	2020年1月19日
		美国	REC先进硅材料有限责任公司	REC Advanced Silicon Materials LLC	57%	2019年1月20日	2020年1月19日
		美国	赫姆洛克半导体公司	Hemlock Semiconductor Corporation	53.3%	2019年1月20日	2020年1月19日
		美国	MEMC帕萨迪纳有限公司	MEMC Pasadena,Inc.	53.6%	2019年1月20日	2020年1月19日
		美国	AE Polysilicon Corporation	AE Polysilicon Corporation	57%	2019年1月20日	2020年1月19日
		美国	其他美国公司	All Others	57%	2019年1月20日	2020年1月19日
		韩国	熊津多晶硅有限公司	Woongjin Polysilicon Co.,Ltd.	113.8%	2019年1月20日	2020年1月19日
		韩国	OCI株式会社	OCI Company Ltd.	4.4%	2019年1月20日	2020年1月19日
		韩国	韩国硅业株式会社	Hankook Silicon Co.,Ltd.	9.5%	2019年1月20日	2020年1月19日
		韩国	KCC Corp. and Korean Advanced Materials	KAM Corp.	113.8%	2019年1月20日	2020年1月19日
		韩国	Innovation Silicon Co.,Ltd.	Innovation Silicon Co.,Ltd.	113.8%	2019年1月20日	2020年1月19日
		韩国	其他韩国公司	All Others	88.7%	2019年1月20日	2020年1月19日
		国(地)别不详	国(地)别不详	国(地)别不详	113.8%	2019年1月20日	2020年1月19日
		韩国	韩华化学株式会社	HanwhaChemicalCorporation	8.9%	2019年1月20日	2020年1月19日
		韩国	SMP株式会社	SMPLtd.	88.7%	2019年1月20日	2020年1月19日
2804619093	含硅量≥99.99%的太阳能级多晶硅废碎料(CIQ码:999)	美国	REC太阳能级硅有限责任公司	REC Solar Grade Silicon LLC	57%	2019年1月20日	2020年1月19日
		美国	REC先进硅材料有限责任公司	REC Advanced Silicon Materials LLC	57%	2019年1月20日	2020年1月19日
		美国	赫姆洛克半导体公司	Hemlock Semiconductor Corporation	53.3%	2019年1月20日	2020年1月19日
		美国	MEMC帕萨迪纳有限公司	MEMC Pasadena,Inc.	53.6%	2019年1月20日	2020年1月19日
		美国		AE Polysilicon Corporation	57%	2019年1月20日	2020年1月19日
		美国	其他美国公司	All Others	57%	2019年1月20日	2020年1月19日
		韩国	熊津多晶硅有限公司	Woongjin Polysilicon Co.,Ltd.	113.8%	2019年1月20日	2020年1月19日
		韩国	OCI株式会社	OCI Company Ltd.	4.4%	2019年1月20日	2020年1月19日
		韩国	韩国硅业株式会社	Hankook Silicon Co.,Ltd.	9.5%	2019年1月20日	2020年1月19日
		韩国		KAM Corp.	113.8%	2019年1月20日	2020年1月19日
		韩国	Innovation Silicon Co.,Ltd.	Innovation Silicon Co.,Ltd.	113.8%	2019年1月20日	2020年1月19日
		韩国	其他韩国公司	All Others	88.7%	2019年1月20日	2020年1月19日
		国(地)别不详	国(地)别不详	国(地)别不详	113.8%	2019年1月20日	2020年1月19日
		韩国	韩华化学株式会社	HanwhaChemicalCorporation	8.9%	2019年1月20日	2020年1月19日
		韩国	SMP株式会社	SMPLtd.	88.7%	2019年1月20日	2020年1月19日
2811199010	氢碘酸(CIQ码:999)	美国	艾菲纳化工有限公司	IofinaChemical,Inc.	123.4%	2018年10月16日	2023年10月15日
		美国	其他美国公司	All Others	123.4%	2018年10月16日	2023年10月15日
		日本	其他日本公司	All Others	41.1%	2018年10月16日	2023年10月15日
		国(地)别不详的	国(地)别不详的	国(地)别不详的	123.4%	2018年10月16日	2023年10月15日

HS 编码	商品名称	原产国名称	厂商中文名称	厂商英文名称	反倾销税率	反倾销开始时间	反倾销结束日期
2902500000	苯乙烯(CIQ码:301;)	韩国	韩华道达尔株式会社	HANWHATOTALPETRO-CHEMICALCO.,LTD.	6.2%	2018年6月23日	2023年6月22日
		韩国	丽川NCC株式会社	YeochunNCCCo.,Ltd	6.2%	2018年6月23日	2023年6月22日
		韩国	乐天化学株式会社	LOTTECHEMICALCORPO-RATION	7.5%	2018年6月23日	2023年6月22日
		韩国	(株)LG化学	LGChem,Ltd	6.6%	2018年6月23日	2023年6月22日
		韩国	SK综合化学株式会社	SKglobalchemicalCo.,Ltd	6.6%	2018年6月23日	2023年6月22日
		韩国	其他韩国公司	All Others	7.5%	2018年6月23日	2023年6月22日
		台湾	台湾化学纤维股份有限公司	HANWHATOTALPETRO-CHEMICALCO.,LTD.	3.8%	2018年6月23日	2023年6月22日
		台湾	其他台湾地区公司	All Others	4.2%	2018年6月23日	2023年6月22日
		美国	利安德化学品公司	LyondellChemicalCompany	13.9%	2018年6月23日	2023年6月22日
		美国	美国华美苯乙烯公司	WestlakeStyreneLL	13.7%	2018年6月23日	2023年6月22日
		美国	英力士苯领美国有限责任公司	INEOS Styrolution America LLC	13.9%	2018年6月23日	2023年6月22日
		美国	美洲苯乙烯公司	AmericasStyrenicsLLC	13.9%	2018年6月23日	2023年6月22日
		美国	其他美国公司	All Others	55.7%	2018年6月23日	2023年6月22日
		国(别)不地详	国(别)不地详	国(别)不地详	55.7%	2018年6月23日	2023年6月22日
2903230000	四氯乙烯(CIQ码:999)	欧盟	陶氏德国设施有限公司	Dow Deutschland Anlagengesell-schaft mbH	27.6%	2019年5月31日	2020年5月30日
		欧盟	法国苏威公司	SOLVAY BENVIC EUROPE—FRANCE S.A.S.	27.6%	2019年5月31日	2020年5月30日
		欧盟	其他欧盟公司	All Others	27.6%	2019年5月31日	2020年5月30日
		美国	西方化学公司	Occidental Chemical Corporation	71.8%	2019年5月31日	2020年5月30日
		美国	埃克塞尔公司	Axiall Corporation	71.8%	2019年5月31日	2020年5月30日
		美国	陶氏化学公司	The Dow Chemical Company	71.8%	2019年5月31日	2020年5月30日
		美国	美国PPG工业公司	PPG Industries	71.8%	2019年5月31日	2020年5月30日
		美国	其他美国公司	All Others	71.8%	2019年5月31日	2020年5月30日
		国(地)别不详	国(地)别不详	国(地)别不详	71.8%	2019年5月31日	2020年5月30日
2903911000	邻二氯苯(CIQ码:999)	日本	其他日本公司	All Others	70.4%	2019年1月23日	2024年1月22日
		印度	其他印度公司	All Others	31.9%	2019年1月23日	2024年1月22日
		日本	株式会社吴羽	KUREHACORPORATION	70.4 %	2019年1月23日	2024年1月22日
		国(地)别不详	国(地)别不详	国(地)别不详	70.4 %	2019年1月23日	2024年1月22日
2905130000	正丁醇(CIQ码:301:易燃液体,需申报仅用于工业用途不用于食品添加剂无检疫要求,302:属于危险化学品的食品添加剂)	台湾	塑胶工业股份有限公司	FORMOSA PLASTICS COR-PORATION	6.0%	2018年12月29日	2023年12月28日
		台湾	其他台湾地区公司	All Others	56.1%	2018年12月29日	2023年12月28日
		马来西亚	国油石化衍生公司/马石化营销(纳闽)有限公司	PETRONAS CHEMICALS DE-RIVATIVES SDN BHD)/(PETRONAS CHEMICALS MARKETING (LABUAN) LTD)	12.7%	2018年12月29日	2023年12月28日
		马来西亚	巴斯夫马来西亚国油化学私人有限公司	BASF PETRONAS Chemicals Sdn Bhd	26.7%	2018年12月29日	2023年12月28日
		马来西亚	奥伯帝莫马来西亚化学公司	Optimal Chemicals Sdn Bhd	26.7%	2018年12月29日	2023年12月28日
		马来西亚	其他马来西亚公司	All Others	26.7%	2018年12月29日	2023年12月28日
		美国	欧季亚公司	OXEA CORPORATION	52.2%	2018年12月29日	2023年12月28日
		美国	伊士曼化学公司	Eastman Chemical Company	139.3%	2018年12月29日	2023年12月28日
		美国	道化学公司	The Dow Chemical Company	139.3%	2018年12月29日	2023年12月28日
		美国	巴斯夫公司	BASF Corporation	139.3%	2018年12月29日	2023年12月28日
		美国	其他美国公司	All Others	139.3%	2018年12月29日	2023年12月28日
		国(地)别不详	国(地)别不详的	国(地)别不详	139.3%	2018年12月29日	2023年12月28日

HS编码	商品名称	原产国名称	厂商中文名称	厂商英文名称	反倾销税率	反倾销开始时间	反倾销结束日期
2907111000	苯酚（CIQ码:301:）	美国	英力士美国公司	INEOSAmericasLLC	287.2%	2019－09－06	2024－09－06
		美国	美国兰科运营有限责任公司	BlueCubeCperationsLLC	244.30%	2019－09－06	2024－09－06
		美国	其他美国公司	All Others	287.20%	2019－09－06	2024－09－06
		欧盟	其他欧盟公司	All Others	30.40%	2019－09－06	2024－09－06
		韩国	锦湖P&B化学株式会社	KUMHOP&BCHEMICALS,INC.	12.50%	2019－09－06	2024－09－06
		韩国	(株)LG化学	LGCHEM,LTD.	12.6%	2019－09－06	2024－09－06
		韩国	其他韩国公司	All Others	23.70%	2019－09－06	2024－09－06
		日本	三井化学株式会社	MitsuiChemicals,Inc.	19.30%	2019－09－06	2024－09－06
		日本	其他日本公司	All Others	27.00%	2019－09－06	2024－09－06
		秦国	PTT苯酚有限公司	PTTPhenolCompanyLimited	10.6%	2019－09－06	2024－09－06
		秦国	其他泰国公司	All Others	28.60%	2019－09－06	2024－09－06
		国（地）别不详	国(地)别不详	国(地)别不详	287.2%	2019－09－06	2024－09－06
2907131000	壬基酚、对壬基酚、支链－4－壬基酚(包括4－壬基苯酚、壬基苯酚）（CIQ码:999)	台湾	和益化学工业股份有限公司	Formosan Union Chemical Corporation	6.87%	2019年3月29日	2024年3月28日
		台湾	其他台湾地区公司	All Others	20.38%	2019年3月29日	2024年3月28日
		台湾	中国人造纤维股份有限公司	China Man－Made Fiber Corporation	4.08%	2019年3月29日	2024年3月28日
		印度	其他印度公司	All Others	20.38%	2019年3月29日	2024年3月28日
		印度	印度十拿一赫蒂利亚有限公司	SI GROUP－INDIA LIMITED	12.22%	2019年3月29日	2024年3月28日
		国（地）别不详	国(地)别不详	国(地)别不详	20.38%	2019年3月29日	2024年3月28日
2907210001	间苯二酚(CIQ码:301:)	日本	三井化学株式会社	Mitsui Chem cals,INC.	40.5%	2019年3月23日	2024年3月22日
		日本	住友化学株式会社	Sumitomo Chemical Company, Limited	40.5%	2019年3月23日	2024年3月22日
		日本	其他日本公司	All Others	40.5%	2019年3月23日	2024年3月22日
		美国	茵蒂斯派克化学公司	INDSPEC Chemical Corporation	30.1%	2019年3月23日	2024年3月22日
		美国	其他美国公司	All Others	30.1%	2019年3月23日	2024年3月22日
		国（地）别不详	国(地)别不详	国(地)别不详	40.5%	2019年3月23日	2024年3月22日
2907230001	双酚A(4,4－异亚丙基联苯酚)(CIQ码:999)	韩国	其他韩国公司	All Others	37.1%	2019年8月30日	2024年8月29日
		日本	其他日本公司	All Others	37.1%	2019年8月30日	2024年8月29日
		台湾	其他台湾地区公司	All Others	37.1%	2019年8月30日	2024年8月29日
		新加坡	其他新加坡公司	All Others	37.1%	2019年8月30日	2024年8月29日
		新加坡	三井酚类新加坡公司	MITSUI PHENOLS SINGAPORE PTE. LTD.	5.0%	2019年8月30日	2024年8月29日
		台湾	信昌化学工业股份有限公司	Taiwan Prosperity Chemical Corporation	5.3%	2019年8月30日	2024年8月29日
		韩国	锦湖P&B化学株式会社	KUMHO P&B CHEMICALS, INC.	5.8%	2019年8月30日	2024年8月29日
		台湾	南亚塑胶工业股份有限公司	Nan Ya Plastics Corporation	6.0%	2019年8月30日	2024年8月29日
		台湾	长春人造树脂厂股份有限公司	CHANG CHUN PLASTICS CO., LTD.	6.0%	2019年8月30日	2024年8月29日
		日本	三井化学株式会社	Mitsui Chemicals, Inc.	6.1%	2019年8月30日	2024年8月29日
		日本	三菱化学株式会社	Mitsubishi Chemical Corporation	7.9%	2019年8月30日	2024年8月29日
		韩国	(株)LG化学	LG Chem, Ltd.	4.7%	2019年8月30日	2024年8月29日
		国（地）别不详	国(地)别不详	国(地)别不详	37.1%	2019年8月30日	2024年8月29日
		秦国	PTT苯酚有限公司	PTT Phenol Company Limited	9.7%	2018年3月6日	2023年3月5日
		秦国	其他泰国公司	All Others	31%	2018年3月6日	2023年3月5日
2909430000	乙二醇或二甘醇的单丁醚(CIQ码:101:1,2－二甲氧基乙烷,102:2,2－二甲氧基丙烷)	美国	伊士曼化工公司	Eastman Chemical Company	46.9%	2019年1月28日	2024年1月27日
		美国	陶氏化学公司	The Dow Chemical Company	75.5%	2019年1月28日	2024年1月27日
		美国	益科斯达化工产品有限公司	Equistar Chemicals, LP	37.5%	2019年1月28日	2024年1月27日
		欧盟	沙索德国有限责任公司	Sasol Germany GmbH	10.8%	2019年1月28日	2024年1月27日
		欧盟	沙索溶剂德国有限责任公司	Sasol Solvents Germany GmbH	10.8%	2019年1月28日	2024年1月27日
		欧盟	英力士化学拉瓦拉有限公司	INEOS Chemicals Lavera SAS	43.5%	2019年1月28日	2024年1月27日
		欧盟	巴斯夫欧洲公司	BASF SE	18.8%	2019年1月28日	2024年1月27日
		欧盟	其他欧盟公司	All Others	43.5%	2019年1月28日	2024年1月27日
		国（地）别不详	国(地)别不详	国(地)别不详	75.5%	2019年1月28日	2024年1月27日
		美国	其他美国公司	All Others	75.5%	2019年1月28日	2024年1月27日

HS 编码	商品名称	原产国名称	厂商中文名称	厂商英文名称	反倾销税率	反倾销开始时间	反倾销结束日期
2912499010	间苯氧基苯甲醛	印度		BHARAT RASAYAN LIMITED	56.4%	2018 年 6 月 8 日	2023 年 6 月 7 日
		印度	赫曼尼工业有限公司	Hemani Industries Limited	36.4%	2018 年 6 月 8 日	2023 年 6 月 7 日
		印度	古吉拉特杀虫剂有限公司	Gujarat Insecticides Limited	52%	2018 年 6 月 8 日	2023 年 6 月 7 日
		印度	其他印度公司	All Others	56.9%	2018 年 6 月 8 日	2023 年 6 月 7 日
		国（别）地不详	国(别)地不详	国(别)地不详	56.9%	2018 年 6 月 8 日	2023 年 6 月 7 日
2914110000	丙酮(二甲基甲酮、二甲酮、醋酮、木酮)(CIQ 码：301：二甲基甲酮、二甲酮、醋酮、木酮)	日本	三菱化学株式会社	MITSUBISHI CHEMICAL CORPORATION	12.1%	2019 年 6 月 8 日	2020 年 6 月 7 日
		韩国	(株)LG 化学	LG Chem，Ltd.	5.0%	2019 年 6 月 8 日	2020 年 6 月 7 日
		国（地）别不详	国(地)别不详	国(地)别不详	51.6%	2019 年 6 月 8 日	2020 年 6 月 7 日
		韩国	其他韩国公司	All Others	51.6%	2019 年 6 月 8 日	2020 年 6 月 7 日
		日本	其他日本公司	All Others	51.6%	2019 年 6 月 8 日	2020 年 6 月 7 日
		台湾	其他台湾地区公司	All Others	51.6%	2019 年 6 月 8 日	2020 年 6 月 7 日
		新加坡	其他新加坡公司	All Others	51.6%	2019 年 6 月 8 日	2020 年 6 月 7 日
		台湾	台湾化学纤维股份有限公司	FORMOSA CHEMICALS&FIBRE CORPORATION	6.2%	2019 年 6 月 8 日	2020 年 6 月 7 日
		台湾	信昌化学工业股份有限公司	Taiwan Prosperity Chemical Corporation	6.5%	2019 年 6 月 8 日	2020 年 6 月 7 日
		新加坡	三井酚类新加坡公司	MITSUI PHENOLS SINGAPORE PTE. LTD.	6.7%	2019 年 6 月 8 日	2020 年 6 月 7 日
		日本	三井化学株式会社	Mitsui Chemicals，Inc.	7.2%	2019 年 6 月 8 日	2020 年 6 月 7 日
		台湾	长春人造树脂厂股份有限公司	CHANG CHUN PLASTICS CO.，LTD.	9.4%	2019 年 6 月 8 日	2020 年 6 月 7 日
		韩国	锦湖 P&B 化学株式会社	KUMHO P&B CHEMICALS，INC.	4.3%	2019 年 6 月 8 日	2020 年 6 月 7 日
2914130000	4－甲基－2－戊酮(甲基异丁基(甲)酮)(CIQ 码：999)	韩国	锦湖 P&B 化学株式会社	KUMHOP&BCHEMICALS，INC.	18.5%	2018 年 3 月 20 日	2023 年 3 月 19 日
		韩国	其他韩国公司	All Others	32.3%	2018 年 3 月 20 日	2023 年 3 月 19 日
		日本	三井化学株式会社	MitsuiChemicals,Inc.	45%	2018 年 3 月 20 日	2023 年 3 月 19 日
		日本	三菱化学株式会社	MitsubishiChemicalCorporation	47.80%	2018 年 3 月 20 日	2023 年 3 月 19 日
		日本	其他日本公司	All Others	190.40%	2018 年 3 月 20 日	2023 年 3 月 19 日
		南非	沙索南非有限公司	SasolSouthAfrica(Pty)Ltd.	15.90%	2018 年 3 月 20 日	2023 年 3 月 19 日
		南非	其他南非公司	All Others	34.1%	2018 年 3 月 20 日	2023 年 3 月 19 日
		国（地）别不详	国(地)别不详	国(地)别不详	190.4%	2018 年 3 月 20 日	2023 年 3 月 19 日
2916140010	甲基丙烯酸甲酯(CIQ 码：301：爆炸品，302：易燃液体)	新加坡	璐采特国际(新加坡)有限公司	Lucite International Singapore Pte. Ltd.	10.7%	2018 年 2 月 28 日	2020 年 11 月 30 日
		新加坡		Sumitomo Chemical Singapore Pte Ltd	30.6%	2018 年 2 月 28 日	2020 年 11 月 30 日
		新加坡	其他新加坡公司	All Others	30.6%	2018 年 2 月 28 日	2020 年 11 月 30 日
		泰国	泰国 MMA 单体制造销售公司	THAI MMA CO.，LTD.	32.6%	2018 年 2 月 28 日	2020 年 11 月 30 日
		泰国	PTT 旭化成化学有限公司	PTT Asahi Chemical Company Limited	32.6%	2015 年 12 月 1 日	2020 年 11 月 30 日
		泰国	其他泰国公司	All Others	32.6%	2018 年 2 月 28 日	2020 年 11 月 30 日
		日本	三菱丽阳株式会社	Mitsubishi Rayon Co.，Ltd.	34.8%	2018 年 2 月 28 日	2020 年 11 月 30 日
		日本	旭化成化学株式会社	ASAHI KASEI CHEMICALS CORPORATION	34.8%	2018 年 2 月 28 日	2020 年 11 月 30 日
		日本	日本住友化学株式会社	Sumitomo Chemical Company，Limited	34.8%	2018 年 2 月 28 日	2020 年 11 月 30 日
		日本	可乐丽株式会社	KURARAY CO.，LTD.	34.6%	2015 年 12 月 1 日	2020 年 11 月 30 日
		日本	三菱瓦斯化学株式会社	Mitsubishi Gas Chemical Co.，Inc.	34.6%	2015 年 12 月 1 日	2020 年 11 月 30 日
		日本	三井化学株式会社	Mitsui Chemicals，Inc.	34.6%	2015 年 12 月 1 日	2020 年 11 月 30 日
		日本	其他日本公司	All Others	34.6%	2015 年 12 月 1 日	2020 年 11 月 30 日
		国（地）别不详	国(地)别不详	国(地)别不详	34.8%	2015 年 12 月 1 日	2020 年 11 月 30 日

HS 编码	商品名称	原产国名称	厂商中文名称	厂商英文名称	反倾销税率	反倾销开始时间	反倾销结束日期
2917120001	己二酸(CIQ 码:999)	韩国	其他韩国公司	All Others	16.7%	2014年11月2日	2020年11月1日
		欧盟	其他欧盟公司	All Others	16.7%	2014年11月2日	2020年11月1日
		美国		Ascend Performance Materials LLC	16.8%	2014年11月2日	2020年11月1日
		国(地)别不详	国(地)别不详	国(地)别不详	35.4%	2014年11月2日	2020年11月1日
		美国	其他美国公司	All Others	35.4%	2014年11月2日	2020年11月1日
		韩国	旭化成化学韩国	Asahi Kasei Chemicals Korea Co.	5%	2014年11月2日	2020年11月1日
		欧盟	兰蒂奇化工德国有限公司	RADICI CHIMICA DEUTSH-LAND GMBH	7.4%	2014年11月2日	2020年11月1日
		欧盟	兰蒂奇化工有限公司	RADICI CHIMICA S.P.A	7.4%	2014年11月2日	2020年11月1日
		欧盟		BASF SE	9.8%	2014年11月2日	2020年11月1日
		韩国	罗地亚韩国有限公司	Rhodia Korea Co., Ltd.	16.7%	2014年11月2日	2020年11月1日
		韩国	索尔维化学韩国有限公司	Solvay Chemicals Korea Co., Ltd.	5.9%	2014年11月2日	2020年11月1日
2917361100	精对苯二甲酸(白色针状结晶或粉末,密度1.510,主要技术指标为4—羧基苯甲醛(4—CBA)≤25PPM)(CIQ 码:999)	韩国	SK 油化株式会社	SK Petrochemical Co., Ltd	11.2%	2016年8月11日	2021年8月10日
		韩国	其他韩国公司	All Others	11.2%	2016年8月11日	2021年8月10日
		泰国	TPT 石化大众有限公司	TPT Petrochemicals Public Company Limited	12.9%	2016年8月11日	2021年8月10日
		泰国	Indorama 石化有限公司	Indorama Petrochem Limited	16.9%	2016年8月11日	2021年8月10日
		韩国	KP 化学公司	KP CHEMICAL CORPORA-TION	11.2%	2016年8月11日	2021年8月10日
		韩国	三星石油化学株式会社	Samsung Petrochemical Compa-ny Limited	11.2%	2016年8月11日	2021年8月10日
		韩国	泰光产业(株)	TAEKWANG INDUSTRIAL CO.,LTD	2.4%	2016年8月11日	2021年8月10日
		韩国	株式会社晓星	Hyosung Corporation	2.6%	2016年8月11日	2021年8月10日
		国(地)别不详	国(地)别不详	国(地)别不详	20.1%	2016年8月11日	2021年8月10日
		泰国	其他泰国公司	All Others	20.1%	2016年8月11日	2021年8月10日
		韩国	三南石油化学株式会社	Samnam Petrochemical Co., LTD.	3.7%	2016年8月11日	2021年8月10日
		泰国	Siam 三井 PTA 有限公司	Siam Mitsui PTA Co., Ltd.	6.0%	2016年8月11日	2021年8月10日
		韩国	韩国乐天化学株式会社	LOTTE CHEMICAL CORPO-RATION	2.0%	2016年8月11日	2021年8月10日
		韩国	韩华综合化学株式会社	Hanwha General Chemical Co., Ltd.	2.0%	2016年8月11日	2021年8月10日
2921420020	邻氯对硝基苯胺(CIQ 码:999)	印度	阿迪工业有限公司	AartiIndustries Limited	31.4%	2018年2月13日	2023年2月12日
		印度	其他印度公司	All Others	49.9%	2018年2月13日	2023年2月12日
		国(地)别不详	国(地)别不详	国(地)别不详	49.9%	2018年2月13日	2023年2月12日
2921430001	间甲苯胺或对甲苯胺(CIQ 码:999)	欧盟	朗盛德国有限责任公司	LANXESS Deutschland GmbH	19.6%	2019年6月28日	2024年6月27日
		欧盟	其他欧盟公司	All Others	36.9%	2019年6月28日	2024年6月27日
		国(地)别不详	国(地)别不详	国(地)别不详	36.9%	2019年6月28日	2024年6月27日

HS 编码	商品名称	原产国名称	厂商中文名称	厂商英文名称	反倾销税率	反倾销开始时间	反倾销结束日期
2922110001	单乙醇胺(CIQ 码:301:1—氨基乙醇,无检疫要求食品添加剂,302:1—氨基乙醇,一般化学品,需申报仅用于工业用途不用于食品添加剂无检疫要求,303:N,N—二甲基乙醇胺,易燃液体,需申报仅用于工业用途不用于食品添加剂无检疫要求,304:2—氨基乙醇,腐蚀性物质,需申报仅用于工业用途不用于食品添加剂无检疫要求,305:属于危险化学品的食品添加剂)	美国	陶氏化学公司	TheDowChemicalCompany	76.0%	2018 年 10 月 30 日	2023 年 10 月 29 日
		美国	英力士美国公司	INEOSAmericasLLC	97.1%	2018 年 10 月 30 日	2023 年 10 月 29 日
		美国	亨斯迈石化有限公司	HuntsmanPetrochemicalLLC	97.1%	2018 年 10 月 30 日	2023 年 10 月 29 日
		美国	其他美国公司	All Others	97.1%	2018 年 10 月 30 日	2023 年 10 月 29 日
		马来西亚	国油石化衍生公司	PETRONASCHEMICALS-DERIVATIVESSDNBHD	18.3%	2018 年 10 月 30 日	2023 年 10 月 29 日
		马来西亚	其他马来西亚公司	All Others	20.3%	2018 年 10 月 30 日	2023 年 10 月 29 日
		沙特阿拉伯	沙特基础工业公司	SaudiBasicIndustriesCorporation	10.1%	2018 年 10 月 30 日	2023 年 10 月 29 日
		沙特阿拉伯	其他沙特阿拉伯公司	All Others	27.9%	2018 年 10 月 30 日	2023 年 10 月 29 日
		泰国	TOC 乙二醇有限公司	TOCGLYCOLCOMPANYLIMITED	37.6%	2018 年 10 月 30 日	2023 年 10 月 29 日
		泰国	其他泰国公司	All Others	37.6%	2018 年 10 月 30 日	2023 年 10 月 29 日
		国(地)别不详的	国(地)别不详的	国(地)别不详的	97.1%	2018 年 10 月 30 日	2023 年 10 月 29 日
2922120001	二乙醇胺	美国	陶氏化学公司	TheDowChemicalCompany	76.0%	2018 年 10 月 30 日	2023 年 10 月 29 日
		美国	英力士美国公司	INEOSAmericasLLC	97.1%	2018 年 10 月 30 日	2023 年 10 月 29 日
		美国	亨斯迈石化有限公司	HuntsmanPetrochemicalLLC	97.1%	2018 年 10 月 30 日	2023 年 10 月 29 日
		美国	其他美国公司	All Others	97.1%	2018 年 10 月 30 日	2023 年 10 月 29 日
		马来西亚	国油石化衍生公司	PETRONASCHEMICALS-DERIVATIVESSDNBHD	18.3%	2018 年 10 月 30 日	2023 年 10 月 29 日
		马来西亚	其他马来西亚公司	All Others	20.3%	2018 年 10 月 30 日	2023 年 10 月 29 日
		沙特阿拉伯	沙特基础工业公司	SaudiBasicIndustriesCorporation	10.1%	2018 年 10 月 30 日	2023 年 10 月 29 日
		沙特阿拉伯	其他沙特阿拉伯公司	All Others	27.9%	2018 年 10 月 30 日	2023 年 10 月 29 日
		泰国	TOC 乙二醇有限公司	TOCGLYCOLCOMPANYLIMITED	37.6%	2018 年 10 月 30 日	2023 年 10 月 29 日
		泰国	其他泰国公司	All Others	37.6%	2018 年 10 月 30 日	2023 年 10 月 29 日
		国(地)别不详的	国(地)别不详的	国(地)别不详的	97.1%	2018 年 10 月 30 日	2023 年 10 月 29 日
2922150000	三乙醇胺(CIQ 码:999)	美国	陶氏化学公司	TheDowChemicalCompany	76.0%	2018 年 10 月 30 日	2023 年 10 月 29 日
		美国	英力士美国公司	INEOSAmericasLLC	97.1%	2018 年 10 月 30 日	2023 年 10 月 29 日
		美国	亨斯迈石化有限公司	HuntsmanPetrochemicalLLC	97.1%	2018 年 10 月 30 日	2023 年 10 月 29 日
		美国	其他美国公司	All Others	97.1%	2018 年 10 月 30 日	2023 年 10 月 29 日
		马来西亚	国油石化衍生公司	PETRONASCHEMICALS-DERIVATIVESSDNBHD	18.3%	2018 年 10 月 30 日	2023 年 10 月 29 日
		马来西亚	其他马来西亚公司	All Others	20.3%	2018 年 10 月 30 日	2023 年 10 月 29 日
		沙特阿拉伯	沙特基础工业公司	SaudiBasicIndustriesCorporation	10.1%	2018 年 10 月 30 日	2023 年 10 月 29 日
		沙特阿拉伯	其他沙特阿拉伯公司	All Others	27.9%	2018 年 10 月 30 日	2023 年 10 月 29 日
		泰国	TOC 乙二醇有限公司	TOCGLYCOLCOMPANYLIMITED	37.6%	2018 年 10 月 30 日	2023 年 10 月 29 日
		泰国	其他泰国公司	All Others	37.6%	2018 年 10 月 30 日	2023 年 10 月 29 日
		国(地)别不详的	国(地)别不详的	国(地)别不详的	97.1%	2018 年 10 月 30 日	2023 年 10 月 29 日

HS编码	商品名称	原产国名称	厂商中文名称	厂商英文名称	反倾销税率	反倾销开始时间	反倾销结束日期
2933710000	6－己内酰胺（CIQ码:999）	美国	帝斯曼化学品北美公司	DSM Chemicals North America, Inc.	24.2%	2017年10月22日	2022年10月21日
		欧盟	帝斯曼纤维中间体公司	DSM Fibre Intermediates B.V.	25.5%	2017年10月22日	2022年10月21日
		美国	巴斯夫美国公司	BASF Corporation	2.5%	2017年10月22日	2021年10月21日
		欧盟	宇部化学欧洲有限公司	UBE CHEMICAL EUROPE, S.A	2.6%	2017年10月22日	2022年10月21日
		美国	其他美国公司	All Others	24.2%	2017年10月22日	2022年10月21日
		国（地）别不详	国(地)别不详	国(地)别不详	25.5%	2017年10月22日	2021年10月21日
		欧盟	其他欧盟公司	All Others	25.5%	2017年10月22日	2022年10月21日
		欧盟	巴斯夫安特卫普公司	BASF ANTWERPEN N.V.	3.1%	2017年10月22日	2022年10月21日
		欧盟	道默有限公司	DOMO Caproleuna GmbH	3.2%	2017年10月22日	2022年10月21日
		欧盟	朗盛比利时公司	LANXESS NV	3.4%	2017年10月22日	2022年10月21日
		美国	霍尼韦尔树脂和化学品责任有限公司	Honeywell Resins & Chemicals LLC	24.2%	2018年6月9日	2022年10月21日
		欧盟	波兰普瓦维股份公司	Zaklady Azotowe "Pulawy" S.A.	4.4%	2017年10月22日	2022年10月21日
		欧盟	波兰阿佐提塔诺股份公司	Zaklady Azotowe w Tarnowie－Moscicach S.A.	4.9%	2017年10月22日	2022年10月21日
		美国	Fibrant有限责任公司	Fibrant, LLC	2.2%	2017年10月22日	2022年10月21日
		欧盟	Fibrant公司	Fibrant B.V.	2.3%	2017年10月22日	2022年10月21日
		美国	艾德凡斯树脂和化学品责任有限公司	AdvanSix Resins & Chemicals LLC	3.6%	2017年10月22日	2022年10月21日
3703101000	成卷未曝光的宽幅感光纸及纸板(宽幅指成卷宽度＞610毫米)（CIQ码:999）	欧盟	柯达有限公司	Kodak Limited	19.4%	2018年3月23日	2023年3月22日
		欧盟	富士胶片制造(欧洲)有限公司	FUJIFILM Manufacturing Europe B.V.	23.5%	2018年3月23日	2023年3月22日
		欧盟	其他欧盟公司	All Others	19.4%	2018年3月23日	2023年3月22日
		美国	富士胶片制造(美国)有限公司	FUJIFILM Manufacturing U.S.A., Inc.	23.6%	2018年3月23日	2023年3月22日
		美国	其他美国公司	All Others	28.8%	2018年3月23日	2023年3月22日
		日本	其他日本公司	All Others	28.8%	2018年3月23日	2023年3月22日
		国（别）地不详	国(别)地不详	国(别)地不详	28.8%	2018年3月23日	2023年3月22日
3703201000	未曝光的彩色感光纸及纸板(成卷的宽幅感光纸及纸板除外)（CIQ码:999）	欧盟	柯达有限公司	Kodak Limited	19.4%	2018年3月23日	2023年3月22日
		欧盟	富士胶片制造(欧洲)有限公司	FUJIFILM Manufacturing Europe B.V.	23.5%	2018年3月23日	2023年3月22日
		欧盟	其他欧盟公司	All Others	19.4%	2018年3月23日	2023年3月22日
		美国	富士胶片制造(美国)有限公司	FUJIFILM Manufacturing U.S.A., Inc.	23.6%	2018年3月23日	2023年3月22日
		美国	其他美国公司	All Others	28.8%	2018年3月23日	2023年3月22日
		日本	其他日本公司	All Others	28.8%	2018年3月23日	2023年3月22日
		国（别）地不详	国(别)地不详	国(别)地不详	28.8%	2018年3月23日	2023年3月22日
3703901000	其他未曝光的非彩色感光纸及纸板(成卷的宽幅感光纸及纸板除外)（CIQ码:999）	欧盟	柯达有限公司	Kodak Limited	19.4%	2018年3月23日	2023年3月22日
		欧盟	富士胶片制造(欧洲)有限公司	FUJIFILM Manufacturing Europe B.V.	23.5%	2018年3月23日	2023年3月22日
		欧盟	其他欧盟公司	All Others	19.4%	2018年3月23日	2023年3月22日
		美国	富士胶片制造(美国)有限公司	FUJIFILM Manufacturing U.S.A., Inc.	23.6%	2018年3月23日	2023年3月22日
		美国	其他美国公司	All Others	28.8%	2018年3月23日	2023年3月22日
		日本	其他日本公司	All Others	28.8%	2018年3月23日	2023年3月22日
		国（别）地不详	国(别)地不详	国(别)地不详	28.8%	2018年3月23日	2023年3月22日
3904500010	偏二氯乙烯－氯乙烯共聚树脂（CIQ码:999）	日本	株式会社吴羽	KUREHA CORPORATION	47.1%	2017年4月20日	2022年4月19日
		日本	旭化成株式会社	ASAHI KASEI CHEMICALS CORP.	47.1%	2017年4月20日	2022年4月19日
		日本	其他日本公司	All Others	47.1%	2017年4月20日	2022年4月19日
		国（地）别不详	国(地)别不详	国(地)别不详	47.1%	2017年4月20日	2022年4月19日

HS编码	商品名称	原产国名称	厂商中文名称	厂商英文名称	反倾销税率	反倾销开始时间	反倾销结束日期
3907101010	聚甲醛(均聚聚甲醛及改性聚甲醛除外)(CIQ码:999)	韩国	韩国工程塑料株式会社	KOREA ENGINEERING PLASTICS CO., LTD	30.0%	2017年10月24日	2022年10月23日
		韩国	(株)可隆塑胶股份有限公司	KOLON PLASTICS,INC.	6.2%	2017年10月24日	2022年10月23日
		韩国	其他韩国公司	All Others	30.4%	2017年10月24日	2022年10月23日
		泰国	泰国聚甲醛有限公司	THAI POLYACETAL CO.,LTD	18.5%	2017年10月24日	2022年10月23日
		泰国	其他泰国公司	All Others	34.9%	2017年10月24日	2022年10月23日
		马来西亚	宝理塑料(亚太)公司	PolyplasticsAsiaPacificSdn.Bhd	8%	2017年10月24日	2022年10月23日
		马来西亚	其他马来西亚公司	All Others	9.5%	2017年10月24日	2022年10月23日
		国(地)别不详	国(地)别不详	国(地)别不详	34.9%	2017年10月24日	2022年10月23日
3907109010	共聚聚甲醛(改性聚甲醛除外)(CIQ码:999)	韩国	韩国工程塑料株式会社	KOREAENGINEERINGPLASTICSCO.,LTD	30.0%	2017年10月24日	2022年10月23日
		韩国	(株)可隆塑胶股份有限公司	KOLONPLASTICS,INC。	6.2%	2017年10月24日	2022年10月23日
		韩国	其他韩国公司	All Others	30.4%	2017年10月24日	2022年10月23日
		泰国	泰国聚甲醛有限公司	THAI POLYACETAL CO., LTD.	18.5%	2017年10月24日	2022年10月23日
		泰国	其他泰国公司	All Others	34.9%	2017年10月24日	2022年10月23日
		马来西亚	宝理塑料(亚太)公司	PolyplasticsAsiaPacificSdn.Bhd.	8%	2017年10月24日	2022年10月23日
		马来西亚	其他马来西亚公司	All Others	9.5%	2017年10月24日	2022年10月23日
		国(地)别不详	国(地)别不详	国(地)别不详	34.9%	2017年10月24日	2022年10月23日
3908101101	聚酰胺—6,6切片(CIQ码:999)	法国	其他法国公司	All Others	20.9%	2015年10月13日	2020年10月12日
		台湾	台湾地区公司	All Others	20.9%	2015年10月13日	2020年10月12日
		意大利	其他意大利公司	All Others	20.9%	2015年10月13日	2020年10月12日
		美国	英威达有限责任公司	INVISTA S.A R.L.	25.2%	2015年10月13日	2020年10月12日
		美国	Ascend Performance Materials LLC	Ascend Performance Materials LLC	31.4%	2015年10月13日	2020年10月12日
		国(地)别不详	国(地)别不详	国(地)别不详	37.5%	2015年10月13日	2020年10月12日
		美国	其他美国公司	All Others	37.5%	2015年10月13日	2020年10月12日
		意大利	意大利兰蒂奇化工有限公司	RADICI CHIMICA S.p.A	5.3%	2015年10月13日	2020年10月12日
3908101200	聚酰胺—6切片(锦纶6切片)(CIQ码:999)	俄罗斯	其他俄罗斯公司	All Others	23.9%	2011年1月1日	2021年4月21日
		欧盟	其他欧盟公司	All Others	23.9%	2011年1月1日	2021年4月21日
		台湾	其他台湾地区公司	All Others	23.9%	2011年1月1日	2021年4月21日
		美国	巴斯夫美国公司	BASF Corporation.	29.3%	2011年1月1日	2021年4月21日
		美国	霍尼韦尔树脂和化学品责任有限公司	Honeywell Resins&Chemical LLC	96.5%	2018年6月9日	2021年4月21日
		台湾	台湾化学纤维股份有限公司	FORMOSA CHEMICALS&FIBER CORPORATION	4.0%	2011年1月1日	2021年4月21日
		台湾	华隆股份有限公司	HUALON CORPORATION	4.2%	2011年1月1日	2021年4月21日
		台湾	集盛实业股份有限公司	Zig sheng Industrial Co.,Ltd.	4.2%	2011年1月1日	2021年4月21日
		台湾	太洋尼龙股份有限公司	Tai—Young Nylon Co.,Ltd	4.2%	2011年1月1日	2021年4月21日
		台湾	展颂股份有限公司	CHAIN YARN CO.,LTD.	4.2%	2011年1月1日	2021年4月21日
		台湾	中国石油化学工业开发股份有限公司	China Petrochemical Development Corporation	4.2%	2011年1月1日	2021年4月21日
		台湾	力鹏企业股份有限公司	Li Peng Enterprise Co.,Ltd.	4.3%	2011年1月1日	2021年4月21日
		俄罗斯	古比雪夫氮开放式股份公司	Open Joint Stock Company "KuibyshevAzot"	23.9%	2017年3月16日	2021年4月21日
		欧盟	巴斯夫安特卫普公司	BASF ANTWERPEN N.V.	8.0%	2011年1月1日	2021年4月21日
		欧盟	巴斯夫欧洲公司	BASF SE	8.2%	2011年1月1日	2021年4月21日
		欧盟	道默有限公司	DOMO Caproleuna GmbH	8.2%	2011年1月1日	2021年4月21日
		欧盟	帝斯曼工程塑料公司	DSM Engineering Plastics B.V.	8.2%	2011年1月1日	2021年4月21日
		欧盟	波兰阿佐提塔诺股份公司	Zaklady Azotowe w Tarnowie—Moscicach,S.A.	9.7%	2011年1月1日	2021年4月21日
		国(地)别不详	国(地)别不详	国(地)别不详	96.5%	2011年1月1日	2021年4月21日
		美国	其他美国公司	All Others	96.5%	2011年1月1日	2021年4月21日
		俄罗斯	古比雪夫氮公众股份有限公司	Public Joint Stock Company "KuibyshevAzot	5.9%	2017年3月16日	2021年4月21日
		欧盟	朗盛德国有限公司	LANXESS Deutschland GmbH	8.2%	2017年7月21日	2021年4月21日
		欧盟	朗盛比利时有限公司	LANXESS N.V.	8.2%	2017年7月21日	2021年4月21日
		美国	艾德凡斯树脂和化学品责任有限公司	AdvanSix Resins & Chemicals LLC	36.2%	2018年6月9日	2021年4月21日

HS编码	商品名称	原产国名称	厂商中文名称	厂商英文名称	反倾销税率	反倾销开始时间	反倾销结束日期
4002391000	初级形状的其他卤代丁基橡胶（CIQ码:999）	美国	埃克森美孚公司	ExxonMobilChemicalLimited	75.5%	2018年8月20日	2023年8月19日
		美国	其他美国公司	All Others	75.5%	2018年8月20日	2023年8月19日
		欧盟	埃克森美孚化工有限公司	ExxonMobilChemicalLimited	71.9%	2018年8月20日	2023年8月19日
		欧盟	阿朗新科比利时有限公司	ARLANXEOBelgiumNV	27.4%	2018年8月20日	2023年8月19日
		欧盟	其他欧盟公司	All Others	71.9%	2018年8月20日	2023年8月19日
		新加坡	阿朗新科新加坡私人有限公司	ARLANXEOSINGAPOREPTE.LTD	23.1%	2018年8月20日	2023年8月19日
		新加坡	其他新加坡公司	All Others	45.2%	2018年8月20日	2023年8月19日
		国（地）别不详的	国(地)别不详的	国(地)别不详的	75.5%	2018年8月20日	2023年8月19日
4002399000	卤代丁基橡胶板、片、带（CIQ码:999）	美国	埃克森美孚公司	ExxonMobilCorporation	75.5%	2018年8月20日	2023年8月19日
		美国	其他美国公司	All Others	75.5%	2018年8月20日	2023年8月19日
		欧盟	埃克森美孚化工有限公司	ExxonMobilChemicalLimited	71.9%	2018年8月20日	2023年8月19日
		欧盟	阿朗新科比利时有限公司	ARLANXEOBelgiumNV	27.4%	2018年8月20日	2023年8月19日
		欧盟	其他欧盟公司	All Others	71.9%	2018年8月20日	2023年8月19日
		新加坡	阿朗新科新加坡私人有限公司	ARLANXEOSINGAPOREPTE.LTD.	23.1%	2018年8月20日	2023年8月19日
		新加坡	其他新加坡公司	All Others	45.2%	2018年8月20日	2023年8月19日
		国(地)别不详的	国（地）别不详的		75.5%	2018年8月20日	2023年8月19日
4002491000	初级形状的氯丁二烯橡胶（胶乳除外）（CIQ码:999）	美国	其他美国公司	All Others	151%	2017年5月10日	2022年5月9日
		欧盟	其他欧盟公司	All Others	151%	2017年5月10日	2022年5月9日
		欧盟	埃尼橡胶法国有限公司	Polimeri Europa Elastomeres France S.A.	53%	2017年5月10日	2022年5月9日
		国（地）别不详的	国(地)别不详的	国(地)别不详的	151%	2007年5月10日	2022年5月9日
		日本	日本东曹株式会社	TOSOH CORPORATION	10.2%	2017年5月10日	2022年5月9日
		日本	昭和电工株式会社	SHOWA DENKO K.K	20.8%	2017年5月10日	2022年5月9日
		日本	其他日本公司	All Others	43.9%	2017年5月10日	2022年5月9日
		日本	日本电化株式会社	DenkaCompanyLimited	20.8%	2017年5月10日	2022年5月9日
		欧盟	阿朗新科德国有限公司	ARLANXEO Deutschland GmbH	11%	2017年5月10日	2022年5月9日
4002499000	氯丁二烯橡胶板、片、带（CIQ码:999）	美国	其他美国公司	All Others	151%	2017年5月10日	2022年5月9日
		欧盟	其他欧盟公司	All Others	151%	2017年5月10日	2022年5月9日
		欧盟	埃尼橡胶法国有限公司	Polimeri Europa Elastomeres France S.A.	53%	2017年5月10日	2022年5月9日
		国（地）别不详	国(地)别不详	国(地)别不详	151%	2017年5月10日	2022年5月9日
		日本	日本东曹株式会社	TOSOH CORPORATION	10.2%	2017年5月10日	2022年5月9日
		日本	昭和电工株式会社	SHOWA DENKO K.K	20.8%	2017年5月10日	2022年5月9日
		日本	其他日本公司	All Others	43.9%	2017年5月10日	2022年5月9日
		日本	日本电化株式会社	DenkaCompanyLimited	20.8%	2017年5月10日	2022年5月9日
		欧盟	阿朗新科德国有限公司	ARLANXEO Deutschland GmbH	11%	2017年5月10日	2022年5月9日
4002591000	初级形状的丁腈橡胶（胶乳除外）（CIQ码:999）	韩国	锦湖石油化学株式会社	KUMHOPETROCHEMICALCO.,LTD.	12.0%	2018年11月9日	2023年11月8日
		韩国	（株）LG化学	LGCHEM,LTD.	15.0%	2018年11月9日	2023年11月8日
		韩国	其他韩国公司	All Others	37.3%	2018年11月9日	2023年11月8日
		日本	日本瑞翁株式会社	ZeonCorporation	28.1%	2018年11月9日	2023年11月8日
		日本	JSR株式会社	JSRCorporation	16.0%	2018年11月9日	2023年11月8日
		日本	其他日本公司	All Others	56.4%	2018年11月9日	2023年11月8日
		国（地）别不详	国(地)别不详	国(地)别不详	56.4%	2018年11月9日	2023年11月8日
4002599000	丁腈橡胶板、片、带（CIQ码:999）	韩国	锦湖石油化学株式会社	KUMHOPETROCHEMICALCO.,LTD.	12.0%	2018年11月9日	2023年11月8日
		韩国	（株）LG化学	LGCHEM,LTD.	15.0%	2018年11月9日	2023年11月8日
		韩国	其他韩国公司	All Others	37.3%	2018年11月9日	2023年11月8日
		日本	日本瑞翁株式会社	ZeonCorporation	28.1%	2018年11月9日	2023年11月8日
		日本	JSR株式会社	JSRCorporation	16.0%	2018年11月9日	2023年11月8日
		日本	其他日本公司	All Others	56.4%	2018年11月9日	2023年11月8日
		国(地)别不详	国（地）别不详	国（地）别不详	56.4%	2018年11月9日	2023年11月8日

HS编码	商品名称	原产国名称	厂商中文名称	厂商英文名称	反倾销税率	反倾销开始时间	反倾销结束日期
4804210000	未漂白的袋用牛皮纸(成卷或成张的及未经涂布的)(CIQ码:999)	美国	开思通牛皮纸公司	Kapstone Kraft Paper Corporation	14.9%	2016年4月10日	2021年4月9日
		美国	其他美国公司	All Others	14.9%	2016年4月10日	2021年4月9日
		欧盟	毕瑞瑞典公司	BillerudKorsnäsSweden AB	23.5%	2016年4月10日	2021年4月9日
		欧盟	蒙迪斯坦博利斯基有限公司	MondiStambolijski EAD	29.0%	2016年4月10日	2021年4月9日
		欧盟	毕瑞芬兰公司	BillerudKorsnäsFinland Oy	26.2%	2016年4月10日	2021年4月9日
		欧盟	蒙迪弗兰特沙赫有限公司	Mondi Frantschach GmbH	26.2%	2016年4月10日	2021年4月9日
		欧盟	蒙迪斯特缇股份公司	Mondi Steti a.s.	26.2%	2016年4月10日	2021年4月9日
		欧盟	蒙迪狄娜股份公司	Mondi Dynäs Aktiebolag	26.2%	2016年4月10日	2021年4月9日
		欧盟	其他欧盟公司	All Others	29.0%	2016年4月10日	2021年4月9日
		日本	王子制纸株式会社	Oji Paper Co., Ltd.	20.5%	2016年4月10日	2021年4月9日
		日本	王子Materia株式会社	Oji Materia Co., Ltd.	20.5%	2016年4月10日	2021年4月9日
		日本	中越纸浆工业株式会社	Chuetsu Pulp & Paper Co., Ltd.	20.5%	2016年4月10日	2021年4月9日
		日本	大王制纸株式会社		20.5%	2016年4月10日	2021年4月9日
		日本	日本制纸株式会社	Nippon Paper Industries Co., Ltd.	20.5%	2016年4月10日	2021年4月9日
		日本	其他日本公司	All Others	20.5%	2016年4月10日	2021年4月9日
		国(地)别不详	国(地)别不详	国(地)别不详	29%	2016年4月10日	2021年4月9日
4804310020	未漂白的其他薄牛皮纸及纸板(抗张指数(横向+纵向)大于等于69N.M/,撕裂指数(纵向)大于等于10Mn2/g,抗张能量吸收指数(横向)大于等于1.0J/g,抗张能量吸收指数(纵向)大于等于0.8J/g,透气度大于等于3.4um/(pa.s),伸长率(纵向)大于等于2%。(薄纸指每平米重≤150克,成卷或成张未经涂布的)(CIQ码:999)	美国	开思通牛皮纸公司	Kapstone Kraft Paper Corporation	14.9%	2016年4月10日	2021年4月9日
		美国	其他美国公司	All Others	14.9%	2016年4月10日	2021年4月9日
		欧盟	蒙迪斯坦博利斯基有限公司	MondiStambolijski EAD	29.0%	2016年4月10日	2021年4月9日
		欧盟	毕瑞瑞典公司	BillerudKorsnäsSweden AB	23.5%	2016年4月10日	2021年4月9日
		欧盟	毕瑞芬兰公司	BillerudKorsnäsFinland Oy	26.2%	2016年4月10日	2021年4月9日
		欧盟	蒙迪弗兰特沙赫有限公司	Mondi Frantschach GmbH	26.2%	2016年4月10日	2021年4月9日
		欧盟	蒙迪斯特缇股份公司	Mondi Steti a.s.	26.2%	2016年4月10日	2021年4月9日
		欧盟	蒙迪狄娜股份公司	Mondi Dynäs Aktiebolag	26.2%	2016年4月10日	2021年4月9日
		欧盟	其他欧盟公司	All Others	29.0%	2016年4月10日	2021年4月9日
		日本	王子制纸株式会社	Oji Paper Co., Ltd.	20.5%	2016年4月10日	2021年4月9日
		日本	王子Materia株式会社	Oji Materia Co., Ltd.	20.5%	2016年4月10日	2021年4月9日
		日本	中越纸浆工业株式会社	Chuetsu Pulp & Paper Co., Ltd.	20.5%	2016年4月10日	2021年4月9日
		日本	大王制纸株式会社		20.5%	2016年4月10日	2021年4月9日
		日本	日本制纸株式会社	Nippon Paper Industries Co., Ltd.	20.5%	2016年4月10日	2021年4月9日
		日本	其他日本公司	All Others	20.5%	2016年4月10日	2021年4月9日
		国(地)别不详	国(地)别不详	国(地)别不详	29%	2016年4月10日	2021年4月9日
4805911000	电解电容器原纸(每平方米重量≤150克,成卷或成张的)(CIQ码:999)	日本	大福制纸株式会社	Daifuku Seishi Co., Ltd.	15%	2019年4月18日	2024年4月17日
		日本	其他日本公司	All Others	40.83%	2019年4月18日	2024年4月17日
		日本	日本高度纸工业株式会社	NIPPON KODOSHI CORPORATION	22%	2019年4月18日	2024年4月17日
		国(地)别不详	国(地)别不详	国(地)别不详	40.83%	2019年4月18日	2024年4月17日

HS编码	商品名称	原产国名称	厂商中文名称	厂商英文名称	反倾销税率	反倾销开始时间	反倾销结束日期
5501300010	聚丙烯腈制长丝丝束(不包括变性聚丙烯腈制)(CIQ码:999)	日本	日本依克丝兰工业株式会社	JAPAN EXLAN CO., LTD	16.1%	2016年7月14日	2021年7月13日
		日本	三菱丽阳株式会社	Mitsubishi Rayon Co., Ltd.	16.1%	2017年8月5日	2021年7月13日
		日本	东丽株式会社	Toray Industries, Inc.	16%	2016年7月14日	2021年7月13日
		日本	其他日本公司	All Others	16.1%	2016年7月14日	2021年7月13日
		韩国	泰光产业株式会社	TAEKWANG INDUSTRIAL CO., LTD.	8.6%	2018年11月7日	2021年7月13日
		韩国	其他韩国公司	All Others	21.7%	2018年11月7日	2021年7月13日
		土耳其	阿克萨丙烯酸化学工业公司	Aksa Akrilik Kimya Sanayii A.Ş.	8.2%	2016年7月14日	2021年7月13日
		土耳其	其他土耳其公司	All Others	16.1%	2016年7月14日	2021年7月13日
		国(地)别不详	国(地)别不详	国(地)别不详	21.7%	2018年11月7日	2021年7月13日
		日本	三菱化学株式会社	Mitsubishi Chemical Corporation	15.8%	2017年8月5日	2021年7月13日
5503300010	未梳或未经其他纺前加工的聚丙烯腈制短纤维(不包括变性聚丙烯腈制)(CIQ码:999)	日本	日本依克丝兰工业株式会社	JAPAN EXLAN CO., LTD	16.1%	2016年7月14日	2021年7月13日
		日本	三菱丽阳株式会社	Mitsubishi Rayon Co., Ltd.	16.1%	2017年8月5日	2021年7月13日
		日本	东丽株式会社	Toray Industries, Inc.	16%	2016年7月14日	2021年7月13日
		日本	其他日本公司	All Others	16.1%	2016年7月14日	2021年7月13日
		韩国	泰光产业株式会社	TAEKWANG INDUSTRIAL CO., LTD.	8.6%	2018年11月7日	2021年7月13日
		韩国	其他韩国公司	All Others	21.7%	2018年11月7日	2021年7月13日
		土耳其	阿克萨丙烯酸化学工业公司	Aksa Akrilik Kimya Sanayii A.Ş.	8.2%	2016年7月14日	2021年7月13日
		土耳其	其他土耳其公司	All Others	16.1%	2016年7月14日	2021年7月13日
		国(地)别不详	国(地)别不详	国(地)别不详	21.7%	2018年11月7日	2021年7月13日
		日本	三菱化学株式会社	三菱化学株式会社	15.8%	2017年8月5日	2021年7月13日
5506300010	已梳或经其他纺前加工的聚丙烯腈制短纤(不包括变性聚丙烯腈制)(CIQ码:999)	日本	日本依克丝兰工业株式会社	JAPAN EXLAN CO., LTD	16.1%	2016年7月14日	2021年7月13日
		日本	三菱丽阳株式会社	Mitsubishi Rayon Co., Ltd.	16.1%	2017年8月5日	2021年7月13日
		日本	东丽株式会社	Toray Industries, Inc.	16%	2016年7月14日	2021年7月13日
		日本	其他日本公司	All Others	16.1%	2016年7月14日	2021年7月13日
		韩国	泰光产业株式会社	TAEKWANG INDUSTRIAL CO., LTD.	8.6%	2018年11月7日	2021年7月13日
		韩国	其他韩国公司	All Others	21.7%	2018年11月7日	2021年7月13日
		土耳其	阿克萨丙烯酸化学工业公司	Aksa Akrilik Kimya Sanayii A.Ş.	8.2%	2016年7月14日	2021年7月13日
		土耳其	其他土耳其公司	All Others	16.1%	2016年7月14日	2021年7月13日
		国(地)别不详	国(地)别不详	国(地)别不详	21.7%	2018年11月7日	2021年7月13日
		日本	三菱化学株式会社	三菱化学株式会社	15.8%	2017年8月5日	2021年7月13日
7002201000	光导纤维预制棒(CIQ码:999)	日本	信越化学株式会社	Shin-Etsu Chemical Co., Ltd.	8.0%	2018年7月11日	2023年7月10日
		日本	住友电气工业株式会社	Sumitomo Electric Industries, Ltd.	9.1%	2018年7月11日	2023年7月10日
		日本	株式会社藤仓	Fujikura Ltd.	8.5%	2018年7月11日	2023年7月10日
		日本	古河电气工业株式会社	Furukawa Electric Co., Ltd.	8.5%	2018年7月11日	2023年7月10日
		日本	其他日本公司	All Others	9.1%	2018年7月11日	2023年7月10日
		美国	康宁公司	Corning Incorporated	41.7%	2018年7月11日	2023年7月10日
		美国	OFS-费特有限责任公司	OFS Fitel, LLC.	17.4%	2018年7月11日	2023年7月10日
		美国	其他美国公司	All Others	41.7%	2018年7月11日	2023年7月10日
		国(地)别不详	国(地)别不详	国(地)别不详	41.7%	2018年7月11日	2023年7月10日
7218910000	矩形截面的不锈钢半制成品(正方形截面除外)(CIQ码:999)	欧盟	其他欧盟公司	All Others	43.0%	2019-03-23	2019-07-22
		日本	日本冶金工业株式会社	NIPPONYAKINKOGYOCO., LTD	18.1%	2019-07-23	2024-07-22
		日本	其他日本公司	All Others	29.0%	2019-07-23	2024-07-22
		韩国	株式会社POSCO	POSCO	23.1%	2019-07-23	2024-07-22
		韩国	其他韩国公司	All Others	103.1%	2019-07-23	2024-07-22
		印度尼西亚	其他印度尼西亚公司	All Others	20.2%	2019-07-23	2024-07-22
		国(地)别不详	国(地)别不详	国(地)别不详	103.1%	2019-07-23	2024-07-22

HS编码	商品名称	原产国名称	厂商中文名称	厂商英文名称	反倾销税率	反倾销开始时间	反倾销结束日期
7218990000	其他不锈钢半制成品（CIQ码:999）	欧盟	其他欧盟公司	All Others	43.0%	2019－07－23	2024－07－22
		日本	日本冶金工业株式会社	NIPPONYAKINKOGYOCO., LTD	18.1%	2019－07－23	2024－07－22
		日本	其他日本公司	All Others	29.0%	2019－07－23	2024－07－22
		韩国	株式会社 POSCO	POSCO	23.1%	2019－07－23	2024－07－22
		韩国	其他韩国公司	All Others	103.1%	2019－07－23	2024－07－22
		印度尼西亚	其他印度尼西亚公司	All Others	20.2%	2019－07－23	2024－07－22
		国（地）别不详	国(地)别不详	国(地)别不详	103.1%	2019－07－23	2024－07－22
7219110000	（厚度＞10mm热轧不锈钢卷板(除热轧外未经进一步加工宽度≥600mm)（CIQ码:999))	欧盟	其他欧盟公司	All Others	43.0%	2019－07－23	2024－07－22
		日本	日本冶金工业株式会社	NIPPONYAKINKOGYOCO., LTD	18.1%	2019－07－23	2024－07－22
		日本	其他日本公司	All Others	29.0%	2019－07－23	2024－07－22
		韩国	株式会社 POSCO	POSCO	23.1%	2019－07－23	2024－07－22
		韩国	其他韩国公司	All Others	103.1%	2019－07－23	2024－07－22
		印度尼西亚	其他印度尼西亚公司	All Others	20.2%	2019－07－23	2024－07－22
		国（地）别不详	国(地)别不详	国(地)别不详	103.1%	2019－07－23	2024－07－22
7219120990	（4.75mm≤厚≤10mm热轧不锈钢卷板(除热轧外未经进一步加工宽度≥600mm)（CIQ码:999))	欧盟	其他欧盟公司	All Others	43.0%	2019－07－23	2024－07－22
		日本	日本冶金工业株式会社	NIPPONYAKINKOGYOCO., LTD	18.1%	2019－07－23	2024－07－22
		日本	其他日本公司	All Others	29.0%	2019－07－23	2024－07－22
		韩国	株式会社 POSCO	POSCO	23.1%	2019－07－23	2024－07－22
		韩国	其他韩国公司	All Others	103.1%	2019－07－23	2024－07－22
		印度尼西亚	其他印度尼西亚公司	All Others	20.2%	2019－07－23	2024－07－22
		国（地）别不详	国(地)别不详	国(地)别不详	103.1%	2019－07－23	2024－07－22
7219131200	(3mm≤厚＜4.75mm未经酸洗的热轧不锈钢卷板(除热轧外未经进一步加工宽度≥600mm含锰≥5.5%铬锰系不锈钢	欧盟	其他欧盟公司	All Others	43.0%	2019－07－23	2024－07－22
		日本	日本冶金工业株式会社	NIPPONYAKINKOGYOCO., LTD	18.1%	2019－07－23	2024－07－22
		日本	其他日本公司	All Others	29.0%	2019－07－23	2024－07－22
		韩国	株式会社 POSCO	POSCO	23.1%	2019－07－23	2024－07－22
		韩国	其他韩国公司	All Others	103.1%	2019－07－23	2024－07－22
		印度尼西亚	其他印度尼西亚公司	All Others	20.2%	2019－07－23	2024－07－22
		国（地）别不详	国(地)别不详	国(地)别不详	103.1%	2019－07－23	2024－07－22
7219131900	3mm≤厚＜4.75mm未经酸洗的其他热轧不锈钢卷板(除热轧外未经进一步加工宽度≥600mm)（CIQ码:999))	欧盟	其他欧盟公司	All Others	43.0%	2019－07－23	2024－07－22
		日本	日本冶金工业株式会社	NIPPONYAKINKOGYOCO., LTD	18.1%	2019－07－23	2024－07－22
		日本	其他日本公司	All Others	29.0%	2019－07－23	2024－07－22
		韩国	株式会社 POSCO	POSCO	23.1%	2019－07－23	2024－07－22
		韩国	其他韩国公司	All Others	103.1%	2019－07－23	2024－07－22
		印度尼西亚	其他印度尼西亚公司	All Others	20.2%	2019－07－23	2024－07－22
		国（地）别不详	国(地)别不详	国(地)别不详	103.1%	2019－07－23	2024－07－22
7219132200	3mm≤厚＜4.75mm经酸洗的热轧不锈钢卷板(除热轧外未经进一步加工宽度≥600mm含锰≥5.5%铬锰系不锈钢	欧盟	其他欧盟公司	All Others	43.0%	2019－07－23	2024－07－22
		日本	日本冶金工业株式会社	NIPPONYAKINKOGYOCO., LTD	18.1%	2019－07－23	2024－07－22
		日本	其他日本公司	All Others	29.0%	2019－07－23	2024－07－22
		韩国	株式会社 POSCO	POSCO	23.1%	2019－07－23	2024－07－22
		韩国	其他韩国公司	All Others	103.1%	2019－07－23	2024－07－22
		印度尼西亚	其他印度尼西亚公司	All Others	20.2%	2019－07－23	2024－07－22
		国（地）别不详	国(地)别不详	国(地)别不详	103.1%	2019－07－23	2024－07－22

HS编码	商品名称	原产国名称	厂商中文名称	厂商英文名称	反倾销税率	反倾销开始时间	反倾销结束日期
7219132900	3mm≤厚＜4.75mm经酸洗的其他热轧不锈钢卷板(除热轧外未经进一步加工宽度≥600mm)(CIQ码:999))	欧盟	其他欧盟公司	All Others	43.0%	2019－07－23	2024－07－22
		日本	日本冶金工业株式会社	NIPPONYAKINKOGYOCO.,LTD	18.1%	2019－07－23	2024－07－22
		日本	其他日本公司	All Others	29.0%	2019－07－23	2024－07－22
		韩国	株式会社 POSCO	POSCO	23.1%	2019－07－23	2024－07－22
		韩国	其他韩国公司	All Others	103.1%	2019－07－23	2024－07－22
		印度尼西亚	其他印度尼西亚公司	All Others	20.2%	2019－07－23	2024－07－22
		国(地)别不详	国(地)别不详	国(地)别不详	103.1%	2019－07－23,	2024－07－22
7219141200	(厚度＜3mm未经酸洗的热轧不锈钢卷板(除热轧外未经进一步加工宽度≥600mm含锰≥5.5%铬锰系不锈钢)(CIQ码:999)	欧盟	其他欧盟公司	All Others	43.0%	2019－07－23	2024－07－22
		日本	日本冶金工业株式会社	NIPPONYAKINKOGYOCO.,LTD	18.1%	2019－07－23	2024－07－22
		日本	其他日本公司	All Others	29.0%	2019－07－23	2024－07－22
		韩国	株式会社 POSCO	POSCO	23.1%	2019－07－23	2024－07－22
		韩国	其他韩国公司	All Others	103.1%	2019－07－23	2024－07－22
		印度尼西亚	其他印度尼西亚公司	All Others	20.2%	2019－07－23	2024－07－22
		国(地)别不详	国(地)别不详	国(地)别不详	103.1%	2019－07－23	2024－07－22
7219141900	厚度＜3mm未经酸洗的其他热轧不锈钢卷板(除热轧外未经进一步加工宽度≥600mm)(CIQ码:999))	欧盟	其他欧盟公司	All Others	43.0%	2019－07－23	2024－07－22
		日本	日本冶金工业株式会社	NIPPONYAKINKOGYOCO.,LTD	18.1%	2019－07－23	2024－07－22
		日本	其他日本公司	All Others	29.0%	2019－07－23	2024－07－22
		韩国	株式会社 POSCO	POSCO	23.1%	2019－07－23	2024－07－22
		韩国	其他韩国公司	All Others	103.1%	2019－07－23	2024－07－22
		印度尼西亚	其他印度尼西亚公司	All Others	20.2%	2019－07－23	2024－07－22
		国(地)别不详	国(地)别不详	国(地)别不详	103.1%	2019－07－23	2024－07－22
7219142200	(厚度＜3mm经酸洗的热轧不锈钢卷板(除热轧外未经进一步加工宽度≥600mm含锰≥5.5%铬锰系不锈钢)(CIQ码:999))	欧盟	其他欧盟公司	All Others	43.0%	2019－07－23	2024－07－22
		日本	日本冶金工业株式会社	NIPPONYAKINKOGYOCO.,LTD	18.1%	2019－07－23	2024－07－22
		日本	其他日本公司	All Others	29.0%	2019－07－23	2024－07－22
		韩国	株式会社 POSCO	POSCO	23.1%	2019－07－23	2024－07－22
		韩国	其他韩国公司	All Others	103.1%	2019－07－23	2024－07－22
		印度尼西亚	其他印度尼西亚公司	All Others	20.2%	2019－07－23	2024－07－22
		国(地)别不详	国(地)别不详	国(地)别不详	103.1%	2019－07－23	2024－07－22
7219142900	厚度＜3mm经酸洗的其他热轧不锈钢卷板(除热轧外未经进一步加工宽度≥600mm)(CIQ码:999))	欧盟	其他欧盟公司	All Others	43.0%	2019－07－23	2024－07－22
		日本	日本冶金工业株式会社	NIPPONYAKINKOGYOCO.,LTD	18.1%	2019－07－23	2024－07－22
		日本	其他日本公司	All Others	29.0%	2019－07－23	2024－07－22
		韩国	株式会社 POSCO	POSCO	23.1%	2019－07－23	2024－07－22
		韩国	其他韩国公司	All Others	103.1%	2019－07－23	2024－07－22
		印度尼西亚	其他印度尼西亚公司	All Others	20.2%	2019－07－23	2024－07－22
		国(地)别不详	国(地)别不详	国(地)别不详	103.1%	2019－07－23	2024－07－22

HS编码	商品名称	原产国名称	厂商中文名称	厂商英文名称	反倾销税率	反倾销开始时间	反倾销结束日期
7219210000	（厚度＞10mm 热轧不锈钢平板（除热轧外未经进一步加工宽度≥600mm）（CIQ 码：999））	欧盟	其他欧盟公司	All Others	43.0%	2019－07－23	2024－07－22
		日本	日本冶金工业株式会社	NIPPONYAKINKOGYOCO.，LTD	18.1%	2019－07－23	2024－07－22
		日本	其他日本公司	All Others	29.0%	2019－07－23	2024－07－22
		韩国	株式会社 POSCO	POSCO	23.1%	2019－07－23	2024－07－22
		韩国	其他韩国公司	All Others	103.1%	2019－07－23	2024－07－22
		印度尼西亚	其他印度尼西亚公司	All Others	20.2%	2019－07－23	2024－07－22
		国（地）别不详	国（地）别不详	国（地）别不详	103.1%	2019－07－23	2024－07－22
7219220000	4.75mm≤厚≤10mm热轧不锈钢平板（除热轧外未经进一步加工宽度≥600mm）（CIQ 码：999））	欧盟	其他欧盟公司	All Others	43.0%	2019－07－23	2024－07－22
		日本	日本冶金工业株式会社	NIPPONYAKINKOGYOCO.，LTD	18.1%	2019－07－23	2024－07－22
		日本	其他日本公司	All Others	29.0%	2019－07－23	2024－07－22
		韩国	株式会社 POSCO	POSCO	23.1%	2019－07－23	2024－07－22
		韩国	其他韩国公司	All Others	103.1%	2019－07－23	2024－07－22
		印度尼西亚	其他印度尼西亚公司	All Others	20.2%	2019－07－23	2024－07－22
		国（地）别不详	国（地）别不详	国（地）别不详	103.1%	2019－07－23	2024－07－22
7219230000	3mm≤厚＜4.75mm热轧不锈钢平板（除热轧外未经进一步加工宽度≥600mm）（CIQ 码：999））	欧盟	其他欧盟公司	All Others	43.0%	2019－07－23	2024－07－22
		日本	日本冶金工业株式会社	NIPPONYAKINKOGYOCO.，LTD	18.1%	2019－07－23	2024－07－22
		日本	其他日本公司	All Others	29.0%	2019－07－23	2024－07－22
		韩国	株式会社 POSCO	POSCO	23.1%	2019－07－23	2024－07－22
		韩国	其他韩国公司	All Others	103.1%	2019－07－23	2024－07－22
		印度尼西亚	其他印度尼西亚公司	All Others	20.2%	2019－07－23	2024－07－22
		国（地）别不详	国（地）别不详	国（地）别不详	103.1%	2019－07－23	2024－07－22
7219241000	1mm＜厚度＜3mm热轧不锈钢平板（除热轧外未经进一步加工宽度≥600mm）（CIQ 码：999））	欧盟	其他欧盟公司	All Others	43.0%	2019－07－23	2024－07－22
		日本	日本冶金工业株式会社	NIPPONYAKINKOGYOCO.，LTD	18.1%	2019－07－23	2024－07－22
		日本	其他日本公司	All Others	29.0%	2019－07－23	2024－07－22
		韩国	株式会社 POSCO	POSCO	23.1%	2019－07－23	2024－07－22
		韩国	其他韩国公司	All Others	103.1%	2019－07－23	2024－07－22
		印度尼西亚	其他印度尼西亚公司	All Others	20.2%	2019－07－23	2024－07－22
		国（地）别不详	国（地）别不详	国（地）别不详	103.1%	2019－07－23	2024－07－22
7219242000	0.5mm≤厚≤1mm热轧不锈钢平板（除热轧外未经进一步加工宽度≥600mm）（CIQ 码：999））	欧盟	其他欧盟公司	All Others	43.0%	2019－07－23	2024－07－22
		日本	日本冶金工业株式会社	NIPPONYAKINKOGYOCO.，LTD	18.1%	2019－07－23	2024－07－22
		日本	其他日本公司	All Others	29.0%	2019－07－23	2024－07－22
		韩国	株式会社 POSCO	POSCO	23.1%	2019－07－23	2024－07－22
		韩国	其他韩国公司	All Others	103.1%	2019－07－23	2024－07－22
		印度尼西亚	其他印度尼西亚公司	All Others	20.2%	2019－07－23	2024－07－22
		国（地）别不详	国（地）别不详	国（地）别不详	103.1%	2019－07－23	2024－07－22
721924300	厚度＜0.5mm热轧不锈钢平板（除热轧外未经进一步加工宽度≥600mm）（CIQ 码：999））	欧盟	其他欧盟公司	All Others	43.0%	2019－07－23	2024－07－22
		日本	日本冶金工业株式会社	NIPPONYAKINKOGYOCO.，LTD	18.1%	2019－07－23	2024－07－22
		日本	其他日本公司	All Others	29.0%	2019－07－23	2024－07－22
		韩国	株式会社 POSCO	POSCO	23.1%	2019－07－23	2024－07－22
		韩国	其他韩国公司	All Others	103.1%	2019－07－23	2024－07－22
		印度尼西亚	其他印度尼西亚公司	All Others	20.2%	2019－07－23	2024－07－22
		国（地）别不详	国（地）别不详	国（地）别不详	103.1%	2019－07－23	2024－07－22

HS 编码	商品名称	原产国名称	厂商中文名称	厂商英文名称	反倾销税率	反倾销开始时间	反倾销结束日期
7220110000	(热轧不锈钢带材厚度≥4.75mm(除热轧外未经进一步加工宽度＜600mm)(CIQ 码:999))	欧盟	其他欧盟公司	All Others	43.0%	2019－07－23	2024－07－22
		日本	日本冶金工业株式会社	NIPPONYAKINKOGYOCO.,LTD	18.1%	2019－07－23	2024－07－22
		日本	其他日本公司	All Others	29.0%	2019－07－23	2024－07－22
		韩国	株式会社 POSCO	POSCO	23.1%	2019－07－23	2024－07－22
		韩国	其他韩国公司	All Others	103.1%	2019－07－23	2024－07－22
		印度尼西亚	其他印度尼西亚公司	All Others	20.2%	2019－07－23	2024－07－22
		国(地)别不详	国(地)别不详	国(地)别不洋	103.1%	2019－07－23	2024－07－22
7220120000	热轧不锈钢带材厚度＜4.75mm(除热轧外未经进一步加工宽度＜600mm)(CIQ 码:999))	欧盟	其他欧盟公司	All Others	43.0%	2019－07－23	2024－07－22
		日本	日本冶金工业株式会社	NIPPONYAKINKOGYOCO.,LTD	18.1%	2019－07－23	2024－07－22
		日本	其他日本公司	All Others	29.0%	2019－07－23	2024－07－22
		韩国	株式会社 POSCO	POSCO	23.1%	2019－07－23	2024－07－22
		韩国	其他韩国公司	All Others	103.1%	2019－07－23	2024－07－22
		印度尼西亚	其他印度尼西亚公司	All Others	20.2%	2019－07－23	2024－07－22
		国(地)别不详	国(地)别不详	国(地)别不详	103.1%	2019－07－23	2024－07－22
7225110000	取向性硅电钢宽板(宽≥600mm、按重量计含硅量至少为0.6%,含碳量不超过0.08%,可含有不超过1%的铝,所含其他元素的比例并不使其具有其他合金钢的特性;厚度不超过56毫米;呈卷状的,则其可为任何宽度;呈板状的,则其宽度至少是厚度的十倍。)(CIQ 码:999)	日本	JFE 钢铁株式会社	JFE Steel Corporation	39.0%	2016 年 7 月 23 日	2021 年 7 月 22 日
		日本	新日铁住金株式会社	Nippon Steel & Sumitomo Metal Corporation	45.7%	2016 年 7 月 22 日	2021 年 7 月 22 日
		日本	其他日本公司	All Others	45.7%	2016 年 7 月 23 日	2021 年 7 月 22 日
		韩国	株式会社 POSCO	POSCO	37.3%	2016 年 7 月 23 日	2021 年 7 月 22 日
		韩国	其他韩国公司	All Others	37.3%	2016 年 7 月 23 日	2021 年 7 月 22 日
		欧盟	其他欧盟公司	All Others	46.3%	2016 年 7 月 23 日	2021 年 7 月 22 日
		国别(地)不详	国(别)地不详	国(别)地不详	46.3%	2016 年 7 月 23 日	2021 年 7 月 22 日
7226110000	取向性硅电钢窄板(宽＜600mm、按重量计含硅量至少为0.6%,含碳量不超过0.08%,可含有不超过1%的铝,所含其他元素的比例并不使其具有其他合金钢的特性;厚度不超过56毫米;呈卷状的,则其可为任何宽度;呈板状的,则其宽度至少是厚度的十倍。)(CIQ 码:999)	日本	JFE 钢铁株式会社	JFE Steel Corporation	39.0%	2016 年 7 月 23 日	2021 年 7 月 22 日
		日本	新日铁住金株式会社	Nippon Steel & Sumitomo Metal Corporation	45.7%	2016 年 7 月 23 日	2021 年 7 月 22 日
		日本	其他日本公司	All Others	45.7%	2016 年 7 月 23 日	2021 年 7 月 22 日
		韩国	株式会社 POSCO	POSCO	37.3%	2016 年 7 月 23 日	2021 年 7 月 22 日
		韩国	其他韩国公司	All Others	37.3%	2016 年 7 月 23 日	2021 年 7 月 22 日
		欧盟	其他欧盟公司	All Others	46.3%	2016 年 7 月 23 日	2021 年 7 月 22 日
		国(地)别不详	国(地)别不详	国(地)别不详	46.3%	2016 年 7 月 23 日	2021 年 7 月 22 日

HS编码	商品名称	原产国名称	厂商中文名称	厂商英文名称	反倾销税率	反倾销开始时间	反倾销结束日期
7226919910	宽度＜600毫米的铁基非晶合金带材(除热轧外未经进一步加工)(CIQ码:999)	日本	美特格拉斯安来工厂	Metglas Yasugi Works	25.9%	2016年11月18日	2021年11月17日
		日本	其他日本公司	All Others	25.9%	2016年11月18日	2021年11月17日
		美国	美特格拉斯股份有限公司	Metglas, Inc	48.5%	2016年11月18日	2021年11月17日
		美国	其他美国公司	All Others	48.5%	2016年11月18日	2021年11月17日
		国(地)别不详	国(地)别不详	国(地)别不详	48.5%	2016年11月18日	2021年11月17日
7304511001	高温承压用合金钢无缝钢管(抗拉强度≥620MPa、屈服强度≥440MPa)(外径在127mm以上(含127mm),化学成分(wt%)中碳(C)的含量≥0.07且≤0.13、铬(Cr)的含量≥8.5且≤9.5、钼(Mo)的含量≥0.3且≤0.6、钨(W)的含量≥1.5且≤2.0、抗拉强度≥620Mpa、屈服强度≥440Mpa)(CIQ码:101:无缝钢管压力管道,102:无缝钢管)	欧盟	瓦卢瑞克德国公司	Vallourec Deutschland GmbH	57.90%	2019年6月14日	2024年6月13日
		欧盟	瓦卢瑞克法国钢管公司	VALLOUREC TUBES FRANCE	57.90%	2019年6月14日	2024年6月13日
		欧盟	意大利IBF公司	IBF S.P.A.	60.8%	2019年6月14日	2024年6月13日
		欧盟	其他欧盟公司	All Others	60.8%	2019年6月14日	2024年6月13日
		美国	美国威曼高登锻造有限公司	Wyman－Gordon Forgings, Inc.	101.00%	2019年6月14日	2024年6月13日
		美国	其他美国公司	All Others	147.80%	2019年6月14日	2024年6月13日
		国(地)别不详	国(地)别不详	国(地)别不详	147.80%	2019年6月14日	2024年6月13日
7304519001	高温承压用合金钢无缝钢管(抗拉强度≥620MPa、屈服强度≥440MPa)(外径在127mm以上(含127mm),化学成分(wt%)中碳(C)的含量≥0.07且≤0.13、铬(Cr)的含量≥8.5且≤9.5、钼(Mo)的含量≥0.3且≤0.6、钨(W)的含量≥1.5且≤2.0、抗拉强度≥620Mpa、屈服强度≥440Mpa)(CIQ码:101:无缝钢管压力管道,102:无缝钢管)	欧盟	瓦卢瑞克德国公司	Vallourec Deutschland GmbH	57.90%	2019年6月14日	2024年6月13日
		欧盟	瓦卢瑞克法国钢管公司	VALLOUREC TUBES FRANCE	57.90%	2019年6月14日	2024年6月13日
		欧盟	意大利IBF公司	IBF S.P.A.	60.8%	2019年6月14日	2024年6月13日
		欧盟	其他欧盟公司	All Others	60.8%	2019年6月14日	2024年6月13日
		美国	美国威曼高登锻造有限公司	Wyman－Gordon Forgings, Inc.	101.00%	2019年6月14日	2024年6月13日
		美国	其他美国公司	All Others	147.80%	2019年6月14日	2024年6月13日
		国(地)别不详	国(地)别不详	国(地)别不详	147.80%	2019年6月14日	2024年6月13日

HS 编码	商品名称	原产国名称	厂商中文名称	厂商英文名称	反倾销税率	反倾销开始时间	反倾销结束日期
7304591001	高温承压用合金钢无缝钢管(抗拉强度≥620MPa、屈服强度≥440MPa)(外径在127mm以上(含127mm),化学成分(wt%)中碳(C)的含量≥0.07且≤0.13、铬(Cr)的含量≥8.5且≤9.5、钼(Mo)的含量≥0.3且≤0.6、钨(W)的含量≥1.5且≤2.0、抗拉强度≥620Mpa、屈服强度≥440Mpa)(CIQ码:101:无缝钢管压力管道,102:无缝钢管)	欧盟	瓦卢瑞克德国公司	Vallourec Deutschland GmbH	57.90%	2019年6月14日	2024年6月13日
		欧盟	瓦卢瑞克法国钢管公司	VALLOUREC TUBES FRANCE	57.90%	2019年6月14日	2024年6月13日
		欧盟	意大利IBF公司	IBF S.P.A.	60.8%	2019年6月14日	2024年6月13日
		欧盟	其他欧盟公司	All Others	60.8%	2019年6月14日	2024年6月13日
		美国	美国威曼高登锻造有限公司	Wyman－Gordon Forgings, Inc.	101.00%	2019年6月14日	2024年6月13日
		美国	其他美国公司	All Others	147.80%	2019年6月14日	2024年6月13日
		国(地)别不详	国(地)别不详	国(地)别不详	147.80%	2019年6月14日	2024年6月13日
7304599001	高温承压用合金钢无缝钢管(抗拉强度≥620MPa、屈服强度≥440MPa)(外径在127mm以上(含127mm),化学成分(wt%)中碳(C)的含量≥0.07且≤0.13、铬(Cr)的含量≥8.5且≤9.5、钼(Mo)的含量≥0.3且≤0.6、钨(W)的含量≥1.5且≤2.0、抗拉强度≥620Mpa、屈服强度≥440Mpa)(CIQ码:101:无缝钢管压力管道,102:无缝钢管)	欧盟	瓦卢瑞克德国公司	Vallourec Deutschland GmbH	57.90%	2019年6月14日	2024年6月13日
		欧盟	瓦卢瑞克法国钢管公司	VALLOUREC TUBES FRANCE	57.90%	2019年6月14日	2024年6月13日
		欧盟	意大利IBF公司	IBF S.P.A.	60.8%	2019年6月14日	2024年6月13日
		欧盟	其他欧盟公司	All Others	60.8%	2019年6月14日	2024年6月13日
		美国	美国威曼高登锻造有限公司	Wyman－Gordon Forgings, Inc.	101.00%	2019年6月14日	2024年6月13日
		美国	其他美国公司	All Others	147.80%	2019年6月14日	2024年6月13日
		国(地)别不详	国(地)别不详	国(地)别不详	147.80%	2019年6月14日	2024年6月13日
7318120001	非用于民用航空器维护和修理的其他木螺钉(不包括不锈钢紧固件)(CIQ码:999)	国(地)别不详	国(地)别不详	国(地)别不详	26.0%	2016年6月29日	2021年6月28日
		欧盟	其他欧盟公司	All Others	26.0%	2016年6月29日	2021年6月28日
		欧盟	卡马克斯有限两合公司	KAMAX GmbH & Co.KG	6.1%	2016年6月29日	2021年6月28日
		欧盟	皇家内德史罗夫控股有限公司	(Koninklijke Nedschroef Holding B.V.)	5.5%	2017年9月20日	2021年6月28日
		欧盟	内德史罗夫阿尔特纳有限公司	(Nedschroef Altena GmbH)	5.5%	2017年9月20日	2021年6月28日
		欧盟	内德史罗夫福罗劳顿有限公司	Nedschroef Fraulautern GmbH)	5.5%	2017年9月20日	2021年6月28日
		欧盟	内德史罗夫海尔蒙德有限公司	(Nedschroef Helmond B.V.)	5.5%	2017年9月20日	2021年6月28日
		欧盟	内德史罗夫巴塞罗那有限公司	(Nedschroef Barcelona SAU)	5.5%	2017年9月20日	2021年6月28日
		欧盟	内德史罗夫贝京根有限公司	(Nedschroef Beckingen GmbH)	5.5%	2017年9月20日	2021年6月28日

HS编码	商品名称	原产国名称	厂商中文名称	厂商英文名称	反倾销税率	反倾销开始时间	反倾销结束日期
7318140001	非用于民用航空器维护和修理的自攻螺钉(不包括不锈钢紧固件)(CIQ码:999)	国(地)别不详	国(地)别不详	国(地)别不详	26.0%	2016年6月29日	2021年6月28日
		欧盟	其他欧盟公司	All Others	26.0%	2016年6月29日	2021年6月28日
		欧盟	卡马克斯有限两合公司	KAMAX GmbH & Co.KG	6.1%	2016年6月29日	2021年6月28日
		欧盟	皇家内德史罗夫控股有限公司	(Koninklijke Nedschroef Holding B.V.)	5.5%	2017年9月20日	2021年6月28日
		欧盟	内德史罗夫阿尔特纳有限公司	(Nedschroef Altena GmbH)	5.5%	2017年9月20日	2021年6月28日
		欧盟	内德史罗夫福罗劳顿有限公司	(Nedschroef Fraulautern GmbH)	5.5%	2017年9月20日	2021年6月28日
		欧盟	内德史罗夫海尔蒙德有限公司	(Nedschroef Helmond B.V.)	5.5%	2017年9月20日	2021年6月28日
		欧盟	内德史罗夫贝京根有限公司	(Nedschroef Beckingen GmbH)	5.5%	2017年9月20日	2021年6月28日
		欧盟	内德史罗夫巴塞罗那有限公司	(Nedschroef Barcelona SAU)	5.5%	2017年9月20日	2021年6月28日
7318151001	抗拉强度≥800兆帕,杆径＞6mm的其他螺钉及螺栓(不包括不锈钢紧固件)(不论是否带有螺母或垫圈,非用于民用航空器维护和修理的)(CIQ码:999)	国(地)别不详	国(地)别不详	国(地)别不详	26.0%	2016年6月29日	2021年6月28日
		欧盟	其他欧盟公司	All Others	26.0%	2016年6月29日	2021年6月28日
		欧盟	卡马克斯有限两合公司	KAMAX GmbH & Co.KG	6.1%	2016年6月29日	2021年6月28日
		欧盟	皇家内德史罗夫控股有限公司	(KoninklijkeNedschroefHoldingB.V.)	5.5%	2017年9月20日	2021年6月28日
		欧盟	内德史罗夫阿尔特纳有限公司	(Nedschroef Altena GmbH)	5.5%	2017年9月20日	2021年6月28日
		欧盟	内德史罗夫福罗劳顿有限公司	(Nedschroef Fraulautern GmbH)	5.5%	2017年9月20日	2021年6月28日
		欧盟	内德史罗夫海尔蒙德有限公司	(Nedschroef Helmond B.V.)	5.5%	2017年9月20日	2021年6月28日
		欧盟	内德史罗夫巴塞罗那有限公司	(Nedschroef Barcelona SAU)	5.5%	2017年9月20日	2021年6月28日
		欧盟	内德史罗夫贝京根有限公司	(Nedschroef Beckingen GmbH)	5.5%	2017年9月20日	2021年6月28日
7318159001	杆径＞6mm的其他螺钉及螺栓(不包括不锈钢紧固件)(不论是否带有螺母或垫圈,非用于民用航空器维护和修理的)(CIQ码:101:螺钉,102:螺栓)	国(地)别不详	国(地)别不详	国(地)别不详	26.0%	2016年6月29日	2021年6月28日
		欧盟	其他欧盟公司	All Others	26.0%	2016年6月29日	2021年6月28日
		欧盟	卡马克斯有限两合公司	KAMAX GmbH & Co.KG	6.1%	2016年6月29日	2021年6月28日
		欧盟	皇家内德史罗夫控股有限公司	(Koninklijke Nedschroef Holding B.V.)	5.5%	2017年9月20日	2021年6月28日
		欧盟	内德史罗夫阿尔特纳有限公司	(Nedschroef Altena GmbH)	5.5%	2017年9月20日	2021年6月28日
		欧盟	内德史罗夫福罗劳顿有限公司	(Nedschroef Fraulautern GmbH)	5.5%	2017年9月20日	2021年6月28日
		欧盟	内德史罗夫海尔蒙德有限公司	(Nedschroef Helmond B.V.)	5.5%	2017年9月20日	2021年6月28日
		欧盟	内德史罗夫巴塞罗那有限公司	(Nedschroef Barcelona SAU)	5.5%	2017年9月20日	2021年6月28日
		欧盟	内德史罗夫贝京根有限公司	(Nedschroef Beckingen GmbH)	5.5%	2017年9月20日	2021年6月28日
7318210001	弹簧垫圈及其他防松垫圈(不包括不锈钢紧固件)(非用于民用航空器维护和修理的)(CIQ码:999)	国(地)别不详	国(地)别不详	国(地)别不详	26.0%	2016年6月29日	2021年6月28日
		欧盟	其他欧盟公司	All Others	26.0%	2016年6月29日	2021年6月28日
		欧盟	卡马克斯有限两合公司	KAMAX GmbH & Co.KG	6.1%	2016年6月29日	2021年6月28日
		欧盟	皇家内德史罗夫控股有限公司	(Koninklijke Nedschroef Holding B.V.)	5.5%	2017年9月20日	2021年6月28日
		欧盟	内德史罗夫阿尔特纳有限公司	(Nedschroef Altena GmbH)	5.5%	2017年9月20日	2021年6月28日
		欧盟	内德史罗夫福罗劳顿有限公司	(Nedschroef Fraulautern GmbH)	5.5%	2017年9月20日	2021年6月28日
		欧盟	内德史罗夫海尔蒙德有限公司	(Nedschroef Helmond B.V.)	5.5%	2017年9月20日	2021年6月28日
		欧盟	内德史罗夫巴塞罗那有限公司	(Nedschroef Barcelona SAU)	5.5%	2017年9月20日	2021年6月28日
		欧盟	内德史罗夫贝京根有限公司	(Nedschroef Beckingen GmbH)	5.5%	2017年9月20日	2021年6月28日

HS编码	商品名称	原产国名称	厂商中文名称	厂商英文名称	反倾销税率	反倾销开始时间	反倾销结束日期
7318220001	其他垫圈(不包括不锈钢紧固件)(非用于民用航空器维护和修理的)(CIQ码:999)	国(地)别不详	国(地)别不详	国(地)别不详	26.0%	2016年6月29日	2021年6月28日
		欧盟	其他欧盟公司	All Others	26.0%	2016年6月29日	2021年6月28日
		欧盟	卡马克斯有限两合公司	KAMAX GmbH & Co.KG	6.1%	2016年6月29日	2021年6月28日
		欧盟	皇家内德史罗夫控股有限公司	(Koninklijke Nedschroef Holding B.V.)	5.5%	2017年9月20日	2021年6月28日
		欧盟	内德史罗夫阿尔特纳有限公司	(Nedschroef Altena GmbH)	5.5%	2017年9月20日	2021年6月28日
		欧盟	内德史罗夫福罗劳顿有限公司	(Nedschroef Fraulautern GmbH)	5.5%	2017年9月20日	2021年6月28日
		欧盟	内德史罗夫海尔蒙德有限公司	(Nedschroef Helmond B.V.)	5.5%	2017年9月20日	2021年6月28日
		欧盟	内德史罗夫巴塞罗那有限公司	(Nedschroef Barcelona SAU)	5.5%	2017年9月20日	2021年6月28日
		欧盟	内德史罗夫贝京根有限公司	(Nedschroef Beckingen GmbH)	5.5%	2017年9月20日	2021年6月28日
9001100001	非色散位移单模光纤(G.652,包括G652A、G652B、G652C、G652D等)(CIQ码:999)	韩国	其他韩国公司	All Others	46%	2017年1月1日	2021年12月31日
		日本	其他日本公司	All Others	46%	2017年1月1日	2021年12月31日
		国(地)别不详	国(地)别不详	国(地)别不详	46%	2017年4月22日	2022年4月21日
		韩国	大韩光通信株式会社	TAIHAN Fiberoptics CO. LTD.	7.9%	2017年1月1日	2021年12月31日
		美国	德拉克通信美国公司	Draka Communications Americas, Inc.	78.2%	2018年7月11日	2022年4月21日
		美国	康宁公司	Corning Incorporated	37.9%	2018年7月11日	2022年4月21日
		美国	美国OFS-费特有限责任公司	OFS Fitel, LLC	33.3%	2018年7月11日	2022年4月21日
		美国	其他美国公司	All Others	78.2%	2018年7月11日	2022年4月21日
		欧盟	丹麦OFS-费特有限责任公司	OFS Fitel Denmark ApS	29.1%	2017年4月22日	2022年4月21日
		欧盟	德拉克通信法国集团公司	Draka Comteq France SAS	12.9%	2017年4月22日	2022年4月21日
		欧盟	德拉克通信纤维有限公司	Draka Comteq Fibre B.V.	12.9%	2017年4月22日	2022年4月21日
		欧盟	菲布里奥蒂切苏德有限责任公司	Fibre Ottiche Sud -F.O.S.S.r.l.	24.7%	2017年4月22日	2022年4月21日
		欧盟	其他欧盟公司	All Others	29.1%	2017年4月22日	2022年4月21日
		印度	斯德雷特科技有限公司	Sterlite Technologies Limited	7.4%	2019年8月14日	2020年8月13日
		印度	贝拉古河光纤有限公司	Birla Furukawa Fibre Optics Limited	11.4%	2019年8月14日	2020年8月13日
		印度	康宁技术印度有限公司	Corning Technologies India Private Limited	24.5%	2019年8月14日	2020年8月13日
		印度	阿克什光纤有限公司	AkshOptifibre Limited	30.6%	2019年8月14日	2020年8月13日
		印度	菲诺莱克斯电缆有限公司	Finolex Cables Limited	30.6%	2019年8月14日	2020年8月13日
		印度	其他印度公司	All Others	24.5%	2019年8月14日	2020年8月13日
		韩国	韩国LS电线株式会社	LS Cable & System Ltd.	9.1%	2017年1月1日	2021年12月31日
9001100002	其他单模光纤(CIQ码:999)	印度	斯德雷特科技有限公司	STERLITE TECHNOLOGIES LIMITED	7.4%	2019年8月14日	2020年8月13日
		印度	贝拉古河光纤有限公司	Birla Furukawa Fibre Optics Limited	11.4%	2019年8月14日	2020年8月13日
		印度	康宁技术印度有限公司	Corning Technologies India Private Limited	24.5%	2019年8月14日	2020年8月13日
		印度	阿克什光纤有限公司	AkshOptifibre Limited	30.6%	2019年8月14日	2020年8月13日
		印度	菲诺莱克斯电缆有限公司	Finolex Cables Limited	30.6%	2019年8月14日	2020年8月13日
		印度	其他印度公司	All Others	24.5%	2019年8月14日	2020年8月13日
		国(地)别不详	国(地)别不详	国(地)别不详	30.6%	2019年8月14日	2020年8月13日

附表5：中华人民共和国进境物品进口税税率表

税目序号	物品名称	税率(%)
1	书报、刊物、教育用影视资料；计算机、视频摄录一体机、数字照相机等信息技术产品；食品、饮料；金银；家具；玩具，游戏品、节日或其他娱乐用品；药品①	13
2	运动用品(不含高尔夫球及球具)、钓鱼用品；纺织品及其制成品；电视摄像机及其他电器用具；自行车；税目1、3中未包含的其他商品	20
3②	烟、酒；贵重首饰及珠宝玉石；高尔夫球及球具；高档手表；高档化妆品	50

注：①对国家规定减按3%征收进口环节增值税的进口药品，按照货物税率征税。

②税目3所列商品的具体范围与消费税征收范围一致。

5

中华人民共和国海关出口税则

（2020 年 1 月 1 日起实施）

Customs Export Tariff of the People's Republic of China

（Enforced from January 1,2020）

注释：

出口税则也采用《商品名称及编码协调制度》目录，进口税则的归类总规则同样适用于出口税则。

出口商品税率表

序号	EX[①]	税则号列	商品名称(简称)	出口税率(%)	2020 年暂定税率(%)
1		03019210	鳗鱼苗	20	
2		05061000	经酸处理的骨胶原及骨	40	
3		05069011	含牛羊成分的骨粉及骨废料	40	
4		05069019	其他骨粉及骨废料	40	
5		05069090	其他骨及角柱(已脱胶骨、角柱除外)	40	
6	ex	05069090	已脱胶骨、角柱	40	0
7		26070000	铅矿砂及其精矿	30	
8		26080000	锌矿砂及其精矿(氧化锌含量大于 80%的灰色饲料氧化锌除外)	30	
9	ex	26080000	灰色饲料氧化锌(氧化锌 ZnO 含量大于 80%)	30	0
10		26090000	锡矿砂及其精矿	50	20
11		26110000	钨矿砂及其精矿	20	
12		26159010	水合钽铌原料(钽铌富集物)	30	
13		26159090	其他铌钽钒矿砂及其精矿	30	
14		26171010	生锑(锑精矿,选矿产品)	20	
15		28047010	黄磷(白磷)	20	
16		28047090	其他磷	20	10
17	ex	28269090	氟钽酸钾	30	
18		29022000	苯	40	0
19		41039011	经逆鞣处理的山羊板皮	20	
20		41039019	未经逆鞣处理的山羊板皮	20	
21		72011000	非合金生铁,含磷量小于或等于 0.5%(含锰量＜0.08%,含磷量＜0.03%,含硫量＜0.02%,含钛量＜0.03%的高纯生铁除外)	20	
22	ex	72011000	高纯生铁(含锰量＜0.08%,含磷量＜0.03%,含硫量＜0.02%,含钛量＜0.03%)	20	10
23		72012000	非合金生铁,含磷量＞0.5%	20	
24		72015000	合金生铁、镜铁	20	
25		72021100	锰铁,含碳量＞2%	20	
26		72021900	锰铁,含碳量≤2%	20	
27		72022100	硅铁,含硅量＞55%	25	20
28		72022900	硅铁,含硅量≤55%	25	20
29		72023000	硅锰铁	20	
30		72024100	铬铁,含碳量＞4%	40	15
31		72024900	铬铁,含碳量≤4%	40	15
32		72041000	铸铁废碎料	40	
33		72042100	不锈钢废碎料	40	
34		72042900	其他合金钢废碎料	40	
35		72043000	镀锡钢铁废碎料	40	
36		72044100	机械加工中产生的废料	40	
37		72044900	其他钢铁废碎料	40	
38		72045000	供再熔的碎料钢铁锭	40	
39		74020000	未精炼铜、电解精炼用铜阳极	30	15
40	ex	74031111	高纯阴极铜(铜含量不低于 99.9999%)	30	0
41	ex	74031111	高纯阴极铜(铜含量高于 99.9935%,但低于 99.9999%)	30	5
2		74031119	其他阴极精炼铜	30	10
3		74031190	精炼铜阴极型材	30	10
4		74031200	精炼铜的线锭	30	10
		74031300	精炼铜的坯段	30	10
		74031900	其他未锻轧的精炼铜	30	10
		74032100	未锻轧的铜锌合金(黄铜)	30	5
		74032200	未锻轧的铜锡合金(青铜)	30	5
		74032900	其他未锻轧的铜合金(税目 7405 的铜母合金除外)	30	5
		74040000	铜废碎料	30	15
		74071010	铬锆铜制条、杆及型材及异型材	30	0
		74071090	其他精炼铜条、杆及型材及异型材	30	0
		74072111	直线度不大于 0.5 毫米/米铜锌合金条、杆	30	0
		74072119	其他铜锌合金条、杆	30	0

序号	EX[①]	税则号列	商品名称(简称)	出口税率(%)	2020年暂定税率(%)
55		74072190	其他黄铜条、杆及型材及异型材	30	0
56		74072900	其他铜合金条杆、型材及异型材	30	0
57		74081100	最大截面尺寸>6mm 的精炼铜丝	30	0
58		74081900	截面尺寸≤6mm 的精炼铜丝	30	0
59		74082100	黄铜丝	30	0
60		74082210	铜镍锌铅合金(加铅德银)丝	30	0
61		74082290	其他白铜丝或德银(铜镍锌合金)丝	30	0
62		74082900	其他铜合金丝	30	0
63		74091110	"含氧量不超过 10PPM,厚度超过 0.15mm 的盘卷精炼铜板、片、带"	30	0
64		74091190	厚度超过 0.15mm 的其他盘卷精炼铜板、片、带	30	0
65		74091900	其他精炼铜板、片、带	30	0
66		74092100	成卷的黄铜板、片、带	30	0
67		74092900	其他黄铜板、片、带	30	0
68		74093100	成卷的青铜板、片、带	30	0
69		74093900	其他青铜板、片、带	30	0
70		74094000	白铜或德银制板、片、带	30	0
71		74099000	其他铜合金板、片、带	30	0
72		75021010	按重量计镍、钴总量在 99.99%及以上的,但钴含量不超过 0.005%的非合金镍	40	5
73		75021090	其他非合金镍	40	15
74		75022000	未锻轧镍合金	40	15
75		75089010	电镀用镍阳极	40	15
76		76011010	按重量计含铝量在 99.95%及以上的未煅轧非铝合金	30	0
77		76011090	其他未煅轧非铝合金	30	15
78	ex	76012000	碱金属含量(Na+K+Ca)<10ppm,氢含量<0.12ml/100gAl 的低碱精炼铝合金	30	0
79	ex	76012000	其他未锻轧铝合金	30	15
80		76020000	铝废碎料	30	15
81		76041090	非合金铝型材及异形材	20	0
82		76042100	铝合金制空心异型材	20	0
83		76041010	非合金铝条、杆	20	0
84		76042910	截面周长大于等于 210 毫米的铝合金制条、杆	20	0
85		76042990	铝合金型材及异形材	20	0
86		76051100	纯铝制的粗丝	20	0
87		76051900	纯铝制的细丝	20	0
88		76052100	铝合金制的粗丝	20	0
89		76052900	铝合金制的细丝	20	0
90		76061121	0.3mm≤厚度<0.36mm 的非合金铝与塑料复合的矩形板片带	20	0
91		76061129	其他 0.3mm≤厚度<0.36mm 的非合金铝制矩形铝板片带	20	0
92		76061191	0.28mm≤厚度≤0.35mm 的铝合金制矩形铝板片带	20	0
93		76061199	纯铝制矩形的其他板、片及带	20	0
94		76061220	厚度<0.28mm 的铝合金制矩形铝板片带	20	0
95		76061230	0.28mm ≦厚度≤0.35mm 的铝合金制矩形铝板片带	20	0
96		76061251	0.35mm<厚度≤0.4mm 的铝合金与塑料复合的矩形板片带	20	0
97		76061259	其他 0.35mm<厚度≤0.4mm 的铝合金制矩形铝板片带	20	0
98		76061290	厚度>0.4mm 的铝合金制矩形铝板片带	20	0
99		76069100	纯铝制非矩形的板、片及带	20	0
100		76069200	铝合金制非矩形的板、片及带	20	0
101		79011110	按重量计含锌量在 99.995%及以上的未煅轧锌	20	0
102		79011190	含锌量不小于 99.99%,并小于 99.995%的未煅轧锌	20	5
103		79011200	含锌量<99.99%的未锻轧锌	20	15
104		79012000	未锻轧锌合金	20	0
105		81101010	未锻轧锑	20	5
106		81101020	锑粉末	20	
107		81102000	锑废碎料	20	

注①"ex"表示实施暂定税率的商品应在该税号范围内,以具体商品描述为准。

6

中华人民共和国进出口关税税款计算方法

Calculation methods for Import and Export Tax of the People's Republic of China

本书所列计算方法是根据《中华人民共和国关税条例》、《中华人民共和国增值税暂行条例》及《中华人民共和国消费税暂行条例》编制的。

为便于使用，现将有关问题说明如下：

一、所称进口税包括进口关税、进口环节增值税（简称增值税）、进口环节消费税（简称消费税），其中消费税仅对少数商品征收；出口税只含出口关税一项。

二、关税税率分为优惠关税税率和普通关税税率。凡原产地属于世贸组织成员或与我国签定有互惠双边贸易协定的国家或地区进口的商品，其进口关税税率使用优惠关税税率，否则使用普通关税税率。

三、税款计算公式

$$\text{进口关税税额}=\text{到岸价格}\times\text{进口关税税率}$$

$$\text{出口关税税额}=\frac{\text{离岸价格}}{1+\text{出口税税率}}\times\text{出口关税税率}$$

$$\text{增值税税额}=(\text{到岸价}+\text{进口关税额}+\text{消费税额})\times\text{增值税税率}$$

$$\text{从价消费税税额}=\left(\frac{\text{到岸价}+\text{关税额}}{1-\text{消费税税率}}\right)\times\text{消费税税率}$$

$$\text{从量消费税税额}=\text{应征消费税的商品数量}\times\text{消费税单位税额}$$

其中，从量消费税商品计量单位的换算标准（按体积净重计）如下：

啤酒 1 吨＝988 升

黄酒 1 吨＝962 升

汽油 1 吨＝1388 升

柴油 1 吨＝1176 升

$$\text{进口税额}=\text{进口关税}+\text{增值税}+\text{消费税}$$

$$=\left(\frac{\text{进口关税率}+\text{消费税率}+\text{增值税率}+\text{进口关税率}\times\text{增值税率}}{1-\text{消费税税率}}\right)\times\text{到岸价}$$

$$=\text{常数}\times\text{到岸价}$$

四、为便于计算进口税额，本书编制了《进口税计税系数表》，其使用方法如下：

（一）"系数表 1"适用于应征消费税税率不为 0 税率的商品。鉴于此类商品法定增值税率均为 17%，因此在本书中查出该商品的关税税率和消费税税率后，在"表 1"内找出这两个税率交叉栏内的常数，用进口货物的到岸价乘以该常数，即为应纳进口税额。

（二）"系数表 2"适用于消费税税率为 0 的进口商品。首先在本书中查出该商品的关税税率和增值税税率，然后在"表 2"内找出这两个税率的交叉栏内的常数，用进口货物的到岸价乘以该常数即为应纳进口税额。

五、对适用于暂定税率的商品，关税税率应用暂定关税税率。

The Calculation methods in this book is compiled in accordance with Regulations on Customs Tariff of the People's Republic of China, Provisional Regulations on Value-added Tax of the People's Republic of China and Provisional Regulations on Consumption Tax of the People's Republic of China.

For the convenience of usage, relevant explanations are listed below:

1. Import tax we mean consists of import customs duty (ICD), value-added tax (VAT), and consumption tax (CT) among which CT is levied on a few items of goods. Export tax consists of only export customs duty (ECD).

2. Import customs duty rates we mean fall into general duty rates and preferential duty rates. The preferential duty rates apply to goods originally produced or manufactured in countries with which the People's Republic of China has concluded trading agreement. Otherwise, the general duty rates will be applied.

3. Calculation formulae for tax collection

$$\text{ICD}=\text{CIF value}\times\text{ICD rate}$$

$$\text{ECD}=\frac{\text{FOB value}}{1+\text{ECD rate}}\times\text{ECD rate}$$

$$\text{VAT}=(\text{CIF value}+\text{ICD}+\text{CT})\times\text{VAT rate}$$

$$\textit{Ad Valorem CT}=\left(\frac{\text{CIF value}+\text{ICD}}{1-\text{CT rate}}\right)\times\text{CT rate}$$

$$\text{Specific CT}=\text{Quantity of goods}\times\text{unit CT rate}$$

Note: The following is the conversion table of measurements of goods on which specific consumption tax is levied (net bulk)

Beer	1ton＝988 litres
Millet wine	1 ton＝962 litres
Gasoline	1 ton＝1388 litres
Diesel	1 ton＝1176 litres

$$\text{Total Import Tax}=\text{ICD}+\text{VAT}+\text{CT}$$

$$=\left(\frac{\text{ICD rate}+\text{CT rate}+\text{VAT rate}+\text{ICD rate}\times\text{VAT rate}}{1-\text{CT rate}}\right)\times\text{CIF value}$$

$$=\text{Coefficient}\times\text{CIF value}$$

4. To facilitate easy calculation, we compiled tables of import tax coefficients for reference. The following are the exemplary usage methods:

(1) The Table of Import Tax Coefficient (Consumption Taxes Applicable) applies to goods on which the consumption tax is levied. In viewof the statutory VAT rate is 17% for all goods in this table, the user may first find the duty rate and consumption tax rate of a particular type of goods in the table, then find the coefficient where those two rates meet in the table. The import tax payable equals the coefficient times the CIF value.

(2) The Table of Import Tax Cofficients (Consumption Taxes Not Applicable) applies to goods on which no consumption tax is levied. The user may first find the duty rate and VAT rate of a particular type of goods in the table, then find the coefficient where those two rates meet in the table. The total import tax is the coefficient times the CIF value.

5. As far as goods on which Interim Duty Rate is appliable, ICD rate is no other than Interim Duty Rate.

表 1　进口关税与进口环节代征税（消费税）计税常数表

Table of import tariff and import tax (Consumption tax and value added tax)

	关税率	不同消费税税率对应常数										
		1%	3%	5%	9%	10%	12%	15%	20%	25%	30%	40%
增值税 13%	0.0%	14.141%	16.495%	18.947%	24.176%	25.556%	28.409%	32.941%	41.250%	50.667%	61.429%	88.333%
	1.0%	15.283%	17.660%	20.137%	25.418%	26.811%	29.693%	34.271%	42.663%	52.173%	63.043%	90.217%
	2.0%	16.424%	18.825%	21.326%	26.659%	28.067%	30.977%	35.600%	44.075%	53.680%	64.657%	92.100%
	3.0%	17.566%	19.990%	22.516%	27.901%	29.322%	32.261%	36.929%	45.488%	55.187%	66.271%	93.983%
	5.0%	19.848%	22.320%	24.895%	30.385%	31.833%	34.830%	39.588%	48.313%	58.200%	69.500%	97.750%
	6.5%	21.561%	24.067%	26.679%	32.247%	33.717%	36.756%	41.582%	50.431%	60.460%	71.921%	100.575%
	8.0%	23.273%	25.814%	28.463%	34.110%	35.600%	38.682%	43.576%	52.550%	62.720%	74.343%	103.400%
	10.0%	25.556%	28.144%	30.842%	36.593%	38.111%	41.250%	46.235%	55.375%	65.733%	77.571%	107.167%
	11.0%	26.697%	29.309%	32.032%	37.835%	39.367%	42.534%	47.565%	56.788%	67.240%	79.186%	109.050%
	12.5%	28.409%	31.057%	33.816%	39.698%	41.250%	44.460%	49.559%	58.906%	69.500%	81.607%	111.875%
	15.0%	31.263%	33.969%	36.789%	42.802%	44.389%	47.670%	52.882%	62.438%	73.267%	85.643%	116.583%
	16.0%	32.404%	35.134%	37.979%	44.044%	45.644%	48.955%	54.212%	63.850%	74.773%	87.257%	118.467%
	23.0%	40.394%	43.289%	46.305%	52.736%	54.433%	57.943%	63.518%	73.738%	85.320%	98.557%	131.650%
	80.0%	105.455%	109.691%	114.105%	123.516%	126.000%	131.136%	139.294%	154.250%	171.200%	190.571%	239.000%
	100.0%	128.283%	132.990%	137.895%	148.352%	151.111%	156.818%	165.882%	182.500%	201.333%	222.857%	276.667%
	150.0%	185.354%	191.237%	197.368%	210.440%	213.889%	221.023%	232.353%	253.125%	276.667%	303.571%	370.833%

注：

1.所列常数均已包括增值税在内。

2.常数计算公式为：

$$常数=\frac{进口关税税率+消费税税率+增值税税率+进口关税税率\times增值税税率}{1-消费税税率}$$

表 2　进口关税与进口环节代征税（增值税）计税常数表

Table of Import Tariff and Import Tax (Value added Tax)

关税税率	不同增值税税率对应常数		关税税率	不同增值税税率对应常数		关税税率	不同增值税税率对应常数	
	9%	13%		9%	13%		9%	13%
0.0%	9.00%	13.00%	2.0%	11.18%	15.26%	3.5%	12.82%	16.96%
0.4%	9.44%	13.45%	2.1%	11.29%	15.37%	3.8%	13.14%	17.29%
0.5%	9.55%	13.57%	2.3%	11.51%	15.60%	4.0%	13.36%	17.52%
0.8%	9.87%	13.90%	2.5%	11.73%	15.83%	4.2%	13.58%	17.75%
1.0%	10.09%	14.13%	2.6%	11.83%	15.94%	4.3%	13.69%	17.86%
1.1%	10.20%	14.24%	2.7%	11.94%	16.05%	4.4%	13.80%	17.97%
1.3%	10.42%	14.47%	3.0%	12.27%	16.39%	4.5%	13.91%	18.09%
1.5%	10.64%	14.70%	3.1%	12.38%	16.50%	4.7%	14.12%	18.31%
1.7%	10.85%	14.92%	3.2%	12.49%	16.62%	4.8%	14.23%	18.42%
1.8%	10.96%	15.03%	3.3%	12.60%	16.73%	5.0%	14.45%	18.65%
1.9%	11.07%	15.15%	3.4%	12.71%	16.84%	5.3%	14.78%	18.99%

关税税率	不同增值税税率对应常数	
	9%	13%
5.4%	14.89%	19.10%
5.5%	15.00%	19.22%
5.6%	15.10%	19.33%
5.8%	15.32%	19.55%
6.0%	15.54%	19.78%
6.1%	15.65%	19.89%
6.3%	15.87%	20.12%
6.5%	16.09%	20.35%
6.7%	16.30%	20.57%
6.8%	16.41%	20.68%
7.0%	16.63%	20.91%
7.5%	17.18%	21.48%
7.9%	17.61%	21.93%
8.0%	17.72%	22.04%
8.3%	18.05%	22.38%
8.4%	18.16%	22.49%
8.5%	18.27%	22.61%
8.8%	18.59%	22.94%
9.0%	18.81%	23.17%
9.3%	19.14%	23.51%
9.4%	19.25%	23.62%
9.5%	19.36%	23.74%
9.7%	19.57%	23.96%
10.0%	19.90%	24.30%
10.5%	20.45%	24.87%
11.0%	20.99%	25.43%
11.3%	21.32%	25.77%
11.7%	21.75%	26.22%
12.0%	22.08%	26.56%
12.5%	22.63%	27.13%
12.6%	22.73%	27.24%

关税税率	不同增值税税率对应常数	
	9%	13%
12.8%	22.95%	27.46%
13.0%	23.17%	27.69%
13.1%	23.28%	27.80%
13.5%	23.72%	28.26%
13.8%	24.04%	28.59%
14.0%	24.26%	28.82%
14.3%	24.59%	29.16%
14.4%	24.70%	29.27%
15.0%	25.35%	29.95%
15.6%	26.00%	30.63%
16.0%	26.44%	31.08%
16.5%	26.99%	31.65%
17.0%	27.53%	32.21%
17.5%	28.08%	32.78%
18.0%	28.62%	33.34%
18.8%	29.49%	34.24%
19.0%	29.71%	34.47%
19.3%	30.04%	34.81%
20.0%	30.80%	35.60%
21.0%	31.89%	36.73%
21.9%	32.87%	37.75%
22.0%	32.98%	37.86%
22.5%	33.53%	38.43%
23.0%	34.07%	38.99%
23.3%	34.40%	39.33%
24.0%	35.16%	40.12%
24.5%	35.71%	40.69%
25.0%	36.25%	41.25%
26.3%	37.67%	42.72%
27.0%	38.43%	43.51%
28.0%	39.52%	44.64%

关税税率	不同增值税税率对应常数	
	9%	13%
29.0%	40.61%	45.77%
29.2%	40.83%	46.00%
30.0%	41.70%	46.90%
32.0%	43.88%	49.16%
35.0%	47.15%	52.55%
36.0%	48.24%	53.68%
38.0%	50.42%	55.94%
40.0%	52.60%	58.20%
45.0%	58.05%	63.85%
46.0%	59.14%	64.98%
50.0%	63.50%	69.50%
57.0%	71.13%	77.41%
60.0%	74.40%	80.80%
63.0%	77.67%	84.19%
65.0%	79.85%	86.45%
70.0%	85.30%	92.10%
75.0%	90.75%	97.75%
80.0%	96.20%	103.40%
85.0%	101.65%	109.05%
90.0%	107.10%	114.70%
100.0%	118.00%	126.00%
110.0%	128.90%	137.30%
114.0%	133.26%	141.82%
125.0%	145.25%	154.25%
130.0%	150.70%	159.90%
150.0%	172.50%	182.50%
160.0%	183.40%	193.80%
170.0%	194.30%	205.10%
180.0%	205.20%	216.40%
190.0%	216.10%	227.70%
230.0%	259.70%	272.90%
270.0%	303.30%	318.10%

计量单位换算表
Conversion Table

面(地)积换算

公制		英美制			
平方米	平方厘米	平方码	平方英尺	平方英寸	平方尺
1	10000	1.1960	10.7639	1550	9
0.0001	1	0.00012	0.00108	0.155	0.0009
0.8361	8361	1	9	1296	7.525
0.0929	929	0.1111	1	144	0.836
0.00065	6.45	0.00077	0.00694	1	0.0058
0.111	1111	0.133	1.196	172.2	1

长度换算

公制		中国市制	英美制		
米	厘米	尺	码	英尺	英寸
1	100	3	1.094	3.2808	39.37
0.01	1	0.03	0.01094	0.03281	0.3937
0.3333	33.33	1	0.3646	1.094	13.123
0.9144	91.44	2.743	1	3	36
0.3048	30.48	0.9144	0.3334	1	12
0.0254	2.54	0.0762	0.0278	0.833	1

1 米＝100 厘米＝1000 毫米

重量换算(一)

公制	英制	美制	港制
公吨	长吨	短吨	司马担
1	0.9842	1.1023	16.535
1.016	1	1.12	16.8
0.9072	0.8929	1	15
0.05	0.04921	0.0551	0.8267
0.0508	0.05	0.056	0.8402
0.0605	0.0594	0.0667	1

港制 1 司马担＝100 司马斤

公制 1 公吨＝10 公担

英制 1 长吨＝20 英担(CWT)

1 英担＝50.8024 千克

美制 1 短吨＝20 短担(CWT)

1 短担＝100 磅＝45.36 千克

公制	中国市制	英美制
千克	斤	磅
1000	2000	2204.6
1016	2032	2242
907	1814	2000
50	100	110.23
50.8	101.6	112
60.48	120.96	133.33
1	2	2.2046
0.5	1	1.1023
0.4536	0.9072	1

重量换算(二)

公制		英美制常衡		英美制金衡或药衡		中国市制
千克	克	磅	啢	磅	啢	两
1	1000	2.2046	35.2736	2.697	31.1507	20
0.001	1	0.0022	0.03527	0.00268	0.0321	0.02
0.4536	453.59	1	16	1.2153	14.5833	9.072
0.02835	28.35	0.0625	1	0.07595	0.9114	0.567
0.3732	373.24	0.82286	13.1657	1	12	7.465
0.0311	31.10	0.06857	1.0971	0.08333	1	0.622
0.05	50	0.1102	1.76363	0.13396	1.6075	1

宝石:1 克拉＝0.2 克　　1 金衡＝155.5 克拉

容(体)积换算(一)

公制	中国市制	英制	美制
升	升	英加仑	美加仑
1	1	0.22	0.264
4.546	4.546	1	1.201
3.785	3.785	0.833	1

1000 升＝1 立方米　　1 升＝1000 毫升＝1000 立方厘米(c.c.)

英制 1 加仑＝277.42 立方英寸　　英制 1 加仑＝231 立方英寸

容(体)积换算(二)

公制		英美制			中国市制
立方米	立方厘米	立方码	立方英尺	立方英寸	立方尺
1	1000000	1.303	35.3147	61024	27
0.000001	1	0.0000013	0.00004	0.06102	0.000027
0.7636	764555	1	27	46656	20.643
0.02832	28317	0.037	1	1728	0.7646
0.000016	16.387	0.00002	0.00058	1	0.00044
0.037	37037	0.0484	1.308	2260	1

木材体积单位换算

板(Board Foot Measure,BFM)

指厚一英寸、面积一平方英尺的木材

板材的换算:100 板＝2.36 立方米

原木的换算:100 板＝5 立方米(近似值)

功率换算

1 千瓦(kW)＝1.34 英制马力(hp)＝2.36 公制马力(hp)

1 英制马力＝0.746 千瓦(kW)

1 公制马力＝0.735 千瓦(kW)

1 千伏安(kVA)＝$\frac{千瓦(kW)}{0.80}$

粮谷重量容积换算

品名	1 公吨折合蒲式耳	1 蒲式耳折合	
		磅	千克
小麦、大豆	36.743	60	27.216
玉米	39.368	56	25.402
大麦(英制)	44.092	50	22.68
大麦(美制)	45.931	48	21.773

1 英制蒲式耳(1.0321 美制蒲式耳)合 36.3677 升。

石(原)油重量、容积换算

国别	1 公吨折合			
	千升	美制桶	英制加仑	美制加仑
贡国、印度尼西亚	1.18	7.4	259.1	310.6
伊朗、沙特阿拉伯	1.19	7.49	261.8	314.5
日本	1.11	6.99	.244.5	293.3
英国、科威特	1.16	7.31	255.8	306.7
委内瑞拉	1.09	6.84	239.2	287.4

注:世界平均比重的原油通常以 1 公吨＝7.35 桶(每桶为 42 美制加仑)或 1174 升计。

常用度量衡英文名称和简写

名称	英文名称	简写	名称	英文名称	简写
克	gram	g.	码	yard	yd.
千克	kilogram	kg.	英尺	foot	ft.
公担	quintal	q.	英寸	inch	in
公吨	metric ton	m.t.	平方米	square metre	sq.m.
长吨	long ton	l.t.	平方英尺	square foot	sq.ft
短吨	short ton	sh.t.	平方码	square yard	sq.yd
英担	hundredweight	cwt.	立方米	cubic metre	cu.m.
美担	hundredweight	cwt.	立方英尺	cubic toor	cu.ft.
磅	pound	lb.	升	litre	l.
唡(常衡)	ounce	oz.	毫升	millilitre	ml.
(金衡)	ounce	oz.t	加仑	gallon	gal.
司马担	picul		蒲式耳	bushel	bu.
米	metre	m.	克拉	carat	car.
公里	kilomere	km.	马力	horse power	hp.
厘米	centimetre	cm.	千瓦	kilowatt	kw.
毫米	millimetre	mm.	公吨度	metric ton unit	m.t.u.